W9-CFT-807

LIFT
TAKE YOUR STUDYING TO THE NEXT LEVEL.

This book comes with 1-year digital access to the
Examples & Explanations for this course.

Step 1: Go to **www.CasebookConnect.com/LIFT** and redeem your access code to get started.

Access Code:  STXT23599187559

Step 2: Go to your BOOKSHELF and select your online *Examples & Explanations* to start reading, highlighting, and taking notes in the margins of your e-book.

Step 3: Select the STUDY tab in your toolbar to access the questions from your book in interactive format, designed to give you extra practice and help you master the course material.

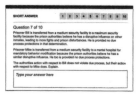

Is this a used casebook? Access code already scratched off?

You can purchase the online *Examples & Explanations* and still access all of the powerful tools listed above. Please visit CasebookConnect.com/Catalog to learn more about Connected Study Aids.

PLEASE NOTE: Each access code provides 12 month access and can only be used once. This code will also expire one year after the discontinuation of the corresponding print title and must be redeemed before then. CCH reserves the right to discontinue this program at any time for any business reason. For further details, please see the Casebook Connect End User Agreement.

PIN: 9111149623

05052

ASPEN CASEBOOK SERIES

ENVIRONMENTAL PROTECTION

Law and Policy

Seventh Edition

Robert L. Glicksman

J.B. & Maurice C. Shapiro Professor of Environmental Law
The George Washington University Law School

David L. Markell

Steven M. Goldstein Professor and Associate Dean for Environmental
Programs
Florida State University College of Law

William W. Buzbee

Professor of Law
Georgetown University Law Center

Daniel R. Mandelker

Howard A. Stamper Professor of Law
Washington University School of Law

Daniel Bodansky

Foundation Professor of Law, Center for Law and Global Affairs'
Faculty Co-Director
Arizona State University Sandra Day O'Connor College of Law

Emily Hammond

Professor of Law
The George Washington University Law School

 Wolters Kluwer

Published by Wolters Kluwer in New York.

Wolters Kluwer serves customers worldwide with CCH, Aspen Publishers, and Kluwer Law International products. (www.wolterskluwerlb.com)

To contact Customer Service, e-mail customer.service@wolterskluwer.com, call 1-800-234-1660, fax 1-800-901-9075, or mail correspondence to:

Wolters Kluwer
Attn: Order Department
PO Box 990
Frederick, MD 21705

Printed in the United States of America.

2 3 4 5 6 7 8 9 0

ISBN 978-1-4548-4935-3

Library of Congress Cataloging-in-Publication Data

Glicksman, Robert L., author.
  Environmental protection : law and policy / Robert L. Glicksman, J.B. & Maurice C. Shapiro Professor of Environmental Law, The George Washington University Law School; David L. Markell, Steven M. Goldstein Professor and Associate Dean for Environmental Programs, Florida State University College of Law; William W. Buzbee, Professor of Law, Georgetown University Law Center; Daniel R. Mandelker, Howard A. Stamper Professor of Law, Washington University School of Law; Daniel Bodansky, Foundation Professor of Law, Center for Law and Global Affairs' Faculty Co-Director, Arizona State University Sandra Day O'Connor College of Law; Emily Hammond, Professor of Law, The George Washington University Law School.—Seventh Edition.
    pages cm.—(Aspen casebook series)
    ISBN 978-1-4548-4935-3
1. Environmental law—United States. I. Markell, David L., author. II. Buzbee, William W., 1960- , author. III. Mandelker, Daniel R., author. IV. Bodansky, Daniel, author. V. Hammond, Emily (Law teacher), author. VI. Title.
    KF3775.G57 2015
    344.7304'6—dc22

                                2014044813

About Wolters Kluwer Law & Business

Wolters Kluwer Law & Business is a leading global provider of intelligent information and digital solutions for legal and business professionals in key specialty areas, and respected educational resources for professors and law students. Wolters Kluwer Law & Business connects legal and business professionals as well as those in the education market with timely, specialized authoritative content and information-enabled solutions to support success through productivity, accuracy and mobility.

Serving customers worldwide, Wolters Kluwer Law & Business products include those under the Aspen Publishers, CCH, Kluwer Law International, Loislaw, ftwilliam.com and MediRegs family of products.

CCH products have been a trusted resource since 1913, and are highly regarded resources for legal, securities, antitrust and trade regulation, government contracting, banking, pension, payroll, employment and labor, and healthcare reimbursement and compliance professionals.

Aspen Publishers products provide essential information to attorneys, business professionals and law students. Written by preeminent authorities, the product line offers analytical and practical information in a range of specialty practice areas from securities law and intellectual property to mergers and acquisitions and pension/benefits. Aspen's trusted legal education resources provide professors and students with high-quality, up-to-date and effective resources for successful instruction and study in all areas of the law.

Kluwer Law International products provide the global business community with reliable international legal information in English. Legal practitioners, corporate counsel and business executives around the world rely on Kluwer Law journals, looseleafs, books, and electronic products for comprehensive information in many areas of international legal practice.

Loislaw is a comprehensive online legal research product providing legal content to law firm practitioners of various specializations. Loislaw provides attorneys with the ability to quickly and efficiently find the necessary legal information they need, when and where they need it, by facilitating access to primary law as well as state-specific law, records, forms and treatises.

ftwilliam.com offers employee benefits professionals the highest quality plan documents (retirement, welfare and non-qualified) and government forms (5500/PBGC, 1099 and IRS) software at highly competitive prices.

MediRegs products provide integrated health care compliance content and software solutions for professionals in healthcare, higher education and life sciences, including professionals in accounting, law and consulting.

Wolters Kluwer Law & Business, a division of Wolters Kluwer, is headquartered in New York. Wolters Kluwer is a market-leading global information services company focused on professionals.

To Emily and Bertie

R.L.G.

To Mona, Rebecca, Jenny, and Rachel,
and in honor of my parents,
William Markell (1923-2009)
and Elaine Markell

D.L.M.

To Lisa, Tian, and Seana, and to my parents,
John and Ellen Buzbee

W.W.B.

To all my children and grandchildren

D.R.M.

To Anne, Maria, and Sarah

D.M.B.

To Joel, Arielle, Landon, and Scarlett

E.H.

SUMMARY OF CONTENTS

CONTENTS

CHAPTER II.   ENVIRONMENTAL FEDERALISM   85

CHAPTER III.   THE ADMINISTRATIVE LAW OF
                  ENVIRONMENTAL PROTECTION   167

CHAPTER IV.   THE NATIONAL ENVIRONMENTAL
                  POLICY ACT   261

CHAPTER VII.   PROTECTING THE WATER RESOURCE   601

CHAPTER IX.   ENVIRONMENTAL CONTAMINATION LIABILITY AND REMEDIATION   913

CHAPTER X.   ENFORCEMENT OF ENVIRONMENTAL LAW   1013

CHAPTER XI.   INTERNATIONAL
                   ENVIRONMENTAL LAW   1095

CHAPTER XII.   CLIMATE CHANGE LAW AND
                 POLICY CHOICES   1171

PREFACE TO THE SEVENTH EDITION

Environmental law continues to be characterized by political ferment and corresponding legal change. Although many central cases and statutory frameworks remain stable, environmental law demands attention to statutory and regulatory amendments, changes in agency policy, and the issuance of important new cases. Regular revision of environmental law casebooks is therefore indispensable to ensure that students are exposed to the current state of the law and its implementation. The seventh edition of this casebook has been thoroughly updated to reflect recent and proposed changes in environmental law.

Several key actors have made significant changes in U.S. environmental law since publication of the sixth edition, many of which relate to the intersection of environmental law and energy production and use. First, administrative agencies have embarked on bold new policy initiatives, such as the federal Environmental Protection Agency's efforts to reduce greenhouse gas emissions that contribute to climate change by adopting regulations that require greater fuel efficiency in cars and trucks and proposed regulations to limit these emissions from fossil fuel-fired power plants. Second, many states and local governments have continued to serve in their fundamental roles as laboratories in developing and implementing innovative environmental policy. California, for example, continued to implement its Global Warming Solutions Act. Third, as has been true since the advent of modern environmental law, the courts at both the federal and state levels have issued decisions that signaled expanded opportunities to promote environmental protection in some cases and narrowed such opportunities in others. The viability of common law causes of action has continued to receive attention, for example, as reflected in the Supreme Court's 2011 decision in American Electric Power Co. v. Connecticut. The seventh edition of this book takes account of developments in all three arenas.

We have not added any new chapters to this edition. We have made significant changes in many of the book's chapters and updated developments in all of them. For example, Chapter 2 assesses the impact of the Supreme Court's 2012 decision addressing the constitutionality of the Affordable Care Act for the application of the Constitution's federalism provisions to environmental law statutory and regulatory programs. We also have moved coverage of dormant Commerce Clause issues from Chapter 8 to Chapter 2, so that students can better understand the relationships among federalist doctrines such as preemption and the dormant Commerce Clause.

We have made significant additions to and revisions of Chapter 6, some in response to suggestions of casebook users. We have moved materials on motor vehicle pollution from the casebook's website to the text and combined that coverage with the materials on regulation of mobile source emissions in nonattainment areas. We also have moved from the website to the text our coverage of hazardous air pollutants and expanded that coverage with excerpts from recent cases involving implementation of the 1990 Clean Air Act Amendments. We have deepened our coverage of the Clean Air Act by better integrating analysis of the relationships among the various statutory programs to control stationary sources, focusing on how these relationships affect strategies of regulators and regulated entities. We added as a new principal case the Supreme Court's 2014 decision in EPA v. EME Homer City Generation, dealing with the intractable problem of interstate air pollution.

In Chapter 7, we reorganized coverage of the threshold questions governing the scope of the Clean Water Act's application, including excerpts from the U.S. Army Corps of Engineers' proposed regulations defining the key term "waters of the United States." In Chapter 8, we have moved coverage of the Federal Insecticide, Fungicide, and Rodenticide Act from the casebook's website to the text and compared and contrasted that statute's regulatory strategies with those of the Toxic Substances Control Act.

Chapter 10 adds the Supreme Court's 2012 decision in Sackett v. EPA as a principal case. This decision addresses important issues concerning the scope of EPA enforcement authority and the availability of judicial review to check agency action. Chapter 10 also covers new innovations in EPA enforcement policy, including the agency's Next Generation Compliance initiative.

Chapter 12's coverage of the science and laws relating to climate change law has been thoroughly updated, including comprehensive coverage of EPA's efforts to address climate change under the Clean Air Act. The chapter now includes as a principal case the Supreme Court's decision in American Electric Power Co., Inc. v. Connecticut, discussed above, and the Court's other important 2014 Clean Air Act decision, Utility Air Regulatory Group v. EPA, which addresses the legality of EPA efforts to regulate greenhouse gas emissions by stationary sources. Chapter 12 also now includes coverage of the Durban Platform, adopted at the Durban Conference of the Parties, which launched negotiations to develop a new legal protocol under the UN Framework Convention on Climate Change.

As we have done in previous editions, we have made an effort to enhance student accessibility and instructor teachability by adding new principal cases and other primary documents that we regard as good teaching vehicles, revising note materials, creating new problems, and enhancing clarity through devices such as visual aids.

We will continue to track recent developments and make our analyses available to casebook users both in the annual professors' updates made available by the publisher every summer and at the casebook's companion website. We plan to provide comprehensive updates of the entire book each summer. In addition, we will provide individual chapter updates, which may appear more frequently. To access these materials, go to the website address, http://www.aspenlawschool.com/books/glicksman_environ7e/default.asp, and click on Professor Materials. You will be asked to type in the password, which is glicksman2015. The annual updates will appear under the heading Updates and Supplemental Materials. Individual chapter updates in two formats will appear directly below the annual updates. Finally, we may post recent cases and other Supplementary Documents on a chapter-by-chapter basis.

Given the dynamic nature of environmental law, it is crucial to bring new perspectives to bear on the subject. Beginning with the third edition, several new co-authors, each with extensive experience in the field and a host of valuable insights, have been added to participate in the composition of the book. With this edition, we welcome our newest co-author, Emily Hammond, Professor of Law at the George Washington University Law School. Before joining the GW Law faculty in 2014, Professor Hammond taught at the University of Oklahoma College of Law and Wake Forest School of Law, and visited at the University of Texas, Florida State University, and the University of Georgia. Professor Hammond teaches and writes in the areas of environmental law, energy law, and administrative law. She has taken over responsibility for preparing Chapter 7, on water pollution, for this edition. A more complete biography is available at the casebook's website or on the faculty page of GW Law School's website.

We have many people to thank for this publication. We start by thanking Carol McGeehan, the initial editor for the casebook and now Publisher at Wolters Kluwer Law & Business. Carol has consistently supported our efforts over the more than thirty years of this book's lifespan. Similarly, we owe much to our current editor, Kathy Langone, who has efficiently and effectively shepherded the book through the publication process and provided all the help we requested, and more. Geoffrey Lokke did excellent work leading the copy editing process. We also thank the Deans at our respective law schools for providing both moral and financial support for our efforts, and our colleagues at other law schools whose interests overlap with ours and whose insights into environmental law have informed our work.

Finally, we would be remiss if we did not take this occasion to thank the casebook's original three authors. The first is Dan Mandelker, the Howard A. Stamper Professor of Law at the Washington University in St. Louis School of Law, and the nation's unparalleled expert on the National Environmental Policy Act. Dan continues to be responsible for preparation of Chapter 4 of this book, on NEPA. The second is Frederick R. Anderson, who passed away this year at far too early an age. Fred had an extraordinary career that included serving as the founding president of the Environmental Law Institute, the founding board chair of the Center for International Environmental Law and the Institute for Governance and Sustainable Development, dean of American University's Washington College of Law, and a partner at the law firms of McKenna Long & Aldridge and Cadwalader, Wickersham & Taft. The third founding author is A. Dan Tarlock, Distinguished Professor of Law and Director of the Program in Environmental and Energy Law at the Illinois Institute of Technology Chicago-Kent College of Law. A prolific author in the fields of environmental law, international environmental law, and water law, Dan served as the chair of a National Academy of Sciences/National Research Council committee to study water management in the western United States, was the principal report writer for the Western Water Policy Review Advisory Committee, and has been a member of a standing National Research Council committee to advise the U.S. Army Corps of Engineers on future challenges such as climate change to their missions. Professors Anderson, Mandelker, and Tarlock are among a very short list of legal academics who helped create the modern field of environmental law. Without their efforts, this book would never have existed and the current authors would not have had the opportunity to contribute to its development. We are all profoundly grateful for that opportunity and for all that the three original authors have taught us. Any errors that appear in the book are of course the responsibility of the current author group.

We encourage users of this casebook to forward their thoughts on and suggestions for improvements on any future editions to any of us. As indicated earlier in this preface, we have benefited from suggestions by casebook users in making changes to the book that appear in this edition. Our e-mail addresses are available at the casebook's website.

Robert L. Glicksman
David L. Markell
William W. Buzbee
Daniel R. Mandelker
Daniel Bodansky
Emily Hammond

Washington, D.C.
Tallahassee, Florida
Washington, D.C.
St. Louis, Missouri
Tempe, Arizona
Washington, D.C.

December 2014

ACKNOWLEDGMENTS

Any casebook is a collaborative effort among many people. Professor Glicksman would like to thank Interim Dean Gregory Maggs and Dean Blake Morant for facilitating work on this project. Professor Markell would like to thank Katie Miller, FSU Research Center, for very helpful research assistance, and Florida State University College of Law and Dean Don Weidner for research support for this project. Professor Hammond would like to thank Alina Buccella, Wake Forest University School of Law 2015. With gratitude, we would like once again to acknowledge Carol McGeehan, Publisher, Wolters Kluwer Law & Business, and our first editor, for her support. We also thank Kathy Langone, our Developmental Editor at The Froebe Group, and Geoffrey Lokke, our Production Editor, for helping us to navigate the publication process for the seventh edition.

The authors gratefully acknowledge the permissions granted to reproduce the following materials.

Bodansky, Daniel M., The Art and Craft of International Environmental Law, adapted and reprinted by permission of the publisher from the Art and Craft of International Environmental Law by Daniel Bodansky, pp. 99, 154-155, 186-187, 192, 206, 208, 210-212, 214-215, 223. Cambridge, Mass.: Harvard University Press, Copyright © 2010 by the President and Fellows of Harvard College.

Climate Change 2007: Synthesis Report. Contribution of Working Groups I, II, and III to the Fourth Assessment Report of the Intergovernmental Panel on Climate Change, Figure I.1; Figure 2.1; Figure 5.2. IPCC, Geneva, Switzerland.

Copenhagen Accord from the Report of the Conference of the Parties on its fifteenth session, held in Copenhagen from 7 to 19 December 2009. Copyright © 2009 by the United Nations Framework Convention on Climate Change (UNFCCC), www.unfccc.int.

Engel, Kirsten H. & Miller, Marc L., State Governance: Leadership on Climate Change, in Agenda for a Sustainable America (Environmental Law Institute, John Dernbach ed., 2009). Copyright © 2009 by the Environmental Law Institute ®. Reprinted with permission of ELI®.

Excerpts from SILENT SPRING by Rachel Carson. Copyright © 1962 by Rachel L. Carson. Copyright © renewed 1990 by Roger Christie. Reprinted by permission of Houghton Mifflin Company and Frances Collin, Trustee. All copying, including electronic, or re-distribution of this text, is expressly forbidden. All rights reserved.

Geoengineering Options, http://www.noc.soton.ac.uk/geo-engineering/. Reprinted with permission of Prof. Richard Lampitt, National Oceanography Centre, UK.

Hardin, Garrett, The Tragedy of the Commons, 162 Science 1243 (1968). Copyright © 1968 by the American Association for the Advancement of Science. Reprinted with permission from AAAS.

I

ENVIRONMENTAL LAW'S FOUNDATIONS

Problem 1-1

Leopold Forest is a private forest that was logged in the nineteenth century and is now a second-growth forest. The forest supports a wide variety of flora and fauna, none of which is subject to an immediate threat of extinction. Global Mining purchased the mineral rights necessary to open a mine in the forest. The mine will comply with all applicable federal, state, and local regulations, but there is substantial concern among local scientists and environmental groups that the mine may change the forest and its watershed. Some scientists think that the yellow mountain daisy community, which supports the purple-tailed hawk, will be eliminated, although no definitive scientific studies exist to support their concern. The plant and purple-tailed hawks are found throughout a four-state region, but the scientists are concerned that the local hawk community is genetically distinct due to its evolution in isolation from other hawk communities. In addition, the mine wastes will change the color of Rushing Creek from a deep blue to a gray-green and will increase the possibility of rapid algae growth near the banks. The mine will also be located between a widely used hiking trail and the Upper Rushing Creek Valley, a scenic vista that was extensively painted in the nineteenth century by the famous Saturday Painting Club, the first group of native-born romantic painters in the United States. A local environmental nongovernmental organization (NGO) is contemplating a legal action to enjoin the operation of the mine and has asked you to assess the nonstatutory legal remedies and theories of relief that might be available to it. The organization also hopes that you will consider arguments that might persuade government decision-makers to modify the mine's plans, even if you, the courts, or regulators ultimately determine that legal victory is uncertain. Your client is concerned with success in minimizing or preventing harms from the mine, not just with victory in the courts. What is your advice?

A. ENVIRONMENTAL LAW'S ROOTS AND RATIONALES

The modern environmental law frameworks that will dominate your attention in this book are primarily statutory and regulatory, with most dating from the early 1970s through 1990, and most passed by the federal government. These modern legislative frameworks did not, however, appear out of nowhere. Nor were environmental harms unknown as a legal problem before that time. Today's environmental laws did not supplant all that came before, but are built on existing frameworks and often explicitly preserve state law and, of particular importance, state common law related to environmental harms and use of environmental amenities.

But a preliminary question should be asked. Is there any need for legal intervention to deal with environmental harms? What rationales justify these modern regulatory statutes or the remedies provided by state statutes or state common law? When should an environmental lawyer or policymaker turn to statutes, regulations, common law, or perhaps arguments rooted in other disciplines, especially economics, political science, and ecology?

To set the stage for the rest of this book, this chapter introduces the reader to the foundations of environmental law. First, the chapter provides readings discussing classic rationales for why environmental harms occur, and why environmental harms should not be ignored or go unremedied by the legal system. This requires review of a handful of basic economic and political concepts that shed light on why environmental ills are so pervasive and why market actions alone are unlikely to deter or correct such harms. Economic and market factors, however, are far from the only justification for legal intervention. Of particular importance are ecological and philosophical justifications for addressing environmental harms, be they from pollution or other modifications of nature. Although less subject to easy categorization, broad-based changes in political and social perspectives also explain the increased focus during the twentieth century on conserving natural resources, discouraging waste, and addressing widespread harms associated with America's rapid industrialization. Especially since the late 1960s, polls consistently reveal broad citizen support for a cleaner environment. See Moore, Most Americans Say Government Is Doing Too Little for the Environment (Gallup News Service, April 6, 2006); Carlson, Public Priorities: Environment vs. Economic Growth: Age and Politics Influence Attitudes (Gallup, April 12, 2005); Dunlap & Scarce, Poll Trends: Environmental Problems and Protection, 55 Pub. Opinion Q. 651 (1991). The era in which polluters might assume that they had a right to pollute is long past. The question now tends to be whether limited pollution and resulting environmental harm should be allowed, along with the related question of how best to assess and limit those harms.

After exploring various rationales for legal intervention to address environmental harms, this chapter turns to long-established and still important common law means to address environmental ills. Despite the creation of the many environmental law statutes that you will study, common law remedies remain a significant part of the environmental lawyer's arsenal and a significant incentive for polluters to avoid causing environmental harms. Few environmental statutes provide monetary relief for those harmed by pollution; common law claims are a critical tool to provide redress, even if regulators fulfill their roles. Common law claims are a foundation of modern environmental law not only because of their continuing viability and importance, but also because their limitations provided a key impetus for modern regulatory statutes.

B. ENVIRONMENTALISM'S REJECTION OF EXPLOITATION EXPECTATIONS

Environmentalism can roughly be defined as the view that the modification of natural systems through resource exploitation and development has substantial and potentially adverse consequences for humankind. Environmental protection has evolved to include three broad objectives: (1) the reduction of the use of air, soil, and water media as sinks for waste disposal; (2) the protection of the public from long-term health and ecosystem degradation risks associated with exposure to toxic and other harmful substances; and (3) the conservation of natural resources and biodiversity. More recently, debates over "environmental justice" have increased sensitivity to the distributional impacts of environmental harms, as well as the distributional impacts of various environmental law regimes.

Environmentalism cuts against the grain of many central tenets and assumptions of Western civilization, which has long promoted material progress through the exploitation of nature's bounty. This change is described by the geographer Gilbert White, in Reflections on Changing Perceptions of the Earth, 19 Ann. Rev. Energy & Env't (1994):

> People around the world in the 1990s are perceiving the earth as more than a globe to be surveyed, or developed for the public good in the short term, or to be protected from threats to its well-being both human and natural. It is all of these to some degree, but has additional dimensions. People in many cultures accept its scientific description as a matter of belief. They recognize a commitment to care for it in perpetuity. They accept reluctantly the obligation to come to terms with problems posed by growth in numbers and appetites. This is not simply an analysis of economic and social consequences of political policies toward environmental matters. The roots are a growing solemn sense of the individual as part of one human family for whom the earth is its spiritual home.

Throughout history, almost all societies have characterized undeveloped nature as a storehouse of raw commodities to be exploited, manipulated, "improved," and transformed through the institutions of government or the market. In modern terms, they "commodified" nature. Undeveloped resources such as a clear stream, a rain or old-growth forest, or a mangrove swamp were not considered resource stocks because they lacked market value and society did not appreciate the functions they performed. Environmentalism teaches that we should value ecosystems either intrinsically or for the beneficial services, such as pollution reduction, provision of species habitat, and flood control, that they provide society. For reasons discussed further below, however, the relationship between ecosystem change and societally unacceptable consequences is much more complex than we thought some 30 years ago.

Environmental law professor Joseph Sax argued that judicial resistance to legal protection of the environment may spring from a refusal to see nature as something of value in its natural state. In critiquing the Supreme Court's "takings" jurisprudence, Professor Sax observed an anti-environmental animus that reflected a "transformative economy" perspective. Justices adhering to this perspective see property as existing to be modified and reworked for human benefit. An "ecological view of property, the economy of nature," would perceive land and nature as "already at work, performing important services in its unaltered state." Sax, Property Rights and the Economy of Nature: Understanding *Lucas v. South Carolina Coastal Council*, 45 Stan. L. Rev. 1433, 1442 (1993). This collision of perspectives frequently divides the Supreme Court and judges on lower and state courts and continues to divide individuals in their views about legal efforts to protect the environment.

Efforts to protect the environment, especially efforts to discourage, limit, or prohibit pollution, destructive modes of resource extraction, and profligate resource use, are often grounded in skepticism or observations that economic growth, markets, and technological progress will, if not subject to some kind of countervailing protective efforts, lead to undue harm to the environment. L. Milbrath, The World Is Relearning Its Story about How the World Works, in Environmental Politics in the International Arena 21, 24-27 (S. Kamieniecki ed., 1993) (calling such views a "New Environmental Paradigm"). Unrestrained growth creates the risk that such "life patterns will swiftly deplete resources and, more importantly, are likely to alter biogeo-chemical earth systems so that they behave unpredictably and injure life systems." Id.

Environmentalism has its roots in an array of disciplines, but most important for students of environmental law and policy is an understanding of basic concepts and terminology of both economics and ecology, as well as ethically based arguments for environmental protection. The next three sections provide an introduction to these concepts.

C.   ECONOMIC PERSPECTIVES ON ENVIRONMENTAL HARMS AND POLICY CHOICE

Problem 1-2

The Institute for Global Environmental Analysis has asked you to prepare a brief economic and legal analysis of global climate change. You are to take as a given that consumption of fossil fuels (coal, oil, and natural gas) emits CO_2 into the atmosphere and that during the twentieth century, the Earth's temperature increased by 0.5°C from these greenhouse gases. You are also to take as a given that the possible adverse impacts include temperature increases and rainfall changes from extreme flood to severe drought events, shifts in ecosystems, more severe storms, and sea level rise. As a result of increasingly frequent heat events, energy demands may rise. Drawing on the materials that follow, explain how the gases produced by energy generation and vehicles should be characterized. Does it follow from economic analysis that the emitters should be responsible for the reduction of CO_2 emissions to "safer" levels? Is the cost of curbing the emissions relevant to the first two questions? What economic arguments can you fashion for (a) why CO_2 emitters should cut back on their emissions and (b) why government intervention will likely be necessary but may be hard to prompt?

1. Introduction: Why We Pollute

When economists tried to find an explanation for the environmental problem, they looked at the same facts that philosopher Aldo Leopold did, but drew the opposite conclusion. To Leopold, whose writing is presented below, the Abrahamic concept of private property had to give way to a land ethic based on "love, respect, and admiration for land, and a high regard for its value." By "value," Leopold meant "something far broader than mere economic value; I mean value in the philosophic sense." A Sand County Almanac, at 223 (1949).

To economists, the problem is not the well-established phenomenon of private property but the opposite—the lack of clearly assigned property rights in common resources. Scarcity, and the discipline and market changes it provokes, may not even be perceived if environmental amenities and their destruction are off the ledger. Economics and ecology have provided us with powerful analyses of the roots and nature of environmental harms. Economists largely ignored adverse environmental impacts until the 1960s, but they quickly made up for lost time and have greatly influenced the public policy debate since the 1970s. The following article by biologist Garrett Hardin, which had its roots in debates over the problem of overpopulation, has substantially influenced economic and environmental thinking about the relationship between property and environmental problems. Many of its basic analytic insights also appeared in the earlier article by Scott Gordon, The Economic Theory of a Common-Property Resource: The Fishery, 62 J. Pol. Econ. 124 (1954). A number of key market imperfections that frequently are linked to environmental harms will be introduced after this classic work on the "tragedy of the commons."

HARDIN, THE TRAGEDY OF THE COMMONS
162 Science 1243, 1243-1248 (1968)

It is fair to say that most people who anguish over the population problem are trying to find a way to avoid the evils of overpopulation without relinquishing any privileges they now enjoy. They think that farming the seas or developing new strains of wheat will solve the problem—technologically. I try to show here that the solution they seek cannot be found. The population problem cannot be solved in a technical way, any more than can the problem of winning the game of tick-tack-toe.

What Shall We Maximize?

Population, as Malthus said, naturally tends to grow "geometrically," or, as we would now say, exponentially. In a finite world this means that the per capita share of the world's goods must steadily decrease. Is ours a finite world?

A fair defense can be put forward for the view that the world is infinite: or that we do not know that it is not. But, in terms of the practical problems that we must face in the next few generations with the foreseeable technology, it is clear that we will greatly increase human misery if we do not, during the immediate future, assume that the world available to the terrestrial human population is finite. "Space" is no escape.

A finite world can support only a finite population; therefore, population growth must eventually equal zero. (The case of perpetual wide fluctuations above and below zero is a trivial variant that need not be discussed.) When this condition is met, what will be the situation of mankind? Specifically, can Bentham's goal of "the greatest good for the greatest number" be realized?

No—for two reasons, each sufficient by itself. The first is a theoretical one. It is not mathematically possible to maximize for two (or more) variables at the same time. This was clearly stated by [two Princeton game theorists in 1947], but the principle is implicit in the theory of partial differential equations, dating back at least to D'Alembert (1717-1783).

The second reason springs directly from biological facts. To live, any organism must have a source of energy (for example, food). This energy is utilized for two purposes: mere maintenance and work. For man, maintenance of life requires about 1600 kilocalories a day ("maintenance calories"). Anything that he does over and above merely staying alive will be defined as work, and is supported by "work calories" which he takes in. Work calories are used not only for what we call work in common speech; they are also required for all forms of enjoyment, from swimming and automobile racing to playing music and writing poetry. If our goal is to maximize population it is obvious what we must do: We must make the work calories per person approach as close to zero as possible. No gourmet meals, no vacations, no sports, no music, no literature, no art. . . . I think that everyone will grant, without argument or proof, that maximizing population does not maximize goods. Bentham's goal is impossible.

In reaching this conclusion I have made the usual assumption that it is the acquisition of energy that is the problem. The appearance of atomic energy has led some to question this assumption. However, given an infinite source of energy, population growth still produces an inescapable problem. The problem of the acquisition of energy is replaced by the problem of its dissipation, as J. H. Fremlin has so wittily shown. The arithmetic signs in the analysis are, as it were, reversed; but Bentham's goal is still unobtainable.

The optimum population is, then, less than the maximum. The difficulty of defining the optimum is enormous; so far as I know, no one has seriously tackled this problem. Reaching an acceptable and stable solution will surely require more than one generation of hard analytical work—and much persuasion. . . .

We can make little progress in working toward optimum population size until we explicitly exorcize the spirit of Adam Smith in the field of practical demography. In economic affairs, The Wealth of Nations (1776) popularized the "invisible hand," the idea that an individual who "intends only his own gain," is, as it were, "led by an individual hand to promote . . . the public interest." . . .

The Tragedy of Freedom in a Commons

The rebuttal to the invisible hand in population control is to be found in a scenario first sketched in a little-known pamphlet in 1833 by a mathematical amateur named William Forster Lloyd (1794-1852). We may well call it "the tragedy of commons," using the word "tragedy" as the philosopher Whitehead used it: "The essence of dramatic tragedy is not unhappiness. It resides in the solemnity of the remorseless working of things." He then goes on to say, "This inevitableness of destiny can only be illustrated in terms of human life by incidents which in fact involve unhappiness. For it is only by them that the futility of escape can be made evident in the drama."

The tragedy of the commons develops in this way. Picture a pasture open to all. It is to be expected that each herdsman will try to keep as many cattle as possible on the commons. Such an arrangement may work reasonably satisfactorily for centuries because tribal wars, poaching, and disease keep the numbers of both man and beast well below the carrying capacity of the land. Finally, however, comes the day of reckoning, that is, the day when the long-desired goal of social stability becomes a reality. At this point, the inherent logic of the commons remorselessly generates tragedy.

As a rational being, each herdsman seeks to maximize his gain. Explicitly or implicitly, more or less consciously, he asks, "What is the utility to me of adding one more animal to my herd?" This utility has one negative and one positive component.

1. The positive component is a function of the increment of one animal. Since the herdsman receives all the proceeds from the sale of the additional animal the positive utility is nearly $+1$.
2. The negative component is a function of the additional overgrazing created by one more animal. Since, however, the effects of overgrazing are shared by all the herdsmen, the negative utility for any particular decisionmaking herdsman is only a fraction of 1.

Adding together the component partial utilities, the rational herdsman concludes that the only sensible course for him to pursue is to add another animal to his herd. And another; and another. But this is the conclusion reached by each and every rational herdsman sharing a commons. Therein is the tragedy. Each man is locked into a system that compels him to increase his herd without limit—in a world that is limited. Ruin is the destination toward which all men rush, each pursuing his own best interest in a society that believes in the freedom of the commons. Freedom in a commons brings ruin to all. . . .

What shall we do? We have several options. We might sell them off as private property. We might keep them as public property, but allocate the right to enter them. The allocation might be on the basis of wealth, by the use of an auction system. It might be on the basis of merit, as defined by some agreed upon standards. It might be by lottery. Or it might be on a first-come, first-served basis, administered to long queues. These, I think, are all the reasonable possibilities. They are objectionable. But we must choose—or acquiesce in the destruction of the commons that we call our National Parks.

Pollution

In a reverse way, the tragedy of the commons reappears in problems of pollution. Here it is not a question of taking out of the commons, but of putting something in—sewage, or chemical, radioactive, and heat wastes into water; noxious and dangerous fumes into the air; and distracting and unpleasant advertising signs into the line of sight. The calculations of utility are much the same as before. The rational man finds that his share of the cost of the wastes he discharges into the commons is less than the cost of purifying his wastes before releasing them. Since this is true for everyone, we are locked into a system of "fouling our own nest," so long as we behave only as independent, rational, free-enterprisers.

The tragedy of the commons as a food basket is averted by private property, or something formally like it. But the air and waters surrounding us cannot readily be fenced, and so the tragedy of the commons as a cesspool must be prevented by different means, by coercive laws or taxing devices that make it cheaper for the polluter to treat his pollutants than to discharge them untreated. We have not progressed as far with the solution of this problem as we have with the first. Indeed, our particular concept of private property, which deters us from exhausting the positive resources of the earth, favor pollution. The owner of a factory on the bank of a stream—whose property extends to the middle of the stream—often has difficulty seeing why it is not his natural right to muddy the waters flowing past his door. The law, always behind the times, requires elaborate stitching and fitting to adapt it to this newly perceived aspect of the commons. . . .

How to Legislate Temperance?

Analysis of the pollution problem as a function of population density uncovers a not generally recognized principle of morality, namely: the morality of an act is a function of the state of the system at the time it is performed. Using the commons as a cesspool does not harm the general public under frontier conditions, because there is no public; the same behavior in a metropolis is unbearable. A hundred and fifty years ago a plainsman could kill an American bison, cut out only the tongue for his dinner, and discard the rest of the animal. He was not in any important sense being wasteful. Today, with only a few thousand bison left, we would be appalled at such behavior.

NOTES ON THE TRAGEDY AND ENVIRONMENTAL POLICY

1. *Post-Hardin Thinking.* Along with Rachel Carson's Silent Spring, which is excerpted below, The Tragedy of the Commons is among the most powerful foundations of environmental law. Hardin's conclusion that commons will inevitably degrade has often been accepted as gospel by the environmental movement, but it has been challenged by political scientists and lawyers who have documented many instances of effective conservation cooperation among commons users, at least in more primitive cultures or small communities. The leading works are E. Ostrom, Governing the Commons: The Evolution of Institutions for Collective Action (1990); E. Ostrom, Rules, Games and Common Pool Resources (1994); National Research Council, Proceedings of a Conference on Common Property Resources Management (1988); and R. Ellickson, Order without Law: How Neighbors Settle Disputes (1991). Bosselman, Limitations Inherent in the Title to Wetlands at Common Law, 15 Stan. Envtl. L.J. 247 (1996), is an insightful case study of how the common law encouraged sustainable use of the fens of northeast England.

2. *Governance Issues.* The commons dilemma is often argued to provide the basis for severe government restrictions on the use of natural sinks for waste disposal or ecosystems for commodity production. But, as Professor James E. Krier has pointed out, Hardin's argument contains a contradiction: "The public has to coerce the government to coerce it, and to do this the public must organize. Yet the inability to

organize or coordinate is the problem to begin with." Krier, The Tragedy of the Commons Part Two, 15 Harv. J.L. & Pub. Pol'y 325, 338 (1992).

As revealed further in this chapter's tracing of the history of environmental protection and in Chapter 2's discussion of environmental federalism, environmental law is pervaded by complex and overlapping legal frameworks and regulatory turfs divided among federal, state, and local governments, and institutions such as legislatures, courts, and agencies. These forms of regulatory overlap, jurisdictional mismatch, and complexity can create a "regulatory commons" problem. Much as the herder in Hardin's work will fail to consider the actions of others and collective repercussions of excessive resource use, the existence of shared, overlapping, or conflicting regulatory turfs may lead both those desiring environmental protection and those who might supply it to fail to perceive the larger picture. Inaction or ineffective action may result. Hence, environmental lawyers and policymakers need to take into account not just unowned commons' natural resources, but regulatory commons where no single regulator has clear primacy over a legal ill, and, instead, many share potential responsibility. See Buzbee, Recognizing the Regulatory Commons: A Theory of Regulatory Gaps, 89 Iowa L. Rev. 1 (2003).

3. *Is Congestion the Key Variable?* Professor Carol Rose has explored many facets of environmental policy through a law and economics perspective. In Rose, Rethinking Environmental Controls: Management Strategies for Common Resources, 1991 Duke L.J. 1, she suggests that the "commons" problem is not the only key variable. She adds congestion as another important cause of environmental problems, stating that some "[c]ongestible resources such as fishing areas are typically the subjects of environmental problems. Their common use seems unproblematic under conditions of low consumption; under these circumstances there is plenty for everyone, and so no one tries to patrol additional fishing. But at some point, if increased fishing makes the resource perceptibly scarcer, and perhaps even threatens the resource with ruin, we collectively start to feel the pinch." Id. at 6-7.

4. *Commons, Property, and the Liberal Tradition.* Most environmental thinking adheres to the liberal tradition and seeks the least intrusive invasion of private property and individual liberty to remedy a scientifically defined problem. See Sagoff, Can Environmentalists Be Liberals? Jurisprudential Foundations of Environmentalism, 16 Envtl. L. 755 (1986); Wandesforde-Smith, Learning from Experience, Planning for the Future: Beyond the Parable (and Paradox) of Environmentalists as Pin-Striped Pantheists, 13 Ecology L.Q. 715 (1986); and Westbrook, Liberal Environmental Jurisprudence, 27 U.C. Davis L. Rev. 619 (1994). W. Ophuls, Ecology and the Politics of Scarcity (1977), dissented from this discourse by suggesting a Platonic alternative: "During the transition from any form of steady state one can envision it would be imperative to use physical resources as efficiently as possible, and this would probably mean greater centralization and expert control in the short term, even if the long-term goal is a technologically simple, decentralized society favorable to a democratic politics."

The second edition of W. Ophuls & A. S. Boyan, Jr., Ecology and the Politics of Scarcity Revisited: The Unraveling of the American Dream 3 (1992), reiterated the book's original thesis that we must move to a steady-state society because "the external reality of ecological scarcity has cut the ground out from under our political system, making reformist politics of ecological management all but useless." But, in an afterword, Ophuls argued that this premise does not lead to the need for antidemocratic solutions. He drew on De Tocqueville's distinction between government and administration and argued that we need more government but not administration. The book called for "[a] decentralized Jeffersonian policy of relatively small, intimate, locally autonomous, and self-governing communities rooted in the land (or other local ecological resource) and affiliated at the federal level only for a few clearly defined purposes." Id. at 302-303. More recently, environmental writers such William McKibben have called for a fundamental change in the economy and modes of production to stem environmental ills. W. McKibben, Oil and Honey: The Education of an Unlikely Environmentalist (2013). It is far from clear, however, that this sort of vision is broadly embraced. During the current era of divided and polarized government, probably the most certain prediction is that any environmentally motivated proposal, even one rooted in strong science or other evidence of need, will have many supporters but also be met with vocal opposition.

5. *Hardin and Pessimism.* As you will see in the succeeding chapters, the United States has responded to the problem of environmental degradation primarily by regulating private choice through prohibitions on major types of pollution or landscape degradation. It has not concentrated on the prohibition of small, cumulative consumer choices. In general, it has simply avoided the problem of population control and any talk of limits. But see G. Hardin, Living Within Limits: Ecology, Economics, and Population Taboos (1993). Nonetheless, the environmental movement has at times had an apocalyptic tone to it. See, e.g., Boulding, The Economics of the Coming Spaceship Earth, in Environmental Quality in a Growing Economy (H. Jarrett ed., 1971). D.H. Meadows et al., The Limits to Growth (1972), argued that the exponential growth rates of population and of industrial production (and thus pollution) would soon press the finite limits of the planet Earth, with catastrophic declines in the welfare of all. The models used in The Limits to Growth were based on J. Forrester, World Dynamics (1971). The Limits to Growth produced a spate of critical responses. See, e.g., Kaysen, The Computer That Printed Out W*O*L*F, 50 Foreign Aff. 660 (1972), and P. Passell & L. Ross, The Retreat from Riches: Affluence and Its Enemies (1973). (A similar document, A Blueprint for Survival, appeared in the January 1972 issue of British Ecologist.) The collapse thesis was thoroughly reevaluated in Thinking About the Future (1973), edited by H.S.D. Cole, C. Freeman, M. Jahoda & K.L.R. Pavitt, an interdisciplinary team from the University of Sussex, in England. Heller, Coming to Terms with Growth and the Environment, in Energy, Economic Growth and the Environment 3 (S. Schurr ed., 1972), is a thoughtful examination of the positive relationship that might exist between economic growth and pollution control. Krier & Gillette, The Uneasy Case for Technological Optimism, 84 Mich. L. Rev. 405 (1985), present a thoughtful argument for reopening the debate about the ability of technology, as promoted and constrained by markets and government intervention, to solve environmental problems.

2.   The Economics Model of Environmental Problems: Key Concepts

Lawyers think lawsuits and regulation. Hardin emerged from training as a biologist, but melded in his work both biological understanding and logic rooted in a focus on incentives and markets. Economists think markets, and analyze environmental ills by seeing how and why markets contribute to these ills and invariably influence efforts to find solutions. Early economists who turned their attention to environmental quality problems started from the premise that environmental quality was simply another example of a resource that had become scarce because demand exceeded supply. For economists, the demand (or taste) for clean air, clean water, minimal risks, or biodiversity is the same as the demand for any other resource, be it mountain bikes, blue corn chips, or Starbucks coffee: How much clean air, clean water, or wilderness should there be, compared with alternative possibilities such as industrial waste disposal sinks, mines, or ski resorts? Economists also generally agree that in an ideal world these resource allocation choices would be made most efficiently and fairly through the operation of the free-market economy. See H. Macaulay & B. Yandle, Environmental Use and the Market (1977). Consumers would vote with their dollars to allocate resources between biodiversity and ski resorts or between levels of risk exposure just as they decide between Coke and Pepsi. However, few people, if any, assert that the market is currently capable of doing this.

Several sorts of market flaws contribute to environmental harms, as well as to efforts to impose remedial measures through political and legal means. Although many environmentalists criticize excessive faith in the power of markets to correct environmental harms, economic concepts actually both explain the pervasiveness of environmental harms and point toward legally based solutions.

a.   Key Terms

A key concept to grasp is that of *externalities*. If you imagine a typical pollution setting, where a factory's emissions cause harm to its neighbors, an externality is implicated. In this setting, we confront a "negative externality," which economists define "as a human-made, un-bargained-for, negative element of the environment. Pollution is termed an externality because it imposes costs on people who are external to the transaction between the producer and consumer of the polluting product." E. Goodstein, Economics and Environment 32-33 (1995). Hence, an economist would not regard the harm that a person caused to herself, or the harm that a person was exposed to as a result of a consensual, informed bargaining process, as an externality. If environmental goods such as air or water may be polluted or used without any cost to the user, economists predict that too much pollution or excessive use will follow. As Goodstein states, if such goods are "'underpriced,' . . . [b]ecause no one owns these resources, in the absence of government regulation or legal protection for pollution victims, businesses will use them up freely, neglecting the external costs imposed on others." In contrast, if such goods were priced such that a polluter had to pay for the harm caused, there might still be pollution, but the activity would no longer be imposing an externality on others. Economists speak of "negative" externalities, in the sense of uncompensated harms, and "positive" externalities, where someone may create a good enjoyed by many, but for which the creator is unpaid. Hence, pollution emissions are often externalities because "those who produce the emissions do not pay for the privilege, and those who are harmed are not compensated." W. Nordhaus, The Climate Casino: Risk, Uncertainty, and Economics for a Warming World 6 (2013).

But externalities and the tragedy of the commons are far from the only key economic concepts important to understanding why environmental harms occur. Efficient markets also depend on market participants having *perfect information* about market choices. Perfect information is, of course, an aspiration and a near impossibility in the real world. Still, environmentally harmful activities are pervaded by information flaws and uncertainties. Pollution producers may not know who or what will be harmed, victims of pollution typically cannot even figure out who caused the harms, and the impacts of contact with environmental pollution are frequently nearly impossible to calculate, if noticed at the time at all. Contact with a pollutant may be followed by a period in which the harms remain latent. Scientific complexities and uncertainties make it very difficult to secure anything more than tentative information about environmental impacts. Deriving an appropriate price for environmental harms, let alone determining who should be part of such bargaining, is also rife with uncertainties.

Furthermore, markets will not function appropriately in allocating goods and services if *transaction costs* prevent people from getting together and coming to consensual solutions. Where pollution affects many people in uncertain ways, high transaction costs, such as costs of negotiation, figuring out appropriate solutions, and finding people who will cooperate, are a substantial hurdle to market solutions.

As political economist Mancur Olson established in his renowned book, The Logic of Collective Action (1965), the high costs of *collective action* explain both many environmental ills and political failures to provide redress. The many victims of pollution are unlikely to act together because they individually often experience small amounts of harm, and the costs of transacting with each other will dwarf any possible recovery. Pollution victims are thus unlikely to bargain for compensation through the market, but they are also unlikely to act collectively in political or legal arenas for the same reason. Relatedly, because environmentally harmful activity usually affects many, those affected will be tempted to hope that others will take the laboring oar and confront the actor causing the harm. This phenomenon is known as the *free rider* problem.

On the other hand, as Olson discusses, those with a concentrated interest in a particular approach, especially potential regulation, are likely to see both pollution and its regulation as creating substantial benefits and potential costs. Producers of risk also tend to be fewer in number and to have a shared interest. The net effect of collective action dynamics is that victims of pollution are far less likely to act effectively in political settings, while those creating risk will be nearly certain to act, due to the higher stakes and relatively small transaction costs associated with acting collectively. The disadvantage faced by victims of environmental harms is exacerbated by the free rider temptation to rely on others' efforts. Still, where an environmental ill is truly localized, is traceable, and causes determinate effects on a small number of actors, and both the causer of harms and the victims are known to each other, market solutions are possible. The problem is that such circumstances are rare.

Despite the market flaws that contribute to environmental ills and confound efforts to find political solutions, economics-oriented scholars and policymakers still tend to look at environmental problems through a market-based lens and seek solutions that use or mimic markets. Since economic activity in markets causes most environmental harms, it would indeed be myopic to ignore the workings of markets and motivations and incentives of market actors in devising solutions. Still, some property rights advocates with a strong animus against regulatory or bureaucratic solutions to environmental ills advocate discarding much of modern environmental law in favor of reliance on markets, coupled with reliance on common law litigation. See T. Anderson & D. Leal, Free Market Environmentalism (2001). The viability of such prescriptions has been strongly challenged, but has nevertheless influenced public discourse. For a symposium issue presenting and critiquing such arguments, see Symposium—Free Market Environmentalism, 15 Harv. J.L. & Pub. Pol'y 297-538 (1992).

Economic analysis of environmental problems is powerful because it not only purports to explain the cause of the problems, but also tends to provide a strong justification for legislative, regulatory, or judicial intervention to solve the problems. Proponents also often see economic insights as useful in determining the means or instruments of intervention, tending to champion regulatory methods that provide flexibility and incentives for improvement. Further, because welfare economics accepts the legitimacy of current patterns of production and consumption, neither its explanations nor its prescriptions for change are radical. Classic environmental regulation is well within the liberal political tradition because it seeks to restrict individual autonomy only when other individuals are seriously harmed by pollution. See Westbrook, Liberal Environmental Jurisprudence, 27 U.C. Davis L. Rev. 619 (1994).

Yet, although the application of economic analysis is increasingly accepted and often legislatively mandated, economic analysis remains controversial, posing two distinct questions. First, how effectively can economic prescriptions be applied? No matter how elegant various explanations and models are, it is not always certain that the information necessary to utilize the models can be collected in order to produce resource allocations superior to those being made by means of messy political and administrative processes. See Cole & Grossman, When Is Command-and-Control Efficient? Institutions, Technology, and the Comparative Efficiency of Alternative Regulatory Regimes for Environmental Protection, 1999 Wis. L. Rev. 887. The second and broader question is, how relevant and helpful is economic analysis compared with other theories and approaches to environmental protection? See D. Driesen, The Economic Dynamics of Environmental Law (2003). For a recent work melding a critique of economic approaches to regulation and literature on commons regulation, see Sinden, The Tragedy of the Commons and the Myth of a Private Property Solution, 78 U. Colo. L. Rev. 533 (2007).

b. Coase's Insights and the "Polluter Pays" Principle

Can one conclude that if a negative environmental externality exists, the discharger must assume financial responsibility for all of the social costs of his activity? In short, is it clear that the polluter must pay? A few economists and many lawyers have drawn this conclusion from new welfare economics, but this normative conclusion was challenged in 1960 in a seminal article that is central to economic analyses of environmental ills.

In The Problem of Social Cost, 3 J.L. & Econ. 1 (1960), Nobel Laureate Ronald Coase argued that it is wrong to think in terms of only one party causing harm to another. According to Coase, the "harmful effects" problem is "a problem of a reciprocal nature" rather than a unilateral one. In his view, "harmful effects" arise when two parties whose resource uses are incompatible compete for the right to use the same resource. Among his key insights is that if the government intervenes and prevents a polluter or cattle rancher (or other causer of harmful effects) from causing harm to a neighbor, then the polluter or cattle rancher is harmed. "The real question that has to be decided is: Should A be allowed to harm B or should B be allowed to harm A." He recast the challenge as one about "avoid[ing] the more serious harm." Coase contended that, viewed from a societal perspective, competing parties are likely to negotiate an efficient allocation of resources if there are "no costs in carrying out market transactions." Id. at 15.

Coase then, however, devoted substantial attention to the reason transaction costs will exist, and in fact will often be the key determinant in whether consensual bargaining will result in socially efficient outcomes. Especially in settings with numerous parties, difficult bargaining points, and an array of activities, bargaining solutions are unlikely. He did not concede that a governmental solution is invariably the answer. Anticipating, if not giving birth to, a more skeptical view of regulation that is prevalent today, as well as to later comparative institutional perspectives, Coase stated that "[a]ll solutions have costs and there is no reason to suppose that government regulation is called for simply because the problem is not well handled by the market or the firm." Id. at 18. For an introduction to "comparative institutional analysis," which calls for comparison of how different institutions will address social ills, see N. Komesar, Imperfect Alternatives: Choosing Institutions in Law, Economics and Public Policy (1994).

Coase's insights have had a wide impact but have not gone unchallenged. Diverse lessons have been drawn from this work. Many advocates of market solutions to social ills focus on Coase's view that without transaction costs, parties will bargain to achieve efficient outcomes. Since some transaction costs will always exist, the question is how often bargaining outcomes will be reached without legal intervention. Coase himself appears to have been of several minds about this, sometimes seeming to assume that consensual bargaining would typically occur and offer the best solution to the "harmful effects" problem, and in other settings claiming that economists had overlooked the magnitude of the transaction costs problem. He stated in a more recent book that "[t]he world of zero transaction costs has often been described as a Coasian world. Nothing could be further from the truth." R.H. Coase, The Firm, the Market, and the Law 174-179 (1988). As Coase further explained:

> The reason why economists went wrong was their theoretical system did not take into account a factor which is essential if one wishes to analyze the effect of a change in the law on the allocation of resources. This missing factor is the existence of transaction costs. . . . Once we take transaction costs into account, the various parties have no incentive (or a reduced incentive) to disclose the information needed to formulate an optimal liability rule. Indeed, this information may not even be known to them, since those who have no incentive to disclose information have no reason for discovering what it is. Information needed for transactions which cannot be carried out will not be collected.

The law plays a critical role in determining the baseline situation and the transaction costs associated with efforts (if any) to reach a consensual solution. In Coase's words, "what incentives will be lacking depends on what the law is, since this determines what contractual arrangements will have to be made to bring about those actions which maximize the value of production. The result brought about by different legal rules is not intuitively obvious and depends on the facts of each particular case." For discussion of whether Coase has often been misconstrued, see Katz, The Strategic Structure of Offer and Acceptance: Game Theory and the Law of Contract Formation, 89 Mich. L. Rev. 215, 219 (1990).

The implications and soundness of Coase's insights remain the subject of considerable debate. Mishan, Pareto Optimality and the Law, 19 Oxford Econ. Papers (n.s.) 255 (1967), and Mishan, The Economics of Disamenity, 14 Nat. Resources J. 55 (1974), mount a detailed technical argument to show that an optimal allocation depends on the existing assignment of rights ("existing law") and that the costs of reaching an ideal solution also depend on the existing assignment of rights. For further critique, see J. Coleman, Markets, Morals and the Law 76-81 (1988).

However, the fundamental insight of Coase—that the presence of externalities does not automatically justify government regulation—has had a profound effect on environmental law. Perhaps for this reason, the principle that the polluter must pay "has not received the broad geographic and subject matter support over the long term accorded to the principle of preventive action, or attention accorded the precautionary principle in recent years." P. Sands, 1 Principles of International Environmental Law 213 (1995). Principle 16 of the 1992 Rio Declaration states only that national authorities should endeavor to promote the internalization of environmental costs and the use of economic instruments, taking into account the approach that the polluter should, in principle, bear the costs of pollution, with due regard to the public interest and without distorting international trade and investment.

If you are advising a federal or state policymaker about whether to regulate a new sort of environmental risk, how does Coase's analysis influence your approach to the problem? At a minimum, these economic concepts and Coase's arguments should lead you to see several potential policy pathways, rather than any single obvious answer. Identify the key variables you would want to examine.

c. Nonuse Values and Incommensurability: Are Some Values Extrinsic or Not Capable of Measurement?

Suppose that the primary external cost of an activity is that it forecloses enjoyment of a scenic vista. If no market exists to measure the opportunity cost of the activity, is the degradation of the vista an external cost that should be internalized? Traditionally, these costs were ignored because no market existed to value them. Is willingness to pay the only criterion for allocating resources? Neo-welfare economics assumes that consumers can measure their preferences rationally when confronted with a range of choices. Measurement is possible because properly established market prices will accurately reveal the value a consumer attaches to a product. Economists now accept the principle that the dichotomy between monetized and nonmonetized costs is not economically rational. The decision to develop or degrade a resource has an opportunity cost—the value forgone by resource development. This value can be reflected in individual preferences and thus is equivalent to preferences revealed through the market. The problem is the measurement of these costs, not whether or not they exist.

In a seminal article, Conservation Reconsidered, 57 Am. Econ. Rev. 777 (1967), John Krutilla advanced the argument that nonuse values exist and can and should be measured. He argued that public intervention to preserve unique natural environments, especially when development would produce irreversible change, was economically justified in order to prevent future shortages caused by a progressive change in taste favoring amenities. It was rational to "purchase" a present option for future use:

> Another reason for questioning the allocative efficiency of the market for the case in hand has been recognized only more recently. This involves the notion of option demand. This demand is characterized as a willingness to pay for retaining an option to use an area or facility that would be difficult or impossible to replace and for which no close substitute is available. Moreover, such a demand may exist even though there is no current intention to use the area or facility in question and the option may never be exercised. If an option value exists for rare or unique occurrences of nature, but there is no means by which a private resource owner can appropriate this value, the resulting allocation may be questioned. [Id. at 780.]

Krutilla subsequently explored the technical problems of developing a dynamic model of valuing option demand and tried to test it by applying it to several case studies.

Resource economists now generally argue that the appropriate measure of the value of a resource is its *total economic value*, which is the sum of its use and nonuse values. Many continue to debate whether these values are in fact "real" compared with pollution damage. However, the debate has shifted from the legitimacy of nonuse values to the comparative merits of different measurement techniques (see Chapter 9, section E). See M. Freeman III, The Measurement of Environmental Resource Values: Theory and Methods (1993).

d. Ethics or Economics?

Is willingness to pay the correct measure of the optimal level of environmental quality? In a fundamental attack on the adequacy of economic approaches to environmental protection, Sagoff, Economic Theory and Environmental Law, 79 Mich. L. Rev. 1393 (1985), argues that public and private preferences are two different logical categories. "The economist asks of objective beliefs a question that is appropriate only to subjective wants." In Principles of Federal Pollution Control Law, 71 Minn. L. Rev. 19 (1986), Sagoff attempts a synthesis of the moral and economic justifications for environmental law and argues that environmental statutes seek to eliminate moral evils, but that economic values operate as a legitimate constraint, and the degree of the constraint is a function of the ethical duty. Thus, costs are less relevant when the government seeks to reduce severe toxic risks and more relevant when it seeks to reduce *de minimis* hazards and background risks.

Even if Sagoff is right, should economic considerations still play a role in addressing environmental harms? Can economic variables be considered without undercutting other justifications for environmental protection? How should policymakers balance economic considerations and other variables? Will policymakers ever be able to ignore markets and economic factors?

e. Cost-Benefit Analysis and Economic Perspectives

The role of economic analysis is especially controversial in the use of cost-benefit analysis (CBA) to evaluate risk minimization standards. Cost-benefit analysis is a formal method of comparing the costs and benefits of public action to determine if public actions or funds result in a net efficiency gain or represent an unjustified subsidy or deadweight loss. Such analysis can be used either to advocate environmental protection or to stifle regulation. Its very underpinnings and supposed neutrality have been the subjects of fierce debate over the past 25 years. For an array of readings concerning CBA, see Chapter 3, section C. CBA is rooted in economic perspectives on regulatory policy because of its focus on costs and market repercussions. Gunningham & Young, Toward Optimal Environmental Policy: The Case of Biodiversity Conservation, 24 Ecology L.Q. 243, 268 (1997), quote a study estimating that 90 cents of every dollar invested in biodiversity conservation protection is spent on undoing perverse incentives to destroy biodiversity. For further introduction to the topic, see F. Ackerman & L. Heinzerling, Priceless: On Knowing the Price of Everything and the Value of Nothing (2004); Driesen, The Societal Cost of Environmental Regulation: Beyond Administrative Cost-Benefit Analysis, 24 Ecology L.Q. 545 (1997); Heinzerling, Regulatory Costs of Mythic Proportions, 107 Yale L.J. 1981 (1998); and Heinzerling, Environmental Law and the Present Future, 87 Geo. L.J. 2025 (1999).

f. What if "Rational Actor" Assumptions are Wrong? The Growing Influence of Behavioral Economics

Much of the economics literature discussed above works from a basic "rational actor" model, assuming that individuals and often institutions will rationally seek to maximize something for their own benefit, and typically that something is wealth. Market-based transactions are part of that analysis, as are assumptions that individuals will act rationally in their self-interest in the market and in political venues. (Modern scholarship on market and especially political behavior tends to assume a broader array of motivations than just wealth maximization.) However, starting with psychological studies and publications dating back to the 1980s, psychologists have found that people are often far from the rational actors they have long been assumed to be. Much of this work traces back to studies and publications of psychologists Amos Tversky and Daniel Kahneman, but legal scholars have further refined these insights' implications for environmental law. This body of work is variously labeled "behavioral economics," or "behavioral law and economics," or "cognitive psychology." Of particular relevance to environmental law are several tendencies that further explain why environmental harms can be hard to address, especially through legislative change. People fear loss more than they value potential gains, and tend to be reluctant to surrender what they have. These linked tendencies are referred to as *loss aversion* and the *status quo bias*. People often also have difficulty in rationally comparing risks, especially low probability risks. And in assessing a choice, people tend to rely on whatever most easily comes to mind, and that often is the most recent or available similar experience or choice. This tendency is referred to as the *availability heuristic*. The implications of these and other related psychological tendencies vary depending on the environmental setting or source of risk, but they further explain why fomenting major change, especially to protect the environment, is difficult. These discoveries and insights have also been used to suggest regulatory strategies that anticipate these tendencies. For a concise distillation of many of these insights and citation to foundational scholarship, see Rachlinski, The Psychology of Climate Change, 2000 U. Ill. L. Rev. 299, 303-313. Sunstein & Reisch, Automatically Green: Behavioral Economics and Environmental Protection, 38 Harv. Envtl. L. Rev. 127 (2014), discuss the use

of behavioral economics to create default rules to address environmental policy problems. See also Sunstein, The Storrs Lectures: Behavioral Economics and Paternal-
ism, 122 Yale L.J. 1826 (2013) (discussing "behaviorally informed regulation"). For
further explorations of these insights, see Chapter 12, section B.

D.   THE ENVIRONMENTAL LESSONS OF ECOLOGY

All disciplines that approach environmental problems systematically have been greatly
influenced by the science of ecology. The word "ecology," derived from the Greek word
oikos ("house" or "place to live"), was not coined until 1869, and the science of ecology
dates from only 1890. Ecology has to do with the structure and function of nature,
considered in a grand perspective. Initially, the science was attractive to policymakers
looking for a quick fix because it was thought to offer scientific laws, or a fairly certain
promise of them, that would translate directly into moral and hence legal imperatives. In
his introduction to a collection of essays, Paul Shepard expressed this idea as follows:
"Ecology may testify as often against our uses of the world, even against conservation
techniques of control and management for sustained yield, as it does for them. Although
ecology may be treated as a science, its greater and overriding wisdom is universal."
Introduction: Ecology and Man—A Viewpoint, in The Subversive Science: Essays
Toward an Ecology of Man 1, 4-5 (P. Shepard & D. McKinley eds., 1969).

However, ecology as a science was ill prepared to realize its potential when the
environmental decade began. Before then, ecology was a nonprestigious branch of
learning. True, it boasted some brilliant scientists and some gifted, almost poetic,
writers, but its focus on systems and large units of analysis became increasingly out
of step with other scientific fields' study of smaller and smaller units of analysis. Odum,
A New Ecology for the Coast, in Coastal Alert: Scientists Speak Out 145 (T. Jackson &
D. Reische eds., 1981). Carpenter, The Scientific Basis of NEPA—Is It Adequate?, 6
Envtl. L. Rep. 50,014 (1976); and Carpenter, Ecology in Court, and Other Disap-
pointments of Environmental Science and Environmental Law, 15 Nat. Resources
Law. 573 (1983), are useful summaries of the gap between the information demands of
regulation and available research. Sagoff, Ethics, Ecology, and the Environment:
Integrating Science and Law, 56 Tenn. L. Rev. 77 (1988), is a thorough review of
the debates within ecology about its mission.

Law has a knack for adopting an idea from another discipline just as the idea is
being questioned and rejected in the discipline. This happened with ecology. Ecology
was attractive because the idea that ecosystems had a natural equilibrium state
provided a normative basis for much of environmental law, from environmental
impact assessment to pollution control. In his widely influential book, Fundamentals
of Ecology 89 (2d ed. 1959), Eugene Odum warned that

> tinkering with basic ecosystems of the world can result either in a glorious future for
> mankind, or in his complete destruction if too many large-scale mistakes are made.
> Although nature has remarkable resilience, the limits of homeostatic mechanisms can
> easily be exceeded by the actions of man. When treated sewage is introduced into a
> stream at a moderate rate, the system is able to "purify itself" and return to the previous
> condition within a comparatively few miles downstream. If the pollution is great or if
> toxic substances for which no natural homeostatic mechanisms have been evolved are

included, the stream may be permanently altered or even destroyed as far as usefulness to man is concerned.

However, the idea of a natural, static or equilibrium state of nature is no longer accepted in ecology. After providing an excerpt from Rachel Carson's hugely influential work that draws on ecological understandings to warn of the broad, systemic harms of chemicals such as DDT, used especially to control pests, we summarize the development of the idea that ecosystems were once naturally in equilibrium, and recent theories that substantially modify this idea.

RACHEL CARSON, SILENT SPRING
1-3, 277-278, 295-297 (1962) (Houghton Mifflin 1994 Ed.)

[As mentioned later in this chapter's tracing of the arc of this country's environmental protection efforts, virtually every historian and scholar of environmentalism mentions Carson's book as being one of several factors that led to a new and widespread concern with environmental protection during the 1960s and 1970s. This excerpt provides just a short portion of her dramatic presentation and clear message against the excessive use of pesticides.]

I. A Fable for Tomorrow

There was once a town in the heart of America where all life seemed to live in harmony with its surroundings. Then a strange blight crept over the area and everything began to change. Some evil spell had settled on the community; mysterious maladies swept the flocks of chickens; the cattle and sheep sickened and died. Everywhere was a shadow of death. The farmers spoke of much illness among their families. In the town the doctors had become more and more puzzled by new kinds of sickness appearing among their patients. There had been several sudden and unexplained deaths, not only among adults but even among children, who would be stricken suddenly while at play and die within a few hours.

There was a strange stillness. The birds, for example—where had they gone? Many people spoke of them, puzzled and disturbed. The feeding stations in the backyards were deserted. The few birds seen anywhere were moribund; they trembled violently and could not fly. It was a spring without voices. . . .

No witchcraft, no enemy action had silenced the rebirth of new life in this stricken world. The people had done it themselves. A grim specter has crept upon us almost unnoticed, and this imagined tragedy may easily become a stark reality we all shall know.

What has already silenced the voices of spring in countless towns in America? This book is an attempt to explain. . . .

17. The Other Road

We stand now where two roads diverge. But unlike the roads in Robert Frost's familiar poem, they are not equally fair. The road we have long been traveling is deceptively easy, a smooth superhighway on which we progress with great speed, but at its end lies disaster. The other fork of the road—the one "less traveled by"—offers our last, our only chance to reach a destination that assures the preservation of our earth.

The choice, after all, is ours to make. If, having endured much, we have at last asserted our "right to know," and if, knowing, we have concluded that we are being asked to take senseless and frightening risks, then we should no longer accept the counsel of those who tell us that we must fill our world with poisonous chemicals; we should look about and see what other course is open to us.

A truly extraordinary variety of alternatives to the chemical control of insects is available. Some are already in use and have achieved brilliant success. Others are in the stage of laboratory testing. Still others are little more than ideas in the minds of imaginative scientists, waiting for the opportunity to put them to the test. All have this in common: they are biological solutions, based on understanding of the living organisms they seek to control, and of the whole fabric of life to which these organisms belong. . . .

Through all these new, imaginative, and creative approaches to the problem of sharing our earth with other creatures there runs a constant theme, the awareness that we are dealing with life—with living populations and all their pressures and counter-pressures, their surges and recessions. Only by taking account of such life forces and by cautiously seeking to guide them into channels favorable to ourselves can we hope to achieve a reasonable accommodation between the insect hordes and ourselves.

NOTE

Carson's book forced citizens and policymakers to consider whether insects, often considered pests deserving of extirpation, needed to be protected, and whether measures to control insects posed equal or greater risks than the insects themselves. Although ecological understandings have radically changed in recent decades, Carson's call for caution and "taking into account such life forces" remains a central tenet of environmentalism today. As you read further into this textbook, note how many environmental amenities protected by the law were once viewed as nuisances worthy of destruction to improve the human condition. Take note, as well, how much judicial resistance to environmental protection measures may spring from judges who are reluctant to toss aside their preconceptions about what kind of natural environments provide value and deserve protection. See Chapter 5 (regarding endangered species protection), Chapter 7 (regarding wetlands protection), and Chapter 8 (regarding chemical, pesticide, and toxic waste regulation).

BOSSELMAN & TARLOCK, THE INFLUENCE OF ECOLOGICAL SCIENCE ON AMERICAN LAW: AN INTRODUCTION
69 Chi.-Kent L. Rev. 847, 854-856, 861-862 (1994)

[The vision of ecology embraced in the 1960s derives from the work of two botanists working in Nebraska during the progressive era: Roscoe Pound, who migrated into law and became one of the towering figures of American jurisprudence, and Frederick Clements. Pound and Clements pioneered the use of the "quadrant" method to survey vegetation patterns on the Nebraska prairie; this work led to a static concept of the landscape that influenced both ecology and the emerging discipline of city planning.]

Clements liked to label his theory of ecology as succession, and he wrote extensively about natural processes by which one plant community replaces another in successive waves. But the part of his theory that had the greatest influence on public policy was not succession itself, but his contention that succession eventually would end in a climax state, at which point succession would cease because the landscape had reached its natural condition of equilibrium. Each plant and animal species would then occupy its niche in perpetual harmony. Of course, fire, flood, or other natural event might disrupt such harmony, but in the long run it would not matter because the process of succession would begin again and eventually return to the climax condition.

The idea of climax and equilibrium fell on fertile ground. For centuries, many theologically inclined students of science had inferred a balance of nature, divinely provided until the disrupters of the Garden of Eden bungled things. They argued that humans should search to fit themselves into the framework of natural processes so that a condition of permanent stability could be re-established. . . .

The idea of climax coincided nicely with the field observations of those biological scientists who were increasingly taking up residence in the more newly settled regions of the country and who, because they could obtain little historical data about landscape changes in their areas, had to rely on snapshot observations, the value of which would be enhanced if it could be assumed that the natural areas that they observed were representative of a permanent climax condition. . . .

The idea that the plants and animals living in a particular area formed an interdependent community was a dramatic breakthrough at the beginning of the twentieth century when most people had been educated to differentiate elements of the biota only by the place of the individual species on the "great chain of being." By the 1930s, however, some ecologists began to question whether even Clements and the other community ecologists had been thinking on too small a scale. Still, the idea of a stable, functioning system remained.

The concept of an ecosystem as a functioning, holistic, and inherently stable system vulnerable to serious and long-term insults from a wide variety of human activities drives the biodiversity branch of modern environmental law as well as a substantial part of the case against toxic pollutants. This ecosystem focus defined the distinctiveness of ecology as a science and provided a concrete, visible rationale for environmental regulation. The story of the idea's triumph is a fascinating example of the power of paradigms which resonate with deeply held non-scientific values to capture the imagination of scientists. It is also a story of the strengths and weaknesses of tying regulatory justifications and resource management programs to science when the science is still in the theoretical and experimental stage.

The ecosystem paradigm replaced Clements' theory that plant communities were an organism rather than a system of individual plants responding to various stimuli. A British ecologist floated the ecosystem concept as a theory in 1935, and within fifteen years it became an established scientific paradigm. Sir Alfred George Tansley, a distinguished Oxbridge ecologist and longtime friend and follower of Clements, was impressed with the progress of physics at the Cavendish Laboratory in Cambridge and proposed a conception, the ecosystem, to focus the science on a system which permitted nonprogressive vegetational change. "From Tansley's new 'systematic' point of view, systems—not organisms—underwent evolution." An ecosystem was defined as the whole system (in the sense of physics), including not only the organism-complex, but also the whole complex of physical factors forming what we call the environment of the biome—the habitat factors in the widest sense. Succession became a process rather than an end-state.

Tansley's shift from an organism to a system also carried with it the longstanding scientific belief that systems tended toward equilibrium. The idea of a "holistic . . . ecological concept that combined living organisms and the physical environment into a system" was a theory in the grand scientific tradition: it was not based on field observations. Two American ecologists, Ralph Lindeman and Eugene Odum, took the next step and made Tansley's theory operational. In so doing, they paved the way for the shift in environmental discourse from the aesthetic and spiritual to the scientific. The two modes of analysis had long been intertwined, but the case for what we now call ecosystem preservation was primarily made on aesthetic or moral grounds. For example, in a 1930 article, Wilderness Esthetics, Robert Marshall, one of the major proponents of wilderness preservation, contrasted the "dynamic beauty" of primitive areas to the static beauty of a Gothic cathedral and argued that "wilderness furnishes perhaps the best opportunity for pure esthetic enjoyment."

The ecosystem concept was made operational in Madison, Wisconsin—a historic center of applied progressivism in the United States. A University of Wisconsin ecologist, Ralph Lindeman, applied the ecosystem concept to the study of a Wisconsin lake and developed the building blocks of modern ecology "such as food webs, food chains, trophic levels, productivity, metabolism, energy flow, and ecological succession."

Ecologists now follow a nonequilibrium paradigm. In Discordant Harmonies: A New Ecology for the Twenty-first Century 189-190 (Oxford University Press 1990), Daniel Botkin, a leading proponent of the new ecology, captures well several key components of this new nonequilibrium paradigm:

> [W]e understand, in spite of our wishes, that nature moves and changes and involves risks and uncertainties and that our judgments of our own actions must be made against this moving image.
>
> There are ranges within which life can persist, and changes that living systems must undergo in order to persist. We can change structural aspects of life within the acceptable ranges. Those changes that are necessary to the continuation of life we must allow to occur, or substitute for them at huge cost the qualities that otherwise would have been achieved. We can engineer nature at nature's rate and in nature's ways; we must be wary when we engineer nature at an unnatural rate and in novel ways. To conserve well is to engineer within the rule of natural changes, patterns, and ambiguities; to engineer well is to conserve, to maintain the dynamics of the living systems. The answer to the question about the human role in nature depends on time, culture, technologies, and peoples. There is no simple, universal (external to all peoples, cultures, times) answer. However, the answer to this question for our time is very much influenced by the fact that we are changing nature at all levels from the local to the global—that we have the power to mold nature into what we want it to be or to destroy it completely, and that we know we have that power.

As Dan Tarlock observes in Slouching Toward Eden: The Eco-Pragmatic Challenges of Ecosystem Revival, 87 Minn. L. Rev. 1173, 1184-1186 (2003), this new perspective calls into question the very concept of ecosystems:

> Some ecologists have drawn a startling conclusion from the new ecology: The current concept of an ecosystem may no longer be a meaningful construct. The reason is

that the new ecology undermines the crucial assumptions of the concept. Ecology has traditionally assumed that an ecosystem has definable boundaries, that it has spatial homogeneity, that we may substitute different flora and fauna and still maintain a sustainable system, that natural selection is relatively unimportant, that we can identify stability levels at different scales, and that humans are not part of ecosystems. These simplistic assumptions are now being recast. . . .

The first lesson of the new ecology and the deconstructed ecosystem for revival is that we can never return to a state of nature; we can only approximate it for an undetermined period of time. The idea that ecosystems are moving rather than fixed targets and must be "mapped" at larger scales will subject the relevant environmental sciences to even greater stress. Scientists must answer questions that require mixed scientific and policy judgments. In contrast, environmental law and policy still have a tendency to view degraded ecosystems as broken machines. We want to know the causal relationship between the installation of a new part, a management action (experiment), and improved performance, an ecologically beneficial outcome. Science can rarely answer the causal relationship with the expected confidence or comfort level because it requires unprecedented and costly levels of data assembly and synthesis and the need to endlessly revisit previous conclusions and judgments.

Professor Lee Breckinridge, in Can Fish Own Water? Envisioning Nonhuman Property in Ecosystems, 20 J. Land Use & Envtl. L. 293 (2005), relates these new perspectives to changing scientific efforts to anticipate effects in systems that must be understood as dynamic and complex:

> Modern understandings of ecosystems reveal dynamic biophysical systems in which organisms interact with each other and with the abiotic components of their environment in complex ways. Feedback mechanisms produce nonlinear results, magnifying some phenomena while minimizing others. Equilibrium conditions exist, but these are dynamic phenomena produced through self-reinforcing patterns of ongoing activity rather than permanent conditions or steady states. A system may shift suddenly from one equilibrium and into another. Much remains uncertain and unpredictable about ecological systems and the organisms within them, precisely because the interactions are so complex and because small events can trigger large changes through nonlinear processes.
>
> The fluid, dynamic, and uncertain characteristics of ecosystems do not mean that meaningful patterns and processes are indecipherable in the midst of the transformation and change. Ecosystems have become the focus of intensive research in complex systems analysis. A key goal is to discern patterns and processes of ecological organization within "chaotic" phenomena.

---

1. *Nonequilibrium Theory's Implications.* What are the legal and ethical implications of Botkin's thesis? Some have read the nonequilibrium paradigm as an argument for not trying to "save" nature. However, the most common reading of Botkin is an argument for the more intense, holistic, and experimental management of "natural" and modified large-scale ecosystems. See S. Budiansky, Nature's Keepers: The New Science of Nature Management (1995). Scientists endorse the concept of adaptive management, which is a decision-making process based on the establishment of ecological performance targets, ecological risk assessment policy, monitoring, feedback, and change or adaptation. More generally, the more holistic emphasis on dynamic large systems leads to a greater appreciation of the need for large-scale landscape management to conserve biodiversity. National Research Council-

National Academy of Sciences, Restoration of Aquatic Ecosystems: Science, Technology and Public Policy 372 (1992). This management will take place at larger scales; see Bosselman, What Lawyers Can Learn from Large-Scale Ecology, 17 Land Use & Envtl. L. 207 (2002), which stresses the very concept of an ecosystem. See O'Neill, Is It Time to Bury the Ecosystem Concept? (With Full Military Honors of Course!), 82 Ecology 3275 (2001).

2. *Complexity and the Need for Flexibility.* In Panarchy: Understanding Transformations in Human and Natural Systems 9-14 (L. Gunderson & C.S. Holling eds., 2002), Gunderson and Hollings suggest that "there is growing evidence that the partial perspectives from [economics, ecology, and organizational or institutional analysis] generate actions that are unsustainable." After highlighting the shortcoming of each discipline standing on its own, and introducing a few "caricatures" of nature that they find inadequate (among them "Nature Flat," "Nature Balanced," "Nature Anarchic," and "Nature Resilient"), they introduce and advocate consideration of a perspective they label "Nature Evolving." Under this view, nature

> is evolutionary and adaptive. It has been given recent impetus by the paradoxes that have emerged in successfully applying the previous more limited views. Complex systems behavior, discontinuous change, chaos and order, self-organization, nonlinear systems behavior, and adaptive evolving systems are all code words characterizing the more recent activities. They are leading to integrative studies that combine insights and people from developmental biology and genetics, evolutionary biology, physics, economics, ecology, and computer science. Nature Evolving is a view of abrupt and transforming change. It is a view that exposes a need for understanding unpredictable dynamics in ecosystems and a corollary focus on institutional and political flexibility.

How are these more complex characterizations of nature, ecology, and governance efforts likely to play out in legal institutions such as legislatures, agencies, and courts? How might you distill these various ecological insights and new perspectives to make effective arguments in legal settings?

E. THE ETHICAL LESSONS OF ECOLOGY

Science is positive, not normative; however, environmentalists generally have drawn normative conclusions from ecology, many of them traceable to the beautifully crafted reflections of Aldo Leopold, first published in 1949. Note that some of Leopold's perspectives are consistent with modern ecological views, but others are not. Despite changing ecological understandings, Leopold's writings, like Rachel Carson's, continue to influence the path of environmental law. In A Sand County Almanac and Sketches Here and There 202-204, 214-216, 220, 224-225 (Oxford University Press paperback ed. 1968), Leopold articulated an argument rooted in ethics for why humans should respect the environment and avoid causing harm. In his view, such an ethical perspective calls for more than arguments rooted merely in property or economics:

> There is as yet no ethic dealing with man's relation to land and to the animals and plants which grow upon it. Land . . . is still property. The land-relation is still strictly economic, entailing privileges but not obligations. . . .

An ethic may be regarded as a mode of guidance for meeting ecological situations so new or intricate, or involving such deferred reactions, that the path of social expediency is not discernible to the average individual. . . . Ethics are possibly a kind of community instinct in-the-making. . . .

The land ethic simply enlarges the boundaries of the community to include soils, waters, plants, and animals, or collectively: the land.

This sounds simple: do we not already sing our love for and obligation to the land of the free and the home of the brave? Yes, but just what and whom do we love? Certainly not the soil, which we are sending helter-skelter downriver. Certainly not the waters, which we assume have no function except to turn turbines, float barges, and carry off sewage. Certainly not the plants, of which we exterminate whole communities without batting an eye. Certainly not the animals, of which we have already extirpated many of the largest and most beautiful species. A land ethic of course cannot prevent the alteration, management, and use of these "resources," but it does affirm their right to continued existence, and, at least in spots, their continued existence in a natural state. . . .

In short, a land ethic changes the role of Homo sapiens from conqueror of the land-community to plain member and citizen of it. It implies respect for his fellow-members, and also respect for the community as such. . . .

A thing is right when it tends to preserve the integrity, stability, and beauty of the biotic community. It is wrong when it tends otherwise. . . .

NOTES AND QUESTIONS

1. *Legal Implications of Stewardship.* What are the implications of A Sand County Almanac for environmental law? Despite Leopold's widespread influence, his direct, and perhaps indirect, legal influence is small. The most common use has been to bolster assertions of the police power to protect the environment. For example, in Application of Christensen, 417 N.W.2d 607, 615 (Minn. 1988), the Minnesota Supreme Court upheld the denial of a wetland drainage permit with this language:

We reaffirm our statements that the state's environmental legislation had given [Leopold's] land ethic the force of law, and imposed on the courts a duty to support the legislative goal of protecting our state's environmental resources. Vanishing wetlands require, even more today than in 1976 when [County of Freeborn v. Bryson, 243 N.W.2d 316 (Minn. 1976)] was decided, the protection and preservation that environmental legislation was intended to provide.

Leopold's thinking is also directly reflected in Department of Cmty. Affairs v. Moorman, 664 So. 2d 930, 932 (Fla. 1995), stating that "[t]he clear policy underlying Florida environmental regulation is that our society is to be a steward of the natural world, not its unreasoning overlord."

Leopold identifies the institution of private property as a primary stumbling block to environmental stewardship. The issue is critical to environmental law because the Fifth and Fourteenth Amendments to the United States Constitution prohibit the taking, which includes excess regulation, of property without just compensation. See Chapter 5, section C below (discussing the law of regulatory takings). In the initial regulation of air, water, and land pollution, constitutional objections to environmental regulation were largely unsuccessful. First-generation environmental regulation by and large codified and extended common law prohibitions against the maintenance of nuisances. Thus, dischargers could not claim the taking of a previously recognized entitlement. As we focus on the preservation of terrestrial bio-diversity, the tension between stewardship and private property increases.

Although actual judicial citation to Leopold remains scarce, his land ethic forms the basis for developing theories of "green property." Green property theory seeks to incorporate the principle of stewardship into the individualistic liberal theories of property. See Goldstein, Green Wood in the Bundle of Sticks: Fitting Environmental Ethics and Ecology into Real Property Law, 25 B.C. Envtl. Aff. L. Rev. 347 (1998). It stresses that the natural interconnectedness of the arbitrary divisions of land produced by the common law justify more stringent limitations on individual parcel use to protect the integrity of remnant ecosystems. However, Leopold himself seems to have intended his land ethic as a call for private landowners to internalize conservation practices. See Freyfogle, The Land Ethic and Pilgrim Leopold, 61 U. Colo. L. Rev. 217, 236 (1990).

2. *Can Ecosystems Have Rights?* Environmental philosophers and others read Leopold as creating a new system of ethics that breaks with the individualistic, anthropocentric bias in Western philosophy and the Anglo-American insistence on a strict separation of fact from value. Environmental ethics posit specific duties, not just a plea for the evolution of changed attitudes, toward nature, although Leopold himself held a dualistic view of the relationship between man and nature. Environmental protection law is a complex mix of scientific and economic consequences constructed on the assertion that we have a moral duty to respect "nature." The insight that human activities that modify natural systems have short- and long-run adverse consequences is a powerful one. However, the question is whether this insight can support new rights that run to natural systems. We usually define rights as relatively absolute entitlements to a consistent outcome, and we limit the competing interests that can be traded off against them.

The argument for new environmental or ecosystem rights starts from the premise that the prevailing theory of Western civilization, that man commands nature, should be replaced with the radical view that he is just a participant in the biotic community. As Roderick Nash has observed, "[I]f Darwin killed dualism, the ecologists presided over its burial." The Rights of Nature: A History of Environmental Ethics 70 (1989). Nash traces the gradual expansion of the circle of rights and speculates on the implication of this expansion for environmentalism. He observes that "environmental ethics created entirely new definitions of what liberty and justice mean on planet earth. It recognized that there can be no individual welfare (or liberty) apart from the ecological matrix in which individual life must exist. A biocentric ethical philosophy . . . can be understood . . . as both the end and a new beginning of the American liberal tradition." Id. at 160.

3. *Leopoldian Ethics and the Western Philosophical Tradition.* The effort to construct a theory of ecological rights faces at least four formidable conceptual hurdles. First, rights are generally limited to sentient beings. This affords some hope for animal rights advocates, but not for the protection of entire ecosystems or landscapes. The best articulations of the possibility of bringing animals within a modified rights framework remain the late R. Nozick's Anarchy, State and Utopia 35-42 (1974) and P. Singer's Animal Rights (1975). But this extension of sentiency offers no help for proponents of ecosystem rights. Second, the argument that moral duties flow from ecological awareness flies in the face of the dominant philosophical view, following Hume, that fact should be separated from value. The distinction is vigorously supported in C. Mann & M. Plummer, Noah's Choice: The Future of Endangered

Species 204-208 (1995). Are the categories truly absolute? Why have we as a society decided to protect the environment? Can one avoid the problem by dissolving the categories and by adopting moral concern for the functioning of the entire ecological system as the value? See generally P. Wenz, Environmental Justice (1988).

4. *Duties to Future Generations.* Can the anthropocentric-nonanthropocentric problem also be avoided by imposing a duty on present generations to protect future generations? The question is central to environmental law because many conflicts revolve around pleas for the deferral, perhaps infinitely, of the consumption of resources to benefit future generations. A major justification for many environmental policies is that the present consumption of resources should be limited to protect the interests of future generations. This debate today arises in conflicts over climate change regulation, where some policymakers and scholars advocate regulation to reduce more severe climate harms that are often many years into the future, while others champion decreasing poverty in the nearer term, even at the price of increased emissions contributing to climate change. Chapter 12 discusses climate regulation battles and choices in detail. Considerable controversy exists among philosophers about whether rights can be possessed by unidentifiable (unborn) individuals and thus whether any duties or moral obligations are owed to those yet to come.[a] How should present as opposed to future consumption be valued? See Heal, Economics and Resources, in Economics of Environmental and Natural Resources Policy 62 (J. A. Butlin ed., 1981). Professor Edith Brown Weiss has argued that the public trust concept is a basis for intergenerational equity as a limitation on present resource consumption. She has expanded her argument in her widely influential book, In Fairness to Future Generations: International Law, Common Patrimony, and Intergenerational Equity (1989). See generally the exchange between professors Weiss and Anthony D'Amato in 84 Am. J. Int'l L. 190 and 198 (1990). For more discussion of the public trust doctrine, see section F.5 below.

5. *Is There a Nonequilibrium Environmental Ethic?* Recall the excerpts from Botkin and others regarding nonequilibrium ecology. One of the major lessons of nonequilibrium ecology is that it is not enough to fence off nature from human contact because nature is too dynamic. Does this underline Leopoldian ethics? Callicott, Do Deconstructive Ecology and Sociobiology Undermine Leopold's Land Ethic?, 18 Envtl. Ethics 353, 372 (1996), offers the following revision of Leopold's ethic:

> In light of more recent developments in ecology, we can add norms of scale to the land ethic for both climatic and ecological dynamics in land-ethically evaluating anthropogenic changes in nature. One hesitates to edit Leopold's elegant prose, but as a stab at formulating a dynamized summary moral maxim for the land ethic, I hazard the following: "A thing is right when it tends to disturb the biotic community only at normal spatial and temporal scales. It is wrong when it tends otherwise."

6. *Religion and Man's Place in Nature.* For a nuanced tracing of how various religious traditions perceive man's place in nature, as well as diverse perceptions regarding the relationship of nature to God, see J. Passmore, Man's Responsibility

---

a. See Kavka, The Paradox of Future Individuals, 11 Phil. & Pub. Aff. 93 (1982); Parfit, Future Generations: Further Problems, 11 Phil. & Pub. Aff. 113 (1982); Farber & Hemmersbaugh, The Shadow of the Future: Discount Rates, Later Generations, and the Environment, 46 Vand. L. Rev. 267 (1993).

for Nature: Ecological Problems and Western Traditions 5-6, 10, 12-14 (1974). He points out that in addition to religious strains of thought that emphasize man's dominion over nature, there is a Western tradition of the stewardship of nature.

F. COMMON LAW, NONSTATUTORY, AND CONSTITUTIONAL REMEDIES FOR ENVIRONMENTAL HARMS

Economic and ecological perspectives on the roots and repercussions of environmental harms point to the same conclusion—environmental harms should be discouraged. From an economics perspective, harmful conduct that creates no liability for the agent of harm will be produced in excess. Such negative externalities need somehow to become internalized, be it through consensual bargaining (as Coase posited might occur in some settings), through regulation prohibiting or limiting the harm in the first instance (the answer adopted by most modern environmental laws), or through long-established common law frameworks that provide rights to injunctive or monetary relief. Such common law frameworks have their roots in English law predating America's independence, but continued on their own somewhat distinct path in the roughly 200 years before the explosion of modern federal environmental laws (starting around 1970). Constitutionally based arguments for a right to a clean environment never took root under the federal Constitution, but under a few state constitutions, limited constitutional rights to a clean environment have been recognized.

This section introduces the reader to the most important common law causes of action for environmental harms, as well as the public trust doctrine, a judicially derived doctrine of somewhat indeterminate origin but with occasionally substantial influence. The section closes with a brief review of constitutionally based arguments for rights to a clean environment. Many of the cases excerpted precede modern federal environmental laws, but, as will also be discussed, most common law causes of action remain viable, typically even when environmentally harmful activity is permitted by federal law. They remain a key foundation of our environmental law, influencing statutory strategies but also remaining a key alternative means to remedy environmental harms when political officials refuse to take action. Common law actions face many hurdles and are viewed by most policymakers and scholars as inadequate to deter most environmental harms, but they remain an important part of the environmental lawyer's arsenal. They are often the sole means for injured citizens to be compensated for their harms.

In working through the following materials, assess which claims, if any, might be effective in deterring or remedying harms from a mine in the circumstances set forth in Problem 1-1. Or you might think about the following hypothetical to sort out the various common law causes of action often available to remedy environmental harms.

Problem 1-3

Power generated through use of modern wind turbines can provide many public and private benefits, especially due to the profitable production of energy without emissions of any greenhouse gases or more localized forms of air pollution such as particulate matter or air toxics. Nevertheless, wind power is not always popular, especially if placed too near homes and buildings. The following exact problem is unlikely due to state and local land use regulations that mandate considerable distance between humans and wind turbines, but contains elements that have actually begun provoking litigation.

Assume that an urban and financially struggling municipality, Greentown, just announced plans to issue a 99-year lease to Windco, a private wind power company, for acreage on the edge of Greentown's Vista Park. Vista Park, which covers about 500 acres, was designed in the late 1800s by a famous landscape architect. Windco plans to put up three towering wind turbines on 50 acres of leased land. The turbines would be placed about 150 feet from Park Edge Road, a busy urban street. The lease revenue would be used to maintain the park, as well as for other government expenses and accumulated debt. Park Edge Road is next to the Parkside neighborhood. Due to Parkside's slight upward slope, Parkside's coveted brownstone row homes often have a view of a sliver or more of the park. Now some residents will see wind turbine towers and, in late afternoon light, sunlight passing through the turbines' blades. In addition, studies of wind turbines' effects indicate that turbine blades at times cause an audible whooshing or rhythmic sound as they cut through the air and emit a low frequency noise that can travel far and can sometimes be heard through building walls. In addition, the operation of turbines sometimes causes a mechanical rumble or hum. Some people are bothered by a strobe-like effect of sunlight passing through blades, air pressure changes from the blades' movement, and the specified types of resulting noises, but others are not. Windco's turbines would be state of the art and, according to Windco, would minimize all noises so, in most conditions and at the distance to the Parkside neighborhood, the turbines would produce noise no louder than a residential refrigerator. Nonetheless, the blades' movement will, in certain conditions, cause sounds, and, with the park's current landscaping, the strobe effect is unavoidable unless the blades are shut down each afternoon. Mechanical noises heard near the wind turbines can be rendered quite minimal with diligent maintenance and investment in sound insulation by the wind company. If Greentown or Windco plant additional trees between the turbines and the road and Parkside, that would further reduce noise and the strobe effect. Unfortunately, such wind turbines also cause some bird deaths, with injured and killed birds dropping from the sky onto neighboring lands. Parkside residents also worry that their homes will lose market value. Others worry about catastrophic failures should a major storm or mechanical malfunction cause parts of the towers, turbine blades, or winter ice on the blades to fall or be thrown. Most of these catastrophic failure risks are remote, but cannot be ruled out. As you read the materials that follow on environmental common law claims, assess which claims might be asserted by unhappy Parkside residents if such wind power turbines were slated to be built or actually built, and what defenses Windco or Greentown would assert.

1. Negligence Claims

When a private or public actor causes an environmental harm, citizens and possibly other governments can experience substantial harms. Although most upper-class law students have studied tort law at great length and immediately think "negligence" when someone is harmed, most environmental harms result from intentional activity that may be just like the activity of many other, similar producers of environmental harms. Harms may flow from ordinary, standard conduct, even conduct that reflects the technological state of the art. In addition, broad-based environmental harms likely to generate litigation tend to be caused by large producers of risk such as manufacturers, refineries, resource extraction industries (e.g., oil drilling operations), power plants, and chemical plants. Thus, for victims of pollution and their lawyers, trying to prove that negligent operations caused a harm presents formidable challenges. For this reason, negligence common law theories tend to be little used for environmental harms unless (a) the harm arises out of what is clearly an accident, such as a spill or facility malfunction; (b) the remedies sought are of a sort recognized only under negligence doctrine, which does tend to have a more nuanced array of recognized remedies and categories of recoverable damage; or (c) insurance held by the causer of harm will pay any recovery, and, as is typically the case, insurance does not cover "intentional" acts. 46 C.J.S. Insurance §1153 (2005).

2. *Public and Private Nuisance Claims*

Rather than negligence claims, public and private nuisance actions are the norm for remedying environmental harms. Such claims are typically rooted in allegations of intentional conduct, although not in the sense of a specific intent to cause harm of a particular sort to a particular victim. Instead, the only intent that the plaintiff must show is that the activity causing the harm was undertaken intentionally. A reduced foreseeability requirement is imposed for such claims, requiring only that harms of the sort caused could reasonably be foreseen by the polluter. In both public and private nuisance cases, the idea that externalized harms should be internalized through an award of damages and injunctive relief is often explicitly cited by courts. See Boomer v. Atlantic Cement Co., 26 N.Y.2d 219, 225-226 (1970). Key to both theories are concepts of unreasonable harm. As you read the following materials, seek to sort out when each sort of claim is most advantageous. When will both sorts of nuisance claims be available?

a. Public Nuisance Claims

Public nuisance claims are often brought by governments on behalf of citizens and to protect lands in the jurisdiction, but also now can be brought by individuals and nongovernmental organizations. Such public nuisance actions typically involve broad-based harms, especially to commonly enjoyed resources. Public nuisance actions allow plaintiffs to aggregate damages and enjoin polluting activities that produce serious cumulative harms, rather than focus merely on individual impacts. Originally, public nuisance claims were based on criminal violations, but the modern theory is that a public nuisance is an unreasonable interference with the rights of the public.

The substantive standards are the same as for a private nuisance, but private parties have historically had standing to sue for a public nuisance only if they suffer special damages. See Bryson & Macbeth, Public Nuisance, The Restatement (Second) of Torts, and Environmental Law, 2 Ecology L.Q. 241 (1972). There has been a limited expansion of the standing rules. In re The Exxon Valdez (Alaska Native Class v. Exxon Corp.), 104 F.3d 1196 (9th Cir. 1997), illustrates the limits of the common law in allowing private actions for many types of pollution, especially diffuse ones. The Restatement of Torts (Second) §821C has a liberal standing rule for injunctive relief and abatement actions. Representatives of the general public, "as a citizen in a citizen's action, or as a member of a class in a class action," have standing. But §821C(1) limits damage actions to those who suffer "harm of a different kind from that suffered by other members of the public exercising the right common to the general public that was the subject of the interference." The court recognized that Native Americans injured by the Exxon Valdez spill had a right to sue for economic damages from lost fishing opportunities, but refused to allow them to sue to recover "cultural damage—damage to the Class members' subsistence way of life"—because the damages were not special. All Alaska residents have a right to subsistence hunting and fishing, and thus "the right to obtain and share wild food, enjoy uncontaminated nature, and cultivate traditional, cultural, spiritual, and physiological benefits in pristine natural surroundings is shared by all Alaskans." Id. at 1198. Compare Miotke v. City of Spokane, 678 P.2d 803 (Wash. 1984) (riparian owners and environmental organization had standing to recover damages for stream pollution because individuals suffered nausea, headaches, and insomnia). See generally Hodas, Private Actions for Public Nuisance: Common Law Citizen Suits for Relief from Environmental Harm, 16 Ecology L.Q. 883 (1989). Antolini, Modernizing Public Nuisance: Solving the Paradox of the Special Injury Rule, 28 Ecology L.Q. 755 (2001), reviews the turbulent history of §821 and the courts' general neglect of it, and proposes a new common law standard consistent with the rise of public law litigation by environmental groups and other NGOs. .

In 1906, the Supreme Court decided Missouri v. Illinois, 200 U.S. 496. The case arose out of Chicago's successful effort to reverse the flow of the Chicago River to shift pollution from Lake Michigan into the Mississippi watershed. The case is a classic example of the limits of the common law of nuisance to deal with diffuse injuries and risks rather than proven damage to person or property. Downstream Missouri sued Illinois for increasing the risk of illness to Mississippi River communities. Justice Holmes's opinion for the Court, however, revealed the difficulty of carrying proof burdens in a case involving multiple pollution sources, risks of harm, and complex questions of causation:

> As to the principle to be laid down, the caution necessary is manifest. It is a question of the first magnitude whether the destiny of the great rivers is to be the sewers of the cities along their banks or to be protected against everything which threatens their purity. To decide the whole matter at one blow by an irrevocable fiat would be at least premature. If we are to judge by what the plaintiff itself permits, the discharge of sewage into the Mississippi by cities and towns is to be expected. We believe that the practice of discharging into the river is general along its banks, except where the levees of Louisiana have led to a different course. The argument for the plaintiff asserts it to be proper within certain limits. These are facts to be considered. . . .
>
> . . . At the outset we cannot but be struck by the consideration that if this suit had been brought fifty years ago it almost necessarily would have failed. There is no pretense that there is a nuisance of the simple kind that was known to the older common law. There is nothing which can be detected by the unassisted senses,—no visible increase of filth, no new smell. On the contrary, it is proved that the great volume of pure water from Lake Michigan, which is mixed with the sewage at the start, has improved the Illinois river in these respects to a noticeable extent. Formerly it was sluggish and ill smelling.

Now it is a comparatively clear stream to which edible fish have returned. Its water is drunk by the fishermen, it is said without evil results. The plaintiff's case depends upon an inference of the unseen. It draws the inference from two propositions. First, that typhoid fever has increased considerably since the change, and that other explanations have been disproved; and second, that the bacillus of typhoid can and does survive the journey and reach the intake of St. Louis in the Mississippi.

We assume the now-prevailing scientific explanation of typhoid fever to be correct. But when we go beyond that assumption, everything is involved in doubt. The data upon which an increase in the deaths from typhoid fever in St. Louis is alleged are disputed. The elimination of other causes is denied. The experts differ as to the time and distance within which a stream would purify itself. No case of an epidemic caused by infection at so remote a source is brought forward and the cases which are produced are controverted. . . .

. . . [T]he defendant's evidence shows a reduction in the chemical and bacterial accompaniments of pollution in a given quantity of water, which would be natural in view of the mixture of nine parts to one from Lake Michigan. It affirms that the Illinois is better or no worse at its mouth than it was before, and makes it at least uncertain how much of the present pollution is due to Chicago and how much to sources further down, not complained of in the bill. It contends that if any bacilli should get through, they would be scattered and enfeebled and would do no harm. The evidence is very strong that it is necessary for St. Louis to take preventive measures, by filtration or otherwise, against the dangers of the plaintiff's own creation or from other sources than Illinois. What will protect against one will protect against another. The presence of causes of infection from the plaintiff's action makes the case weaker in principle as well as harder to prove than one in which all came from a single source. . . .

We might go more into detail, but we believe that we have said enough to explain our point of view and our opinion of the evidence as it stands. What the future may develop, of course we cannot tell. But our conclusion upon the present evidence is that the case proved falls so far below the allegations of the bill that it is not brought within the principles heretofore established in the cause. [Id. at 521-523, 525-526.]

Fears that the dismissal of the *Missouri* case might be a harbinger of general resistance to environmental public nuisance claims quickly proved unfounded.

GEORGIA v. TENNESSEE COPPER CO.
206 U.S. 230 (1907)

HOLMES, J.

This is a bill in equity filed in this court by the state of Georgia, in pursuance of a resolution of the legislature and by direction of the governor of the state, to enjoin the defendant copper companies from discharging noxious gas from their works in Tennessee over the plaintiff's territory. It alleges that, in consequence of such discharge, a wholesale destruction of forests, orchards, and crops is going on, and other injuries are done and threatened in five counties of the state. It alleges also a vain application to the state of Tennessee for relief. A preliminary injunction was denied; but, as there was ground to fear that great and irreparable damage might be done, an early day was fixed for the final hearing, and the parties were given leave, if so minded, to try the case on affidavits. This has been done without objection, and, although the method would be unsatisfactory if our decision turned on any nice question of fact, in the view that we take we think it unlikely that either party has suffered harm.

The case has been argued largely as if it were one between two private parties; but it is not. The very elements that would be relied upon in a suit between fellow-citizens as a ground for equitable relief are wanting here. The state owns very little of the territory alleged to be affected, and the damage to it capable of estimate in money, possibly, at least, is small. This is a suit by a state for an injury to it in its capacity of quasi-sovereign. In that capacity the state has an interest independent of and behind the titles of its citizens, in all the earth and air within its domain. It has the last word as to whether its mountains shall be stripped of their forests and its inhabitants shall breathe pure air. It might have to pay individuals before it could utter that word, but with it remains the final power. The alleged damage to the state as a private owner is merely a makeweight, and we may lay on one side the dispute as to whether the destruction of forests has led to the gullying of its roads.

The caution with which demands of this sort, on the part of a State, for relief from injuries analogous to torts, must be examined is dwelt upon in Missouri v. Illinois, 200 U.S. 496, 520, 521. But it is plain that some such demands must be recognized, if the grounds alleged are proved. When the States by their union made the forcible abatement of outside nuisance impossible to each, they did not thereby agree to submit to whatever might be done. They did not renounce the possibility of making reasonable demands on the ground of their still remaining quasi-sovereign interests; and the alternative to force is a suit in this court. Missouri v. Illinois, 180 U.S. 208, 241. . . .

It is a fair and reasonable demand on the part of a sovereign that the air over its territory should not be polluted on a great scale by sulphurous acid gas, that the forests on its mountains, be they better or worse, and whatever domestic destruction they have suffered, should not be further destroyed or threatened by the act of persons beyond its control, that the crops and orchards on its hills should not be endangered from the same source. If any such demand is to be enforced this must be notwithstanding the hesitation that we might feel if the suit were between private parties, and the doubt whether, for the injuries which they might be suffering to their property, they should not be left to action at law.

The proof requires but a few words. It is not denied that the defendants generate in their works near the Georgia line large quantities of sulphur dioxid[e] which becomes sulphurous acid by its mixture with the air. It hardly is denied and cannot be denied with success that this gas often is carried by the wind great distances and over great tracts of Georgia land. On the evidence the pollution of the air and the magnitude of that pollution are not open to dispute. Without any attempt to go into details immaterial to the suit, it is proper to add that we are satisfied by a preponderance of evidence that the sulphurous fumes cause and threaten damage on so considerable a scale to the forest and vegetable life, if not to health, with the plaintiff State as to make out a case within the requirements of Missouri v. Illinois, 200 U.S. 496. Whether Georgia by insisting upon this claim is doing more harm than good to her own citizens is for her to determine. The possible disaster to those outside the State must be accepted as a consequence of her standing upon her extreme rights.

NOTES AND QUESTIONS

1. *More Recent Cases Affirming State Public Nuisance Authority.* For another, more recent case affirming the right of governments to seek public nuisance relief, see

Machipongo Land and Coal Co. v. Commonwealth, 799 A.2d 751 (Pa. 2002) (holding that the Commonwealth can prohibit coal mining by showing that it has a "high potential" to increase dissolved solids and metal concentrations in trout streams or has a significant potential to disrupt a stream's hydrologic balance by increasing net alkalinity).

2. *Climate Change and Public Nuisance Actions.* Concern about climate change resulting from anthropogenic contributions to greenhouse gases has led to significant litigation and regulatory and legislative activity, with ferment at the federal, state, and local levels. Those developments are covered in Chapter 2 briefly, and in Chapter 12's coverage of climate change law. As with most areas of environmental harm, common law litigation over climate change has accompanied regulatory and legislative activity. Public nuisance claims have been initiated by state governments and private actors against this nation's largest greenhouse gas emitters. Although they initially did not meet with success, such claims scored a major victory in Connecticut v. American Elec. Power Co., 582 F.3d 309 (2d Cir. 2009) (reversing the district's dismissal on political question grounds and upholding such claims in a lengthy decision closely parsing public nuisance history and cases). But see California v. General Motors Corp., 2007 WL 2726871 (N.D. Cal. Sept. 17, 2007) (dismissing public nuisance claims mainly on political-question-related grounds). However, as covered in Chapter 12, section E.5, the Supreme Court in American Elec. Power Co. v. Connecticut, 131 S. Ct. 2527 (2011), reversing the Second Circuit's 2009 decision, largely rejected a public nuisance claim, although focusing in that case on the federal common law claim of public nuisance in light of the existence of the Clean Air Act and the Court's ruling that EPA could regulate greenhouse gas emissions under the Act. The Court recognized that the viability of a state law public nuisance claim raised a different legal issue, but did not resolve it. Further related discussion requires reading of the *Ouellette* case, which is covered below in section G of this chapter. Prior to the Court's ruling in *American Electric Power*, scholars were generally positive about the merits of such cases, due in part to how such litigation can serve as a gap-filling strategy during periods of political inertia and also can prompt needed legislative and regulatory activity. See, e.g., Abate, Automobile Emissions and Climate Change Impacts: Employing Public Nuisance Doctrine as Part of a "Global Warming Solution" in California, 40 Conn. L. Rev. 591 (2008); Klass, Tort Experiments in the Laboratories of Democracy, 50 Wm. & Mary L. Rev. 1501 (2009); Zasloff, The Judicial Carbon Tax: Reconstructing Public Nuisance and Climate Change, 55 UCLA L. Rev. 1827 (2008). Professor Thomas Merrill was more pessimistic about the viability of public nuisance climate change actions. Merrill, Global Warming as a Public Nuisance, 30 Colum. J. Envtl. L. 293 (2005). Chapter 12 offers more related discussion.

b. Private Nuisance Claims

Private nuisance claims remain the bread and butter of environmental common law litigation. Where a citizen's property has been injured by another's pollution or environmental degradation, private nuisance claims are often the answer. The sorts of harms found actionable in private nuisance actions vary greatly, but still are limited. Some jurisdictions, for example, do not recognize interference with aesthetic sensibilities as actionable. See Robie v. Lillis, 299 A.2d 155 (N.H. 1972). Cf. State v. Piemontese, 659 A.2d 1385 (N.J. Super. App. Div. 1995) (ordinance that prohibited "unsightly" hedges and lawns held unconstitutionally vague). A few courts have recognized that such an interference can be a nuisance but have limited the tort to land use pariahs such as junkyards. Foley v. Harris, 286 S.E.2d 186 (Va. 1982); Town of Delafield v. Sharpley, 568 N.W.2d 779 (Wis. App. 1997). But cf. Prah v. Maretti, 321 N.W.2d 182 (Wis. 1982) (interference with solar access).

A private nuisance is a nontrespassory invasion of another's interest in the use and enjoyment of land. The plaintiff must prove that the defendant's conduct is unreasonable and causes a substantial interference with the use and enjoyment of land or causes bodily injury. Nuisance is a hybrid tort that has elements of strict liability and intentional tort. Nuisance differs from negligence. The focus in a nuisance case is on the reasonableness of the activity's effects in a particular place, not on the general reasonableness of the defendant's conduct. Nuisance evaluates the reasonableness of the conduct and its effects by comparing it to the surrounding land uses. Private nuisance claims hence can be a form of judicial zoning, with courts assessing whether a use is environmentally incompatible with the surrounding area. For example, Penland v. Redwood Sanitary Sewer Serv. Dist., 965 P.2d 433 (Or. App. 1998), affirmed a trial court decision that a sewage composting facility, located in a rural residential area on the Rogue River in southern Oregon, and that stank like "500 outhouses at once," was a nuisance. The appellate court quoted the trial judge's remarks after viewing the site. "The day we were out there, there were osprey flying over the river. It's a beautiful, very much a residential" area. The trial judge also noted that the District switched from a sewage treatment facility to a composting facility in 1990 and that the change was not foreseeable and was "akin" to locating an industrial use in the area. Thus, the intentional act is focused not on a specific intent to cause harm, but on the location of intentional activity in an unsuitable place.

The issue of what must be unreasonable, and what should be balanced in making such an assessment, has long confounded courts and led to varying formulations in the Restatements of Torts. The following two case excerpts from Connecticut should give you a feel for arguments and counterarguments over "unreasonable harm."

WALSH v. TOWN OF STONINGTON WATER POLLUTION CONTROL AUTHORITY
250 Conn. 443, 736 A.2d 811 (1999)

[Citizen neighbors of a coastal town's sewage treatment plant sued for damages resulting from the plant's odors. After a jury awarded them damages, the town challenged the trial court's formulation for the jury of how "unreasonableness" should be determined. Only the relevant case discussion is excerpted below.]

NORCOTT, J.

An analysis of the defendants' claims requires us to review the contours of the unreasonable use element of a common-law private nuisance cause of action. As we previously have stated, "'the law will not interfere with a use that is reasonable.' Hurlbut v. McKone, 55 Conn. 31, 42 [1887]. 'It is the duty of every person to make a reasonable use of his own property so as to occasion no unnecessary damage or annoyance to his neighbor.' Nailor v. C.W. Blakeslee & Sons, Inc., 117 Conn. 241, 245 [1933]. A fair test of whether a proposed use constitutes a nuisance is 'the reasonableness of the use of the property in the particular locality under the circumstances of the case.' Wetstone v. Cantor, 144 Conn. 77, 80 [1956]." Nicholson v. Connecticut Half-Way House, Inc., 153 Conn. 507, 510 (1966). The test of unreasonableness is "essentially a weighing process, involving a comparative evaluation of conflicting interests in various situations according to objective legal standards." O'Neill v. Carolina Freight Carriers Corp., 156 Conn. 613, 617-18 (1968), quoting 4 Restatement, Torts §826, comment (b) (1939); see Nair v. Thaw, 156 Conn. 445, 452 (1968). In Maykut v. Plasko, 170 Conn. 310, 314 (1976), we again referred to the weighing process described in the Restatement, in determining whether the trial court had applied the proper test to determine the reasonableness of the defendants' use of their land. We concluded that the trial court had applied the proper test where "[t]he facts outlined in [the] memorandum of decision and set out in the finding include a consideration not only of the interest of the plaintiff, but of the defendants also." Id., at 315.

The charge to the jury in the present case was consistent with our prior holdings on the element of unreasonable use. When viewed in the context of the charge as a whole, the jury instructions concerning unreasonable use conveyed to the jury that it was to take into consideration and weigh the conflicting interests involved. The trial court stated at the outset of the explanation of the unreasonable use element of the claim that the jury "must consider the location of the condition and any other circumstances that you find proven which indicate whether the defendants [were] making a reasonable use of the property." . . . This statement indicates that the jury must take into account a multiplicity of factors. Reference to the fact that the use of the property for a plant is a reasonable use makes clear that the use of the defendants' land to operate a plant is reasonable in and of itself. By then noting that the determination of reasonableness is to be made in the context of odors produced by the plant, the trial court underscored that the weighing process for the jury to conduct is of the reasonableness of use in light of the production of unreasonable odors that the jury had determined existed in its answers to the first four interrogatories. We disagree with the defendants, therefore, that the effect of the jury instruction was to remove the interests of the defendants from the jury's consideration. Rather, we conclude that the trial court's charge provided a reasonably clear instruction that the jury must consider many factors in determining the reasonableness of use, including the reasonableness of use as a plant that creates certain odors in the course of its operation.

Moreover, the defendants' arguments regarding the impropriety of the jury instructions necessarily are unpersuasive because they are based on an inaccurate construction of the concept of unreasonable use. We begin by noting that the defendants' reliance upon the state mandate concerning water pollution control is misplaced. As discussed further in part III of this opinion, the fact that operating a plant is permissible, or even necessary, on the land in question does not necessarily shield the defendants from liability for harm to the land of others that may result from that use. "A municipality which creates a nuisance causing damage to the land of another is not excused from liability on the ground that the act is lawful in itself if, under all the circumstances, it is unreasonable." Cyr v. Brookfield, 153 Conn. 261, 265 (1965). As a result, we reject the defendants' claim that "[w]here a town is undertaking an activity in furtherance of a state goal and pursuant to a state mandate, the charge to the jury should protect the town from liability for actions that are necessary to carry out the state's directives."

The defendants also place much emphasis on our prior statement in Cyr that "[a]n intentional invasion of another's interest in the use and enjoyment of land is unreasonable under the rule stated in §822 [of the Restatement of

Torts],[1] unless the utility of the actor's conduct outweighs the gravity of the harm." Cyr v. Brookfield, *supra*, 153 Conn. at 265-66, quoting 4 Restatement (Second) Torts, §826. On the basis of this statement, the defendants assert that the element of unreasonable use cannot be met in this case unless the harm to the plaintiffs outweighs the social utility of a plant, that is, the harm outweighs the benefit to the residents of the town as a whole. The comments in the Restatement (Second) of Torts on utility versus gravity of harm do not, however, support the interpretation asserted by the defendants. The Restatement (Second) provides the example that "[e]ven though the noise and smoke from a factory cannot feasibly be eliminated, the utility of the factory is not weighed in the abstract. In a suit for damages, the legal utility of the activity may also be greatly reduced by the fact that the actor is operating the factory and producing the noise and smoke without compensating his neighbors for the harm done to them. The conduct for which the utility is being weighed includes both the general activity and what is done about its consequences." 4 Restatement (Second), Torts §826, comment (e) (1979). The defendants' understanding of the balancing requirement does not involve simply the weighing of factors to determine reasonableness as the law requires.[2] Instead, application of the defendants' approach would result in an all-or-nothing scenario wherein the plaintiffs could never prove unreasonable use because their harm could never trump the undisputed need for a town plant. In other words, the plaintiffs would be expected to bear all of the harm without compensation for their damages, while receiving no greater benefits from the continued operation of the plant than any other resident of the town. Such an interpretation goes far beyond the necessary weighing process to be undertaken by the jury.

We conclude that the jury instructions were adequate to guide the jury properly in the determination of the issues.

NOTE AND QUESTION

Clarity or Confusion? Does *Walsh* offer a satisfactory or clear explication of how this balancing is to occur? Note that the court cited several Restatement of Torts formulations of the balancing or assessment of harm that is part of the assessment of "unreasonable" use or harm. Note also how some formulations focus on the conduct of the source of the harm, while others focus on the nature or magnitude of the harm experienced by the victims. After *Walsh*, in Connecticut, was sorting out the relative interests and harms a task for the court, or for a jury?

---

1. Section 822 of the Restatement (Second) of Torts now provides in relevant part: "One is subject to liability for a private nuisance if, but only if, his conduct is a legal cause of an invasion of another's interest in the private use and enjoyment of land, and the invasion is . . . (a) intentional and unreasonable. . . ."

2. In a similar vein, the town also cites to 2 D. Wright & W. Ankerman, Connecticut Jury Instructions (4th ed. 1993) §44, p. 886, for the proposition that "[i]f there was nothing which the defendant could reasonably have done to guard against the danger, it cannot be held to have created a nuisance." This proposed instruction, and the case law from which it was generated, applies to claims of public nuisance wherein the condition or conduct complained of interfered with a right common to the general public. State v. Tippetts-Abbett-McCarthy-Stratton, 204 Conn. 177, 183 (1987). Without addressing the question of whether there was anything further that the town could have done to reduce or eliminate the production of odors, we simply note that such a requirement is irrelevant in the context of the present case.

After Connecticut courts and litigants struggled to make sense of *Walsh*, the state's highest court revisited the issue, not literally overruling *Walsh* but substantially modifying what needs to be considered in assessing reasonableness. Note that in this short case excerpt, which arose out of a conflict between neighbors and a nearby dairy farm generating allegedly offensive odors, the court emphasized a particular Restatement formulation, rather than throwing all of them into the mix.

PETSEY v. CUSHMAN
259 Conn. 345, 788 A.2d 496 (2002)

VERTEFEUILLE, J.

. . . "There is perhaps no more impenetrable jungle in the entire law than that which surrounds the word 'nuisance.' " W. Prosser & W. Keeton . . . §86, p. 616. This court has stated often that a plaintiff must prove four elements to succeed in a nuisance cause of action: "(1) the condition complained of had a natural tendency to create danger and inflict injury upon person or property; (2) the danger created was a continuing one; (3) the use of the land was unreasonable or unlawful; [and] (4) the existence of the nuisance was the proximate cause of the plaintiffs' injuries and damages." These elements developed through a long line of cases that can be described best as public nuisance cases.[3]

Despite its grounding in public nuisance law, this four factor analysis has since been applied without distinction to both public and private nuisance causes of action. Although there are some similarities between a public and a private nuisance, the two causes of action are distinct. Indeed, Professors Prosser and Keeton in their treatise on the law of torts have stated: "The two have almost nothing in common, except that each causes inconvenience to someone, and it would have been fortunate if they had been called from the beginning by different names." W. Prosser & W. Keeton, *supra*, §86, p. 618. Public nuisance law is concerned with the interference with a public right, and cases in this realm typically involve conduct that allegedly interferes with the public health and safety. . . . Private nuisance law, on the other hand, is concerned with conduct that interferes with an individual's private right to the use and enjoyment of his or her land. Showing the existence of a condition detrimental to the public safety, or, as the first two elements of the four factor analysis discussed previously require, showing that the condition complained of had a natural tendency to create a continuing danger, is often irrelevant to a private nuisance claim. In light of the fundamental differences between these two distinct causes of action, we conclude that further attempts to employ the four part test discussed previously herein in the

---

3. Section 821B of the Restatement (Second) of Torts defines a public nuisance as "an unreasonable interference with a right common to the general public." See State v. Tippetts-Abbett-McCarthy-Stratton, 204 Conn. at 183. Whether an interference is unreasonable in the public nuisance context depends, according to the Restatement (Second), on "(a) [w]hether the conduct involves a significant interference with the public health, the public safety, the public peace, the public comfort or the public convenience, or (b) whether the conduct is proscribed by [law]. . . ." 4 Restatement (Second) . . . §821B. The rights common to the general public can include, but certainly are not limited to, such things as the right to use a public park, highway, river, or lake. Id., §821D, comment (c).

assessment of private nuisance causes of action would be imprudent; private nuisance claims simply do not fit comfortably within the same analytical rubric as public nuisance claims. We must restate, therefore, the elements that a plaintiff must prove to prevail on a claim for damages in a common-law private nuisance action.

In prescribing these specific elements, we look to the leading authorities in the field of common-law private nuisance for guidance. According to the Restatement (Second) of Torts, a plaintiff must prove that: (1) there was an invasion of the plaintiff's use and enjoyment of his or her property; (2) the defendant's conduct was the proximate cause of the invasion; and (3) the invasion was either intentional and unreasonable, or unintentional and the defendant's conduct was negligent or reckless. 4 Restatement (Second) . . . §822. Although the language used in this third element does not make the point clearly, under this test, showing unreasonableness is an essential element of a private nuisance cause of action based on negligence or recklessness. See id., §822, comment (k). Professors Prosser and Keeton define the plaintiff's burden in a similar manner. According to their view, a plaintiff in a private nuisance action must demonstrate that: (1) the defendant acted with the intent of interfering with the plaintiff's use and enjoyment of his or her property; (2) the interference with the use and enjoyment of the land was of the kind intended; (3) the interference was substantial; and (4) the interference was unreasonable. W. Prosser & W. Keeton . . . §87, p. 622-25. In the context of a private nuisance, they define a defendant's intent as meaning merely that "the defendant has created or continued the condition causing the interference with full knowledge that the harm to the plaintiff's interests are occurring or are substantially certain to follow." Id., at 625.

This requirement of unreasonableness, a part of the third element in the test set forth in the Restatement (Second) and the fourth element in the test enunciated by Professors Prosser and Keeton, often has been stated, not in terms of whether the interference was unreasonable, but, rather, in terms of whether the defendant's conduct was unreasonable. See, e.g., Walsh v. Stonington Water Pollution Control Authority, 250 Conn. at 446 (determining whether defendants' operation of wastewater treatment plant was " 'unreasonable use' "). In its charge to the jury, the trial court in the present case framed the inquiry in such a manner.

Although similar, "[t]he two concepts—unreasonable interference and unreasonable conduct—are not at all identical." W. Prosser & W. Keeton . . . §87, p. 623. "Confusion has resulted from the fact that the . . . interference with the plaintiff's use of his property can be unreasonable even when the defendant's conduct is reasonable. . . . Courts have often found the existence of a nuisance on the basis of unreasonable use when what was meant is that the interference was unreasonable, i.e., it was unreasonable for the defendant to act as he did without paying for the harm that was knowingly inflicted on the plaintiff. Thus, an industrial enterprise who properly locates a cement plant or a coal-burning electric generator, who exercises utmost care in the utilization of known scientific techniques for minimizing the harm from the emission of noxious smoke, dust and gas and who is serving society well by engaging in the activity may yet be required to pay for the inevitable harm caused to neighbors." Id., §88, p. 629. As this example amply demonstrates, while an unreasonable use and an unreasonable interference often coexist, the two concepts are not equivalent, and it is possible to prove that a defendant's use of his property, while reasonable, nonetheless constitutes a common-law private nuisance because it unreasonably interferes with the use of property by another person. That was the situation in *Walsh*.

In *Walsh*, this court rejected the defendants' argument on appeal that their operation of the wastewater treatment plant in question could not constitute a nuisance since the operation of such a plant was clearly a reasonable use of property. Id., at 457. This court held that the production of odors by the defendants' plant could constitute a nuisance, notwithstanding the fact that operating a wastewater treatment plant was clearly a reasonable use of the property in question. Although the proposition was not stated expressly in *Walsh*, our holding in that case demonstrates that, while the reasonableness of a defendant's conduct is a factor in determining whether an interference is unreasonable, it is not an independent element that must be proven in order to prevail in all private nuisance causes of action. The inquiry is cast more appropriately as whether the defendant's conduct unreasonably interfered with the plaintiff's use and enjoyment of his or her land rather than whether the defendant's conduct was itself unreasonable. Quinnett v. Newman, *supra*, 213 Conn. at 348 (nuisance refers to condition that exists and not to act that creates it). The proper focus of a private nuisance claim for damages, therefore, is whether a defendant's conduct, i.e., his or her use of his or her property, causes an unreasonable interference with the plaintiff's use and enjoyment of his or her property. Herbert v. Smyth, *supra*, 155 Conn. at 81-82; see also Scribner v. Summers, 84 F.3d 554, 559 (2d Cir. 1996); Copart Industries, Inc. v. Consolidated Edison Co. of New York, Inc., 41 N.Y.2d 564, 570 (1977).

On the basis of our reexamination of our case law and upon our review of private nuisance law as described by the leading authorities, we adopt the basic principles of §822 of the Restatement (Second) of Torts and conclude that in order to recover damages in a common-law private nuisance cause of action, a plaintiff must show that the defendant's conduct was the proximate cause of an unreasonable interference with the plaintiff's use and enjoyment of his or her property. The interference may be either intentional; Quinnett v. Newman, 213 Conn. at 348 (nuisance is created intentionally if defendant intends act that brings about condition found to be nuisance); or the result of the defendant's negligence. Id., at 348-49. Whether the interference is unreasonable depends upon a balancing of the interests involved under the circumstances of each individual case. In balancing the interests, the fact finder must take into consideration all relevant factors, including the nature of both the interfering use and the use and enjoyment invaded, the nature, extent and duration of the interference, the suitability for the locality of both the interfering conduct and the particular use and enjoyment invaded, whether the defendant is taking all feasible precautions to avoid any unnecessary interference with the plaintiff's use and enjoyment of his or her property, and any other factors that the fact finder deems relevant to the question of whether the interference is unreasonable. No one factor should dominate this balancing of interests; all relevant factors must be considered in determining whether the interference is unreasonable.

The determination of whether the interference is unreasonable should be made in light of the fact that some level of interference is inherent in modern society. There are few, if any, places remaining where an individual may rest assured that he will be able to use and enjoy his property free from all interference. Accordingly, the interference must be substantial to be unreasonable. See 4 Restatement (Second) . . . §822, comment (g); W. Prosser & W. Keeton . . . §88, p. 626.

Ultimately, the question of reasonableness is whether the interference is beyond that which the plaintiff should bear, under all of the circumstances of the particular case, without being compensated.

NOTES AND QUESTIONS

1. *Recasting the "Unreasonableness" Focus.* Although the *Petsey* court undoubtedly retains some balancing as part of the private nuisance formulation, where is the focus now placed? Is this focus different from that in *Walsh*?

2. *Balancing, Injunctive Relief, and Economic Vitality.* As most students already know from their first-year courses on property law, and the common coverage in many classes of Boomer v. Atlantic Cement Co., 257 N.E.2d 870 (N.Y. 1970) (excerpted in Chapter 10), a court's finding of a nuisance in many jurisdictions has historically led to issuance of an injunction against the conduct causing harm. Hence, the unreasonableness balancing and liability determination can lead to a court-imposed shutdown of manufacturers that may be important to economic vitality and employment. Some states fashioned their common law so that this liability-injunction linkage was severed, at least where damages could still be recovered, see Madison v. Ducktown Sulphur Copper & Iron Co., 83 S.W. 658 (Tenn. 1904), but also, at times, it would lead courts to deny the existence of a nuisance even where it appeared solidly proven.

In *Boomer*, New York refashioned its law to issue a conditional injunction against a cement company's polluting operations until it paid court-set "permanent damages." This case and a few related cases led to publication of one of the law's most influential law review articles, Calabresi & Melamed, Property Rules, Liability Rules, and Inalienability: One View of the Cathedral, 85 Harv. L. Rev. 1089 (1972). Dean Calabresi and his co-author looked at nuisance cases and saw in them four possible modes of resolution, with the key variables being how different resolutions would leave certain tasks either to the court or to private negotiation, and who held the "entitlement" to enjoy or undertake an activity. You have been introduced to all but one of these various resolutions. Can you articulate what they are?

For a case decided virtually simultaneously with this article, and utilizing the less intuitively obvious fourth potential resolution, see Spur Industries, Inc. v. Del E. Webb Dev. Co., 494 P.2d 700 (Ariz. 1972).

3. *The Holdout.* Key to understanding judicial refusal to issue injunctions, or embrace of conditional injunctions with judicially set damages, is the concept of the *holdout.* Just because a defendant might offer a market-priced damages remedy to a pollution victim does not mean the victim will budge and surrender her right to an injunction. Even if a defendant offers well above the actual market value of the damage or outright acquisition of the plaintiff victim's property, the plaintiff might hold out, refusing to sell. The injunction then could become a permanent closure order for a plant of great local value. This possibility has led numerous jurisdictions to abandon the previously mechanical linkage of the finding of a nuisance and the issuance of an injunction.

4. *Nuisance and the Risk of Future Injury.* Advocates of statutory and regulatory answers to environmental ills sometimes describe such public law approaches as different from common law in their preventive focus, seeking to limit or prevent harms before they occur. Certainly they are more decidedly preventive or precautionary in focus, but they also often actually add up to "right to pollute" laws, limiting but allowing pollution.

The preventive versus after-the-fact distinction between regulatory and common law answers is more a difference of degree. Where a proposed land use will become a nuisance, courts may use the apprehended or anticipatory nuisance doctrine to enjoin the proposed use before it begins. 58 Am. Jur. 2d Nuisances §339 (2006). Anticipatory nuisance is a widely recognized cause of action. Smith, Re-validating the Doctrine of Anticipatory Nuisance, 29 Vt. L. Rev. 687, 688 (2005); see Rock Island and Pacific R.R. Co. v. Iowa Dep't of Transp., 756 F.2d 517, 521 (7th Cir. 1985) ("A land use that will create a nuisance can be enjoined in advance, as an alternative to abating the nuisance once it comes into being."); Roach v. Combined Util. Comm'n, 351 S.E.2d 168 (S.C. App. 1986) ("An anticipatory nuisance is an act, occupation or structure which is not a nuisance per se, but which may become a nuisance by reason of circumstances, location or surroundings."). Anticipatory nuisance requires a high burden of proof because it restricts a landowner's freedom to use his land before any harm occurs. Smith, *supra*, at 697. Generally, the plaintiff must demonstrate that "[t]he injury must be practically certain, rather than merely probable." 58 Am Jur. 2d Nuisances §342 (2006). Because of the high burden of proof, the anticipatory nuisance doctrine is seldom used.

3. Trespass Claims

The use of trespass actions to remedy groundwater contamination or air pollution is another example of the limits of the common law to promote a high level of environmental protection. To maintain a trespass claim, a plaintiff must prove that the defendant intended to act in a manner that produced an unlawful invasion and had good reason to know that, for example, the subsurface geology would permit the contamination to migrate beneath plaintiff's land. The discharge of toxic pollutants that migrate beneath another's land can also be a trespass. E.g., Davey Compressor Co. v. City of Delray Beach, 613 So. 2d 60 (Fla. App. 1993), *approved*, 639 So. 2d 595 (Fla. 1994); Sterling v. Velsicol Chem. Corp., 647 F. Supp. 303, 317-319 (W.D. Tenn. 1986), *aff'd*, 855 F.2d 1188, 1198 (6th Cir. 1988). Air pollution historically was not a trespass because the particles did not amount to a direct physical invasion. Indirect injuries had to be redressed as nuisances. However, the "tangible" invasion requirement has been rejected as unscientific in some jurisdictions. Martin v. Reynolds Metals Co., 342 P.2d 790 (Or. 1959); Bradley v. American Smelting and Ref. Co., 709 P.2d 782 (Wash. 1985).

Environmental trespass remains, however, different from a simple unconsented entry onto the land of another. Courts have aligned trespass with negligence and nuisance liability. *Bradley* and other cases require proof of "actual and substantial damages." For example, Chance v. BP Chem., Inc., 670 N.E.2d 985 (Ohio 1996), upheld the dismissal of a trespass, negligence, and nuisance action for injected liquid wastes that allegedly migrated beneath plaintiff's land. The court held that plaintiffs must show an actual interference with a reasonable and foreseeable use of the subsurface beneath their land.

4. Strict Liability Claims

Common law claims rooted in strict liability theory also can provide plaintiffs with significant relief, but typically plaintiffs must convince a court that the activity causing the harm was unusually dangerous, was inherently dangerous in the location in which it occurred, or involved materials that are always inherently dangerous. For example, strict liability is a possibility for the discharge of hazardous waste into aquifers, but the plaintiff must still establish that defendant's conduct in fact caused injury. A New Jersey case, State Dep't of Envtl. Prot. v. Ventron Corp., 468 A.2d 150 (N.J. 1983), imposed common law strict liability on the purchasers of a 40-acre tract from which mercury pollution was seeping into the ground.

Such claims are far from automatic victories for plaintiffs. Section 520 of the Restatement (Second) of Torts and some case law appear to impose a foreseeability requirement for strict liability. A post-*Ventron* New Jersey case indicates that the issue is open, but found that the owner of an industrial site that had processed radium since 1917 was strictly liable because it should have known that radium has always been an abnormally dangerous substance and "the injudicious handling, processing, and disposal of radium has [sic] for decades caused concern. . . ." T & E Indus., Inc. v. Safety Light Corp., 587 A.2d 1249, 1261 (N.J. 1991). Compare Cambridge Water Co. v. Eastern Counties Laeher, PLC (1994), 2 App. Cas. 264 (1994) 1 All E.R. 53, which imposed a foreseeability requirement on strict liability claims for past industrial practices that cause pollution.

The following case not only illuminates how lawyers and judges will seek to push environmental cases into more typical negligence settings, but also illustrates the power of strict liability claims.

BRANCH v. WESTERN PETROLEUM INC.
657 P.2d 267 (Utah 1982)

STEWART, Justice.

The Branches, the plaintiff property owners, sued for damages for the pollution of their culinary water wells caused by percolation of defendant Western Petroleum Inc.'s formation waters (waste waters from oil wells containing various chemical contaminants) into the subterranean water system that feeds the wells. A jury answered questions to special interrogatories, finding, *inter alia*, that the formation waters had contaminated plaintiffs' two wells and awarded damages of $8,050 for pollution of the well water, $700 for trespass, $10,000 for "mental suffering, discomfort and annoyance," and $13,000 punitive damages. The jury, over objection, was instructed on the theory of negligence; however, the trial court entered judgment on the basis of strict liability for the above amounts, except that damages for mental suffering, discomfort, and annoyance were disallowed.

Western appeals, arguing that the trial court erred in awarding damages for pollution of the wells on the basis of strict liability. It contends that negligence is the only valid legal theory upon which the judgment can be sustained and that the trial court erred (1) in not instructing on proximate cause; and (2) in not directing the jury to find the percentage of negligence attributable to each party as required by the Utah Comparative Negligence Act, U.C.A., 1953, §78-27-38. . . .

I

In December 1975, Western purchased forty acres of land in a rural area north of Roosevelt, Utah, which had previously been used as a gravel pit. Western used the property solely for the disposal of formation water, a waste water produced by oil wells while drilling for oil. Formation water contains oil, gas and high concentrations of salt and chemicals, making it unfit for culinary or agricultural uses. The formation water was transported by truck from various oil-producing sites and emptied into the disposal pit with the intent that the toxic water would dissipate through evaporation into the air and percolation into the ground. Alternative sites for disposing of the water were available to Western, but at a greater expense.

In 1976, the Branches purchased a parcel of property immediately adjacent to, and at an elevation of approximately 200 to 300 feet lower than, Western's property. The twenty-one acre parcel had on it a "diligence" well, which had been in existence since 1929, some outbuildings, and a home. After acquiring the property, the Branches made some $60,000 worth of improvements to the home and premises. Prior owners of the property used the water from the well for a grade A dairy and later a grade B dairy. Both dairy operations required that the water be approved for fitness and purity by appropriate state agencies. The Branches, as had all prior owners since 1929, used water from the diligence well for culinary purposes. The water from the diligence well was described as being sweet to the taste and of a high quality until December of 1976.

Two months after purchasing the property, the Branches noticed that the well water began to take on a peculiar taste and had the distinctive smell of petroleum products. Soap added to the water would no longer form suds. They observed that polluted water from Western's disposal pit was running onto the surface of the Branches' property and, on one occasion, reached their basement, causing damage to food stored there. After testing the diligence well water and finding it unfit for human consumption, and after their rabbits and one hundred chickens had died, apparently from the polluted water, the Branches began trucking water to their property from outside sources. In November, 1977, the Branches dug an additional well south of their home. Water from the new well was tested and found safe for culinary purposes. But after a few months, the new well also ceased producing potable water, and on advice of the State Health Department, the Branches ceased using the new well for culinary purposes and hauled water to their property almost until the time of trial.

The Branches requested Western to cease dumping formation water in the disposal pit, but Western refused unless the Branches would post a bond to cover the costs. Western did, however, agree to build a pond on its property to contain the escaping surface water and prevent it from flowing onto the Branches' land. In doing so, Western failed to establish the proper boundary line and built part of the pond on the Branches' land. After the Branches hired a surveyor to establish that Western had built the pond on their land, Western built another containing pond on its own property. The pond, however, was only partially successful in preventing the run-off onto the Branches' land from the disposal pit. Western caused additional damage by permitting its trucks to enter the Branches' property for the purpose of pumping out the containment ponds. When the discharge nozzles on the trucks were left open, polluted water was sprayed directly onto the Branches' land.

As a consequence of the unavailability of culinary water in her home, plaintiff Jeanne Branch returned to her original home in Colorado for a three or four month period so that she could "pull herself together." During this time, Lloyd Branch made weekly trips to and from Colorado to be with his family and otherwise tried to keep in contact with his wife on the telephone while he maintained his contracting business in Roosevelt.

Western's agents admitted that they did not know, and made no attempt to ascertain, what state law was with respect to permitting formation waters to seep or percolate into subsurface waters. Even after Western became aware of the laws relative to dumping, it still took no affirmative action to obtain approval of its ponds. . . .

[The jury] found, in response to special interrogatories, that "defendant's use of the evaporation pit for the dumping of formation water [was] a cause of the pollution of the water in plaintiffs' [wells]," and that Western caused 66 percent of the pollution in Branches' original well and 52 percent of the pollution in the new well. The rest of the pollution was found to be caused by other unspecified "parties or conditions." The jury also found that Western was "negligent . . . in dumping formation waters in its evaporation pit," and had also committed a "trespass upon plaintiffs' land . . . other than the claimed pollution of [the] wells."

II

The major substantive dispute is whether the trial court erred in entering judgment against Western on the basis of strict liability for pollution of the Branches' wells. Western argues that other states have based liability for pollution of subterranean waters on either negligence, nuisance, or trespass, and that since the Branches failed to allege nuisance or trespass, "the only accepted theory upon which this case could be based is negligence." Therefore, according to Western, the trial court erred in entering judgment on the basis of strict liability. Western further submits that since the court did not instruct the jury on proximate cause and comparative negligence, the judgment cannot stand. The Branches, on the other hand, take the position that Western created an abnormally dangerous condition by collecting contaminated water on its land for the purpose of having it seep or percolate into the groundwater and that, therefore, the law of strict liability controls. . . .

Two doctrines have developed in the common law to provide a remedy to a private landowner for nontrespassory injuries caused by another. The landmark case of Rylands v. Fletcher, 3 H. & C. 774, 159 Eng. Rep. 737 (1865), rev'd in Fletcher v. Rylands, L.R. 1 Ex. 265 (1866), aff'd in Rylands v. Fletcher, L.R. 3 H.L. 330 (1868), held that one who uses his land in an unnatural way and thereby creates a dangerous condition or engages in an abnormal activity may be strictly liable for injuries resulting from that condition or activity. Whether a condition or activity is considered abnormal is defined in terms of whether the condition or activity is unduly dangerous or inappropriate to the place where it is maintained. W. Prosser, Law of Torts §78, at 506 (4th ed. 1971). That doctrine was the genesis of §519 of the Restatement of Torts (1939), which, however, limited strict liability to "ultrahazardous activities." Prosser, *supra*, at 512.

Although Rylands v. Fletcher was initially rejected by a number of states, its influence has been substantial in the United States. According to the latest edition of Dean Prosser's treatise on torts, only seven American jurisdictions have rejected the rule of that case, while some thirty jurisdictions have essentially approved the rule. Id. at 509. Indeed, the strict liability rule of the Restatement of Torts was broadened in §519 of the Restatement (Second) of Torts by making it applicable to "abnormally dangerous activities."

Nuisance law also protects property interests from nontrespassory invasions. Unlike most other torts, it is not centrally concerned with the nature of the conduct causing the damage, but with the nature and relative importance of the interests interfered with or invaded. The doctrine of nuisance "has reference to the interests invaded, to the damage or harm inflicted, and not to any particular kind of action or omission which has led to the invasion." W. Prosser, *supra*, §87 at 73-75. Since it is not the nature of one's conduct that generally is essential to an action for nuisance, a person whose interests have been invaded may have a claim for relief based both on nuisance and on the nature of the conduct producing the damage. See Cities Service Oil Co. v. Merritt, Okl., 332 P.2d 677, 684 (1958); Wood v. Picillo, R.I., 443 A.2d 1244 (1982). As the court in *Wood* stated:

> The essential element of an actionable nuisance is that persons have suffered harm or are threatened with injuries that they ought not have to bear. Citizens for Preservation of Waterman Lake v. Davis, R.I., 420 A.2d 53, 59 (1980). Distinguished from negligence liability, liability in nuisance is predicated upon unreasonable injury rather than upon unreasonable conduct. Braun v. Iannotti, 54 R.I. 469, 471, 175 A. 656, 657 (1934). Thus, plaintiffs may recover in nuisance despite the otherwise nontortious nature of the conduct which creates the injury. . . .

It is of no consequence that a business which causes a nuisance is a lawful business. Mowrer v. Ashland Oil & Refining Co., *supra*, at 661. The production of formation water is a natural and necessary incident to the business of producing oil and gas. A business such as Western, which collects and disposes of formation water, conducts a wholly legitimate business. But that does not give it a license to dispose of waste in a manner that for practical purposes appropriates the property of others by making it impossible for them to use water which they are entitled to use. North Point C.I. Co. v. Utah & Salt Lake Canal Co., 52 P. 168 (Utah 1898). . . .

There are two separate, although somewhat related, grounds for holding Western strictly liable for the pollution of the Branches' wells. First, the facts of the case support application of the rule of strict liability because the ponding of the toxic formation water in an area adjacent to the Branches' wells constituted an abnormally dangerous and inappropriate use of the land in light of its proximity to the Branches' property and was unduly dangerous to the Branches' use of their well water. Several cases on comparable facts have applied strict liability due to the abnormal danger of polluting activity. For example, Mowrer v. Ashland Oil & Refining Co., Inc., 518 F.2d 659 (7th Cir. 1975), applied strict liability to the leakage of crude oil and salt water into a fresh water well; Yommer v. McKenzie, 257 A.2d 138 (Md. 1969), applied the same rule to the seepage of gasoline from an underground tank into an adjoining landowner's well; Cities Service Co. v. Florida, 312 So. 2d 799 (Fla. App. 1975), applied strict liability to the escape of phosphate slime into a creek and river. See also Bumbarger v. Walker, 164 A.2d 144 (Pa. Super. 1960) (strict liability for well pollution caused by defendant's mine blasting). See generally Clark-Aiken Co. v. Cromwell-Wright Co., 323 N.E.2d 876 (Mass. 1975) (strict liability applied to escape of impounded water); Indiana Harbor Belt R.R. Co. v. American Cynamid Co., 517 F. Supp. 314 (N.D. Ill. 1981) (strict liability applied to spillage of toxic chemical that resulted in property damage and pollution of water supply); W. Prosser, *supra*, §78 at 512-13 and cases there cited. See also Atlas Chem. Indus., Inc. v. Anderson, 514 S.W.2d 309 (Tex. Civ. App. 1974), aff'd, 524 S.W.2d 681 (1975), where the Texas court, distinguishing a case relied upon by Western, Turner v. Big Lake Oil Co., 96 S.W.2d 221 (Tex. 1936), held the defendant strictly liable for polluting surface streams with industrial wastes. The strict liability rule of Rylands v. Fletcher was held to apply to pollution cases "in which the defendant has set the substance in motion for escape, such as the discharge of the harmful effluent or the emission of a harmful gas or substance."[6] *Atlas Chemical, supra*, at 314.

In concluding that strict liability should govern in that case, the court in *Atlas Chemical* reasoned that the common law rules of tort liability in pollution cases "should be in conformity with the public policy of this state as declared by the Legislature in the Texas Water Code. . . ." Id. at 315. The court also found support for the rule of strict liability in the policy consideration that an industry should not be able to use its property in such a way as to inflict injury on the property of its neighbors because to do so would result in effect in appropriating the neighbor's property to one's own use. An industrial polluter can and should assume the costs of pollution as a cost of doing business rather than charge the loss to a wholly innocent party. The court in *Atlas Chemical* stated:

> We know of no acceptable rule of jurisprudence which permits those engaged in important and desirable enterprises to injure with impunity those who are engaged in enterprises of lesser economic significance. The costs of injuries resulting from pollution must be internalized by industry as a cost of production and borne by consumers or shareholders, or both, and not by the injured individual. Id. at 316.

We think these reasons adequately support application of the rule of strict liability in this case.

NOTES AND QUESTIONS

1. *Who Was There First?* Note that in this case, the defendant was in its location prior to the plaintiffs. That fact was not dispositive. Should it be? Why or why not?

2. *Economics in Action.* Quoting *Atlas Chemical*, the court brought in the concept of internalizing the costs associated with a harmful activity. Would Coase agree with this statement? Can you construct a more sophisticated argument for why Western Petroleum should pay?

3. *The Facts.* Be sensitive to all of the facts that plaintiffs' counsel gathered to make their case. What sorts of facts would you need to gather if you were to bring a similar case for a client?

4. *Damages and the Punitive Damages Remedy.* As noted earlier and in the principal case, plaintiffs bring common law actions, especially private nuisance actions, in the usual hope that they will obtain both injunctive and compensatory relief. The possible right to receive injunctive relief versus court-set damages is discussed in note 2 after the *Petsey* case above.

Where the injuries from environmental harms are substantial, especially where the conduct causing the harm shows recklessness, willfulness, or other reprehensible or egregious misconduct, the common law of most states allows for the possibility of a punitive damages award. That possibility can create substantial plaintiff and attorney incentives to bring suit: the plaintiff might receive a substantial award far outstripping provable economic losses or pain and suffering, while the plaintiff's attorney could

---

6. Even if Western did not know that the formation water would enter the aquifer and cause damage to plaintiffs' wells, it could have determined the likelihood of that consequence. . . .

earn a percentage of a substantial punitive damages award. Several recent developments, however, have diminished the prospect of huge punitive damage awards. First, many states by statute cap the amount that can be received in a punitive damages award. Second, the Supreme Court in several recent cases has imposed a federal constitutional limitation on punitive damage awards rooted in the Due Process Clause of the Constitution. See, e.g., BMW of N. Am. v. Gore, 517 U.S. 559 (1996) (limiting punitive damages award in setting of consumer claiming deceptive selling of a repaired car). The Court further articulated this federal court role in State Farm Mut. Auto. Ins. Co. v. Campbell, 538 U.S. 408, 425 (2003), stating that few punitive damage awards exceeding a single-digit ratio of 9 to 1 of punitive to compensatory damages will be constitutional, and also indicating that 4 to 1 will be the more typical limit. The two main exceptions identified were settings in which harms are hard to detect or an "egregious act" that has resulted in only small compensatory damages.

The large punitive damages award arising out of the massive spill of oil from the supertanker Exxon Valdez led to the Supreme Court's most watched environmental harm punitive damages decision, in Exxon Shipping Co. v. Baker, 554 U.S. 471 (2008). By the time the case was before the Supreme Court, the punitive damages award had been reduced by the Ninth Circuit to $2.5 billion, with a compensatory award to fishermen of $287 million. The Supreme Court again reduced the punitive damages award, this time with language stating that "in maritime cases . . . a one-to-one ratio . . . is a fair upper limit." Due to the Supreme Court's emphasis on the case as rooted in federal maritime law and not the Due Process Clause, but with little actual attention to maritime law, it is not yet clear whether an even lower cap will be applied by courts in non-maritime cases. For discussion of the use of punitive damage remedies in environmental harm settings, see Klass, Punitive Damages and Valuing Harm, 92 Minn. L. Rev. 83 (2007) (analyzing the major Supreme Court precedents and calling for adjustment of due process caps for undervalued harms such as environmental damages that are not borne by plaintiffs); see also Kerr, Comment, Exxon Shipping Company v. Baker: The Perils of Judicial Punitive Damages Reform, 59 Emory L.J. 727 (2010) (focusing on the Exxon Valdez case and questioning the economic logic of the Supreme Court). These cases will be of substantial importance in state common law actions brought against BP and other defendants linked to the huge Deepwater Horizon oil spill that occurred during the spring and summer of 2010.

5.   *The Public Trust Doctrine*

Since the late 1960s, environmentalists have been searching for a substantive theory of environmental protection. Statutory and nuisance claims are typically now the first place lawyers turn for environmental damages, but the public trust doctrine continues to provide a source of argument and relief when other claims might fail.

The public trust doctrine was transformed through scholarship and cases starting in the 1960s, but arguably has its roots in antiquity. Briefly, Roman and English common law posited that the beds of navigable rivers were held in trust for the public to protect the public right of navigation and associated uses, such as fishing and, later, recreation. Note, The Public Trust in Tidal Areas: A Sometimes Submerged Traditional Doctrine, 79 Yale L.J. 762 (1970). The doctrine became important in the nineteenth century as large harbors were filled to build new cities. Most courts held that states could terminate the trust in some unspecified percentage of tideland areas, but in 1892 the U.S. Supreme Court, citing not a single precedent and refusing to explain whether its decision was based on the Constitution or state law, held that the Illinois state legislature could not convey the submerged lands along Chicago's lakefront to a railroad because the grant violated the public trust:

> Such abdication is not consistent with the exercise of that trust which requires the government of the State to preserve such waters for the use of the public. The trust devolving upon the State for the public, and which can only be discharged by the management and control of property in which the public has an interest, cannot be relinquished by a transfer of the property. The control of the State for the purposes of the trust can never be lost, except as to such parcels as are used in promoting the interests of the public therein, or can be disposed of without any substantial impairment of the public interest in the lands and waters remaining. It is only by observing the distinction between a grant of such parcels for the improvement of the public interest, or which when occupied do not substantially impair the public interest in the lands and waters remaining, and a grant of the whole property in which the public is interested, that the language of the adjudged cases can be reconciled. General language sometimes found in opinions of lands under navigable waters, irrespective of any trust as to their use and disposition, must be read and construed with reference to the special facts of the particular cases. A grant of all lands under the navigable waters of a State has never been adjudged to be within the legislative power; and any attempted grant of the kind would be held, if not absolutely void on its face, as subject to revocation. The State can no more abdicate its trust over property in which the whole people are interested, like navigable waters and soils under them, so as to leave them entirely under the use and control of private parties, except in the instance of parcels mentioned for the improvement of the navigation and use of the waters, or when parcels can be disposed of without impairment of the public interest in what remains, than it can abdicate its police powers in the administration of government and the preservation of the peace. [Illinois Central R. Co. v. Illinois, 146 U.S. 387 (1892).]

For a reexamination of the case that calls into question some of its key conclusions, see Kearney & Merrill, The Origins of the American Public Trust Doctrine: What Really Happened in *Illinois Central*, 71 U. Chi. L. Rev. 799 (2004).

Illinois Central, its progeny, and state public trust cases raise as many questions as they resolve. As you read the notes and cases that follow, try to answer the following questions. Does the doctrine really create an insurmountable substantive barrier against land dispositions as occurred in *Illinois Central*? When can governments allow the development or sale of natural resources previously held by the government? Can procedural steps allow what would otherwise be judicially rejected? The following paragraphs offer some answers to these questions, but because the public trust doctrine has developed differently in different states, only careful research in each state can reveal the restrictions imposed by the public trust doctrine.

Environmentalists have built on *Illinois Central* to argue that the trust imposes both domestic and international law stewardship duties to manage all resources, especially public ones. E. Weiss, In Fairness to Future Generations: International Law, Common Patrimony, and Intergenerational Equity (1989). There is some precedent to extend it to public lands, but precedent is slim. For example, during the progressive conservation era, the Supreme Court invoked the public trust doctrine to reject the perennial western states' argument that the federal government lacked the power to retain and manage public lands for national forests, parks, and other public use classifications. Light v. United States, 220 U.S. 523 (1911). The Court repeated an earlier statement that "[a]ll the public lands are held in trust for the people of the whole country, United States v. Trinidad Coal & Coking Co., 137 U.S. 160," but rejected any judicial role in policing the trust. "And it is not for the courts to say how the trust shall be administered. That is for Congress to determine."

Two environmental interpretations of *Illinois Central* have emerged. The first, articulated by Professor Joseph Sax, argues that the trust is a procedural doctrine that allows courts to (a) decide if political decisions to reallocate public resources were made after a reasonable consideration of all alternatives and (b) to remand to the legislature if the political process failed to do so for reasons such as undue special interest influence. Sax, The Public Trust Doctrine in Natural Resources Law: Effective Judicial Intervention, 68 Mich. L. Rev. 471 (1970). The second theory eschews the indirect procedural-process route and posits that the trust contains a hierarchy of values with ecosystem stability at the top.

California's Supreme Court first said in dictum that the trust included ecosystem stability and recreation, Marks v. Whitney, 491 P.2d 374 (Cal. 1971), and then it applied the public trust doctrine to reallocate a vested water right whose exercise disrupted a delicate ecosystem. As you read the following case excerpt, assess whether California is adopting one of these two theories or a hybrid.

NATIONAL AUDUBON SOCIETY v. SUPERIOR COURT OF ALPINE COUNTY
658 P.2d 709 (Cal. 1983)

[As the movie *Chinatown* graphically illustrates, to sustain its growth, Los Angeles turned to the eastern slope of the Sierra Nevada mountains in the early 1900s after it had exhausted local water supplies. The Los Angeles Department of Water and Power eventually perfected appropriations to the tributary creeks to Mono Lake, a unique closed basin. As the city exercised its rights, the diversions lowered the lake by some 44 feet, altering the lake ecosystem by increasing the salinity of the lake. These alterations threatened the brine shrimp population that fed the birds that gathered on islands in the lake, and they dried up the bed between islands in the lake so that predators could now reach these former refuges. California's highest court held that the public trust required a reallocation of water to raise the lake level, although no specific level was specified by the California Supreme Court's opinion. Its key articulation of California's formulation of the public trust doctrine follows.]

BROUSSARD, J. . . .

a. The state as sovereign retains continuing supervisory control over its navigable waters and the lands beneath those waters. This principle, fundamental to the concept of the public trust, applies to rights in flowing waters as well as to rights in tidelands and lakeshores; it prevents any party from acquiring a vested right to appropriate water in a manner harmful to the interest protected by the public trust.

b. As a matter of current and historical necessity, the Legislature, acting directly through an authorized agency such as the Water Board, has the power to grant usufructuary licenses that will permit an appropriator to take water from flowing streams and use that water in a distant part of the state, even though this taking does not promote, and may unavoidably harm, the trust uses at the source stream. The population and economy of this state depend upon the appropriation of vast quantities of water for uses unrelated to in-stream trust values. California's Constitution, its statutes, decisions, and commentators all emphasize the need to make efficient use of California's limited water resources: all recognize, at least implicitly, that efficient use requires diverting water from in-stream uses. Now that the economy and population centers of this state have developed in reliance upon appropriated water, it would be disingenuous to hold that such appropriations are and have always been improper to the extent that they harm public trust uses, and can be justified only upon theories of reliance or estoppel.

c. The state has an affirmative duty to take the public trust into account in the planning and allocation of water resources, and to protect public trust uses whenever feasible. Just as the history of this state shows that appropriation may be necessary for efficient use of water despite unavoidable harm to public trust values, it demonstrates that an appropriative water rights system administered without consideration of the public trust may cause unnecessary and unjustified harm to trust interests. As a matter of practical necessity the state may have to approve appropriations despite foreseeable harm to public trust uses. In so doing, however, the state must bear in mind its duty as trustee to consider the effect of taking on the public trust (see United Plainsmen v. N.D. State Water Con. Commission (N.D. 1976) 247 N.W.2d 457-463) and to preserve, so far as consistent with the public interest, the uses protected by the trust.

NOTE AND QUESTIONS

1. *The* Mono Lake *Denouement.* Ultimately, a trial court fixed the lake level at 2 feet above the level at the time the litigation was initiated. This new level is approximately 25 feet below the prediversion level, but is considered sufficient to restore the ecosystem to something close to its prediversion functions. See also In re Water Use Permit Applications, Petitions for Interim Instream Flow Standard Amendments, and Petitions for Water Reservations for the Waiahole Ditch, 9 P.3d 409 (Haw. 2000) (public trust requires state to allocate abandoned water to instream and ecosystem restoration purposes before reallocating the supply for consumptive uses and to adopt a conservative margin of safety in setting instream and ecosystem restoration requirements).

Questions still abound: Does the trust extend to dry land? One district court held that the government had a trust duty to acquire enough land to buffer the Redwood National Park, Sierra Club v. Department of Interior, 376 F. Supp. 90, 398 F. Supp. 284 (N.D. Cal. 1974), but subsequent courts have refused to extend the trust to public lands. The decided cases have confined it to navigable waters and associated areas such as beaches and stream access. Can one derive an operational principle of ecosystem stability from the public trust doctrine? Is prehuman intervention background the trust standard? What is background? Is it the predevelopment ecosystem in the area? Is it the prehuman settlement landscape? If not, what is the standard? In the *Mono Lake* case, the California Supreme Court did not use the prediversion level of a navigable lake as the standard. Can you articulate a general standard other than pre-anthropocentric change background? For a case seeing a municipal park as subject to the public trust doctrine, but allowing open legislative action to modify the parkland's use to educational purposes, see Paepke v. Public Bldg. Comm'n, 263 N.E.2d 11 (Ill. 1970).

For additional discussion of the public trust doctrine, see generally Lazarus, Changing Conceptions of Property and Sovereignty in Natural Resources: Questioning the Public Trust Doctrine, 71 Iowa L. Rev. 631 (1986); and Araiza, Democracy, Distrust, and the Public Trust: Process-Based Constitutional Theory, the Public Trust Doctrine, and the Search for a Substantive Environmental Value, 45 UCLA L. Rev. 385 (1997).

2. *New Energy Sources and Common Law Claims.* Between periodic energy crises, changing technologies, and likely climate change and energy legislation, there is likely to be a boom in the construction of new energy sources, especially wind power and increased natural gas production. These newer or at least substantially more pervasive forms of energy production or extraction can provide great benefits in the market and also help shift energy production away from more carbon-intensive and polluting energy sources. Nonetheless, as you probably already figured out in studying this body of law, and in light of the common law claims in Problem 1-3, noise and view impairment caused by wind turbines can give rise to private nuisance claims. For a thorough survey of legal issues surrounding use of wind power, including discussion of nuisance claims, see Andriano, The Power of Wind: Current Legal Issues in Siting for Wind Power, 61 Planning and Envtl. L. 3, 7-10 (May 2009). Similarly, vastly increased production of natural gas through fracturing techniques—often called "fracking"—can pose risks to private and public amenities, including groundwater aquifers, as well as cause other risks from spills, air pollution, and discomforts to neighbors from the activities inherent in setting up and operating such drilling and extraction operations. For discussion of possible legal responses to resulting risks and harms, see Merrill & Schizer, The Shale Oil and Gas Revolution, Hydraulic Fracturing, and Water Contamination: A Regulatory Strategy, 98 Minn. L. Rev. 145 (2013).

6. *Constitutionally Rooted Environmental Claims*

Environmental law has evolved and even flourished without judicial recognition of federal constitutional rights to a clean environment. Lazarus, Restoring What's Environmental About Environmental Law in the Supreme Court, 47 UCLA L. Rev. 703 (2000). Indeed, in recent years, constitutional law doctrines have been wielded by litigators and recognized in the courts to weaken environmental protections. Percival, "Greening" the Constitution—Harmonizing Environmental and Constitutional Values, 32 Envtl. L. 809 (2002).

The basic reason for the lack of constitutional footing for an affirmative constitutionally based right to a clean environment is that the Constitution is primarily a charter of negative rights, rather than of affirmative government duties and individual entitlements to government action. In addition, a right to a decent environment does not fit within the classic paradigm of a constitutional right. Proponents of environmental protection are typically not an isolated minority subject to serious, long-terms risks of severe discrimination by legislatures indifferent or hostile to their concerns, and effective access to the legislative process is not blocked.

For these reasons, persistent arguments that the Supreme Court should recognize an implied right to environmental quality have met the same fate as most calls for constitutional change. In 1965, the Supreme Court, in a concurrence by Mr. Justice Goldberg in Griswold v. Connecticut, 381 U.S. 479 (1965), suggested that the Ninth Amendment and its penumbra could be the source of new implied constitutional rights. Nonetheless, courts quickly rejected arguments that the Fifth, Ninth, and Fourteenth Amendments could be the basis of an implied constitutional right to environmental quality. In United States v. 247.37 Acres, 2 Env't Rep. Cas. (BNA) 20154 (S.D. Ohio 1972), a landowner challenged the condemnation of his farm for a U.S. Army Corps of Engineers flood control reservoir, arguing that the Ninth Amendment guarantees "the preservation of their property and its surrounding environs in its natural state." The court declined the invitation to make new constitutional law because that function, it stated, was the sole province of the Supreme Court. Other courts reached the same result because of the lack of textual support and precedent, Ely v. Velde, 451 F.2d 1130 (4th Cir. 1971), or because of separation of powers considerations. "Such a construction would be ahistorical and would represent essentially a policy decision. In effect, plaintiffs invite this Court to enact a law. Since our system reserves to the legislative branch the task of legislating, this Court must decline the invitation." Tanner v. Armco Steel, 340 F. Supp. 532 (S.D. Tex. 1972).

If a right existed, what would it look like? For example, what level of public health protection would it guarantee? Zero risk? Most proponents of environmental protection reject this approach as irrational because some degree of risk is inevitable. See C. Sunstein, After the Rights Revolution: Reconceiving the Regulatory State (1990); Farber, Playing the Baseline: Civil Rights, Environmental Law, and Statutory Interpretation, 91 Colum. L. Rev. 676 (1991).

Despite resistance to recognition of federal constitutional rights to a clean environment, several states have constitutional provisions that recognize environmental rights. The Constitution of the Commonwealth of Pennsylvania, Article 1, §27, provides that "[t]he people have a right to clean air, pure water, and to the preservation of the natural, scenic, historic and esthetic values of the environment." However, the state supreme court refused to enjoin a 300-foot tower overlooking the Gettysburg battlefield. The majority held that the amendment was not self-executing, but the opinions of two concurring justices indicate that the real concern was the lack of standards to guide courts in making aesthetic judgments and the resulting unfairness that the increased risk of litigation, which had no basis at common law, created for property owners. Pennsylvania courts subsequently held that the amendment was self-executing, Commonwealth v. National Gettysburg Battlefield Tower, Inc., 311 A.2d 588 (Pa. 1973); Payne v. Kassab, 312 A.2d 86 (Pa. Commw. 1973), aff'd, 361 A.2d 263 (Pa. 1976). And in Robinson Twp. v. Commonwealth of Pa., 83 A.3d 901 (Pa. 2013), the state supreme court concluded that a state statute preempting the authority of localities to regulate hydrofracking operations to address environmental concerns amounted to an unauthorized use of public trust assets in violation of Article I, §27. See Daly & May, Robinson Township: A Model for Environmental Constitutionalism, 21 Widener L. Rev. _____ (forthcoming). Cf. Machipongo Land and Coal Co. v. Commonwealth, 799 A.2d 751 (Pa. 2002) (Commonwealth can defend against takings claim arising from prohibition of coal mining in watershed if it can prove that proposed mine plan has a high potential to increase dissolved solids and metal concentrations in stream.). Other states have applied the public doctrine more narrowly. See, e.g., Glisson v. City of Marion, 720 N.E.2d 1034 (Ill. 1999) (state constitutional provision is limited to protection against pollution only and thus does not extend to biodiversity conservation).

Another leading case illustrating the potential of state constitutional law as a source of expanded environmental protection is Montana Envtl. Info. Ctr. v. Department of Envtl. Quality, 988 P.2d 1236 (Mont. 1999). The state supreme court held that Articles II and IX of the state constitution, which guarantee a right to a clean and healthful environment, rendered unconstitutional a state water quality statute that exempted well monitoring from nondegradation review. The issue was whether open-pit gold mining into shallow aquifers, which served as mixing zones, near two high-quality rivers was subject to nondegradation review because the state's arsenic levels in the river might be exceeded. The Department of Environmental Quality concluded that the water would be diluted below state levels when it reached the river. The court held that the right to a clean and healthful environmental was fundamental and that no demonstrated harm to public health had to be established by the plaintiffs because the right "is implicated based on Plaintiff's demonstration that pumping tests proposed by . . . [the mine] would have added a known carcinogen . . . to the environment in concentrations greater than the conditions present in the receiving water." Id. at 1249.

Despite the lack of recognition of affirmative constitutional rights under the federal Constitution, the student must be aware that there are three increasingly important constitutional dimensions to environmental law that serve as resistance to environmental protection. First, the Supreme Court's active redrawing of federalism doctrine in recent years has implications for the extent of federal environmental powers under statutory law. See Chapter 2. Second, environmental protection can clash with long-recognized property entitlements and lead to regulatory takings claims. See Chapter 5, section C. Finally, state efforts to protect state amenities and, especially, regulate and encourage safe handling of waste, can run afoul of dormant Commerce Clause doctrine. See Chapter 2, section F. See also Percival, "Greening the Constitution"—Harmonizing Environmental and Constitutional Values, 32 Envtl. L. 809 (2002).

In contrast to the United States' view of a constitution as an eternal guide to the process of political organization, most other countries view constitutions as a reflection of contemporary political and social priorities. Many new constitutions contain affirmative environmental protection and ecologically sustainable development mandates that contemplate further legislative action. E.g., Constitution of the Federative Republic of Brazil, Article 225 (1988); Constitution of the Republic of South Africa, Section 24 (1996). What is the value of a constitutional provision that imposes a broad affirmative duty on the state to protect environmental quality? See Krier, The Environment, the Constitution, and the Coupling Policy, 32 Mich. L. Quadrangle Notes 35 (1988); Ruhl, The Metrics of Constitutional Amendments, and Why Proposed Environmental Quality Amendments Don't Measure Up, 74 Notre Dame L. Rev. 245 (1999).

Environmental law in Europe has been found to have roots in the protection of human dignity. See Lopez Ostra v. Spain, European Court of Human Rights (A/303/C) 20 European Human Right Reports 277 (1994) (finding that the failure of a Spanish town to protect plaintiff from odors and emissions of a group of tanning plants violated §8 of the European Convention on Human Rights).

7. *Environmental Justice Theories*

Over the past 25 years, lawyers, policymakers, environmentalists, and civil rights advocates have turned their focus to the distributional consequences of environmental protection efforts on minority, poor, and at-risk groups, such as those for whom existing pollution standards are insufficiently stringent or who live near pollution "hot spots." "Environmental justice" is now one of the standards against which environmental protection programs and policy instruments must be measured. Also known by the monikers of "environmental equity" and "environmental racism," this new area of policy ferment has changed from a problem going virtually unrecognized to an issue that has spawned dozens of books, articles, cases, and an important Executive Order. What it has not spawned, however, is any recasting of constitutional doctrine to recognize any rights to environmental justice. Claims of discrimination by recipients of federal funds have been found actionable under Title VI, but basic Equal Protection claims or affirmative constitutional claims have not met with success. The environmental justice body of law and activity remains today in part a political movement, in part a category of claims, and in part a sort of grievance to which a handful of effective legal theories have at times been applied.

Executive Order 12,898, 59 Fed. Reg. 7629 (1994), mandates that each federal agency "shall make achieving environmental justice part of its mission." Executive Orders do not impose duties outside the government and, as in this instance and in most such orders, do not create any judicially cognizable cause of actions. Instead, such orders establish internal rules and priorities for the executive branch. Any president can undo a previous president's order with a countermanding order, but many remain well-established law. Executive Order 12,898 is an important addition to federal environmental policy because it legitimizes the environmental justice movement and ensures that environmental justice will be a factor to be considered in the administration of existing programs and the development of new ones. Executive Order 12,898 was drafted and signed in direct response to the growing political strength of the environmental justice movement. It is informed by the belief that there are defined population groups and communities that are insufficiently protected by existing environmental programs. Thus, disproportionate impact is the only substantive standard the Order adopts to measure existing regulatory programs. All federal agencies must now develop agency-wide justice strategies that identify and address the "disproportionately high and adverse human health or environmental effects of its programs, policies, and activities on minority populations and low-income populations." Other theories have also been tested, meeting with notable success or failure in the courts and other political settings. See Foster, Justice from the Ground Up: Distributive Inequities, Grassroots Resistance, and the Transformative Politics of the Environmental Justice Movement, 86 Cal. L. Rev. 775 (1998); Rechtschaffen, Advancing Environmental Justice Norms, 37 U.C. Davis L. Rev. 95 (2003). For additional coverage of environmental justice issues, see Chapter 8, section F, covering siting battles.

G. COMMON LAW AND OTHER THEORIES DURING THE STATUTORY ENVIRONMENTAL ERA

As will quickly become apparent to students, environmental law is pervaded by statutory and regulatory edicts. An issue with which lawyers, legislators, and judges must often grapple concerns what is left of common law and other claims in areas that are now overwhelmingly statutory. As a related matter, why not rely on common law and the other theories discussed above to rectify environmental harms?

Advocates of market-based approaches to environmental protection generally disfavor reliance on statutory, regulatory, and bureaucratic responses to environmental harms. Instead, they prefer private bargaining or, where necessary, common law claims, because they rely on individual initiative and monetary incentives, and they tend not to make radical changes in legal rules that can disrupt expectations and markets. Several such advocates have asserted that common law claims have been replaced, not supplemented, by statutory schemes. See Meiners & Yandle, Common Law and the Conceit of Modern Environmental Policy, 7 Geo. Mason L. Rev. 923 (1999); Anderson, Enviro-Capitalism v. Enviro-Socialism, 4 Kan. J.L. & Pub. Pol'y 35, 39 (1995) (describing public law as an impediment to private law remedies). While the law has taken some twists and turns, the proposition that statutory schemes have generally replaced common law claims is most definitely in error. Only rarely do federal environmental laws displace state common law claims.

Note that in *Western Petroleum*, and also in *Walsh* and *Petsey*, defendants argued that their conduct was lawful in all respects, yet the courts rejected the defense. Defendants frequently argue that activity that is lawful and often explicitly permitted under state or federal statutes should not give rise to common law liability. Perhaps counterintuitively for lawyers new to this field, such a defense is typically rejected. The reasons are several and are significant to understanding environmental common law claims as well as environmental federalism, which is covered primarily in Chapter 2.

First, most major federal environmental statutes contain explicit "savings" clauses that preserve common law claims. Thus, judicial elimination of a common law remedy would run counter to explicit statutory mandate. See, e.g., Her Majesty the Queen v. City of Detroit, 874 F.2d 332, 342-343 (6th Cir. 1989) (Clean Air Act does not preempt claims under state pollution statute); Gutierrez v. Mobil Oil Corp., 789 F. Supp. 1280, 1285-1286 (W.D. Tex. 1992) (Clean Air Act does not preempt state common law claims); Ouellette v. International Paper Co., 666 F. Supp. 58, 60-62 (D. Vt. 1987) (holding common law nuisance claim not preempted by Clean Air Act). For more coverage of savings clauses, see Chapter 2, section E.1.

Second, the fact that statutes allow an activity does not mean that victims of harm should go remediless. Note that the *Western Petroleum* and *Petsey* cases both refer to the need to provide remedies for unreasonable harm, regardless of the reasonableness of the activity causing harm.

Third, as noted in *Western Petroleum*, economic incentives for less harmful polluting conduct are created when previously externalized harms are "internalized."

Some of the confusion concerning the effect of federal statutory frameworks on common law claims arises out of a trio of Supreme Court cases, two of which dealt with *federal* common law claims, while the third dealt ultimately with the question of which state's common law to apply. Economists advocating common law and market-based approaches to deal with environmental harms have misconstrued these cases and perhaps statutes to preclude ongoing reliance on common law claims. As explored in Thompson, Free Market Environmentalism and the Common Law: Confusion, Nostalgia and Inconsistency, 45 Emory L.J. 1329, 1330 (1996), common law claims do generally remain viable under both statutory language and case law. Any shortage of such claims is not a result of federal statutory edict, but of state law choices and other practical barriers to the efficacy of common law claims. Thompson explains how confusion likely results from the following case, and cases cited therein. As you read, carefully note the distinctions drawn among federal common law, state common law from the source or affected state, and language regarding the effect of federal statutory law. You will again encounter similar issues in *American Electric Power*, in Chapter 12, although that case focuses on federal common law claims of public nuisance.

INTERNATIONAL PAPER CO. v. OUELLETTE
479 U.S. 481 (1987)

Justice POWELL delivered the opinion of the Court.

This case involves the pre-emptive scope of the Clean Water Act, 86 Stat. 816, as amended, 33 U.S.C. §1251 et seq. (CWA or Act). The question presented is whether the Act pre-empts a common-law nuisance suit filed in a Vermont court under Vermont law, when the source of the alleged injury is located in New York.

I

[Petitioner International Paper Company (IPC) operated a pulp and paper mill on the New York side of Lake Champlain. IPC discharged waste into the lake through a pipe that runs through the water and ends just before reaching the state border with Vermont, which divides the lake. Respondents were a group of property owners who owned or leased land on the Vermont shore. In 1978, the owners filed a class action suit against IPC, claiming that the discharge constituted a "continuing nuisance" under Vermont common law. They alleged that the pollutants diminished both the quality of the water and the value of their property. The action was filed in State Superior Court and later removed to Federal District Court for the District of Vermont.]

II

A brief review of the regulatory framework is necessary to set the stage for this case. Until fairly recently, federal common law governed the use and misuse of interstate water. This principle was called into question in the context of water pollution in 1971, when the Court suggested in dicta that an interstate dispute between a State and a private company should be resolved by reference to state nuisance law. Ohio v. Wyandotte Chemicals Corp., 401 U.S. 493, 499, n.3 (1971) ("[A]n action such as this, if otherwise cognizable in federal district court, would have to be adjudicated under state law.") (citing Erie R. Co. v. Tompkins, 304 U.S. 64 (1938)).

We had occasion to address this issue in the first of two Supreme Court cases involving the dispute between Illinois and Milwaukee. In *Milwaukee I*, the State moved for leave to file an original action in this Court, seeking to enjoin the city from discharging sewage into Lake Michigan. Illinois v. Milwaukee, 406 U.S. 91 (1972). The Court's opinion in that case affirmed the view that the regulation of interstate water pollution is a matter of federal, not state, law, thus overruling the contrary suggestion in *Wyandotte*. The Court was concerned, however, that the existing version of the Act was not sufficiently comprehensive to resolve all interstate disputes that were likely to arise. *Milwaukee I* therefore held that these cases should be resolved by reference to federal common law; the implicit corollary of this ruling was that state common law was preempted.[8] The Court noted, though, that future action by Congress to regulate water pollution might pre-empt federal common law as well. 406 U.S., at 107.

Congress thereafter adopted comprehensive amendments to the Act. We considered the impact of the new legislation when Illinois and Milwaukee returned to the Court several years later. Milwaukee v. Illinois, 451 U.S. 304 (1981) (*Milwaukee II*). There the Court noted that the amendments were a " 'complete rewriting' " of the statute considered in *Milwaukee I*, and that they were " 'the most comprehensive and far reaching' " provisions that Congress ever had passed in this area. 451 U.S., at 317-318. Consequently, the Court held that federal legislation now occupied the field, pre-empting all federal common law. The Court left open the question of whether injured parties still had a cause of action under state law. Id., at 310, n.4. The case was remanded for further consideration; the result on remand was the decision of the Court of Appeals for the Seventh Circuit in *Milwaukee III*. . . .

While source States have a strong voice in regulating their own pollution, the CWA contemplates a much lesser role for States that share an interstate waterway with the source (the affected States). Even though it may be harmed by the discharges, an affected State only has an advisory role in regulating pollution that originates beyond its borders. Before a federal permit may be issued, each affected State is given notice and the opportunity to object to the proposed standards at a public hearing. 33 U.S.C. §1341(a)(2); *Milwaukee III*, [731 F.2d 403, 412 (7th Cir. 1984)]. An affected State has similar rights to be consulted before the source State issues its own permit; the source State must send notification, and must consider the objections and recommendations submitted by other States before taking action. §1342(b). Significantly, however, an affected State does not have the authority to block the issuance of the permit if it is dissatisfied with the proposed standards. An affected State's only recourse is to apply to the EPA Administrator, who then has the discretion to disapprove the permit if he concludes that the discharges will have an undue impact on interstate waters. §1342(d)(2). Also, an affected State may not establish a separate permit system to regulate an out-of-state source. Thus the Act makes it clear that affected States occupy a subordinate position to source States in the federal regulatory program.

III

With this regulatory framework in mind, we turn to the question presented: whether the Act pre-empts Vermont common law to the extent that law may impose liability on a New York point source. . . .

A.

Although Congress intended to dominate the field of pollution regulation, the [CWA's] saving clause negates the inference that Congress "left no room" for state causes of action. Respondents read the language of the saving clause broadly to

8. Although the Court's opinion could be read as distinguishing rather than overruling that part of *Wyandotte*, a later decision made it clear that state common-law actions did not survive *Milwaukee I. See Milwaukee II*, 451 U.S., at 327, n.19; see also Glicksman [Federal Preemption and Private Legal Remedies for Pollution, 134 U. Penn. L. Rev.] 156, n.176 (1985).

preserve both a State's right to regulate its waters, 33 U.S.C. §1370, and an injured party's right to seek relief under "any statute *or common law*," §1365(e) (emphasis added). They claim that this language and selected portions of the legislative history compel the inference that Congress intended to preserve the right to bring suit under the law of any affected State. We cannot accept this reading of the Act.

To begin with, the plain language of the provisions on which respondents rely by no means compels the result they seek. Section 505(e) merely says that "[n]othing *in this section*," i.e., the citizen-suit provisions, shall affect an injured party's right to seek relief under state law; it does not purport to preclude pre-emption of state law by other provisions of the Act. Section 510, moreover, preserves the authority of a State "with respect to the waters (including boundary waters) of such Stat[e]." This language arguably limits the effect of the clause to discharges flowing *directly* into a State's own waters, i.e., discharges from within the State. The savings clause, then, does not preclude pre-emption of the law of an affected State.

Given that the Act itself does not speak directly to the issue, the Court must be guided by the goals and policies of the Act in determining whether it in fact pre-empts an action based on the law of an affected State. Cf. City of Rome v. United States, 446 U.S. 156, 199 (1980) (Powell, J., dissenting) ("We resort to legislative materials only when the congressional mandate is unclear on its face."). After examining the CWA as a whole, its purposes and its history, we are convinced that if affected States were allowed to impose separate discharge standards on a single point source, the inevitable result would be a serious interference with the achievement of the "full purposes and objectives of Congress." See Hillsborough County v. Automated Medical Laboratories, Inc., *supra*, 471 U.S. at 713. Because we do not believe Congress intended to undermine this carefully drawn statute through a general saving clause, we conclude that the CWA precludes a court from applying the law of an affected State against an out-of-state source.

B.

In determining whether Vermont nuisance law "stands as an obstacle" to the full implementation of the CWA, it is not enough to say that the ultimate goal of both federal and state law is to eliminate water pollution. A state law also is pre-empted if it interferes with the methods by which the federal statute was designed to reach this goal. See Michigan Canners & Freezers Assn. v. Agricultural Marketing & Bargaining Bd., 467 U.S. 461, 477 (1984). In this case the application of Vermont law against IPC would allow respondents to circumvent the NPDES permit system, thereby upsetting the balance of public and private interests so carefully addressed by the Act. . . .

An interpretation of the saving clause that preserved actions brought under an affected State's law would disrupt this balance of interests. If a New York source were liable for violations of Vermont law, that law could effectively override both the permit requirements and the policy choices made by the source State. The affected State's nuisance laws would subject the point source to the threat of legal and equitable penalties if the permit standards were less stringent than those imposed by the affected State. Such penalties would compel the source to adopt different control standards and a different compliance schedule from those approved by the EPA, even though the affected State had not engaged in the same weighing of the costs and benefits. This case illustrates the problems with such a rule. If the Vermont court ruled that

respondents were entitled to the full amount of damages and injunctive relief sought
in the complaint, at a minimum IPC would have to change its methods of doing
business and controlling pollution to avoid the threat of ongoing liability. In suits such
as this, an affected-state court also could require the source to cease operations by
ordering immediate abatement. Critically, these liabilities would attach even though
the source had complied fully with its state and federal permit obligations. The inevitable result of such suits would be that Vermont and other States could do indirectly
what they could not do directly—regulate the conduct of out-of-state sources.

Application of an affected State's law to an out-of-state source also would undermine the important goals of efficiency and predictability in the permit system. The
history of the 1972 amendments shows that Congress intended to establish "clear and
identifiable" discharge standards. See S. Rep. No. 92-414, p.81 (1971). As noted above,
under the reading of the saving clause proposed by respondents, a source would be
subject to a variety of common-law rules established by the different States along the
interstate waterways. These nuisance standards often are "vague" and "indeterminate."
The application of numerous States' laws would only exacerbate the vagueness and
resulting uncertainty. The Court of Appeals in *Milwaukee III* identified the problem
with such an irrational system of regulation:

> For a number of different states to have independent and plenary regulatory authority
> over a single discharge would lead to chaotic confrontation between sovereign states.
> Dischargers would be forced to meet not only the statutory limitations of all states
> potentially affected by their discharges but also the common law standards developed
> through case law of those states. It would be virtually impossible to predict the standard
> for a lawful discharge into an interstate body of water. Any permit issued under the Act
> would be rendered meaningless. 731 F.2d, at 414.

It is unlikely—to say the least—that Congress intended to establish such a chaotic
regulatory structure.

Nothing in the Act gives each affected State this power to regulate discharges.
The CWA carefully defines the role of both the source and affected States, and
specifically provides for a process whereby their interests will be considered and balanced by the source State and the EPA. This delineation of authority represents
Congress' considered judgment as to the best method of serving the public interest
and reconciling the often competing concerns of those affected by the pollution. It
would be extraordinary for Congress, after devising an elaborate permit system that sets
clear standards, to tolerate common-law suits that have the potential to undermine this
regulatory structure.

C.

Our conclusion that Vermont nuisance law is inapplicable to a New York point
source does not leave respondents without a remedy. The CWA precludes only those
suits that may require standards of effluent control that are incompatible with those
established by the procedures set forth in the Act. The saving clause specifically
preserves other state actions, and therefore nothing in the Act bars aggrieved individuals from bringing a nuisance claim pursuant to the law of the source State. By its
terms the CWA allows States such as New York to impose higher standards on their
own point sources, and in *Milwaukee II* we recognized that this authority may include
the right to impose higher common-law as well as higher statutory restrictions. 451

U.S., at 328 (suggesting that "States may adopt more stringent limitations . . . through state nuisance law, and apply them to in-state dischargers"); see also Committee for Jones Falls Sewage System v. Train, 539 F.2d 1006, 1009, and n.9 (CA4 1976) (CWA preserves common-law suits filed in source State). . . .

An action brought against IPC under New York nuisance law would not frustrate the goals of the CWA as would a suit governed by Vermont law.[19] First, application of the source State's law does not disturb the balance among federal, source-state, and affected-state interests. Because the Act specifically allows source States to impose stricter standards, the imposition of source-state law does not disrupt the regulatory partnership established by the permit system. Second, the restriction of suits to those brought under source-State nuisance law prevents a source from being subject to an indeterminate number of potential regulations. Although New York nuisance law may impose separate standards and thus create some tension with the permit system, a source only is required to look to a single additional authority, whose rules should be relatively predictable. Moreover, States can be expected to take into account their own nuisance laws in setting permit requirements.

IV

The District Court correctly denied IPC's motion for summary judgment and judgment on the pleadings. Nothing in the Act prevents a court sitting in an affected State from hearing a common-law nuisance suit, provided that jurisdiction otherwise is proper. Both the District Court and the Court of Appeals erred, however, in concluding that Vermont law governs this litigation. The application of affected-State laws would be incompatible with the Act's delegation of authority and its comprehensive regulation of water pollution. The Act pre-empts state law to the extent that the state law is applied to an out-of-state point source.

19. The District Court concluded that the interference with the Act is insignificant, in part because respondents are seeking to be compensated for a specific harm rather than trying to "regulate" *IPC*, 602 F. Supp. 264, 271-272 (Vt. 1985). The Solicitor General, on behalf of the United States as *amicus curiae*, adopts only a portion of this view. He acknowledges that suits seeking punitive or injunctive relief under affected-state law should be pre-empted because of the interference they cause with the CWA. The Government asserts that compensatory damages actions, however, may be brought under the law of the State where the injury occurred. The Solicitor General reasons that compensatory damages only require the source to pay for the external costs created by the pollution, and thus do not "regulate" in a way inconsistent with the Act. The Government cites Silkwood v. Kerr-McGee Corp., 464 U.S. 238 (1984), for the proposition that in certain circumstances a court may find pre-emption of some remedies and not others.

We decline the Government's invitation to draw a line between the types of relief sought. There is no suggestion of such a distinction in either the Act or the legislative history. As the Court noted in *Silkwood*, unless there is evidence that Congress meant to "split" a particular remedy for pre-emption purposes, it is assumed that the full cause of action under state law is available (or as in this case, pre-empted). Id., at 255. We also think it would be unwise to treat compensatory damages differently under the facts of this case. If the Vermont court determined that respondents were entitled only to the requested compensatory relief, IPC might be compelled to adopt different or additional means of pollution control from those required by the Act, regardless of whether the purpose of the relief was compensatory or regulatory. See Perez v. Campbell, 402 U.S. 637, 651-652 (1971) (effect rather than purpose of a state statute governs pre-emption analysis). As discussed, this result would be irreconcilable with the CWA's exclusive grant of authority to the Federal Government and the source State. Cf. Chicago & North Western Transportation Co. v. Kalo Brick & Tile Co., 450 U.S. 311, 324-325 (1981).

The decision of the Court of Appeals is affirmed in part and reversed in part. The case is remanded for further proceedings consistent with this opinion.

NOTES AND QUESTIONS

1. Does the text of the two savings CWA clauses cited by the Court, §§505(e) and 510, support reaching different results on the CWA's preemptive effect on source state and affected state common law remedies? For further discussion of savings clauses and common law and state law claims, see Chapter 2.

2. For a recent case interpreting and applying *Ouellette* in the setting of a public nuisance action by the State of North Carolina against Tennessee Valley Authority (TVA) coal-fired plants in Alabama and Tennessee, see North Carolina v. Tennessee Valley Authority, 615 F.3d 291 (4th Cir. 2010). North Carolina sought to use public nuisance law to force the TVA plants, through injunctive orders, to reduce pollution below levels permitted under the federal Clean Air Act. The Fourth Circuit concluded that the trial court's grant of relief, and underlying experts testifying for North Carolina, heavily relied on North Carolina law. The Fourth Circuit reversed the district court, finding several underlying legal errors. Despite the Clean Air Act's savings clauses that, like the Clean Water Act provision discussed in *Ouellette,* "saved" state common law, the *Ouellette* case logic called for application of source state law to determine if a public nuisance claim was viable. Neither Tennessee nor Alabama law allowed public nuisance claims for injunctive relief for non-negligent behavior authorized by law, so state law–rooted public nuisance claims were not viable. The Fourth Circuit also discussed at some length problems with allowing state public nuisance claims to compel pollution reductions below Clean Air Act requirements and expert agency judgments following participatory process, building on *Ouellette*'s language that a claim will be preempted if it "interferes with the methods by which the federal statute was designed to reach [its] goal." The opinion was ultimately a bit unclear whether the public nuisance claim would have been held contrary to federal law even if Alabama and Tennessee law did not on their own undercut North Carolina's claims. The court also did not discuss private nuisance claims or how it would have viewed claims for damages. See Chapter 9, section D.3 and its coverage of the Oil Pollution Act and *Deepwater Horizon* decision for further application of *Ouellette* in assessing the viability of damage claims arising out of the BP Gulf of Mexico oil spill. In addition, as mentioned earlier in the public nuisance materials and in coverage in Chapter 12, *Ouellette* was also relevant to the Supreme Court's ruling in the *American Electric Power* case concerning public nuisance claims for climate change–related harms. For another recent decision interpreting *Ouellette* and resolving preemption claims, this time under the Clean Air Act in a case involving private nuisance allegations and other claims for damages, see Bell v. Cheswick Generating Station, 734 F.3d 188 (3d Cir. 2013) (holding that "source state" common law claims were not preempted).

A NOTE REGARDING HURDLES TO COMMON LAW SUCCESS

Federal statutory provisions, Supreme Court case law, and state court decisions overwhelmingly confirm that state common law environmental claims remain part of the arsenal of the environmental lawyer. Such claims are so uncommon, however, that market-oriented economists writing about environmental law have apparently concluded that the shortage of such claims must reflect a legal prohibition. Why are these claims brought with such infrequency? Perhaps more important, what is lacking in common law regimes such that the massive modern array of federal environmental laws is needed?

Professors Sidney A. Shapiro & Robert L. Glicksman, in Risk Regulation at Risk: Restoring a Pragmatic Approach 5-6 (2003), capture well many of the hurdles faced by torts plaintiffs complaining of environmental injuries such as cancers resulting from toxic exposures:

> The importance of protecting human life and the environment led the 1960s reformers to reject tort law as the basis of government regulation of technological risks. In a tort system, persons who have been injured by corporate behavior have the burden of initiating expensive legal action to prove that their injury was caused by the defendant's actions. Moreover, someone who anticipates a potential injury usually cannot obtain protection against that risk. Although injunctive relief is theoretically available in actions such as private nuisance to avoid harms alleged to be the imminent result of technological development, the courts are reluctant to enjoin such "anticipatory nuisances" on the basis of the plaintiff's speculation.
>
> In light of its evidentiary burdens, tort law starts with the baseline assumption that individuals and corporations that operate in private markets should be free from government regulation until and unless a plaintiff can compile convincing proof that their conduct has caused an injury to a person or that person's property. This baseline comports with traditional liberalism and its emphasis on limited government, private autonomy, and the protection of private markets.
>
> The impotence of tort law was vividly demonstrated in the 1960s by the various prominent accidents and environmental injuries that occurred. Tort law failed in part because of what Talbot Page has called "ignorance of mechanism." The tort system will not compensate an individual unless that person has convincing evidence that the defendant caused the plaintiff's injury. If, however, the injury is allegedly caused by exposure to chemicals or other by-products of technological activity, few plaintiffs will be able to meet their burden of proof because the mechanisms of cancer are still not very well understood. Scientists and policy-makers understood even less about how disease is caused and develops in the 1970s, when most risk-reduction statutes were adopted. The "ignorance of mechanism" is exacerbated by the long latency period that typically elapses between exposure to the disease and its manifestation. By the time the disease appears it is often impossible to isolate its cause or causes; the long latency period means that years if not decades worth of exposure have already occurred by then. Plaintiffs who sue over environmental injuries face an even more difficult task. Scientific understanding of the manner in which the by-products of technological development adversely affect the ecosystems into which they are discharged is, if anything, even more inadequate than our understanding of cancer mechanisms.
>
> Risk regulation was a paradigm shift from the common law because Congress authorized regulators to act on the basis of anticipated harm, which permitted regulators to reduce personal and environmental risks despite an "ignorance of mechanism."

Common law cases are certainly still brought, especially where a plaintiff has experienced a substantial personal or property injury and needs compensation. It will be the rare plaintiff, however, who can trace the source of injury and prove that contact with a pollutant caused the alleged injury. Even rarer will be the setting where plaintiffs experience sufficiently serious injuries that the transaction costs of bringing suit, especially in light of uncertainties about an ultimate victory, do not dwarf a possible recovery. The broader the harm, the more likely it is that no single plaintiff will find it worth litigating. The use of contingency arrangements or class action devices may make financing such litigation feasible, but in a highly polluted environment, proof burdens will often be insurmountable. In addition, use of a class action arrangement buys plaintiffs a virtually certain additional layer of intensive motion practice over the suitability of class treatment. For a concise cataloguing of barriers to such private common law suits, see Brunet, Debunking Wholesale Private Enforcement of Environmental Rights, 15 Harv. J.L. & Pub. Pol'y 311 (1992).

H. THE HISTORICAL ARC OF ENVIRONMENTAL LAW

The succeeding chapters will toss readers into a large and complex body of primarily statutory law, with a fair bit of constitutional and some international law as well. Much of this complexity is due to the way our nation's environmental laws have developed and been recast repeatedly over the past three decades. But even today's modern environmental statutes were built on the foundation of earlier conservation movements and prior laws and provisions, many of which live on today, even if little utilized. The closing two sections of this chapter offer a quick historical sketch of the development of America's environmental laws. The chapter closes by reviewing the sorts of regulatory strategies utilized in the laws that will be studied in depth in the succeeding chapters.

1. Reconceiving Wilderness and Natural
Resource Values

From an environmental perspective, "[t]he problem for human societies has been to balance their various demands against the ability of ecosystems to withstand the resulting pressures." C. Ponting, A Green History of the World: The Environment and the Collapse of Great Civilizations 17 (1992). Thus, many societies ultimately rise or fall as a result of the choices they make about their stocks of natural resources.

Environmental history has emerged as a major historical area and has refocused attention on the role of landscape and climate in shaping societies. In his book Landscape and Memory (1995), the historian Simon Schama sums up the dismal lessons of these new histories. Although environmental history offers some of the most original and challenging accounts now being written, it often relates the same dismal tale—of land taken, exploited, and exhausted; of traditional cultures reportedly living in a relation of sacred reverence with the soil displaced by the reckless individualist, the capitalist aggressor. W. Cronon, Changes in the Land: Indians, Colonists and the Ecology of New England (1983), is a classic example of the genre.

The more interesting question is how a new, anti-exploitation or stewardship narrative arose. Until the early eighteenth century, wilderness was the opposite of paradise. "When Adam and Eve were driven from the garden, the world they entered was a wilderness that only their labor and pain could redeem. Wilderness, in short, was a place to which one came only against one's will, and always in fear and trembling." Cronon, The Trouble with Wilderness or, Getting Back to the Wrong Nature, in Uncommon Ground: Toward Reinventing Nature 69, 71 (W. Cronon ed., 1995). By the end of the eighteenth century, wilderness had become a sublime place where one could encounter the divine.

In the United States, the nineteenth-century New England Transcendentalists were among the first to voice romantic reactions to the social disruption caused by the Industrial Revolution. They blended the Jeffersonian pastoral ideal of self-sufficient yeomen with the claim that nature "enjoyed its own morality which, when understood, could lead the sympathetic and responsive human being to a new spiritual awareness of his own potential, his obligations to others, and his responsibilities to the life-supporting processes of his natural surroundings." T.O. Riordan, Environmentalism 3 (2d ed. 1980). L. Marx, The Machine in the Garden: Technology and the Pastoral Ideal in America (1967), is a full exploration of the tension between pastoral visions and the realities of an industrialized society. See also R. Tomalin, W.H. Hudson: A Biography (1982), and L.K. Thomas, Man and the Natural World: A History of Modern Sensibility (1983). Environmentalism has become progressively more science-based, but the romantic origins of environmentalism still occasionally surface.

2. The Conservation and Preservation Movements

Environmentalism can be traced both to a changed perception of "nature" and to the production and dissemination of information about the consequences of the unrestrained exploitation of nature. Starting in the nineteenth century, industrialized societies began to appreciate the adverse consequences of unrestrained resource exploitation and set new limits on resource use. From the Transcendentalists' attempts to develop a theory of the relationship between democracy and nature came two major resource use philosophies or movements that have greatly influenced the modern environmental era: the conservation and preservation movements.

Initially, the preservation movement was primarily concerned with preserving large areas of public lands that remained wilderness areas as national parks, either to prove that America had scenic beauty comparable to that of Europe, or to allow individuals to find in the wilderness the spiritual fulfillment that no longer seemed attainable in modern society. See R. Nash, Wilderness and the American Mind (3d ed. 1982), and J. Sax, Mountains Without Handrails: Reflections on the National Parks (1980). Until the late 1960s, the preservation movement, based on ambiguous claims about the morality of nature and the beauty of undisturbed areas, was an influential but minor strain in the second, and dominant, resource use philosophy, conservationism.

The conservation movement was part of a deeper, progressive effort to make science compatible with democratic values and thus counter then-prevailing theories of social Darwinism. As historian Edward A. Purcell explains in The Crisis of Democratic Theory: Scientific Naturalism and the Problem of Value 10 (1973), this led progressives to the notion that all environments can be bettered by scientific resource use.

The intellectual roots of the conservation movement are usually traced to a book written in 1864 by a lawyer, diplomat, and self-trained scientist, George Perkins Marsh, but they can also be traced to the scientific surveys of the West in the middle of the nineteenth century, which ultimately led to federal retention and management of much of the public domain:

> The geologists and topographers were members of a newer elite community which was fast replacing that informed by the old army. As such, they often saw the West in terms of the scientific rather than the military problems involved. And where they were called upon to apply their knowledge, they thought largely in terms of efficiency and waste. This was in sharp contrast to the ideas of Western legislators and the demands of Western citizens, who had always thought of the West as a place to live in and develop and exploit. To them the geologist was not much different from a fur trader's guide, or a wagon master. His job was to lead them to the promised land and show them the way to the riches. . . .
>
> The new West was, by implication, the "resource West," to be revealed by the scientific explorer, but also to be guarded when the occasion demanded against reckless exploitation and the rampant, often illicit speculation that came to characterize the Grant administration, both in the East and in the West. Thus it became clear that in an age which depended upon and demanded exploitation and speculation, the explorer was once again ahead of his time and even running counter to it. Out of his Western experience came conservation and the first great national agencies dedicated to that proposition. [W. Goetzman, Exploration and Empire 356 (1966).]

Marsh's Man and Nature, republished ten years later as The Earth Modified by Human Action, was the first popular book to use what we now call the ecological perspective to draw attention to the consequences of overusing resources and to reach the normative conclusion that natural resource use policy should be based on use — rather than abuse — of nature's "spontaneous arrangements."

Man and Nature contributed significantly to the growth of interest in conservation. Conservationism was, and is, concerned with moderating the rate of present resource use to ensure plentiful supplies of needed commodities in the foreseeable future. Preservationism and conservationism, like the Anglican and Roman communions, share certain principles, but the two movements have retained a fair degree of separation because of a historic split. In the 1880s the founding fathers of the two movements, John Muir of the preservation movement and Gifford Pinchot of the conservation movement, split over forest use and later over water use policy. The defining moment was the battle to stop the Hetch Hetchy dam. Hetch Hetchy Valley is located north of Yosemite Valley and was almost as spectacular. In 1913, President William Howard Taft made the decision to allow the city of San Francisco to flood the valley to develop a secure public water supply, which it enjoys today. As one of the leading new Western historians explains, the controversy was actually a three-way battle:

> In the battle over Hetch Hetchy, Pinchot and the conservationists believed that they confronted two sets of enemies: preservationists such as Muir and western entrepreneurs and speculators who cared nothing about Hetch Hetchy but who sought to stop the creation of municipally owned water and power companies. Muir and his allies pointed out that there were other possible reservoir sites for San Francisco, but conservationists and most urban progressives rejected the sites because they were in the hands of private developers who could hold the city at ransom. Conservationists believed that for the public good, San Francisco had to develop Hetch Hetchy. One side made preserving Hetch Hetchy a symbol of ethical, spiritual, and aesthetic standards; the other made destroying it a symbol of the victory of the public goods — also a matter of ethics — over the

greedy interests of private developers. Both sides phrased the issue in terms of a managed West. Utility and public development won; preservation of nature lost. [R. White, "It's Your Misfortune and None of My Own": A History of the American West 413 (1991).]

The conservation movement, which stressed the use of scientific principles to make rational resource use choices, established two once-controversial fundamental principles that have had a great influence on environmental law. First, resource management is a legitimate public function and should be based on science and promote the efficient allocation of resources. Second, the state may legitimately restrain the use of private property when private initiative wastes and degrades natural resources. Progressive conservationism was a powerful political force in the first two decades of the twentieth century and helped to shape the structure and thrust of federal and state resource use programs. Powerful government agencies were established to develop resources for the purpose of reclamation of arid lands, flood control, and public power. In the debate over how best to use natural resources, preservationists became dissenters who lobbied Congress on an ad hoc basis to block certain projects or federal actions. See generally J. Petulla, American Environmental History: The Exploitation and Conservation of Natural Resources (2d ed. 1987); Hargrove, The Historical Foundations of American Environmental Attitudes, 1 Envtl. Ethics 209 (1979). The standard history of the conservation movement is the superb S. Hays, Conservation and the Gospel of Efficiency: The Progressive Conservation Movement 1890-1920 (1959); see also D. Strong, The Conservationists (1971).

Under the leadership of John Muir, the preservation movement scored a number of important political successes in setting aside national parks and curbing excessive use of public lands, but it lacked the breadth of vision acceptable to the American mind to displace scientific conservation as the dominant resource use policy. John Muir's ecological vision was perhaps too advanced for his time:

> Hetch Hetchy was a part of the flow of Nature. It was filled with waterfalls, and was the path of the Tuolumne River. It was the path of ancient glaciers, and a path new life had taken as it entered the mountains. And damming it was an act by men which bespoke their arrogance. Men who built dams believed they could control and harness the flow of Nature. Hetch Hetchy was also a consummation, as all the inseparable sections of the flow were. It was not an "exceptional" creation, since none of God's gardens were. It was part of a larger whole, an edenic valley. Yet when men chose to stop its flowing life, and did so not for the farmers of the Central Valley, but for the businessmen of the City of San Francisco, Muir saw in this action civilization's willingness to kill Nature for its own convenience. In theory—for the young Muir certainly—all dams in all valleys were arrogant gestures by men.
> . . . The entire idea behind Yosemite Park, an idea so long in taking shape, was to hold inviolate the whole watersheds of the Merced and Tuolumne rivers. To violate that precedent was to damage the concept of a national park as more than a collection of scenic features. So it was that the principle of a national park as an ecological whole was also at stake. [M. Cohen, The Pathless Way: John Muir and the American Wilderness 330-331 (1984).]

According to conventional wisdom, it was not until the twentieth century that the full consequences of man's powers over nature began to portend disaster. As a result of the factors enumerated above, by the 1970s concern over resource use had secured a prominent place on political agendas, and the notion of resource mismanagement had acquired a sense of urgency it had lacked previously. The working assumption of the modern environmental movement was set forth by Barbara Ward and René Dubos in their book Only One Earth (1972):

> What is certain is that our sudden, vast accelerations—in numbers, in the use of energy and new materials, in urbanization, in consumptive ideals, in consequent pollution—have set technological man on a course which could alter dangerously and perhaps irreversibly, the natural systems of his planet upon which his biological survival depends. [Id. at 11.]

3.   *The Political Emergence of the Modern Environmental Era*

The subordination of preservationism to conservationism continued until 1969-1970, when what is now referred to as the environmental decade began. Suddenly, debates over environmental quality shifted from a near exclusive focus on public lands protection or reservoir construction issues, or a local air or water pollution problem, to a national political issue. Environmental protection became a sometimes diffuse, but typically broad-based and enduring, national political priority that triggered an unprecedented legislative response from Congress. Council on Environmental Quality, Tenth Annual Report 1-15 (1979), offers several reasons for the sudden emergence of environmental quality as a major political priority. The first of the two most important long-range trends was the post–World War II growth of affluence, which allowed many people to relocate in suburban communities. Many of those who moved to the suburbs witnessed firsthand the degradation of the very amenities they had relocated to enjoy.

The second major long-range trend was the growth of the synthetic organic chemical industry. As the synthetic chemical industry grew, and as more sophisticated monitoring devices were developed, it became increasingly clear that pollution posed a serious threat to human health. In this connection, an event of signal importance was the 1962 publication of Rachel Carson's brief against DDT, Silent Spring, which was provided in excerpt form earlier in this chapter. Silent Spring "began an educational process by which ecological precepts entered the common vocabulary," S. Udall, The Quiet Crisis and the Next Generation 203 (1988), and a continuing effort to document the adverse health effects of exposure to chemicals released into the air, water, and soil. See S. Steingraber, Living Downstream: An Ecologist Looks at Cancer and the Environment (1997), for an example of Carson's legacy. A more recent book draws on Carson and traces changing perceptions of industrial production and risk in recounting the history of PCB production and resulting pollution harms and environmental justice disputes in Anniston, Alabama. E. Spears, Baptized in PCBs: Race, Pollution, and Justice in an All-American Town (2014).

Many have observed that crises are necessary to trigger political responses, see B. Adam, Timescapes of Modernity: The Environment and Invisible Hazards (1988). Reactions to the Santa Barbara oil spill that immediately preceded Earth Day in April 1970 showed the breadth of the environmental movement. L. Dye, Blowout at Platform A: A Crisis That Awakened a Nation (1971), contains a useful account of the reactions of the citizens of Santa Barbara to the spill. The mood of the late 1960s is described in Editors of Fortune, The Environment: A National Mission for the

Seventies (1970). It is paradoxical that this spill, which took no human lives, caused no permanent impairment of human health, and seems to have produced no long-range ecological damage, became a national crisis that "brought home to a great many Americans a feeling that protection would not simply happen, but required their active support and involvement," Council on Environmental Quality, Tenth Annual Report, at 12. Subsequent disasters such as the radiation fallout from the fire in the nuclear reactor at the Chernobyl plant near Kiev in Ukraine, spills on the Rhine and in Spain, and the Exxon Valdez oil spill in Alaska, as well as concerns about global climate change, helped to internationalize the environmental movement and to focus public attention on the need for better environmental protection. The massive Gulf Coast BP oil spill of 2010 similarly prompted calls for legislative change and stronger regulatory protection.

Finally, a major catalyst for the birth of the environmental movement was the transfer of political energy from the bitterly controversial and often violent civil rights and anti–Vietnam War movements to a movement that was clean, enjoyed widespread support, and promised to transcend old ideological issues.

But the exact reasons modern environmental law frameworks emerged when they did remain subject to debate. Richard Lazarus acknowledges that the "original 1970 Earth Day looks very much like a 'republican moment,'" coming at a time of "such heightened civic-mindedness that it is possible to overcome substantial institutional and political obstacles to potentially radical social change." Lazarus, The Making of Environmental Law 43-44 (2004). Lazarus, however, suggests that a more incremental change actually occurred, with modern frameworks building on earlier social movements and changing federal and state environmental laws. Environmental historian Richard N.L. Andrews similarly suggests that a combination of galvanizing events and incrementally increasing state, local, and federal environmental roles set the stage for the environmental decade's emergence around 1970. In addition, he observes that as states and municipalities began to respond to citizen environmental unrest and enact their own early environmental laws, industry opposition to federal regulation softened. "[A]s a few leading states and cities began to toughen their air pollution control regulations—though only a few . . . —key industries themselves acquired a powerful new interest in obtaining moderate and uniform federal standards that would preempt more stringent and inconsistent state and local standards." R. Andrews, Managing the Environment, Managing Ourselves: A History of American Environmental Policy 209 (1999). As discussed further below and in Chapter 2, industry willingness to countenance federal regulation did not mean it controlled such regulation; the modern environmental laws actually enacted often were stringent and also typically preserved state regulatory roles, especially the right to be more stringent than federal standards require.

4. A Brief Chronology of the Development of Modern Environmental Laws and Political Trends

The previous sections provided a broad overview of social attitudes and linked political movements that led to modern environmental law frameworks. This closing historical section picks up with the development of modern environmental laws. It also offers a slightly different focus, emphasizing the linkages between political trends and the particular forms of environmental laws that resulted. The eras of environmental protection are, like all historical lines, arbitrary, but we offer them as a rough guide to bracket the statutes, regulations, and cases that you will study in this course. As covered at length earlier in this chapter, common law claims and background principles of environmental law exist and influence statutory frameworks, but environmental law is primarily positive law, that is, law created by actions of legislatures and agencies. The environmental law that you will study for most of the remainder of this book, and work with as an attorney or policymaker, reflects legislative, regulatory, and judicial perceptions of the diverse environmental problems confronting this country. Recent environmental history can be roughly divided into the following phases.

A. *State and Federal Law before 1968.* Environmental law as we know it today did not exist before 1968. Pollution control legislation existed before the 1960s and momentum for the federalization of pollution control had been building since the 1930s, but the common law of nuisance was the principal legal method to force the internalization of environmental "insults." Environmental concerns, as we now define them, existed, but they were largely aesthetic or spiritual claims asserted to preserve public lands from more intensive use and commodity production (e.g., the national park and wilderness preservation systems) or were public-health based. Pollution was perceived as a local or state problem, although there were exceptions. The Ohio Valley had an interstate program going back to the 1930s to stop untreated discharges into the Ohio River. In the main, environmental values were either ignored or clearly subordinate to economic development.

Scattered instances of federal regulation existed. The Refuse Act of 1899 prohibited the discharge of refuse in navigable waters because a clear federal interest— interstate and foreign navigation—was threatened by large debris discharges into harbors. Untreated sewage discharges were identified as a serious local and interstate problem in the 1930s, but the initial post–World War II federal involvement was limited to federal grants to states. Still, as environmental ills began to loom larger in the national consciousness, and states and cities began to respond, national environmental politics began to change.

Some of that change was independent of activities in the courts, but a few key early cases provided a rough template for the enforcement structures that would later become a central element in modern environmental laws. It is perilous to describe any single case as "the" critical or defining moment leading to political change, yet the regulatory battles, legal challenges, and court decision in Scenic Hudson Pres. Conference v. FPC, 354 F.2d 608 (2d Cir. 1965), proved to be greatly influential. It has been called the first environmental law case. Rabin, Federal Regulation in Historical Perspective, 38 Stan. L. Rev. 1189, 1298 (1986). In the case, citizens successfully challenged a proposal to modify the landscape of the Hudson River's highlands to accommodate a power generation facility that would pump water from the Hudson River to a huge reservoir, which then would be released to power turbines during times of high energy demand. The landscape's beauty and fishery resources were threatened by the plan. As the Second Circuit noted, the citizen plaintiffs' claims were based on statutory and agency language allowing the Federal Power Commission to issue a license only if it could find that

> a prospective project [met] the statutory test of being "best adapted to a comprehensive plan for improving or developing a waterway," Federal Power Act §10(a),

16 U.S.C. §803(a). In framing the issue before it, the Federal Power Commission properly noted:

> We must compare the Cornwall project with any alternatives that are available. If on this record Con Edison has available an alternative source for meeting its power needs which is better adapted to the development of the Hudson River for all beneficial uses, including scenic beauty, this application should be denied. . . .

"Recreational purposes" are expressly included among the beneficial public uses to which the statute [§10(a)] refers. The phrase undoubtedly encompasses the conservation of natural resources, the maintenance of natural beauty, and the preservation of historic sites. See Namekagon Hydro Co. v. Federal Power Comm., 216 F.2d 509, 511-512 (7th Cir. 1954). All of these "beneficial uses," the Supreme Court has observed, "while unregulated, might well be contradictory rather than harmonious." Federal Power Comm. v. Union Electric Co., 381 U.S. 90, 98 (1965). In licensing a project, it is the duty of the Federal Power Commission properly to weigh each factor. . . .

This role does not permit it to act as an umpire blandly calling balls and strikes for adversaries appearing before it; the right of the public must receive active and affirmative protection at the hands of the Commission.

This court cannot and should not attempt to substitute its judgment for that of the Commission. But we must decide whether the Commission has correctly discharged its duties, including the proper fulfillment of its planning function in deciding that the "licensing of the project would be in the overall public interest." The Commission must see to it that the record is complete. The Commission has an affirmative duty to inquire into and consider all relevant facts. . . .

Although the *Scenic Hudson* case did not break new doctrinal ground or interpret a pathbreaking statute, its emphasis on citizen and court willingness to look at all of a statute's language, and enforce language focused on environmental quality, provided a virtual template for environmental actions that continue today. For the first time, a court remanded an agency decision because it failed to consider adequately a trio of interests—aesthetics, fish and wildlife, and recreation—that constituted "environmental quality" circa the mid-1960s, and suggested that agencies had an affirmative duty to take these interests into account in their decisions. In his memorial to Judge Hays, Judge Henry J. Friendly described the case as "Judge Hays' most influential opinion for the court." In Memoriam, 635 F.2d lxi (1981). In his article, The Most Creative Moments in Environmental Law, 2000 Ill. L. Rev. 1, Professor William Rodgers lists *Scenic Hudson* as the second most creative moment in environmental law, behind Rachel Carson's Silent Spring.

Scenic Hudson established the fundamental pattern of environmental litigation that continues to this day. The case is distinguished by five important characteristics. First, it was initiated by an ad hoc citizen's group, which was forced to use the judicial process after political and administrative avenues failed. Nongovernmental organization (NGO) participation in the development of environmental law and policy is a feature of U.S. environmental law that has been admired and emulated all over the world, although this nation's citizen litigation options are less broadly embraced. Second, standing was a major barrier, but the Second Circuit's liberal understanding of the interests that qualified for standing was echoed in part in the foundational Supreme Court standing case Sierra Club v. Morton, excerpted in Chapter 3, section A. Third, the plaintiff association was faced with the problem that there were no constitutional, common law, or statutory substantive theories that would allow it to argue that the FPC's decision to license the pump storage plant violated a right possessed by it. Fourth, plaintiffs were thus forced to craft a primarily procedural rather than substantive administrative law theory that would convince a court at least to reverse and remand the administrative decision. Post–New Deal administrative law was not promising. Decisions such as those delegated to the FPC were seen as best made by agency experts with minimal judicial supervision. Plaintiffs crafted a strategy that built on the traditional criticism of the administrative state: the rule of law demands strict fidelity to congressional mandates. This principle was combined with the theory that the injury was not substantive, in the sense that there was no principled basis for a court to order the agency to prefer preservation of Storm King Mountain over the pump storage plant, but procedural. The crux of the injury was a procedural error caused by the agency's failure to afford plaintiffs a meaningful opportunity to present a wide range of evidence about environmental degradation and, more important, to argue that alternatives to the project existed. The limits of procedural theories and relief are illustrated by the fact that the FPC reissued the license and the decision was upheld. Scenic Hudson Pres. Conf. v. FPC, 453 F.2d 463 (2d Cir. 1971). Fifth, *Scenic Hudson* illustrated the potential of more intrusive judicial review.

In the following years, both in legislative provisions and in battles over implementation of and compliance with environmental laws, NGOs came to rely heavily on courts to shape as well as enforce environmental law. One of the *Scenic Hudson* lawyers, David Sive, a seminal figure in early modern environmental law, drew on his experience in the case to articulate a more general theory of judicial supervision of mission agencies. Sive, Some Thoughts of an Environmental Lawyer in the Wilderness of Administrative Law, 70 Colum. L. Rev. 612 (1970). See also A. Talbot, Power Along the Hudson: The Storm King Case and the Birth of Environmentalism (1972) (recounting the legal and political history of the Storm King battles).

B. *The Environmental Moment: 1968-1973*. This represents the formative period of environmental law. Pollution control through technology-based regulation emerged as a national priority, and the idea of ecosystem stability became the guiding principle behind NEPA and environmental impact assessment generally. NEPA, the Clean Air Act and Clean Water Act, risk-based pesticide regulation, and the Endangered Species Act were passed during this period, and federal pesticide law was transformed from a consumer protection to a cancer risk prevention law.

This particular burst of activity and, especially, the stringency of the laws enacted, resulted from a brief period of time when the Democrat-controlled Congress, led by Senators Edmund Muskie of Maine and Henry Jackson of Washington State, competed with the Republican President Nixon to out-"green" each other. Elliott et al., Toward a Theory of Statutory Evolution: The Federalization of Environmental Law, 1 J.L. Econ. & Org. 313, 316, 327 (1985). M. Landy et al., The Environmental Protection Agency: Asking the Wrong Questions from Nixon to Clinton 22-33 (1994), explain the competition in the broader context of both major political parties' efforts to appeal to suburban voters who responded positively to the growing media accounts of middle-class victims of environmental degradation.

During this period, the control and prevention of gross nuisances shifted from the courts to the newly created EPA and state agencies. The assumption was that air and water pollution problems were attributable to (1) industrial and municipal discharges, (2) the emission of soot from factories, and (3) automobile emissions that caused smog. This era also saw the adoption of the idea of performing a comprehensive environmental assessment before public works and important regulatory activities were undertaken. NEPA and "little NEPAs" enacted by states and municipalities, coupled with active and sympathetic judicial review by courts, especially the D.C. Circuit Court of Appeals, became important tools to contest activities that were previously virtually immune from judicial review.

During the early years of this period, there was a widespread perception that the mission agencies such as the then Atomic Energy Commission, Federal Power Commission, the U.S. Army Corps of Engineers, the Bureau of Reclamation, the federal land management agencies, and the Federal Highway Administration, were making decisions without any consideration of the "environmental consequences" of these decisions or alternative, less environmentally destructive ways of achieving the mission's objective. It was difficult to challenge these decisions in court. The resource management laws contained broad delegations of discretion that virtually immunized them from judicial control. Courts typically applied the bedrock principle of administrative law that courts should defer to the exercise of administrative expertise to uphold most of these challenged management decisions unless the action was outside the scope of the statute. Moreover, the underlying question, to develop or to preserve, had long been considered a political rather than a legal question. Thus, there were few legal standards to apply, and challengers faced difficult standing issues.

Nevertheless, building on the more skeptical and intrusive sort of review utilized in the *Scenic Hudson* case mentioned above, by the late 1960s, courts had begun to manifest a far more rigorous attitude, scrutinizing the actions of governments and polluters and enforcing the often aspirational language of the many new and amended environmental laws.

C. *Extension and Refinements: 1973-1980.* The period between 1969 and 1980 is referred to as the environmental decade. The 1970s saw the extension of legislative protection to a wide range of public health risks and the completion of the environmental moment despite mounting arguments that environmental protection should be "traded off" against other social objectives such as energy security. Legislative regulation of pollutants continued, but the emphasis shifted from gross nuisances to the identification and minimization of toxic risks. Questions over the balance between environmental protection and continued development became more important. Cancer became a proxy for many human health–related environmental problems. Congress enacted programs to control the entry of toxic substances in commerce (the Toxic Substances Control Act); to protect the human use of resources (the Safe Drinking Water Act); to regulate the transportation, treatment, storage, and disposal of hazardous wastes (the Resource Conservation and Recovery Act); and to clean up orphaned waste dumps, broadly defined (the Comprehensive Environmental Response, Compensation, and Liability Act (CERCLA or Superfund)).

The environmental movement weathered the energy crisis of the 1970s, and the principle that environmental protection is a core value seems to have become a widely accepted and perhaps permanent political reality. For example, after the 1973 OPEC oil embargo, the executive branch and Congress tried to stimulate increased coal production at a time when there was great concern about the environmental impacts of surface mining. After intense controversy, Congress enacted the Surface Mining Control and Reclamation Act (SMCRA) in 1977. SMCRA preserves some environmentally sensitive public and private lands from mining and requires that mined lands be reclaimed. See L. McBride & J. Pendergrass, Coal, in Environmental Law from Resources to Recovery 635 (C. Campbell-Mohn ed., 1993).

D. *The Bipartisan Consensus Begins to Crumble: 1980-1988.* This period can be characterized domestically as the period when the environmentally oriented biparti-san consensus started crumbling, and internationally as the time when the globaliza-tion of environmental issues became apparent. Globalization led to two important ideas that influence both international and domestic law. The first is the concept of global commons, such as polluted or stressed airsheds—related to such phenomena as acid rain and global climate change—and rain forests, along with the older commons, the seas. Second is the rise of the idea that biodiversity preservation is a transcendent value that should be broadly pursued. Biodiversity conservation, which is not self-defining, has provided a new focus for programs such as the Endangered Species Act and public land management. This focus helped, along with the divided Congress and executive, preserve the 1970s programs from major congressional revision.

Domestically, the period from 1980 to1988 was a testing ground. Initially, the Reagan administration (1981-1989) sought to roll back many of the gains of the previous decade; however, this strategy failed, and many programs were actually strengthened. Despite the lack of success in the legislature, President Reagan did issue a strong Executive Order mandating that most major regulations be subjected to cost-benefit analysis. Overall, the idea of environmental protection became more contingent and contested.

E. *Little Progress, with Attack and Gridlock: 1988-Present.* The period extending from 1988 into the twenty-first century is difficult to characterize because it is marked by several divergent but overlapping trends. Politically, there has been little innovation in environmental programs. We continue to live off the intellectual capital of the active first 15 years of the modern environmental movement. The Clean Air Act amendments of 1990 represent the last successful major federal legislative initiatives. Congress has intervened in many specific controversies, but has done little more than reauthorize and make minor adjustments to the main federal laws. A partisan logjam in Congress continues to thwart efforts to amend this nation's environmental laws. See Richard J. Lazarus, The Making of Environmental Law (2004), at Chapter 10, for a discussion of this partisan blockage and its implications.

The other prominent exception to federal legislative inaction concerns hazard-ous waste and oil spill laws. CERCLA was amended both in the late 1990s and early in the presidency of George W. Bush, but in ways intended to reduce liability uncertain-ties for, respectively, the lending industry and those involved with "brownfield" prop-erties. Also, after the Alaska Exxon Valdez oil spill, Congress enacted the Oil Pollution Act of 1990, creating a new liability scheme for oil spills, but in ways that provide new potential relief while at the same time acting to protect polluters from large-scale liability. The huge Deepwater Horizon BP oil spill in the Gulf of Mexico in 2010 prompted several ultimately unsuccessful legislative proposals, some to amend the Oil Pollution Act. Apart from so far ill-fated efforts to enact new laws or amendments to deal with the issue of climate change and greenhouse gases, or to pass narrow amend-ments to the Clean Water Act to respond to two Supreme Court opinions narrowing the law's reach, along with sporadic amendments of agricultural laws to encourage sounder environmental conduct, there are no major new domestic environmental statutory programs on the political agenda.

The major international initiatives centered on the implementation of the 1992 Rio Biodiversity Convention and on finding ways for nations to share the burden of rolling back greenhouse gas emissions to implement the United Nations Framework Convention on Climate Change, but little tangible progress has been made in implementing them since the 1992 Rio Summit. The ten-year follow-up conference held in Johannesburg was a virtual nonevent in the wake of September 11, 2001. See generally Stumbling Toward Sustainability (J. Dernbach ed., 2002). Similarly, a Copenhagen summit held in 2009 to create a new international framework to address climate change, which would have largely supplanted the earlier Kyoto Accord, ended in disarray, with little more than an informal commitment of the world's largest polluters to take steps to reduce emissions of greenhouse gases. See Chapter 12, section F.

Polls show public support for environmental protection to be consistently strong, but some question the depth of that support. There is a growing consensus that we are entering the second generation of environmental law, which is characterized by a highly politicized atmosphere that makes rational assessment of first-generation approaches difficult. Richard Lazarus has traced the increasingly polarized nature of national legislative politics, finding few signs of any reemerging bipartisan environmental coalitions. Lazarus, A Different Kind of "Republican Moment" in Environmental Law, 87 Minn. L. Rev. 999 (2003). Environmental law in the 1980s became highly politicized because of the tension between the Reagan and Bush administrations and the Democratic Congress. This politicization continued during the early 1990s with the combination of Democratic President Clinton and a Republican-controlled Congress.

In 1994, Republicans captured both houses of Congress for the first time since 1952. Republicans centered their campaign on their highly publicized "Contract with America." Claiming the public's approval for change, they advocated more rigorous cost-benefit analyses to roll back existing and proposed new regulations, reliance on "sound" as opposed to allegedly speculative science, the elimination of unfunded state and local mandates, and greater protection for private property. See Glicksman & Chapman, Regulatory Reform and (Breach of) the Contract with America, 5 Kan. J.L. & Pub. Pol'y 9 (1996). This initiative produced a substantial pro–environmental protection backlash; as a result, few substantive changes were made. For more extensive discussion of cost-benefit analysis and this period, see Chapter 3, sections B and C.

After the second President Bush assumed office, in 2001, and continuing into the Obama administration, environmental protection has remained an area of dispute. The era of federal bipartisan work to improve the environment and its laws remains only a memory. The result has been an increasingly sterile debate, with each side reaching for a kill, only to be beaten back, as happened in 1995-1996. The Republican Party's triumph in the 2002 midterm legislative elections broke the political deadlock, but one-party rule was delayed for a time by Vermont Senator James Jeffords's switch from Republican to Independent status, preserving a bare Democratic majority in the Senate. During the next elections, in 2004, the Republican Party secured control of all three branches, with a Republican president, control of both houses, and a majority of federal judges having been appointed by Republican presidents. Despite this period of exclusive rule by a party long dedicated to "reforming" federal environmental laws, major statutory rollbacks did not occur. Some of this may result from a post-9/11 focus on national security issues and the United States' war in Iraq, but it also appears that overt attacks on environmental laws remain a political risk. A sufficient number of Republicans opposed environmental rollbacks so that the narrow Republican majority was insufficient to overcome opposition from Democrats and a small number of allied Republicans. The Democrats' recapturing of the House and the Senate in the 2006 midterm elections further reduced the risk of environmental rollbacks. But with the White House still in Republican control, Democrats were unable to strengthen any environmental laws.

Barack Obama assumed office with solid Democratic majorities in both houses of Congress, but because of increased bloc voting by Republicans and some Democrats ambivalent about environmental legislative change, no major changes in environmental law were passed during the first two years of the Obama administration. President Obama and the Democrat-led Congress were also occupied with a major economic and financial crisis and the resulting recession that affected the United States and much of the world, as well as wars in Afghanistan and Iraq, and the passage of major health and financial regulation bills. Legislators proposed climate and energy legislation, amendments to toxic substances law, and a focused fix to the Clean Water Act following two major Supreme Court decisions, but none of these proposals are yet law. With the Republican's gaining solid control of the House after two years of the Obama presidency, and Democrats maintaining only a narrow Senate majority, neither Democrats nor Republicans have met with success in their efforts to change the nation's environmental laws. The logjam remains.

During the periods of Republican ascendancy in the White House and for a number of years during the Republican control of Congress, weakening of federal environmental laws did occur, but through less overt means than direct, major statutory amendments. Instead, where statutory changes were made, it was often through language in appropriations riders that were subject to little or no advance public notification or legislative discussion. Through such riders, for example, the Information (or Data) Quality Act was passed, giving citizens, industries, and any other stakeholders the ability to challenge information utilized by administrative agencies. See Chapter 3, section B. Similarly, appropriations riders have exempted certain activities and sometimes particular geographic areas from the law's usual protections and requirements, especially where endangered species protections conflicted with use of natural resources for profit. See id. (discussing appropriations bills restricting judicial review of timber harvest plans in the Pacific Northwest). Amendments to CERCLA in the 1990s that provided lenders with new exemptions from liability were also passed through an appropriations rider. Amendments to encourage reuse of brownfield sites were among the few openly enacted changes to federal environmental laws since 1990.

Environmental laws have also been undercut by judicial actions. In decisions focused on standing doctrine, federalism-influenced statutory interpretations limiting federal regulatory power, and administrative law doctrines preserving executive discretion not to act, the Supreme Court and lower courts have in a broad array of areas weakened environmental laws, or at least made their enforcement less likely. Even focused corrective legislation, such as proposed laws to amend the Clean Water Act in response to adverse or confusing Supreme Court decisions, failed to pass even when Democrats controlled the White House and both houses of Congress.

The legislative and Republican-Democrat political gridlock has stimulated innovation in the shadow of existing regulatory programs. There is considerable vertical and horizontal power sharing through collaborative public-private stakeholder processes. See Freeman, Collaborative Governance in the Administrative State, 45 UCLA L. Rev. 1 (1997); Seidenfeld, Empowering Stakeholders: Limits on Collaboration as the Basis for Flexible Regulation, 41 Wm. & Mary L. Rev. 411 (2000). The pros and cons of collaborative decisionmaking as well as the implications for environmental lawyers are perceptively discussed in Karkkainen, Environmental Lawyering in the Age of Collaboration, 2002 Wis. L. Rev. 555. See also C. Powers & M. Chertow, Industrial Ecology: Overcoming Policy Fragmentation, in Thinking Ecologically: The Next Generation of Environmental Policy 20, 23 (M. Chertow & D. Esty eds., 1997).

In addition, some states, often through their attorneys general, during periods of federal inaction have become more active in challenging federal regulatory rollbacks and have also stepped more actively into enforcement roles. States have also legislatively innovated in such areas as brownfields policy after the federal government proved slow to amend hazardous waste laws to address widely perceived flaws. Buzbee, Contextual Environmental Federalism, 14 N.Y.U. Envtl. L.J. 108 (2005). In dealing with the risks of greenhouse gases and climate change, several states have taken the lead. See Chapters 2 and 12 for discussion of these state enactments and innovations. As discussed at greater length in Chapter 2's coverage of the "race to the bottom," the extent and nature of state environmental protection efforts remain subject to fierce debate.

F. *The Roots of Ongoing Policy Ferment.* The political deadlock from the 1990s to the present masks a major intellectual ferment among academics and other policy analysts aimed at taking stock of the first generation of environmental protection, assessing more rationally its strengths and weaknesses, and devising strategies to maintain a sound level of environmental quality. Federal legislative gridlock has also contributed to creative local and regional ad hoc environmental conservation and ecosystem restoration experiments. In 1994, the National Environmental Policy Act reached its twenty-fifth anniversary, and this event triggered much thoughtful reassessment of initial efforts. E.g., Symposium, Twenty-Five Years of Environmental Regulation, 27 Loyola L.A. L. Rev. 3 (1994).

The fundamental tensions of environmentalism remain unresolved. Although it may have seemed that we were moving into a more consensus-based preventive era, frustration continues with the politics of environmentalism, independent of narrow partisan politics. There are two principal strains of this frustration. The first is the sustained industry and development opposition to all forms of government regulation—except for subsidies—which is having a strong run, especially in the intermountain West. See J. Switzer, Green Backlash: The History and Politics of Environmental Opposition in the U.S. (1997), and W. Graf, Wilderness Preservation and the Sagebrush Rebellions (1990). This has been augmented by efforts of critics of environmental regulation to equate environmentalism and "Soviet-style" governance. For such critics, environmental regulation represents inefficient and sometimes unconstitutional interference with the natural right to exploit resources; overly centralized regulations, critics contend, impose regulatory burdens that are inadequately attuned to local conditions. See Chapter 2. It is becoming almost acceptable to question the validity of the basic principle of environmental quality.

The second strain is a more general unease with the growing disconnect between environmentalism and traditional concepts of rationality and our modern technology-based civilization. This is the subject of M. Lewis, Green Delusions: An Environmentalist Critique of Radical Environmentalism (1992). G. Easterbrook's controversial book A Moment on Earth: The Coming Age of Environmental Optimism (1995) chastises the environmental movement for its efforts to maintain itself solely through claims that environmental catastrophes are imminent and for not keeping up with scientific developments. See also the controversial B. Lomberg, The Skeptical

Environmentalist: Measuring the Real State of the World (2001). For a critical response to Lomberg, see Kysar, Some Realism about Environmental Skepticism: The Implications of Bjorn Lomborg's *The Skeptical Environmentalist* for Environmental Law and Policy, 30 Ecology L.Q. 223 (2003).

On the environmentalist side, citizens and policymakers look at problems such as climate change and associated greenhouse gases, environmental inequities, ongoing struggles to clean America's many areas plagued by degraded rivers and substandard air quality, as well as widespread failure to enforce existing laws, and see unfinished business and unaddressed ills. Calls for greater energy conservation continue to fall mostly on deaf ears, and gaps between statutory aspirations and implemented reality persist. Still, over the past few decades, far greater attention has begun to be paid to "sustainability" goals, the growth of a "green economy," green building, alternative energy sources, less-polluting transportation, and perils of climate change. For a small sampling of the burgeoning literature influencing these movements, see P. Hawken et al., Natural Capitalism: Creating the Next Industrial Revolution (1999); P. Hawken, The Ecology of Commerce: A Declaration of Sustainability (1994); W. McDonough & M. Braungart, Cradle to Cradle: Remaking the Way We Make Things (2002). Whether changing public discourse on environmental issues will translate into actual improvements in legislation and results remains to be seen. The massive BP Deepwater Horizon oil spill in the Gulf of Mexico during 2010 caused significant long-term harm to the environment and also to businesses and nearby residents dependent on fishery resources and tourism. Past environmental crises have often served as a catalyst for new or corrective legislation, but not this time. Despite legislative hearings about the causes of the disaster and discussion of amendments to the National Environmental Policy Act (NEPA) and the Oil Pollution Act, as well as changes to the administrative agencies overseeing offshore oil drilling, no major legislative changes followed. The BP spill did, however, at least temporarily quiet claims that environmental laws go too far and should be weakened.

In short, persistent, fundamental divides among the dominant political parties and among the nation's regions continue to complicate environmental law and politics. Little is certain at this point, other than a climate of ongoing ferment and resulting policy debate.

I.   ENVIRONMENTAL POLICY AND REGULATORY DESIGN CHOICE

As you dig more deeply into this nation's environmental laws and regulations, you may find yourself puzzled. Little in the way of uniform goals or regulatory approaches will be evident. Even within a single law, you will find several different goals and regulatory strategies. This statutory diversity is the result of several factors. First, most laws have been amended on numerous occasions. Although assembled as a single law in the United States Code or a book of environmental statutes, most laws reflect the goals of different political coalitions, different states of knowledge about the efficacy of particular regulatory designs, and responses to different events prompting statutory enactment or amendment. Sometimes laws have been triggered by a galvanizing environmental catastrophe or by risks highlighted by a popular book. Each major statutory amendment tends to incorporate effective regulatory approaches utilized in other laws, but seldom are old statutory provisions jettisoned. At other times, laws have been amended in response to legal developments, such as an unexpected and environmentally destructive court decision, or regulatory failures to act during a time of divided government, or particular electoral cycles that prompted short-lived coalitions to enact a new law. Compromises and partial efforts to achieve goals are the norm. As the chapter on international law states, "sustainability" is becoming an increasingly influential goal in international law, but it neither explains the passage of this nation's laws nor justifies their particular schemes.

As will quickly become evident, this lack of a unifying goal or regulatory approach, coupled with their frequent amendment, means that these laws are both best explained and perhaps justified as the result of pragmatic, incremental adjustments. For such a defense, see S. Shapiro & R. Glicksman, Risk Regulation at Risk: Restoring a Pragmatic Approach (2003).

As discussed above, the rigor with which modern environmental laws were enacted starting in the late 1960s is attributable to an array of factors. Few, however, would dispute that this nation's environmental laws are in many respects a political economic miracle; today's laws, still largely reflecting the laws enacted during the "environmental decade," protect dispersed citizens and environmental interests, often to the detriment of industries with concentrated interests in avoiding substantial regulatory costs. See Farber, Politics and Procedure in Environmental Law, 8 J.L. Econ. & Org. 59 (1992); Schroeder, Rational Choice versus Republican Moment — Explanations for Environmental Law, 1969-1973, 9 Duke Envtl. L. & Pol'y F. 29 (1998).

Many of this nation's laws remain impressive and surprisingly effective, but they are often difficult work. Do not expect comprehensive coverage or consistency across statutes, but do be sensitive to the array of regulatory choices reflected in this nation's laws.

To highlight a few key aspects of the laws you will study, this chapter closes by highlighting in brief form several important statutory attributes. First, this section identifies the several sorts of *goals* evident in environmental laws. Second, it identifies key *triggers* that justify action under the statutes. Third, it identifies the most common *regulatory strategies or designs* utilized in the field we call environmental law. You have already been introduced to two strategies manifest in common law approaches to environmental ills — reliance on private bargaining to resolve conflicts, and the award of damages or injunctive relief following proof of environmental harm. Modern environmental statutes use a wider array of strategies.

1. Environmental Law Goals, Triggers, and Strategies

Environmental laws all share some sort of connection with the environment, but often have little focus on the environment in the sense of ecological health. Other laws are focused overwhelmingly on a cleaner environment. Sometimes the three statutory elements that we suggest require analysis — goals, triggers, and regulatory strategies or designs — are somewhat collapsed. Modern environmental laws share little other than a general rejection of the common law strategy of providing remedies after a harm has occurred, but even that generalization is only partly accurate. Several major statutes, chiefly laws dealing with spills and disposal of hazardous materials and oil, do utilize after-the-fact imposition of monetary liability both to pay for cleanups and discourage future mishandling of such wastes. Most of our environmental laws, however, share the goal of preventing or addressing risks before harm occurs. Most laws also rely on regulatory agencies to turn statutory aspirations and often broadly articulated mandates into implemented reality. Exactly what institutions play particular regulatory roles varies widely across statutes.

This brief catalogue of goals, triggers, and regulatory designs or strategies is not meant to provide a comprehensive identification of which statutes utilize which regulatory features. Instead, it highlights major salient features in laws by way of examples. The Clean Air Act could be used to illustrate virtually every paragraph that follows; in its cumbersome several hundred pages, it employs almost every feature described. The same is true of other laws. The provisions mentioned highlight major statutory features and strategies that you will encounter and must learn to recognize.

a. Goals

A Clean Environment. Several laws have as their overarching goal cleaning up the environment or preserving the natural environment's attributes, especially biological integrity or biodiversity. The Clean Water Act and Endangered Species Act share these goals, while the Clean Air Act is more focused on health, with a somewhat secondary focus on the environment. CERCLA, also known as the Superfund law, has the goal of cleaning up contaminated lands, but primarily for health reasons. Several of its provisions, however, also require assessment of environmental impacts.

The goal of a clean environment is itself an aspiration that will probably never be reached. Instead, a major question is assessing just "how clean is clean," and how far a statute requires movement toward a clean environment. Seldom is a pristine, prehuman environment the goal. Instead, most laws allow varying degrees of environmental degradation, with current or anticipated uses often influencing the requisite level of pollution control. In addition, other goals such as protection of health are often considered in conjunction with clean environment goals.

Public Health. The Clean Air Act and CERCLA share a focus on cleaning up pollution to prevent or minimize risks to health. Similarly, pesticide and food laws and chemicals regulation focus on public health, as does the Safe Drinking Water Act. As with cleanliness goals, the significant regulatory choice relates to the relevant proxies or measures for health, and at what level of protection standards should be set.

Fairness or Remedying of Damages. The central goal of common law schemes is provision of a remedy or award of damages. Perhaps surprisingly, little in statutory environmental law other that oil spill laws shares these goals. Most laws focus on reducing certain risks and preserve the right to bring common law actions, but do not include their own separate right to a damages remedy. CERCLA allows for cost recovery actions when governments or individuals undertake a cleanup of hazardous waste contributed to by others, as do several other laws related to spills and hazardous materials, but the relief provided does not actually amount to damages. Instead, it is a judicial award of some or all of the costs of cleanup. Frequently, monetary remedies are combined with rights to injunctive relief mandating action or cessation of harmful activity.

b. Triggers

Triggers for regulatory actions and obligations vary in form. Some triggers create obligations for the government to act, whereas others call for polluters to take remedial steps or report a pollution incident.

No Threshold Risk Determination. Some laws, such as food regulation, contain provisions that authorize protective government action against certain additives without proof of any risk in their regulated use. Similarly, certain types of unreported releases of hazardous substances can justify government sanctions, even without proof of any resulting risk or harm. In addition, some laws require improved environmental performance for certain sources of risk based on what can be technologically achieved, with little or no focus on or proof of risk before or after regulation. Especially for known carcinogens, laws sometimes require actions without any prior proof of manifested harms.

Risk-Based Thresholds. More common are laws that allow government action only upon a determination that risk exceeds some statutory threshold, usually some sort of risk to health or the environment. The degree of risk that must be shown can vary from minimal risk to a high proof threshold. The quintessential example of such a law is the Clean Air Act. Its various provisions reflect dramatically different sorts of risk-based triggers. Pervasive ambient air pollutants threatening health must be regulated to preserve health, allowing an adequate margin of safety, while stationary sources of pollution, such as factories, can be regulated if they can be reasonably anticipated to endanger public health or welfare. The main law governing pesticides, in contrast, requires regulatory scrutiny to determine if pesticide use will cause unreasonable health effects. Note, however, that how regulatory burdens are allocated can differ, with some laws requiring government proof of risk and other laws requiring industry proof of safety before a product can be entered into commerce. Note also that the stringency of and criteria for setting those regulatory restrictions is a different matter addressed below. Several laws that utilize technology-based standards with little or no regard to risk contain provisions that bring risk evaluations back into the picture in later assessments of whether technology-based standards and resulting pollution permits leave unacceptable levels of residual risk. Prime examples of such schemes are found in the Clean Water Act's water quality and total maximum daily load provisions, and in the Clean Air Act's provisions regarding hazardous air pollutants.

c. Regulatory Designs and Strategies

Regulatory designs and strategies are many, and they are often utilized in tandem in the same statute and sometimes even within the same programs. They nevertheless have distinct attributes.

Economic Incentives and Market-Based Strategies. Both the oldest environmental law schemes, namely common law approaches, and the most modern schemes, such as those found in the 1990 amendments to the Clean Air Act, use economic incentives. These can range from awards of damages to "internalize" otherwise externalized harms, to taxing of harmful activity to create an incentive for improved performance, to the subsidizing of desired conduct. In addition, both existing Clean Air Act provisions and most domestic and international climate change proposals utilize a variant on "cap-and-trade" strategies, an innovation rooted in economic insights about the benefits of market-based strategies. Instead of telling polluters how to control pollution, or even uniformly imposing regulatory burdens on all similar polluters, a cap-and-trade strategy sets an overall cap for a pollutant and then creates a market by allowing private trading of pollution allowances or permit rights. The hope is that potential profits from pollution trading will encourage all polluters to do better, will help achieve environmental goals at lower cost, and will rely less on government omniscience about how best to achieve environmental goals.

Technology-Based Standards. Since the early 1970s, both the Clean Air and Clean Water Acts have embraced strategies that require regulators to determine, against carefully crafted benchmarks and criteria, what level of pollution reduction or emission level is able to be accomplished through technological means. The age of the polluting facility, the nature of the pollutant, and assessments of cost all usually influence what must be accomplished. Other such provisions can require little more than meeting what are common performance measures for an industry. Despite often being derided as inefficient "command and control" regulation, technology-based standards typically do not mandate the use of any particular technology, but instead require achieving the performance level of the benchmark group. The standards are typically later rolled into source-specific permits. A risk-averse industry will often simply adopt the technology considered by federal regulators in setting the required standard, but this is seldom the result of any technology mandate.

Technology-Forcing Provisions. Technology-forcing provisions are a variant of technology-based provisions. Instead of looking at what has been achieved, regulators typically determine what can be accomplished through the use of innovative technologies or sometimes (in less ambitious forms of technology forcing) through mandates to meet the accomplishments of the least polluting similar sources or the most effective tested pollution control technology, even if not yet in industrial use. In some instances, especially those concerning motor vehicle pollution under the Clean Air Act, legislative provisions have required ambitious levels of pollution reduction without advance knowledge of the particular means to the legislative end. Such provisions force the development of new pollution control technologies.

Technology Mandates. Rarely, and typically only as a fallback mechanism, some laws do require agencies to determine what technology is best to achieve a specific goal, and then mandate its use. Such mandates usually require that pollution control obligations later be rolled into a permit specific to each pollution source.

Risk- or Ambient-Environment-Based Standard Setting. In both the Clean Air and Clean Water Acts, provisions require regulators to set standards for what constitutes an adequately clean or safe environment. Once this level of ambient environmental cleanliness or level of acceptable risk is determined, then regulators must, in effect, engage in a reverse engineering sort of calculation. Sources contributing to the particular ambient environment must meet levels of pollution so that the ambient environment will at least move toward the specified level of cleanliness or risk. The quintessential example of such provisions is in the Clean Air Act's state implementation plan provisions and their linkage to attainment of National Ambient Air Quality Standards.

Information-Based Schemes. In numerous laws, governments or private actors, or both, must prepare and make public information about their environmental activities or the environmental impacts of proposed activities. This is seen most prominently in NEPA as well as in later amendments to CERCLA requiring industry revelation of toxic releases. As interpreted by the Supreme Court, NEPA does not require the adoption of any particular environmentally sound outcome. Other laws with analogous or simultaneously applicable provisions, such as the Endangered Species Act, create substantial regulatory risks if information about possible harms is ignored. Even standard permit-based schemes such as the Clean Water Act industrial-discharge-permit program require that all stages of the permit process, from application to periodic compliance reports, be publicly accessible. Failure to provide required information, or the provision of false information, is subject to potentially severe penalties. Information-based schemes are particularly favored by economists and market-oriented policymakers because they facilitate informed market choice.

Liability-Based Schemes. CERCLA, or the Superfund law, as it is colloquially known, is designed to deter future creation of dangerous hazardous waste sites, but it achieves this goal not through advance permitting but through the imposition of huge cleanup liabilities on contributors to such sites. It is much like common law schemes, using monetary incentives to encourage environmentally sound behavior. CERCLA and some similar provisions in the Oil Pollution Act can require cleanup actions by responsible parties, not just payment for the costs of cleanup. CERCLA also utilizes more standard regulatory procedures for the process of determining how to categorize and clean up particular sites.

Phase-Outs and Prohibitions. Less common, but still highly effective at times, are laws and regulatory actions that require the phasing out of risky products or activities or prohibitions or presumptive prohibitions on certain activities.

Constrained Balancing Standards. Professors Shapiro and Glicksman, in their book, Risk Regulation at Risk, *supra*, identify a number of laws as utilizing a "constrained balancing standards" approach. Id. at 37. Such provisions may embrace a health or environmental goal, but then require consideration of regulatory repercussions such as cost, economic impacts, what can be achieved in a certain time frame, or what is technologically feasible. Many technology-based forms of regulation, which are described above, utilize a variant of constrained balancing.

Cost-Benefit–Influenced Standard Setting. Although championed by many vocal critics of the modern regulatory state, few laws at this time subject regulatory actions to a cost-benefit analysis test. An Executive Order does so when consistent with underlying statutory law, and one regulatory reform law focused on unfunded mandates imposes a limited requirement of cost-benefit analysis, but most environmental laws merely require attention to costs or economic impacts among many other variables. Portions of major laws, especially a key provision in the Clean Air Act focused on health, do not allow attention to costs or benefits. The ferment on whether to require greater attention to costs and benefits of regulatory action will surely continue.

2.   *Implementation and Enforcement Design Choice*

The preceding paragraphs focus on what regulatory strategies are imposed on polluters and others who might harm the environment. A different sort of regulatory design choice focuses on what regulatory institutions will play implementation and enforcement roles. The exact mix of roles varies in the statutory schemes you will study, but you should be sensitive to the following regulatory design choices.

Are provisions self-implementing or delegated to agencies? and how are requirements imposed on polluters? Although some major environmental laws impose burdens directly on regulatory targets and hence are self-implementing, most delegate implementation tasks to governmental institutions. Typically, federal agencies such as the

U.S. Environmental Protection Agency (EPA) are statutorily delegated initial implementation obligations, such as issuing regulations following notice and comment rulemakings. Some laws, however, hand presumptive implementation authority to state actors. Even then, a dense web of regulations usually exists to guide policymakers. The criteria to be applied in delegations to agencies are often the most important statutory language guiding government conduct and allowing for oversight and judicial challenge. A further layer of delegation and articulation of legal obligations is contained in government-issued permits. Under most major statutes, agencies roll regulatory obligations and specification of permitted activities into source-specific permits. Compliance with such permits is often the key to translating environmental aspirations into implemented reality. Due to the centrality of this multi-level delegation process, virtually every stage is subject to citizen participation rights, judicial challenge, and enforcement by all levels of government and by citizens as well.

Do key provisions provide for elective or mandatory action? Be sensitive to the language of mandate, such as the use of "shall" or the imposition of statutory deadlines for action. Note also when laws provide criteria or goals, but do not require action in specified circumstances. Statutes vary wildly in the specificity of their language, sometimes granting broad discretionary authority, and other times micro-managing all that will occur. As you will see in the administrative law chapter and in many cases that follow, courts respond very differently to language of mandate or statutes that leave agencies with a substantial range of discretionary choices. A statutory allocation of tasks may make clear which institution is to act, but whether the action is elective or required often determines whether the statutory language leads to actual implementation or to delay.

Who can enforce the law? Most environmental laws empower several enforcers, with federal authorities, states, and citizens all handed potential enforcement authority, at least if the other does not act. In addition, allegedly "arbitrary and capricious" agency action or allegedly erroneous statutory interpretations are subject to challenge under well-established administrative law doctrines.

What creates enforceable legal obligations? Enforceable obligations can arise at different points for different actors. For example, it is quite common for a federal agency to have an initial obligation to promulgate a regulation, with states then able to assume implementation or enforcement roles, either in lieu of or in addition to federal agencies. Next, legal obligations are rolled into permits that are themselves subject to challenge in regulatory proceedings or later in court. Finally, violations of permit obligations by a polluter are separately subject to enforcement actions. Few laws or even sections of laws create anything close to a single clear obligation. The complex regulatory statutes you will study set a sequence of regulatory actions in motion, generating many settings where lawyers seek to influence outcomes. Hence, a public interest lawyer concerned about mercury air pollution, for example, will typically monitor national regulations regarding such pollution, implementation at the state or regional level, levels of pollution control imposed on pollution sources in their permits, and actual compliance with such permits. Each regulatory stage specifying legal requirements allows for participation and comment by interested entities, including citizens and public interest groups, as well as the possibility of challenge in the courts.

As is apparent in this review of regulatory strategies and designs, a critical element in all environmental laws is how federal and state governments fill their implementation and enforcement roles. Chapter 2 turns to that topic.

II

ENVIRONMENTAL FEDERALISM

Environmental laws seldom contain direct, clear mandates. Instead, modern environmental statutory schemes work within the complex constraints of our federalist form of government. Modern environmental laws preserve certain roles for federal agencies, seek to enlist state and local government actors to play assisting or perhaps primary delegated roles, and preserve the possibility of additional state and local environmental laws and common law regimes. In addition, background constitutional law doctrines influence how these laws are interpreted, implemented, and enforced. This layering of environmental laws, coupled with doctrines influencing the roles federal and state actors can play, pervades environmental law. At each level of government, administrative law doctrines, which are the subject of Chapter 3, further influence how statutory aspirations are implemented in practice.

This chapter focuses on environmental federalism. To work effectively as an environmental lawyer or policymaker, one must develop facility with environmental federalism's wrinkles and choices. Multilayered law, entailing the possibility of conflict, cooperation, overlap, and fundamental challenges to governmental actors' authority, is the norm, not the exception. Constitutional law courses provide most environmental law students with a solid grounding in federalism doctrine. Nevertheless, the Supreme Court's active recent recasting of federalism doctrine, coupled with particular challenges likely to arise in connection with environmental protection, require the inclusion of a separate chapter highlighting environmental federalism's many facets. Some of the subjects covered are constitutional in nature, but many involve questions of regulatory choice within areas under the largely unquestioned authority of federal and state actors.

This chapter examines environmental federalism law in the following order. First, we will look at the *rationales* for federal environmental regulation. When should an environmental problem be addressed by the federal government or the states? This fundamental question remains a subject of active policy and scholarship debate. Even if the federal government has power to act, should it?

Next, we turn to the question of *federal power* to protect the environment. This question primarily involves analysis of federal power under the Commerce Clause of the U.S. Constitution. The Supreme Court's varying approaches and persistent analytical divisions leave the question of federal power open to challenge and certain litigation in the coming years. This debate over the reach of federal or state power also influences how courts will interpret legislation.

We then examine means by which the federal government can *enlist or encourage state assistance*. Building off of this analysis, we next look briefly at the ways statutes

deal with the reality of federal and state actors and multilayered laws. Most significantly, this section examines *delegated program federalism* (a form of *cooperative federalism*) and *savings clauses* that preserve existing law, typically state common law and
parallel or completely independent, nonconflicting bodies of state law.

Federalism doctrine also provides opportunities for challenges to federal or state
regulatory power, particularly where federal and state actors collide. Although the
Constitution's Supremacy Clause clearly provides that federal law will trump
conflicting state law, controversy over conflicting laws implicates several doctrines
that can serve to undercut state or federal law.

Sovereign immunity doctrine can potentially immunize states from monetary
liabilities and has been an area of substantial Supreme Court activity since the
1990s. State sovereign immunity doctrine is rooted in language from the Tenth
and Eleventh Amendments, although it is justified in large part on claimed pre-
constitutional understandings. As you will see, even if private actions against states
are barred, states are still subject to potential liability and litigation.

Dormant Commerce Clause doctrine can prohibit state actions that could
impede interstate commerce, even in the absence of any expressly conflicting federal
law.

Preemption doctrine sets limits on what kinds of state actions are permitted in
areas addressed by federal law; as you will see, preemption doctrine's many facets
make it an area where the basic law is more easily stated than applied. Preemption law
became a source of recent regulatory and judicial ferment when, starting around 2005,
numerous Bush administration administrative agencies started aggressively asserting
preemptive power and effect, often leading to claims that state common law protections were preempted. This led to extensive policy and scholarship debate, litigation,
and a reversal of policy early in the Obama administration. These debates are also of
great significance to climate and energy policy. During a period of federal inaction
due to both executive branch opposition and legislative partisan divisions, states and
regions began to enact climate-related legislation. This state leadership, in turn, provoked substantial debate that continues today over what state and local roles should be
retained if federal climate and energy legislation is enacted.

In short, environmental federalism law remains an area of great complexity and
ongoing debate. Environmental federalism law is about much more than just power or
lack of power. Federalism frameworks influence strategic decisions by public and
private actors. Familiarity with the different doctrines, rationales, and common
choices manifested in this nation's environmental laws is critical to working effectively
in the field of environmental law.

Problem 2-1

You are counsel for Greenbuild Inc., a large, national company interested in
developing abandoned and possibly moderately contaminated real property, often in
urban areas. These sites, typically referred to as *brownfield sites*, have often been
abandoned or underutilized due to liability fears, but also often due to tax liens,
disputes over ownership, and perhaps other easements and covenants related to conservation limiting how these sites will be used. Furthermore, site-specific agreements
and orders under federal, state, and local laws sometimes limit permitted land uses due
to concerns about exposure to hazardous substances and other pollutants. Your

company has found that these many sorts of title and use uncertainties are hindering redevelopment efforts and reducing profitability. State and local governments also would like to see such brownfield properties redeveloped. Following a visit from a U.S. senator interested in strengthening her environmental and business reputation, your company's president has sought your guidance. In particular, she and the visiting senator want to know if federal legislation could survive challenges if it required all levels of government to input information into a shared national database that would record all use limitations on parcels of property over ten acres in size. Applying the materials that follow in this chapter, sketch your analysis of the constitutionality of such a law, paying special attention to how it might best be structured to pass constitutional muster and also to work effectively.

A. RATIONALES FOR FEDERAL ENVIRONMENTAL REGULATION

Even if the federal assertion of regulatory power can survive a direct constitutional attack, and even if such an assertion is beyond dispute, the question remains whether federal regulatory power should be asserted. Despite the broad perception since the late 1960s that the federal government is the chief environmental innovator and the level of government responsible for most major environmental improvements, recent influential scholarship questions the accuracy of that perception. Scholarly reexamination of the rationales for federal environmental regulation, as well as related historical analysis, continues today, influencing the worlds of academe and policy. Presumptions against federal regulation, or in favor of the preservation of certain areas as primarily ruled by state law, surface periodically in court decisions. Familiarity with the rationales for federal or state regulatory primacy, or for overlapping implementation and enforcement regimes, can be essential to success as a lawyer or policymaker. The following readings and notes provide an introduction to these debates and competing rationales.

1. Interstate Externalities

Perhaps the most widely accepted rationale for federal over state environmental standard setting is the interstate movement of pollution externalities. Since many forms of pollution, especially air and water pollution, as well as environmental threats to animals, plants, or endangered species, and the species themselves, can and typically do move across state borders, the primacy of federal regulation is often accepted. Stewart, Pyramids of Sacrifice? Problems of Federalism in Mandating State Implementation of National Environmental Policy, 86 Yale L.J. 1210, 1215 (1977) (discussing how interstate "spillovers . . . generate conflicts and welfare losses not easily remedied under a decentralized regime"). Other influential analyses include Merrill, Golden Rules for Transboundary Pollution, 46 Duke L.J. 931 (1997); Revesz, Federalism and Interstate Externalities, 144 U. Pa. L. Rev. 2341 (1996). States have little incentive to abate their own interstate pollution or that caused by their industries unless some higher level of government imposes such a requirement. As seen in

Chapter 1, states can pursue public nuisance claims, but they often face difficult proof hurdles and generally will not succeed if there are many polluters contributing to a pollution stream.

Some scholars focus almost exclusively on the physical location or nature of the pollution and hence advocate the "matching principle," arguing that the regulator with jurisdiction most commensurate with the pollution's effects should have regulatory primacy. Butler & Macey, Externalities and the Matching Principle: The Case for Reallocating Environmental Regulatory Authority, 14 Yale L. & Pol'y Rev. 23 (1996). Others suggest that interstate business dynamics, resources that exceed a single jurisdiction, or interjurisdictional competition also can weigh in favor of federal regulation. See Buzbee, Recognizing the Regulatory Commons: A Theory of Regulatory Gaps, 89 Iowa L. Rev. 1, 25 (2003); see also Adler, Jurisdictional Mismatch in Environmental Federalism, 14 N.Y.U. Envtl. L.J. 130 (2005) (exploring the problem of jurisdictional mismatch, with an emphasis on limiting federal regulation to areas of clear federal institutional advantage).

2.   Economies of Scale and Information

Where effective regulation requires substantial investigation of technological capabilities, links between pollutants and health impacts, or comprehensive assessment of diverse jurisdictions' pollution control efforts, economies of scale and free rider concerns will favor a federal role in such information-generating tasks. Otherwise, no individual state will have the incentive to gather these sorts of valuable statistics, and other states will be tempted to "free ride" at the expense of any state that does make such an investment. For exploration of the "free rider" problem, see Chapter 1, at page 12. Federal leadership also reduces the risk of duplicative regulatory investigation, and placing research capabilities in a single institution's hands likely will help that institution develop experience and expertise. For this reason, federal gathering and dissemination of information about pollution impacts and pollution control has long been part of federal environmental law. Due to the widely shared view that federal action benefits from economies of scale, one seldom encounters calls for the federal government to surrender these informational roles.

3.   The Race to the Bottom

One of the most common justifications for federalizing environmental regulation is the fear that, without federal standards, the states will engage in a game of competitive deregulation or lowering of regulatory standards—a phenomenon typically called "race to the bottom" or race to laxity. This argument surfaces in Judge Wilkinson's opinion in Gibbs v. Babbitt, excerpted below. He identifies this dynamic as a justification for federal regulation that influenced Congress to enact environmental laws such as the Endangered Species Act. Stated most basically, race-to-the-bottom theory posits that without federal regulation, states will relax their standards in order to attract industrial development, with its attendant employment and tax benefits. Under this theory, each jurisdiction will end up sacrificing its citizens' preferred level of environmental cleanliness. In short, this competition results in suboptimal levels of environmental protection. See Stewart, supra, at 1211-1212;

Stewart, The Development of Administrative and Quasi-Constitutional Law in Judicial Review of Environmental Decisionmaking: Lessons from the Clean Air Act, 62 Iowa L. Rev. 713, 747 (1977).[a]

In a 1992 article, New York University law professor Richard Revesz challenged the theoretical underpinnings of race-to-the-bottom theory. Rehabilitating Interstate Competition: Rethinking the "Race to the Bottom" Rationale for Federal Environmental Regulation, 67 N.Y.U. L. Rev. 1210 (1992). Revesz asserts that there is no formal support for the conclusion that interstate competition tends to lead to a race to the bottom in social welfare. Rather, using neoclassical economic models to simulate the effects of interstate competition, he argues that competition among states, like competition within industry, tends to produce socially efficient outcomes. Revesz questions the assumption that federal minima in the area of environmental regulation will prevent a race to the bottom; even if constrained by federal environmental standards, states could still choose to compete by lowering standards in other areas that remain under their control. Hence, he does not explicitly deny that environmental standards may drop due to such dynamics, but that social welfare may be reduced by taking nonuniform levels of environmental stringency off the table of state policy options. Though not intended "as a definitive refutation to race-to-the-bottom arguments," Revesz argues that the forces of interstate competition are at least "presumptively beneficial." Id. at 1253.

His examination of the issue touched off a lively debate among legal scholars. Several critics challenged Revesz's theoretical framework, charging that it rested on assumptions that do not closely reflect real-world conditions. See Esty, Revitalizing Environmental Federalism, 95 Mich. L. Rev. 570 (1996) ("In the end, Revesz's theoretical dismissal of the race to the bottom depends on heroic assumptions, including perfect government rationality."); Swire, The Race to Laxity and the Race to Undesirability: Explaining Failures in Competition among Jurisdictions in Environmental Law, 14 Yale J. on Reg. 67 (1996) ("Environmental law is largely defined by the very factors that are assumed away in the models, such as many interstate externalities, deep public choice problems, and intractable theoretical and practical obstacles to measuring the social utility of environmental regulations.").

Others have taken a more empirical approach. Most notably, in 1996, Professor Kirsten Engel published the results of a study in which 400 state environmental, economic, and legislative officials, along with selected interest groups, were polled regarding the existence of race-to-the-bottom behavior. Engel, State Environmental Standard-Setting: Is There a "Race" and Is It "to the Bottom"?, 48 Hastings L.J. 271 (1997). Among her findings: 57 out of 65 state regulators stated that concern over industry relocation affected environmental decisionmaking in their states; 47 out of

a. Literature on the dynamics of interjurisdictional competition and its benefits and costs is also prominent outside the environmental area. See, e.g., Cary, Federalism and Corporate Law: Reflections upon Delaware, 83 Yale L.J. 663 (1974) (corporate law); Butler & Macey, The Myth of Competition in the Dual Banking System, 73 Cornell L. Rev. 677 (1988) (banking law); Kaplow, Fiscal Federalism and the Deductibility of State and Local Taxes Under the Federal Income Tax, 82 Va. L. Rev. 413, 458-560 (1996) (tax law); Brown, Competitive Federalism and the Legislative Incentives to Recognize Same-Sex Marriage, 68 S. Cal. L. Rev. 745, 816-818 (1995) (family law); Been, Exit as a Constraint on Land Use Exactions: Rethinking the Unconstitutional Conditions Doctrine, 91 Colum. L. Rev. 473 (1991) (land use); Esty & Geradin, Market Access, Competitiveness, and Harmonization: Environmental Protection in Regional Trade Agreements, 21 Harv. Envtl. L. Rev. 269 (1997) (environmental protection in the context of free trade); Zelinsky, Against a Federal Patients' Bill of Rights, 21 Yale L. & Pol'y Rev. 443 (2003) (health care law).

80 regulators believed that the degree of environmental regulation was a fairly or a very important factor in determining industry location/relocation; and 48 percent of state regulators reported that their state or agency had done something to lower their environmental standards in response to concerns over industry relocation. Among those officials reporting that industry relocation had played no role whatsoever in environment policymaking, most attributed this to the presence of federal standards that limited their ability to deregulate. Engel's findings provide strong empirical support for race-to-the-bottom theorists, as well as renewed support for the rationale for federal standard setting. She also strongly questions Revesz's basic assumption that the world of environmental standard setting resembles an efficient market. She points out that competition among states for industrial siting is characterized by small numbers of states and corporations, and is rife with imperfect information.

Professor Jerome Organ in 1995 examined state willingness to enact environmental standards more stringent than the presumptive federal standard, as specifically allowed under most federal statutes. He discovered that many states have enacted laws either prohibiting or creating procedural or substantive hurdles constraining environmental regulators from exceeding federal standards. Organ, Limitations on State Agency Authority to Adopt Environmental Standards More Stringent than Federal Standards: Policy Considerations and Interpretive Problems, 54 Md. L. Rev. 1373 (1995). He observes that the pervasiveness of these enactments confirms the theory that fears of competitive disadvantage, a central tenet of race-to-the-bottom theory, remain important to states. Id. at 1393 n.91.

Revesz responded to many of these criticisms in The Race to the Bottom and Federal Environmental Regulation: A Response to Critics, 82 Minn. L. Rev. 535 (1997), distilling and sharpening some of his main points. The following statement makes clear that he is not necessarily disputing the claim that environmental standards may drop in response to competition, but is positing that federal standards might induce a reduction in social welfare:

> I argue that even if states systematically enacted suboptimally lax environmental standards, federal environmental regulation would not necessarily improve the situation. If states cannot compete over environmental regulation because it has been federalized, they will compete along other regulatory dimensions, leading to suboptimally lax standards in other areas, or along the fiscal dimension, leading to the underprovision of public goods. Thus, the reduction in social welfare implicit in race-to-the-bottom arguments would not be eliminated merely by federalizing environmental regulation: federalization of all regulatory and fiscal decisions would be necessary to solve the problem. [Id. at 541.]

4. Centralization versus Decentralization

The benefits or costs of centralized or decentralized regulatory standard setting and implementation is a fourth variable weighed in most federalism discussions. Here arguments cut both ways, with advocates of decentralization favoring state primacy and advocates of centralization favoring a federal role. As you will see, most environmental laws adopt hybrid schemes, with both centralized and decentralized elements. Most numerical standard setting, however, whether for ambient environmental levels or by category of industry, is federally set. As Professors Rubin and Feeley argue forcefully, decentralization arguments and federalism arguments are not the same, although the two are often confused. Rubin & Feeley, Federalism: Some Notes on a National Neurosis, 41 UCLA L. Rev. 903 (1994).

Decentralization Arguments. Professor Stewart has articulated well the arguments in favor of decentralized environmental regulation:

> This presumption [in favor of decentralization] serves utilitarian values because decisionmaking by state and local governments can better reflect geographical variations in preferences for collective goods like environmental quality and similar variations in the costs of providing such goods. Noncentralized decisions also facilitate experimentation with differing governmental policies, and enhance individuals' capacities to satisfy their different tastes in conditions of work and residence by fostering environmental diversity.
>
>   Important nonutilitarian values are also served by noncentralized decisionmaking. It encourages self-determination by fragmenting governmental power into local units of a scale conducive to active participation in or vicarious identification with the processes of public choice. This stimulus to individual and collective education and self-development is enriched by the wide range of social, cultural and physical environments which noncentralized decisionmaking encourages. [Stewart, Pyramids, *supra*, at 1210-1211.]

Stewart and others also point out that reliance on an overly large regulator can lead to "diseconomies of scale" because the regulator will not be sensitive to smaller-scale variations and differences in priorities. In addition, in literature overlapping with "race-to-the-bottom" analyses, theorists posit that with many jurisdictions in competition for citizens, businesses, and revenues, competition will lead to more efficient delivery of government services.

Centralization Arguments. Without a more centralized regulatory authority that views environmental harms as internal costs, and that will answer to constituents both causing and harmed by pollution, these harms may go unaddressed. In addition, many environmental ills and citizen demands for a safe and clean environment are rooted in the concept of the right to a clean environment, or at least the argument that a certain degree of environmental protection should be uniformly guaranteed across the nation. Finally, centralized environmental regulation can reduce the number of venues in which policy and legal battles occur. This can be particularly advantageous for groups with scant resources. As Daniel Esty states, with a "centralized" regulatory structure, "environmental groups find it easier to reach critical mass and thereby to compete on more equal footing with industrial interests." Esty, *supra*, at 650 n.302. This is linked to "public choice" rationales for federal or state regulation, discussed below.

Of course, a multiplicity of potential regulators can lead to confusion over lines of responsibility and to dissipation or misdirection of demands for regulatory protection, see Buzbee, *supra*, but the more clearly responsible a single regulator is for an environmental ill, the more likely it is that action will be taken. As mentioned above, economies of scale in gathering or creating information also favor a centralized governmental role.

Mixed Regimes with Centralized and Decentralized Regulatory Roles. Because of the many varieties of environmental ills, scholars such as Daniel Esty advocate "multi-tier regulatory structure[s] capable of mixing and matching decision levels depending on the issue at hand." Esty, *supra*, at 652. The Clean Air Act represents such a mixed regime, with its reliance on federal information gathering, federal standard setting, local implementation, and overlapping enforcement roles. Given the risk of under-enforcement due to lack of resources or political will, shared enforcement roles can create a more credible deterrent to polluters. See Buzbee, Contextual Environmental Federalism, 14 N.Y.U. Envtl. L.J. 108, 121-126 (2005).

5.   Political, Economic, and Historical Rationales for Federal (or State) Regulation

A separate rationale for federal regulation, or perhaps state regulation, is rooted in observations about political and economic dynamics at the federal or state level. This is sometimes characterized as a "public choice" rationale that uses economic "rational actor" assumptions to predict how political and market actors will behave in political settings to further their goals. Others look at the history of environmental law and politics and make normative arguments about which level of government can and should address environmental harms.

Based on empirical observations about environmental politics, in an argument closely linked to the centralization arguments discussed above, Professor Stewart in 1977 posited that environmental groups might fare better in national politics than in state venues:

> Much of the politics of pollution control involves conflict between environmental groups and industrial and union interests. There are persuasive grounds for believing that, on the whole, environmental groups have a comparatively greater impact on policy decisions at the national level, even disregarding "commons" factors that make state and local governments particularly vulnerable to industry and union pressures. It is therefore not surprising that environmental groups should favor determination of environmental policies by the federal government, and that increased public support for environmental protection should translate into increased legislation and regulation at the federal level. [Stewart, Pyramids, *supra*, at 1213.]

Stewart further suggested that appeals to morals and self-sacrifice may work better in national politics. In such settings "there are effective assurances that others are making sacrifices too. National policies can provide such assurances and can also facilitate appeals to sublimate parochial interests in an embracing national crusade." Id. at 1217.

In recent years, the idea that the federal venue is the most advantageous for environmental interests has been debated on both theoretical and historical grounds. Professor Daniel Esty built on Stewart's argument, stating that

> asymmetries in information and the concentration of regulatory costs and benefits may give rise to asymmetries of political activity and influence between polluters and pollutees or between common-resource users and the public owners of these resources. Because these asymmetries may be more significant at the state and local levels, decentralization may represent a strategy to advance deregulation for the benefit of certain special interests. [Esty, *supra*, at 598.]

The preference for national regulation is not invariably associated with the environmentalist side. Once states start regulating in an area, industry may prefer federal regulation either to promote a uniform approach that will facilitate compliance economies of scale, or perhaps to secure a weaker preemptive action. See id. at 602. Still, the general perception remains that the federal legislative venue has been more willing to confront environmental harms with laws that have teeth. This perception has perhaps led to a "first mover" advantage for federal leadership, with federal legislators having long been perceived as the place to turn for responses to environmental problems. See Buzbee, Brownfields, Environmental Federalism, and Institutional Determinism, 21 Wm. & Mary L. Rev. 1, 27-58 (1997) (developing the "first mover" hypothesis in analysis focused on hazardous waste policies). In addition, political science scholarship indicates that federal politics is characterized by greater attention to issues, more press coverage, and increased surveying of citizen preferences. Id. at 44-46. Local and state politics, in contrast, are marked by less attention to issues and reduced awareness of both politician and citizen views. Id.; see also P. Peterson, City Limits 116-130 (1981). With polls consistently revealing broad-based support for environmental protection, the federal level, where issues-based politics is prevalent, likely is a venue more favorable to environmental interests than state or local fora.

More recently, several scholars have begun to question the story of past federal environmental leadership. Professor Jonathan Adler suggests that states were more active in addressing environmental ills in the pre-1970 period than is commonly acknowledged. Adler, The Fable of Federal Environmental Regulation: Reconsidering the Federal Role in Environmental Protection, 55 Case W. Res. L. Rev. 93 (2004); Adler, Fables of the Cuyahoga: Reconstructing a History of Environmental Protection, 14 Fordham Envtl. L.J. 89 (2002). Professor Revesz, in a recent article exploring "public choice rationales" for federal regulation, points to areas of recent state environmental activism to challenge the assumption that the federal government is more environmentally protective. Revesz, Federalism and Environmental Regulation: A Public Choice Analysis, 115 Harv. L. Rev. 553 (2001). He also finds unconvincing arguments that environmental interests will be disadvantaged in regulatory schemes that are less federally dominated, disputing long-standing arguments by Stewart, Esty, and others, as well as legislative assumptions underlying environmental law frameworks created between 1969 and the present.

In partial response to these arguments against a leading federal role, others suggest that analysts look more closely at the context leading to state activity, pointing out that much state activity during the early 2000s reflects efforts to enforce federal law or to deal with out-of-state pollution not yet adequately undertaken by federal actors. Much state environmental law also reflects imitation of federal regulatory approaches. Similarly, state innovations have often been prompted by pressures to attain federal standards. See Buzbee, Contextual Federalism, *supra.*

Still, it is indisputable that some states do, at times, innovate and take a more proactive role in protecting the environment. California, for example, in the fall of 2006, enacted a law designed to ratchet back greenhouse gases contributing to climate change, while the federal government continued to resist any such requirement. For a discussion of greenhouse gas regulation and California's new law, see coverage of climate change law in Chapter 12. For a discussion of preemption implications and other assessment of the benefits of federal and state activity regarding greenhouse gases, see discussion within section E.4, below.

6. Using Competing Federalism Rationales

Little is certain in the world of environmental federalism. Apart from widespread acceptance of a federal role in gathering and generating environmental information, federalism rationales tend to engender debate. Sensitivity to how these competing rationales apply in the settings of diverse environmental ills is part of effective legal advocacy, whether one is working in a legislative, regulatory, or judicial venue. These rationales do not provide answers, but provide important artillery for legal advocacy.

B. THE QUESTION OF FEDERAL COMMERCE POWER

The federal government has limited, specified powers under the Constitution. The federal government's power to control federal land use is rooted in the Constitution's Property Clause. That power has been broadly construed and subject to little debate. Instead, this section focuses on an area of active revision and debate—the limits of power under the Commerce Clause. Most modern environmental laws were passed pursuant to federal authority claimed under the Commerce Clause to "regulate Commerce . . . among the several states." U.S. Constitution, art. I, §8, cl. 3. The Supreme Court long ago abandoned the dualist presumption that federal and state governments had no overlapping authority; it also long ago abandoned rigid and narrow definitions of commerce that rendered the federal government unable to deal with a complex national economy. Nevertheless, what counts as commerce and thus as potentially subject to federal regulation remains contested. Especially in environmental law areas such as efforts to preserve biodiversity, protect wetlands, and save endangered species, arguments over federal power continue.

The following case introduces Commerce Clause doctrine and a recent series of related Supreme Court cases as they apply to one of the hot-button areas of federal power, endangered species protection. Note in particular the analytical differences between the appellate court's opinion and the dissent.

GIBBS v. BABBITT
214 F.3d 483 (4th Cir. 2000)

WILKINSON, C.J.

In this case we ask whether the national government can act to conserve scarce natural resources of value to our entire country. Appellants challenge the constitutionality of a Fish and Wildlife Service (FWS) regulation that limits the taking of red wolves on private land. The district court upheld the regulation as a valid exercise of federal power under the Commerce Clause. We now affirm because the regulated activity substantially affects interstate commerce and because the regulation is part of a comprehensive federal program for the protection of endangered species. Judicial deference to the judgment of the democratic branches is therefore appropriate. . . .

The red wolf, *Canis rufus*, is an endangered species whose protection is at issue in this case. The red wolf was originally found throughout the southeastern United States. It was once abundant in the "riverine habitats of the southeast," and was especially numerous near the "canebrakes" that harbored large populations of swamp and marsh rabbits, the primary prey of the red wolf. 51 Fed. Reg. 41,790, 41,791 (1986). The FWS found that "the demise of the red wolf was directly related to man's activities, especially land changes, such as the drainage of vast wetland areas for agricultural purposes . . . and predator control efforts at the private, State, and Federal levels." Id. . . .

In 1986, the FWS issued a final rule outlining a reintroduction plan for red wolves in the 120,000-acre Alligator River National Wildlife Refuge in eastern North Carolina. See 51 Fed. Reg. 41,790. This area was judged the ideal habitat within the red wolf's historic range. Between 1987 and 1992, a total of 42 wolves were released in the Refuge. In 1993, the reintroduction program was expanded to include the release of red wolves in the Pocosin Lakes National Wildlife Refuge in Tennessee. Since reintroduction, some red wolves have wandered from federal refuges onto private property. From available data, as of February 1998 it was estimated that about 41 of the approximately 75 wolves in the wild may now reside on private land.

This case raises a challenge to 50 C.F.R. §17.84(c), a regulation governing the experimental populations of red wolves reintroduced into North Carolina and Tennessee pursuant to section 10(j). The FWS has extended the takings prohibitions of section 9(a)(1) to the experimental red wolf populations with certain exceptions. See 50 C.F.R. §17.84(c) (1998). As noted above, the taking provision of section 9(a)(1) prevents landowners from harassing, harming, pursuing, hunting, shooting, wounding, killing, trapping, capturing, or collecting any endangered species. See 16 U.S.C. §1532(19). However, in order to insure that other agencies and the public would accept the proposed reintroduction, the FWS relaxed the taking standards for wolves found on private land under its authority over experimental populations. . . .

In October, 1990, plaintiff, Richard Lee Mann, shot a red wolf that he feared might threaten his cattle. The federal government prosecuted Mann under §17.84(c), and Mann pled guilty. Mann's prosecution triggered some opposition to the red wolf program in the surrounding communities. After the program was in place for several years, the FWS held meetings with local governments and the public to receive feedback about the reintroductions. The Service contended that most people who commented expressed support for the program and that the reintroductions were generally supported by local, state and federal agencies, and elected officials. See 58 Fed. Reg. 62,086, 62,088 (1993). In addition, owners of nearly 200,000 acres of private land have permitted red wolves onto their land through agreements with the FWS. Nonetheless, Hyde and Washington Counties, and the towns of Belhaven and Roper, passed resolutions opposing the reintroductions of the wolves. The resolutions appeared to be based on the farming community's fears of prohibitions on private land use.

In response to discontent with the reintroduction program, the North Carolina General Assembly passed a bill entitled "An Act to Allow the Trapping and Killing of Red Wolves by Owners of Private Land." The Act makes it lawful to kill a red wolf on private property if the landowner has previously requested the FWS to remove the red wolves from the property. See 1994 N.C. Sess. Laws Ch. 635, amended by 1995 N.C. Sess. Laws Ch. 83. This law facially conflicts with the federal regulation. . . .

Appellants Charles Gibbs, Richard Mann, Hyde County, and Washington County filed the instant action challenging the federal government's authority to protect red wolves on private land. They seek a declaration that the anti-taking regulation, 50 C.F.R. §17.84(c), as applied to the red wolves occupying private land in eastern North Carolina, exceeds Congress's power under the interstate Commerce Clause, U.S. Const. art. I, §8, cl. 3 ("Congress shall have Power . . . To regulate Commerce . . . among the several States . . ."). Appellants also seek an injunction against continued enforcement of the anti-taking regulation on non-federal land. Appellants claim that the red wolves have proven to be a "menace to citizens and animals in the Counties." They further allege that because of the federal regulatory protections surrounding the wolves, North Carolinians cannot effectively defend their property.

On cross-motions for summary judgment, the United States District Court for the Eastern District of North Carolina held that Congress's power to regulate interstate commerce includes the power to regulate conduct that might harm red wolves on private land. See Gibbs v. Babbitt, 31 F. Supp. 2d 531 (E.D.N.C., 1998). . . .

II.

We consider this case under the framework articulated by the Supreme Court in United States v. Lopez, 514 U.S. 549 (1995), and United States v. Morrison, 529 U.S. 598 (2000), *aff'g* Brzonkala v. Virginia Polytechnic Inst. and State Univ., 169 F.3d 820 (4th Cir. 1999). While Congress's power to pass laws under the Commerce Clause has been interpreted broadly, both *Lopez* and *Morrison* reestablish that the commerce power contains "judicially enforceable outer limits." . . . It is essential to our system of government that the commerce power not extend to effects on interstate commerce that are so remote that we "would effectually obliterate the distinction between what is national and what is local." National Labor Relations Bd. v. Jones & Laughlin Steel Corp., 301 U.S. 1, 37 (1937). . . .

While this is rational basis review with teeth, the courts may not simply tear through the considered judgments of Congress. Judicial restraint is a long and honored tradition and this restraint applies to Commerce Clause adjudications. "Due respect for the decisions of a coordinate branch of Government demands that we invalidate a congressional enactment only upon a plain showing that Congress has exceeded its constitutional bounds." *Morrison,* 529 U.S. at 607. In fact, "[t]he substantial element of political judgment in Commerce Clause matters leaves our institutional capacity more in doubt than when we decide cases, for instance, under the Bill of Rights." *Lopez*, 514 U.S. at 579 (Kennedy, J., concurring). . . .

The *Lopez* Court recognized three broad categories of activity that Congress may regulate under its commerce power. "First, Congress may regulate the use of the channels of interstate commerce. Second, Congress is empowered to regulate and protect the instrumentalities of interstate commerce, or persons or things in interstate commerce, even though the threat may come only from intrastate activities. Finally, Congress' commerce authority includes the power to regulate those activities having a substantial relation to interstate commerce, i.e., those activities that substantially affect interstate commerce." Id. at 558-59.

Section 17.84(c) is "not a regulation of the use of the channels of interstate commerce, nor is it an attempt to prohibit the interstate transportation of a commodity through the channels of commerce." *Lopez*, 514 U.S. at 559. The term "channel of interstate commerce" refers to, *inter alia*, "navigable rivers, lakes, and canals of the United States; the interstate railroad track system; the interstate highway system; . . . interstate telephone and telegraph lines; air traffic routes; television and radio broadcast frequencies." United States v. Miles, 122 F.3d 235, 245 (5th Cir. 1997). This regulation of red wolf takings on private land does not target the movement of wolves or wolf products in the channels of interstate commerce.

This case also does not implicate *Lopez*'s second prong, which protects things in interstate commerce. Although the Service has transported the red wolves interstate for the purposes of study and the reintroduction programs, this is not sufficient to make the red wolf a "thing" in interstate commerce. See, e.g., . . . National Assoc. of Home Builders v. Babbitt, 130 F.3d 1041, 1046 (D.C. Cir. 1997) ("*NAHB*") (rejecting notion that Delhi Sands Flower-Loving Fly was a "thing" in interstate commerce). Therefore, if 50 C.F.R. §17.84(c) is within the commerce power, it must be sustained under the third prong of *Lopez*.

Under the third *Lopez* test, regulations have been upheld when the regulated activities "arise out of or are connected with a commercial transaction, which viewed in the aggregate, substantially affects interstate commerce." *Lopez*, 514 U.S. at 561. . . .

Although the connection to economic or commercial activity plays a central role in whether a regulation will be upheld under the Commerce Clause, economic activity must be understood in broad terms. Indeed, a cramped view of commerce would cripple a foremost federal power and in so doing would eviscerate national authority. The *Lopez* Court's characterization of the regulation of homegrown wheat in Wickard v. Filburn, 317 U.S. 111 (1942), as a case involving economic activity makes clear the breadth of this concept. The Court explained that "[e]ven *Wickard*, which is perhaps the most far reaching example of Commerce Clause authority over intrastate activity, involved economic activity in a way that the possession of a gun in a school zone does not." *Lopez*, 514 U.S. at 560. . . .

III.

Appellants argue that the federal government cannot limit the taking of red wolves on private land because this activity cannot be squared with any of the three categories that Congress may regulate under its commerce power. Appellants assert that 50 C.F.R. §17.84(c) is therefore beyond the reach of congressional authority under the Commerce Clause.

We disagree. It was reasonable for Congress and the Fish and Wildlife Service to conclude that §17.84(c) regulates economic activity. The taking of red wolves implicates a variety of commercial activities and is closely connected to several interstate markets. The regulation in question is also an integral part of the overall federal scheme to protect, preserve, and rehabilitate endangered species, thereby conserving valuable wildlife resources important to the welfare of our country. Invalidating this provision would call into question the historic power of the federal government to preserve scarce resources in one locality for the future benefit of all Americans. . . .

Unlike the Violence Against Women Act (VAWA) in *Morrison* and the Gun-Free School Zones Act (GFSZA) in *Lopez*, §17.84(c) regulates what is in a meaningful sense economic activity. . . . The relationship between red wolf takings and interstate commerce is quite direct—with no red wolves, there will be no red wolf related tourism, no scientific research, and no commercial trade in pelts. We need not "pile inference upon inference," *Lopez*, 514 U.S. at 567, to reach this conclusion. While a beleaguered species may not presently have the economic impact of a large commercial enterprise, its eradication nonetheless would have a substantial effect on interstate commerce. And through preservation the impact of an endangered species on commerce will only increase.

Because the taking of red wolves can be seen as economic activity in the sense considered by *Lopez* and *Morrison*, the individual takings may be aggregated for the purpose of Commerce Clause analysis. See *Morrison*, 529 U.S. at 611, n.4. While the taking of one red wolf on private land may not be "substantial," the takings of red wolves in the aggregate have a sufficient impact on interstate commerce to uphold this regulation. This is especially so where, as here, the regulation is but one part of the broader scheme of endangered species legislation.

Further, §17.84(c) is closely connected to a variety of interstate economic activities. Whether the impact of red wolf takings on any one of these activities qualifies as a substantial effect on interstate commerce is something we need not address. We have no doubt that the effect of the takings on these varied activities in combination qualifies as a substantial one. The first nexus between the challenged regulation and interstate commerce is tourism. The red wolves are part of a $29.2 billion national wildlife-related recreational industry that involves tourism and interstate travel. . . . Many tourists travel to North Carolina from throughout the country for "howling events"—evenings of listening to wolf howls accompanied by educational programs. These howlings are a regular occurrence at the Alligator River National Wildlife Refuge. According to a study conducted by Dr. William E. Rosen of Cornell University, the recovery of the red wolf and increased visitor activities could result in a significant regional economic impact. Rosen estimates that northeastern North Carolina could see an increase of between $39.61 and $183.65 million per year in tourism-related activities, and that the Great Smoky Mountains National Park could see an increase of between $132.09 and $354.50 million per year. This is hardly a trivial impact on interstate commerce. Appellants understandably seek to criticize the Rosen study, but concede that the howling events attract interstate tourism and that red wolf program volunteers come from all around the country.

Appellants argue that the tourism rationale relates only to howling events on national park land or wildlife refuges because people do not travel to private land. They reason that without tourism on private land the regulated activity does not substantially affect interstate commerce. Yet this argument misses the mark. Since reintroduction, red wolves have strayed from federal lands onto private lands. Indeed, wolves are known to be "great wanderers." See 60 Fed. Reg. 18,940, 18,943 (1995). In 1998, it was estimated that 41 of the 75 wolves in the wild now live on private land. Because so many members of this threatened species wander on private land, the regulation of takings on private land is essential to the entire program of reintroduction and eventual restoration of the species. Such regulation is necessary to conserve enough red wolves to sustain tourism. Appellants in fact seem unmindful of the history of endangered species regulation. The Endangered Species Acts of 1966 and 1969 initially targeted conservation efforts only on federal lands, but they met with limited success. See Note, Evolution of Wildlife Legislation in the United States: An Analysis of the Legal Efforts to Protect Endangered Species and the Prospects for the Future, 5 Geo. Int'l Envtl. L. Rev. 441, 449-53 (1993). The Endangered Species Act of 1973 was motivated in part by the need to extend takings regulation beyond the limited confines of federal land. The prohibition of takings on private land was critical to the overall success of the ESA in halting and reversing the near extinction of numerous species. See 16 U.S.C. §1538(a)(1). The success of many commercial enterprises depends on some regulation of activity on private land, and interstate tourism is no exception.

Tourism, however, is not the only interstate commercial activity affected by the taking of red wolves. The regulation of red wolf takings is also closely connected to a second interstate market—scientific research. Scientific research generates jobs. It also deepens our knowledge of the world in which we live. . . . Protection of the red wolves on private land thus encourages further research that may have inestimable future value, both for scientific knowledge as well as for commercial development of the red wolf. . . .

When enacting the ESA, various legislators expressed these exact concerns, namely that species be conserved for future scientific development:

> The value of this genetic heritage is, quite literally, incalculable. . . . From the most narrow possible point of view, it is in the best interests of mankind to minimize the losses of genetic variations. The reason is simple: they are potential resources. . . . Who knows, or can say, what potential cures for cancer or other scourges, present or future, may lie locked up in the structures of plants which may yet be undiscovered, much less analyzed? . . . Sheer self-interest impels us to be cautious. [H.R. Rep. No. 93-412, at 4-5 (1973).]

B.

This regulation is also sustainable as "an essential part of a larger regulation of economic activity, in which the regulatory scheme could be undercut unless the intrastate activity were regulated." *Lopez*, 514 U.S. at 561. The Supreme Court in Hodel v. Indiana stated: "A complex regulatory program . . . can survive a Commerce Clause challenge without a showing that every single facet of the program is independently and directly related to a valid congressional goal. It is enough that the challenged provisions are an integral part of the regulatory program and that the regulatory scheme when considered as a whole satisfies this test." 452 U.S. 314, 329 n.17 (1981). . . .

IV.

Upholding this regulation is consistent with the "first principles" of a Constitution that establishes a federal government of enumerated powers. See *Lopez*, 514 U.S. at 552. *Lopez* and *Morrison* properly emphasize that we must carefully evaluate legislation in light of our federal system of government. "The Constitution requires a distinction between what is truly national and what is truly local." *Morrison*, 529 U.S. at 617-18. We must particularly scrutinize regulated activity that "falls within an area of the law where States historically have been sovereign and countenance of the asserted federal power would blur the boundaries between the spheres of federal and state authority." *Brzonkala*, 169 F.3d at 837.

A.

It is imperative to set forth at the outset the historic roles of federal and state authority in this area. The regulated activity at issue here does not involve an "area of traditional state concern," one to which "States lay claim by right of history and expertise." *Lopez*, 514 U.S. at 580, 583 (Kennedy, J., concurring).

Appellants argue that the regulation infringes on the traditional state control over wildlife. We are cognizant that states play a most important role in regulating wildlife—many comprehensive state hunting and fishing laws attest to it. State control over wildlife, however, is circumscribed by federal regulatory power. In Minnesota v. Mille Lacs Band of Chippewa Indians, the Supreme Court recently reiterated that "[a]lthough States have important interests in regulating wildlife and natural resources within their borders, this authority is shared with the Federal Government when the Federal Government exercises one of its enumerated constitutional powers." 526 U.S. 172, 204 (1999). In *Mille Lacs*, the Court upheld Chippewa Indian rights under an 1837 treaty that allowed the Chippewa to hunt, fish, and gather free of territorial, and later state, regulation. These Indian treaty rights were found to be "reconcilable with state sovereignty over natural resources." Id. at 205.

It is true that in the nineteenth century courts followed the legal precept that wildlife was the property of the state. See Geer v. Connecticut, 161 U.S. 519 (1896) (upholding a Connecticut statute that prohibited the interstate transportation of game birds that had been killed within the state). But the principles in *Geer* were modified early in the twentieth century. See Hughes v. Oklahoma, 441 U.S. 322, 329 (1979) ("The erosion of *Geer* began only 15 years after it was decided."). *Geer* was finally overruled in 1979 by Hughes v. Oklahoma, which held that states do not own the wildlife within their borders and that state laws regulating wildlife are circumscribed by Congress's commerce power. 441 U.S. at 326, 335. In light of *Mille Lacs* and *Hughes*, the activity regulated by §17.84(c)—the taking of red wolves on private property—is not an area in which the states may assert an exclusive and traditional prerogative in derogation of an enumerated federal power.

Appellants next argue that the application of this regulation to private land intrudes on the state's traditional police power to regulate local land use. Of course, states and localities possess broad regulatory and zoning authority over land within their jurisdictions. See Village of Euclid v. Ambler Realty Co., 272 U.S. 365 (1926). It is well established, however, that Congress can regulate even private land use for environmental and wildlife conservation. Courts have consistently upheld Congress's authority to regulate private activities in order to conserve species and protect the environment. For example, in a post-*Lopez* challenge to CERCLA, the Eleventh Circuit held that the private, on-site, intrastate disposal of hazardous waste was within Congress's authority to regulate because such disposal "significantly impacts interstate commerce." United States v. Olin Corp., 107 F.3d 1506, 1510 (11th Cir. 1997). In *Sweet Home*, the Supreme Court upheld a FWS regulation defining "harm" in the Endangered Species Act to include "significant habitat modification." 515 U.S. at 697. The regulation applied equally to private and public land. See id. at 692 (challenge brought by small landowners and logging companies). Here, the FWS similarly acted within its authority in determining that conservation of the red wolf population requires prohibiting certain takings on private land surrounding the refuges. See 51 Fed. Reg. 41,790, 41,792-93 (1986). . . .

In contrast to gender-motivated violence or guns in school yards, the conservation of scarce natural resources is an appropriate and well-recognized area of federal regulation. The federal government has been involved in a variety of conservation efforts since the beginning of this century. In 1900, Congress passed the Lacey Act, which provided penalties for the taking of wildlife in violation of state laws. See 16 U.S.C. §701. The Migratory Bird Treaty Act of 1918 forbade all takings of numerous bird species and explicitly preempted state laws. See 16 U.S.C. §§703-12. Furthermore, Congress has regulated wildlife on nonfederal property through numerous statutes, including the Bald Eagle Protection Act of 1940, which prohibits, *inter alia*, the taking, possession, selling, or exporting of bald eagles or any of their parts. See 16 U.S.C. §§668-668d. Similarly, the Marine Mammal Protection Act of 1972 regulates the taking of marine mammals and restricts the importing of marine mammals and their products through an elaborate system of permits. See 16 U.S.C. §§1361-1421h. The Magnuson Fishery Conservation and Management Act of 1976 provides national standards for fishery conservation and management along with an elaborate system of enforcement. See 16 U.S.C. §§1801-1883.

The Supreme Court has repeatedly upheld these statutes and the conservation efforts of Congress with regard to a variety of animal species. In Missouri v. Holland, the Court upheld the Migratory Bird Treaty Act as a necessary and proper means of executing Congress's treaty power. The conservation of endangered wildlife, Justice Holmes stated, was a "matter[] of the sharpest exigency for national well being." 252 U.S. 416, 432-33 (1920). In 1977, the Supreme Court held that Congress had the power under the Commerce Clause to grant federal fishing licenses for use in state waters, thereby preempting conflicting state laws. See Douglas v. Seacoast Products, Inc., 431 U.S. 265 (1977). Later in Andrus v. Allard, the Court emphasized that the "assumption that the national commerce power does not reach migratory wildlife is clearly flawed." 444 U.S. 51, 63 n.19 (1979).

Post-*Lopez* cases addressing wildlife conservation statutes do not call these cases into question, but rather uphold the exercise of agency power over private land use in order to conserve endangered species. In *Sweet Home*, for example, the Court upheld the Service's broad definition of "harm" in the ESA as including "significant habitat modification." 515 U.S. at 708. The lower courts have followed suit, both before and after *Lopez*. For example, in United States v. Hartsell, this court reaffirmed that Congress retains authority to regulate even non-navigable waters under the Commerce Clause. 127 F.3d 343, 348 & n.1 (4th Cir. 1997). The Ninth Circuit reaffirmed that the Bald Eagle Protection Act is a valid exercise of the commerce power because Congress had a rational basis for concluding that "extinction of the eagle would have a substantial effect on interstate commerce." See *Bramble*, 103 F.3d at 1482. In sum, it is clear from our laws and precedent that federal regulation of endangered wildlife does not trench impermissibly upon state powers. Rather, the federal government possesses a historic interest in such regulation—an interest that has repeatedly been recognized by the federal courts.

B.

It is important not simply to point to the historic fact of federal efforts in the area of resource conservation. Courts have respected the justifications for these federal efforts as well.

The Supreme Court has recognized that protection of natural resources may require action from Congress. This general point holds true where endangered species are concerned. Species conservation may unfortunately impose additional costs on private concerns. States may decide to forgo or limit conservation efforts in order to lower these costs, and other states may be forced to follow suit in order to compete. The Supreme Court has held that Congress may take cognizance of this dynamic and arrest the "race to the bottom" in order to prevent interstate competition whose overall effect would damage the quality of the national environment. In Hodel v. Virginia Surface Mining and Reclamation Ass'n, the Court upheld provisions of the Surface Mining Control and Reclamation Act of 1977 that regulated intrastate mining activities. 452 U.S. 264 (1981). The Court deferred to a congressional finding that nationwide standards were "essential" to insuring that competition in interstate commerce among sellers of coal would not be used to undermine environmental standards. See id. at 281-82. Congress expressed concern that such competition would disable states from improving and maintaining "adequate standards on coal mining operations within their borders." Id. The Court emphasized, "The prevention of this sort of destructive interstate competition is a traditional role for congressional action under the commerce clause." . . .

[The majority then addressed the arguments of Judge Luttig's dissent, closing with the following statement.]

Of course natural resource conservation is economic and commercial. If we were to decide that this regulation lacked a substantial effect on commerce and therefore was invalid, we would open the door to standardless judicial rejection of democratic initiatives of all sorts. Courts need not side with one party or the other on the wisdom of this endangered species regulation. We hold only as a basic maxim of judicial restraint that Congress may constitutionally address the problem of protecting endangered species in the manner undertaken herein. The political, not the judicial, process is the appropriate arena for the resolution of this particular dispute. The judgment of the district court is accordingly Affirmed.

LUTTIG, J., dissenting.

[After providing a recapitulation of the majority's arguments and his own distillation of the Supreme Court's major federalism decisions, the dissent continues as follows.]

That these [majority opinion] conclusions are not even arguably sustainable under *Lopez*, *Morrison*, and *Brzonkala*, much less for the reasons cobbled together by the majority, is evident from the mere recitation of the conclusions. The killing of even all 41 of the estimated red wolves that live on private property in North Carolina would not constitute an economic activity of the kind held by the Court in *Lopez* and in *Morrison* to be of central concern to the Commerce Clause, if it could be said to constitute an economic activity at all. *Morrison*, 529 U.S. at 610 ("[A] fair reading of *Lopez* shows that the noneconomic, criminal nature of the conduct at issue was central to our decision in that case."). It is for this reason that the majority's attempted aggregation is impermissible: "While we need not adopt a categorical rule against aggregating the effects of any noneconomic activity in order to decide these cases, thus far in our Nation's history our cases have upheld Commerce Clause regulation of intrastate activity only where that activity is economic in nature." Id. at 613. But even assuming that such is an economic activity, it certainly is not an activity that has a substantial effect on interstate commerce. The number of inferences (not even to mention the amount of speculation) necessary to discern in this activity a substantial effect on interstate commerce is exponentially greater than the number necessary in *Lopez* to show a substantial effect on interstate commerce from the sale of guns near schools or in *Morrison* to show a substantial effect on interstate commerce from domestic assault. The number (and the speculation) is even greater than that necessary in Wickard v. Filburn, 317 U.S. 111 (1942). And, it bears reminding, the regulated activity in *Lopez* and *Wickard* at least was in some sense economic in character.

In a word, the expansive view of the Commerce power expressed by the majority today is . . . a view far more expansive than that expressed by any of the dissenting Justices in either *Lopez* or *Morrison*—a fact confirmed by the dissents in *Morrison*, ironically the case for which the majority herein unnecessarily held this case in abeyance. See Order of April 21, 2000 (Luttig, J., dissenting from abeyance order). . . .

Indeed, if the Supreme Court were to render tomorrow the identical opinion that the majority does today (not necessarily the decision, but the opinion, worded capaciously as it is), both *Lopez* and *Morrison* would be consigned to aberration. . . .

Nor, in the wake of *Lopez* and *Morrison*, can I accept my colleagues' view of the appropriate role of the judiciary in Commerce Clause disputes. As Judge Wilkinson's view of *Lopez* mirrors that of the dissenters in *Lopez* and *Morrison*, so also does my colleagues' view of the judiciary's role in Commerce Clause conflicts mirror that of the *Lopez* and *Morrison* dissenters. The majority herein, like the dissents in both *Lopez* and *Morrison*, takes the view that the political processes are the safeguard against federal encroachment upon the states. . . . The majority of the Supreme Court in *Lopez* and *Morrison* has left no doubt, however, that the interpretation of this clause of the Constitution, no less so than any other, must ultimately rest not with the political branches, but with the judiciary. See *Lopez*, 514 U.S. 549, 557 n.2 ("[W]hether particular operations affect interstate commerce sufficiently to come under the constitutional power of Congress to regulate them is ultimately a judicial rather than a legislative question, and can be settled finally only by this Court.") (quoting Heart of Atlanta Motel v. United States, 379 U.S. 241, 273, 85 (1964) (Black, J., concurring)); *Morrison*, 529 U.S. at 616 n.7 ("Departing from their parliamentary past, the Framers adopted a written Constitution that further divided authority at the federal level so that the Constitution's provisions would not be defined solely by the political branches nor the scope of legislative power limited only by public opinion and the legislature's self-restraint. See, e.g., Marbury v. Madison, 1 Cranch 137, 176 (1803) (Marshall, C.J.).").

Accordingly, I would faithfully apply in this case the Supreme Court's landmark decisions in *Lopez* and *Morrison*, as I would in any other case. The affirmative reach and the negative limits of the Commerce Clause do not wax and wane depending upon the subject matter of the particular legislation under challenge.

NOTES AND QUESTIONS: POWER AND THE ANALYTICAL FRAMEWORK

1. *Is the ESA Constitutional?* For discussions of the constitutionality of the ESA, see Mank, Protecting Intrastate Threatened Species: Does the Endangered Species Act Encroach on Traditional State Authority and Exceed the Outer Limits of the Commerce Clause?, 36 Ga. L. Rev. 723 (2002); and Nagle, The Commerce Clause Meets the Delhi Sands Flower-Loving Fly, 97 Mich. L. Rev. 174 (1998). See also note 3 below, discussing recent cases upholding actions under the ESA with substantial reliance on Gonzales v. Raich, 545 U.S. 1 (2006).

2. *Analytical Frameworks and Perspectives in Commerce Clause Challenges.* When writing their *Gibbs* opinions, Judge Wilkinson and former Judge Luttig were both renowned conservative judges. Both were mentioned as potential Supreme Court Justices when President George W. Bush filled vacancies with Chief Justice Roberts and Justice Alito. Nevertheless, they disagree about far more than just the conclusion in this case. How does each approach his Commerce Clause analysis? Do they each assume that the Commerce Clause requires judicial scrutiny of one sort of "activity," or numerous sorts of activities implicated by the law? Which sort of review

empowers the courts, and which leads to a more deferential mode of review? See Schapiro & Buzbee, Unidimensional Federalism: Power and Perspective in Commerce Clause Adjudication, 88 Cornell L. Rev. 1199 (2003), arguing that the judicial search for the relevant "activity" should consider the "impetus" for the legislation, "political motivation" for the law, and the activity "targeted" by the legislation — typically activity that causes harm or requires modification to maximize social welfare — as well as benefits and other effects that would flow from regulation. Under this view, a law will usually implicate several sorts of activities that might suffice to pass Commerce Clause muster. Which judge adopts a similar approach?

A second major issue concerns whether judges should assess constitutionality under the Commerce Clause by looking at activities in the aggregate or as part of a comprehensive scheme of regulation or (at the other end of the spectrum) application by application. What difference do these two approaches make? See note 3, which follows, for more regarding the "comprehensive scheme" rationale.

3. Raich *and the Issue of "Comprehensive Schemes" and Aggregation: Classes of Activities, or an Individualized Focus?* Since *Gibbs,* and several years after *Lopez* and *Morrison,* the Supreme Court decided Gonzales v. Raich, 545 U.S. 1 (2006), a case involving a challenge to the constitutionality of a federal law, the Controlled Substances Act, criminalizing local and home-grown marijuana use for medicinal purposes, even where allowed by a California state law. In language that surely would have influenced the terms of the earlier *Gibbs* majority and dissenting opinions, the Court rejected the challenge, stating:

> Our case law firmly establishes Congress' power to regulate purely local activities that are part of an economic "class of activities" that have a substantial effect on interstate commerce. See, e.g., *Perez,* 402 U.S., at 151; Wickard v. Filburn, 317 U.S. 111, 128-129 (1942). As we stated in *Wickard,* "even if appellee's activity be local and though it may not be regarded as commerce, it may still, whatever its nature, be reached by Congress if it exerts a substantial economic effect on interstate commerce." Id., at 125. We have never required Congress to legislate with scientific exactitude. When Congress decides that the " 'total incidence' " of a practice poses a threat to a national market, it may regulate the entire class. See Perez v. United States, 402 U.S. [146], at 154-155 [1971]. . . . *Wickard* thus establishes that Congress can regulate purely intrastate activity that is not itself "commercial," in that it is not produced for sale, if it concludes that failure to regulate that class of activity would undercut the regulation of the interstate market in that commodity. . . . Here [as in *Wickard*], Congress had a rational basis for concluding that leaving home-consumed marijuana outside federal control would similarly affect price and market conditions. . . .
>
> In assessing the scope of Congress' authority under the Commerce Clause, we stress that the task before us is a modest one. We need not determine whether respondents' activities, taken in the aggregate, substantially affect interstate commerce in fact, but only whether a "rational basis" exists for so concluding. *Lopez,* 514 U.S., at 557. Given the enforcement difficulties that attend distinguishing between marijuana cultivated locally and marijuana grown elsewhere, 21 U.S.C. §801(5), and concerns about diversion into illicit channels, we have no difficulty concluding that Congress had a rational basis for believing that failure to regulate the intrastate manufacture and possession of marijuana would leave a gaping hole in the CSA. . . .
>
> . . . Here, respondents ask us to excise individual applications of a concededly valid statutory scheme. In contrast, in both *Lopez* and *Morrison,* the parties asserted that a particular statute or provision fell outside Congress' commerce power in its entirety. This distinction is pivotal for we have often reiterated that "[w]here the class

of activities is regulated and that class is within the reach of federal power, the courts have no power 'to excise, as trivial, individual instances' of the class." *Perez*, 402 U.S., at 154. [*Raich*, 545 U.S. at 17-23.]

In light of *Raich*, do you think Judge Luttig or Chief Judge Wilkinson has the better argument? What are the implications of *Raich* for attacks on environmental laws viewed as being at the cusp of federal power? See Blumm & Kimbrell, Gonzales v. Raich, the "Comprehensive Scheme" Principle, and the Constitutionality of the Endangered Species Act, 35 Envtl. L. 491 (2005).

For cases applying *Raich* to uphold actions under the Endangered Species Act, see Alabama-Tombigbee Rivers Coal. v. Kempthorne, 477 F.3d 1250 (11th Cir. 2007), where the Eleventh Circuit rejected a coalition's constitutional challenge to the endangered species designation of the Alabama sturgeon, allegedly a purely intra-state species with little commercial value and unconnected with a commercial trans-action. Relying on *Raich*, the court reasoned that the Alabama sturgeon, while a purely intrastate species, was part of a general regulatory scheme to protect all endan-gered species and thus the "de minimis character of the individual instance" was irrelevant. Id. at 1272-1273 (quoting Gonzales v. Raich, 545 U.S. at 17 (2006)). Relying on *Raich*, the court held that Congress need only "rationally conclude" that protecting species like the Alabama sturgeon was an "essential part of the larger regulatory scheme." Id. at 1274 (quoting *Raich*, 545 U.S. at 26-27). See also San Luis & Delta-Mendota Water Auth. v. Salazar, 638 F.3d 1163 (9th Cir. 2011) (sim-ilarly relying on *Raich* in upholding application of the ESA's no jeopardy and taking prohibitions to the delta smelt).

4. *The Unclear Role of Legislative Findings and a Supporting Legislative Record.* In *Raich*, the Court stated the following about the effect of legislative findings:

> Findings in the introductory sections of the CSA explain why Congress deemed it appropriate to encompass local activities within the scope of the CSA. The submissions of the parties and the numerous amici all seem to agree that the national, and international, market for marijuana has dimensions that are fully comparable to those defining the class of activities regulated by the Secretary pursuant to the 1938 statute. Respondents nonetheless insist that the CSA cannot be constitutionally applied to their activities because Congress did not make a specific finding that the intrastate cultivation and possession of marijuana for medical purposes based on the recommendation of a physician would substantially affect the larger interstate marijuana market. Be that as it may, we have never required Congress to make particularized findings in order to leg-islate, see *Lopez*, 514 U.S., at 562; *Perez*, 402 U.S., at 156, absent a special concern such as the protection of free speech, see, e.g., Turner Broadcasting System, Inc. v. FCC, 512 U.S. 622, 664-668 (1994) (plurality opinion). While congressional findings are certainly helpful in reviewing the substance of a congressional statutory scheme, particularly when the connection to commerce is not self-evident, and while we will consider congressional findings in our analysis when they are available, the absence of particularized findings does not call into question Congress' authority to legislate. [545 U.S. at 20-21.]

This language about findings appears to be less a resolution than yet another salvo in an ongoing Court battle about how, if at all, Congress needs to create a record or include findings for its laws to satisfy constitutional scrutiny. This question has arisen in straightforward Commerce Clause attacks, as in *Lopez* and *Raich*, but also in cases involving claims of state discrimination and, therefore, constitutional scrutiny under §5 of the Fourteenth Amendment.[b] The lack of an adequate "record" has proved fatal in several recent cases, see, e.g., United States v. Morrison, 529 U.S. 598 (2000); Board of Trustees of the Univ. of Ala. v. Garrett, 531 U.S. 356 (2001); but in Nevada v. Hibbs, 538 U.S. at 721 (2003), over scathing dissents, the record was found adequate in an opinion authored by Chief Justice Rehnquist to justify holding states liable for violation of the Family Medical Leave Act. This vote and opinion were a surprise to many; Rehnquist had in numerous cases since *Lopez* joined four other Justices in striking down federal laws.

While the Court has repeatedly said "findings" are not required, this new judicial scrutiny of the record has changed how courts review the basis for legislative action, especially in settings implicating federalism concerns. Numerous scholars have questioned the appropriateness of such record review in light of the realities of the legislative process and the capabilities of the courts:

> Legislative record review . . . represents a novel mode of judicial review that limits congressional power in crucial respects. This kind of review threatens to impose procedural and substantive constraints on legislative action that have no support in precedent or in constitutional text or structure. Moreover, the Court's reliance on the concept of "the legislative record," in the sense of a comprehensive set of documents reflecting the full scope of congressional deliberations underlying a statute, is fundamentally flawed on the most basic level. This kind of "legislative record" simply does not exist. The entire concept of a legislative record constitutes an inappropriate importation from different institutional settings of the expectation that a written record will justify a legal judgment. Congress acts on the basis of a wide variety of information, concerns, and interests. Informal contacts and latent policy judgments serve as key determinants of legislative conduct. The Court's new legislative record review seeks to reduce the legislative crucible to a written, comprehensive record. Such a process will not be "legislative" as we currently understand that term. In short, "the legislative record" is fundamentally incoherent. To render the concept coherent would require a transformation of legislation. [Buzbee & Schapiro, Legislative Record Review, 54 Stan. L. Rev. 87, 90 (2001).][c]

If the Court returns to engaging in close scrutiny of legislative findings and the so-called record, what might the implications be for challenges to environmental laws that were generally passed over a decade ago, many involving legislative judgments made despite great uncertainty about their underlying science?

5. *The Losing Track Record of Commerce Clause Challenges to Environmental Laws.* Despite the Supreme Court's federalism revival imposing new limits on federal

---

b. As you may recall from your constitutional law courses, where state sovereignty is implicated, especially where citizens seek damages from a state, federal power under the Commerce Clause is not the end of the necessary analysis. State sovereign immunity still must be overcome, requiring judicial scrutiny under §5 of the Fourteenth Amendment to see if Congress had an adequate basis for impinging on state sovereignty. City of Boerne v. Flores, 521 U.S. 507 (1997); Seminole Tribe v. Florida, 517 U.S. 44 (1996). See "A Note Regarding Sovereign Immunity," below, at page 125, for further discussion.

c. For other critiques of the Court's new scrutiny of findings and the record, see Bryant & Simeone, Remanding to Congress: The Supreme Court's New "On the Record" Constitutional Review of Federal Statutes, 86 Cornell L. Rev. 328 (2001); Colker & Brudney, Dissing Congress, 100 Mich. L. Rev. 80 (2001); Frickey, The Fool on the Hill: Congressional Findings, Constitutional Adjudication, and United States v. Lopez, 46 Case W. Res. L. Rev. 695 (1996); Frickey & Smith, Judicial Review, the Congressional Process, and the Federalism Cases: An Interdisciplinary Critique, 111 Yale L.J. 1707 (2002); Post & Siegel, Equal Protection by Law: Federal Antidiscrimination Legislation After *Morrison* and *Kimel*, 110 Yale L.J. 441, 461 (2000).

power, Commerce Clause challenges to federal environmental laws have so far failed. For example, largely due to hazardous wastes' largely stationary state, the federal CERCLA law was challenged as being beyond federal power. The Eleventh Circuit rejected that argument, focusing on how on- or off-site disposal of hazardous wastes can substantially affect commerce. United States v. Olin, 107 F.3d 1506 (11th Cir. 1997). Other Endangered Species Act challenges have, as in *Gibbs*, met with little success. See Rancho Viejo v. Norton, 323 F.3d 1062 (D.C. Cir. 2003); National Ass'n of Homebuilders v. Babbitt, 130 F.3d 1041 (D.C. Cir. 1997). As covered in the next section, constitutional challenges to the reach of the Clean Water Act have also failed in direct attacks, but nevertheless changed the reach of the law by influencing statutory interpretation of the Act. See also note 3 above, discussing courts applying *Raich* to uphold the Endangered Species Act.

NOTE ON THE AFFORDABLE CARE ACT CHALLENGE AND FEDERAL POWER TO PROTECT THE ENVIRONMENT

In the Supreme Court's 2012 ruling on the constitutionality of new federal health care legislation (the Patient Protection and Affordable Care Act of 2010, or "ACA"), Nat'l Fed'n of Indep. Business v. Sebelius, 132 S. Ct. 2566 (2012), the Court addressed several constitutional hot-button issues relevant to environmental law. How far does Commerce Clause power extend? In particular, under the Commerce Clause, could the federal government impose an "individual mandate" on citizens not at the time active in the health care system or health care insurance market, forcing them to enter private health insurance markets? Even if not authorized under the Commerce Clause alone, might the law survive due to the Constitution's additional grant of power to the federal government to "make all laws which shall be necessary and proper for carrying into Execution" the powers enumerated under the Constitution? Could the federal government's power under the Constitution's grant of authority to "lay and collect Taxes" justify such a mandate where it was enforced through something denominated as a "penalty"? The case also involved another major issue and source of federal power: Could the federal government use inducements under the Spending Clause (discussed in New York v. United States, excerpted at page 114 below), to incentivize states to expand health coverage for the poor, either by threatening states with the loss of all federal Medicaid support, or by withholding newly expanded federal support for states that declined to go along? (Two other issues, regarding the applicability of the Anti-Injunction Act and regarding the severability of parts of the law that were struck down, are of lesser relevance to environmental law and are not addressed here.)

The Court's ruling and fractured set of opinions broke new constitutional law ground on one issue and set the stage for new constitutional arguments. It will become a much-cited case in environmental federalism–related challenges because it touched on so many central questions, although only on one issue did it break new ground or speak with such clarity that it will likely change the path of the law. The case resulted in two clear majority outcomes, one of which commanded a clear, unified majority opinion.

First, the individual mandate was upheld under the federal tax power. The mandate was defensible under the taxing power because the law enforced the mandate through the tax code, the size of penalties (if any) was tied to income levels, and case law has for years allowed tax laws to create behavioral incentives in addition to generating revenue. That it was called a "penalty," not a "tax," was not dispositive. Chief Justice John Roberts joined the four more liberal Justices (Justices Ruth Bader Ginsburg, Stephen Breyer, Sonia Sotomayor, and Elena Kagan) in an opinion section reaching this conclusion. The second majority outcome did not result in a single opinion, but section II-C of Chief Justice Roberts's opinion was joined by Justices Breyer and Kagan. This section concluded that the ACA's use of spending power inducements slipped into impermissible coercion when it threatened states with loss of all federal Medicaid funding if they did not expand coverage to the poor as sought under the Act. Expanded federal support under the ACA could be withheld from uncooperative states. Justices Antonin Scalia, Anthony Kennedy, Clarence Thomas, and Samuel Alito wrote their own opinion reaching a similar conclusion, but did not join any of the Roberts opinion. Nevertheless, due to the analytical similarities, seven Justices agreed with this result. Both opinions emphasized the unusually massive amount of federal support under the existing Medicaid program. Levels of state dependence varied, but (assuming the Justices' sources were accurate) as much as 10 to 16 percent of some states' entire budgets was derived from existing federal Medicaid program dollars. To threaten what the Roberts opinion saw as massive funding under another program was "a gun to the head" of the states, or "economic dragooning," and hence was "impermissibly coercive."

Although these two rulings eliminated the need for an opinion from the Chief Justice regarding the Commerce Clause power and the "individual mandate," he nevertheless wrote one, concluding that such a mandate lacked constitutional justification rooted in the Commerce Clause. He also concluded that it could not be justified under the "Necessary and Proper" Clause. The four conservative Justices agreed with these views, but did not join the opinion. Justice Ginsburg, joined by Justices Breyer, Sotomayor, and Kagan, dissented on both the Commerce Clause and Necessary and Proper Clause analysis, and questioned the need for any opinion on the issue at all. But since five Justices agreed with this result, even if in reality it is dicta or an advisory opinion, it may indicate future paths of the law. Neither the Roberts opinion nor the Scalia opinion disputed that health care was imbued with commerce, and that decisions of individuals not to obtain health insurance had effects on the market. These opinions, at their heart, emphasized that it was unheard of for the federal government to compel someone who is economically inactive to do something, even if for the common good. The federal government could not force someone not actively in the health care market to buy health insurance. Roberts and the Scalia bloc emphasized the uninsured's lack of market activity, even contrasting that person with the wheat farmer who was growing for home consumption but who was found within the reach of the commerce power in Wickard v. Filburn, 317 U.S. 111 (1942). In Chief Justice Roberts's words, the government cannot compel activity under the Commerce Clause "whenever enough [individuals] are not doing something the Government would have them do." The Necessary and Proper Clause could not be used to allow this compelled entry into private markets.

So what effects will these rulings have on environmental law, if any?

The Commerce Power. Most federal environmental laws were enacted with explicit reliance on the commerce power. Almost all polluting and environmentally destructive activity results from economic *activity*, and so will seldom raise "individual mandate" sorts of concerns. And the opinions finding no authority under the Commerce Clause emphasized the coercion of individuals; would corporations and businesses, which by their nature engage in commerce, be subject to similar analysis? The question marks, as usual, will likely arise where environmental laws impose burdens on individuals, especially in compelling action that individuals would otherwise decline to undertake. Where small-scale, individual, noncommercial activities on wetlands cause harms or result in "fill" under the Clean Water Act, would a prohibition create arguments under the ACA decision? See coverage of the dredge and fill permit program in section C of this chapter and section C.1 of Chapter 7. Perhaps, but they would be unlikely to succeed. First, actions causing harms of a magnitude sufficient to trigger enforcement concern without some commercial or real estate–related motivation are and would be rare. Second, a prohibition on harmful action is arguably distinct from compelling an inactive individual to enter private markets; it was this latter problem that most concerned the Chief Justice and the aligned Scalia bloc. What about forcing an individual to address the flow of hazardous substances under his land under "passive migration" theories under federal hazardous waste law? See section C.3.a of Chapter 9. If such a mandate involved truly innocent, noncommercial actors who played no role in the creation of the hazardous materials risk, compelling regulatory action might create concerns. Litigants seeking to resolve this unsettled question will likely cite the ACA decision, perhaps calling for a limiting read of the Comprehensive Environmental Response, Compensation, and Liability Act (CERCLA) to avoid a constitutional concern. In the past, either "necessary and proper" justifications or "comprehensive scheme" and "aggregation" rationales (see Notes and Questions: Power and the Analytical Framework at p. 103 above) would likely have allowed reaching an individually small action that fell within a larger scheme of regulation. Under the new categorical approach of the Chief Justice and his aligned Justices, none of these sorts of rationales seem to provide additional federal authority if the regulatory scheme works by compelling individuals not engaged in economic activity to enter markets for the larger good.

It thus appears the key problem variables for future cases involving Commerce Clause arguments will be: regulation (a) targeted at the individual, (b) where the individual is not active in the relevant market and is not engaged in economic activity, and (c) where federal law would compel that individual to enter the market to help address some larger social ill. But these aligned opinions are also laden with language expressing concern with limitless federal power. That language will also become part of future efforts to weaken environmental or risk regulation.

The Spending Power. New law was definitely made here, with seven Justices for the first time finding that federal spending inducements tipped into impermissible coercion. Given that conditional federal spending is common under federal environmental laws, and is of especial importance under the Clean Air Act due to its threat of loss of federal highway funds if a state fails to address nonattainment air pollution problems (see Clean Air Act, 42 U.S.C. §§7410(c), 7410(m), 7509(b) and section D.2 of Chapter 6), will this decision lead to new challenges to federal authority? The ACA decision emphasized the extreme magnitude of the threat, and states were threatened with loss of all of funding from the existing Medicaid program, which the Court viewed as distinct from the 2010 extension. It was a "gun to the head" of the states because the threatened loss of federal funds far exceeded the new spending inducements within the ACA that were upheld. Look at the Clean Air Act highway sanction language in 42 U.S.C. §7509(b); note the language making highway sanctions elective, and notice, as well, how even a sanctioned jurisdiction remains eligible for a wide variety of federal highway funding. It appears likely that threatened highway funding would rarely, if ever, approach the huge importance to states of existing federal Medicaid funding. Furthermore, given the direct programmatic linkage between pollution resulting from new highways and nonattainment woes, perhaps highway sanctions would be viewed as different from sanctions found excessive and unrelated in the ACA case. In addition, the huge Medicaid funding stream and less certain federal highway appropriations might be seen as constitutionally different. And, in reality, states and federal authorities have typically worked out Clean Air Act clashes well before imposition of any onerous highway sanctions. Nevertheless, states reluctant to invest in clean air or interested in scoring political points by rebelling against federal regulatory burdens may use the ACA decision to challenge the EPA's sanctioning power. A complete state refusal to act and an onerous EPA highway sanction could create a clash where new spending power limitations under *Sebelius* would become the most authoritative relevant law. For further analysis, see Ryan, The Spending Power and Environmental Law After *Sebelius*, 85 U. Colo. L. Rev. 1003 (2014).

C. FEDERAL POWER AND INTERPRETATION: COMMERCE CONCERNS AS A TIEBREAKER

So far, direct attacks on the Commerce Clause basis for federal environmental legislation have generally failed to elicit judicial declarations of unconstitutionality. Even if this continues to happen, it would be a mistake to assume that Commerce Clause arguments are therefore of little importance. As you will see in the following short excerpts from two recent Supreme Court cases, Commerce Clause concerns and claims that federal power is at its limit have the potential to make a major difference. These two cases are excerpted and covered at greater length in Chapter 7, among materials about the Clean Water Act and §404 "dredge and fill" permits. Section 404's requirements greatly limit the circumstances in which wetlands and other waters can be destroyed or impaired. Due to real estate, industry, and agricultural interest in developing or using areas classified as wetlands or "waters of the United States," under the Clean Water Act, §404 has been repeatedly subjected to constitutional attack.

SOLID WASTE AGENCY OF NORTHERN COOK COUNTY v. U.S. ARMY CORPS OF ENGINEERS
531 U.S. 159 (2001)

Chief Justice REHNQUIST delivered the opinion of the Court.

... Respondents—relying upon all of the arguments addressed above—contend that, at the very least, it must be said that Congress did not address the precise question of §404(a)'s scope with regard to nonnavigable, isolated, intrastate waters, and that, therefore, we should give deference to the "Migratory Bird Rule." See, e.g., Chevron U.S.A. Inc. v. Natural Resources Defense Council, Inc., 467 U.S. 837 (1984). We find §404(a) to be clear, but even were we to agree with respondents, we would not extend *Chevron* deference here.

Where an administrative interpretation of a statute invokes the outer limits of Congress' power, we expect a clear indication that Congress intended that result. See Edward J. DeBartolo Corp. v. Florida Gulf Coast Building & Constr. Trades Council, 485 U.S. 568, 575 (1988). This requirement stems from our prudential desire not to needlessly reach constitutional issues and our assumption that Congress does not casually authorize administrative agencies to interpret a statute to push the limit of congressional authority. This concern is heightened where the administrative interpretation alters the federal-state framework by permitting federal encroachment upon a traditional state power. See United States v. Bass, 404 U.S. 336, 349 (1971) ("[U]nless Congress conveys its purpose clearly, it will not be deemed to have significantly changed the federal-state balance."). Thus, "where an otherwise acceptable construction of a statute would raise serious constitutional problems, the Court will construe the statute to avoid such problems unless such construction is plainly contrary to the intent of Congress." *DeBartolo, supra,* at 575.

Twice in the past six years we have reaffirmed the proposition that the grant of authority to Congress under the Commerce Clause, though broad, is not unlimited. See United States v. Morrison, 529 U.S. 598 (2000); United States v. Lopez, 514 U.S. 549 (1995). Respondents argue that the "Migratory Bird Rule" falls within Congress' power to regulate intrastate activities that "substantially affect" interstate commerce. They note that the protection of migratory birds is a "national interest of very nearly the first magnitude," Missouri v. Holland, 252 U.S. 416, 435 (1920), and that, as the Court of Appeals found, millions of people spend over a billion dollars annually on recreational pursuits relating to migratory birds. These arguments raise significant constitutional questions. For example, we would have to evaluate the precise object or activity that, in the aggregate, substantially affects interstate commerce. This is not clear, for although the Corps has claimed jurisdiction over petitioner's land because it contains water areas used as habitat by migratory birds, respondents now, *post litem motam,* focus upon the fact that the regulated activity is petitioner's municipal landfill, which is "plainly of a commercial nature." Brief for Federal Respondents 43. But this is a far cry, indeed, from the "navigable waters" and "waters of the United States" to which the statute by its terms extends.

These are significant constitutional questions raised by respondents' application of their regulations, and yet we find nothing approaching a clear statement from Congress that it intended §404(a) to reach an abandoned sand and gravel pit such as we have here. Permitting respondents to claim federal jurisdiction over ponds and mudflats falling within the "Migratory Bird Rule" would result in a significant impingement of the States' traditional and primary power over land and water use. See, e.g., Hess v. Port Auth. Trans-Hudson Corp., 513 U.S. 30, 44 (1994) ("[R]egulation of land use [is] a function traditionally performed by local governments."). Rather than expressing a desire to readjust the federal-state balance in this manner, Congress chose to "recognize, preserve, and protect the primary responsibilities and rights of States . . . to plan the development and use . . . of land and water resources. . . ." 33 U.S.C. §1251(b). We thus read the statute as written to avoid the significant constitutional and federalism questions raised by respondents' interpretation, and therefore reject the request for administrative deference.

RAPANOS v. UNITED STATES
547 U.S. 715 (2006)

[*Rapanos* and its companion case in the courts below, *Carabell*, also involve questions about the statutory and constitutional reach of the Clean Water Act. In these consolidated cases, the Court had to construe the statutory definition of "navigable waters" as "waters of the United States" in connection with federal claims of jurisdiction over tributaries and wetlands adjacent to tributaries feeding into navigable-in-fact waters. The Court ended up splitting into a confusing 4-1-4 grouping, with five Justices agreeing to a judgment requiring the courts and likely agency below on remand to better establish its jurisdiction, but no opinion for the Court. The middle opinion, by Justice Kennedy, agreed with this judgment but disagreed with virtually all of Justice Scalia's opinion, instead repeatedly adopting logic and language from the four-Justice dissenting opinion penned by Justice Stevens. For reasons that will be explored in greater depth in the Chapter 7 coverage of wetlands protection, Justice Kennedy's opinion is viewed by most as the key opinion for future application by agencies and lower courts. Still, the disagreement between Justices Scalia and Kennedy concerning how federalism concerns should drive certain interpretations provides a strong reminder of how federalism concerns can have great power, even without any declaration of unconstitutionality.]

Justice SCALIA announced the judgment of the court, delivered an opinion, which THE CHIEF JUSTICE, Justice THOMAS and Justice ALITO join.

. . . Even if the phrase "the waters of the United States" were ambiguous as applied to intermittent flows, our own canons of construction would establish that the Corps' interpretation of the statute is impermissible. As we noted in *SWANCC*, the Government's expansive interpretation would "result in a significant impingement of the States' traditional and primary power over land and water use." 531 U.S., at 174. Regulation of land use, as through the issuance of the development permits sought by petitioners in both of these cases, is a quintessential state and local power. See FERC v. Mississippi, 456 U.S. 742, 768, n.30 (1982); Hess v. Port Auth. Trans-Hudson Corp., 513 U.S. 30, 44 (1994). The extensive federal jurisdiction urged by the Government would authorize the Corps to function as a de facto regulator of immense stretches of intrastate land—an authority the agency has shown its willingness to exercise with the scope of discretion that would befit a local zoning board. See 33 CFR §320.4(a)(1) (2004). We ordinarily expect a "clear and manifest" statement from Congress to authorize an unprecedented intrusion into traditional state authority. See BFP v. Resolution Trust Corp., 511 U.S. 531, 544 (1994). The phrase "the waters of the United States" hardly qualifies.

Likewise, just as we noted in *SWANCC*, the Corps' interpretation stretches the outer limits of Congress's commerce power and raises difficult questions about the ultimate scope of that power. See 531 U.S., at 173. (In developing the current regulations, the Corps consciously sought to extend its authority to the farthest reaches of the commerce power. See 42 Fed. Reg. 37,127 (1977).) Even if the term "the waters of the United States" were ambiguous as applied to channels that sometimes host ephemeral flows of water (which it is not), we would expect a clearer statement from Congress to authorize an agency theory of jurisdiction that presses the envelope of constitutional validity. See Edward J. DeBartolo Corp. v. Florida Gulf Coast Building & Constr. Trades Council, 485 U.S. 568, 575 (1988).[9] . . .

   Justice KENNEDY, concurring in the judgment. . . .

   . . . With these concerns in mind, the Corps' definition of adjacency is a reasonable one, for it may be the absence of an interchange of waters prior to the dredge and fill activity that makes protection of the wetlands critical to the statutory scheme.

   In sum the plurality's opinion is inconsistent with the Act's text, structure, and purpose. As a fallback the plurality suggests that avoidance canons would compel its reading even if the text were unclear. . . . In SWANCC, as one reason for rejecting the Corps' assertion of jurisdiction over the isolated ponds at issue there, the Court observed that this "application of [the Corps'] regulations" would raise significant questions of Commerce Clause authority and encroach on traditional state land-use regulation. 531 U.S., at 174. As SWANCC observed, and as the plurality points out here, the Act states that "[i]t is the policy of the Congress to recognize, preserve, and protect the primary responsibilities and rights of States to prevent, reduce, and eliminate pollution, [and] to plan the development and use . . . of land and water resources," 33 U.S.C. §1251(b). The Court in SWANCC cited this provision as evidence that a clear statement supporting jurisdiction in applications raising constitutional and federalism difficulties was lacking. 531 U.S., at 174.

   The concerns addressed in SWANCC do not support the plurality's interpretation of the Act. In SWANCC, by interpreting the Act to require a significant nexus with navigable waters, the Court avoided applications—those involving waters without a significant nexus—that appeared likely, as a category, to raise constitutional difficulties and federalism concerns. Here, in contrast, the plurality's interpretation does not fit the avoidance concerns it raises. On the one hand, when a surface-water connection is lacking, the plurality forecloses jurisdiction over wetlands that abut navigable-in-fact waters—even though such navigable waters were traditionally subject to federal authority. On the other hand, by saying the Act covers wetlands (however remote) possessing a surface-water connection with a continuously flowing stream (however small), the plurality's reading would permit applications of the statute as far from traditional federal authority as are the waters it deems beyond the statute's reach. Even assuming, then, that federal regulation of remote wetlands and nonnavigable waterways would raise a difficult Commerce Clause issue notwithstanding those waters' aggregate effects on national water quality, but cf. Wickard v. Filburn, 317 U.S. 111 (1942); . . . the plurality's reading is not responsive to this concern. As for States' "responsibilities and rights," §1251(b), it is noteworthy that 33 States plus the District

---

9. Justice Kennedy objects that our reliance on these two clear-statement rules is inappropriate because "the plurality's interpretation does not fit the avoidance concerns that it raises"—that is, because our resolution both eliminates some jurisdiction that is clearly constitutional and traditionally federal, and retains some that is questionably constitutional and traditionally local. But a clear-statement rule can carry one only so far as the statutory text permits. Our resolution, unlike Justice Kennedy's, keeps both the overinclusion and the underinclusion to the minimum consistent with the statutory text. Justice Kennedy's reading—despite disregarding the text—fares no better than ours as a precise "fit" for the "avoidance concerns" that he also acknowledges. He admits that "the significant nexus requirement may not align perfectly with the traditional extent of federal authority" over navigable waters—an admission that "tests the limits of understatement," Gonzales v. Oregon, 126 S. Ct. 904, 932 (2005) (Scalia, J., dissenting)—and it aligns even worse with the preservation of traditional state land-use regulation.

of Columbia have filed an amici brief in this litigation asserting that the Clean Water Act is important to their own water policies. These amici note, among other things, that the Act protects downstream States from out-of-state pollution that they cannot themselves regulate. . . .

NOTE

In his *SWANCC* dissent, joined by three other Justices, Justice Stevens disputed the majority's characterization of §404 as intruding on a traditional area of state regulation of land use. Instead, he characterized the Clean Water Act and §404 as targeting water pollution. Do you see any problems with the Supreme Court's interpretations of federal environmental laws hinging on how they characterize the nature of that law, as well as on how the Court characterizes related or overlapping areas of state law? How about the Court's use of provisions preserving state roles? Is this area of law predictable? What incentives does the *SWANCC* Court create for legislators eager to pass federal law but also willing to preserve state authority?

D.   SECURING STATE COOPERATION

Even if the federal government has the power to enact federal law, a separate issue is how the federal government can secure state cooperation in achieving federal goals. As this section and the sections that follow establish, states stand in a special, privileged position under our Constitution. Especially during the past couple of decades, an array of Supreme Court decisions has solidified the states' special status and the federal government's limited ability to impinge on state interests. This section starts with one of the most important federalism cases, New York v. United States, 505 U.S. 144 (1992), and the Court's articulation of the means by which the federal government can secure state cooperation without running afoul of principles of state sovereignty and a federal government of limited power. We then, in notes, look at successor cases to *New York*, as well as undertake a closer examination of these additional means through which the federal government can attempt to entice states to cooperate.

NEW YORK v. UNITED STATES
505 U.S. 144 (1992)

O'CONNOR, J., delivered the opinion of the Court.

These cases implicate one of our Nation's newest problems of public policy and perhaps our oldest question of constitutional law. The public policy issue involves the disposal of radioactive waste: In these cases, we address the constitutionality of three provisions of the Low-Level Radioactive Waste Policy Amendments Act of 1985, 42 U.S.C. §2021b et seq. The constitutional question is as old as the Constitution: It consists of discerning the proper division of authority between the Federal Government and the States. We conclude that while Congress has substantial power under the Constitution to encourage the States to provide for the disposal of the radioactive waste generated within their borders, the Constitution does not confer upon Congress the ability simply to compel the States to do so. We therefore find that only two of the Act's three provisions at issue are consistent with the Constitution's allocation of power to the Federal Government.

I.

[Concerned about the possibility of a shortage of disposal sites for low-level radioactive waste, Congress enacted the Low-Level Radioactive Waste Policy Amendments Act of 1985. In its provisions, states that had borne the brunt of the nation's disposal responsibilities agreed to continue to accept waste for seven more years. In exchange, states without their own disposal sites agreed to end their reliance on the other states by 1992. The Act provided three types of incentives to ensure that the unsited states met their obligations under the bargain. States that met the statutory deadlines received monetary rewards. States that failed to make progress by certain dates were subject to reduced access to disposal sites. States that failed to account for all the waste generated within their borders by 1996 were required, upon the request of the generator of the waste, "[to] take title to the waste, be obligated to take possession of the waste, and shall be liable for all damages directly or indirectly incurred by such generator or owner as a consequence of the failure of the State to take possession of the waste. . . ." §2021e(d)(2)(C). Petitioners argued that the Act was unconstitutional under the Tenth Amendment and the Guarantee Clause.]

. . . The Act provides three types of incentives to encourage the States to comply with their statutory obligation to provide for the disposal of waste generated within their borders.

1. *Monetary incentives.* One quarter of the surcharges collected by the sited States must be transferred to an escrow account held by the Secretary of Energy. §2021e(d)(2)(A). The Secretary then makes payments from this account to each State that has complied with a series of deadlines. . . . Each State that has not met the 1993 deadline must either take title to the waste generated within its borders or forfeit to the waste generators the incentive payments it has received. §2021e(d)(2)(C).

2. *Access incentives.* The second type of incentive involves the denial of access to disposal sites. States that fail to meet the July 1986 deadline may be charged twice the ordinary surcharge for the remainder of 1986 and may be denied access to disposal facilities thereafter. §2021e(e)(2)(A). States that fail to meet the 1988 deadline may be charged double surcharges for the first half of 1988 and quadruple surcharges for the second half of 1988, and may be denied access thereafter. §2021e(e)(2)(B). States that fail to meet the 1990 deadline may be denied access. §2021e(e)(2)(C). Finally, States that have not filed complete applications by January 1, 1992, for a license to operate a disposal facility, or States belonging to compacts that have not filed such applications, may be charged triple surcharges. §§2021e(e)(1)(D), 2021e(e)(2)(D).

3. *The take title provision.* The third type of incentive is the most severe. The Act provides:

> If a State (or, where applicable, a compact region) in which low-level radioactive waste is generated is unable to provide for the disposal of all such waste generated within such State or compact region by January 1, 1996, each State in which such waste is generated, upon the request of the generator or owner of the waste, shall take title to the waste, be

obligated to take possession of the waste, and shall be liable for all damages directly or indirectly incurred by such generator or owner as a consequence of the failure of the State to take possession of the waste as soon after January 1, 1996, as the generator or owner notifies the State that the waste is available for shipment. §2021e(d)(2)(C).

These three incentives are the focus of petitioners' constitutional challenge. . . .

Petitioners have abandoned their due process and Eleventh Amendment claims on their way up the appellate ladder; as the cases stand before us, petitioners claim only that the Act is inconsistent with the Tenth Amendment and the Guarantee Clause.

II.

A.

In 1788, in the course of explaining to the citizens of New York why the recently drafted Constitution provided for federal courts, Alexander Hamilton observed: "The erection of a new government, whatever care or wisdom may distinguish the work, cannot fail to originate questions of intricacy and nicety; and these may, in a particular manner, be expected to flow from the establishment of a constitution founded upon the total or partial incorporation of a number of distinct sovereignties." The Federalist No. 82, p. 491 (C. Rossiter ed. 1961). Hamilton's prediction has proved quite accurate. While no one disputes the proposition that "[t]he Constitution created a Federal Government of limited powers," Gregory v. Ashcroft, 501 U.S. 452, 457 (1991); and while the Tenth Amendment makes explicit that "[t]he powers not delegated to the United States by the Constitution, nor prohibited by it to the States, are reserved to the States respectively, or to the people"; the task of ascertaining the constitutional line between federal and state power has given rise to many of the Court's most difficult and celebrated cases. . . .

It is in this sense that the Tenth Amendment "states but a truism that all is retained which has not been surrendered." United States v. Darby, 312 U.S. 100, 124 (1941). As Justice Story put it, "[t]his amendment is a mere affirmation of what, upon any just reasoning, is a necessary rule of interpreting the constitution. Being an instrument of limited and enumerated powers, it follows irresistibly, that what is not conferred, is withheld, and belongs to the state authorities." 3 J. Story, Commentaries on the Constitution of the United States 752 (1833). This has been the Court's consistent understanding: "The States unquestionably do retai[n] a significant measure of sovereign authority . . . to the extent that the Constitution has not divested them of their original powers and transferred those powers to the Federal Government." Garcia v. San Antonio Metropolitan Transit Authority, supra, 469 U.S., at 549.

Congress exercises its conferred powers subject to the limitations contained in the Constitution. Thus, for example, under the Commerce Clause Congress may regulate publishers engaged in interstate commerce, but Congress is constrained in the exercise of that power by the First Amendment. The Tenth Amendment likewise restrains the power of Congress, but this limit is not derived from the text of the Tenth Amendment itself, which, as we have discussed, is essentially a tautology.

Instead, the Tenth Amendment confirms that the power of the Federal Government is subject to limits that may, in a given instance, reserve power to the States. The

Tenth Amendment thus directs us to determine, as in this case, whether an incident of state sovereignty is protected by a limitation on an Article I power. . . .

The Federal Government undertakes activities today that would have been unimaginable to the Framers in two senses; first, because the Framers would not have conceived that any government would conduct such activities; and second, because the Framers would not have believed that the Federal Government, rather than the States, would assume such responsibilities. Yet the powers conferred upon the Federal Government by the Constitution were phrased in language broad enough to allow for the expansion of the Federal Government's role. Among the provisions of the Constitution that have been particularly important in this regard, three concern us here.

First, the Constitution allocates to Congress the power "[t]o regulate Commerce . . . among the several States." Art. I, §8, cl. 3. . . .

Second, the Constitution authorizes Congress "to pay the Debts and provide for the . . . general Welfare of the United States." Art. I, §8, cl. 1. As conventional notions of the proper objects of government spending have changed over the years, so has the ability of Congress to "fix the terms on which it shall disburse federal money to the States." Pennhurst State School and Hospital v. Halderman, 451 U.S. 1, 17 (1981). Compare, e.g., United States v. Butler, *supra*, 297 U.S., at 72-75 (spending power does not authorize Congress to subsidize farmers), with South Dakota v. Dole, 483 U.S. 203 (1987) (spending power permits Congress to condition highway funds on States' adoption of minimum drinking age). While the spending power is "subject to several general restrictions articulated in our cases," id., at 207, these restrictions have not been so severe as to prevent the regulatory authority of Congress from generally keeping up with the growth of the federal budget.

The Court's broad construction of Congress' power under the Commerce and Spending Clauses has of course been guided, as it has with respect to Congress' power generally, by the Constitution's Necessary and Proper Clause, which authorizes Congress "[t]o make all Laws which shall be necessary and proper for carrying into Execution the foregoing Powers." U.S. Const., Art. I, §8, cl. 18. . . .

Finally, the Constitution provides that "the Laws of the United States . . . shall be the supreme Law of the Land . . . any Thing in the Constitution or Laws of any State to the Contrary notwithstanding." U.S. Const., Art. VI, cl. 2. As the Federal Government's willingness to exercise power within the confines of the Constitution has grown, the authority of the States has correspondingly diminished to the extent that federal and state policies have conflicted. See, e.g., Shaw v. Delta Air Lines, Inc., 463 U.S. 85 (1983). We have observed that the Supremacy Clause gives the Federal Government "a decided advantage in th[e] delicate balance" the Constitution strikes between state and federal power. Gregory v. Ashcroft, 501 U.S., at 460.

The actual scope of the Federal Government's authority with respect to the States has changed over the years, therefore, but the constitutional structure underlying and limiting that authority has not. In the end, just as a cup may be half empty or half full, it makes no difference whether one views the question at issue in these cases as one of ascertaining the limits of the power delegated to the Federal Government under the affirmative provisions of the Constitution or one of discerning the core of sovereignty retained by the States under the Tenth Amendment. Either way, we must determine whether any of the three challenged provisions of the Low-Level Radioactive Waste Policy Amendments Act of 1985 oversteps the boundary between federal and state authority.

B.

Petitioners do not contend that Congress lacks the power to regulate the disposal of low level radioactive waste. Space in radioactive waste disposal sites is frequently sold by residents of one State to residents of another. Regulation of the resulting interstate market in waste disposal is therefore well within Congress' authority under the Commerce Clause. Cf. Philadelphia v. New Jersey, 437 U.S. 617, 621-623 (1978); Fort Gratiot Sanitary Landfill, Inc. v. Michigan Dept. of Natural Resources, 504 U.S. 353, 359 (1992). Petitioners likewise do not dispute that under the Supremacy Clause Congress could, if it wished, pre-empt state radioactive waste regulation. Petitioners contend only that the Tenth Amendment limits the power of Congress to regulate in the way it has chosen. Rather than addressing the problem of waste disposal by directly regulating the generators and disposers of waste, petitioners argue, Congress has impermissibly directed the States to regulate in this field. . . .

This litigation instead concerns the circumstances under which Congress may use the States as implements of regulation; that is, whether Congress may direct or otherwise motivate the States to regulate in a particular field or a particular way. Our cases have established a few principles that guide our resolution of the issue.

1.

As an initial matter, Congress may not simply "commandee[r] the legislative processes of the States by directly compelling them to enact and enforce a federal regulatory program." Hodel v. Virginia Surface Mining & Reclamation Ass'n, Inc., 452 U.S. 264, 288 (1981). In *Hodel*, the Court upheld the Surface Mining Control and Reclamation Act of 1977 precisely because it did not "commandeer" the States into regulating mining. The Court found that "the States are not compelled to enforce the steep-slope standards, to expend any state funds, or to participate in the federal regulatory program in any manner whatsoever. If a State does not wish to submit a proposed permanent program that complies with the Act and implementing regulations, the full regulatory burden will be borne by the Federal Government." Ibid.

The Court reached the same conclusion the following year in FERC v. Mississippi, *supra*. At issue in *FERC* was the Public Utility Regulatory Policies Act of 1978, a federal statute encouraging the States in various ways to develop programs to combat the Nation's energy crisis. We observed that "this Court never has sanctioned explicitly a federal command to the States to promulgate and enforce laws and regulations." Id., 456 U.S., at 761-762. As in *Hodel*, the Court upheld the statute at issue because it did not view the statute as such a command. . . .

These statements in *FERC* and *Hodel* were not innovations. While Congress has substantial powers to govern the Nation directly, including in areas of intimate concern to the States, the Constitution has never been understood to confer upon Congress the ability to require the States to govern according to Congress' instructions.

In providing for a stronger central government, therefore, the Framers explicitly chose a Constitution that confers upon Congress the power to regulate individuals, not States. As we have seen, the Court has consistently respected this choice. We have always understood that even where Congress has the authority under the Constitution to pass laws requiring or prohibiting certain acts, it lacks the power directly to compel the States to require or prohibit those acts. . . . The allocation of power contained in the Commerce Clause, for example, authorizes Congress to regulate interstate commerce directly; it does not authorize Congress to regulate state governments' regulation of interstate commerce.

2.

This is not to say that Congress lacks the ability to encourage a State to regulate in a particular way, or that Congress may not hold out incentives to the States as a method of influencing a State's policy choices. Our cases have identified a variety of methods, short of outright coercion, by which Congress may urge a State to adopt a legislative program consistent with federal interests. Two of these methods are of particular relevance here.

First, under Congress' spending power, "Congress may attach conditions on the receipt of federal funds." South Dakota v. Dole, 483 U.S., at 206. Such conditions must (among other requirements) bear some relationship to the purpose of the federal spending, id., at 207-208, and n.3; otherwise, of course, the spending power could render academic the Constitution's other grants and limits of federal authority. Where the recipient of federal funds is a State, as is not unusual today, the conditions attached to the funds by Congress may influence a State's legislative choices. See Kaden, Politics, Money, and State Sovereignty: The Judicial Role, 79 Colum. L. Rev. 847, 874-881 (1979). Dole was one such case: The Court found no constitutional flaw in a federal statute directing the Secretary of Transportation to withhold federal highway funds from States failing to adopt Congress' choice of a minimum drinking age. Similar examples abound. . . .

Second, where Congress has the authority to regulate private activity under the Commerce Clause, we have recognized Congress' power to offer States the choice of regulating that activity according to federal standards or having state law pre-empted by federal regulation. Hodel v. Virginia Surface Mining & Reclamation Ass'n, Inc., supra, 452 U.S., at 288. See also FERC v. Mississippi, supra, 456 U.S., at 764-765. This arrangement, which has been termed "a program of cooperative federalism," Hodel, supra, 452 U.S., at 289, is replicated in numerous federal statutory schemes. These include the Clean Water Act, 33 U.S.C. §1251 et seq.; see Arkansas v. Oklahoma, 503 U.S. 91, 101 (1992) (Clean Water Act "anticipates a partnership between the States and the Federal Government, animated by a shared objective"); the Occupational Safety and Health Act of 1970, 29 U.S.C. §651 et seq.; see Gade v. National Solid Wastes Mgmt. Ass'n, 505 U.S. 88, 97 (1992); the Resource Conservation and Recovery Act of 1976, 42 U.S.C. §6901 et seq.; see Department of Energy v. Ohio, 503 U.S. 607, 611-612 (1992); and the Alaska National Interest Lands Conservation Act, 16 U.S.C. §3101 et seq.; see Kenaitze Indian Tribe v. Alaska, 860 F.2d 312, 314 (CA9 1988).

By either of these methods, as by any other permissible method of encouraging a State to conform to federal policy choices, the residents of the State retain the ultimate decision as to whether or not the State will comply. If a State's citizens view federal policy as sufficiently contrary to local interests, they may elect to decline a federal grant. If state residents would prefer their government to devote its attention and resources to problems other than those deemed important by Congress, they may choose to have the Federal Government rather than the State bear the expense of a federally mandated regulatory program, and they may continue to supplement that program to the extent state law is not pre-empted. Where Congress encourages state regulation rather than compelling it, state governments remain responsive to the local electorate's preferences; state officials remain accountable to the people.

By contrast, where the Federal Government compels States to regulate, the accountability of both state and federal officials is diminished. If the citizens of New York, for example, do not consider that making provision for the disposal of radioactive waste is in their best interest, they may elect state officials who share their view. That view can always be pre-empted under the Supremacy Clause if it is contrary to the national view, but in such a case it is the Federal Government that makes the decision in full view of the public, and it will be federal officials that suffer the consequences if the decision turns out to be detrimental or unpopular.

But where the Federal Government directs the States to regulate, it may be state officials who will bear the brunt of public disapproval, while the federal officials who devised the regulatory program may remain insulated from the electoral ramifications of their decision. Accountability is thus diminished when, due to federal coercion, elected state officials cannot regulate in accordance with the views of the local electorate in matters not pre-empted by federal regulation. See Merritt, 88 Colum. L. Rev., at 61-62; La Pierre, Political Accountability in the National Political Process—The Alternative to Judicial Review of Federalism Issues, 80 Nw. U. L. Rev. 577, 639-665 (1985).

With these principles in mind, we turn to the three challenged provisions of the Low-Level Radioactive Waste Policy Amendments Act of 1985.

III.

The parties in these cases advance two quite different views of the Act. . . .

Construed as a whole, the Act comprises three sets of "incentives" for the States to provide for the disposal of low level radioactive waste generated within their borders. We consider each in turn.

A.

The first set of incentives works in three steps. First, Congress has authorized States with disposal sites to impose a surcharge on radioactive waste received from other States. Second, the Secretary of Energy collects a portion of this surcharge and places the money in an escrow account. Third, States achieving a series of milestones receive portions of this fund.

The first of these steps is an unexceptionable exercise of Congress' power to authorize the States to burden interstate commerce. While the Commerce Clause has long been understood to limit the States' ability to discriminate against interstate commerce, see, e.g., Wyoming v. Oklahoma, 502 U.S. 437, 454-455 (1992); Cooley v. Board of Wardens of Port of Philadelphia ex rel. Society for Relief of Distressed Pilots, 12 How. 299 (1852), that limit may be lifted, as it has been here, by an expression of the "unambiguous intent" of Congress. Wyoming, supra, 502 U.S., at 458; Prudential Ins. Co. v. Benjamin, 328 U.S. 408, 427-431 (1946). Whether or not the States would be permitted to burden the interstate transport of low level radioactive waste in the absence of Congress' approval, the States can clearly do so with Congress' approval, which is what the Act gives them.

The second step, the Secretary's collection of a percentage of the surcharge, is no more than a federal tax on interstate commerce, which petitioners do not claim to be an invalid exercise of either Congress' commerce or taxing power. Cf. United States v.

Sanchez, 340 U.S. 42, 44-45 (1950); Steward Machine Co. v. Davis, 301 U.S. 548, 581-583 (1937).

The third step is a conditional exercise of Congress' authority under the Spending Clause: Congress has placed conditions—the achievement of the milestones—on the receipt of federal funds. Petitioners do not contend that Congress has exceeded its authority in any of the four respects our cases have identified. See generally South Dakota v. Dole, 483 U.S., at 207-208. The expenditure is for the general welfare, Helvering v. Davis, 301 U.S. 619, 640-641 (1937); the States are required to use the money they receive for the purpose of assuring the safe disposal of radioactive waste. 42 U.S.C. §2021e(d)(2)(E). The conditions imposed are unambiguous, Pennhurst State School and Hospital v. Halderman, 451 U.S., at 17; the Act informs the States exactly what they must do and by when they must do it in order to obtain a share of the escrow account. The conditions imposed are reasonably related to the purpose of the expenditure, Massachusetts v. United States, 435 U.S., at 461; both the conditions and the payments embody Congress' efforts to address the pressing problem of radioactive waste disposal. Finally, petitioners do not claim that the conditions imposed by the Act violate any independent constitutional prohibition. Lawrence County v. Lead-Deadwood School Dist. No. 40-1, 469 U.S. 256, 269-270 (1985).

Petitioners contend nevertheless that the form of these expenditures removes them from the scope of Congress' spending power. . . . The Constitution's grant to Congress of the authority to "pay the Debts and provide for the . . . general Welfare" has never, however, been thought to mandate a particular form of accounting. A great deal of federal spending comes from segregated trust funds collected and spent for a particular purpose. . . . The Spending Clause has never been construed to deprive Congress of the power to structure federal spending in this manner. . . . That the States are able to choose whether they will receive federal funds does not make the resulting expenditures any less federal; indeed, the location of such choice in the States is an inherent element in any conditional exercise of Congress' spending power.

The Act's first set of incentives, in which Congress has conditioned grants to the States upon the States' attainment of a series of milestones, is thus well within the authority of Congress under the Commerce and Spending Clauses. Because the first set of incentives is supported by affirmative constitutional grants of power to Congress, it is not inconsistent with the Tenth Amendment.

B.

In the second set of incentives, Congress has authorized States and regional compacts with disposal sites gradually to increase the cost of access to the sites, and then to deny access altogether, to radioactive waste generated in States that do not meet federal deadlines. As a simple regulation, this provision would be within the power of Congress to authorize the States to discriminate against interstate commerce. See Northeast Bancorp, Inc. v. Board of Governors, FRS, 472 U.S. 159, 174-175 (1985). Where federal regulation of private activity is within the scope of the Commerce Clause, we have recognized the ability of Congress to offer States the choice of regulating that activity according to federal standards or having state law pre-empted by federal regulation. See Hodel v. Virginia Surface Mining & Reclamation Ass'n, Inc., 452 U.S., at 288; FERC v. Mississippi, 456 U.S., at 764-765.

This is the choice presented to nonsited States by the Act's second set of incentives: States may either regulate the disposal of radioactive waste according to federal standards by attaining local or regional self-sufficiency, or their residents who produce radioactive waste will be subject to federal regulation authorizing sited States and regions to deny access to their disposal sites. The affected States are not compelled by Congress to regulate, because any burden caused by a State's refusal to regulate will fall on those who generate waste and find no outlet for its disposal, rather than on the State as a sovereign. A State whose citizens do not wish it to attain the Act's milestones may devote its attention and its resources to issues its citizens deem more worthy; the choice remains at all times with the residents of the State, not with Congress. The State need not expend any funds, or participate in any federal program, if local residents do not view such expenditures or participation as worthwhile. Cf. *Hodel*, *supra*, 452 U.S., at 288. Nor must the State abandon the field if it does not accede to federal direction; the State may continue to regulate the generation and disposal of radioactive waste in any manner its citizens see fit.

The Act's second set of incentives thus represents a conditional exercise of Congress' commerce power, along the lines of those we have held to be within Congress' authority. As a result, the second set of incentives does not intrude on the sovereignty reserved to the States by the Tenth Amendment.

C.

The take title provision is of a different character. This third so-called "incentive" offers States, as an alternative to regulating pursuant to Congress' direction, the option of taking title to and possession of the low level radioactive waste generated within their borders and becoming liable for all damages waste generators suffer as a result of the States' failure to do so promptly. In this provision, Congress has crossed the line distinguishing encouragement from coercion. . . .

The take title provision offers state governments a "choice" of either accepting ownership of waste or regulating according to the instructions of Congress. Respondents do not claim that the Constitution would authorize Congress to impose either option as a freestanding requirement. On one hand, the Constitution would not permit Congress simply to transfer radioactive waste from generators to state governments. Such a forced transfer, standing alone, would in principle be no different than a congressionally compelled subsidy from state governments to radioactive waste producers. The same is true of the provision requiring the States to become liable for the generators' damages. Standing alone, this provision would be indistinguishable from an Act of Congress directing the States to assume the liabilities of certain state residents. Either type of federal action would "commandeer" state governments into the service of federal regulatory purposes, and would for this reason be inconsistent with the Constitution's division of authority between federal and state governments. On the other hand, the second alternative held out to state governments — regulating pursuant to Congress' direction — would, standing alone, present a simple command to state governments to implement legislation enacted by Congress. As we have seen, the Constitution does not empower Congress to subject state governments to this type of instruction.

Because an instruction to state governments to take title to waste, standing alone, would be beyond the authority of Congress, and because a direct order to regulate, standing alone, would also be beyond the authority of Congress, it follows that Congress lacks the power to offer the States a choice between the two. Unlike the first two sets of incentives, the take title incentive does not represent the conditional exercise of any congressional power enumerated in the Constitution. In this provision, Congress has not held out the threat of exercising its spending power or its commerce power; it has instead held out the threat, should the States not regulate according to one federal instruction, of simply forcing the States to submit to another federal instruction. A choice between two unconstitutionally coercive regulatory techniques is no choice at all. Either way, "the Act commandeers the legislative processes of the States by directly compelling them to enact and enforce a federal regulatory program," Hodel v. Virginia Surface Mining & Reclamation Ass'n, Inc., *supra*, 452 U.S., at 288, an outcome that has never been understood to lie within the authority conferred upon Congress by the Constitution.

Respondents emphasize the latitude given to the States to implement Congress' plan. The Act enables the States to regulate pursuant to Congress' instructions in any number of different ways. States may avoid taking title by contracting with sited regional compacts, by building a disposal site alone or as part of a compact, or by permitting private parties to build a disposal site. States that host sites may employ a wide range of designs and disposal methods, subject only to broad federal regulatory limits. This line of reasoning, however, only underscores the critical alternative a State lacks: A State may not decline to administer the federal program. No matter which path the State chooses, it must follow the direction of Congress.

The take title provision appears to be unique. No other federal statute has been cited which offers a state government no option other than that of implementing legislation enacted by Congress. Whether one views the take title provision as lying outside Congress' enumerated powers, or as infringing upon the core of state sovereignty reserved by the Tenth Amendment, the provision is inconsistent with the federal structure of our Government established by the Constitution.

IV.

Respondents raise a number of objections to this understanding of the limits of Congress' power. . . .

Respondents note that the Act embodies a bargain among the sited and unsited States, a compromise to which New York was a willing participant and from which New York has reaped much benefit. Respondents then pose what appears at first to be a troubling question: How can a federal statute be found an unconstitutional infringement of state sovereignty when state officials consented to the statute's enactment?

The answer follows from an understanding of the fundamental purpose served by our Government's federal structure. The Constitution does not protect the sovereignty of States for the benefit of the States or state governments as abstract political entities, or even for the benefit of the public officials governing the States. To the contrary, the Constitution divides authority between federal and state governments for the protection of individuals. State sovereignty is not just an end in itself: "Rather, federalism secures to citizens the liberties that derive from the diffusion of sovereign power." Coleman v. Thompson, 501 U.S. 722, 759 (1991) (Blackmun, J., dissenting). "Just as the separation and independence of the coordinate branches of the Federal Government serves to prevent the accumulation of excessive power in any one branch, a healthy balance of power between the States and the Federal Government will reduce the risk of tyranny and abuse from either front." Gregory v. Ashcroft, 501 U.S., at 458 (1991). See The Federalist No. 51, p. 323 (C. Rossiter ed. 1961).

Where Congress exceeds its authority relative to the States, therefore, the departure from the constitutional plan cannot be ratified by the "consent" of state officials. An analogy to the separation of powers among the branches of the Federal Government clarifies this point. The Constitution's division of power among the three branches is violated where one branch invades the territory of another, whether or not the encroached-upon branch approves the encroachment. . . .

State officials thus cannot consent to the enlargement of the powers of Congress beyond those enumerated in the Constitution. . . .

VII.

States are not mere political subdivisions of the United States. State governments are neither regional offices nor administrative agencies of the Federal Government. The positions occupied by state officials appear nowhere on the Federal Government's most detailed organizational chart. The Constitution instead "leaves to the several States a residuary and inviolable sovereignty," The Federalist No. 39, p. 245 (C. Rossiter ed. 1961), reserved explicitly to the States by the Tenth Amendment.

Whatever the outer limits of that sovereignty may be, one thing is clear: The Federal Government may not compel the States to enact or administer a federal regulatory program. The Constitution permits both the Federal Government and the States to enact legislation regarding the disposal of low level radioactive waste. The Constitution enables the Federal Government to pre-empt state regulation contrary to federal interests, and it permits the Federal Government to hold out incentives to the States as a means of encouraging them to adopt suggested regulatory schemes. It does not, however, authorize Congress simply to direct the States to provide for the disposal of the radioactive waste generated within their borders. While there may be many constitutional methods of achieving regional self-sufficiency in radioactive waste disposal, the method Congress has chosen is not one of them. The judgment of the Court of Appeals is accordingly.

Affirmed in part and reversed in part.

[The dissents of Justice White (joined by Justices Blackmun and Stevens) and Justice Stevens are omitted.]

NOTES AND QUESTIONS

1. *Enticement Techniques.* For a federal legislator eager to enlist the states' assistance, what techniques remain constitutional after *New York*?

2. *The Limits of New York.* After *New York*, courts and analysts wondered about the implications of the case. What sorts of actions, short of legislative action, might the federal government order states to undertake? *New York* was quickly extended when a closely divided Court in Printz v. United States, 521 U.S. 898 (1997), declared unconstitutional a federal requirement under the Brady Handgun Violence Protection Act that state law enforcement officials perform statutorily required duties, including background checks and handling related forms. A unanimous Court limited the reach of *New York* and *Printz* in Reno v. Condon, 528 U.S. 141 (2000), where it upheld a federal law restricting the ability of states or others to market drivers'

registration information without the consent of the driver. The Court distinguished the *Reno* setting from those in *New York* and *Printz* by stating it did not involve "commandeering" state governmental actors or processes, but regulated states among others, restricting all in the marketing of driver information.

How should courts assess federal laws that mandate certain conduct by states in providing public amenities such as water and sewage treatment?

A NOTE ON STATE SOVEREIGN IMMUNITY

States engage in numerous types of conduct subject to federal law, ranging from serving as an employer, to running public facilities such as universities, prisons, and sewage treatment plants, to building large infrastructure projects. Through these and many other activities, states and state agencies create an array of pollution streams that can violate the law. *New York* and its progeny make clear that states can be subjected to regulation as are other individuals, with the caveat that at least some sorts of governmental functions or actions, especially legislative functions, cannot be "commandeered" by the federal government. But that is not the end of required federalism analysis.

Since the Court in *Lopez* started recasting the lines of federalism doctrine, virtually all areas of federalism doctrine have undergone change. One significant area of change, or at least substantial refinement, has been the Supreme Court's sovereign immunity case law. The importance of the Eleventh Amendment as a key text for federalist revisionism emerged in Seminole Tribe v. Florida, 517 U.S. 44 (1996). The text of the Eleventh Amendment appears to be quite specific and limited:

> The judicial power of the United States shall not be construed to extend to any suit in law or equity, commenced or prosecuted against one of the United States by Citizens of another State, or by Citizens or Subjects of any Foreign State.

In *Seminole Tribe*, however, the Supreme Court overruled Pennsylvania v. Union Gas, 491 U.S. 1 (1989), a case that had upheld federal power by allowing citizens to sue states to compel payment for cleanup costs under CERCLA. Although *Seminole Tribe* involved Indian gaming and not environmental liability, five Justices concurred in a result holding that "the Eleventh Amendment prevents congressional authorization of suit by private parties against unconsenting States" in federal court. 517 U.S. at 72. Although some language appeared broadly to immunize states from suits by private parties in federal court, other language focused on immunity from claims seeking monetary relief.

In 1999, the Court issued three opinions, often identified as the *Alden* trio, on interrelated questions of sovereign immunity doctrine. All three reflected enduring federalism divisions on the Rehnquist Court, each garnering a narrow 5-4 majority. Due to their somewhat limited impact on federal environmental law, they are summarized here, along with commentary explaining why their impact is likely to be limited.

In *Alden*, the Court held that Congress lacks the power under Article I to subject nonconsenting states to private suits for damages in state courts. Alden v. Maine, 527

U.S. 706, 712 (1999). In *Alden*, state probation officers filed suit against the state of Maine in federal court seeking compensation and liquidated damages, alleging that Maine had violated the overtime provisions of the Fair Labor Standards Act (FLSA). After the district court dismissed the suit based on *Seminole Tribe*, the probation officers refiled the suit in state court. Although the FLSA authorized private actions against states in their own courts, the trial court dismissed the suit on the ground that it was barred by sovereign immunity.

Writing for the Court, Justice Kennedy, over the dissent of four Justices, concluded that the Constitution's structure and history, along with the Court's authoritative interpretations, demonstrate that states' sovereign immunity is rooted in the sovereignty they enjoyed before the Constitution's ratification and is retained today except as altered by certain amendments. Justice Kennedy explained that "the Eleventh Amendment confirmed rather than established sovereign immunity as a constitutional principle; it follows that the scope of the States' immunity from suit is demarcated not by the text of the Amendment alone but by fundamental postulates inherent in the constitutional design." Id. at 728-729.

Justice Kennedy next addressed whether Congress has the power to abrogate states' sovereign immunity in state courts from suits by private parties based on federal law. He concluded that even though the words of the Eleventh Amendment do not apply to suits against states in state court, neither the Constitution's text nor the Court's recent sovereign immunity decisions suggest that Congress has the authority to abrogate state immunity in state courts under the Constitution. Id. at 754.

However, Justice Kennedy pointed out that state sovereign immunity in state courts "does not confer upon the state a concomitant right to disregard the Constitution or valid federal law." Id. at 754-755. Justice Kennedy proceeded to identify reasons states may still comply with federal law: the good faith of the states; voluntary state consent to suits for violations of federal law, including "consent" obtained by Congress's exercise of its spending power; suits by another state or the federal government in federal court; Congress's power to abrogate states' sovereign immunity pursuant to its Fourteenth Amendment §5 powers to enforce due process and equal protection; suits against municipal governments or another government entity that is not an arm of the state; and *Ex parte Young*–type suits for injunctive relief directed against individual state officials.

In two other cases decided on the same day, the Court restricted the scope of Congress's enforcement authority under the Fourteenth Amendment, limiting two of the mechanisms by which states could be sued for retrospective relief. The Court, in College Sav. Bank v. Florida Prepaid Postsecondary Educ. Expense Bd., 527 U.S. 666, 672-690 (1999), held that §5 of the Fourteenth Amendment does not give Congress the authority to abrogate states' sovereign immunity in federal court for violations of federal trademark statutes. Writing for the Court, Justice Scalia found that under *Seminole Tribe*, Congress cannot rely on its commerce power to abrogate Eleventh Amendment immunity and that, under City of Boerne v. Flores, 521 U.S. 507 (1997), §5 of the Fourteenth Amendment gives Congress the power to abrogate state immunity only to remedy or prevent constitutional violations. The Court rejected plaintiff's arguments that the right to be free from a business competitor's false advertising about its own product and a generalized right to be secure in one's business interests were constitutionally cognizable protected property rights. After determining that Congress did not abrogate Florida's right to sovereign immunity, the Court found that Florida did not voluntarily waive its sovereign immunity by actively engaging in interstate commerce. In doing so, the Court expressly overruled *Parden v. Terminal RR. Co. of Alabama Docks Dep't*, 377 U.S. 184 (1964), which had held that where Congress conditioned the right to operate a railroad in interstate commerce upon amenability to suit in federal court, the state of Alabama consented to suit by operating a railroad in interstate commerce. A state's consent to waive its sovereign immunity requires an unequivocal and express waiver. The Court also stated that Congress might be able to accomplish the same result using its spending power. Id. at 686-687 ("Congress has no obligation to use its Spending Clause power to disburse funds to the states; such funds are gifts. In the present case however, what Congress threatens if the state refuses to agree to its condition is not the denial of a gift or gratuity, but a sanction: exclusion of the state from otherwise permissible activity.").

Similarly, in Florida Prepaid Postsecondary Educ. Expense Bd. v. College Sav. Bd., 527 U.S. 627, 630 (1999), the Court held that Congress lacks the authority under §5 of the Fourteenth Amendment to abrogate states' Eleventh Amendment immunity from suit in federal court for alleged violations of federal patent statutes. Chief Justice Rehnquist, writing for the Court, held that Congress clearly made known its intent to abrogate a state's sovereign immunity in the Patent and Plant Variety Protection Remedy Clarification Act. The second inquiry, however, is whether Congress acted pursuant to a valid exercise of power. The Court found that Congress did not have the authority under the Commerce Clause or Article I patent authority because Congress may not abrogate state sovereign immunity pursuant to Article I powers. To invoke §5, the Court reiterated that under *City of Boerne*, Congress must identify state conduct transgressing the Fourteenth Amendment's substantive provisions and must tailor the federal legislative scheme for remedying or preventing such state conduct. In passing the Act, Congress failed to identify a pattern of such state infringement, let alone a pattern of constitutional violations.

Recognizing that patents may well be considered "property" for Fourteenth Amendment purposes, the Court determined that Congress did not find state remedies inadequate, and the legislative record indicated that the Act did not respond to a history of widespread and persisting deprivation of constitutional rights—conditions that are required of Congress in enacting legislation under §5. Finally, the Court concluded that even if some abrogation of state immunity was appropriate in this context, the statutory provision before the Court was too broad to withstand constitutional scrutiny. Congress did not limit the Act's coverage to cases involving arguable constitutional violations or confine its reach by limiting the remedy to certain types of infringement. Thus, the Court held that in light of the historical record and scope of coverage of the Act, the law could not be sustained under §5 of the Fourteenth Amendment.

Taken together, the *Alden* trio and the earlier *Seminole Tribe* decision raise questions about Congress's ability to provide for reliable enforcement of federal environmental laws. Clearly, the rulings limit the ability of citizens to obtain monetary relief against nonconsenting states. However, as you will see in Chapters 3 and 10, on administrative law and enforcement, most environmental "citizen suit" provisions do not provide for damages relief, but generally provide causes of action for injunctive relief, penalties, and attorneys' fees and costs. Citizens have played a critical adjunct role in environmental enforcement, often stepping in to enforce the law when federal or state actors have declined to act. What is the impact of these cases on such actions? Professors McAllister and Glicksman, in State Liability for Environmental Violations:

The U.S. Supreme Court's "New" Federalism, 29 Envtl. L. Rep. 10665, 10667 (1999), conclude that

> a variety of enforcement mechanisms and options remain available. [T]he Court's recent federalism decisions may make implementation and the enforcement of federal environmental laws more complicated and difficult in some instances but the decisions do not ultimately appear to preclude Congress from regulating environmental matters in any significant measure.

For a somewhat more pessimistic appraisal, see Araiza, Alden v. Maine and the Web of Environmental Law, 33 Loy. L.A. L. Rev. 1513 (2000).

It is clear that as a result of the *Alden* trio, state violators of environmental laws have a substantially reduced risk of liability if the federal government lacks interest in punishing those violations. See Burnette v. Carothers, 192 F.3d 52 (2d Cir. 1999) (applying these cases and dismissing citizen suit claims under three environmental statutes, finding monetary relief precluded by sovereign immunity doctrine). For scholarly critiques of the effect of the *Alden* trio, see Adler, Judicial Federalism and the Future of Federal Environmental Regulation, 90 Iowa L. Rev. 377, 397-402, 431-433 (2005); Babcock, The Effect of the United States Supreme Court's Eleventh Amendment Jurisprudence on Clean Water Act Citizen Suits: Muddied Waters, 83 Or. L. Rev. 47 (2004).

E.   THE POWER ALLOCATION CHOICE: SAVINGS CLAUSES, DELEGATED PROGRAMS, AND PREEMPTION

Validly enacted federal law can trump contrary state laws under the Constitution's Supremacy Clause, which states in Article VI, "This Constitution, and the Laws of the United States which shall be made in Pursuance thereof . . . shall be the supreme Law of the Land." The Court's abundant, although confusing, body of preemption doctrine sets forth how and when federal law will preempt state law. In federal environmental laws, however, most major statutes explicitly preserve state law and even welcome more stringent state laws. Buzbee, Asymmetrical Regulation: Risk, Preemption, and the Floor/Ceiling Distinction, 82 N.Y.U. L. Rev. 1547 (2007); Lehner, Act Locally: Municipal Enforcement of Environmental Law, 12 Stan. Envtl. L.J. 50, 78-79 (1993); Spence & Murray, The Law, Economics, and Politics of Federal Preemption Jurisprudence: A Quantitative Analysis, 87 Cal. L. Rev. 1125, 1146-1150 (1999). For chapter essays analyzing the many facets of the preemption choice and linked doctrine, see Preemption Choice: The Theory, Law, and Reality of Federalism's Core Question (W. Buzbee ed., (2009). This section briefly discusses these "savings" clauses as well as the less common preempting provisions in federal environmental laws. It also provides a brief introduction to "delegated program" provisions in federal environmental law, under which states can assume substantial implementation and enforcement roles. This part closes by examining the basics of preemption case law, looking at the Court's *Engine Manufacturers* and *Bates* decisions, as well as noting several more recent regulatory preemption cases, to illustrate preemption doctrine's importance to environmental law.

1. Savings Clauses

As covered in Chapter 1, especially in materials concerning the *Ouellette* case, federal environmental laws generally do not displace all state laws, but in various ways retain or dovetail with state law. Federal laws that retain state law do so in provisions that are often characterized as *savings clauses*. Although each new statute has its particular formulations, this section reviews a few paradigmatic savings clause provisions. Keep in mind that statutes with savings clauses often also contain preemptive provisions, and that courts can still find a preemptive effect even when a statute contains a savings clause.

The Clean Water Act arguably contains the greatest number of savings clauses; some were perhaps drafted to mollify legislators concerned with expanded federal power, but others contain direct, clear content. Section 1251, the law's opening "declaration of goals and policy," contains a broad statement of "the policy of Congress to recognize, preserve, and protect the primary responsibilities and rights of States to prevent, reduce, and eliminate pollution, to plan the development and use . . . of land and water resources, and to consult with" EPA's administrator. 33 U.S.C. §1251(b). This subsection goes on to state the legislative intent to have states administer construction grant and permit programs under the statute's chief provisions, and also to have the federal government provide assistance with research, technical services, and funding. These initial provisions are more broad statements of policy than operative clauses or provisions that will resolve conflicts, but they certainly serve as broad anti-preemption statements. Nevertheless, as is evident in the excerpts from *SWANCC* and *Rapanos* above, at times the Supreme Court has looked at broad declarations regarding intent to preserve state power as grounds for limiting federal power, even in massive new federal anti-pollution legislation such as the Clean Water Act. The intent not to displace state riparian rights law is made with unusual clarity (and a fair bit of repetition in clauses not quoted here); it is stated to be the "policy of Congress that the authority of each State to allocate quantities of water shall not be superseded, abrogated or otherwise impaired by this Chapter." §1251(g).

Section 1365(e) explicitly preserves "any right which any person . . . may have under any statute or common law to seek enforcement of any effluent standard or to seek any other relief." This provision, you may recall, was significant in the *Ouellette* opinion excerpted in Chapter 1.

Of equal importance is the typical savings clause language of §1370, specifying that federal anti-pollution standards are a floor, constituting the minimum level of stringency or protection that must be provided by states and political subdivisions. States can pass additional "standard[s] or limitation[s]," or "any requirement respecting control or abatement of pollution," as long as they are not "less stringent" than federal requirements.

Other statutes have similar savings clauses, some containing both general statements about states' retained regulatory power, such as 42 U.S.C. §7401(a)(3) (the Clean Air Act) or 42 U.S.C. §6901(a)(4) (the Resource Conservation and Recovery Act (RCRA)), and provisions preserving states' rights to protect the environment with more stringent protections. Compare 42 U.S.C. §6929 (allowing "more stringent" regulation under RCRA) and 42 U.S.C. §7416 (allowing additional state regulation of air pollution, other than that related to "moving sources," as long as it is not "less stringent" than federal requirements).

As covered in Chapter 9's materials on oil spills, savings clauses in both the Clean Water Act and Oil Pollution Act, 33 U.S.C. §2718(a) and (c), appear to save state common law claims, but leave room for argument about preemption or at least choice of law, especially when the physical realities of spills and the laws' provisions are examined in light of the *Ouellette* case covered in Chapter 1. See the discussion of these issues in section D.3 of Chapter 9; In re Deepwater Horizon, 745 F.3d 157 (5th Cir. 2014) (finding claims based on the affected state's laws preempted but stating that claims remain possible under federal law or the law of the pollution source state).

The net effect of these many federal savings clauses is that, other than in the rare explicitly preempting provisions, federal law serves as a stringency floor, not a ceiling; states can enact additional, parallel laws or more stringent protections. Choice of law questions may remain. See Buzbee, Asymmetrical Regulation, *supra*; Glicksman, From Cooperative to Inoperative Federalism: The Perverse Mutation of Environmental Law and Policy, 41 Wake Forest L. Rev. 719, 737-743 (2006); Percival, Environmental Federalism: Historical Roots and Contemporary Models, 54 Md. L. Rev. 1141, 1175 (1995).

2. Delegated Programs

Intertwined with savings clauses are provisions that are perhaps of greatest importance to understanding this nation's environmental laws. These are the quintessential *cooperative federalism* provisions, providing that states or their subdivisions can retain or assume responsibility for implementing and enforcing federal programs. These are often described as *delegated programs* because they involve broad delegation of federal regulatory power and obligations to states. As you will see in Chapter 10's discussion of environmental law enforcement, statutes and court decisions vary in terms of how much federal enforcement or "overfiling" power is retained when a state takes over a federal program; this hot-button issue is covered separately below.

Most major programs of this nation's pollution control legislation provide for the delegated program option. Indeed, this is such a pervasive feature, often contained in numerous provisions of a law, that this introduction to federalism will cover only a few to emphasize their most significant features. Natural resource laws, however, less frequently incorporate such cooperative federalism structures. Fischman, Cooperative Federalism and Natural Resources Law, 14 N.Y.U. Envtl. L.J. 179 (2005).

You will learn in depth about the two most significant delegated programs in subsequent chapters on the Clean Air and Clean Water Acts (Chapters 6 and 7). However, a brief summary of these provisions' key attributes is provided here. Under the Clean Water Act, the industrial discharge permitting program (the National Pollution Discharge Elimination System, or NPDES), lies presumptively in the hands of federal agencies, but states can pass laws and make other commitments to establish that they are qualified to assume the permit implementation and enforcement roles. Under §402(b) and (c), the governor and state attorney general can submit to the Administrator of EPA a description of the program they propose to implement, with evidence that it conforms to federal statutory and regulatory requirements regarding stringency, participatory rights, permit duration, sanctions, and an array of other requirements. 33 U.S.C. §1342(b). State programs need not exactly duplicate what the federal government would choose to do or had been doing. The onus is on the EPA Administrator to find that a state's program is inadequate: "The Administrator shall approve each such submitted program unless he determines that adequate authority does not exist" to carry out the specified regulatory obligations. States can lose this authority if, after federal notification and an opportunity for state correction, EPA determines that the state program, as written or in actual implementation, is no longer consistent with federal law. Id. §1342(c).

The Clean Air Act's state implementation plan (SIP) provisions, especially §110, 42 U.S.C. §7410, are much like those of the Clean Water Act NPDES program in setting forth an array of criteria states must meet to be primarily responsible for implementation plans designed to bring regions into compliance with federally set ambient air quality standards. In contrast to the NPDES provisions, the authorization to adopt SIPs places initial regulatory power in the hands of the states. Only if federal regulators or a court determine that a state is failing to comply with this provision's requirements can the state lose that power. As with the NPDES program, loss of state implementation power can occur only following notice and an opportunity for cure.

As you delve into the intricacies of the Clean Air Act, be sensitive to the wide variety of ways in which states can fail to meet federal goals or requirements and the nuanced series of procedural steps and sanctions that can follow. As you will see, the Clean Air Act distinguishes among failure to plan, failure to attain ambient air quality levels, failure to implement plans, and failure to enforce the law and plan commitments.

Many delegated programs are linked to monetary incentives. Partial federal underwriting of state efforts is common, often as an enticement for state participation, as allowed for in New York v. United States under well-established "conditional federal spending" powers. In addition, when a state falls short in carrying out its regulatory obligations, it can lose federal funds. Under the Clean Air Act, for example, the fear of loss of federal highway funding is a substantial motivator for states that might otherwise give federal clean air goals low priority. 42 U.S.C. §7509(b). Under many statutes, especially the Clean Water Act NPDES program, federal monetary support seldom covers more than a fraction of state costs. States nevertheless jealously guard and seek to preserve their planning and permitting authority. Whether it involves highly discretionary Clean Air Act planning for air quality control regions or more technical negotiations over industrial water pollution permits, states fight to preserve their regulatory roles rather than surrender them to federal regulators, who are perceived to be less sensitive to state and local conditions and politics.

3. *Preempting Clauses and Regulatory Actions*

Preemption doctrine generates a great deal of disagreement, although most courts, lawyers, and scholars readily agree that "[m]odern preemption jurisprudence is a muddle." Caleb Nelson, Preemption, 86 Va. L. Rev. 225, 233 (2000). Professor Nelson questions "the usefulness of dividing . . . into separate analytical categories . . . 'express' preemption, 'field' preemption, and 'conflict' preemption. The Supreme Court itself has been unable to keep these categories 'rigidly distinct,' and they only get in the way of its analysis." Id. at 262 (citing to English v. General Elec. Co., 496 U.S. 72, 79 n.5 (1990)). Despite the uncertainties associated with these imperfect categories, they remain the starting point for preemption argument. Before turning to recent policy developments, cases, and notes illuminating preemption's influence on environmental law, this section lays out the basics of preemption doctrine.

In Crosby v. National Foreign Trade Council, 530 U.S. 363 (2000), the Supreme Court reviewed many of the central tenets of preemption doctrine. Congress undoubtedly has the power to preempt state law under the Constitution, but a finding of preemption does not require an explicit legislative statement of such intent:

> Even without an express provision for preemption, we have found that state law must yield to a congressional Act in at least two circumstances. When Congress intends federal law to "occupy the field," state law in that area is preempted. . . . And even if Congress has not occupied the field, state law is naturally preempted to the extent of any conflict with a federal statute. . . . We will find preemption where it is impossible for a private party to comply with both state and federal law, see, e.g., Florida Lime & Avocado Growers, Inc. v. Paul, 373 U.S. 132, 142-143 (1963), and where "under the circumstances of [a] particular case, [the challenged state law] stands as an obstacle to the accomplishment and execution of the full purposes and objectives of Congress." . . . What is a sufficient obstacle is a matter of judgment, to be informed by examining the federal statute as a whole and identifying its purpose and intended effects: "For when the question is whether a Federal act overrides a state law, the entire scheme of the statute must of course be considered and that which needs must be implied is of no less force than that which is expressed. If the purpose of the act cannot otherwise be accomplished—if its operation within its chosen field else must be frustrated and its provisions be refused their natural effect—the state law must yield to the regulation of Congress within the sphere of its delegated power." [Id. at 372-373 (2000).]

In Gade v. National Solid Wastes Mgmt. Ass'n, 505 U.S. 88 (1992), the Court articulated with a bit more specificity when preemption might be found, even in the absence of explicitly preemptive language: "Absent explicit pre-emptive language, we have recognized at least two types of implied pre-emption: field pre-emption, where the scheme of federal regulation is 'so pervasive as to make reasonable the inference that Congress left no room for the States to supplement it,' . . . and conflict pre-emption, where 'compliance with both federal and state regulations is a physical impossibility' . . . or where state law 'stands as an obstacle to the accomplishment and execution of the full purposes and objectives of Congress.' . . . Our ultimate task in any pre-emption case is to determine whether state regulation is consistent with the structure and purpose of the statute as a whole." Id. at 98.

In Louisiana Pub. Serv. Comm'n v. FCC, 476 U.S. 355, 368-369 (1986), the Court explained that "[p]re-emption may result not only from action taken by Congress itself; a federal agency acting within the scope of its congressionally delegated authority may pre-empt state regulation." As discussed in the notes below, the agency power to preempt has recently become of great importance.

Although it is uncommon, federal environmental laws do at times explicitly preempt state laws. This occurs most frequently when federal law imposes a design requirement or calls for major design investments by industry. In such settings, a uniform federal standard can provide stability and a fixed regulatory target. The most notable preemptive provisions in federal environmental law relate to automobile emissions. As is evident in the following case, even apparently clear preemption provisions can, due to linguistic uncertainties or other, related provisions, create uncertainty and thus generate litigation. As you read *Engine Manufacturers*, a decision garnering eight supporting Justices, be sensitive to how different interpretive techniques might lead to different outcomes. Does this case result in a sensible policy?

ENGINE MANUFACTURERS ASSOCIATION v. SOUTH COAST AIR QUALITY MANAGEMENT DISTRICT
541 U.S. 246 (2004)

Justice SCALIA delivered the opinion of the Court.

Respondent South Coast Air Quality Management District (District) is a political subdivision of California responsible for air pollution control in the Los Angeles metropolitan area and parts of surrounding counties that make up the South Coast Air Basin. It enacted six Fleet Rules that generally prohibit the purchase or lease by various public and private fleet operators of vehicles that do not comply with stringent emission requirements. The question in this case is whether these local Fleet Rules escape pre-emption under §209(a) of the Clean Air Act (CAA), 81 Stat. 502, as renumbered and amended, 42 U.S.C. §7543(a), because they address the purchase of vehicles, rather than their manufacture or sale. . . .

II.

Section 209(a) of the CAA states:

> No State or any political subdivision thereof shall adopt or attempt to enforce any standard relating to the control of emissions from new motor vehicles or new motor vehicle engines subject to this part. No State shall require certification, inspection, or any other approval relating to the control of emissions . . . as condition precedent to the initial retail sale, titling (if any), or registration of such motor vehicle, motor vehicle engine, or equipment. [42 U.S.C. §7543(a).]

The District Court's determination that this express pre-emption provision did not invalidate the Fleet Rules hinged on its interpretation of the word "standard" to include only regulations that compel manufacturers to meet specified emission limits. This interpretation of "standard" in turn caused the court to draw a distinction between purchase restrictions (not pre-empted) and sale restrictions (pre-empted). Neither the manufacturer-specific interpretation of "standard" nor the resulting distinction between purchase and sale restrictions finds support in the text of §209(a) or the structure of the CAA.

"Statutory construction must begin with the language employed by Congress and the assumption that the ordinary meaning of that language accurately expresses the legislative purpose." Park 'N Fly, Inc. v. Dollar Park & Fly, Inc., 469 U.S. 189, 194 (1985). Today, as in 1967 when §209(a) became law, "standard" is defined as that which "is established by authority, custom, or general consent, as a model or example; criterion; test." Webster's Second New International Dictionary 2455 (1945). The criteria referred to in §209(a) relate to the emission characteristics of a vehicle or engine. To meet them the vehicle or engine must not emit more than a certain amount of a given pollutant, must be equipped with a certain type of pollution-control device, or must have some other design feature related to the control of emissions. This interpretation is consistent with the use of "standard" throughout Title II of the CAA (which governs emissions from moving sources) to denote requirements such as numerical emission levels with which vehicles or engines must comply, e.g., 42 U.S.C. §7521(a)(3)(B)(ii), or emission-control technology with which they must be equipped, e.g., §7521(a)(6).

Respondents, like the courts below, engraft onto this meaning of "standard" a limiting component, defining it as only "[a] *production* mandat[e] that require[s] *manufacturers* to ensure that the vehicles they produce have particular emissions characteristics, whether individually or in the aggregate." Brief for Respondent South Coast Air Quality Management District 13 (emphases added). This confuses standards with the means of enforcing standards. Manufacturers (or purchasers) can be made responsible for ensuring that vehicles comply with emission standards, but the standards themselves are separate from those enforcement techniques. While standards target vehicles or engines, standard-enforcement efforts that are proscribed by §209 can be directed to manufacturers or purchasers.

The distinction between "standards," on the one hand, and methods of standard enforcement, on the other, is borne out in the provisions immediately following §202. These separate provisions enforce the emission criteria—i.e., the §202 standards. Section 203 prohibits manufacturers from selling any new motor vehicle that is not covered by a "certificate of conformity." 42 U.S.C. §7522(a). Section 206 enables manufacturers to obtain such a certificate by demonstrating to the Environmental Protection Agency that their vehicles or engines conform to the §202 standards. §7525. Sections 204 and 205 subject manufacturers, dealers, and others who violate the CAA to fines imposed in civil or administrative enforcement actions. §§7523-7524. By defining "standard" as a "production mandate directed toward manufacturers," respondents lump together §202 and these other distinct statutory provisions, acknowledging a standard to be such only when it is combined with a mandate that prevents manufacturers from selling noncomplying vehicles.

That a standard is a standard even when not enforced through manufacturer-directed regulation can be seen in Congress's use of the term in another portion of the CAA. As the District Court recognized, CAA §246 (in conjunction with its accompanying provisions) requires state-adopted and federally approved "restrictions on the purchase of fleet vehicles to *meet clean-air standards*." 158 F. Supp. 2d, at 1118 (emphasis added); see also 42 U.S.C. §§7581-7590. (Respondents do not defend the District's Fleet Rules as authorized by this provision; the Rules do not comply with all of the requirements that it contains.) Clearly, Congress contemplated the enforcement of emission standards through purchase requirements. . . .

Respondents contend that their qualified meaning of "standard" is necessary to prevent §209(a) from pre-empting "far too much" by "encompass[ing] a broad range of state-level clean-air initiatives" such as voluntary incentive programs. But it is hard to see why limitation to mandates on manufacturers is necessary for this purpose; limitation to mandates on manufacturers and purchasers, or to mandates on anyone, would have the same salvific effect. We need not resolve application of §209(a) to voluntary incentive programs in this case, since all the Fleet Rules are mandates.

In addition to having no basis in the text of the statute, treating sales restrictions and purchase restrictions differently for pre-emption purposes would make no sense. The manufacturer's right to sell federally approved vehicles is meaningless in the absence of a purchaser's right to buy them. It is true that the Fleet Rules at issue here cover only certain purchasers and certain federally certified vehicles, and thus do not eliminate all demand for covered vehicles. But if one State or political subdivision may enact such rules, then so may any other; and the end result would undo Congress's carefully calibrated regulatory scheme.

A command, accompanied by sanctions, that certain purchasers may buy only vehicles with particular emission characteristics is as much an "attempt to enforce" a "standard" as a command, accompanied by sanctions, that a certain percentage of a manufacturer's sales volume must consist of such vehicles. We decline to read into §209(a) a purchase/sale distinction that is not to be found in the text of §209(a) or the structure of the CAA.

III.

The dissent expresses many areas of disagreement with our interpretation, but this should not obscure its agreement with our answer to the question "whether these local Fleet Rules escape pre-emption . . . because they address the purchase of vehicles, rather than their manufacture or sale." The dissent joins us in answering "no." See opinion of Souter, J. It reaches a different outcome in the case because (1) it feels free to read into the unconditional words of the statute a requirement for the courts to determine which purchase restrictions in fact coerce manufacture and which do not; and (2) because it believes that Fleet Rules containing a "commercial availability" proviso do not coerce manufacture.

As to the first point: The language of §209(a) is categorical. It is (as we have discussed) impossible to find in it an exception for standards imposed through purchase restrictions rather than directly upon manufacturers; it is even more inventive to discover an exception for only that subcategory of standards-imposed-through-purchase-restrictions that does not coerce manufacture. But even if one accepts that invention, one cannot conclude that these "provisos" save the day. For if a vehicle of the mandated type were commercially available, thus eliminating application of the proviso, the need to sell vehicles to persons governed by the Rule would effectively coerce manufacturers into meeting the artificially created demand. To say, as the dissent does, that this would be merely the consequence of "market demand and free competition" is fanciful. The demand is a demand, not generated by the market but compelled by the Rules, which in turn effectively compels production. To think that the Rules are invalid until such time as one manufacturer makes a compliant vehicle available, whereupon they become binding, seems to us quite bizarre. . . .

Finally, the dissent says that we should "admit" that our opinion pre-empts voluntary incentive programs. Voluntary programs are not at issue in this case, and are significantly different from command-and-control regulation. Suffice it to say that nothing in the present opinion necessarily entails pre-emption of voluntary programs. It is at least arguable that the phrase "adopt or attempt to enforce any standard" refers only to standards that are enforceable—a possibility reinforced by the fact that the prohibition is imposed only on entities (States and political subdivisions) that have power to enforce. . . .

The judgment is vacated, and the case is remanded for further proceedings consistent with this opinion.

[Justice Souter's dissenting opinion is omitted.]

NOTES AND QUESTIONS

1. *Manufacturing Economies of Scale.* In *Engine Manufacturers*, the Court saw little difference between a standard requiring particular engine designs or performance, and state or local regulation limiting what sorts of vehicles can be purchased.

Given the Clean Air Act's goals and the frequent focus in preemption law on avoiding the imposition of impossible, conflicting requirements, how would you have argued for a contrary outcome? After you have studied the Clean Air Act in depth in later chapters, look again at *Engine Manufacturers*. Is the Court's ruling consistent with long-established law regarding divisions of federal, state, and local authority under the Clean Air Act?

2. *Textualism and Policy Repercussions.* Seven Justices joined the majority opinion, an opinion that focuses overwhelmingly on language, interrelated provisions, and dictionaries. First, is this outcome compelled by statutory language? Second, when one is facing a court or judge that tends to use textualist modes of interpretation, are there any means by which an attorney can bring policy repercussions and broader statutory goals into the argument without losing the textualist judge or Justice?

Many recent cases have dealt with various forms of product and risk regulation, often in connection with federal design or labeling requirements. Typically, the question is whether room is left for related state regulation or state common law claims over the design or safety of the product. Many of the laws giving rise to these cases contain both savings clauses and preemption clauses. These provisions do not, however, explicitly address the status of state common law liabilities. As a result of the tension between savings and preemptive provisions, and the failure explicitly to address common law liabilities, as well as the often substantial injuries that can flow from regulated products, this has become a fertile area of litigation. *Bates* is among the most recent cases dealing with these questions. As you will see in citations within the decision and in the following notes, this particular line of cases leaves a great deal of legal uncertainty for future similar cases.

BATES v. DOW AGROSCIENCES LLC
544 U.S. 431 (2005)

Justice STEVENS delivered the opinion of the Court.

[Petitioners contended that their peanut crops were damaged by the application of respondent's pesticide ("Strongarm"). Strongarm's label asserted that the pesticide would be safe for use "in all areas where peanuts are grown." The petitioners alleged fraud, breach of warranty, tort claims, as well as violations of the Texas Deceptive Trade Practices–Consumer Protection Act (DTPA). The question at issue in this case was whether the Federal Insecticide, Fungicide, and Rodenticide Act (FIFRA) preempted their state law claims.]

III.

Against this background, we consider whether petitioners' claims are pre-empted by §136v(b), which, again, reads as follows: "Such State shall not impose or continue in effect any requirements for labeling or packaging in addition to or different from those required under this subchapter."

The introductory words of §136v(b) — "Such State" — appear to limit the coverage of that subsection to the States that are described in the preceding subsection (a). Texas is such a State because it regulates the sale and use of federally registered pesticides and does not permit any sales or uses prohibited by FIFRA. It is therefore beyond dispute that subsection (b) is applicable to this case.

The prohibitions in §136v(b) apply only to "requirements." An occurrence that merely motivates an optional decision does not qualify as a requirement. The Court of Appeals was therefore quite wrong when it assumed that any event, such as a jury verdict, that might "induce" a pesticide manufacturer to change its label should be viewed as a requirement. The Court of Appeals did, however, correctly hold that the term "requirements" in §136v(b) reaches beyond positive enactments, such as statutes and regulations, to embrace common-law duties. Our decision in *Cipollone* supports this conclusion. See 505 U.S., at 521 (plurality opinion) ("The phrase '[n]o requirement or prohibition' sweeps broadly and suggests no distinction between positive enactments and common law; to the contrary, those words easily encompass obligations that take the form of common-law rules."); see also id., at 548-549 (Scalia, J., concurring in judgment in part and dissenting in part). While the use of "requirements" in a pre-emption clause may not invariably carry this meaning, we think this is the best reading of §136v(b).

That §136v(b) may pre-empt judge-made rules, as well as statutes and regulations, says nothing about the scope of that pre-emption. For a particular state rule to be pre-empted, it must satisfy two conditions. First, it must be a requirement "for labeling or packaging"; rules governing the design of a product, for example, are not pre-empted. Second, it must impose a labeling or packaging requirement that is "in addition to or different from those required under this subchapter." A state regulation requiring the word "poison" to appear in red letters, for instance, would not be pre-empted if an EPA regulation imposed the same requirement.

It is perfectly clear that many of the common-law rules upon which petitioners rely do not satisfy the first condition. Rules that require manufacturers to design reasonably safe products, to use due care in conducting appropriate testing of their products, to market products free of manufacturing defects, and to honor their express warranties or other contractual commitments plainly do not qualify as requirements for "labeling or packaging." None of these common-law rules requires that manufacturers label or package their products in any particular way. Thus, petitioners' claims for defective design, defective manufacture, negligent testing, and breach of express warranty are not pre-empted.

To be sure, Dow's express warranty was located on Strongarm's label. But a cause of action on an express warranty asks only that a manufacturer make good on the contractual commitment that it voluntarily undertook by placing that warranty on its product. Because this common-law rule does not require the manufacturer to make an express warranty, or in the event that the manufacturer elects to do so, to say anything in particular in that warranty, the rule does not impose a requirement "for labeling or packaging." See id., at 525-526 (plurality opinion).

In arriving at a different conclusion, the court below reasoned that a finding of liability on these claims would "induce Dow to alter [its] label." 332 F.3d, at 332. This effects-based test finds no support in the text of §136v(b), which speaks only of "requirements." A requirement is a rule of law that must be obeyed; an event, such as a jury verdict, that merely motivates an optional decision is not a requirement. The proper inquiry calls for an examination of the elements of the common-law duty at issue, see *Cipollone*, 505 U.S., at 524; it does not call for speculation as to whether a jury verdict will prompt the manufacturer to take any particular action (a question, in any event, that will depend on a variety of cost/benefit calculations best left to the manufacturer's accountants).

The inducement test is unquestionably overbroad because it would impeach many "genuine" design defect claims that Dow concedes are not pre-empted. A design defect claim, if successful, would surely induce a manufacturer to alter its label to reflect a change in the list of ingredients or a change in the instructions for use necessitated by the improvement in the product's design. Moreover, the inducement test is not entirely consistent with §136v(a), which confirms the State's broad authority to regulate the sale and use of pesticides. Under §136v(a), a state agency may ban the sale of a pesticide if it finds, for instance, that one of the pesticide's label-approved uses is unsafe. This ban might well induce the manufacturer to change its label to warn against this questioned use. Under the inducement test, however, such a restriction would anomalously qualify as a "labeling" requirement. It is highly unlikely that Congress endeavored to draw a line between the type of indirect pressure caused by a State's power to impose sales and use restrictions and the even more attenuated pressure exerted by common-law suits. The inducement test is not supported by either the text or the structure of the statute.

Unlike their other claims, petitioners' fraud and negligent-failure-to-warn claims are premised on common-law rules that qualify as "requirements for labeling or packaging." These rules set a standard for a product's labeling that the Strongarm label is alleged to have violated by containing false statements and inadequate warnings. While the courts of appeal have rightly found guidance in *Cipollone*'s interpretation of "requirements," some of those courts too quickly concluded that failure-to-warn claims were pre-empted under FIFRA, as they were in *Cipollone*, without paying attention to the rather obvious textual differences between the two pre-emption clauses.

Unlike the pre-emption clause at issue in *Cipollone*, §136v(b) prohibits only state-law labeling and packaging requirements that are "in addition to or different from" the labeling and packaging requirements under FIFRA. Thus, a state-law labeling requirement is not pre-empted by §136v(b) if it is equivalent to, and fully consistent with, FIFRA's misbranding provisions. Petitioners argue that their claims based on fraud and failure-to-warn are not pre-empted because these common-law duties are equivalent to FIFRA's requirements that a pesticide label not contain "false or misleading" statements, §136(q)(1)(A), or inadequate instructions or warnings. §§136(q)(1)(F), (G). We agree with petitioners insofar as we hold that state law need not explicitly incorporate FIFRA's standards as an element of a cause of action in order to survive pre-emption. As we will discuss below, however, we leave it to the Court of Appeals to decide in the first instance whether these particular common-law duties are equivalent to FIFRA's misbranding standards.

The "parallel requirements" reading of §136v(b) that we adopt today finds strong support in Medtronic, Inc. v. Lohr, 518 U.S. 470 (1996). In addressing a similarly worded pre-emption provision in a statute regulating medical devices, we found that "[n]othing in [21 U.S.C.] §360k denies Florida the right to provide a traditional damages remedy for violations of common-law duties when those duties parallel federal requirements." Id., at 495. As Justice O'Connor explained in her separate opinion, a state cause of action that seeks to enforce a federal requirement "does not impose a requirement that is 'different from, or in addition to,' requirements under federal law. To be sure, the threat of a damages remedy will give manufacturers an additional cause to comply, but the requirements imposed on them under state and federal law do not differ. Section 360k does not preclude States from imposing different or additional remedies, but only different or additional requirements." Id., at 513 (opinion concurring in part and dissenting in part). Accordingly, although FIFRA does not provide a federal remedy to farmers and others who are injured as a result of a manufacturer's violation of FIFRA's labeling requirements, nothing in §136v(b) precludes States from providing such a remedy.

Dow, joined by the United States as amicus curiae, argues that the "parallel requirements" reading of §136v(b) would "give juries in 50 States the authority to give content to FIFRA's misbranding prohibition, establishing a crazy-quilt of anti-misbranding requirements different from the one defined by FIFRA itself and intended by Congress to be interpreted authoritatively by EPA." Brief for Respondent 16. In our view, however, the clear text of §136v(b) and the authority of *Medtronic* cannot be so easily avoided. Conspicuously absent from the submissions by Dow and the United States is any plausible alternative interpretation of "in addition to or different from" that would give that phrase meaning. Instead, they appear to favor reading those words out of the statute, which would leave the following: "Such State shall not impose or continue in effect any requirements for labeling or packaging." This amputated version of §136v(b) would no doubt have clearly and succinctly commanded the pre-emption of all state requirements concerning labeling. That Congress added the remainder of the provision is evidence of its intent to draw a distinction between state labeling requirements that are pre-empted and those that are not.

Even if Dow had offered us a plausible alternative reading of §136v(b)—indeed, even if its alternative were just as plausible as our reading of that text—we would nevertheless have a duty to accept the reading that disfavors pre-emption. "[B]ecause the States are independent sovereigns in our federal system, we have long presumed that Congress does not cavalierly pre-empt state-law causes of action." *Medtronic*, 518 U.S., at 485. In areas of traditional state regulation, we assume that a federal statute has not supplanted state law unless Congress has made such an intention " 'clear and manifest.' " New York State Conf. of Blue Cross & Blue Shield Plans v. Travelers Ins. Co., 514 U.S. 645, 655 (1995) (quoting Rice v. Santa Fe Elevator Corp., 331 U.S. 218, 230 (1947)); see also *Medtronic*, 518 U.S., at 485. Our reading is at once the only one that makes sense of each phrase in §136v(b) and the one favored by our canons of interpretation. The notion that FIFRA contains a nonambiguous command to pre-empt the types of tort claims that parallel FIFRA's misbranding requirements is particularly dubious given that just five years ago the United States advocated the interpretation that we adopt today.

The long history of tort litigation against manufacturers of poisonous substances adds force to the basic presumption against pre-emption. If Congress had intended to deprive injured parties of a long available form of compensation, it surely would have expressed that intent more clearly. See Silkwood v. Kerr-McGee Corp., 464 U.S. 238, 251 (1984). Moreover, this history emphasizes the importance of providing an incentive to manufacturers to use the utmost care in the business of distributing inherently dangerous items. See *Mortier*, 501 U.S., at 613 (stating that the 1972 amendments' goal was to "strengthen existing labeling requirements and ensure that these requirements were followed in practice"). Particularly given that Congress amended FIFRA to allow EPA to waive efficacy review of newly registered pesticides (and in the course of those amendments made technical changes to §136v(b)), it seems unlikely that Congress considered a relatively obscure provision like §136v(b) to give pesticide manufacturers virtual immunity from certain forms of tort liability. Overenforcement of FIFRA's misbranding prohibition creates a risk of imposing unnecessary financial burdens on manufacturers; under-enforcement creates not only financial risks for consumers, but risks that affect their safety and the environment as well.

Finally, we find the policy objections raised against our reading of §136v(b) to be unpersuasive. . . .

In sum, under our interpretation, §136v(b) retains a narrow, but still important, role. In the main, it pre-empts competing state labeling standards—imagine 50 different labeling regimes prescribing the color, font size, and wording of warnings—that would create significant inefficiencies for manufacturers. The provision also pre-empts any statutory or common-law rule that would impose a labeling requirement that diverges from those set out in FIFRA and its implementing regulations. It does not, however, pre-empt any state rules that are fully consistent with federal requirements.

Having settled on our interpretation of §136v(b), it still remains to be decided whether that provision pre-empts petitioners' fraud and failure-to-warn claims. Because we have not received sufficient briefing on this issue, which involves questions of Texas law, we remand it to the Court of Appeals. We emphasize that a state-law labeling requirement must in fact be equivalent to a requirement under FIFRA in order to survive pre-emption. For example, were the Court of Appeals to determine that the element of falsity in Texas' common-law definition of fraud imposed a broader obligation than FIFRA's requirement that labels not contain "false or misleading statements," that state-law cause of action would be pre-empted by §136v(b) to the extent of that difference. State-law requirements must also be measured against any relevant EPA regulations that give content to FIFRA's misbranding standards. For example, a failure-to-warn claim alleging that a given pesticide's label should have stated "DANGER" instead of the more subdued "CAUTION" would be pre-empted because it is inconsistent with 40 CFR §156.64 (2004), which specifically assigns these warnings to particular classes of pesticides based on their toxicity.

In undertaking a pre-emption analysis at the pleadings stage of a case, a court should bear in mind the concept of equivalence. To survive pre-emption, the state-law requirement need not be phrased in the identical language as its corresponding FIFRA requirement; indeed, it would be surprising if a common-law requirement used the same phraseology as FIFRA. If a case proceeds to trial, the court's jury instructions must ensure that nominally equivalent labeling requirements are genuinely equivalent. If a defendant so requests, a court should instruct the jury on the relevant FIFRA misbranding standards, as well as any regulations that add content to those standards. For a manufacturer should not be held liable under a state labeling requirement subject to §136v(b) unless the manufacturer is also liable for misbranding as defined by FIFRA.

The judgment of the Court of Appeals is vacated, and the case is remanded for further proceedings consistent with this opinion.

NOTES

1. Bates *and Earlier Pro-Preemption Cases.* Bates upholds the validity of the challenged state common law actions, but the Court's preemption jurisprudence has been far from a model of consistency or clarity. As is evident in the *Bates* Court's

distinguishing of *Medtronic* and other cases, it has sometimes been willing broadly to preempt state law claims. See, e.g., Geier v. American Honda Motor Co., 529 U.S. 861 (2000) (narrowly construing a savings clause and finding that National Traffic and Motor Vehicle Safety Act of 1966 preempted a design defect state tort claim). For a thorough canvassing of recent cases involving preemption claims in the setting of risk, pesticide, and product safety, see Vladeck, Preemption and Regulatory Failure, 33 Pepp. L. Rev. 95 (2005).

   2. *And the Court Returns to a Strong Preemptive Approach.* In Riegel v. Medtronic, 552 U.S. 312 (2008), the Court again encountered similar preemption issues, although this time in a non–environmental law case deciding what kind of preemptive effect to give to language in the Medical Device Amendments of 1976. As in *Bates*, "requirement" language proved critical, although in a regulatory regime requiring far more advance premarket review and postmarketing reporting by manufacturers of a medical device causing injury. The question was whether state common law liabilities for injuries caused by a Food and Drug Administration (FDA)-approved device constituted preempted "requirements." Emphasizing the rigor of the pre-sale review and post-sale disclosure obligations imposed on manufacturers, and emphasizing language in *Cipollone* while barely noting contrary language in *Bates*, the Court concluded that common law liabilities were preempted. It included broad language, stating that "[a]bsent other indication, reference to a State's 'requirements' includes its common-law duties." In contrast to *Bates*, the Court stated that the incentives created by common law liabilities "disrupt[] the federal scheme no less than state regulatory law to the same effect." The Court also expressed concern with trusting a jury, stating a jury "sees only the cost of a more dangerous design, and is not concerned with its benefits; the patients who reaped those benefits are not represented in court." The Court noted that its conclusions were aligned with those advocated by the Bush administration FDA, which for several years pushed an aggressive view of its own preemptive authority. The Court declined to resolve the ongoing question of whether agency preemption views deserve ordinary sorts of judicial deference. Standards of review for judicial review of agency action are covered in Chapter 3.

   3. *The Supreme Court's Ongoing Preemption Vacillations.* The tensions between *Riegel* and *Bates* were on display again in the much-awaited decision in Wyeth v. Levine, 555 U.S. 555 (2009), which involved arguments over the preemptive effect of federal drug label approvals on state common law failure-to-warn tort claims. The *Wyeth* Court distinguished *Riegel* due to the different underlying statutory language, and especially the absence of express language supporting a preemption claim by industry or a claim of preemptive power by the FDA. It denied arguments that state common law should be found preempted, rejecting both conflict preemption arguments rooted in a claim of "impossibility" preemption and arguments rooted in obstacle preemption jurisprudence. Critical to the outcome was the Court's close parsing of the FDA's previous long-standing view that federal drug label approvals did not preempt common law claims and the lack of evidence that state common law really was posing an obstacle to federal ends. The FDA had supported industry's preemption claim in its own supporting briefs and in a 2006 regulatory preamble. In that 2006 preamble, the FDA for the first time articulated the argument that its label approvals should preempt state common law claims. The Court acknowledged that agency action can provide the basis for a federal preemption outcome, but distinguished that result from the question of the court's deference to "an agency's *conclusion* that state law is pre-empted." Id. at 576. Despite acknowledging that agencies

have a "unique understanding" of statutes they administer, the Court concluded the FDA's views in its regulatory preamble and brief did not "merit deference." The Court explained this lack of deference by noting that there was no express grant of agency preemptive power, that the agency declared its claim of preemptive impact without any advance notice and opportunity for comment, and that there was no convincing record establishing the existence of a conflict as there were in earlier cases upholding obstacle preemption claims. The Court went further in tracing the rationale for the long-standing previous anti-preemption view of the FDA, including the argument that state law works as a "complementary form" of regulation, creates incentives for industry's rapid disclosure of risks, and can complement the FDA's statutory role. The Court noted that the FDA has often been found to lack necessary resources and in 2006 may have acted in ways sympathetic to industry due to pressure from political appointees, despite contrary forceful views of career staff. Id. at 578 & n.11. The Court concluded that the FDA's new pro-preemption view was "entitled to no weight." Id. at 581. For analysis of *Riegel* and standards of judicial review to apply to agency claims of preemptive power, including arguments that fact- and policy-based assertions claimed to justify agency preemption should be subjected to "hard look review" by courts, see Buzbee, Preemption Hard Look Review, Regulatory Interaction, and the Quest for Stewardship and Intergenerational Equity, 77 Geo. Wash. L. Rev. 1521 (2009); Sharkey, Federalism Accountability: Agency-Forcing Measures, 58 Duke L.J. 2125 (2009).

For a recent book tracing preemption battles and developments in agencies and the courts, especially during the second term of the Bush administration, see T. McGarity, The Preemption War: When Federal Bureaucracies Trump Local Juries (2008).

4. Environmental Preemption in the Courts. The growing body of preemption jurisprudence from the Supreme Court has unsurprisingly generated preemption-based litigation in the lower courts, plus one recent Supreme Court decision. Several recent lower court decisions have, like *Engine Manufacturers*, adopted fairly expansive preemptive interpretations of federal law, mostly under "obstacle" preemption theory.

a. Recent Comprehensive Environmental Response Compensation and Liability Act (CERCLA) Challenges. In CTS Corp. v. Waldburger, 134 S. Ct. 2175 (2014), the Court dealt with somewhat technical language and a history-heavy question: Did CERCLA preempt a North Carolina "statute of repose" due to CERCLA's language in 42 U.S.C. §9658 adopting a federal "discovery rule" and preempting contrary state statutes of limitations? The Court, in an opinion by Justice Kennedy, concluded it did not, finding statutes of limitations and repose to be distinct, due in substantial part to language usage in an underlying legislatively mandated report about the adequacy of existing common law and statutory remedies for hazardous substance release harms. That report, the Court appears to have concluded, influenced the language in subsequently amended CERCLA §9658. Finding the question close, Justice Kennedy, joined by only two other Justices, wrote that the Court's decision should also be influenced by the presumption against preemption, stating that where there is more than one "plausible reading," courts disfavor the preemptive interpretation, especially when Congress has legislated in an area, such as torts, traditionally "governed by the States' police powers." The Court thereby allowed North Carolina law to block a damage action brought 24 years after a property sale where the property contained stored contaminants. The decision provoked a separate concurring opinion by Justice

Scalia and three other Justices calling for resolution of the question without reliance on the presumption against preemption. Justices Ginsburg and Breyer dissented.

While CERCLA was not intended to be the exclusive source of compensation for injury caused by hazardous substances, recent state law claims have been found preempted. In Niagara Mohawk Power Corp. v. Chevron U.S.A., Inc., 596 F.3d 112 (2d Cir. 2010), a responsible party's state contribution, indemnification, and unjust enrichment claims for cleanup expenses were held preempted by CERCLA under the logic that CERCLA was meant to "avoid the possibility of fifty different state statutory schemes" regulating the "duties and obligations" of non-settling potentially liable parties under federal law; CERCLA was held "to provide the only contribution avenue for parties with response costs incurred under CERCLA." Id. at 138.

b. *Clean Air Act Preemption of Trading Restrictions.* The Second Circuit held that state efforts to preclude sales of federally created tradable pollution allowances to upwind states, where pollution would blow back into New York, were preempted by the CAA. Clean Air Mkts. Group v. Pataki, 338 F.3d 82 (2d Cir. 2003). Such trades were allowable under the CAA, plus federal regulations stated that states "shall not restrict or interfere with allowance trading." The court concluded that the state law "creat[ed] an obstacle to the accomplishment and execution of the full purpose and objectives of Congress." Id. at 87.

c. *Green Building and Urban Air Quality Efforts Meet the Preemptive Power of the Energy Policy and Conservation Act (EPCA).* Despite a long tradition of building code regulation as the province of state and local governments, local attempts to increase energy efficiency have sometimes been found preempted as conflicting with EPCA's express preemption provision, prohibiting state or local regulations "concerning energy efficiency . . . of any covered products." 1987 amendments to EPCA created a multi-factored carveout from preemption for state and local building codes aimed at improving energy efficiency. Although EPCA does not regulate homes as products, it does regulate heating and air conditioning (HVAC) systems. The City of Albuquerque could not impose overall efficiency requirements for homes that the court concluded effectively required the installation of HVAC products with efficiencies greater than the federal standard. See Air Conditioning, Heating and Refrigeration Inst. v. City of Albuquerque, 2008 WL 5586316, at *1 (D.N.M. Oct. 3, 2008). However, a Washington State law that appeared much like the Albuquerque law was upheld, with the court finding the Washington law did not impose prohibited conflicting "requirements," but (relying heavily on *Bates, supra*) created "incentives" and offered several compliant "options" other than installation of HVAC systems exceeding federal standards. Building Indus. Ass'n of Washington v. Washington State Bldg. Code Council, 683 F.3d 1144 (9th Cir. 2012).

A New York City rule requiring new taxicabs to meet a minimum miles-per-gallon rating was preempted under EPCA, which expressly preempts state or local actions "related to fuel economy standards." Metro. Taxicab Bd. of Trade v. City of New York, 2008 WL 4866021 (S.D.N.Y. Oct. 31, 2008). New York City's second attempt to avoid EPCA's preemptive effect by passing regulations that created incentives for fleet owners to purchase hybrid taxicabs also failed under EPCA. See Metro. Taxicab Bd. of Trade v. City of New York, 633 F. Supp. 2d 83, 105-106 (S.D.N.Y. 2009) (finding regulations were de facto mandates that related to fuel economy standards, and also finding preemption based on the CAA), *aff'd*, 615 F.3d 152 (2d Cir. 2010) (agreeing with preemption conclusion under EPCA and upholding preliminary injunction against city); see also Ophir v. City of Boston, 647 F. Supp. 2d 86 (D. Mass. 2009) (holding Boston ordinance requiring hybrid taxicabs was "related to" fuel economy standards and thus preempted under EPCA's preemption provision even though the ordinance did not include a specific miles-per-gallon standard). However, some state actions relating to EPCA fuel economy standards have been held permissible. See, e.g., Paduano v. American Honda Motor Co. Inc., 169 Cal. App. 4th 1453 (Cal. Dist. Ct. App. 2009) (allowing state false-advertising claims relating to fuel efficiency standards).

4.   *Preemption by Agency Declaration*

In *Engine Manufacturers* and *Bates*, the Court worked primarily with arguments made in briefs, as well as with close parsing of statutory language and structure. As evident in the discussion in notes 2 and 3 above regarding *Riegel* and *Wyeth*, around the spring of 2006 numerous federal agencies started articulating a new and aggressive view of their own preemptive authority. Most regulatory scholars and journalists assumed that this simultaneous assertion of strong preemptive authority represented a concerted new legal view of the Bush administration, not mere coincidence. Sometimes these views were articulated in briefs, but they also at times were asserted in the Federal Register, often in preamble statements that followed the give-and-take of notice and comment rulemaking, but were not themselves subject to public opportunities for comment. Several of these preemption claims included claimed authority to preempt state common law liabilities that could arise out of harms from products subject to federal agency regulatory approvals.

This sort of "preambular preemption" was unusual. First, the mode of declaration—in Federal Register regulatory preambles (that is, in explanatory regulatory materials typically in the Federal Register)—was unusual in form, especially following little or no advance notice of the intent to make such a declaration. These declarations also appeared to follow no process of the sort anticipated by Executive Order 13,132, 64 Fed. Reg. 43,255 (1999), which calls on agencies to engage in consultation with affected states before preempting state regulation. Finally, the few somewhat similar Federal Register declarations regarding preemption have, under earlier presidential administrations, tended to declare an intent to preserve, not preempt, state regulation or common law. These actions engendered criticism, and were part of the backdrop to and ruling in *Wyeth*, discussed above in note 3. See Buzbee, Asymmetrical Regulation, *supra*, at 1552-1554; Sharkey, Preemption by Preamble: Federal Agencies and the Federalization of Tort Law, 56 DePaul L. Rev. 227 (2007); Vladeck, *supra*, at 122-126.

In the early months of his administration, President Obama issued a Presidential Memorandum for the Heads of Executive Departments and Agencies, 74 Fed. Reg. 24,693 (May 22, 2009). He articulated a general policy against agency preemption of state law, and directed that claims of preemption should "be undertaken only with full consideration of the legitimate prerogatives of the States and with a sufficient legal basis for preemption." He directed departments and agencies not to declare preemptive effect in regulatory preambles unless preemptive provisions were in the codified regulation itself. He also required departments and agencies to review the previous ten years of regulatory actions for any claims of preemptive power and effect. As evident in these seesawing policy changes regarding regulatory preemption power, agency authority to assert preemptive effect remains contested. The following notes and questions illuminate related questions.

NOTES AND QUESTIONS

1. *Deference and Federalism Rationales.* The recent actions cited above raise a variety of issues. Should agency declarations in briefs or regulatory preambles receive deference? What kind of deference? After reading the excerpts in Chapter 3 of key cases articulating how courts should review agency action, consider which cases should apply in this setting. Should often-declared presumptions against preemption apply here, or should agencies receive some sort of deference when they declare their views on the preemptive impact of a law or regulation? Finally, think through basic federalism rationales and consider arguments for and against such preemption declarations. For a discussion of how preemption presumptions apply when an agency interprets a statute to have a preemptive effect, see Mendelson, A Presumption Against Agency Preemption, 102 Nw. U. L. Rev. 695 (2008); Mendelson, *Chevron* and Preemption, 102 Mich. L. Rev. 737 (2004); Sharkey, Products Liability Preemption: An Institutional Approach, 76 Geo. Wash. L. Rev. 449 (2008). And how should the policy and factual claims underpinning an agency's claim of preemptive power and effect be reviewed? See Buzbee, Preemption Hard Look Review, *supra*; Sharkey, Federalism Accountability, *supra*. See also Galle & Seidenfeld, Administrative Law's Federalism: Preemption, Delegation, and Agencies at the Edge of Federal Power, 57 Duke L.J. 1933 (2008) (analyzing the relative merits of preemption by legislative versus agency action and also discussing frameworks to review preemption claims); Young, Executive Preemption, 102 Nw. U. L. Rev. 869 (2008) (also exploring agency claims of preemptive power, but with focus on constitutional law's lessons for how such claims should be reviewed).

2. *Agency Inertia, Regulatory Failure, and Broad Preemption Declarations.* If agencies consistently had abundant resources and implementation and enforcement zeal, broad preemption might pose little problem. Professor David Vladeck and other observers of risk and environmental regulation find that budgetary limitations, political pressures, interest group influence, and ideological leanings all can result in agency failure to act. See Vladeck, Preemption and Regulatory Failure Risks, in Preemption Choice, *supra*, at 54-77. If inaction is a pervasive problem, and regulatory action by others is preempted, then regulatory accomplishment may fall far short of statutory aspirations. As discussed below in note 3, broad preemption declarations also can leave citizens unprotected. Supporters of these declarations, however, see the elimination of legal uncertainty created by additional potential state law liabilities as a means to facilitate commerce. As the Consumer Products Safety Commission explained in 2006 about its mattress flammability regulation, "[s]tate requirements . . . have the potential to undercut the Commission's uniform national flammability standard, create impediments for manufacturers . . . , establish requirements that make dual state and federal compliance physically impossible, and cause confusion among consumers. . . ." 16 C.F.R. Part 1633, Section N, discussed and quoted in 71 Fed. Reg. 13,471, 13,496-13,497 (2006).

3. *Rights Without Remedies? And Damages?* Where citizens have been harmed by a product, perhaps in violation of federal regulatory requirements or perhaps as a result of some other product problem not addressed by regulation, citizens will often

seek common law damages relief. Most regulatory statutes, and almost all environmental laws, provide no such damages remedy. If agency preemption declarations regarding state law and state common law liabilities are given broad effect, then injured citizens may be left with no remedy, even in the face of underlying legal violations. As Professor Sharkey observes in her DePaul Law Review article, *supra*, the Supreme Court has made it quite clear that implied causes of action will rarely be recognized. See Alexander v. Sandoval, 532 U.S. 275 (2001). Because many laws regarding product safety and labeling do not contain "citizen suit" provisions, as do most environmental laws directed at pollution or protection of natural resources, as opposed to products like pesticides, this combination of agency declarations and Court precedent threatens to leave citizens and states (which are granted rights commensurate with those of other people) with no statutory or common law remedies for legal violations causing harms.

4. *Greenhouse Gases and State Power, in the Absence of Federal Climate Legislation.* During a period of federal regulatory and legislative inaction regarding climate change, numerous states, municipalities, and even multi-state regions stepped into the void and began regulating large greenhouse gas emitters, set up their own "cap-and-trade" schemes to reduce emissions but allow trading of pollution rights, and initiated numerous "green economy" measures to reduce energy consumption and related pollution. For reflections on these efforts and their prospects, see Carlson, Federalism, Preemption, and Greenhouse Gas Emissions, 37 U.C. Davis L. Rev. 281 (2003); Engel, Who's Afraid of Overlapping Federal and State Jurisdiction?: Harnessing the Benefits of Dynamic Federalism in Environmental Law, 56 Emory L.J. 159 (2006); Kysar & Meyler, Like a Nation State, 55 UCLA L. Rev. 1621 (2008); Glicksman & Levy, A Collective Action Perspective on Ceiling Preemption by Federal Environmental Regulation: The Case of Global Climate Change, 102 Nw. U. L. Rev. 579 (2008). A few recent decisions have addressed federal constitutional challenges to such state efforts. One is excerpted below in section F, and further related discussion is in Chapter 12's coverage of climate change law.

5. *Federal Climate Change Legislation and the Preemption Question.* During 2009 and 2010, the battle lines over federal climate change legislation were becoming clear. Recently elected President Obama strongly stated his support for federal climate and energy legislation, but did not champion his own bill or demand that such legislation contain particular provisions. Representatives Waxman and Markey introduced a comprehensive bill, as did Senators Kerry and Lieberman, along with numerous other legislators with less comprehensive bills. Key legislative provisions and legislative dividing lines are discussed *infra* in Chapter 12's coverage of climate change. A major issue both before and after these bills were released was how they would handle federalism issues. Given state, local, and regional measures to address climate change that are already up and running, the question of ongoing state authority is a substantial one. With slightly different language, the leading, most comprehensive bills would have preempted state and regional cap-and-trade regimes for six years, but otherwise preserve state and local power to take other steps to regulate greenhouse gas emissions. Chapter 12, discussing climate change law and policy, delves more deeply into these questions. For a sampling of the growing body of scholarship analyzing federalism and often preemption issues with a substantial focus on climate change legislation and regulation, see pages 1208-10 and note a on 1209, and accompanying text discussion.

F. DORMANT COMMERCE CLAUSE LIMITATIONS ON STATE REGULATION

As noted in virtually all constitutional law classes, state regulatory activity can be blocked by arguments rooted in dormant Commerce Clause doctrine. It is also sometimes called the "negative Commerce Clause." Most Supreme Court dormant Commerce Clause cases in recent years arise from state or municipal efforts to control and handle waste, especially efforts to ensure the existence of markets adequate to finance local waste-handling facilities. The problem occurs when one jurisdiction's efforts have the effect of precluding interstate commerce, by limiting the movement of goods either into or out of the jurisdiction, or perhaps by creating what is in effect extraterritorial regulation. Such efforts do not require federal law or regulations to create an express conflict. Instead, it is a court's finding of a prohibited form of regulation or an undue burden on interstate commerce that leads to invalidation on dormant Commerce Clause grounds. Thus, federalism concerns do not just cut against federal power, or arise only when federal statutes or regulations come into conflict with state law. State and local activities can be struck down as unconstitutional based solely on court determinations about their adverse impact on interstate commerce.

The case excerpts that follow show the power of dormant Commerce Clause claims, as well as several of the common factors arising in such cases. The first case concerns state regulation of waste. The second case links to efforts to deal with fuel and transportation–related pollution. California's efforts to incentivize use of fuels and fuel-linked transportation modes that would result in low greenhouse gas emissions to reduce climate impacts were challenged under several prongs of dormant Commerce Clause jurisdiction.

UNITED HAULERS ASSOCIATION, INC. v. ONEIDA-HERKIMER SOLID WASTE MANAGEMENT AUTHORITY
550 U.S. 330 (2007)

ROBERTS, C.J., delivered the opinion of the Court, except as to Part II-D. SOUTER, GINSBURG, and BREYER, JJ., joined that opinion in full. SCALIA, J., filed an opinion concurring as to Parts I and II-A through II-C. THOMAS, J., filed an opinion concurring in the judgment. ALITO, J., filed a dissenting opinion, in which STEVENS and KENNEDY, JJ., joined.

"Flow control" ordinances require trash haulers to deliver solid waste to a particular waste processing facility. In C & A Carbone, Inc. v. Clarkstown, 511 U.S. 383 (1994), this Court struck down under the Commerce Clause a flow control ordinance that forced haulers to deliver waste to a particular *private* processing facility. In this case, we face flow control ordinances quite similar to the one invalidated in *Carbone*. The only salient difference is that the laws at issue here require haulers to bring waste to facilities owned and operated by a state-created public benefit corporation. We find this difference constitutionally significant. Disposing of trash has been a traditional government activity for years, and laws that favor the government in such areas—but treat every private business, whether in-state or out-of-state, exactly the same—do not discriminate against interstate commerce for purposes of the Commerce Clause. Applying the Commerce Clause test reserved for regulations that do not discriminate against interstate commerce, we uphold these ordinances because any incidental burden they may have on interstate commerce does not outweigh the benefits they confer on the citizens of Oneida and Herkimer Counties.

I

[Oneida and Herkimer Counties in New York contain about 306,000 residents.] By the 1980's, the Counties confronted what they could credibly call a solid waste "crisis." Many local landfills were operating without permits and in violation of state regulations. Sixteen were ordered to close and remediate the surrounding environment, costing the public tens of millions of dollars. These environmental problems culminated in a federal clean-up action against a landfill in Oneida County; the defendants in that case named over 600 local businesses and several municipalities and school districts as third-party defendants.

The "crisis" extended beyond health and safety concerns. The Counties had an uneasy relationship with local waste management companies, enduring price fixing, pervasive overcharging, and the influence of organized crime. Dramatic price hikes were not uncommon. . . .

Responding to these problems, the [state legislature] created the Oneida-Herkimer Solid Waste Management Authority (Authority), a public benefit corporation. The Authority is empowered to collect, process, and dispose of solid waste generated in the Counties. To further the Authority's governmental and public purposes, the Counties may impose "appropriate and reasonable limitations on competition" by, for instance, adopting "local laws requiring that all solid waste . . . be delivered to a specified solid waste management-resource recovery facility."

In 1989, the Authority and the Counties entered into a Solid Waste Management Agreement, under which the Authority agreed to manage all solid waste within the Counties. Private haulers would remain free to pick up citizens' trash from the curb, but the Authority would take over the job of processing the trash, sorting it, and sending it off for disposal. To fulfill its part of the bargain, the Authority agreed to purchase and develop facilities for the processing and disposal of solid waste and recyclables generated in the Counties.

The Authority collected "tipping fees" to cover its operating and maintenance costs for these facilities.[1] The tipping fees significantly exceeded those charged for waste removal on the open market, but they allowed the Authority to do more than the average private waste disposer. In addition to landfill transportation and solid waste disposal, the fees enabled the Authority to provide recycling of 33 kinds of materials, as well as composting, household hazardous waste disposal, and a number of other services. If the Authority's operating costs and debt service were not recouped through tipping fees and other charges, the agreement provided that the Counties would make up the difference.

1. Tipping fees are disposal charges levied against collectors who drop off waste at a processing facility. They are called "tipping" fees because garbage trucks literally tip their back end to dump out the carried waste. . . .

As described, the agreement had a flaw: Citizens might opt to have their waste hauled to facilities with lower tipping fees. To avoid being stuck with the bill for facilities that citizens voted for but then chose not to use, the Counties enacted "flow control" ordinances requiring that all solid waste generated within the Counties be delivered to the Authority's processing sites. Private haulers must obtain a permit from the Authority to collect waste in the Counties. Penalties for noncompliance with the ordinances include permit revocation, fines, and imprisonment.

Petitioners are United Haulers Association, Inc., a trade association made up of solid waste management companies, and six haulers that operated in Oneida and Herkimer Counties when this action was filed. In 1995, they sued the Counties and the Authority under 42 U.S.C. §1983, alleging that the flow control laws violate the Commerce Clause by discriminating against interstate commerce. They submitted evidence that without the flow control laws and the associated $86-per-ton tipping fees, they could dispose of solid waste at out-of-state facilities for between $37 and $55 per ton, including transportation. . . .

II

A

The Commerce Clause provides that "Congress shall have Power . . . [t]o regulate Commerce with foreign Nations, and among the several States." U.S. Const., Art. I, §8, cl. 3. Although the Constitution does not in terms limit the power of States to regulate commerce, we have long interpreted the Commerce Clause as an implicit restraint on state authority, even in the absence of a conflicting federal statute.

To determine whether a law violates this so-called "dormant" aspect of the Commerce Clause, we first ask whether it discriminates on its face against interstate commerce. Fort Gratiot Sanitary Landfill, Inc. v. Michigan Dept. of Natural Resources, 504 U.S. 353, 359 (1992). In this context, "'discrimination' simply means differential treatment of in-state and out-of-state economic interests that benefits the former and burdens the latter." Oregon Waste Systems, Inc. v. Department of Environmental Quality of Ore., 511 U.S. 93, 99 (1994). Discriminatory laws motivated by "simple economic protectionism" are subject to a "virtually per se rule of invalidity," Philadelphia v. New Jersey, 437 U.S. 617, 624 (1978), which can only be overcome by a showing that the State has no other means to advance a legitimate local purpose, Maine v. Taylor, 477 U.S. 131, 138 (1986).

B

. . . [T]he haulers argue vigorously that the Counties' ordinances discriminate against interstate commerce under Carbone. In Carbone, the town of Clarkstown, New York, hired a private contractor to build a waste transfer station. According to the terms of the deal, the contractor would operate the facility for five years, charging an above-market tipping fee of $81 per ton; after five years, the town would buy the facility for one dollar. The town guaranteed that the facility would receive a certain volume of trash per year. To make good on its promise, Clarkstown passed a flow control ordinance requiring that all nonhazardous solid waste within the town be deposited at the transfer facility.

This Court struck down the ordinance, holding that it discriminated against interstate commerce by "hoard[ing] solid waste, and the demand to get rid of it, for the benefit of the preferred processing facility." The dissent pointed out that all of this Court's local processing cases involved laws that discriminated in favor of private entities, not public ones. According to the dissent, Clarkstown's ostensibly private transfer station was "essentially a municipal facility," and this distinction should have saved Clarkstown's ordinance because favoring local government is by its nature different from favoring a particular private company. The majority did not comment on the dissent's public-private distinction.

The parties in this case draw opposite inferences from the majority's silence. The haulers say it proves that the majority agreed with the dissent's characterization of the facility, but thought there was no difference under the dormant Commerce Clause between laws favoring private entities and those favoring public ones. The Counties disagree, arguing that the majority studiously avoided the issue because the facility in *Carbone* was private, and therefore the question whether public facilities may be favored was not properly before the Court.

We believe the latter interpretation of *Carbone* is correct. As the Second Circuit explained, "in *Carbone* the Justices were divided over the *fact of whether* the favored facility was public or private, rather than on the import of that distinction." 261 F.3d, at 259 (emphasis in original).

The *Carbone* majority viewed Clarkstown's flow control ordinance as "just one more instance of local processing requirements that we long have held invalid." It then cited six local processing cases, every one of which involved discrimination in favor of private enterprise. . . .

The *Carbone* majority stated that "[t]he *only conceivable distinction*" between the laws in the local processing cases and Clarkstown's flow control ordinance was that Clarkstown's ordinance favored a single local business, rather than a group of them. 511 U.S., at 392 (emphasis added). If the Court thought Clarkstown's processing facility was public, that additional distinction was not merely "conceivable"—it was conceived, and discussed at length, by three Justices in dissent. *Carbone* cannot be regarded as having decided the public-private question.

C

The flow control ordinances in this case benefit a clearly public facility, while treating all private companies exactly the same. Because the question is now squarely presented on the facts of the case before us, we decide that such flow control ordinances do not discriminate against interstate commerce for purposes of the dormant Commerce Clause.

Compelling reasons justify treating these laws differently from laws favoring particular private businesses over their competitors. "Conceptually, of course, any notion of discrimination assumes a comparison of substantially similar entities." General Motors Corp. v. Tracy, 519 U.S. 278, 298 (1997). But States and municipalities are not private businesses—far from it. Unlike private enterprise, government is vested with the responsibility of protecting the health, safety, and welfare of its citizens.

Given these differences, it does not make sense to regard laws favoring local government and laws favoring private industry with equal skepticism. As our local processing cases demonstrate, when a law favors in-state business over out-of-state competition, rigorous scrutiny is appropriate because the law is often the product of "simple economic protectionism." Wyoming v. Oklahoma, 502 U.S. 437, 454 (1992); Philadelphia v. New Jersey, 437 U.S., at 626-627. Laws favoring local government, by contrast, may be directed toward any number of legitimate goals unrelated to protectionism. Here the flow control ordinances enable the Counties to pursue particular policies with respect to the handling and treatment of waste generated in the Counties, while allocating the costs of those policies on citizens and businesses according to the volume of waste they generate.

The contrary approach of treating public and private entities the same under the dormant Commerce Clause would lead to unprecedented and unbounded interference by the courts with state and local government. The dormant Commerce Clause is not a roving license for federal courts to decide what activities are appropriate for state and local government to undertake, and what activities must be the province of private market competition. In this case, the citizens of Oneida and Herkimer Counties have chosen the government to provide waste management services, with a limited role for the private sector in arranging for transport of waste from the curb to the public facilities. The citizens could have left the entire matter for the private sector, in which case any regulation they undertook could not discriminate against interstate commerce. But it was also open to them to vest responsibility for the matter with their government, and to adopt flow control ordinances to support the government effort. It is not the office of the Commerce Clause to control the decision of the voters on whether government or the private sector should provide waste management services. "The Commerce Clause significantly limits the ability of States and localities to regulate or otherwise burden the flow of interstate commerce, but it does not elevate free trade above all other values." Maine v. Taylor, 477 U.S., at 151.

We should be particularly hesitant to interfere with the Counties' efforts under the guise of the Commerce Clause because "[w]aste disposal is both typically and traditionally a local government function." 261 F.3d, at 264 (case below) (Calabresi, J., concurring). Congress itself has recognized local government's vital role in waste management, making clear that "collection and disposal of solid wastes should continue to be primarily the function of State, regional, and local agencies." Resource Conservation and Recovery Act of 1976, 42 U.S.C. §6901(a)(4). The policy of the State of New York favors "displac[ing] competition with regulation or monopoly control" in this area. N.Y. Pub. Auth. Law Ann. §2049-tt(3). We may or may not agree with that approach, but nothing in the Commerce Clause vests the responsibility for that policy judgment with the Federal Judiciary.

Finally, it bears mentioning that the most palpable harm imposed by the ordinances—more expensive trash removal—is likely to fall upon the very people who voted for the laws. Our dormant Commerce Clause cases often find discrimination when a State shifts the costs of regulation to other States, because when "the burden of state regulation falls on interests outside the state, it is unlikely to be alleviated by the operation of those political restraints normally exerted when interests within the state are affected." Southern Pacific Co. v. Arizona ex rel. Sullivan, 325 U.S. 761, 767-768, n.2 (1945). Here, the citizens and businesses of the Counties bear the costs of the ordinances. There is no reason to step in and hand local businesses a victory they could not obtain through the political process.

We hold that the Counties' flow control ordinances, which treat in-state private business interests exactly the same as out-of-state ones, do not "discriminate against interstate commerce" for purposes of the dormant Commerce Clause.

D

The Counties' flow control ordinances are properly analyzed under the test set forth in Pike v. Bruce Church, Inc., 397 U.S. 137, 142 (1970), which is reserved for laws "directed to legitimate local concerns, with effects upon interstate commerce that are only incidental." Philadelphia v. New Jersey, 437 U.S., at 624. Under the *Pike* test, we will uphold a nondiscriminatory statute like this one "unless the burden imposed on [interstate] commerce is clearly excessive in relation to the putative local benefits." 397 U.S., at 142.

. . . We find it unnecessary to decide whether the ordinances impose any incidental burden on interstate commerce because any arguable burden does not exceed the public benefits of the ordinances.

The ordinances give the Counties a convenient and effective way to finance their integrated package of waste-disposal services. While "revenue generation is not a local interest that can justify *discrimination* against interstate commerce," *Carbone*, 511 U.S., at 393 (emphasis added), we think it is a cognizable benefit for purposes of the *Pike* test.

At the same time, the ordinances are more than financing tools. They increase recycling in at least two ways, conferring significant health and environmental benefits upon the citizens of the Counties. First, they create enhanced incentives for recycling and proper disposal of other kinds of waste. Solid waste disposal is expensive in Oneida-Herkimer, but the Counties accept recyclables and many forms of hazardous waste for free, effectively encouraging their citizens to sort their own trash. Second, by requiring all waste to be deposited at Authority facilities, the Counties have markedly increased their ability to enforce recycling laws. If the haulers could take waste to any disposal site, achieving an equal level of enforcement would be much more costly, if not impossible. For these reasons, any arguable burden the ordinances impose on interstate commerce does not exceed their public benefits. . . .

The Counties' ordinances are exercises of the police power in an effort to address waste disposal, a typical and traditional concern of local government. The haulers nevertheless ask us to hold that laws favoring public entities while treating all private businesses the same are subject to an almost *per se* rule of invalidity, because of asserted discrimination. In the alternative, they maintain that the Counties' laws cannot survive the more permissive *Pike* test, because of asserted burdens on commerce. There is a common thread to these arguments: They are invitations to rigorously scrutinize economic legislation passed under the auspices of the police power. There was a time when this Court presumed to make such binding judgments for society, under the guise of interpreting the Due Process Clause. See Lochner v. New York, 198 U.S. 45 (1905). We should not seek to reclaim that ground for judicial supremacy under the banner of the dormant Commerce Clause. . . .

[Justices Scalia and Thomas each wrote a concurring opinion expressing discomfort with the whole body of dormant Commerce Clause jurisprudence. Justice Scalia argued that the body of law should not expanded beyond its "existing domain," while Justice Thomas bluntly stated that the "negative Commerce Clause has no basis in the Constitution and has proved unworkable in practice." Justice Alito, in a dissent joined by Justices Stevens and Kennedy, saw the case as ruled by *Carbone* and hence thought the ordinance should have been declared unconstitutional. In his view, "[W]e have never treated discriminatory legislation with greater deference simply because

the entity favored by that legislation was a government-owned enterprise. . . ."
He argued that there should not be any "exception for discrimination in favor of a
state-owned entity. . . ."]

NOTES AND QUESTIONS

1. How did the majority distinguish *Carbone*? Why is discrimination against
interstate commerce that is impermissible if engaged in by a private waste management company less objectionable if it is engaged in by a publicly owned facility? Is
there an argument that discrimination by a public entity is worse than discrimination
by a private entity?

2. *The Dormant Commerce Clause and Economic Protectionism.* State public
health quarantines have long been an exception to the general rule that a state cannot
discriminate against interstate commerce. Bowman v. Chicago & N.W. Ry. Co., 12
U.S. 465 (1888). Although efforts to prohibit or make more costly the disposal of out-
of-state wastes could be characterized as quarantines, the Supreme Court has consistently invalidated as protectionist waste import bans or laws that subject out-of-state
wastes to differential costs or otherwise distort interstate markets. In Philadelphia v.
New Jersey, 437 U.S. 617 (1978), the Court invalidated a New Jersey law that prohibited the import of out-of-state waste for disposal in New Jersey landfills. The law was
not a quarantine because the danger arose after disposal, thus negating any difference
between in- and out-of-state wastes. The statute was facially discriminatory and thus
subject to the Court's "virtually per se rule of invalidity."

One justification for *Philadelphia* is that waste is an article of commerce and
must be allocated exclusively by national markets that increase efficiency and promote
a national union. The counter-theory is that waste import bans and similar laws reflect
not economic protectionism but environmental externality prevention. The externality theory has not impressed the Court. Oregon Waste Sys., Inc. v. Department of
Envtl. Quality, 511 U.S. 93 (1994); Chemical Waste Mgmt. v. Hunt, 504 U.S. 334
(1992). In each case the Court invalidated waste disposal laws that imposed
differential fees on the disposal or treatment of out-of-state wastes. Alabama attempted
in *Hunt* to justify its additional fee on out-of-state waste as a health and safety measure,
but the Court found "absolutely no evidence" that out-of-state wastes are more dangerous than in-state wastes. Chief Justice Rehnquist dissented in both cases because
the results presented states with a Hobson's choice: either ban all landfills or accept all
wastes, thus increasing risks to the public.

3. *Resource versus Economic Protectionism.* The Court's antiprotectionist jurisprudence applies to *intrastate* discrimination, too. Fort Gratiot Sanitary Landfill,
Inc. v. Michigan Dep't of Natural Res., 504 U.S. 353 (1992), applied *Philadelphia*
to a state statute that barred counties from accepting out-of-county wastes unless their
mandatory solid waste plan explicitly authorized it. While the statute allowed counties
to accept out-of-state wastes, one county denied an application to accept out-of-state
waste because the plan did not authorize out-of-county waste. Michigan argued,
relying on Pike v. Bruce Church, that the statute regulated evenhandedly to achieve
local interests and that any burden it imposed on interstate commerce was not clearly
excessive in relation to those benefits; the Court, however, found the statute as
protectionist as New Jersey's import ban. The fact that some Michigan counties

accepted out-of-state waste did not adequately distinguish the case from *Philadelphia*. The Court did suggest that a state could determine a safe capacity level and limit the amount of wastes that landfill operators accept per year based on this projection. But in *Oregon Waste Sys., supra*, the Court rejected Oregon's argument that conserving scarce landfill space for home-generated waste was resource, not economic, protectionism; a state may not give its own citizens preferred access to its natural resources over out-of-state consumers.

In Pacific Merchant Marine Shipping Ass'n v. Goldstene, 639 F.3d 1154 (9th Cir. 2011), the court addressed a dormant Commerce Clause challenge to a California regulation requiring vessel operators calling at a California port (and not just passing through the area 24 nautical miles off the state's coastline) to use clean marine fuels in diesel engines and auxiliary boilers when they operate within that 24-mile zone. The court upheld the regulation under the Pike v. Bruce Church balancing test. Can you re-create the court's analysis?

4. *Extraterritorial Legislation*. If a court determines that a local measure has extraterritorial effect, it is likely to strike it down as violative of the dormant Commerce Clause. See, e.g., National Solid Wastes Mgmt. Ass'n v. Meyer, 165 F.3d 1151 (7th Cir. 1999) (striking down as an improper "clog on interstate commerce" a Wisconsin statute allowing out-of-state waste to be disposed of in Wisconsin only if the community where the waste originates adopts an ordinance incorporating the mandatory components of Wisconsin's recycling program). Compare National Solid Wastes Mgmt. Ass'n v. Granholm, 344 F. Supp. 2d 559 (E.D. Mich. 2004) (requirements that out-of-state jurisdictions impose limits on solid waste disposal in landfills comparable to those in Michigan to be eligible for disposal in Michigan, and that out-of-state solid waste be inspected before being deposited in Michigan landfill, did not discriminate against out-of-state waste). The case that follows further discusses the problem of extraterritorial regulation.

5. *Economic Protectionism versus Environmental Justice*. One rationale for the Court's dormant Commerce Clause jurisprudence is that facially discriminatory legislation is a good indicator that out-of-state interests have been excluded from the political process. Engel, Reconsidering the National Market in Solid Waste: Trade-offs in Equity, Efficiency, Environmental Protection and State Autonomy, 73 N.C. L. Rev. 1481 (1995), finds that waste exports move from richer, generally eastern states to poorer, southern and midwestern ones. Is there an environmental justice case for abandoning the *Philadelphia* per se rule? See Verchick, The Commerce Clause, Environmental Justice and the Interstate Garbage Wars, 70 So. Cal. L. Rev. 1239 (1997).

6. *Market Participation*. The market participation doctrine, which is discussed in Justice Alito's dissent in *Oneida-Herkimer*, exempts direct state participation in the market from dormant Commerce Clause scrutiny. See BFI Waste Sys. of N. Am., Inc. v. Broward County, 265 F. Supp. 2d 1332 (2003) (finding that contract between county and solid waste hauler requiring hauler to deliver waste it collected to designated facilities was exempt from Commerce Clause scrutiny because the county was acting as a market participant in both the solid waste collection and disposal markets). The state, however, cannot impose conditions on the sale of state-owned natural resources. South-Central Timber Dev., Inc. v. Wunnicke, 467 U.S. 82 (1984), held that an Alaskan statute requiring that all timber purchased from the state be processed in-state violated the Commerce Clause.

7. *Funding Hazardous Waste Remediation.* State schemes for financing the cleanup of hazardous waste sites also may run afoul of the dormant Commerce Clause. See, e.g., CWM Chem. Serv., L.L.C. v. Roth, 787 N.Y.S.2d 780 (N.Y. App. Div. 2004) (holding New York law unconstitutional), *aff'd as modified,* 846 N.E.2d 448 (N.Y. 2006). Cf. American Trucking Ass'ns, Inc. v. New Jersey, 852 A.2d 142 (N.J. 2004) (holding that hazardous waste transporter registration fee discriminated against interstate commerce by charging a flat fee unrelated to the transporter's level of activity in the state).

8. *New Jersey versus Pennsylvania.* In 2003, the states exporting the most waste were New York, New Jersey, Missouri, Illinois, and Maryland. Pennsylvania was the largest importer, with most of its imports coming from New York and New Jersey. In 2006, Pennsylvania remained the largest importer of garbage, importing 9.2 million tons. Virginia was second, at about 7.3 million tons.

As the case and notes that follow illustrate, the dormant Commerce Clause has become an important battleground as states seek to reduce energy use or reduce greenhouse gas (GHG) emissions. Due to the interconnectedness of energy grids and the risk that efforts to reduce GHGs will lead to movement or increases of polluting activity outside the jurisdiction—a risk referred to by scholars as "leakage"—state regulatory schemes generally have some impacts on commerce in other states, thereby provoking dormant Commerce Clause challenges. This issue is further addressed in Chapter 12's coverage of climate change law, but the case that follows further illuminates dormant Commerce Clause doctrine while also discussing federalism precepts, benefits, risks, and congressional choices reflected in laws like the Clean Air Act.

ROCKY MOUNTAIN FARMERS UNION V. COREY
730 F.3d 1070 (9th Cir. 2013), *reh'g en banc denied,* 740 F.3d. 507 (9th Cir. 2014)

GOULD, Circuit Judge:

Whether global warming is caused by carbon emissions from our industrialized societies is a question for scientists to ponder. Whether, if such a causal relationship exists, the world can fight or retard global warming by implementing taxes or regulations that deter carbon emissions is a question for economists and politicians to decide. Whether one such regulatory scheme, implemented by the State of California, is constitutional under the United States Constitution's Commerce Clause is the question that we consider in this opinion.

Plaintiffs-Appellees Rocky Mountain Farmers' Union et al. ("Rocky Mountain") and American Fuels & Petrochemical Manufacturers Association et al. ("American Fuels") separately sued Defendant-Appellant California Air Resources Board ("CARB"), contending that the Low Carbon Fuel Standard ("Fuel Standard" [or LCFS]), Cal. Code Regs. tit. 17, §§95480-90 (2011), violated the dormant Commerce Clause. . . .

We hold that the Fuel Standard's regulation of ethanol does not facially discriminate against out-of-state commerce, and its initial crude-oil provisions (the "2011 Provisions") did not discriminate against out-of-state crude oil in purpose or practical effect. Further, the Fuel Standard does not violate the dormant Commerce Clause's prohibition on extraterritorial regulation. . . .

I

A

California has long been in the vanguard of efforts to protect the environment, with a particular concern for emissions from the transportation sector. Since 1957, California has acted at the state level to regulate air pollution from motor vehicles. Motor & Equip. Mfrs. Ass'n v. EPA ("*MEMA*"), 627 F.2d 1095, 1109 n. 26 (D.C. Cir. 1979) (citing 1957 Cal. Stats., chap. 239, §1). Based on this expertise, "[t]he first federal emission standards were largely borrowed from California." Id. at 1110 & n. 34.

When instituting uniform federal regulations for air pollution in the Clean Air Act, "Congress consciously chose to permit California to blaze its own trail with a minimum of federal oversight." Ford Motor Co. v. EPA, 606 F.2d 1293, 1297 (D.C. Cir. 1979). Section 209(a) of the Clean Air Act expressly prohibited state regulation of emissions from motor vehicles. 42 U.S.C. §7543(a). But the same section allowed California to adopt its own standards if it "determine[d] that the State standards will be, in the aggregate, at least as protective of public health and welfare as applicable Federal standards." Id. §7543(b). Other states could choose to follow either the federal or the California standards, but they could not adopt standards of their own. Id. §7507. The auto industry strenuously objected to this waiver provision and was "adamant that the nature of [its] manufacturing mechanism required a single national standard in order to eliminate undue economic strain on the industry." *MEMA*, 627 F.2d at 1109 (quoting S. Rep. No. 403, at 33 (1967)). But Congress decided to encourage California "to continue and expand its pioneering efforts at adopting and enforcing motor vehicle emission standards different from and in large measure more advanced than the corresponding federal program; in short, to act as a kind of laboratory for innovation." Id. at 1111. So California's role as a leader in developing air-quality standards has been explicitly endorsed by Congress in the face of warnings about a fragmented national market.

Continuing its tradition of leadership, the California legislature enacted Assembly Bill 32, the Global Warming Solutions Act of 2006. The legislature found that "[g]lobal warming poses a serious threat to the economic well-being, public health, natural resources, and the environment of California." Cal. Health & Safety Code §38501(a). These threats included "exacerbation of air quality problems, a reduction in the quality and supply of water to the state from the Sierra snowpack, [and] a rise in sea levels resulting in the displacement of thousands of coastal businesses and residences." Id. This environmental damage would have "detrimental effects on some of California's largest industries, including agriculture, wine, tourism, skiing, recreational and commercial fishing and forestry" and would "increase the strain on electricity supplies." Id. §38501(b).

Faced with these threats, California resolved to reduce its greenhouse gas ("GHG") emissions to their 1990 level by the year 2020, and it empowered CARB to design emissions-reduction measures to meet this goal. . . .

. . . Given the relative import of these emissions, CARB adopted a three-part approach designed to lower GHG emissions from the transportation sector: (1) reducing emissions at the tailpipe by establishing progressively stricter emissions limits for new vehicles ("Tailpipe Standards"), Cal. Code Regs. tit. 13, §1961.1 (2001); (2) integrating regional land use, housing, and transportation planning to reduce the number of "vehicle miles traveled" each year ("VMT Standards"), see Cal. Gov't Code §65080; and (3) lowering the embedded GHGs in transportation fuel by adopting the Fuel Standard to reduce the quantity of GHGs emitted in the production of transportation fuel, Cal. Code Regs. tit. 17, §§95480-90.

The Tailpipe and VMT Standards work on the demand side: they aim to lower the consumption of GHG-generating transportation fuels. The Fuel Standard, by contrast, is directed at the supply side, creating an alternate path to emissions reduction by reducing the carbon intensity[1] of transportation fuels that are burned in California.

B

. . . The Fuel Standard . . . applies to nearly all transportation fuels currently consumed in California and any fuels developed in the future. Id. §95480.1(a). In 2010, regulated parties were required to meet the Fuel Standard's reporting requirements but were not bound by a carbon intensity cap. Id. §95482(a). Beginning in 2011, the Fuel Standard established a declining annual cap on the average carbon intensity of California's transportation-fuel market. Id. §95482(b). By setting a predictable path for emissions reduction, the Fuel Standard is intended to spur the development and production of low-carbon fuels, reducing overall emissions from transportation.

To comply with the Fuel Standard, a fuel blender must keep the average carbon intensity of its total volume of fuel below the Fuel Standard's annual limit. Id. §95482(a). Fuels generate credits or deficits, depending on whether their carbon intensity is higher or lower than the annual cap. Id. §95485(a). . . . To build a durable and effective marketplace to stimulate the development of alternative fuels, the Fuel Standard created a market for trading, banking, and borrowing Fuel Standard credits. Id. CARB expects that the demand for credits will encourage producers, wherever they are located, to develop fuels with lower carbon intensities for use within the California market.

i

The Fuel Standard uses a "lifecycle analysis" to determine the total carbon intensity of a given transportation fuel. Because GHGs mix in the atmosphere, all emissions [emitted anywhere in the country or world] related to transportation fuels used in California pose the same local risk to California citizens. . . . Without lifecycle analysis, all GHGs emitted before the fuel enters a vehicle's gas tank would be excluded from California's regulation. Similarly, the climate-change benefits of bio-fuels such as ethanol, which mostly come before combustion, would be ignored if

---

1. A fuel's carbon intensity is the amount of lifecycle greenhouse gas emissions caused by production and transportation of the fuel, per unit of energy of fuel delivered, expressed in grams of carbon dioxide equivalent per megajoule (gCO_2e/MJ). See Cal. Code Regs. tit. 17, §95481(16). Carbon dioxide is the namesake gas of carbon intensity values, but it is not the only GHG. Others, such as methane, exert a more potent greenhouse effect than carbon dioxide. A fuel's "carbon dioxide equivalent" refers to the total greenhouse potency of all the GHG emissions attributable to a fuel, expressed in terms of the amount of carbon dioxide that would exert the same greenhouse effect in the atmosphere. See CARB's Initial Statement of Reasons for the Fuel Standard ("ISOR") IV–1 (2009).

CARB's regulatory focus were limited to emissions produced when fuels are consumed in California.

With a one-sided focus on consumption, even strong tailpipe-emissions standards would let GHG emissions rise during fuel production. . . .

To avoid these perverse shifts, CARB designed the Fuel Standard to account for emissions associated with all aspects of the production, refining, and transportation of a fuel, with the aim of reducing total, well-to-wheel GHG emissions. See id. §95481(a)(38). When these emissions are measured, CARB assigns a cumulative carbon intensity value to an individual fuel lifecycle, which is called a "pathway." Id. §95481(a)(14). . . .

An accurate comparison [of different "feedstocks" and production processes] is possible only when it is based on the entire lifecycle emissions of each fuel pathway.

Recognizing the need for a reliable method to compare the lifecycle emissions of diverse fuels, the Argonne National Laboratory developed the Greenhouse Gases, Regulated Emissions, and Energy Use in Transportation Model ("GREET"). . . . [Regulated parties can comply with its reporting requirements either by using CARB's "default pathways" or by coming up with their own "individualized pathways."]

ii

[The court then reviewed ethanol's entire lifecycle, including transportation, and summarized factors going into "carbon intensity values for each ethanol pathway." Because transportation is included, ethanol coming from distant places, often other states, is penalized due to its location. However,] emissions from transporting the feedstock and the refined fuel are related to location, but they are not directly proportionate to distance traveled. . . . As shown in [two tables omitted here], California's combination of more efficient plants and greater access to low-carbon electricity outweighs Midwest ethanol's lower transportation emissions. . . .

iii

The Fuel Standard also regulates crude oil and derivatives sold in California. . . . [The court reviewed the science and regulatory strategies for crude oil in analysis tracking much of its ethanol discussion.]

III

Plaintiffs contend that the Fuel Standard's ethanol and crude-oil provisions discriminate against out-of-state commerce and regulate extraterritorial activity. CARB disagrees . . .

The Commerce Clause provides that "Congress shall have Power . . . [t]o regulate Commerce . . . among the several States." U.S. Const., art. I, §8, cl. 3. This affirmative grant of power does not explicitly control the several states, but it "has long been understood to have a 'negative' aspect that denies the States the power unjustifiably to discriminate against or burden the interstate flow of articles of commerce." Or. Waste Sys., Inc. v. Dep't of Envtl. Quality of State of Or., 511 U.S. 93 (1994) (citing Wyoming v. Oklahoma, 502 U.S. 437, 454 (1992)). Known as the "negative" or "dormant" Commerce Clause, this aspect is not a perfect negative, as "the Framers' distrust of economic Balkanization was limited by their federalism favoring a degree of local autonomy." Dep't of Revenue of Ky. v. Davis, 553 U.S. 328, 338 (2008). Within the federal system, a "courageous state may, if its citizens choose, serve as a laboratory; and try novel social and economic experiments without risk to the rest of the country." New State Ice Co. v. Liebmann, 285 U.S. 262, 311 (1932) (Brandeis, J., dissenting). If successful, those experiments may often be adopted by other states without Balkanizing the national market or by the federal government without infringing on state power.

"The modern law of what has come to be called the dormant Commerce Clause is driven by concern about 'economic protectionism—that is, regulatory measures designed to benefit in-state economic interests by burdening out-of-state competitors.'" *Davis*, 553 U.S. at 337-38 (quoting New Energy Co. of Ind. v. Limbach, 486 U.S. 269, 273-74 (1988)). For dormant Commerce Clause purposes, economic protectionism, or discrimination, "simply means differential treatment of in-state and out-of-state economic interests that benefits the former and burdens the latter." *Or. Waste Sys., Inc.*, 511 U.S. at 99. "[O]f course, any notion of discrimination assumes a comparison of substantially similar entities." Gen. Motors Corp. v. Tracy, 519 U.S. 278, 298 (1997). If a statute discriminates against out-of-state entities on its face, in its purpose, or in its practical effect, it is unconstitutional unless it "serves a legitimate local purpose, and this purpose could not be served as well by available nondiscriminatory means." Maine v. Taylor, 477 U.S. 131, 138 (1986). Absent discrimination, we will uphold the law "unless the burden imposed on [interstate] commerce is clearly excessive in relation to the putative local benefits." *Pike*, 397 U.S. at 142.

A

The district court concluded that the Fuel Standard facially discriminated against out-of-state corn ethanol by (1) differentiating between ethanol pathways based on origin and (2) discriminating against out-of-state ethanol based on factors within the CA-GREET formula that were "inextricably intertwined with origin." *Rocky Mountain Ethanol*, 843 F. Supp. 2d at 1087. . . .

ii

Under the dormant Commerce Clause, distinctions that benefit in-state producers cannot be based on state boundaries alone. But a regulation is not facially discriminatory simply because it affects in-state and out-of-state interests unequally. If California is to assign different carbon intensities to ethanol from different regions, there must be "some reason, apart from their origin, to treat them differently." Philadelphia v. New Jersey, 437 U.S. 617, 627 (1978).

Following this logic, the Supreme Court has consistently recognized facial discrimination where a statute or regulation distinguished between in-state and out-of-state products and no nondiscriminatory reason for the distinction was shown. . . .

Unlike these discriminatory statutes, the Fuel Standard does not base its treatment on a fuel's origin but on its carbon intensity. The Fuel Standard performs life-cycle analysis to measure the carbon intensity of all fuel pathways. When it is relevant to that measurement, the Fuel Standard considers location, but only to the extent that location affects the actual GHG emissions attributable to a default pathway. Under dormant Commerce Clause precedent, if an out-of-state ethanol pathway does impose higher costs on California by virtue of its greater GHG emissions, there is a nondiscriminatory reason for its higher carbon intensity value. Stated another way, if producers of out-of-state ethanol actually cause more GHG emissions for each unit produced, because they use dirtier electricity or less efficient plants, CARB can base its regulatory treatment on these emissions. If California is to successfully promote low-carbon-intensity fuels, countering a trend towards increased GHG output and rising world temperatures, it cannot ignore the real factors behind GHG emissions.

The Fuel Standard does not isolate California and protect its producers from competition. To date, the lowest ethanol carbon intensity values, providing the most beneficial market position, have been for pathways from the Midwest and Brazil. . . . Yet Plaintiffs contend (1) that certain factors in the CA-GREET analysis are inherently discriminatory against out-of-state ethanol and (2) that the regional categories and default pathways shown in Table 6 discriminate against out-of-state ethanol based on origin. We address these arguments at more length, as they are the crux of the challenges by Rocky Mountain and American Fuels to CARB's regulatory scheme.

iii

The district court held that two of the CA-GREET factors, transportation and electricity source, were "inextricably intertwined with origin" and that CARB's use of those factors was impermissible under the dormant Commerce Clause. *Rocky Mountain Ethanol*, 843 F. Supp. 2d at 1088-89. To reach this conclusion, the district court reasoned first that any factor correlated with origin is "inextricably intertwined with geography" and second that any otherwise neutral factor becomes discriminatory if it is intertwined with geography, even if that factor measures real variations in emissions from different methods and locations of ethanol production. This reasoning is incorrect.

As explained above, these factors bear on the reality of GHG emissions, with resulting consequences for California. Unless and until either the United States Supreme Court or the Congress forbids it, California is entitled to proceed on the understanding that global warming is being induced by rising carbon emissions and attempt to change that trend. California, if it is to have any chance to curtail GHG emissions, must be able to consider all factors that cause those emissions when it assesses alternative fuels.

Plaintiffs contend that any consideration of emissions from the transportation of feedstocks and fuels is forbidden. They cite Fort Gratiot Sanitary Landfill, Inc. v. Michigan Department of Natural Resources, 504 U.S. 353 (1992), and Dean Milk Co. v. City of Madison, 340 U.S. 349 (1951), but neither case stands for that proposition. . . . In both of these cases, the Supreme Court found discrimination based on the communities' decision to isolate themselves and direct business to local processors, not based on the use of distance for sound reasons correlating with the purposes of the regulation.

CARB's attention to emissions from transportation has no such isolating effect. We "view[] with particular suspicion state statutes requiring business operations to be performed in the home State that could more efficiently be performed elsewhere." *Pike*, 397 U.S. at 145. But transporting raw corn produces more emissions than importing refined ethanol, driving up a fuel pathway's carbon intensity and making local processing less attractive. This is not a form of discrimination against out-of-state producers. Even if California were to someday produce significant amounts of corn for ethanol, the CA-GREET transportation factor would remain non-discriminatory to the extent it applies evenly to all pathways and measures real differences in the harmful effects of ethanol production. See *Or. Waste Sys., Inc.*, 511 U.S. at 101 n.5.

Plaintiffs also contend that the carbon intensity of electricity is "inextricably intertwined with geography." California's mix of electricity generation is weighted toward lower-carbon sources such as natural gas, nuclear, and hydroelectric, and California ethanol producers pay more for electricity with fewer emissions than the national average. By contrast, Midwest producers have largely located their plants near cheap and carbon-intensive sources of coal-fired electricity generation. The default pathways reflect the resulting difference in the average carbon intensity of electricity available in the region where producers are located. . . .

But ethanol producers in the Midwest are not hostage to these regional electricity-generating portfolios. Many ethanol plants in the Midwest generate some or all of their own electricity and use the waste heat as a source of thermal energy, reducing emissions. See 75 Fed. Reg. at 14745. Drawing electricity from the coal-fired grid might be the easiest and cheapest way to power an ethanol plant. But the dormant Commerce Clause does not guarantee that ethanol producers may compete on the terms they find most convenient. . . .

The Fuel Standard does not "artificially encourag[e] in-state production even when the same goods could be produced at lower cost in other States." *See W. Lynn Creamery*, 512 U.S. at 193. It creates a market in which the monetary cost of ethanol better reflects the full costs of ethanol production, taking into account the harms from GHG emissions. After accounting for those costs, Midwest ethanol has attained both the highest and the lowest carbon intensity values, and Brazilian ethanol boasts the default pathway with the lowest carbon intensity. The dormant Commerce Clause does not require California to ignore the real differences in carbon intensity among out-of-state ethanol pathways, giving preferential treatment to those with a higher carbon intensity. These factors are not discriminatory because they reflect the reality of assessing and attempting to limit GHG emissions from ethanol production.

We conclude: (1) that all sources of ethanol compete in the California market and are therefore relevant to comparison; (2) that all of the factors included in CA-GREET's lifecycle analysis are relevant to determining which forms of ethanol are similarly situated — not just those factors that are uncorrelated with location; (3) that the CA-GREET lifecycle analysis used by CARB, including the specific factors to which Plaintiffs object, does not discriminate against out-of-state commerce. We next address Plaintiffs' challenge to the regional categories and average values that form the default pathways in Table 6.

iv

[The court found them reasonable, concluding as follows:]

Just as a state law need not "be drafted explicitly along state lines in order to demonstrate its discriminatory design," Amerada Hess Corp. v. N.J. Dep't of Treasury, 490 U.S. 66, 76 (1989), California's reasonable decision to use regional categories in its default pathways and in the text of Table 6 does not transform its evenhanded treatment of fuels based on their carbon intensities into forbidden discrimination.

That decision does not empower out-of-state ethanol producers to eliminate the factors of lifecycle analysis that do not favor them while keeping those that do. We hold that CARB's use of categories in Table 6 does not facially discriminate against out-of-state ethanol.

Our conclusion is reinforced by the grave need in this context for state experimentation. Congress of course can act at any time to displace state laws that seek to regulate the carbon intensity of fuels, but Congress has expressly empowered California to take a leadership role as to air quality. If GHG emissions continue to increase, California may see its coastline crumble under rising seas, its labor force imperiled by rising temperatures, and its farms devastated by severe droughts. To be effective, California's effort to combat these harms must not be so complicated and costly as to be unworkable. California's regulatory experiment seeking to decrease GHG emissions and create a market that recognizes the harmful costs of products with a high carbon intensity does not facially discriminate against out-of-state ethanol. [The court also upheld the crude oil regulations.]

IV

In addition to discrimination based on origin, the dormant Commerce Clause holds that any "statute that directly controls commerce occurring wholly outside the boundaries of a State exceeds the inherent limits of the enacting State's authority." Healy v. Beer Inst., 491 U.S. 324, 336 (1989). Under *Healy*, the "critical inquiry is whether the practical effect of the regulation is to control conduct beyond the boundary of the state." Id. To determine the practical effect of the regulation, we consider not only the direct consequences of the statute itself, but also "how the challenged statute may interact with the legitimate regulatory regimes of other States and what effect would arise if not one, but many or every, State adopted similar legislation." Id.

The district court held that the Fuel Standard regulated extraterritorial conduct because: (1) by treating fuels based on lifecycle emissions, it "attempts to control" out-of-state conduct, *Rocky Mountain Ethanol*, 843 F. Supp. 2d at 1091; (2) California's attempt to take "legal and political responsibility" for worldwide carbon emissions caused by transportation fuels used in California was an improper extension of California's police power to other states; (3) the Fuel Standard regulates the channels of interstate commerce by compelling producers to submit changes in their transportation routes to CARB to qualify for an altered pathway; and (4) if each state enacted a regulation similar to the Fuel Standard, it would result in economic Balkanization. We disagree. The Fuel Standard regulates only the California market. Firms in any location may elect to respond to the incentives provided by the Fuel Standard if they wish to gain market share in California, but no firm must meet a particular carbon intensity standard, and no jurisdiction need adopt a particular regulatory standard for its producers to gain access to California.

A

In the modern era, the Supreme Court has rarely held that statutes violate the extraterritoriality doctrine. The two most prominent cases where a violation did occur both involved similar price-affirmation statutes. In *Brown-Forman*, . . . the Court explained that "[f]orcing a merchant to seek regulatory approval in one State before undertaking a transaction in another directly regulates interstate commerce." [476 U.S.] at 582. . . .

Courts have extended the rule from *Healy* and *Brown-Forman* to cases where the "price" floor being imposed on another jurisdiction was not monetary but rather a minimum standard of environmental protection. Plaintiffs contend that the Fuel Standard is forbidden by the Supreme Court's statement in *Carbone* that "[s]tates and localities may not attach restrictions to exports or imports in order to control commerce in other States." 511 U.S. at 393 (citing *Baldwin*, 294 U.S. at 511). . . .

The Fuel Standard imposes no analogous conditions on the importation of ethanol. It says nothing at all about ethanol produced, sold, and used outside California. . . .

These credits and caps instead resemble the incentives in a more recent case in which the "alleged harm to interstate commerce would be the same regardless of whether manufacturer compliance is completely voluntary or the product of coercion." Pharm. Research & Mfrs. of Am. v. Walsh, 538 U.S. 644, 669 (2003). . . .

Plaintiffs are right that—like any government—California cannot exceed its powers. California's police power does not allow it to "invade [another state] to force reductions in greenhouse gas emissions." *Massachusetts*, 549 U.S. at 519. It cannot peacefully impose its own regulatory standards on another jurisdiction. *Nat'l Solid Wastes Mgmt. Ass'n*, 63 F.3d at 658-62. But California may regulate with reference to local harms, structuring its internal markets to set incentives for firms to produce less harmful products for sale in California. Plaintiffs point to no extraterritoriality cases where differences in the physical structure of a product was a prerequisite to regulation. In non-extraterritoriality cases where physical properties were relevant, it was because those properties determined the degree of harm inflicted on the regulating state. See, e.g., *Chem. Waste*, 504 U.S. at 344 n.7. Here, California properly based its regulation on the harmful properties of fuel. It does not control the production or sale of ethanol wholly outside California.

B

The district court next concluded that by requiring blenders to report any material change to a pathway's production and transportation process before it can generate Fuel Standard credits, CARB "forc[es] a merchant to seek regulatory approval in one State before undertaking a transaction in another." *Rocky Mountain Ethanol*, 843 F. Supp. 2d at 1092 (quoting *Brown-Forman*, 476 U.S. at 582). But the Fuel Standard requires fuel distributors to seek regulatory approval in California before undertaking a transaction also in California—the sale of fuel that generates Fuel Standard credits. States do not regulate transactions occurring wholly out of state when they impose reporting requirements that out-of-state producers must meet before making in-state sales. *See Baldwin*, 294 U.S. at 524 (holding that states may exact certificates from out-of-state producers).

C

As an alternative basis for invalidating the Fuel Standard as an extraterritorial regulation, the district court concluded that widespread adoption of comparable legislation by other states would Balkanize the fuels market in two ways. First, the district court explained that the Fuel Standard encourages a producer to "either relocate its operations in the State of largest use, or sell only locally to avoid transportation and other penalties." [843 F. Supp. 2d] at 1093. . . .

Second, the district court concluded that the Fuel Standard raised the danger of inconsistent regulation, warning that ethanol producers would "be hard-pressed to satisfy the requirements of 50 different [Fuel Standards]." Id. at 1093-94. A few jurisdictions are considering legislation similar to the Fuel Standard, but these would be complementary, encouraging similar reductions in carbon intensity across the board. To show the threat of inconsistent regulation, Plaintiffs "must either present evidence that conflicting, legitimate legislation is already in place or that the threat of such legislation is both actual and imminent." S.D. Myers v. City of San Francisco, 253 F.3d 461, 469-70 (9th Cir. 2001) (citing Huron Portland Cement Co. v. City of Detroit, 362 U.S. 440, 448 (1960)). . . .

The Fuel Standard does not "place[] a financial barrier around the State of [California]." [American Trucking Assocations v. Scheiner, 483 U.S. 266, 284 (1987)]. If similar standards were adopted nationwide, they would not create the interlocking problems of cross-border price setting or out-of-state approval that appeared in *Healy* and *Edgar*. . . .

If we were to invalidate regulation every time another state considered a complementary statute, we would destroy the states' ability to experiment with regulation. Successful experiments inspire imitation both vertically, as when the federal government followed California's lead on air pollution, and horizontally, as shown by the federal Organic Foods Production Act of 1990, 7 U.S.C. §§6501-23, adopted after twenty-two states, starting with Oregon, enacted organic food labeling standards. See Or. Rev. Stat. §632.925 (1973); S. Rep. No. 357, *reprinted in* 1990 U.S.C.C.A.N. 4656, 4943. After nearly half of the states acted, Congress provided a uniform standard. . . . [T]he possibility that many states might perform lifecycle analysis on fuel sold within their borders does not risk the "competing and interlocking local economic regulation that the Commerce Clause was meant to preclude." *Healy*, 491 U.S. at 337.

With the Fuel Standard, California "has essentially assumed legal and political responsibility for emissions of carbon resulting from the production and transport, regardless of location, of transportation fuels actually used in California." *Rocky Mountain Ethanol*, 843 F. Supp. 2d at 1092. . . . The Fuel Standard has incidental effects on interstate commerce, but it does not control conduct wholly outside the state. Those effects may be considered under *Pike* on remand. 397 U.S. at 142.

[Due to earlier circuit precedent, the court declined to find that §211(c)(4)(b) of the Clean Air Act authorized the Fuel Standard under the Commerce Clause.]

VI

. . . To combat . . . tremendous risks [climate change poses to California], the California legislature and its regulatory arm CARB chose to institute a market-based solution that recognizes the costs of harmful carbon emissions. For any such system to work, two conditions must be met. First, the market must have full and accurate information about the real extent of GHG emissions. Second, the compliance costs of entering the market must not be so great as to prevent participation. Plaintiffs attack the lifecycle analysis and default pathways that fulfill these conditions, relying on archaic formalism to prevent action against a new type of harm. It has been sagely observed by Justice Jackson that the constitutional Bill of Rights is not a "suicide pact." See Terminiello v. City of Chicago, 337 U.S. 1, 37 (1949) (Jackson, J., dissenting). Nor is the dormant Commerce Clause a blindfold. It does not invalidate by strict scrutiny state laws or regulations that incorporate state boundaries for good and non-discriminatory reason. It does not require that reality be ignored in lawmaking.

California should be encouraged to continue and to expand its efforts to find a workable solution to lower carbon emissions, or to slow their rise. If no such solution is found, California residents and people worldwide will suffer great harm. We will not at the outset block California from developing this innovative, nondiscriminatory regulation to impede global warming. If the Fuel Standard works, encouraging the development of alternative fuels by those who would like to reach the California market, it will help ease California's climate risks and inform other states as they attempt to confront similar challenges.

VII

The Fuel Standard's ethanol provisions are not facially discriminatory, so we reverse that portion of the district court's decision and remand for entry of partial summary judgment in favor of CARB. We also reverse the district court's decision that the Fuel Standard is an impermissible extraterritorial regulation and we direct that an order of partial summary judgment be entered in favor of CARB on those grounds. We remand the case for the district court to determine whether the ethanol provisions discriminate in purpose or effect and, if not, to apply the *Pike* balancing test. . . .

[The partial concurrence and partial dissent of Judge Murguia is omitted.]

NOTE AND QUESTIONS

1. If another state enacted a body of law modeled on California's Low Carbon Fuel Standard, how much of the Ninth Circuit's logic or opinion building blocks would remain relevant in a subsequent dormant Commerce Clause challenge? (In answering this question, remember that generally, one circuit's rulings are only persuasive precedent in another circuit; inter-circuit disagreement is common.) Exactly how is California's long-standing special treatment under the CAA relevant to this dormant Commerce Clause challenge? How might challengers have used that treatment to fashion arguments against California's LCFS?

2. What is the distinction the court makes between regulation that controls and regulation that creates incentives? Why is this distinction so important to the court's conclusions?

3. Since this case brings to a close this chapter's introduction of environmental federalism, look again at the case and see if you can identify the types of federalism benefits and risks that the court considered as it weighed the legality of California's LCFS.

4. Not all state zeal in addressing the causes and complex regulatory challenges of climate change has survived constitutional challenge. As briefly discussed in section E.2 of Chapter 12's coverage of climate change federalism, Minnesota's Renewable Portfolio Standard was found to constitute unconstitutional "extraterritorial" regulation violating the Commerce Clause in North Dakota v. Heydinger, 2014

WL 1612331 (D. Minn. Apr. 18, 2014). Minnesota had sought to address the risk that constraints on in-state power-related emissions would lead to purchases increasing energy production in other states, but in doing so, the court held, Minnesota was engaging in prohibited "extraterritorial" regulation of transactions occurring in other jurisdictions. The court distinguished *Rocky Mountain* primarily by noting the "boundary-less nature of the energy grid" compared to regulation targeted at tangible fuels and products, but also stated that the California LCFS "applied only to fuel blenders in California and the producers who contracted with them." In summarizing the *Rocky Mountain* decision, the court appeared to agree that California's regulation was both more targeted in-state and less likely to cause Balkanization than Minnesota's regulatory scheme.

III

THE ADMINISTRATIVE LAW OF
ENVIRONMENTAL PROTECTION

Environmental law, like all administrative law, is heavily influenced by the process by which it is adopted. Accordingly, it is helpful to survey some of the important issues raised by the processes that govern environmental decisionmaking before addressing, in the remainder of this book, the substance of environmental law that emerges from those processes.

Administrative law is largely concerned with two great questions. First, it is concerned with the roles of the three branches of government established by the Constitution in the creation and implementation of law and policy. Second, it is concerned with the procedures followed by the executive or independent agencies to which legislative and non–Article III judicial authority has been delegated. Because administrative agencies have no explicit constitutional footing, their legal status has always been ambiguous and subject to intense debate. Criticisms of the "headless fourth branch of government" have been raised since the explosion of the administrative state during the New Deal in the 1930s. More recently, the impetus toward deregulation among academics, economists, and legislators that began during the 1980s fueled a renewed interest in fundamental administrative law questions such as the constitutional legitimacy of agencies and the role of the courts, Congress, and the executive branch in promoting greater accountability by agency decisionmakers. This chapter focuses on selected examples of how these debates have played out in the context of environmental law.

Those who are dissatisfied with agency decisions concerning environmental matters often seek to invoke the aid of the courts in reversing decisions they perceive to deviate from legislative mandates. But judicial assistance is available only if litigants have access to the courts. Accordingly, this chapter begins with a survey of various doctrines, such as standing to sue, which serve to limit that access. The issue is particularly resonant in the environmental law area because it was in large part the skillful advocacy by environmental interests that was responsible for the root-and-branch alteration of American administrative law during the 1970s. Two Supreme Court decisions in the 1970s facilitated the access of these groups to the courts and essentially eliminated standing as a serious obstacle to judicial review of environmental matters in the federal courts for nearly two decades. Another pair of formalist Supreme Court decisions in the early 1990s reopened the issue of standing and threatened to restrict significantly judicial review at the behest of environmental groups as a constraint on agency decisionmaking.

Even if access to the courts is available, judicial review will not limit agency discretion unless the courts take seriously the task of reviewing the merits of agency decisions. Section A of this chapter is therefore also devoted to a study of the standards that govern judicial review of agency interpretation and implementation of statutes. The materials reflect the continuing conflict between judicial inclinations to defer to administrative expertise and to provide meaningful review of agency decisions to ensure that they conform to legislative mandates.

Congress also plays an active role in confining administrative discretion. The agencies that make decisions that affect the environment are all creatures of statute. Congress has a variety of tools for placing limits on how agencies make those decisions, including drafting statutes that confine agency discretion through specific mandates and holding hearings to oversee agency performance. Congress also can cut appropriations to express dissatisfaction with agency decisions or place restrictions on the ability of agencies to expend appropriated funds for disfavored purposes or projects. Congress also has enacted statutes, applicable to all or most administrative agencies, which either require that agencies engage in analytical processes or apply substantive standards that further restrict agency discretion. Section B of this chapter briefly surveys these congressional oversight techniques.

Finally, the executive branch can rein in the discretion of regulatory agencies such as EPA. Section C covers executive review of administrative agency decisionmaking and touches on the policy and legal issues raised by efforts within the White House to control implementation of statutes enacted by Congress.

Not surprisingly, agencies whose discretion has been narrowed have responded to these kinds of oversight (especially by the courts and the executive branch) by seeking to recapture some of their independence. The final section of this chapter illustrates a tendency by agencies to shift from decisionmaking through formal mechanisms (such as rulemaking) that are subject to judicial, legislative, and executive branch review to more informal processes not saddled by those review procedures. Among the questions raised by that shift is whether the new methods of doing business threaten to reduce the ability of those affected by agency decisions to have meaningful input into the decisionmaking process, and therefore to weaken the legitimacy of those decisions.

A. JUDICIAL CONTROL OF ADMINISTRATIVE ENVIRONMENTAL DECISIONMAKING

1. Access to the Courts: Standing and Related Preclusion Doctrines

Frequently, an administrative decision that is claimed to have negative environmental impacts is challenged by organizations or individuals who did not initiate the agency decisionmaking process. For example, if the Interior Department enters into a lease with a private company for mining on public lands, both parties to the lease probably will be satisfied with this decision (unless, of course, the agency imposes environmentally protective or other conditions that are unacceptable to the lessee).

In such a case, judicial review will be sought, if at all, only by third parties concerned about the adverse environmental consequences of the Department's action.

Third parties who seek judicial review of agency actions must have standing to sue or they will be denied access to the courts. These third-party plaintiffs traditionally have faced difficult standing problems because of the rule that a plaintiff must show injury to a common law or statutory legal interest. That theory of access left no room for the generally concerned citizen representing a broad public interest, such as a public policy concern that was ecological or even philosophical in nature. In the leading case of Associated Indus., Inc. v. Ickes, 134 F.2d 694 (2d Cir. 1943), however, Judge Frank held that Congress could constitutionally authorize "so to speak, private Attorney Generals" to bring suit to prevent an administrative official from acting in violation of statutory power. The major constitutional argument against such a public action is that it violates the "case or controversy" requirement of Article III of the Constitution. See Berger, Standing to Sue in Public Actions: Is It a Constitutional Requirement?, 78 Yale L.J. 816 (1969). The decisions reproduced and discussed in this section illustrate how the courts have swung back and forth between the theory that administrative standing should be based on private rights, created by common law or statute, and the theory that public actions can legitimately be policed by members of the public, which were intended to be the beneficiaries of regulatory programs.

SIERRA CLUB v. MORTON
405 U.S. 727 (1972)

Mr. Justice STEWART delivered the opinion of the Court.

I

The Mineral King Valley is an area of great natural beauty nestled in the Sierra Nevada Mountains in Tulare County, California, adjacent to Sequoia National Park. It has been part of the Sequoia National Forest since 1926, and is designated as a national game refuge by special Act of Congress. Though once the site of extensive mining activity, Mineral King is now used almost exclusively for recreational purposes. Its relative inaccessibility and lack of development have limited the number of visitors each year, and at the same time have preserved the valley's quality as a quasi-wilderness area largely uncluttered by the products of civilization.

[The U.S. Forest Service invited bids from private developers for the construction and operation of a combination ski resort and summer recreation area in the national forest. In January 1969, it approved a plan by Walt Disney Enterprises for "a $35 million complex of motels, restaurants, swimming pools, parking lots, and other structures designed to accommodate 14,000 visitors daily. This complex is to be constructed on 80 acres of the valley floor under a 30-year use permit from the Forest Service." The agency issued another permit for construction of ski lifts, ski trails, a cog-assisted railway, and utility installations. Access to the resort required construction by California of a 20-mile highway, a section of which would traverse Sequoia National Park. A proposed high-voltage power line needed to provide electricity for the resort would also cut through the park. Approval of the Department of the

Interior, which administers the park, was required for both the highway and the power line.

In June 1969, the Sierra Club sought a declaratory judgment in federal district court that the proposed development violated federal statutes and regulations governing management of the national parks and forests. It also sought to enjoin the agencies involved from issuing the permits necessary for development. It sued as a membership corporation with "a special interest in the conservation and the sound maintenance" of the national parks and forests. The district court issued a preliminary injunction, ruling that the Sierra Club had standing to sue. After the Ninth Circuit reversed, the Club appealed.]

II

The first question presented is whether the Sierra Club has alleged facts that entitle it to obtain judicial review of the challenged action. Whether a party has a sufficient stake in an otherwise justiciable controversy to obtain judicial resolution of that controversy is what has traditionally been referred to as the question of standing to sue. Where the party does not rely on any specific statute authorizing invocation of the judicial process, the question of standing depends upon whether the party has alleged such a "personal stake in the outcome of the controversy," Baker v. Carr, 369 U.S. 186, 204, as to ensure that "the dispute sought to be adjudicated will be presented in an adversary context and in a form historically viewed as capable of judicial resolution." Flast v. Cohen, 392 U.S. 83, 101. Where, however, Congress has authorized public officials to perform certain functions according to law, and has provided by statute for judicial review of those actions under certain circumstances, the inquiry as to standing must begin with a determination of whether the statute in question authorizes review at the behest of the plaintiff.

The Sierra Club relies upon §10 of the Administrative Procedure Act (APA), 5 U.S.C. §702, which provides: "A person suffering legal wrong because of agency action, or adversely affected or aggrieved by agency action within the meaning of a relevant statute, is entitled to judicial review thereof." Early decisions under this statute interpreted the language as adopting the various formulations of "legal interest" and "legal wrong" then prevailing as constitutional requirements of standing. But, in Association of Data Processing Service Organizations, Inc. v. Camp, 397 U.S. 150, and Barlow v. Collins, 397 U.S. 159, . . . we held more broadly that persons had standing to obtain judicial review of federal agency action under §10 of the APA where they had alleged that the challenged action had caused them "injury in fact," and where the alleged injury was to an interest "arguably within the zone of interests to be protected or regulated" by the statutes that the agencies were claimed to have violated.[5]

. . . [P]alpable economic injuries [of the kind allegedly suffered by the plaintiffs in *Data Processing* and *Barlow*] have long been recognized as sufficient to lay the basis for standing, with or without a specific statutory provision for judicial review. [But] neither *Data Processing* nor *Barlow* addressed itself to the question . . . as to what must

---

5. In deciding this case we do not reach any questions concerning the meaning of the "zone of interests" test or its possible application to the facts here presented.

be alleged by persons who claim injury of a noneconomic nature to interests that are widely shared. That question is presented in this case.

III

The injury alleged by the Sierra Club will be incurred entirely by reason of the change in the uses to which Mineral King will be put, and the attendant change in the aesthetics and ecology of the area. Thus, in referring to the road to be built through Sequoia National Park, the complaint alleged that the development "would destroy or otherwise adversely affect the scenery, natural and historic objects and wildlife of the park and would impair the enjoyment of the park for future generations." We do not question that this type of harm may amount to an "injury in fact" sufficient to lay the basis for standing under §10 of the APA. Aesthetic and environmental well-being, like economic well-being, are important ingredients of the quality of life in our society, and the fact that particular environmental interests are shared by the many rather than the few does not make them less deserving of legal protection through the judicial process. But the "injury in fact" test requires more than an injury to a cognizable interest. It requires that the party seeking review be himself among the injured.

The impact of the proposed changes in the environment of Mineral King will not fall indiscriminately upon every citizen. The alleged injury will be felt directly only by those who use Mineral King and Sequoia National Park, and for whom the aesthetic and recreational values of the area will be lessened by the highway and ski resort. The Sierra Club failed to allege that it or its members would be affected in any of their activities or pastimes by the Disney development. Nowhere in the pleadings or affidavits did the Club state that its members use Mineral King for any purpose, much less that they use it in any way that would be significantly affected by the proposed actions of the respondents.[8]

---

8. The only reference in the pleadings to the Sierra Club's interest in the dispute is contained in paragraph 3 of the complaint, which reads in its entirety as follows:

Plaintiff Sierra Club is a non-profit corporation . . . with its principal place of business in San Francisco, California since 1892. Membership of the club is approximately 78,000 nationally, with approximately 27,000 members residing in the San Francisco Bay Area. For many years the Sierra Club by its activities and conduct has exhibited a special interest in the conservation and the sound maintenance of the national parks, game refuges and forests of the country, regularly serving as a responsible representative of persons similarly interested. One of the principal purposes of the Sierra Club is to protect and conserve the national resources of the Sierra Nevada Mountains. Its interests would be vitally affected by the acts hereinafter described and would be aggrieved by those acts of the defendants as hereinafter more fully appears.

[An amicus brief asserted that the Sierra Club conducted regular camping trips into the Mineral King area and that its members continued to use the area for recreational purposes. The Court noted that these allegations were not presented to either court below.] Moreover, the Sierra Club in its reply brief specifically declines to rely on its individualized interest, as a basis for standing. See n.15, *infra*. Our decision does not, of course, bar the Sierra Club from seeking in the District Court to amend its complaint by a motion under Rule 15, Federal Rules of Civil Procedure.

The Club apparently regarded any allegations of individualized injury as superfluous, on the theory that this was a "public" action involving questions as to the use of natural resources, and that the Club's longstanding concern with and expertise in such matters were sufficient to give it standing as a "representative of the public."[9] This theory reflects a misunderstanding of our cases involving so-called "public actions" in the area of administrative law. . . .

Taken together, [the Court's previous decisions] established a dual proposition: the fact of economic injury is what gives a person standing to seek judicial review under the statute, but once review is properly invoked, that person may argue the public interest in support of his claim that the agency has failed to comply with its statutory mandate. It was in the latter sense that the "standing" of the appellant in [a previous case] existed only as a "representative of the public interest." It is in a similar sense that we have used the phrase "private attorney general" to describe the function performed by persons upon whom Congress has conferred the right to seek judicial review of agency action.

The trend of cases arising under the APA and other statutes authorizing judicial review of federal agency action has been toward recognizing that injuries other than economic harm are sufficient to bring a person within the meaning of the statutory language, and toward discarding the notion that an injury that is widely shared is ipso facto not an injury sufficient to provide the basis for judicial review. We noted this development with approval in *Data Processing*. . . . But broadening the categories of injury that may be alleged in support of standing is a different matter from abandoning the requirement that the party seeking review must himself have suffered an injury.

Some courts have indicated a willingness to take this latter step by conferring standing upon organizations that have demonstrated "an organizational interest in the problem" of environmental or consumer protection. It is clear that an organization whose members are injured may represent those members in a proceeding for judicial review. But a mere "interest in a problem," no matter how longstanding the interest and no matter how qualified the organization is in evaluating the problem, is not sufficient by itself to render the organization "adversely affected" or "aggrieved" within the meaning of the APA. The Sierra Club is a large and long-established organization, with a historic commitment to the cause of protecting our Nation's natural heritage from man's depredations. But if a "special interest" in this subject were enough to entitle the Sierra Club to commence this litigation, there would appear to be no objective basis upon which to disallow a suit by any other bona fide "special interest" organization however small or short-lived. And if any group with a bona fide "special interest" could initiate such litigation, it is difficult to perceive why any individual citizen with the same bona fide special interest would not also be entitled to do so.

The requirement that a party seeking review must allege facts showing that he is himself adversely affected does not insulate executive action from judicial review, nor

9. This approach to the question of standing was adopted by the Court of Appeals for the Second Circuit in Citizens Committee for Hudson Valley v. Volpe, 425 F.2d 97, 105:

> We hold, therefore, that the public interest in environmental resources—an interest created by statutes affecting the issuance of this permit—is a legally protected interest affording these plaintiffs, as responsible representatives of the public, standing to obtain judicial review of agency action alleged to be in contravention of that public interest.

does it prevent any public interests from being protected through the judicial process.[15] It does serve as at least a rough attempt to put the decision as to whether review will be sought in the hands of those who have a direct stake in the outcome. That goal would be undermined were we to construe the APA to authorize judicial review at the behest of organizations or individuals who seek to do no more than vindicate their own value preferences through the judicial process. The principle that the Sierra Club would have us establish in this case would do just that.

. . . [T]he Court of Appeals was correct in its holding that the Sierra Club lacked standing to maintain this action. . . .

[The dissenting opinions of Justices Blackmun, Brennan, and Douglas are omitted.]

NOTES AND QUESTIONS

1. Did the Court's "user standing" rule place any serious limitations on the standing of plaintiffs with ideological interests? Do you see why *Sierra Club* in retrospect may be viewed as a victory for environmental interests, even though the Club did not prevail? The Club had no difficulty amending its complaint to allege facts sufficient to confer standing. Sierra Club v. Morton, 348 F. Supp. 219 (N.D. Cal. 1972). Why do you think the Club chose not to assert individualized injury to itself or its members?[a]

2. *Injury in Fact and* SCRAP. *Sierra Club*'s relaxed user standard appeared to afford access to the courts to environmental public interest groups on the basis of third-party standing. But because the plaintiff in that case did not allege individualized injury to itself or its members, it was not clear at what point the link between the challenged project and the claimed environmental harm would become so attenuated as to defeat the plaintiff's standing. United States v. Students Challenging Regulatory Agency Procedures (*SCRAP I*), 412 U.S. 669 (1973), provided an answer. A student group and environmental organization brought suit challenging a rate increase by the Interstate Commerce Commission (ICC). They argued that the increase would discourage the use of recycled materials by subjecting them to higher transportation charges than those applicable to virgin materials, and they sought to compel the ICC to prepare an environmental impact statement. The Supreme Court held that the plaintiffs had standing:

> Unlike the specific and geographically limited federal action of which the petitioner complained in *Sierra Club*, the challenged agency action in this case is applicable to

---

15. In its reply brief, after noting the fact that it might have chosen to assert individualized injury to itself or to its members as a basis for standing, the Sierra Club states:

> The Government seeks to create a "heads I win, tails you lose" situation in which either the courthouse door is barred for lack of assertion of a private, unique injury or a preliminary injunction is denied on the ground that the litigant has advanced private injury which does not warrant an injunction adverse to a competing public interest. Counsel have shaped their case to avoid this trap.

The short answer to this contention is that the "trap" does not exist. The test of injury in fact goes only to the question of standing to obtain judicial review. Once this standing is established, the party may assert the interests of the general public in support of his claims for equitable relief.

a. For a critique of *Sierra Club*, see Sax, Standing to Sue: A Critical Review of the Mineral King Decision, 13 Nat. Resources J. 76 (1973).

substantially all of the Nation's railroads, and thus allegedly has an adverse environmental impact on all the natural resources of the country. Rather than a limited group of persons who used a picturesque valley in California, all persons who utilize the scenic resources of the country, and indeed all who breathe its air, could claim harm similar to that alleged by the environmental groups here. But we have already made it clear that standing is not to be denied simply because many people suffer the same injury. . . . To deny standing to persons who are in fact injured simply because many others are also injured, would mean that the most injurious and widespread Government actions could be questioned by nobody. We cannot accept that conclusion.

But the injury alleged here is also very different from that at issue in *Sierra Club* because here the alleged injury to the environment is far less direct and perceptible. The petitioner there complained about the construction of a specific project that would directly affect the Mineral King Valley. Here, the Court was asked to follow a far more attenuated line of causation to the eventual injury of which appellees complained—a general rate increase would allegedly cause increased use of nonrecyclable commodities as compared to recyclable goods, thus resulting in the need to use more natural resources to produce such goods, some of which resources might be taken from the Washington area, and resulting in more refuse that might be discarded in national parks in the Washington area. The railroads protest that the appellees could never prove that a general increase in rates would have this effect, and they contend that these allegations were a ploy to avoid the need to show some injury in fact.

Id. at 687-688. The Court responded that the pleadings alleged facts sufficient to show standing; if the railroads believed that the allegations in the pleadings were untrue, they should have moved for summary judgment.

3. *The Fall of the Standing Barrier.* The SCRAP I decision appeared to reduce the injury in fact requirement to a fiction. Occasionally, the government and other defendants attempted to disprove plaintiffs' allegations of injury, but such attempts generally did not succeed. Taken together, *Sierra Club* and *SCRAP* sent clear signals to the lower courts that those seeking to enforce federal environmental legislation should be afforded relatively unhindered access to the courts. Eventually, the Justice Department stopped vigorously asserting lack of standing in environmental cases.

4. *The Erection of New Standing Obstacles:* Lujan I. Nearly two decades after the *SCRAP* decision, statutory beneficiaries were confronted with a reinvigorated standing barrier as a result of two cases decided by the Supreme Court in 1990 and 1992. The first decision was Lujan v. National Wildlife Fed'n, 497 U.S. 871 (1990) (*Lujan I*). The NWF sued the Bureau of Land Management (BLM), alleging that it violated the Federal Land Policy and Management Act (FLPMA) and the National Environmental Policy Act (NEPA) in implementing what the NWF called the "land withdrawal review program." The BLM had revoked some withdrawals of public lands, thereby reopening them to developmental uses such as mining and oil and gas leasing. Two NWF members filed affidavits alleging adverse effects on their recreational use and aesthetic enjoyment of federal lands in the vicinity of the lands reopened to those activities. The NWF relied on §10 of the APA to establish a right to review because neither FLPMA nor NEPA provides a private right of action. A plaintiff invoking §10 must show that it is suffering legal wrong or has been adversely affected or aggrieved by "agency action" and that the action is "final." 5 U.S.C. §704. The government claimed that the NWF lacked standing.

The affidavits appeared to satisfy the "user standing" requirements set forth in *Sierra Club*, as interpreted in *SCRAP I* and applied in subsequent lower court cases.

The Court, in an opinion by Justice Scalia joined by four other Justices, decided otherwise. It found that the affidavits did not satisfy the requirements of Rule 56 of the Federal Rules of Civil Procedure, which governs summary judgment motions, because they stated only that the NWF's members had used

> unspecified portions of an immense tract of territory, on some portions of which mining activity has occurred or probably will occur by virtue of [the challenged] governmental action. It will not do to "presume" the missing facts because without them the affidavits would not establish the injury they generally allege.

497 U.S. at 889. Taking a swipe at *SCRAP I*, the Court averred that its "expansive expression of what would suffice for [review of agency action under §10 of the APA] under its particular facts has never since been emulated by this Court." Id. Further, *SCRAP I* was irrelevant because it arose in the context of a Rule 12(b) motion to dismiss rather than a Rule 56 motion for summary judgment.

The majority found that the district court also lacked jurisdiction because the BLM's so-called "land withdrawal review program" did not constitute "agency action" for purposes of the APA, much less final agency action. It characterized the BLM's 1250 or so individual revocation and land classification decisions instead as "the continuing (and thus constantly changing) operations of the BLM" in carrying out its responsibilities under FLPMA of reviewing withdrawals and classifications and developing land use plans. Although the NWF alleged rampant violations of the law in the implementation of the program, the Court refused to permit it to "seek wholesale improvement of this program by court decree, rather than in the offices of the Department or the halls of Congress, where programmatic improvements are normally made." Id. at 891.

What is the status of Sierra Club v. Morton and *SCRAP* after *Lujan I*? What would the NWF's members have had to allege to survive a motion for summary judgment on the standing issue? *Lujan I* is often cited as precedent for the proper interpretation of Article III's "case or controversy" provision. What role did that provision and separation of powers concerns play in the Court's decision? What is the likely effect of *Lujan I* on the ability of environmental groups to challenge the BLM's implementation of FLPMA? Farber, A Place-Based Theory of Standing, 55 UCLA L. Rev. 1505 (2008), suggests that a plaintiff with an appropriate personal connection to a specific geographic area should have standing to contest environmental violations involving that area.

The Court's retrenchment of environmental standing continued in the following case.

LUJAN v. DEFENDERS OF WILDLIFE
504 U.S. 555 (1992)

Justice SCALIA delivered the opinion of the Court with respect to Parts I, II, III-A, and IV, and an opinion with respect to Part III-B, in which THE CHIEF JUSTICE, Justice WHITE, and Justice THOMAS join.

[In 1978, the Fish and Wildlife Service (FWS) and the National Marine Fisheries Service (NMFS) issued a joint regulation stating that the obligations imposed by

§7(a)(2) of the Endangered Species Act of 1973 (ESA) extend to actions taken in foreign nations. Section 7(a)(2) requires federal agencies, in consultation with the Secretary of the Interior, to ensure that their actions are not likely to jeopardize the continued existence of any endangered or threatened species or result in the destruction of critical habitat. In 1986, the agencies revised the regulation to require consultation only for actions taken in the United States or on the high seas. The Defenders of Wildlife sued the Secretary, seeking a declaratory judgment that the new regulation was inconsistent with §7(a)(2) and an injunction requiring the Secretary to reissue the original regulation. The district court dismissed for lack of standing, but the Eighth Circuit reversed. On remand, the district court denied the Secretary's motion for summary judgment and granted Defenders' motion on the standing issue, concluding that the Eighth Circuit had already ruled on the question. The Secretary sought review.]

II

. . . [T]he Constitution of the United States . . . limits the jurisdiction of federal courts to "Cases" and "Controversies[.]" . . . One of [the Constitutional] landmarks, setting apart the "Cases" and "Controversies" that are of the justiciable sort referred to in Article III—"serv[ing] to identify those disputes which are appropriately resolved through the judicial process," Whitmore v. Arkansas, 495 U.S. 149 (1990)—is the doctrine of standing. Though some of its elements express merely prudential considerations that are part of judicial self-government, the core component of standing is an essential and unchanging part of the case-or-controversy requirement of Article III.

Over the years, our cases have established that the irreducible constitutional minimum of standing contains three elements. First, the plaintiff must have suffered an "injury in fact"—an invasion of a legally protected interest which is (a) concrete and particularized;[1] and (b) "actual or imminent, not 'conjectural' or 'hypothetical.'" Second, there must be a causal connection between the injury and the conduct complained of—the injury has to be "fairly . . . trace[able] to the challenged action of the defendant, and not . . . th[e] result [of] the independent action of some third party not before the court." Simon v. Eastern Ky. Welfare Rights Org., 426 U.S. 26, 41-42 (1976). Third, it must be "likely," as opposed to merely "speculative," that the injury will be "redressed by a favorable decision."

The party invoking federal jurisdiction bears the burden of establishing these elements. . . . [E]ach element must be supported in the same way as any other matter on which the plaintiff bears the burden of proof, i.e., with the manner and degree of evidence required at the successive stages of the litigation. At the pleading stage, general factual allegations of injury resulting from the defendant's conduct may suffice, for on a motion to dismiss we "presum[e] that general allegations embrace those specific facts that are necessary to support the claim." [Lujan v. National Wildlife Federation, 497 U.S. 871, 889 (1990).] In response to a summary judgment motion, however, the plaintiff can no longer rest on such "mere allegations," but must "set forth" by affidavit or other evidence "specific facts," Fed. Rule Civ. Proc. 56(e), which for purposes of the summary judgment motion will be taken to be true. And at the final

---

1. By particularized, we mean that the injury must affect the plaintiff in a personal and individual way.

stage, those facts (if controverted) must be "supported adequately by the evidence adduced at trial."

When the suit is one challenging the legality of government action or inaction, the nature and extent of facts that must be averred (at the summary judgment stage) or proved (at the trial stage) in order to establish standing depends considerably upon whether the plaintiff is himself an object of the action (or forgone action) at issue. If he is, there is ordinarily little question that the action or inaction has caused him injury, and that a judgment preventing or requiring the action will redress it. When, however, as in this case, a plaintiff's asserted injury arises from the government's allegedly unlawful regulation (or lack of regulation) of someone else, much more is needed. In that circumstance, causation and redressability ordinarily hinge on the response of the regulated (or regulable) third party to the government action or inaction—and perhaps on the response of others as well. The existence of one or more of the essential elements of standing "depends on the unfettered choices made by independent actors not before the courts and whose exercise of broad and legitimate discretion the courts cannot presume either to control or to predict," ASARCO Inc. v. Kadish, 490 U.S. 605, 615 (1989) (opinion of Kennedy, J.); and it becomes the burden of the plaintiff to adduce facts showing that those choices have been or will be made in such manner as to produce causation and permit redressability of injury. Thus, when the plaintiff is not himself the object of the government action or inaction he challenges, standing is not precluded, but it is ordinarily "substantially more difficult" to establish.

III

A

Respondents' claim to injury is that the lack of consultation with respect to certain funded activities abroad "increas[es] the rate of extinction of endangered and threatened species." Of course, the desire to use or observe an animal species, even for purely esthetic purposes, is undeniably a cognizable interest for purpose of standing. See, e.g., Sierra Club v. Morton, 405 U.S., at 734. "But the 'injury in fact' test requires more than an injury to a cognizable interest. It requires that the party seeking review be himself among the injured." Id. at 734-35. To survive the Secretary's summary judgment motion, respondents had to submit affidavits or other evidence showing, through specific facts, not only that listed species were in fact being threatened by funded activities abroad, but also that one or more of respondents' members would thereby be "directly" affected apart from their " 'special interest' in th[e] subject."

With respect to this aspect of the case, the Court of Appeals focused on the affidavits of two Defenders' members—Joyce Kelly and Amy Skilbred. Ms. Kelly stated that she traveled to Egypt in 1986 and "observed the traditional habitat of the endangered Nile crocodile there and intend[s] to do so again, and hope[s] to observe the crocodile directly," and that she "will suffer harm in fact as the result of [the] American . . . role . . . in overseeing the rehabilitation of the Aswan High Dam on the Nile. . . ." Ms. Skilbred averred that she traveled to Sri Lanka in 1981 and "observed th[e] habitat" of "endangered species such as the Asian elephant and the leopard" at what is now the site of the Mahaweli project funded by the Agency for International Development (AID). [Ms. Skilbred averred that, although she did not see any endangered species in 1981, the Mahaweli project "will seriously reduce" endangered species habitat in areas that she visited, which might accelerate the extinction of those species. She averred that this threat harmed her because she intended to return to Sri Lanka "in the future" and hoped to spot elephants and leopards on that trip. At a subsequent deposition, Ms. Skilbred claimed that "I intend to go back to Sri Lanka," but had no current plans to do so: "I don't know [when]. There is a civil war going on right now. I don't know. Not next year, I will say. In the future."]

We shall assume . . . that these affidavits contain facts showing that certain agency-funded projects threaten listed species—though that is questionable. They plainly contain no facts, however, showing how damage to the species will produce "imminent" injury to Mses. Kelly and Skilbred. That the women "had visited" the areas of the projects before the projects commenced proves nothing. As we have said in a related context, " 'Past exposure to illegal conduct does not in itself show a present case or controversy regarding injunctive relief . . . if unaccompanied by any continuing, present adverse effects.' " Los Angeles v. Lyons, 461 U.S. 95, 102 (1983). And the affiants' profession of an "inten[t]" to return to the places they had visited before—where they will presumably, this time, be deprived of the opportunity to observe animals of the endangered species—is simply not enough. Such "some day" intentions—without any description of concrete plans, or indeed even any specification of when the some day will be—do not support a finding of the "actual or imminent" injury that our cases require.

Besides relying upon the Kelly and Skilbred affidavits, respondents propose a series of novel standing theories. The first, inelegantly styled "ecosystem nexus," proposes that any person who uses any part of a "contiguous ecosystem" adversely affected by a funded activity has standing even if the activity is located a great distance away. This approach, as the Court of Appeals correctly observed, is inconsistent with our opinion in *National Wildlife Federation*, which held that a plaintiff claiming injury from environmental damage must use the area affected by the challenged activity and not an area roughly "in the vicinity" of it. It makes no difference that the general-purpose section of the ESA states that the Act was intended in part "to provide a means whereby the ecosystems upon which endangered species and threatened species depend may be conserved," 16 U.S.C. §1531(b). To say that the Act protects ecosystems is not to say that the Act creates (if it were possible) rights of action in persons who have not been injured in fact, that is, persons who use portions of an ecosystem not perceptibly affected by the unlawful action in question.

Respondents' other theories are called, alas, the "animal nexus" approach, whereby anyone who has an interest in studying or seeing the endangered animals anywhere on the globe has standing; and the "vocational nexus" approach, under which anyone with a professional interest in such animals can sue. Under these theories, anyone who goes to see Asian elephants in the Bronx Zoo, and anyone who is a keeper of Asian elephants in the Bronx Zoo, has standing to sue because the Director of [AID] did not consult with the Secretary regarding the AID-funded project in Sri Lanka. This is beyond all reason. Standing is not "an ingenious academic exercise in the conceivable," United States v. Students Challenging Regulatory Agency Procedures (SCRAP), 412 U.S. 669, 688 (1973), but as we have said requires, at the summary judgment stage, a factual showing of perceptible harm. It is clear that the person who observes or works with a particular animal threatened by a federal decision is facing perceptible harm, since the very subject of his interest will no longer exist. It is even plausible—though it goes to the outermost limit of plausibility—to think that a person who observes or works with animals of a particular species in the very area of the world where that species is threatened by a federal decision is facing such harm, since some animals that might have been the subject of his interest will no longer exist. It goes beyond the limit, however, and into pure speculation and fantasy, to say that anyone who observes or works with an endangered species, anywhere in the world, is appreciably harmed by a single project affecting some portion of that species with which he has no more specific connection.

B

Besides failing to show injury, respondents failed to demonstrate redressability. Instead of attacking the separate decisions to fund particular projects allegedly causing them harm, respondents chose to challenge a more generalized level of Government action (rules regarding consultation), the invalidation of which would affect all overseas projects. This programmatic approach has obvious practical advantages, but also obvious difficulties insofar as proof of causation or redressability is concerned. . . .

The most obvious problem in the present case is redressability. Since the agencies funding the projects were not parties to the case, the District Court could accord relief only against the Secretary: He could be ordered to revise his regulation to require consultation for foreign projects. But this would not remedy respondents' alleged injury unless the funding agencies were bound by the Secretary's regulation, which is very much an open question. . . . When the Secretary promulgated the regulation at issue here, he thought it was binding on the agencies. The Solicitor General, however, has repudiated that position here, and the agencies themselves apparently deny the Secretary's authority. . . .

[Even if the district court had ruled that the regulation bound other federal agencies, such a decision] would not have remedied respondents' alleged injury anyway, because it would not have been binding upon the agencies. They were not parties to the suit, and there is no reason they should be obliged to honor an incidental legal determination the suit produced. . . . The short of the matter is that redress of the only injury in fact respondents complain of requires action (termination of funding until consultation) by the individual funding agencies; and any relief the District Court could have provided in this suit against the Secretary was not likely to produce that action.

A further impediment to redressability is the fact that the agencies generally supply only a fraction of the funding for a foreign project. AID, for example, has provided less than 10% of the funding for the Mahaweli project. Respondents have produced nothing to indicate that the projects they have named will either be suspended, or do less to listed species, if that fraction is eliminated. . . . [I]t is entirely conjectural whether the nonagency activity that affects respondents will be altered or affected by the agency activity they seek to achieve. There is no standing.

IV

The Court of Appeals found that respondents had standing for an additional reason: because they had suffered a "procedural injury." The so-called "citizen-suit" provision of the ESA provides, in pertinent part, that "any person may commence a civil suit on his own behalf (A) to enjoin any person, including the United States and any other governmental instrumentality or agency . . . who is alleged to be in violation of any provision of this chapter." 16 U.S.C. §1540(g). The court held that, because §7(a)(2) requires interagency consultation, the citizen-suit provision creates a "procedural righ[t]" to consultation in all "persons"—so that anyone can file suit in federal court to challenge the Secretary's (or presumably any other official's) failure to follow the assertedly correct consultative procedure, notwithstanding his or her inability to allege any discrete injury flowing from that failure. To understand the remarkable nature of this holding one must be clear about what it does not rest upon: This is not a case where plaintiffs are seeking to enforce a procedural requirement the disregard of which could impair a separate concrete interest of theirs (e.g., the procedural requirement for a hearing prior to denial of their license application, or the procedural requirement for an environmental impact statement before a federal facility is constructed next door to them).[7] Nor is it simply a case where concrete injury has been suffered by many persons, as in mass fraud or mass tort situations. Nor, finally, is it the unusual case in which Congress has created a concrete private interest in the outcome of a suit against a private party for the government's benefit, by providing a cash bounty for the victorious plaintiff. Rather, the court held that the injury-in-fact requirement had been satisfied by congressional conferral upon all persons of an abstract, self-contained, noninstrumental "right" to have the Executive observe the procedures required by law. We reject this view.

We have consistently held that a plaintiff raising only a generally available grievance about government—claiming only harm to his and every citizen's interest in proper application of the Constitution and laws, and seeking relief that no more directly and tangibly benefits him than it does the public at large—does not state an Article III case or controversy. . . .

To be sure, our generalized-grievance cases have typically involved Government violation of procedures assertedly ordained by the Constitution rather than the Congress. But there is absolutely no basis for making the Article III inquiry turn on the source of the asserted right. Whether the courts were to act on their own, or at the invitation of Congress, in ignoring the concrete injury requirement described in our cases, they would be discarding a principle fundamental to the separate and distinct constitutional role of the Third Branch—one of the essential elements that identifies those "Cases" and "Controversies" that are the business of the courts rather than of the political branches. "The province of the court," as Chief Justice Marshall said in Marbury v. Madison, 5 U.S. (1 Cranch) 137, 170 (1803), "is, solely, to decide on the rights of individuals." Vindicating the public interest (including the public interest in Government observance of the Constitution and laws) is the function of Congress and the Chief Executive. The question presented here is whether the public interest in proper administration of the laws (specifically, in agencies' observance of a particular,

---

7. There is this much truth to the assertion that "procedural rights" are special: The person who has been accorded a procedural right to protect his concrete interests can assert that right without meeting all the normal standards for redressability and immediacy. Thus, under our case law, one living adjacent to the site for proposed construction of a federally licensed dam has standing to challenge the licensing agency's failure to prepare an environmental impact statement, even though he cannot establish with any certainty that the statement will cause the license to be withheld or altered, and even though the dam will not be completed for many years. (That is why we do not rely, in the present case, upon the Government's argument that, even if the other agencies were obliged to consult with the Secretary, they might not have followed his advice.) What respondents' "procedural rights" argument seeks, however, is quite different from this: standing for persons who have no concrete interests affected—persons who live (and propose to live) at the other end of the country from the dam.

statutorily prescribed procedure) can be converted into an individual right by a statute that denominates it as such, and that permits all citizens (or, for that matter, a subclass of citizens who suffer no distinctive concrete harm) to sue. If the concrete injury requirement has the separation-of-powers significance we have always said, the answer must be obvious: To permit Congress to convert the undifferentiated public interest in executive officers' compliance with the law into an "individual right" vindicable in the courts is to permit Congress to transfer from the President to the courts the Chief Executive's most important constitutional duty, to "take Care that the Laws be faithfully executed," Art. II, §3. It would enable the courts, with the permission of Congress, "to assume a position of authority over the governmental acts of another and co-equal department," and to become "'virtually continuing monitors of the wisdom and soundness of Executive action.'" [Allen v. Wright, 468 U.S. 737, 760 (1984)]. We have always rejected that vision of our role. . . .

Nothing in this contradicts the principle that "[t]he . . . injury required by Art. III may exist solely by virtue of 'statutes creating legal rights, the invasion of which creates standing.'" Warth v. Seldin, 422 U.S. 490, 500 (1975). . . . As we said in *Sierra Club*, "[Statutory] broadening [of] the categories of injury that may be alleged in support of standing is a different matter from abandoning the requirement that the party seeking review must himself have suffered an injury." 405 U.S., at 738. Whether or not the principle set forth in *Warth* can be extended beyond that distinction, it is clear that in suits against the Government, at least, the concrete injury requirement must remain.

We hold that respondents lack standing to bring this action and that the Court of Appeals erred in denying the summary judgment motion filed by the United States. . . .

Justice KENNEDY, with whom Justice SOUTER joins, concurring in part and concurring in the judgment. . . .

I agree with the Court's conclusion in Part III-A that, on the record before us, respondents have failed to demonstrate that they themselves are "among the injured." . . .

While it may seem trivial to require that Mses. Kelly and Skilbred acquire airline tickets to the project sites or announce a date certain upon which they will return, this is not a case where it is reasonable to assume that the affiants will be using the sites on a regular basis, see Sierra Club v. Morton, *supra*, 405 U.S., at 735, n.8, nor do the affiants claim to have visited the sites since the projects commenced. With respect to the Court's discussion of respondents' "ecosystem nexus," "animal nexus," and "vocational nexus" theories, I agree that on this record respondents' showing is insufficient to establish standing on any of these bases. I am not willing to foreclose the possibility, however, that in different circumstances a nexus theory similar to those proffered here might support a claim to standing. See Japan Whaling Ass'n v. American Cetacean Soc'y, 478 U.S. 221, 231, n.4 (1986) ("[R]espondents . . . undoubtedly have alleged a sufficient 'injury in fact' in that the whale watching and studying of their members will be adversely affected by continued whale harvesting.").

In light of the conclusion that respondents have not demonstrated a concrete injury here sufficient to support standing under our precedents, I would not reach the issue of redressability that is discussed by the plurality in Part III-B.

I also join Part IV of the Court's opinion with the following observations. As Government programs and policies become more complex and far reaching, we must be sensitive to the articulation of new rights of action that do not have clear analogs in our common-law tradition. . . . In my view, Congress has the power to define injuries and articulate chains of causation that will give rise to a case or controversy where none existed before, and I do not read the Court's opinion to suggest a contrary view. In exercising this power, however, Congress must at the very least identify the injury it seeks to vindicate and relate the injury to the class of persons entitled to bring suit. The citizen-suit provision of the Endangered Species Act does not meet these minimal requirements, because while the statute purports to confer a right on "any person . . . to enjoin . . . the United States and any other governmental instrumentality or agency . . . who is alleged to be in violation of any provision of this chapter," it does not of its own force establish that there is an injury in "any person" by virtue of any "violation." 16 U.S.C. §1540(g)(1)(A).

The Court's holding that there is an outer limit to the power of Congress to confer rights of action is a direct and necessary consequence of the case and controversy limitations found in Article III. I agree that it would exceed those limitations if, at the behest of Congress and in the absence of any showing of concrete injury, we were to entertain citizen suits to vindicate the public's nonconcrete interest in the proper administration of the laws. While it does not matter how many persons have been injured by the challenged action, the party bringing suit must show that the action injures him in a concrete and personal way. . . .

Justice STEVENS, concurring in the judgment.

Because I am not persuaded that Congress intended the consultation requirement in §7(a)(2) of the Endangered Species Act to apply to activities in foreign countries, I concur in the judgment of reversal. I do not, however, agree with the Court's conclusion that respondents lack standing. . . .

. . . An injury to an individual's interest in studying or enjoying a species and its natural habitat occurs when someone (whether it be the Government or a private party) takes action that harms that species and habitat. . . .

[In responding to Part III-B of Justice Scalia's opinion, Justice Stevens asserted that the Court] must presume that if this Court holds that §7(a)(2) requires consultation, all affected agencies would abide by that interpretation and engage in the requisite consultations. Certainly the Executive Branch cannot be heard to argue that an authoritative construction of the governing statute by this Court may simply be ignored by any agency head. Moreover, if Congress has required consultation between agencies, we must presume that such consultation will have a serious purpose that is likely to produce tangible results. . . . [I]t is not mere speculation to think that foreign governments, when faced with the threatened withdrawal of United States assistance, will modify their projects to mitigate the harm to endangered species. . . .

Justice BLACKMUN, with whom Justice O'CONNOR joins, dissenting.

. . . I question the Court's breadth of language in rejecting standing for "procedural" injuries. I fear the Court seeks to impose fresh limitations on the constitutional authority of Congress to allow citizen suits in the federal courts for injuries deemed "procedural" in nature. . . .

The Court . . . concludes that injury is lacking, because respondents' allegations of "ecosystem nexus" failed to demonstrate sufficient proximity to the site of the environmental harm. To support that conclusion, the Court mischaracterizes our decision in Lujan v. National Wildlife Federation, 497 U.S. 871 (1990), as establishing a general rule that "a plaintiff claiming injury from environmental damage must use the area affected by the challenged activity." In *National Wildlife Federation*, the Court required specific geographical proximity because of the particular type of harm alleged in that case: harm to the plaintiff's visual enjoyment of nature from mining activities. One cannot suffer from the sight of a ruined landscape without being close enough to see the sites actually being mined. Many environmental injuries, however, cause harm distant from the area immediately affected by the challenged action. Environmental destruction may affect animals traveling over vast geographical ranges, see, e.g., Japan Whaling Ass'n v. American Cetacean Soc'y, 478 U.S. 221 (1986) (harm to American whale watchers from Japanese whaling activities), or rivers running long geographical courses. It cannot seriously be contended that a litigant's failure to use the precise or exact site where animals are slaughtered or where toxic waste is dumped into a river means he or she cannot show injury. . . .

I have difficulty imagining this Court applying its rigid principles of geographic formalism anywhere outside the context of environmental claims. As I understand it, environmental plaintiffs are under no special constitutional standing disabilities. Like other plaintiffs, they need show only that the action they challenge has injured them, without necessarily showing they happened to be physically near the location of the alleged wrong. . . .

The Court . . . rejects the view that the "injury-in-fact requirement [is] satisfied by congressional conferral upon all persons of an abstract, self-contained, noninstrumental 'right' to have the Executive observe the procedures required by law." Whatever the Court might mean with that very broad language, it cannot be saying that "procedural injuries" as a class are necessarily insufficient for purposes of Article III standing.

Most governmental conduct can be classified as "procedural." Many injuries caused by governmental conduct, therefore, are categorizable at some level of generality as "procedural" injuries. Yet, these injuries are not categorically beyond the pale of redress by the federal courts. When the Government, for example, "procedurally" issues a pollution permit, those affected by the permittee's pollutants are not without standing to sue. Only later cases will tell just what the Court means by its intimation that "procedural" injuries are not constitutionally cognizable injuries. In the meantime, I have the greatest of sympathy for the courts across the country that will struggle to understand the Court's standardless exposition of this concept today.

The Court expresses concern that allowing judicial enforcement of "agencies' observance of a particular, statutorily prescribed procedure" would "transfer from the President to the courts the Chief Executive's most important constitutional duty, to 'take Care that the Laws be faithfully executed,' Art. II, §3." In fact, the principal effect of foreclosing judicial enforcement of such procedures is to transfer power into the hands of the Executive at the expense—not of the courts—but of Congress, from which that power originates and emanates.

Under the Court's anachronistically formal view of the separation of powers, Congress legislates pure, substantive mandates and has no business structuring the procedural manner in which the Executive implements these mandates. . . . In complex regulatory areas, however, Congress often . . . sets forth substantive policy goals and provides for their attainment by requiring Executive Branch officials to follow certain procedures, for example, in the form of reporting, consultation, and certification requirements. . . .

. . . Just as Congress does not violate separation of powers by structuring the procedural manner in which the Executive shall carry out the laws, surely the federal courts do not violate separation of powers when, at the very instruction and command of Congress, they enforce these procedures. . . .

. . . [The] acknowledgment of an inextricable link between procedural and substantive harm does not reflect improper appellate factfinding. It reflects nothing more than the proper deference owed to the judgment of a coordinate branch—Congress—that certain procedures are directly tied to protection against a substantive harm. . . .

In conclusion, I cannot join the Court on what amounts to a slash-and-burn expedition through the law of environmental standing. In my view, "[t]he very essence of civil liberty certainly consists in the right of every individual to claim the protection of the laws, whenever he receives an injury." Marbury v. Madison, 1 Cranch 137, 163 (1803). . . .

NOTES AND QUESTIONS

1. *Injury in Fact.* Why is "much more" needed to demonstrate standing where the plaintiff's asserted injury arises from the government's allegedly unlawful regulation of a third party? Is *Defenders of Wildlife*, like Sierra Club v. Morton, an example of inartful drafting of pleadings and affidavits by the plaintiff's attorneys, and thus easily avoided in future cases? What, if anything, does *Defenders of Wildlife* add to *Lujan I*? Why didn't the plaintiff have standing based on procedural injury? What role did the separation of powers doctrine and Article II's "take Care" clause play in the Court's ruling on this issue?

2. *Legal Rights, Statutes, and Injuries in Fact.* Before 1940, the predominant approach to standing was the "legal right" doctrine. Under that doctrine, a plaintiff had standing only if agency action impaired a "legal right" specifically granted by statute or common law. A nineteenth-century private right was a predicate for judicial intervention. As a result, courts were unable to "redress the systemic or probabilistic harms that Congress intended regulatory schemes to prevent." Sunstein, Standing and the Privatization of Public Law, 88 Colum. L. Rev. 1432, 1433 (1988). The doctrine was abandoned when the courts began to grant standing to intended statutory beneficiaries as well as to regulated entities. See, e.g., Scenic Hudson Pres. Conf. v. FPC, 354 F.2d 608, 615-617 (2d Cir. 1965). Is the net effect of the two *Lujan* cases to return to a regime in which it will be more difficult for intended regulatory beneficiaries than for regulated entities to establish standing to sue? See Sunstein, *supra*, at 1435-1436, 1458, 1463; Weinberg, Are Standing Requirements Becoming a Great Barrier Reef against Environmental Actions?, 7 N.Y.U. Envtl. L.J. 1 (1999) (decrying "[a]rchaic standing rules that hearken back to the era of special pleading"). What appears to be Justice Kennedy's view of the legal right approach? The lower courts have resisted a return to that approach. See, e.g., Cantrell v. City of Long Beach, 241 F.3d 674, 681 (9th Cir. 2001) ("That the litigant's interest must be greater than that of the public at large does not imply that the interest must be a substantive right sounding in property or contract.").

An important issue raised by the Court's treatment of procedural injury in *Defenders of Wildlife* is whether Congress can create injury in fact where none existed before. Justice Scalia's opinion seems to indicate that it cannot. Other cases point in a different direction, however. In Federal Election Comm'n v. Akins, 524 U.S. 11 (1998), a group of voters with views opposed to those of the American Israel Public Affairs Committee (AIPAC) challenged the FEC's determination that AIPAC was not subject to statutory reporting requirements. The Court held that the group had standing under Article III. Justice Breyer, writing for the majority, reasoned that

> Congress has specifically provided in FECA that "[a]ny person who believes a violation of this Act . . . has occurred, may file a complaint with the Commission." It has added that "[a]ny party aggrieved by an order of the Commission dismissing a complaint filed by such party . . . may file a petition" in district court seeking review of that dismissal. History associates the word "aggrieved" with a congressional intent to cast the standing net broadly beyond the common-law interests and substantive statutory rights upon which "prudential" standing traditionally rested. . . .
>
> Given the language of the statute and the nature of the injury, we conclude that Congress, intending to protect voters such as respondents from suffering the kind of injury here at issue, intended to authorize this kind of suit. [Id. at 19-20.]

Is *Akins* consistent with *Defenders of Wildlife*, or has the Court erected more burdensome obstacles to standing in environmental law cases than in other areas? How did Justice Blackmun address this question in *Defenders of Wildlife*? Professor Buzbee has argued that "the 'statutory universe' of legislatively created goals, procedures and incentives remains central to standing analysis." He endorses recent Supreme Court decisions, including the next principal case, *Laidlaw*, that "embrac[e] the persistent, albeit contested, strain in standing jurisprudence that calls for a more limited and deferential judicial standing role. Legislative judgments about statutory goals and means [referred to in the article as the statutory universe] receive substantial deference by courts under this consistent line of standing analysis." Buzbee criticizes a competing conception of standing, consistently reflected in Justice Scalia's opinions, in which "the statutory interests Congress has sought to further in a statute conferring a cause of action" are ignored or belittled. Buzbee, Standing and the Statutory Universe, 11 Duke Envtl. L. & Pol'y F. 247, 249-250 (2001). See also Buzbee, The Story of *Laidlaw*: Standing and Citizen Enforcement, in Environmental Law Stories 201 (R. Lazarus & O. Houck eds., 2005) (describing *Laidlaw* as a case that "embrace[d] a legislation-centered view of injury"); Murphy, Abandoning Standing: Trading a Rule of Access for a Rule of Deference, 60 Admin. L. Rev. 943 (2008) (arguing that the Supreme Court "cannot forge a consensus regarding the nature of the injury requirement because the Justices fundamentally disagree over whether the basic purpose of standing doctrine is to block federal courts from usurping the policymaking power of the political branches").

Some courts have accepted the view that Congress has a role in defining justiciable injuries. In Maine People's Alliance v. Mallinckrodt, Inc., 471 F.3d 277 (1st Cir. 2006), for example, the court stated that while "it would be a usurpation of legislative prerogative for a court to assume policymaking control over environmental regulation, it would be no less offensive a usurpation for a court to refuse to undertake a task validly entrusted to it by Congress. In the last analysis, Article III requires a cognizable injury; it does not speak to the wisdom of the legislature's actions in providing redress for that injury." Id. at 286. Which view of the relevance of statutory goals and provisions to Article III standing analysis do you find more persuasive?

3. *Procedural or Informational Injury*. To what extent does footnote 7 of *Defenders of Wildlife* allow litigants to rely on procedural injury to show injury in fact? In Sierra Club v. Johnson, 436 F.3d 1269 (11th Cir. 2006), an environmental group had standing to challenge EPA's failure to object to a state permit issued under the CAA that did not comply with statutory public participation requirements based on a member's allegation that additional public input could have led to improvements in

the permit that could have reduced the harm caused by the permittee's air pollution. See also Sierra Club v. U.S. Army Corps of Eng'rs, 645 F.3d 978, 986-989 (8th Cir. 2011) (hunting club and environmental group whose members lived near utility granted CWA dredge and fill permit allegedly issued in violation of NEPA had standing). Other courts have been more reluctant to credit claims of procedural injury. Florida Audubon Soc'y v. Bentsen, 94 F.3d 658 (D.C. Cir. 1996), rejected claims of procedural injury due to an agency's failure to prepare an environmental impact statement on the effects of issuing a tax credit for the use of alternative fuel additives because the plaintiffs failed to show a sufficient geographic nexus to any asserted environmental injury. Judge Rogers dissented, charging the majority with effectively making it impossible for anyone to bring a NEPA claim concerning a rulemaking with diffuse impact.

After *Defenders of Wildlife* and *Akins*, when can a plaintiff rely on informational injury to show injury in fact? Suppose that an individual who used lands in a national forest in the past submitted comments on logging projects proposed by the Forest Service. The agency, in accordance with statutory and regulatory procedures for administrative appeals, mailed to the individual a copy of the agency's decision and informed her of her right to appeal it. The notice, however, provided the wrong due date for the appeal—it was one day too late. When the individual filed her appeal by the date set forth in the notice, the Forest Service dismissed it as untimely. The individual sues the Forest Service, claiming that it is estopped from dismissing her appeal. To support her standing, the plaintiff relies on both procedural injury (the denial of her right to participate in the appeals process) and informational injury (the right to have access to the additional information that would have been generated if the Forest Service had allowed the appeal). What results? See Bensman v. U.S. Forest Serv., 408 F.3d 945 (7th Cir. 2005). Compare Center for Biological Diversity, Inc. v. BP Am. Prod. Co., 704 F.3d 413, 418-421 (5th Cir. 2013) (holding that environmental group suffered a redressable, concrete informational injury as a result of BP's failure to submit reports on hazardous substance releases in connection with the Deepwater Horizon oil spill under the Emergency Planning and Community Right-to-Know Act) with Foundation on Economic Trends v. Lyng, 943 F.2d 79, 84 (D.C. Cir. 1991) (refusing to allow standing based on damage to a group's interest in disseminating the data expected to appear in an EIS). According to one court, informational injury "arises only in very specific statutory contexts where a statutory provision has explicitly created a right to information." A plaintiff alleging informational injury must (1) identify a statute that directly requires the defendant to disclose the information that plaintiff has a right to obtain, (2) show that it has been denied the information to which it is entitled, and (3) provide a credible claim that the information would be helpful to it. WildEarth Guardians v. Salazar, 859 F. Supp. 2d 83, 92-93 (D.D.C. 2012).

4. *The Functions of Standing Doctrine.* The courts use standing rules to serve more than one purpose. See generally Nichol, Rethinking Standing, 72 Cal. L. Rev. 68 (1984). They use it to ensure that litigants are truly adverse and thus likely to present the case effectively and that those most directly concerned are able to litigate the issues in a case. As late as 1968, the Supreme Court stated that standing law

does not by its own force raise separation of powers problems related to improper judicial interference in areas committed to other branches of the Federal Government. . . . Thus, in terms of Article III limitations on federal court jurisdiction, the question of standing is related only to whether the dispute sought to be adjudicated will be presented in an adversary context and in a form historically viewed as capable of judicial resolution. It is for that reason that the emphasis in standing problems is on whether the party invoking federal court jurisdiction has "a personal stake in the outcome of the controversy," and whether the dispute touches upon "the legal relations of parties having adverse legal interests."

Flast v. Cohen, 392 U.S. 83, 100 (1968). By 1984, the Court had declared that standing doctrine could be understood by reference to a "single basic idea—the idea of separation of powers." Allen v. Wright, 468 U.S. 737, 752 (1984). Since then, the Court's standing cases have been suffused with discussion of that idea. While the earlier, instrumental justifications are still advanced, they appear to have become secondary to some Justices. Cf. American Bottom Conservancy v. U.S. Army Corps of Eng'rs, 650 F.3d 652, 655-656 (7th Cir. 2011) (asserting that "[s]ome of the most frequently mentioned grounds for the constitutional doctrine of standing are tenuous," and that "the solidest grounds are practical (just like the avowedly prudential grounds for judge-made supplements to the Article III standard," including the need "to limit premature judicial interference with legislation, to prevent the federal courts from being overwhelmed by cases, and to ensure that the legal remedies of primary victims of wrongful conduct will not be usurped by persons trivially or not harmed at all by the wrong complained of").

Justice Scalia has remarked that the standing requirement excludes from the courts those interests that are likely to lose (or that have lost) in the political process (such as potential hikers and campers who would be harmed by construction of a new ski resort). Scalia, Rulemaking as Politics, 34 Admin. L. Rev. v, vi (1982).[b] Is it possible that standing restrictions will actually interfere with the democratic process? See Poisner, Comment, Environmental Values and Judicial Review After *Lujan*: Two Critiques of the Separation of Powers Theory of Standing, 18 Ecology L.Q. 335, 372 (1991) (judicial review may compensate for antidemocratic tendencies of the bureaucracy by lessening the danger of agency capture, equalizing bargaining power between regulated industries and public interest plaintiffs, and heightening public scrutiny of agency decisions). Elliott, The Functions of Standing, 61 Stan. L. Rev. 459 (2008), identifies three different ways in which the Supreme Court has invoked separation of powers principles in standing cases, and argues that the Court's failure to distinguish among these three functions has created confusion so that current standing law serves none of these functions well.

5. *Standing Doctrine and Citizen Suits.* What effect will *Defenders of Wildlife* have on the ability of private citizens to seek redress of allegedly unlawful government activity under the citizen suit provisions of the environmental laws (which are analyzed more thoroughly in Chapter 10, section C.4)? Professor Sunstein has claimed that, "[r]ead for all it is worth," *Defenders of Wildlife* invalidated the citizen suit provisions as they apply to actions to force agencies to perform nondiscretionary duties. Sunstein, What's Standing After *Lujan*: Of Citizen Suits, "Injuries," and Article III, 91 Mich. L. Rev. 163, 165 (1992). Does the Court's holding necessarily

---

b. See also Community Nutrition Inst. v. Block, 698 F.2d 1239, 1256 (D.C. Cir. 1983) (Scalia, J., concurring in part and dissenting in part), rev'd, 467 U.S. 340 (1984) ("Governmental mischief whose effects are widely distributed is more readily remedied through the political process, and does not call into play the distinctive function of the courts as guardians against oppression of the few by the many.").

sweep that broadly? The lower courts have not interpreted the case that way and have continued to reach the merits in citizen suits against EPA.

Justice Scalia based his analysis in *Defenders of Wildlife* on Article II as well as Article III. He has argued elsewhere that executive nonimplementation of statutes is part of a well-functioning democratic process, keeping law current with existing views. Scalia, The Doctrine of Standing as an Essential Element of the Separation of Powers, 17 Suffolk U. L. Rev. 881, 897 (1983). Professor Sunstein responds that the "take Care" clause does not authorize the executive to violate the law through insufficient action any more than it does so through overzealous enforcement. Sunstein, *supra*, 88 Colum. L. Rev. at 1471.

> If administrative action is legally inadequate or if the agency has violated the law by failing to act at all, there is no usurpation of executive prerogatives in a judicial decision to that effect. Such a decision is necessary in order to vindicate congressional directives, as part of the judicial function "to say what the law is." The "take Care" clause and concerns of separation of powers argue in favor of rather than against a judicial role when statutory beneficiaries challenge agency behavior as legally inadequate.

Id. at 1471-1472, citing Marbury v. Madison, 5 U.S. (1 Cranch) 137, 177 (1803).

6. *Causation and Redressability.* The other two prongs of Article III standing are causation and redressability. What evidence must a plaintiff introduce to trace impaired water used by its members to an upstream point source? See Piney Run Pres. Ass'n v. County Comm'rs, 268 F.3d 255 (4th Cir. 2001) (plaintiff need not show to a scientific certainty that defendant's effluent caused its harm, but only that defendant discharges a pollutant that causes or contributes to the kinds of injuries alleged). Compare Friends of the Earth, Inc. v. Crown Central Petroleum Corp., 95 F.3d 358 (5th Cir. 1996), in which the plaintiff alleged that the defendant had discharged pollutants and failed to monitor compliance in violation of the CWA. The court concluded that the plaintiff, whose members used a body of water located three tributaries and 18 miles downstream from the defendant's refinery, failed to show causation.

Justice Scalia stated in *Defenders of Wildlife* that when the existence of one or more elements of standing depends on the decisions of "independent actors" who are not before the court, it is ordinarily "substantially more difficult" to establish standing. This barrier has blocked access to the courts by some environmental groups. In Wilderness Soc'y v. Norton, 434 F.3d 584 (D.C. Cir. 2006), for example, a plaintiff alleging decreased enjoyment of wilderness areas in a national park lacked standing because the relief it sought—orders requiring the Park Service to complete wilderness recommendations to the President, a description of wilderness boundaries, and wilderness suitability assessments—would not necessarily change agency wilderness management practices. In National Parks Conservation Ass'n v. Manson, 414 F.3d 1 (D.C. Cir. 2005), however, an environmental group had standing to challenge the Interior Department's finding that construction of a power plant would not adversely affect visibility in nearby Yellowstone National Park, in violation of the CAA. A finding of adverse effect by Interior precludes the state pollution agency from issuing a permit under the Act. Given this "formal legal relationship" between Interior and the state agency, the latter was "not the sort of truly independent actor who could destroy the causation required for standing." Id. at 6.

How does Justice Scalia's opinion in *Defenders of Wildlife* facilitate the ability of plaintiffs alleging procedural injury to show causation and redressability? Consider

Ohio Forestry Ass'n, Inc. v. Sierra Club, 523 U.S. 726 (1998). In dismissing an environmental group's challenge to a Forest Service land and resource management plan as unripe, the Court noted that "a person with standing who is injured by a failure to comply with the NEPA procedure may complain of that failure at the time the failure takes place, for the claim can never get riper." Id. at 737. Does this statement encourage the lower courts to find that environmental groups alleging procedural injuries due to noncompliance with NEPA have satisfied Article III?

7. *Associational Standing.* An association may sue on behalf of its members if the members have standing to sue in their own right, the interests the association seeks to protect are germane to its purposes, and neither the claim asserted nor the relief requested requires the participation of individual members in the lawsuit. Hunt v. Washington State Apple Advertising Comm'n, 432 U.S. 333, 343 (1977). For a good discussion of the function of associational standing doctrine, see Coho Salmon v. Pacific Lumber Co., 30 F. Supp. 2d 1231 (N.D. Cal. 1998). In Building and Constr. Trades Council v. Downtown Dev., Inc., 448 F.3d 138 (2d Cir. 2006), the court explained that the "germaneness" condition requires a court to assess whether an association's lawsuit, if successful, would reasonably tend to further the general interests that individual members sought to vindicate in joining the association and whether the lawsuit bears a reasonable connection to the association's knowledge and experience. Under that test, a labor union could sue to abate waste disposal practices that allegedly created health risks for its members. An organization also may establish standing by showing that the defendant's action caused a concrete injury to its activities that is more than simply a setback to its abstract social interests. Havens Realty Corp. v. Coleman, 455 U.S. 363 (1982). In ASPCA v. Feld Entertainment, Inc., 659 F.3d 13 (D.C. Cir. 2011), the ASPCA failed to make that showing because the record did not support its claim that a circus's use of bullhooks and chains on elephants fostered a public impression (that the ASPCA spent money combating) that these practices are harmless.

NOTE ON STANDING TO SUE IN OTHER NATIONS

The United States was a world leader in the development of environmental law in the 1970s, and its legislation provided a model for the adoption of standards elsewhere. It is somewhat ironic that access to the courts in environmental law cases in some other countries has become more accommodating than in the United States. The decision of the Supreme Court of the Philippines in Oposa v. Secretary of the Dep't of Env't & Natural Res. Fulgencio Factoran, G.R. No. 101083, July 30, 1993, 33 I.L.M. 173 (1994), is illustrative. The court held that a group of Filipino minors seeking to halt destruction of the country's natural rain forest had a right to sue on behalf of future generations. The explicit constitutional right to a healthful ecology reflected the "well founded fears of [the Constitution's] framers" that unless that right were recognized and enforced, future generations would "stand to inherit nothing but parched earth incapable of sustaining life." Does the Filipino court's decision represent a sounder approach to environmental standing than that reflected in the U.S. Constitution, as interpreted by the U.S. Supreme Court?[c]

c. See generally Owens, Comparative Law and Standing to Sue: A Petition for Redress to the Environment, 7 Envtl. Law. 321 (2001).

The High Court of Australia endorsed broad citizen access to its courts in Truth About Motorways Pty Ltd. v. Macquarie Infrastructure Mgmt. Ltd. [2000] HCA 11 (9 March 2000). The issue was whether a corporation claiming no special interest in the subject matter of the dispute and that had suffered no loss or damage as a result of the defendant's conduct could sue under the Trade Practices Act, which prohibits misleading or deceptive conduct in trade or commerce. The Court concluded that the plaintiff had standing and that the provisions of the Act enabling the corporation to sue did not violate the Constitution. According to Gleeson, C.J., and McHugh, J., "Parliament, by conferring standing upon any person to invoke the jurisdiction of the court has, at one time, created the potential for a justiciable controversy and conferred jurisdiction to determine the controversy." Further, the separation of powers reasoning relied on in *Defenders of Wildlife* does not apply in Australia, where ministers of the executive branch sit in the Parliament. Canada's courts also have recognized "public interest standing" in environmental cases. See Friends of the Earth v. Canada (Governor in Council), 2008 FC 1183, 2008 CarswellNat 3763 (Fed. Ct. Vancouver, B.C. 2008) (finding that environmental group satisfied public interest standing because it had a genuine interest in the subject matter raised, it presented a serious issue, and there was no other reasonable and effective way to bring the matter before the court).

Suppose that an environmental group brings a citizen suit, alleging violations of CWA permits. Assuming the plaintiff can show that its members are suffering actual harm as a result of the defendant's discharges, it would have standing to seek an injunction barring further discharges in violation of the CWA because that relief would redress the alleged injuries. Would it also have standing to sue for the imposition of civil penalties, which are payable to the government, rather than the plaintiff? Consider the following case.

FRIENDS OF THE EARTH, INC. v. LAIDLAW ENVIRONMENTAL SERVICES (TOC), INC.
528 U.S. 167 (2000)

GINSBURG, J., delivered the opinion of the Court, in which REHNQUIST, C. J., and STEVENS, O'CONNOR, KENNEDY, SOUTER, and BREYER, JJ., joined. STEVENS, J., and KENNEDY, J., filed concurring opinions. SCALIA, J., filed a dissenting opinion, in which THOMAS, J., joined.

Justice GINSBURG delivered the opinion of the Court.

This case presents an important question concerning the operation of the citizen-suit provisions of the Clean Water Act. Congress authorized the federal district courts to entertain Clean Water Act suits initiated by "a person or persons having an interest which is or may be adversely affected." 33 U.S.C. §§1365(a), (g). To impel future compliance with the Act, a district court may prescribe injunctive relief in such a suit; additionally or alternatively, the court may impose civil penalties payable to the United States Treasury. §1365(a). In the Clean Water Act citizen suit now before us, the District Court determined that injunctive relief was inappropriate because the defendant, after the institution of the litigation, achieved substantial compliance with the terms of its discharge permit. The court did, however, assess a civil penalty of $405,800. The "total deterrent effect" of the penalty would be adequate to forestall future violations, the court reasoned, taking into account that the defendant "will be required to reimburse plaintiffs for a significant amount of legal fees and has, itself, incurred significant legal expenses."

The Court of Appeals vacated the District Court's order. The case became moot, the appellate court declared, once the defendant fully complied with the terms of its permit and the plaintiff failed to appeal the denial of equitable relief. "[C]ivil penalties payable to the government," the Court of Appeals stated, "would not redress any injury Plaintiffs have suffered." . . .

We reverse the judgment of the Court of Appeals. The appellate court erred in concluding that a citizen suitor's claim for civil penalties must be dismissed as moot when the defendant, albeit after commencement of the litigation, has come into compliance. In directing dismissal of the suit on grounds of mootness, the Court of Appeals incorrectly conflated our case law on initial standing to bring suit, see, e.g., Steel Co. v. Citizens for Better Environment, 523 U.S. 83 (1998), with our case law on post-commencement mootness. A defendant's voluntary cessation of allegedly unlawful conduct ordinarily does not suffice to moot a case. The Court of Appeals also misperceived the remedial potential of civil penalties. Such penalties may serve, as an alternative to an injunction, to deter future violations and thereby redress the injuries that prompted a citizen suitor to commence litigation.

[Section 402 of the CWA, 33 U.S.C. §1342, provides for the issuance by EPA or authorized states of National Pollutant Discharge Elimination System (NPDES) permits, which limit the discharge of pollutants and establish related monitoring and reporting requirements. Noncompliance with a permit constitutes a violation of the Act.

The South Carolina environmental agency issued an NPDES permit to Laidlaw, which owned a wastewater treatment plant in the state. The permit authorized Laidlaw to discharge treated water into the North Tyger River but placed limits on Laidlaw's discharge of several pollutants, including mercury, "an extremely toxic pollutant." The permit also imposed monitoring and reporting obligations. Laidlaw's discharges exceeded the permit limits for mercury nearly 500 times between 1987 and 1995, when the last recorded mercury discharge violation occurred.

In June 1992, FOE filed a citizen suit against Laidlaw, alleging noncompliance with the discharge limitations in Laidlaw's permit, as well as the related monitoring and reporting obligations. It sought declaratory and injunctive relief and an award of civil penalties. Laidlaw moved for summary judgment on the ground that FOE lacked Article III standing. The district court denied the motion, finding "by the very slimmest of margins," that FOE had standing.

In January 1997, the district court imposed on Laidlaw a civil penalty of $405,800, finding that it would have an adequate deterrent effect, even though Laidlaw had gained a total economic benefit of $1,092,581 as a result of its extended period of noncompliance with the discharge limit. The court denied injunctive relief because Laidlaw had been in "substantial compliance" with its permit since at least August 1992.

FOE appealed the civil penalty judgment, arguing that it was inadequate, but not the denial of injunctive relief. Laidlaw cross-appealed, arguing that FOE lacked standing. The Fourth Circuit assumed without deciding that FOE initially had standing to bring the action, but held that the case had since become moot. Citing Steel Co., that court found the case moot because "the only remedy currently available to [FOE]—civil penalties payable to the government—would not redress any injury

[FOE has] suffered." The court remanded with instructions to dismiss. After that decision, Laidlaw permanently closed its facility, dismantled it, and put it up for sale. According to Laidlaw, all discharges from the facility permanently ceased.]

II

A

The Constitution's case-or-controversy limitation on federal judicial authority, Art. III, §2, underpins both our standing and our mootness jurisprudence, but the two inquiries differ in respects critical to the proper resolution of this case, so we address them separately. Because the Court of Appeals was persuaded that the case had become moot and so held, it simply assumed without deciding that FOE had initial standing. But because we hold that the Court of Appeals erred in declaring the case moot, we have an obligation to assure ourselves that FOE had Article III standing at the outset of the litigation. . . .

Laidlaw contends first that FOE lacked standing from the outset even to seek injunctive relief, because the plaintiff organizations failed to show that any of their members had sustained or faced the threat of any "injury in fact" from Laidlaw's activities. In support of this contention Laidlaw points to the District Court's finding . . . that there had been "no demonstrated proof of harm to the environment" from Laidlaw's mercury discharge violations.

The relevant showing for purposes of Article III standing, however, is not injury to the environment but injury to the plaintiff. To insist upon the former rather than the latter as part of the standing inquiry (as the dissent in essence does) is to raise the standing hurdle higher than the necessary showing for success on the merits in an action alleging noncompliance with an NPDES permit. Focusing properly on injury to the plaintiff, the District Court found that FOE had demonstrated sufficient injury to establish standing. For example, FOE member Kenneth Lee Curtis averred in affidavits that he lived a half-mile from Laidlaw's facility; that he occasionally drove over the North Tyger River, and that it looked and smelled polluted; and that he would like to fish, camp, swim, and picnic in and near the river between 3 and 15 miles downstream from the facility, as he did when he was a teenager, but would not do so because he was concerned that the water was polluted by Laidlaw's discharges. . . .

These sworn statements, as the District Court determined, adequately documented injury in fact. We have held that environmental plaintiffs adequately allege injury in fact when they aver that they use the affected area and are persons "for whom the aesthetic and recreational values of the area will be lessened" by the challenged activity. Sierra Club v. Morton, 405 U.S. 727, 735 (1972). . . .

. . . [T]he affidavits and testimony presented by FOE in this case assert that Laidlaw's discharges, and the affiant members' reasonable concerns about the effects of those discharges, directly affected those affiants' recreational, aesthetic, and economic interests. These submissions present dispositively more than the mere "general averments" and "conclusory allegations" found inadequate in [Lujan I]. Nor can the affiants' conditional statements—that they would use the nearby North Tyger River for recreation if Laidlaw were not discharging pollutants into it—be equated with the speculative " 'some day' intentions" to visit endangered species halfway around the world that we held insufficient to show injury in fact in [Defenders of Wildlife] . . .

Laidlaw argues next that even if FOE had standing to seek injunctive relief, it lacked standing to seek civil penalties. Here the asserted defect is not injury but redressability. Civil penalties offer no redress to private plaintiffs, Laidlaw argues, because they are paid to the government, and therefore a citizen plaintiff can never have standing to seek them.

Laidlaw is right to insist that a plaintiff must demonstrate standing separately for each form of relief sought. But it is wrong to maintain that citizen plaintiffs facing ongoing violations never have standing to seek civil penalties.

We have recognized on numerous occasions that "all civil penalties have some deterrent effect." Hudson v. United States, 522 U.S. 93, 102 (1997). More specifically, Congress has found that civil penalties in Clean Water Act cases do more than promote immediate compliance by limiting the defendant's economic incentive to delay its attainment of permit limits; they also deter future violations. This congressional determination warrants judicial attention and respect. "The legislative history of the Act reveals that Congress wanted the district court to consider the need for retribution and deterrence, in addition to restitution, when it imposed civil penalties. . . . [The district court may] seek to deter future violations by basing the penalty on its economic impact." Tull v. United States, 481 U.S. 412, 422-423 (1987).

It can scarcely be doubted that, for a plaintiff who is injured or faces the threat of future injury due to illegal conduct ongoing at the time of suit, a sanction that effectively abates that conduct and prevents its recurrence provides a form of redress. Civil penalties can fit that description. To the extent that they encourage defendants to discontinue current violations and deter them from committing future ones, they afford redress to citizen plaintiffs who are injured or threatened with injury as a consequence of ongoing unlawful conduct.

The dissent argues that it is the availability rather than the imposition of civil penalties that deters any particular polluter from continuing to pollute. This argument misses the mark in two ways. First, it overlooks the interdependence of the availability and the imposition; a threat has no deterrent value unless it is credible that it will be carried out. Second, it is reasonable for Congress to conclude that an actual award of civil penalties does in fact bring with it a significant quantum of deterrence over and above what is achieved by the mere prospect of such penalties. A would-be polluter may or may not be dissuaded by the existence of a remedy on the books, but a defendant once hit in its pocketbook will surely think twice before polluting again.[2]

We recognize that there may be a point at which the deterrent effect of a claim for civil penalties becomes so insubstantial or so remote that it cannot support citizen standing. The fact that this vanishing point is not easy to ascertain does not detract from the deterrent power of such penalties in the ordinary case. . . . In this case we need not explore the outer limits of the principle that civil penalties provide sufficient deterrence to support redressability. Here, the civil penalties sought by FOE carried with them a deterrent effect that made it likely, as opposed to merely speculative, that the penalties would redress FOE's injuries by abating current violations and

---

2. The dissent suggests that there was little deterrent work for civil penalties to do in this case because the lawsuit brought against Laidlaw by DHEC had already pushed the level of deterrence to "near the top of the graph." This suggestion ignores the District Court's specific finding that the penalty agreed to by Laidlaw and DHEC was far too low to remove Laidlaw's economic benefit from noncompliance, and thus was inadequate to deter future violations. And it begins to look especially farfetched when one recalls that Laidlaw itself prompted the DHEC lawsuit, paid the filing fee, and drafted the complaint.

preventing future ones—as the District Court reasonably found when it assessed a penalty of $405,800.

Laidlaw contends that the reasoning of our decision in *Steel Co.* directs the conclusion that citizen plaintiffs have no standing to seek civil penalties under the Act. We disagree. *Steel Co.* established that citizen suitors lack standing to seek civil penalties for violations that have abated by the time of suit. We specifically noted in that case that there was no allegation in the complaint of any continuing or imminent violation, and that no basis for such an allegation appeared to exist. In short, *Steel Co.* held that private plaintiffs, unlike the Federal Government, may not sue to assess penalties for wholly past violations, but our decision in that case did not reach the issue of standing to seek penalties for violations that are ongoing at the time of the complaint and that could continue into the future if undeterred.[4]

B

. . . [W]e turn to the question of mootness.

The only conceivable basis for a finding of mootness in this case is Laidlaw's voluntary conduct—either its achievement by August 1992 of substantial compliance with its NPDES permit or its more recent shutdown of the Roebuck facility. It is well settled that "a defendant's voluntary cessation of a challenged practice does not deprive a federal court of its power to determine the legality of the practice." *City of Mesquite*, 455 U.S., at 289. "[I]f it did, the courts would be compelled to leave '[t]he defendant . . . free to return to his old ways.'" Id., at 289, n.10. . . . "A case might become moot if subsequent events made it absolutely clear that the allegedly wrongful behavior could not reasonably be expected to recur." United States v. Concentrated Phosphate Export Ass'n, Inc., 393 U.S. 199, 203 (1968). The "heavy burden of per-sua[ding]" the court that the challenged conduct cannot reasonably be expected to start up again lies with the party asserting mootness.

The Court of Appeals justified its mootness disposition by reference to *Steel Co.*, which held that citizen plaintiffs lack standing to seek civil penalties for wholly past violations. In relying on *Steel Co.*, the Court of Appeals confused mootness with standing. The confusion is understandable, given this Court's repeated statements that the doctrine of mootness can be described as "the doctrine of standing set in a time frame: The requisite personal interest that must exist at the commencement of the litigation (standing) must continue throughout its existence (mootness)." [Arizonans for Official English v. Arizona, 520 U.S. 43, 68 n.22 (1997).]

Careful reflection on the long-recognized exceptions to mootness, however, reveals that the description of mootness as "standing set in a time frame" is not comprehensive. As just noted, a defendant claiming that its voluntary compliance moots a case bears the formidable burden of showing that it is absolutely clear the allegedly wrongful behavior could not reasonably be expected to recur. By contrast, in a lawsuit

---

4. . . . The dissent's . . . charge that citizen suits for civil penalties under the Act carry "grave implications for democratic governance," seems to us overdrawn. Certainly the federal Executive Branch does not share the dissent's view that such suits dissipate its authority to enforce the law. In fact, the Department of Justice has endorsed this citizen suit from the outset, submitting amicus briefs in support of FOE in the District Court, the Court of Appeals, and this Court. As we have already noted, the Federal Government retains the power to foreclose a citizen suit by undertaking its own action. 33 U.S.C. §1365(b)(1)(B). And if the Executive Branch opposes a particular citizen suit, the statute allows the Administrator of the EPA to "intervene as a matter of right" and bring the Government's views to the attention of the court. §1365(c)(2).

brought to force compliance, it is the plaintiff's burden to establish standing by demonstrating that, if unchecked by the litigation, the defendant's allegedly wrongful behavior will likely occur or continue, and that the "threatened injury [is] certainly impending." Whitmore v. Arkansas, 495 U. S. 149, 158 (1990). . . . The plain lesson of these cases is that there are circumstances in which the prospect that a defendant will engage in (or resume) harmful conduct may be too speculative to support standing, but not too speculative to overcome mootness. . . .

Standing doctrine functions to ensure, among other things, that the scarce resources of the federal courts are devoted to those disputes in which the parties have a concrete stake. In contrast, by the time mootness is an issue, the case has been brought and litigated, often (as here) for years. To abandon the case at an advanced stage may prove more wasteful than frugal. This argument from sunk costs does not license courts to retain jurisdiction over cases in which one or both of the parties plainly lacks a continuing interest, as when the parties have settled or a plaintiff pursuing a nonsurviving claim has died. But the argument surely highlights an important difference between the two doctrines.

. . . Denial of injunctive relief does not necessarily mean that the district court has concluded there is no prospect of future violations for civil penalties to deter. Indeed, it meant no such thing in this case. The District Court denied injunctive relief, but expressly based its award of civil penalties on the need for deterrence. . . .

. . . The facility closure, like Laidlaw's earlier achievement of substantial compliance with its permit requirements, might moot the case, but—we once more reiterate—only if one or the other of these events made it absolutely clear that Laidlaw's permit violations could not reasonably be expected to recur. The effect of both Laidlaw's compliance and the facility closure on the prospect of future violations is a disputed factual matter. FOE points out, for example—and Laidlaw does not appear to contest—that Laidlaw retains its NPDES permit. These issues have not been aired in the lower courts; they remain open for consideration on remand. . . .

[Justice Stevens's concurring opinion is omitted.]

Justice KENNEDY, concurring.

Difficult and fundamental questions are raised when we ask whether exactions of public fines by private litigants, and the delegation of Executive power which might be inferable from the authorization, are permissible in view of the responsibilities committed to the Executive by Article II of the Constitution of the United States. The questions presented in the petition for certiorari did not identify these issues with particularity; and neither the Court of Appeals in deciding the case nor the parties in their briefing before this Court devoted specific attention to the subject. In my view these matters are best reserved for a later case. With this observation, I join the opinion of the Court.

Justice SCALIA, with whom Justice THOMAS joins, dissenting.

The Court begins its analysis by finding injury in fact on the basis of vague affidavits that are undermined by the District Court's express finding that Laidlaw's discharges caused no demonstrable harm to the environment. It then proceeds to marry private wrong with public remedy in a union that violates traditional principles of federal standing—thereby permitting law enforcement to be placed in the hands of private individuals. Finally, the Court suggests that to avoid mootness one needs even less of a stake in the outcome than the Court's watered-down requirements for initial standing. I dissent from all of this. . . .

I

. . .

Typically, an environmental plaintiff claiming injury due to discharges in violation of the Clean Water Act argues that the discharges harm the environment, and that the harm to the environment injures him. This route to injury is barred in the present case, however, since the District Court concluded after considering all the evidence that there had been "no demonstrated proof of harm to the environment," [and] that the "permit violations at issue in this citizen suit did not result in any health risk or environmental harm." . . .

The Court finds [that] "[t]he relevant showing for purposes of Article III standing . . . is not injury to the environment but injury to the plaintiff." This statement is correct, as far as it goes. We have certainly held that a demonstration of harm to the environment is not enough to satisfy the injury-in-fact requirement unless the plaintiff can demonstrate how he personally was harmed. E.g., [*Defenders of Wildlife*,] *supra*, at 563. In the normal course, however, a lack of demonstrable harm to the environment will translate, as it plainly does here, into a lack of demonstrable harm to citizen plaintiffs. While it is perhaps possible that a plaintiff could be harmed even though the environment was not, such a plaintiff would have the burden of articulating and demonstrating the nature of that injury. . . . Plaintiffs here have made no attempt at such a showing, but rely entirely upon unsupported and unexplained affidavit allegations of "concern." . . .

Inexplicably, the Court is untroubled by this. . . . Although we have previously refused to find standing based on the "conclusory allegations of an affidavit" [*Lujan I*], the Court is content to do just that today. By accepting plaintiffs' vague, contradictory, and unsubstantiated allegations of "concern" about the environment as adequate to prove injury in fact, and accepting them even in the face of a finding that the environment was not demonstrably harmed, the Court makes the injury-in-fact requirement a sham. If there are permit violations, and a member of a plaintiff environmental organization lives near the offending plant, it would be difficult not to satisfy today's lenient standard.

II

The Court's treatment of the redressability requirement—which would have been unnecessary if it resolved the injury-in-fact question correctly—is equally cavalier. As discussed above, petitioners allege ongoing injury consisting of diminished enjoyment of the affected waterways and decreased property values. They allege that these injuries are caused by Laidlaw's continuing permit violations. But the remedy petitioners seek is neither recompense for their injuries nor an injunction against future violations. Instead, the remedy is a statutorily specified "penalty" for past violations, payable entirely to the United States Treasury. Only last Term, we held that such penalties do not redress any injury a citizen plaintiff has suffered from past violations. Steel Co. v. Citizens for Better Environment, 523 U.S. 83, 106-107 (1998). The Court nonetheless finds the redressability requirement satisfied here, [holding] that a penalty payable to the public "remedies" a threatened private harm, and suffices to sustain a private suit.

That holding has no precedent in our jurisprudence . . . . Even if it were appropriate, moreover, to allow Article III's remediation requirement to be satisfied by the indirect private consequences of a public penalty, those consequences are entirely too speculative in the present case. The new standing law that the Court makes—like all expansions of standing beyond the traditional constitutional limits—has grave implications for democratic governance. . . .

. . . [I]t is my view that a plaintiff's desire to benefit from the deterrent effect of a public penalty for past conduct can never suffice to establish a case or controversy of the sort known to our law. Such deterrent effect is, so to speak, "speculative as a matter of law." . . .

By permitting citizens to pursue civil penalties payable to the Federal Treasury, the Act does not provide a mechanism for individual relief in any traditional sense, but turns over to private citizens the function of enforcing the law. A Clean Water Act plaintiff pursuing civil penalties acts as a self-appointed mini-EPA. Where, as is often the case, the plaintiff is a national association, it has significant discretion in choosing enforcement targets. Once the association is aware of a reported violation, it need not look long for an injured member, at least under the theory of injury the Court applies today. And once the target is chosen, the suit goes forward without meaningful public control. The availability of civil penalties vastly disproportionate to the individual injury gives citizen plaintiffs massive bargaining power—which is often used to achieve settlements requiring the defendant to support environmental projects of the plaintiffs' choosing. Thus is a public fine diverted to a private interest.

To be sure, the EPA may foreclose the citizen suit by itself bringing suit. 33 U.S.C. §1365(b)(1)(B). This allows public authorities to avoid private enforcement only by accepting private direction as to when enforcement should be undertaken—which is no less constitutionally bizarre. Elected officials are entirely deprived of their discretion to decide that a given violation should not be the object of suit at all, or that the enforcement decision should be postponed. This is the predictable and inevitable consequence of the Court's allowing the use of public remedies for private wrongs. . . .

NOTES AND QUESTIONS

1. *Injury in Fact.* Why were the plaintiffs in *Laidlaw* able to prove injury in fact whereas the plaintiffs in *Defenders of Wildlife* were not? Was it simply a matter of providing more detailed affidavits? How did the plaintiffs demonstrate injury, given the district court's finding that the defendant's discharge did not harm the quality of the receiving water? Farber, Environmental Litigation after *Laidlaw*, 30 Envtl. L. Rep. 10516 (2000), argues that the effect of *Laidlaw* is to shift the focus of standing analysis under Article III in citizen suits against polluters from the impact of the defendant's activities on the plaintiff alone to the disruption of the plaintiff's relationship with the affected natural resources.[d]

2. *Fear, Risk, and Injury in Fact.* The plaintiffs in *Laidlaw* based their claim of injury in fact on their unwillingness to use the river due to concerns that Laidlaw's discharges were polluting it. Did the alleged injury arise from their fear of exposure to polluted river water or from a risk that if they did use the water, they would suffer adverse health effects?

d. Symposium, Citizen Suits and the Future of Standing in the 21st Century: From *Lujan* to *Laidlaw* and Beyond, 11 Duke Envtl. L. & Pol'y F. No. 2 (2001); 12 Duke Envtl. L. & Pol'y F. No. 1 (2001), analyzes the state of standing law after *Laidlaw* from a variety of perspectives.

If a plaintiff relies on fear of the adverse consequences of exposure to pollution to show injury in fact, must it show that the fear is reasonable? How can it do so? Friends of the Earth, Inc. v. Gaston Copper Recycling Corp., 204 F.3d 149 (4th Cir. 2000), addressed those questions. The defendant was a metals-smelting facility alleged to be violating the CWA by discharging metals in excess of permit limits. One of the plaintiff's members (Shealy) lived four miles downstream from the facility on property that included a lake formed behind a dam on the creek into which the metals were discharged. Shealy alleged that the defendant's pollution adversely affected his use and enjoyment of the lake. He was concerned that defendant's discharges polluted the lake and that the discharged metals had lodged in fish there. He also alleged that the discharges caused a decline in the value of his property. The court held that the plaintiff had standing. Shealy produced evidence of actual or threatened injury to a waterway in which he had a legally protected interest, given that he was a property owner whose lake lay in the path of the defendant's discharge. He and his family fished and swam in the lake. He presented ample evidence that his fears were reasonable and not based on mere conjecture. The defendant's discharge limits were set at the level necessary to protect the designated uses of the receiving waterways. As a result, "their violation necessarily means that these uses may be harmed." Id. at 157. The court also indicated that threatened injury can satisfy Article III's standing requirements. "Threats or increased risk thus constitutes cognizable harm. Threatened environmental injury is by nature probabilistic. And yet other circuits have had no trouble understanding the injurious nature of risk itself." Id. at 160. By demanding more than that by way of proof of injury, the district court engaged in "a judicial evisceration of the Clean Water Act's protections. And separation of powers will not countenance it." Id. at 161. After Shealy's death, the Fourth Circuit allowed the suit to proceed on the basis of another group member, Jones, who was the president of a company that provided guided canoe and kayak trips on the river. The company provided fewer trips due to concern that runoff from Gaston's facility was polluting the water. Jones himself had conducted some of the trips, so that he used the area affected by the discharges. Friends of the Earth, Inc. v. Gaston Copper Recycling Corp., 629 F.3d 387 (4th Cir. 2011).

Suppose that an environmental group files suit alleging that EPA's approval of a CAA permit creates uncertainty among the group's members, who live near the permitted sources, as to whether the sources' emissions are harming their health. Are these allegations sufficient to demonstrate injury in fact under Article III? See New York Pub. Interest Research Group v. Whitman, 321 F.3d 316 (2d Cir. 2003). Compare Pollack v. U.S. Dep't of Justice, 577 F.3d 736 (7th Cir. 2009) (holding that environmental organization and its members lacked standing to challenge operation of gun range involving discharge of bullets into the environment, finding allegations that member intended to drink water that he feared was contaminated by lead were insufficient).

Justice Scalia stated in Defenders of Wildlife that to satisfy Article III, a plaintiff must allege injuries that are actual or imminent rather than conjectural or hypothetical. May a risk of future harm suffice under this standard? NRDC v. EPA, 464 F.3d 1 (D.C. Cir. 2006), held that NRDC's members alleged sufficient injury to challenge an EPA regulation exempting emissions of methyl bromide from CAA provisions designed to protect the stratospheric ozone layer. The court confirmed that increases in risk can suffice to confer standing, noting that environmental and health injuries often are "purely probabilistic." To prevent this category of injury from becoming "too expansive," the court generally requires plaintiffs to demonstrate a "substantial probability" that they will be injured. NRDC met that test based on expert testimony showing a lifetime risk of about 1 in 200,000 that an individual would develop nonfatal skin cancer as a result of EPA's rule. See also NRDC v. EPA, 735 F.3d 873, 878-879 (9th Cir. 2013) (finding that environmental group had standing to challenge EPA's registration of pesticide under FIFRA based on "credible threat" that members' children would be exposed to the pesticide if it were approved, making alleged injury actual or imminent); Northwest Envtl. Def. Ctr. v. Owens Corning Corp., 434 F. Supp. 2d 957 (D. Or. 2006) (finding standing based on allegation that defendant's emissions of HCFCs would contribute to ozone depletion, heightening the risk that plaintiff's members would be exposed to damaging levels of ultraviolet radiation). Compare Sierra Club v. EPA, 754 F.3d 995 (D.C. Cir. 2014) (plaintiffs alleging harm from EPA memo directing states how to implement CAA's interstate pollution provisions failed to meet substantial probability test).

In other cases, the courts have stepped back from broad recognition of increased risk as injury in fact. In Utility Air Regulatory Group v. EPA, 471 F.3d 1333 (D.C. Cir. 2006), the court warned parties not to rely on statistical evidence when they have better evidence at hand, although the size of the group's membership in that case was enough to indicate a "substantial probability" of injury. In Public Citizen, Inc. v. NHTSA, 513 F.3d 234, 241 (D.C. Cir. 2008), the court found that the imminence requirement demands "a very strict understanding of what increases in risk and overall risk levels will support injury in fact." In Summers v. Earth Island Inst., 555 U.S. 488 (2009), the Supreme Court, in holding that environmental groups lacked standing to challenge the Forest Service's exemption of salvage timber sales from statutory public notice, comment, and appeal procedures, refused to "replace the requirement of imminent harm . . . with the requirement of a *realistic* threat that reoccurrence of the challenged activity would cause the plaintiff harm in the reasonably near future." Id. at 499-500. The Court rejected the dissent's "hitherto unheard-of test for organizational standing: whether, accepting the organization's self-description of the activities of its members, there is a statistical probability that some of those members are threatened with concrete injury." Id. at 497. In Monsanto Co. v. Geertson Seed Farms, 561 U.S. 139, 153-156 (2010), however, the Court ruled that farmers seeking to block marketing of a genetically altered pesticide met the injury in fact requirement by showing a substantial risk (reasonable probability) that their crops would be infected with the engineered gene. What is the difference between the two cases, other than that *Summers* involved an environmental plaintiff and *Geertson* involved an economic plaintiff? Compare Chamber of Commerce of the U.S. v. EPA, 642 F.3d 192 (D.C. Cir. 2011) (holding that auto dealers claiming that EPA's grant of a waiver to California of the CAA's preemption of state authority to regulate new motor vehicle emissions would cause them to lose sales lacked standing because their allegations of future injury were speculative and injury was not imminent). Most recently, the Supreme Court referred to "the well-established requirement that threatened injury must be 'certainly impending.'" Clapper v. Amnesty Int'l, USA, 133 S. Ct. 1138, 1143 (2013). It is not clear whether the lower courts will interpret this case as narrowing standing based on threats of future harm. See, e.g., Sierra Club v. EPA, 755 F.3d 968, 973 (D.C. Cir. 2014) (emphasis added) (stating that an allegation of threatened injury may suffice if it is "certainly impending *or* there is a substantial risk that harm will occur").

Cases involving climate change are particularly likely to give rise to allegations of risk-based injuries given the uncertainties surrounding the contributions of individual emission sources of greenhouse gases and the effects of climate change. The Supreme Court held that states had standing to challenge EPA's denial of their petition to regulate greenhouse gas emissions from motor vehicles in Massachusetts v. EPA, 549 U.S. 497 (2007). Standing issues surrounding climate change are discussed in section E of Chapter 12.

3. *Causation and Redressability.* The CWA's citizen suit provision authorizes the payment of civil penalties exclusively to the government. How, then, were the plaintiffs in *Laidlaw* able to demonstrate that the imposition of civil penalties would redress their alleged injury? How did the majority distinguish the *Steel Co.* case? If the penalty payment winds up in the public coffers, how can it be said that the result of *Laidlaw* is that "a public fine is diverted to a private interest"? Is a citizen suit plaintiff really "self-appointed," given that Congress has authorized individuals or groups with standing to bring citizen suits?

Even after *Laidlaw*, environmental plaintiffs may have difficulty establishing causation and redressability. In American Petroleum Inst. v. EPA, 216 F.3d 50 (D.C. Cir. 2000), environmental groups challenged EPA's decision not to classify unleaded gas storage tank sediment (UGSTS) as a hazardous waste under the Resource Conservation and Recovery Act. The court held that the groups lacked standing because they failed to establish either a substantial probability that the shipments to the landfills located near members' properties contained UGSTS or a link between such deposits and the specific harms alleged by their members. Because the petitioners failed to connect their alleged injuries to UGSTS, they could not establish a likelihood that the alleged injuries would be redressed by a favorable decision requiring listing either.

Suppose that owners and operators of air pollution sources sue EPA to challenge its approval of a state implementation plan for achieving the national ambient air quality standards under the CAA, which regulates those sources. EPA claims that the plaintiffs lack standing because any injuries they suffer will result from the specific control measures adopted by the state in the plan, and not from any action by EPA. What would be the result? See BCCA Appeal Group v. EPA, 355 F.3d 817 (5th Cir. 2003). Compare Texas v. EPA, 726 F.3d 180 (D.C. Cir. 2013) (holding that industrial petitioners lacked standing to challenge EPA rule requiring permits for sources emitting greenhouse gases because the statutory permit requirement is self-implementing and the rule mitigated the petitioners' harms in that without it, the sources could not operate at all). Suppose that an environmental group sues EPA, alleging that it failed to comply with a statutory duty to issue regulations limiting discharges of water pollutants under the CWA. The members' affidavits state that they regularly use rivers and lakes that are polluted by industries that would be subject to the regulations if EPA issued them. What arguments can EPA make that the group has not met either the injury in fact or redressability requirements?

4. *Standing and Mootness.* According to the majority in *Laidlaw*, how do the inquiries into standing and mootness differ? Are the purposes of the two doctrines different? Why wasn't the case moot given that the defendant had ceased discharging and shut down the offending facility? Suppose that a company violates its NPDES permit but sells the point source at which the violation occurred before the filing of a citizen suit seeking payment of civil penalties. Is the case moot? See San Francisco Baykeeper, Inc. v. Tosco Corp., 309 F.3d 1153 (9th Cir. 2002). Suppose an environmental group sues a point source for discharging without a permit. After the complaint is filed, the state pollution control agency issues a permit that covers the point source's

discharges. Is the case moot? May the court assess civil penalties for the discharges that occurred before issuance of the permit? See Mississippi River Revival, Inc. v. City of Minneapolis, 319 F.3d 1013 (8th Cir. 2003).

NOTE ON PRUDENTIAL AND STATUTORY STANDING REQUIREMENTS

For years, the courts have referred to "prudential limitations" on standing that may provide a basis for denying standing even if a plaintiff satisfies the three-part Article III test. These courts identified three such non-constitutional limits. First, the harm asserted by the plaintiff must not represent a "generalized grievance" shared in substantially equal measure by all or a large class of citizens. Suppose plaintiffs alleging a violation of the CAA's stratospheric ozone protection provisions claim that the defendant, the operator of a landfill, released CFCs into the environment because the landfill was improperly managed and that the release created an increased risk that the plaintiffs would get skin cancer because of the depletion of the ozone layer caused by the CFCs. Is this the kind of generalized grievance that the court should refuse to hear? See Covington v. Jefferson County, 358 F.3d 626, 649-655 (9th Cir. 2004) (Gould, J., concurring) (reading Supreme Court standing cases as rejecting the proposition that "injury to all is injury to none"); Northwest Envtl. Def. Ctr. v. Owens Corning Corp., 434 F. Supp. 2d 957, 969 (D. Or. 2006) (concluding that "issues such as global warming and ozone depletion may be of 'wide public significance' but they are neither 'abstract questions' nor mere 'generalized grievances'"). It now appears that the bar on adjudication of generalized grievance may be of constitutional origin, however. In Lexmark Int'l, Inc. v. Static Control Components, Inc., 134 S. Ct. 1377, 1387 n.3 (2014), the Court stated that "[w]hile we have at times grounded our reluctance to entertain [suits involving generalized grievances] in the 'counsels of prudence' (albeit counsels 'close[ly] relat[ed] to the policies reflected in' Article III), we have since held that such suits do not present constitutional 'cases' or 'controversies.'" They are barred for constitutional reasons, not 'prudential' ones."

Second, the plaintiff generally must assert his or her own legal rights and interests rather than those of third parties.

> Without such limitations—closely related to Art. III concerns but essentially matters of judicial self-governance—the courts would be called upon to decide abstract questions of wide public significance even though other governmental institutions may be more competent to address the questions and even though judicial intervention may be unnecessary to protect individual rights. [Warth v. Seldin, 422 U.S. 490, 500 (1975).]

Third, the plaintiff's alleged injury must be within the zone of interest protected or regulated by the constitutional or statutory provision in question. When the plaintiff relies on the APA rather than a substantive statute for its right to seek review, the zone of interest test is a judicial gloss on §702 of the APA, which provides that a person "adversely affected or aggrieved by agency action *within the meaning of a relevant statute*" may seek review (emphasis added). The zone of interest test also applies to claims based on substantive statutes such as the ESA. Although the term "prudential" standing rules is sometimes used to refer to court-created limits, the Court in *Lexmark*

Int'l made it clear that, however denominated, the zone of interest test (except when a cause of action is based on the Constitution itself) is of statutory origin, not a creature of judicial invention: "Although we admittedly have placed [the zone of interest] test under the 'prudential' rubric in the past, it does not belong there: . . . Whether a plaintiff comes within 'the "zone of interests"'' is an issue that requires us to determine, using traditional tools of statutory interpretation, whether a legislatively conferred cause of action encompasses a particular plaintiff's claim." 134 S. Ct. at 1387.

Environmental plaintiffs have had little difficulty satisfying the zone of interest test in post-*Lujan* cases. Is the zone of interest requirement likely to provide a significant obstacle to developmental interests? The Supreme Court addressed the issue in Bennett v. Spear, 520 U.S. 154 (1997). The Bureau of Reclamation (BoR), which administered the Klamath irrigation project, consulted under the ESA with the FWS after informing the FWS that the project's operation might affect two species of endangered fish. The FWS issued a biological opinion finding it likely that operation would jeopardize the fish and describing "reasonable and prudent alternatives" (RPAs) to avoid jeopardy, including maintenance of minimum water levels in some lakes and reservoirs. The BoR agreed to abide by these RPAs. Two irrigation districts that received water from the project and two ranches within those districts sued the FWS, but not the BoR, denying that the project was responsible for any decline in fish populations or that minimum water levels would benefit the fish. The plaintiffs alleged that these deficiencies violated §7 of the ESA, which requires each federal agency to ensure that its actions not be likely to jeopardize the continued existence of any listed species or result in the destruction or adverse modification of its critical habitat. They also alleged that the FWS violated §4 of the ESA, which governs the listing and critical habitat designation process, by failing to consider the economic impact of critical habitat designation, and that the agency acted in an arbitrary and capricious fashion in violation of the APA. The plaintiffs claimed that their use of Klamath project water for recreational, aesthetic, and commercial purposes (including irrigation) would be damaged by implementation of the RPAs through reduction of the amounts of water available to them. The lower courts found no standing because these purposes did not fall within the ESA's zone of interest, but the Supreme Court reversed.

The Court held first that, by adopting the ESA's broadly worded citizen suit provision, 16 U.S.C. §1540(g), which authorizes "any person" to sue to enforce the Act, Congress repealed the zone of interest limitation on standing. Justice Scalia read that provision literally because

> the overall subject matter of this legislation is the environment (a matter in which it is common to think all persons have an interest) and . . . the obvious purpose of the particular provision in question is to encourage enforcement by so-called "private attorneys general." . . . The statutory language . . . is . . . clear[], and the subject of the legislation makes the intent to permit enforcement by everyman even more plausible.
>
> It is true that the plaintiffs here are seeking to prevent application of environmental restrictions rather than to implement them. But the "any person" formulation applies to all the causes of action authorized by §1540(g)—not only to actions against private violators of environmental restrictions, and not only to actions against the Secretary asserting underenforcement under §1533, but also to actions against the Secretary asserting overenforcement under §1533. . . . [Id. at 165-166.]

After finding that the plaintiffs had constitutional standing, the Court concluded that the ESA authorized review of the petitioners' claim that the FWS failed to take economic impact into account in designating critical habitat. It also held, however, that the ESA's citizen suit provision did not vest the district court with jurisdiction of claims alleging that the FWS violated §7 of the ESA by acting without adequate supporting data. Judicial review of those claims was nevertheless available under the APA, provided the plaintiffs had standing. In defining the zone of interests within which plaintiffs' interests had to fall, the Court looked to the substantive statutory provisions allegedly violated by the FWS, §7 of the ESA. The district court found no standing because the plaintiffs were not directly regulated by the ESA and did not seek to vindicate its "overarching purpose of species preservation." But the Court stated that the scope of the statutory zone of interests must be assessed by reference to the particular provision whose violation forms the basis for the complaint. Section 7 of the ESA requires that each agency "use the best scientific and commercial data available" in ensuring that its actions not jeopardize listed species or adversely affect their critical habitat. The Court found that the purpose of that provision is

> to ensure that the ESA not be implemented haphazardly, on the basis of speculation or surmise. While this no doubt serves to advance the ESA's overall goal of species preservation, we think it readily apparent that another objective (if not indeed the primary one) is to avoid needless economic dislocation produced by agency officials zealously but unintelligently pursuing their environmental objectives. That economic consequences are an explicit concern of the Act is evidenced by §1536(h), which provides exemption from §1536(a)(2)'s no-jeopardy mandate where there are no reasonable and prudent alternatives to the agency action and the benefits of the agency action clearly outweigh the benefits of any alternatives. We believe the "best scientific and commercial data" provision is similarly intended, at least in part, to prevent uneconomic (because erroneous) jeopardy determinations. Petitioners' claim that they are victims of such a mistake is plainly within the zone of interests that the provision protects. . . .

Id. at 176-177. Accordingly, the plaintiff's §4 claim was reviewable under the ESA's citizen suit provision and its §7 claims were reviewable under the APA. Buzbee, Expanding the Zone, Tilting the Field: Zone of Interests and Article III Standing Analysis after *Bennett v. Spear*, 49 Admin. L. Rev. 763, 764-765 (1997), maintains that *Bennett* results in "skewed standing criteria, or what I refer to as a 'tilted standing playing field,' disfavoring claims brought by the beneficiaries of regulation."

Do nonhuman environmental resources, such as animals, have standing to sue? In Cetacean Cmty. v. Bush, 386 F.3d 1169 (9th Cir. 2004), the court concluded that nothing in Article III prevents Congress from authorizing suits to be brought on behalf of animals. It also concluded, however, that Congress did not provide such authorization in the ESA, the Marine Mammal Protection Act, NEPA, or the APA.

Section 102(2)(C) of NEPA requires that federal agencies prepare environmental impact statements before proceeding with any major federal action significantly affecting the quality of the environment. Does a plaintiff asserting economic injury have standing to challenge an agency's noncompliance with this NEPA obligation? In Ashley Creek Phosphate Co. v. Norton, 420 F.3d 924 (9th Cir. 2005), the court held that a plaintiff whose interests are purely economic in nature is not within NEPA's zone of interests. Accordingly, the court ruled that

Ashley Creek did not have standing to challenge the BLM's decision to issue a phosphate lease to a manufacturer of phosphate-based fertilizer. Ashley Creek had challenged the decision on the basis of an alleged NEPA violation, asserting that the BLM should have considered as an alternative to issuance of the lease the possibility that the lessee could get all the phosphate it needed by purchasing phosphate mined by Ashley Creek, 250 miles away from the lease site. The Supreme Court held in Monsanto Co. v. Geertson Seed Farms, 561 U.S. 139, 153-156 (2010), that farmers alleging NEPA noncompliance fell within the statute's zone of interests, even if they sought to avoid economic harms, because they also sought to prevent significant environmental harms stemming from the use of genetically modified crops.

Will regulated entities who complain that their competitors are being treated too leniently by EPA be able to satisfy the zone of interest test? See, e.g., Honeywell Int'l, Inc. v. EPA, 374 F.3d 1363 (D.C. Cir. 2004).

Problem 3-1

The Clean Air Act requires that each state achieve national ambient air quality standards (NAAQS) designed to protect the public health with an adequate margin of safety. EPA has established NAAQS for ozone, among other air pollutants. After finding that the states in the Northeast have not yet achieved the ozone NAAQS and are unlikely to do so under current regulatory requirements, EPA issued a regulation requiring each state in the Northeast to implement a low-emission vehicle (LEV) plan that was already being implemented in California. California's LEV plan requires that 25 percent of the new car sales by each car manufacturer selling cars in that state be composed of cars that meet California's emission controls for two precursors of ozone pollution, hydrocarbons and oxides of nitrogen. California's controls are more stringent than the vehicle emission standards otherwise applicable to the auto manufacturers under the statute.

The Hot Rod Club of New Jersey (Hot Rod), a group of car racing enthusiasts devoted to attending and participating in amateur car races, filed suit on May 1, 2002, in the appropriate federal Court of Appeals challenging the validity of EPA's regulation. For a variety of reasons, it charged that the regulation is beyond EPA's statutory authority. Several of Hot Rod's members filed affidavits claiming that, as a result of the LEV requirement, the car manufacturers will be required to market in New Jersey a certain percentage of cars that comply with the stringent LEV emission standards. These cars have higher sticker prices than cars built to conform to the normal EPA standards because the emission control technology they contain is expensive for the manufacturers to install. Further, according to the affidavits, the requirement that 25 percent of sales comprise LEV vehicles will increase consumer competition for the remaining, lower-priced 75 percent of the market, thus driving up the prices of non-LEV cars as well. For both of these reasons, it will be more difficult for Hot Rod's members to find the kinds of cars they want and to afford to purchase them if and when they find them.

The Justice Department, which is representing the United States and EPA in the litigation commenced by Hot Rod, has moved to dismiss the suit on the ground that Hot Rod lacks standing. As an attorney for the Justice Department, what arguments can you make to support that motion to dismiss?

NOTE ON EXHAUSTION OF ADMINISTRATIVE REMEDIES,
PRIMARY JURISDICTION, AND RIPENESS

In addition to the standing doctrine, a number of other administrative law doctrines can defeat judicial review of administrative agency decisions and thus are important to environmental litigants. Generally, these doctrines require judicial deference to agency decisionmaking when agency action is considered necessary to establish a basis for judicial review.

Exhaustion of Administrative Remedies. Exhaustion is a defense to judicial review when the agency has not had an opportunity to consider the plaintiff's claim for relief. The exhaustion doctrine allows the agency to perform functions within its "special competence," such as specialized factfinding, interpretations of disputed technical subject matter, and resolution of disputes concerning the meaning of agency regulations. Affording the agency the first opportunity to perform these functions promotes administrative autonomy and efficiency and facilitates judicial review. See Izaak Walton League of Am. v. St. Clair, 497 F.2d 849 (8th Cir. 1974) (remanding to allow the Forest Service to determine the extent of mining activity in a wilderness area and whether a permit with protective conditions should be issued).

A court may not dismiss a claim for relief under the APA on exhaustion grounds unless the enabling statute or agency regulations involved specifically mandate exhaustion as a prerequisite to judicial review. Darby v. Cisneros, 509 U.S. 137 (1993), interpreting 5 U.S.C. §704. For claims not based on the APA, the exhaustion doctrine applies as a matter of judicial discretion. Some statutes bar litigants from asserting arguments not specifically raised during informal rulemaking or other administrative proceedings (a requirement sometimes referred to as issue exhaustion). E.g., 42 U.S.C. §7607(d)(7)(B) (CAA). What if a litigant fails to raise an issue during the administrative proceedings but the agency considers the issue on its own initiative, or because another party raised it; may the litigant challenge the agency's disposition of the issue in court? See Engine Mfrs. Ass'n v. EPA, 88 F.3d 1075, 1084 (D.C. Cir. 1996). May an agency waive an otherwise available exhaustion defense? See Ciba-Geigy Corp. v. Sidamon-Eristoff, 3 F.3d 40, 46 (2d Cir. 1993).

The courts have refused to apply the exhaustion doctrine when an agency acts in excess of its delegated powers, when administrative remedies are deemed to be inadequate, when it would be futile to require the litigants to pursue those remedies, or when the question is a purely legal one. See, e.g., Western Radio Serv. Co. v. Espy, 79 F.3d 896 (9th Cir. 1996). Statutory review provisions, however, may limit the availability of these exceptions. E.g., Texas Mun. Power Agency v. EPA, 89 F.3d 858, 876 (D.C. Cir. 1996) (refusing to invoke the futility exception). Courts frequently have made exceptions to the doctrine in NEPA cases. See Jette v. Bergland, 579 F.2d 59, 62 (10th Cir. 1978) ("[e]xceptions to the requirement of exhaustion [may] outweigh the advantages in the circumstances of a particular case").

Primary Jurisdiction. The related defense of primary jurisdiction arises when a court has original jurisdiction of a claim requiring the resolution of issues also placed within the competence of an agency. If the court recognizes the agency's primary jurisdiction, it suspends the judicial process until the agency can resolve the issues. The relative competence of agency and court to decide complex technical issues often underlies application of this defense. As a result, the defense is less likely to be invoked successfully where the issue is a purely legal one. E.g., Environmental Tech. Council v. Sierra Club, 98 F.3d 774, 789 (4th Cir. 1996). The need for uniformity in the interpretation of regulatory legislation is another basis for the rule. See Massachusetts v. Blackstone Valley Elec. Co., 67 F.3d 981, 992-993 (1st Cir. 1995) (remanding to EPA question of whether substance qualified as hazardous under Superfund law). The existence of explicit statutory rights of action cuts against application of the primary jurisdiction defense. See, e.g., Raritan Baykeeper v. NL Indus., Inc., 660 F.3d 686 (3d Cir. 2011) (refusing to dismiss citizen suit under the Resource Conservation and Recovery Act to remediate river contamination, despite state agency's prior determination that remedial actions at the site should be part of a regional approach, which had not yet been implemented when suit was filed).

Suppose that an individual exposed to pesticides registered by EPA brings a personal injury action under state law against the manufacturer, requesting damages but not injunctive relief. Should the court dismiss the action on primary jurisdiction grounds? See Ryan v. Chemlawn Corp., 935 F.2d 129 (7th Cir. 1991). Cf. Southern Utah Wilderness Alliance v. BLM, 425 F.3d 735 (10th Cir. 2005) (holding that the BLM does not have primary jurisdiction over determination of statutory rights-of-way over public lands); Interfaith Cmty. Org. v. Honeywell Int'l, Inc., 399 F.3d 248, 267-268 (3d Cir. 2005) (concluding that federal district court's injunction to abate endangerment to health and the environment in citizen suit under the Resource Conservation and Recovery Act did not improperly usurp EPA's power). Compare B.H. v. Gold Fields Mining Corp., 506 F. Supp. 2d 792 (N.D. Okla. 2007) (relying on the primary jurisdiction doctrine to stay common law claims for injunctive relief against mining activities alleged to cause health problems due to potential for interference with ongoing CERCLA cleanup action).

Finality and Ripeness. We have already seen an example in *Lujan I* of a case in which the Supreme Court refused to reach the merits because the agency whose decisions were challenged had not yet engaged in the "final agency action" required by §704 of the APA. Agency actions are not final if they create no rights, obligations, or legal consequences, e.g., National Pork Producers Council v. EPA, 635 F.3d 738 (5th Cir. 2011), or if they represent an intermediate step in a larger agency process, e.g., Ocean County Landfill Corp. v. EPA, 631 F.3d 652 (3d Cir. 2011). The "final action" rule also has been codified or implied in various environmental statutes. See, e.g., 42 U.S.C. §6976(a). In Sackett v. EPA, 132 S. Ct. 1367 (2012), the Court held that EPA engaged in final agency action when it issued an administrative compliance order under the CWA which determined that property owners had illegally filled wetlands without a permit under §404 of the CWA. The property owners, without waiting for EPA to enforce the order, brought suit challenging EPA's determination that their land contained wetlands covered by §404. EPA argued that it had not engaged in final agency action for purposes of the APA, but the Court disagreed. But cf. Belle Co., L.L.C. v. U.S. Army Corps of Eng'rs, 761 F.3d 383 (5th Cir. 2014) (Corps' jurisdictional determination that property contained wetlands subject to regulation under the CWA's dredge and fill permit program was not a final agency action). Does issuance of a notice of violation under §113 of the CAA qualify as final agency action? See Luminant Generation Co., L.L.C. v. EPA, 757 F.3d 439 (5th Cir. 2014) (distinguishing *Sackett*). *Sackett* is excerpted in section C.2 of Chapter 10.

The ripeness doctrine is also intended to prevent judicial consideration of controversies before the administrative agency has made a final decision that puts the case in a concrete context. Ripeness determinations turn on the fitness of the issues for judicial resolution and the hardship to the parties of withholding court consideration. In National Ass'n of Home Builders v. U.S. Army Corps of Eng'rs, 440 F.3d 459 (D.C.

Cir. 2006), the court held that a challenge to an EPA regulation defining the circumstances in which the CWA's dredge and fill permit requirement applies was ripe because the issues were purely legal, and industry faced hardship if forced to apply for a permit despite believing it was not required to do so, or to ignore permit requirements and face civil or criminal penalties. The extent to which judicial review would inappropriately interfere with administrative action and the court would benefit from further factual development of the issues presented are also relevant considerations. See, e.g., Texas Indep. Producers and Royalty Owners Ass'n v. EPA, 410 F.3d 964 (5th Cir. 2005). Ripeness problems can arise when plaintiffs challenge agency policies that provide the basis for agency actions but do not challenge a specific agency decision.

If the agency has taken a final position on an issue but has not yet begun an enforcement action, is there any reason to deny pre-enforcement judicial review? Abbott Laboratories v. Gardner, 387 U.S. 136 (1967), answered this question no, substituting crystallization of the agency position for the "final order" rule. A statutory provision authorizing pre-enforcement review may tip the balance toward review when the agency's position is fully crystallized and the issues are purely legal ones.

Does the ripeness doctrine bar judicial review of agency plans immediately upon adoption? The Forest Service must issue land and resource management plans for individual forest units in accordance with regulations designed to ensure optimal forest management. Subsequent decisions, such as the issuance of permits or timber contracts, must conform to the plan. 16 U.S.C. §1604(i). In Ohio Forestry Ass'n v. Sierra Club, 523 U.S. 726 (1998), the plaintiffs challenged the validity of portions of a plan authorizing logging on 126,000 acres in an Ohio national forest. The Court held that the challenge was not ripe for review. The plan itself did not inflict significant practical harm on the plaintiffs because site-specific environmental assessment, which could be challenged by the plaintiffs later on, was a prerequisite to logging activity. Won't it be more difficult, time-consuming, and expensive for a group like the Sierra Club to attack a multitude of site-specific timber sales than to seek invalidation of the plan pursuant to which those sales may be implemented? The Court also concluded that immediate judicial review of the lawfulness of logging would hinder the efforts of the Forest Service to refine its policies through plan revisions and application of the plan in practice. Finally, judicial review would be more meaningful in the context of a particular logging proposal. Agency decisions to implement land use plans may be ripe for review even if a challenge to the plan itself is not.

Problem 3-2

The federal Clean Air Act (CAA) requires that certain major stationary sources of air pollution apply for operating permits. The statute requires that states administering the permit program apply rigorous emission controls that are not required for nonmajor sources. A source is regarded as major, and therefore subject to the permit program, if it emits or has the potential to emit 100 tons per year or more of any air pollutant. 42 U.S.C. §7602(j). EPA regulations provide that in calculating a source's annual emissions, it will aggregate emissions from multiple facilities that are (1) under common control, (2) belong to the same industrial grouping, and (3) "are located on one or more contiguous or adjacent properties." 40 C.F.R. §71.2. For years, EPA, in applying that regulation, determined whether two or more facilities are "adjacent" based on a "common sense" notion of a source and the functional interrelationship of the facilities, rather than simply on the physical distance between the facilities. Recently, the Court of Appeals for the Sixth Circuit ruled that this approach violates the plain meaning of the statute, which mandates that EPA determine adjacency based on physical proximity alone. Following that decision, EPA's General Counsel sent a memorandum to the agency's regional offices directing the office located in the Sixth Circuit to abide by the court's decision, but directing all offices outside the Sixth Circuit to continue to apply the approach invalidated by the court.

American Industry Rocks (AIR), an association of manufacturing companies that own sources regulated under the CAA, sued EPA to challenge the validity of the memorandum. Assume that the suit was properly brought under the APA rather than under the CAA's judicial review provisions. AIR argued that EPA is required to apply a uniform definition of adjacency in administering the permit program, and that the Sixth Circuit's decision provides a definitive interpretation of that term that applies throughout the country. Further, AIR claimed that the memorandum puts its members owning sources located outside the Sixth Circuit at a competitive disadvantage with respect to sources located in the jurisdiction of the Sixth Circuit because those sources are subject to a more expansive definition of adjacency, which will subject more of them to the permit program than if EPA had adhered to the Sixth Circuit's ruling on a nationwide basis.

EPA has moved to dismiss the association's suit. It has argued that AIR lacks standing to sue, that there is no reviewable final agency action, and that AIR's challenge is not ripe. EPA argues that AIR lacks standing because until a regional office determines under §71.2, as interpreted and applied by EPA before the Sixth Circuit's decision, whether a particular source is major, no member of AIR will suffer any injury. Instead, the alleged injuries at this point are speculative and not imminent. EPA also argues that the memorandum did not cause any injury to AIR's members because all it does is retain the status quo legal regime facing sources outside the Sixth Circuit before the court's decision. EPA argues that the memorandum does not qualify as final agency action because the memorandum states that EPA "continues to assess what additional actions, if any, are necessary in response to the Sixth Circuit's decision, and EPA's deliberations on the proper approach to defining the scope of CAA permit programs are ongoing." Finally, EPA argues that the case is not ripe because it is speculative how the memorandum will affect any particular source, and that EPA's approach to applying §71.2 requires case-by-case determinations on the functional interrelationships among multiple, commonly owned sources. As a result, any challenge to the memorandum is premature until EPA actually determines whether a specific source located outside the Sixth Circuit is required to apply for a permit.

You represent AIR. What arguments can you make in response to EPA's motion to dismiss?

NOTE ON RECOVERY OF ATTORNEYS' FEES

Even if a plaintiff can satisfy applicable threshold justiciability requirements, it must have the wherewithal to finance the litigation. The costs of paying an attorney sometimes comprise a formidable obstacle, particularly to nonprofit public interest groups. Although attorneys' fees are not usually available to prevailing parties under the so-called American rule, some federal courts developed a "private attorney general" exception that permitted the recovery of attorneys' fees in public interest litigation, such as environmental litigation. The Supreme Court rejected this exception in Alyeska Pipeline Serv. Co. v. Wilderness Soc'y, 421 U.S. 240 (1975), but Congress has since authorized the award of attorneys' fees under most environmental statutes. E.g., Clean Air Act §304(d). The courts have not always been receptive to these fee-shifting provisions. In Ruckelshaus v. Sierra Club, 463 U.S. 680 (1983), the Supreme Court interpreted a similar provision of the CAA, which authorized the award of fees "whenever [the court] determines that such award is appropriate," to bar recovery by anyone other than a party who prevailed at least in part. At least one lower court refused to award fees to a financially able party whose economic interests motivated it to sue, particularly because its successful challenge to an EPA decision under the CAA did not promote statutory goals. Western States Petroleum Ass'n v. EPA, 87 F.3d 280 (9th Cir. 1996). How can a successful challenge to agency action fail to promote statutory objectives? In New Jersey v. EPA, 663 F.3d 1279 (D.C. Cir. 2011), the court held, over a dissent, that issuance of a fee award under the CAA to a party that had intervened in a successful challenge to EPA regulations was appropriate, even though the court in its ruling on the merits had not addressed the specific arguments raised by the intervenors. The court reasoned that any other result would discourage interventions that play a useful role because it is impossible to determine in advance which issues the court will reach.

Reimbursement for attorneys' fees may be available even under statutes that do not themselves authorize fee shifting. The Equal Access to Justice Act (EAJA), 28 U.S.C. §2412, authorizes the mandatory award of attorneys' fees and expenses to any party "prevailing" against the United States unless a court finds "that the position of the United States was substantially justified or that special circumstances make an award unjust." Can a party qualify as a "prevailing party" if the case is settled before a final judicial resolution? In Buckhannon Bd. and Care Home, Inc. v. West Virginia Dep't of Health and Human Res., 532 U.S. 598 (2001), the Supreme Court held that a party is a "prevailing party" for purposes of the Fair Housing Act Amendments of 1988 and the Americans with Disabilities Act only if it secures a judgment on the merits or a court-ordered consent decree. The Court disavowed the "catalyst theory," under which a plaintiff can qualify as "prevailing" if it achieves the desired result because a lawsuit brought about a voluntary change in the defendant's conduct. The Court concluded that the catalyst theory improperly allowed fee awards absent a "judicially sanctioned change in the legal relationship of the parties." Id. at 605.

The Buckhannon holding presumably applies to the EAJA, which also limits fee awards to "prevailing parties." See BARK v. Larsen, 423 F. Supp. 2d 1135, 1139-1140 (D. Or. 2006). Does it apply, however, to the numerous environmental statutes that allow courts to award fees without requiring that the fee recipient be a "prevailing party"? The ESA, like the CAA, authorizes fee awards "whenever [the court] determines that such award is appropriate." 16 U.S.C. §1540(g)(4). In Loggerhead Turtle v. County Council, 307 F.3d 1318 (11th Cir. 2002), the court held that the catalyst theory survived Buckhannon under this provision. The court found that Congress intended that a plaintiff whose suit furthers the goals of a "whenever . . . appropriate" statute be entitled to recover attorneys' fees. In addition, the Court in Buckhannon had discounted the argument that, if the catalyst theory were rejected, "mischievous defendants" could avoid liability for attorneys' fees in a meritorious suit by voluntarily changing their conduct. That strategy would not work, the Court reasoned, because as long as the plaintiffs retain a cause of action for damages, the defendant's change in conduct would not moot the case. Under citizen suit provisions such as the ESA's, however, the only relief that may be sought is equitable relief; damages are not available. Accordingly, rejection of the catalyst theory would induce rational defendants to voluntarily change their conduct to avoid fee liability if defeat seemed imminent. Such an outcome would "cripple the citizen suit provision of the [ESA,] in derogation of Congress's 'abundantly clear' intent to 'afford[] endangered species the highest of priorities.'" Id. at 1327. Suppose a statute authorizes fee awards "to any prevailing or substantially prevailing party, whenever the court determines such award is appropriate." Does the catalyst theory apply? See Kasza v. Whitman, 325 F.3d 1178 (9th Cir. 2003); Amigos Bravos v. EPA, 324 F.3d 1166, 1171 (10th Cir. 2003). Cf. City of Waukesha v. PDQ Food Stores, Inc., 500 F. Supp. 2d 1119 (E.D. Wis. 2007) (holding that the *Buckhannon* approach applies to CERCLA judicial review provision authorizing award of fees to a prevailing or substantially prevailing party).

2. *Standards of Review*

Once environmental plaintiffs clear applicable threshold jurisdictional hurdles, the issue becomes how thoroughly the courts will review the outcome of the agency's decisionmaking process. As indicated below, the answer tends to be context-specific, varying in accordance with the nature of the decision being challenged and the procedural context in which the agency made it. This section first briefly describes the kinds of decisions administrative agencies make and then explores how the courts approach the task of reviewing those decisions.

a. The Types of Reviewable Administrative Action

Generally speaking, administrative lawmaking oscillates between the two extremes represented by courts and legislators. If the existing rights of one or a few individuals are challenged, the judicial model usually applies and the agency acts more like a court, sometimes conducting a trial-type hearing on the record with cross-examination and other procedural formalities. If noncompetitive governmental permissions or broad policies that will apply prospectively to large numbers of organizations or individuals are in question, the freewheeling informality of the legislative model usually applies.

Procedural rules governing agency decisionmaking may derive from the statute delegating to the agency its authority to act, the APA, the agency's own regulations, and even the Due Process Clause of the Constitution. The applicability of the Due Process Clause depends largely on the kind of administrative proceeding involved. The Supreme Court has adhered to a distinction between quasi-judicial agency "adjudication" and quasi-legislative agency "rulemaking." In United States v. Florida E. Coast Ry., 410 U.S. 224 (1973), the Court held that an agency did not have to hold an on-the-record, trial-type hearing before issuing a "rule" under a statute requiring that the decision be made "after hearing." The regulated parties had no constitutional right to a trial-type hearing because the factual inferences relied on by the agency were used in "the formulation of a basically legislative-type judgment, for prospective application only, rather than in adjudicating a particular set of disputed facts." Id. at 246.

The Court explained the distinction between rulemaking and adjudication by referring to two seminal due process cases. Londoner v. Denver, 210 U.S. 373 (1908), held that a landowner challenging an assessment for street paving who was allowed to file written objections but not to be heard orally was denied due process. But in Bi-Metallic Inv. Co. v. State Bd. of Equalization, 239 U.S. 441 (1915), due process did not require any hearing before state tax officers increased the valuation of all taxable property. The Court distinguished *Londoner* as a case in which few persons were affected on individual grounds. The two cases thus distinguished between "proceedings for the purpose of promulgating policy-type rules or standards, on the one hand, and proceedings designed to adjudicate disputed facts in particular cases, on the other." 410 U.S. at 245.

Today, most administrative actions fall into five categories: (1) formal rulemaking, (2) informal notice-and-comment rulemaking, (3) formal adjudication, (4) informal adjudication or other informal action (such as approval of the location and funding of an interstate highway, as the *Overton Park* case, reproduced below, indicates), and (5) informal actions that require minimal procedural formalities (e.g., nonbinding policy statements). As section D of this chapter reveals, the fifth category appears to be growing.

Many agency decisions concerning the environment take the form of informal rulemaking under statutes like those addressed in Chapters 5-9. Consider the following explanation of the process:

> Agency decision making in regulating to protect health, safety, and the environment is overwhelmingly of the legislative sort, with a frequent dash of extra formality. It involves selecting and implementing statute-like policies that will apply prospectively to large classes of manufacturers, employers, and polluters. In developing their policies through standards, guidelines, and regulations—or *rules*, as they are collectively called—agencies follow a more or less standard process that is often called notice-and-comment rule making. First, they provide notice about what they want to require regulatees to do by publishing their proposed rules in the Federal Register. A period for public comment and counterproposal follows, which may include informal public hearings. . . . If they are doing their jobs properly, agencies respond in detail to the public commentary in the Federal Register when they issue rules in final form. Sometimes they propose significantly modified rules and reopen the comment period. . . . [Anderson, Human Welfare and the Administered Society: Federal Regulation in the 1970s to Protect Health, Safety, and the Environment, in Environmental and Occupational Medicine 835, 856-857 (W. Rom ed., 1983).]

As Anderson points out, rulemaking is often "the fastest, least expensive, and politically most expedient way for agencies" to implement statutory policies. Id. Occasionally, the environmental statutes require formal rulemaking, which provides affected parties with more extensive participatory opportunities, including limited rights to cross-examine agency officials. Permit applications are resolved in adjudicatory proceedings, which tend to be relatively informal. Administrative enforcement also is an adjudicatory process, which may be formal or informal depending on the requirements of agency organic statutes.

NOTES AND QUESTIONS

1. *The Hybrid Rulemaking Experiment.* For a time during the 1970s, some lower federal courts required agencies to abide by "hybrid" procedures, including the use of

cross-examination, that were more extensive than the informal notice-and-comment procedures dictated by §553 of the APA, and to explain their decisions more thoroughly—in short, to require a more trial-like record. See, e.g., International Harvester Co. v. Ruckelshaus, 478 F.2d 615 (D.C. Cir. 1973). The Supreme Court, however, prohibited this approach in Vermont Yankee Nuclear Power Corp. v. NRDC, 435 U.S. 519, 523 (1978). It explained that the APA "settled long-continued and hard-fought contentions, and enact[ed] a formula upon which opposing social and political forces have come to rest." Referring to §553, the Court stated:

> . . . [G]enerally speaking this section of the Act established the maximum procedural requirements which Congress was willing to have the courts impose upon agencies in conducting rulemaking procedures. Agencies are free to grant additional procedural rights in the exercise of their discretion, but reviewing courts are generally not free to impose them if the agencies have not chosen to grant them. This is not to say necessarily that there are no circumstances which would ever justify a court in overturning agency action because of a failure to employ procedures beyond those required by the statute. But such circumstances, if they exist, are extremely rare. [Id.]

2. *Hybrid Rulemaking and the Federal Pollution Control Laws. Vermont Yankee* precludes the courts from adding to the procedures specified in the APA, but it does not bar Congress from supplementing or supplanting those procedures in substantive legislation or the agencies themselves from voluntarily going beyond statutory procedural mandates, and Congress has exercised this authority. Section 307(d) of the CAA, for example, provides more formalized rulemaking procedures for the adoption of many of the rules authorized by the Act. It requires EPA to develop a decision record that includes a summary of the factual data on which the rule is based, as well as "the major legal interpretations and policy considerations underlying the proposed rule." The Toxic Substances Control Act is another statute that grafts some of the procedural requirements characteristic of formal rulemaking or adjudication onto the adoption of rules. See 15 U.S.C. §2605(c)(2)-(3). We explore some of the consequences of these procedures in connection with the *Corrosion Proof Fittings* case in Chapter 8, section E.1.

3. *Comparing Informal and Hybrid Rulemaking.* Well before *Vermont Yankee,* Judge Bazelon, writing for the court in EDF v. Ruckelshaus, 439 F.2d 584, 598 (D.C. Cir. 1971), claimed that "[w]hen administrators provide a framework for principled decision-making, the result will be to diminish the importance of judicial review by enhancing the integrity of the administrative process, and to improve the quality of judicial review in those cases where judicial review is sought." Professor Joseph Sax characterized that view as a "dubious example of wishful thinking. I know of no solid evidence to support the belief that requiring articulation, detailed findings or reasoned opinions enhances the integrity or propriety of administrative decisions." Sax, The (Unhappy) Truth about NEPA, 26 Okla. L. Rev. 239, 239 (1973).

Professor McGarity has argued that, although "informal rulemaking is still an exceedingly effective tool for eliciting public participation in administrative policy-making, it has not evolved into the flexible and efficient process that its early supporters originally envisioned," and that it has become "increasingly rigid and burdensome." McGarity, Some Thoughts on "Deossifying" the Rulemaking Process, 41 Duke L.J. 1385, 1385 (1992). He attributes the "ossification" of the rulemaking process in large part to the imposition of analytical requirements by both the courts and Congress. Others have criticized notice-and-comment rulemaking on the ground that, in practice, it tends to be dominated by input from regulated entities, with significantly less participation by representatives of regulatory beneficiaries. See, e.g., Wagner et al., Rulemaking in the Shade: An Empirical Study of EPA's Air Toxic Emission Standards, 63 Admin. L. Rev. 99 (2011). Sections B and C of this chapter explore the requirements imposed on the agencies by Congress and the executive branch.

b. Judicial Review of Statutory Interpretation

A different standard of judicial review may apply if a litigant asserts that an agency misinterpreted its enabling legislation than if it claims that the agency improperly implemented a statute whose meaning is agreed upon in a given situation. The first question is basically a question of law, while the second requires the application of law or policy to the fact situation before the agency. During the 1960s, the Supreme Court afforded deference to agency statutory interpretations and even greater deference to agency interpretations of their own regulations. See Udall v. Tallman, 380 U.S. 1 (1965). Due to a combination of faith in the legislative process, suspicion that administrative agencies were susceptible to capture by the interests they were responsible for regulating, and a sense that environmental values were special, the courts in the 1970s were willing to engage in fairly rigorous review of both kinds of questions in environmental cases. See Glicksman & Schroeder, EPA and the Courts: Twenty Years of Law and Politics, 54. Law & Contemp. Probs. 249 (Autumn 1991).

The Supreme Court ushered in a new era of deference to agency statutory interpretations in the following case.

CHEVRON U.S.A. INC. v. NATURAL RESOURCES DEFENSE COUNCIL, INC.
467 U.S. 837 (1984)

Justice STEVENS delivered the opinion of the Court. . . .

In the Clean Air Act Amendments of 1977, Congress enacted certain requirements applicable to States that had not achieved the national air quality standards established by the Environmental Protection Agency (EPA) pursuant to earlier legislation. [Section 172(c)(5)[e] of the] amended Clean Air Act required these "nonattainment" States to establish a permit program regulating "new or modified major stationary sources" of air pollution. . . . The EPA regulation promulgated to implement this permit requirement allows a State to adopt a plantwide definition of the term "stationary source."[2] Under this definition, an existing plant that contains several pollution-emitting devices may install or modify one piece of equipment without

---

e. [At the time of this case, the relevant provision was §172(b)(6).—*Eds.*]

2. "(i) 'Stationary source' means any building, structure, facility, or installation which emits or may emit any air pollutant subject to regulation under the Act." "(ii) 'Building, structure, facility, or installation' means all of the pollutant-emitting activities which belong to the same industrial grouping, are located on one or more contiguous or adjacent properties, and are under the control of the same person (or persons under common control) except the activities of any vessel." 40 C.F.R. §§51.18(j)(1)(i) and (ii) (1983).

meeting the permit conditions if the alteration will not increase the total emissions from the plant. The question presented by these cases is whether EPA's decision to allow States to treat all of the pollution-emitting devices within the same industrial grouping as though they were encased within a single "bubble" is based on a reasonable construction of the statutory term "stationary source."

[The Court of Appeals set aside the 1981 regulations containing the plantwide definition of the term "stationary source" in NRDC v. Gorsuch, 685 F.2d 718 (D.C. Cir. 1982). Finding neither the statutory language nor the legislative history dispositive, that court resorted to "the purposes of the nonattainment program." The court had addressed the applicability of the bubble concept to other CAA programs twice before in Alabama Power Co. v. Costle, 636 F.2d 323 (D.C. Cir. 1979), and ASARCO Inc. v. EPA, 578 F.2d 319 (D.C. Cir. 1978). Based on these precedents, the court reasoned that the bubble concept was "mandatory" in programs designed merely to maintain existing air quality, but "inappropriate" in programs whose purpose was to improve air quality. Because the purpose of the nonattainment provisions is to improve air quality, the court held that the bubble concept was prohibited.]

II

When a court reviews an agency's construction of the statute which it administers, it is confronted with two questions. First, always, is the question whether Congress has directly spoken to the precise question at issue. If the intent of Congress is clear, that is the end of the matter; for the court, as well as the agency, must give effect to the unambiguously expressed intent of Congress.[9] If, however, the court determines Congress has not directly addressed the precise question at issue, the court does not simply impose its own construction on the statute, as would be necessary in the absence of an administrative interpretation. Rather, if the statute is silent or ambiguous with respect to the specific issue, the question for the court is whether the agency's answer is based on a permissible construction of the statute.

"The power of an administrative agency to administer a congressionally created . . . program necessarily requires the formulation of policy and the making of rules to fill any gap left, implicitly or explicitly, by Congress." Morton v. Ruiz, 415 U.S. 199, 231 (1974). If Congress has explicitly left a gap for the agency to fill, there is an express delegation of authority to the agency to elucidate a specific provision of the statute by regulation. Such legislative regulations are given controlling weight unless they are arbitrary, capricious, or manifestly contrary to the statute. Sometimes the legislative delegation to an agency on a particular question is implicit rather than explicit. In such a case, a court may not substitute its own construction of a statutory provision for a reasonable interpretation made by the administrator of an agency.

We have long recognized that considerable weight should be accorded to an executive department's construction of a statutory scheme it is entrusted to administer, and the principle of deference to administrative interpretations

9. The judiciary is the final authority on issues of statutory construction and must reject administrative constructions which are contrary to clear congressional intent. If a court, employing traditional tools of statutory construction, ascertains that Congress had an intention on the precise question at issue, that intention is the law and must be given effect.

has been consistently followed by this Court whenever decision as to the meaning or reach of a statute has involved reconciling conflicting policies, and a full understanding of the force of the statutory policy in the given situation has depended upon more than ordinary knowledge respecting the matters subjected to agency regulations. . . . United States v. Shimer, 367 U.S. 374, 382 (1961). . . .

In light of these well-settled principles it is clear that the Court of Appeals misconceived the nature of its role in reviewing the regulations at issue. Once it determined . . . that Congress did not actually have an intent regarding the applicability of the bubble concept to the permit program, the question before it was not whether in its view the concept is "inappropriate" in the general context of a program designed to improve air quality, but whether the Administrator's view that it is appropriate in the context of this particular program is a reasonable one. . . . [W]e agree with the Court of Appeals that Congress did not have a specific intention on the applicability of the bubble concept in these cases, and conclude that the EPA's use of that concept here is a reasonable policy choice for the agency to make. . . .

V

The legislative history of the portion of the 1977 Amendments dealing with nonattainment areas does not contain any specific comment on the "bubble concept" or the question whether a plantwide definition of a stationary source is permissible under the permit program. It does, however, plainly disclose that in the permit program Congress sought to accommodate the conflict between the economic interest in permitting capital improvements to continue and the environmental interest in improving air quality. Indeed, the House Committee Report identified the economic interest as one of the "two main purposes" of this section of the bill. It stated:

> Section 117 of the bill, adopted during full committee markup, establishes a new section 127 of the Clean Air Act. The section has two main purposes: (1) to allow reasonable economic growth to continue in an area while making reasonable further progress to assure attainment of the standards by a fixed date; and (2) to allow States greater flexibility for the former purpose than EPA's present interpretative regulations afford. . . .[25] [H.R. Rep. No. 95-294, at 211 (1977), 1977 U.S. Code Cong. & Admin. News 1077, 1290.]

VI

As previously noted, prior to the 1977 Amendments, the EPA had adhered to a plantwide definition of the term "source" under a NSPS program. . . .

In August 1980, however, the EPA adopted a regulation that, in essence, applied the basic reasoning of the Court of Appeals in these cases. The EPA took particular note of the two then-recent Court of Appeals decisions, which had created the bright-line rule that the "bubble concept" should be employed in a program designed to maintain air quality but not in one designed to enhance air quality. Relying heavily on

---

25. . . . [T]he second "main purpose" of the provision—allowing the States "greater flexibility" than the EPA's interpretative Ruling— . . . is entirely consistent with the view that Congress did not intend to freeze the definition of "source" contained in the existing regulation into a rigid statutory requirement.

those cases, EPA adopted a dual definition of "source" for nonattainment areas that required a permit whenever a change in either the entire plant, or one of its components, would result in a significant increase in emissions even if the increase was completely offset by reductions elsewhere in the plant. The EPA expressed the opinion that this interpretation was "more consistent with congressional intent" than the plantwide definition because it "would bring in more sources or modifications for review," 45 Fed. Reg. 52,697 (1980), but its primary legal analysis was predicated on the two Court of Appeals decisions.

In 1981 a new administration took office and initiated a "Government-wide reexamination of regulatory burdens and complexities." 46 Fed. Reg. 16,281. In the context of that review, the EPA reevaluated the various arguments that had been advanced in connection with the proper definition of the term "source." . . .

In explaining its conclusion, the EPA first noted that the definitional issue was not squarely addressed in either the statute or its legislative history and therefore that the issue involved an agency "judgment as how to best carry out the Act." It then set forth several reasons for concluding that the plantwide definition was more appropriate. It pointed out that the dual definition "can act as a disincentive to new investment and modernization by discouraging modifications to existing facilities" and "can actually retard progress in air pollution control by discouraging replacement of older, dirtier processes or pieces of equipment with new, cleaner ones." Moreover, the new definition "would simplify EPA's rules by using the same definition of 'source' for PSD, nonattainment new source review and the construction moratorium. This reduces confusion and inconsistency." Finally, the agency explained that additional requirements that remained in place would accomplish the fundamental purposes of achieving attainment with NAAQS's as expeditiously as possible. . . .

VII

In this Court respondents expressly reject the basic rationale of the Court of Appeals' decision. That court . . . interpreted the policies of the statute . . . to mandate the plantwide definition in programs designed to maintain clean air and to forbid it in programs designed to improve air quality. Respondents . . . contend that the text of the Act requires the EPA to use a dual definition [in the context of both the PSD and nonattainment area permit programs].

STATUTORY LANGUAGE

The definition of the term "stationary source" in §111(a)(3) refers to "any building, structure, facility, or installation" which emits air pollution. This definition is applicable only to the NSPS program by the express terms of the statute; the text of the statute does not make this definition applicable to the permit program. Petitioners therefore maintain that there is no statutory language even relevant to ascertaining the meaning of stationary source in the permit program aside from §302(j), which defines the term "major stationary source." We disagree. . . .

The definition in §302(j) tells us what the word "major" means—a source must emit at least 100 tons of pollution to qualify—but it sheds virtually no light on the meaning of the term "stationary source." It does equate a source with a facility—a "major emitting facility" and a "major stationary source" are synonymous under

§302(j). The ordinary meaning of the term "facility" is some collection of integrated elements which has been designed and constructed to achieve some purpose. Moreover, it is certainly no affront to common English usage to take a reference to a major facility or a major source to connote an entire plant as opposed to its constituent parts. Basically, however, the language of §302(j) simply does not compel any given interpretation of the term "source."

Respondents recognize that, and hence point to §111(a)(3). Although the definition in that section is not literally applicable to the permit program, it sheds as much light on the meaning of the word "source" as anything in the statute. As respondents point out, use of the words "building, structure, facility, or installation," as the definition of source, could be read to impose the permit conditions on an individual building that is a part of a plant. . . . The language may reasonably be interpreted to impose the requirement on any discrete, but integrated, operation which pollutes. This gives meaning to all of the terms — a single building, not part of a larger operation, would be covered if it emits more than 100 tons of pollution, as would any facility, structure, or installation. Indeed, the language itself implies a "bubble concept" of sorts: each enumerated item would seem to be treated as if it were encased in a bubble. While respondents insist that each of these terms must be given a discrete meaning, they also argue that §111(a)(3) defines "source" as that term is used in §302(j). The latter section, however, equates a source with a facility, whereas the former defines "source" as a facility, among other items.

We are not persuaded that parsing of general terms in the text of the statute will reveal an actual intent of Congress. We know full well that this language is not dispositive; the terms are overlapping and the language is not precisely directed to the question of the applicability of a given term in the context of a larger operation. To the extent any congressional "intent" can be discerned from this language, it would appear that the listing of overlapping, illustrative terms was intended to enlarge, rather than to confine, the scope of the agency's power to regulate particular sources in order to effectuate the policies of the Act.

LEGISLATIVE HISTORY . . .

. . . We find that the legislative history as a whole is silent on the precise issue before us. It is, however, consistent with the view that the EPA should have broad discretion in implementing the policies of the 1977 Amendments.

More importantly, that history plainly identifies the policy concerns that motivated the enactment; the plantwide definition is fully consistent with one of those concerns — the allowance of reasonable economic growth — and, whether or not we believe it most effectively implements the other, we must recognize that the EPA has advanced a reasonable explanation for its conclusion that the regulations serve the environmental objectives as well. Indeed, its reasoning is supported by the public record developed in the rulemaking process, as well as by certain private studies.[37]

---

37. "Economists have proposed that economic incentives be substituted for the cumbersome administrative-legal framework. The objective is to make the profit and cost incentives that work so well in the marketplace work for pollution control. . . . [The 'bubble' or 'netting' concept] is a first attempt in this direction. By giving a plant manager flexibility to find the places and processes within a plant that control emissions most cheaply, pollution control can be achieved more quickly and cheaply." L. Lave & G. Omenn, Cleaning Air: Reforming the Clean Air Act 28 (1981).

Our review of the EPA's varying interpretations of the word "source"—both before and after the 1977 Amendments—convinces us that the agency primarily responsible for administering this important legislation has consistently interpreted it flexibly—not in a sterile textual vacuum, but in the context of implementing policy decisions in a technical and complex arena. The fact that the agency has from time to time changed its interpretation of the term "source" does not, as respondents argue, lead us to conclude that no deference should be accorded the agency's interpretation of the statute. An initial agency interpretation is not instantly carved in stone. On the contrary, the agency, to engage in informed rulemaking, must consider varying interpretations and the wisdom of its policy on a continuing basis. Moreover, the fact that the agency has adopted different definitions in different contexts adds force to the argument that the definition itself is flexible, particularly since Congress has never indicated any disapproval of a flexible reading of the statute. . . .

POLICY

The arguments over policy that are advanced in the parties' briefs create the impression that respondents are now waging in a judicial forum a specific policy battle which they ultimately lost in the agency and in the 32 jurisdictions opting for the "bubble concept," but one which was never waged in the Congress. Such policy arguments are more properly addressed to legislators or administrators, not to judges.[38]

In these cases, the Administrator's interpretation represents a reasonable accommodation of manifestly competing interests and is entitled to deference: the regulatory scheme is technical and complex, the agency considered the matter in a detailed and reasoned fashion, and the decision involves reconciling conflicting policies. Congress intended to accommodate both interests, but did not do so itself on the level of specificity presented by these cases. Perhaps that body consciously desired the Administrator to strike the balance at this level, thinking that those with great expertise and charged with responsibility for administering the provision would be in a better position to do so; perhaps it simply did not consider the question at this level; and perhaps Congress was unable to forge a coalition on either side of the question, and those on each side decided to take their chances with the scheme devised by the agency. For judicial purposes, it matters not which of these things occurred.

Judges are not experts in the field, and are not part of either political branch of the Government. Courts must, in some cases, reconcile competing political interests, but not on the basis of the judges' personal policy preferences. In contrast, an agency to which Congress has delegated policy-making responsibilities may, within the limits of that delegation, properly rely upon the incumbent administration's views of wise policy to inform its judgments. While agencies are not directly accountable to the people, the Chief Executive is, and it is entirely appropriate for this political branch of the Government to make such policy choices—resolving the competing interests which Congress itself either inadvertently did not resolve, or intentionally left to be

---

38. Respondents point out if a brand new factory that will emit over 100 tons of pollutants is constructed in a nonattainment area, that plant must obtain a permit pursuant to [§172(c)(5)] and in order to do so, it must satisfy the §173 conditions. . . . Respondents argue if an old plant containing several large emitting units is to be modernized by the replacement of one or more units emitting over 100 tons of pollutant with a new unit emitting less—but still more than 100 tons—the result should be no different simply because "it happens to be built not at a new site, but within a pre-existing plant."

resolved by the agency charged with the administration of the statute in light of everyday realities.

When a challenge to an agency construction of a statutory provision, fairly conceptualized, really centers on the wisdom of the agency's policy, rather than whether it is a reasonable choice within a gap left open by Congress, the challenge must fail. In such a case, federal judges—who have no constituency—have a duty to respect legitimate policy choices made by those who do. The responsibilities for assessing the wisdom of such policy choices and resolving the struggle between competing views of the public interest are not judicial ones: "Our Constitution vests such responsibilities in the political branches." TVA v. Hill, 437 U.S. 153, 195 (1978).

We hold that the EPA's definition of the term "source" is a permissible construction of the statute which seeks to accommodate progress in reducing air pollution with economic growth. . . .

The judgment of the Court of Appeals is reversed.

NOTES AND QUESTIONS

1. How is a court to tell whether the statute is clear on the "precise question at issue"? Do the "traditional tools of statutory construction" include reference to legislative history, statutory purposes, canons of statutory construction, or previous judicial decisions interpreting the statute, or is the reviewing court confined to an analysis of statutory text? Compare Kmart Corp. v. Cartier, Inc., 486 U.S. 281 (1988) with Neal v. United States, 516 U.S. 284 (1996); Dole v. United Steelworkers of Am., 494 U.S. 26 (1990). In FDA v. Brown & Williamson Tobacco Corp., 529 U.S. 120, 132 (2000), the Supreme Court indicated that at step 1 of *Chevron*, a reviewing court "should not confine itself to examining a particular statutory provision in isolation. The meaning—or ambiguity—of certain words or phrases may only become evident when placed in context." In that case, the "context" included the agency's past interpretations of the scope of its own authority, the adoption of other statutes concerning the regulation of tobacco products, and the economic and political magnitude of the policy decision at issue. Jellum, *Chevron*'s Demise: A Survey of *Chevron* from Infancy to Senescence, 59 Admin. L. Rev. 725 (2007), argues that the Supreme Court now applies step 1 of *Chevron* as a search for statutory clarity, not congressional intent.

Assume that the "object and policy" of a statute are relevant in assessing the reasonableness of an agency's statutory construction under step 2 of *Chevron*. Is it reasonable for an agency to interpret a CAA provision that requires compliance with technology-based controls "as expeditiously as practicable" to require industries burning hazardous waste as fuels to cease using that waste within two years, even if the agency cannot demonstrate that compliance with the requirement will result in any air quality benefits? See Chemical Mfrs. Ass'n v. EPA, 217 F.3d 861 (D.C. Cir. 2000). See also NRDC v. Abraham, 355 F.3d 179, 195 (2d Cir. 2004). In Entergy Corp. v. Riverkeeper, 556 U.S. 208 (2009), the Court deferred under *Chevron* step 2 to EPA's conclusion that §316(b) of the CWA allows EPA to rely on cost-benefit analysis in determining the appropriate level of controls for cooling water intake structures at power plants. Are pragmatic considerations relevant to judicial assessment of an agency's interpretation at step 2? See Utility Air Regulatory Group v. EPA, 134 S. Ct. 2427, 2444 (2014) (stating that the fact that an agency's interpretation "would place plainly excessive demands on limited governmental resources is alone a good reason for rejecting it").

2. *The Source of* Chevron *Deference.* Is *Chevron* compelled by separation of powers principles? Seidenfeld, *Chevron's* Foundations, 86 Notre Dame L. Rev. 273 (2011), argues that *Chevron* deference is better grounded in the exercise of judicial self-restraint than in the fiction of congressional delegation of interpretive primacy. Is the gap-filling function of agencies endorsed by the Court consistent with the constitutional law nondelegation doctrine, which forbids Congress from delegating authority to an administrative agency without ascertainable legislative standards to guide agency discretion? See United States v. Henry, 136 F.3d 12, 16-17 (1st Cir. 1998). Once Congress authorizes the exercise of broad agency discretion, has it authorized the executive to interpret the statute as it chooses? Garry, Accommodating the Administrative State: The Interrelationship Between the *Chevron* and Nondelegation Doctrines, 38 Ariz. St. L.J. 921 (2006), argues that the courts' failure to enforce the nondelegation doctrine has made the *Chevron* doctrine virtually inevitable.

How does the impact of a statutory interpretation on the allocation of power between the federal government and the states affect the application of *Chevron*? Does a special version of *Chevron* apply in contexts with federalism implications? See Solid Waste Agency of N. Cook County v. U.S. Army Corps of Eng'rs, 531 U.S. 159 (2001). In Wyeth v. Levine, 555 U.S. 555, 573-581 (2009), the Court refused to defer to the FDA's determination that the agency's drug labeling requirements preempted state law product liability claims based on inadequate warning. See generally Mendelson, *Chevron* and Preemption, 102 Mich. L. Rev. 737 (2004) (discussing the degree to which courts should defer to agency determinations that federal statutes preempt state law, in light of the general presumption against preemption).

3. *The Influence of Public Choice Theory.* Professor Richard Stewart has argued that the administrative law that developed at the beginning of modern environmental law in the 1970s rejected the view that agency decisions reflect the disinterested application of expertise. Instead, agencies resolve conflicts between antagonistic stakeholders, thus requiring that they be shielded from crass political influence. This changing conception of the role of agencies affected judicial review of their decisions by changing the focus from preventing unauthorized intrusions on private autonomy to assuring fair representation for all affected interests before the agency.

> Implicit in this development is the assumption that there is no ascertainable, transcendent "public interest," but only the distinct interests of various individuals and groups in society. Under this assumption, legislation represents no more than compromises struck between competing interest groups.[206] This analysis suggests that if agencies were to function as a forum for all interests affected by agency decisionmaking, bargaining leading to compromises generally acceptable to all might result, thus replicating the process of legislation. Agency decisions made after adequate consideration of all affected interests would have, in microcosm, legitimacy based on the same principle as legislation and therefore the fact that statutes cannot control agency discretion would become largely irrelevant. [Stewart, The Reformation of American Administration Law, 88 Harv. L. Rev. 1669, 1712 (1975).]

206. . . . See, e.g., . . . D. Truman, The Governmental Process (1951). In the extreme form of this view, there is no objective, independent yardstick by which one can measure the content of compromise; compromises are legitimated by the process of their negotiation. For criticism of such analysis, see T. Lowi, [The Poverty of Liberalism (1968)]; R. Wolff, [The End of Liberalism (1969)]. . . .

Professor Stewart's argument presaged a shift in political thought based on the application of public choice theory to the legislative process. That theory assumes that legislators, like everyone else, are motivated by self-interest. Public choice theorists and judges stressed the need for judges to view legislative delegations as interest group bargains struck by Congress and further argued that courts should generally uphold such bargains by limiting their inquiry into the meaning of the statute.[f] One court, for example, opined that even if a broad policy goal "is the animating force driving the legislation, achievement of actual passage invariably requires compromise and accommodation." NRDC v. EPA, 822 F.2d 104, 113 (D.C. Cir. 1987). Such compromises may entail agreeing to let the agency resolve disputed issues over which a consensus failed to emerge. See NRDC v. EPA, 859 F.2d 156, 199 (D.C. Cir. 1988) ("it falls to the agency to reconcile competing legislative goals"). As a result, the courts should be wary of relying on broadly stated objectives to overturn an agency's statutory interpretation because doing so risks tearing apart the legislative compromise. See American Mining Cong. v. EPA, 824 F.2d 1177, 1185 n.10 (D.C. Cir. 1987). Underlying such arguments is a loss of faith in the ability of Congress to be other than a conduit for special interests. Does *Chevron* reflect this deferential review posture?

NOTE ON THE SCOPE AND IMPACT OF THE CHEVRON DEFERENCE DOCTRINE

Should the degree of deference due an agency's statutory interpretation differ depending upon the procedural context in which it was rendered? In Christensen v. Harris County, 529 U.S. 576 (2000), the Court held that an interpretation contained in an opinion letter did not warrant *Chevron*-style deference. Similarly, in United States v. Mead Corp., 533 U.S. 218 (2001), the Court held that

> administrative implementation of a particular statutory provision qualifies for *Chevron* deference when it appears that Congress delegated authority to the agency generally to make rules carrying the force of law, and that the agency interpretation claiming deference was promulgated in the exercise of that authority. Delegation of such authority may be shown in a variety of ways, as by an agency's power to engage in adjudication or notice-and-comment rulemaking, or by some other indication of a comparable congressional intent. [Id. at 226-227.]

In Barnhart v. Walton, 535 U.S. 212 (2002), however, the Court concluded (arguably in dictum) that the fact that an agency's long-standing interpretation had been reached "through means less formal than 'notice and comment' rulemaking does not automatically deprive that interpretation of the judicial deference otherwise its due," citing *Chevron*. It added that, even if *Christensen* suggested an "absolute rule to the contrary," *Mead* indicated that the degree of deference owed "depends in significant part upon the interpretive method used and the nature of the question at issue." In *Barnhart*, "the interstitial nature of the legal question, the related expertise of the

f. See Easterbrook, Statutes' Domains, 50 U. Chi. L. Rev. 533 (1983); Posner, Economics, Politics, and the Reading of Statutes and the Constitution, 49 U. Chi. L. Rev. 263 (1982). For further reading, see Farber & Frickey, The Jurisprudence of Public Choice, 65 Tex. L. Rev. 873 (1987); Pierce, The Role of Constitutional and Political Theory in Administrative Law, 64 Tex. L. Rev. 469 (1985).

Agency, the importance of the question to administration of the statute, the complexity of that administration, and the careful consideration the Agency has given the question over a long period of time all indicate that *Chevron* provides the appropriate legal lens through which to view the legality of the Agency interpretation here at issue." Id. at 221-222.

An agency interpretation that does not qualify for *Chevron* deference may nevertheless be entitled to some deference. The *Mead* Court recognized that judicial deference may still be appropriate, depending on factors such as "the degree of the agency's care, its consistency, formality, and relative expertness, and . . . the persuasiveness of the agency's position." Id. at 228 (citing Skidmore v. Swift & Co., 323 U.S. 134, 139-140 (1944)). See Luminant Generation Co., L.L.C. v. EPA, 675 F.3d 917, 928 (5th Cir. 2012) (determining that affording *Chevron* deference to EPA interpretation contained in appellate brief was "out of the question," and that the interpretation was not even entitled to *Skidmore* deference).

Limitations on the scope of an agency's power to promulgate rules may narrow the application of the *Chevron* doctrine. See, e.g., Gonzales v. Oregon, 546 U.S. 243 (2006) (holding that attorney general's interpretation of Controlled Substances Act was not entitled to *Chevron* deference because the Act does not authorize him to issue a rule declaring illegitimate a medical standard for care and treatment of patients that is specifically authorized by law). *Chevron* deference applies, however, to an agency's interpretation of statutory ambiguity that concerns the scope of the agency's regulatory authority (i.e., its jurisdiction). City of Arlington, Texas v. FCC, 133 S. Ct. 1863 (2013). For discussion of when *Chevron* applies, see Sunstein, Chevron Step Zero, 92 Va. L. Rev. 187 (2006).

Suppose that an agency publishes a draft policy statement in the Federal Register, upon which it solicits comments. Before the agency issues the statement in final form, the propriety of one of the legal issues addressed in the statement becomes the subject of judicial review. What degree of deference, if any, should a court afford to an interpretation reflected in the policy statement? See Southern Utah Wilderness Alliance v. Dabney, 222 F.3d 819 (10th Cir. 2000). Should agency interpretations contained in litigation briefs be afforded *Chevron* deference? See Talk Am., Inc. v. Michigan Bell Tel. Co. dba AT&T Michigan, 131 S. Ct. 2254 (2011); Chase Bank USA N.A. v. McCoy, 131 S. Ct. 871, 880-882 (2011). Is an agency interpretation entitled to *Chevron* deference if it conflicts with a previous judicial interpretation of the same statutory provision? See Nat'l Cable & Telecommc'ns Ass'n v. Brand X Internet Servs., 545 U.S. 967 (2005); Masur, Judicial Deference and the Credibility of Agency Commitments, 60 Vand. L. Rev. 1021 (2007).

Has *Chevron* affected how courts review agency statutory interpretations? A study of federal appellate court review during the 1990s of EPA decisions found that in cases decided under step 1 of *Chevron*, EPA lost 59.1 percent of the time. Schroeder & Glicksman, *Chevron, State Farm*, and EPA in the Courts of Appeals during the 1990s, 31 Envtl. L. Rep. 10371 (2001). During the same period, courts resolving challenges to EPA statutory interpretations under step 2 ruled in favor of the agency more than 92 percent of the time.

Another study finds "a strong relationship between the justices' ideological predispositions and the probability that they will validate agency determinations," and concludes that "[i]f judicial decisions under the *Chevron* framework are assessed in crudely political terms, the voting patterns of Supreme Court justices fit with the conventional groupings of the justices along political lines—a clear signal that the

Chevron framework is not having the disciplining effect that it is supposed to have." Sunstein & Miles, Do Judges Make Regulatory Policy? An Empirical Investigation of *Chevron*, 73 U. Chi. L. Rev. 823, 826 (2006). Eskridge & Baer, The Continuum of Deference: Supreme Court Treatment of Agency Statutory Interpretations from *Chevron* to *Hamdan*, 96 Geo. L.J. 1083 (2008), conclude "that there has not been a *Chevron* 'revolution' at the Supreme Court level" and that *Chevron* was applied in only 8.3% of Supreme Court cases evaluating agency statutory interpretations" during the period studied. The authors found that "the Court employed *a continuum of deference regimes*" and that in the majority of cases (53.6 percent), the Court applied no deference regime at all. "Instead, it relies on ad hoc judicial reasoning of the sort that typifies the Court's methodology in regular statutory interpretation cases." Id. at 1090. The authors argue that the degree of deference afforded an agency's statutory interpretation should be governed by (1) whether the interpretation is made pursuant to a congressional delegation of lawmaking authority (*Chevron/Mead*), (2) whether the agency is applying special expertise (*Skidmore*), and (3) whether the interpretation is consistent with larger public norms, including constitutional values (*Gonzales*).

c. Judicial Review of Statutory Implementation

Once an agency determines what a statute means, it must apply the statute, as so interpreted, to the factual situation before it. What is the judicial role in resolving challenges to such mixed determinations of fact, law, and policy? Is the court likely to be more or less deferential than when it reviews agency statutory interpretations? Does the nature of the agency action (rulemaking, adjudication, or other informal action) affect the standard of review? The next case addresses these and other questions.

CITIZENS TO PRESERVE OVERTON PARK, INC. v. VOLPE
401 U.S. 402 (1971)

Opinion of the Court by Mr. Justice MARSHALL, announced by Mr. Justice STEWART. . . .

[Overton Park was a 342-acre city-owned park located near the center of Memphis that included recreational facilities and 170 acres of forest. After Tennessee acquired a right-of-way on both sides of the park, the Secretary of Transportation agreed with local officials that part of I-40, a six-lane interstate highway, should be built through the park. In 1969, the state acquired a 250- to 400-foot wide right-of-way inside the park from the city. The Secretary approved both the route and design of the project later that year. The proposed highway would sever the zoo from the rest of the park, destroying 26 acres of the park even though the roadway would be largely depressed below ground level. When completed, I-40 would provide Memphis with a major east-west expressway that would allow easier access to downtown Memphis from the residential areas on the eastern edge of the city.

Section 4(f) of the Department of Transportation Act of 1966 and §18(a) of the Federal-Aid Highway Act of 1968, 23 U.S.C. §138, prohibited the Secretary from authorizing the use of federal funds to finance the construction of highways through public parks if a "feasible and prudent" alternative route exists. Absent such a route, the statutes allowed the Secretary to approve construction through parks only if there had been "all possible planning to minimize harm" to the park. Section 4(f) barred distribution of federal funds for the part of the highway slated to go through Overton Park until the Secretary determined whether the statute's requirements had been met, but federal funds for the rest of the project were not so restricted. When the Secretary announced his approval of the route and design of I-40, he did not issue any factual findings under §4(f) or §18(a) as to why he believed there were no feasible and prudent alternative routes or why design changes could not be made to reduce harm to the park.

Local and national conservation organizations, as well as private citizens from the Overton Park area, sued the Secretary, asserting that he violated §§4(f) and 18(a) by authorizing the expenditure of federal funds for the construction of the highway through the park. The lower courts ruled for the Secretary.]

Petitioners contend that the Secretary's action is invalid without [formal findings under §4(f)] and that the Secretary did not make an independent determination but merely relied on the judgment of the Memphis City Council. They also contend that it would be "feasible and prudent" to route I-40 around Overton Park either to the north or to the south. And they argue that if these alternative routes are not "feasible and prudent," the present plan does not include "all possible" methods for reducing harm to the park. Petitioners claim that I-40 could be built under the park by using either of two possible tunneling methods,[18] and they claim that, at a minimum, by using advanced drainage techniques the expressway could be depressed below ground level along the entire route through the park. . . .

Respondents argue that it was unnecessary for the Secretary to make formal findings, and that he did, in fact, exercise his own independent judgment which was supported by the facts. . . .

A threshold question—whether petitioners are entitled to any judicial review—is easily answered. Section 701 of the Administrative Procedure Act [APA] provides that the action of "each authority of the Government of the United States," which includes the Department of Transportation, is subject to judicial review except where there is a statutory prohibition on review or where "agency action is committed to agency discretion by law." In this case, there is no indication that Congress sought to prohibit judicial review and there is most certainly no "showing of 'clear and convincing evidence' of a . . . legislative intent" to restrict access to judicial review. Abbott Laboratories v. Gardner, 387 U.S. 136, 141 (1967).

Similarly, the Secretary's decision here does not fall within the exception for action "committed to agency discretion." This is a very narrow exception. The legislative history of the [APA] indicates that it is applicable in those rare instances where "statutes are drawn in such broad terms that in a given case there is no law to apply." S. Rep. No. 752, 79th Cong., 1st Sess., 26 (1945).

[Referring to the "feasible and prudent" and "all possible planning" language of §4(f), the Court stated:] This language is a plain and explicit bar to the use of federal funds for construction of highways through parks—only the most unusual situations are exempted.

Despite the clarity of the statutory language, respondents argue that the Secretary has wide discretion. They recognize that the requirement that there be no "feasible"

18. Petitioners argue that either a bored tunnel or a cut-and-cover tunnel, which is a fully depressed route covered after construction, could be built. Respondents contend that the construction of a tunnel by either method would greatly increase the cost of the project, would create safety hazards, and because of increases in air pollution would not reduce harm to the park.

alternative route admits of little administrative discretion. For this exemption to apply the Secretary must find that as a matter of sound engineering it would not be feasible to build the highway along any other route. Respondents argue, however, that the requirement that there be no other "prudent" route requires the Secretary to engage in a wide-ranging balancing of competing interests. They contend that the Secretary should weigh the detriment resulting from the destruction of parkland against the cost of other routes, safety considerations, and other factors, and determine on the basis of the importance that he attaches to these other factors whether, on balance, alternative feasible routes would be "prudent."

[The Court denied that Congress intended such a "wide-ranging endeavor." Use of parkland for highway construction will almost always minimize cost (because the public already owns the land and there will be no need to pay for right-of-way) and community disruption (because if a highway is built through a parkland, homes and businesses need not be moved).]

Congress clearly did not intend that cost and disruption of the community were to be ignored by the Secretary. But the very existence of the statutes indicates that protection of parkland was to be given paramount importance. The few green havens that are public parks were not to be lost unless there were truly unusual factors present in a particular case or the cost or community disruption resulting from alternative routes reached extraordinary magnitudes. If the statutes are to have any meaning, the Secretary cannot approve the destruction of parkland unless he finds that alternative routes present unique problems.

Plainly, there is "law to apply" and thus the exemption for action "committed to agency discretion" is inapplicable. But the existence of judicial review is only the start: the standard for review must also be determined. For that we must look to §706 of the [APA], which provides that a "reviewing court shall . . . hold unlawful and set aside agency action, findings, and conclusions found" not to meet six separate standards. . . .

[Petitioners argued that the Secretary's approval of the construction of I-40 was subject to §706(2)(E) or (F), which the Court characterized as "standards of limited applicability." The Court found neither standard to be applicable.]

Review under the substantial-evidence test is authorized only when the agency action is taken pursuant to a rulemaking provision of the [APA] itself, 5 U.S.C. §553, or when the agency action is based on a public adjudicatory hearing. See 5 U.S.C. §§556, 557. The Secretary's decision to allow the expenditure of federal funds to build I-40 through Overton Park was plainly not an exercise of a rulemaking function. And the only hearing that is required by either the [APA] or the statutes regulating the distribution of federal funds for highway construction is a public hearing conducted by local officials for the purpose of informing the community about the proposed project and eliciting community views on the design and route. 23 U.S.C. §128. The hearing is nonadjudicatory, quasi-legislative in nature. It is not designed to produce a record that is to be the basis of agency action—the basic requirement for substantial-evidence review.

Petitioners' alternative argument also fails. De novo review of whether the Secretary's decision was "unwarranted by the facts" is authorized by §706(2)(F) in only two circumstances. First, such de novo review is authorized when the action is adjudicatory in nature and the agency factfinding procedures are inadequate. And, there may be independent judicial factfinding when issues that were not before the agency are raised in a proceeding to enforce nonadjudicatory agency action. H.R. Rep. No. 1980, 79th Cong., 2d Sess. Neither situation exists here.

Even though there is no de novo review in this case and the Secretary's approval of the route of I-40 does not have ultimately to meet the substantial-evidence test, the generally applicable standards of §706 require the reviewing court to engage in a substantial inquiry. Certainly, the Secretary's decision is entitled to a presumption of regularity. See, e.g., Pacific States Box & Basket Co. v. White, 296 U.S. 176, 185 (1935). But that presumption is not to shield his action from a thorough, probing, in-depth review.

The court is first required to decide whether the Secretary acted within the scope of his authority. This determination naturally begins with a delineation of the scope of the Secretary's authority and discretion. As has been shown, Congress has specified only a small range of choices that the Secretary can make. Also involved in this initial inquiry is a determination of whether on the facts the Secretary's decision can reasonably be said to be within that range. The reviewing court must consider whether the Secretary properly construed his authority to approve the use of park-land as limited to situations where there are no feasible alternative routes or where feasible alternative routes involve uniquely difficult problems. And the reviewing court must be able to find that the Secretary could have reasonably believed that in this case there are no feasible alternatives or that alternatives do involve unique problems.

Scrutiny of the facts does not end, however, with the determination that the Secretary has acted within the scope of his statutory authority. Section 706(2)(A) requires a finding that the actual choice made was not "arbitrary, capricious, an abuse of discretion, or otherwise not in accordance with law." 5 U.S.C. §706(2)(A). To make this finding the court must consider whether the decision was based on a consideration of the relevant factors and whether there has been a clear error of judgment. Although this inquiry into the facts is to be searching and careful, the ultimate standard of review is a narrow one. The court is not empowered to substitute its judgment for that of the agency. . . .

The lower courts based their review on the litigation affidavits that were presented. These affidavits were merely "post hoc" rationalizations, Burlington Truck Lines v. United States, 371 U.S. 156, 168-169 (1962), which have traditionally been found to be an inadequate basis for review. SEC v. Chenery Corp., 318 U.S. 80, 87 (1943). And they clearly do not constitute the "whole record" compiled by the agency: the basis for review required by §706 of the Administrative Procedure Act.

Thus it is necessary to remand this case to the District Court for plenary review of the Secretary's decision. That review is to be based on the full administrative record that was before the Secretary at the time he made his decision. But since the bare record may not disclose the factors that were considered or the Secretary's construction of the evidence it may be necessary for the District Court to require some explanation in order to determine if the Secretary acted within the scope of his authority and if the Secretary's action was justifiable under the applicable standard.

The court may require the administrative officials who participated in the decision to give testimony explaining their action. Of course, such inquiry into the mental processes of administrative decisionmakers is usually to be avoided. United States v. Morgan, 313 U.S. 409, 422 (1941). And where there are administrative findings that were made at the same time as the decision, . . . there must be a strong showing of bad faith or improper behavior before such inquiry may be made. But here there are no such formal findings and it may be that the only way there can be effective judicial review is by examining the decisionmakers themselves.

The District Court is not, however, required to make such an inquiry. It may be that the Secretary can prepare formal findings . . . that will provide an adequate explanation for his action. Such an explanation will, to some extent, be a "post hoc rationalization" and thus must be viewed critically. . . .

NOTES AND QUESTIONS

1. *The Fate of Overton Park and §4(f)*. I-40 was never built through Overton Park because, on remand from the district court, the Secretary refused to approve the route, based on the record then before him, and attempts by the state to force him to specify an acceptable route were rebuffed. Citizens to Preserve Overton Park v. Volpe, 357 F. Supp. 846 (W.D. Tenn. 1973), rev'd, 494 F.2d 1212 (6th Cir. 1974). For discussion of the background and consequences of *Overton Park*, see Gibson, Not in My Neighborhood: Memphis and the Battle to Preserve Overton Park, 41 U. Mem. L. Rev. 725 (2011). For a case finding no violation of §4(f) in which the court emphasized the discretionary nature of agency analytical duties, particularly in determining the prudence of alternatives, see Prairie Band Pottawatomie Nation v. Federal Highway Admin., 684 F.3d 1002 (10th Cir. 2012).

Congress amended §4(f) in the 2005 Safe Accountable, Flexible, Efficient Transportation Equity Act: A Legacy for Users. The statute now provides that the alternative consideration and harm minimization requirements will be deemed satisfied if the Secretary determines that a transportation project or program will have a *de minimis* impact on historic properties or on parks, recreation areas, or wildlife or waterfowl refuges. The Secretary may make a finding of *de minimis* impact only by determining, after public notice and an opportunity for public comment, that the program or project will not adversely affect the activities, features, and attributes of the area, and the officials with jurisdiction over the park, recreation area, or refuge concur with that finding. 23 U.S.C. §138(b). Further, the Secretary must issue regulations clarifying the factors and standards relevant to determining the prudence and feasibility of alternatives. 23 U.S.C. §138 note.

2. Overton Park, Vermont Yankee, *and Judicial Review of Deregulation*. Does *Overton Park* in effect require agencies to compile records of decision in informal rulemaking and adjudication that are just as detailed as they must be in formal proceedings? Can you reconcile *Overton Park* with the Supreme Court's later decision in *Vermont Yankee*, discussed in section A.2.a above?

Vermont Yankee preceded the deregulation movement in the 1980s. Does the fact that the agency is relaxing a previous regulatory burden have any influence on the standard of review? The issue raised in Motor Vehicle Mfrs. Ass'n v. State Farm Mut. Auto. Ins. Co., 463 U.S. 29 (1983), was whether the Department of Transportation could rescind a previously adopted rule requiring passive restraints (airbags) in new cars. The auto industry argued that the decision to rescind should be governed by the same standard of review that applies to a decision not to adopt a rule in the first instance. But the Court, unanimously holding that the rescission was arbitrary and capricious, took the position that rescission of a previously adopted rule is different from a decision not to adopt a rule because there is a presumption that congressional policies contained in the enabling statute will be served best by a settled rule. "Accordingly, an agency changing its course by rescinding a rule is obligated to supply a reasoned analysis for change beyond that which may be required when an agency does not act in the first instance." Id. at 42. DOT acted arbitrarily because it offered no reasons to reject airbags, given their safety benefits.

More generally, *State Farm* provides guidance on the factors to be considered in determining whether an agency's statutory implementation is arbitrary and capricious:

> Normally, an agency rule would be arbitrary and capricious if the agency has relied on factors which Congress has not intended it to consider, entirely failed to consider an important aspect of the problem, offered an explanation for its decision that runs counter to the evidence before the agency, or is so implausible that it could not be ascribed to a difference in view or the product of agency expertise. [Id. at 43.]

See, e.g., Portland Cement Ass'n v. EPA, 665 F.3d 177 (D.C. Cir. 2011) (invalidating CAA regulation because in promulgating it, EPA relied on information it knew would soon be irrelevant).

3. *Arbitrary and Capricious Decisions and Offshore Drilling.* A striking example of the application of the arbitrary and capricious standard is Hornbeck Offshore Servs., L.L.C. v. Salazar, 696 F. Supp. 2d 627 (E.D. La. 2010). After the blowout of the drilling platform at the Deepwater Horizon offshore oil well in the Gulf of Mexico led to a massive oil spill in 2010, the Interior Secretary announced a six-month moratorium on offshore drilling operations at new and currently permitted deepwater wells under the Outer Continental Shelf Lands Act. The Secretary based the moratorium on his findings that offshore drilling posed "an unacceptable threat of serious and irreparable harm to wildlife and the marine, coastal, and human environment," and that the installation of additional safety or environmental protection equipment was necessary to prevent injury or loss of life and property and environmental damage. The court held the moratorium to be arbitrary and capricious because it was "unable to divine or fathom a relationship between the findings and the immense scope of the moratorium." Id. at 637. The decision lacked any analysis of the asserted fear or threat of irreparable injury or safety hazards posed by rigs that already had permits. In addition, the decision was "incident-specific and driven. Deepwater Horizon and [British Petroleum] only. None others." Id. Is there anything wrong with relying on a particular incident to draw general conclusions about the wisdom of existing practices in a broader context? The court also took the Secretary to task for failing to explain why the moratorium applied to drilling 500 feet or more below the sea surface, even though the studies on which he relied involved drilling at 1,000 feet or more below the surface. The court found no evidence that the Secretary balanced the concern for safety and environmental protection with the statutory policy of making leases available for development or considered less drastic curtailment on permitting. Which aspects of the *State Farm* test were at issue in this case? The Interior Secretary responded to *Hornbeck* by issuing a more comprehensive justification for the moratorium, which could be avoided if a drilling rig's owner could show it had adequate plans to shut down an out-of-control well, that blowout preventers were in place, and that sufficient resources would be available in the event of a spill. Decision Memorandum Regarding the Suspension of Certain Offshore Permitting and Drilling Activities on the Outer Continental Shelf (July 12, 2010).

4. *Arbitrary and Capricious versus Substantial Evidence Review.* Section 706(2) of the APA provides that certain agency decisions are reviewable under the substantial evidence test, while others trigger arbitrary and capricious review. The substantial evidence standard, discussed in *Overton Park*, was developed for review of formal

adjudications, for which a trial-type hearing record was available to the reviewing court. The arbitrary and capricious standard applies to quasi-legislative or informal decision-making, for which a "proper" record and hearing were not required. Congress has required application of the substantial evidence test to review of some EPA regulations. E.g., 15 U.S.C. §2618(c)(1)(B)(i) (Toxic Substances Control Act). Although the substantial evidence test has long been viewed as the more searching of the two standards, it is not clear what, if any, meaningful differences exist between the two. See, e.g., Pennaco Energy, Inc. v. U.S. Dep't of the Interior, 377 F.3d 1147, 1156 n.6 (10th Cir. 2004) (stating that "[w]hen the arbitrary and capricious test is performing [the] function of assuring factual support [for the agency's decision], there is no substantive difference between what it requires and what would be required by the substantial evidence test, since it is impossible to conceive of a nonarbitrary factual judgment supported only by evidence that is not insubstantial in the APA sense").

The strictest standards in §706(2) of the APA are those calling for de novo review. According to *Overton Park*, under what circumstances does §706(2)(F) apply? Why didn't that standard apply in *Overton Park* itself? Section 706(2)(F) rarely applies in environmental cases.

5. *Substantive Review in Practice.* Schroeder & Glicksman, *Chevron, State Farm, and EPA in the Courts of Appeals during the 1990s,* 31 Envtl. L. Rep. 10371 (2001), analyze judicial review of statutory implementation in the federal Courts of Appeals during the 1990s. They conclude that although the courts often cite *Overton Park, State Farm,* or both, when engaged in review of EPA's statutory implementation decisions, neither case has achieved the "iconic status" that *Chevron* has in the context of judicial review of statutory interpretation. The study found that litigants attacking EPA's methodology for collecting and interpreting scientific data rarely succeed, perhaps largely due to the judges' awareness of the relatively greater competence that agency decisionmakers have to make such judgments. Attacks on EPA's reasoning process are more likely to succeed, particularly when a litigant convinces a court that the agency has failed to provide any evidence to support its technical determinations, relied on evidence that conflicts with the stated views of its own experts, relied on technical models or methodologies that are obviously ill-suited to the task for which they were employed, failed to explain in any way an apparently illogical conclusion, left a gap in logic in its explanation, or engaged in internally inconsistent reasoning. For criticism of judicial "super deference" to agency scientific determinations, see Hammond Meazell, Super Deference, the Science Obsession, and Judicial Review as Translation of Agency Science, 109 Mich. L. Rev. 733 (2011).

6. *The Relationship between* Chevron *and* Overton Park/State Farm. How does the judicial function differ if the question is (1) whether an agency's interpretation of an ambiguous statute is reasonable (a *Chevron* step 2 issue) and (2) whether an agency's statutory implementation is arbitrary and capricious (a question governed by the *Overton Park* standard, as modified by *State Farm*)? The answer is far from clear. In Arent v. Shalala, 70 F.3d 610 (D.C. Cir. 1995), the majority and concurring opinions agreed that *Chevron* review and arbitrary and capricious review overlap "at the margins." They disagreed, however, on which standard of review applied in that case. See also Judulang v. Holder, 132 S. Ct. 476, 483 n.7 (2011) ("[U]nder *Chevron* step two, we ask whether an agency interpretation is " 'arbitrary or capricious in substance.' "); Mayo Found. for Medical Educ. and Research v. United States, 131 S. Ct. 704, 711 (2011) (stating that under "*Chevron* step two, . . . we may not disturb an agency rule unless it is arbitrary or capricious in substance, or manifestly contrary to the statute").

NOTE ON THE ORIGINS OF HARD LOOK REVIEW

The statement in *Overton Park* that courts applying the APA's arbitrary and capricious standard must engage in a "searching and careful" inquiry—"a thorough, probing, in-depth review" of the full administrative record—raised considerably the level of judicial review under that standard. Before *Overton Park*, the arbitrary and capricious standard was widely believed to be highly indulgent toward the exercise of administrative discretion. After this case, the "hard look" doctrine of judicial review became common in judicial review of environmental decisionmaking.

The phrase "hard look review" originated in Greater Boston Television Corp. v. FCC, 444 F.2d 841, 851 (D.C. Cir. 1970), in which Judge Harold Leventhal remarked that the supervisory function of the courts calls on them "to intervene not merely in case of procedural inadequacies, or bypassing of the mandate in the legislative charter, but more broadly if the court becomes aware . . . that the agency has not really taken a hard look at the salient problems, and has not genuinely engaged in reasoned decision-making." Even though Judge Leventhal used the term "hard look" to describe the agency's obligation to review the issues before it, the term soon came to describe the relatively rigorous review that courts applied to agency decisions to ensure that these decisions were not arbitrary and capricious. This gloss on the arbitrary and capricious standard thrust courts into an examination of the methodology and substance of agency decisions to ensure that they had adequate factual support.

But what if complex scientific and technical matters arise, as they often do under the environmental statutes; are the courts competent to "second-guess" agency determinations under the rubric of arbitrary and capricious review? The judges of the D.C. Circuit engaged in a spirited debate in the 1970s about the proper role of the courts in environmental litigation. In Ethyl Corp. v. EPA, 541 F.2d 1 (D.C. Cir. 1976) (excerpted in Chapter 8, section C), Chief Judge Bazelon argued that the best way for the courts in highly technical cases to guard against erroneous agency decisions is not to scrutinize the technical merits of the decision. Instead, the courts should "establish a decisionmaking process that assures a reasoned decision that can be held up to the scrutiny of the scientific community and the public."[g] Id. at 66.

Two other judges endorsed substantive review of some sort. Judge Wright took the position that, although the arbitrary and capricious standard is "highly deferential" and presumes the validity of agency action, the courts should not merely "rubberstamp the agency decision." Careful perusal of the technical record enables the court "to satisfy itself that the agency has exercised a reasoned discretion, with reasons that do not deviate from or ignore ascertainable legislative intent." The court's task is to "understand enough about the problem confronting the agency to comprehend the meaning of the evidence," the questions addressed, and the choices made. But Judge Wright warned courts to defer to the agency's expertise, not supplant it. The judicial

---

g. Bazelon asserted that judges who address the merits risk making "plausible-sounding, but simplistic judgments. . . . Because substantive review of mathematical and scientific evidence by technically illiterate judges is dangerously unreliable, I continue to believe we will do more to improve administrative decisionmaking by concentrating our efforts on strengthening administrative procedures." 541 F.2d at 66-67. How free are the courts to follow Judge Bazelon's recommendations after *Vermont Yankee*, discussed in section A.2.a above?

role is to exercise "our narrowly defined duty of holding agencies to certain minimal standards of rationality."[h] Id. at 35-36.

Judge Leventhal also supported substantive review, arguing that Congress delegated its legislative powers to agencies, and courts had upheld those delegations, only on the condition that judicial review is available to ensure that agencies rationally exercise the delegated power within statutory limits. The courts therefore had a responsibility to engage in substantive review. Warning against "a charade that gives the imprimatur without the substance of judicial confirmation that the agency is not acting unreasonably," Leventhal summarized his views as follows: "Restraint, yes, abdication, no."[i] Id. at 69.

Hard Look Review and the Nondelegation Doctrine. In the *Ethyl* case, both Judges Wright and Leventhal justified "hard look" judicial review by noting the willingness of the federal courts to uphold broad delegations of legislative power to administrative agencies. During the 1930s, the Supreme Court invalidated congressional legislation as standardless delegations of the legislature's core policymaking function, but it has not done so since then. See Whitman v. American Trucking Ass'ns, Inc., 531 U.S. 457 (2001), reproduced in Chapter 6, section D.1.b. Both the "hard look" and nondelegation doctrines "are grounded upon similar insights about the deficiencies of broadly written regulatory legislation," such as lack of notice to affected parties, lack of opportunity to participate in rule formulation, and "legislative cowardice in handing over lawmaking power while retreating to the role of second-guessing opportunist." Rodgers, Judicial Review of Risk Assessments: The Role of Decision Theory in Unscrambling the *Benzene* Decision, 11 Envtl. L. 301, 317 (1981). Does intensive judicial procedural review compensate for overbroad congressional delegation? What about intensive substantive judicial review?

NOTE ON REVIEWABILITY

Section 704 of the APA provides that "[a]gency action made reviewable by statute and final agency action for which there is no adequate remedy in a court are subject to judicial review." But §701(a) recognizes two exceptions to the reviewability of agency action to the extent that "(1) statutes preclude judicial review; or (2) agency action is committed to agency discretion by law." Justice Marshall had no trouble holding in *Overton Park* that neither of these two provisions made the Secretary of Transportation's decision unreviewable. There was no evidence that Congress sought to prohibit judicial review and the decision was not "committed to agency discretion" because §4(f) constituted "law to apply." The Secretary claimed that §4(f) had enacted a balancing test. Why is this relevant to the "committed to agency discretion" problem?

h. See also Shapiro & Levy, Heightened Scrutiny of the Fourth Branch: Separation of Powers and the Requirement of Adequate Reasons for Agency Decisions, 1987 Duke L.J. 387 (endorsing "rationalist" review, which requires agencies to provide adequate reasons for their decisions, as required by the separation of powers, and claiming that it has become the primary method of constraining agency discretion).

i. See also Leventhal, Environmental Decision Making and the Role of the Courts, 122 U. Pa. L. Rev. 509, 555 (1974) (explaining that the central role of the courts in environmental cases is ensuring that "mission-oriented agencies . . . will take due cognizance of environmental matters" and that environmental protection agencies implement statutory mandates that "environmental concerns be reconciled with other social and economic objectives").

In Block v. Community Nutrition Inst., 467 U.S. 340, 351 (1984), the Court held that the presumption of reviewability created by §§702 and 704 of the APA may be overcome for purposes of §701(a)(1) "whenever the congressional intent to preclude review is 'fairly discernable from the statutory scheme.'" Congress has rarely precluded review in the environmental statutes. In High Country Citizens Alliance v. Clarke, 454 F.3d 1177 (10th Cir. 2006), however, the court concluded that the General Mining Law of 1872 precludes a person not claiming a property interest in the affected land from attacking the validity of a mineral patent issued by the BLM. According to the court, allowing such a suit would conflict with Congress's intent, reflected in the legislative history, to provide finality in the patent process to induce miners to invest the necessary time and capital to develop the industry. See also NRDC v. Johnson, 461 F.3d 164 (2d Cir. 2006) (Federal Food, Drug, and Cosmetic Act precluded review in district court of EPA decision to leave tolerances for pesticide residues on food in effect).

The mere existence of agency discretion is insufficient to invoke the second exception to judicial review in §701(a)(2). After all, §706(2)(A) authorizes courts to set aside agency action that is "arbitrary, capricious, an abuse of discretion, or otherwise not in accordance with law." See American Canoe Ass'n v. EPA, 30 F. Supp. 2d 908, 925 (E.D. Va. 1998) (discussing the "uneasy tension" that exists between §§701(a)(2) and 706(2)(A)). The courts typically have little difficulty finding "law to apply" in the statutes delegating discretionary authority to an agency. The agency's own output, such as regulations or land use plans, also may constrain agency discretion sufficiently to furnish the necessary "law to apply." See Kola, Inc. v. United States, 882 F.2d 361 (9th Cir. 1989) (Forest Service special use permit decision reviewable).

The courts are most likely to invoke §701(a)(2) to preclude review where a litigant challenges an agency decision not to enforce a statute or regulation. See Heckler v. Chaney, 470 U.S. 821 (1985). See also Sierra Club v. Jackson, 648 F.3d 848 (D.C. Cir. 2011) (holding that challenge to EPA's decision not to prevent construction of stationary sources despite issuance of permits under invalid state implementation plan was committed to agency discretion by law under provision providing that EPA "shall . . . take such measures . . . as necessary to prevent the construction"). Should the same approach apply to a challenge to an agency refusal to initiate rulemaking proceedings in response to a private party's petition to do so? In Massachusetts v. EPA, 549 U.S. 497, 527 (2007), the Court identified "key differences between a denial of a petition for rulemaking and an agency's decision not to initiate an enforcement action," including the fact that rulemaking petitions are less frequent, more likely to involve legal, not factual analysis, and more likely to be subject to the requirement to provide a formal, public explanation. Cf. Sierra Club v. Yeutter, 911 F.2d 1405, 1414 (10th Cir. 1990) (Forest Service's decision not to assert federal reserved water rights in wilderness areas in state water rights adjudications was nonreviewable).

The reviewability of agency inaction was also at issue in the following case.

NORTON v. SOUTHERN UTAH WILDERNESS ALLIANCE
542 U.S. 55 (2004)

Justice SCALIA delivered the opinion of the Court.

In this case, we must decide whether the authority of a federal court under the Administrative Procedure Act (APA) to "compel agency action unlawfully withheld or unreasonably delayed," 5 U.S.C. §706(1), extends to the review of the United States

Bureau of Land Management's stewardship of public lands under certain statutory provisions and its own planning documents.

I

[The Federal Land Policy and Management Act of 1976 (FLPMA) delegates to the Bureau of Land Management (BLM) the authority to manage the public lands. FLPMA dictates that the BLM adhere to a multiple use, sustained yield management standard.] "Multiple use management" is a deceptively simple term that describes the enormously complicated task of striking a balance among the many competing uses to which land can be put, "including, but not limited to, recreation, range, timber, minerals, watershed, wildlife and fish, and [uses serving] natural scenic, scientific and historical values." 43 U.S.C. §1702(c). . . . "[S]ustained yield" requires BLM to control depleting uses over time, so as to ensure a high level of valuable uses in the future. §1702(h). To these ends, FLPMA establishes a dual regime of inventory and planning. Sections 1711 and 1712, respectively, provide for a comprehensive, ongoing inventory of federal lands, and for a land use planning process that "project[s]" "present and future use," §1701(a)(2), given the lands' inventoried characteristics.

Of course not all uses are compatible. Congress made the judgment that some lands should be set aside as wilderness at the expense of commercial and recreational uses. A pre-FLPMA enactment, the Wilderness Act of 1964, provides that designated wilderness areas, subject to certain exceptions, "shall [have] no commercial enterprise and no permanent road," no motorized vehicles, and no manmade structures. 16 U.S.C. §1133(c). The designation of a wilderness area can be made only by Act of Congress, see 43 U.S.C. §1782(b).

Pursuant to §1782, the Secretary of the Interior has identified so-called "wilderness study areas" (WSAs), roadless lands of 5,000 acres or more that possess "wilderness characteristics," as determined in the Secretary's land inventory. §1782(a); see 16 U.S.C. §1131(c). As the name suggests, WSAs . . . have been subjected to further examination and public comment in order to evaluate their suitability for designation as wilderness. In 1991, out of 3.3 million acres in Utah that had been identified for study, 2 million were recommended as suitable for wilderness designation. This recommendation was forwarded to Congress, which has not yet acted upon it. Until Congress acts one way or the other, FLPMA provides that "the Secretary shall continue to manage such lands . . . in a manner so as not to impair the suitability of such areas for preservation as wilderness." 43 U.S.C. §1782(c). This nonimpairment mandate applies to all WSAs identified under §1782, including lands considered unsuitable by the Secretary.

Aside from identification of WSAs, the main tool that BLM employs to balance wilderness protection against other uses is a land use plan—what BLM regulations call a "resource management plan." Land use plans, adopted after notice and comment, are "designed to guide and control future management actions," [43 C.F.R. §1601.0-2 (2003)]. Generally, a land use plan describes, for a particular area, allowable uses, goals for future condition of the land, and specific next steps. Under FLPMA, "[t]he Secretary shall manage the public lands under principles of multiple use and sustained yield, in accordance with the land use plans . . . when they are available." 43 U.S.C. §1732(a).

Protection of wilderness has come into increasing conflict with another element of multiple use, recreational use of so-called off-road vehicles (ORVs), which include vehicles primarily designed for off-road use, such as lightweight, four-wheel "all-terrain vehicles," and vehicles capable of such use, such as sport utility vehicles. According to the United States Forest Service's most recent estimates, some 42 million Americans participate in off-road travel each year, more than double the number two decades ago. . . . The use of ORVs on federal land has negative environmental consequences, including soil disruption and compaction, harassment of animals, and annoyance of wilderness lovers. Thus, BLM faces a classic land use dilemma of sharply inconsistent uses, in a context of scarce resources and congressional silence with respect to wilderness designation.

[Southern Utah Wilderness Alliance (SUWA) filed suit in federal district court against the BLM and the Secretary of the Interior, seeking] declaratory and injunctive relief for BLM's failure to act to protect public lands in Utah from damage caused by ORV use. SUWA made three claims that are relevant here: (1) that BLM had violated its nonimpairment obligation under §1782(a) by allowing degradation in certain WSAs; (2) that BLM had failed to implement provisions in its land use plans relating to ORV use; (3) that BLM had failed to take a "hard look" at whether, pursuant to the National Environmental Policy Act of 1969 (NEPA), it should undertake supplemental environmental analyses for areas in which ORV use had increased. SUWA contended that it could sue to remedy these three failures to act pursuant to the APA's provision of a cause of action to "compel agency action unlawfully withheld or unreasonably delayed." 5 U.S.C. §706(1).

[The district court dismissed all three claims, but the Tenth Circuit reversed, concluding that the plaintiffs had alleged the BLM's failure to perform nondiscretionary duties, including FLPMA's nonimpairment obligation.]

II

All three claims at issue here involve assertions that BLM failed to take action with respect to ORV use that it was required to take. Failures to act are sometimes remediable under the APA, but not always. We begin by considering what limits the APA places upon judicial review of agency inaction.

The APA authorizes suit by "[a] person suffering legal wrong because of agency action, or adversely affected or aggrieved by agency action within the meaning of a relevant statute." 5 U.S.C. §702. Where no other statute provides a private right of action, the "agency action" complained of must be "*final* agency action." §704 (emphasis added). "Agency action" is defined in §551(13) to include "the whole or a part of an agency rule, order, license, sanction, relief, or the equivalent or denial thereof, or *failure to act*." (Emphasis added.) The APA provides relief for a failure to act in §706(1): "The reviewing court shall . . . compel agency action unlawfully withheld or unreasonably delayed."

Sections 702, 704, and 706(1) all insist upon an "agency action," either as the action complained of (in §§702 and 704) or as the action to be compelled (in §706(1)). The definition of that term begins with a list of five categories of decisions made or outcomes implemented by an agency—"agency rule, order, license, sanction [or] relief." §551(13). All of those categories involve circumscribed, discrete agency actions, as their definitions make clear [citing 5 U.S.C. §§551(4), (6), (8), (10), (11)].

The terms following those five categories of agency action are not defined in the APA: "or the equivalent or denial thereof, or failure to act." §551(13). But an "equivalent . . . thereof" must also be discrete (or it would not be equivalent), and a "denial thereof" must be the denial of a discrete listed action (and perhaps denial of a discrete equivalent).

The final term in the definition, "failure to act," is in our view properly understood as a failure to take an *agency action*—that is, a failure to take one of the agency actions (including their equivalents) earlier defined in §551(13). Moreover, even without this equation of "act" with "agency action" the interpretive canon of *ejusdem generis* would attribute to the last item ("failure to act") the same characteristic of discreteness shared by all the preceding items. A "failure to act" is not the same thing as a "denial." The latter is the agency's act of saying no to a request; the former is simply the omission of an action without formally rejecting a request—for example, the failure to promulgate a rule or take some decision by a statutory deadline. The important point is that a "failure to act" is properly understood to be limited, as are the other items in §551(13), to a discrete action.

A second point central to the analysis of the present case is that the only agency action that can be compelled under the APA is action legally *required*. This limitation appears in §706(1)'s authorization for courts to "compel agency action *unlawfully* withheld." . . . As described in the Attorney General's Manual on the APA, a document whose reasoning we have often found persuasive, §706(1) empowers a court only to compel an agency "to perform a ministerial or non-discretionary act," or "to take action upon a matter, without directing *how* it shall act." Attorney General's Manual on the Administrative Procedure Act 108 (1947) (emphasis added).

Thus, a claim under §706(1) can proceed only where a plaintiff asserts that an agency failed to take a *discrete* agency action that it is *required to take*. These limitations rule out several kinds of challenges. The limitation to discrete agency action precludes the kind of broad programmatic attack we rejected in Lujan v. National Wildlife Federation, 497 U.S. 871 (1990). There we considered a challenge to BLM's land withdrawal review program, couched as unlawful agency "action" that the plaintiffs wished to have "set aside" under §706(2). We concluded that the program was not an "agency action":

> [R]espondent cannot seek *wholesale* improvement of this program by court decree, rather than in the offices of the Department or the halls of Congress, where programmatic improvements are normally made. Under the terms of the APA, respondent must direct its attack against some particular "agency action" that causes it harm. Id., at 891 (emphasis in original).

The plaintiffs in *National Wildlife Federation* would have fared no better if they had characterized the agency's alleged "failure to revise land use plans in proper fashion" and "failure to consider multiple use," in terms of "agency action unlawfully withheld" under §706(1), rather than agency action "not in accordance with law" under §706(2).

The limitation to *required* agency action rules out judicial direction of even discrete agency action that is not demanded by law (which includes, of course, agency regulations that have the force of law). Thus, when an agency is compelled by law to act within a certain time period, but the manner of its action is left to the agency's discretion, a court can compel the agency to act, but has no power to specify what the action must be. . . .

III

A

With these principles in mind, we turn to SUWA's first claim, that by permitting ORV use in certain WSAs, BLM violated its mandate to "continue to manage [WSAs] . . . in a manner so as not to impair the suitability of such areas for preservation as wilderness," 43 U.S.C. §1782(c). SUWA relies not only upon §1782(c) but also upon a provision of BLM's Interim Management Policy for Lands Under Wilderness Review, which interprets the nonimpairment mandate to require BLM to manage WSAs so as to prevent them from being "degraded so far, compared with the area's values for other purposes, as to significantly constrain the Congress's prerogative to either designate [it] as wilderness or release it for other uses."

Section 1782(c) is mandatory as to the object to be achieved, but it leaves BLM a great deal of discretion in deciding how to achieve it. It assuredly does not mandate, with the clarity necessary to support judicial action under §706(1), the total exclusion of ORV use.

SUWA argues that §1782 does contain a categorical imperative, namely the command to comply with the nonimpairment mandate. It contends that a federal court could simply enter a general order compelling compliance with that mandate, without suggesting any particular manner of compliance. [But g]eneral deficiencies in compliance . . . lack the specificity requisite for agency action.

The principal purpose of the APA limitations we have discussed—and of the traditional limitations upon mandamus from which they were derived—is to protect agencies from undue judicial interference with their lawful discretion, and to avoid judicial entanglement in abstract policy disagreements which courts lack both expertise and information to resolve. If courts were empowered to enter general orders compelling compliance with broad statutory mandates, they would necessarily be empowered, as well, to determine whether compliance was achieved—which would mean that it would ultimately become the task of the supervising court, rather than the agency, to work out compliance with the broad statutory mandate, injecting the judge into day-to-day agency management. . . . The prospect of pervasive oversight by federal courts over the manner and pace of agency compliance with such congressional directives is not contemplated by the APA.

B

SUWA's second claim is that BLM failed to comply with certain provisions in its land use plans, thus contravening the requirement that "[t]he Secretary shall manage the public lands . . . in accordance with the land use plans . . . when they are available." 43 U.S.C. §1732(a). . . .

[SUWA claimed that, "in light of damage from ORVs in the Factory Butte area," the applicable resource management plan obligated the BLM to conduct "an intensive ORV monitoring program." The plan stated that the area open to ORV use "will be monitored and closed if warranted."] SUWA does not contest BLM's assertion in the court below that informal monitoring has taken place for some years, but it demands continuing implementation of a monitoring *program*. By this it apparently means to insist upon adherence to [a plan provision stating that] "[r]esource damage will be documented and recommendations made for corrective action," "[m]onitoring in open areas will focus on determining damage which may necessitate a change in designation," and "emphasis on use supervision will be placed on [limited and closed areas]." . . .

The statutory directive that BLM manage "in accordance with" land use plans, and the regulatory requirement that authorizations and actions "conform to" those plans, prevent BLM from taking actions inconsistent with the provisions of a land use plan. Unless and until the plan is amended, such actions can be set aside as contrary to law pursuant to 5 U.S.C. §706(2). The claim presently under discussion, however, would have us go further, and conclude that a statement in a plan that BLM "will" take this, that, or the other action, is a binding commitment that can be compelled under §706(1). In our view it is not—at least absent clear indication of binding commitment in the terms of the plan.

FLPMA describes land use plans as tools by which "present and future use is *projected*." 43 U.S.C. §1701(a)(2) (emphasis added). The implementing regulations make clear that land use plans are a preliminary step in the overall process of managing public lands—"designed to guide and control future management actions and the development of subsequent, more detailed and limited scope plans for resources and uses." 43 CFR §1601.0-2 (2003). The statute and regulations confirm that a land use plan is not ordinarily the medium for affirmative decisions that implement the agency's "project[ions]." 43 U.S.C. §1712(e) provides that "[t]he Secretary may issue management decisions to implement land use plans"—the decisions, that is, are distinct from the plan itself. Picking up the same theme, . . . [t]he BLM's Land Use Planning Handbook specifies that land use plans are normally not used to make site-specific implementation decisions. . . .

Quite unlike a specific statutory command requiring an agency to promulgate regulations by a certain date, a land use plan is generally a statement of priorities; it guides and constrains actions, but does not (at least in the usual case) prescribe them. It would be unreasonable to think that either Congress or the agency intended otherwise, since land use plans nationwide would commit the agency to actions far in the future, for which funds have not yet been appropriated. Some plans make explicit that implementation of their programmatic content is subject to budgetary constraints. While the plan [in this case] does not contain such a specification, we think it must reasonably be implied. A statement by BLM about what it plans to do, at some point, provided it has the funds and there are not more pressing priorities, cannot be plucked out of context and made a basis for suit under §706(1).

Of course, an action called for in a plan may be compelled when the plan merely reiterates duties the agency is already obligated to perform, or perhaps when language in the plan itself creates a commitment binding on the agency. But allowing general enforcement of plan terms would lead to pervasive interference with BLM's own ordering of priorities. . . . And while such a decree might please the environmental plaintiffs in the present case, it would ultimately operate to the detriment of sound environmental management. Its predictable consequence would be much vaguer plans from BLM in the future—making coordination with other agencies more difficult, and depriving the public of important information concerning the agency's long-range intentions.

We therefore hold that the Henry Mountains plan's statements to the effect that BLM will conduct "use supervision and monitoring" in designated areas—like other "will do" projections of agency action set forth in land use plans—are not a legally binding commitment enforceable under §706(1). That being so, we find it unnecessary to consider whether the action envisioned by the statements is sufficiently discrete to be amenable to compulsion under the APA.

IV

Finally, we turn to SUWA's contention that BLM failed to fulfill certain obligations under NEPA. Before addressing whether a NEPA-required duty is actionable under the APA, we must decide whether NEPA creates an obligation in the first place. NEPA requires a federal agency to prepare an environmental impact statement (EIS) as part of any "proposals for legislation and other major Federal actions significantly affecting the quality of the human environment." 42 U.S.C. §4332(2)(C). Often an initial EIS is sufficient, but in certain circumstances an EIS must be supplemented. See Marsh v. Oregon Natural Resources Council, 490 U.S. 360, 370-374 (1989). A regulation of the Council on Environmental Quality requires supplementation where "[t]here are significant new circumstances or information relevant to environmental concerns and bearing on the proposed action or its impacts." 40 CFR §1502.9(c)(1)(ii) (2003). In *Marsh*, we interpreted §4332 in light of this regulation to require an agency to take a "hard look" at the new information to assess whether supplementation might be necessary.

SUWA argues that evidence of increased ORV use is "significant new circumstances or information" that requires a "hard look." We disagree. As we noted in *Marsh*, supplementation is necessary only if "there remains 'major Federal actio[n]' to occur," as that term is used in §4332(2)(C). 490 U.S., at 374. In *Marsh*, that condition was met: the dam construction project that gave rise to environmental review was not yet completed. Here, by contrast, although the "[a]pproval of a [land use plan]" is a "major Federal action" requiring an EIS, 43 CFR §1601.0-6 (2003) (emphasis added), that action is completed when the plan is approved. The land use plan is the "proposed action" contemplated by the regulation. There is no ongoing "major Federal action" that could require supplementation (though BLM *is* required to perform additional NEPA analyses if a plan is amended or revised).

The judgment of the Court of Appeals is reversed, and the case is remanded for further proceedings consistent with this opinion.

NOTES AND QUESTIONS

1. *The Nonimpairment Mandate.* Is the analysis in the *SUWA* case limited to situations involving claims of allegedly improper agency inaction, or does it apply more broadly to allegedly improper actions as well? What is the significance of the requirement that a suit seeking review under §706(1) of the APA allege failure to perform a "discrete" agency action? What is the source of the requirement that the action be discrete? Is there any other limitation on the kinds of inaction covered by §706(1)? Why wasn't SUWA's claim that the BLM failed to comply with FLPMA's nonimpairment mandate justiciable? What is a "general deficiency" in compliance? What is the policy rationale for limiting judicial supervision of compliance with "broad statutory mandates"?

2. *Land Use Plans: Scope of Review Questions.* One of the casebook authors has observed that, "[a]t a minimum, [BLM and Forest Service land use plans] should provide bases for judicial review requiring the agency to explain seeming departures from plan provisions." 2 G. Coggins & R. Glicksman, Public Natural Resources Law §16:1 (2d ed. 2007). Does the *SUWA* case contradict that observation? Would the result in *SUWA* have been different if the BLM's plan had stated that the agency

"must" monitor for the effects of ORV use, instead of stating that the agency "will" do so? Does *SUWA* affect judicial review of agency decisions to allow site-specific activities that are prohibited by land use plans?

3. *Land Use Plans: Incentives for Planning Specificity.* Professors Coggins and Glicksman feared that the federal land management agencies might adopt plans so general as to be meaningless as limitations on agency discretion in making subsequent management decisions. "[A]gencies may prefer to write motherhood generalities rather than blueprints for future resource allocation and protection." Id. The Court in *SUWA* argued that the "predictable consequence" of allowing general enforcement of BLM plans "would be much vaguer plans from BLM in the future—making coordination with other agencies more difficult, and depriving the public of important information concerning the agency's long-range intentions." Won't the Court's decision in *SUWA* have precisely those consequences?

4. *Statutory Deadlines.* One way to accelerate the pace of agency regulatory decisions is for Congress to adopt deadlines by which agencies must make those decisions. In an empirical study of the deadlines used to structure agency decisions, Gersen & O'Connell, Deadlines in Administrative Law, 156 U. Pa. L. Rev. 923 (2008), conclude that deadlines generally increase the pace of agency action, but only modestly, and that most deadlines apply to just a handful of agencies, including EPA. The article considers the benefits and disadvantages of agency-forcing deadlines. See also Shapiro & Glicksman, Congress, the Supreme Court, and the Quiet Revolution in Administrative Law, 1988 Duke L.J. 819.

5. *Supplemental EISs.* Under the Court's decision, will federal agencies ever be obligated to prepare a supplemental EIS for a land use plan based on changed conditions?

6. For criticism of *SUWA*, see Glicksman, "Judicial Review of Agency Inaction (and Action) in the Wake of *Norton v. Southern Utah Wilderness Alliance*," in Strategies for Environmental Success in an Uncertain Judicial Climate 163 (M. Wolf ed., 2005); Flournoy, "Following the Court Off-Road in *Norton v. Southern Utah Wilderness Alliance*," id. at 215. See generally Biber, Two Sides of the Same Coin: Judicial Review of Administrative Agency Action and Inaction, 26 Va. Envtl. L.J. 461 (2008).

B.   CONGRESSIONAL CONTROL OF ADMINISTRATIVE ENVIRONMENTAL DECISIONMAKING

Agencies like EPA may issue and enforce regulations and take other actions to protect the environment only if authorized to do so by Congress. Although Congress has been willing to vest in many agencies decisionmaking authority over environmental matters, it has various techniques for limiting the scope of that authority.[j] One technique is

---

j. See generally Beermann, Congressional Administration, 43 San Diego L. Rev. 61 (2006) (analyzing the influence over the execution of the laws that results from Congress's "intimate" involvement, both formal and informal, in that process); Lazarus, The Neglected Question of Congressional Oversight of EPA: *Quis Custodiet Ipsos Custodes* (Who Shall Watch the Watchers Themselves)?, 54 Law & Contemp. Probs. 205 (Autumn 1991).

to limit the President's authority to appoint and remove agency decisionmakers. Such limits may prevent the President from appointing officials whose positions conflict with congressionally adopted policies or from removing those implementing those policies in a manner unsatisfactory to the Chief Executive. The Senate has the constitutional authority to advise and consent to the appointment of the heads of agencies with environmental responsibilities, but it may not impose its own selections on the President. See Buckley v. Valeo, 424 U.S. 1 (1976). Congress has substantially more authority to limit presidential removal of executive officials by restricting the conditions under which it may occur, but even that authority may not be exercised if its effect is to interfere with the core functions of the executive branch. E.g., Free Enter. Fund v. Public Co. Accounting Oversight Bd., 561 U.S. 477 (2010); Morrison v. Olson, 487 U.S. 654 (1988).

Of greater practical, day-to-day relevance are the use of the appropriations process and the imposition of substantive statutory decisionmaking criteria as means for Congress to confine agency discretion. Traditionally, an agency's authorizing legislation delineates the standards it must apply in making decisions. Appropriations legislation provides the funds that permit the agency to implement its substantive mandates. But Congress has resorted to appropriations bills to limit agency substantive authority. The first subsection below considers some examples of this technique for controlling agency discretion. The second subsection deals with the use of substantive legislation to constrain that discretion. It focuses on statutes that require agencies to conduct analytical processes and make findings to support their decisions.

1.   Control Through the Appropriations Process

Congress has always used the appropriations process to induce agencies to conform their decisions to desired legislative norms. Agencies that perform in a way that legislators deem acceptable may be rewarded with higher funding levels, while those whose performance is disappointing may wind up with slashed appropriations. But Congress also has used the appropriations process more directly. It has incorporated into appropriations bills provisions that supplement or override agency enabling statutes and environmental legislation such as NEPA and the Endangered Species Act. These provisions can either expand or contract the discretion otherwise available to the affected agency. Sometimes, these provisions raise serious constitutional questions.

The controversies over the environmental effects of timber harvesting in the Pacific Northwest provide the backdrop for some of the most prominent examples of the use of appropriations bills to control agency decisionmaking (and limit judicial authority to mandate agency compliance with previously enacted legislation). Environmentalists tried throughout the 1980s to prevent liquidation of the old growth forests in this region, claiming that timber contracts awarded by the Forest Service and the BLM were inconsistent with a host of environmental laws. Beginning in 1984, Congress passed a series of appropriations riders that restricted judicial review of timber harvest plans adopted by the two land management agencies. A rider enacted in 1989, for example, provided that if the agencies abided by standards set forth in the rider (such as the specification of the number of board feet of timber to be cut) in managing thirteen national forests known to contain northern spotted owls (which were listed as threatened under the ESA), they would be deemed in compliance with statutes such as NEPA and the ESA. Pub. L. No. 101-121, §318, 103 Stat. 701, 745-750 (1989). Agency noncompliance with those statutes had been alleged in several suits pending at the time the rider was passed. The rider also provided that compliance with its guidelines for timber management would not be subject to judicial review. Environmental groups challenged the rider, claiming that congressional specification of the results of pending litigation violated the separation of powers by infringing on judicial authority. The Supreme Court in Robertson v. Seattle Audubon Soc'y, 503 U.S. 429 (1992), upheld the rider on the ground that it affected a change in the underlying substantive law that governed timber harvesting rather than commanded the outcome of pending litigation. See also Mount Graham Coal. v. Thomas, 89 F.3d 554 (9th Cir. 1996) (exemption from NEPA and the ESA for construction of astrophysical observatory upheld).

After the rider expired in 1990, the Ninth Circuit virtually shut down timber harvesting on federal lands in Washington and Oregon due to Forest Service and BLM noncompliance with the ESA and NEPA. See Seattle Audubon Soc'y v. Espy, 998 F.2d 699 (9th Cir. 1993). In a 1995 supplemental appropriations bill, Congress restricted judicial review of the legality of timber sales with potentially serious environmental impacts. Pub. L. No. 104-19, §2001, 109 Stat. 194, 240 (1995). The bill authorized the two agencies to conduct timber sales "notwithstanding any other provision of law." Id. §2001(b)(1). Finally, the bill precluded any court from enjoining certain categories of timber sales and provided that sales conducted in accordance with specified procedures would "be deemed to satisfy" laws such as NEPA, the ESA, and "[a]ll other applicable Federal environmental and natural resources laws." Id. §2001(i). Constitutional attacks on the rider failed, e.g., Northwest Forest Res. Council v. Pilchuck Audubon Soc'y, 97 F.3d 1161, 1165 (9th Cir. 1996), as did efforts to halt sales on the basis of alleged noncompliance with other statutory requirements. Idaho Conservation League v. Thomas, 91 F.3d 1345 (9th Cir. 1996) (approving sale that conflicted with established Forest Service policies for watershed protection); Inland Empire Pub. Lands Council v. Glickman, 88 F.3d 697 (9th Cir. 1996) (refusing to halt sale conducted in violation of grizzly bear management standards).

The appropriations process has been used to constrict, as well as augment, agency discretion. Congress has used appropriations bills to adopt a moratorium on the issuance of new patents for hardrock minerals on the federal lands. E.g., Pub. L. No. 103-322, §§112-113, 108 Stat. 2499, 2519 (1994). Former EPA Administrator William Reilly described the use of the appropriations process to redirect EPA discretion as "a guaranteed recipe for disillusionment on the part of the public." Former EPA Chief Criticizes Congress's Methods for Changing Agency, Inside EPA, Sept. 15, 1995, at 2.

2. *Control Through Substantive Standards and Analytical Requirements*

The traditional reliance on agency expertise prompted Congress to delegate broad powers to federal agencies during the New Deal and in subsequent years. It was not uncommon for the enabling statute of an agency such as the Interstate Commerce Commission to state simply that the agency was to regulate in the "public interest, convenience, and necessity" or for the Federal Trade Commission to be charged with preventing "unfair trade practices." The environmental legislation of the 1970s, such as the Clean Air and Water Acts, was always more specific than that, due in part to the fear of agency capture that prompted Congress to rein in agency discretion. When Congress disagreed with EPA's implementation of the statutes governing hazardous waste management and remediation during the 1980s, it made the relevant statutes even more prescriptive, further reducing EPA's discretion. Congress imposed deadlines to limit the agency's discretion to forestall issuing regulations and taking other measures, and it specified detailed decisionmaking criteria to curtail EPA's discretion to craft the content of regulations and other decisions. See generally Shapiro & Glicksman, Congress, the Supreme Court, and the Quiet Revolution in Administrative Law, 1988 Duke L.J. 819. Nevertheless, environmental and natural resource management statutes still left agencies considerable room to maneuver.

The election of conservative majorities in Congress during the 1990s ushered in a new wave of legislative limitations on agency discretion. Legislators, convinced that the pendulum had swung too far in the direction of rigorous environmental controls on industrial activity and development, introduced bills to require agencies such as EPA and the Occupational Safety and Health Administration (OSHA) to temper health, safety, and environmental protection goals with a greater consciousness of countervailing considerations such as cost. Some of these bills included analytical requirements that supplemented the factors agencies were authorized to consider under existing legislation, but others were designed to redirect agency priorities in response to what the bills' supporters perceived as misplaced regulatory emphasis. See generally S. Shapiro & R. Glicksman, Risk Regulation at Risk: Restoring a Pragmatic Approach, ch. 7 (2003).

The first of these bills to be adopted was the *Unfunded Mandates Reform Act of 1994*, Pub. L. No. 104-4, 109 Stat. 48 (1995), which requires each federal agency, unless otherwise prohibited by law, to assess the effects of its regulatory actions on state, local, and tribal governments and the private sector. Before an agency issues a regulation that includes any "federal mandate" (defined as a regulation that would impose an enforceable duty on state, local, or tribal governments, other than a condition of federal assistance) that may result in the expenditure by governments in the aggregate or by the private sector of $100 million or more in any one year, it must prepare a regulatory impact statement. The statement must include a qualitative and quantitative assessment of the anticipated costs and benefits of the mandate, estimate future compliance costs of the mandate, and estimate the effect of the rule on the national economy if it is feasible to do so. 2 U.S.C. §1532. The Act also requires that the agency consider alternatives and select from among them "the least costly, most cost-effective or least burdensome alternative" for state and local governments and the private sector that achieves the rule's objective. Id. §1535(a). An agency need not comply with this requirement if it explains why it did not adopt the identified alternative or is precluded from doing so by law. Id. §1535(b). Neither failure to prepare a regulatory impact statement nor preparation of an inadequate statement provides a basis for judicial invalidation of agency regulations. Id. §1571(a)(3), (b). Failure to prepare a statement can render agency regulations arbitrary and capricious, but not if the substantive legislation precludes consideration of the costs of regulatory implementation.[k]

Other statutes also require analytical support for regulations that goes beyond what is required by the APA. The *Regulatory Flexibility Act*, adopted in 1980 and amended by the Small Business Regulatory Enforcement Fairness Act, Pub. L. No. 104-121, 110 Stat. 847, 857-874 (1996), requires agencies proposing rules that will have a "significant economic impact on a substantial number" of small businesses or governments to prepare and make available to the public a regulatory flexibility analysis (RFA). The analysis must describe the projected reporting, recordkeeping, and other compliance requirements of the proposed rule; estimate the affected classes of small entities; describe the steps the agency has taken to minimize significant economic impact on small entities; and justify selecting the alternative chosen. 5 U.S.C. §§603-604.

Although noncompliance with the statute initially was not judicially reviewable, the 1996 amendments provided that any small entity that is adversely affected or aggrieved by final agency action is entitled to judicial review of agency compliance with these requirements. Courts may now order an agency to take "corrective action," including remanding the rule to the agency or deferring enforcement of the rule against small entities. Id. §611(a)(4). But cf. National Ass'n of Home Builders v. EPA, 682 F.3d 1032, 1041-1043 (D.C. Cir. 2012) (relying on §611(c) of the RFA to hold that challenge to EPA's alleged failure to convene a small business advocacy panel before amending rule controlling exposure to lead was unreviewable). Litigants have had little success derailing agency actions on the basis of failure to comply with the Act's analytical requirements. In some cases, the courts defer to an agency's certification that it need not prepare an RFA because its action would not have a significant economic impact on a substantial number of small entities. See, e.g., Washington v. Daley, 173 F.3d 1158, 1170 (9th Cir. 1999). See also Michigan v. EPA, 213 F.3d 663, 689-690 (D.C. Cir. 2000) (EPA need not prepare RFA in requiring revision of CAA state implementation plans because EPA did not establish "requirements" applicable to anyone, including small entities; instead, it required states to devise emission reductions necessary to mitigate interstate pollution). See generally Holman, The Regulatory Flexibility Act at 25: Is the Law Achieving Its Goal?, 33 Fordham Urb. L.J. 119 (2006).

The 1996 amendments, codified as the *Congressional Review Act*, 5 U.S.C. §§801-808, also established a procedure for congressional disapproval of agency rules. For a time, Congress relied on the legislative veto mechanism to control agency regulatory discretion by adopting statutes vesting in the entire Congress, one House of Congress, or even congressional committees the power to overturn agency regulations. The Supreme Court declared the legislative veto unconstitutional in INS v. Chadha, 462 U.S. 919 (1983), reasoning that the exercise of the veto is a legislative function that fails to comply with Article I's bicameralism and presentment requirements. Congress

k. See generally Adler, Unfunded Mandates and Fiscal Federalism: A Critique, 50 Vand. L. Rev. 1137 (1997) (arguing that the propriety of unfunded mandates should be determined on a case-by-case basis through the political process rather than through the creation of "procedural road-blocks" like those in the 1995 Act); Dana, The Case for Unfunded Environmental Mandates, 69 S. Cal. L. Rev. 1 (1995) (arguing that a prohibition on unfunded mandates is unlikely to promote political accountability); Steinzor, Unfunded Environmental Mandates and the "New (New) Federalism": Devolution, Revolution, or Reform?, 81 Minn. L. Rev. 97 (1996) (arguing that dismantling of federal bureaucracies and devolution of power to states and localities is unlikely to result in adequate protection of the environment).

tried to recoup some of the control it lost as a result of *Chadha* by enacting the Congressional Review Act. The Act prohibits any "major rule" from taking effect until 60 legislative days after the agency submitted the regulation and explanatory documents to both Houses of Congress. An agency's determination that a rule is not major is not subject to judicial review. 5 U.S.C. §805; In re Operation of the Missouri River Sys. Litig., 363 F. Supp. 2d 1145, 1173 (D. Minn. 2004), *aff'd in part and vacated in part on other grounds*, 421 F.3d 618 (8th Cir. 2005). The 60-day window affords Congress the opportunity to enact a joint resolution of disapproval pursuant to expedited procedures that minimize the opportunities for obstructive efforts by supporters of the regulation. Because such a resolution is not effective absent majority support in both Houses of Congress and the President's signature, the Congressional Review Act is not vulnerable to the constitutional deficiencies that doomed the legislative veto in *Chadha*. An agency may not reissue a disapproved rule in substantially the same form unless it is specifically reauthorized by a law enacted after the joint resolution of disapproval. 5 U.S.C. §801(a)(3), (b)(2). Although Congress has rarely invoked the Act to invalidate agency regulations, it is most likely to come into play when a rule issued at the end of one presidential administration is opposed by a successor whose party controls both Houses of Congress.

The *Paperwork Reduction Act*, 44 U.S.C. §§3501-3520, requires that agencies seeking to impose reporting or recordkeeping requirements on the private sector justify them as necessary for the performance of agency functions and nonduplicative of information available from other sources, and demonstrate that they have taken steps to minimize the burden of collecting information through the use of automated collection techniques and other means. Agency noncompliance with the Act does not prevent promulgation of a rule, but it may prevent enforcement. Dithiocarbamate Task Force v. EPA, 98 F.3d 1394, 1405 (D.C. Cir. 1996).

The *Information Quality Act*, 44 U.S.C. §3516 note, requires the Office of Management and Budget (OMB) to issue guidelines providing "policy and procedural guidance" to federal agencies "for ensuring and maximizing the quality, objectivity, utility, and integrity of information (including statistical information) disseminated by Federal agencies." The IQA requires agencies to issue their own guidelines and establish administrative mechanisms allowing affected persons to seek and obtain correction of information that does not comply with the OMB guidelines. The IQA's applicability to informal rulemaking is unclear. Relying on its authority to implement the IQA, OMB has required extensive peer review of regulatory information before its dissemination, including information used in rulemaking. Final Information Quality Bulletin for Peer Review, 70 Fed. Reg. 2664 (2005). According to one analysis, this approach "is likely to stifle the government's efforts to provide useful information to the public about their safety and health risks and about risks to the environment." Shapiro, OMB's Dubious Peer Review Procedures, 34 Envtl. L. Rep. 10064 (2004).[1]

The availability of judicial review of an agency's rejection of individual complaints about data quality is also unclear. One court held that the IQA does not create a private cause of action and that agency compliance with the IQA is "committed to agency discretion by law," and therefore immune from judicial review under 5 U.S.C.

1. See generally Shapiro, The Information Quality Act and Environmental Protection: The Perils of Reform by Appropriations Rider, 28 Wm. & Mary Envtl. L. & Pol'y Rev. 339 (2004); Johnson, Junking the "Junk Science" Law: Reforming the Information Quality Act, 58 Admin. L. Rev. 37 (2006).

§701(a)(2). See *Missouri River Sys. Litig., supra,* 363 F. Supp. 2d at 1174-1175. See also Family Farm Alliance v. Salazar, 749 F. Supp. 2d 1083 (E.D. Cal. 2010). Cf. Habitat for Horses v. Salazar, 745 F. Supp. 2d 438, 455-456 (S.D.N.Y. 2010) (noting that courts have found no private right of action under the IQA). Another court held that a trade association of salt producers lacked standing to bring a suit under the IQA. The plaintiffs had alleged that the Department of Health and Human Services violated the IQA by reporting on its website and in medical journals the results of studies showing that decreased use of salt could lower blood pressure and by recommending that all Americans limit salt intake. Salt Inst. v. Thompson, 440 F.3d 156 (4th Cir. 2006). The court concluded that because the IQA does not create a legal right of access to information or to the correctness of information relied upon by a federal agency, the business plaintiffs failed to establish injury in fact.

In Prime Time Int'l Co. v. Vilsack, 599 F.3d 678 (D.C. Cir. 2010), the court ruled that the Department of Agriculture did not violate the IQA by failing to respond to a cigar manufacturer's request to disclose and correct certain information relating to assessments on manufacturers and importers of tobacco products that were designed to compensate for the repeal of statutory quotas and price supports for tobacco production. The court did not address the justiciability of IQA challenges. Instead, it ruled for the agency based on the OMB's guidelines, which do not apply to an agency's findings and determinations in the course of adjudications involving specific parties. In doing so, the court characterized the guidelines as binding. Some observers interpreted that reference as an endorsement of the position that IQA challenges are judicially reviewable.

In 2009, President Obama issued a memorandum to the heads of executive departments and agencies on "Scientific Integrity" in an attempt to guarantee scientific integrity throughout the executive branch, http://www.whitehouse.gov/the__press__office/Memorandum-for-the-Heads-of-Executive-Departments-and-Agencies-3-9-09.

Other legislation requires the use of cost-benefit and risk assessment procedures. E.g., the *Accountable Pipeline Safety and Partnership Act of 1996,* 49 U.S.C. §60102 (requiring the use of these analytical techniques in connection with the adoption of standards governing gas pipeline safety and the transportation of hazardous liquids). The controversy surrounding these techniques is discussed in the Note on Cost-Benefit Analysis later in this chapter and in Chapter 8.

C.   EXECUTIVE CONTROL OF ADMINISTRATIVE ENVIRONMENTAL DECISIONMAKING

Like Congress, the President has an interest in putting his policy stamp on the implementation of the environmental protection and natural resource management statutes. Although the President can influence the decisions of administrative agencies such as EPA by removing high-level agency appointees, his ability to dictate substantive decisions entrusted to agencies by statute may be limited. See, e.g., Percival, Presidential Management of the Administrative State: The Not-So-Unitary Executive, 51 Duke L.J. 963 (2001).

The President may influence the substance of agency decisions by requiring agencies to clear their regulatory proposals with an official responsible to the

President. President Reagan's Executive Order No. 12,291, 3 C.F.R. 127 (1982), *reprinted in* 5 U.S.C. §601 note, required agencies to conduct cost-benefit analyses for major rules. The Order assigned the responsibility for overseeing agency compliance to the Office of Information and Regulatory Affairs (OIRA) within the OMB, a part of the Executive Office of the President. It prohibited agencies from issuing any regulation whose benefits did not exceed its costs, unless their substantive enabling statutes required otherwise. OIRA could block publication of a major rule pending review for compliance with the Order. Executive Order No. 12,498, 3 C.F.R. 323 (1986), *reprinted in* 5 U.S.C. §601 note, extended the scope of executive oversight by requiring that agencies submit an annual regulatory plan for OIRA review and restricting the agencies' ability to pursue actions not included on the agenda.

President Clinton's Executive Order No. 12,866, 58 Fed. Reg. 51,735 (1993), *reprinted in* 5 U.S.C. §601 note, revoked the previous orders but continued to require federal agencies to engage in cost-benefit analysis. The Order requires that, in choosing among alternative regulatory approaches, agencies select those that maximize net benefits, unless a statute requires another regulatory approach. To the extent permitted by law, agencies should adhere to "principles of regulation" that include designing regulations in the most cost-effective manner, proposing and adopting only those regulations whose benefits are reasonably determined to justify their costs, and tailoring regulations to impose the least burden on society. Id. §1(b). Agencies must provide OIRA with a list of planned regulatory actions. If either the agency proposing the action or OIRA decides that a particular action is significant (because, for example, it may have an annual effect on the economy of $100 million or more or adversely affect in a material way the economy, productivity, jobs, the environment, or public health or safety), the proposing agency must furnish to OIRA a detailed explanation. The explanation must describe the need for the regulatory action, assess potential costs and benefits of the proposal and potentially effective and reasonably feasible alternatives, and explain why the planned action is preferable to the identified alternatives. OIRA must provide "meaningful guidance and oversight so that each agency's actions are consistent with applicable law, the President's priorities, and the principles set forth in [the] Executive Order." Id. §6(b). What if these sources of guidance conflict; which should prevail? To the extent permitted by law, conflicts between the agency and OIRA should be resolved by the President or the Vice President. Id. §7. Compliance with the provisions of the Executive Order is not judicially reviewable. Id. §10. See Idaho Mining Ass'n, Inc. v. Browner, 90 F. Supp. 2d 1078, 1102 (D. Idaho 2000).

President George W. Bush amended Executive Order 12,866 by signing Executive Order No. 13,422, 72 Fed. Reg. 2763 (2007), which required agencies to identify specific market failures (such as externalities or lack of information) and assess whether they warranted new regulation. It also expanded assessment obligations to guidance documents and sought tighter presidential control over agency policy by generally barring significant regulatory actions without the approval of the agency's Regulatory Policy Officer, which had to be a presidential appointee.

President Obama repealed the changes and reinstated the Clinton Order. Exec. Order No. 13,497, 74 Fed. Reg. 6113 (Feb. 4, 2009). President Obama then issued Executive Order No. 13,563, 76 Fed. Reg. 3821 (Jan. 18, 2011), to supplement the Clinton Order. The 2011 Order required executive agencies to propose or adopt a regulation only if its benefits justify its costs; tailor regulations to impose the least burden on society and select regulatory approaches which maximize net benefits; rely on performance rather than design standards, if feasible; and identify and assess alternatives to direct regulation, such as market mechanisms and information disclosure. The Order directs agencies to quantify anticipated benefits and costs as accurately as possible, but also authorizes them, to the extent permitted by law, to consider qualitatively values that are difficult or impossible to quantify, including equity, human dignity, fairness, and distributive impacts. It requires agencies to ensure the objectivity of scientific and technological information used to support regulatory actions, and to engage in retrospective review to help identify outmoded, ineffective, insufficient, or excessively burdensome regulations, and modify, streamline, expand, or repeal them accordingly. See also Exec. Order No. 13,610, 77 Fed. Reg. 28,469 (May 14, 2012). Yet another Obama Order stated that independent agencies "should" engage in similar retrospective review and develop "a plan, consistent with law and reflecting its resources and regulatory priorities and processes," to determine whether existing regulations should be changed to make them more effective or less burdensome. Exec. Order No. 13,579, §2, 76 Fed. Reg. 41,587 (July 14, 2011). This Order disclaims any intention to impair or affect authority granted by law to an agency. Id. §3(b).

Presidential attempts to confine agency discretion in making regulatory decisions have not been confined to the imposition of cost-benefit analytical requirements. President Reagan's Executive Order No. 12,630, 53 Fed. Reg. 8859 (1988), directed federal agencies to avoid regulatory actions that would amount to takings of property without just compensation. Compliance with the Order is not judicially reviewable, however. See Duval Ranching Co. v. Glickman, 965 F. Supp. 1427, 1446 (D. Nev. 1997). Executive Order No. 12,612, 52 Fed. Reg. 41,685 (1987), requires agencies to consider principles of federalism in regulatory decisionmaking processes. President Obama restricted federal agency preemption of state law, directing agencies not to include preemption provisions in codified regulations unless doing so is "justified under legal principles governing preemption." Preemption: Memorandum for the Heads of Executive Departments and Agencies, 74 Fed. Reg. 24,693 (May 20, 2009). For brief discussion of executive orders affecting environmental rulemaking, see Seidenfeld, A Table of Requirements for Federal Administrative Rulemaking, 27 Fla. St. U. L. Rev. 533 (2000).

These efforts to subject regulatory decisions to review by the President or by officials close to him raise both policy and legal questions. The ultimate policy issue is who should control the cabinet and independent regulatory agencies. Professor Sidney Shapiro asserts that the effectiveness of regulatory policy deteriorated as a result of presidential and legislative oversight that impaired political accountability and failed to take advantage of agency expertise and experience. Shapiro, Political Oversight and the Deterioration of Regulatory Policy, 46 Admin. L. Rev. 1 (1994). Professor Percival concluded that Executive Office oversight of EPA decisionmaking resulted in delays in rulemaking, imposed pressure to weaken environmental regulation, and reduced the public's ability to monitor the rulemaking process and influence regulatory decisions. Percival, Checks Without Balance: Executive Office Oversight of the Environmental Protection Agency, 54 Law & Contemp. Probs. 127, 201 (Autumn 1991). According to Percival, "fidelity to statutory requirements, rather than to the preferences of the president or the regulated community, should be the touchstone of regulatory decisionmaking" on environmental issues. For another critical review of OMB review of agency rulemaking, see Bressman & Vandenbergh, Inside the Administrative State: A Critical Look at the Practice of Presidential Control, 105 Mich. L. Rev. 47 (2006).

Other observers endorse the theory of executive oversight while recognizing the potential for abuse. Strauss & Sunstein, The Role of the President and OMB in Informal Rulemaking, 38 Admin. L. Rev. 181 (1986), assert that regulatory review can improve interagency coordination and increase accountability. See also Sunstein, The Office of Information and Regulatory Affairs: Myths and Realties, 126 Harv. L. Rev. 1838 (2013) (written by one of OIRA's former heads). Others claim that cost-benefit analysis and related techniques can improve the substance of agency decision-making on regulatory matters. See, e.g., DeMuth & Ginsburg, White House Review of Agency Rulemaking, 99 Harv. L. Rev. 1075 (1986). Finally, proponents of centralized review argue that it can serve as a palliative for agency capture by well-organized special interests such as environmental groups. Id. at 1081; Miller et al., A Note on Centralized Regulatory Review, 43 Pub. Choice 83 (1984). Bagley & Revesz, 106 Colum. L. Rev. 1260 (2006), respond that "[e]ven if the regulatory state were in fact characterized by zealous agencies captured by powerful interest groups, . . . OMB review is a poorly designed solution to that problem for the simple reason that OMB's location within the Executive Office of the President does not immunize it from any pathologies that affect other agencies." Id. at 1263.

The principal legal issue is whether executive branch oversight violates separation of powers principles because Congress has delegated the rulemaking function to a specific agency rather than to the Executive Office. Olson, The Quiet Shift of Power: Office of Management and Budget Supervision of Environmental Protection Agency Rulemaking under Executive Order 12,291, 4 Va. J. Nat. Resources L. 1 (1984), argues that Executive Order 12,291 may have violated separation of powers principles and given OMB unwarranted authority to encroach on discretion delegated to agencies by Congress.[m]

A few cases have addressed the impact of executive oversight on EPA. Several courts have concluded that OMB lacks the power to delay the issuance of EPA regulations beyond congressionally established deadlines in order to complete the review processes dictated by executive order. In EDF v. Thomas, 627 F. Supp. 566, 570 (D.D.C. 1986), the district court held that, even though "[a] certain degree of deference must be given to the authority of the President to control and supervise executive policymaking," OMB lacks the power to delay compliance with congressional mandates because such delay "is incompatible with the will of Congress." See also NRDC v. EPA, 797 F. Supp. 194 (E.D.N.Y. 1992). Cases involving challenges to the substantive impact of executive oversight have been rare. In one such case, New York v. Reilly, 969 F.2d 1147 (D.C. Cir. 1992), the court remanded to EPA for further explanation the decision, made under pressure from a body chaired by the Vice-President, not to impose a ban on the combustion of lead-acid batteries.

Executive branch officials also may try to influence agency regulatory decisions on a less formal basis. Such attempts may give rise to some of the same objections raised in response to the activities of OIRA. The APA restricts ex parte communications[n] between "interested persons" and agency officials engaged in adjudication.

---

m. See generally Herz, Imposing Unified Executive Branch Statutory Interpretation, 15 Cardozo L. Rev. 219 (1993) (arguing that the constitutional argument for executive oversight is strongest in relation to agency statutory interpretations); Colloquium, The Council on Competitiveness: Executive Oversight of Agency Rulemaking, 7 Admin. L.J. Am. U. 297 (1993).

n. The APA defines an ex parte communication as "an oral or written communication not on the public record with respect to which reasonable prior notice to all parties is not given, but it shall not include requests for status reports. . . ." 5 U.S.C. §551(14).

5 U.S.C. §557(d). What is the rationale for such restrictions? In Portland Audubon Soc'y v. Endangered Species Comm., 984 F.2d 1534 (9th Cir. 1993), environmental groups challenged a decision by the Endangered Species Committee to exempt a series of timber sales proposed by the BLM from the requirements of the ESA. They asserted that President Bush's domestic policy adviser engaged in ex parte contacts with Committee members, including the Interior Secretary and the EPA Administrator, before the Committee made its decision. Is the president or his domestic policy adviser an "interested person" subject to §557(d) of the APA? The government argued that if the APA's ex parte communications ban encompasses the President and his aides it violates the doctrine of separation of powers, but the court rejected the argument "out of hand." Id. at 1546. Congress's important objectives in restricting ex parte contacts outweighed any *de minimis* impact on presidential power. The court therefore held that the communications were improper and remanded for an evidentiary hearing to determine their nature, extent, and effect. The APA's restrictions on ex parte communications have little applicability, however, to rulemaking proceedings. See, e.g., Sierra Club v. Costle, 657 F.2d 298, 400 (D.C. Cir. 1981) ("the concept of ex parte contacts is of more questionable utility" as applied to policy decisions reflected in informal rulemaking).

NOTE ON COST-BENEFIT ANALYSIS

The Rationale for Cost-Benefit Analysis. Why might Congress or the President choose to require that regulatory agencies engage in cost-benefit analysis? The technique is premised on the belief that rational choice is impossible without a full awareness of the consequences of a decision. Cost-benefit analysis also builds on the central tenet of economic theory that society's resources are limited and that the allocation of resources to achieve one objective necessarily precludes other allocations. Cost-benefit analysis implies that regulatory tasks should be ranked and that those regulations that show the highest cost-benefit ratios should be undertaken first, so that limited government resources may be applied first to tasks yielding the highest marginal return in public health and environmental protection. Putting it slightly differently, cost-benefit analysis seeks to replicate the result that would have occurred as a result of free-market bargaining between those who generate and those who are adversely affected by environmental externalities in the absence of transaction costs by requiring a reduction in environmental damage up to the point at which the costs and benefits of such a reduction are equal.

The Methodology of Cost-Benefit Analysis. Formal cost-benefit analysis assumes that one can (1) identify correctly and put accurate money prices on the social benefits of an activity (e.g., producing a product, building a public works project, regulating a dangerous substance), and (2) identify and price the things ("costs") whose value or alternative uses must be reduced to produce the benefits (e.g., raw materials, the natural environment, capital, and labor), so that one can (3) predict quantitatively the net posture of the activity, which may be expressed either as a ratio of benefits to costs or as the net increase in social utility one hopes to maximize. In the context of environmental regulation, the agency must compute costs, including compliance costs (capital equipment, maintenance, monitoring, etc.), the social benefits lost as a result of constraints on regulated activities, and arguably the transaction costs incurred by the agency in promulgating the regulation. Then the agency must undertake the harder task of placing a money value on benefits, e.g., the health injuries averted (cancers, mutations, diseases, other systematic disorders) and environmental degradation avoided.[o] Because these harms obviously have no established market prices that can be inserted into the agency's computations, studies must be performed to develop surrogate prices by imputing to affected individuals their willingness to pay to avoid these costs (e.g., from the payments they make for medical treatment or to move away from a hazardous neighborhood) or their willingness to be paid to risk harm (e.g., hazardous duty pay, reduced rent). The "willingness-to-pay" criterion is used by economists to ensure that "priceless" items are valued in the same way as articles in everyday commerce.

Difficulties in Identifying Costs and Benefits. Several aspects of using cost-benefit analysis as a device for determining the appropriate amount of environmental regulation are problematic. Preparation of a cost-benefit analysis requires identification of the prospective costs and benefits of the regulatory action contemplated. This preliminary step may present knotty problems. In inventorying relevant costs and benefits, the benefit of workdays saved by disease prevention should be counted. Likewise, the lives of children and other non–wage earners are indisputably valuable, although traditional cost-benefit analysis focused only on wage losses averted. Should the benefits also include a dollar estimate of the reduced need for special diets for patients? Transportation costs to obtain medical treatment? Should victims' anxieties, nervous system disorders, and genetic injury be included? Important effects may be neglected or deliberately ignored, especially in light of the high administrative costs of identifying and computing "remote" effects, the possibility that quantifying speculative but potentially disastrous factors might tip the scales against an activity with definite immediate economic benefits, and the reluctance to include factors for which a firm causal nexus with the harm regulated has not yet been established.

Difficulties of Quantification. Even if the costs and benefits have been identified adequately, they may be extremely difficult to quantify. Often the best one can say about the benefits of controlling carcinogenic substances at a given exposure level, for example, is that the number of cancers varies within a range of several orders of magnitude (factors of ten). If a quantitative risk assessment of numbers of deaths, diseases, injuries, and other impacts cannot be made, they cannot be assigned more than a range of dollar values (e.g., "the health injury averted by this regulation may be between $1 million and $10 billion"). More fundamentally, "[p]erhaps the most significant objection to cost-benefit analysis is the inability of economic analysis to reduce the benefits of regulation to dollar equivalents to compare with regulatory costs." McGarity, A Cost-Benefit State, 50 Admin. L. Rev. 1, 63 (1998).

A particularly sensitive area of risk quantification concerns the dollar value of losing (or saving) a human life as a consequence of regulation. The valuation problem is similar for loss of an endangered species or a symbolic or unique aesthetic resource. Agencies are understandably uneasy about overtly assigning a dollar value to human life in their cost-benefit analyses, but those that do not do so overtly do so impliedly because there is no other way to reduce the costs and benefits of life-saving regulation to a common money measure. See Sagoff, On Markets for Risk, 41 Md. L. Rev. 755, 767 (1982). OMB guidance has suggested monetizing reductions in fatality risks

o. Note that the words "benefit" and "cost" require that the context of their usage be clearly stated. Otherwise, the "benefits" of reduced health risks may be confused with the economic "costs" of abatement or the "benefits" of not regulating an activity may be entered on the "benefits" side of the analysis rather than on the "costs" side, where they belong.

attributable to regulation according to the willingness-to-pay approach, which is meant to reflect opportunity cost by measuring what individuals are willing to forgo to enjoy a particular benefit (in this case, a reduction in the risk of premature death).

An alternative is to express all non-health-related costs and benefits in dollars, but reduce all health-related matters (e.g., cases of disease and injury, days of restricted activity) to the common unit of lives saved (or lost) (or portions of lives saved or lost) by regulating (or refusing to regulate), without ever assigning a dollar value to them. This approach would create two bases for cost-benefit comparisons: dollars and lives. Decisionmakers would then decide whether or how strictly to regulate by comparing both dollar costs averted and lives saved. To some, however, framing the lives to be protected by regulation in such "statistical" terms "dehumanize[s] the suffering and death that scientific risk assessments tell us will occur due to particular hazards." Heinzerling, The Rights of Statistical People, 24 Harv. Envtl. L. Rev. 189, 207 (2000).

Adler, Fear Assessment: Cost-Benefit Analysis and the Pricing of Fear and Anxiety, 79 Chi.-Kent L. Rev. 977 (2004), argues that the failure by agencies to price distressing mental states (such as fear, anxiety, panic, or dread) that are causally connected to environmental hazards when they perform cost-benefit analyses creates an inappropriate asymmetry and that fear assessment should be a component of such analyses. Adler discusses how best to measure psychological distress that could be averted through regulation on a monetary scale.

The Discounting Controversy and Equitable Considerations. The selection of an appropriate discount rate raises additional issues. In formal cost-benefit analysis, whenever a benefit of regulation is to be enjoyed in the future, its future value is deflated or "discounted" to its present value. The benefits of regulation may be worth a lot in the future to us or to persons yet unborn, but because our present enjoyment of a future benefit exists only as an expectation that may never be enjoyed, the theory is that we will want to value it less now. As a National Academy of Sciences report pointed out, if the discount rate were 5 percent, one toxic poisoning case in 1975 would be valued the same as 1733 cases in 200 years, or the same as the world population in 450 years. Decision Making for Regulating Chemicals in the Environment 43 (1975). The issue is important to cost-benefit analysis of health and safety regulation because the injuries caused by some activity may not be realized for generations, or even centuries. Thus, the discounting controversy involves distributional considerations, which may entail a balancing of the interests of the living and the unborn. See J. Rawls, A Theory of Justice 284 (1971). Kysar, Discounting on Stilts, 74 U. Chi. L. Rev. 119 (2007), contends that cost-benefit analysis is incapable of taking adequate account of the needs and interests of future generations. That article is part of a symposium on Intergenerational Equity and Discounting, 74 U. Chi. L. Rev. 1-246 (2007). Revesz & Shahabian, Climate Change and Future Generations, 84 S. Cal. L. Rev. 1097 (2011), argue that discounting the interests of future generations is ethically indefensible, and that "we cannot simply reduce all of our ethical qualms to the choice of a discount rate and then mechanically discount future benefits of climate change mitigation at the market rate of return."

Professor Lisa Heinzerling has asserted that the tendency of the beneficial consequences of environmental regulation to range along a continuum stretching from the immediate present to the distant future makes discounting in general, and the use of life-years saved as a measure of the benefits of life-saving rules in particular, inappropriate. Discounting skews cost-benefit analysis because deflating life-saving benefits greatly inflates costs per life saved.[p] The concept of "quality-adjusted life years" (QALYs) has been proposed as a means of assessing the cost-effectiveness of regulatory (or nonregulatory) alternatives without the need to quantify the value of a human life. Supporters of this approach argue that the goal ought to be to deliver the greatest number of QALYs at the lowest possible cost. Critics charge, however, that assessment of regulatory alternatives based on the QALYs each will yield discriminates against the elderly and the disabled, whose lives are valued lower than those who are young and healthy. See F. Ackerman & L. Heinzerling, Priceless: On Knowing the Price of Everything and the Value of Nothing 98-102 (2004).

According to some critics of cost-benefit analysis, the equitable concerns raised by discounting represent only one aspect of its downgrading of equitable considerations:

[C]ost-benefit analysis ignores the question of *who* suffers as a result of environmental problems and, therefore, threatens to reinforce existing patterns of economic and social inequality. Cost-benefit analysis treats questions about equity as, at best, side issues, contradicting the widely shared view that equity should count in public policy. Poor countries, communities, and individuals are likely to express less "willingness to pay" to avoid environmental harms simply because they have fewer resources. Therefore, cost-benefit analysis would justify imposing greater environmental burdens on them than on their wealthier counterparts. With this kind of analysis, the poor get poorer. [L. Heinzerling & F. Ackerman, Pricing the Priceless: Cost-Benefit Analysis of Environmental Protection 2 (2001).]

Cost-Benefit Analysis and Transparency. Some cost-benefit analysis supporters claim that it is a useful way to inform thoughtful decisionmaking, provided disaggregated cost and benefit data are disclosed. Pildes & Sunstein, Reinventing the Regulatory State, 62 U. Chi. L. Rev. 1, 72 (1995). Others contest that view. Sinden, Cass Sunstein's Cost-Benefit Lite: Economics for Liberals, 29 Colum. J. Envtl. L. 191, 193 (2004), argues that rather than promoting transparency, "CBA will obscure the inevitable policy choices and value judgments that underlie government decision-making behind a veil of numbers and render the decision-making process inaccessible to those without a Ph.D. in economics." See also Mendelson, Disclosing Political Oversight of Agency Decisionmaking, 108 Mich. L. Rev. 1127 (2010) (urging greater disclosure of the impact of executive branch oversight).

Cost-Benefit Analysis and Value Selection. Ultimately, the critics charge, consistent application of the economic view creates a tendency among policy analysts to view arms, health, life, and environmental resources as part of a smoothly interchangeable mix, in which dollar evaluations allow regulators to trade off items that are entirely different in nature. Any tradeoffs based on a weighing of toxicant reduction and economic and technological considerations is "fundamentally flawed," in this view, because when applied to "matters of intense personal interest" such as risk to life and highly valued environmental amenities, such tradeoffs ignore the "almost universal recognition that citizens of this country have a 'right' to a healthy environment and workplace, at least insofar as the societal pursuit of that right is not technologically impossible or prohibitively expensive." McGarity, Media-Quality,

p. See Heinzerling, Discounting Our Future, 34 Land & Water L. Rev. 39 (1999); Heinzerling, Environmental Law and the Present Future, 87 Geo. L.J. 2025 (1999).

Technology, and Cost-Benefit Balancing Strategies for Health and Environmental Regulation, 46 Law & Contemp. Probs. 159, 163 (Summer 1983).

Similarly, Mark Sagoff argues in On Markets for Risk, *supra*, that environmental legislation reflects a desire to promote autonomy, not efficiency, in the sense that it seeks to control the conditions under which we live. Thus, an efficiency-based justification for the use of cost-benefit analysis in environmental decisionmaking is not persuasive. "People want to determine the background level of risk; they do not want the working conditions of their lives to be determined by others. It does not matter how cost-beneficial risks are; it is a question, rather, of who controls them." Id. at 764. In short, "[v]irtues like altruism, dignity, equity, fairness (in both the procedural and substantive senses), decency, mutuality, tolerance, and empathy that are highly valued in a civilized society are belittled or ignored entirely in a cost-benefit regulatory regime in which allocative efficiency is the only goal." McGarity, A Cost-Benefit State, *supra*, at 72.

Michaelson, Note, Rethinking Regulatory Reform: Toxics, Politics, and Ethics, 105 Yale L.J. 1891, 1919 (1996), argues that "cost-benefit analysis reorders risk allocation" by "shift[ing] regulation from a proxy liability rule in which persons receive the entitlement to their body to a proxy property rule in which toxics producers receive the entitlement to produce a profitable amount of poison. . . . [C]ost-benefit risk determination gives toxic producers the right to kill until the entitlement price (that point at which it 'pays' not to kill) is paid by the number of injured people."

Supporters of cost-benefit analysis claim that it measures the benefits of protecting the environment based on the willingness of individuals to pay for such protection, and that market prices reflect altruistic as well as self-interested concerns. Thus, cost-benefit analysis reflects more than just utilitarian values.

Are the Benefits of EPA Regulations Worth the Costs? The OMB concluded that the estimated annual benefits of all major EPA regulations reviewed by it between October 1, 2003 and September 30, 2013 ranged between $164.8 and $849.5 billion, while the costs of those regulations ranged between $38.2 and $46.1 billion (all in 2010 dollars). OMB, 2014 Draft Report to Congress on the Benefits and Costs of Federal Regulations and Unfunded Mandates on State, Local, and Tribal Entities 10 (2014). Thus, the highest cost estimate was less than a third of the lowest benefit estimate, while the highest benefit estimate was nearly twenty times even the highest cost estimate.

Problem 3-3

You are an attorney and policy analyst in the office of a centrist member of the U.S. Senate who regards herself as an independent-thinking legislator interested in sound policy, not partisan politics. A prominent economics think tank has dropped a proposed piece of legislation pertaining to cost-benefit analysis at your senator's office. The bill, if passed into law, would subject all federal agencies responsible for implementing "a program designed to protect human health, safety, or the environment" to a statutory obligation to undertake cost-benefit analysis before adopting "major regulations" (defined as those likely to result in an annual increase in costs of $25 million or more). In particular, the bill, whose requirements would "supplement, not supersede" the provisions of preexisting regulatory statutes, would require the relevant agencies to determine whether the "identified benefits of the regulation are likely to exceed the identified costs of the regulation." Based on that analysis, the agency would have to certify before proceeding with a major regulation that the benefits of the regulation "will be likely to justify, and be reasonably related to, the incremental costs incurred by State, local, and tribal governments, the Federal Government, and other public and private entities as a result of the regulation." In addition, the bill would require that the agency adopt the regulatory alternative that is both feasible and that would create the "greatest net benefits." The bill defines the term "costs" as "the direct and indirect costs to the United States Government, to State, local, and tribal governments, and to the private sector, wage earners, consumers, and the economy, of implementing and complying with a regulation or alternative strategy." It defines benefits to mean "the reasonably identifiable significant health, safety, environmental, social, and economic benefits that are expected to result directly or indirectly from implementation of a regulation or alternative strategy."

The senator has set up a meeting at which the two of you and the rest of her staff will discuss the implications of the proposed bill for federal agencies engaged in the promulgation of rules that are designed to protect health, safety, or the environment, as well as likely responses to the bill by industry, agencies, and environmentalists. Be prepared to advise the senator whether to oppose, support, or seek amendments to the bill. If you suggest amendments or clarifications, be prepared to explain the reasoning behind your suggestions.

D.   AVOIDING CONTROL THROUGH INFORMAL DECISIONMAKING

Many of the techniques for controlling agency discretion described above apply to agency attempts to implement policy through rulemaking. The cost-benefit requirements of Executive Order 12,866, for example, are triggered whenever an agency issues a regulation with an annual effect on the economy of $100 million or more. The analytical procedures of the Unfunded Mandates Act apply to regulatory provisions that impose enforceable duties, and the Regulatory Flexibility Act's procedures govern rules with a significant impact on small business. Regulations issued by agencies such as EPA are, of course, subject to judicial review under the arbitrary and capricious or substantial evidence standards.

What has been the impact of this aggregation of analytical overlays on agency decisionmaking processes? Consider the following assessment by Professor McGarity.

McGARITY, THE COURTS AND THE OSSIFICATION OF RULEMAKING: A RESPONSE TO PROFESSOR SEIDENFELD
75 Texas L. Rev. 525, 528, 533-535 (1997)

By the end of the 1980s, it was becoming increasingly clear that the informal rulemaking model was not faring very well. Its great virtue had been the efficiency with which federal agencies could implement regulatory policy and the degree to which affected members of the public could participate in the policymaking process. Throughout the late 1970s and early 1980s, however, the executive branch and, to a more limited extent, Congress added analytical requirements and review procedures, often at the behest of the regulated industries. These initiatives and the continuing scrutiny of reviewing courts under the hard look doctrine caused the rulemaking process to "ossify" to a disturbing degree. By the mid-1990s, it has become so difficult for agencies to promulgate major rules that some regulatory programs have ground to a halt and others have succeeded only because agencies have resorted to alternative policymaking vehicles. . . .

In today's regulatory climate it is very difficult for an agency to promulgate a rule. The "program office" responsible for the rule must gather (by contract or otherwise) information, conduct technical and economic analyses, assemble decision packages and preambles, and convince skeptical agency employees in other offices of the desirability of the program office's preferred alternatives. The rulemaking exercise is often considerably complicated by the absence of information on relevant questions and the corresponding need to draw inferences from existing data. The program office staff often relies upon impenetrable computer models to make predictions about the probable beneficial and adverse consequences of the proposal. Large uncertainties becloud all of these analytical exercises. . . .

If the agency leadership is persuaded that the rule should go forward, it must be circulated to the Office of Management and Budget (OMB) for review by OMB economists, many of whom are well-known and persistent critics of existing regulatory regimes. The agency must then publish the proposed rule and preamble in the Federal Register and make supporting documents available for public review and comment. The program office staff must then review and respond to the voluminous comments, many of which are prepared by sophisticated employees or consultants of the regulated industries. The supporting documents and analyses must then be revised in light of the comments, and the package must be circulated again through the agency and sent to OMB for further review. For any rulemaking initiative that may have a substantial impact on small businesses, the final rule and supporting documentation must then be sent to the relevant congressional committees to give them an opportunity (potentially extending for several months) to enact legislation disapproving the rule. Finally, any adversely affected person may challenge in court the propriety of the agency's rulemaking procedures, the correctness of its interpretations of its statute, and the rationality of its factual and policy conclusions in light of the information and analysis in the record. . . .

. . . Uncertainty about how reviewing courts will view both agency reliance upon its own expertise and agency rejections of arguments raised by outside commentators unquestionably adds to the ossification of the rulemaking process. Because agency staffers have no way of knowing how reviewing judges will react to their responses to blunderbuss attacks, their tendency is to adopt the cautious approach of commissioning expensive quantitative modeling exercises to support predictions and of responding to every conceivable argument raised in blunderbuss attacks.

The ossification complaint, however, goes beyond uncertainty about how judges will react to agency rulemaking efforts. Far more troublesome, in my view, is the tendency of reviewing courts to demand too much by way of explanation and analysis from the regulatory agencies. An agency can be certain that some judges will demand more than the agency can reasonably produce under existing resource constraints. Many currently sitting judges were appointed by presidents who took great pains to ensure that the appellate judiciary was populated with judges who were not sympathetic to governmental intervention into private economic

arrangements. Far from neutral civic republican arbiters of agreed-upon conceptions of rationality, these judges are not at all reluctant to impose demanding informational and analytical requirements on agencies before allowing them to impose
costly regulations upon an unwilling private sector. Even judges who do not share
this antigovernment ideological perspective are often attracted to the synoptic paradigm and are therefore unduly demanding of the agencies. The real problem with
judicial review under the hard look doctrine is not uncertainty—it is the inability of
agencies to meet judicial expectations while still providing the protections that
Congress intended.

NOTES AND QUESTIONS

1. *The Impact of "Ossification."* In an earlier article, Professor McGarity argued
that the "ossification" of the rulemaking process described in the preceding excerpt
has had additional undesirable consequences, including inefficient regulation,
reduced agency flexibility, and, ultimately, frustration of legislative policy objectives:

> In addition to frustrating congressional policy goals, the ossification of the informal
> rulemaking process deprives it of one of its greatest virtues—administrative
> efficiency. . . . To be sure, other societal goals, such as fairness, allocative efficiency,
> and factual accuracy, may demand more deliberative rulemaking procedures, analyt-
> ical exercises, and other quality control requirements. And the extent to which a more
> burdensome rulemaking process reflects an appropriate balance among these compet-
> ing goals is a matter on which reasonable minds can differ. Nevertheless, the fact that
> the ossification of the informal rulemaking process frustrates statutory goals is a
> primary reason for inquiring into the causes of and cures for the ossification
> phenomenon.
>
> The ossification of the informal rulemaking process also reduces agency incentives
> to experiment with flexible or temporary rules. Experimentation is welcome in an atmo-
> sphere in which rules can be undone if they do not produce the anticipated changes or
> cause unanticipated side effects. But experimentation is riskier in an atmosphere in
> which any change is likely to be irreversible. This inflexibility is especially unfortunate
> in the context of programs in which agencies must regulate on the "frontiers of scientific
> knowledge" with particularly treacherous "facts." New scientific discoveries can erode
> the technical basis for a rule that was promulgated only a few years ago. New technologies
> can make available fresh alternatives that were not considered at the time the agency first
> examined the issues. However, the agencies are understandably reluctant to rock the boat
> when to do so requires an enormously expensive rulemaking in which a successful
> outcome is by no means assured. . . . [McGarity, Some Thoughts on "Deossifying"
> the Rulemaking Process, 41 Duke L.J. 1385, 1391-1392 (1992).]

Not everyone agrees with Professor McGarity's evaluation of the relative merits
and demerits of the judicial, congressional, and executive branch control techniques
which, according to McGarity, have led to rulemaking "ossification." Professor Seidenfeld claims, for example, that easing up on the rigors of judicial review of agency
decisions is likely to reduce the usefulness of this check on agency arbitrariness.
Greater judicial deference may fail to reduce agency incentives to engage in excessive
data collection because the chances of a rule surviving judicial review will still be
greater with a more extensive supporting record. Still worse, more deferential review
might harm agency deliberative processes by making it easier for an agency to adopt

rules to benefit narrow interest groups.[q] The materials in section C above summarize the arguments in defense of continued executive branch oversight.

2. *Agency Response to Limits on Discretion*. How have agencies reacted to the analytical burdens that congressional, executive, and judicial oversight of informal rulemaking has produced? One way to avoid the analytical processes mandated by the executive orders and statutes reviewed in the previous two sections is to make policy through a form other than rulemaking. Some agencies, like the Forest Service, have for years used handbooks and manuals, sometimes developed without public input, to guide agency decisionmakers. The courts have struggled to ascertain the legal status of such documents.[r] EPA routinely includes disclaimers in its guidance documents under statutes such as the Comprehensive Environmental Response, Compensation, and Liability Act to the effect that the documents are intended solely for internal agency use and create neither legal rights for those who rely upon them nor legal duties for the agency to follow. Nevertheless, the documents are typically available to the public (EPA often publishes notice of their availability in the Federal Register or posts them on its website) and the regulated community uses them to try to persuade the agency to make favorable decisions.

Another way to avoid the need to comply with the analytical procedures applicable to regulations is to adopt or implement policy through an interpretive rule or policy statement. If an agency issues an interpretive rule or a general statement of policy, as opposed to a substantive or legislative regulation, it need not comply with APA notice-and-comment rulemaking procedures. 5 U.S.C. §553(b)(A). See Beazer East, Inc. v. EPA, 963 F.2d 603 (3d Cir. 1992). What is the difference between an interpretive rule or a policy statement and a legislative rule? Interpretive rules are those which purport to "clarify" existing law or regulations, while policy statements announce how the agency hopes to implement policy in the future through subsequent rulemakings or adjudications. Phillips Petroleum Co. v. Johnson, 22 F.3d 616 (5th Cir. 1994).

In Appalachian Power Co. v. EPA, 208 F.3d 1015 (D.C. Cir. 2000), the court chastised the "familiar" agency practice of "making law" without notice and comment, public participation, or publication in the Federal Register through guidance documents, purported policy statements, and the like. It refused to allow this "lawmaking" practice to be immune from judicial review.[s] Mendelson, Regulatory Beneficiaries and Informal Agency Policymaking, 92 Cornell L. Rev. 397 (2007), argues that the use of guidance documents and other forms of informal agency policymaking harms the

q. Seidenfeld, Demystifying Deossification: Rethinking Recent Proposals to Modify Judicial Review of Notice and Comment Rulemaking, 75 Tex. L. Rev. 483 (1997). See also Seidenfeld, Cognitive Loafing, Social Conformity, and Judicial Review of Agency Rulemaking, 87 Cornell L. Rev. 486 (2002) (arguing that judicial review under the arbitrary and capricious standard encourages decisionmaking that reduces the probability of bias).

r. Compare Western Radio Serv. Co. v. Espy, 79 F.3d 896 (9th Cir. 1996) (Forest Service manual provision lacked the independent force and effect of law) with Stone Forest Indus., Inc. v. United States, 973 F.2d 1548, 1551 (Fed. Cir. 1992) (manual provision is evidence of the custom and practice of the agency). See also NRDC v. EPA, 643 F.3d 311, 320-321 (D.C. Cir. 2011) (holding that purported CAA guidance document was actually a legislative rule adopted in violation of APA rulemaking procedures).

s. See also Croplife Am. v. EPA, 329 F.3d 876 (D.C. Cir. 2003) (holding that press release announcing that EPA would not consider third-party studies in evaluating the safety of pesticides was a binding regulation, not a policy statement); Chamber of Commerce v. U.S. Dep't of Labor, 174 F.3d 206 (D.C. Cir. 1999) ("directive" subjecting employers to an inspection by OSHA was a legislative rule, not a procedural rule or a policy statement).

interests of regulatory beneficiaries by reducing access to judicial review and the ability to participate in agency decisionmaking.

3. *The "No Surprises" Policy.* Regulated entities may seek to block what they perceive to be an end run around statutory procedures or analytical requirements by disputing the agency's characterization of its actions. In 1994, the FWS and several other federal agencies issued a "no surprises" policy under their authority to implement the ESA. This policy was designed to promote Congress's goal of assuring developers who agree to abide by habitat conservation plans to protect endangered species that they will not be subject to additional land use restrictions, even if unforeseen circumstances arise after issuance that makes the need for further mitigation efforts clear. The agencies incorporated the policy into a draft Handbook for Habitat Conservation Planning and Incidental Take Permitting Process. When they proposed to finalize the handbook, commenters complained that the policy should have been issued as a regulation, with all of the attendant procedural safeguards. The agencies disagreed, asserting that "it [was not] necessary to codify the 'No Surprises' policy as a specific regulation, because it is simply a statement of policy." 61 Fed. Reg. 63,854, 63,856 (1996). They nevertheless claimed that the policy had been subjected to procedures similar to those used in issuing regulations, including a public review process when a notice of availability was published in the Federal Register for the draft handbook.

The agencies were sued by litigants claiming that the policy was invalid because it did not qualify for the APA exemption for interpretive rules or general statements of policy. In 1997, the agencies relented and agreed in a settlement of that suit to codify the policy in a proposed rule. They issued the final rule the following year. 63 Fed. Reg. 8,859 (1998). In Spirit of the Sage Council v. Norton, 294 F. Supp. 2d 67 (D.D.C. 2003), the court vacated a rule specifying the circumstances in which the Interior Department may revoke an incidental take permit due to the agency's failure to comply with notice-and-comment informal rulemaking procedures. Because the agency had relied on the "No Surprises" rule to defend the validity of the permit revocation rule, the court also remanded the "No Surprises" rule for reconsideration as a whole with the permit revocation rule. For litigation over the agency's decision on remand, see Spirit of the Sage Council v. Kempthorne, 511 F. Supp. 2d 31 (D.D.C. 2007).

4. *Regulatory Negotiation.* Widespread dissatisfaction with existing processes for resolving environmental issues, including formal adjudication, informal rulemaking, and lawsuits, have prompted increased resort to mediation and arbitration to resolve resource allocation controversies. These efforts involve consensus building among interested parties through the use of "facilitators" and focus groups. In another form of collaborative governance, regulatory negotiation (or reg-neg), federal agencies and major stakeholders negotiate to develop a consensus on the shape of regulation. Stakeholders may then agree not to challenge the resulting solution.

> Negotiated rule making is a consensus-based process, usually convened by an agency, through which stakeholders negotiate the substance of a rule. It represents the importation of alternative dispute resolution principles and strategies into the public policy context. In 1982, Philip Harter . . . proposed reg-neg as a response to the failures of the adversarial rule-making process, arguing that direct stakeholder negotiation of rules would restore legitimacy to rule making. [The ensuing debate] now consists of two distinct sides: those who argue that reg-neg is preferable to traditional rule making in

terms of the cost, implementability, and legitimacy of the rules produced, and those suspicious of its potential to subvert the public interest by granting inordinate power to unaccountable private groups. However, there is broad agreement even among ardent supporters on at least two limitations on the process. First, reg-neg should be used only under specific conditions when the incentives are conducive to producing agreement. Second, there should be plenty of safeguards against agency capture, including post-consensus notice and comment, and judicial review. [Freeman, Collaborative Governance in the Administrative State, 45 UCLA L. Rev. 1, 34-35 (1997).]

Experiments in stakeholder collaboration raise substantial constitutional and statutory authority questions. Collaborative governance may be characterized as an unconstitutional delegation of public lawmaking authority to private parties under *Carter v. Carter Coal Co.*, 298 U.S. 238 (1936). To work, these experiments require each side to take risks and for the public participants to exercise a kind of prosecutorial discretion not to seek full enforcement of existing laws. See also Rossi, Participation Run Amok: The Costs of Mass Participation in Deliberative Agency Decisionmaking, 92 Nw. U. L. Rev. 173 (1997).

5. *Decisionmaking by Inaction.* An agency may avoid judicial review by failing to take any "action" at all. As both the *Lujan I* and *Southern Utah Wilderness Alliance* cases discussed earlier in this chapter indicate, those dissatisfied with the agency's inaction may find it difficult to secure judicial review of the failure to act.

6. *Assessing the Informalization of Agency Policymaking.* Is the tendency of federal agencies to implement environmental policy through less and less formal means a laudable development? Professor McGarity contends that it is not:

> Frustrated agencies are beginning to explore techniques for avoiding notice-and-comment rulemaking altogether, such as establishing rules in adjudications. . . . To the extent that agencies establish rules in adjudications in order to avoid informal rulemaking, regulatees are not put on notice of the standards of conduct that such agencies are applying to them. As a result, both regulatees and regulatory beneficiaries are deprived of the open opportunity that informal rulemaking provides to influence the agencies' thinking. [McGarity also mentioned increased use of policy statements, interpretative rules, manuals, and other informal devices, all of which] are promulgated without the benefit of comments by an interested public. . . .
>
> If all this leads the frustrated potential regulatee to wonder whether "secret law" is at play here, those fears may be well founded. . . .

McGarity, Some Thoughts on "Deossifying" the Rulemaking Process, 41 Duke L.J. 1385, 1393-1395 (1992). See also Anthony, Interpretive Rules, Policy Statements, Guidances, Manuals, and the Like—Should Federal Agencies Use Them to Bind the Public?, 41 Duke L.J. 1311 (1992).

IV

THE NATIONAL ENVIRONMENTAL POLICY ACT

A. NEPA'S ROLE IN ENVIRONMENTAL MANAGEMENT

1. An Environmental Magna Carta

The National Environmental Policy Act of 1969 (NEPA) is one of the earliest and most influential environmental laws, and is often called an environmental Magna Carta. By injecting environmental concerns into federal agency decisionmaking, and by allowing litigation to verify compliance with the statute, NEPA moved concern about environmental problems to a high level. It covers state and local governments and even private actions when there is a federal connection.

Congress's reasons for adopting NEPA are not entirely clear, but the consensus is that it adopted NEPA to limit so-called program- or mission-oriented agencies that carry out their mandates at the expense of the environment. Highways are an example. Federal highway legislation once required highways to take the shortest distance between two points. As one commentator explained at the time, "[e]xisting agencies were established to supervise the development of our natural resources consistent with the ethic which has prevailed throughout this country's history and, thus, they tended to overstress the benefits of development and to explore insufficiently the less environmentally damaging alternatives to current methods of meeting their programmed objectives." Tarlock, Balancing Environmental Considerations and Energy Demands: A Comment on *Calvert Cliffs' Coordinating Committee, Inc. v. AEC*, 47 Ind. L. Rev. 645, 658 (1972).

Unlike other federal environmental laws, NEPA does not include substantive mandates. A law adopted the year before NEPA was enacted established substantive requirements for federally funded transportation projects that affect parks and other sensitive resources, see the *Overton Park* case in Chapter 3, *supra*, but NEPA requires only the consideration of environmental values in agency decisionmaking. The key statutory requirement is in §102(2)(C):

> The Congress authorizes and directs that, to the fullest extent possible: . . . (2) all agencies of the Federal Government shall—
>
> (C) include in every recommendation or report on proposals for legislation and other major Federal actions significantly affecting the quality of the human environment, a detailed statement by the responsible official on—

(i) the environmental impact of the proposed action,

(ii) any adverse environmental effects which cannot be avoided should the proposal be implemented,

(iii) alternatives to the proposed action,

(iv) the relationship between local short-term uses of man's environment and the maintenance and enhancement of long-term productivity, and

(v) any irreversible and irretrievable commitments of resources which would be involved in the proposed action should it be implemented.

Other paragraphs in §102(2) legislate additional environmental responsibilities for federal agencies, but only the requirement for a "detailed statement" contained in §102(2)(C) is meaningful. The "detailed statement" referred to in that paragraph is now known as the environmental impact statement (EIS).

Legislative History. The environmental impact statement requirement was not included in early drafts of the bill. They merely authorized setting up a research program on environmental problems and created an advisory Council on Environmental Quality (CEQ) within the executive branch, modeled on the President's Council of Economic Advisors. The late Lynton K. Caldwell, a professor of political science at Indiana University, introduced what became the environmental impact statement requirement at a Senate hearing, using language that included the requirement of an agency "finding" of environmental impact. A later Senate amendment substituted language calling for a "detailed statement."

The House approved its counterpart of the Senate NEPA bill without the detailed statement requirement. The conference committee reconciled this difference by keeping the impact statement requirement, but adding language ordering federal agencies to follow this procedure "to the fullest extent possible." This language was a compromise between the House sponsor's view that NEPA did not change agency statutory mandates, and Senator Jackson's intention to ensure across-the-board compliance by federal agencies. Though the conference report stated that the "fullest extent" phrase qualified NEPA's duties, a statement by the House conference committee managers claimed that the compromise adopted Senator Jackson's strict view of compliance. 115 Cong. Rec. 39,703 (1969). Senator Jackson was the bill's chief sponsor in the Senate.

Both Houses hurriedly approved the conference report, with most of the debate centering on the executive reorganization required by creation of CEQ. Few members of Congress understood the meaning of the action-forcing provisions. See R. Andrews, Environmental Policy and Administrative Change: Implementation of the National Environmental Policy Act ch. 2 (1976), for an analysis of NEPA's legislative history.

NOTES AND QUESTIONS

1. *Alternative Strategies.* Was NEPA the only legislative strategy available to protect environmental resources? One commentator suggested the following three alternatives:

a. Agency decisionmakers could be required to consider additional information, including information on environmental consequences. NEPA adopted this approach.

b. Congress could withdraw designated natural resource areas from development or give environmentally sensitive agencies a veto over development. This technique is used for resource areas, such as floodplains and wetlands.

c. Agencies could be authorized to adopt environmental standards and prohibit development that violates these standards. Congress adopted this approach in the Clean Air and Water Acts and the Resource Conservation and Recovery (solid and toxic wastes) Acts. [Tarlock, *supra*, at 659.]

The critical student will want to contrast the environmentally sensitive decision-making process mandated by NEPA with the other alternatives suggested by Professor Tarlock.

2. *Assumptions.* NEPA appears to have been based on a number of assumptions. These included a faith in rational decisionmaking, and assumptions that the natural environment is a static system injured by man's incursions, that environmental values can be sufficiently defined, and that the science of ecology can provide the necessary information to permit the environmental evaluations NEPA requires. See L.K. Caldwell, Environment: A Challenge to Modern Society 101-102 (1970). One author summarized the abandonment of these assumptions:

NEPA was born in an era that had faith in bureaucratic comprehensive rationality, the idea that predictive analysis of a broad class of administrative decisions would produce a rational decision making that would consider environmental impacts. This hope disappeared with the understanding that environmental systems are complex, dynamic, non-linear, and mutually independent, making environmental prediction a much more difficult task. These complexities make the application of NEPA to actions and programs a much more difficult problem than initially expected. A statute and its regulations that assumed a more predictive and less complicated environment do not work well in an environment that has multiple ecological dimensions where change is not measured easily. [Mandelker, The National Environmental Policy Act: A Review of Its Experience and Problems, 32 Wash. U. J.L. & Pol'y 293, 294 (2010).]

On the prediction problem consider the following, written soon after NEPA was enacted:

Ecology has not yet achieved a predictive capacity to the extent that other natural sciences such as chemistry and physics have. There are few established "principles" of ecology upon which to construct a prediction. Most importantly, ecology by its very definition involves such a broad and complex number of things and interactions that adequate knowledge for practical application is very difficult to obtain. [Carpenter, The Scientific Basis of NEPA—Is It Adequate? 6 Envtl. L. Rep. (ELI) 50014, 50017 (1976).]

Do these criticisms mean that NEPA is not an effective statute, or can they be addressed? Can monitoring help? See also Rodgers, NEPA's Insatiable Optimism, 39 Envtl. L. Rep. 10618 (2009).

3. *CEQ and the NEPA Regulations.* The Council on Environmental Quality (CEQ) in the executive office of the President is the primary enforcer of NEPA, and it has adopted regulations for the statute. Implementation is carried out by the various federal agencies, whose NEPA regulations are expected to comply with CEQ's regulations. Because NEPA applies to and supplements the statutory authority of all

federal agencies, it is known as "crosscutting" legislation. CEQ no longer has a three-person council, as the statute requires, but is headed by a chairperson.

CEQ initially was authorized to adopt advisory guidelines for the statute, but President Carter issued an executive order giving CEQ authority to issue regulations to replace the guidelines, Exec. Order No. 11,990, 42 Fed. Reg. 26,967 (1977). CEQ issued regulations pursuant to the order in late 1978. For discussion, see Fisher, The CEQ Regulations: New Stage in the Evolution of NEPA, 3 Harv. Envtl. L. Rev. 347 (1979). The regulations have been amended only once, and CEQ now issues guidance documents on implementation issues that supplement the regulations.

The Supreme Court defers to CEQ's interpretation of the statute, as in Robertson v. Methow Valley Citizens Council, 490 U.S. 332 (1989), where it deferred to CEQ's revocation of its worst-case analysis regulation. However, the authority conferred on CEQ to adopt regulations may be entitled to less deference, because it is the federal agencies with program and project responsibilities that directly administer and apply the law.

4. *Questions about NEPA.* As you read the cases and materials that follow, you should ask yourself the following questions: What was the objective of NEPA's drafters? Did they expect that existing mission agencies would self-destruct? If the answer to this question is obviously no, what did the drafters expect would be gained by the passage of a general charter of environmental goals, coupled with what Senate staff members admitted was an undefined action-forcing impact statement? Note that NEPA creates no general extra-agency enforcement mechanism, except for CEQ. Thus, the reader of the impact statement will be the superior of the preparers. What assumptions did the drafters make about the reader's reaction to the information contained in the impact statement?

One commentator identified six reform ideas that were important in the debate over NEPA's purposes. Perhaps most important, "rational systems analysts wished to reform so-called incrementalist agency behavior." Second, "environmental scientists believed resources decisions were made with little or no recognition of complex ecosystem relationships or state-of-the-art scientific understanding of those relationships." Third, "[k]ey staffers and members of the Senate Interior Committee were frustrated by the absence of alternatives in agency proposals presented to Congress." Fourth, "a group of reformers in the legal community wished to counteract the power conveyed in broad delegations of rulemaking authority to administrative agencies." Fifth, "environmental and citizens group leaders championed public participation in resources policy decision processes." Finally, agencies adopted public participation programs as a means of obtaining support for their decisions. Culhane, NEPA's Impacts on Federal Agencies, Anticipated and Unanticipated, 20 Envtl. L. 681, 684-687 (1990).

2.   *The* Calvert Cliffs *Decision: Judicial Enforcement*

The drafters of NEPA, especially Professor Caldwell, expected Congress and the executive branch of the government, especially the Office of Management and Budget, to be the primary enforcers of NEPA. Federal agencies would consider NEPA's environmental commands in their decisionmaking and would make the necessary changes

2011 NEPA Case Dispositions

Judgment for defendant	79
Dismissal w/o settlement	20
Settlement	18
Adverse dispositions	29
Temporary restraining order	0
Preliminary injunction	5
Permanent injunction	3
Remand	21

FIGURE 4-1
A Profile of Recent NEPA Cases

Source: Department of Energy 2011 Litigation Survey, available at http://energy.gov/nepa/downloads/nepa-litigation-surveys.

to incorporate environmental values. The Senate report supports this interpretation, see S. Rep. No. 91-296, at 21 (1969), although commentators disagree about whether Congress contemplated judicial enforcement. See Dreyfus & Ingram, The National Environmental Policy Act: A View of Intent and Practice, 16 Nat. Resources J. 243 (1976). Congress may also have counted on external pressure from the public and from agencies with environmental expertise. The statute expressly requires comments from these sources on environmental impact statements.

Despite these assumptions, the federal courts have assumed the major role in enforcing NEPA, even though NEPA does not expressly provide for judicial review (see Figure 4-1 for a profile of recent NEPA cases). This activist judicial role began with the first major NEPA case to reach the courts, Calvert Cliffs' Coordinating Comm., Inc. v. United States Atomic Energy Comm'n, 449 F.2d 1109 (D.C. Cir. 1971). The District of Columbia Court of Appeals was then an activist court that used NEPA as one of several opportunities to tell agencies how they should interpret their duties toward the public. *Calvert Cliffs* considered a conflict between the Atomic Energy Commission (AEC)—later the Nuclear Regulatory Commission (NRC)— and protestors over AEC rules that limited the AEC's duty to consider environmental impacts in the licensing of nuclear power plants. The court, in a forceful decision by Judge Skelly Wright, used this occasion to consider the judicial enforceability of NEPA. Implicit in Judge Wright's decision is rejection of the Commission's argument that "the vagueness of the NEPA mandate and delegation" exempted federal agency actions under NEPA from judicial review as agency decisions "committed to agency discretion by law." The following excerpts from Judge Wright's opinion give the flavor of his response:

> NEPA, first of all, makes environmental protection a part of the mandate of every federal agency and department. The Atomic Energy Commission, for example, had continually asserted, prior to NEPA, that it had no statutory authority to concern itself with the adverse environmental effects of its actions. Now, however, its hands are no longer tied. It is not only permitted, but compelled, to take environmental values into account. Perhaps the greatest importance of NEPA is to require the Atomic Energy Commission to consider environmental issues just as they consider other matters within their mandates. . . . Senator Jackson, NEPA's principal sponsor, stated that "[n]o agency will [now] be able to maintain that it has no mandate or no requirement to consider

the environmental consequences of its actions." He characterized the requirements of Section 102 as "action-forcing" and stated that "[o]therwise, these lofty declarations [in Section 101] are nothing more than that." . . .

[T]he procedural duties of Section 102 must be fulfilled to the fullest extent possible. . . . They must be complied with to the fullest extent, unless there is a clear conflict of statutory authority. Considerations of administrative difficulty, delay or economic cost will not suffice to strip the section of its fundamental importance. . . .

We conclude, then, that Section 102 of NEPA mandates a particular sort of careful and informed decisionmaking process and creates judicially enforceable duties. . . . As one District Court has said of Section 102 requirements: "It is hard to imagine a clearer or stronger mandate to the Courts." [449 F.2d at 1112-1115.]

NOTES AND QUESTIONS

1. *What the Decision Means.* Judge Wright's decision in *Calvert Cliffs* is important for its holding that agency duties under NEPA are judicially enforceable. Reread the Supreme Court's *Overton Park* decision, reproduced in Chapter 3, which declined to apply the "committed to agency discretion" exemption to a somewhat different environmental statute. Does *Overton Park* support Judge Wright's holding on this point? Note that an agency's compliance with NEPA is judicially reviewable even though its actions under its enabling legislation may be "committed to agency discretion." See Schiffler v. Schlesinger, 548 F.2d 96 (3d Cir. 1977).

Calvert Cliffs is also important for its interpretation of NEPA's statutory mandate. Judge Wright discussed the "procedural" duties imposed by NEPA. What are they? Do they refer to the duty to prepare an impact statement when one is required or to the rules that courts are to apply when they determine whether an impact statement is adequate?

2. *Independent NEPA Review.* Another issue the court considered in *Calvert Cliffs* was whether NEPA required the AEC to consider the water quality impacts of nuclear power plants. In brief, the AEC claimed the law allowed it merely to incorporate water quality standards adopted by EPA into its license. The court adopted the argument of protestors, who argued that NEPA required an independent evaluation of water quality impacts beyond compliance with EPA-approved water quality standards. Congress overruled this part of the *Calvert Cliffs* decision in subsequent amendments to the Clean Water Act. See §511(c)(2), 33 U.S.C. §1371(c)(2). See also §104 of NEPA, which states that NEPA does not "in any way affect the specific statutory obligations of any federal agency."

3. *NEPA Today.* The *Calvert Cliffs* decision came in the early days of NEPA, when the statute had taken agencies by surprise, and they were still struggling to interpret the statute and often resisted compliance with its requirements. Agencies today are more mature, and their NEPA documents usually are a good faith attempt to comply with the statute. For this reason the role of the courts is quite different, and the problem may be a disconnect between the environmental data and an agency's refusal to listen, rather than an attempt to avoid statutory environmental disclosure obligations. For a case in which the disconnect problem led to invalidation of an impact statement for a major west-side highway along the Hudson River in New York City, see Sierra Club v. United States Army Corps of Eng'rs (I), 701 F.2d 1011 (2d Cir. 1983). The district court found, for example, "that the [Final Environmental Impact Statement] contained false statements depicting the interpier region as 'biologically

impoverished' and as a 'biological wasteland,' when in fact the interpier area in winter harbored a concentration of juvenile striped bass." The highway was eventually abandoned.

B. WHEN DOES NEPA APPLY? EXEMPTIONS, NONDISCRETIONARY ACTIONS, AND CATEGORICAL EXCLUSIONS

NEPA, in theory, applies to all federal agencies and federal programs, and is a crosscutting statute for this reason. Statutes and court cases have limited NEPA's reach, however. Courts have exempted some statutory programs from NEPA, and Congress has adopted several statutory exemptions and modifications of the statute. Neither does NEPA apply to the nondiscretionary actions of federal agencies. CEQ regulations also allow agencies to exempt an action from NEPA by finding that it is categorically excluded.

1. Exemptions

CATRON COUNTY BOARD OF COMMISSIONERS v. UNITED STATES FISH AND WILDLIFE SERVICE
75 F.3d 1429 (10th Cir. 1996)

KELLY, Circuit Judge.

The United States Fish and Wildlife Service and various governmental officials (FWS, Secretary or Appellants) appeal the district court's order granting Catron County's (County or Appellee) motion for partial summary judgment in the County's action alleging that the Secretary of Interior (Secretary or Appellants), acting on behalf of the FWS, failed to comply with the National Environmental Policy Act of 1969 (NEPA), in designating certain lands within the County as critical habitat for the spikedace and loach minnow. In addition, the district court granted the County's motion for injunctive relief but stayed its order pending appeal. We exercise jurisdiction under 28 U.S.C. §1292(a)(1) and affirm.

I. Background

In 1985, the Secretary proposed listing the spikedace and loach minnow as threatened species and establishing a critical habitat for them. . . . In March 1994, the Secretary issued notice of final designation of critical habitat, which became effective on April 7, 1994. In April 1994, the County filed its motion for injunctive relief claiming that the Secretary had failed to comply with NEPA and seeking to prevent the Secretary from implementing and enforcing its designation of critical habitat. The district court granted Appellants' motion to consolidate for consideration both the County's motion for injunctive relief and the parties' motions for partial summary judgment.

On October 13, 1994, finding that the Secretary had failed to comply with NEPA in designating critical habitat, the district court granted the County's motions for partial summary judgment and injunctive relief.

II. *Discussion*

. . .

B. STATUTORY FRAMEWORK

[The court discussed NEPA and the Endangered Species Act.]

C. NEPA'S APPLICABILITY TO ESA

. . .

2. RELEVANT PRECEDENT

Compliance with NEPA is excused when there is a statutory conflict with the agency's authorizing legislation that prohibits or renders compliance impossible. See H.R. Conf. Rep. No. 91-765, 91st Cong., 1st Sess. (1969); see also Flint Ridge Dev. Co. v. Scenic Rivers Ass'n, 426 U.S. 776. Judicial interpretation of what constitutes a "conflict" with NEPA has varied, however. Courts have approved noncompliance with NEPA on the basis of statutory conflict after finding either (i) an unavoidable conflict between the two statutes that renders compliance with both impossible; or (ii) duplicative procedural requirements between the statutes that essentially constitute "functional equivalents," rendering compliance with both superfluous.

In *Flint Ridge*, the Supreme Court addressed a conflict between NEPA and the Interstate Land Sales Full Disclosure Act (Disclosure Act), which imposes a statutory duty upon the Secretary of Housing and Urban Development (HUD) to allow statements of record to go into effect within 30 days of filing unless the Secretary of HUD acts affirmatively within that time to suspend it for inadequate disclosure. See 15 U.S.C. §1706. Finding it "inconceivable that an environmental impact statement could, in 30 days, be drafted, circulated, commented upon, and then reviewed and revised," the Supreme Court held that a "clear and fundamental conflict of statutory duty" existed between NEPA and the Disclosure Act that prevented simultaneous compliance with both statutes. *Flint Ridge*, 426 U.S. at 788-91. In light of the "clear and unavoidable conflict in statutory authority," the Supreme Court held that "NEPA must give way . . . '[as] NEPA was not intended to repeal by implication any other statute.'" Id. at 788 (quoting United States v. SCRAP, 412 U.S. 669, 694).

NEPA compliance has also been excused by some courts where the particular action being undertaken is subject to rules and regulations that essentially duplicate the NEPA inquiry. See, e.g., Merrell v. Thomas, 807 F.2d 776, 778 (9th Cir. 1986) (holding that to require registration procedures under both NEPA and Federal Insecticide, Fungicide, and Rodenticide Act would be superfluous); Pacific Legal Foundation v. Andrus, 657 F.2d 829, 835 (6th Cir. 1981) (NEPA conflicts with ESA provisions regarding listing of species as endangered or threatened); Portland

Cement Ass'n v. Ruckelshaus, 486 F.2d 375, 384 (D.C. Cir. 1973) (EPA not required to comply with NEPA when promulgating standards under §111 of the Clean Air Act). In view of the focus of the ESA critical habitat designation, we do not believe that the NEPA inquiry has been duplicated, nor do we believe the statutes are mutually exclusive. We rejected an analogous argument in Davis v. Morton, 469 F.2d 593 (10th Cir. 1972). We declined to find an unavoidable, irreconcilable conflict between NEPA and 25 U.S.C. §415, a statute that regulates secretarial approval of leases on Indian lands. Section 415 provided that "prior to approval of any lease [on Indian land] . . . the Secretary of Interior shall first satisfy himself that adequate consideration has been given to . . . the effect on the environment of the uses to which the leased lands will be subject." 25 U.S.C. §415. The government argued that NEPA did not apply to §415 because the latter statute required the Bureau of Indian Affairs (BIA) to consider the environmental ramifications of its authorization of leases. Davis, 469 F.2d at 598. We disagreed, noting that, unlike NEPA, §415 did not require substantive and in depth environmental consideration but rather a more focused analysis of issues concerning the lease of Indian land. We concluded that "unless the obligations of another statute are clearly mutually exclusive with the mandates of NEPA, the specific requirements of NEPA will remain in force." Id.

The Secretary relies upon Douglas County v. Babbitt, 48 F.3d 1495 (9th Cir. 1995), and urges us to adopt its holding. After careful consideration, we believe our precedent and analysis require a different result. In Douglas County, the Ninth Circuit addressed the precise issue before us. That case arose after the Secretary attempted to designate critical habitat for the Spotted Owl, a species he listed as threatened in June 1990 pursuant to the ESA. In May 1991, the Secretary issued a proposal designating over 11 million acres as critical habitat, asserting that he need not comply with NEPA's documentation requirements. See 48 Fed. Reg. 49,244 (1983) (letter from the Council on Environmental Quality (CEQ) indicating that the Secretary may cease complying with NEPA for actions under §1533 of ESA). After Douglas County filed suit claiming that the Secretary had failed to comply with NEPA, the Secretary issued a final habitat designation comprising almost 7 million acres of exclusively federal land. The district court held that Douglas County had standing to sue, granted Douglas' motion for summary judgment finding that NEPA did apply to the Secretary's decision to designate critical habitat under the ESA and, sua sponte, stayed the order pending appeal.

The Ninth Circuit affirmed in part and reversed in part, holding that while Douglas County did have standing, NEPA did not apply. Douglas County, 48 F.3d at 1507-08. We disagree with the panel's reasoning. First, given the focus of the ESA together with the rather cursory directive that the Secretary is to take into account "economic and other relevant impacts," we do not believe that the ESA procedures have displaced NEPA requirements. Secondly, we likewise disagree with the panel that no actual impact flows from the critical habitat designation. Merely because the Secretary says it does not make it so. The record in this case suggests that the impact will be immediate and the consequences could be disastrous. The preparation of an EA will enable all involved to determine what the effect will be. Finally, we believe that compliance with NEPA will further the goals of the ESA, and not vice versa as suggested by the Ninth Circuit panel. For these reasons and in view of our own circuit precedent, we conclude that the Secretary must comply with NEPA when designating critical habitat under ESA.

3. FACTUAL ANALYSIS

Appellants do not allege that compliance with both statutes is impossible due to an unavoidable, irreconcilable conflict between §1533 of ESA and NEPA's documentation requirements. Rather, Appellants argue that the similarity of the statutes' procedures, together with congressional failure to respond to judicial and executive announcements of NEPA noncompliance, evidence Congress' implicit intent to "displace[] NEPA's procedural and informational requirements."

It is clear that the provisions of the ESA governing the designation of critical habitat instruct the Secretary to follow procedures that to some extent parallel and perhaps overlap the requirements imposed by NEPA. Together, the ESA requirements for notice and environmental consideration partially fulfill the primary purposes of NEPA, namely, "to inject environmental consideration into the federal agency's decisionmaking . . . [and] inform the public that the agency" has considered the environment. [Weinberger v. Catholic Action of Hawaii, 454 U.S. 139, 143 (1981).]

Partial fulfillment of NEPA's requirements, however, is not enough. The plain language of NEPA makes clear that "to the fullest extent possible" federal agencies must comply with the act and prepare an impact statement for all major federal actions significantly affecting the environment. 42 U.S.C. §4332(2)(C). NEPA does not require particular results but rather a particular process. Robertson v. Methow Valley Citizens Council, 490 U.S. 332, 350 (1989). NEPA ensures that a federal agency makes informed, carefully calculated decisions when acting in such a way as to affect the environment and also enables dissemination of relevant information to external audiences potentially affected by the agency's decision.

By contrast, ESA's core purpose is to prevent the extinction of species by preserving and protecting the habitat upon which they depend from the intrusive activities of humans. See 16 U.S.C. §1531(b). While the protection of species through preservation of habitat may be an environmentally beneficial goal, Secretarial action under ESA is not inevitably beneficial or immune to improvement by compliance with NEPA procedure. The designation of critical habitat effectively prohibits all subsequent federal or federally funded or directed actions likely to affect the habitat. Id. at §1536(a)(2). The short- and long-term effects of the proposed governmental action (and even the governmental action prohibited under ESA designation) are often unknown or, more importantly, initially thought to be beneficial, but after closer analysis determined to be environmentally harmful. Furthermore, that the Secretary believes the effects of a particular designation to be beneficial is equally immaterial to his responsibility to comply with NEPA. "Even if the Federal agency believes that on balance the effect [of the action] will be beneficial," regulations promulgated by the Council on Environmental Quality (CEQ) nonetheless require an impact statement. 40 C.F.R. §1508.27(b)(1). NEPA's requirements are not solely designed to inform the Secretary of the environmental consequences of his action. NEPA documentation notifies the public and relevant government officials of the proposed action and its environmental consequences and informs the public that the acting agency has considered those consequences. A federal agency could not know the potential alternatives to a proposed federal action until it complies with NEPA and prepares at least an EA.

To interpret NEPA as merely requiring an assessment of detrimental impacts upon the environment would significantly diminish the act's fundamental purpose — to "help public officials make decisions that are based on understanding of environmental consequences, and take actions that protect, restore, and enhance the environment." 40 C.F.R. §1500.1(c). Appellants' theory would cast the judiciary as final arbiter of what federal actions protect or enhance the environment, a role for which the courts are not suited.

Here, the County alleges that the proposed designation will prevent continued governmental flood control efforts, thereby significantly affecting nearby farms and ranches, other privately owned land, local economies and public roadways and bridges. These claims, if proved, constitute a significant effect on the environment the impact of which and alternatives to which have not been adequately addressed by ESA. Furthermore, unlike the county in Douglas County, Catron County actually owns land potentially affected by the designation; the final designation in Douglas County included only federal land. It is true that after complying with NEPA's documentation requirements, the Secretary nonetheless may adhere to his proposed designation, Regardless, NEPA is clear: "to the fullest extent possible," federal agencies must comply with the act and prepare an impact statement for "major Federal actions significantly affecting the quality of the human environment." 42 U.S.C. §4332(2)(C), (E). . . .

[The court rejected an argument "that congressional failure to reverse or revise prior judicial and secretarial announcements of NEPA noncompliance evidences congressional endorsement of such noncompliance."]

AFFIRMED.

NOTES AND QUESTIONS

1. *NEPA's Reach.* NEPA's sweeping environmental mandate would seem to apply, without exception, to the statutory obligations of all federal agencies, because NEPA provides that federal agencies shall comply with NEPA "to the fullest extent possible," and that NEPA supplements existing federal legislation. A basis for exemption can be found only in §104, discussed earlier, which states that NEPA is not to affect the "specific statutory obligations" of federal agencies. In *Calvert Cliffs*, the court held that §104 relieves an agency of compliance with NEPA only when its "specific statutory obligations" are clearly mutually exclusive of NEPA's requirements. *Calvert Cliffs* also held that §104 does not prohibit agencies from considering stricter water pollution controls than those required by EPA under the Clean Water Act. This holding can require agencies to consider environmental impacts under NEPA, even though their enabling legislation does not require it. Ocoee River Council v. Tennessee Valley Auth., 540 F. Supp. 788 (E.D. Tenn. 1981) (TVA must consider environmental impact of power decisions).

The leading case on direct conflict is Flint Ridge Dev. Co. v. Scenic Rivers Ass'n, 426 U.S. 776 (1976), discussed in the principal decision. The Interstate Land Sales Full Disclosure Act, 15 U.S.C. §§1701-1720, requires developers to submit full disclosure statements on their land developments with the Department of Housing and Urban Development (HUD). A disclosure statement becomes effective 30 days after it is filed if it is complete and accurate on its face. The HUD Secretary may not substantively evaluate a developer's project but may only suspend the statement's effective date if the statement is procedurally defective.

HUD first claimed NEPA did not apply to its actions under the disclosure act because NEPA applies only to agencies "that have the ability to react to environmental consequences when taking action." Since HUD could not review the environmental impact of a proposed development, it claimed NEPA did not apply. The Court did not decide this question because it found HUD exempt under NEPA §102, requiring federal agencies to comply only "to the fullest extent possible." The disclosure act made the developer's statement effective 30 days after filing, unless the HUD Secretary acted affirmatively to suspend the statement. It was inconceivable, the Court concluded, that an impact statement could be drafted, reviewed, and revised within that period. The Court found a "clear and fundamental conflict of a statutory duty." As an afterthought, it noted that the disclosure act authorized the HUD Secretary "to incorporate a wide range of environmental information into property reports." Is this a functional equivalence rule?

Compare Jones v. Gordon, 792 F.2d 821 (9th Cir. 1986). The court rejected an argument that statutory time limits imposed on the issuance of permits for the capture of whales precluded compliance with NEPA. The court distinguished *Flint Ridge* by holding the statute authorized the agency to control the "triggering act for the statutory timetable" to allow compliance with NEPA.

2. *Conflict in Statutory Purpose.* In *Catron County*, the issue was a conflict in statutory purpose. How did the court use NEPA's legislative purpose to support a ruling that it applies to a habitat designation under the ESA, which is discussed in Chapter 5? As the court noted, there is a conflict in the cases on this issue. Notice that the environmental impact of habitat designations need not be considered under the ESA, and that a habitat designation is arguably a benign environmental action. This problem did not trouble the court. For a different view on a different issue under the ESA, see Pacific Legal Found. v. Andrus, 657 F.2d 829 (6th Cir. 1981), where the court held that an EIS is not required on the listing of an endangered species under the ESA. It held that the agency did not have discretion to consider environmental impacts, that the statutory criteria for listing endangered species precluded consideration of environmental impacts, and that the listing of an endangered species furthered NEPA's purposes.

3. *Functional Equivalence.* The courts have also implied a "functional equivalence" exemption from NEPA for agency actions that protect rather than harm the environment, but have applied it only to actions taken by EPA in its environmental regulation programs. A leading case is Portland Cement Ass'n v. Ruckelshaus, 486 F.2d 375 (D.C. Cir. 1973), which held that EPA need not prepare an impact statement prior to its adoption of air pollution emissions standards under §111 of the Clean Air Act. The court noted that §111 required an emissions standard reflecting "the best system of emission reduction," and mandated the EPA Administrator to take "into account the cost of achieving such reduction." It interpreted these criteria to require the Administrator to consider both the adverse environmental effects and the costs to industry of a proposed standard, and to prepare a statement of reasons explaining EPA's environmental review to accompany the proposal through the remainder of the rulemaking process. The court held that although this procedure "may not import the complete advantages of the structured determinations of NEPA into the decision-making of EPA, it does . . . strike a workable balance between some of the advantages and disadvantages of full application of NEPA." EPA's proposed rule and the reasons for adopting it could provide an "alert" to environmental issues. Actions taken by the EPA under the Clean Air Act are now explicitly exempt from NEPA. 15 U.S.C. §793(c).

Courts have applied the functional equivalence exception to other EPA programs where there is no explicit exemption, such as the regulation of pesticides under the Federal Insecticide, Fungicide and Rodenticide Act. State of Wyoming v. Hathaway, 525 F.2d 66 (10th Cir. 1975). The court held that "an organization like EPA whose regulatory activities are necessarily concerned with environmental consequences need not stop in the middle of its proceedings in order to issue a separate and distinct impact statement just to be issuing it. To so require would decrease environmental protection activity rather than increase it." Id. at 71-72. Does the functional equivalence rule seem consistent with NEPA's purposes? If an action is covered by NEPA, CEQ regulations require that the benign environmental effects of the action must be considered. 40 C.F.R. §1508.27(b)(1). What does the *Catron* case suggest on this issue?

4. *Appropriations and Legislation.* The Supreme Court held that requests for appropriations are exempt from NEPA in Andrus v. Sierra Club, 442 U.S. 347 (1979). It noted, in part, that an EIS requirement at the appropriation stage would be redundant because it "would merely recapitulate the EISs that should have accompanied the initial proposals of the programs." These "proposals" may have included a proposal for legislation, as legislative proposals are covered by NEPA. Though potentially helpful as a means of providing Congress with information necessary to review the environmental impact of federal programs, the application of NEPA to legislative proposals is NEPA's neglected mandate. Very few have been submitted. Is a report on legislation a "proposal" for legislation? See Citizens for the Mgmt. of Alaska Lands v. Department of Agric., 447 F. Supp. 753 (D. Alaska 1978) (holding no, because to hold otherwise would violate the political question doctrine). For discussion, see Note, NEPA's Forgotten Clause: Impact Statements for Legislative Proposals, 58 B.U. L. Rev. 560 (1978).

5. *National Security Exemption.* In Weinberger v. Catholic Action of Hawaii, 454 U.S. 139 (1981), the U.S. Navy invoked the Freedom of Information Act (FOIA), 5 U.S.C. §552, to claim an impact statement was not required for the construction of new ammunition and weapons storage facilities in which the plaintiff claimed that nuclear weapons would be stored. FOIA applies to NEPA, §102(2)(C). The court of appeals required the preparation of a hypothetical EIS that would hypothesize, but not concede, that the facilities would be used for nuclear weapons storage. The Supreme Court reversed. It held that classified national defense matters were exempt from disclosure under FOIA, and that information on the storage of nuclear weapons fell in this category. For national security reasons, the Navy could neither admit nor deny that it proposed to store nuclear weapons, and so a court could not determine whether the Navy had taken an action to which NEPA applied. The Court added that if the Navy proposed to store nuclear weapons at the facility the Defense Department regulations "can fairly be read to require that an EIS be prepared solely for internal purposes, even though such a document cannot be disclosed to the public." 454 U.S. at 146.

The cases have read *Catholic Action* to require preparation of an EIS when FOIA does not apply, and have held that the application of NEPA to national security activities is a justiciable question. See No Gwen Alliance v. Aldridge, 855 F.2d 1380 (9th Cir. 1988) (holding, however, that nexus between radio emergency network and nuclear war was too tenuous to require discussion); Romer v. Carlucci, 847 F.2d 445 (8th Cir. 1988) (court can review EIS on MX missile deployment for compliance with NEPA). Reread §101. Are these decisions consistent with the statutory intent? See Dycus, NEPA's Secrets, 2 N.Y.U. Envtl. L.J. 300 (1993).

2. Nondiscretionary Actions

NEPA does not make a distinction between actions that are discretionary and those that are not, but the courts have concluded that NEPA does not apply if agency action is nondiscretionary. In an early leading case, South Dakota v. Andrus, 614 F.2d 1190 (8th Cir. 1980), the court held NEPA did not apply to the Department of Interior's decision to issue a mineral patent for mining claims in a national forest, which it held to be a ministerial action. Reasoning that the primary purpose of NEPA was to aid agency decisionmaking, the court held the statute did not apply to ministerial acts. See also Citizens Against Rails-to-Trails v. Surface Transp. Bd., 267 F.3d 1144 (D.C. Cir. 2001) (issuance of Certificate of Interim Trail Use held ministerial).

The Supreme Court considered this problem in Department of Transportation v. Public Citizen, 541 U.S. 742 (2004). After the President announced his intent to lift a moratorium on the operation of Mexican trucks in the United States, the Federal Motor Carrier Safety Administration (FMCSA) adopted regulations allowing Mexican trucks to operate in the United States. The Court held the agency did not have to consider the environmental effects of an increase in Mexican truck operations in the United States resulting from the adoption of the regulations. Plaintiff argued that the adoption of the regulations would "cause" an increase in truck volume as a reasonably foreseeable effect. The Court rejected this argument because the agency had no authority to prevent the entry of Mexican trucks. It was required by statute to issue permits when applicants complied with statutory safety and financial responsibility requirements. See Quechan Indian Tribe v. United States Dep't of the Interior, 547 F. Supp. 2d 1033 (D. Ariz. 2008) (Bureau of Land Management need not consider effects of an oil refinery to be built on land transferred out of federal ownership; agency lacked authority to control existence, location, or construction of refinery). Compare Humane Soc'y of the United States v. Johanns, 520 F. Supp. 2d 8 (D.D.C. 2007) (agency had discretion to adopt regulations for horse slaughter).

3. Categorical Exclusions

Categorical exclusions are an option provided by CEQ regulations that allows agencies to opt out of NEPA by excluding actions they believe are not covered by NEPA. CEQ regulations define a categorical exclusion, known as a CATX, as "a category of actions which do not individually or cumulatively have a significant effect on the human environment." 40 C.F.R. §1508.4. Federal agencies have adopted lists of actions they consider to be exempt as categorical exclusions, as well as regulations that echo the generic CEQ exemption. Agencies can make decisions on categorical exclusions with much less documentation than they prepare for an impact statement, an approach CEQ has encouraged, but some agencies provide substantial documentation as a defensive measure. The Council on Environmental Quality estimates that many NEPA analyses are categorical exclusions.

One court has explained:

> Categorical exclusions are classes of actions that an agency has determined do not "have a significant effect on the human environment." 40 C.F.R. §1508.4. Application of a categorical exclusion is not an exemption from NEPA; rather, it is a form of

NEPA compliance, albeit one that requires less than where an environmental impact statement or an environmental assessment is necessary. Id. Indeed, even where an action falls into a categorical exclusion, an agency must nevertheless provide procedures for determining whether "extraordinary circumstances" exist, such that the action, though "normally excluded" from full NEPA analysis, "may have a significant environmental effect." Id. [Center for Biological Diversity v. Salazar, 706 F.3d 1085, 1096 (9th Cir. 2013).]

The effect of the regulation is that agencies can categorically exclude actions they decide will never have significant environmental effects. Courts reviewing a categorical exclusion must then decide whether this decision is correct. They apply the usual arbitrary and capricious standard of judicial review and often defer to agency decisions. For example, agencies typically classify minor actions that are not expected to have significant environmental effects as categorical exclusions, and courts uphold these decisions if they are not arbitrary. See, e.g., Bicycle Trails of Marin v. Babbitt, 82 F.3d 1445 (9th Cir. 1996) (closing off-road areas in national parks to bicycle use). Major categorical exclusions may not be tolerated. A district court, for example, invalidated a categorical exclusion adopted by the Forest Service that excluded proposals to develop, amend, or revise forest management plans. Citizens for Better Forestry v. United States Dep't of Agric., 481 F. Supp. 2d 1059 (N.D. Cal. 2007).

As noted earlier, CEQ regulations provide that an agency may not designate an action as a CATX if there are "extraordinary circumstances in which a normally excluded action may have a significant environmental effect." 40 C.F.R. §1508.4. Judicial challenges to a CATX often argue this exception to claim a CATX has been made improperly. Compare Town of Marshfield v. Federal Aviation Admin., 552 F.3d 1 (1st Cir. 2008) (finding no extraordinary circumstances in exclusion of airport departure, routing, and approach procedures) with Wilderness Watch v. Mainella, 375 F.3d 1085 (11th Cir. 2004) (decision to transport busloads of tourists through wilderness area not eligible as CATX for "routine and continuing government business").

Categorical exclusions have received a lot of attention because agencies see them as a way of escaping NEPA entirely. The exploration plan for the oil well that created the BP Gulf oil spill, for example, was handled as a categorical exclusion. CEQ has issued a guidance on how categorical exclusions should be used. 75 Fed. Reg. 75,628 (2010). Congress has also acted and in several statutes has expanded agency authority to adopt a CATX. For an article claiming that categorical exclusions create a "gaping hole" in NEPA requirements see Note, Circumventing the National Environmental Policy Act: Agency Abuse of the Categorical Exclusion, 79 N.Y.U. L. Rev. 2312 (2004).

C. THRESHOLD ISSUES: MUST AN IMPACT STATEMENT BE PREPARED?

If an agency's action is not categorically excluded, the agency must decide whether to prepare an impact statement. This issue is the threshold issue. Courts asked to decide the threshold issue must consider questions of interpretation raised by NEPA's somewhat vague language in §102(2)(C), which requires an impact statement on "major federal actions significantly affecting the quality of the human environment." The materials that follow examine the meaning of these statutory terms. The question here is to determine when actions covered by NEPA require the preparation of an impact statement. Figure 4-2 diagrams the NEPA process in which this decision is made.

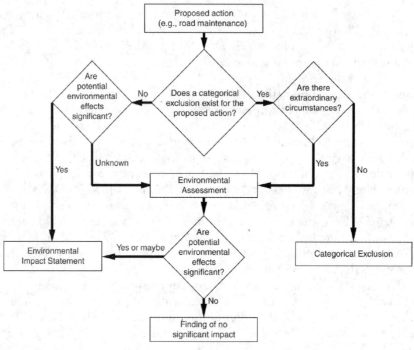

Source: GAO.

FIGURE 4-2
Process for Implementing National Environmental Policy Act Requirements

Source: U.S. General Accountability Office, National Environmental Policy Act: Little Information Exists on NEPA Analyses 5 (2014), available at http://www.gao.gov/products/GAO-14-370.

Environmental Assessments. If an action is not categorically excluded, an agency must prepare an environmental impact statement or, in the alternative, prepare an environmental assessment to decide whether an environmental impact statement is required. In practice, environmental impact statements are prepared in a relatively small number of cases. Although definite figures are not available, most estimates suggest that agencies usually decide to prepare an environmental assessment. An environmental assessment must include brief discussions of the need for the proposed action, alternatives to the proposed action, the environmental impacts of the proposed action, any alternatives, and a list of agencies and persons consulted during the environmental assessment process. 40 C.F.R. §1508.9. It is a "concise public document" which is to "[b]riefly provide sufficient analysis and evidence for determining" whether the agency should prepare an impact statement or make a Finding of No Significant Impact (FONSI) as the basis for a decision that an impact statement is not necessary. Id. §1508.9. A FONSI is a document "briefly presenting the reasons" an impact statement is not necessary. Id. §1508.13.

Agencies usually make a FONSI determination based on mitigation requirements that are accepted as the basis for concluding that the action will not have significant environmental effects. This strategy is called a mitigated FONSI, and this approach, rather than the preparation of an environmental impact statement, has become the most common method of achieving NEPA compliance.

Comparison with the EIS. The Fifth Circuit has explained the difference between an environmental assessment (EA) and an environmental impact statement (EIS):

> An EIS must contain "a detailed statement of the expected adverse consequences of an action, the resource commitments involved in it, and the alternatives to it." An EA, on the other hand, is prepared in order to determine whether an EIS is required. An EA is a rough-cut, "low budget environmental impact statement" intended to determine whether effects are significant enough to warrant preparation of an EIS. An EA must include "brief discussions of the need for the proposal, of alternatives . . . of the impacts of proposed action and alternatives, and a listing of agencies and persons consulted." 40 C.F.R. §1508.9(b). [Sierra Club v. Espy, 38 F.3d 792, 802-803 (5th Cir. 1994).]

The following problem will introduce you to the legal questions raised by NEPA, including the threshold environmental assessment issue. Transportation and highway projects rank high in the preparation of environmental documents under NEPA, and their NEPA compliance is frequently litigated.

Problem 4-1

The State Department of Transportation has had a major limited-access highway connector, called the Outstate Connector, in the planning stages for over 20 years. A corridor map adopted by the Department shows the general location of the connector on the state's long-range transportation plan. The connector will go from Metro City, the capital city of the state, to River Junction, a smaller city. The hope is that building the new highway will open up economic opportunities in River Junction and in the area between that city and the capital.

The state has used federal funding to conduct preliminary planning and engineering studies for the Outstate Connector. To help with planning, the state Department of Transportation divided the highway into three segments. The first segment goes from the capital to an intersection with Interstate Highway 54, about 20 miles away. This segment crosses high-quality agricultural land. The second segment goes from this intersection another 50 miles to Wildlake, a small resort town. This segment crosses a major wildlife preserve; bridges over the preserve are necessary at some points. The third and final segment goes from Wildlake another 100 miles to River Junction. This segment crosses numerous wetlands.

The Department has issued a FONSI on the first segment of the Outstate Connector based on an environmental assessment that the segment will not have significant environmental impacts. The environmental assessment considered a number of alternatives, including a "no-action" alternative and alternatives that would modify the design of the project but not its location. The Department has adopted the second segment as part of the state highway system, but does not plan to submit it to the Federal Highway Administration (FHWA) or to do an environmental assessment of this part of the highway. The status of the third segment is uncertain at this time.

An environmental organization, Save Our State (SOS), has opposed the Out-state Connector for some time. It especially opposes segments two and three because of the impact they will have on natural resource lands, and has suggested a number of alternatives. One alternative is an alternative route that would avoid prime agricultural and other natural resource lands. Another alternative would abandon the highway altogether in favor of a new rail line to River Junction.

As counsel to SOS, what would you advise? Would you advise litigation challenging the FONSI on the first segment? Would you include the other two segments in this lawsuit? If so, how? On what basis would you challenge the conclusion that the environmental effects of the connector are not significant? The failure to consider additional alternatives? As counsel to the Department of Transportation, what defenses would you suggest if this suit is brought?

1. Is It Federal?

The first requirement for inclusion under NEPA is whether an action is federal. Activities that federal agencies carry out, such as federal construction projects, are clearly federal. Federal agency decisions on projects carried out by private entities fall within NEPA as "federal" actions if there is the necessary federal nexus. An example is a federal permit for a project in wetlands. Projects carried out by state and local governments can also be "federal" actions if funded by federal assistance, or if they are under federal control or supervision. 40 C.F.R. §1508.18. See generally D. Mandelker et al., NEPA Law & Litigation §§8:18-8:22 (2014 ed.) (hereinafter NEPA Law).

Categories of Federal Actions. CEQ regulations do not define federal actions, but indicate the categories in which these actions "tend to fall." 40 C.F.R. §1508.18(b). These categories include:

1. The adoption of official policies, such as rules and regulations.
2. The adoption of "formal plans . . . which guide or prescribe alternative uses of federal resources, upon which future agency actions will be based."
3. The adoption of "programs, such as a group of concerted actions to implement a specific policy or plan" or "allocating agency resources to implement" a statutory program or executive directive.
4. The approval of specific projects such as "actions approved by permit or other regulatory decision as well as federal and federally assisted activities."

Can you think of examples that fit each of these categories? Federal approval can be minimal.

Projects Funded by Federal Assistance. Under one federal assistance format, a state or local agency submits and the federal agency approves a specific project. NEPA clearly applies when a federal agency approves project assistance. Sierra Club v. U.S. Dep't of Agric., 777 F. Supp. 2d 44 (D.D.C. 2011) (debt restructuring and release of lien that facilitated utility's ability to expand a coal-fired power plant; significant assistance provided). However, funding for preliminary studies is not usually enough because there is no final action. Macht v. Skinner, 916 F.2d 13 (D.C. Cir. 1990). Block grants are another type of federal assistance. In block grant programs, federal assistance is made available to states and local governments under a statutory formula for use in programs authorized by the statute. Congress sometimes requires compliance with NEPA in block grant programs. See, e.g., Housing and Community Development Act of 1974, 42 U.S.C. §5304(g).

Whether NEPA applies to block grant programs if not expressly made applicable depends on the program and the extent of the federal commitment. In one case, a court did not require an EIS on the construction of a new prison not funded with federal assistance. It rejected a claim that an EIS was required because the federal government provided general support for the state prison system. Citizens for a Better St. Clair County v. James, 648 F.2d 246 (5th Cir. 1981).

Federal Approvals, Permits, and Control. NEPA reaches outside the federal government through federal permits and approvals, such as permits for private development in wetlands that bring an action under NEPA even if the project is to be carried out by a state or local government or private entity:

> [T]here is "Federal action" within the meaning of the statute not only when an agency proposes to build a facility itself, but also whenever an agency makes a decision which permits action by other parties which will affect the quality of the environment. NEPA's impact statement procedure has been held to apply where a federal agency approves a lease of land to private parties, grants licenses and permits to private parties, or approves and funds state highway projects. In each of these instances the federal agency took action affecting the environment in the sense that the agency made a decision which permitted some other party—private or governmental—to take action affecting the environment. [Scientists' Inst. for Pub. Info., Inc. v. AEC (SIPI), 481 F.2d 1079, 1088-1089 (D.C. Cir. 1973).]

The "Small Handle" Problem. How strong must the federal link be? Cases raise what is known as the "small handle" problem when the federal link is not strong enough. In Winnebago Tribe v. Ray, 621 F.2d 269 (8th Cir. 1980), for example, a power company proposed to construct a 67-mile transmission line. The line required a permit from the U.S. Army Corps of Engineers for a 1.25-mile segment that crossed the Missouri River. An environmental assessment prepared by the Corps considered only the environmental impacts of the river crossing. The court rejected a "but for" argument by the tribe that NEPA applied to the entire transmission line because the line could not be constructed without the river-crossing permit. Contra: Colorado River Indian Tribes v. Marsh, 605 F. Supp. 1425 (C.D. Cal. 1985) (NEPA applied to 156-acre development project when the only federal action was a federal permit that was required for riprap to stabilize a riverbank). Is this case consistent with *Winnebago Tribe?*

State and local projects can also present this problem. In Maryland Conservation Council v. Gilchrist, 808 F.2d 1039 (4th Cir. 1986), the court held a state-funded highway project was federalized because federal approval was needed to allow the highway to cross a park. NEPA applied "[b]ecause of the inevitability of the need for at least one federal approval." Applying a narrower test, Southwest Williamson Cmty. Ass'n v. Slater, 243 F.3d 270 (6th Cir. 2001), found federal control insufficient when the federal agency had control over highway interchanges but not a connecting corridor. The court held the federal agency must be able to influence the outcome of a project through sufficient control and responsibility.

How important is it to extend NEPA to marginal situations? Is there a danger that the environmental mandate of the statute will be weakened through overextension? Consider, if you are inclined to narrow NEPA's reach, that a strict reading might exempt a series of small federal actions in a region even though their cumulative impact is significant. Does the policy underlying NEPA's enactment suggest a "cumulative federal impact" theory as the basis for applying the statute? Can this problem be handled by program impact statements, which are discussed below? See Fitzgerald, Comment, Small Handles, Big Impacts: When Should the National Environmental Policy Act Require an Environmental Impact Statement?, 23 B.C. Envtl. Aff. L. Rev. 437 (1996).

2. Is It a Federal "Action"?

The Proposal Requirement. Section 102(2)(C) of NEPA requires an impact statement on "every recommendation or report on proposals for . . . major federal actions." The Supreme Court has emphasized the "proposal" requirement: "The committee report [on NEPA] made clear that the impact statement was required in conjunction with specific proposals for action." Kleppe v. Sierra Club, 427 U.S. 390, 401 n.12 (1976). The questions are how specific a proposal must be, and when in the agency's decisionmaking process a proposal occurs that is subject to NEPA. CEQ has ambiguously defined a "proposal" as "that stage in the development of an action when an agency subject to the Act has a goal and is actively preparing to make a decision on one or more alternative means of accomplishing that goal and the effects can be meaningfully evaluated." 40 C.F.R. §1508.23. The *Kleppe* case, where the proposal requirement is discussed, is reproduced below.

Inaction. Whether an impact statement is required for federal agency inaction presents another controversial issue. Consider the following problem: though the states have primary authority for the management of wildlife on federal lands, the Department of the Interior "may" designate areas where no hunting is permitted. The state of Alaska decided to order a wolf kill in a substantial area of its federal lands. When requested to intervene, the Department refused to act and also refused to file an impact statement on its decision. Suit was then brought to require the preparation of an impact statement.

In Defenders of Wildlife v. Andrus, 627 F.2d 1238 (D.C. Cir. 1980), the court held the Department's failure to act was federal "inaction" for which an impact statement was not required. Because the federal statute did not compel the Department to act, the court believed it had no obligation to prepare an impact statement on its failure to act in a particular instance. As the court explained, "in no published opinion of which we have been made aware has a court held that there is 'federal action' where an agency has done nothing more than fail to prevent the other party's action from occurring." Id. at 1244. See also Drakes Bay Oyster Co. v. Jewell, 747 F.3d 1073 (9th Cir. 2014) (refusal to renew permit for commercial oyster farming). The inaction problem also arises when agencies are given statutory responsibilities they fail to carry out. In Norton v. Southern Utah Wilderness Alliance (SUWA), 542 U.S. 55 (2004), the Court held that NEPA does not apply to an agency's neglect of its statutory duties when such neglect is not a deliberate decision not to act. The Federal Land Policy and Management Act places a duty on the Secretary of Interior to manage federal lands identified as potential wilderness areas "so as not to impair the suitability of such areas for preservation as wilderness" while they are under review for designation and until Congress has determined otherwise. The Court held that an action for judicial review under the Administrative Procedure Act did not lie for the agency's failure to carry out its statutory mandate to preserve potential wilderness areas from impairment. Though the Act defines an agency action subject to judicial review to include a "failure to act," the Court held the agency's refusal to carry out this statutory mandate was not judicially reviewable. Judicial review would be available only when an agency refused to take an action it was required to take. *SUWA* may also reduce the number of cases in which NEPA applies. See Greater Yellowstone Coal. v. Tidwell, 572 F.3d 1115 (10th Cir. 2009) (failure to exercise discretion reserved in special use permit to revise conditions under which the state could use national forests as elk feed grounds).

How should these issues be resolved? Federal agencies necessarily engage in a decisionmaking process in which they decide whether to take or authorize action that may have an environmental impact. If an agency decides not to undertake or authorize a project, has it necessarily engaged in "inaction" not subject to NEPA? See Fergenson, The Sin of Omission: Inaction as Action under Section 102(2)(C) of the National Environmental Policy Act of 1969, 53 Ind. L.J. 497 (1978).

3. Is It a Major Federal Action Significantly Affecting the Environment?

An agency action does not fall under NEPA simply because it is federal. It must also be "major" and "significant." Under a dual standard, an action must meet both requirements. Under a unitary standard, an action is considered major if it is held to be significant. CEQ regulations adopt the unitary standard, and provide that the word "major" "reinforces but does not have a meaning independent of significant." 40 C.F.R. §1508.18. Whether an action is "major" has not received much attention in recent cases. However, see Florida Wildlife Fed'n v. United States Army Corps of Eng'rs, 401 F. Supp. 2d 1298 (S.D. Fla. 2005) (dredge and fill permit held to be major action).

The next step is to decide whether an agency action is significant. The "significance" requirement is critical. It imposes a threshold test of significant environmental impact that must be met before a federal agency is required to prepare an impact statement on a major federal action. As noted earlier, agencies usually prepare an environmental assessment in which they decide that their action will not have significant environmental effects. Objectors can then challenge this agency finding in court, claiming that an environmental impact statement should be prepared. A typical case follows:

OCEAN ADVOCATES v. UNITED STATES ARMY CORPS OF ENGINEERS
402 F.3d 846 (9th Cir. 2004)

D.W. Nelson, Senior Circuit Judge: . . .

Factual and Procedural Background

I. Cherry Point Marine Terminal

Cherry Point is an approximately ten-mile stretch of coastline located in the Strait of Georgia in northeast Puget Sound. It has been described as "a shoreline of statewide significance," by the Whatcom County Hearing Examiner.

BP first constructed a refinery to process Alaskan North Slope crude oil in Cherry Point, south of Point Whitehorn, in 1971. The 1969 permit authorizing this project allowed BP to construct a dock to which tankers would deliver crude oil. [This comment apparently refers to a permit issued under the Clean Water Act.] The dock design included two platforms: one for unloading crude oil and one for loading refined product. Just before construction began, BP opted to build only the southern platform and deferred building the northern platform until production at the refinery reached capacity or the loading and unloading of tankers began to interfere with refinery operations. Physical adjustments enabled the southern platform both to unload crude oil and to load refined product so that the dock could function as it would have with both platforms. . . . [BP submitted and then withdrew an application for an expansion permit in 1977.]

II. The Permit at Issue

BP again applied for a permit to build the northern platform in 1992. The additional platform would double the refinery's berthing capacity. The existing southern platform would cease to serve the dual functions of unloading crude oil and loading refined oil. Instead, the southern platform would only receive crude oil, while the northern addition would only load refined product.

The Corps provided public notice of the application on June 3, 1992, and received substantive responses from the U.S. Fish and Wildlife Service (FWS), the Lummi Indian Nation, and the Nooksack Indian Tribe.

The FWS raised concerns about the cumulative impact of the construction and operation of the pier when considered together with similar industrial projects in the Strait of Georgia. The FWS worried that the additional platform would facilitate an increase in tanker traffic and product handling, thereby increasing the likelihood of a major oil spill. Three years after the public notice, but before the permit was issued, the FWS requested an environmental impact statement (EIS) to assess increased traffic and the cumulative impact of the additional platform.

In response, BP insisted that the dock expansion would decrease the risk of oil spills because the new dock would reduce the amount of time tankers spent anchored at sea while waiting to dock. Therefore, BP argued, the additional dock would diminish the potential for oil spills "during anchorage and bunkering," when ships are most vulnerable. BP also noted that in the event of a spill, the new dock would contain "state of the art" oil spill containment equipment. . . .

Meanwhile, the marbled murrelet was listed as a threatened species under the Endangered Species Act, 16 U.S.C. §§1531-44. See 50 C.F.R. §17.11 (2002). The Corps accordingly asked BP to consider how the dock addition would affect this bird. BP concluded that although "marbled murrelet[s] are susceptible to death or injury from oil spills" and although "oil spills are chance events that could have an impact on local populations of murrelets near Cherry Point," an oil spill containment boom made that already "remote" threat "negligible."

The Corps granted the permit on March 1, 1996, concluding that constructing the northern platform probably would not result in adverse cumulative impacts to fish and wildlife resources in the Cherry Point area. The Corps also agreed with BP that the project would reduce the chance of oil spills while ships anchored because the pier extension would decrease tanker wait time. Moreover, the Corps found that the additional pier likely would diminish the devastation associated with an oil spill during bunkering of tankers at dock because oil spill containment booms would surround the new platform. The Corps also made a Finding of No Significant Impact (FONSI), determining that the pier addition "will not significantly affect the quality of the human environment," and that an EIS therefore was not required.

OA contacted the Corps on October 9, 1997, asking it to reopen the permit granted BP and requesting a more complete evaluation of the cumulative impacts that the new platform would have on vessel traffic safety. . . . The Corps declined to reopen or reconsider the permit.

In July 1999, the Washington State Department of Natural Resources (WSDNR) issued a Screening Level Ecological Risk Assessment (SLERA). This report concluded that additional ship traffic associated with the expanded pier would elevate the probability of an oil spill. Although the reduction in temporary anchoring while waiting to dock would decrease the chance of an oil spill, the SLERA noted that the number of vessels using the pier would increase eighteen to thirty-six percent over five years, which would increase the likelihood of an oil spill. This increase in ship traffic would occur, according to the SLERA, whether or not BP built the pier extension.

OA contacted the Corps on September 29, 1999, and again asked it to reconsider the permit. OA argued that the Corps' previous denial of its request to reopen the permit relied on inaccurate information, including that the refinery was operating "at capacity." New data demonstrated that the refinery had increased its output and that the project would promote additional tanker traffic and an increased potential for an oil spill. For these reasons, OA . . . requested a "full" EIS.

The Corps asked BP to address OA's concerns. BP continued to allege that the dock extension would benefit the environment by reducing the risk of oil spills; any further environmental analysis was unnecessary. . . .

III. BP's REQUEST FOR A PERMIT EXTENSION

[The Corps granted the extension and again determined that an EIS was not necessary.]

IV. THE DISTRICT COURT'S DECISION

OA brought this action against the Corps on November 21, 2000. The district court allowed BP to intervene as a defendant, and the parties filed cross-motions for summary judgment. The district court granted summary judgment for the Corps and BP as to OA's environmental claims. In doing so, the court found that NEPA did not require an EIS because the pier extension was intended to alleviate existing tanker traffic and because tanker traffic would increase with or without the dock extension. . . .

Standard of Review

We review de novo the district court's grant of summary judgment. We "must determine, viewing the evidence in the light most favorable to the nonmoving party, whether the district court correctly applied the relevant substantive law and whether there are any genuine issues of material fact." Balint v. Carson City, 180 F.3d 1047, 1050 (9th Cir. 1999) (en banc).

The Administrative Procedure Act (APA) governs our review of the Corps' action, conclusions, and findings of fact. Section 10(a), 5 U.S.C. §702, sets out the standard for judicial review of decisions involving NEPA. . . . We must set aside the Corps' actions, findings, or conclusions if they are "arbitrary, capricious, an abuse of discretion, or otherwise not in accordance with law." 5 U.S.C. §706(2)(A).

This review is "searching and careful," but the arbitrary and capricious standard is narrow, and we cannot substitute our own judgment for that of the Corps. Citizens to Preserve Overton Park, Inc. v. Volpe, 401 U.S 402 (1971). We ask "whether the [Corps'] decision was based on a consideration of the relevant factors and whether there has been a clear error of judgment." *Citizens to Preserve Overton Park*, [id.] at 416. We also "must determine whether the [Corps] articulated a rational connection between the facts found and the choice made." Ariz. Cattle Growers' Ass'n v. United States Fish & Wildlife Serv., 273 F.3d 1229, 1236 (9th Cir. 2001). Our review "must not 'rubber-stamp' . . . administrative decisions that [we] deem inconsistent with a statutory mandate or that frustrate the congressional policy underlying a statute." Id.

Discussion

I. STANDING

[The court found that Ocean Advocates had standing.]

II. LACHES

[The court dismissed a claim of laches.]

III. NEPA

OA challenges the Corps' failure to prepare an EIS prior to granting BP's permit application and permit extension application.

The relevant provision of NEPA provides that "all agencies of the Federal Government shall . . . include in every recommendation or report on . . . major Federal actions significantly affecting the quality of the human environment, a detailed statement by the responsible official." 42 U.S.C. §4332(2)(C). This report, or EIS, considers the environmental impact of the proposed project.

Not every project necessitates an EIS. Where an EIS is not categorically required, the agency must prepare an Environmental Assessment to determine whether the environmental impact is significant enough to warrant an EIS. 40 C.F.R. §§1501.3, 1508.9. If the action will significantly affect the environment, an EIS must be prepared, while if the project will have only an insignificant effect, the agency issues a FONSI. 40 C.F.R. §§1501.3, 1501.4.

NEPA aims to establish procedural mechanisms that compel agencies, such as the Corps, to take seriously the potential environmental consequences of a proposed action. We have termed this crucial evaluation a "hard look." The Corps cannot avoid preparing an EIS by making conclusory assertions that an activity will have only an insignificant impact on the environment. If an agency, such as the Corps, opts not to prepare an EIS, it must put forth a "convincing statement of reasons" that explain why the project will impact the environment no more than insignificantly. Blue Mountains

Biodiversity Project v. Blackwood, 161 F.3d 1208, 1212 (9th Cir. 1998). This account proves crucial to evaluating whether the Corps took the requisite "hard look" at the potential impact of the dock extension. Id.

"An EIS must be prepared if 'substantial questions are raised as to whether a project . . . may cause significant degradation of some human environmental factor.'" Idaho Sporting Cong. v. Thomas, 137 F.3d 1146, 1149 (9th Cir. 1998). "To trigger this requirement a 'plaintiff need not show that significant effects will in fact occur,' [but] raising 'substantial questions whether a project may have a significant effect' is sufficient." Id. at 1150.

The Council on Environmental Quality has adopted regulations governing the implementation of NEPA. In determining whether a federal action requires an EIS because it significantly affects the quality of the human environment, an agency must consider what "significantly" means. The regulations give it two components: context and intensity. 40 C.F.R. §1508.27. Context refers to the setting in which the proposed action takes place, in this case Cherry Point. See id. §1508.27(a). Intensity means "the severity of the impact." Id. §1508.27(b).

In considering the severity of the potential environmental impact, a reviewing agency may consider up to ten factors that help inform the "significance" of a project, such as the unique characteristics of the geographic area, including proximity to an ecologically sensitive area; whether the action bears some relationship to other actions with individually insignificant but cumulatively significant impacts; the level of uncertainty of the risk and to what degree it involves unique or unknown risks; and whether the action threatens violation of an environmental law. Id. §508.27(b)(3), (5), (7), (10). We have held that one of these factors may be sufficient to require preparation of an EIS in appropriate circumstances. See Nat'l Parks & Conservation Ass'n v. Babbit, 241 F.3d 722, 731 (9th Cir. 2001).

The Corps has failed to provide the requisite convincing statement of reasons explaining why the dock extension would have only a negligible impact on the environment and therefore has left us unpersuaded that it took a "hard look" at the environmental impact of the dock extension. Moreover, the permit necessitated an EIS because OA raised a substantial question as to whether the dock extension may cause significant degradation of the environment.

A. CONVINCING STATEMENT OF REASONS

In granting the 1996 permit, the Corps made a finding of no significant impact:

Performance of this work, in accordance with the standard conditions of the permit, will not significantly affect the quality of the human environment. Further, [the Corps has] determined that the issuance of this particular permit is a Federal action not having a significant impact on the environment. [The Corps has] thus concluded that the preparation of a formal Environmental Impact Statement is not required.

This finding fails to provide any reason, let alone a convincing one, why the Corps refrained from preparing an EIS. The only portion of the 1996 permit that might be considered a statement of reasons—if construed quite liberally—is the Corps' discussion of the FWS' concern about the cumulative impact of the pier extension. We conclude, however, that this neither qualifies as a statement of reasons nor convinces us that a comprehensive environmental impact report was unnecessary.

The Corps recounted the concerns that the FWS raised, namely increased tanker traffic that would raise the risk of an oil spill, and BP's response to those concerns in the text of the 1996 permit. The Corps then concluded:

> The new pier also should reduce the chance of oil spills during bunkering of tankers at dock, as the ships will be surrounded with containment booms while moored at the dock. The project will also reduce turnaround time for tankers at anchorage, thus reducing the chance for oil spills while at anchor. The Corps concludes that the proposed facility should result in a reduction in the chances for oil spills.

We find this determination unsatisfactory, even if it could be interpreted as a statement of reasons obviating the need for an EIS. First, the Corps never explicitly adopted the claim that the project could result in an increase in tanker traffic, leaving us to guess whether it took a hard look at, or even considered, this obvious potential impact. Second, the Corps notes in its summation of BP's arguments that the dock "will not lead to an increase in the [BP] refinery capacity, as the refinery is already working at maximum capacity." This statement cannot possibly qualify as a fully informed and well-reasoned basis for failing to give more careful attention to the potential for increased traffic. BP alleged that its refinery was operating "at capacity," but the Corps never explicitly adopted or relied on this contention, and OA later disproved this claim when it sought to reopen the permit. A patently inaccurate factual contention can never support an agency's determination that a project will have "no significant impact" on the environment. Third, the Corps relied wholly on BP's claims that the project would reduce oil spills because of containment booms and reduced anchoring time to conclude that the dock extension would decrease the potential for an oil spill. This claim alone, without a reasoned evaluation of the potential for increased traffic, which is at least in part due to the Corps' erroneous conclusion that the refinery was operating at full capacity, does not inspire any confidence that the Corps took the hard look that we require.

The permit extension granted in 2000 proves equally deficient. Again, the Corps made a finding of no significant impact:

> [The Corps has] determined that performance of the work, as revised and extended in accordance with the conditions of the permit, will not significantly affect the quality of the human environment. Further, [the Corps has] determined that the revision and extension of this particular permit is a Federal action not having a significant impact on the environment and thus [has] concluded that the preparation of a formal Environmental Impact Statement is not required.

Here, too, the Corps failed to provide any reason why an EIS was unnecessary. As before, even a generous reading of the rest of the permitting decision as a statement of reasons supporting the Corps' decision not to prepare an EIS, fails to convince us that the Corps took the obligatory hard look.

In discussing OA's concern that the project would have adverse cumulative effects on the Cherry Point area, the Corps reasoned:

> In the original permit review for the [BP] project, the Corps made a determination of no significant impact and determined that an EIS was not necessary. [The Corps has] again reviewed possible cumulative impacts of this project and again determined that an EIS is not necessary to review those cumulative impacts.

Before coming to this conclusion, the Corps cited to a Biological Evaluation (BE) that BP had prepared, which found that the dock extension would not increase vessel traffic, and a letter from BP stating that only market forces, and not the additional pier, would increase total vessel traffic. The permitting decision includes absolutely no discussion about the tenability or reasonableness of BP's self-serving claims that the dock extension would not increase vessel traffic. While the designation of Cherry Point as an aquatic reserve—an action that prohibited additional terminals in the area—necessarily reduces the future cumulative impact from all projects in the area, the Corps still failed to demonstrate in the 2000 permit extension that it critically evaluated the potential increase in tanker traffic from the dock extension alone. Common sense suggests that BP may have hoped that its sizable investment in the dock would facilitate its ability to handle a greater number of tankers a day, thereby increasing tanker traffic to the facility. The Corps' failure to look through BP's claims that it wanted only to increase its efficiency in handling existing congestion and its consequent failure to consider increased vessel traffic as a likely result of the project is unreasonable and insufficiently explained. Given evidence of increasing tanker traffic throughout the 1990s and BP's admission that demand for refined product may increase considerably, the Corps at a minimum should have analyzed and evaluated BP's claims that vessel traffic would not increase.

B. SUBSTANTIAL QUESTION AS TO A "SIGNIFICANT" IMPACT ON THE ENVIRONMENT

OA has raised a substantial question as to the dock extension's potential significant impact on the environment. As just discussed, the Corps did not consider the potential for increased tanker traffic when it granted the 1996 permit, other than to mention—erroneously—in its recitation of BP's contentions that the dock extension would not result in increased tanker traffic because the refinery was operating at maximum capacity. The 2000 permit extension decision did not revisit this omission, instead relying exclusively on BP's expedient assertion that the project would not increase tanker traffic.

Without even considering the factors outlined by the Council on Environmental Quality, OA has raised a substantial question about the intensity of the impact that increased tanker traffic would have on Puget Sound; in fact, the "severity of the impact" would be unquestionably severe. The Corps ignored record evidence that the dock could not handle much additional traffic. In its 1992 permit application, BP noted that the use of the pier increased incrementally since the mid-1980s and that the pier was operating at seventy-four percent of its capacity, a figure it termed "a very high utilization rate that is considered close to, if not maximum practical utilization." In addition, a report that BP commissioned from an outside consultant expected "marine traffic, especially tanker traffic" to increase upon project completion. Because the new platform would double the berthing capacity of the dock, this factor also would contribute to an increase in the number of vessels able to and actually accessing the refinery. When added to the other traffic demands on the Cherry Point area, the cumulation of tanker traffic may well have a significant impact on the environment, and OA has raised a substantial question about this effect.

We agree with the Corps and BP that market forces also would increase tanker traffic to the BP facility. The dock extension, however, also increases the facility's ability to handle increased tanker traffic. Were the dock extension never constructed,

BP could handle some additional tanker traffic caused by increasing market demands. With the dock extension, though, the BP facility can handle even greater increases in traffic, should market forces dictate such increases. Because a "reasonably close causal relationship" exists between the Corps' issuance of the permit, the environmental effect of increased vessel traffic, and the attendant increased risk of oil spills, the Corps had a duty to explore this relationship further in an EIS. Public Citizen v. Dep't of Transp., 541 U.S. 752 (2004) (quoting Metropolitan Edison Co. v. People Against Nuclear Energy, 460 U.S. 766, 774, (1983)).

Increased tanker traffic elevates the risk of oil spills—an undeniable and patently apparent risk of harm to Puget Sound. An oil spill could destroy and disrupt ecosystems and kill or injure critical numbers of threatened and endangered species that live, and thrive, in the Cherry Point Region. The Corps failed to appreciate that the permitted activity would lead to increased tanker traffic, an error about the fundamental nature and severity of the impact that the dock extension would have. The obvious severity of the impact that increased tanker traffic poses is enough to warrant reversal on OA's NEPA claim. . . .

i. Cumulatively Significant Impact

The impact of an action is severe "if it is reasonable to anticipate a cumulatively significant impact on the environment." 40 C.F.R. §1508.27(b)(7). . . . [The court found that cumulatively significant impacts could be anticipated.]

ii. Uncertainty

Where the environmental effects of a proposed action are highly uncertain or involve unique or unknown risks, an agency must prepare an EIS. 40 C.F.R. §1508.27(b)(5); *Nat'l Parks*, 241 F.3d at 731-32. "Preparation of an EIS is mandated where uncertainty may be resolved by further collection of data or where the collection of such data may prevent 'speculation on potential . . . effects. The purpose of an EIS is to obviate the need for speculation. . . .'" *Nat'l Parks*, 241 F.3d at 732.

The amount that tanker traffic might increase in relation to the dock extension was largely unknown. Presumably, data collection or projection analysis could have determined the likely increase in tanker traffic, considering market forces, the dock extension, and the cumulative impact of the existing and pending facilities in the area. No such analysis is evident in the EA, nor is there a "'justification regarding why more definitive information could not be provided.'" *Blue Mountains*, 161 F.3d at 1213. The Corps' "lack of knowledge does not excuse the preparation of an EIS; rather it requires [the Corps] to do the necessary work to obtain it." *Nat'l Parks*, 241 F.3d at 733. Concluding that a general risk, but not one attendant to the pier, exists, does not qualify as a hard look that would allow the Corps to skirt preparing an EIS. . . .

The Corps' position was based entirely on BP's unsupported assertions, and the record reflects no convincing reason for the Corps' decision. The Corps should have realized that uncertainty surrounded the potential for increased traffic based on the undetermined additional berthing capacity at the BP refinery, the magnitude of this change and its relationship to the increased risk of oil spills, and unknown, long-term projections for increased traffic and the risk of an oil spill. OA has raised a substantial question about these uncertainties, and the Corps acted arbitrarily and capriciously in failing to gather this quantifiable data. . . .

NOTES AND QUESTIONS

1. *Beating the Odds.* What decided the principal case? The court considered a marginal addition to an existing facility, thus raising the question of how NEPA applies to incremental actions. The case also involved a project by a private entity. The federal permit federalized the project for NEPA purposes. This link is not uncommon, but raised questions concerning the relationship of BP with the federal agency. Did the Corps simply rubber-stamp what BP told it? Why didn't the decline in offshore standbys and the inclusion of a containment boom support a finding of no significant impact despite the increase in traffic? Alternatively, was the EA inadequate because the Corps simply refused to consider the effects of an increase in traffic? Was the EA conclusory? The case also raises a baseline problem. Did the court implicitly accept a baseline from which it measured the environmental impacts of the dock extension? If so, what was it? Was this a natural or an urban environment? See Hanly v. Mitchell, 460 F.2d 640, 647 (2d Cir. 1972) (*Hanly I*) (NEPA "must be construed to include protection of the quality of life for city residents").

Idaho Sporting Cong. v. Thomas, 137 F.3d 1146 (9th Cir. 1998), a timber sale case, shows how a court can require an impact statement when environmental impacts are considered but there are omissions in the EA analysis. It agreed with the plaintiff "that an EIS is necessary because there are substantial questions as to whether the timber sales will have a significant effect on the water quality of" two creeks, and that the report on which the EA relied "failed to conduct standard factual and scientific site specific analysis, and failed to provide the analytical data necessary for any public challenge to the proposed sale." The agency was not entitled to rely solely on expert opinion without hard data.

The cumulative impact issue, and the duty to consider indirect impacts and project alternatives, also arise in the preparation of an EIS. These issues are considered later in connection with EIS questions.

2. *Winning and Losing.* A count of the cases indicates federal agencies are more likely to win than lose a case challenging a finding of no significance, despite the importance of the threshold decision. In fact, CEQ statistics show that the government wins in about 68 percent of all NEPA cases. Typically, when an agency conducts a comprehensive study and fully considers all of the environmental impacts, a court will uphold an EA. For example, in Earth Protector, Inc. v. Jacobs, 993 F. Supp. 701 (D. Minn. 2001), the court held an EIS was not necessary on a timber sale in a national forest and stressed the importance of comprehensive study:

> The administrative record of the Forest Service's decisionmaking process is voluminous. The process involved consultation with over 20 experts in various fields. The final EA demonstrates that the interdisciplinary team conducting the Environmental Assessment considered each of the concerns and values plaintiff raises before the Court, as well as many others, in a comprehensive and thorough manner. [Id. at 707.]

What was different in the principal case? See also Spiller v. White, 352 F.3d 235 (5th Cir. 2003), upholding the adequacy of a 2,400-page environmental assessment.

3. *The Standard of Judicial Review.* The principal case applied the arbitrary and capricious standard of judicial review for the significance decision, adopted in

Marsh v. Oregon Natural Res. Council, 490 U.S. 360 (1989), that settled a split in the circuits. The Court held this standard applied to an Army Corps of Engineers' decision that a supplemental impact statement was not necessary on a proposed Elk Creek dam in the Rogue River Basin in southwest Oregon. It noted that the decision on whether to prepare a supplemental impact statement was similar to the decision on whether to prepare an impact statement in the first instance. Courts thus apply the arbitrary and capricious standard adopted in *Marsh* to agency decisions that an EIS is not required.

The Court held the arbitrary and capricious standard that requires deference to agency decisions was the appropriate judicial review standard because the significance decision "in this case is a classic example of a factual dispute." The dispute turned on whether new information undermined the conclusions contained in the impact statement, whether the information was accurate, and whether the review of the information by the agency's experts was incomplete, inconclusive, or inaccurate. Because the analysis of the relevant documents required a high level of expertise, the Court deferred to and upheld the agency's decision that a supplemental impact statement was not necessary.

The Court quoted and reaffirmed language from its *Overton Park* decision that judicial review must be searching and careful, but that the ultimate standard of review is narrow. When specialists express conflicting views, the Court noted, the agency must have discretion to rely on the "reasonable opinions of its own qualified experts" even if a court might find contrary views more persuasive as an original matter. Yet the Court added language that appeared to confirm the "hard look" doctrine. It held that courts "should not automatically defer" to agency decisions without reviewing the record and deciding whether the agency had made a reasoned decision. "A contrary approach would not simply render judicial review generally meaningless, but would be contrary to the demand that courts ensure that agency decisions are founded on a reasoned evaluation 'of the relevant factors.'" 490 U.S. at 378. The court in the principal case also relied on the hard look doctrine. Does its decision square with the standard of judicial review as explained in *Marsh*?

Judicial review is complicated in NEPA cases because a district court proceeding intervenes between an agency's decision not to file an impact statement and an appeal to a court of appeals. As one court of appeals pointed out, it is not clear whether it is to review the agency's decision on the basis of the administrative record or to review the district court's decision under the usual "clearly erroneous" test. Sierra Club v. Marsh, 769 F.2d 868 (1st Cir. 1985). The court's pragmatic answer was to defer to district court findings of fact but to review more vigorously the district court's review of the agency's administrative record.

4. *Tests for Deciding Significance*. The courts have also adopted tests to determine whether the environmental impact of an action is significant. The Ninth Circuit held in the principal case that an "[a]n EIS must be prepared if 'substantial questions are raised as to whether a project . . . may cause significant degradation of some human environmental factor.'" It also held it is not necessary to show that significant effects will occur. Some circuits refer to this test as a "substantial possibility" test. City of Waltham v. United States Postal Serv., 11 F.3d 235, 240 (1st Cir. 1993). Other circuits require more. Greater Yellowstone Coal. v. Flowers, 359 F.3d 1257 (10th Cir. 2004) (clear error of judgment test).

5. *The Mitigated FONSI.* Though not attempted in the principal case, the mitigated FONSI is a common and frequently used strategy to claim that an action or project will not have a significant environmental impact, though not all agencies use this term. In the principal case, for example, the agency could have formally adopted a plan in which it agreed to mitigate impacts by providing the containment boom and reducing offshore standbys.

CEQ regulations authorize mitigation measures for impact statements and do not authorize mitigated FONSIs, but CEQ indicated in a guidance document that federal agencies can include enforceable mitigation measures when they conclude an action is not significant. Council on Environmental Quality, "Forty Most Asked Questions Concerning CEQ's National Environmental Policy Act Regulations," Question 39, 46 Fed. Reg. 18,026, 18,037 (1981). An agency that prepares a FONSI can adopt mitigation measures as enforceable permit conditions or as part of its final decision.

The courts have approved the use of mitigation measures to support FONSIs. In Cabinet Mountains Wilderness/Scotchman's Peak Grizzly Bears v. Peterson, 685 F.2d 678 (D.C. Cir. 1982), a case considering the effect of exploratory mining on grizzly bears, the court held that mitigation measures can "compensate completely" for any adverse effects of the proposal. An EA does not require as full and "reasonably complete" discussion of mitigation measures as is required in an impact statement, however. Akiak Native Cmty. v. United States Postal Serv., 213 F.3d 1140 (9th Cir. 2000). Nevertheless, a court must consider whether mitigation measures are an adequate buffer against negative impacts, and must decide whether they make these impacts so minor that an impact statement is not required. National Parks & Conservation Ass'n v. Babbitt, 241 F.3d 722 (9th Cir. 2001) (citing cases). The mere listing of mitigation measures without any analytical data is not enough. Klamath-Siskiyou Wildlands Ctr. v. United States Forest Serv., 373 F. Supp. 2d 1069 (D. Cal. 2004). Spiller v. White, *supra*, is a case where the court held that specific mitigation measures, described in detail in the EA, lowered the identified risk to acceptable levels. Could mitigation measures in the principal case have made a difference? See generally Herson, Project Mitigation Revisited: Most Courts Approve Findings of No Significant Impact Justified by Mitigation, 13 Ecology L.Q. 51 (1986) (noting that courts have usually imposed a heavy burden on agencies to show that environmental impacts have been mitigated).

CEQ has published a guidance on mitigation, Appropriate Use of Mitigation and Monitoring and Clarifying the Appropriate Use of Mitigated Findings of No Significant Impact (2011). The Guidance recommends that mitigation measures be clearly described, actually implemented, and monitored.

6. *Uncertainty.* As the principal case indicates, CEQ regulations state that an agency must prepare an EIS if environmental impacts are uncertain. National Parks & Conservation Ass'n v. Babbitt, cited there, is a leading decision. The agency was uncertain about the environmental impacts of an increase in the number of ships allowed in Glacier Bay in Alaska. The court held the "[p]reparation of an EIS is mandated where uncertainty may be resolved by further collection of data." For discussion, see Snowden, Judicial Review and Environmental Analysis under NEPA: "Timing Is Everything," 33 Envt. L. Rep. 10050 (2002). May an agency then refuse to discuss, an uncertain impact in an EIS? Uncertainty problems in impact statements are covered by a regulation on how to handle incomplete and unavailable information. See section D.2, *infra*.

7. *Commenting.* The agency appeared to have received comments in the principal case, but the commenting process was not detailed. NEPA has minimal statutory requirements for public participation, which is an essential part of the NEPA process, and CEQ regulations give them more content. For environmental assessments they state that "[t]he agency shall involve environmental agencies, applicants, and the public, to the extent practicable, in preparing assessments," 40 C.F.R. §1501.4(b). They also state that an agency shall make a FONSI available for public review "30 days before the agency makes its final determination whether to prepare an environmental impact statement and before the action may begin . . . [when] (i) [t]he proposed action is, or is closely similar to, one which normally requires the preparation of an environmental impact statement . . . , or (ii) [t]he nature of the proposed action is one without precedent." Id. §1501.4(e)(2). The regulations do not require public participation in every case, and a number of courts have not required circulation of an EA for public comment. E.g., Alliance to Protect Nantucket Sound v. United States Dep't of the Army, 398 F.3d 105 (1st Cir. 2005). Other courts have relied on more general CEQ regulations to require agencies to provide notice of and solicit comments on environmental assessments. These include a requirement that agencies shall make "diligent efforts to involve the public in preparing and implementing their NEPA procedures." 40 C.F.R. §1506.6(a). See Western Watersheds Project v. Bennett, 392 F. Supp. 2d 1217 (D. Idaho 2005).

The Ninth Circuit adopted a middle position. Bering Strait Citizens for Responsible Res. Dev. v. United States Army Corp of Eng'rs, 524 F.3d 938 (9th Cir. 2008). The court held that "[a]n agency, when preparing an [environmental assessment], must provide the public with sufficient environmental information, considered in the totality of circumstances, to permit members of the public to weigh in with their views and thus inform the agency decision-making process." Id. at 953. See NEPA Law, §7:14.20. Should the extensive use of mitigated FONSIs require a more robust public participation process?

NOTE ON ENVIRONMENTAL EFFECTS AND OTHER ISSUES THAT MUST BE CONSIDERED IN MAKING THE SIGNIFICANCE DECISION

Controversial Actions. As the principal case indicates, CEQ regulations require agencies to consider the intensity and severity of environmental impacts when they make a significance decision. CEQ regulations also state, in a provision not involved in the principal case, that agencies should consider "[t]he degree to which the effects on the quality of the human environment are likely to be highly controversial" when evaluating the intensity of environmental impacts to decide whether they are significant. 40 C.F.R. §1508.27(b)(4). This regulation introduces the degree of public opposition into the consideration of significance, and does not quite square with NEPA's direction that it is the effect of an action on the quality of the human environment that must be considered. An early decision put an interpretive gloss on the controversial action requirement that has generally been accepted:

[T]he term "controversial" apparently refers to cases where a substantial dispute exists as to the size, nature or effect of the major federal action rather than to the existence of opposition to a use, the effect of which is relatively undisputed. . . . The suggestion that "controversial" must be equated with neighborhood opposition has also been rejected by others. [Hanly v. Kleindienst (*Hanly II*), 471 F.2d 823, 830 (2d Cir. 1972).]

Mere opposition to or disagreement about a project is not enough. Nor is an action controversial if an agency makes a good faith effort to satisfy the concerns of commentators on an EA by answering all comments and by making modifications in its proposal. Foundation for N. Am. Wild Sheep v. United States Dep't of Agric., 681 F.2d 1172 (9th Cir. 1982), is a leading case that establishes what is required to make an action controversial. The Forest Service did not prepare an EIS on a permit to reopen a road for mining operations in a national forest, though the Foundation claimed it would have an adverse effect on the habitat of one of the few remaining herds of desert bighorn sheep. Numerous responses from conservationists, biologists, and state agencies disagreed with the decision not to prepare an impact statement. The court believed "that this is precisely the type of 'controversial' action for which an . . . [impact statement] must be prepared." How should the line be drawn?

Greenhouse Gases and Climate Change. Climate change issues raise new problems for NEPA, because the impact an action has in aggravating climate change problems arguably is an environmental impact that environmental assessments and impact statements must consider. This issue can arise, for example, in highway projects that increase motor vehicle traffic and with it an increase in the greenhouse gases that create the climate change problem. NEPA may not be implicated because the link between the agency action and climate change may be too tenuous, but Center for Biological Diversity v. National Highway Traffic Safety Admin., 538 F.3d 1172 (9th Cir. 2008), held the agency violated NEPA by failing to consider in its environmental assessment the impact of a rule revising Corporate Fuel Economy (CAFE) standards on greenhouse gas emissions:

> Moreover, the CAFE standard will affect the level of the nation's greenhouse gas emissions and impact global warming. . . . NHTSA does not dispute that light trucks account for a significant percentage of the U.S. transportation sector, that the U.S. transportation sector accounts for about six percent of the world's greenhouse gases, and that "fuel economy improvements could have a significant impact on the rate of CO_2 accumulation in the atmosphere," which would affect climate change. [Id. at 1213.]

The court also held the environmental assessment was inadequate:

> While the EA quantifies the expected amount of CO_2 emitted from light trucks MYs 2005-2011, it does not evaluate the "incremental impact" that these emissions will have on climate change or on the environment more generally in light of other past, present, and reasonably foreseeable actions such as other light truck and passenger automobile CAFE standards. [Id.]

Other courts have not required discussion of global warming in environmental assessments for small-scale projects, where the effects on global warming would not be significant. Hapner v. Tidwell, 621 F.3d 1239 (9th Cir. 2010) (thinning of small amount of forestland). Should consideration of climate change be governed by a *de minimis* rule?

CEQ proposed but then revoked a guidance on the consideration of climate change in NEPA reviews. See also McAliley, NEPA and Assessment of Greenhouse Gas Emissions, 41 Envtl. L. Rptr. 10197 (2011). Climate change issues, including the role of NEPA, are discussed in Chapter 12.

Terrorist Risks. The cases are divided on whether a risk of terrorist attacks is an environmental impact that must be considered in NEPA reviews. Considering terrorist risks is problematic because the risk is created by an intervening third party, not the agency undertaking the action. NEPA does not cover speculative impacts or risks, and most courts have held that terrorist risks are speculative risks that are not covered. See City of New York v. United States Dep't of Transp., 715 F.2d 732 (2d Cir. 1982) (threat of sabotage to interstate shipments of radioactive materials held an unascertainable and remote risk; court deferred to agency's decision to adopt Nuclear Regulatory Commission security requirements); NEPA Law, §8:47.20.

San Luis Obispo Mothers for Peace v. Nuclear Regulatory Comm'n, 449 F.3d 1016 (9th Cir. 2006), held differently. The court held the risk of terrorism had to be considered in the licensing of an interim spent fuel storage site at a nuclear power plant. It found there was a causal relationship between the licensing decision and the risk of terrorism, that the probability of a terrorist attack need not be numerically quantifiable, and that there was "no support for the use of security concerns as an excuse from NEPA's compliance." On remand, the court found no significant impact on the environment. 653 F.3d 1109 (9th Cir. 2011). A later case, New Jersey Dep't of Envtl. Prot. v. United States Nuclear Regulatory Comm'n, 561 F.3d 132 (3d Cir. 2009), disagreed. The question was whether NEPA applied to the Nuclear Regulatory Commission's relicensing of a nuclear power plant that could aggravate the risk of a potential aircraft attack by terrorists on the plant. The court could not find a reasonably close causal relationship between the relicensing and the potential attack. It distinguished *San Luis Obispo* because that case involved the construction of a new facility, a change in the physical environment with a closer causal relationship to a potential terrorist attack.

Causation. The terrorist risk cases raised a causation problem, an issue considered in *Ocean Advocates*: what link must be shown between an agency action and the environmental effect that is claimed to fall under NEPA? In Metropolitan Edison Co. v. People Against Nuclear Energy (PANE), 460 U.S. 766 (1983), the Nuclear Regulatory Commission (NRC) authorized a restart of TMI-1, one of the nuclear reactors located on the site of the earlier and catastrophic Three Mile Island accident, but not the reactor that failed. PANE was an association of residents in the area who opposed the operation of either reactor. It claimed NEPA required NRC to consider the "severe psychological health damage to persons living in the vicinity" that would be caused by a restart of TMI-1, because the restart would remind residents of the nuclear accident and would raise the possibility that an accident could happen again. The Court disagreed, holding that NEPA was limited to impacts on the physical environment, and that the statute should "be read to include a requirement of a reasonably close causal relationship between a change in the physical environment and the effect at issue." The Court also suggested that PANE's objections reflected a "policy disagreement" best resolved in the political process. Justice Brennan, concurring, distinguished cases in which a psychological injury arose "out of the direct sensory change in the environment." See Glass Packaging Inst. v. Regan, 737 F.2d 1083 (D.C. Cir. 1984) (NEPA does not cover environmental effects caused by criminal acts of third parties).

The Supreme Court in *Public Citizen*, discussed *supra*, read *PANE* to mean a "but for" causal relationship is not sufficient to bring an action under NEPA, and held that the "rule of reason" inherent in NEPA likewise made this clear. Most cases, like

Ocean Advocates, have not applied *Public Citizen* to find a lack of causation that bars the application of NEPA. See NEPA Law, §8:38.

   Effect of Other Statutes. As *Ocean Advocates* indicates, NEPA applies to decisions and actions taken under other statutes, in that case a permit granted under the Clean Water Act. An agency must comply with NEPA even if it has complied with its own statute. For example, an action can have a significant effect on the environment even though the continued existence of an endangered species is not jeopardized within the meaning of the Endangered Species Act. Greater Yellowstone Coal. v. Flowers, 359 F.3d 1257 (10th Cir. 2004).

D. IF AN IMPACT STATEMENT MUST BE PREPARED, HOW IS IT DONE, AND WHAT IS ITS SCOPE?

   When a federal agency decides or has been ordered by a court to prepare an impact statement, the next step is to determine its scope. This problem has several dimensions. One concerns the range of alternatives an agency must take into account. NEPA requires the consideration of "alternatives" to a proposed action, a requirement that compels agencies to consider options to their proposal they would not otherwise consider. There is also a physical dimension. Agencies may divide proposed projects into more than one segment, so they can minimize consideration of the environmental impacts by analyzing a project one part at a time. An example is a highway project that is divided into several parts. The question is whether this kind of segmentation is allowable under NEPA.

   Actions and projects that agencies consider may also be interrelated. A federal agency, for example, may authorize coal-mining leases throughout a large area of public land. May the agency then prepare an impact statement on each lease separately, or must it prepare an impact statement on all of the leases as a single group? Another option in this situation is a program impact statement that can evaluate entire programs for their environmental impact before individual project decisions are made. The materials that follow first discuss the procedures through which an impact statement is prepared, and then consider questions concerning scope.

1. How Environmental Impact Statements Are Prepared

   If an agency decides to prepare an impact statement, it must first file a Notice of Intent (NOI) in the Federal Register. 40 C.F.R. §1508.22. The NOI must briefly describe the proposed action, possible alternatives, and the proposed scoping process and provide the name of a lead agency contact. Figure 4-3 presents the basic EIS preparation process. The scoping process occurs next. Scoping determines the scope of the issues to be addressed in the impact statement and identifies the significant issues related to the proposed action. The process is to "eliminate from detailed study the issues which are not significant or which have been covered by prior environmental review." Id. §1501.7(a)(3).

After the agency completes the scoping process it prepares a draft environmental impact statement (DEIS) "in accordance with the scope decided upon in the scoping process." Id. §1502.09(a). NEPA requires an EIS to be circulated for comments, and CEQ has interpreted this requirement to apply to draft impact statements. The commenting process is an important part of NEPA's full disclosure requirement. The statute requires circulation for comment to federal, state, and local agencies, and CEQ has extended the comment requirement by requiring comments from any agency that has requested copies of the DEIS, from the applicant, from the public, and from "interested or affected" persons or organizations. Id. §1503.1(a). Additional consultation with the federal wildlife agencies is required by the Fish and Wildlife Coordination Act, 16 U.S.C. §662(a).

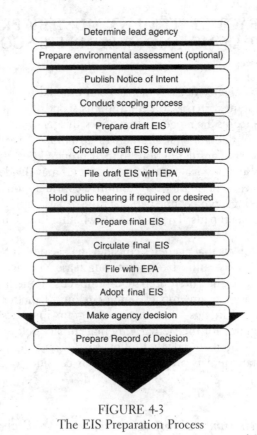

FIGURE 4-3
The EIS Preparation Process

Owen L. Schmidt, NEPA Models and Case Lists (3d ed. 2009), p.18. Reprinted with permission of Owen L. Schmidt. Copyright © 2009.

The agency then prepares a final impact statement (FEIS), in which it must respond to comments on the draft statement. The final impact statement must respond to comments in the following ways: modifying the proposed action or alternatives; proposing a new action or alternatives; developing or evaluating new alternatives; supplementing, modifying, or improving its analysis; making factual corrections; or explaining why the comments do not warrant further response. 40 C.F.R. §1503.4(a). The FEIS is circulated in the same manner as the draft EIS. If the agency prepares an impact statement it must also prepare a "concise public record of decision." Id. §1505.2. The record of decision must state what the decision was, discuss alternatives considered, and state whether "all practicable means" to avoid or minimize harm from the alternative selected have been adopted and if not, why not.

Agencies must prepare a supplemental environmental impact statement (SEIS) when "significant" new circumstances or information, or substantial changes, affect the proposed action or its environmental impact. Id. §1502.9(c). Scoping is not required if an agency decides to prepare a supplemental impact statement, but the statement is prepared, filed, and circulated in the same manner as a draft or final impact statement.

Go back and read the statute and notice how CEQ has extended the statutory requirements. Do you agree with the decisionmaking process CEQ has created? Note how many checkpoints there are in the system. What are they? Are there too many? Too few? Consider how the structure of this decisionmaking process affects the way in which NEPA's requirements are applied to agency actions. How are decisions made concerning the scope and content of impact statements? What is the balance between the role of commenting entities and the role of the agency? What recourse does a commenting entity have if its comments are ignored or pushed aside?

In 2012, CEQ issued a Memorandum for Heads of Federal Departments and Agencies in which its discussed ways for agencies to engage in efficient and timely conduct of their NEPA responsibilities. Memorandum for Heads of Federal Departments and Agencies from Nancy H. Sutley, on Improving the Process for Preparing Reviews under the National Environmental Policy Act (2012), available at http://www.whitehouse.gov/sites/default/files/microsites/ceq/nepa_improving_efficiencies_06mar2012.pdf. The guidance implements an executive order. See Improving Regulation and Regulatory Review, Exec. Order No. 13,563, 76 Fed. Reg. 3821 (2011), available at http://www.gpo.gov/fdsys/pkg/DCPD-201100031.pdf.

NOTES AND QUESTIONS

1. *Commenting.* The commenting process is an important element in the EIS process, and the courts have required compliance with commenting procedures. They have invalidated an impact statement, for example, when an agency modifies its project subsequent to the draft impact statement but does not amend the draft EIS to afford opportunity for comment. California v. Block, 690 F.2d 753 (9th Cir. 1982). The commenting procedure does not authorize a veto by the commenting agency. Sierra Club v. Callaway, 499 F.2d 982, 993 (5th Cir. 1974). Compare Warm Springs Dam Task Force v. Gribble, 565 F.2d 549, 554 (9th Cir. 1977): "[T]here is no requirement that the responsible agency alter its project or perform new studies in response to comments."

2. *EPA Review.* A potentially powerful requirement that can provide a supplementary environmental review is in §309 of the Clean Air Act, 42 U.S.C. §7609. It states that "[t]he Administrator [of EPA] shall review and comment in writing on the environmental impact of . . . any major Federal agency action (other than a project for construction) to which section 102(2)(C) of NEPA applies." In most cases, the normal NEPA commenting process is a substitute for a §309 intervention. EPA carries out its reviews under a 1984 Policy and Procedures for the Review of Federal Actions

Impacting the Environment that requires an evaluation of the draft EIS and the environmental merits of the action covered by the EIS. It includes Rating Systems Criteria under which EPA can decide whether EPA has no objections, has environmental concerns or objections, or finds the EIS unsatisfactory, a finding that is seldom made. The agency must take corrective steps if there are objections or concerns, and must not proceed if the EIS is unsatisfactory. EPA has published a number of Guidance documents for its reviews. See Sierra Club v. Morton, 379 F. Supp. 1254 (D. Colo. 1974) (reviewing legislative history of provision); Tzoumis & Finegold, Looking at the Quality of Draft Environmental Impact Statements over Time: Have the Ratings Improved?, 29 Envtl. Impact Assess. Rev. 527 (2000) (reviewing quality of EPA reviews over the years).

There is little authority on the legal effect of an unsatisfactory EPA review. Alaska v. Andrus, 580 F.2d 465 (D.C. Cir. 1978), suggested in dictum that an unsatisfactory review "did give rise to a heightened obligation on . . . [the agency's] part to explain clearly and in detail its reasons for proceeding," and that an agency that decides to proceed in the face of an unsatisfactory EPA determination "must articulate clearly its reasons for doing so." Is the agency obligation procedural or substantive? EPA must publish an unsatisfactory determination and refer it to CEQ.

3. *Delegation.* Federal agencies may delegate the preparation of an EIS. When this occurs there is a possibility for bias if the preparer is an applicant for a federal permit or would like to obtain work required by a project that is considered in an EIS. Do the following cases, regulations, and statutes adequately handle this problem?

Impact statements may not be prepared by applicants for a federal permit or other approval. Greene County Planning Bd. v. Federal Power Comm'n, 455 F.2d 412 (2d Cir. 1972), held an EIS was self-serving because it was prepared by an applicant that applied for a federal approval. However, an applicant may submit environmental information needed for an EIS as outlined by the agency, which must independently evaluate the information. Sierra Club v. Lynn, 502 F.2d 43 (5th Cir. 1974). See 40 C.F.R. §1506.5(a).

CEQ regulations authorize the delegation of impact statement preparation to contractors. 40 C.F.R. §1506.5(c). Contractors are to "avoid" conflicts of interest and submit a disclosure that they have no financial or other interest in the project. If a contractor prepares an EIS, the regulations require the federal agency to furnish guidance, participate in EIS preparation, evaluate the EIS independently, and take responsibility for its scope and content. See Associations Working for Aurora's Residential Env't v. Colorado Dep't of Transp., 153 F.3d 1122 (10th Cir. 1998) (federal oversight sufficient; contractor with enforceable promise or guarantee of work has conflict of interest, but contractor who merely has expectation does not).

Congress authorized a delegation of impact statement preparation under §104(g) of the Housing and Community Development Act of 1974, 42 U.S.C. §5304(g). The courts have interpreted this provision as only conferring procedural responsibilities on the federal Department of Housing and Urban Development. It is not required to independently review impact statements submitted by local governments or prepare its own impact statement. See Brandon v. Pierce, 725 F.2d 555 (10th Cir. 1984). There is also a provision in NEPA, §102(2)(D), that authorizes the delegation of impact statements on federally funded highways to state highway agencies. See Frank, Comment, Delegation of Environmental Impact Statement Preparation: A Critique of NEPA's Enforcement, 13 B.C. Envtl. Aff. L. Rev. 79 (1985).

4. *Lead and Cooperating Agencies.* In many cases in which NEPA applies, a single action or project may require approval from more than one agency. CEQ

regulations in this situation require the designation of a lead agency for NEPA compliance and provide a number of factors to be considered in the lead agency designation. 40 C.F.R. §1501.5. See National Wildlife Fed'n v. Benn, 491 F. Supp. 1234 (S.D.N.Y. 1980). Where both the Corps and EPA had jurisdiction over ocean dumping, the court held the Corps could prepare the impact statement either in conjunction with or with partial reliance on EPA reports.

CEQ regulations also provide a role for cooperating agencies when more than one agency has an interest in an action that requires environmental review. 40 C.F.R. §1501.6 (lead agency must request cooperation). The lead and cooperating agency requirement has problems. For example, a cooperating agency may proceed with its action before the lead agency prepares the impact statement, thus frustrating the environmental review process. See Upper Pecos Ass'n v. Stans, 452 F.2d 1233 (10th Cir. 1971), *vacated*, 409 U.S. 1021 (1972). Exclusion of a cooperating agency from the decisionmaking process can result in a violation of NEPA. E.g., Wyoming v. United States Dep't of Agric., 570 F. Supp. 2d 1309 (D. Wyo. 2008). The 2003 NEPA Task Force Report to CEQ, Modernizing NEPA Implementation, recommended methods to increase collaboration among agencies, including guidance suggesting the elements of successful collaborative agreements. Id. at 33. CEQ's concern about collaboration among agencies led it to issue a memorandum on this subject in 2004.

NOTE ON STATUTORY EXEMPTIONS FROM AND MODIFICATIONS OF NEPA

Though Congress sometimes makes NEPA explicitly applicable to an agency program, see Energy Security Act, 16 U.S.C. §2705(b), it has also granted full or partial exemption from NEPA in several statutes. For example, Congress overruled *Calvert Cliffs* by prohibiting federal agencies from requiring stricter pollution controls than required by established water quality standards under the Clean Water Act. Under §511(c)(1) of the Act, only certain limited actions by EPA are subject to NEPA, such as the dredge and fill permit required for development in wetlands. For an argument that Congress is weakening NEPA through exemptions, see Sher & Hunting, Eroding the Landscape, Eroding the Laws: Congressional Exemption from Judicial Review of Environmental Laws, 15 Harv. Envtl. L. Rev. 435 (1991).

Here is a selected list of statutes that contain full or partial exemptions from NEPA:

Deep Seabed Hard Mineral Resources Act: U.S.C. §1419(d)
Disaster Relief Act: 42 U.S.C. §5159
Endangered Species Act: 16 U.S.C. §1536(k)
Energy Supply and Environmental Coordination Act: 15 U.S.C §793(c)(2)
National Forest Management Act: 16 U.S.C. §544o(f)
Nuclear Waste Policy Act: 42 U.S.C. §10141(c)
Power Plant & Industrial Fuel Use Act: 42 U.S.C. §8473
Surface Mining Control & Reclamation Act: 30 U.S.C. §1292(d)

Other statutes have modified the environmental review process for important federal programs. Here are some examples:

Safe, Accountable, Flexible, Efficient Transportation Equity Act. Congress adopted this Act in 2005, Pub. L. No. 109-59, 119 Stat. 1144 (2005), and The Moving Ahead for Progress in the 21st Century Act [Map-21], 112 Pub. L. No. 141, 126 Stat. 405 (2012) (variously codified), substantially modify the application of NEPA to transportation projects by requiring a modified environmental review process. They require a coordination plan to guide the process, and assurances from participating agencies that environmental review decisions will be made on an established schedule. A failure to meet the schedule incurs fines. For highways, the Federal Highway Administration may convene a meeting to assure the project is on schedule, with later referrals to the Secretary of Transportation, CEQ, and the President if schedules are not met. The authority to make categorical exclusions is delegated to the states. Changes made in agency responsibilities to discuss alternatives are discussed later in this chapter. There is a six-month statute of limitations for judicial review running from the publication of a Federal Register notice announcing that a permit, license, or approval is final. These statutes build on an earlier executive streamlining order. For a similar recent order, see Presidential Memorandum, Modernizing Federal Infrastructure Review and Permitting Regulations, Policies, and Procedures (May 17, 2013), available at http://www.whitehouse.gov/the-press-office/2013/05/17/presidential-memorandum-modernizing-federal-infrastructure-review-and-pe.

Aviation Streamlining Approval Process Act of 2003. This Act, 49 U.S.C. §47171, requires the Secretary of Transportation to develop an "expedited and coordinated environmental review process for airport capacity enhancement projects." It requires that there be better coordination among governmental agencies, that all required environmental reviews be conducted concurrently, and that all required environmental reviews and approvals be completed in a time period specified by the Secretary. Environmental reviews in the streamlining process must be given high priority, and procedures for carrying out these reviews are specified. The Federal Aviation Administration as lead agency is "responsible for defining the scope and content of the environmental impact statement, consistent with regulations issued by the Council on Environmental Quality." See Berger, False Promises: NEPA's Role in Airport Expansions and the Streamlining of the Environmental Review Process, 18 J. Envt. L. & Litig. 279 (2003).

Healthy Forests Restoration Act of 2003. This statute, 42 U.S.C. §9607(f), expedites environmental reviews under NEPA for authorized hazardous fuel reduction projects in national forests, such as thinning, the establishment of strategic fuel breaks, and prescribed fires. The statute prescribes the alternatives that must be considered and contains requirements for public notice, public meeting, and public collaboration requirements. Judicial review is available only if administrative remedies are exhausted, and (with some exceptions) may only raise issues considered in a required predecisional administrative review process. Judicial review must be expeditious, and the time period for injunctions is limited. See Wildwest Inst. v. Bull, 472 F.3d 587, 589 (9th Cir. 2006) (upholding fuel reduction project under the Act).

Energy Policy Act of 2005. This Act, Pub. L. No. 109-54, 119 Stat. 594 (2005) (variously codified), enacted a number of modifications to NEPA as it applies to energy projects. It legislates a rebuttable presumption, 42 U.S.C. §15942, that a categorical exclusion is appropriate for activities carried out under the Mineral Leasing Act, 30 U.S.C. Ch. 3A, including surface disturbances of less than five acres but subject to certain limitations, such as a requirement that a site-specific analysis pursuant to NEPA must have been completed previously. A report by the Government Accountability Office found that the Bureau of Land Management had improperly used this statutory authority to grant categorical exclusions under the Act. Energy Policy Act of 2005: Greater Clarity Needed to Address Concerns with Categorical Exclusions for Gas Development under Section 309 of the Act (2009), available at www.gao.gov/products/GAO-09-812.

Other provisions authorize a Federal Permit Streamlining Pilot Project in designated western states. They authorize memoranda of understanding between the states and relevant federal agencies to designate corridors for oil, gas, and hydrogen pipelines and electricity transmission and distribution facilities. A similar program applies to environmental reviews relating to proposed or existing utility facilities on public lands. The Act amends the Mineral Leasing Act to provide deadlines on the consideration of permit applications.

Statutes modifying NEPA procedures for agency programs maintain NEPA's requirements, but modify compliance responsibilities by delegating them to agencies that have program responsibility for actions that are subject to NEPA. This modification is a statutory change that weakens the environmental responsibility that NEPA places on mission agencies, because the agency responsible for an action decides whether NEPA compliance has been achieved. This problem also arises under provisions that modify the consideration of alternatives, discussed later in this chapter. Streamlining NEPA procedures can weaken NEPA compliance by not providing enough time for environmental analysis.

2. The Alternatives Requirement

One of NEPA's major expectations was that federal agencies, directed by statute to carry out narrowly conceived missions, would consider alternatives they might not otherwise examine that were less environmentally damaging. Highway projects are a good example. The federal government funds state highways to meet expected highway needs. State transportation agencies may not select a location of a new highway with the least damaging environmental impacts, or may not consider alternatives, such as mass transit.

NEPA requires the consideration of alternatives, as the statute requires discussion of "alternatives to the proposed action." §102(2)(C)(iii). Both the courts and CEQ have characterized the alternatives requirement as the "heart" of the NEPA process. Another section of NEPA provides independently for the consideration of alternatives. It requires agencies of the federal government to "study, develop, and describe appropriate alternatives to recommended courses of action in any proposal which involves unresolved conflicts concerning alternative uses of available resources." §102(2)(E). This requirement applies even though an impact statement is not prepared.

Alternatives may be primary or secondary. A primary alternative is a substitute for agency action that accomplishes the action in another manner. Mass transit as an alternative for a highway is an example. Other alternatives would keep but modify the proposed action. These can be called secondary alternatives. Are agencies better equipped to evaluate primary or secondary alternatives? Which type of alternative is likely to lie outside the agency's jurisdiction to implement? Should this factor be considered by courts and agencies in the evaluation of alternatives?

The Court of Appeals for the District of Columbia Circuit expansively interpreted the alternatives requirement in an early leading case and required consideration of a primary alternative. NRDC v. Morton, 458 F.2d 827 (D.C. Cir. 1972). The Secretary of the Interior announced a general sale of oil and gas tract leases on the Outer Continental Shelf of eastern Louisiana, in response to an energy supply message by President Nixon. The impact statement prepared for the lease announcement stated the elimination of then-existing oil import quotas might be an alternative to offshore leasing, but required a consideration of complex factors, including national security, beyond the scope of the impact statement. The court disagreed. It stated that "[w]hen the proposed action is an integral part of a coordinated plan to deal with a broad problem, the range of alternatives that must be evaluated is broadened. While the Department of the Interior does not have the authority to eliminate or reduce oil import quotas, such action is within the purview of both Congress and the President, to whom the impact statement goes." Id. at 837. The court also held that an alternative is not automatically disqualified from consideration because it requires legislative change, but that discussion of alternatives "so remote from reality as to depend on, say, the repeal of the anti-trust laws" was not required. Id.

The Supreme Court had an opportunity to consider *Morton's* "reasonably available" rule in a nuclear power plant licensing case. The Court's decision follows:

VERMONT YANKEE NUCLEAR POWER CORP. v. NATURAL RESOURCES DEFENSE COUNCIL, INC.
435 U.S. 519 (1978)

Justice REHNQUIST delivered the opinion of the Court.

[The Court consolidated for review two decisions by the now-superseded Atomic Energy Commission. Commission licensing procedures at this time were as follows: The utility first filed a preliminary safety analysis report, an environmental report, and information on antitrust implications. This information was reviewed by Commission staff, the Advisory Committee on Reactor Safeguards (ACRS), and a group of atomic energy experts. Both the ACRS and the experts submitted their evaluations to the Commission. A NEPA review was carried out by Commission staff, which prepared a draft and final impact statement. A three-member Atomic Safety and Licensing Board then held a public adjudicatory hearing, with the option of appeal to an appeal board and, in the board's discretion, to the Commission. The final agency decision was appealable to the federal Court of Appeals. Generally, the same procedure applied for an application for a license to operate a nuclear power plant.]

I

. . .

C

In January 1969, petitioner Consumers Power Co. applied for a permit to construct two nuclear reactors in Midland, Mich. Consumers Power's application was examined by the Commission's staff and the ACRS. The ACRS issued reports which discussed specific problems and recommended solutions. It also made reference to "other problems" of a more generic nature and suggested that efforts should be made to resolve them with respect to these as well as all other projects. Two groups, one called Saginaw and another called Mapleton, intervened and opposed the application. Saginaw filed with the Board a number of environmental contentions, directed over 300 interrogatories to the ACRS, attempted to depose the chairman of the ACRS, and requested discovery of various ACRS documents. The Licensing Board denied the various discovery requests directed to the ACRS. Hearings were then held on numerous radiological health and safety issues. Thereafter, the Commission's staff issued a draft environmental impact statement. Saginaw submitted 119 environmental contentions which were both comments on the proposed draft statement and a statement of Saginaw's position in the upcoming hearings. The staff revised the statement and issued a final environmental statement in March 1972. Further hearings were then conducted during May and June 1972. Saginaw, however, choosing not to appear at or participate in these latter hearings, indicated that it had "no conventional findings of fact to set forth" and had not "chosen to search the record and respond to this proceeding by submitting citations of matters which we believe were proved or disproved." But the Licensing Board, recognizing its obligations to "independently consider the final balance among conflicting environmental factors in the record," nevertheless treated as contested those issues "as to which intervenors introduced affirmative evidence or engaged in substantial cross examination."

At issue now are 17 of those 119 contentions which are claimed to raise questions of "energy conservation." The Licensing Board indicated that as far as appeared from the record, the demand for the plant was made up of normal industrial and residential use. It went on to state that it was "beyond our province to inquire into whether the customary uses being made of electricity in our society are 'proper' or 'improper.'" With respect to claims that Consumers Power stimulated demand by its advertising the Licensing Board indicated that "[n]o evidence was offered on this point and absent some evidence that Applicant is creating abnormal demand, the Board did not consider the question." The Licensing Board also failed to consider the environmental effects of fuel reprocessing or disposal of radioactive wastes. The Appeal Board ultimately affirmed the Licensing Board's grant of a construction permit and the Commission declined to further review the matter.

At just about the same time, the Council on Environmental Quality revised its regulations governing the preparation of environmental impact statements. The regulations mentioned for the first time the necessity of considering in impact statements energy conservation as one of the alternatives to a proposed project. The new guidelines were to apply only to final impact statements filed after January 28, 1974. Thereafter, on November 6, 1973, more than a year after the record had been closed in the Consumers Power case and while that case was pending before the Court of Appeals, the Commission ruled in another case that while its statutory power to compel conservation was not clear, it did not follow that all evidence of energy conservation issues should therefore be barred at the threshold. In re Niagara Mohawk Power Corp., 6 A.E.C. 995 (1973). Saginaw then moved the Commission to clarify its ruling and reopen the Consumers Power proceedings.

In a lengthy opinion, the Commission declined to reopen the proceedings. The Commission first ruled it was required to consider only energy conservation alternatives which were "reasonably available," would in their aggregate effect curtail demand for electricity to a level at which the proposed facility would not be needed, and were susceptible of a reasonable degree of proof. It then determined, after a thorough examination of the record, that not all of Saginaw's contentions met these threshold tests. It further determined that the Board had been willing at all times to take evidence on the other contentions. Saginaw had simply failed to present any such evidence. The Commission further criticized Saginaw for its total disregard of even those minimal procedural formalities necessary to give the Board some idea of exactly what was at issue. The Commission emphasized that "[p]articularly in these circumstances, Saginaw's complaint that it was not granted a hearing on alleged energy conservation issues comes with ill grace." And in response to Saginaw's contention that regardless of whether it properly raised the issues, the Licensing Board must consider all environmental issues, the Commission basically agreed, as did the Board itself, but further reasoned that the Board must have some workable procedural rules and these rules

> in this setting must take into account that energy conservation is a novel and evolving concept. NEPA "does not require a 'crystal ball' inquiry." Natural Resources Defense Council v. Morton, 458 F.2d 827, 837 (1972). This consideration has led us to hold that we will not apply *Niagara* retroactively. As we gain experience on a case-by-case basis and hopefully, feasible energy conservation techniques emerge, the applicant, staff, and licensing boards will have obligations to develop an adequate record on these issues in appropriate cases, whether or not they are raised by intervenors.
>
> However, at this emergent stage of energy conservation principles, intervenors also have their responsibilities. They must state clear and reasonably specific energy conservation contentions in a timely fashion. Beyond that, they have a burden of coming forward with some affirmative showing if they wish to have these novel contentions explored further.

Respondents then challenged the granting of the construction permit in the Court of Appeals for the District of Columbia Circuit. . . .

We now turn to the Court of Appeals' holding "that rejection of energy conservation on the basis of the 'threshold test' was capricious and arbitrary," and again conclude the court was wrong.

The Court of Appeals ruled that the Commission's "threshold test" for the presentation of energy conservation contentions was inconsistent with NEPA's basic mandate to the Commission. The Commission, the court reasoned, is something more than an umpire who sits back and resolves adversary contentions at the hearing stage. 547 F.2d, at 627. And when an intervenor's comments "bring 'sufficient attention to the issue to stimulate the Commission's consideration of it,'" the Commission must "undertake its own preliminary investigation of the proffered alternative sufficient to reach a rational judgment whether it is worthy of detailed consideration in the EIS. Moreover, the Commission must explain the basis for each conclusion that further consideration of a suggested alternative is unwarranted." 547 F.2d, at 628, quoting from Indiana & Michigan Electric Co. v. FPC, 502 F.2d 336, 339 (1974).

While the court's rationale is not entirely unappealing as an abstract proposition, as applied to this case we think it basically misconceives not only the scope of the agency's statutory responsibility, but also the nature of the administrative process, the thrust of the agency's decision, and the type of issues the intervenors were trying to raise.

There is little doubt that under the Atomic Energy Act of 1954, state public utility commissions or similar bodies are empowered to make the initial decision regarding the need for power. The Commission's prime area of concern in the licensing context, on the other hand, is national security, public health, and safety. And it is clear that the need, as that term is conventionally used, for the power was thoroughly explored in the hearings. Even the Federal Power Commission, which regulates sales in interstate commerce, agreed with Consumers Power's analysis of projected need.

NEPA, of course, has altered slightly the statutory balance, requiring "a detailed statement by the responsible official on . . . alternatives to the proposed action." But, as should be obvious even upon a moment's reflection, the term "alternatives" is not self-defining. To make an impact statement something more than an exercise in frivolous boilerplate the concept of alternatives must be bounded by some notion of feasibility. As the Court of Appeals for the District of Columbia Circuit has itself recognized:

> There is reason for concluding that NEPA was not meant to require detailed discussion of the environmental effects of "alternatives" put forward in comments when these effects cannot be readily ascertained and the alternatives are deemed only remote and speculative possibilities, in view of basic changes required in statutes and policies of other agencies — making them available, if at all, only after protracted debate and litigation not meaningfully compatible with the timeframe of the needs to which the underlying proposal is addressed. [Natural Resources Defense Council v. Morton, 458 F.2d 827, 837-838 (1972).]

Common sense also teaches us that the "detailed statement of alternatives" cannot be found wanting simply because the agency failed to include every alternative device and thought conceivable by the mind of man. Time and resources are simply too limited to hold that an impact statement fails because the agency failed to ferret out every possible alternative, regardless of how uncommon or unknown that alternative may have been at the time the project was approved.

With these principles in mind we now turn to the notion of "energy conservation," an alternative the omission of which was thought by the Court of Appeals to have been "forcefully pointed out by Saginaw in its comments on the draft EIS." 547 F.2d, at 625. Again, as the Commission pointed out, "the phrase 'energy conservation' has a deceptively simple ring in this context. Taken literally, the phrase suggests a virtually limitless range of possible actions and developments that might, in one way or another, ultimately reduce projected demands for electricity from a particular proposed plant." Moreover, as a practical matter, it is hard to dispute the observation that it is largely the events of recent years that have emphasized not only the need but also a large variety of alternatives for energy conservation. Prior to the drastic oil shortages incurred by the United States in 1973, there was little serious thought in most Government circles of energy conservation alternatives. Indeed, the Council on Environmental Quality did not promulgate regulations which even remotely suggested the need to consider energy conservation in impact statements until August 1, 1973. And even then the guidelines were not made applicable to draft and final statements filed with the Council before January 28, 1974. The Federal Power Commission likewise did not require consideration of energy conservation in applications to build hydroelectric facilities until June 19, 1973. And these regulations were not made retroactive either. All this occurred over a year and a half after the draft environmental statement for Midland had been prepared, and over a year after the final environmental statement had been prepared and the hearings completed.

We think these facts amply demonstrate that the concept of "alternatives" is an evolving one, requiring the agency to explore more or fewer alternatives as they become better known and understood. This was well understood by the Commission, which, unlike the Court of Appeals, recognized that the Licensing Board's decision had to be judged by the information then available to it. And judged in that light we have little doubt the Board's actions were well within the proper bounds of its statutory authority. Not only did the record before the agency give every indication that the project was actually needed, but also there was nothing before the Board to indicate to the contrary.

We also think the court's criticism of the Commission's "threshold test" displays a lack of understanding of the historical setting within which the agency action took place and of the nature of the test itself. In the first place, while it is true that NEPA places upon an agency the obligation to consider every significant aspect of the environmental impact of a proposed action, it is still incumbent upon intervenors who wish to participate to structure their participation so that it is meaningful, so that it alerts the agency to the intervenors' position and contentions. This is especially true when the intervenors are requesting the agency to embark upon an exploration of uncharted territory, as was the question of energy conservation in the late 1960's and early 1970's.

> [C]omments must be significant enough to step over a threshold requirement of materiality before any lack of agency response or consideration becomes of concern. The comment cannot merely state that a particular mistake was made . . . ; it must show why the mistake was of possible significance in the results. . . . Portland Cement Assn. v. Ruckelshaus, 486 F.2d 375, 394 (1973).

Indeed, administrative proceedings should not be a game or a forum to engage in unjustified obstructionism by making cryptic and obscure reference to matters that "ought to be" considered and then, after failing to do more to bring the matter to the agency's attention, seeking to have that agency determination vacated on the ground that the agency failed to consider matters "forcefully presented." In fact, here the agency continually invited further clarification of Saginaw's contentions. Even without such clarification it indicated a willingness to receive evidence on the matters. But not only did Saginaw decline to further focus its contentions, it virtually declined to participate, indicating that it had "no conventional findings of fact to set forth" and that it had not "chosen to search the record and respond to this proceeding by submitting citations of matter which we believe were proved or disproved."

We also think the court seriously mischaracterized the Commission's "threshold test" as placing "heavy substantive burdens . . . on intervenors. . . ." On the contrary, the Commission explicitly stated: "We do not equate this burden with the civil litigation concept of a prima facie case, an unduly heavy burden in this setting. But the showing should be sufficient to require reasonable minds to inquire further." We think this sort of agency procedure well within the agency's discretion.

In sum, to characterize the actions of the Commission as "arbitrary or capricious" in light of the facts then available to it as described at length above, is to deprive those words of any meaning. As we have said in the past:

> Administrative consideration of evidence . . . always creates a gap between the time the record is closed and the time the administrative decision is promulgated [and, we might add, the time the decision is judicially reviewed]. . . . If upon the coming down of the order litigants might demand rehearings as a matter of law because some new circumstance has arisen, some new trend has been observed, or some new fact discovered, there would be little hope that the administrative process could ever be consummated in an order that would not be subject to reopening. ICC v. Jersey City, 322 U.S. 503, 514 (1944).

We have also made it clear that the role of a court in reviewing the sufficiency of an agency's consideration of environmental factors is a limited one, limited both by the time at which the decision was made and by the statute mandating review. "Neither the statute nor its legislative history contemplates that a court should substitute its judgment for that of the agency as to the environmental consequences of its actions." Kleppe v. Sierra Club, 427 U.S., at 410 n.21. We think the Court of Appeals has forgotten that injunction here and accordingly its judgment in this respect must also be reversed.

NOTES AND QUESTIONS

1. *What* Vermont Yankee *Means.* Though the Supreme Court in *Vermont Yankee* quoted the "speculative alternative" language from *Morton*, it ignored *Morton*'s more expansive reading of the alternatives requirement discussed above. Has the Supreme Court overruled *Morton*? Is the standard adopted by *Vermont Yankee* procedural or substantive? Did the Supreme Court imply that an agency does not have to consider alternatives that require an amendment of its basic enabling legislation? Or does the case simply mean an agency need not consider remote and speculative alternatives?

For a critical view of *Vermont Yankee*, which takes the position that the Court misapplied the *Morton* decision, see Rodgers, A Hard Look at *Vermont Yankee*: Environmental Law Under Strict Scrutiny, 67 Geo. L.J. 699 (1979). Professor Rodgers claims *Vermont Yankee* qualified the important "balls and strikes" doctrine. Under this doctrine, an agency does not sit as an umpire, calling balls and strikes, but must affirmatively seek out issues relevant to the case that may not have occurred to the parties. *Vermont Yankee* qualified this doctrine, he claims, by holding that "the energy conservation alternative did not have to be addressed because the intervenors did not raise their objections with sufficient support and precision." Id. at 720. Rodgers argued that the burden placed on intervenors "means a great deal . . . in the case of arguable or partial alternatives, such as energy conservation, which is within a reasonable, albeit ambitious, range of policy options." Id. at 721. A panel of the Court of Appeals for the D.C. Circuit has since suggested that *Morton* is no longer good law because it is qualified by *Vermont Yankee*. City of Alexandria v. Slater, 198 F.3d 862, 869 n.4 (D.C. Cir. 1999).

CEQ regulations require federal agencies to consider the no-action alternative, other "reasonable courses of action," and mitigation measures not in the proposed action. 40 C.F.R. §1508.25(b). The regulations also require agencies to consider "reasonable alternatives" not within their jurisdiction. Id. §1502.14(b). Are these regulations consistent with *Vermont Yankee*?

2. *Purpose, Need, and Statutory Objectives.* CEQ regulations require an impact statement to "briefly specify the underlying purpose and need of the project for which it is responding in proposing alternatives." Id. §1502.13. Defining purpose and need will define the character of the project and thus the type of alternatives that have to be considered. Assume a project to expand the number of lanes in an expressway. Is the purpose and need "expanding highway capacity" or "improving transportation facilities in the region"? How does either alternative affect the choice of alternatives to be considered? Agencies will try the narrowing tack because narrowing the statement of purpose will narrow the number of alternatives that have to be considered.

Courts often defer to an agency's decision on purpose and need but have cautioned that agencies must take a middle ground:

> [A]n agency may not define the objectives of its action in terms so unreasonably narrow that only one alternative from among the environmentally benign ones in the agency's power would accomplish the goals of the agency's action, and the EIS would become a foreordained formality. Nor may an agency frame its goals in terms so unreasonably broad that an infinite number of alternatives would accomplish those goals and the project would collapse under the weight of the possibilities. [Citizens Against Burlington, Inc. v. Busey, 938 F.2d 190, 196 (D.C. Cir. 1991).]

How should these guidelines be interpreted? In City of Alexandria v. Slater, *supra*, the court held the agency did not have to consider a 10-lane alternative to a 12-lane replacement of a congested 6-lane bridge over the Potomac in Washington, D.C. The court accepted a definition of purpose and need that focused on traffic and safety issues rather than on the future transportation needs of the region. Would this broader statement of purpose and need have required consideration of the 10-lane alternative?

Compare Davis v. Mineta, 302 F.3d 1104, 1119 (10th Cir. 2002). The court held that the purpose and need statement for a highway project required a crossing of the Jordan River, but commented that "if the Project did narrowly express its purposes and needs as requiring a new crossing across the Jordan River at 11400 South, we would conclude that such a narrow definition of Project needs would violate NEPA given the more general overarching objective of improving traffic flow in the area." Id. at 1119. Are the cases distinguishable?

3. *The No-Action Alternative.* CEQ regulations require consideration of a no-action alternative. 40 C.F.R. §1502.14(2). The no-action alternative provides a baseline against which the proposed alternative is evaluated. A no-action alternative must be meaningful. It is meaningless if it assumes the existence of the very plan being proposed. Friends of Yosemite Valley v. Kempthorne, 520 F.3d 1024 (9th Cir. 2007). Neither may it be identical to the proposed alternative. Muckleshoot Indian Tribe v. U.S. Forest Serv., 177 F.3d 800 (9th Cir. 1999). A no-action alternative must include a discussion of reasonably foreseeable development that would result from its adoption. Young v. General Servs. Admin., 99 F. Supp. 2d 59 (D.D.C. 2000). For example, a decision not to build a new highway could result in very different development patterns.

Nevertheless, the courts have been generous in approving agency decisions that reject no-action alternatives, though they have not given much guidance when discussion of a no-action alternative is required. In some of these cases they rejected the no-action alternative because it would not meet project purposes. For example, courts have rejected a no-action alternative in highway cases because it would not satisfy the purpose and need of the project, which was to provide highway improvements. See North Buckhead Civic Ass'n v. Skinner, 903 F.2d 1533 (11th Cir. 1990). For an example of a no-action alternative rejected by the court as "cursory," see Southeast Alaska Conservation Council v. FHA, 649 F.3d 1050 (9th Cir. 2011) (three paragraphs explaining existing ferry service as no-action alternative to highway and other transportation improvements).

4. *Primary Alternatives*. In most cases, courts reject arguments that an agency failed to discuss a primary alternative, or that a discussion of a primary alternative was inadequate. For example, in North Buckhead Civic Ass'n v. Skinner, *supra*, the court upheld a refusal to consider mass transit as an alternative to a highway. Though admitting that agencies have an obligation to discuss an alternative that partially satisfies the need and purpose of a proposed project, the court held "[t]here is no evidence here that heavy rail transit alone is a reasonable alternative to the construction of the Georgia 400 extension in the North Atlanta corridor. While mass transit lines would provide additional transportation capacity in the corridor, the problems of surface street congestion would remain completely unresolved." Id. at 1542. Has the court simply defined away the environmental problem? See also Coalition for Better Veterans Care, Inc. v. Veterans Admin., 16 Env't Rep. Cas. (BNA) 1685 (D. Or. 1981) (rejecting alternative of private treatment as alternative to hospital construction as an "assault on basic policy").

Some courts require agencies to consider primary alternatives. See *Southeast Alaska Conservation Council, supra* (failure to consider improvement of existing ferry services as alternative to construction of new roads, ferries, or terminals).

5. *Secondary Alternatives*. When an agency has considered secondary alternatives, the courts usually find the discussion adequate, sometimes dismissing alternatives not considered because they would be environmentally disruptive or would not be environmentally superior. Courts will require the consideration of alternate ways of carrying out a project, however, when an alternative appears reasonable. In Dubois v. United States Dep't of Agric., 103 F.3d 1273 (1st Cir. 1996), for example, the court held the federal agency did not adequately consider an alternative of using artificial water storage units instead of a natural pond as a snowmaking source for a ski resort. The court noted that taking water from the pond would be environmentally devastating, that the federal agency had required construction of artificial ponds for another ski area, and that the resort owner held land on which it could feasibly construct artificial ponds. Noting that several commenters had proposed artificial ponds as an alternative, the court held that "[t]he agency did not in any way explain its reasoning or provide a factual basis for its refusal to consider, in general, the possibility of alternatives to using Loon Pond for snowmaking, or . . . [a] reasonably thoughtful proposal in particular." Id. at 1288. See also Utahns for Better Transp. v. U.S. Dep't of Transp., 319 F.3d 1207 (10th Cir. 2003), where the court required consideration of a different highway alignment, a narrower highway configuration, and a mass transit alternative as alternatives to a major parkway.

Alternatives must also be considered in environmental assessments. In the *Ocean Advocates* case, reproduced above, were there any alternatives the agency could be required to consider?

6. *Range of Alternatives That Must Be Considered*. An important question an agency must decide is how many alternatives it has to consider, and to what extent they must differ in the options they provide. NEPA's environmental mandate is not met if an agency is allowed to excessively restrict the number of alternatives it is willing to

consider. However, the courts have usually accepted agency decisions limiting the range of alternatives under a feasibility test if they appear sufficiently comprehensive and there is no attempt to eliminate alternatives that present viable options. See, e.g., Friends of the Boundary Waters Wilderness v. Dombeck, 164 F.3d 1115 (8th Cir. 1999). One court has described the limiting rules:

> An agency's discussion of alternatives must be bound by some notion of "feasibility." In addition, an agency need not consider every available alternative. The range of alternatives is reviewed under a rule of reason that requires an agency to set forth only those alternatives necessary to permit a reasoned choice. NEPA does not require a separate analysis of alternatives which are not significantly distinguishable from alternatives actually considered, or which have substantially similar consequences. However, NEPA does require federal agencies to rigorously explore and objectively evaluate all reasonable alternatives. [Navajo Nation v. United States Forest Serv., 408 F. Supp. 2d 866 (D. Ariz. 2006) (ski area upgrade), *rev'd in part and remanded on other grounds*, 479 F.3d 1024 (9th Cir. 2007), *opinion adopted en banc*, 535 F.3d 1058 (9th Cir. 2008).]

Compare California v. Block, 690 F.2d 753 (9th Cir. 1982), where the Forest Service reviewed the future use of 62 million acres of roadless national forest land. All serious alternatives considered in its impact statement contemplated the development of some of this land, and no alternative would have retained more than 34 percent of the area in a wilderness condition. The court held the alternatives considered were inadequate, noting "it is puzzling why the Forest Service did not seriously consider an alternative that allocated more than a third of the . . . acreage to Wilderness." Id. at 768. What if the Forest Service had decided, as a matter of policy, that all of the wilderness area under consideration should be released for development? Could the agency then eliminate the wilderness alternative from consideration?

NOTE ON STATUTORY MODIFICATIONS OF THE ALTERNATIVES REQUIREMENT

Legislation that has modified compliance with NEPA in several agency programs includes provisions that shift decisions on the alternatives requirement to the lead project agency. For example, the Department of Transportation (DOT) is made the lead agency for NEPA compliance for transportation projects under the Safe, Accountable, Flexible, Efficient Transportation Equity Act, Pub. L. No. 109-59, 119 Stat. 1144 (2005) (variously codified). DOT makes the purpose and need decision that determines the alternatives that must be considered, which may include achieving a transportation objective identified in a statewide or metropolitan transportation plan, or that supports "land use, economic development or growth objectives" established in federal, state, local, or tribal plans. 23 U.S.C. §139(f)(2-3). DOT also has the authority to determine the "range of alternatives" to be considered in any environmental document, §139(f)(4)(B), and is to "determine" the methodologies to be used and the level of detail required to analyze alternatives, §139(f)(4)(c). The preferred alternative, in DOT's discretion, can be developed at a higher level of detail than other alternatives, if DOT determines that developing a higher level of detail will not prevent it from making an impartial decision on whether to accept another alternative that is being considered in the environmental review process. §139(f)(4)(D).

Comparable provisions appear in the Aviation Streamlining Approval Process Act of 2003, 49 U.S.C. §47171. See Berger, False Promises: NEPA's Role in Airport Expansions and the Streamlining of the Environmental Review Process, 18 J. Envtl. L. & Litig. 279 (2003). The Federal Aviation Agency is made the lead agency for aviation projects. The definition of purpose and need by the Secretary of Transportation in any environmental review for these projects is binding on other agencies. 49 U.S.C. §47171(j). The statute also provides that the Secretary shall determine the reasonable alternatives for airport capacity enhancement projects. Other agencies participating in a coordinated environmental review process can consider only those alternatives to the project the Secretary determines to be reasonable. 49 U.S.C. §47171(k). Similar provisions appear in the Healthy Forests Restoration Act of 2003. See 16 U.S.C. §§6514, 9604. These statutes undercut NEPA's legislative purpose, which was to provide an environmental override on decisions by mission agencies that often neglected environmental concerns.

3. *Segmentation*

The scope of an impact statement is defined by the geographic extent of the "action" covered, as well as by the environmental impacts that must be discussed. Many governmental projects are constructed in stages, and deciding on how to identify separate stages of a project for coverage in an impact statement is often difficult. Highways are a good example. Major highways are divided into segments for purposes of federal funding. The question is whether these individual segments may be separated for impact statement preparation. Objectors may complain that this kind of "piecemealing" allows the highway agency to minimize environmental impacts by avoiding discussion of the cumulative impacts of a highway project. Agencies argue that widening the scope of the impact statement to include related projects is impractical, and may compel the agency to consider the speculative impacts of projects not yet approved.

The following case considers a typical segmentation issue:

FLORIDA KEYS CITIZENS COALITION, INC. v.
UNITED STATES ARMY CORPS OF ENGINEERS
374 F. Supp. 2d 1116 (S.D. Fla. 2005)

PAUL C. HUCK, District Judge.

[This case considered a highway safety improvement project for U.S. Highway 1, which is the principal highway that goes through the Florida Keys. The project originally was to be four lanes but was reduced to two lanes. It also provided for the replacement of an existing bascule bridge with a high-level, fixed span bridge over a creek.] The [Federal Highway Administration (FHWA)] approved the bridge replacement portion of the 2LSP ("Bridge Replacement Project") over Jewfish Creek and Lake Surprise under NEPA by finding that it presented no impacts not known and scrutinized by the FEIS. The FHWA approved the remainder of the 2LSP, consisting primarily of roadway safety improvements ("Road Safety Improvements"), pursuant to a categorical exclusion under NEPA. Specifically, the FHWA found that the Road Safety Improvements are the type of safety improvements that are generally considered to be "categorically excluded" from detailed environmental review under NEPA, "such as shoulders for emergency use and bridge replacements and attendant environmental mitigation," which do not increase traffic capacity. . . .

[Plaintiffs contend] that the Project, and specifically the Bridge Replacement Project, has been improperly segmented from other projects or actions in order to limit the scope of the FEIS and the Reevaluation's environmental impact evaluation. The FHWA has promulgated regulations concerning environmental analysis of roadway systems "in order to ensure meaningful evaluation of alternatives and to avoid commitments to transportation improvements before they are fully evaluated. . . ." 23 C.F.R. §771.111(f). These regulations and the related judicial interpretations require a stand-alone project to: (1) connect logical termini and be of sufficient length to address environmental matters on a broad scope; (2) have independent utility or independent significance; and (3) not restrict consideration of alternatives for other reasonably foreseeable transportation improvements. The "independent utility" factor is the most important. Moreover, in determining whether these criteria are met, a central question is whether the project "will serve a significant purpose even if a second related project is not built. . . . Only when a given project effectively commits decisionmakers to a future course of action will this form of linkage argue strongly for joint environmental evaluation." Coalition on Sensible Transp., Inc. v. Dole, 826 F.2d 60, 69 (D.C. Cir. 1987). In turn, the question of whether a decision-maker is committed to a future course of action will largely turn upon whether the project irretrievably commits more public funding to other, future projects. Finally, courts have held that an agency's determination of the scope of a project is entitled to deference, and the regulations direct that an EIS's analysis of cumulative actions is required to cover only proposed actions rather than actions that are only a theoretical possibility. See 40 C.F.R. §1508.25(a)(2).

With the foregoing criteria in mind, the Court must determine whether the FHWA has impermissibly "segmented" the Bridge Replacement Project. To begin, the Bridge Replacement Project has independent utility, because it is designed to replace an obsolete bridge structure that is in need of replacement regardless of whether the Road Safety Improvements are also made. The record establishes that the existing bridge is more than 60 years old, in need of frequent repairs, subject to frequent mechanical failures, and considered "functionally obsolete," not to mention that standing alone it constitutes an identifiable major safety problem. Moreover, the Plaintiffs have not established that the completion of the Bridge Replacement Project will irretrievably commit the FHWA to the funding of other future projects identified in the Miller Study [of the project], which Plaintiffs contend should have been considered in the evaluation. Finally, the administrative record reflects that at least a portion of the projects recommended by the Miller Study are only in the planning stages and, therefore, do not qualify as proposed action.

Although, as indicated above, the Road Safety Improvements ultimately were approved pursuant to a categorical exclusion rather than by reliance upon the FEIS and Reevaluation, the extensive analysis of the Road Safety Improvements in these documents is sufficient for satisfying the cumulative impacts analysis required for the improved bridge. These documents do not, however, attempt to assess the full cumulative impacts from all future highway improvements that may eventually be completed to improve evacuation times out of the Florida Keys. Regardless, Plaintiffs have failed to establish that such a requirement falls within the NEPA requirements relating to cumulative impacts. See [Preserve Endangered Areas of Cobb's History v. United States Army Corps of Eng'rs, 87 F.3d 1242 (11th Cir. 1996)] ("Just because the project at issue connects existing highways does not mean that it must be considered as part of a larger highway project; all roads must begin and end somewhere."). Any attempt to assess the cumulative impacts from such future projects would be pure speculation and is not required. See 40 CFR §1508.25(a)(2). Accordingly, for all of the foregoing reasons, the Court concludes that the FHWA did not improperly segment the Bridge Replacement Project. See Village of Los Ranchos de Albuquerque v. Barnhart, 906 F.2d 1477, 1482-84 (10th Cir. 1990) (holding that a project for the construction of two highway bridges was properly deemed independent of the connecting highway interchange project because the bridges had logical termini, substantial independent utility, did not foreclose alternatives for future projects, and did not commit funds for any related projects). See also Conservation Law Found. v. FHWA, 24 F.3d 1465, 1472 (1st Cir. 1994) ("Two bridges on either side of an island appear to be perfectly logical termini. . . ."). Notwithstanding the foregoing, the record reflects that the FDOT and the FHWA recognized the reality that the Bridge Replacement Project was not designed in a vacuum, but rather is considered an "indivisible part" of the Road Safety Improvements. . . .

Accordingly, the Court will enter a final judgment against the Plaintiffs and in favor of all Defendants.

NOTES AND QUESTIONS

1. *The Segmentation Problem.* The segmentation problem is to define the action the agency must consider when carrying out its environmental review. This problem is closely tied to the question of when a comprehensive "program" impact statement must be prepared for related projects, an issue considered in the *Kleppe* case, reproduced next. A decision prohibiting segmentation will increase the geographic scope of an action and, presumably, the extent of its possibly significant environmental impacts.

2. *Highway Segmentation.* The segmentation issue is especially troublesome in highway projects, which often are part of a comprehensive system difficult to disentangle, as in the principal case. The Federal Highway Administration regulation quoted in the principal case is long-standing, and courts apply it when deciding whether segmentation in a particular case is acceptable. Since U.S. 1 is the only highway through the narrow Florida Keys, the decision to segment the bridge seems difficult to accept, though the court's decision is consistent with other segmentation decisions.

Highway segmentation is usually approved. In metropolitan areas, where highway systems are interdependent and interconnected, courts sometimes avoid segmentation problems by holding that the major issue to be considered is independent utility. See Save Barton Creek Ass'n v. Federal Highway Admin., 950 F.2d 1129 (5th Cir. 1992), finding independent utility, inter alia, because the highway connected two expressways and relieved transportation congestion. Is this correct?

Deciding whether a segment of a larger project has "independent utility" can be difficult. Assume a proposed and relatively short new segment of an interstate highway intended to provide a bypass around a small community. Can the segment be isolated for review in the impact statement because its primary purpose is to provide traffic relief for the community? Or is its primary purpose to provide a link in the interstate highway system? See Daly v. Volpe, 514 F.2d 1106 (9th Cir. 1975) (adopting the former view). Does this holding allow agencies to adopt any self-serving justification for a project segment?

Highway agencies sometimes lose segmentation cases, though not often. In Western N. Carolina Alliance v. North Carolina Dep't of Transp., 312 F. Supp. 2d 765 (E.D.N.C. 2003), the court rejected segmentation because there were no logical termini, connection with another highway would create congestion, there was an admission that the highway had to be segmented to avoid environmental problems, segmentation would restrict consideration of alternatives, and all of the projects were under consideration at the same time.

3. *Interrelated Projects.* Segmentation problems also arise when a federal agency plans to develop or approves a project that contains several related but different components. In Hudson River Sloop Clearwater, Inc. v. Department of the Navy, 836 F.2d 760 (2d Cir. 1988), for example, the Navy planned to build a new port for its ships together with associated housing. The court held that the Navy could segment the port for purposes of preparing an EIS because the port would be operational even though the Navy decided not to build the housing.

4. *Staged Projects.* Segmentation problems also arise when agencies plan to build projects in stages. County of Suffolk v. Secretary of Interior, 562 F.2d 1368 (2d Cir. 1977), is a leading case. The court held an impact statement on an offshore oil and gas lease sale did not have to discuss the environmental impacts of the onshore transportation routes, including onshore pipelines that would transport any oil that might be found. Any discussion of these environmental effects was speculative because the building of the pipelines was at least three years away and transportation routes would not be known until oil was discovered. Is a three-year planning horizon too much to expect of an agency?

4.   *Regional and Program Impact Statements*

Discussion of the segmentation problem leads naturally to another option that can take into account the interrelated impacts of a number of related projects: the program impact statement. The following Supreme Court case considers the circumstances under which program impact statements are required under NEPA.

KLEPPE v. SIERRA CLUB
427 U.S. 390 (1976)

Mr. Justice POWELL delivered the opinion of the Court.

I

Respondents, several organizations concerned with the environment, brought this suit in July 1973 in the United States District Court for the District of Columbia. The defendants in the suit, petitioners here, were the officials of the Department and other federal agencies responsible for issuing coal leases, approving mining plans, granting rights-of-way, and taking the other actions necessary to enable private companies and public utilities to develop coal reserves on land owned or controlled by the Federal Government. Citing widespread interest in the reserves of a region identified as the "Northern Great Plains region," and an alleged threat from coal-related operations to their members' enjoyment of the region's environment, respondents claimed that the federal officials could not allow further development without preparing a "comprehensive environmental impact statement" under §102(2)(C) on the entire region. They sought declaratory and injunctive relief. . . .

[The district court, on the basis of extensive findings of fact and conclusions of law, granted petitioners' motions for summary judgment. On appeal, the Court of Appeals for the District of Columbia reversed and remanded for further proceedings. The Supreme Court then granted certiorari.]

II

. . .

The Northern Great Plains region identified in respondents' complaint encompasses portions of four States—northeastern Wyoming, eastern Montana, western North Dakota, and western South Dakota. There is no dispute about its richness in coal, nor about the waxing interest in developing that coal, nor about the crucial role the federal petitioners will play due to the significant percentage of the coal to which they control access. The Department has initiated, in this decade, three studies in areas either inclusive of or included within this region. The North Central Power Study was addressed to the potential for coordinated development of electric power in an area encompassing all or part of 15 States in the North Central United States. It aborted in 1972 for lack of interest on the part of electric utilities. The Montana-Wyoming Aqueducts Study, intended to recommend the best use of water resources for coal development in southeastern Montana and northeastern Wyoming, was suspended in 1972 with the initiation of the third study, the Northern Great Plains Resources Program (NGPRP).

While the record does not reveal the degree of concern with environmental matters in the first two studies, it is clear that the NGPRP was devoted entirely to the environment. It was carried out by an interagency, federal-state task force with public participation, and was designed "to assess the potential social, economic and environmental impacts" from resource development in five States—Montana, Wyoming, South Dakota, North Dakota, and Nebraska. Its primary objective was "to provide an analytical and informational framework for policy and planning decisions at all levels of government" by formulating several "scenarios" showing the probable consequences for the area's environment and culture from the various possible techniques and levels of resource development. The final interim report of the NGPRP was issued August 1, 1975, shortly after the decision of the Court of Appeals in this case.

In addition, since 1973 the Department has engaged in a complete review of its coal-leasing program for the entire Nation. On February 17 of that year the Secretary announced the review and announced also that during study a "short-term leasing policy" would prevail, under which new leasing would be restricted to narrowly defined circumstances and even then allowed only when an environmental impact statement had been prepared if required under NEPA. The purpose of the program review was to study the environmental impact of the Department's entire range of coal-related activities and to develop a planning system to guide the national leasing program. The impact statement, known as the "Coal Programmatic EIS," went through several drafts before issuing in final form on September 19, 1975 — shortly before the petitions for certiorari were filed in this case. The Coal Programmatic EIS proposed a new leasing program based on a complex planning system called the Energy Minerals Activity Recommendation System (EMARS), and assessed the prospective environmental impact of the new program as well as the alternatives to it. We have been informed by the parties to this litigation that the Secretary is in the process of implementing the new program.

Against this factual background, we turn now to consider the issues raised by this case in the status in which it reached this Court.

[In part III of its opinion, the Court held that "there is no evidence in the record of an action or a proposal for an action of regional scope." It noted that the district court had found that "there was no existing or proposed plan or program on the part of the Federal Government for the regional development" of the Northern Great Plains area.]

IV

A

The Court of Appeals, in reversing the District Court, did not find that there was a regional plan or program for development of the Northern Great Plains region. It accepted all of the District Court's findings of fact, but concluded nevertheless that the petitioners "contemplated" a regional plan or program. The court thought that the North Central Power Study, the Montana-Wyoming Aqueducts Study, and the NGPRP all constituted "attempts to control development" by individual companies on a regional scale. It also concluded that the interim report of the NGPRP, then expected to be released at any time, would provide the petitioners with the information needed to formulate the regional plan they had been "contemplating." The Court therefore remanded with instructions to the petitioners to inform the District Court of their role in the further development of the region within 30 days after the NGPRP interim report issued; if they decided to control that development, an impact statement would be required.

We conclude that the Court of Appeals erred in both its factual assumptions and its interpretation of NEPA. We think the court was mistaken in concluding, on the record before it, that the petitioners were "contemplating" a regional development plan or program. It considered the several studies undertaken by the petitioners to represent attempts to control development on a regional scale. This conclusion was based on a finding by the District Court that those studies, as well as the new national coal-leasing policy, were "attempts to control development by individual companies in a manner consistent with the policies and procedures of the National Environmental Policy Act of 1969." But in context, that finding meant only that the named studies were efforts to gain background environmental information for subsequent application in the decisionmaking with respect to individual coal-related projects. This is the sense in which the District Court spoke of controlling development consistently with NEPA. Indeed, in the same paragraph containing the language relied upon by the

Court of Appeals, the District Court expressly found that the studies were not part of a plan or program to develop or encourage development.

Moreover, at the time the Court of Appeals ruled there was no indication in the record that the NGPRP was aimed toward a regional plan or program, and subsequent events have shown that this was not its purpose. The interim report of the study, issued shortly after the Court of Appeals ruled, described the effects of several possible rates of coal development but stated in its preface that the alternatives "are for study and comparison only; they do not represent specific plans or proposals." All parties agreed in this Court that there still exists no proposal for a regional plan or program of development.

Even had the record justified a finding that a regional program was contemplated by the petitioners, the legal conclusion drawn by the Court of Appeals cannot be squared with the Act. The court recognized that the mere "contemplation" of certain action is not sufficient to require an impact statement. But it believed the statute nevertheless empowers a court to require the preparation of an impact statement to begin at some point prior to the formal recommendation or report on a proposal. The Court of Appeals accordingly devised its own four-part "balancing" test for determining when, during the contemplation of a plan or other type of federal action, an agency must begin a statement. The factors to be considered were identified as the likelihood and imminence of the program's coming to fruition, the extent to which information is available on the effects of implementing the expected program and on alternatives thereto, the extent to which irretrievable commitments are being made and options precluded "as refinement of the proposal progresses," and the severity of the environmental effects should the action be implemented.

The Court of Appeals thought that as to two of these factors—the availability of information on the effects of any regional development program, and the severity of those effects—the time already was "ripe" for an impact statement. It deemed the record unclear, however, as to the likelihood of the petitioners' actually producing a plan to control the development, and surmised that irretrievable commitments were being avoided because petitioners had ceased approving most coal-related projects while the NGPRP study was underway. The court also thought that the imminent release of the NGPRP interim report would provide the officials with sufficient information to define their role in development of the region, and it believed that as soon as the NGPRP was completed the petitioners would begin approving individual projects in the region, thus permitting irrevocable commitments of resources. It was for this reason that the court in its remand required the petitioners to report to the District Court their decision on the federal role with respect to the Northern Great Plains as a region within 30 days after issuance of the NGPRP report.

The Court's reasoning and action find no support in the language or legislative history of NEPA. The statute clearly states when an impact statement is required, and mentions nothing about a balancing of factors. Rather, as we noted last Term, under the first sentence of §102(2)(C) the moment at which an agency must have a final statement ready "is the time at which it makes a recommendation or report on a *proposal* for federal action." Aberdeen & Rockfish R. Co. v. SCRAP, 422 U.S. 289, 320 (1975) (*SCRAP II*) (emphasis in original). The procedural duty imposed upon agencies by this section is quite precise, and the role of the courts in enforcing that duty is similarly precise. A court has no authority to depart from the statutory language and, by a balancing of court-devised factors, determine a point during the germination process of a potential proposal at which an impact statement should be prepared. Such an assertion of judicial authority would leave the agencies uncertain as to their procedural duties under NEPA, would invite judicial involvement in the day-to-day decisionmaking process of the agencies, and would invite litigation. As the contemplation of a project and the accompanying study thereof do not necessarily result in a proposal for major federal action, it may be assumed that the balancing process devised by the Court of Appeals also would result in the preparation of a good many unnecessary impact statements. . . .

V

Our discussion thus far has been addressed primarily to the decision of the Court of Appeals. It remains, however, to consider the contention now urged by respondents. They have not attempted to support the Court of Appeals' decision. Instead, respondents renew an argument they appear to have made to the Court of Appeals, but which that court did not reach. Respondents insist that, even without a comprehensive federal plan for the development of the Northern Great Plains, a "regional" impact statement nevertheless is required on all coal-related projects in the region because they are intimately related.

There are two ways to view this contention. First, it amounts to an attack on the sufficiency of the impact statements already prepared by the petitioners on the coal-related projects that they have approved or stand ready to approve. As such, we cannot consider it in this proceeding, for the case was not brought as a challenge to a particular impact statement and there is no impact statement in the record. It also is possible to view the respondents' argument as an attack upon the decision of the petitioners not to prepare one comprehensive impact statement on all proposed projects in the region. This contention properly is before us, for the petitioners have made it clear they do not intend to prepare such a statement.

We begin by stating our general agreement with respondents' basic premise that §102(2)(C) may require a comprehensive impact statement in certain situations where several proposed actions are pending at the same time. NEPA announced a national policy of environmental protection and placed a responsibility upon the Federal Government to further specific environmental goals by "all practicable means, consistent with other essential considerations of national policy." §101(b). Section 102(2)(C) is one of the "action-forcing" provisions intended as a directive to "all agencies to assure consideration of the environmental impact of their actions in decisionmaking." Conference Report on NEPA, 115 Cong. Rec. 40416 (1969). By requiring an impact statement Congress intended to assure such consideration during the development of a proposal or—as in this case—during the formulation of a position on a proposal submitted by private parties. A comprehensive impact statement may be necessary in some cases for an agency to meet this duty. Thus, when several proposals for coal-related actions that will have cumulative or synergistic environmental impact upon a region are pending concurrently before an agency, their environmental consequences must be considered together. Only through comprehensive consideration of pending proposals can the agency evaluate different courses of action.[21]

21. Neither the statute nor its legislative history contemplates that a court should substitute its judgment for that of the agency as to the environmental consequences of its actions. See Scenic Hudson Preservation Conference v. FPC, 453 F.2d 463, 481 (2d Cir. 1971), *cert. denied*, 407 U.S.

Agreement to this extent with respondents' premise, however, does not require acceptance of their conclusion that all proposed coal-related actions in the Northern Great Plains region are so "related" as to require their analysis in a single comprehensive impact statement. Respondents informed us that the Secretary recently adopted an approach to impact statements on coal-related actions that provides:

> As a general proposition, and as determined by the Secretary, when action is proposed involving coal development such as issuing several coal leases or approving mining plans in the same region, such actions will be covered by a single EIS rather than by multiple statements. In such cases, the region covered will be determined by basin boundaries, drainage areas, areas of common reclamation problems, administrative boundaries, areas of economic interdependence, and other relevant factors.

At another point, the document containing the Secretary's approach states that a "regional EIS" will be prepared "if a series of proposed actions with interrelated impacts are involved . . . unless a previous EIS has sufficiently analyzed the impacts of the proposed action[s]." Thus, the Department has decided to prepare comprehensive impact statements of the type contemplated by §102(2)(C), although it has not deemed it appropriate to prepare such a statement on all proposed actions in the region identified by respondents.

Respondents conceded at oral argument that to prevail they must show that petitioners have acted arbitrarily in refusing to prepare one comprehensive statement on this entire region, and we agree. The determination of the region, if any, with respect to which a comprehensive statement is necessary requires the weighing of a number of relevant factors, including the extent of the interrelationship among proposed actions and practical considerations of feasibility. Resolving these issues requires a high level of technical expertise and is properly left to the informed discretion of the responsible federal agencies. Cf. *SCRAP II*, 422 U.S., at 325-26. Absent a showing of arbitrary action, we must assume that the agencies have exercised this discretion appropriately. Respondents have made no showing to the contrary.

Respondents' basic argument is that one comprehensive statement on the Northern Great Plains is required because all coal-related activity in that region is "programmatically," "geographically," and "environmentally" related. Both the alleged "programmatic" relationship and the alleged "geographic" relationship resolve, ultimately, into an argument that the region is proper for a comprehensive impact statement because the petitioners themselves have approached environmental study in this area on a regional basis. Respondents point primarily to the NGPRP, which they claim—and petitioners deny—focused on the region described in the complaint. The precise region of the NGPRP is unimportant, for its irrelevance to the delineation of an appropriate area for analysis in a comprehensive impact statement has been well stated by the Secretary:

> Resource studies [like the NGPRP] are one of many analytical tools employed by the Department to inform itself as to general resource availability, resource need and general environmental considerations so that it can intelligently determine the scope of

---

926 (1972). The only role for a court is to insure that the agency has taken a "hard look" at environmental consequences; it cannot "interject itself within the area of discretion of the executive as to the choice of the action to be taken." Natural Resources Defense Council v. Morton, 458 F.2d 827, 838 (1972).

environmental analysis and review specific actions it may take. Simply put, resource studies are a prelude to informed agency planning, and provide the data base on which the Department may decide to take specific actions for which impact statements are prepared. The scope of environmental impact statements seldom coincide[s] with that of a given resource study, since the statements evolve from specific proposals for federal action while the studies simply provide an educational backdrop.

As for the alleged "environmental" relationship, respondents contend that the coal-related projects "will produce a wide variety of cumulative environmental impacts" throughout the Northern Great Plains region. They described them as follows: Diminished availability of water, air and water pollution, increases in population and industrial densities, and perhaps even climatic changes. Cumulative environmental impacts are, indeed, what require a comprehensive impact statement. But determination of the extent and effect of these factors, and particularly identification of the geographic area within which they may occur, is a task assigned to the special competency of the appropriate agencies. Petitioners dispute respondents' contentions that the interrelationship of environmental impacts is regionwide and, as respondents' own submissions indicate, petitioners appear to have determined that the appropriate scope of comprehensive statements should be based on basins, drainage areas, and other factors. We cannot say that petitioners' choices are arbitrary. Even if environmental interrelationships could be shown conclusively to extend across basins and drainage areas, practical considerations of feasibility might well necessitate restricting the scope of comprehensive statements.

In sum, respondents' contention as to the relationships between all proposed coal-related projects in the Northern Great Plains region does not require that petitioners prepare one comprehensive impact statement covering all before proceeding to approve specific pending applications. As we already have determined that there exists no proposal for regionwide action that could require a regional impact statement, the judgment of the Court of Appeals must be reversed, and the judgment of the District Court reinstated and affirmed. The case is remanded for proceedings consistent with this opinion. . . .

NOTES AND QUESTIONS

1. *Understanding* Kleppe. The *Kleppe* litigation was an attempt to overcome the limitation in NEPA that agencies are required to consider the environmental impacts of their actions one at a time. The balancing test rejected by the Court was adopted in an earlier NEPA case, Scientists' Inst. for Pub. Info., Inc. v. AEC (*SIPI*), 481 F.2d 1079 (D.C. Cir. 1973), but did not clarify what is required to show that a "proposal" exists. And, since *Kleppe* did not consider a multi-segmented single project of the kind considered in the segmentation cases, the impact of *Kleppe* on segmentation doctrine also is unclear. For an extended discussion of *Kleppe*, see Johnston, Kleppe v. Sierra Club: An Environmental Planning Catch-22?, 1 Harv. Envtl. L. Rev. 182 (1976).

CEQ published what amounted to an official case note on the *Kleppe* opinion in the Federal Register. 42 Fed. Reg. 61,066, 61,069 (1977). CEQ stated that "the most useful principles for defining the scope of comprehensive environmental statements" were precedent-setting effect, interdependence, cumulation of impact, and availability of information. Id. at 61,071. Does this advice properly reflect the holding in *Kleppe*?

2. *CEQ Regulations.* CEQ regulations deal with program impact statements by suggesting that agencies might find it useful to prepare statements on "broad actions." These include actions in the same general location, and actions that generically have "relevant similarities." 40 C.F.R. §1502.4(c). They add that statements on technological development programs are to be prepared "before the program has reached a stage of investment or commitment to implementation likely to determine subsequent development or restrict later alternatives." Id. §1502.4(c)(3). This regulation reflects *SIPI*. Does it meet the *Kleppe* tests?

3. *Applying* Kleppe. Ambiguities latent in the *Kleppe* decision make it difficult to apply, and case law is limited. The Supreme Court's decision not to require an impact statement at the program planning stage, and the deference it paid to agency exercise of discretion, suggest that agencies may be able to avoid impact statement preparation until they are sufficiently comfortable with their plans to be able to formalize them in proposal form. See Texas Comm. on Natural Res. v. Bergland, 573 F.2d 201 (5th Cir. 1978) (upholding agency decision not to file program impact statement on timber management program).

Kleppe may confine the impact statement requirement to incremental project decisions rather than to agency planning programs. As one commentator noted, "the less overall articulation of planning an agency undertakes (in the form of concrete proposals) the less actual environmental planning (in the form of impact statements) it can be compelled to perform." Johnston, *supra*, at 200. Compare NRDC, Inc. v. Hodel, 435 F. Supp. 590 (D. Or. 1977), *aff'd on other grounds sub nom.* Natural Res. Def. Council, Inc. v. Munro, 626 F.2d 134 (9th Cir. 1980). The federal Bonneville Power Administration and a number of private and public utilities entered into a cooperative program for the allocation of electric power throughout the Pacific Northwest. The court held an impact statement was required on an extension of this program, which included plans for the construction of additional thermal power plants, as well as a number of agreements on purchasing and power allocation strategies. The court distinguished *Kleppe*, and held that "[t]he program contains] specific plans for regional development, hammered out after long negotiations and embodied in published documents. Individual projects undertaken by the federal government, by public and private utilities, and by industry are interrelated according to an integrated plan." Id. at 600. See also Environmental Def. Fund, Inc. v. Andrus, 596 F.2d 848 (9th Cir. 1979) (programmatic impact statement required for Interior Department industrial water marketing plan for federally controlled reservoir).

4. *Post-Program Impact Statements and Tiering.* Does the preparation of a program impact statement eliminate the need to prepare an impact statement later on a site-specific action included within the program when the program impact statement is not sufficiently detailed to cover all aspects of the site-specific action? A CEQ regulation encourages "tiering," and states that when an EIS or EA is prepared on an action included within the program statement, "the subsequent statement or environmental assessment need only summarize the issues discussed in the broader statement and incorporate discussions from the broader statement by reference and shall concentrate on the issues specific to the subsequent action." 40 C.F.R. §1502.20. See also id. §1502.28. See Town of Superior v. United States Fish & Wildlife Serv., 913 F. Supp. 2d 1087 (D. Colo. 2012) (agency did not duplicate earlier broad analysis and instead focused on the details of the submitted proposals); Chemical Weapons Working Group v. United States Dep't of Def., 655 F. Supp. 2d 18 (D.D.C. 2009) (approved preparation of both a programmatic impact statement for the entire

chemical weapons destruction project, and site-specific statements for each disposal facility that incorporated the analysis included in the programmatic statement).

5. *Connected, Cumulative and Similar Actions.* Another CEQ regulation deals with the problem of when a group of actions must be considered together in the same impact statement. It requires consideration in the same impact statement of connected, cumulative, or similar actions. 40 C.F.R. §1508.25. Actions are "connected" if they "(i) Automatically trigger other actions which may require environmental impact statements. (ii) Cannot or will not proceed unless other actions are taken previously or simultaneously. (iii) Are interdependent parts of a larger action and depend on the larger action for their justification." Id. §1508.25(a)(1). Cumulative actions are those "which when viewed with other proposed actions have cumulatively significant impacts and should therefore be discussed in the same impact statement." Id. §1508.25(a)(2). Similar actions are those which have "similarities that provide a basis for evaluating their environmental consequences together." Id. §1508.25(a)(3).

The Ninth Circuit applied these regulations in a leading case, Thomas v. Peterson, 753 F.2d 754 (9th Cir. 1985). The Forest Service prepared an environmental assessment on a road in a national forest, and decided no impact statement was necessary because the road would not cause significant environmental impacts. Subsequently, the Service issued environmental assessments for proposed timber sales that would use the new road, and concluded these sales also would not have significant environmental impact. The court decided these two projects had to be considered together. It held that "[t]he construction of the road and the sale of the timber in the Jersey Jack area meet the second and third, as well as perhaps the first of these [connected action] criteria. It is clear that the timber sales cannot proceed without the road, and the road would not be built but for the contemplated timber sales." The court also held the two projects had to be considered together as cumulative actions. "The record in this case contains considerable evidence to suggest that the road and the timber sales will have cumulatively significant impacts." Most of the cases have not found connected, cumulative, or similar actions that had to be considered together, however. See, e.g., Coalition on W. Valley Nuclear Wastes v. Chu, 592 F.3d 303 (2d Cir. 2009) (off-site disposal of nuclear waste and later closure facilities not connected); Quechan Tribe of the Fort Yuma Indian Reservation v. United States Dep't of Interior, 927 F. Supp. 2d 921 (S.D. Cal. 2013) (wind farm project; renewable energy projects across 25 million acres of land). A court reached a different result when a group of projects was closely integrated. Delaware Riverkeeper Network v. FERC, 753 F.3d 1304 (D.C. Cir. 2014).

NOTE ON NEPA's EXTRATERRITORIAL IMPACT AND ENVIRONMENTAL ASSESSMENT IN OTHER COUNTRIES

NEPA Abroad. Whether NEPA applies to the extraterritorial impacts of federal agency actions has produced a protracted controversy, still not entirely resolved. NEPA does not expressly exclude or include extraterritorial environmental impacts, though the statute does require federal agencies to "recognize the worldwide . . . character of environmental problems." §102(2)(F). CEQ regulations do not address this problem, which is covered by an executive order issued by President Carter. Exec. Order No. 12,114, 44 Fed. Reg. 1957 (1979). The order, though not based on NEPA, requires an environmental review of the extraterritorial environmental impacts of federal agency actions. This review is not as extensive as the environmental review covered by NEPA, and the order contains a number of exemptions, primarily for national security actions.

The Supreme Court adopted the key principle that determines whether NEPA applies extraterritorially in Equal Employment Opportunity Comm'n v. Arabian Am. Oil Co., 499 U.S. 244 (1991), which reaffirmed the rule establishing a presumption against the extraterritorial application of statutes. Despite this presumption, Environmental Def. Fund, Inc., v. Massey, 986 F.2d 528 (D.C. Cir. 1993), held NEPA applied to a decision by the National Science Foundation to incinerate wastes in Antarctica without preparing an impact statement. The court applied an exception, also adopted in *Arabian Am. Oil*, that the presumption against extraterritoriality applies with significantly less force when there is no potential for conflict with the laws of another country. It also held this exception applied because Antarctica was a "sovereign-less" country, and that the United States has "some measure of legislative control" there through control over research installations and air transportation. Accord Hirt v. Richardson, 127 F. Supp. 2d 833 (W.D. Mich. 1999) (NEPA applies to shipments of mixed oxide fuel intended for research power plant in Canada).

Recent cases have not applied NEPA extraterritorially, however, and later Supreme Court decisions have placed the precedential importance of *Massey* in doubt. See Smith v. United States, 507 U.S. 197 (1993) (extraterritorial jurisdiction did not apply to tort claims in Antarctica). In Basel Action Network v. Maritime Admin., 370 F. Supp. 2d 57 (D.D.C. 2005), for example, the court held NEPA did not apply to the towing of vessels for scrapping to the United Kingdom. It distinguished *Massey* because the United States does not have legislative control over the high seas, and because the presumption against extraterritoriality applies only in "sovereign-less" areas. Accord NEPA Coal. of Japan v. Aspin, 837 F. Supp. 466 (D.D.C. 1993) (impact statement not required on military bases in Japan subject to complex treaty arrangements). See Lewis, It's a Small World After All: Making the Case for Extraterritorial Application of the National Environmental Policy Act, 25 Cardozo L. Rev. 2143 (2004).

President Carter issued an Executive Order in 1979 on the Environmental Effects Abroad of Major Federal Actions. Exec. Order No. 12,114, 44 Fed. Reg. 1957 (1979). The Order is based on independent executive authority rather than NEPA, and requires less rigorous environmental assessment procedures, rather than an environmental impact statement, for most of the actions it covers. The Order excludes social and economic impacts from its definition of "environment," expressly provides that it does not create a "cause of action," and does not preempt the application of NEPA extraterritorially.

Environmental Assessment in Other Countries. Should the question of NEPA's extraterritorial scope be informed by the knowledge that environmental impact assessment is now an environmental policy instrument widely used throughout the world to examine the likely adverse environmental impacts of a wide class of activities before they are undertaken? In 1985, the European Economic Community adopted a Directive, which came into force in 1988, mandating environmental impact assessment (EIA) throughout the EU. 85/337/EEC. The duty to conduct an assessment for covered projects is mandatory.

Unlike NEPA, the EU Directive applies to projects rather than governmental agencies, and applies to both public and private projects "which are likely to have significant effects on the environment." Art. 1(1). Amendments to the Directive are under review. The Directive authorizes member states to integrate EIA into procedures for the approval of development projects, into other procedures, or into procedures established to comply with the Directive. For discussion see E. Wood, Environmental Impact Assessment: A Comparative Review (2d ed. 2003). England did not pass new complying legislation but integrated EIA into its planning and land use regulation procedures. The Directive must be given a "direct effect" in member states. This means that legislation and regulations in member states must comply with it. See Regina v. North Yorkshire County Council, [1999] 1 All E.R. 969 (H.L.), an English House of Lords decision.

Environmental impact assessment was endorsed in Agenda 21 adopted by the 1992 Rio Conference. The Rio Declaration on Environment and Development, Principle 17, A/CONF.151.5/Rev.1, 31 I.L.M. 874 (1992). The practice has become so widespread that it can now be said to be customary international law. See Argentina v. Uruguay (International Court of Justice 2010), available at icj-cij.org/docket/files/135/15877.pdf.

E. WHEN IS AN ENVIRONMENTAL IMPACT STATEMENT ADEQUATE?

1. The Substantive versus the Procedural Problem

The Problem. Once an agency has decided to prepare an environmental impact statement, it must meet the requirements of §102(2)(C). Ultimately, the courts must consider whether the impact statement is adequate, and the question they must resolve is this: Assuming that decisionmakers will seriously read and react to the information in the impact statement, is the statement likely to further the basic goal of NEPA, which is the promotion of more environmentally enlightened decisions? This question is troublesome for federal courts. At a minimum, as the decisions indicate, the impact statement is a full disclosure document, much like a Securities and Exchange Commission prospectus, and must fully disclose the environmental impacts of the proposed action. But, because the federal courts also take a "hard look" at agency decisions that have environmental consequences, more than mere disclosure may be required.

To understand the cases on the adequacy of an impact statement and the scope of judicial review, a basic distinction must be kept in mind, and that is the distinction between a challenge to the adequacy of an impact statement and a challenge to the merits of the decision. A NEPA plaintiff's first two challenges are to allege that an impact statement should have been prepared, if one has not been, and that if one was prepared, it is inadequate. The remedies for successful plaintiffs in these cases are the preparation of an initial, new, or supplemental impact statement. A challenge to the merits of the decision is based upon an unsatisfactory impact statement, but the impact statement is only one—although a very important—piece of evidence the decisionmaker must consider in making a final decision. The link between an unsatisfactory impact statement and the assertion that the final decision is arbitrary is the argument that, given the unsatisfactory impact statement, an informed decisionmaker could reach no other conclusion but that the proposed action should be rejected or modified. Supreme Court decisions indicate that this is an impossible argument to win.

Courts and commentators usually refer to the duty to prepare an adequate impact statement as NEPA's "procedural" duty. They refer to the agency's responsibility to reject or modify a proposal for action because of an unsatisfactory impact statement as NEPA's "substantive" duty. The term "procedural duty" does not refer to the duty to observe hearing procedures or other procedures in the preparation of an impact statement; it refers instead to the duty to comply sufficiently with the procedures mandated by NEPA for the preparation of an impact statement, so that the statement will contain a reasoned analysis on which the decisionmaker can base his or her decision. Courts ask whether an impact statement is "adequate" when they consider NEPA's procedural duty. The adequacy inquiry includes the following questions: Have all environmental impacts and alternatives been considered? If all alternatives and impacts have been considered, have they been adequately discussed and evaluated? What rules should the agency apply in discussing and evaluating alternatives and impacts?

Supreme Court Decisions. Whether NEPA should be given a substantive effect turns, in the words of *Overton Park*, on whether the statute has enacted "law to apply." Early court decisions concluded that NEPA had done just that. The leading case was Environmental Def. Fund, Inc. v. Corps of Engineers, 470 F.2d 289 (8th Cir. 1972), reviewing an impact statement prepared for Gillham Dam, a dam authorized to be constructed for flood control purposes in Arkansas. However, the Supreme Court soon laid to rest any expectancy that NEPA conferred substantive review.

At this point, reread the *Vermont Yankee* and *Kleppe* opinions, reproduced above. Recall that in footnote 21 of *Kleppe* the Court observed that "[n]either the statute nor its legislative history contemplates that a court should substitute its judgment for that of the agency as to the environmental consequences of its actions." And in *Vermont Yankee* the Court observed that "NEPA does set forth significant substantive goals for the nation, but its mandate is essentially procedural." See also Strycker's Bay Neighborhood Council v. Karlen, 444 U.S. 223 (1980) (affirming *Kleppe* footnote). The issue was finally settled in Robertson v. Methow Valley Citizens Council, reproduced below. The Supreme Court, citing *Strycker's Bay*, stated that although NEPA procedures are "almost certain" to affect substantive decisions, "it is now well settled that NEPA itself does not mandate particular results, but simply prescribes the necessary process." See Winter v. NRDC, Inc., 555 U.S. 7 (2008); Kalen, The Devolution of NEPA: How the APA Transformed the Nation's Environmental Policy, 33 Wm. & Mary Envtl. L. & Pol'y Rev. 483 (2009).

NOTES AND QUESTIONS

1. *Understanding Judicial Review.* As the critical observer must have realized by now, "the procedural and substantive theories are interrelated, for a procedural requirement of a reasoned analysis, especially as applied to broad policies and programs, must ultimately lead to holdings that some justifications for an activity are acceptable while others are not. This is especially true if the standard of procedural adequacy is coupled with a detailed and probing analysis of the factual basis of the impact statement." C. Meyers & A.D. Tarlock, Water Resource Management 586 (2d

ed. 1980). For a thoughtful analysis of judicial review problems by a late judge of the D.C. Circuit Court of Appeals who did much to bring about the "new" administrative law, see Leventhal, Environmental Decisionmaking and the Role of the Courts, 122 U. Pa. L. Rev. 509 (1974).

2. *Judicial Tests for the Review of Impact Statements*. The Supreme Court adopted the arbitrary and capricious standard of judicial review authorized by the Administrative Procedure Act for agency decisions on whether to prepare an impact statement. Marsh v. Oregon Natural Res. Council, 490 U.S. 360 (1989). Courts have applied this standard when reviewing the adequacy of impact statements, but also reference a "rule of reason" that was applied pre-*Marsh*. For example, the Ninth Circuit rule of reason asks whether an impact statement "contains a reasonably thorough discussion of the significant aspects of the probable environmental consequences." Idaho Conservation League v. Mumma, 956 F.2d 1508, 1519 (9th Cir. 1992).

Courts frequently repeat the statement that the standard of judicial review is a "narrow one." A court cannot decide whether an agency made the "right" decision, but can only determine whether the agency followed the procedures required by NEPA in making its decision. E.g., Habitat Educ. Ctr. v. United States Forest Serv., 603 F. Supp. 2d 1176 (E.D. Wis. 2009). One court has summarized the rules and held that the standards for judicial review are not precise, and that a pragmatic judgment is required. Courts must not "flyspeck" a document and look for minor or technical flaws, but must take a holistic view. Judicial review must also be deferential, especially for scientific and technical matters. However, "courts must ensure that agencies carry out their duties under NEPA, make reasoned choices, and provide a discussion that fully and frankly explains the environmental consequences of a proposed action." Highway J Citizens Group v. U.S. Dep't of Transp., 656 F. Supp. 2d 868, 885 (E.D. Wis. 2009).

A much-quoted early case, Silva v. Linn, 482 F.2d 1282 (1st Cir. 1973), adopted a three-part test that elaborates the judicial review standard. An EIS must allow the court to determine whether the agency made a "good faith effort" to take environmental values into account. Second, it must provide an "environmental full disclosure" to members of the public through an appropriate balance of nontechnical and scientific information. It may not contain vague, general, and conclusory reasoning. Finally, the EIS must ensure the integrity of the decisionmaking process by preventing problems and criticisms from being "swept under the rug," an admonition also contained in the previous quotation. All of this suggests more than minimal judicial attention.

3. *Injunctions*. Judicial intervention to ensure compliance with NEPA requires a remedy, and the traditional remedy in NEPA cases is a court-ordered injunction. NEPA plaintiffs usually seek a preliminary injunction to preserve the status quo in a case until the court can make a final decision. If the court does not issue a preliminary injunction, the plaintiff takes the risk that the defendant agency may proceed with its project, and may later convince the court the case is moot because the project is substantially or entirely completed. Courts asked to order preliminary injunctions normally balance the equities, usually requiring the plaintiff to show probable success on the merits, irreparable injury, and that the injunction is in the public interest.

Some courts applied a "NEPA exception" and granted a preliminary injunction without considering the usual equity factors. Other courts relaxed the irreparable harm rule in NEPA cases and found irreparable harm in the damage that would be done to NEPA's statutory purposes if the court refused all injunctions. See NEPA Law, §§4:53-4:61. The Supreme Court's decisions in Weinberger v. Romero-Barcelo, 456 U.S. 305 (1982), and Amoco Prod. Co. v. Village of Gambell, 480 U.S. 531 (1987), changed this. The Court held that traditional principles applied to injunctions in environmental cases and that courts should not presume environmental harm, but added that the "balance of harms" will usually favor the issuance of an injunction. These were not NEPA cases, but the courts have applied them in NEPA cases. See Rubinstein, Injunctions Under NEPA After Weinberger v. Romero-Barcelo and Amoco Production Co. v. Village of Gambell, 5 Wis. Envtl. L.J. 1 (1998).

In Winter v. Natural Res. Def. Council, Inc., 555 U.S. 7 (2008), a complex and fact-based case involving Navy sonar exercises, a split Court reiterated that plaintiffs seeking preliminary relief must show "that irreparable injury is likely unless an injunction is granted." On the facts, the Court held that a balancing of the equities and the public interest favored the Navy. See Eubanks, Damage Done? The Status of NEPA After Winter v. NRDC and Answers to Lingering Questions Left Open by the Court, 33 Vt. L. Rev. 649 (2009). Monsanto Co. v. Geertson Seed Farms, 561 U.S. 139 (2010), applied the traditional four-factor test for permanent injunctions, and held under those tests that it was improper to enjoin the planting of a genetically engineered crop until an impact statement was prepared. The Court rejected a presumption that "injunction is the proper remedy for a NEPA violation except in unusual circumstances."

2.   What Is an "Adequate" Impact Statement?

Compliance with NEPA requires agencies to prepare an environmental impact statement that is an adequate "full disclosure" document. We will now consider what an impact statement must contain in order to meet the adequacy requirement.

SIERRA CLUB v. BOSWORTH
199 F. Supp. 2d 971 (N.D. Cal. 2002)

MAXINE M. CHESNEY, United States District Judge . . .

Before the Court are cross-motions for summary judgment, filed pursuant to Rule 56 of the Federal Rules of Civil Procedure. . . . Having considered the papers filed in support of and in opposition to the motions and the arguments of counsel, the Court rules as follows.

BACKGROUND

In the instant action, plaintiffs challenge the adequacy of the Final Environmental Impact Statement ("EIS" or "FEIS") prepared by the Forest Service in connection with the Fuels Reduction for Community Protection project ("Fuels Reduction Project") on the Six Rivers National Forest ("Six Rivers"). In August, 1999, three small fires known as the Megram, Fawn, and Onion fires (collectively the "Big Bar Complex Fires") ignited on the Shasta-Trinity National Forest. After merging with the Fawn fire, the Megram fire burned approximately 59,220 acres of the Six Rivers National Forest, as well as many acres of the adjacent National Forests, an Indian Reservation, and private lands, before the fire was controlled on November 4, 1999.

The fire created extensive areas of dead and dying trees and shrubs which the Forest Service believes may become fuels for future fires. In an effort to reduce the intensity and severity of future wild fires within Six Rivers, the Forest Service has proposed numerous commercial logging projects designed to construct "strategic fuel breaks" and to "reduce fuels" in already burned areas.[1] In the instant action, plaintiffs challenge the EIS prepared in connection with Phase 1 of the Fuels Reduction Project ("Phase 1"), asserting that the EIS violates the National Environmental Policy Act (NEPA), and the National Forest Management Act ("NFMA").

[The court discussed the arbitrary and capricious standard of judicial review it would apply, and explained the rules that apply to motions for summary judgment.] . . .

DISCUSSION

A. Violations of NEPA

NEPA requires that impacts of "major Federal actions significantly affecting the quality of the human environment" be considered and disclosed in a detailed EIS. See 42 U.S.C. §4332(2)(C). NEPA, therefore, "ensures that the agency . . . will have available, and will carefully consider, detailed information concerning significant environmental impacts; it also guarantees that the relevant information will be made available to the larger audience." See Robertson v. Methow Valley Citizens Council, 490 U.S. 332, 349 (1989). Under NEPA, the Court must "ensure that the procedure followed by the Service resulted in a reasoned analysis of the evidence before it, and that the Service made the evidence available to all concerned." See Friends of Endangered Species, Inc. v. Jantzen, 760 F.2d 976, 986 (9th Cir. 1985).

Plaintiffs claim that the EIS prepared for Phase 1 violates NEPA "because it . . . fails to disclose and address the scientific evidence that directly contradicts both the statement of need and environmental analysis for the proposed action". . . .

1. Purpose and Need

A. LACK OF SUPPORTING EVIDENCE

The Forest Service states that the purpose of Phase I is to "protect[] local communities from catastrophic wildfires and extended exposure to smoke" by "reducing fuels." AR 246. According to the Forest Service, the Phase I project will reduce the intensity of future wildfires by removing the "fuels" that help to spread the fires.

Plaintiffs assert that the EIS violates NEPA by failing to disclose the lack of scientific evidence supporting the Forest Service's belief that the Phase I logging

1. A fuel break is "a strategically located wide block, or strip, on which a cover of dense, heavy, or flammable vegetation has been permanently changed to one of lower fuel volume or reduced flammability." AR [Administrative Record] 9397.

project will reduce the intensity of future wildfires and by failing to address reports that contradict the Forest Service's belief. See Seattle Audubon Society v. Lyons, 871 F. Supp. 1291, 1318 (W.D. Wash. 1994) (holding EIS must "disclose responsible scientific opinion in opposition to the proposed action, and make a good faith, reasoned response to it."). In particular, plaintiffs note that the EIS fails to disclose or discuss that a "Literature Review" of post-fire logging studies, completed by the Forest Service's Pacific Northwest Research Station in 2000, "found no studies documenting a reduction in fire intensity in a stand that had previously burned and then been logged." Plaintiffs also assert that the EIS fails to disclose and analyze an independent report on ecologically sound post-fire salvage logging, known as the "Beschta report," which also concluded that "no evidence supporting the contention that leaving large dead woody material significantly increases the probability of reburn." Plaintiffs point out that the Forest Service, in its Literature Review, acknowledged there is an "intense debate" over post-fire logging and yet the EIS, plaintiffs' assert, fails to disclose or analyze the contrary opinions and fails to "address the uncertainties surrounding the scientific opinion upon which the entire project is founded."

In response, the Forest Service does not contend that the EIS discloses or analyzes the scientific evidence that supports or that contradicts the goals of the Phase 1 project. Rather, the Forest Service contends that evidence supporting its position can be found within the administrative record and that its scientists did, in fact, consider contrary opinions, including the Beschta report.

It is not an adequate alternative, however, to merely include scientific information in the administrative record. NEPA requires that the EIS itself "make explicit reference . . . to the scientific and other sources relied upon for conclusions in the statement." See 40 C.F.R. §1502.24; see also Grazing Fields Farm v. Goldschmidt, 626 F.2d 1068, 1072 (1st Cir. 1980) ("We find no indication in [NEPA] that Congress contemplated that studies or memoranda contained in the administrative record, but not incorporated in any way into an EIS, can bring into compliance with NEPA an EIS that by itself is inadequate"); Blue Mountains Biodiversity Project v. Blackwood, 161 F.3d 1208, 1214 (9th Cir. 1998) (holding Environmental Assessment ("EA") inadequate where EA contained "virtually no reference to any material in support of or in opposition to its conclusions;" deficiency not cured by support contained in administrative record.)

Nor does the fact that the Forest Service's scientists may have considered contrary opinions, such as the Beschta report, constitute sufficient compliance with NEPA where the EIS fails to disclose or analyze such opinions. See Seattle Audubon Society v. Moseley, 798 F. Supp. 1473, 1482 (W.D. Wash. 1992) ("NEPA requires that the agency candidly disclose in its EIS the risks of its proposed action, and that it respond to the adverse opinions held by respected scientists."); Lyons, 871 F. Supp. at 1318 ("An EIS must . . . candidly disclose the risks and any scientific uncertainty. It must also disclose responsible scientific opinion in opposition to the proposed action, and make a good faith, reasoned response to it.").

Accordingly, the Court concludes that the Phase 1 EIS violates NEPA by failing to disclose and analyze scientific opinion in support of and in opposition to the conclusion that the Phase 1 project will reduce the intensity of future wildfires in the project area.

B. CONTRARY SCIENTIFIC EVIDENCE

Plaintiffs also assert that the EIS fails to disclose and analyze scientific opinion that is directly opposed to post-fire logging on the ground that it has a detrimental effect on the environment. Specifically, plaintiffs assert that the Forest Service erred in failing to disclose and analyze studies, such as the Beschta report, which recommended that no salvage logging occur in sensitive areas including severely burned areas and erosive sites. According to plaintiffs, the "EIS does not mention or discuss the substantial weight of scientific evidence that opposes logging in the aftermath of intense wildfire" and, thus, members of the public who are reviewing the EIS "would be unaware that there is a considerable controversy and debate surrounding the potential impacts of post-fire logging."

In response, the Forest Service does not contend that the "considerable controversy and debate" identified by plaintiffs does not exist. Nor does the Forest Service explain its failure to identify or address in the EIS the scientific opinion that opposes post-fire logging. Rather, the Forest Service merely challenges the importance of and applicability of the Beschta report for the Six Rivers region. The Forest Service's critique of this one report, however, does not explain why the Forest Service failed to disclose or address any contrary scientific opinion in the EIS. See *Lyons*, 871 F. Supp. at 1318 ("An EIS must . . . candidly disclose the risks and any scientific uncertainty. It must also disclose responsible scientific opinion in opposition to the proposed action, and make a good faith, reasoned response to it.") Although the Forest Service is not required to adopt the recommendations contained within the Beschta report and may rely on other expert opinion instead, the Phase 1 EIS fails, "not because experts disagree, but because the FEIS lacks reasoned discussion of major scientific objections." See *Moseley*, 798 F. Supp. 1473, 1482.

Accordingly, the Court concludes that the EIS violates NEPA by failing to disclose scientific opinion that opposes post-fire logging. . . . [The court granted plaintiff's motion for summary judgment and denied defendant's motion for summary judgment.]

NOTES AND QUESTIONS

1. *The Duty to Disclose.* NEPA is a disclosure statute, and the principal case explains the requirement that an impact statement must disclose responsible scientific opinion that supports its conclusions. Failure to disclose can be fatal. CEQ regulations detail this responsibility. They require that opposing scientific views be disclosed and discussed and require agencies to "make every effort to disclose and discuss at appropriate points . . . all major points of view on the environmental impacts of the proposed action." 40 C.F.R. §1502.9(a). As the principal case also notes, when there is conflicting evidence, agencies must explain the considerations they find persuasive when choosing one expert over another. Less is required if an agency makes full disclosure. There is no requirement that a methodology be peer-reviewed and published in a credible source. Lands Council v. Martin, 529 F.3d 1219 (9th Cir. 2008). Neither is it a court's function to resolve disagreements among scientific experts. As the Supreme Court stated in a NEPA case, "[w]hen specialists express conflicting views, an agency must have discretion to rely on the reasonable opinions of its own

experts, even if a court may find contrary views more persuasive." Marsh v. Oregon Natural Resources Council, 490 U.S. 360, 376 (1989). And as another court put it:

> NEPA does not require that we decide whether an EIR is based on the best scientific methodology available, nor does NEPA require us to resolve disagreements among various scientists as to methodology. . . . Our task is simply to ensure that the procedure followed by the Service resulted in a reasoned analysis of the evidence before it, and that the Service made the evidence available to all concerned. [Friends of Endangered Species, Inc. v. Jantzen, 760 F.2d 976, 986 (9th Cir. 1985).]

From these cases it seems clear an agency cannot ignore respectable expert opinion contrary to its conclusions, but once the agency identifies a reasonable range of opinion, it need do little more than state that no consensus exists on the issue at hand. In fact, the more candid the agency is about adverse impacts, the better its chances are of successfully resisting a judicial ruling that the impact statement is inadequate. What if a plaintiff claims that important elements of an analysis are missing? In National Indian Youth Council v. Andrus, 501 F. Supp. 649 (D.N.M. 1980), *aff'd on other grounds sub nom.* National Indian Youth Council v. Watt, 664 F.2d 220 (10th Cir. 1981), a case dealing with the adequacy of surface mining rec-lamation techniques, the plaintiff claimed there was a void of discussion of the "state of the art" of reclamation and revegetation, among other problems. The court answered: "As for the 'state of the art' contention, there simply is no requirement in Section 102(2)(C), or elsewhere in NEPA, that the 'state of the art' of a scientific discipline be explicitly discussed in an EIS, especially as an autonomous category." Id. at 668. What should have been done to remedy the problems identified in the principal case?

2. *Uncertainty and Worst-Case Analysis.* What if the information the plaintiff wanted in the principal case was unavailable, or could not be made available because of excessive cost? This lack of information would create an uncertainty problem. In the *Ocean Advocates* case, reproduced *supra*, the court held an agency could not use uncertainty as a reason for not preparing an impact statement. What is an agency's responsibility at the impact statement stage? CEQ originally had a "worst-case" ana-lysis rule that applied to impact statements and that was intended to deal with the uncertainty problem. An example is the situation where the environmental impacts of an agency project or action have a low probability of occurrence, but would be disastrous if they occurred. Agencies were supposed to analyze these consequences in view of this uncertainty. A catastrophic oil spill was the classic example, a possibility proved all too real by the BP 2010 Gulf spill. See Sierra Club v. Sigler, 695 F.2d 957 (5th Cir. 1983), requiring a worst-case analysis of an oil spill for a multipurpose deepwater port and oil distribution system under the former rule. CEQ revoked the worst-case rule in 1986 because it was inconsistent with the rule of reason, and because it was considered an unproductive and inefficient technique that could breed endless hypothesis and speculation. The Supreme Court upheld CEQ's revocation of the worst-case regulation in the *Robertson* case, reproduced below. Under the new regulation, agencies must disclose incomplete or unavailable information and obtain it "if the incomplete information relevant to reasonably foreseeable significant adverse impacts is essential to a reasoned choice among alternatives and the overall costs of doing so are not exorbitant." 40 C.F.R §1502.22 (a). This is a commonsense rule that requires disclosure when it is not burdensome. See Cabinet Res. Group v. United States Fish and Wildlife Serv., 465 F. Supp. 2d 1067 (D. Mont. 2006) (missing

information about species habitat and mortality essential to reasoned choice of alternatives to rule allowing motorized access to forests). If the information is essential and can be obtained without exorbitant cost, it must be included in the impact statement.

If costs are exorbitant or the means to obtain it are unknown, agencies must state the relevance of the information to evaluating reasonably foreseeable significant environmental impacts, summarize "credible scientific evidence" relating to these impacts, and evaluate these impacts based on generally accepted theoretical approaches or research methods in the scientific community. Courts will reverse agencies if they find compliance inadequate. E.g., Mid States Coal. for Progress v. Surface Transp. Bd., 345 F.3d 520 (8th Cir. 2003) (computer models were available that could be used). See Fitzgerald, The Rise and Fall of Worst Case Analysis, 18 U. Dayton L. Rev. 1 (1992). Should the regulation be strengthened?

3. *Commenting and Responses to Comments.* One of NEPA's purposes is to require agencies to adequately explain and disclose the basis for their environmental analysis, as the principal case points out, so that other agencies and interested parties can provide comments. Agencies must then provide a response. CEQ regulations suggest that responses can include a modification of alternatives, new alternatives, and improvements in the environmental analysis. 40 C.F.R. §1504.3(a). Agencies cannot ignore the conflicting comments of other agencies with expertise and must make a reasoned and detailed response. See North Carolina Wildlife Fed'n v. North Carolina DOT, 677 F.3d 596 (4th Cir. 2012) (public commentators repeatedly asked agencies whether "no build" baseline assumed construction of connector, but agencies either failed to address underlying issue or stated facts incorrectly). Compare WildWest Inst. v. Bull, 547 F.3d 1162 (9th Cir. 2008) (Forest Service summarized nature of comments received and primary concerns raised, and provided specific substantive responses). Responses to comments may not be perfunctory. A mere tabulation of comments is not enough. Neither is a "mere admission of some impact." National Wildlife Fed'n v. Andrus, 440 F. Supp. 1245, 1253 (D.D.C. 1977). See 40 C.F.R. §1503.4 (agency must explain why comments do not warrant further response). However, agencies need not accept the comments or suggestions of other agencies. Custer County Action Ass'n v. Garvey, 256 F.3d 1024 (10th Cir. 2001).

What if objections to an EIS are not made at the comment stage? *Vermont Yankee*, reproduced above, held that parties must make objections to agency actions at an appropriate time or be precluded from making them at the litigation stage. Courts apply this rule to preclude objections by parties in court if they fail to make objections to comments on an EIS. Oregon Natural Desert Ass'n v. McDaniel, 751 F. Supp. 2d 1151 (D. Or. 2011) (contains extensive discussion). Some courts, however, have not applied a preclusion rule in NEPA cases. Sierra Club v. Bosworth, 352 F. Supp. 2d 909 (D. Minn. 2005).

4. *Cost-Benefit Analysis.* It is by now reasonably well settled by court decisions that NEPA does not require a cost-benefit analysis. A strong statement rejecting this requirement can be found in Trout Unlimited v. Morton, 509 F.2d 1276 (9th Cir. 1974). CEQ does not require a cost-benefit analysis in impact statements, and does not require that costs and benefits be given monetary values. 40 C.F.R. §1502.23. Cost-benefit analysis has been most extensively used in water resource and flood control projects, in which it has been institutionalized by congressional and administrative directives. For these and other projects for which cost-benefit analysis is used, the technique provides a rule of decision that contrasts with the open-ended review of costs and benefits that NEPA contemplates.

Courts will review a cost-benefit analysis if an agency decides to do one, however, though an agency analysis may be hard to rebut if it is complete and bona fide. In rare cases, rebuttal is possible. In Hughes River Watershed Conservancy v. Glickman, 81 F.3d 437 (4th Cir. 1996), for example, plaintiffs sought judicial review of a decision approving construction of a dam on the North Fork of the Hughes River in northwestern West Virginia. A study commissioned for the dam estimated gross, rather than net, economic benefits, as required in the study contract. The court held the agencies relied on the gross benefit calculation, and that this reliance impaired the environmental analysis of the project. The court also held that reliance on gross benefits prevented the public from obtaining accurate information about the project.

After remand, the agencies calculated benefits relying on net economic benefits, and determined the project would have an overall positive net cost-benefit ratio. The court of appeals affirmed. Hughes River Watershed Conservancy v. Johnson, 165 F.3d 283 (4th Cir. 1999). See also Webster v. United States Dep't of Agric., 685 F.3d 411 (4th Cir. 2012) (dam; 100-year project life acceptable, costs and benefits of individual site not masked, inclusion of incidental recreation benefits acceptable). Compare Texas Comm. on Natural Res. v. Marsh, 736 F.2d 262 (5th Cir. 1984) (economic values not weighted against environmental concerns); Sierra Club v. Sigler, 695 F.2d 957 (5th Cir. 1983) (agency excluded a number of environmental costs from its cost-benefit analysis).

5. *Judicial Relief for Noncompliance.* What if an impact statement calls for environmentally protective measures that the agency does not carry out when it completes its project? Is judicial relief available? The courts have denied post-completion relief on a number of grounds, some holding the case was moot because the project had been completed. Other courts refused to read into NEPA an implied cause of action to enforce an impact statement. See Noe v. Metropolitan Atlanta Rapid Transit Auth., 644 F.2d 434 (5th Cir. 1981) (noise from construction of rapid transit station exceeded noise levels predicted in impact statements). Commentators have been critical of these cases, suggesting that courts should require agencies to file a supplemental impact statement when they deviate from an approved impact statement. See Note, EIS Supplements for Improperly Completed Projects: A Logical Extension of Judicial Review Under NEPA, 81 Mich. L. Rev. 221 (1982).

3. Cumulative Impacts

Problem 4-2

Review Problem 4-1. Now assume the Federal Highway Administration (FHWA) has considered all three segments of the highway in one EIS. Save Our State now argues that FHWA should also have considered the improvement of a primary state highway in its EIS that provides access to the proposed Outstate Connector near Metro City. FHWA has refused to do so, claiming the highway is only in the planning stage. Save Our State also argues that FHWA should consider in its EIS the effect the Outstate Connector will have in encouraging new development at two interchanges along its route. FHWA again refuses, claiming the Connector is only intended to serve existing traffic needs, and that no additional population growth is expected in the area served by the highway. How would you evaluate these arguments?

The following case considers a cumulative impact problem that arose in an environmental assessment, but the same issues arise in the preparation of environmental impact statements.

GRAND CANYON TRUST v. FEDERAL AVIATION ADMINISTRATION
290 F.3d 339 (D.C. Cir. 2002)

ROGERS, Circuit Judge:

The Grand Canyon Trust petitions for review of the decision of the Federal Aviation Administration ("FAA") approving the federal actions necessary to allow the city of St. George, Utah, to construct a replacement airport near Zion National Park. The Trust challenges the adequacy of the FAA's environmental assessment under §102(2)(C) of the National Environmental Policy Act of 1969 ("NEPA") and the FAA's conclusion that there would be no significant environmental impacts from the project necessitating preparation of an environmental impact statement under NEPA. Focusing on the noise impacts on the Park, the Trust principally contends that the FAA failed adequately to consider the cumulative impact on the natural quiet of the Park and instead addressed only the incremental impact of the replacement airport. We grant the petition.

I.

In 1995, the FAA began working with the City of St. George, Utah, to determine the feasibility of continuing use of the existing airport as compared to development of a new airport at a new site. A growing retirement community and projected air-traffic demand was outstripping the capacity of the existing airport, which could not be expanded due to geographic constraints. Three sites in addition to a no-action alternative were examined. In response to comments on a draft environmental assessment, the FAA conducted a Supplemental Noise Analysis on the potential noise impacts of the replacement airport on Zion National Park ("the Park"). The Park is located approximately 25 miles northeast of St. George and the preferred replacement airport alternative.

The FAA concluded that the noise impacts on the Park from the replacement airport would be negligible and insignificant. On January 30, 2001, the FAA approved the final environmental assessment, concluding that an environmental impact statement was unnecessary, and issued the record of decision, setting forth actions, determinations, and approvals that will allow St. George to construct the replacement airport. It is the determination underlying this record of decision, that the proposed action will not significantly affect the environment of the Park, that the Trust challenges.

II.

The essential disagreement between the parties is whether the FAA was required in its environmental assessment to address more than the incremental impact of the replacement airport as compared to the existing airport. NEPA requires federal agencies to prepare an environmental impact statement ("EIS") for "every . . . major Federal action[] significantly affecting the quality of the human environment." An environmental assessment ("EA") is made for the purpose of determining whether an EIS is required. See 40 C.F.R. §1508.9. "If any 'significant' environmental impacts might result from the proposed agency action then an EIS must be prepared before agency action is taken." Sierra Club v. Peterson, 717 F.2d 1409, 1415 (D.C. Cir. 1983) ("*Peterson*"). . . .

The Trust does not dispute that the FAA properly defined the relevant environmental concern of noise impacts from aircraft on the Park. Rather, the Trust contends that the FAA cannot be said to have taken a "hard look" at the problem when it considered only the incremental impacts of the replacement airport and not the total noise impact that will result from the relocated airport. The Trust notes that the EA does not address the cumulative impact in light of other air flights over the Park, air tours in or near the Park, and reasonably foreseeable future aircraft activity and airport expansions that will contribute to the cumulative noise impact on the Park. Indeed, the EA's statement on cumulative impact is, in full: "There are no known factors that could result in cumulative impacts as a result of the proposed St. George Replacement Airport." Further, the Trust notes, the FAA's Supplemental Noise Analysis disregards cumulative impacts. The FAA responds that it adequately considered the cumulative impact when it compared noise impacts associated with the replacement airport with the no-action alternative of continued use of the existing airport. It rejects the Trust's position that it was required in an EA to compare the project to an environmental baseline of natural quiet and to consider the total impact of aircraft noise on the Park.

The issue dividing the parties is settled by regulations promulgated by the Council on Environmental Quality ("CEQ") to implement NEPA and by case law applying those regulations. "The CEQ regulations, which . . . are entitled to substantial deference, impose a duty on all federal agencies." Marsh v. Oregon Natural Res. Council, 490 U.S. 360, 372 (1989). The CEQ regulations define each term within NEPA's requirement of an EIS for "every . . . major Federal action significantly affecting the quality of the human environment." The term "significantly" is defined as those actions "with individually insignificant but cumulatively significant impacts. Significance exists if it is reasonable to anticipate a cumulatively significant impact on the environment." 40 C.F.R. §1508.27(b)(7). "Cumulative impact," in turn, is defined as:

> the impact on the environment which results from the incremental impact of the action when added to other past, present, and reasonably foreseeable future actions regardless of what agency (Federal or non-Federal) or person undertakes such other actions. Cumulative impacts can result from individually minor but collectively significant actions taking place over a period of time. 40 C.F.R. §1508.7. . . .

The courts, in reviewing whether a federal agency has acted arbitrarily and capriciously in finding no significant environmental impact, have given effect to the plain language of the regulations. While the factual settings differ in some respects from the instant case, the consistent position in the case law is that, depending on the environmental concern at issue, the agency's EA must give a realistic evaluation of the total impacts and cannot isolate a proposed project, viewing it in a vacuum. For example, in Coalition on Sensible Transportation v. Dole, 826 F.2d 60 (D.C. Cir. 1987) ("*Dole*"), this court stated that the CEQ regulations on cumulative impact "provide a distinct meaning to the concept" separate and apart from the notion of improper segmentation of agency action. Noting that the regulatory definition of cumulative impact specifies that the "'incremental impact of the action' [at issue]" must be considered "'when added to other past, present, and reasonably foreseeable future actions,'" id. (quoting 40 C.F.R. §1508.7), the court observed that, consistent with the regulation and purpose of NEPA, "it makes sense to consider the 'incremental impact' of a project for possible cumulative effects by incorporating the effects of other projects into the background 'data base' of the project at issue." The point, the court stated, was to provide in the EA "sufficient [information] to alert interested members of the public to any arguable cumulative impacts involving . . . other projects." . . . Natural Resources Defense Council, Inc. v. Hodel, 865 F.2d 288 (D.C. Cir. 1988), is to the same effect. There, the agency had failed to consider the cumulative impact, as defined in the CEQ regulations, of simultaneous development in the region on "species, particularly whales and salmon, that migrate through the different planning areas" when it considered only the effect on those species "within the Planning Area" rather than "the interregional effects." Id. at 297-99. Other circuits take a similar approach in applying the regulations. . . .

The FAA, in finding that the St. George replacement airport would have no significant impact on the environment of the Park, concluded that "there is little discernible increased noise intrusion to the Park" from the proposed replacement airport as compared to the existing airport, and that "the increase in noise levels that would result from the development of a replacement airport is negligible [because] aircraft traffic will increase even if the replacement airport is not constructed." The FAA's analysis appears principally in a Supplemental Noise Analysis attached to the EA, and proceeds on the basis of a comparison of the noise impacts from predicted air traffic at the existing airport and predicted air traffic at the larger replacement airport. . . . Comparing the predicted noise impact on the Park from the existing and replacement airports, the FAA found that Day-Night Noise Level ("DNL") would increase "due to the implementation of the replacement airport over the use of the existing airport" by no more than 3.5 dBA in 2008 and 3.2 dBA in 2018, which the FAA characterized as "extremely low" increases. The FAA concluded that "there will be little difference associated with the replacement airport, as compared with the existing airport, in the long-term based on the DNL metric."

The FAA also examined in the Supplemental Noise Analysis the peak hour Equivalent Noise Level ("LEQ") based on a threshold of 45 dBA, when aircraft would be clearly audible and noticeable in the Park. . . . The FAA concluded that "there will be little difference in noise between the existing and replacement airport."

In a section of the EA entitled "Impacts to Natural Quiet of the Park," the FAA did acknowledge the existence of "overflights" that pass over the Park. Noting that NPS had completed ambient noise monitoring in Zion National Park, the FAA stated that the results showed that "the background or ambient noise levels vary, but are often in the low 20 dBA." Finding that the typical peak or maximum noise levels from aircraft from either the existing or proposed St. George airport sites ranged from 45 to 65 dBA when passing directly overhead, the FAA concluded that, because "these aircraft are at or near cruise altitude, or in the case of jets [are] above 20,000 feet, the peak or maximum noise levels will remain the same for either airport site." While recognizing that these overflights constitute noise events that are higher than background natural quiet during periods when ambient noise levels are low, the FAA focused on the incremental impact, stating that it was "important to illustrate that the development of the St. George replacement airport has little effect on the overall aircraft noise levels in the Park." The FAA referred to the 250 overflights following established flight paths near or over the Park that are not associated with St. George Airport in concluding that "the replacement airport has very little contribution to the cumulative number of aircraft over flights over Zion National Park." . . . The FAA concluded that the existing St. George airport would contribute only 11% of all existing flights using instrument flight rules over or near the Park, and that the increased flights from the replacement airport would represent only approximately 2% of the total aircraft flights using instrument flight rules over or near the Park.

The FAA's noise analysis in the EA, including the Supplemental Noise Analysis, may, in fact, be a splendid incremental analysis, but it fails to address what is crucial if the EA is to serve its function. While, as the FAA stresses, the EA is not intended to be a lengthy document, it must at a minimum address the considerations relevant to determining whether an EIS is required. NEPA regulations require that an agency consider cumulative impacts and the FAA's EA fails to address the total noise impact that will result from the replacement airport. Indeed, the FAA's own NEPA policy calls for consideration of cumulative impact, parroting the language of the NEPA regulations to include proposed projects and past, present, and reasonably foreseeable future actions. Comments on the draft EA called the FAA's attention to the need to consider mitigation measures in view of the results of the study of noise-annoyance to persons in the Park; the EA does not respond and provides no analysis of the 2% to 9% or the 4% to 15% level of annoyance shown in the NPS study. Yet, as the FAA was aware, the NPS had identified Zion National Park as among the nine national parks of "highest priority" for attention to noise impact on their natural quiet from overflights. Comments also expressed concern about the total impacts of noise on the Park and on Park visitors, yet the EA contains no analysis of the impact of 54 daily flights in 2008 and 69 in 2018 associated with St. George.

The Trust maintains that each flight may be responsible for a noise level of 45 to 65 dBA and points to expert testimony that an increase of 10 dBA correlates to a doubling of loudness such that a commercial jet overflight at the Park may be 4 to 23 times as loud as the natural soundscape. Even in the absence of the regulatory definitions it would be difficult to understand how an agency could determine that an EIS is not required if it had not evaluated existing noise impacts as well as those planned impacts that will exist by the time the new facility is constructed and in operation. As the Trust gleans from case law:

> a meaningful cumulative impact analysis must identify (1) the area in which the effects of the proposed project will be felt; (2) the impacts that are expected in that area from the proposed project; (3) other actions—past, present, and proposed, and reasonably foreseeable—that have had or are expected to have impacts in the same area; (4) the impacts or expected impacts from these other actions; and (5) the overall impact that can be expected if the individual impacts are allowed to accumulate. Petitioner's Reply Br. at 3.

The analysis in the EA, in other words, cannot treat the identified environmental concern in a vacuum, as an incremental approach attempts. Although the replacement airport may contribute only a 2% increase to the amount of overflights near or over the Park, there is no way to determine from the FAA's analysis in the EA whether, deferring to the FAA's expert calculations, a 2% increase, in addition to other noise impacts on the Park, will "significantly affect[]" the quality of the human environment in the Park. At no point does the FAA's EA aggregate the noise impacts on the Park. The analysis in the EA does not address the accumulated, or total, incremental impacts of various man-made noises, such as the 250 daily aircraft flights near or over the Park that originate at, or have as their destination, airports other than that in St. George. Neither does the EA consider in any manner the air tours near and over the Park originating from the St. George airport. Nor does the EA address the impact, much less the cumulative impact, of noise in the Park as a result of other activities, such as the planned expansions of other regional airports that have flights near or over the Park. Without analyzing the total noise impact on the Park as a result of the construction of the replacement airport, the FAA is not in a position to determine whether the additional noise that is projected to come from the expansion of the St. George airport facility at a new location would cause a significant environmental impact on the Park and, thus, to require preparation of an EIS. . . .

We remand the case because the record is insufficient for the court to determine whether an EIS is required. On remand, the FAA must evaluate the cumulative impact of noise pollution on the Park as a result of construction of the proposed replacement airport in light of air traffic near and over the Park, from whatever airport, air tours near or in the Park, and the acoustical data collected by NPS in the Park in 1995 and 1998 mentioned in comments on the draft EA. Other data may also prove relevant. . . .

NOTES AND QUESTIONS

1. *What Impacts Are Cumulative?* Notice the difference between the cumulative impact problem and the segmentation problem. The segmentation problem is whether an agency must discuss related projects in a single impact statement. The cumulative impact problem is whether an EA or EIS must discuss the environmental impacts of other actions because they are cumulative and add to the impacts of the action considered in the EA or EIS. In the principal case, for example, the question was whether the impact of other flights had to be considered in the EA on the replacement airport. There was no improper segmentation of other projects. The question was whether the scope of the agency's cumulative impact analysis was correct.

Scope cases fall into several categories. In the principal case the issue was whether the agency had to consider a nonadjacent but similar effect. Compare Selkirk Conservation Alliance v. Forsgren, 336 F.3d 944 (9th Cir. 2003) (need not consider similar logging project in adjacent national forest). In another type of case the claim is that a nonadjacent but dissimilar action should have been considered. See People v. United States Dep't of Transp., 260 F. Supp. 2d 969 (N.D. Cal. 2003) (airport expansion project must address cumulative impact of other nearby projects, including hotel construction). Claims can also be made that the impact of a project on an adjacent area must be considered. Earth Island Inst. v. United States Forest Serv., 351 F.3d 1291 (9th Cir. 2003) (must consider impact of timber sale on spotted owl species in neighboring forest).

A related question is whether an agency must consider the cumulative effects of an action that is later in time. Selkirk Conservation Alliance v. Forsgren, 336 F.3d 944 (9th Cir. 2003), held that a three-year analysis period for cumulative impacts in an EIS for a road easement through national forest land with an endangered grizzly bear population was correct.

To decide scope cases, the Ninth Circuit uses an "independent utility" test similar to that used in segmentation cases, but the Tenth Circuit holds this is only one factor to consider. City of Oxford v. Federal Aviation Admin., 428 F.3d 1346 (10th Cir. 2005). Most cases do not attempt to develop a deciding principle. What test would you adopt?

2. *Considering Cumulative Impacts.* The requirement that an agency must consider cumulative impacts usually adds to the environmental impacts an environmental assessment or impact statement must review, because additional actions and projects are brought into the analysis. This can make the agency's job more difficult, as the principal case illustrates, because the cumulative effects of an action may aggravate its environmental impact.

Another issue in the consideration of cumulative impacts is whether the discussion was adequate. Courts apply the "rule of reason" they use when considering the adequacy of any analysis in an EIS. Kern v. U.S. Bureau of Land Mgmt., 284 F.3d 1062 (9th Cir. 2002), summarizes the rules that apply in that circuit:

> Consideration of cumulative impacts requires "some quantified or detailed information; . . . general statements about 'possible' effects and 'some risk' do not constitute a 'hard look' absent a justification regarding why more definitive information could not be provided." The cumulative impact analysis must be more than perfunctory; it must provide a "useful analysis of the cumulative impacts of past, present, and future projects." Finally, cumulative impact analysis must be timely. It is not appropriate to defer consideration of cumulative impacts to a future date when meaningful consideration can be given now. When an agency's determination of what are "reasonably foreseeable future actions" and appropriate "component parts" is "'fully informed and well-considered,'" we will defer to that determination. But we "need not forgive a 'clear error in judgment.'" [Id. at 1075.]

This statement reflects judicial review standards usually applied. A requirement that all "reasonably foreseeable" actions that have potential environmental effects must be addressed is contained in the CEQ regulations.

The cumulative impact requirement is heavily litigated, and courts are frequently asked to consider whether a discussion of cumulative impacts is adequate. For a case holding the cumulative effects of a wind energy project were adequately analyzed, see Quechan Tribe of the Fort Yuma Indian Reservation v. U.S. Dep't of Interior, 927 F. Supp. 2d 921 (S.D. Cal. 2013). A Ninth Circuit case created problems concerning the level of detail required in the discussion of past cumulative impacts, but this problem has been addressed by a CEQ Guidance on the Consideration of Past Actions in Cumulative Impacts Analysis (2005).

The principal case considered the discussion of cumulative impacts in an environmental assessment. Note the somewhat different role they play there, and that an agency must also consider other NEPA requirements, such as the alternatives requirement, in its EAs. For additional discussion of why an environmental assessment must discuss cumulative impacts, see the *Kern* case, discussed above.

3. *The Proposal Problem*. Another problem that arises in the consideration of cumulative impacts is whether an agency must discuss the cumulative impact of projects still in the planning stage on which no final "proposal" has been made. The Supreme Court's Kleppe v. Sierra Club decision, reproduced above, held that only actions on which a "proposal" has been made fall under NEPA. The question is whether *Kleppe* means agencies do not have to discuss the cumulative impacts of actions that have not been proposed.

Several courts have held they do not. See WildEarth Guardians v. Jewell, 738 F.3d 298 (D.C. Cir. 2013) (coal mine lease; need not consider eleven other pending lease applications). But see Fritiofson v. Alexander, 772 F.2d 1225 (5th Cir. 1985), holding that *Kleppe* does not apply when an agency is assessing the environmental impacts of an action to decide whether an impact statement should be prepared. What is the policy issue here? Relatedly, a court may decide the cumulative impacts of an action that has not reached the proposal stage need not be considered because they are not "reasonably foreseeable" as required by CEQ regulations. See Theodore Roosevelt Conservation P'ship v. Salazar, 616 F.3d 497 (D.C. Cir. 2010) (gas field development).

4. *The CEQ Study*. CEQ published a study, Considering Cumulative Impacts under the National Environmental Policy Act (1997), that provides guidance to agencies on cumulative impact analysis. The study recommends the delineation of "project impact zones" as the basis for studying cumulative impacts:

> Project impact zones for a proposed action are likely to vary for different resources and environmental media. For water, the project impact zone would be limited to the hydrologic system that would be affected by the proposed action. . . . Land-based effects may occur within some set distance from the proposed action. In addition, the boundaries for an individual resource should be related to the resource's dependence on different environmental media. [Id. at 15.]

5. *Indirect Impacts*. CEQ regulations also require consideration of the indirect impacts of an action. 40 C.F.R. §1508.3(b). These are impacts that are "caused by the action and are later in time or further removed in distance, but are still reasonably foreseeable. Indirect effects may include growth inducing effects and other effects related to induced changes in land use patterns, population density or growth rate, and related effects on air and water and other natural systems, including ecosystems." An example is a project, such as a highway project, that encourages growth in the surrounding area. City of Davis v. Coleman, 521 F.2d 661 (9th Cir. 1975), is a leading example. A federally funded highway interchange was planned in a rural area near the city to service and stimulate new industrial development. The court held an impact statement was required. The agency had not discussed the inevitable industrial development and population increase that would have a potentially detrimental impact on the city's controlled growth policy, and that would create a demand for residential and commercial development and the beginning of urban sprawl.

City of Carmel-by-the-Sea v. U.S. Dep't of Transp., 123 F.3d 1142 (9th Cir. 1997), distinguished *City of Davis* because there the highway was planned only to meet existing needs, and other cases have also not required a discussion of growth-inducing effects when a project met existing needs. In other cases the courts found circumstances indicating that future growth would not occur. Northwest Bypass Group v. U.S. Army Corps of Eng'rs, 470 F. Supp. 2d 30 (D.N.H. 2007) (need not consider effect of connector road on development, much of adjacent area in wetlands and some tracts were subject to conservation easements; *City of Davis* distinguished).

Does the requirement to consider indirect impacts turn NEPA analysis into a planning exercise? Agencies doing NEPA reviews must consider growth problems but do not have the authority to plan for and regulate it. Agencies can rely on local plans and zoning, however, as the basis for a decision that growth-inducing impacts would not occur. In *City of Carmel*, for example, the EIS admitted that some development might occur, but did not discuss it because it was planned, accounted for, and properly analyzed in a local master plan. State and regional transportation plans developed with federal funds are an example of land use plans that can be relied on by agencies in making decisions about growth-inducing effects. See Federal Highway Admin. & Federal Transit Admin., Integration of Planning and NEPA Processes (2005). Is this enough? See Mandelker, Growth-Induced Land Development Caused by Highway and Other Projects as an Indirect Effect Under NEPA, 43 Envtl. L. Rptr. 11068 (2013).

6. *Trying the NEPA Case.* This is a good place to discuss how a NEPA case is tried. Often the parties make cross-motions for summary judgment on the pleadings, usually to avoid the expense and time of a trial and to take advantage of pleading claims. If the case goes to trial, the usual practice is to try the case on the record. NEPA decisions are informal. There is no adjudicative hearing that produces a disciplined record for an appeal, so the record usually consists of a messy accumulation of documents and files that the court must examine.

If a NEPA case is tried on the record the agency makes, may the plaintiff introduce extra-record evidence at trial? Review the cases reproduced and discussed in this chapter and try to see where the record has been supplemented by trial evidence. The decision on whether a plaintiff can supplement the record is critical in NEPA litigation. Without supplementation, the plaintiff will not be able to challenge an agency's conclusions with its own evidence.

In *Overton Park*, reproduced in Chapter 3, section A.2.c, the Supreme Court held that district courts should usually limit their review to the administrative record, and indicated a plaintiff may introduce extra-record evidence only when the record is incomplete or not clear. NEPA cases have applied these exceptions, Soda Mountain Wilderness Council v. U.S. Bureau of Land Mgmt., 945 F. Supp. 2d 1162 (D. Or. 2013) (admitting map but not other documents to help determine whether agency considered relevant factors in approving timber sale). However, the circuits are sharply divided on whether extra-record evidence should be allowed, and some take a restrictive view. County of Suffolk v. Secretary of the Interior, 562 F.2d 1368 (2d Cir. 1977), is a leading case for applying an exception allowing extra-record evidence when an agency fails to raise an important environmental issue in an impact statement. Some courts apply other exceptions, as when the extra-record evidence is supplemental or cumulative. A court will allow limited discovery to determine whether a record is complete. Bar MK Ranches v. Yeutter, 994 F.2d 735 (10th Cir. 1993). See NEPA Law §4:38; Comment, Judicial Review of the Administrative Record in NEPA Litigation, 81 Cal. L. Rev. 929 (1993). Success in getting extra-record evidence in at trial may be critical for a plaintiff if the impact statement (or assessment) does not present a clear and accurate assessment of environmental impacts.

4. *Mitigation*

Mitigation issues arise at the EIS stage, in which the question is whether the agency has adequately mitigated the significant environmental impacts it has discussed in its impact statement. The following case considers whether mitigation is required, and what this requirement means.

ROBERTSON v. METHOW VALLEY CITIZENS COUNCIL
490 U.S. 332 (1989)

Justice STEVENS delivered the opinion of the Court.

We granted certiorari to decide two questions of law. As framed by petitioners, they are:

1. Whether the National Environmental Policy Act requires federal agencies to include in each environmental impact statement: (a) a fully developed plan to mitigate environmental harm; and (b) a "worst case" analysis of potential environmental harm if relevant information concerning significant environmental effects is unavailable or too costly to obtain.
2. Whether the Forest Service may issue a special use permit for recreational use of national forest land in the absence of a fully developed plan to mitigate environmental harm.

Concluding that the Court of Appeals for the Ninth Circuit misapplied the National Environmental Policy Act of 1969 (NEPA), and gave inadequate deference to the Forest Service's interpretation of its own regulations, we reverse and remand for further proceedings.

I

. . .

The Forest Service is authorized to manage the national forests for a number of purposes, including "outdoor recreation." It has issued approximately 170 special use permits pursuant to that authority for alpine and nordic ski areas. These permits are major federal actions that must be preceded by the preparation of an impact statement. . . .

[Methow Recreation was awarded a special use permit to develop and operate a proposed Early Winters Ski Resort on Sandy Butte, a 6000-foot mountain in Okanogan National Forest, Washington, and on an adjacent 1,165 acre parcel. Sandy Butte, "like the Methow Valley it overlooks, is an unspoiled, sparsely populated area that the district court characterized as 'pristine.'" The Forest Service cooperated with state and county officials to prepare an impact statement known as the Early Winters Alpine Winter Sports Study.]

The Early Winters Study is a printed document containing almost 150 pages of text and 12 appendices. It evaluated five alternative levels of development of Sandy Butte that might be authorized, the lowest being a "no action" alternative and the highest being development of a 16-lift ski area able to accommodate 10,500 skiers at one time. The Study considered the effect of each level of development on water resources, soil, wildlife, air quality, vegetation and visual quality, as well as land use and transportation in the Methow Valley, probable demographic shifts, the economic market for skiing and other summer and winter recreational activities in the Valley, and the energy requirements for the ski area and related developments. The Study's discussion of possible impacts was not limited to on-site effects, but also, as required by Council on Environmental Quality (CEQ) regulations, see 40 CFR §1502.16(b) (1987), addressed "off-site impacts that each alternative might have on community facilities, socioeconomic and other environmental conditions in the Upper Methow Valley." As to off-site effects, the Study explained that "due to the uncertainty of where other public and private lands may become developed," it is difficult to evaluate offsite impacts, and thus the document's analysis is necessarily "not site-specific." Finally, the Study outlined certain steps that might be taken to mitigate adverse effects, both on Sandy Butte and in the neighboring Methow Valley, but indicated that these proposed steps are merely conceptual and "will be made more specific as part of the design and implementation stages of the planning process." . . .

[The study concluded that although the ski resort would not have an adverse effect on air quality, off-site development that would accompany the resort would reduce air quality below state standards unless mitigation measures were taken. This impact would be created by increased automobile, fireplace, and wood stove use.] . . .

[As mitigation measures t]he Study suggested that Okanogan County develop an air quality management plan, requiring weatherization of new buildings, limiting the number of wood stoves and fireplaces, and adopting monitoring and enforcement measures. In addition, the Study suggested that the Forest Service require that the master plan include procedures to control dust and to comply with smoke management practices.

In its discussion of adverse effects on area wildlife, the EIS concluded that no endangered or threatened species would be affected by the proposed development and that the only impact on sensitive species was the probable loss of a pair of spotted owls and their progeny. With regard to other wildlife, the Study considered the impact on 75 different indigenous species and predicted that within a decade after development vegetational change and increased human activity would lead to a decrease in population for 31 species, while causing an increase in population for another 24 species on Sandy Butte. Two species, the pine marten and nesting goshawk, would be eliminated altogether from the area of development.

In a comment in response to the draft EIS, the Washington Department of Game voiced a special concern about potential losses to the State's largest migratory deer herd, which uses the Methow Valley as a critical winter range and as its migration route. The state agency estimated that the total population of mule deer in the area most likely to be affected was "better than 30,000 animals" and that "the ultimate impact on the Methow deer herd could exceed a 50 percent reduction in numbers." The agency asserted that "Okanogan County residents place a great deal of importance on the area's deer herd." In addition, it explained that hunters had "harvested" 3,247 deer in the Methow Valley area in 1981, and that in 1980 hunters on average spent $1,980 for each deer killed in Washington, and they had contributed over $6 million to the State's economy. Because the deer harvest is apparently proportional to the size of the herd, the state agency predicted that "Washington business can expect to lose over $3 million annually from reduced recreational opportunity." The Forest Service's own analysis of the impact on the deer herd was more modest. It first concluded that the actual operation of the ski hill would have only a "minor" direct impact on the herd,[7] but then recognized that the off-site effect of the development "would noticeably reduce numbers of deer in the Methow [Valley] with any alternative." Although its estimate indicated a possible 15 percent decrease in the size of the herd, it summarized the State's contrary view in the text of the EIS, and stressed that off-site effects are difficult to estimate due to uncertainty concerning private development.

As was true of its discussion of air quality, the EIS also described both on-site and off-site mitigation measures. Among possible on-site mitigation possibilities, the Study recommended locating runs, ski lifts, and roads so as to minimize interference with wildlife, restricting access to selected roads during fawning season, and further examination of the effect of the development on mule deer migration routes.[8] Off-site options discussed in the Study included the use of zoning and tax incentives to limit development on deer winter range and migration routes, encouragement of conservation easements, and acquisition and management by local government of critical tracts of land. As with the measures suggested for mitigating the off-site effects on air quality, the proposed options were primarily directed to steps that might be taken by state and local government.

Ultimately, the Early Winters Study recommended the issuance of a permit for development at the second highest level considered—a 16-lift ski area able to accommodate 8,200 skiers at one time. On July 5, 1984, the Regional Forester decided to issue a special use permit as recommended by the Study. [To mitigate secondary impacts on air quality and a reduction in mule deer range the Forester directed the forest supervisor to implement mitigation measures "both independently and in cooperation with local officials."] . . .

[The plaintiffs appealed to the Chief Forester, who affirmed the Regional Forester's decision. They then brought suit claiming violations of NEPA. The suit was assigned to a Magistrate, who found that the impact statement was adequate. The court of appeals reversed. It held the agency could not rely on mitigation measures to

7. Id., at 76. The Study predicted that development of the ski area would diminish available summer range for the deer by between 5 and 10 percent, depending on the level of development chosen. Moreover, it recognized that although disturbance would be greatest during fawning season, "[f]awning would not be adversely affected with implementation of mitigation measures." Id., at 75-76.

8. The EIS listed the following opportunities for on-site mitigation:

a) Locate runs, lifts, roads, and other facilities to minimize disturbance of blue grouse wintering areas (primarily ridgetops).
b) Leave dead and defective trees standing in timbered areas where skier safety can be protected.
c) Restrict activities and travel on selected roads during the fawning season (June).
d) Locate new service roads away from water sources and fawning cover.
e) Evaluate impact to mule deer migration routes in review of Master Plan.
f) Design and harvest nearby, off-site timber sales to retain adequate travel corridors, foraging, roosting, and nesting sites for spotted owls.
g) Protect other likely migration routes between summer and winter habitats for spotted owls.
h) Restrict other activities within the spotted owls home range.
i) Springs and riparian areas in the permit area will be protected as water sources and wildlife habitat. . . . Id., at 16-17.

The Study further noted that additional mitigation opportunities might result from review of the master plan. Id., at 77.

support its finding that the effect on mule deer would be minor because these measures had not been developed. With respect to air quality, the court held the agency had an affirmative duty to develop necessary mitigation measures before the permit was granted. It read NEPA as imposing a substantive requirement that "action be taken to mitigate the adverse effects of major federal actions."]

II

Section 101 of NEPA declares a broad national commitment to protecting and promoting environmental quality. To ensure that this commitment is "infused into the ongoing programs and actions of the Federal Government, the act also establishes some important 'action-forcing' procedures." 115 Cong. Rec. 40416 (remarks of Sen. Jackson). . . . [The Court then quoted §102.]

The statutory requirement that a federal agency contemplating a major action prepare such an environmental impact statement serves NEPA's "action-forcing" purpose in two important respects. It ensures that the agency, in reaching its decision, will have available and will carefully consider detailed information concerning significant environmental impacts; it also guarantees that the relevant information will be made available to the larger audience that may also play a role in both the decisionmaking process and the implementation of that decision.

Simply by focusing the agency's attention on the environmental consequences of a proposed project, NEPA ensures that important effects will not be overlooked or underestimated only to be discovered after resources have been committed or the die otherwise cast. Moreover the strong precatory language of §101 of the Act and the requirement that agencies prepare detailed impact statements inevitably bring pressure to bear on agencies "to respond to the needs of environmental quality." 115 Cong. Rec. 40425 (1969) (remarks of Sen. Muskie).

Publication of an EIS, both in draft and final form, also serves a larger informational role. It gives the public the assurance that the agency "has indeed considered environmental concerns in its decision making process," Baltimore Gas & Electric [Co. v. NRDC, Inc., 462 U.S. 87, 97 (1983)], and, perhaps more significantly, provides a springboard for public comment, see L. Caldwell, Science and the National Environmental Policy Act 72 (1982). Thus, in this case the final draft of the Early Winters Study reflects not only the work of the Forest Service itself, but also the critical views of the Washington State Department of Game, the Methow Valley Citizens Council, and Friends of the Earth, as well as many others, to whom copies of the draft Study were circulated. Moreover, with respect to a development such as Sandy Butte, where the adverse effects on air quality and the mule deer herd are primarily attributable to predicate off-site development that will be subject to regulation by other governmental bodies, the EIS serves the function of offering those bodies adequate notice of the expected consequences and the opportunity to plan and implement corrective measures in a timely manner.

The sweeping policy goals announced in §101 of NEPA are thus realized through a set of "action-forcing" procedures that require that agencies take a "'hard look' at environmental consequences," Kleppe [v. Sierra Club, 427 U.S. 390, 410 n.21 (1976)], and that provide for broad dissemination of relevant environmental information. Although these procedures are almost certain to affect the agency's substantive decision, it is now well settled that NEPA itself does not mandate particular results, but simply prescribes the necessary process. See Stryker's Bay Neighborhood Council, Inc. v. Karlen, 444 U.S. 223, 227-228 (1980) (per curiam); Vermont Yankee Nuclear Power Corp. v. Natural Resources Defense Council, Inc., 435 U.S. 519, 558 (1978). If the adverse environmental effects of the proposed action are adequately identified and evaluated, the agency is not constrained by NEPA from deciding that other values outweigh the environmental costs. See ibid.; *Strycker's Bay Neighborhood Council, Inc., supra,* at 227-228; *Kleppe,* 427 U.S., at 410, n.21. In this case, for example, it would not have violated NEPA if the Forest Service, after complying with the Act's procedural prerequisites, had decided that the benefits to be derived from downhill skiing at Sandy Butte justified the issuance of a special use permit, notwithstanding the loss of 15 percent, 50 percent, or even 100 percent of the mule deer herd. Other statutes may impose substantive environmental obligations on federal agencies, but NEPA merely prohibits uninformed—rather than unwise—agency action.

   To be sure, one important ingredient of an EIS is the discussion of steps that can be taken to mitigate adverse environmental consequences. The requirement that an EIS contain a detailed discussion of possible mitigation measures flows from both the language of the Act and, more expressly, from CEQ's implementing regulations. Implicit in NEPA's demand that an agency prepare a detailed statement on "any adverse environmental effects which cannot be avoided should the proposal be implemented," 42 U.S.C. §4332(C)(ii), is an understanding that the EIS will discuss the extent to which adverse effects can be avoided. See D. Mandelker, NEPA Law and Litigation §10:38 (1984). More generally, omission of a reasonably complete discussion of possible mitigation measures would undermine the "action-forcing" function of NEPA. Without such a discussion, neither the agency nor other interested groups and individuals can properly evaluate the severity of the adverse effects. An adverse effect that can be fully remedied by, for example, an inconsequential public expenditure is certainly not as serious as a similar effect that can only be modestly ameliorated through the commitment of vast public and private resources. Recognizing the importance of such a discussion in guaranteeing that the agency has taken a "hard look" at the environmental consequences of proposed federal action, CEQ regulations require that the agency discuss possible mitigation measures in defining the scope of the EIS, 40 CFR §1508.25(b) (1987), in discussing alternatives to the proposed action, §1502.14(f), and consequences of that action, §1502.16(h), and in explaining its ultimate decision, §1505.2(c).

   There is a fundamental distinction, however, between a requirement that mitigation be discussed in sufficient detail to ensure that environmental consequences have been fairly evaluated, on the one hand, and a substantive requirement that a complete mitigation plan be actually formulated and adopted, on the other. In this case, the off-site effects on air quality and on the mule deer herd cannot be mitigated unless nonfederal government agencies take appropriate action. Since it is those state and local governmental bodies that have jurisdiction over the area in which the adverse effects need be addressed and since they have the authority to mitigate them, it would be incongruous to conclude that the Forest Service has no power to act until the local agencies have reached a final conclusion on what mitigating measures they consider necessary. Even more significantly, it would be inconsistent with NEPA's reliance on procedural mechanisms—as opposed to substantive, result-based standards—to demand the presence of a fully developed plan that will mitigate environmental harm before an agency can act. Cf. *Baltimore Gas & Electric Co.,* 462 U.S., at 100 ("NEPA does not require agencies to adopt any particular internal decision making structure").

We thus conclude that the Court of Appeals erred, first, in assuming that "NEPA requires that 'action be taken to mitigate the adverse effects of major federal actions,'" and, second, in finding that this substantive requirement entails the further duty to include in every EIS "a detailed explanation of specific measures which will be employed to mitigate the adverse impacts of a proposed action."

III

[The Court held that CEQ had properly amended its NEPA regulations to delete the requirement for a "worst case" analysis. The Court also held that the Forest Service's failure to develop a complete mitigation plan did not violate its own regulations.]

V

In sum, we conclude that NEPA does not require a fully developed plan detailing what steps will be taken to mitigate adverse environmental impacts. . . . The judgment of the Court of Appeals is accordingly reversed and the case is remanded for further proceedings consistent with this opinion. . . .

NOTES AND QUESTIONS

1. *The Role of Mitigation.* Mitigation is important in the NEPA environmental assessment process. It gives the agency an opportunity to proceed with its action by modifying it, or by including additional measures that will prevent the action from having significant environmental effects. *Robertson* was willing to imply an obligation to consider mitigation measures but not an obligation actually to formulate and adopt them. The Court's holding on mitigation is a replay of the substantive versus procedural debate. For different views of the decision compare Mandelker, NEPA Alive and Well: The Supreme Court Takes Two, 19 Envtl. L. Rep. 10385 (1989) (approving), with Rossmann, NEPA: Not So Well at Twenty, 20 Envtl. L. Rep. 10174 (1990) (disapproving).

CEQ has issued guidance on the use of mitigation and monitoring. Memorandum for Heads of Federal Agencies, Appropriate Use of Mitigation and Monitoring and Clarifying the Appropriate Use of Mitigated Findings of No Significant Impact (2011), available at https://ceq.doe.gov/current_developments/docs/Mitigation_ and_Monitoring_Guidance_14Jan2011.pdf. The guidance, which applies to the preparation of both environmental assessments and EISs, provides that agencies may use commitments to perform (or ensure the performance of) mitigation measures to support a finding of no significant impact. Agencies should not commit to mitigation measures, however, if there are insufficient legal authorities or if sufficient resources to implement the measures are unlikely to be available. The guidance also provides that agencies should take steps to ensure that mitigation measures are actually implemented by clearly identifying commitments to them in their decision documents. They should establish clear expectations by specifying measurable performance standards or clear results. Agencies should also establish a time frame for the agency action and mitigation measures, so that the start date and duration of the mitigation commitment are clear. The guidance endorses the use of adaptive management.

2. *Adequacy of Mitigation Measures.* The Court in *Robertson* did not discuss the adequacy of the mitigation measures in that case, but emphasized that "omission of a reasonably complete discussion of possible mitigation measures would undermine the 'action forcing' function of NEPA." The adequacy of mitigation measures is frequently litigated. As explained in High Sierra Hikers Ass'n v. U.S. Dep't of Interior, 848 F. Supp. 2d 1036 (N.D. Cal. 2012), information must be detailed and easily accessible. Listing is not enough. An agency must explain why mitigation measures are effective, but need not actually mitigate environmental harms.

Desert Protective Council v. U.S. Dep't of Interior, 927 F. Supp. 2d 949 (S.D. Cal. 2013), is an example of a case where mitigation measures were held adequate. For a utility-scale wind power project they included advanced conservation practices to minimize the risk of collision with birds pre-construction, during construction, and during operation and management. They also included a special eagle conservation plan, which requires Advanced Conservation Practices designed to curtail turbines if and when golden eagles approached. The plan included monitoring, adaptive management, and reporting procedures. There was no time frame as the guidance requires, but the mitigation measures appeared to be ongoing.

South Fork Band Council of W. Shoshone of Nev. v. U.S. Dep't of Interior, 588 F.3d 718 (9th Cir. 2009), is an example of a case where mitigation measures were held inadequate. The court held that the Bureau of Land Management did not conduct an appropriate mitigation analysis for the extensive removal of groundwater that would be caused by a gold mining project. A number of local springs and streams were expected to dry up. The impact statement explained only that the "[f]easibility and success of mitigation would depend on site-specific conditions and details of the mitigation plan." Nothing was said about whether mitigation measures would avoid any of the anticipated harms, which had to be considered even though they were uncertain. The court stated that "[e]ven if the discussion must necessarily be tentative or contingent, NEPA requires that the agency give some sense of whether the drying up of these water resources could be avoided." Id. at 727. What mitigation measures could prevent this result?

See also Neighbors of Cuddy Mountain v. United States Forest Serv., 137 F.3d 1372 (9th Cir. 1998). The Forest Service admitted a timber sale would negatively affect an endangered fish species because of increased sedimentation in three creeks, but provided only a perfunctory description of mitigation measures that could avoid this effect. The court held that the "broad generalizations and vague references to mitigation measures in relation to the streams affected" did not satisfy the "hard look" required by NEPA.

3. *Adaptive Management.* The enforcement or follow-up on a NEPA document after it has been accepted is a weak point in NEPA implementation. CEQ regulations encourage agencies to monitor compliance, and lead agencies must report monitoring and mitigation information "upon request." 40 C.F.R. §1505.3. This requirement applies, however, only if an agency commits to mitigation and other conditions in its decision. Id. §§1505.2(c), 1505.3. Agencies must decide whether post-decision monitoring and enforcement are "applicable for any mitigation."

A NEPA task force report published by CEQ called for the use of adaptive management strategy as a means of monitoring decisions under NEPA. The report described the traditional environmental review process as one involving prediction, mitigation, and implementation, a one-time process that does not provide for unanticipated change. Adaptive management remedies this problem by including post-decision responses to conditions and circumstances related to an action. It adds a monitoring and adaptation element that allows agencies to address unanticipated results and adjust decisions accordingly. NEPA Task Force Report to the Council on Environmental Quality: Modernizing NEPA Implementation 47-49 (2003), available at https://ceq.doe.gov/ntf/report/finalreport.pdf. This can be done without triggering the need for a supplemental EIS, discussed below in note 5. See 43 C.F.R. §46.145 (Interior Department regulation recognizing adaptive management). Cases have upheld the use of adaptive management. Western Watershed Project v. U.S. Forest Serv., 780 F. Supp. 2d 1115 (D. Idaho 2011) (approving reliance on adaptive management for sheep grazing that required monitoring, set goals, and required management changes if goals were not met).

For discussion see Ruhl, Regulation by Adaptive Management: Is It Possible?, 7 Minn. J.L. Sci. & Tech. 21 (2005); Karkkainen, Toward a Smarter NEPA: Monitoring and Managing Environmental Performance, 102 Colum. L. Rev. 903 (2002). For a skeptical view, see Biber, Adaptive Management and the Future of Environmental Law, 46 Akron L. Rev, 933 (2013). CEQ also issued a guide in 2007 to assist agencies in linking the NEPA process with environmental management systems (EMS). Aligning National Environmental Policy Act Processes with Environmental Management Systems: A Guide for NEPA and EMS Practitioners (2007), available at https://ceq .doe.gov/publications/nepa_and_ems.html. It is intended to assist federal agencies in recognizing the complementary relationship of EMS and NEPA and to help them align EMS elements with the NEPA analysis and decision processes.

4. *Environmental Justice Executive Order.* An environmental justice Executive Order issued by President Clinton requires each federal agency, "to the greatest extent practicable," to make "achieving environmental justice part of its mission." Executive Order 12,898, 50 Fed. Reg. 7629 (1994). Agencies are to achieve this objective by identifying and addressing any disproportionately "high and adverse human health or environmental effects of its programs, policies, and activities on minority and low-income populations." A White House memorandum implementing the Order requires federal agencies to analyze the human health, economic, and social effects of their actions, including effects on minority and low-income communities, when NEPA requires this analysis. Memorandum of Feb. 11, 1994.

CEQ Guidance states that the Executive Order "does not change the prevailing legal thresholds and statutory interpretations under NEPA and existing case law." Environmental Justice: Guidance under the National Environmental Policy Act 8 (1998). However, the guidance adds that the identification of disproportionately high and adverse effects on minority and low-income populations "should heighten agency attention to alternatives (including alternative sites), mitigation strategies, monitoring needs, and preferences expressed by the affected community or population." Id.

The Executive Order prohibits judicial review, and some courts have refused to hear cases claiming that the Order has been violated. E.g., Sur Contra La Contaminacion v. EPA, 202 F.3d 443, 449 (1st Cir. 2000). Some courts have reviewed these claims, however, but have usually not found a violation. See Communities Against Runway Expansion, Inc. v. Federal Aviation Admin., 355 F.3d 678 (D.C.

Cir. 2004) (correct comparison community selected for environmental justice analysis of noise from airport project). The court held the agency's environmental justice determination was subject to review under NEPA and the APA even though the order expressly states it does not provide for a private right of action.

5. *Supplemental Environmental Impact Statements.* Even though an impact statement may adequately discuss the environmental impacts of a proposed action, circumstances may arise in which a supplemental impact statement is necessary. CEQ regulations require the preparation of supplemental statements when

(i) The agency makes substantial changes in the proposed action that are relevant to environmental concerns; or

(ii) There are significant new circumstances or information relevant to environmental concerns and bearing on the proposed action or its impacts. [40 C.F.R. §1502.9(c)(1).]

In Marsh v. Oregon Natural Res. Council, 490 U.S. 360 (1989), the Supreme Court upheld the regulation, even though NEPA does not require supplemental statements, noting it would defeat the purpose of the statute if an action could escape additional review when new impacts were discovered. The Court held that agencies should apply a "rule of reason" to the decision whether to prepare a supplemental statement and give a "hard look" to the environmental effects of an action even after they have given initial approval of a project. The Court also held it would apply the arbitrary and capricious standard of judicial review to an agency's decision that a supplemental impact statement was not necessary. It rejected a claim that new information required a supplemental statement in that case because it held the information was neither new nor accurate.

Most of the cases rejected arguments that supplemental impact statements were necessary. They held that supplemental statements were not necessary because of new circumstances or information when the original impact statement adequately discussed the circumstances claimed to be new. E.g., Tinicum Twp. Pa. v. U.S. Dep't of Transp., 685 F.3d 288 (3d Cir. 2012) (airport expansion, post-decision air quality studies). Compare Friends of the Clearwater v. Dombeck, 222 F.3d 552 (9th Cir. 2000). The court found that the Forest Service failed to prepare or even consider and evaluate the need for a supplemental impact statement on timber sales because of seven new sensitive species designations, and held that its recognition that old growth and snag standards on which the original impact statement relied were inadequate. Wisconsin v. Weinberger, 745 F.2d 412 (7th Cir. 1984), a pre-*Marsh* case, held a supplemental statement is not necessary unless "new information provides a seriously different picture of the environmental landscape such that another hard look is necessary."

A supplemental impact statement is not required when substantial change is adequately discussed in the impact statement. Great Old Broads for Wilderness v. Kimbell, 709 F.3d 836 (9th Cir. 2013) (road repair; selected alternative primarily made of elements from alternatives analyzed in final impact statement, and several mitigating modifications adopted). Neither is supplementation required if the change is minor or not significant, or when the final impact statement does not add to the objectives discussed in the draft impact statement. Compare New Mexico ex rel. Richardson v. Bureau of Land Mgmt., 565 F.3d 683 (10th Cir. 2009). A supplemental EIS was required when an agency substantially modified the alternatives it was considering for oil and gas development.

6. *What Does It Take to Win a NEPA Case?* The federal courts are the major enforcers of NEPA, so this is the place to ask what it takes to win a NEPA case. Because the courts defer to the agencies on many NEPA issues, and because agencies have matured in their compliance with NEPA, litigation may not seem useful. Distinctions must be made, however, between questions of law, questions of fact, and questions of mixed law and fact. Courts will intervene if an agency has not interpreted NEPA correctly. An example is a decision to segment projects that should be considered together, or to reject an alternative that should have been evaluated. Environmental assessments and EISs require the collection and evaluation of environmental information. Courts will not intervene if an agency has done this job well. They will intervene, however, if an agency omits information or scientific opinion it should have considered or does not fully explain its conclusions. Review the issues discussed in this chapter and identify those that are most likely to receive careful judicial review.

NOTE ON STATE ENVIRONMENTAL POLICY LEGISLATION

Fifteen states, the District of Columbia, and Puerto Rico have state environmental policy acts (SEPAs) similar to NEPA, which require environmental assessments and the preparation of environmental impact statements. Most of these statutes are carbon copies of NEPA. However, the California Environmental Quality Act (CEQA) is unique as a lengthy, detailed prescription of how the environmental review process should be carried out. CEQA also uses the term environmental "report" to describe the document that must be prepared. Some of the statutes apply only to state governments, but some apply to local governments as well. The California and New York statutes are heavily litigated and they, as well as the Washington statute, apply to private development. Most states have adopted regulations that interpret the statute. See Weiner, NEPA and State NEPAs: Learning from the Past, Foresight for the Future, 39 Envtl. L. Rep. 10675 (2009). A summary table of the statutes is at NEPA Law, §12.2.

Environmental reviews under SEPAs raise issues similar to those raised under NEPA. State judicial interpretations of SEPAs are usually comparable, though some of the state decisions have held that the state law is to be more broadly applied. A few SEPAs specify a judicial review standard, e.g., Cal. Pub. Res. Code §21168.5 (prejudicial abuse of discretion). The test for determining when an action is significant may be more relaxed. The test in California is "whenever it can be fairly argued on the basis of substantial evidence that the project may have significant environmental impact." No Oil, Inc. v. City of Los Angeles, 529 P.2d 66, 75 (Cal. 1975).

Actions and Projects Covered and Exemptions. Many of the state statutes follow NEPA by using the term "major action" to designate what is covered by the statute, though some differ. CEQA differs, and requires public agencies to prepare impact reports on "any project they propose to carry out or approve." Projects need not be major. Cal. Pub. Res. Code §21100. Some states, through regulations, classify actions into various categories, which can include a category of actions not subject to the statute, and a category of actions for which an EIS is always required.

Some SEPAs contain extensive exemptions. For example, a certified state agency regulatory program is exempt if it requires the preparation of written documentation containing the environmental analysis required by Cal. Pub. Res. Code §21080.5. The program must involve the issuance of a permit or similar approval, or adoption or approval of standards, rules, regulations, or plans. A statute may also authorize the adoption of categorical exclusions. Id. §21084(a).

Land Use Planning and Regulation. SEPAs can apply to local land use planning and land use decisions, such as rezonings and project approvals, as in California, New York, and Washington. See Friends of Mammoth v. Board of Supervisors of Mono County, 502 P.2d 1049 (Cal. 1972). The New York law particularly defines an "action" as a project or activity directly undertaken or funded by an agency or "involving the issuance . . . of a lease, permit, license, certificate or other entitlement for use or permission to act by one or more agencies." NY Envtl. Conserv. Law §8-0105(4)(ii). Only discretionary, not ministerial, actions are covered. See Friends of Westwood, Inc. v. City of Los Angeles, 235 Cal. Rptr. 788 (Cal. App. 1987) (building permit approval for high-rise office building subject to special "plan-check" review held discretionary).

The environmental review process required by a SEPA is as important as review under the land use process. This overlap can be troublesome, and has been addressed through court decisions and remedial legislation. In Citizens of Goleta Valley v. Board of Supervisors, 801 P.2d 1161 (Cal. 1990), for example, a county considered but rejected a number of alternatives for a shorefront hotel development. Objectors argued the county should have taken an optimal view of alternative sites throughout the region, but the court disagreed. It held the county's comprehensive land use and coastal plans addressed these issues, and added that an impact report "is not ordinarily an occasion for the reconsideration or overhaul of fundamental land use policy." California, New York, and Washington have adopted reforms that attempt to integrate the planning and land use control process with SEPA environmental reviews. See Mandelker, Melding State Environmental Policy Acts with Land-Use Planning and Regulation, Land Use L. & Zoning Dig., Vol. 49, No. 3, at 3 (1997). One option provides that SEPA reviews are to rely on an environmental analysis carried out in the land use planning process. See also Cal. Code Regs. tit. 14, §15183.3 (streamlines CEQA process for urban infill projects and exempts these projects where environmental impacts have already been evaluated in planning level documents, or where uniform development standards apply that mitigate environmental impacts).

Substantive Effect. In a landmark opinion, the Washington Supreme Court gave a decisively substantive effect to its environmental policy act. Polygon Corp. v. City of Seattle, 578 P.2d 1309 (Wash. 1978), noted in 54 Wash. L. Rev. 693 (1979). A developer applied for a building permit to construct a high-rise condominium onone of Seattle's seven hills. The impact statement disclosed a number of adverse environmental effects, including view obstruction, excessive bulk and scale, and noise and shadow effects. The city building superintendent relied on these adverse effects to deny the building permit, and the court affirmed, even though the building was a permitted use under the city's zoning ordinance. A subsequent legislative amendment qualified *Polygon* by authorizing denials only on the basis of "formally designated" local policies. Wash. Rev. Code §43.21C.060. Any such action is appealable to the local legislative authority. The cases have approved project rejections based on specifically identified policies, even when the zoning code allowed the project. E.g., Victoria Tower P'ship v. City of Seattle (II), 800 P.2d 380 (Wash. App. 1990) (approving rejection of project based on city growth policy). California's law allows agencies to approve impact reports only if they make findings that "changes or alterations have been required in, or incorporated into, the project which mitigate the significant effects on the environment." Cal. Pub. Res. Code §2181. The cases seem to have taken the position that the statute does not require selection of an environmentally superior alternative if modifications to a project mitigate its environmental impacts to an "acceptable" level. Laurel Hills Homeowners Ass'n v. City Council, 147 Cal. Rptr. 841 (Cal. App. 1978).

Climate Change. Some states have taken steps to incorporate climate change into their environmental review processes. California legislation, for example, provides that guidelines shall be prepared for the mitigation of greenhouse gas emissions. Cal. Pub. Res. Code §21083.05. The guidelines have been amended to include these concerns. 14 Cal. Code Reg. §15064.4. See Crockett, Addressing the Significance of Greenhouse Gas Emissions Under CEQA: California's Search for Regulatory Certainty in an Uncertain World, 4 Golden Gate U. Envtl. L.J. 203 (2011).

Communities for a Better Env't v. City of Richmond, 108 Cal. Rptr. 3d 478 (Cal. App. 2010), considered an environmental report under CEQA on new equipment that would allow an oil refinery to process crude oil with a higher sulfur content. The court held that proposed mitigation measures for greenhouse gases were not too vague, even though knowledge about greenhouse gases was expanding during the environmental review period. The novelty of greenhouse gas mitigation measures was an important reason why they should be timely set forth, and why environmental information should be complete and relevant. A revised environmental report should analyze "potential greenhouse gas emissions and their cumulative impact on climate change, as well as defining legally adequate mitigation measures to avoid those impacts." The court referenced the new state regulation restricting greenhouse gas emissions.

F. WHERE IS NEPA TODAY? A CRITIQUE AND RECOMMENDATIONS FOR REFORM

1. Evaluation of the NEPA Process

The Issues. Ultimately, some essential questions must be asked: Has NEPA worked? Has it made a difference in agency decisionmaking? Has it eliminated or at least mitigated the environmental impacts of agency projects and actions? As might be expected, the answers to these questions vary. Supporters of NEPA view it as having made a modest but important contribution to informed environmental decisionmaking. They report improvements in agency procedures for environmental evaluation, and believe NEPA has brought about the mitigation if not the elimination of negative environmental impacts from agency actions.

Critics see NEPA as a statute that requires unnecessary paperwork that delays or even eliminates beneficial projects. They criticize impact statements as self-serving and bulky justifications for projects that agencies plan to undertake whatever the environmental analysis reveals. They also view impact statements as collections of irrelevant data with a blurred focus that do not contribute to informed evaluation.

Here is a helpful summary of both views:

In the view of NEPA's admirers, this simple information disclosure mandate forces agency managers to identify and confront the environmental consequences of their actions, about which they otherwise would remain ignorant. It also opens governmental decisions to an unprecedented level of public scrutiny, with consequent political impli-cations that decisionmakers ignore only at their peril. NEPA's supporters argue that this combustible blend of information, transparency, and political accountability creates powerful pressures on agency decisionmakers to avoid the most environmentally damag-ing courses of action, and to mitigate environmental harms when it is cost effective to do so.

Critics, on the other hand, variously bemoan the length and cost of the NEPA process, the spottiness and low overall quality of the information it generates, the high triggering threshold before an EIS is required (with the result that few actions receive full NEPA scrutiny), and the temporal and functional gulf that separates the ritualized procedures of EIS production from agencies' real decisionmaking processes. From the critics' vantage point, NEPA appears to demand burdensome procedural for-malities while accomplishing little or nothing of substance. [Karkkainen, Toward a Smarter NEPA: Monitoring and Managing Government's Environmental Performance, 102 Colum. L. Rev. 903, 904-905 (2002).]

NEPA in Practice. A number of studies examine how agencies respond to and internalize their responsibilities under NEPA. See NEPA Law, §11.5. An early and one of the most comprehensive studies of the Forest Service and the Corps of Engi-neers, S. Taylor, Making Bureaucracies Think: The Environmental Impact Statement Strategy of Administrative Reform (1984), answered with a "complicated and contingent" yes the question of whether the "average" agency project is better than it might have been before NEPA applied. Taylor noted that project outcomes varied depending on whether a project could gain from incorporating environmental miti-gation measures, and on whether the project had enough "slack" to incorporate such measures, yet still be viable. Taylor also noted that uncertainties in the NEPA process gave environmental groups additional leverage to challenge the adequacy of agency impact statements, and compensated for CEQ's relatively weak oversight role. For an earlier study of the Corps, see D. Mazmanian & J. Nienaber, Can Organizations Change? Environmental Protection, Citizen Participation, and the Corps of Engi-neers (1979).

A more recent study of eight agencies with major NEPA responsibilities, however, showed that funding for NEPA compliance decreased at the same time that NEPA workloads increased, NEPA training and staff positions were reduced, and "most agency headquarters NEPA offices lack an ongoing national tracking sys-tem to monitor the numbers or types of NEPA documents that their agency is pre-paring or has completed." Smythe & Isber, NEPA in the Agencies 1 (National Resources Council of America, 2002). Workload increased because the number of federal actions subject to NEPA increased, which expands the role of nonfederal cooperating agencies. In addition, "[t]here is a pervasive tendency for senior policy officials to place more emphasis on reducing the time, costs, and paperwork associated with NEPA compliance than on assuring the quality and adequacy of the analysis." Id. at 2.

Commentary evaluating NEPA compliance is extensive. Some is critical. See M. Lindstrom & Z. Smith, The National Environmental Policy Act: Judicial Misconstruction, Legislative Indifference & Executive Neglect (2001). W. Buzbee, Westway: Environmental Law, Citizen Activism and the Regulatory War that Trans-formed New York City (2014), is a fascinating study of how the NEPA review process for a proposed major highway in New York City was mismanaged. The highway was litigated and abandoned after the court found fatal flaws in the NEPA process and substantive CWA §404 Compliance. Compare Borgstrom, Integrating NEPA into Long-Term Planning at DOE, 30 Envtl. L. Rep. 10640 (2009) (documenting successes at the Department of Energy with programmatic impact statements).

Recommendations for Improvement. There is extensive commentary on NEPA that provides recommendations for improvement. See, especially, Environmental Policy and NEPA: Past Present and Future (R. Clark & L. Canter eds., 1997), and articles by Dinah Bear, for many years General Counsel for the Council on Environmental Quality. E.g., Some Modest Suggestions for Improving Implementation of the National Environmental Policy Act, 43 Nat. Resources J. 931 (2003). A survey of 31 academics, the majority of whom had over 20 years of experience with NEPA in teaching, research, and practice, provides some insight on what needs to be done. Canter & Clark, NEPA Effectiveness—A Survey of Academics, 17 Envtl. Impact Assess. Rev. 313 (1997).

The survey identified several accepted strengths of the NEPA process, including an opening up of the decisionmaking process and its fulfillment of the need to think about environmental consequences before agencies commit resources. Survey participants also prioritized five important needs for improvement, some of which will be familiar. These were (1) to follow up post-EIS to monitor implementation of mitigation measures, ecosystem management, and environmental auditing; (2) to improve methodology for considering cumulative impacts and reduce institutional barriers to the analysis of these impacts; (3) to train federal personnel who implement NEPA; (4) to consider NEPA earlier in project planning and decisionmaking; and (5) to integrate consideration of biophysical and socioeconomic sciences along with risk assessment.

One of the authors of this casebook has suggested that the three alternatives presently available for NEPA compliance—the categorical exclusion, environmental assessment, and environmental impact statement—are overlapping and confusing and should be modified. Mandelker, The National Environmental Policy Act: A Review of Its Experience and Problems, 32 Wash. U. J.L. & Pol'y 293 (2010).

2. Reports on NEPA's Effectiveness and the Need for Reform

The CEQ NEPA Effectiveness Study. CEQ carried out an effectiveness study of NEPA's first 25 years that included organizations and individuals who were experienced in NEPA's performance. Council on Environmental Quality, The National Environmental Policy Act: A Study of Its Effectiveness After Twenty-Five Years (1997). The report noted that NEPA helps agencies to make better decisions, produce better results, and build trust in communities, but often is triggered too late to be fully effective. It found problems in interagency coordination, and suggested that agencies can improve environmental protection, get projects started earlier, and dramatically reduce NEPA compliance costs by monitoring and modifying project management rather than by discussing environmental impacts before project approval. The report criticized the heavy reliance on environmental assessments, which creates a danger of diminished public participation and creates a risk that individual minor actions may not require impact statements even though they may have major adverse cumulative effects. See the discussion of mitigated FONSIs earlier in this chapter.

The CEQ Task Force Report. CEQ later convened a task force whose report made a number of recommendations for improvements in NEPA practice. The NEPA Task Force Report to the Council of Environmental Quality: Modernizing NEPA Implementation (2003). Practice areas included technology and information management security, federal and intergovernmental collaboration, programmatic analysis and tiering, adaptive management and monitoring, categorical exclusions, and environmental assessments. CEQ has implemented some of these recommendations.

The former CEQ chair issued a Memorandum including recommendations for improving the implementation of NEPA that were based on the task force report. Memorandum to Heads of Federal Agencies from James L. Connaughton on Implementing Recommendations to Modernize NEPA (May 2, 2005). For discussion, see 36 Env't Rep. (BNA) 1355 (2005). The memorandum suggests principles for modernizing NEPA implementation, while recognizing the need to "[e]nsure timely and cost effective environmental reviews while maintaining environmentally sound decision-making that helps achieve the Nation's environmental, social and economic objectives" and maintain "effective environmental impact assessment processes already in existence."

CEQ also released a Compendium of Useful Practices to improve the implementation of NEPA in September 2005. It defines a useful practice as "those processes, techniques, or innovative uses of resources that have either demonstrated actual improvements or have the potential to improve the cost, schedule, quality, performance, or some other factor that impacts [NEPA] implementation." The compendium contains a discussion of adaptive management and monitoring, collaboration, environmental management systems, programmatic analysis, and tiering and technology. Case studies illustrate the recommendations for these topics. It is available at http://ceq.hss.doe.gov/ntf/compendium.

NOTES AND QUESTIONS

1. *Which Way for NEPA?* Concerns about NEPA's performance, and reports from CEQ outlining areas that need improvement, raise questions about NEPA's future. Some have suggested amendments to the statute, but this seems unlikely. The statute has remained unchanged through several administrations, except for an amendment authorizing the delegation of limited authority to the states. Recent statutes, discussed earlier, amended NEPA's requirements as applied to significant federal programs, and additional legislation limiting NEPA may be adopted. Amendment of the regulations also is unlikely. The 1978 regulations, which were adopted at the close of the Carter administration, were the product of a long and comprehensive collaborative process, and there does not seem to be much interest in disturbing them. The only amendment that was adopted was the change in the worst-case regulation. CEQ has decided instead to issue a series of guidances that provide advice on a number of issues that arise in NEPA practice. The guidances are published only after extensive consultation and are sent out for comment in draft form, but they are not rules and do not go through the notice-and-comment procedure required for regulations. Examples are the guidances issued to explain when a cumulative

impacts analysis must discuss past actions, which was discussed earlier, and the guidance on environmental justice. A Ninth Circuit case upheld the past actions guidance, and held it was not plainly erroneous or inconsistent with CEQ's cumulative impact regulation. League of Wilderness Defenders v. United States Forest Serv., 549 F.3d 1211 (9th Cir. 2008).

Recent guidances are expected to provide advice on how to carry out the NEPA environmental review process. One deals with mitigation and monitoring in the NEPA process. Another deals with the use of categorical exclusions. The guidances build on the CEQ regulations and explain how they can be implemented by agencies. Public tools for reporting on NEPA activities are also being enhanced.

2. *The Litigation Record.* Is the success rate in NEPA litigation affected by the political affiliations of the judges on the federal courts hearing NEPA cases? One study found that the political affiliation of the administration that appointed the judge deciding the case affected the outcome of NEPA cases. Between January 2001 and June 2004, there were 217 federal district court NEPA cases, with environmental plaintiffs achieving success 59.2 percent of the time when appearing before a Democrat-appointed judge, and only 28.4 percent of the time when appearing before a Republican-appointed judge. During the same period, the overall success rate before courts of appeal was 31.8 percent. Environmental plaintiffs were more than six times likely to prevail before majority Democrat-appointed panels than they were before majority Republican-appointed panels. If all three members of a panel were Democrat-appointed, the success rate was 75 percent, compared to a success rate of 11 percent if all of the judges were Republican-appointed. J. Austin et al., Judging NEPA: A "Hard Look" at Judicial Decision Making under the National Environmental Policy Act, Environmental Law Institute 8, 9 (Nov. 2004), available at www.eli-org/research-reports.

A recent study of Forest Service litigation found the Service won nearly 58 percent of its cases and lost about 21 percent. Many of these cases involved NEPA. Keele et al., Forest Service Land Management Litigation 1989-2002, 104 J. Forestry 196 (2006). Seventeen percent of the cases settled, which the study found was an important dispute resolution tool. Another study found similar results. Miner et al., Twenty Years of National Forest Service National Environmental Policy Act Litigation, 12 Envtl. Practice 116 (2010).

3. *References.* For evaluations of the role and future of NEPA, see L. Caldwell, The National Environmental Policy Act: An Agenda for the Future (1998); Symposium, NEPA at 40: How a Visionary Statute Confronts 21st Century Impacts, 39 Envtl. L. Rep. 10615 (2009); Luther, CRS Report for Congress, The National Environmental Policy Act: Background and Implementation CRS-34-35 (2008), available at http://www.enviro-lawyer.com/NEPASummary.pdf; Connaughton, Modernizing the National Environmental Policy Act: Back to the Future, 12 N.Y.U. Envtl. L.J. 1 (2003) (author was chair of CEQ); Trip & Alley, Streamlining NEPA's Environmental Review Process: Suggestions for Agency Reform, 12 N.Y.U. Envtl. L.J. 74 (2003). For studies of NEPA practices in federal agencies see Funk, NEPA at Energy: An Exercise in Legal Narrative, 20 Envtl. L. 759 (1990); Note, Federal Highways and Environmental Litigation: Toward a Theory of Public Choice and Administrative Reaction, 27 Harv. J. Legis. 229 (1990).

V

BIODIVERSITY CONSERVATION

Problem 5-1

The northern spitfire beetle lives on the edge of Ice Age Lake. It inhabits the Ice Age dunes, a 10,000-acre area of sand dunes and scrub forest land, and is found only in this ecosystem. One-half of the land is in a national forest, one-fourth lies in a state park, and the rest is privately owned. The beetle lives for three weeks in late August and then dies. There are over 290,000 varieties of beetles in the world, and the northern spitfire beetle is distinguished from similar species by a burnt-orange shell, which has been copied by jewelry designers in Budapest. The beetle does not support any other species in the ecosystem. Eco-tours has purchased 1,000 acres of private land to build a luxury eco-lodge. For $1,000 per night (food, but not alcohol, included), eco-tourists will be able to explore the Ice Age dunes, fish for Ice Age pike, and view wildlife in the area. Scientists are concerned that the lodge will shrink the beetle's habitat by about 15 percent and thus increase the risk of extinction. They are also concerned that global climate change may cause the beetle to migrate northward into areas where human-caused habitat fragmentation will make its survival more problematic in the coming decades. An entomologist at State University has proposed that the beetle be listed as a threatened or endangered species. The local lumber company has located a scientist who has published two papers arguing that the northern spitfire beetle is no more than a subspecies of the much more common northern orange stinging beetle. At a public hearing, local residents, who will have the opportunity to work in the lodge, ask representatives of the federal government why the beetle should be listed, what a listing would mean for the area, and, more generally, why they should be concerned about biodiversity. What is your answer?

A. INTRODUCTION TO BIODIVERSITY CONSERVATION

I keep waiting each day to make friends with the Forest Service. . . . The agency harbors, as a rotting log harbors nutrients and hope for the future, some of the country's best and most passionate hydrologists, entomologists, range managers, recreation specialists, ornithologists, wilderness specialists, and big game biologists. But the gears and levers of the agency are still pulled and fitted in Washington, in an agency run by a Congress . . . run . . . by the corporations that funded their election campaigns.

Rick Bass, Ecosystem Management, Wallace Stegner, and the Yaak Valley of
Northwestern Montana, in Reclaiming the Native Home of Hope: Community,
Ecology and the American West 50 (R. Keiter ed., 1998).

Two major objectives of environmental law are the prevention of pollution,
especially toxic pollutants, and the conservation of biodiversity. The two objectives
are, of course, related but they raise different ethical issues and often require different
policy instruments. The objective of biodiversity protection is to conserve species
richness. This can be done ex situ (via zoos and research facilities) or in situ (with
the conservation of natural habitats). Biologist Edward O. Wilson in his book The
Diversity of Life 333 (1992) argues that "ex situ methods will save a few species
otherwise beyond hope, but the light and way for the world's biodiversity is the preservation of natural ecosystems." The general objective of biodiversity conservation
may seem clear, but the scientific questions involved in deciding just what biodiversity
we want to conserve and devising effective strategies to do so are extraordinarily, if not
maddeningly, complex. Bosselman, A Dozen Biodiversity Puzzles, 12 N.Y.U. Envtl.
L.J. 364 (2004), lays out the questions for lawyers.

Biodiversity protection did not emerge as a policy focus until the mid-1980s. For
this reason, few laws expressly use the construct. Biodiversity is thus often a post hoc
rationale for existing program objectives. In the 1990s, for example, the Endangered
Species Act (ESA) evolved from a law designed to protect individual species that face
extinction to regulations governing the protection of representative ecosystems. The
ESA is the primary biodiversity protection mechanism in the United States. The
conservation of biodiversity is also now an international concern. Article 8(d) of
the Convention on Biological Diversity defines biodiversity conservation as "the protection of ecosystems, natural habitats and the maintenance of viable populations of
species in natural surroundings."

Biodiversity conservation is an effort to preserve the dynamics of evolution, but
immediate priorities are driven by efforts to arrest the loss of ecosystems and the
extinction of flora and fauna. Biodiversity loss is ultimately a function of human
population growth and resource consumption. The most important cause is habitat
fragmentation through development and road building, although the introduction of
exotic species into ecosystems, overhunting, overfishing, and global climate change
also play a role. The adverse effects of climate change are likely to become increasingly
prominent. R. Noss & A. Cooperrider, Saving Nature's Legacy: Protecting and Restoring Biodiversity (1994), describe how habitat fragmentation and loss can affect native
species. In the early stages of the process, large carnivores, furbearers, and the other
species subject to human exploitation or persecution are likely to be most affected. As
human activity increases, gaps in the original natural habitat matrix become larger and
more species are adversely affected, though species such as weedy plants, insects,
fungi, microbes, and some small vertebrates may persist and even thrive. Id. at
32-33. At any rate, modification of natural systems by human activity affects the
mix of species present.

Some scientists have concluded that a sixth mass extinction (there have been five
previous ones over the last 540 million years) may be underway, highlighting the need
for effective conservation measures. See Dirzo et al., Defaunation in the Anthropo-
cene, 345 Science 401, 405 (July 25, 2014) (concluding that "systematic defaunation
threatens to fundamentally alter basic ecological functions and is contributing to push
us towards global-scale 'tipping points' from which we may not be able to return");

Barnosky et al., Has the Earth's Sixth Mass Extinction Already Arrived?, 471 Nature 51 (Mar. 3, 2011) (concluding that this is the first wave attributable to human activities). See also E. Kolbert, The Sixth Extinction: An Unnatural History (2014). Pimm et al., The Biodiversity of Species and Their Rates of Extinction, Distribution, and Protection, 344 Science no. 987 (May 30, 2014), find that the current rate of extinction of plant and animal species is at least 1,000 times faster than the background extinction rate (before humans arrived), which is about ten times higher than previously believed.

Why do we value biodiversity?

DOREMUS, PATCHING THE ARK: IMPROVING LEGAL PROTECTION OF BIOLOGICAL DIVERSITY
18 Ecology L.Q. 265, 269-273 (1991)

1. The Utilitarian Basis for Preservation of Diversity

The utilitarian justification for the preservation of diversity rests on the direct and indirect usefulness of biological resources to humanity. Individual species provide us with a number of direct benefits. For example, we have domesticated our food crops, both plant and animal, from wild species. Other species can also provide a source of useful genetic traits. As breeding and genetic engineering technologies improve, such traits are becoming transferable across ever wider taxonomic distances.

Biological diversity is also a useful source of new medical drugs. Chemicals derived from higher plants form the major ingredient in about a quarter of all prescriptions written in the United States; chemicals derived from lower plants and microbes account for another eighth. Many of these drugs can be produced more cheaply by extraction than by chemical synthesis. Numerous species have yet to be examined for their medical properties. Thus, many useful chemicals may exist in the natural world. . . .

Nature may also serve more subtle needs. Human beings may have "a deep-rooted need" for contact with other living things. Such contact may promote both mental and physical health.

Besides the direct benefits above, ecosystems provide a number of indirect benefits to humanity. These "ecosystem services" include climate control, oxygen production, removal of carbon dioxide from the atmosphere, soil generation, nutrient cycling, and purification of freshwater supplies. Some of these functions could probably be performed by managed systems, at least on a small scale, but management of such systems on a global scale is presently beyond our technological capability. Moreover, some of these processes, such as nutrient cycling, are highly complex and not yet fully understood. . . .

2. The Esthetic Basis for Preservation of Diversity

Many people find beauty in the natural world, viewing natural objects, both living and nonliving, with a sense of admiration, wonder, or awe. Esthetic interest in nature is demonstrated in a variety of ways. For example, millions of Americans visit national parks and wildlife refuges every year. Some sixty million Americans participate in bird watching and millions more engage in other forms of wildlife-related recreation. Nature photography and gardening are enormously popular hobbies. A perennial audience exists for television nature documentaries.

Individual species and specific natural areas may also come, over time, to be imbued with powerful symbolic value. They may embody the cultural or political identity of a people. The bald eagle is one such symbolic species; Mt. Fuji is an example of a symbolic natural feature. This symbolism provides further evidence of the esthetic attractions of nature. . . .

3. *The Ethical Basis for Preservation of Diversity*

In 1949, Aldo Leopold advocated the extension of ethical obligations to the relations between man and nature, calling for the development of an "ecological conscience" reflecting "a conviction of individual responsibility for the health of the land." Since then, several commentators have argued that nonhuman organisms, and even non-living natural objects, have or should have rights based on their intrinsic value. Under such a view, human beings have an ethical obligation not to destroy these creatures and objects, at least in the absence of a strong countervailing value.

NOTE ON ECOSYSTEM SERVICES PROVISION AS A RATIONALE FOR BIODIVERSITY PROTECTION

The utilitarian rationale for biodiversity conservation has become the predominant one as a new concept—ecosystem services provision—has emerged to justify many biodiversity conservation initiatives.[a] A United Nations report links biodiversity conservation and ecosystem services. Millennium Ecosystem Assessment, Living Beyond Our Means: Natural Assets and Well Being 12 (Statement of the Board 2005). E. Chivian & A. Bernstein, Sustaining Life: How Human Health Depends on Biodiversity (2008), describe how a loss of biodiversity can eliminate potential sources of antibiotics and other disease-curing drugs. Ecosystems provide services from which humans benefit, such as pollution filtering, species maintenance, flood protection, recreation, or just the pleasure that knowledge of the existence of a system gives. If one then seeks to put a monetary value on these services, assuming that doing so is possible, the numbers can be huge. A widely cited but controversial article estimated the value of 17 ecosystems as between 16 and 44 trillion dollars. Costanza et al., The Value of the World's Ecosystem Services and Natural Capital, 387 Nature 253 (May 15, 1997). Updates to that study estimate the value of total global ecosystem services in 2011 at between 125 and 145 trillion dollars a year, and calculate the loss of ecosystem services from 1997 to 2011 due to land use change at 4.3 to 20.2 trillion dollars a year. Costanza et al., Changes in the Global Value of Ecosystem Services, 26 Global Envtl. Change 152 (May 2014).

a. See H. Monney & P. Ehrlich, Ecosystem Services: A Fragmentary History, in Nature's Services: Societal Dependence on Natural Systems (G. Daily ed., 1997); Thompson, Ecosystem Services and Natural Capital: Reconceiving Environmental Management, 17 N.Y.U. Envtl. L.J. 460 (2008); Ruhl, The Law and Policy Beginnings of Ecosystem Services, 22 J. Land Use & Envtl. L. 157 (2007); Salzman, A Field of Green? The Past and Future of Ecosystem Services, 21 J. Land Use & Envtl. L. 133 (2006).

Two important legal consequences follow. First, if these numbers are taken into account in the preparation of analyses such as EISs or decision documents such as public land use plans, the relative values of ecosystem protection and exploitation can change dramatically. As a result, the traditional bias in favor of exploitation created by ignoring "off-balance-sheet values" can be partially reversed. Second, markets may be created in ecosystem service provision, which also reduces exploitation pressure. This utilitarian rationale for ecosystem and biodiversity protection reflects the capture of much of the environmental policy discourse by science and welfare economics and has the potential to appeal to a wide variety of interests. Appeals to "hard" monetary dollar values are less polarizing than appeals to "soft" higher spiritual and aesthetic values.

Important questions remain. The first is whether the focus on monetizable services will cause society to ignore the conservation of biodiversity that currently provides no service to humanity. Operational and ethical questions follow. For example, it is not easy to connect service providers to beneficiaries. If an ecosystem owner has historically chosen to impair a service, is it fair now to compel her to provide the service, or should the government subsidize the service provision by paying her to forgo exploitation? See Salzman, Creating Markets for Ecosystem Services: Notes from the Field, 80 N.Y.U. L. Rev. 870 (2005). If markets are created, they will often be used to offset exploitation in a system. Hard questions may arise about whether the alleged service is in fact being provided and whether it justifies reducing the service capacity of an ecosystem. See Salzman & Ruhl, Currencies and the Commodification of Environmental Law, 53 Stan. L. Rev. 607 (2000); Glicksman, Regulatory Safeguards for Accountable Ecosystem Service Markets in Wetlands Development, 62 U. Kan. L. Rev. 943 (2014).

SIERRA CLUB v. MARITA
46 F.3d 606 (7th Cir. 1995)

FLAUM, Circuit Judge.

[Environmental NGOs sued the U.S. Forest Service to enjoin timber harvesting, road construction or reconstruction, and the creation of wildlife openings at two national forests in northern Wisconsin, the Nicolet and Chequamegon National Forests. Until the mid-1800s, both forests were old-growth forests consisting primarily of northern hardwoods. Due to logging, forest fires and fire control, and replanting, the forests no longer reflected pre-1800 "natural" conditions, but included trees that were more diverse in type and age. The two forests served various uses, including hiking, skiing, snowmobiling, logging, fishing, hunting, sightseeing, and scientific research. They supported both tourism and the forest product industries in Wisconsin.

The National Forest Management Act (NFMA), the Forest Service's organic statute, requires the agency to develop land and resource management plans (LRMPs) to guide management of resources within the national forests. The statute requires the Forest Service to develop guidelines for LRMPs which, among other things, must "provide for diversity of plant and animal communities based on the suitability and capability of the specific land area in order to meet overall multiple-use objectives . . . [and] provide, where appropriate to the degree practicable, for steps to be taken to preserve diversity of tree species similar to that existing in the region controlled by the plan." 16 U.S.C. §1604(g)(3)(B). The plaintiffs claimed that the agency violated both the NFMA and NEPA in developing forest management plans for the two forests by failing to consider properly certain ecological principles of biological diversity. The district court granted summary judgment to the government.]

III.

The Sierra Club claims that the Service violated the NFMA and NEPA by using scientifically unsupported techniques to address diversity concerns in its management plans and by arbitrarily disregarding certain principles of conservation biology in developing those plans. The Sierra Club asserts that the Service abdicated its duty to take a "hard look" at the environmental impact of its decisions on biological diversity in the forests on the erroneous contentions that the Sierra Club's proposed theories and predictions were "uncertain" in application and that the Service's own methodology was more than adequate to meet all statutory requirements. According to the Sierra Club, the Service, rather than address the important ecological issues the plaintiffs raised, stuck its head in the sand. The result, the Sierra Club argues, was a plan with "predictions about diversity directly at odds with the prevailing scientific literature." . . .

B.

The Service . . . defined diversity as "the distribution and abundance of different plant and animal communities and species within the area covered by the Land and Resource Management Plan." The Service assumed that "an increase in the diversity of habitats increases the potential livelihood of diverse kinds of organisms."

The Service focused its attention first on vegetative diversity. Diversity of vegetation was measured within tree stands as well as throughout the forest, noting that such diversity is "desirable for diverse wildlife habitat, visual variety, and as an aid to protecting the area from wildfire, insects, and disease." The Service assessed vegetative diversity based on vegetative types, age class structure of timber types, within-stand diversity of tree species, and the spatial distribution pattern of all these elements across the particular forest. The Service also factored in other considerations, including the desirability of "large areas of low human disturbance" and amount of "old-growth" forest, into its evaluations. Using these guidelines, the Service gathered and analyzed data on the current and historical composition of the forests to project an optimal vegetative diversity.

The Service assessed animal diversity primarily on the basis of vegetative diversity. Pursuant to the regulations, the Service identified all rare and uncommon vertebrate wildlife species as well as those species identified with a particular habitat and subject to significant change through planning alternatives. The Service grouped these species with a particular habitat type, identifying 14 categories in the Nicolet and 25 (reduced to 10 similar types) in the Chequamegon. For each of these habitat types, the Service selected MIS [Management Indicator Species] (33 in the Nicolet and 18 in the Chequamegon) to determine the impact of management practices on these species in particular and, by proxy, on other species in general. For each MIS, the Service calculated the minimum viable population necessary in order to ensure the continued reproductive vitality of the species. Factors involved in this calculation included a determination of population size, the spatial distribution across the forest needed to ensure fitness and resilience, and the kinds, amounts and pattern of habitats needed to support the population.

Taking its diversity analysis into consideration, along with . . . its numerous other mandates, the Service developed a number of plan alternatives for each of the forests. . . . Each alternative emphasized a different aspect of forest management, including cost efficiency, wildlife habitat, recreation, and hunting, although all were considered to be "environmentally, technically, and legally feasible." In the Nicolet, the Service selected the alternative emphasizing resource outputs associated with large diameter hardwood and softwood vegetation; in the Chequamegon an alternative emphasizing recreational opportunities, quality sawtimber, and aspen management was chosen.

C.

The Sierra Club argues that the [NFMA] diversity statute and regulations, as well as NEPA, required the Service to consider and apply certain principles of conservation biology in developing the forest plan. These principles, the Sierra Club asserts, dictate that diversity is not comprehensible solely through analysis of the numbers of plants and animals and the variety of species in a given area. Rather, diversity also requires an understanding of the relationships between differing landscape patterns and among various habitats. That understanding, the Sierra Club says, has led to the prediction that the size of a habitat—the "patch size"—tends to affect directly the survival of the habitat and the diversity of plant and animal species within that habitat.

A basic generalization of conservation biology is that smaller patches of habitat will not support life as well as one larger patch of that habitat, even if the total area of the smaller patches equals the total area of the large patch. This generalization derives from a number of observations and predictions. [The court noted that populations in a larger patch have a better chance of survival. Smaller patches can be destroyed by edge effects, which occur when one habitat's environment suffers because it is surrounded by a different type of habitat. Distance between habitats makes it less likely that organisms can migrate from one habitat to another in the event of a local disturbance. Consequently, fewer organisms will survive such a disturbance and diversity will decline.] On the basis of these submissions, the Sierra Club desires us to rule that to perform a legally adequate hard look at the environmental consequences of landscape manipulation across the hundreds of thousands of hectares of a National Forest, a federal agency must apply in some reasonable fashion the ecological principles identified by well accepted conservation biology. Species-by-species techniques are simply no longer enough. Ecology must be applied in the analysis, and it will be used as a criterion for the substantive results.

As a way of putting conservation biology into practice, the Sierra Club suggested that large blocks of land (at least 30,000 to 50,000 acres per block), so-called "Diversity Maintenance Areas" ("DMAs"), be set aside in each of the forests. . . . In these areas, which would have included about 25 percent of each forest, habitats were to be undisturbed by new roads, timber sales, or wildlife openings. Neither forest plan, however, ultimately contained a DMA. . . .

The Sierra Club contends that the Service ignored its submissions, . . . simply disregard[ing] extensive documentary and expert testimony, including over 100 articles and 13 affidavits supporting the Sierra Club's assertions, and thereby shirked its legal duties.

The Service replies that . . . while the theories of conservation biology in general and of island biogeography in particular were "of interest, . . . there is not sufficient justification at this time to make research of the theory a Forest Service priority." . . .

IV . . .

[T]he Sierra Club asserts that the Service failed in its responsibility under NEPA to utilize "high quality" science in preparing EISs and evaluating diversity in them. 40 C.F.R. §1500.1. The Sierra Club believes that it more than adequately demonstrated that conservation biology is (and was at the time the Service prepared its FEISs) an essential element of any proper scientific evaluation of diversity in the Nicolet and Chequamegon. The Sierra Club also points to a mountain of literature, as well as thirteen experts, that demonstrate its point. . . .

[W]e disagree. The Service is entitled to use its own methodology, unless it is irrational. The Service . . . developed an appropriate method of analyzing diversity. The Sierra Club is correct that the Service did not employ conservation biology in its final analysis. However, the Service appropriately considered conservation biology and ultimately determined that science to be uncertain in application. With regard to the Service's assumption that human intervention in the form of cuttings could aid diversity, the Service notes that it was precisely its intervention in the past fifty years that permitted the forests to rejuvenate after the logging and fires prior to the 1930s. Moreover, the Service proposes, without some intervention, the forests would return to their pre-1800s, climax hardwood composition, a composition less diverse than at present. We cannot conclude from the record and these explanations that the Service acted irrationally. . . .

[T]he Sierra Club [also] contends that the rejection of its "high quality" science argument on the basis of "uncertainty" in the application of conservation biology was unscrupulous. The Sierra Club asserts that conservation biology represented well-accepted and well-respected science even at the time the Service developed its management plans in the mid-1980s and that this evidence was before the Service when it drafted the forest plans. Thus, if the Service's only argument against applying the "high quality" science of conservation biology was its uncertainty, the Service has utterly failed to respond to the challenge of conservation biology.

A brief look at available evidence suggests that the district court's understanding of uncertainty was correct and the Service's explanation principled. The Service, in looking at island biogeography, noted that it had been developed as a result of research on actual islands or in the predominantly old-growth forests of the Pacific Northwest and therefore did not necessarily lend itself to application in the forests of Wisconsin. Literature submitted by the Sierra Club to the Service was not unequivocal in stipulating how to apply conservation biology principles in the Nicolet and Chequamegon. . . . Even recent literature has recognized that "new legislation may be necessary" in order to force the Service to adopt conservation biology. Robert B. Keiter, Conservation Biology and the Law: Assessing the Challenges Ahead, 69 Chi.-Kent L. Rev. 911, 916 (1994). Perhaps the Service "has the ability to reinterpret [its] own governing mandates to give species protection priority over visitor services and other concerns," id. at 921, but that is not and was not required. . . .

Amici, like the Sierra Club, misapprehend the "uncertainty" of which the Service and the district court spoke. We agree that an agency decision to avoid a science should not escape review merely because a theory is not certain. But, however valid a general theory may be, it does not translate into a management tool unless one can apply it to a concrete situation. The Service acknowledged the developments in conservation biology but did not think that they had been shown definitively applicable to forests like the Nicolet or the Chequamegon. Thus, circumstances did not warrant setting aside a large portion of these forests to study island biogeography and related theories at the expense of other forest-plan objectives. Given that uncertainty, we appropriately defer to the agency's method of measuring and maintaining diversity. See Baltimore Gas & Elec. Co. v. Natural Resources Defense Council, Inc., 462 U.S. 87 (1983).

[F]inally, the Sierra Club argues that even if the application of conservation biology was uncertain, the district court overlooked the dispositive NEPA regulation regarding scientific uncertainty, 40 C.F.R. §1502.22. . . . The Sierra Club contends that once the Service determined that the application of conservation biology was uncertain, §1502.22 obligated the agency to conduct and disclose its own evaluation of the effects of its management practices as predicted by conservation biology.

. . . [The record clearly shows that the Service sufficiently complied with this regulation. The Service looked at and disclosed the foreseeable environmental effects of the proposed alternatives and discussed them at length. . . . Nor did §1502.22 require the Service to use a methodology it reasonably found lacking in certainty of application. "NEPA does not require that we decide whether an [EIS] is based on the best scientific methodology available, nor does NEPA require us to resolve disagreements among various scientists as to methodology." Friends of Endangered Species, Inc. v. Jantzen, 760 F.2d 976, 986 (9th Cir. 1985).

To the extent §1502.22 did mandate a discussion of conservation biology, the Service more than adequately complied. The Service . . . determined that while the theory was "of interest," there was "conflicting scientific evidence regarding the necessity of providing large areas of old growth habitat," especially in a region like the Lake States area. Thus, "there is not sufficient justification available to make this study a priority for Forest Service research at this time." The Service allowed for the possibility that such a research proposal could be presented at a later date under the management plan as a site-specific proposal. This analysis of conservation biology appears to us to more than adequately meet whatever burden §1502.22 placed on the Service. . . .

For the foregoing reasons, we affirm the decisions of the district court.

NOTES AND QUESTIONS

1. *Baselines and Adaptive Management.* Ecosystem management often seeks to protect and restore a system's biological diversity by defining a baseline against which existing and future land uses will be measured. For discussion of the problems of defining ecological baselines, see Patten, Restoration as the Order of the 21st Century: An Ecologist's Perspective, 18 J. Land, Resources & Envtl. L. 31 (1998). What baseline did the court implicitly adopt in *Marita*? Prehuman intervention? The forest as it existed after the lumber booms of the mid-nineteenth century? A computer model of the ecosystem? Glisson v. United States Forest Serv., 138 F.3d 1181 (7th Cir. 1998), involved the issue of how to define the baseline in ecosystems that have been substantially modified over time. The Forest Service proposed to restore 10,500 acres in the Shawnee National Forest in Illinois. The ecological restoration project plan

required the removal of stands of shortleaf pines, a listed endangered species under state law. The removal of the pines, planted in the project area in the 1930s, would also impact the pine warblers, but the Forest Service defined "natural" as "native to the project area." Judge Posner concluded that the pines were "too recent to satisfy the Service's conception of what it means for a plant or animal to be 'native' to an area." Id. at 1183.

Ecosystem management also increases the importance of adaptive management as the major resource management strategy. A National Research Council–National Academy of Sciences study captures the essence of adaptive management:

> Adaptive planning and management involve a decision making process based on trial, monitoring, and feedback. Rather than developing a fixed goal and an inflexible plan to achieve the goal, adaptive management recognizes the imperfect knowledge of inter-dependencies existing within and among natural and social systems, which requires plans to be modified as technical knowledge improves.

Committee on Restoration of Aquatic Ecosystems, National Research Council, Restoration of Aquatic Ecosystems: Science, Technology, and Public Policy 357 (1992). See also Craig & Ruhl, Designing Administrative Law for Adaptive Management, 67 Vand. L. Rev. 1 (2014) (explaining adaptive management's theory and limits).

2. *The Scientific Case Against* Marita. Students of conservation biology objected to *Marita* and the Forest Service's focus on protecting management indicator species because of the resulting threats to biodiversity. Management for select species may result in the conversion of lands to habitats favored by these species at the expense of other flora and fauna that contribute to biodiversity. "Such restricted approaches to conserving 'wildlife' or boosting quite local 'alpha' diversity have led us to chop up many managed landscapes into small fragments with abundant edge." Waller, Biodiversity as the Basis for Conservation Efforts, in Biodiversity and the Law 16, 22-23 (W. Snape III ed., 1996). Waller specifically objected to the Forest Service's measurement of forest diversity by the number of age classes represented within each area of the forest because it perversely (though perhaps intentionally) promoted clearcutting to promote a variety of early age classes, such as young aspen, which were already abundant in the two Wisconsin forests. He argued that selective cutting and the harvest of individual trees would have better regenerated the mixed hardwood forest that once dominated the area. Compare League of Wilderness Defenders–Blue Mountains Biodiversity Project v. Allen, 615 F.3d 1122, 1125 (9th Cir. 2010) (describing indicator species as "bellwethers" for the other species that have the same special habitat or population characteristics).

NOTE ON SOURCES OF BIODIVERSITY CONSERVATION LAW

Biodiversity law draws from various sources of preexisting laws with related objectives. Society has long worried about the extinction of commercially valuable species. Fish and game laws have historically aimed at maintaining viable populations of species that are hunted or fished commercially and for sport by restricting hunting and fishing. See T. Lund, American Wildlife Law (1980). Biodiversity conservation law builds on the tradition of state regulation of wildlife. Under Roman law, wildlife was deemed unowned until an individual acquired ownership through capture. In nineteenth-century America, the same reasoning was used to justify state regulation of capture. Courts accepted the fiction, at a time when assertions of the police power were suspect, that the state "owned" wildlife in trust for the benefit of its citizens. Geer v. Connecticut, 161 U.S. 519 (1896). The Supreme Court rejected the concept of state ownership of wildlife in Hughes v. Oklahoma, 441 U.S. 322 (1979). A California case summarizes the modern law of wildlife ownership:

> California wildlife is publicly owned and is not held by owners of private land where wildlife is present. . . . It is this state's policy to conserve and maintain wildlife for citizens' use and enjoyment, for their intrinsic and ecological values, and for aesthetic, educational and nonappropriative uses.

Betchart v. California State Dep't of Fish and Game, 205 Cal. Rptr. 135, 136 (1984). In contrast to fauna, flora is treated as part of the land subject to private ownership.

The primary thrust of modern biodiversity law is to promote species survival through habitat conservation. This goal moves beyond the traditional rationale for state wildlife regulation because it both seeks to impose new management mandates on public land managers and to regulate the use of "ecologically sensitive" private land. Biodiversity conservation strategies generally use existing federal and state laws to create public and mixed public and private institutions to manage large areas of functionally connected habitat as a single ecosystem. As the *Marita* case illustrates, a major legal problem is that ecosystem management is a scientific rather than a legal construct that must be superimposed over existing political jurisdictions and specific federal and state agency mandates. Public land management statutes date from an era when commodity production was the preeminent public land use. Modern statutes often permit biodiversity conservation on public lands, but they provide little guidance as to how this objective is to be integrated with older, commodity production mandates. Ecosystem protection strategies must overcome the fragmented, incomplete, and shared regulatory authority that exists both among the three levels of government and within these levels, as well as the lack of integration among water and land management regulatory programs that impact biodiversity. The wetlands protection program created under §404 of the Clean Water Act, for example, is not necessarily an ecosystem management program as currently structured and administered because of the narrow geographic focus on individual wetlands. Other programs have the same problem. See generally Keiter, Beyond the Boundary Line: Constructing a Law of Ecosystem Management, 65 U. Colo. L. Rev. 293 (1994); Tarlock, Biodiversity Federalism, 54 Md. L. Rev. 1315 (1995).

Domestic biodiversity conservation efforts are supported by the emerging international biodiversity conservation regime. The international biodiversity conservation regime is based on the Convention on International Trade in Endangered Species (CITES) and the 1992 Convention on Biological Diversity. CITES is an international treaty that seeks to preserve species, but not their habitats, threatened by trade. The major focus has been on elephants, tropical birds, and reptiles. For example, the CITES ban on ivory products from southern African elephants has been implemented in the United States by the ESA and by the African Elephant Conservation Act, 16 U.S.C. §§1361-1407, which bans the sale of most ivory products derived from these animals. See Favre, The Risk of Extinction: A Risk Analysis of the Endangered Species Act as Compared to CITES, 6 N.Y.U. Envtl. L.J. 341 (1998).

The Convention on Biological Diversity adopted at the 1992 Rio de Janeiro Conference on Environment and Economic Development entered into force at the end of 1993. The Convention is acceptable to the international community because it attempts to blend the pro-preservation view of the North with the pro-development views of the South. Efforts to "balance" these concerns diluted the Convention. For example, the Preamble affirms that "the conservation of biological diversity is a common concern of mankind" rather than a common (and thus shared) heritage of mankind, as some nations advocated, and conservation duties are tempered by a capacity defense. But Article 6 posits that biological conservation is a national mandate. Article 8 reflects a preference for in situ (e.g., reserves) rather than ex situ conservation, and it provides a set of benchmarks against which national programs can be measured. This preference is reinforced by recent criticisms of the effectiveness of captive breeding programs. Articles 23-27 create a potential enforcement and information dissemination scheme. A Convention Secretariat and Conference are created, and the possibility of international disputes is recognized.

What are the primary lessons of conservation biology that can be applied to the design of habitat reserves? One source identifies species diversity and endemism as the two principal criteria for assessing the conservation value of sites, but notes that other criteria include naturalness, rarity, extent of habitat, threat of human interface, amenity and scientific value, and representation. The use of "representation" as a conservation criterion derives from the idea that a reserve network that includes every possible species is necessary to preserve maximum biological diversity.

> [R]epresentation, as we see it, means capturing the full spectrum of biological and environmental variation with the understanding that this variation is dynamic and not easily classified. Because diversity occurs at multiple levels of organization, conservation programs ideally should seek to represent all genotypes, species, ecosystems, and landscapes in protected areas. In practice, vegetation usually provides a good surrogate for the rest of biodiversity in the short term, so long as variation within classified types is recognized and sensitive and endemic species are given the extra attention they deserve. [R. Noss & A. Cooperrider, Saving Nature's Legacy, *supra*, at 104-105.]

Over time, the Forest Service has adapted the manner in which it uses management indicator species as surrogates for biodiversity. Consider the following case.

NATIVE ECOSYSTEMS COUNCIL v. U.S. FOREST SERVICE
428 F.3d 1233 (9th Cir. 2005)

McKEOWN, Circuit Judge.

[The Forest Service approved the Jimtown Vegetation Project in the Helena National Forest, whose objective was to lower the risk of a catastrophic fire by thinning, prescribed burning, and weed management. Parts of the forest consisted of dry ponderosa pine stands, within what the Forest Service characterized as "fire dependent ecosystems." Past efforts by the agency to prevent low-intensity, periodic fires had led to an increase in the likelihood of large, stand-replacing fires. The proposed project was located very close to a nest area used by a pair of northern goshawks. The Forest Service had designated goshawks as a sensitive species, which required that it prepare a Biological Evaluation to consider the potential impact of proposed forest management actions on the goshawks. The Forest Service's Evaluation concluded that the project might impact individual goshawks or their habitat, but was unlikely to contribute to a loss of species viability. It also concluded that the primary threat to goshawks is loss of habitat due to logging and fire.

The Helena National Forest Plan also designated goshawks as a management indicator species (MIS) for old-growth stands in that forest. Forest Service planning regulations required the Forest Service to select MIS for the purpose of monitoring the effects of management activities in various types of habitat. Although the project did not include any old growth, the Forest Service took the position that the project would contribute to the development of a sustainable old-growth forest in the project area.

Native Ecosystems challenged the project, alleging that the Forest Service violated the NFMA because it threatened the forest-wide viability of the goshawk. The district court granted the Forest Service's motion for summary judgment, finding that the agency did not act arbitrarily in concluding that the project would not impact goshawk viability under the NFMA.]

NFMA creates a two-step process for the management of our national forests. The Forest Service must first develop a Land Resource Management Plan ("Forest Plan") for each unit of the National Forest System. 16 U.S.C. §1604(f)(1). For individual management actions within a forest unit, all relevant plans, contracts, or permits must be consistent with each forest's overall management plan. Id. §1604(i).

In addition, NFMA imposes substantive requirements on the Forest Service's management of the national forests. NFMA requires that forest plans "provide for diversity of plant and animal communities based on the suitability and capability of the specific land area." 16 U.S.C. §1604(g)(3)(B). The Forest Service's NFMA regulations further require:

> Fish and wildlife habitat shall be managed to maintain viable populations of existing native and desired non-native vertebrate species in the planning area. For planning purposes, a viable population shall be regarded as one which has the estimated numbers and distribution of reproductive individuals to insure its continued existence is well distributed in the planning area. In order to insure that viable populations will be maintained, habitat must be provided to support, at least, a minimum number of reproductive individuals and that habitat must be well distributed so that those individuals can interact with others in the planning area.

36 C.F.R. §219.19 (2000). The duty to ensure viable populations "applies with special force" to sensitive species. Inland Empire Pub. Lands Council v. U.S. Forest Serv., 88 F.3d 754, 759 (9th Cir. 1996).

Native Ecosystems claims the Forest Service failed to comply with the substantive wildlife requirements of the NFMA. Specifically, Native Ecosystems claims the Forest Service failed to ensure goshawk viability, in violation of the NFMA, by failing to discuss forest-wide goshawk population trends and the impacts the Jimtown Project would have on goshawk viability and population trends. The 1986 Helena National Forest Plan designated goshawks as a management indicator species, and the Forest Service considers the goshawk to be a "sensitive species." As a result, Native Ecosystems contends the Forest Service had a substantive duty under NFMA to ensure forest-wide goshawk viability before approving a project that would impact goshawk habitat.

Although Native Ecosystems admits that the Forest Service has monitored goshawks in the Helena National Forest for more than eight years, Native Ecosystems claims this monitoring fails to establish the existence of a viable population of goshawks. The record contains a 2002 Goshawk Nest Monitoring Report that chronicles goshawk sightings and goshawk nests from 1995 through 2002 in the Helena National Forest. The record also contains a 2003 chart listing goshawk sightings and nests from 1992 through 2003. On the basis of these reports, Native Ecosystems claims that there is not a viable population of goshawks in the Helena National Forest, or at least that goshawk viability cannot be presumed based on these charts. According to Native Ecosystems, the Forest Service must positively demonstrate forest-wide goshawk viability before proceeding with the Jimtown Project.

In contrast, the Forest Service views its responsibility under NFMA to ensure the viability of animal species as a duty to ensure adequate habitat for wildlife species, not an obligation to ensure the actual viability of a species in every locale. See 36 C.F.R. §219.19 (2000) ("[H]abitat shall be managed to maintain viable populations. . . ."); see also id. §219.19(a)(6) ("Population trends of the management indicator species will be monitored and relationships to habitat changes determined."). Because the Forest Service concluded that the Jimtown Project will not have a significant effect on goshawk habitat, the Forest Service concludes that the project meets NFMA's species viability requirement by preserving goshawk habitat. In addition, the Forest Service contends Native Ecosystems misinterpreted the two goshawk observation charts and argues that the charts demonstrate a nearly fifty percent occupancy rate of potential goshawk home ranges.

Our case law permits the Forest Service to meet the wildlife species viability requirements by preserving habitat, but only where both the Forest Service's knowledge of what quality and quantity of habitat is necessary to support the species and the Forest Service's method for measuring the existing amount of that habitat are reasonably reliable and accurate. Compare Idaho Sporting Cong. v. Thomas, 137 F.3d 1146, 1154 (9th Cir. 1998) (holding that under the circumstances of that case the Forest Service could use habitat as a proxy for population if the Forest Service performed further analysis and showed that "no appreciable habitat disturbance" would result from the planned activity), and Idaho Sporting Cong. v. Rittenhouse, 305 F.3d 957, 967-68, 972-73 (9th Cir. 2002) (holding that use of habitat as a proxy for population monitoring of the management indicator species was arbitrary and capricious where record indicated that the Forest Service's habitat standard and measurements were erroneous).

We recently explained the proxy-on-proxy approach to ensuring species viability under the NFMA:

> We have, in appropriate cases, allowed the Forest Service to avoid studying the population trends of the Indicator Species by using Indicator Species habitat as a proxy for Indicator Species population trends in a so-called "proxy on proxy" approach. Crucial to this approach, however, is that the methodology for identifying the habitat proxy be sound. If the habitat trend data is flawed, the proxy on proxy result, here population trends, will be equally flawed. [Lands Council v. Powell, 395 F.3d 1019, 1036 (9th Cir. 2005).]

The record does not demonstrate any flaws in the methodology used by the Forest Service to identify goshawk habitat. . . . The Forest Service's habitat analysis revealed that even if the Jimtown Project thinning area is not used by the nearby goshawk pair, there will be ample habitat available to them. A goshawk home range should contain approximately 5,400 acres of foraging habitat. The Jimtown Project will diminish the goshawk foraging habitat in the goshawk home range by approximately 480 acres (720 acres prior to the Jimtown Fire), leaving at least 6,780 acres of suitable foraging habitat in the relevant goshawk home range. The remaining foraging habitat exceeds the [scientific experts'] recommendation of 5,400 acres of foraging habitat per goshawk home range. Given that the Jimtown Project area does not contain old-growth forest and is designed to create an ecosystem that can support old growth in the long-term, and given that the NEPA documents incorporate the [experts'] habitat recommendations, we conclude that the Forest Service satisfied NFMA's species viability requirements by demonstrating that adequate goshawk habitat is preserved.

While the Forest Service experts predict that goshawks will use the thinned area of the Jimtown Project for foraging, there will still be sufficient foraging habitat even if the goshawks avoid the project area after thinning. The long-term benefit of preventing stand-replacing fires, which completely destroy goshawk habitat, is preferable over any short-term benefit the goshawks might receive from retaining the dense forest structure in the project area. The Forest Service considered the relevant factors and there has not been a clear error of judgment.

Consequently, we uphold the agency action under the APA's arbitrary and capricious standard.

NOTES AND QUESTIONS

1. What did the NFMA and the Forest Service planning regulations require the agency to do to preserve diversity within the national forests? In what sense was the Forest Service's approach in this case a "proxy-on-proxy" approach? Why did the court approve it? One of the casebook authors has explained the agency's motivation for using MIS as surrogates for biodiversity:

> The benefit of the proxy-on-proxy simulation approach is that it avoids the need to do any population monitoring. The agency can fulfill its responsibility to protect biodiversity through the planning process simply by assuming that if sufficient habitat acreage for the MIS (as defined by the agency's scientists) remains following a particular management action such as a timber harvest, then a viable population of the MIS must also exist. Because the MIS is a surrogate for the other species present in the area affected, a viable population of MIS necessarily translates into plant and animal diversity sufficient to satisfy the NFMA planning provisions. It may not even be necessary for the habitat to exist in any particular location or condition.

Glicksman, Bridging Data Gaps Through Modeling and Evaluation of Surrogates: Use of the Best Available Science to Protect Biological Diversity Under the National Forest Management Act, 83 Ind. L.J. 465, 497 (2008).

2. *The "Proxy-on-Proxy" Approach in Other Jurisdictions.* Other courts have refused to allow the Forest Service to rely on the proxy-on-proxy approach at all. In Sierra Club v. Martin, 168 F.3d 1 (11th Cir. 1999), for example, the court concluded that habitat analysis did not comply with the regulatory requirement that the Forest Service monitor population trends of MIS and their relationships to habitat changes. It held that the agency's approval of timber sales was arbitrary and capricious because it failed to gather quantitative data on MIS and use that data to measure the impact of habitat changes on the forest's diversity. Other courts agreed that the 1982

regulations did not permit the Forest Service to substitute habitat information for actual, quantitative population data. See, e.g., Utah Envtl. Cong. v. Bosworth, 439 F.3d 1184, 1191 (10th Cir. 2006).

In Lands Council v. McNair, 537 F.3d 981 (9th Cir. 2008), the Ninth Circuit clarified some of its own jurisprudence concerning the Forest Service's obligations under the NFMA's diversity provision. The court refused to impose a bright-line rule on the Forest Service concerning particular means that it must take in every case to demonstrate compliance with the NFMA. It endorsed, as it had in past cases, the Forest Service's use of the amount of suitable habitat for a particular species as a proxy for the viability of that species. The court summarized its position on the validity of the proxy approach, stating that "when the Forest Service decides, in its expertise, that habitat is a reliable proxy for species' viability in a particular case, the Forest Service nevertheless must both describe the quantity and quality of habitat that is necessary to sustain the viability of the species in question and explain its methodology for measuring this habitat." Id. at 997-998. The court will defer to the Forest Service's decision to use habitat as a proxy unless the agency makes a clear error of judgment that makes its decision arbitrary and capricious. That may occur if an environmental impact statement states that the relationship between the species at issue and the habitat is unclear, the record fails to describe the type or amount of habitat that is necessary to sustain the viability of the species in question, or the record indicates that the Forest Service based its habitat calculations on outdated or inaccurate information. See also Lands Council v. McNair, 629 F.3d 1070 (9th Cir. 2010) (upholding use of proxy-on-proxy approach, even though no MIS were detected in the habitat used as proxy, because the species were difficult to detect and the Forest Service used available scientific data to reach its conclusions).

3. *Forest Service Planning Regulations.* The Forest Service amended its planning regulations in 2012. 77 Fed. Reg. 21,162 (Apr. 9, 2012). It adopted "a complementary ecosystem and species-specific approach" to protecting diversity of plant and animal communities in the national forests. The ecosystem (or coarse filter) approach would suffice to protect most species, but the species-specific (or fine filter) approach would provide a "safety net" for species whose habitat needs are not met by the ecosystem approach. The Forest Service also eliminated the requirement that each LRMP designate MIS, concluding that "[t]he concept of MIS as a surrogate for the status of other species is not supported by current science, and population trends are difficult and sometimes impossible to determine within the lifetime of a plan." Id. at 21,175. Instead, the regulations require monitoring of "focal species," which, though not surrogates for the status of other species, provide information regarding the effectiveness of a plan in providing the ecological conditions needed to maintain diversity of plant and animal communities and persistence of native species in the plan area. Appropriate monitoring methods include measures of abundance, distribution, reproduction, presence/absence, area occupied, and survival rates.

4. *Biodiversity and the Federal Land Management Agencies.* Congress has sought to protect biological diversity in the management of other categories of federal lands. See, e.g., 16 U.S.C. §460aaa (national monument establishment); 16 U.S.C. §460bbb-3(a)(6) (national recreation area). Karkkainen, Biodiversity and Land, 83 Cornell L. Rev. 1 (1997), urges federal acquisition of privately owned lands as the centerpiece of a federal biodiversity protection strategy, supplemented by federal regulation of private lands adjacent to core federal reserves. The article finds efforts by each federal land management agency to protect biodiversity to be inadequate.

*NOTE ON CLIMATE CHANGE, BIODIVERSITY PROTECTION,
AND ASSISTED MIGRATION*

Global climate change poses substantial challenges to biodiversity protection and the administration of the ESA as species migrate out of protected habitats or become extinct. See Ruhl, Climate Change and the Endangered Species Act: Building Bridges to the No-Analog Future, 88 B.U. L. Rev. 1 (2008). The federal government and the states may be forced to address the relationship between climate change and biodiversity conservation more systematically. Camacho, Assisted Migration: Redefining Nature and Natural Resource Law Under Climate Change, 27 Yale J. on Reg. 171 (2010), argues that assisted migration of species whose viability is threatened by climate change may be the best management alternative for promoting healthy ecosystems. Professor Camacho further contends that assisted migration illustrates how climate change requires the reinvention of natural resource management to better reflect and manage a dynamic world, and that policymakers should develop regulatory institutions that help reduce uncertainty and teach agencies how to better manage ecological change over time. The impact of climate change on biodiversity is considered further in Chapter 12 below.

B. THE ENDANGERED SPECIES ACT

The centerpiece of U.S. biodiversity conservation law is the Endangered Species Act (ESA). Its primary focus is the prevention of individual species extinction, but such prevention often requires habitat reserves. The presence of an endangered species on public or private land is often necessary to trigger efforts not only to preserve the species but to protect other species as well. The ESA is administered by the Fish and Wildlife Service (FWS), in the Department of the Interior, and the National Marine Fisheries Service (NMFS, sometimes referred to as the NOAA Fisheries), in the Department of Commerce. The latter has jurisdiction over ocean and anadromous fisheries, which comprise fish that migrate from fresh- to saltwater sources and then back so that they may swim upstream to their birth waters to spawn. For purposes of simplicity, most references in this chapter are to the FWS, but the statutory duties of the two agencies are the same.

1. *An Overview of the Endangered Species Act*

The first ESA case to reach the Supreme Court addressed how the Act balances the obligations of federal agencies under the ESA with the responsibilities they derive from their organic statutes. It also addressed the scope of judicial discretion to fashion remedies for violations of the ESA by those agencies.

TENNESSEE VALLEY AUTHORITY v. HILL
437 U.S. 153 (1978)

Mr. CHIEF JUSTICE BURGER delivered the opinion of the Court.

[The case is a classic story of an effort to stop an economically dubious public works project in the face of strong regional political support. In 1967,

Tennessee Valley Authority (TVA) began constructing the Tellico Dam on the Little Tennessee River, a shallow, fast-moving river, for hydroelectric power generation, flood control, recreation, and regional development. Opponents first succeeded in preventing the dam's opening because the EIS was inadequate, but this injunction was subsequently lifted when TVA filed an adequate statement. Shortly before the NEPA injunction was lifted, a University of Tennessee scientist discovered a three-inch, previously unknown species of perch, the snail darter. In 1975, the Secretary of the Interior listed the snail darter as an endangered species, noting that "the snail darter is a living entity which is genetically distinct and reproductively isolated from other fishes," and that it was unique to the reach of the Little Tennessee, which would be inundated by the dam. The fish would be adversely affected by the dam because it requires a swift-flowing aquatic habitat.

Due to efforts from Tennessee's congressional representatives, Congress appropriated funds for the dam's completion a month after the listing of the snail darter. A House Appropriations Committee report in 1975 recommended that an additional $29 million be appropriated for the dam, stating: "The Committee directs that the project, for which an environmental impact statement has been completed and provided [to] the Committee, should be completed as promptly as possible." After the President signed the appropriations legislation, the plaintiffs filed a citizen suit under the ESA. The district court found that completion of the dam would result in adverse modification or destruction of the snail darter's habitat, but it refused to enjoin a substantially completed project. The Sixth Circuit reversed, holding that the Act did not permit a court to balance the equities. Congress nevertheless continued to fund the project after members of TVA's Board of Directors testified at hearings that TVA was successfully relocating the species and after the House Appropriations Committee concluded that the ESA did not apply to substantially completed projects. TVA's general budget, which included funds for Tellico, was passed, and President Carter signed the bill on August 7, 1977.]

I

. . .

Until recently the finding of a new species of animal life would hardly generate a cause célèbre. This is particularly so in the case of darters, of which there are approximately 130 known species, 8 to 10 of these having been identified only in the last five years. The moving force behind the snail darter's sudden fame came some four months after its discovery, when the Congress passed the Endangered Species Act of 1973 (Act), 16 U.S.C. §1531 et seq. This legislation, among other things, authorizes the Secretary of the Interior to declare species of animal life "endangered"[8] and to

8. An "endangered species" is defined by the Act to mean "any species which is in danger of extinction throughout all or a significant portion of its range other than a species of the Class Insecta determined by the Secretary to constitute a pest whose protection under the provisions of this chapter would present an overwhelming and overriding risk to man." 16 U.S.C. §1532(4). [The Court noted that the ESA covers animal and plant species, subspecies, and populations throughout the world needing protection, that about 1.4 million animal species and 600,000 plant species existed, and that as many as 10 percent of them—some 200,000—might qualify as endangered or threatened. That number could increase by three to five times if subspecies and populations were counted.]

identify the "critical habitat" of these creatures.[9] When a species or its habitat is so listed, the following portion of the Act—relevant here—becomes effective:

> The Secretary [of the Interior] shall review other programs administered by him and utilize such programs in furtherance of the purposes of this chapter. All other Federal departments and agencies shall, in consultation with and with the assistance of the Secretary, utilize their authorities in furtherance of the purposes of this chapter by carrying out programs for the conservation of endangered species and threatened species listed pursuant to section 1533 of this title and *by taking such action necessary to insure that actions authorized, funded, or carried out by them do not jeopardize the continued existence of such endangered species and threatened species or result in the destruction or modification of habitat of such species* which is determined by the Secretary, after consultation as appropriate with the affected States, to be critical. 16 U.S.C. §1536 (1976 ed.) (emphasis added). . . .

II

We begin with the premise that operation of the Tellico Dam will either eradicate the known population of snail darters or destroy their critical habitat. Petitioner does not now seriously dispute this fact. In any event, under §4(a)(1) of the Act, 16 U.S.C. §1533(a)(1), the Secretary of the Interior is vested with exclusive authority to determine whether a species such as the snail darter is "endangered" or "threatened" and to ascertain the factors which have led to such a precarious existence. By §4(d) Congress has authorized—indeed commanded—the Secretary to "issue such regulations as he deems necessary and advisable to provide for the conservation of such species." 16 U.S.C. §1533(d). . . .

. . . [T]wo questions are presented: (a) Would TVA be in violation of the Act if it completed and operated the Tellico Dam as planned? (b) If TVA's actions would offend the Act, is an injunction the appropriate remedy for the violation? For the reasons stated hereinafter, we hold that both questions must be answered in the affirmative.

(A)

It may seem curious to some that the survival of a relatively small number of three-inch fish among all the countless millions of species extant would require the permanent halting of a virtually completed dam for which Congress has expended more than $100 million. The paradox is not minimized by the fact that Congress continued to appropriate large sums of public money for the project, even after congressional Appropriations Committees were apprised of its apparent impact upon the

---

9. The Act does not define "critical habitat," but the Secretary of the Interior has administratively construed the term:

> "Critical habitat" means any air, land, or water area (exclusive of those existing man-made structures or settlements which are not necessary to the survival and recovery of a listed species) and constituent elements thereof, the loss of which would appreciably decrease the likelihood of the survival and recovery of a listed species or a distinct segment of its population. The constituent elements of critical habitat include, but are not limited to: physical structures and topography, biota, climate, human activity, and the quality and chemical content of land, water, and air. Critical habitat may represent any portion of the present habitat of a listed species and may include additional areas for reasonable population expansion. 43 Fed. Reg. 874 (1978) (to be codified as 50 CFR §402.02).

survival of the snail darter. We conclude, however, that the explicit provisions of the Endangered Species Act require precisely that result.

One would be hard pressed to find a statutory provision whose terms were any plainer than those in §7 of the Endangered Species Act. Its very words affirmatively command all federal agencies "to *insure* that *actions authorized, funded, or carried out* by them do not jeopardize the continued existence" of an endangered species or "*result* in the destruction or modification of habitat of such species. . . ." 16 U.S.C. §1536. (Emphasis added.) This language admits of no exception. Nonetheless, petitioner urges, as do the dissenters, that the Act cannot reasonably be interpreted as applying to a federal project which was well under way when Congress passed the Endangered Species Act of 1973. To sustain that position, however, we would be forced to ignore the ordinary meaning of plain language. It has not been shown, for example, how TVA can close the gates of the Tellico Dam without "carrying out" an action that has been "authorized" and "funded" by a federal agency. Nor can we understand how such action will "*insure*" that the snail darter's habitat is not disrupted. Accepting the Secretary's determinations, as we must, it is clear that TVA's proposed operation of the dam will have precisely the opposite effect, namely the *eradication* of an endangered species.

Concededly, this view of the Act will produce results requiring the sacrifice of the anticipated benefits of the project and of many millions of dollars in public funds. But examination of the language, history, and structure of the legislation under review here indicates beyond doubt that Congress intended endangered species to be afforded the highest of priorities. . . .

> The dominant theme pervading all Congressional discussion of the proposed [Endangered Species Act of 1973] was the overriding need *to devote whatever effort and resources were necessary* to avoid further diminution of national and worldwide wildlife resources. Much of the testimony at the hearings and much debate was devoted to the biological problem of extinction. Senators and Congressmen uniformly deplored the irreplaceable loss to aesthetics, science, ecology, and the national heritage should more species disappear. Coggins, Conserving Wildlife Resources: An Overview of the Endangered Species Act of 1973, 51 N.D. L. Rev. 315, 321 (1975). (Emphasis added.)

The legislative proceedings in 1973 are, in fact, replete with expressions of concern over the risk that might lie in the loss of *any* endangered species. . . .

In shaping legislation to deal with the problem thus presented, Congress started from the finding that "[t]he two major causes of extinction are hunting and destruction of natural habitat." S. Rep. No. 93-307, p. 2 (1973). Of these twin threats, Congress was informed that the greatest was destruction of natural habitats. . . . Witnesses recommended, among other things, that Congress require all land-managing agencies "to avoid damaging critical habitat for endangered species and to take positive steps to improve such habitat." Virtually every bill introduced in Congress during the 1973 session responded to this concern by incorporating language similar, if not identical, to that found in the present §7 of the Act. These provisions were designed, in the words of an administration witness, "for the first time [to] *prohibit* [a] federal agency from taking action which does jeopardize the status of endangered species" [hearings on S. 1592 and S. 1983, 93d Cong., 1st Sess., 68 (1973) (emphasis added)]. . . .

As it was finally passed, the [ESA] represented the most comprehensive legislation for the preservation of endangered species ever enacted by any nation. Its stated purposes were "to provide a means whereby the ecosystems upon which endangered species and threatened species depend may be conserved," and "to provide a program for the conservation of such . . . species. . . ." 16 U.S.C. §1531(b). In furtherance of these goals, Congress expressly stated in §2(c) that "all Federal departments and agencies *shall* seek to *conserve endangered species* and threatened species. . . ." 16 U.S.C. §1531(c). (Emphasis added.) Lest there be any ambiguity as to the meaning of this statutory directive, the Act specifically defined "conserve" as meaning "to use and the use of *all methods and procedures which are necessary to bring any endangered species* or threatened species to the point at which the measures provided pursuant to this chapter are no longer necessary." §1532(2). (Emphasis added.) Aside from §7, other provisions indicated the seriousness with which Congress viewed this issue: Virtually all dealings with endangered species, including taking, possession, transportation, and sale, were prohibited, 16 U.S.C. §1538, except in extremely narrow circumstances, see §1539(b). The Secretary was also given extensive power to develop regulations and programs for the preservation of endangered and threatened species.[25] §1533(d). Citizen involvement was encouraged by the Act, with provisions allowing interested persons to petition the Secretary to list a species as endangered or threatened, §1533(c)(2), and bring civil suits in United States district courts to force compliance with any provision of the Act, §§1540(c) and (g).

Section 7 of the Act . . . provides a particularly good gauge of congressional intent. . . . [T]his provision had its genesis in the Endangered Species Act of 1966, but that legislation qualified the obligation of federal agencies by stating that they should seek to preserve endangered species only "*insofar as is practicable and consistent with the[ir] primary purposes. . . .*" Likewise, every bill introduced in 1973 contained a qualification similar to that found in the earlier statutes. . . .

What is very significant in this sequence is that the final version of the 1973 Act carefully omitted all of the reservations described above. . . .

It is against this legislative background that we must measure TVA's claim that the Act was not intended to stop operation of a project which, like Tellico Dam, was near completion when an endangered species was discovered in its path. While there is no discussion in the legislative history of precisely this problem, the totality of congressional action makes it abundantly clear that the result we reach today is wholly in accord with both the words of the statute and the intent of Congress. The plain intent of Congress in enacting this statute was to halt and reverse the trend toward species extinction, whatever the cost. This is reflected not only in the stated policies of the Act, but in literally every section of the statute. . . .

Furthermore, it is clear Congress foresaw that §7 would, on occasion, require agencies to alter ongoing projects in order to fulfill the goals of the Act. . . .

One might [argue] that in this case the burden on the public through the loss of millions of unrecoverable dollars would greatly outweigh the loss of the snail darter. But neither the Endangered Species Act nor Art. III of the Constitution provides federal courts with authority to make such fine utilitarian calculations. On the contrary, the plain language of the Act, buttressed by its legislative history, shows clearly that Congress viewed the value of endangered species as "incalculable." Quite obviously, it would be difficult for a court to balance the loss of a sum

25. A further indication of the comprehensive scope of the 1973 Act lies in Congress' inclusion of "threatened species" as a class deserving federal protection. Threatened species are defined as those which are "likely to become an endangered species within the foreseeable future throughout all or a significant portion of [their] range." 16 U.S.C. §1532(15).

certain—even $100 million—against a congressionally declared "incalculable" value, even assuming we had the power to engage in such a weighing process, which we emphatically do not.

[The Court next concluded that the continuing appropriations for the dam did not expressly repeal the ESA, and repeals by implication are not favored, especially for appropriations. "When voting on appropriations measures, legislators are entitled to operate under the assumption that the funds will be devoted to purposes which are lawful and not for any purpose forbidden. Without such an assurance, every appropriations measure would be pregnant with prospects of altering substantive legislation, repealing by implication any prior statute which might prohibit the expenditure."]

(B)

Having determined that there is an irreconcilable conflict between operation of the Tellico Dam and the explicit provisions of §7 of the [ESA], we must now consider what remedy, if any, is appropriate. It is correct, of course, that a federal judge sitting as a chancellor is not mechanically obligated to grant an injunction for every violation of law. This Court made plain in Hecht Co. v. Bowles, 321 U.S. 321, 329 (1944), that "[a] grant of jurisdiction to issue compliance orders hardly suggests an absolute duty to do so under any and all circumstances." As a general matter it may be said that "[s]ince all or almost all equitable remedies are discretionary, the balancing of equities and hardships is appropriate in almost any case as a guide to the chancellor's discretion." D. Dobbs, Remedies 52 (1973). . . .

But these principles take a court only so far. Our system of government is, after all, a tripartite one, with each branch having certain defined functions delegated to it by the Constitution. While "[i]t is emphatically the province and duty of the judicial department to say what the law is," Marbury v. Madison, 1 Cranch 137, 177 (1803), it is equally—and emphatically—the exclusive province of the Congress not only to formulate legislative policies and mandate programs and projects, but also to establish their relative priority for the Nation. Once Congress, exercising its delegated powers, has decided the order of priorities in a given area, it is for the Executive to administer the laws and for the courts to enforce them when enforcement is sought.

Here we are urged to view the Endangered Species Act "reasonably," and hence shape a remedy "that accords with some modicum of common sense and the public weal." But is that our function? We have no expert knowledge on the subject of endangered species, much less do we have a mandate from the people to strike a balance of equities on the side of the Tellico Dam. Congress has spoken in the plainest of words, making it abundantly clear that the balance has been struck in favor of affording endangered species the highest of priorities, thereby adopting a policy which it described as "institutionalized caution."

Our individual appraisal of the wisdom or unwisdom of a particular course consciously selected by the Congress is to be put aside in the process of interpreting a statute. Once the meaning of an enactment is discerned and its constitutionality determined, the judicial process comes to an end. We do not sit as a committee of review, nor are we vested with the power of veto. . . .

We agree with the Court of Appeals that in our constitutional system the commitment to the separation of powers is too fundamental for us to pre-empt congressional action by judicially decreeing what accords with "common sense and the public weal." Our Constitution vests such responsibilities in the political branches.

NOTES

The ESA has long been the subject of frequent political attacks, and efforts to weaken it through statutory amendments routinely occur. Property owners subject to the Act's constraints and other litigants have also attacked the constitutionality of the Act, alleging primarily that the statute exceeds the scope of Congress's authority to regulate interstate commerce. The judicial response to those attacks is discussed in Chapter 2's coverage of Gibbs v. Babbitt, 214 F.3d 483 (4th Cir. 2000), and the accompanying notes.[b] Although the Supreme Court took the position in TVA v. Hill that it was compelled to uphold the issuance of an injunction once a statutory violation had been proven, it has not taken a similarly restrictive view of the scope of judicial remedial discretion in the face of violations of other environmental statutes. See, e.g., Winter v. NRDC, 555 U.S. 7 (2008).

2. Listing and Critical Habitat Designation

ARIZONA CATTLE GROWERS' ASSOCIATION v. SALAZAR
606 F.3d 1160 (9th Cir. 2010)

FLETCHER, Circuit Judge:

[The Interior Department listed the Mexican Spotted Owl as a threatened species under the ESA in 1993. The FWS issued a rule in 2004 designating approximately 8.6 million acres of critical habitat for the owl. The Arizona Cattle Growers Association sued to set aside the rule, arguing, among other things, that the FWS failed to account properly for the economic impacts of the critical habitat designation. The district court granted summary judgment to the government. The Association appealed.]

The decision to list a species as endangered or threatened is made without reference to the economic effects of that decision. See N.M. Cattle Growers Ass'n v. U.S. Fish & Wildlife Serv., 248 F.3d 1277, 1282 (10th Cir. 2001). Listing alone results in certain protections for the species, including a requirement that federal agencies "insure that any action authorized, funded, or carried out by such agency . . . is not likely to jeopardize the continued existence of any endangered species or threatened species." 16 U.S.C. §1536(a)(2); see also, e.g., id. §1538. These protections may impose economic burdens.

In contrast to the listing decision, under the ESA the agency may designate critical habitat only after considering the economic impact of the designation on any particular area. Id. §1533(b)(2). The agency has discretion to exclude any area from the designation if the agency determines "that the benefits of such exclusion outweigh the benefits of specifying such area as part of the critical habitat," unless exclusion would result in extinction of the species. Id. This can be a delicate balancing act. After critical habitat is designated, the ESA requires that federal agencies "insure that any action authorized, funded, or carried out by such agency . . . is not likely to . . . result in the destruction or adverse modification" of critical habitat. Id.

b. For further discussion of the constitutionality of the ESA, see Mank, After Gonzales v. Raich: Is the Endangered Species Act Constitutional Under the Commerce Clause?, 78 U. Colo. L. Rev. 375 (2007); Nagle, The Commerce Clause Meets the Delhi Sands Flower-Loving Fly, 97 Mich. L. Rev. 174 (1998).

§1536(a)(2); see also [Gifford Pinchot Task Force v. U.S. Fish and Wildlife Serv., 378 F.3d 1059, 1069 (9th Cir. 2004)].

The crux of the parties' dispute over the FWS's economic analysis is whether the FWS was required to attribute to the critical habitat designation economic burdens that would exist even in the absence of that designation. The parties agree that the FWS applied the "baseline" approach to the economic analysis. Under this approach, any economic impacts of protecting the owl that will occur regardless of the critical habitat designation—in particular, the burdens imposed by listing the owl—are treated as part of the regulatory "baseline" and are not factored into the economic analysis of the effects of the critical habitat designation.[12] Arizona Cattle, relying on the Tenth Circuit's decision in [New Mexico Cattle Growers Ass'n], argues that this was error and that the FWS was required to apply a "co-extensive" approach to the economic analysis. Under the co-extensive approach, the agency must ignore the protection of a species that results from the listing decision in considering whether to designate an area as critical habitat. Any economic burden that designating an area would cause must be counted in the economic analysis, even if the same burden is already imposed by listing the species and, therefore, would exist even if the area were not designated.

In New Mexico Cattle Growers, the Tenth Circuit held that the baseline approach was impermissible under the ESA. See 248 F.3d at 1285. It did so, however, relying on an FWS regulation that defined "destruction or adverse modification" as effectively identical to the standard for determining whether an agency action places a species in "jeopardy." See id. at 1283-85; see also Gifford Pinchot, 378 F.3d at 1069-70.[13] The Tenth Circuit held that this regulation rendered an economic analysis relying on the baseline approach "virtually meaningless" because it allowed the agency, in all cases, to find no economic impact to the critical habitat designation. See N.M. Cattle Growers Ass'n, 248 F.3d at 1283-85. Our court and others have since found the agency's definition of "adverse modification" too narrow. See Gifford Pinchot, 378 F.3d at 1070; see also Ctr. for Biological Diversity v. BLM, 422 F. Supp. 2d 2f1115, 1151-53 (N.D. Cal. 2006). We therefore reject the Tenth Circuit's approach in New Mexico Cattle Growers as relying on a faulty premise and hold that the FWS may employ the baseline approach in analyzing the critical habitat designation.

The baseline approach is, if anything, more logical than the co-extensive approach. The very notion of conducting a cost/benefit analysis is undercut by incorporating in that analysis costs that will exist regardless of the decision made.[14] Moreover, the practical relevance of the economic analysis under the ESA is to determine the benefits of excluding or including an area in the critical habitat

---

12. For example, suppose that the decision to list the owl as endangered resulted in a ban on logging in a particular area, and that designating that area as critical habitat would independently result in the same ban. Because the listing decision would result in the logging ban even if the agency did not designate critical habitat in that area, the baseline approach would not treat the ban as a burden that was imposed by the critical habitat designation.

13. The Tenth Circuit declined to address whether the FWS's definition of "adverse modification" was invalid. See N.M. Cattle Growers, 248 F.3d at 1283-85.

14. We note further the confusion engendered by the co-extensive approach on the "benefit" side of the equation. If the FWS must consider "burdens" imposed by the critical habitat designation as if there were no protections imposed by the listing decision, must it also assume that in the absence of the critical habitat designation the species is entirely unprotected in considering the "benefits" of designating a particular area? The co-extensive approach runs the risk of becoming a purely academic exercise.

designation: if there is no net benefit (such as a reduction in economic impacts) to excluding the area, the agency must designate it. See 16 U.S.C. §1533(b)(2). The baseline approach, in contrast to the co-extensive approach, reflects this purpose.

Congress has directed the FWS to list species, and thus impose a regulatory burden, without consideration of the costs of doing so. See 16 U.S.C. §1533(a); *N.M. Cattle Growers*, 248 F.3d at 1282. It would be strange to conclude that Congress intended the FWS to consider costs at the critical habitat phase that the agency was barred from considering at the listing phase where, as a result, the analysis would bear little relationship to reality.[15] It would also be strange to conclude that Congress intended to use the critical habitat designation to require the agency to consider the previously irrelevant costs of listing the species, particularly given that the decision to exclude an area from critical habitat for economic reasons is discretionary. See 16 U.S.C. §1533(b)(2); Bennett v. Spear, 520 U.S. 154, 172 (1997). The simpler explanation is that the economic analysis of the critical habitat designation is exactly what it sounds like and is not intended to incorporate the burdens imposed by listing the species.

Arizona Cattle argues that if the FWS designated critical habitat at the same time as it listed the species, see 16 U.S.C. §1533(a)(3), there would be no baseline to which to compare the critical habitat designation. Even if the FWS lists the species concurrently with designating critical habitat, however, listing the species is a necessary antecedent to designating habitat. We see little inconsistency with the FWS's considering the burdens imposed by the critical habitat designation while taking into account those necessarily imposed by the listing decision even in these circumstances.

Finally, Arizona Cattle argues that the baseline approach allows the FWS to treat the economic analysis as a mere procedural formality. We reject the argument that, as a matter of course, the FWS will neglect its duty to perform a thorough economic analysis. To hold otherwise would amount to a presumption that the FWS will act in an arbitrary and capricious fashion, a presumption that is inconsistent with the deference the court affords agencies. See, e.g., Smith v. U.S. Forest Serv., 33 F.3d 1072, 1077 n.2 (9th Cir. 1994). Furthermore, contrary to Arizona Cattle's contention that the impact of designating critical habitat cannot be negligible, the costs of a critical habitat designation could, in fact, be subsumed by the burdens imposed by listing the species—any burden that is entirely "co-extensive" with the listing decision will reflect exactly such a case.

We hold that the FWS permissibly applied the baseline approach in conducting the economic analysis of the effects of the designation. . . .

. . . Arizona Cattle [also] asserts that the FWS's economic analysis ignored the difference between the jeopardy and adverse modification standard in light of *Gifford Pinchot*, and should have considered the economic impacts of additional consultations and project modifications that the adverse modification standard imposes. Arizona Cattle did not make this argument at the district court level and we therefore do not consider it now.[16] . . .

15. Although the Tenth Circuit is likely correct that inclusion of the costs of listing in the critical habitat analysis does not affect the FWS's listing process, see *N.M. Cattle Growers*, 248 F.3d at 1285, it has clear potential to distort the critical habitat analysis.

16. Although we need not reach it, we note that this argument appears fundamentally inconsistent with Arizona Cattle's primary complaint regarding the FWS's application of the baseline approach. The baseline approach counts precisely these economic impacts and Arizona Cattle's disagreement with the baseline approach is, in fact, that it counts only impacts like these.

NOTES AND QUESTIONS

1. What is the role of economic impact in ESA listing and critical habitat decisions? What is the difference between the baseline and co-extensive approaches to habitat designation? How did the court's view of the validity of the baseline approach differ from that of the Tenth Circuit in *New Mexico Cattle Growers*?

In Cape Hatteras Access Pres. Alliance v. U.S. Dep't of Interior, 344 F. Supp. 2d 108, 128-130 (D.D.C. 2004), which the court cited in *Arizona Cattle Growers*, the court discussed the relationship between the baseline approach and the "functional equivalence" approach. Under the latter approach, the designation of critical habitat serves a minimal additional function separate from species listing in that the effects of designation are mainly a subset of the effects of listing. The FWS explained that "a project that is unlikely to jeopardize the continued existence of a species is not likely to destroy or adversely modify critical habitat. Therefore, . . . consultations and project modifications are likely to flow from the listing of the species, and no additional consultations or project modifications are likely to result as a 'but for' effect of the critical habitat designation." The court then addressed the relationship of the two approaches:

> When the [FWS] employs functional equivalence and baseline analysis in tandem to predict the economic impact of future Section 7 consultations, the result is syllogistic: no additional consultations or project modifications are likely to result from designations, the world before and after designations will likely have the same number of consultations and modifications, therefore, designations have no incremental economic impact related to these consultations and modifications.
>
> Circuit courts are uncomfortable with this syllogism that threatens to, as a practical matter, remove from consideration the economic analysis required by statute.

Id. at 127. The Tenth Circuit reacted by invalidating the baseline approach. The Fifth and Ninth Circuits instead rejected functional equivalence on the ground that it rested on the agency's definitions of the terms "jeopardize" and "adverse modification" for purposes of §7(a)(2) of the ESA. The two definitions referred, respectively, to agency actions that appreciably reduce "the likelihood of both the survival and recovery of a listed species," and to those that appreciably diminish "the value of critical habitat for both the survival and recovery of a listed species." The problem was that both definitions required consultation under §7(a) only when a species' survival was at stake, not just when its recovery was at stake. As the court explained in *Cape Hatteras*, "[t]he definition of the adverse modification standard, then, fails to account for the ESA's command that critical habitat be designated for 'conservation,' and not merely survival. 16 U.S.C. §1532(5)(A)." Id. at 129. The court reasoned that once functional equivalence is eliminated, "[t]he baseline approach is a reasonable method for assessing the actual costs of a particular critical habitat designation." Id. at 130. As the district court decision in *Arizona Cattle Growers* put it, "[w]ith the revitalized definition of 'adverse modification,' the Service must consider recovery when consulting on critical habitat, distinguishing those consultations initiated pursuant to the jeopardy standard. Accordingly, additional economic impacts will be associated with Section 7 consultations concerning critical habitat, and the two can no longer be considered functionally equivalent." Arizona Cattle Growers' Ass'n v. Kempthorne, 534 F. Supp. 2d 1013, 1034 (D. Ariz. 2008), *aff'd*, 606 F.3d 1160 (9th Cir. 2010).

In 2014, in response to cases such as *Gifford Pinchot*, the FWS proposed to amend the regulatory definition of "destruction or adverse modification" to mean "a direct or indirect alteration that appreciably diminishes the conservation value of critical habitat for listed species. Such alterations may include, but are not limited to, effects that preclude or significantly delay the development of physical or biological features that support the life-history needs of the species for recovery." 79 Fed. Reg. 27,060, 27,066 (May 12, 2014) (proposed §402.02). Does this proposal address the problem identified in *Gifford Pinchot*? If so, how?

2. *To List or Not to List.* The first step in the protection of a species is the FWS's decision to list it as threatened or endangered. The difference between the two classifications is the degree and immediacy of the risk of extinction. Compare §§3(6) and 3(20). Section 4(b)(1)(A) requires that listing decisions be based on "the best scientific and commercial data available." Economic considerations are not relevant. In re Polar Bear Endangered Species Act Listing and §4(d) Rule Litig., 748 F. Supp. 2d 19 (D.D.C. 2010), concluded that the distinction between endangered and threatened species is not based solely on the imminence of the species' anticipated extinction. Although imminence is relevant, the FWS has broad discretion to decide that other factors outweigh it in making listing decisions. Whether a species is endangered must be determined on a case-by-case basis, taking into account all relevant factors, including the present or threatened destruction or modification of habitat or range, overutilization, disease or predation, inadequacy of existing regulatory mechanisms, and other natural or manmade factors affecting the species' continued existence.

The listing decision is crucial because, as TVA v. Hill teaches, the listing of a species triggers the government's duty to protect the species if federal actions put it in jeopardy. Courts generally overturn FWS decisions to list or to refuse only when the agency departs substantially from the scientific mandate of the statute or violates statutory procedures.[c] The FWS may resolve questions of scientific uncertainty with the same margin of safety accorded EPA in setting water and air pollution standards. See, e.g., City of Las Vegas v. Lujan, 891 F.2d 927 (D.C. Cir. 1989). See also Alabama-Tombigbee Rivers Coal. v. Kempthorne, 477 F.3d 1250 (11th Cir. 2007) (rejecting contention that the FWS failed to rely on the best available scientific evidence in listing the Alabama sturgeon); Alaska v. Lubchenco, 825 F. Supp. 2d 209, 220-223 (D.D.C. 2011) (holding that the NMFS relied on the best available scientific data in listing beluga whale as endangered, and stating that "even if plaintiffs can poke some holes in the agency's models, that does not necessarily preclude a conclusion that these models are the best available science").

How much spatial risk must exist before a species can be listed? The Act provides that a species is endangered if it "is in danger of extinction throughout all or a significant portion of its range." §3(6). In Tucson Herpetological Soc'y v. Salazar, 566 F.3d 870 (9th Cir. 2009), the court rejected the FWS's contention that it need not consider lost historical habitat in making listing decisions because it is largely irrelevant to the recovery of species. The agency must develop some rational explanation for why the lost and threatened portions of a species' range are insignificant before deciding not to list the species for protection. See also Defenders of Wildlife v. Norton,

c. See 3 G. Coggins & R. Glicksman, Public Natural Resources Law §§29:3 to 29:11 (2d ed. 2007), for a full discussion of the cases reviewing the FWS's listing discretion.

258 F.3d 1136 (9th Cir. 2001). The FWS and the NMFS issued a binding policy interpreting the term "significant portion of its range." 79 Fed. Reg. 37,578 (July 1, 2014).

3. *What Is a Species?* The issue of how to define the species that qualify for protection is an increasingly critical one as the FWS tries to protect species specific to a stressed ecosystem. Section 3(16) of the ESA extends the definition of species to subspecies and distinct populations, even though the latter is not a scientific term. See Doremus, Listing Decisions Under the Endangered Species Act: Why Better Science Isn't Always Better Policy, 75 Wash. U. L.Q. 1029 (1997). In National Ass'n of Home Builders v. Norton, 340 F.3d 835 (9th Cir. 2003), the court held that the FWS improperly designated a population of cactus ferruginous pygmy-owls in Arizona as a distinct population segment (DPS). The court found that the agency failed to support its finding that the gap created by the loss of the Arizona owl population would be significant to the taxon as a whole.

In Humane Society v. Kempthorne, 579 F. Supp. 2d 7 (D.D.C. 2008), the court remanded the FWS's decision to designate a cluster of gray wolves in the western Great Lakes region as a DPS and then remove that DPS from the list of endangered species. The court ruled that the ESA does not permit the FWS to use the DPS tool to remove the statute's protections from a healthy subpopulation of a listed species, even if that subpopulation was neither designated as a DPS nor listed as endangered or threatened beforehand. See also Greater Yellowstone Coal., Inc. v. Servheen, 665 F.3d 1015 (9th Cir. 2011) (invalidating the FWS's decision to designate a DPS for the Greater Yellowstone grizzly bear and then remove that DPS from the threatened species list).

In Modesto Irrigation Dist. v. Gutierrez, 619 F.3d 1024 (9th Cir. 2010), the plaintiffs argued that the ESA makes interbreeding the single, definitive characteristic of a DPS. Because steelhead and rainbow trout interbreed to some extent, the plaintiffs claimed the NMFS erred in designating the steelhead as a DPS. The court deferred to the NMFS's view that interbreeding is a necessary but not exclusive condition for qualification as a DPS. According to the NMFS, a DPS also must be distinct. The NMFS determined that the differences between steelhead and rainbow trout set the former apart from other Pacific salmon. Despite reproductive exchanges between steelhead and rainbow trout, the two kinds of fish are physically, physiologically, ecologically, and behaviorally distinct. In re Polar Bear Endangered Species Act Listing and Section 4(d) Rule Litig., 709 F.3d 1 (D.C. Cir. 2013), rejected an attack on the FWS's decision to list polar bears as threatened. It was undisputed that that the bear is dependent on sea ice for its survival; that sea ice is declining; and that climate change has begun reducing the extent and quality of ice to a degree sufficient to jeopardize bear populations. The court upheld the FWS's determination that the species was threatened throughout its range, and disagreed that the FWS should have divided the species into DPSs. The agency supported its conclusion that physiology, demographics, behavior, and life history strategies of the species were insufficient to distinguish population segments.

4. *Critical Habitat Designation.* Must the Interior Secretary designate critical habitat whenever a species is listed as endangered or threatened? Section 4 seems to mandate that designation occur concurrently with a listing "to the maximum extent prudent and determinable." Only a small percentage of listings are in fact accompanied by critical habitat designation, however. Some courts have accepted as a justification for the FWS's refusal to designate critical habitat

the likelihood that designation will encourage species destruction. See, e.g., Fund for Animals v. Babbitt, 903 F. Supp. 96 (D.D.C. 1995), *amended*, 967 F. Supp. 6 (D.D.C. 1997). Other cases suggest that it will be difficult to justify a refusal to designate. In NRDC v. United States Dep't of Interior, 113 F.3d 1121 (9th Cir. 1997), the court found the "increased threat" rationale for not designating to be inconsistent with the FWS's obligation under §4(b)(2) to balance the pros and cons of designation. Section 4(b)(2) allows the FWS to exclude portions of habitat from critical habitat designation only if it "determines that the benefits of such exclusion outweigh the benefits of specifying such area as part of the critical habitat." The FWS never weighed the benefits and risks of designation and did not show that designation would cause more landowners to destroy, rather than protect, gnatcatcher sites. How does the FWS conduct the "delicate balancing act" called for by §4(b)(2)? The FWS issued a draft policy in 2014 explaining how it will consider private or other non-federal conservation plans or partnerships, habitat conservation plans adopted pursuant to §10(a)(1)(B) of the ESA, the federal government's trust responsibilities to tribes, national security concerns, and the duties of federal land managers in deciding whether to exclude areas from critical habitat. 79 Fed. Reg. 27,052 (May 12, 2014). See also 79 Fed. Reg. 27,066, 27,071 (May 12, 2014) (proposing to amend the regulations governing habitat designation to reduce regulatory burdens "in rare circumstances" in which designation does not contribute to species conservation, and providing examples of factors relevant to determining whether designation would benefit species).

What is the consequence of failing to designate critical habitat concurrently with listing? Should a court invalidate the listing until the FWS is ready to designate critical habitat? See Alabama-Tombigbee Rivers Coal. v. Kempthorne, 477 F.3d 1250 (11th Cir. 2007). Nondesignation does not excuse noncompliance with §7 of the ESA. Jeopardy can still be found if there is no designation. United States v. Glenn-Colusa Irrigation Dist., 788 F. Supp. 1126 (E.D. Cal. 1992). But the failure to designate makes it somewhat easier to find no jeopardy. Pyramid Lake Paiute Tribe v. United States Dep't of the Navy, 898 F.2d 1410 (9th Cir. 1990).

Section 3(5) limits the extent of land that can be designated as "critical habitat." The term is defined as "the specific areas within the geographical area occupied by the species, at the time it is listed." Specific areas outside of this area may also be designated if they are "essential for the conservation of the species," but the statute warns that "[e]xcept in those circumstances determined by the Secretary, critical habitat shall not include the entire geographical area which can be occupied by the threatened or endangered species."

Home Builders Ass'n of N. Cal. v. U.S. Fish and Wildlife Serv., 616 F.3d 983 (9th Cir. 2010), ruled that a critical habitat designation need not determine the point in time at which the ESA's protections will no longer be necessary to protect the species. The court found no reason why the FWS should not be able to determine what elements are necessary to conserve a species without determining exactly when conservation will be complete. It also pointed out that §4(f) of the ESA does require a determination of criteria for measuring when a species will be conserved when adopting a recovery plan. The absence of such a requirement in the statute's critical habitat designation provisions indicates that Congress did not intend to require identification of time of recovery in that context.

3. *Substantive and Procedural Duties for Federal Agencies under Section 7*

NATIONAL ASSOCIATION OF HOME BUILDERS v. DEFENDERS OF WILDLIFE
551 U.S. 644 (2007)

ALITO, J., delivered the opinion of the Court.

These cases concern the interplay between two federal environmental statutes. Section 402(b) of the Clean Water Act requires that the Environmental Protection Agency transfer certain permitting powers to state authorities upon an application and a showing that nine specified criteria have been met. Section 7(a)(2) of the Endangered Species Act of 1973 provides that a federal agency must consult with agencies designated by the Secretaries of Commerce and the Interior in order to "insure that any action authorized, funded, or carried out by such agency . . . is not likely to jeopardize the continued existence of any endangered species or threatened species." The question presented is whether §7(a)(2) effectively operates as a tenth criterion on which the transfer of permitting power under the first statute must be conditioned. We conclude that it does not. The transfer of permitting authority to state authorities—who will exercise that authority under continuing federal oversight to ensure compliance with relevant mandates of the Endangered Species Act and other federal environmental protection statutes—was proper. . . .

I

A

. . .

The Clean Water Act of 1972 (CWA) established a National Pollution Discharge Elimination System (NPDES) that is designed to prevent harmful discharges into the Nation's waters. The Environmental Protection Agency (EPA) initially administers the NPDES permitting system for each State, but a State may apply for a transfer of permitting authority to state officials. If authority is transferred, then state officials—not the federal EPA—have the primary responsibility for reviewing and approving NPDES discharge permits, albeit with continuing EPA oversight.

Under §402(b) of the CWA, "the Governor of each State desiring to administer its own permit program for discharges into navigable waters within its jurisdiction may submit to [the EPA] a full and complete description of the program it proposes to establish and administer under State law or under an interstate compact," as well as a certification "that the laws of such State . . . provide adequate authority to carry out the described program." 33 U.S.C. §1342(b). The same section provides that the EPA "shall approve each submitted program" for transfer of permitting authority to a State "unless [it] determines that adequate authority does not exist" to ensure that nine specified criteria are satisfied. These criteria all relate to whether the state agency that will be responsible for permitting has the requisite authority under state law to administer the NPDES program. If the criteria are met, the transfer must be approved. . . .

Section 7 of the ESA prescribes the steps that federal agencies must take to ensure that their actions do not jeopardize endangered wildlife and flora. Section 7(a)(2) provides that "[e]ach Federal agency shall, in consultation with and with the assistance of the Secretary [of Commerce or the Interior], insure that any action authorized, funded, or carried out by such agency (hereinafter in this section referred to as an 'agency action') is not likely to jeopardize the continued existence of any endangered species or threatened species." 16 U.S.C. §1536(a)(2).

[When the consultation process is completed, §7(b)(3)(A) requires the Secretary to give the agency a biological opinion that details how the agency action affects the species or its critical habitat. If the Secretary concludes that the action would place the listed species in jeopardy or adversely modify its critical habitat, the Secretary "shall" suggest reasonable and prudent alternatives (RPAs) that would not violate §7(a)(2) and that can be taken by the agency in implementing its action. §7(b)(3)(A). Regulations promulgated jointly by the Secretaries of Commerce and the Interior provide that an RPA must be capable of implementation in a way "consistent with the scope of the Federal agency's legal authority and jurisdiction." §402.02. After issuance of a "jeopardy" opinion, the agency must either terminate the action, implement the proposed RPA, or seek an exemption from the Endangered Species (or "God") Committee under §7(e). The regulations also provide that "Section 7 and the requirements of this part apply to all actions in which there is discretionary Federal involvement or control." 50 CFR §402.03.]

B

. . .

[Arizona applied for EPA authorization to administer the NPDES program. EPA consulted with the FWS to determine whether the transfer of permitting authority would adversely affect any listed species. The FWS concluded that the transfer would not cause any direct impact on water quality that would adversely affect listed species. It was concerned, however, that the transfer could result in the issuance of more discharge permits, which would lead to more development, which could have an indirect adverse effect on the habitat of upland species such as the cactus ferruginous pygmy-owl and the Pima pineapple cactus. Specifically, the FWS feared that, because §7(a)(2)'s consultation requirement does not apply to permitting decisions by state authorities, the transfer of authority would empower Arizona officials to issue individual permits without considering and mitigating their indirect impact on these species. The FWS therefore urged that, in considering the proposed transfer of permitting authority, those involved in the consultation process should take these potential indirect impacts into account.

EPA disagreed, maintaining that the link between the transfer of permitting authority and the potential harm that could result from increased development was too attenuated. EPA also concluded that the mandatory nature of §402(b), which states that EPA "shall approve" a transfer request if the nine statutory criteria are met, deprived it of authority to disapprove a transfer based on any other factors.

After dispute resolution between the two agencies, the FWS issued a biological opinion, concluding that the transfer would not cause jeopardy to listed species because "the loss of section 7-related conservation benefits . . . is not an indirect effect of the authorization action." Instead, the absence of any requirement that states issuing NPDES permits consult with the FWS "reflects Congress' decision to grant States the right to administer these programs under state law provided the State's program meets the requirements of [§]402(b) of the Clean Water Act." Moreover, the FWS concluded that EPA's continuing oversight of Arizona's permit program would adequately protect listed species and their habitats after the transfer. EPA then concluded that Arizona had met all nine statutory criteria listed in §402(b) and approved the transfer of permitting authority.

Respondents Defenders of Wildlife challenged the transfer in the Ninth Circuit, which allowed the National Association of Homebuilders to intervene in support of the government. Defenders of Wildlife filed a separate action in federal district court challenging the FWS's biological opinion under the ESA. The district court transferred that claim to the Ninth Circuit, which consolidated the two cases.]

A divided panel of the Ninth Circuit held that the EPA's approval of the transfer was arbitrary and capricious. . . . [It held that] the ESA granted the EPA both the power and the duty to determine whether its transfer decision would jeopardize threatened or endangered species. The panel did not dispute that Arizona had met the nine criteria set forth in §402(b) of the CWA, but the panel nevertheless concluded that §7(a)(2) of the ESA provided an "affirmative grant of authority to attend to [the] protection of listed species," in effect adding a tenth criterion to those specified in §402(b). . . .

The Ninth Circuit's construction of §7(a)(2) is at odds with that of other Courts of Appeals. . . . We . . . reverse. . . .

III

A

. . . [T]he substantive statutory question raised by the petitions . . . requires us to mediate a clash of seemingly categorical—and, at first glance, irreconcilable— legislative commands. Section 402(b) of the CWA provides, without qualification, that the EPA "shall approve" a transfer application unless it determines that the State lacks adequate authority to perform the nine functions specified in the section. 33 U.S.C. §1342(b). By its terms, the statutory language is mandatory and the list exclusive; if the nine specified criteria are satisfied, the EPA does not have the discretion to deny a transfer application. Neither respondents nor the Ninth Circuit has ever disputed that Arizona satisfied each of these nine criteria.

The language of §7(a)(2) of the ESA is similarly imperative: it provides that "[e]ach Federal agency shall, in consultation with and with the assistance of the Secretary, insure that any action authorized, funded, or carried out by such agency . . . is not likely to jeopardize" endangered or threatened species or their habitats. 16 U.S.C. §1536(a)(2). This mandate is to be carried out through consultation and may require the agency to adopt an alternative course of action. As the author of the panel opinion below recognized, applying this language literally would "ad[d] one [additional] requirement to the list of considerations under the Clean Water Act permitting transfer provision." That is, it would effectively repeal the mandatory and exclusive list of criteria set forth in §402(b), and replace it with a new, expanded list that includes §7(a)(2)'s no-jeopardy requirement. . . .

B

[The Court cited cases establishing that "repeals by implication are not favored" and will not be inferred "unless the later statute expressly contradict[s] the original act or unless such a construction is absolutely necessary . . . in order that [the] words [of the later statute] shall have any meaning at all." Traynor v. Turnage, 485 U.S. 535, 548 (1988).]

Here, reading §7(a)(2) as the Court of Appeals did would effectively repeal §402(b)'s statutory mandate by engrafting a tenth criterion onto the CWA. Section 402(b) of the CWA commands that the EPA "shall" issue a permit whenever all nine exclusive statutory prerequisites are met. Thus, §402(b) does not just set forth *minimum* requirements for the transfer of permitting authority; it affirmatively mandates that the transfer "shall" be approved if the specified criteria are met. The provision operates as a ceiling as well as a floor. By adding an additional criterion, the Ninth Circuit's construction of §7(a)(2) raises that floor and alters §402(b)'s statutory command.

The Ninth Circuit's reading of §7(a)(2) would not only abrogate §402(b)'s statutory mandate, but also result in the implicit repeal of many additional otherwise categorical statutory commands. Section 7(a)(2) by its terms applies to "any action authorized, funded, or carried out by" a federal agency—covering, in effect, almost anything that an agency might do. Reading the provision broadly would thus partially override every federal statute mandating agency action by subjecting such action to the further condition that it pose no jeopardy to endangered species. See, e.g., Platte River Whooping Crane Critical Habitat Maintenance Trust v. FERC, 962 F.2d, at 33-34 (considering whether §7(a)(2) overrides the Federal Power Act's prohibition on amending annual power licenses). While the language of §7(a)(2) does not explicitly repeal any provision of the CWA (or any other statute), reading it for all that it might be worth runs foursquare into our presumption against implied repeals.

C

1

The agencies charged with implementing the ESA have attempted to resolve this tension through regulations implementing §7(a)(2). The NMFS and FWS . . . have promulgated a regulation stating that "Section 7 and the requirements of this part apply to all actions in which there is *discretionary* Federal involvement or control." 50 CFR §402.03 (emphasis added). Pursuant to this regulation, §7(a)(2) would not be read as impliedly repealing nondiscretionary statutory mandates, even when they might result in some agency action. Rather, the ESA's requirements would come into play only when an action results from the exercise of agency discretion. This interpretation harmonizes the statutes by giving effect to the ESA's no-jeopardy mandate whenever an agency has discretion to do so, but not when the agency is forbidden from considering such extrastatutory factors. . . .

We must therefore read §7(a)(2) of the ESA against the statutory backdrop of the many mandatory agency directives whose operation it would implicitly abrogate or repeal if it were construed as broadly as the Ninth Circuit did below. When §7(a)(2) is read this way, we are left with a fundamental ambiguity that is not resolved by the statutory text. An agency cannot simultaneously obey the differing mandates set forth in §7(a)(2) of the ESA and §402(b) of the CWA, and consequently the statutory language—read in light of the canon against implied repeals—does not itself provide clear guidance as to which command must give way.

In this situation, it is appropriate to look to the implementing agency's expert interpretation, which cabins §7(a)(2)'s application to "actions in which there is discretionary Federal involvement or control." 50 CFR §402.03. This reading harmonizes the statutes by applying §7(a)(2) to guide agencies' existing discretionary authority, but not reading it to override express statutory mandates.

2

We conclude that this interpretation is reasonable in light of the statute's text and the overall statutory scheme, and that it is therefore entitled to deference under *Chevron*. Section 7(a)(2) requires that an agency "insure" that the actions it authorizes, funds, or carries out are not likely to jeopardize listed species or their habitats. To "insure" something—as the court below recognized—means "[t]o make certain, to secure, to guarantee (some thing, event, etc.)." 420 F.3d, at 963 (quoting 7 Oxford English Dictionary 1059 (2d ed. 1989)). The regulation's focus on "discretionary" actions accords with the commonsense conclusion that, when an agency is *required* to do something by statute, it simply lacks the power to "insure" that such action will not jeopardize endangered species. . . .

3

The court below simply disregarded §402.03's interpretation of the ESA's reach, dismissing "the regulation's reference to 'discretionary . . . involvement'" as merely "congruent with the statutory reference to actions 'authorized, funded, or carried out' by the agency." 420 F.3d, 968. But this reading cannot be right. Agency discretion presumes that an agency can exercise "judgment" in connection with a particular action. See Citizens to Preserve Overton Park, Inc. v. Volpe, 401 U.S. 402, 415-416 (1971); see also Random House Dictionary of the English Language 411 (unabridged ed. 1967) ("discretion" defined as "the power or right to decide or act according to one's own judgment; freedom of judgment or choice"). As the mandatory language of §402(b) itself illustrates, not every action authorized, funded, or carried out by a federal agency is a product of that agency's exercise of discretion.

The dissent's interpretation of §402.03 is similarly implausible. The dissent would read the regulation as simply clarifying that discretionary agency actions are included within the scope of §7(a)(2), but not confining the statute's reach to such actions. But this reading would render the regulation entirely superfluous. Nothing in either §7(a)(2) or the other agency regulations interpreting that section, see §402.02, suggests that discretionary actions are *excluded* from the scope of the ESA, and there is thus no need for a separate regulation to bring them within the statute's scope. On the dissent's reading, §402.03's reference to "discretionary" federal involvement is mere surplusage, and we have cautioned against reading a text in a way that makes part of it redundant. . . .

In short, we read §402.03 to mean what it says: that §7(a)(2)'s no-jeopardy duty covers only discretionary agency actions and does not attach to actions (like the NPDES permitting transfer authorization) that an agency is *required* by statute to undertake once certain specified triggering events have occurred. This reading not only is reasonable, inasmuch as it gives effect to the ESA's provision, but also comports with the canon against implied repeals because it stays §7(a)(2)'s mandate where it would effectively override otherwise mandatory statutory duties.

D

Respondents argue that our opinion in TVA v. Hill, 437 U.S. 153 (1978), supports their contrary position. . . . In language on which respondents rely, the Court concluded that "the ordinary meaning" of §7 of the ESA contained "no exemptions" and reflected "a conscious decision by Congress to give endangered species priority over the 'primary missions' of federal agencies." Id., at 173, 185, 188.

TVA v. Hill, however, had no occasion to answer the question presented in these cases. That case was decided almost a decade before the adoption in 1986 of the regulations contained in 50 CFR §402.03. And in any event, the construction project at issue in TVA v. Hill, while expensive, was also discretionary. The TVA argued that by continuing to make lump-sum appropriations to the TVA, some of which were informally earmarked for the Tellico Dam project, Congress had implicitly repealed §7's no-jeopardy requirement as it applied to that project. The Court rejected this argument, concluding that "[t]he Appropriations Acts did not themselves identify the projects for which the sums had been appropriated" and that reports by congressional committees allegedly directing the TVA to complete the project lacked the force of law. Id., at 189, n.35. Central to the Court's decision was the conclusion that Congress did not *mandate* that the TVA put the dam into operation; there was no statutory command to that effect; and there was therefore no basis for contending that applying the ESA's no-jeopardy requirement would implicitly repeal another affirmative congressional directive.

TVA v. Hill thus supports the position, expressed in §402.03, that the ESA's no-jeopardy mandate applies to every *discretionary* agency action—regardless of the expense or burden its application might impose. But that case did not speak to the question whether §7(a)(2) applies to *non*-discretionary actions, like the one at issue here. The regulation set forth in 50 CFR §402.03 addressed that question, and we defer to its reasonable interpretation.

IV

Finally, respondents and their *amici* argue that, even if §7(a)(2) is read to apply only to "discretionary" agency actions, the decision to transfer NPDES permitting authority to Arizona represented such an exercise of discretion. They contend that the EPA's decision to authorize a transfer is not entirely mechanical; that it involves some exercise of judgment as to whether a State has met the criteria set forth in §402(b); and that these criteria incorporate references to wildlife conservation that bring consideration of §7(a)(2)'s no-jeopardy mandate properly within the agency's discretion.

The argument is unavailing. While the EPA may exercise some judgment in determining whether a State has demonstrated that it has the authority to carry out §402(b)'s enumerated statutory criteria, the statute clearly does not grant it the discretion to add another entirely separate prerequisite to that list. Nothing in the text of §402(b) authorizes the EPA to consider the protection of threatened or endangered species as an end in itself when evaluating a transfer application. And to the extent that some of the §402(b) criteria may result in environmental benefits to marine species, there is no dispute that Arizona has satisfied each of those statutory criteria. . . . [11]

11. Respondents also contend that the EPA has taken, or will take, other discretionary actions apart from the transfer authorization that implicate the ESA. For example, they argue that the EPA's alleged provision of funding to Arizona for the administration of its clean water programs is the kind of discretionary agency action that is subject to §7(a)(2). However, assuming this is true, any such

Applying *Chevron*, we defer to the agency's reasonable interpretation of ESA §7(a)(2) as applying only to "actions in which there is discretionary Federal involvement or control." 50 CFR §402.03. Since the transfer of NPDES permitting authority is not discretionary, but rather is mandated once a State has met the criteria set forth in §402(b) of the CWA, it follows that a transfer of NPDES permitting authority does not trigger §7(a)(2)'s consultation and no-jeopardy requirements. Accordingly, the judgment of the Court of Appeals for the Ninth Circuit is reversed, and these cases are remanded for further proceedings consistent with this opinion.

Justice STEVENS, with whom Justice SOUTER, Justice GINSBURG, and Justice BREYER join, dissenting. . . .

When faced with competing statutory mandates, it is our duty to give full effect to both if at all possible. The Court fails at this task. Its opinion unsuccessfully tries to reconcile the CWA and ESA by relying on a federal regulation, 50 CFR §402.03 (2006), which it reads as limiting the reach of §7(a)(2) to *only* discretionary federal actions. Not only is this reading inconsistent with the text and history of §402.03, but it is fundamentally inconsistent with the ESA itself.

In the celebrated "snail darter" case, TVA v. Hill, 437 U.S. 153 (1978), we held that the ESA "reveals a conscious decision by Congress to give endangered species priority over the 'primary missions' of federal agencies," id., at 185. Consistent with that intent, Chief Justice Burger's exceptionally thorough and admirable opinion explained that §7 "admits of no exception." Id., at 173. Creating precisely such an exception by exempting nondiscretionary federal actions from the ESA's coverage, the Court whittles away at Congress' comprehensive effort to protect endangered species from the risk of extinction and fails to give the Act its intended effect. . . .

Our opinion in *Hill* explained at length why §7 imposed obligations on "all federal agencies" to ensure that "actions authorized, funded, or carried out by them do not jeopardize the continued existence of endangered species." Not a word in the opinion stated or suggested that §7 obligations are inapplicable to mandatory agency actions that would threaten the eradication of an endangered species. Nor did the opinion describe the Tennessee Valley Authority's (TVA) attempted completion of the Tellico Dam as a discretionary act. How could it? After all, if the Secretary of the Interior had not declared the snail darter an endangered species whose critical habitat would be destroyed by operation of the Tellico Dam, the TVA surely would have been obligated to spend the additional funds that Congress appropriated to complete the project.[2] Unconcerned with whether an agency action was mandatory or discretionary, we simply held that §7 of the ESA

---

funding decision is a separate agency action that is outside the scope of this lawsuit. Respondents also point to the fact that, following the transfer of permitting authority, the EPA will retain oversight authority over the state permitting process, including the power to object to proposed permits. But the fact that the EPA may exercise discretionary oversight authority—which may trigger §7(a)(2)'s consultation and no-jeopardy obligations—after the transfer does not mean that the decision authorizing the transfer is itself discretionary.

2. . . . Justice Alito maintains that *Hill* held that the "acts appropriating funds to the TVA . . . did *not require* the agency to use any of the generally appropriated funds to complete the Tellico Dam project." But *Hill* said no such thing. That case only held that the *subsequent* appropriation of funds for the Tellico Dam Project could not overcome the mandatory requirements of §7 of the ESA; it did not hold that the TVA would not have been required to spend any and all appropriated funds if the ESA had never been passed. If the ESA had never been enacted and did not stand in the way of the completion of the Tellico Dam, there is no doubt that the TVA would have finished the project that Congress had funded.

reveals an explicit congressional decision to require agencies to afford *first priority* to the declared national policy of saving endangered species. The pointed omission of the type of qualifying language previously included in endangered species legislation reveals a conscious decision by Congress to give endangered species *priority over the "primary missions" of federal agencies*. [Id., at 185 (emphasis added).] . . .

. . . Moreover, after observing that the ESA creates only a limited number of "hardship exemptions," see 16 U.S.C. §1539—none of which would apply to federal agencies—we applied the maxim *expressio unius est exclusio alterius* to conclude that "there are no exemptions in the Endangered Species Act for federal agencies," 437 U.S., at 188.

Today, however, the Court countenances such an exemption. It erroneously concludes that the ESA contains an unmentioned exception for nondiscretionary agency action. . . . But both the text of the ESA and our opinion in *Hill* compel the contrary determination that Congress intended the ESA to apply to "all federal agencies" and to all "actions authorized, funded, or carried out by them." Id., at 173. . . .

Given our unequivocal holding in *Hill* that the ESA has "first priority" over all other federal action, if any statute should yield, it should be the CWA. But no statute must yield unless it is truly incapable of coexistence. Therefore, assuming that §402(b) of the CWA contains its own mandatory command, we should first try to harmonize that provision with the mandatory requirements of §7(a)(2) of the ESA.

[Justice Stevens asserted that the majority misread §402.03, whose coverage is not limited to discretionary actions. He argued that the regulation "surely does not . . . say (as the Court does) that the duty 'does not attach to actions (like the NPDES permitting transfer authorization) that an agency is *required* by statute to undertake once certain specified triggering events have occurred.' If the drafters of the regulation had intended such a far-reaching change in the law, surely they would have said so by using language similar to that which the Court uses today."]

As for the final rule's explanation for the scope of the term "action" in §402.01, that too is fully consistent with my interpretation of §402.03. That explanation plainly states that "*all* Federal actions including 'conservations programs' are subject to the consultation requirements of section 7(a)(2) if they 'may affect' listed species or their critical habitats." 51 Fed. Reg. 19929 (emphasis added). The regulation does not say all "discretionary" federal actions, nor does it evince an intent to limit the scope of §7(a)(2) in any way. Rather, it just restates that the ESA applies to "all" federal actions. . . .

[Justice Stevens next argued that there are two other ways to reconcile the CWA and the ESA "without privileging one statute over the other." First, in the event of a conflict between the ESA and the CWA, the FWS could include in its biological opinion RPAs that would enable EPA to develop a substitute that would allow a transfer of permitting authority without jeopardizing endangered species. If no such RPA were available, EPA could apply to the Endangered Species Committee under §1536(e) for an exemption from §7(a)(2). Second, EPA regulations vest in it the duty to oversee delegated state NPDES programs and allow it to veto a state permit if it is "outside the guidelines and the requirements" of the CWA. 33 U.S.C. §1342(d)(2). EPA had adopted regulation that requires a state to enter into a Memorandum of Agreement (MOA), which "may include other terms, conditions, or agreements" that are "relevant to the administration and enforcement of the State's regulatory program." MOAs thus provided a potential mechanism for giving effect to §7 of the ESA while also allowing the transfer of permitting authority to a state.

Finally, Justice Stevens argued that EPA's decision whether to approve a transfer of NPDES permitting authority is discretionary.] The first criterion [of §402(b)], for example, requires the EPA Administrator to examine five other statutes and ensure that the State has adequate authority to comply with each. 33 U.S.C. §1342(b)(1)(A). One of those five statutes, in turn, expressly directs the Administrator to exercise his "judgment." §1312. . . . The Court plainly acknowledges that EPA exercises discretion when deciding whether to transfer permitting authority to a State. If we are to take the Court's approach seriously, once any discretion has been identified—as it has here—§7(a)(2) must apply. . . .

Justice BREYER, dissenting. . . .

. . . [T]he majority cannot possibly be correct in concluding that the structure of §402(b) precludes application of §7(a)(2) to the EPA's discretionary action. That is because grants of discretionary authority always come with *some* implicit limits attached. See L. Jaffe, Judicial Control of Administrative Action 359 (1965) (discretion is "a power to make a choice" from a "permissible class of actions"). And there are likely numerous instances in which, prior to, but not after, the enactment of §7(a)(2), the statute might have implicitly placed "species preservation" outside those limits. . . .

NOTES AND QUESTIONS

1. How do the majority and the dissenting opinions differ in describing the scope of the obligation imposed on federal agencies by §7(a)(2) of the ESA to consult with the FWS or the NMFS to determine the impact of proposed agency actions on listed species or their critical habitat? How did Justices Alito and Stevens each interpret TVA v. Hill and its implications for this case? Which treatment of *Hill* do you find more convincing? Why was the FWS's regulation defining the scope of §7(a) relevant to the analysis?

2. *Substantive and Procedural Protection Duties.* Assuming that an agency "action" is involved, an agency's substantive protection duties under §7(a)(2) are primarily implemented through the procedural obligation to consult with the FWS. An agency whose actions "*may affect* listed species or critical habitat" must consult with the FWS. 50 C.F.R. §402.14(a) (emphasis added). The FWS must determine whether listed species are present in the area and whether the proposed action is *likely to affect* a species or its habitat. If the answer to either question is negative, the FWS can end informal consultation and the acting agency's ESA duties are satisfied. If the answer is affirmative, the FWS must begin a formal consultation process and prepare a biological opinion assessing whether the proposed action is *likely to jeopardize listed species or adversely affect critical habitat*. Id. §402.14(g)(4). An affirmative answer requires that the opinion include reasonable and prudent alternatives (RPAs) to avoid jeopardy. Although the acting agency is not bound to implement the RPAs contained in a biological opinion, deviation from the terms of the opinion increases the risk that the agency will be deemed in violation of the ESA. E.g., Tribal Village of Akutan v. Hodel, 869 F.2d 1185, 1193 (9th Cir. 1988).

Negative impacts on critical habitat need not be permanent to amount to adverse modification for purposes of §7(a)(2). According to one court, any biological opinion that plans to allow short-term habitat degradation "must carefully consider the life cycles and behavioral patterns of the species to avoid crippling . . . recovery. It is not enough that the habitat will recover in the future if there is a serious risk that when that future arrives the species will be history." Miccosukee Tribe of Indians v. United States, 566 F.3d 1257, 1271 (11th Cir. 2009).

3. *The Role and Scope of the Consultation Duty.* Defenders of Wildlife v. Salazar, 842 F. Supp. 2d 181, 188 (D.D.C. 2012), explained the rationale for §7(a)(2)'s requirement that federal agencies consult with the FWS or the NMFS on the possible impacts of their project on listed species and critical habitat:

> [T]he Service Agencies play a unique role vis-a-vis the Action Agencies. Most critically they are independent from the Action Agencies. The job of the Action Agencies is, naturally enough, to get their projects accomplished. They cannot help but put their major efforts into completion of their statutory mission. The Service Agencies on the other hand approach the ESA issues with an independent, impartial, and objective eye. Their experts for many years have informally consulted with Action Agencies on . . . many . . . listed species, and have made it clear that eliminating their individual project review would inevitably have a serious adverse impact on listed species . . . .

Karuk Tribe of Calif. v. U.S. Forest Serv., 681 F.3d 1006 (9th Cir. 2012), specified a two-part test for determining whether ESA consultation obligations apply: (1) whether a federal agency affirmatively authorized, funded, or carried out the underlying activity; and (2) whether the agency had some discretion to influence or change the activity for the benefit of a protected species. Both requirements were met when the Forest Service allowed gold mining operations in a national forest on the condition that mining activity comply with criteria for the protection of coho salmon. The agency's decision to approve a request to mine is a discretionary determination through which it can influence those activities to benefit listed species. The court in *Karuk Tribe* concluded that the Forest Service's approval of mining met §402.14(a)'s relatively low trigger for consultation because mining activities might cause disturbance of surface resources. The trigger for consultation is lower than for a violation of the taking prohibition, §9(a)(1)(B). As the next principal case illustrates, takings liability normally turns on evidence that a listed species has in fact been injured.

Do actions that result in greenhouse gas emissions linked to climate change trigger §7(a)(2)? The FWS has taken the position that the emission of greenhouse gases from a federal action cannot trigger §7(a) consultation requirements because "there is currently no way to determine how the emissions from a specific action both influence climate change and then subsequently affect specific listed species, including polar bears. As we now understand them, the best scientific data currently available do not draw a causal connection between GHG emissions resulting from a specific Federal action and effects on listed species or critical habitat by climate change." Endangered and Threatened Wildlife and Plants; Special Rule for the Polar Bear, 73 Fed. Reg. 76,249, 76,266 (Dec. 16, 2008). Chapter 12, section E.4.b contains further discussion of the application of the ESA to activities that contribute to climate change.

4. *Judicial Review of Biological Opinions.* Biological opinions are subject to judicial review under the "arbitrary and capricious" standard. The court rejected a NMFS biological opinion in Idaho Dep't of Fish & Game v. National Marine Fisheries Serv., 850 F. Supp. 886, 891-893 (D. Or. 1994), *remanded as moot*, 56 F.3d 1071 (9th Cir. 1995). The NMFS inquired whether hydropower operations would result in a "significant" reduction in salmon mortality relative to a 1986-1990 base period

chosen because: (a) it represented the most recent series of years before consideration of the species for listing; (b) it was long enough to encompass a full life cycle; (c) and it reflected relatively consistent management practices. The court found the base period to be unreasonable. It was significantly shorter than base periods used in prior years; a longer base period that included years of higher salmon abundance levels would have resulted in a higher species protection goal. The period 1986-1990 constituted record-low years for the species due to drought conditions in the area. Finally, the NMFS failed to consider alternative baselines. Compare Consolidated Salmonid Cases, 791 F. Supp. 2d 802, 848 (E.D. Cal. 2011) (stating that "even if the baseline itself causes jeopardy to the species, only if the project causes additional harm can the project be found to jeopardize the species' continued existence. This determination requires an evaluation of the project's effects, separate from the conditions that would exist if the project were not carried out.").

Suppose that the BLM consults with the FWS on its proposed issuance of a right of way across public lands and surface waters that provide habitat for listed fish species. The FWS issues a biological opinion containing a no-jeopardy finding, relying on an agreement with the BLM in which the private company proposing to build the pipe-line promised to take specified conservation measures to protect the fish during pipe-line construction. The biological opinion, however, does not include those measures as RPAs or make the company liable for takings under §9 if it fails to implement the conservation measures, resulting in fish deaths. If an environmental group challenges the opinion, should the court uphold or vacate it? See Center for Biological Diversity v. U.S. Bureau of Land Mgmt., 698 F.3d 1101 (9th Cir. 2012) (vacating the opinion).

Gifford Pinchot Task Force v. U.S. Fish and Wildlife Serv., 378 F.3d 1059 (9th Cir. 2004), was a challenge to a series of biological opinions that allowed incidental takes of spotted owls in the Pacific Northwest. Plaintiffs objected to the use of habitat proxies to determine jeopardy and argued that the FWS had to conduct on-the-ground population surveys. The court responded as follows:

> The test for whether the habitat proxy is permissible in this case is whether it "reasonably ensures" that the proxy results mirror reality. . . . Though it is a close case, we conclude that the habitat models used here reasonably ensure that owl population projections from the habitat proxy are accurate.
>
> . . . [T]he use of habitat as a proxy for species in this case makes sense. The habitat analysis here is not just a simplistic "x number acres = y number of owls" type of equation. Rather, the habitat proxy takes into account type of land, extent of degradation of the habitat, relationship between different habitats, the owls' distribution, and the owls' range. The jeopardy analysis also takes into account non-habitat factors, including competition from other species, forest insects, and disease. This detailed model for owl population is sufficient to ensure that the FWS's habitat proxy reasonably correlates to the actual population of owls. Finally, the habitat proxy does not exist in a vacuum: The FWS has a program of demographic studies that supplements and verifies the habitat results. . . .
>
> Second, Appellants argue that the statutory scheme does not allow a habitat proxy method for jeopardy assessment even if habitat proxy is a sound method. . . . Appellants argue that because "habitat" is already accounted for in the adverse modification prong of Section 7 analysis, any analysis of jeopardy to species must look to the actual species themselves instead of simply analyzing habitat, or at the very least, must continually verify habitat models by on-the-ground population verifications.

We reject this argument. Focus on actual species count is an overly narrow interpretation of what is required under the jeopardy prong. The FWS asserts that it uses different methodologies when it analyzes habitat under jeopardy and adverse modification, limiting potential overlap. Importantly, if the habitat proxy is used correctly, it can evaluate a species's habitat that has not been designated as "critical habitat," and thus is indirectly evaluating species that live outside the critical habitat. In the ordinary course, any endangered or threatened species may have some habitat that is not deemed critical habitat. See 16 U.S.C. §1532(5)(C) (noting that, [with exceptions,] "critical habitat shall not include the entire geographical area which can be occupied by the threatened or endangered species"). Further, if habitat models are sufficiently accurate and are robust, in the sense that the results are accurate in many cases, then the models function as if the FWS were counting spotted owls. Because the ESA does not prescribe how the jeopardy prong is to be determined, nor how species populations are to be estimated, we hold that it is a permissible interpretation of the statute to rest the jeopardy analysis on a habitat proxy. [Id. at 1066-1067.]

Compare the court's treatment of the "proxy-on-proxy" issue in the context of national forest management in the *Northwest Ecosystem Council* case.

Wild Fish Conservancy v. Salazar, 628 F.3d 513 (9th Cir. 2010), found fault with a FWS no jeopardy finding concerning the effects of the FWS's own operation of a salmon fish hatchery on bull trout. The first issue was whether the FWS properly defined the scope of the agency action as ongoing operation of the hatchery during a five-year period. The court stated that §7(a)(2) requires a biological opinion to analyze the effect on the species of "the entire agency action." The FWS failed to justify the choice of five years, as the court reasoned that artificial division of a continuing operation into a series of short terms can undermine the ability to determine accurately the species' likelihood of survival and recovery and mask the possibility that nonappreciable impact in each subdivided period could amount to appreciable impact on a cumulative basis. Is this problem similar to the segmentation problem under NEPA? The agency action had to be long enough to make a meaningful determination as to whether ongoing operation of the hatchery would be expected to reduce appreciably the likelihood of survival and recovery of the trout. Further, the duty to reinitiate consultation in the future did not diminish the FWS's obligation to prepare a comprehensive biological opinion now.

The court also held that even if a five-year period were proper, the FWS failed to explain how its conclusion that operation of the hatchery was likely to produce continuing long-term negative population trends in the affected trout population was consistent with its ultimate determination that operations could not reasonably be expected to reduce appreciably the survival and recovery of the fish. Finally, the court held that the incidental take statement that accompanied the biological opinion pursuant to §7(b)(4) did not include adequate monitoring requirements. Although the FWS set a clear numerical cap on the allowable incidental take, it did not specify monitoring and reporting requirements or select a surrogate trigger that could be monitored, thereby vitiating the usefulness of the numerical cap.

Arizona Cattle Growers' Ass'n v. U.S. Fish and Wildlife Serv., 273 F.3d 1229 (9th Cir. 2001), held that the FWS may use ecological conditions rather than numbers to define the trigger for exceeding the taking authorized by an incidental take statement included in a biological opinion under §7(b)(4) only if it establishes that "no such numerical value could be practically obtained." The FWS later proposed rules addressing the use of surrogates to express the amount or extent of anticipated incidental take. Under the proposal, surrogates could be used if the statement (1) describes the causal link between the surrogate and take of listed species; (2) describes why it is not practical to express the amount or extent of anticipated take or to monitor take-related impacts in terms of individual species members; and (3) sets a clear standard for determining when the extent of taking has been exceeded. The regulations would also clarify the requirements for issuance of incidental take statements for programmatic actions where implementation requires later authorization, funding, or implementation of site-specific actions that will be subject to future consultation and incidental take statements. 78 Fed. Reg. 54,437 (Sept. 4, 2013).

5. *The "Affirmative Conservation" Duty.* Section 7(a)(1) of the ESA requires agencies to conserve listed species. This "affirmative conservation" duty is separate from the duty to avoid jeopardy or adverse impacts on critical habitat. The §7(a)(1) duty is the subject of less litigation than the §7(a)(2) duty. Defenders of Wildlife v. Secretary, U.S. Dep't of the Interior, 354 F. Supp. 2d 1156 (D. Or. 2005), illustrates the potential impact of §7(a)(1). Environmental groups challenged the FWS's decision to downlist (and thereby provide less protection to) two distinct population segments of the gray wolf. They argued that the downlisting constituted a violation of the affirmative conservation duty because the FWS was not using all methods necessary to conserve the wolf. The FWS responded that §7(a)(1) does not apply to the FWS because the agency's implementation of the ESA is a program, in and of itself, that is designed to effectuate the conservation of listed species. The court found the argument to be inconsistent with the plain language of §7(a)(1), which makes "all" federal agencies subject to the affirmative conservation duty. The court also held, however, that the FWS did not violate the duty because it had implemented specific and concrete conservation and recovery programs for the gray wolf. The court in Defenders of Wildlife v. Andrus, 428 F. Supp. 167 (D.D.C. 1977), found that the FWS violated the duty by failing to determine, before it issued regulations governing the sport hunting of migratory game birds, whether misidentification due to poor visibility would result in the mistaken killing of listed bird species.

Suppose that global climate change is altering the habitat of an endangered species by destroying the plants upon which it depends for food. Does the affirmative conservation duty require a federal agency such as the Forest Service to take steps to move remaining members of the species to other lands managed by the agency in cooler climates that may enhance the prospects for the species' survival? Conservation biologists have begun to debate the appropriateness of such "assisted migration" efforts. See Joy & Fuller, Advising Noah: A Legal Analysis of Assisted Migration, 39 Envtl. L. Rep. 10413 (2009); Camacho, Assisted Migration: Redefining Nature and Natural Resource Law under Climate Change, 27 Yale J. on Reg. 171 (2010); Fischman & Hyman, The Legal Challenge of Protecting Animal Migrations as Phenomena of Abundance, 28 Va. Envtl. L.J. 173 (2010).

4. *The Section 9 Taking Prohibition*

TVA v. Hill and *National Association of Home Builders* involved §7 of the ESA, which applies only to the federal government. Section 9 prohibits "any person," which includes both federal agencies and private individuals, from "taking" an endangered species. §9(a)(1)(B). The killing of a listed species clearly qualifies as a "take," but what about habitat destruction? The following case addresses this issue.

BABBITT v. SWEET HOME CHAPTER OF
COMMUNITIES FOR A GREAT OREGON
515 U.S. 687 (1995)

STEVENS, J., delivered the opinion of the Court, in which O'CONNOR, KENNEDY, SOUTER, GINSBURG, and BREYER, JJ., joined. O'CONNOR, J., filed a concurring opinion. SCALIA, J., filed a dissenting opinion, in which REHNQUIST, C.J., and THOMAS, J., joined.

Justice STEVENS delivered the opinion of the Court.

. . . Section 9 of the Act makes it unlawful for any person to "take" any endangered or threatened species. The Secretary has promulgated a regulation that defines the statute's prohibition on takings to include "significant habitat modification or degradation where it actually kills or injures wildlife." This case presents the question whether the Secretary exceeded his authority under the Act by promulgating that regulation.

I

Section 9(a)(1) of the Endangered Species Act provides the following protection for endangered species:

> Except as provided in sections 1535(g)(2) and 1539 of this title, with respect to any endangered species of fish or wildlife listed pursuant to section 1533 of this title it is unlawful for any person subject to the jurisdiction of the United States to— . . .
>
>> (B) take any such species within the United States or the territorial sea of the United States[.] 16 U.S.C. §1538(a)(1).

Section 3(19) of the Act defines the statutory term "take":

> The term "take" means to harass, harm, pursue, hunt, shoot, wound, kill, trap, capture, or collect, or to attempt to engage in any such conduct. 16 U.S.C. §1532(19).

The Act does not further define the terms it uses to define "take." The Interior Department regulations that implement the statute, however, define the statutory term "harm":

> Harm in the definition of "take" in the Act means an act which actually kills or injures wildlife. Such act may include significant habitat modification or degradation where it actually kills or injures wildlife by significantly impairing essential behavioral patterns, including breeding, feeding, or sheltering. 50 CFR §17.3 (1994).

This regulation has been in place since 1975.

A limitation on the §9 "take" prohibition appears in §10(a)(1)(B) of the Act, which Congress added by amendment in 1982. That section authorizes the Secretary to grant a permit for any taking otherwise prohibited by §9(a)(1)(B) "if such taking is incidental to, and not the purpose of, the carrying out of an otherwise lawful activity." 16 U.S.C. §1539(a)(1)(B). . . .

Respondents advanced three arguments to support their submission that Congress did not intend the word "take" in §9 to include habitat modification, as the

Secretary's "harm" regulation provides. First, they correctly noted that language in the Senate's original version of the ESA would have defined "take" to include "destruction, modification, or curtailment of [the] habitat or range" of fish or wildlife, but the Senate deleted that language from the bill before enacting it. Second, respondents argued that Congress intended the Act's express authorization for the Federal Government to buy private land in order to prevent habitat degradation in §5 to be the exclusive check against habitat modification on private property. Third, because the Senate added the term "harm" to the definition of "take" in a floor amendment without debate, respondents argued that the court should not interpret the term so expansively as to include habitat modification.

[The district court dismissed plaintiffs' complaint. The D.C. Circuit reversed, establishing a split among the circuits.] We granted certiorari to resolve the conflict. Our consideration of the text and structure of the Act, its legislative history, and the significance of the 1982 amendment persuades us that the Court of Appeals' judgment should be reversed.

II

Because this case was decided on motions for summary judgment, we may appropriately make certain factual assumptions in order to frame the legal issue. First, we assume respondents have no desire to harm either the red-cockaded woodpecker or the spotted owl; they merely wish to continue logging activities that would be entirely proper if not prohibited by the ESA. On the other hand, we must assume, *arguendo*, that those activities will have the effect, even though unintended, of detrimentally changing the natural habitat of both listed species and that, as a consequence, members of those species will be killed or injured. Under respondents' view of the law, the Secretary's only means of forestalling that grave result—even when the actor knows it is certain to occur[9]—is to use his §5 authority to purchase the lands on which the survival of the species depends. The Secretary, on the other hand, submits that the §9 prohibition on takings, which Congress defined to include "harm," places on respondents a duty to avoid harm that habitat alteration will cause the birds unless respondents first obtain a permit pursuant to §10.

The text of the Act provides three reasons for concluding that the Secretary's interpretation is reasonable. First, an ordinary understanding of the word "harm" supports it. The dictionary definition of the verb form of "harm" is "to cause hurt or damage to: injure." Webster's Third New International Dictionary 1034 (1966). In the context of the ESA, that definition naturally encompasses habitat modification that results in actual injury or death to members of an endangered or threatened species.

Respondents argue that the Secretary should have limited the purview of "harm" to direct applications of force against protected species, but the dictionary definition does not include the word "directly" or suggest in any way that only direct or willful

---

9. . . . [T]he Secretary's definition of "harm" is limited to "act[s] which actually kil[l] or injur[e] wildlife." 50 CFR §17.3 (1994). . . . We do not agree with the dissent that the regulation covers results that are not "even foreseeable . . . no matter how long the chain of causality between modification and injury." Respondents have suggested no reason why . . . the "harm" regulation itself . . . should not be read to incorporate ordinary requirements of proximate causation and foreseeability. . . .

action that leads to injury constitutes "harm."[10] Moreover, unless the statutory term "harm" encompasses indirect as well as direct injuries, the word has no meaning that does not duplicate the meaning of other words that §3 uses to define "take." A reluctance to treat statutory terms as surplusage supports the reasonableness of the Secretary's interpretation.[11]

Second, the broad purpose of the ESA supports the Secretary's decision to extend protection against activities that cause the precise harms Congress enacted the statute to avoid. In TVA v. Hill, 437 U.S. 153 (1978), we described the Act as "the most comprehensive legislation for the preservation of endangered species ever enacted by any nation." . . .

Third, the fact that Congress in 1982 authorized the Secretary to issue permits for takings that §9(a)(1)(B) would otherwise prohibit, "if such taking is incidental to, and not the purpose of, the carrying out of an otherwise lawful activity," strongly suggests that Congress understood §9(a)(1)(B) to prohibit indirect as well as deliberate takings. The permit process requires the applicant to prepare a "conservation plan" that specifies how he intends to "minimize and mitigate" the "impact" of his activity on endangered and threatened species, §10(a)(2)(A), making clear that Congress had in mind foreseeable rather than merely accidental effects on listed species. No one could seriously request an "incidental" take permit to avert §9 liability for direct, deliberate action against a member of an endangered or threatened species, but respondents would read "harm" so narrowly that the permit procedure would have little more than that absurd purpose. . . . Congress' addition of the §10 permit provision supports the Secretary's conclusion that activities not intended to harm an endangered species, such as habitat modification, may constitute unlawful takings under the ESA unless the Secretary permits them.

The Court of Appeals made three errors in asserting that "harm" must refer to a direct application of force because the words around it do.[15] First, the court's premise

10. Respondents and the dissent emphasize what they portray as the "established meaning" of "take" in the sense of a "wildlife take," a meaning respondents argue extends only to "the effort to exercise dominion over some creature, and the concrete effect of [sic] that creature." This limitation ill serves the statutory text, which forbids not taking "some creature" but "tak[ing] any [endangered] species"—a formidable task for even the most rapacious feudal lord. More importantly, Congress explicitly defined the operative term "take" in the ESA, no matter how much the dissent wishes otherwise, thereby obviating the need for us to probe its meaning as we must probe the meaning of the undefined subsidiary term "harm." Finally, Congress' definition of "take" includes several words—most obviously "harass," "pursue," and "wound," in addition to "harm" itself—that fit respondents' and the dissent's definition of "take" no better than does "significant habitat modification or degradation."

11. In contrast, if the statutory term "harm" encompasses such indirect means of killing and injuring wildlife as habitat modification, the other terms listed in §3—"harass," "pursue," "hunt," "shoot," "wound," "kill," "trap," "capture," and "collect"—generally retain independent meanings. Most of those terms refer to deliberate actions more frequently than does "harm," and they therefore do not duplicate the sense of indirect causation that "harm" adds to the statute. In addition, most of the other words in the definition describe either actions from which habitat modification does not usually result (e.g., "pursue," "harass") or effects to which activities that modify habitat do not usually lead (e.g., "trap," "collect"). To the extent the Secretary's definition of "harm" may have applications that overlap with other words in the definition, that overlap reflects the broad purpose of the Act.

15. The dissent makes no effort to defend the Court of Appeals' reading of the statutory definition as requiring a direct application of force. Instead, it tries to impose on §9 a limitation of liability to "affirmative conduct intentionally directed against a particular animal or animals." Under the dissent's interpretation of the Act, a developer could drain a pond, knowing that the act would extinguish an endangered species of turtles, without even proposing a conservation plan or

was flawed. Several of the words that accompany "harm" in the §3 definition of "take," especially "harass," "pursue," "wound," and "kill," refer to actions or effects that do not require direct applications of force. Second, to the extent the court read a requirement of intent or purpose into the words used to define "take," it ignored §9's express provision that a "knowing" action is enough to violate the Act. Third, the court employed *noscitur a sociis* to give "harm" essentially the same function as other words in the definition, thereby denying it independent meaning. The canon, to the contrary, counsels that a word "gathers meaning from the words around it." Jarecki v. G. D. Searle & Co., 367 U.S. 303, 307 (1961). The statutory context of "harm" suggests that Congress meant that term to serve a particular function in the ESA, consistent with but distinct from the functions of the other verbs used to define "take." The Secretary's interpretation of "harm" to include indirectly injuring endangered animals through habitat modification permissibly interprets "harm" to have "a character of its own not to be submerged by its association." Russell Motor Car Co. v. United States, 261 U.S. 514, 519 (1923).

Nor does the Act's inclusion of the §5 land acquisition authority and the §7 directive to federal agencies to avoid destruction or adverse modification of critical habitat alter our conclusion. Respondents' argument that the Government lacks any incentive to purchase land under §5 when it can simply prohibit takings under §9 ignores the practical considerations that attend enforcement of the ESA. Purchasing habitat lands may well cost the Government less in many circumstances than pursuing civil or criminal penalties. In addition, the §5 procedure allows for protection of habitat before the seller's activity has harmed any endangered animal, whereas the Government cannot enforce the §9 prohibition until an animal has actually been killed or injured. . . . [17]

We need not decide whether the statutory definition of "take" compels the Secretary's interpretation of "harm," because our conclusions that Congress did not unambiguously manifest its intent to adopt respondents' view and that the Secretary's interpretation is reasonable suffice to decide this case. See generally Chevron U.S.A. Inc. v. Natural Resources Defense Council, Inc., 467 U.S. 837 (1984). The latitude the ESA gives the Secretary in enforcing the statute, together with the degree of regulatory expertise necessary to its enforcement, establishes that we owe some degree of deference to the Secretary's reasonable interpretation. [18] . . .

---

applying for a permit under §9(a)(1)(B); unless the developer was motivated by a desire "to get at a turtle," no statutory taking could occur. Because such conduct would not constitute a taking at common law, the dissent would shield it from §9 liability, even though the words "kill" and "harm" in the statutory definition could apply to such deliberate conduct. We cannot accept that limitation. In any event, our reasons for rejecting the Court of Appeals' interpretation apply as well to the dissent's novel construction.

17. Congress recognized that §§7 and 9 are not coextensive as to federal agencies when, in the wake of our decision in *Hill* in 1978, it added §7(o), 16 U.S.C. §1536(o), to the Act. That section provides that any federal project subject to exemption from §7, 16 U.S.C. §1536(h), will also be exempt from §9.

18. Respondents also argue that the rule of lenity should foreclose any deference to the Secretary's interpretation of the ESA because the statute includes criminal penalties. The rule of lenity is premised on two ideas: first, "a fair warning should be given to the world in language that the common world will understand, of what the law intends to do if a certain line is passed"; second, "legislatures and not courts should define criminal activity." United States v. Bass, 404 U.S. 336, 347-350 (1971). . . . We have never suggested that the rule of lenity should provide the standard for reviewing facial challenges to administrative regulations whenever the governing statute authorizes

IV

When it enacted the ESA, Congress delegated broad administrative and interpretive power to the Secretary. See 16 U.S.C. §§1533, 1540(f). . . . The proper interpretation of a term such as "harm" involves a complex policy choice. When Congress has entrusted the Secretary with broad discretion, we are especially reluctant to substitute our views of wise policy for his. See *Chevron*, 467 U.S., at 865-866. In this case, that reluctance accords with our conclusion, based on the text, structure, and legislative history of the ESA, that the Secretary reasonably construed the intent of Congress when he defined "harm" to include "significant habitat modification or degradation that actually kills or injures wildlife."

In the elaboration and enforcement of the ESA, the Secretary and all persons who must comply with the law will confront difficult questions of proximity and degree; for, as all recognize, the Act encompasses a vast range of economic and social enterprises and endeavors. These questions must be addressed in the usual course of the law, through case-by-case resolution and adjudication.

The judgment of the Court of Appeals is reversed. . . .

Justice O'CONNOR, concurring.

My agreement with the Court is founded on two understandings. First, the challenged regulation is limited to significant habitat modification that causes actual, as opposed to hypothetical or speculative, death or injury to identifiable protected animals. Second, even setting aside difficult questions of scienter, the regulation's application is limited by ordinary principles of proximate causation, which introduce notions of foreseeability. These limitations, in my view, call into question . . . many of the applications derided by the dissent. Because there is no need to strike a regulation on a facial challenge out of concern that it is susceptible of erroneous application, however, and because there are many habitat-related circumstances in which the regulation might validly apply, I join the opinion of the Court.

In my view, the regulation is limited by its terms to actions that actually kill or injure individual animals. Justice Scalia disagrees, arguing that the harm regulation "encompasses injury inflicted, not only upon individual animals, but upon populations of the protected species." At one level, I could not reasonably quarrel with this observation; death to an individual animal always reduces the size of the population in which it lives, and in that sense, "injures" that population. But by its insight, the dissent means something else. Building upon the regulation's use of the word "breeding," Justice Scalia suggests that the regulation facially bars significant habitat modification that actually kills or injures hypothetical animals (or, perhaps more aptly, causes potential additions to the population not to come into being). Because "[i]mpairment of breeding does not 'injure' living creatures," Justice Scalia reasons, the regulation must contemplate application to "a population of animals which would otherwise have maintained or increased its numbers."

I disagree. As an initial matter, I do not find it as easy as Justice Scalia does to dismiss the notion that significant impairment of breeding injures living creatures. To raze the last remaining ground on which the piping plover currently breeds, thereby making it impossible for any piping plovers to reproduce, would obviously

---

criminal enforcement. Even if there exist regulations whose interpretations of statutory criminal penalties provide such inadequate notice of potential liability as to offend the rule of lenity, the "harm" regulation, which has existed for two decades and gives a fair warning of its consequences, cannot be one of them.

injure the population (causing the species' extinction in a generation). But by completely preventing breeding, it would also injure the individual living bird, in the same way that sterilizing the creature injures the individual living bird. . . .

. . . I see no indication that Congress, in enacting [§9(a)(1)], intended to dispense with ordinary principles of proximate causation. Strict liability means liability without regard to fault; it does not normally mean liability for every consequence, however remote, of one's conduct. See generally W. Keeton et al., Prosser and Keeton on The Law of Torts 559-560 (5th ed. 1984) (describing "practical necessity for the restriction of liability within some reasonable bounds" in the strict liability context).

. . .

Proximate causation is not a concept susceptible of precise definition. It is easy enough, of course, to identify the extremes. The farmer whose fertilizer is lifted by tornado from tilled fields and deposited miles away in a wildlife refuge cannot, by any stretch of the term, be considered the proximate cause of death or injury to protected species occasioned thereby. At the same time, the landowner who drains a pond on his property, killing endangered fish in the process, would likely satisfy any formulation of the principle. . . . I note, at the least, that proximate cause principles inject a foreseeability element into the statute, and hence, the regulation, that would appear to alleviate some of the problems noted by the dissent. . . .

NOTES AND QUESTIONS

1. *What Habitat Modification Is a §9 Taking?* What limitations does the majority opinion impose on defining habitat destruction or modification as a §9 taking? Does *Sweet Home* require proof that the species' habitat has previously been harmed? The issue arose in Marbled Murrelet v. Babbitt, 83 F.3d 1060, 1066 (9th Cir. 1996), which concluded that "[a] reasonably certain threat of imminent harm to a protected species is sufficient for issuance of an injunction." According to the Ninth Circuit, under *Sweet Home*, habitat modification that significantly impairs the breeding and sheltering of a protected species amounts to "harm." Harm therefore includes the threat of future harm. *Marbled Murrelet* adopts a risk-margin of safety analysis similar to that adopted by courts in air and water pollution cases. See also Forest Conservation Council v. Rosboro Lumber Co., 50 F.3d 781, 784 (9th Cir. 1995). But cf. NWF v. Burlington N. R.R., 23 F.3d 1508, 1512 n.8 (9th Cir. 1994); American Bald Eagle v. Bhatti, 9 F.3d 163, 165-167 (1st Cir. 1993).

2. *Takings of Threatened Species.* The take prohibition of §9(a)(1)(B) applies on its face only to endangered species of fish and wildlife. Section 4(d), however, authorizes the Interior Secretary to issue "such regulations as he deems necessary and advisable to provide for the conservation" of threatened species. The agency's default position is that the take prohibition applies to threatened species to the same extent as to endangered species. After the FWS listed polar bears as threatened, however, it adopted a "special rule" refusing to apply the take prohibitions to activities currently authorized or exempted under other laws such as the Marine Mammal Protection Act (MMPA) or to activities occurring outside the range of the species that may incidentally impact polar bears. The court upheld that decision In re Polar Bear Endangered Species Act Listing and §4(d) Rule Litigation, 818 F. Supp. 2d 214 (D.D.C. 2011), although it invalidated the §4(d) rule due to noncompliance with NEPA. With respect to the MMPA exemption, the court concluded that the FWS

reasonably chose to minimize administrative redundancy because doing so would not sacrifice significant conservation benefits. The court's response to the agency's decision to exempt activities outside the bear's range is discussed in Chapter 12, §E.4.b. After conducting a NEPA analysis, the FWS reissued the §4(d) rule for the polar bear. 78 Fed. Reg. 11,766 (Feb. 20, 2013).

3. *Incidental Take Permits.* Section 9 is the most controversial section of the ESA because it has the potential to stop a great deal of private real estate development in biodiversity hot spots such as California, Florida, and Texas. Any land clearing could be a "taking." In 1982, Congress added §10 to deal with this problem. Section 10 allows the creation of Department of Interior–approved Habitat Conservation Plans (HCPs). An HCP was originally a single species land reserve program funded by developer exactions and public funds. An approved HCP is the basis for the issuance of an incidental take permit. The permit allows a development to proceed on the theory that "the taking will not appreciably reduce the likelihood of the survival and recovery of the species" because of efficacy of the HCP. §10(a)(2)(B)(iv).[d] Habitat planning has since become more proactive and moved toward large-scale bio-regional ecosystem management experiments.[e]

The majority opinion in *Sweet Home* refers to the FWS's authority under §10(a)(1)(B) to issue incidental take permits. Must an incidental take permit specify the number of animals killed that will trigger a take determination? Can the FWS issue an incidental take permit to a private party when its own findings indicate that species losses need to be mitigated, the developer has rejected a key mitigation alternative, and no map of the developer's mitigation habitat dedication is available? See Gerber v. Norton, 294 F.3d 173 (D.C. Cir. 2002). May the FWS issue an incidental take permit that threatens the recovery of a listed species? See Spirit of the Sage Council v. Kempthorne, 511 F. Supp. 2d 31, 41-44 (D.D.C. 2007) (concluding that it may, but citing cases to the contrary).

HCP creation and management raise constitutional taking issues discussed in the notes following Lucas v. South Carolina Coastal Council, excerpted in the next section. See Thompson, The Endangered Species Act: A Case Study in Takings and Incentives, 49 Stan. L. Rev. 305 (1997). It is therefore not surprising that the federal government has sought to create incentives for voluntary land and financial contributions to create reserve systems. The major incentive for landowner participation in these voluntary species protection efforts is the assurance that participation will meet all ESA obligations. In 1994 the Department of the Interior promulgated its "no surprises" policy, which promises that once an HCP is approved, no new reserve additions for subsequently listed species will be required except in extraordinary circumstances.[f] Can the government in effect promise not to "prosecute" future ESA violations? Bosselman, The Statutory and Constitutional Mandate for a No Surprises Policy, 24 Ecology L.Q. 707 (1997), argues that §10 authorizes the policy and that United States v. Winstar Corp., 518 U.S. 839 (1996), supports the proposition

d. See Ruhl, How to Kill Endangered Species, Legally: The Nuts and Bolts of Endangered Species Act "HCP" Permits for Real Estate Development, 5 Envtl. Law. 345 (1999).

e. See Lin, Participants' Experiences with Habitat Conservation Plans and Suggestions for Streamlining the Process, 23 Ecology L.Q. 369 (1996); Karkkainen, Collaborative Ecosystem Governance: Scale, Complexity, and Dynamism, 21 Va. Envtl. L.J. (2002); Ruhl, Biodiversity Conservation and the Ever-Expanding Web of Federal Laws Regulating Nonfederal Lands: Time for Something Completely Different?, 66 U. Colo. L. Rev. 555 (1995); Symposium, The Ecosystem Approach: New Departures for Land and Water, 24 Ecology L.Q. 619 (1997).

f. The subsequent procedural history is discussed in Chapter 3, section D.

that the federal government may bind itself to assume the costs of changes in future regulations.

4. *So What?* The ultimate question is whether the ESA is effective in preventing species extinction. The Act's effectiveness is a source of continuing scientific and political controversy. The basic scientific criticism is that the species-by-species approach neither prevents extinction nor promotes biodiversity conservation. See C. Mann & M. Plummer, Noah's Choice: The Future of Endangered Species (1995). S. Budiansky, Nature's Keepers 171 (1995), sets out the oft-repeated criticism of the Act.

> Of the more than fourteen hundred species listed as endangered or threatened since . . . 1966, only twenty-two have ever been "delisted." Of those, eight were removed from the list because it was found that the original data used to justify the listing was in error, usually when additional populations were discovered; seven were removed from the list because of extinction. That leaves seven supposedly bone fide success stories: the Pacific grey whale, the American alligator, the Arctic peregrine falcon, the Rydberg milk vetch (a plant found in Utah), and three birds found on a single Pacific island. But even here the evidence is not clear-cut. The milk vetch and alligator were thought to have been listed in error and never to have been truly endangered; grey whale populations have been increasing steadily since the nineteenth century, as demand for whale products evaporated; and the birds of Palau Islands may have recovered largely due to the (unassisted) regrowth of vegetation wiped out in bombing during World War II.

Professor Rachlinski, on the other hand, provides empirical data to support his evaluation that the ESA has succeeded at saving species and would be even more successful if Congress provided sufficient funds to implement it. Rachlinski, Noah by the Numbers: An Empirical Investigation of the Endangered Species Act, 82 Cornell L. Rev. 356 (1997). Doremus, The Endangered Species Act: Static Law Meets Dynamic World, 32 Wash. U. J.L. & Pol'y 175 (2010), contends that the ESA's failure to take account of nature's dynamic qualities has hampered its effectiveness.

C.   THE REGULATORY TAKING PROBLEM

LUCAS v. SOUTH CAROLINA COASTAL COUNCIL
505 U.S. 1003 (1992)

Justice SCALIA delivered the opinion of the Court.

In 1986, petitioner David H. Lucas paid $975,000 for two residential lots on the Isle of Palms in Charleston County, South Carolina, on which he intended to build single-family homes. In 1988, however, the South Carolina Legislature enacted the Beachfront Management Act, which had the direct effect of barring petitioner from erecting any permanent habitable structures on his two parcels. . . .

[A 1977 state statute required owners of coastal zone land that qualified as a "critical area" (which included beaches and immediately adjacent sand dunes) to obtain a permit from a state agency, the South Carolina Coastal Council (Council), before committing the land to a "use other than the use the critical area was devoted to" on the the effective date of the statute. At the time, no portion of Lucas's lots, located approximately 300 feet from the beach, qualified as a "critical area." Statutory amendments in 1988 brought Lucas's lots within the critical area, prohibiting his construction of occupiable improvements. Lucas sued, charging that the statutory ban on construction amounted to a taking of his property without just compensation.]

Prior to Justice Holmes's exposition in Pennsylvania Coal Co. v. Mahon, 260 U.S. 393 (1922), it was generally thought that the Takings Clause reached only a "direct appropriation" of property, Legal Tender Cases, 12 Wall. 457, 551 (1871), or the functional equivalent of a "practical ouster of [the owner's] possession." . . . Justice Holmes recognized in *Mahon*, however, that if the protection against physical appropriations of private property was to be meaningfully enforced, the government's power to redefine the range of interests included in the ownership of property was necessarily constrained by constitutional limits. . . . These considerations gave birth in that case to the oft-cited maxim that "while property may be regulated to a certain extent, if regulation goes too far it will be recognized as a taking." . . .

The trial court found Lucas's two beachfront lots to have been rendered valueless by respondent's enforcement of the coastal-zone construction ban. [According to the South Carolina Supreme Court, however, the statute represented an exercise of the state's police powers to mitigate the harm to the public interest that Lucas's use of his land might cause. The court treated Lucas's failure to challenge the statute's purposes as a concession that the beach/dune area along the South Carolina coast is a valuable public resource, that the erection of new construction contributes to the destruction of that resource, and that discouraging new construction near the beach/dune area was necessary to prevent great public harm. It held that these concessions triggered the application of a line of cases holding that regulation of property uses that are akin to public nuisances are not compensable takings.]

. . . The "harmful or noxious uses" principle was the Court's early attempt to describe in theoretical terms why government may, consistent with the Takings Clause, affect property values by regulation without incurring an obligation to compensate—a reality we nowadays acknowledge explicitly with respect to the full scope of the State's police power. . . .

Where the State seeks to sustain regulation that deprives land of all economically beneficial use, we think it may resist compensation only if the logically antecedent inquiry into the nature of the owner's estate shows that the proscribed use interests were not part of his title to begin with. This accords, we think, with our "takings" jurisprudence, which has traditionally been guided by the understandings of our citizens regarding the content of, and the State's power over, the "bundle of rights" that they acquire when they obtain title to property. It seems to us that the property owner necessarily expects the uses of his property to be restricted, from time to time, by various measures newly enacted by the State in legitimate exercise of its police powers; "[a]s long recognized, some values are enjoyed under an implied limitation and must yield to the police power." Pennsylvania Coal Co. v. Mahon, 260 U.S., at 413. . . . In the case of land, however, we think the notion pressed by the Council that title is somehow held subject to the "implied limitation" that the State may subsequently eliminate all economically valuable use is inconsistent with the historical compact recorded in the Takings Clause that has become part of our constitutional culture. . . .

. . . We believe similar treatment must be accorded confiscatory regulations, i.e., regulations that prohibit all economically beneficial use of land: Any limitation so severe cannot be newly legislated or decreed (without compensation), but must inhere in the title itself, in the restrictions that background principles of the State's law of property and nuisance already place upon land ownership. A law or decree with such an effect must, in other words, do no more than duplicate the result that could have been achieved in the courts—by adjacent landowners (or other uniquely affected persons) under the State's law of private nuisance, or by the State under its complementary power to abate nuisances that affect the public generally, or otherwise.

On this analysis, the owner of a lake-bed, for example, would not be entitled to compensation when he is denied the requisite permit to engage in a landfilling operation that would have the effect of flooding others' land. Nor the corporate owner of a nuclear generating plant, when it is directed to remove all improvements from its land upon discovery that the plant sits astride an earthquake fault. Such regulatory action may well have the effect of eliminating the land's only economically productive use, but it does not proscribe a productive use that was previously permissible under relevant property and nuisance principles. The use of these properties for what are now expressly prohibited purposes was always unlawful, and (subject to other constitutional limitations) it was open to the State at any point to make the implication of those background principles of nuisance and property law explicit. In light of our traditional resort to "existing rules or understandings that stem from an independent source such as state law" to define the range of interests that qualify for protection as "property" under the Fifth and Fourteenth Amendments, Board of Regents of State Colleges v. Roth, 408 U.S. 564, 577 (1972), this recognition that the Takings Clause does not require compensation when an owner is barred from putting land to a use that is proscribed by those "existing rules or understandings" is surely unexceptional. When, however, a regulation that declares "off-limits" all economically productive or beneficial uses of land goes beyond what the relevant background principles would dictate, compensation must be paid to sustain it.

The "total taking" inquiry we require today will ordinarily entail (as the application of state nuisance law ordinarily entails) analysis of, among other things, the degree of harm to public lands and resources, or adjacent private property, posed by the claimant's proposed activities, see, e.g., Restatement (Second) of Torts §§826, 827, the social value of the claimant's activities and their suitability to the locality in question, see, e.g., id., §§828(a) and (b), 831, and the relative ease with which the alleged harm can be avoided through measures taken by the claimant and the government (or adjacent private landowners) alike, see, e.g., id., §§827(e), 828(c), 830. The fact that a particular use has long been engaged in by similarly situated owners ordinarily imports a lack of any common-law prohibition (though changed circumstances or new knowledge may make what was previously permissible no longer so), see id., §827, Comment g. So also does the fact that other landowners, similarly situated, are permitted to continue the use denied to the claimant. . . .

[To avoid a taking on remand,] South Carolina must identify background principles of nuisance and property law that prohibit the uses [Lucas] now intends in the circumstances in which the property is presently found. . . .

Justice BLACKMUN, dissenting.

Today the Court launches a missile to kill a mouse. . . .

If the state legislature is correct that the prohibition on building in front of the setback line prevents serious harm, then, under this Court's prior cases, the Act is constitutional. "Long ago it was recognized that all property in this country is held under the implied obligation that the owner's use of it shall not be injurious to the community, and the Takings Clause did not transform that principle to one that requires compensation whenever the State asserts its power to enforce it." Keystone Bituminous Coal Assn. v. DeBenedictis, 480 U.S. 470, 491-492 [(1987)]. . . .

. . . In determining what is a nuisance at common law, state courts make exactly the decision that the Court finds so troubling when made by the South Carolina General Assembly today: They determine whether the use is harmful. Common-law public and private nuisance law is simply a determination whether a particular use causes harm. There is nothing magical in the reasoning of judges long dead. They determined a harm in the same way as state judges and legislatures do today. If judges in the 18th and 19th centuries can distinguish a harm from a benefit, why not judges in the 20th century, and if judges can, why not legislators? . . .

. . . Nothing in the discussions in Congress concerning the Takings Clause indicates that the Clause was limited by the common-law nuisance doctrine. Common-law courts themselves rejected such an understanding. They regularly recognized that it is "for the legislature to interpose, and by positive enactment to prohibit a use of property which would be injurious to the public." [Commonwealth v. Tewksbury, 11 Metc., at 57 (Mass. 1846).] . . . Commonwealth v. Parks, 155 Mass. 531, 532 (1892) (Holmes, J.) ("[T]he legislature may change the common law as to nuisances, and may move the line either way, so as to make things nuisances which were not so, or to make things lawful which were nuisances").

In short, I find no clear and accepted "historical compact" or "understanding of our citizens" justifying the Court's new takings doctrine. Instead, the Court seems to treat history as a grab bag of principles, to be adopted where they support the Court's theory, and ignored where they do not. If the Court decided that the early common law provides the background principles for interpreting the Takings Clause, then regulation, as opposed to physical confiscation, would not be compensable. If the Court decided that the law of a later period provides the background principles, then regulation might be compensable, but the Court would have to confront the fact that legislatures regularly determined which uses were prohibited, independent of the common law, and independent of whether the uses were lawful when the owner purchased. What makes the Court's analysis unworkable is its attempt to package the law of two incompatible eras and peddle it as historical fact.

NOTES AND QUESTIONS

1. *What Happened to Mr. Lucas's Exposed House?* After the case, South Carolina purchased the lot from Lucas. The Coastal Council then sold the lot to new owners, who constructed a house. See generally Been, Lucas v. The Green Machine: Using the Takings Clause to Promote More Efficient Regulation?, in Property Stories (G. Korngold & A. Morriss eds., 2d ed. 2009).

2. *The Historical Basis for Physical and Regulatory Takings.* Is the concept of a regulatory taking consistent with the original intent of the drafters of the Constitution? Most students of takings history argue that the Fifth Amendment was intended to apply only to physical appropriations.[g] Proponents of Justice Scalia's approach in *Lucas* agree that the history of the Fifth Amendment is thin but argue that it reflects Lockean

g. Hart, Colonial Land Use Law and Its Significance for Modern Takings Doctrine, 109 Harv. L. Rev. 1252 (1996); Treanor, The Original Understanding of the Takings Clause and the Political Process, 95 Colum. L. Rev. 782 (1995); Treanor, The Origins and Significance of the Just Compensation Clause of the Fifth Amendment, 94 Yale L.J. 694 (1985).

respect for private property. See, e.g., R. Epstein, Takings: Private Property and the Power of Eminent Domain (1985).

   3. *Is a Coherent Takings Doctrine Possible?* Assuming that regulation that does not involve physical expropriation may amount to a taking, when does it do so? Academic commentators have tried to guide courts on how to decide when regulations that severely diminish the economic value of a tract of land constitute a taking either by looking at the purpose of the regulation or by applying criteria to evaluate the fairness of not compensating an impacted property owner. One influential answer distinguished between government activities designed to prevent a landowner from undertaking an activity that harms other landowners and those intended to force a landowner to benefit others. Dunham, A Legal and Economic Basis for City Planning, 58 Colum. L. Rev. 650, 664 (1958). Much subsequent commentary is a variation on this theme.[h] How would you classify a land use regulation intended to conserve biodiversity? The relationship between the harm-benefit approach and the *Lucas* analytical framework has been described as follows:

> Although *Lucas* purported to reject the harm-benefit test as neither "objective" nor "value-free," *Lucas* itself incorporated common law nuisance into takings law.[i] Both the harm-benefit test and the approach adopted in *Lucas* share the notion of harm as socially defined. The critical difference between the two approaches is that the *Lucas* inquiry attempts to enshrine common law historical understandings of harm into the takings doctrine, whereas the harm-benefit test looks to contemporary community norms, which are influenced but not dictated by historical allocations of rights. [Lin, The Unifying Role of Harm in Environmental Law, 2006 Wis. L. Rev. 897, 934.]

   Commentators who find the harm-benefit distinction to be too indeterminate to decide whether a compensable taking has occurred have sought to ascertain when compensation is justly due as a result of governmental interference with recognized property relationships. Some have invoked Jeremy Bentham, who defined property as a settled expectation of undisturbed use and enjoyment, and then asked when the government can legitimately claim that a regulation does not frustrate legitimate

---

   h. Professor Sax recast the harm-benefit test as an arbitration-enterprise versus appropriation test and then as a conflict resolution versus expropriation test. Sax, Takings and the Police Power, 74 Yale L.J. 36, 67 (1964); Sax, Takings: Private Property and Public Rights, 81 Yale L.J. 149, 172 (1971).

   i. In rejecting the harm-benefit test as a viable means of determining when land use regulation amounts to a taking, Justice Scalia asserted that "the distinction between 'harm-prevent-ing' and 'benefit-conferring' regulation is often in the eye of the beholder. It is quite possible, for example, to describe in either fashion the ecological, economic, and esthetic concerns that inspired the South Carolina Legislature in the present case. One could say that imposing a servitude on Lucas's land is necessary in order to prevent his use of it from 'harming' South Carolina's ecological resources; or, instead, in order to achieve the 'benefits' of an ecological preserve." *Lucas,* 505 U.S. at 1024. He added that "[a] given restraint will be seen as mitigating 'harm' to the adjacent parcels or securing a 'benefit' for them, depending upon the observer's evaluation of the relative importance of the use that the restraint favors." Id. at 1025. According to Scalia, the constitutionality of land use regulations should not depend on whether statutes like the South Carolina law contain findings that the targets of regulation are inflicting harm on the community. "Since such a justification can be formulated in practically every case, this amounts to a test of whether the legislature has a stupid staff. We think the Takings Clause requires courts to do more than insist upon artful harm-preventing characterizations." Id. at 1025 n.12.

expectations. Relying both on utilitarian and Rawlsian justifications for property and the legitimacy of state regulation, a classic article framed the critical issue as whether the state gave fair prior notice that it would not recognize individual claims to exploit the resource. Michelman, Property, Utility, and Fairness: Comments on the Ethical Foundations of Just Compensation Law, 80 Harv. L. Rev. 1165 (1967).

The Supreme Court summarized the different bases for finding a regulatory taking in Lingle v. Chevron U.S.A., Inc., 544 U.S. 528 (2005). It explained that a plaintiff seeking to challenge a government regulation as a compensable taking of private property may proceed under one of three theories. The claimant may assert that the regulation (1) amounts to a "physical" taking; (2) amounts to a *Lucas*-type, per se "total regulatory taking"; (3) amounts to a regulatory taking under the multi-factor balancing test announced in Penn Central Transp. Co. v. New York City, 438 U.S. 104 (1978), which applies when an owner has suffered adverse economic impact that does not amount to a complete denial of all economically viable use; or (4) takes the form of a land use exaction that violates the standards set forth in Nollan v. California Coastal Comm'n, 483 U.S. 825 (1987), and Dolan v. City of Tigard, 512 U.S. 374 (1994). The first three tests, at least, "share a common touchstone. Each aims to identify regulatory actions that are functionally equivalent to the classic taking in which government directly appropriates private property or ousts the owner from his domain. Accordingly, each of these tests focuses directly upon the severity of the burden that government imposes upon private property rights." *Lingle*, 544 U.S. at 539. The Court also described the first two categories as "relatively narrow." Koontz v. St. Johns River Water Mgmt. Dist., 133 S. Ct. 2586 (2013), extended the fourth category to monetary exactions charged developers as the price for issuance of land development permits. Land dedication requirements and monetary exactions may trigger takings liability if a "nexus" and "rough proportionality" between the property that the government demands and the social costs of a permit applicant's development proposal is lacking. Id. at 2595.

May a judicial decision amount to a taking? In Stop the Beach Renourishment, Inc. v. Florida Dep't of Envtl. Prot., 560 U.S. 702, 715 (2010), a divided Court concluded that it may if it "declares that what was once an established right of private property no longer exists." The Court held, however, that a state court decision concerning the effect of accretions and relictions on littoral rights did not amount to a taking under that standard. For a collection of articles on *Stop the Beach*, see Symposium, 61 Syracuse L. Rev. 203-314 (2011). See also Blumm & Dawson, The Florida Beach Case and the Road to Judicial Takings, 35 Wm. & Mary Envtl. L. & Pol'y Rev. 713 (2011) (characterizing *Stop the Beach* as a radical departure from judicial restraint and the original meaning of the takings clause, and as an obstacle to state courts' ability to adapt state property law to changing circumstances).

4. *The Green Critique.* Strong, exclusive property rights have long been regarded as a keystone of commerce and nonarbitrary government. See Rose, Property as a Keystone Right, 71 Notre Dame L. Rev. 329 (1996). In contrast, the basic environmental critique of *Lucas* is that the Court's concept of property is too individualistic and insufficiently communitarian. In A Sand County Almanac, Aldo Leopold identified the institution of private property as a primary stumbling block to environmental stewardship. This argument and his land ethic form the basis for developing theories of "green property." Green property theory seeks to incorporate the principle of

stewardship into the individualistic liberal theories of property. It stresses that the natural interconnectedness of the arbitrary divisions of land produced by the common law justify more stringent limitations on individual parcel use to protect the integrity of remnant ecosystems.[j]

5. Lucas *Defenses.* Are there any justifications for not requiring compensation for a regulation whose application results in a deprivation of all economically viable use? The *Lucas* majority offers such a justification. Most of the attention has been focused on Justice Scalia's statement that a landowner has no right to compensation if the regulation duplicates a restriction that inheres "in the title itself, in the restrictions that background principles of the State's law of property or nuisance already place on land ownership." In his concurring opinion, Justice Kennedy suggested that the background principles justification was intended by Justice Scalia to be very narrow because it looks backward to a natural-law Blackstonian vision of the common law, which imposes minimal restraints on land development and thus excludes contemporary biodiversity regulation. He suggested, however, that the state could recognize other limitations through legislation.[k] The background principles test may be broader than Justice Scalia envisions because many common law doctrines (such as the public trust doctrine) limit legitimate investment-backed expectations. Ruhl, Making Nuisance Ecological, 58 Case W. Res. L. Rev. (2008), urges recognition of a nuisance cause of action based on the disruption of ecosystem services.

6. *Timing Questions.* Suppose that a property owner asserting a regulatory takings claim purchased the property after the adoption of the regulatory scheme being challenged. Should that fact alone preclude the owner from demonstrating a sufficient interference with investment-backed expectations to support a claim for compensation? In Palazzolo v. Rhode Island, 533 U.S. 606, 627 (2001), Justice Kennedy's majority opinion rejected the contention that those who purchase after a regulation goes into effect are automatically barred from asserting a successful takings claim under *Lucas* based on adverse economic impact, concluding that "the state may not put so potent a Hobbesian stick into the Lockean bundle." Justice O'Connor's concurring opinion, however, posited that the timing of the purchase may be relevant under the multi-factor balancing test enunciated in *Penn Central.* A person who acquires property knowing that it is already regulated may have a difficult time convincing a court that the regulation interferes with his or her legitimate expectations at the time of purchase.

7. *Defining the Regulated Parcel. Lucas* establishes that a regulation that deprives property of all economically viable use is a per se taking. In order to apply that test, one must ascertain what the regulated "property" is. Similarly, courts applying the *Penn Central* balancing test must ascertain, among other things, the degree of the economic impact that the regulation has on the property of the takings claimant. Again, how

j. See Freyfogle, Property and Liberty, 34 Harv. Envtl. L. Rev. 75 (2010); Goldstein, Green Wood in the Bundle of Sticks: Fitting Environmental Ethics and Ecology into Real Property Law, 25 B.C. Envtl. Aff. L. Rev. 347 (1998); Sax, Property Rights and the Economy of Nature: Understanding Lucas v. South Carolina Coastal Council, 45 Stan. L. Rev. 1433, 1447-1448 (1993).

k. For discussion of cases recognizing statutory or regulatory enactments as "background principles" for purposes of the *Lucas* exception, see Glicksman, Making a Nuisance of Takings Law, 3 Wash. U. J.L. & Pol'y 149 (2000); Ruhl, The "Background Principles" of Natural Capital and Ecosystem Services—Did *Lucas* Open Pandora's Box?, 22 J. Land Use & Envtl. L. 525 (2007). Blumm & Ritchie, *Lucas*'s Unlikely Legacy: The Rise of Background Principles as Categorical Takings Defenses, 29 Harv. Envtl. L. Rev. 321 (2005), argue that courts have recognized a wide variety of categorical nuisance defenses to takings claims.

should courts define the "property"? At least as far back as *Penn Central*, the Supreme Court has directed courts to base takings analysis on the impact of regulation on the "parcel as a whole." The Court reaffirmed that approach in Tahoe-Sierra Pres. Council, Inc. v. Tahoe-Sierra Regional Planning Agency, 535 U.S. 302 (2002). The issue was whether a moratorium on development imposed during the process of devising a comprehensive land use plan triggered takings liability under the *Lucas* per se test. The Tahoe Regional Planning Agency (TRPA) imposed the moratorium for 32 months to maintain the status quo pending completion of a study on the impact of development on Lake Tahoe, which Mark Twain described as "not merely transparent, but dazzlingly, brilliantly so," and the adoption of a strategy for environmentally sound growth around the Lake.

The owners of property subject to the moratorium initiated a facial attack on the moratorium. They claimed that the enactment of a temporary regulation that, while in effect, denies a property owner all viable economic use amounts to a per se taking under *Lucas*, requiring the payment of compensation equal to the use value of the property for the period the moratorium is in effect. The Court had stated in *Penn Central* that takings jurisprudence

> does not divide a single parcel into discrete segments and attempt to determine whether rights in a particular segment have been entirely abrogated. In deciding whether a particular governmental action has effected a taking, this Court focuses rather both on the character of the action and on the nature and extent of the interference with rights in the parcel as a whole.

438 U.S. at 130-131. In *Tahoe-Sierra*, the Court applied that principle to reject the *Lucas* claim:

> Certainly, our holding that the permanent "obliteration of the value" of a fee simple estate constitutes a categorical taking does not answer the question whether a regulation prohibiting any economic use of land for a 32-month period has the same legal effect. Petitioners seek to bring this case under the rule announced in *Lucas* by arguing that we can effectively sever a 32-month segment from the remainder of each landowner's fee simple estate, and then ask whether that segment has been taken in its entirety by the moratoria. Of course, defining the property interest taken in terms of the very regulation being challenged is circular. With property so divided, every delay would become a total ban; the moratorium and the normal permit process alike would constitute categorical takings. Petitioners' "conceptual severance" argument is unavailing because it ignores *Penn Central*'s admonition that in regulatory takings cases we must focus on "the parcel as a whole." We have consistently rejected such an approach to the "denominator" question. See [Keystone Bituminous Coal Ass'n v. DeBenedictis, 480 U.S. 470, 495 (1987)]. The starting point for the court's analysis should have been to ask whether there was a total taking of the entire parcel; if not, then *Penn Central* was the proper framework.
>
> An interest in real property is defined by the metes and bounds that describe its geographic dimensions and the term of years that describes the temporal aspect of the owner's interest. Both dimensions must be considered if the interest is to be viewed in its entirety. Hence, a permanent deprivation of the owner's use of the entire area is a taking of "the parcel as a whole," whereas a temporary restriction that merely causes a diminution in value is not. Logically, a fee simple estate cannot be rendered valueless by a temporary prohibition on economic use, because the property will recover value as soon as the prohibition is lifted.

Neither *Lucas* . . . nor any of our other regulatory takings cases compels us to accept petitioners' categorical submission. In fact, these cases make clear that the categorical rule in *Lucas* was carved out for the "extraordinary case" in which a regulation permanently deprives property of all value; the default rule remains that, in the regulatory taking context, we require a more fact specific inquiry. [535 U.S. at 330-332.]

8. *The Relevance of Ends-Means Fit.* In *Lingle*, a unanimous Court eliminated one method of demonstrating a regulatory taking. It repudiated oft-cited dicta that originated in Agins v. City of Tiburon, 447 U.S. 255 (1981), and held that a regulation that does not substantially advance the purported government interest does not amount to a taking. The absence of such a fit between the ends sought and the means chosen to achieve them is irrelevant to the takings inquiry because it provides no information about the magnitude or distribution of the regulatory burden. Pearson, Some Thoughts on the Role of Substantive Due Process in the Federal Constitutional Law of Property Rights Protection, 25 Pace Envtl. L. Rev. 1 (2008), applauds *Lingle* and supports the erosion of the influence of substantive due process on takings law.

9. *Takings and the ESA.* In 1992-1993, California and the federal Bureau of Reclamation (BoR) reduced water deliveries to state permit holders and federal contractees to comply with a NMFS biological opinion. Tulare Lake Basin Water Storage Dist. v. United States, 49 Fed. Cl. 313 (2001), held that a three percent reduction of federal contract entitlements over a two-year period constituted a per se physical taking, rather than a regulatory taking, because the government substituted itself for the contract project beneficiary. *Tulare Lake* rejected the argument that the state's public trust doctrine was a background title limitation.

Another decision reached the opposite result. Irrigators supplied by a federal irrigation project sued the federal government for $1 billion after irrigation deliveries were substantially cut off during a drought in 2001 to conserve listed fish and birds. Klamath Irrigation Dist. v. United States, 67 Fed. Cl. 504 (2005), found no physical taking and held that individual farmers had only contract and not property rights in unappropriated water. In addition, many reclamation contracts, including the ones in that case, absolved the government of liability for "water shortages—hydrological, regulatory, or hybrid—that may occur within the system." The court also suggested that even if the contracts did not specifically provide for delivery interruptions, the ESA could be characterized as a sovereign act that overrode the BoR's duties under the Reclamation Act. See also Seiber v. United States, 364 F.3d 1356 (Fed. Cir. 2004) (denial of incidental take permit was not a temporary Fifth Amendment taking). But in Casitas Mun. Water Dist. v. United States, 543 F.3d 1276 (Fed. Cir. 2008), *reh'g and reh'g en banc denied*, 556 F.3d 1329 (Fed. Cir. 2009), the court found a physical taking arising from the physical diversion of water away from the District's reservoir into a fish ladder to facilitate fish migration.

A NOTE ON STATE AND FOREIGN TAKINGS PROTECTIONS

Some state statutes protect regulated property owners to a greater extent than federal constitutional requirements. In 2004, for example, Oregon voters approved Ballot Measure 37, codified at Or. Rev. Stat. Ann. §197.352, which required the state and local governments to either provide just compensation to landowners for reductions in the fair market value of private property whose use is restricted by "land use regulations" or modify, remove, or not apply those regulations. It defined "land use regulations" broadly to include any statute regulating the use of land or any interest in land; local government comprehensive plans; zoning, land division, and transportation ordinances; and statutes and administrative rules regulating farming and forest practices. Property owners whose neighbors were exempted from land use regulation as a result of the adoption of Ballot Measure 37 filed a declaratory judgment action, alleging that the statute improperly intruded on the power of the legislature, violated the separation of powers principles of the state constitution, and violated the Due Process Clause of the 14th Amendment to the U.S. Constitution. The Oregon Supreme Court upheld the statute. MacPherson v. Department of Admin. Serv., 130 P.3d 308 (Or. 2006). It reasoned that Oregon's legislative bodies did not divest themselves of the right to enact future land use regulations, so that the measure did not impair the legislature's plenary power or the people's exercise of their initiative power. The court also ruled that the measure did not violate either procedural or substantive due process guaranteed by the U.S. Constitution:

> The people, in exercising their initiative power, were free to enact Measure 37 in furtherance of policy objectives such as compensating landowners for a diminution in property value resulting from certain land use regulations or otherwise relieving landowners from some of the financial burden of certain land use regulations. Neither policy is irrational; no one seriously can assert that Measure 37 is not reasonably related to those policy objectives. [Id. at 322.]

What are the likely effects of statutes such as Measure 37 on land use and environmental regulation? According to one critic, "[i]n the face of Measure 37, there is a tangible threat of a regulation rollback on a property-by-property basis, leading to an incoherent patchwork of land use regulations and reluctance by state, regional, or local governments to undertake most new land use regulations because of the Measure." Sullivan, Year Zero: The Aftermath of Measure 37, 38 Urb. Law. 237, 272 (2006).

In 2007, Oregon voters approved Measure 49 (HB 3540), which narrowed the scope of the compensation requirements established by Measure 37. The amended legislation limits Measure 37 to regulations restricting residential development or agricultural or forestry practices. See Hirokawa, Property Pieces in Compensation Statutes: Law's Eulogy for Oregon's Measure 37, 38 Envtl. L. 1111 (2008) (arguing that Measure 37 created anomalies in the meaning of property throughout the legal system). Bowers v. Whitman, 671 F.3d 905 (9th Cir. 2012), held that Measure 49 did not amount to a taking or a violation of substantive due process by eliminating the ability of property owners to seek a "waiver" under Measure 39 allowing them to continue to use their land for uses permitted at the time of acquisition but subsequently precluded by regulation.

Echeverria & Hansen-Young, The Track Record on Takings Legislation: Lessons from Democracy's Laboratories (Georgetown Envtl. Law & Pol'y Inst. 2008), analyze Oregon's takings legislation (and Florida property rights legislation that creates a judicially enforceable right to compensation stemming from regulatory restrictions on land use). The authors claim that the two states' measures undermine community protection, primarily benefit special interests (such as timber companies, real estate developers, and corporate landowners), generate land use conflicts, confer windfalls on landowners by absolving them of responsibilities applicable to the rest of the community, and undermine local democracy.

Other countries do not always provide the same degree of protection for landowners affected by regulation as the United States does. See, e.g., Christy, A Tale of Three Takings: Taking Analysis in Land Use Regulation in the United States, Australia, and Canada, 13 Brook. J. Int'l L. 343 (2007).

VI

PROTECTING THE AIR RESOURCE

Natural defenses protect our lungs from germs and large particles dust and pollen. Air pollution harms lung tissue directly and bypasses or weakens those important defenses. Air pollution can make your eyes water, irritate your nose, mouth, and throat, and make you cough and wheeze. But most important, it can worsen lung diseases like asthma, bronchitis, and emphysema. It can even kill.

American Lung Association, Impacts on Your Health, http://www.lungusa.org/ healthy-air/outdoor/protecting-your-health/impacts-on-your-health.

The problem of air pollution prompted Congress, after 15 years of study, to enact a complex, expansive, and pervasive federal regulatory statute, the Clean Air Act of 1970 (CAA). The Act, the first of the many pollution statutes enacted during the environmental decade, regulates all new vehicles and hundreds of thousands of large and small stationary sources throughout the nation. It is appropriate for several reasons to select the CAA as the first major pollution control legislation to be analyzed in this casebook. First, the Act was the model for other federal environmental programs. Second, it relies on a variety of regulatory techniques (including ambient, performance, and design standards), allowing us to assess the strengths and weaknesses of the regulatory approaches used throughout environmental law.

Third, the CAA was the first federal pollution control statute to incorporate economic incentive–based approaches, such as marketable permits, emissions fees, and other provisions that allow or require trading among pollution sources, as an important component of the arsenal Congress chose to achieve its environmental protection goals. In his classic book Pollution, Property and Prices (1968), the Canadian economist John Dales argued that the most efficient way to control pollution is to charge for the right to emit amounts up to a government-established ceiling and to create markets in pollution rights. Supporters of this approach assert that it minimizes the costs involved in controlling pollution. The tradable SO_2 permit program adopted by Congress in the 1990 CAA amendments, which many believe has efficiently mitigated the adverse effects of acid rain, has led to other experiments in market environmentalism, under the CAA and elsewhere. That program's successes were critical to proposals to address climate change via cap-and-trade legislation, as covered in Chapter 12.

Fourth, the CAA provides an opportunity to examine the evolution of an environmental regulatory program as it responds to unanticipated implementation obstacles and the discovery of previously unknown environmental risks. Despite the considerable improvement in air quality that has been achieved in response to the Act's mandates, the CAA has not eliminated air pollution in urban centers, particularly in the most intractable areas, such as the Los Angeles basin. The persistence of these pockets of air pollution has raised difficult policy questions about the most efficient and equitable means of achieving the CAA's health-related goals by bringing the nation into compliance with the statute's fundamental feature, the national ambient air quality standards. In addition, the nation has faced air quality issues that were unforeseen at the time of the Act's adoption in 1970 and that were thus unaddressed in the original version of the statute. These include acid rain, stratospheric ozone depletion, and climate change (the last of which we address in Chapter 12).

Fifth, the CAA provides an example of a regulatory program whose implementation requires deciding how to provide equitable treatment of the different kinds of sources that contribute to an environmental problem. The Act has prompted significant emissions reductions from stationary sources such as industrial facilities. It has been less successful at combating pollution from automobiles. Should the focus of future emission reduction efforts shift from stationary to mobile sources? The pursuit of rigorous efforts to reduce pollution from cars and trucks has the potential to affect individual lifestyle choices by constraining, for example, the use of automobiles for commuting. Is the American public willing to adjust to such changes? See, e.g., Kentucky Res. Council, Inc. v. EPA, 304 F. Supp. 2d 920, 923 (W.D. Ky. 2004) (stating that "many believe that [an automobile vehicle emission testing program] was 'intrusive and wasteful'"). As the materials in this chapter indicate, the fate of several provisions of the 1990 CAA amendments designed to crack down on mobile-source emissions casts serious doubt on more rigorous mobile-source regulation that would impinge on individual choice.

Sixth, the CAA raises difficult questions of environmental federalism involving the choice of the level of government to which the responsibility for formulating pollution control policies should be allocated. Many of these questions are addressed in Chapter 2, which covers the topic of federalism and environmental law in a variety of contexts. Federalism questions arising under the CAA are noted throughout this chapter.

Finally, air pollution creates transboundary disputes (both interstate and international) that pose difficult technical and political problems. For example, even if emissions reduction in a polluted area requires aggressive steps, ambient concentrations of pollution in the area may remain higher than the levels mandated by the national ambient air quality standards because of emissions in upwind states and cities. Is it fair to require costly further reductions in upwind sources when the benefits of those reductions will not be enjoyed by those who bear the costs? Is it fair to require those living in the affected areas to bear the brunt of eliminating pollution attributable to activities from which they do not benefit? Policymakers responsible for implementing the CAA continue to grapple with these and similar dilemmas.

A. AIR POLLUTION: TYPES, SOURCES, IMPACTS, AND CONTROL TECHNIQUES

1. Pollutants and Their Sources

Like much of environmental law, air pollution control law relies on a factual foundation that is more scientifically sophisticated than those underpinning many other legal regimes. Chemistry, engineering, medicine, and meteorology interact with law in the production of modern air quality control policies. Scientific understanding of air pollution is constantly in flux, which challenges air quality management schemes to remain ever ready for change.

Air pollution consists of particles and gases in the air that, for various reasons, are viewed as undesirable. Whether a substance is a pollutant necessarily involves a social judgment; an air pollutant may be a valuable resource that is simply out of place in the air. Urban air pollutants include carbon monoxide, oxides of sulfur and nitrogen, a great variety of hydrocarbon compounds, and trace amounts of industrial materials such as lead, mercury, asbestos, and chlorine.

Not all pollution is man-made. For example, hydrocarbons and hydrogen sulfide (later becoming sulfur oxides) form when organic materials decompose; forest fires and volcanoes release tons of carbon monoxide, hydrocarbons, and particulate matter into the air; naturally occurring "background" radiation (including radon gas) augments radiation caused by human activities; and the introduction of lead into the environment by humans adds to levels occurring naturally. Although widely derided, President Reagan's assertion that trees cause pollution has some validity, 19 Env't Rep. (BNA) 1086 (1988). The story is not nearly that simple, however. Plants emit gaseous volatile organic compounds (VOCs) called terpenes. Although these substances were not a problem a century ago, today they react with oxides of nitrogen from car exhaust to generate ground-level ozone.[a] Trees, of course, are also beneficial to the environment, both directly and indirectly. They produce oxygen; help move carbon dioxide from the air to the soil, where it can be dissolved in water; and filter airborne particulates that settle on their leaves and are washed to the ground by rain. See, e.g., Nowak et al., Modeled $PM_{2.5}$ Removal by Trees in Ten U.S. Cities and Associated Health Effects, 178 Envtl. Pollution 395 (2013) (documenting health benefits resulting from removal of fine particulate pollution from the air by trees in urban areas). They also lower the temperature on hot days, which can reduce the demand for electricity-dependent air conditioning, whose generation causes air pollution.

Major Conventional Pollutants. Several air pollutants appear in such quantities or cause such serious harm that they have received major regulatory attention over the past several decades. Table 6-1 summarizes some of the adverse health effects of air pollutants currently regulated as so-called criteria pollutants under the CAA. The odorless and colorless gas carbon monoxide (CO) forms when fossil fuels do not burn completely. Vehicles are its major source, and because of its weight, CO tends to collect in city street "canyons." CO bonds strongly with hemoglobin in the blood, and as a result impairs mental functions and fetal development, and aggravates cardiovascular diseases. Effective control of motor vehicle emissions requires proper engine tuning and catalytic or thermal exhaust gas conversion.

Nitrogen oxides form when air is heated, principally in motor vehicle engines and high-temperature power plant furnaces. Nitrogen dioxide (NO_2) is a pungent, brownish-red gas that aggravates respiratory and cardiovascular diseases, causes kidney

---

a. See, e.g., Di Carlo et al., Missing OH Reactivity in a Forest: Evidence for Unknown Reactive Biogenic VOCs, 304 Science 722 (2004); Hickman et al., Kudzu (*Pueraria montana*) Invasion Doubles Emissions of Nitric Oxide and Increases Ozone Pollution, 107 PNAS 10115 (June 1, 2010) (finding that the spread of kudzu in the southeastern United States has the potential to raise ozone levels in the region by increasing nitric oxide emissions from soils). See also Virginia v. EPA, 108 F.3d 1397, 1400 n.1 (D.C. Cir. 1997) (citing the "heightened appreciation of the importance of reactive [VOCs] emitted by vegetation").

inflammation, impairs visibility, and retards plant growth. Long-term exposure to high levels of NO_2 (along with fine particulate matter) has been correlated to hospitalization for pneumonia. Neupane et al., Long-Term Exposure to Ambient Air Pollution and Risk of Hospitalization with Community-Acquired Pneumonia in Older Adults, 181 Am. J. Respiratory & Critical Care Med. 47 (2010); Raaschou-Nielsen, Lung Cancer Incidence and Long-Term Exposure to Air Pollution from Traffic, 119 Envtl. Health Perspectives 860 (2011) (finding association between lung cancer risk and exposure to NO_x and other air pollutants in those residing near traffic routes). Abatement techniques, which are less effective than those for other pollutants, include catalytic control of motor vehicle emissions and "scrubbing" of stack gases with caustic substances or urea.

TABLE 6-1
Health Effects of the Regulated Air Pollutants

Criteria Pollutants	Health Concerns
Ozone	Respiratory tract problems such as difficulty breathing and reduced lung function. Asthma, eye irritation, nasal congestion, reduced resistance to infection, and possible premature aging of lung tissue.
Particulate matter	Eye and throat irritation, bronchitis, lung damage, and impaired visibility.
Carbon monoxide	Ability of blood to carry oxygen impaired. Cardiovascular, nervous, and pulmonary systems affected.
Sulfur dioxide	Respiratory tract problems and permanent harm to lung tissue.
Lead	Retardation and brain damage, especially in children.
Nitrogen dioxide	Respiratory illnesses and lung damage.

Source: EPA, Environmental Progress and Challenges, EPA's Update (Aug. 1988), at 13.

Like CO, gaseous and particulate hydrocarbon compounds (HCs) form when fuels or other carbon-bearing substances are burned. Vehicle engines and fuel evaporation are the major sources of these volatile organic compounds (VOCs), but they can also escape during the manufacture or handling of asphalt, rubber, and petroleum products. (VOCs and HCs are largely overlapping categories.) Rotting organic materials, home fireplaces, and forest fires also generate HCs. VOCs contribute to the health problems and visibility impairment associated with smog because they are major precursors in the formation of photochemical oxidants through atmospheric reactions. HC control techniques are analogous to those for CO emissions.

Photochemical oxidants are formed when precursor pollutants such as HCs and NO_x react with each other and with atmospheric gases in the presence of sunlight. In combination, they produce smog, whose principal oxidant component is ozone (O_3).[b] Photochemical oxidants aggravate respiratory and cardiovascular illnesses. Exposure to ozone for six to seven hours at relatively low concentrations can significantly reduce lung function and induce respiratory inflammation in healthy individuals during periods of moderate exercise. EPA, National Air Quality and Emissions

b. "Although ozone in the lower atmosphere harms ambient (breathable) air quality, ozone in the stratosphere prevents cancers caused by overexposure to the sun's ultraviolet radiation. Ironically, destruction of stratospheric ozone tends to increase ambient ozone levels by permitting more ultraviolet radiation to reach the surface of the Earth." Virginia v. United States, 74 F.3d 517, 519 n.1 (4th Cir. 1996).

Trend Report, 1993 Executive Summary. The National Research Council concluded in a 2008 study that short-term exposure to low levels of ambient ozone can exacerbate lung conditions and contribute to heart disease, resulting in increased illnesses, hospitalization, and even death.[c] An earlier study found that exposure to short-term spikes in ground-level ozone concentrations may be linked to thousands of deaths a year in the United States. Bell et al., Ozone and Short-Term Mortality in 95 US Urban Communities, 1987-2000, 292 JAMA 2372 (2004).[d] Ozone also contributes to visibility impairment; damages rubber, textiles, and paints; and causes plants to drop their leaves and fruit prematurely. Control of ozone pollution requires reductions in NO_x, HC, and possibly sulfur dioxide emissions.

Lead, a ubiquitous, naturally occurring element, appears in the air as an oxide aerosol or dust. The principal source of ambient lead used to be emissions from motor vehicles that burned leaded gasoline. Today, lead smelting and processing, the manufacture of lead products, the combustion of coal and refuse, and the use of pesticides containing lead continue to contribute to ambient lead pollution. Lead accumulates in body organs and impairs bone growth and the development and functioning of the nervous, circulatory, and renal systems. Lead exposure also can accelerate the aging process. It also has been linked to hyperactivity in children. Exposure has been reduced by eliminating lead additives from gasoline and paint and lead soldering from tin cans and by instituting dietary controls.

A colorless gas with a pungent odor, sulfur dioxide (SO_2) forms when coal and oil are burned in power plants or space heaters, or when sulfur-bearing metal ores such as lead and copper are smelted (see Figure 6-1). Electric utilities produce a major portion of the SO_2 emitted in the United States. SO_2 aggravates respiratory diseases and irritates the eyes. Asthmatics, individuals with cardiovascular disease or chronic lung disease (such as bronchitis or emphysema), children,[e] and the elderly are

c. Committee on Estimating Mortality Risk Reduction Benefits from Decreasing Tropospheric Ozone Exposure, National Research Council, Estimating Mortality Risk Reduction and Economic Benefits from Controlling Ozone Air Pollution (2008). According to one study, if anthropogenic ozone precursor emissions were reduced by a fifth worldwide, more than 20,000 cardiopulmonary mortalities could be avoided. Anenberg, Intercontinental Impacts of Ozone Pollution on Human Mortality, 43 Envtl. Sci. & Tech. 6482 (2009). Researchers have found links between exposure to ozone pollution and other criteria pollutants and increased incidence of appendicitis. See Kaplan et al., Effect of Ambient Air Pollution on the Incidence of Appendicitis, 9 Can. Med. Ass'n J. 181 (Oct. 27, 2009). See also Devlin et al., Exposure to Ozone Causes Cardiovascular Effects in Healthy Young Adults, 185 Am. J. of Respiratory and Critical Care Med. A3199 (2012). Mustafić, Main Air Pollutants and Myocardial Infarction, 307 J. Am. Med. Ass'n 713 (Feb. 15, 2012), similarly found significant association between exposure to CO, NOx, SO_2, and $PM_{2.5}$ and near-term risk of myocardial infarction.

d. For every 10 parts per billion increase in daily ozone levels, the death rate over the next three days goes up about 0.85-0.87 percent. Older people and people living in cities without air conditioning seem to be at particular risk. See, e.g., Bell et al., A Meta-Analysis of Time-Series Studies of Ozone and Mortality with Comparison to the National Morbidity, Mortality, and Air Pollution Study, 16 Epidemiology 436 (2005). One study concluded that exposure of healthy young adults to 0.06 ppm ozone (a lower concentration than the CAA's national ambient air quality standard allows) for 6.6 hours causes significant pulmonary function and airway inflammation. Kim et al., Lung Function and Inflammatory Responses in Healthy Young Adults Exposed to 0.06 ppm Ozone for 6.6 Hours, 183 Am. J Respiratory & Critical Care Med. 1215 (May 1, 2011).

e. Researchers have linked increased concentrations of particulate matter, carbon dioxide, and nitrogen dioxide to a greater incidence of death among infants from respiratory causes and sudden infant death syndrome. Ritz et al., Air Pollution and Infant Death in Southern California, 1989-2000, 118 Pediatrics 493 (August 2006). Research also links exposure of pregnant women to air pollution and increased risk of autism in their children. Volk et al., Autism Spectrum Disorder:

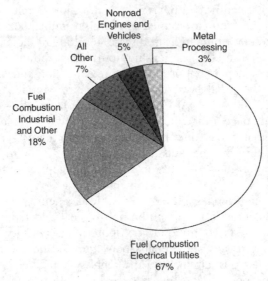

FIGURE 6-1

SO$_2$: What Is It? Where Does It Come from?

Source: www.epa.gov/air/urbaniar/so2what1./html (removed).

particularly susceptible. SO$_2$ emissions have been successfully reduced by using low-sulfur fuels, removing sulfur before fuel use, scrubbing stack gases with lime, and using catalytic technology to convert SO$_2$ to sulfuric acid.

The public has a fairly good understanding of the polluting nature of total suspended particulates (TSPs), the collection of solid or liquid particles such as dust, pollen, soot, metals, and chemical compounds dispersed in the atmosphere. Cinders and soot from urban waste incinerators are common sources, but any burning or abrasion of a solid or splashing of a liquid typically contributes to TSPs. Particle size and weight vary dramatically, from visible soot to air particles detectable only under an electron microscope. Power plant particulates are small, spherical, glassy particles usually smaller than 50 microns in diameter, the same as a typical human hair (see Figure 6-2). The composition as well as the size of the particle may be determinative of the degree of the public health risk it poses when inhaled.

Particulates exacerbate asthma and other respiratory or cardiovascular symptoms, sully and damage building materials, impair visibility, contribute to cloud formation, and interfere with plant growth.[f] Researchers believe that settleable particles (50 microns and larger) present few health risks compared with aerosols (smaller than

---

Interaction of Air Pollution with the MET Receptor Tyrosine Kinase Gene, 25 Epidemiology 44 (Jan. 2014). EPA has issued annual reports on the effect of its regulatory actions on reducing risks to children's health. See, e.g., America's Children and the Environment (3d ed. Jan. 25, 2013), http://www.epa.gov/ace/

f. Exposure to particulate matter also may cause heritable mutations in DNA. See Somers et al., Reductions in Particulate Air Pollution Lowers the Risk of Heritable Mutations in Mice, 304 Science 1008 (2004). Studies have also linked exposure to PM$_{2.5}$ to increased diabetes risk. Pearson et al., Association Between Fine Particulate Matter and Diabetes Prevalence in the U.S., 33 Diabetes Care 2196 (2010). See also Kravchenko et al., Long-term Dynamics of Death Rates of Emphysema, Asthma, and Pneumonia and Improving Air Quality, 9 Int'l J. of COPD 613 (2014).

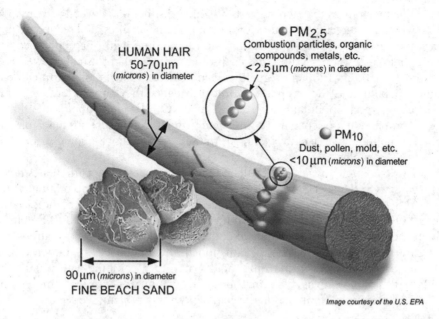

PM2.5
Combustion particles, organic
compounds, metals, etc.
< 2.5 μm (*microns*) in diameter

HUMAN HAIR
50-70 μm
(*microns*) in diameter

PM10
Dust, pollen, mold, etc.
<10 μm (*microns*) in diameter

90 μm (*microns*) in diameter
FINE BEACH SAND

Image courtesy of the U.S. EPA

FIGURE 6-2
How Big is Particle Pollution?

Source: http://www.epa.gov/pm/basic.html.

50 microns) and fine particulates (smaller than 3 microns in diameter). Fine particulates, which can penetrate deeply into the lungs, may be carcinogenic, while many of the larger particulates now regulated are caught in the nose and pulmonary mucous membranes and eventually excreted. Studies have found that increased concentrations of fine particulates are associated with an increased risk of death from cardiopulmonary and respiratory causes.[g] TSPs are reduced by up to 99.75 percent by cleaning stack gases with electrostatic precipitators, scrubbers, or fabric filters. "Fugitive" emissions can be controlled by spraying construction and demolition sites with water. Some of the highest particulate concentrations in the world are in Asia. In January 2014, monitors measured $PM_{2.5}$ concentrations in Beijing as high as 671 micrograms/m^3. The World Health Organization considers concentrations above 10 micrograms/m^3 to create health risks.

g. See Jerrett et al., Long-Term Exposure and Ozone Mortality, 360 New Eng. J. Med. 1085 (Mar. 12, 2009); Dominici et al., Fine Particulate Air Pollution and Hospital Admission for Cardiovascular and Respiratory Diseases, 295 JAMA 1127 (2006). Exposure to fine particulates is linked to increased lung cancer risk, especially among nonsmokers. See Puett et al., Particulate Matter Air Pollution Exposure, Distance to Road, and Incident Lung Cancer in the Nurses' Health Study Cohort, 122 Envtl. Health Perspectives 926 (Sept. 2014); Raaschou-Nielsen et al., Air Pollution and Lung Cancer Incidence in 17 European Cohorts: Prospective Analyses from the European Study of Cohorts for Air Pollution Effects (ESCAPE), 14 The Lancet Oncology 813 (Aug. 2013). Compare Pope et al., Fine-Particulate Air Pollution and Life Expectancy in the United States, 360 New Eng. J. Med. 376 (Jan. 22, 2009) (concluding that "[a] reduction in exposure to ambient fine-particulate air pollution contributed to significant and measurable improvements in life expectancy in the United States").

The foregoing discussion suggests a natural distinction between primary pollutants, which are directly emitted as a result of human activities, and secondary pollutants, which form when human emissions combine with naturally occurring
atmospheric gases, water vapor, and each other, with sunlight usually powering the
chemical reactions. Although regulators' main concern may be the harm caused by
secondary pollutants such as photochemical oxidants, they have to reduce them by
controlling primary pollutants such as HC and NO_x. (Readers should note that this
use of "primary" and "secondary" is unrelated to the use of those terms in regulation of
"criteria" pollutants subject to "National Ambient Air Quality Standards," as covered
later in this chapter.)

Evidence now suggests that sulfates, very small secondary particulates derived
from gaseous SO_2, may be primarily responsible for the health effects originally attributed to SO_2 and large primary particulates. Similarly, fine nitrate particles formed
from NO_2 may cause many of the health effects once attributed to NO_2. Sulfate and
nitrate aerosols are formed when chemical reactions occur in the atmosphere,
sometimes days after the aerosols' emission from smokestacks or motor vehicles.
The aerosols form sulfuric and nitric acids when they combine with water. These
acids may then show up as acid rain, snow, or dew hundreds of miles from the source
responsible for them. For more on the acid deposition problem, see section I.2 of this
chapter.

Many other air pollutants endanger health or the environment only under
certain conditions and in particular locales. These pollutants include toxic metals
such as arsenic, beryllium, cadmium, and mercury; minerals such as asbestos; gases
such as chlorine; radioactive substances; and scores of organic compounds. EPA has
estimated that, based on 2005 data, all 285 million people in the U.S. have an
increased cancer risk of greater than 10 in one million as a result of exposure to air
toxics, 13.8 million people have an increased cancer risk of greater than 100 in a
million, and the average national cancer risk is 50 in a million. As a result, about 1 in
every 20,000 people living in the U.S. has an increased likelihood of contracting
cancer as a result of breathing air toxics from outdoor sources if they are exposed to
2005 emission levels over the course of their lifetime. EPA, The 2005 National-Scale
Air Toxics Assessment (2011). Adelman, The Collective Origins of Toxic Air Pollution: Implications for Greenhouse Gas Trading and Toxic Hotspots, 88 Ind. L.J. 273
(2013), interprets EPA data as showing that mobile sources (such as cars and trucks)
and small point sources (such as dry cleaners, gas stations, and landfills) dominate
toxic emissions and health risks in most jurisdictions.

2.   Documenting the Health Effects of Air Pollution

Air pollution chiefly threatens human health. Marshaling the medical proof that
emissions harm human health often defies the best efforts of scientists:

> [W]e know that the most massive health problem with air pollution is not associated with
> identifiable episodes but in the gradual erosion of health by frequent and long-term
> exposures. Hypotheses linking this type of exposure with specific illness require
> murky assumptions and estimates that are easily attacked piecemeal by dissenters. . . .
>   Most victims of air pollution will not die during an air episode. They will contract a
> respiratory disease or another symptom associated with air pollution, gradually weaken,

and then typically die from pneumonia, a heart attack, or failure of some other vital organ. Or they will bear a child with a birth defect that future medical research will link to an air pollutant. Or perhaps they will develop a disease, such as cancer, caused by a dimly understood set of factors with air pollution as only one possible component. [G. Sewell, Environmental Quality Management 168-170 (1975).]

Despite these uncertainties, many studies describe the benefits of controlling air pollution. One study, for example, found that a reduction of one microgram of soot per cubic meter of air is associated with a 3 percent decline in death rates from cardio-vascular disease, respiratory illness, and lung cancer. Each such decrease may extend the lives of 75,000 Americans per year. Laden et al., Reduction in Fine Particulate Air Pollution and Mortality, 173 Am. J. Respiratory & Critical Care Med. 667 (2006). Figure 6-3 presents a continuum of risks associated with various forms of air pollution.

3. The Evolving Mix of Emissions Sources

The contributions of various emissions sources to air pollution have shifted since the adoption of the CAA in 1970. In that year, transportation sources accounted for 46.7 percent of VOC emissions in the United States, while industrial sources con-tributed 32.5 percent of the total. By 2002, a higher percentage of VOCs was associ-ated with utilization of solvents than with highway vehicles. Similarly, the contribution by transportation sources to lead pollution has fallen dramatically due to the removal of lead from gasoline, but primary metal smelters and electric utilities continue to emit large quantities of lead.[h] Emissions of sulfur oxides due to fuel combustion at electric utilities fell between 1970 and 2008 (from 15.8 million tons to 7.5 million tons), and emissions of nitrogen oxides from those sources fell during the same period from 4.4 million to 3 million tons a year. 1996 Statistical Abstract of the United States, at 234; 2012 Statistical Abstract of the United States, Table 375.

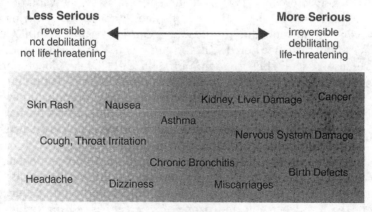

FIGURE 6-3
Which Risks Are of Greatest Concern?

Source: www.epa.gov/oar/oaqps/air_risc/3_90_022.html.

h. See Commission for Environmental Cooperation, Taking Stock (2005), available at http://www.cec.org/takingstock/index.cfm?varlan=english.

The relative contributions of mobile sources must be examined against the backdrop of growth in the number of motor vehicles in use and vehicle miles traveled. Between 1970 and 2010, the number of vehicles (automobiles, buses, and trucks) registered increased significantly, as did the numbers of vehicle miles traveled each year (showing a 91 percent increase between 1980 and 2008), Americans who commuted to work by automobile, and gallons of fuel consumed in the United States by motor vehicles. Compare Figure 6-4. These figures are sensitive to the price of gasoline and to economic conditions, however. For example, Americans reduced their driving by more than 112 billion miles over a 13-month period during 2007 and 2008 due to factors that included high unemployment, housing price declines, and a desire to reduce carbon footprints. Americans Cut Driving by More than 112B Miles, Greenwire, Jan. 23, 2009. According to one report, the absolute number of vehicles in the U.S. reached a maximum in 2008, but the rate of vehicle ownership per person, household, and licensed drivers peaked two years earlier. The number of vehicle miles traveled on a per person, household, and licensed driver basis peaked in 2004. M. Sivak, Has Motorization in the U.S. Peaked? (Univ. of Michigan Transportation Inst. UMTRI-20-13-17) (June 2013). Recent declines resulted in part from automakers' responses to tightened fuel efficiency standards adopted by the Obama administration. Despite per vehicle emissions reductions, mobile sources remain the largest cause of air pollution-related deaths in the U.S. See Caiazzo, Air Pollution and Early Deaths in the U.S., Part I: Quantifying the Impact of Major Sectors in 2005, 79 Atmospheric Env't 198 (Nov. 2013) (finding that the largest contributors for air pollutant-related mortalities is road transportation, causing about 58,000 early deaths per year from exposure to $PM_{2.5}$ and ozone).

Among the tasks facing air pollution control policymakers is to determine how to reduce emissions in persistent problem areas from mobile and stationary sources alike. Bedsworth et al., Driving Change: Reducing Vehicle Miles Traveled in California (2011), concluded that the best strategy for reducing vehicle miles traveled involves a combination of greater commercial development around transit stations, investments in alternatives to solo driving (such as mass transit, biking, walking, and carpooling), and increases in road use fees. The installation of E-ZPass highway toll programs has reduced premature birth rates and low birth rates among mothers living near toll plazas by reducing emissions during auto idling. Currie & Walker, Traffic Congestion and Infant Health: Evidence from E-ZPass, 3 Am. Econ. J: Applied Economics (1): 65 (2011). See also Federal Highway Administration, 2011 Urban Congestion Trends: Improving Travel Reliability with Operations, FHWA-HOP-12-09 (2012).

4.   The State of Air Quality and Its Improvement

Pollution levels for the six major conventional air pollutants have declined in recent years. EPA reported that ambient levels of the criteria pollutants declined by the following percentages between 1980 and 2012: lead, 91 percent; CO, 83 percent; SO_2, 78 percent; NO_2, 60 percent; and ozone, 25 percent based on eight-hour data. Between 1990 and 2012, concentrations of PM_{10} (measured on a 24-hour basis) fell by 39 percent. Emissions of all of the criteria pollutants fell between 1980 and 2008, and between 2000 and 2012, $PM_{2.5}$ concentrations fell by 33 percent.[i] Despite

i. The percentage decreases for the criteria pollutants and their precursors were as follows: CO, 56; NOx, 40; PM_{10}, 68; SO_2, 56; VOCs, 47; and lead, 99. EPA, Air Quality Trends, http://www.epa.gov/airtrends/aqtrends.html.

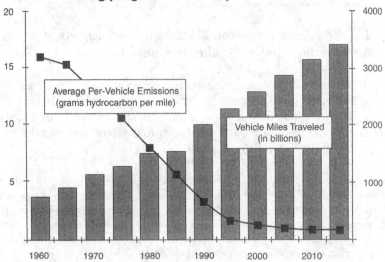

Cars are getting cleaner, but people are driving more, offsetting progress in ozone pollution control

Average Per-Vehicle Emissions (grams hydrocarbon per mile)

Vehicle Miles Traveled (in billions)

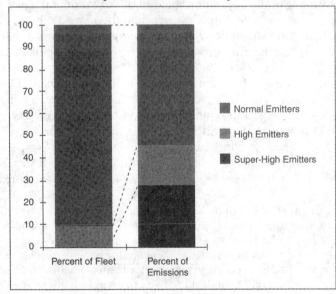

A large amount of hydrocarbon pollution comes from relatively few cars with "dirty" exhaust

Normal Emitters

High Emitters

Super-High Emitters

Percent of Fleet

Percent of Emissions

FIGURE 6-4

Source: www.epa.gov/oms/04-ozone.htm (removed).

these improvements, EPA reported that in 2008, more than 142 million Americans continued to live in counties with concentrations of the criteria pollutants above levels required by EPA's national ambient air quality standards. More than 133 million lived in areas not in compliance with the ozone standard.[j] EPA, Air Quality Trends, http://www.epa.gov/airtrends/aqtrends.html.

5.   The Economic Impact and Distributional Effects of Air Pollution and Air Pollution Control

The relationship between the economic costs and benefits of air pollution control is a matter of sharp controversy. L. Lave & E. Seskin, Air Pollution and Human Health (1977), found that the initial benefits of the CAA ($23 billion) exceeded its costs ($15 billion). EPA concluded in a report assessing the impact of the first 20 years of the CAA that

> [w]hen the human health, human welfare, and environmental effects which could be expressed in dollar terms were added up for the entire 20-year period, the total benefits of Clean Air Act programs were estimated to range from about $6 trillion to about $50 trillion, with a mean estimate of about $22 trillion. . . . By comparison, the actual costs of achieving the pollution reductions observed over the 20 year period were $523 billion, a small fraction of the estimated monetary benefits.[k]

The agency's figures have not gone unchallenged. Crandall et al., Clearing the Air: EPA's Self-Assessment of Clean-Air Policy, 1996 Regulation #4, at 35, claim (1) that a draft version of the EPA study failed to show that the marginal benefits of most clean-air policies are equal to or greater than the marginal costs, (2) that the true health benefits attributable to reduced pollution levels are much less than EPA claims, and (3) that the true costs of control are much higher than EPA's figures indicate.

In a subsequent study, EPA's central estimate of the benefits of the CAA between 1990 and 2020 exceeded costs by a factor of more than 30 to one, the high benefits estimate exceeded costs by 90 times, and even the low benefits estimate exceeded costs by about three to one. EPA, Benefits and Costs of the Clean Air Act, Second Prospective Study—1990 to 2020, http://www.epa.gov/air/sect812/prospective2.html. EPA pegged the net economic benefits of regulation under the 1990 amendments at $1,886 billion. EPA characterized its findings as "robust" for several reasons.

> First, the benefits of improved morbidity and improved visibility alone are more than twice the estimated cost of compliance with 1990 Clean Air Act Amendment requirements; so even if one chose to ignore the substantial reductions in mortality risk achieved by these programs or assigned them a value of zero, benefits would still be projected to exceed costs. Second, many beneficial outcomes involving human health or environmental improvement could not be expressed in terms of economic values

j. The American Lung Association (ALA) reported that 47 percent of Americans lived in areas with unhealthy air quality between 2010 and 2012. ALA, State of the Air 2014. In early 2014, six of the eight U.S. cities with the worst ozone pollution were in California (with Los Angeles leading the list). The others were Houston and the D.C.-Baltimore area. California cities also dominated the list of cities with the worst particulate pollution. ALA, Most Polluted Cities, http://www.stateoftheair .org/2014/city-rankings/most-polluted-cities.html.

k. EPA, Retrospective Study Design and Summary of Results, http://www.epa.gov/oar/ sect812/design.html.

> because the scientific and economic studies to support such valuations remain inadequate or unavailable. If methods were available to quantify these omitted effects, the estimate of net benefits would further increase. Some components of cost are also subject to uncertainty or omission, but cost uncertainties are comparatively minor in number and significance relative to uncertainties on the benefit side of the ledger. Finally, the in-depth assessment of key uncertainties described in the full report indicates that the chances are extremely small that uncertainties in the analysis could lead to a scenario in which costs exceed benefits. [EPA, Office of Air and Radiation, The Benefits and Costs of the Clean Air Act from 1990 to 2020, Summary Report 19-20 (March 2011).]

See also OMB, 2014 Draft Report to Congress on the Benefits and Costs of Federal Regulations and Unfunded Mandates on State, Local, and Tribal Entities 12-13 (2014) (finding that the benefits of EPA's CAA regulations between 2003 and 2013 ranged between $162 and $839 billion, while the costs ranged from $37.5 to 45.1 billion; of EPA's rules during this period, its $PM_{2.5}$ NAAQS provided the highest benefits, with a range of $19 to $167 billion per year). EPA's 2006 national ambient air quality standards for PM yielded estimated benefits ranging from $4 billion to $40 billion per year and estimated costs of $3 billion per year.

The burdens and benefits of air quality control policies are almost certainly unevenly distributed among classes of emitters and receptors. Some studies indicate that the poor benefit more than the rich from these policies. See, e.g., Gianessi et al., The Distributional Effects of Uniform Air Pollution Policy, 93 Q.J. Econ. 281 (1979). Other researchers have found that residents of low- and middle-income areas in the South Coast Air Basin of California were exposed to higher levels of ozone and particulate pollution than residents of wealthier districts. Brajer & Hall, Recent Evidence on the Distribution of Air Pollution Effects, 10 Contemp. Pol. Issues 2, at 63 (April 1992). Another study concluded that racial minority groups tend to live in counties with higher emissions levels than those to which whites are exposed. Perlin et al., Distribution of Industrial Air Emissions by Income and Race in the United States: An Approach Using the Toxic Release Inventory, 29 Envtl. Sci. & Tech. 1, at 69 (January 1995). See also Kahn, The Beneficiaries of Clean Air Act Regulation, 24 Reg. Mag. 1 (2001) (concluding that "it appears that regulation under the Clean Air Act has helped, and not economically harmed, the 'have nots'").

B.   THE HISTORY OF AIR POLLUTION: FROM COMMON LAW NUISANCE TO THE CLEAN AIR ACT

Although air pollution was scarcely acknowledged as a national problem before World War II and did not move to the top of the public agenda until the end of the 1960s, the legal foundations of air pollution control were laid centuries earlier in England. The earliest relief from air pollution was provided through private common law nuisance actions; a public nuisance broadly affecting the community was subject to abatement following a jury trial. The common law crime of public nuisance is the earliest example of quasi-statutory intervention by local government to protect environmental quality.

1. Beginnings

The first smoke abatement ordinance appears to have been enacted in 1273 in London. Smoke ordinances enacted in the United States in the late nineteenth century required the manufacture of furnaces that could consume their own smoke, or forbade the burning of high-sulfur coal. The more sophisticated ordinances empowered municipal health officials and the courts to specify performance levels for air pollution controls and, occasionally, to specify the equipment needed to achieve them. They also authorized action even in the absence of proof of actual harm. Indicators such as dense smoke or the burning of soft coal became legal surrogates for actual harm. As a result, the legislature could adopt controls as a precaution without having to wait for scientific evidence to accumulate. Modern pollution control laws make extensive use of devices that foreclose inquiry into the extent and nature of the injury on which regulatory programs are predicated. Today, a regulation prohibiting particulate emissions "visible by an observer . . . beyond the property line of the source" might be too vague to be enforceable. See McEvoy v. IEI Barge Serv., Inc., 622 F.3d 671 (7th Cir. 2010).

2. Early Legislation

After World War II, air pollution slowly increased, as did congressional frustration with ineffectual state efforts to combat the problem. In 1955, the federal government entered the field for the first time with a modest program of research and technical assistance directed primarily at the causes and effects of air pollution, which had not been established. Air Pollution Control Act, Pub. L. No. 84-159, 69 Stat. 322. In the 1950s, the smog in Los Angeles was linked to automobile emissions. After that, the motor vehicle became the central focus of air pollution legislation. In 1960, Congress enacted a research and technical assistance program for motor vehicles. Motor Vehicle Act of 1960, Pub. L. No. 86-493, 74 Stat. 162.

Congress expanded the federal role throughout the 1960s. In 1963, it required the Department of Health, Education, and Welfare (HEW) (now called the Department of Health and Human Services) to provide the states with scientific information, called "criteria documents," on the effects of various air pollutants. Clean Air Act, Pub. L. No. 88-206, 77 Stat. 392. These studies would eventually provide the technical basis for HEW's establishment of mandatory uniform national ambient air quality standards. The 1963 legislation also empowered the secretary of HEW to initiate enforcement proceedings if pollution "endangered the health or welfare of persons." Responsibility was so diffused, however, that no effective enforcement actions were ever mounted under the 1963 Act. The Motor Vehicle Air Pollution Control Act, Pub. L. No. 89-272, 79 Stat. 992 (1965), authorized HEW to establish emissions standards for new motor vehicles and engines based on "technological feasibility and economic costs." The Air Quality Act, Pub. L. No. 90-148, 81 Stat. 485 (1967), authorized HEW to designate geographic air quality control regions. The states were to adopt ambient air quality standards for each major pollutant, subject to HEW approval, which would define the maximum levels of pollution necessary to maintain health and welfare in each region. Each state also had to adopt an implementation plan, again subject to HEW approval, specifying emissions limitations for individual sources necessary to enable the state to achieve the standards.

The 1967 Act failed completely in practice, partly because of the difficult scientific and institutional problems the federal and state agencies faced in preparing implementation plans and enforcing standards. The states lacked adequate resources for these tasks, and federal subsidies did not make up the difference. The states nevertheless accumulated considerable experience in using technology-based standards. They pioneered the use of permits that enabled regulators to obtain a specific, written agreement in advance that sources would comply with abatement requirements. See generally Currie, State Pollution Statutes, 48 U. Chi. L. Rev. 27 (1981).

3. *The 1970 Act*

In 1970, Congress overhauled federal air pollution control with vote margins that rivaled those on declarations of war (Senate 73-0; House of Representatives 374-1). Yet just beneath the surface of this apparent unanimity, deep conflicts lurked:

> The prevailing wisdom is that the current federal air pollution policy was chosen irrationally. . . . Scientists argue that the [Clean Air Act] is based on misconceptions about biological and physical systems. Atmospheric chemists suggest that the notion of threshold levels of emissions that are damaging to health is not supported by research. Physicists believe that the diffusion of pollutants and their chemical interaction are much more complex than can be appropriately handled by the simple standards in the 1970 act. Engineers claim that the deadlines set by the legislation are not technically realistic. Economists, the most outspoken of critics, condemn federal regulations as inefficient, inequitable, and ineffectual. [Ingram, The Political Rationality of Innovation: The Clean Air Act Amendments of 1970, in Approaches to Controlling Air Pollution 12, 12-13 (A. Friedlaender ed., 1978).]

As the materials throughout this chapter indicate, many of these same charges continue to be raised.

4. *Conflicting Goals*

The apparent "irrationality" of federal air pollution control begins with the failure at the outset to concur on what the term "air pollution" means. Its meaning hinges on which of two major pollution reduction goals is adopted. The conservation goal defines air pollution as any concentration that degrades air below the "background" levels of substances in the ambient air as a result of natural processes; pollution is any change produced artificially. The economic goal defines pollution in terms of the costs of degradation; any proposed reduction of damages from pollution must yield tangible benefits in excess of the tangible costs of achieving cleaner air. This chapter will use the term "air pollution" to refer to air quality levels above those allowed by a legislature, agency, or court. The conflict between the conservation and economic strategies remains intense. The conservation strategy is based in part on moral and philosophical grounds. Conservationists argue that natural environments should be preserved or restored for aesthetic or moral reasons. See Nagle, The Idea of Pollution, 43 U.C. Davis L. Rev. 1 (2009) (discussing the moral concerns that contributed to the original meaning of pollution as defilement). The rational imperative of the economic goal suggests that, in a society of limited resources, the objective should be to adopt efficient pollution control levels and cost-effective reduction strategies. This can be done by converting the benefits of air pollution control, to the greatest extent possible, to monetary values, after which it becomes possible to compare at the margin the costs of emission reduction with the benefits achieved.

Proponents of the economic approach were singularly ineffectual in 1970 in convincing the public that costly air pollution controls would sacrifice other valuable social benefits that the money spent on air pollution control might bring. Most members of Congress seemed uninterested in calculating the opportunity costs of emission reductions. Further, Congress apparently ignored the likelihood that air pollution control costs vary among regions and that an efficient policy would correlate regional reduction levels and control costs.

5.   *The 1977 Amendments*

Private stationary sources did a passable job under the 1970 version of the CAA in reducing total emissions of some air pollutants (notably TSP, SO_2, and HC) nationwide. At the same time, the clean-air program threatened to hamper economic growth in the more developed regions of the country by making it difficult to build new sources. The 1970 Act itself gave few hints as to how new industrial facilities were to be rationally accommodated with the goal of reducing air pollution.

The initial effort by states to control mobile-source pollutants was less successful. The deadlines for achieving national ambient air quality standards were too optimistic in light of the serious ozone and CO problems in some urban areas. In addition, the emissions standards for new vehicles did not fulfill the central abatement function expected of them because vehicle manufacturers were able to delay compliance deadlines. The manufacturers' failures forced the states to rely on transportation control strategies such as dispersing traffic, providing incentives for people to take mass transit or not to drive, instituting inspection and maintenance programs, and setting standards for older vehicles. These techniques directly affected the driving public, sometimes in ways that were viewed as exceedingly restrictive and intrusive. When states and cities balked at secondary controls, EPA tried to force them to implement transportation control plans (TCPs). The results were a political disaster. A series of lawsuits and congressional amendments to the Act quickly brought the EPA initiatives to a standstill. See, e.g., EPA v. Brown, 431 U.S. 99 (1977) (declaring challenges to TCPs moot because EPA agreed to eliminate the requirement that states adopt TCPs).

In 1977 Congress adopted a pragmatic set of "midcourse corrections" in recognition of the shortcomings of its original approach. By then Congress's pro-environmental ardor had cooled somewhat, the opposition to strong air pollution controls had rallied, the OPEC oil embargo had occurred, certain components of air pollution programs had foundered on political shoals, and industry and consumers had begun to absorb the costs of controlling air pollution. On the one hand, industry secured delays in meeting the 1970 vehicle emissions standards along with concessions for coal-burning power plants and other industries. Congress endorsed extensions of the deadlines for meeting the national ambient air quality standards and provided relief from the burdensome traffic management strategies EPA had imposed to control smog. On the other hand, Congress established controls over new construction in both clean- and dirty-air areas (through a process called new source review) and took steps to prevent the erosion of existing high air quality, protect visibility, and strengthen enforcement provisions.

The 1970 Act did not include a program specifically designed to protect the pristine air quality of places like the American Southwest, where the relatively common 80-mile scenic vistas were being threatened by the growing number of coal-fired power plants in the region. The Act did state that its purpose was to "protect and enhance" the nation's air resources, a phrase the courts interpreted as requiring EPA to produce a plan for maintaining air quality in clean-air areas. After EPA responded by creating a program intended to prevent degradation of areas with clean air, in 1977, Congress endorsed that program by making it a statutory requirement. The Prevention of Significant Deterioration program mandates a detailed preconstruction review procedure and permits for major new stationary sources seeking to locate in clean air areas.

6. *The 1990 Amendments*

Following the adoption of the 1977 amendments, the localization of air quality problems gave rise to increasing regional conflict. The northeastern states supported legislation on acid rain, but it was stalled by congressional representatives of states that were sources of high-sulfur coal, whose mining jobs would be threatened by acid rain control measures. Detroit automakers fought the enactment of more stringent controls necessary to deal with smog problems in cities like Los Angeles and Houston.

A series of factors combined to produce a set of statutory amendments in 1990 that greatly increased the length, specificity, and scope of the Act. These factors included the failure of industrial critics of the Act to accommodate their often conflicting interests; concerns that the Act failed to ensure that the costs of emission controls were justified by the benefits of cleaner air, and that the laborious process of obtaining permits for new construction hampered economic growth; and charges that EPA's implementation of the statute in the 1980s was overly solicitous of industry wish lists and insufficiently protective of the public health. See G. Bryner, Blue Skies, Green Politics: The Clean Air Act of 1990, at 88 (1993). The 1990 amendments imposed new deadlines for compliance with the national ambient air quality standards and prescribed in greater detail the means to which the states had to resort to achieve compliance, including the imposition of limits on vehicle use. The amendments transformed the mechanism for controlling hazardous air pollutants from a health-based to a primarily technology-based model in recognition of EPA's inability or unwillingness to limit emissions under the original approach. Congress adopted a new set of controls on precursors of acid deposition, which included an innovative emissions trading program. Congress phased out the production and use of ozone-depleting chemicals in an effort to protect the integrity of the stratospheric ozone layer. Finally, Congress created a federal permit program to facilitate both compliance with and enforcement of the Act's multifarious obligations.

The amended Act almost immediately came under attack as being too costly, insufficiently attentive to state and local concerns, and overly intrusive into the everyday affairs of businesses and vehicle users. Beginning in 1995, Congress adopted a series of minor amendments to the Act that eliminated some of the more objectionable provisions regarding automobile inspection and maintenance and mandatory employer van pooling.

C.   A SUMMARY OF THE CLEAN AIR ACT TODAY

The Clean Air Act, as amended in 1970, 1977 (Pub. L. No. 95-95, 91 Stat. 685), and 1990 (Pub. L. No. 101-549, 104 Stat. 2399), provides the basic framework for modern air pollution control. The summary that follows highlights the key elements of this massive and complex Act. You may want to consult this summary from time to time to maintain your perspective as you move through the remaining materials in this chapter.

The Regulatory Provisions: A Preview. The CAA depends on two very different types of regulatory standards (ambient and technology-based) and two very different governmental roles (federal standard setting and state implementation). The paramount goals of the Act are to clean up dirty air to an acceptable level and to maintain high air quality where it still exists. See §101(b)(1). The federal ambient standards and state implementation plans are shaped to accomplish these goals. Other provisions, however, are keyed to the ability of air pollution control technology to reduce emissions from stationary or mobile sources at an acceptable cost. Standards and implementation procedures vary depending on two additional factors: whether sources are stationary or mobile, and whether sources are located in clean-air or dirty-air areas of the country. When you fully understand the interaction of these four pairs of components (ambient versus technology-based standards, federal versus state implementation, stationary versus mobile sources, clean-air versus dirty-air areas), you will have a firm grasp on the bulk of the regulatory programs established by the Act.

Ambient Air Quality Standards. Ambient standards specify maximum pollutant concentrations deemed to be safe for exposure over various time periods. Because they do not specify limitations that must be placed on actual sources, ambient standards cannot constitute a complete basis for air pollution control; they must be coupled with measures limiting individual source emissions. Sections 108 and 109 of the CAA authorize EPA to promulgate national ambient air quality standards (NAAQS) by regulation after the agency has gathered the necessary scientific information in the criteria documents first required by the 1963 legislation. EPA must set primary NAAQS to protect human health with an adequate margin of safety; secondary standards are designed to protect additional environmental values such as plant and animal life, property, and aesthetic sensibilities. Standards currently exist for six "criteria pollutants." See Table 6-2. For additional information on the NAAQS, see http://www.epa.gov/ttn/naaqs.

The primary emphasis of the CAA is on the "attainment" of these ambient standards. Although the Act now calls for direct federal regulation of some pollution sources, primarily large new or modified stationary sources and mobile sources via emissions restrictions, it requires states to select and implement the combination of emissions limitations on stationary and mobile sources necessary to ensure that they meet and maintain the ambient standards. The states make these choices through the adoption (subject to EPA approval) of a separate state implementation plan (SIP) for each of the criteria pollutants.

Emissions Standards. Technology-based uniform national emissions standards specify the pollution control performance levels expected from particular types of air pollution sources. The Act contains four types of federally uniform emissions standards. (Three additional emissions standards that have been combined, somewhat untidily, with the ambient standards approach are covered later in this discussion.)

First, it includes technology-based standards for vehicle emissions. The 1970 Act set deadlines of five years for vehicle manufacturers to reduce CO, HC, and NO$_x$ emissions by 90 percent from 1970 levels; the deadlines, however, were extended through a series of administrative and congressional actions. The statute currently requires that EPA issue and periodically revise standards for vehicle emissions that, in the agency's judgment, cause or contribute to a level of air pollution that may reasonably be anticipated to endanger public health or welfare. §202(a)(1). The 1990 amendments required EPA for the first time to control vehicle emissions of hazardous air pollutants such as benzene and formaldehyde. §202(*l*). The statute prevents states (except California) from setting standards for new vehicles different from those set by Congress. §209. It also regulates the use of fuels whose emissions cause or contribute to public health or welfare risks (§211(c)(1)), and prohibits the use of leaded gasoline (§211(g)) and the sale of diesel fuel with excessive sulfur content (§211(i)). State vehicle inspections and traffic management plans supplement these mechanisms.

Second, the Act requires EPA to set by regulation nationally uniform new source performance standards (NSPS) for various categories of stationary sources. Once promulgated, these standards require emissions levels no higher than those that could be achieved through the application of the best system of emissions reduction that, taking into account such factors as cost, EPA determines has been adequately demonstrated. §111(a)(1). The NSPS cover all types of emissions that "may reasonably be anticipated to endanger public health or welfare." §111(b)(1)(A).

Third, §112 of the Act provides uniform national emission standards for hazardous air pollutants (NESHAP). Under the 1970 version of the Act, EPA was to issue standards for those pollutants at the level that would provide "an ample margin of safety to protect the public health." Although hundreds of hazardous substances appeared to qualify for regulation, EPA listed only a handful of substances between 1970 and 1990 for NESHAPs preparation. The 1990 amendments completely overhauled the program for regulating hazardous air pollutants. Congress itself established a list of 189 hazardous air pollutants. §112(b)(1). EPA must determine which source categories pose a threat of adverse human health or environmental effects through their emissions of a listed pollutant and establish emission standards for each such category. §112(c)(2). The statute authorizes two rounds of standards. The first round consists of technology-based standards that require the maximum degree of reduction that EPA determines is achievable. §112(d)(2). The standards for new sources are designed to be more stringent than those for existing sources. EPA must assess and report to Congress on any risks to the public health that remain after application of the round 1 standards. If Congress fails to act on the agency's recommendations for further legislation to address those risks, EPA must issue a second round of controls, if necessary, to provide an ample margin of safety to protect the public health or prevent adverse environmental effects. The statute requires the issuance of round 2 standards for any source category of carcinogenic emissions if the round 1 standards do not reduce the lifetime excess cancer risk to the most exposed individual to less than one in a million. §112(f)(2)(A).

Fourth, the statute requires that existing sources in nonattainment areas (those that have not yet achieved the NAAQS) install, at a minimum, "reasonably available control technology" (RACT). §172(c)(1).

Although federal law imposes additional pollution control obligations on large new and modified stationary sources of pollution and linked permit review and approval obligations on state or federal officials, they are not "uniform" or dictated

TABLE 6-2
National Ambient Air Quality Standards

Pollutant [final rule cite]	Primary/ Secondary	Averaging Time	Level	Form
Carbon Monoxide [76 FR 54294, Aug 31, 2011]	Primary	8-hour	9 ppm	Not to be exceeded more than once per year
		1-hour	35 ppm	
Lead [73 FR 6694, Nov 12, 2008]	Primary and Secondary	Rolling 3-month average	0.15 $\mu g/m^3$ [1]	Not to be exceeded
Nitrogen Dioxide [75 FR 6474, Feb 9, 2010]	Primary	1-hour	100 ppb	98th percentile, averaged over 3 years
[61 FR 5282, Oct. 8, 1996]	Primary and Secondary	Annual	53 ppb [2]	Annual mean
Ozone [73 FR 16436, Mar 27, 2008]	Primary and Secondary	8-hour	0.075 ppm [3]	Annual fourth-highest daily maximum 8-hour concentration, averaged over 3 years
Particle Pollution PM$_{2.5}$ Dec 14, 2012	Primary	Annual	12 $\mu g/m^3$	Annual mean, averaged over 3 years
	Secondary	Annual	15 $\mu g/m^3$	Annual mean, averaged over 3 years
PM$_{10}$	Primary and Secondary	24-hour	35 $\mu g/m^3$	98th percentile, averaged over 3 years
	Primary and Secondary	24-hour	150 $\mu g/m^3$	Not to be exceeded more than once per year on average over 3 years
Sulfur Dioxide [75 FR 35520, Jun 22, 2010] [38 FR 25678, Sept 14, 1973]	Primary	1-hour	75 ppb [4]	99th percentile of 1-hour daily maximum concentrations, averaged over 3 years
	Secondary	3-hour	0.5 ppm	Not to be exceeded more than once per year

[1] Final rule signed October 15, 2008. The 1978 lead standard (1.5 $\mu g/m^3$ as a quarterly average) remains in effect until one year after an area is designated for the 2008 standard, except that in areas designated nonattainment for the 1978 standard, the 1978 standard remains in effect until implementation plans to attain or maintain the 2008 standard are approved.

[2] The official level of the annual NO_2 standard is 0.053 ppm, equal to 53 ppb, which is shown here for the purpose of clearer comparison to the 1-hour standard.

[3] Final rule signed March 12, 2008. The 1997 ozone standard (0.08 ppm, annual fourth-highest daily maximum 8-hour concentration, averaged over 3 years) and related implementation rules remain in place. In 1997, EPA revoked the 1-hour ozone standard (0.12 ppm, not to be exceeded more than once per year) in all areas, although some areas have continued obligations under that standard ("anti-backsliding"). The 1-hour ozone standard is attained when the expected number of days per calendar year with maximum hourly average concentrations above 0.12 ppm is less than or equal to 1.

[4] Final rule signed June 2, 2010. The 1971 annual and 24-hour SO_2 standards were revoked in that same rulemaking. However, these standards remain in effect until one year after an area is designated for the 2010 standard, except in areas designated nonattainment for the 1971 standards, where the 1971 standards remain in effect until implementation plans to attain or maintain the 2010 standard are approved.

Source: http://www.epa.gov/air/criteria.html.

by regulation to the same extent as the four categories just summarized. Exactly what is required depends on air quality and is set on a case-by-case basis with reference to federal databases and categorical, uniform regulation of similar new sources, but also to other sources of information about pollution control capabilities and accomplishments. More about those provisions follows.

State Implementation Plans. The nationally applicable emission standards for new vehicles and stationary sources described above constitute a principal line of attack against air pollution, but achievement of the NAAQS remains the CAA's paramount objective. The states have the primary responsibility for designing and implementing plans to achieve the ambient standards. §§107(a), 110(a)(2). In designing a SIP, state officials make many controversial decisions detailing the steps industrial plants, businesses, mobile-source owners, airports, highway departments, and local traffic control officials must take to bring the state's air quality control regions (of which the nation has been divided into more than 200) into compliance with the NAAQS. Once approved by EPA, SIPs are enforceable by state and federal authorities and citizens or public interest groups. §113.

The 1977 amendments distinguished for the first time "clean-air" and "dirty-air" areas of the nation. Since then, the CAA has applied different requirements to regions that have yet to attain the NAAQS and regions that have relatively clean or even pristine air quality. The Act's nonattainment program provisions spell out SIP requirements for the former, while Congress addressed clean-air regions in the provisions dealing with the prevention of significant deterioration (PSD) of air quality. §§160-169A. The different SIP requirements for PSD and nonattainment regions apply to each SIP-controlled pollutant individually. In effect, a separate "sub-SIP" applies to each pollutant depending on its PSD or nonattainment status. Thus, the statute now divides, or "zones," the United States into PSD and nonattainment areas on a pollutant-by-pollutant basis, with overlapping designations when an area has attained the NAAQS for one pollutant but not for another.

The Nonattainment Provisions. Because many areas had still not met the NAAQS by the time it adopted the 1990 amendments, Congress tackled the nonattainment program more vigorously than it had previously. In doing so, it removed some of the discretion the states had to develop whatever mix of controls they deemed best suited to achieving the NAAQS. The amendments crafted a new set of NAAQS deadlines that differ depending on the degree to which pollutant concentrations exceed the NAAQS. See §§181(a)(1) (ozone), 186(a)(1) (CO), 188(c) (PM_{10}), 192(a) (other criteria pollutants). Los Angeles, for example, had until 2010 to comply with the NAAQS for ozone.

The statute now imposes on states with nonattainment areas a set of general requirements and a series of pollutant-specific requirements whose stringency varies in relation to the severity of the nonattainment problem. The general requirements, set forth in §172(c) of the Act, include the RACT requirement for existing sources mentioned above and a requirement that SIPs make reasonable further progress (defined as annual incremental reductions in emissions) toward compliance with the relevant NAAQS. In addition, the SIP of a state with a nonattainment area must require a permit for the construction and operation of any new or modified major stationary source in the area. To qualify for a permit, the applicant must comply with a strict technology-based emissions standard defined by the "lowest achievable emission rate" (LAER) for the applying facility. If the state's SIP does not require existing sources to reduce emissions enough to accommodate new construction without exceeding the NAAQS, the applicant itself must purchase or secure from existing sources a reduction in emissions more than sufficient to offset new emissions from the proposed facility. §173(a).

The pollutant-specific requirements supplement or increase the severity of these general requirements. The statute categorizes nonattainment areas based on the degree to which ambient concentrations exceed the NAAQS. Ozone nonattainment areas, for example, are divided into marginal, moderate, serious, severe, and extreme classifications. The stringency of the required controls (such as the amount of offset needed to qualify for a new source permit) increases with pollutant concentrations. SIPs for ozone nonattainment areas must provide for reductions in emissions of VOCs and NO_x by specified amounts.

As for controls on mobile sources, the 1990 amendments reversed a trend begun in the mid-1970s. In 1974 and 1975, Congress prohibited EPA from imposing parking surcharges and from spending federal funds to tax or regulate parking facilities. The 1977 amendments further restricted federal authority. They prohibited, for example, federal controls on indirect sources that attract large numbers of vehicles, including shopping centers, sports complexes, and airports. The 1990 amendments, on the other hand, appeared to recognize that additional reductions in stationary-source emissions would be more expensive and difficult to achieve, and that mobile-source reductions were necessary if the NAAQS for ozone and CO were ever going to be satisfied. Accordingly, the 1990 amendments cracked down on vehicle usage in nonattainment areas. Gasoline vapor recovery systems, clean-fuel vehicle programs, transportation controls, and traffic control measures were all required in certain ozone nonattainment areas. The requirements for CO nonattainment areas were similar.

The 1990 amendments subject states that fail to comply with their nonattainment area obligations to a variety of sanctions. These include the withholding of federal grants in support of air pollution planning and control programs and highway construction, and the imposition of multiple offset requirements that make it harder to construct new or modified major stationary sources that may be important to a state's economic development. §179. The 1990 amendments contain additional pollutant-specific sanctions that include the imposition of penalty fees calculated on the basis of the level of emissions of VOCs. §185.

Prevention of Significant Deterioration. The 1990 amendments did not affect the PSD program. Under that program, major emitting facilities must install the "best available control technology" (BACT), to be determined for each facility, and demonstrate that plant operation will not cause ambient air to be "significantly" degraded. §§165(a)(4), 169(3). What constitutes a significant increment depends on the exact location of the proposed facility. §163. All clean-air areas of the country are placed in one of three classes. The increment of deterioration in ambient concentrations allowed within Class I areas, which mainly consist of major national parks and wilderness areas, is quite small, necessarily constricting new industrial development near the southwestern parklands. Class III increments were set generously at approximately half the NAAQS levels, and Class II increments fall in between. Visibility is protected separately, with "best available retrofit technology" (BART) to be applied as needed to existing sources that impair visibility. §169A.

The Act's "Hybrid" Emission Standards. The three emission standards applicable to sources that are required to apply for permits under the nonattainment, PSD, and visibility protection programs—LAER, BACT, and BART—are not technology-based in the same sense as the mobile-source standards, the NSPS, and RACT for existing sources. These three standards are not applied uniformly, but on a case-by-case basis. In setting them, the states are supposed to play a larger role than EPA, depending on PSD and nonattainment SIP needs. Perhaps these hybrid standards—partly ambient quality oriented and partly technology oriented—can best be viewed as technical guidelines for officials as they negotiate with source operators on the extent of abatement necessary to achieve local air quality goals. In this process NSPS have provided a benchmark; ordinarily BACT and even the stricter LAER are set close to the NSPS baseline.

Acid Deposition Control. Under a program added in 1990, Congress set a goal of reducing annual emissions of SO_2 by 10 million tons and emissions of NO_x by 2 million tons from 1980 levels. Beginning in 2000, annual emissions of SO_2 were capped nationwide at 8.9 million tons. Title IV of the Act requires that EPA allocate SO_2 emission allowances to electric utility plants with fossil fuel–fired combustion devices. It is unlawful for any regulated source to emit SO_2 in excess of the allowances it holds. Each allowance entitles its holder to emit one ton of SO_2. However, the statute authorizes the transfer of allowances among regulated sources as well as among non-regulated persons. A regulated utility, therefore, may purchase additional allowances instead of reducing its emissions, and environmental groups may purchase allowances and retire them from the system. Industrial sources of SO_2 may opt into the program.

Stratospheric Ozone Protection. Based on evidence of an ever-expanding hole in the stratospheric ozone layer (initially detected over Antarctica but now present in the Northern Hemisphere as well), Congress adopted a new Title VI in 1990 aimed at eliminating ozone-depleting chemicals. The statute required a gradual phasing out of the production of chlorofluorocarbons by 2001. EPA was obliged to phase out use of these substances during the same period. Beginning in 2015, the statute limited the production and use of hydrochlorofluorocarbons. EPA may accelerate these schedules if practicable or if necessary to prevent harmful effects on the ozone layer. §606(a).

Global Climate Change. Unlike acid rain and ozone depletion, climate change is not addressed by a set of specific CAA provisions. The Supreme Court held in 2007 that CO_2 qualifies as a pollutant so that EPA has the authority to establish motor vehicle emission standards for CO_2 and other greenhouse gases (GHGs). Since 2009, EPA has begun addressing GHG emissions under various provisions of the CAA, with a backdrop of partisan division in Congress over whether EPA should address climate change at all, and, if so, how. Chapter 12 covers climate change and regulatory responses to it, and section E.1 of that chapter addresses the role of the CAA.

Permits. Title V of the CAA, adopted in 1990, establishes for the first time a federal CAA permit program that covers sources regulated under the acid deposition control provisions of the statute, sources subject to NSPS or NESHAPs, sources required to have either a nonattainment or a PSD permit, and other major sources. The states must develop permit programs that conform to minimum EPA requirements and are subject to sanctions for failure to do so. EPA may establish and administer a permit program for a state that fails to submit an acceptable program of its own. Permit applicants must submit plans detailing how they will comply with applicable regulatory requirements. Permits must include enforceable emission limitations and schedules of compliance with applicable requirements, including those derived from the SIP. EPA may veto state-issued permits.

Enforcement. The statute provides an array of enforcement mechanisms to redress noncompliance with its various obligations. Section 113 allows the federal government to seek civil or criminal penalties for statutory or regulatory violations. Section 304 allows private citizens to step in if neither the federal government nor the states are adequately enforcing the law. If adequate statutory notice has been given, §304 allows "any person" to commence a civil action on his own behalf against emitters alleged to be in violation of emissions standards or limitations or alleged to have failed to obtain the necessary permits for new facility construction under the Act's nonattainment and PSD provisions. Citizens may sue to compel EPA to perform nondiscretionary duties.

Upon receiving evidence that air pollution is presenting "an imminent and substantial endangerment to the health of persons" and that local government has not acted to remedy the problem, EPA may issue administrative orders or sue in federal district court to abate the dangerous condition under §303. This authority allows EPA to secure prompt relief from a dangerous condition before the Act's primary but more cumbersome regulatory programs take effect.

Judicial Review. Judicial review of EPA's actions under the CAA is available under §307 in the federal courts of appeals. Section 307(d) establishes special procedures for EPA rulemaking that supplant the provisions of the Administrative Procedure Act.

NOTE ON PROTECTION OF INDOOR AIR QUALITY

Research has revealed that the air within homes and other "weatherized" and "energy-efficient" structures often contains significantly higher concentrations of many pollutants than does outdoor air. The sources of these pollutants are items and products very common in the home or office: asbestos (from insulation); formaldehyde and other toxic compounds (from cleaning products and chemical processes such as dry cleaning); tobacco smoke (which contains over 2,000 chemicals, many known carcinogens); heating fuels; pesticides; volatile organic compounds from such varied sources as hot water, deodorizers, and paints; plastics; biological contaminants such as microorganisms, molds, and mildews; and outdoor air pollutants that enter buildings through ventilation. These substances may cause human health problems ranging from allergies to asthma to cancer. See Reitze & Carof, The Legal Control of Indoor Air Pollution, 25 B.C. Envtl. Aff. L. Rev. 247, 248-251 (1998).

One troublesome indoor air pollutant is radon, a decay product of uranium that is found in many homes and is a known cancer-causing agent. According to a report issued by EPA's Office of Inspector General, More Action Needed to Protect Public from Indoor Radon Risks, Rep. No. 08-P-0174 (June 2, 2008), indoor radon is the second leading cause of lung cancer in America, after smoking, and the leading cause of lung cancer among nonsmokers. About 20,000 lung cancer deaths occur each year in the United States due to radon exposure. The combination of radon exposure and smoking appears to be particularly lethal. EPA administers a voluntary Indoor Radon Program to promote testing and mitigation. Testing is largely driven by real estate transactions. The program is authorized by the 1988 Indoor Radon Abatement Act (IRAA), a statute that seeks to achieve radon levels in buildings equal to outdoor levels. 15 U.S.C. §2661. The report concluded that the program has failed to achieve the IRAA's goal. Instead, the number of homeowners potentially exposed to excessive radon (for which there is no safe threshold level of exposure) has increased each year. The problems include the disincentives for real estate sellers and brokers to test for radon and for builders to build homes using radon-resistant techniques.

EPA has long interpreted the CAA as vesting it with the power to regulate only outdoor air pollution. See 40 C.F.R. §50.1(e). This position has never been definitively confirmed or refuted. Congress has delegated authority to various federal agencies—including EPA under other laws, the Consumer Product Safety Commission, and the Occupational Safety and Health Administration—to take steps to limit exposure to particular kinds of indoor air pollution threats. But no statute gives any agency the broad regulatory authority to address indoor air pollution across the board that the CAA vests in EPA for outdoor air pollution.

D. UNIFORM NATIONAL PRIMARY AND SECONDARY AMBIENT AIR QUALITY STANDARDS

In developing uniform primary and secondary national ambient air quality standards (NAAQS), EPA faces the formidable task of determining, for each of the major air pollutants, separate numerical, time-limited ambient concentration levels that can be tolerated without endangering health and welfare anywhere in the nation. The following subsection introduces the problem of setting numerical standards to protect public health under conditions of scientific uncertainty.

Once EPA has promulgated ambient standards, responsibility under the CAA shifts from the federal government to the states. Each state must submit a SIP that specifies emission limitations and other measures necessary to attain the standards by the various statutory deadlines contained in the Act. Subsection 2 below addresses the constraints that apply to the states in carrying out that task.

1. Establishment of the NAAQS

a. Listing of Criteria Pollutants

As the preceding discussion indicates, the only air pollutants for which NAAQS currently exist are those listed in Table 6-2. What is the scope of EPA's discretion in selecting pollutants for promulgation of the NAAQS? In NRDC v. Train, 411 F. Supp. 864 (S.D.N.Y. 1976), NRDC brought a citizen suit under §304(a)(2) to force EPA to list lead as a criteria pollutant under §108 of the Act. NRDC argued that the agency had a mandatory duty to list lead once it determined that the pollutant "has an adverse effect on public health or welfare"[1] and comes from the requisite numerous or diverse sources. EPA conceded that lead met both tests, but claimed that §108(a)(1)(C), which requires that EPA "plan[] to issue air quality criteria," left the decision to list or not list within the Administrator's sole discretion. According to EPA, discretion was

---

1. The statute has since been amended; EPA must now list a pollutant under §108 if, among other things, its emissions, "in [EPA's] judgment, cause or contribute to air pollution which may reasonably be anticipated to endanger public health or welfare." §108(a)(1)(A).

necessary because the choice of regulating lead under different sections of the Act involved "complex considerations." In particular, EPA had to consider whether to list lead as a criteria pollutant under §108 or establish standards restricting the lead content of gasoline under §211(c)(1). EPA chose §211 because it would be simpler and more efficient and would not add to the burdens imposed on the states by the obligation to adopt SIPs for the other criteria pollutants.

EPA's choices were not easy. On the one hand, at the time EPA was considering the optimal strategy for limiting exposure to lead, gasoline combustion accounted for about 88 percent of airborne lead; smelters contributed just under 4 percent. Smelters are not very numerous and usually are located in less populous regions. EPA observed that some lead and copper smelters might be "severely strained economically" if regulated under SIPs as a means of meeting any NAAQS ultimately adopted. 43 Fed. Reg. 46,256 (1978). Do these facts support the policy of concentrating on mobile-source lead pollution and letting the smelters go? On the other hand, under the ambient approach, nothing would have to be done in the vast regions of the country where lead is not a problem, whereas the §211(c)(1) approach required the imposition of costly controls on lead in gasoline throughout the nation. The ambient approach theoretically permitted selective land use planning to regulate the spacing and timing of lead emissions as needed, whereas fuel controls blanketed the nation. Was regulation of lead under §111 an additional available alternative? See §111(b)(1)(A), (d).

The court in NRDC ruled for the plaintiff. It interpreted §108 as requiring EPA to list a pollutant under the two enumerated conditions in §108(a)(1)(A)-(B), "one factual and one judgmental." According to the court, §§108 and 211(c) are "neither mutually exclusive nor alternative provisions." The court pointed out that any reductions in lead resulting from §211(c) regulations would make the states' task of achieving the NAAQS for lead easier. On appeal, the district court's judgment was affirmed in NRDC v. Train, 545 F.2d 320 (2d Cir. 1976). The court agreed that Congress did not give EPA the discretion to list only the pollutants for which the Administrator thought ambient standards were the most appropriate strategy. It concluded that Congress intended the ambient standard and SIP strategy to be the linchpin of the Act and built safeguards into the Act (such as citizen suits) to prevent delays: "Congress sought to eliminate, not perpetuate, opportunity for administrative foot-dragging." Id. at 328. NRDC v. Train forced a basic change in EPA's air quality management strategy for lead. Other important CAA policy changes also began with a §304 suit challenging EPA's failure to perform a nondiscretionary duty. Why haven't more pollutants been listed as criteria pollutants under §108 since the forced listing of lead?

Despite being forced to promulgate an ambient standard for lead, EPA continued to place primary reliance on its regulations limiting the lead content of gasoline. Congress ultimately banned all lead in gasoline as of December 31, 1995. §211(g)(1), (n). Largely as a result, blood lead levels in children between 1 and 5 years old in the United States dropped to an average of 1-2 micrograms per deciliter (μg/dL) in the early 2000s, compared to about 15 μg/dL from 1976 to 1980. Americans nevertheless continue to be exposed to lead from many sources, as indicated in Figure 6-5. EPA has identified reports showing associations between relatively low blood lead levels (scientists have not detected any safe level of lead in blood) and increased risk of cardiovascular and cancer-related mortality among the general

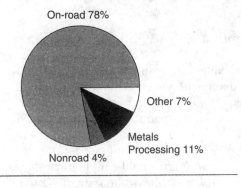

1970 Lead Emissions Sources
221,000 tons

On-road 78%

Other 7%

Metals Processing 11%

Nonroad 4%

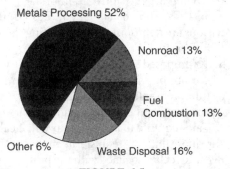

1997 Lead Emissions Sources
3,915 tons

Metals Processing 52%

Nonroad 13%

Fuel Combustion 13%

Other 6%

Waste Disposal 16%

FIGURE 6-5

Source: http://www.epa.gov/air/urbanair/lead/what/html (removed).

U.S. population.[m] Young children continue to be exposed to lead primarily through lead in household dust and lead-based paint. Studies show brain damage to children at exposure levels as low as 0.02 µg/dL. Researchers have found correlations between neurobehavioral damage due to lead exposure in the first year of life and violent crime, age-specific arrest, and incarceration trends. The data also suggest that murder is associated with severe cases of childhood lead poisoning.[n] Adults are primarily exposed along roads due to vehicle brake particles, road dust, and emissions from cars and trucks that still burn leaded gasoline. Adults 20 years or older had a geometric mean blood lead level of 1.6 µg/dL during 2001-2002. EPA's Report on the

m. See Air Quality Criteria for Lead (Second External Review Draft), available at http://cfpub.epa.gov/ncea/cfm/recordisplay.cfm?deid=154041.

n. Nevin, Understanding International Crime Trends: The Legacy of Preschool Lead Exposure, 104 Envtl. Res. 315 (July 2007). Chandramouli et al., Effects of Early Childhood Lead Exposure on Academic Performance and Behaviour of School Age Children, Archives Disease Childhood 2009, 94:844-848 (Sept. 21, 2009), concluded that exposure to lead early in childhood has effects on subsequent educational attainment, even at blood levels below 10 µg/dL. Fadrowski, Blood Lead Level and Kidney Function in U.S. Adolescents, 170 Archives Internal Med. 75 (Jan. 11, 2010), found kidney damage in adolescents with blood lead levels of 2.0 µg/dL.

Environment: 2008 (May 2008), at 5-11. Adults can experience adverse health effects (including cardiovascular disease, tooth decay, miscarriage, kidney disease, cognitive problems, and cataracts) decades after exposure.

b.   The Adoption of NAAQS

The second step, after listing, in promulgating an ambient standard is the preparation of a criteria document, which is not a standard that sources must meet, but rather a document describing the latest scientific knowledge concerning the injury to public health or welfare that the pollutant may cause. See §108(a)(2). The third step, required by §109(a)(2), to occur simultaneously with the publication of the criteria document, is for EPA to issue proposed numerical primary and secondary NAAQS and, after soliciting and considering public input, final standards. The NAAQS must be based on the criteria document. Section 109(d)(1) requires EPA to review the existing air quality criteria and NAAQS at least once every five years. It also requires EPA to make such revisions in the criteria and NAAQS "as may be appropriate in accordance with" §7408. When are revisions "appropriate"? In Center for Biological Diversity v. EPA, 749 F.3d 1079, 1087-89 (D.C. Cir. 2014), an environmental group argued that NAAQS revisions are appropriate if the existing standards are not adequate to protect the public health or welfare. EPA responded that if EPA cannot make a "reasoned judgment" that a proposed standard would comply with §108(b) because of scientific uncertainty, it cannot be "appropriate" for EPA to make the revision. The court deferred to EPA's interpretation of the statute.

Section 109(b)(1) provides that the primary standards are those that, "allowing an adequate margin of safety, are requisite to protect the public health." Under §109(b)(2), the secondary standards are those that are "requisite to protect the public welfare from any known or anticipated adverse effects associated with the presence of such pollutant in the ambient air." After EPA promulgated NAAQS for lead in 1978, the Lead Industries Association challenged the standards in Lead Indus. Ass'n, Inc. v. EPA, 647 F.2d 1130 (D.C. Cir. 1980). One of the issues was whether EPA erred by refusing to consider economic and technological feasibility in setting the standards. The court held that it did not, because "the statute and its legislative history make clear that economic considerations play no part in the promulgation of ambient air quality standards under Section 109." Id. at 1148. That ruling went undisturbed for more than 20 years, after which time the same issue arose before the Supreme Court in the second principal case below.

In November 2008, EPA revised the NAAQS for lead for the first time in 30 years. Those standards were challenged in the following case.

COALITION OF BATTERY RECYCLERS ASSOCIATION v. EPA
604 F.3d 613 (D.C. Cir. 2010)

ROGERS, Circuit Judge:

[EPA's revised NAAQS for lead altered the permissible level of lead in ambient air and the averaging time over which the level must be met. National Ambient Air Quality Standards for Lead, 73 Fed. Reg. 66,964 (Nov. 12, 2008) (Final Rule). The Coalition of Battery Recyclers Association challenged the standard, contending EPA action was arbitrary and capricious.]

I.

. . . Lead ("Pb") emitted into the air can be inhaled or ingested and then absorbed into the bloodstream, potentially leading to a broad range of adverse health effects including adverse neurological effects in children. In 1978 EPA established primary and secondary NAAQS for lead of 1.5 micrograms of lead per cubic meter of air ($\mu g/m^3$) averaged over a calendar quarter. At this time, adverse neurocognitive effects in children had not been shown for blood lead levels below 50 micrograms of lead per deciliter of blood ($\mu g/dL$), and the 1978 NAAQS aimed to prevent most children from exceeding a blood lead level of 30 $\mu g/dL$. However, later studies showed adverse neurocognitive effects in children with blood lead levels below 10 $\mu g/dL$.

EPA began reviewing the NAAQS for lead in 2004, considering some 6,000 studies and concluding "there is now no recognized safe level of Pb in children's blood." As part of its review, EPA produced a "Criteria Document" assessing the latest scientific information regarding health effects associated with lead in the ambient air. EPA's review "shift[ed] focus from identifying an appropriate target population mean blood lead level and instead focuse[d] on the magnitude of effects of air-related Pb on neurocognitive functions." EPA developed an "evidence-based framework" that examined published studies addressing the relationship between IQ loss in children and air lead levels. EPA relied to a lesser extent on risk estimates derived from risk assessment models. Through its review, EPA sought to identify an air lead level "that would prevent air-related IQ loss (and related effects) of a magnitude judged by the Administrator to be of concern in populations of children exposed to the level of the standard."

To relate IQ loss to air lead levels, EPA used its evidence-based framework to determine relationships between air lead levels and blood lead levels (the "air-to-blood ratio") and between blood lead levels and IQ loss (the "concentration-response" relationship). EPA concluded that for each $\mu g/m^3$ increase of lead in air, children's blood lead levels increase by 5-10 $\mu g/dL$, i.e., the air-to-blood ratio ranged from 1:5 to 1:10. EPA selected an air-to-blood ratio of 1:7 "as a generally central value within this range." EPA also concluded that the concentration-response relationship is nonlinear, with greater incremental IQ loss occurring at lower blood lead levels, and thus that analyses of children with blood lead levels closest to those of children in the United States today were most relevant. EPA determined that the most recently measured mean blood lead level of U.S. children five years old and younger was 1.8 $\mu g/dL$, and selected four study groups involving children with mean blood lead levels between 2.9 and 3.8 $\mu g/dL$ rather than groups with higher mean blood lead levels. To "avoid[] focus on a single estimate that may be unduly influenced by one single analysis," each of the four selected groups was from a different study. Id. Using each group's reported mean IQ point decrease per $\mu g/dL$ increase in blood lead levels, i.e., using the slope of the concentration-response relationship for each group, EPA calculated the median concentration-response slope to be -1.75 $\mu g/dL$. Id.

. . . EPA concluded that an allowable airborne lead-related loss of two IQ points should be used to set the NAAQS standard. . . . Combining the blood-to-air ratio of 1:7, the concentration-response slope of -1.75 $\mu g/dL$, and the allowable air-related IQ loss of 2 points, EPA concluded that an air lead level standard of 0.15 $\mu g/m^3$ "would be sufficient to protect public health with an adequate margin of safety" and "is neither more nor less stringent than necessary for this purpose."

EPA also concluded that the appropriate averaging time for the air lead level standard is a rolling three-month period with a maximum (not-to-be-exceeded) form evaluated over a period of three years. EPA based its conclusion on scientific evidence indicating that blood lead levels increase quickly in response to increased lead exposure, that blood lead levels measured at the same time as an IQ test ("concurrent blood lead levels") are most strongly associated with IQ response, and that these concurrent blood lead levels reflect lead exposure over the past one to three months. On November 12, 2008, EPA published the final rule, revising the primary and secondary NAAQS for lead to 0.15 $\mu g/m^3$ averaged over a rolling three-month period.

II.

Petitioners assert that the revised primary lead NAAQS is overprotective, contending that (A) EPA did not provide sufficient record support for basing the standard on preventing a decrease of more than two IQ points, . . . and (C) selection of a lead standard of 0.15 $\mu g/m^3$ was arbitrary and capricious when measured as an average over a rolling three-month period. Consistent with our standard of review, see Lead Indus. Ass'n v. EPA, 647 F.2d 1130, 1145-48 (D.C. Cir. 1980); 42 U.S.C. §7607(d)(9), we conclude these contentions lack merit because there is substantial record evidence to support EPA's conclusions that the population of children exposed to air lead levels above the revised NAAQS could suffer, and should be prevented from suffering, average losses of more than two IQ points, that greater incremental IQ loss occurs at lower relative blood levels and the more relevant IQ analyses are those of children with blood levels closest to today's population of children, and that a standard of 0.15 $\mu g/m^3$ measured as a three-month rolling average is required to protect public health with an adequate margin of safety.

A.

Sensitive populations; focus on IQ decrements. Petitioners' assertion that the revised lead NAAQS is overprotective because it is more stringent than necessary to protect the entire population of young U.S. children ignores that the Clean Air Act allows protection of sensitive subpopulations. Primary NAAQS are those "which in the judgment of the Administrator, . . . allowing an adequate margin of safety, are requisite to protect the public health." 42 U.S.C. §7409(b)(1). . . . [T]his court has held that "NAAQS must protect not only average healthy individuals, but also 'sensitive citizens'" such as children, and "[i]f a pollutant adversely affects the health of these sensitive individuals, EPA must strengthen the entire national standard." Am. Lung Ass'n v. EPA, 134 F.3d 388, 389 (D.C. Cir. 1998) (quoting S. Rep. No. 91-1196 at 10); see also Lead Indus. Ass'n, 647 F.2d at 1152-53.

In the Final Rule EPA explained that the scientific evidence showing the impact of lead exposure in young children in the United States led it "to give greater prominence to children as the sensitive subpopulation in this review," and to focus its revision of the lead NAAQS on "the sensitive subpopulation that is the group of children living near [lead emission] sources and more likely to be exposed at the level of the standard." Given the recent scientific evidence on which it relied, EPA's decision to base the revised lead NAAQS on protecting the subset of children likely to be exposed to airborne lead at the level of the standard was not arbitrary or capricious.

Petitioners' suggestion that EPA failed to explain adequately its shift in focus, from blood lead levels in the original 1978 lead NAAQS to IQ decrements in children in the revised NAAQS, is without merit. In the rulemaking EPA explained that although the 1978 NAAQS was based on determining a maximum safe blood lead level for children, current scientific evidence no longer recognized a safe blood lead level, and EPA consequently adopted a different focus when revising the lead NAAQS. EPA further explained that epidemiological studies of cognitive effects and lead exposure commonly use IQ scores and that the scientific literature supports the conclusion that lead exposure causes IQ loss in children. As EPA noted in its brief, EPA does not view blood lead levels as adverse health effects under the Clean Air Act, and both the 1978 and 2008 lead NAAQS focused on preventing adverse health effects such as neurocognitive effects.

Petitioners further contend EPA's use of IQ decrements to revise the lead NAAQS was arbitrary and capricious because IQ measurements are more uncertain than blood lead level measurements. They assert that confounding factors such as environmental factors affect IQ scores and that the population significance of IQ loss is imprecise. However, EPA explained that a large number of high quality studies support the inference that lead exposure causes population IQ loss, and that animal studies in which confounding factors are not present show that low levels of lead cause neurobehavioral effects. Petitioners claim that EPA has acknowledged the standard error of measurement for IQ is between three and four IQ points, and so assert that an IQ decrement of two points therefore "cannot be detected at the level of an individual." This assertion confuses the "'critical' distinction between population and individual risk," wherein a small change in IQ at the level of an individual is a substantial change at the level of a population, as noted by EPA when citing the discussion of the differences between individual-level and population-level data in the Criteria Document. . . .

Petitioners also protest . . . that EPA did not provide adequate record support for its decision to protect against a population loss of more than two IQ points. In the Final Rule and the Criteria Document EPA explained that a mean population loss of two IQ points would cause both a substantial decrease in the percentage of the population achieving very high IQ scores and a substantial increase in the percentage achieving very low scores. . . . EPA cited the comments of the American Academy of Pediatrics and state health agencies that such a loss should be prevented. These explanations sufficiently support EPA's decision to prevent a population loss of more than two IQ points. . . .

For these reasons we conclude that EPA adequately justified its decision to prevent a loss of more than two IQ points in the population of children exposed to the level of the revised NAAQS. . . .

C.

Non-conversion with three-month rolling average. Petitioners contend EPA was arbitrary and capricious not in selecting a rolling three-month averaging period, but in failing to convert the 0.15 $\mu g/m^3$ air lead level from an annual basis to a three-month basis. This contention lacks merit. EPA based its selection of a rolling three-month average on different studies than its selection of the 0.15 $\mu g/m^3$ standard. From the studies considered in determining the averaging period, EPA concluded that the scientific evidence "does not specify the duration of a sustained air concentration associated with a particular blood Pb contribution" but does "support[] the importance of time periods on the order of three months or less." Petitioners' characterization of the 0.15 μg/m³ standard as the product of a unit conversion error is thus inapt. . . .

Petitioners erroneously conclude that because EPA's risk assessment models could accept inputs only of annual average ambient air lead concentrations, EPA calculated the 0.15 μg/m³ level based on annual average air lead exposure rather than three-month exposure. As detailed in EPA's Criteria Document, the annual average values were used in the risk assessment models to estimate blood lead levels rather than IQ responses to blood lead levels. However, as EPA explained, the use of annual average ambient air lead concentrations in the risk assessment modeling was an artifact of the models themselves, and EPA adjusted the input annual concentrations to correspond to monthly or quarterly averaging times.

The rulemaking thus demonstrates that EPA adequately explained that it did not determine the 0.15 μg/m³ air lead level by assuming exposure to that level over a period of one year, and that EPA reasonably concluded and adequately explained that a lead NAAQS of 0.15 μg/m³ measured as a three-month rolling average is requisite to protect public health with an adequate margin of safety. . . .

NOTES AND QUESTIONS

1. Why did the court reject petitioners' contention that the revised lead NAAQS were overly protective? On what basis did the court uphold EPA's switch in focus from blood lead levels in the 1978 lead NAAQS to IQ decrements in the 2008 rules?

What is the function of the margin of safety requirement? Mississippi v. EPA, 744 F.3d 1334, 1353 (D.C. Cir. 2013), explained that "[b]y requiring an 'adequate margin of safety,' Congress was directing EPA to build a buffer to protect against uncertain and unknown dangers to human health."

2. What was the basis for petitioners' challenge to EPA's use of a three-month rolling averaging period to determine air lead levels? Why did the court uphold this aspect of the rule? What does this case tell you about the need for attorneys involved in litigation with EPA over major rules to understand the technical and scientific aspects of EPA regulatory decisions?

3. *Sensitive Populations and Genetic Susceptibility.* Note EPA's duty to protect sensitive individuals. Compare American Farm Bureau Fed'n v. EPA, 559 F.3d 512, 520-524 (D.C. Cir. 2009) (remanding NAAQS for PM$_{2.5}$ because EPA failed to explain how the standard would provide an adequate margin of safety for vulnerable populations, such as children, the elderly, or those otherwise subject to greater risk upon exposure to fine particles). To what extent (and in what manner) should EPA factor in the increased sensitivity to air pollution exposure that some individuals have as a result of their genetic makeup? See Marchant, Genetic Susceptibilities: The Future Driver of Ambient Air Quality Standards?, 43 Ariz. St. L.J. 791 (2011).

WHITMAN v. AMERICAN TRUCKING ASSOCIATIONS, INC.
531 U.S. 457 (2001)

Justice SCALIA delivered the opinion of the Court.

These cases present the following questions: (1) Whether §109(b)(1) of the Clean Air Act (CAA) delegates legislative power to [EPA]. (2) Whether the [EPA]

Administrator may consider the costs of implementation in setting national ambient air quality standards (NAAQS) under §109(b)(1). . . .

I

. . . These cases arose when, on July 18, 1997, the Administrator revised the NAAQS for particulate matter (PM) and ozone. American Trucking Associations, Inc., and its co-respondents . . . —which include, in addition to other private companies, the States of Michigan, Ohio, and West Virginia—challenged the new standards in the Court of Appeals for the District of Columbia Circuit, pursuant to 42 U.S.C. §7607(b)(1).

The District of Columbia Circuit accepted some of the challenges and rejected others. It agreed with [the respondents] that §109(b)(1) delegated legislative power to the Administrator in contravention of the United States Constitution, Art. I, §1, because it found that the EPA had interpreted the statute to provide no "intelligible principle" to guide the agency's exercise of authority. American Trucking Ass'ns, Inc. v. EPA, 175 F.3d 1027, 1034 (1999). The court thought, however, that the EPA could perhaps avoid the unconstitutional delegation by adopting a restrictive construction of §109(b)(1), so instead of declaring the section unconstitutional the court remanded the NAAQS to the agency. . . . The Court of Appeals [also] unanimously rejected respondents' argument that the court should depart from the rule of Lead Industries Ass'n, Inc. v. EPA, 647 F.2d 1130, 1148 (CADC 1980), that the EPA may not consider the cost of implementing a NAAQS in setting the initial standard. . . .

The Administrator and the EPA petitioned this Court for review of the first . . . question[] described in the first paragraph of this opinion. Respondents conditionally cross-petitioned for review of the second question. . . .

II

In Lead Industries, the [D.C.] Circuit held that "economic considerations [may] play no part in the promulgation of ambient air quality standards under Section 109" of the CAA. In the present cases, the court adhered to that holding, as it had done on many other occasions. See, e.g., American Lung Ass'n v. EPA, 134 F.3d 388, 389 (1998); NRDC v. EPA, 902 F.2d 962, 973 (1990); American Petroleum Inst. v. Costle, 665 F.2d 1176, 1185 (CADC 1981). Respondents argue that these decisions are incorrect. We disagree; and since the first step in assessing whether a statute delegates legislative power is to determine what authority the statute confers, we address that issue of interpretation first and reach respondents' constitutional arguments in Part III, *infra*.

Section 109(b)(1) instructs the EPA to set primary ambient air quality standards "the attainment and maintenance of which . . . are requisite to protect the public health" with "an adequate margin of safety." 42 U.S.C. §7409(b)(1). Were it not for the hundreds of pages of briefing respondents have submitted on the issue, one would have thought it fairly clear that this text does not permit the EPA to consider costs in setting the standards. The language, as one scholar has noted, "is absolute." D. Currie, Air Pollution: Federal Law and Analysis 4-15 (1981). The EPA, "based on" the information about health effects contained in the technical "criteria" documents compiled under §108(a)(2), is to identify the maximum airborne concentration of a pollutant that the public health can tolerate, decrease the concentration to provide an "adequate" margin of safety, and set the standard at that level. Nowhere are the costs of achieving such a standard made part of that initial calculation.

Against this most natural of readings, respondents make a lengthy, spirited, but ultimately unsuccessful attack. They begin with the object of §109(b)(1)'s focus, the "public health." When the term first appeared in federal clean air legislation—in the [1955 Air Pollution Control Act]—which expressed "recognition of the dangers to the public health" from air pollution—its ordinary meaning was "[t]he health of the community." Webster's New International Dictionary 2005 (2d ed. 1950). Respondents argue, however, that §109(b)(1), as added by the [1970 Act], meant to use the term's secondary meaning: "[t]he ways and means of conserving the health of the members of a community, as by preventive medicine, organized care of the sick, etc." Words that can have more than one meaning are given content, however, by their surroundings, and in the context of §109(b)(1) this second definition makes no sense. Congress could not have meant to instruct the Administrator to set NAAQS at a level "requisite to protect" "the art and science dealing with the protection and improvement of community health." Webster's Third New International Dictionary 1836 (1981). We therefore revert to the primary definition of the term: the health of the public.

Even so, respondents argue, many more factors than air pollution affect public health. In particular, the economic cost of implementing a very stringent standard might produce health losses sufficient to offset the health gains achieved in cleaning the air—for example, by closing down whole industries and thereby impoverishing the workers and consumers dependent upon those industries. That is unquestionably true, and Congress was unquestionably aware of it. . . . The 1970 Congress . . . not only anticipated that compliance costs could injure the public health, but provided for that precise exigency. Section 110(f)(1) of the CAA permitted the Administrator to waive the compliance deadline for stationary sources if, *inter alia*, sufficient control measures were simply unavailable and "the continued operation of such sources is *essential . . . to the public health or welfare.*" 84 Stat. 1683 (emphasis added). Other provisions explicitly permitted or required economic costs to be taken into account in implementing the air quality standards. Section 111(b)(1)(B), for example, commanded the Administrator to set "standards of performance" for certain new sources of emissions that as specified in §111(a)(1) were to "reflec[t] the degree of emission limitation achievable through the application of the best system of emission reduction which (taking into account the cost of achieving such reduction) the Administrator determines has been adequately demonstrated." Section 202(a)(2) prescribed that emissions standards for automobiles could take effect only "after such period as the Administrator finds necessary to permit the development and application of the requisite technology, giving appropriate consideration to the cost of compliance within such period." . . . Subsequent amendments to the CAA have added many more provisions directing, in explicit language, that the Administrator consider costs in performing various duties. See, e.g., 42 U.S.C. §7545(k)(1) (reformulate gasoline to "require the greatest reduction in emissions . . . taking into consideration the cost of achieving such emissions reductions"); §7547(a)(3) (emission reduction for nonroad vehicles to be set "giving appropriate consideration to the cost" of the standards). We have therefore refused to find implicit in ambiguous sections of the CAA an authorization to consider costs that has elsewhere, and so often, been expressly granted. See Union Elec. Co. v. EPA, 427 U.S. 246, 257 n.5 (1976).

Accordingly, to prevail in their present challenge, respondents must show a textual commitment of authority to the EPA to consider costs in setting NAAQS under §109(b)(1). And because §109(b)(1) and the NAAQS for which it provides are the engine that drives nearly all of Title I of the CAA, 42 U.S.C. §§7401-7515, that textual commitment must be a clear one. Congress, we have held, does not alter the fundamental details of a regulatory scheme in vague terms or ancillary provisions—it does not, one might say, hide elephants in mouseholes. Respondents' textual arguments ultimately founder upon this principle.

Their first claim is that §109(b)(1)'s terms "adequate margin" and "requisite" leave room to pad health effects with cost concerns. . . . [W]e find it implausible that Congress would give to the EPA through these modest words the power to determine whether implementation costs should moderate national air quality standards.

The same defect inheres in respondents' next two arguments: that while the Administrator's judgment about what is requisite to protect the public health must be "based on [the] criteria" documents developed under §108(a)(2), see §109(b)(1), it need not be based *solely* on those criteria; and that those criteria themselves, while they must include "effects on public health or welfare which may be expected from the presence of such pollutant in the ambient air," are not necessarily *limited* to those effects. Even if we were to concede those premises, we still would not conclude that one of the unenumerated factors that the agency can consider in developing and applying the criteria is cost of implementation. That factor is *both* so indirectly related to public health and so full of potential for canceling the conclusions drawn from direct health effects that it would surely have been expressly mentioned in §§108 and 109 had Congress meant it to be considered. Yet while those provisions describe in detail how the health effects of pollutants in the ambient air are to be calculated and given effect, see §108(a)(2), they say not a word about costs.

Respondents point, finally, to a number of provisions in the CAA that *do* require attainment cost data to be generated. Section 108(b)(1), for example, instructs the Administrator to "issue to the States," simultaneously with the criteria documents, "information on air pollution control techniques, which information shall include data relating to the cost of installation and operation." And §109(d)(2)(C)(iv) requires the Clean Air Scientific Advisory Committee to "advise the Administrator of any adverse public health, welfare, social, economic, or energy effects which may result from various strategies for attainment and maintenance" of NAAQS. Respondents argue that these provisions make no sense unless costs are to be considered in setting the NAAQS. That is not so. These provisions enable the Administrator to assist the States in carrying out their statutory role as primary *implementers* of the NAAQS. It is to the States that the Act assigns initial and primary responsibility for deciding what emissions reductions will be required from which sources. See 42 U.S.C. §§7407(a), 7410 (giving States the duty of developing implementation plans). It would be impossible to perform that task intelligently without considering which abatement technologies are most efficient, and most economically feasible—which is why we have said that "the most important forum for consideration of claims of economic and technological infeasibility is before the state agency formulating the implementation plan," Union Elec. Co. v. EPA, 427 U.S., at 266. Thus, federal clean air legislation has, from the very beginning, directed federal agencies to develop and transmit implementation data, including cost data, to the States. That Congress chose to carry forward this research program to assist States in choosing the means through which they would implement the standards is perfectly sensible, and has no bearing upon whether cost considerations are to be taken into account in formulating the standards.[3]

. . . The text of §109(b), interpreted in its statutory and historical context and with appreciation for its importance to the CAA as a whole, unambiguously bars cost considerations from the NAAQS-setting process. . . . [4] We therefore affirm the judgment of the Court of Appeals on this point.

III

Section 109(b)(1) of the CAA instructs the EPA to set "ambient air quality standards the attainment and maintenance of which in the judgment of the Administrator, based on [the] criteria [documents of §108] and allowing an adequate margin of safety, are requisite to protect the public health." The Court of Appeals held that this section as interpreted by the Administrator did not provide an "intelligible principle" to guide the EPA's exercise of authority in setting NAAQS. "[The] EPA," it said, "lack[ed] any determinate criteria for drawing lines. It has failed to state intelligibly how much is too much." 175 F.3d, at 1034. The court hence found that the EPA's interpretation (but not the statute itself) violated the nondelegation doctrine. We disagree.

In a delegation challenge, the constitutional question is whether the statute has delegated legislative power to the agency. Article I, §1, of the Constitution vests "[a]ll legislative Powers herein granted . . . in a Congress of the United States." This text permits no delegation of those powers, and so we repeatedly have said that when Congress confers decisionmaking authority upon agencies *Congress* must "lay down by legislative act an intelligible principle to which the person or body authorized to [act] is directed to conform." J.W. Hampton, Jr., & Co. v. United States, 276 U.S. 394, 409 (1928). We have never suggested that an agency can cure an unlawful delegation of legislative power by adopting in its discretion a limiting construction of the statute. . . . The idea that an agency can cure an unconstitutionally standardless delegation of power by declining to exercise some of that power seems to us internally contradictory. The very choice of which portion of the power to exercise—that is to say, the prescription of the standard that Congress had omitted—would *itself* be an exercise of the forbidden legislative authority. Whether the statute delegates legislative power is a question for the courts, and an agency's voluntary self-denial has no bearing upon the answer.

We agree with the Solicitor General that the text of §109(b)(1) of the CAA at a minimum requires that "[f]or a discrete set of pollutants and based on published air quality criteria that reflect the latest scientific knowledge, [the] EPA must establish uniform national standards at a level that is requisite to protect public health from the adverse effects of the pollutant in the ambient air." Requisite, in turn, "mean[s]

3. . . . For many of the same reasons described in the body of the opinion, as well as the text of §109(b)(2), . . . we conclude that the EPA may not consider implementation costs in setting the secondary NAAQS.

4. Respondents' speculation that the EPA is secretly considering the costs of attainment without telling anyone is irrelevant to our interpretive inquiry. If such an allegation could be proved, it would be grounds for vacating the NAAQS, because the Administrator had not followed the law. See, e.g., Chevron U.S.A. Inc. v. Natural Resources Defense Council, Inc., 467 U.S. 837, 842-843 (1984). It would not, however, be grounds for this Court's changing the law.

sufficient, but not more than necessary." These limits on the EPA's discretion are strikingly similar to the ones we approved in [previous cases].

The scope of discretion §109(b)(1) allows is in fact well within the outer limits of our nondelegation precedents. In the history of the Court we have found the requisite "intelligible principle" lacking in only two statutes, one of which provided literally no guidance for the exercise of discretion, and the other of which conferred authority to regulate the entire economy on the basis of no more precise a standard than stimulating the economy by assuring "fair competition." See Panama Refining Co. v. Ryan, 293 U.S. 388 (1935); A.L.A. Schechter Poultry Corp. v. United States, 295 U.S. 495 (1935). . . . [W]e have found an "intelligible principle" in various statutes authorizing regulation in the "public interest." See, e.g., National Broadcasting Co. v. United States, 319 U.S. 190, 225-226 (1943) (FCC's power to regulate airwaves). In short, we have "almost never felt qualified to second-guess Congress regarding the permissible degree of policy judgment that can be left to those executing or applying the law." Mistretta v. United States, 488 U.S. 361, 416 (1989) (Scalia, J., dissenting).

It is true enough that the degree of agency discretion that is acceptable varies according to the scope of the power congressionally conferred. While Congress need not provide any direction to the EPA regarding the manner in which it is to define "country elevators," which are to be exempt from new-stationary-source regulations governing grain elevators, see §7411(i), it must provide substantial guidance on setting air standards that affect the entire national economy. But even in sweeping regulatory schemes we have never demanded, as the Court of Appeals did here, that statutes provide a "determinate criterion" for saying "how much [of the regulated harm] is too much." 175 F.3d, at 1034. . . . It is therefore not conclusive for delegation purposes that, as respondents argue, ozone and particulate matter are "nonthreshold" pollutants that inflict a continuum of adverse health effects at any airborne concentration greater than zero, and hence require the EPA to make judgments of degree. "[A] certain degree of discretion, and thus of lawmaking, inheres in most executive or judicial action." Mistretta v. United States, *supra*, at 417 (Scalia, J., dissenting). Section 109(b)(1) of the CAA, which to repeat we interpret as requiring the EPA to set air quality standards at the level that is "requisite"—that is, not lower or higher than is necessary—to protect the public health with an adequate margin of safety, fits comfortably within the scope of discretion permitted by our precedent.

We therefore reverse the judgment of the Court of Appeals remanding for reinterpretation that would avoid a supposed delegation of legislative power. It will remain for the Court of Appeals—on the remand that we direct for other reasons—to dispose of any other preserved challenge to the NAAQS under the judicial-review provisions contained in 42 U.S.C. §7607(d)(9). . . .

Justice THOMAS, concurring. . . .

. . . Although this Court since 1928 has treated the "intelligible principle" requirement as the only constitutional limit on congressional grants of power to administrative agencies, the Constitution does not speak of "intelligible principles." Rather, it speaks in much simpler terms: "*All* legislative Powers herein granted shall be vested in a Congress." U.S. Const., Art. 1, §1 (emphasis added). I am not convinced that the intelligible principle doctrine serves to prevent all cessions of legislative power. I believe that there are cases in which the principle is intelligible and yet the significance of the delegated decision is simply too great for the decision to be called anything other than "legislative."

. . . On a future day . . . I would be willing to address the question whether our delegation jurisprudence has strayed too far from our Founders' understanding of separation of powers.

Justice STEVENS, with whom Justice SOUTER joins, concurring in part and concurring in the judgment.

. . . I wholeheartedly endorse the Court's result [on the nondelegation issue] and endorse its explanation of its reasons, albeit with the following caveat. [Justice Stevens urged the Court "to admit that agency rulemaking authority is 'legislative power.'"]

The proper characterization of governmental power should generally depend on the nature of the power, not on the identity of the person exercising it. . . . If the NAAQS that the EPA promulgated had been prescribed by Congress, everyone would agree that those rules would be the product of an exercise of "legislative power." The same characterization is appropriate when an agency exercises rulemaking authority pursuant to a permissible delegation from Congress. . . .

It seems clear that an executive agency's exercise of rulemaking authority pursuant to a valid delegation from Congress is "legislative." As long as the delegation provides a sufficiently intelligible principle, there is nothing inherently unconstitutional about it. . . . I would hold that when Congress enacted §109, it effected a constitutional delegation of legislative power to the EPA.

Justice BREYER, concurring in part and concurring in the judgment.

. . . In order better to achieve regulatory goals—for example, to allocate resources so that they save more lives or produce a cleaner environment—regulators must often take account of all of a proposed regulation's adverse effects, at least where those adverse effects clearly threaten serious and disproportionate public harm. Hence, I believe that, other things being equal, we should read silences or ambiguities in the language of regulatory statutes as permitting, not forbidding, this type of rational regulation.

In this case, however, other things are not equal. Here, legislative history, along with the statute's structure, indicates that §109's language reflects a congressional decision not to delegate to the agency the legal authority to consider economic costs of compliance.

For one thing, the legislative history shows that Congress intended the statute to be "technology forcing." Senator Edmund Muskie, the primary sponsor of the 1970 amendments to the Act, introduced them by saying that Congress' primary responsibility in drafting the Act was not "to be limited by what is or appears to be technologically or economically feasible," but "to establish what the public interest requires to protect the health of persons," even if that means that *industries will be asked to do what seems to be impossible at the present time.*" 116 Cong. Rec. 32901-32902 (1970) (emphasis added). . . .

To read this legislative history as meaning what it says does not impute to Congress an irrational intent. Technology-forcing hopes can prove realistic. Those persons, for example, who opposed the 1970 Act's insistence on a 90% reduction in auto emission pollutants, on the ground of excessive cost, saw the development of catalytic converter technology that helped achieve substantial reductions without the economic catastrophe that some had feared. . . .

At the same time, the statute's technology-forcing objective makes regulatory efforts to determine the costs of implementation both less important and more difficult. It means that the relevant economic costs are speculative, for they include the cost of unknown future technologies. It also means that efforts to take costs into account can breed time-consuming and potentially unresolvable arguments about the accuracy and significance of cost estimates. Congress could have thought such efforts not worth the delays and uncertainties that would accompany them. . . .

. . . [T]his interpretation of §109 does not require the EPA to eliminate every health risk, however slight, at any economic cost, however great, to the point of "hurtling" industry over "the brink of ruin," or even forcing "deindustrialization." American Trucking Assns., Inc. v. EPA, 175 F.3d 1027, 1037, 1038 n.4 (CADC 1999). . . .

Section 109(b)(1) directs the Administrator to set standards that are "requisite to protect the public health" with "an adequate margin of safety." But these words do not describe a world that is free of all risk—an impossible and undesirable objective. See Industrial Union Dept., AFL-CIO v. American Petroleum Inst., 448 U.S. 607, 642 (1980) (plurality opinion) (the word "safe" does not mean "risk-free"). Nor are the words "requisite" and "public health" to be understood independent of context. . . . And what counts as "requisite" to protecting the public health will similarly vary with background circumstances, such as the public's ordinary tolerance of the particular health risk in the particular context at issue. The Administrator can consider such background circumstances when "decid[ing] what risks are acceptable in the world in which we live." NRDC v. EPA, 824 F.2d 1146, 1165 (CADC 1987).

The statute also permits the Administrator to take account of comparative health risks. That is to say, she may consider whether a proposed rule promotes safety overall. A rule likely to cause more harm to health than it prevents is not a rule that is "requisite to protect the public health." For example, as the Court of Appeals held and the parties do not contest, the Administrator has the authority to determine to what extent possible health risks stemming from reductions in tropospheric ozone (which, it is claimed, helps prevent cataracts and skin cancer) should be taken into account in setting the ambient air quality standard for ozone. See 175 F.3d, at 1050-1053 (remanding for the Administrator to make that determination). . . .

NOTES AND QUESTIONS

1. *The Role of Cost in Standard Setting.* What roles do economic impact and feasibility play in EPA's decision about the degree of strictness with which to set the primary NAAQS? According to the respondents, what words in §109(b)(1) are broad enough to encompass cost concerns? Why did the Court disagree? How did the Court interpret the provision requiring that the primary NAAQS be based on criteria documents issued under §108(a)(2)? How could the ambient air quality standards be set through analysis that takes costs into account? Oren, The Supreme Court Forces a U-Turn: The Fate of *American Trucking*, 34 Envtl. L. Rep. 10687 (2004), argues that the Court reached the correct result using unpersuasive reasoning.

As Union Elec. Co. v. EPA, excerpted at page 469, demonstrates, the statute permits consideration of economic impact at various stages of the implementation of the standards. Compare White Stallion Energy Ctr., LLC v. EPA, 748 F.3d 1222, 1236-1241 (D.C. Cir. 2014) (upholding EPA's decision not to consider cost in determining whether regulation of hazardous air pollutants by electric generating units under §112(n)(1)(A) of the CAA was "appropriate and necessary") with Sierra Club v. EPA, 375 F.3d 537, 541 (7th Cir. 2004) ("when the statute is ambiguous the EPA is free to take costs into account"). Suppose that a statute authorizes consideration of "cost" in the adoption of regulatory standards. May the agency consider the cost-effectiveness of regulatory options or is it only authorized to take into account whether a regulatory option is too expensive for industry to afford? See NRDC v. EPA, 749 F.3d 1055, 1060-61 (D.C. Cir. 2014).

Sinden, In Defense of Absolutes: Combating the Politics of Power in Environmental Law, 90 Iowa L. Rev. 1405 (2005), refers to "absolute" (or cost-blind) standards as those that are gauged only to the protection of human health or the environment and that prohibit any consideration of economic costs, such as the CAA's NAAQS. She claims that such standards, by treating environmental interests as trumps that override cost considerations except in extraordinary circumstances, perform a crucial "power-shifting function" by helping to counteract the power imbalance between diffuse citizen interests and moneyed corporate interests that tend to distort agency decisions on environmental issues.

2. *The Benefits of Ozone Pollution.* Can ozone pollution be good for public health and the environment? That issue was raised in a portion of the D.C. Circuit's decision in *American Trucking* that was not appealed to the Supreme Court. Industry argued that, in setting the primary NAAQS for ozone, EPA improperly ignored the health benefits of tropospheric ozone in acting as a shield from the harmful effects of the sun's ultraviolet rays, including cataracts and skin cancers. The court explained why EPA disregarded any such benefits:

> EPA explained its decision first as a matter of statutory interpretation. Under the Clean Air Act, EPA's ambient standards for any pollutant are to be "based on [the] criteria" that EPA has published for that pollutant. 42 U.S.C. §7409(b)(1) & (2). The "criteria," in turn, are to "reflect the latest scientific knowledge useful in indicating the kind and extent of all identifiable effects on public health or welfare which may be expected from the presence of such pollutant in the ambient air, in varying quantities." Id. §7408(a)(2). The reference to "all identifiable effects" would seem on its face to include beneficent effects.
>
> EPA attempts to avoid this straightforward reading in several ways. First, it points to the term "such pollutant," arguing that the statute requires it to focus exclusively on the characteristics that make the substance a "pollutant." But the phrase "pollutant" is simply a label used to identify a substance to be listed and controlled by the statute. While it is perfectly true that a substance known to be utterly without adverse effects could not make it onto the list, this fact of nomenclature does not visibly manifest a congressional intent to banish consideration of whole classes of "identifiable effects."
>
> EPA also relies on the fact that two of the three specified considerations under §108(a)(2)'s general mandate refer to "adverse effect[s]." . . . EPA's argument would be of uncertain force even if all three types of effects specifically required to be considered were spoken of as "adverse effects"; there is no reason to read "adverse" back into the "all identifiable effects" of §108(a)(2). But as one of the three specified classes refers to "effects" unmodified, id. §7408(a)(2)(A), we can reject EPA's argument without even reaching that issue. That Congress qualified "effects" in clauses (B) and (C) with "adverse" seems only to strengthen the supposition that in (A)—and in the general mandate—it intended to cover all health or welfare effects. Therefore if petitioners' contentions are right, clause (A) applies to ozone: the presence of ultraviolet radiation at various levels "alter[s] the effects [of ozone] on public health or welfare" by making them on the whole less malign—perhaps even beneficial.
>
> EPA next argues that Title VI of the Clean Air Act, id. §§7671-7671q, which mandates certain measures to preserve stratospheric ozone, represents a complete consideration of ozone's beneficial role as a UV shield. Petitioners' claim, however, is that ground-level (tropospheric) ozone—the subject of this rule—has a UV-screening

function independent of the ozone higher in the atmosphere. EPA points to nothing in the statute that purports to address tropospheric ozone.

[The court concluded that the statute is not ambiguous, but even if it were, EPA's interpretation of it would be unreasonable.] [I]t seems bizarre that a statute intended to improve human health would, as EPA claimed at argument, lock the agency into looking at only one-half of a substance's health effects in determining the maximum level for that substance [such as in this case, where ozone "evidently impedes breathing but provides defense against various cancers."].

Legally, then, EPA must consider positive identifiable effects of a pollutant's presence in the ambient air in formulating air quality criteria under §108 and NAAQS under §109. . . . [American Trucking Ass'ns, Inc. v. EPA, 175 F.3d 1027, 1051-1052 (D.C. Cir. 1999).]

On remand, EPA concluded that the alleged health benefits of ground-level ozone in reducing exposure to ultraviolet radiation are too uncertain to justify any relaxation in the ozone NAAQS. 67 Fed. Reg. 614 (2003).

3. *The Nondelegation Issue.* What is the source of the nondelegation doctrine? What intelligible principle did the Court discern in §109(b)(1)? How does the scope of the regulatory program bear on application of the nondelegation doctrine? For another environmental law case implicating the nondelegation doctrine, see the *Industrial Union Dep't* case, excerpted in Chapter 8, section D.2. For discussion of the relationship between cost-benefit analysis and the nondelegation doctrine, see Flatt, The "Benefits" of Non-Delegation: Using the Non-Delegation Doctrine to Bring More Rigor to Cost-Benefit Analysis, 15 Wm. & Mary Bill Rts. J. 1087 (2007).

4. *Risk-Based and Precautionary Regulation.* In the *Lead Industries Ass'n* case, industry argued that Congress intended that the NAAQS protect the public health only against effects known to be "clearly harmful to health" as a means to ensure that EPA would not adopt excessively stringent standards. The court disagreed that EPA's authority was limited in that manner, emphasizing "the preventive or precautionary nature" of the CAA's mandate to establish ambient quality standards.

It may be . . . LIA's view that the Administrator must show that there is a "medical consensus that (the effects on which the standards were based) are harmful." . . . If so, LIA is seriously mistaken. This court has previously noted that some uncertainty about the health effects of air pollution is inevitable. And we pointed out that "[a]waiting certainty will often allow for only reactive, not preventive regulat[ory action]." Ethyl Corp. v. EPA, [541 F.2d 1, 25 (D.C. Cir. 1976)]. Congress apparently shares this view; it specifically directed the Administrator to allow an adequate margin of safety to protect against effects which have not yet been uncovered by research and effects whose medical significance is a matter of disagreement. . . . Congress' directive to the Administrator to allow an "adequate margin of safety" alone plainly refutes any suggestion that the Administrator is only authorized to set primary air quality standards which are designed to protect against health effects that are known to be clearly harmful.

Furthermore, we agree with the Administrator that requiring EPA to wait until it can conclusively demonstrate that a particular effect is adverse to health before it acts is inconsistent with both the Act's precautionary and preventive orientation and the nature of the Administrator's statutory responsibilities. Congress provided that the Administrator is to use his judgment in setting air quality standards precisely to permit him to act in the face of uncertainty. And as we read the statutory provisions and the legislative history, Congress directed the Administrator to err on the side of caution in making the necessary decisions. We see no reason why this court should put a gloss on Congress' scheme by requiring the Administrator to show that there is a medical consensus that the effects on which the lead standards were based are "clearly harmful to health." All that is required by the statutory scheme is evidence in the record which substantiates his conclusions about the health effects on which the standards were based. Accordingly, we reject LIA's claim that the Administrator exceeded his statutory authority. . . . [647 F.2d at 1154-1157.]

In effect, then, the court concluded that Congress intended to vest EPA with the authority to protect the public "against effects that research has not yet uncovered" (i.e., against risk).

The precautionary approach to regulation was fully articulated in two landmark decisions, Reserve Mining Co. v. EPA, 514 F.2d 492 (8th Cir. 1975), and Ethyl Corp. v. EPA, 541 F.2d 1 (D.C. Cir. 1976), which are discussed further in Chapter 8. These opinions posit that whenever a statute instructs a regulator to protect the public from exposure to the danger (risk) of possible harm, as opposed to harm certain to occur unless exposure is prevented, Congress intended for the regulator to weigh subjectively the magnitude of the harm (if it did occur) against the probability that it will occur at all and then decide what regulatory action is warranted in light of the seriousness of the risk presented. In Ethyl Corp., the court upheld EPA's adoption of standards under §211(c)(1)(A) of the CAA that phased out the use of lead in gasoline. The statute authorized EPA to regulate the lead content if it determined that emissions "will endanger" public health, without providing any guidance on how strict the standard had to be. Similarly, Lead Industries reveals that the precautionary standard in §109 gives EPA great leeway to set standards despite scientific uncertainty. See also American Petroleum Inst. v. EPA, 684 F.3d 1342, 1353 (D.C. Cir. 2012) (relying on EPA's "duty to err on the side of caution" to uphold new primary NAAQS for NO_2). But cf. Center for Biological Diversity v. EPA, 749 F.3d 1079, 1090 (D.C. Cir. 2014) ("[The CAA's] preference for preventive—and thus potentially speculative—regulation is not absolute. . . . [N]ew rules must be based on reasoned judgment. Reasoned judgment may at times permit—and the Act may at times require—action in the face of uncertainty, lest 'the precautionary purpose of the statute' be undermined. Ethyl Corp., 541 F.2d at 28. But, at some point, action infected by enough uncertainty cannot be called reasoned. Distinguishing among these degrees is emphatically the province of EPA.").

5. Peer Review of the NAAQS. The 1977 CAA amendments established the Clean Air Scientific Advisory Committee (CASAC), a seven-member independent advisory committee authorized to review ambient standards and criteria documents every five years. CASAC must publicly review any proposed EPA standard under §109, 111, or 112. §109(d)(2). According to one court, "Congress intended that CASAC's expert scientific analysis aid not only EPA in promulgating NAAQS but also the courts in reviewing EPA's decision." Mississippi v. EPA, 744 F.3d 1344, 1355 (D.C. Cir. 2013). Nevertheless, as indicated below, the court in Mississippi upheld EPA's 2008 primary NAAQS for ozone even though EPA set the standard above the range recommended by CASAC.

6. Unanswered Questions. The Court in American Trucking remanded the case to the Court of Appeals. In the following decision, the D.C. Circuit addressed claims by industry and a group of states that the particulate matter and ozone standards were arbitrary and capricious.

AMERICAN TRUCKING ASSOCIATIONS, INC. v. EPA
283 F.3d 355 (D.C. Cir. 2002)

TATEL, Circuit Judge: . . .

III . . .

State and Business Petitioners urge us to vacate the primary NAAQS [for PM$_{2.5}$] because EPA "did not apply *any* legal standard, much less the correct standard." . . . Petitioners claim [that] EPA asserted that it had no obligation to determine a "safe level" of PM$_{2.5}$ prior to adopting a primary NAAQS. . . . As Petitioners see it, [this "concession" proves] that EPA failed to set the primary NAAQS at levels " 'requisite' — that is, not lower or higher than . . . necessary — to protect the public health with an adequate margin of safety," as mandated by *Whitman*, 531 U.S. at 475-76.

Petitioners' argument suffers from two significant flaws. First, the final PM rule makes neither alleged concession. In the first passage, which Petitioners cite as evidence that EPA failed to identify a "safe level" of PM$_{2.5}$, the Agency merely disclaimed any obligation to set primary NAAQS by means of a two-step process, identifying a "safe level" and then applying an additional margin of safety. Instead, EPA stated, it "may take into account margin of safety considerations throughout the process as long as such considerations are fully explained and supported by the record." Nothing in this statement implies that EPA failed to determine "safe levels" for fine particulate matter; indeed, the Agency's establishment of new primary NAAQS demonstrates that it did reach a conclusion regarding "safe" daily and annual-average PM$_{2.5}$ levels. . . .

Petitioners' argument that EPA neither identified nor applied the proper legal standard also exaggerates the Agency's obligation to quantify its decisionmaking. The argument relies on two statements from the rulemaking and one from [the D.C. Circuit's initial decision in *American Trucking* (ATA I)]: EPA's assertion that it need not "determine a 'safe level' " of PM$_{2.5}$ before calculating a margin of safety; the Agency's "disavow[al]" of certain "specific risk estimates"; and finally, the Agency's claim that "there is no threshold 'amount of scientific information or degree of certainty' required to promulgate or revise a NAAQS." [The court rejected the Petitioners' contention that American Lung Ass'n v. EPA, 134 F.3d 388 (D.C. Cir. 1998), requires EPA "to identify perfectly safe levels of pollutants, to rely on specific risk estimates, or to specify threshold amounts of scientific information."]

Although we recognize that the Clean Air Act and circuit precedent require EPA qualitatively to describe the standard governing its selection of particular NAAQS, we have expressly rejected the notion that the Agency must "establish a measure of the risk to safety it considers adequate to protect public health every time it establishes a [NAAQS]." NRDC v. EPA, 902 F.2d 962, 973 (D.C. Cir. 1990), *vacated in part*, 921 F.2d 326 (D.C. Cir. 1991). Such a rule would compel EPA to leave hazardous pollutants unregulated unless and until it completely understands every risk they pose, thus thwarting the Clean Air Act's requirement that the Agency err on the side of caution by setting primary NAAQS that "allow[] an adequate margin of safety[.]" 42 U.S.C. §7409(b)(1). The Act requires EPA to promulgate protective primary NAAQS even where, as here, the pollutant's risks cannot be quantified or "precisely identified as to nature or degree," 62 Fed. Reg. at 38,653. For its part, *American Lung Ass'n* requires only that EPA "engage in reasoned decision-making," not that it definitively identify pollutant levels below which risks to public health are negligible.

Thus, EPA's inability to guarantee the accuracy or increase the precision of the $PM_{2.5}$ NAAQS in no way undermines the standards' validity. Rather, these limitations indicate only that significant scientific uncertainty remains about the health effects of fine particulate matter at low atmospheric concentrations. As the exhaustive rulemaking process makes clear, EPA set the primary NAAQS notwithstanding that uncertainty, just as the Act requires.

We are equally unpersuaded by State and Business Petitioners' argument that EPA should have considered whether reducing atmospheric concentrations of fine particles would increase levels of "'ozone or . . . a different fine particle component,' potentially *increasing* [overall] health risk[s]." 61 Fed. Reg. at 65,768. Petitioners apparently believe EPA may not regulate one pollutant without determining how that regulation would affect the levels of all other pollutants with which the first could react. Given the complexity of atmospheric chemistry, however, imposing such a requirement would hamstring the Agency, preventing it from complying with the Clean Air Act's mandate to set protective primary NAAQS. We might feel differently about EPA's obligations in this regard had Petitioners pointed to clear evidence that lowering atmospheric $PM_{2.5}$ levels will necessarily increase levels of other pollutants. Petitioners cite no such evidence, however. . . .

IV . . .

American Trucking Associations and the other Ozone Petitioners challenge the NAAQS [for ozone] along several lines. To begin with, just as State and Business Petitioners argued with respect to the NAAQS for particulate matter, Ozone Petitioners contend that EPA neither identified nor applied "*any* legal standard" in setting the ozone NAAQS. . . . [The court rejected that argument for the same reasons as it rejected the attack on the $PM_{2.5}$ standard.]

Petitioners raise two specific arguments regarding the primary ozone NAAQS. First, they assert that EPA "failed to determine whether attainment of the [old, one-hour-average, primary ozone] standard would leave unacceptable public health risk," and relatedly, that "none of the alternative [eight]-hour standards [considered by EPA] is significantly more protective of the public health than the [old] [one]-hour NAAQS." We disagree. As noted earlier, not only is the record replete with references to studies demonstrating the inadequacies of the old one-hour standard, but EPA discussed at length the advantages of a longer averaging time, including reduced risk of prolonged exposures to unhealthy ozone levels and increased uniformity of protection across different urban areas. Moreover, EPA specifically cited CASAC's "consensus . . . that an [eight]-hour standard [is] more appropriate for a human health-based standard than a [one]-hour standard" and its recommendation that "the present . . . standard be eliminated and replaced with an [eight]-hour standard." Given this record evidence, our deferential standard of review, and the Clean Air Act's requirement that EPA must either follow CASAC's advice or explain why the proposed rule "differs . . . from . . . [CASAC's] recommendations," 42 U.S.C. §7607(d)(3), Petitioners cannot seriously expect us to second-guess EPA's conclusion regarding the inadequacy of the old, one-hour-average standard.

Though somewhat more persuasive, Petitioners' second specific challenge also falls short. They argue that in selecting a level of 0.08 ppm rather than 0.09 or 0.07, EPA reached "inconsistent conclusions regarding specific health risks," thus "demonstrat[ing] that [the Agency's] decision to revise the NAAQS lacks a rational basis and therefore is arbitrary and capricious." In support of this point, Petitioners challenge EPA's three justifications for selecting 0.08 rather than 0.07: that no CASAC member supported a standard below 0.08; that health effects at ozone levels below 0.08 are transient and reversible; and that 0.07 would be too close to peak background levels. As to the first point, Petitioners observe that "most members of the CASAC panel who expressed an opinion on standard level supported a level *above* . . . 0.08 ppm." . . . In addition, Petitioners point out, *ATA I* expressly discredits the contention that ozone health effects are more transient and reversible at concentrations below 0.08 ppm than at concentrations between 0.08 and 0.09. 175 F.3d at 1035 (. . . "it is far from apparent that any health effects existing above [0.08 ppm] are permanent or irreversible"). Petitioners finally note that proximity to peak background levels is an indeterminate standard that points to no particular level for the primary NAAQS.

Although we think Petitioners' individual criticisms have some force, we are satisfied that in selecting a level of 0.08 rather than 0.07 (or, for that matter, 0.09), EPA "engage[d] in reasoned decision-making." *American Lung Ass'n*, 134 F.3d at 392. For one thing, CASAC's inability to reach consensus is hardly dispositive; EPA is entitled to give "significant weight" to the fact that no committee member advocated a level of 0.07 ppm, particularly as eight of the ten panel members who expressed opinions advocated a level of 0.08 ppm or greater, while the remaining two simply "endorsed the [0.07-0.09 ppm] range presented by the Agency . . . and stated that the [final] selection should be a policy decision." Also, although relative proximity to peak background ozone concentrations did not, in itself, necessitate a level of 0.08, EPA could consider that factor when choosing among the three alternative levels. Most convincing, though, is the absence of *any* human clinical studies at ozone concentrations below 0.08. This lack of data amply supports EPA's assertion that the most serious health effects of ozone are "less certain" at low concentrations, providing an eminently rational reason to set the primary standard at a somewhat higher level, at least until additional studies become available. Overall, therefore, we disagree with Petitioners that in selecting 0.08 ppm rather than a lower or higher level, EPA reached "inconsistent conclusions." The Agency could reasonably conclude that existing data support a standard below 0.09 but do not yet justify a standard below 0.08.

This brings us, finally, to Petitioners' challenges to the secondary ozone NAAQS. According to Petitioners, the secondary NAAQS are unlawful because EPA failed to account for factors other than ozone—including "temperature, rainfall, and pests"—that affect crop-yield. This is unreasonable. EPA had no more obligation to consider climatic conditions and pests in "evaluat[ing] whether its new [secondary] standard would measurably improve crop yield," than to consider automobile accidents and malnutrition in evaluating whether its new primary standard would measurably improve public health. The Clean Air Act directs EPA to protect public welfare from adverse effects of ozone and other pollutants; the Agency cannot escape that directive simply because ozone wreaks less havoc than temperature, rainfall, and pests. . . .

NOTES AND QUESTIONS

1. *The PM$_{2.5}$ Standard.* To what extent is EPA required to quantify the level of exposure to a criteria pollutant that is "safe"? What would such a quantification requirement mean in the context of efforts to regulate non-threshold pollutants? Does the statute mandate that EPA tack on the required "margin of safety" in any particular fashion? The D.C. Circuit decided in *Lead Indus. Ass'n* that the CAA does not require that EPA add on one margin of safety at the end of its effort to ascertain the "requisite" level of public health protection, instead of building multiple margins of safety into the standards at various points of analysis.

In 2006, EPA revised the NAAQS for PM, lowering the primary standard for PM$_{2.5}$ from 65 to 35 $\mu g/m^3$ averaged over 24 hours. It rejected the recommendation of CASAC, however, that it adopt even more stringent standards. It refused to tighten the standard for PM$_{2.5}$ averaged on an annual basis (which remained at 15 $\mu g/m^3$, but which CASAC recommended be reduced to 13 or 14 $\mu g/m^3$) or the short-term standard for PM$_{10}$. It also revoked the annual standard for coarse particles. EPA set the secondary PM standards equal in all respects to the primary standards. 71 Fed. Reg. 61,144 (Oct. 17, 2006). In 2013, EPA again revised the PM NAAQS. It lowered the annual primary PM$_{2.5}$ standard to 12.0 μ/m^3 but retained the 24-hour standard for PM$_{2.5}$, the 24-hour PM$_{10}$ primary standard, and the secondary standards for both PM$_{2.5}$ and PM$_{10}$. 78 Fed. Reg. 3086 (Jan. 15, 2013). National Ass'n of Mfrs. v. EPA, 750 F.3d 921 (D.C. Cir. 2014), upheld the standard. Among other things, the court accepted EPA's rationale for lowering the level to somewhat below the lowest long-term mean concentration shown by epidemiological studies to cause adverse health effects. It also rejected an attack on EPA's decision to eliminate spatial averaging to measure compliance because such averaging would allow areas in which sensitive individuals are likely to live to exceed the NAAQS for periods of time.

2. *The Ozone Standard.* How did EPA justify selection of a level of 0.08 ppm rather than 0.07 or 0.09? Why did the court reject Petitioners' attack on the secondary NAAQS for ozone? In 2008, EPA revised the ozone NAAQS again. 73 Fed. Reg. 16,437 (Mar. 27, 2008). EPA set the level of the 8-hour standard at 0.075 ppm and made the secondary standard identical to the primary standard. CASAC had recommended a more stringent primary standard. Mississippi v. EPA, 744 F.3d 1334 (D.C. Cir. 2013), largely upheld those revisions. The court rejected arguments by some states and industry that the primary standard was too stringent (not "requisite" to protect the public health), deferring to EPA's interpretation of the scientific evidence in the record and to the policy judgments EPA made in light of that evidence. It also rejected the claim by a different group of states and environmental groups that the primary standard was not stringent enough. The court concluded that the primary standard included the required adequate margin of safety, and that EPA adequately explained its decision not to follow CASAC's recommendation that EPA adopt a primary standard between 0.60 and 0.70 ppm. The court found it impossible to determine whether CASAC's recommendation rested on a scientific conclusion or on public health policy considerations. EPA's policy judgments are entitled to judicial deference, even if they differ from CASAC's. The court remanded (without vacating) EPA's decision to set the secondary standard equal to the primary standard, however. Relying on American Farm Bureau Fed'n v. EPA, 559 F.3d 512 (D.C. Cir. 2009), the court held that it was insufficient for EPA merely to compare the level of protection afforded by the primary standard to a possible

seasonal secondary standard and find the two roughly equivalent. Rather, EPA was required (but failed) to specify why the secondary standard it chose as the basis for this comparison was "requisite to protect the public welfare." The primary standard offered less protection than other seasonal levels within the range recommended by CASAC and EPA staff. EPA should have explained why it looked at only one potential seasonal secondary standard.

   3. *Judicial Consideration of Other NAAQS Decisions.* In 1996, EPA decided not to revise the annual and 24-hour primary standards for SO_2. It admitted that a substantial portion (at least 20 percent) of mild to moderate asthmatics were being exposed to SO_2 concentrations that could be expected to cause adverse respiratory symptoms, and that repeated occurrences of such effects should be regarded as a significant health issue. But the agency also concluded that the problem was not a "broad public health problem when viewed from a national perspective." Rather, the localized, infrequent, and site-specific risks involved would be better addressed at the state level. Instead of revising the NAAQS, therefore, EPA announced that it would rely largely on state control of short-term peak SO_2 levels. If a state had reason to believe that ambient levels of SO_2 may constitute an imminent and substantial endangerment, it could consider taking immediate action to protect the public health. EPA reserved the right to act in the event the state failed to address an imminent and substantial endangerment or if EPA had evidence that SO_2 levels caused an endangerment due to their frequency, magnitude, and reported health impacts.

   Is this approach to public health protection authorized by §109? By any other provision of the CAA? See §303. Consider American Lung Ass'n v. EPA, 134 F.3d 388 (D.C. Cir. 1998), which remanded this EPA decision not to revise the primary SO_2 standard to control exposure to high-level SO_2 bursts of five or more minutes for lack of an adequate explanation. The Administrator concluded that no national public health problem had been identified because the bursts were infrequent and site-specific. The bursts affect asthmatics, who are subject to bronchoconstriction, but the effects range from short-term discomfort to rare instances of death when individuals are exposed to SO_2 concentrations below 1.0 ppm while they are engaged in strenuous activity. The medical community was split regarding the medical significance of the effects, and research studies on the number of asthmatics who suffer stress from repeated bursts were inconclusive:

   . . . [W]e think the Administrator has failed to explain [her conclusion] that SO_2 bursts do not amount to a "public health" problem within the meaning of the Act. The link between this conclusion and the factual record as interpreted by EPA—that "repeated" exposure is "significant" and that thousands of asthmatics are exposed more than once a year—is missing. Why is the fact that thousands of asthmatics can be expected to suffer atypical physical effects from repeated five-minute bursts of high-level sulfur dioxide not a public health problem? Why are from 180,000 to 395,000 annual "exposure events" . . . so "infrequent" as to warrant no regulatory action? Why are disruptions of ongoing activities, use of medication, and hospitalization not "adverse health effects" for asthmatics? Answers to these questions appear nowhere in the administrative record.

      In her only statement resembling an explanation for her conclusion that peak SO_2 bursts present no public health hazard, the Administrator characterizes the bursts as "localized, infrequent and site-specific." But nothing in the Final Decision explains away the possibility that "localized," "site-specific" or even "infrequent" events might nevertheless create a public health problem. . . . [Id. at 392.]

Given the lack of scientific consensus and the fact that most adverse effects of SO_2 bursts appear to be reversible, was it not reasonable for EPA to defer the setting of a more stringent standard until further research resolved some of the uncertainties? Suppose the agency had found that SO_2 bursts caused adverse health effects for asthmatics. Would it have been required to amend the NAAQS? How does the "margin of safety" requirement of §109(b)(1) bear on this question? Based on *Battery Recyclers*, excerpted at the beginning of this section, is EPA obliged to protect sensitive individuals? In another portion of the opinion, the court stated that

> Congress defined the public health broadly. NAAQS must protect not only average healthy individuals, but also "sensitive citizens"—children, for example, or people with asthma, emphysema, or other conditions rendering them particularly vulnerable to air pollution. If a pollutant adversely affects the health of these sensitive individuals, EPA must strengthen the entire national standard. [Id. at 389.]

In National Envtl. Dev. Ass'n's Clean Air Project v. EPA, 686 F.3d 803 (D.C. Cir. 2012), the court upheld EPA's regulations on remand from *American Lung Ass'n*, which were the first set of SO_2 NAAQS revisions since 1971, and which were intended to prevent asthmatics from being exposed to short-term bursts of SO_2 capable of impairing lung function. The court held that EPA has discretion to set a NAAQS at a concentration below a level demonstrated to have a statistically significant association with negative health effects. The evidence showed that current levels of SO_2 caused respiratory effects in some areas that met the preexisting NAAQS.

EPA has fared better in defending its decisions not to amend other NAAQS. See Center for Biological Diversity v. EPA, 749 F.3d 1079 (D.C. Cir. 2014) (upholding EPA's decision to retain current NO_2 and SO_2 secondary standards protecting against the direct effects on vegetation resulting from exposure to these pollutants, and deferring to EPA's conclusion that uncertainties made it impossible to gauge the degree of protection that would be afforded by a multi-pollutant standard to protect against adverse deposition-related effects associated with these pollutants on sensitive aquatic and terrestrial ecosystems); Communities for a Better Env't v. EPA, 748 F.3d 333 (D.C. Cir. 2014) (upholding EPA decision not to amend CO NAAQS).

4. *More on Cost Considerations.* The D.C. Circuit in *American Trucking* cited NRDC v. EPA, 902 F.2d 962 (D.C. Cir. 1990), which rejected a challenge by the American Iron & Steel Institute (AISI) to EPA's 24-hour and annual primary standards for SO_2. Among other things, AISI argued that EPA violated §109(b)(1) by failing to consider the adverse consequences to the public health that would result from the unemployment attributable to efforts to comply with the standard. But the court found the argument to be meritless. "Consideration of costs associated with alleged health risks from unemployment would be flatly inconsistent with the statute, legislative history, and case law on this point." Id. at 973.

2. Achievement of the NAAQS Through State Implementation Plans

The CAA makes the states primarily responsible for ensuring adequate air quality within their geographic areas. Each state must submit for EPA approval a state implementation plan (SIP) that specifies the manner in which the NAAQS will be achieved and maintained within each air quality control region (AQCR) within the state. §107(a). This section describes how states designate AQCRs and develop, submit for EPA approval, and revise their SIPs.

a. Designation of Air Quality Control Regions

Although different problems face "clean-air" and "dirty-air" areas, the 1970 Act made no distinction among types of AQCR based on the severity of air pollution. The 1977 amendments divided the country into nonattainment areas, where the NAAQS have not been met, and attainment areas (also known as clean-air or nondegradation or PSD areas), where the quality of the air is better than the ambient standards require. Sections F and G below elaborate on the different control strategies for these two types of regions and describe how the broad discretion initially vested in the states to achieve the NAAQS has been circumscribed by the provisions of the 1977 and 1990 amendments that govern nonattainment or PSD areas. For now, the essential point is that each state is responsible for meeting the ambient standards for its AQCRs, and the SIPs detail the means the state will use to do so.

The Act requires that, within one year of issuance or revision of a NAAQS, each state submit to EPA a list of AQCRs within the state divided into three categories: nonattainment, attainment, and unclassifiable. §107(d)(1)(A). EPA must review these submissions and approve them (with whatever modifications EPA deems necessary) within two years of issuance or revision of the NAAQS. §107(d)(1)(B). In determining whether to modify a state's choice of boundary lines for AQCRs, EPA tends to defer to the governor's recommendations. See, e.g., Pennsylvania v. EPA, 429 F.3d 1125 (D.C. Cir. 2005). EPA may also initiate the process of redesignation on the basis of planning or air quality–related considerations. §107(d)(3). EPA has advised the states to take nine factors into account in making AQCR designations: (1) emission data, (2) air quality data, (3) population density and degree of urbanization, (4) traffic and commuting patterns, (5) growth rates and patterns, (6) meteorology, (7) geography/topography (e.g., mountain ranges and other air basin boundaries), (8) jurisdictional boundaries, and (9) level of control of emission sources. The factors are neither mandatory nor an exclusive list of the types of relevant information. ATK Launch Sys., Inc. v. EPA, 669 F.3d 330, 334 (D.C. Cir. 2012).

The category into which an AQCR falls is important because the controls that apply to air pollution sources within the area, the nature of the state's obligations in formulating its SIP, and the sanctions available to the government for noncompliance with the NAAQS all differ depending on the status of an AQCR. The extent to which new stationary sources must apply for a construction and operating permit, for example, differs between nonattainment and attainment areas, as do the substantive criteria for permit issuance. Some states have tried to upgrade from nonattainment to attainment status to avoid the constraints and sanctions that apply only to the former. Ohio v. Ruckelshaus, 776 F.2d 1333 (6th Cir. 1985), upheld EPA's refusal to allow the state to carve out and redesignate as an ozone attainment area an upwind county that was part of the Cleveland nonattainment area. The state argued that the county qualified as an attainment area because air quality monitoring data indicated that the NAAQS was being achieved there. At the time, §171(2) of the statute defined a nonattainment area as "an area which is shown by monitored data or which is calculated by air quality modeling ... to exceed any [NAAQS] for such pollutant."

EPA refused the state's request for redesignation because nearly 20 percent of ozone precursors in Cleveland, where the ozone NAAQS was not being achieved, originated in the upwind county. How would this case be decided under the current statute? See §§171(2), 107(d)(1), (3)(E), (4)(A)(iv)-(v). Cf. Montana Sulphur & Chem. Co. v. EPA, 666 F.3d 1174, 1185 (9th Cir. 2012) (concluding that the 1990 amendments were not meant to eliminate the use of modeling or statistical extrapolation in requiring states to remedy inadequate SIPs).

Section 107(d)(3)(E) sets forth the requirements for redesignation of an AQCR. These include the approval of a maintenance plan for the area that complies with §175A. The plan must provide for the maintenance of the NAAQS for at least ten years after the redesignation and contain "such additional measures, if any, as may be necessary to ensure such maintenance." §175A(a). A state seeking redesignation also must submit a SIP revision that contains contingency measures, including a requirement that the state implement all control measures contained in the SIP for the area before its redesignation as attainment. §175A(d). How specific must the description of the contingency measures in the maintenance plan be? See Sierra Club v. EPA, 375 F.3d 537 (7th Cir. 2004).

b.   Formulation, Approval, and Revision of SIPs

Section 110(a)(1) requires each state to adopt and submit a SIP to EPA within three years (or any shorter period prescribed by EPA) of EPA's issuance of the NAAQS. SIPs must contain "enforceable emission limitations and other control measures, means, or techniques . . . as may be necessary or appropriate" to meet and maintain the NAAQS. §110(a)(2)(A). Although SIPs and SIP revisions do not take effect as federal law until EPA approves them, §110(k)(3), the Supreme Court made it clear early on that Congress meant to leave the choice of emissions limitations for existing air pollution sources to the states, as long as the combination of measures selected was sufficient to achieve compliance with the NAAQS:

> The Act gives . . . [EPA] no authority to question the wisdom of a State's choices of emissions limitations if they are part of a plan which satisfies the standards of §110(a)(2). . . . Thus, so long as the ultimate effect of a State's choice of emission limitations is compliance with the national standards for ambient air, the state is at liberty to adopt whatever mix of emission limitations it deems best suited to its particular situation. [Train v. NRDC, Inc., 421 U.S. 60, 79 (1975).]

The following case, decided a year later, confirms this initial understanding of the relationship between federal and state authority to craft an emission control strategy and also addresses the scope of state discretion to push harder than the statute requires in controlling emissions. The failure of some states to comply with the NAAQS induced Congress in both the 1977 and 1990 amendments to remove some of the states' discretion. As you study the CAA, take note of how the statute and EPA's implementation of it strike a balance between expeditious pursuit of acceptable air quality and a distaste for intruding too heavily on state prerogatives or on the ability of individuals to choose how, when, and where they may drive their cars and trucks. Note that in the much-cited case that follows, several of the §110 references are to subsections that have now been changed or moved in the current Act. Nevertheless, because the Act's basic structure and allocations of authority are still the same, the case remains of great importance to actions under the 1990 CAA.

UNION ELECTRIC COMPANY v. EPA
427 U.S. 246 (1976)

Mr. Justice Marshall delivered the opinion of the Court.

[After the expiration of variances issued by Missouri to Union Electric for three of its coal-fired generating plants, EPA notified the company that its SO_2 emissions violated the state's SIP. Section 307(b)(1) allowed petitions for review of EPA's approval of a SIP to be filed in the federal courts of appeals more than 30 days after such approval only if the petition was "based solely on grounds arising after such 30th day." Union Electric claimed in a petition to the Eighth Circuit that economic and technological difficulties that had arisen more than 30 days after EPA's approval made compliance with the emission limitations impossible and hence could be challenged long after those 30 days. The Eighth Circuit held that it lacked jurisdiction because only matters that would justify setting aside EPA's initial approval of a SIP are properly reviewable after the initial 30-day review period. Because EPA lacked the power to reject a SIP based on claims of economic and technological infeasibility, such claims could not serve at any time as the basis for a court's overturning an approved plan.]

I

[T]he Clean Air Amendments of 1970 . . . reflect congressional dissatisfaction with the progress of existing air pollution programs and a determination to "tak[e] a stick to the States," [Train v. NRDC, Inc., 421 U.S. 60, 64 (1975)], in order to guarantee the prompt attainment and maintenance of specified air quality standards. The heart of the Amendments is the requirement that each State formulate, subject to EPA approval, an implementation plan designed to achieve national primary ambient air quality standards—those necessary to protect the public health—"as expeditiously as practicable but . . . in no case later than three years from the date of approval of such plan." §110(a)(2)(A). The plan must also provide for the attainment of national secondary ambient air quality standards—those necessary to protect the public welfare—within a "reasonable time." Each State is given wide discretion in formulating its plan, and the Act provides that the Administrator "shall approve" the proposed plan if it has been adopted after public notice and hearing and if it meets eight specified criteria. §110(a)(2). . . .

II

[The Court held that if "new grounds" are alleged for an appeal more than 30 days after the approval or promulgation of a SIP, "they must be such that, had they been known at the time the plan was presented to the Administrator for approval, it would have been an abuse of discretion for the Administrator to approve the plan."]

Since a reviewing court—regardless of when the petition for review is filed—may consider claims of economic and technological infeasibility only if the Administrator may consider such claims in approving or rejecting a state implementation plan, we must address ourselves to the scope of the Administrator's responsibility. The Administrator's position is that he has no power whatsoever to reject a state implementation plan on the ground that it is economically or technologically infeasible. . . . [W]e agree that Congress intended claims of economic and technological infeasibility to be wholly foreign to the Administrator's consideration of a state implementation plan.

As we have previously recognized, the 1970 Amendments to the Clean Air Act were a drastic remedy to what was perceived as a serious and otherwise uncheckable problem of air pollution. The Amendments place the primary responsibility for formulating pollution control strategies on the States, but nonetheless subject the States to strict minimum compliance requirements. These requirements are of a "technology-forcing character," and are expressly designed to force regulated sources to develop pollution control devices that might at the time appear to be economically or technologically infeasible.

This approach is apparent on the face of §110(a)(2). The provision sets out eight criteria that an implementation plan must satisfy, and provides that if these criteria are met, . . . the Administrator "shall approve" the proposed state plan. The mandatory "shall" makes it quite clear that the Administrator is not to be concerned with factors other than those specified, and none of the eight factors appears to permit consideration of technological or economic infeasibility.[5] . . .

It is suggested that consideration of claims of technological and economic infeasibility is required by the first criterion that the primary air quality standards be met "as expeditiously as practicable but . . . in no case later than three years" . . . and that the secondary air quality standards be met within a "reasonable time." §110(a)(2)(A). The argument is that what is "practicable" or "reasonable" cannot be determined without assessing whether what is proposed is possible. This argument does not survive analysis.

Section 110(a)(2)(A)'s three-year deadline for achieving primary air quality standards . . . leaves no room for claims of technological or economic infeasibility. The 1970 congressional debate . . . centered on whether technology forcing was necessary and desirable in framing and attaining air quality standards sufficient to protect the public health, standards later termed primary standards. . . . The Senate bill . . . flatly required that, possible or not, health-related standards be met "within three years."

The Senate's stiff requirement was intended to foreclose the claims of emission sources that it would be economically or technologically infeasible for them to achieve emission limitations sufficient to protect the public health within the specified time. As Senator Muskie, manager of the Senate bill, explained to his chamber:

The first responsibility of Congress is not the making of technological or economic judgments or even to be limited by what is or appears to be technologically or

5. Comparison of the eight criteria of §110(a)(2) with other provisions of the [Act] bolsters this conclusion. Where Congress intended the Administrator to be concerned about economic and technological infeasibility, it expressly so provided. Thus, §§110(a), 110(f), 111(a)(1), 202(a), 211(c)(2)(A), and 231(b) of the Amendments all expressly permit consideration [of the cost of compliance]. Section 110(a)(2) contains no such language.

economically feasible. Our responsibility is to establish what the public interest requires to protect the health of persons. This may mean that people and industries will be asked to do what seems to be impossible at the present time. [116 Cong. Rec. 32901-32902 (1970).]

This position reflected that of the Senate committee:

In the Committee discussions, considerable concern was expressed regarding the use of the concept of technical feasibility as the basis of ambient air standards. The Committee determined that 1) the health of people is more important than the question of whether the early achievement of ambient air quality standards protective of health is technically feasible; and 2) the growth of pollution load in many areas, even with application of available technology, would still be deleterious to public health.

Therefore, the Committee determined that existing sources of pollutants either should meet the standard of the law or be closed down. . . . [S. Rep. No. 91-1196, at 2-3 (1970).]

The Conference Committee and, ultimately, the entire Congress accepted the Senate's three-year mandate for the achievement of primary air quality standards, and the clear import of that decision is that the Administrator must approve a plan that provides for attainment of the primary standards in three years even if attainment does not appear feasible. [H]owever, the conferees strengthened the Senate version. The Conference Committee made clear that the States could not procrastinate until the deadline approached. Rather, the primary standards had to be met in less than three years if possible; they had to be met "as expeditiously as practicable." §110(a)(2)(A). Whatever room there is for considering claims of infeasibility in the attainment of primary standards must lie in this phrase, which is, of course, relevant only in evaluating those implementation plans that attempt to achieve the primary standard in less than three years. . . .

Secondary air quality standards . . . were subject to far less legislative debate than the primary standards. . . . The final Amendments . . . adopted the House's requirement that [the secondary standards] be met within a "reasonable time." §§109(b), 110(a)(2)(A). Thus, technology forcing is not expressly required in achieving standards to protect the public welfare.

It does not necessarily follow, however, that the Administrator may consider claims of impossibility in assessing a state plan for achieving secondary standards. . . . [T]he scope of the Administrator's power to reject a plan depends on whether the State itself may decide to engage in technology forcing and adopt a plan more stringent than federal law demands.[7]

Amici Appalachian Power Co. et al. argue . . . that the States are precluded from submitting implementation plans more stringent than federal law demands by §110(a)(2)'s second criterion that the plan contain such control devices "as may be necessary" to achieve the primary and secondary air quality standards. §110(a)(2)(B). The contention is that an overly restrictive plan is not "necessary" for attainment of the national standards and so must be rejected by the Administrator. . . .

---

7. A different question would be presented if the Administrator drafted the plan himself pursuant to §110(c). Whether claims of economic or technical infeasibility must be considered by the Administrator in drafting an implementation plan is a question we do not reach.

We read the "as may be necessary" requirement of §110(a)(2)(B) to demand only that the implementation plan submitted by the State meet the "minimum conditions" of the Amendments.[13] Beyond that, if a State makes the legislative determination that it desires a particular air quality by a certain date and that it is willing to force technology to attain it or lose a certain industry if attainment is not possible such a determination is fully consistent with the structure and purpose of the Amendments, and §110(a)(2)(B) provides no basis for the EPA Administrator to object to the determination on the ground of infeasibility.[14]

In sum, we have concluded that claims of economic or technological infeasibility may not be considered by the Administrator in evaluating a state requirement that primary ambient air quality standards be met in the mandatory three years. And, since we further conclude that the States may submit implementation plans more stringent than federal law requires and that the Administrator must approve such plans if they meet the minimum requirements of §110(a)(2), it follows that the language of §110(a)(2)(B) provides no basis for the Administrator ever to reject a state implementation plan on the ground that it is economically or technologically infeasible. Accordingly, a court of appeals reviewing an approved plan under §307(b)(1) cannot set it aside on those grounds, no matter when they are raised.

III

Our conclusion is bolstered by recognition that the Amendments do allow claims of technological and economic infeasibility to be raised in situations where consideration of such claims will not substantially interfere with the primary congressional purpose of prompt attainment of the national air quality standards. Thus, we do not hold that . . . sources unable to comply with emission limitations must inevitably be shut down.

Perhaps the most important forum for consideration of claims of economic and technological infeasibility is before the state agency formulating the implementation plan. So long as the national standards are met, the State may select whatever mix of control devices it desires, and industries with particular economic or technological problems may seek special treatment in the plan itself. Moreover, if the industry is not exempted from, or accommodated by, the original plan, it may obtain a variance, as petitioner did in this case; and the variance, if granted after notice and a hearing, may be submitted to the EPA as a revision of the plan. Lastly, an industry denied an exemption from the implementation plan, or denied a subsequent variance, may

13. Economic and technological factors may be relevant in determining whether the minimum conditions are met. Thus, the Administrator may consider whether it is economically or technologically possible for the state plan to require more rapid progress than it does. If he determines that it is, he may reject the plan as not meeting the requirement that primary standards be achieved "as expeditiously as practicable" or as failing to provide for attaining secondary standards within "a reasonable time."

14. In a literal sense, of course, no plan is infeasible since offending sources always have the option of shutting down if they cannot otherwise comply with the standard of the law. Thus, there is no need for the Administrator to reject an economically or technologically "infeasible" state plan on the ground that anticipated noncompliance will cause the State to fall short of the national standards. Sources objecting to such a state scheme must seek their relief from the State.

be able to take its claims of economic or technological infeasibility to the state courts.[16] . . .

Even if the State does not intervene on behalf of an emission source, technological and economic factors may be considered in at least one other circumstance. When a source is found to be in violation of the state implementation plan, the Administrator may, after a conference with the operator, issue a compliance order rather than seek civil or criminal enforcement. Such an order must specify a "reasonable" time for compliance with the relevant standard, taking into account the seriousness of the violation and "any good faith efforts to comply with applicable requirements." §113(a)(4). Claims of technological or economic infeasibility, the Administrator agrees, are relevant to fashioning an appropriate compliance order under §113(a)(4).[18]

In short, the Amendments offer ample opportunity for consideration of claims of technological and economic infeasibility. Always, however, care is taken that consideration of such claims will not interfere substantially with the primary goal of prompt attainment of the national standards. Allowing such claims to be raised by appealing the Administrator's approval of an implementation plan, as petitioner suggests, would frustrate congressional intent. It would permit a proposed plan to be struck down as infeasible before it is given a chance to work, even though Congress clearly contemplated that some plans would be infeasible when proposed. And it would permit the Administrator or a federal court to reject a State's legislative choices in regulating air pollution, even though Congress plainly left with the States, so long as the national standards were met, the power to determine which sources would be burdened by regulation and to what extent. Technology forcing is a concept somewhat new to our national experience and it necessarily entails certain risks. But Congress considered those risks in passing the 1970 [Act] and decided that the dangers posed by uncontrolled air pollution made them worth taking. Petitioner's theory would render that considered legislative judgment a nullity, and that is a result we refuse to reach.

Affirmed.

[Justice Powell, concurring, agreed with the majority's interpretation of the Act, but believed that it might lead to economically disastrous consequences. He found it "difficult to believe that Congress would adhere to its absolute position if faced with the potentially devastating consequences to the public" that might arise from the shutdown of a public utility, and asserted the belief that "Congress, if fully aware of this Draconian possibility, would strike a different balance."]

16. Of course, the [Act does] not require the States to formulate their implementation plans with deference to claims of technological or economic infeasibility, to grant variances on those grounds, or to provide judicial review of such actions. Consistent with Congress' recognition of the primary role of the States in controlling air pollution, the [Act leaves] all such decisions to the States. . . .

18. If he chooses not to seek a compliance order, or if an order is issued and violated, the Administrator may institute a civil enforcement proceeding. §113(b). Additionally, violators of an implementation plan are subject to criminal penalties under §113(c) and citizen enforcement suits under §304. Some courts have suggested that in criminal or civil enforcement proceedings the violator may in certain circumstances raise a defense of economic or technological infeasibility. We do not address this question here.

NOTES AND QUESTIONS

1. *Statutory Interpretation.* What provisions of the Act helped the Court to reach the result it did? Several of the provisions referred to in *Union Elec.* have since been amended, Section 110(a)(2) no longer specifies the deadlines for compliance with the primary and secondary NAAQS. Those deadlines now appear at several places in the statute. AQCRs not designated as nonattainment areas must achieve the primary NAAQS within three years after adoption of the 1990 amendments or within five years of a finding by EPA that a SIP was substantially inadequate under the pre-1990 version of §110(a)(2). §110(n)(2). A nonattainment area is obliged to comply with the primary NAAQS "as expeditiously as practicable," but no later than five years from the date the area was designated nonattainment (or ten years, if EPA so provides, based on the severity of nonattainment and the feasibility of control measures). §172(a)(2)(A). A nonattainment area must comply with the secondary NAAQS "as expeditiously as practicable" after the date it was designated nonattainment. §172(a)(2)(B). These deadlines do not apply if the statute provides other dates for compliance in nonattainment areas, §172(a)(2)(D). See §§181(a), 186(a), 188(c), 192. The list of mandatory SIP requirements in §110(a)(2) now includes 13 rather than 8 elements, and the "as may be necessary" phrase is now a part of §110(a)(2)(A) instead of §110(a)(2)(B). EPA's obligation to approve a SIP containing each of these elements now appears in §110(k)(3) rather than in §110(a)(2). Do any of these changes alter the result in *Union Elec.*?

2. *Other Contexts for Consideration of Feasibility.* The Court in *Union Elec.* discussed various contexts in which regulated entities could raise claims of "technological and economic infeasibility." What is the relationship between those two different kinds of feasibility? See Honeywell Int'l, Inc. v. EPA, 374 F.3d 1363, 1372-1373 (D.C. Cir. 2004). The availability of other forums for raising feasibility concerns obviously made the Court more comfortable with its holding. As the Court indicated, several options exist for individual polluters to elude or delay compliance with stringent emissions limitations contained in state plans. The earliest and strategically most effective opportunity is when the state selects the regionwide combination of emissions limitations for all sources that will achieve the SIP goals within the statutory deadlines.

If a source fails to obtain an emissions limitation acceptable to it when the SIP is first prepared, it may seek a variance from the state pollution control agency if applicable state legislation authorizes variances. A state variance usually operates as an amendment to the SIP. In Train v. NRDC, 421 U.S. 60 (1975), the Supreme Court held that a variance could be approved only if it did not cause a violation of the NAAQS or prevent a state from meeting the SIP compliance deadline. EPA review of SIP revisions is now governed by §110(k)(3) and (*l*). What approach do those provisions take to the conditions under which variances may be approved as SIP revisions? See Hall v. EPA, 273 F.3d 1146 (9th Cir. 2001) (considering whether §110(*l*) permits approval of SIP amendments based simply on a showing that the amendments do not relax preexisting SIP rules). As *Union Elec.* points out, a party also may take its claim of infeasibility to a state court. In Kentucky Res. Council, Inc. v. EPA, 467 F.3d 986 (6th Cir. 2006), the court upheld EPA's approval of a SIP revision that moved a motor vehicle inspection and maintenance (I&M) program for an ozone nonattainment area from the active portion to the contingency measures portion of the

SIP. The revision did not violate §110(*l*) because it would not make air quality worse. EPA properly allowed the state to make up for lost emissions reductions from the I&M program by approving reductions elsewhere. As a result, the revision did not "interfere" with an applicable requirement concerning attainment.

3. *More on SIP Revisions.* A state may not revise an EPA-approved SIP without further EPA approval. In General Motors Corp. v. United States, 496 U.S. 530 (1990), the state approved a SIP revision and was awaiting EPA approval. EPA took enforcement action against GM under the old SIP. The Supreme Court ruled that EPA was allowed to do so because the Act allows EPA to enforce violations of "an applicable implementation plan," §113(b)(2), and a SIP revision does not "apply" until EPA approves it. A source may be able to rely on EPA's delay in ruling on the SIP revision as a mitigating factor in an enforcement action, however. See also Sierra Club v. TVA, 430 F.3d 1337, 1346-1350 (11th Cir. 2005) (holding that §110(i) of the CAA prevents a state from unilaterally modifying SIP provisions, and that defendant was liable for violating unmodified provision).

In Luminant Generation Co., LLC v. EPA, 675 F.3d 917, 921 (5th Cir. 2012), a challenge to EPA's disapproval of revisions to Texas's SIP, the court, citing §110(k)(3), explained that the CAA "confines the EPA to the ministerial function of reviewing SIPs for consistency with the Act's requirements." See also Luminant Generation Co. LLC v. EPA, 714 F.3d 841, 846 (5th Cir. 2013). Is that a convincing, or even plausible reading of the statute? The court in the first *Luminant* case held that EPA may not invalidate SIP revisions on the basis of noncompliance with state, as opposed to federal law. The court in Texas v. EPA, 690 F.3d 670 (5th Cir. 2012), invalidated EPA's rejection of other revisions to Texas's SIP authorizing the use of "flexible" permit programs. The court characterized EPA's action as insistence on a particular control measure that violated the cooperative federalism principles that are an essential part of the CAA.

Section 110(k)(6) allows EPA to revise a SIP unilaterally if it determines that previous approval "was in error." See Alabama Envtl. Council v. EPA, 711 F.3d 1277 (11th Cir. 2013) (vacating EPA's disapproval of SIP revision based on EPA's failure to identify the error that justified rejection of approved plan).

4. *Feasibility as a Defense in Enforcement Proceedings.* Although the Supreme Court left the issue open in *Union Elec.*, it now seems clear that a noncomplying source may not raise a defense of economic and technological infeasibility in an enforcement action. Navistar Int'l Transp. Corp. v. EPA, 858 F.2d 282 (6th Cir. 1988); NRDC v. Thomas, 705 F. Supp. 1 (D.D.C. 1988). But cf. Union Elec. Co. v. EPA, 593 F.2d 299 (8th Cir. 1979) (leaving the question open). Can Congress constitutionally foreclose all consideration of economic and technological feasibility?

Section 110(k)(5) authorizes EPA to require a state to revise its SIP (by issuing a "SIP call") if the existing SIP is "substantially inadequate to attain or maintain" the NAAQS. EPA required revision of a Utah SIP because it exempted facilities from enforcement actions when they suffer an unexpected and unavoidable equipment malfunction. EPA objected because the SIP could be interpreted as precluding injunctive relief for exempted activity, which would render emission controls less than continuous in violation of §110(a)(2)(A) and (C). In addition, the SIP could be interpreted to allow Utah officials to decide that exempted activity does not amount to a violation, precluding not only Utah, but also EPA and private citizens from pursuing enforcement action, thereby undermining the CAA's enforcement structure.

US Magnesium, LLC v. EPA, 690 F.3d 1157 (10th Cir. 2012), upheld EPA's SIP call. In Luminant Generation Co., LLC v. EPA, 714 F.3d 841 (5th Cir. 2013), the court upheld EPA's approval of a Texas SIP provision creating an affirmative defense against civil penalties for excess emissions during unplanned startup, shutdown, and maintenance/malfunction (SSM) events, as well as its disapproval of a provision creating the same affirmative defense for planned SSM events.

5. *Conditional Approval of SIPs.* What if EPA deems certain provisions of a SIP acceptable but regards others as insufficient; may it approve part of the plan or approve the entire plan subject to the condition that the state remedy the defective provisions? See §110(k)(3)-(4). May EPA approve a SIP on the condition that the state adopt measures specified by EPA, rather than simply require that the state take whatever steps it desires to achieve the NAAQS? In Virginia v. EPA, 108 F.3d 1397 (D.C. Cir. 1997), EPA, acting under §110(k)(5), declared the SIPs of 12 states to be substantially inadequate to attain the NAAQS for ozone. EPA required these states to revise their SIPs by adopting a low-emission vehicle (LEV) program (already in effect in California) to reduce motor vehicle emissions of NO_x and VOCs. The court ruled that EPA may not condition approval of a SIP on the state's adoption of control measures chosen by EPA, concluding that the 1990 amendments did not eliminate a state's "liberty to 'adopt whatever mix of emission limitations it deems best suited to its particular situation.' Train v. NRDC, 421 U.S. at 79." 108 F.3d at 1408-1409. EPA argued that §110(k)(5) authorizes it, upon a finding of inadequacy, to require the states to include in their SIPs whatever measures EPA deems "necessary" to correct the inadequacy. But the court found that the "as necessary" language of §110(k)(5) restricts, not broadens EPA's authority: EPA may only call for the revisions that are necessary to correct the problem rather than require that a state adopt a "wholesale revision of its entire plan." Id. at 1409-1410. The court also held that §184(c)(5) provides EPA with the authority to condition SIP approval on the adoption of particular control measures, but that §§177 and 202 forbid EPA from conditioning approval on the adoption of California's LEV program.

May EPA conditionally approve SIPs that contain no specific remedial measures but that promise to adopt such measures within a year? See NRDC v. EPA, 22 F.3d 1125 (D.C. Cir. 1994); Sierra Club v. EPA, 356 F.3d 296 (D.C. Cir. 2004) (rejecting claim that state may qualify for conditional approval by committing to adopt specific enforceable measures by a certain date, even if the state does not tell EPA what those measures are, or even know what they are). BCCA Appeal Group v. EPA, 355 F.3d 817 (5th Cir. 2004), however, upheld EPA's determination that a state's enforceable commitment to adopt unspecified control measures on a fixed schedule as part of an overall control strategy was an "appropriate" technique or timetable for compliance under §110(a)(2)(A). Environmental Def. v. EPA, 369 F.3d 193 (2d Cir. 2004), endorsed EPA's test for determining whether a commitment is appropriate: (1) whether it addresses a limited portion of the reductions needed for attainment, (2) whether the state can fulfill it, and (3) whether it is for a reasonable time. The court distinguished the 1994 NRDC decision because, in this case, the state's SIP included a comprehensive and detailed plan for attainment.

6. *Formulation of Implementation Plans by EPA.* Section 110(c) still authorizes EPA to issue a federal implementation plan (FIP) (as defined in §302(y)) for a state that has not complied with its obligations. See Oklahoma v. EPA, 723 F.3d 1201, 1223 (10th Cir. 2013) (EPA not required to defer issuing a FIP when state submitted a SIP

after EPA had already found that it had failed to make timely submission). Must EPA issue a FIP after it disapproves a state's discretionary SIP revision? See §110(c)(1)(B); Association of Irritated Residents v. EPA, 686 F.3d 668 (9th Cir. 2012) (yes). Suppose EPA fails to issue a FIP within two years of its disapproval of a SIP. Has it lost the authority to do so? See Montana Sulphur & Chem. Co. v. EPA, 666 F.3d 1174, 1190-1191 (9th Cir. 2012) (no). The Court, in footnote 7 of *Union Elec.*, left open the question of whether EPA must consider claims of economic or technological infeasibility when it is formulating a FIP. What arguments support such an obligation? Are there contrary arguments?

7. *More Stringent State Requirements.* Suppose that a SIP imposes emission limitations on non-criteria pollutants that need not be regulated as a matter of federal law. After EPA approves the SIP, are those limitations enforceable by EPA or in a citizen suit? See Washington Envtl. Council v. Sturdevant, 834 F. Supp. 2d 1209 (W.D. Wash. 2011), *rev'd for lack of standing,* 732 F.3d 1131 (9th Cir. 2013).

8. *Conflicting SIP Interpretations.* Suppose that after EPA approves a SIP, EPA and the state disagree on the proper interpretation of one of its provisions. Whose interpretation controls? See United States v. Duke Energy Corp., 981 F. Supp. 2d 435, 450-455 (M.D.N.C. 2013) (EPA's).

9. *Justice Powell Triumphant.* Justice Powell's views in *Union Elec.* essentially prevailed in Sierra Club v. Georgia Power Co., 180 F.3d 1309 (11th Cir. 1999). For discussion of the SIP process, including suggestions for why it has failed to achieve the NAAQS in many areas, see Reitze, Air Quality Protection Using State Implementation Plans—Thirty-seven Years of Increasing Complexity, 15 Vill. Envtl. L.J. 209 (2004).

NOTE ON TALL STACKS AND OTHER DISPERSION TECHNIQUES

Although the CAA requires SIPs to contain enforceable emission limitations, it also authorizes such other measures, means, or techniques "as may be necessary." §110(a)(2)(A). Must a state rely primarily on emissions limitations on existing sources, or may it rely on other techniques to meet the NAAQS? Are any techniques forbidden? Can a facility disperse pollution by constructing tall stacks? NRDC v. EPA, 489 F.2d 390 (5th Cir. 1974), *rev'd on other grounds,* Train v. NRDC, Inc., 421 U.S. 60 (1975), invalidated this technique because it did not reduce emissions; instead, it merely distributed them over a wider area. Two other courts extended that rationale to "intermittent" controls (which distribute emissions temporally instead of geographically), disapproving efforts to reduce operations at the source or switch to less-polluting fuel when atmospheric conditions cause high pollution levels. Kennecott Copper Corp. v. Train, 526 F.2d 1149 (9th Cir. 1975); Big Rivers Elec. Corp. v. EPA, 523 F.2d 16 (6th Cir. 1975). Do the 1977 amendments prohibit intermittent control technique strategies such as closing the plant or switching to less-polluting fuels?

The legislative history of the 1990 amendments discusses the tall stacks issue:

The [1970] Act was written at a time when the interstate transport of air pollution was not widely acknowledged. Indeed, it was the implementation of the Clean Air Act which created a substantial number of the interstate pollution problems. Rather than reducing their emissions of sulfur dioxide, electric utilities proposed the use of "tall stacks" to inject pollution into the upper atmosphere where it could be diluted and transported over long distances. Although illegal, this policy was expressly approved by the first Administrator of the Environmental Protection Agency, William D. Ruckelshaus, and quickly led to the widespread use of super-tall smokestacks.

Although the Congress enacted curbs on the use of tall stacks in [1977, and enacted provisions] to control interstate air pollution[, these provisions] largely failed to achieve the congressionally intended goal of curbing and controlling interstate air pollution. Thus, the law remains . . . keyed almost entirely to achieving local ambient air quality standards. [S. Rep. No. 101-228, at 553 (1989).]

The 1977 amendments addressed the dispersion techniques controversy in §123, which provides that the "degree of emission limitation" is not to be affected by stack height in excess of "good engineering practice" or by any dispersion technique. "Dispersion technique" is defined to mean "any intermittent or supplemental control of air pollutants varying with atmospheric conditions." In addition, §302(k) defines an emission limitation as a requirement that "limits the quantity, rate, or concentration of emissions of air pollutants on a continuous basis." Section 123 does not prohibit the building of tall stacks. It merely limits the extent to which a polluter can take credit for tall stacks in meeting its emission limitations.

Section 123 defines "good engineering practice" as that height "necessary" to ensure that emissions will not cause local "excessive concentration" due to atmospheric downwash from "nearby" structures or terrain. Montana Sulphur & Chem. Co. v. EPA, 666 F.3d 1174, 1186 (9th Cir. 2012), explained the function of §123 as follows:

> The basic concern with stack height is this: a pollution source can lower ground-level, measured concentrations of pollution by raising the height of its stack and dispersing the pollution further into the atmosphere. Concerned that such a dispersion technique does not actually reduce the amount of pollution but merely spreads it around, Congress adopted 42 U.S.C. §7423 to regulate the use of tall stacks. Rather than completely prohibiting the use of tall stacks, which do prevent some harmful downwash of pollutants near the source, the statute and regulations seek to strike a balance between elevating stack height to disperse pollution away from a source and preventing relocation of pollution from one site to others.

See also Sierra Club v. EPA, 719 F.2d 436 (D.C. Cir. 1983) (holding that EPA must adopt an absolute, health-based standard in defining excessive concentrations); NRDC v. Thomas, 838 F.2d 1224 (D.C. Cir. 1988) (upholding regulations issued on remand from *Sierra Club* that modified the methods for determining good-engineering-practice stack height credit).

Unfortunately, the tall stacks problem is not merely a relic of a bygone era when neither regulators nor sources knew how emissions from tall stacks affect air quality. According to the GAO, 284 tall smokestacks operated at 172 coal-fired power plants in 34 states at the end of 2010. More than 200 of these stacks were 500 to 699 feet tall and 14 were 1,000 feet tall or higher. One Indiana stack was nearly as tall as the Eiffel Tower and nearly twice as high as the Washington Monument. Many of these stacks had been operating for less than 4 years. Of the 48 tall stacks built since 1988, 17 exceeded their GEP height, though some did so for legitimate reasons, such as protection against downwash or to help emissions clear local geographic features. The GAO found that tall stacks contributed to the interstate transport of air pollution, but that stack height represents just one variable in this process. U.S. Government Accountability Office, Information on Tall Smokestacks and Their Contribution to Interstate Transport of Air Pollution, GAO-11-473 (May 2011).

c. Monitoring and Modeling

As the preceding discussion indicates, the CAA requires each state to determine whether its AQCRs should be classified as nonattainment or attainment. To achieve the NAAQS in a nonattainment area, a state must impose emissions controls on individual sources of the nonattainment pollutant or its precursors that are sufficient to reduce ambient concentrations by the necessary amounts. Once a state has set individual emission limitations, it must enforce them. EPA has developed air quality monitoring and modeling techniques to assist in each of these tasks. Although the courts generally defer to EPA's selection of modeling techniques, in a few cases they have set aside EPA's application of these models.

Monitoring, Modeling, and AQCR Designation. The statute authorizes EPA to use monitoring or modeling in the designation of AQCRs. The agency need not base its designation on actual rather than model-predicted air quality. PPG Indus., Inc. v. Costle, 630 F.2d 462 (6th Cir. 1980) (but holding that modeling was based on erroneous data). Because of the uncertainties inherent in air quality modeling, EPA allows the use of supplemental analysis to demonstrate attainment in cases where modeling shows ambient concentration levels in excess of the NAAQS. See ATK Launch Systems, Inc. v. EPA, 669 F.3d 330, 339 (D.C. Cir. 2012) ("By confirming the modeling results with on-the-ground data, EPA 'took reasonable steps to ensure that' [the model's] limitations were considered, 'and its choices are not arbitrary or capricious.'"). See also Sierra Club v. EPA, 356 F.3d 296 (D.C. Cir. 2004) (construing §182(c)(2)(A) to allow EPA to adjust results of photochemical grid modeling to ensure consistency with real-world observations).

May EPA base an AQCR designation on predicted growth in pollution as well as on present air quality? See *PPG Indus., supra*, which upheld EPA's view that §107(d)(1) (before it was amended in 1990) allows consideration of "projected future violations" as the basis for a nonattainment area designation. Is this result still appropriate under the current version of §107(d)(1)? On the problems involved in ambient monitoring, see generally Biber, The Problem of Environmental Monitoring, 83 U. Colo. L. Rev. 1 (2011).

Monitoring, Modeling, and SIP Formulation. EPA at first used the "rollback" model, which is based on "the commonsensical proposition that pollutants will be reduced proportionally to reductions in their chemical precursors," to review SIPs. Texas v. EPA, 499 F.2d 289, 301 (5th Cir. 1974). EPA later adopted more sophisticated diffusion models. In Cleveland Elec. Illuminating Co. v. EPA, 572 F.2d 1150 (6th Cir. 1978), the court upheld a FIP drafted by EPA for Ohio, despite the availability of more advanced models than the one EPA used, the existence of monitoring data inconsistent with the model's predictions, and evidence that the model systematically overpredicted emissions. In Environmental Def. v. EPA, 369 F.3d 193 (2d Cir. 2004), the issue was whether EPA's approval of New York's SIP complied with §182(c)(2)(A), which requires that attainment demonstrations for ozone nonattainment areas be "based on photochemical grid modeling." The court upheld EPA's approval, even though New York demonstrated attainment through a "weight of the evidence" approach that adjusted the results of the grid modeling to correct for inaccuracies. The court interpreted the statute as requiring only that grid modeling form the "foundation and principal component of the attainment demonstration." See also Montana Sulphur & Chem. Co. v. EPA, 666 F.3d 1174 (9th Cir. 2012) (upholding EPA's reliance on computer models in adopting FIP for control of SO_2 emissions from sulfur recovery plant); BCCA Appeal Group v. EPA, 355 F.3d 817 (5th Cir. 2004) (upholding EPA's reliance on photochemical grid model in approving Texas's demonstration that Houston's SIP would attain NAAQS, despite the model's inability to replicate the city's unique meteorological conditions).

In other cases, the courts have rejected EPA or state models. E.g., Sierra Club v. EPA, 671 F.3d 955 (9th Cir. 2012) (reliance on emission inventory data EPA knew were outdated and inaccurate at the time of SIP approval); Columbus & S. Ohio Elec. Co. v. Costle, 638 F.2d 910 (6th Cir. 1980) (invalid assumptions concerning weather stability conditions); Ohio v. EPA, 784 F.2d 224 (6th Cir. 1986) (arbitrary reliance on model for stack emissions without testing it against actual monitoring data).

Monitoring and Enforcement. Finally, disputes over the appropriate kind and extent of monitoring can arise in enforcement proceedings. In United States v. Louisiana Pac. Corp., 925 F. Supp. 1484 (D. Colo. 1996), the state issued a permit requiring the defendants to install continuous opacity monitoring (COM) systems. The defendant argued that §110(a)(2)(F) does not require that every source install and use monitoring devices and that, absent EPA-issued emissions monitoring guidance for a source category, the state lacked the power to require monitoring. The court held that §§110(a)(2)(A) and (F) and 114 allow the states to implement and enforce emission monitoring requirements not prescribed by EPA to ensure the enforceability of emissions limitations. See also Grand Canyon Trust v. Public Serv. Co., 294 F. Supp. 2d 1246 (D.N.M. 2003) (COM is relevant but not necessarily determinative evidence of CAA violations); United States v. Comunidades Unidas Contra la Contaminación, 106 F. Supp. 2d 216 (D.P.R. 2000) (upholding EPA finding that utility violated monitoring requirements because it used improper methodology in conducting opacity readings).

NOTE ON CONTINUOUS EMISSIONS MONITORING AND "ALL CREDIBLE EVIDENCE"

Although EPA has taken the position that the CAA does not limit its authority to use any type of information to prove a violation, some courts have interpreted EPA regulations that refer to specific test methods for determining compliance as precluding the agency's reliance on evidence obtained through other methods. EPA sought to broaden the evidentiary basis for proving violations when it adopted the "all credible evidence" rule. 62 Fed. Reg. 8314 (1997). It clarified that the inclusion in a SIP of enforceable test methods for emissions limits does not preclude enforcement based on other credible evidence relevant to whether a source would have satisfied applicable requirements if the appropriate compliance test procedures or methods had been performed. EPA cited as authority for the new rule §113(a) and (e)(1) of the CAA. What language in these two provisions supports EPA's interpretation? See also §§114(a)(3), 504(b).

EPA emphasized that the rule addressed an evidentiary issue and would not have the effect of increasing the stringency of underlying emission standards. It simply removed what had been construed as a regulatory bar to the admission of non-reference test data to prove the violation of an emission standard, regardless of the credibility and probative value of those data. Thus, according to the agency, the rule did not affect whether emission standards require intermittent or continuous compliance.[o] The rule would allow EPA and the states (but not citizen suit plaintiffs; see Sierra Club v. TVA, 430 F.3d 1337 (11th Cir. 2005)) to use a wider range of evidence to assess compliance status and respond to noncompliance. Regulated sources also would benefit by being able to use the same, broader range of evidence to contest allegations of noncompliance.

EPA explained the advantage of the non-reference test data made available by the rule to those seeking to enforce CAA obligations:

> Reference tests may not yield a representative emissions picture because the sources typically schedule, set up and run the tests themselves. This allows sources to "fine tune" their operations and emissions control processes prior to the tests, and generate results that may not be typical of day-to-day source operations. Reference tests can also be expensive and burdensome: They can cost up to $100,000, and take a week or more to complete. . . .
>
> Where available, continuous emission monitoring (CEM) data [which measure and record the chemical composition of a waste stream at regular intervals within smokestacks] and well-chosen parametric monitoring data . . . generally provide accurate data regarding a source's compliance with emission limits and standards. [62 Fed. Reg. at 8315.]

Industry was not nearly as sanguine about the purpose or potential impact of the "all credible evidence" rule. They asserted that CEM distorts a source's compliance status due to the inevitability of occasional violations despite the source's having average emissions levels that comply fully with applicable limitations. As a result, companies will have to take steps to ensure that emissions always fall below those limitations. The practical effect would be a 50 percent tightening of standards. Industry's challenge to the rule was deemed unripe in NRDC v. EPA, 194 F.3d 130 (D.C. Cir. 1999). The rule remains in effect. 40 C.F.R. §§52.12(c), 52.33(a).

The D.C. Circuit rejected EPA's position that state permitting authorities are prohibited from adding new monitoring requirements if a CAA Title V permit already contains some periodic monitoring requirements, even if they are insufficient. In Sierra Club v. EPA, 536 F.3d 673 (D.C. Cir. 2008), the court vacated the rules, holding that EPA's interpretation of Title V conflicts with clear statutory language that compels EPA to allow state permitting authorities to supplement inadequate monitoring requirements in a Title V permit.

---

o. The notion that monitoring requirements do not affect the substance of the emission standards to which they relate was rejected in Appalachian Power Co. v. EPA, 208 F.3d 1015 (D.C. Cir. 2000). Regulations that specify test methods and frequency of testing for compliance are substantive in nature in that they impose duties on regulated entities. Changes in monitoring methods can affect the stringency of the relevant emission limitation. Monitoring requirements also impose significant compliance costs.

E. NATIONALLY UNIFORM EMISSION STANDARDS FOR NEW SOURCES: CONTROLLING NEW STATIONARY SOURCE POLLUTION BY CATEGORICAL REGULATION

Although Congress enshrined attainment of the NAAQS as the overall goal of the CAA, it subjected a variety of mobile and stationary sources to uniform federal emissions standards. Emissions standards are direct limitations on the emissions that regulated sources can discharge. Thus, despite the important SIP planning role of states, such direct federal regulation means that some sources are subject to pollution restrictions that are not up for debate in SIP planning. Resulting emissions reductions will of course influence air quality, a jurisdiction's air status, and the challenges faced by regulators and other pollution sources. In contrast to the health-based ambient air quality approach, most CAA emissions standards issued by EPA are technology-based because they require EPA to determine the technical and engineering feasibility of pollution control by sources that use similar production processes. Based on its feasibility studies, EPA sets performance-oriented standards that specify the quantity of pollutant that may be emitted per unit of product, raw material, or fuel input. It is thus important to note that they are based substantially on technology-based assessment, but do not actually mandate use of a technology. At least in theory, the standards pressure regulated sources to make improvements in pollution control by installing control technologies and by changing to fuels, raw materials, and manufacturing processes that emit less pollution. The new source performance standards (NSPS) authorized by §111 are one example of a technology-based standard.

A *Note Regarding Stationary Source Regulation.* As this chapter continues, it will introduce readers to several other CAA sections that require regulation of stationary sources. Although under the CAA's design and logic these various sections are programmatically quite distinct and use different regulatory strategies, it is important to keep in mind that the stationary source (and its lawyers) in the end will need to sort out how these overlapping and intertwined sections work. Who is the principal regulator? Which section or sections are triggered in a particular setting? Does the stringency of regulation applicable to a stationary source require review of regulatory materials or performance achieved in practice? Are regulatory obligations set in a promulgated regulation or set on a case-by-case basis to be memorialized in a permit? How does the pollutant emitted influence the source's regulatory obligations? And, across all of these provisions applicable to stationary sources, the physical size and nature of the source and pollution quantities often matter, as will a stationary source's characterization as "existing," "new," or "modified." And because the CAA is often criticized and proposed for amendment, a question for policymakers (and students) is whether there are better ways to juggle the diverse goals reflected in the Act, especially ways to address incentives for regulatory stasis, ongoing improved environmental performance, or ongoing operation of old, high polluting facilities.

Hence, a lawyer working with a stationary source of air pollution will need to keep straight regulatory obligations determined by or under the following sections: NSPS set by regulation under §111 and linked follow-on regulation of existing sources; nonattainment area new source permitting; attainment area new source permitting under the "Prevention of Significant Deterioration" program; and regulation of hazardous air pollutant emissions through regulations issued under §112.

The Scope of the New Source Performance Standards. Section 111(e) requires new and modified stationary sources to comply with technology-based NSPS. A "new source" is defined in §111(a)(2). What factors may EPA consider in establishing NSPS? See §111(a)(1). For purposes of §111, EPA has defined modification as "any physical or operational change to an existing facility which results in an increase in the emission rate to the atmosphere of any pollutant to which a standard applies." 40 C.F.R. §60.14(a). The extension of "new source" review to modified sources is critical because it sweeps changes in operation in existing sources into new source review (NSR) programs (discussed in section F below). The addition or use of any system or device whose primary function is the reduction of air pollutants does not constitute a modification, except when an emission control system is removed or replaced by a system EPA determines to be less environmentally beneficial. Id. §60.14(e)(5). How far does this definition stretch? See National-Southwire Aluminum Co. v. EPA, 838 F.2d 835 (6th Cir. 1988) (turning off pollution control equipment is modification); Hawaiian Elec. Co. v. EPA, 723 F.2d 1440 (9th Cir. 1984) (change to fuel containing more sulfur than allowed by existing permit is modification for purposes of NSR). Section 111(b) describes the categories of sources for which EPA must issue NSPS.

The Rationale for the NSPS. The idea of imposing uniform national emission standards dates back to the hearings on the 1967 amendments. The reasons offered in support of uniform emission standards for new sources included (1) the unreliability of ambient standards, (2) the elimination of regional pollution havens and "hot spots" as discussed in the "race-to-the-bottom" materials in Chapter 2, (3) the inability of states to take necessary action, (4) the rapidity with which emission standards could be adopted, (5) simplicity of enforcement, (6) due consideration of economic and technical factors, and (7) the reduction of atmospheric transport of pollutants to distant polluted areas that would result.

The wisdom of the CAA's reliance on nationally uniform new source emission controls, however, has since been called into question. The Act arguably creates an incentive for sources to keep older, dirtier plants in operation as long as possible in order to avoid triggering the more rigorous controls applicable to new plants. The result is arguably bad not only for the environment, but also for the economy, as the construction of newer, more efficient and productive plants is delayed. See Ackerman & Stewart, Reforming Environmental Law, 37 Stan. L. Rev. 1333, 1335-1336 (1985). The issue is salient because coal-fired power plants constructed as much as 70 years ago are still operating. The average coal plant in the U.S. is 42 years old. See Mufson, These Coal-Fired Power Plants Could Be Collecting Social Security, Wash. Post, June 15, 2014, at G1.

Technology Forcing and NSPS. Are §111 NSPS technology forcing? The §111 requirement that technology be "adequately demonstrated," taking various costs into account, seems on its face to preclude technology forcing that would require a higher level of performance than current technology is capable of producing. Cf. §111(j). Portland Cement Ass'n v. Ruckelshaus, 486 F.2d 375 (D.C. Cir. 1973), indicated that Congress did not require a technology to be in routine use before it can be adopted. To be "adequately demonstrated" means to be "available" at a future date when the technology may reasonably be expected to be installed and to work: "Section 111 looks toward what may fairly be projected for the regulated future, rather than the state of the art at present." Id. at 391-392. But the cases do not seem to allow EPA to add a "margin for striving" on top of its forecast of routine technological development. See National Lime Ass'n v. EPA, 627 F.2d 416 (D.C. Cir. 1980) (remand of NSPS because

EPA failed to show that the standard was "achievable" for the industry as a whole). EPA may compensate for a shortage of data, however, by extrapolating a technology's performance in one industry in determining its availability in another. Lignite Energy Council v. EPA, 198 F.3d 930 (D.C. Cir. 1999) (upholding NSPS for coal-fired industrial boilers based on extrapolation from studies of utility boilers).

Despite the NSPS name and focus on "new" and "modified" sources, it contains §111(d), a provision that acts as a follow-on provision requiring regulation of existing sources in categories subject to a NSPS. Although this provision has provoked little debate and attention during the early decades of the modern Act, it has come to the fore in battles over regulation of greenhouse gases, especially from power plants. As this book goes to press, EPA has issued proposed §111(d) regulations for such sources. Look at the language of this section. What process does it call for? Why might its cross-references matter in debates over the latitude it provides for pollution trading and other flexible regulatory strategies? Section E.1.d of Chapter 12 addresses the application of §111(d) to greenhouse gas emissions that contribute to climate change.

NSPS for Coal-Fired Electricity-Generating Facilities. Sierra Club v. Costle, 657 F.2d 298 (D.C. Cir. 1981), sustained a controversial NSPS for electric utilities. The standard required utilities to employ some form of flue gas desulfurization (or "scrubbing") technology, a relatively expensive means of reducing emissions, instead of simply increasing their use of low-sulfur coal. EPA enacted the NSPS sustained in *Sierra Club* in response to amendments to §111(a)(1) adopted in 1977. Those amendments defined a "standard of performance" applicable to any air pollutant emitted from fossil fuel–fired stationary sources as a standard that (1) established allowable emission limitations and (2) required "the achievement of a percentage reduction in the emissions from [those categories] of sources from the emissions which would have resulted from the use of fuels which are not subject to treatment prior to combustion." Thus, utilities could not meet the standards by limiting the hours or levels of plant operation or by burning untreated low-sulfur coal; they had to use scrubbers or other technological controls.

Critics charged that the scrubber-based NSPS for coal-fired power plants would cost billions more than standards that could be achieved primarily through coal washing and the burning of low-sulfur coal. See, e.g., B. Ackerman & W. Hassler, Clean Coal/Dirty Air or How the Clean Air Act Became a Multibillion-Dollar Bailout for High-Sulfur Coal Producers and What Should Be Done About It (1981). They viewed the amended §111(a)(1) as an unwarranted subsidy to eastern high-sulfur coal interests because it required that the emissions from low-sulfur western coal be scrubbed despite the relatively low SO_2 levels produced by the burning of that coal.

The issue was put to rest when Congress amended §111(a)(1) again in 1990. A Senate report on the amendments explained that "[t]he original intention of the provision was to prevent western low sulfur coal from shutting eastern high sulfur coal out of the fuel market," but that this subsidy was no longer necessary because the provisions of the 1990 amendments that limited SO_2 emissions to abate acid deposition would induce new utility sources to reduce their emissions as much as possible. The report added that the amendments would remain in effect only as long as acid rain control provisions remain in effect. S. Rep. No. 101-228, at 656 (1989). For further discussion of the acid deposition control provisions adopted in 1990, see section I.2 below.

Multiple Emissions Points, Bubbles, and Efficiency. A power *plant* may consist of several boiler *units*, each of which emits pollutants and is presently subject to NSPS.

Other industrial subcategories subject to NSPS also may emit pollutants from several locations within a plant. For NSPS purposes, should the entire plant be considered the source, or should each piece of emissions-generating equipment within the plant be considered a separate source? See §111(a)(3). The same question has arisen under the NSR provisions discussed in sections F and G below.

The issue of how to define a "source" that is subject to NSPS or NSR is crucial because a broader definition of the term allows plant operators more leeway in deciding the level of control at individual units, thus promoting efficient operation. Marginal emissions control costs vary widely among pieces of plant equipment that emit the same pollutants. Substantial cost savings may be possible if plant operators are allowed to reduce emissions the most in the units for which control is the cheapest. Hahn & Hester, Where Did All the Markets Go? An Analysis of EPA's Emissions Trading Program, 6 Yale J. on Reg. 109 (1989).

In 1975, EPA authorized regulators and plant operators to consider the entire plant to be the source subject to NSPS. 40 Fed. Reg. 58,416. EPA imagined the plant to be covered by a "bubble," with only one emissions point at the top. Under this "plantwide" definition of a source, NSPS would apply only if a physical or operational change resulted in an increase in emissions from that point; increases in individual contributing units beneath the bubble would not trigger NSPS if they were offset by emissions reductions elsewhere under the bubble. The D.C. Circuit in ASARCO Inc. v. EPA, 578 F.2d 319 (D.C. Cir. 1978), invalidated the NSPS bubble policy. It concluded that the plantwide definition, by permitting in-plant modifications that did not increase overall plantwide emissions to elude or "net out" of the NSPS requirements, might retard the application of new technology that met the strict NSPS criteria and therefore delay the improvement in air quality that §111 was designed to achieve.

The same court accepted the plantwide definition for purposes of the PSD program in Alabama Power Co. v. Costle, 636 F.2d 323 (D.C. Cir. 1980). Later, in the *Chevron* case, incorporated by reference below in section F.4 (where the merits and disadvantages of the bubble concept and similar regulatory techniques are discussed in greater detail), the Supreme Court upheld the use of the bubble for modified sources in nonattainment areas, indicated its disapproval of *ASARCO*, and refused to overturn *Alabama Power*. EPA subsequently reinstated the bubble under certain circumstances for the NSPS program. See 58 Fed. Reg. 28,780 (1993) (discussing "compliance bubbles").

F. NONATTAINMENT AREAS: THE SPECIAL PROBLEMS OF DIRTY-AIR AREAS

1. *The Scope of the Nonattainment Problem*

Many areas of the country, particularly industrialized urban areas, were not able to meet the deadlines for achieving the NAAQS established in the 1970 version of the CAA for one or more criteria pollutants. Problems included the technical and economic challenge of effective pollution control, the inadequacy of some SIPs, the intransigence of some sources, inadequate enforcement, and litigation that delayed the implementation of some state regulations.

The problems differed from pollutant to pollutant. For sulfur oxides or TSP, the primary causes of missed deadlines were high concentrations of sources in industrialized eastern and midwestern areas (requiring a larger percentage reduction by each source) and the difficulties of adequately controlling emissions at large smelters and electricity-generating facilities located primarily in the West. "Dirty-air" areas therefore feared that the CAA would foreclose most new growth.

The main reasons for missing the deadlines for mobile-source pollutant ambient standards were more complex. First, the deadlines were hopelessly optimistic in view of the magnitude of the ozone and CO problem in some urban areas. Second, Congress extended the deadlines for achieving the 1975 and 1976 emissions standards for new vehicles into the late 1970s. Even if the states had the will, the Act allowed only California to set more stringent emissions standards for new vehicles. Instead, to control mobile-source emissions, the statute thrust the states back to secondary strategies such as dispersing traffic, providing incentives not to drive or to take mass transit, policing the performance of new car emissions control systems through inspection and maintenance programs, and (in theory more than in practice) setting retrofit standards for older vehicles. Third, the secondary techniques directly affected the driving public, sometimes in ways that drivers viewed as exceedingly restrictive. As a result, these nontechnological control alternatives crumbled one by one under the political reality of the average American's daily dependence on the automobile.

Against this backdrop, EPA attempted to provide for new industrial growth with its 1975 "offset" program. This program allowed new sources to build in nonattainment areas if they could offset their new emissions by cutting back emissions at other existing facilities or by paying other existing sources to reduce emissions. EPA also confronted the automobile head-on. For example, it promulgated, and the Ninth Circuit approved, draconian gas rationing regulations for Los Angeles, explaining that NAAQS attainment for some mobile-source pollutants would require an 82 percent reduction in summer automobile traffic in the city. City of Santa Rosa v. EPA, 534 F.2d 150 (9th Cir. 1976). The rules were subsequently withdrawn.

To avoid the need for such strategies, EPA sought direct legislative relief. Congress responded by amending the CAA in 1977. On the one hand, the amendments gave EPA and regulated sources the delays they sought; states now had until 1982 or 1987 (in the case of some areas that were designated nonattainment for ozone or CO) to meet the NAAQS. On the other hand, Congress imposed new constraints on the states in the implementation and enforcement of SIPs in nonattainment areas to facilitate compliance. The amendments established a permit program for the construction of major stationary sources in nonattainment areas, for example, including a codification of the offset policy.

These constraints notwithstanding, many urban areas were still not in compliance with the NAAQS by the end of the 1980s. More than 90 percent of these areas, for example, had failed to attain the NAAQS for ozone by 1989. Virginia v. United States, 74 F.3d 517, 520 (4th Cir. 1996). Congress responded by amending the Act in 1990. The 1990 amendments extended the deadlines again and imposed still more rigorous obligations on states containing nonattainment areas, with the effect of reducing still further the initial flexibility afforded the states to design whatever mix of emission controls they desired to achieve the NAAQS. As indicated below, the obligations, the deadlines for compliance with the NAAQS, and the sanctions for noncompliance differ depending on the severity of the nonattainment problem.

As you study the nonattainment coverage, consider what steps should be taken in the event that implementation of the 1990 amendments fails to result in compliance with the NAAQS. Should Congress impose further restrictions on the discretion of the states in selecting how to reduce emissions, or should it move in an entirely different direction? Should it continue moving, as it did in the 1990 amendments, toward increased reliance on economic incentives as a supplement to or substitute for more traditional regulatory techniques? How much of the burden of reducing emissions further should come from stationary and from mobile sources?

NOTE ON THE OZONE AND CARBON MONOXIDE NONATTAINMENT PROBLEM

Excessive concentrations of ozone (smog) and carbon monoxide are the major nonattainment problems in urban areas. As shown in Figure 6-6, VOCs and NO_x are both important precursors to ozone formation in the atmosphere. The major sources of VOCs include industrial processes, transportation, and solvent uses, while NO_x are generated largely by transportation sources and utility and industrial boilers. Hydrocarbons (HCs) are an important type of VOC.

The multiple sources of ozone precursors make control difficult. Emission reductions of VOCs or NO_x may or may not decrease ozone concentrations, depending on the amounts of the various kinds of pollutants, the background concentrations of ozone and its precursors, and meteorological conditions. U.S. Office of Technology Assessment, Urban Ozone and the Clean Air Act 58 (1988). Consumer and commercial products also contribute to ozone pollution through emissions of VOCs. Section 183(e) of the CAA authorizes EPA to regulate VOC emissions from categories of consumer and commercial products through application of the "best available controls." §183(e)(3)(A). Allied Local and Regional Mfrs. Caucus v. EPA, 215 F.3d 61 (D.C. Cir. 2000), held that, in regulating the manufacture and distribution of paints and architectural coatings, EPA need not determine the reactivity of each individual VOC species, but may assess reactivity on the basis of industrial category. The court also ruled that EPA may regulate product sales nationwide based on the agency's conclusion that VOC emissions in attainment areas can contribute to nonattainment elsewhere.

Carbon monoxide, unlike ozone, is directly emitted. As indicated in section A.1 above, it results from the combustion of carbon-containing materials in power plants, furnaces, fires, and engines. Most violations of the CO NAAQS occur in high-concentration "hot spots" near major traffic arteries.

2. *Deadlines for Achieving the NAAQS*

When Congress amended the CAA in 1990, it recognized that a uniform set of deadlines for achieving the NAAQS was not appropriate due to the differences in the nature, extent, and sources of pollution problems across the country. Section 172(a)(2)(A) provides that the date for complying with the primary NAAQS for an area that is designated nonattainment for the first time after adoption of the

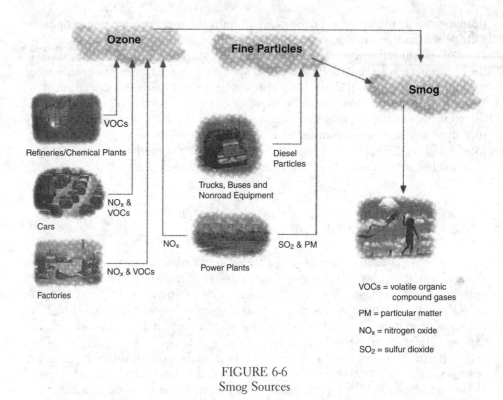

FIGURE 6-6
Smog Sources

Source: http://www.epa.gov/oar/oaqps/regusmog/smog.html (removed).

amendments is the date by which attainment can be achieved as expeditiously as practicable, but not more than five years after designation. See also §192(a). EPA may extend the deadline for up to ten years based on the severity of nonattainment and the availability and feasibility of control measures. The secondary standards must be achieved in these areas as expeditiously as practicable. §172(a)(2)(B). These same deadline provisions apply to nonattainment areas for pollutants newly added to the §108(a) list of criteria pollutants, and to criteria pollutants for which EPA revises the NAAQS after adoption of the 1990 amendments. The deadlines contained in §172(a) apply only if the CAA does not specifically provide different attainment dates. §172(a)(2)(D).

The scheme for compliance in areas that were already designated as nonattainment before the 1990 amendments is considerably more complex, but is becoming increasingly irrelevant as EPA amends more of the NAAQS that were in effect in 1990. The deadlines for these preexisting nonattainment areas depend on the criteria pollutant involved and the severity of the nonattainment problem. The statute divides ozone nonattainment areas, for example, into five classifications (marginal, moderate, serious, severe, and extreme) based on increasing "design values," or ambient concentrations, of that pollutant. The deadlines for compliance with the primary ozone NAAQS ranged from 1993 to 2010, with limited extensions available. §181(a)(1), Table 1. When Congress adopted the 1990 amendments, the Los Angeles area was the only spot that qualified as an extreme ozone nonattainment area. What deadlines apply to areas that, although once designated as attainment or unclassifiable, subsequently fall out of attainment status? See §§181(b), 192(c). The statute establishes a similar range of deadlines for CO (§186) and particulate matter (§188(c)). The states had to achieve the primary NAAQS for the other criteria pollutants as expeditiously as practicable, but not later than 1995. See §192(b).

3. General State Implementation Plan Requirements for Nonattainment Areas

Specifying new deadlines for achieving the NAAQS is one thing; actually achieving them is another. Under §107(a), the primary responsibility for achieving the NAAQS remains with the states, but the CAA constrains the discretion of the states in developing control strategies to allocate required reductions among sources. Some of the constraints apply to all states with AQCRs designated as nonattainment. A plethora of others vary, like the amended NAAQS deadlines, in accordance with the criteria pollutant for which an AQCR is classified as nonattainment and the severity of the nonattainment problem. States with nonattainment areas were required to revise their SIPs to conform to the requirements of the 1990 amendments. §172(b). The amended SIPs had to comply not only with the minimal requirements for all SIPs set forth in §110(a)(2), but also with plan provisions unique to nonattainment areas.

The general nonattainment area provisions are described in §172(c). Each state with a nonattainment area must include in its SIP an updated inventory of actual emissions from all sources of the nonattainment pollutant. §172(c)(3). The SIP must provide for reasonable further progress (RFP), defined as annual incremental reductions in emissions for the purpose of ensuring timely attainment of the NAAQS. §§172(c)(2), 171(1). Nonattainment states must implement all reasonably available control measures (RACM) as expeditiously as practicable, including emissions reductions from existing sources obtainable through the application of reasonably available control technology (RACT). §172(c)(1). May EPA define RACM as limited to those measures that would advance the date at which an area reaches attainment? See BCCA Appeal Group v. EPA, 355 F.3d 817, 847-848 (5th Cir. 2004); Sierra Club v. EPA, 314 F.3d 735 (5th Cir. 2002); Sierra Club v. EPA, 294 F.3d 155, 162 (D.C. Cir. 2002). NRDC v. EPA, 571 F.3d 1245 (D.C. Cir. 2009), held that EPA could define RACT that way. The court in Ober v. Whitman, 243 F.3d 1190 (9th Cir. 2001), upheld EPA's decision to exempt *de minimis* sources from transportation control measures.

The SIP for a state with nonattainment areas also must require permits for the construction and operation of new or modified major stationary sources in the area. §172(c)(5). This permit program, along with a similar permit program for PSD areas, is referred to as new source review (NSR).[p] It is the focus of the next subsection. Understanding how the NSR program and NSPS provisions and resulting regulatory actions intertwine and differ is critical to understanding the Act and its diverse yet overlapping strategies to reduce pollution from stationary sources.

---

p. Be careful not to confuse NSR with NSPS. Both apply to certain new or modified stationary sources. NSPS are nationally uniform technology-based standards adopted by EPA for categories of stationary sources that pose health risks. See section E of this chapter. NSR is a permit program for new or modified major stationary sources in nonattainment and PSD areas that has components of both ambient quality- and technology-based approaches to pollution control. Permit requirements are crafted to the conditions applying to the particular source seeking a permit and the area in which it is located.

Nonattainment SIPs must include other enforceable emission limitations and control techniques, including economic incentives such as emission fees and marketable permits, as well as compliance timetables. §172(c)(6). They also must include contingency measures that go into effect automatically if a nonattainment area fails to make RFP or attain the NAAQS by the applicable deadline. §172(c)(9).

The statutory provisions dealing with specific criteria pollutants may supplement or supplant these more general requirements. As ambient concentrations increase, the Act reduces the discretion of state SIP planners and imposes both more stringent controls and more mandatory plan elements. Thus, for example, SIPs that cover moderate ozone nonattainment areas must require reductions in emissions of VOCs of at least 15 percent from amounts emitted in 1990. §182(b)(1)(A). NRDC v. EPA, 571 F.3d 1245 (D.C. Cir. 2009), made it clear that ozone nonattainment areas that had complied with the 15 percent reduction requirement under the 1-hour ozone standard in effect in 1990 need not do so again now that EPA has replaced that standard with an 8-hour primary NAAQS. In serious ozone nonattainment areas, compliance with the RFP mandate entails annual reductions in emissions of VOCs of three percent from 1990 levels, with some exceptions. §182(c)(2)(B). Not surprisingly, most of the special SIP provisions for carbon monoxide nonattainment areas deal with the use of automobiles. See §187. The provisions applicable to both CO and particulate matter nonattainment areas contain annual emission reductions (called milestones) that elaborate on the RFP requirement for those areas. See, e.g., §§187(d), 189(c).

The 1990 amendments divided nonattainment areas for particulate matter into two categories, moderate and serious. SIPs for moderate areas must include provisions to ensure implementation of "reasonably available control measures." §189(a)(1)(C). SIPs for serious areas also must include provisions to ensure implementation of the "best available control measures." §189(b)(1)(B). Although the statute does not define either term, EPA has defined the latter as the maximum degree of emissions reduction of PM, determined on a case-by-case basis, taking into account economic impacts and other costs. Vigil v. Leavitt, 381 F.3d 826 (9th Cir. 2004), upheld EPA's approval of an Arizona SIP that required farmers to adopt one of a group of best management practices (BMPs) designed to reduce PM emissions. The court concluded that the "best" measures did not require farmers to adopt more than one form of BMPs. But it also held that EPA failed to explain adequately its rejection of reformulated diesel fuel required by the California Air Resources Board since 1993 as a best available control measure.

Problem 6-1

Suppose a county that is currently designated as a moderate nonattainment area for ozone pursuant to §181(a)(1) of the CAA demonstrates that, for each of the last three years, it has been in compliance with the NAAQS. The county has filed a petition with EPA to be redesignated as an attainment area under §107(d)(3)(E), but EPA has not yet ruled on the petition. EPA nevertheless issues a rule in which it declares that the county need not comply with the 15 percent RFP and attainment demonstration requirements of §182(b)(1)(A)(i) or the contingency measures requirement of §172(c)(9). In addition, EPA rules that the state will not be subject to sanctions for failure to submit SIP revisions that address these requirements. A local environmental group challenges the validity of the rule, asserting that it is inconsistent with the statutory language and purposes and with EPA's decision to continue to require the county to adhere to some nonattainment area requirements (including RACT and a vehicle I&M program). The complaint also alleges that §107(d)(3)(E) provides the exclusive means of redesignating an area from nonattainment to attainment. What arguments can EPA make to support its rule?

4. Controlling Emissions from Stationary Sources in Nonattainment Areas

a. The Scope of the New Source Review Permit Program

One of the mandatory components of a SIP that covers nonattainment areas is a permit program for the construction and operation of new or modified major stationary sources. §172(c)(5). The CAA contains a similar program for PSD areas, which is covered in section G.2 below. Together, the two permit programs are often referred to as the new source review (NSR) program. These provisions, along with §111 NSPS, §112 regulation of hazardous air pollutants, and the Title V permit program, comprise the regulatory requirements faced by many stationary pollution sources.

The *Chevron* case, reproduced in Chapter 3, and the notes that follow it deal with the scope of the nonattainment portion of the NSR program. *Chevron* also focuses on the bubble concept, to which you were introduced in section E in connection with the new source performance standards of §111. The *New York* case and the *Duke Energy* case (reproduced in section G. 2 below) also deal with the scope of NSR, in both the nonattainment and PSD contexts. The next subsection, which includes the *CARE* case, addresses the substantive requirements of the nonattainment area permit program. Because one of those, the offset requirement, raises issues similar to those that relate to the bubble concept, detailed consideration of the merits of the bubble concept and of incorporating other economic incentives into the CAA's regulatory scheme is deferred until after the *CARE* case.

CHEVRON U.S.A. INC. v. NATURAL RESOURCES DEFENSE COUNCIL, INC.
467 U.S. 837 (1984)

[See Chapter 3, page 213.]

NOTES AND QUESTIONS

1. *Chevron* stands as a strong statement on the need for deference to agency interpretations of statutes. For additional discussion of the administrative law aspects of *Chevron*, see Chapter 3, section A.2.b.

2. Why did the Court of Appeals hold that the bubble concept was inappropriate in the context of the nonattainment area program? What was the source of the "bright line" distinction upon which it relied? How do you think NRDC tried to take advantage of that distinction before the Court of Appeals? How had EPA approached

the bubble concept before it issued the regulations reviewed in this case? How did EPA explain its endorsement of the bubble concept in 1981? How convincing is the Court's reading of the legislative history of the nonattainment area permit program?

3. *The Bubble After 1990.* The 1990 amendments to the CAA explicitly endorse the bubble concept but make it more difficult to "bubble out" of NSR in certain nonattainment areas. A stationary source located in a serious ozone nonattainment area that emits or has the potential to emit fewer than 100 tons per year of VOCs, for example, may not use the bubble concept to avoid the permit program unless the increase in emissions that results from a physical change or change in the method of operation of any discrete operation, unit, or other pollutant-emitting activity at the source is offset by emissions reductions of at least 1.3 times that amount. §182(c)(7). If such a source emits or has the potential to emit 100 tons per year or more of VOCs, it may not use the bubble at all to avoid the permit program, although it may be able to avoid the stringent technology-based requirements of the permit program (described below) by achieving an internal offset ratio of at least 1.3:1. §182(c)(8). See also §182(e)(2).

4. *"Major" Sources. Chevron* focused on the issue of whether a major stationary source had been modified, thereby becoming subject to the permit requirement of §172(c)(5). But what constitutes a major stationary source for purposes of the non-attainment area permit program? The answer differs depending on the criteria pollutant for which the area is designated nonattainment and the severity of the nonattainment problem. In a serious ozone nonattainment area, for example, a major stationary source is one that emits or has the potential to emit at least 50 tons of VOCs per year. §182(c). In an extreme area the threshold is 10 tons per year. §182(e). Why did Congress lower the threshold qualifications for a major stationary source as the concentration of ozone in nonattainment areas increased?

Suppose that a business is considering constructing a warehouse that will not emit any pollutants, but will be serviced by trucks that emit CO and ozone precursors (oxides of nitrogen). The warehouse will be located in a moderate nonattainment area for both CO and ozone. If the emissions from the trucks will exceed the 100-ton threshold of §302(j), will the business have to apply for a nonattainment area permit? See Village of Oconomowoc Lake v. Dayton Hudson Corp., 24 F.3d 962 (7th Cir. 1994).

5. *What Is a Physical Change?* For years EPA has exempted from NSR physical or operational changes that qualify as "routine maintenance, repair, and replacement." In 2003, EPA adopted regulations that expanded the scope of the exemption. The following case addressed the legality of the changes.

NEW YORK v. EPA
443 F.3d 880 (D.C. Cir. 2006)

ROGERS, Circuit Judge.

In New York v. EPA, 413 F.3d 3 (D.C. Cir. 2005) ("*New York I*"), the court addressed the first of two rules promulgated by the Environmental Protection Agency providing ways for stationary sources of air pollution to avoid triggering New Source Review ("NSR"). . . . We now address the second rule, the Equipment Replacement Provision ("ERP"), which amends the Routine Maintenance, Repair, and Replacement Exclusion ("RMRR") from NSR requirements. Under [§111(a)(4) of the CAA], sources that undergo "any physical change" that increases emissions are required to undergo the NSR permitting process [under both the nonattainment and PSD permit programs]. The exclusion has historically provided that routine maintenance, repair, and replacement do not constitute changes triggering NSR. The ERP both defined and expanded that exclusion. EPA explained:

> [The] rule states categorically that the replacement of components with identical or functionally equivalent components that do not exceed 20% of the replacement value of the process unit and does not change its basic design parameters is not a change and is within the RMRR exclusion.

Hence, the ERP would allow sources to avoid NSR when replacing equipment under the twenty-percent cap notwithstanding a resulting increase in emissions. . . . We now vacate the ERP because it is contrary to the plain language of section 111(a)(4) of the Act.

. . . Since the inception of NSR, RMRR has been excluded from the definition of "modification." Heretofore, EPA applied the RMRR exclusion through "a case-by-case determination by weighing the nature, extent, purpose, frequency, and cost of the work as well as other factors to arrive at a common sense finding." Consistent with *Alabama Power Co. v. Costle*, 636 F.2d 323 (D.C. Cir. 1979), which recognized EPA's discretion to exempt from NSR "some emission increases on grounds of *de minimis* or administrative necessity," EPA has for over two decades defined the RMRR exclusion as limited to "*de minimis* circumstances." The ERP provides a bright-line rule and expands the traditional scope of the RMRR by exempting certain equipment replacements from NSR. See, e.g., 40 C.F.R. §52.21(cc) (2005).[2]

The government and environmental petitioners contend that the ERP is contrary to the plain text of the Act because the statutory definition of "modification" applies unambiguously to any physical change that increases emissions, necessarily including the emission-increasing equipment replacements excused from NSR by the rule. They maintain that the word "any," when given its natural meaning, requires that the phrase "physical change" be read broadly, such that EPA's attempt to read "physical change" narrowly would relegate the word "any" to an insignificant role. . . .

The petitioners and EPA agree that the phrase "physical change" is susceptible to multiple meanings, each citing dictionary definitions. However, "the sort of ambiguity giving rise to *Chevron* deference 'is a creature not of definitional possibilities, but of statutory context.'" *American Bar Ass'n v. FTC*, 430 F.3d 457, 469 (D.C. Cir. 2005). As the parties point out, the ordinary meaning of "physical change" includes activities that "make different in some particular," "make over to a radically different

---

2. The ERP provides:

> Without regard to other considerations, routine maintenance, repair and replacement includes, but is not limited to, the replacement of any component of a process unit with an identical or functionally equivalent component(s), and maintenance and repair activities that are part of the replacement activity, provided that all of the requirements in paragraphs (cc)(1) through (cc)(3) of this section are met.

40 C.F.R. §52.21(cc). Paragraph (cc)(1) establishes that the fixed capital cost of the replacement component cannot exceed twenty percent of the replacement value of the process unit. Paragraph (cc)(2) states that the replacement cannot change the basic design parameters of the process unit. Paragraph (cc)(3) requires that the replacement activity not cause the process unit to exceed any independent, legally enforceable emission limitation.

form," or "replace with another or others of the same kind or class." Webster's Third New International Dictionary 373 (1981). To say that it is "physical," in this context, indicates that the change must be "natural or material," rather than "mental, moral, spiritual, or imaginary." The parties agree that in "[r]eal-world, common-sense usage," "physical change" includes equipment replacements. They further agree that the ERP would excuse from NSR requirements certain emission-increasing activities that EPA has historically considered to be "physical changes."

The parties' essential disagreement, then, centers on the effect of Congress's decision in defining "modification" to insert the word "any" before "physical change." According to the petitioners, the word "any" means that the phrase "physical change" covers any activity at a source that could be considered a physical change that increases emissions. According to EPA, "any" does nothing to resolve ambiguity in the phrase it modifies. EPA maintains that because "physical change" is "susceptible to multiple meanings," "identifying activities that are 'changes' for NSR purposes . . . requires an exercise of Agency expertise," "the classic situation in which an agency is accorded deference under *Chevron*." Under this approach, once EPA has identified an activity as a "physical change," the word "any" requires that the activity be subject to NSR. We conclude that the differences between the parties' interpretations of the role of the word "any" are resolved by recognizing that "[r]ead naturally, the word 'any' has an expansive meaning, that is, 'one or some indiscriminately of whatever kind,'" United States v. Gonzales, 520 U.S. 1, 5 (1997), and that courts must give effect to each word of a statute. Because Congress used the word "any," EPA must apply NSR whenever a source conducts an emission-increasing activity that fits within one of the ordinary meanings of "physical change." . . .

Although EPA is correct that the meaning of "any" can differ depending upon the statutory setting, the context of the Clean Air Act warrants no departure from the word's customary effect. . . . [T]he question of statutory interpretation here does not arise in a setting in which the Supreme Court has required heightened standards of clarity to avoid upsetting fundamental policies. EPA points to no "strange and indeterminate results" that would emerge from adopting the natural meaning of "any" in section 111(a)(4) of the Act. Given Congress's goal in adopting the 1977 amendments of establishing a balance between economic and environmental interests, see Wisconsin Elec. Power Co. v. Reilly, 893 F.2d 901, 909-10 (7th Cir. 1990) ("WEPCo"), it is hardly "farfetched" for Congress to have intended NSR to apply to any type of physical change that increases emissions. In this context, there is no reason the usual tools of statutory construction should not apply and hence no reason why "any" should not mean "any." Indeed, EPA's interpretation would produce a "strange," if not an "indeterminate," result: a law intended to limit increases in air pollution would allow sources operating below applicable emission limits to increase significantly the pollution they emit without government review.

Even without specific reliance on the effect of "any," this court has construed the definition of "modification" broadly. In *Alabama Power*, the court explained that "the term 'modification' [in section 111(a)(4)] is nowhere limited to physical changes exceeding a certain magnitude." 636 F.2d at 400. . . . More recently, in *New York I*, the court looked to the plain meaning of section 111(a)(4) and the absence of contrary legislative history in holding that even pollution control projects constituted "physical changes." Likewise, the Seventh Circuit concluded in *WEPCo* that the purposes of the 1977 amendments to the Act required an expansive reading of the plain language of section 111(a)(4). . . .

... EPA's approach to interpreting "physical change," as well as a similar approach by industry intervenors that focuses on the thirty-nine words following "any," contravenes several rules of statutory interpretation. EPA's position is that the word "any" does not affect the expansiveness of the phrase "physical change"; it only means that, once the agency defines "change" as broadly or as narrowly as it deems appropriate, everything in the agency-defined category is subject to NSR. To begin, that reading, contrary to "a cardinal principle of statutory construction," would make Congress's use of the word "any" "insignificant" if not "superfluous." Reading the definition in this way makes the definition function as if the word "any" had been excised from section 111(a)(4); there is virtually no role for "any" to play. Additionally, the approaches of EPA and industry would require Congress to spell out all the applications covered by a definition before a court could conclude that Congress had directly spoken regarding a particular application, ignoring the fact that a definition, like a general rule, need not list everything it covers. EPA's approach would ostensibly require that the definition of "modification" include a phrase such as "regardless of size, cost, frequency, effect," or other distinguishing characteristic. Only in a Humpty Dumpty world[3] would Congress be required to use superfluous words while an agency could ignore an expansive word that Congress did use. We decline to adopt such a world-view.

In contrast, the petitioners' approach, by adopting an expansive reading of the phrase "any physical change," gives natural effect to all the words used by Congress and reflects both their common meanings and Congress's purpose in enacting the 1970 and 1977 amendments. To improve pollution control programs in a manner consistent with the balance struck by Congress in 1977 between "the economic interest in permitting capital improvements to continue and the environmental interest in improving air quality," *Chevron*, 467 U.S. at 851, Congress defined the phrase "physical change" in terms of increases in emissions. After using the word "any" to indicate that "physical change" covered all such activities, and was not left to agency interpretation, Congress limited the scope of "any physical change" to changes that "increase[] the amount of any air pollutant emitted by such source or which result[] in the emission of any air pollutant not previously emitted." 42 U.S.C. §7411(a)(4). Thus, only physical changes that do not result in emission increases are excused from NSR. Because Congress expressly included one limitation, the court must presume that Congress acted "intentionally and purposely," Barnhart v. Sigmon Coal Co., 534 U.S. 438, 452 (2002), when it did not include others. So construed, each word in the phrase "any physical change" has a meaning consonant with congressional intent and the scope of the definitional phrase is limited only by Congress's determination that such changes be linked to emission increases.

... EPA, through its historical practice and its words, has acknowledged that the equipment replacements covered by the ERP are "physical changes" under one of the ordinary meanings of the phrase. EPA may not choose to exclude that "[r]eal-world, common-sense usage of the word 'change.'" Moreover, a physical change is not the sole criterion for triggering NSR under the definition of "modification." The expansive meaning of "any physical change" is strictly limited by the requirement that the change increase emissions. See 42 U.S.C. §7411(a)(4).[4]

3. See TVA v. Hill, 437 U.S. 153, 173 n.18 (1978) (quoting Through the Looking Glass, in The Complete Works of Lewis Carroll 196 (1939)).
4. The court has no occasion to decide whether part replacements or repairs necessarily constitute a "modification" under the definition taken as a whole.

The fact that EPA, through the RMRR exclusion, has historically interpreted "any physical change" to exclude changes of trivial regulatory concern on a *de minimis* rationale, does not demonstrate that the meaning of "physical change" is ambiguous. Rather, it reflects an agency's inherent power to overlook "trifling matters." . . . Reliance on the *de minimis* doctrine invokes congressional intent that agencies diverge from the plain meaning of a statute only so far as is necessary to avoid its futile application. . . . [T]he court [in *Alabama Power*] explained that *de minimis* standards served to alleviate "severe" administrative and economic burdens by lifting requirements on "minuscule" emission increases. While the court today expresses no opinion regarding EPA's application of the *de minimis* exception, given the limits on the scope of the *de minimis* doctrine, EPA appropriately has not attempted to justify the ERP as an exercise of *de minimis* discretion. As EPA has disclaimed the assertion that its prior expansive interpretations of "any physical change" were "absurd or futile," it is in no position to claim that the ERP is necessary to avoid absurdity. . . .

. . . EPA cannot show that historical fact prevents a broad reading of "any physical change" inasmuch as EPA for decades has interpreted that phrase to mean "virtually all changes, even trivial ones, . . . generally interpret[ing] the [RMRR] exclusion as being limited to *de minimis* circumstances." 68 Fed. Reg. at 61,272.

As for logic, EPA cannot show any incoherence in Congress requiring NSR for equipment replacements that increase emissions while allowing replacements that do not increase emissions to avoid NSR. EPA acknowledges the reasonableness of its past expansive interpretation of "any physical change." To the extent that EPA relies on the argument that allowing ERP projects has the potential to lower overall emissions through increased efficiency even if emissions increase at a source, the court in *New York I* rejected EPA's similar argument in support of an exemption from NSR for pollution control projects. The court stated that "Congress could reasonably conclude, for example, that tradeoffs between pollutants are difficult to measure, and thus any significant increase in emissions of any pollutant should be subject to NSR." *New York I*, 413 F.3d at 41. Absent a showing that the policy demanded by the text borders on the irrational, EPA may not "avoid the Congressional intent clearly expressed in the text simply by asserting that its preferred approach would be better policy." *Engine Mfrs.*, 88 F.3d at 1089.

Likewise, EPA offers no reason to conclude that the structure of the Act supports the conclusion that "any physical change" does not mean what it says. EPA does not address the Act's structure except in defending the reasonableness of the ERP as a policy choice. In that context, EPA points to the Act's "many other systematic air programs," particularly "model market-based programs," as support for its view that economic and environmental interests can be effectively balanced while limiting the application of NSR to existing sources. Although EPA might prefer market-based methods of controlling pollution, Congress has chosen a different course with NSR.

Accordingly, we hold that the ERP violates section 111(a)(4) of the Clean Air Act in two respects. First, Congress's use of the word "any" in defining a "modification" means that all types of "physical changes" are covered. Although the phrase "physical change" is susceptible to multiple meanings, the word "any" makes clear that activities within each of the common meanings of the phrase are subject to NSR when the activity results in an emission increase. As Congress limited the broad meaning of "any physical change," directing that only changes that increase emissions will trigger NSR, no other limitation (other than to avoid absurd results) can be implied. The definition of "modification," therefore, does not include only physical changes that are costly or major. Second, Congress defined "modification" in terms of emission increases, but the ERP would allow equipment replacements resulting in non–*de minimis* emission increases to avoid NSR. Therefore, because it violates the Act, we vacate the ERP.

NOTES AND QUESTIONS

1. According to the court, how would its acceptance of EPA's approach have required Congress to alter its statutory drafting? Why didn't *Alabama Power*'s recognition of EPA's inherent authority to exempt *de minimis* effects from regulation support EPA's approach?

2. New York I. The court in the principal case cited New York v. EPA, 413 F.3d 3 (D.C. Cir. 2005) (*New York I*), in support of its holding that EPA's ERP rule violated the CAA. In *New York I*, the court invalidated an EPA rule that exempted sources that qualified as Clean Units from NSR, even if they were modified so as to result in an increase in emissions. The regulation defined a Clean Unit as one that had installed state-of-the-art pollution control technology as a result of undergoing NSR within the previous ten years or that could show that it had installed control technology comparable to what would have been required if NSR had occurred during that time. The court struck down the rule because §111(a)(4) defines a "modification" as *any* physical or operational change that results in an increase in emissions, yet EPA's rule allowed a change that concededly resulted in increases in emissions to escape NSR, simply because the source involved had previously made changes that triggered NSR or installed certain kinds of technologies that nevertheless would not prevent an increase in emissions at the source. In United States v. Westvaco Corp., 675 F. Supp. 2d 524 (D. Md. 2009), the court ruled that improvements to coal-fired power boilers at a paper mill triggered NSR in a PSD area. The owner claimed that the project did not qualify as a "modification" because EPA regulations exclude from that term the addition of systems whose primary function is to reduce air pollution. The mill argued that controlling emissions through the new boilers was more environmentally beneficial than the previous method of incinerating noncondensible gases, but the court found that the primary purpose of the new equipment was not to reduce emissions.

The court in *New York I* invalidated another portion of the rule that required a source making physical or operational changes to keep records and report to EPA on its emissions only if it made a determination that any physical or operational change would not significantly increase the source's emissions, thereby triggering NSR, and it nevertheless stated its belief that there was a "reasonable possibility that [the] project . . . may result in a significant emissions increase." The court found the rule to be arbitrary and capricious because EPA failed to explain how, absent record-keeping, it would be able to determine after the fact whether sources had accurately concluded that they had no reasonable possibility of significantly increased emissions.

3. *More on Routine Maintenance.* The courts have grappled with other aspects of the RMRR exemption. One issue is whether to assess what is "routine" by reference to a particular plant or to the entire industry of which it is a part. The courts have disagreed. In United States v. Ohio Edison Co., 276 F. Supp. 2d 829 (S.D. Ohio 2003), the court deferred to EPA's view that the determination of what is routine should be made on a plant-by-plant basis, taking into account the nature, extent, purpose, frequency, and cost of the activity. See also United States v. Cinergy

Corp., 495 F. Supp. 2d 909 (S.D. Ind. 2007) (project was not routine because it was a massive renovation of the plant, was designed to add 30 years of service to the plant, and cost more than $16 million, compared to average annual boiler and plant maintenance costs of $2 to $3 million). In United States v. Southern Indiana Gas and Elec. Co., 258 F. Supp. 2d 884, 886 (S.D. Ind. 2003), however, the court reasoned that "[a]lthough the routine maintenance exemption does not turn on whether a certain type of project is prevalent within industry as a whole, the frequency with which similar projects take place throughout industry" is relevant to whether the RMMR exemption applies. The court in National Parks Conservation Ass'n v. TVA, 618 F. Supp. 2d 815, 825 (E.D. Tenn. 2009), adopted the industry-wide test, but later considered whether the changes were routine by examining projects in both the industry and at the specific plant. National Parks Conservation Ass'n v. TVA, 2010 WL 1291335 (E.D. Tenn. 2010). See also United States v. Alabama Power Co., 681 F. Supp. 2d 1292 (N.D. Ala. 2008).

4. *Remedy.* What is the appropriate remedy in a case finding that a plant required to apply for a NSR permit failed to do so? See United States v. Cinergy Corp., 618 F. Supp. 2d 942 (S.D. Ind. 2009) (requiring plant shutdown, surrender of SO_2 emission allowances under the CAA's acid rain emissions trading program, payment of civil penalties, and installation of a continuous emissions monitor).

5. *What Is an "Increase"?* A "modification" of a major stationary source triggering NSR occurs only if there is a physical or operational change that results in an increase in emissions. How does one calculate whether such an increase has taken place? We return to that question in the materials introducing you to the Prevention of Significant Deterioration (PSD) program. In the *Duke Energy* case, excerpted below, industry litigants challenged EPA's approach by linking NSPS language and regulations and PSD cross-references.

b.   The Substantive Requirements of the Nonattainment Area Permit Program

The owner of a major stationary source whose construction or operation in a nonattainment area is subject to the permit program under §172(c)(5) must satisfy the program's substantive requirements to qualify for a permit. Those requirements are described in §173. Under §173(a)(2), the permit applicant will have to comply with the lowest achievable emission rate (LAER), as defined in §171(3). While §111's NSPS regulate new and modified sources by industry category and are set forth in regulations in the Code of Federal Regulations, nonattainment permit LAER determinations are made by the states on a case-by-case basis for each permit, subject to public comment and federal oversight. LAER was intended to be the strictest of the CAA's technology-based standards—stricter than the "best available control technology" (BACT), which is applicable to sources applying for PSD permits, and which in turn is stricter than the NSPS under §111.

A permit applicant also must demonstrate that all major stationary sources owned or operated by it (or by an affiliated company) are in compliance or on a schedule of compliance with all applicable emission limitations under the CAA. §173(a)(3). See Sierra Club v. Leavitt, 368 F.3d 1300 (11th Cir. 2004) (remanding to EPA to consider whether it was appropriate for state to approve nonattainment permit of partial owner of noncompliant major stationary source, where the part owned by the applicant was in compliance), *appeal after remand*, 496 F.3d 1182 (11th Cir. 2007) (affirming EPA's order approving state permit). A permit must be denied if EPA finds that the applicable SIP is not being properly implemented for the non-attainment area that includes the proposed source. §173(a)(4). Under §173(a)(5), the proposed source must be justified on cost-benefit grounds.

The potential economic benefits of the construction of new or modified major stationary sources make it easy to understand why states may want to encourage industry to undertake such projects. But how can authorization to construct and operate a major new or modified source of the nonattainment pollutant avoid exacerbating the existing nonattainment problem? How is it possible to accommodate the dual economic growth and environmental improvement objectives of the nonattainment program to which the Supreme Court referred in *Chevron*? EPA's response took the form of its offset policy, initially formulated in 1976, 41 Fed. Reg. 55,524, and later incorporated into the 1977 amendments. The statute authorizes two ways of permitting the construction and operation of major stationary sources without jeopardizing the air quality improvement objectives of the nonattainment provisions. Under §173(a)(1)(B), the so-called growth allowance provision, the state can extract from existing stationary sources and mobile sources enforceable emissions reductions greater than those that would otherwise be required by the "reasonable further progress" requirements and that would be projected as necessary to achieve timely compliance with the NAAQS deadlines. The excess reductions can then be doled out to new sources seeking permission to operate in the nonattainment area.

If the state does not build this kind of growth allowance into its SIP, then it is up to the source seeking a permit to accommodate the economic growth and air quality improvement objectives. Section 173(a)(1)(A) authorizes it to do so by securing, from whatever currently emitting sources it can, an enforceable reduction in emissions more than sufficient to offset the new emissions from the proposed facility. This type of emissions trading is called an *extra-source offset*, to distinguish it from the "bubbles," or intra-source offsets, that enable existing sources to avoid NSR altogether. EPA has explained the extra-source offset as follows:

> In *nonattainment* areas, major new stationary sources and major modifications are subject to a preconstruction permit requirement that they secure sufficient surplus emission reductions to more than "offset" their emissions. This requirement is designed to allow industrial growth in nonattainment areas without interfering with attainment and maintenance of ambient air quality standards. [51 Fed. Reg. 43,814, 43,830 (1986).]

Generally speaking, a permit applicant must secure its offset from an existing plant located in the same nonattainment area. §173(c)(1). What is the purpose of this limitation? The pollutant-specific nonattainment area provisions impose special offset requirements in certain instances. Permit applicants whose plants will be located in marginal ozone nonattainment areas, for example, must extract 1.1 pounds of reductions from existing sources for each pound of VOCs they will emit. §182(a)(4). The ratio of reductions from existing sources to emissions from the newly permitted source is 1.15:1 for moderate ozone nonattainment areas (§182(b)(5)), 1.2:1 for serious areas (§182(c)(10)), 1.3:1 for severe areas (§182(d)(2)), and 1.5:1 for extreme areas (§182(e)(1)), with some exceptions.

Problem 6-2

A frequent complaint about regulation, especially many areas of federal environmental regulation, is that neither regulated polluters nor regulators have incentives to make ongoing changes and improvements in applicable regulations or facility operations. Look at the nonattainment permit program and LAER requirements. In what ways does the Act in these provisions create, over time, regulatory dynamism, movement toward greater regulatory stringency, and regulator (and likely environmentalist) attention to best-performing polluters or jurisdictions? Do any of these provisions address or change incentives for jurisdictions to engage in a "race" to the regulatory bottom, as covered in Chapter 2?

Offset Games and Risks. One of the issues raised by extra-source offsets is whether they represent real reductions in emissions or are spurious "paper" reductions with no beneficial impact. Section 173(c)(2) addresses this issue by prohibiting the use of emissions reductions that are already required by the statute or by federal or state regulations to satisfy the offset requirement. The next case also considers this issue. A citizens group opposed plans to locate a large oil refinery in Portsmouth, Virginia due to the anticipated increase in HC emissions. The area already violated the since-repealed NAAQS for HC. Local officials, on the other hand, welcomed the prospect of new jobs and a significant annual increase in property tax income. The case arose under an Interpretive Ruling that preceded the adoption of the 1990 amendments, but the challenges and risks inherent in determining baseline emission levels and determining whether emissions offsets are truly new continue to be relevant under the current Act and under any law or program allowing use of pollution offsets. (We return to this issue in Chapter 12's coverage of climate change law.)

CITIZENS AGAINST THE REFINERY'S EFFECTS, INC. v. EPA
643 F.2d 183 (4th Cir. 1981)

K.K. HALL, Circuit Judge. . . .

[Before the 1977 amendments, the CAA] created a no-growth environment in areas where the clean air requirements had not been attained. EPA recognized the need to develop a program that encouraged attainment of clean air standards without discouraging economic growth. Thus the agency proposed an Interpretive Ruling in 1976 which allowed the states to develop an "offset program" within the State Implementation Plans. 41 Fed. Reg. 55,524 (1976). The offset program, later codified by Congress in the 1977 Amendments to the Clean Air Act, permits the states to develop plans which allow construction of new pollution sources where accompanied by a corresponding reduction in an existing pollution source. 42 U.S.C. §7502(b)(6) [since recodified at §7502(c)(5)] and §7503. In effect, a new emitting facility can be built if an existing pollution source decreases its emissions or ceases operations as long as a positive net air quality benefit occurs. [The 1976 ruling required calculation of a base time period to determine how much reduction is needed in existing pollutants to offset the new source. The ruling defined the base period as the first year of the SIP or, where the state has not yet developed a SIP, as the year in which a construction permit application is filed.]

If the proposed factory will emit carbon monoxide, sulfur dioxide, or particulates, the EPA requires that the offsetting pollution source be within the immediate vicinity of the new plant. The other two pollutants, hydrocarbons and nitrogen oxide, are less "site-specific," and thus the ruling permits the offsetting source to locate anywhere within a broad vicinity of the new source.

The Refinery

[Hampton Roads Energy Company (HREC)] proposes to build a petroleum refinery and offloading facility in Portsmouth, Virginia. Portsmouth has been unable to reduce air pollution enough to attain the national standard for one pollutant, photochemical oxidants, which is created when hydrocarbons are released into the atmosphere and react with other substances. Since a refinery is a major source of hydrocarbons, the Clean Air Act prevents construction of the HREC plant until the area attains the national standard.

[In 1975, HREC applied to a state agency (the Virginia Board, or the Board) for a refinery construction permit. The agency issued the permit in 1975 and later extended it. In an effort to facilitate its ruling for HREC, the Board proposed to use the offset ruling to comply with the CAA. In 1977, the Board submitted a SIP to EPA that included the HREC permit. The Board] proposed to offset the new HREC hydrocarbon pollution by reducing the amount of cutback asphalt[5] used for road paving operations in three highway districts by the Virginia Department of Highways. By switching from "cutback" to "emulsified" asphalt, the state can reduce hydrocarbon pollutants by the amount necessary to offset the pollutants from the proposed refinery.[6] [EPA approved the Virginia offset plan, with some modifications, despite critical comments by Citizens Against the Refinery's Effects (CARE).] . . .

The Geographic Area

CARE contends that the state plan should not have been approved by EPA since the three highway-district area where cutback usage will be reduced to offset refinery emissions was artificially developed by the state. The ruling permits a broad area (usually within one AQCR) to be used as the offset basis. . . .

The agency action in approving the use of three highway districts was neither arbitrary, capricious, nor outside the statute. First, Congress intended that the states and the EPA be given flexibility in designing and implementing SIPs. Such flexibility allows the states to make reasoned choices as to which areas may be used to offset new pollution and how the plan is to be implemented. Second, the offset program was initiated to encourage economic growth in the state. Thus a state plan designed to reduce highway department pollution in order to attract another industry is a reasonable contribution to economic growth without a corresponding increase in pollution. Third, to be sensibly administered the offset plan had to be divided into districts which could be monitored by the highway department. Use of any areas other than highway districts would be unwieldy and difficult to administer. Fourth, the scientific

5. "Cutback" asphalt has a petroleum base which gives off great amounts of hydrocarbons. "Emulsified" asphalt uses a water base which evaporates, giving off no hydrocarbons.
6. The three highway districts so designated comprise almost the entire eastern one-third of the state. This area cuts across four of the seven Virginia Air Quality Control Regions (AQCR).

understanding of ozone pollution is not advanced to the point where exact air transport may be predicted. Designation of the broad area in which hydrocarbons may be transported is well within the discretion and expertise of the agency.

The Legally Binding Plan

For several years, Virginia has pursued a policy of shifting from cutback asphalt to the less expensive emulsified asphalt in road-paving operations. The policy was initiated in an effort to save money, and was totally unrelated to a State Implementation Plan. Because of this policy, CARE argues that hydrocarbon emissions were decreasing independent of this SIP and therefore are not a proper offset against the refinery. They argue that there is not, in effect, an actual reduction in pollution.

The Virginia voluntary plan is not enforceable and therefore is not in compliance with the 1976 Interpretive Ruling which requires that the offset program be enforceable. The EPA, in approving the state plan, obtained a letter from the Deputy Attorney General of Virginia in which he stated that the requisites had been satisfied for establishing and enforcing the plan with the Department of Highways. Without such authority, no decrease in asphalt-produced pollution is guaranteed.[8] In contrast to the voluntary plan, the offset plan guarantees a reduction in pollution resulting from road-paving operations. . . . [The court affirmed EPA's approval of the SIP.]

NOTES AND QUESTIONS

1. *Subsequent Developments.* In 1997, EPA approved a request by Virginia's congressional delegation to redesignate Hampton Roads to attainment status for ozone. The area had not violated the NAAQS for three years. The delegation feared that continuing the area's nonattainment status would disrupt the Navy's plan to move jet fighter squadrons from closed bases in California and Florida to bases in the Hampton Roads area. To what extent should national security considerations factor into implementation of environmental statutes such as the Clean Air Act? See §173(e)(3). See also §§112(i)(4), 604(f); Winter v. NRDC, 555 U.S. 7 (2009); Kasza v. Browner, 133 F.3d 1159 (9th Cir. 1998); Center for Biological Diversity v. Pirie, 201 F. Supp. 2d 113 (D.D.C. 2002).

2. *Creating Emission Reduction Credits.* EPA's 1986 Emission Trading Policy Statement addressed concerns about spurious offsets. It limited emissions trading in nonattainment areas that lack a demonstrated plan to achieve attainment to trades that would produce a net air quality benefit resulting in interim progress toward attaining the NAAQS. According to EPA:

> Emission reduction credits (ERCs) are the common currency of all trading activity. ERCs may be created by reductions from either stationary, area, or mobile sources. To assure that emissions trades do not contravene relevant requirements of the Clean Air Act, only reductions which are *surplus, enforceable, permanent,* and *quantifiable* can qualify as ERCs and be banked or used in an emissions trade. [51 Fed. Reg. 43,814, 43,831 (1986).]

8. Despite the fact that the voluntary plan has been in force for several years, 1977 was the year of the highest consumption of cutback asphalt.

Did the emissions trade in *CARE* meet these requirements? EPA studies in the early 1970s revealed that water-based paving asphalt was rapidly replacing petroleum-based asphalt for energy conservation and cost reasons. By 1977, EPA had recognized water-based asphalt as a minimum "reasonably available control technology" (RACT) that existing sources of air pollution might adopt, yet EPA did not require states to impose RACT in nonattainment areas until 1979. Under the *CARE* decision, Virginia and other resourceful states could generously offer as "legally binding" offsets reduced petroleum-based asphalt use between 1976 and 1979 even though water-based asphalt was cheaper; offered a better energy conservation strategy; was a readily available, soon-to-be-required emission control technology; and was destined for highway use whether or not CAA offsets were created.

Sierra Club v. Georgia Power Co., 365 F. Supp. 2d 1287 (N.D. Ga. 2004), rejected a challenge to a state agency's issuance of a Title V CAA permit to a power company, concluding that the offsets met the state agency's requirement that they be "real, permanent, quantifiable, enforceable, and surplus." Under the state's regulations, offsets were real if they resulted in a reduction in actual emissions. They were enforceable if the state agency could enforce them as operating permit conditions. They were permanent if they were guaranteed for the life of the corresponding emission reduction credit through an enforceable mechanism such as a permit condition. They were surplus if they were not required by local, state, or federal regulations and were in excess of reductions used by the state agency in issuing other permits or to demonstrate attainment of the NAAQS or reasonable further progress toward achieving the NAAQS. In NRDC v. EPA, 571 F.3d 1245 (D.C. Cir. 2009), the court struck down portions of EPA's regulations implementing the 8-hour ozone NAAQS that allowed emission reductions occurring before a permit application to qualify for offset credits if the proposed source replaced the productive capacity represented by the proposed offset credit. The regulations included no safe-guards to ensure that issuing a permit would be consistent with §173's mandate that total reductions represent reasonable further progress.

Can a source use emission reduction credits created by the shutdown of another plant? The 1986 policy statement allowed credits for shutdowns subject to "stringent qualitative review" to ensure consistency with SIP planning goals, such as avoidance of double counting and shifting demand. Motivation was not a factor, but it had to be shown that there was an application to make the shutdown state enforceable through a banking mechanism before the shutdown occurred. The same rules applied to curtailments.

3. *The Offset Area.* The court allowed Virginia to include in the offset highways selected from any area into which HC might in time be transported, rather than confining the offsets to the urban area around the new source. Yet the Interpretive Ruling favored keeping offsets at least within the same AQCR as the proposed source. How would the Hampton Refinery offset fare after the 1990 amendments? See §173(c)(1).

4. *Establishing a Dependable and Fair Supply of Marketable Offsets.* Without a fixed, dependable base of allowable emissions, emitters will be reluctant to purchase offsets at high prices, only to be faced with the possibility of finding them plentiful and cheap the next day. Sources that can provide relatively cheap offsets (i.e., sources with inherently low emission control costs) will not want to part with their emissions rights if they believe that they will need them themselves imminently or because offsets may increase greatly in value. An EPA-approved SIP relaxation would automatically create

new offset possibilities, and a SIP constriction would potentially extinguish them. In markets in which the government prints new money or restricts money supply, prices fluctuate and the outcomes of economic transactions become less predictable. Offset transactions are sensitive to the same risks. See T. Tietenberg, Emissions Trading ch. 6 (1985).

5. *The Relationship Between LAER and the Offset Requirement.* If the offset policy is in effect, why should LAER be required? Recall that NSPS would also apply. With the offset policy in effect, are NSPS necessary? In fact, if total area-wide annual emissions quotas are set at levels adequate to ensure "reasonable further progress" and eventual attainment of the NAAQS, and if offsets within the quota can be freely bought and sold, is there a need for additional regulatory controls at all?

NOTES AND QUESTIONS ON BUBBLES, OFFSETS, AND OTHER ECONOMIC INCENTIVE–BASED REGULATORY TECHNIQUES

1. *Kinds of Economic Incentive–Based Techniques for Controlling Pollution.* Before addressing the relative merits and disadvantages, theoretical and practical, of the use of economic incentives instead of or in addition to traditional regulation to achieve emission reductions, it is helpful to review the various types of incentive-based mechanisms that have been or may be authorized under the CAA.

EPA's Emission Trading Policy Statement, 51 Fed. Reg. 43,814 (1986), endorsed the use of several kinds of emission trading. The first kind, to which you were introduced in connection with the *Chevron* case, is called netting. This form of trading enables the owner or operator of an existing source to avoid having to comply with the requirements of a permit program applicable to modifications of major stationary sources by compensating for increased emissions at some points within a source by reducing emissions elsewhere within the source to produce emission reduction credits (ERCs). A source that nets out of NSR must still comply with NSPS requirements.

A related mechanism is the bubble concept. In *Chevron*, the Supreme Court deferred to EPA's view that the bubble concept was an appropriate device to escape the nonattainment area permit program. But use of the bubble is not limited to avoidance of NSR. Existing firms can offset emissions increases and decreases in a similar manner. EPA's bubble policy for existing sources, first published in 1979, allowed a source with multiple emission points (e.g., stacks or vents), each of which is subject to specific emissions limitation requirements in an EPA-approved SIP, to meet its total SIP emissions control requirements for a given criteria pollutant with a mix of controls different from the combination mandated by its existing SIP obligations.

The nonattainment area permit program relies on a third kind of emission trading. The offset mechanism of §173(a)(1)(A), which was the subject of the *CARE* case, requires new or modified major stationary sources to extract from existing sources enforceable emission reductions that more than offset the increased emissions attributable to the permitted source.

A fourth concept, emission credit banking, "encompasses the processes of creating, certifying and storing ERCs" for later use in trading transactions. Dudek & Palmisano, Emissions Trading: Why Is This Thoroughbred Hobbled?, 13 Colum. J. Envtl. L. 217, 227 (1988). The bank purchases offsets or other emission reduction credits and holds them until an applicant needs them. EPA's Tier 2 rules establishing limits on the sulfur content of gasoline, issued under §211(c) of the Act, include a program for banking and selling sulfur reduction credits. 64 Fed. Reg. 6698 (2000). EPA regulations require crude oil refiners to meet a corporate average gasoline sulfur cap. A refinery may generate bankable credits by reducing sulfur at least 10 percent below its 1990 baseline level.

2. *The Theoretical Advantages of Emission Trading.* The primary theoretical advantage of emission trading is that it holds out the prospect for more economically efficient control of pollution than does a traditional system of regulation. Emission trading affords plant managers greater choice in deciding how to reduce emissions so that they can take advantage of the differing marginal costs of reducing emissions at different sources. Economists argue that, if left alone, plant managers will choose to reduce emissions the most in plant components with the lowest marginal emissions control costs. This strategy allows them to reduce emissions at the lowest possible cost, freeing the money saved from less efficient approaches for income-producing investment elsewhere. The application of different legal requirements to different units in a plant deprives managers of the opportunity to make these cost-minimizing choices. As EPA has recognized, the problem with traditional source-specific emission standards, such as RACT, is that

> [e]ven though set as performance standards, these regulations have a tendency to treat all sources within a category the same and to be oriented toward the lowest common denominator, that is, toward sources within the class that have the greatest difficulty and/or greatest cost of control. Such standards simultaneously miss substantial opportunities for cheap emissions controls by "better" sources, and impose a disproportionately high cost (per ton of pollutant reduced) on a smaller group of sources. Government frequently lacks information on untapped but cost-effective control options, and sources have no incentive to be forthcoming. Government also tends to overlook smaller or unconventional sources. [Open Market Trading Rule for Ozone Smog Precursors, 60 Fed. Reg. 39,668, 39,670 (1995).]

The bubble concept and offsets may allow efficient emission reductions within a plant and an area, respectively. If the total emissions allowed to escape through one imaginary vent at the top of the hypothetical bubble over a plant were projected to be equal to or less than the total approved emissions from all emissions points within the plant, the plant's operator might be able to achieve the level of control at less expense by placing relatively more control on emissions points with low marginal costs of control and less on points with high costs. With respect to offsets:

> The offset price is set by the parties. . . . [E]ach polluter will hold his rights until the offset price is greater than his costs of emission abatement. If the price of an offset is more than the cost of abatement, the rational profit-motivated decision would be to abate emissions and sell an offset. Theoretically, trading would continue until each polluter's cost of an additional reduction would equal the cost of an additional offset right. Prices would reach this equilibrium because each polluter would reduce pollution by purchasing abatement equipment until the next (marginal) reduction would be equally as costly as purchasing the right to emit pollutants. Limiting the amount of offsets through control of the supply of pollution rights would ensure that the equilibrium price would be relatively high, stimulating voluntary reductions. The allocation of rights would be economically efficient when no source could benefit from a trade without greater cost to another source. [Mendrick, Note, Regulating with a Carrot: Experimenting with Incentives for Clean Air, 31 Buff. L. Rev. 193, 204-205 (1982).]

3. *Cap-and-Trade Programs.* Cap-and-trade (or emission budget) systems set an overall cap on the amount of emissions permitted under a regulatory program as a whole. Emissions are then apportioned to sources, which can use them for compliance or sell them to other sources. This approach is used in EPA's acid rain program, which is discussed in section I.2 below. EPA has attempted to include cap-and-trade programs in other regulatory contexts without explicit statutory authorization, with mixed success. See the materials on the Clean Air Act Interstate Rule in section I.2.a of this chapter. Cap-and-trade systems tend to have lengthy startup periods because they require agreement on matters such as baseline emissions levels, the size of the cap, and the allocation of allowances. These programs historically tended to be limited to well-measured pollutants from relatively uniform industrial sectors with a comparatively small number of sources. Although not enacted, several major climate change bills sought to reduce GHG pollution through a cap-and-trade strategies, which would have applied to a wide range of numerous and disparate sources. See Chapter 12.

4. *Economic Incentive Programs.* In addition to establishing a cap-and-trade program to assist in achieving reductions in the emission of pollutants that contribute to acid rain, the 1990 amendments also endorsed the use of economic incentives in the nonattainment provisions. One of the sanctions available if a state fails to achieve RFP or comply with an applicable emission reduction milestone is the requirement that it adopt an economic incentive program (EIP), which may authorize the use of emissions fees and marketable permits. §182(g)(3). Similar requirements apply to CO nonattainment areas. See §187(d)(3). In 1994, EPA issued rules to govern the content of EIPs. Economic Incentive Program Rules, 59 Fed. Reg. 16,690. A well-designed EIP, according to EPA, will allow emission sources facing differential costs of control to lower overall control costs through emission trading and will encourage sources already able to meet their emission caps to find ways to reduce emissions beyond what traditional regulatory programs would otherwise require.

The EIP rules authorize emission trading between stationary sources subject to the RACT requirement and any sources (stationary, mobile, or area) not subject to RACT if trading will result in an "exceptional environmental benefit," defined as a level of reductions that is significantly greater than RACT-level amounts. Is this authorization consistent with §172(c)(1) of the Act? Does that provision require each existing source subject to RACT to itself make the reductions achievable by the application of RACT? Or may a source subject to RACT comply with its obligations under a SIP by making no reductions itself, but instead purchasing excess emission reductions from other sources, including mobile sources? Which interpretation of §172(c)(1) is more consistent with the concept of technology forcing? Which is more consistent with the economically efficient reduction of emissions? If these two goals conflict, which should take precedence?

5. *Objections to Emission Trading.* Despite its potential for achieving emission reductions more efficiently than more traditional regulation can, emission trading has not been universally lauded. Some environmentalists have argued that emission trading programs tend to subordinate environmental quality objectives to the pursuit of economic efficiency. Others have objected to emission trading on moral grounds, claiming that clean air is a right that should not be for sale at any price. They complain that "[a]llowing firms to trade emission rights sends a message that decisions about tradeoffs between economics and environmental quality can be left to the polluters." Hahn, Regulatory Reform at EPA: Separating Fact from Illusion, 4 Yale J. on Reg. 173, 179-80 (1986).

Trading proposals have been attacked on both economic and environmental grounds. Since avoiding NSPS or NSR would allow an existing plant to continue to pollute at the same level while expanding or rebuilding, the bubble and kindred schemes create an incentive to keep an old plant in operation long past its optimal lifetime and discourage the opening of new plants. Thus, two very important national goals—one environmental and one economic—are frustrated: (1) as a general rule, new plants emit less pollution than existing ones; and (2) new plants are more productive because they are built to reflect changing markets, population shifts, fluctuations in resources and labor supplies, and competitive opportunity. But some regard as the source of the problem the core traditional regulatory programs, not the trading components added onto them. In this view, the difficulty arises

> where emission control is typically far more expensive, per unit of pollution, when accomplished by retrofitting old plants than by including state-of-the-art control technology in new ones. In the interests of reasonable thrift, such regulation inevitably imposes more demanding standards on the new. But that provides an incentive for firms to string out the life of old plants. Indefinite plant life is impossible without modifications, however, so the statute conditions modifications on the firm's use of technological improvements. This in turn replicates the original dilemma: a broad concept of modification extends both the scope of the mandate for improved technology and the incentive to keep the old. By contrast, emissions charges or marketable pollution entitlements provide incentives for firms to use—*at any and every plant*—all pollution control methods that cost less per unit than the emissions charge or the market price of an entitlement, as the case may be. [New York v. EPA, 413 F.3d 3, 45 (D.C. Cir. 2005) (Williams, J., concurring).]

Another environmental objection to emissions trading is based on the possibility that trades will result in the development of "hot spots" of pollution, where concentrations of the traded pollutant are dangerously high or otherwise interfere with statutory ambient quality objectives.

The use of economic incentives as a substitute for or supplement to traditional regulation has been hailed as a means of increasing governmental accountability. Professors Ackerman, Stewart, and Sunstein all have argued that trading programs are preferable to traditional regulation because they require as a starting point an explicit decision concerning what levels of pollution are acceptable. Debate over appropriate levels of pollution control rather than over appropriate control technologies will be more accessible, and for that reason will inspire broader public participation and promote reasoned governmental decisionmaking regarding environmental goals. The effect will be to shift responsibility for pollution control decisions from bureaucrats and self-interested factions to the affected public.[r] But this claim has prompted skepticism as well.

> [The history of the adoption of the acid rain provisions of the 1990 amendments to the CAA] challenges the view that establishing a system of marketable pollution permits will promote . . . democratic values, such as deliberation, decentralization, and freedom from faction. . . . In reality, Congress paid little attention to the overall limit on sulfur

r. See, e.g., Ackerman & Stewart, Reforming Environmental Law: The Democratic Case for Market Incentives, 13 Colum. J. Envtl. L. 171 (1988); Sunstein, Administrative Substance, 1991 Duke L.J. 607; Sunstein, Democratizing America Through Law, 25 Suffolk L. Rev. 949 (1991).

dioxide emissions set by the 1990 Amendments. . . . Moreover, the market system created by the 1990 Amendments owes much of its content to the influence of special interest groups. . . . Thus, the legislative process that created this new market system appears to have been exactly the kind of process which proponents of market-based regulation had hoped to move beyond. . . .

. . . [T]he elimination of democracy-based justifications for pollution trading requires us to face squarely the distributional objections to pollution trading. . . . If pollution trading programs are indeed more democratic . . . , then the distributional objection is of little moment because one might assume that citizens effectively agreed to the distributional mechanism through their participation in the decisionmaking process. However, if pollution trading programs do not assure meaningful citizen participation in decisions about the environment, then the distributional objection goes unmet: some unconsenting citizens must endure greater pollution, in the service of reducing the overall costs of environmental compliance. [Heinzerling, Selling Pollution, Forcing Democracy, 14 Stan. Envtl. L.J. 300, 318, 343 (1995).]

Johnson, Economics v. Equity: Do Market-Based Environmental Reforms Exacerbate Environmental Injustice?, 56 Wash. & Lee L. Rev. 111 (1999), claims that market-based reforms will probably exacerbate environmental justice problems.

6. *Emission Trading in Practice.* Some reports indicate that early source bubbles did not decrease emissions and resulted in little technological innovation. Driesen, The Economic Dynamics of Environmental Law: Cost-Benefit Analysis, Emissions Trading, and Priority-Setting, 31 B.C. Envtl. Aff. L. Rev. 501, 519 (2004), argues that "[t]rading reduces the incentive for high-cost sources to apply new technology. In theory, emissions trading probably weakens net incentives for innovation." Others have concluded that "paper trades" of emission credits that never really existed or that would have happened anyway (such as a credit resulting from a plant shutdown or a credit resulting from plant-controlled emissions that are lower than RACT) in some cases may have actually increased rather than lowered emissions. Similarly, despite its theoretical promise, the offset mechanism is rarely used. See Reitze, A Century of Air Pollution Control Law: What's Worked; What's Failed; What Might Work, 21 Envtl. L. 1549, 1628 (1991).

Netting out to avoid NSR has been a more popular form of emission trading and seems to have produced substantial cost savings. Hahn & Hester, *supra*, at 132-136. Netting does not appear to have had much of an effect on environmental quality, primarily because the nonattainment problem in the areas in which netting has occurred is due principally to mobile sources. Because netting is an internal trade, it may actually dampen the market for external trades if a source can accomplish the same objective internally.

Why has industry not embraced emission trading to the extent that its proponents predicted? Uncertainties in the process may have inhibited trading. Professor Reitze asserts, for example, that information is often lacking about both baseline and actual current emissions. Banking, which allows businesses to save emission reduction credits for future use, has been "almost nonexistent." Reitze, *supra*, at 1628-1629. The failure to take advantage of available banking mechanisms is due in large part to fears that regulators will tighten emission control requirements and thus effectively eliminate what once was an emission surplus. High transaction costs attributable to the need of potential traders to negotiate trade terms and to secure the approval of regulators also discourage trading. Inertia and concerns over the legality of particular trades are additional culprits.

Some state emission trading programs have not fared well. New Jersey environmental officials announced plans in 2002 to end a highly touted trading program, characterizing it as "an experiment that failed." The program's critics had complained that it resulted in a shifting of emissions from one source to another but not in emissions reductions. See DeMarco, The Origin and Demise of New Jersey's Open Market Emissions Trading Program, 35 Envtl. L. Rep. 10032 (2005) (arguing that the program was plagued by an "absence of real safeguards and numerical targets essential to achieving substantiated environmental improvements"). A California trading program has been called "an unmitigated disaster from both a public health and an administrative perspective." Steinzor, "You Just Don't Understand!"—The Right and Left in Conversation, 32 Envtl. L. Rep. 11109 (2002).[s] Monitoring and enforcement costs incurred by the states under these cap-and-trade programs tend to be higher than they are under the acid rain program covered in section I.2.b of this chapter (and in some cases higher than similar costs in administering traditional regulatory programs) because of the diversity of the participating sources. See McAllister, Beyond Playing "Banker": The Role of the Regulatory Agency in Emissions Trading, 59 Admin. L. Rev. 269 (2008).

7. *Emission Trading and the Constitution.* Does the government risk incurring liability under the taking clause if it authorizes emission trading, such as the banking of emission reduction credits, and subsequently renders such banked credits worthless by reducing permissible emission levels? What are the arguments for and against the conclusion that a compensable regulatory taking has occurred in those circumstances? Consider §403(f) of the CAA, which deals with the trading scheme that forms a part of the acid deposition control provisions of the statute. See generally Austin, Comment, Tradable Emissions Programs: Implications Under the Takings Clause, 26 Envtl. L. 323 (1996).

8. *Beyond Emission Trading.* The incentive-based techniques discussed above all involve the engrafting of trading schemes onto more traditional regulatory programs. Would it be possible to scrap those programs altogether and substitute a new strategy that relies wholly on the economics-based approach? One such strategy would rely on emissions fees or taxes instead of regulatory restrictions. See W. Baumol & W. Oates, The Theory of Environmental Policy 135 (1975); J. Dales, Pollution, Property, and Prices (1968).

A pure emissions fee would not be based on achieving predetermined levels of ambient air quality; rather, it would be set by comparing the dollar value of the *marginal* (additional or incremental) damage to health and welfare caused by the last unit of pollutant emitted with the emitter's *marginal* investment in emissions control equipment that will abate that additional unit of pollution. The fee for each unit of pollutant emitted should be set equal to the dollar amount at which the marginal damage and marginal abatement costs are equal. In Figure 6-7, for example, as Plant 1's SO_x emissions increase (right to left) to hypothetical maximum uncontrolled emissions of 100 tons, the marginal health and other environmental injury, expressed in dollars, increases with each marginal ton of emissions (MD). But as Plant 1 installs more emissions control equipment or otherwise reduces sulfur emissions, its marginal costs of controlling each additional ton rise (MC, left to right).

---

s. For a discussion of emission trading programs in a variety of air pollution and other contexts, see Environmental Trading, 20 Nat. Resources & Env't 1 (Summer 2005) (entire issue devoted to analysis of emission trading).

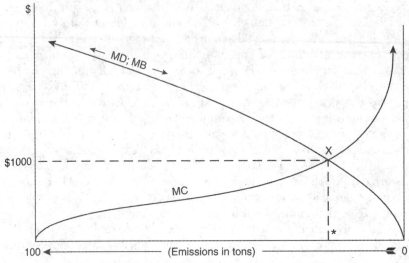

FIGURE 6-7
Plant 1: SO$_x$ Emissions

Source: http://www.epa.gov/oar/oaqps/regusmog/smog.html (removed).

The MC curve becomes especially steep as it approaches very low emissions levels. Abatement may proceed in phases, as large units of pollution control equipment are added, one after the other, so that the MC curve becomes a staircase. The MD curve also plots the marginal benefits (MB) of increased abatement, read as reduced damages from left to right. It arguably represents the willingness of receptors to "bribe" Plant 1 to reduce emissions or the amount receptors should be willing to invest to avoid injury to themselves.

At X, marginal damage equals marginal abatement cost. The emissions fee should be set equal to $1,000 per ton—no more, no less. A higher fee would reduce emissions and cause more to be spent on pollution control, but the additional pollution control costs would exceed the additional benefits (in terms of reduced damage) from the increased abatement. A lower fee would not stimulate Plant 1 to control all possible emissions of pollutant for which abatement is cheaper than the injury the emissions inflict.

The practical problems of calculating the dollar value of marginal damage and abatement costs for individual sources in thousands of specific settings are overwhelming. The pure emissions fee, therefore, remains more of an ideal than a concrete proposal for legislative action. A more practical variant, *averaging* marginal abatement costs across entire categories of emitters, has attracted numerous proponents. On the injury side, even the most serious fee system advocates concede the difficulty of computing regional or national environmental injury costs associated with varying pollution levels. For analysis of the use of a carbon tax to address global climate change, see the symposium The Reality of Carbon Taxes in the 21st Century, 10 Vt. J. Envtl. L. 1-179 (2008).

5. *Sanctions for Failure to Comply with Nonattainment Area Requirements*

The issue of what steps to take against states failing to comply with the obligations imposed on them to achieve the NAAQS has long been a troublesome one. The 1977 amendments imposed a ban on new construction of major stationary sources in nonattainment areas if the state did not attain the standards by 1983. EPA also could withhold the state's sewage treatment funding if SIP submission and compliance deadlines were not met. §316.

The 1990 amendments represented both a loosening and a tightening of the screws on states with persistent nonattainment problems. Congress repealed EPA's authority to impose the most dreaded sanction, the moratorium on the construction of major stationary sources, although in some instances moratoria imposed before 1990 remained in effect. §110(n)(3). But §179(a) of the amended Act confirmed EPA's power to impose sanctions on states that fail to submit required SIP revisions, submit unacceptable revisions, or fail to implement approved SIP provisions, absent timely corrective action by the state within 18 months. In these circumstances, EPA may withhold federal grants for air pollution planning and control programs, prohibit the award of federal highway construction funds, or increase the ratio of emission reductions from existing sources to emission increases from new or modified major stationary sources needed to satisfy the offset requirement of §173(a)(1). How much sense does the first of these sanctions make? Compare §179(b)(1)(B). Section 179(d)(2) requires that when EPA makes a finding of nonattainment, the affected state must revise its SIP to include "all measures that can be feasibly implemented in the area in light of technological achievability." In Latino Issues Forum v. EPA, 558 F.3d 936 (9th Cir. 2009), the court held that EPA has the discretion to choose which measures among those that are feasible to require the state to include in its SIP.

In addition to these general sanctions, the statute provides for special sanctions that apply to noncompliance with the ozone, CO, and particulate matter nonattainment provisions. If a severe ozone nonattainment area fails to achieve the primary NAAQS on time, major stationary sources of VOCs within the area become subject to penalty fees for each ton emitted. §185(a)-(b). The statute requires that, under certain circumstances, EPA reclassify nonattainment areas that do not meet the NAAQS attainment deadlines (e.g., from serious to severe). §181(b)(2)(A). EPA may adjust statutory deadlines (other than attainment dates) when it reclassifies an ozone nonattainment area. §182(i). Suppose that a serious ozone nonattainment area fails to meet the applicable compliance deadline because of emissions that originate in another state. May EPA extend the deadline for compliance without reclassifying the area as severe? See Southern Organizing Comm. for Econ. and Soc. Justice v. EPA, 333 F.3d 1288 (11th Cir. 2003); Sierra Club v. EPA, 311 F.3d 853 (7th Cir. 2002). In those cases, the courts struck down EPA's policy of allowing extensions of compliance deadlines for nonattainment areas adversely affected by upwind emissions of ozone precursors. Cf. Sierra Club v. EPA, 356 F.3d 296 (D.C. Cir. 2004) (approving EPA's decision to extend deadline for submitting revised SIP for severe area). The sanctions for defaulting CO and particulate matter nonattainment areas are similar to those for ozone. See §§186(b)(2)(A), 187(d)(3), (g), 188(b)(2), 189(d).

G.   PREVENTION OF SIGNIFICANT DETERIORATION

1.   *Origins and Purposes of the PSD Program*

The Origins of PSD. Lurking in the background in the early 1970s was the issue of whether air quality in areas of the nation that already enjoyed air cleaner than that required by the NAAQS should be allowed to deteriorate to the ambient standards. Congress did not address the nondegradation issue until 1977. In the meantime, motivated primarily to protect the unique vistas in the western national parks, the Sierra Club sued EPA in 1972 to force it to do so. It adopted a simple legal argument: Congress plainly stated in §101 that a purpose of the CAA was to "protect" as well as "enhance" air resources. The Club thought that EPA had to take Congress at its cryptic word.

Relying on §101, legislative history from the 1960s, and prior federal commitments to maintain existing air quality, a federal district court held that EPA had a nondiscretionary duty to adopt measures that would improve air quality and prevent all but nonsignificant deterioration of existing high air quality levels. The circuit court affirmed without issuing an opinion, and the Supreme Court also affirmed, without opinion, dividing 4-4 on the issue. Sierra Club v. Ruckelshaus, 344 F. Supp. 253 (D.D.C. 1972), *aff'd per curiam without opinion*, 2 Envtl. L. Rep. (ELI) 20656 (D.C. Cir. 1972), *aff'd by an equally divided Court*, 412 U.S. 541 (1973). Congress endorsed that result in the 1977 amendments.

The Purposes of PSD. The PSD program, §§160-169A, was designed to achieve several goals. One justification was health-based: the primary NAAQS might turn out to be insufficient to protect against known or suspected adverse effects of ambient concentrations of the criteria pollutants. Limiting pollutant concentrations in so-called clean-air areas might also reduce adverse health and welfare effects, such as acid rain and visibility impairment, resulting from long-range transport of air pollutants. The PSD program sought to provide special protection to scenic vistas in pristine areas of the West. It also responded to fears that, absent protection of air quality better than that required by the NAAQS, states with clean air could compete for industrial expansion using the ability to degrade air quality as a bargaining chip. Thus, a PSD program would equalize the burden of air pollution controls among more and less industrialized areas. See H.R. Rep. No. 95-294, at 103-141 (1977).

The leading study of the justifications for a nondegradation policy is still Hines, A Decade of Nondegradation Policy in Congress and the Courts: The Erratic Pursuit of Clean Air and Clean Water, 62 Iowa L. Rev. 643 (1977). According to Professor Hines, the policy responds to "the historical evidence that, unless restrained by some external force or internal command, mankind incessantly exploits and ultimately despoils or destroys natural environments" and recognizes that "it is morally necessary to think about what kind of world will be passed along to future generations." Id. at 649. Thus, "[w]hile the nondegradation principle does not rely solely on philosophical grounds for its justification, . . . the ethical force of the idea best explains the action taken." Id.

Development of the Regulatory Program for PSD. EPA issued its first set of PSD regulations in 1974. After adoption of the 1977 amendments to the CAA, EPA issued a second set of PSD guidelines (43 Fed. Reg. 26,380), which was immediately challenged in court. The reviewing court's decision in Alabama Power Co. v. Costle, 636

F.2d 323 (D.C. Cir. 1979), provided a kind of environmental lawyer's PSD hornbook. *Alabama Power* reshaped the PSD program to an appreciable extent. To implement the decision, EPA revised its regulations again. 45 Fed. Reg. 52,676 (1980).

2. The Current PSD Program: An Overview

The following excerpt describes the highlights of the current PSD program.[u] Keep in mind that an AQCR can be a PSD area for one or more pollutants even though it is a nonattainment area for other pollutants, and no part of the country is nonattainment for all pollutants. The PSD regulations are at 40 C.F.R. §52.21.

NATIONAL RESEARCH COUNCIL OF THE NATIONAL ACADEMY OF SCIENCES, ON PREVENTION OF SIGNIFICANT DETERIORATION OF AIR QUALITY
5-18 (1981)

In the Clean Air Act Amendments of 1977, Congress specified the initial classification of the lands for PSD purposes. [Under §162(a),][c]ertain lands, where existing good air quality is deemed to be of national importance, were designated Class I and may not be reclassified. These mandatory Class I areas include all international parks, national wilderness areas larger than 5,000 acres, national memorial parks larger than 5,000 acres, and national parks larger than 6,000 acres that were in existence when the amendments were passed. [Under §162(b), a]ll other areas to which the PSD provisions apply were initially designated Class II. . . . [The Act provides procedures for reclassification to Class I or III.[v]]

Defining Significant Deterioration

[Section 163 of][t]he Act defines significant deterioration due to the presence of sulfur dioxide (SO_2) and total suspended particulate matter (TSP) by setting maximum allowable increases over baseline concentrations (increments) for these pollutants for each of three classes of land, subject to the restriction that the allowed increases may not result in concentrations that exceed either the primary or the secondary NAAQS. Increments for SO_2 and TSP called Set I pollutants are defined for both a long-term (annual) average concentration and maximum concentrations over short periods of time. . . .

As a result of the decision in Alabama Power v. Costle, the baseline concentration includes (a) the ambient concentration resulting from actual emissions from existing sources at the time of the first application for a permit to construct a major emitting facility in a PSD area, and (b) the projected emissions from major stationary

---

u. For a thorough review of the program, see Oren, Prevention of Significant Deterioration: Control-Compelling v. Site-Shifting, 74 Iowa L. Rev. 1 (1988).

v. Congress intended that the federal government play a limited role in reviewing decisions by state governments or Indian tribes to redesignate areas as Class I or Class III on social, economic, or environmental grounds. See, e.g., Arizona v. EPA, 151 F.3d 1205 (9th Cir. 1998), *amended*, 170 F.3d 870 (9th Cir. 1999). No state has redesignated a PSD area as Class III.

sources that began construction before January 6, 1975, but had not begun operation by the time of the first permit application. [See §169(4).] . . .

The 1977 Amendments also require EPA to devise means for preventing significant deterioration of air quality from other pollutants regulated under the Act. [These are called the Set II pollutants; see §166.]

Preconstruction Review

To assess the potential consequences of emissions from new sources for ambient air quality and the consumption of increments, proposed sources of pollution must be reviewed before construction [under §165(a)]. However, not all sources are subject to preconstruction review for PSD purposes. Only major stationary sources or major modifications to existing stationary sources in areas in which the PSD provisions apply are subject to review. As a result of the decision in Alabama Power v. Costle, a major source located in a nonattainment area is not subject to PSD review even if emissions from the source adversely affect air quality in a PSD area, unless the affected PSD area and the source are in different states.

There are two classes of major stationary sources. In one class are all stationary sources that emit or have the potential to emit 250 or more tons per year of any pollutant regulated under the Act. In the other class are any stationary sources from a list of 28 types of industrial facilities that emit or have the potential to emit 100 tons or more per year of any regulated pollutant. . . . [Section 169(1) contains the list.]

In EPA's earlier regulations, the potential for a source to emit pollutants was to be judged without taking into account any air pollution control equipment. The decision in *Alabama Power* overturned this interpretation, and thus potential to emit now means the maximum capacity of a source to emit pollutants under its actual physical and operational design, which includes any air pollution control equipment. . . .

Major modifications of existing sources are defined as physical or operational changes that result in a significant net increase in emissions of any pollutant regulated under the Act. Regulations specify what a significant increase is for each pollutant. . . .

Stationary point sources that are not large enough to be classified as major sources and distributed sources such as urban growth . . . , including emissions from mobile sources that accompany this growth, are not subject to preconstruction review; however, changes in air quality due to emissions from such sources are to be counted against the increments. It is up to the permitting authorities to maintain inventories of the nonmajor sources as well as the major sources and to assess the effects of emissions from both major and nonmajor sources. . . .

The AQRV [Air Quality—Related Values] Test for Class I Areas

To represent the national interest in Class I areas that encompass federal lands, federal officials have been given special roles in the preconstruction review of proposed facilities that may affect those lands. Under the Act, the federal land manager and the federal official who is directly responsible for managing federal land in a Class I area have an affirmative responsibility to protect AQRVs in that land. One way of discharging that responsibility is to determine whether a proposed major source will adversely affect those values. The federal land manager is the secretary of the department with authority over the federal land in question. Other than visibility, the Act does not specify what AQRVs are.

Even if Class I increments have not been consumed and a proposed new source would not cause or contribute to concentrations of pollutants that exceed the increments, a construction permit cannot be issued if the federal land manager demonstrates to the satisfaction of the state that the proposed facility would nonetheless have adverse consequences for AQRVs on the federal lands in question.

Conversely, when Class I increments have been consumed or when a proposed source would cause or contribute to concentrations of pollutants that do exceed the increments, a permit may still be issued if the applicant can demonstrate to the satisfaction of the federal land manager that the emissions from the facility will not have adverse consequences for AQRVs on federal lands in the Class I area. The burden of proof in these circumstances is on the applicant. When such waivers of the Class I increments are granted, the Act specifies new maximum allowable increases over ambient concentrations, which are the same as the increments for Class II areas. . . .

Neither the AQRV test nor waivers and variances are applicable to Class II and III areas. [This report goes on to discuss provisions to protect visibility in such mandatory Class I areas. Section G.3 below includes further discussion of those provisions.]

PSD Stationary Source Permitting. As in other contexts involving regulation of stationary pollution sources, disputes over the stringency of resulting regulation often involve a mix of statutory parsing about performance levels and questions about the roles of citizens, states, federal regulators, and the courts. The following case raises all of these issues, with a substantial federalism overlay.

ALASKA DEPARTMENT OF ENVIRONMENTAL CONSERVATION v. EPA
540 U.S. 461 (2004)

Justice GINSBURG delivered the opinion of the Court.

[The issue in this case was whether EPA could block construction of a new major pollutant-emitting facility to which the Alaska Department of Environmental Conservation (ADEC) had issued a PSD permit on the ground that ADEC's best available control technology (BACT) determination was unreasonable in light of §169(3).

Under §165(a)(1) of the CAA, no "major emitting facility" may be constructed or modified unless a permit prescribing emission limitations has been issued for the facility. Alaska's SIP imposed an analogous requirement, and in particular, it required a PSD permit for a modification that increased nitrogen oxide (NO_x) emissions by more than 40 tons per year. Among other things, §165(a)(4) bars issuance of a PSD permit unless "the proposed facility is subject to the best available control technology" (BACT), as defined in §169(a)(3), for each pollutant subject to regulation that is emitted from the facility. Alaska regulations defined BACT in similar terms as "the emission limitation that represents the maximum reduction achievable for each regulated air contaminant, taking into account energy, environmental and economic impacts, and other costs."

Cominco operated a zinc mine, the Red Dog Mine, in northwest Alaska. The mine was the region's largest private employer and it supplied a quarter of the area's wage base. In 1988, ADEC issued a PSD permit to Cominco to operate the mine, which qualified as a "major emitting facility" under the CAA and Alaska's SIP. In 1996, Cominco initiated a project that would expand zinc production by 40 percent and increase NO_x emissions by more than 40 tons per year. It applied to ADEC for a PSD permit to allow increased electricity generation by one of its standby generators, MG-5. On March 3, 1999, ADEC proposed to define BACT for MG-5 as an emission control technology known as selective catalytic reduction (SCR),[5] which reduces NO_x emissions by 90 percent. Cominco responded by proposing as BACT an alternative control technology—Low NO_x[6]—that achieves a 30 percent reduction in NO_x pollutants.

ADEC staff initially concluded that SCR was BACT for MG-5. It found that SCR "is the most stringent" technology and that it was technically and economically feasible. It also pointed out that "SCR has been installed on similar diesel-fired engines throughout the world." Despite the staff's conclusion that SCR was "techno-logically, environmentally, and economically feasible" for Cominco, ADEC endorsed the use of Low NO_x in a draft PSD permit. EPA objected to ADEC's failure to designate SCR as BACT. In response, ADEC issued a second draft permit on September 1, 1999, again finding Low NO_x to be BACT. Contradicting the staff's previous conclusion that SCR was "technically and economically feasible," ADEC found that SCR imposed "a disproportionate cost" on the mine. According to ADEC, requiring SCR for a rural Alaska utility would lead to a 20 percent price increase, and, in comparison with other BACT technologies, SCR came at a "significantly higher" cost. ADEC's technical analysis contained no economic basis for a comparison between the mine and a rural utility.

EPA protested again, stating in a letter to ADEC that "Cominco has not ade-quately demonstrated any site-specific factors to support their claim that the installa-tion of [SCR] is economically infeasible" at the mine, and that ADEC's refusal to designate SCR as BACT on cost-effectiveness grounds was erroneous. EPA suggested that ADEC analyze whether requiring SCR would have adverse economic impacts on Cominco. Cominco declined to submit financial data to ADEC, stating that such an inquiry was unnecessary and expressing "concerns related to confidentiality." Cominco asserted that its debt was high despite continuing profits and invoked the need for "[i]ndustrial development in rural Alaska."

On December 10, 1999, ADEC issued the final permit, approving Low NO_x as BACT. ADEC failed to include the economic analysis EPA had suggested, con-ceding that it had made "no judgment . . . as to the impact of . . . [SCR's] cost on the operation, profitability, and competitiveness of the Red Dog Mine." ADEC relied on SCR's adverse effect on the mine's "impact on the economic diversity" of the region and on the venture's "world competitiveness." ADEC did not explain how it could assess adverse effects on the region's economy or the mine's "world competitiveness" without financial information showing SCR's impact on the oper-ation of the mine.

5. SCR requires injections of "ammonia or urea into the exhaust before the exhaust enters a catalyst bed made with vanadium, titanium, or platinum. The reduction reaction occurs when the flue gas passes over the catalyst bed where the NO_x and ammonia combine to become nitrogen, oxygen, and water. . . ."

6. In Low NO_x, changes are made to a generator to improve fuel atomization and modify the combustion space to enhance the mixing of air and fuel.

EPA issued two orders to ADEC under §§113(a)(5) and 167. The first prohibited ADEC from issuing a PSD permit to Cominco "unless ADEC satisfactorily documents why SCR is not BACT." The second prohibited Cominco from commencing construction or modification at the mine. ADEC and Cominco sought review of EPA's orders in the Ninth Circuit, which held that §§113(a)(5) and 167 authorized EPA to issue the orders and that it had properly exercised its discretion in doing so. It stated that EPA had "authority to determine the reasonableness or adequacy of the state's justification for its decision." EPA did not abuse its discretion because (1) Cominco failed to "demonstrat[e] that SCR was economically infeasible" and (2) "ADEC failed to provide a reasoned justification for its elimination of SCR as a control option."]

III

Centrally at issue in this case is the question whether EPA's oversight role, described by Congress in CAA §§113(a)(5) and 167, extends to ensuring that a state permitting authority's BACT determination is reasonable in light of the statutory guides. . . . In notably capacious terms, Congress armed EPA with authority to issue orders stopping construction when "a State is not acting in compliance with any [CAA] requirement or prohibition . . . relating to the construction of new sources or the modification of existing sources," §7413(a)(5), or when "construction or modification of a major emitting facility . . . does not conform to the requirements of [the PSD program]," §7477. . . .

All parties agree that one of the "many requirements in the PSD provisions that the EPA may enforce" is "that a [PSD] permit contain a BACT limitation." It is therefore undisputed that the Agency may issue an order to stop a facility's construction if a PSD permit contains no BACT designation.

EPA reads the Act's definition of BACT, together with CAA's explicit listing of BACT as a "[p]reconstruction requiremen[t]," to mandate not simply a BACT designation, but a determination of BACT faithful to the statute's definition. In keeping with the broad oversight role §§113(a)(5) and 167 vest in EPA, the Agency maintains, it may review permits to ensure that a State's BACT determination is reasonably moored to the Act's provisions. We hold . . . that the Agency has rationally construed the Act's text and that EPA's construction warrants our respect and approbation.

BACT's statutory definition requires selection of an emission control technology that results in the "maximum" reduction of a pollutant "achievable for [a] facility" in view of "energy, environmental, and economic impacts, and other costs." 42 U.S.C. §7479(3). This instruction, EPA submits, cabins state permitting authorities' discretion by granting only "authority to make *reasonable* BACT determinations," i.e., decisions made with fidelity to the Act's purpose "to insure that economic growth will occur in a manner consistent with the preservation of existing clean air resources," 42 U.S.C. §7470(3). Noting that state permitting authorities' statutory discretion is constrained by CAA's strong, normative terms "maximum" and "achievable," §7479(3), EPA reads §§113(a)(5) and 167 to empower the federal Agency to check a state agency's unreasonably lax BACT designation.

EPA stresses Congress' reason for enacting the PSD program—to prevent significant deterioration of air quality in clean-air areas within a State and in neighboring States. §§7470(3), (4). That aim, EPA urges, is unlikely to be realized absent an

EPA surveillance role that extends to BACT determinations. The Agency notes in this regard a House Report observation:

> Without national guidelines for the prevention of significant deterioration a State deciding to protect its clean air resources will face a double threat. The prospect is very real that such a State would lose existing industrial plants to more permissive States. But additionally the State will likely become the target of "economic-environmental blackmail" from new industrial plants that will play one State off against another with threats to locate in whichever State adopts the most permissive pollution controls. [H.R. Rep. No. 95-294, p. 134 (1977).]

. . . Federal agency surveillance of a State's BACT designation is needed, EPA asserts, to restrain the interjurisdictional pressures to which Congress was alert. . . .

ADEC argues that the statutory definition of BACT, §7479(3), unambiguously assigns to "the permitting authority" alone determination of the control technology qualifying as "best available." Because the Act places responsibility for determining BACT with "the permitting authority," ADEC urges, CAA excludes federal Agency surveillance reaching the substance of the BACT decision. EPA's enforcement role, ADEC maintains, is restricted to the requirement "that the permit contain a BACT limitation."

Understandably, Congress entrusted state permitting authorities with initial responsibility to make BACT determinations "case-by-case." §7479(3). A state agency, no doubt, is best positioned to adjust for local differences in raw materials or plant configurations, differences that might make a technology "unavailable" in a particular area. But the fact that the relevant statutory guides—"maximum" pollution reduction, considerations of energy, environmental, and economic impacts—may not yield a "single, objectively 'correct' BACT determination," surely does not signify that there can be no unreasonable determinations. Nor does Congress' sensitivity to site-specific factors necessarily imply a design to preclude in this context meaningful EPA oversight under §§113(a)(5) and 167. EPA claims no prerogative to designate the correct BACT; the Agency asserts only the authority to guard against unreasonable designations.

Under ADEC's interpretation, EPA properly inquires whether a BACT determination appears in a PSD permit, but not whether that BACT determination "was made on reasonable grounds properly supported on the record." Congress, however, vested EPA with explicit and sweeping authority to enforce CAA "requirements" relating to the construction and modification of sources under the PSD program, including BACT. We fail to see why Congress, having expressly endorsed an expansive surveillance role for EPA in two independent CAA provisions, would then implicitly preclude the Agency from verifying substantive compliance with the BACT provisions and, instead, limit EPA's superintendence to the insubstantial question whether the state permitting authority had uttered the key words "BACT." . . .[7]

7. According to the Agency, "[i]t has proven to be relatively rare that a state agency has put EPA in the position of having to exercise [its] authority," noting that only two other reported judicial decisions concern EPA orders occasioned by States' faulty BACT determinations [Allsteel, Inc. v. EPA, 25 F.3d 312 (6th Cir. 1994); Solar Turbines Inc. v. Seif, 879 F.2d 1073 (3d Cir. 1989)]. EPA's restrained and moderate use of its authority hardly supports the dissent's speculation that the federal Agency will "displac[e]" or "degrad[e]" state agencies or relegate them to the performance of "ministerial" functions. Nor has EPA ever asserted authority to override a state-court judgment. . . .

Even if the Act imposes a requirement of reasoned justification for a BACT determination, ADEC ultimately argues, such a requirement may be enforced only through state administrative and judicial processes. . . .

It would be unusual, to say the least, for Congress to remit a federal agency enforcing federal law solely to state court. We decline to read such an uncommon regime into the Act's silence. EPA, the expert federal agency charged with enforcing the Act, has interpreted the BACT provisions and its own §§113(a)(5) and 167 enforcement powers not to require recourse to state processes before stopping a facility's construction. That rational interpretation, we agree, is surely permissible. . . .

In sum, EPA interprets the Act to allow substantive federal Agency surveillance of state permitting authorities' BACT determinations subject to federal court review. We credit EPA's longstanding construction of the Act and confirm EPA's authority, pursuant to §§113(a)(5) and 167, to rule on the reasonableness of BACT decisions by state permitting authorities.

IV . . .

We turn finally, and more particularly, to the reasons why we conclude that EPA properly exercised its statutory authority in this case. . . .

We do not see how ADEC, having acknowledged that no determination "[could] be made as to the impact of [SCR's] cost on the operation . . . and competitiveness of the [mine]," could simultaneously proffer threats to the mine's operation or competitiveness as reasons for declaring SCR economically infeasible. ADEC, indeed, forthrightly explained why it was disarmed from reaching any judgment on whether, or to what extent, implementation of SCR would adversely affect the mine's operation or profitability: Cominco had declined to provide the relevant financial data, disputing the need for such information and citing "confidentiality" concerns. No record evidence suggests that the mine, were it to use SCR for its new generator, would be obliged to cut personnel, or raise zinc prices. Absent evidence of that order, ADEC lacked cause for selecting Low NO_x as BACT based on the more stringent control's impact on the mine's operation or competitiveness.

[The Court found that ADEC provided no other valid justification for its choice of Low NO_x. ADEC itself had previously found that SCR's control costs per ton were "well within what ADEC and EPA considers economically feasible." EPA appropriately rejected ADEC's comparison between the mine and a rural utility because there was no evidence to suggest that the economic impact of the cost of SCR on a large and profitable zinc producer "would be anything like its impact on a rural, non-profit utility that must pass costs on to a small base of individual consumers." ADEC's readiness to support Cominco's project for increasing mine production and Cominco's "contributions to the region" did not satisfy ADEC's own standards of a "source-specific . . . economic impac[t]" that demonstrated SCR to be inappropriate as BACT. In short,] . . . EPA validly issued stop orders because ADEC's BACT designation simply did not qualify as reasonable in light of the statutory guides. . . .

Affirmed.

Justice KENNEDY, with whom The CHIEF JUSTICE, Justice SCALIA, and Justice THOMAS join, dissenting.

The majority, in my respectful view, rests its holding on mistaken premises, for its reasoning conflicts with the express language of the [CAA], with sound rules of administrative law, and with principles that preserve the integrity of States in our federal system. . . . [EPA] sought to overturn the State's decision, not by the process of judicial review, but by administrative fiat. The Court errs, in my judgment, by failing to hold that EPA, based on nothing more than its substantive disagreement with the State's discretionary judgment, exceeded its powers in setting aside Alaska's BACT determination. . . .

The majority holds that, under the CAA, state agencies are vested with "initial responsibility for identifying BACT in line with the Act's definition of that term" and that EPA has a "broad oversight role" to ensure that a State's BACT determination is "reasonably moored to the Act's provisions." The statute, however, contemplates no such arrangement. It directs the "permitting authority"—here, the Alaska Department of Environmental Conservation (ADEC)—to "determine" what constitutes BACT. To "determine" is not simply to make an initial recommendation that can later be overturned. It is "[t]o decide or settle . . . conclusively and authoritatively." American Heritage Dictionary 495 (4th ed. 2000). . . .

To be sure, §§113(a) and 167 authorize EPA to enforce requirements of the Act. These provisions, however, do not limit the States' latitude and responsibility to balance all the statutory factors in making their discretionary judgments. If a State has complied with the Act's requirements, §§113(a)(5) and 167 are not implicated and can supply no separate basis for EPA to exercise a supervisory role over a State's discretionary decision. . . . When the statute is read as a whole, it is clear that the CAA commits BACT determinations to the discretion of the relevant permitting authorities. . . .

EPA insists it needs oversight authority to prevent a "race to the bottom," where jurisdictions compete with each other to lower environmental standards to attract new industries and keep existing businesses within their borders. Whatever the merits of these arguments as a general matter, EPA's distrust of state agencies is inconsistent with the Act's clear mandate that States bear the primary role in controlling pollution and, here, the exclusive role in making BACT determinations. In "cho[osing] not to dictate a Federal response to balancing sometimes conflicting goals" at the expense of "[m]aximum flexibility and State discretion," H.R. Rep. No. 95-294, p. 146 (1977), Congress made the overriding judgment that States are more responsive to local conditions and can strike the right balance between preserving environmental quality and advancing competing objectives. . . .

. . . As EPA concedes, States, by and large, take their statutory responsibility seriously, and EPA sees no reason to intervene in the vast majority of cases. In light of this concession, EPA and amici not only fail to overcome the established presumption that States act in good faith, but also admit that their fears about a race to the bottom bear little relation to the real-world experience under the statute. . . .

[The dissent pointed out that the CAA contains "safeguards to correct arbitrary and capricious BACT decisions when they do occur." EPA may not approve a state's PSD permit program unless the program provides an opportunity for state judicial review. States must allow interested persons, including EPA, to submit comments on proposed PSD permits, §165(a)(2), and inform EPA of every action taken in the permit approval process, §175(d). Any person who participated in the comment process, including EPA, can file an administrative appeal and judicial review in state court of the state's decision. According to the dissent, the availability of judicial review negated the argument that, "absent EPA's oversight, there is a legal vacuum where BACT decisions are not subject to review." Moreover, "EPA followed none of the normal procedures here."]

There is a further, and serious, flaw in the Court's ruling. Suppose, before EPA issued its orders setting aside the State's BACT determination, an Alaska state court had reviewed the matter and found no error of law or abuse of discretion in ADEC's determination. The majority's interpretation of the statute would allow EPA to intervene at this point for the first time, announce that ADEC's determination is unreasoned under the CAA, and issue its own orders nullifying the state court's ruling. This reworking of the balance between State and Federal Governments, not to mention the reallocation of authority between the Executive and Judicial Branches, shows the implausibility of the majority's reasoning. . . .

. . . Under the majority's holding, decisions by state courts would be subject to being overturned, not just by any agency, but by an agency established by a different sovereign. We should be reluctant to interpret a congressional statute to deny to States the judicial independence guaranteed by their own constitutions. . . . The Federal Government is free, within its vast legislative authority, to impose federal standards. For States to have a role, however, their own governing processes must be respected. New York v. United States, 505 U.S. 144 (1992). . . .

The broader implication of today's decision is more unfortunate still. The CAA is not the only statute that relies on a close and equal partnership between federal and state authorities to accomplish congressional objectives. Under the majority's reasoning, these other statutes, too, could be said to confer on federal agencies ultimate decisionmaking authority, relegating States to the role of mere provinces or political corporations, instead of coequal sovereigns entitled to the same dignity and respect. If cooperative federalism is to achieve Congress' goal of allowing state governments to be accountable to the democratic process in implementing environmental policies, federal agencies cannot consign States to the ministerial tasks of information gathering and making initial recommendations, while reserving to themselves the authority to make final judgments under the guise of surveillance and oversight. . . .

NOTES AND QUESTIONS

1. What was the statutory basis for EPA's issuance of the two orders to ADEC and Cominco? What is the scope of EPA's review of state PSD permitting decisions, according to EPA and ADEC? Why did the Court, but not the dissent, approve of EPA's interpretation? Did the dissenters accurately depict the allocation of decision-making authority between EPA and the states that Congress intended? Is there really an "equal partnership between federal and state authorities"? Does the majority opinion present Tenth Amendment problems?

2. The NRC excerpt that precedes the *ADEC* case stated that BACT "is at least as stringent as an applicable NSPS, but in general is not as stringent as the LAER requirement to which the new source would be subject in a nonattainment area." New or modified nonmajor stationary sources in PSD areas are not subject to NSR (or BACT), but may be subject to NSPS under §111. Cf. Sierra Club v. EPA, 499 F.3d

653 (7th Cir. 2007) (upholding EPA's refusal to require PSD permit applicant to redesign plant to accommodate cleaner-burning fuel).

NOTES AND QUESTIONS ON THE SCOPE OF THE PSD NSR PERMIT PROGRAM

The PSD permit program applies to any "major emitting facility on which construction is commenced after August 7, 1977 [the effective date of the 1977 amendments] in any area to which this part applies." §165(a)(1). This deceptively simple phrase gives rise to a host of questions concerning the scope of the PSD permit program. The notes and questions that follow flesh out some of these threshold questions. If the permit program applies, a permit applicant must satisfy the substantive requirements of §165(a) in order to qualify for a permit. The notes that begin on page 530 address exactly what those requirements are.

1. *"Major" Facilities and "Potential to Emit."* What is a "major emitting facility"? See §169(1). A facility may escape being classified as "major" "if either of two different forces limits its rate of emission of air pollutants to below a specified amount: first, physical or mechanical limits constraining its rate of emission; and second, legal limits, in the form of legal restrictions on its rate of emission or hours of operation. 40 C.F.R. §51.166(b)(4)." United States v. Marine Shale Processors, 81 F.3d 1329, 1352 (5th Cir. 1996).

Suppose that a proposed new facility would engage in two different kinds of industrial activities, one of which (chemical processing) is among the kinds of activities subject to the 100-ton-per-year threshold for a "major emitting facility" in §169(1), and the other of which (waste processing) is subject to the default 250-ton-per-year threshold. If the facility emits more than 100 tons but less than 250 tons per year of air pollutants, is it a major emitting facility subject to the PSD permit program? See LaFleur v. Whitman, 300 F.3d 256 (2d Cir. 2002).

Is a facility's "potential to emit" assessed on the basis of uncontrolled or controlled emission levels? According to the NRC excerpt, how did the *Alabama Power* case dispose of this issue? See 636 F.2d at 352-355; United States v. Louisiana-Pacific Corp., 682 F. Supp. 1122, 1141 (D. Colo. 1987) (EPA may not base "potential to emit" on operation not contemplated by design of plant).

Suppose an electric utility decides to replace an old, inefficient peak load generator that operates only a few days each year with a modern generator. It could operate the new generator every day but almost certainly will not. Only if the generator were operated every day would emissions of SO_2 exceed 100 tons annually. The utility is hesitant to promise EPA that it will never increase actual emissions above the levels emitted from the existing generator because of uncertainties about the precise nature of future electricity demand. Must the utility apply for a PSD permit? Is it fair for EPA to compare actual emissions from existing operations with potential emissions from proposed replacement operations in determining the applicability of the PSD permit program? See Puerto Rican Cement Co. v. EPA, 889 F.2d 292 (1st Cir. 1989).

Suppose that a proposed plant will emit less than 100 tons per year of particulates from its smokestack but will release more than that amount in fugitive emissions. Fugitive emissions are derived primarily from traffic on unpaved roads and from wind erosion. They account for most of the air pollution generated at certain kinds of industrial operations. Will the plant have to apply for a PSD permit? In 1984, EPA issued a list of 27 categories of industrial stationary sources for which fugitive emissions must be included in determining whether a source is major for purposes of the PSD permit program. Surface coal mining was excluded from the list because, according to EPA, the costs of regulation would exceed the benefits. NRDC challenged that determination on the grounds that cost-benefit analysis is not the correct standard. In NRDC v. EPA, 937 F.2d 641 (D.C. Cir. 1991), the court concluded that §302(j) vests sufficiently broad discretion in EPA that it may decide whether to include fugitive emissions on cost-benefit grounds. Why did §302(j) apply instead of §169(1)? See also 75 Fed. Reg. 16,102 (2010) (soliciting comments on whether to include fugitive emissions in determining applicability of NSR in PSD areas).

2. *Plant Location.* Suppose that a proposed major particulate-emitting facility will be located in a nonattainment area for particulates, but its emissions will adversely affect air quality in a nearby attainment area for particulates; may the facility be constructed without a PSD permit? As a result of *Alabama Power*, unless a facility is located in a PSD or unclassifiable area in the same state as the area in which it will degrade air quality, it need not apply for a PSD permit. If both the nonattainment and PSD areas are located in the same state, there may be other mechanisms in the statute by which adverse impacts on the air quality in the PSD area can be avoided. See, e.g., §161. The problem is more serious, however, if the two areas are located in different states. *Alabama Power* blocks reaching over a state boundary to apply the PSD requirements, no matter how severely the proposed facility impairs air quality in a neighboring state. The problem is not confined to short distances. Even distant new sources 200 to 300 miles away could be linked to local loss of air quality.

Because both PSD and nonattainment requirements apply on the basis of individual pollutants, a major new plant may want to locate in an area that is nonattainment for one pollutant but is PSD for others. Even a dense urban area can be a Class II PSD area, despite serious nonattainment problems, if ambient levels of a single criteria pollutant fall under the NAAQS. As a result, a plant seeking to locate in an industrialized zone often must undergo nonattainment review for ozone and PSD review for pollutants such as CO and NO_x.

3. *The Definition of a "Modification" in the PSD Permit Program (and Under the NSPS regulations).* When is a proposed plant modification subject to PSD permit review? See §§165(a)(1), 169(2)(C). What level of emissions from a unit added to an existing plant will trigger PSD review? *Alabama Power* held that a modification that increases emissions to *any* extent (except for *de minimis* increases) requires PSD review, invalidating an EPA regulation limiting PSD review to the same 100- or 250-ton-per-year threshold Congress established in defining a "major emitting facility." 636 F.2d at 400. In Great Basin Mine Watch v. EPA, 401 F.3d 1094 (9th Cir. 2005), the court ruled that EPA did not act arbitrarily in refusing to aggregate the increases caused by three modifications to the same facility in a single year and in concluding that no permit was necessary because no single modification caused a 40-ton-per-year increase in emissions.

Should the existence of an "increase" be determined by the rate of emissions, or by actual emissions resulting from operation? Industry challenged EPA's different approaches under different stationary source–linked provisions and programs in the following case.

ENVIRONMENTAL DEFENSE v. DUKE ENERGY CORP.
549 U.S. 561 (2007)

Justice SOUTER delivered the opinion of the Court.

In the 1970s, Congress added two air pollution control schemes to the Clean Air Act: New Source Performance Standards (NSPS) and Prevention of Significant Deterioration (PSD), each of them covering modified, as well as new, stationary sources of air pollution. The NSPS provisions define the term "modification," 42 U.S.C. §7411(a)(4), while the PSD provisions use that word "as defined in" NSPS, §7479(2)(C). The Court of Appeals concluded that the statute requires the Environmental Protection Agency (EPA) to conform its PSD regulations on "modification" to their NSPS counterparts, and that EPA's 1980 PSD regulations can be given this conforming construction. We hold that the Court of Appeals's reading of the 1980 PSD regulations, intended to align them with NSPS, was inconsistent with their terms and effectively invalidated them; any such result must be shown to comport with the Act's restrictions on judicial review of EPA regulations for validity.

I

The Clean Air Amendments of 1970 . . . dealing with NSPS authorized EPA to require operators of stationary sources of air pollutants to use the best technology for limiting pollution, both in newly constructed sources and those undergoing "modification," 42 U.S.C. §7411(a)(2). Section 111(a) of the 1970 amendments defined this term within the NSPS scheme as "any physical change in, or change in the method of operation of, a stationary source which increases the amount of any air pollutant emitted by such source or which results in the emission of any air pollutant not previously emitted," 42 U.S.C. §7411(a)(4).

EPA's 1975 regulations implementing NSPS provided generally that "any physical or operational change to an existing facility which results in an increase in the emission rate to the atmosphere of any pollutant to which a standard applies shall be considered a modification within the meaning of [S]ection 111." 40 CFR §60.14(a) (1976). Especially significant here is the identification of an NSPS "modification" as a change that "increase[s] . . . the emission rate," which "shall be expressed as kg/hr of any pollutant discharged into the atmosphere." §60.14(b).[1]

NSPS, however, did too little to "achiev[e] the ambitious goals of the 1970 Amendments," and the Clean Air Act Amendments of 1977 included the PSD provisions, which aimed at giving added protection to air quality in certain parts of the country "notwithstanding attainment and maintenance of" the NAAQS. 42 U.S.C. §7470(1). The 1977 amendments required a PSD permit before a "major emitting facility" could be "constructed" in an area covered by the scheme. §7475(a). As originally enacted, PSD applied only to newly constructed sources, but soon a technical amendment added the following subparagraph: "The term 'construction' when used in connection with any source or facility, includes the modification (as defined in [S]ection 111(a)) of any source or facility." 42 U.S.C. §7479(2)(C); see also New York v. EPA, 413 F.3d 3, 13 (C.A. D.C. 2005). In other words, the "construction"

---

1. EPA's 1975 NSPS regulations did not specify that the "rate" means the maximum rate possible for the technology, but the parties all read the regulations this way.

requiring a PSD permit under the statute was made to include (though it was not limited to) a "modification" as defined in the statutory NSPS provisions.

In 1980, EPA issued PSD regulations, which "limited the application of [PSD] review" of modified sources to instances of "'major' modificatio[n]," defined as "any physical change in or change in the method of operation of a major stationary source that would result in a significant net emissions increase of any pollutant subject to regulation under the Act." 40 CFR §51.166(b)(2)(I) (1987). Further regulations in turn addressed various elements of this definition, three of which are to the point here. First, the regulations specified that an operational change consisting merely of "[a]n increase in the hours of operation or in the production rate" would not generally constitute a "physical change or change in the method of operation." §51.166(b)(2)(iii)(f). For purposes of a PSD permit, that is, such an operational change would not amount to a "modification" as the Act defines it. Second, the PSD regulations defined a "net emissions increase" as "[a]ny increase in actual emissions from a particular physical change or change in the method of operation," net of other contemporaneous "increases and decreases in actual emissions at the source." §51.166(b)(3). "Actual emissions" were defined to "equal the average rate, in tons per year, at which the unit actually emitted the pollutant during a two-year period which precedes the particular date and which is representative of normal source operation." §51.166(b)(21)(ii). "[A]ctual emissions" were to be "calculated using the unit's actual operating hours [and] production rates." Ibid. Third, the term "significant" was defined as "a rate of emissions that would equal or exceed" one or another enumerated threshold, each expressed in "tons per year." §51.166(b)(23)(I).

It would be bold to try to synthesize these statutory and regulatory provisions in a concise paragraph, but three points are relatively clear about the regime that covers this case:

(a) The Act defines modification of a stationary source of a pollutant as a physical change to it, or a change in the method of its operation, that increases the amount of a pollutant discharged or emits a new one.
(b) EPA's NSPS regulations require a source to use the best available pollution-limiting technology only when a modification would increase the rate of discharge of pollutants measured in kilograms per hour.
(c) EPA's 1980 PSD regulations require a permit for a modification (with the same statutory definition) only when it is a major one and only when it would increase the actual annual emission of a pollutant above the actual average for the two prior years.

The Court of Appeals held that Congress's provision defining a PSD modification by reference to an NSPS modification caught not only the statutory NSPS definition, but also whatever regulatory gloss EPA puts on that definition at any given time (for the purposes of the best technology requirement). When, therefore, EPA's PSD regulations specify the "change" that amounts to a "major modification" requiring a PSD permit, they must measure an increase in "the amount of any air pollutant emitted," 42 U.S.C. §7411(a)(4), in terms of the hourly rate of discharge, just the way NSPS regulations do. Petitioners and the United States say, on the contrary, that when EPA addresses the object of the PSD scheme it is free to put a different regulatory interpretation on the common statutory core of "modification," by measuring increased emission not in terms of hourly rate but by the actual, annual discharge of a pollutant that will follow the modification, regardless of rate per hour. This disagreement is the nub of the case.

II

Respondent Duke Energy Corporation runs 30 coal-fired electric generating units at eight plants in North and South Carolina. The units were placed in service between 1940 and 1975, and each includes a boiler containing thousands of steel tubes arranged in sets. Between 1988 and 2000, Duke replaced or redesigned 29 tube assemblies in order to extend the life of the units and allow them to run longer each day.

The United States filed this action in 2000, claiming, among other things, that Duke violated the PSD provisions by doing this work without permits. [Several environmental groups] intervened as plaintiffs and filed a complaint charging similar violations.

Duke moved for summary judgment, one of its positions being that none of the projects was a "major modification" requiring a PSD permit because none increased hourly rates of emissions. The District Court agreed with Duke's reading of the 1980 PSD regulations. It reasoned that their express exclusion of "[a]n increase in the hours of operation" from the definition of a "physical change or change in the method of operation" implied that "post-project emissions levels must be calculated assuming" preproject hours of operation. Consequently, the District Court said, a PSD "major modification" can occur "only if the project increases the hourly rate of emissions." The District Court found further support for its construction of the 1980 PSD regulations in one letter and one memorandum written in 1981 by EPA's Director of the Division of Stationary Source Enforcement, Edward E. Reich.

The United States and intervenor-plaintiffs (collectively, plaintiffs) subsequently stipulated "that they do not contend that the projects at issue in this case caused an increase in the maximum hourly rate of emissions at any of Duke Energy's units." Rather, their claim "is based solely on their contention that the projects would have been projected to result in an increased utilization of the units at issue." Duke, for its part, stipulated to plaintiffs' right to appeal the District Court's determination that projects resulting in greater operating hours are not "major modifications" triggering the PSD permit requirement, absent an increase in the hourly rate of emissions. The District Court then entered summary judgment for Duke on all PSD claims.

The Court of Appeals for the Fourth Circuit affirmed, "albeit for somewhat different reasons." "[T]he language and various interpretations of the PSD regulations . . . are largely irrelevant to the proper analysis of this case," reasoned the Court of Appeals, "because Congress' decision to create identical statutory definitions of the term 'modification'" in the NSPS and PSD provisions of the Clean Air Act "has affirmatively mandated that this term be interpreted identically" in the regulations promulgated under those provisions. . . .

III

The Court of Appeals understood that it was simply construing EPA's 1980 PSD regulations in a permissible way that left them in harmony with their NSPS counterpart and, hence, the Act's single definition of "modification." The plaintiffs say that the

Court of Appeals was rewriting the PSD regulations in a way neither required by the Act nor consistent with their own text.

It is true that no precise line runs between a purposeful but permissible reading of the regulation adopted to bring it into harmony with the Court of Appeals's view of the statute, and a determination that the regulation as written is invalid. But the latter occurred here, for the Court of Appeals's efforts to trim the PSD regulations to match their different NSPS counterparts can only be seen as an implicit declaration that the PSD regulations were invalid as written.

A

In applying the 1980 PSD regulations to Duke's conduct, the Court of Appeals thought that, by defining the term "modification" identically in its NSPS and PSD provisions, the Act required EPA to conform its PSD interpretation of that definition to any such interpretation it reasonably adhered to under NSPS. But principles of statutory construction are not so rigid. Although we presume that the same term has the same meaning when it occurs here and there in a single statute, the Court of Appeals mischaracterized that presumption as "effectively irrebuttable." We also understand that "[m]ost words have different shades of meaning and consequently may be variously construed, not only when they occur in different statutes, but when used more than once in the same statute or even in the same section." Atlantic Cleaners & Dyers, Inc. v. United States, 286 U.S. 427, 433 (1932). . . . A given term in the same statute may take on distinct characters from association with distinct statutory objects calling for different implementation strategies.

The point is the same even when the terms share a common statutory definition, if it is general enough. . . .

In fact, . . . we recently declined to require uniformity when resolving ambiguities in identical statutory terms. . . . United States v. Cleveland Indians Baseball Co., 532 U.S. 200 (2001). . . . There is, then, no "effectively irrebuttable" presumption that the same defined term in different provisions of the same statute must "be interpreted identically." Context counts.

It is true that the Clean Air Act did not merely repeat the term "modification" or the same definition of that word in its NSPS and PSD sections; the PSD language referred back to the section defining "modification" for NSPS purposes. 42 U.S.C. §7479(2)(C). But . . . we do not see the distinction as making any difference here. Nothing in the text or the legislative history of the technical amendments that added the cross-reference to NSPS suggests that Congress had details of regulatory implementation in mind when it imposed PSD requirements on modified sources; the cross-reference alone is certainly no unambiguous congressional code for eliminating the customary agency discretion to resolve questions about a statutory definition by looking to the surroundings of the defined term, where it occurs. . . . Absent any iron rule to ignore the reasons for regulating PSD and NSPS "modifications" differently, EPA's construction need do no more than fall within the limits of what is reasonable, as set by the Act's common definition.

B

The Court of Appeals's reasoning that the PSD regulations must conform to their NSPS counterparts led the court to read those PSD regulations in a way that seems to us too far a stretch for the language used. The 1980 PSD regulations on "modification" simply cannot be taken to track the agency's regulatory definition under the NSPS.

True, the 1980 PSD regulations may be no seamless narrative, but they clearly do not define a "major modification" in terms of an increase in the "hourly emissions rate." On its face, the definition in the PSD regulations specifies no rate at all, hourly or annual, merely requiring a physical or operational change "that would result in a significant net emissions increase of any" regulated pollutant. 40 CFR §51.166(b)(2)(I). But even when a rate is mentioned, as in the regulatory definitions of the two terms, "significant" and "net emissions increase," the rate is annual, not hourly. Each of the thresholds that quantify "significant" is described in "tons per year," §51.166(b)(23)(I), and a "net emissions increase" is an "increase in actual emissions" measured against an "average" prior emissions rate of so many "tons per year." §§51.166(b)(3) and (21)(ii). And what is further at odds with the idea that hourly rate is relevant is the mandate that "[a]ctual emissions shall be calculated using the unit's actual operating hours," §51.166(b)(21)(ii), since "actual emissions" must be measured in a manner that looks to the number of hours the unit is or probably will be actually running. What these provisions are getting at is a measure of actual operations averaged over time, and the regulatory language simply cannot be squared with a regime under which "hourly rate of emissions," 411 F.3d, at 550, is dispositive.

The reasons invoked by the Court of Appeals for its different view are no match for these textual differences. The appellate court cited two authorities ostensibly demonstrating that the 1980 PSD regulations "can be interpreted consistently" with the hourly emissions test, the first being the analysis of the District Court in this case. The District Court thought that an increase in the hourly emissions rate was necessarily a prerequisite to a PSD "major modification" because a provision of the 1980 PSD regulations excluded an "'increase in the hours of operation or in the production rate'" from the scope of "'[a] physical change or change in the method of operation.'" 278 F. Supp. 2d, at 640-641 (quoting 40 CFR §§51.166(b)(2)(iii)(f) and (3)(I)(a) (1987)). The District Court read this exclusion to require, in effect, that a source's hours of operation "be held constant" when preproject emissions are being compared with postproject emissions for the purpose of calculating the "net emissions increase."

We think this understanding of the 1980 PSD regulations makes the mistake of overlooking the difference between the two separate components of the regulatory definition of "major modification": "[1] any physical change in or change in the method of operation of a major stationary source that [2] would result in a significant net emissions increase of any pollutant subject to regulation under the Act." §51.166(b)(2)(I); cf. New York [I], 413 F.3d, at 11 ("[The statutory] definition requires both a change—whether physical or operational—and a resulting increase in emissions of a pollutant" (emphasis in original)); Wisconsin Electric Power Co. v. Reilly, 893 F.2d 901, 907 (C.A.7 1990) (same). The exclusion of "increase in . . . hours . . . or . . . production rate," §51.166(b)(2)(iii)(f), speaks to the first of these components ("physical change . . . or change in . . . method," §51.166(b)(2)(I)), but not to the second ("significant net emissions increase," ibid.). As the preamble to the 1980 PSD regulations explains, forcing companies to obtain a PSD permit before they could simply adjust operating hours "would severely and unduly hamper the ability of any company to take advantage of favorable market conditions." 45 Fed. Reg. 52704. In other words, a mere increase in the hours of operation, standing alone, is not a "physical change or change in the method of operation." 40 CFR §51.166(b)(2)(iii).

But the District Court took this language a step further. It assumed that increases in operating hours (resulting in emissions increases at the old rate per hour) must be ignored even if caused or enabled by an independent "physical change . . . or change in the method of operation." §51.166(b)(2)(i). That reading, however, turns an exception to the first component of the definition into a mandate to ignore the very facts that would count under the second, which defines "net emissions increase" in terms of "actual emissions," §51.166(b)(3), during "the unit's actual operating hours," §51.166(b)(21)(ii); see also 57 Fed. Reg. 32328 (1992) ("[A]n increase in emissions attributable to an increase in hours of operation or production rate which is the result of a construction-related activity is not excluded from [PSD] review. . . ."). . . . [7]

In sum, the text of the 1980 PSD regulations on "modification" doomed the Court of Appeals's attempt to equate those regulations with their NSPS counterpart. . . .

QUESTION

Why did the replacement or redesign of the tube assemblies at Duke's coal-fired power plants between 1988 and 2000 qualify as modifications under the plaintiffs' interpretation of the PSD statutory and regulatory provisions, but not under the interpretations of the district court and the Court of Appeals? According to the Supreme Court, what are the "two separate components of the regulatory definition of 'major modification'" and how did the district court misconstrue them? Which interpretation of the NSR provisions, Duke's or the government's, is more consistent with the purposes of the NSR program?

Problem 6-3

An electric power plant owned and operated by National Electric Company (NECO) consists of five coal-fired steam-generating units that were placed in operation between 1935 and 1950. Over the years, the performance of some of the units has declined due to age-related deterioration. NECO proposes to repair and replace the turbine-generators, boilers, mechanical and electrical auxiliaries, and the common plant support facilities. EPA's NSPS for coal-fired electric power plants have been in effect for some time. NECO's proposed repair and replacement program would cause emissions of SO_2 to increase from the deteriorated plant's current levels, but only if the plant were operated at full capacity, 24 hours a day. NECO has never operated its plant at full capacity on a round-the-clock basis in the past.

---

7. Two Courts of Appeals agree. See United States v. Cinergy Corp., 458 F.3d 705, 708 (C.A.7 2006) ("[M]erely running the plant closer to its maximum capacity is not a major modification because it does not involve either a physical change or a change in the method of operation. If, however, a physical change enables the plant to increase its output, then, according to the EPA's interpretation, the exclusion for merely operating the plant for longer hours is inapplicable." (emphasis in original)); Wisconsin Electric Power Co. v. Reilly, 893 F.2d 901, 916, n.11 (C.A.7 1990) (the regulatory exclusion for increases in the hours of operation "was provided to allow facilities to take advantage of fluctuating market conditions, not construction or modification activity"); Puerto Rican Cement Co. v. EPA, 889 F.2d 292, 298 (C.A.1 1989) ("[T]here is no logical contradiction in rules that, on the one hand, permit firms using existing capacity simply to increase their output and, on the other, use the potential output of *new* capacity as a basis for calculating an increase in emissions levels.").

If NECO decides to proceed with its proposed repair and replacement program, will the renovated plant be subject to NSR for coal-fired electric power plants?

NOTES AND QUESTIONS ON THE SUBSTANTIVE REQUIREMENTS OF THE PSD PERMIT PROGRAM

1. *Construction or Operation?* Does a source violate §165(a)(1) if it operates without a PSD permit, or only if it commences construction without one? See Sierra Club v. Otter Tail Corp., 615 F.3d 1008 (8th Cir. 2010); United States v. Midwest Generation, LLC, 694 F. Supp. 2d 999 (N.D. Ill. 2010) (discussing cases addressing this question).

2. *The Baselines and Increment Consumption.* Section 165(a)(3) requires a PSD permit applicant to demonstrate that emissions from the proposed major emitting facility will neither cause nor contribute to violations of maximum allowable increases, maximum allowable concentrations, the NAAQS, or any other applicable emission standard. Congress established the maximum allowable increases, or PSD increments, for SO_2 and particulates in §163(b). The PSD increments for Class I areas are the smallest and those for Class III areas are the largest.

The maximum allowable concentrations are determined by adding the maximum allowable increases to the baseline concentration of either SO_2 or particulates. See §163(b)(4). How is the baseline concentration calculated? See §169(4). What purpose is served by allowing baseline determinations to be postponed until the time of the first PSD permit application? The EPA could see none and tried to fix the baseline determination date at August 7, 1977, the date of enactment of the 1977 amendments. The *Alabama Power* court disagreed with EPA's reading of the statute and mandated the "first applicant" policy. 636 F.2d at 374-376. Is it possible that the PSD increment may be consumed before the first PSD permit application for a particular PSD area is even filed? What incentives does this situation create for those considering the construction of a major emitting facility in a PSD area? EPA and most states allocate the available PSD increments on a first-come, first-served basis.

3. *Monitoring, Modeling, and the Rationality of the PSD Baseline Increment Analysis.* To determine the projected impact of a proposed major emitting facility, it is necessary to gauge the air quality in the affected PSD area before construction is permitted to begin. Section 165(a)(2), (e) requires an analysis that includes at least one year of preconstruction air quality monitoring to determine whether emissions from the proposed facility will result in violations of the maximum allowable increases or maximum allowable concentrations.

The administration of the PSD increment system is anything but straightforward.[w] As the NRC excerpt explains, under the 1977 amendments the baseline and the increments are computed from a mishmash of monitoring data and regulatory fiats about hypothetical and actual emissions that must be (or cannot be) counted. The result is that actual air quality in PSD areas may bear little resemblance to what the regulatory accounting system says it is.

---

w. See generally Stensvaag, Preventing Significant Deterioration under the Clean Air Act: Baselines, Increments, and Ceilings—Part I, 35 Envtl. L. Rep. 10807 (2005); Part II, 36 Envtl. L. Rep. 10017 (2006).

EPA has attempted to overcome these problems through modeling. But modeling capability is far from perfect and tends to be least successful in situations where increment exceedance is likely. The courts nevertheless have been deferential to the efforts of EPA and the states to address the shortcomings of models. See Sur Contra la Contaminación v. EPA, 202 F.3d 443 (1st Cir. 2000); *Alabama Power*, 636 F.2d at 381-388. PSD permit holders also may be required to conduct post-construction monitoring, presumably to correct errors in the predicted level of increment consumption and to help EPA refine its models. §165(a)(7). The court in *Alabama Power* held that EPA has the discretion not to require post-construction monitoring. 636 F.3d at 373.

4. *The BACT Determination.* Suppose that a proposed facility, to be located in a PSD area for particulates, will emit not only particulates, but also SO_2 and NO_x. To which of these pollutants will the BACT requirement at issue in the *ADEC* case apply? See §165(a)(4). What if the plant will emit heavy metals listed as hazardous air pollutants under §112 in amounts less than 10 tons per year; will those pollutants also be subject to BACT?

A source comes under nonattainment review only for the particular pollutants for which nonattainment violations exist and only if the proposed plant exceeds the size cutoff for each of those pollutants. But PSD review occurs for all pollutants subject to regulation under the CAA that will be emitted by a major facility in any amount, so long as one pollutant exceeds the 100- to 250-ton PSD trigger emissions level. According to *Alabama Power*, EPA must apply BACT to each pollutant regulated for any purpose under any provision of the CAA, 636 F.2d at 403, although the agency may exempt *de minimis* amounts.

Must the permit-issuing agency prepare a BACT analysis for CO_2, which is not a criteria pollutant? Utility Air Regulatory Group v. EPA, 134 S. Ct. 2427 (2014), which is excerpted as a principal case in Chapter 12, section E.1, addresses the application of the PSD permit program to GHGs.

The *ADEC* case provides some insights into how BACT is determined. Does §169(3) rule out switching fuel or reducing or interrupting operations to meet BACT? Compare NSPS under §111. Administration of the BACT requirement historically has been lenient, as in *ADEC*. Critics have charged that BACT determinations exacerbate a basic flaw of the CAA by putting the heaviest cleanup burden on the newest sources and that they yield inefficient controls by restricting emissions control options, leading to wide discrepancies between the marginal costs of control among sources. Is the determination of BACT made as of the date of permit application or permit issuance? What if EPA has issued regulations requiring more stringent controls between those dates? See Sierra Club v. EPA, 762 F.3d 971 (9th Cir. 2014) (construing §§110(j), 175(a)(3)-(4)).

NOTE ON THE APPLICATION OF PSD TO THE SET II POLLUTANTS

The Clean Air Act establishes PSD increments only for SO_2 and particulates. Section 166 of the statute required EPA to issue PSD regulations for the other criteria pollutants (referred to as the Set II pollutants) by 1979. Those regulations were to "provide specific numerical measures against which a permit application may be evaluated," as well as protect air quality values and "fulfill the goals" of §§101 and

160 of the Act. §166(c). The statute also requires that these regulations "provide specific measures at least as effective as the increments in [§163] to fulfill such goals and purposes." §166(d).

EPA issued PSD regulations for NO_x in 1988. It adopted the same three-tiered classification of PSD areas reflected in §§162 and 164. It also relied on the same increment consumption mechanism that the statute established for the Set I pollutants, with calculation of the permissible increments based on the NAAQS. As a result, EPA adopted PSD regulations only for nitrogen dioxide (NO_2), the only oxide of nitrogen for which EPA had established a NAAQS. EPA afforded states the option, however, of seeking approval of alternative approaches that do not rely on increments, as long as those approaches satisfy the requirements of §166(c) and (d). After years of litigation and delay, the court in Environmental Def. v. EPA, 489 F.3d 1320 (D.C. Cir. 2007), upheld that approach.

3. Control of Visibility Impairment

The Values at Stake. The spacious western sky is a striking natural and cultural asset that has played an important role in mobilizing public support for the national park system. Visibility has increased in some areas of the West, such as the Grand Canyon, Las Vegas, and Phoenix, since 1970, apparently as a result of measures required by the CAA. On the other hand, visibility has declined in some parts of the East, such as the Great Smoky Mountains National Park, largely due to increased emissions of man-made fine sulfur particulate matter.

Causes and Types of Visibility Impairment. Particles and gases impair visibility by scattering or absorbing light. Pollution impairs visibility in several ways, each of which presents a different regulatory challenge. The first—plume blight from a single source, such as a coal-fired power plant—is the most obvious. In areas closest to a plant, light scattering by fly ash and discoloration by NO_2 are the dominant processes. Further away, after colorless SO_2 has been transformed to sulfate particles, sulfates and NO_2 determine the visible character of the plume. The first astronauts reported that the plume from the Four Corners Power Plant in northeastern New Mexico, which stretched for over 1,000 miles, was the most striking human artifact visible from space. Wang et al., Clear Sky Visibility Has Decreased over Land Globally from 1973 to 2007, 323 Science 1468 (Mar. 13, 2009), discuss the phenomenon of "global dimming," which involves reduction in visibility through the presence of aerosols in the atmosphere.

At the opposite extreme, thoroughly diffused "older" pollutants may cause a second form of visibility-impairing pollution: large-scale regional haze. Sulfates are the chief culprit. In the southwestern national parks, 90 percent of regional sulfate haze originates hundreds of miles away, chiefly at copper smelters in Arizona, New Mexico, Texas, and possibly the Los Angeles area. A third visibility-impairing phenomenon, intermediate between plumes and regional haze, consists of small pockets of haze that form in valleys or around other land forms, usually in layered bands of discoloration. Urban smog, eastern high-humidity haze, and pollution pockets generated by unique western geological features (especially high terrain) are examples.

Visibility and the PSD Permit Program. The CAA protects visibility through a two-tier scheme. A state must deny a PSD permit to a major new emitting facility even though Class I increments are not violated if the facility is expected to have an "adverse impact" on "air quality–related values" (AQRVs). See §165(d)(2). The CAA defines neither of these phrases. Conversely, a source that would violate the increments may obtain a permit if it can show that AQRVs are not violated. Visibility is the principal air quality–related value that must be reviewed under §165 before a major new source can be sited near a Class I area. In Montana Envtl. Info. Ctr. v. Montana Dep't of Envtl. Quality, 112 P.3d 964 (Mont. 2005), the court held that the state agency had an independent responsibility to determine whether a proposed power plant would adversely affect visibility in Class I areas, and could not simply defer to the federal land manager's conclusion that it would not.

Visibility Protection for Mandatory Class I PSD Areas. A separate visibility protection program not technically part of PSD is provided by §169A for mandatory Class I areas in which EPA designates visibility as an important value. All but two of the mandatory Class I areas are on the EPA list. See 40 C.F.R. §§81.401-81.437. Section 169A requires states to adopt long-term strategies for making "reasonable progress" toward the goal of remedying and preventing impairment of visibility from air pollution in mandatory Class I areas. §169A(b)(2)(B). The affected states must revise their SIPs to identify existing major stationary sources whose emissions cause or contribute to visibility impairment. Each such source must install the "best available retrofit technology" (BART) if built after 1962. §169A(b)(2)(A).

Regulation of "Reasonably Attributable" Visibility Impairment. In 1980, EPA issued regulations under §169A to control visibility impairment reasonably attributable to a single existing stationary source or a small group of such sources. EPA deferred addressing regional haze because of the difficulty of identifying, measuring, and controlling that kind of visibility impairment. In Central Ariz. Water Conservation Dist. v. EPA, 990 F.3d 1531 (9th Cir. 1993), the court approved a federal implementation plan requiring a 90 percent reduction in SO_2 emissions at an Arizona power plant that, according to EPA, was contributing to visibility impairment at the Grand Canyon. The plan represented the first time that an existing source was forced to reduce its emissions as a result of the 1980 regulations.

Regulation of Regional Haze. In 1999, EPA issued regulations that required all states to submit regional haze SIP revisions. 64 Fed. Reg. 35,714 (1999). American Corn Growers Ass'n v. EPA, 291 F.3d 1 (D.C. Cir. 2002), upheld in part and vacated in part those regulations. The court held that EPA violated the statute by requiring the states to consider the degree of improvement in visibility anticipated to result from the use of BART on a group or area-wide basis instead of a source-specific basis. It rejected industry's claim, however, that EPA exceeded its authority by adopting the achievement of "natural visibility" as the goal of the regional haze program. Finding the same flaw in a plan for reducing visibility impairment in the Grand Canyon region, the court in Center for Energy and Econ. Dev. v. EPA, 398 F.3d 653 (D.C. Cir. 2005), invalidated EPA's approval of the plan. The plan calculated the degree by which BART would improve visibility (so that it could establish milestones that were equivalent to that degree of improvement) by reference to all sources affecting an area, rather than by reference to individual plants. The court regarded this methodology as inconsistent with the definition of BART in §169A(g)(2).

EPA responded to *American Corn Growers* by issuing revised regional haze regulations. The regulations provide several approaches by which the states may determine which stationary sources cause or contribute to visibility impairment, and thus are subject to BART. In deciding on the appropriate type and level of control for reducing emissions for individual sources, the states may take into account the degree of improvement in visibility that may result from the use of BART on a source-by-source basis. 70 Fed. Reg. 39,104 (2005). In 2009, EPA issued a finding that 37 states had failed to submit required SIPs for improving visibility in national parks and wilderness areas. Finding of Failure to Submit State Implementation Plans Required by the 1999 Regional Haze Rule, 74 Fed. Reg. 2392 (Jan. 15, 2009). That finding required EPA to develop federal implementation plans if affected states did not file acceptable plans within two years.

H. MOTOR VEHICLE EMISSION CONTROLS

As the description of air pollution sources in section A of this chapter indicates, the persistence of the nation's air pollution problems is due in significant part to emissions from mobile sources, such as cars, trucks, and planes. This section covers the CAA provisions that are designed to mitigate mobile-source pollution. The first subsection describes the provisions that authorize the issuance of technology-based emission standards that apply to the manufacturers of new motor vehicles. The second subsection deals with the requirements with which states must comply in adopting state implementation plans to deal with air quality control regions that are nonattainment for automotive criteria pollutants.

1. Vehicle Emission Standards

Motor vehicles remain heavy contributors to air pollution despite more than 40 years of substantial emission controls. Cars and trucks in urban areas in particular emit VOCs and NO_x, which contribute to ozone pollution, and CO. See Reitze, Mobile Source Air Pollution Control, 6 Envtl. Law. 309, 314-315 (2000). Although significant reductions of emissions of ozone precursors and CO from mobile sources have occurred since 1970, growth in the number of vehicles on the road and longer commutes for workers, among other factors, have contributed to continuing high levels of automotive pollution.

Emission Standards for Cars, Trucks, and Buses. In 1970, seeing persistent high pollution linked to motor vehicles in several major cities, Congress ordered automobile manufacturers to curtail new vehicle emissions of ozone precursors and CO by 90 percent within five to six years. The auto manufacturers claimed that emissions control technology capable of meeting the new standards did not exist and could not be developed by the statutory deadline. In rejecting that argument, Congress chose to adopt strict standards that would give industry an overwhelming incentive to invest in the necessary research and development, forcing an acceleration in the pace of technological innovation. The statute authorized EPA to extend the deadlines for compliance by the auto manufacturers. When EPA refused to do so, the court in International Harvester Co. v. Ruckelshaus, 478 F.2d 615, 648 (D.C. Cir. 1973), glossed over the concept of technology-forcing and remanded to the agency for further consideration given its "grave doubts" as to the soundness of EPAs prediction that the necessary technology would be available in time to meet the standards. The Note on the Concept of Technology-Forcing that appears later in this subsection further addresses the fate of this effort to force the development of better motor vehicle emission control technology.

The current statute contains a general mandate that EPA regulate emissions of any air pollutant from classes of new motor vehicles or new motor vehicle engines which, in its judgment, cause or contribute to air pollution which may reasonably be anticipated to endanger public health or welfare. These standards must apply for the useful life of the vehicles or engines. §202(a)(1). The Act defines the useful life requirement for light duty (passenger car) vehicles and engines as ten years or 100,000 miles, whichever occurs first. §202(d)(1). It also imposes more specific requirements for emissions of particular pollutants. See, e.g., §202(g)(1)-(2) (phasing in reductions in tailpipe emissions of nonmethane hydrocarbons, CO, NO_x, and particulates). EPA has the authority to determine whether further emissions reductions by light duty cars and trucks are appropriate based on the need for further reductions, the future availability of more effective emission control technology, and the cost-effectiveness of further reductions. §202(i)(3)(C). The 1990 amendments for the first time required EPA to control emissions of hazardous air pollutants from motor vehicles and motor vehicle fuels. §202(*l*).

Trains, Planes, Vessels and Other Equipment. For years, there were no emission standards for trains or seagoing vessels, which contribute relatively small amounts of HC, CO, or NO_x to the nation's air pollution problem. The 1990 amendments extended federal regulation to nonroad pollution sources. §213; Engine Mfrs. Ass'n v. EPA, 88 F.3d 1075 (D.C. Cir. 1996) (upholding EPA's implementing regulations). See also §§231 to 234 (concerning aircraft emission standards).

Certification of Prototype Vehicles. To facilitate enforcement of its vehicle emission standards, the CAA requires that each new vehicle sold be covered by a certificate of conformity indicating that it meets applicable emissions standards. §206(a)(1). The sale of vehicles not covered by a certificate is prohibited and subjects the manufacturer to civil penalties. §§203(a)(1), 205. To obtain federal certification, a manufacturer must submit a prototype of its new model vehicles to EPA for testing. If the prototype meets the emissions standards, EPA provides a certificate of conformity approving the prototype for mass production. The actual testing is ordinarily performed by the manufacturer itself, in accordance with detailed test procedures, although EPA may conduct confirmatory tests itself. Congress required EPA in 1990 to add tests capable of determining whether light duty vehicles, when properly maintained and used, will pass the inspection methods and procedures used to determine whether vehicles in actual use comply with applicable emission standards. §206(a)(4)(A).

Recalls. The CAA authorizes EPA to recall, at the manufacturer's expense, entire classes of vehicles when "a substantial number of any class or category of vehicles or engines, although properly maintained, do not conform to" applicable emission standards. §207(c)(1). In General Motors Corp. v. Ruckelshaus, 742 F.2d 1561 (D.C. Cir. 1984), the court endorsed EPA's view that this language provided for "classwide remedies of classwide defects." EPA could thus require manufacturers to recall and repair all members of a recall class even though some vehicles would have exceeded their natural lives. The court disapproved an EPA plan that allowed a manufacturer to offset pollution from a nonconforming class by attaining more-than-required emissions from future model years. It reasoned that offsets would not remedy the conformity of the recall vehicles, and that Center for Auto Safety v. Ruckelshaus, 747 F.2d 1 (D.C. Cir. 1984), requires recall and repair as the only statutory remedy for nonconformity.

Defect Warranties. Section 207(a) requires manufacturers to provide purchasers with defect warranties that cover the design and workmanship of emissions control components. The warranty remains in effect for the statutory useful life of the vehicle. If a covered defect causes the vehicle to exceed the emissions standards during that period, the manufacturers must make the necessary repairs at no cost to the owner. Manufacturers also must warrant that if a vehicle that has been maintained and used in accordance with the manufacturer's instructions fails an emissions test in a properly enforced state inspection and maintenance program, the manufacturer will repair the vehicle at no cost to the owner. §207(b). These provisions create a warranty relationship between the manufacturer and the vehicle owner, but EPA has the power to enforce the warranty provision and to prosecute manufacturers who fail to honor valid claims. See Motor Vehicle Mfrs. Ass'n v. Costle, 647 F.2d 675 (6th Cir. 1981).

State Regulation. The CAA generally preserves the rights of the states to adopt air pollution control standards that are more stringent than those enacted by EPA. See §116. Section 209(a) of the Act, however, with an exception noted below, prohibits states from adopting or attempting to enforce *any* motor vehicle emission controls, regardless of whether they are stronger or weaker than EPA's. The reason for that prohibition is as follows:

> Congress clearly enunciated the view that uniform federal pollution standards would reduce the transaction costs of regulated entities when it decided in the 1960s to regulate automotive emissions. A 1965 Senate committee report explained that federal regulation of automotive emissions was warranted because "it would be more desirable to have national standards rather than for each State to have a variation in standards and requirements which could result in chaos insofar as manufacturers, dealers, and users are concerned." Two years later, a House committee . . . rejected the suggestion that auto manufacturers would be able to meet any diverse standards that resulted from state regulation by manufacturing vehicles that comply with the most stringent controls on the ground that "this would lead to increased costs to consumers nationwide, with benefit only to those in one section of the country." [Glicksman & Levy, A Collective Action Perspective on Ceiling Preemption by Federal Environmental Regulation: The Case of Global Climate Change, 102 Nw. U. L. Rev. 579, 599 (2008).]

The statute allows California, however, to seek a waiver of §209(a)'s preemption provision from EPA. Congress decided to afford special treatment to California because it began controlling automotive pollution before the federal government did, and Congress was loath to divest the state of its authority to provide leadership on auto pollution control, and because California experienced some of the most severe automotive pollution problems in the 1960s and 1970s, and therefore needed the authority to adopt controls more stringent than federal standards. See H.R. Rep. No. 90-278, at 42 (1967) (referring to "the unique problems facing California as a result of its climate and topography"). One court described the resulting statutory structure:

> When instituting uniform federal regulations for air pollution in the [CAA], "Congress consciously chose to permit California to blaze its own trail with a minimum of federal oversight." Ford Motor Co. v. EPA, 606 F.2d 1293, 1297 (D.C .Cir. 1979). Section 209(a) of the Clean Air Act expressly prohibited state regulation of emissions from motor vehicles. 42 U.S.C. §7543(a). But the same section allowed California to adopt its own standards if it "determine[d] that the State standards will be, in the aggregate, at

least as protective of public health and welfare as applicable Federal standards." Id. §7543(b) [§209(b))]. Other states could choose to follow either the federal or the California standards, but they could not adopt standards of their own. Id. §7507. The auto industry strenuously objected to this waiver provision and was "adamant that the nature of [its] manufacturing mechanism required a single national standard in order to eliminate undue economic strain on the industry." Motor & Equip. Mfrs. Ass'n v. EPA, 627 F.2d 1095, 1109 (D.C. Cir. 1979). But Congress decided to encourage California "to continue and expand its pioneering efforts at adopting and enforcing motor vehicle emission standards different from and in large measure more advanced than the corresponding federal program; in short, to act as a kind of laboratory for innovation." Id. at 1111. So California's role as a leader in developing air-quality standards has been explicitly endorsed by Congress in the face of warnings about a fragmented national market.

Rocky Mountain Farmers Union v. Corey, 730 F.3d 1070, 1078-1079 (9th Cir. 2013). Over the years, EPA routinely approved California's more stringent standards. It refused to do so when the state sought to adopt motor vehicle emission standards for greenhouse gases before EPA regulated those pollutants, but after a change in presidential administration, EPA approved California's standards. See section E.1.c of Chapter 12, below. The *Engine Manufacturers* case reproduced in section E.3 of Chapter 2 deals with the scope of §209(b)'s preemption waiver.

Fuel Economy Standards. In the Energy Policy and Conservation Act of 1975 (EPCA), Pub. L. No. 94–163, 89 Stat. 871, Congress authorized the Secretary of Transportation to reduce the contribution of auto exhaust emissions to air pollution problems by adopting corporate average fuel economy (CAFE) standards. At least 18 months before the beginning of each model year, the Secretary must prescribe standards reflecting the maximum feasible average fuel economy level that manufacturers can achieve in that model year. 42 U.S.C. §32902(a). As section E.1.c of Chapter 12 indicates, EPA (using its CAA authority) and the Department of Transportation (operating under EPCA) have jointly issued emission control/CAFE standards to reduce emissions of greenhouse gases from motor vehicles by forcing the manufacture of more fuel-efficient cars that consume less energy for each vehicle mile traveled.

NOTE ON THE CONCEPT OF TECHNOLOGY FORCING

Technology-Based and Technology-Forcing Standards. The Supreme Court in *American Trucking*, excerpted in section D.1 of this chapter, described the CAA as "technology forcing" in character. The Court had previously found that the Act was "expressly designed to force regulated sources to develop pollution control devices that might at the time appear to be economically or technologically infeasible." Union Elec. Co. v. EPA, 427 U.S. 246, 257 (1976). Technology-forcing standards are based on the recognition that industry often lacks incentives to solve engineering problems, often has greater knowledge of the cause of such problems than EPA, and is capable of figuring out the most efficient ways of integrating potential solutions into current methods of operation. In addition, "[i]f a government-imposed emission limit is scheduled to take effect on a certain date, the one who finds a solution has a ready-made market for his invention." J. Bonine, The Evolution of Technology-Forcing in the Clean Air Act, 6 Env't Rep. (BNA) Monograph No. 21, at 2 (July 25, 1975).

The concept of technology forcing emerged most clearly in the context of the statutory provisions designed to reduce emissions from mobile sources. See Central Valley Chrysler-Jeep, Inc. v. Goldstene, 529 F. Supp. 2d 1151, 1178 (E.D. Cal. 2007) (stating that "[t]he 'technology-forcing goals' of . . . the portion of the [CAA] that establishes emissions standards for moving vehicles, are well recognized"), *reconsideration denied*, 563 F. Supp. 2d 1158 (E.D. Cal. 2008).

The scope of EPA's discretion to force the development of new technologies was at issue in NRDC v. Thomas, 805 F.2d 410 (D.C. Cir. 1986). NRDC challenged EPA's 1985 regulations to reduce heavy-duty motor vehicle emissions of particulate matter (some of it coated with carcinogenic compounds) and NO_x as too lenient, and the Engine Manufacturers Association attacked them as too stringent. Congress did not establish emission standards for heavy-duty engines. Instead, it ordered EPA to set "standards which reflect the greatest degree of emission reduction achievable through the application of technology which the Administrator determines will be available for the model year to which such standards apply." §202(a)(3)(A)(iii). In issuing those standards, EPA was to give "appropriate consideration to the cost of applying such technology within the period of time available to manufacturers and to noise, energy, and safety factors associated with the application of such technology." Id.

NRDC claimed that EPA improperly failed to set the standards at levels based on what the most advanced engine, the technological leader in the industry, was capable of achieving. EPA instead devised its regulations on the basis of what the engine manufacturing industry as a whole could accomplish. The court sided with EPA, concluding that the statute did not mandate "a leader-specific balancing" process. Industry fared no better in its attack on the particulate standards as being too stringent. Section 202(a)(3)(A)(iii) required EPA to set standards based on technology that "will be available" for the applicable model year. Industry argued that the statute did not envision technology forcing. The court disagreed:

> The agency describes technology-forcing standards as those that "are to be based upon that technology which the Administrator determines will be available, and not necessarily that technology which is *already available*. The adoption of such standards helps to encourage and hasten the development of new technology." 49 Fed. Reg. 40,258, 40,258 (1984). On the other hand, an adequately demonstrated technology "is one which has been *shown* to be reasonably reliable, reasonably efficient, and which can reasonably be expected to serve the interests of pollution control without becoming exorbitantly costly in an economic or environmental way." Essex Chem. Corp. v. Ruckelshaus, 486 F.2d 427, 433 (D.C. Cir. 1973). . . . As we pointed out in NRDC v. EPA, 655 F.2d 318, 328 (D.C. Cir. 1981):
>
> > The legislative history of both the 1970 and the 1977 amendments demonstrates that Congress intended the agency to project future advances in pollution control capability. It was "expected to press for the development and application of improved technology rather than be limited by that which exists today." S. Rep. No. 1196, 91st Cong., 2d Sess. 24 (1970). . . . [Id. at 429 n.30.]

Compare Bluewater Network v. EPA, 370 F.3d 1 (D.C. Cir. 2004) (concluding that under §213(a)(3), EPA may rely on cost and other statutory factors to set emission standards for snowmobiles at a level less stringent than reflected by across-the-fleet implementation of advanced technologies).

The court in NRDC v. Thomas distinguished between technology-forcing standards and those based on adequately demonstrated technology, concluding that Congress intended in the context of heavy-duty vehicle emission controls to authorize the imposition of the former. In a subsequent case, NRDC v. Reilly, 983 F.2d 259 (D.C. Cir. 1993), the same court characterized this distinction as one between "absolute" and technology-based standards. The discussion arose in the context of a challenge to EPA's failure to issue regulations under §202(a)(6) to control vehicle refueling emissions through on-board devices. EPA regarded on-board refueling vapor recovery (ORVR) as inherently and unreasonably unsafe.

> We have previously noted a distinction between provisions in the [CAA] that are "technology-based" and those that are "absolute." See NRDC v. EPA, 655 F.2d 318, 322 & 332 n.25 (D.C. Cir. 1981). Technology-based provisions require EPA to promulgate standards only after finding that the requisite technology exists or may be feasibly developed. Absolute standards, on the other hand, require compliance with statutorily prescribed standards and time tables, irrespective of present technologies. Absolute standards presume that industry can be driven to develop the requisite technologies.[12] In this case, the use of the word "systems" in section 202(a)(6), in combination with the statutorily fixed time table, indicates that this provision falls into the "absolute" category and, hence, is technology-forcing. There is nothing in the section warranting EPA's decision to limit its consideration of ORVR to a single existing technology. Moreover, this statutory command was not, EPA's protestations to the contrary notwithstanding, unrealistic. While it is true that alternative control methods are not production-ready, several are beyond the conceptualization stage and should have been amenable to engineering evaluation. [Id. at 268-269.]

The court found it significant that EPA did not conclude that ORVR systems were incapable of being made safe, and held that the agency's failure to issue the regulations conflicted with the technology-forcing intent of §202(a)(6). What is the role of technology forcing under a statute that orders EPA to adopt emission control standards that "achieve the greatest degree of emission reduction achievable through the application of technology which [EPA] determines will be available," but also requires that EPA consider "the lead time necessary to permit the development and application of the requisite technology"? See Bluewater Network, supra (upholding regulations issued under §213(a)(3), (b)). In American Petroleum Inst. v. EPA, 706 F.3d 474 (D.C. Cir. 2013), the court rejected an effort by EPA to apply pressure to one industry (petroleum refiners) to increase the manufacture of alternative fuels by another industry (the cellulosic biofuel industry) over which it had no control. The court found that this effort was "not 'technology-forcing' in the same sense as other innovation-minded regulations that we have upheld." Id. at 480.

How is EPA supposed to distinguish between an "absolute" and a more modest technology-based statutory mandate? How revealing is the statutory language likely to be? What were the statutory terms that led the courts in the two NRDC cases to

12. This results in the so-called "technology-forcing" character of the CAA. See Union Elec. Co. v. EPA, 427 U.S. 246, 257 (1976); NRDC v. Thomas, 805 F.2d 410, 429 (D.C. Cir. 1986); see also 116 Cong. Rec. 42,381, 42,382 (1970) (claims of technological impossibility not sufficient to avoid standards under the CAA) (comments of Senator Muskie). It is the nature of technology-forcing sections that technical problems, including those involving safety, are ironed out in the course of the statutorily spurred process of research and development. It is not necessary, or even anticipated, that required systems will be absolutely safe at the prototype stage of development.

conclude that Congress intended to force the development of vehicle emission control technology? Which of the following vehicle emission control provisions appear to be technology forcing in nature: §§202(a)(3)(A)(i), 202(a)(3)(D), 202(a)(4)(A)-(B), 202(a)(6), 202(g)(1), 202(i)(3)(B)?

The Role of Risk Reduction in Technology Forcing. What is the relationship between the health protection goals of a statute like the CAA and the objective of technology forcing? If a technology-forcing mandate is based on a decision to press industry to perform better, the question remains how hard to press for improved emission controls. In Sierra Club v. Costle, 657 F.2d 298 (D.C. Cir. 1981), Judge Wald opined that EPA cannot decide meaningfully how much marginal pollution reduction to require at very high levels of control—at which each new increment of pollution control secures much less pollution reduction than the preceding one—without examining whether the small pollution control gain is worth its high cost in terms of health protection "purchased." Even if a statute does not explicitly require that health be considered in setting technology-based standards, it may be impossible for EPA to exclude it entirely from the judgment process. For more on technology forcing, see generally La Pierre, Technology-Forcing and Federal Environmental Protection Statutes, 62 Iowa L. Rev. 771 (1977).

2. Controlling Emissions from Mobile Sources in Nonattainment Areas

Given that mobile-source emissions are a major component of the nonattainment problem for ozone and CO, one might expect to see EPA aggressively seeking to limit those emissions. EPA has indeed tried to crack down on mobile-source emissions to accelerate attainment of the NAAQS, but those efforts have a checkered history at best. A critical element in EPA's pre-1977 mobile-source strategy was the Transportation Control Plan (TCP), through which it sought in some areas to impose dramatic controls on automobile usage. The TCP aimed at reducing the use of automobiles through controls ranging from the encouragement of carpooling to improvements in public mass transit. These measures are known as Transportation Control Measures (TCMs).

Public opposition to EPA's attempts to control car and truck use by means of TCPs and TCMs was prompt and vociferous. Congress responded in the 1977 amendments by curtailing federal authority to control mobile-source pollution through TCPs and by suspending existing TCP provisions for private vehicle retrofitting, gas rationing, parking supply reduction, and bridge tolls. The 1977 legislation also prohibited the imposition of federal controls on indirect sources that attract large numbers of vehicles.

The 1977 amendments required that the SIPs of states with ozone or CO nonattainment areas include a "specific schedule" for imposition of an auto emissions control inspection and maintenance (I&M) program. I&M programs soon became a key TCP strategy. The states persuaded EPA that in meeting the extended NAAQS deadlines they should be allowed to rely heavily on the emissions reductions that were supposed to occur under EPA's motor vehicle emission standards discussed above. But the effectiveness of emissions controls declines rapidly soon after vehicles go into service, and the number of vehicles on the road increased even as the pollutant amounts emitted by each vehicle fell. As a result, the vehicle emission standards proved just as ineffective in eliminating ozone and CO nonattainment problems after 1977 as they had been before.

When Congress amended the CAA again in 1990, it restored some of EPA's authority to require measures in ozone and CO nonattainment areas that, if implemented, would restrict vehicle use. The worse the nonattainment problem, the greater is EPA's authority to require significant changes in activities with the potential to generate mobile-source emissions of ozone precursors or CO. The existence of that authority on paper, however, does not necessarily translate into effective controls in the real world. EPA and any states seeking to constrain mobile-source emissions must still deal with the love affair between the average American and his or her car(s). As the discussion below indicates, Congress has backtracked on several mandates included in the 1990 amendments to limit mobile-source emissions. It remains to be seen whether meaningful measures to control these emissions are feasible.

The remainder of this subsection explores some of the provisions of the 1990 amendments that relate to mobile-source emissions in nonattainment areas and the legal and practical issues that the application of those provisions has raised or may present in the future.

a. Vehicle Inspection and Maintenance Programs

I&M programs have been at the center of political and legal controversy over the implementation of nonattainment plans. Although they are capable of reducing automotive pollution, they are costly to implement and tend to be regarded as intrusive. Kentucky's vehicle emission testing program, for example, "has always generated more than its share of controversy. By necessity, it imposes a certain amount of inconvenience and expense upon citizens whose vehicles regularly meet its standards. Not surprisingly, many people find the testing requirements intrusive and wasteful." Kentucky Res. Council, Inc. v. EPA, 304 F. Supp. 2d 920, 923 (W.D. Ky. 2004).

The 1990 amendments required states with marginal or moderate ozone nonattainment areas to implement a basic I&M program that conforms to EPA guidance. §182(a)(2)(B)(i), (b)(4). A basic program involves visual inspection of pollution control devices and measurement of exhaust during engine idling. States with serious, severe, or extreme areas had to establish more costly enhanced I&M programs to reduce HC and NO_x emissions, which include computerized on-road testing devices, denial of registration for noncomplying vehicles, and operation of the program on a centralized basis instead of through local gasoline service stations. E.g., §182(c)(3)(A), (C).

EPA favored centralized I&M facilities that lack the authority to make repairs in deficient vehicles because it regarded centralized testing as more accurate and less likely to result in the issuance of undeserved waivers based on the high cost of repairs. State officials tended to support decentralized programs run by local service station operators, claiming that centralization would provide car owners with fewer testing stations to choose from, require that they wait in longer lines, and impose on them the inconvenience of having to fix noncomplying cars elsewhere before returning for retesting. The states also wanted to protect the investments that service station owners had made in testing equipment. See Dwyer, The Practice of Federalism Under the Clean Air Act, 54 Md. L. Rev. 1183, 1212 (1995). Ultimately, Congress adopted the National Highway System Designation Act of 1995, Pub. L. No. 104-59, §348, 109 Stat. 568, which bars EPA from requiring states with ozone nonattainment areas to establish centralized testing facilities and authorizes states to resort to test-and-repair facilities. EPA subsequently took additional steps "to provide greater flexibility to states to tailor their I/M programs to better meet local needs." 65 Fed. Reg. 45,526, 45,527 (2000).

What does this tale indicate about Congress's willingness to adhere to vigorous requirements to reduce vehicle exhaust and about the willingness of state and local governments to help achieve motor vehicle emission reductions? See McGarity, Regulating Commuters to Clear the Air: Some Difficulties in Implementing a National Program at the Local Level, 27 Pac. L.J. 1521, 1620 (1996) ("The history of federal I/M programs plainly demonstrates that the states are entirely unwilling to implement such programs voluntarily," couching opposition in the "rhetoric of state sovereignty."). EPA's Inspector General reported in 2006 that EPA failed to provide effective oversight of state vehicle emissions testing programs, even though more than a third of 34 states operating I&M programs failed to file reports on their effectiveness between 2001 and 2006.

b. Gasoline Vapor Recovery

Another control strategy is the recovery of gasoline vapor hydrocarbon VOCs that escape during refueling. The entry of gasoline vapor into the atmosphere during refueling can be limited by reducing the gasoline's volatility, capturing gasoline vapors in a container "on board" the vehicle, or capturing gasoline vapors by routing them back to the station's main tank.

In 1990, Congress ordered EPA to issue standards requiring new cars to be equipped with onboard controls. §202(a)(6). EPA balked, concluding that the safety risks were unreasonable. Although the agency claimed that it had discretion to pursue this option, the court in NRDC v. Reilly, 983 F.2d 259 (D.C. Cir. 1993), found EPA's duty to issue the standards to be mandatory. On remand, EPA phased in onboard controls. 59 Fed. Reg. 16,262 (1994). Congress also required SIPs in all but marginal ozone nonattainment areas to require controls at the pump. §182(b)(3).

c. Alternative Fuels

The 1990 amendments sought to encourage or mandate the use of alternative fuels with lower pollution potential than motor gasoline derived from crude oil. See Figure 6-8. Exxon Mobil Corp. v. EPA, 217 F.3d 1246 (9th Cir. 2000), upheld EPA's approval of a Nevada SIP revision requiring that all gasoline sold in the winter have an oxygen content of at least 3.5 percent. The 1990 amendments also sought to encourage the use of ethanol (which is primarily made from corn) as an oxygenate to reduce emissions of CO, but Congress repealed the oxygenate requirements in the Energy Policy Act of 2005, Pub. L. No. 109-58, §1504, 119 Stat. 594, 1077.

Congress sought to accelerate the use of alternative fuels as an energy conservation measure in the Energy Independence and Security Act of 2007, Pub. L. No. 110-140, 121 Stat. 1492. The Act amends the CAA to require EPA to revise its regulations governing the use of fuels or fuel additives "to ensure that transportation fuel sold or introduced into commerce in the United States . . . , on an annual basis, contains at least the applicable volume of renewable fuel, advanced biofuel, cellulosic

FUEL	ADVANTAGES	DISADVANTAGES
ELECTRICITY	• Potential for zero vehicle emissions • Power plant emissions easier to control • Can recharge at night when power demand is low	• Current technology is limited • Higher vehicle cost; lower vehicle range, performance • Less convenient refueling
ETHANOL	• Excellent automotive fuel • Very low emissions of ozone-forming hydrocarbons and toxics • Made from renewable sources • Can be domestically produced	• High fuel cost • Somewhat lower vehicle range
METHANOL	• Excellent automotive fuel • Very low emissions of ozone-forming hydrocarbons, and toxics • Can be made from a variety of feedstocks, including renewables	• Fuel could initially be imported • Somewhat lower vehicle range
NATURAL GAS (METHANE)	• Very low emissions of ozone-forming hydrocarbons, toxics and carbon monoxide • Can be made from a variety of feedstocks, including renewables • Excellent fuel, especially for fleet vehicles	• Higher vehicle cost • Lower vehicle range • Less convenient refueling
PROPANE	• Cheaper than gasoline today • Most widely available clean fuel today • Somewhat lower emissions of ozone-forming hydrocarbons and toxics • Excellent fuel, especially for fleet vehicles	• Cost will rise with demand • Limited supply • No energy security or trade balance benefits
REFORMULATED GASOLINE	• Can be used in all cars without changing vehicles or fuel distribution system • Somewhat lower emissions of ozone-forming hydrocarbons, nitrogen oxides, and toxics	• Somewhat higher fuel cost • Few energy security or trade balance benefits

FIGURE 6-8

Summary Table of Alternative Fuel Advantages and Disadvantages

Source: http://www.epa.gov/otaq/06-clean.htm (removed).

biofuel, and mass-based diesel." 42 U.S.C. §7545(o)(2)(A)(i). EPA has limited authority to adjust the statutory percentages for required reductions in life cycle GHG emissions up or down based on factors such as cost and feasibility. §7545(o)(4). The statute authorizes the trading of credits for additional renewable fuels. §7545(o)(5)(E). For a description of the program, see Monroe Energy, LLC v. EPA, 750 F.3d 909, 912-913 (D.C. Cir. 2014).

d. Clean-Fuel Vehicles

Under the 1990 amendments, states with specified ozone or CO nonattainment areas must revise their SIPs to establish a clean-fuel vehicle program for covered fleets. §246(a)(1); Figure 6-9. See also §182(c)(4) (serious ozone nonattainment areas). Clean-fuel vehicles must meet standards issued by EPA under §242. Revised SIPs must require an increasing percentage of all new covered fleet vehicles (ten or more vehicles owned or operated by a single person) to use clean alternative fuels when operating in a covered nonattainment area. §246(b). The SIP also must require fuel providers to make clean alternative fuels available to covered fleet operators at central

Clean-Fueled Vehicles and Potential Ozone Reductions in a Typical City

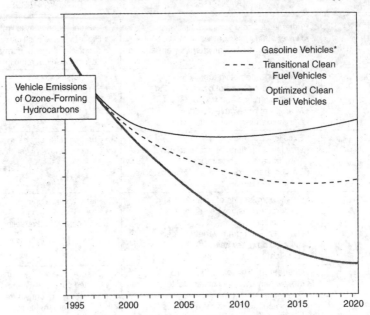

FIGURE 6-9

Source: http://www.epa.gov/oms/04-ozone.htm (removed).

fueling locations. §246(e). See generally Bale, The Newest Frontier in Motor Vehicle Emission Control: The Clean Fuel Vehicle, 15 Va. Envtl. L.J. 213 (1995-1996).

e.   Transportation Controls and Related Measures

Stung by its experience during the mid-1970s, EPA was reluctant to require transportation control measures (TCMs) of the sort described in §108(f)(1) after the 1977 amendments. E.g., Delaney v. EPA, 898 F.2d 687 (9th Cir. 1990) (EPA's refusal to require reasonably available TCMs was arbitrary). The states resisted implementing them even when they were required. The 1990 amendments enhanced EPA's authority to require states to include TCMs in their SIPs. States with serious and severe ozone nonattainment areas had to submit to EPA periodic demonstrations that aggregate vehicle mileage, vehicle emissions, and congestion levels were consistent with projections in the SIP for attaining the NAAQS. If actual figures exceeded the projections, the state had to revise its SIP to include a TCM program to reduce emissions of ozone precursors. §182(c)(5). See also §§182(e)(4), 187(b)(2).

The fate of the employee trip reduction program under the 1990 amendments raises doubts about whether these requirements will amount to anything. The amendments obligated states with ozone nonattainment areas to require large employers to increase average passenger occupancy per vehicle commuting between home and the workplace during peak travel periods by at least 25 percent. Congress anticipated that employers would either provide van pools for their employees or provide incentives for employees to carpool or take public transportation to work. But businesses resented their new obligations, complaining that they should not be forced to redress past state failures to achieve the NAAQS. In 1995, Congress barred EPA from financing the program. Pub. L. No. 104-19, 109 Stat. 194. It later gave states the *discretion* to revise their SIPs to require employers to implement programs to reduce work-related vehicle trips and miles traveled by employees. §182(d)(1)(B).[t]

The Safe, Accountable, Flexible, Efficient Transportation Equity Act: A Legacy for Users (SAFETEA-LU), Pub. L. No. 109-59, §6001(a), 119 Stat. 1144 (2005), prohibits the use of federal funds on any highway project in an urbanized area with a population of over 200,000 people that is classified as nonattainment for either ozone or CO if the project would significantly increase carrying capacity for single-occupant vehicles, unless the project is subject to a process designed to manage traffic congestion through travel demand reduction and operational management strategies. 49 U.S.C. §5303(n)(1).

f.   Indirect Source Review

The 1977 amendments eliminated federal measures for improving air quality through land use controls on the spacing and location of facilities that attract large numbers of vehicles. These "indirect sources" include highways, airports, parking garages and lots, shopping centers, and large office and apartment buildings. States are free to adopt indirect source review (ISR) requirements, but EPA may not require that they be included in SIPs.

All facilities that could be subjected to parking supply reductions—parking lots, garages, and other existing off-street facilities—are clearly excluded from EPA-imposed control. But the Act makes it equally clear that EPA could impose controls on new or existing on-street parking and other TCMs. §110(a)(5)(C), (E). Do exclusive bus and carpool lanes and other traffic flow improvement strategies that involve modifying highways or highway use (e.g., bike lanes) fit the definition of indirect sources? Suppose that a major city located on a river proposes to build a tunnel underneath the river. The city will vent CO from the tunnel through a ventilation building located nearby. The city is part of a nonattainment area for CO. Is the ventilation building a major stationary source for which the city must file a permit under §172(c)(5), or is it an indirect source whose regulation is left to the discretion of the state? See Sierra Club v. Larson, 2 F.3d 462 (1st Cir. 1993). Suppose that a state agency adopts a regulation requiring developers of large residential or commercial real estate projects to reduce NO_x and particulate matter emissions from construction equipment by specified percentages or pay emissions fees that the agency will then use to fund emissions reductions elsewhere. Is the rule an indirect source review program authorized by §110(a)(5)(A) or an effort to regulate emissions from nonroad engines that is preempted by §209(e)(2)? See National Ass'n of Home Builders v. San Joaquin Valley Unified Air Pollution Control Dist., 627 F.3d 730 (9th Cir. 2010).

---

t. For a discussion of the reasons for the failure of the trip reduction program, see Professor Oren's trilogy, Getting Commuters out of Their Cars: What Went Wrong?, 17 Stan. Envtl. L.J. 141 (1998); Detail and Implementation: The Example of Employee Trip Reduction, 17 Va. Envtl. L.J. 123 (1998); How a Mandate Came from Hell: The Makings of the Federal Employee Trip Reduction Plan, 28 Envtl. L. 267 (1998).

The ISR provisions of the Act were not amended in 1990. ISR apparently is even more abhorrent than the extremely unpopular TCMs. In prohibiting ISR in 1977, Congress sought to avoid effectively divesting control over land use siting decisions from the local governments that had traditionally exercised them. H.R. Rep. No. 95-294, at 1301 (1977). Localities have the power under some state laws to impose fees on those responsible for mobile-source pollution from indirect sources. See, e.g., California Bldg. Indus. Ass'n v. San Joaquin Valley Air Pollution Control Dist., 178 Cal. App. 4th 120 (2009).

I. CONTROL OF OTHER POLLUTANTS

1. Hazardous Air Pollutants

The Clean Air Act regulates hazardous air pollutants through a lengthy single section, §112. Federal regulation of hazardous air pollutants has, since the CAA's 1970 enactment, undergone fundamental changes due to a major legislative amendment in 1990 and different presidential administrations' varying approaches to such regulation. Before 1990, the CAA required that EPA issue national emission standards for hazardous air pollutants, which were defined as pollutants that "may reasonably be anticipated to result in an increase" in serious illness or mortality. Under the 1970 Act, hazardous air pollution standards had to be set "at the level which in [the Administrator's] judgment provide[d] an ample margin of safety to protect the public health." Most of the pollutants that EPA considered regulating under this authority were known or suspected carcinogens. EPA struggled with the proper analytical methodology for setting standards for these substances in light of its view that it was impossible to establish a safe threshold level of exposure to them and its obligation to provide "an ample margin of safety."

In NRDC v. EPA, 824 F.2d 1146 (D.C. Cir. 1987), the court rejected NRDC's argument that the statute required a complete prohibition on emissions whenever EPA was incapable of establishing a safe threshold level. According to Judge Bork, speaking for the court, "Congress' use of the word 'safety' . . . is significant evidence that it did not intend to require the Administrator to prohibit all emissions of non-threshold pollutants. . . . '[S]afe' does not mean 'risk-free.' Instead, something is 'unsafe' only when it threatens humans with 'a significant risk of harm.'" Id. at 1152. The court also held, however, that EPA's chosen methodology for setting emission levels for non-threshold pollutants was improper because the agency substituted technological feasibility for health protection as the primary consideration. Precluded from placing significant emphasis on cost, EPA virtually abandoned efforts to regulate hazardous air pollutants. The 1990 Amendments discussed below sought to address this regulatory dysfunction. Congress amended the statute by authorizing EPA in §112 to adopt a technology-based approach to regulation of hazardous air pollutants. It retained risk-based standards as a backup in the event that technology-based controls did not reduce the risks of exposure to acceptable levels. One court has described the difference between technology-based and risk-based standards as follows: "A technology-based approach . . . focuses on the achievable level of pollutant reduction given current technology, whereas a hazard-based approach seeks to identify known hazards or contaminants in the [environment] and to reduce the prevalence of those hazards." Our Children's Earth Found. v. EPA, 527 F.3d 842, 845 (9th Cir. 2008).

Regulation of hazardous air pollutants from coal and oil-fired electricity generators (often referred to as electric utility steam generating units, or EGUs) has been a particularly contentious ongoing source of flux and litigation under §112, much as EGUs have been at the center of battles over new source regulation under other CAA provisions and, especially, recent regulation of greenhouse gas emissions for their climate impacts. (Section E.1 of Chapter 12 covers those climate-linked EGU actions and court opinions.) The following case summarizes §112's history and its changing strategies, parses its key provisions, and also reviews subsections focused upon EGUs. In addition, between the majority and dissent the case provides an excellent example of choices and disputes arising in setting emissions standards for hazardous air pollutants, as well as fundamental statutory interpretation and administrative law precepts shaping such battles.

WHITE STALLION ENERGY CENTER, LLC v. EPA
748 F.3d 1222 (D.C. Cir. 2014)

Before: GARLAND, Chief Judge, and ROGERS and KAVANAUGH, Circuit Judges.
PER CURIAM:

In 2012, the Environmental Protection Agency promulgated emission standards for a number of listed hazardous air pollutants emitted by coal- and oil-fired electric utility steam generating units. In this complex case, we address the challenges to the Final Rule. . . . [W]e deny the petitions challenging the Final Rule. [This excerpt focuses primarily on the challenges by the State, Industry, and Labor petitioners, as well as one of the challenges of the Environmental petitioners, and distills portions of the lengthy, mostly dissenting, Judge Kavanagh opinion.]

I.

In 1970, Congress enacted §112 of the Clean Air Act to reduce hazardous air pollutants ("HAPs"). . . . The statute defined HAPs as "air pollutant[s] . . . which in the judgment of the Administrator [of the Environmental Protection Agency ("EPA")] cause, or contribute to, air pollution which may reasonably be anticipated to result in an increase in mortality or an increase in serious irreversible, or incapacitating reversible, illness." §112(a)(1), 84 Stat. at 1685. In its original form, §112 required EPA to publish a list containing "each hazardous air pollutant for which [it] intends to establish an emission standard." §112(b)(1)(A). EPA then was to promulgate, within 360 days, emission standards "provid[ing] an ample margin of safety to protect the public health" for each listed HAP, unless EPA found that a particular listed substance was in fact not hazardous. §112(b)(1)(B). Over the next eighteen years, EPA listed only eight HAPs, established standards for only seven, and as to these seven addressed only a limited selection of possible pollution sources. See New Jersey v. EPA, 517 F.3d 574, 578 (D.C. Cir. 2008); S. Rep. No. 101-228, at 131 (1989).

To remedy the slow pace of EPA's regulation of HAPs, Congress amended the Clean Air Act in 1990 by eliminating much of EPA's discretion in the process. In the amended §112, Congress itself listed 189 HAPs that were to be regulated, see CAA §112(b), 42 U.S.C. §7412(b), and directed EPA to publish a list of "categories and subcategories" of "major sources" and certain "area sources" that emit these pollutants, §112(c). Once listed, a source category may only be delisted (with one exception not relevant here) if EPA determines that "no source" in that category emits HAPs in quantities exceeding specified thresholds. §112(c)(9)(B). For each listed "category or subcategory of major sources and area sources" of HAPs, EPA must promulgate emission standards. §112(d)(1). Section 112(d) provides, as relevant, that emission standards

> shall require the *maximum degree of reduction in emissions* of the hazardous air pollutants subject to this section (including a prohibition on such emissions, where achievable) that the Administrator, taking into consideration the cost of achieving such emission reduction, and any non-air quality health and environmental impacts and energy requirements, determines is achievable[.]

§112(d)(2) (emphasis added). For existing sources, these "maximum achievable control technology" ("MACT") standards may not be less stringent—regardless of cost or other considerations—"than [ ] the average emission limitation achieved by the best performing [ ] sources" in the relevant category or subcategory. §112(d)(3)(A)-(B); see Nat'l Lime Ass'n v. EPA, 233 F.3d 625, 629 (D.C. Cir. 2000). EPA refers to minimum-stringency MACT standards as "floors." Standards more stringent than the floors, determined pursuant to §112(d)(2), are called "beyond-the-floor" limits.

For electric utility steam generating units ("EGUs"), however, Congress directed that prior to any listing EPA conduct a study of "the *hazards to public health* reasonably anticipated to occur as a result of [EGU HAP emissions] after imposition of the requirements of this Chapter [i.e., Chapter 85 Air Pollution Prevention and Control]." §112(n)(1)(A) (emphasis added). The results of this "Utility Study" were to be reported to Congress within three years. Id. Further, Congress directed that:

> The Administrator shall regulate [EGUs] under this section, if the Administrator finds such regulation is *appropriate and necessary* after considering the results of the study required by this subparagraph.

Id. (emphasis added). Congress also directed EPA to conduct two other studies on mercury emissions: the "Mercury Study" on "the rate and mass of such emissions, the health and environmental effects of such emissions, technologies which are available to control such emissions, and the costs of such technologies," to be reported to Congress in four years, and the National Institute of Environmental Health Sciences "study to determine the threshold level of mercury exposure below which adverse human health effects are not expected to occur," to be reported to Congress in three years. See §112(n)(1)(A)-(C).

In December 2000, on the basis of the Utility Study and other data subsequently gathered, EPA issued a notice of regulatory finding "that regulation of HAP emissions from coal- and oil-fired electric utility steam generating units under section 112 of the CAA is appropriate and necessary." Regulatory Finding on the Emissions of Hazardous Air Pollutants from Electric Utility Steam Generating

Units, 65 Fed. Reg. 79,825, 79,826 (Dec. 20, 2000) ("2000 Finding"). EPA found that EGUs "are the largest source of mercury emissions in the U.S." and that "[m]ercury is highly toxic, persistent, and bioaccumulates in food chains." Id. at 79,827. Specifically, "[m]ercury emitted from [EGUs] . . . is transported through the atmosphere and eventually deposits onto land or water bodies" where it then changes into "a highly toxic" substance called methylmercury. Id. Methylmercury "biomagnifies in the aquatic food chain," meaning that it becomes concentrated in the bodies of predatory fish which absorb the methylmercury their food sources contained. When humans eat these contaminated fish, they also are exposed; the methylmercury from the fish is absorbed into the bloodstream and "distributed to all tissues including the brain." Id. at 79,829. The risks are greatest for women of childbearing age, EPA explained, because methylmercury "readily passes . . . to the fetus and fetal brain," id., and "the developing fetus is most sensitive to the effects of methylmercury," id. at 79,827. Children born to women who were exposed to methylmercury during pregnancy have exhibited neurological abnormalities and developmental delays. Id. at 79,829.

EPA concluded that "the available information indicate[d] that mercury emissions from [EGUs] . . . are a threat to public health and the environment," notwithstanding "uncertainties regarding the *extent* of the risks due to electric utility mercury emissions." Id. (emphasis added). EPA also identified several other metal and acid gas emissions from EGUs that were "of potential concern," namely arsenic, chromium, nickel, cadmium, dioxins, hydrogen chloride, and hydrogen fluoride. EPA therefore determined that it was "appropriate" to regulate coal-and oil-fired EGUs under §112 because of the health and environmental hazards posed by mercury emissions from EGUs, and the availability of a number of control options to effectively reduce such emissions. EPA further determined that it was "necessary" to regulate EGUs under §112 because implementation of other provisions of the CAA would "not adequately address" the public health and environmental hazards found. Therefore, EPA added "coal- and oil-fired electric utility steam generating units to the list of source categories under section 112(c) of the CAA." Id.

In 2005, EPA reversed its 2000 Finding and removed coal- and oil-fired EGUs from the list of source categories under §112(c). See Revision of December 2000 Regulatory Finding on the Emissions of Hazardous Air Pollutants from Electric Utility Steam Generating Units and the Removal of Coal- and Oil-Fired Electric Utility Steam Generating Units from the Section 112(c) List, 70 Fed. Reg. 15,994, 15,994 (Mar. 29, 2005) ("2005 Delisting Decision"). This change was based on EPA's revised interpretation of §112(n)(1)(A) and, to some extent, on a revised assessment of the results of the Utility Study. EPA concluded that it lacked authority under §112(n)(1)(A) to regulate on the basis of non-health hazards (e.g., environmental harms), and should "focus solely" on the health effects directly attributable to EGU emissions, rather than on EGUs' contribution to overall pollutant levels. Further, EPA decided it could consider other relevant, "situation-specific factors, including cost" that may affect whether regulation under §112 is "appropriate." Critically, EPA determined that it must make its "appropriate and necessary" finding by reference to health hazards that will remain "*after* imposition of the requirements of" the CAA. Id. at 15,998 (emphasis added) (quoting CAA §112(n)(1)(A)). EPA interpreted these other "requirements" to include "not only those requirements already imposed and in effect, but also those requirements that EPA reasonably anticipates will be implemented" and which "could either directly or indirectly result in reductions of utility HAP emissions." Id. at 15,999. Concluding that regulation under other provisions of the CAA would adequately address EGU emissions of mercury and other HAPs, EPA determined that regulation under §112 was neither "appropriate" nor "necessary." Id. at 16,002–08. In responding to comments, EPA stated that if it *were* to regulate EGU emissions, then it would regulate *only* those substances for which it had made a specific "appropriate and necessary" determination. States and other groups petitioned for review and this court vacated the 2005 Listing Decision, *New Jersey*, 517 F.3d at 583, holding that EPA's attempt to reverse its December 2000 listing decision was unlawful because Congress had "unambiguously limit[ed] EPA's discretion to remove sources, including EGUs, from the section 112(c)(1) list once they have been added to it."

In 2012, after notice and comment, EPA "confirm[ed]" its 2000 Finding that regulation of EGU emissions under §112 is "appropriate and necessary." Final Rule, 77 Fed. Reg. 9304, 9310–11. . . . Although of the view that no further evidence was required to affirm the 2000 Finding, EPA had conducted additional quantitative and qualitative analyses "confirm[ing] that it remains appropriate and necessary today to regulate EGUs under CAA section 112." Id. at 24,986. With respect to the term "appropriate," EPA explained that it was "chang[ing] the position taken in 2005 that the appropriate finding could not be based on environmental effects alone"; "revisiting the 2005 interpretation that required the Agency to consider HAP emissions from EGUs without considering the cumulative impacts of all sources of HAP emissions"; "revising the 2005 interpretation that required the Agency to evaluate the hazards to public health after imposition of the requirements of the CAA"; and "rejecting the 2005 interpretation that authorizes the Agency to consider other factors (e.g., cost), even if the agency determines that HAP emitted by EGUs pose a hazard to public health (or the environment)." Id. at 24,989. With respect to the term "necessary," EPA rejected as "unreasonable" its interpretation in 2005 that regulation under §112 was "necessary" only if *no* other provision in the CAA—whether implemented or only anticipated—could "directly or indirectly" reduce HAP emissions to acceptable levels. Id. at 24,992.

EPA explained that it interpreted §112(n)(1)(A)

> to require the Agency to find it *appropriate* to regulate EGUs under CAA section 112 if the Agency determines that the emissions of one or more HAP emitted from EGUs pose an identified or potential hazard to public health or the environment at the time the finding is made. If the Agency finds that it is *appropriate* to regulate, it must find it *necessary* to regulate EGUs under section 112 if the identified or potential hazards to public health or the environment will not be adequately addressed by the imposition of the requirements of the CAA. Moreover, it may be *necessary* to regulate utilities under section 112 for a number of other reasons, including, for example, that section 112 standards will assure permanent reductions in EGU HAP emissions, which cannot be assured based on other requirements of the CAA.

Id. at 24,987–88. EPA also affirmed that coal- and oil-fired EGUs were properly listed as a source category under §112(c). See id. at 24,986. EPA adhered to these interpretations in the Final Rule, 77 Fed. Reg. at 9311. Accordingly, on February 16, 2012, EPA promulgated emission standards for a number of listed HAPs emitted by coal- and oil-fired EGUs. See id. at 9487–93.

Several petitions for review challenge the Final Rule. . . .

II.

State, Industry, and Labor petitioners challenge EPA's interpretation and application of the "appropriate and necessary" requirement in §112(n)(1)(A). . . .

    B.

    The crux of [State, Industry, and Labor petitioners'] challenge to the Final Rule focuses on EPA's interpretation of the phrase "appropriate and necessary" in §112(n)(1)(A). The context of this phrase is as follows. In a special subsection on EGUs, Congress first directed: "The Administrator shall perform a *study of the hazards to public health* reasonably anticipated to occur as a result of emissions by electric utility steam generating units of pollutants listed under subsection (f) after imposition of the requirements of this Act." §112(n)(1)(A) (emphasis added). Congress then directed: "The Administrator shall regulate electric utility steam generating units under this section, if the Administrator finds such regulation is *appropriate and necessary after considering the results of the study* required by this subparagraph." Id. (emphasis added). Apart from the instruction to "consider[ ] the results of the [Utility Study]" on public health hazards from EGU emissions, the statute offers no express guidance regarding what factors EPA is required or permitted to consider in deciding whether regulation under §112 is "appropriate and necessary." Neither does it define the words "appropriate" or "necessary." See NPRM, 76 Fed. Reg. at 24,986; 2005 Listing Decision, 70 Fed. Reg. at 15,997. Petitioners object to how EPA chose to fill these gaps.

    In matters of statutory interpretation, the court applies the familiar two part test under *Chevron.* . . .

    To the extent petitioners' challenge concerns EPA's *change* in interpretation from that in 2005, our approach is the same because "[a]gency inconsistency is not a basis for declining to analyze the agency's interpretation under the *Chevron* framework." Nat'l Cable & Telecomms. Ass'n v. Brand X Internet Servs., 545 U.S. 967, 981 (2005). That is, "if the agency adequately explains the reasons for a reversal of policy, change is not invalidating, since the whole point of *Chevron* is to leave the discretion provided by the ambiguities of a statute with the implementing agency." Id. And while "[u]nexplained inconsistency" may be "a reason for holding an interpretation to be an arbitrary and capricious change from agency practice," id., our review of a change in agency policy is no stricter than our review of an initial agency action, see FCC v. Fox Television Stations, Inc., 556 U.S. 502, 514–16 (2009). Thus, although an agency may not "depart from a prior policy *sub silentio* or simply disregard rules that are still on the books," the agency "need not demonstrate to a court's satisfaction that the reasons for the new policy are *better* than the reasons for the old one." Id. at 515. Rather, "it suffices that the new policy is permissible under the statute, that there are good reasons for it, and that the agency *believes* it to be better." Id.

    1. Reliance on delisting criteria. In the Final Rule, EPA concluded that it is "appropriate and necessary" to regulate HAP emissions on the basis, *inter alia*, that EGU emissions of certain HAPs pose a cancer risk higher than the standard set forth in the §112(c)(9) delisting criteria (i.e., greater than one in a million for the most exposed individual). See Final Rule, 77 Fed. Reg. at 9311; NPRM, 76 Fed. Reg. at 24,998. Petitioners contend that by so doing EPA wrongly conflated the delisting criteria with the "appropriate and necessary" determination. . . .

EPA explained that it was relying upon the delisting criteria to interpret an ambiguous term in §112(n)(1)(A), namely, "hazards to public health," see Final Rule, 77 Fed. Reg. at 9333–34; NPRM, 76 Fed. Reg. at 24,992–93, because the phrase "hazards to public health" is nowhere defined in the CAA. EPA looked to the delisting criteria, which specify the risk thresholds below which a source category need not be regulated, as evidence of congressional judgment as to what *degree* of risk constitutes a health hazard. . . .

EPA reasonably relied on the §112(c)(9) delisting criteria to inform its interpretation of the undefined statutory term "hazard to public health." Congress did not specify what types or levels of public health risks should be deemed a "hazard" for purposes of §112(n)(1)(A). By leaving this gap in the statute, Congress delegated to EPA the authority to give reasonable meaning to the term. Cf. *Chevron*, 467 U.S. at 843–44. . . .

2. *Costs of regulation.* Noting that in 2005 EPA construed §112(n)(1)(A) to allow consideration of costs in determining whether regulation of EGU HAP emissions is "appropriate," petitioners contend that EPA's new interpretation to "preclude consideration of costs," "unreasonably constrains the language of §112(n)(1)(A)." . . .

In the Final Rule, EPA stated that "it is reasonable to make the listing decision, including the appropriate determination, without considering costs." Final Rule, 77 Fed. Reg. at 9327. EPA reasoned that §112(n)(1)(A) would have included an "express statutory requirement that the Agency consider costs in making the appropriate determination" if Congress wanted to require EPA to do so. Id. EPA also noted that "[t]o the extent [its] interpretation differs from the one set forth in 2005," it had "fully explained the basis for such changes." Id. at 9323 (citing NPRM, 76 Fed. Reg. at 24,986–93). . . .

On its face, §112(n)(1)(A) neither requires EPA to consider costs nor prohibits EPA from doing so. Indeed, the word "costs" appears nowhere in subparagraph A. In the absence of any express statutory instruction regarding costs, petitioners rely on the dictionary definition of "appropriate"—meaning "especially suitable or compatible" or "suitable or proper in the circumstances"—to argue that EPA was required "to take into account costs to the nation's electricity generators when deciding whether to regulate EGUs." SIL Br. 39 (citing Merriam-Webster's Online Dictionary; New Oxford American Dictionary (2d ed. 2005)). Yet these definitions, which do not mention costs, merely underscore that the term "appropriate" is "open-ended," "ambiguous," and "inherently context-dependent." Sossamon v. Texas, 131 S. Ct. 1651, 1659 (2011); cf. Nat'l Ass'n of Clean Air Agencies v. EPA, 489 F.3d 1221, 1229 (D.C. Cir. 2007).

Even if the word "appropriate" might require cost consideration in *some* contexts, such a reading of "appropriate" is unwarranted here, where Congress directed EPA's attention to the conclusions of the study regarding public health hazards from EGU emissions. Throughout §112, Congress mentioned costs explicitly where it intended EPA to consider them. Cf. §112(d)(2), 112(d)(8)(A)(i), 112(f)(1)(B), 112(f)(2)(A), 112(n)(1)(B), 112(s)(2). Indeed, in the immediately following subparagraph of §112(n), Congress expressly required costs to be considered. §112(n)(1)(B). The contrast with subparagraph A could not be more stark. "Where Congress includes particular language in one section of a statute but omits it in another section of the same Act, it is generally presumed that Congress acts intentionally . . . in the disparate inclusion or exclusion." Russello v. United States, 464 U.S. 16, 23 (1983); cf. Catawba

Cnty., N.C. v. EPA, 571 F.3d 20, 36 (D.C. Cir. 2009). Petitioners offer no compelling reason why Congress, by using only the broad term "appropriate," would have intended the same result—that costs be considered—in §112(n)(1)(A). The legislative history the dissent claims "establishes" the point, consists of a Floor statement by a single Congressman that at best is ambiguous. For these reasons, we conclude that the statute does not evince unambiguous congressional intent on the specific issue of whether EPA was required to consider costs in making its "appropriate and necessary" determination under §112(n)(1)(A).

Turning to EPA's approach, its position that "nothing about the definition of ['appropriate'] compels a consideration of costs," Final Rule, 77 Fed. Reg. at 9327, is clearly permissible. In Whitman v. American Trucking Ass'ns, 531 U.S. 457 (2001), Justice Scalia, writing for a unanimous Court, noted that the Supreme Court has "refused to find implicit in ambiguous sections of the CAA an authorization to consider costs that has elsewhere, and so often, been expressly granted." Id. at 467. . . . Petitioners cannot point to a single case in which this court has *required* EPA to consider costs where the CAA does not expressly so instruct. In Michigan v. EPA, this court merely held that "the agency was *free* to consider . . . costs" under CAA §110(a)(2)(D), as EPA had urged in that case. 213 F.3d at 679 (emphasis added).

EPA's interpretation is also consistent with the purpose of the 1990 Amendments, which were aimed at remedying "the slow pace of EPA's regulation of HAPs" following the initial passage of the CAA. *New Jersey*, 517 F.3d at 578. To ensure that HAP emissions would be reduced to at least minimally-acceptable levels, Congress, among other things, listed 189 HAP substances for regulation and "restrict[ed] the opportunities for EPA and others to intervene in the regulation of HAP sources." Id. The overall purpose of the 1990 Amendments was to spur EPA to action. Although Congress gave EGUs a three-year pass when it instructed EPA to conduct a further study before regulating EGUs, see §112(n)(1)(A), there is no indication that Congress did *not* intend EPA to regulate EGUs if and when their public health hazards were confirmed by the study, as they were here.

Petitioners, and our dissenting colleague, suggest that EPA's interpretation is unreasonable because the notion that Congress would have authorized EPA to regulate without *any* consideration of regulatory costs is implausible. But this argument rests on a false premise. Here, as in *Whitman*, interpreting one isolated provision not to require cost consideration does not indicate that Congress was unconcerned with costs altogether, because Congress accounted for costs elsewhere in the statute. Section 112(d)(2) expressly requires EPA to "tak[e] into consideration the cost of achieving . . . emission reduction[s]" when setting the *level* of regulation under §112. §112(d)(2). It is true that this cost consideration requirement does not apply with respect to MACT floors. Yet even for MACT floors, costs are reflected to some extent because the floors correspond (by definition) to standards that better-performing EGUs have *already achieved*, presumably in a cost efficient manner. See §112(d)(3)(A). . . .

Basically, petitioners and our dissenting colleague seek to impose a requirement that Congress did not. What they ignore is that Congress sought, as a threshold matter, to have EPA confirm the nature of public health hazards from EGU emissions. That is the clear focus of §112(n)(1)(A). After that, Congress left it to the expertise and judgment of EPA whether or not to regulate. For EPA to focus its "appropriate and necessary" determination on factors relating to public health hazards, and not industry's objections that emission controls are costly, properly puts the horse before the cart, and not the other way around as petitioners and our dissenting colleague urge.

Given Congress's efforts in the 1990 Amendments to promote regulation of hazardous pollutants, EPA's interpretation of §112(n)(1)(A) appears consistent with Congress's intent. Recall that only EGUs' hazardous emissions were relieved of regulation until completion of a study, and once the study confirmed the serious public health effects of hazardous pollutants from EGUs, Congress gave no signal that the matter should end if remediation would be costly. . . .

For these reasons, we hold that EPA reasonably concluded it need not consider costs in making its "appropriate and necessary" determination under §112(n)(1)(A).

3. *Environmental harms.* Petitioners also contend that EPA was constrained to consider only public health hazards, not environmental or other harms, in making its "appropriate and necessary" determination. In their view, §112(n)(1)(A) unambiguously forecloses the consideration of non-health effects because the statute requires EPA to make its "appropriate and necessary" determination after considering the results of the Utility Study, which is focused exclusively on identifying "hazards to public health" caused by EGU HAP emissions. Petitioners insist that in 2005 EPA followed the health-only approach. . . .

EPA did not err in considering environmental effects alongside health effects for purposes of the "appropriate and necessary" determination. Although petitioners' interpretation of §112(n)(1)(A) is plausible, the statute could also be read to treat consideration of the Utility Study as a mere condition precedent to the "appropriate and necessary" determination. EPA has consistently adopted this latter interpretation, including in 2005. See 2005 Delisting Decision, 70 Fed. Reg. at 16,002. In the absence of any limiting text, and considering the context (including §112(n)(1)(B)) and purpose of the CAA, EPA reasonably concluded that it could consider environmental harms in making its "appropriate and necessary" determination. The court need not decide whether environmental effects *alone* would allow EPA to regulate EGUs under §112, because EPA did not base its determination *solely* on environmental effects. As we explain, . . . EPA's decision to list EGUs can be sustained on the basis of its findings regarding health hazards posed by EGU HAP emissions. . . .

6. *Regulation of all HAP emissions.* In the Final Rule, EPA claimed authority to promulgate standards for all listed HAPs emitted by EGUs, not merely for those HAPs it has expressly determined to cause health or environmental hazards. See, e.g., 77 Fed. Reg. at 9325–26. Petitioners challenge this approach, maintaining that §112(n)(1)(A) limits regulation to those individual HAPs that are "appropriate and necessary" to regulate. Petitioners also object that EPA's interpretation contradicts its 2005 rulemaking when it supported a substance-by-substance approach to regulation.

EPA explained its disagreement with petitioners' proposed approach. First, EPA reiterated its view that once an "appropriate and necessary" determination is properly made, "EGUs should be regulated under section 112 in the same manner as other categories for which the statute requires regulation." Final Rule, 77 Fed. Reg. at 9326. EPA then reasoned that this court's decision in *National Lime*, 233 F.3d at 633, "requires [EPA] to regulate *all* HAP from major sources of HAP emissions once a source category is added to the list of categories under CAA section 112(c)." Id. (emphasis added). In other words, EPA concluded that if EGUs are to be regulated in the same manner as other source categories, then *all* HAPs emitted by EGUs should be subject to regulation. See id.

EPA did not err by concluding that it may regulate all HAP substances emitted by EGUs. . . . Although petitioners attempt to distinguish *National Lime* on grounds that it concerned "major sources" rather than EGUs, they have not provided any compelling reason why EGUs should not be regulated the same way as other sources once EPA has determined that regulation under §112 is "appropriate and necessary." It also bears emphasis that the plain text of §112(n)(1)(A) directs the Administrator to "regulate electric utility steam generating units"—not to regulate their *emissions*, as petitioners suggest. This source-based approach to regulating EGU HAPs was affirmed in *New Jersey*, 517 F.3d at 582, which held that EGUs could not be delisted without demonstrating that EGUs, as a category, satisfied the delisting criteria set forth in §112(c)(9). The notion that EPA must "pick and choose" among HAPs in order to regulate only those substances it deems most harmful is at odds with the court's precedent. . . .

In view of the above, EPA's conclusion that it may regulate *all* HAP emissions from EGUs must be upheld.

III.

A.

Petitioners assert that even if EPA has correctly interpreted §112(n)(1)(A), the emission standards that EPA promulgated in the Final Rule are flawed in several respects.

1. Appropriate and necessary determination. Petitioners first contend that the agency's determination that it was "appropriate and necessary" to regulate EGUs is arbitrary and capricious. Consistent with their position on the proper interpretation of §112(n)(1)(A), petitioners take a HAP-by-HAP approach to criticizing EPA's Finding. But, as we explained above, EPA reasonably interprets the CAA as allowing it to regulate *all* EGU HAP emissions pursuant to the usual MACT program once it makes the threshold "appropriate and necessary" determination. The question then is whether EPA reasonably found it appropriate and necessary to regulate EGUs based on all the record evidence before it.

EPA's "appropriate and necessary" determination in 2000, and its reaffirmation of that determination in 2012, are amply supported by EPA's findings regarding the health effects of mercury exposure. Mercury exposure has adverse effects on human health, primarily through consumption of fish in which mercury has bioaccumulated. And EGUs are the largest domestic source of mercury emissions. Petitioners . . . take issue with whether EPA has sufficiently quantified the contribution of EGU mercury emissions to overall mercury exposure. Our case law makes clear, however, that EPA is not obligated to conclusively resolve every scientific uncertainty before it issues regulation. See Coal. for Responsible Regulation v. EPA, 684 F.3d 102, 121 (D.C. Cir. 2012) ("If a statute is precautionary in nature and designed to protect the public health, and the relevant evidence is difficult to come by, uncertain, or conflicting because it is on the frontiers of scientific knowledge, EPA need not provide rigorous step-by-step proof of cause and effect to support an endangerment finding."). Instead, "[w]hen EPA evaluates scientific evidence in its bailiwick, we ask only that it take the scientific record into account in a rational manner." Id. at 122.

EPA did so here. As explained in the technical support document (TSD) accompanying the Final Rule, EPA determined that mercury emissions posed a significant threat to public health based on an analysis of women of child-bearing age who consumed large amounts of freshwater fish. See Mercury TSD; NPRM, 76 Fed.

Reg. at 25,007; Final Rule, 77 Fed. Reg. at 9311–17. The design of EPA's TSD was neither arbitrary nor capricious; the study was reviewed by EPA's independent Science Advisory Board, which stated that it "support[ed] the overall design of and approach to the risk assessment" and found "that it should provide an objective, reasonable, and credible determination of the potential for a public health hazard from mercury emitted from U.S. EGUs." . . .

3. *Mercury* MACT *floor.* Petitioners next challenge EPA's standards for mercury emissions from existing coal-fired EGUs. Petitioners maintain that in calculating the MACT floor for those units, EPA collected emissions data from only those EGUs that were best-performing for mercury emissions. Consequently, petitioners insist, the mercury MACT standard reflects the results achieved by the "best of the best" EGUs, and not the results of the best 12% of all EGUs, as required by statute.

Petitioners' assertions of a biased or irrational data collection process are not supported by a review of the record. "EPA typically has wide latitude in determining the extent of data-gathering necessary to solve a problem." Sierra Club v. EPA, 167 F.3d 658, 662 (D.C. Cir. 1999). Here, EPA determined that a three-pronged approach was appropriate for developing the mercury MACT standard. . . .

Based on the results of its ICR, covering a total of 388 EGUs, EPA chose "the average emission limitation achieved by the best performing 12 percent" of all existing sources "for which [it] ha[d] emissions information," as authorized by §112(d)(3)(A). See NPRM, 76 Fed. Reg. at 25,022–23. Although, as EPA acknowledges, it would be arbitrary and capricious for EPA to set a MACT floor based on intentionally skewed data, the facts indicate that EPA did not do so here. Nor does the record suggest that EPA's data collection efforts resulted in unintentional bias. As previously noted, EPA collected data from a wide range of EGUs because the agency concluded that it could not identify units representing the best-performing 12 percent of mercury emitters. That conclusion is borne out by the data in the record, which showed that some of the best-performing units for particulate matter control were among the worst performing units for mercury control. See generally MACT Floor Analysis Spreadsheets. Similarly, many of the mercury best performers (32 of the best performing 126 units) were not drawn from the pool of units that EPA targeted as best performers for particulate matter. In short, EPA's data-collection process was reasonable, even if it may not have resulted in a perfect dataset. . . .

IV.

We turn to the challenges by Environmental petitioners. . . .

A.

Environmental petitioners challenge the provisions of the Final Rule that allow compliance with emission standards to be demonstrated through (1) emissions averaging and (2) options for non-mercury metal HAP emissions monitoring. . . .

1. *Averaging.* Under the Final Rule, existing contiguous, commonly-controlled EGUs in the same subcategory can demonstrate compliance by averaging their emissions as an alternative to meeting certain requirements on an individual basis. Final Rule, 77 Fed.Reg. at 9384, 9473–76 (codified at 40 C.F.R. §63.10009). Averaging is permissible only between the same types of pollutants, individual EGUs that are part of the same affected source, EGUs subject to the same emission standard, and existing

(not new) EGUs. Each facility intending to use emissions averaging must develop an emissions averaging plan identifying "(1) [a]ll units in the averaging group; (2) the control technology installed; (3) the process parameter that will be monitored; (4) the specific control technology or pollution prevention measure to be used; (5) the test plan for the measurement of the HAP being averaged; and (6) the operating parameters to be monitored." Id. at 9385–86.

Environmental petitioners contend the averaging alternative is unlawful because it relaxes the stringency of the MACT floor standards. . . .

EPA permissibly interpreted §112(d) to allow emissions averaging as provided for in the Final Rule. See *Chevron*, 467 U.S. at 843. That section neither expressly allows nor disallows emissions averaging among multiple units. . . .

Viewing averaging as "an equivalent, more flexible, and less costly alternative" to requiring units to demonstrate compliance individually, EPA explained that permitting averaging is part of its "general policy of encouraging the use of flexible compliance approaches where they can be properly monitored and enforced." Id. . . .

KAVANAUGH, Circuit Judge, concurring in part and dissenting in part:

Suppose you were the EPA Administrator. You have to decide whether to go forward with a proposed air quality regulation. Your only statutory direction is to decide whether it is "appropriate" to go forward with the regulation. Before making that decision, what information would you want to know? You would certainly want to understand the benefits from the regulations. And you would surely ask how much the regulations would cost. You would no doubt take both of those considerations—benefits and costs—into account in making your decision. That's just common sense and sound government practice.

So it comes as a surprise in this case that EPA excluded any consideration of costs when deciding whether it is "appropriate"—the key statutory term—to impose significant new air quality regulations on the Nation's electric utilities. In my view, it is unreasonable for EPA to exclude consideration of costs in determining whether it is "appropriate" to impose significant new regulations on electric utilities. To be sure, EPA could conclude that the benefits outweigh the costs. But the problem here is that EPA did not even consider the costs. And the costs are huge, about $9.6 billion a year—that's billion with a b—by EPA's own calculation. . . .

[After parsing the statute and discussing his views on regulatory consideration of costs, Judge Kavanagh continues:]

In this case, whether one calls it an impermissible interpretation of the term "appropriate" at *Chevron* step one, or an unreasonable interpretation or application of the term "appropriate" at *Chevron* step two, or an unreasonable exercise of agency discretion under *State Farm*, the key point is the same: It is entirely unreasonable for EPA to exclude consideration of costs in determining whether it is "appropriate" to regulate electric utilities under the MACT program.

To begin with, consideration of cost is commonly understood to be a central component of ordinary regulatory analysis, particularly in the context of health, safety, and environmental regulation. And Congress legislated against the backdrop of that common understanding when it enacted this statute in 1990. Put simply, as a matter of common sense, common parlance, and common practice, determining whether it is "appropriate" to regulate requires consideration of costs. . . .

In upholding EPA's cost-blind approach, the majority opinion points to other statutory provisions that expressly reference cost and invokes the familiar interpretive canon that "[w]here Congress includes particular language in one section of a statute but omits it in another section of the same Act, it is generally presumed that Congress acts intentionally and purposely in the disparate inclusion or exclusion." Russello v. United States, 464 U.S. 16, 23 (1983). The majority opinion assigns particular weight to the Supreme Court's decision in Whitman v. American Trucking Associations, 531 U.S. 457 (2001), which referenced that canon when construing a different section of the Clean Air Act. See id. at 467 ("We have therefore refused to find implicit in ambiguous sections of the CAA an authorization to consider costs that has elsewhere, and so often, been expressly granted."). As in Whitman, according to the majority opinion, Congress's decision not to explicitly mention cost in Section 112(n)(1)(A), despite doing so in other parts of the Act, creates a negative implication that costs are an unnecessary consideration.

But I respectfully believe the majority opinion is misreading—or at least over-reading—Whitman. Whitman was a textualist decision written for a unanimous Court by Justice Scalia. It stands for the basic proposition that consideration of costs cannot be jammed into a statutory factor that, by its terms, otherwise would not encompass "costs," particularly when other provisions of the Act expressly reference costs. See [Entergy Corp. v. Riverkeeper, Inc., 556 U.S. 208, 223 (2008)] (Whitman "stands for the rather unremarkable proposition that sometimes statutory silence, when viewed in context, is best interpreted as limiting agency discretion.").

In Whitman itself, the statutory factor was a provision of the Clean Air Act, Section 109(b)(1), that directed EPA to set ambient air quality standards at levels "requisite to protect the public health" with "an adequate margin of safety." The dispute concerned whether those "modest words" granted EPA "the power to determine whether implementation costs should moderate national air quality standards." 531 U.S. at 468. Concluding that EPA had not been granted such power, the Court speaking through Justice Scalia observed that cost "is *both* so indirectly related to public health *and* so full of potential for canceling the conclusions drawn from direct health effects that it would surely have been expressly mentioned in §§108 and 109 had Congress meant it to be considered." Id. at 469.

The statutory provision at issue in Whitman differs significantly from the statute at issue here. The statutory provision in Whitman tied regulation solely to "public health," which is typically a critical factor *on the other side of the balance* from costs, not a factor that includes costs. Here, by contrast, the key statutory term is "appropriate"—the classic broad and all-encompassing term that naturally and traditionally includes consideration of all the relevant factors, health and safety benefits on the one hand and costs on the other. To unblinkingly rely on Whitman here is to overlook the distinct language of the relevant statutes. . . .

To sum up: All significant regulations involve tradeoffs, and I am very mindful that Congress has assigned EPA, not the courts, to make many discretionary calls to protect both our country's environment and its productive capacity. In this case, if EPA had decided, in an exercise of its judgment, that it was "appropriate" to regulate electric utilities under the MACT program because the benefits outweigh the costs, that decision would be reviewed under a deferential arbitrary and capricious standard of review. See American Radio Relay League, Inc. v. FCC, 524 F.3d 227, 247–48 (D.C. Cir. 2008) (separate opinion of Kavanaugh, J.). But before we assess the merits of any cost-benefit balancing, this statutory scheme requires that we first ensure that EPA has actually considered the costs. See State Farm, 463 U.S. at 42–43. In my view, whether we call it a Chevron problem or a State Farm problem, it is unreasonable for

EPA to exclude consideration of costs when deciding whether it is "appropriate" to regulate electric utilities under the MACT program. I respectfully dissent from the majority opinion's contrary conclusion.

NOTES AND QUESTIONS

1. Both the majority and dissent hinge much of their analysis on the Whitman v. American Trucking Ass'ns decision, even relying on similar portions of the opinion. What is the source of their disagreement?

2. In the court's review of the history of §112, it refers to the 2005 decision to "delist" EGU's as a §112 category, and the subsequent rejection by the D.C. Circuit of that action in New Jersey v. EPA, 517 F.3d 574 (D.C. Cir. 2008). That decision hinged on the relationship of §112(n)(1)(A) and 112(c)(9). Which provision applies to initial "listing" decisions and which to "delisting" decisions? Look at §112(c)(9) and identify language that cuts against the 2005 delisting action. What criteria must be satisfied before a delisting? The court characterized the delisting effort without observance of the requirements of §112(c)(9) as "deploy[ing] the logic of the Queen of Hearts, substituting EPA's desires for the plain text of section 112(c)(9)."

3. *From Risk-Based Regulation to Technology-Based, and Back Again.* The *White Stallion* court reviewed old §112's risk-based strategy and the implementation challenges it caused. While the 1990 CAA amendments shifted §112 so it has much more in common now with other technology-based standard setting such as New Source Performance Standards under §111, and Congress itself designated an initial 189 HAPs, it did not eliminate reliance on risk-based regulation. As discussed in the following case, Congress set up a process and regulatory obligations for EPA to follow in addressing "residual risk" left after reliance on technology-based standard setting.

NRDC v. EPA
529 F.3d 1077 (D.C. Cir. 2008)

SILBERMAN, Senior Circuit Judge.

Synthetic organic chemicals have few direct consumer uses, but they often serve as raw materials in the production of plastics, rubbers, fibers, protective coatings, and detergents. Petitioners, the Natural Resources Defense Council and the Louisiana Environmental Action Network, challenge EPA's residual risk rulemaking under subsection 112(f) of the Clean Air Act for facilities that use or produce synthetic organic chemicals ("the industry"). Petitioners also challenge EPA's technology review under subsection 112(d)(6). In a rather unusual bit of rulemaking, the agency determined by rule not to change its previous rule, which gave rise to petitioners' challenge. We deny the petition.

I.

[The court described the history of §112 of the CAA and, post-1990 requiring EPA in §112(d)(2)-(3) to adopt technology-based standards (based on the "maximum achievable control technology" or "MACT") in the first instance for each listed pollutant.]

After setting the "floor"—i.e., the minimum required reduction in emissions for a new or existing source—EPA has discretion to require an even greater reduction in emissions, taking into account costs, health effects, environmental effects, and energy requirements.[2] Id. §112(d)(2).

In the second stage of regulation, EPA was obliged to review any residual health risks that had not been eliminated by the initial technology-based standards. Id. §7412(f). This second stage is described as "risk-based" or "health-based" because it requires EPA to set a standard based on a medical assessment of a given pollutant's health risks (as was true of the pre-1990 statute), rather than the current state of control technology. Within six years of promulgating the technology-based standards, EPA was required to prepare a report to Congress analyzing any residual health risks. If Congress did not act on the report, then EPA was to conduct residual risk analysis under subsection 112(f)(2).

EPA initially promulgated technology-based emission standards for the industry in 1994 (there are 238 facilities in the United States that produce or use synthetic organic chemicals). Those standards required the use of control technologies such as recovery devices, thermal oxidizers, carbon absorbers, and steam strippers. After submitting the required report to Congress in 1999, the agency commenced residual risk rulemaking, apparently because—as we discuss below—it read the statute as requiring a rulemaking proceeding to consider whether to revise the technology-based standards, since the industry's emissions pose lifetime excess cancer risks of greater than one-in-one million.

In the notice of proposed rulemaking, EPA listed two options for the residual risk rulemaking, one of which would have imposed somewhat stricter standards. But the other, which EPA adopted in the final rule, 71 Fed. Reg. 76,603 (2006), was a reaffirmation of the existing rule. EPA determined that under the existing technology-based standard, no individual would face an excess lifetime cancer risk of greater than 100-in-one million, which EPA regards as the "presumptively acceptable" level under its precedents. In the same regulatory procedure, EPA sought to satisfy another statutory requirement, subsection 112(d)(6), which commands the Administrator to "review, and revise as necessary" the technology-based standards in light of technological developments at least every eight years. 42 U.S.C. §7412(d)(6). It concluded there were no such developments.

Petitioners challenge EPA's actions on several grounds. Their primary argument is one of statutory construction. They contend that the statute obliged EPA, in the residual risk rulemaking, to tighten the standards for the industry so that the lifetime excess cancer risk to exposed persons would be no greater than one-in-one million. It is also argued that in reviewing the technology-based standards, EPA violated subsection 112(d)(6) by taking costs into account. Alternatively, even if EPA complied with the statute, petitioners claim that the rulemaking violated the APA, as arbitrary and capricious, because it relied on faulty data and overlooked significant sources of emission.

---

2. Although EPA considered costs . . . in setting its technology-based standards, we subsequently held that it was not appropriate to consider costs in establishing the maximum achievable control technology "floor" (although the agency is permitted to consider cost in deciding whether to require further "beyond the floor" reductions). See Nat'l Lime Ass'n v. EPA, 233 F.3d 625, 640 (D.C. Cir. 2000); see also NRDC v. EPA, 489 F.3d 1364, 1375-76 (D.C. Cir. 2007).

II.

A.

Petitioners contend that subsection 112(f)(2)(A) obliged EPA to revise industry standards to reduce lifetime excess cancer risk to one-in-one million. Petitioners rely primarily on the last sentence of that subsection, whereas EPA looks to the whole subsection. That provision states in full:

> If Congress does not act on any recommendation submitted under paragraph (1), the Administrator shall, within 8 years after promulgation of standards for each category or subcategory of sources pursuant to subsection (d) of this section, promulgate standards for such category or subcategory if promulgation of such standards is required in order to provide an ample margin of safety to protect public health in accordance with this section (as in effect before November 15, 1990) or to prevent, taking into consideration costs, energy, safety, and other relevant factors, an adverse environmental effect. Emissions standards promulgated under this subsection shall provide an ample margin of safety to protect public health in accordance with this section (as in effect before November 15, 1990), unless the Administrator determines that a more stringent standard is necessary to prevent, taking into consideration costs, energy, safety, and other relevant factors, an adverse environmental effect. If standards promulgated pursuant to subsection (d) of this section and applicable to a category or subcategory of sources emitting a pollutant (or pollutants) classified as a known, probable or possible human carcinogen do not reduce lifetime excess cancer risks to the individual most exposed to emissions from a source in the category or subcategory to less than one in one million, the Administrator shall promulgate standards under this subsection for such source category. [§112(f)(2)(A).]

It is undisputed that facilities that produce or use synthetic organic chemicals emit carcinogens and are, therefore, within the reach of the last sentence. It is also undisputed that, in light of the fact that existing technology-based standards do not reduce the risk to less than one-in-one million, EPA was obliged to "promulgate standards" under subsection 112(f). Petitioners contend that the third sentence obviously means that residual risk standards must meet the threshold test—i.e., EPA must reduce such risks to one-in-one million. That may well be a possible interpretation, but the sentence contains a glaring omission; it does not say what petitioners would like us to infer. Rather, that sentence instructs the Administrator to "promulgate standards," but it says nothing about the substantive content of those standards. If Congress had wished to set a "bright line" standard, it would have been rather easy for the draftsmen to say just that. The failure to do so could not have been accidental. In light of the rest of the subsection's language (and other provisions), it seems to us that the subsection was drafted as a deliberately ambiguous compromise.[4]

We reach that conclusion because the second sentence, which sets forth the substantive standard to be applied, simply calls for standards that "provide an ample margin of safety to protect public health" (unless the Administrator wishes to go further to avoid adverse environmental effects). No distinction is drawn between carcinogens and non-carcinogens. The third sentence, on which petitioners rely, not only lacks the language that petitioners ask us to infer; it also specifically states

---

4. Congress rejected the Senate version of the bill—which mandated a bright line standard for carcinogens—in favor of the House version, which gave the Secretary more discretion under the "ample margin of safety" standard.

that if the one-in-one million trigger is met, the Administrator must promulgate standards "under this subsection," which, perforce, takes us back to the second sentence. EPA's construction of the subsection is bolstered by another paragraph, 112(f)(2)(B), which states:

> Nothing in subparagraph (A) or in any other provision of this section shall be construed as affecting, or applying to the Administrator's interpretation of this section, as in effect before November 15, 1990, and set forth in the Federal Register of September 14, 1989 (54 Federal Register 38044).

§112(f)(2)(B). The cited item in the Federal Register is EPA's emission standard for benzene, which is a carcinogenic hazardous air pollutant. In the *Benzene* rulemaking, EPA set forth its interpretation of "ample margin of safety," as that term was used in the 1970 version of the Clean Air Act. It said that the "ample margin" was met if as many people as possible faced excess lifetime cancer risks no greater than one-in-one million, and that no person faced a risk greater than 100-in-one million (one-in-ten thousand). In other words, the *Benzene* standard established a maximum excess risk of 100-in-one million, while adopting the one-in-one million standard as an aspirational goal. This standard, incorporated into the amended version of the Clean Air Act, undermines petitioners' assertion that EPA must reduce residual risks to one-in-one million for all sources that emit carcinogenic hazardous air pollutants.

Petitioners respond that subsection 112(f)(2)(B) is a savings clause that only preserves EPA's specific regulations regarding benzene. But the text belies this contention. Subsection 112(f)(2)(B) makes clear that nothing in subparagraph (A) shall be construed as "affecting, or applying to the Administrator's interpretation" of section 112, as set forth in the *Benzene* standard. The word "interpretation" indicates that the savings clause is not limited to EPA's benzene-specific determinations, but applies broadly to the agency's construction of the Clean Air Act in the *Benzene* standard. Petitioners also contend that subsection (B) should only be read as applying to non-carcinogens, but this is not persuasive. Subsection 112(f)(2)(B) incorporates EPA's "interpretation" of the Clean Air Act from the *Benzene* standard, and the text of this provision draws no distinction between carcinogens and non-carcinogens. Indeed, benzene is itself a carcinogen, so it would make little sense for Congress to incorporate this standard only for non-carcinogens.

The parenthetical clause in the second sentence of subsection 112(f)(2)(A) lends further support to EPA's position. That sentence states "[e]missions standards promulgated under this subsection shall provide an ample margin of safety to protect public health in accordance with this section (as in effect before November 15, 1990). . . ." EPA interprets the parenthetical as a "shorthand reference" to the *Benzene* standard, given that subsection (B) uses almost identical language, incorporating "the Administrator's interpretation of this section, as in effect before November 15, 1990, and set forth in the Federal Register. . . ." The phrase "this section (as in effect before November 15, 1990)" is certainly broad enough to encompass EPA's prior interpretations of "this section" as well as the text itself. In fact, the operative provision of the pre-1990 version of section 112 uses the exact same "ample margin of safety" language as subsection 112(f)(2)(A) currently uses. See *Sierra Club*, 353 F.3d at 979-80. Thus, the parenthetical must refer to something more than the bare text of "this section," or else it would be surplusage.

Petitioners insist that EPA's interpretation renders the third sentence effectively meaningless. To be sure, the third sentence, as EPA interprets it, seems relatively anodyne; it lacks substantive force. But, at least as EPA reads it, the word "promulgate" means the agency is obliged to conduct a rulemaking to consider residual risks for sources that emit carcinogens. That extra procedural step is not a trivial obligation. Congress often imposes procedural requirements without dictating substantive outcomes. See, e.g., Strycker's Bay Neighborhood Council v. Karlen, 444 U.S. 223, 227-28 (1980) (discussing the National Environmental Policy Act). We also disagree with petitioners' argument that EPA did not "promulgate standards" under subsection 112(f)(2) because it simply readopted the initial standards. This position finds no support in the text of the statute. Subsection 112(f)(2) only mandates that residual risk standards "provide an ample margin of safety to protect public health." If EPA determines that the existing technology-based standards already provide an "ample margin of safety," then the agency is free to readopt those standards during a residual risk rulemaking.

Finally, petitioners argue that EPA unlawfully considered cost while setting the "ample margin of safety" in the residual risk standards. Petitioners are correct that the Supreme Court has "refused to find implicit in ambiguous sections of the [Clean Air Act] an authorization to consider costs that has elsewhere, and so often, been expressly granted." Whitman v. Am. Trucking Ass'n, 531 U.S. 457, 467 (2001). In this case, however, we believe the clear statement rule has been satisfied. As explained above, subsection 112(f)(2)(B) expressly incorporates EPA's interpretation of the Clean Air Act from the *Benzene* standard, complete with a citation to the Federal Register. In that rulemaking, EPA set its standard for benzene "at a level that provides 'an ample margin of safety' in consideration of all health information . . . as well as other relevant factors *including costs and economic impacts*, technological feasibility, and other factors relevant to each particular decision." 54 Fed. Reg. at 38,045 (emphasis added). EPA considered cost in *Benzene*, and subsection 112(f)(2)(B) makes clear that nothing in the amended version of the Clean Air Act shall "affect[ ]" the agency's interpretation of the statute from that rulemaking.

In sum, we conclude that EPA's interpretation of subsection 112(f)(2), although not an inevitable one, certainly is, at least, a reasonable construction of the statute. See Chevron U.S.A., Inc. v. NRDC, 467 U.S. 837, 843 (1984).

B.

Petitioners' second statutory argument is based on subsection 112(d)(6), which states:

> The Administrator shall review, and revise as necessary (taking into account developments in practices, processes, and control technologies), emissions standards promulgated under this section no less often than every 8 years.

42 U.S.C. §7412(d)(6). It is argued that EPA was obliged to completely recalculate the maximum achievable control technology — in other words, to start from scratch. We do not think the words "review, and revise as necessary" can be construed reasonably as imposing any such obligation. Even if the statute did impose such an obligation, petitioners have not identified any post-1994 technological innovations that EPA has overlooked.

More troublesome, however, is petitioners' assertion that the agency improperly considered costs in considering whether to revise the standards. EPA did, in fact, state in its notice of proposed rulemaking that "leakless components" should not be considered the "maximum achievable control technology" because of the high cost of replacing existing components. That could be thought in tension with our cases holding that EPA may not consider costs in setting the maximum achievable control technology "floors," but only in determining whether to require "beyond the floor" reductions in emissions.[6] EPA may have done just that in setting the initial floors. Yet the time period for challenging those standards has long since passed, 42 U.S.C. §7607(b)(1), which raises the question whether EPA's reaffirmation of its cost-based reasoning in its technology review gives rise to a new opportunity for petitioners to challenge this apparent defect.

Fortunately, we do not have to decide this question because in its final rule, EPA squarely found that there were no "significant developments in practices, processes and control technologies," and petitioners do not challenge this conclusion. Since that is the core requirement of subsection 112(d)(6) and EPA's finding satisfies that requirement, it is irrelevant whether EPA considered costs in arriving at the initial MACT floor and reaffirming that standard in the residual risk rulemaking. Petitioners argue that EPA's consideration of cost somehow "tainted" the entire technology review. But under the deferential "arbitrary and capricious" standard, we may not set aside an agency's factual finding based on amorphous allegations of "taint."

III.

There remains petitioners' claim that EPA's analysis of the residual health risks from facilities that use or produce synthetic organic chemicals was arbitrary and capricious (unreasonable). In conducting its risk assessment, EPA relied upon industry-supplied data — collected by the American Chemistry Council — that was submitted on a questionnaire approved by the agency. Based on this data, EPA determined that no source presented a lifetime cancer risk of greater than 100-in-one million, and that only two sources presented a risk equal to that threshold. Petitioners argue that EPA should have handled the data collection itself, and that the industry-supplied data was defective in several respects.

[The court rejected the argument. It interpreted §114(a), under which EPA "may require" the owner of an emissions source to keep records, make reports, install monitoring equipment, take emissions samples, and "provide such other information as the Administrator may reasonably require," as affording EPA the discretion to decide what types of data should be used for a risk assessment. Because it is costly and time-consuming to issue information requests under §114, it was not unreasonable for EPA "to decline to invoke its section 114 authority when more efficient data-collection methods were available."]

Nevertheless, petitioners assert that the industry-supplied data was flawed. They contend that many of the questionnaires were incomplete, and that the data will understate health risks because high-emissions sources have an incentive to withhold data from the agency. Although there were some gaps in the data, EPA ultimately

---

6. As we indicated, *supra*, costs may be considered in appraising risk—i.e., the "ample margin of safety." 42 U.S.C. §7412(f)(2)(B).

received responses from 44% of all sources, including sources with both low and high emissions levels. The agency also explained that when certain data points were missing, EPA used "environmentally protective defaults" in its models. . . . In other words, EPA acknowledged that the data was not comprehensive, but compensated for this uncertainty by erring on the side of protecting public health. We think that is a reasonable position.

[The court also disagreed with petitioners' assertion that the emissions data was unreliable.] EPA compared the industry-supplied data to the National Emissions Inventory, which is a database of air emissions information supplied by state and local air agencies, tribes, and industry sources. The agency determined that the two data sets yield similar results in terms of maximum risk. Petitioners challenge this conclusion, pointing to specific facilities in which the Emissions Inventory data show higher risks than the industry-supplied data. But EPA explained that the Emissions Inventory data for each facility includes hazardous air pollutants other than synthetic organic chemicals, which means that the Emissions Inventory is likely to show higher risks than the industry-supplied data. Intervenors further emphasize that in at least one of the three "high risk" facilities in the Emissions Inventory data, the emissions of synthetic organic chemicals were less than half of the facility's overall emissions. EPA noted that the Emissions Inventory included conservative assumptions that caused this data set to overstate the risks from synthetic organic chemicals. . . .

Be that as it may, EPA's analysis of the Emissions Inventory data was only used to check the agency's risk analysis based on the industry-supplied data. . . .

In sum, petitioners' arguments boil down to one simple point: EPA could have used better data in conducting its risk analysis. Whether or not this is true, it misstates the inquiry under the arbitrary and capricious standard. As we have explained:

> EPA typically has wide latitude in determining the extent of data-gathering necessary to solve a problem. We generally defer to an agency's decision to proceed on the basis of imperfect scientific information, rather than to invest the resources to conduct the perfect study.

Sierra Club v. EPA, 167 F.3d 658, 662 (D.C. Cir. 1999). In other words, the sole question before us is whether EPA has acted reasonably, not whether it has acted flawlessly. On the record before us, EPA explained why it chose to rely on industry-supplied data, and it reasonably responded to petitioners' objections to its data analysis. . . .

For the aforementioned reasons, the petition for review is denied.

NOTES AND QUESTIONS

1. How persuasive is the court's interpretation of the phrase in the last sentence of §112(f)(2)(A) requiring EPA to "promulgate standards under this subsection" if EPA finds that the technology-based standards adopted under §112(d) do not reduce lifetime excess cancer risk to the most exposed individual to less than one in a million? Why was EPA's *Benzene* standard, adopted in 1989 under the original version of §112, relevant to the validity of the residual risk rulemaking in this case? What is the basis for the court's conclusion that, under that standard, the one-in-one million standard referred to in §112(f)(2)(A) was but an "aspirational goal"? Compare 42 U.S.C.

§300g-1(b)(4)(A)-(B) (Safe Drinking Water Act). Why shouldn't the parenthetical phrase in §112(f)(2)(A) include pre-1990 judicial, as well as EPA interpretations of §112? Assuming that it does, what affect would that have on the court's analysis? Consider the *Vinyl Chloride* case, NRDC v. EPA, 824 F.2d 1146 (D.C. Cir. 1987), discussed in the introduction to this section.

Is readoption of preexisting technology-based standards after a residual risk determination tantamount to "promulgation" of standards under the third sentence of §112(f)(2)(A), or does such an interpretation sap that provision of all meaning? How did the court distinguish Whitman v. American Trucking Ass'ns on the question of the relevance of cost to residual risk determinations? Why was it irrelevant for purposes of §112(d)(2) that EPA considered costs in arriving at the initial MACT floor? Should it have been?

Why did the court reject petitioners' claim that EPA's decision was arbitrary and capricious on the basis of the information EPA considered, even if EPA did not misinterpret the statute?

2. Flatt, Gasping for Breath: The Administrative Flaws of Hazardous Air Pollutant Regulation and What We Can Learn from the States, 34 Ecology L.Q. 107 (2007), analyzes the flaws in §112 and suggests how a revised approach to the regulation of hazardous air pollutants, modeled after state programs, might improve public health protection.

2. *Interstate Pollution and Acid Deposition*

a. **The Difficulty of Controlling Interstate Pollution**

The 1970 CAA reflected the assumption that local, easily identifiable sources cause most air pollution problems and that an adequate SIP will enable a state to achieve the NAAQS within its own borders. But it soon became apparent that air pollution does not respect political boundaries. Emissions from out-of-state sources may prevent a downwind state from designing a SIP that achieves the NAAQS through controls on its own sources at a reasonable cost. Interstate air pollution problems occur, for example, where state boundaries pass through or near urban areas, creating intergovernmental conflicts over the responsibility for pollution abatement.

Only two sections of the pre-1990 CAA directly addressed interstate air pollution. Section 110(a)(2)(E) (recodified as amended at §110(a)(2)(D))[x] required that every SIP contain adequate provisions restricting interstate air pollution and §126 authorized states to petition EPA for a finding that another state was violating these restrictions. If EPA issued the requested finding, it would be a violation of the applicable SIP of the source state to operate in violation of §110(a)(2)(E)(i). Even if the source state did not enforce that SIP violation, EPA or a private citizen could. In practice, this petitions process was of limited success. See Glicksman, Watching the River Flow: The Prospects for Improved Interstate Water Pollution Control, 43 Wash. U. J. Urb. & Contemp. L. 119, 167-168 (1993). In response, as explained in the

___

x. The cross-reference in §126(b) should be to §110(a)(2)(D)(i), not §110(a)(2)(D)(ii). Congress inadvertently substituted (ii) for (i) in the course of a routine renumbering process occasioned by the adoption of the 1990 amendments. See Appalachian Power Co. v. EPA, 249 F.3d 1032, 1043 (D.C. Cir. 2001).

next principal case, Congress amended the statute in 1990 in an effort to ease the burden of states seeking to curb pollution originating in upwind states.

Professor Revesz attributes the CAA's failures to control interstate pollution to a variety of factors. Revesz, Federalism and Interstate Environmental Externalities, 144 U. Pa. L. Rev. 2341 (1996). The technology-based provisions, such as the NSPS, fail to regulate the number or location of sources within a particular state. The NAAQS do not bar a state meeting those standards from exporting pollution to downwind states from stationary sources located near the border. The acid rain provisions discussed below are limited in scope: they deal with only two pollutants and, for the most part, one kind of facility (electric utilities). The effectiveness of §§110(a)(2)(D) and 126 has been impaired by EPA's refusal to acknowledge predictions of the effects of emissions beyond a range of 50 kilometers, to establish NAAQS for sulfates, and to recognize the cumulative impacts of upwind sources. Revesz urges the adoption of tougher controls on activities generating interstate externalities through a marketable permit system allowing interstate coordination that would be difficult to accomplish through non-market-based federal regulation.

In 2011, EPA issued its Cross-State Air Pollution Rule, 76 Fed. Reg. 48,208 (Aug. 8, 2011), under the 1990 CAA amendments. Among other things, the rule allows allowance trading among power plants, using a market infrastructure based on existing, successful allowance trading programs. Trading among power plants within the same state is freely permitted, but interstate trades are more tightly controlled. The following case addressed the validity of the rule.

EPA v. EME HOMER CITY GENERATION, L.P.
134 S. Ct. 1584 (2014)

Justice GINSBURG delivered the opinion of the Court.

These cases concern the efforts of Congress and the Environmental Protection Agency (EPA or Agency) to cope with a complex problem: air pollution emitted in one State, but causing harm in other States. Left unregulated, the emitting or upwind State reaps the benefits of the economic activity causing the pollution without bearing all the costs. Conversely, downwind States to which the pollution travels are unable to achieve clean air because of the influx of out-of-state pollution they lack authority to control. To tackle the problem, Congress included a Good Neighbor Provision in the Clean Air Act (Act or CAA). That provision, in its current phrasing, instructs States to prohibit in-state sources "from emitting any air pollutant in amounts which will . . . contribute significantly" to downwind States' "nonattainment . . . , or interfere with maintenance," of any EPA-promulgated national air quality standard. 42 U.S.C. §7410(a)(2)(D)(i).

Interpreting the Good Neighbor Provision, EPA adopted the Cross-State Air Pollution Rule (commonly and hereinafter called the Transport Rule). The rule calls for consideration of costs, among other factors, when determining the emission reductions an upwind State must make to improve air quality in polluted downwind areas. The Court of Appeals for the D.C. Circuit vacated the rule in its entirety. It held, 2 to 1, that the Good Neighbor Provision requires EPA to consider only each upwind State's physically proportionate responsibility for each downwind State's air quality problem. That reading is demanded, according to the D.C. Circuit, so that no State will be required to decrease its emissions by more than its ratable share of downwind-state pollution.

In Chevron U.S.A. Inc. v. Natural Resources Defense Council, Inc., 467 U.S. 837 (1984), we reversed a D.C. Circuit decision that failed to accord deference to EPA's reasonable interpretation of an ambiguous Clean Air Act provision. Satisfied that the Good Neighbor Provision does not command the Court of Appeals' cost-blind construction, and that EPA reasonably interpreted the provision, we reverse the D.C. Circuit's judgment.

I

A

Air pollution is transient, heedless of state boundaries. Pollutants generated by upwind sources are often transported by air currents, sometimes over hundreds of miles, to downwind States. As the pollution travels out of state, upwind States are relieved of the associated costs. Those costs are borne instead by the downwind States, whose ability to achieve and maintain satisfactory air quality is hampered by the steady stream of infiltrating pollution.

For several reasons, curtailing interstate air pollution poses a complex challenge for environmental regulators. First, identifying the upwind origin of downwind air pollution is no easy endeavor. Most upwind States propel pollutants to more than one downwind State, many downwind States receive pollution from multiple upwind States, and some States qualify as both upwind and downwind. The overlapping and interwoven linkages between upwind and downwind States with which EPA had to contend number in the thousands.

Further complicating the problem, pollutants do not emerge from the smoke-stacks of an upwind State and uniformly migrate downwind. Some pollutants stay within upwind States' borders, the wind carries others to downwind States, and some subset of that group drifts to States without air quality problems. "The wind bloweth where it listeth, and thou hearest the sound thereof, but canst not tell whence it cometh, and whither it goeth." The Holy Bible, John 3:8 (King James Version). In crafting a solution to the problem of interstate air pollution, regulators must account for the vagaries of the wind.

Finally, upwind pollutants that find their way downwind are not left unaltered by the journey. Rather, as the gases emitted by upwind polluters are carried downwind, they are transformed, through various chemical processes, into altogether different pollutants. The offending gases at issue in these cases—nitrogen oxide (NO_x) and sulfur dioxide (SO_2)—often develop into ozone and fine particulate matter ($PM_{2.5}$) by the time they reach the atmospheres of downwind States. Downwind air quality must therefore be measured for ozone and $PM_{2.5}$ concentrations. EPA's chore is to quantify the amount of upwind gases (NO_x and SO_2) that must be reduced to enable downwind States to keep their levels of ozone and $PM_{2.5}$ in check.

B

Over the past 50 years, Congress has addressed interstate air pollution several times and with increasing rigor. In 1963, Congress directed federal authorities to "encourage cooperative activities by the States and local governments for the prevention and control of air pollution." U.S.C. §1857a (1964 ed.).

In 1977, Congress amended the Good Neighbor Provision to require more than "cooperation." It directed States to submit SIPs that included provisions "adequate" to "prohibi[t] any stationary source within the State from emitting any air pollutant in amounts which will . . . prevent attainment or maintenance [of air quality standards] by any other State." Ibid. The amended provision thus explicitly instructed upwind States to reduce emissions to account for pollution exported beyond their borders. As then written, however, the provision regulated only individual sources that, considered alone, emitted enough pollution to cause nonattainment in a downwind State. Because it is often "impossible to say that any single source or group of sources is the one which actually prevents attainment" downwind, S. Rep. No. 101-228, p. 21 (1989), the 1977 version of the Good Neighbor Provision proved ineffective, see ibid. (noting the provision's inability to curb the collective "emissions [of] multiple sources").

Congress most recently amended the Good Neighbor Provision in 1990. The statute, in its current form, requires SIPs to "contain adequate provisions . . . prohibiting . . . any source or other type of emissions activity within the State from emitting any air pollutant in amounts which will . . . contribute significantly to non-attainment in, or interfere with maintenance by, any other State with respect to any . . . [NAAQS]." §7410(a)(2)(D)(i). The controversy before us centers on EPA's most recent attempt to construe this provision.

C

Three times over the past two decades, EPA has attempted to delineate the Good Neighbor Provision's scope by identifying when upwind States "contribute significantly" to nonattainment downwind. In 1998, EPA issued a rule known as the "NO_x SIP Call." That regulation limited NO_x emissions in 23 upwind States to the extent such emissions contributed to nonattainment of ozone standards in downwind States. In Michigan v. EPA, 213 F.3d 663 (2000), the D.C. Circuit upheld the NO_x SIP Call, specifically affirming EPA's use of costs to determine when an upwind State's contribution was "significan[t]" within the meaning of the statute.

In 2005, EPA issued the Clean Air Interstate Rule, or CAIR. CAIR regulated both NO_x and SO_2 emissions, insofar as such emissions contributed to downwind nonattainment of two NAAQS, both set in 1997, one concerning the permissible annual measure of $PM_{2.5}$, and another capping the average ozone level gauged over an 8-hour period. The D.C. Circuit initially vacated CAIR as arbitrary and capricious. See North Carolina v. EPA, 531 F.3d 896, 921 (2008) (per curiam). On rehearing, the court decided to leave the rule in place, while encouraging EPA to act with dispatch in dealing with problems the court had identified. See North Carolina v. EPA, 550 F.3d 1176, 1178 (2008) (per curiam).

The rule challenged here—the Transport Rule—is EPA's response to the D.C. Circuit's North Carolina decision. Finalized in August 2011, the Transport Rule curtails NO_x and SO_2 emissions of 27 upwind States to achieve downwind attainment of three different NAAQS: the two 1997 NAAQS previously addressed by CAIR, and the 2006 NAAQS for $PM_{2.5}$ levels measured on a daily basis.

Under the Transport Rule, EPA employed a "two-step approach" to determine when upwind States "contribute[d] significantly to nonattainment," and therefore in "amounts" that had to be eliminated. At step one, called the "screening" analysis, the Agency excluded as de minimis any upwind State that contributed less than one percent of the three NAAQS to any downwind State "receptor," a location at which EPA measures air quality. If all of an upwind State's contributions fell below the one-percent threshold, that State would be considered not to have "contribute[d] significantly" to the nonattainment of any downwind State. States in that category were screened out and exempted from regulation under the rule.

The remaining States were subjected to a second inquiry, which EPA called the "control" analysis. At this stage, the Agency sought to generate a cost-effective allocation of emission reductions among those upwind States "screened in" at step one.

The control analysis proceeded this way. EPA first calculated, for each upwind State, the quantity of emissions the State could eliminate at each of several cost thresholds. Cost for these purposes is measured as cost per ton of emissions prevented, for instance, by installing scrubbers on powerplant smokestacks. EPA estimated, for example, the amount each upwind State's NO_x emissions would fall if all pollution sources within each State employed every control measure available at a cost of $500 per ton or less. The Agency then repeated that analysis at ascending cost thresholds.

Armed with this information, EPA conducted complex modeling to establish the combined effect the upwind reductions projected at each cost threshold would have on air quality in downwind States. The Agency then identified "significant cost threshold[s]," points in its model where a "noticeable change occurred in downwind air quality, such as . . . where large upwind emission reductions become available because a certain type of emissions control strategy becomes cost-effective." For example, reductions of NO_x sufficient to resolve or significantly curb downwind air quality problems could be achieved, EPA determined, at a cost threshold of $500 per ton (applied uniformly to all regulated upwind States). "Moving beyond the $500 cost threshold," EPA concluded, "would result in only minimal additional . . . reductions [in emissions]."

Finally, EPA translated the cost thresholds it had selected into amounts of emissions upwind States would be required to eliminate. For each regulated upwind State, EPA created an annual emissions "budget." These budgets represented the quantity of pollution an upwind State would produce in a given year if its in-state sources implemented all pollution controls available at the chosen cost thresholds. If EPA's projected improvements to downwind air quality were to be realized, an upwind State's emissions could not exceed the level this budget allocated to it, subject to certain adjustments not relevant here.

Taken together, the screening and control inquiries defined EPA's understanding of which upwind emissions were within the Good Neighbor Provision's ambit. In short, under the Transport Rule, an upwind State "contribute[d] significantly" to downwind nonattainment to the extent its exported pollution both (1) produced one percent or more of a NAAQS in at least one downwind State (step one) and (2) could be eliminated cost-effectively, as determined by EPA (step two). Upwind States would be obliged to eliminate all and only emissions meeting both of these criteria.[9]

For each State regulated by the Transport Rule, EPA contemporaneously promulgated a FIP allocating that State's emission budget among its in-state sources.[10]

9. Similarly, upwind States EPA independently determined to be "interfer[ing] with [the] maintenance" of NAAQS downwind were required to eliminate pollution only to the extent their emissions satisfied both of these criteria.

10. These FIPs specified the maximum amount of pollution each in-state pollution source could emit. Sources below this ceiling could sell unused "allocations" to sources that could not reduce emissions to the necessary level as cheaply. This type of "cap-and-trade" system cuts costs while still reducing pollution to target levels.

For each of these States, EPA had determined that the State had failed to submit a SIP adequate for compliance with the Good Neighbor Provision. These determinations regarding SIPs became final after 60 days, see §7607(b)(1), and many went unchallenged. EPA views the SIP determinations as having triggered its statutory obligation to promulgate a FIP within two years, see §7410(c), a view contested by respondents.

D

A group of state and local governments (State respondents), joined by industry and labor groups (Industry respondents), petitioned for review of the Transport Rule in the U.S. Court of Appeals for the D.C. Circuit. Over the dissent of Judge Rogers, the Court of Appeals vacated the rule in its entirety. See 696 F.3d 7, 37 (2012).

EPA's actions, the appeals court held, exceeded the Agency's statutory authority in two respects. By promulgating FIPs before giving States a meaningful opportunity to adopt their own implementation plans, EPA had, in the court's view, upset the CAA's division of responsibility between the States and the Federal Government. In the main, the Court of Appeals acknowledged, EPA's FIP authority is triggered at the moment the Agency disapproves a SIP. Thus, when a State proposes a SIP inadequate to achieve a NAAQS, EPA could promulgate a FIP immediately after disapproving that SIP.

But the Court of Appeals ruled that a different regime applies to a State's failure to meet its obligations under the Good Neighbor Provision. . . . EPA had an implicit statutory duty, the court held, to give upwind States a reasonable opportunity to allocate their emission budgets among in-state sources before the Agency's authority to issue FIPs could be triggered.

The D.C. Circuit also held that the Agency's two-part interpretation of the Good Neighbor Provision ignored three "red lines . . . cabin[ing the] EPA's authority." Id., at 19. First, the D.C. Circuit interpreted the Good Neighbor Provision to require upwind States to reduce emissions in "a manner proportional to their contributio[n]" to pollution in downwind States. Id., at 21. The Transport Rule, however, treated all regulated upwind States alike, regardless of their relative contribution to the overall problem. It required all upwind States "screened in" at step one to reduce emissions in accord with the uniform cost thresholds set during the step two control analysis. Imposing these uniform cost thresholds, the Court of Appeals observed, could force some upwind States to reduce emissions by more than their "fair share." Id., at 27.

According to the Court of Appeals, EPA had also failed to ensure that the Transport Rule did not mandate up-wind States to reduce pollution unnecessarily. The Good Neighbor Provision, the D.C. Circuit noted, "targets [only] those emissions from upwind States that 'contribute significantly to *nonattainment*'" of a NAAQS in downwind States. Id., at 22. Pollution reduction beyond that goal was "unnecessary over-control," outside the purview of the Agency's statutory mandate. Ibid. Because the emission budgets were calculated by reference to cost alone, the court concluded that EPA had done nothing to guard against, or even measure, the "over-control" potentially imposed by the Transport Rule.

Finally, by deciding, at the screening analysis, that upwind contributions below the one-percent threshold were insignificant, EPA had established a "floor" on the Agency's authority to act. Again pointing to the rule's reliance on costs, the Court of Appeals held that EPA had failed to ensure that upwind States were not being forced to reduce emissions below the one-percent threshold. . . .

II . . .

Once EPA has calculated emission budgets, the D.C. Circuit held, the Agency must give upwind States the opportunity to propose SIPs allocating those budgets among in-state sources before issuing a FIP. As the State respondents put it, a FIP allocating a State's emission budget "must issue after EPA has quantified the States' good-neighbor obligations [in an emission budget] and given the States a reasonable opportunity to meet those obligations in SIPs." Brief for State Respondents 20. . . .

. . . [W]e hold that the text of the statute supports EPA's position. As earlier noted, the CAA sets a series of precise deadlines to which the States and EPA must adhere. Once EPA issues any new or revised NAAQS, a State has three years to adopt a SIP adequate for compliance with the Act's requirements. See §7410(a)(1). Among those requirements is the Act's mandate that SIPs "shall" include provisions sufficient to satisfy the Good Neighbor Provision. §7410(a)(2). . . .

. . . [O]nce EPA has found a SIP inadequate, the Agency has a statutory duty [under §110(c)(1)] to issue a FIP "at any time" within two years (unless the State first "corrects the deficiency," which no one contends occurred here).

The D.C. Circuit, however, found an unwritten exception to this strict time prescription for SIPs aimed at implementing the Good Neighbor Provision. . . . [It] required EPA, after promulgating each State's emission budget, to give the State a "reasonable" period of time to propose SIPs implementing its budget.

However sensible (or not) the Court of Appeals' position, a reviewing court's "task is to apply the text [of the statute], not to improve upon it." Pavelic & LeFlore v. Marvel Entertainment Group, Div. of Cadence Industries Corp., 493 U.S. 120, 126 (1989). Nothing in the Act differentiates the Good Neighbor Provision from the several other matters a State must address in its SIP. Rather, the statute speaks without reservation: Once a NAAQS has been issued, a State "shall" propose a SIP within three years, §7410(a)(1), and that SIP "shall" include, among other components, provisions adequate to satisfy the Good Neighbor Provision, §7410(a)(2).

Nor does the Act condition the duty to promulgate a FIP on EPA's having first quantified an upwind State's good neighbor obligations. . . . After EPA has disapproved a SIP, the Agency can wait up to two years to issue a FIP, during which time the State can "correc[t] the deficiency" on its own. Ibid. But EPA is not obliged to wait two years or postpone its action even a single day: The Act empowers the Agency to promulgate a FIP "at any time" within the two-year limit. Ibid. Carving out an exception to the Act's precise deadlines, as the D.C. Circuit did, "rewrites a decades-old statute whose plain text and structure establish a clear chronology of federal and State responsibilities." 696 F.3d, at 47 (Rogers, J., dissenting).

The practical difficulties cited by the Court of Appeals do not justify departure from the Act's plain text. When Congress elected to make EPA's input a prerequisite to state action under the Act, it did so expressly. States developing vehicle inspection and maintenance programs under the CAA, for example, must await EPA guidance before issuing SIPs. §7511a(c)(3)(B). A State's obligation to adopt a SIP, moreover, arises only after EPA has first set the NAAQS the State must meet. §7410(a)(1). Had Congress intended similarly to defer States' discharge of their obligations under the Good Neighbor Provision, Congress, we take it, would have included a similar direction in that section.

In short, nothing in the statute places EPA under an obligation to provide specific metrics to States before they undertake to fulfill their good neighbor obligations. By altering the schedule Congress provided for SIPs and FIPs, the D.C. Circuit stretched out the process. It allowed a delay Congress did not order and placed an information submission obligation on EPA Congress did not impose. The D.C. Circuit, we hold, had no warrant thus to revise the CAA's action-ordering prescriptions. . . .

III . . .

B

We routinely accord dispositive effect to an agency's reasonable interpretation of ambiguous statutory language. Chevron U.S.A. Inc. v. Natural Resources Defense Council, Inc., 467 U.S. 837 (1984), is the pathmarking decision, and it bears a notable resemblance to the cases before us. . . .

We conclude that the Good Neighbor Provision delegates authority to EPA at least as certainly as the CAA provisions involved in *Chevron.* The statute requires States to eliminate those "amounts" of pollution that "contribute significantly to *nonattainment*" in downwind States. §7410(a)(2)(D)(i) (emphasis added). Thus, EPA's task is to reduce upwind pollution, but only in "amounts" that push a downwind State's pollution concentrations above the relevant NAAQS. As noted earlier, however, the nonattainment of downwind States results from the collective and interwoven contributions of multiple upwind States. The statute therefore calls upon the Agency to address a thorny causation problem: How should EPA allocate among multiple contributing upwind States responsibility for a downwind State's excess pollution?

A simplified example illustrates the puzzle EPA faced. Suppose the Agency sets a NAAQS, with respect to a particular pollutant, at 100 parts per billion (ppb), and that the level of the pollutant in the atmosphere of downwind State A is 130 ppb. Suppose further that EPA has determined that each of three upwind States—X, Y, and Z— contributes the equivalent of 30 ppb of the relevant pollutant to State A's airspace. The Good Neighbor Provision, as just observed, prohibits only upwind emissions that contribute significantly to downwind nonattainment. EPA's authority under the provision is therefore limited to eliminating a total of 30 ppb, i.e., the overage caused by the collective contribution of States X, Y, and Z.[17]

How is EPA to divide responsibility among the three States? Should the Agency allocate reductions proportionally (10 ppb each), on a per capita basis, on the basis of the cost of abatement, or by some other metric? Under *Chevron,* we read Congress' silence as a delegation of authority to EPA to select from among reasonable options. See United States v. Mead Corp., 533 U.S. 218, 229 (2001).[18]

17. For simplicity's sake, the hypothetical assumes that EPA has not required any emission reductions by the downwind State itself.

18. The statutory gap identified also exists in the Good Neighbor Provision's second instruction. That instruction requires EPA to eliminate amounts of upwind pollution that "interfere with maintenance" of a NAAQS by a downwind State. §7410(a)(2)(D)(i). This mandate contains no qualifier analogous to "significantly," and yet it entails a delegation of administrative authority of the same character as the one discussed above. Just as EPA is constrained, under the first part of the Good Neighbor Provision, to eliminate only those amounts that "contribute . . . to *nonattainment*," EPA is limited, by the second part of the provision, to reduce only by "amounts" that "interfere with *maintenance*," i.e., by just enough to permit an already-attaining State to maintain satisfactory air quality. (Emphasis added.) With multiple upwind States contributing to the maintenance problem,

Yet the Court of Appeals believed that the Act speaks clearly, requiring EPA to allocate responsibility for reducing emissions in "a manner proportional to" each State's "contributio[n]" to the problem. 696 F.3d, at 21. Nothing in the text of the Good Neighbor Provision propels EPA down this path. Understandably so, for as EPA notes, the D.C. Circuit's proportionality approach could scarcely be satisfied in practice. See App. in No. 11-1302 etc. (CADC), p. 2312 ("[W]hile it is possible to determine an emission reduction percentage if there is a single downwind [receptor], most upwind states contribute to multiple downwind [receptors] (in multiple states) and would have a different reduction percentage for each one.") [The Court then discussed illustrative challenges created by this regulatory task.]

Persuaded that the Good Neighbor Provision does not dictate the particular allocation of emissions among contributing States advanced by the D.C. Circuit, we must next decide whether the allocation method chosen by EPA is a "permissible construction of the statute." *Chevron*, 467 U.S., at 843. As EPA interprets the statute, upwind emissions rank as "amounts [that] . . . contribute significantly to nonattainment" if they (1) constitute one percent or more of a relevant NAAQS in a nonattaining downwind State and (2) can be eliminated under the cost threshold set by the Agency. In other words, to identify which emissions were to be eliminated, EPA considered both the magnitude of upwind States' contributions and the cost associated with eliminating them.

The Industry respondents argue that, however EPA ultimately divides responsibility among upwind States, the final calculation cannot rely on costs. The Good Neighbor Provision, respondents and the dissent emphasize, "requires each State to prohibit only those '*amounts*' of air pollution emitted within the State that 'contribute significantly' to another State's nonattaintment." Brief for Industry Respondents 23 (emphasis added). The cost of preventing emissions, they urge, is wholly unrelated to the actual "amoun[t]" of air pollution an upwind State contributes. Because the Transport Rule considers costs, respondents argue, "States that contribute identical 'amounts' . . . may be deemed [by EPA] to have [made] substantially *different*" contributions. Id., at 30.

But, as just explained, the Agency cannot avoid the task of choosing which among equal "amounts" to eliminate. The Agency has chosen, sensibly in our view, to reduce the amount easier, i.e., less costly, to eradicate, and nothing in the text of the Good Neighbor Provision precludes that choice.

Using costs in the Transport Rule calculus, we agree with EPA, also makes good sense. Eliminating those amounts that can cost-effectively be reduced is an efficient and equitable solution to the allocation problem the Good Neighbor Provision requires the Agency to address. Efficient because EPA can achieve the levels of attainment, i.e., of emission reductions, the proportional approach aims to achieve, but at a much lower overall cost. Equitable because, by imposing uniform cost thresholds on regulated States, EPA's rule subjects to stricter regulation those States that have done relatively less in the past to control their pollution. Upwind States that have not yet implemented pollution controls of the same stringency as their neighbors will be

---

however, EPA confronts the same challenge that the "contribute significantly" mandate creates: How should EPA allocate reductions among multiple upwind States, many of which contribute in amounts sufficient to impede downwind maintenance? Nothing in *either* clause of the Good Neighbor Provision provides the criteria by which EPA is meant to apportion responsibility.

stopped from free riding on their neighbors' efforts to reduce pollution. They will have to bring down their emissions by installing devices of the kind in which neighboring States have already invested. . . .

Obligated to require the elimination of only those "amounts" of pollutants that contribute to the nonattainment of NAAQS in downwind States, EPA must decide how to differentiate among the otherwise like contributions of multiple upwind States. EPA found decisive the difficulty of eliminating each "amount," i.e., the cost incurred in doing so. Lacking a dispositive statutory instruction to guide it, EPA's decision, we conclude, is a "reasonable" way of filling the "gap left open by Congress." *Chevron*, 467 U.S., at 866.[21]

C

The D.C. Circuit stated two further objections to EPA's cost-based method of defining an upwind State's contribution. Once a State was screened in at step one of EPA's analysis, its emission budget was calculated solely with reference to the uniform cost thresholds the Agency selected at step two. The Transport Rule thus left open the possibility that a State might be compelled to reduce emissions beyond the point at which every affected downwind State is in attainment, a phenomenon the Court of Appeals termed "over-control." 696 F.3d, at 22. Second, EPA's focus on costs did not foreclose, as the D.C. Circuit accurately observed, the possibility that an upwind State would be required to reduce its emissions by so much that the State no longer contributed one percent or more of a relevant NAAQS to any downwind State. This would place the State below the mark EPA had set, during the screening phase, as the initial threshold of "significan[ce]."

We agree with the Court of Appeals to this extent: EPA cannot require a State to reduce its output of pollution by more than is necessary to achieve attainment in every downwind State or at odds with the one-percent threshold the Agency has set. If EPA requires an upwind State to reduce emissions by more than the amount necessary to achieve attainment in every downwind State to which it is linked, the Agency will have overstepped its authority, under the Good Neighbor Provision, to eliminate those "amounts [that] contribute . . . to nonattainment." Nor can EPA demand reductions that would drive an upwind State's contribution to every downwind State to which it is linked below one percent of the relevant NAAQS. Doing so would be counter to step one of the Agency's interpretation of the Good Neighbor Provision.

Neither possibility, however, justifies wholesale invalidation of the Transport Rule. First, instances of "over-control" in particular downwind locations, the D.C. Circuit acknowledged, may be incidental to reductions necessary to ensure

---

21. The dissent relies heavily on our decision in Whitman v. American Trucking Assns., Inc., 531 U.S. 457 (2001). In *Whitman*, we held that the relevant text of the CAA "unambiguously bars" EPA from considering costs when determining a NAAQS. Id., at 471. Section 7409(b)(1) commands EPA to set NAAQS at levels "requisite to protect the public health" with "an adequate margin of safety." This mandate, we observed in *Whitman*, was "absolute," and precluded any other consideration (e.g., cost) in the NAAQS calculation. Id., at 465. Not so of the Good Neighbor Provision, which grants EPA discretion to eliminate "amounts [of pollution that] . . . contribute significantly to nonattainment" downwind. On the particular "amounts" that should qualify for elimination, the statute is silent. Unlike the provision at issue in *Whitman*, which provides express criteria by which EPA is to set NAAQS, the Good Neighbor Provision, as earlier explained, fails to provide any metric by which EPA can differentiate among the contributions of multiple upwind States.

attainment elsewhere. Because individual upwind States often "contribute significantly" to nonattainment in multiple downwind locations, the emissions reduction required to bring one linked downwind State into attainment may well be large enough to push other linked downwind States over the attainment line. As the Good Neighbor Provision seeks attainment in *every* downwind State, however, exceeding attainment in one State cannot rank as "over-control" unless unnecessary to achieving attainment in any downwind State. Only reductions unnecessary to downwind attainment *anywhere* fall outside the Agency's statutory authority.

Second, while EPA has a statutory duty to avoid over-control, the Agency also has a statutory obligation to avoid "under-control," i.e., to maximize achievement of attainment downwind. For reasons earlier explained, a degree of imprecision is inevitable in tackling the problem of interstate air pollution. Slight changes in wind patterns or energy consumption, for example, may vary downwind air quality in ways EPA might not have anticipated. The Good Neighbor Provision requires EPA to seek downwind attainment of NAAQS notwithstanding the uncertainties. Hence, some amount of over-control, i.e., emission budgets that turn out to be more demanding than necessary, would not be surprising. Required to balance the possibilities of under-control and over-control, EPA must have leeway in fulfilling its statutory mandate.

Finally, in a voluminous record, involving thousands of upwind-to-downwind linkages, respondents point to only a few instances of "unnecessary" emission reductions, and even those are contested by EPA.

If any upwind State concludes it has been forced to regulate emissions below the one-percent threshold or beyond the point necessary to bring all downwind States into attainment, that State may bring a particularized, as-applied challenge to the Transport Rule, along with any other as-applied challenges it may have. Satisfied that EPA's cost-based methodology, on its face, is not "arbitrary, capricious, or manifestly contrary to the statute," *Chevron,* 467 U.S., at 844, we uphold the Transport Rule. The possibility that the rule, in uncommon particular applications, might exceed EPA's statutory authority does not warrant judicial condemnation of the rule in its entirety.

In sum, we hold that the CAA does not command that States be given a second opportunity to file a SIP after EPA has quantified the State's interstate pollution obligations. We further conclude that the Good Neighbor Provision does not require EPA to disregard costs and consider exclusively each upwind State's physically proportionate responsibility for each downwind air quality problem. EPA's cost-effective allocation of emission reductions among upwind States, we hold, is a permissible, workable, and equitable interpretation of the Good Neighbor Provision. . . .

Justice SCALIA, with whom Justice THOMAS joins, dissenting.

Too many important decisions of the Federal Government are made nowadays by unelected agency officials exercising broad lawmaking authority, rather than by the people's representatives in Congress. With the statute involved in the present cases, however, Congress did it right. It specified quite precisely the responsibility of an upwind State under the Good Neighbor Provision: to eliminate those *amounts of pollutants* that it contributes to downwind problem areas. But the Environmental Protection Agency was unsatisfied with this system. Agency personnel, perhaps correctly, thought it more efficient to require reductions not in proportion to the *amounts of pollutants* for which each upwind State is responsible, but on the basis of how *cost-effectively* each can decrease emissions.

Today, the majority approves that undemocratic revision of the Clean Air Act. The Agency came forward with a textual justification for its action, relying on a farfetched meaning of the word "significantly" in the statutory text. That justification is so feeble that today's majority does not even recite it, much less defend it. The majority reaches its result ("Look Ma, no hands!") without benefit of text, claiming to have identified a remarkable "gap" in the statute, which it proceeds to fill (contrary to the plain logic of the statute) with cost-benefit analysis—and then, with no pretended textual justification at all, simply extends cost-benefit analysis beyond the scope of the alleged gap. . . .

I. The Transport Rule . . .

. . . The statute addresses solely the environmental consequences of emissions, *not* the facility of reducing them; and it requires States to shoulder burdens in proportion to the size of their contributions, *not* in proportion to the ease of bearing them. EPA's utterly fanciful "from each according to its ability" construction sacrifices democratically adopted text to bureaucratically favored policy. It deserves no deference under [*Chevron*].

A. Alleged Textual Support: "Significantly" . . .

. . . [T]he statute does not focus on whether the upwind State has "achieved significantly"; it asks whether the State has "contributed significantly" to downwind pollution. The provision addresses the physical effects of physical causes, and it is only the magnitude of the relationship sufficient to trigger regulation that admits of some vagueness. Stated differently, the statute is ambiguous as to *how much* of a contribution to downwind pollution is "significant," but it is not at all ambiguous as to whether factors unrelated to the *amounts of pollutants* that make up a contribution affect the analysis. Just as "[i]t does not matter whether the word 'yellow' is ambiguous when the agency has interpreted it to mean 'purple,' " United States v. Home Concrete & Supply, LLC, 132 S. Ct. 1836, 1847, n.1 (2012) (SCALIA, J., concurring in part and concurring in judgment), it does not matter whether the phrase "amounts which . . . contribute significantly [to downwind NAAQS nonattainment]" is ambiguous when EPA has interpreted it to mean "amounts which are inexpensive to eliminate." . . .

B. The Alleged "Gap"

To fill the void created by its abandonment of EPA's "significantly" argument, the majority identifies a supposed gap in the text, which EPA must fill: While the text says that each upwind State must be responsible for its own contribution to downwind pollution, it does not say how responsibility is to be divided among multiple States when the total of their combined contribution to downwind pollution in a particular area exceeds the reduction that the relevant NAAQS requires. In the example given by the majority, when each of three upwind States contributes 30 units of a pollutant to a downwind State but the reduction required for that State to comply with the NAAQS is only 30 units, how will responsibility for that 30 units be apportioned? Wow, that's a hard one—almost the equivalent of asking who is buried in Grant's Tomb. If the criterion of responsibility is *amounts of pollutants*, then surely shared responsibility must be based upon *relative amounts of pollutants*—in the majority's example, 10 units for each State. The statute makes no sense otherwise. The Good Neighbor Provision contains a gap only for those who blind themselves to the obvious in order to pursue a preferred policy. . . .

C. Our Precedent

The majority agrees with EPA's assessment that "[u]sing costs in the Transport Rule calculus . . . makes good sense." Its opinion declares that "[e]liminating those amounts that can cost-effectively be reduced is an efficient and equitable solution to the allocation problem the Good Neighbor Provision requires the Agency to address." Ibid. Efficient, probably. Equitable? Perhaps so, but perhaps not. But the point is that whether efficiency should have a dominant or subordinate role is for Congress, not this Court, to determine.

This is not the first time parties have sought to convert the Clean Air Act into a mandate for cost-effective regulation. Whitman v. American Trucking Assns., Inc., 531 U.S. 457, (2001), confronted the contention that EPA should consider costs in setting NAAQS. The provision at issue there, like this one, did not expressly bar cost-based decisionmaking—and unlike this one, it even contained words that were arguably ambiguous in the relevant respect. Specifically, §7409(b)(1) instructed EPA to set primary NAAQS "the attainment and maintenance of which . . . are requisite to protect the public health" with "an adequate margin of safety." One could hardly overstate the capaciousness of the word "adequate," and the phrase "public health" was at least equally susceptible (indeed, much more susceptible) of permitting cost-benefit analysis as the word "significantly" is here. As the respondents in *American Trucking* argued, setting NAAQS without considering costs may bring about failing industries and fewer jobs, which in turn may produce poorer and less healthy citizens. But we concluded that "in the context of" the entire provision, that interpretation "ma[de] no sense." Ibid. [W]e said that Congress "does not alter the fundamental details of a regulatory scheme in vague terms or ancillary provisions—it does not . . . hide elephants in mouseholes." Id., at 468.

In *American Trucking*, the Court "refused to find implicit in ambiguous sections of the [Clear Air Act] an authorization to consider costs that has elsewhere, and so often, been expressly granted," id., at 467, citing a tradition dating back to Union Elec. Co. v. EPA, 427 U.S. 246, 257, & n.5 (1976). There are, indeed, numerous Clean Air Act provisions explicitly permitting costs to be taken into account. See, e.g., §7404(a)(1); §7521(a)(2); §7545(c)(2); §7547(a)(3); §7554(b)(2); §7571(b); §7651c(f)(1)(A). *American Trucking* thus demanded "a textual commitment of authority to the EPA to consider costs," 531 U.S., at 468—a hurdle that the Good Neighbor Provision comes nowhere close to clearing. Today's opinion turns its back upon that case and is incompatible with that opinion.

II. Imposition of Federal Implementation Plans . . .

. . . "[N]othing in the statute," the majority says, "places EPA under an obligation to provide specific metrics to States before they undertake to fulfill their good neighbor obligations." This remarkably expansive reasoning makes a hash of the Clean Air Act, transforming it from a program based on cooperative federalism to one of centralized federal control. Nothing in the Good Neighbor Provision suggests such a stark departure from the Act's fundamental structure. . . .

The Good Neighbor Provision is one of the requirements with which SIPs must comply. §7410(a)(2)(D)(i)(I). The statutory structure described above plainly demands that EPA afford States a meaningful opportunity to allocate reduction responsibilities among the sources within their borders. But the majority holds that EPA may in effect force the States to guess at what those responsibilities might be by requiring them to submit SIPs before learning what the Agency regards as a "signif- ican[t]" contribution—with the consequence of losing their regulatory primacy if they guess wrong. EPA asserts that the D.C. Circuit "was wrong as a factual matter" in reasoning that States cannot feasibly implement the Good Neighbor Provision without knowing what the Agency considers their obligations to be. That is literally unbelievable. . . .

Call it "punish[ing] the States for failing to meet a standard that EPA had not yet announced and [they] did not yet know," 696 F.3d, at 28; asking them "to hit the target . . . before EPA defines [it]," id., at 32; requiring them "to take [a] stab in the dark," id., at 35; or "set[ting] the States up to fail," id., at 37. Call it "hid[ing] the ball," Brief for State Respondents 20; or a "shell game," id., at 54. Call it "pin the tail on the donkey." Tr. of Oral Arg. 24. As we have recently explained:

> It is one thing to expect regulated parties to conform their conduct to an agency's inter- pretations once the agency announces them; it is quite another to require regulated parties to divine the agency's interpretations in advance or else be held liable when the agency announces its interpretations for the first time . . . and demands deference." Christopher v. SmithKline Beecham Corp., 132 S. Ct. 2156, 2168 (2012).

That principle applies *a fortiori* to a regulatory regime that rests on principles of cooperative federalism. . . .

. . . The Good Neighbor Provision does not expressly state that EPA must pub- lish target quantities before the States are required to submit SIPs—even though the Clean Air Act does so for NAAQS more generally and for vehicle inspection and maintenance programs, see §7511a(c)(3)(B). From that premise, the majority reasons that "[h]ad Congress intended similarly to defer States' discharge of their obligations under the Good Neighbor Provision, Congress . . . would have included a similar direction in that section." Perhaps so.

The negative implication suggested by a statute's failure to use consistent terminology can be a helpful guide to determining meaning, especially when all the provisions in question were enacted at the same time (which is not the case here). But because that interpretive canon, like others, is just one clue to aid construction, it can be overcome by more powerful indications of meaning elsewhere in the statute. It is, we have said, "no more than a rule of thumb that can tip the scales when a statute could be read in multiple ways." Sebelius v. Auburn Regional Med- ical Center, 133 S. Ct. 817, 825 (2013). The Clean Air Act simply cannot be read to make EPA the primary regulator in this context. The negative-implication canon is easily overcome by the statute's state-respecting structure—not to mention the sheer impossibility of submitting a sensible SIP without EPA guidance. Negative impli- cation is the tiniest mousehole in which the majority discovers the elephant of federal control. . . .

NOTES AND QUESTIONS

1. What were the provisions that, under *Chevron*, EPA and the Court relied on so that EPA received the benefit of deference in its statutory interpretation?

2. The dissenting opinion strongly rejects EPA's approach, as well as the majority's opinion. What judicial review frame does the dissent utilize? Can you place its various points within the familiar *Chevron* two-step?

3. *More on the Relationship Between Interstate Pollution Abatement and Other CAA Programs.* In 2000, in response to petitions filed by a group of northeastern states under §126, EPA found that large electric utilities and industrial boilers and turbines located in upwind states violated §110(a)(2)(D)'s ban on one state's significant contribution to air pollution in other states. It ordered nearly 400 facilities in 12 states (including some of the petitioning states) and the District of Columbia to reduce annual emissions by more than 500,000 tons from 2007 levels. A group of states from the Midwest and the Southeast and operators of electric generating facilities sued, arguing that the CAA precluded EPA from making any findings in response to the northeastern states' §126 petition while the NO_x call at issue in the *Michigan* case was pending. According to the petitioners, principles of cooperative federalism dictate that the states be allowed the opportunity to decide how to reduce NO_x emissions without direction from EPA. In Appalachian Power Co. v. EPA, 249 F.3d 1032 (D.C. Cir. 2001), the court held that the statute does not require that proceedings under either §110 or §126 be completed before the agency may proceed with action under the other provision. See also Genon Rema, LLC v. EPA, 722 F.3d 513 (3d Cir. 2013) (holding that the "prohibition" referred to in §126(b) is not dependent on a standard established in a SIP that has already been approved or is in the process of being revised). In the alternative, the petitioners argued that although EPA may act under either §110 or §126, it may not impose §126 findings and a SIP call simultaneously. The court deferred, however, to EPA's determination that the two provisions operate independently. The court nevertheless remanded to EPA to explain further the manner in which it allocated NO_x allowances to the upwind states. On remand, EPA decided to retain the previously determined results but to provide a fuller explanation. The court in West Virginia v. EPA, 362 F.3d 861 (D.C. Cir. 2004), deemed EPA's explanation reasonable.

4. *Interstate Air Pollution and the Common Law.* In North Carolina v. TVA, 615 F.3d 291 (4th Cir. 2010), the court reversed a district court decision holding that emissions of ozone precursors and PM_{10} from TVA power plants in Alabama and Tennessee created a public nuisance and imposing an injunction requiring installation of pollution controls. It reasoned that such an injunction would scuttle the CAA's carefully crafted regulatory structure for abating interstate pollution, displace judgments about the appropriate degree of pollution control derived from the application of EPA's scientific expertise, and create uncertainty for regulated entities by subjecting them to a welter of potentially conflicting court decrees. A public nuisance remedy might even lead to increased air pollution by creating perverse incentives for power companies to use plants in regions subject to less stringent judicial decrees, and triggering rushed plant alterations instead of allowing system-wide analysis of where changes would do the most good. The court indicated that its reversal would not leave North Carolina without the ability to protect its residents' health from out-of-state emissions because it could resort to the §126

petition process or bring citizen suits under §304. Are these remedies likely to be effective?

5. *International Air Pollution.* Section 179B exempts from some of the statute's enforcement mechanisms for nonattainment areas those states that are able to establish that they would have attained the NAAQS but for emissions of ozone, CO, or PM_{10} emanating from outside the United States. See Sierra Club v. EPA, 346 F.3d 955 (9th Cir. 2003) (California unable to establish that it would have attained the NAAQS for PM_{10} but for emissions generated in Mexico).

b. The Acid Deposition Controversy

CLEAN AIR ACT AMENDMENTS OF 1990, REPORT OF THE COMMITTEE ON ENERGY AND COMMERCE, U.S. HOUSE OF REPRESENTATIVES, ON H.R. 3030
H.R. Rep. No. 101-490, pt. 1, at 157-158 (1990)

The Clean Air Act was originally designed mainly to reduce high pollution levels that tend to occur near major pollution sources. It did not contemplate that long-distance transport of air pollutants could cause widespread adverse impacts.

Scientists have since learned that SO_2 and NO_x pollution from power plants, factories, and other sources can be carried hundreds or even thousands of miles through the atmosphere, chemically transformed in the process, and eventually returned to earth as sulfuric and nitric acids. These acids often [are] picked up in droplets of rain or snow, but sometimes the particles simply fall back as "dry deposition." . . . [S]uch acid pollution has been associated with a variety of harmful effects, on health, especially to those with respiratory ailments; lakes; forests; and man-made materials, such as buildings, bridges, statuary, and car finishes. . . .

The small acidic sulfate and nitrate particles (acid aerosols) which form in the atmosphere from SO_2 and NO_x pollution irritate the lungs, causing constricted breathing. They pose risks to asthmatics and others with already impaired breathing abilities. Some epidemiological studies have suggested that acid aerosols increase the incidence of chronic cough and bronchitis and death rates.

Acidification of lakes and streams in the U.S. is another widespread effect of acid deposition. Although there are some natural acidic water bodies, "most of the acidity comes from acid deposition," according to findings of [the National Acid Precipitation Assessment Program (NAPAP)]. Nationally, acid deposition has reportedly acidified over one thousand large lakes (greater than 10 acres) and thousands of miles of streams. According to [the Office of Technology Assessment], thousands more lakes and streams are "extremely vulnerable" to further acidification. . . .

Acid deposition has been implicated in the damage of some forests. Contact with highly acidified rain or fog can directly injure leaves and needles. And over the long term, acid deposition may stunt tree growth by altering soil chemistry, both by washing away vital nutrients, such as magnesium and calcium, and by contaminating the soil with heavy metals like aluminum, that are freed from soil particles.

The red spruce forests along the crest of the Appalachian Mountains, which stretch from Maine to Georgia, have been the most damaged. These forests have suffered widespread decline, including the death of 40-70 percent of the spruce on some mountaintops in Vermont, New York, and North Carolina. NAPAP has found that regular exposure to extremely acidic clouds (average pH of 3.6) is contributing to the decline, along with exposure to ozone, disease, insects, and unusual weather conditions.

The pollutants that create acid deposition also have a major impact on visibility. The sulfate particles that form from SO_2 emissions scatter light and reduce visibility. The problem is particularly great during summer months, because high humidity and temperatures promote sulfate formation. . . .

Finally, acid deposition causes substantial economic impacts by eroding man-made building materials, such as steel, stones, and paint. According to some estimates, the cost of damage in 17 Eastern States alone could be as high as $2 billion per year.

NOTES AND QUESTIONS

1. *Scientific Uncertainty.* This excerpt from the legislative history of the 1990 amendments fails to disclose the controversy that surrounded the debate over whether—and if so, how—to control emissions of the precursors of acid deposition. Uncertainty attended the questions of whether there is a linear relationship between precursor gases and sulfate or nitrate formation and the nature of the relationship between sources and receptors.

Research conducted since the 1990 amendments reduced this uncertainty and confirmed the severity of the problem. A 1999 report, for example, concluded that soil in high-elevation forests in the Colorado Front Range, the Allegheny Mountains in West Virginia, the Great Smoky Mountains in Tennessee, and the San Gabriel Mountains near Los Angeles was becoming more acidic due to excess nitrogen; that excess nitrogen in the Chesapeake Bay was causing algae blooms that suffocate other life forms; and that lakes and streams in the Sierra Nevada, Cascade, Rocky, and Adirondack mountains were suffering from chronically high acidity. Dao, Study Sees Acid Rain Threat in Adirondacks and Beyond, N.Y. Times, Apr. 5, 1999, at A19.

The court in Center for Biological Diversity v. EPA, 749 F.3d 1079 (D.C. Cir. 2014), in upholding EPA's decision not to revise the secondary NAAQS for oxides of nitrogen and oxides of sulphur to address acid rain, described scientific understanding (or lack thereof) of the mechanisms that contribute to acid deposition.

2. *Political Obstacles to Control of Acid Deposition.* Acid rain control highlights the important distributive judgments that often accompany air pollution control efforts. The fact that acid deposition is a long-range phenomenon meant that efforts to control it would have different impacts in various regions of the country. Because evidence of acidified lakes was strong in New York's Adirondack Mountains and New England, northeastern states supported efforts to control emissions of acid rain precursors. They charged that the predominant cause of the problem was the concentration of old electric power plants in the Midwest. But some feared that forcing coal-fired power plants to control acid rain precursors would significantly increase electric rates in states such as Ohio. One way for power plants to reduce SO_2 emissions and the resulting formation of sulfates is to switch from coal with a high sulfur content to coal with a low sulfur content or to other low-sulfur fuels. States with large deposits of high-sulfur coal, such as West Virginia and Kentucky, therefore feared that requirements to reduce SO_2 emissions would decimate the local coal mining industry. States

farther west with thriving low-sulfur coal industries anticipated reaping the benefits of a new acid rain control program.

These divisive regional conflicts prevented an agreement over acid deposition control amendments to the CAA throughout the 1980s. The logjam broke when Congress amended the CAA in 1990. By then, the public viewed acid rain as a serious problem. In addition, the new program was relatively narrow, subjecting only coal-fired power plants, the very industry that had long opposed any compromises, to regulation. Finally, the program authorized emissions trading, a market-oriented approach that some conservative legislators then favored because it was "decentralized, flexible, and efficient." Bryner, Blue Skies, Green Politics: The Clean Air Act of 1990, at 95-96 (1993).

3. *The Costs and Benefits of Control.* In 1995, EPA reported that the health benefits (primarily reductions in premature deaths and new cases of chronic bronchitis) of controlling emissions of SO_2 under the acid rain provisions of the 1990 amendments in the 31 eastern states would amount to between $3 and $11 billion in 1997. These benefits would far exceed the estimated costs of control, which were substantially lower than the earlier worst-case estimates: $1.2 billion in 1997 and $2.4 billion in 2010. EPA Press Advisory, 1995 WL 740253 (Dec. 15, 1995). EPA estimated that by 2010, annual health benefits would fall within a range of $12 to $40 billion, which would be 5 to 17 times the costs of implementing SO_2 controls.

Fears that acid rain control would adversely affect the high-sulfur coal mining industry proved justified. Many mines in Appalachia and other coal-mining areas east of the Mississippi closed, resulting in a decline in coal mine employment in these areas. While coal production in the east fell, production in the west increased. The 1990 amendments authorized the payment of unemployment compensation and retraining benefits to miners who lost jobs, but hard-hit mining communities tended to regard these efforts as insufficient. Kilborn, East's Coal Towns Wither in the Name of Cleaner Air, N.Y. Times, Feb. 15, 1996, at A1.

c. Emissions Trading and the Control of Acid Deposition

INDIANAPOLIS POWER & LIGHT CO. v. EPA
58 F.3d 643 (D.C. Cir. 1995)

Title IV of the Clean Air Act establishes an acid rain program to reduce emissions of sulfur dioxide and nitrogen oxides, the primary precursors of acid rain. See 42 U.S.C. §§7651-7651o. Title IV imposes a national cap of 8.90 million tons of sulfur dioxide emissions per year on electric utilities. 42 U.S.C. §§7651b(a)(1), 7651d(a)(3). The emissions reductions are to occur in two phases. [See Figure 6-10.] In Phase I, ... 110 utilities with the largest coal-fired utility electric generating units must reduce their emissions to 2.50 pounds of sulfur dioxide per million British thermal units (Btus) of fuel consumed by each power-generating unit in the "baseline" years of 1985, 1986 and 1987. 42 U.S.C. §7651c. Each utility unit is allocated a number of fully marketable pollution allowances so that it may emit sulfur dioxide at this level. 42 U.S.C. §7651c. Each allowance authorizes the emission of one ton of sulfur dioxide during one calendar year and may be bought, sold, traded or banked for future use or resale. 42 U.S.C. §§7651a(3), 7651b(b).

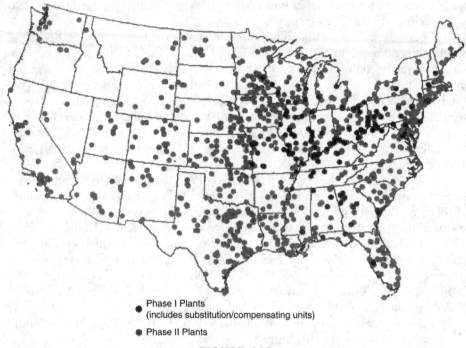

Phase I Plants
(includes substitution/compensating units)

Phase II Plants

FIGURE 6-10
Affected Sources Under the Acid Rain Program

Source: http://www.epa.gov/airmarkets/cmap/mapgallery/mg_affected_sources.html (removed).

Beginning in 1995, the emissions from each Phase I unit may not exceed the number of allowances that unit holds. 42 U.S.C. §7651c(a). Emissions from a Phase I unit that exceed the number of allowances allocated to it are unlawful and are subject to various fines and penalties. 42 U.S.C. §§7651b(g), 7651j. To comply with Title IV requirements and ensure that its emissions do not exceed its allowances, a utility has three options. A utility can switch from coal with a high sulfur content to low-sulfur coal, purchase allowances from other utilities or install costly sulfur dioxide control technology known as "scrubbers." Congress encouraged the installation of scrubbers by establishing an extension allowance program. 42 U.S.C. §7651c(d).

MADISON GAS & ELECTRIC CO. v. EPA
25 F.3d 526 (7th Cir. 1994)

Under Phase II of the statutory program, . . . the EPA is required to award, effective in the year 2000, SO_2 emission allowances to each of the nation's 2,200 electric utilities. §7651d. Each allowance permits the emission of one ton of SO_2 per year. The allowances can be bought and sold. §7651b(b). This is the novel feature of the acid rain program. A market in pollution is created. Clean utilities can make money selling their excess allowances and dirty utilities that do not want to expend the resources necessary to become clean can instead buy allowances from the clean utilities.

NOTES AND QUESTIONS

1. *Statutory Purposes.* Congress sought in the 1990 amendments to reduce the adverse effects of acid deposition through reductions in annual emissions of SO_2 by 10 million tons and of NO_x by about 2 million tons from 1980 emission levels. The program was also designed to encourage energy conservation, the use of renewable and clean alternative technologies, and pollution prevention. §401(a). How might the program accomplish these goals? According to the statute, the allowance program described in the *Indianapolis Power & Light Co.* excerpt "allocates the costs of achieving the required reductions in emissions . . . among sources in the United States. Broad-based taxes and emissions fees that would provide for payment of the costs of achieving required emissions reductions by any party or parties other than the sources required to achieve the reductions are undesirable." Pub. L. No. 101-549, §407, 104 Stat. 2399 (1990). Undesirable from an economic or a political perspective?

2. *The Potential Inequities of an Allowance System Based on Historical Usage.* How were the allowances that authorize emissions of SO_2 by electric power plants initially allocated? See §§404 (Phase I), 405 (Phase II). The use of a historical "baseline" to determine regulatory rights creates the potential for inequity. Given that allowances were doled out primarily on the basis of historical operating practice and that the statute prohibits SO_2 emissions in excess of the allowances held by a power plant, for example, how will a new utility procure the allowances sufficient to cover its emissions? See Dennis, Comment, Smoke for Sale: Paradoxes and Problems of the Emissions Trading Program of the Clean Air Act Amendments of 1990, 40 UCLA L. Rev. 1101, 1116-1117 (1993). See also Texas Mun. Power Agency v. EPA, 89 F.3d 858 (D.C. Cir. 1996) (EPA acted properly in relying on an emission rate calculated from a statewide average in determining the allowances to be received by a utility unit whose emission rate was not included in the relied-upon database).

EPA must establish a pool of reserve allowances to use for the grant of extension allowances and other purposes, but such allowances are capped at 3.5 million. §404(a)(2). How should EPA dole out these allowances? By lottery? On a first-come, first-served basis?

3. *Allowances and Property Rights.* The statute describes an allowance as "a limited authorization to emit SO_2," which "does not constitute a property right." §403(f). What do you suppose was the rationale behind this provision? Might it be advisable to reduce the number of available allowances? What legal problems might be caused by an attempt to do so by EPA? See Dennis, *supra,* at 1126-1127.

4. *Allowance Trading in Practice.* Several years after adoption of the 1990 amendments, the General Accounting Office reported that utilities had tended to take advantage of cost-saving opportunities within their own plants (such as switching from high- to low-sulfur coal) rather than to use trading to meet requirements.[y] At the same time, the price of an allowance was far below what utility lobbyists had predicted. One explanation was that the market was not working. But another was that industry lobbyists had engaged in "gaming"—intentionally overestimating the costs of control (and the price of an allowance) in an attempt to dissuade Congress from adopting stringent controls. As a result, the regulatory burden Congress thought it was imposing on utilities was far less than originally predicted. To put it another way,

---

y. U.S. General Accounting Office, Air Pollution—Allowance Trading Offers an Opportunity to Reduce Emissions at Less Cost, GAO/RCED 95-30, 1994 WL 792389 (Dec. 16, 1994).

Congress could have purchased far more pollution control for the amount it was willing to force industry to commit to the problem than the statute actually accomplished. Compare Coniff, The Political History of Cap and Trade, Smithsonian Mag., July 2009 (noting that utility executives estimated the cost of the acid rain control program at between $5 and $25 billion per year, but that it actually turned out to cost only $3 billion per year). A third explanation involved the low price of coal. How is that price relevant? As the deadline for Phase II limits approached, creating more potential buyers, the market heated up and sales of allowances increased.

5. *Allowance Trading, Hot Spots, and Environmental Justice.* Given the risk discussed at page 507 above that emissions trading can create hot spots of high pollutant concentrations, has the acid deposition control program done so? Ringquist, Trading Equity for Efficiency in Environmental Protection? Environmental Justice Effects from the SO_2 Allowance Trading Program, 92 Social Science Q. 297 (2011), concluded that the 1990 CAA program did not concentrate SO_2 emissions in black or Hispanic neighborhoods, but that it did transfer emissions into poorly educated communities.

6. *State Efforts to Control Acid Deposition.* Is it possible that the trading of allowances will make the acid rain problem worse rather than better, at least in some areas? What is the likely result of a trade of allowances from a New York utility to a power plant in the Midwest? In 2000, the New York legislature adopted the Air Pollution Mitigation Law, which assessed an "air pollution mitigation offset" equal to any sum received for the sale or trade of SO_2 allowances to a unit in an upwind state. Any amount received by a regulated unit for such an allowance was forfeited to the state public utility commission. The offset could be avoided only with the attachment of a restrictive covenant to a transfer of SO_2 allowances prohibiting their later transfer to and usage in an upwind state. Clean Air Markets Group v. Pataki, 338 F.3d 82 (2d Cir. 2003), held that the CAA preempted New York's law because the latter interfered with the method selected by Congress for regulating SO_2 emissions, including a nationwide allowance transfer system. The state statute effectively banned allowance sales to utilities in upwind states. The court did not reach the issue of whether the state statute violated the dormant Commerce Clause.

7. *Limits on Emissions of NO_x by Utilities.* The acid deposition control provisions limit emissions of NO_x as well as SO_2. §407. A utility may avoid the prescribed emission limits by requesting from EPA an alternative emission limit on the basis of its inability to meet the regulatory limit through the use of low NO_x burner technology. §407(d).

8. *Has the Program Worked?* According to one court, "[s]ince 1980, the national average SO_2 concentration has dropped 78 percent. EPA, Air Trends, http://www.epa.gov/air/airtrends/sulfur.html (last updated Sept. 3, 2013). This is the result, at least in part, of the cap-and-trade program established by the Acid Rain Program. The level of NO_x has also declined, but these reductions have been 'offset by increases in emissions from automobiles.'" Center for Biological Diversity v. EPA, 749 F.3d 1079, 1084 (D.C. Cir. 2014).

A 2005 White House report to Congress[z] indicated that sulfate deposition dropped by 40 percent in the Northeast between 1990 and 2002. But the report also indicated that many water bodies in the region (except in the Adirondack

z. The National Acid Precipitation Assessment Program Report to Congress: An Integrated Assessment, available at http://www.cleartheair.org/documents/NAPAP_FINAL_print.pdf.

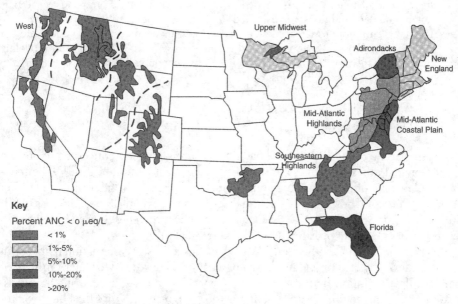

Key

Percent ANC < o μeq/L

- < 1%
- 1%-5%
- 5%-10%
- 10%-20%
- >20%

Source: NAPAP 1991, 1990 Integrated Assessment Report

FIGURE 6-11
Acidic Surface Waters in Surveyed Regions

Source: http://www.epa.gov/airmarkets/cmap/mapgallery/mg_acidic_waters.html (removed).

Mountains) had not shown signs of recovery from acidic conditions. See Figure 6-11. Wet nitrate deposition did not decline during the same period. A report issued by EPA in 2007 found that SO_2 emissions from electric power generators dropped below 10 million tons for the first time in 2006. NO_x emissions fell by more than 3 million tons between 1990 and 2006. See EPA's Report on the Environment: 2008, at 2-38 to 2-43. Compare Strock et al., Decadal Trends Reveal Recent Acceleration in the Rate of Recovery from Acidification in the Northeastern U.S., 48 Envtl. Sci. Tech. 4681 (May 6, 2014), who reported that reductions in sulfate concentrations in lakes in upstate New York and New England were accelerating (at a rate three times faster between 2002-2010 than in the 1980s and 1990s). While soil pH levels in some of these areas fell, others increased or were static. These uneven results may have been due to other human activities, such as development and the use of road salts.

Burns, et al., National Acid Precipitation Assessment Program Report to Congress 2011: An Integrated Assessment (2011), assesses the impact of the 1990 acid precipitation control program. A summary of the report states:

Title IV has been successful in reducing emissions of SO_2 and NO_x from power generation to the levels set by Congress. In fact, by 2009, SO_2 emissions from power plants were already 3.25 million tons lower than the final 2010 cap level of 8.95 million tons, and NO_x emissions were 6.1 million tons less than the projected level in 2000 without the [acid rain program], or more than triple the Title IV NO_x emission-reduction objective. As a result of these emission reductions, air quality has improved, providing significant human health benefits, and acid deposition has decreased to the extent that some acid-sensitive areas are beginning to show signs of recovery. Current emission reductions and

588 Chapter VI. Protecting the Air Resource

the passage of time, which is needed for affected ecosystems to respond to the new environmental conditions, are expected to allow more acid-sensitive areas to recover. However, current emission-reduction levels (rules finalized as of spring 2005) are not sufficient to allow full recovery of acid-sensitive ecosystems. Estimates from modeling presented in this report show that additional emission reductions are necessary in order to protect acid-sensitive ecosystems.

NOTE ON THE INTERNATIONAL IMPLICATIONS OF ACID DEPOSITION

The Nature of the Problem. Canada has historically been concerned about the impact of acid rain on its lakes and forests. Before the adoption of the 1990 amendments, Canadian officials estimated that about 60 percent of the acid rain that falls on Canada came from the United States and that U.S. sources contribute 4 times as much SO_2 and 11 times as much NO_x to Canada's eastern provinces as the United States receives from Canada. 12 Env't Rep. (BNA) 648 (1981).

The Legal Approach. Section 115 of the CAA addresses international air pollution. Paradoxically, it affords Canada a somewhat stronger ground to attack Ohio River Valley sulfate pollution than it affords New York. Do you see why? Canadian legislation satisfies the section's requirement that the foreign country give the United States equal treatment.

The province of Ontario and several states and environmental groups petitioned EPA for a rulemaking under §115 that would result in the issuance of endangerment and reciprocity findings with respect to U.S. emissions that allegedly result in harmful levels of acid deposition in Canada. EPA argued that it need not make an endangerment finding until it was able to identify the sources of pollution. Because EPA could not trace pollutants adversely affecting Canada to specific sources in the United States, it was not obliged to do anything. The petitioners claimed that §115 mandated abatement measures even if EPA could not pinpoint particular sources. In Her Majesty the Queen in Right of Ontario v. EPA, 912 F.2d 1525 (D.C. Cir. 1990), the court concluded that judicial review was premature. EPA had neither made a final decision on whether endangerment and reciprocity findings could be made, nor conclusively determined whether it could adequately trace pollutants to specific sources.

The Diplomatic Approach. The Canada—United States Air Quality Agreement, 30 I.L.M. 676 (1991), committed the two nations to reductions of both SO_2 and NO_x. Canada fully implemented its treaty commitments by 1994, reducing SO_2 emissions by more than 50 percent in the seven eastern provinces. The United States would comply with its obligations primarily by implementing the 1990 CAA amendments. The treaty set up an International Joint Commission to conduct five-year reviews of progress in reducing transboundary air pollution. By 2010, the United States had reduced total SO_2 emissions from covered sources by 67 percent from 1990 levels, while Canada's total SO_2 emissions decreased by 57 percent in 2010 from 1990 emission levels. Between 2000 and 2010, the United States reduced total NO_x emissions by 42 percent in the transboundary ozone region, while Canada's emissions fell by 40 percent. United States-Canada Air Quality Agreement Progress Report 2012, at 1.

For an example of another effort to control transboundary pollution involving Canada and the United States, see Chapter 11, section B's coverage of the Trail

Smelter Arbitration (United States v. Canada) (1941), 3 U.N.R.I.A.A. 1938 (1949), in which the United States alleged that SO_2 emissions from a Canadian smelting plant caused damage in the United States.

3. *Protection of Stratospheric Ozone*

a. The Problem of Ozone Depletion

CLEAN AIR ACT AMENDMENTS OF 1989
S. Rep. No. 101-228, at 383-385 (1989)

In 1985, scientists discovered a significant loss of ozone over a portion of the southern hemisphere that was about the size of North America. The collapse of the ozone layer was not predicted by any of the scientific theories or models. Measurements of what has become a seasonal phenomenon have revealed losses greater than 50 percent in the total column and greater than 95 percent [for] an altitude of 15 to 20 kilometers (9 to 12 miles). The discovery of this "Hole" in the stratospheric ozone layer over Antarctica gave renewed impetus to international efforts to understand and protect the ozone layer.

In September 1987, the Montreal Protocol on Substances That Deplete the Ozone Layer (the Protocol) [26 I.L.M. 1550 (1987); amended by 32 I.L.M. 874 (1992)] was negotiated and signed by more than two dozen nations. The Protocol entered into force in January 1989 and approximately 50 nations are now Parties to the Protocol.

Signatories to the Protocol, including the United States, agreed to respond to this threat by imposing limits on consumption (defined as production plus imports minus exports of bulk quantities) of [chlorofluorocarbons (CFCs)] and halons. Production and use of CFCs and halons are being curtailed worldwide because of the risks that current production levels and use patterns pose to human health and the environment. The current version of the Protocol requires industrialized countries such as the United States to (1) limit CFC consumption, beginning in 1989, (2) reduce CFC consumption 50 percent by 1998, and (3) limit halon consumption, beginning in 1992.

Since the Montreal Protocol was negotiated and signed in 1987, the causal link between CFCs and the Antarctic ozone "Hole" has been substantiated. In addition, recent scientific studies have demonstrated that destruction of the ozone layer is not limited to remote, uninhabited portions of Antarctica. Scientists have observed and measured losses of ozone on a global scale. Losses of ozone since 1970 have been measured during the winter months on a worldwide basis, including losses ranging from 2.3 percent to 6.2 percent over densely-populated portions of the Northern Hemisphere. . . .

These measurements of actual ozone loss are significantly greater than computer models had predicted and raise serious questions about the adequacy of the control measures set forth in the Montreal Protocol and existing EPA regulations. Recent reports from Antarctica showing that this year's "Hole" has grown and now covers 10 *million* square miles, in addition to reports from the Arctic indicating the possible formation of a Northern Hemisphere "Hole," lend a new sense of urgency to ongoing negotiations to amend and strengthen the Montreal Protocol.

By waiting for measurements of actual ozone loss, by failing to take appropriate action on the basis of credible scientific theory, governments around the world allowed a manageable environmental threat to become an environmental crisis. As a result of atmospheric lag time and the persistence of CFCs and similar ozone-depleting and greenhouse-forcing gases, it is too late to prevent additional damage to the ozone layer or human-induced global climate change. Our challenge is to take action as rapidly as possible that will, to the greatest extent possible, (1) reduce the threat of additional damage to the ozone layer and (2) reduce the rate and magnitude of human-induced global climate change.

NOTES AND QUESTIONS

1. *How Much Is Gone?* Between 1980 and 1995, more than 6 percent of global ozone was destroyed. 17 Discover (Jan. 1996), at 78. In 1995 ozone levels were about 40 percent of what they were in the 1960s, and 2000 witnessed the largest hole ever measured (more than 11 million square miles, or three times larger than the United States), appearing earlier in the season than usual. National Oceanic and Atmospheric Administration (NOAA) scientists measured the second-largest hole in the ozone layer over Antarctica in 2003. 34 Env't Rep. (BNA) 2239 (2003).

2. *How Do CFCs and Other Chemicals Attack the Ozone Layer?* Before 1990 CFCs were widely used in the United States as coolants for air conditioners and refrigerators, as propellants for aerosol sprays, and as cleansers for computer micro-chips and other electronic parts. In Covington v. Jefferson County, 358 F.3d 626, 649 (9th Cir. 2004) (Gould, J., concurring), one federal judge explained that CFCs can have an atmospheric lifetime of 45-100 years:

> In that extensive time span, each CFC, converted to chlorine monoxide (ClO) after reactions with sunlight, can destroy hundreds of molecules of stratospheric ozone because the ClO is a catalyst. ClO first reacts with an oxygen atom (O) to form a chlorine atom (Cl) and an oxygen molecule (O_2). The chlorine atom (Cl) reacts with an ozone molecule (O_3) to re-form ClO along with an oxygen molecule (O_2). The ClO, then, is ready to begin the ozone-depletion cycle once more. Once released, CFCs by natural processes create ClO, which is an unrelenting destroyer of ozone. Because this process occurs at the molecular level, it is difficult for us to fathom the cumulative impact of repetitive small destructions of ozone, but science knows that the impact of this process, if unrestrained, will be devastating to all life on earth.

See Figure 6-12. According to one study, strong thunderstorms that pump water as high as twelve miles into the upper atmosphere through a process called convective injection can raise air temperatures so as to trigger the chemical reactions that destroy stratospheric ozone. To the extent that climate change increases the incidence of strong thunderstorms, it may have a role in depleting the ozone layer. See Anderson et al., UV Dosage Levels in Summer: Increased Risk of Ozone Loss from Convectively Injected Water Vapor, 337 Science 835 (Aug. 17, 2012).

3. *What Difference Does It Make?* The stratospheric ozone layer shields the Earth's surface from ultraviolet radiation. Exposure to ultraviolet radiation can cause skin cancer and cataracts and impair the functioning of the human immune system.

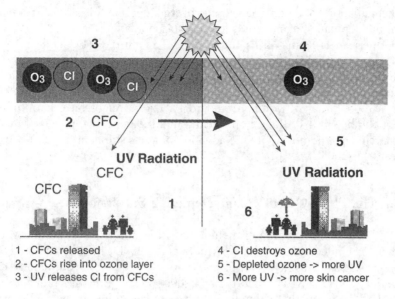

FIGURE 6-12
The Process of Ozone Depletion

Source: http:/www.epa.gov/ozone/science/process.html.

NASA scientists confirmed that levels of harmful ultraviolet radiation on Earth increased steadily from 1979 to 1992. Daily Env't Rep. 150 (BNA), Aug. 5, 1996, at A-7. According to EPA, each 1 percent decline in atmospheric ozone is capable of increasing nonmalignant skin cancer rates by 5 percent and malignant skin cancer rates by 2 percent. Dutch researchers concluded that in the absence of controls on chemicals that deplete stratospheric ozone, skin cancer rates in the United States and northwest Europe would more than triple by 2100. 27 Env't Rep. (BNA) 1590 (1996).

4. *The Montreal Protocol.* In light of evidence of a worsening of the ozone depletion problem, the signatories to the Montreal Protocol agreed in 1990 to eliminate production and use of CFCs by 2000. Developing countries were afforded an extra ten years to comply, with the possibility of further extensions for halons. What justification might there be for providing this kind of leeway to developing countries? See also CAA §604c(e). In 1992, the parties to the Protocol again accelerated the phase-out deadline for developed countries for CFCs, methyl chloroform, and carbon tetrachloride and established a schedule for phasing out hydrochlorofluorocarbons (HCFCs) by 2030. The Montreal protocol is discussed further in Chapter 11, section D.3.

5. *Tropospheric and Stratospheric Ozone.* Is it possible that the reduction of ground-level (or tropospheric) ozone will have some of the same adverse effects on the environment as depletion of stratospheric ozone? The Department of Energy and the Office of Management and Budget have raised concerns that reducing ozone levels pursuant to a tightening of the NAAQS would increase the public's exposure to ultraviolet radiation by lowering levels of tropospheric ozone, which blocks

ultraviolet radiation. What criteria should govern a decision to trade off risks for one group of the population against risks for another population segment?

In American Trucking Ass'ns, Inc. v. EPA, 175 F.3d 1027 (D.C. Cir. 1999), *rev'd on other grounds*, 531 U.S. 457 (2001), the court remanded EPA's 1997 revisions to the NAAQS for ozone in part because EPA disregarded evidence that tropospheric ozone blocks ultraviolet radiation from the sun. The agency therefore failed to consider whether a more stringent primary standard for ozone might have harmful effects on the public health. EPA found on remand that the beneficial effects of increased ground-level ozone do not justify the adoption of a less stringent ozone NAAQS. 67 Fed. Reg. 614 (2003).

b.   The Phase-Out of Ozone-Depleting Substances

The 1990 CAA amendments include provisions that correspond to the responsibilities of the United States under the Montreal Protocol. The statute phased out the production of Class I ozone-depleting substances (including CFCs, halons, carbon tetrachloride, and methyl chloroform) by 2000. §604(a). Effective January 1, 2000 (January 1, 2002, for methyl chloroform), it was unlawful for any person to produce any amount of a Class I substance. §604(b). What exceptions does the statute provide? See §604(e)-(g); NRDC v. EPA, 464 F.3d 1 (D.C. Cir. 2006) (rejecting a challenge to EPA regulation implementing the "critical use" exemption because side agreement to the Montreal Protocol that was not ratified by Congress was not "the law of the land," enforceable in the federal courts). The statute required EPA to issue regulations to ensure that the consumption of Class I substances is phased out in accordance with the same schedule. §604(c).

Beginning January 1, 2015, it became unlawful to introduce into interstate commerce any Class II ozone-depleting substances (HCFCs) that has not been recycled, used, and entirely consumed in the production of other chemicals or used as a refrigerant in appliances manufactured before January 1, 2020. §605(a). The production of Class II substances will be banned effective January 1, 2030, §605(b)(2), and EPA must issue regulations phasing out consumption on the same schedule. §605(c). EPA may accelerate the production or consumption phase-out schedules for Class I or Class II substances if necessary to protect health and the environment against harmful effects on stratospheric ozone, if an accelerated phase-out is practicable (taking into account factors such as technological achievability and safety), or if the Montreal Protocol is modified to speed up the ban on production, consumption, or use of ozone-depleting chemicals. §606(a). President George H.W. Bush accelerated the phase-out of the production of Class I substances to January 1, 1996. 58 Fed. Reg. 65,018 (1993). At the 20th Anniversary Meeting of the parties to the Montreal Protocol in 2007, 191 industrialized and developing nations agreed to accelerate the phase-out of HCFCs, which not only damage the ozone layer but also contribute significantly to global warming. The 25th Meeting of the Parties in 2012 addressed proposals to include hydrofluorocarbons (HFCs) under the Protocol, but consensus eluded the parties.

The statute requires EPA to issue regulations governing the issuance of transferable allowances for the production of Class I and II substances. What conditions does the statute impose on "emission trading" of ozone-depleting substances? See §607. In Arkema, Inc. v. EPA, 618 F.3d 1 (D.C. Cir. 2010), the court invalidated

EPA's effort to restrict intra-company, inter-pollutant allowance transfers on the ground that it amounted to improper retroactive rulemaking. See also Honeywell Int'l, Inc. v. EPA, 705 F.3d 470 (D.C. Cir. 2013).

To the maximum extent practicable, Class I and II substances must be replaced by chemicals, product substitutes, or alternative manufacturing processes that reduce overall risks to human health and the environment. §612(a). EPA must issue rules making it unlawful to replace any Class I or II substances with any substitute substance EPA determines may present adverse effects to human health or the environment, where EPA has identified an alternative to that replacement that reduces overall risk and is currently or potentially available. §612(c).

Is It Working? Scientists at the NOAA found in 1996 that the amount of ozone-depleting chemicals in the lower atmosphere had declined for the first time since measurements began. They credited the Montreal Protocol for the improvement. The United Nations Environment Program reported in 2002 that levels of ozone-depleting gases were at or near their projected peak in the stratosphere and had begun a slow decline in the troposphere. Scientists again attributed the improvement to the Montreal Protocol, but warned that noncompliance could result in increased threats to the integrity of the ozone layer.

In early 2007, scientists reported that the hole in the ozone layer over the Antarctic had once again increased, equaling its record size of 2001. The increase may have been due to an unusually cold Antarctic winter, but scientists were concerned that a huge increase in demand for air conditioners in developing nations such as India and China may pose obstacles to long-term efforts to prevent stratospheric ozone depletion. The refrigerants being used in those countries (such as HCFC-22) are already banned in Europe, though the Montreal Protocol allows developing nations to continue using HCFC-22 until 2040. See Bradsher, The Price of Keeping Cool in Asia, N.Y. Times, Feb. 23, 2007, at C1. For the first time in 2011, scientists found that ozone destruction over the Arctic was comparable to that in the Antarctic. They attributed that finding to unusually long-lasting cold conditions in the Arctic lower stratosphere, which caused persistent enhancement in ozone-destroying forms of chlorine and unprecedented ozone loss. Manney et al., Unprecedented Arctic Ozone Loss in 2011, 478 Nature 469 (Oct. 27, 2011). In addition, scientists have discovered the presence of CFCs and HCFCs whose manufacture began relatively recently and that are not covered by the Montreal Protocol. See Laube et al., Newly Detected Ozone-Depleting Substances in the Atmosphere, 7 Nature Geoscience 266 (2014).

Scientists at NOAA reported in 2009 that nitrous oxide is the dominant ozone-depleting substance now being emitted (as well as being a potent greenhouse gas). Because nitrous oxide remains in the atmosphere for about a century, current emissions will have long-term adverse effects. See Ravishankara et al., Nitrous Oxide (N_2O): The Dominant Ozone-Depleting Substance Emitted in the 21st Century, 326 Science 123 (Oct. 2, 2009). Waugh et al., Recent Changes in the Ventilation of the Southern Oceans, 339 Science 568 (Feb. 1, 2013), concluded that the ozone hole over Antarctica has changed wind patterns, which in turn have shifted ocean currents. The altered currents are bringing deeper water to the surface. The problem is that this water is rich in carbon and unable to absorb as much carbon from the air as water previously closer to the surface. As less carbon is absorbed by the water, more will remain in the air, exacerbating warming caused by climate change.

J. FACILITATING ENFORCEMENT: CLEAN AIR ACT PERMITS

As the materials on water pollution in Chapter 7 indicate, the federal Clean Water Act (CWA) centers around a comprehensive permit program for all point sources of water pollution. The 1970 version of the CAA lacked a similar broad-reaching national operating permit mechanism. Most changes in emission limits for individual sources had to be processed by the states as SIP revisions, subject to EPA approval. This led to delays as minor revisions tended to pile up in EPA regional offices. The 1990 amendments created a new permit program. §§501-507. The Senate Report on the amendments explained that the program would facilitate enforcement by clarifying the obligations of individual sources and making it easier to track compliance, and by expediting implementation of new control requirements. A source's pollution control obligations were often scattered throughout "numerous, often hard-to-find provisions of the SIP or other Federal regulations," and often it was never made clear in a SIP how its general regulation applied to a specific source. The new permit program would collect all of a source's CAA obligations in one permit document and clarify how the SIP's general rules apply to the permit holder. EPA, the states, and the public would benefit because they would find it easier to identify the requirements applicable to a source and determine its compliance status. Regulated sources would benefit from the greater certainty provided by the permit's identification of relevant obligations. By identifying the baseline requirements for each source, permits would also facilitate emissions trading. Regulated sources also would benefit because the permit program would simplify and expedite procedures for modifying a source's pollution obligations. Before 1990, most such changes took the form of SIP amendments, subject to lengthy EPA review. The new permit program placed time limits on EPA review of state permit decisions. Finally, the permit program would assist states in implementing their CAA programs by imposing fees on permit applicants to offset program administration costs. See S. Rep. No. 101-228, at 346-348 (1989).

The D.C. Circuit described the need for the Title V permit program and part of its structure as follows:

> Under the regulatory regime established by the Clean Air Act ("Act"), emission limits for pollutants and monitoring requirements that measure compliance applicable to any given stationary source of air pollution are scattered throughout rules promulgated by states or EPA, such as state implementation plans, id. §7410, new source performance standards, id. §7411, and national emission standards for hazardous air pollutants, id. §7412. Before 1990, regulators and industry were left to wander through this regulatory maze in search of the emission limits and monitoring requirements that might apply to a particular source. Congress addressed this confusion in the 1990 Amendments by adding Title V of the Act, which created a national permit program that requires many stationary sources of air pollution to obtain permits that include relevant emission limits and monitoring requirements. Id. §§7661-7661f. Congress intended that EPA and state and local permitting authorities administer the permit program together. Title V gives EPA a supervisory role over the program, which includes the duty to identify its "minimum elements," id. §7661a(b), the power to establish new compliance procedures, id. §7661c(b), and the opportunity to object to permits that do not comply with the Act, id. §7661d(b). State and local authorities are assigned the task of issuing permits in their jurisdictions but can do so only if EPA has approved their proposals for how to implement the permit program.

Id. §7661a(d)(1). If a permitting authority fails to propose an acceptable program, responsibility for issuing permits falls to EPA. Id. §7661a(d)(3).

Sierra Club v. EPA, 536 F.3d 673, 674 (D.C. Cir. 2008).

COMMONWEALTH OF VIRGINIA v. BROWNER
80 F.3d 869 (4th Cir. 1996)

MICHAEL, Circuit Judge:

[Virginia sought review of EPA's disapproval of the state's proposed program for issuing air pollution permits. It contested EPA's finding that the state failed to comply with Title V of the CAA, §§501-507, because the proposal lacked adequate provisions for judicial review of the state's permitting decisions. Virginia also charged that the Act's sanctions provisions, CAA §§179(b) & 502(d), violated the Tenth Amendment and the spending clause of the Constitution.]

I.

Title V's key provision, CAA §502, prohibits major stationary sources of air pollution from operating either without a valid permit or in violation of the terms of a permit. The permit is crucial to the implementation of the Act: it contains, in a single, comprehensive set of documents, all CAA requirements relevant to the particular polluting source. In a sense, a permit is a source-specific bible for Clean Air Act compliance. . . .

States are directed to submit for EPA approval their own programs for issuing permits. CAA §502(d)(1). EPA may not approve a proposed permit program unless it meets certain minimum criteria set out in CAA §502(b). Among other things, states must . . . provide for review in state courts of permitting decisions (§502(b)(6)).

If a state fails to submit a permit program, or submits a permit program that EPA disapproves for failure to comply with CAA §502(b), the state becomes subject to sanctions designed to encourage compliance. CAA §502(d).

One sanction deprives states of certain federal highway funds. CAA §179(b)(1). However, the state loses no funds that would be spent in regions that are in "attainment" within the meaning of the Act. CAA §179(b)(1)(A). . . . CAA §179(b)(1)(B).

A second sanction increases the pollution offset requirements already imposed on private polluters within ozone nonattainment areas. Normally, new [or modified] major stationary sources of pollution may not be operated within nonattainment areas . . . unless pollution from other sources is reduced to offset increased pollution from the new or modified source. [§182(a)(4), (b)(5), (c)(10), (d)(2), (e)(1).] . . . The sanction supersedes these normal ratios by increasing the ratio in all ozone nonattainment areas to 2:1, requiring 200 tons of old pollutants to be eliminated for every 100 tons of new pollutants allowed. CAA §179(b)(2). The offset sanction, therefore, could slow the rate of industrial development within a noncomplying state.

A third sanction eliminates the state's ability to manage its own pollution control regime. If the state does not gain approval for its permit program, EPA develops and implements its own Title V permitting program within the noncomplying state. CAA §502(d)(3). . . .

III.

Virginia claims that EPA erroneously determined that Virginia's permit program contained inadequate judicial review provisions. . . . We find that EPA correctly determined that Virginia's proposed judicial review provisions do not comply with the Act. . . .

. . . [Under §502(b)(6), a] state permit program will be disapproved unless the state submits a legal opinion stating that the proposed Title V program allows state court review of permitting decisions upon the request of "the [permit] applicant, any person who participated in the public participation process . . . and any other person who could obtain judicial review of such actions under State laws." 40 C.F.R. §70.4(b)(3)(x). EPA interprets the statute and regulation to require, at a minimum, that states provide judicial review of permitting decisions to any person who would have standing under Article III of the United States Constitution.

Virginia law grants standing to seek judicial review of permitting decisions to "[a]ny owner aggrieved by" such decisions. Va. Code §10.1-1318(A). This provision satisfies CAA §502(b)(6)'s requirement that the permit "applicant" be allowed to seek judicial review. But §502(b)(6) also requires that states grant certain standing rights to members of the public, and here is where Virginia's judicial review provision falls short of the mark. Under Virginia's provision, a member of the public "who is aggrieved by a final [permitting decision] who participated, in person or by submittal of written comments, in the public comment process" may only seek judicial review of a permitting decision if he can establish that

> (i) [he] has suffered an actual, threatened, or imminent injury; (ii) such injury is an invasion of an immediate, legally protected, *pecuniary and substantial* interest which is concrete and particularized; (iii) such injury is fairly traceable to the [permitting decision] and not the result of the action of some third party not before the court; and (iv) such injury will likely be redressed by a favorable decision of the court.

Va. Code §10.1-1318(B) (emphasis supplied).

According to EPA, this provision is too restrictive: limiting availability of review to those persons with "pecuniary and substantial" interests violates CAA §502(b)(6). We agree with EPA. . . .

As Virginia reads the statute, the final clause, "who could obtain judicial review of that action under applicable [state] law," modifies all three categories of persons earlier described as being allowed to seek judicial review: "the applicant," "any person who participated in the public comment process," and "any other person." Thus, according to Virginia, §506(b)(6) requires states to grant standing to participants in the public comment process only if those persons would otherwise have standing under existing state law.

Virginia's proposed reading is contrary to ordinary principles of statutory construction and to the rules of English usage. The clause, "who could obtain judicial review of that action under applicable law," modifies only the immediately preceding category, "any other person." . . .

Properly read, the final clause simply allows the states to grant broader standing rights than those otherwise required under federal law. . . .

[The court next rejected Virginia's contention that its "pecuniary and substantial interest" requirement satisfied the statute.]

IV.

Having determined that EPA had a valid reason to disapprove Virginia's permit program, we now examine whether Title V and its sanctions provisions are constitutional. Virginia claims that Title V and its sanctions provisions are unconstitutional because they impinge upon a fundamental element of state sovereignty, the state's right to articulate its own rules of judicial standing. . . .

We agree that Congress lacks power to impinge upon "the core of sovereignty retained by the States." New York v. United States, 505 U.S. 144, 158-60 (1992). We also agree that an important aspect of a state's sovereignty is the administration of its judicial system. Thus, a state cannot be required to create a court with power to decide federal claims, if no court otherwise exists. Similarly, a state may apply neutral venue rules to require that federal claims be brought in a particular state court. But the Supremacy Clause compels state judges to apply federal law, if such law is applicable. U.S. Const. art. VI, cl. 2. Furthermore, to require an existing state administrative body to adjudicate a dispute arising under federal law does not unreasonably interfere with state sovereignty. Testa v. Katt, 330 U.S. 386 (1947) (state court must entertain civil action arising under federal Emergency Price Control Act).

. . . [W]e find that the CAA does not compel the states to modify their standing rules; it merely induces them to do so. The CAA is constitutional because although its sanctions provisions potentially burden the states, those sanctions amount to inducement rather than "outright coercion." See *New York*, 505 U.S. at 165-67. . . .

Two sources of Congressional power allow use of the highway sanction. Because the elimination of air pollution promotes the general welfare, Congress may tie the award of federal funds to the states' efforts to eliminate air pollution. . . . U.S. Const. art. I, §8, cl. 1. Furthermore, the Commerce Clause, U.S. Const. art. I, §8, cl. 3, gives Congress the power to regulate "activities causing air or water pollution, or other environmental hazards that may have effects in more than one State." Hodel v. Virginia Surface Mining & Reclamation Ass'n, 452 U.S. 264, 282 (1981).

Generally, Congress may use the power of the purse to encourage states to enact particular legislation. This power, however, is not limitless. Exercise of the power to the point of "outright coercion" violates the Constitution. . . . Also, it has been suggested that federal funds may be subject to conditions "only in ways reasonably related to the purpose for which the funds are expended." [South Dakota v. Dole, 483 U.S. 203, 213 (1987) (O'Connor, J., dissenting).] No court, however, has ever struck down a federal statute on grounds that it exceeded the Spending Power.

The highway sanction here does not rise to the level of "outright coercion." First, a state does not lose any highway funds that would be spent in areas of the state that are in attainment. CAA §179(b)(1)(A). Second, even within nonattainment areas, federal highway funds may be spent on projects designed to promote safety or designed to reduce air pollution. CAA §179(b)(1). More severe funding restrictions than those at issue here have been upheld. . . .

And contrary to what Virginia claims, the conditions on spending are reasonably related to the goal of reducing air pollution. The CAA as a whole is a comprehensive scheme to cope with the problem of air pollution from all sources. Congress may ensure that funds it allocates are not used to exacerbate the overall problem of air pollution. It is therefore of no consequence that a highway sanction, which will have the effect of reducing emissions from mobile pollution sources, is being used to induce compliance with a portion of the Act designed to reduce emissions from stationary sources.

We hold that the highway sanction, CAA §179(b)(1), is a valid exercise of the Spending Power. As a valid exercise of that power, it also comports with the requirements of the Tenth Amendment. Congress has not overstepped its bounds here. . . .

The offset sanction, CAA §179(b)(2), which limits new construction or modification of major stationary sources of air pollution, is constitutional because it regulates private pollution sources, not states.

The burden of the offset sanction falls on private parties. The more stringent offset requirements will likely make it more difficult for individual pollution sources (manufacturers, utilities, and the like) to upgrade or modify existing plants and equipment or to open new plants. Thus, although the sanction may burden some Virginia citizens, it does not burden Virginia as a governmental unit. For this reason, the sanction does not violate the principles of federalism embodied in the Tenth Amendment. . . .

The final sanction, federal permit program implementation, CAA §502(d)(3), also is constitutional. The essence of a Tenth Amendment violation is that the state is commanded to regulate. Here, Virginia is not commanded to regulate; the Commonwealth may choose to do nothing and let the federal government promulgate and enforce its own permit program within Virginia. Because "the full regulatory burden will be borne by the Federal Government," the sanction is constitutional. *Hodel*, 452 U.S. at 288.

. . . If anything, the CAA's method—to give the states a chance first to avoid imposition of any federal plan by promulgating satisfactory regulations—seems less coercive than [a statute upheld in a previous case; that statute adopted an environmental regulatory program but allowed each state to opt out of federal regulation by establishing its own program that met federal standards]. The CAA simply "establishes a program of cooperative federalism that allows the States, within limits established by federal minimum standards, to enact and administer their own regulatory programs, structured to meet their own particular needs." *Hodel*, 452 U.S. at 289.

Because Congress may choose to preempt state law completely, it may also take the less drastic step of allowing the states the ability to avoid preemption by adopting and implementing their own plans that sufficiently address congressional concerns. . . .

Finally, the CAA's sanctions provisions maintain unity between regulation and political accountability. If sanctions are imposed, it will be "the Federal Government that makes the decision in full view of the public, and it will be federal officials that suffer the consequences if the decision turns out to be detrimental or unpopular." *New York*, 505 U.S. at 168. The sanctions provisions are constitutional.

NOTES AND QUESTIONS

1. Why did Virginia's permit program provide insufficient access to the state courts for review of permitting decisions? What are the potential consequences of a state's failure to establish an operating permit program that complies with the CAA? Why did the court reject Virginia's constitutional attacks on each of the three applicable sanctions?

2. *Scope of the Title V Permit Program.* After the effective date of an approved state permit program, it is unlawful for any person required to apply for a permit issued under Title V to operate except in compliance with such a permit. §502(a). To whom

does the permit requirement apply? See id. EPA may exempt categories of nonmajor sources from the permit program if it finds that compliance is impracticable, not feasible, or unnecessarily burdensome. See also Western States Petroleum Ass'n v. EPA, 87 F.3d 280 (9th Cir. 1996) (overturning EPA's disapproval of state's attempt to exempt insignificant emissions units from Title V monitoring, reporting, and record-keeping requirements).

3. *Substantive Permit Requirements.* What must a source do to qualify for a permit? See §503. What requirements must a permit impose on the applicant? See §504(a)-(c). Under what circumstances may EPA veto a state permit? See §505(b). May EPA issue a permit despite noncompliance with Title V require-ments on the ground that the defects amounted to "harmless error"? See §505(b)(2); New York Pub. Interest Research Group, Inc. v. Whitman, 321 F.3d 316 (2d Cir. 2003). In New York Pub. Research Interest Group, Inc. v. Johnson, 427 F.3d 172 (2d Cir. 2005), EPA failed to object to New York's issuance of operating permits to two coal-fired power plants that had previously received notices of violation from the state environmental agency. The court held that EPA erred in approving them despite their failure to include compliance schedules. In addition, the imposition of quarterly reporting requirements did not comply with the requirement in §503(b)(2) that per-mittees "promptly report any deviations from permit requirements." Compare Wild-Earth Guardians v. EPA, 728 F.3d 1075 (10th Cir. 2013) (holding that the existence of a previously issued notice of violation does not, by itself, demonstrate noncompliance for purposes of §505(b)(2) or create a presumption of noncompliance and shift the burden of rebutting it to EPA). EPA has sought to promote flexibility (and market responsiveness) in Title V permitting by allowing permitted sources to make certain types of physical or operational changes without further review or approval by per-mitting authorities. Operating Permit Programs: Flexible Air Permitting Rules, 74 Fed. Reg. 51,418 (Oct. 6, 2009).

What is the effect of compliance with a properly issued permit? See §504(f). According to EPA, this "permit shield" is not available for noncompliance with appli-cable requirements that occurred before or continue after submission of a permit application.

VII

PROTECTING THE WATER RESOURCE

The river must have been wonderful when he was young. The shad would run up it in the spring and there was a run of salmon also. Now it had an oily odor from the cotton mills upstream.

J.P. Marquand, Wickford Point 92-93 (1939)

The nation's water resources have immeasurable value. . . . The *extent* of water resources (their amount and distribution) and their *condition* (physical, chemical, and biological attributes) are critical to ecosystems, human uses, and the overall function and sustainability of the hydrologic cycle.

U.S. EPA, EPA's Report on the Environment 3-3 (May 2008)

INTRODUCTION

This chapter reviews the Clean Water Act's (CWA) legal framework for controlling water pollution. A central component of the CWA is the permitting program Congress established in §402 to regulate discharges of pollutants into the waters of the United States. Much of the chapter focuses on the jurisdictional boundaries of this permitting program and on how it sets limits on pollutant discharges. The chapter covers several other significant components of the CWA as well, including the §404 permitting program, which imposes limitations on activities that involve "dredging" and "filling" wetlands and other navigable waters.

While the CWA is the centerpiece of the nation's efforts to protect our waters, numerous other federal, state, and local laws also are intended to protect these waters. These include the Safe Drinking Water Act (intended to protect U.S. water supplies), the Resource Conservation and Recovery Act (RCRA) (intended to prevent the release of hazardous wastes into our waters in certain cases; see Chapter 8), and various cleanup authorities, such as the Oil Pollution Act of 1990 and the Comprehensive Environmental Response, Compensation, and Liability Act (CERCLA) (see Chapter 9 for coverage of remediation-type approaches to environmental law).

TABLE 7-1
Conventional Pollutants: Descriptions and Examples of Impacts

Pollutant	Description	Examples of Impacts
Total suspended solids (TSS)	Organic or inorganic particles that are suspended in the water; biological solids like algal cells, bacteria	Aesthetic degradation; provides adsorption sites for various toxics like pesticides; lowers ability of light to reach bottoms of water bodies; impedes aquatic photosynthesis; clogs fish gills; biological solids may cause disease
Biochemical oxygen demand (BOD)	The amount of oxygen consumed by microbial use of organics	When more oxygen is used than is replenished, natural water bodies develop anaerobic conditions that severely impact ecology
pH	Measure of how acidic or basic the water is	pH determines how easily nutrients, heavy metals, and other constituents can be dissolved in water and made available biologically; aquatic organisms require particular pH ranges to function
Fecal coliforms	Bacteria that live in warm-blooded animals and are excreted in feces	Presences of fecal coliforms indicates possible presence of illness-causing microbes
Oil and grease	Petroleum hydrocarbons, vegetable oils, natural oils (e.g., fats)	Possible toxic impacts; clogging of sewer pipes

A.   WATER POLLUTANTS AND THE STATE OF THE NATION'S WATERS

Common Water Pollutants. Water pollution can be just as varied as air pollution, as described in Chapter 6. However, it is helpful to be familiar with a few different types of water pollutants. Table 7-1 sets forth conventional pollutants, their descriptions, and examples of their impacts. See 40 C.F.R. §401.16 (listing conventional pollutants). Other important pollutants are temperature, color, nutrients (such as nitrogen and phosphorous, both of which can lead to the degradation of water bodies), and toxics.

Causes and Sources of Impairment. The causes and sources of impairment of our nation's waters vary by type of water body. EPA's chart depicting the major causes and sources of impairment is reproduced as Table 7-2.

As Table 7-2 reflects, there are significant differences between types of water bodies in terms of the causes and sources of impairment. Moreover, there is insufficient information to determine some sources. Once again, full evaluations are expensive and difficult to obtain. As you read about the CWA framework in the materials that follow, ask yourself how regulation under that statute could be tailored to better obtain data as well as to address water-body-specific causes and sources of impairment.

TABLE 7-2

Leading Causes of Impairment in Assessed Rivers, Lakes, and Estuaries and Leading Sources of Impairment in Assessed Rivers, Lakes, and Estuaries

	Rivers and Streams	*Lakes, Ponds, and Reservoirs*	*Estuaries*
Causes	Pathogens	Mercury	Pathogens
	Habitat alterations	PCBs	Organic enrichment
	Organic enrichment	Nutrients	Mercury
Sources	Agriculture	Atmospheric deposition	Atmospheric deposition
	Hydromodification	Unknown/unspecified	Unknown/unspecified
	Unknown/unspecified*	Agriculture	Municipal discharges

* Source unknown or undocumented due to insufficient information.

Source: EPA, National Water Quality Inventory: Report to Congress for the 2004 Reporting Cycle—A Profile (Jan. 2009).

Impacts. EPA describes the impacts of water pollution on public and environmental health as follows:

> Water pollution threatens public health both directly through the consumption of contaminated food or drinking water, and indirectly through skin exposure to contaminants present in recreational or bathing waters. Contaminants that threaten human health include toxic chemicals and waterborne disease-causing pathogens such as viruses, bacteria, and protozoans.
>
> Some of the problems caused by toxic and pathogen contamination include fish, wildlife, and shellfish consumption advisories, drinking water closures, and recreational (e.g., swimming) restrictions. [EPA, National Water Quality Inventory 2000 Report, ES-4.]

A Look at the Quality of Our Nation's Waters. Over 40 years of regulatory efforts under the CWA to reduce water pollution have achieved considerable progress, at considerable cost. Major municipal and industrial sources, in particular, have installed required technology and eliminated billions of tons of sewage, chemicals, and trash from the nation's waterways, at a cost of billions of dollars. See Stoner, Celebrate the 40th Anniversary of the Clean Water Act, http://blog.epa.gov/blog/2012/10/cwa40 (Oct. 18, 2012). As Professor Robert Adler notes, "[a]s far as it goes, the CWA has been among the nation's more successful environmental statutes. . . . [T]he law has resulted in significant progress in improving the quality of the Nation's waters." Adler, Resilience, Restoration, and Sustainability: Revisiting the Fundamental Principles of the Clean Water Act, 32 Wash U. J.L. & Pol'y 139, 172 (2010); see also Houck, The Clean Water Act TMDL Program: Law, Policy, and Implementation 3-4 (ELI 2d ed. 2002) [hereafter Houck, TMDL] (lauding CWA's accomplishments).

Despite this progress, however, our waters remain impaired. In a 2009 report based on the most recent inventory of our nation's waters, EPA reported that 44 percent of assessed stream miles, 64 percent of assessed lake acres, and 30 percent of assessed bay and estuarine square miles were "not clean enough to support uses such as fishing and swimming." EPA, National Water Quality Inventory: Report to Congress, 2004 Reporting Cycle—A Profile (Jan. 2009) [hereinafter NWQI 2004]. Table 7-3 presents EPA's summary of the quality of assessed rivers, lakes, and estuaries.

TABLE 7-3
Summary of the Quality of Assessed Rivers, Lakes, and Estuaries

Water Body Type*	Total Size	Amount Assessed (% of Total)	Good (% of Assessed)	Good but Threatened (% of Assessed)	Polluted (% of Assessed)
Rivers (miles)	3,533,205	563,955 (16)	302,255 (53)	15,698 (3)	246,002 (44)
Lakes (acres)	41.7 million	16,230,384 (39)	5,619,221 (35)	159,761 (1)	10,451,402 (64)
Estuaries (sq. miles)	87,791	25,399 (29)	17,721 (70)	37 (<1)	7,641 (30)

* Includes water bodies assessed as not attainable for one or more uses.

Note: Percentages may not add up to 100 due to rounding.

Source: EPA, National Water Quality Inventory: Report to Congress for the 2004 Reporting Cycle—A Profile (Jan. 2009).

As Table 7-3 reflects, data concerning the quality of our nation's waters is extremely limited. Notice that the "Amount Assessed" column shows that the data above include only 16 percent of the nation's miles of rivers and streams, 39 percent of the nation's lakes, ponds, and reservoirs, and 29 percent of the nation's bays and estuaries. Thus, fewer than 30 percent of all the nation's waters were part of this water quality inventory. In its report, EPA suggested that non-assessed waters are actually more likely than assessed waters to meet designated uses because "many states target their limited monitoring resources to waters that they suspect are impaired. . . ." Id. at 1. Professor Oliver Houck offers a more critical interpretation: "[w]e have been spared knowing how polluted our waters are by the simple fact that we have not made a serious effort to find out." Houck, TMDL, at 4. There are, of course, many reasons for the incompleteness of the inventory. Water systems are expansive and complex, and it can be difficult to distinguish chronic from transient impairment. Obtaining credible, quality-controlled data, with properly calibrated and operated equipment, requires substantial resources.

NOTES AND QUESTIONS ON THE QUALITY OF OUR NATION'S WATERS

1. *"Big Picture" Assessments of the CWA and the Status of Our Nation's Waters.* The modern version of the CWA was adopted more than 40 years ago, in 1972. Several retrospectives have been published that provide varied perspectives on the progress that has been made and the challenges that remain. See, e.g., Adler, *supra*; Andreen, Success and Backlash: the Remarkable (Continuing) Story of the Clean Water Act, 4 J. of Energy & Envtl. L. 25 (Winter 2013); Glicksman & Batzel, Science, Politics, Law, and the Arc of the Clean Water Act: The Role of Assumptions in the Adoption of a Pollution Control Landmark, 32 Wash U. J.L. & Pol'y 99 (2010); Symposium: The Clean Water Act at 40, 4 Geo. Wash. J. Energy & Envtl. L. 1 (2013). EPA's 2014 Report on the Environment assesses trends in the quality of the nation's waters, evaluates causes of water quality concerns, and identifies possible effects of water pollution. See http://www.epa.gov/roe. Clean Water: Foundation of Healthy Communities

and a Healthy Environment (April 2011), summarizes ongoing initiatives by a variety of federal agencies, including EPA, the Army Corps of Engineers, USDA, and DOI, to preserve water quality.[a]

2. *The Need for More and Better Data.* Data gathering concerning the quality of our nation's waters extends far beyond EPA and state National Water Quality Inventory reporting. For example, EPA issued a draft National Lakes Assessment in December 2009, which the agency characterized as the first statistical survey of the condition of U.S. lakes, ponds, and reservoirs. 41 Env't Rep. (BNA) 25 (Jan. 1, 2010). But others argue that much more is needed. See, e.g., The H. John Heinz Center for Science, Economics, and the Environment, The State of the Nation's Ecosystems: Measuring the Lands, Waters, and Living Resources of the United States (2008), at 2 ("In too many cases, information on the state of our surroundings is isolated, overly technical, not comparable from one place to another, or simply unavailable.").

3. *Protecting Our Waters Is an Expensive Enterprise.* EPA has estimated that the nation's water quality needs exceed $298.1 billion. EPA, Clean Watersheds Needs Survey 2008: Report to Congress (June 2010), at v. These funds are needed mainly for infrastructure rehabilitation, increasing water quality standards, and responding to population growth. Id. at vi. Indeed, overall infrastructure—much of it related to water resources and water quality—is in need of upgrading and rehabilitation. In its 2013 report card, for example, the American Society of Civil Engineers gave an overall grade of "D" to the nation's wastewater treatment infrastructure. 2013 Report Card for America's Infrastructure, http://www.infrastructurereportcard.org/a/#p/overview/executive-summary.

Yet substantial funds have already been spent on water treatment. Total public and private spending on water pollution control between 1972 and 1996 is estimated at $700 billion. J.C. Davies & J. Mazurek, Pollution Control in the United States: Evaluating the System 70 (1998). Under the 1987 amendments to the CWA, EPA, in conjunction with the states, administers a Clean Water State Revolving Fund, which provides loans for water-related infrastructure upgrades, nonpoint source management activities, and other water-protection projects. Further, the 2009 stimulus bill, the American Recovery and Reinvestment Act (ARRA), included significant sums for clean water and drinking water infrastructure funding. A May 2011 EPA report indicated that, of the $6 billion in ARRA funds provided to EPA for clean water and drinking water state revolving funds, a total of $5.6 billion in agreements had been signed by March 2010 for a total of 3,200 assistance grants. $3.8 billion is being used for wastewater projects and $1.8 billion for drinking water projects.[b] Yet a January 2013 American Society of Civil Engineers report indicated that "[i]f current trends continue, $126 billion will be needed for drinking water and wastewater infrastructure by 2020, leaving an anticipated funding gap of $84 billion. . . ." Infrastructure Deficit

a. For a National Association of Clean Water Agencies assessment of trends in water quality and steps needed to improve conditions, see NACWA, Money Matters, Smarter Investment to Advance Clean Water: Two Sides of the Same Coin, Increased Investment & Regulatory Prioritization (March 2011). For a recent EPA take, see EPA, Coming Together for Clean Water: EPA's Strategy to Protect America's Waters (March 28, 2011), https://blog.epa.gov/waterforum/wp-content/uploads/2011/04/ComingTogether-for-Clean-Water-FINAL.pdf. Another perspective is provided in Charting New Waters, Financing Sustainable Infrastructure (Jan. 2012), http://www.johnsonfdn.org/sites/default/files/reports_publications/WaterInfrastructure.pdf.

b. EPA, Implementation of the American Recovery & Reinvestment Act of 2009: Clean Water & Drinking Water State Revolving Fund Programs 4, 5, 7 (May 2011). http://water.epa.gov/aboutow/eparecovery/upload/epa-WEB-ar-arra-May2011.pdf.

Will Be $84 Billion by 2020 Unless Measures Taken, ASCE Says, 44 Env't Rep. (BNA) 164 (Jan. 18, 2013). See ASCE, Failure to Act: the Impact of Current Infrastructure Investment on America's Economic Future (Jan. 2013), http://www .asce.org/economicstudy.

4. *Is It Worth It?* Determining the benefits and costs of pollution control strategies is complex. The challenges associated with evaluating the appropriateness of expenditures are illustrated by a 1994 EPA study aimed at calculating the marginal costs and benefits of improvements in water pollution control, such as control of urban sewer and stormwater overflow and the reduction of toxic pollutants. The study found that quantified benefits did not exceed the costs but that reduction initiatives should proceed because of cost calculation uncertainties and the number of benefits for which monetary estimates have not been developed. Davies & Mazurek, *supra*, at 132-133.

This study raises the issue of how difficult it can be to monetize costs and benefits. Metrics other than dollars can be important. For example, an EPA study framed improvements in terms of impacts to the population when it stated that, while capital expenditures are increasingly needed, the nation is "making significant progress in providing wastewater treatment. . . . [T]he number of people provided with advanced wastewater treatment increased dramatically (from 7.8 million people in 1972 to 113.0 million people in 2008). Moreover, the population served by less-than-secondary treatment decreased from more than 50 million in 1972 to 3.8 million in 2008." EPA, Clean Watershed Needs Survey 2008: Report to Congress (June 2010), at ix.

5. *Where Are We Going?* The first generation of CWA administration assumed that the major sources of pollution were industrial and municipal discharges and that pollution could be substantially reduced through technology. We now recognize that a more integrated pollution control approach is necessary to achieve healthy aquatic ecosystems because other sources of pollution, including land use practices, continue to frustrate attainment of the CWA's goals. New objectives include restoring degraded aquatic ecosystems, establishing baselines for the maintenance of ecologically functioning systems, and controlling nonpoint source pollution. See Adler, *supra*. Professor Adler suggests that "our virtually exclusive implementation focus on the discharge of chemical pollutants has been at the expense of efforts to redress other forms of pollution. . . . Spending limited resources tilting at the zero discharge windmill while ignoring so many other sources of impairment may not reflect the best use of society's resources. . . ." Id. at 150.

Efforts to reduce concentrations of phosphorus and nitrogen have received considerable attention in recent years and have been a source of tension between EPA and several states. Environmental, agricultural, and industrial interests have raised concerns about developments in this arena as well, including development of numeric criteria as benchmarks. For a 2011 framework-level take on the challenges involved, see Nancy K. Stoner, Memorandum, EPA Acting Assistant Administrator, Working in Partnership with States to Address Phosphorus and Nitrogen Pollution Through Use of a Framework for State Nutrient Reductions (March 16, 2011).

6. *Security Issues.* As one might expect, because of the attacks on September 11, 2001, and their aftermath, the government has focused attention on the security of the nation's water infrastructure. The Council on Foreign Relations, for example, has concluded that "drinking water remains vulnerable to mass destruction." Drinking Water: U.S. Water Supply Vulnerable to Attacks, Council on Foreign Relations

Report Says, 214 Daily Env't Rep. (BNA) A-9 (Nov. 5, 2002). Congress enacted the Public Health Security and Bioterrorism Preparedness and Response Act of 2002, which, among other things, amends the Safe Drinking Water Act to require larger utilities to assess the vulnerability of their systems to terrorism and to file those assessments with EPA. In 2003, EPA established a "permanent homeland security office" to be housed in the Office of the Administrator. A 2006 survey of the U.S. Conference of Mayors found that security relating to drinking water and wastewater facilities, as well as the need to update the aging infrastructure of such facilities, are major concerns. Mayors List Aged Infrastructure, Supply, Security Among Chief Water Priorities, 17 Daily Env't Rep. (BNA) A-12 (Jan. 26, 2006). EPA has created an "action plan" to address water security issues and in 2005 issued a progress report on the action plan. http://www.epa.gov/nhsrc/pubs/600r05104.pdf.

7. *The Possible Impacts of Climate Change on Our Water Resources.* EPA actively considers possible ways to mitigate the adverse impacts of climate change on water resources. Beginning in 2008, it has issued recurring reports on responding to climate change as well as updates on progress already made. See, e.g., EPA National Water Program 2012 Strategy: Response to Climate Change, http://water.epa.gov/scitech/climatechange/2012-National-Water-Program-Strategy.cfm. States have also been active in planning for, and responding to climate change. For an overview of some of the approaches, see Chapter 12, section E.3.

B. BACKGROUND ON WATER POLLUTION REGULATION

In 1607, the first English colonists in the Chesapeake Bay region drew their drinking water from the often-brackish James River estuary, which ebbed and flowed past the shores of the swampy island that was to be called Jamestown. In doing so, they exposed themselves to disease-carrying bacteria from their own wastes (according to a theory of a twentieth century historian) and subjected themselves to gradual salt poisoning from the brackish water. Those who sickened and died may have been the first recorded victims of water pollution in the Bay. [F. Capper et al., Governing Chesapeake Waters: A History of Water Quality Controls on Chesapeake Bay, 1607-1972 (1983), citing C. Earle, Environment, Disease and Mortality in Early Virginia, in The Chesapeake in the Seventeenth Century 96 (T. Tate & D. Ammorman eds., 1979).]

1. Nineteenth-Century Water Pollution Problems and Legal Responses

Until the nineteenth century, the major water pollution problem was fecal contamination. Cities relied on the natural waste-assimilative capacity of oceans, lakes, and rivers or on cesspools, privy vaults, and scavenger systems. As a seventeenth-century English visitor to Venice observed, "Though the flood or ebb of salt water bee [sic] small, yet with that motion it carried away the filth of the city." C. Hibbert, Venice: The Biography of a City 131 (1989). Other cities, such as London, were not so lucky, experiencing virulent cholera epidemics as a result of contamination of drinking water supplies by human waste. Eventually the discovery of the relationship between germs and illness, and specifically the role of polluted water in spreading infections, led to widespread sanitation efforts to eliminate germs or to avoid contact with their sources. By 1920, most large public drinking water supplies were using chlorination to kill disease-causing microbes. See J. Tarr, The Search for the Ultimate Sink: Urban Pollution in Historical Perspective (1996). Using chlorine to disinfect drinking water was a great public health advance (it is now recognized that some chlorination by-products are also carcinogens; EPA regulates their concentrations). See S. Putnam & J. Wiener, Seeking Safe Drinking Water, in Risk versus Risk: Tradeoffs in Protecting Health and the Environment 124 (J. Graham & J. Wiener eds., 1995); see also EPA, Stage 2 Disinfectants and Disinfection Byproducts Rule, 71 Fed. Reg. 388 (Jan. 4, 2006). But until the mid-twentieth century industrial waste practices were virtually unrestrained because industrial pollution was not seen as a major public health threat.

2.   *The Twentieth-Century Evolution of Federal Water Pollution Control Policy*

Until after World War II, pollution control was assumed to be a local and state responsibility. Chapter 6 traced the evolution of the shift from local and state to federal responsibility in air pollution regulation. The shift is similar for water pollution, although the federal interest in the quality of navigable waters precedes its interest in air pollution.

Federal water pollution control policy has moved through three stages and is moving into a fourth. The first three stages were (1) post hoc federal actions against those who had discharged substances into navigable waters; (2) a federal-state effort to dedicate different waters to varying levels of waste assimilation, with federal enforcement as a last resort; and (3) a federal effort to reduce pollution by imposing technology-based standards on effluent discharges, as opposed to setting standards for the quality of receiving waters, with state enforcement of federal policy. The technology-based effluent limitations strategy, put in place in 1972, is at the heart of CWA. But increasing emphasis is being given to ambient-based strategies and to the protection of healthy ecosystems. See R. Adler, Integrated Approaches to Water Pollution: Lessons from the Clean Air Act, 23 Harv. Envtl. L. Rev. 203 (1999).

a.   Post Hoc Actions Against Discharges

Because of the federal government's traditional interest in protecting navigation, federal water pollution control legislation existed long before air pollution control legislation. The oldest surviving statute of current interest is §13 of the Rivers and Harbors Act of 1899. This simple statute, which grew out of efforts to regulate potential obstructions to navigation, prohibits the discharge of "any refuse matter of any kind or description whatever other than that flowing from streets and sewers and passing therefrom in a liquid state," without a permit from the Secretary of the Army, 33 U.S.C. §407. The measurement and control of water pollution have become much more scientific and technical, but the Rivers and Harbors Act's legacy establishing pollution as any discharge of a foreign substance into a body of water had a profound influence on CWA jurisprudence.

b. Water Use Zoning

Until 1948, the federal government's role in pollution control was limited to special problems, such as refuse discharged into navigable waters and oil spills. The Federal Water Pollution Control Act of 1948 expanded the federal government's role. The surgeon general was authorized to conduct investigations; make grants to state and local agencies for research; make loans for the construction of treatment works; and declare interstate pollution a public nuisance, although the necessary investigation to determine if a nuisance in fact existed could not begin unless the local agency authorized it. In 1956 federal efforts were strengthened when Congress began to subsidize the construction of sewage treatment works. See Wilson, Legal Aspects of Water Pollution Control, in U.S. Department of Health, Education, and Welfare, Proceedings: The National Conference on Water Pollution 354, 364-369 (1961).

By the end of the 1950s, a consensus was emerging among key legislators that would expand the federal role. See Federal-State Relations in Transition: Implications for Environmental Policy, A Report Prepared by the Congressional Research Service of the Library of Congress for the Committee on Environment and Public Works, S. Rep. No. 87-52, at 3-32 (1962). Northern states, which had so-so track records for cleaning up their waters, became increasingly concerned that southern and western states were trying to lure industry with their low water quality standards, and thus the industrialized states began to support the idea of minimum standards for federal water quality. See D. Carr, Death of the Sweet Waters: The Politics of Pollution (1966). The idea also found some support among industry. A similar tolerance—or even preference—among the large firms in an industry for federal regulation as a means of eliminating competition from smaller firms was first noted in G. Kolko, The Triumph of Conservatism (1960), and this observation was applied to the pollution field in W. Tucker, Progress and Privilege: America in the Age of Environmentalism (1982).

At an important National Conference on Water Pollution in 1959, the assistant surgeon general offered the following reason for the emergence of water pollution as a national problem:

> Prior to 1940, there was a somewhat orderly transition from a rural to an industrial economy. Cities were still separate entities, generally with appreciable distances between shocks of pollution. Industries were in or near cities. Pollution, for the most part, was natural organic materials with concentrations of biological contaminants. Improvements in water treatment and extension of waste treatment kept the scales reasonably in balance. Excessive pollution, where it occurred, was still largely localized and over short stretches of streams.
>
> Since 1940, three major influences have aggravated the pollution situation. All three are World War II related:
>
> 1. There was a fantastically increased tempo in the transition to metropolitan and industrial development—the formation of gigantic metropolitan complexes extending

> hundreds of miles generally following major watercourses. Industries go where there is water and populations build up where there is industry.
> 2. There was practically no construction of municipal or industrial waste treatment works over the period 1940 to 1947. Men and materials were needed for the war effort.
> 3. The avalanche of technological progress brought with it a whole array of new-type contaminants, such as synthetic chemicals and radioactive wastes. Production and use of such materials continue upward at substantial rates. [Hollis, The Water Pollution Image, in Proceedings of the National Conference on Water Pollution 30, 32 (1961).]

The Water Quality Act of 1965 required all states to enact water quality standards for interstate navigable waters, although many states already had such standards in place. It empowered the federal government to convene a conference and to investigate pollution problems and remedies, if the pollution substantially endangered the health of citizens in another state or if substantial injury would result in those attempting to market shellfish in interstate commerce. The governor of an injured state could request and thereby trigger a federal government conference. If the pollution was wholly intrastate, the governor had the exclusive right to determine if a federal conference would be convened. Amendments in 1966 increased the federal contribution to sewage treatment plants and initiated funding of water quality planning programs.

Professor N. William Hines described the 1965 Act's "water quality standards zone" approach of allocating assimilative uses for different reaches of a stream.

> The water quality standards . . . involve three essential components: First, a determination is made concerning the present and future uses to be made of each body or stretch of interstate water. . . . Second, the specific water quality characteristics allowed or required for such uses must be identified and descriptive or numerical values established for each of them. . . . The third component of the standards is a precise, detailed plan for achieving and preserving the criteria established, including such ingredients as preventive steps, construction schedules, enforcement actions, surveillance and monitoring. [Hines, Controlling Industrial Water Pollution: Color the Problem Green, 9 B.C. Indus. & Com. L. Rev. 553, 585-586 (1968).]

Professor Hines has written the definitive history of the evolution of federal water pollution control policy prior to the Clean Water Act of 1972: Nor Any Drop to Drink: Public Regulation of Water Quality, Part I: State Pollution Control Programs, 52 Iowa L. Rev. 186 (1966); Part II: Interstate Arrangements for Pollution Control, 52 Iowa L. Rev. 432 (1966); Part III: The Federal Effort, 52 Iowa L. Rev. 799 (1967).

c. The Clean Water Act: An Overview

(1) Goals

In 1972, Congress concluded that the water quality approach was not working. The amendments it adopted that year departed from the 1965-1966 legislation in three major ways. First, Congress substituted the goal of no pollution discharges for the goal of calibrating discharges to water use. Second, a two-tiered system of progressively higher technology-based effluent limitations supplemented existing water quality standards. Third, the federal role in setting water pollution policy was expanded substantially, though states were assigned a significant role if they enacted qualifying programs.

In the Senate debate, Senator Edmund Muskie likened water pollution to cancer and offered the following explanation for a control-at-any-cost strategy:

> Can we afford clean water? Can we afford rivers and lakes and streams and life itself? Those questions were never asked as we destroyed the waters of our Nation, and they deserve no answers as we finally move to restore and renew them. These questions answer themselves. [Senate Consideration of the Report of the Conference Comm., Oct. 4, 1972, reprinted in Senate Comm. on Public Works, 1 Legislative History of the Water Pollution Control Act Amendments of 1972, S. Rep. No. 93-1, at 164 (1973) (hereinafter cited as 1972 Legislative History).]

The structure of the CWA can be analyzed in terms of multiple levels of commands. First, the lofty objective of CWA §101(a) is "to restore and maintain the chemical, physical, and biological integrity of the Nation's waters." Only slightly less lofty are the national goal in CWA §101(a)(1) "that the discharge of pollutants into the navigable waters be eliminated by 1985" and the §101(a)(2) interim goal that by 1983, "wherever attainable," waters be made fishable and swimmable. The national objective and the interim goal, however, are not directly enforceable. Rather, Congress chose to further achievement of these goals indirectly, in part through creation of technology-based effluent limitation standards. These standards also were to serve as objectives in and of themselves:

> The Congressional debate makes it clear that supporters of the 1972 amendments saw them as an explicit rejection of ambient water quality standards, either as a feasible basis for determining effluent reduction or as a basis for enforcement. Rather, if technology allows an effluent limitation to be achieved, it should be done. [Freeman, Air and Water Pollution Policy, in Current Issues in U.S. Environmental Policy 12, 48 (1978).]

Was it a good idea for Congress to establish unenforceable and unachievable objectives and goals? The major environmentalist argument for unenforceable goals has been that they help to hold Congress's and regulators' feet to the fire. The contrary case is that symbolic legislation obscures the difficult policy choices that must be made to achieve the objective and delays the rational resolution of regulatory problems. Dwyer, The Pathology of Symbolic Legislation, 17 Ecology L.Q. 233 (1990); see also Lazarus, The Tragedy of Distrust in the Implementation of Federal Environmental Law, 54 Law & Contemp. Probs. 311 (1991).

(2) Structure

What the Act Regulates. The CWA divides pollution into two fundamental categories: (1) pollution from point sources; and (2) pollution from nonpoint sources. The legal definition of a point source is complicated (see section C.2 of this chapter), but for our immediate purposes it can be defined as a confined discharge; envision a pipe emptying treated wastewater into a large lake or river. Point sources are subjected to a two-level reduction standard that initially relies on the adopting effluent reduction technology, with limited consideration of the costs versus the benefits of effluent reduction. In addition to "technology-based controls," point sources also may be subject to water quality–based controls if necessary for the receiving waters to meet water quality standards.

Point sources are regulated under the National Pollutant Discharge Elimination System (NPDES) permit program. Under the "new federalism" in vogue in the early 1970s, states were permitted to administer their own programs if they met federal standards. The vast majority of states (currently 46) now are authorized to administer the NPDES permit program. http://cfpub.epa.gov/npdes/statestats.cfm. NPDES permits establish the effluent limitations a discharger must meet and the deadline for meeting them. Applications for NPDES permits are considered by the relevant state agency or EPA in adjudicatory proceedings. Federal regulations for federally issued NPDES permits can be found at 40 C.F.R. §122.

The CWA focuses primarily on two classes of point sources, municipal sewage treatment plants and industrial discharges. Both types of point sources must apply for, and operate in compliance with, an NPDES permit issued by either the federal government or a qualified state program. Sewage treatment works are subject to technology-based standards known as "primary" and "secondary" treatment. CWA §301(b)(1)(B). Publicly owned sewage treatment plants (POTWs) at first were eligible for grants to upgrade their treatment systems, but these grants have given way to a revolving loan program. POTWs accept wastewater from industries as well as households; industries that discharge pollutants into POTWs are known as "indirect dischargers" (because the industrial entity is not discharging its effluent directly into a navigable water, but is instead sending the effluent to a POTW for treatment before it is discharged). Indirect industrial dischargers may be required to pretreat their effluent before sending it to a POTW. Indirect dischargers are to control their effluent discharges into the POTWs so that they do not interfere with the operation of the POTW or contribute to or cause exceedance of the POTW's permit limits. CWA §307(b)(1); 40 C.F.R. §403.5. Municipal sewage treatment plants are discussed in more detail in section G below.

Direct industrial dischargers have been subject to various levels of technology-based controls and treatment over the years. The minimum level of treatment required is known as best practicable control technology currently available (BPT). Dischargers initially were to be in compliance with limits based on such technologies by 1977. Dischargers then were to meet limits based on more stringent technology-based standards, known as best available technology economically achievable (BAT or BATEA), by 1983 (§301(b)(2)(A)). These deadlines have been extended over the years.

Technology-Based Standards. The 1977 amendments divided pollutants into three classes: conventional, nonconventional, and toxic. BAT is still required for nonconventional and toxic pollutants, but conventional pollutants are subject to a less rigorous treatment standard, BCT (best conventional pollutant control technology). EPA categorizes conventional pollutants as biochemical oxygen demand (BOD), total suspended solids, fecal coliform bacteria, pH, and oil and grease. The BCT limitations for pollutants must be at least as stringent as BPT limits. In addition to BPT, BAT, and BCT, there are new source performance standards known as BADT (best available demonstrated control technology), which are similar in some ways to those in the Clean Air Act (described in Chapter 6). CWA §306. Determining the technology (or technologies) qualifying as BPT, BAT, and so on, often is no easy matter. Congress has provided somewhat different methodologies for EPA to use in making these determinations, and EPA's judgments often are subject to legal challenge, as discussed in more detail below. Technology-based standards for direct industrial dischargers are covered in more detail in section D below.

Water Quality Standards. The CWA establishes a second line of defense to water pollution, known as "water quality standards," to complement technology-based standards. Water quality-based controls are known as the "safety net" feature of the CWA regulatory scheme because the Act requires that permits be based on more stringent water quality-based standards when technology-based standards fail to achieve applicable water quality standards. CWA §301(b)(1)(C). The Supreme Court explains that "[t]hese state water quality standards provide 'a supplementary basis . . . so that . . . point sources, despite individual compliance with [technology-based] effluent limitations, may be further regulated to prevent water quality from falling below acceptable levels.' " PUD No. 1 of Jefferson County v. Washington Dep't of Ecology, 511 U.S. 700, 704 (1994) (quoting EPA v. California ex rel. State Water Res. Control Bd., 426 U.S. 200, 205 (1976)). In addition, water quality standards embody a concept known as "antidegradation," which is intended to limit, and in some cases prevent, degradation in the quality of waters that meet water quality standards. Many observers expect water quality–based controls to play an increasingly important role in managing discharges to address the remaining deficiencies in water quality. Implementing a water quality–based approach will not be simple or fast. As indicated at the outset, Congress focused on implementation of a technology-based approach in 1972 in part because of the failure of the ambient-based approach that had been used up to that point. Two of the outstanding questions at this point are (1) whether we have learned enough over the past 40 years to produce better results with an ambient-based approach than we achieved the last time, and (2) whether the tools the CWA provides are adequate to enable us to achieve our goals. Water quality standards are discussed in more detail in section E below.

Nonpoint sources have long been considered less amenable to add-on technologies because they require changes in land use activities—such as agriculture, mining, forestry, and construction—that cause runoff into streams. The CWA traditionally has subjected nonpoint source controls to softer, state-run planning and management programs and best practice standards. See section H below.

Section 404 Permits. The CWA also includes a second permitting scheme, in §404, that covers discharges of dredge and fill material (see section I below) and the Act addresses oil spills as well, in a separate section, §311, 33 U.S.C. §1321. A series of spills in 1989 revived interest in this section and in the natural resources damage assessment standards developed under Superfund. See Chapter 9, section D.3. In response to the *Exxon Valdez* and other spectacular oil spills, Congress enacted the Oil Pollution Act of 1990, Pub. L. No. 101-380, 104 Stat. 484. The Oil Pollution Act retains prior federal legislation, but liability is now determined by the Act. The 2010 oil spill in the Gulf of Mexico triggered renewed interest in liability for spills. Liability- or remediation-based approaches to environmental regulation of the sort embodied by §311 and the OPA are covered in detail in Chapter 9. Some of the enforcement issues are covered in Chapter 10.

C.   THE CWA'S NPDES PERMIT PROGRAM FOR POINT SOURCES: JURISDICTIONAL BOUNDARIES

Section 301 of the Clean Water Act generally makes unlawful the discharge of any pollutant. This general proscription, however, is subject to several qualifications. This section focuses on one of the most significant exceptions, notably that a party may discharge pollutants if it has obtained a NPDES permit under CWA §402 that authorizes the discharge.

NPDES permitting jurisdiction extends to discharges that satisfy the following four elements: (1) addition (2) of a pollutant (3) from a point source (4) into a navigable water. See CWA §§502(7), (12), (14). The rest of this section explores all four elements in reverse order. The definition of "navigable waters" in particular has raised significant issues concerning the scope of congressional power under the Commerce Clause.

1.   *"Navigable Waters"*

A major element required to trigger NPDES jurisdiction is that a discharge be to "navigable waters," defined in CWA §502(7) as "waters of the United States. . . ." Issues of constitutional as well as statutory interpretation have been in the forefront of efforts to determine the types of waters that Congress intended, and is empowered, to reach in the exercise of its regulatory powers.

a.   Constitutional Power to Regulate Water Pollution

All federal environmental regulation must be grounded in an enumerated power of the Constitution. The most obvious source of federal power to regulate water pollution is the Commerce Clause, art. 1, §8, cl. 3. For several decades the constitutional power of Congress to regulate any form of point or nonpoint pollution of surface water, wetlands, and groundwater under the Commerce Clause was assumed to rest on Wickard v. Filburn, 317 U.S. 111 (1942), which upheld regulation of intrastate activities that cumulatively had a substantial effect on interstate commerce, and the Court's post–New Deal era deference to congressional conclusions about the nexus between a regulated activity and interstate commerce. However, in 1995, the Court refused to defer to Congress for the first time in 59 years. United States v. Lopez, 514 U.S. 549 (1995), held that Congress lacked the authority under the Commerce Clause to enact the Gun-Free School Zones Act, which made it a federal crime to possess a firearm in a school zone.

What are the constitutional boundaries on Congress's ability to define the scope of navigable waters? This question has become central to defining the jurisdictional boundaries of the CWA. As you will see from the materials that follow, the U.S. Supreme Court has avoided the question by adopting limiting interpretations of the term "navigable waters." But understanding that this issue is lurking behind the Court's opinions is important to fully appreciating their meaning. Indeed, it is impossible to separate entirely questions of constitutional interpretation from issues of statutory construction; thus, while we introduce the former here, we address them to some extent below as well.

b. Statutory Boundaries on the Regulation of Water Pollution

Why did the constitutional question arise? The key lies in the CWA's definition of navigable waters: "waters of the United States." CWA §502(7). This definition is perplexing when viewed against the history of the term. Consider this early definition:

> Those rivers must be regarded as public navigable rivers in law which are navigable in fact. And they are navigable in fact when they are used, or are susceptible of being used, in their ordinary condition, as highways for commerce, over which trade and travel are or may be conducted in the customary modes of trade and travel on water. And they constitute navigable waters of the United States within the meaning of the acts of Congress, in contradistinction from the navigable waters of the States, when they form in their ordinary condition by themselves, or by uniting with other waters, a continued highway over which commerce is or may be carried on with other States or foreign countries in the customary modes in which such commerce is conducted by water.

The Daniel Ball, 77 U.S. 557, 563 (1870). The Rivers and Harbors Act incorporated this definition of navigability—that is, as meaning "navigable in fact." Although the meaning of navigability was refined over the years, see United States v. Appalachian Elec. Power Co., 311 U.S. 377 (1940), it continued to carry this basic meaning.

But by using the broad definition "waters of the United States," Congress seemingly meant to reach more broadly than it had in the past. But how broadly? Has Congress exercised the full extent of its Commerce Clause power by using this definition? If so, where does that power end?

This issue has presented a conundrum for the federal agencies charged with administering the CWA (that is, both EPA and the Army Corps of Engineers (the Corps)). Both agencies have struggled to establish workable boundaries that are consistent with congressional direction and constitutional limits. It is widely recognized that the courts have muddied the waters considerably. The Supreme Court has issued three prominent opinions on this issue, in 1985 (Riverside Bayview), 2001 (SWANCC), and 2006 (Rapanos). Each case considered the definition of navigable waters in the context of the CWA §404 program, administered by the Corps and discussed below, but this definition is also relevant to the scope of the NPDES permit program, the TMDL program, and water quality certifications.

Riverside Bayview. In the first of these decisions, United States v. Riverside Bayview Homes, Inc., 474 U.S. 121 (1985), the Court considered the Corps' requirement that landowners obtain §404 permits before discharging fill material into wetlands adjacent to navigable bodies of water and their tributaries. Although the Corps had initially interpreted "navigable waters" in the CWA to mean navigable in fact, it revised its definition in 1975 to also cover, among other things, tributaries to such waters, interstate waters and their tributaries, and wetlands adjacent to other covered waters. The respondents in the case owned 80 acres of marshy land in Michigan, which they began filling in preparation for constructing a housing development. The Corps believed the property was an adjacent wetland, and filed suit to enjoin filling the property without a permit.

The Court upheld the Corps' definition. Recognizing that it is not always obvious where the division between dry land and "waters" lies, and considering the CWA's broad purposes of restoring and maintaining water quality, the Court reasoned that a view of "waters" that includes ecosystems and the hydrologic cycle was consistent with the Act's purpose. Thus, the Court recognized that the Congress intended "navigable waters" to include "at least some waters that would not be deemed 'navigable' under the classical understanding of that term." Id. at 133. The Court wrote:

> We cannot say that the Corps' conclusion that adjacent wetlands are inseparably bound up with the "waters" of the United States—based as it is on the Corps' and EPA's technical expertise—is unreasonable. In view of the breadth of federal regulatory authority contemplated by the Act itself and the inherent difficulties of defining precise bounds to regulable waters, the Corps' ecological judgment about the relationship between waters and their adjacent wetlands provides an adequate basis for a legal judgment that adjacent wetlands may be defined as waters under the Act.

Id. at 134. Following its decision in *Riverside Bayview*, in 2001 the Supreme Court again had occasion to consider the scope of the term "navigable waters," this time in the context of the Corps' definition of such waters to include those used as habitat by migratory birds.

SOLID WASTE AGENCY OF NORTHERN COOK COUNTY v. UNITED STATES ARMY CORPS OF ENGINEERS
531 U.S. 159 (2001)

Chief Justice REHNQUIST delivered the opinion of the Court.

. . . The United States Army Corps of Engineers (Corps) has interpreted §404(a) to confer federal authority over an abandoned sand and gravel pit in northern Illinois which provides habitat for migratory birds. We are asked to decide whether the provisions of §404(a) may be fairly extended to these waters, and, if so, whether Congress could exercise such authority consistent with the Commerce Clause, U.S. Const., art. I, §8, cl. 3. We answer the first question in the negative and therefore do not reach the second.

Petitioner, the Solid Waste Agency of Northern Cook County (SWANCC), is a consortium of 23 suburban Chicago cities and villages that united in an effort to locate and develop a disposal site for baled nonhazardous solid waste. The Chicago Gravel Company informed the municipalities of the availability of a 533-acre parcel, . . . which had been the site of a sand and gravel pit mining operation for three decades up until about 1960. Long since abandoned, the old mining site eventually gave way to a successional stage forest, with its remnant excavation trenches evolving into a scattering of permanent and seasonal ponds of varying size (from under one-tenth of an acre to several acres) and depth (from several inches to several feet).

The municipalities decided to purchase the site for disposal of their baled nonhazardous solid waste. . . . [B]ecause the operation called for the filling of some of the permanent and seasonal ponds, SWANCC contacted federal respondents (hereinafter respondents), including the Corps, to determine if a federal landfill permit was required under §404(a) of the CWA. . . .

In 1986, in an attempt to "clarify" the reach of its jurisdiction, the Corps stated that §404(a) extends to intrastate waters:

    a. Which are or would be used as habitat by birds protected by Migratory Bird Treaties; or

    b. Which are or would be used as habitat by other migratory birds which cross state lines. . . . 51 Fed. Reg. 41217.

This last promulgation has been dubbed the "Migratory Bird Rule."

The Corps . . . ultimately asserted jurisdiction over the balefill site pursuant to subpart (b) of the "Migratory Bird Rule." The Corps found that approximately 121 bird species had been observed at the site, including several known to depend upon aquatic environments for a significant portion of their life requirements. Thus, . . . the Corps formally "determined that the seasonally ponded, abandoned gravel mining depressions located on the project site, while not wetlands, did qualify as 'waters of the United States' . . . based upon the following criteria: (1) the proposed site had been abandoned as a gravel mining operation; (2) the water areas and spoil piles had developed a natural character; and (3) the water areas are used as habitat by migratory bird [sic] which cross state lines." . . .

[The Corps ultimately refused to issue a §404 permit.]

Relevant here, §404(a) authorizes respondents to regulate the discharge of fill material into "navigable waters," which the statute defines as "the waters of the United States, including the territorial seas." Respondents have interpreted these words to cover the abandoned gravel pit at issue here because it is used as habitat for migratory birds. We conclude that the "Migratory Bird Rule" is not fairly supported by the CWA.

This is not the first time we have been called upon to evaluate the meaning of §404(a). In *United States v. Riverside Bayview Homes, Inc.*, . . . we held that the Corps had §404(a) jurisdiction over wetlands that actually abutted on a navigable waterway. In so doing, we noted that the term "navigable" is of "limited import" and that Congress evidenced its intent to "regulate at least some waters that would not be deemed 'navigable' under the classical understanding of that term." . . . But our holding was based in large measure upon Congress' unequivocal acquiescence to, and approval of, the Corps' regulations interpreting the CWA to cover wetlands adjacent to navigable waters. . . . We found that Congress' concern for the protection of water quality and aquatic ecosystems indicated its intent to regulate wetlands "inseparably bound up with the 'waters' of the United States. . . ."

It was the significant nexus between the wetlands and "navigable waters" that informed our reading of the CWA in *Riverside Bayview Homes*. Indeed, we did not "express any opinion" on the "question of the authority of the Corps to regulate discharges of fill material into wetlands that are not adjacent to bodies of open water. . . ." In order to rule for respondents here, we would have to hold that the jurisdiction of the Corps extends to ponds that are *not* adjacent to open water. But we conclude that the text of the statute will not allow this. . . .

We . . . decline respondents' invitation to take what they see as the next ineluctable step after *Riverside Bayview Homes*: holding that isolated ponds, some only seasonal, wholly located within two Illinois counties, fall under §404(a)'s definition of "navigable waters" because they serve as habitat for migratory birds. As counsel for respondents conceded at oral argument, such a ruling would assume that "the use of the word navigable in the statute . . . does not have any independent significance." . . . We cannot agree that Congress' separate definitional use of the phrase "waters of the United States" constitutes a basis for reading the term "navigable waters" out of the statute. We said in *Riverside Bayview Homes* that the word "navigable" in the statute was of "limited effect" and went on to hold that §404(a) extended to nonnavigable wetlands adjacent to open waters. But it is one thing to give a word limited effect and quite another to give it no effect whatever. The term "navigable" has at least the import of showing us what Congress had in mind as its authority for enacting the CWA: its traditional jurisdiction over waters that were or had been navigable in fact or which could reasonably be so made. . . .

Respondents contend that . . . at the very least, it must be said that Congress did not address the precise question of §404(a)'s scope with regard to nonnavigable, isolated, intrastate waters, and that, therefore, we should give deference to the "Migratory Bird Rule." See, e.g., Chevron U.S.A. Inc. v. Natural Resources Defense Council, Inc., 467 U.S. 837 (1984). We find §404(a) to be clear, but even were we to agree with respondents, we would not extend *Chevron* deference here.

Where an administrative interpretation of a statute invokes the outer limits of Congress' power, we expect a clear indication that Congress intended that result. This requirement stems from our prudential desire not to needlessly reach constitutional issues and our assumption that Congress does not casually authorize administrative agencies to interpret a statute to push the limit of congressional authority. This concern is heightened where the administrative interpretation alters the federal-state framework by permitting federal encroachment upon a traditional state power. . . . Thus, "where an otherwise acceptable construction of a statute would raise serious constitutional problems, the Court will construe the statute to avoid such problems unless such construction is plainly contrary to the intent of Congress." . . .

These are significant constitutional questions raised by respondents' application of their regulations, and yet we find nothing approaching a clear statement from Congress that it intended §404(a) to reach an abandoned sand and gravel pit such as we have here. Permitting respondents to claim federal jurisdiction over ponds and mudflats falling within the "Migratory Bird Rule" would result in a significant impingement of the States' traditional and primary power over land and water use. . . . Rather than expressing a desire to readjust the federal-state balance in this manner, Congress chose to "recognize, preserve, and protect the primary responsibilities and rights of States . . . to plan the development and use . . . of land and water resources. . . ." 33 U.S.C. §1251(b). We thus read the statute as written to avoid the significant constitutional and federalism questions raised by respondents' interpretation, and therefore reject the request for administrative deference.

We hold that 33 CFR §328.3(a)(3) (1999), as clarified and applied to petitioner's balefill site pursuant to the "Migratory Bird Rule," exceeds the authority granted to respondents under §404(a) of the CWA. The judgment of the Court of Appeals for the Seventh Circuit is therefore

Reversed.

In 2006 the Supreme Court handed down its most recent decision concerning the scope of "navigable waters" in two consolidated cases, *Rapanos v. United States* and *Carabell v. U.S. Army Corps of Engineers*. Ever since, the courts have expressed "bafflement" over how they are supposed to apply *Rapanos*. United States v. Cundiff, 555 F.3d 200, 208 (6th Cir. 2009). The decision has wreaked havoc with the government's efforts to implement the §404 program. EPA's Office of Inspector General indicated that "EPA maintain[s] that the effect of the *Rapanos* and SWANCC decisions on the §404 enforcement program cannot be overstated." EPA OIG, Congressionally Requested Report on Comments Related to Effects of Jurisdictional Uncertainty on Clean Water Act Implementation, Report No. 09-N-0149 (April 30, 2009); EPA OIG, EPA Needs a Better Strategy to Identify Violations of Section 404 of the Clean Water Act, Report No. 10-P-0009 (Oct. 26, 2009), at 10. The OIG indicated that the Supreme Court decisions have caused EPA to shift its caseload to minimize cases with jurisdictional uncertainty and to drop numerous cases because of uncertainty about jurisdiction. According to Corps officials, it takes government officials considerably longer to make jurisdictional decisions now than was the case pre-*Rapanos* because of the complexity *Rapanos* added. Clean Water Act Jurisdictional Decisions Slower, More Complex, Army Corps Says, 97 Daily Env't Rep. (BNA) A-3 (May 20, 2008).

In spring 2014, EPA and the Corps jointly released a proposed rule to clarify the reach of the CWA in light of *Riverside Bayview*, *SWANCC*, and *Rapanos*. Definition of "Waters of the United States" under the Clean Water Act, 79 Fed. Reg. 22,188 (Apr. 21, 2014). An excerpt of the proposed rule is set forth following the *Rapanos* decision. As you read *Rapanos*, pay careful attention to how each Justice would define "navigable waters." Which view or views made its way into the subsequently proposed regulation?

RAPANOS v. UNITED STATES
547 U.S. 715 (2006)

Justice SCALIA announced the judgment of the Court, and delivered an opinion, in which THE CHIEF JUSTICE, Justice THOMAS, and Justice ALITO join. . . .

I

The Corps' current regulations interpret "the waters of the United States" to include, in addition to traditional interstate navigable waters, 33 CFR §328.3(a)(1) (2004), "[a]ll interstate waters including interstate wetlands," §328.3(a)(2); "[a]ll other waters such as intrastate lakes, rivers, streams (including intermittent streams), mudflats, sandflats, wetlands, sloughs, prairie potholes, wet meadows, playa lakes, or natural ponds, the use, degradation, or destruction of which could affect interstate or foreign commerce," §328.3(a)(3); "[t]ributaries of [such] waters," §328.3(a)(5); and "[w]etlands adjacent to [such] waters [and tributaries] (other than waters that are themselves wetlands)," §328.3(a)(7). The regulation defines "adjacent" wetlands as those "bordering, contiguous [to], or neighboring" waters of the United States. §328.3(c). It specifically provides that "[w]etlands separated from other waters of the United States by man-made dikes or barriers, natural river berms, beach dunes, and the like are 'adjacent wetlands.'"

II

In these consolidated cases, we consider whether four Michigan wetlands, which lie near ditches or man-made drains that eventually empty into traditional navigable waters, constitute "waters of the United States" within the meaning of the Act. Petitioners in No. 04-1034, the Rapanos and their affiliated businesses, deposited fill material without a permit into wetlands on three sites near Midland, Michigan: the "Salzburg site," the "Hines Road site," and the "Pine River site." The wetlands at the Salzburg site are connected to a man-made drain, which drains into Hoppler Creek, which flows into the Kawkawlin River, which empties into Saginaw Bay and Lake Huron. The wetlands at the Hines Road site are connected to something called the "Rose Drain," which has a surface connection to the Tittabawassee River. And the wetlands at the Pine River site have a surface connection to the Pine River, which flows into Lake Huron. It is not clear whether the connections between these wetlands and the nearby drains and ditches are continuous or intermittent, or whether the nearby drains and ditches contain continuous or merely occasional flows of water.

The United States brought civil enforcement proceedings against the Rapanos petitioners. The District Court found that the three described wetlands were "within federal jurisdiction" because they were "adjacent to other waters of the United States. . . ." On appeal, the United States Court of Appeals for the Sixth Circuit affirmed, holding that there was federal jurisdiction over the wetlands at all three sites because "there were hydrological connections between all three sites and corresponding adjacent tributaries of navigable waters."

Petitioners in No. 04-1384, the Carabells, were denied a permit to deposit fill material in a wetland located on a triangular parcel of land about one mile from Lake St. Clair. A man-made drainage ditch runs along one side of the wetland, separated from it by a 4-foot-wide man-made berm. The berm is largely or entirely impermeable to water and blocks drainage from the wetland, though it may permit occasional overflow to the ditch. The ditch empties into another ditch or a drain, which connects to Auvase Creek, which empties into Lake St. Clair.

. . . The District Court ruled that there was federal jurisdiction because the wetland "is adjacent to neighboring tributaries of navigable waters and has a significant nexus to 'waters of the United States.'" Again the Sixth Circuit affirmed, holding that the Carabell wetland was "adjacent" to navigable waters.

We granted certiorari and consolidated the cases to decide whether these wetlands constitute "waters of the United States" under the Act, and if so, whether the Act is constitutional.

III

. . . We have twice stated that the meaning of "navigable waters" in the Act is broader than the traditional understanding of that term, SWANCC, *Riverside Bayview*. We have also emphasized, however, that the qualifier "navigable" is not devoid of significance. SWANCC.

We need not decide the precise extent to which the qualifiers "navigable" and "of the United States" restrict the coverage of the Act. Whatever the scope of these qualifiers, the CWA authorizes federal jurisdiction only over "waters." The only natural definition of the term "waters," our prior and subsequent judicial constructions of it, clear evidence from other provisions of the statute, and this Court's canons of construction all confirm that "the waters of the United States" in §1362(7) cannot bear the expansive meaning that the Corps would give it.

The Corps' expansive approach might be arguable if the C[W]A defined "navigable waters" as "water of the United States." But "the waters of the United States" is something else. The use of the definite article ("the") and the plural number ("waters") show plainly that §1362(7) does not refer to water in general. In this form, "the waters" refers more narrowly to water "[a]s found in streams and bodies forming geographical features such as oceans, rivers, [and] lakes," or "the flowing or moving masses, as of waves or floods, making up such streams or bodies." Webster's New International Dictionary 2882 (2d ed. 1954) (hereinafter Webster's Second). On this definition, "the waters of the United States" include only relatively permanent, standing or flowing bodies of water. . . . All of these terms connote continuously present, fixed bodies of water, as opposed to ordinarily dry channels through which water occasionally or intermittently flows. . . . None of these terms encompasses transitory puddles or ephemeral flows of water.

The restriction of "the waters of the United States" to exclude channels containing merely intermittent or ephemeral flow also accords with the commonsense understanding of the term. In applying the definition to "ephemeral streams," "wet meadows," storm sewers and culverts, "directional sheet flow during storm events," drain tiles, man-made drainage ditches, and dry arroyos in the middle of the desert, the Corps has stretched the term "waters of the United States" beyond parody. The plain language of the statute simply does not authorize this "Land Is Waters" approach to federal jurisdiction. . . .

. . . [T]he CWA itself categorizes the channels and conduits that typically carry intermittent flows of water separately from "navigable waters," by including them in the definition of "'point source.'" The Act defines "'point source'" as "any discernible, confined and discrete conveyance, including but not limited to any . . . ditch, channel, tunnel, [or] conduit . . . from which pollutants are or may be discharged." It also defines "discharge of a pollutant" as "any addition of any pollutant *to* navigable waters *from* any point source." The definitions thus conceive of "point sources" and "navigable waters" as separate and distinct categories. The definition of "discharge" would make little sense if the two categories were significantly overlapping. The separate classification of "ditch[es], channel[s], and conduit[s]"—which are terms ordinarily used to describe the watercourses through which *intermittent* waters typically flow—shows that these are, by and large, *not* "waters of the United States."

Moreover, only the foregoing definition of "waters" is consistent with the CWA's stated "policy of Congress to recognize, preserve, and protect the primary responsibilities and rights of the States to prevent, reduce, and eliminate pollution, [and] to plan the development and use (including restoration, preservation, and enhancement) of land and water resources. . . ." §1251(b). . . .

[T]he Government's expansive interpretation would "result in a significant impingement of the States' traditional and primary power over land and water use." Regulation of land use, as through the issuance of the development permits sought by petitioners in both of these cases, is a quintessential state and local power. The extensive federal jurisdiction urged by the Government would authorize the Corps to function as a *de facto* regulator of immense stretches of intrastate land—an authority the agency has shown its willingness to exercise with the scope of discretion that would befit a local zoning board. See 33 CFR §320.4(a)(1) (2004). We ordinarily expect a "clear and manifest" statement from Congress to authorize an unprecedented intrusion into traditional state authority. The phrase "the waters of the United States" hardly qualifies.

Likewise, . . . the Corps' interpretation stretches the outer limits of Congress's commerce power and raises difficult questions about the ultimate scope of that power. Even if the term "the waters of the United States" were ambiguous as applied to channels that sometimes host ephemeral flows of water (which it is not), we would expect a clearer statement from Congress to authorize an agency theory of jurisdiction that presses the envelope of constitutional validity.

In sum, on its only plausible interpretation, the phrase "the waters of the United States" includes only those relatively permanent, standing or continuously flowing bodies of water "forming geographic features" that are described in ordinary parlance as "streams[,] . . . oceans, rivers, [and] lakes." The phrase does not include channels through which water flows intermittently or ephemerally, or channels that periodically provide drainage for rainfall. The Corps' expansive interpretation of the "the waters of the United States" is thus not "based on a permissible construction of the statute."

IV

In *Carabell*, the Sixth Circuit held that the nearby ditch constituted a "tributary" and thus a "water of the United States" under 33 CFR §328.3(a)(5) (2004). Likewise in *Rapanos*, the Sixth Circuit held that the nearby ditches were "tributaries" under §328(a)(5). But *Rapanos II* also stated that, even if the ditches were not "waters of the United States," the wetlands were "adjacent" to *remote* traditional navigable waters in virtue of the wetlands' "hydrological connection" to them. This statement reflects the practice of the Corps' district offices, which may "assert jurisdiction over a wetland without regulating the ditch connecting it to a water of the United States." We therefore address in this Part whether a wetland may be considered "adjacent to" remote "waters of the United States," because of a mere hydrologic connection to them. . . .

[O]nly those wetlands with a continuous surface connection to bodies that are "waters of the United States" in their own right, so that there is no clear demarcation between "waters" and wetlands, are "adjacent to" such waters and covered by the Act. Wetlands with only an intermittent, physically remote hydrologic connection to "waters of the United States" do not implicate the boundary-drawing problem of *Riverside Bayview*, and thus lack the necessary connection to covered waters that we described as a "significant nexus" in SWANCC. Thus, establishing that wetlands such as those at the Rapanos and Carabell sites are covered by the Act requires two findings: First, that the adjacent channel contains a "wate[r] of the United States," (*i.e.*, a relatively permanent body of water connected to traditional interstate navigable waters); and second, that the wetland has a continuous surface connection with that water, making it difficult to determine where the "water" ends and the "wetland" begins. . . .

VIII

[T]he lower courts should determine, in the first instance, whether the ditches or drains near each wetland are "waters" in the ordinary sense of containing a relatively permanent flow; and (if they are) whether the wetlands in question are "adjacent" to these "waters" in the sense of possessing a continuous surface connection that creates the boundary-drawing problem we addressed in *Riverside Bayview.*

We vacate the judgments of the Sixth Circuit in both No. 04-1034 and No. 04-1384, and remand both cases for further proceedings.

It is so ordered.

Chief Justice ROBERTS, concurring.

Five years ago, this Court rejected the position of the Army Corps of Engineers on the scope of its authority to regulate wetlands under the Clean Water Act. [SWANCC]. The Corps had taken the view that its authority was essentially limitless; this Court explained that such a boundless view was inconsistent with the limiting terms Congress had used in the Act. . . .

Agencies delegated rulemaking authority under a statute such as the Clean Water Act are afforded generous leeway by the courts in interpreting the statute they are entrusted to administer. Given the broad, somewhat ambiguous, but none-theless clearly limiting terms Congress employed in the Clean Water Act, the Corps and the EPA would have enjoyed plenty of room to operate in developing *some* notion of an outer bound to the reach of their authority.

[While the Corps and EPA initiated a rulemaking to consider "issues associated with the scope of waters that are subject to the Clean Water Act (CWA), in light of the U.S. Supreme Court decision in [SWANCC]," "the proposed rulemaking went nowhere." Instead, the "Corps chose to adhere to its essentially boundless view of the scope of its power. The upshot today is another defeat for the agency."]

It is unfortunate that no opinion commands a majority of the Court on precisely how to read Congress' limits on the reach of the Clean Water Act. Lower courts and regulated entities will now have to feel their way on a case-by-case basis. This situation is certainly not unprecedented. What is unusual in this instance, perhaps, is how readily the situation could have been avoided.

Justice KENNEDY, concurring in the judgment.

These consolidated cases require the Court to decide whether the term "navi-gable waters" in the Clean Water Act extends to wetlands that do not contain and are not adjacent to waters that are navigable in fact. In [SWANCC], the Court held, under the circumstances presented there, that to constitute "navigable waters" under the Act, a water or wetland must possess a "significant nexus" to waters that are or were nav-igable in fact or that could reasonably be so made. In the instant cases neither the plurality opinion nor the dissent by Justice Stevens chooses to apply this test; and though the Court of Appeals recognized the test's applicability, it did not consider all the factors necessary to determine whether the lands in question had, or did not have, the requisite nexus. In my view the cases ought to be remanded to the Court of Appeals for proper consideration of the nexus requirement.

I

. . .

A

. . . The statutory term to be interpreted and applied in the two instant cases is the term "navigable waters." The outcome turns on whether that phrase reasonably describes certain Michigan wetlands the Corps seeks to regulate. Under the Act "[t]he term 'navigable waters' means the waters of the United States, including the territorial seas." §1362(7). In a regulation the Corps has construed the term "waters of the United States" to include not only waters susceptible to use in interstate commerce—the traditional understanding of the term "navigable waters of the United States[]"— but also tributaries of those waters and, of particular relevance here, wetlands adjacent to those waters or their tributaries. 33 CFR §§328.3(a)(1), (5), (7) (2005). The Corps views tributaries as within its jurisdiction if they carry a perceptible "ordinary high water mark." §328.4(c); 65 Fed. Reg. 12,823 (2000). An ordinary high-water mark is a "line on the shore established by the fluctuations of water and indicated by physical characteristics such as clear, natural line impressed on the bank, shelving, changes in the character of soil, destruction of terrestrial vegetation, the presence of litter and debris, or other appropriate means that consider the characteristics of the surrounding areas." 33 CFR §328.3(e).

. . . Under the Corps' regulations, wetlands are adjacent to tributaries, and thus covered by the Act, even if they are "separated from other waters of the United States by man-made dikes or barriers, natural river berms, beach dunes and the like." §328.3(c). . . .

II

Twice before the Court has construed the term "navigable waters" in the Clean Water Act. In *United States v. Riverside Bayview Homes, Inc.*, the Court upheld the Corps' jurisdiction over wetlands adjacent to navigable-in-fact waterways. The property in *Riverside Bayview*, like the wetlands in the *Carabell* case now before the Court, was located roughly one mile from Lake St. Clair, though in that case, unlike *Carabell*, the lands at issue formed part of a wetland that directly abutted a navigable-in-fact creek. In regulatory provisions that remain in effect, the Corps had concluded that wetlands perform important functions such as filtering and purifying water draining into adjacent water bodies, slowing the flow of runoff into lakes, rivers, and streams so as to prevent flooding and erosion, and providing critical habitat for aquatic animal species. Recognizing that "[a]n agency's construction of a statute it is charged with enforcing is entitled to deference if it is reasonable and not in conflict with the expressed intent of Congress," the Court held that "the Corps' ecological judgment about the relationship between waters and their adjacent wetlands provides an adequate basis for a legal judgment that adjacent wetlands may be defined as waters under the Act." The Court reserved, however, the question of the Corps' authority to regulate wetlands other than those adjacent to open waters.

In SWANCC, the Court considered the validity of the Corps' jurisdiction over ponds and mudflats that were isolated in the sense of being unconnected to other waters covered by the Act. The property at issue was an abandoned sand and gravel pit mining operation where "remnant excavation trenches" had "evolv[ed] into a scattering of permanent and seasonal ponds." Asserting jurisdiction pursuant to a regulation called the "Migratory Bird Rule," the Corps argued that these isolated ponds were "waters of the United States" (and thus "navigable waters" under the Act) because they were used as habitat by migratory birds. The Court rejected this theory. "It was the significant nexus between wetlands and 'navigable waters,'" the Court held, "that informed our reading of the [Act] in *Riverside Bayview Homes*." Because such a nexus was lacking with respect to isolated ponds, the Court held that the plain text of the statute did not permit the Corps' action.

Riverside Bayview and SWANCC establish the framework for the inquiry in the cases now before the Court: Do the Corps' regulations, as applied to the wetlands in *Carabell* and the three wetlands parcels in *Rapanos*, constitute a reasonable interpretation of "navigable waters" as in *Riverside Bayview* or an invalid construction as in SWANCC? Taken together these cases establish that in some instances, as exemplified by *Riverside Bayview*, the connection between a nonnavigable water or wetland and a navigable water may be so close, or potentially so close, that the Corps may deem the water or wetland a "navigable water" under the Act. In other instances, as exemplified by SWANCC, there may be little or no connection. Absent a significant nexus, jurisdiction under the Act is lacking. Because neither the plurality nor the dissent addresses the nexus requirement, this separate opinion, in my respectful view, is necessary.

A

. . . As the plurality points out, and as *Riverside Bayview* holds, in enacting the Clean Water Act Congress intended to regulate at least some waters that are not navigable in the traditional sense. *Riverside Bayview*, SWANCC. This conclusion is supported by "the evident breadth of congressional concern for protection of water quality and aquatic ecosystems." It is further compelled by statutory text, for the text is explicit in extending the coverage of the Act to some nonnavigable waters. . . . [33 U.S.C. §1344(g)(1).] . . .

From this reasonable beginning the plurality proceeds to impose two limitations on the Act; but these limitations, it is here submitted, are without support in the language and purposes of the Act or in our cases interpreting it. First, . . . the plurality would conclude that the phrase "navigable waters" permits Corps and EPA jurisdiction only over "relatively permanent, standing or flowing bodies of water[]"—a category that in the plurality's view includes "seasonal" rivers, that is, rivers that carry water continuously except during "dry months," but not intermittent or ephemeral streams. Second, the plurality asserts that wetlands fall within the Act only if they bear "a continuous surface connection to bodies that are 'waters of the United States' in their own right"—waters, that is, that satisfy the plurality's requirement of permanent standing water or continuous flow. . . .

As a fallback the plurality suggests that avoidance canons would compel its reading even if the text were unclear. In SWANCC, as one reason for rejecting the Corps' assertion of jurisdiction over the isolated ponds at issue there, the Court observed that this "application of [the Corps'] regulations" would raise significant questions of Commerce Clause authority and encroach on traditional state land-use regulation. As SWANCC observed, and as the plurality points out here, the Act states that "[i]t is the policy of the Congress to recognize, preserve, and protect the primary responsibilities and rights of States to prevent, reduce, and eliminate pollution, [and] to plan the development and use . . . of land and water resources." The Court in SWANCC cited this provision as evidence that a clear statement supporting jurisdiction in applications raising constitutional and federalism difficulties was lacking.

The concerns addressed in SWANCC do not support the plurality's interpretation of the Act. In SWANCC, by interpreting the Act to require a significant nexus with navigable waters, the Court avoided applications—those involving waters without a significant nexus—that appeared likely, as a category, to raise constitutional difficulties and federalism concerns. Here, in contrast, the plurality's interpretation does not fit the avoidance concerns it raises. On the one hand, when a surface-water connection is lacking, the plurality forecloses jurisdiction over wetlands that abut navigable-in-fact waters—even though such navigable waters were traditionally subject to federal authority. On the other hand, by saying the Act covers wetlands (however remote) possessing a surface-water connection with a continuously flowing stream (however small), the plurality's reading would permit applications of the statute as far from traditional federal authority as are the waters it deems beyond the statute's reach. Even assuming, then, that federal regulation of remote wetlands and nonnavigable waterways would raise a difficult Commerce Clause issue notwithstanding those waters' aggregate effects on national water quality, [the] plurality's reading is not responsive to this concern. As for States' "responsibilities and rights," §1251(b), it is noteworthy that 33 States plus the District of Columbia have filed an *amici* brief in this litigation asserting that the Clean Water Act is important to their own water policies. These *amici* note, among other things, that the Act protects downstream States from out-of-state pollution that they cannot themselves regulate. . . .

Finally, it should go without saying that because the plurality presents its interpretation of the Act as the only permissible reading of the plain text, the Corps would lack discretion, under the plurality's theory, to adopt contrary regulations. The Chief Justice suggests that if the Corps and EPA had issued new regulations after SWANCC they would have "enjoyed plenty of room to operate in developing *some* notion of an outer bound to the reach of their authority" and thus could have avoided litigation of the issues we address today. That would not necessarily be true under the opinion the Chief Justice has joined. New rulemaking could have averted the disagreement here only if the Corps had anticipated the unprecedented reading of the Act that the plurality advances.

B

While the plurality reads nonexistent requirements into the Act, the dissent reads a central requirement out—namely, the requirement that the word "navigable" in "navigable waters" be given some importance. Although the Court has held that the statute's language invokes Congress' traditional authority over waters navigable in fact or susceptible of being made so, the dissent would permit federal regulation whenever wetlands lie alongside a ditch or drain, however remote and insubstantial, that eventually may flow into traditional navigable waters. The deference owed to the Corps' interpretation of the statute does not extend so far. . . .

Consistent with SWANCC and *Riverside Bayview* and with the need to give the term "navigable" some meaning, the Corps' jurisdiction over wetlands depends upon the existence of a significant nexus between the wetlands in question and navigable waters in the traditional sense. The required nexus must be assessed in terms of the statute's goals and purposes. Congress enacted the law to "restore and maintain the chemical, physical, and biological integrity of the Nation's waters," and it pursued that objective by restricting dumping and filling in "navigable waters." With respect to wetlands, the rationale for Clean Water Act regulation is, as the Corps has recognized, that wetlands can perform critical functions related to the integrity of other waters—functions such as pollutant trapping, flood control, and runoff storage. Accordingly, wetlands possess the requisite nexus, and thus come within the statutory phrase "navigable waters," if the wetlands, either alone or in combination with similarly situated lands in the region, significantly affect the chemical, physical, and biological integrity of other covered waters more readily understood as "navigable." When, in contrast, wetlands' effects on water quality are speculative or insubstantial, they fall outside the zone fairly encompassed by the statutory term "navigable waters." . . .

The Corps' existing standard for tributaries, however, provides no such assurance [of ecological interconnection]. As noted earlier, the Corps deems a water a tributary if it feeds into a traditional navigable water (or a tributary thereof) and possesses an ordinary high-water mark, defined as a "line on the shore established by the fluctuations of water and indicated by [certain] physical characteristics." This standard presumably provides a rough measure of the volume and regularity of flow. Assuming it is subject to reasonably consistent application, it may well provide a reasonable measure of whether specific minor tributaries bear a sufficient nexus with other regulated waters to constitute "navigable waters" under the Act. Yet the breadth of this standard—which seems to leave wide room for regulation of drains, ditches, and streams remote from any navigable-in-fact water and carrying only minor water-volumes towards it—precludes its adoption as the determinative measure of whether adjacent wetlands are likely to play an important role in the integrity of an aquatic system comprising navigable waters as traditionally understood. Indeed, in many cases wetlands adjacent to tributaries covered by this standard might appear little more related to navigable-in-fact waters than were the isolated ponds held to fall beyond the Act's scope in *SWANCC*.

When the Corps seeks to regulate wetlands adjacent to navigable-in-fact waters, it may rely on adjacency to establish its jurisdiction. Absent more specific regulations, however, the Corps must establish a significant nexus on a case-by-case basis when it seeks to regulate wetlands based on adjacency to nonnavigable tributaries. Given the potential overbreadth of the Corps' regulations, this showing is necessary to avoid unreasonable applications of the statute. Where an adequate nexus is established for a particular wetland, it may be permissible, as a matter of administrative convenience or necessity, to presume covered status for other comparable wetlands in the region. That issue, however, is neither raised by these facts nor addressed by any agency regulation that accommodates the nexus requirement outlined here.

This interpretation of the Act does not raise federalism or Commerce Clause concerns sufficient to support a presumption against its adoption. To be sure, the significant-nexus requirement may not align perfectly with the traditional extent of federal authority. Yet in most cases regulation of wetlands that are adjacent to tributaries and possess a significant nexus with navigable waters will raise no serious constitutional or federalism difficulty. As explained earlier, moreover, and as exemplified by *SWANCC*, the significant-nexus test itself prevents problematic applications of the statute. . . .

Justice STEVENS, with whom Justice SOUTER, Justice GINSBURG, and Justice BREYER join, dissenting. . . .

In my view, the proper analysis is straightforward. The Army Corps has determined that wetlands adjacent to tributaries of traditionally navigable waters preserve the quality of our Nation's waters by, among other things, providing habitat for aquatic animals, keeping excessive sediment and toxic pollutants out of adjacent waters, and reducing downstream flooding by absorbing water at times of high flow. The Corps' resulting decision to treat these wetlands as encompassed within the term "waters of the United States" is a quintessential example of the Executive's reasonable interpretation of a statutory provision. See Chevron U.S.A. Inc. v. Natural Resources Defense Council, Inc., 467 U.S. 837 (1984). . . .

I

. . . Prior to their destruction, the wetlands at all three sites had surface connections to tributaries of traditionally navigable waters. The Salzburg wetlands connected to a drain that flows into a creek that flows into the navigable Kawkawlin River. The Hines Road wetlands connected to a drain that flows into the navigable Tittabawassee River. And the Pine River wetlands connected with the Pine River, which flows into Lake Huron.

At trial, the Government['s] . . . wetland expert . . . testified that the wetlands at these three sites provided ecological functions in terms of "habitat, sediment trapping, nutrient recycling, and flood peak diminution." He explained:

> [G]enerally for all of the . . . sites we have a situation in which the flood water attenuation in that water is held on the site in the wetland . . . such that it does not add to flood peak. By the same token it would have some additional water flowing into the rivers during the drier periods, thus, increasing low water flow.

> . . . By the same token on all of the sites to the extent that they slow the flow of water of the site they will also accumulate sediment and thus trap sediment and hold nutrients for use in those wetland systems later in the season as well. . . .

II

Our unanimous opinion in *Riverside Bayview* squarely controls these cases. There, we evaluated the validity of the very same regulations at issue today. These regulations interpret "waters of the United States" to cover all traditionally navigable waters; tributaries of these waters; and wetlands adjacent to traditionally navigable waters or their tributaries. Although the particular wetland at issue in *Riverside Bayview* abutted a navigable creek, we framed the question presented as whether the Clean Water Act "authorizes the Corps to require landowners to obtain permits from the Corps before discharging fill material into wetlands adjacent to navigable bodies of water *and their tributaries.*"

We held that . . . the Corps' decision to interpret "waters of the United States" as encompassing such wetlands was permissible. We recognized the practical difficulties in drawing clean lines between land and water, and deferred to the Corps' judgment that treating adjacent wetlands as "waters" would advance the "congressional concern for protection of water quality and aquatic ecosystems."

Contrary to the plurality's revisionist reading today, *Riverside Bayview* nowhere implied that our approval of "adjacent" wetlands was contingent upon an understanding that "adjacent" means having a "continuous surface connection" between the wetland and its neighboring creek. Instead, we acknowledged that the Corps defined "adjacent" as including wetlands "that form the border of or are in reasonable proximity to other waters" and found that the Corps reasonably concluded that adjacent wetlands are part of the waters of the United States. . . .

[W]e emphasized that the scope of the Corps' asserted jurisdiction over wetlands had been specifically brought to Congress' attention in 1977, that Congress had rejected an amendment that would have narrowed that jurisdiction, and that even proponents of the amendment would not have removed wetlands altogether from the definition of "waters of the United States."

Disregarding the importance of *Riverside Bayview*, the plurality relies heavily on the Court's subsequent opinion in [SWANCC]. In stark contrast to *Riverside Bayview*, however, SWANCC had nothing to say about wetlands, let alone about wetlands adjacent to traditionally navigable waters or their tributaries. Instead, SWANCC dealt with a question specifically reserved by *Riverside Bayview*, namely, the Corps' jurisdiction over isolated waters — "waters that are *not* part of a tributary system to interstate waters or to navigable waters of the United States, the degradation or destruction of which could affect interstate commerce." At issue in SWANCC was "an abandoned sand and gravel pit . . . which provide[d] habitat for migratory birds" and contained a few pools of "nonnavigable, isolated, intrastate waters." The Corps had asserted jurisdiction over the gravel pit under its 1986 Migratory Bird Rule, which treated isolated waters as within its jurisdiction if migratory birds depended upon these waters. The Court rejected this jurisdictional basis since these isolated pools, unlike the wetlands at issue in *Riverside Bayview*, had no "significant nexus" to traditionally navigable waters. In the process, the Court distinguished *Riverside Bayview*'s reliance on Congress' decision to leave the Corps' regulations alone when it amended the Act in 1977, since "[i]n both Chambers, debate on the proposals to narrow the definition of navigable waters centered largely on the issue of wetlands preservation" rather than on the Corps' jurisdiction over truly isolated waters.

Unlike SWANCC and like *Riverside Bayview*, the cases before us today concern wetlands that are adjacent to "navigable bodies of water [or] their tributaries." Specifically, these wetlands abut tributaries of traditionally navigable waters. As we recognized in *Riverside Bayview*, the Corps has concluded that such wetlands play important roles in maintaining the quality of their adjacent waters, and consequently in the waters downstream. Among other things, wetlands can offer "nesting, spawning, rearing and resting sites for aquatic or land species"; "serve as valuable storage areas for storm and flood waters"; and provide "significant water purification functions." These values are hardly "*independent*" ecological considerations as the plurality would have it — instead, they are integral to the "chemical, physical, and biological integrity of the Nation's waters." Given that wetlands serve these important water quality roles and given the ambiguity inherent in the phrase "waters of the United States," the Corps has reasonably interpreted its jurisdiction to cover non-isolated wetlands. . . .

The Corps' exercise of jurisdiction is reasonable even though not every wetland adjacent to a traditionally navigable water or its tributary will perform all (or perhaps any) of the water quality functions generally associated with wetlands. *Riverside*

Bayview made clear that jurisdiction does not depend on a wetland-by-wetland inquiry. Instead, it is enough that wetlands adjacent to tributaries generally have a significant nexus to the watershed's water quality. If a particular wetland is "not significantly intertwined with the ecosystem of adjacent waterways," then the Corps may allow its development "simply by issuing a permit." . . .

IV

While I generally agree with Parts I and II-A of Justice Kennedy's opinion, I do not share his view that we should replace regulatory standards that have been in place for over 30 years with a judicially crafted rule distilled from the term "significant nexus" as used in SWANCC. To the extent that our passing use of this term has become a statutory requirement, it is categorically satisfied as to wetlands adjacent to navigable waters or their tributaries. . . .

I think it clear that wetlands adjacent to tributaries of navigable waters generally have a "significant nexus" with the traditionally navigable waters downstream. Unlike the "nonnavigable, isolated, intrastate waters" in SWANCC, these wetlands can obviously have a cumulative effect on downstream water flow by releasing waters at times of low flow or by keeping waters back at times of high flow. This logical connection alone gives the wetlands the "limited" connection to traditionally navigable waters that is all the statute requires—and disproves Justice Kennedy's claim that my approach gives no meaning to the word "navigable[.]" Similarly, these wetlands can preserve downstream water quality by trapping sediment, filtering toxic pollutants, protecting fish-spawning grounds, and so forth. While there may exist categories of wetlands adjacent to tributaries of traditionally navigable waters that, taken cumulatively, have no plausibly discernible relationship to any aspect of downstream water quality, I am skeptical. And even given Justice Kennedy's "significant nexus" test, in the absence of compelling evidence that many such categories do exist I see no reason to conclude that the Corps' longstanding regulations are overbroad.

. . . Justice Kennedy's approach will have the effect of creating additional work for all concerned parties. Developers wishing to fill wetlands adjacent to ephemeral or intermittent tributaries of traditionally navigable waters will have no certain way of knowing whether they need to get §404 permits or not. And the Corps will have to make case-by-case (or category-by-category) jurisdictional determinations, which will inevitably increase the time and resources spent processing permit applications. These problems are precisely the ones that *Riverside Bayview*'s deferential approach avoided. Unlike Justice Kennedy, I see no reason to change *Riverside Bayview*'s approach—and every reason to continue to defer to the Executive's sensible, bright-line rule.

V

. . . I would affirm the judgments in both cases, and respectfully dissent from the decision of five Members of this Court to vacate and remand. I close, however, by noting an unusual feature of the Court's judgments in these cases. It has been our practice in a case coming to us from a lower federal court to enter a judgment commanding that court to conduct any further proceedings pursuant to a specific mandate. That prior practice has, on occasion, made it necessary for Justices to join a judgment that did not conform to their own views. In these cases, however, while both the plurality and Justice Kennedy agree that there must be a remand for further proceedings, their respective opinions define different tests to be applied on remand. Given that all four Justices who have joined this opinion would uphold the Corps' jurisdiction in both of these cases—and in all other cases in which either the plurality's or Justice Kennedy's test is satisfied—on remand each of the judgments should be reinstated if *either* of those tests is met.

NOTES AND QUESTIONS

1. The *Rapanos* opinions raise a host of issues. Which opinion or opinions control? What rule(s) of law does the controlling opinion (or do the controlling opinions) announce? What options do the opinions leave regulators to try to bring greater clarity to, or to revise, the definition of navigable waters? What are Congress's options in light of *Rapanos*? What role do possible constitutional issues play in the various opinions?

2. The Circuit courts split on how to apply *Rapanos*. One article found that the Seventh, Ninth, and Eleventh Circuits have applied Justice Kennedy's test; the First and Eighth Circuits have held that there is CWA jurisdiction "whenever either Justice Kennedy's or the plurality's test is met"; and the Fifth and Sixth Circuits have "finessed" the issue. Johnston & Sendek-Smith, Muddy Waters: Recent Developments under the Clean Water Act, Nat. Resources & Env't 31, 34 (Winter 2010). For another of many takes on the scope of navigable waters, see Strand & Rothschild, What Wetlands Are Regulated? Jurisdiction of the §404 Program, 40 Envtl. L. Rep. 10372 (April 2010).

As indicated above, SWANCC and especially *Rapanos* made jurisdictional determinations under the CWA much more difficult. EPA and the Corps issued joint guidance following *Rapanos*, but they were criticized for making things more complicated rather than alleviating confusion. See, e.g., ECOS Resolution No. 08-2, Clean Water Act Jurisdiction Issues Require Clarification from Congress (Apr. 14, 2008). EPA and the Corps proposed a new rule in 2014:

PROPOSED RULE, DEFINITION OF "WATERS OF THE UNITED STATES" UNDER THE CLEAN WATER ACT
79 Fed. Reg. 22,188 (Apr. 16, 2014)

. . .

The SWANCC and *Rapanos* decisions resulted in [EPA and the Corps] evaluating the jurisdiction of waters on a case-specific basis far more frequently than is best for clear and efficient implementation of the CWA. This approach results in confusion and uncertainty to the regulated public and results in significant resources being allocated to these determinations by Federal and State regulators. . . .

In light of the Supreme Court decisions in SWANCC and *Rapanos*, the scope of regulatory jurisdiction in this proposed rule is narrower than that under the existing regulations. See 40 CFR 122.2 (defining "waters of the United States").

. . .

A. *Executive Summary*

. . .

The proposed rule would revise the existing definition of "waters of the United States" consistent with the science and the above Supreme Court cases. The proposed rule retains much of the structure of the agencies' longstanding definition of "waters of the United States," and many of the existing provisions of that definition where revisions are not required in light of Supreme Court decisions or other bases for revision. As a result of the Supreme Court decisions in *SWANCC* and *Rapanos*, the scope of regulatory jurisdiction of the CWA in this proposed rule is narrower than that under the existing regulations.

The most substantial change is the proposed deletion of the existing regulatory provision that defines "waters of the United States" as all other waters such as intrastate lakes, rivers, streams (including intermittent streams), mudflats, sandflats, wetlands, sloughs, prairie potholes, wet meadows, playa lakes, or natural ponds, the use, degradation or destruction of which could affect interstate or foreign commerce including any such waters: Which are or could be used by interstate or foreign travelers for recreational or other purposes; from which fish or shellfish are or could be taken and sold in interstate or foreign commerce; or which are used or could be used for industrial purposes by industries in interstate commerce. 33 CFR 328.3(a)(3); 40 CFR 122.2. Under the proposed rule, these "other waters" (those which do not fit within the proposed categories of waters jurisdictional by rule) would only be jurisdictional upon a case-specific determination that they have a significant nexus as defined by the proposed rule. Waters in a watershed in which there is no connection to a traditional navigable water, interstate water or the territorial seas would not be "waters of the United States." In addition, the proposed rule would for the first time explicitly exclude some features and waters over which the agencies have not generally asserted jurisdiction and in so doing would eliminate the authority of the agencies to determine in case specific circumstances that some such waters are jurisdictional "waters of the United States."

. . .

Under the proposed first section of the regulation, section (a), the agencies propose to define the "waters of the United States" for all sections (including sections 301, 311, 401, 402, 404) of the CWA to mean:

- All waters which are currently used, were used in the past, or may be susceptible to use in interstate or foreign commerce, including all waters which are subject to the ebb and flow of the tide;
- All interstate waters, including interstate wetlands;
- The territorial seas;
- All impoundments of a traditional navigable water, interstate water, the territorial seas or a tributary;
- All tributaries of a traditional navigable water, interstate water, the territorial seas or impoundment;
- All waters, including wetlands, adjacent to a traditional navigable water, interstate water, the territorial seas, impoundment or tributary; and
- On a case-specific basis, other waters, including wetlands, provided that those waters alone, or in combination with other similarly situated waters, including wetlands, located in the same region, have a significant nexus to a traditional navigable water, interstate water or the territorial seas.

As discussed in further detail below, the rule would not change the following provisions of the existing rule (although some provisions have been renumbered): Traditional navigable waters; interstate waters; the territorial seas; and impoundments of "waters of the United States." In paragraph (a)(5) of the proposed rule, the agencies propose that all tributaries as defined in the proposed rule are "waters of the United States." While tributaries are "waters of the United States" under the existing regulation, the rule would for the first time include a regulatory definition of "tributary."

With this proposed rule, the agencies conclude, based on existing science and the law, that a significant nexus exists between tributaries (as defined in the proposed rule) and the traditional navigable waters, interstate waters, and the territorial seas into which they flow; and between adjacent water bodies (as defined in the proposed rule) and traditional navigable waters, interstate waters, and the territorial seas, respectively. Consequently, this rule establishes as "waters of the United States," all tributaries (as defined in the proposal), of the traditional navigable waters, interstate waters, and the territorial seas, as well as all adjacent waters (including wetlands). This will eliminate the need to make a case-specific significant nexus determination for tributaries or for their adjacent waters because it has been determined that as a category, these waters have a significant nexus and thus are "waters of the United States."

In paragraph (a)(6) of the proposed rule, the rule would clarify that adjacent waters, rather than simply adjacent wetlands, are "waters of the United States." The rule would further clarify the meaning of "adjacent" by defining one of its elements, "neighboring." The related terms of "riparian area" and "floodplain" are also defined in the proposed rule.

The rule states that on a case-specific basis "other waters" that have a significant nexus to a traditional navigable water, interstate water or the territorial seas are "waters of the United States." Unlike the categories of waters in paragraphs (a)(1) through (6), which would be jurisdictional by definition, these "other waters" would not be "waters of the United States" by definition; rather, these "other waters" would only be jurisdictional provided that they have been determined on a case-specific basis to have a significant nexus to a paragraph (a)(1) through (a)(3) water. Therefore, the rule also includes a definition of "significant nexus."

"Significant nexus" is not itself a scientific term. The relationship that waters can have to each other and connections downstream that affect the chemical, physical, or biological integrity of traditional navigable waters, interstate waters, or the territorial seas is not an all or nothing situation. The existence of a connection, a nexus, does not by itself establish that it is a "significant nexus." There is a gradient in the relation of waters to each other, and this is documented in the Report. The agencies propose a case-specific analysis in establishing jurisdiction over these "other waters" as consistent with the current science, the CWA, and the caselaw. A case-specific analysis allows for a determination of jurisdiction at the point on the gradient in the relationship that constitutes a "significant nexus." In the proposed regulation the rule defines the following terms: adjacent, neighboring, riparian area, floodplain, tributary, wetlands, and significant nexus. However, the agencies also recognize that relying on a case-specific analysis provides less certainty to the regulated public on the jurisdictional status of other waters and is considering other approaches, as discussed later in this preamble.

The proposed section (b) excludes specified waters and features from the definition of "waters of the United States." Waters and features that are determined to be excluded under section (b) of the proposed rule will not be jurisdictional under any of the categories in the proposed rule under section (a), even if they would otherwise satisfy the regulatory definition. Those waters and features that would not be "waters of the United States" are:

- Waste treatment systems, including treatment ponds or lagoons, designed to meet the requirements of the Clean Water Act.
- Prior converted cropland. Notwithstanding the determination of an area's status as prior converted cropland by any other Federal agency, for the purposes of the Clean Water Act the final authority regarding Clean Water Act jurisdiction remains with EPA.
- Ditches that are excavated wholly in uplands, drain only uplands, and have less than perennial flow.
- Ditches that do not contribute flow, either directly or through another water, to a traditional navigable water, interstate water, the territorial seas or an impoundment of a jurisdictional water.
- The following features:
  - Artificially irrigated areas that would revert to upland should application of irrigation water to that area cease;
  - artificial lakes or ponds created by excavating and/or diking dry land and used exclusively for such purposes as stock watering, irrigation, settling basins, or rice growing;
  - artificial reflecting pools or swimming pools created by excavating and/or diking dry land;
  - small ornamental waters created by excavating and/or diking dry land for primarily aesthetic reasons;
  - water-filled depressions created incidental to construction activity;
  - groundwater, including groundwater drained through subsurface drainage systems; and
  - gullies and rills and non-wetland swales.

. . .

A review of the scientific literature, including the Report of the peer-reviewed science, shows that tributaries and adjacent waters play an important role in maintaining the chemical, physical, and biological integrity of traditional navigable waters, interstate waters, and the territorial seas—and of other jurisdictional waters—because of their hydrological and ecological connections to and interactions with those waters. Therefore, it is appropriate to protect all tributaries and adjacent waters, because the tributaries, adjacent waters, and the downstream traditional navigable waters, interstate waters, and the territorial seas function as an integrated system. Water flows through tributaries to downstream traditional navigable waters, interstate waters, and the territorial seas, and that water carries pollutants that affect the chemical, physical, and biological integrity of the (a)(1) through (a)(3) waters, including water quality, fisheries, recreation, and other ecological services.

In discussing the significant nexus standard, Justice Kennedy stated: "The required nexus must be assessed in terms of the statute's goals and purposes. Congress enacted the [CWA] to 'restore and maintain the chemical, physical, and biological integrity of the Nation's waters. . . .' " 547 U.S. at 779. To protect the integrity of the waters subject to the CWA, the significant nexus standard must be implemented in a manner that restores and maintains any of these three attributes of traditional navigable waters, interstate waters, or the territorial seas. Waters adjacent to tributaries also provide ecological functions that, in conjunction with the functions provided by the tributaries they are adjacent to, have a significant influence on the chemical, physical, and biological integrity of downstream traditional navigable waters, interstate waters, and the territorial seas.

Examples of the important functions provided by adjacent waters are the sequestering or transformation of pollutants to reduce inputs to tributaries and subsequently to downstream (a)(1) through (a)(3) waters, water storage, and sediment trapping. Thus, in some instances, the significance of adjacent waters is to prevent or delay a hydrological connection with downstream waters and store water and/or pollutants. Given the large scale systematic interactions that occur, and the substantial effects that result, among tributaries, adjacent waters, and the downstream traditional navigable waters, interstate waters, or the territorial seas, a significant nexus exists that warrants making those categories of waters jurisdictional by rule. . . .

QUESTIONS

1. Is the proposed rule consistent with *Riverside Bayview*? *SWANCC*? *Rapanos*? To what extent does the proposed rule rely on the traditional "navigable in fact" definition of navigable waters?

2. Think back to the *Rapanos* opinions. In what ways did they impact the agencies' approach to the proposed rule? The proposed rule says that it narrows the scope of CWA jurisdiction and will be easier for permitting authorities to implement. Do you agree? For further analysis, see Copeland, EPA and the Army Corps' Proposed Rule to Define "Waters of the United States," Cong. Res. Serv. 7-5700 (June 10, 2014).

Problem 7-1

You represent the American Farm Bureau Federation ("Farm Bureau"), which is a national public-interest group dedicated to representing the interests of farmers and ranchers. Your client is concerned that the proposed rule, if finalized, would vastly expand the jurisdiction of EPA and the Corps, giving the agencies power to dictate land use decisions as well as farming practices. For example, the Farm Bureau worries that building a fence across a ditch, filling mud puddles with soil, and deciding where to create a new pond for livestock would all be potentially subject to CWA jurisdiction. The Farm Bureau is planning to submit a comment to the proposed rule, and has asked you to draft a paragraph of the letter that would explain why the proposed rule would expand CWA jurisdiction to potentially reach these traditional farming activities. How would you draft the comment? If you wish, refer to the Farm Bureau's website, www.fb.org, to gain a better understanding of your client's interests.

2. Definition of a Point Source

As noted earlier, the Clean Water Act divides pollution sources into two categories: point and nonpoint. There is no biological rationale for this division. Pesticide residues, for example, are just as harmful whether they enter a drinking water supply from a chemical company's outfall or as the result of agricultural runoff. The reason for the distinction is technological and political. Congress expressed great faith in the ability of engineers to limit what came out of pipes but less faith in their ability to control nonpoint pollution:

> There is no effective way as yet, other than land use control, by which you can intercept that runoff and control it in the way that you do a point source. We have not yet developed technology to deal with that kind of problem. We need to find ways to deal with it, because a great quantity of pollutants is discharged by runoff, not only from agriculture but from construction sites, from streets, from parking lots, and so on, and we have to be concerned with developing controls for them. [Senate Debate on S. 2770, Nov. 2, 1971, reported in 1972 Legislative History, at 1315.]

Further, to move aggressively against nonpoint sources of pollution, the federal government would have had to mandate new local land use control and agricultural practices standards. In 1972 Congress was unwilling to do this directly, so it attempted to address local land use and agricultural management by shifting the responsibility for nonpoint pollution control to the states, subject to federal planning standards.

The legal consequence of characterizing water pollution as "point source" pollution is significant. If a source is a point source and the other required jurisdictional elements are met, a discharger must obtain an NPDES permit and comply with applicable effluent limitations. CWA §502(14) defines "point source" as follows (it does not define the term "nonpoint source"):

> any discernible, confined and discrete conveyance, including but not limited to any pipe, ditch, channel, tunnel, conduit, well, discrete fissure, container, rolling stock, concentrated animal feeding operation, or vessel or other floating craft, from which pollutants are or may be discharged. This term does not include agricultural stormwater discharges and return flows from irrigated agriculture.

EPA perceived from the beginning that what came out of a pipe did not exhaust the definition of point source, but it chose not to specify the extent of "non-outfall" point sources. Initially, EPA sought to exempt the most controversial, potential non-pipe point sources from the NPDES permit program. These sources include all silvicultural point sources, all confined animal feedlots, and all irrigation return flows from less than 3,000 acres. NRDC v. Costle, 568 F.2d 1369 (D.C. Cir. 1977), rejected EPA's argument that it could avoid regulating these sources because doing so would be administratively infeasible. The court did hold, however, that EPA could introduce flexibility into its program by issuing general area-wide permits for classes of point source dischargers.

The question of what kinds of activities qualify as point sources has arisen in a wide variety of contexts, as the following case reflects.

UNITED STATES v. PLAZA HEALTH LABORATORIES, INC.
3 F.3d 643 (2d Cir. 1993)

GEORGE C. PRATT, Circuit Judge: . . .

Facts and Background

[Defendant Villegas co-owned and served as vice president of Plaza Health Laboratories, Inc., a blood-testing laboratory in Brooklyn, New York. Between April and September 1988, Villegas loaded containers of numerous vials of human blood generated from his business into his personal car and drove to his residence at the Admirals Walk Condominium in Edgewater, New Jersey. Once at his condominium complex, Villegas removed the containers from his car and carried them to the edge of the Hudson River. On one occasion he carried two containers of the vials to the bulkhead that separates his condominium complex from the river, and placed them at low tide within a crevice in the bulkhead that was below the high-water line. Numerous vials subsequently were discovered in the water and along the shore. Ten of the retrieved vials contained blood infected with the hepatitis-B virus. All of the vials recovered were eventually traced to Plaza Health Laboratories.

Based on the discovery of the vials, Plaza Health Laboratories and Villegas were indicted on counts of violating §309(c)(2) and (3) of the Clean Water Act. Villegas contends that one element of the CWA crime, knowingly discharging pollutants from a "point source," was not established in his case because the CWA §502(14) definition of "point source" does not include discharges that result from the individual acts of human beings.]

Discussion

. . .

A. NAVIGATING THE CLEAN WATER ACT

The basic prohibition on discharge of pollutants is in 33 U.S.C. §1311(a), which states:

> Except as in compliance with this section and sections 1312, 1316, 1317, 1328, 1342, and 1344 of this title, the *discharge* of any *pollutant* by any person shall be unlawful.

Id. (emphasis added).

The largest exception to this seemingly absolute rule is found in 33 U.S.C. §1342, which establishes the CWA's national pollutant discharge elimination system, or NPDES:

> (a) Permits for discharge of pollutants
>
> > (1) Except as provided in sections 1328 [aquaculture] and 1344 [dredge and fill permits] of this title, the Administrator may, after opportunity for public hearing, issue a permit for the discharge of any pollutant . . . *notwithstanding section 1311(a) of this title,* upon condition that such discharge will meet . . . all applicable requirements under sections 1311, 1312, 1316, 1317, 1318, and 1343 of this title. . . .

33 U.S.C. §1342(a) (emphasis added).

Reading §1311(a), the basic prohibition, and §1342(a)(1), the permit section, together, we can identify the basic rule, our rhumb line to clean waters, that, absent a permit, "the discharge of any pollutant by any person" is unlawful. 33 U.S.C. §1311(a).

We must then adjust our rhumb line by reference to two key definitions— "pollutant" and "discharge." "Pollutant" is defined, in part, as "biological materials . . . *discharged* into water." 33 U.S.C. §1362(6) (emphasis added). "Discharge," in turn, is "any addition of any pollutant to navigable waters *from any point source* . . ." (emphasis added). 33 U.S.C. §1362(12).

As applied to the facts of this case, then, the defendant "added" a "pollutant" (human blood in glass vials) to "navigable waters" (the Hudson River), and he did so without a permit. The issue, therefore, is whether his conduct constituted a "discharge," and that in turn depends on whether the addition of the blood to the Hudson River waters was "from any point source." For this final course adjustment in our navigation, we look again to the statute.

> The term "point source" means any discernible, confined and discrete conveyance, including but not limited to any pipe, ditch, channel, tunnel, conduit, well, discrete fissure, container, rolling stock, concentrated animal feeding operation, or vessel or other floating craft, from which pollutants are or may be discharged. This term does not include agricultural stormwater discharges and return flows from irrigated agriculture.

33 U.S.C. §1362(14). . . .

[T]he question is "whether a human being can be a point source." Both sides focus on the district court's conclusion in its *rule* 29 memorandum that, among other things, the requisite "point source" here could be Villegas himself. . . .

Simply put, . . . this statute was never designed to address the random, individual polluter like Villegas.

To determine the scope of the CWA's "point source" definition, we first consider the language and structure of the act itself. If the language is not plain, an excursion into legislative history and context may prove fruitful. Judicial interpretations of the term can be instructive as well, as may be interpretive statements by the agency in charge of implementing the statute. If we conclude after this analysis that the statute is ambiguous as applied to Villegas, then the rule of lenity may apply.

1. LANGUAGE AND STRUCTURE OF ACT

Human beings are not among the enumerated items that may be a "point source." Although by its terms the definition of "point source" is nonexclusive, the words used to define the term and the examples given ("pipe, ditch, channel, tunnel, conduit, well, discrete fissure," etc.) evoke images of physical structures and instrumentalities that systematically act as a means of conveying pollutants from an industrial source to navigable waterways.

In addition, if every discharge involving humans were to be considered a "discharge from a point source," the statute's lengthy definition of "point source" would have been unnecessary. It is elemental that Congress does not add unnecessary words to statutes. Had Congress intended to punish any human being who polluted navigational waters, it could readily have said: "any person who places pollutants in navigable waters without a permit is guilty of a crime."

The Clean Water Act generally targets industrial and municipal sources of pollutants, as is evident from a perusal of its many sections. Consistent with this focus, the term "point source" is used throughout the statute, but invariably in sentences referencing industrial or municipal discharges. . . .

This emphasis was sensible, as "industrial and municipal point sources were the worst and most obvious offenders of surface water quality. They were also the easiest to address because their loadings emerge from a discrete point such as the end of a pipe."

Finally on this point, we assume that Congress did not intend the awkward meaning that would result if we were to read "human being" into the definition of "point source." Section 1362(12)(A) defines "discharge of a pollutant" as "any addition of any pollutant to navigable waters from any point source." Enhanced by this definition, §1311(a) reads in effect "the addition of any pollutant to navigable waters *from any point source by any person* shall be unlawful" (emphasis added). But were a human being to be included within the definition of "point source," the prohibition would then read: "the addition of any pollutant to navigable waters *from any person by any person* shall be unlawful," and this simply makes no sense. As the statute stands today, the term "point source" is comprehensible only if it is held to the context of industrial and municipal discharges.

2. LEGISLATIVE HISTORY AND CONTEXT

. . . The legislative history of the CWA, while providing little insight into the meaning of "point source," confirms the act's focus on industrial polluters. Congress required NPDES permits of those who discharge from a "point source." The term "point source," introduced to the act in 1972, was intended to function as a means of identifying industrial polluters—generally a difficult task because pollutants quickly disperse throughout the subject waters. The senate report for the 1972 amendments explains:

> In order to further clarify the scope of the regulatory procedures in the Act the Committee had added a definition of point source to distinguish between control requirements where there are *specific confined conveyances, such as pipes*, and control requirements which are imposed to control runoff. The control of pollutants from runoff is applied pursuant to section 209 and the authority resides in the State or other local agency.

S. Rep. No. 92-414, reprinted in 1972 U.S.C.C.A.N. 3668, 3744.
Senator Robert Dole added his comments to the committee report:

> Most of the problems of agricultural pollution deal with non-point sources. Very simply, a non-point source of pollution is one that does not confine its polluting discharge to one fairly specific outlet, such as a sewer pipe, a drainage ditch or a conduit; thus, a feedlot would be considered to be a non-point source as would pesticides and fertilizers.

Id. at 3760 (supplemental views).

We find no suggestion either in the act itself or in the history of its passage that Congress intended the CWA to impose criminal liability on an individual for the myriad, random acts of human waste disposal, for example, a passerby who flings a candy wrapper into the Hudson River, or a urinating swimmer. Discussions during the passage of the 1972 amendments indicate that Congress had bigger fish to fry. . . .

[The court here compared the CWA to the permitting scheme in the Rivers and Harbors Act of 1899.]

3. CASELAW

Our search for the meaning of "point source" brings us next to judicial constructions of the term.

The "point source" element was clearly established in the few CWA criminal decisions under §1319(c) that are reported.

With the exception of *Oxford Royal Mushroom*, [487 F. Supp. 852, 854 (E.D. Pa. 1980),] the cases that have interpreted "point source" have done so in civil-penalty or licensing settings, where greater flexibility of interpretation to further remedial legislative purposes is permitted, and the rule of lenity does not protect a defendant against statutory ambiguities. *See, e.g.,* Avoyelles Sportsmen's League, Inc. v. Marsh, 715 F.2d 897, 922 (5th Cir. 1983) ("point source" includes bulldozing equipment that discharged dredged materials onto wetland). . . .

The government relies on broad dicta in another civil case, United States v. Earth Sciences, Inc., 599 F.2d 368, 373 (10th Cir. 1979), in which the court held "[t]he concept of a point source was designed to further this [permit regulatory] scheme by embracing the broadest possible definition of any identifiable conveyance from which pollutants might enter the waters of the United States." We do not find this *Earth Sciences* dicta persuasive here, however, because that court found a "point source" in a ditch used in the mining operation—certainly not a far leap when "ditch" also is an expressly listed example of a "point source." We cannot, however, make the further leap of writing "human being" into the statutory language without doing violence to the language and structure of the CWA.

4. REGULATORY STRUCTURE

Finally, not even the EPA's regulations support the government's broad assertion that a human being may be a "point source." The EPA stresses that the discharge be "through pipes, sewers, or other conveyances."

Discharge of a pollutant means:

(a) Any addition of any "pollutant" or combination of pollutants to "waters of the United States" from any "point source." . . .

This definition includes additions of pollutants into waters of the United States from

surface runoff which is collected or channelled by man; *discharges through pipes, sewers, or other conveyances* owned by a State, municipality, or other person which do not lead to a treatment works; and discharges through pipes, sewers, or other conveyances, leading into privately owned treatment works. This term does not include an addition of pollutants by any "indirect discharger."

40 C.F.R. §122.2 (1992) (emphasis supplied).

In sum, although Congress had the ability to so provide, §1362(14) of the CWA does not expressly recognize a human being as a "point source"; nor does the act make structural sense when one incorporates a human being into that definition. The legislative history of the act adds no light to the muddy depths of this issue, and cases urging a broad interpretation of the definition in the civil-penalty context do not persuade us to do so here, where Congress has imposed heavy criminal sanctions. Adopting the government's suggested flexibility for the definition would effectively read the "point source" element of the crime out of the statute, and not even the EPA has extended the term "point source" as far as is urged here.

We accordingly conclude that the term "point source" as applied to a human being is at best ambiguous.

B. RULE OF LENITY

[The court concluded that, because it was not clear that a human being is a "point source" under the CWA, the criminal provisions of the CWA did not clearly proscribe Villegas's conduct and did not accord him fair warning of the sanctions the law placed on that conduct. As a result, under the rule of lenity, it dismissed the prosecutions against him.]

OAKES, Circuit Judge, dissenting:

. . . [B]ecause I do not agree that a person can never be a point source, and because I believe that Mr. Villegas' actions, as the jury found them, fell well within the bounds of activity proscribed by the Clean Water Act's bar on discharge of pollutants into navigable waters, I am required to dissent. . . .

I begin with the obvious, in hopes that it will illuminate the less obvious: the classic point source is something like a pipe. This is, at least in part, because pipes and similar conduits are needed to carry large quantities of waste water, which represents a large proportion of the point source pollution problem. Thus, devices designed to convey large quantities of waste water from a factory or municipal sewage treatment facility are readily classified as point sources. Because not all pollutants are liquids, however, the statute and the cases make clear that means of conveying solid wastes to be dumped in navigable waters are also point sources. See, e.g., 33 U.S.C. §1362(14) ("rolling stock," or railroad cars, listed as an example of a point source); Avoyelles Sportsmen's League, Inc. v. Marsh, 715 F.2d 897, 922 (5th Cir. 1983) (backhoes and bulldozers used to gather fill and deposit it on wetlands are point sources).

What I take from this look at classic point sources is that, at the least, an organized means of channeling and conveying industrial waste in quantity to navigable waters is a "discernible, confined and discrete conveyance." The case law is in accord: courts have deemed a broad range of means of depositing pollutants in the country's navigable waters to be point sources. See, e.g., . . . Sierra Club v. Abston Constr. Co., 620 F.2d 41, 45 (5th Cir. 1980) (spill of contaminated runoff from strip mine, if collected or channeled by the operator, is point source discharge). . . .

In short, the term "point source" has been broadly construed to apply to a wide range of polluting techniques, so long as the pollutants involved are not just human-made, but reach the navigable waters by human effort or by leaking from a clear point at which waste water was collected by human effort. From these cases, the writers of one respected treatise have concluded that such a "man-induced gathering mechanism plainly is the essential characteristic of a point source" and that a point source, "put simply, . . . is an identifiable conveyance of pollutants." 5 Robert E. Beck, Waters & Water Rights §53.01(b)(3) at 216-17 (1991). . . . See . . . Appalachian Power Co. v. Train, 545 F.2d 1351, 1373 (EPA may regulate channeled runoff, but not unchanneled runoff). In explaining why a broad definition was needed, the *Kennecott Copper* court, quoting American Petroleum Inst. v. EPA, 540 F.2d 1023, 1032 (10th Cir. 1976), noted that the statute sets as its goal the "attainment of the no discharge objective," and that this objective could not be achieved if the term "point source" were read narrowly. 612 F.2d at 1243.

This broad reading of the term "point source" is essential to fulfill the mandate of the Clean Water Act, in that

> [t]he touchstone of the regulatory scheme is that those needing to use the waters for waste distribution must seek and obtain a permit to discharge that waste, with the quantity and quality of the discharge regulated. The concept of a point source was designed to further this scheme by embracing the broadest possible definition of any identifiable conveyance from which pollutants might enter the waters of the United States. . . .
>
> We believe it contravenes the intent of FWPCA and the structure of the statute to exempt from regulation any activity that emits pollution from an identifiable point.

Earth Sciences, 599 F.2d 368, 373.

Nonetheless, the term "point source" sets significant definitional limits on the reach of the Clean Water Act. Fifty percent or more of all water pollution is thought to come from nonpoint sources. . . . So, to further refine the definition of "point source," I consider what it is that the Act does not cover: nonpoint source discharges.

Nonpoint source pollution is, generally, runoff: salt from roads, agricultural chemicals from farmlands, oil from parking lots, and other substances washed by rain, in diffuse patterns, over the land and into navigable waters.[3] The sources are many, difficult to identify and difficult to control. Indeed, an effort to greatly reduce nonpoint source pollution could require radical changes in land use patterns which Congress evidently was unwilling to mandate without further study. The structure of the statute—which regulates point source pollution closely, while leaving nonpoint source regulation to the states under the Section 208 program—indicates that the term "point source" was included in the definition of discharge so as to ensure that nonpoint source pollution would *not* be covered. Instead, Congress chose to regulate first that which could easily be regulated: direct discharges by identifiable parties, or point sources. . . .

While Villegas' activities were not prototypical point source discharges—in part because he was disposing of waste that could have been disposed of on land, and so did not need a permit or a pipe—they much more closely resembled a point source discharge than a nonpoint source discharge. First, Villegas and his lab were perfectly capable of avoiding discharging their waste into water: they were . . . a "controllable" source.

3. According to the EPA, nonpoint source pollution is caused by diffuse sources that are not regulated as point sources and normally is associated with agricultural, silvicultural, and urban runoff, runoff from construction activities, etc. Such pollution results in the human-made or human-induced alteration of the chemical, physical, biological, and radiological integrity of water. In practical terms, nonpoint source pollution does not result from a discharge at a specific, single location (such as a single pipe) but generally results from land runoff, precipitation, atmospheric deposition, or percolation. EPA Office of Water, Office of Water Regulations and Standards, Nonpoint Source Guidance 3 (1987).

Furthermore, the discharge was directly into water, and came from an identifiable point, Villegas. Villegas did not dispose of the materials on land, where they could be washed into water as nonpoint source pollution. Rather, he carried them, from his firm's laboratory, in his car, to his apartment complex, where he placed them in a bulkhead below the high tide line. I do not think it is necessary to determine whether it was Mr. Villegas himself who was the point source, or whether it was his car, the vials, or the bulkhead: in a sense, the entire stream of Mr. Villegas' activity functioned as a "discrete conveyance" or point source. The point is that the source of the pollution was clear, and would have been easy to control. Indeed, Villegas was well aware that there were methods of controlling the discharge (and that the materials were too dangerous for casual disposal): his laboratory had hired a professional medical waste handler. He simply chose not to use an appropriate waste disposal mechanism.

Villegas' method may have been an unusual one for a corporate officer, but it would undermine the statute—which, after all, sets as its goal the elimination of discharges, 33 U.S.C. §1311(a)—to regard as "ambiguous" a Congressional failure to list an unusual method of disposing of waste. I doubt that Congress would have regarded an army of men and women throwing industrial waste from trucks into a stream as exempt from the statute. Since the Act contains no exemption for de minimus [sic] violations—since, indeed, many Clean Water Act prosecutions are for a series of small discharges, each of which is treated as a single violation—I cannot see that one man throwing one day's worth of medical waste into the ocean differs (and indeed, with this type of pollution, it might be that only a few days' violations could be proven even if the laboratory regularly relied on Villegas to dispose of its waste by throwing it into the ocean). A different reading would encourage corporations perfectly capable of abiding by the Clean Water Act's requirements to ask their employees to stand between the company trucks and the sea, thereby transforming point source pollution (dumping from trucks) into nonpoint source pollution (dumping by hand). Such a method is controllable, easily identifiable, and inexcusable. To call it nonpoint source pollution is to read a technical exception into a statute which attempts to define in broad terms an activity which may be conducted in many different ways. . . .

My colleagues suggest that a person can never be a point source, relying heavily on the supposed redundancy produced when the Act's language barring the "discharge of any pollutant by any person" is read with the definitional terms placed in terms of the linguistic variables, as follows: "any addition of any pollutant to navigable waters from a person by a person." Granted, this sounds odd. But I believe the oddity is an artifact of assuming that the term "person" means the same thing in both parts of the sentence, and that in both cases it means what it means in everyday language.

The apparent oddness disappears when one grasps that the first term "person" in the peculiar sentence means "a person acting as a point source"[6] and that the second term "person" has been defined, typically for statutes imposing responsibility on a variety of parties, but not typically for ordinary speech, as a responsible party. As the linguistic hint "any" before both "person" and "point source" suggests, the terms are to be construed broadly. . . .

6. In my view, persons can be both point and nonpoint sources of pollution. They may be point sources when they deposit waste directly into water; they may be nonpoint sources when they, for example, spread fertilizer on the ground or deposit oil in a driveway, leaving it to be washed into nearby rivers. Thus, to say that the Clean Water Act bars persons polluting, rather than point sources polluting, would be too broad.

Having resorted to the language and structure, legislative history and motivating policies of the Clean Water Act, I think it plain enough that Congress intended the statute to bar corporate officers from disposing of corporate waste into navigable waters by hand as well as by pipe. . . .

NOTES AND QUESTIONS

1. Determining the appropriate line between point and nonpoint source pollution has not been easy. Which of the following might be a point source? Trash from a riverfront industrial building? Rainwater that leaks into the building and enters the river as runoff? Compare Hudson Riverkeeper Fund, Inc. v. Harbor at Hastings Ass'n, 917 F. Supp. 251 (S.D.N.Y. 1996), with Hudson River Fishermen's Ass'n v. Arcuri, 862 F. Supp. 73 (S.D.N.Y. 1994). A trap-shooting facility on the edge of a navigable body of water? See Stone v. Naperville Park Dist., 38 F. Supp. 2d 651 (N.D. Ill. 1999); Connecticut Coastal Fishermen's Ass'n v. Remington Arms Co., 989 F.2d 1305 (2d Cir. 1993); Cordiano v. Metacon Gun Club, Inc., 575 F.3d 199, 219 (2d Cir. 2009) (holding that "[l]imiting the scope of the term point source to surface runoff that is collected or channeled by human beings is consistent with the CWA's definition of point sources . . .").

2. What about runoff from logging roads that is collected in ditches, culverts, and channels and makes its way into a navigable water? The following saga reflects that the debate continues about where the boundaries should be set for point source dischargers. In Northwest Envtl. Def. Ctr. v. Brown, 617 F.3d 1176 (9th Cir. 2010), the Ninth Circuit held that, under CWA §502(14), NPDES permits are required under such circumstances, despite EPA's rule governing runoff from silvicultural operations contained in 40 C.F.R. §122.27. The court rejected EPA's interpretation that under the CWA and the agency's regulations, natural runoff from silvicultural operations does not qualify as a point source, regardless whether it is channeled and controlled through a discernible, confined, and discrete conveyance. The court expressed confidence that, even though EPA had "not had occasion to establish a permitting process" for such discharges, the agency "will be able to do so effectively and relatively expeditiously." Id. at 1198. The Ninth Circuit withdrew and replaced this opinion, but in its second opinion, the court maintained its view that "stormwater runoff from logging roads that is collected by and then discharged from a system of ditches, culverts, and channels is a point source discharge for which an NPDES permit is required." It remanded the case to the district court for further proceedings in light of that decision. Northwest Envtl. Def. Ctr. v. Brown, 640 F.3d 1063 (9th Cir. 2011). In 2012, the Supreme Court agreed to review the Ninth Circuit's decision, shortly after EPA proposed a notice of intent to revise its stormwater regulations to specify that an NPDES permit is not required for stormwater discharges from logging roads. 77 Fed. Reg. 30,473 (May 23, 2012).

In November 2012, in response to the *Brown* decision, EPA revised its stormwater regulations to clarify that an NPDES permit is not required for stormwater discharges from logging roads. Revisions to Stormwater Regulations to Clarify That an NPDES Permit Is Not Required for Stormwater Discharges from Logging Roads, 77 Fed. Reg. 72,970 (Dec. 7, 2012).

The agency explained the purpose of the rule as follows:

The final rule clarifies that, for the purposes of assessing whether stormwater dischargers are "associated with industrial activity," the only facilities under SIC code 2411 [covering logging] that are "industrial" are: rock crushing, gravel washing, log sorting, and log storage. This clarifies, contrary to the Ninth Circuit's decision in *NEDC*, that discharges from stormwater from silviculture facilities other than the four specifically named silviculture facilities identified above do not require an NPDES permit.

In March 2013, the Supreme Court reversed the Ninth Circuit's decision in *Brown*, based on the earlier version of the EPA stormwater rule; the Court did not interpret the amended regulation. The Court held that, under the Clean Water Act:

> [P]etitioners were required to secure NPDES permits for the discharges of channeled stormwater runoff only if the discharges were "associated with industrial activity," 33 U.S.C. §1342(p)(2)(B), as that statutory term is defined in the preamendment version of the Industrial Stormwater Rule, 30 C.F.R. §122.26(b)(14)(2006). Otherwise, the discharges fall within the Act's general exemption of "discharges composed entirely of stormwater" from the NPDES permitting scheme. 33 U.S.C. §1342(p)(1).

Decker v. Northwest Envtl. Def. Ctr., 133 S. Ct. 1326, 1336 (2013). The Court concluded that "the preamendment version of the Industrial Stormwater rule, as permissibly construed by the agency, exempts discharges of channeled stormwater from logging roads from the NPDES permitting scheme." Id. at 1337. It reversed the Ninth Circuit's decision in *Brown* and remanded the case for proceedings consistent with the Court's opinion. (See the discussion of stormwater carried by municipal treatment systems below in section G.4.)

Following the Court's decision in *Decker*, the Ninth Circuit held that wood preservatives from utility poles released into the environment ("pollutant-bearing storm water runoff") were not point source pollution because the stormwater was not "discretely collected and conveyed to waters of the United States," the poles themselves were not "conveyances" under 33 U.S.C. §1362(14), and the stormwater runoff was not a discharge associated with industrial activity. *Ecological Rights Found. v. Pac. Gas & Elec.*, 713 F.3d 502, 509-512 (9th Cir. 2013).

3. *Pollutant*

The next element required to trigger NPDES jurisdiction is that the material discharged be a "pollutant." Courts generally interpret the definition of "pollutant," contained in CWA §502(6) and 40 C.F.R. §122.2, broadly. In Sierra Club Lone Star Chapter v. Cedar Point Oil Co., 73 F.3d 546, 564-568 (5th Cir. 1996), the Fifth Circuit held that the list of substances in the definition of "pollutant" in CWA §502(6) is not exclusive: "[I]t seems clear that, while the listing of a specific substance in the definition of pollutant may be significant, the fact that a substance is not specifically included does not remove it from the coverage of the statute." The court further held that courts are empowered to make independent determinations that a particular substance is (or is not) a pollutant. In Romero-Barcelo v. Brown, 478 F. Supp. 646, 665 (D.P.R. 1979), the court defined "pollutant" to include unexploded bombs that the military fired into the ocean during training exercises. On the other hand, the Ninth Circuit has held that mussel shells and their by-products are not "pollutants" on the ground that they are the "natural biological processes of the mussels, not the waste product of a transforming human process." Ass'n to Protect Hammersley, Eld & Totten Inlets v. Taylor Res., Inc., 299 F.3d 1007, 1017 (9th Cir. 2002). This issue has arisen in the context of aerial spraying of pesticides, discussed in more detail in the notes and comments below.

4. Addition

The word "addition" is not defined by the CWA, but its meaning first became an issue in the context of dams. Dams can have substantial adverse environmental impacts on the stream system that they impound and modify. The theory of dams adding pollutants is that they transfer water from the impoundment to the flowing stream below the dam; this might result, for example, in additional nutrients, temperature changes, and lower dissolved oxygen being transferred to the stream below the dam. EPA took the position, however, that the changes dams caused were not pollutants, and even if they were, they were not additions because the water from the impoundments would eventually go downstream. In National Wildlife Fed'n v. Gorsuch, 693 F.2d 156 (D.C. Cir. 1982), the court granted deference to EPA's interpretation. See also Los Angeles Cnty. Flood Control Dist. v. Natural Res. Def. Council, Inc., 133 S. Ct. 710 (2013) ("the flow of water from [one portion of a waterway into another] does not qualify as a discharge of pollutants under the CWA" because there is no "addition" of a pollutant as required by the Act).

The Gorsuch decision did not reach an important but related controversy: whether water transfers from one water body to another, through diversion systems, pumps, and other mechanisms, qualify as "addition" of pollutants. Such transfers are key components of the U.S. water infrastructure, providing drinking water and serving agricultural and industrial purposes as well. One approach advanced by some litigants but rejected by several courts was the "unitary waters" theory. See Friends of the Everglades v. South Fla. Water Mgmt. Dist., 570 F.3d 1210, 1217-1218 (11th Cir. 2009) (collecting sources). That is, moving water from one navigable source to another is not an "addition" where only preexisting pollutants are moved. As the Supreme Court has described the theory, "If one takes a ladle of soup from a pot, lifts it above the pot, and pours it back into the pot, one has not 'added' soup or anything else to the pot." South Fla. Water Mgmt. Dist. v. Miccosukee Tribe, 541 U.S. 95, 110 (2004).

Although the unitary waters rule was disfavored, EPA adopted it through notice-and-comment rulemaking. NPDES Water Transfers Rule, 73 Fed. Reg. 33,697, 33,699 (June 13, 2008). Because the prior court decisions had been rendered before EPA's adoption of the water transfers rule, the Eleventh Circuit determined that Chevron deference applied to its review of EPA's interpretation. Friends of the Everglades, 570 F.3d at 1218. Ultimately, the court concluded that EPA's interpretation was reasonable and upheld it. The unitary waters theory, though the governing law, continues to be criticized. See Reagen, Comment, The Water Transfers Rule: How an EPA Rule Threatens to Undermine the Clear Water Act, 83 U. Colo. L. Rev. 307 (2011).

NOTES AND QUESTIONS ON NPDES JURISDICTION

1. *General Permits.* Our focus in the text is primarily on issuing individual NPDES permits to specific facilities. A party that is subject to NPDES individual permitting requirements is supposed to apply for such a permit from EPA or the authorized state. The permitting authority then drafts a permit for that discharger for public comment. The authority then issues a final permit to the discharger, with the permit having a specific expiration date (not to exceed five years from the date of issuance). Permittees are expected to apply for renewal of such a permit before it expires. See, e.g., EPA, Draft National Pollutant Discharge Elimination System (NPDES) Pesticide General Permit for Point Source Discharges from the Application of Pesticides, 75 Fed. Reg. 31,775 (June 4, 2010).

The CWA also empowers EPA to issue "general permits." These permits cover multiple facilities within a specific category, again for a specific period of time not to exceed five years. EPA develops and issues a general permit, again subject to public comment. Following EPA's issuance of a general permit, dischargers engaging in the activity covered by the permit must submit a Notice of Intent (NOI) in order to be covered. 40 C.F.R. §122.28. General permits serve administrative efficiency because they permit EPA to address only once an issue that would otherwise recur redundantly. The courts have approved EPA's use of general permits. See, e.g., Envtl. Def. Ctr., Inc. v. EPA, 344 F.3d 832, 853 (9th Cir. 2003).

A 2009 report suggests that EPA and state regulators are "increasingly relying" on general permits as a way to regulate a rapidly expanding regulatory universe. Regulators Eye General Permits to Address Growing CWA Universe, www.insideepa.com (April 28, 2009). Recent court rulings concerning discharges from vessels and spraying pesticides on or near water have required that the NPDES program nearly double in size, from approximately 400,000 facilities (45,000 covered by an individual NPDES permit and 350,000 covered by a general permit) to roughly 830,000 (an additional 435,000 discharges). Regulators Eye General Permits to Address Growing CWA Universe, Envtl. Policy Alert, www.insideepa.com (May 6, 2009), at 13. EPA makes the same point in its October 2009 Clean Water Act Enforcement Action Plan, noting that "[t]he sheer magnitude of the expanding universe of the NPDES program itself, from roughly 100,000 traditional point sources to nearly a million sources—95 percent of which are covered by general permits—presents challenges in how we regulate and enforce the laws of this country." Id. at 1. The use of general permits poses important issues concerning accountability and flexibility, while the expanding universe of permittees obviously poses challenges for the traditional approach of issuing facility-specific NPDES permits.

2. *Groundwater.* Groundwater is not explicitly dealt with in the CWA. Federal courts are split on whether discharges into aquifers that are hydrologically connected to jurisdictional surface streams require NPDES permits. Two cases that provide fairly thorough discussions of this issue came out on opposite sides. Compare Umatilla Water Quality Protective Ass'n v. Smith Frozen Foods, 962 F. Supp. 1312 (D. Or. 1997) (holding that the CWA does not apply to discharges into groundwater hydrologically connected to surface water), with Idaho Rural Council v. Bosma, 143 F. Supp. 2d 1169, 1178-1181 (D. Idaho 2001) (holding that the CWA does apply to groundwater that is hydrologically connected to surface water). Hernandez v. Esso Standard Oil Co. (Puerto Rico), 599 F. Supp. 2d 175 (D.P.R. 2009), includes a summary of the case law.

3. *The Relationship Between the NPDES Permit Scheme and the Jurisdictional Reach of Other Environmental Laws.* Under some circumstances, the existence of NPDES jurisdiction potentially exempts a discharger from obligations that it otherwise might face under other environmental laws. For example, RCRA §1004(27) exempts from its definition of solid waste some discharges regulated under the CWA (see Chapter 8), and CERCLA §107(j) limits liability for federally permitted releases (see Chapter 9). In National Ass'n of Homebuilders v. Defenders of Wildlife, 551 U.S. 644 (2007) (excerpted as a principal case in Chapter 5), the Court held that the CWA requirements for authorizing a state to implement the NPDES program are exclusive in the sense that EPA need not consider ESA-related issues in deciding whether to approve a request for authorization. The Supreme Court addressed the relationship between the NPDES permit scheme and the CWA §404 permit scheme in Coeur Alaska, Inc. v. Southeast Alaska Conservation Council, 557 U.S. 261 (2009) (see section I below).

4. *A Special Note on Aerial Spraying of Pesticides.* The issue of what is a "pollutant" under the CWA (as well as the question of what is a "point source") has received considerable attention in the context of application of federally registered pesticides. It is undisputed that aerial spraying of pesticides in and near bodies of water results in pesticide residues remaining in those waters. As the text in this section reflects, to trigger NPDES permitting jurisdiction, such spraying must qualify as a "discharge of a pollutant"—that is, the addition of a pollutant from a point source into a navigable water. In recent years, proponents of such spraying sought to avoid coverage of the NPDES permit scheme by arguing that such spraying operations do not qualify as a "point source." They have further argued that the pesticides do not qualify as "pollutants," in part because they are being applied for a legitimate purpose (they are products, not "chemical wastes") and their use (application) is subject to FIFRA (the Federal Insecticide, Fungicide and Rodenticide Act, covered in Chapter 8), which imposes a variety of limits on the application of pesticides. E.g., Nat'l Cotton Council of Am. v. EPA, 553 F.3d 927, 934-935 (6th Cir. 2009).

EPA sought to bring clarity to these issues on several occasions. In a 2006 regulation, the agency provided that application of pesticides to, or over, waters does not require a NPDES permit in two circumstances, so long as the application is consistent with FIFRA: (1) the application of pesticides directly to water in order to control pests (e.g., mosquito larvae); and (2) the application of pesticides to control pests that are present over (including near) water where a portion of the pesticides will unavoidably be deposited to the water to target the pests (e.g., applying pesticides near water to control adult mosquitoes or other pests). 40 C.F.R. §122.3(h). Challenges to EPA's regulation were filed in all 11 circuit courts. In 2009, the Sixth Circuit vacated the rule, holding that application of pesticides from the air is a point source. Further, the court held that the CWA unambiguously includes within its definition of "pollutant" (specifically as "chemical wastes and biological materials") "biological pesticides," and "chemical pesticides" that leave a residue. *National Cotton Council*, 553 F.3d at 935-938.

EPA estimated the Sixth Circuit decision would "apply to 5.6 million annual pesticide applications performed by 365,000 applicants." Despite Senators' Call, EPA Plans Narrow NPDES Spraying Permit, Envtl. Policy Alert, www.insideepa.com (May 6, 2009, at 18). EPA sought and received a two-year stay of the mandate from the Sixth Circuit, until April 2011, so that it could develop general permits for application of pesticides and work with states to develop new state-level permitting plans. Case

No. 06-4630 (6th Cir. June 8, 2009). In the interim, the application of pesticides consistent with EPA's regulation was lawful. The Second Circuit in Peconic Baykeeper, Inc. v. Suffolk County, 600 F.3d 180, 187 (2d Cir. 2010), deferred to the Sixth Circuit decision, holding that "[s]praying that occurs prior to expiration of the Sixth Circuit's stay of mandate, and is consistent with the EPA-approved FIFRA labeling, remains in compliance with the Final Rule. Once the stay of mandate expires a yet-to-be finalized CWA permitting system will govern the application of pesticides."

EPA issued a Pesticide General Permit (PGP) for discharges from the application of pesticides in 2011. Final NPDES Pesticide for Point Source Discharges from the Application of Pesticides, 76 Fed. Reg. 68,750 (Nov. 7, 2011). The PGP covers four specific applications of biological pesticides and chemical pesticides that leave a residue: (1) spraying to control mosquito and other flying insect pests that create public health and nuisance concerns and that develop or are present during a portion of their life cycle in or above standing or flowing water; (2) spraying to control weeds and algae in water and at water's edge; (3) spraying to control invasive or other nuisance species in water and at water's edge; and (4) spraying over a forest canopy to control the population of a pest species (e.g., insects) where to target the pest effectively a portion of the pesticide unavoidably will be applied over and deposited to water.

Problem 7-2

Assume that you are a staff attorney with a Gulf-state regulatory agency that has been authorized to administer the NPDES program. Your main responsibility involves working with technical staff in the Department to interpret and apply the Clean Water Act. A new inspector has joined your unit. The new person approaches you one day and says:

> I was driving across the bridge at the State Wildlife Refuge last weekend. The bridge is currently undergoing some maintenance work. It's being painted, and there's also some reinforcement work being done. There were a few workers out there over the weekend, and I noticed that some liquid material from the containers the workers were using was spilling occasionally into the marsh below the bridge. The marsh serves as habitat for migratory birds and is hydrologically connected to the Gulf of Mexico.

Analyze whether this maintenance operation is subject to Clean Water Act permitting authority.

D. ESTABLISHING TECHNOLOGY-BASED EFFLUENT LIMITATIONS

"Technology-based controls" are one of the most important tools in the environmental regulatory mechanisms. Under Subchapter III of the CWA, EPA develops technology-based effluent limitations on a national basis for different industries, and sometimes regulates more precisely by industrial subcategory. CWA §§304(b), (m), 306. Chemical Manufacturers Ass'n v. NRDC, 470 U.S. 116, 120 (1985), makes it clear that the agency has considerable discretion to establish such subcategories—subcategories are necessarily "rough hewn." The agency develops standards by looking at the existing state of the art in an industry and potential advances in waste treatment technology. The process of establishing national standards for a particular industry is often expensive and time consuming. If there is not a national rule in place, the permitting agency uses "best professional judgment" (BPJ) to establish permit limits for facilities as needed. CWA §402(a)(1)(B); 40 C.F.R. §122.44(a). The permit writer, in determining BPJ, considers the same factors as EPA considers in establishing nationwide effluent limits. 40 C.F.R. §125.3(d).

Technology-based regulation requires point sources to use the best available technology to treat their wastes, rather than requiring levels of treatment based on water quality goals. This has led to charges that the standards impede economic efficiency because they discourage or prohibit adopting the least costly treatment alternative. See Note, Technology-Based Emission and Effluent Standards and the Achievement of Ambient Environmental Standards, 91 Yale L.J. 792 (1982). Critics have charged that this approach of establishing national technology-based categorical standards for various industries is inefficient because it employs a "one size fits all" approach to regulation. This issue came up in Weyerhaeuser Co. v. Costle, 590 F.2d 1011 (D.C. Cir. 1978), discussed below at page 655, in which regulated parties that challenged EPA regulations argued, among other things, that the agency is obligated to take into account the actual environmental impact on receiving waters in setting permit limits for particular dischargers. One commentator's succinct summary and criticism of this centerpiece of the CWA regulatory scheme is that the technology-based approach

> is not finely tuned to the condition of the specific waterbody nor does it vary based on the relationship between the discharge and water quality. Rather, a technology based approach imposes similar limitations on similar dischargers irrespective of the effect of the discharge on water quality or the specific waterbody. Consequently, although "end of pipe" controls frequently improve stream conditions, the technology-based approach may under or over regulate the affected discharger.

Warren, Total Maximum Daily Loads: A Watershed Approach to Improved Water Quality, ALI-ABA Course of Study Clean Water Act: Law and Regulations 115 (Oct. 23-25, 2002).

The NPDES permit program's reliance on national, technology-based pollution control limits includes three crucial distinctions. First, the CWA establishes distinct technology-based standards for different types of dischargers. The primary focus in this chapter is on direct industrial dischargers—that is, industrial facilities that discharge directly into a water body. The CWA also imposes technology-based standards on sewage treatment plants, often referred to as publicly owned treatment works or POTWs. 33 U.S.C. §1311(b)(1)(B). And it imposes a different set of standards on "pretreaters," industrial dischargers that discharge into a sewage treatment system rather than directly into a navigable water. We have included a note on municipal treatment systems that provides a brief overview of regulatory treatment of the latter two types of dischargers (see section G). Second, the CWA provides for different treatment of existing and new direct industrial dischargers, as does the Clean Air Act. Third, pollutants are divided into four categories for purposes of standard setting and compliance deadlines: (1) conventional pollutants, generally those that are biodegradable; (2) toxic pollutants, those that are not biodegradable and create a risk of substantial human health impairment; (3) nonconventional, nontoxic pollutants; and (4) heat, which is treated as a separate category because its adverse impacts are more site-specific than those of the first three categories.

The 1972 CWA anticipated that technology-based standards for direct industrial dischargers would become increasingly stringent over time. The CWA required existing dischargers initially to install BPT (the best practicable control technology currently available) by 1977, 33 U.S.C. §1311(b)(1). It then required existing direct dischargers to install more effective technology, BAT (the best available technology economically achievable). Congress extended the deadline for implementing BAT until 1989. Id. §1311(b)(2). New sources were subject to BADT (best available demonstrated control technology) and were required to meet new source performance standards (NSPS). Congress anticipated that BADT limits would be the most stringent of the technology-based controls, expecting that new sources could reduce discharges more cost-effectively than could existing plants. See, e.g., CPC Int'l, Inc. v. Train, 540 F.2d 1329 (8th Cir. 1976). In 1977, Congress amended the CWA to require dischargers of "conventional" pollutants to meet BCT (best conventional technology) limits rather than the more stringent BAT, thus creating an intermediate level of technology-based controls between BPT and BAT. EPA is required periodically to review and update its technology-based standards. For one of many overviews of technology-based standards, see Notice of Availability of Preliminary 2010 Effluent Guidelines Program Plan, 74 Fed. Reg. 68,599 (Dec. 28, 2009).

Once EPA establishes technology-based regulations for an industrial category, these regulations operate as floors—not ceilings—that must be incorporated into all NPDES permits (subject to limited variances in the Act). Effluent limitations may specify, among other things, (1) numerical limits on the discharge from individual units of production, (2) maximum daily and 30-day average permissible concentrations in unit waste streams of listed pollutants, and (3) specific treatment and process modification designs that must be employed. R. Zener, Guide to Federal Environmental Law 96 (1981). Permits issued to individual sources also may require monitoring and reporting for pollutants for which numerical limits are not set. The CWA includes a series of variance provisions that create a limited degree of flexibility in this national program.

1. A National, Industry-Wide Approach

An early issue concerned whether EPA could issue uniform industry-wide limitations that would bind all permittees. The Supreme Court approved this approach in the following case.

E.I. DU PONT DE NEMOURS & CO. v. TRAIN
430 U.S. 112 (1977)

Mr. Justice STEVENS delivered the opinion of the Court.

Inorganic chemical manufacturing plants operated by the eight petitioners . . . discharge various pollutants into the Nation's waters and therefore are "point sources" within the meaning of the Federal Water Pollution Control Act (Act). . . . The Environmental Protection Agency has promulgated industry wide regulations imposing three sets of precise limitations on petitioners' discharges. The first two impose progressively higher levels of pollution control on existing point sources after July 1, 1977, and after July 1, 1983, respectively. The third set imposes limits on "new sources" that may be constructed in the future.

[The Court noted that these cases present important questions of statutory construction, including: (1) whether EPA has the authority under §301 of the Act to issue industry-wide regulations limiting discharges by existing plants; and (2) whether the new-source standards issued under §306 must allow variances for individual plants.]

The Statute

The statute, enacted on October 18, 1972, authorized a series of steps to be taken to achieve the goal of eliminating all discharges of pollutants into the Nation's waters by 1985, §101(a)(1).

The first steps required by the Act are described in §304, which directs the Administrator to develop and publish various kinds of technical data to provide guidance in carrying out responsibilities imposed by other sections of the Act. Section 304(b) goes into great detail concerning the contents of these regulations. They must identify the degree of effluent reduction attainable through use of the best practicable or best available technology for a class of plants. The guidelines must also "specify factors to be taken into account" in determining the control measures applicable to point sources within these classes. A list of factors to be considered then follows. The Administrator was also directed to develop and publish, within one year, elaborate criteria for water quality accurately reflecting the most current scientific knowledge, and also technical information on factors necessary to restore and maintain water quality. §304(a). . . .

Section 306 directs the Administrator to publish within 90 days a list of categories of sources discharging pollutants and, within one year thereafter, to publish regulations establishing national standards of performance for new sources within each category. Section 306 contains no provision for exceptions from the standards for individual plants; on the contrary, subsection (e) expressly makes it unlawful to operate a new source in violation of the applicable standard of performance after its effective date. The statute provides that the new-source standards shall reflect the greatest degree of effluent reduction achievable through application of the best available demonstrated control technology.

Section 301(b) defines the effluent limitations that shall be achieved by existing point sources in two stages. By July 1, 1977, the effluent limitations shall require the application of the best practicable control technology currently available; by July 1, 1983, the limitations shall require application of the best available technology economically achievable. The statute expressly provides that the limitations which are to become effective in 1983 are applicable to "categories and classes of point sources"; this phrase is omitted from the description of the 1977 limitations. While §301 states that these limitations "shall be achieved," it fails to state who will establish the limitations.

Section 301(c) authorizes the Administrator to grant variances from the 1983 limitations. Section 301(e) states that effluent limitations established pursuant to §301 shall be applied to all point sources. . . .

The Regulations

The various deadlines imposed on the Administrator were too ambitious for him to meet. For that reason, the procedure which he followed in adopting the regulations applicable to the inorganic chemical industry and to other classes of point sources is somewhat different from that apparently contemplated by the statute. Specifically, as will appear, he did not adopt guidelines pursuant to §304 before defining the effluent limitations for existing sources described in §301(b) or the national standards for new sources described in §306. This case illustrates the approach the Administrator followed in implementing the Act.

EPA began by engaging a private contractor to prepare a Development Document. This document provided a detailed technical study of pollution control in the industry. The study first divided the industry into categories. For each category, present levels of pollution were measured and plants with exemplary pollution control were investigated. Based on this information, other technical data, and economic studies, a determination was made of the degree of pollution control which could be achieved by the various levels of technology mandated by the statute. The study was made available to the public and circulated to interested persons. It formed the basis of "effluent limitation guideline" regulations issued by EPA after receiving public comment on proposed regulations. These regulations divide the industry into 22 subcategories. Within each subcategory, precise numerical limits are set for various pollutants. The regulations for each subcategory contain a variance clause, applicable only to the 1977 limitations. . . .

The Issues

The broad outlines of the parties' respective theories may be stated briefly. EPA contends that §301(b) authorizes it to issue regulations establishing effluent limitations for classes of plants. The permits granted under §402, in EPA's view, simply incorporate these across-the-board limitations, except for the limited variances allowed by the regulations themselves and by §301(c). The §304(b) guidelines, according to EPA, were intended to guide it in later establishing §301 effluent-limitation regulations. Because the process proved more time-consuming than Congress assumed when it established this two-stage process, EPA condensed the two stages into a single regulation.

In contrast, petitioners contend that §301 is not an independent source of authority for setting effluent limitations by regulation. Instead, §301 is seen as merely a description of the effluent limitations which are set for each plant on an individual basis during the permit-issuance process. Under the industry view, the §304 guidelines serve the function of guiding the permit issuer in setting the effluent limitations. . . .

I

We think §301 itself is the key to the problem. The statutory language concerning the 1983 limitations, in particular, leaves no doubt that these limitations are to be set by regulation. Subsection (b)(2)(A) of §301 states that by 1983 "effluent limitations *for categories and classes* of point sources" are to be achieved which will require "application of the best available technology economically achievable for such *category or class.*" (Emphasis added.) These effluent limitations are to require elimination of all discharges if "such elimination is technologically and economically achievable for a *category or class* of point sources." (Emphasis added.) This is "language difficult to reconcile with the view that individual effluent limitations are to be set when each permit is issued." The statute thus focuses expressly on the characteristics of the "category or class" rather than the characteristics of individual point sources. Normally, such classwide determinations would be made by regulation, not in the course of issuing a permit to one member of the class.

Thus, we find that §301 unambiguously provides for the use of regulations to establish the 1983 effluent limitations. Different language is used in §301 with respect to the 1977 limitations. Here, the statute speaks of "effluent limitations for point sources," rather than "effluent limitations for categories and classes of point sources." Nothing elsewhere in the Act, however, suggests any radical difference in the mechanism used to impose limitations for the 1977 and 1983 deadlines. For instance, there is no indication in either §301 or §304 that the §304 guidelines play a different role in setting 1977 limitations. Moreover, it would be highly anomalous if the 1983 regulations and the new-source standards were directly reviewable in the Court of Appeals, while the 1977 regulations based on the same administrative record were reviewable only in the District Court. The magnitude and highly technical character of the administrative record involved with these regulations makes it almost inconceivable that Congress would have required duplicate review in the first instance by different courts. We conclude that the statute authorizes the 1977 limitations as well as the 1983 limitations to be set by regulation, so long as some allowance is made for variations in individual plants, as EPA has done by including a variance clause in its 1977 limitations.

The question of the form of §301 limitations is tied to the question whether the Act requires the Administrator or the permit issuer to establish the limitations. Section 301 does not itself answer this question, for it speaks only in the passive voice of the achievement and establishment of the limitations. But other parts of the statute leave little doubt on this score. Section 304(b) states that "[f]or the purpose of adopting or revising effluent limitations . . . the Administrator shall" issue guideline regulations; while the judicial-review section, §509(b)(1), speaks of "the Administrator's action . . . in approving or promulgating any effluent limitation or other limitation under section 301. . . ." And §101(d) requires us to resolve any ambiguity on this score in favor of the *Administrator.* (Emphasis added.) It provides that "(e)xcept as otherwise expressly provided in this Act, the *Administrator* of the Environmental Protection Agency . . . shall administer this Act." (Emphasis added.) In sum, the language of the statute supports the view that §301 limitations are to be adopted by the Administrator, that they are to be based primarily on classes and categories, and that they are to take the form of regulations. . . .

What, then, is the function of the §304(b) guidelines? As we noted earlier, §304(b) requires EPA to identify the amount of effluent reduction attainable through use of the best practicable or available technology and to "specify factors to be taken into account" in determining the pollution control methods "to be applicable to point sources . . . within such categories or classes." These guidelines are to be issued "[f]or the purpose of adopting or revising effluent limitations under this Act." As we read it, §304 requires that the guidelines survey the practicable or available pollution-control technology for an industry and assess its effectiveness. The guidelines are then to describe the methodology EPA intends to use in the §301 regulations to determine the effluent limitations for particular plants. . . .

III

The remaining issue in this case concerns new plants. Under §306, EPA is to promulgate "regulations establishing Federal standards of performance for new sources. . . ." §306(b)(1)(B). A "standard of performance" is a "standard for the control of the discharge of pollutants which reflects the greatest degree of effluent reduction which the Administrator determines to be achievable through application of the best available demonstrated control technology, . . . including, where practicable, a standard permitting no discharge of pollutants." §306(a)(1). In setting the standard, "[t]he Administrator may distinguish among classes, types, and sizes within categories of new sources . . . and shall consider the type of process employed (including whether batch or continuous)." §306(b)(2).

   . . . [The Court also determined that Congress] intended these [new source] regulations to be absolute prohibitions. The use of the word "standards" implies as much. So does the description of the preferred standard as one "permitting *no* discharge of pollutants." (Emphasis added.) It is "unlawful for *any* owner or operator of *any* new source to operate such source in violation of any standard of performance applicable to such source." §306(e) (emphasis added). In striking contrast to §301(c), there is no statutory provision for variances, and a variance provision would be inappropriate in a standard that was intended to insure national uniformity and "maximum feasible control of new sources."

2. *Relevant Factors in Setting National Standards*

   With the Supreme Court having established that EPA may issue industry-wide technology-based standards, numerous questions arose concerning interpretation and application of the legal framework for establishing such standards. As might be expected, EPA regulations establishing such national standards were challenged on a wide variety of grounds. Prominent issues included the role that cost should play in EPA's analysis, and the role of "receiving water capacity"—that is, the extent to which "dilution could be the solution to pollution." The following case addresses these questions.

WEYERHAEUSER CO. v. COSTLE
590 F.2d 1011 (D.C. Cir. 1978)

McGowan, Circuit Judge: . . .

   [The pulp and paper mill industry challenged EPA's BPT standards. The court's description of the pulp and paper waste disposal process and its disposition of the industry's two major challenges to the regulations follow.]

B.

To make paper from trees is an old art; to do it without water pollution is a new science. In papermaking, logs or wooden chips must be ground up or "cooked" in one of several processes until only cellulose pulp is left. The pulp is bleached and made into various types and grades of paper. The cooking solutions and wash water that are left contain a variety of chemicals produced during "cooking" and other processes, including acids and large quantities of dissolved cellulose-breakdown products. Indeed, in some pulping processes, more of the wood is discarded in the waste water than is used to make paper. EPA has selected three parameters for measuring the pollutant content of the industry's effluent, all of which have been used extensively in this and other industries' measurements: total suspended solids (TSS), biochemical oxygen demand (BOD), and pH. TSS reflects the total amount of solids in solution, while BOD reflects the amount of biodegradable material in solution, and pH measures the acidity of the solution.

EPA has divided this segment of the industry into 16 subcategories, and further subdivided it into 66 subdivisions, for the purposes of its rulemaking effort. As noted, some of petitioners' challenges concern all of the regulations for the whole industry, while other challenges are directed to regulations for particular industry subcategories. Actually, of the 16 subcategories in the whole industry, only the three that use some form of the "sulfite process" have evoked particularized challenges. The reaction of sulfite mill operators stems from the limitations' greater economic impact on them. That impact in turn results from the fact that the sulfite process creates one of the highest pollution loads of any industrial process, and certainly the highest within the pulping industry. In fact, the Act's legislative history focused in particular on injury to shellfish in rivers and bays caused by sulfite wastes. A Legislative History of the Water Pollution Control Act Amendments of 1972 718-21 (1973) [hereinafter referred to as Legislative History]. . . .

V. The Agency's Interpretation of the Statute

. . .

1.

Some of the paper mills that must meet the effluent limitations under review discharge their effluents into the Pacific Ocean. Petitioners contend that the ocean can dilute or naturally treat effluent, and that EPA must take this capacity of the ocean ("receiving water capacity") into account in a variety of ways. They urge what they term "common sense," i.e., that because the amounts of pollutant involved are small in comparison to bodies of water as vast as Puget Sound or the Pacific Ocean, they should not have to spend heavily on treatment equipment, or to increase their energy requirements and sludge levels, in order to treat wastes that the ocean could dilute or absorb.[41]

41. Apart from this simple "common sense" version of the argument, there is a more sophisticated economic version called the "optimal pollution" theory. This economic theory contends that there is a level or type of pollution that, while technologically capable of being controlled, is uneconomic to treat because the benefit from treatment is small and the cost of treatment is large. See generally W. Baxter, People or Penguins: The Case for Optimal Pollution (1974); B. Ackerman, S. Rose-Ackerman, J. Sawyer & D. Henderson, The Uncertain Search for Environmental Quality (1974). These economic theories are premised on a view that we have both adequate information about the effects of pollution to set an optimal test, and adequate political and

EPA's secondary response to this claim was that pollution is far from harmless, even when disposed of in the largest bodies of water. As congressional testimony indicated, the Great Lakes, Puget Sound, and even areas of the Atlantic Ocean have been seriously injured by water pollution. Even if the ocean can handle ordinary wastes, ocean life may be vulnerable to toxic compounds that typically accompany those wastes. In the main, however, EPA simply asserted that the issue of receiving water capacity could not be raised in setting effluent limitations because Congress had ruled it out. We have examined the previous legislation in this area, and the 1972 Act's wording, legislative history, and policies, as underscored by its 1977 amendments. These sources, which were thoroughly analyzed in a recent opinion of the administrator of the Agency, fully support EPA's construction of the Act. They make clear that based on long experience, and aware of the limits of technological knowledge and administrative flexibility, Congress made the deliberate decision to rule out arguments based on receiving water capacity. . . .

Moreover, by eliminating the issue of the capacity of particular bodies of receiving water, Congress made nationwide uniformity in effluent regulation possible. Congress considered uniformity vital to free the states from the temptation of relaxing local limitations in order to woo or keep industrial facilities.[46] In addition, national uniformity made pollution clean-up possible without engaging in the divisive task of favoring some regions of the country over others.

More fundamentally, the new approach implemented changing views as to the relative rights of the public and of industrial polluters. Hitherto, the right of the polluter was pre-eminent, unless the damage caused by pollution could be proven. Henceforth, the right of the public to a clean environment would be pre-eminent, unless pollution treatment was impractical or unachievable. The Senate Committee declared that "[t]he use of any river, lake, stream or ocean as a waste treatment system is unacceptable" regardless of the measurable impact of the waste on the body of water in question. Legislative History at 1425 (Senate Report). The Conference Report stated that the Act "specifically bans pollution dilution as an alternative to waste treatment." Id. at 284. This new view of relative rights was based in part on the hard-nosed assessment of our scientific ignorance: "[W]e know so little about the ultimate consequences of injection of new matter into water that (the Act requires) a presumption of pollution. . . ." Id. at 1332 (remarks of Sen. Buckley). It also was based on the widely shared conviction that the nation's quality of life depended on its natural bounty, and that it was worth incurring heavy cost to preserve that bounty for future generations. . . .

The Act was passed with an expectation of "mid-course corrections," Legislative History, at 175 (statement of Sen. Muskie), and in 1977 Congress amended the Act, although generally holding to the same tack set five years earlier. Pub. L. No. 95-217, 91 Stat. 1584. Notably, during those five years, representatives of the paper industry had appeared before Congress and urged it to *change* the Act and to incorporate receiving water capacity as a consideration. (Emphasis added.) Nonetheless, Congress was satisfied with this element of the statutory scheme. . . .

---

administrative flexibility to keep polluters at that level once we allow any pollution to go untreated. As discussed in this section, it appears that Congress doubted these premises.

46. "[T]he greatest political barrier to effective pollution control is the threat by industrial polluters to move their factories out of any State that seriously tries to protect its environment." Legislative History, at 577 (remarks of Rep. Reuss). "Varying local revenue capabilities, economic pressures, and citizen interest have often stagnated community and State initiative." Id. at 156 (remarks of EPA Administrator Ruckelshaus). See American Frozen Food Inst. v. Train, 539 F.2d 107, 129 (1976).

2.

Petitioners also challenge EPA's manner of assessing two factors that all parties agree must be considered: cost and non–water quality environmental impacts. They contend that the Agency should have more carefully balanced costs versus the effluent reduction benefits of the regulations, and that it should have also balanced those benefits against the non–water quality environmental impacts to arrive at a "net" environmental benefit conclusion. Petitioners base their arguments on certain comments made by the Conferees for the Act, and on the fact that the Act lists non–water quality environmental impacts as a factor the Agency must "take into account."

In order to discuss petitioners' challenges, we must first identify the relevant statutory standard. Section 304(b)(1)(B) of the Act identifies the factors bearing on BPCTCA in two groups. First, the factors shall

> include consideration of the total cost of application of technology in relation to the effluent reduction benefits to be achieved from such application,

and second, they

> shall also take into account the age of equipment and facilities involved, the process employed, the engineering aspects of the application of various types of control techniques, process changes, non–water quality environmental impact (including energy requirements), and such other factors as the Administrator deems appropriate[.]

The first group consists of two factors that EPA must compare: total cost versus effluent reduction benefits. We shall call these the "comparison factors." The other group is a list of many factors that EPA must "take into account": age, process, engineering aspects, process changes, environmental impacts (including energy), and any others EPA deems appropriate. We shall call these the "consideration factors." Notably, section 304(b)(2)(B) of the Act, which delineates the factors relevant to setting 1983 BATEA limitations, tracks the 1977 BPCTCA provision before us except in one regard: in the 1983 section, *all* factors, including costs and benefits, are consideration factors, and no factors are separated out for comparison. (Emphasis added.)

Based on our examination of the statutory language and the legislative history, we conclude that Congress mandated a particular structure and weight for the 1977 comparison factors, that is to say, a "limited" balancing test.[52] In contrast, Congress did not mandate any particular structure or weight for the many consideration factors. Rather, it left EPA with discretion to decide how to account for the consideration factors, and how much weight to give each factor. In response to these divergent

---

52. Senator Muskie described the "limited" balancing test:

The modification of subsection 304(b)(1) is intended to clarify what is meant by the term "practicable." The balancing test between total cost and effluent reduction benefits is intended to limit the application of technology only where the additional degree of effluent reduction is wholly out of proportion to the costs of achieving such marginal level of reduction for any class or category of sources.

The Conferees agreed upon this limited cost-benefit analysis in order to maintain uniformity within a class and category of point sources subject to effluent limitations, and to avoid imposing on the Administrator any requirement to consider the location of sources within a category or to ascertain water quality impact of effluent controls, or to determine the economic impact of controls on any individual plant in a single community.

Legislative History, at 170 (emphasis added).

congressional approaches, we conclude that, on the one hand, we should examine EPA's treatment of cost and benefit under the 1977 standard to assure that the Agency complied with Congress' "limited" balancing directive. On the other hand, our scrutiny of the Agency's treatment of the several consideration factors seeks to assure that the Agency informed itself as to their magnitude, and reached its own express and considered conclusion about their bearing. More particularly, we do not believe that EPA is required to use any specific structure such as a balancing test in assessing the consideration factors, nor do we believe that EPA is required to give each consideration factor any specific weight.

Our conclusions are based initially on the section's wording and apparent logic. By singling out two factors (the comparison factors) for separate treatment, and by requiring that they be considered "in relation to" each other, Congress elevated them to a level of greater attention and rigor. Moreover, the comparison factors are a closed set of two, making it possible to have a definite structure and weight in considering them and preventing extraneous factors from intruding on the balance.

By contrast, the statute directs the Agency only to "take into account" the consideration factors, without prescribing any structure for EPA's deliberations. As to this latter group of factors, the section cannot logically be interpreted to impose on EPA a specific structure of consideration or set of weights because it gave EPA authority to "upset" any such structure by exercising its discretion to add new factors to the mix. Instead, the listing of factors seems aimed at noting all of the matters that Congress considered worthy of study before making limitation decisions, without preventing EPA from identifying other factors that it considers worthy of study. So long as EPA pays some attention to the congressionally specified factors, the section on its face lets EPA relate the various factors as it deems necessary.

The legislative history reveals that clear congressional policies support the section's facial structure. The original House and Senate versions of the section differed significantly. A major point of contention between the two versions involved the House's stronger concern over the economic effects of imposing stringent effluent limitations. Ultimately a compromise was reached at Conference and accepted by both houses. It provided, first, that the Agency must use "limited" cost-benefit balancing in deriving 1977 standards, but not in arriving at the 1983 standards. Legislative History, at 170 (statement of Sen. Muskie). A "midcourse" evaluation was then to occur in the mid- to late-1970's, after the Act had been in effect for several years but before full implementation of the 1983 standards. Id. at 175. The latter step was designed to allow Congress to rewrite the 1983 standards in order to continue the cost-benefit balancing during that period as well, if Congress found after early experience that such a course was necessary. Section 315 of the Act (establishing a National Study Commission to consider mid-course changes).

Thus the fact that Congress indicated its greater concern for cost-benefit calculation in the short run by making cost and benefit "comparison factors" for 1977, but only "consideration factors" for 1983, demonstrates the more relaxed view it took of EPA's treatment of consideration factors relevant to both the 1977 and 1983 standards. Indeed, after studying the need for mid-course correction, Congress decided to retain the 1972 arrangement, which, except for limited modifications not germane here, gives the Agency more complete discretion in considering the relevant factors in the future.[53]

Judicial decisions have carefully observed that the cost and benefit factors require more rigorous EPA consideration of cost versus benefit in the 1977 standards than in the 1983 standards. *American Paper Inst., supra*, 543 F.2d at 338 (cost-benefit balancing in 1977, not in 1983). Since the consideration factors specified in the 1977 provision track the language of all of the factors including cost and benefit in the 1983 provision, these cases support a lower level of administrative rigor and judicial review with respect to the 1977 consideration factors than with respect to the costs and benefit factors relevant to that year's limitations. We are fortified in this view by its coincidence with the Agency's interpretation. As the Supreme Court held last year, the EPA's construction of this Act is entitled to some deference. *Du Pont, supra*, 430 U.S. at 134-35.

Consequently, we must review the comparison factors to determine if EPA weighed them through the "limited" balancing test as intended by Congress. On the other hand, we may review the consideration factors only to determine if EPA was fully aware of them and reached its own express conclusions about them. Since the two types of factors are separate, we divide our discussion accordingly.

A.

Petitioners do not challenge the cost-benefit analysis for the whole industry. They do, however, challenge the analysis for the sulfite sector, contending that EPA used an "overall" instead of an "incremental" method of balancing, and that its figures on the cost of BPCTCA for the dissolving sulfite subcategory were underestimates. We uphold EPA's determination against both contentions.

EPA's approach was similar to the one we upheld in *American Paper Inst., supra*, 543 F.2d at 338-39. The Agency assessed the costs of internal and external effluent treatment measures, not only for the industry, but also for each subcategory. This included a separate cost assessment for the sulfite subcategories. An economic analysis was prepared to determine the impact of the costs on the industry. It found that the industry as a whole would readily absorb the cost of compliance with the 1977 standards, estimated at $1.6 billion. Out of 270 mills employing 120,000 people, eight mills would likely be closed and 1800 people laid off. The Agency noted that the impact on the three heavily polluting sulfite subcategories would be the greatest. Of less than 30 sulfite mills, three would probably close, resulting in 550 people being laid off.

53. When the mid-course study by the National Study Commission was completed and congressional hearings were held, Congress concluded that "little contained in the study of the Commission could be construed as justifying major change in the direction established in 1972. . . . With respect to the industrial program (which includes the regulations at issue in this case), the committee recognizes and applauds the significant success that most of the Nation's major industries have attained." S. Rep. No. 370, 95th Cong., 1st Sess. 1. Reprinted in (1977) U.S. Code Cong. & Admin. News pp. 4326, 4327. Accordingly, the 1977 amendments did not change the factors involved in §304(b)(2).

Against these costs, EPA balanced the main effluent reduction benefit: overall 5,000 fewer tons per day of BOD discharged into the nation's waters. EPA refined this balance by calculating the cost per pound of BOD removed for each subcategory. Although sulfite mills must make large investments in waste treatment facilities, the cost-benefit balance is favorable for the limitations on these mills, because of the large volume of waste they produce and thus the greater treatment efficiency.

Petitioners' first contention is that EPA not only should have calculated the overall cost-benefit balance, but also should have made an "incremental" calculation of that balance. More precisely, they contend that EPA must undertake to measure the costs and benefits of each additional increment of waste treatment control, from bare minimum up to complete pollution removal. In support of this contention, they point to Senator Muskie's description of cost-benefit balancing, which suggests a focus on the "additional degree" or "marginal" amount of effluent reduction. See note 52 *supra.* Petitioners concede that we accepted EPA's calculation of the overall cost-benefit balance, without any further marginal or incremental analysis, in *American Paper Inst., supra,* 543 F.2d at 338. Nonetheless, they suggest that the present case can be distinguished, because in these proceedings, unlike in *American Paper Inst.,* industry representatives submitted an incremental breakdown of costs and benefits to the Agency.

The failure of *American Paper Inst.* to require EPA to perform its own incremental analysis is justified for a number of reasons beyond some oversight on the part of paper industry petitioners in that case. While EPA has no discretion to avoid cost-benefit balancing for its 1977 standards, it does have some discretion to decide how it will perform the cost-benefit balancing task. "[E]ven with th[e] 1977 standard, the cost of compliance was not a factor to be given primary importance," *American Iron & Steel Inst., supra,* 526 F.2d at 1051, and, as such, cost need not be balanced against benefits with pinpoint precision. A requirement that EPA perform the elaborate task of calculating incremental balances would bog the Agency down in burdensome proceedings on a relatively subsidiary task. Hence, the Agency need not on its own undertake more than a net cost-benefit balancing to fulfill its obligation under section 304.

However, when an incremental analysis has been performed by industry and submitted to EPA, it is worthy of scrutiny by the Agency, for it may "avoid the risk of hidden imbalances between cost and benefit." Id. at 1076 n.19 (Adams, J., concurring). If such a "hidden imbalance" were revealed here, and if the Agency had ignored it, we might remand for further consideration. But in this case the incremental analysis proffered by industry showed that the last and most expensive increment of BOD treated in sulfite mills cost less than $.15 per pound of BOD removed, which is below the average cost of treatment in most of the industry's subcategories. We would be reluctant to find that EPA had ignored a "hidden imbalance" when the most unfavorable incremental cost-benefit balance that is challenged falls well within the range of averages for the industry as a whole. . . .

While *Weyerhaeuser* focused on a technology-based approach to setting BPT-based limits, the following case applies this approach with respect to BAT-based limits.

ASSOCIATION OF PACIFIC FISHERIES v. EPA
615 F.2d 794 (9th Cir. 1980)

KENNEDY, Circuit Judge:

In 1972 Congress, intending "to restore and maintain the chemical, physical, and biological integrity of the Nation's waters," amended the Federal Water Pollution Control Act (Act), 33 U.S.C. §1251 et seq. Congress established national pollution goals to be achieved by specific dates. By July 1, 1977, industries discharging pollutants into the nation's waters were to have achieved "the best practicable control technology currently available (BPT)." Section 301(b)(1)(A). By 1983, industry is to achieve "the best available technology economically achievable (BEA)." Section 301(b)(2)(A). The Environmental Protection Agency (EPA or Agency) was entrusted with the responsibility of defining and policing the efficient and prompt achievement of these goals. Section 304.

This case involves a challenge to regulations promulgated by the Agency establishing effluent guidelines for the Canned and Preserved Seafood Processing Point Source Category. 40 C.F.R. §§408.10 et seq. Petitioner Association of Pacific Fisheries is a trade association representing canners and fresh and frozen fish processors in affected subcategories. The remaining petitioners process seafood in all the subcategories at issue on this appeal.

The EPA's regulations governing the fish processing industry were promulgated in two phases. . . . [P]etitioners challenge several of the regulations promulgated during phase II of the Agency's proceedings. These phase II regulations covered nineteen separate subcategories. The subcategories were determined by the species of fish being processed; whether there was mechanization in the processing technique; for Alaska processors, the location of the plant, i.e., whether the plant was located in a "population or processing center"; and in some cases, the production capacity of the plant. At issue are the regulations which apply to Alaskan hand-butchered salmon (Subpart P), Alaskan mechanized salmon (Subpart Q), west coast hand-butchered salmon (Subpart R), west coast mechanized salmon (Subpart S), Alaskan bottomfish (Subpart T), west coast bottomfish (Subparts U and V), Alaskan scallops (Subpart AC), and herring fillets (Subparts AE and AF). See 40 C.F.R. §§408.160-408.226, 408.290-408.296, 408.310-408.326.

The effluent which is the subject of the regulations consists of unused fish residuals. This discharge includes heads, tails, and internal residuals of the processed fish. Substantial quantities of water are used at various stages of the plant operations. This water comes into contact with the fish residuals and contains pollutants when discharged. The regulations prescribe limitations on discharge, and utilize three measures of pollution: five-day biochemical oxygen demand (BOD_5); total suspended solids (TSS); and oil and grease (O & G).[2] The regulations establish daily maximum

---

2. BOD_5, five-day biochemical oxygen demand, is a measure of the oxygen-consuming potentialities of organic matter in the effluent. The BOD_5 test measures the extent to which the biological degradation of organic waste matter over a five-day period removes oxygen from the water. This test does not identify what kind of organic material is present in the effluent, but merely indicates the presence of biodegradable matter.

TSS describes the quantity of undissolved solid matter suspended in the effluent. As with BOD, the TSS measure does not identify the nature or the physical and chemical characteristics of the matter present in the effluent.

Oil and grease describes the volume of naturally-occurring fish oil in the effluent.

levels and monthly average levels for each subcategory, and are measured in terms of the amount of pollutant per thousand pounds of fish processed. . . .

By 1983 the fisheries must comply with more rigorous technology requirements and effluent limitations. For nonremote facilities, the Agency directed that a dissolved air flotation unit be installed at each location and that the end-of-pipe effluent be channeled through this system before it is discharged into the receiving water. These regulations apply to all nonremote subcategories except Subpart V, Conventional Bottomfish. There, the Administrator has prescribed aerated lagoons. . . . Remote Alaska fish processors will be required by the 1983 regulations to screen the effluent before discharging it into the receiving waters. . . .

1983 Regulations

The regulations promulgated by the Administrator for 1983 are to reflect the "best available technology economically achievable." Section 301(b)(2)(A). For the regulations to be affirmed, the Agency must demonstrate that the technology required is "available" and the effluent limitations are "economically achievable."

A. DISSOLVED AIR FLOTATION UNIT

A dissolved air flotation unit is the prescribed technology for the following subcategories: west coast hand-butchered salmon (Subpart R), west coast mechanized salmon (Subpart S), non-Alaskan mechanized bottomfish (Subpart V), and non-Alaskan herring fillet (Subpart AF).

The system operates as follows: Effluent passes into a holding tank. Air enters the effluent under pressure and attaches to solid particles. Buoyed by the air, the particles rise to the surface and are skimmed off. The particles can be used as animal feed or fertilizer. The clarified water is withdrawn from the bottom of the tank. Before entering the receiving waters, this effluent remainder must be within certain maximum limitations. The regulations set forth limitations for BOD_5, TSS, O & G, and acidity for each category.

The numerical limitations were based on the assumption that a DAF unit will reduce BOD_5 by 75%, TSS by 90%, and O & G by 90%. Petitioners claim these figures were the result of a single study conducted by the British Columbia seafood industry in conjunction with the Canadian Fisheries Research Board. The study measured the amount of reduced pollutants in the effluent from a salmon processing plant. The DAF unit reduced the BOD_5 by 80%, the TSS by 90%, and the oil and grease by 95%. Petitioners argue that the Agency was arbitrary and capricious in basing its 1983 technology regulations on a single study.

The legislative history of the 1983 regulations indicates that regulations establishing BEA can be based on statistics from a single plant. The House Report states:

> It will be sufficient for the purposes of setting the level of control under available technology, that there be one operating facility which demonstrates that the level can be achieved or that there is sufficient information and data from a relevant pilot plant or semi-works plant to provide the needed economic and technical justification for such new source.

L.H. at 798.

Although only one salmon study was in the record, the Administrator also considered numerous other DAF studies involving herring, groundfish, stickwater, sardines, shrimp, tuna, mackerel, scabbard, yellow croaker, and menhaden bailwater. Each of these studies revealed a substantial reduction in pollution levels. Although the pollution reduction in some studies was not as dramatic as others, the EPA is not charged with burden of showing that all DAF units could meet the limitations, but rather that the best existing DAF units can meet the limitations. Further, to the extent that some of these studies are best viewed as implicating "transfer technology," the Agency did not misuse its discretion in finding the technology to be transferable to the subcategories at issue. The EPA's data base was sufficient to show that the technology required to meet the 1983 limitations is "available." . . .

The next question is whether the Agency properly evaluated the costs of meeting the 1983 guidelines. In describing the role of costs in promulgating BEA, the Conference Report stated:

> While cost should be a factor in the Administrator's judgment, no balancing test will be required. The Administrator will be bound by a test of reasonableness. In this case, the reasonableness of what is "economically achievable" should reflect an evaluation of what needs to be done to move toward the elimination of the discharge of pollutants and what is achievable through the application of available technology without regard to cost.

L.H. at 170. Although the wording of the statute clearly states that the 1983 limitations must be "economically achievable," there is some disagreement among the circuits as to whether the costs of compliance should be considered in a review of the 1983 limitations. We hold, in agreement with the court in *Weyerhaeuser, supra,* 590 F.2d at 1044-45, that the EPA must consider the economic consequences of the 1983 regulations, along with the other factors mentioned in section 304(b)(2)(B).

Petitioners maintain that the Agency must balance the ecological benefits against the associated costs in determining whether the technology is economically achievable. They cite in support of this proposition *Appalachian Power Co. v. Train, supra.* In remanding the 1983 regulations affecting electrical power companies, the court there stated:

> [I]n choosing among alternative strategies, EPA must not only set forth the cost of achieving a particular level of heat reduction but must also state the expected environmental benefits, that is to say the effect on the environment, which will take place as a result of reduction, for it is only after EPA has fully explicated its course of conduct in this manner that a reviewing court can determine whether the agency has, in light of the goal to be achieved, acted arbitrarily or capriciously in adopting a particular effluent reduction level.

Id. at 1364-65. According to petitioners, the Agency did not consider the incremental benefit to the environment to be achieved by the dissolved air flotation units, and the regulations must be set aside. We cannot agree. As noted by the court in *Weyerhaeuser, supra,* 590 F.2d at 1045-46, the language of the statute indicates that the EPA's consideration of costs in determining BPT and BEA was to be different. In prescribing the appropriate 1977 technology, the Agency was to "include consideration of the total cost of application of *technology in relation to the effluent reduction benefits to be achieved from such application.*" Section 304(b)(1)(B) (emphasis added).

In determining the 1983 control technology, however, the EPA must "take into account . . . the cost of achieving such effluent reduction," along with various other factors. Section 304(b)(2)(B). The conspicuous absence of the comparative language contained in section 304(b)(1)(B) leads us to the conclusion that Congress did not intend the Agency or this court to engage in marginal cost-benefit comparisons.

The intent of Congress is stated in 33 U.S.C. §1251(a)(1): "(I)t is the national goal that the discharge of pollutants into the navigable waters be eliminated by 1985. . . ." The regulations that will be applied in 1983 are intended to result "in reasonable further progress toward the national goal of eliminating the discharge of all pollutants. . . ." 33 U.S.C. §1311(b)(2)(A). These express declarations of congressional intent cannot be ignored in determining the reasonableness of the 1983 regulations. So long as the required technology reduces the discharge of pollutants, our inquiry will be limited to whether the Agency considered the cost of technology, along with the other statutory factors, and whether its conclusion is reasonable. Of course, at some point extremely costly more refined treatment will have a de minimis effect on the receiving waters. But that point has not been reached in these BEA regulations.

The record discloses that the Agency studied the cost of complying with the 1983 regulations. It set forth the cost of compliance for plants that produced various amounts of effluent per minute, both in terms of capital costs and operation and maintenance costs. The projections include estimates of the costs of construction, labor, power, chemicals and fuel. Although land acquisition costs were not considered, the amount of land necessary for the air flotation unit is minimal. In contrast to our conclusion regarding aerated lagoons, the Agency was not arbitrary in concluding that the DAF unit could be installed on existing plant locations without necessitating additional land acquisitions.

Finally, it does not appear that the cost of complying with the 1983 regulations is unreasonable. The cost of compliance for the Northwest Canned Salmon subcategory, for example, is estimated to be $157,000 for initial investment and $32,000 of annual expenditures for the average size plants. According to the EPA's economic analysis, the total annual costs of pollution abatement averaged between one and two percent of the total sales figures of each subcategory. Depreciation is available for the capital outlays and tax deductions are available for business expenses. The Agency concluded that the benefits justified the costs, and petitioners have not shown that conclusion to be arbitrary or capricious.

Although the number of plants estimated to close as a result of the 1983 regulations was not stated clearly to us, it appears to be a lesser proportion of affected plants than that which we approved for the 1977 regulations. Since Congress contemplated the closure of some marginal plants, we do not consider the regulations to be arbitrary and capricious.

For these reasons, we conclude that the 1983 regulations requiring dissolved air flotation units for West Coast fish processors should be upheld.

B. AERATED LAGOONS

The aerated lagoon is the required technology for the non-Alaskan conventional bottomfish subcategory. 40 C.F.R. §408.213. Aerated lagoons are still ponds in which waste water is treated biologically. They are usually three to four feet deep. With oxidation taking place in the upper eighteen inches, the water will remain in the lagoon from three to fifty days. Mechanically aerated lagoons are between six and twenty feet deep and receive oxygen from a floating aerator. Because of the length of detention time, the lagoons must be large in relation to the square footage of a processing plant to handle peak wasteload production.

Petitioners contend that the data are insufficient to determine if the limitations are achievable. The Agency relied on one study conducted with perch and smelt wastewater. Although the record also makes a vague reference to a shrimp processing lagoon in Florida, the record contains no information about its similarities to or differences from the technology at issue. The record does not disclose the analytic approach utilized, the transferability of the technology, or even the person or persons who conducted the study. Therefore, we limit our discussion to the smelt and perch wastewater study.

Although the 1983 regulations can be based on information from a single model plant, the study must demonstrate the effectiveness of the required technology. The smelt perch study does not reach this standard. The study measured the BOD_5 and TSS contained in the wastewater before entry to the lagoon (BOD_5 4.5, TSS 2.3), but the record reveals only the reduction in BOD_5 in the effluent leaving the lagoon. Although the BOD_5 level would comply with the 1983 limitations, there is no indication as to whether the TSS and O & G levels would be sufficiently reduced.

The Agency is charged with the duty of articulating the reasons for its determination. Since there are no data upon which to determine that the TSS and O & G levels will be reduced sufficiently to comply with the 1983 limitations, we remand these regulations to the Agency for further findings.

The final question presented is whether the Agency gave adequate consideration to costs in the determination that aerated lagoons are achievable technology. The major disadvantage of aerated lagoons is that they require large amounts of readily accessible land. The Agency did not consider the cost of acquiring land in determining the economic impact of the regulations. The reason given for this omission is that the costs of acquiring land are "site-specific" and vary depending upon the location and surrounding area. Although this may be true, it does not follow that the cost of acquiring land should be completely ignored in determining whether the technology is achievable. Where a significant amount of land proximate to a plant is an inherent requirement of a control technology, the Agency must attempt to determine the economic impact of acquiring the land. The Agency may set forth the amount of land necessary for various size plants, the average cost of land in the vicinity of identified processing plants, and, finally, whether it is reasonable to conclude that land will be available for the aerated lagoons.

We recognize this holding may be at odds with American Iron and Steel Inst. v. EPA, 526 F.2d 1027, 1053 (3d Cir. 1976). The court there determined that the cost of land acquisition should not be considered because it is "inherently site-specific" and that petitioners have the burden of showing "the magnitude of these excluded costs factors." Id. at 1053. We respectfully disagree on both counts.

The Agency has successfully projected other average costs that might be termed "site-specific" such as the cost of in-plant process changes, the cost of barging and screening and the cost of other control technology. Each of these costs is subject to variability, depending on plant design and location. Similarly, when a significant amount of land is required for implementation of the regulation, we think the Agency must take land availability or land cost into account in some manner before it can make a reasoned determination that the regulations are economically achievable, especially when actual plant sites can be studied for this purpose. Failure to do so results in an incomplete consideration of the economic impact of the regulations. This is especially true where, as here, it appears many plant sites are located on waterfront areas where proximate land is not available or is in all probability expensive. That the cost or practicality of acquiring land is difficult to discern does not excuse the Agency from making some estimate of those factors. The amount of land necessary for this control technology is quite significant, and we think it is essential that the Agency give express consideration to that aspect of the 1983 regulations. . . .

The agency must show that the regulations are achievable. These regulations, based on data that fail to consider land acquisition cost or availability, are not the result of reasoned decisionmaking.

We therefore remand the regulation requiring aerated lagoons to the Agency in order that it may promulgate new 1983 regulations for the non-Alaskan conventional bottomfish subcategory. The remaining regulations are sustained upon the reasoning set forth above.

AFFIRMED in part and REMANDED in part.

NOTES AND QUESTIONS

1. *Challenges to EPA's Technology-Based Standards.* Du Pont upholds EPA's discretion to promulgate uniform national effluent standards, and *Weyerhaeuser* and *APF* explore some of the issues associated with establishing such standards. Within the parameters of this framework, establishing effluent limitations has been extremely difficult and involves considerable judgment by the agency. First, the agency must rely on the regulated community for much of its data on available technologies, reduction rates, and the costs of achieving possible discharge levels. Industry has naturally had incentives to withhold data, inflate costs, and challenge EPA's methodologies for making each of these judgments. Second, the agency must constantly balance what is technically feasible with cost considerations and deal with the problem of being unable to quantify the environmental benefits of the mandated effluent limitations. Third, these limitations are established through informal notice-and-comment rulemaking. Regulations frequently are challenged on procedural grounds, as ultra vires, or as arbitrary because they failed to adequately consider relevant data or statutory factors.

2. *Good, Better, Best.* In setting BPT and BAT regulations, can EPA base the regulations solely on the performance of the best plants, or must all plants within an industrial subcategory be considered in setting an effluent limitation? Hooker Chemical & Plastics Corp. v. Train, 537 F.2d 620, 632 (2d Cir. 1976), holds that the agency correctly limited the range of plants to the more technologically advanced ones because the legislative history supported the use of "the average of the best existing performance." *National Crushed Stone* affirms this holding. Chemical Manufacturers Ass'n v. EPA, 870 F.2d 177, 207-211 (5th Cir.), *clarified on reh'g*, 885 F.2d 253 (5th Cir. 1989), followed these cases to hold that EPA could base BPT for the organic chemical, plastics, and synthetic fiber industry on its use by 99 out of 304 plants, and further could use the practice of 71 plants as the "average of the best" and need not distinguish between cold- and warm-weather plants. Cold-weather-area plants could apply biological treatment, but warm-weather ones needed design and

operations changes. Kennecott v. EPA, 780 F.2d 445, 453 (4th Cir. 1985), summarized and applied the law of inter-industry technology transfers, concluding that "Congress contemplated that EPA might use technology from other industries to establish the Best Available Technology."

The issue of the availability of foreign and hypothetical technologies arose early in the administration of the CWA. Is a technology that is not in actual use in any plant within the United States "available" for the purpose of establishing BAT? See Kennecott v. EPA, 780 F.2d 445 (4th Cir. 1985); American Frozen Food Inst. v. Train, 539 F.2d 107 (D.C. Cir. 1976). A technology is not per se unavailable just because it is not in use in any plant, but the agency's burden of justification increases. In *Hooker Chemical & Plastics Corp.*, 537 F.2d 620, the court found that the agency's record was inadequate on the issue of feasibility because EPA had failed to specify adequately the facts underlying its conclusion that technologies would become commercially feasible and thus available. It is difficult for industry to show that the technology is not technically available if a model plant meets the EPA standard. See CPC Int'l, Inc. v. Train, 540 F.2d 1329 (8th Cir. 1976), in which the wet corn milling industry was faced with a plant that met BOD standards and was thus reduced to the unsuccessful argument that the capital and operating costs were excessive.

A zero-discharge BAT effluent limitations guideline for water and sand discharges from the coastal oil and gas industry, with the exception of Cook Inlet, Alaska, was upheld in Texas Oil & Gas Ass'n v. EPA, 161 F.3d 923, 934 (5th Cir. 1998). The court noted that the industry petitions

> face an especially difficult challenge . . . given the proportion of dischargers already practicing zero discharge at the time of rulemaking. The EPA found that 100 percent of coastal oil and gas facilities outside of Cook Inlet, Louisiana, and Texas, and at least 62 percent of facilities in Louisiana and Texas, were practicing zero discharge by 1992.

What does this decision tell us about the technology-forcing nature of BAT in at least some cases? For a case in which the court approved EPA's choosing a BAT that allows various requirements to be implemented on a case-by-case basis because of variability in topography, climate, and other factors, and that similarly approved EPA's rejection of a treatment option that would be "economically prohibitive" and not likely to result in significant environmental benefits, see Waterkeeper Alliance, Inc. v. EPA, 399 F.3d 486 (2d Cir. 2005).

3. The Supreme Court recently addressed technology-based standards under the CWA, albeit in a different context than we cover in the text in this chapter. In Entergy Corp. v. Riverkeeper, Inc., 556 U.S. 208 (2009), the Court held that under CWA §316(b), EPA may consider benefits and costs in setting standards for certain cooling water intake structures. The operative standard in the statute, in §316(b), is that EPA is to set standards for such structures that "reflect the best technology available for minimizing adverse environmental impact." Id. at 1500. The Second Circuit had held that this §316(b) standard does not allow the agency to conduct a cost-benefit analysis in determining appropriate standards. The Supreme Court, based on *Chevron*, deferred to EPA's view that the agency may consider costs in establishing standards under §316(b). The text reflects that other provisions in the CWA that

establish the ground rules for EPA's creation of technology-based standards explicitly identify a role for costs (see, e.g., the excerpt from *Association of Pacific Fisheries* above).

4. *Permit Shields.* A discharge in excess of the amount specified in an NPDES permit is a violation of the Act and potentially makes the discharger vulnerable to the enforcement sections discussed in Chapter 10. The converse is also true. Atlantic States Legal Found. v. Eastman Kodak Co., 12 F.3d 353 (2d Cir. 1994), held that an NPDES permit operates as a shield from citizen suits for discharges that comply with the terms of the permit. "Once within the NPDES or SPDES [State Pollutant Discharge Elimination System] scheme, . . . polluters may discharge pollutants not specifically listed in their permits so long as they comply with the appropriate reporting requirements and abide by any new limitations when imposed on such pollutants." EPA interprets *Kodak* to apply to pollutants for which no limits exist in the permit but that were identified during the permit process. Piney Run Preservation Ass'n v. County Comm'rs of Carroll County, 268 F.3d 255 (4th Cir. 2001), upheld EPA's interpretation of §402(k)'s permit shield provision, notably the position that a discharger is not liable for the discharge of pollutants not listed in the permit but disclosed to the permitting authorities.

3. *Variances*

As discussed above, one of the criticisms of the national categorical standards framework is that its "one size fits all" approach is inefficient and unfair. The CWA contains a number of "variance" provisions that are intended to provide some relief from this framework. The Supreme Court's decision in the following case addresses the issue of "variances."

EPA v. NATIONAL CRUSHED STONE ASSOCIATION
449 U.S. 64 (1980)

Justice WHITE delivered the opinion of the Court.

In April and July 1977, the Environmental Protection Agency (EPA), acting under the Federal Water Pollution Control Act (Act), as amended, promulgated pollution discharge limitations for the coal mining industry and for that portion of the mineral mining and processing industry comprising the crushed-stone, construction-sand, and gravel categories. Although the Act does not expressly authorize or require variances from the 1977 limitation, each set of regulations contained a variance provision. . . .

To obtain a variance from the 1977 uniform discharge limitations a discharger must demonstrate that the "factors relating to the equipment or facilities involved, the process applied, or other such factors relating to such discharger are fundamentally different from the factors considered in the establishment of the guidelines." Although a greater than normal cost of implementation will be considered in acting on a request for a variance, economic ability to meet the costs will not be considered.[5] A variance, therefore, will not be granted on the basis of the applicant's economic inability to meet the costs of implementing the uniform standard. . . .

We granted certiorari to resolve the conflict between the decisions below and Weyerhaeuser Co. v. Costle, 590 F.2d 1011 (D.C. Cir. 1978), in which the variance provision was upheld.

I

. . .

Section 301(c) of the Act explicitly provides for modifying the 1987 (BAT) effluent limitations with respect to individual point sources. A variance under §301(c) may be obtained upon a showing "that such modified requirements (1) will represent the maximum use of technology within the economic capability of the owner or operator; and (2) will result in reasonable further progress toward the elimination of the discharge of pollutants." Thus, the economic ability of the individual operator to meet the costs of effluent reductions may in some circumstances justify granting a variance from the 1987 limitations.

No such explicit variance provision exists with respect to BPT standards, but in E.I. du Pont de Nemours & Co. v. Train, 430 U.S. 112 (1977), we indicated that a variance provision was a necessary aspect of BPT limitations applicable by regulations to classes and categories of point sources. The issue in this case is whether the BPT variance provision must allow consideration of the economic capability of an individual discharger to afford the costs of the BPT limitation. For the reasons that follow, our answer is in the negative.

II

The plain language of the statute does not support the position taken by the Court of Appeals. Section 301(c) is limited on its face to modifications of the 1987 BAT limitations. It says nothing about relief from the 1977 BPT requirements. Nor does the language of the Act support the position that although §301(c) is not itself applicable to BPT standards, it requires that the affordability of the prescribed 1977 technology be considered in BPT variance decisions. This would be a logical reading of the statute only if the factors listed in §301(c) bore a substantial relationship to the considerations underlying the 1977 limitations as they do to those controlling the 1987 regulations. This is not the case.

The two factors listed in §301(c) — "maximum use of technology within the economic capability of the owner or operator" and "reasonable further progress toward the elimination of the discharge of pollutants" — parallel the general definition of BAT

5. EPA has explained its position as follows:

Thus a plant may be able to secure a BPT variance by showing that the plant's own compliance costs with the national guideline limitation would be x times greater [than] the compliance costs of the plants EPA considered in setting the national BPT limitation. A plant may not, however, secure a BPT variance by alleging that the plant's own financial status is such that it cannot afford to comply with the national BPT limitation. 43 Fed. Reg. 50,042 (1978).

standards as limitations that "require application of the best available technology economically achievable for such category or class, which will result in reasonable further progress toward . . . eliminating the discharge of all pollutants. . . ." §301(b)(2). A §301(c) variance, thus, creates for a particular point source a BAT standard that represents for it the same sort of economic and technological commitment as the general BAT standard creates for the class. As with the general BAT standard, the variance assumes that the 1977 BPT standard has been met by the point source and that the modification represents a commitment of the maximum resources economically possible to the ultimate goal of eliminating all polluting discharges. No one who can afford the best available technology can secure a variance.

There is no similar connection between §301(c) and the considerations underlying the establishment of the 1977 BPT limitations. First, §301(c)'s requirement of "reasonable further progress" must have reference to some prior standard. BPT serves as the prior standard with respect to BAT. There is, however, no comparable, prior standard with respect to BPT limitations. Second, BPT limitations do not require an industrial category to commit the maximum economic resources possible to pollution control, even if affordable. Those point sources already using a satisfactory pollution control technology need take no additional steps at all. The §301(c) variance factor, the "maximum use of technology within the economic capability of the owner or operator," would therefore be inapposite in the BPT context. It would not have the same effect there that it has with respect to BAT's, i.e., it would not apply the general requirements to an individual point source.

More importantly, to allow a variance based on the maximum technology affordable by the point source, even if that technology fails to meet BPT effluent limitations, would undercut the purpose and function of BPT limitations. Rather than the 1987 requirement of the best measures economically and technologically feasible, the statutory provisions for 1977 contemplate regulations prohibiting discharges from any point source in excess of the effluent produced by the best practicable technology currently available in the industry. . . .

NOTES AND QUESTIONS

1. *Variances from Technology-Based Standards.* As noted above, Congress has established a limited number of variances from technology-based standards. See, e.g., CWA §301(c), (*l*), and (n); 40 C.F.R. §125. Variances are intended to provide flexibility in what otherwise was thought to be a rigid scheme of national regulation, as the *Train* decision, *supra*, reflects. The availability of variances depends to some extent on the type of pollutant involved. Section 301(*l*), added in 1977, provided: "The Administrator may not modify any requirement of this section as it applies to any specific pollutant which is on the toxic pollutant list under section 307(a)(1) of this title." Chemical Manufacturers Ass'n v. NRDC, 470 U.S. 116 (1985), however, held that EPA's decision to grant variances on the ground that the discharger's situation was fundamentally different from its industrial class was within its discretion:

> Section 301(*l*) states that EPA may not "modify" any requirement of §301 insofar as toxic materials are concerned. EPA insists that §301(*l*) prohibits only those modifications expressly permitted by other provisions of §301, namely, those that §301(c) and §301(g) would allow on economic or water-quality grounds. Section 301(*l*), it is

urged, does not address the very different issue of FDF variances. This view of the agency charged with administering the statute is entitled to considerable deference; and to sustain it, we need not find that it is the only permissible construction that EPA might have adopted but only that EPA's understanding of this very "complex statute" is a sufficiently rational one to preclude a court from substituting its judgment for that of EPA. Train v. NRDC, 421 U.S. 60, 75, 87, (1975). . . .

Id. at 125. In 1987 Congress ratified *Chemical Manufacturers Ass'n.* See CWA §301(*l*), (n).

Problem 7-3

EPA has developed BAT effluent limitations for the dry cleaning industry. This industry's effluent consists primarily of two pollutants, PERC and TCE. EPA's national survey identified one plant that could achieve the PERC limit EPA set, and another plant that could achieve the TCE limit EPA set. No plant that EPA studied could achieve both limitations. The industry has challenged EPA's effluent limitations. Who would you expect to prevail in this challenge?

E. WATER QUALITY STANDARDS

1. Theory and Current Function

Water quality standards were the heart of the pre-1972 federal regulatory program, as discussed in the introduction to this chapter. The theory did not pan out. States dragged their feet in submitting standards, and enforcement was nil. By 1971, despite considerable efforts by the states to control pollution through water quality standards, Congress concluded that this approach was hopelessly flawed and that a switch to technology-based effluent limitations was necessary. The Senate report went on to pinpoint the major flaw in a receiving water quality approach: "Water quality standards, in addition to their deficiencies in relying on the assimilative capacity of receiving water, often cannot be translated into effluent limitations defendable by court tests because of the imprecision of models for water quality and the effects of effluents in most waters." Id. at 18. Professor Bill Andreen summarizes Congress's reasoning in his review of the development of the 1972 legislation, noting that shifting to a technology-based approach from a water quality–based approach "was crucial if water pollution was actually going to be tackled effectively . . . since the implementation of water quality standards was fraught with so many technical and policy problems." Andreen, The Evolution of Water Pollution Control in the United States—State, Local, and Federal Efforts, 1789-1972: Part I, 22 Stan. Envtl. L.J. 145, 158 (2003).

Many members of the Senate wanted to drop the water quality standards approach entirely, but in the end, the Senate accepted a House amendment to continue and expand the program. Thus, the technology-based effluent limitations imposed by §301(b), and discussed in section D of this chapter, were superimposed on the water quality–based approach. Under today's CWA, permittees must meet technology-based requirements; but under CWA §301(b)(1)(C), they also must comply with "any more stringent limitation, including those necessary to meet water quality standards. . . ." Thus, if implementation of technology-based requirements will not suffice to protect a particular body of water adequately, in theory, the permitting agency is obligated to include in the dischargers' permits more stringent controls that will suffice. Water quality standards, in short, are intended to serve as a "safety net" or "supplementary basis" for the protection of our nation's waters. See EPA v. California ex rel. State Water Res. Control Bd., 426 U.S. 200, 205 n.12 (1976).

In recent years the role of water quality standards has increased significantly. Even greater reliance on such standards, and the strategies to achieve them, likely is in store for the future. This is because of the substantial improvements still needed in the quality of our waters, and the likelihood that the application of technology-based controls will not be enough to protect our waters for the uses for which we would like them to be available (swimming, fishing, drinking, etc.). Thus, effective implementation of the "safety net" embodied by the water quality standards approach is needed if we are to achieve our clean water goals.

Setting and Reviewing Water Quality Standards: Required Elements and Distribution of Responsibility. It is up to the states in the first instance to establish water quality or ambient standards for waters in their jurisdiction. CWA §303. All of the states have assumed this responsibility. EPA Office of Inspector General, Water: Proactive Approach Would Improve EPA's Water Quality Standards Program i (Sept. 29, 2000). EPA must approve state water quality standards. The federal agency is obligated to promulgate its own standards under some circumstances if it determines that the state standards are deficient. See, e.g., CWA §303(b), (c)(3).

The first step a state must take in developing water quality standards is to designate uses for its water bodies. CWA §303(c)(2)(A) directs states to consider a series of possible uses, including "public water supplies, propagation of fish and wildlife, recreational purposes, and agricultural, industrial, and other purposes, and also taking into consideration their use and value for navigation." EPA's regulations currently provide some boundaries for the states' designation of uses. Among them, a state may (1) designate several uses for a water body, and (2) establish a "higher quality use" than what is currently in place. The CWA limits a state's ability to alter use designations to make them less demanding. 40 C.F.R. §131.10(g), (h). Further, states are supposed to set their water quality standards so that waters leaving a state do not undermine the ability of downstream states to meet their own water quality standards. 40 C.F.R. §131.10(b). The Supreme Court offered its gloss on this last obligation in its 1991 decision in Arkansas v. Oklahoma, excerpted below.

In addition to designating uses for a water body, a state must establish "water quality criteria" that are sufficient to protect the designated uses. 40 C.F.R. §131.11(a)(1). Criteria are "elements of State water quality standards, expressed as constituent concentrations, levels, or narrative statements, representing a quality of water that supports a particular use." 40 C.F.R. §131.3(b). CWA §304(a)(1) requires EPA to develop its own water quality criteria to help states determine appropriate water quality standards for particular designated uses. The agency has done so periodically—for example, in 1973 it issued its "Blue Book;" in 1976 it issued the "Red Book;" in 1999 it published a compilation of nationally recommended water quality criteria for 157 pollutants (EPA, National Recommended Water Quality Criteria—Correction 1 (April 1999)); and in January 2003 it announced nine "ecoregional nutrient criteria." Nutrient Criteria Development; Notice of Ecoregional Nutrient Criteria, 68 Fed. Reg. 557 (2003). These criteria are based on the "latest scientific knowledge" concerning the relationships between "pollutant concentrations and environmental and human health effects." EPA, National Recommended Water Quality Criteria—Correction 1 (April 1999). When EPA recommends criteria, states often rely on them in setting their own, but do not always do so.

Based on the designated uses each state has established and its water quality criteria, which must protect the designated uses, each state establishes water quality standards for the water bodies in its jurisdiction. States submit proposed water quality standards to EPA for review; EPA either approves the state standards or rejects them on the ground that they are inconsistent with the CWA, in which case EPA may promulgate its own standards. CWA §303(b), (c)(4)(A); 40 C.F.R. §131.22(b). The CWA requires states to engage in a triennial review of their water quality standards and directs them to refine the standards as appropriate. CWA §303(c); 40 C.F.R. §131.20.

A final significant aspect of the legal framework governing the establishment of water quality standards involves a concept known as "antidegradation." 40 C.F.R. §131.12(a)(1). As EPA explains, the Agency's antidegradation policy "ensures that existing water quality is maintained and protected." EPA, Water Quality Criteria and Standards Plan—Priorities for the Future 5 (June 1998). That is, the policy protects *existing* uses of water bodies. It might be helpful to think of antidegradation as an *ex ante* approach to water quality protection—the idea is to protect water quality before it is degraded so that the waters are available for designated uses. In contrast, the other aspect of water quality standards serves as a tool to promote steps to improve water quality *ex post*—after waters have been degraded. Some commentators have suggested that antidegradation holds special promise as a proactive tool to prevent waters from becoming "unusable" in the first place, comparing it to the reactive approach of the TMDL program (discussed in the following section) of cleaning up water bodies after they are no longer available for designated uses. See, e.g., Dernbach, Why Lawyers Should Care, Envtl. F. 30, 46 (July/August 2002); Hersh, The Clean Water Act's Antidegradation Policy and Its Role in Watershed Protection in Washington State, 15 Hastings W.-Nw. J. Envtl. L. & Pol'y 217 (2009). For recommendations on how to improve antidegradation policies, see Zellmer & Glicksman, Improving Water Quality Antidegradation Policies, 20 Geo. Wash. J. of Energy & Envtl Law. 1 (2013).

EPA requires each state to adopt an antidegradation policy, and the Agency provides basic ground rules that states must meet. In particular, federal antidegradation rules require three levels of water quality protection: Tier I, Tier II, and Tier III. Tier I protection establishes *minimum* water quality standards for all of a state's waters. It requires that "[e]xisting instream water uses and the level of water quality necessary to protect the existing uses shall be maintained and protected." 40 C.F.R. §131.12(a)(1).

Tier II protection is required when "the quality of the waters exceed[s] levels necessary to support propagation of fish, shellfish, and wildlife and recreation in and on the water." 40 C.F.R. §131.12(a)(2). The government is required to maintain and protect the quality of such waters "unless the State finds . . . that allowing lower water quality is necessary to accommodate important economic or social development in the area. . . ." Id. Even in such cases, however, the state must adequately protect existing uses, and it must "assure . . . the highest statutory and regulatory requirements for all new and existing point sources and all cost effective and reasonable best management practices for non-point sources." Id. §131.12(a)(2).

Tier III protection requires that "[w]here high quality waters constitute an outstanding National resource, such as waters of National and State parks and wildlife refuges and waters of exceptional recreational or ecological significance, that water quality shall be maintained and protected." Id. §131.12(a)(3).

To sum up, water quality standards have become increasingly important, particularly as EPA and the states struggle with controlling discharges into impaired waters. One of the key questions involves the respective roles of these federalism partners in determining the appropriate content of such standards—what the standards should be for a particular water body. In Mississippi Comm'n on Natural Res. v. Costle, 625 F.2d 1269 (5th Cir. 1980), the Fifth Circuit upheld EPA's refusal to approve Mississippi's water quality standard for dissolved oxygen, which is necessary for the protection and propagation of fish and aquatic life, and the agency's imposition of its own, more stringent standards instead. The court explained the legal framework as follows:

> For EPA to promulgate a water quality standard, it must determine that the state's standard "is not consistent with the applicable requirements of (the Act)" or that "a revised or new standard is necessary to meet the requirements of (the Act)." 33 U.S.C. §1313(c)(3), (c)(4)(B) (1976). Review is therefore centered around two issues: first, whether EPA's disapproval of Mississippi's DO [dissolved oxygen] standard was proper; and second, whether EPA properly promulgated the substitute standard.
>
> Congress did place primary authority for establishing water quality standards with the states [citing §101(b)]. . . . [T]he legislative history reflects congressional concern that the Act not place in the hands of a federal administrator absolute power over zoning watershed areas. The varied topographies and climates in the country call for varied water quality solutions.
>
> Despite this primary allocation of power, the states are not given unreviewable discretion to set water quality standards. All water quality standards must be submitted to the federal Administrator. 33 U.S.C. §1313(c)(2) (1976). The state must review its standards at least once every three years and make the results of the review available to the Administrator. Id. §1313(c)(1). EPA is given the final voice on the standard's adequacy [under §303(c)(3)]. . . . In addition, EPA can override state water quality standards by changing the effluent limits in NPDES permits whenever a source interferes with water quality. Id. §1312.
>
> EPA's role also is more dominant when water quality criteria are in question. Although the designation of uses and the setting of criteria are interrelating chores, the specification of a waterway as one for fishing, swimming, or public water supply is closely tied to the zoning power Congress wanted left with the states. The criteria set for a specific use are more amenable to uniformity. Congress recognized this distinction by placing with EPA the duty to develop and publish water quality criteria reflecting the latest scientific knowledge shortly after the amendment's passage and periodically thereafter. Id. §1314(a)(1). EPA correctly points out that by leaving intact the Mississippi use designations it has acted in the manner least intrusive of state prerogatives. . . .
>
> We conclude that EPA did not exceed its statutory authority in disapproving the state water quality standard.

For a more recent consideration of the CWA's allocation of responsibility between EPA and the states concerning water quality standards, see Defenders of Wildlife v. EPA, 415 F.3d 1121 (10th Cir. 2005). In a 2009 report, EPA's Office of Inspector General expressed significant concerns about the status of water quality standards for nutrients and EPA's oversight of state performance:

EPA's 1998 National Strategy and Plan to promote State adoption of nutrient water quality standards (which better protect aquatic life and human health) has been ineffective. In 1998, EPA stated that a critical need existed for improved water quality standards, given the number of waters that were impaired from nutrients. In the 11 years since EPA issued its strategy, half the States still had no numeric nutrient standards. States have not been motivated to create these standards because implementing them is costly and often unpopular with various constituencies. EPA has not held the States accountable to committed milestones. The current approach does not assure that States will develop standards that provide adequate protection for downstream waters. Until recently, EPA has not used its Clean Water Act authority to promulgate water quality standards for States.

EPA Office of Inspector General, EPA Needs to Accelerate Adoption of Numeric Nutrient Water Quality Standards (August 26, 2009), http://www.epa.gov/oig/reports/2009/20090826-09-P-0223.pdf.

NOTES AND QUESTIONS

1. *EPA's Responsibilities as Part of the Triennial Review of State Water Quality Standards.* The D.C. Circuit considered EPA's role in National Wildlife Fed'n v. Browner, 127 F.3d 1126, 1130 (D.C. Cir. 1997), holding that while states must submit existing water quality standards to EPA upon completion of their triennial review,

> EPA, however, is not automatically required under the Act to review and approve those standards. Instead, EPA observes, the agency is granted discretionary authority under §303(c)(4)(B) of the Act to force a state to accept "a revised or new standard . . . [if] necessary to meet the requirements of" the Act. 33 U.S.C. §1313(c)(4)(B) (1988). This discretionary power is reflected as well in the agency's regulations. Therefore, under §131.20 of the regulations states are only required to submit existing water quality standards to EPA to enable it to make an informed decision about whether to exercise its discretion to supplant the state standards. . . .

For an example of an EPA determination that a state's water quality standards are deficient and require revision, see the May 2011 letter from Nancy Stoner, Acting Assistant Administrator for EPA's Office of Water, to Lisa Bonnett, Interim Director, Illinois Environmental Protection Agency, http://www.epa.gov/region5/chicagoriver/pdfs/caws-determination-letter-20110511.pdf.

2. *Challenges Remain in Implementing Water Quality–Based Approaches.* As this section reflects, EPA and the states have struggled in their efforts to implement the water quality standards–based approach to water protection contained in the Clean Water Act. See, e.g., EPA, Strategy for Water Quality Standards and Criteria: Strengthening the Foundation of Programs to Protect and Restore the Nation's Waters (EPA-823-R-03-010, August 2003). In a June 2003 report, the GAO recommended that EPA simplify the changing of designated uses and enhance uniformity in the process. U.S. Government Accountability Office, Water Quality: The EPA Should Improve Guidance and Support to Help States Develop Standards that Better Target Cleanup Efforts (2003).

2. *Spillover Effects and Treatment of New Dischargers to Impaired Waters*

Two important questions that have been raised concerning water quality standards–based approaches involve (1) how to treat "spillover" effects (i.e., the impacts of pollution spilling over from one state to another) and (2) the circumstances in which a new discharge is allowable into a water body that exceeds water quality standards. The following Supreme Court case discusses both issues.

ARKANSAS v. OKLAHOMA
503 U.S. 91 (1991)

Justice STEVENS delivered the opinion of the Court.

Pursuant to the Clean Water Act, the Environmental Protection Agency (EPA or Agency) issued a discharge permit to a new point source in Arkansas, about 39 miles upstream from the Oklahoma state line. The question presented in this litigation is whether the EPA's finding that discharges from the new source would not cause a detectable violation of Oklahoma's water quality standards satisfied the EPA's duty to protect the interests of the downstream State. Disagreeing with the Court of Appeals, we hold that the Agency's action was authorized by the statute.

I

In 1985, the city of Fayetteville, Arkansas, applied to the EPA, seeking a permit for the city's new sewage treatment plant under the National Pollution Discharge Elimination System (NPDES). After the appropriate procedures, the EPA, pursuant to §402(a)(1) of the Act, 33 U.S.C. §1342(a)(1), issued a permit authorizing the plant to discharge up to half of its effluent (to a limit of 6.1 million gallons per day) into an unnamed stream in northwestern Arkansas. That flow passes through a series of three creeks for about 17 miles, and then enters the Illinois River at a point 22 miles upstream from the Arkansas-Oklahoma border.

The permit imposed specific limitations on the quantity, content, and character of the discharge and also included a number of special conditions, including a provision that if a study then underway indicated that more stringent limitations were necessary to ensure compliance with Oklahoma's water quality standards, the permit would be modified to incorporate those limits.

Respondents challenged this permit before the EPA, alleging, inter alia, that the discharge violated the Oklahoma water quality standards. Those standards provide that "no degradation [of water quality] shall be allowed" in the upper Illinois River, including the portion of the river immediately downstream from the state line.

Following a hearing, the Administrative Law Judge (ALJ) concluded that the Oklahoma standards would not be implicated unless the contested discharge had "something more than a mere de minimis impact" on the State's waters. He found that the discharge would not have an "undue impact" on Oklahoma's waters and, accordingly, affirmed the issuance of the permit.

On a petition for review, the EPA's Chief Judicial Officer first ruled that §301(b)(1)(C) of the Clean Water Act "requires an NPDES permit to impose any effluent limitations necessary to comply with applicable state water quality standards." He then held that the Act and EPA regulations offered greater protection for the downstream State than the ALJ's "undue impact" standard suggested. He explained the proper standard as follows:

> [A] mere theoretical impairment of Oklahoma's water quality standards—i.e., an infinitesimal impairment predicted through modeling but not expected to be actually detectable or measurable—should not by itself block the issuance of the permit. In this case, the permit should be upheld if the record shows by a preponderance of the evidence that the authorized discharges would not cause an actual detectable violation of Oklahoma's water quality standards.

On remand, the ALJ made detailed findings of fact and concluded that the city had satisfied the standard set forth by the Chief Judicial Officer. Specifically, the ALJ found that there would be no detectable violation of any of the components of Oklahoma's water quality standards. The Chief Judicial Officer sustained the issuance of the permit.

Both the petitioners (collectively Arkansas) and the respondents in this litigation sought judicial review. Arkansas argued that the Clean Water Act did not require an Arkansas point source to comply with Oklahoma's water quality standards. Oklahoma challenged the EPA's determination that the Fayetteville discharge would not produce a detectable violation of the Oklahoma standards.

The Court of Appeals did not accept either of these arguments. The court agreed with the EPA that the statute required compliance with Oklahoma's water quality standards, and did not disagree with the Agency's determination that the discharges from the Fayetteville plant would not produce a detectable violation of those standards. Nevertheless, relying on a theory that neither party had advanced, the Court of Appeals reversed the Agency's issuance of the Fayetteville permit. The court first ruled that the statute requires that "where a proposed source would discharge effluents that would contribute to conditions currently constituting a violation of applicable water quality standards, such [a] proposed source may not be permitted." Then the court found that the Illinois River in Oklahoma was "already degraded," that the Fayetteville effluent would reach the Illinois River in Oklahoma, and that effluent could "be expected to contribute to the ongoing deterioration of the scenic [Illinois R]iver" in Oklahoma even though it would not detectably affect the river's water quality. . . .

II

Interstate waters have been a font of controversy since the founding of the Nation. E.g., Gibbons v. Ogden, 9 Wheat. 1 (1824). This Court has frequently resolved disputes between States that are separated by a common river, e.g., that border the same body of water, or that are fed by the same river basin, see, e.g., New Jersey v. New York, 283 U.S. 336 (1931).

Among these cases are controversies between a State that introduces pollutants to a waterway and a downstream State that objects. See, e.g., Missouri v. Illinois, 200 U.S. 496. In such cases, this Court has applied principles of common law tempered by a respect for the sovereignty of the States. Compare id., at 521, with Georgia v. Tennessee Copper Co., 206 U.S. 230, 237 (1907). In forging what "may not improperly be called interstate common law," Illinois v. Milwaukee, 406 U.S. 91, 105-106 (1972) (*Milwaukee I*), however, we remained aware "that new federal laws and new federal regulations may in time pre-empt the field of federal common law of nuisance." Id., at 107.

In Milwaukee v. Illinois, 451 U.S. 304 (1981) (*Milwaukee II*), we held that the Federal Water Pollution Control Act Amendments of 1972 did just that. In addressing Illinois' claim that Milwaukee's discharges into Lake Michigan constituted a nuisance, we held that the comprehensive regulatory regime created by the 1972 amendments pre-empted Illinois' federal common law remedy. We observed that Congress had addressed many of the problems we had identified in *Milwaukee I* by providing a downstream State with an opportunity for a hearing before the source State's permitting agency, by requiring the latter to explain its failure to accept any recommendations offered by the downstream State, and by authorizing the EPA, in its discretion, to veto a source State's issuance of any permit if the waters of another State may be affected. *Milwaukee II*, 451 U.S., at 325-326.

In *Milwaukee II*, the Court did not address whether the 1972 amendments had supplanted state common law remedies as well as the federal common law remedy. See id., at 310, n.4. On remand, Illinois argued that §510 of the Clean Water Act, 33 U.S.C. §1370, expressly preserved the State's right to adopt and enforce rules that are more stringent than federal standards. The Court of Appeals accepted Illinois' reading of §510, but held that that section did "no more than to save the right and jurisdiction of a state to regulate activity occurring within the confines of its boundary waters." Illinois v. Milwaukee, 731 F.2d 403, 413 (CA7 1984), *cert. denied*, 469 U.S. 1196 (1985).

This Court subsequently endorsed that analysis in International Paper Co. v. Ouellette, 479 U.S. 481 (1987), in which Vermont property owners claimed that the pollution discharged into Lake Champlain by a paper company located in New York constituted a nuisance under Vermont law. The Court held the Clean Water Act taken "as a whole, its purposes and its history" pre-empted an action based on the law of the affected State and that the only state law applicable to an interstate discharge is "the law of the State in which the point source is located." Id., at 493, 487. Moreover, in reviewing §402(b) of the Act, the Court pointed out that when a new permit is being issued by the source State's permit-granting agency, the downstream State

> does not have the authority to block the issuance of the permit if it is dissatisfied with the proposed standards. An affected State's only recourse is to apply to the EPA Administrator, who then has the discretion to disapprove the permit if he concludes that the discharges will have an undue impact on interstate waters. §1342(d)(2). . . . Thus the Act makes it clear that affected States occupy a subordinate position to source States in the federal regulatory program. Id., at 490-491.

Unlike the foregoing cases, this litigation involves not a state-issued permit, but a federally issued permit. To explain the significance of this distinction, we comment further on the statutory scheme before addressing the specific issues raised by the parties.

III

The Clean Water Act anticipates a partnership between the States and the Federal Government, animated by a shared objective: "to restore and maintain the chemical, physical, and biological integrity of the Nation's waters." 33 U.S.C. §1251(a). Toward this end, the Act provides for two sets of water quality measures [effluent limitations and water quality standards]. . . .

IV

The parties have argued three analytically distinct questions concerning the interpretation of the Clean Water Act. First, does the Act require the EPA, in crafting and issuing a permit to a point source in one State, to apply the water quality standards of downstream States? Second, even if the Act does not require as much, does the Agency have the statutory authority to mandate such compliance? Third, does the Act provide, as the Court of Appeals held, that once a body of water fails to meet water quality standards no discharge that yields effluent that reach[es] the degraded waters will be permitted?

In these cases, it is neither necessary nor prudent for us to resolve the first of these questions. In issuing the Fayetteville permit, the EPA assumed it was obligated by both the Act and its own regulations to ensure that the Fayetteville discharge would not violate Oklahoma's standards. As we discuss below, this assumption was permissible and reasonable and therefore there is no need for us to address whether the Act requires as much. . . .

Our decision not to determine at this time the scope of the Agency's statutory obligations does not affect our resolution of the second question, which concerns the Agency's statutory authority. Even if the Clean Water Act itself does not require the Fayetteville discharge to comply with Oklahoma's water quality standards, the statute clearly does not limit the EPA's authority to mandate such compliance.

Since 1973, EPA regulations have provided that an NPDES permit shall not be issued "[w]hen the imposition of conditions cannot ensure compliance with the applicable water quality requirements of all affected States." 40 CFR §122.4(d) (1991). Those regulations—relied upon by the EPA in the issuance of the Fayetteville permit—constitute a reasonable exercise of the Agency's statutory authority.

Congress has vested in the Administrator broad discretion to establish conditions for NPDES permits. Section 402(a)(2) provides that for EPA-issued permits "[t]he Administrator shall prescribe conditions . . . to assure compliance with the requirements of [§402(a)(1)] and *such other requirements as he deems appropriate*." 33 U.S.C. §1342(a)(2) (emphasis added). Similarly, Congress preserved for the Administrator broad authority to oversee state permit programs: "No permit shall issue . . . if the Administrator . . . objects in writing to the issuance of such permit as being outside the guidelines and requirements of this chapter." 33 U.S.C. §1342(d)(2).

The regulations relied on by the EPA were a perfectly reasonable exercise of the Agency's statutory discretion. The application of state water quality standards in the interstate context is wholly consistent with the Act's broad purpose "to restore and maintain the chemical, physical, and biological integrity of the Nation's waters." 33 U.S.C. §1251(a). Moreover, as noted above, §301(b)(1)(C) expressly identifies the achievement of state water quality standards as one of the Act's central objectives. The Agency's regulations conditioning NPDES permits are a well-tailored means of achieving this goal.

Notwithstanding this apparent reasonableness, Arkansas argues that our description in *Ouellette* of the role of affected States in the permit process and our characterization of the affected States' position as "subordinate," see 479 U.S., at 490-491, indicates that the EPA's application of the Oklahoma standards was error. We disagree. Our statement in *Ouellette* concerned only an affected State's input into the permit process; that input is clearly limited by the plain language of §402(b). Limits on an affected State's direct participation in permitting decisions, however, do not in any way constrain the EPA's authority to require a point source to comply with downstream water quality standards. . . .

Similarly, we agree with Arkansas that in the Clean Water Act Congress struck a careful balance among competing policies and interests, but do not find the EPA regulations concerning the application of downstream water quality standards at all incompatible with that balance. Congress, in crafting the Act, protected certain sovereign interests of the States; for example, §510 allows States to adopt more demanding pollution-control standards than those established under the Act. Arkansas emphasizes that §510 preserves such state authority only as it is applied to the waters of the regulating State. Even assuming Arkansas' construction of §510 is correct, that section only concerns state authority and does not constrain the EPA's authority to promulgate reasonable regulations requiring point sources in one State to comply with water quality standards in downstream States.

For these reasons, we find the EPA's requirement that the Fayetteville discharge comply with Oklahoma's water quality standards to be a reasonable exercise of the Agency's substantial statutory discretion.

V

The Court of Appeals construed the Clean Water Act to prohibit any discharge of effluent that would reach waters already in violation of existing water quality standards. We find nothing in the Act to support this reading. . . .

Although the Act contains several provisions directing compliance with state water quality standards, see, e.g., §1311(b)(1)(C), the parties have pointed to nothing that mandates a complete ban on discharges into a waterway that is in violation of those standards. The statute does, however, contain provisions designed to remedy existing water quality violations and to allocate the burden of reducing undesirable discharges between existing sources and new sources. See, e.g., §1313(d). Thus, rather than establishing the categorical ban announced by the Court of Appeals—which might frustrate the construction of new plants that would improve existing conditions—the Clean Water Act vests in the EPA and the States broad authority to develop long-range, area-wide programs to alleviate and eliminate existing pollution. See, e.g., §1288(b)(2).

To the extent that the Court of Appeals relied on its interpretation of the Act to reverse the EPA's permitting decision, that reliance was misplaced.

VI

The Court of Appeals also concluded that the EPA's issuance of the Fayetteville permit was arbitrary and capricious because the Agency misinterpreted Oklahoma's water quality standards. The primary difference between the court's and the Agency's interpretation of the standards derives from the court's construction of the Act.

Contrary to the EPA's interpretation of the Oklahoma standards, the Court of Appeals read those standards as containing the same categorical ban on new discharges that the court had found in the Clean Water Act itself. Although we do not believe the text of the Oklahoma standards supports the court's reading (indeed, we note that Oklahoma itself had not advanced that interpretation in its briefs in the Court of Appeals), we reject it for a more fundamental reason—namely, that the Court of Appeals exceeded the legitimate scope of judicial review of an agency adjudication. . . .

As discussed above, an EPA regulation requires an NPDES permit to comply "with the applicable water quality requirements of all affected States." 40 CFR §122.4(d) (1991). This regulation effectively incorporates into federal law those state-law standards the Agency reasonably determines to be "applicable." In such a situation, then, state water quality standards—promulgated by the States with substantial guidance from the EPA and approved by the Agency—are part of the federal law of water pollution control.

Two features of the body of law governing water pollution support this conclusion. First, as discussed more thoroughly above, we have long recognized that interstate water pollution is controlled by federal law. Recognizing that the system of federally approved state standards as applied in the interstate context constitutes federal law is wholly consistent with this principle. Second, treating state standards in interstate controversies as federal law accords with the Act's purpose of authorizing the EPA to create and manage a uniform system of interstate water pollution regulation.

Because we recognize that, at least insofar as they affect the issuance of a permit in another State, the Oklahoma standards have a federal character, the EPA's reasonable, consistently held interpretation of those standards is entitled to substantial deference. In these cases, the Chief Judicial Officer ruled that the Oklahoma standards—which require that there be "no degradation" of the upper Illinois River—would only be violated if the discharge effected an "actually detectable or measurable" change in water quality.

This interpretation of the Oklahoma standards is certainly reasonable and consistent with the purposes and principles of the Clean Water Act. As the Chief Judicial Officer noted, "unless there is some method for measuring compliance, there is no way to ensure compliance." Moreover, this interpretation of the Oklahoma standards makes eminent sense in the interstate context: If every discharge that had some theoretical impact on a downstream State were interpreted as "degrading" the downstream waters, downstream States might wield an effective veto over upstream discharges. . . .

In its review of the EPA's interpretation and application of the Oklahoma standards, the Court of Appeals committed three mutually compounding errors.

First, the court failed to give due regard to the EPA's interpretation of its own regulations, as those regulations incorporate the Oklahoma standards. Instead the court voiced its own interpretation of the governing law and concluded that "where a proposed source would discharge effluents that would contribute to conditions currently constituting a violation of applicable water quality standards, such [a] proposed source may not be permitted." 908 F.2d, at 620. As we have already pointed out, that reading of the law is not supported by the statute or by any EPA regulation. The Court of Appeals sat in review of an agency action and should have afforded the EPA's interpretation of the governing law an appropriate level of deference.

Second, the court disregarded well-established standards for reviewing the factual findings of agencies and instead made its own factual findings. The troubling nature of the court's analysis appears on the face of the opinion itself: At least four times, the court concluded that "there was substantial evidence before the ALJ to support" particular findings which the court thought appropriate, but which were contrary to those actually made by the ALJ. Although we have long recognized the "substantial evidence" standard in administrative law, the court below turned that analysis on its head. A court reviewing an agency's adjudicative action should accept the agency's factual findings if those findings are supported by substantial evidence on the record as a whole. The court should not supplant the agency's findings merely by identifying alternative findings that could be supported by substantial evidence.

Third, the court incorrectly concluded that the EPA's decision was arbitrary and capricious. This error is derivative of the court's first two errors. Having substituted its reading of the governing law for the Agency's, and having made its own factual findings, the Court of Appeals concluded that the EPA erred in not considering an important and relevant fact—namely, that the upper Illinois River was (by the court's assessment) already degraded. . . .

In sum, the Court of Appeals made a policy choice that it was not authorized to make. Arguably, as that court suggested, it might be wise to prohibit any discharge into the Illinois River, even if that discharge would have no adverse impact on water quality. But it was surely not arbitrary for the EPA to conclude—given the benefits to the river from the increased flow of relatively clean water and the benefits achieved in Arkansas by allowing the new plant to operate as designed—that allowing the discharge would be even wiser. It is not our role, or that of the Court of Appeals, to decide which policy choice is the better one, for it is clear that Congress has entrusted such decisions to the Environmental Protection Agency.

Accordingly, the judgment of the Court of Appeals is REVERSED.

NOTES AND QUESTIONS

1. *Dirty Hands.* Is *Oklahoma* a classic case of lack of clean hands or, alternatively, a *de minimis* injury case? Suppose a state adopts a nondegradation standard for its portion of an interstate watercourse and enforces it against its own dischargers. A discharge in an adjoining state threatens to migrate across state lines and violate the host state's antidegradation standard. Does EPA have a mandatory duty to deny or condition the NPDES permit? See Lininger, Narrowing the Preemptive Scope of the Clean Water Act as a Means of Enhancing Environmental Protection, 20 Harv. Envtl. L. Rev. 165, 178-179 (1996). Professor Merrill argues that the federal common law and international law should be that a state can protect its resources from extraterritorial pollution only if the pollution would violate rules that the state has adopted and enforced against its own citizens. Merrill, Golden Rules for Transboundary Pollution, 46 Duke L.J. 931 (1997). How does this differ from the standard for EPA denial of upstream NPDES permits adopted in *Oklahoma*?

2. *Did Downstream States Win or Lose?* More generally, is Arkansas v. Oklahoma the last word on contributions to impaired waters? Professor Glicksman argues that the apparent opportunity that the Court's decision in Arkansas v. Oklahoma provides downstream states to preserve the quality of water resources shared

with other states may be illusory for several reasons. First, the Court refused to decide whether the statute requires rather than merely permits EPA to apply affected-state water quality standards to source-state point sources. Second, political factors may make EPA reluctant to impose significant constraints on source-state industries for the benefit of downstream users. Third, the threshold showing that a downstream state must make to force an upstream discharger to comply with its water quality standards is likely to be insurmountable due to the difficulty of tracing adverse effects on the state's water quality to one out of a number of upstream dischargers. Glicksman, Watching the River Flow: The Prospects for Improved Interstate Water Pollution Control, 43 Wash. U. J. Urb. & Contemp. L. 119, 144-145, 166-174 (1993).

3. *Additional Perspectives on Contributions to Impaired Waters.* Several cases have now taken a stab at interpreting EPA regulations intended to address contributions to impaired waters. In Friends of Pinto Creek v. EPA, 504 F.3d 1007 (9th Cir. 2007), the Ninth Circuit vacated a permit that EPA had issued to a mining company that would have allowed the company to discharge copper into a water body listed as impaired for copper, on the ground that issuance of the permit was inconsistent with 40 C.F.R. §122.4. Section 122.4 allows issuance of permits to new dischargers into an impaired water body under limited circumstances, and the court held that it was not clear that those circumstances had been met. Among other things, it was not clear that "existing dischargers into that segment are subject to compliance schedules designed to bring the segment into compliance with applicable water quality standards." Id. §122.4(i)(2). To clear up the ambiguity, the court found that existing dischargers are not subject to such compliance schedules and, therefore, the mining company had not shown that §122.4(i) had been met. For a different perspective, in which the court allowed a new source because the discharge of the pollutant involved (phosphorus) would be offset by an annual reduction in discharge of that pollutant from another source, see In re Cities of Annandale and Maple Lake, 731 N.W.2d 502 (Minn. 2007).

Problem 7-4

In early 2014, EPA objected to a proposed modification of a wastewater treatment plant permit in Vermont that involved discharge of nitrogen to the Connecticut River. That discharge results in the addition of nitrogen to Long Island Sound, which is already listed as impaired for nitrogen. In supporting its objection, the agency indicated that, to comply with 40 C.F.R. §§122.4(d) and 122.44(d), which apply to state approved programs pursuant to 40 C.F.R. §123.25, the permit must require treatment that will "prevent an increase in total nitrogen compared to the existing average daily load." The agency further indicated that "[a]ny increase in nitrogen loading from the facility would clearly result in an additional contribution to a water quality standards violation and would be inconsistent with [the above-referenced CFR provisions]." EPA Region 1 January 15, 2014, and February 12, 2014, letters to Vermont DEC. What would EPA argue in support of its position? What about the wastewater treatment plant seeking the permit modification? How should a court rule on whether a permit modification should be granted? What facts would be most helpful to each side in this proceeding?

3. The Role of TMDLs in Achieving Water Quality Standards

a. Overview

As we have learned, states are required to establish water quality standards that will protect the designated uses of waters within their jurisdictions. EPA oversees the states; in some cases, the Agency takes on the job itself if a state's performance is inadequate. As we also have learned, the CWA quite clearly (in §301(b)(1)(C)) requires that NPDES permits specify limits that will meet these standards. Yet the reality is that, despite the regulatory and other efforts undertaken over the past 40 years, a substantial percentage of the nation's assessed waters do not meet water quality goals.

Total maximum daily loads (TMDLs) represent, in one commentator's view, the "new frontier" in accomplishing the CWA's goal of restoring and protecting our nation's waters. Warren, Total Maximum Daily Loads: A Watershed Approach to Improved Water Quality, ALI-ABA Course of Study Clean Water Act: Law and Regulations 115 (Oct. 23-25, 2002). The characterization of TMDLs as a "new frontier" might seem surprising given the inclusion of the TMDL provisions in the 1972 version of the CWA and the fact that the TMDL program's focus on ambient conditions harks back to pre-1972 water pollution initiatives. Professor Houck's apt phrase is that "[t]he TMDL process represents, in the short life of environmental law, an ancient approach to pollution control. . . . From the very first hint of federal involvement in water pollution control 50 years ago, states and pollution dischargers have fought a running battle to defend and, where lost, return to the local primacy and utilitarianism of regulation by water quality standards." O. Houck, The Clean Water Act TMDL Program: Law, Policy, and Implementation 12 (ELI 2d ed., 2002). The explanation lies in the limited progress made in implementing TMDLs for the first couple of decades of implementation of the CWA, and in the importance many attach to TMDLs, despite the track record of water quality–based approaches, as a potentially useful mechanism for advancing the CWA's goals.

The TMDL program contains three key components. First, CWA §303(d) obligates states to identify and develop a priority ranking of waters where effluent limitations are not stringent enough to achieve an applicable water quality standard. The priority ranking is to be based on the "severity of the pollution and the uses to be made of such waters." CWA §303(d)(1)(A). This list of impaired waters is sometimes referred to as the "CWA 303(d) list." Second, the government must set TMDLs for specified pollutants for these waters—the maximum pollutant loading that the water body can handle without violating water quality standards. The TMDL is to take into account seasonal variations and incorporate a margin of safety that takes into account "any lack of knowledge concerning the relationship between effluent limitations and water quality." CWA §303(d)(1)(C). Third, the government authorities must allocate the TMDL among the various sources discharging into the water. Congress added §304(*l*) in 1987 to establish a time frame for implementing control strategies for point sources that discharge toxins.

b.   Progress to Date in Implementing the TMDL Program

Progress in implementing the water quality–based TMDL program was slow during the first 20-plus years of the CWA. Professor Houck offers the following summary of the theory and reality of TMDL development, and the reason for the slow pace of early implementation:

> Section 303(d) provided a structure for water quality-based regulation. States would identify waters that remained polluted after the application of technology standards, they would determine the . . . TMDLs of pollutants that would bring these waters up to grade, and they would then allocate these loads among discharge sources in discharge permits and state water quality plans. If the states did not do it, EPA would.
>
> Only the states did none of it, and neither did EPA—until a series of federal court cases in the late 1980s and early 1990s began to crack the defenses, catching EPA and the states by surprise. A wave of litigation followed, state by state, compelling listings of impaired waters and schedules for first-ever TMDLs. [O. Houck, *supra*, at 5.]

The pace of TMDL development has picked up considerably over the past decade, in part because of citizen suits, although adoption and implementation of TMDLs remains very much a work in progress. As of 2012, EPA's website indicates that states have listed more than 42,000 waters as impaired (compared with the list of 22,000 impaired waters in December 2002).[c] As of 2012, EPA had approved nearly 52,000 TMDLs, a significant increase over the 6,853 TMDLs the agency had approved as of December 2002.[d]

c.   A More In-Depth Look at the TMDL Program

Each phase of the TMDL process has proven challenging to implement. The first step in the §303 process is listing (although we divide the TMDL process into three basic steps, the grouping is artificial to some extent and there is overlap among the categories). There has been considerable inconsistency among the states in their approach to exercising this responsibility. For example, some states fail to include waters that do not meet water quality standards because of atmospheric deposition or temperature problems. National Clarifying Guidance for 1998 State and Territory Clean Water Act Section 303(d) Listing Decisions, http://www.epa.gov/OWOW/tmdl/lisgid.html. There has also been litigation over the listing process. The Ninth Circuit, for example, has upheld EPA's view that a state's §303(d) list should include all impaired waters, including waters impaired by nonpoint sources. Pronsolino v. Nastri, 291 F.3d 1123 (9th Cir. 2002).

Indiana's experience with its listing process reflects the dynamic and imprecise nature of the lists. Based on its five-year assessment of its water bodies, in 2002 Indiana's Department of Environmental Management more than doubled its number of impaired waters, from 209 to 428; in doing so, it made clear that the increase "does not necessarily mean the state's waterways have become more polluted but is merely a reflection of the assessment process being completed. . . ." The state indicated that the

c. http://iaspub.epa.gov/waters10/attains_nation_cy.control?p_report_type=T.
d. http://iaspub.epa.gov/waters10/attains_nation_cy.control?p_report_type=T#status_of_data.

increase in the number of impaired waters is due to the collection of additional data. State to Develop Remediation Plans as Number of Impaired Waterways Grows, 33 Env't Rep. (BNA) 2658 (Dec. 6, 2002).

Determining the TMDLs and allocating the total allowable loading among point sources and nonpoint sources have proven enormously difficult as well. Assessing the assimilative capacity of a water body can be extremely challenging technically, requiring consideration of flow and a wide variety of other factors. A TMDL is composed of waste load allocations (WLAs, or point source contributions), load allocations (LAs, or nonpoint source contributions), natural background, and a margin of safety. 40 C.F.R. §130.32. Each of these may be enormously complex. The National Research Council, for example, found that determination of the required "margin of safety" has proved contentious. National Research Council, Assessing the TMDL Approach to Water Quality Management 76 (2001). More generally, even the regulations seem to acknowledge the likelihood of significant variability in implementation, providing that load allocations are "best estimates . . . which may range from reasonably accurate estimates to gross allotments, depending on the availability of data and appropriate techniques for predicting the loading." 40 C.F.R. §130.2(g). TMDLs for water bodies for which narrative (rather than numeric) water quality standards have been established raise an additional set of challenges.

The Ninth Circuit's 2002 *Pronsolino* decision, which follows, addresses a threshold question concerning the types of waters a state must include in its §303(d) list and, in particular, whether §303(d) covers waters impaired solely by nonpoint sources.

PRONSOLINO v. NASTRI
291 F.3d 1123 (9th Cir. 2002)

BERZON, Circuit Judge: . . .

II. Factual and Procedural Background

A. THE GARCIA RIVER TMDL

In 1992, California submitted to the EPA a list of waters pursuant to §303(d)(1)(A). Pursuant to §303(d)(2), the EPA disapproved California's 1992 list because it omitted seventeen water segments that did not meet the water quality standards set by California for those segments. Sixteen of the seventeen water segments, including the Garcia River, were impaired only by nonpoint sources of pollution. After California rejected an opportunity to amend its §303(d)(1) list to include the seventeen sub-standard segments, the EPA, again acting pursuant to §303(d)(2), established a new §303(d)(1) list for California, including those segments on it. California retained the seventeen segments on its 1994, 1996, and 1998 §303(d)(1) lists.

California did not, however, establish TMDLs for the segments added by the EPA. Environmental and fishermen's groups sued the EPA in 1995 to require the EPA to establish TMDLs for the seventeen segments, and in a March 1997 consent decree the EPA agreed to do so. According to the terms of the consent decree, the EPA set March 18, 1998, as the deadline for the establishment of a TMDL for the Garcia River. When California missed the deadline despite having initiated public comment on a draft TMDL and having prepared a draft implementation plan, the EPA established a TMDL for the Garcia River. The EPA's TMDL differed only slightly from the state's draft TMDL.

The Garcia River TMDL for sediment is 552 tons per square mile per year, a sixty percent reduction from historical loadings. The TMDL allocates portions of the total yearly load among the following categories of nonpoint source pollution: a) "mass wasting" associated with roads; b) "mass wasting" associated with timber-harvesting; c) erosion related to road surfaces; and d) erosion related to road and skid trail crossings.

B. The Appellants

In 1960, appellants Betty and Guido Pronsolino purchased approximately 800 acres of heavily logged timber land in the Garcia River watershed. In 1998, after regrowth of the forest, the Pronsolinos applied for a harvesting permit from the California Department of Forestry ("Forestry").

In order to comply with the Garcia River TMDL, Forestry and/or the state's Regional Water Quality Control Board required, among other things, that the Pronsolinos' harvesting provide for mitigation of 90% of controllable road-related sediment run-off and contain prohibitions on removing certain trees and on harvesting from mid-October until May 1. The Pronsolinos' forester estimates that a large tree restriction will cost the Pronsolinos $750,000.

Larry Mailliard, a member of the Mendocino County Farm Bureau, submitted a draft harvesting permit on February 4, 1998, for a portion of his property in the Garcia River watershed. Forestry granted a final version of the permit after incorporation of a 60.3% reduction of sediment loading, a requirement included to comply with the Garcia River TMDL. Mr. Mailliard's forester estimates that the additional restrictions imposed to comply with the Garcia River TMDL will cost Mr. Mailliard $10,602,000. . . .

C. Proceedings Below

. . . The Pronsolinos challenged the EPA's authority to impose TMDLs on rivers polluted only by nonpoint sources of pollution and sought a determination of whether the Act authorized the Garcia River TMDL. . . .

On August 6, 2000, the district court entered final judgment in favor of the EPA. The Pronsolinos timely filed this appeal.

III. Analysis

A. Deference to the EPA

. . . The EPA regulations pertinent to §303(d)(1) lists and TMDLs focus on the attainment of water quality standards, whatever the source of any pollution. For instance, the EPA's regulations define TMDLs as the "sum of the individual WLAs [wasteload allocations] for point sources and LAs [load allocations] for nonpoint sources and natural background." 40 C.F.R. §130.2(i). Section 130.2 also defines a "wasteload allocation" as the "portion of a receiving water's loading capacity that is allocated to one of its existing or future point sources of pollution," §130.2(h), and a "load allocation" as the "portion of a receiving water's loading capacity that is attributed either to one of its existing or future nonpoint sources of pollution or to natural background sources," §130.2(g). The load allocation regulation also advises that, if possible, "natural and nonpoint source loads should be distinguished." Id. No reason appears why, under this TMDL definition, the amount of either point source loads or nonpoint source loads cannot be zero. If the wasteload allocation is zero, then the TMDL would cover only the nonpoint sources and natural background sources. So read, the regulation provides that a TMDL can apply where there is no wasteload allocation for point source pollution. . . .

Section 130.7 evinces the same understanding. That regulation directs states to identify those waters listed pursuant to §303(d)(1) that still require the establishment of TMDLs if:

> (i) Technology-based effluent limitations required by sections 301(b), 306, 307, or other sections of the Act; (ii) More stringent effluent limitations (including prohibitions) required . . . ; and (iii) Other pollution control requirements (e.g., best management practices) required by local, States, or Federal authority are not stringent enough to implement any water quality standards . . . applicable to such waters.

§130.7(b)(1). "Best management practices" pertain to nonpoint sources of pollution. So, again, section 130.7 does not distinguish between sources of pollution for purposes of applying the TMDL requirement. Instead, control requirements applicable to either type of pollution receive equal treatment in the quest to achieve water quality standards.

Also consistent with application of the §303(d)(1) listing and TMDL requirements to waters impaired only by nonpoint sources is the regulation addressing water quality standards. Section 130.3 explains that "such standards serve the dual purposes of establishing the water quality goals for a specific water body and serving as the regulatory basis for establishment of water quality–based treatment controls and strategies beyond the technology-based level of treatment required. . . ." 40 C.F.R. §130.3. One purpose of water quality standards therefore—and not surprisingly—is to provide federally approved goals to be achieved *both* by state controls and by federal strategies *other* than point-source technology-based limitations. This purpose pertains to waters impaired by both point and nonpoint source pollution. The regulations addressing states' water quality management plans, intended to attain the promulgated water quality standards, confirm this understanding. Such plans must include, among other things, TMDLs, effluent limitations, and "*nonpoint* source management and control." 40 C.F.R. §130.6 (emphasis added).

In short, the EPA's regulations concerning §303(d)(1) lists and TMDLs apply whether a water body receives pollution from point sources only, nonpoint sources only, or a combination of the two. The EPA has issued directives concerning the states' CWA §303(d) requirements in conformity with this understanding of its regulations. See, e.g., Memorandum from Geoffrey Grubbs, Director, EPA Assessment and Watershed Protection Division, to Water Quality Branch Chiefs and TMDL Coordinators (Aug. 13, 1992) (Section 303(d)(1)(A) "applies equally to segments affected by point sources only, a combination of point and nonpoint sources, and nonpoint sources only."); EPA, National Clarifying Guidance for 1998 State and Territory Clean Water Act Section 303(d) Listing Decisions 6 (1997) ("Consistent with long-standing EPA policy, regulations, and practice, States should include waterbodies impaired by nonpoint sources alone on 1998 section 303(d)(1)(A) lists. . . .").

[After reviewing EPA's position, the court decided that this position warranted judicial deference.]

B. PLAIN MEANING AND STRUCTURAL ISSUES

1. THE COMPETING INTERPRETATIONS

Section 303(d)(1)(A) requires listing and calculation of TMDLs for "those waters within [the state's] boundaries for which the effluent limitations required by section [301(b)(1)(A)] and section [301(b)(1)(B)] of this title *are not stringent enough to implement any water quality standard* applicable to such waters." §303(d) (emphasis added). The precise statutory question before us is whether, as the Pronsolinos maintain, the term "not stringent enough to implement . . . water quality standards" as used in §303(d)(1)(A) must be interpreted to mean *both* that application of effluent limitations will not achieve water quality standards *and* that the waters at issue are subject to effluent limitations. As only waters with point source pollution are subject to effluent limitations, such an interpretation would exclude from the §303(d) listing and TMDL requirements waters impaired only by nonpoint sources of pollution.

The EPA, as noted, interprets "not stringent enough to implement . . . water quality standards" to mean "not adequate" or "not sufficient . . . to implement any water quality standard," and does not read the statute as implicitly containing a limitation to waters initially covered by effluent limitations. According to the EPA, if the use of effluent limitations will not implement applicable water quality standards, the water falls within §303(d)(1)(A) regardless of whether it is point or nonpoint sources, or a combination of the two, that continue to pollute the water.

2. THE LANGUAGE AND STRUCTURE OF §303(D)

Whether or not the appellants' suggested interpretation is entirely implausible, it is at least considerably weaker than the EPA's competing construction. The Pronsolinos' version necessarily relies upon: (1) understanding "stringent enough" to mean "strict enough" rather than "thoroughgoing enough" or "adequate" or "sufficient";[14] (2) reading the phrase "not stringent enough" in isolation, rather than with reference to the stated goal of implementing "any water quality standard applicable to such waters." Where the answer to the question "not stringent enough for what?" is "to implement any [applicable] water quality standard," the meaning of "stringent" should be determined by looking forward to the broad goal to be attained, not backwards at the inadequate effluent limitations. One might comment, for example, about a teacher that her standards requiring good spelling were not stringent enough to assure good writing, as her students still used bad grammar and poor logic. Based

---

14. Stringent means "rigorous, strict, thoroughgoing; rigorously binding or coercive." Oxford English Dictionary Online (2001). Defining "stringent" as "rigorous" or "strict" would lend support to the Pronsolinos' interpretation. If "stringent" means "thoroughgoing," however, §303(d)(1)(A) would encompass the EPA's broader reading of the statute. Also, "stringent enough" may have a slightly different meaning from "stringent" standing alone, such as "adequate" or "sufficient." See 1 Legislative History of the Water Pollution Control Act Amendments of 1972 at 792 (1973) (Legislative History) (H.R. Rep. 92-911 to accompany H.R. 11896 (March 11, 1972)) (using the term "are inadequate" in place of "not stringent enough").

on the language of the contested phrase alone, then, the more sensible conclusion is that the §303(d)(1) list must contain any waters for which the particular effluent limitations will not be adequate to attain the statute's water quality goals.

Placing the phrase in its statutory context supports this conclusion. Section 303(d) begins with the requirement that each state identify those waters within its boundaries. . . . §303(d)(1)(A). So the statute's starting point for the listing project is a compilation of each and every navigable water within the state. Then, only those waters that will attain water quality standards after application of the new point source technology are excluded from the §303(d)(1) list, leaving all those waters for which that technology will not "implement any water quality standard applicable to such waters." §303(d)(1)(A); see American Wildlands v. Browner, 260 F.3d 1192, 1194 (10th Cir. 2001) ("Each state is required to identify all of the waters within its borders not meeting water quality standards and establish [TMDLs] for those waters.") (citing §303(d)); Pronsolino, 91 F. Supp. 2d at 1347. The alternative construction, in contrast, would begin with a subset of all the state's waterways, those that have point sources subject to effluent limitations, and would result in a list containing only a subset of that subset—those waters as to which the applicable effluent limitations are not adequate to attain water quality standards.

The Pronsolinos' contention to the contrary notwithstanding, no such odd reading of the statute is necessary in order to give meaning to the phrase "for which the effluent limitations required by section [301(b)(1)(A)] and section [301(b)(1)(B)] . . . are not stringent enough." The EPA interprets §303(d)(1)(A) to require the identification of any waters not meeting water quality standards only if specified effluent limitations would not achieve those standards. 40 C.F.R. §130.2(j). If the pertinent effluent limitations would, if implemented, achieve the water quality standards but are not in place yet, there need be no listing and no TMDL calculation. Id.

So construed, the meaning of the statute is different than it would be were the language recast to state only that "[e]ach State shall identify those waters within its boundaries . . . [not meeting] any water quality standard applicable to such waters." Under the EPA's construction, the reference to effluent limitations reflects Congress' intent that the EPA focus initially on implementing effluent limitations and only later avert its attention to water quality standards. . . .

Given all these language considerations, it is not surprising that the only time this court addressed the reach of §303(d)(1)(A), it rejected a reading of §303(d)(1)(A) similar to the one the Pronsolinos now proffer. In Dioxin, 57 F.3d at 1526-27, the plaintiffs argued that the phrase "not stringent enough" prohibited the EPA from listing under §303(d)(1)(A) and establishing TMDLs for toxic pollutants, until after the implementation and proven failure of §301(b)(1)(A) "best practicable technology" effluent limitations. Toxic pollutants, however, are not subject to "best practical technology" controls, but to more demanding "best available technology," precisely because of their toxicity. Id.

The court in Dioxin held that the EPA acted within its statutory authority in setting TMDLs for toxic pollutants, even though the effluent limitations referenced by §303(d)(1)(A) did not apply to those pollutants. 57 F.3d at 1528. The court explained that, since best practical technology effluent limitations do not apply to toxic pollutants, those limitations are, as a matter of law, "not stringent enough" to achieve water quality standards. Id. In other words, Dioxin read §303(d)(1)(A) as applying to all waters in the state, not only to the subset covered by certain kinds of effluent controls, and it understood "not stringent enough" to mean "not adequate for" or "inapplicable to."

Nothing in §303(d)(1)(A) distinguishes the treatment of point sources and non-point sources as such; the only reference is to the "effluent limitations required by" §301(b)(1). So if the effluent limitations required by §301(b)(1) are "as a matter of law" "not stringent enough" to achieve the applicable water quality standards for waters impaired by point sources not subject to those requirements, then they are also "not stringent enough" to achieve applicable water quality standards for other waters not subject to those requirements, in this instance because they are impacted only by nonpoint sources. Additionally, the *Dioxin* court, applying *Chevron* deference, upheld the EPA's interpretation of §303(d) "as requiring TMDLs where existing pollution controls will not lead to attainment of water standards," 57 F.3d at 1527; *see also* 40 C.F.R. §130.7(b), a holding that directly encompasses waters polluted by nonpoint sources.

3. THE STATUTORY SCHEME AS A WHOLE

The Pronsolinos' objection to this view of §303(d), and of *Dioxin*, is, in essence, that the CWA as a whole distinguishes between the regulatory schemes applicable to point and nonpoint sources, so we must assume such a distinction in applying §§303(d)(1)(A) and (C). We would hesitate in any case to read into a discrete statutory provision something that is not there because it is contained elsewhere in the statute. But here, the premise is wrong: There is no such general division throughout the CWA.

Point sources are treated differently from nonpoint sources for many purposes under the statute, but not all. In particular, there is no such distinction with regard to the basic purpose for which the §303(d) list and TMDLs are compiled, the eventual attainment of state-defined water quality standards. Water quality standards reflect a state's designated *uses* for a water body and do not depend in any way upon the source of pollution. See §303(a)-(c). . . .

Additionally, §303(d) follows the subsections setting forth the requirements for water quality standards, §303(a)-(c)—which, as noted above, apply without regard to the source of pollution—and precedes the "continuing planning process" subsection, §303(e), which applies broadly as well. Thus, §303(d) is structurally part of a set of provisions governing an interrelated goal-setting, information-gathering, and planning process that, unlike many other aspects of the CWA, applies without regard to the source of pollution.

True, there are, as the Pronsolinos point out, two sections of the statute as amended, §208 and §319, that set requirements exclusively for nonpoint sources of pollution. But the structural inference we are asked to draw from those specialized sections—that no *other* provisions of the Act set requirements for waters polluted by nonpoint sources—simply does not follow. Absent some irreconcilable contradiction between the requirements contained in §§208 and 319, on the one hand, and the listing and TMDL requirements of §303(d), on the other, both apply.

There is no such contradiction. Section 208 provides for federal grants to encourage the development of state areawide waste treatment management plans for areas with substantial water quality problems, §208(a), (f), and requires that those plans include a process for identifying and controlling nonpoint source pollution "to the extent feasible." §208(b)(2)(F). Section 319, added to the CWA in 1987, directs states to adopt "nonpoint source management programs"; provides grants for nonpoint source pollution reduction; and requires states to submit a report to the EPA that "identifies those navigable waters within the State which, without additional action to control nonpoint sources of pollution, cannot reasonably be expected to attain or maintain applicable water quality standards or the goals and requirements of this chapter." §319(a)(1)(A). This report must also describe state programs for reducing nonpoint source pollution and the process "to reduce, to the maximum extent practicable, the level of pollution" resulting from particular categories of non-point source pollution. §319(a)(1)(C), (D).

The CWA is replete with multiple listing and planning requirements applicable to the same waterways (quite confusingly so, indeed), so no inference can be drawn from the overlap alone. See, e.g., §208(b); §303(d)(1)(A), (d)(1)(B), (d)(3), (e); CWA §304(*l*); §319(a). Nor are we willing to draw the more discrete inference that the §303(d) listing and TMDL requirements cannot apply to nonpoint source pollutants because the planning requirements imposed by §208 and §319 are qualified ones—"to the extent feasible" and "to the maximum extent practicable"—while the §303(d) requirements are unbending. For one thing, the water quality standards set under §303 are functional and may permit more pollution than it is "feasible" or "practicable" to eliminate, depending upon the intended use of a particular waterway. For another, with or without TMDLs, the §303(e) plans for attaining water quality standards must, without qualification, account for elimination of nonpoint source pollution to the extent necessary to meet those standards. §303(e)(3)(F). . . .

Essentially, §319 encourages the states to institute an approach to the elimination of nonpoint source pollution similar to the federally mandated effluent controls contained in the CWA, while §303 encompasses a water quality based approach applicable to all sources of water pollution. As various sections of the Act encourage different, and complementary, state schemes for cleaning up nonpoint source pollution in the nation's waterways, there is no basis for reading any of those sections—including §303(d)—out of the statute.

There is one final aspect of the Act's structure that bears consideration because it supports the EPA's interpretation of §303(d): The list required by §303(d)(1)(A) requires that waters be listed if they are impaired by a combination of point sources and nonpoint sources; the language admits of no other reading. Section 303(d)(1)(C), in turn, directs that TMDLs shall be established at a level necessary *to implement* the applicable water quality standards. . . . Id. (emphasis added). So, at least in blended waters, TMDLs must be calculated with regard to nonpoint sources of pollution; otherwise, it would be impossible "to implement the applicable water quality standards," which do not differentiate sources of pollution. This court has so recognized. *Browner*, 20 F.3d at 985 ("Congress and the EPA have already determined that establishing TMDLs is an effective tool for achieving water quality standards in waters impacted by non-point source pollution.").

Nothing in the statutory structure—or purpose—suggests that Congress meant to distinguish, as to §303(d)(1) lists and TMDLs, between waters with one insignificant point source and substantial nonpoint source pollution and waters with only nonpoint source pollution. Such a distinction would, for no apparent reason, require the states or the EPA to monitor waters to determine whether a point source had been added or removed, and to adjust the §303(d)(1) list and establish TMDLs accordingly. There is no statutory basis for concluding that Congress intended such an irrational regime.

Looking at the statute as a whole, we conclude that the EPA's interpretation of §303(d) is not only entirely reasonable but considerably more convincing than the one offered by the plaintiffs in this case.

C. FEDERALISM CONCERNS

The Pronsolinos finally contend that, by establishing TMDLs for waters impaired only by nonpoint source pollution, the EPA has upset the balance of federal-state control established in the CWA by intruding into the state's traditional control over land use. That is not the case.

The Garcia River TMDL identifies the maximum load of pollutants that can enter the Garcia River from certain broad categories of nonpoint sources if the river is to attain water quality standards. It does not specify the load of pollutants that may be received from particular parcels of land or describe what measures the state should take to implement the TMDL. Instead, the TMDL expressly recognizes that "implementation and monitoring" "are state responsibilities" and notes that, for this reason, the EPA did not include implementation or monitoring plans within the TMDL.

Moreover, §303(e) requires—separately from the §303(d)(1) listing and TMDL requirements—that each state include in its continuing planning process "adequate implementation, including schedules of compliance, for revised or new water quality standards" "for all navigable waters within such State." §303(e)(3). The Garcia River TMDL thus serves as an informational tool for the creation of the state's implementation plan, independently—and explicitly—required by Congress.

California chose both *if* and *how* it would implement the Garcia River TMDL. States must implement TMDLs only to the extent that they seek to avoid losing federal grant money; there is no pertinent statutory provision otherwise requiring implementation of §303 plans or providing for their enforcement. *See* CWA §309; CWA §505.[19]

Finally, it is worth noting that the arguments that the Pronsolinos raise here would apply equally to nonpoint source pollution controls for blended waters. Yet, as discussed above, Congress definitely required that the states or the EPA establish TMDLs for all pollutants in waters on §303(d)(1) lists, including blended waters.

We conclude that the Pronsolinos' federalism basis for reading §303 against its own words and structure is unfounded.

IV. Conclusion

For all the reasons we have surveyed, the CWA is best read to include in the §303(d) listing and TMDLs requirements waters impaired only by nonpoint sources of

---

19. See also Professor Houck's summary:

> Within the statutory scheme §319 is the carrot, funding state programs for nonpoint source abatement statewide, for all waters whether they are currently above standard or below. In keeping with its broad sweep, §319's provisions are voluntary. States may choose to participate or not. . . . Section 303(d), on the other hand, addresses a narrower and more nasty job: the chronically polluted waters of the United States. For this problem zone, enter a stick: quantified pollution load allocations. The nature of the allocations and of the implementing controls remains up to the states, but states do have to come up with them. [The Clean Water Act TMDL Program 62.]

pollution. . . . We therefore hold that the EPA did not exceed its statutory authority in identifying the Garcia River pursuant to §303(d)(1)(A) and establishing the Garcia River TMDL, even though the river is polluted only by nonpoint sources of pollution.

The decision of the district court is AFFIRMED.

NOTES AND QUESTIONS

1. *Additional Issues Relating to Listing.* Numerous issues have arisen concerning the nature of states' listing authority and responsibility and EPA's oversight obligations. For example, under what circumstances may a state decline to list a water body on the basis that the data supporting listing are problematic? When do listing decisions trigger ESA consultation requirements? See American Littoral Soc'y v. EPA, 199 F. Supp. 2d 217 (D.N.J. 2002); Sierra Club v. EPA, 162 F. Supp. 2d 406 (D. Md. 2001). See Sierra Club, Inc. v. Leavitt, 488 F.3d 904 (11th Cir. 2007), for a decision involving several challenges to EPA's approval of Florida's impaired waters list.

2. *Federalism Issues: EPA's Responsibility in Setting TMDLs.* One of the most frequently litigated issues has concerned when EPA must step in to set TMDLs. Several courts, including the Ninth and Tenth Circuits, rejected challenges under numerous theories to lack of progress in setting TMDLs. See, e.g., San Francisco Baykeeper v. Whitman, 297 F.3d 877 (9th Cir. 2002); Hayes v. Whitman, 264 F.3d 1017 (10th Cir. 2001). A law professor and attorney for environmental groups in several TMDL cases characterizes the state of the case law as follows:

> [R]egardless of legal theory (constructive submission, mandatory duty, arbitrary and capricious, abuse of discretion, unreasonable delay, etc.), [several circuit and district courts] declined to order EPA to step in to set TMDLs. The standard for ordering EPA to comply is nearly insurmountable, requiring both (1) an explicit refusal by a state to take *any* TMDL action, and (2) unreasonable EPA delay in declaring such refusal a "constructive submission" of no TMDLs. Not surprisingly, no state is so bold as to declare the intent to refuse to participate in the TMDL program, and EPA has many reasons for delay. Thus, despite the hype, the constructive submission doctrine and related theories appear moribund.

May, Recent Developments in TMDL Litigation 1999-2002 135 (ALI-ABA Course on Clean Water Act Course of Study Materials, Oct. 23-25, 2002).

3. *The Role of Consent Decrees.* EPA has negotiated consent decrees in numerous states to resolve TMDL-related litigation. These cases typically establish schedules for the involved state to complete its responsibilities, but may involve a host of substantive and other issues as well. EPA maintains information concerning these decrees and other developments in TMDL litigation on its website. http://www.epa.gov/owow/tmdl/lawsuit.html.

4. *Outstanding Issues.* In theory, TMDLs are to be allocated in part to point sources, and the permits of these sources are to be modified to reflect the load allocated to them. It remains to be seen how effective this mechanism will be in implementing this scenario, but the mechanism is fairly well established. EPA has stated that "[w]hen a TMDL is developed for waters impaired by point sources only, the issuance of a . . . (NPDES) permit(s) provides the reasonable assurance that the wasteload allocations contained in the TMDL will be achieved." EPA, Guidelines for Reviewing TMDLs Under Existing Regulations Issued in 1992 (May 20, 2002).

The waters are murkier when it comes to the application of TMDLs in the nonpoint source context. The TMDL program is intended to identify nonpoint pollution as a source of impairment. See, e.g., *Pronsolino*, *supra*. EPA contemplates that states, in developing and allocating a TMDL, may allocate a portion of the total load to nonpoint sources. 40 C.F.R. §130.32(b)(7). How much of a burden is the government likely to impose on nonpoint sources? Will this burden be sufficient to achieve the TMDL program's goals of achieving WQSs? Are the government's current tools adequate for it to ensure that nonpoint sources' discharges conform to the amounts allocated to them in the TMDL process (the "load allocations")? EPA explains how the approach is supposed to work, and that the end result is supposed to be that the TMDL will achieve water quality standards, as follows:

> When a TMDL is developed for waters impaired by both point and nonpoint sources, and the WLA is based on an assumption that nonpoint source load reductions will occur, EPA's 1991 TMDL Guidance states that the TMDL should provide reasonable assurances that nonpoint source control measures will achieve expected load reductions in order for the TMDL to be approvable. This information is necessary for EPA to determine that the TMDL, including the load and wasteload allocations, has been established at a level necessary to implement water quality standards. [EPA, Guidelines for Reviewing TMDLs Under Existing Regulations Issued in 1992 (May 20, 2002).]

Professor Robert Adler questions the likely efficacy of the TMDL process, suggesting that the TMDL provision "designed to provide a mechanism for states or EPA to redress water quality standards violations, provides no clear mechanism for imposing requirements other than numeric water quality-based effluent limits for point sources. . . ." Adler, Resilience, Restoration, and Sustainability: Revisiting the Fundamental Principles of the Clean Water Act, 32 Wash U. J.L. & Pol'y 139, 152 (2010).

The devil is likely to be in the details, in short. A state is required to provide assurances persuading EPA that the state's nonpoint source control measures will achieve the expected load reductions. Key implementation questions, therefore, will include: (a) the types of assurances states are providing; (b) the level of EPA scrutiny of such assurances; (c) EPA action in cases where the assurances do not pass muster; and (d) monitoring and follow-up on the implementation end to determine whether the allocated reductions are actually occurring and, if not, the adequacy of steps taken to put the program on the intended track. Pursuant to a settlement agreement, EPA issued what it characterized as the "largest, most complex TMDL in the country" in September 2009, for the Chesapeake Bay. Preliminary Notice of TMDL Development for Chesapeake Bay, 74 Fed. Reg. 47,792, 47,793 (Sept. 17, 2009). The TMDL is currently the subject of pending litigation. See American Farm Bureau Fed'n v. EPA, 984 F. Supp. 2d 289 (M.D. Pa. 2013), *appeal docketed*, No. 13-4079 (3d Cir.).

5. *Bubbles and Effluent Credit Trading.* In January 2003, EPA issued its Water Quality Trading Policy Statement, 68 Fed. Reg. 1608 (2003). The agency characterized water quality trading as a "voluntary, incentive-based approach that can offer greater efficiency in restoring or protecting water bodies." EPA established several ground rules for trading schemes, including (1) demarcating areas in which trades may take place ("within a watershed or a defined area for which a TMDL has been approved"); (2) identifying the types of pollutants that may be traded (generally, nutrients or sediment loads, though EPA indicated that it may support trades of

other pollutants as well under certain circumstances); (3) highlighting the need to establish baselines for trading; and (4) reviewing the circumstances in which trading may occur (e.g., to maintain water quality where WQSs are attained, and intra-plant trading). Id. at 1610-1611. In an October 2008 report, EPA concluded that "[d]espite the theoretical promise of water quality trading . . . WQT . . . has met with limited practical success." EPA, Water Quality Trading Evaluation Final Report ES-1 (2008).

One concern with trading schemes is the possible toleration of localized "hot spots." Further, trades between point and nonpoint sources are likely to be particularly challenging for a variety of reasons. Issues to watch include the extent to which trading schemes create enforceable obligations under the CWA for nonpoint sources, and the degree to which these schemes make point sources accountable for reductions by nonpoint sources. Stephenson, Shabman & Geyer, Toward an Effective Watershed-Based Effluent Allowance Trading System: Identifying the Statutory and Regulatory Barriers to Implementation, 5 Envtl. Law. 775 (1999), argue that the CWA limits watershed-based effluent allowance trading and suggest amendments to remove barriers to an effective trading scheme. For an example of a water trading initiative at the state level, Pennsylvania has authorized and begun to implement a new trading program intended to generate nutrient reduction credits as part of the state's effort to reduce nitrogen, phosphorus, and sediment pollution in the Chesapeake Bay watershed. First Sale of Nutrient Credits Executed Under Pennsylvania Trading Program, 218 Daily Env't Rep. (BNA) A-10 (November 13, 2006).

4. Section 401 Certifications

Section 401 of the CWA gives states another tool to advance water protection goals. Certain types of projects that may discharge pollutants into waters, such as power plants, are subject to federal permitting. Section 401 gives states a special "seat at the table" in such proceedings. In S.D. Warren Co. v. Maine Bd. of Envtl. Prot., 547 U.S. 370 (2006), the Court unanimously held that state regulators have authority under §401 of the CWA to require water flowing through dams to meet their water quality standards. The Court held that water passing through a dam constitutes a "discharge" that triggers the §401 certification requirement. The Court distinguished §401 "discharges" from §402 "discharges of a pollutant," holding that the latter but not the former require "addition" of a "pollutant." At least one commentator has concluded that, as a result, the Warren case is "not likely to have significant implications for the scope of state NPDES permit authority." Glick, State Authority & Hydropower, Water Rep. No. 28 (June 15, 2006). The following case explores the parameters of this mechanism.

PUD NO. 1 OF JEFFERSON COUNTY v. WASHINGTON DEPARTMENT OF ECOLOGY
511 U.S. 700 (1994)

Justice O'CONNOR delivered the opinion of the Court.

Petitioners, a city and a local utility district, want to build a hydroelectric project on the Dosewallips River in Washington State. We must decide whether respondent state environmental agency (hereinafter respondent) properly conditioned a permit for the project on the maintenance of specific minimum stream flows to protect salmon and steelhead runs. . . .

I

The State of Washington has adopted comprehensive water quality standards intended to regulate all of the State's navigable waters. The State created an inventory of all the State's waters, and divided the waters into five classes. Wash. Administrative Code 173-201-045. Each individual fresh surface water of the State is placed into one of these classes. The Dosewallips River is classified AA, extraordinary. . . .

In addition to these specific standards applicable to Class AA waters, the State has adopted a statewide antidegradation policy. That policy provides:

(a) Existing beneficial uses shall be maintained and protected and no further degradation which would interfere with or become injurious to existing beneficial uses will be allowed.

(b) No degradation will be allowed of waters lying in national parks, national recreation areas, national wildlife refuges, national scenic rivers, and other areas of national ecological importance. . . .

(c) In no case, will any degradation of water quality be allowed if this degradation interferes with or becomes injurious to existing water uses and causes long-term and irreparable harm to the environment. 173-201-035(8).

As required by the Act, EPA reviewed and approved the State's water quality standards. See 33 U.S.C. §1313(c)(3). Upon approval by EPA, the state standard became "the water quality standard for the applicable waters of that State." 33 U.S.C. §1313(c)(3).

States are responsible for enforcing water quality standards on intrastate waters. §1319(a). In addition to these primary enforcement responsibilities, §401 of the Act requires States to provide a water quality certification before a federal license or permit can be issued for activities that may result in any discharge into intrastate navigable waters. 33 U.S.C. §1341. Specifically, §401 requires an applicant for a federal license or permit to conduct any activity "which may result in any discharge into the navigable waters" to obtain from the State a certification "that any such discharge will comply with the applicable provisions of sections [1311, 1312, 1313, 1316, and 1317 of this title]." 33 U.S.C. §1341(a). Section 401(d) further provides that "[a]ny certification . . . shall set forth any effluent limitations and other limitations, and monitoring requirements necessary to assure that any applicant . . . will comply with any applicable effluent limitations and other limitations, under section [1311 or 1312 of this title] . . . and with any other appropriate requirement of State law set forth in such certification." 33 U.S.C. §1341(d). The limitations included in the certification become a condition on any federal license. Ibid.

II

Petitioners propose to build the Elkhorn Hydroelectric Project on the Dosewallips River. If constructed as presently planned, the facility would be located just outside the Olympic National Park on federally owned land within the Olympic National Forest.

The project would divert water from a 1.2-mile reach of the river (the bypass reach), run the water through turbines to generate electricity and then return the water to the river below the bypass reach. Under the Federal Power Act, 16 U.S.C. §791a et seq., the Federal Energy Regulatory Commission (FERC) has authority to license new hydroelectric facilities. As a result, petitioners must get a FERC license to build or operate the Elkhorn Project. Because a federal license is required, and because the project may result in discharges into the Dosewallips River, petitioners are also required to obtain state certification of the project pursuant to §401 of the Clean Water Act, 33 U.S.C. §1341.

[The river supports coho and chinook salmon and steelhead trout. The Washington State Department of Ecology imposed a minimum stream flow require-ment of 100 to 200 cubic feet per second. A state administrative appeals board rejected the condition because it was imposed to enhance, not maintain, the fishery and thus was outside the scope of §401. The state supreme court upheld the minimum flow requirements, and the Supreme Court accepted certiorari to resolve a conflict among state supreme courts about the scope of §401.]

III

The principal dispute in this case concerns whether the minimum stream flow requirement that the State imposed on the Elkhorn Project is a permissible condition of a §401 certification under the Clean Water Act. To resolve this dispute we must first determine the scope of the State's authority under §401. We must then determine whether the limitation at issue here, the requirement that petitioners maintain minimum stream flows, falls within the scope of that authority.

A

There is no dispute that petitioners were required to obtain a certification from the State pursuant to §401. Petitioners concede that, at a minimum, the project will result in two possible discharges—the release of dredged and fill material during the construction of the project, and the discharge of water at the end of the tailrace after the water has been used to generate electricity. Petitioners contend, however, that the minimum stream flow requirement imposed by the State was unrelated to these specific discharges, and that as a consequence, the State lacked the authority under §401 to condition its certification on maintenance of stream flows sufficient to protect the Dosewallips fishery.

If §401 consisted solely of subsection (a), which refers to a state certification that a "discharge" will comply with certain provisions of the Act, petitioners' assessment of the scope of the State's certification authority would have considerable force. Section 401, however, also contains subsection (d), which expands the State's authority to impose conditions on the certification of a project. Section 401(d) provides that any certification shall set forth "any effluent limitations and other limitations . . . necessary to assure that *any applicant*" will comply with various provisions of the Act and appropriate state law requirements. 33 U.S.C. §1341(d) (emphasis added). The language of this subsection contradicts petitioners' claim that the State may only impose water quality limitations specifically tied to a "discharge." The text refers to the compliance of the applicant, not the discharge. Section 401(d) thus allows the State to impose "other limitations" on the project in general to assure compliance with various provisions of the Clean Water Act and with "any other appropriate requirement of State law." Although the dissent asserts that this interpretation of §401(d) renders §401(a)(1) superfluous, we see no such anomaly. Section 401(a)(1) identifies the category of activities subject to certification—namely, those with discharges. And §401(d) is most reasonably read as authorizing additional conditions and limitations on the activity as a whole once the threshold condition, the existence of a discharge, is satisfied. . . .

We agree with the State that ensuring compliance with §303 is a proper function of the §401 certification. Although §303 is not one of the statutory provisions listed in §401(d), the statute allows States to impose limitations to ensure compliance with §301 of the Act, 33 U.S.C. §1311. Section 301 in turn incorporates §303 by reference. See 33 U.S.C. §1311(b)(1)(C); see also H.R. Conf. Rep. No. 95-830, p. 96 (1977), U.S. Code Cong. & Admin. News 1977, pp. 4326, 4471 ("Section 303 is always included by reference where section 301 is listed."). As a consequence, state water quality standards adopted pursuant to §303 are among the "other limitations" with which a State may ensure compliance through the §401 certification process. This interpretation is consistent with EPA's view of the statute. . . .[3]

B

Having concluded that, pursuant to §401, States may condition certification upon any limitations necessary to ensure compliance with state water quality standards or any other "appropriate requirement of State law," we consider whether the minimum flow condition is such a limitation. Under §303, state water quality standards must "consist of the designated uses of the navigable waters involved and the water quality criteria for such waters based upon such uses." 33 U.S.C. §1313(c)(2)(A). In imposing the minimum stream flow requirement, the State determined that construction and operation of the project as planned would be inconsistent with one of the designated uses of Class AA water, namely "[s]almonid [and other fish] migration, rearing, spawning, and harvesting." App. to Pet. for Cert. 83a-84a. The designated use of the river as a fish habitat directly reflects the Clean Water Act's goal of maintaining the "chemical, physical, and biological integrity of the Nation's waters." 33 U.S.C. §1251(a). Indeed, the Act defines pollution as "the man-made or man induced alteration of the chemical, physical, biological, and radiological integrity of water." §1362(19). Moreover, the Act expressly requires that, in adopting water quality standards, the State must take into consideration the use of waters for "propagation of fish and wildlife." §1313(c)(2)(A).

Petitioners assert, however, that §303 requires the State to protect designated uses solely through implementation of specific "criteria." According to petitioners, the State may not require them to operate their dam in a manner consistent with a

---

3. The dissent asserts that §301 is concerned solely with discharges, not broader water quality standards. Although §301 does make certain discharges unlawful, see 33 U.S.C. §1311(a), it also contains a broad enabling provision which requires States to take certain actions, to wit: "In order to carry out the objective of this chapter [viz. the chemical, physical, and biological integrity of the Nation's water] there shall be achieved . . . not later than July 1, 1977, any more stringent limitation, including those necessary to meet water quality standards, . . . established pursuant to any State law or regulations. . . ." 33 U.S.C. §1311(b)(1)(C). This provision of §301 expressly refers to state water quality standards, and is not limited to discharges.

designated "use"; instead, say petitioners, under §303 the State may only require that the project comply with specific numerical "criteria."

We disagree with petitioners' interpretation of the language of §303(c)(2)(A). Under the statute, a water quality standard must "consist of the designated uses of the navigable waters involved *and* the water quality criteria for such waters based upon such uses." 33 U.S.C. §1313(c)(2)(A) (emphasis added). The text makes it plain that water quality standards contain two components. We think the language of §303 is most naturally read to require that a project be consistent with both components, namely, the designated use and the water quality criteria. Accordingly, under the literal terms of the statute, a project that does not comply with a designated use of the water does not comply with the applicable water quality standards.

Consequently, pursuant to §401(d) the State may require that a permit applicant comply with both the designated uses and the water quality criteria of the state standards. In granting certification pursuant to §401(d), the State "shall set forth any . . . limitations . . . necessary to assure that [the applicant] will comply with any . . . limitations under [§303] . . . and with any other appropriate requirement of State law." A certification requirement that an applicant operate the project consistently with state water quality standards—i.e., consistently with the designated uses of the water body and the water quality criteria—is both a "limitation" to assure "compl[iance] with . . . limitations" imposed under §303, and an "appropriate" requirement of state law. . . .

The State also justified its minimum stream flow as necessary to implement the "antidegradation policy" of §303, 33 U.S.C. §1313(d)(4)(B). When the Clean Water Act was enacted in 1972, the water quality standards of all 50 States had antidegradation provisions. These provisions were required by federal law. By providing in 1972 that existing state water quality standards would remain in force until revised, the Clean Water Act ensured that the States would continue their antidegradation programs. See 33 U.S.C. §1313(a). EPA has consistently required that revised state standards incorporate an antidegradation policy. And, in 1987, Congress explicitly recognized the existence of an "antidegradation policy established under [§303]." §1313(d)(4)(B).

EPA has promulgated regulations implementing §303's antidegradation policy. . . . These regulations require States to "develop and adopt a statewide antidegradation policy and identify the methods for implementing such policy." 40 CFR §131.12 (1993). These "implementation methods shall, at a minimum, be consistent with the . . . [e]xisting instream water uses and the level of water quality necessary to protect the existing uses shall be maintained and protected." Ibid. EPA has explained that under its antidegradation regulation, "no activity is allowable . . . which could partially or completely eliminate any existing use." EPA, Questions and Answers on Antidegradation 3 (Aug. 1985). Thus, States must implement their antidegradation policy in a manner "consistent" with existing uses of the stream. The State of Washington's antidegradation policy in turn provides that "[e]xisting beneficial uses shall be maintained and protected and no further degradation which would interfere with or become injurious to existing beneficial uses will be allowed." WAC 173-201-035(8)(a) (1986). The State concluded that the reduced stream flows would have just the effect prohibited by this policy. The Solicitor General, representing EPA, asserts, and we agree, that the State's minimum stream flow condition is a proper application of the state and federal antidegradation regulations, as it ensures that an "existing in-stream water us[e]" will be "maintained and protected." 40 CFR §131.12(a)(1) (1993).

Petitioners also assert more generally that the Clean Water Act is only concerned with water "quality," and does not allow the regulation of water "quantity." This is an artificial distinction. In many cases, water quantity is closely related to water quality; a sufficient lowering of the water quantity in a body of water could destroy all of its designated uses, be it for drinking water, recreation, navigation or, as here, as a fishery. In any event, there is recognition in the Clean Water Act itself that reduced stream flow, i.e., diminishment of water quantity, can constitute water pollution. First, the Act's definition of pollution as "the man-made or man induced alteration of the chemical, physical, biological, and radiological integrity of water" encompasses the effects of reduced water quantity. 33 U.S.C. §1362(19). This broad conception of pollution—one which expressly evinces Congress' concern with the physical and biological integrity of water—refutes petitioners' assertion that the Act draws a sharp distinction between the regulation of water "quantity" and water "quality." Moreover, §304 of the Act expressly recognizes that water "pollution" may result from "changes in the movement, flow, or circulation of any navigable waters . . . , including changes caused by the construction of dams." 33 U.S.C. §1314(f). This concern with the flowage effects of dams and other diversions is also embodied in the EPA regulations, which expressly require existing dams to be operated to attain designated uses.

Petitioners assert that two other provisions of the Clean Water Act, §§101(g) and 510(2), 33 U.S.C. §§1251(g) and 1370(2), exclude the regulation of water quantity from the coverage of the Act. Section 101(g) provides "that the authority of each State to allocate quantities of water within its jurisdiction shall not be superseded, abrogated or otherwise impaired by this chapter." 33 U.S.C. §1251(g). Similarly, §510(2) provides that nothing in the Act shall "be construed as impairing or in any manner affecting any right or jurisdiction of the States with respect to the waters . . . of such States." 33 U.S.C. §1370. In petitioners' view, these provisions exclude "water quantity issues from direct regulation under the federally controlled water quality standards authorized in §303."

This language gives the States authority to allocate water rights; we therefore find it peculiar that petitioners argue that it prevents the State from regulating stream flow. In any event, we read these provisions more narrowly than petitioners. Sections 101(g) and 510(2) preserve the authority of each State to allocate water quantity as between users; they do not limit the scope of water pollution controls that may be imposed on users who have obtained, pursuant to state law, a water allocation. In California v. FERC, 495 U.S. 490, 498 (1990), construing an analogous provision of the Federal Power Act, we explained that "minimum stream flow requirements neither reflect nor establish 'proprietary rights' " to water. Moreover, the certification itself does not purport to determine petitioners' proprietary right to the water of the Dosewallips. . . .

IV

Petitioners contend that we should limit the State's authority to impose minimum flow requirements because FERC has comprehensive authority to license hydroelectric projects pursuant to the FPA, 16 U.S.C. §791a et seq. In petitioners' view, the minimum flow requirement imposed here interferes with FERC's authority under the FPA. . . .

No such conflict with any FERC licensing activity is presented here. FERC has not yet acted on petitioners' license application, and it is possible that FERC will eventually deny petitioners' application altogether. Alternatively, it is quite possible, given that FERC is required to give equal consideration to the protection of fish habitat when deciding whether to issue a license, that any FERC license would contain the same conditions as the state §401 certification. Indeed, at oral argument the Deputy Solicitor General stated that both EPA and FERC were represented in this proceeding, and that the Government has no objection to the stream flow condition contained in the §401 certification. . . .

In summary, we hold that the State may include minimum stream flow requirements in a certification issued pursuant to §401 of the Clean Water Act insofar as necessary to enforce a designated use contained in a state water quality standard. The judgment of the Supreme Court of Washington, accordingly, is Affirmed.

While the Court held that a state may set minimum flow standards in exercising its §401 certification requirements, must it do so? See, e.g., Great Basin Mine Watch v. Hankins, 456 F.3d 955 (9th Cir. 2006). Though the Supreme Court in the preceding case appeared to give a broad reading to a state's authority under §401 to protect its waters, in the following case the Ninth Circuit identified limits on this authority, notably that it does not empower the states to address nonpoint source releases. For a Ninth Circuit case also concluding that §401 does not apply to nonpoint source pollution, and that such a conclusion is consistent with the Supreme Court's decision in *S.D. Warren* (discussed briefly above at page 697), see Oregon Natural Desert Ass'n v. United States Forest Serv., 550 F.3d 778 (9th Cir. 2008).

OREGON NATURAL DESERT ASSOCIATION v. DOMBECK
172 F.3d 1092 (9th Cir. 1998)

SCHROEDER, Circuit Judge:

[The question in the case is whether nonpoint source pollution from cattle grazing, notably waste, increased sedimentation, and increased temperature is subject to the certification requirement of §401 of the Clean Water Act, 33 U.S.C. §1341. The court framed the issue as whether the term "discharge" in §1341 includes releases from nonpoint sources as well as releases from point sources. The court concluded from the language and structure of the Act that the certification requirement of §1341 was meant to apply only to point source releases. As a result, the Forest Service did not violate 33 U.S.C. §1341 by issuing a grazing permit without first obtaining the state of Oregon's certification that the grazing would not violate the state's water quality standards.]

The crux of this case is whether the Burrils' Forest Service grazing permit requires certification from the State of Oregon. The resolution of this question hinges on the interpretation of the term "discharge" as used in §1341. . . .

The appellees argued before us and the district court that "discharge" in §1341 refers to pollution from both point sources and nonpoint sources. In accepting this argument below, the district court relied exclusively on §502 [(12), (16)] of the Act. . . . The district court reasoned that because the unqualified term "discharge" is defined as including, but not limited to, point source releases, it must include releases from nonpoint sources as well. The court therefore concluded that the term "discharge" encompassed nonpoint source pollution like runoff from grazing. It rejected the government's position that the unqualified term "discharge" is limited to point sources but includes both polluting and nonpolluting releases. . . .

The Clean Water Act, when examined as a whole, cannot support the conclusion that §1341 applies to nonpoint sources. . . .

The Clean Water Act . . . overhauled the regulation of water quality. Direct federal regulation now focuses on reducing the level of effluent that flows from point sources. This is accomplished through the issuance of permits under the National Pollutant Discharge Elimination System (NPDES). See 33 U.S.C. §1342. The Act prohibits the release of pollutants from point sources except in compliance with an NPDES permit. 33 U.S.C. §1311. . . .

We must reach the same conclusion with regard to the scope of the term "discharge" in §1341. Prior to 1972, the provision required the state to certify that a licensed activity would "not violate applicable water quality standards." Now, the statute requires certification that any discharge from the licensed activity "will comply with the applicable provisions of sections 1311, 1312, 1313, 1316, and 1317" of Title 33. 33 U.S.C. §1341(a)(1). The statute was thus amended "to assure consistency with the bill's changed emphasis from water quality standards to effluent limitations based on the elimination of any discharge of pollutants." The term "discharge" in §1341 is limited to discharges from point sources.

All of the sections cross-referenced in §1341 relate to the regulation of point sources. Appellees contend section 1313, requiring states to establish water quality standards, relates to nonpoint source pollution because it addresses water quality standards and implementation plans. The section does not itself regulate nonpoint source pollution. Water quality standards are established in part to regulate point source pollution. They provide "a supplementary basis . . . so that numerous point sources, despite individual compliance with effluent limitations, may be further regulated to prevent water quality from falling below acceptable levels." EPA v. California ex. rel. State Water Resources Control Bd., 426 U.S. 200, 205 n.12 (1976). In Oregon Natural Resources Council [v. United States Forest Service, 834 F.2d 842, 850 (9th Cir. 1987)], we held that the reference to water quality standards in §1311(b)(1)(C) did not sweep nonpoint sources into the scope of §1311. For similar reasons, §1313 does not sweep nonpoint sources into the scope of §1341.

Appellees' reliance on the Supreme Court's decision in PUD No. 1 v. Washington Dep't of Ecology, 511 U.S. 700 (1994), is similarly misplaced. In that case, the State of Washington issued a §1341 certification for a dam, conditioned on minimum stream flows in order to protect fisheries. The Court held that such a condition was permissible under §1341 even though it did not relate to an effluent discharge from the dam. Thus, a state is free to impose such water-quality limitations "once the threshold condition, the existence of a discharge, is satisfied." Id. at 712. The Supreme Court in PUD No. 1 did not broaden the meaning of the term "discharge" under §1341. . . .

The terminology employed throughout the Clean Water Act cuts against ONDA's argument that the term "discharge" includes nonpoint source pollution like runoff from grazing. Neither the phrase "nonpoint source discharge" nor the phrase "discharge from a nonpoint source" appears in the Act. Rather, the word "discharge" is used consistently to refer to the release of effluent from a point source. By contrast, the term "runoff" describes pollution flowing from nonpoint sources. The term "runoff" is used throughout 33 U.S.C. §1288, describing urban wastewater plans, and 33 U.S.C. §1314(f), providing guidelines for identification of nonpoint sources of pollution. Section 1341 contains no reference to runoff.

Had Congress intended to require certification for runoff as well as discharges, it could easily have written §1341 to mirror the language of §1323, which directs federal agencies "engaged in any activity which may result in the discharge or runoff of pollutants" to comply with applicable water quality standards. 33 U.S.C. §1323(a). Section 1323 plainly applies to nonpoint sources of pollution on federal land. ONDA does not seek relief under this provision, however, because absent the issuance of an NPDES permit under §1342, a citizen suit under the Clean Water Act may not be based on a violation of 33 U.S.C. §1323. See 33 U.S.C. §1365(f).

We have recognized the distinction between the terms "discharge" and "runoff":

> Nonpoint source pollution is not specifically defined in the Act, but is pollution that does not result from the "discharge" or "addition" of pollutants from a point source. Examples of nonpoint source pollution include runoff from irrigated agriculture and silvicultural activities. [*Oregon Natural Resources Council*, 834 F.3d at 849 n. 9.]

We have further noted that "Congress had classified nonpoint source pollution as runoff caused primarily by rainfall around activities that employ or create pollutants. Such runoff could not be traced to any identifiable point of discharge." [Trustees for Alaska v. EPA, 749 F.2d 549, 558 (9th Cir. 1984). The court held that certification was not required.]

In the following sections, we include notes on particular sources of pollution that have received particular attention. We first provide an overview of agricultural pollution, next we turn to municipal operations, and finally we include an overview of some of the issues involving nonpoint source pollution.

F.   AGRICULTURAL POLLUTION, INCLUDING CAFOS

Agricultural operations have long been a significant source of environmental degradation. Ruhl, Farms, Their Environmental Harms, and Environmental Law, 27 Ecology L.Q. 265 (2000). This is particularly true in the arena of water pollution. State inventories suggest that agriculture impacts approximately 25 percent of the rivers and streams (by mileage) identified as impaired in the United States.

Regulation of farms under the federal environmental laws has been quite limited, despite their significant environmental impacts. In some cases, legislatures have created "safe harbor" provisions that exempt farming operations from regulation that otherwise might apply. In the NPDES permit program, for example, Congress has defined point sources to exclude "return flows from irrigated agriculture" and "agricultural stormwater discharges," CWA §502(14), and it makes it clear in §402(*l*)(1) that EPA may not "require a permit . . . for discharges composed entirely of return flows from irrigated agriculture. . . ." The scope of these exemptions has been subject to litigation. See, e.g., Waterkeeper Alliance, Inc. v. EPA, 399 F.3d 486 (2d Cir. 2005) (discussed in more detail below); Fishermen Against the Destruction of the Env't, Inc. v. Closter Farms, 300 F.3d 1294 (11th Cir. 2002); Concerned Area Residents for the Env't v. Southview Farms, 34 F.3d 114 (2d Cir. 1994).

Many have ascribed this light regulatory hand to the "special status of farming in American society. American ideology tends to romanticize farms, focusing on the Jeffersonian agro-society roots of democracy, the plight of dust bowl farmers, and the peacefully bucolic farm by the side of the road." Ruhl, *supra*, at 269 n.9. The difficulty in addressing certain types of farm pollution has also impeded national efforts to regulate it.

Certain agricultural operations, known by the acronym CAFOs (concentrated animal feeding operations), are subject to the NPDES program and must obtain permits in order to discharge wastewater. CWA §502(14) specifically includes CAFOs in its definition of a "point source." EPA summarizes the need for more rigorous regulation of CAFOs because of the increasing concentration of what it refers to as "animal production industries" as follows:

> The continued trend toward fewer but larger operations, coupled with greater emphasis on more intensive production methods and specialization, is concentrating more manure nutrients and other animal waste constituents within some geographic areas. These large operations often do not have sufficient land to effectively use the manure as fertilizer. Furthermore, there is limited land acreage near the CAFO to effectively use the manure. This trend has coincided with increased reports of large-scale discharges from CAFOs, as well as continued runoff that is contributing to the significant increase in nutrients and resulting impairment of many U.S. water bodies. [NPDES Permit Regulation and Effluent Limitation Guidelines and Standards for CAFOs, 68 Fed. Reg. 7176, 7180 (2003).]

EPA first regulated CAFOs under the NPDES program in the mid-1970s, but it promulgated extensive regulations in 2003. 68 Fed. Reg. 7176 (Feb. 12, 2003). As is often the case, the 2003 regulations were subject to judicial challenge by various stakeholders. Key issues included the question of jurisdictional boundaries (e.g., to what types of dischargers did the NPDES permitting requirements apply) and that of content (e.g., what types of controls were regulated parties required to implement and what results were they required to achieve). In Waterkeeper Alliance, Inc. v. EPA, 399 F.3d 486 (2d Cir. 2005), the Second Circuit upheld parts of the rule but vacated and remanded others in response to challenges by each group of petitioners, dealing with features of the permitting scheme the rule established and the rule's treatment of nutrient management plans, among other issues. Id. at 498-506, 524 (discussing some aspects of the rule the court invalidated). EPA finalized issued revised rules in 2008. Revised NPDES Permit Regulation and Effluent Limitation Guidelines and Standards for CAFOs in Response to the *Waterkeeper* Decision, 73 Fed. Reg. 70,418 (Nov. 20, 2008). The agency estimated that approximately 15,500 CAFOs would require NPDES permits and detailed the types of actions they must take to limit pollution. Id. at 70,469.

EPA's 2008 regulations were also challenged, and the suit ultimately settled. NRDC v. EPA, No. 08-61093 (5th Cir. May 25, 2010). EPA agreed to propose additional regulations covering CAFOs within a year, which would require CAFOs to provide information to EPA about their operations. EPA also issued a guidance document a few days after the settlement that was intended to facilitate implementing the CAFO regulations. EPA, Implementation Guidance on CAFO Regulations—CAFOs That Discharge or Are Proposing to Discharge (May 28, 2010), EPA-833-R-10-006.

The Fifth Circuit provided an overview of the 2003 EPA CAFO rule, and the *Waterkeeper* decision, in National Pork Producers v. EPA, 635 F.3d 738 (5th Cir. 2011). That court also reviewed aspects of EPA's 2008 rule and guidance documents EPA had issued after promulgating the 2008 rule. While upholding various parts of the rule, the court held that EPA overreached in establishing the universe of CAFOs that must apply for permits. In particular, it held that "there must be an actual discharge to navigable waters to trigger the CWA's requirements and the EPA's authority." Id. at 751. In other words, EPA's authority "is limited to the regulation of CAFOs that discharge." Id. The court held that EPA has the authority to require such CAFOs to apply for permits, but it vacated the portions of the rule that create liability for failing to apply for an NPDES permit.

In July 2012, EPA amended its CAFO regulations to conform to the *National Pork Producers* decision. The agency eliminated the requirement that an owner or operator of a CAFO that "proposes to discharge" apply for an NPDES permit. The rule "also removes the voluntary certification option for unpermitted CAFOs because removal of the proposal to discharge requirement renders the certification option unnecessary." NPDES Permit Regulations for CAFOs: Removal of Vacated Elements in Response to 2011 Court Decision, 77 Fed. Reg. 44,494 (July 30, 2012). Of procedural interest, in amending the regulations EPA determined that a notice-and-comment rulemaking was unnecessary and not in the public interest because its action was ministerial in nature. In particular, the agency indicated that it was accepting the decision of the court in the *Pork Producers* case that EPA lacked discretion to reach a different conclusion, and therefore providing an opportunity for public comment was unnecessary and would not serve the public interest. Id. at 44,496

Beyond the NPDES permit program, the CWA's nonpoint source authorities (§§208 and 319) provide mechanisms for addressing agricultural pollution. The TMDL program also offers some promise in this area. As we discuss in the sections covering those aspects of the CWA, the prospects for success under either authority for significant reductions in discharges are uncertain. Beyond the CWA, other authorities that potentially address agricultural pollution include the Coastal Zone Management Act and the Endangered Species Act. For a discussion of these authorities, see Ruhl, *supra.* For suggestions for addressing agricultural pollution as nonpoint source pollution, see Zaring, Federal Legislative Solutions to Agricultural Nonpoint Source Pollution, 26 Envtl. L. Rep. 10,128 (1996).

G. MUNICIPAL TREATMENT OPERATIONS

As explained at the start of the chapter, the development of sanitary sewer systems was a major public health advance. In her posthumously published novel Thrones, Dominations, the late British mystery writer Dorothy Sayers has Lord Peter Wimsey explain the construction of London's subterranean sewers, after the Great Stink of 1858, to his new wife:

> 'Whatever was the Great Stink?' asked Harriet, charmed.
> 'A stench so awful from the tidal mudbanks in the Thames that curtains soaked in chloride of lime had to be hung at the windows of the Palace of Westminister to allow MPs to get through necessary parliamentary business.'

'So they had to do something about it?'

'Yes. An engineer called Joseph Bazalgette, whose name would be immortal and known to every schoolboy if there were any justice in the world, built intercepting sewers, running parallel with the Thames at three levels, that carried away the muck to outfalls below London.'

D. Sayers & J. Walsh, Thrones, Dominations 52 (St. Martin's Press 1998).

Following London's lead, most cities chose to discharge the effluent they collected directly into the nearest body of water. By the 1960s, many cities had invested in primary treatment, which involves using basic filtration and settling ponds to separate solids from liquids. The settled sludge traditionally has been disposed of in landfills, dewatered and incinerated, composted, or barged and disposed of in the ocean. The supernatant (liquid) is treated with chlorine and disposed of in the receiving waters.

This section summarizes some of the efforts under the CWA to improve wastewater treatment and management, and some of the environmental and regulatory issues that such operations pose. There have been several interesting twists and turns in management approaches that have the potential to provide insights concerning the use of various tools to promote desired environmental ends.

1.   A Case of Federal Subsidies: The Construction Grants Program and State Revolving Funds

As is the case for industrial dischargers, the CWA requires municipal treatment plants to implement technology-based controls. These controls, known as secondary treatment, involve the use of bacteria or chemicals to remove additional organic material. CWA §301(b)(1)(B). Further, as also is the case for industrial dischargers, CWA §301(b)(1)(C) allows EPA or states to impose additional requirements necessary to meet applicable water quality standards.

To address the enormous costs associated with upgrading municipal wastewater treatment plants, Congress enacted Title II of the CWA, which attempted to reduce municipal discharges of pollution through a subsidy program to finance the construction of POTWs. EPA reports that it spent about $60 billion in the 1970s and 1980s to support the construction grants program. http://www.epa.gov/OWM/cwfinance/construction.htm. In 1987 Congress responded to the mounting budget deficit and continuing criticisms that Title II was not cost-effective by virtually phasing out the construction grants program.

Instead of relying on federal grants, states must now set up revolving loan funds. These funds are supposed to be supported by federal grants and eventually become self-supporting. 33 U.S.C. §§1381-1384. Investments in secondary treatment have produced important improvements, including thousands of communities upgrading and replacing their wastewater treatment plants, correcting combined and sanitary sewer overflows, and preventing contaminated runoff from entering waterways at a much lower cost than they would have incurred through conventional financing. But affordability continues to be a very significant issue. In January 2013, EPA's Acting Assistant Administrator for the Office of Water issued a memorandum that indicates EPA's commitment to continue to work with local governments "to clarify how the financial capability of a community will be considered when developing schedules for municipal projects necessary to meet Clean Water Act obligations."[e] In June 2012, EPA also released its "Integrated Municipal Stormwater and Wastewater Planning Approach Framework," discussed below, in order to address financial and other issues associated with municipal wastewater treatment.

The sewer grant program illustrates some of the challenges in trying to ensure that a program achieves desired improvements in environmental quality. An early charge against the program was that funds were disbursed in such a way that only part of a watercourse's wastewater was treated, so that often there was no net improvement in water quality. Title II and other sections of the CWA tried to make the grants more cost-effective by requiring that states have a priority schedule for POTWs based on the relative severity of a pollution problem; that a planned facility be in conformity with the regional §208 plan; and that Title II grants be subject to NEPA. See Bosco v. Beck, 475 F. Supp. 1029 (D.N.J. 1979), *aff'd*, 614 F.2d 769 (3d Cir. 1980).

In addition to the challenge of bringing POTWs into compliance with their secondary treatment obligations, EPA has focused on the following issues: (1) pretreatment standards for industrial dischargers that discharge into municipal systems, (2) the disposal of sewage sludge, and (3) handling of stormwater.

2. Pretreatment

Industrial discharges into sewers have been singled out for special regulation. CWA §307(b). EPA has developed "National Pretreatment Standards" in an effort to control such discharges. The agency has articulated three objectives in developing such standards: (1) "[t]o prevent the introduction of pollutants into POTWs which will interfere with the operation of a POTW"; (2) "[t]o prevent the introduction of pollutants into POTWs which will pass through the treatment works . . ."; and (3) "to improve opportunities to recycle and reclaim municipal and industrial wastewaters and sludges." 40 C.F.R. §403.2; see also 40 C.F.R. §403.5. The agency refers to its prohibitions against "pass through" and "interference" as general prohibitions. 40 C.F.R. §403.5(a). The regulations also include "specific prohibitions," which include discharges of pollutants that are likely to cause fires or explosions, give off toxic vapors, or would be incompatible with the POTW's treatment processes. 40 C.F.R. §403.5(b). In addition, EPA has promulgated national categorical pretreatment standards that impose limits to industrial users in specific industrial categories. 40 C.F.R. Part 403; Streamlining the General and Pretreatment Regulations for Existing and New Sources of Pollution, 70 Fed. Reg. 60,135 (Oct. 14, 2005). For an EPA summary of the pretreatment program and of the role that different entities play in it, see id. at 60,134.

3. Disposal of Sewage Sludge

The National Research Council defines sewage sludge, a product of wastewater treatment operations, as "the solid, semisolid, or liquid residue generated during

---

e. See Memorandum from Nancy Stoner, Acting Assistant Administrator Office of the Water, Assessing Financial Capability for Municipal Clean Water Act Requirements (January 18, 2013), available at http://insideepa.com//index.php?option=com_iwpfile&file=jan2013/epa2013_0119.pdf.

treatment of domestic sewage." National Research Council, Biosolids Applied to Land: Advancing Standards and Practices 1 (National Academy Press 2002) (Biosolids Report). Sewage sludge is handled in various ways. Approximately 60 percent of the 5.6 million dry tons of sludge generated nationwide each year is land applied, 20 percent is incinerated, and 17 percent is sent to landfills for disposal. Water Pollution, Management of Biosolids Should Be Covered by Water Act Rules Pending EPA Action Plan, Daily Env't Rep. 214 (BNA) A-4 (2002). Historically, some municipal sludge was disposed of in the ocean, but the Ocean Dumping Ban Act of 1988 prohibited such dumping.

The National Research Council explains the increased emphasis given to land application of sewage sludge as follows:

> Since the early 1970s, [EPA] and the wastewater treatment industry have promoted recycling of sewage sludge. With the prohibition of ocean disposal . . . , the use of sewage sludge as soil amendments (soil conditions or fertilizers) or for land reclamation has been increased to reduce the volume of sewage sludge that must be landfilled, incinerated, or disposed of at surface sites. . . . Depending on the extent of treatment, sewage sludge may be applied where little exposure of the general public is expected to occur on the sites, such as on agricultural land, forests, and reclamation sites, or on public-contact sites, such as parks, golf courses, lawns, and home gardens. EPA estimates that sewage sludge is applied to approximately 0.1% of available agricultural land in the United States on an annual basis. [Biosolids Report, at 1.]

EPA has promulgated management practices, concentration limits, loading rates, and the like for applying sewage sludge to land, 40 C.F.R. Part 503, but these restrictions have by no means ended debate about the safety of such practices. As NRC notes, these requirements "are intended to protect public health and the environment from any reasonably anticipated adverse effects [but] [o]ver the past decade, questions have been raised about the adequacy of the chemical and pathogen standards for protecting public health." Biosolids Report, *supra*, at Preface. EPA asked the National Research Council to address questions about the protectiveness of the Part 503 standards and in its July 2002 report, referenced above, the NRC offered several observations and recommendations. The NRC

> Recognize[d] that land application of biosolids, [which it defines as sewage sludge treated to meet land-application standards] is a widely used, practical option for managing the large volume of sewage sludge generated at wastewater treatment plants that otherwise would largely need to be disposed of at landfills or by incinerations.

It continued:

> There is no documented scientific evidence that [EPA's] Part 503 rule has failed to protect public health [the NRC noted at page 2 that it was not asked to judge the adequacy of the individual standards in protecting human health]. However, additional scientific work is needed to reduce persistent uncertainty about the potential for adverse human health effects from exposure to biosolids.

Id. at 3. EPA issued a response to the NRC Report in December 2003. EPA Office of Water, Use and Disposal of Biosolids (Sewage Sludge), 68 Fed. Reg. 75,531 (Dec. 31, 2003).

4. Stormwater: Combined Sewer Overflows (CSOs) and Sanitary Sewer Systems

Stormwater runoff is a leading source of water quality impairment. EPA, National Water Quality Inventory: 2004 Report to Congress (EPA 841-R-08-001, January 2009). It carries pollutants like mud and sediment, suspended solids, nutrients, heavy metals, bacteria, pathogens, toxins, and oil and grease. This section briefly highlights some of the features of the effort to address stormwater carried by municipal treatment systems. The main two types of sewer systems are known as combined sewers (using a single set of pipes to collect storm and sanitary flows and deliver this flow to a treatment plant) and sanitary sewer systems (using two sets of pipes—one collects sanitary sewage and sends it to a POTW, while the other collects stormwater but does not send it to a POTW before discharge). (Stormwater not collected into municipal systems runs off, untreated, as nonpoint source pollution; see below.)

Regardless of the type of system, each experiences overflows under some circumstances (e.g., heavy rains, infrastructure flaws such as cracks in pipes or blockages in the system caused by tree roots, and illegal connections to sewer systems). EPA's Clean Watersheds Needs Survey, Report to Congress (January 2008) puts at over $200 billion the country's total financial need for upgrading POTWs, including those for combined sewer overflows (CSO) and sanitary sewer overflows (SSO).

Combined Sewer Overflows. As their name suggests, combined sewers are structured to collect not just untreated domestic wastewater, but also pretreated industrial discharges and stormwater runoff. This combined wastewater is normally transported to a POTW. But because stormwater volume varies significantly (after all, it results from precipitation), combined sewers as well as POTWs must be designed to handle greatly fluctuating flows. When flows exceed capacity, the systems are designed to overflow—releasing directly into waterways or discharging back onto the surface. Located primarily in older, urban communities—most were built prior to the 1950s—CSOs are an important source of water pollution that causes significant impacts.

The 1987 amendments to the CWA directed EPA to establish a stormwater permitting program for POTWs that would include CSO overflow points (points where CSOs are expected to discharge to various water bodies such as streams, rivers, or lakes without treatment once flows reach a certain level) in NPDES permits. 33 U.S.C. §1342(p); 40 C.F.R. §122.26. EPA issued a CSO Control Strategy in 1989, and then issued a follow-up policy in 1994. Streamlining the General Pretreatment Regulations for Existing and New Sources of Pollution, 59 Fed. Reg. 18,688 (1994). Congress codified the 1994 policy in 2000 amendments to the CWA as part of EPA's fiscal 2001 funding bill, requiring each permit, order, or decree issued after December 21, 2000, to conform to the policy. §402(q)(1).

The policy incorporates three central objectives:

1. To ensure that if CSOs occur, they are as a result only of wet weather;
2. To bring all wet weather CSO discharge points into compliance with the technology-based and water quality–based requirements of the CWA; and
3. To minimize water quality, aquatic biota, and human health impacts from CSOs.

The policy's strategy for achieving reductions contains two main prongs. First, it directs permittees with CSOs to demonstrate that they have implemented nine minimum controls to reduce flows. These include steps such as "proper operation and regular maintenance programs" for the system; maximizing the use of storage capacity; and maximizing flow to the POTW for treatment. 59 Fed. Reg. at 18,691. In addition, permittees must develop and implement long-term CSO control plans (LTCPs).

To address affordability issues, some states have created CSO grant programs under which the state typically bears a percentage of the cost of eligible projects. The Inspector General has also found that educating the public helps to spur public support for CSO projects, which in turn makes it easier to raise the funds needed to implement them. CSO Overflows, *supra*, at 20-22. A February 2002 report of the Association of Metropolitan Sewerage Agencies indicated, on average, that almost 37 percent of their capital improvement plan budgets for CSO controls. Id. at 13. The State Revolving Fund established under the CWA to provide low-cost financing for qualifying projects has served as an important, if imperfect, funding mechanism for work in this area. CSO Overflows, *supra*, at 14. Finally, there have been a number of strategies that have proved quite successful from a technical standpoint in reducing stormwater flow relatively cost-effectively, and opportunities for cross-fertilization of ideas clearly exist.

Significant challenges in controlling CSO releases remain. EPA has estimated that at least an additional $50.6 billion is needed to capture 85 percent of the CSO by volume, and an additional $88.8 billion is needed to control SSOs over the next 20 years. Report to Congress (August 2004), Executive Summary, ES-10. Similarly, financial problems facing some local governments that need to upgrade their surface water runoff infrastructure, such as a declining tax base, undermine local governments' ability to pay for such controls. CSO Overflows, *supra*, at 13. Another impediment is the challenge of finding sites for needed facilities. CSO projects such as retention basins often require large parcels of land; impediments include lack of land availability, community opposition, and competing land usage. Id. at i, 15-16.

To conclude with a point that reinforces the conviction of many that holistic approaches are needed to address water pollution adequately, the Association of Metropolitan Sewerage Agencies survey found that 78 percent of respondents believe that even full implementation of long-term CSO controls will not cure exceedances of water quality standards during wet weather conditions, and that "parallel efforts to address other controlled and uncontrolled upstream sources must be greatly expanded." CSO Overflows, *supra*, at 31. For an EPA follow-up effort to pursue a more watershed-based approach, see EPA, Watershed-Based National Pollutant Discharge Elimination System (NPDES) Permitting Implementation Guidance (2003), http://www.epa.gov/npdespub/pubs/watershedpermitting_finalguidance.pdf.

Sanitary Sewage Systems. CWA §402(p) requires NPDES permits for: (1) industrial stormwater discharges; (2) discharges from large and medium-sized municipal storm sewer systems; and (3) other discharges that the permitting authority determines "contribute to a violation of a water quality standard or is a significant contributor of pollutants to waters of the United States." CWA §402(p)(2)(B)-(E). Another mechanism used to handle stormwater is municipal separate storm sewer systems (sometimes referred to as MS4s or storm sewers). Congress established a two-phase schedule that EPA was to follow in promulgating regulations that would govern stormwater discharges.

EPA adopted Phase I regulations in 1990. In these regulations it established rules for large and medium discharge sources. The regulations require the covered parties to file stormwater permit applications and to develop and implement Storm Water

Management Programs. 40 C.F.R. §122.26(d)(1)(i)-(v). EPA issued Phase II rules for the stormwater program in December 1999. These rules expand the regulated party universe by requiring some small municipal separate storm sewer systems and other operations to obtain NPDES permits. The Phase II rule was challenged on 22 grounds; in Environmental Defense Ctr., Inc. v. EPA, 344 F.3d 832 (9th Cir. 2003), the court affirmed the vast majority of the rule, remanding only aspects of the rule relating to the issuance of notices of intent under the rule's general permitting scheme. Among other things, the court rejected the argument that EPA lacked authority, because of Tenth Amendment limitations on federal authority, to subject small MS4s to NPDES permitting. EPA's Office of Wastewater Management issued a "field test version" of its MS4 Program Evaluation Guidance in January 2007 to facilitate evaluation of the quality of MS4 programs.

For a 2009 review of EPA initiatives to manage stormwater that focuses especially on sanitary sewage systems and construction discharges, see Effluent Limitation Guidelines and Standards for the Construction and Development Point Source Category, 74 Fed. Reg. 62,996 (Dec. 1, 2009). See also U.S. GAO, Further Implementation and Better Cost Data Needed to Determine Impact of EPA's Storm Water Program on Communities 16 (May 2007). For a brief overview of stormwater regulatory efforts generally, including for construction and industrial activities as well as CSOs and SSOs, see Knight et al., EPA Prescribes a "Pollution Diet" for the Impaired Chesapeake Bay, Envtl. Liability, Enforcement & Penalties Rep. Argent Comm. Group, August/September 2010, at 259.

5.   Green Infrastructure and Low Impact Development (LID) Strategies and Practices

In recent years EPA and others have begun to push "green infrastructure" approaches to reduce wet weather water management concerns. EPA has defined green infrastructure as follows:

> Green infrastructure is a comprehensive approach to water quality protection defined by a range of natural and built systems that can occur at the regional, community, and site scales. At the larger regional or watershed scale, green infrastructure is the interconnected network of preserved or restored natural lands and waters that provide essential environmental functions. Large-scale green infrastructure may include habitat corridors and water resource protection. At the community and neighborhood scale, green infrastructure incorporates planning and design approaches such as compact, mixed-use development, parking reductions strategies and urban forestry that reduces impervious surfaces and creates walkable, attractive communities. At the site scale, green infrastructure mimics natural systems by absorbing stormwater back into the ground (infiltration), using trees and other natural vegetation to convert it to water vapor (evapotranspiration), and using rain barrels or cisterns to capture and reuse stormwater. These natural processes manage stormwater runoff in a way that maintains or restores the site's natural hydrology.

EPA, Water Quality Scorecard: Incorporating Green Infrastructure Practices at the Municipal, Neighborhood, and Site Scales 2 (2009).

The agency has entered into agreements with other key stakeholders to move forward on such approaches, which can be more cost-effective than traditional engineering approaches. See, e.g., Green Infrastructure Statement of Intent (EPA,

National Association of Clean Water Agencies, Natural Resources Defense Council, Low Impact Development Center, and Association of State and Interstate Water Pollution Control Administrators (April 19, 2007)). Working with all of the stakeholders listed above as well as American Rivers, EPA issued an Action Strategy in January 2008, entitled Managing Wet Weather with Green Infrastructure. The Action Strategy anticipates significant benefits from a greater emphasis on green infrastructure, including improved water and air quality, reduced urban temperatures, increased energy efficiency, and reduced costs. The strategy is intended to be a key part of EPA's climate change agenda. Id. at 8; see also EPA, Green Infrastructure in Arid and Semi-Arid Climates 2 (EPA 833-B-10-002, May 2010). For more information on how green infrastructure techniques to manage stormwater and CSOs can be incorporated into discharge permits and enforcement actions under the CWA, see EPA's six factsheets and three supplements on green infrastructure, available at http://water.epa.gov/infrastructure/greeninfrastructure/gi_regulatory.cfm.

H. NONPOINT SOURCE POLLUTION

As noted above, Congress makes an extraordinarily important jurisdictional distinction in the CWA between point sources and nonpoint sources. As is evident from the material above, the CWA defines point source and specifically exempts some discharges from that definition. §502(14). But the Act does not include a definition of "nonpoint source pollution" (NPSP). The scientific and technical community generally defines NPSP as water, like precipitation, that runs over the land surface and ultimately into bodies of water.

The sources of NPSP are numerous, and may include:

- Excess fertilizers, herbicides, and insecticides from agricultural lands and residential areas;
- Oil, grease, and toxic chemicals from urban runoff and energy production;
- Sediment from improperly managed construction sites, crop and forest lands, and eroding streambanks;
- Salt from irrigation practices and acid drainage from abandoned mines;
- Bacteria and nutrients from livestock, pet wastes, and faulty septic systems; and
- Atmospheric deposition and hydromodification.

EPA, What is Nonpoint Source Pollution, http://water.epa.gov/polwaste/nps/whatis.cfm.

NPDES jurisdiction attaches to discharges from point sources but not to discharges from nonpoint sources. See Friends of the Everglades v. South Fla. Water Mgmt. Dist., 570 F.3d 1210, 1227 (11th Cir. 2009) (the "NPDES program does not even address nonpoint source pollution."); Kentucky Waterways Alliance v. EPA, 540 F.3d 466, 471 (6th Cir. 2008) (similar); Gaba, New Sources, New Growth and the Clean Water Act, 55 Ala. L. Rev. 651, 662 (2004). Instead, NPSP controls are comprised of a "patchwork of state and local control programs, many of which are voluntary or poorly enforced." Adler, Resilience, Restoration, and Sustainability: Revisiting the Fundamental Principles of the Clean Water Act, 32 Wash. U. J.L. & Pol'y 139, 161 (2010).

In part because of the progress made through the NPDES program in addressing point source pollution, NPSP is the largest cause of water quality impairment in the country. So why did Congress refuse to aggressively regulate NPSP? It was not because Congress was unaware of the problem. Id. at 158. Instead, Congress's approach can be explained in two ways, one technical and the other political. First, the diffuse nature of nonpoint sources makes it harder to control them—they are not susceptible to controls in the same way as effluents running through pipes. Second, the primary means of controlling NPSP—called best management practices (BMP)—usually relate to land-use controls. Federalism concerns made Congress hesitant to intrude on state and local governments' long-held domain. Glicksman & Batzel, Science, Politics, Law, and the Arc of the Clean Water Act: The Role of Assumptions in the Adoption of a Pollution Control Landmark, 32 Wash. U. J.L. & Pol'y 99, 115-116 (2010).

While the legal divide between point and nonpoint source pollution is not always clear, the legal consequences of falling on one side or the other can be dramatic. In marked contrast to the permit-driven approach taken to regulate point sources, "[e]fforts to address nonpoint source water pollution in the CWA . . . have been feeble, unfocused, and underfunded." Ruhl, Farms, Their Environmental Harms, and Environmental Law, 27 Ecology L.Q. 265, 298 (2000). Prof. Mandelker similarly notes that CWA efforts "have not remedied the nonpoint pollution problem." Mandelker, Controlling Nonpoint Source Water Pollution: Can It Be Done?, 65 Chi.-Kent L. Rev. 479 (1989).

Congress's initial approach in the 1972 CWA for controlling nonpoint sources of pollution contemplated that states would develop and submit to EPA area-wide waste treatment management plans that included a process for identifying nonpoint sources and for establishing procedures and methods to control the pollution from such sources to the extent feasible. CWA §208. Federal funds and technical assistance would be available to help states with the planning process. This program became moribund in the early 1980s; it resulted in numerous studies and no real improvement. See O. Houck, The Clean Water Act TMDL Program: Law, Policy, and Implementation 30 (ELI 2d ed., 2002) (attributing failures to the "fundamental political difficulty of dealing with agriculture, silviculture, and municipalities").

Congress tried again in 1987. The rhetoric was ambitious. Congress's goal was to control nonpoint sources of pollution "in an expeditious manner so as to enable the goals of this Act to be met through the control of both point and non-point sources of pollution." Water Quality Act of 1987, Pub. L. No. 100-4, §319. Section 319 served as the statutory home for this goal of invigorating the effort to control nonpoint sources. It is an example of a voluntary approach to devolution, presumably to be accompanied by fiscal support that would provide incentives to the states to implement the scheme set forth in the section. It was supposed to offer attractive (primarily financial) carrots to induce state engagement but did not carry much of a stick.

Section 319 required each state to prepare and submit to EPA an "assessment report" that (1) identifies navigable waters that, "without additional action to control nonpoint sources of pollution, cannot reasonably be expected" to attain WQSs; (2) identifies categories of nonpoint sources and particular nonpoint sources that are significant contributors to these impaired waters; (3) describes the process that the state would use to identify BMPs to reduce, "to the maximum extent practicable, the level of pollution" resulting from these sources; and (4) identifies and describes the state programs for controlling nonpoint source pollution. §319(a). Section 319 also required each state to prepare and submit to EPA a "management program" for controlling nonpoint source pollution. This program was supposed to detail, among other things, the BMPs the state was going to use to address nonpoint source pollution, identify how the state would implement its BMP approach, and provide a timetable for implementing the program. §319(b). These reports were due no later than the fall of 1988, and Congress gave EPA 180 days after receipt to review and approve or disapprove them. §319(c), (d). Congress offered the prospect of financial and technical assistance as an incentive for states to undertake these reporting and management program development activities, and by 1991 all 50 states and the territories had received EPA approval (by 1995 seven tribes had done so as well). EPA, Nonpoint Source Management Program, Pointer No. 4, EPA841-F-96-004D.

But the §319 initiative produced limited environmental results—multiple studies and limited progress. O. Houck, *supra*, at 31; Ruhl, *supra*, 27 Ecology L.Q. at 299. EPA, on the other hand, reported that as of 1995 the agency had awarded states, territories, and tribes $370 million under §319 to implement NPS pollution controls, and it catalogued several projects in which various efforts to reduce pollution from nonpoint sources paid environmental dividends. EPA, Nonpoint Source Management Program, Pointer No. 4 (1996); EPA, Section 319 Success Stories (1994), http://www.epa.gov/owow/nps/Success319. At the end of 2005, EPA issued a guidance document intended to encourage and help states, local governments, and others to manage urban runoff from parking lots, buildings, and homes in particular. EPA, National Management Measures to Control Nonpoint Source Pollution from Urban Areas (2005), http://water.epa.gov/polwaste/nps/urban/.

In addition to the possible role of the TMDL program, discussed above, in spurring efforts to control nonpoint source pollution, another interesting issue to watch concerns the extent to which the trading schemes that EPA is encouraging will create enforceable obligations under the CWA for nonpoint sources, or perhaps make point sources accountable for reductions by nonpoint sources. See Water Quality Trading Policy, 68 Fed. Reg. 1608 (Jan. 13, 2003); EPA, Water Quality Trading Assessment Handbook, http://www.epa.gov/owow/watershed/trading.htm. EPA officials have expressed their hope that such trading schemes will stimulate reductions in nonpoint source pollution. As noted above, EPA established a TMDL for the Chesapeake Bay in 2010, and it views water quality trading programs as a potential tool for meeting the TMDL. http://www.epa.gov/chesapeakebaytmdl/EnsuringResults.html?tab2=1. Some states have used trading to facilitate nonpoint source controls as well. Klahn, TMDLs: Another New Regulation?, TRENDS, July/August 2003, at 12.

The cost of addressing nonpoint sources is significant. The GAO reports that total federal annual spending for nonpoint-related programs is about $3 billion, but also notes EPA's estimate that roughly $9 billion is needed annually to tackle the issues effectively. U.S. GAO, Water Quality, Federal Role in Addressing—and Contributing to—Nonpoint Source Pollution 3-4 (Feb. 1999). According to the GAO, even this substantial annual funding requirement understates the actual amounts of money needed, since it does not include some potentially significant sources of NPS pollution; nor does it include the operation and maintenance costs associated with the BMPs EPA believes are needed.

Beyond the CWA, several other initiatives have the potential to address nonpoint source pollution. In 1990 Congress amended the Coastal Zone Management

Act to require that any state with a federally approved coastal zone management plan develop a coastal nonpoint pollution program subject to federal review and approval. Other federal agencies, such as USDA and DOI, have contributed substantial amounts to addressing NPS pollution and have undertaken a wide variety of programs to address such pollution. See U.S. GAO, Water Quality, Federal Role in Addressing—and Contributing to—Nonpoint Source Pollution 6 (Feb. 1999).

I. THE §404 PROGRAM

1. *The Problem: From Hazard to Ecosystem*

Throughout most of our history, marshes and swamps have been considered health menaces, and much effort has been devoted to draining and filling these lands. At the national level, the nation's chief construction agency, the U.S. Army Corps of Engineers, acquired jurisdiction over many wetlands in the late nineteenth century for the purpose of navigation protection. The Corps historically exercised this jurisdiction by allowing all dredging and filling that did not impair the navigable capacity of rivers and harbors. One-half of the 215 million acres of wetlands that existed at the time of European settlement were drained and filled.

Over the past few decades the environmental movement has increasingly focused on the ecological value of wetlands. In 1987, the Conservation Foundation convened a National Wetlands Policy Forum, which issued a report that proposed the adoption of a "no net loss" goal for wetlands conversion. Both the Clinton administration and the first Bush administration adopted "no net loss" as the guiding wetlands policy, and the second Bush administration affirmed this commitment. Bush Administration's Interagency National Wetlands Mitigation Action Plan, 34 Env't Rep. (BNA) 55 (Dec. 27, 2002). On Earth Day 2004, then-President Bush announced a goal of moving beyond "no net loss" of wetlands and achieving an "overall increase in the amount and quality of wetlands in America." Council on Envtl. Quality, Conserving America's Wetlands 2006: Two Years of Progress Implementing the President's Goal (Apr. 2006).

While the actual extent of wetlands protection has been the subject of some controversy, the U.S. Fish & Wildlife Service and the National Marine Fisheries Service estimate that from 1998 to 2004, there was a 32,000-acre increase in wetlands in the coterminous United States. Stedman & Dahl, Status and Trends of Wetlands in the Coastal Watershed of the Eastern United States 1998 to 2004, at 5 (2008). The Council on Environmental Quality has estimated that more than 4.5 million acres of wetlands were protected between 2004 and Earth Day 2009. CEQ, *supra*.

The "no net loss (or better)" concept has helped to focus a spotlight on a wide array of questions relating to wetlands, such as how they should be delineated, the appropriate parameters for mitigation when natural wetlands are converted under §404, and restoring degraded wetlands. This section briefly reviews three aspects of the §404 program: (1) the allocation of regulatory jurisdiction for its implementation; (2) its jurisdictional boundaries; and (3) the substantive criteria used to make §404 decisions.

2. The Allocation of Regulatory Jurisdiction

EPA and the Corps share responsibility under §404 of the CWA for regulating activities that may adversely impact wetlands. The Corps continues to exercise its historical jurisdiction to issue dredge and fill permits. EPA, however, has a significant role in the process. Among other things, it has established guidelines that the Corps must follow in considering projects (see discussion of §404(b) below). EPA also has the authority to veto any permit that would have an unreasonable adverse effect on water supplies, fish, wildlife, or recreation areas. §404(c).

EPA has used its authority sparingly. In January 2011, EPA issued what it characterized as its second veto in the past 40 years of a CWA §404 permit after the permit had already been issued by the Corps of Engineers.[f] The permit had authorized the Mingo Logan Coal Company to discharge dredge or fill material from a mountaintop coal mine into three streams and their tributaries. EPA had declined to exercise its veto authority during the pre-2007 permit process. In 2011, EPA withdrew the specifications of two of the streams and their tributaries as disposal sites, which had the effect of prohibiting Mingo Logan from discharging into the streams. EPA exercised its authority under §404(c), which allows EPA to withdraw a disposal site "whenever [EPA] determines . . . that the discharge . . . will have an 'unacceptable adverse effect.' . . ." The D.C. Circuit upheld EPA's action, deciding that §404 "imposes no temporal limit" on EPA's authority to withdraw the Corps' specification of a disposal site. Mingo Logan Coal Co. v. EPA, 714 F.3d 608 (D.C. Cir. 2013). For another recent decision involving EPA's exercise of its veto authority under §404, see Board of Mississippi Levee Comm'rs v. EPA, 674 F.3d 409 (5th Cir. 2012).

While Congress has authorized states to assume primary authority for implementing the §404 permitting program, only Michigan and New Jersey have done so. This is in marked contrast to the NPDES §402 permit program, in which nearly all the states have permitting authority. Why the difference?

3. Activities Regulated Under CWA §404

The "discharge of dredged or fill material into . . . navigable waters" triggers a permit scheme contained in §404 of the CWA. 33 U.S.C. §1344(a). Thus, the three key elements are (1) the discharge (2) of dredged or fill material (3) into navigable waters.

Section C.1 above discusses the third element, the definition of "navigable waters." As that discussion reflects, the debate over the appropriate scope of navigable waters continues. The Supreme Court has weighed in on several occasions, as have numerous lower courts, but the consensus view seems to be that these decisions have confused rather than clarified how the statute should be interpreted. As two commentators have noted, "[j]udicial interpretations of the scope of the program have exacerbated rather than resolved" confusion about the jurisdictional boundaries of the program. Glicksman & Batzel, Science, Politics, Law and the Arc of the Clean Water Act: The Role of Assumptions in the Adoption of a Pollution Control

---

f. EPA, Final Determination of U.S. Environmental Protection Agency Pursuant to §404(c) of the Clean Water Act Concerning the Spruce No. 1 Mine, Logan County, West Virginia 99 (January 2011), http://water.epa.gov/lawsregs/guidance/cwa/dredgdis/upload/Spruce_No-_1_Mine_ Final_Determination_011311_signed.pdf.

Landmark, 32 Wash. U. J.L. & Pol'y 99 (2010). EPA and the Corps' draft rule on "waters of the United States," which is intended to resolve some of the difficulties, is detailed in section C.1.b above.

The first element required to create §404 jurisdiction, the definition of "discharge," has also been the subject of litigation. One issue has been how to handle "fallback," that is, material that is removed from the waters of the United States but that happens to fall back into that same water. In the early 1990s, the Corps adopted the *Tulloch* rule (named after the case that precipitated its development, North Carolina Wildlife Fed'n v. Tulloch, No. C90-713-CIV-5-B0 (E.D.N.C. 1992)), which included various incidental discharges or redeposits of dredged material as discharges subject to §404 jurisdiction. 33 C.F.R. §323.2(d)(1)(iii). In 1998, the D.C. Circuit invalidated the *Tulloch* rule, holding that activities that involve "incidental fallback" are not discharges because they do not involve "addition" of a pollutant. National Mining Ass'n v. U.S. Army Corps of Eng'rs, 145 F.3d 1399 (D.C. Cir. 1998). The court stated that "the straightforward statutory term 'addition' cannot reasonably be said to encompass the situation in which material is removed from the waters of the United States and a small portion of it happens to fall back. Because incidental fallback represents a net withdrawal, not an addition, of material, it cannot be a discharge." But the court also observed that since §404 "sets out no bright line between incidental fallback . . . and regulable redeposits . . . a reasoned attempt by the agencies to draw such a line would be entitled to considerable deference." Id. at 1405.

EPA and the Corps have continued to work to define the difference between incidental fallback and regulable redeposits in several rulemakings since the *National Mining Ass'n* decision. The agencies issued a rule in 2008 in which they reaffirmed their intent to distinguish between incidental fallback (which is not regulated), and regulable deposits (which will be evaluated on a case-by-case basis). Revisions to the Clean Water Act Regulatory Definition of "Discharge of Dredged Material," 73 Fed. Reg. 79,641 (Dec. 30, 2008).

For two decisions finding that activities qualify as discharges triggering §404 jurisdiction, see United States v. Deaton, 209 F.3d 331 (4th Cir. 2000) (holding that a landowner who dug a ditch across a wetland on his property and sidecast dirt excavated from the ditch into a wetland violated the CWA), and Borden Ranch P'ship v. U.S. Army Corps of Eng'rs, 261 F.3d 810 (9th Cir. 2001) (holding that a process known as "deep ripping" requires a §404 permit). The "deep ripping" involved dragging four- to seven-foot-long prongs through soil in wetland areas, among others, in order to convert a ranch to a vineyard and orchard, and resulted in the excavation and redeposition of wetland soils. The court held that the destruction of wetlands resulting from this practice qualified as a discharge and triggered §404 jurisdiction. The Supreme Court affirmed, in a one-sentence, 4-4 decision (Justice Kennedy not participating). Borden Ranch P'ship v. U.S. Army Corps of Eng'rs, 537 U.S. 99 (2002). In Save Our Community v. EPA, 971 F.2d 1155 (5th Cir. 1992), the Fifth Circuit held that *draining* a wetland does not require a permit because it does not involve the discharge of material.

The definitions of dredged and fill material have likewise been the subject of controversy. One important question concerning the scope of §404 jurisdiction involves the relationship between §404 and the NPDES CWA §402 permitting program discussed in section C above. In other words, when is material "dredge-and-fill" rather than the "discharge of a pollutant"? For example, in Resource Investments, Inc. v. U.S. Army Corps of Eng'rs, 151 F.3d 1162 (9th Cir. 1998), the court held that construction of a landfill in wetlands is not subject to Corps jurisdiction because it deposits solid waste, not material excavated or dredged from waters of the United States. But in Kentuckians for the Commonwealth, Inc. v. Rivenburgh, 317 F.3d 425 (4th Cir. 2003), the court considered and affirmed the agencies' judgment that §404, rather than §402, applies to the deposition of overburden from mountain coal mining into navigable streams.

The Supreme Court weighed in on this CWA jurisdictional boundaries question involving the types of activities that each of the statute's permitting programs (§402 and §404) covers in the following case.

COEUR ALASKA, INC. v. SOUTHEAST
ALASKA CONSERVATION COUNCIL
557 U.S. 261 (2009)

Justice KENNEDY delivered the opinion of the Court.

[The Court considered two issues in this case: (1) whether the CWA authorizes EPA or the Corps of Engineers to issue a permit for the discharge of mining waste, called slurry; and (2) whether, when the Corps issued such a permit, it was obligated to ensure compliance with new source performance standards contained in CWA §306. This excerpt focuses on the first issue, the jurisdictional boundaries question, and the definition of fill material.]

With regard to the first question, §404(a) of the CWA grants the Corps the power to "issue permits . . . for the discharge of . . . fill material." 33 U.S.C. §1344(a). But the EPA also has authority to issue permits for the discharge of pollutants. Section 402 of the Act grants the EPA authority to "issue a permit for the discharge of any pollutant" "[e]xcept as provided in" §404. 33 U.S.C. §1342(a). We conclude that because the slurry Coeur Alaska wishes to discharge is defined by regulation as "fill material," 40 CFR §232.2 (2008), Coeur Alaska properly obtained its permit from the Corps of Engineers, under §404, rather than from the EPA, under §402.

I

A

Petitioner Coeur Alaska plans to reopen the Kensington Gold Mine, located some 45 miles north of Juneau, Alaska. The mine has been closed since 1928, but Coeur Alaska seeks to make it profitable once more by using a technique known as "froth flotation." Coeur Alaska will churn the mine's crushed rock in tanks of frothing water. Chemicals in the water will cause gold-bearing minerals to float to the surface, where they will be skimmed off.

At issue is Coeur Alaska's plan to dispose of the mixture of crushed rock and water left behind in the tanks. This mixture is called slurry. Some 30 percent of the slurry's volume is crushed rock, resembling wet sand, which is called tailings. The rest is water.

The standard way to dispose of slurry is to pump it into a tailings pond. The slurry separates in the pond. Solid tailings sink to the bottom, and water on the surface returns to the mine to be used again.

Rather than build a tailings pond, Coeur Alaska proposes to use Lower Slate Lake, located some three miles from the mine in the Tongass National Forest. This lake is small—800 feet at its widest crossing, 2,000 feet at its longest, and 23 acres in area. Though small, the lake is 51 feet deep at its maximum. The parties agree the lake is a navigable water of the United States and so is subject to the CWA. They also agree there can be no discharge into the lake except as the CWA and any lawful permit allow.

Over the life of the mine, Coeur Alaska intends to put 4.5 million tons of tailings in the lake. This will raise the lakebed 50 feet—to what is now the lake's surface—and will increase the lake's area from 23 to about 60 acres. To contain this wider, shallower body of water, Coeur Alaska will dam the lake's downstream shore. The transformed lake will be isolated from other surface water. Creeks and stormwater runoff will detour around it. Ultimately, lakewater will be cleaned by purification systems and will flow from the lake to a stream and thence onward.

B

Numerous state and federal agencies reviewed and approved Coeur Alaska's plans. At issue here are actions by two of those agencies: the Corps of Engineers and the EPA.

1

The CWA classifies crushed rock as a "pollutant." 33 U.S.C. §1362(6). On the one hand, the Act forbids Coeur Alaska's discharge of crushed rock "[e]xcept as in compliance" with the Act. CWA §301(a), 33 U.S.C. §1311(a). Section 404(a) of the CWA, on the other hand, empowers the Corps to authorize the discharge of "dredged or fill material." 33 U.S.C. §1344(a). The Corps and the EPA have together defined "fill material" to mean any "material [that] has the effect of . . . [c]hanging the bottom elevation" of water. 40 CFR §232.2. The agencies have further defined the "discharge of fill material" to include "placement of . . . slurry, or tailings or similar mining-related materials." Ibid.

In these cases the Corps and the EPA agree that the slurry meets their regulatory definition of "fill material." On that premise the Corps evaluated the mine's plan for a §404 permit. After considering the environmental factors required by §404(b), the Corps issued Coeur Alaska a permit to pump the slurry into Lower Slate Lake.

[The Court here addressed the CWA's §404 substantive criteria and held that the Corps followed the steps set forth by §404.]

2

The EPA had the statutory authority to veto the Corps permit, and prohibit the discharge, if it found the plan to have "an unacceptable adverse effect on municipal water supplies, shellfish beds and fishery areas . . . , wildlife, or recreational areas." CWA §404(c), 33 U.S.C. §1344(c). By declining to exercise its veto, the EPA in effect deferred to the judgment of the Corps on this point.

The EPA's involvement extended beyond the agency's veto consideration. The EPA also issued a permit of its own—not for the discharge from the mine into the lake but for the discharge from the lake into a downstream creek. Section 402 grants the

EPA authority to "issue a permit for the discharge of any pollutant," "[e]xcept as provided in [CWA §404]." 33 U.S.C. §1342(a). The EPA's §402 permit authorizes Coeur Alaska to discharge water from Lower Slate Lake into the downstream creek, subject to strict water-quality limits that Coeur Alaska must regularly monitor.

The EPA's authority to regulate this discharge comes from a regulation, termed a "new source performance standard," that it has promulgated under authority granted to it by §306(b) of the CWA. Section 306(b) gives the EPA authority to regulate the amount of pollutants that certain categories of new sources may discharge into the navigable waters of the United States. 33 U.S.C. §1316(b). Pursuant to this authority, the EPA in 1982 promulgated a new source performance standard restricting discharges from new froth-flotation gold mines like Coeur Alaska's. The standard is stringent: It allows "no discharge of process wastewater" from these mines. 40 CFR §440.104(b)(1).

Applying that standard to the discharge of water from Lower Slate Lake into the downstream creek, the EPA's §402 permit sets strict limits on the amount of pollutants the water may contain. The permit requires Coeur Alaska to treat the water using "reverse osmosis" to remove aluminum, suspended solids, and other pollutants. Coeur Alaska must monitor the water flowing from the lake to be sure that the pollutants are kept to low, specified minimums.

C

SEACC brought suit against the Corps of Engineers and various of its officials in the United States District Court for the District of Alaska. In SEACC's view, the permit was issued by the wrong agency—Coeur Alaska ought to have sought a §402 permit from the EPA, just as the company did for the discharge of water from the lake into the downstream creek.

II

The question of which agency has authority to consider whether to permit the slurry discharge is our beginning inquiry. We consider first the authority of the EPA and second the authority of the Corps. Our conclusion is that under the CWA the Corps had authority to determine whether Coeur Alaska was entitled to the permit governing this discharge.

A

Section 402 gives the EPA authority to issue "permit[s] for the discharge of any pollutant," with one important exception: The EPA may not issue permits for fill material that fall under the Corps' §404 permitting authority. Section 402(a) states:

> *Except as provided in* [CWA §404], the Administrator may . . . issue a permit for the discharge of any pollutant, . . . notwithstanding [§301(a)], upon condition that such discharge will meet . . . (A) all applicable requirements under [CWA §§301, 302, 306, 307, 308, and 403].

Section 402 thus forbids the EPA from exercising permitting authority that is "provided [to the Corps] in" §404.

This is not to say the EPA has no role with respect to the environmental consequences of fill. The EPA's function is different, in regulating fill, from its function in regulating other pollutants, but the agency does exercise some authority. Section 404 assigns the EPA two tasks in regard to fill material. First, the EPA must write guidelines for the Corps to follow in determining whether to permit a discharge of fill material. CWA §404(b); 33 U.S.C. §1344(b). Second, the Act gives the EPA authority to "prohibit" any decision by the Corps to issue a permit for a particular disposal site. CWA §404(c); 33 U.S.C. §1344(c). We, and the parties, refer to this as the EPA's power to veto a permit.

The Act is best understood to provide that if the Corps has authority to issue a permit for a discharge under §404, then the EPA lacks authority to do so under §402.

Even if there were ambiguity on this point, the EPA's own regulations would resolve it. Those regulations provide that "[d]ischarges of dredged or fill material into waters of the United States which are regulated under section 404 of CWA" "do not require [§402] permits" from the EPA. 40 CFR §122.3.

In the agencies' view the regulation essentially restates the text of §402, and forbids the EPA from issuing permits for discharges that "are regulated under section 404." 40 CFR §122.3(b). . . . Before us, the EPA confirms this reading of the regulation. The agency's interpretation is not "plainly erroneous or inconsistent with the regulation"; and so we accept it as correct. . . .

The question whether the EPA is the proper agency to regulate the slurry discharge thus depends on whether the Corps of Engineers has authority to do so. If the Corps has authority to issue a permit, then the EPA may not do so. We turn to the Corps' authority under §404.

B

Section 404(a) gives the Corps power to "issue permits . . . for the discharge of dredged or fill material." 33 U.S.C. §1344(a). As all parties concede, the slurry meets the definition of fill material agreed upon by the agencies in a joint regulation promulgated in 2002. That regulation defines "fill material" to mean any "material [that] has the effect of . . . [c]hanging the bottom elevation" of water—a definition that includes "slurry, or tailings or similar mining-related materials." 40 CFR §232.2.

SEACC concedes that the slurry to be discharged meets the regulation's definition of fill material. Its concession on this point is appropriate because slurry falls well within the central understanding of the term "fill," as shown by the examples given by the regulation. See 40 CFR §232.2 ("Examples of such fill material include, but are not limited to: rock, sand, soil, clay. . . ."). The regulation further excludes "trash or garbage" from its definition. Ibid. SEACC expresses a concern that Coeur Alaska's interpretation of the statute will lead to §404 permits authorizing the discharges of other solids that are now restricted by EPA standards (listing, for example, "feces and uneaten feed," "litter," and waste produced in "battery manufacturing"). But these extreme instances are not presented by the cases now before us. If, in a future case, a discharger of one of these solids were to seek a §404 permit, the dispositive question for the agencies would be whether the solid at issue—for instance, "feces and uneaten feed"—came within the regulation's definition of "fill." SEACC cites no instance in which the agencies have so interpreted their fill regulation. If that instance did arise, and the agencies were to interpret the fill regulation as SEACC fears, then SEACC could challenge that decision as an unlawful interpretation of the fill regulation; or SEACC could claim that the fill regulation as interpreted is an unreasonable interpretation of §404. The difficulties are not presented here, however, because the slurry meets the regulation's definition of fill.

Rather than challenge the agencies' decision to define the slurry as fill, SEACC instead contends that §404 contains an implicit exception. According to SEACC, §404 does not authorize the Corps to permit a discharge of fill material if that material is subject to an EPA new source performance standard.

But §404's text does not limit its grant of power in this way. Instead, §404 refers to all "fill material" without qualification. Nor do the EPA regulations support SEACC's reading of §404. The EPA has enacted guidelines, pursuant to §404(b), to guide the Corps permitting decision. 40 CFR pt. 230. Those guidelines do not strip the Corps of power to issue permits for fill in cases where the fill is also subject to an EPA new source performance standard.

SEACC's reading of §404 would create numerous difficulties for the regulated industry. As the regulatory regime stands now, a discharger must ask a simple question—is the substance to be discharged fill material or not? The fill regulation, 40 CFR §232.2, offers a clear answer to that question; and under the agencies' view, that answer decides the matter—if the discharge is fill, the discharger must seek a §404 permit from the Corps; if not, only then must the discharger consider whether any EPA performance standard applies, so that the discharger requires a §402 permit from the EPA.

Under SEACC's interpretation, however, the discharger would face a more difficult problem. The discharger would have to ask—is the fill material also subject to one of the many hundreds of EPA performance standards, so that the permit must come from the EPA, not the Corps? The statute gives no indication that Congress intended to burden industry with that confusing division of permit authority.

The regulatory scheme discloses a defined, and workable, line for determining whether the Corps or the EPA has the permit authority. Under this framework, the Corps of Engineers, and not the EPA, has authority to permit Coeur Alaska's discharge of the slurry. . . .

Justice BREYER, concurring.

As I understand the Court's opinion, it recognizes a legal zone within which the regulating agencies might reasonably classify material either as "dredged or fill material" subject to §404 of the Clean Water Act, 33 U.S.C. §1344(a), or as a "pollutant," subject to §§402 and 306, 33 U.S.C. §§1342(a), 1316(a). Within this zone, the law authorizes the environmental agencies to classify material as the one or the other, so long as they act within the bounds of relevant regulations, and provided that the classification, considered in terms of the purposes of the statutes and relevant regulations, is reasonable.

This approach reflects the difficulty of applying §§402 and 306 literally to *every* new-source-related discharge of a "pollutant." The Environmental Protection Agency (EPA) applies §306 new source "performance standards" to a wide variety of discharges, ranging, for example, from those involved in the processing of apples into apple juice or apple cider, 40 CFR §407.10 (2008); to the manufacturing of cement, §411.10; to the production of fresh meat cuts by a meat cutter, §432.60; and to the manufacture of pharmaceutical products by fermentation, §439.10. See generally 40 CFR pts. 405-471 (containing more than 800 pages of "new source performance" and effluent limitation regulations). At the same time the regulations for any one point source often regulate numerous chemicals, minerals, and other substances produced by that point source; in the case of fermentation products, for example, the regulations provide performance standards for roughly 30 different chemicals. §439.15. These "standards of performance" "reflect the greatest degree of effluent reduction which the Administrator determines to be achievable through application of the best available demonstrated control technology . . . including, where practicable, a standard permitting no discharge of pollutants." 33 U.S.C. §1316(a)(1).

To literally apply these performance standards so as to forbid the use of any of these substances as "fill," even when, say, they constitute no more than trace elements in dirt, crushed rock, or sand that is clearly being used as "fill" to build a levee or to replace dirt removed from a lake bottom may prove unnecessarily strict, cf. §1362(6) (defining "pollutant" to include "rock"), to the point that such application would undermine the objective of §404, which foresees the use of "dredged or fill material" in certain circumstances and with approval of the relevant agencies. §1344. At minimum, the EPA might reasonably read the statute and the applicable regulations as allowing the use of such material, say crushed rock, as "fill" in some of these situations.

At the same time, I recognize the danger that Justice Ginsburg warns against, namely, that "[w]hole categories of regulated industries" might "gain immunity from a variety of pollution-control standards," if, say, a §404-permit applicant simply adds "sufficient solid matter" to a pollutant "to raise the bottom of a water body," thereby turning a "pollutant" governed by §306 into "fill" governed by §404.

Yet there are safeguards against that occurring. For one thing, as the Court recognizes, it is not the case that *any* material that has the " 'effect of . . . [c]hanging the bottom elevation' " of the body of water is automatically subject to §404, not §402. The EPA has never suggested that it would interpret the regulations so as to turn §404 into a loophole, permitting evasion of a "performance standard" simply because a polluter discharges enough pollutant to raise the bottom elevation of the body of water. For another thing, even where a matter is determined reasonably to be "fill" and consequently falls within §404, the EPA can retain an important role in the permitting process. That is because the EPA may veto any §404 plan that it finds has an "unacceptable adverse effect on municipal water supplies, shellfish beds and fishery areas . . . , wildlife, or recreational areas." §1344(c). Finally, EPA's decision not to apply §306, but to allow permitting to proceed under §404, must be a reasonable decision; and court review will help assure that is so. 5 U.S.C. §706.

In these cases, it seems to me that the EPA's interpretation of the statute as permitting the EPA/Corps of Engineers "fill" definition to apply to the cases at hand is reasonable, hence lawful. Lower Slate Lake, located roughly three miles from the Kensington Gold Mine, is 51 feet deep, 800 feet wide, and 2,000 feet long; downstream from the lake is Slate Creek. Faced with a difficult choice between creating a huge pile of slurry on nearby wetlands or using part of the lake as a storage facility for mine tailings, the EPA arrived at a compromise. On the one hand, it would treat mine tailings placed directly into the lake as "fill" under the §404 permitting program. The tailings, the EPA recognized, would have the "immediate effect of filling the areas of water into which they are discharged." But it would also treat any spillover of the tailings, or chemicals from the tailings, into any nearby waterway, most particularly Slate Creek (running out of Slate Lake) as requiring a §402 permit. The EPA's §306 "performance standard" would apply and that standard insists upon *no discharge of process wastewater at all*. [S]ee also 40 CFR §440.104(b). The EPA reached this result because it recognized that, even though pollutants discharged into the creek might come "in the form of suspended and settleable solids," such solids would "have, at most, an incidental filling effect." The EPA thereby sought to apply the distinction it had previously recognized between discharges that have the immediate effect of raising the bottom elevation of water, and those that only have the "associated effect, over time, of raising the bottom elevation of a water due to settling of waterborne pollutants." See 67 Fed. Reg. 31135 (2002) (concluding that §402 applies to the latter). . . .

4. Substantive Criteria

Some have expressed concern that *Coeur Alaska* drew the jurisdictional boundaries for the §§402 and 404 permit programs in the wrong place. This concern is at least partly rooted in the substantive criteria used to consider and issue permits under each program. In a part of the *Coeur Alaska* opinion not included in the excerpt in the preceding section, the Court held that the EPA's §306 new source performance standard that would apply under §402 does not apply to the discharge of fill material subject to §404. As a result, an EPA new source performance standard that prohibited mines like Coeur Alaska's from discharging "process wastewater" into navigable waters did not apply to the discharge at issue in the case, even though it would apply if a §402 permit were required. Thus, the substantive criteria used to make §404 decisions differ significantly from the criteria used to make §402 permitting decisions.

Professor Adler compares and contrasts the substantive criteria used to consider §402 permits (discussed above in sections D and E) with those used in the §404 context as follows:

> [T]he *Coeur Alaska* case and the history of section 404 implementation generally suggest a much more troubling question. For those cases in which section 404 does properly apply . . . , why are some waters allowed to be destroyed (or "filled") entirely, while discharges permitted under section 402 require absolute protection via either strict technology-based controls (with a goal of zero discharge wherever technologically and economically feasible) or through absolute attainment of applicable water quality standards adequate to protect all existing and designated water body uses? Indeed, how can permits allowing dischargers to destroy entire wetlands . . . be reconciled with the underlying statutory goal to "restore and maintain the chemical, physical, and biological integrity of the Nation's waters?"

Adler, Resilience, Restoration, and Sustainability: Revisiting the Fundamental Principles of the Clean Water Act, 32 Wash U. J.L. & Pol'y 139, 169 (2010).

This section provides a brief overview of key substantive criteria used to determine whether a §404 permit should be issued. For projects that are subject to §404 jurisdiction, the Corps must determine whether a permit is in the "public interest." 33 C.F.R. Part 320. The scope of the Corps' discretion to make this determination is considerable. See Water Works & Sewer Bd. of the City of Birmingham v. U.S. Army Corps of Eng'rs, 983 F. Supp. 1052, 1067 (N.D. Ala. 1997) (scope of §404 "public interest review is essentially the same as the extent of review permitted under NEPA analysis"). 33 C.F.R. §320.4(a)(1) directs the Corps as follows:

> All factors which may be relevant to the proposal must be considered including the cumulative effects thereof: among those are conservation, economics, aesthetics, general

environmental concerns, wetlands, historic properties, fish and wildlife values, flood hazards, floodplain values, land use, navigation, shore erosion and accretion, recreation, water supply and conservation, water quality, energy needs, safety, food and fiber production, mineral needs, considerations of property ownership and, in general, the needs and welfare of the people.

33 C.F.R. §320.4(a) and (b) highlight the value of wetlands and, consistent with CWA §404(b)(1), require the Corps, in exercising its §404 authority for projects involving wetlands, to adhere to regulations that EPA has developed. See 40 C.F.R. Part 230. In those regulations, EPA provides several environmental guidelines concerning when a §404 permit should be issued. EPA's regulations, set forth in 40 C.F.R. §230.12(a)(3)(i)-(iv), limit the permitting agency's flexibility by providing that a proposed discharge site falls short when

 (i) there is a practicable alternative to the proposed discharge that would have less adverse effect on the aquatic ecosystem, so long as such alternative does not have other significant adverse environmental consequences; or
 (ii) the proposed discharge will result in significant degradation of the aquatic ecosystem under §230.10(b) or (c); or
 (iii) the proposed discharge does not include all appropriate and practicable measures to minimize potential harm to the aquatic ecosystem; or
 (iv) there does not exist sufficient information to make a reasonable judgment as to whether the proposed discharge will comply with these Guidelines.

See also id. §230.10.

Probably the most important substantive criterion is the Corps' water dependency standard. Before the Corps can approve a non-water-dependent activity, it must determine whether a practicable alternative site is available that would cause less damage to wetlands. Id. §230.10(a). The regulations define "practicable" as "available and capable of being done after taking into consideration cost, existing technology, and logistics in light of overall project purposes." Id. §230.3(q).

For non-water-dependent projects, it is "presumed" that a practicable alternative exists. This presumption does not rise to the level of an automatic bar to issuance of a permit, but the applicant has the burden of demonstrating otherwise. Utahns for Better Transp. v. U.S. Dep't of Transp., 305 F.3d 1152, 1162, 1186-1190 (10th Cir. 2002), held that an applicant must make a "persuasive showing concerning the lack of alternatives" if it is to overcome the CWA's presumption for non-water-dependent projects that there is a practicable alternative to dredging or filling wetlands. See also Sierra Club v. Van Antwerp, 362 Fed. Appx. 100 (11th Cir. 2010); W. Want, Law of Wetlands Regulation §§6:17-6:21 (2010) (reviewing judicial and agency decisions applying this criterion).

A second important issue that has arisen in the permitting context involves the circumstances in which it is appropriate to allow mitigation—that is, replacement of wetlands lost or damaged by a project. The steps for mitigation are typically three-fold. First, a prospective permittee must show that it is using the alternative that would be least damaging to the environment. Second, the applicant must show a plan that would minimize unavoidable environmental harm. Finally, the applicant must compensate for any harm that could not be avoided. To compensate, the applicant pays to enhance, restore, create, or preserve wetlands either on or off the site of the project. Gardner, Banking on Entrepreneurs: Wetlands, Mitigation Banking, and Takings, 81

Iowa L. Rev. 527, 535-536 (1996). To promote mitigation, EPA and the Corps also recognize "mitigation banking."

The track record of mitigation efforts is mixed. The National Research Council (NRC), in a report Compensating for Wetland Losses Under the Clean Water Act (June 2001), indicated that annually from 1993 to 2000, 24,000 acres of wetlands were permitted to be filled, and 42,000 acres were required as compensatory mitigation (1.8 acres mitigated or gained for every acre permitted or lost). It notes that if the mitigation conditions in permits were observed, the result would be a net gain in jurisdictional wetland area and function. But the NRC committee was not convinced that commitments on paper are being translated into reality because, among other things, "the literature on compensatory mitigation suggests that required mitigation projects often are not undertaken or fail to meet permit conditions." It said that "the magnitude of the shortfall [compared with the goal of no net loss] is not precisely known and cannot be determined from current data." Id. at 3.

EPA and the Corps issued a rule on March 31, 2008, governing compensatory mitigation projects. Compensatory Mitigation for Losses of Aquatic Resources, 73 Fed. Reg. 19,594 (April 10, 2008). For a brief summary of the rule, see EPA, Army Corps Issue Final Rule to Mitigate Loss of Wetlands, Streams, 39 Env't Rep. (BNA) 662 (Apr. 4, 2008). The National Mitigation Banking Association, composed of companies that create compensatory wetlands, issued recommendations on implementing the new rule. Wetland Bankers Detail Implementation Plan for EPA Mitigation Rule, Environmental Policy Alert (Inside EPA) 21 (May 21, 2008). The Ninth Circuit applied the rule in Butte Envtl. Council v. U.S. Army Corps of Eng'rs, 620 F.3d 936 (9th Cir. 2010). For a review of some mitigation initiatives, see Environmental Law Inst., The Status and Character of In-Lieu Fee Mitigation in the United States, 2006 http://www.epa.gov/owow/wetlands/pdf/ELI_ILF_Study06.pdf.

The following case identifies some of the key issues that often arise in §404 permit proceedings.

NORTHWEST ENVIRONMENTAL DEFENSE CENTER v. WOOD
947 F. Supp. 1371 (D. Or. 1996)

Judge HOGAN delivered the opinion of the Court.

Plaintiffs bring this action challenging the Army Corps of Engineers' decision to issue a permit allowing Hyundai Electronics of America to fill 10.4 acres of wetlands. Plaintiffs argue that the issuance of the permit violates the Clean Water Act, 33 U.S.C. §1344, and that the Army Corps of Engineers' decision not to prepare an Environmental Impact Statement with regard to the issuance of the permit violates the National Environmental Policy Act, 42 U.S.C. §4321, et seq.

Facts

Hyundai Electronics of America (Hyundai) entered into a contract with D.A.G. Trusts Partnership (DAG) to purchase a 205-acre parcel of land located in the Willow Creek

Industrial Park. . . . The Hyundai/DAG contract is contingent on DAG obtaining necessary permits, including a wetlands fill permit as required under the Clean Water Act (CWA). . . .

On December 20, 1995, the Corps issued wetlands fill permit number 95-00482, signed by Colonel Wood. . . . [T]he Corps determined that the project purpose was to construct "a large semiconductor facility in the Eugene area." The Corps also found that

> while the project is not water-dependent and includes the placement of fill in . . . wetlands, it has been clearly demonstrated that there are no available, practicable alternatives having less adverse impact on the aquatic ecosystem and without other significant adverse environmental consequences that do not involve discharges into "waters of the United States" or at other locations within these waters.

Finally, the Corps found that issuance of the permit was not contrary to the public interest and would not have a significant impact on the human environment, especially given the limitations and conditions imposed by the permit.

. . . The amount of wetlands to be filled was . . . 10.4 acres. In addition, the permit required Hyundai to restore 13 acres of wetlands and enhance 6.9 acres of wet prairie lands.

Discussion

I. STANDARDS OF REVIEW

The Corps' decisions to issue the wetlands fill permit and to forego an Environmental Impact Statement are subject to an arbitrary and capricious standard of review under the Administrative Procedure Act, 5 U.S.C. §706. Under this standard, an agency decision must be upheld unless it is "arbitrary, capricious, an abuse of discretion, or otherwise not in accordance with law." 5 U.S.C. §706(2). . . .

III. SUMMARY JUDGMENT MOTIONS

A. CLEAN WATER ACT

1. Practicable Alternatives Test

The Corps may not issue a wetlands fill permit without complying with the guidelines promulgated under section 404(b)(1) of the Clean Water Act. 33 C.F.R. §320.4(a)(1). One such guideline requires the Corps to apply a "practicable alternatives" test, under which the Corps must deny a fill permit

> if there is a practicable alternative to the proposed discharge which would have less adverse impact on the aquatic ecosystem, so long as the alternative does not have other significant adverse environmental consequences. [40 C.F.R. §230.10(a).]

When the proposed project is not water dependent, the guidelines place the burden on the applicant to "clearly demonstrate" that there are no practicable, less damaging sites. 40 C.F.R. §230.10(a)(3). The regulations define "practicable" to mean "available and capable of being done after taking into consideration cost, existing technology, and logistics in light of the overall project purpose." 40 C.F.R. §230.10(a)(2); 230.3(q).

The regulations contemplate a certain degree of flexibility in an agency's application of the practicable alternatives test under certain circumstances. The preamble to 40 C.F.R. §230.10 provides:

> Although all requirements in §230.10 must be met, the compliance evaluation procedures will vary to reflect the seriousness of the potential for adverse impacts on the aquatic ecosystems posed by the specific . . . activities.

In addition, the guidelines require the Corps to consider planning processes relevant to a proposed site:

> To the extent that practicable alternatives have been identified and evaluated under a . . . planning process, such evaluation shall be considered . . . as part of the consideration of alternatives under the Guidelines. [40 C.F.R. §230.10(a)(5).]

a. Project Purpose

In order to conduct a practicable alternatives test, the Corps must first determine the "overall project purposes." 40 C.F.R. §230.10(a)(2). While the Corps may not manipulate the project purpose so as to exclude alternative sites, "the Corps has a duty to take into account the objectives of the applicant's project."

Plaintiffs contend the Corps erred in its application of the practicable alternatives test by defining the project purpose too narrowly. The Corps determined that Hyundai's project purpose was to "develop a large semiconductor fabrication plant in the Eugene area." Plaintiffs contend that because Hyundai is a multinational company with national and international customer bases, there was no need to restrict the project purpose to Eugene; rather, the scope of alternate sites should have been national, or at least state-wide. Plaintiffs argue that Hyundai failed to clearly demonstrate that the project purpose should be restricted to the Eugene area.

The administrative record contains detailed explanations for Hyundai's desire to build its plant in the Eugene area. These include proximity to customers, suppliers, and competitors; availability of quality, trainable labor; proximity to a major university; access to adequate transportation facilities; availability of sufficiently large sites in an urban area with adequate utilities, proper zoning and other conditions appropriate for semiconductor manufacturing; land-use planning and regulatory support in the community; and the availability of financial and tax incentives. The decision document states that the Corps "reviewed and evaluated . . . the documents and factors concerning this permit application." In light of the substantial evidence in the record regarding Hyundai's legitimate economic reasons for choosing to construct its project in Eugene, the Corps' decision to restrict the project purpose to "the Eugene area" was neither arbitrary nor capricious.

b. Practicability of Alternatives

After determining the project purpose, the Corps must consider alternatives that are "available and capable of being done after taking into consideration cost, existing technology, and logistics in light of the overall project purpose." 40 C.F.R. §230.10(a)(2). As noted above, the overall project purpose here was to "develop a large semiconductor fabrication plant in the Eugene area." Under the regulations, Hyundai had the burden to show by clear and convincing evidence that, given cost, technology, and logistical factors, its overall project purpose could not be achieved on an alternative site with less damage to the aquatic ecosystem.

Hyundai considered seven sites within the Eugene area's "Special Light Industrial" zoning designation. . . .

The Corps concluded that "it has been clearly demonstrated that there are no available, practicable alternatives having less adverse impact on the aquatic ecosystem and without other significant adverse environmental consequences. . . ." It is apparent that this conclusion was based in part on the substantial evidence submitted by Hyundai with regard to practicable, alternative sites. . . .

Section 230.10 also allows a more flexible procedural approach with respect to projects that the Corps deems to be less serious threats to wetlands. The Corps promulgates nationwide permits for activities having "minimal impacts" on the waters of the United States. 33 C.F.R. §330.1(b). One such permit is available for activities which fill no more than ten acres of wetlands. 33 C.F.R. Pt. 330, App. A ¶26. Where the activity displaces less than ten but more than one acre of water, the permittee must notify the Corps but may proceed with the project after 30 days unless otherwise notified by the Corps. 33 C.F.R. §330.1(e).

While there are factors and concerns that point to this project's impact on the subject wetlands, the Corps' nationwide permit regulations, promulgated with the benefit of rulemaking procedures and agency expertise, suggest that any wetlands impact resulting from the fill of 10.4 acres is likely to be at the low end of the spectrum. Under 40 C.F.R. §230.10, the proposed fill of 10.4 acres is close enough to what the Corps considers to be a "minimal" impact to warrant a more procedurally flexible alternatives review procedure. This authorized flexibility supports the court's conclusion that the Corps did not abuse its discretion by basing its decision in part on the project's conformance with the WEWP. [WEWP, or West Eugene Wetlands Plan, was an effort that began in the early 1990s to conserve and restore the wetlands in the area.] . . .

In sum, there is substantial evidence in the record that the Corps thoroughly considered the alternative sites analysis submitted by Hyundai in addition to the Corps' own prior analysis regarding WEWP alternatives. Given the substantial information in the record, it was not arbitrary or capricious for the Corps to conclude that "it has been clearly demonstrated that there are no available, practicable alternatives having less adverse impact on the aquatic ecosystem and without other significant adverse environmental consequences that do not involve discharges into 'waters of the United States' or at other locations within these waters."

2. Public Interest Analysis

The Corps' general regulatory procedures require permit decisions to "be based on an evaluation of the probable impacts, including cumulative impacts, of the proposed activity . . . on the public interest." 33 C.F.R. §320.4(a). This public interest evaluation requires a "general balancing" of the project's benefits and detriments, taking into account (1) "the public and private need" for the project; (2) "the practicability of using reasonable alternative locations and methods"; and (3) "the extent and permanence of the beneficial and/or detrimental effects. . . ." 33 C.F.R. §320.4(a)(2)(i)-(iii).

Plaintiffs contend that "any public or private need for the proposed chip plant is outweighed by the public interest in protecting the wetland resource on the site." The Corps, of course, did not reach this conclusion, finding issuance of the permit to be

> based on thorough analysis and evaluation of the various factors affecting the public interest; that there are no reasonable alternatives available to the applicant that will achieve the purposes for which the work is being constructed; that the proposed work is not contrary to the public interest as reflected in the comments of Federal, State and local agencies and the general public; that the proposed work is deemed to comply with established State and local laws, regulations and codes; that the issuance of this permit is consonant with national policy, statutes, and administrative directives; and that on balance the activity is not contrary to the public interest. . . .

Moreover, the decision document explicitly addresses alternative sites (as described above); the minimization of wetland impacts; the effects on water, soil, and drainage; the effects on wildlife (including endangered and threatened species) and other biological characteristics; the effects on "human use characteristics" such as recreation, aesthetics, transportation, general safety, air quality, noise levels, cultural sites, economics, and adjacent private property owners; secondary and cumulative effects; the comments of agencies, including the Fish and Wildlife Service, the Environmental Protection Agency, the Oregon Division of State Lands, the Oregon Department of Environmental Quality, the Oregon Department of Fish and Wildlife, the Oregon Department of Transportation; and the comments of the public, including the Nature Conservancy and individuals who provided input via the 1200 comment letters and 200 public hearing testimonials.

The Corps' decision that issuance of the permit was in the public interest was based on a careful balancing of relevant public concerns and thousands of pages of public and agency input. Though it may have differed from plaintiffs' opinion, the Corps' decision that issuance of the permit was in the public interest was not arbitrary or capricious or in violation of applicable law. . . .

NOTES AND QUESTIONS

1. *Where Should the Jurisdictional Boundary Line Be Drawn Between the CWA §§402 and 404 Permitting Programs?* Professor Adler argues that the Court got it wrong in *Coeur Alaska* in establishing the respective jurisdictional boundaries of the §§402 and 404 permitting programs, suggesting that the CWA gives EPA (and authorized states) the "primary authority to issue permits for discharges of pollutants under the Act;" that Congress delegated the Corps authority to issue permits "only for a narrowly defined category of pollutants" ("dredged or fill material . . . at specified disposal sites"); and that the Court's opinion "turned the exception into the rule. . . ." Adler, Resilience, Restoration, and Sustainability: Revisiting the Fundamental Principles of the Clean Water Act, 32 Wash U. J.L. & Pol'y 139, 168 (2010).

2. *The ESA Operates as a Limit on the Corps' §404 Authority.* As noted in Chapter 5, 16 U.S.C. §1536(a)(2) requires that all federal agencies ensure that their actions will not jeopardize the continued existence of species listed as threatened or endangered. Once a federal action is found to jeopardize a listed species, the agency has an absolute mandate to prevent the destruction of the listed species, TVA v. Hill,

437 U.S. 153 (1978), unless a cabinet-level committee exempts the species from the Act. 16 U.S.C. §1536(e)-(h). See Riverside Irrigation Dist. v. Andrews, 568 F. Supp. 583 (D. Colo. 1983), aff'd, 758 F.2d 508 (10th Cir. 1985) (dam developer may not discharge sand and gravel pursuant to a permit during the construction of a dam because the operation of the dam and the altered water flow might have an adverse impact on a whooping crane habitat 250 to 300 miles downstream). The agencies' duties to protect species are well outlined in Roosevelt Campobello Park Comm'n v. EPA, 684 F.2d 1041 (1st Cir. 1982). See generally Tarlock, The Endangered Species Act & Western Water Rights, 20 Land & Water L. Rev. 1 (1985). Section 9 of the ESA prohibits private parties from taking a species. Water diversions may be a §9 taking, United States v. Glenn-Colusa Irrigation Dist., 788 F. Supp. 1126 (E.D. Cal. 1992), and the Supreme Court has upheld regulations that define habitat destruction as a taking under some circumstances. Babbitt v. Sweet Home Chapter of Cmtys. for a Great Or., 515 U.S. 687 (1995). See Chapter 5.

3. *General Permits as an Alternative Regulatory Approach.* The CWA authorizes the Corps to issue general permits under §404(e) if the Agency determines that "the activities in such category are similar in nature, will cause only minimal adverse environmental effects when performed separately, and will have only minimal cumulative adverse effect on the environment." 33 U.S.C. §1344(e)(1). In one case, the Eleventh Circuit upheld a general permit to cover suburban development over a 48,000 acre area on the ground that the special conditions included in the permit "effectively cabin the scope of permitted activities and mitigate any environmental impacts. . . ." Sierra Club v. U.S. Army Corps of Eng'rs, 508 F.3d 1332, 1334 (11th Cir. 2007). Two commentators estimate that the "mean individual permit application costs over $271,596 to prepare (ignoring the cost of mitigation, design changes, costs of carrying capital and other costs), while the cost of preparing a nationwide permit application averages $28,915." D.L. Sunding & D. Zilberman, Non-Federal and Non-Regulatory Approaches to Wetlands Conservation: A Post-SWANCC Exploration of Conservation Alternatives 7 (2003).

J. WATERSHED OR "PLACE-BASED" APPROACHES TO WATER PROTECTION

The preceding sections of this chapter make three fundamental points: (1) in addition to expressing a commitment to cleaning up our nation's waters by reducing discharges of pollutants into them, the CWA (as well as other statutes) provides a series of tools for accomplishing this goal; (2) use of these tools over the past 40-plus years has produced substantial reductions in discharges of various types of pollutants, which in turn has yielded many significant improvements in water quality; (3) but considerably more needs to be done if we are to come close to the goal of cleaning up our waters so that they can be available for such seemingly basic uses as fishing, swimming, drinking, and various forms of recreation. Watershed or "place-based" approaches continue to gain popularity as a possible framework for taking on some of the remaining challenges.

This section briefly reviews three features of watershed-based approaches to water protection. It begins with a definition of the concept. It then offers examples of the substantial support that seems to have emerged for such approaches. Finally, the section summarizes some of the insights gleaned to date from experimenting with watershed-based approaches.

EPA defines a watershed-based approach as one that "focuses multi-stakeholder efforts within hydrologically defined boundaries to protect and restore our aquatic resources and ecosystems. . . ." Mem. from G. Tracy Mehan, III, U.S. EPA Assistant Administrator, Office of Water, Committing EPA's Water Program to Advancing the Watershed Approach (Dec. 3, 2002). The agency has also described a watershed as a "geographic area in which all the falling water drains to a common water body, i.e., river, lake or stream." It notes that watersheds may be "as small as a few acres or larger than several states." And it suggests that, based on U.S. Geological Survey data, the country can be "divided into 2,149 medium-sized watersheds, averaging about 1,700 square miles in each area." EPA, Watershed Success Stories: Applying the Principles and Spirit of the Clean Water Action Plan 3, 4 (Sept. 2000). The agency has elaborated on this definition in the context of state watershed approaches by characterizing such approaches as having five key components:

> (1) the delineation of a state into natural geographic (e.g., watershed/basin) management areas; (2) a series of management steps or phases to guide regulatory and non-regulatory actions within geographic areas (i.e., monitoring, assessment, planning, implementation); (3) the integration of CWA and other water resource programs through the coordinated implementation of management steps and the formation of partnerships; (4) a process for involving stakeholders; and (5) a focus on environmental results. [EPA, A Review of Statewide Watershed Management Approaches, Final Report 1 (April 2002).]

EPA has placed considerable hope in watershed-based approaches as a tool for improving water quality. This was evident during the Clinton administration, as reflected in its 1998 Clean Water Action Plan and the 2000 Success Stories report cited above, and Bush administration EPA officials took much the same view. The Obama administration's treatment of the Chesapeake Bay is an example of its apparent commitment to such an approach as well. See, e.g., Exec. Order No. 13,508 (2009).

Many state officials appear to share EPA's enthusiasm for watershed approaches. A Wisconsin official, for example, lauds such approaches because they can help focus stakeholders' attention on the watershed's particular needs, which helps integrate the various jurisdictional lines (e.g., federal, state, and local) that cover that watershed, maximize financial resources and avoid duplication, and provide a sense of ownership to those most directly impacted by the measures taken to protect the watershed. Sylvester, The Watershed Approach: The Path to Further Progress, ECOStates 10, 11 (Spring 2000).

EPA reports that more than 20 states have adopted statewide watershed management approaches. EPA, A Review of Statewide Watershed Management Approaches, Final Report (April 2002). Based on case studies of 8 such states (Kentucky, Massachusetts, New Jersey, North Carolina, Ohio, Oregon, Texas, and Washington), EPA offered the following five conclusions:

- State managers and staff are overwhelmingly supportive of the statewide watershed management approach despite a number of programmatic and institutional barriers.

- The key to a successful statewide watershed program[] appears to be one that recognizes the important value of inter-agency and state-local partnerships and is supported by an adequate coordination infrastructure.
- The rotating basin approach to statewide watershed management should be viewed as a framework for focusing resources and coordinating activities and not an end in itself. [EPA explains that the "most common form of statewide watershed management" is the "5-year, 5-step rotating basin approach. . . ."]
- EPA needs to focus more resources and attention on improving federal-state oversight and building state watershed management capacity as part of its strategy to support the watershed approach.
- EPA and states need to begin documenting the resource and environmental gains attributed to the statewide watershed management approach. [Id. at 41-45.]

EPA's study identified numerous barriers to the success of state watershed strategies. These include, at a programmatic level, (1) "state-level program management barriers" (e.g., the reality that state managers have specific responsibilities for implementing the NPDES program or other features of the CWA that may compete with watershed-related activities for priority attention); (2) "EPA program management barriers" (EPA's fragmented and output-oriented approach to oversight undermines efforts to operate in an integrated and environmental results–driven fashion); (3) difficulties in coordinating across programs and among agencies (a barrier that will resonate with anyone who has sought to design and implement a joint initiative); and (4) challenges in engaging the public and coordinating with local governments. Id. at 15-27.

At a practical level, what effect does "watershed" management have on a state's use of the specific tools and strategies embodied in the state monitoring and permitting programs discussed in this chapter, and vice versa? EPA offers some interesting insights about this relationship. It found that "statewide watershed management has resulted in dramatic improvements in both the quantity and quality of data," although it identified numerous deficiencies in basin-wide monitoring. In contrast, the agency found little overlap between watershed management approaches and states' obligations to develop water quality standards because of a number of factors, including the different cycles involved (triennial review for WQSs and five-year basin cycles used for watershed management). EPA found that "TMDL development and statewide watershed approaches can provide mutual benefits." For example, key elements of watershed management, such as interagency collaboration, stakeholder involvement, and intensive monitoring, can "provide benefits and set the stage for more effective TMDL programs."

States appear to have had mixed experiences in their efforts to integrate or coordinate NPDES permitting efforts with watershed management. Some states apparently found that basin-wide NPDES permitting was a net positive because it proved more strategic and efficient, while many states experienced significant difficulties in pursuing such permitting (because of uneven permitting workloads across basins, special EPA initiatives that divert attention from basin-oriented approaches, etc.). Finally, EPA found that states have not fully integrated their nonpoint source programs into their watershed management approaches. Again, the reasons vary, but in part the lack of integration stems from the multitude of actors involved (e.g., state officials may be focusing on one aspect of the pollution while local officials are focused on another). Id. at 4-6; see also Adler, *supra* at 154 (summarizing mixed success of watershed-based programs).

In short, the jury is very much still out as to the extent to which watershed management is likely to change significantly the regulatory and nonregulatory landscape for reducing water pollution. The opportunity to consider the possibilities for integrating such approaches with the types of tools outlined in the rest of this chapter, in a way that advances the goals of water protection and minimizes some of the obstacles identified above, is part of what makes environmental law such an interesting field to study.

NOTES AND QUESTIONS

1. Case studies have been developed of several watershed-based efforts. See, e.g., EPA, Watershed Success Stories: Applying the Principles and Spirit of the Clean Water Action Plan (Sept. 2000) (reviewing experiences with respect to 30 watersheds throughout the United States); ECOStates 10, 12, 13 (Spring 2000) (brief case studies of such efforts in Florida, Louisiana, and Wisconsin). The National Research Council issued a January 2005 report in which it recommended a "watershed"-type approach to handle water-related issues in southwestern Pennsylvania. Natural Research Council, Regional Cooperation for Water Quality Improvement in Southwestern Pennsylvania (2005). An April 2008 report issued by a consortium of organizations brought together by EPA and the New York Academy of Sciences contains recommendations for controlling pollution in the New York/New Jersey Harbor estuary. Organizations Issue Final Research on New York/New Jersey Harbor Estuary, 39 Env't Rep. (BNA) 664 (Apr. 4, 2008). Efforts to restore the Chesapeake Bay watershed have received enormous attention over the past several decades and continue to do so. 74 Fed. Reg. 23,097 (May 15, 2009) (Executive Order 13,508—Chesapeake Bay Protection and Restoration).

A 2008 EPA report provides guidance for performing watershed ecological risk assessments. Application of Watershed Ecological Risk Assessment Methods to Watershed Management, 73 Fed. Reg. 20,047 (Apr. 14, 2008). Also in April 2008, EPA issued a Handbook for Developing Watershed Plans to Restore and Protect Our Waters, http://water.epa.gov/polwaste/nps/handbook_index.cfm. In August 2007, EPA issued its Watershed-Based National Pollutant Discharge Elimination System (NPDES) Permitting Technical Guidance, EPA-833-B-07-004 (Aug. 2007). A 2013 report that reviews the investments the United States has made in protecting watersheds indicates that the country spent about $360 million in 2011. Ecosystem Marketplace, Charting New Waters: State of Watershed Payments 2012 (2013), http://www.forest-trends.org/documents/files/doc_3308.pdf.

2. Watershed approaches inherently contemplate place-based, place-tailored strategies to reduce pollution. We referred above to criticisms that the CWA is overly rigid. To what extent do the CWA and other laws provide the tools needed to implement such strategies? How good, in short, is the match between current statutory authority and the design and implementation of watershed strategies? What types of changes need to be made to the environmental laws to facilitate the implementation of such strategies? See, e.g., Stephenson, Shabman & Geyer, Toward an Effective Watershed-Based Effluent Allowance Trading System: Identifying the Statutory and Regulatory Barriers to Implementation, 5 Envtl. Law. 775 (1999). For a summary of EPA's efforts to use existing strategies to clean up the Chesapeake Bay, see Knight et al., EPA Prescribes a "Pollution Diet" for the Impaired

Chesapeake Bay, Envtl. Liability Enforcement & Penalties Rep., August/September 2010, at 259.

For "beyond watershed" approaches involving plans to reduce mercury concentrations, EPA approved a Minnesota statewide plan and also approved a plan by the northeast states for New England and New York. See Minnesota Mercury Plan Gets Approval from New EPA, Touted as Model for Others, 38 Env't Rep. (BNA) 867 (Apr. 13, 2007); EPA Approves Plan by Northeast States to Lower Mercury Levels in Fish, Envtl. Liability Enforcement & Penalties Rep. 78 (Feb. 2008).

VIII

CONTROLLING TOXIC SUBSTANCES AND HAZARDOUS WASTES

Chapters 6 and 7 examined the two basic media protection programs, the Clean Air and Clean Water Acts. This chapter addresses the health and environmental risks posed by the management of toxic substances. The focus is on the manufacture, use, and discharge of substances that create significant health risks in the workplace, in the outdoor environment, through the use of products, or through the consumption of food and water. Several agencies are responsible for protecting the public against these health risks under a host of statutes that sometimes overlap, but that also leave troublesome gaps in protection.

Congress enacted the Clean Air and Clean Water Acts in 1970 and 1972. The assumption regarding the core of the pollution problem was that a fairly small number of environmental pollutants that were present in large quantities were causing a limited amount of harm to large numbers of people (e.g., SO_2 was a respiratory irritant and waterborne bacteria caused infectious diseases). In a few situations, however, a few persons were apparently threatened with severe harm from being exposed to small quantities of a few pollutants (e.g., a heavy metal in the air or water might cause cancer; SO_2 could cause emphysema in sensitive population groups). Brief provisions were added, almost as an afterthought, to the Clean Air and Clean Water Acts to handle pollutants that could not be adequately regulated under the ambient and technology-based provisions of those laws. By the mid-1970s, policymakers had begun to realize that their perspective on the pollution problem might be wrong—that there may in fact be hundreds or thousands of environmental contaminants that might cause severe harm to large numbers of persons if exposure even to trace quantities should occur over long periods of time, no matter what the pathway.

These observations raise the problem, which we address throughout this chapter and the next, of how a "hazardous" or "toxic" pollutant is any different from the pollutants that are the focus of most of the regulatory programs encountered in Chapters 6 and 7. A pollutant may irritate the skin or mucous membranes; depress the functions of the nervous system; damage blood, liver, kidney, or brain cells; interfere with important enzyme systems; or cause damage to the reproductive system. Most effects of this type are reversible; generally, when the exposure stops, the individual gradually returns to normal. To take a simple example, alcohol-induced central nervous system depression disappears a few hours after a person stops drinking. The effects of many conventional pollutants are reversible under most conditions of exposure. But essentially nonreversible effects also may occur, sometimes after

739

prolonged exposure at low levels. Examples include mutations that are passed on to succeeding generations, teratogens that deform the developing fetus—and cancer.

In the public mind, cancer is the most important harm produced by the discharge of toxic substances. The prevention of increased cancer risk has been the driving force behind toxic or hazardous substances regulation since the start of the environmental movement. The basic "environmentalist" thesis is that the majority of human cancers are caused by human exposure to specific substances and that these cancers are potentially preventable by eliminating or reducing exposure levels. See Proctor, Cancer Wars: How Politics Shapes What We Know and Don't Know About Cancer 35-53 (1995). In this chapter, we will examine the theories of cancer causation that lie behind toxic substances regulation as well as inquire whether recent developments in cancer theory suggest a need to reexamine basic regulatory assumptions.

Concern related to exposure to toxic substances emerged in part because the chemical industry expanded after World War II. The industry produced thousands of new chemicals, most of which are organic (carbon-containing) compounds. Because life itself is based in part on carbon compounds, interference by newly invented compounds with evolutionary ones may play havoc with human life processes if exposure occurs. See Colburn et al., Our Stolen Future (1996) (discussing the effects of endocrine-disrupting chemicals). See also Jones, Endocrine Disruptors and Risk Assessment: Potential for a Big Mistake, 17 Vill. Envtl. L.J. 357 (2006) (arguing that traditional risk assessment methodologies may be inadequate for regulating endocrine-disrupting chemicals because of their potential cumulative action).

The key questions for environmental policymakers are: What compounds are dangerous to humans in the quantities in which they are likely to be encountered? What regulatory responses are appropriate? In particular, how should prolonged low-level, low-risk exposures to chemicals be addressed? Although many hazardous compounds are capable of inducing disease or causing death, the effects of everyday low-level exposures on human health are extremely difficult to determine. The Surgeon General stated long ago, "We believe that toxic chemicals are adding to the disease burden of the United States in a significant, although as yet not precisely defined, way. In addition, we believe that this problem will become more important in the years ahead." Senate Comm. on Env't and Pub. Works, 96th Cong., 2d Sess., Health Effects of Toxic Pollution: A Report from the Surgeon General iii (Comm. Print 1980). The uncertainty that caused the Surgeon General to describe the problem as not "precisely defined" represents the major issue awaiting you in this chapter.

A.   DEFINING THE PROBLEM: RISK AND UNCERTAINTY

1.   *The Nature of Environmental Risk*

PAGE, A GENERIC VIEW OF TOXIC CHEMICALS
AND SIMILAR RISKS
7 Ecology L.Q. 207, 207-223 (1978)

A new type of environmental problem is emerging which differs in nature from the more familiar pollution and resource depletion problems. This type of problem, which may be called *environmental risk*,[1] has rapidly increased in importance over the last few decades and may indeed become the dominant type of environmental problem. Environmental risk problems are exemplified by: the risk of leakage and contamination in the disposal of nuclear wastes [and] the production of synthetic chemicals which may be toxic, carcinogenic, mutagenic, or teratogenic. . . . [Environmental risk possesses nine characteristics, discussed below. The first four emphasize scientific uncertainty and often are the focus of cost-benefit analysis. The remaining five concern regulatory management of risk.]

Ignorance of mechanism is the first characteristic of environmental risk problems. The present state of knowledge of the mechanisms by which a risk is effected is both limited and limiting. Ignorance of mechanism may be present at any number of levels of risk creation, from the generation of the hazard (e.g., the release of radiation from the nuclear fuel cycle) or transmission of the hazard's effect (e.g., dispersion of radiation in the ambient environment or food chain) to an organism's response to exposure, particularly health-related responses (e.g., sensitivity to "hot particles" and other forms of radiation). The mechanisms of generation, transmission, and response are understood so poorly that any management of these problems is truly decision making under pervasive uncertainty. . . .

The *potential for catastrophic costs* is the second common characteristic of environmental risk. What little is known about mechanism in each case establishes that each is a gamble with high stakes. But what is known about mechanism precludes specification of just how catastrophic and likely the costs might be. Ignorance of mechanism colors the next two characteristics as well.

The third characteristic is a *relatively modest benefit* associated with environmental risk gamble. . . . [T]here appears to be at some level a strong asymmetry between potential costs and benefits . . . for most . . . environmental risks. . . . The situation with spray cans and ozone depletion is . . . clear cut. The benefit of fluorocarbons can be directly measured in markets in terms of a cheaper and finer spray compared with the alternatives, which include pump spray. These benefits accrue regardless of the potential effects of the fluorocarbons on the ozone layer. They appear modest indeed compared with the potentially catastrophic costs which might result from ozone depletion. Correspondingly, for the potentially toxic chemical Red Dye No. 40, the benefit is the cosmetic effect the color provides in foods. Again this benefit is modest compared with the potential of the chemical as a carcinogen. This asymmetry in the orders of magnitude of potential costs and benefits has important implications for environmental decision making in terms of the degree of proof necessary to warrant precautionary action.

An environmental risk gamble may be thought of as a seesaw with the potential costs on one side of the pivot and the potential benefits on the other. The distances from the pivot represent the relative magnitudes of benefits and costs. Figure 8-1 illustrates the freon propellant example. The distance from zero to B represents the benefit of the convenience of using propellants. Forgoing this convenience is the cost of opting out of the gamble. The distance from zero to C–B represents the net cost of taking the gamble and losing. The net cost is the potential, relatively large "catastrophic" cost reduced by the comparatively small benefit of using propellants that will accrue even if propellants do deplete the ozone.

1. "Environmental risk" will be defined specifically in terms of nine characteristics discussed *infra*. "Risk" has several distinct meanings depending on its usage. In "environmental risk," the term draws attention to the potential adverse consequences, for which the underlying probability may be highly uncertain. . . .

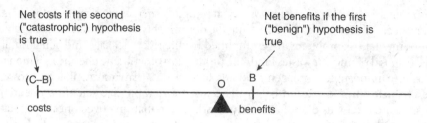

FIGURE 8-1
Net Costs and Benefits Associated with Two Hypotheses

In Figure 8-1 the potential costs, due to their magnitude, are considerably farther from the pivot than the modest benefits. If both hypotheses were of equal weight the seesaw would tip toward the potentially great loss. Common sense then suggests that the gamble is too risky to undertake.

However, there is a dilemma. There often are reasons to believe that the probabilities of the safe and catastrophic hypotheses are not equal and that the catastrophic outcome is considerably less likely than the favorable outcome. For many potentially toxic chemicals, . . . what little is known about mechanism suggests that the probability of the catastrophic outcome is low, much lower than the probability of the favorable outcome. Just how low is impossible to say with confidence, because of the incomplete knowledge of mechanism. Due to the fragmentary knowledge of mechanism, the likelihood of the catastrophic hypotheses cannot be determined objectively, but must be assessed subjectively, based upon whatever knowledge is available.

Low subjective probability of the catastrophic outcome is the fourth characteristic of environmental risk. Common sense suggests that the low subjective probability of the catastrophic costs should be taken into account in balancing costs and benefits. In terms of the seesaw illustration, the probabilities of the benign and catastrophic hypotheses can be thought of as weight placed upon the seesaw at distances from the pivot equal to the magnitude of the respective potential costs and benefits. A heavy weight close to the pivot can more than balance a light weight farther from the pivot. With a low subjective probability of the catastrophic outcome and a high subjective probability of the favorable outcome, it is no longer clear which way the seesaw will tip. The fourth characteristic, low subjective probability of the potential catastrophe, introduces a second asymmetry which tends to counterbalance the asymmetry of potential high costs and modest benefits.

Whether the greater likelihood of the favorable outcome compensates for its smaller relative size is a fundamental question of environmental risk management. In the extreme case, the problem is called a "zero-infinity dilemma": a virtually zero probability of a virtually infinite catastrophe.

In the seesaw illustration, common sense may suggest that an environmental risk is worth taking as long as the seesaw, with the probability of weights added, tips in the direction of benign hypothesis. This interpretation is formally equivalent to the expected value criterion, which says that a gamble is worth taking only if the product of the benefits and their likelihood is greater than the product of the adverse outcome and its likelihood. The analogy to the seesaw is used to suggest that the expected value criterion has some natural appeal as a way of balancing potential costs and benefits and their probabilities.

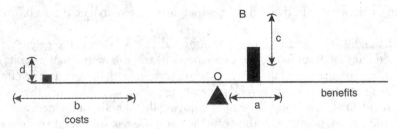

FIGURE 8-2
Costs and Benefits Weighted by Probability

There are obvious limitations to the expected value criterion. It focuses on outcomes rather than processes; because of the uncertainties involved it may be difficult or even impossible to estimate the magnitudes of the outcomes or their probabilities. The various uncertainties surrounding the quantification of costs, benefits, and probabilities are illustrated in Figure 8-2. The range of uncertainty associated with benefits, represented by a, is the uncertainty of *efficacy*. . . . The corresponding range of uncertainty associated with *costs*, represented by b, is typically much larger than the uncertainty of efficacy. In addition, there is uncertainty as to the *likelihood* of each hypothesis (c and d).

The uncertainties surrounding the potential costs, benefits, and probabilities often are so strong that the decision maker avoids numerical quantification altogether. Even so, the magnitudes of the costs, benefits, and probabilities are essential considerations in environmental risk decision making, and informal estimations of costs, benefits, and probabilities cannot be avoided. Moreover, a decision to forgo a final verdict on a chemical's use and to allow, or prevent, its use pending the collection of more information, is still a decision made under uncertainty. . . .

The five remaining characteristics common to environmental risk problems bear more directly on the institutional problems encountered in their management. The first of these is the *internal transfer of benefits* associated with these risks. In the case of the freon propellants, the benefits—added convenience and possibly lower manufacturing costs—are transferred through markets and reflected in product prices. The economic term for costs and benefits thus transferred is "internal."

In contrast to an internal transfer, the adverse effects of environmental risk gambles usually are transferred directly through the environment rather than through the market. A direct, non-market transfer of an effect is called an economic externality. The *external transfer of costs* is the sixth characteristic of environmental risk. The failure of markets to internalize these potentially catastrophic costs is the primary reason for regulation of environmental risk problems. . . .

The seventh characteristic of environmental risk, *collective risk*, is also related to the environmental transfer of effect. A risk is collective when it is borne by many people simultaneously. Since environmental transfer often means a diffusion of effect, major environmental risk problems have the potential to affect millions of people at the same time. The effectiveness of insurance, liability law, and other traditional compensatory mechanisms in protecting against loss resulting from risk is limited in the case of collective risk. The larger the potential loss and the more widespread its effects, the more difficult it is to insure. Society is more [averse] to collective risks than to individual risks, which often are managed through insurance markets.

The eighth characteristic of environmental risk is *latency*, the extended delay between the initiation of hazard, or exposure to it, and the manifestation of its effect. For many carcinogens, the latency is 20 to 30 years. Indeed, the mutagenic effect of a chemical may not show up for several generations. As a result of latency, those bearing environmental risks may not be the ones enjoying the benefits of the decision. Moreover, in most cases, latency is sufficiently long and the risk sufficiently diffuse so that the risk is borne involuntarily, if not unknowingly. Since an acute, or short-term, effect usually is much easier to discover and trace than a chronic, or long-term, effect, long latencies increase the likelihood that the potential effects of environmental risks will be masked by other factors.

The ninth characteristic of environmental risk is *irreversibility*. Even when an effect is theoretically reversible, as a practical matter there are important elements of irreversibility when reversal of the effect inescapably requires a long time, especially when reversal entails a high cost in addition to a long time. Irreversibility can be essentially absolute, as is the case with plutonium's half-life of 24,000 years. It can also be measured on a scale of tens of generations, as is the case with mutagens. In the freon propellant example, the stratospheric effects of ozone depletion might last a hundred years after fluorocarbon emissions are stopped. Within this essentially irreversible period of stratospheric change, however, the resulting climate modification could produce further irreversible effects, such as species extinction.

The last two characteristics, latency and irreversibility of effect, have profound ethical and institutional implications. They raise questions concerning fair distributions of risk over time and how institutions can be designed to anticipate adverse effects, rather than merely to react to existing, known effects. . . .

NOTES AND QUESTIONS

1. Page asserts that the risks to those exposed to toxic substances possess a series of common characteristics that distinguish them from other kinds of risks. Why is ignorance of mechanism arguably the predominant such characteristic? What are the implications of ignorance of mechanism for application of the expected value criterion described by Page? Which of the common characteristics arguably justify governmental intervention to assist in risk reduction efforts?

2. Assuming that those responsible for setting public policy on environmental matters determine that government intervention to reduce the risks created by exposure to toxic substances is appropriate, the next logical question is what form that intervention should take. The issue of whether a risk is serious enough to warrant action (be it public or private) is often called the risk assessment question. The issue of how to manage the risk, once it is decided that it crosses some threshold level of significance that has been established to trigger risk-reducing action, is often referred to as the risk management question. The first excerpt below describes the risk assessment process as it applies to toxic substances. The second excerpt describes EPA's current approach to assessing the risk of exposure to potentially carcinogenic substances.

2. *Risk Assessment, Risk Management, Cancer, and the Environment*

ADLER, AGAINST "INDIVIDUAL RISK": A SYMPATHETIC CRITIQUE OF RISK ASSESSMENT
153 U. Pa. L. Rev. 1121, 1133-1139, 1161-1162 (2005)

Risk assessment, generically, is a set of techniques for quantifying the fatalities or fatality risks resulting from various hazards. These techniques can also be used to quantify nonfatal illness or injury, or the risk of nonfatal illness or injury. . . . [D]eath is the central and paradigmatic harm addressed by health and safety regulators. . . . The best-developed variant of risk assessment, in current regulatory practice, is *toxic* risk assessment: a quantitative description of the fatalities and fatality risks caused by toxic chemicals. But risk assessment with respect to a much wider array of death's causes is also possible and, to some extent, practiced.

Let's start with the toxins. Toxic risk assessment is, in effect, quantitative toxicology and dates from the nineteenth century. Toxic risk assessment by U.S. governmental entities is more recent than that, but still has a substantial history. Toxic risk assessment at the federal level was pioneered by [the federal Food and Drug Administration (FDA)]. This agency is charged with implementing a statute that generally precludes foods containing "poisonous or deleterious" substances and that imposes even stricter standards on "food additives": such additives must be "safe," and carcinogenic food additives are flatly prohibited by the (in)famous "Delaney Clause." . . . As for the threat of cancer: there are various escape routes around the absolutism of the Delaney Clause—for example, FDA takes the position that the Clause does not apply to the nonfunctional carcinogenic constituents of additives—and in the 1970s FDA commenced a practice of quantifying the potency of certain food carcinogens. The 1 in 1 million cutoff for individual cancer risk derives from FDA practice during this period.

The widespread use of toxic risk assessment at other federal agencies began in the 1980s. This development had multiple triggers, including three apparent ones: (1) the *Industrial Union* case [excerpted at page 799 below], which forced OSHA to follow FDA's lead and, more generally, made clear that the courts would not permit federal agencies engaged in health and safety regulation to impose large costs on the regulated entities without some effort to justify such costs through a quantification of benefits, even in cases (as with OSHA) where the underlying statute was quite pro-safety; (2) the 1983 appointment, as EPA administrator, of William Ruckelshaus, who made risk assessment his top priority and actually succeeded in infusing such techniques into administrative routines throughout the large EPA bureaucracy; and (3) the publication, also in 1983, of a seminal study by the National Research Council, Risk Assessment in the Federal Government: Managing the Process (the so-called Red Book), which further popularized the practice of risk assessment and, perhaps more importantly, did much to standardize it. By the 1990s, risk assessment had become such a familiar feature of the regulatory landscape that OMB, in its guidance to federal agencies regarding Executive Order 12,866, instructed that the regulatory impact analysis required by this Executive Order prior to the issuance of major rules should include a "risk assessment":

> Estimating the benefits and costs of risk-reducing regulations [requires, inter alia,] . . . a risk assessment that . . . characterizes the probabilities of occurrence of outcomes of interest. . . .

. : . The risk assessment should generate a credible, objective, realistic, and scientifically balanced analysis; present information on hazard, dose-response, and exposure (or analogous material for non-health assessments); and explain the confidence in each assessment. . . .

So risk assessment is now standard practice for federal agencies that regulate toxins, as well as other health and safety agencies, at the major rulemaking stage. But the practice of toxic risk assessment is really much broader than that. For example, the overwhelming majority of EPA risk assessments do not involve major rules, but other categories of administrative decision, such as clean-up decisions with respect to individual Superfund sites.

The Red Book framework for toxic risk assessment has been the canonical framework since its publication and runs as follows. There are four parts to toxic risk assessment: hazard identification, dose-response assessment, exposure assessment, and risk characterization. Hazard identification is a preliminary step: the risk analyst verifies that the allegedly toxic substance is indeed a toxin, that there is sufficient evidence of a causal link to disease and death. If so, the analysis moves on to the two central parts of the risk-assessment inquiry, namely dose-response assessment and exposure assessment. Dose-response assessment means quantifying the link between different doses of the toxin and premature death. This inquiry is, in effect, *physiological*: it seeks to determine how frequently the ingestion, inhalation, or dermal uptake of the toxin, into humans' bodies, leads to cancer or other fatal illnesses. This physiological inquiry is almost always grounded in two types of data—rodent bioassays, in which the differing rates of fatal illness in groups of rodents fed different doses of the toxin are measured, and human epidemiological data—and eventuates in a dose-response curve. The X-axis of the curve represents human doses of the toxin; the Y-axis, the risk to a person exposed to that dose of dying prematurely as a result.

Exactly how to draw this curve, based on the animal or epidemiological evidence, is a technical (but important!) issue in risk assessment. While dose-response assessment [see Figure 8-3] is physiological, exposure assessment [see Figure 8-4] is

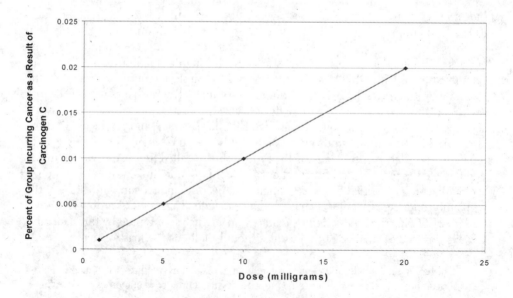

FIGURE 8-3
Dose-Response Curve for Carcinogen C

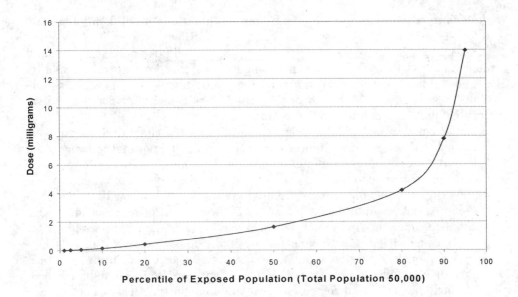

FIGURE 8-4
Exposure Assessment for Carcinogen C in Source S

topographical and *demographic*. The aim here is to characterize the pattern of exposures to the toxin that will occur under various contingencies (for regulatory purposes, as a result of different regulatory options, including the status quo option of inaction). This assessment depends on where the toxin is located; on how much toxin currently exists, and would be produced under various contingencies, at the source; on the toxin's so-called "fate and transport," i.e., how the toxin migrates through the air, the water, and other environmental pathways; and on how the human population is distributed at varying distances from the source of the toxin. What "source" means depends, of course, on the toxin and the regulatory program. It might be a single waste dump, a group of smokestacks (for example all smokestacks in factories in a given industrial category), a food type (in which case the relevant pathway is direct ingestion by food consumers), containers of hazardous workplace chemicals (in which case the relevant pathway is air transport to workers or direct worker contact with the containers), and so on. A relatively complete exposure assessment will predict the dose of the toxin that each member of the population will receive as a result of the evaluated source. Typically, members of the population will not be identified by name, but rather by their doses. That is: a relatively complete exposure assessment will produce a predicted distribution, by numbers and percentiles, of lifetime doses resulting from the analyzed source, for the status quo option of regulatory inaction and, ideally, for each regulatory contingency being assessed. . . .

The final stage of risk assessment [is] risk characterization. . . . "Risk characterization" means combining the dose-response assessment (which correlates doses and fatality risks) and the exposure assessment (which predicts doses, across the population or at least for some segment) so as to generate a prediction of the fatalities and fatality risks resulting from the toxin under various contingencies. The risk assessment jargon for total fatalities, as I have already noted, is "population risk"; the jargon for the risk of death incurred by one or another individual is "individual risk." Using the dose-response assessment and exposure assessment to predict "population risk" is somewhat laborious. In general, to do that, the analyst needs a full population distribution of doses, and even then the analyst cannot simply "read" an estimate of total deaths off the dose-response curve, but instead must use probability theory to generate a probability distribution of total deaths and then a point estimate of "population risk" equaling the mean number of total deaths.

Generating a prediction of "individual risk" is more straightforward. For example, if the analyst possesses a full or truncated exposure assessment showing the dosage of the toxin to the "maximally exposed" individual, then the "individual risk" to that person is simply the risk corresponding to that dosage given by the dose-response curve. And if the analyst possesses a full or truncated exposure assessment showing the exposure to the "representative" individual—the person at the median or mean of the dosage distribution—then the "individual risk" incurred by this "ordinary Joe" is the risk for his dosage predicted by our physiological graph, the dose-response curve. . . .

Traditionally, non-cancer and cancer risk assessments have been performed somewhat differently. Toxic effects other than cancer have been seen to have a physiological threshold. The difference, crudely, stems from the special causal mechanism for cancer—DNA damage to some cells, followed by proliferation of those cells—such that a dose so small as to be genotoxic to but a single cell might, in unfortunate circumstances, lead to fatal cancer for the organism.

Dose-response evaluation is therefore performed differently for non-cancer toxicity than for cancers. Experiments and epidemiological studies are still used to produce dose-response data points pairing doses of the toxin with incremental risks (frequencies) of death or some other adverse effect, relative to background. But instead of fitting a linear function to these data points, or some other function without a threshold, the analyst instead identifies the so-called NOAEL ("no observed adverse effect level"): the "highest tested dose at which no statistically significant elevation over background in the incidence of the adverse effect was observed." So-called safety factors are then applied to the NOAEL dose to produce a conservative estimate of the physiologically safe level. Typically, this means dividing the NOAEL dose by a factor of 10, 100, or 1000. The resultant dose, termed the "reference dose" (RfD) by EPA, is the physiologically safe dose, to a high degree of certainty: that dose, and lower doses, do not (it can be said with great confidence) produce an incremental risk of death.

This difference between the procedure for estimating non-cancer and cancer risk leads to a difference in how "individual risks" for noncarcinogens are expressed. The "individual risk" incurred by a particular person, given her exposure to a non-carcinogen, is expressed as a ratio of the dose to the RfD—not as a probability number. For example, if the RfD for the toxin is a lifetime dose of 100 grams, and the exposure assessment predicts that the maximally exposed individual will receive a lifetime dose of 25 grams, she will be ascribed an "individual risk" index of 1/4. If the exposure assessment instead predicts a maximal exposure of 200 grams, the "individual risk" index to the maximally exposed person is 2. These nonprobabilistic indices of "individual risk" are less meaningful than the probabilistic indices employed for carcinogens. All that a nonprobabilistic index number less than 1 means is this: to a high degree of certainty, the incremental fatality risk incurred by that person is zero. All that a nonprobabilistic index number greater than 1 means is the negation, namely it cannot be stated with a high degree of confidence that the individual incurs a zero incremental fatality risk. . . .

NOTES AND QUESTIONS

1. Risk assessment is the process of deciding how dangerous a substance is. It draws on a variety of disciplines, including toxicology, biostatistics, epidemiology, economics, and demography. Its objective is to ascertain the nature of the adverse effects of exposure and to produce quantitative estimates of the probability that an individual will experience those effects as a result of a specified exposure, the consequences of exposure to an entire population (i.e., the number of cases of disease or death), or both. Carnegie Commission on Science, Technology, and Government, Risk and the Environment: Improving Regulatory Decision Making, June 1993, at 76. See also Shere, The Myth of Meaningful Environmental Risk Assessment, 19 Harv. Envtl. L. Rev. 409, 412 (1995). Risk assessment serves a screening function by helping to guide regulators in making decisions on which substances and activities merit regulation. Risk management is the process of deciding what to do about an assessed risk or group of risks. Unlike traditional risk assessment, it "explicitly involves consideration of a wide range of legal, economic, political, and sociological factors." Carnegie Commission, *supra*, at 32. "The 'conventional wisdom' (which some believe needs rethinking) stresses that risk management must not influence the processes and assumptions made in risk assessment, so the two functions must be kept conceptually and administratively separate." Id. at 76.

2. What is the relationship among risk assessment, risk management, and regulation? In Flue-Cured Tobacco Coop. Stabilization Corp. v. EPA, 4 F. Supp. 2d 435 (M.D.N.C. 1998), representatives of the tobacco industry sued to invalidate an EPA report concluding that secondhand or environmental tobacco smoke (ETS) causes lung cancer in humans. They argued that issuance of the report violated the Radon Gas and Indoor Air Quality Research Act of 1986, Pub. L. No. 99-499, 100 Stat. 1758-1760 (1986), which authorizes EPA to develop a research program on indoor air pollutants, but not "to carry out any regulatory program or any activity other than research, development, and related reporting, information dissemination, and coordination activities specified in [the Act]." According to the plaintiffs, the risk assessment reflected in the report amounted to regulatory, not research, activity because under EPA's own Guidelines for Carcinogen Risk Assessment, 51 Fed. Reg. 33,992 (1986), regulatory decisionmaking involves two components — risk assessment and risk management — and because EPA had issued regulations for every other substance it had classified as a Group A human carcinogen.

The court refused to equate risk assessment with regulation. The Radon Act authorized EPA to engage in research on the effects of indoor air pollution, and "researching health effects is indistinguishable from assessing risk to health. Congress' directives to research the effects of indoor air pollution on human health and disseminate the findings encompass risk assessment. . . . " 4 F. Supp. 2d at 441-442. Although "[r]isk assessment is a component of regulation[,] . . . Congress' prohibition of regulation is not a prohibition against the components comprising regulation." Id. at 443. The Fourth Circuit later vacated the judgment, concluding that the report was not a judicially reviewable final agency action. 313 F.3d 852 (4th Cir. 2002). In the meantime, a subcommittee of the National Toxicology Program's Board of Scientific Counselors had voted unanimously to endorse the conclusion that ETS is carcinogenic. Subsequent studies have found correlations between exposure to ETS and increased cardiovascular mortality and dementia. See, e.g., Chen et al., Association Between Environmental Tobacco Smoke Exposure and Dementia Syndromes, 70 Occupational and Envtl. Med. 63 (2012).

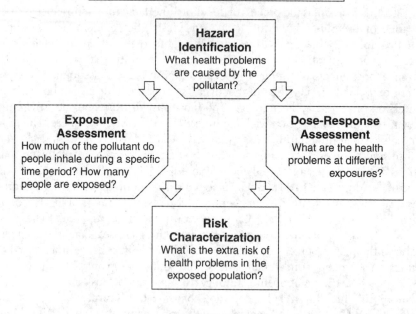

FIGURE 8-5
What Is Risk Assessment?

3. In response to a request by EPA to improve risk analysis approaches, the National Research Council issued a report, Science and Decisions: Advancing Risk Assessment (2010) (referred to as the Silver Book). The NRC asserted that risk assessment "is at a crossroads, and its credibility is being challenged." Id. at 3. It added that the risk assessment process is bogged down (assessments for some chemicals take more than ten years), as is decisionmaking based on risk assessment. It urged retention of the approach to risk assessment reflected in the Red Book, which is referred to in the Adler excerpt. But it recommended using risk assessment to evaluate the relative merits of risk management options rather than as an end in itself. Agencies therefore should pose the risk management questions that risk assessment will address before engaging in risk assessment. In particular, the report recommended a three-step framework for risk-based decisionmaking: (1) enhanced problem formulation and scoping, in which available risk management options are identified; (2) planning and assessment, using the traditional four-step risk assessment process described in the Red Book (and depicted in Figure 8-5) to determine risks under existing conditions and potential risk management options; and (3) risk management, involving integration of risk and nonrisk information to inform choices among policy options. That approach has the potential to increase the influence of risk assessment on decisions because it entails more front-end planning to ensure that risk assessment is relevant to the regulatory issues being addressed. Does it, however, also subject risk assessments to greater political manipulation? The NRC noted concerns about political interference in risk assessment, but indicated that its revised approach maintains the conceptual distinction between risk assessment and risk management. It nevertheless stated that it is "imperative that risk assessments used to evaluate risk-management options not be inappropriately influenced by the preferences of risk managers." Id. at 12.

4. In 2005, EPA revised its risk assessment guidelines for exposure to carcinogens:

ENVIRONMENTAL PROTECTION AGENCY, NOTICE OF AVAILABILITY; DOCUMENTS ENTITLED GUIDELINES FOR CARCINOGEN RISK ASSESSMENT AND SUPPLEMENTAL GUIDANCE FOR ASSESSING SUSCEPTIBILITY FROM EARLY-LIFE EXPOSURE TO CARCINOGENS
70 Fed. Reg. 17,766 (2005)

In the 1983 Risk Assessment in the Federal Government: Managing the Process, the National Academy of Sciences recommended that Federal regulatory agencies establish "inference guidelines" to promote consistency and technical quality in risk assessment, and to ensure that the risk assessment process is maintained as a scientific effort separate from risk management. A task force within EPA accepted that recommendation and requested that EPA scientists begin to develop such guidelines. [These guidelines replace those published by EPA in 1986.]

Features of the Guidelines

Use of default options—Default options are approaches that EPA can apply in risk assessments when scientific information about the effects of an agent on human health is unavailable, limited, or of insufficient quality. Under the final Guidelines, EPA's approach begins with a critical analysis of available information, and then invokes defaults if needed to address uncertainty or the absence of critical information.

Consideration of mode of action—Cancer refers to a group of diseases involving abnormal, malignant tissue growth. Research has revealed that the development of cancer involves a complex series of steps and that carcinogens may operate in a number of different ways. The final Guidelines emphasize the value of understanding the biological changes and how these changes might lead to the development of cancer. They also discuss ways to evaluate and use such information, including information about an agent's postulated mode of action [MOA], or the series of steps and processes that lead to cancer formation. Mode-of-action data, when available and of sufficient quality, may be used to draw conclusions about the potency of a chemical, its potential effects at low doses, whether findings in animals are relevant to humans, and which populations or lifestages may be particularly susceptible.

Fuller characterization of carcinogenic potential—In the final Guidelines, an agent's human carcinogenic potential is described in a weight-of-evidence narrative. The narrative summarizes the full range of available evidence and describes any conditions associated with conclusions about an agent's hazard potential. For example, the narrative may explain that a chemical appears to be carcinogenic by some routes of exposure but not by others (e.g., by inhalation but not ingestion). Similarly, a hazard may be attributed to exposures during sensitive life-stages of development but not at other times. The narrative also summarizes uncertainties and key default options that have been invoked. . . .

Consideration of differences in susceptibility—The Guidelines explicitly recognize that variation may exist among people in their susceptibility to carcinogens. Some subpopulations may experience increased susceptibility to carcinogens throughout their life, such as people who have inherited predisposition to certain cancer types or reduced capacity to repair genetic damage. Also, during certain lifestages the entire population may experience heightened susceptibility to carcinogens. In particular, EPA notes that childhood may be a lifestage of greater susceptibility for a number of reasons: rapid growth and development that occurs prenatally and after birth, differences related to an immature metabolic system, and differences in diet and behavior patterns that may increase exposure. . . .

Risk Assessment Guidelines at EPA . . .

1.3.   KEY FEATURES OF THE CANCER GUIDELINES

1.3.1.   CRITICAL ANALYSIS OF AVAILABLE INFORMATION AS THE STARTING POINT FOR EVALUATION

As an increasing understanding of carcinogenesis is becoming available, these cancer guidelines adopt a view of default options that is consistent with EPA's mission to protect human health while adhering to the tenets of sound science. Rather than viewing default options as the starting point from which departures may be justified by new scientific information, these cancer guidelines view a critical analysis of all of the available information that is relevant to assessing the carcinogenic risk as the starting point from which a default option may be invoked if needed to address uncertainty or the absence of critical information. . . . The primary goal of EPA actions is protection of human health; accordingly, as an Agency policy, risk assessment procedures, including default options that are used in the absence of scientific data to the contrary, should be health protective.

Use of health-protective risk assessment procedures as described in these cancer guidelines means that estimates, while uncertain, are more likely to overstate than understate hazard and/or risk. [The National Research Council (NRC)] reaffirmed the use of default options as "a reasonable way to cope with uncertainty about the choice of appropriate models or theory." . . .

Encouraging risk assessors to be receptive to new scientific information, NRC discussed the need for departures from default options when a "sufficient showing" is made. . . . NRC envisioned that principles for choosing and departing from default options would balance several objectives, including "protecting the public health, ensuring scientific validity, minimizing serious errors in estimating risks, maximizing incentives for research, creating an orderly and predictable process, and fostering openness and trustworthiness." . . .

The basis for invoking a default option depends on the circumstances. Generally, if a gap in basic understanding exists or if agent-specific information is missing, a default option may be used. If agent-specific information is present but critical analysis reveals inadequacies, a default option may also be used. . . .

In the absence of sufficient data or understanding to develop . . . a robust, biologically based model, an appropriate policy choice is to have a single preferred curve-fitting model for each type of data set. Many different curve-fitting models have been developed, and those that fit the observed data reasonably well may lead to several-fold differences in estimated risk at the lower end of the observed range. In addition, goodness-of-fit to the experimental observations is not by itself an effective means of discriminating among models that adequately fit the data. To provide some measure of consistency across different carcinogen assessments, EPA uses a standard curve-fitting procedure for tumor incidence data. Assessments that include a different approach should provide an adequate justification and compare their results with those from the standard procedure. Application of models to data should be conducted in an open and transparent manner.

1.3.2. MODE OF ACTION

The use of mode of action[3] in the assessment of potential carcinogens is a main focus of these cancer guidelines. This area of emphasis arose because of the significant scientific advances that have developed concerning the causes of cancer induction. . . . Significant information should be developed to ensure that a scientifically justifiable mode of action underlies the process leading to cancer at a given site. In the absence of sufficiently, scientifically justifiable mode of action information, EPA generally takes public health–protective, default positions regarding the interpretation of toxicologic and epidemiologic data: Animal tumor findings are judged to be relevant to humans, and cancer risks are assumed to conform with low dose linearity.

Understanding of mode of action can be a key to identifying processes that may cause chemical exposures to differentially affect a particular population segment or lifestage. Some modes of action are anticipated to be mutagenic and are assessed with a linear approach. This is the mode of action of radiation and several other agents that are known carcinogens. Other modes of action may be modeled with either linear or nonlinear[4] approaches after a rigorous analysis of available data under the guidance provided in the framework for mode of action analysis.

1.3.3. WEIGHT OF EVIDENCE NARRATIVE

The cancer guidelines emphasize the importance of weighing all of the evidence in reaching conclusions about the human carcinogenic potential of agents. This is accomplished in a single integrative step after assessing all of the individual lines of evidence, which is in contrast to the step-wise approach in the 1986 cancer guidelines. Evidence considered includes tumor findings, or lack thereof, in humans and laboratory animals; an agent's chemical and physical properties; its structure-activity

3. The term "mode of action" is defined as a sequence of key events and processes, starting with interaction of an agent with a cell, proceeding through operational and anatomical changes, and resulting in cancer formation. A "key event" is an empirically observable precursor step that is itself a necessary element of the mode of action or is a biologically based marker for such an element. Mode of action is contrasted with "mechanism of action," which implies a more detailed understanding and description of events, often at the molecular level, than is meant by mode of action. . . . There are many examples of possible modes of carcinogenic action, such as mutagenicity, mitogenesis, inhibition of cell death, cytotoxicity with reparative cell proliferation, and immune suppression.

4. The term "nonlinear" is used here in a narrower sense than its usual meaning in the field of mathematical modeling. In these cancer guidelines, the term "nonlinear" refers to threshold models (which show no response over a range of low doses that include zero) and some nonthreshold models (e.g., a quadractic model, which shows some response at all doses above zero). . . . Use of nonlinear approaches does not imply a biological threshold dose below which the response is zero. Estimating thresholds can be problematic; for example, a response that is not statistically significant can be consistent with a small risk that falls below an experiment's power of detection.

relationships (SARs) as compared with other carcinogenic agents; and studies addressing potential carcinogenic processes and mode(s) of action, either *in vivo* or *in vitro*. Data from epidemiologic studies are generally preferred for characterizing human cancer hazard and risk. However, all of the information discussed above could provide valuable insights into the possible mode(s) of action and likelihood of human cancer hazard and risk. . . .

The weight of evidence narrative to characterize hazard summarizes the results of the hazard assessment and provides a conclusion with regard to human carcinogenic potential. The narrative explains the kinds of evidence available and how they fit together in drawing conclusions, and it points out significant issues/strengths/limitations of the data and conclusions. Because the narrative also summarizes the mode of action information, it sets the stage for the discussion of the rationale underlying a recommended approach to dose-response assessment.

In order to provide some measure of clarity and consistency in an otherwise free-form, narrative characterization, standard descriptors are used as part of the hazard narrative to express the conclusion regarding the weight of evidence for carcinogenic hazard potential. There are five recommended standard hazard descriptors: *"Carcinogenic to Humans," "Likely to Be Carcinogenic to Humans," "Suggestive Evidence of Carcinogenic Potential," "Inadequate Information to Assess Carcinogenic Potential,"* and *"Not Likely to Be Carcinogenic to Humans."* . . .

1.3.5.   SUSCEPTIBLE POPULATIONS AND LIFESTAGES

An important use of mode of action information is to identify susceptible populations and lifestages. It is rare to have epidemiologic studies or animal bioassays conducted in susceptible individuals. This information need can be filled by identifying the key events of the mode of action and then identifying risk factors, such as differences due to genetic polymorphisms, disease, altered organ function, lifestyle, and lifestage, that can augment these key events. . . .

2. Hazard Assessment

2.1.   OVERVIEW OF HAZARD ASSESSMENT AND CHARACTERIZATION

2.1.1.   ANALYSES OF DATA

The purpose of hazard assessment is to review and evaluate data pertinent to two questions: (1) Whether an agent may pose a carcinogenic hazard to human beings, and (2) under what circumstances an identified hazard may be expressed. Hazard assessment involves analyses of a variety of data that may range from observations of tumor responses to analysis of structure-activity relationships (SARs). . . .

2.2.   ANALYSIS OF TUMOR DATA

Evidence of carcinogenicity comes from finding tumor increases in humans or laboratory animals exposed to a given agent or from finding tumors following exposure to structural analogues to the compound under review. The significance of observed or anticipated tumor effects is evaluated in reference to all the other key data on the agent. . . .

2.2.1. HUMAN DATA

Human data may come from epidemiologic studies or case reports. . . . The most common sources of human data for cancer risk assessment are epidemiologic investigations. Epidemiology is the study of the distribution of disease in human populations and the factors that may influence that distribution. The goals of cancer epidemiology are to identify distribution of cancer risk and determine the extent to which the risk can be attributed causally to specific exposures to exogenous or endogenous factors. Epidemiologic data are extremely valuable in risk assessment because they provide direct evidence on whether a substance is likely to produce cancer in humans, thereby avoiding issues such as: species-to-species inference, extrapolation to exposures relevant to people, [and] effects of concomitant exposures due to lifestyles. Thus, epidemiologic studies typically evaluate agents under more relevant conditions. When human data of high quality and adequate statistical power are available, they are generally preferable over animal data and should be given greater weight in hazard characterization and dose-response assessment, although both can be used.

Null results from epidemiologic studies alone generally do not prove the absence of carcinogenic effects because such results can arise either from an agent being truly not carcinogenic or from other factors such as: inadequate statistical power, inadequate study design, imprecise estimates, or confounding factors. . . . [But] data from a well designed and well conducted epidemiologic study that does not show positive results, in conjunction with compelling mechanistic information, can lend support to a conclusion that animal responses may not be predictive of a human cancer hazard.

2.2.2. ANIMAL DATA

Various whole-animal test systems are currently used or are under development for evaluating potential carcinogenicity. Cancer studies involving chronic exposure for most of the lifespan of an animal are generally accepted for evaluation of tumor effects (. . . but see Ames and Gold, 1990). . . . Other studies of special design are useful for observing formation of preneoplastic lesions or tumors or investigating specific modes of action. Their applicability is determined on a case-by-case basis.

2.2.2.1. Long-Term Carcinogenicity Studies

The objective of long-term carcinogenesis bioassays is to determine the potential carcinogenic hazard and dose-response relationships of the test agent. Carcinogenicity rodent studies are designed to examine the production of tumors as well as preneoplastic lesions and other indications of chronic toxicity. . . . Current standardized carcinogenicity studies in rodents test at least 50 animals per sex per dose group in each of three treatment groups and in a concurrent control group, usually for 18 to 24 months, depending on the rodent species tested. The high dose in long-term studies is generally selected to provide the maximum ability to detect treatment-related carcinogenic effects while not compromising the outcome of the study through excessive toxicity or inducing inappropriate toxicokinetics (e.g., overwhelming absorption or detoxification mechanisms). The purpose of two or more lower doses is to provide some information on the shape of the dose-response curve. . . .

2.2.2.1.1.   *Dosing Issues*

With regard to the appropriateness of the high dose, an adequate high dose would generally be one that produces some toxic effects without unduly affecting mortality from effects other than cancer or producing significant adverse effects on the nutrition and health of the test animals. . . .

2.2.3.   STRUCTURAL ANALOGUE DATA

For some chemical classes, there is significant available information, largely from rodent bioassays, on the carcinogenicity of analogues. Analogue effects are instructive in investigating carcinogenic potential of an agent as well as in identifying potential target organs, exposures associated with effects, and potential functional class effects or modes of action. . . . Confidence in conclusions is a function of how similar the analogues are to the agent under review in structure, metabolism, and biological activity. It is important to consider this confidence to ensure a balanced position. . . .

2.3.5.   EVENTS RELEVANT TO MODE OF CARCINOGENIC ACTION

Knowledge of the biochemical and biological changes that precede tumor development (which include, but are not limited to, mutagenesis, increased cell proliferation, inhibition of programmed cell death, and receptor activation) may provide important insight for determining whether a cancer hazard exists and may help inform appropriate consideration of the dose-response relationship below the range of observable tumor response. Because cancer can result from a series of genetic alterations in the genes that control cell growth, division, and differentiation, the ability of an agent to affect genotype (and hence gene products) or gene expression is of obvious importance in evaluating its influence on the carcinogenic process. . . .

Furthermore, carcinogenesis involves a complex series and interplay of events that alter the signals a cell receives from its extracellular environment, thereby promoting uncontrolled growth. Many, but not all, mutagens are carcinogens, and some, but not all, agents that induce cell proliferation lead to tumor development. Thus, understanding the range of key steps in the carcinogenic process upon which an agent might act is essential for evaluating its mode of action. . . .

2.4.   MODE OF ACTION—GENERAL CONSIDERATIONS AND FRAMEWORK FOR ANALYSIS

2.4.1.   GENERAL CONSIDERATIONS

The interaction between the biology of the organism and the chemical properties of the agent determine whether there is an adverse effect. Thus, mode of action analysis is based on physical, chemical, and biological information that helps to explain key events in an agent's influence on development of tumors. . . .

Information for mode of action analysis generally includes tumor data in humans and animals and among structural analogues, as well as the other key data. The more complete the data package and the generic knowledge about a given mode of action, the more confidence one has and the more one can rely on assessment of available data rather than reverting to default options to address the absence of information on mode of action. . . . Many times there will be conflicting data and gaps in the information base; it is important to carefully evaluate these uncertainties before reaching any conclusion. . . .

3. Dose-Response Assessment . . .

3.3.1. CHOOSING AN EXTRAPOLATION APPROACH

The approach for extrapolation below the observed data considers the understanding of the agent's mode of action at each tumor site. Mode of action information can suggest the likely shape of the dose-response curve at lower doses. The extent of inter-individual variation is also considered, with greater variation spreading the response over a wider range of doses.

Linear extrapolation should be used when there are MOA data to indicate that the dose-response curve is expected to have a linear component below the [point of departure (POD)]. . . .

When the weight of evidence evaluation of all available data are insufficient to establish the mode of action for a tumor site and when scientifically plausible based on the available data, linear extrapolation is used as a default approach, because linear extrapolation generally is considered to be a health-protective approach. Non-linear approaches generally should not be used in cases where the mode of action has not been ascertained. Where alternative approaches with significant biological support are available for the same tumor response and no scientific consensus favors a single approach, an assessment may present results based on more than one approach.

A *nonlinear approach* should be selected when there are sufficient data to ascertain the mode of action and conclude that it is not linear at low doses and the agent does not demonstrate mutagenic or other activity consistent with linearity at low doses. . . .

3.3.2. EXTRAPOLATION USING A LOW-DOSE, LINEAR MODEL

Linear extrapolation should be used in two distinct circumstances: (1) when there are data to indicate that the dose-response curve has a linear component below the POD, or (2) as a default for a tumor site where the mode of action is not established. For linear extrapolation, a line should be drawn from the POD to the origin, corrected for background. This implies a proportional (linear) relationship between risk and dose at low doses. (Note that the dose-response curve generally is not linear at higher doses.) . . .

3.3.3. NONLINEAR EXTRAPOLATION TO LOWER DOSES

A nonlinear extrapolation method can be used for cases with sufficient data to ascertain the mode of action and to conclude that it is not linear at low doses but with not enough data to support a toxicodynamic model that may be either nonlinear or linear at low doses. Nonlinear extrapolation having a significant biological support may be presented in addition to a linear approach when the available data and a weight of evidence evaluation support a nonlinear approach, but the data are not strong enough to ascertain the mode of action applying the Agency's mode of action framework. If the mode of action and other information can support chemical-specific modeling at low doses, it is preferable to default procedures. . . .

3.4.   EXTRAPOLATION TO DIFFERENT HUMAN EXPOSURE SCENARIOS

. . . [S]pecial problems arise when the human exposure situation of concern suggests exposure regimens, e.g., route and dosing schedule, that are substantially different from those used in the relevant animal studies. Unless there is evidence to the contrary in a particular case, the cumulative dose received over a lifetime, expressed as average daily exposure prorated over a lifetime, is recommended as an appropriate measure of exposure to a carcinogen. That is, the assumption is made that a high dose of a carcinogen received over a short period of time is equivalent to a corresponding low dose spread over a lifetime. This approach becomes more problematical as the exposures in question become more intense but less frequent, especially when there is evidence that the agent has shown dose-rate effects. . . .

NOTES AND QUESTIONS

1. *Competing Theories of Cancer Causation.* Theories about the causes of cancer have changed over time, with scientists pointing to viruses, environmental exposure to industrial chemicals, and lifestyle and diet as the major determinants of cancer incidence. Table 8-1 presents one effort, published in 1981, to quantify the role of these causes. See also Trichopoulos et al., What Causes Cancer?, Sci. Am. (Sept. 1996), at 80 (noting view that environmental exposure is responsible for no more than two percent of annual cancer deaths). The President's Cancer Panel, Reducing Environmental Cancer Risk 2 (April 2010), characterized the figures in Table 8-1 as "woefully out of date, given our current understanding of cancer. . . ." It concluded that the fractions of the cancer burden attributed to occupation and industrial products significantly understate the percentage of cancers related to those exposures. The study summarized in Table 8-1 also failed to account for the interactions between multiple environmental contaminants and between those contaminants and avoidable causes of cancer. Efforts to link cancer to a cause illustrate the need to analyze environmental regulatory questions in the context of what Talbot Page called ignorance of mechanism. In this case, the stakes are high: according to the 2010 report, about 21 million Americans die from cancer each year. The 2010 report recommended strengthening the regulations that control workplace and environmental exposure to carcinogenic substances. Many occupational correlations exist—for example, mesothelioma (cancer of the lung lining) with asbestos, angiosarcoma (liver cancer) with polyvinylchloride, and leukemia with benzene.[a] What position did EPA take in its 2005 guidelines on the different risks facing sensitive subpopulations and the general population?

---

a. See, e.g., Freeman et al., Mortality from Lymphohematopoietic Malignancies Among Workers in Formaldehyde Industries: The National Cancer Institute Cohort, 101 J. Nat'l Cancer Inst. 751 (May 20, 2009) (discussing possible link between formaldehyde exposure and leukemia).

TABLE 8-1
Cancer Deaths in the United States

Attribution	Percent
Diet	35
Tobacco	30
Infection (speculative)	10
Sexual/reproductive behavior	7
Occupational	4
Alcohol	3
Geophysical (sunlight, radiation)	3
Pollution	2
Other and unknown	6

Source: Based on Doll & Peto, The Causes of Cancer: Quantitative Estimates of Avoidable Risks of Cancer in the United States Today, 66 J. Nat'l Cancer Inst (1981).

The American Cancer Society assessed the causes of cancer in the U.S. in 2012 as follows:

> Exposure to carcinogenic agents in occupational, community, and other settings is thought to account for a relatively small percentage of cancer deaths—about 4% from occupational exposures and 2% from environmental pollutants (man-made and naturally occurring). Although the estimated percentage of cancers related to occupational and environmental carcinogens is small compared to the cancer burden from tobacco smoking (30%) and the combination of poor nutrition, physical inactivity, and obesity (35%), the relationship between such agents and cancer is important for several reasons. First, even a small percentage of cancers can represent many deaths: 6% of cancer deaths in the US in 2011 correspond to approximately 34,320 deaths. Second, the burden of exposure to occupational and environmental carcinogens is borne disproportionately by lower-income workers and communities, contributing to disparities in the cancer burden across the US population. Third, although much is known about the relationship between occupational and environmental exposure and cancer, some important research questions remain. These include the role of exposures to certain classes of chemicals (such as hormonally active agents) during critical periods of human development and the potential for pollutants to interact with each other, as well as with genetic and acquired factors.

American Cancer Society, Cancer Facts and Figures 2012, at 51 (2012). Compare Parkin et al., 105 British J. of Cancer S77 (2011) (concluding that one-third of all cancers in the United Kingdom are caused by common lifestyle factors (tobacco, diet, alcohol, and obesity).

Some argue that genetic susceptibility justifies more stringent regulation to protect target populations—if they can be scientifically and ethically identified. Defective genes may be inherited or healthy genes may be subject to damage by external forces, such as exposure to sunlight or chemicals, which tends to accumulate over time. According to Professor Tarlock,

> [M]odern genetic theory suggests that cancer is in part caused by the genetic susceptibility of individuals. In short, cancer is more likely to be the result of multiple hits rather than a single hit as previously assumed. But, the one-hit hypothesis may still be valid in some circumstances. [Tarlock, Is There a There There in Environmental Law?, 19 J. Land Use & Envtl. L. 213, 247-248 (2004).]

Scientists assert that they have begun to better understand cancer's mechanisms of action. In Tozzi v. U.S. Dep't of Health and Human Servs. 271 F.3d 301 (D.C. Cir. 2001), the court rejected the claim that the Department of Health and Human Services and the National Institute of Environmental Health Sciences erroneously relied on mechanistic evidence (evidence of the actual biochemical processes by which a substance causes cancer) in upgrading dioxin from a chemical that is reasonably anticipated to be a human carcinogen to one that is known to be a human carcinogen under the National Toxicology Program's biennial Report on Carcinogens, published under the Public Health Service Act.

2. *The Role of Smoking.* Smoking is by far the single most important preventable cause of death in the United States and the leading cause of death by cancer in both sexes. "[T]obacco kills more people every year than alcohol, illicit drugs, automobile accidents, violent crime, and AIDS combined." Hanson & Logue, The Costs of Cigarettes: The Economic Case for Ex Post Incentive-Based Regulation, 107 Yale L.J. 1163, 1167 (1998). Tobacco smoke, which causes genetic mutations, contains numerous chemical carcinogens. According to the American Cancer Society, tobacco use is responsible for nearly one in five deaths in the U.S. (about 443,000 premature deaths each year). "[A]n estimated 8.6 million people suffer from chronic conditions related to smoking, such as chronic bronchitis, emphysema, and cardiovascular diseases. Smoking accounts for at least 30% of all cancer deaths and 80% of lung cancer deaths." American Cancer Society, Cancer Facts and Figures 2012, at 36 (2012). Smoking also has been linked to Lou Gehrig's disease, diabetes, arthritis, impaired immune function, and ectopic pregnancy, among other conditions. See Wang et al., Smoking and Risk of Amyotrophic Lateral Sclerosis, 68 Archives of Neurology 207 (2011); Tavernise, List of Smoking-Related Illnesses Grows Significantly in U.S. Report, N.Y. Times, Jan. 17, 2014.

As noted above, exposed nonsmokers are at risk. In 1992, EPA classified secondhand smoke (also known as environmental tobacco smoke, or ETS) as a human carcinogen. The Surgeon General of the United States reported in 2006 that ETS "has immediate adverse effects on the cardiovascular system and causes coronary heart disease and lung cancer," and that there is no risk-free level of exposure to it. Segregation of smokers and nonsmokers does not eliminate the risk; only complete elimination of indoor smoking fully protects nonsmokers.[b] The World Health Organization reported that more than 600,000 deaths annually worldwide are caused by passive smoking (one percent of all deaths) and that around 165,000 of those killed are children. See Oberg et al., Worldwide Burden of Disease from Exposure to Secondhand Smoke: A Retrospective Analysis of Data from 192 Countries, 37 The Lancet 139 (Jan. 2011). Even tobacco smoke that lingers on furniture and clothing (thirdhand smoke) may react with indoor air pollution to form potential carcinogens.

3. *The Role of Diet.* Some scientists contend that the human body is awash in naturally occurring carcinogens and mutagens. See, e.g., Ames, Dietary Carcinogens and Anticarcinogens, 221 Science 1256, 1258 (1983). Foods may also play a positive role, however. Cancer is thwarted by natural cell repair mechanisms and cancer-inhibiting chemicals in common foods that contain vitamin E, carotene, selenium, and ascorbic and uric acids. Id. at 1259. Certain foods can increase the activity of enzymes that convert chemicals to carcinogens, while other foods inactivate enzymes

b. See Department of Health and Human Services, The Health Consequences of Involuntary Exposure to Tobacco Smoke (2006).

that detoxify chemicals. Some researchers advocate increased consumption of fruits, vegetables, antioxidants, and fiber and decreased consumption of fat (along with not smoking) as the best way to reduce cancer risks.[c] Nelson et al., Alcohol-Attributable Cancer Deaths and Years of Potential Life Lost in the United States, 103 Am. J. on Pub. Health 641 (Apr. 2013), concluded that alcohol is a major contributor to cancer mortality, that higher consumption increases risk, but that there is no safe threshold for alcohol and cancer risk.

Richard Merrill, former General Counsel of the FDA, suggested shifting the emphasis from the regulation of dietary carcinogens to requiring labels on foods that cannot practically be eliminated from the diet. Merrill, Reducing Diet-Induced Cancer Through Federal Regulation: Opportunities and Obstacles, 38 Vand. L. Rev. 513 (1985). Are there any legal obstacles to regulation requiring information disclosure? See Philip Morris, Inc. v. Reilly, 312 F.3d 24 (1st Cir. 2002) (analyzing whether state statute requiring tobacco product manufacturers to report for potential public disclosure the constituents of each brand effected an unconstitutional taking). What about the First Amendment? R.J. Reynolds Tobacco Co. v. FDA, 696 F.3d 1205 (D.C. Cir. 2012), invalidated FDA regulations adopted pursuant to the Family Smoking Prevention and Tobacco Control Act, Pub. L. No. 111-31, 123 Stat. 1776 (2009), which required tobacco companies to include on their packaging color graphics and textual warnings about the risks of smoking. The court concluded that the First Amendment requires the government to show both a substantial interest justifying a regulation on commercial speech and that its regulation directly advances that goal. The FDA "failed to present any data—much less the substantial evidence required under the APA—showing that enacting their proposed graphic warnings will accomplish the agency's stated objective of reducing smoking rates." Id. at 1222.

4. *The Role of Exercise.* Exercise and weight also may affect cancer risk. Stewart et al., Forecasting the Effects of Obesity and Smoking on U.S. Life Expectancy, 361 New Eng. J. Med. 2252 (Dec. 3, 2009), concluded that the negative effects of increasing body mass index were overwhelming the positive effects of smoking declines in the U.S. The American Cancer Society estimates that about one-third of U.S. cancer deaths can be traced to "poor nutrition, physical inactivity, and excess weight. Maintaining a healthy body weight, being physically active on a regular basis, and eating a healthy diet are as important as not using tobacco products in reducing cancer risk." Cancer Facts and Figures 2012, *supra*, at 48. See also Eheman et al., Annual Report to the Nation on the Status of Cancer, 1975-2008, Featuring Cancers Associated with Excess Weight and Lack of Sufficient Physical Activity, 118 Cancer 2338 (May 1, 2012).

5. *Competing Cancer Reduction Strategies.* What do the previous notes suggest should be the prevailing strategy for reducing cancer mortality in the United States? Should the focus of regulation shift to dietary and other lifestyle choices? Do the data

c. Ames & Gold, Too Many Rodent Carcinogens: Mitogenesis Increases Mutagenesis, 249 Science 970 (1990). See also Key et al., Cancer Incidence in British Vegetarians, 101 Brit. J. Cancer 192 (2009) (finding that the incidence of some cancers may be lower in fish eaters and vegetarians than in meat eaters). Compare Kolata, Which of These Foods Will Stop Cancer? (Not So Fast), N.Y. Times, Sept. 27, 2005, at D1 (stating that "scientists say they really do not know whether dietary changes will make a difference" and that "[i]t is turning out to be much more difficult than anyone expected to discover if diet affects cancer risk. Hypotheses abound, but convincing evidence remains elusive.").

suggest that regulators should reexamine their assumption that no threshold dose exists for regulated carcinogens? Is it possible to conduct meaningful cancer risk assessments in light of the data? For one view, see generally Calabrese & Blain, A Single Exposure to Many Carcinogens Can Cause Cancer, 28 Envtl. L. Rep. 10254 (1998).

6. *Good Science, Bad Science, and Ignorance of Mechanism.* The critics of prevailing methodologies have claimed that government officials misuse science to bolster predetermined positions and that the public overreacts to environmental health threats because the government rarely explains them properly. Professor Tarlock noted the hope of some that "good science" would provide objective criteria for making regulatory decisions about toxic risks. He argued, however, that science is often so uncertain that it provides inadequate guidance to legislatures and agencies engaged in risk assessment and risk management. As a result, "the questions are framed as scientific questions when they are actually scientifically informed value judgments. Scientists are pushed to give answers to questions that are framed as positive or verifiable, but the questions are normative because a decision must be made before acceptable verification procedures can be followed." Tarlock, The Non-Equilibrium Paradigm in Ecology and the Partial Unraveling of Environmental Law, 27 Loy. L.A. L. Rev. 1121, 1133-1134 (1994).

7. *Framing the Issues.* Consider the following questions as you move through this chapter and the next: To what extent will economic markets and common law liability provide sufficient incentives to keep hazardous substances in check? Would changes in the common law have to be made (e.g., in allocation of the burden of proof, statutes of limitations, the standard of liability, and causation requirements) to render common law actions a sufficient mechanism for controlling exposure to toxic substances? Should regulatory decisions depend on whether risks, injuries, and other costs exceed the benefits of further use of the toxic substance in question? Should the burden rest on the agency to prove risk, or should an agency be able to require that a suspect substance be strictly contained or removed from commerce pending a demonstration that satisfies the agency that the substance is safe?

NOTE ON ANIMAL TEST METHODOLOGIES AND CANCER RISK ASSESSMENTS

Animal Tests. The insufficiency of data (particularly epidemiological data) concerning the risks of exposure to carcinogens at commonly experienced low levels, coupled with insufficient understanding of the etiology of carcinogenesis, creates the need for the controversial risk assessment default assumptions. Federal regulation relies overwhelmingly on rodent bioassay data. To demonstrate low-level cancer risk, regulators have to somehow extrapolate from the high-dose region of the dose-response curve of an actual animal experiment, where tumor rates run 5 to 50 percent, to the low-dose region of a hypothetical human dose-response curve, where there is a projected incidence of one cancer per 100 thousand to 100 million people. This process is probably the "most contentious judgment in carcinogen risk assessment." Rosenthal et al., Legislating Acceptable Cancer Risk from Exposure to Toxic Chemicals, 19 Ecology L.Q. 269, 287 (1992). The cancer risks found by applying different extrapolation models to the same animal bioassay data can differ by a factor of 100,000 in terms of the dose size that creates a risk of one cancer per million subjects. See Figure 8-6.

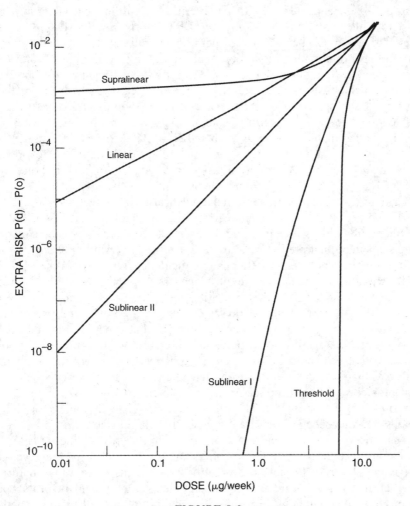

FIGURE 8-6
Results of Alternative Extrapolation Models for the Same Experimental Data

Some scientists are not willing to accept the chain of inferences upon which a conclusion that a substance is carcinogenic to humans depends—animal evidence, large-dose experiments, the one-hit no-threshold theory, and so on.[d] Other scientists question the premises reflected in the linear, no-threshold model that some risk is present at all levels of exposure above zero, and that the risk estimates at low levels should be calculated by linear extrapolation from observed data at higher doses. See, e.g., Goldman, Cancer Risk of Low-Level Exposure (Chemical and Radiation

---

d. For example, some scientists question the legitimacy of using rodent bioassays to assess cancer risks to humans. Bender, Societal Risk Reduction: Promise and Pitfalls, 3 N.Y.U. Envtl. L.J. 255, 290 n.158 (1995). See also Baxter Healthcare Corp. v. Denton, 15 Cal. Rptr. 3d 430 (Cal. Ct. App. 2004) (upholding trial court's judgment declaring that chemical plasticizer contained in medical devices posed no significant risk of causing cancer in humans, even though it was undisputed that the substance causes liver cancer in rats and mice, because a preponderance of the evidence demonstrated that the biological mechanism by which the substance causes liver cancer in laboratory animals does not function in humans).

Exposure), 271 Science 1821 (1996). Such criticisms can prove troublesome to regulators. In Chlorine Chemistry Council v. EPA, 206 F.3d 1285 (D.C. Cir. 2000), excerpted in section E.3 below, industry petitioners challenged EPA's decision to set a zero-level maximum contaminant level goal under the Safe Drinking Water Act for chloroform, even though the agency conceded that recent evidence supported the conclusions that there is a safe threshold level of exposure to that chemical and that the chloroform dose-response curve should be considered nonlinear. The court vacated EPA's action on the ground that it was inconsistent with its obligation to act on the basis of the best available evidence. Compare Schultz v. Akzo Nobel Paints, LLC, 721 F.3d 426 (7th Cir. 2013), which reversed a trial judge's decision in a toxic tort case to exclude an oncologist's expert testimony on the ground that the "no threshold" theory, which the expert endorsed, is "merely a hypothesis."

Critics of extrapolation from animal test data also charge that high-dose testing is flawed. Exposure of test animals to massive or maximum tolerated doses (MTDs) may cause cell proliferation, which itself increases the risk of cell mutation and cancer, and of toxic side effects that predispose animals to cancers that would not occur at lower doses. It is therefore not clear whether cancer incidence in test animals is attributable to the inherent carcinogenicity of the substance tested or to the use of MTDs. Ames & Gold, Too Many Rodent Carcinogens: Mitogenesis Increases Mutagenesis, 249 Science 970 (1990). Most scientists, however, support the continued use of animal bioassays because, in the absence of epidemiological data, they are the best available method of assessing carcinogenic potential, their results are representative of the results of workplace exposures, and their usefulness has been verified: all chemicals known to induce cancer in humans that have been studied under adequate experimental protocols also have induced cancer in laboratory animals. See, e.g., Baxter Healthcare Corp. v. Denton, 15 Cal. Rptr. 3d 430, 435 (Cal. Ct. App. 2004) ("There is a 'broad scientific acceptance of the inference that carcinogenicity in other animals means carcinogenicity in humans.'"). Supporters of linearity, including EPA, assert that it has been validated in studies of both humans and rodents and that, even if this model is not strictly defensible on scientific grounds, its conservative nature can compensate for unknown differences between rodents and humans and protect potentially sensitive subpopulations. Finkel, A Second Opinion on an Environmental Misdiagnosis: The Risky Prescriptions of Breaking the Vicious Circle, 3 N.Y.U. Envtl. L.J. 295, 342 (1995); Rosenthal et al., supra, at 287-289.

Nevertheless, some courts continue to be skeptical of the relevance of animal test results to assessments of human disease risk, at least in the context of toxic tort litigation. See, e.g., Johnson v. Arkema, Inc., 685 F.3d 452, 463 (5th Cir. 2012) (noting the "very limited usefulness of animal studies" to questions of a substance's toxicity to humans, and stating that such studies "must be carefully qualified in order to have explanatory potential for human beings").

What position do the 2005 EPA guidelines take on the relevance of animal studies to human cancer risk assessments, on the appropriateness of testing at MTDs, and on the validity of the linear model of cancer formation? To what extent do the 2005 guidelines reflect the precautionary principle? The "core idea" of that principle is that policymakers "need not wait for conclusive evidence of environmental damage or the impairment of public health before regulating an activity that poses credible risks of substantial future damage." Tarlock, Biodiversity Conservation in the United States: A Case Study in Incompleteness and Indirection, 32 Envtl. L. Rep. 10529 (2002).

B. RISK AND THE COMMON LAW

The common law offers many forms of relief to a plaintiff who can prove that the defendant has caused or is causing actual harm: damages, injunctions, and other equitable relief. But what about the plaintiff who is merely endangered and cannot yet show any actual harm? This section addresses the relief the common law offers to persons who are threatened but not yet injured by the low probability, delayed, but potentially serious harms that hazardous substances may cause.

VILLAGE OF WILSONVILLE v. SCA SERVICES, INC.
86 Ill. 2d 1, 426 N.E.2d 824 (1981)

CLARK, Justice . . .

[SCA hauled away chemical wastes generated by its customers and delivered them to its chemical waste disposal site, which it had operated since 1977 within and adjacent to the village. These wastes included substances that can cause pulmonary diseases, cancer, brain damage, and birth defects to exposed individuals. After testing waste samples, SCA deposited the waste in steel drums, which it placed in large 15-foot-deep trenches. It then placed uncompacted clay between groups of containers and between the top drum and the top clay level of the trench.

The landfill was bordered on three sides by farmland and on the fourth by the village. The mine site, the village, and much of the surrounding area was located above an abandoned coal mine. About 50 percent of the coal was left in pillars to support the earth above the mine. Testimony at trial established that pillar failure might occur in any mine where there was a readjustment of stress. The 73 water wells in the village were used mostly to water gardens and wash cars, but one was used for drinking water. The trenches were built in an area with a surface layer of about 10 feet of wind-blown silt and clay material. Beneath that material was 40-65 feet of dense and relatively impermeable glacial till composed of a thin sand layer that contained groundwater.

The village sued to enjoin operation of the waste disposal site on the ground that it presented a public nuisance. The trial court ordered the defendant to close the site, remove the wastes and the contaminated soil, and restore the site to its former condition. The Supreme Court upheld the trial court's findings that chemical wastes had spilled from the metal drums and paper bags in which they were transported to the site, that explosions and fires might result from chemical interactions, that chemicals might overflow the trenches or migrate down to groundwater through the soil, and that subsidence in the abandoned mine could hasten waste migration and infiltration into groundwater. The defendant relied on the testimony of Raymond Harbison, a pharmacology professor at Vanderbilt University and consultant to EPA (referred to by the court as USEPA), who called the site the most advanced scientific landfill in the country and stated that the "absolute confinement" of the materials to the site made it impossible for the chemicals to interact. The trial court had discounted Harbison's testimony in the light of the other evidence presented.]

The trial court herein concluded that defendant's chemical-waste-disposal site constitutes both a private and a public nuisance. Professor Prosser has defined a private nuisance as "a civil wrong, based on a disturbance of rights in land" (Prosser, Torts sec. 86, at 572 (4th ed. 1971)). . . . [A] public nuisance is ". . . the doing of or the failure to do something that injuriously affects the safety, health or morals of the public, or works some substantial annoyance, inconvenience or injury to the public." (Id. sec. 88, at 583 n.29.) It is generally conceded that a nuisance is remediable by injunction or a suit for damages. . . .

[The court found that Illinois law required that before a court may find a prospective nuisance, it must balance the social utility of the defendant's activity against the plaintiff's right to use its property without deleterious effects. The trial court conducted such a balancing process, contrary to the defendant's assertions. The defendant did not dispute a trial court's authority to enjoin a prospective nuisance, but it argued that the trial court erred by failing "to require a showing of a substantial risk of certain and extreme future harm before enjoining operation of the defendant's site."] The defendant argues that the proper standard to be used is that an injunction is proper only if there is a "dangerous probability" that the threatened or potential injury will occur. The defendant further argues that the appellate court looked only at the potential consequences of not enjoining the operation of the site as a nuisance and not at the likelihood of whether harm would occur. . . .

We agree with the defendant's statement of the law, but not with its urged application to the facts of this case. Again, Professor Prosser has offered a concise commentary. He has stated that

> [o]ne distinguishing feature of equitable relief is that it may be granted upon the threat of harm which has not yet occurred. The defendant may be restrained from entering upon an activity where it is highly probable that it will lead to a nuisance, although if the possibility is merely uncertain or contingent he may be left to his remedy after the nuisance has occurred.

(Prosser, Torts sec. 90, at 603 (4th ed. 1971).) This view is in accord with Illinois law. In [Fink v. Board of Trustees, 218 N.E.2d 240 (1966)], . . . [t]he court stated:

> While, as a general proposition, an injunction will be granted only to restrain an actual, existing nuisance, a court of equity may enjoin a threatened or anticipated nuisance, where it clearly appears that a nuisance will necessarily result from the contemplated act or thing which it is sought to enjoin. This is particularly true where the proof shows that the apprehension of material injury is well grounded upon a state of facts from which it appears that the danger is real and immediate. While care should be used in granting injunctions to avoid prospective injuries, there is no requirement that the court must wait until the injury occurs before granting relief.

(71 Ill. App. 2d 226, 281-82.) We agree.

In this case there can be no doubt but that it is highly probable that the chemical-waste-disposal site will bring about a substantial injury. . . . [W]e think it is sufficiently clear that it is highly probable that the instant site will constitute a public nuisance if, through either an explosive interaction, migration, subsidence, or the "bathtub effect," the highly toxic chemical wastes deposited at the site escape and contaminate the air, water, or ground around the site. That such an event will occur was positively attested to by several expert witnesses. A court does not have to wait for it to happen before it can enjoin such a result. Additionally, the fact is that the condition of a nuisance is already present at the site due to the location of the site and the manner in which it has been operated. Thus, it is only the damage which is prospective. Under these circumstances, if a court can prevent any damage from occurring, it should do so.

The defendant next asserts that error occurred in the courts below when they failed to defer to the [Illinois Environmental Protection Agency (IEPA)] and the USEPA, as well as when they failed to give weight to the permits issued by the IEPA. This assertion has no merit, however, because the data relied upon by the IEPA in deciding to issue a permit to the defendant were data collected by the defendant, data which have been proved at trial to be inaccurate. In particular, defendant's experts concluded that any subsidence at the site would be negligible. The IEPA (as well as the USEPA) adopted this inaccurate conclusion in deciding to issue a permit to the defendant. . . .

The next issue we consider is whether the trial court erroneously granted a permanent injunction. The defendant argues . . . that the courts below did not balance the equities in deciding to enjoin the defendant from continuing to operate the waste-disposal site. Defendant cites Harrison v. Indiana Auto Shredders Co. (7th Cir. 1975), 528 F.2d 1107, for the proposition that the court must balance the relative harm and benefit to the plaintiff and defendant before a court may enjoin a nuisance. . . .

In *Harrison*, . . . [t]he court stated:

> Reasonableness is the standard by which the court should fashion its relief in ordinary nuisance cases, . . . and reasonableness is also the appropriate standard for relief from environmental nuisance. Ordinarily a permanent injunction will not lie unless (1) either the polluter seriously and imminently threatens the public health or (2) he causes non-health injuries that are substantial and the business cannot be operated to avoid the injuries apprehended. . . .

(Id. at 1123.) The court concluded in *Harrison* that since the defendant was not in violation of any relevant zoning standards, and since the [activity] did not pose an imminent hazard to the public health, the defendant should not be prevented from continuing to operate. The court then ordered that the defendant be permitted a reasonable time to "launder its objectionable features." (528 F.2d 1107, 1125.)

This case is readily distinguishable for the reason that the gist of this case is that the defendant is engaged in an extremely hazardous undertaking at an unsuitable location, which seriously and imminently poses a threat to the public health. We are acutely aware that the service provided by the defendant is a valuable and necessary one. We also know that it is preferable to have chemical-waste-disposal sites than to have illegal dumping in rivers, streams, and deserted areas. But a site such as defendant's, if it is to do the job it is intended to do, must be located in a secure place, where it will pose no threat to health or life, now, or in the future. This site was intended to be a permanent disposal site for the deposit of extremely hazardous chemical-waste materials. Yet this site is located above an abandoned tunneled mine where subsidence is occurring several years ahead of when it was anticipated. Also, the permeability-coefficient samples taken by defendant's experts, though not conclusive alone, indicate the soil is more permeable at the site than expected. Moreover, the spillage, odors, and dust caused by the presence of the disposal site indicate why it was inadvisable to locate the site so near the plaintiff village.

Therefore, we conclude that in fashioning relief in this case the trial court did balance relative hardship to be caused to the plaintiffs and defendant, and did fashion reasonable relief when it ordered the exhumation of all material from the site and the reclamation of the surrounding area. The instant site is akin to Mr. Justice Sutherland's observation that "Nuisance may be merely a right thing in a wrong place — like a pig in the parlor instead of the barnyard." Village of Euclid v. Ambler Realty Co. (1926), 272 U.S. 365, 388.

We are also cognizant of amicus USEPA's suggestion in its brief and affidavits filed with the appellate court which urge that we remand to the circuit court so that alternatives to closure of the site and exhumation of the waste materials may be considered. The USEPA states:

> Heavy equipment may damage drums, releasing wastes and possibly causing gaseous emissions, fires, and explosions. Repackaging and transporting damaged drums also risks releasing wastes. Workers performing the exhumation face dangers from contact with or inhalation of wastes; these risks cannot be completely eliminated with protective clothing and breathing apparatus. Nearby residents may also be endangered.

It is ironic that the host of horribles mentioned by the USEPA in support of keeping the site open includes some of the same hazards which the plaintiffs have raised as reasons in favor of closing the site.

The USEPA continues that while it is not suggesting a specific alternative remedy to closure, possible alternative remedies exist:

> A proper cap of low permeability can ensure that little or no rain water can infiltrate the site, and thus that little leachate will be formed. Leachate-collection sumps can also be installed to remove whatever leachate is formed. Ground water monitoring can generally detect any migration of waste constituents, and counterpumping of contaminated ground water (or other measures) can protect against further migration.

We note, however, that the USEPA does not suggest how the location of the disposal site above an abandoned tunneled mine and the effects of subsidence can be overcome. . . .

Affirmed and remanded.

RYAN, Justice, concurring. . . .

I am concerned that the holding of *Fink*, quoted by the majority, may be an unnecessarily narrow view of the test for enjoining prospective tortious conduct in general. . . .

I believe that there are situations where the harm that is potential is so devastating that equity should afford relief even though the possibility of the harmful result occurring is uncertain or contingent. The Restatement's position applicable to preventative injunctive relief in general is that "[t]he more serious the impending harm, the less justification there is for taking the chances that are involved in pronouncing the harm too remote." (Restatement (Second) of Torts sec. 933, at 561, comment b (1979).) If the harm that may result is severe, a lesser possibility of it occurring should be required to support injunctive relief. Conversely, if the potential harm is less severe, a greater possibility that it will happen should be required. Also, in the balancing of competing interests, a court may find a situation where the potential harm is such that a plaintiff will be left to his remedy at law if the possibility of it occurring is slight. This balancing test allows the court to consider a wider range of factors and avoids the anomalous result possible under a more restrictive alternative where a person engaged in an ultrahazardous activity with potentially catastrophic results would be allowed to continue until he has driven an entire community to the brink of certain disaster. A court of equity need not wait so long to provide relief.

Although the "dangerous probability" test has certainly been met in this case, I would be willing to enjoin the activity on a showing of probability of occurrence substantially less than that which the facts presented to this court reveal, due to the extremely hazardous nature of the chemicals being dumped and the potentially catastrophic results.

NOTES AND QUESTIONS

1. *Imminence.* Traditionally, injunctive relief is appropriate only if a damage remedy would not be adequate. According to one source, a damage remedy is inadequate if the plaintiff will suffer imminent, substantial, and irreparable injury in the absence of an injunction. Irreparable harm includes damage for which adequate compensation cannot be provided. Injury is "imminent," according to the majority view, if there is "a threat that harm will occur in the immediate future" and "the anticipated harm is 'practically certain' to result from the act which [the plaintiff] seeks to enjoin." Hellerich, Note, Imminent Irreparable Injury: A Need for Reform, 45 S. Cal. L. Rev. 1025, 1031-1032 (1972). Did the *Wilsonville* court apply this version of the black letter law? Which is the sounder test of the power to issue injunctions to enjoin risky hazardous waste disposal practices—the rule that Justice Clark applied or the approach of Justice Ryan's concurring opinion? Does Talbot Page's risk "seesaw" (see section A.1 above) offer a better standard for injunctions than the *Wilsonville* majority or concurrence did? Which of the following situations would be enjoinable under each of the three approaches: (1) an ax poised to fall on your wrist, (2) exposure to smallpox, (3) exposure to asbestos dust?

Congress has authorized the federal district courts to enjoin activities that pose imminent threats to health or the environment. Under §7002(a)(1)(B) of the Resource Conservation and Recovery Act, for example, private citizens may sue to enjoin any person contributing to waste management activities "which may present an imminent and substantial endangerment to health or the environment." In Interfaith Cmty. Org. v. Honeywell Int'l, Inc., 399 F.3d 248 (3d Cir. 2005), the court upheld the district court's injunction requiring the defendant to excavate and remove 1.5 million tons of solid waste that had been deposited at a tidal wetlands site. The court found no credible evidence that either a containment cap or shallow groundwater treatment, the remedies favored by the defendant, would be effective. It also found that the district court crafted a "reasonable and narrow" injunction that was only what was necessary to abate the endangerment and was consistent with the public interest.

2. *Public Nuisance and Equitable Relief.* Historically, courts of equity, sitting without a jury, ordered abatement of a public nuisance only under unusual circumstances. When evidence of injury to the public was conflicting or doubtful, equity would not intervene but would leave the issue of fact to trial by jury. Should courts show a similar reluctance today? See Mugler v. Kansas, 123 U.S. 623, 673 (1887).

How broad is the public nuisance cause of action in environmental litigation? Does it cover a suit by a state against paint manufacturers whose product, which for years contained lead, allegedly caused harm to children exposed to it? See Rhode Island v. Lead Indus. Ass'n, 951 A.2d 428 (R.I. 2008) (overturning jury's damage award). What about a suit against electric utilities and coal, oil, and gas producers on the ground that their activities contribute to global climate change? See the materials in Chapter 12, section E.5.

3. *Private Nuisance and Trespass.* Private nuisance, which is designed to protect the right to use and enjoy private property, and trespass, which is designed to protect a person's right to exclusive possession of land, are causes of action that plaintiffs in environmental and toxic tort cases often rely upon. In Cook v. Rockwell Int'l Corp., 618 F.3d 1127 (10th Cir. 2010), the owners of land near the Rocky Flats Nuclear Weapons Plant sued the facility's operators, alleging private nuisance and trespass arising from the release of plutonium particles onto their properties. The court held that the trial court should have instructed the jury that, under Colorado law, recovery is not permitted based on a finding of interference with use and enjoyment arising from anxiety or fear of health risks that is not supported by some scientific evidence. No reasonable jury could find that irrational anxiety about a risk that cannot be scientifically verified makes an interference unreasonable. The court also held that the district court erred by failing to require plaintiffs to prove physical damage to the property to prevail in trespass. Although proof of actual physical damage is not normally required in Colorado to prevail in trespass, it is required for "intangible trespass," which involves "impalpable and imperceptible" invasions. The entry of plutonium particles onto the plaintiffs' land was impalpable and imperceptible by the senses.

4. *Resolving Uncertainty and Proving Causation.* According to one account, cases such as *Wilsonville* provide courts with broad discretion "to resolve the uncertainty issue in the public's favor when hazardous wastes are involved." Tarlock, Anywhere but Here: An Introduction to State Control of Hazardous Waste Facility Location, 2 UCLA J. Envtl. L. & Pol'y 1, 21 (1981). The courts have not always exercised that discretion in favor of plaintiffs in hazardous waste management cases, however. In Adkins v. Thomas Solvent Co., 487 N.W.2d 715 (Mich. 1992), for example, the plaintiffs claimed that toxic chemicals released at the defendant's property had contaminated groundwater in the area. Although the chemicals had not polluted the plaintiffs' property, the plaintiffs alleged that the releases had caused a diminution in value of their land because of public concern about contaminants in the general area. The court refused to "relax" the boundaries of traditional nuisance doctrine to permit damage recovery. It concluded that the plaintiffs did not demonstrate a risk of illness or a threat to safety, that property depreciation alone is an insufficient basis to impose liability, and that negative publicity resulting in unfounded fears did not constitute a significant interference with the use and enjoyment of land. A damage award might result in "a reordering of a polluter's resources for the benefit of persons who have suffered no cognizable harm at the expense of those claimants who have been subjected to a substantial and unreasonable interference." Id. at 727.[e]

---

e. See also Adams v. Star Enter., 51 F.3d 417 (4th Cir. 1995) (attachment of stigma to community and decline in property values linked to underground oil plume was too speculative to support imposition of liability on oil distribution facility); Smith v. Kansas Gas Serv. Co., 169 P.3d 1052, 1062 (Kan. 2007) (private nuisance liability requires interference with use and enjoyment of property beyond diminished property value due to marketplace fear or stigma); Duff v. Morgantown Energy Ass'n, 421 S.E.2d 253 (W. Va. 1992) (refusing to enjoin operation of proposed cogeneration facility because neighbors failed to prove that it would result in "devastating harm or is certain to result in serious damages or irreparable injury"); In re TVA Ash Spill Litig., 805 F. Supp. 2d 468, 488-489 (E.D. Tenn. 2011) (mere proximity of plaintiffs' properties to toxic coal ash spill or decrease in property value due to negative stigma "does not, without a finding that a legally protectable property interest was invaded, result in a finding of a [private] nuisance"). In re Tutu Wells Contamination Litig., 909 F. Supp. 991, 998 (D.V.I. 1995), criticized the *Adams* approach as likely to lead to "underdeterrence of environmental contamination."

Other courts have been more accommodating to the plaintiffs in toxics cases. In Walker Drug Co. v. La Sal Oil Co., 972 P.2d 1238 (Utah 1998), the court ruled that a nuisance suit would not lie for unsubstantiated fears of third persons concerning contamination of adjacent property, but that stigma damages are recoverable when a plaintiff demonstrates that defendants caused temporary physical injury to plaintiff's land, and repair of that injury would not return the value of the property to its prior level "because of a lingering negative public perception." Cf. Bradley v. Armstrong Rubber Co., 130 F.3d 168 (5th Cir. 1997) (recognizing the propriety of awarding stigma damages for permanent physical injury to the land to promote policy of redressing economic loss).

The difficulty of proving causation often stymies common law tort actions resulting from toxic substance exposures. See, e.g., Anglado v. Leaf River Forest Prod., Inc., 716 So. 2d 543 (Miss. 1998), where the court granted summary judgment to a pulp mill operator on trespass and nuisance claims filed by downstream riparian owners because the plaintiffs failed to prove that the dioxin and other chemicals to which they were exposed came from the defendant's pulp mill. The dissenting justice complained that the plaintiffs' burden of proof should not require such "fingerprinting" of the defendant's waste. See also Golden v. CH2M Hill Hanford Group, Inc., 528 F.3d 681 (9th Cir. 2008) (finding that employee at nuclear facility failed to prove that accident resulting in toxic liquid splash caused physical injuries).

5. *Regulatory Compliance.* Is it significant that the site in *Wilsonville* was fully authorized under state and federal law? Compare North Carolina v. TVA, 615 F.3d 291, 296 (4th Cir. 2010) (holding that TVA's operation of power plants was not a public nuisance, in part because "it is difficult to understand how an activity expressly permitted and extensively regulated by both federal and state government could somehow constitute a public nuisance") with Barrette v. Ciment du St-Laurent Inc., 2008 SCC 64, 2008 CarswellQue 11070 (S.C.R. Nov. 28, 2008) (holding in class action against cement company that compliance with government regulations did not preclude damage award in nuisance action). See also Green v. Castle Concrete Co., 509 P.2d 588 (Colo. 1973); Armory Park Neighborhood Ass'n v. Episcopal Cmty. Serv., 712 P.2d 914, 921-922 (Ariz. 1985). Does it make a difference whether the plaintiff files a private or a public nuisance claim? See Desruisseau v. Isley, 553 P.2d 1242, 1245-1246 (Ariz. App. 1976). Cf. City of Sunland Park v. Harris News, Inc., 124 P.3d 566, 578 (N.M. Ct. App. 2005) (stating that, while violation of a municipal ordinance is not sufficient to prove either a nuisance in fact or a nuisance per se in a public nuisance action, violation of a state statute declaring certain conduct to be a public nuisance will be considered a nuisance per se). What is the effect of proof of a regulatory violation on a negligence cause of action? See Regional Airport Auth. v. LFG, LLC, 255 F. Supp. 2d 688 (W.D. Ky. 2003), *aff'd on other grounds*, 460 F.3d 697 (6th Cir. 2006). Klass, Common Law and Federalism in the Age of the Regulatory State, 92 Iowa L. Rev. 545, 548 (2007), urges development of a new state common law that incorporates data, standards, and policy principles developed under regulatory programs to increase health and environmental protection.

Some state statutes foreclose the courts from enjoining the construction or operation of a hazardous waste disposal facility that conforms to the state's hazardous waste facility siting statute. Landowners are instead limited to seeking compensation in an inverse condemnation action for loss of property value or use at the time a facility is constructed. E.g., Utah Code Ann. §19-6-206. It is unclear whether the statute allows recovery of damages for personal injury. If not, does the statute unconstitutionally foreclose potential plaintiffs' right to bring an action at common law? See Duke Power Co. v. Carolina Envtl. Study Group, Inc., 438 U.S. 59 (1978); Bormann v. Board of Supervisors, 584 N.W.2d 309 (Iowa 1998). But see Moon v. North Idaho Farmers Ass'n, 96 P.3d 637 (Idaho 2004) (holding that statute immunizing crop residue burning from nuisance or trespass liability was not a taking of property of grower's neighbors because plaintiff's land was not appropriated, they did not lose access or complete use of the property, and the right to maintain a nuisance is not an easement under Idaho law).

A subcategory of environmental tort cases—toxic tort cases—has raised a series of difficult questions concerning the kinds of interests that the legal system should protect against harm resulting from the conduct of others. Consider the following analysis.

LIN, THE UNIFYING ROLE OF HARM IN ENVIRONMENTAL LAW
2006 Wis. L. Rev. 897, 922-930, 945-946, 955-968, 984

. . . Harm is the most widely accepted justification for the exercise of police power, and it is the rationale most applicable to environmental regulation.

At first glance, harm may appear to be a simple and objective concept, capable of ready definition. But . . . the concept is surprisingly elusive. One possible conception, for example, would define harm with respect to utilitarian goals of maximizing happiness, pleasure, or the fulfillment of subjective preferences. In this framework, harm would be synonymous with pain or the frustration of one's preferences. Such an account of harm, however, is simply too subjective to provide a workable basis for defining the permissible scope of government power. A harm principle [which Professor Lin defines as "jurisdictional in nature" in that "it is a touchstone for identifying one class of conduct that society has the power to regulate"] based on this conceptualization of harm would be boundless because "[a]ny sort of conduct to which some people object will inflict pain of various sorts and will interfere with the satisfaction of some people's preferences."

[John Stuart Mill] suggested that harm involves "encroachment" on others' rights, or the injuring of "certain interests" of another, "which, either by express legal provision or by tacit understanding, ought to be considered as rights." . . . As commentators have pointed out, Mill's distinctions rely heavily on unstated moral and social assumptions that may not be universally shared. . . .

[Others have suggested that the concept of harm entails a wrongful violation of another's rights.] Intuitive notions of harm, however, do not necessarily incorporate wrongfulness. For example, . . . harm in environmental law—whether in nuisance, regulatory law, or otherwise—does not always require wrongdoing. Consider the operation of a brickyard in a residential area. If the brickyard's presence long predates construction of the neighboring residences, and if the brickyard complies with applicable regulations, its operations could hardly be termed wrongful. Yet the noise and dust it generates surely harm its neighbors, and the brickyard's operations would almost certainly qualify as a nuisance. Likewise, the release of pollutants by a power plant during normal operations may harm nearby residents, even if such releases are lawful under the plant's permit and subject to the most advanced emission control devices available.

Including wrongfulness in the concept of harm thus seems contingent on the criminal law context of [the] inquiry. The primary purpose of criminal law is to punish and to deter wrongful conduct that has resulted in or is likely to result in harm if allowed to proceed. Civil law, however, has a broader reach: tort law seeks to compensate for harm and to foster corrective justice as well as to deter; and public law seeks to accomplish these aims and others as well. The differences between criminal and civil law suggest that . . . [in the context of environmental harm], the element of wrongfulness [should be] set aside. Consistent with this approach, and perhaps reflecting the origins of environmental law, the Restatement (Second) of Torts defines harm as a "loss or detriment in fact of any kind to a person resulting from any cause.". . .

If harm is a setback to one's interests, the obvious question is as follows: what sort of interests can give rise to harm? . . .

The definition of harm found in the Restatement (Second) of Torts hints at the wide range of interests that might be implicated:

> [H]arm . . . is the detriment or loss to a person which occurs by virtue of, or as a result of, some alteration or change in his person, or in physical things, and also the detriment resulting to him from acts or conditions which impair his physical, emotional, or aesthetic well-being, his pecuniary advantage, his intangible rights, his reputation, or his other legally recognized interests.

With respect to environmental harm in particular, one commentator has suggested various classes of harm: immediate and future physical injury to people, emotional distress from fear of future injury, social and economic disruption, remediation costs, property damage, ecological damage, and regulatory harms.

The variety of interests just mentioned raises a number of issues. First, the absence of an obvious unifying theme suggests that the task of determining what interests matter is a subjective one—perhaps hopelessly so. . . . Even physical injuries . . . qualify as harms "not because harm is a matter of unadorned fact," but because most reasonable normative accounts of harm would encompass such injuries. The Restatement's definition, which limits the interests that can be harmed to "legally recognized interests," underscores the normative nature of harm and begs the question of what interests are to be legally recognized.

Second, if a setback to any interest qualified as a harm, the harm principle might become useless as a limit on societal jurisdiction. And if indirect harms—that is, setbacks to interests that flow from long chains of causation—are considered regardless of their magnitude, virtually any activity could be said to be "harmful." . . . Thus, implicit in the harm principle may be limits as to the types and the insignificance of interests that the principle will protect. Absent such limits, harm may lose its force and utility as a critical principle for determining the legitimacy of government action, regulation, or judicial intervention. . . .

[Professor Lin asserts that physical injury, emotional injury, and damage to property represent "easy, core cases of harm." His primary interest is several contexts "that present more difficult questions of harm." In each context, "society has not conclusively determined that harm is present, and there is debate over if and how society should respond." According to Lin, "[u]nderstanding how these cutting-edge issues of harm might be resolved will help shape future environmental law."]

. . . [F]ear, anxiety, and other emotional injuries constitute serious setbacks to welfare interests. In the environmental context, the fear that may accompany toxic exposure can debilitate individuals and communities. The term "dread" is often used to describe this kind of fear, which is a serious and substantial setback to the affected individuals' welfare interests. The latent hazards characteristic of environmental problems are dreaded not only because of their involuntary nature, catastrophic potential, and fatal consequences, but also because they often have no clearly defined end. People exposed to invisible contaminants, unlike victims of natural disasters such as floods or hurricanes, may be left without closure for years or decades. . . . [T]he emotional impacts may ultimately include loss of trust in society's institutions and fracturing of the affected community.

Various trends likely will draw more attention to psychological injury in the future. First, rapidly developing technologies will give rise to new fears. New technologies with the potential for significant, unprecedented, and wide-ranging impacts include nanotechnology, biotechnology, and cloning. Potentially catastrophic environmental risks posed by the use or misuse of these technologies are already beginning to arouse widespread concern. . . .

Despite the potentially devastating impacts and growing importance of psychological injury, Congress and the Environmental Protection Agency (EPA) generally have not recognized fear as a harm in environmental statutes. . . . Nuisance actions against environmental pollution, for example, cannot rely on emotional injuries alone. . . . For most environmental statutes, Congress did not expressly consider fear as a harm. Rather, the more direct, tangible, and easily quantified health effects have driven the regulatory process. . . . Absent adequate justification for differential treatment, environmental law should address fear in a manner consistent with other areas of law. . . .

Exposure to toxics can give rise not only to fear, of course, but also to various physical changes in the body. Technological advances have enhanced scientists' ability to detect subcellular changes—such as chromosomal aberrations—and other potential precursors of toxic illness. These advances pose the question of whether the existence of such precursors, in the absence of a clinical diagnosis of illness, constitutes harm.

Existing safety and environmental regulations may limit the level and duration of exposure to toxic substances, but they do not eliminate all exposure or risk. Thus, an exposed individual may appear healthy, having no physical injuries or symptoms of illness, yet face a heightened level of risk. Because no physical harm is manifest—at least not yet—some might say there is no harm at all. Although courts increasingly allow plaintiffs in cases of toxic exposure to recover medical monitoring costs, such people are otherwise uncompensated for their heightened risk.

Technological advances in the detection and measurement of biomarkers will force reconsideration of such cases and of the nature of harm. Biomarkers are chemical substances or events in the human body that provide concrete evidence of exposure to a chemical, the effects of such exposure, and a person's susceptibility to disease. . . . These cellular responses to toxic exposure may signal or even increase the risk of adverse health consequences. As scientists develop more sophisticated analyses of biomarkers of effect, they will be able to measure bodily changes that are quantitatively or qualitatively predictive of health impairment resulting from toxic exposure. . . .

The question posed by such developments is whether the exposed individual has suffered harm. In contrast to the cancer victim, a person having high levels of [chromosomal aberrations (CAs)] has not yet suffered an obvious setback to welfare interests. Nevertheless, our growing knowledge about CAs may soon give rise to the ability to diagnose disease in such people before any symptoms appear. This development will blur the line between good health and disease, and that blurring will have implications for the law. For instance, tort law generally requires that a potential plaintiff be harmed before bringing suit. Whether high CA levels constitute harm may determine who can bring an action, as well as when an action can or must be brought. . . .

Illness is harm because it is a setback to physical well-being. Subcellular damage per se, however, does not constitute illness. Rather, it is a physical effect that may be a precursor or predictor of illness. Cancer, for instance, develops in a multistage process in which four to six critical genes must mutate before a malignant tumor appears. . . . Cancer results when a "sufficient number of mutations" have occurred in the "genes that control a cell's replication and repair functions so that the cell reproduces endlessly." As the process of cancer development illustrates, the presence of subcellular damage hardly guarantees that an individual will become ill.

There is thus a very significant qualitative difference between a person who has subcellular damage and a person who has cancer, as the judicial skepticism of subcellular injury claims reflects. Subcellular damage is extremely common, and it does not have the same impacts as a cancer diagnosis on daily life or on one's more ultimate interests. Moreover, it is the relative frequency of chromosomal aberrations, and not simply their presence or absence, that has predictive force. Because even single low-level exposures to carcinogens may cause damage to DNA, and because people who will never develop cancer nonetheless have cells containing damaged DNA, a view that any subcellular damage qualifies as harm means that virtually any activity—such as living in a house with ordinary background levels of radiation or breathing in cigarette smoke while visiting a casino—could be deemed harmful.

Even so, the difficulty of drawing a line between good health and disease cautions against an outright rejection of subcellular damage as harm. . . .

. . . The ultimate question . . . is whether particular levels of subcellular damage make a difference to the welfare of the exposed individual. The answer to that question depends on whether any risk associated with subcellular damage is a harm. . . .

The question of whether risk constitutes harm is particularly important to toxic tort claims. Tort law has traditionally demanded physical, emotional, or economic injury as a prerequisite to recovery. Negligent behavior that imposes risk on another person, but causes no such injury, does not give rise to a cause of action. This is in contrast to preventative environmental regulation, which inherently regulates the risk of harm. Risk of harm is the inevitable object of regulation because regulation generally seeks to prevent harm before it occurs. Such regulation is consistent with the harm principle because reducing or eliminating the risk of physical harm protects one's fundamental welfare interest in not being physically injured. Tort law, however, requires proof of harm that has actually occurred. The question is whether risk alone can satisfy that requirement. [Lin explains that he is referring to "risk" as an objective conception—"that is, risk that has some objective existence in the physical world."]

. . . [W]e begin with a relatively simple case: if a sufficiently large population is exposed to a toxic substance, we might predict that a certain number of illnesses and deaths will result. In such a case, where risk is spread across a population, the harm is certain, although the victims are indeterminate. This is a clear instance of harm, because physical harm almost certainly will occur.

Such harm is distinct from "risk harm," which presents the more difficult question of whether there is harm when an individual is exposed to a one in one-hundred risk of cancer, but ultimately does not develop the disease. Here, the answer is less obvious because one cannot rely on the indisputably harmful nature of physical injuries. On the one hand, everyday activities are filled with numerous unrealized risks—risks that result in no physical harm and provide no recognized basis for a tort action. We simply accept such risks as part of daily life. . . . The adage "no harm, no foul" would seem to suggest that risk harm is no harm at all.

On the other hand, even when the risked physical harm does not come to pass, being subjected to risk by others is an unsettling matter, particularly when the risk exposure occurs without one's knowledge or consent. . . . [A] person who only after the fact becomes aware of high-level radiation exposure might still claim harm, even if no radiation-induced illness ever develops. [Professor Claire] Finkelstein contends that people subjected to such risks have been harmed because they have suffered an objective setback to their interests; the person exposed to radiation is now in a class of people with a higher risk of developing cancer, and thus is doing substantially less well in life. . . .

Ultimately, whether a risk constitutes harm depends on factors in addition to the probability and magnitude of harm. Because harm is a normative concept, society may reach very different judgments about the harmfulness of quantitatively similar risks. Indeed, gaps between public perceptions of risk and probabilistic notions of risk have widened over the last few decades. . . . Studies of expressed preferences have found that public perceptions of risk depend on factors such as controllability, voluntariness, and equity, not just on raw probabilities. . . .

The risks to the individual exposed to toxic substances . . . are very different from the risks involved in skydiving. Risks from exposure to environmental toxins are not voluntary, readily observable, well understood, or equally distributed among the population. Even if it is theoretically possible to avoid such risks, it is often prohibitively difficult or costly to do so. These factors point toward a low social tolerance for such risks, and hence a judgment that such risks qualify as harm. Indeed, the involuntary nature of such risks may explain why they constitute harm: the imposition of involuntary risks infringes on individual autonomy, which is the core value that the harm principle seeks to promote.

The conclusion that involuntary risk is a harm does not necessarily dictate the recognition of a tort action. The use of substances that generate health or environmental risks, such as preservatives or pesticides, may reduce other risks. And government regulation may be a more appropriate response to risk than an enforceable "right" against risk, particularly for broadly distributed, low-level risks. . . . Notwithstanding the variety of possible responses to harm, the point remains: the imposition of significant involuntary risk is a serious setback to one's welfare because it interferes with one's autonomy. . . .

Some commentators within and outside of environmental law have bemoaned the expansion of the concept of harm. The main complaint is that the harm principle, originally set forth by Mill as a limit on government power, is often employed to justify the regulation of morals under the guise of preventing harm. If harm is too broadly understood, jurisdiction to legislate might extend to almost any behavior. The expansion of the traditional concept of harm in environmental law beyond physical injury, however, does not—for the most part—pose such a danger. Rather, it reflects a more sophisticated understanding of the relationship between humans and the environment. . . .

[The realization that "many of our activities can, and do, cause harm to others"] does not dictate government involvement wherever harm is present; case-by-case policy decisions are still necessary. In such decisions, the nature and extent of harm at issue should be a critical consideration—as should interests in autonomy and other factors. . . . [T]he harm principle is not without limits even in our more informed and interconnected world. Most of modern environmental law is not really about deontological harm to the environment; it is about setbacks to fundamental human interests. These setbacks lie firmly within the harm principle. . . .

NOTE ON THE COMMON LAW APPROACH TO RISK AS INJURY

As the materials in this chapter demonstrate, one of the major innovations of environmental law has been to use the concept of risk as a proxy for injury, rather than following the common law's insistence that injury be established by proof that an action in fact caused demonstrable harm. This is a controversial departure from the common law baseline reflected in Restatement of Torts (Second) §433B, which requires that a plaintiff prove that defendant's conduct is a substantial factor in bringing about harm. To recover for a "toxic tort," a plaintiff must generally prove (1) exposure in an amount and over a period of time sufficient to cause the disease complained of, (2) the occurrence of the disease, (3) the elapse of an appropriate time interval between exposure and the disease, (4) a scientifically recognized relationship between the chemicals and the disease, and (5) the absence of alternative, equally probable explanations. See In re Paoli R.R. Yard PCB Litig., 916 F.2d 829 (3d Cir. 1990).

The required demonstration of causation of harm has been more rigorous in the tort context, including toxic tort cases, than in regulatory contexts. In In re "Agent Orange" Product Liab. Litig., 597 F. Supp. 740, 781 (E.D.N.Y. 1984), aff'd, 818 F.2d 145 (2d Cir. 1987), Judge Weinstein stated that in a tort action as opposed to an action to review a risk-based regulation, "a far higher probability (greater than 50%) is required since the law believes it unfair to require an individual to pay for another's tragedy unless it is shown that it is more likely than not that he caused it." The moral basis of the necessity to prove cause in fact is expressed most clearly in criminal law, which adopts a "beyond a reasonable doubt" standard and a presumption of innocence to reduce the risk of factual error and preserve the moral force of the criminal law by preserving individual freedom. In re Winship, 397 U.S. 358, 363 (1970).

Nevertheless, the courts have developed novel theories of liability and causes of action addressing some of the forms of "harm" covered in the Lin excerpt, and litigants have sought to establish others that would facilitate the ability of plaintiffs to seek relief in toxic tort cases.

Market Share Liability. When regulators began to implement the modern environmental statutes, they had to confront what scientists have long known: most environmental decisions must be made under conditions of extreme uncertainty (Page's "ignorance of mechanism"). Beginning with EPA's decision to cancel DDT's pesticide registration based on the chemical's human health risks, the agency increasingly accepted risk as a sufficient basis to justify regulation, rather than insisting upon proof of past harm. Such probabilistic cause has a limited basis in the common law. The leading case is Sindell v. Abbott Lab., 607 P.2d 924 (Cal. 1980). Plaintiff alleged that she developed a malignant bladder tumor from DES, an anti-miscarriage drug.

Because the plaintiff could not identify the manufacturer of the drug that she ingested, she sued the entire industry. To allow the plaintiff to recover, the California Supreme Court created a new rule of market share liability, relying on Summers v. Tice, 199 P.2d 1 (Cal. 1948). In *Summers*, one of two hunters shot the plaintiff, and the court shifted the burden to the two defendants to absolve themselves. The court's approach is sometimes referred to as the alternative liability approach. Under the Restatement (Second) of Torts §433B(3), "[w]here the conduct of two or more actors is tortious, and it is proved that harm has been caused to the plaintiff by only one of them, but there is uncertainty as to which one has caused it, the burden is upon each such actor to prove that he has not caused the harm." The *Sindell* court applied the alternative liability theory:

> . . . [W]e hold it to be reasonable in the present context to measure the likelihood that any of the defendants supplied the product which allegedly injured plaintiff by the percentage which the DES sold by each of them for the purpose of preventing miscarriage bears to the entire production of the drug sold by all for that purpose. . . .
>
> The presence in the action of a substantial share of the appropriate market . . . provides a ready means to apportion damages among the defendants. Each defendant will be held liable for the proportion of the judgment represented by its share of that market unless it demonstrates that it could not have made the product which caused plaintiff's injuries. . . . Once plaintiff has met her burden of joining the required defendants, they in turn may cross-complaint against other DES manufacturers, not joined in the action, which they can allege might have supplied the injury-causing product. [607 P.2d at 937.]

Sindell has been adopted in several other states, but other courts have rejected it. For example, Smith v. Eli Lilly & Co., 560 N.E.2d 324 (Ill. 1990), rejected market share liability because it is difficult to make allocations, there is a high risk that they will be arbitrary, and the rule provides a disincentive to disclose and recall products on the market. Multiple causal agent cases are different from the usual toxic tort case where the consequence of exposure is uncertain. Does this explain the New Jersey Supreme Court's rejection of a collective liability approach in favor of one that requires toxic tort plaintiffs to establish factual proof of frequent, regular, and proximate exposure to a product and medical and/or scientific proof of a nexus between exposure and plaintiff's condition? James v. Bessemer Processing Co., 714 A.2d 898 (N.J. 1998). Compare Conde v. Velsicol Chem. Corp., 24 F.3d 809 (6th Cir. 1994) (expert testimony that exposure to chlordane was "consistent with" the plaintiffs' health problems did not demonstrate that the exposure caused their injuries).

An analogous theory is the risk contribution doctrine, which provides that if all products of the type that injured the plaintiff are fungible and present the identical danger, an injured plaintiff may recover by showing that the defendant produced the type of product that caused the injury at a time that it could reasonably have caused the injury. See, e.g., Stokes v. American Cyanamid Co., 787 F. Supp. 2d 828 (E.D. Wis. 2011) (holding that modification of the burden of proof under risk contribution doctrine did not violate due process or amount to a compensable taking).

Commingled Product Theory. In re Methyl Tertiary Butyl Ether ("MTBE") Products Liab. Litig., 379 F. Supp. 2d 348 (S.D.N.Y. 2005), local governments and public and private water suppliers sought tort relief from companies that designed, manufactured, or distributed gasoline containing methyl tertiary butyl ether (MTBE), which had contaminated local groundwater supplies. Because the plaintiffs could not identify the offending product due to its fungible nature and the commingling of many suppliers' petroleum products during transportation and distribution, the issue was whether they could recover based on some collective liability theory.

The court described market share liability as "uniquely suited to fungible product cases because such products (1) create the problem of non-identification in the first place, and (2) pose equal risks of harm to those exposed to the product." Id. at 376. The MTBE cases suggested the need to modify market share liability by incorporating "elements of concurrent wrongdoing." Id. The court described its new theory of "commingled product" market share liability as follows:

> When a plaintiff can prove that certain gaseous or liquid products (e.g., gasoline, liquid propane, alcohol) of many suppliers were present in a completely commingled or blended state at the time and place that the risk of harm occurred, and the commingled product caused a single indivisible injury, then each of the products should be deemed to have caused the harm. [Id. at 377-378.]

Accordingly, if a defendant's indistinct product was present in the area of contamination and was commingled with the products of other suppliers, all of the suppliers can be held severally liable for any harm arising from an incident of contamination. Damages would be apportioned by reference to a defendant's share of the market at the time a risk of harm was created to a class of potential victims. A defendant may exculpate itself by proving that its product was not present at the relevant time and place and therefore could not have been part of the new commingled or blended product. See also In re Methyl Tertiary Butyl Ether ("MTBE") Prods. Liab. Litig., 643 F. Supp. 2d 461 (S.D.N.Y. 2009) (concluding that liability in a commingled products case is several, not joint and several; that the burden of production and persuasion is on the defendant; and that the defendant must show only a reasonable basis for apportionment).

As the Lin article indicates, persons claiming exposure to toxic chemicals have sought recovery for a variety of alleged harms, including the increased risk of future injury stemming from the exposure, immune system impairment, the costs of medical monitoring, the fear of contracting cancer, and post-traumatic stress disorder. Endorsement of these novel causes of action is another route to recognition of probabilistic cause. According to Lin, what is the unifying thread that provides the basis for deciding whether or not these should be recognized as legitimate causes of action? Which of the causes of action does his analysis support? Judicial receptivity has been mixed.

Fear of Illness. In Sterling v. Velsicol Chem. Corp., 855 F.2d 1188 (6th Cir. 1988), plaintiffs established defendant's liability for personal injuries sustained as a result of drinking and using well water contaminated by organic chemical toxicants from defendant's negligent operation of a nearby hazardous waste disposal site. Unlike the plaintiff in *Wilsonville*, the plaintiffs in *Sterling* had already sustained a variety of physical injuries. The court nevertheless required the plaintiffs to show to "a reasonable medical certainty" that the contaminated water caused bodily harm. Damages may not be "speculative or conjectural" and may not be based on a mere "probability" or "likelihood," especially for diseases that may result from a variety of causes that "inflict society at random, often with no known specific origin." Id. at 1200. How does this test compare to the test in *Wilsonville*?

Applying the reasonable medical certainty test, the court in *Sterling* held that fear of increased risk of cancer was "clearly" a present injury and compensable, but only for "reasonable" fear. The court denied damages for immune system impairment and learning disorders entirely because no generally accepted scientific theory of causation exists for these injuries. It also denied damage awards for post-traumatic stress disorder, holding that drinking the contaminated water was not sufficiently stressful and that no recurring fear existed. Compare In re Berg Litig., 293 F.3d 1127 (9th Cir. 2002) (Price Anderson Act does not allow claims for emotional distress or medical monitoring absent present physical injury). Even if a court refuses to recognize a separate cause of action for fear of illness or other injury, it may allow a plaintiff who prevails on a more traditional cause of action (such as trespass, nuisance, or negligence) to recover for emotional distress as an element of damages for that claim. See, e.g., Nnadili v. Chevron U.S.A. Inc., 435 F. Supp. 2d 93 (D.D.C. 2006).

Medical Monitoring. The leading case of Ayers v. Township of Jackson, 525 A.2d 287 (N.J. 1987), rejected the creation of a new tort of "cancerphobia," in part because the damages were too speculative and it would be difficult to adjudicate damage claims. The court did recognize a right to recover damages for the medical expenses necessary to monitor the enhanced risk caused by exposure. Theer v. Philip Carey Co., 628 A.2d 724 (N.J. 1993), however, limited *Ayers* to cases of direct exposure where the plaintiff suffered some injury. Bower v. Westinghouse Elec. Corp., 522 S.E.2d 424 (W. Va. 1999), endorsed a cause of action for medical monitoring costs as "a well-grounded extension of traditional common-law tort principles" in the sense that a claim for medical monitoring is essentially a claim for future damages. The court did not insist that the plaintiff seeking such costs demonstrate any present physical harm or even the probable likelihood that a serious disease will result from the exposure because "significant economic harm may be inflicted on those exposed to toxic substances, notwithstanding the fact that the physical harm resulting from such exposure is often latent." Id. at 429. Thus, the exposure itself and the concomitant need for testing constitute the injury. Rhodes v. E.I. du Pont de Nemours and Co., 636 F.3d 88 (4th Cir. 2011), interpreted *Bower* to require proof in a medical monitoring claim of a significantly increased risk of contracting a particular disease relative to the risk that would exist in the absence of exposure. The West Virginia Supreme Court refused to extend *Bower* to recognize a separate cause of action for the recovery of the costs of future inspection and monitoring of real property located next to a chemical dump, where the plaintiffs had not yet demonstrated that their properties had been exposed to a hazardous substance. Carter v. Monsanto Co., 575 S.E.2d 342 (W. Va. 2002).

Other courts have resisted recognition of this cause of action. Hinton v. Monsanto Co., 813 So. 2d 827, 830 (Ala. 2001), reasoned that recognition of a cause of action for medical monitoring based only on an increased risk that an injury or an illness might occur would premise liability on "nothing more than speculation and conjecture." Similarly, in Henry v. Dow Chem. Co., 701 N.W.2d 784 (Mich. 2005), the court concluded that recognition of a cause of action for medical monitoring in the absence of present physical injuries could drain resources needed to compensate those with manifest physical injuries and a more immediate need for medical care. The court expressed concern that recognizing the cause of action could wreak "enormous harm" on Michigan's citizens and economy. Id. at 697. A dissenting judge chastised the majority for "inexcusably" subordinating the plaintiffs' physical health to defendant's economic health. "Sadly, this Court has resorted to a cost-benefit analysis to determine and, consequently, degrade the value of human life." Id. at 715.

Even when a court recognizes a medical monitoring cause of action, it may reject as insufficient the plaintiffs' showing that exposure caused a sufficient increased risk of disease to justify a medical monitoring remedy. See, e.g., Hirsch v. CSX Transp., Inc., 656 F.3d 359, 364 (6th Cir. 2011) (dioxin exposure created risk that "border[ed] on legal insignificance"). Further, restrictions on the ability to bring class actions may make the theory unattractive to plaintiffs' attorneys. See, e.g., Gates v. Rohm & Haas Co., 655 F.3d 255 (3d Cir. 2011). For an argument that medical monitoring may be a transitional remedy in the law of torts, see Grodsky, Genomics and Toxic Torts: Dismantling the Risk-Injury Divide, 59 Stan. L. Rev. 1671 (2007).

Increased Risk. Potter v. Firestone Tire & Rubber Co., 863 P.2d 795 (Cal. 1993), recognized a limited tort of enhanced risk exposure. Firestone maintained a toxic landfill that contaminated plaintiffs' wells. Plaintiffs manifested no immediate injuries but sued for fear of an increased risk of cancer. The court held that there is a tort of increased risk of cancer that does not require a showing of physical injury. But it adopted a very high objective standard to prevent medical research into products like prescription drugs from being chilled, to prevent liability insurance for toxic liability risks from becoming unavailable or unaffordable, and to ensure that compensation remains available for those individuals who actually develop cancer or other physical harms. Plaintiff must prove that it is more likely than not that cancer will develop, except in cases of fraud, oppression, or malice. This exception applied to Firestone because it ignored warnings about the dangers of careless waste disposal practices. Compare Rhodes v. E.I. du Pont de Nemours and Co., 636 F.3d 88 (4th Cir. 2011) (increased risk of illness from drinking contaminated water was not sufficient to support liability; plaintiffs must show that detrimental effects on health have actually occurred or are reasonably certain to occur due to a present harm); Bonnette v. Conoco, Inc., 837 So. 2d 1219 (La. 2003) (declining to allow damage recovery for a "slightly" increased risk of developing cancer due to asbestos exposure); Alsteen v. Wauleco Inc., 802 N.W.2d 212 (Wis. App. 2011) ("mere exposure to a dangerous substance does not constitute an actual injury," nor does an increased risk of injury).

The Maryland Court of Appeals addressed several of these causation-alleviating causes of action in Exxon Mobil Corp. v. Albright, 71 A.3d 30 (Md. App. 2013), *on reconsideration in part*, 71 A.3d 151 (Md. App. 2013). It held that to recover damages for fear of contracting a latent disease, a plaintiff must show that (1) he or she was actually exposed to a toxic substance due to the defendant's tortious conduct; (2) which led him or her to fear objectively and reasonably that he or she would contract a disease; and (3) as a result of the objective and reasonable fear, he or she manifested a physical injury capable of objective determination. It ruled that subcellular change produced by exposure to toxic chemicals—without manifested symptoms of a disease or actual impairment—is not a compensable "injury" under Maryland law. In addition, the court endorsed recovery for medical monitoring costs if a plaintiff can show:

> (1) that the plaintiff was significantly exposed to a proven hazardous substance through the defendant's tortious conduct; (2) that, as a proximate result of significant exposure, the plaintiff suffers a significantly increased risk of contracting a latent disease; (3) that increased risk makes periodic diagnostic medical examinations reasonably necessary; and (4) that monitoring and testing procedures exist which make the early detection and treatment of the disease possible and beneficial.

> To determine what is a "significantly increased risk of contracting a latent disease" for a particular plaintiff, the court may consider quantifiable and reliable medical expert testimony that indicates the plaintiff's chances of developing the disease had he or she not been exposed, compared to the chances of the members of the public at large of developing the disease.

Id. at 81-82. See also Exxon Mobil Corp. v. Ford, 71 A.3d 105 (Md. App. 2013).

Preconception Injury. Suppose that plaintiffs seek compensation in a negligence action for injuries allegedly caused by chemical exposures of parents, grandparents, or great-grandparents before the plaintiffs were conceived. Is such a cause of action viable? What elements of a negligence action might prove problematic for such plaintiffs? See Avila v. Willits Envtl. Remediation Trust, 633 F.3d 828 (9th Cir. 2011). Compare Junk v. Terminix Int'l Co., 628 F.3d 439 (8th Cir. 2010) (affirming dismissal of various tort and breach of warranty actions against pesticide manufacturer and distributor by plaintiffs claiming that their son's severe neurological problems were caused by spraying of the family home while the mother was pregnant).

Other Torts. Would battery be an appropriate tort cause of action to bring against those whose activities expose others to potentially harmful toxic substances? See C. Cranor, Legally Poisoned: How the Law Puts Us at Risk from Toxicants (Harvard Univ. Press 2011) (reviewed in Lyndon, The Toxicity of Low-Dose Chemical Exposures: A Status Report and a Proposal, 52 Jurimetrics J. 457 (2012)) (recommending that the distribution of suspect pollutants, without prior research on their toxicity, be considered the intentional cause of an offensive contact). May a person who drank contaminated water sue the responsible polluter in battery or trespass? See Rhodes v. E.I. du Pont de Nemours and Co., 636 F.3d 88 (4th Cir. 2011).

DAUBERT v. MERRELL DOW PHARMACEUTICALS, INC.
509 U.S. 579 (1993)

Justice BLACKMUN delivered the opinion of the Court.

In this case we are called upon to determine the standard for admitting expert scientific testimony in a federal trial.

[Petitioners, minor children born with serious birth defects, and their parents sued Merrell Dow (Merrell or respondent), alleging that the birth defects had been caused by the mothers' ingestion of Bendectin, a prescription antinausea drug marketed by Merrell. Merrell moved for summary judgment, contending that Bendectin does not cause birth defects in humans and that petitioners would not be able to come forward with any admissible evidence that it does. Merrell relied on an affidavit of a physician and epidemiologist, Dr. Lamm, with expertise on the risks from exposure to various chemical substances. In his review of the literature on Bendectin and human birth defects, he located no study finding Bendectin to be capable of causing malformations in fetuses, and concluded that maternal use of Bendectin during the first trimester of pregnancy had not been shown to be a risk factor for human birth defects.

Instead of contesting this characterization of the published record, petitioners submitted the testimony of eight more well-credentialed experts, all of whom concluded that Bendectin can cause birth defects. Petitioners' experts relied on "in vitro" (test tube) and "in vivo" (live) animal studies; "pharmacological studies of the chemical structure of Bendectin that purported to show similarities between the structure of the drug and that of other substances known to cause birth defects; and the 'reanalysis' of previously published epidemiological (human statistical) studies."

The district court awarded summary judgment to Merrell, stating that scientific evidence is admissible only if the principle upon which it is based is "sufficiently established to have general acceptance in the field to which it belongs." Petitioners' evidence did not meet this standard.] Given the vast body of epidemiological data concerning Bendectin, the court held, expert opinion which is not based on epidemiological evidence is not admissible to establish causation. Thus, the animal-cell studies, live-animal studies, and chemical-structure analyses on which petitioners had relied could not raise by themselves a reasonably disputable jury issue regarding causation. Petitioners' epidemiological analyses, based as they were on recalculations of data in previously published studies that had found no causal link between the drug and birth defects, were ruled to be inadmissible because they had not been published or subjected to peer review.

[The Ninth Circuit affirmed. Citing Frye v. United States, 293 F. 1013 (D.C. Cir. 1923), it] stated that expert opinion based on a scientific technique is inadmissible unless the technique is "generally accepted" as reliable in the relevant scientific community. The court declared that expert opinion based on a methodology that diverges "significantly from the procedures accepted by recognized authorities in the field . . . cannot be shown to be 'generally accepted as a reliable technique.'" . . .

II

A

In the 70 years since its formulation in the *Frye* case, the "general acceptance" test has been the dominant standard for determining the admissibility of novel scientific evidence at trial. . . .

The *Frye* test has its origin in a short and citation-free 1923 decision concerning the admissibility of evidence derived from a systolic blood pressure deception test, a crude precursor to the polygraph machine. In what has become a famous (perhaps infamous) passage, the then Court of Appeals for the District of Columbia described the device and its operation and declared:

> Just when a scientific principle or discovery crosses the line between the experimental and demonstrable stages is difficult to define. Somewhere in this twilight zone the evidential force of the principle must be recognized, and while courts will go a long way in admitting expert testimony deduced from a well-recognized scientific principle or discovery, *the thing from which the deduction is made must be sufficiently established to have gained general acceptance in the particular field in which it belongs.* 293 F., at 1014 (emphasis added). . . .

[Petitioners contended that the *Frye* test was superseded by the Federal Rules of Evidence.] Here there is a specific Rule that speaks to the contested issue. Rule 702, governing expert testimony, provides:

> If scientific, technical, or other specialized knowledge will assist the trier of fact to understand the evidence or to determine a fact in issue, a witness qualified as an expert by knowledge, skill, experience, training, or education, may testify thereto in the form of an opinion or otherwise.

Nothing in the text of this Rule establishes "general acceptance" as an absolute prerequisite to admissibility. Nor does respondent present any clear indication that Rule 702 or the Rules as a whole were intended to incorporate a "general acceptance" standard. The drafting history makes no mention of *Frye*, and a rigid "general acceptance" requirement would be at odds with the "liberal thrust" of the Federal Rules and their "general approach of relaxing the traditional barriers to 'opinion' testimony." Beech Aircraft Corp. v. Rainey, 488 U.S., at 169 (citing Rules 701 to 705). See also Weinstein, Rule 702 of the Federal Rules of Evidence Is Sound; It Should Not Be Amended, 138 F.R.D. 631 (1991) ("The Rules were designed to depend primarily upon lawyer-adversaries and sensible triers of fact to evaluate conflicts."). Given the Rules' permissive backdrop and their inclusion of a specific rule on expert testimony that does not mention "general acceptance," the assertion that the Rules somehow assimilated *Frye* is unconvincing. *Frye* made "general acceptance" the exclusive test for admitting expert scientific testimony. That austere standard, absent from, and incompatible with, the Federal Rules of Evidence, should not be applied in federal trials.

B

That the *Frye* test was displaced by the Rules of Evidence does not mean, however, that the Rules themselves place no limits on the admissibility of purportedly scientific evidence. Nor is the trial judge disabled from screening such evidence. To the contrary, under the Rules the trial judge must ensure that any and all scientific testimony or evidence admitted is not only relevant, but reliable.

The primary locus of this obligation is Rule 702, which clearly contemplates some degree of regulation of the subjects and theories about which an expert may testify. "*If scientific*, technical, or other specialized *knowledge will assist the trier of fact* to understand the evidence or to determine a fact in issue" an expert "may testify *thereto*." (Emphasis added.) The subject of an expert's testimony must be "scientific . . . knowledge." The adjective "scientific" implies a grounding in the methods and procedures of science. Similarly, the word "knowledge" connotes more than subjective belief or unsupported speculation. The term "applies to any body of known facts or to any body of ideas inferred from such facts or accepted as truths on good grounds." Webster's Third New International Dictionary 1252 (1986). Of course, it would be unreasonable to conclude that the subject of scientific testimony must be "known" to a certainty; arguably, there are no certainties in science. See, e.g., Brief for American Association for the Advancement of Science et al. as Amici Curiae 7-8 ("Science is not an encyclopedic body of knowledge about the universe. Instead, it represents a *process* for proposing and refining theoretical explanations about the world that are subject to further testing and refinement."). But, in order to qualify as "scientific knowledge," an inference or assertion must be derived by the scientific method. Proposed testimony must be supported by appropriate validation—i.e., "good grounds," based on what is known. In short, the requirement that an expert's testimony pertain to "scientific knowledge" establishes a standard of evidentiary reliability. . . .

C

Faced with a proffer of expert scientific testimony, then, the trial judge must determine at the outset, pursuant to Rule 104(a), whether the expert is proposing to testify to (1) scientific knowledge that (2) will assist the trier of fact to understand or determine a fact in issue. This entails a preliminary assessment of whether the reasoning or methodology underlying the testimony is scientifically valid and of whether that reasoning or methodology properly can be applied to the facts in issue. We are confident that federal judges possess the capacity to undertake this review. Many factors will bear on the inquiry, and we do not presume to set out a definitive checklist or test. But some general observations are appropriate.

Ordinarily, a key question to be answered in determining whether a theory or technique is scientific knowledge that will assist the trier of fact will be whether it can be (and has been) tested. "Scientific methodology today is based on generating hypotheses and testing them to see if they can be falsified; indeed, this methodology is what distinguishes science from other fields of human inquiry." Green 645. See also K. Popper, Conjectures and Refutations: The Growth of Scientific Knowledge 37 (5th ed. 1989) ("[T]he criterion of the scientific status of a theory is its falsifiability, or refutability, or testability.").

Another pertinent consideration is whether the theory or technique has been subjected to peer review and publication. Publication (which is but one element of peer review) is not a *sine qua non* of admissibility; it does not necessarily correlate with reliability, and in some instances well-grounded but innovative theories will not have been published. Some propositions, moreover, are too particular, too new, or of too limited interest to be published. But submission to the scrutiny of the scientific community is a component of "good science," in part because it increases the likelihood that substantive flaws in methodology will be detected. The fact of publication (or lack thereof) in a peer reviewed journal thus will be a relevant, though not dispositive, consideration in assessing the scientific validity of a particular technique or methodology on which an opinion is premised.

Additionally, in the case of a particular scientific technique, the court ordinarily should consider the known or potential rate of error, and the existence and maintenance of standards controlling the technique's operation.

Finally, "general acceptance" can yet have a bearing on the inquiry. A "reliability assessment does not require, although it does permit, explicit identification of a relevant scientific community and an express determination of a particular degree of acceptance within that community." United States v. Downing, 753 F.2d, at 1238. Widespread acceptance can be an important factor in ruling particular evidence admissible, and "a known technique which has been able to attract only minimal support within the community," id. at 1238, may properly be viewed with skepticism.

The inquiry envisioned by Rule 702 is, we emphasize, a flexible one. Its overarching subject is the scientific validity—and thus the evidentiary relevance and reliability—of the principles that underlie a proposed submission. The focus, of course, must be solely on principles and methodology, not on the conclusions that they generate. . . .

III

. . . Respondent expresses apprehension that abandonment of "general acceptance" as the exclusive requirement for admission will result in a "free-for-all" in which befuddled juries are confounded by absurd and irrational pseudoscientific assertions. In this regard respondent seems to us to be overly pessimistic about the capabilities of the jury and of the adversary system generally. Vigorous cross-examination, presentation of contrary evidence, and careful instruction on the burden of proof are the traditional and appropriate means of attacking shaky but admissible evidence. Additionally, in the event the trial court concludes that the scintilla of evidence presented supporting a position is insufficient to allow a reasonable juror to conclude that the position more likely than not is true, the court remains free to direct a judgment, Fed. Rule Civ. Proc. 50(a), and likewise to grant summary judgment, Fed. Rule Civ. Proc. 56. . . . These conventional devices, rather than wholesale exclusion under an uncompromising "general acceptance" test, are the appropriate safeguards where the basis of scientific testimony meets the standards of Rule 702.

Petitioners and, to a greater extent, their amici exhibit a different concern. They suggest that recognition of a screening role for the judge that allows for the exclusion of "invalid" evidence will sanction a stifling and repressive scientific orthodoxy and will be inimical to the search for truth. It is true that open debate is an essential part of both legal and scientific analyses. Yet there are important differences between the quest for truth in the courtroom and the quest for truth in the laboratory. Scientific conclusions are subject to perpetual revision. Law, on the other hand, must resolve disputes finally and quickly. The scientific project is advanced by broad and wide-ranging consideration of a multitude of hypotheses, for those that are incorrect will eventually be shown to be so, and that in itself is an advance. Conjectures that are probably wrong are of little use, however, in the project of reaching a quick, final, and binding legal judgment—often of great consequence—about a particular set of events in the past. We recognize that, in practice, a gatekeeping role for the judge, no matter how flexible, inevitably on occasion will prevent the jury from learning of authentic insights and innovations. That, nevertheless, is the balance that is struck by Rules of Evidence designed not for the exhaustive search for cosmic understanding but for the particularized resolution of legal disputes. . . .

NOTES AND QUESTIONS

1. *The Scope of the* Daubert *Ruling.* Does *Daubert* require a higher standard for reviewing the trial judge's admissibility rulings on expert testimony than the standard that applies to other evidentiary rulings? General Elec. Co. v. Joiner, 522 U.S. 136 (1997), holds that *Daubert* does not modify the prior abuse-of-discretion standard. In Weisgram v. Marley Co., 528 U.S. 440 (2000), the Court held that if the court of appeals decides that the district court should have excluded the plaintiff's expert testimony and that the remaining evidence is insufficient to justify a jury verdict for the plaintiff, the appellate court may instruct the district court to enter judgment against the plaintiff. *Weisgram* describes the standards for the admissibility of expert testimony set forth in *Daubert* and its progeny as "exacting standards of reliability." Id. at 455. In Kumho Tire Co. v. Carmichael, 526 U.S. 1377 (1999), the Court extended *Daubert* to the testimony of engineers and other experts who are not scientists.

In 2000, Rule 702 was amended by the addition of the following language at the end of the previous version of the rule: "if (1) the testimony is based upon sufficient facts or data, (2) the testimony is the product of reliable principles and methods, and (3) the witness has applied the principles and methods reliably to the facts of the case." The Advisory Committee notes indicate that the amendment "affirms the trial court's role as gatekeeper and provides some general standards that the trial court must use to assess the reliability and helpfulness of proffered expert testimony." It added that the "standards set forth in the amendment are broad enough to require consideration of any or all of the specific *Daubert* factors where appropriate." Additional factors also may be relevant.

The test for admissibility of scientific expert testimony in state courts is not necessarily the same as for federal court. In Goeb v. Tharaldson, 615 N.W.2d 800 (Minn. 2000), the court refused to abandon the *Frye* general acceptance test, as modified by previous Minnesota Supreme Court decisions to require an additional showing that the particular evidence derived from a novel scientific test has a foundation that is scientifically reliable, even though the applicable Minnesota rule of evidence was identical to Rule 702 of the federal rules. The court reasoned that *Daubert* confers upon "judges uneducated in science the authority to determine what is scientific," whereas *Frye* "ensures that the persons most qualified to assess scientific validity of a technique have the determinative voice." Id. at 813. See also Donalson v. Central Ill. Pub. Serv. Co., 767 N.E.2d 314, 323 (2002) (retaining *Frye*).

2. *The Impact of* Daubert. Consider the following assessment of *Daubert*:

> [*Daubert*] lowered a veil over civil litigation. The law, dense and esoteric as it is, has become much more so because many cases of alleged wrongful injuries are being decided as if they were the outcome of scientific seminars. Tort law has become increasingly cloaked behind the arcana of scientific evidence and legally subtle discussions of admissibility and pre-trial hearings. . . . In short, our legal system has become less comprehensible to ordinary citizens than it was previously. [C. Cranor, Toxic Torts 367 (2006).]

A study by the RAND Institute for Civil Justice found that the proportion of expert evidence that district courts have excluded increased after *Daubert*. L. Dixon & B. Gill, Changes in the Standards for Admitting Expert Evidence in Federal Civil Cases since the *Daubert* Decision (2001).

3. *Independence, Peer Review, and Other Factors.* A trial court ruling on the admissibility of expert scientific testimony need not take into account all of the factors the Court mentioned in *Daubert* as being relevant to the question of whether the testimony represents scientific knowledge. In Ellis v. Gallatin Steel Co., 390 F.3d 461 (6th Cir. 2004), the court concluded that the failure to consider the absence of peer review or scholarly writing did not preclude admission of testimony relating to an assessment of a local real estate market. On remand in *Daubert*, however, the plaintiffs' proffered evidence was found inadmissible. The Ninth Circuit indicated that one significant factor in determining reliability is

> whether the experts are proposing to testify about matters growing naturally and directly out of research they have conducted independent of the litigation, or whether they have developed their opinions expressly for purposes of testifying. . . .
>
> That an expert testifies based on research he has conducted independent of the litigation provides important, objective proof that the research comports with the dictates of good science. For one thing, experts whose findings flow from existing research are less likely to have been biased toward a particular conclusion by the promise of remuneration; when an expert prepares reports and findings before being hired as a witness, that record will limit the degree to which he can tailor his testimony to serve a party's interests. Then, too, independent research carries its own indicia of reliability, as it is conducted, so to speak, in the usual course of business and must normally satisfy a variety of standards to attract funding and institutional support. Finally, there is usually a limited number of

scientists actively conducting research on the very subject that is germane to a particular case, which provides a natural constraint on parties' ability to shop for experts who will come to the desired conclusion. . . . [Daubert v. Merrell Dow Pharmaceuticals, Inc., 43 F.3d 1311, 1317 (9th Cir. 1995).]

None of the plaintiffs' experts based their testimony concerning Bendectin's effect on birth defects on research conducted before they were hired to testify in *Daubert* or related cases. Because the plaintiffs' proffered expert testimony was not based on independent research, they had to produce other evidence that was objective and verifiable, such as scrutiny through peer review and publication. But none of the plaintiffs' experts had published their work on Bendectin in scientific journals, and no other scientists had verified, refuted, or commented on that work. "It's as if there were a tacit understanding within the scientific community that what's going on here is not science at all, but litigation." Id. at 1318. For other post-*Daubert* cases in which expert testimony was excluded, see Johnson v. Arkema, Inc., 685 F.3d 452 (5th Cir. 2012) (toxicologist's expert testimony on causal link between allegedly defective hood to shield workers from chemical exposures and worker's restrictive lung disease and pulmonary fibrosis); Barrett v. Rhoda, Inc., 606 F.3d 975 (8th Cir. 2010) (testimony on whether exposure to chemical caused brain injuries based on assumption, without scientific testing or exposure analysis). Compare City of Pomona v. SQM N. Am. Corp., 750 F.3d 1046 (9th Cir. 2014) (overturning exclusion of expert testimony on grounds of lack of general acceptance because "scientific methods that are subject to 'further testing and refinement' may be generally accepted and sufficiently reliable, and quoting *Daubert*'s statement that there are "no certainties in science").

In Milward v. Acuity Specialty Prod. Group, Inc., 639 F.3d 11 (1st Cir. 2011), the court ruled that plaintiff's expert's testimony on whether exposure to benzene-containing products manufactured by the defendants could have caused plaintiff's leukemia should have been admitted. The physician based his opinion on causation on a "weight of the evidence" approach, which the court described as a mode of logical reasoning based on "inference to the best explanation." The fact that scientific judgment is involved in applying that approach does not make it any less "scientific" than other causation methodologies. The physician relied on his knowledge and experience in the field of toxicology and molecular epidemiology and on five bodies of evidence drawn from the peer-reviewed scientific literature on benzene and leukemia. The opinion rested on a scientifically sound and methodologically reliable foundation, as required by *Daubert*. The possibility that an explanation other than the one offered by the expert might be correct did not justify excluding his testimony. The alleged flaws went to the weight, not admissibility of the expert's testimony. Nor was it determinative that relevant epidemiological studies did not offer conclusive statistically significant evidence either way. For a collection of articles on the impact of *Milward*, see Symposium: Toxic Tort Litigation After Milward v. Acuity Products, 3 Wake Forest J.J. & Pol'y 1-190 (2013). See also Schultz v. Akzo Nobel Paints, LLC, 721 F.3d 426 (7th Cir. 2013) (holding that trial court erred in excluding testimony of oncologist who relied on differential diagnosis—in which an expert rules out alternative causes and eliminates the possibility that the etiology of the disease is unknown—in concluding that decedent's exposure to paints manufactured by defendant that contained benzene was a substantial factor in causing the decedent's leukemia). Compare Pluck v. BP Oil Pipeline Co., 640 F.3d 671 (6th Cir. 2011) (upholding exclusion of testimony on causation because the expert failed to address whether plaintiff was exposed to benzene at a high enough level to cause illness and failed to rule out alternative causes, as required by differential diagnosis methodology).

    4. *Science and Risk Regulation.* Courts in toxic tort cases have used *Daubert* to exclude the kind of evidence routinely used to set toxic exposure standards, extrapolations from animal studies. See In re Paoli R.R. Yard PCB Litig., 35 F.3d 717, 743 (3d Cir. 1994). Does *Daubert* preclude regulators from relying on new fields of applied science? Should the standard of proof of causation be less for public health-based regulation than for tort liability? Environmental regulators may ask scientists to answer questions that they consider nonscientific, or at least to answer questions that arise in a form different from the way they arise within traditional scientific research. The answers often involve moral judgments about resource worth. Does *Daubert* make such judgments unscientific, and therefore insufficient to justify regulatory action? Must environmental standards be grounded in the scientific method as applied in *Daubert*? Does the last part of Justice Blackmun's opinion adequately address these concerns?[f]

C.   EARLY STATUTORY EXAMPLES OF PRECAUTIONARY REGULATION OF RISK

Environmental legislation often goes beyond the common law in authorizing the abatement of dangers posed by hazardous substances. Professor Applegate has summarized one rationale for shifting the focus of concern from harm to risk to redress the deficiencies in common law standards in controlling health and environmental risks.

> [R]egulation of risk instead of harm . . . contrasts with, and is a reaction to, the traditional tort law rule that damages can be recovered only for actual harm or for the definite likelihood of future harm to the individual plaintiff. Toxic effects are extremely difficult to prove under the preponderance of the evidence standard of civil litigation because of the great uncertainty caused by the passage of time (latency), the relative unlikelihood of causation (rarity of effect), and the possibility of other causes (nonsignature diseases) present in most toxic substances cases. As a result, tort law fails to internalize these costs and serves as a poor deterrent to toxic risk creation.
>
>   An important impetus for governmental regulation was the desire to overcome this obstacle to successful recovery for toxic injury. . . . Risk is an expression of uncertainty; it is easier to prove than actual harm. Regulation based on risk permits regulatory action based on *ex ante* collective danger rather than *ex post* individual injury, and also operates preventively to avert injury to the public as a whole. [Applegate, The Perils of Unreasonable Risk: Information, Regulatory Policy, and Toxic Substances Control, 91 Colum. L. Rev. 261, 271-273 (1991).]

---

    f. See Doremus, Data Gaps in Natural Resource Management: Sniffing for Leaks Along the Information Pipeline, 83 Ind. L.J. 407, 440 (2008) (arguing that, despite industry efforts to import *Daubert* into the administrative process, "[t]he *Daubert* standard is specific to the courtroom, both as a matter of law and as a matter of principle"); Kelly, The Dangers of *Daubert* Creep in the Regulatory Realm, 14 J.L. & Pol'y 165 (2006) (addressing the "danger that *Daubert* can undermine administrative law by fostering an attitude of skepticism of agency action based upon science and creating a rhetorical weapon with which to attack agency policy-making").

The question of whether Congress intended to depart from common law standards was raised in two landmark cases. In each case, brief federal statutes authorized the abatement of conditions that "endangered" the public health. In each, the strict common law approach denying abatement of risks was first embraced by the majority of a three-judge panel and then rejected on fuller consideration en banc. The second of the two cases, *Ethyl Corp.*, is excerpted below. The first case, Reserve Mining Co. v. EPA, 514 F.2d 492 (8th Cir. 1975), is discussed in the notes following *Ethyl Corp.*

ETHYL CORP. v. EPA
541 F.2d 1 (D.C. Cir. 1976)

[Section 211(c)(1)(A) of the Clean Air Act authorized the Administrator of EPA to regulate gasoline additives if their emissions products "will endanger the public health or welfare." After rulemaking proceedings in which EPA reviewed a number of inconclusive scientific studies indicating that lead emissions harmed the health of urban populations, particularly children, the Administrator determined that leaded gasoline emissions presented "a significant risk of harm," thereby endangering the public health within the meaning of the statute. The Administrator therefore set standards requiring an annual reduction in the lead content of gasoline.

In upholding those standards, the court, in an opinion by Judge Skelly Wright, made the following observations about the meaning of the critical statutory language and the scope of the agency's decisionmaking authority:]

. . . Case law and dictionary definition agree that endanger means something less than actual harm. When one is endangered, harm is *threatened*; no actual injury need ever occur. Thus, for example, a town may be "endangered" by a threatening plague or hurricane and yet emerge from the danger completely unscathed. A statute allowing for regulation in the face of danger is, necessarily, a precautionary statute. Regulatory action may be taken before the threatened harm occurs; indeed, the very existence of such precautionary legislation would seem to *demand* that regulatory action precede, and, optimally, prevent, the perceived threat. As should be apparent, the "will endanger" language of Section 211(c)(1)(A) makes it such a precautionary statute.

The Administrator read it as such, interpreting "will endanger" to mean "presents a significant risk of harm." We agree with the Administrator's interpretation. . . .

. . . While the dictionary admittedly settles on "probable" as its measure of danger, we believe a more sophisticated case-by-case analysis is appropriate. Danger, the Administrator recognized, is not set by a fixed probability of harm, but rather is composed of reciprocal elements of risk and harm, of probability and severity. Cf. Reserve Mining Co. v. EPA, [514 F.2d 492, 519-520 (8th Cir. 1975)]. That is to say, the public health may properly be found endangered both by a lesser risk of a greater harm and by a greater risk of a lesser harm.[32] Danger depends upon the relation

---

32. This proposition must be confined to reasonable limits, however. In Carolina Environmental Study Group v. United States, 510 F.2d 796 (1975), a division of this court found the possibility of a Class 9 nuclear reactor disaster, a disaster of ultimate severity and horrible consequences, to be so low that the Atomic Energy Commission's minimal consideration of the effects of such a disaster in an environmental impact statement prepared for a new reactor was sufficient. Likewise, even the absolute certainty of de minimis harm might not justify government action. Under §211 the threatened harm must be sufficiently significant to justify health-based regulation of national impact. . . .

between the risk and harm presented by each case, and cannot legitimately be pegged to "probable" harm, regardless of whether that harm be great or small. . . .

. . . Where a statute is precautionary in nature, the evidence difficult to come by, uncertain, or conflicting because it is on the frontiers of scientific knowledge, the regulations designed to protect the public health, and the decision that of an expert administrator, we will not demand rigorous step-by-step proof of cause and effect. Such proof may be impossible to obtain if the precautionary purpose of the statute is to be served. Of course, we are not suggesting that the Administrator has the power to act on hunches or wild guesses. . . . The Administrator may apply his expertise to draw conclusions from suspected, but not completely substantiated, relationships between facts, from trends among facts, from theoretical projections from imperfect data, from probative preliminary data not yet certifiable as "fact," and the like. We believe that a conclusion so drawn—a risk assessment—may, if rational, form the basis for health-related regulations under the "will endanger" language of Section 211.[58]

All this is not to say that Congress left the Administrator free to set policy on his own terms. To the contrary, the policy guidelines are largely set, both in the statutory term "will endanger" and in the relationship of that term to other sections of the Clean Air Act. These prescriptions direct the Administrator's actions. Operating within the prescribed guidelines, he must consider all of the information available to him. Some of the information will be factual, but much more of it will be speculative—scientific estimates and "guesstimates" of probable harm, hypotheses based on still-developing data, etc. Ultimately, he must act, in part on "factual issues," but largely "on choices of policy, on an assessment of risks, [and] on predictions dealing with matters on the frontiers of scientific knowledge. . . ." Amoco Oil Co. v. EPA, [501 F.2d 722, 741

---

58. . . . Petitioners argue that the Administrator must decide that lead emissions "will endanger" the public health solely on "facts," or . . . by a "chain of scientific facts or reasoning leading [the Administrator] ineluctably to this conclusion. . . ." Petitioners demand sole reliance on *scientific* facts, on evidence that reputable scientific techniques certify as certain. Typically, a scientist will not certify evidence unless the probability of error, by standard statistical measurement, is less than 5%. That is, scientific fact is at least 95% certain. Such certainty has never characterized the judicial or the administrative process. It may be that the "beyond a reasonable doubt" standard of criminal law demands 95% certainty. But the standard of ordinary civil litigation, a preponderance of the evidence, demands only 51% certainty. A jury may weigh conflicting evidence and certify as adjudicative (although not scientific) fact that which it believes is more likely than not. . . . Inherently, such a standard is flexible; inherently, it allows the fact-finder to assess risks, to measure probabilities, to make subjective judgments. Nonetheless, the ultimate finding will be treated, at law, as fact and will be affirmed if based on substantial evidence, or, if made by a judge, not clearly erroneous. The standard before administrative agencies is no less flexible. Agencies are not limited to scientific fact, to 95% certainties. Rather, they have at least the same fact-finding powers as a jury, particularly when, as here, they are engaged in rule-making. "Looking to the future, and commanded by Congress to make policy, a rule-making agency necessarily deals less with 'evidentiary' disputes than with normative conflicts, projections from imperfect data, experiments and simulations, educated predictions, differing assessments of possible risks, and the like." Amoco Oil Co. v. EPA, 501 F.2d at 735. An agency's finding of fact differs from that of a jury or trial judge primarily in that it is accorded more deference by a reviewing court. Thus, as a matter of administrative law, the Administrator found as fact that lead emissions "will endanger" the public health. That in so doing he did not have to rely solely on proved scientific fact is inherent in the requirements of legal fact-finding. Petitioners' assertions of the need to rely on "fact" confuse the two terminologies. We must deal with the terminology of law, not science. At law, unless the administrative or judicial task is peculiarly factual in nature, or Congress expressly commands a more rigorous finding, assessment of risks as herein described typifies both the administrative and the judicial fact-finding function, and is not the novel or unprecedented theory that petitioners contend.

(D.C. Cir. 1974)]. A standard of danger—fear of uncertain or unknown harm—contemplates no more.

[After reviewing the evidence in the administrative record, Judge Wright concluded that EPA complied with all statutory requirements and that its reasons provided a rational basis for its actions. Judge Wilkey dissented, contending that "the paucity of scientific evidence pointing to any firm conclusion, [and] the gaps in logic supporting the Administrator's analysis" rendered the regulations arbitrary and capricious. He argued that, by dispensing with any requirement that EPA rely on proof of actual harm which has already occurred, that is, by countenancing risk assessment, the majority had "grant[ed] the plainest license for the wildest speculation."]

NOTES AND QUESTIONS

1. *The Terminology of Risk Assessment.* Footnote 58 of *Ethyl* is an excellent statement of the jurisprudence of risk assessment. Judge Wright referred to both risk and uncertainty. According to Professor Hornstein, risk exists when one can calculate an outcome's "expected value" with reasonable confidence by multiplying its magnitude by its probability. Uncertainty exists when one's understanding of the underlying probabilities is "so shaky that expected values (losses) cannot be calculated with much confidence at all." Hornstein, Reclaiming Environmental Law: A Normative Critique of Comparative Risk Analysis, 92 Colum. L. Rev. 562, 571 (1992). See also Sunstein, Irreversible and Catastrophic, 91 Cornell L. Rev. 841, 848 (2006). Footnote 58 also distinguishes between legal and scientific "facts." Is a 51 to 94 percent certainty sufficient to support either kind of "fact"?

2. *Reserve Mining.* The *Reserve Mining* litigation involved an attempt to halt the company's discharge of mine tailings (the crushed rock residue discarded in the mining process) resembling asbestos fibers into Lake Superior. Concern that discharge of the fibers into the air and water created a cancer risk for those exposed to them prompted the United States, the states of Michigan, Wisconsin, and Minnesota, and several environmental groups to bring suit in federal district court to enjoin further discharges into either medium. The effort to halt discharges into the water was based in part on a provision of the pre-1972 Federal Water Pollution Control Act (FWPCA) authorizing the United States to secure abatement of discharges into interstate waters that, among other things, "endanger[ed] . . . the health or welfare of persons." 33 U.S.C. §1160(g)(1).

The district court ordered Reserve's facility to shut down, holding that its operation violated the FWPCA and state air pollution regulations, and that both the air and water discharges constituted common law nuisances. After a panel of the Eighth Circuit stayed the decision, the entire court, sitting en banc, modified the order and remanded. Focusing on the discharges into Lake Superior, the court remarked that:

> [i]n assessing probabilities in this case, it cannot be said that the probability of harm is more likely than not. Moreover, the level of probability does not readily convert into a prediction of consequences. On this record it cannot be forecast that the rates of cancer will increase from drinking Lake Superior water or breathing Silver Bay air. The best that can be said is that the existence of this asbestos contaminant in air and water gives rise to a reasonable medical concern for the public health. The public's exposure to asbestos fibers in air and water creates some health risk. Such a contaminant should be removed. [514 F.2d at 520.]

The issue under §1160(g)(1) was whether the discharges "endangered" the public health or welfare. The court found that Congress used the term "in a precautionary or preventive sense, and, therefore, evidence of potential harm as well as actual harm comes within the purview of that term." Id. at 528. The appellate court confirmed the district court's finding that, due to "an acceptable but unproved theory" that the tailings might be carcinogenic, the discharges constituted an endangerment subject to abatement. Id. at 529.

Nevertheless, the court refused to order an immediate shutdown of the plant, basing its decision on the need to "strike a proper balance between the benefits conferred and the hazards created" by the facility. Id. at 535. The benefits of the plant included a $350 million capital investment, construction of two company towns, jobs for more than 3,000 employees, and payment of substantial state and local taxes. The mine was responsible for 12 percent of total U.S. production of taconite. On the other hand, the probability of harm from exposure to tailings discharged into the water was low because, even though "[s]erious consequences could result" if the risk materialized, the probability did "not rest on a history of past health harm attributable to ingestion but on a medical theory implicating the ingestion of asbestos fibers as a causative factor in increasing the rates of gastrointestinal cancer among asbestos workers." Id. at 536. In addition, the court credited the intervening union's claim that ill health effects resulting from prolonged unemployment should the plant shut down might be more certain than the harm attributable to exposure to the tailings. Ultimately, the court concluded:

> Some pollution and ensuing environmental damage are, unfortunately, an inevitable concomitant of a heavily industrialized economy. In the absence of proof of a reasonable risk of imminent or actual harm, a legal standard requiring immediate cessation of industrial operations will cause unnecessary economic loss, including unemployment, and, in a case such as this, jeopardize a continuing domestic source of critical metals without conferring adequate countervailing benefits.
>
> We believe that on this record the district court abused its discretion by immediately closing this major industrial plant. In this case, the risk of harm to the public is potential, not imminent or certain, and Reserve says it earnestly seeks a practical way to abate the pollution. A remedy should be fashioned which will serve the ultimate public weal by insuring clean air, clean water, and continued jobs in an industry vital to the nation's welfare. . . . [Id. at 537.]

The court therefore gave Reserve "a reasonable time to stop discharging its wastes into Lake Superior," during which the company would arrange for land disposal of its waste. Id.

3. Village of Wilsonville, Ethyl Corp., *and* Reserve Mining *Compared.* What standards did the courts use in *Village of Wilsonville* and *Reserve Mining* to decide whether to enjoin the alleged risk-creating activities? Would the danger factually documented in *Reserve Mining* have justified injunctive relief under the standard applied by the majority in *Wilsonville*? Under the standard adopted by the concurrence in *Wilsonville*? Which of the three approaches is closest to that suggested by the Page excerpt at the beginning of this chapter?

The statutory standards at issue in *Ethyl Corp.* and *Reserve Mining* are quite similar. What differences, if any, do you detect in the two courts' interpretations and applications of the "endangerment" standard? The result of considering both the *probability* that actual harm will eventually occur and the *magnitude* or severity of that harm if it does occur sometimes is called "risk," but it is also sometimes called "danger." As Judge Wright indicates, "danger . . . is not set by a fixed probability of harm, but rather is composed of reciprocal elements of . . . probability and severity." *Ethyl Corp.*, 541 F.2d at 18.

If danger or risk depends on two interdependent factors, probability and magnitude of harm, and neither factor can be considered in isolation, then what was the court in *Reserve Mining* doing when, in addressing the remedies to be applied, it reassessed the "probabilities of harm" and then refused to sustain the trial court's injunction? Was it incorrectly applying its own analytic framework by permitting the timing of relief to hinge on probability alone? See Henderson & Pearson, Implementing Federal Environmental Policies: The Limits of Aspirational Commands, 78 Colum. L. Rev. 1429, 1453-1456 (1978).

To justify its refusal to grant an immediate injunction, the *Reserve Mining* court contrasted the "potential" threat to the public health it found to exist with an "imminent" danger to public health. The implication is that only an "imminent" hazard merits immediate relief, and Reserve's discharges did not present one. Yet is it correct to say that the danger in *Reserve* was not imminent? If Reserve Mining was almost ready to open the mine and dump the first load of tailings into the lake, the danger could have been imminent. But in the actual case, the danger existed, and the statute said nothing about showing imminent *harm* before relief could be granted.

The courts have relied on *Ethyl Corp.* in endorsing EPA's precautionary approach in other water pollution cases. In Upper Blackstone Water Pollution Abatement Dist. v. EPA, 690 F.3d 9 (1st Cir. 2012), for example, the court rejected an attack on effluent limitations imposed by EPA on a sewage treatment plant discharging into an impaired water body. The plant argued that EPA should have waited to impose limits until a new computer model of discharges into the river was available. The court deferred, however, to EPA's "risk analysis of the consequences of waiting." It noted that "[i]n almost every case, more data can be collected, models further calibrated to match real world conditions; the hope or anticipation that better science will materialize is always present, to some degree, in the context of science-based agency decisionmaking. Congress was aware of this when it nonetheless set a firm deadline for issuing new permits." Id. at 23. The court concluded that "[a]s in many science-based policymaking contexts, under the CWA the EPA is required to exercise its judgment even in the face of some scientific uncertainty. . . . The EPA did not act irrationally here by issuing the permit in the face of some scientific uncertainty." Id.

4. *The Role of Public Input.* What should be the role of those who live near and those who work in a plant engaged in activities alleged to create risks similar to those involved in *Reserve Mining* in deciding the fate of those activities? One view is that "it is more important in a democracy that the public have the decision it wants, rationally or irrationally, right or wrong, than that the 'correct' decision be made." Green, Limitations on the Implementation of Technology Assessment, 14 Atomic Energy L.J. 59, 82 (1972). In 1983, EPA held public workshops in Tacoma, Washington, in which it informed the public that a copper smelter's emissions of arsenic, a known carcinogen, created a cancer risk for workers and nearby residents. The plant's employees responded that unemployment and the emotional and economic stress resulting from it created worse health risks than those posed by the plant's operation. While some residents and editorialists argued that the issue was too sophisticated for public input, EPA Administrator William Ruckelshaus concluded that the community reached some sort of consensus and that the agency was informed by the public's nontechnical concerns. Pildes & Sunstein, Reinventing the Regulatory State, 62 U. Chi. L. Rev. 1, 89-90 (1995). The plant was closed, but the overcapacity of the copper

industry may have played at least as great a role as environmental factors. Sunstein, On the Divergent American Reactions to Terrorism and Climate Change, 107 Colum. L. Rev. 503 (2007), contends that the divergence between the belief of many Americans that aggressive action to reduce the risks of terrorist events is worth taking, but that aggressive action to reduce the risk of global climate change is not, is based on intuitive cost-benefit analysis, affected by bounded rationality.

5. *The Impact of* Ethyl Corp. *and* Reserve Mining. In 1970, before the adoption of a spate of environmental legislation, Professor James Krier wrote that "burden of proof rules at present have an inevitable bias against protection of the environment. . . ." Krier, Environmental Litigation and the Burden of Proof, in Law and the Environment 105, 107 (M. Baldwin & J. Page eds., 1970). *Ethyl Corp.* and *Reserve Mining* have decisively influenced judicial interpretation of practically all subsequently adopted regulatory statutes that attempt to protect health and the environment before actual harm occurs. Indeed, the rationale that they provide stretches across the breadth of pollution control legislation, from the provisions contained in all the major pollution control statutes for direct abatement by court action when the federal government can show that "imminent and substantial endangerment" to health and the environment exists, to the threshold showing of danger necessary to trigger regulation under conventional ambient and emissions standards provisions. Interestingly, the statutory provisions at issue in both cases have since been amended. Look at §211(c)(1) of the Clean Air Act and §504(a) of the Clean Water Act. Do they endorse or refute the courts' respective decisions in *Ethyl Corp.* and *Reserve Mining*? See also H.R. Rep. No. 95-294 (1977) (explaining the amendments to §211(c)(1)).

6. *False Positives and False Negatives.* Debate over the advisability of precautionary regulation often revolves around the distinction between false positives and false negatives. A false positive arises when a regulation to address an environmental risk turns out, after the accumulation of more information, to have been unnecessary. A false negative occurs when information reveals that a decision not to regulate was premised on the erroneous conclusion that the risk presented either did not exist or was acceptably low. Overregulation based on a false positive imposes costs on the regulated community and on the consumers of the products and services they produce. Underregulation based on a false negative imposes costs on those who incur risk as a result of exposure to the unregulated substance or activity. C. Cranor, Regulating Toxic Substances: A Philosophy of Science and the Law 8 (1993). One argument for precautionary regulation is that the costs imposed by a false positive tend to be less (or less serious) than the often irreversible costs emanating from a false negative. What are some examples that support this view? See Guruswamy, Global Warming: Integrating United States and International Law, 32 Ariz. L. Rev. 221 (1990). The opposing view is that false positives may pose greater threats to public health than false negatives because regulation may induce conduct or the use of alternative substances that pose even greater risks than those being regulated. Banning a pesticide may allow the proliferation of molds that create health risks. A crackdown on nuclear power plant operating practices may require more frequent shutdowns and start-ups, even though these activities are the stages of operation that pose the greatest risk of an accident. See Cross, The Public Role in Risk Control, 24 Envtl. L. 887 (1994).

7. *A Postscript on* Ethyl Corp. After the decision in *Ethyl Corp.*, studies revealed that combustion of lead-containing fuels was the principal source of lead in the environment, that the blood lead level of urban children directly correlated with the lead content of gasoline, and that high blood lead levels caused psychological and

behavioral problems in those children. In the 1990 Clean Air Act amendments, Congress banned the sale of leaded gasoline for use as fuel in any motor vehicle effective January 1, 1996. 42 U.S.C. §7545(n).

D. DEALING WITH RISK THROUGH COMPARATIVE RISK ASSESSMENT AND COST-BENEFIT ANALYSIS

Much of the rest of this chapter concerns federal regulatory statutes that at least in part shift the burden of proving safety to risk creators. Although the details differ from statute to statute, a common analytical framework for regulating risk applies in a variety of contexts. For each statute, Congress had to answer two key questions. The first is the risk assessment question: what criteria should the agency with responsibility to implement the statute apply in deciding whether to regulate a particular activity or substance, or, stated otherwise, what is the threshold showing of risk that will suffice to trigger the agency's authority to regulate? The second major question is the risk management question: once the agency has decided to regulate a particular risk, what standards should it apply in choosing the appropriate method and extent of regulation?

Subsequent sections of this chapter and the next address the details of how Congress and regulatory agencies such as EPA have answered these questions. This section provides an overview of some of the issues raised by the use of the two fundamental concepts traced in section A.2 of this chapter—risk assessment (particularly the comparative and quantitative varieties) and risk management—in regulation that is designed to address the health and environmental risks posed by the generation, use, and management of toxic materials.

1. The Rationale for Comparative Risk Assessment

The Diagnosis. Federal environmental regulation began in earnest in 1970, with the passage of NEPA and the Clean Air Act. Collectively, the many environmental statutes adopted by Congress during the next two decades applied to activities that used toxic substances in otherwise useful endeavors and that generated hazardous waste in every environmental medium—air, water, and land.

By the 1990s, however, it was clear to many that more regulation did not always mean better regulation. In particular, critics of this accretion of risk-regulating commands charged that federal environmental regulation had resulted in a misallocation of expenditures both by regulators and the regulated community. See generally Glicksman & Chapman, Regulatory Reform and (Breach of) the Contract with America: Improving Environmental Policy or Destroying Environmental Protection?, 5 Kan. J.L. & Pub. Pol'y (Winter 1996), at 9, 13-15. The principal problem was how to set regulatory priorities by ranking the health and environmental risks agencies had identified. Irrational or haphazard priority setting could result in overregulation of some hazards and underregulation of others.

One forceful critic was then–Circuit Judge Stephen Breyer, whose book Breaking the Vicious Circle: Toward Effective Risk Regulation (1993), argued that regulation often focused on the wrong risks. One result was that even though cancer is "the engine that drives much of health risk regulation," id. at 6, regulation prevented only a small portion of annual U.S. cancer deaths. Breyer described three problems. First, regulation often reflects too much of a good thing. By seeking to eliminate the last 10 percent of the risk, regulators impose enormous costs without achieving significant incremental risk reductions. What if an increase in pollutant concentrations in the blood at low levels is found to have greater adverse effects on human health than an increase of the same magnitude at higher concentration levels? What effect would that finding have on Justice Breyer's "too much of a good thing" argument? See Warren, The Little Engine that Could Poison, N.Y. Times, June 22, 2007 (discussing findings concerning the effects of lead concentrations in human blood). In addition, agencies rarely select the least-cost means of regulation. Second, agencies such as EPA lack a rational agenda selection mechanism. Breyer's charge echoed a 1987 report, Unfinished Business: A Comparative Assessment of Environmental Problems, in which EPA concluded that its regulatory efforts tended to be more responsive to public perceptions of risk severity than to the views of its own scientific experts. The report described a mismatch between EPA's focus on medium to low risks, such as groundwater pollution, and the inadequacy of its efforts to address serious risks such as indoor air pollution and global warming. Third, different agencies use different methods to assess risks and too often ignore the effect of regulation of one environmental medium upon another.

Breyer attributed these problems to irrational public perceptions of risk, overly prescriptive and compartmentalized legislation, and the use by regulators of excessively conservative assumptions to deal with uncertainty. That conservative posture exacerbates public concern, which contributes to continuing irrationality in the perception of risk and to inappropriate responses by legislators and regulators alike.

The Prescription. The analytical technique that emerged as the most promising candidate for reallocating risk reduction efforts was comparative risk assessment (CRA), the process by which scientists determine which environmental risks are the most serious. The goal of this ranking process is to assign priorities to environmental problems so that limited resources are directed at the most serious risks first. Better allocation of these resources will spread them further and generate a higher rate of return on the regulatory investment. Ideally, CRA would take the form of "societal risk reduction" analysis, a comparison of *all* health and safety risks, so that, for example, risk reduction investments could be rechanneled from environmental regulation to expanded childhood vaccinations and crime prevention measures, if those initiatives would provide greater risk reduction payoffs. See generally Bender, Societal Risk Reduction: Promise and Pitfalls, 3 N.Y.U. Envtl. L.J. 255 (1995). Breyer urged the creation of a centralized, multidisciplinary team of experts to conduct CRA. Regulatory decisions based on the scientific underpinnings of CRA could prevent capture of regulators by the supporters of an irrational risk reduction agenda.

"Risk-Risk" Analysis. Some proponents of CRA argue that regulation can cause as well as avert harm and that, before deciding to regulate, agencies should compare the harms attributable to and avoided by regulation to ensure that the former does not exceed the latter and that regulation is not counterproductive. According to this theory, sometimes referred to as "risk-risk" or "richer is safer" analysis,

> [i]ndividuals with more disposable income are less likely to die, to become ill, or to suffer accidental injuries. Thus, a regulation that reduces disposable income might have an incidental effect of increasing death, illness, and injury. Consequently, a regulation that imposes significant costs could produce a negative health effect that more than

counteracts the positive health effect from reduced exposure to harmful substances. [Cross, When Environmental Regulations Kill: The Role of Health/Health Analysis, 22 Ecology L.Q. 729, 731 (1995).][g]

By one estimate, each $7.25 million spent on regulation will cause one death. Keeney, Mortality Risks Induced by Economic Expenditures, 10 Risk Analysis 147 (1990).

In International Union, UAW v. OSHA, 938 F.2d 1310 (D.C. Cir. 1991), Judge Stephen Williams, concurring, relied on both the theory and Keeney's figures to conclude that less stringent regulations under the Occupational Safety and Health (OSH) Act would not necessarily adversely affect worker health and safety. In American Dental Ass'n v. Martin, 984 F.2d 823 (7th Cir. 1993), the court rejected an attack on regulations under the OSH Act limiting workplace exposure to blood-borne pathogens based on OSHA's failure to use risk-risk analysis. Although the court accepted the theoretical basis for risk-risk analysis, it concluded that the challengers failed to quantify such "indirect" costs of regulation as increased costs of medical care, and therefore that the agency's decision to ignore those costs was not arbitrary. The intervening union in *Reserve Mining* also relied on a rudimentary version of risk-risk analysis in arguing against plant closure. What was the union's argument? See also NRDC v. EPA, 902 F.2d 962, 972-973 (D.C. Cir. 1990) (rejecting argument that standards limiting ambient lead concentrations under the Clean Air Act were flawed because EPA failed to consider the adverse health consequences of unemployment that would result from issuance of the standards); United States v. Vertac Chem. Corp., 33 F. Supp. 2d 769, 779-780 (E.D. Ark. 1998) (rejecting challenge to hazardous substance cleanup based on EPA's failure to consider risks of injuries and fatalities to workers involved in the cleanup), *vacated on other grounds*, 247 F.3d 706 (8th Cir. 2001). In Union Elec. Co. v. EPA, 427 U.S. 246 (1976), reproduced in Chapter 6, Justice Powell concurred with the majority's holding that EPA lacked the authority to reject a state implementation plan under the Clean Air Act on the ground that it was infeasible. He added, however, that the adverse effects on public health that would result from shutting down an electric utility might outweigh the adverse health effects attributable to continued air pollution, and that "Congress, if fully aware of this Draconian possibility, would strike a different balance." Id. at 271. For a statutory analogue of risk-risk analysis, see 42 U.S.C. §7412(f)(1)(C).

2. *Quantitative Risk Assessment*

NATIONAL RESEARCH COUNCIL OF THE NATIONAL ACADEMIES, SCIENCE AND DECISIONS: ADVANCING RISK ASSESSMENT
19 (2010)

Whatever the decision context, the goal of risk assessment is to describe the probability that adverse health or ecosystem effects of specific types will occur

g. See also Wildavsky, Richer Is Safer, 60 Pub. Int. 23 (1980); Calandrillo, Responsible Regulation: A Sensible Cost-Benefit, Risk versus Risk Approach to Federal Health and Safety Regulation, 81 B.U. L. Rev. 957, 964 (2001) (risk-risk analysis "simply means that the risks unintentionally created by the imposition of a new regulation should never outweigh the risks reduced or alleviated by that regulation").

under specified conditions of exposure to an activity or an agent (chemical, biologic, radiologic, or physical), to describe the uncertainty in the probability estimate, and to describe how risk varies among populations. To be most useful in decision-making, risk assessment would consider the risks associated with existing conditions (that is, the probability of harm under the "take no action" alternative) and the risks that would remain if each of various possible actions were taken to alter the conditions. There would also be a need for some commonality in the uncertainty analysis goals and assumptions that are applied to each of the analyses so that the different policy options can be compared. The conduct of risk assessment in the broadest practicable risk-management context brings to light the fullest possible picture of net public-health and environmental benefits.

INDUSTRIAL UNION DEPARTMENT, AFL-CIO v. AMERICAN PETROLEUM INSTITUTE
448 U.S. 607 (1980)

Mr. Justice STEVENS announced the judgment of the Court and delivered an opinion, in which The CHIEF JUSTICE and Mr. Justice STEWART joined and in [parts] of which Mr. Justice POWELL joined.

. . . This litigation concerns a standard promulgated by the Secretary of Labor [under the Occupational Safety and Health Act of 1970] to regulate occupational exposure to benzene, a substance which has been shown to cause cancer at high exposure levels. The principal question is whether such a showing is a sufficient basis for a standard that places the most stringent limitation on exposure to benzene that is technologically and economically possible.

The Act delegates broad authority to the Secretary to promulgate different kinds of standards. The basic definition of an "occupational safety and health standard" is found in §3(8), which provides: "The term 'occupational safety and health standard' means a standard which requires conditions, or the adoption or use of one or more practices, means, methods, operations, or processes, reasonably necessary or appropriate to provide safe or healthful employment and places of employment." 29 U.S.C. §652(8). . . . Where toxic materials or harmful physical agents are concerned, a standard must also comply with §6(b)(5), which provides [that] "[t]he Secretary, in promulgating standards dealing with [such materials], shall set the standard which most adequately assures, to the extent feasible, on the basis of the best available evidence, that no employee will suffer material impairment of functional capacity even if such employee has regular exposure for the period of his working life." 29 U.S.C. §655(b)(5). . . .

[After finding a causal connection between benzene exposure and leukemia (a cancer of the white blood cells), the Secretary set an exposure limit on airborne concentrations of one part benzene per million parts of air (1 ppm). The Fifth Circuit held that the regulation was invalid because the Occupational Safety and Health Administration (OSHA) failed to show that the exposure limit was "reasonably necessary or appropriate to provide safe or healthful employment" as required by §3(8), and because §6(b)(5) does "not give OSHA the unbridled discretion to adopt standards designed to create absolutely risk-free workplaces regardless of costs." The court read the two provisions as requiring the agency to assess whether the benefits expected from the standard bore a reasonable relationship to the costs it imposed. Although OSHA estimated the costs of compliance, it did not demonstrate substantial evidence of any discernible benefits.]

We agree with the Fifth Circuit's holding that §3(8) requires the Secretary to find, as a threshold matter, that the toxic substance in question poses a significant health risk in the workplace and that a new, lower standard is therefore "reasonably necessary or appropriate to provide safe or healthful employment and places of employment." . . .

I

[Benzene, a liquid that evaporates rapidly under ordinary atmospheric conditions, was produced in large quantities by the petroleum, petrochemical, and steel industries. It was used to manufacture products that included motor fuels, solvents, detergents, and other organic chemicals. "The entire population of the United States is exposed to small quantities of benzene, ranging from a few parts per billion to 0.5 ppm, in the ambient air. Over one million workers are subject to additional low-level exposures as a consequence of their employment." Most of those workers were employed in a limited number of occupations, including gasoline service stations, benzene production operations, chemical processing, and rubber manufacturing.]

Benzene is a toxic substance. . . . [T]he principal risk of harm comes from inhalation of benzene vapors. When these vapors are inhaled, the benzene diffuses through the lungs and is quickly absorbed into the blood. Exposure to high concentrations produces an almost immediate effect on the central nervous system. Inhalation of concentrations of 20,000 ppm can be fatal within minutes; exposures in the range of 250 to 500 ppm can cause vertigo, nausea, and other symptoms of mild poisoning. Persistent exposures at levels above 25-40 ppm may lead to blood deficiencies and diseases of the blood-forming organs, including aplastic anemia, which is generally fatal.

. . . As early as 1928, some health experts theorized that there might . . . be a connection between benzene in the workplace and leukemia. In the late 1960's and early 1970's a number of epidemiological studies were published indicating that workers exposed to high concentrations of benzene were subject to significantly increased risk of leukemia. In a 1974 report . . . , the National Institute for Occupational Safety and Health (NIOSH), OSHA's research arm, noted that these studies raised the "distinct possibility" that benzene caused leukemia. . . .

[NIOSH interpreted additional studies published between 1974 and 1976 as providing "conclusive" proof of a causal connection between benzene and leukemia. Acknowledging that the dose-response data it had found lacking earlier were still not available, NIOSH nevertheless recommended that the exposure limit be set as low as possible. OSHA responded in 1977 by issuing a permanent standard that reduced the benzene exposure limit from 10 to 1 ppm. OSHA explained that benzene had been shown to cause leukemia at exposures below 25 ppm and that a 1 ppm exposure limit was feasible.]

In its published statement giving notice of the proposed permanent standard, OSHA did not ask for comments as to whether or not benzene presented a significant health risk at exposures of 10 ppm or less. Rather, it asked for comments as to whether 1 ppm was the minimum feasible exposure limit. [T]his formulation of the issue . . . was consistent with OSHA's general policy with respect to carcinogens. Whenever a carcinogen is involved, OSHA will presume that no safe level of exposure exists in the absence of clear proof establishing such a level and will accordingly set the exposure limit at the lowest level feasible. . . . Given OSHA's cancer policy, it was in fact irrelevant whether there was any evidence at all of a leukemia risk at 10 ppm. The important point was that there was no evidence that there was not some risk, however small, at that level. . . .

. . . [T]he benzene standard is an expensive way of providing some additional protection for a relatively small number of employees. . . . [O]nly 35,000 employees would gain any benefit from the regulation in terms of a reduction in their exposure to benzene. [The record indicated that compliance costs would be $1,390 per employee in the rubber industry and $82,000 per employee in the petroleum refining industry.]

. . . [I]t appears from the economic impact study done at OSHA's direction that [the benefits of regulation] may be relatively small. . . . [T]he actual exposures outlined in that study are often considerably lower [than the current 10 ppm standard]. For example, for the period 1970-1975 the petrochemical industry reported that, out of a total of 496 employees exposed to benzene, only 53 were exposed to levels between 1 and 5 ppm and only 7 (all at the same plant) were exposed to between 5 and 10 ppm.

II

. . . The written explanation of the standard . . . demonstrates that there is ample justification for regulating occupational exposure to benzene and that the prior limit of 10 ppm, with a ceiling of 25 ppm (or a peak of 50 ppm) was reasonable. It does not, however, provide direct support for the Agency's conclusion that the limit should be reduced from 10 ppm to 1 ppm.

The evidence in the administrative record of adverse effects of benzene exposure at 10 ppm is sketchy at best. OSHA noted that there was "no dispute" that certain nonmalignant blood disorders . . . could result from exposures of 25-40 ppm. It then stated that several studies had indicated that relatively slight changes in normal blood values could result from exposures below 25 ppm and perhaps below 10 ppm. OSHA did not attempt to make any estimate based on these studies of how significant the risk of nonmalignant disease would be at exposures of 10 ppm or less. Rather, it stated that because of the lack of data concerning the linkage between low-level exposures and blood abnormalities, it was impossible to construct a dose-response curve at this time.[33] OSHA did conclude, however, that the studies demonstrated that the current 10 ppm exposure limit was inadequate to ensure that no single worker would suffer a nonmalignant blood disorder as a result of benzene exposure. Noting that it is "customary" to set a permissible exposure limit by applying a safety factor of 10-100 to the lowest level at which adverse effects had been observed, the Agency stated that the evidence supported the conclusion that the limit should be set at a point "substantially less than 10 ppm" even if benzene's leukemic effects were not

---

33. "A dose-response curve shows the relationship between different exposure levels and the risk of cancer [or any other disease] associated with those exposure levels. Generally, exposure to higher levels carries with it a higher risk, and exposure to lower levels is accompanied by a reduced risk." 581 F.2d, at 504, n.24. OSHA's comments with respect to the insufficiency of the data were addressed primarily to the lack of data at low exposure levels. OSHA did not discuss whether it was possible to make a rough estimate, based on the more complete epidemiological and animal studies done at higher exposure levels, of the significance of the risks attributable to those levels, nor did it discuss whether it was possible to extrapolate from such estimates to derive a risk estimate for low-level exposures.

considered. OSHA did not state, however, that the nonmalignant effects of benzene exposure justified a reduction in the permissible exposure limit to 1 ppm.

[The plurality described the evidence of an increased cancer risk due to benzene exposure as "even sketchier." The agency cited no empirical evidence to support the conclusion that exposure to benzene at or below 10 ppm "had ever in fact caused leukemia."] In the end OSHA's rationale for lowering the permissible exposure limit to 1 ppm was based, not on any finding that leukemia has ever been caused by exposure to 10 ppm of benzene and that it will not be caused by exposure to 1 ppm, but rather on a series of assumptions indicating that some leukemias might result from exposure to 10 ppm and that the number of cases might be reduced by reducing the exposure level to 1 ppm. In reaching that result, the Agency first unequivocally concluded that benzene is a human carcinogen. Second, it concluded that industry had failed to prove that there is a safe threshold level of exposure to benzene below which no excess leukemia cases would occur. . . .

Third, the Agency applied its standard policy with respect to carcinogens, concluding that, in the absence of definitive proof of a safe level, it must be assumed that any level above zero presents some increased risk of cancer. . . . [T]here are a number of scientists and public health specialists who subscribe to this view, theorizing that a susceptible person may contract cancer from the absorption of even one molecule of a carcinogen like benzene.[41]

Fourth, the Agency reiterated its view of the Act, stating that it was required by §6(b)(5) to set the standard either at the level that has been demonstrated to be safe or at the lowest level feasible, whichever is higher. If no safe level is established, as in this case, the Secretary's interpretation of the statute automatically leads to the selection of an exposure limit that is the lowest feasible. . . . [T]he Agency selected 1 ppm as a workable exposure level, and then determined that compliance with that level was technologically feasible and that "the economic impact of . . . [compliance] will not be such as to threaten the financial welfare of the affected firms or the general economy." 43 Fed. Reg. 5939 (1978). It therefore held that 1 ppm was the minimum feasible exposure level within the meaning of §6(b)(5) of the Act.

Finally, [OSHA] . . . concluded that some benefits were likely to result from reducing the exposure limit from 10 ppm to 1 ppm. This conclusion was based, again, not on evidence, but rather on the assumption that the risk of leukemia will decrease as exposure levels decrease. Although the Agency had found it impossible to construct a dose-response curve that would predict with any accuracy the number of leukemias that could be expected to result from exposures at 10 ppm, at 1 ppm, or at any intermediate level, it nevertheless "determined that the benefits of the proposed standard are likely to be appreciable." 43 Fed. Reg. 5941 (1978). . . .

It is noteworthy that at no point in its lengthy explanation did the Agency quote or even cite §3(8) of the Act. It made no finding that any of the provisions of the new

---

41. The so-called "one hit" theory is based on laboratory studies indicating that one molecule of a carcinogen may react in the test tube with one molecule of DNA to produce a mutation. The theory is that, if this occurred in the human body, the mutated molecule could replicate over a period of years and eventually develop into a cancerous tumor. . . . In light of the improbability of a person's contracting cancer as a result of a single hit, a number of the scientists testifying on both sides of the issue agreed that every individual probably does have a threshold exposure limit below which he or she will not contract cancer. The problem, however, is that individual susceptibility appears to vary greatly and there is no present way to calculate each and every person's threshold. Thus, even industry witnesses agreed that if the standard must ensure with absolute certainty that every single worker is protected from any risk of leukemia, only a zero exposure limit would suffice.

standard were "reasonably necessary or appropriate to provide safe or healthful employment and places of employment." Nor did it allude to the possibility that any such finding might have been appropriate.

III

Our resolution of the issues in these cases turns, to a large extent, on the meaning of and the relationship between §3(8) . . . and §6(b)(5). . . .

In the Government's view, §3(8)'s definition of the term "standard" has no legal significance or at best merely requires that a standard not be totally irrational. It takes the position that §6(b)(5) is controlling and that it requires OSHA to promulgate a standard that either gives an absolute assurance of safety for each and every worker or reduces exposures to the lowest level feasible. The Government interprets "feasible" as meaning technologically achievable at a cost that would not impair the viability of the industries subject to the regulation. The respondent industry representatives, on the other hand, argue that the Court of Appeals was correct in holding that the "reasonably necessary and appropriate" language of §3(8), along with the feasibility requirement of §6(b)(5), requires the Agency to quantify both the costs and the benefits of a proposed rule and to conclude that they are roughly commensurate.

. . . [W]e think . . . that §3(8) . . . requires the Secretary, before issuing any standard, to determine that it is reasonably necessary and appropriate to remedy a significant risk of material health impairment. Only after the Secretary has made the threshold determination that such a risk exists with respect to a toxic substance, would it be necessary to decide whether §6(b)(5) requires him to select the most protective standard he can consistent with economic and technological feasibility, or whether, as respondents argue, the benefits of the regulation must be commensurate with the costs of its implementation. Because the Secretary did not make the required threshold finding in these cases, we have no occasion to determine whether costs must be weighed against benefits in an appropriate case. . . .

. . . [W]e think it is clear that the statute was not designed to require employers to provide absolutely risk-free workplaces whenever it is technologically feasible to do so, so long as the cost is not great enough to destroy an entire industry. Rather, both the language and structure of the Act, as well as its legislative history, indicate that it was intended to require the elimination, as far as feasible, of significant risks of harm. . . .

By empowering the Secretary to promulgate standards that are "reasonably necessary or appropriate to provide safe or healthful employment and places of employment," the Act implies that, before promulgating any standard, the Secretary must make a finding that the workplaces in question are not safe. But "safe" is not the equivalent of "risk-free." There are many activities that we engage in every day — such as driving a car or even breathing city air — that entail some risk of accident or material health impairment; nevertheless, few people would consider these activities "unsafe." Similarly, a workplace can hardly be considered "unsafe" unless it threatens the workers with a significant risk of harm.

Therefore, before he can promulgate any permanent health or safety standard, the Secretary is required to make a threshold finding that a place of employment is unsafe — in the sense that significant risks are present and can be eliminated or lessened by a change in practices. This requirement applies to permanent standards promulgated pursuant to §6(b)(5) . . . [f]or there is no reason why §3(8)'s definition of a standard should not be deemed incorporated by reference into §6(b)(5). . . .

In the absence of a clear mandate in the Act, it is unreasonable to assume that Congress intended to give the Secretary the unprecedented power over American industry that would result from the Government's view of §§3(8) and 6(b)(5), coupled with OSHA's cancer policy. . . . In light of the fact that there are literally thousands of substances used in the workplace that have been identified as carcinogens or suspect carcinogens, the Government's theory would give OSHA power to impose enormous costs that might produce little, if any, discernible benefit.

If the Government was correct in arguing that neither §3(8) nor §6(b)(5) requires that the risk from a toxic substance be quantified sufficiently to enable the Secretary to characterize it as significant in an understandable way, the statute would make such a "sweeping delegation of legislative power" that it might be unconstitutional under the Court's reasoning in A.L.A. Schechter Poultry Corp. v. United States, 295 U.S. 495, 539, and Panama Refining Co. v. Ryan, 293 U.S. 388. A construction of the statute that avoids this kind of open-ended grant should certainly be favored. . . .

Given the conclusion that the Act empowers the Secretary to promulgate health and safety standards only where a significant risk of harm exists, the critical issue becomes how to define and allocate the burden of proving the significance of the risk in a case such as this, where scientific knowledge is imperfect and the precise quantification of risks is therefore impossible. The Agency's position is that there is substantial evidence in the record to support its conclusion that there is no absolutely safe level for a carcinogen and that, therefore, the burden is properly on industry to prove, apparently beyond a shadow of a doubt, that there is a safe level for benzene exposure. The Agency argues that, because of the uncertainties in this area, any other approach would render it helpless, forcing it to wait for the leukemia deaths that it believes are likely to occur before taking any regulatory action.

We disagree. As we read the statute, the burden was on the Agency to show, on the basis of substantial evidence, that it is at least more likely than not that long-term exposure to 10 ppm of benzene presents a significant risk of material health impairment. Ordinarily, it is the proponent of a rule or order who has the burden of proof in administrative proceedings. See 5 U.S.C. §556(d). In some cases involving toxic substances, Congress has shifted the burden of proving that a particular substance is safe onto the party opposing the proposed rule. The fact that Congress did not follow this course in enacting the [OSH] Act indicates that it intended the Agency to bear the normal burden of establishing the need for a proposed standard. [The Court concluded that OSHA failed to carry its burden of proof.] . . .

Contrary to the Government's contentions, imposing a burden on the Agency of demonstrating a significant risk of harm will not strip it of its ability to regulate carcinogens, nor will it require the Agency to wait for deaths to occur before taking any action. First, the requirement that a "significant" risk be identified is not a mathematical straitjacket. It is the Agency's responsibility to determine, in the first instance, what it considers to be a "significant" risk. Some risks are plainly acceptable and others are plainly unacceptable. If, for example, the odds are one in a billion that a person will die from cancer by taking a drink of chlorinated water, the risk clearly could not be considered significant. On the other hand, if the odds are one in a thousand that regular inhalation of gasoline vapors that are 2% benzene will be fatal, a reasonable person might well consider the risk significant and take appropriate steps to decrease or eliminate it. Although the Agency has no duty to calculate the exact probability of harm, it does have an obligation to find that a significant risk is present before it can characterize a place of employment as "unsafe."[62]

Second, OSHA is not required to support its finding that a significant risk exists with anything approaching scientific certainty. Although the Agency's findings must be supported by substantial evidence, 29 U.S.C. §655(f), §6(b)(5) specifically allows the Secretary to regulate on the basis of the "best available evidence." . . . [T]his provision requires a reviewing court to give OSHA some leeway where its findings must be made on the frontiers of scientific knowledge. Thus, so long as they are supported by a body of reputable scientific thought, the Agency is free to use conservative assumptions in interpreting the data with respect to carcinogens, risking error on the side of overprotection rather than underprotection. . . .

. . . We express no opinion on what . . . factual determinations would warrant a conclusion that significant risks are present which make promulgation of a new standard reasonably necessary or appropriate. . . .

In this case the record makes it perfectly clear that the Secretary relied squarely on a special policy for carcinogens that imposed the burden on industry of proving the existence of a safe level of exposure, thereby avoiding the Secretary's threshold responsibility of establishing the need for more stringent standards. . . .

The judgment of the Court of Appeals remanding the petition for review to the Secretary for further proceedings is affirmed. . . .

[Justice Powell joined all portions of the plurality opinion quoted above except that dealing with allocation of the burden of proof. He took the position that, even if OSHA had met its threshold burden, the regulations would have been invalid because OSHA failed to determine that the economic impact of the benzene standard bore a reasonable relationship to the expected benefits. The standard "is neither 'reasonably necessary' nor 'feasible,' as required by statute, if it calls for expenditures wholly disproportionate to the expected health and safety benefits."

Justice Rehnquist concurred in the judgment, concluding that §6(b)(5) violated the nondelegation doctrine by failing to provide OSHA with any guidance on the appropriate level of control for hazardous substances for which a "safe" level is either unknown or impractical.]

Mr. Justice MARSHALL, with whom Mr. Justice BRENNAN, Mr. Justice WHITE, and Mr. Justice BLACKMUN join, dissenting. . . .

. . . The critical problem in cases like the ones at bar is scientific uncertainty. While science has determined that exposure to benzene at levels above 1 ppm creates a definite risk of health impairment, the magnitude of the risk cannot be quantified at the present time. . . . [T]he existing evidence may frequently be inadequate to enable the Secretary to make the threshold finding of "significance" that the Court requires today. . . .

. . . [T]he Secretary concluded that benefits will result, that those benefits "may" be appreciable, but that the dose-response relationship of low levels of benzene exposure and leukemia, nonmalignant blood disorders, and chromosomal damage was impossible to determine. The question presented is whether, in these circumstances, the Act permits the Secretary to take regulatory action, or whether he must allow continued exposure until more definitive information becomes available.

62. . . . [W]hile the Agency must support its finding that a certain level of risk exists by substantial evidence, we recognize that its determination that a particular level of risk is "significant" will be based largely on policy considerations. At this point we have no need to reach the issue of what level of scrutiny a reviewing court should apply to the latter type of determination.

. . . Nothing in the Act purports to prevent the Secretary from acting when definitive information as to the quantity of a standard's benefits is unavailable. Where, as here, the deficiency in knowledge relates to the extent of the benefits rather than their existence, I see no reason to hold that the Secretary has exceeded his statutory authority. . . .

. . . The plurality does not show how [the significant risk] requirement can be plausibly derived from the "reasonably necessary or appropriate" clause. . . . In short, the plurality's standard is a fabrication bearing no connection with the acts or intentions of Congress. . . .

Under these circumstances, the plurality's requirement of identification of a "significant" risk will have one of two consequences. If the plurality means to require the Secretary realistically to "quantify" the risk in order to satisfy a court that it is "significant," the record shows that the plurality means to require him to do the impossible. But the regulatory inaction has very significant costs of its own. The adoption of such a test would subject American workers to a continuing risk of cancer and other serious diseases; it would disable the Secretary from regulating a wide variety of carcinogens for which quantification simply cannot be undertaken at the present time. . . .

. . . [T]he record amply demonstrates that in light of existing scientific knowledge, no purpose would be served by requiring the Secretary to take steps to quantify the risk of exposure to benzene at low levels. Any such quantification would be based not on scientific "knowledge" as that term is normally understood, but on considerations of policy. For carcinogens like benzene, the assumptions on which a dose-response curve must be based are necessarily arbitrary. To require a quantitative showing of a "significant" risk, therefore, would either paralyze the Secretary into inaction or force him to deceive the public by acting on the basis of assumptions that must be considered too speculative to support any realistic assessment of the relevant risk. . . .

NOTES AND QUESTIONS

1. *Nondelegation and Precautionary Regulation.* In his concurrence in *Benzene*, Justice Rehnquist contended that §6(b)(5) of the OSH Act constituted an impermissible delegation of legislative authority to OSHA. The court in American Trucking Ass'ns, Inc. v. EPA, 175 F.3d 1027 (D.C. Cir. 1999), had this to say about the role of the nondelegation doctrine in the *Benzene* plurality opinion:

> To be sure, the plurality in the *Benzene* case ostensibly relied on the doctrine to support its interpretation of the [OSH] Act. But a careful reading of the plurality opinion . . . reveals that the doctrine was only a makeweight, tossed into the analysis, in light of Justice Rehnquist's concurrence, to help justify the result. The plurality, disturbed at the seemingly draconian impact of the Secretary of Labor's standard as applied to several industries, analytically conflated the scope of the Secretary's discretion—the legitimate concern of the nondelegation doctrine—with the regulatory consequences of his interpretation of the statute. The latter concern is not really germane to the doctrine. . . . Accordingly, the *Benzene* plurality opinion gives only lip service to the nondelegation doctrine. . . . [American Trucking Ass'ns, Inc. v. EPA, 195 F.3d 4, 14 (D.C. Cir. 1999).]

The Supreme Court reversed the D.C. Circuit on a nondelegation issue that arose under the Clean Air Act in Whitman v. American Trucking Ass'ns, Inc., 531 U.S. 457 (2001), reproduced in Chapter 6, section D.1.b. The Court ruled that it is not necessary for Congress to provide a "determinate criterion" for saying how much of a regulated harm is too much. For further consideration of the application of the nondelegation doctrine to the OSH Act, see Sunstein, Is OSHA Unconstitutional?, 94 Va. L. Rev. 1407 (2008).

2. *The Functions of Risk Assessment.* Risk assessment can help a regulator determine whether a risk is acceptable or should be reduced through regulation of the activities that create it. On what grounds did the Fifth Circuit and the plurality opinion conclude that OSHA's risk assessment did not support issuance of the benzene standard? Risk assessment also serves to inform the agency whether the costs of regulation justify the benefits and whether the regulatory method being considered is cost-effective. Did OSHA quantify the costs and benefits of reducing permissible workplace exposure levels for benzene? Did it compare the costs and benefits of reducing PELs from 10 to 1 ppm? Why did OSHA establish a PEL of 1 ppm rather than, say, 5 or 3 ppm?

3. According to OSHA and industry, what is the relationship between §§3(8) and 6(b)(5) of the OSH Act? According to the plurality, what standards did Congress provide for OSHA's application of risk assessment and risk management inquiries?

4. According to the plurality, how did Congress intend to allocate the burden of proof in situations involving uncertainty concerning the level of risk presented by workplace exposure to toxic substances such as benzene? Which statutory provisions were determinative? How did Justice Marshall's interpretation of congressional intent differ? Do the two interpretations correspond to the approaches reflected in the Page excerpt, *Wilsonville, Reserve Mining,* or *Ethyl Corp.*? Latin, The "Significance" of Toxic Health Risks: An Essay on Legal Decisionmaking Under Uncertainty, 10 Ecology L.Q. 339 (1982), argues that the Supreme Court's approach in *Benzene* to allocation of the burden of proof in the face of scientific uncertainty seriously misinterpreted the statute, which was designed to resolve uncertainty on the side of precautionary action.

One observer has concluded that "OSHA learned its lesson" after *Benzene* and began to use mathematical models to quantify the risks posed by exposure to low concentrations of toxic materials such as ethylene oxide. Shere, The Myth of Meaningful Environmental Risk Assessment, 19 Harv. Envtl. L. Rev. 409, 425 (1995). These models relied on conservative assumptions to extrapolate the data observed in animal experiments to the low-dose regions of the dose-response curve relevant to human exposure. The ethylene oxide PEL was upheld in Public Citizen Health Research Group v. Tyson, 796 F.2d 1479 (D.C. Cir. 1986). See also Graham, The Risk Not Reduced, 3 N.Y.U. Envtl. L.J. 382, 386 (1995) (*Benzene* was "[t]he turning point for quantitative risk assessment."). Professor Adler, whose description of the risk assessment process appears earlier in this chapter, postulates that the *Benzene* case left OSHA with room to maneuver:

> *Industrial Union*'s linkage between significant risk and "individual risk" might have been rejected as dictum. An agency more self-confident than OSHA might have read the case as mandating a de minimis threshold but permitting that to be specified in "population risk" terms—as some number of premature deaths that would be caused by the workplace toxin absent OSHA intervention. Instead, OSHA's practice in regulating workplace carcinogens has been to follow the letter of *Industrial Union*: the agency determines

whether the existing concentration of a workplace carcinogen is a "significant risk," warranting OSHA intervention, by determining whether a worker exposed to that concentration for his entire working lifetime (forty-five years of exposure, five days a week, eight hours a day) would incur an "individual risk" of premature death that exceeds, or at least is not too far below, 1 in 1000. [Adler, Against "Individual Risk": A Sympathetic Critique of Risk Assessment, 153 U. Pa. L. Rev. 1121, 1170-1171 (2005).]

5. The agency learned its lesson with respect to benzene as well. In 1987, OSHA amended the benzene standard again by reducing the permissible exposure limit to an eight-hour time-weighted average of 1 ppm. 52 Fed. Reg. 34,460. It based that action on a finding that employees exposed to benzene face a significant health risk (in the form of aplastic anemia, leukemia, and other blood disorders) and that the standard would substantially reduce that risk. The current standard, which is still 1 ppm, is at 29 C.F.R. §1910.1028(c)(1).

6. The *Benzene* decision can be read to require OSHA to determine acceptable risk levels solely on the basis of health concerns, before considering factors such as cost and technological feasibility. "[I]t is difficult to imagine how one could go about rationally making a choice between acceptable risks without relying on nonhealth factors like cost and technology. . . . [W]e accept risk precisely on account of nonhealth factors." Applegate, The Perils of Unreasonable Risk: Information, Regulatory Policy, and Toxic Substances Control, 91 Colum. L. Rev. 261, 275-276 (1991). Is there some other basis upon which an agency could premise a decision that an unregulated risk is acceptable? Does quantitative risk assessment perform an allocative function?

3.   Criticisms of Comparative and Quantitative Risk Assessment

Instrumental Criticisms. Despite its appeal as a screening mechanism for determining which risks merit regulation and as an allocative mechanism for ordering regulatory priorities, risk assessment, especially in its comparative and quantitative forms, has come under heavy attack from various perspectives. The uncertainties that surround the use of comparative risk assessment are well known. "Risk comparisons assume that a great deal is known about the relationship between risk factors and human disease, and that risk assessment methods have a high degree of quantitative validity and predictability. Unfortunately, neither assumption is well established." Silbergeld, The Risks of Comparing Risks, 3 N.Y.U. Envtl. L.J. 405, 408 (1995). Information is often lacking, for example, about the physical processes that give rise to toxic risks. As a result of these uncertainties, cancer risk assessors possess considerable discretion to choose extrapolation models and exposure assumptions and to interpret data. Because of the many controversial assumptions and extrapolation models built into the risk assessment process, "each of which may skew the analysis by a factor of ten or more, . . . [t]he hard fact is that quantitative risk assessment generates numbers that are meaningless." Shere, The Myth of Meaningful Environmental Risk Assessment, 19 Harv. Envtl. L. Rev. 409, 413-414 (1995). The consequences of the exercise of that discretion, however, are a matter of debate.

On the one hand, critics charge that the use of overly conservative assumptions in risk assessment models generates overregulation and unwarranted public concern.

E.g., Viscusi, Equivalent Frames of Reference for Judging Risk Regulation Policies, 3 N.Y.U. Envtl. L.J. 431 (1995). On the other hand, supporters of regulation based on current practices contend that the biases reflected in risk assessments are not uniformly pro-regulatory in nature. Carcinogenesis tends to be the primary if not exclusive focus of many risk assessments. See Heinzerling, Reductionist Regulatory Reform, 8 Fordham Envtl. L.J. 459, 489 (1997). Because carcinogenesis may not be the most sensitive endpoint, this focus may fail to account for the risk of other adverse health effects, such as neurotoxic and teratogenic effects. Further, substance-by-substance risk assessments may fail to factor synergistic effects into the analysis. Hornstein, Reclaiming Environmental Law: A Normative Critique of Comparative Risk Analysis, 92 Colum. L. Rev. 562, 572 (1992). Because risk assessments have tended to assume that all people are equally susceptible to the risk of adverse effects, and "have generally failed to examine susceptibility as a function of race, ethnicity, and income," they have produced regulations that fail to protect particularly sensitive subgroups. Israel, An Environmental Justice Critique of Risk Assessment, 3 N.Y.U. Envtl. L.J. 469, 503 (1995).

Environmentalists and other supporters of regulation have attacked increased reliance on CRA on other grounds. They claim that the evidence does not support the contention that the regulatory budget has been misallocated. They question the assertion that regulation has been directed at trivial risks, both because the number of cancer deaths attributed by Justice Breyer and others to certain activities may be understated and because society has expressed concern over smaller numbers of fatalities caused by other activities, such as the use of handguns. They claim that the costs of regulatory compliance tend to be overstated because cost estimates typically do not take into account economies of scale as demand for control technology increases, cost savings attributable to technological innovation, or the productive economic uses (such as substitute products) that regulatory expenditures generate. Finkel, A Second Opinion on an Environmental Misdiagnosis: The Risky Prescriptions of Breaking the Vicious Circle, 3 N.Y.U. Envtl. L.J. 295, 307, 369, 372 (1995).

Critics of CRA charge that the need to generate sufficient reliable data to enable decisionmakers to compare the costs and benefits of risk reduction alternatives would impose a crushing analytical burden that would paralyze agencies such as EPA. Applegate, Worst Things First: Risk, Information, and Regulatory Structure in Toxic Substances Control, 9 Yale J. on Reg. 277, 325 (1992). "The fact that much of the information is within the control of the regulated industry, which has every incentive to delay new regulations, only exacerbates the potential for delay." McGarity, A Cost-Benefit State, 50 Admin. L. Rev. 1, 26 (1998). The critics also argue that legislation prescribing the methodology of CRA may limit analytical flexibility and hinder the development of more accurate risk assessment techniques.

Proposals to increase reliance on risk-risk analysis and societal risk reduction have been particularly controversial. Risk-risk analysis has been characterized as everything from "a provocative thesis worthy of further research [that] is currently far too speculative to serve as a firm foundation" for regulatory policy decisions, Bender, Societal Risk Reduction: Promise and Pitfalls, 3 N.Y.U. Envtl. L.J. 255, 283 (1995), to "close to analysis gone haywire." Finkel, supra, at 324. For a particularly jaundiced view of risk-risk analysis, see Watkins, Pollution Can Save Your Life, N.Y. Times, June 19, 1997, at A15. One report criticized the Office of Information and Regulatory Affairs within the OMB, which endorsed the use of risk-risk analysis in the early 1990s, for failing to recognize that a correlation between wealth and health may not be causal in nature. GAO, Risk-Risk Analysis: OMB's Review of a Proposed OSHA Rule, GAO/PEMD-92-93 (1992). In other words, "wealthy people might be wealthy partly because they are healthy, rather than the other way around." Heinzerling, *supra*, at 479. In addition, risk-risk analysis improperly assumes that money spent on regulation yields no economic gains such as new jobs. Heinzerling & Ackerman, The Humbugs of the Anti-Regulatory Movement, 87 Cornell L. Rev. 650, 669 (2002). Even those who support risk-risk analysis as a theoretical matter have characterized as implausible the $7.25 million figure often used as the amount of regulatory expenditure that corresponds to each death attributable to lost income: "either the implicit value of life estimate is too high or the amount of expenditure that will lead to the loss of a statistical life is too low." Viscusi, *supra*, at 458. Societal risk reduction is a flawed analytical technique, according to its critics, because its use would free up relatively little money for more efficient risk reduction, given that environmental regulatory expenditures are much smaller than the resources (e.g., defense expenditures) devoted to other risk-producing activities. Finkel, *supra*, at 373-374. In addition, most resources saved by directing risk reduction efforts away from environmental regulation would be private compliance costs, not government expenditures. As a result, absent new taxes on risk-creating activities, much of the money saved might not be committed to alternative risk reduction projects. Bender, *supra*, at 275-276.

Normative Criticisms. The attacks on CRA have extended beyond qualms over data availability and the validity of current analytical methodology to broader policy-based critiques. EPA's 1987 Unfinished Business report noted the discrepancy between public and expert perceptions of risk. Justice Breyer advocated the creation of a centralized administrative group whose function would be the rationalization of the process by which environmental risks are targeted. Breyer, Breaking the Vicious Circle: Toward Effective Risk Regulation 60-63 (1993). Critics of CRA, however, contend that reliance on public perceptions of risk to set the regulatory agenda is far from irrational. The differences between public and expert perceptions of risk may be due to differences in perspective rather than to ignorance or irrationality. The experts tend to view risk in terms of the total number of fatalities expected to result from the activities under consideration. The public tends to consider a wider range of factors, such as whether the risk is voluntarily or involuntarily incurred, familiar or unfamiliar, concentrated or disbursed, natural or man-made, preventable or unpreventable, reversible or irreversible, and chronic or catastrophic. See Sandman, A Formula for Effective Risk Communication (1991); Freeman & Godsil, The Question of Risk: Incorporating Community Perceptions into Environmental Risk Assessments, 21 Fordham Urb. L.J. 547 (1994). Cognitive error theory postulates, for example, that because people tend to weigh the probability of an event by the ease with which relevant information comes to mind, they may overestimate low risks of catastrophic events but underestimate higher risks of more diffuse, chronic harms. Similarly, critics of CRA contest its tendency to ignore equitable considerations by focusing on aggregate effects and downplaying society's distaste for risks that disproportionately affect the poor, the elderly, children, racial minorities, and future generations. Hornstein, *supra*, at 600-601.

What are the consequences of these differing perceptions for the development of a mechanism for ranking the severity of risks? At the very least, public perceptions arguably should not be excluded from the debate through exclusive reliance on the risk rankings of technocratic experts. Because the debate involves "competing rationalities,"

> it unarguably follows that the choice of approach is an ethical and political one that technical experts have neither the knowledge nor the authority to dictate, because the issue transcends technocratic expertise. Were we to defer to agencies simply on the basis of their technical proficiency, the ethical-political question would be begged entirely. Agencies could be expected to resort to methods the use of which denies the very values at stake . . . [and] methodological proclivities would bias agency risk processing in the direction of too much public risk—as viewed from the public's perspective. [Gillette & Krier, Risk, Courts, and Agencies, 138 U. Pa. L. Rev. 1027, 1085 (1990).]

In short, the tradeoffs "are not resolvable as technocratic exercises" and the delegation to an expert body of authority to determine which risks are "reasonable" "both avoids and obscures the real policy decision being made. These decisions are fundamentally political and must be based on broader sets of values, many of which are not quantifiable." Applegate, *supra*, at 300. See also Kahan, Two Conceptions of Emotion in Risk Regulation, 156 U. Pa. L. Rev. 741 (2008) (comparing the "irrational weigher" and "cultural evaluator" theories of public perceptions of risk).

Why not simply increase public participation in the risk assessment process? Although the use of comparative risk assessment does not necessarily preclude public input that reflects values other than utilitarianism, the technical nature of the process may discourage such input, and the experts responsible for ranking risks, who may deride the public's irrationality toward risk, may subordinate these values to the more concrete considerations reflected in aggregate risk reduction figures. A process that fails to incorporate public concerns in this manner is likely to be perceived as illegitimate and undemocratic. See Finkel, *supra*, at 357. Moreover, the kind of body of experts envisioned by Justice Breyer may insulate itself from everyone except representatives of special interest groups. The information-intensive nature of risk-based decisionmaking tends to favor such resource-rich groups in producing the information relied on by the experts in making their decisions. The decisionmaking process also tends to be more accessible to these groups because of its length and complexity. As a result, "risk-based decisionmaking can itself become a device by which politically powerful groups can effectuate their interests—now clothed as merely the objective determinations of 'science'—at the expense of less powerful groups." Hornstein, Lessons from Federal Pesticide Regulation on the Paradigms and Politics of Environmental Law Reform, 10 Yale J. on Reg. 369, 416 (1993).

Finally, the skeptics contend that CRA tends to pose "false choices" by encouraging decisionmakers to trade off one environmental risk against another instead of developing alternative, creative solutions that seek to reduce all of those risks.

> Comparative risk analysis tends to undermine [the] forward-looking enterprise [of current environmental law]. . . . By tending to compare environmental risks with each other, rather than to alternative possibilities, comparative risk analysis emphasizes the wrong risk baseline, one that fails to capture the law's moral direction (as well as its abhorrence of market externalities). The result is an ideological scheme, based on an inward-looking set of comparisons, that is decidedly biased toward the status quo. . . . By exacerbating uncertainty in the current standing of a given risk, comparative risk analysis can dramatically complicate the willingness or ability of entrepreneurs to capitalize improvements such as pollution-control processes or environmentally benign products. [Hornstein, Reclaiming Environmental Law, *supra*, at 616-617.]

Further Reading. For more on risk assessment as a mechanism for improving environmental policy and on the usefulness of comparative risk assessment, see Risk Symposium, 63 U. Cin. L. Rev. 1533 (1995), and Symposium, Risk in the Republic: Comparative Risk Analysis and Public Policy, 8 Duke Envtl. L. & Pol'y F. 1-180 (1997).

4. Comparing the Costs and Benefits of Hazardous Substance Control

Quantification of regulatory benefits may be relevant to risk management as well as risk assessment. Once the agency decides it is authorized to regulate, it must decide how to trade off health benefits against the economic costs of hazardous substances control. Quantification places a numerical value on risk that can be compared with regulatory costs, allowing the agency to choose the regulatory option that produces the greatest net benefit. The following case addresses the question that the Supreme Court left open in the *Benzene* case: whether the OSH Act requires OSHA to engage in cost-benefit analysis when promulgating health standards for toxic materials.

AMERICAN TEXTILE MANUFACTURERS INSTITUTE, INC. v. DONOVAN
452 U.S. 490 (1981)

Justice BRENNAN delivered the opinion of the Court.

[In 1978, OSHA issued a standard limiting occupational exposure to cotton dust, an airborne particle by-product of the preparation and manufacture of cotton products, exposure to which may cause a respiratory illness known as byssinosis, or "brown lung" disease. OSHA determined that exposure to cotton dust represents a significant health hazard to employees, and that the standard, which the agency deemed both technologically and economically feasible, would lead to a significant reduction in the prevalence of byssinosis.[25] Representatives of the cotton industry challenged the validity of the standard.]

II

The principal question presented in these cases is whether the Occupational Safety and Health Act requires the Secretary, in promulgating a standard pursuant to §6(b)(5) of the Act, 29 U.S.C. §655(b)(5), to determine that the costs of the standard bear a reasonable relationship to its benefits. Relying on §§6(b)(5) and 3(8) of the Act,

---

25. ... OSHA expressly found that "exposure to cotton dust presents a significant health hazard to employees," and that "cotton dust produced significant health effects at low levels of exposure." ... OSHA relied on dose-response curve data (the Merchant Study) showing that 25% of employees suffered at least Grade 1/2 byssinosis at a 500 $\mu g/m^3$ PEL standard. ... OSHA concluded that the "prevalence of byssinosis should be significantly reduced" by the 200 $\mu g/m^3$ PEL. It is difficult to imagine what else the agency could do to comply with this Court's decision in [*Benzene*].

29 U.S.C. §§655(b)(5) and 652(8), petitioners urge not only that OSHA must show that a standard addresses a significant risk of material health impairment, see Industrial Union Dept. v. American Petroleum Institute, 448 U.S., at 639 (plurality opinion), but also that OSHA must demonstrate that the reduction in risk of material health impairment is significant in light of the costs of attaining that reduction. Respondents on the other hand contend that the Act requires OSHA to promulgate standards that eliminate or reduce such risks "to the extent such protection is technologically and economically feasible." . . .

A

. . . Although their interpretations differ, all parties agree that the phrase "to the extent feasible" contains the critical language in §6(b)(5) for purposes of these cases.

The plain meaning of the word "feasible" supports respondents' interpretation of the statute. According to Webster's Third New International Dictionary of the English Language 831 (1976), "feasible" means "capable of being done, executed, or effected." Thus, §6(b)(5) directs the Secretary to issue the standard that "most adequately assures . . . that no employee will suffer material impairment of health," limited only by the extent to which this is "capable of being done." In effect then, . . . Congress itself defined the basic relationship between costs and benefits, by placing the "benefit" of worker health above all other considerations save those making attainment of this "benefit" unachievable. Any standard based on a balancing of costs and benefits by the Secretary that strikes a different balance than that struck by Congress would be inconsistent with the command set forth in §6(b)(5). Thus, cost-benefit analysis by OSHA is not required by the statute because feasibility analysis is.[29]

When Congress has intended that an agency engage in cost-benefit analysis, it has clearly indicated such intent on the face of the statute. . . . Congress uses specific language when intending that an agency engage in cost-benefit analysis. See Industrial Union Dept. v. American Petroleum Institute, 448 U.S. at 710, n.27 (Marshall, J., dissenting). Certainly in light of its ordinary meaning, the word "feasible" cannot be construed to articulate such congressional intent. We therefore reject the argument that Congress required cost-benefit analysis in §6(b)(5).

B

Even though the plain language of §6(b)(5) supports this construction, we must still decide whether §3(8), the general definition of an occupational safety and health standard, either alone or in tandem with §6(b)(5), incorporates a cost-

---

29. In these cases we are faced with the issue whether the Act requires OSHA to balance costs and benefits in promulgating a single toxic material and harmful physical agent standard under §6(b)(5). Petitioners argue that without cost-benefit balancing, the issuance of a single standard might result in a "serious misallocatio[n] of the finite resources that are available for the protection of worker safety and health," given the other health hazards in the workplace. This argument is more properly addressed to other provisions of the Act which may authorize OSHA to explore costs and benefits for deciding between issuance of several standards regulating different varieties of health and safety hazards, e.g., §6(g) of the Act, 29 U.S.C. §655(g); or for promulgating other types of standards not issued under §6(b)(5). We express no view on these questions.

benefit requirement for standards dealing with toxic materials or harmful physical agents. Section 3(8) of the Act, 29 U.S.C. §652(8) (emphasis added), provides:

> The term "occupational safety and health standard" means a standard which requires conditions, or the adoption or use of one or more practices, means, methods, operations, or processes, *reasonably necessary or appropriate* to provide safe or healthful employment and places of employment.

Taken alone, the phrase "reasonably necessary or appropriate" might be construed to contemplate some balancing of the costs and benefits of a standard. Petitioners urge that, so construed, §3(8) engrafts a cost-benefit analysis requirement on the issuance of §6(b)(5) standards, even if §6(b)(5) itself does not authorize such analysis. We need not decide whether §3(8), standing alone, would contemplate some form of cost-benefit analysis. For even if it does, Congress specifically chose in §6(b)(5) to impose separate and additional requirements for issuance of a subcategory of occupational safety and health standards dealing with toxic materials and harmful physical agents: it required that those standards be issued to prevent material impairment of health to the extent feasible. Congress could reasonably have concluded that health standards should be subject to different criteria than safety standards because of the special problems presented in regulating them.

Agreement with petitioners' argument that §3(8) imposes an additional and overriding requirement of cost-benefit analysis on the issuance of §6(b)(5) standards would eviscerate the "to the extent feasible" requirement. Standards would inevitably be set at the level indicated by cost-benefit analysis, and not at the level specified by §6(b)(5). For example, if cost-benefit analysis indicated a protective standard of 1,000 µg/m^3 PEL, while feasibility analysis indicated a 500 µg/m^3 PEL, the agency would be forced by the cost-benefit requirement to choose the less stringent point. We cannot believe that Congress intended the general terms of §3(8) to countermand the specific feasibility requirement of §6(b)(5). Adoption of petitioners' interpretation would effectively write §6(b)(5) out of the Act. We decline to render Congress' decision to include a feasibility requirement nugatory, thereby offending the well-settled rule that all parts of a statute, if possible, are to be given effect. . . .[32]

[The Court concluded that the record contained substantial evidence to support the conclusion that the cotton dust standard was feasible because, even though some marginal employers might shut down rather than comply, the standard would not threaten the industry as a whole.]

---

32. This is not to say that §3(8) might not require the balancing of costs and benefits for standards promulgated under provisions other than §6(b)(5) of the Act. . . . Furthermore, the mere fact that a §6(b)(5) standard is "feasible" does not mean that §3(8)'s "reasonably necessary or appropriate" language might not impose additional restraints on OSHA. For example, all §6(b)(5) standards must be addressed to "significant risks" of material health impairment. In addition, if the use of one respirator would achieve the same reduction in health risk as the use of five, the use of five respirators was "technologically and economically feasible," and OSHA thus insisted on the use of five, then the "reasonably necessary or appropriate" limitation might come into play as an additional restriction on OSHA to choose the one-respirator standard. In this case we need not decide all the applications that §3(8) might have, either alone or together with §6(b)(5).

NOTES AND QUESTIONS

1. The Court relied on the plain meaning of the word "feasible" in §6(b)(5) to conclude that OSHA need not engage in cost-benefit analysis when it promulgates occupational safety and health standards for toxic materials. Did the Court rely on the plain meaning of the word "safe" in the *Benzene* case? Was the Court's interpretation of the relationship between §§6(b)(5) and 3(8) in *Cotton Dust* consistent with its interpretation of the same relationship in *Benzene*? Why might cost-benefit analysis be required when OSHA issues occupational safety and health standards that do not deal with toxic materials? See International Union, UAW v. OSHA, 37 F.3d 665 (D.C. Cir. 1994); International Union, UAW v. OSHA, 938 F.2d 1310 (D.C. Cir. 1991).

2. The cotton industry argued that, absent a requirement that OSHA engage in cost-benefit analysis, agency standards might result in a misallocation of worker protection resources. Why? What was the Court's response to this argument? Does §6(g) of the OSH Act provide a model for requiring comparative risk assessment? Cf. American Iron and Steel Inst. v. OSHA, 182 F.3d 1261 (11th Cir. 1999) (judicial review of OSHA's priority setting in determining the appropriate subjects of regulation is deferential).

3. *Different Approaches to Risk Management.* We have now examined a number of attempts by courts, legislatures, and regulatory agencies to respond to the economic impact of efforts to reduce risks. In *Wilsonville*, the court took the costs and benefits of closing the hazardous waste disposal site into account in enjoining further operation of the facility. In *Reserve Mining* and *Ethyl Corp.*, the statutes at issue required abatement if public health was "endangered," without explicitly requiring the high costs involved to be taken into account in any particular manner, if at all. But in *Reserve Mining* the court explicitly took the economic costs of enjoining taconite discharges into Lake Superior into account in fashioning delayed injunctive relief, and in *Ethyl Corp.*, EPA took costs into account in scheduling the phase-in of its gasoline lead content standards.

Do these cases and other federal environmental statutory provisions reveal a consistent pattern in the treatment of the costs and benefits of risk reduction? A former general counsel of the Food and Drug Administration (FDA) discerns three categories of legislation for preventing human exposure to carcinogenic substances. First, some statutes reflect a "no risk" policy, which requires the implementing agency to prevent any human exposure. Second, some laws restrict the agency to the regulation of significant risks. Third, some statutes require that other criteria, such as the technological capabilities of regulated industries, moderate agency efforts to protect health. The differences in these approaches stem from a mix of considerations, including the fact that most of the statutes are directed at the reduction of other health hazards in addition to cancer. R. Merrill, Federal Regulation of Cancer-Causing Chemicals, Report to the Administrative Conference of the United States 22-32 (1982). Where in Professor Merrill's taxonomy do the statutory provisions discussed in *Reserve Mining, Ethyl Corp., Benzene,* and *Cotton Dust* belong? Professor Rodgers posits a different categorization scheme: the cost-oblivious, cost-effective, cost-sensitive, and strict cost-benefit models. Rodgers, Benefits, Costs, and Risks: Oversight of Health and Environmental Decision Making, 4 Harv. Envtl. L. Rev. 191 (1980). Cost-benefit analysis is not the same as cost-effectiveness analysis, which serves the allied but more limited purpose of ensuring that the agency selects the least costly method for attaining a predetermined goal. More cost-effective solutions produce better cost-benefit ratios. For another attempt to discern patterns in the role Congress has assigned to cost considerations in the health and safety protection statutes, see S. Shapiro & R. Glicksman, Risk Regulation at Risk: Restoring a Pragmatic Approach ch. 3 (2003) (concluding that Congress typically requires that agencies consider costs in some fashion, but not by engaging in cost-benefit analysis).

4. What is the rationale for cost-benefit analysis in the environmental regulatory context, and what are its advantages and disadvantages from practical and normative points of view? See the note on cost-benefit analysis in Chapter 3, section C.

E. PREVENTING THE ENTRY OF TOXIC SUBSTANCES INTO THE STREAM OF COMMERCE

Over the years, agencies and programs have been established to deal with hazardous substances, with recent focus on deleterious long-term effects, such as cancer, of these substances. A detailed analysis of the legislative acts enacted by Congress concerning toxic substances [Table 8-2] reveals an evolution of thought in that each reflects the scientific views that existed at the time of enactment. Consequently, these acts are not uniform in their view of the disease, the role chemical substances might play in its incidence, and what ought to be done about potential toxic substances and potential carcinogens. [Office of Science and Technology Policy, Chemical Carcinogens: Review of the Science and Its Associated Principles, 50 Fed. Reg. 10,372, 10,373 (1985).]

More can be done to control hazardous substances than bringing common law actions to enjoin a nuisance or setting emissions and effluent standards, using the classic approach of the Clean Air and Clean Water Acts. Commerce in all substances that pre-market screening shows to be likely to subject the public to unacceptable hazards may be restricted or banned. The Toxic Substances Control Act (TSCA) of 1976, which purports to screen all existing and new toxic substances, authorizes EPA to regulate the manufacture and use of toxic substances in this manner. Another strategy allows a product to be marketed (sometimes with the requirement of a registration or a license) until its hazards become known and then restricts its marketing to the extent necessary to protect the public. Federal regulation of pesticides under the Federal Insecticide, Fungicide, and Rodenticide Act (FIFRA) exemplifies this approach.

As the OST excerpt quoted above indicates, Congress has delegated to several agencies the power to restrict the manufacture of toxic chemicals and their incorporation into otherwise useful products. These delegations reflect diverse approaches to risk assessment and risk management. Some of the statutory schemes listed in Table 8-2, such as the Clean Air and Clean Water Acts and the Occupational Safety and Health Act, are covered in earlier portions of this book. Others, those that regulate and impose liability for hazardous waste management, are treated in section F of this chapter and in Chapter 9. This section focuses on representative examples of the regulation of the manufacture and use of toxic chemicals authorized by federal law. As you study these materials, consider what approaches to risk assessment and risk management Congress has chosen, why it may have chosen them, and whether the choices are appropriate.

TABLE 8-2
Federal Laws Related to Exposures to Toxic Substances*

Legislation	Agency	Area of Concern
Food, Drug, and Cosmetic Act	FDA	Food, drugs, food additives, color additives, new drugs, animal and feed additives, and medical devices
Federal Insecticide, Fungicide, and Rodenticide Act	EPA	Pesticides
Dangerous Cargo Act	DOT, USCG	Water shipment of toxic materials
Atomic Energy Act	NRC	Radioactive substances
Federal Hazardous Substances Act	CPSC	Toxic household products
Federal Meat Inspection Act	USDA	Food, feed, color additives, and pesticide residues
Poultry Products Inspection Act		
Egg Products Inspection Act		
Occupational Safety and Health Act	OSHA, NIOSH	Workplace toxic chemicals
Poison Prevention Packaging Act	CPSC	Packaging of hazardous household products
Clean Air Act	EPA	Air pollutants
Hazardous Materials Transportation Uniform Safety Act	DOT	Transport of hazardous materials
Clean Water Act	EPA	Water pollutants
Marine Protection, Research, and Sanctuaries Act	EPA	Ocean dumping
Consumer Product Safety Act	CPSC	Hazardous consumer products
Lead-Based Paint Poison Prevention Act	CPSC, HEW (HHS), HUD	Use of lead paint in federally assisted housing
Safe Drinking Water Act	EPA	Drinking water contaminants
Resource Conservation and Recovery Act	EPA	Solid waste, including hazardous wastes
Toxic Substances Control Act	EPA	Hazardous chemicals not covered by other laws, including pre-market review
Federal Mine Safety and Health Act	DOL, NIOSH	Toxic substances in coal and other mines
Comprehensive Environmental Response, Compensation, and Liability Act	EPA	Hazardous substances, pollutants, and contaminants

*Dates of enactment and amendment omitted.

1.   Regulation of Chemical Manufacturing and Use

a.   The Toxic Substances Control Act

MARKELL, AN OVERVIEW OF TSCA, ITS HISTORY AND KEY UNDERLYING ASSUMPTIONS, AND ITS PLACE IN ENVIRONMENTAL REGULATION
32 Wash. U. J.L. & Pol'y 333, 340-341, 344-347, 349 (2010)

During the 1970s, policy makers and others increasingly paid attention to the risks that toxic substances posed to human health and the environment. Some of the

[Council on Environmental Quality (CEQ)] reports during this era demonstrate this. [A 1971 CEQ report] observed that significant numbers of new chemicals enter commercial use annually, that use of these chemicals is growing rapidly, and that, while "many of these substances are not toxic, the sheer number of them, their increasing diversity and use, and the environmental problems already encountered from some indicate the existence of a problem." [A 1975 CEQ report suggested] that "[a] disconcerting, growing body of evidence indicates that subtle, manmade hazards are supplanting famine and infectious disease as significant determinants of life expectancy in 20th century developed nations." The CEQ 1977 Annual Report notes that the "importance of dealing with toxic substances comprehensively and systematically has been highlighted in recent years by growing recognition of the environmental — and, in particular, chemical — contributions to cancer." The CEQ 1978 Annual Report similarly identifies a "[h]eightened awareness of toxic chemical problems" and refers to the "urgency of the toxics problem."

The legislative history of TSCA is to the same effect. It reflects that Congress enacted TSCA because of its growing concern about the risks that chemicals used in commerce posed to public health and the environment. For example, during a March 26, 1976, Senate debate about TSCA, Senator Pearson, one of the bill's sponsors, stated that:

> We can no longer operate under the assumption that what we do not know about a chemical substance cannot hurt us. Tragic results associated with too many toxic substances have taught us that lesson all too well. Chemicals, not people, must be put to the test. . . .

Congress's view in adopting TSCA was that existing legislation had significant shortcomings that TSCA would help to cure. . . . First, existing legislation tended to have an "after-the-fact" focus. The CEQ's 1971 report . . . highlights this concern, noting that existing legislation "generally deal[s] with a problem only *after* it is manifest," and asserts that "[w]e should no longer be limited to repairing the damage after it has been done." . . .

An important congressional objective in TSCA was to complement the after-the-fact character of the primary regulatory statutes by focusing attention on toxics earlier in their development and use. In enacting TSCA Congress created a regulatory focus that did not yet exist — regulation of chemicals before they were manufactured. As the 1978 CEQ Report notes: "The intent of [TSCA] is that the harmful effects of chemicals produced in the future shall be investigated and if possible discovered in the laboratory rather than turning up in injuries to human beings or the environment after full-scale production has begun." Some commentators have referred to this goal as one of "creating 'upstream' protections against the introduction of new chemicals."

Second, existing legislation tended to be media-focused. It did not take a holistic or comprehensive approach to pollution control. [According to the CEQ,] "the media-based pollution laws, primarily air and water, did not adequately account for individuals' total exposure to chemicals or for chemical pollution that shifts among media. . . . By regulating chemicals *per se*, TSCA was supposed to avoid these gaps or to fill them when they appear, as well as to regulate more efficiently and effectively." . . .

The felt need for additional information on toxic chemicals, while related to each of these two motivations for TSCA, was on its own a strong impetus for Congress's decision to enact TSCA. . . . Congress believed there was a significant need for additional information about toxic substances—about their toxicity, the possibility of exposure, and the risk they posed. [EPA Administrator Russell Train] highlighted the information gaps as follows:

> [W]e know so little—so abysmally little—about these chemicals. We know little about their health effects. . . . We know little about how many humans are exposed, and how and to what degree. We do not even know precisely how many—much less precisely which—new chemical compounds are made and marketed every year. . . .

In sum, while Congress's enactment of TSCA was informed by a variety of goals and then-extant understandings of hazard and risk assessment, from a big picture perspective, three of Congress's key assumptions in adopting TSCA were that we needed to: (1) embrace a more proactive or preventative approach to understanding toxics and limiting their risks; (2) approach risks from toxics in a holistic rather than fragmented way; and (3) develop a great deal of information in order to increase understanding about the toxicity of toxics and the risks they posed.

---

(1) Introduction

In 1976, Congress passed the Toxic Substances Control Act (TSCA), 15 U.S.C. §§2601-2629, which empowers EPA to regulate the manufacture of most of the chemical substances not already regulated, based on the health or environmental risks they pose. Rather than focusing on the use of products or the disposal of wastes (although it reaches that far), TSCA's emphasis falls high in the stream of commerce, at the premanufacture phase. EPA is supposed to review each new chemical marketed, as well as the approximately 62,000 chemicals in commerce shortly after TSCA was enacted, to determine if they "may present an unreasonable risk of injury to health or the environment." §4(a)(1)(A)(i). By 2010, more than 84,000 chemicals were available for sale and use in the United States. Markell, *supra*, at 352. TSCA exempts some materials because they are regulated under other statutes and others because political lobbies were powerful enough to secure their exclusion. §3(2)(B).

Despite these exemptions, TSCA on its face represents the closest thing to a comprehensive chemical substance control statute that Congress has ever enacted. Yet TSCA has disappointed its proponents, who do not believe that its testing and pre-manufacture review provisions have improved chemical product safety. The following materials address whether TSCA succeeds as a legal device for shifting the burden of proof of safety to chemical manufacturers, and whether the test of "unreasonable risk," which appears repeatedly in TSCA, can be applied with a balanced emphasis on health protection and economic productivity.[h]

(2) A Summary of TSCA

TSCA is not difficult to summarize. See Figure 8-7. Subject to some important exemptions, it requires that manufacturers or others engaging in commerce in a new chemical substance, or making a significant new use of an existing chemical

---

h. For more extensive coverage of the practical aspects of TSCA's applications, see generally Hathaway et al., A Practitioner's Guide to the Toxic Substances Control Act: Parts I, II, and III, 24 Envtl. L. Rep. 10,207 (May 1994); id. at 10,285 (June 1994); id. at 10,357 (July 1994).

substance, give EPA premanufacturing notice (PMN) of data and test results regarding the substance. EPA then determines if the new chemical presents an unreasonable risk or if testing must be done to enable that determination to be made. §5. EPA must compile an inventory of chemicals already in commerce and determine if the chemicals on the inventory present unreasonable risks. Manufacturers or others responsible for putting chemicals in commerce must perform tests on both new and existing chemical substances and mixtures if EPA determines that they present unreasonable risks or that existing information is insufficient to allow an informed preliminary assessment to be made. §4. EPA may limit or forbid the manufacture of new or existing chemicals that studies have shown present an unreasonable risk to health or the environment. §6. These provisions were intended to put the burden of proof on the manufacturer whenever EPA raises the issue of a chemical's safety. In theory, this burden may be difficult to meet. In practice, however, critics charge that EPA still assumes, or has been forced to assume, most of the burden of showing that a chemical presents an unreasonable risk.

(3) Premanufacturing Notice for New Chemicals

No one may manufacture a new chemical substance (i.e., one not on the inventory of existing chemicals) or manufacture or process an existing chemical substance for a "significant new use" without providing at least 90 days prior notice to EPA. §5(a)(1). This premanufacture notification of intent to manufacture or make a significant new use may have to be accompanied by existing data and, in theory at least, new information. For specific requirements, see §§8(a)(2), 5(b)(1)-(2), 5(d)(1). The statute affords trade secrets protection to those who submit these PMNs. See §14; section E.2 below. If the data submitted to EPA are insufficient to permit a reasoned conclusion about the health and environmental risks posed by the substance, and allowing commerce in the chemical may present an unreasonable risk, EPA may issue an administrative order or seek a court injunction to limit or prohibit its use. §5(e). Manufacturers sometimes withdraw PMNs to avoid the issuance of §5(e) orders or interim regulations under §5(f) to protect against unreasonable risks.

Suppose that EPA is considering requiring PMN for newly developed nanomaterial. Nanotechnology is "a collection of technologies for building materials and devices 'from the bottom up,' atom by atom." Van Lente, Note, Building the World of Nanotechnology, 38 Case W. Res. J. Int'l L. 173, 174 (2006). It involves the design, production, and application of structures and devices by controlling shape and size at the nanoscale (a nanometer encompasses about 8-10 atoms).[i] Representatives of the nanotechnology industry argue that if the molecular structure of a nanomaterial is identical to that of a substance on EPA's inventory of existing chemicals (discussed below), it is not subject to PMN. Under this view, carbon nanotubes would not require PMN because graphite is an existing chemical on the TSCA inventory. Environmental groups respond that unless a chemical substance has not only the same molecular structure, but also the same physical and chemical properties as a listed

---

i. See also Lemley, Patenting Nanotechnology, 58 Stan. L. Rev. 601, 602 (2005) ("Nanotechnology is the study and use of the unique characteristics of materials at the nanometer scale, between the classical large-molecule level to which traditional physics and chemistry apply and the atomic level in which the bizarre rules of quantum mechanics take effect.").

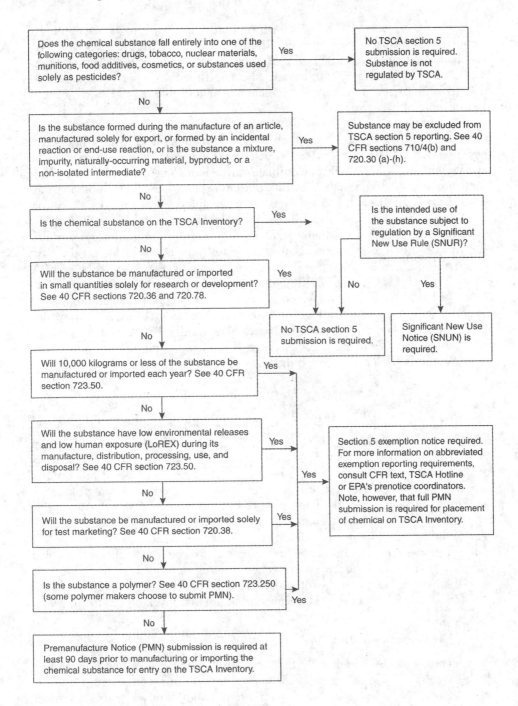

FIGURE 8-7

Steps for Determining Whether a Premanufacture Submission Is Required
for a Chemical Substance

Source: http://www.epa.gov/oppt/newchems/pubs/pmnchart.htm.

Chapter VIII. Controlling Toxic Substances and Hazardous Wastes

substance, it is subject to PMN. Which conception of the PMN program as applied to nanomaterials is correct? See generally Rudd, Regulating the Impacts of Engineered Nanoparticles Under TSCA: Shifting Authority from Industry to Government, 33 Colum. J. Envtl. L. 215 (2008); Mandel, Nanotechnology Governance, 59 Ala. L. Rev. 1323 (2008) (reviewing existing regulation of nanotechnology by federal agencies and suggesting improvements).

EPA estimates that it reviews an average of 2,300 new chemical substances each year under the PMN process. Nevertheless, the information that must be submitted by those subject to PMN review has hardly been comprehensive. Many PMNs contain no toxicological test data at all. By one estimate, only about 15 percent of PMNs include health or safety test data. Woolf, Why Modernization of the U.S. Toxic Substance Law Is Good for Public Health and Business, 6 Sustainable Dev. & Pol'y L. #3 (Spring 2006), at 6. Agency scientists assess the risk posed by substances for which there are no toxicological data based on their structural similarity to known toxic chemicals (known as a structure-activity relationship). Is this practice justifiable on the basis of a desire to allocate scarce investigative resources efficiently? See EDF v. EPA, 598 F.2d 62 (D.C. Cir. 1978) (EPA justified regulation of less-chlorinated PCBs under §307(a) of the Clean Water Act on the basis of available information concerning more-chlorinated PCBs). About 90 percent of chemicals for which PMNs are submitted wind up not being restricted under TSCA. Hanan, Pushing the Environmental Regulatory Focus a Step Back: Controlling the Introduction of New Chemicals Under the Toxic Substances Control Act, 18 Am. J.L. & Med. 395 (1992).

(4) Screening Existing Chemicals

EPA must supplement the original TSCA chemical inventory by adding all new chemicals for which PMN notices are filed. §8(b). Although TSCA does not specifically require that EPA systematically study this backlog to determine which chemicals may pose an unreasonable risk, the inventory requirement would be pointless without such a review. Section 8(d) requires that EPA issue rules forcing manufacturers to submit copies and lists of unpublished health and safety studies conducted by, known to, or reasonably ascertainable by them on the listed chemicals they manufacture, import, or process. Based on available information, EPA may decide that a chemical requires additional testing or that it presents significant risks that warrant regulation. Of the inventoried chemicals, however, relatively few receive more than cursory attention. As of 2005, EPA had performed internal reviews on only about two percent of the chemicals on the original inventory. Markell, *supra*, at 355.

(5) The Issuance of Test Rules

Section 4 of TSCA authorizes EPA to require testing of both new and existing chemical substances to determine their safety. Once a test is completed, EPA may carry out its PMN duties under §5 or make a determination of unreasonable risk under §6 and adopt rules limiting or banning the chemical's use. Each test rule must include standards for the development of test data for the substance or mixture being tested. §4(b)(1)(B). TSCA specifies a list of effects (e.g., carcinogenesis, mutagenesis), characteristics (e.g., acute and chronic toxicity), and methodologies that may be used in formulating standards. §4(b)(2)(A). The tests required under §4 are referred to collectively as the chemical's "test rule" because TSCA specifies notice-and-comment rulemaking procedures.

What must EPA demonstrate to justify issuance of a test rule? Section 4 authorizes testing requirements in two situations. First, EPA may issue a test rule if it finds that (1) the manufacture, distribution in commerce, processing, use, or disposal of a chemical substance may present an unreasonable risk of injury to health or the environment, (2) there are insufficient data to reasonably assess the effects of those activities on health or the environment, and (3) testing is necessary to develop the data. §4(a)(1)(A). In Chemical Mfrs. Ass'n v. EPA, 859 F.2d 977 (D.C. Cir. 1988), CMA challenged a test rule for 2-ethylhexanoic acid (EHA). The court upheld EPA's view that TSCA authorizes issuance of a test rule where EPA finds that there is "a more-than-theoretical basis for concluding that the substance is sufficiently toxic, and human exposure to it is sufficient in amount, to generate" an unreasonable risk. EPA can establish the existence and extent of human exposure based on inferences drawn from the circumstances of the substance's manufacture and use. It must rebut industry-supplied evidence attacking those inferences only if that evidence renders the probability of exposure in the amount found by EPA "no more than theoretical or speculative. The probability of infrequent or even one-time exposure to individuals can warrant a test rule, so long as there is a more-than-theoretical basis for determining that exposure in such doses presents an 'unreasonable risk of injury to health.'" Id. at 979.

Because the standard of judicial review of test rules is the substantial evidence test, §19(c)(1)(B)(i), Professor Applegate has described §4(a)(1)(A) test rules as predicated on

> a third order probability: EPA must promulgate a test rule when it finds a probability (substantial evidence) of a probability (may present) of a probability (risk). Moreover, each probability is a very different type of calculation: risk is a statement of frequency of effect; "may present" is a statement of the confidence in the induction from known data to frequency; and substantial evidence is a statement of the overall certainty with which the foregoing statements are made. Risk and "may present" take an *ex ante* perspective; substantial evidence is an *ex post* evaluation. [Applegate, The Perils of Unreasonable Risk: Information, Regulatory Policy, and Toxic Substances Control, 91 Colum. L. Rev. 261, 322 (1991).]

Second, EPA may issue a test rule if a chemical substance is or will be produced in substantial quantities and "(I) it enters or may reasonably be anticipated to enter the environment in substantial quantities or (II) there is or may be significant or substantial exposure to such substance or mixture," provided again that insufficient data exist to assess the risk, and testing is necessary to supply the data. §4(a)(1)(B). Chemical Mfrs. Ass'n v. EPA, 899 F.2d 344 (5th Cir. 1990), involved the scope of EPA's authority under this provision. The chemical industry challenged a regulation requiring manufacturers of the chemical cumene to engage in toxicological testing. EPA based its rule on the following finding:

> Under [§4(a)(1)(B)], EPA finds that cumene is produced in substantial quantities and that there is substantial environmental release with the potential for substantial human exposure from manufacturing, processing, use, and disposal. . . . Workers potentially exposed to cumene range between 700 [and] 800. During manufacturing, processing, and use an estimated 3 million pounds of cumene are lost to the atmosphere per year in

fugitive emissions. Although this amount is only approximately one-fifth the estimated atmospheric release of cumene from land transportation vehicles, the industrial releases are localized and may result in more significant exposures to the general population living near these facilities than the more ubiquitous vehicle emissions. Over half of the cumene manufacturing and processing plants are located in two major metropolitan areas, thus increasing the potential human exposure to 15 to 16 million people. [Id. at 348-349.]

CMA argued (1) that a finding of "substantiality" under either clause (I) or (II) of §4(a)(1)(B)(i) requires a showing that the quantity or level of exposure is such that if the chemical were "highly toxic" it could "realistically be expected" to cause health or environmental harm; (2) that in order to make a proper finding under §4(a)(1)(B)(i)(I) of entry into the environment in substantial quantities, EPA must determine not only that the substance will enter the environment in such quantities, but also that it will persist there; and (3) that whether "human exposure" is "substantial" depends on more than simply the number of persons exposed, no matter how brief the exposure or how small its quantity or what the circumstances are in which the exposure occurs.

The court rejected all three assertions, but remanded the regulations to EPA on the basis of CMA's fourth argument. CMA contended that EPA did not articulate any understandable basis—either in the form of a general definition of or a set of criteria respecting the statutory term "substantial," or in its analysis of the specific evidence respecting cumene—for its ultimate determinations that the quantities of cumene that entered the environment from the facilities in question were "substantial" and that the potentially resulting human exposure to cumene was "substantial." The court ordered the agency to explain the basis on which its §4(a)(1)(B)(i)(I) and (II) "substantiality" findings were made. The court added:

> Under the statutory wording, it is clear that mere entry into the environment of some quantities of the chemical does not suffice for clause (I), rather the quantities entering must be "substantial"; likewise, for clause (II), just any human exposure to the chemical does not suffice, for that human exposure must be "substantial" (or "significant," but here there is no "significant" finding). A focus on quantity, without more, is hence of little help in understanding what is meant by "substantial."
>
> We recognize that "substantial" is an inherently imprecise word. We are also aware that in this context no definition or group of criteria can be established which will function like a mathematical formula, so that for every given set of facts a specific, predictable answer will always be forthcoming. Room must be left for the exercise of judgment. [899 F.2d at 359.]

On remand, EPA adopted a 1 million–pound threshold for "substantial production" under §4(a)(1)(B)(i), and a threshold value for "substantial releases" of 1 million pounds per year or the release of 10 percent or more of total production volume, whichever is lower. The agency also determined that "substantial exposure" means exposure to large numbers of people, which it described as 1,000 workers, 10,000 consumers, and/or 100,000 persons in the general population. Finally, it concluded that it lacked sufficient experience to define generic criteria for making a finding of "significant" human exposure. Instead, a finding of "significant" exposure would generally be made on a case-by-case basis, taking into consideration, among other factors, the manner of use, substance-specific physical properties, concentration levels, and the duration and frequency of the exposure to the substance. Exposure might be "significant" where the potential exposed population is not large but the conditions of exposure are unique and create unusually great concern about the substance's potential for adverse effects. 58 Fed. Reg. 28,736 (1993). Under what circumstances may EPA order chemical testing under §4(a)(1)(B) in which it would not be able to order testing under §4(a)(1)(A)?

EPA's implementation of the test rule provisions, like its use of the PMN process, has been disappointing. As of 2010, EPA had required testing of only about one percent of chemicals in commerce. President's Cancer Panel, Reducing Environmental Cancer Risk: What We Can Do Now 22 (2010). Compare Markell, *supra*, at 355 (reporting GAO finding that EPA had required testing for only about 200 chemicals since TSCA's adoption). One congressional staffer has argued that §4(a)(1)

> creates a classic "Catch-22" situation. The Agency must already have sufficient data to demonstrate that a chemical poses an unreasonable risk of injury to human health or the environment before it can start a data collection rulemaking. Based on the circular logic of this provision, EPA must already have the data needed to evaluate a chemical's risk in order to compel companies to submit the missing data.

Woolf, *supra*, at 6. Is this an accurate characterization of EPA's authority under §4(a)(1)?

(6) Regulation of Chemical Substances under TSCA

If the results of testing, PMN review, or screening of the inventory of existing chemicals indicate that there is a "reasonable basis to conclude" that commerce in a chemical "presents or will present" an unreasonable risk to health or the environment, the Administrator may impose a variety of restraints on the marketing of a chemical, including absolute bans, production quotas, bans or limitations on particular uses or at certain concentrations, and labeling requirements. §6(a). See also §6(b).

If time is of the essence, a §6 rule may be made effective almost immediately. §§5(f)(2), 6(d)(2)(B). If even faster action seems necessary, the Administrator may file a civil action for immediate seizure of "an imminently hazardous chemical substance or mixture" or for other temporary or permanent relief necessary to "protect health or the environment from the unreasonable risk associated with" the substance or mixture. §7(a)(1), (b). What is an "imminently hazardous chemical substance or mixture"? See §7(f).

TSCA specifically regulates polychlorinated biphenyls (PCBs), the only chemicals singled out for special attention in the Act. PCBs have long been used for their chemical stability, fire resistance, and electrical resistance properties in products such as electrical transformers, but they are toxic to humans and wildlife. TSCA prohibits the manufacture, processing, and sale of PCBs, with limited exemptions. With certain exceptions, §6(e) permits PCBs to be used only in conditions of total enclosure. EPA may authorize unenclosed uses that "present no unreasonable risk of injury to health or the environment." See EDF v. EPA, 636 F.2d 1267 (D.C. Cir. 1980), where the court upheld EPA's use of §6(c)(1) criteria, including adverse economic impacts, in determining unreasonable risk of injury under §6(e)(2)(B).

The following case deals with the scope of EPA's authority under §6(a) to regulate other chemical substances not banned by the statute itself, but that present unreasonable risks.

CORROSION PROOF FITTINGS v. EPA
947 F.2d 1201 (5th Cir. 1991)

Jerry E. Smith, Circuit Judge.

[EPA issued a final rule under §6(a) of TSCA prohibiting the manufacture, importation, processing, and distribution of asbestos in almost all products. Petitioners claimed that the rulemaking procedures were flawed and that the rule was not based on substantial evidence. The court agreed and remanded to EPA.]

I

Asbestos is a naturally occurring fibrous material that resists fire and most solvents. Its major uses include heat-resistant insulators, cements, building materials, fireproof gloves and clothing, and motor vehicle brake linings. Asbestos is a toxic material, and occupational exposure to asbestos dust can result in mesothelioma, asbestosis, and lung cancer. . . .

[Based on its review of more than one hundred studies, EPA concluded that asbestos is a potential carcinogen at all levels of exposure, regardless of the type of asbestos or the size of the fiber. It issued a rule prohibiting the manufacture, importation, processing, and distribution in commerce of most asbestos-containing products. Based on its finding that asbestos constituted an unreasonable risk to health and the environment, it also promulgated a staged ban of most commercial uses of asbestos. The ban was to go into effect in three stages, depending upon how toxic each substance was and how soon adequate substitutes would be available. EPA estimated that the rule would save either 202 or 148 lives, depending upon whether the benefits were discounted, at a cost of approximately $450-800 million, depending upon the price of substitutes.]

III.   Rulemaking Defects

[The court concluded that the rule was procedurally flawed for two reasons. First, EPA should have afforded interested parties full cross-examination on all of its major witnesses. "Precluding cross-examination of EPA witnesses—even a minority of them—is not the proper way to expedite the finish of a lengthy rulemaking procedure." Second, EPA failed to provide notice that it intended to use "analogous exposure" data to calculate the expected benefits of certain product bans. "EPA should not hold critical analysis in reserve and then use it to justify its regulation despite the lack of public comment on the validity of its basis. Failure to seek public comment on such an important part of the EPA's analysis deprived its rule of the substantial evidence required to survive judicial scrutiny."]

IV. *The Language of TSCA*

A. STANDARD OF REVIEW

. . . TSCA provides that a reviewing court "shall hold unlawful and set aside" a final rule promulgated under §6(a) "if the court finds that the rule is not supported by substantial evidence in the rulemaking record . . . taken as a whole." 15 U.S.C. §2618(c)(1)(B)(i). . . .

Contrary to the EPA's assertions, the arbitrary and capricious standard found in the APA and the substantial evidence standard found in TSCA are different standards, even in the context of an informal rulemaking. . . . "The substantial evidence standard mandated by [TSCA] is generally considered to be more rigorous than the arbitrary and capricious standard normally applied to informal rulemaking," Environmental Def. Fund v. EPA, 636 F.2d 1267, 1277 (D.C. Cir. 1980), and "affords a considerably more generous judicial review" than the arbitrary and capricious test. Abbott Laboratories v. Gardner, 387 U.S. 136 (1967). The test "imposes a considerable burden on the agency and limits its discretion in arriving at a factual predicate." Mobil Oil Corp. v. FPC, 483 F.2d 1238, 1258 (D.C. Cir. 1973). . . .

B. THE EPA'S BURDEN UNDER TSCA

. . . We conclude that the EPA has presented insufficient evidence to justify its asbestos ban. We base this conclusion upon two grounds: the failure of the EPA to consider all necessary evidence and its failure to give adequate weight to statutory language requiring it to promulgate the least burdensome, reasonable regulation required to protect the environment adequately. . . .

1. LEAST BURDENSOME AND REASONABLE

TSCA requires that the EPA use the least burdensome regulation to achieve its goal of minimum reasonable risk. This statutory requirement can create problems in evaluating just what is a "reasonable risk." Congress' rejection of a no-risk policy, however, also means that in certain cases, the least burdensome yet still adequate solution may entail somewhat more risk than would other, known regulations that are far more burdensome on the industry and the economy. The very language of TSCA requires that the EPA, once it has determined what an acceptable level of non-zero risk is, choose the least burdensome method of reaching that level.

In this case, the EPA banned, for all practical purposes, all present and future uses of asbestos—a position the petitioners characterize as the "death penalty alternative," as this is the most burdensome of all possible alternatives listed as open to the EPA under TSCA. TSCA not only provides the EPA with a list of alternative actions, but also provides those alternatives in order of how burdensome they are. The regulations thus provide for EPA regulation ranging from labeling the least toxic chemicals to limiting the total amount of chemicals an industry may use. Total bans head the list as the most burdensome regulatory option.

By choosing the harshest remedy given to it under TSCA, the EPA assigned to itself the toughest burden in satisfying TSCA's requirement that its alternative be the least burdensome of all those offered to it. Since, both by definition and by the terms of TSCA, the complete ban of manufacturing is the most burdensome alternative—for even stringent regulation at least allows a manufacturer the chance to invest and meet the new, higher standard—the EPA's regulation cannot stand if there is any other regulation that would achieve an acceptable level of risk as mandated by TSCA. . . .

The EPA considered, and rejected, such options as labeling asbestos products, thereby warning users and workers involved in the manufacture of asbestos-containing products of the chemical's dangers, and stricter workplace rules. EPA also rejected controlled use of asbestos in the workplace and deferral to other government agencies charged with worker and consumer exposure to industrial and product hazards, such as OSHA, the [Consumer Product Safety Commission], and the [Mine Safety and Health Administration]. The EPA determined that deferral to these other agencies was inappropriate because no one other authority could address all the risk posed "throughout the life cycle" by asbestos, and any action by one or more of the other agencies still would leave an unacceptable residual risk.[16]

Much of the EPA's analysis is correct, and the EPA's basic decision to use TSCA as a comprehensive statute designed to fight a multi-industry problem was a proper one that we uphold today on review. What concerns us, however, is the manner in which the EPA conducted some of its analysis. TSCA requires the EPA to consider, along with the effects of toxic substances on human health and the environment, "the benefits of such substance[s] or mixture[s] for various uses and the availability of substitutes for such uses," as well as "the reasonably ascertainable economic consequences of the rule, after consideration of the effect on the national economy, small business, technological innovation, the environment, and public health." Id. §2605(c)(1)(C)-(D).

The EPA presented two comparisons in the record: a world with no further regulation under TSCA, and a world in which no manufacture of asbestos takes place. The EPA rejected calculating how many lives a less burdensome regulation would save, and at what cost. Furthermore the EPA, when calculating the benefits of its ban, explicitly refused to compare it to an improved workplace in which currently available control technology is utilized. This decision artificially inflated the purported benefits of the rule by using a baseline comparison substantially lower than what currently available technology could yield.

Under TSCA, the EPA was required to evaluate, rather than ignore, less burdensome regulatory alternatives. TSCA imposes a least-to-most-burdensome hierarchy. In order to impose a regulation at the top of the hierarchy—a total ban of asbestos—the EPA must show not only that its proposed action reduces the risk of the product to an adequate level, but also that the actions Congress identified as less burdensome also would not do the job. The failure of the EPA to do this constitutes a failure to meet its burden of showing that its actions not only reduce the risk but do so in the Congressionally mandated *least burdensome* fashion. . . .

This comparison of two static worlds is insufficient to satisfy the dictates of TSCA. While the EPA may have shown that a world with a complete ban of asbestos

16. EPA argues that OSHA can only deal with workplace exposures to asbestos and that the CPSC and MSHA cannot take up the slack, as the CPSC can impose safety standards for asbestos products based only upon the risk to consumers, and MSHA can protect against exposure only in the mining and milling process. These agencies leave unaddressed dangers posed by asbestos exposure through product repair, installation, wear and tear, and the like.

might be preferable to one in which there is only the current amount of regulation, the EPA has failed to show that there is not some intermediate state of regulation that would be superior to both the currently regulated and the completely banned world. Without showing that asbestos regulation would be ineffective, the EPA cannot discharge its TSCA burden of showing that its regulation is the least burdensome available to it.

Upon an initial showing of product danger, the proper course for the EPA to follow is to consider each regulatory option, beginning with the least burdensome, and the costs and benefits of regulation under each option. The EPA cannot simply skip several rungs, as it did in this case, for in doing so, it may skip a less-burdensome alternative mandated by TSCA. Here, although the EPA mentions the problems posed by intermediate levels of regulation, it takes no steps to calculate the costs and benefits of these intermediate levels. Without doing this it is impossible, both for the EPA and for this court on review, to know that none of these alternatives was less burdensome than the ban in fact chosen by the agency. . . .

2.   THE EPA'S CALCULATIONS

[The court expressed concern over EPA's failure to compute the costs and benefits of its ban past the year 2000.] In performing its calculus, the EPA only included the number of lives saved over the next thirteen years, and counted any additional lives saved as simply "unquantified benefits." The EPA and intervenors now seek to use these unquantified lives saved to justify calculations as to which the benefits seem far outweighed by the astronomical costs. For example, the EPA plans to save about three lives with its ban of asbestos pipe, at a cost of $128-227 million (i.e., approximately $43-76 million per life saved). Although the EPA admits that the price tag is high, it claims that the lives saved past the year 2000 justify the price.

Such calculations not only lessen the value of the EPA's cost analysis, but also make any meaningful judicial review impossible. While TSCA contemplates a useful place for unquantified benefits beyond the EPA's calculation, unquantified benefits never were intended as a trump card allowing the EPA to justify any cost calculus, no matter how high.

The concept of unquantified benefits, rather, is intended to allow the EPA to provide a rightful place for any remaining benefits that are impossible to quantify after the EPA's best attempt, but which still are of some concern. But the allowance for unquantified costs is not intended to allow the EPA to perform its calculations over an arbitrarily short period so as to preserve a large unquantified portion.

Unquantified benefits can, at times, permissibly tip the balance in close cases. They cannot, however, be used to effect a wholesale shift on the balance beam. Such a use makes a mockery of the requirements of TSCA that the EPA weigh the costs of its actions before it chooses the least burdensome alternative. . . .

3.   REASONABLE BASIS

In addition to showing that its regulation is the least burdensome one necessary to protect the environment adequately, the EPA also must show that it has a reasonable basis for the regulation. 15 U.S.C. §2605(a). . . .

Most problematical to us is the EPA's ban of products for which no substitutes presently are available. In these cases, the EPA bears a tough burden indeed to show that under TSCA a ban is the least burdensome alternative, as TSCA explicitly instructs the EPA to consider "the benefits of such substance or mixture for various uses and the availability of substitutes for such uses." Id. §2605(c)(1)(C). These words are particularly appropriate where the EPA actually has decided to ban a product, rather than simply restrict its use, for it is in these cases that the lack of an adequate substitute is most troubling under TSCA.

As a general matter, we agree with the EPA that a product ban can lead to great innovation, and it is true that an agency under TSCA, as under other regulatory statutes, "is empowered to issue safety standards which require improvements in existing technology or which require the development of new technology." Chrysler Corp. v. Department of Transp., 472 F.2d 659, 673 (6th Cir. 1972). As even the EPA acknowledges, however, when no adequate substitutes currently exist, the EPA cannot fail to consider this lack when formulating its own guidelines. Under TSCA, therefore, the EPA must present a stronger case to justify the ban, as opposed to regulation, of products with no substitutes.

We note that the EPA does provide a waiver provision for industries where the hoped-for substitutes fail to materialize in time. Under this provision, if no adequate substitutes develop, the EPA temporarily may extend the planned phase-out.

The EPA uses this provision to argue that it can ban any product, regardless of whether it has an adequate substitute, because inventive companies soon will develop good substitutes. The EPA contends that if they do not, the waiver provision will allow the continued use of asbestos in these areas, just as if the ban had not occurred at all.

The EPA errs, however, in asserting that the waiver provision will allow a continuation of the status quo in those cases in which no substitutes materialize. By its own terms, the exemption shifts the burden onto the waiver proponent to convince the EPA that the waiver is justified. As even the EPA acknowledges, the waiver only "may be granted by [the] EPA in very limited circumstances." 54 Fed. Reg. at 29,460. . . .

We also are concerned with the EPA's evaluation of substitutes even in those instances in which the record shows that they are available. The EPA explicitly rejects considering the harm that may flow from the increased use of products designed to substitute for asbestos, even where the probable substitutes themselves are known carcinogens. The EPA justifies this by stating that it has "more concern about the continued use and exposure to asbestos than it has for the future replacement of asbestos in the products subject to this rule with other fibrous substitutes." Id. at 29,481. The agency thus concludes that any "[r]egulatory decisions about asbestos which poses well-recognized, serious risks should not be delayed until the risk of all replacement materials are fully quantified." Id. at 29,483. . . .

[T]he EPA cannot say with any assurance that its regulation will increase workplace safety when it refuses to evaluate the harm that will result from the increased use of substitute products. While the EPA may be correct in its conclusion that the alternate materials pose less risk than asbestos, we cannot say with any more assurance than that flowing from an educated guess that this conclusion is true.

Considering that many of the substitutes that the EPA itself concedes will be used in the place of asbestos have known carcinogenic effects, the EPA not only cannot assure this court that it has taken the least burdensome alternative, but cannot even prove that its regulations will increase workplace safety. Eager to douse the dangers of asbestos, the agency inadvertently actually may increase the risk of injury

Americans face. The EPA's explicit failure to consider the toxicity of likely substitutes thus deprives its order of a reasonable basis. [The court construed TSCA to require that, when interested parties introduce credible studies and evidence showing the toxicity of substitutes, EPA consider whether its regulations would represent a net increase in safety or whether the increased risk resulting from dangerous substitutes renders regulation unreasonable.]

4. UNREASONABLE RISK OF INJURY

The final requirement the EPA must satisfy before engaging in any TSCA rulemaking is that it only take steps designed to prevent "unreasonable" risks. In evaluating what is "unreasonable," the EPA is required to consider the costs of any proposed actions and to "carry out this chapter in a reasonable and prudent manner [after considering] the environmental, economic, and social impact of any action." 15 U.S.C. §2601(c). . . .

That the EPA must balance the costs of its regulations against their benefits further is reinforced by the requirement that it seek the least burdensome regulation. While Congress did not dictate that the EPA engage in an exhaustive, full-scale cost-benefit analysis, it did require the EPA to consider both sides of the regulatory equation, and it rejected the notion that the EPA should pursue the reduction of workplace risk at any cost. See *American Textile Mfrs. Inst.*, 452 U.S. at 510 n.30 ("unreasonable risk" statutes require "a generalized balancing of costs and benefits[")]. . . .

Even taking all of the EPA's figures as true, and evaluating them in the light most favorable to the agency's decision (non-discounted benefits, discounted costs, analogous exposure estimates included), the agency's analysis results in figures as high as $74 million per life saved. . . .

While we do not sit as a regulatory agency that must make the difficult decision as to what an appropriate expenditure is to prevent someone from incurring the risk of an asbestos-related death, we do note that the EPA, in its zeal to ban any and all asbestos products, basically ignored the cost side of the TSCA equation. The EPA would have this court believe that Congress, when it enacted its requirement that the EPA consider the economic impacts of its regulations, thought that spending $200-300 million to save approximately seven lives (approximately $30-40 million per life) over thirteen years is reasonable. . . .

The EPA's willingness to argue that spending $23.7 million to save less than one-third of a life reveals that its economic review of its regulations, as required by TSCA, was meaningless. As the petitioners' brief and our review of EPA case law reveals, such high costs are rarely, if ever, used to support a safety regulation. If we were to allow such cavalier treatment of the EPA's duty to consider the economic effects of its decisions, we would have to excise entire sections and phrases from the language of TSCA. Because we are judges, not surgeons, we decline to do so.[23] . . .

---

23. . . . As the petitioners point out, the EPA regularly rejects, as unjustified, regulations that would save more lives at less cost. For example, over the next 13 years, we can expect more than a dozen deaths from ingested toothpicks—a death toll more than twice what the EPA predicts will flow from the quarter-billion dollar bans of asbestos pipe, shingles, and roof coatings. See L. Budnick, Toothpick-Related Injuries in the United States, 1979 Through 1982, 252 J. Am. Med. Ass'n, Aug. 10, 1984, at 796 (study showing that toothpick-related deaths average approximately one per year).

NOTES AND QUESTIONS

1. Did EPA make a finding that asbestos posed an unreasonable risk? What factors did the agency consider in reaching that conclusion? Did EPA consider the availability of substitutes for the products it banned? What were the flaws in the agency's reasoning process? For a more sympathetic and deferential review of EPA's consideration of regulatory alternatives in a Clean Air Act rulemaking, see Allied Local and Regional Mfrs. Caucus v. EPA, 215 F.3d 61, 74 (D.C. Cir. 2000) (characterizing industry's argument that the regulation of VOC emissions might have counterproductive consequences as "a series of theoretical possibilities" rather than "fact-based predictions"). What role do unquantified benefits play in determinations of the reasonableness of risk under TSCA? What must EPA do on remand to abide by the court's interpretation of §6(a)?

On what basis did the court in *Corrosion Proof Fittings* conclude that the asbestos ban rule might inadvertently increase the risk of injury? Is this portion of the court's opinion an example of the risk-risk analysis described at pages 797-98, *supra*? Relying on an article written by Justice Scalia before he became a judge, two observers suggest that judicial review of the substantive validity of risk regulation ought to revolve around the basic precept that agency action is justifiable only if it "does more good than harm." See Warren & Marchant, "More Good than Harm": A First Principle for Environmental Agencies and Reviewing Courts, 20 Ecology L.Q. 379 (1993).

2. *The Meaning of "Unreasonable Risk."* TSCA repeatedly instructs EPA to apply the standard of "unreasonable risk of injury to health or the environment" in making decisions. If "unreasonable risk" is suspected or determined to be present, EPA may, among other things, issue a test rule (§4(a), (b)), place a chemical on a list for priority attention (§4(e)), require PMN of new chemicals (§5(b)(2)(B)), regulate chemicals under §6, and regulate imminent hazards (§7). See Table 8-3.

Other sections apply slightly different standards to agency determinations under TSCA. Under §4(f), EPA has a nondiscretionary duty to take action within six months under other TSCA provisions if available data indicate that "there may be a reasonable basis to conclude that a chemical substance or mixture presents a significant risk of serious or widespread harm to human beings from cancer, gene mutations, or birth defects." What is the difference between the "unreasonable risk" and "significant risk" standards? EPA at times has taken the position that the "significant risk" standard is stricter than the "unreasonable risk" standard. Can you devise an argument that, while economic considerations are relevant to determinations of unreasonable risk, they have no bearing on determinations of significant risk under §4(f)?

3. Corrosion Proof Fittings *and the Standard of Judicial Review Under TSCA.* Do the hybrid rulemaking procedures, the substantial evidence standard of judicial review, and the unreasonable risk standard, as interpreted in *Corrosion Proof Fittings*, make regulation under §6 impossible to sustain? Consider the following:

> The court's analysis shows the basic flaw in evaluating regulations based on complex scientific analysis under the substantial evidence standard of review. In many instances, qualitative indicators of risk may suggest regulation. However, these qualitative indicators of risk may prove, as the EPA noted in its final asbestos rule, "unquantifiable" . . . because of technological limitations or limited agency resources. It is entirely possible that, at one level of practical scientific investigation, a reasonable conclusion could be

TABLE 8-3
Summary of EPA's Authority Under TSCA

Source of EPA's Authority	Nature of EPA's Authority	Conditions for Exercise of EPA's Authority
§4(a)	Require testing on health and environmental effects of chemical substances	Chemical substance may present an unreasonable risk of injury to health or the environment, or chemical substance is or will be produced in substantial quantities with substantial human or environmental exposure
§4(f)	Take action under §§5, 6, or 7 of TSCA to prevent or reduce risk or publish a finding that a risk is not unreasonable	Reasonable basis to conclude that chemical substance presents or will present a significant risk of serious or widespread harm to human beings from cancer, gene mutations, or birth defects
§5(e)	Issue orders prohibiting or limiting manufacture, use, etc. of chemical substances pending development of further information	Finding that chemical substance is manufactured or produced in the United States
§5(f)	Issue orders or regulations or apply to federal court for injunction prohibiting or limiting manufacture, use, etc. of chemical substance	Finding of reasonable basis to conclude that manufacture, use, etc. of chemical substance subject to premanufacture notification under §5 presents or will present an unreasonable risk of injury to health or the environment before EPA can regulate under §6
§6(a)	Regulate chemical substances, including a prohibition on manufacture, use, etc. to the extent necessary to protect adequately against the risk, using the least burdensome requirements	Finding of reasonable basis to conclude that manufacture, use, etc. of chemical substance presents or will present an unreasonable risk of injury to health or the environment
§7(a)	Commence civil action in federal court for seizure of imminently hazardous chemical substance or for other relief	Finding that chemical substance presents an imminent and unreasonable risk of serious or widespread injury to health or the environment
§8(b)	Compile inventory of substances subject to premanufacture notification requirements of §5(a)	Finding that chemical substance is manufactured or processed in the United States

drawn that a risk exists and is potentially large. To go to the next level of scientific investigation and actually calculate these risks with precision, however, may be completely impractical. . . . In the final analysis, the substantial evidence standard of review removes judicial deference to agency expertise when EPA deems it impractical and unsafe to waive regulation in order to make further scientific findings. Rather, it is in these situations that deference to agency expertise is warranted. [Hanan, Pushing the Environmental Regulatory Focus a Step Back: Controlling the Introduction of New Chemicals Under the Toxic Substances Control Act, 18 Am. J.L. & Med. 395, 415-416 (1992).]

Central and South West Serv., Inc. v. EPA, 220 F.3d 683 (5th Cir. 2000), interpreted §6(e) of TSCA to create a rebuttable presumption that all PCB uses present an unreasonable risk of injury to health and the environment. This interpretation dictated the conclusion that §19(c)(1)(B)(i)'s substantial evidence standard of review applies only when a petitioner challenges EPA's decision to depart from the ban and to permit or expand the use of PCBs. A petitioner challenging a rule restricting or prohibiting the use of PCBs is subject to the "arbitrary and capricious" standard of review. Does this result make sense as a matter of policy? Is it consistent with §19(c)(1)(B)(i)?

4. *The Impact of* Corrosion Proof Fittings. Between TSCA's adoption and 2010, EPA issued regulations under §6 to control only five chemicals, none after 1989. President's Cancer Panel, *supra*, at 22; Woolf, *supra*, at 6-7. By one account, TSCA "may be the most egregious example of ineffective regulation on environmental contaminants." President's Cancer Panel, *supra*, at 20. The GAO in 2009 deemed TSCA to be at "high risk" of failure because it does not provide EPA with enough authority to effectively regulate chemicals. Id. at 22-23. How much of the problem is intrinsic to TSCA and how much is due to *Corrosion Proof Fittings*? See Woolf, *supra,* at 7 (claiming that "many TSCA practitioners believ[e] that EPA could never meet the statutory standard as interpreted by the court"); McGarity, The Courts and the Ossification of Rulemaking: A Response to Professor Seidenfeld, 75 Tex. L. Rev. 525, 541-548 (1997) (arguing that the court "sent EPA on a potentially endless analytical crusade in search of the holy grail of *the* least burdensome alternative that still protected adequately against unreasonable risk," that the court afforded "not one whit" of deference to EPA's interpretation of the statute, and that the opinion left EPA with the choice of adopting regulations "that were sufficiently inoffensive to the regulated industry to avoid legal challenge or . . . giving up the quest altogether").

Following the Fifth Circuit's decision, EPA turned primarily to market-based mechanisms to control the use of asbestos. In the meantime, all forms of asbestos were banned in 52 countries because of its known health effects. More than 2 million tons continue to be produced each year in nations that include Russia, China, Brazil, and Canada. LaDou et al., The Case for a Global Ban on Asbestos, 118 Envtl. Health Persp. 897 (2010). For discussion of the history of regulation of asbestos in the U.S., see Garlow, Asbestos—The Long-Lived Mineral, 19 Nat. Resources & Env't No. 4 (Spring 2005), at 36.

Applegate, Synthesizing TSCA and REACH: Practical Principles for Chemical Regulation Reform, 35 Ecology L.Q. 721 (2008), suggests amending TSCA, based in part on comparisons to Europe's comprehensive system for the regulation of industrial chemicals throughout Europe: Registration, Evaluation, and Authorization of Chemicals (REACH). Do common law tort actions have the potential to plug the gaps in TSCA's coverage? Is a public nuisance action a viable vehicle for compelling chemical testing? See Lin, Deciphering the Chemical Soup: Using Public Nuisance to Compel Chemical Testing, 85 Notre Dame L. Rev. 955 (2010).

NOTE ON INTEGRATION OF TSCA WITH OTHER REGULATORY SCHEMES

TSCA §9 is intended to prevent regulatory activity under that law from overlapping with or duplicating regulation under other federal statutes. If EPA has a reasonable basis to conclude that certain activities involving chemical substances or mixtures present an unreasonable risk, and it determines that the risk may be prevented or reduced to a sufficient extent under another law not within EPA jurisdiction, EPA must submit to the agency administering that law a report describing the risk and the activities presenting it. If the other agency either declares that the activities do not present an unreasonable risk or decides to regulate them, EPA is barred by §9(a) from acting under §§6 or 7 of TSCA. Section 9(b) requires EPA to coordinate actions taken under TSCA with actions taken under other EPA-administered statutes. If EPA determines that a health or environmental risk could be addressed sufficiently under such other statutes, it must regulate under those laws unless, in EPA's discretion, TSCA regulation would be in the public interest. See also §6(c)(1). Section 9(c) provides that the exercise of EPA's authority under TSCA will not be regarded as the issuance or enforcement of occupational health and safety standards under the OSH Act. In issuing its asbestos ban regulations, did EPA make the findings required by §9? Did the court in *Corrosion Proof Fittings* second-guess EPA's determinations?

Ruggerio, Referral of Toxic Chemical Regulation Under the Toxic Substances Control Act: EPA's Administrative Dumping Ground, 17 B.C. Envtl. Aff. L. Rev. 75, 77 (1989), argues that §9 is "an escape hatch for the EPA to avoid regulatory responsibility that it should legitimately exercise." She claims that EPA's referral to OSHA of regulatory responsibility for toxic substances in the workplace has increased health risks because the OSH Act is weaker than TSCA.

Problem 8-1

In 2010, EPA began receiving complaints that people working in buildings with new carpets were experiencing headaches, nausea, skin rashes, and other symptoms. In 2013, X-Pose-A, Inc., a private laboratory in Massachusetts, issued a report on a recently completed animal bioassay in which the lab had exposed mice to emissions from several brands of new carpets treated with flame retardants. The report indicated that neurotoxicity, pulmonary irritation, and death had occurred in a small but statistically significant percentage of the exposed animals. EPA scientists received permission to repeat the carpet emissions tests on the X-Pose-A premises. The results were similar to the ones produced in the tests conducted by X-Pose-A scientists. EPA scientists were unable to replicate the findings in subsequent tests in EPA's own labs, however. Those tests did not even indicate mild toxicity: no deaths, no severe or moderate sensory irritation, and no clear evidence of neurotoxicity arose. In 2014, EPA sent the three sets of test results to a panel of scientists unaffiliated with either EPA or any carpet manufacturers for peer review. The panel recently concluded that the findings were irreconcilable. The panel also indicated that it was unable to detect methodological flaws in any of the tests.

EPA is considering whether to take action to control the risks to the public health posed by exposure to carpet emissions in the workplace. Does it have sufficient information to make that decision? If not, how may it solicit more information? If so, should it regulate or refer the matter to another agency? If it decides to regulate, should it regulate under TSCA or another statute? If it decides to regulate under TSCA, what is the threshold showing necessary to justify regulation?

b. Regulation of Pesticide Use: The Federal Insecticide, Fungicide, and Rodenticide Act

Modern agriculture depends heavily on two chemical technologies: fertilizers and pesticides. Some 40,000 registered pesticides contain 600 active ingredients. Pesticide use in the United States increased by 250 percent between 1964 and 1993. Kahn, Comment, New Developments in Pesticide Regulation, 13 Temple Envtl. L. & Tech. J. 309 (1994). Of the 1 billion pounds of pesticides sold annually in the U.S., 80 percent are used in agriculture, 15 percent in industry and government, and 5 percent in homes. General Accounting Office, Carcinogens: EPA's Formidable Task to Assess and Regulate Their Risk 10 (1986). But even among farmers, the distribution of pesticide use varies by region and crop:

> [H]alf of all insecticides used in agriculture are applied to non-food crops, such as cotton or tobacco, grown primarily in the Southeast. Pesticides are applied to more than seventy-five percent of the total acreage of relatively few crops, mainly fruits and vegetables. On a per acre basis, only seventeen percent of total U.S. cropland is treated with herbicides, six percent with insecticides, and less than one percent with fungicides. Thus, the benefits of pesticide use are distributed among farmers who control a relatively small amount of total agricultural production acreage. [Carlucci, Note, Reforming the Law on Pesticides, 14 Va. Envtl. L.J. 189, 197 (1994).]

The application of large amounts of chemical pesticides (a generic name for three different classes of chemicals and compounds: fungicides, insecticides, and rodenticides) became controversial after the publication of Rachel Carson's book Silent Spring (1962). Her book touched off a reevaluation of one of the most widely hailed benefits of World War II technology, synthetic organic pesticides. Initially, environmentalists focused their attention on eliminating the use of DDT. Out of the DDT cancellation proceeding emerged many of the core concepts that continue to control the assessment of toxic chemicals because that proceeding first illustrated the use of cancer risk as a proxy for other environmental injuries.

Pesticide regulation remains controversial. On the one hand are those who assert that, although pesticide use is often effective over the short run, productivity gains "are not sustained over the long run due to the counterproductive tendency of pesticides to induce genetic 'resistance' to target pests and to destroy beneficial insects that previously had helped to check target pest populations." Hornstein, Lessons from Federal Pesticide Regulation on the Paradigms and Politics of Environmental Law Reform, 10 Yale J. on Reg. 369, 393 (1993). The significant environmental risks posed by pesticide use outweigh these marginal economic benefits.

> EPA's Science Advisory Board concluded in 1990 that, when compared with dozens of other risks, pesticides presented one of the country's more widespread and severe environmental problems. Apart from accelerating the development of resistant pests,

pesticides can cause at least eight other broad types of unintended effects: acute or chronic health effects among workers in the manufacturing process; acute or chronic effects on third parties due to accidents in manufacturing or transport; acute and chronic health problems among applicators and farmworkers; contamination of groundwater due to leaching; contamination of surface waters from farm run-off; poisoning of wildlife; acute and chronic health problems among consumers due to residues on food; and contamination of the environment due to improper disposal of unused pesticides and their containers.

Id. at 394-395. Pesticides are present in 15 percent of wastes at sites remediated under CERCLA, id. at 395, and studies of wildlife exposed to pesticides reveal a risk of adverse impacts on immuno-competency, neurotoxicity, and endocrine function. Meyers & Colborn, Blundering Questions, Weak Answers Lead to Poor Pesticide Policies, Chem. & Engineering News, Jan. 7, 1991, at 40, 41. On the other hand are those who downplay the size of the risk and insist that food production would decline drastically in the absence of pesticide use, significantly increasing the risk of starvation and malnutrition. "Rather than debate the risk of pesticides versus the benefit of pesticides, we should consider the risk of pesticides versus the risk of not having them." Carpenter, Insignificant Risks Must Be Balanced Against Great Benefits, Chem. & Engineering News, Jan. 7, 1991, at 37, 38. The interconnections between food and drug law and pesticide control law are discussed at section E.1.d below.

Pesticide use is supported by a powerful constituency of industry, agricultural associations, and much (but not all) of the agricultural research establishment. Not surprisingly, Congress has tried to balance the desire to protect public health against the economic and other benefits of pesticide use. EPA has broad authority to take both risks and economic impacts into account.

(1) The Evolution of Pesticide Regulations: From Classic Consumer Protection to DDT

Pesticides were first regulated in 1910 to prevent consumer fraud after users complained of adulterated goods. Insecticide Act of 1910, Pub. L. No. 61-152, 36 Stat. 331. In 1947 Congress responded to the increasing use of more sophisticated, synthetic compounds by passing the Federal Insecticide, Fungicide, and Rodenticide Act (FIFRA), 7 U.S.C. §§136-136y. The Federal Food, Drug, and Cosmetic Act (FFDCA) and FIFRA relied largely on the same model: drugs and pesticides should be efficacious; any public health or "environmental" problems are caused by misuse, which labeling will prevent. FIFRA required the Department of Agriculture to register all pesticides; the chief restriction on entry to the market took the form of labeling requirements explaining how to use the compound effectively and safely. Until 1964, a pesticide to which the Department of Agriculture objected could be registered under protest. Once a pesticide was registered, it could be marketed unless the registration was suspended under an interim administrative procedure, pending the initiation of lengthy proceedings to cancel the registration.

The Department's administration of FIFRA was examined and found wanting when public attention focused on DDT. See Rodgers, The Persistent Problem of the Persistent Pesticides: A Lesson in Environmental Law, 70 Colum. L. Rev. 567 (1970). In 1969 the Environmental Defense Fund (EDF) asked the Department to suspend the registration of DDT. A 1964 amendment to FIFRA required the agency to suspend a registration if necessary to prevent an "imminent hazard." The Secretary responded by refusing to suspend the registration for the major use of DDT, the suppression of cotton pests. (A pesticide is registered not by chemical compound, but by use.) The Department issued notices to cancel four minor uses and promised additional notices after further study. In the interim, two significant events occurred. The administration of FIFRA was given to the newly created EPA, and the D.C. Circuit held that EPA had a duty to suspend a registration when a substantial question of an "imminent hazard" existed. EDF v. Ruckelshaus, 439 F.2d 584 (D.C. Cir. 1971). The DDT litigation provides a case study in the power and limits of appellate courts to control an agency agenda and discretion within the constraints of separation of powers principles. The crucial opinions in addition to EDF v. Ruckelshaus are EDF v. Hardin, 428 F.2d 1093 (D.C. Cir. 1970); Wellford v. Ruckelshaus, 439 F.2d 598 (D.C. Cir. 1971); and EDF v. EPA, 465 F.2d 528 (D.C. Cir. 1972).

By the time the DDT cancellation hearing began on August 17, 1971, the focus of public concern and of the administrative proceeding against DDT had shifted from general environmental damage to carcinogenicity, although Carson's Silent Spring had focused entirely on ecosystem effects. The hearing examiner refused cancellation, finding that DDT was neither carcinogenic nor mutagenic and that it did not have a deleterious effect on freshwater fish, estuarine organisms, wild birds, or other wildlife. After finding that DDT did present significant risks and balancing all of the risks and benefits of DDT use, EPA Administrator William Ruckelshaus canceled almost all of the pesticide's registrations. His decision was sustained on appeal, partly because an agency head can ignore the decision of the hearing examiner when the issue involves a policy judgment. EDF v. EPA, 489 F.2d 1247 (D.C. Cir. 1973). See generally McGarity, Substantive and Procedural Discretion in Administrative Resolution of Science Policy Questions: Regulating Carcinogens in EPA and OSHA, 67 Geo. L.J. 729 (1979). For an argument that "DDT may remain the best hope for saving and improving millions of lives," see Mulliken et al., DDT: A Persistent Lifesaver, 19 Nat. Resources & Env't #4 (Spring 2005), at 3.

(2) The Current Law

In 1972, Congress amended FIFRA with the Federal Environmental Pesticide Control Act (FEPCA). FEPCA supplements FIFRA's initial consumer protection philosophy with public health regulation for more subtle risks. FEPCA requires that the risks and benefits of pesticide use be considered at four stages of decisionmaking (registration, restricted registration, suspension, and cancellation), but the definition of risk and benefit is not the same at each stage. See generally Spector, Regulation of Pesticides by the Environmental Protection Agency, 5 Ecology L.Q. 223 (1976); Fischer, et al., A Practitioner's Guide to the Federal Insecticide, Fungicide and Rodenticide Act: Parts I, II, and III, 24 Envtl. L. Rep. 10,449 (Aug. 1994), id. at 10,507 (Sept. 1994), and id. at 10,629 (Nov. 1994). Angelo, Embracing Uncertainty, Complexity, and Change: An Eco-Pragmatic Reinvention of a First-Generation Environmental Law, 33 Ecology L.Q. 105, 108 (2006), argues that FIFRA "has not changed significantly with regard to ecological matters since 1972 and remains primarily a consumer protection statute not well-suited for ecological protection." Professor Angelo recommends changes to improve FIFRA's ability to protect ecological integrity.

(a) Registration, Restricted Registration, and Re-Registration

Registration. EPA must register a pesticide[j] if the Administrator determines that its chemical composition seems to justify the efficacy claims made for it, that the manufacturer has complied with FIFRA labeling and data submission requirements, and that the pesticide will not cause "unreasonable adverse effects on the environment" when used as intended and "in accordance with widespread and commonly recognized practice." §136a(c)(5). FIFRA defines the term "unreasonable adverse effects on the environment" to mean "(1) any unreasonable risk to man or the environment, taking into account the economic, social, and environmental costs and benefits of the use of any pesticide, or (2) a human dietary risk from residues that result from a use of a pesticide in or on food" that is inconsistent with standards established under the food and drug laws. §136(bb). In 1978 Congress allowed EPA to grant conditional registrations for pesticides that are "identical or substantially similar" to registered pesticides and that do not significantly increase the risk of any unreasonable adverse effects on the environment. §136a(c)(7). See NRDC v. EPA, 735 F.3d 873 (9th Cir. 2013) (disapproving conditional registration of pesticides containing nanosilver particles because EPA's finding that they did not pose health concerns was inconsistent with its own regulations).

How should EPA assess reasonableness? FIFRA requires a fuller balancing of costs and benefits than do most other environmental statutes. The balancing stops just short of a formal cost-benefit analysis. See Rodgers, Benefits, Costs, and Risks: Oversight of Health and Environmental Decisionmaking, 4 Harv. Envtl. L. Rev. 191, 207 (1980); Headwaters, Inc. v. Talent Irrigation Dist., 243 F.3d 526, 532 (9th Cir. 2001) ("FIFRA registration is a cost-benefit analysis"). A tension exists between a full balancing and EPA's policy of using sensitive cancer triggers to determine risk. Earlier drafts of the 1972 amendments required a showing of substantial adverse effects before registration could be denied, but the more environmentally oriented Senate Commerce Committee changed the language to the present formula to ensure that a court would not hold "that a 'substantial' level of adversity must be reached before [EPA] invokes the necessary balancing of risk versus benefit in determining whether a pesticide ought to be registered." S. Rep. No. 92-970, at 10 (1972). Does this mean that EPA need not make a threshold finding of significant risk, as OSHA must in regulating under the OSH Act? How does the standard for registration compare with TSCA's unreasonable risk standard?

FIFRA requires EPA to consider the benefits of pesticide use. Although EPA is not required to do so, it has tried to adapt formal cost-benefit analysis for application in pesticide decisions. See Office of Pesticide Programs, Office of Water and Hazardous Materials, A Benefit-Cost System for Chemical Pesticides (1975). Judicial consideration of EPA benefit decisions is relatively unenlightening (e.g., EDF v. EPA, 510 F.2d 1292, 1302-1303 (D.C. Cir. 1975)), and nagging unresolved issues remain regarding whether the agency knows how to develop and apply benefit data. For example, EPA refused to cancel most uses of chlorobenzilate, used primarily to control citrus rust mites, because the failure to control the mite in Florida, Texas,

j. FIFRA defines a pesticide, in part, as a substance or mixture "intended for preventing, destroying, repelling, or mitigating any pest," or "intended for use as a plant regulator, defoliant, or desiccant." §136(u). Occasionally, controversies arise over the scope of the definition. See, e.g., Turner v. EPA, 848 F. Supp. 711 (S.D. Miss. 1994) (upholding EPA order preventing further sales of mound leveler without registration because EPA had reasonable basis for concluding that the product, which was marketed to kill fire ants, was a pesticide rather than a plant nutrient).

and California would have significant adverse effects on fruit size, appearance, crop yield, and treestock stamina. A National Academy of Sciences (NAS) study found in a subsequent independent literature search that the Department of Agriculture, which has a formal role in supplying benefit data, had failed to bring to EPA's attention "eight additional studies of the effect of chemical miticides on citrus yields. None of these additional studies . . . found a statistically significant difference in yields between sprayed and unsprayed plots that could be attributed to rust mites." National Academy of Sciences, Regulating Pesticides 192 (1980). More startling, the NAS concluded that estimated increased pest control costs from canceling the uses of chlorobenzilate would range between $2.4 and 9.2 million per year rather than $57 million a year, as EPA had projected. Id. at 209-210. Compare Love v. Thomas, 838 F.2d 1059 (9th Cir. 1988) (remanding suspension of registration for dinoseb because EPA failed to investigate adequately the adverse economic impacts of suspension, and therefore could not do even a rough cost-benefit balancing).

The issue in Merrell v. Thomas, 807 F.2d 776 (9th Cir. 1986), was whether EPA must comply with the National Environmental Policy Act (NEPA) when it registers pesticides under FIFRA. The court held that it need not do so because the application of NEPA would increase the regulatory burdens of registration, contrary to Congress's intention in the 1978 amendments to FIFRA to do the opposite, and because the application of NEPA would upset the compromise between environmental and economic considerations reflected in FIFRA's standard for registration. Cf. Washington Toxics Coal. v. EPA, 413 F.3d 1024 (9th Cir. 2005) (EPA's registration of a pesticide under FIFRA does not excuse EPA from complying with the consultation requirements of the Endangered Species Act).

Restricted Registration. Under §136a(d)(1)(B), if EPA decides that a pesticide, when properly used, will not generally cause unreasonable adverse effects on the environment, it will classify the pesticide (or certain of its uses) for general use. But under §136a(d)(1)(C), if a pesticide so used may generally cause those effects, EPA must classify it (or certain of its uses) for restricted use. A pesticide that is classified for restricted use may only be applied by or under the direct supervision of a certified applicator, as defined in §136(e)(1). In addition, under certain conditions, EPA may subject pesticides classified for restricted use to whatever other restrictions EPA deems appropriate. See §136a(d)(1)(C)(ii). What is the function of classifying a pesticide for restricted use? How does restriction for classified use relate to initial registration and cancellation decisions?

Re-Registration. Approximately 50,000 pesticides were registered under the permissive pre-1972 requirements. Examination of all these pesticides proved impossible by the 1976 deadline for re-registration decisions imposed by the 1972 FEPCA. The 1988 FIFRA amendments established a new, nine-year re-registration schedule, provided funding through $150 million in fees to be collected from registrants, shifted numerous tasks to registrants, and streamlined the process. From 1989 to 1991, more than 40,000 studies were submitted to EPA pursuant to the 1988 re-registration process. W. Rodgers, Environmental Law 435 (2d ed. 1994). But the process continued to move slowly. By 2005, EPA had completed 229 Reregistration Eligibility Decisions and begun to process an additional 152. Beyond Pesticides/National Coal. Against the Misuse of Pesticides v. Johnson, 407 F. Supp. 2d 38 (D.D.C. 2005) (holding that EPA's delay in responding to petitions to suspend or cancel wood preservative pesticides was not unreasonable in light of its obligation to review other pesticides as part of the re-registration process).

Among the provisions of the 1978 amendments intended to facilitate EPA's review of previously approved pesticides was the one authorizing data call-ins. If EPA determines that additional data are required to maintain in effect an existing registration, it may issue a Data Call-In Notice (DCI) requiring the registrant to produce evidence that it is taking steps to gather the requested information. If the registrant fails to follow through in an appropriate manner, EPA may issue a notice of intent to suspend the pesticide's registration. §136a(c)(2)(B)(iv). EPA establishes priorities for DCIs on the basis of the extent of human exposure. Hornstein, Reclaiming Environmental Law: A Normative Critique of Comparative Risk Analysis, 92 Colum. L. Rev. 562, 568 n.21 (1992). See also Bergeson & Hutton, FIFRA—Chemical Testing Issues, 35 Envtl. L. Rep. 10141 (2005). Atochem N. Am., Inc. v. EPA, 759 F. Supp. 861 (D.D.C. 1991), held that EPA may require registrants to conduct monitoring in response to a DCI, and that §136a(c)(2)(B) does not require EPA to perform a cost-benefit analysis in issuing a DCI by balancing the need for information on the risks posed by a pesticide against the possibility that the product might cease to be produced if the data requirements are enforced.

Congress amended FIFRA in 1996 to require EPA to establish procedures for the periodic review of pesticides, stating a goal that each registration would be reviewed every 15 years. Registrations may not be canceled as a result of the review process, however, absent compliance with both the substantive and procedural requirements of §136d, discussed below. §136a(g)(1)(A). EPA's review of organophosphates under the 1996 amendments produced an agreement between the agency and manufacturers of chlorpyrifos to eliminate use of the chemical in places where children might be exposed and to limit its use on fruits eaten frequently by children. EPA, Citing Risks to Children, Sharply Limits a Chief Pesticide, N.Y. Times, June 9, 2000. The 1996 amendments also established expedited registration procedures for antimicrobial pesticides (those designed to disinfect microbiological organisms such as bacteria or fungi). §136a(h).

In West Harlem Envtl. Action v. EPA, 380 F. Supp. 2d 289 (S.D.N.Y. 2005), the court reviewed EPA's decision to rescind two mitigation requirements imposed on rodenticide manufacturers as part of EPA's reregistration of the rodenticides in question. The court deferred to EPA's decision to rescind the requirement that the rodenticides contain an indicator dye that would help identify whether children or pets had consumed the chemicals. It reversed EPA's decision, however, to rescind a requirement that the rodenticides include a bittering agent to reduce consumption by children and pets. The court found that EPA's explanation for the rescission of the bittering agent requirement lacked even a "scintilla" of supporting evidence.

(b) Suspension, Cancellation, and Related Matters

Suspension. FIFRA guarantees the registrant of a pesticide an adjudicatory hearing before cancellation, which may take place whenever it appears that "a pesticide or its labeling or other material required to be submitted does not comply with . . . [this Act] or when used in accordance with widespread and commonly recognized practice, [the pesticide] . . . generally causes unreasonable adverse effects on the environment." §136d(b). If EPA determines that an "imminent hazard" is posed by continued use during the time required for cancellation, the agency may immediately suspend the pesticide's registration. §136d(c)(1). The test for imminent hazard is whether "unreasonable adverse effects on the environment," the familiar criterion for initial registration and for cancellation, are likely to result during the interim period if suspension does not occur. §136(*l*), (bb). Compare TSCA §5(e)(1), (f)(1). The registrant may request that EPA convene an expedited hearing, which delays the effective date of the suspension. §136d(c)(2). If EPA determines that an emergency exists, it may issue a suspension that goes into effect even before the registrant has the opportunity to request an expedited hearing and remains in effect pending disposition of that hearing. §136d(c)(3). The statute does not define what constitutes an emergency. FIFRA provides for immediate judicial review of an emergency suspension, but the reviewing court has only two choices: uphold the suspension or stay it pending a final decision on cancellation. §136d(c)(4). The court may not impose conditions on the pesticide's use to prevent adverse effects pending a decision on cancellation. See Love v. Thomas, 838 F.2d 1059 (9th Cir. 1988).

The first judicial interpretations of FIFRA focused on its suspension provisions. These cases set the tone for the courts' interpretation of other provisions of FIFRA as well. Although the courts initially intimated that suspension should be reserved for substantial irreparable harm to the public, after 1970 they concluded that for a suspension only a preliminary assessment indicating possible public harm was required. The decision to suspend would be upheld if it was supported by respectable scientific authority. EDF v. EPA, 465 F.2d 528 (D.C. Cir. 1972). This interpretation effectively placed the burden of proving the safety of a pesticide on the registrant. This tilt toward precaution was made explicit in suspension proceedings for the pesticides heptachlor and chlordane. EPA regulations placed the burden of going forward on the agency and the burden of persuasion on the registrant:

> In urging that the ultimate burden of proof in a suspension proceeding rests on the Administrator, Velsicol and USDA assert that the suspension decision is a drastic step differing fundamentally from both the registration and cancellation decisions made under FIFRA. But we have already cautioned that the "imminent hazard" requisite for suspension is not limited to a concept of crisis: "It is enough if there is *substantial likelihood* that serious harm will be experienced during the year or two required in any realistic projection of the administrative process."[15] "FIFRA confers broad discretion" on the Administrator to find facts and "to set policy in the public interest." Wellford v. Ruckelshaus, 439 F.2d 598, 601 (1971). This broad discretion was conferred on the implicit assumption that interim action may be necessary to protect against the risk of harm to the environment and public health while a fuller factual record is developed in the cancellation proceeding. This avenue of protective relief would be effectively foreclosed if we accepted Velsicol's argument that the Administrator must *prove* imminent hazard—apparently in some sense of weight of the evidence going beyond substantial likelihood. But as we have already pointed out, the basic statutory directive requires affirmance of the Administrator's decision if supported by substantial evidence, and this requires "something less than the weight of the evidence." We reject that renewed invitation to exercise increased substantive control over the agency decision process.

EDF v. EPA, 548 F.2d 998, 1004-1005 (D.C. Cir. 1976). See generally McCarey, Note, Pesticide Regulation: Risk Assessment and Burden of Proof, 45 Geo. Wash. L.

15. EDF v. EPA, 510 F.2d at 1297, quoting EDF v. EPA, 465 F.2d at 540.

Our en banc decision in Ethyl Corp. v. EPA, 541 F.2d 1 at 16, n.28 (1976), considered this standard as more rigorous than the standard involved in *Ethyl*; we have not sought to engage in a comparative analysis of the differences that may be discernible in these two statutory standards, but have rested with applying the "substantial likelihood" standard to the facts of this case.

Rev. 1066 (1977). How does this allocation of the burden of proof compare with the allocation in the context of TSCA §6 regulation, as interpreted in *Corrosion Proof Fittings?*

Cancellation and the "Rebuttable Presumption Against Registration" (RPAR). The DDT case discussed above, EDF v. Ruckelshaus, interpreted FIFRA to require EPA to commence a cancellation proceeding whenever a "substantial question" exists about health hazards caused by a registered pesticide. The difficulty came in establishing workable guidelines for the health hazards that would "trigger" cancellation and in bringing the long adjudicatory proceedings to a successful conclusion. To aid it in achieving both these objectives, in 1975 EPA issued a policy statement that declared that a rebuttable presumption against registration (RPAR) would arise if certain types of data suggested that the pesticide was acutely or chronically toxic or no effective emergency treatment was available in case of human exposure. See Atochem N. Am., Inc. v. EPA, 759 F. Supp. 861, 864 n.7 (D.D.C. 1991). Evidence of chronic toxicity that would trigger the RPAR included, in addition to epidemiological data, acceptance of mutagenic or benign tumorigenic effects discovered through animal experiments. This policy not only formalized the acceptance of animal experiment data on carcinogenicity but ignored for precautionary purposes the distinction between benign and malignant tumors. Any tumors in laboratory animals potentially would trigger an RPAR. 40 Fed. Reg. 28,242 (1975). Did the RPAR process reflect the adoption of default assumptions of the kind discussed in section A.2 of this chapter?

In 1976, EPA published a broader and more polished statement of its RPAR "cancer principles," indicating that it intended to apply them not only in pesticide regulation but in its remaining regulatory programs as well. 41 Fed. Reg. 21,402 (1976). EPA was careful not to propose that its principles be adopted as binding rules. The 1976 "interim" guidelines recognized four types of evidence of carcinogenicity: (1) epidemiological studies in humans confirmed with animals tests (the "best evidence"); (2) animal tests in which malignant tumors appear, including benign tumors recognized as early stages of malignancy ("substantial evidence"); (3) indirect tests of tumorigenic activity and animal tests revealing only non-life-shortening benign tumors ("suggestive evidence"); and (4) studies relating chemical structure to carcinogenicity ("ancillary evidence"). The significance that these types of evidence may carry in a decision to register or cancel a pesticide is more likely to turn on EPA's assessment of overall risks and benefits than merely on the evidence of carcinogenicity. Under FIFRA's cost-benefit standards, EPA may permit even a known human carcinogen to be registered if it determines that the benefits of its use outweigh its health risks. The courts have responded sympathetically to EPA's attempt to "prejudge" the acceptability of various categories of evidence before a particular pesticide has even been singled out for cancellation proceedings. See EDF v. EPA, 548 F.2d 998, 1006-1007 (D.C. Cir. 1976).

In 1985, EPA renamed the RPAR "Special Review." 40 C.F.R. §154.7; 50 Fed. Reg. 49,015 (1985). The concept remained the same, but third parties could now initiate a second look at a compound. See 59 Fed. Reg. 60,412 (1994). From time to time, EPA issues notices of intent to cancel registrations based on the results of the Special Review process. E.g., 60 Fed. Reg. 50,338 (1995) (noting carcinogenic potential of dichlorvos). In addition, formulators sometimes voluntarily cancel their registrations. E.g., 60 Fed. Reg. 46,592 (1995).

The ultimate test for cancellation is whether a pesticide, "when used in accordance with widespread and commonly recognized practice, generally causes unreasonable adverse effects on the environment." §136d(b). In Ciba-Geigy v. EPA, 874 F.2d 277 (5th Cir. 1989), EPA canceled the registration of diazinon for use on sod farms and golf courses, rejecting the manufacturer's contention that cancellation is justified only if a product causes unreasonable adverse effects most of the time it is used. EPA claimed authority to cancel a pesticide's registration upon a finding that it causes unreasonable risk, regardless of the frequency of that risk. The court remanded the cancellation to EPA:

> The Administrative Law Judge concluded that bird kills due to diazinon may be an "unusual occurrence." Ciba-Geigy asserts, therefore, that even if diazinon sometimes causes adverse environmental effects, it does not do so "generally" as the statute requires.
>
> Ciba-Geigy's argument focuses on a single word in the statutory phrase, ignoring the meaning of the phrase as a whole. FIFRA provides that the Administrator may cancel the registration of a pesticide if it appears to him that, "when used in accordance with widespread and commonly recognized practice, (it) generally causes unreasonable adverse effects on the environment." The statute defines "unreasonable adverse effects on the environment" to mean "any unreasonable risk to man or the environment, taking into account the . . . costs and benefits."
>
> Neither the statute nor its legislative history explains the word "generally," but, as the numerous dictionary definitions that the parties have quoted to us make clear, it means "usually," "commonly," or "with considerable frequency," though not necessarily "more likely than not." Interpreting the statutory standard as a whole, therefore, the Administrator may cancel a registration if it appears to him that the pesticide commonly causes unreasonable risks.
>
> Because FIFRA defines "adverse effects" as "unreasonable risks," the Administrator need not find that use of a pesticide commonly causes undesirable consequences, but only that it commonly creates a significant probability that such consequences may occur. FIFRA therefore does not oblige the Administrator to maintain the registration of a pesticide that might not generally have adverse effects but, say, killed children on 30% of the occasions on which it was used. A 30% risk that children might be killed is plainly an "unreasonable risk" more than sufficient to justify cancellation of the noxious pesticide. Similarly, a significant risk of bird kills, even if birds are actually killed infrequently, may justify the Administrator's decision to ban or restrict diazinon use.
>
> Nevertheless, the Administrator improperly read the word "generally" out of FIFRA [§136d(b)]. The word is not superfluous: it requires the Administrator to determine that the use of a pesticide in a particular application creates unreasonable risks, though not necessarily actual adverse consequences, with considerable frequency, and thus requires the Administrator to consider whether he has defined the application he intends to prohibit sufficiently narrowly. If the use of diazinon creates an unreasonable risk of killing birds on only 10% of the golf courses on which it is used, for example, the Administrator should define the class of golf courses on which its use is to be prohibited more narrowly. Without attempting to interpret the vast administrative record ourselves, therefore, we grant Ciba-Geigy's petition to the extent of remanding this case to the Administrator for application of the correct legal standard.

874 F.2d at 279-280. What is the function and significance of each of the key words in §§136(bb) and 136d(b)—"generally," "unreasonable," and "risk"?

On remand from the decision in *Ciba-Geigy*, EPA concluded that

> diazinon use on golf courses and sod farms causes an unreasonable risk to birds *commonly and with considerable frequency*. . . . [T]he number and frequency of bird kills that have

occurred, or that could be expected in the future, cannot be precisely quantified. None-theless, continued diazinon use . . . would generally pose a serious risk of regularly repeated bird kills, a risk that the Agency unquestionably views as unreasonable in light of the safer alternatives to diazinon for effective turf pest control, the negligible benefits of continued diazinon use, and the absence of any economic dislocations that would attend cancellation.

55 Fed. Reg. 31,138 (1990). EPA reasoned that, even if Ciba-Geigy implemented a series of proposals to reduce the risk of adverse effects, waterfowl and songbirds would continue to be generally exposed to lethal levels of diazinon residues, and individual deaths would likely be repeated on a fairly consistent basis. Diazinon use posed an unreasonable risk "with considerable frequency," and Ciba-Geigy failed to prove that any proposal short of a complete prohibition of diazinon use on sod farms and golf courses would constitute an adequate response to the risk.

Indemnification, Disposal, and Management of Existing Stocks. The 1972 law, FEPCA, required EPA to indemnify producers, distributors, and others for economic loss when EPA canceled or suspended a registration. A Senate Committee estimated claims for dinoseb, whose cancellation was upheld in Northwest Food Processors Ass'n v. Reilly, 886 F.2d 1075 (9th Cir. 1989), at about $40 million. S. Rep. No. 100-346, at 7 (1988). To eliminate the chilling effect on regulation caused by assessing these sums against the EPA operating budget, the 1988 amendments trans-ferred liability to the Federal Judgment Fund, which relies on general appropriations to pay claims against the federal government. §136m(b)(3). The pre-1988 FIFRA also required EPA to bear the costs of disposing of canceled pesticides. The amendments shifted responsibility for disposal to the pesticide industry. See generally Ferguson & Gray, 1988 FIFRA Amendments: A Major Step in Pesticide Regulation, 19 Envtl. L. Rep. 10070 (1989).

Section 136d(a)(1) authorizes EPA to permit the continued sale and use of existing stocks of a pesticide whose registration has been suspended or canceled, provided EPA determines that those activities are not inconsistent with FIFRA's purposes. In National Coal. Against the Misuse of Pesticides v. EPA, 867 F.2d 636 (D.C. Cir. 1989), the Coalition challenged EPA's decision to permit sales, commercial uses, and commercial application of existing stocks of two termiticides (chlordane and heptachlor) following the producer's voluntary agreement to cancel registration. When EPA issued a draft notice of intent to cancel registration, the Coalition brought suit, seeking not only cancellation, but also emergency suspen-sion. In the meantime, Velsicol, the company that had registered chlordane, agreed voluntarily to cancel certain registered uses, temporarily suspend others pending analysis of ongoing studies, and cease all manufacture, distribution, and sale of chlordane. In return, EPA agreed to authorize the sale and use of existing stocks of chlordane already outside the company's control. Relying on §136d(a)(1), EPA reasoned that, in the absence of this settlement, the only way to get chlordane off the market would be to proceed with formal cancellation and suspension hear-ings. While those proceedings were pending, additional amounts of the pesticide would flow onto the market. According to EPA, the amount of existing stocks it authorized in the settlement was less than the amount of chlordane that would have entered the market during formal cancellation proceedings. As a result, the risk to health and the environment posed by continued sale and use of the existing stocks would be less than the risk posed by delaying cancellation.

After EPA and Velsicol entered the agreement, the Coalition amended its complaint and sought to restrain EPA from permitting any use of the existing stocks covered by the agreement. The district court agreed with the Coalition that EPA should not have taken into account the amounts of chlordane that would have entered the market during any cancellation proceedings that would have been necessary in the absence of a settlement with Velsicol. Instead, before deciding whether to authorize continued sale and use of existing stocks under §136d(a)(1), EPA should have assumed that the cancellation order had already been issued, and that, therefore, no more chlordane would be entering the market. The appellate court reversed. Even if the statute was unclear on the scope of EPA's authority under the existing stocks provision, Congress clearly wanted to encourage settlements. EPA's interpretation of §136d(a)(1) facilitates settlements, while the Coalition's and the district court's would do the opposite. If EPA could not authorize the continued use and sale of existing stocks in exchange for voluntary cancellation, registrants would have incentives to drag out the cancellation proceedings. Even if they did not prevail, they would buy additional time to dispose of existing stocks. The Court of Appeals therefore approved of EPA's comparative risk assessment rationale.

c.   Regulation of Drinking Water Supplies: The Safe Drinking Water Act

The Nature of the Problem. Drinking water distribution may contribute to the dissemination of harmful substances. Ingestion of water contaminated by pathogens such as cryptosporidium, giardia, legionella, and *E. coli* can cause severe diarrhea, abdominal cramps, vomiting, and fever. Thousands of people experience illness and some die each year in the United States as the result of pathogenic organisms in drinking water. See S. Rep. No. 104-169, at 6 (1995); 44 Env't Rep. (BNA) 2885 (2013). Chemical pollution is also a concern. According to a Senate committee, "[a]bout 10 percent of ground water wells supplying drinking water systems are contaminated with man-made chemicals—an estimated 3 percent at levels above EPA health standards." Id. at 7. A 2006 study concluded that an increased risk of bladder cancer was associated with the intake of tap water in the U.S., Canada, Finland, France, and Italy, and suggested the presence of carcinogenic chemicals as the reason. Villanueva et al., Total and Specific Fluid Consumption as Determinants of Bladder Cancer Risk, 118 Int'l J. Cancer 2040 (2006).[k]

Drinking Water Regulations. The Safe Drinking Water Act (SDWA) of 1974, 42 U.S.C. §§300f to 300j-26, established a federal regulatory system to ensure the safety of public drinking water systems. The Act authorizes EPA to issue maximum contaminant level goals (MCLGs) and subject most public water systems to national primary drinking water regulations (NPDWRs). These regulations identify contaminants with

---

k. See also Aschengrau et al., Affinity for Risky Behaviors Following Prenatal and Early Childhood Exposure to Tetrachloroethylene (PCE)-Contaminated Drinking Water: A Retrospective Cohort Study, 10 Envtl. Health 1186 (2011) (finding that exposure to PCE-contaminated drinking water increases risky behavior, including illegal drugs and alcohol use); Getz et al., Prenatal and Early Childhood Exposure to Tetrachloroethylene and Adult Vision, 120 Envtl. Health Perspectives 1327 (2012) (finding link between the same kinds of PCE exposure and long-term subclinical visual dysfunction in adulthood).

potential adverse effects on public health and specify maximum contaminant levels (MCLs) or treatment techniques. §§300g, 300f(1). A "contaminant" is broadly defined to include "any physical, chemical, biological, or radiological substance or matter in water." §300f(6). A public water system is "a system for the provision to the public of piped water for human consumption . . . if such system has at least fifteen service connections or regularly serves at least twenty-five individuals." §300f(4)(A). United States v. Ritz, 772 F. Supp. 2d 1017 (S.D. Ind. 2011), *appeal dismissed*, 721 F.3d 825 (7th Cir. 2013), held that spigots at a campground qualified as "service connections." "Human consumption" includes bathing, showering, cooking, dishwashing, and maintaining oral hygiene. United States v. Midway Heights County Water Dist., 695 F. Supp. 1072 (E.D. Cal. 1988).

In 1986, Congress amended the statute to force more aggressive EPA regulation. It required EPA to publish MCLGs and promulgate NPDWRs for 83 listed contaminants by 1989 and to publish a priority list every three years of contaminants "known or anticipated to occur in public water systems" that require NPDWRs. By the end of 1995, EPA had issued or proposed NPDWRs for 88 contaminants and identified an additional 25 substances for regulation. S. Rep. No. 104-169, *supra*, at 9-10. But the provision requiring EPA to regulate a specified number of contaminants provoked widespread criticism.

> This single provision of the Safe Drinking Water Act has provoked more critical comment than virtually any other element of environmental law. Some of the 83 contaminants for which standards are required occur so infrequently in public water systems that the costs of monitoring (for a substance not present) far outweigh any health benefit that could be realized at the few systems that may detect the contaminant. In other cases, the available science is so uncertain that standards incorporate extravagant margins of safety (30,000-fold for one contaminant), making it impossible to assert that expenditures to implement the regulation are a public health necessity. Finally, the mandate that EPA set standards for an additional 25 contaminants every 3 years regardless of the threat posed by these contaminants in drinking water is for many the quintessential example of an arbitrary Federal law imposing burdens on consumers and the taxpayers of other governments with no rational relationship to the public benefits that might be realized. [Id. at 12-13.]

In short, the statute "unintentionally discourages EPA from concentrating its resources on regulating contaminants that pose the highest health risks," requiring instead that the agency "regulate a long list of contaminants, regardless of the seriousness of the threat they pose to public health and regardless [of] the frequency with which they occur in drinking water." Id. at 1.

Congress set out to "give EPA flexibility to set drinking water standards based on peer-reviewed science and the benefits and risks associated with contaminants," and to minimize the impact of the statute on local drinking water systems struggling to keep up with the growing burdens imposed by the Act's regulatory requirements. Id. at 2. In the Safe Drinking Water Act Amendments of 1996, Pub. L. No. 104-182, 110 Stat. 1613, Congress required that EPA issue MCLGs and NPDWRs for each contaminant that may have an adverse effect on health and that is known or is substantially likely to occur in public water systems "with a frequency and at levels of public health concern," provided that, in the sole judgment of the Administrator, regulation "presents a meaningful opportunity for health risk reduction for persons served by public water systems." 42 U.S.C.

§300g-1(b)(1)(A). EPA must periodically publish a list of contaminants not subject to NPDWRs that are known or are anticipated to occur in public water systems and that may require regulation. EPA's decision to list or not list a particular contaminant is exempt from judicial review. §300g-1(b)(1)(B)(i). As for unregulated contaminants, EPA must select for consideration those that present the greatest public health concern, taking into consideration the effects of the contaminants on subgroups that are at greater risk of adverse health effects than the general population. §300g-1(b)(1)(C). Between 2000 and 2009, EPA did not list a single additional contaminant. Duhigg, That Tap Water Is Legal but May Be Unhealthy, N.Y. Times, Dec. 17, 2009.

What is the relationship between the MCLGs and the NPDWRs? See Figure 8-8. The MCLGs must be set "at the level at which no known or anticipated adverse effects on the health of persons occur and which allows an adequate margin of safety." §300g-1(b)(4)(A). Is the margin of safety concept well suited to the regulation of carcinogenic drinking water contaminants? In International Fabricare Inst. v. EPA, 972 F.2d 384 (D.C. Cir. 1992), chemical companies and an association of dry cleaning businesses challenged the establishment of MCLGs and MCLs for 38 organic and inorganic chemicals. The petitioners attacked the MCLGs on the ground, among others, that EPA's decision to set zero-level MCLGs for known or probable carcinogens failed to take into account new scientific evidence concerning the possibility that there are threshold levels of exposure to the substances regulated. The court rejected the attack, concluding that the petitioners' "evidence" amounted to nothing more than the opinions of a few scientists who were out of the mainstream. The court was also not persuaded that EPA placed undue reliance on animal studies. Compare that result with the following case.

CHLORINE CHEMISTRY COUNCIL v. EPA
206 F.3d 1286 (D.C. Cir. 2000)

STEPHEN F. WILLIAMS, Circuit Judge:

[Chloroform is a nonflammable, colorless liquid that is one of four compounds classified as total trihalomethanes (TTHMs), which are by-products of chlorination, a widely used technique for ensuring the safety of drinking water. Although chlorination plays a significant role in the control of microbial pathogens, EPA concluded on the basis of rodent tumor data that chloroform, a by-product of this process, is a probable human carcinogen. In particular, EPA concluded in 1998 that chloroform exhibits a "nonlinear mode of carcinogenic action."] In other words, exposures to chloroform below some threshold level pose no risk of cancer. But in promulgating the MCLG [under the SDWA] it retained the existing standard of zero, which was based on the previously held assumption that there was no safe threshold. EPA justified its action on a variety of grounds, including an alleged need to consult the report of its Science Advisory Board ("SAB"), which would not be available until after the statutory deadline for rulemaking had expired. Petitioners, including the Chlorine Chemistry Council, a trade association comprised of chlorine and chlorine product manufacturers, petitioned this court for review, arguing that EPA violated its statutory mandate to use the "best available" evidence when implementing the provisions of the Safe Drinking Water Act. 42 U.S.C. §300g-1(b)(3)(A). We agree. . . .

Appcicability (§300g-1(b) (1) (A)). EPA must set a maximum
contaminant level goal (MCLG) for a contaminant if
  (i) the contaminant may have an adverse effect on the health of
      persons;
 (ii) the contaminant is known to occur or there is a substantial
      likelihood that it will occur in public water systems with a
      frequency and at levels of public health concern; and
(iii) in the sole judgment of EPA regulation presents a meaningful
      opportunity for public health risk reduction.

Regulatory Goal (§300g-1(b)(4)(A)). EPA must set the
contaminant level goal MCLG at the level at which no known or
anticipated adverse effects on the health of persons occur and
which allows an adequate margin of safety.

Regulatory Standard (§300g-1(b)(4)(B)). EPA must set maximum
contaminant level (MCL) as close to the MCLG as is feasible
(as defined in §300g-1(b)(4)(D)), with exceptions specified in
§300g-1(b)(5)-(6).

FIGURE 8-8
National Primary Drinking Water Regulations Under the SDWA

On July 29, 1994, EPA issued a proposed rule on disinfectants and disinfection byproducts in water. This included a zero MCLG for chloroform, based on EPA's finding of an *absence* of data to suggest a threshold level below which there would be no potential carcinogenic effects. The Agency's default method of inferring risk at exposure levels for which it has no adequate data is linear extrapolation from cancer incidence inferred at exposures for which it does have data. [Citing EPA's 1996 Proposed Guidelines for Carcinogen Risk Assessment.] Thus, either if the evidence supports linearity, *or* if there is "insufficient" evidence of nonlinearity, EPA assumes that if a substance causes cancer at *any* exposure it will do so at *every* nonzero exposure (though with cancer incidence declining with exposure). But EPA acknowledges its authority "to establish nonzero MCLGs for carcinogens if the scientific evidence" indicates that a "safe threshold" exists. And petitioners here assume the validity of the linear default assumption.

[The 1996 amendments to the SDWA included a timetable for EPA's issuance of rules relating to disinfectants and disinfection by-products associated with water treatment. 42 U.S.C. §300g-1(b)(2)(C). The deadline for regulating chloroform was November 1998. Based on the findings and recommendations of an advisory group formed by EPA in 1997 to collect and analyze new information, EPA published two Notices of Data Availability specific to chloroform. The Notices discussed the findings of the experts, which had been subjected to peer review, that although chloroform was "a likely carcinogen to humans above a certain dose range, [it was] unlikely to be carcinogenic below a certain dose range." The experts recommended "the nonlinear or margin of exposure approach [as] the preferred approach to quantifying the cancer risk associated with chloroform exposure."]

EPA agreed. It said that "[a]lthough the precise mechanism of chloroform carcinogenicity is not established," nevertheless "the chloroform dose-response should be considered nonlinear." Rather than operating through effects on DNA, which is consistent with linearity, chloroform evidently works through "cytotoxicity" (i.e., damage to the cells) followed by regenerative cell proliferation. Employing the threshold approach that it found was entailed by chloroform's mode of action, EPA then calculated an MCLG of 600 parts per billion ("ppb"), based solely on carcinogenicity. This level built in a 1000-fold margin of error in relation to the maximum safe dosage implied from the animal studies used by EPA. But because even lower chlorine doses cause liver toxicity (a non-cancer effect), EPA proposed an MCLG of 300 ppb.

When EPA came to promulgate its final rule in December 1998, however, its MCLG was again zero. It stuck with 1994's zero level despite its explicit statement that it now "believe[d] that the underlying science for using a nonlinear extrapolation approach to evaluate the carcinogenic risk from chloroform is well founded." It justified the action on the basis that "additional deliberations with the Agency's SAB on the analytical approach used" and on the underlying scientific evidence were needed "prior to departing from a long-held EPA policy." It could not complete such additional deliberations by the November 1998 statutory deadline, and, moreover, the rulemaking would not affect the enforceable MCL for TTHMs. . . .

On February 11, 2000, the day of oral argument, EPA released a draft report by the SAB on chloroform. The report concluded that chloroform exhibits a "cytotoxic" mode of action. Such a mode of action (unlike a "genotoxic" mechanism, which acts directly on a cell's DNA) involves no carcinogenic effects at low doses; thus a nonlinear approach is "scientifically reasonable." . . .

. . . [P]etitioners argue that EPA's decision to adopt a zero MCLG in the face of scientific evidence establishing that chloroform is a threshold carcinogen was inconsistent with the Safe Drinking Water Act. Section 300g-1(b)(3)(A) of the Act states unequivocally that "to the degree that an Agency action is based on science, the Administrator shall use . . . the best available, peer-reviewed science and supporting studies conducted in accordance with sound and objective scientific practices." In promulgating a zero MCLG for chloroform EPA openly overrode the "best available" scientific evidence, which suggested that chloroform is a threshold carcinogen.

EPA provides several arguments in defense of its action. First, it argues that to establish a nonzero MCLG would be a "precedential step," that represents "a major change in the substance of regulatory decisions related to chloroform." We do not doubt that adopting a nonzero MCLG is a significant step, one which departs from previous practice. But this is a change in result, not in policy. The change in outcome occurs simply as a result of steadfast application of the relevant rules: first, the statutory mandate to set MCLGs at "the level at which no known or anticipated adverse effect on the health of persons occur," 42 U.S.C. §300g-1(b)(4)(A), as determined on the basis of the "best available" evidence; and second, EPA's Carcinogen Risk Assessment guidelines, stating that when "adequate data on mode of action show that linearity is not the most reasonable working judgment and provide sufficient evidence to support a nonlinear mode of action," the default assumption of linearity drops out. The fact that EPA has arrived at a novel, even politically charged, outcome is of no significance either for its statutory obligation or for fulfillment of its adopted policy.

Second, and similarly, EPA supports its action on the basis that "it could not complete the deliberations with the SAB" before the November 1998 deadline. But however desirable it may be for EPA to consult an SAB and even to revise its conclusion in the future, that is no reason for acting against its own science findings in the meantime. The statute requires the agency to take into account the "best *available*" evidence. 42 U.S.C. §300g-1(b)(3)(A) (emphasis added). EPA cannot reject the "best available" evidence simply because of the possibility of contradiction in the future by evidence unavailable at the time of action—a possibility that will *always* be present. . . .

. . . All scientific conclusions are subject to some doubt; future, hypothetical findings always have the potential to resolve the doubt (the new resolution itself being subject, of course, to falsification by later findings). What is significant is Congress's requirement that the action be taken on the basis of the best available evidence *at the time* of the rulemaking. The word "available" would be senseless if construed to mean "expected to be available at some future date." . . .

NOTES AND QUESTIONS

1. Under EPA's 1996 proposed cancer risk guidelines, how did EPA ascertain the level of risk at exposure levels for which it lacked adequate data? Under what circumstances did EPA apply the linear, no-threshold approach to ascertaining the risk of exposure to a carcinogenic substance? How did EPA attempt to defend its decision to set a zero-level MCLG in this case? What provision of the statute did the court find that EPA violated? Compare City of Waukesha v. EPA, 320 F.3d 228 (D.C. Cir. 2003) (rejecting assertion that EPA failed to use the best available scientific evidence in issuing national primary drinking water standards for radionuclides). What is EPA's approach to choosing an extrapolation approach under the 2005 carcinogen risk assessment guidance excerpted in section A.2 of this chapter?

2. The MCLG for a drinking water contaminant is not binding on public water systems. It is the MCL that establishes the maximum concentration of the relevant contaminant in drinking water that may be distributed. Nevertheless, EPA sometimes uses MCLGs to set remediation levels for cleanups under the Comprehensive Environmental Response, Compensation, and Liability Act. Industry in the principal case faced liability for the cleanup of chloroform at Superfund sites across the country, and thus faced higher cleanup costs under a zero-level than under a higher MCLG.

Before the 1996 amendments, the NPDWRs[1] had to specify a MCL "which is as close to the [MCLG] as is feasible." This provision generated three principal

1. EPA also has the authority to issue secondary drinking water regulations to protect against contaminants that may adversely affect the odor or appearance of drinking water or otherwise adversely affect the public welfare. §§300g-1(c), 300f(2).

criticisms. First, small drinking water systems might not be able to afford compliance with MCLs arrived at using this methodology, even if larger systems could. Second, compliance costs might outweigh the resulting benefits for some contaminants, particularly low-potency carcinogens. "The only identifiable benefit that can be stated for some standards is to prevent a handful of cancer cases nationwide, in some cases at costs that exceed tens of millions of dollars per cancer case avoided." S. Rep. No. 104-169, *supra*, at 14. Third, treatment technologies needed to achieve the MCLs might increase the risks posed by other contaminants. For example, chlorine, which is used to kill pathogenic organisms, might increase the cancer risk from disinfection by-products. "Read literally, the statute requires EPA to 'over control' some contaminants to a degree that overall public health risks from drinking water would be greater using the best available technology that is feasible than risks would be if the standard were set at a less stringent level." Id.

In response to these concerns, the 1996 amendments altered the manner in which EPA sets MCLs. Section 300g-1(b)(3)(C)(i) now requires that, in promulgating MCLs, EPA analyze the quantifiable and nonquantifiable health risk reduction benefits and costs likely to occur as a result of regulation, as well as the incremental costs and benefits associated with each alternative contaminant level considered. Based on this analysis, EPA must determine when it proposes a NPDWR whether the benefits of an MCL that represents the maximum feasible level of control justify the costs. §300g-1(b)(4)(C). What does "feasible" mean in this context? See §300g-1(b)(4)(D); City of Portland v. EPA, 507 F.3d 706, 712 (D.C. Cir. 2007) (holding that a "feasible" treatment technique is one that is "technically possible and affordable," not one whose benefits outweigh its costs). If EPA decides that they do not, it may establish an MCL that "maximizes health risk reduction benefits at a cost that is justified by the benefits." §300g-1(b)(6)(A). EPA also may set an MCL at a level other than the feasible level if the technology, treatment techniques, and other means used to determine the feasible level would result in an increase in the health risk from drinking water by increasing the concentration of other contaminants in drinking water or interfering with the efficacy of drinking water treatment techniques used to comply with other NPDWRs. §300g-1(b)(5)(A). In this situation, EPA must choose a level for the MCL that minimizes the overall risk posed by exposure to the contaminant being regulated and the other affected contaminants. §300g-1(b)(5)(B). Is this provision an example of "risk-risk" analysis?

Even before the 1996 amendments, EPA could issue NPDWRs that require the use of treatment techniques in lieu of establishing an MCL if it is not economically or technologically feasible to ascertain the level of the contaminant. §§300g-1(b)(7)(A), 300f(1)(C)(ii). This authority remains intact. American Water Works Ass'n v. EPA, 40 F.3d 1266 (D.C. Cir. 1994), involved challenges to EPA's pre-1996 NPDWRs for lead. NRDC challenged EPA's decisions to establish a treatment technique instead of an MCL. It argued that because it was economically and technologically feasible to ascertain the level of lead in water, EPA was obliged to set an MCL for lead. According to NRDC, "feasible" means "physically capable of being done at reasonable cost." EPA, however, argued that "feasible" means "capable of being accomplished in a manner consistent with the SDWA," and that subjecting public water systems to an MCL for lead would frustrate the statute's goals. If public water systems were required to comply with an MCL for lead, they would have to undertake corrosion control techniques that would increase the levels of other contaminants at the same time that they were reducing the amount of lead leached from customers' plumbing. The court deferred to EPA's interpretation:

The Congress clearly contemplated that an MCL would be a standard by which both the quality of the drinking water and the public water system's efforts to reduce the contaminant could be measured. See 42 U.S.C. §300g-1(b)(5). Because lead generally enters drinking water from corrosion in pipes owned by customers of the water system, an MCL for lead would be neither; ascertaining the level of lead in water at the meter (i.e., where it enters the customer's premises) would measure the public water system's success in controlling the contaminant but not the quality of the public's drinking water (because lead may still leach into the water from the customer's plumbing), while ascertaining the level of lead in water at the tap would accurately reflect water quality but effectively hold the public water system responsible for lead leached from plumbing owned by its customers.

. . . A single national standard (i.e., an MCL) for lead is not suitable for every public water system because the condition of plumbing materials, which are the major source of lead in drinking water, varies across systems and the systems generally do not have control over the sources of lead in their water. In this circumstance the EPA suggests that requiring public water systems to design and implement custom corrosion control plans for lead will result in optimal treatment of drinking water overall, i.e., treatment that deals adequately with lead without causing public water systems to violate drinking water regulations for other contaminants. [40 F.3d at 1271.]

Enforcement. EPA delegates primary enforcement responsibility to the states, provided they comply with EPA drinking water standards. 40 C.F.R. §142.10. EPA may assume enforcement if the state fails to commence appropriate enforcement action. §300g-3(a)(1)(A). Yet a 2009 report indicated that more than 20 percent of municipal water treatment systems supplying water to more than 49 million people had violated the SDWA within the previous five years, but less than six percent of the violators were fined or punished by federal or state officials. The DOJ conceded that the government is often reluctant to bring enforcement actions against cash-strapped local governments, which would pass liability costs onto local taxpayers. Duhigg, Millions in U.S. Drink Dirty Water, Records Show, N.Y. Times, Dec. 8, 2009. Subsequently, researchers found that the incidence of noncompliance was lower than initially reported because the data included tests on water that public water systems never supplied for human consumption. Ruff, Some Data in Water Report Is Off Base, Omaha World-Herald, Jan. 2, 1010. Data on levels of drinking water contaminants at water systems across the U.S. are available at http://projects.nytimes.com/toxic-waters/contaminants.

The SDWA also authorizes EPA to bring a civil action in federal district court to require statutory compliance. The court may provide such relief "as protection of the public health may require." §300g-3(b). In United States v. Massachusetts Water Res. Auth., 256 F.3d 36 (1st Cir. 2001), the court affirmed the district court's refusal to require the Authority to build a filtration plant to treat water drawn from a reservoir to supply the Boston area. The district court had agreed with the Authority that a less expensive system of ozonation and chloramination would adequately protect against the risk of disease from waterborne pathogens, and that the expenditure of $180 million for a plant that would achieve less than a one percent improvement in treatment capacity was unwarranted. United States v. Alisal Water Corp., 431 F.3d 643 (9th Cir. 2005), upheld as an appropriate exercise of judicial discretion under §300g-3(b) the district court's order requiring the owners of various private water systems to divest themselves of some of their systems based on their numerous violations of SDWA regulations.

The SDWA authorizes EPA to take whatever actions it deems necessary to protect the public health if it finds that a contaminant that is present in or is likely to enter a public water system or underground source of drinking water may present an imminent and substantial endangerment to health. §300i. United States v. Midway Heights County Water Dist., 695 F. Supp. 1072 (E.D. Cal. 1988), held that to prove that the water system "may present" such an endangerment, the government need not show that the failure to comply with MCLs had already caused illness. The Act "authorizes preventative actions. . . . This court need not wait to exercise its authority until water district customers have actually fallen ill from drinking Midway Heights water." Id. at 1076. Similarly, Trinity Am. Corp. v. EPA, 150 F.3d 389 (4th Cir. 1998), upheld an emergency order requiring a polyurethane foam plant located above a groundwater aquifer to sample groundwater near its property and provide bottled water to anyone with access to groundwater not meeting the standards. It made no difference that there was no evidence that anyone was actually drinking contaminated water. As long as the risk of harm was imminent, the harm itself need not be. Compare W.R. Grace & Co. v. EPA, 261 F.3d 330 (3d Cir. 2001), where the court vacated and remanded a §300i emergency order that required Grace to conduct a long-term cleanup of an aquifer contaminated by ammonia. The court found that EPA failed to provide a rational basis for its determination that cleanup to the specified level was necessary to protect health or that the remedial approach chosen (the removal of excess ammonia) was necessary.

The GAO reported in 2011 that EPA has not effectively implemented the 1996 amendments' requirement to prioritize regulation of contaminants that present the greatest public health concern. EPA often lacked sufficient occurrence and health effects data to support regulatory determinations and its presentation of health effects information on some contaminants lacked clarity, consistency, and transparency. Part of the problem may have been that decisions on whether to regulate were made largely by high-level political officials, not career agency science experts. Safe Drinking Water Act: Improvements in Implementation Are Needed to Better Assure the Public of Safe Drinking Water, GAO-11-803T (July 2011).

Problem 8-2

Section 300g-1(b)(1)(B)(i)(I) of the SDWA requires that EPA compile a list once every five years of contaminants not already covered by NPDWRs "which are known or anticipated to occur in public water systems, and which may require regulation" under the SDWA. EPA must then decide whether or not to regulate each of the listed contaminants. EPA recently published one such list, including on it 20 contaminants. EPA explained that it had excluded 10 other contaminants (contaminants A-J) not already subject to regulation but known to occur in public water systems because it concluded that the financial burdens imposed on local governments operating public water systems were already onerous and that requiring local governments to monitor and regulate those 10 contaminants would not be financially feasible. EPA indicated that it would consider including the 10 excluded substances on the next five-year list.

Several months later, EPA decided to issue NPDWRs for 4 of the contaminants included on the previous list. The agency indicated that it had decided not to issue NPDWRs for 9 of the listed contaminants (contaminants K-S) on the ground that requiring public water systems to comply with MCLs for them would impose economic costs on those systems that would exceed the environmental benefits attributable to regulation. EPA chose not to regulate 5 other contaminants on the list (contaminants T-X) on the ground that no evidence had been presented to EPA that exposure to the contaminants would cause adverse health effects. Finally, it chose not to regulate 2 other contaminants (contaminants Y and Z) because, although exposure to those contaminants might create adverse effects, EPA determined that local governments operating public water systems could achieve higher levels of public health protection by devoting the resources that would be required to comply with NPDWRs for contaminants Y and Z to providing better facilities for the disposal of solid waste in landfills located near public drinking water supplies.

EPA has just issued final NPDWRs for the first of the remaining 4 listed contaminants, hexaflurgapilon-1,2,3. EPA conceded that this substance is a suspected human carcinogen. It nevertheless established a maximum contaminant level goal (MCLG) above zero for that contaminant because it was unable to determine that there is no safe threshold level of exposure to hexaflurgapilon-1,2,3. Further, EPA established the MCL for hexaflurgapilon-1,2,3 at 10 percent above the MCLG, even though it would have been feasible for public water systems to reduce concentrations further to 5 percent above the MCLG. EPA justified that decision on the ground that the 10 percent level produced a better cost-benefit ratio than the 5 percent level.

An environmental public interest group, Better Water's Our Only Game (BWOOG), filed petitions for review of each of these EPA decisions. It attacked the validity of the following decisions: (1) EPA's decision to exclude contaminants A-J from the five-year list of unregulated contaminants; (2) EPA's decisions not to issue NPDWRs for contaminants K-S, T-X, and Y-Z; and (3) EPA's decisions to set an MCLG for hexaflurgapilon-1,2,3 at an above-zero level and to set an MCL for hexaflurgapilon-1,2,3 at 10 percent instead of 5 percent above the MCLG. How should the court resolve BWOOG's challenges?

d. Regulation of Chemicals in Food: The Federal Food, Drug, and Cosmetic Act

LES v. REILLY
968 F.2d 985 (9th Cir. 1992)

SCHROEDER, Circuit Judge:

[EPA denied an administrative petition requesting that it revoke a final order permitting the use of four pesticides as food additives although they had been found to induce cancer. The petitioners challenged the order on the ground that it violated the Delaney clause, 21 U.S.C. §348(c)(3), which prohibits the use of any food additive that is found to induce cancer.]

The Federal Food, Drug, and Cosmetic Act (FFDCA), 21 U.S.C. §§301-394, is designed to ensure the safety of the food we eat by prohibiting the sale of food that is "adulterated." 21 U.S.C. §331(a). Adulterated food is in turn defined as food containing any unsafe food "additive." 21 U.S.C. §342(a)(2)(C). A food "additive" is defined broadly as "any substance the intended use of which results or may reasonably be expected to result . . . in its becoming a component . . . of any food." 21 U.S.C.

§321(s). A food additive is considered unsafe unless there is a specific exemption for the substance or a regulation prescribing the conditions under which it may be used safely. 21 U.S.C. §348(a).

Before 1988, the four pesticide chemicals with which we are here concerned—benomyl, mancozeb, phosmet and trifluralin—were all the subject of regulations issued by the EPA permitting their use. In October 1988, however, the EPA published a list of substances, including the pesticides at issue here, that had been found to induce cancer. Regulation of Pesticides in Food: Addressing the Delaney Paradox Policy Statement, 53 Fed. Reg. 41,104, 41,119 (1988). As known carcinogens, the four pesticides ran afoul of a special provision of the FFDCA known as the Delaney clause, which prescribes that additives found to induce cancer can never be deemed "safe" for purposes of the FFDCA. The Delaney clause is found in FFDCA section 409, 21 U.S.C. §348. That section limits the conditions under which the Secretary may issue regulations allowing a substance to be used as a food additive:

> No such regulation shall issue if a fair evaluation of the data before the Secretary—
> (A) fails to establish that the proposed use of the food additive, under the conditions of use to be specified in the regulation, will be safe: Provided, That no additive shall be deemed to be safe if it is found to induce cancer when ingested by man or animal, or if it is found, after tests which are appropriate for the evaluation of the safety of food additives, to induce cancer in man or animal. . . . [21 U.S.C. §348(c)(3).]

The FFDCA also contains special provisions which regulate the occurrence of pesticide residues on raw agricultural commodities. Section 402 of the FFDCA, 21 U.S.C. §342(a)(2)(B), provides that a raw food containing a pesticide residue is deemed adulterated unless the residue is authorized under section 408 of the FFDCA, 21 U.S.C. §346a, which allows tolerance regulations setting maximum permissible levels and also provides for exemption from tolerances under certain circumstances. When a tolerance or an exemption has been established for use of a pesticide on a raw agricultural commodity, then the FFDCA allows for the "flow-through" of such pesticide residue to processed foods, even when the pesticide may be a carcinogen. This flow-through is allowed, however, only to the extent that the concentration of the pesticide in the processed food does not exceed the concentration allowed in the raw food. The flow-through provisions are contained in section 402 which provides:

> That where a pesticide chemical has been used in or on a raw agricultural commodity in conformity with an exemption granted or a tolerance prescribed under section 346a of this title [FFDCA section 408] and such raw agricultural commodity has been subjected to processing such as canning, cooking, freezing, dehydrating, or milling, the residue of such pesticide chemical remaining in or on such processed food shall, notwithstanding the provisions of sections 346 and 348 of this title [FFDCA sections 406 and 409], not be deemed unsafe if such residue in or on the raw agricultural commodity has been removed to the extent possible in good manufacturing practice and the concentration of such residue in the processed food when ready to eat is not greater than the tolerance prescribed for the raw agricultural commodity.

21 U.S.C. §342(a)(2)(C). It is undisputed that the EPA regulations at issue in this case allow for the concentration of cancer-causing pesticides during processing to levels in excess of those permitted in the raw foods.

[I]n October 1988 . . . EPA announced a new interpretation of the Delaney clause: the EPA proposed to permit concentrations of cancer-causing pesticide residues greater than that tolerated for raw foods so long as the particular substances posed only a "de minimis" risk of actually causing cancer. Finding that benomyl, mancozeb, phosmet and trifluralin (among others) posed only such a de minimis risk, the Agency announced that it would not immediately revoke its previous regulations authorizing use of these substances as food additives.

The issue before us is whether the EPA has violated section 409 of the FFDCA, the Delaney clause, by permitting the use of carcinogenic food additives which it finds to present only a de minimis or negligible risk of causing cancer. The Agency acknowledges that its interpretation of the law is a new and changed one. From the initial enactment of the Delaney clause in 1958 to the time of the rulings here in issue, the statute had been strictly and literally enforced. . . .

The language is clear and mandatory. The Delaney clause provides that no additive shall be deemed safe if it induces cancer. 21 U.S.C. §348(c)(3). The EPA states in its final order that appropriate tests have established that the pesticides at issue here induce cancer in humans or animals. The statute provides that once the finding of carcinogenicity is made, the EPA has no discretion. As a leading work on food and drug regulation notes:

> [T]he Delaney Clause leaves the FDA room for scientific judgment in deciding whether its conditions are met by a food additive. But the clause affords no flexibility once FDA scientists determine that these conditions are satisfied. A food additive that has been found in an appropriate test to induce cancer in laboratory animals may not be approved for use in food for any purpose, at any level, regardless of any "benefits" that it might provide. [R. Merrill & P. Hutt, Food and Drug Law 78 (1980).] . . .

The Agency asks us to look behind the language of the Delaney clause to the overall statutory scheme governing pesticides, which permits the use of carcinogenic pesticides on raw food without regard to the Delaney clause. Yet section 402 of the FFDCA, 21 U.S.C. §342(a)(2)(C), expressly harmonizes that scheme with the Delaney clause by providing that residues on processed foods may not exceed the tolerance level established for the raw food. The statute unambiguously provides that pesticides which concentrate in processed food are to be treated as food additives, and these are governed by the Delaney food additive provision contained in section 409. If pesticides which concentrate in processed foods induce cancer in humans or animals, they render the food adulterated and must be prohibited.

The legislative history, too, reflects that Congress intended the very rigidity that the language it chose commands. The food additive Delaney clause was enacted in response to increasing public concern about cancer. It was initially part of a bill, introduced in the House of Representatives in 1958 by Congressman Delaney, to amend the FFDCA. The bill, intended to ensure that no carcinogens, no matter how small the amount, would be introduced into food, was at least in part a response to a decision by the FDA to allow a known carcinogen, the pesticide Aramite, as an approved food additive. Of the FDA's approval for sale of foods containing small quantities of Aramite, Congressman Delaney stated:

> The part that chemical additives play in the cancer picture may not yet be completely understood, but enough is known to put us on our guard. The safety of the public health

demands that chemical additives should be specifically pretested for carcinogenicity, and this should be spelled out in the law. The precedent established by the Aramite decision has opened the door, even if only a little, to the use of carcinogens in our foods. That door should be slammed shut and locked. That is the purpose of my anticarcinogen provision.

The scientific witnesses who testified before Congress stressed that because current scientific techniques could not determine a safe level for carcinogens, all carcinogens should be prohibited. . . . Thus, the legislative history supports the conclusion that Congress intended to ban all carcinogenic food additives, regardless of amount or significance of risk, as the only safe alternative.

Throughout its 30-year history, the Delaney clause has been interpreted as an absolute bar to all carcinogenic food additives. . . . Further, Congress has repeatedly ratified a strict interpretation of the Delaney clause by reenacting all three FFDCA provisions which contain Delaney clauses without changing the Agency's interpretation. See 21 U.S.C. [§§348, 360b, 376].

The EPA contends that the legislative history shows that Congress never intended to regulate pesticides, as opposed to other additives, with extraordinary rigidity under the food additives provision. The Agency is indeed correct that the legislative history of the food additive provision does not focus on pesticides, and that pesticides are regulated more comprehensively under the Federal Insecticide, Fungicide, and Rodenticide Act (FIFRA). Nevertheless, the EPA's contention that Congress never intended the food additive provision to encompass pesticide residues is belied by the events prompting passage of the provision into law: FDA approval of Aramite was the principal impetus for the food additive Delaney clause and Aramite was itself a regulated pesticide. Thus, Congress intended to regulate pesticides as food additives under section 409 of the FFDCA, at least to the extent that pesticide residues concentrate in processed foods and exceed the tolerances for raw foods.

Finally, the EPA argues that a de minimis exception to the Delaney clause is necessary in order to bring about a more sensible application of the regulatory scheme. It relies particularly on a recent study suggesting that the criterion of concentration level in processed foods may bear little or no relation to actual risk of cancer, and that some pesticides might be barred by rigid enforcement of the Delaney clause while others, with greater cancer-causing risk, may be permitted through the flow-through provisions because they do not concentrate in processed foods. See National Academy of Sciences, Regulating Pesticides in Food: The Delaney Paradox (1987). . . . Revising the existing statutory scheme, however, is neither our function nor the function of the EPA. . . . If there is to be a change, it is for Congress to direct.

The EPA's refusal to revoke regulations permitting the use of benomyl, mancozeb, phosmet and trifluralin as food additives on the ground the cancer risk they pose is de minimis is contrary to the provisions of the Delaney clause prohibiting food additives that induce cancer. . . .

NOTES AND QUESTIONS

1. *Tolerances for Pesticide Residues.* At the time of the *Les* decision, §408 of the Federal Food, Drug, and Cosmetic Act (FFDCA), 21 U.S.C. §346a, authorized EPA to issue tolerances for residues on raw agricultural commodities of pesticides not generally recognized as safe, taking into account the necessity for the production of

an adequate and economical food supply and the ways in which consumers might be affected by those pesticides or by related deleterious substances. EPA granted tolerances for residues of pesticides that induced tumors in laboratory animals when it perceived the risks to humans as relatively small (generally, less than one in a million). Hornstein, Lessons from Federal Pesticide Regulation on the Paradigms and Politics of Environmental Law Reform, 10 Yale J. on Reg. 369, 389-390 (1993). The Food and Drug Administration (FDA) is responsible for enforcing these tolerances. EPA's discretion in approving pesticide residues on processed foods was narrower. Section 402(a)(2)(C) of the FFDCA, 21 U.S.C. §342(a)(2)(C), allowed for the flow-through of such residues, notwithstanding §409 (which contains the food additive Delaney clause), 21 U.S.C. §348, but only in amounts not exceeding the tolerance prescribed for the raw agricultural commodity. How did EPA explain its October 1988 decision to approve concentrations of pesticide residues in processed foods that exceeded those amounts?

2. *The Delaney Clause and Comparative Risk Assessment.* EPA's concern that the literal application of the food additive Delaney clause might prevent the use of less risky products helps to explain its reliance on the *de minimis* doctrine in *Les*:

> Because pesticides approved in earlier decades were not adequately tested to identify their carcinogenic potential and were grandfathered in under earlier standards, EPA is concerned that strict application of the Delaney Clause to new pesticides prevents the replacement of more dangerous older chemicals with safer new ones. Because EPA does not have the administrative flexibility to approve new pesticides that are carcinogenic, older high risk pesticides are retained on the market while less toxic alternatives are discouraged because the smaller risk they pose might still trigger a registration rejection. [Rosenthal et al., Legislating Acceptable Cancer Risk from Exposure to Toxic Chemicals, 19 Ecology L.Q. 269, 299 (1992).]

What is the "paradox" referred to in the 1987 NAS study cited by the court in *Les*? See 139 Cong. Rec. S12139 (daily ed. Sept. 21, 1993) (statement of Senator Nickles). Compare Turner, Delaney Lives! Reports of Delaney's Death Are Greatly Exaggerated, 28 Envtl. L. Rep. 10003, 10006 (1998) (characterizing the paradox as "a nonexistent legal inconsistency").

3. *EPA's Coordination Policy.* Were the FFDCA provisions governing the marketing of foods containing carcinogenic pesticide residues consistent with the treatment of carcinogenic pesticides under FIFRA? What risk management approach did each statute employ?

> The consequences of [the] "flow through" provision [of 21 U.S.C. §342(a)(2)(C)] are in fact more severe than what is statutorily mandated. When the pesticide registrant seeks a section 408 tolerance for a specific crop, it must address the need for a section 409 food additive tolerance by showing whether the residues concentrate during specific processes such as drying, milling, or juicing. The EPA coordinates its regulatory decisions under sections 408 and 409 of the FFDCA by revoking a section 408 tolerance where section 409 regulations are needed but cannot be established. The EPA also coordinates its regulatory actions under FIFRA and the FFDCA by not permitting under FIFRA a pesticide use that would result in adulterated food. Therefore, when a section 409 tolerance is revoked, EPA revokes both the section 408 tolerance and the FIFRA registration for that use. This is referred to as EPA's "coordination policy." [Curme, Regulation of Pesticide Residues in Foods: Proposed Solutions to Current Inadequacies Under FFDCA and FIFRA, 49 Food & Drug L.J. 609, 614-615 (1994).]

Does the coordination policy "unlawfully incorporate[] the Delaney clause into the standard for raw product tolerances"? See Ely, An Obscure EPA Policy Is to Blame, EPA J., Jan./Feb./Mar. 1993, at 44. How did the *Les* court respond to EPA's use of FIFRA to justify its 1988 regulations?

Shortly after the decision in *Les*, various associations of food processors and fresh fruit and vegetable growers filed a petition with EPA challenging its policies linking its regulatory activities under the various pesticide provisions of FIFRA and the FFDCA. The petition charged that the coordination policy was both unnecessary and unlawful, in that it required that the agency ignore the risk/benefit standards of FIFRA and FFDCA §408. The petitioners requested repeal of the coordination policy so that §408 tolerances could remain in effect (or be established) for pesticide uses even when, under the *Les* decision, the associated §409 tolerances had to be revoked (or could not be established).

The agency largely denied the petition. It retained most aspects of the coordination policy intact because, although the Delaney clause does not directly govern §408 tolerances or FIFRA registrations, EPA has a responsibility to avoid inconsistent action under FIFRA and the FFDCA. "Legally used pesticides should not result in illegal food." The Pesticide Coordination Policy; Response to Petitions, 61 Fed. Reg. 2378, 2379 (1996). EPA noted its willingness, however, to consider an exception to the coordination approach to avert severe economic disruption:

> EPA, in making the risk/benefit balancing determination called for under FIFRA and section 408 for a carcinogenic pesticide, takes into account the likelihood that residues of the pesticide will exceed the section 408 tolerance in processed food and the added weight such overtolerance residues are due in light of the Delaney clause.
>
> Additionally, in evaluating the benefits provided by use of a pesticide in the FIFRA and section 408 risk/benefit decision, EPA must consider the extent to which use of a pesticide could result in adulterated food. Adulterated food resulting from use of a pesticide would decrease any benefits the pesticide provided to society. Thus, the Delaney clause's effect of denying a [tolerance] for carcinogenic pesticides affects benefits determinations as well as risk evaluations under FIFRA and section 408. . . .
>
> . . . EPA cannot rule out the possibility that . . . application of the coordination policy may result in the cancellation of a use or group of uses that is so central to the production of a certain crop that the revocation of that use or uses would severely disrupt domestic production of that commodity with attendant consequences to the price and availability of food to the consumer. In these circumstances, EPA believes it may be appropriate to allow an exception to the coordination policy. [Id. at 2380-2381.]

4. *Scientific Advances and Zero Tolerance.* Have scientific advances in methodologies for measuring trace amounts of chemicals in foods made the Delaney clause obsolete? Senator Edward Kennedy thought so when he remarked in 1995 that:

> there has been a revolution in food science and biochemistry since 1958, when the Delaney clause was enacted. We now have the technology to identify cancer-causing chemicals in foods, in far smaller trace amounts than possible 40 years ago. We also understand that animals may develop tumors from certain chemicals through pathways of animal biology that humans do not have. Zero tolerance, therefore, means something different today than it did in 1958. . . . In 1958, testing equipment might have considered zero risk to be a 1 in 100,000 chance of causing cancer. Today, we have scientific instruments that can detect risk levels as low as 1 in 1 billion. Clearly a modern standard of risk is warranted. [141 Cong. Rec. S10267 (daily ed. July 19, 1995).]

The *Les* decision put dozens of tolerances and pesticide registrations at risk of revocation. See Hornstein, *supra*, at 445.

5. *The 1996 FFDCA Amendments.* Concerns over the economic impact of a literal application of the food additive Delaney clause and over its questionable scientific underpinnings culminated in adoption of the Food Quality Protection Act of 1996, Pub. L. No. 104-170, 110 Stat. 1489, which amended the FFDCA. Section 408 of the FFDCA now provides that a pesticide chemical residue is unsafe, and subject to the prohibition on adulterated food in §402(a)(2)(B), unless it is in compliance with a tolerance or covered by an exemption issued by EPA. For purposes of the amended §408, "food" means either a raw agricultural commodity or processed food. What effect does this definition have on the dual standard for tolerances previously in effect under §§408 and 409? For a good description of the relationship between FIFRA and the FFDCA after the 1996 amendments, see NRDC v. Johnson, 461 F.3d 164 (2d Cir. 2006). EPA may issue a tolerance only if it regards exposure to food with pesticide residues that comply with the tolerance as safe. To reach that conclusion, EPA must determine "that there is a reasonable certainty that no harm will result from aggregate exposure" to the residue. See National Corn Growers Ass'n v. EPA, 613 F.3d 266 (D.C. Cir. 2010) (largely upholding EPA's revocation of FFDCA tolerances for pesticide residues EPA regarded as not safe). If EPA is unable to determine a level of exposure at which a residue will not cause or contribute to a known or anticipated harm to human health, it may leave a tolerance in effect only if it finds either that use of the pesticide that produces the residue protects consumers from adverse health effects that would pose a greater risk than the dietary risk from the residue, or that use of the pesticide is necessary to avoid a significant disruption in domestic production of an adequate, wholesome, and economical food supply.

The 1996 amendments also responded to a study finding that physiological differences between adults and children make children more sensitive to pesticide exposure. National Academy of Sciences, Board on Agriculture, Pesticides in the Diets of Infants and Children (1993). Under amended §408(b)(2)(C), when EPA issues or modifies a tolerance, it must assess the risks of the pesticide residue on infants and children, given their "special susceptibility," and ensure that there is a reasonable certainty that no harm will result to them from aggregate exposure to the residue. EPA must build into a tolerance an additional tenfold margin of safety for infants and children to account for pre- and postnatal toxicity. Suppose the agency adopts a presumption that the extra tenfold margin of safety is needed to protect infants and children, but allows the presumption to be rebutted on a case-by-case basis if test and exposure data indicate that an additional uncertainty factor is unnecessary. Does the statute permit such an approach? Section 408(b)(2)(C) allows EPA to remove the additional safety factor for infants and children and use the normal margin "if, on the basis of reliable data, such margin will be safe for infants and children." What constitutes "reliable data"? See NRDC v. EPA, 658 F.3d 200 (2d Cir. 2011) (rejecting NRDC's argument that, regardless of other evidence, EPA must apply the tenfold margin of safety factor unless it relies on data from its estrogen disruptor screening program, but holding that EPA failed to justify using threefold safety factor instead of tenfold factor). May EPA use computer modeling instead of actual drinking water sampling? See Northwest Coal. for Alternatives to Pesticides (NCAP) v. EPA, 544 F.3d 1043 (9th Cir. 2008).

What effect does the amended FFDCA have on the food additive Delaney clause of §409(c)(3)(A)? Weinstein et al., The Food Quality Protection Act: A New Way of

Looking at Pesticides, 28 Envtl. L. Rep. 10555, 10556 (1998), explain that the amended Act exempts pesticide residues from §409 and the Delaney clause by removing them from the definition of food additives, but that the prohibition against establishing tolerances for carcinogenic food additives otherwise remains in place. Although the 1996 Act did not amend §409 of the FFDCA, it provides that regulations establishing tolerances for pesticide residues on processed food issued under §409 before adoption of the 1996 amendments will be treated as §408 regulations and subject to modification under that section. 21 U.S.C. §346a(j)(2). Does the amended FFDCA afford EPA more flexibility in its regulation of food additives? Too much flexibility? Is the "reasonable certainty of no harm" standard too vague? Does it make sense to impose a uniform level of risk, regardless of the benefits afforded by pesticide use? Or does the new standard for tolerances take account of the degree of benefits provided by a pesticide?

Section 408(a)(2) now provides that if a tolerance is in effect for a pesticide residue on a raw agricultural commodity, a residue present on processed food because the food is made from that commodity will not be regarded as unsafe within the meaning of §402(a)(2)(B), even if EPA has not established a tolerance for the processed food, if the pesticide has been used on the raw commodity in conformity with a §408 tolerance, the residue has been removed to the extent possible in good manufacturing practice, and the concentration of the pesticide in the processed food is not greater than the tolerance for the residue in the raw commodity. What is the relationship between this provision and the pre-1996 version of §402(a)(2)(C), which was repealed by the 1996 amendments? Do the provisions of the 1996 law affect the coordination policy? Amended §408(l)(1) provides that, to the extent practicable, when EPA suspends or revokes a tolerance for a pesticide residue on food, it must coordinate that action with "any related necessary action" under FIFRA. Under §408(l)(2)-(3), if EPA cancels or suspends a pesticide registration under FIFRA due to dietary risks to humans posed by the presence of residues on food, it must revoke any tolerance that allows the presence in food of the pesticide or any residue that results from its use. Do the 1996 amendments protect consumers against the cumulative risks of ingesting the residues of many different pesticides in raw and processed foods? See Weinstein et al., *supra*, at 10557-10558 (the statute requires consideration of aggregate exposure from dietary and nondietary sources).

2. Proprietary Rights to Information versus the Public's Right to Know

a. Market Failure and the Availability of Information on Toxic Substances

WAGNER, COMMONS IGNORANCE: THE FAILURE OF ENVIRONMENTAL LAW TO PRODUCE NEEDED INFORMATION ON HEALTH AND THE ENVIRONMENT
53 Duke L.J. 1619, 1622, 1631-1634, 1639-1641, 1650-1651, 1653-1654, 1656-1657, 1663-1664, 1670, 1677-1679, 1699 (2004)

Rational choice theory and the large body of laws premised on it understand that those who inflict invisible and costly harms on others are disinclined to document the problems, much less take responsibility for them. Indeed, rational choice theory predicts that if wrongdoers are going to invest in research at all, they will dedicate resources to concealing and contesting incriminating information and producing exculpatory excuses and alibis. The criminal justice system is certainly familiar with this natural reaction to culpability. Yet, for some reason, environmental law has largely failed to come to grips with this inescapable feature of human nature. Instead, environmental law innocently assumes that information linking actors to resulting invisible harms will arise serendipitously, and, even more surprising, that the actors will either volunteer or accept this incriminating information without fuss or fanfare. . . .

[Professor Wagner discusses the "pervasive ignorance" about how hazardous substances affect health and the environment.] So, what accounts for this pervasive commons ignorance in the United States? The complexity of the systems is an important impediment to producing better information. But this is not the whole explanation. Research in other fields is also complex, and yet discoveries in health care and technology greatly outpace the minimal advancements in assessing man's impact on health and the environment.

Much of the blame belongs to industry's rational and vigorous resistance to producing information about the damage that it may cause to the commons. In other areas of scientific inquiry, private actors contribute substantially to advancements in public knowledge because the research promises to provide simultaneous private gains. No equivalent benefit attaches to research on the adverse effects of human activities on health or the environment. Rather than presenting the opportunity for private profit, these questions pose the opposite equation for private actors generating externalities. These actors vastly prefer ignorance over research because most documentation of externalities will ultimately affect them negatively. Thus, rather than contribute to enlightenment, actors seem more willing to contribute to, and even invest in, the perpetuation of ignorance.

Although it is rarely noticed, ignorance regarding the harm that private actors are causing health and the environment is just another external cost of their activities that they are able to pass on to society. The common law courts have sometimes appreciated this, requiring actors to disprove that they caused harm when they are best situated to know how their activities might affect others. Similarly, externality theory supports requiring actors to internalize the costs of researching an externality, because these costs are imposed on society by the actor's conduct. As long as there are predictable, nonobvious harms that flow from an activity, it is the actors' duty to investigate and disclose these harms before taking action. Otherwise, the externality and the ignorance surrounding it will be self-perpetuating. . . .

In Professor Mary Lyndon's classic article about the lack of safety research on toxic products [Lyndon, Information Economics and Chemical Toxicity: Designing Laws to Produce and Use Data, 87 Mich. L. Rev. 1795 (1989)], she details the ways in which the market discourages manufacturers from conducting research on the long-term safety of potentially toxic products. . . .

According to Professor Lyndon, there are at least three reasons that actors will not find it in their interest to document the potential harm from their products or polluting activities. First, the out-of-pocket (direct) costs associated with conducting safety research are not only expensive but also may not produce definitive results. Indeed, even after protracted testing, the results generally cannot completely exonerate a product or activity, nor do they enable the manufacturer to quantify risks in a definitive way. Given the lack of inexpensive screening tests, actors will rarely be able to obtain information about the harms created by their product or activity at low cost. Thus, financial realities and lack of research efficacy combine to explain why long-term safety testing is generally not an attractive investment for actors.

Second, virtually no market benefits accrue to actors who produce research on the long-term safety of products or activities. Professor Lyndon demonstrates that when safety representations cannot be easily validated or compared, consumers are unlikely to make purchasing or investment decisions based upon a manufacturer's self-serving statements about safety. Moreover, given that the results are rarely determinative, even thorough safety research will seldom provide a clear market signal of "safety." Even if research results were definitive and comparable between different products and activities, advertising that a product or activity did not cause cancer in animals might not impress consumers or be received positively in the marketplace.

Third, for toxicity and safety testing, there are few guarantees about what the testing will reveal. Any possible good news, moreover, is always tempered by looming uncertainties. Most screening tests produce false positives by design. Yet even when "no effect" is observed in a toxicity study, the testing cannot ensure that the product is safe—only that it did not cause a few types of adverse effects (e.g., cancer) in one exposure setting (e.g., ingestion by rats). On the other hand, a bad result is almost always definitive in the following sense: When a substance does cause cancer in laboratory animals, uncertainty about how those results could or should be extrapolated to humans does not materially diminish the impact of the adverse result. The best that can be said is that bad news encourages more testing to refine and improve the outlook for the product or activity.

Beyond the lack of market incentives for developing information on externalities, actors also have legitimate concerns about increased tort liability that could result from producing incriminating information about the harms caused by their products or activities. Common law tort liability is generally imposed only after injured parties prove that the defendant's activity caused their harm. Producing and publicizing internal research on such harms is, therefore, a risky proposition. Once plaintiffs' attorneys seize on a firm's internal research suggesting that harm may result from the firm's products or activities, catastrophic liability may follow. Under such information-triggered common law regimes, actors benefit from knowing nothing, in part because it deprives plaintiffs of the evidence that they need to bring their case.

That remaining ignorant about the impact of their products and activities is an effective strategy is evident in practice. Industries do not volunteer information on the long-term safety of their products and activities, and they lobby against laws requiring them to share even basic internal information. . . . [I]gnorance is not merely a byproduct of a market system that fails to offer incentives to provide this information; ignorance actually represents a willful, strategic choice. . . .

. . . In addition, whatever positive incentives may exist are mitigated because the information—once produced and publicized—becomes a public good. Thus actors producing useful information, unless it pertains exclusively to them, will be unable to capture its full benefit. Any good news that safety testing may yield is of little value to a manufacturer unless it is publicized. But once publicized, competitors can capitalize on the information without bearing any of the costs of producing it. . . .

If actors believe that information about their activities has a negative value, they might not only resist producing this information, but also may make it more difficult for third parties to produce it. . . . Actors will invest as much in obstructing research as they expect to lose if the information is made publicly available. Moreover, to the extent that actors enjoy superior access to or control over information essential to assess externalities, they may be able to increase the costs of third-party research simply by preventing access to key information. If actors believe that they have much to lose from public enlightenment about externalities—particularly, for example, if there is a potential for mass liability—they might even take affirmative steps to discredit or counter the claims made by third parties. Even if these efforts ultimately fail, the actors benefit by postponing the ultimate "day of reckoning"—sometimes indefinitely. . . .

Actors have developed a number of imaginative approaches to obscure or discredit potentially troublesome third-party research suggesting that their activities cause harm. The easiest approach is for an actor simply to publicize only the positive information about a product or activity, while keeping potentially damaging information private. Because actors control access to key information, this tactic allows them to present a misleadingly positive account of the externalities associated with their products and activities that helps to offset damaging research produced by outsiders. . . .

More aggressive efforts to manufacture uncertainty . . . generally involve either blatant, underhanded attacks on third-party research or investments in "counter-research" carefully designed to produce results more favorable to an actor's interests. . . . Many actors have launched a frontal assault on academic or public research that documents how their products or activities harm the public health or the environment. . . . These "hired gun" attacks on third-party research are common in high-stakes cases when acceptance of the results could lead to shattering liability and publicity. . . .

In addition to attacking the credibility of the research and in some cases the researcher, affected actors have also financed counter-research designed to refute third-party research, either by producing different results or by suggesting that the results of the independent research cannot be reproduced—a devastating critique within the scientific community. By hiring scientists willing to "collaborate" closely with the sponsoring industry (under contracts that require sponsor control of the research), sponsors historically have been able to exert dramatic control over the outcome of research, to the point of designing studies, framing research questions, and even editing and ghostwriting articles. . . .

Most environmental laws do aspire to ensure that needed information on environmental harms is developed and, in some cases, the laws even demand that actors bear full responsibility for producing this information. . . .

[With certain exceptions, however], actors are generally off the hook when it comes to identifying and analyzing the harms created by their products and activities. . . . Typically actors are only required to provide information about the nature of the activity and not information about its possible adverse effects. . . . It is instead left to the public, particularly government agencies, to collect and assess this information. . . .

It is bad enough that environmental laws—contrary to their promise—fail to require actors to produce information needed to assess their externalities. But some environmental laws lead to a still worse state of affairs: the laws sometimes reward actors for their ignorance, penalize them for producing useful knowledge, and provide mechanisms for them to attack damaging public science that suggests they are causing harm. . . .

Under the current regulatory system, volunteering adverse information on the effects or even the existence of harms associated with one's product or activity is equivalent to shooting oneself in the foot. Regulation and enforcement increase in lockstep with the availability of public information on adverse effects. Whereas no information means no regulation, a solid body of uncontested, adverse information will almost certainly lead to intrusive regulation, enforcement activity, and sometimes even a ban on the activity or product. . . . [A]s long as information is neither required nor rewarded but instead is used punitively by the regulatory system, the decision about whether to voluntarily conduct and report research on one's product's or activity's externalities is an easy one. Ignorance is bliss. . . .

With such strong reasons to resist producing information, it is no surprise that actors . . . actively seek legal protections to limit the disclosure of the incriminating information. By claiming broad protections, actors can raise the costs to others of accessing this information or, in some cases, can even bar access completely. [Professor Wagner goes on to describe legal protections that allow actors to claim confidentiality for privately held, damaging information and that bar most public access to the information, often, even by EPA. These include protection for trade secrets or confidential business information, privacy protections, litigation settlements, nondisclosure contracts, state privilege laws, and national security legislation. She also points out that several laws, such as the Information Quality Act (which is discussed in the notes below) "actually facilitate the ability of actors to disparage credible research" by providing "opportunities for private actors to contest the quality of research and taint the integrity of researchers, even when the actors' charges are without scientific merit."]

NOTES

1. *Information Sources.* Other observers agree that neither workers nor consumers are likely to generate significant amounts of information concerning toxic risks because of the high cost and low individual benefit involved. The tort system is an inadequate means of remedying the resulting data deficiency due to the absence of information, the inability to generate data, and the institutional incompetence of the judiciary. That leaves government regulation as the best source of the data necessary for effective regulation of toxic substances. Shifting the cost of generating the data to those who manufacture and use toxic chemicals in their products is both efficient (because internalization of the cost of detecting externalities will result in prices that more accurately reflect the true cost of their production) and equitable (because the primary beneficiaries of the chemicals ought to pay for the cost of ascertaining the extent of the risks they impose). See Applegate, The Perils of Unreasonable Risk: Information, Regulatory Policy, and Toxic Substances Control, 91 Colum. L. Rev. 261 (1991). On the impacts of legal obstacles to public disclosure of information on environmental risk, see Symposium, Sequestered Science: The Consequences of Undisclosed Knowledge, 69-WTR Law & Contemp. Probs. 1-186 (2006).

2. Among the corrective mechanisms that Professor Wagner recommends to the problems she has identified is legislation that would make it illegal to invoke trade secret and other protections to classify information about the adverse effects of products and activities that threaten public health and the environment, and the adoption of a requirement, backed by civil and criminal sanctions, that all health-related information be reported to the government. She also supports sanctions for those who abuse litigation and administrative mechanisms to delay regulation and "harass and discredit

public scientists." Wagner, *supra*, at 1734. She recommends creation of incentives to produce information by basing environmental regulatory standards on worst-case predictions and reducing regulation when credible information suggests that harms have been overestimated.

3. *The Information Quality Act.* The Information Quality Act (IQA), referred to by Professor Wagner, requires OMB to issue guidelines to federal agencies "for ensuring and maximizing the quality, objectivity, utility, and integrity of information (including statistical information) disseminated by Federal agencies." 44 U.S.C. §3516 note. Each agency to which the guidelines apply must issue its own, similar guidelines and establish administrative mechanisms allowing affected persons to seek and obtain correction of information that does not comply with the guidelines. In one case, a trade association of companies that produce salt for food and other uses alleged that the Department of Health and Human Services violated the IQA by reporting on its website, in medical journals, and in at least one report the results of studies showing that decreased use of salt by all Americans could lower blood pressure and by recommending that people limit salt intake. In Salt Inst. v. Thompson, 440 F.3d 156 (4th Cir. 2006), the court held that the plaintiffs lacked standing to bring a suit under the IQA to challenge HHS's dissemination of the information. For further discussion of the IQA, see pages 244-245.

b. Trade Secrets and Information Property

The federal statutes requiring chemical manufacturers and users to disclose information about those substances to the government give rise to a potential conflict between the desire to protect industry investments in proprietary information and the need for the dissemination of sufficient information to the government and the public. The government needs information about toxic substances to make appropriate regulatory decisions. The public needs the information to make informed choices about matters such as whether to live near a risk-producing activity and whether to consume a product containing a potentially toxic substance.

The stakes can be high on both sides. It may cost as much as $15 million annually to develop a potential commercial pesticide, for example, and the development process may take 20 years. Further, "f[o]r every manufacturing-use pesticide the average company finally markets, it will have screened and tested 20,000 others." Ruckelshaus v. Monsanto Co., 467 U.S. 986, 998 (1984). The information generated by a pesticide manufacturer and submitted to EPA in support of its application for registration is typically valuable to the manufacturer "beyond its instrumentality in gaining that particular application. Monsanto uses this information to develop additional end-use products and to expand the uses of its registered products. The information would also be valuable to Monsanto's competitors. For that reason, Monsanto has instituted stringent security measures to ensure the secrecy of the data." What is at stake for members of the public is the ability to participate meaningfully in the regulatory process and to make informed choices about the degree of exposure risk they are willing to incur.

Both TSCA and FIFRA require the submission of large quantities of technical data. Both also provide significant protection to proprietary information that constitutes trade secrets, confidential business information, or privileged information under the Trade Secrets Act, 18 U.S.C. §1905; the Freedom of Information Act, 5 U.S.C.

§552; or state statutes or common law. TSCA removes this protection from data that EPA determines must be disclosed to protect health or the environment against an unreasonable risk of injury, and from certain health and safety studies submitted for regulatory purposes. TSCA §14(a)(3), (b). Section 14(b) bars EPA from disclosing processes used in the manufacture or processing of a chemical substance or mixture. From 1977 to 1990, EPA treated more than 90 percent of all PMNs for new chemicals under TSCA as confidential business information. Bass & MacLean, Enhancing the Public's Right-to-Know About Environmental Issues, 4 Vill. Envtl. L.J. 287, 310 (1993). As a result, the health risks posed by some chemicals on the market appear to be cloaked in secrecy. See Layton, Use of Potentially Harmful Chemicals Kept Secret Under Law, Wash. Post, Jan. 4, 2010.

Under FIFRA, EPA may not disclose trade secrets and commercial or financial information. Information concerning test results on registered pesticides or the effects of pesticides on the environment is available to the public, except for information that discloses manufacturing or quality control processes, the details of testing methods, or the identity or percentages of inert ingredients. That information, however, may be disclosed if in EPA's judgment it is necessary to protect against unreasonable risks. §136h(d)(1). Both TSCA and FIFRA provide stiff penalties for the willful disclosure of protected information by agency personnel.

Both statutes permit subsequent reliance on data submitted in connection with earlier health and safety studies, but with protections accorded the company that first generated the information. Under TSCA, for a five-year period after its submission of data, a manufacturer may obtain EPA-adjudicated "fair and equitable" reimbursement from companies that rely upon its test results in their own submissions to EPA. TSCA §4(c)(3). Under FIFRA, the operation of a more complex exclusive use and compensation scheme turns on how long the information has existed—for 10 years post-1978, no use; for the next 15 years, compensated use. FIFRA §136a(c)(1)(F).

The Supreme Court addressed the constitutionality of FIFRA's data use provisions in *Ruckelshaus, supra*. It held that EPA's use of health data submitted by Monsanto after the effective date of the 1978 FIFRA amendments to assist the agency's consideration of another applicant's request for registration was not a taking. Monsanto had no reasonable expectation that EPA would regard the information as confidential beyond the limits prescribed in the amended statute. The requirement that a registrant give up its property interest in the data did not amount to an unconstitutional condition on the right to a valuable government benefit (registration). See also Sygenta Crop Prot., Inc. v. EPA, 444 F. Supp. 2d 435 (M.D.N.C. 2006) (holding that similar use by EPA of one company's data to rule on another's registration request did not deprive the submitter of procedural or substantive due process or equal protection).

c. Public Disclosure Requirements and Right-to-Know Acts

OSHA's Hazard Communication Standard. OSHA's Hazard Communication Standard, 29 C.F.R. §1910.1200, adopted in 1974, is one of the first examples of federally mandated disclosure of the risks of exposure to toxic substances. Its purpose is to ensure evaluation of the hazards of produced or imported chemicals and transmission to employers and employees of information concerning known chemical hazards. Employers need not perform tests on the health effects of exposure, but they must develop and implement at each workplace a hazard communication program that includes a list of the hazardous chemicals known to be present, disclosure of the methods the employer will use to inform employees of the hazards, labeling of containers of hazardous substances leaving the workplace, and preparation of material safety data sheets (MSDSs) with information about chemicals in the workplace.

The Emergency Planning and Community Right-to-Know Act. Perhaps the most important federal disclosure program today is the 1986 Emergency Planning and Community Right-to-Know Act (EPCRA), 42 U.S.C. §§11001-11050. The Act was passed in response to the 1984 disaster at Union Carbide's plant in Bhopal, India, where thousands of people were killed or injured as a result of the accidental release of methyl isocyanide into the air. (Twenty-five years after the accident at Bhopal, the site of the leak remained contaminated with 390 metric tons of toxics without any plan for safe disposal having been developed.) EPCRA requires local and federal governments and industry to prepare emergency response plans and to disclose the manufacture or use of hazardous chemicals. The following excerpt analyzes the potential benefits of EPCRA's reporting and disclosure requirements.

KARKKAINEN, INFORMATION AS ENVIRONMENTAL REGULATION: TRI AND PERFORMANCE BENCHMARKING, PRECURSOR TO A NEW PARADIGM?
89 Geo. L.J. 257, 260-263, 270, 277, 284, 294-295 (2001)

. . . Conventional environmental reporting typically demands only the minimum information necessary to gauge compliance with a fixed regulatory standard. Like the regulations they are designed to support, reported data are fragmentary and narrowly tailored to program requirements that vary by medium, industry, pollutant, and source. Consequently, data are difficult to aggregate, compare, rank, or track over time. In contrast, [the Toxic Release Inventory (TRI)] establishes a broadly accessible, objective, open-ended, cross-media metric of facility-level environmental performance that is not tied to any particular regulatory standard. Because TRI data are reported in standard units, they can be aggregated to produce profiles and performance comparisons at the level of the facility, firm, industrial sector, community, metropolitan region, state, watershed or other critical ecosystem, and the nation as a whole. . . .

By creating this performance metric, TRI both compels and enables facilities and firms to monitor their own environmental performance. It also encourages them to compare, rank, and track performance among production processes, facilities, operating units, and peer or competitor firms. By enabling an unprecedented degree of self-monitoring, aggregation, disaggregation, comparison, ranking, and tracking of environmental performance, TRI produces information that is far more valuable to reporting entities than that produced by conventional forms of environmental reporting. It enables managers to engage in both internal and comparative benchmarking to establish performance baselines, set improvement targets, track progress toward those targets, and hold operational units within the firm accountable for meeting them. In this way, TRI empowers managers to translate the firm's general environmental goals into specific performance objectives, and to incorporate environmental management almost seamlessly into their overall business strategy and ongoing operations. . . . [I]n contrast to fixed regulatory standards that effectively become performance ceilings as well as floors, TRI-induced benchmarking creates an implicit open-ended performance standard that demands continuous improvement in relation to one's peers and to one's own past performance. . . .

The ready availability of TRI data also enhances transparency and accountability to external parties. It subjects the environmental performance of facilities and firms to an unprecedented degree of scrutiny by their peers, competitors, investors, employees, consumers, community residents, environmental organizations, activists, elected officials, regulators, and the public in general. . . . These external monitors often have powerful tools at their disposal, including political, market, community, and regulatory pressures, which they use to discipline poor performers and reward superior performance outcomes as measured by TRI. . . .

Conventional approaches to environmental regulation are nearing a dead end, limited by the capacity of regulators to acquire the information necessary to set regulatory standards and keep pace with rapid changes in knowledge, technology, and environmental conditions. A pervasive information bottleneck constrains the extent, effectiveness, efficiency, and responsiveness of the regulatory system.

. . . Many leading advocates of market-based reforms explicitly recognize that the problems of conventional command regulation stem largely from the inability of the regulator to acquire sufficient information. But upon closer examination, market-based substitutes turn out to suffer from similar information problems, limiting their usefulness as a corrective. . . .

Neither conventional regulation nor tradeable permits are inherently well-suited to institutional learning and adaptation to new information. Both approaches presume that, by amassing sufficient scientific and technical information prior to setting the regulatory standard, the regulator can get the right standard the first time, essentially making a permanent judgment as to the appropriate level of pollution. If conventional regulations are based on erroneous judgments or produce unintended consequences, they can be suspended or modified, tightened or relaxed, either as a formal matter or de facto, by adjusting the pace and stringency of the enforcement effort. But these adjustments are slow, painful, cumbersome, and costly to both regulators and regulated entities, and they occur infrequently. This places a heavy burden on the regulator to "get it right" the first time so as to avoid having to make costly corrections, further raising the information bar to regulation in the first instance, and slowing the pace of regulatory change. . . .

. . . TRI works by establishing an objective, quantifiable, standardized (and therefore comparable), and broadly accessible metric that transforms the firm's understanding of its own environmental performance, while facilitating unprecedented levels of transparency and accountability. Firms and facilities are compelled to self-monitor and, therefore, to "confront disagreeable realities" concerning their environmental performance. . . . Simultaneously, they are subjected to the scrutiny of a variety of external parties, including investors, community residents, and regulators, any of whom may desire improved environmental performance and exert powerful pressures on poor performers to up-grade their performance as measured by the TRI yardstick.

NOTES AND QUESTIONS

1. According to Professor Karkkainen, how does the TRI represent an improvement over conventional statutory reporting requirements in terms of the kinds of

information it will generate? How will the reporting requirements of EPCRA yield improved environmental performance rather than just increased information to the government and the public?

2. *The Toxic Release Inventory.* EPCRA §313's annual toxic chemical release reporting program requires facilities covered by it to submit to EPA annual reports describing each toxic chemical on a list published by EPA that was manufactured, processed, or otherwise used at the facility during the preceding calendar year in quantities exceeding the threshold quantities designated pursuant to §313(f). The first annual Toxic Release Inventory (TRI) compiled by EPA covered reports filed by 18,500 companies on releases of 329 chemicals to the environment in 1987. These companies released 10.4 billion pounds of toxic substances. EPA reported in 2010 that 20,904 facilities reported disposals and other releases of 3.93 billion pounds of toxic materials. The metal mining sector was responsible for 41 percent of all TRI-reported releases, while the electricity utility and chemical manufacturing sectors ranked second and third at 18 percent and 13 percent, respectively. In 2011, toxic releases increased by 8 percent to 4.09 billion pounds, mostly because of land disposal at metal mines. Of that amount, 2.44 billion were released or disposed of on land. EPA, 2011 Toxic Release Inventory National Analysis Overview, http://www.epa.gov/tri/tridata/tri10/nationalanalysis/overview/2010TRINAOverview.pdf.

Section 313(d) of EPCRA authorizes EPA to add chemicals to or delete chemicals from the TRI list. In Troy Corp. v. Browner, 120 F.3d 277 (D.C. Cir.), *reh'g denied*, 129 F.3d 1200 (D.C. Cir. 1997), the court largely upheld the addition of 286 chemicals to the TRI under §313(d)(2)(B). It rejected the contention that the statute requires EPA to consider the likelihood of human exposure to listed chemicals that pose risks of chronic adverse effects. Why might EPA choose not to consider this factor? Would the result be the same if EPA were considering listing a substance under §313(d)(2)(A)? See also Fertilizer Inst. v. Browner, 163 F.3d 774 (3d Cir. 1998) (upholding listing of nitrate compounds based on long-term consequences of exposure rather than long-term exposure).

In American Chemistry Council v. Johnson, 406 F.3d 738 (D.C. Cir. 2005), an industry trade association challenged EPA's denial of its petition to remove methyl ethyl ketone (MEK) from the TRI list. Exposure to MEK itself (which is a volatile organic compound) does not cause adverse health effects. Rather, MEK is a precursor to the formation of tropospheric ozone, which causes adverse health effects. The issue was whether a chemical may meet the "chronic health effects" requirement of §313(d)(2)(B) or the "significant adverse effect on the environment" requirement of §313(d)(2)(C) on the basis of its contribution to the formation of tropospheric ozone. The court held that a chemical may not be listed solely on the basis of its contribution to the creation of a toxic chemical; it must cause harm via exposure to qualify for listing.

TRI release forms are available publicly (except for protected trade secrets), §§313(h)-(j), 322(a)(1), (2)(A), (b). Does the decline in annual releases since 1987 indicate that public dissemination of information on releases has induced reporting companies to reduce the volumes of their releases to avoid adverse publicity? Should statutory disclosure requirements substitute for some or all of the regulations designed to control the manufacture and use of toxic substances discussed in the preceding sections of this chapter?

3. *Other Reporting Requirements Under the EPCRA.* Under EPCRA §302, EPA must publish a list of extremely hazardous substances. If a release of such a

substance in an amount above reportable quantities under CERCLA occurs at a facility at which the chemical is produced, used, or stored, the facility must notify the local emergency planning committee in the affected area. §304(a)(1), (b). In Huls Am., Inc. v. Browner, 83 F.3d 445 (D.C. Cir. 1996), the petitioner argued that EPA improperly denied its petition under §302(a)(4) to remove isophorone diisocyanate (IPDI) from the list of extremely hazardous substances. Huls argued that by focusing primarily upon one factor, toxicity, in deciding that IPDI should remain on the list, EPA improperly ignored other statutory factors, which include reactivity, volatility, dispersibility, combustibility, and flammability. The court deferred to EPA's view that it need not consider all of the factors in every case. What single word in §302(a)(4) supports that holding? Huls also argued that EPA acted arbitrarily by relying on toxicity data derived from animal tests conducted by the National Institute of Occupational Safety and Health (NIOSH) because it extrapolated the NIOSH data from animal studies conducted under extreme conditions that were unlikely to occur in reality and bore no relationship to the accidental releases addressed by §304. The court characterized the validity of extrapolation of the results of toxicity tests conducted at high concentrations as the type of technical question that merits deference.

4. *State Disclosure Laws.* States such as California and New Jersey have imposed additional disclosure requirements on businesses and landowners involved with toxic materials. California's Safe Drinking Water and Toxic Enforcement Act of 1986 (Proposition 65), Cal. Health and Safety Code §§25180.7, 25249.5-25249.13, prohibited any business from knowingly and intentionally exposing any individual to a chemical known to the state to cause cancer or reproductive toxicity without first giving a clear and reasonable warning. §25249.6. Proposition 65 exempted exposure that poses no significant risk assuming lifetime exposure. §25249.10(c). In Baxter Healthcare Corp. v. Denton, 15 Cal. Rptr. 3d 430 (Cal. Ct. App. 2004), the court upheld a trial court's finding that a chemical used in medical devices qualified for the exemption because a preponderance of the evidence demonstrated that, even though it was undisputed that the chemical causes liver cancer in rats and mice, the biological mechanism by which it causes liver cancer in laboratory animals does not function in humans.

Do the EPCRA and California's Proposition 65 reflect the same approach? Consider the following:

> While Proposition 65 may induce close self-monitoring on the part of polluting firms to ensure that their activities do not exceed thresholds that might expose them to Proposition 65 liability, it does not produce a TRI-like stream of generally available and comparable performance data. Consequently, it does not promote the kinds of performance monitoring, bench marking, and transparency that are so central to TRI's operative success. It is the latter, TRI-inspired approach that appears from this vantage point to hold the greater potential to change the face of environmental regulation. [Karkkainen, *supra*, at 347.]

5. *Mandatory Disclosure and National Security Concerns.* The public dissemination of information about industrial chemical use creates a risk that information about the whereabouts and content of dangerous chemicals could become available to potential terrorists. In the Chemical Safety Information, Site Security and Fuels Regulatory Relief Act, Pub. L. No. 106-40, 113 Stat. 207 (1999), Congress required that EPA assess the increased risk of terrorist and other criminal activity associated with

the posting on the Internet or the compilation in government electronic databases of information contained in risk management plans filed under §112(r) of the Clean Air Act. Based on that assessment, EPA must issue regulations to minimize the risk of terrorist and criminal activity by restricting access to the information.

Following the terrorist attacks of September 11, 2001, some federal agencies, including EPA, removed information from their websites to reduce national security risks. In the Homeland Security Act of 2002, Pub. L. No. 107-296, §214(a), 116 Stat. 2135, Congress exempted from disclosure under the Freedom of Information Act "critical infrastructure information" that is voluntarily submitted to the Department of Homeland Security (DHS). No level of government may use information submitted in good faith absent the submitter's consent. Nor may any third party use it in a civil action arising under federal or state law. The Act defines "critical infrastructure information" in part to mean "information not customarily in the public domain and related to the security of critical infrastructure," but it does not define "critical infrastructure." Environmental groups feared that the Act could induce regulated entities to voluntarily submit information concerning violations of environmental laws to preclude its use to support government or private enforcement action.

6. For further reading, see Symposium, Harnessing the Power of Information for the Next Generation of Environmental Law, 86 Tex. L. Rev. 1347-1876 (2008); Durham-Hammer, Left to Wonder: Reevaluating, Reforming, and Implementing the Emergency Planning and Community Right-to-Know Act of 1986, 29 Colum. J. Envtl. L. 323 (2004).

F. PREVENTING HARM FROM HAZARDOUS WASTE

Human and environmental exposure to chemical wastes creates the same kinds of risks as those considered in previous sections of this chapter. Chemical wastes may explode, ignite, or bring instant death from inhalation of their fumes during generation, treatment, storage, transportation, or disposal processes. More often, they work incrementally, like other toxic substances, revealing their effects over longer periods. Human exposure occurs via direct contact with the skin, inhalation, or ingestion of contaminated drinking water and food. Potential adverse health impacts range from acute and chronic damage to the respiratory, nervous, alimentary, and urological systems to cancer, birth defects, and permanent genetic impairment. Environmental disruption can range from the instant death of exposed plant and animal life to long-term disruption of ecological systems.

Chemical waste dumps probably account for a large degree of the popular consciousness of the risks created by improper hazardous waste management. Although these dumps contain industrial wastes, they also may include infectious organic materials from hospitals and scientific laboratories. As time passes, storage containers, ponds, and burial grounds are adversely affected by corrosion, breakage, natural processes, and acts of vandalism, so that the waste material disperses in ground and surface waters, soil, and the air.

The Love Canal dump site near Niagara Falls, New York, illustrates the pitfalls of haphazard waste management. Until the early 1940s, the Hooker Chemical Company dumped wastes that included benzene, PCBs, and pesticides into a mile-long, abandoned hydroelectric canal. After Hooker abandoned and bulldozed the site, it sold it in 1953 to the Niagara Falls Board of Education for one dollar. The Board built a school and playground on the site, and over one hundred residences were built near the school. Health problems eventually plagued area residents, even though dumping had ceased decades earlier. The afflictions included cancer; spontaneous abortion; malformed fetal organ systems; and skin, neurological, kidney, and liver disorders. In 1977, chemicals that had accumulated for several years in the clay-lined canal appeared in residents' basements. See M. Brown, Laying Waste (1980). The resulting publicity was a crucial impetus for the adoption of CERCLA, discussed in the next chapter.

Although the federal Clean Air Act and Clean Water Act are discussed in detail in Chapters 6 and 7, the special provisions for hazardous emissions and effluents considered there also place them conceptually among the statutes Congress has adopted for regulating hazardous wastes. The bulk of this section, however, is devoted to a study of the regulation of the management of hazardous waste under the Resource Conservation and Recovery Act (RCRA).

1.   Regulation of Hazardous Air Pollutants Under the Clean Air Act

[See Chapter 6, section I.1.]

2.   Regulation of Toxic Water Pollutants Under the Clean Water Act

[See Chapter 7, section D.]

3.   Regulation of Hazardous Waste Management Under the Resource Conservation and Recovery Act

a.   Introduction to the Management of Hazardous Waste

Each year millions of tons of hazardous waste are generated in the United States by large industrial facilities such as chemical manufacturers, electroplating companies, petroleum refineries, and by smaller businesses such as dry cleaners, auto repair shops, exterminators, and photo-processing centers. The hazardous waste disposal problem is largely a groundwater protection problem. Groundwater trapped in underground aquifers supplies one-quarter of all fresh water used in the U.S. The "most pernicious" consequence of land disposal is that improperly maintained waste sites have caused many drinking water wells to be closed, sacrificing millions of dollars' worth of usable groundwater. H.R. Rep. No. 94-1491, at 89 (1976).

NOTE ON POLLUTION PREVENTION

There are three basic strategies for minimizing the risks created by hazardous wastes: (1) treatment, storage, or disposal; (2) process changes, to reduce waste stream volume; and (3) resource recovery (e.g., recycling). Congress has relied mostly on the first strategy, assuming that little can be done to reduce the volume of waste generated if we want to preserve the benefits of the chemical era. Further, Congress has chosen to avoid mandating the adoption of the specific technologies used in resource recovery. Many policymakers now agree that the second and third strategies represent the best long-term options.

Despite their focus on waste management, both Congress and EPA have recognized that it is better to prevent the generation of waste in the first place than to control how it is managed. In 1990, Congress enacted the Pollution Prevention Act (PPA), 42 U.S.C. §§13101-13109. The Act enunciates a national policy to prevent or reduce pollution at the source whenever feasible, to recycle in an environmentally sound manner pollution that cannot be prevented, and to dispose of or release pollution into the environment only as a last resort. §13101(b). The PPA requires that EPA establish a pollution prevention office, authorizes it to make grants to states to promote the use of source reduction techniques by businesses, and expands its authority to collect data to better track source reduction activities. §§13103-13107.

When EPA published its Pollution Prevention Strategy, 56 Fed. Reg. 7849 (1991), it cited studies showing that pollution prevention can be the most effective and cost-efficient way to reduce risks; it therefore harmonizes environmental protection and economic efficiency. EPA announced its intention to work with industry to achieve reasonable prevention goals (such as a 50 percent reduction in environmental releases) by assisting in the identification of opportunities to profit from prevention. It also stated that a strong regulatory and enforcement program under existing statutory authorities is necessary to provide further incentives to prevent pollution. EPA therefore would build pollution prevention principles into its regulatory programs to help overcome limitations in traditional approaches to pollution control, such as the use of treatment technologies that solve one pollution problem while creating a new one in a different medium. It stated that "[p]revention reduces emissions, discharges or wastes released to all parts of the ecosystem, thereby eliminating a potential cross-media 'shell-game.'" Id. at 7853. Pollution prevention also could help to address the problems caused by dispersed sources such as nonpoint sources of water pollution for which treatment technologies may not be practical or economical.

Neither the PPA nor EPA's pollution prevention strategy have generated any significant litigation, but the courts have cited the statute and the strategy in interpreting other statutes. In Monsanto Co. v. EPA, 19 F.3d 1201 (7th Cir. 1994), the company petitioned for review of EPA's denial of its request for additional time to comply with national emission standards for hazardous air pollutants issued under §112 of the Clean Air Act. EPA granted Monsanto a two-year extension under §112(c)(1)(B)(ii) to allow the company to install water-scrubbing equipment. When the equipment did not work as well as anticipated, Monsanto requested an additional extension so that it could install a secondary filtration system to catch harmful emissions not captured by the primary system. The court found EPA's denial of this second request to be contrary to the PPA and EPA's own pollution prevention strategy because it would induce companies to adopt "quick fixes" that change the form of the problem (by removing the environmental hazard from the air but creating a hazardous waste disposal problem) rather than eliminate it. If a company like Monsanto has a choice between two control strategies, EPA may grant a waiver for a pollution prevention strategy even if that strategy would take slightly longer to implement than the less desirable strategy.

Although RCRA, to which we turn next, focuses primarily on traditional techniques for regulating hazardous waste management, it also fosters pollution prevention. RCRA requires that all hazardous waste generators certify in the manifest that must accompany waste shipments that they have established a program to reduce the volume or toxicity of their waste to the extent economically practicable. §3002(b)(1). In addition, a generator applying for a permit for treatment, storage, or disposal of hazardous waste on the generating premises must provide an annual certification that such a program is in place. §3005(h)(1). See generally Guidance to Hazardous Waste Generators on the Elements of a Waste Minimization Program, 58 Fed. Reg. 31,114 (1993); Strasser, Cleaner Technology, Pollution Prevention and Environmental Regulation, 9 Fordham Envtl. L.J. 1 (1997) (urging multimedia regulatory approach to encourage pollution prevention).

b.   A Summary of RCRA

Local, state, and federal laws have controlled hazardous wastes piecemeal for decades. The techniques included public nuisance laws and emergency health measures, although a few states adopted more comprehensive legislation. Tort suits also acted as a deterrent to negligent hazardous waste management. In the 1970s, however, the inadequacy of these predominantly local or stopgap strategies prompted Congress to adopt the Solid Waste Disposal Act, better known as the Resource Conservation and Recovery Act (RCRA), 42 U.S.C. §§6901-6991i.

RCRA distinguishes between nonhazardous solid waste and hazardous waste, each of which is subject to a separate regulatory program. Subtitle D authorizes EPA to establish guidelines for state regulation of nonhazardous solid waste disposal facilities. As initially adopted, Subtitle D envisioned federal financial and technical assistance to the states, with a minimal federal regulatory presence. Subtitle C, on the other hand, which addresses hazardous waste, fully reflects the regulatory paradigm for pollution control. EPA has promulgated thousands of pages of regulations under Subtitle C. As a result, environmental practitioners in this field must immerse themselves in a regulatory exegesis. Frankly, the experience is not for everyone.

Touted as a comprehensive, "cradle to grave" system, Subtitle C of RCRA provides for the listing of specific wastes as hazardous and the identification of characteristics that subject nonlisted wastes to the regulatory scheme. Hazardous waste generators must comply with recordkeeping, reporting, and container labeling requirements, as well as assist federal and state regulators in tracking the movement of hazardous waste through the preparation of manifests to accompany waste shipments. Waste transporters must abide by regulatory standards issued under the Hazardous Materials Transportation Uniform Safety Act as well as RCRA. The most extensive controls apply to those engaged in the treatment, storage, or disposal of hazardous waste (TSD facilities). These entities may not operate without a permit, which requires compliance with performance standards for location, design, construction, operation, closure, and post-closure care. RCRA bars or severely restricts disposal on land of certain untreated hazardous wastes. The usual civil and criminal sanctions apply to violators. As it has elsewhere, Congress authorized the states to run their own hazardous waste regulatory programs, so long as they satisfy or exceed minimum federal requirements. The states may adopt more stringent requirements. Table 8-4 summarizes EPA's authority to implement Subtitle C of RCRA.

TABLE 8-4
Summary of EPA's Regulatory Authority Under Subtitle C of RCRA

Source of Regulatory Authority	*Nature of Regulatory Authority*
§3001	Identify and list hazardous wastes
§3002	Promulgate standards applicable to hazardous waste generators "as may be necessary to protect human health and the environment"
§3003	Promulgate standards applicable to hazardous waste transporters "as may be necessary to protect human health and the environment"
§3004	Promulgate performance standards applicable to facilities that treat, store, or dispose of hazardous waste (TSD facilities) "as may be necessary to protect human health and the environment"
	Implement land disposal restrictions (LDRs) on particular hazardous wastes
	Issue treatment standards for hazardous wastes subject to LDRs
	Require corrective action for releases of hazardous wastes or their constituents
§3005	Require permits for TSD facilities
	Issue TSD facility permits
§3006	Authorize states to issue TSD facility permits
§3007	Inspect and obtain samples from sources that generate, transport, treat, store, or dispose of hazardous waste
§3008	Pursue civil or criminal enforcement of Subtitle C

As the statute's name suggests, RCRA is designed to encourage the recovery of useful materials through process substitution and properly conducted recycling and reuse, thereby minimizing the amount of waste generated, as well as to ensure the proper management of hazardous waste. §1003(a)(4), (6). It declares a national policy of reducing or eliminating the generation of hazardous waste as expeditiously as possible, "wherever feasible," and of managing waste that is nevertheless generated in a manner that minimizes threats to health and the environment. §1003(b). Although these objectives seem complementary in theory, in practice there is considerable tension between them.

c.   Distinguishing Waste from Useful Materials: Legitimate versus Sham Recycling

The potential for activities that increase reuse to thwart the statute's safe management objective is reflected in EPA's efforts to define waste. Neither Subtitle C nor Subtitle D applies to materials unless they qualify as solid wastes. (Hazardous wastes are a subset of solid wastes. See §1004(5).) Whether a material is or is not a waste is probably the single most perplexing question raised by RCRA. Its resolution is the crucial determinant of the statute's scope. The statute defines solid waste in §1004(27). EPA's definition, located at 40 C.F.R. §261.2 (and reproduced in part after the second principal case in this section), is considerably more complex, if not convoluted. The following case reviews some of the history of EPA's interpretation of the parameters of the term "solid waste."

OWEN ELECTRIC STEEL CO. OF SOUTH CAROLINA, INC. v. BROWNER
37 F.3d 146 (4th Cir. 1994)

RUSSELL, Circuit Judge:

The sole issue in this case is whether the "slag" produced by petitioner Owen Electric Steel Company ("Owen") at its Cayce, South Carolina, facility as a byproduct of steel production is "discarded," and therefore constitutes a "solid waste" under 42 U.S.C. §6903(27). . . .

. . . Owen is engaged in the production of steel. The steel is produced in an electric arc furnace. In the course of production, crushed limestone (calcium carbonate) is added to the furnace to remove certain non-ferrous constituents from the molten metal. In this process, the non-ferrous constituents bind with the limestone, creating "slag," which is essentially limestone and dolomite (magnesium carbonate) with trace amounts of metallic oxides. The slag then floats to the surface of the molten metal and is removed.

The slag is continuously processed at the Owen's plant. . . . Following processing, the slag is placed in holding bays, where the slag lies on bare soil for tempering and weathering. During this process, known as "curing," the slag is hydrated and undergoes phase changes where its bulk increases volumetrically. This curing process generally takes six months. After this time, the slag becomes dimensionally stable and, as a result, amenable for use as a construction aggregate. The slag generated at Owen's Cayce facility is sold to the construction industry for use as a road base material or for other commercial purposes. . . .

[RCRA requires that an operator of a facility that treats, stores, or disposes of hazardous wastes (a TSD facility, or TSDF) obtain a permit from EPA or an authorized state. Owen applied for and received a TSDF permit for its Cayce facility. The permit identified the slag processing area (SPA) as a solid waste management unit (SWMU). Owen challenged that classification.]

We must determine whether the EPA properly classified the SPA as an SWMU. . . . The legislative history . . . unequivocally states: "[T]he term 'solid waste management unit' [in amended RCRA §3004] is used to reaffirm the Administrator's responsibility to examine all units at [a TSDF] from which hazardous constituents might migrate, irrespective of whether the units were intended for the management of solid and/or hazardous waste." H.R. Rep. No. 98-198, pt. 1, at 60 (1983). Accordingly, in order to conclude that the SPA is an SWMU, the EPA need only find that Owen's slag is a "solid waste" [under §1004(27)].

. . . At issue is whether Owen's slag constitutes "other discarded material." Owen argues that its slag is not a "discarded material" because it is ultimately recycled and used in roadbeds. EPA counters that, because the slag lies dormant, exposed, on the ground for six months before such use, it is discarded even if it is later "picked up" and used in another capacity. . . .

A series of cases have addressed the meaning of "discarded material." In American Mining Cong. v. EPA, 824 F.2d 1177 (D.C. Cir. 1987) ("AMC I"), the District of Columbia Circuit was faced with the question of

> whether, in light of [Congress's] expressly stated objectives and the underlying problems that motivated it to enact RCRA in the first instance, Congress was using the term "discarded" in its ordinary sense—"disposed of" or "abandoned"—or whether Congress

was using it in a much more open-ended way, so as to encompass materials no longer useful in their original capacity though destined for immediate reuse in another phase of the industry's ongoing production process.

Id. at 1185. The court of appeals settled upon the former option, emphasizing that it found the statutory language unambiguous. The court observed that the legislative history and policies underlying RCRA supported its conclusion. In the court's opinion, only materials that are "disposed of" or "abandoned" "become part of the waste disposal problem," id. at 1186, with which RCRA is concerned.

Were *AMC I* the final case offering interpretation of the phrase "discarded material," Owen might be victorious here: because Owen's slag is eventually recycled, it cannot be said to have been discarded. Subsequent cases, however, have read *AMC I* narrowly. First, in American Petroleum Inst. v. EPA, 906 F.2d 729 (D.C. Cir. 1990), the EPA asserted that the District of Columbia Circuit's holding in *AMC I* precluded it from regulating as waste hazardous slag that was delivered to a plant for metal reclamation. The court of appeals held otherwise, explaining:

> The issue in *AMC [I]* was whether the EPA could, under the RCRA, treat as "solid wastes" "materials that are recycled and reused in an *ongoing* manufacturing or industrial process." [*AMC I*, 824 F.2d at 1186.] We held that it could not because
>
>> [t]hese materials have not yet become part of the waste disposal problem; rather, *they are destined for beneficial reuse or recycling in a continuous process by the generating industry itself.*
>
> Id. Materials subject to such a process were not "discarded" because they were never "disposed of, abandoned, or thrown away."
>
> *AMC [I]* is by no means dispositive of EPA's authority to regulate K061 slag. Unlike the materials in question in *AMC [I]*, K061 is indisputably "discarded" *before* being subject to metals reclamation. Consequently, it *has* "become part of the waste disposal problem."

American Petroleum Inst., 906 F.2d at 741 (emphasis provided by the *American Petroleum Inst.* court).

Next, in American Mining Cong. v. EPA, 907 F.2d 1179 (D.C. Cir. 1990) ("*AMC II*"), petitioners, relying on *AMC I*, claimed that three hazardous wastes were not solid wastes on the basis that "sludges [containing the wastes] from wastewater that are stored in surface impoundments and that *may* at some time in the future be reclaimed are not 'discarded.'" *AMC II*, 907 F.2d at 1186 (emphasis in original). The court of appeals rejected petitioners' reading of *AMC I*, stating:

> Petitioners read *AMC [I]* too broadly. *AMC [I]*'s holding concerned only materials that are "destined for *immediate reuse* in another phase of the industry's ongoing production process," and that "have not yet become part of the waste disposal problem." Nothing in *AMC [I]* prevents the agency from treating as "discarded" the wastes at issue in this case, which are managed in land disposal units that *are* part of wastewater treatment systems, which have therefore become "part of the waste disposal problem," and which are not part of the ongoing industrial processes.

Finally, in United States v. ILCO, Inc., 996 F.2d 1126 (11th Cir. 1993), ILCO, Inc. ("ILCO") purchased spent batteries from various sources and then recycled them. ILCO contended that, because it recycled the spent batteries, they had not been discarded and, therefore, were not solid waste. The Eleventh Circuit rejected this argument, stating:

> ILCO argues that it has never "discarded" the plates and groups [of the batteries] and, therefore, the material it recycles is not "solid waste" as defined in §6903(27). The lead plates and groups are, no doubt, valuable feedstock for a smelting process. Nevertheless, EPA, with congressional authority, promulgated regulations that classify these materials as "discarded solid waste." *Somebody* has discarded the battery in which these components are found. This fact does not change just because a reclaimer has purchased or finds value in the components.[4]

From these cases, we glean that the fundamental inquiry in determining whether a byproduct has been "discarded" is whether the byproduct is *immediately* recycled for use in the same industry; if not, then the byproduct is justifiably seen as "part of the waste disposal problem," *AMC I*, 824 F.2d at 1186, and therefore as a "solid waste." We think it reasonable and permissible . . . for the EPA to adhere to this inquiry in determining whether a material is "discarded."

Moreover, we find no abuse of discretion in EPA's conclusion that, under this interpretation, Owen's slag constitutes "discarded material" and therefore "solid waste." The slag is not immediately used in Owen's production process; rather, the slag must sit, untouched, for some six months before it is sold to other entities. The EPA is justified in finding that, where a byproduct sits untouched for six months, it cannot be said that the material was "*never* 'disposed of, abandoned, or thrown away.'" *American Petroleum Inst.*, 906 F.2d at 741 (emphasis added) (quoting *AMC I*, 824 F.2d at 1193). The EPA is also justified to conclude that, because the slag is sold to others for use in roadbed construction, it is not "destined for beneficial reuse or recycling in a continuous process by the generating industry itself," *AMC I*, 824 F.2d at 1186. In short, the EPA did not abuse its discretion in concluding that Owen's slag is "part of the waste disposal problem." . . .

We conclude that Owen's slag is "solid waste" and that, therefore, the SPA was appropriately determined to be an SWMU. Owen's petition for relief is therefore denied.

QUESTIONS

What is the "ordinary sense" of the terms "disposed of" and "abandoned"? How did the *AMC I* court appear to interpret those terms? How long after generation may the agency properly regard a material as a waste under that approach? When does a material generated by a production process become "part of the waste disposal problem"? How did the decisions in *American Petroleum Inst.* and *AMC II* alter the inquiry? Had Owen used its slag in one of its own production processes, would the result in the principal case have been different?

---

4. . . . The crucial element of the Eleventh Circuit's reasoning is that the batteries became, in the words of *AMC I*, "part of the waste disposal problem," as soon as the various owners of the batteries discarded them. That ILCO, a third party, then agreed to recycle the batteries, thereby, at least in some sense, ameliorating the waste disposal problem, is irrelevant in the sense that that subsequent act does not divest the EPA of jurisdiction over the waste. In other words, once the batteries were discarded they became classified as solid waste; subsequent treatment is irrelevant.

AMERICAN PETROLEUM INSTITUTE v. EPA (*API II*)
216 F.3d 50 (D.C. Cir. 2000)

Before: WILLIAMS, SENTELLE and ROGERS, Circuit Judges . . .
PER CURIAM:

[Petroleum refiners, including the American Petroleum Institute (API), and petrochemical manufacturers, including the Chemical Manufacturers Association (CMA), challenged EPA's decision to regulate under Subtitle C of RCRA certain materials generated by the petroleum refining industry.]

In petroleum refining, impurities are removed and usable hydrocarbon fractions are isolated from crude oil feedstock. Large quantities of water are used, and the resulting wastewaters contain a small percentage of residual oil. These "oil-bearing wastewaters" are destined for ultimate discharge, but only after a three-step treatment process is first applied. The first phase of treatment, known as "primary treatment," removes certain materials including the oil. This phase has at least two beneficial consequences: (1) it meets a Clean Water Act requirement that refineries remove oil from their wastewater, and (2) it allows refineries to recover a not insignificant quantity of oil (up to 1,000 barrels a day across the industry) which is cycled back into the refinery production process.

Industry petitioners and EPA disagree over when these wastewaters become discarded for purposes of the solid waste definition. While no one disputes that discard has certainly occurred by the time the wastewaters move into the later phases of treatment, the question is whether discard happens before primary treatment, allowing regulation of wastewater as solid waste at that point, or not until primary treatment is complete and oil has been recovered for further processing.

EPA's initial proposal excluded oil-bearing wastewaters. However, it changed its mind in 1994 and concluded that even before the oil is recovered in primary treatment, "the wastewaters are discarded materials and hence solid wastes subject to regulation under RCRA." EPA stated: "Primary wastewater treatment operations exist to treat plant wastewaters." It noted that the percentage of oil in the wastewater is very small and "not significant in the context of a refinery's overall production activities," and that the Clean Water Act mandates such treatment. For these stated reasons, EPA concluded that "[c]learly, wastewater treatment is the main purpose of the systems in question, and any oil recovery is of secondary import." . . .

Industry petitioners . . . contend that . . . oil-bearing wastewaters cannot be regulated because they are (as claimed in API's *AMC I* brief) unquestionably in-process materials not yet discarded. Alternately, . . . [p]etitioners emphasize that primary treatment yields valuable oil that is reinserted into the refining processes in a continuous operation. They also claim that oil recovery operations began long before Clean Water Act regulations required it. In sum, they contend that oil recovery in primary treatment is a part of in-process oil production.

At bottom, the parties disagree over the proper characterization of primary treatment. Is it simply a step in the act of discarding? Or is it the last step in a production process before discard? Our prior cases have not had to draw a line for deciding when discard has occurred. . . .

It may be permissible for EPA to determine that the predominant purpose of primary treatment is discard. Legal abandonment of property is premised on determining the intent to abandon, which requires an inquiry into facts and circumstances. Where an industrial by-product may be characterized as discarded or "in process" material, EPA's choice of characterization is entitled to deference. See *AMC II*, 907 F.2d at 1186. However, the record must reflect that EPA engaged in reasoned decisionmaking to decide which characterization is appropriate. The record in this case is deficient in that regard. EPA has noted two purposes of primary treatment and concludes, "[c]learly, wastewater treatment is the main purpose." As English teachers have long taught, a conclusion is not "clear" or "obvious" merely because one says so.

EPA points out that primary treatment only recovers a small amount of oil relative to the entire output of a typical refining facility. However, the oil is still valuable and usable, so that reason alone cannot show discard. The rock of a diamond mine may only contain a tiny portion of precious carbon, but that is enough to keep miners busy. In the refining industry, the net amount of oil recovered may reach 1,000 barrels a day. It is plausible to claim, as industry petitioners do, that refiners engage in primary treatment first and foremost to recover this usable resource. At the very least, EPA cannot merely rely on the small relative amount of oil recovered from primary treatment without further explanation.

EPA also notes that the Clean Water Act requires primary treatment before discharge. If refiners got nothing from primary treatment, this might be a compelling rationale because it would be hard to explain why, other than to discard, refiners would engage in a costly treatment activity with no economic benefits. However, petitioners claim they would engage in primary treatment regardless of the treatment standards in order to recover the desired oil. EPA does not explain why this possibly valid motivation is not compelling. EPA makes no attempt to balance the costs and benefits of primary treatment, or otherwise to explain why the Clean Water Act requirements are the real motivation behind primary treatment. Indeed, without further explanation, it is not inherently certain why a substance is definitively "discarded" if its possessor is continuing to process it, even though the possessor's decision to continue processing may have been influenced, or even predominantly motivated, by some external factor. Otherwise put, it is not so obvious as EPA would have us hold that if the industry petitioners conceded that their overriding motivation in further processing the wastewaters was compliance with Clean Water Act regulations that they would then conclusively be discarding the material in question even while further processing it. If the non–Clean Water Act benefits of the initial treatment are enough to justify firms' incurring the costs (petitioners point to material in the record that may support such a proposition), the EPA would have to reconcile that fact with any conclusion that the Clean Water Act purpose was primary.

In short, EPA has not set forth why it has concluded that the compliance motivation predominates over the reclamation motivation. Perhaps equally importantly it has not explained why that conclusion, even if validly reached, compels the further conclusion that the wastewater has been discarded. Therefore, because the agency has failed to provide a rational explanation for its decision, we hold the decision to be arbitrary and capricious. We therefore vacate the portion of EPA's decision declining to exclude oil-bearing wastewaters from the statutory definition of solid waste, and remand for further proceedings. We do not suggest any particular result on remand, only a reasoned one demonstrating when discard occurs if EPA wishes to assert jurisdiction.

NOTES AND QUESTIONS

1. Why didn't *AMC I* or *AMC II* control the result in this case? How did the purpose of the activities of the petroleum refining industry bear on the proper characterization of the wastewaters that contained residual oil? What defects did the court identify in EPA's justification for subjecting the oil-bearing wastewaters to RCRA regulation?

2. In another portion of the principal case, the court addressed EPA's decision to regulate as hazardous waste under RCRA certain residual oil, known as "petrochemical recovered oil," that results from the use of refined petroleum products and other feedstocks to produce petrochemical products such as organic chemicals. This residual oil can be inserted back into the petroleum refining process. EPA was concerned that if extra materials were added to petrochemical recovered oil that provide no benefit to the industrial process, petrochemical producers would be engaged in an act of discard under the guise of recycling. EPA raised this concern because some of the residual oil samples it tested were contaminated with chlorinated or other halogenated materials that were unexpected. Industry argued that EPA lacks the authority to regulate any petrochemical recovered oil under any circumstances because such materials are not "discarded." The court disagreed and upheld EPA's approach, concluding that EPA can regulate material "discarded" through sham recycling even though it cannot regulate under RCRA materials that are not discarded.

3. *A Timing Question: When Is Immediate Not Imminent?* The *AMC I* court required that recycled materials be "destined for immediate reuse" in an ongoing production process to avoid characterization as discarded material. Both the *AMC II* and *Owen Elec.* cases emphasized that aspect of *AMC I.* But what does "immediate reuse" mean? In Association of Battery Recyclers, Inc. v. EPA, 208 F.3d 1047 (D.C. Cir. 2000), the mineral processing industry challenged an EPA regulation that regarded as solid waste secondary materials destined for recycling in its production processes if they exhibit a characteristic of hazardous waste and are stored by means other than tanks, containers, buildings, or properly maintained pads. Such materials were solid wastes regardless of the length of their storage before recycling. The petitioners relied on *AMC I*, but EPA argued that subsequent cases had sharply limited the scope of that case. EPA claimed it was prohibited from treating secondary materials as discarded only if "reclamation is continuous in the sense that there is no interdiction in time" in that materials move from one step of a recovery process to another without a break in the process for storage.

The court invalidated the regulation. First, it concluded that the materials destined for recycling were neither thrown away nor abandoned. Thus, *AMC I* precluded EPA from characterizing them as discarded. Remarkably, the court added that "[l]ater cases in this court do not limit *AMC I,* as EPA supposes." Id. at 1054. *AMC II,* for example, stands only for the proposition that EPA may regulate as solid waste materials that "may at some time in the future be reclaimed." The secondary materials at issue in this case *would* be reclaimed. Second, the court contested EPA's assumption that "immediate," as the court in *AMC I* used that word, means "at once." Instead, the court concluded that it means "direct," as in "the immediate cause of the accident." In this case, EPA improperly regulated materials that were not a by-product of solid waste, but rather a direct by-product of industrial processes that were destined for reuse as part of a continuous industrial process. EPA thus exceeded the scope of its authority by regulating these in-process secondary materials.

4. *Recycling Between Industries.* Suppose that secondary materials generated by one industry are destined for recycling in another industry. Are those materials necessarily "discarded" and therefore solid wastes under §1003(27) of RCRA? In *Safe Food and Fertilizer v. EPA*, 350 F.3d 1263 (D.C. Cir. 2003), *remanded on reh'g*, 365 F.3d 46 (D.C. Cir. 2004), the issue was whether secondary materials recycled to make zinc fertilizer, as well as the zinc fertilizer itself, were solid wastes under RCRA. The court accepted EPA's argument that they were not, based on two factors. First, market participants treated the recycled feedstocks more like valuable products than like negatively valued wastes, managing them in ways inconsistent with treatment of discarded materials. Second, the fertilizers derived from the recycled feedstocks were chemically indistinguishable from analogous commercial products made from virgin materials (the court referred to this as the "identity principle"). Under EPA's regulations, feedstocks were exempt from Subtitle C regulation if they were not speculatively accumulated and met certain storage, recordkeeping, and notice requirements consistent with the use of feedstocks as valued commodities rather than wastes.

In response to the court decisions on the definition of solid waste discussed above, EPA amended its regulations defining solid waste "to encourage safe, environmentally sound recycling and resource conservation." 73 Fed. Reg. 64,669 (2008). Relevant portions are reproduced here:

HAZARDOUS WASTE MANAGEMENT SYSTEM
40 C.F.R. Part 260 [EPA's RCRA Regulations]

§261.2 Definition of solid waste

(a)(1) A *solid waste* is any discarded material that is not excluded under §261.4(a)[m] . . . or that is not excluded by a non-waste determination under §§260.30 and 260.34.

(2)(i) A *discarded material* is any material which is:

(A) Abandoned, as explained in paragraph (b) of this section; or

(B) Recycled,[n] as explained in paragraph (c) of this section; or

(C) Considered inherently waste-like, as explained in paragraph (d) of this section. . . .

(ii) A hazardous secondary material is not discarded if it is generated and reclaimed under the control of the generator as defined in §260.10, it is not speculatively accumulated as defined in §261.1(c)(8), it is handled only in

---

m. Section 261.4 provides that certain materials "are not solid wastes" for purposes of Subtitle C, including domestic sewage, industrial wastewater discharges that are point source discharges subject to regulation under the Clean Water Act's NPDES permit program, irrigation return flows, certain nuclear material regulated under the Atomic Energy Act, and materials subjected to in-situ mining techniques which are not removed from the ground as part of the extraction process. Finally, §261.4(a)(8) excludes from the definition of a solid waste certain "secondary materials that are reclaimed and returned to the original process or processes in which they were generated where they are reused in the production process."

n. Section 261.c(7) provides that "[a] material is 'recycled' if it is used, reused, or reclaimed."

non-land based units and is contained in such units; . . . and the reclamation of the material is legitimate, as specified under §260.43. . . .

(b) Materials are solid waste if they are *abandoned* by being:

(1) Disposed of; or

(2) Burned or incinerated; or

(3) Accumulated, stored, or treated (but not recycled) before or in lieu of being abandoned by being disposed of, burned, or incinerated.

(c) Materials are solid wastes if they are *recycled*—or accumulated, stored, or treated before recycling—as specified in paragraphs (c)(1) through (c)(4) of this section.

(1) *Used in a manner constituting disposal.*[o] . . .

(2) *Burning for energy recovery.* . . .

(3) *Reclaimed.*[p] . . .

(4) *Accumulated speculatively.* . . .

(d) *Inherently waste-like materials.* The following are solid wastes when they are recycled in any manner [listed as such in the regulations].

(e) *Materials that are not solid waste when recycled.*

(1) Materials are not solid wastes when they can be shown to be recycled by being:

(i) Used or reused[q] as ingredients in an industrial process to make a product, provided the materials are not being reclaimed; or

(ii) Used or reused as effective substitutes for commercial products; or

(iii) Returned to the original process from which they are generated, without first being reclaimed or land disposed. The material must be returned as a substitute for feedstock materials. In cases where the original process to which the material is returned is a secondary process, the materials must be managed such that there is no placement on the land. . . .

(2) The following materials are solid wastes, even if the recycling involves use, reuse, or return to the original process (described in paragraphs (e)(1)(i)-(iii) of this section):

(i) Materials used in a manner constituting disposal, or used to produce products that are applied to the land; or

(ii) Materials burned for energy recovery, used to produce a fuel, or contained in fuels; or

(iii) Materials accumulated speculatively; or

(iv) Materials listed in paragraphs (d)(1) and (d)(2) of this section.

---

o. This includes materials that are "[a]pplied to or placed on the land in a manner that constitutes disposal" or "[u]sed to produce products that are applied to or placed on the land or are otherwise contained in products that are applied to or placed on the land (in which cases the product itself remains a solid waste)." §261.2(c)(1)(i).

p. Section 261.1(c)(4) provides that "[a] material is 'reclaimed' if it is processed to recover a usable product, or if it is regenerated. Examples are recovery of lead values from spent batteries and regeneration of spent solvents. . . ."

q. Section 261.1(c)(5) provides that "[a] material is 'used or reused' if it is either: (i) Employed as an ingredient (including use as an intermediate) in an industrial process to make a product (for example, distillation bottoms from one process used as feedstock in another process). However, a material will not satisfy this condition if distinct components of the material are recovered as separate end product (as when metals are recovered from metal-containing secondary materials); or (ii) Employed in a particular function or application as an effective substitute for a commercial product (for example, spent pickle liquor used as phosphorous precipitant and sludge conditioner in wastewater treatment)."

§260.30 Non-waste determinations and variances from classification as a solid waste

In accordance with the standards and criteria in §260.31 and §260.34 and the procedures in §260.33, the Administrator may determine on a case-by-case basis that the following recycled materials are not solid wastes:

(a) Materials that are accumulated speculatively without sufficient amounts being recycled (as defined in §261.1(c)(8) of this chapter);

(b) Materials that are reclaimed and then reused within the original production process in which they were generated;

(c) Materials that have been reclaimed but must be reclaimed further before the materials are completely recovered;

(d) Hazardous secondary materials that are reclaimed in a continuous industrial process; and

(e) Hazardous secondary materials that are indistinguishable in all relevant aspects from a product or intermediate. . . .

§260.34 Standards and criteria for non-waste determinations

(a) An applicant may apply to the Administrator for a formal determination that a hazardous secondary material is not discarded and therefore not a solid waste. The determinations will be based on the criteria contained in paragraph (b) or (c) of this section, as applicable. . . .

(b) The Administrator may grant a non-waste determination for hazardous secondary material which is reclaimed in a continuous industrial process if the applicant demonstrates that the hazardous secondary material is a part of the production process and is not discarded. The determination will be based on whether the hazardous secondary material is legitimately recycled as specified in §260.43 and on the following criteria:

(1) The extent that the management of the hazardous secondary material is part of the continuous primary production process and is not waste treatment;

(2) Whether the capacity of the production process would use the hazardous secondary material in a reasonable time frame and ensure that the hazardous secondary material will not be abandoned (for example, based on past practices, market factors, the nature of the hazardous secondary material, or any contractual arrangements);

(3) Whether the hazardous constituents in the hazardous secondary material are reclaimed rather than released to the air, water or land at significantly higher levels from either a statistical or from a health and environmental risk perspective than would otherwise be released by the production process; and

(4) Other relevant factors that demonstrate the hazardous secondary material is not discarded.

(c) The Administrator may grant a non-waste determination for hazardous secondary material which is indistinguishable in all relevant aspects from a product or intermediate if the applicant demonstrates that the hazardous secondary material is comparable to a product or intermediate and is not discarded. The determination will be based on whether the hazardous secondary material is legitimately recycled as specified in §260.43 and on the following criteria:

(1) Whether market participants treat the hazardous secondary material as a product or intermediate rather than a waste (for example, based on the current

positive value of the hazardous secondary material, stability of demand, or any contractual arrangements);

(2) Whether the chemical and physical identity of the hazardous secondary material is comparable to commercial products or intermediates;

(3) Whether the capacity of the market would use the hazardous secondary material in a reasonable time frame and ensure that the hazardous secondary material will not be abandoned (for example, based on past practices, market factors, the nature of the hazardous secondary material, or any contractual arrangements);

(4) Whether the hazardous constituents in the hazardous secondary material are reclaimed rather than released to the air, water or land at significantly higher levels from either a statistical or from a health and environmental risk perspective than would otherwise be released by the production process; and

(5) Other relevant factors that demonstrate the hazardous secondary material is not discarded. . . .

§260.43 Legitimate recycling of hazardous secondary materials regulated under §260.34 . . .

(a) Persons regulated under §260.34 or claiming to be excluded from hazardous waste regulation under §261.2(a)(2)(ii) . . . because they are engaged in reclamation must be able to demonstrate that the recycling is legitimate. Hazardous secondary material that is not legitimately recycled is discarded material and is a solid waste. In determining if their recycling is legitimate, persons must address the requirements of §260.43(b) and must consider the requirements of §260.43(c) below.

(b) Legitimate recycling must involve a hazardous secondary material that provides a useful contribution to the recycling process or to a product or intermediate of the recycling process, and the recycling process must produce a valuable product or intermediate.

(1) The hazardous secondary material provides a useful contribution if it

(i) Contributes valuable ingredients to a product or intermediate; or

(ii) Replaces a catalyst or carrier in the recycling process; or

(iii) Is the source of a valuable constituent recovered in the recycling process; or

(iv) Is recovered or regenerated by the recycling process; or

(v) Is used as an effective substitute for a commercial product.

(2) The product or intermediate is valuable if it is

(i) Sold to a third party; or

(ii) Used by the recycler or the generator as an effective substitute for a commercial product or as an ingredient or intermediate in an industrial process.

(c) The following factors must be considered in making a determination as to the overall legitimacy of a specific recycling activity.

(1) The generator and the recycler should manage the hazardous secondary material as a valuable commodity. Where there is an analogous raw material, the hazardous secondary material should be managed, at a minimum, in a manner consistent with the management of the raw material. Where there is no analogous raw material, the hazardous secondary material should be contained. Hazardous secondary materials that are released to the environment and are not recovered immediately are discarded.

(2) The product of the recycling process does not

(i) Contain significant concentrations of any hazardous constituents . . . that are not found in analogous products; or

(ii) Contain concentrations of any hazardous constituents . . . at levels that are significantly elevated from those found in analogous products; or

(iii) Exhibit a hazardous characteristic (as defined in part 261 subpart C) that analogous products do not exhibit.

(3) In making a determination that a hazardous secondary material is legitimately recycled, persons must evaluate all factors and consider legitimacy as a whole. If, after careful evaluation of these other considerations, one or both of the factors are not met, then this fact may be an indication that the material is not legitimately recycled.

However, the factors in this paragraph do not have to be met for the recycling to be considered legitimate. In evaluating the extent to which these factors are met and in determining whether a process that does not meet one or both of these factors is still legitimate, persons can consider the protectiveness of the storage methods, exposure from toxics in the product, the bioavailability of the toxics in the product, and other relevant considerations.

QUESTIONS

1. Should the materials involved in *Owen Elec.* or any of the cases cited in that opinion have qualified for exclusion from regulation under §261.4(a)(8)? More generally, do you think the revised regulations respond appropriately to the cases concerning the definition of solid waste? Do the revisions simplify the concepts involved in determining whether a material is a solid waste? Do they strike an appropriate balance between the desire to encourage "legitimate" recycling and to preclude resort to "sham" recycling as a means of avoiding Subtitle C regulation?

2. *Spent Materials.* Under EPA's regulations, materials are solid wastes if they are recycled in certain ways, including "spent materials" that are applied to or placed on the land in a manner that constitutes disposal. 40 C.F.R. §261.2(c)(1)(i). A "spent material" is "any material that has been used and as a result of contamination can no longer serve the purpose for which it was produced without processing." Id. §261.1(c)(1). Suppose that a product manufactured as a cleaning agent becomes too contaminated to be used in that way but is then sent to a fertilizer manufacturer for use as an ingredient in making fertilizer. Is the material "spent" when it can no longer be used as a cleaning agent, or only after it has served its additional function as a fertilizer ingredient? Does the answer depend on whether the word "purpose" in the definition of "spent material" encompasses all purposes for which the material may be used at the time of manufacture, or only the first use made after its production? See Howmet Corp. v. EPA, 614 F.3d 544 (D.C. Cir. 2010).

3. *The Definition of Solid Waste and Its Relevance to Other Statutes.* Section 129 of the CAA requires EPA to establish performance standards to control air pollution from solid waste incineration units. The statute provides that the term "solid waste" has the same meaning as under RCRA. 42 U.S.C. §7429(g)(6). EPA has issued regulations identifying which nonhazardous secondary materials, when used as fuels or ingredients in combustion units, qualify as solid waste for purposes of RCRA, and therefore for purposes of §129. Identification of Non-Hazardous Secondary Materials that Are Solid Waste, 76 Fed. Reg. 15,456 (Mar. 21, 2011).

NOTE ON FURTHER SOLID WASTE DEFINITIONAL ISSUES

Legitimate versus Sham Recycling. Even before EPA adopted §§260.30, 260.34, and 260.43, it sought to determine which recycled materials are subject to regulation as solid wastes by distinguishing between legitimate and sham recycling. In United States v. Marine Shale Processors, 81 F.3d 1361 (5th Cir. 1996), the issue was whether soil contaminated with toxic wastes generated at a wood treatment facility (SWP) was solid waste, given that SWP sent it to a hazardous waste recycler. The recycler burned the soil in a rotary kiln as part of its manufacturing process, producing air particles that contained carcinogenic metals. EPA argued that SWP was engaged in sham recycling, so that the soil was solid waste subject to regulation. Under EPA's approach, sham recycling occurs when the hazardous waste purportedly recycled contributes in no significant way to the production of the product allegedly resulting from the recycling. The sham versus legitimate recycling inquiry therefore focused on the purpose or function the hazardous waste allegedly serves in the production process. If the waste does not in fact serve its alleged function in the process, then sham recycling is occurring. SWP was engaged in legitimate recycling only if its hazardous waste "feed-stocks" were not "simply . . . along for the ride." The court rejected the notion that soil contaminated with organic waste is a fundamentally distinct substance from the organic waste itself. "Incineration does not cease to be incineration when one dumps the waste to be incinerated into a temporary medium like soil." Id. at 1366.

Would SWP's soil qualify as solid waste under the EPA regulations reproduced above? EPA has proposed revisions to the definition of legitimacy in §260.43, including (1) applying the definition to all regulated recycling activities; (2) making all legitimacy factors mandatory, with a petition process for instances where a factor is not met, but the recycling is still legitimate; and (3) requiring documentation of legitimacy. Rulemaking on the Definition of Solid Waste; Proposed Rule, 76 Fed. Reg. 44,094 (July 22, 2011).

A State Approach to Defining Waste. In Waste Mgmt. of the Desert, Inc. v. Palm Springs Recycling Ctr., Inc., 869 P.2d 440 (Cal. 1994), the court held that recyclable materials did not qualify as "wastes" within the meaning of a state statute authorizing cities to grant exclusive franchises for "solid waste" handling services. The analysis revolved around whether the materials were (1) discarded and (2) had economic value.

> The commonly understood meaning of "waste" is something discarded "as worthless or useless." (Amer. Heritage Dict. (1985) p. 1365, col. 1.) If the owner sells his property— that is, receives value for it—the property cannot be said to be worthless or useless in an economic sense and is thus not waste from the owner's perspective. Conversely, if the owner voluntarily disposes of the property without receiving compensation or other consideration in exchange—that is, throws it away—the obvious conclusion is that the property has no economic value to the owner. The concept of value is in this sense related to the manner in which the property is disposed. . . .
>
> [The statute defined the term "solid waste" to include enumerated materials and "other discarded solid and semisolid wastes." Thus, the court reasoned, "an item is not waste until it is discarded."] This returns us to the concept of value. Property that is sold for value—for example, a recyclable—is not "discarded" under any traditional understanding of the term. "Discard" means "to throw away." (Amer. Heritage Dict. (2d college ed. 1982) p. 402, col. 1.) It is not synonymous with the broader term "dispose," which means "To transfer or part with, as by giving or selling." (Id., at p. 407, col. 2.) A homeowner, for example, can dispose of used furniture, clothing, or

automobiles by discarding them or by selling them, but either method of disposition necessarily precludes the other. If he sells the property, he cannot discard it; and if he discards it, he cannot sell it. That "discard" connotes throwing away or abandoning has been well recognized in cases dealing with waste and related issues. [*AMC 1*] (D.C. Cir. 1987) 824 F.2d 1177, 1184. . . .

The proper rule is this: If the owner of property disposes of it for compensation—in common parlance, sells it—it is not waste because it has not been discarded. . . . Discarding the property renders the property waste and subjects it to the Act. [869 P.2d at 442-445.]

Would the recyclable materials in *Waste Mgmt. of the Desert* be "solid waste" under RCRA? If RCRA's definition of solid waste were governed by the economic value and valuable materials concepts from *Waste Mgmt. of the Desert*, would the decisions in *Owen Elec.*, *API II*, or the other cases cited in the notes following the last two principal cases have been different? Should Congress amend RCRA §1003(27) to define solid waste as material that has no economic value and that has been discarded as opposed to being disposed of for compensation? What would be the benefits of adopting such a definition? Compare *Safe Air for Everyone v. Meyer*, 373 F.3d 1035, 1043 n.8 (9th Cir. 2004) ("[T]he issue of monetary value does not affect the analysis of whether materials are 'solid waste' under RCRA").

Nonindustrial Solid Wastes. RCRA solid wastes can turn up in unlikely places. In Connecticut Coastal Fishermen's Ass'n v. Remington Arms Co., 989 F.2d 1305 (2d Cir. 1993), the court concluded that debris in Long Island Sound from lead shot and clay targets discharged by patrons of a gun club was solid waste under RCRA. Without deciding how long materials must accumulate after serving their original, intended purpose but before they are discarded, the court held that the lead shot and clay targets had accumulated long enough to qualify as solid waste. Compare Cordiano v. Metacon Gun Club, Inc., 575 F.3d 199 (2d Cir. 2009) (deferring to EPA's view that lead shot put to its ordinary use—discharge at a shooting range—is not solid waste because the shot has not been discarded); Military Toxics Project v. EPA, 146 F.3d 948 (D.C. Cir. 1998) (deferring to EPA's view that military munitions that, after being fired, hit the ground and remain there are not discarded because they are used for their intended purpose).

If a city decides to undertake an insecticide spraying program to control mosquito-borne diseases, would implementation of the program involve disposal of solid waste under RCRA? See No Spray Coal., Inc. v. City of New York, 252 F.3d 148 (2d Cir. 2001). In Ecological Rights Found. v. Pacific Gas and Elec. Co., 713 F.3d 502 (9th Cir. 2013), the court held that chemical preservatives which entered the environment from utility poles due to wind and rain through normal wear and tear were not discarded materials, and therefore solid wastes.

Suppose farmers who grow bluegrass harvest bluegrass seed by cutting the crop close to the ground, after which it dries out and ripens. They then separate the seed from the straw, leaving the straw on the field. They prepare the seed for commercial distribution, but leave the straw and stubble (the part of the crop not cut from the ground) on the field. The farmers then burn the straw and stubble in a practice called "open burning." Environmental groups claim that burning of the straw and stubble amounts to the disposal of solid waste that may endanger the health of nearby residents. They argue that the primary purpose of open burning is to remove the straw and stubble to maintain high future bluegrass seed yields. The growers respond that open burning (1) extends the productive life of their fields; (2) restores beneficial minerals and fertilizers to the fields (allowing them to purchase less of these materials than they would otherwise have to do to produce a bountiful crop); (3) reduces or eliminates insects, reducing the need for pesticide use; and (4) blackens the soil, which maximizes sunlight absorption and increases future crop yields. Accordingly, the growers contend, the straw and stubble are not solid wastes. Which side has the better argument? See Safe Air for Everyone v. Meyer, 373 F.3d 1035 (9th Cir. 2004).

Problem 8-3

For years the cement industry has lined its kilns with refractory bricks containing chromium. The bricks sometimes leach chromium in amounts sufficient to render the material hazardous under EPA's toxicity characteristic leaching procedure (described in the next section). When a kiln reached the end of its useful life (due to cracking of the bricks, for example), kiln owners often would crush the bricks from the inactive kiln and use the pulverized bricks as a raw material in the manufacture of cement. The manufacturing process involved burning the raw materials in industrial furnaces. Initially, EPA took the position that spent bricks are not solid wastes when they are reused as ingredients in an industrial process. When the agency adopted land disposal restrictions for hazardous debris under §3004 of RCRA, however, it defined hazardous debris to include chromium-containing spent bricks from cement kilns. The regulations also precluded thermal destruction as an acceptable treatment method for spent bricks, and defined thermal destruction to include the use of industrial furnaces at cement plants.

ABC Cement Company no longer manufactures kilns with chromium-containing refractory bricks, but it has a considerable inventory of these bricks. Some of them are in active kilns that will one day be taken out of service, some are in inactive kilns that have not yet been dismantled, and some have never been used and are stored in the company's warehouse. The company is considering challenging EPA's regulations barring the use of pulverized refractory brick as raw materials in cement manufacturing through treatment in industrial furnaces. The company would claim that the bricks do not constitute solid waste, are therefore not hazardous waste, and are therefore not subject to regulation under §3004. Is ABC likely to prevail in such a challenge?

d.   Identification and Listing of Hazardous Wastes

Overview of the Hazardous Waste Designation Process. The trigger for regulatory action under Subtitle C of RCRA is formal designation of a solid waste as hazardous. The statute defines a hazardous waste as a solid waste that, because of its quantity, concentration, or characteristics, may cause or significantly contribute to an increase in mortality or serious illness or pose a substantial hazard to human health or the environment when improperly managed. §1004(5). EPA must issue criteria for identifying the characteristics of hazardous waste and for listing particular hazardous wastes, taking into account factors such as toxicity, persistence, degradability in nature, potential for accumulation in tissue, flammability, and corrosiveness. §3001(a). It must then issue regulations that actually identify the characteristics of hazardous waste and list particular wastes that are hazardous and therefore subject to regulation under Subtitle C. §3001(b)(1).

EPA's regulations establish several mechanisms by which a solid waste may qualify as hazardous.[r] First, a solid waste is hazardous if it is specifically listed as such by EPA. 40 C.F.R. §261.3(a)(2)(ii). This method, which is reflected in the statutes of some states and European countries,[s] simply requires a generator to consult the lists published by EPA to see if a substance is regulated under Subtitle C. See id. §262.11(b). Second, a waste is hazardous if it meets any of the characteristics of a hazardous waste: ignitability, corrosivity, reactivity, or toxicity. Id. §§261.3(a)(2)(i), 261.20. A generator of a solid waste that is not listed as hazardous must determine whether the waste is nevertheless regulated under Subtitle C on the basis of its characteristics by testing the waste using EPA-approved methods, or by "[a]pplying knowledge of the waste in light of the materials or the processes used." Id. §262.11(c)(2). Third, a mixture of a listed hazardous waste and another solid waste is hazardous unless EPA has specifically excluded it. Id. §261.3(a)(2)(iv). Fourth, a mixture of a waste that is hazardous because of its characteristics and a nonhazardous solid waste is hazardous if the resulting mixture exhibits any of the characteristics of a hazardous waste. Id. §261.3(a)(2)(iii). Fifth, the "derived from" rule provides that, with certain exceptions, any solid waste generated from the treatment, storage, or disposal of a hazardous waste is hazardous. Id. §261.3(c)(2)(i). The "derived from" rule was meant to prevent hazardous waste generators and owners of treatment, storage, and disposal facilities from evading regulation by "minimally processing or managing a hazardous waste and claiming that resulting residue was no longer the listed waste, despite the continued hazards that could be posed by the residue even though it does not exhibit a [hazardous waste] characteristic." 60 Fed. Reg. 66,344, 66,346 (1995).

Listing and Delisting of Hazardous Wastes. EPA relies on listing as the predominant strategy for bringing wastes into the RCRA scheme because testing by generators for characteristics such as carcinogenicity, mutagenicity, and teratogenicity is generally impractical. This difficulty explains at least in part why EPA has not expanded the list of characteristics that render a waste hazardous beyond the existing four. Instead, EPA listed the constituents of hazardous waste streams that have been shown in reputable scientific studies to have toxic, carcinogenic, mutagenic, or teratogenic effects on human or other forms of life and generally required that these waste streams be managed under Subtitle C. 40 C.F.R. Part 261, Appendices VII-VIII. EPA has listed scores of hazardous waste streams, typical waste sources, and hazardous waste–generating processes, as well as hundreds of specific hazardous substances. See id. §§261.31-261.33, 261.35. In Dithiocarbamate Task Force v. EPA, 98 F.3d 1394 (D.C. Cir. 1996), the court invalidated a series of waste listings because EPA failed to consider all of the regulatory factors for determining whether a waste containing toxic constituents is capable of posing a substantial threat to health or the environment when improperly managed. But in Environmental Def. Fund v. EPA, 210 F.3d 396 (D.C. Cir. 2000), the court upheld EPA's decision not to list 14 solvent wastes as hazardous, rejecting the claim that EPA violated its own regulations by examining

r. Certain solid wastes, such as household waste, waste generated by the growing or harvesting of crops or the raising of animals, mining overburden returned to the mine site, some geologically sequestered CO_2, and wastes associated with the exploration or production of crude oil, natural gas, or geothermal energy, are excluded from the definition of hazardous waste. 40 C.F.R. §261.4. See also RCRA §§3001(b)(2)-(3), 8002.

s. State law definitions of hazardous waste may be more expansive than RCRA definitions. See 42 U.S.C. §6929.

only the toxicity of the spent solvents and not the toxicity of other constituents that might mix with the solvents to form a larger waste stream.

RCRA authorizes waste generators to petition the agency to delist their wastes. §3001(f). To succeed, the petitioner must demonstrate that a specific waste generated by an individual facility is not hazardous because of plant-specific variations in raw materials, processes, or other factors.

Characteristic Hazardous Wastes. Of the four characteristics, toxicity has proven the most difficult to apply. Cf. United States v. Elias, 269 F.3d 1003 (9th Cir. 2001) (rejecting the claim that the regulatory definition of reactive waste was so vague as to render criminal convictions for its violation unconstitutional). Initially, EPA established an extraction procedure (EP) leach test for measuring toxicity. Under the EP test, the toxicity of a waste was determined by measuring the potential for its toxic constituents to leach out and contaminate groundwater at levels that would create health or environmental concerns under conditions of improper management. See 45 Fed. Reg. 33,110 (1980). In 1990, the agency replaced that test with the Toxicity Characteristic Leaching Procedure (TCLP) test. The TCLP test still aims to determine whether a waste poses a threat to health or the environment if it is mismanaged, but EPA added 25 organic chemicals to the list of toxic constituents of concern. For a more extensive description of how the TCLP test is conducted, see Association of Battery Recyclers, Inc. v. EPA, 208 F.3d 1047 (D.C. Cir. 2000).

The Mixture and "Derived from" Rules. As indicated above, the mixture rule sweeps within Subtitle C any solid waste that is mixed with a listed hazardous waste. The "derived from" rule provides that a waste derived from the treatment, storage, or disposal of a listed waste is also hazardous. In Shell Oil Co. v. EPA, 950 F.2d 741 (D.C. Cir. 1991), the court stunned EPA by vacating both rules on procedural grounds more than a dozen years after their adoption. EPA reissued the rules in 2001, asserting that they continue to be necessary to protect against unacceptable risks. In American Chemistry Council v. EPA, 337 F.3d 1060 (D.C. Cir. 2003), the court upheld the 2001 version of the mixture and "derived from" rules. It was reasonable for EPA to assume that all mixtures of and derivatives from hazardous wastes are themselves hazardous until it can be shown otherwise. Placing the burden on the regulated entity to show the lack of a hazardous characteristic in a mixture or derivative avoids placing on EPA the nearly impossible burden of anticipating the hazardousness or nonhazardousness of every conceivable mixture or derivative that a generator might create. In addition, Congress wanted EPA to err on the side of caution, and the rules were a reasonable exercise of such caution.

NOTE ON MUNICIPAL WASTE COMBUSTION ASH

Many local governments burn their solid wastes. Some do so to recover energy. EPA described the waste produced by waste-to-energy (WTE) facilities as follows:

> Approximately 25 percent (dry weight) of the waste that is combusted remains as ash, amounting to around eight million tons of municipal waste combustor (MWC) ash generated annually. While the ash may be collected at a number of locations within a WTE facility, it typically is characterized as either "bottom ash" or "fly ash." Bottom ash collects at the bottom of the combustion unit and comprises approximately 75-80% of the total ash by weight. Fly ash collects in the air pollution control devices that "clean" the

gases produced during the combustion of the waste and comprises around 20-25% of the total by weight. The fly ash from a WTE facility's different air pollution control devices typically is consolidated and then combined with the bottom ash via enclosed conveyors at the bottom of the MWC where it is cooled and conveyed to a storage area. EPA estimates that nearly 80% of WTE facilities routinely combine their ash. [60 Fed. Reg. 6666, 6666-6667 (1995).]

The issue facing EPA in 1980 was whether to treat MWC ash generated by a WTE facility as a Subtitle C hazardous waste or as a nonhazardous solid waste that could be disposed of in state-regulated, Subtitle D landfills. Why would EPA consider treating the ash that results from the burning of nonhazardous, municipal solid waste as hazardous? The Seventh Circuit explained:

> To borrow a phrase from computer programmers, resource recovery quite literally is "garbage in, garbage out," but the garbage that emerges from the incineration process— ash—is fundamentally different in its chemical composition from the plastic, paper, and other rubbish that goes in. It does not follow that the generation of hundreds of tons of a whole new substance with the characteristic of a hazardous waste should be exempt from regulation just because Congress wanted to spare individual households and municipalities from a complicated scheme if they inadvertently handled hazardous waste. [EDF v. City of Chicago, 948 F.2d 345, 351 (7th Cir. 1991).]

EPA's 1980 regulations excluded "household waste." Although most waste generated by households is nonhazardous in nature, a small portion—such as cleaning fluids and batteries—would have qualified as hazardous under RCRA absent the exclusion. The regulations provided that residues remaining after treatment of household wastes, including incineration, also would be exempt from Subtitle C. As a result, a WTE facility burning only household waste could dispose of the resulting MWC ash in a Subtitle D landfill. If a facility burned nonhazardous industrial waste along with household waste, however, any incinerator ash it produced was deemed hazardous, even though the raw material input was not.

In 1984, Congress enacted §3001(i) of RCRA, titled "Clarification of Household Waste Exclusion." An environmental group sued Chicago in a RCRA citizen suit, claiming that it was illegally disposing of more than 100,000 tons of MWC ash annually at Subtitle D landfills. The issue in City of Chicago v. EDF, 511 U.S. 328 (1994), was whether EPA correctly interpreted §3001(i) as continuing to exempt MWC ash from the definition of hazardous waste. If not, the city would have to dispose of its MWC ash in Subtitle C landfills.

The Court refused to defer to EPA's interpretation. "[S]o long as a facility recovers energy by incineration of the appropriate wastes, it (the facility) is not subject to Subtitle C regulation as a facility that treats, stores, disposes of, or manages hazardous waste. The provision quite clearly does not contain any exclusion for the ash itself." Id. at 334. Citing §1003(b), the Court refused to "interpret the statute to permit MWC ash sufficiently toxic to qualify as hazardous to be disposed of in ordinary landfills." Id. at 335. In short, "while a resource recovery facility's management activities are excluded from Subtitle C regulation, its generation of toxic ash is not." Id. at 337. Justice Stevens dissented, arguing that under §3001(i), both the input and the output of a WTE facility are nonhazardous. Chicago eventually decided to close its municipal garbage incinerators rather than retrofit them with environmental controls.

NOTES AND QUESTIONS

1. *Dueling Objectives.* The desire to both encourage legitimate recycling and prevent activities that pose threats to health and the environment is part of the reason that EPA has had such difficulty ascertaining the appropriate scope of the term "solid waste" under RCRA. Both the majority and dissenting opinions in *City of Chicago* recognized that the same tension affected EPA's implementation of the household waste exclusion. How did EPA's interpretation resolve that tension? What arguments were available to the city to make its case that its activities were exempt from regulation under Subtitle C? Do RCRA's definitions shed light on the persuasiveness of these arguments?

2. *Contingent Management.* Some critics of RCRA have urged the adoption of a "contingent management" approach based on the theory that the risk posed by a waste depends not only on its chemical composition, but also on how it is managed. A waste stream otherwise subject to Subtitle C (because it satisfies a hazardous waste characteristic) would be exempt if its management mitigated the health and environmental risks it poses. EPA endorsed a form of "contingent management" when it relied on §3004(y) of RCRA to exempt from Subtitle C nonchemical military munitions transported or stored in compliance with waste management regulations issued by the Departments of Defense and Transportation. In Military Toxics Project v. EPA, 146 F.3d 948 (D.C. Cir. 1998), the court upheld the exemption. Narrowly construed, the decision does not extend to conditional exemption for wastes managed by the generating industry without oversight by another agency. But the court's rationale may support such an extension. The court interpreted §§3001(a), 3002(a), 3003(a), and 3004(a) as authorizing EPA to decide whether Subtitle C applies based on whether regulation is needed to protect health and the environment.

e. Regulation of Hazardous Waste Generation and Transportation

Regulation of Hazardous Waste Generation Under RCRA. Each generator of solid waste is responsible for determining whether its wastes qualify as hazardous. 40 C.F.R. §262.11. If a generator contracts to have its hazardous waste moved off-site for treatment or disposal, for each waste shipment, it must: originate a detailed manifest, select responsible transporters, specify a fully permitted TSD facility to which delivery is to be made, and report irregularities if receipt is not confirmed. It also must comply with packaging, labeling, and placarding requirements. Generally, hazardous waste generators may not accumulate waste on-site for more than 90 days without engaging in storage requiring a TSD facility permit. §3002; 40 C.F.R. Part 262. Certain small-quantity generators are subject to less onerous requirements.

The Hazardous Waste Electronic Manifest Establishment Act, Pub. L. No. 112-195, 126 Stat. 1452 (2012) (codified at 42 U.S.C. §6939g), required EPA to establish an electronic hazardous waste manifest system for use by hazardous waste generators, transporters, and TSD facility owners or operators. EPA may impose reasonable user fees to cover its costs in developing and operating the system and must deposit such fees in a new fund to be used to establish, operate, manage, and oversee the system. The new system must provide, to the same extent that the paper system does, the ability to track and maintain legal accountability of those certifying that the information provided in a manifest is accurate, acknowledgment of receipt of the manifest, and access by states and the public to information in the manifest. In 2014, EPA issued regulations to facilitate the transition from paper to electronic manifests and to govern operation of the new system. See 79 Fed. Reg. 7518 (Feb. 7, 2014).

   Regulation of Hazardous Waste Transportation Under RCRA and HMTUSA. Tank car explosions or derailments typify the kinds of accidents that can occur during hazardous waste transportation. Subtitle C's requirements for transporters are designed to ensure that wastes remain within the regulated waste handling system. Section 3003, which is aimed at "midnight dumping" by "gypsy haulers," requires compliance with recordkeeping and labeling regulations as well as participation in the manifest system. The implementation of §3003 must be consistent with the requirements of the Hazardous Materials Transportation Uniform Safety Act (HMTUSA) (codified as amended at 49 U.S.C. §§5101-5127). HMTUSA's purpose is to protect against "the risks to life and property arising from the transportation of hazardous material in commerce. §5101. The Secretary of Transportation may designate materials as hazardous and regulate them if their transportation may pose an unreasonable risk to health and safety or property. §5103(a). The Director of the Transportation Security Administration must develop and implement a process for carrying out background checks for drivers hauling hazardous materials. §5103a(g). Motor carriers may transport hazardous materials in commerce only if they have a safety permit, which requires compliance with motor carrier safety rules and financial responsibility requirements. §5109(a). The Secretary must issue standards for states to implement highway routing requirements designed to enhance public safety. §5112(b).

   HMTUSA preempts state and local requirements if compliance with both them and federal requirements is impossible or if compliance with the state or local provision is an obstacle to the implementation of HMTUSA. §5125(a). Some state or local laws (such as those dealing with designation or packaging of hazardous material and container design and manufacture) are preempted if they are "not substantively the same" as ones promulgated under HMTUSA. §5125(b)(1). States may not establish designations for highway routes over which hazardous materials may be transported except in accordance with HMTUSA. §5125(c). The Secretary may waive the preemptive effect of HMTUSA if the state or local requirement is at least as protective as HMTUSA and does not unreasonably burden interstate commerce. §5125(e).

f. Regulation of Hazardous Waste Treatment, Storage, and Disposal

(1) TSD Facility Permits and Performance Standards

   RCRA's most complicated provisions are those that establish a permit system for on- or off-site treatment, storage, and disposal (TSD) of hazardous waste and require compliance by TSD facilities with an extensive array of regulatory requirements. Section 3005(a) prohibits the treatment, storage, or disposal of hazardous waste, or the construction of a new TSD facility, except in accordance with a permit. Disposal begins with an act of disposal, not with a subjective decision to dispose of hazardous waste. United States v. Humphries, 728 F.3d 1028 (9th Cir. 2013). Center for Cmty. Action and Envtl. Justice v. BNSF Ry. Co., 764 F.3d 1019 (9th 2014), held that a railyard operator did not "dispose" of hazardous waste by allowing diesel particulate matter present at the site as a result of train traffic to be blown by wind and air currents offsite to nearby land and waters. Can you recreate the analysis the court could have used to support this conclusion based on relevant RCRA definitions?

EPA (or a state authorized by EPA to administer the TSD facility permit program under §3006) may issue a permit only if the applicant demonstrates compliance with §§3004 and 3005 (§3005(c)(1)), and it may revoke a permit upon finding that the permit holder is not complying with the permit or the requirements of §3004. §3005(d). EPA has authorized most states to implement at least some aspects of the TSD facility permit program. The regulations issued by EPA under §3004 are those that the agency deems "necessary to protect human health and the environment." §3004(a). Suppose a TSD facility violates a state restriction on hazardous waste that federal RCRA regulations do not impose. The regulation was adopted by a state authorized by EPA to administer RCRA's TSD facility permit program. May the United States seek criminal sanctions for violations of the state restriction? See United States v. Southern Union Co., 630 F.3d 17, 28-31 (1st Cir. 2010) (yes).

EPA's regulations prescribe location, design, and construction standards aimed at preventing waste releases during the life of the facility and thereafter. They also establish performance standards for groundwater protection implemented through monitoring and, if necessary, corrective action (i.e., remediation of a contaminated TSD facility). Some of these requirements apply to all kinds of TSD facilities (e.g., 40 C.F.R. Part 264, Subparts A-I), while others apply to specific kinds of facilities, such as surface impoundments, waste piles, landfills, and incinerators (id., Subparts J-O). The TSD facility regulations are meant to prevent landfill leachate from leading to another Love Canal, discussed in the introduction to section F of this chapter. The regulations require that permit holders comply with detailed requirements for chemical treatment, restrictions on the disposal of liquids, site location (away from wetlands and other critical areas), and final site closure. Liner systems must be designed to prevent migration of wastes into adjacent soils or groundwater or surface water during facility life and during a post-closure period, generally 30 years. Certain facilities must have a monitoring program to determine the facility's impact on groundwater. §3004(p).

Upon closing, landfills must be covered and storage and treatment facilities must be decontaminated. Post-closure plans must include an extended period of groundwater monitoring and maintenance activities to ensure the integrity of the final ground cover or containment structures. Deed restrictions required by the regulations in effect create an easement or restrictive covenant that runs with land containing a closed hazardous waste facility. The restrictions must inform subsequent purchasers that the facility is under post-closure RCRA status. The post-closure restriction may be released only if all wastes, waste residues, and contaminated soils are removed from the facility. See 40 C.F.R. §264.119.

The owner or operator of a TSD facility that exists on the effective date of statutory or regulatory changes that first subject it to Subtitle C regulation, that notifies EPA of its operations, and that applies for a permit is treated as if it had a permit until EPA or an authorized state rules on the permit application. §3005(e)(1). These "interim status" facilities must comply with standards that are analogous to but in many respects less stringent than those applicable to finally permitted facilities. 40 C.F.R. Part 264.

(2) Land Disposal Restrictions and Treatment Requirements

Dissatisfied with EPA's progress in promulgating RCRA regulations, Congress adopted the Hazardous and Solid Waste Amendments of 1984 (HSWA). The motivating force behind these amendments to RCRA was a desire to restrict the disposal of hazardous wastes on land. Congress declared that:

> certain classes of land disposal facilities are not capable of assuring long-term containment of certain hazardous wastes, and to avoid substantial risk to human health and the environment, reliance on land disposal should be minimized or eliminated, and land disposal, particularly landfill and surface impoundment, should be the least favored method for managing hazardous waste.

§1002(b)(7). Congress also found that the extent of improper hazardous waste management would likely require expensive, complex, and time-consuming corrective action. §1002(b)(6). RCRA's objectives therefore were expanded to include ensuring that hazardous waste management practices are conducted in a manner that protects health and the environment, requiring proper waste management to reduce the need for corrective action, and minimizing hazardous waste generation and land disposal of hazardous waste through treatment and other means. §1003(a)(4)-(6).

The RCRA provisions designed to achieve those goals reflect the same technology-forcing approach reflected in the Clean Air and Clean Water Acts. HSWA requires, for example, that permits issued after its adoption compel the use by certain kinds of land disposal facilities of liners (described in incredible detail in §3004(o)(5)(B)) and leachate collection systems. §3004(o)(1). The centerpiece of the 1984 amendments, however, is a series of provisions (known collectively as the land disposal restrictions, or LDRs) that limit the land disposal of hazardous wastes. HSWA bans the placement of non-containerized or bulk liquid hazardous wastes in salt dome formations, salt bed formations, underground mines, and caves until EPA finds that those activities are protective of health and the environment and issues performance and permitting standards. §3004(b)(1). It also prohibits the placement of these wastes in landfills. §3004(c)(1).

HSWA also prohibits the land disposal of certain dioxin-containing wastes and halogenated and nonhalogenated solvents. Land disposal includes placement of hazardous waste in facilities such as landfills, surface impoundments, and injection wells. §3004(k). EPA may lift the ban by issuing a finding that the prohibition of one or more methods of land disposal of these wastes "is not required in order to protect human health and the environment for as long as the waste remains hazardous," taking into account the long-term uncertainties associated with land disposal; the goal of managing hazardous waste in an appropriate manner in the first instance; and the persistence, toxicity, mobility, and bioaccumulation propensity of the wastes and their hazardous constituents. The statute precludes such a finding for an untreated hazardous waste unless EPA determines, "to a reasonable degree of certainty, that there will be no migration of hazardous constituents for as long as the waste remains hazardous." §3004(e)(1). A similar set of restrictions applies to the land disposal of liquid hazardous wastes containing free cyanides, metals above specified concentrations, PCBs, and halogenated organic compounds. §3004(d)(1).

HSWA required that EPA review all of the hazardous wastes subject to the restrictions of §3004(d)-(e) that are disposed of by underground injection into deep injection wells. The agency was then to issue regulations by 1988 prohibiting such disposal if "it may reasonably be determined" that it may not be protective of health and the environment, taking into account the same factors that apply to land disposal of the wastes listed in §3004(d)-(e). If EPA failed to make a timely determination for a particular waste, the statute automatically barred its disposal into a deep injection well. §3004(f)(3). The 1984 amendments also compelled EPA to issue LDRs for all other hazardous wastes listed under §3001 in accordance with a statutory schedule. If EPA failed to issue timely restrictions or determine that restrictions are unnecessary, the statute itself, in a series of so-called hammer provisions, either restricted or banned land disposal. §3004(g)(6).

The scope of the LDRs was at issue in NRDC v. EPA, 907 F.2d 1146 (D.C. Cir. 1990). The chemical industry claimed that EPA could not ban the disposal of hazardous waste by deep injection under §3004(f)-(g) and require site-specific deep injection permits because it had failed to make the determination, required by §§3004(f)(2) and 3004(g)(5), that absent a site-specific permitting process, deep injection of hazardous waste might not be protective of human health and the environment for as long as the wastes remain hazardous. But the court found that EPA may ban any method of land disposal of wastes governed by §3004(g) without first determining that the method is not protective of human health and the environment. Indeed, RCRA commands EPA to impose LDRs unless it has made an affirmative determination of safety. Industry also challenged EPA's application of the no-migration standard to the prohibition on disposal by deep injection on the ground that §3004(f) does not contain a no-migration standard similar to the ones found in §3004(d)(1), (e)(1), and (g)(5). The court rejected the attack, holding that it was within EPA's discretion to decide that a disposal method would not be sufficiently protective of health and the environment for purposes of §3004(f)(2) unless it satisfied the no-migration standard.

The issue raised by NRDC in the same case was whether the no-migration standard would be violated if hazardous constituents seeped out of a storage area at a time when some of the stored wastes were still hazardous, but not those actually escaping from the area. Hazardous *constituents*, which are chemical compounds listed in 40 C.F.R. Part 261, Appendix VIII, are defined by molecular formulae without reference to their concentrations. A *waste* is hazardous only if various factors, including the concentration of its hazardous constituents, actually make it hazardous to human health or the environment. NRDC supported a literal reading of the no-migration standard: the migration of even a single molecule would preclude a finding that a land disposal method is protective of health and the environment, even if migrating waste was itself not hazardous. But the court found the phrase "as long as the wastes remain hazardous" to be ambiguous. Because the consistency of wastes may vary throughout an injection zone or disposal unit, wastes near the perimeter may no longer be hazardous even though wastes in another part still are. It was not clear whether hazardous constituents in those nonhazardous wastes could migrate without violating the no-migration standard or whether migration of hazardous constituents was barred until all wastes throughout the injection zone were no longer hazardous. EPA interpreted "the wastes" to refer to the wastes containing the hazardous constituents that are leaving the injection zone. The court deferred to EPA's position that hazardous constituents may migrate so long as they do not do so in high enough concentrations to be hazardous wastes. Does the statutory language support this result?

Section 3004(j) prohibits the storage of hazardous waste subject to the LDRs, unless it is solely for the purpose of accumulating waste quantities necessary to facilitate proper recovery, treatment, or disposal. EPA took the position that the storage of hazardous waste pending development of treatment capacity is not exempt from that prohibition. In Edison Elec. Inst. v. EPA, 996 F.2d 326 (D.C. Cir. 1993), the petitioners argued that when treatment capacity is not available, the only way to "facilitate proper recovery, treatment, or disposal" is to accumulate and store the waste until sufficient capacity becomes available. The court agreed with EPA that §3004(j) does not authorize the indefinite storage of wastes pending development of treatment methods or disposal capacity. Which HSWA policy does this result arguably promote?

The LDRs are not absolute. The statute requires EPA to issue treatment standards simultaneously with the issuance of regulations to implement the LDRs. These standards must specify "those levels or methods of treatment, if any, which substantially diminish the toxicity of the waste or substantially reduce the likelihood of migration of hazardous constituents from the waste so that short-term and long-term threats to human health and the environment are minimized." §3004(m)(1). A hazardous waste that has been treated to the level, or by a method, specified in these treatment regulations is no longer subject to the LDRs. §3004(m)(2). Thus, HSWA in effect · imposes a ban on the land disposal of *untreated* hazardous waste.

COLUMBIA FALLS ALUMINUM CO. v. EPA
139 F.3d 914 (D.C. Cir. 1998)

RANDOLPH, Circuit Judge:

[Small manufacturers of aluminum challenged regulations adopted by EPA under §3004 of RCRA that established a treatment standard for "spent potliner"—a by-product of primary aluminum reduction—and prohibited the land disposal of untreated spent potliner. Aluminum is produced by dissolving aluminum oxide in a molten cryolite bath and introducing a direct electric current to produce aluminum metal. The process occurs in electrolytic steel cells, or pots, lined with brick and carbon. The lining serves as the cathode for the electrolysis process. Over the useful life of the pots, the carbon lining absorbs the cryolite solution and degrades. When the liner cracks, the pot is removed and the steel shell is stripped away, leaving the spent potliner.

At the time EPA issued its regulations, only Reynolds Metals Company was engaged in full-scale treatment of spent potliner. Reynolds' treatment process involved crushing spent potliner to particle size and adding limestone, which reacted with the fluoride in spent potliner to transform it into relatively insoluble calcium fluoride. The mixture was fed into a rotary kiln and heated, after which it was cooled and deposited in an on-site monofill. EPA's treatment standard did not specify a particular technology, but EPA understood that Reynolds provided virtually all capacity for treating spent potliner. EPA expressed the treatment standard in terms of numerical concentration limits for constituents in the waste, including cyanide, toxic metals such as arsenic, polycyclic aromatic hydrocarbons (PAHs), and fluoride. The standards for cyanide and the PAHs were based on a "total composition concentration analysis." For fluoride and the metals, treatment standards were expressed in terms of the TCLP.]

. . . The TCLP is designed to simulate the mobility or leachability of toxic constituents into groundwater following disposal of a hazardous waste in a municipal solid waste landfill. In 1990 EPA adopted the TCLP as the required test for measuring the mobility of toxic metals in all solid wastes.

For solid wastes, the TCLP involves reducing a sample of the waste to particle size and mixing it with an extraction fluid. One of two extraction fluids is used depending on the alkalinity of the waste being tested. Any solid is then discarded and the remaining liquid, called the TCLP extract, is analyzed for toxic contaminants. A solid waste exhibits the characteristic of toxicity if it contains any one of a number of contaminants specified by EPA at a concentration equal to or greater than the regulatory level. . . .

[EPA postponed the effective date of the treatment standard and the prohibition on land disposal of untreated spent potliner. According to the agency, even though the wastes as tested using the TCLP would have complied with the treatment standards for one of the wastes, actual sampling data showed potentially high concentrations of hazardous constituents in the leachate from Reynolds' landfill. Eventually, though, EPA concluded that Reynolds' treatment represented an improvement over the disposal of untreated spent potliner, and it allowed the prohibition on land disposal of untreated potliner to go into effect. The aluminum manufacturers claimed that it was arbitrary and capricious for EPA to continue using the TCLP to measure compliance with the treatment standard once it knew that the test did not accurately predict the mobility of toxic constituents in the actual leachate.]

As discussed above, the concentration limits for fluoride and the toxic metals in spent potliner are expressed in terms of the TCLP. Thus the TCLP cannot be divorced from the standard itself. Because these constituents cannot be destroyed, the goal of treatment is to minimize their mobility. The treatment standard is in fact a model intended to predict the degree to which these constituents will leach following disposal. The problem, as EPA has admitted, is that the model does not work. The leachate "generated from actual disposal of the treatment residues is more hazardous than initially anticipated." 62 Fed. Reg. at 37,695. When tested by the TCLP, the treated spent potliner exhibited numbers that were lower than the regulatory levels for toxic constituents, but tests of the actual leachate revealed numbers above the concentration limits. . . . In its proposal to revoke the delisting of Reynolds' treated spent potliner, EPA described the "residue leachate concentrations" as "orders of magnitude higher than the average predicted TCLP leachate values." 62 Fed. Reg. 41,005, 41,008-09 (1997).

EPA attributes the failure of the TCLP to several factors. It acknowledged . . . that the "extreme alkaline pH conditions that exist in [Reynolds'] monofill were not anticipated by the Agency and are not analogous to" conditions simulated by the TCLP. The TCLP is premised on a "generic mismanagement scenario" in which hazardous waste is deposited in a municipal solid waste landfill, where other wastes would act as buffer agents. Reynolds disposes of treated spent potliner in a monofill—a landfill receiving only spent potliner—where the high pH level remains undiluted. . . . EPA stated:

> In hindsight, it is now apparent that spent potliners are themselves highly alkaline and contain cyanide, arsenic, and fluoride—constituents which are most soluble under alkaline pH. . . . EPA had failed to take into account the effect of alkaline disposal conditions on potliners and potliner treatment residues when promulgating . . . the treatment standard for [the wastes involved]. . . .

62 Fed. Reg. at 37,695. Despite these flaws, the Agency concluded: "Although it is now apparent that the TCLP is not a good model for disposal conditions to which [the

wastes] would be subject, the treatment standard still requires use of the TCLP and any results so obtained that do not exceed the treatment standard are in compliance." 62 Fed. Reg. at 37,696 n.12.

We cannot make sense of EPA's conclusion. Why should the treatment standard for spent potliner be maintained when that standard has no correlation to the actual fate of toxic constituents upon disposal? Petitioners ask this question; EPA gives no good answer. An agency's use of a model is arbitrary if that model "bears no rational relationship to the reality it purports to represent." American Iron & Steel Inst. v. EPA, 115 F.3d 979, 1005 (D.C. Cir. 1997). Models need not fit every application perfectly, nor need an agency "justify the model on an ad hoc basis for every chemical to which the model is applied." Chemical Mfrs. Ass'n v. EPA, 28 F.3d 1259, 1265 (D.C. Cir. 1994). If, however, "the model is challenged, the agency must provide a full analytical defense." Eagle-Picher Indus., Inc. v. EPA, 759 F.2d 905, 921 (D.C. Cir. 1985). Furthermore, EPA "retains a duty to examine key assumptions as part of its affirmative burden of promulgating and explaining a non-arbitrary, noncapricious rule." Small Refiner Lead Phase-Down Task Force v. EPA, 705 F.2d 506, 534 (D.C. Cir. 1983). Here EPA knows that "key assumptions" underlying the TCLP are wrong and yet has offered no defense of its continued reliance on it. . . .

In this case, there is not only no evidence that treated spent potliner is exposed to the disposal conditions that the TCLP simulates, but all available evidence indicates that the treated residue is disposed of in quite different circumstances. It is impossible to say at this point whether the TCLP would be an inaccurate predictor for spent potliner's leachability following all forms of treatment. Certain aspects of the Reynolds treatment process—disposal in a dedicated monofill and the additives it uses—increase alkalinity. The TCLP may or may not work well for other spent potliner treatment technologies. . . .

We therefore conclude that EPA's use of the TCLP is arbitrary and capricious. As a result, we must vacate the treatment standard itself because the concentration limits for fluoride and the metals, including arsenic, are expressed only in terms of the TCLP. . . . Vacating the treatment standard for spent potliner also requires us to vacate the prohibition on land disposal. Contrary to EPA's arguments on appeal, we believe Congress intended treatment standards and land disposal restrictions to operate in tandem. The statutory language indicates as much. RCRA §3004(m) requires that "simultaneously" with the promulgation of prohibitions on land disposal, the Administrator of the EPA shall "promulgate regulations specifying" treatment standards. 42 U.S.C. §6924(m)(1). These regulations are to "become effective on the same date" as any land disposal prohibition. Id. §6924(m)(2).

Pragmatic considerations also strongly suggest that the treatment standard and land disposal restriction are intended to work together. Banning land disposal is a relatively simple task, one that could be accomplished by administrative fiat, but promulgating treatment standards is more complicated. To ensure that EPA would act promptly, Congress enacted an absolute deadline of May 8, 1990—the so-called "hard hammer"—for all hazardous wastes listed or identified as of the time of the 1984 Amendments. This was a powerful incentive for regulatory action because a ban on land disposal without a means of treatment would threaten the closure of entire industries. Under RCRA §3004(j), generators of a waste prohibited from land disposal are also barred from storing it. If we were to vacate the treatment standard for spent potliner without vacating the prohibition on land disposal, aluminum manufacturers might be forced to cease production. . . .

. . . The spent potliner treatment standard and the prohibition on land disposal are vacated and remanded.

Our decision leaves EPA without a regulation governing spent potliner. If EPA wishes to promulgate an interim treatment standard, the Agency may file a motion in this court to delay issuance of this mandate in order to allow it a reasonable time to develop such a standard.

NOTES AND QUESTIONS

1. What was the flaw in EPA's treatment standard for spent potliner? Does the *Columbia Falls* decision threaten the viability of other treatment standards issued under §3004(m)? What relief did the court grant? Should it have left the LDRs in effect despite invalidation of the spent potliner treatment standard? EPA reissued numerical treatment standards on remand "to assure that spent potliners remain prohibited from land disposal." 63 Fed. Reg. 51,254, 51,256 (1998). For another case involving alleged misapplication of the TCLP, see Association of Battery Recyclers, Inc. v. EPA, 208 F.3d 1047 (D.C. Cir. 2000).

EPA approved a new protocol, the Leaching Environmental Assessment Framework (LEAF), to replicate better than the TCLP test leaching that would occur in the natural environment (instead of in a lined landfill) when solid material is exposed to weather conditions and acid rain. Although EPA regards the new test as particularly useful in testing coal ash produced at electric power plants, LEAF will not fully displace the TCLP test. Coal Ash Reuse Tests Mark Early Application of New EPA Leaching Model, Envtl. Policy Alert, Inside EPA, Feb. 5, 2014, at 4.

2. *Risk-Based versus Technology-Based Treatment Standards.* The courts have been called on in other instances to review the legality of §3004(m) treatment standards and the LDRs with which they are associated. In Hazardous Waste Treatment Council v. EPA, 886 F.2d 355 (D.C. Cir. 1989), the legality of EPA regulations governing land disposal of solvents and dioxins under §3004(e) was at issue. The court concluded that §3004(m) authorizes EPA to base treatment standards on either risk-based screening levels or best demonstrated available technology, as long as the effect is to minimize short-term and long-term threats to health and the environment. Which provisions in §3004(m) might the court have relied on to support that reading of the statute? The court remanded the treatment regulations because EPA did not adequately explain why it chose technology-based rather than risk-based screening levels. In particular, EPA impermissibly relied on criticism by members of Congress of the agency's proposal to use risk-based screening levels. On remand, EPA expressed a preference for risk-based treatment levels. Why would risk-based levels arguably be preferable as a matter of policy to technology-based treatment standards? Despite this preference, EPA adopted technology-based standards for solvents and dioxins because it was not yet able, due to the scientific uncertainties involved, to identify constituent concentration levels at which wastes no longer pose risks. See 55 Fed. Reg. 6640 (1990).

3. *Land Treatment.* In American Petroleum Inst. v. EPA, 906 F.2d 729 (D.C. Cir. 1990), the court held that RCRA bars EPA from authorizing land treatment of petroleum refining hazardous wastes under §3004(m). Land treatment involves placing hazardous waste on the ground with the expectation that the hazardous constituents will become less hazardous over time. Citing §3004(k), EPA concluded that it is a type

of land disposal. In a land treatment facility, the treatment of hazardous waste occurs only after the waste has been land disposed. But RCRA requires that hazardous wastes be treated *before* land disposal. What language of §3004(m) supports this analysis?

In Louisiana Envtl. Action Network v. EPA, 172 F.3d 65 (D.C. Cir. 1999), the court upheld an EPA regulation allowing variances under §3004(m) from treatment standards if treatment would likely discourage aggressive remediation. The agency was concerned that the application of overly stringent treatment requirements to waste already in a landfill could discourage excavation and thus prevent any treatment at all. The court distinguished the *API* case, discussed in the previous paragraph, on the ground that it did not address whether EPA, in measuring whether treatment will substantially diminish toxicity or substantially reduce the likelihood of migration, may look beyond the predisposal context.

4. *Treatment of Characteristic Hazardous Wastes.* Both industry and environmental groups challenged the treatment standards for certain characteristic hazardous wastes in Chemical Waste Mgmt. v. EPA, 976 F.2d 2 (D.C. Cir. 1992). Industry argued that EPA lacks the authority to mandate treatment of these wastes beyond the point at which they cease to display hazardous characteristics, claiming that, once a waste ceases to meet the regulatory definition of a hazardous waste, it ceases to be subject to Subtitle C. The court, siding with the agency, held that EPA may bar land disposal of certain wastes unless they have been treated to reduce risks beyond those presented by the characteristics themselves. Environmental petitioners challenged EPA's endorsement of dilution as an acceptable method of treatment. They argued that RCRA requires the use of technological treatment because dilution does not minimize threats to health and the environment or substantially reduce waste toxicity. The court concluded that dilution can constitute an acceptable form of treatment for ignitable, corrosive, or reactive characteristic hazardous wastes, but only if it removes the characteristic and reduces hazardous constituents to concentrations that no longer pose a threat to health or the environment. EPA's justification for the use of dilution sufficed only for corrosive wastes, and, even for those wastes, only to the extent that the wastes do not contain hazardous constituents that, following dilution, would themselves present a continuing danger to health or the environment.

RCRA allows characteristic hazardous waste to escape RCRA treatment requirements if it is disposed of at facilities regulated under the Clean Water Act or the Safe Drinking Water Act, provided the waste no longer exhibits a hazardous characteristic at the time of disposal. §3004(g)(7)-(11).

NOTE ON SITING TSD FACILITIES AND ENVIRONMENTAL JUSTICE

Until the 1970s, location of TSD facilities was regulated, if at all, by local communities through zoning laws. Many communities welcomed such facilities because they added jobs and increased tax revenues. After Love Canal, the perception of the value of these facilities changed and TSD facilities became paradigm examples of the NIMBY ("not in my backyard") syndrome. TSD facilities are widely regarded as LULUs (locally undesirable land uses), which are land uses that pose a higher level of market failure than that usually associated with a land use entering a neighborhood. Fear of the risks that TSD facilities may pose has sparked opposition that cuts across geographical, political, and social class lines. The federal government's approach has been to rely on state siting powers subject to minimal EPA oversight. However, §3004(o)(7) of RCRA requires that EPA promulgate criteria for acceptable TSD location "necessary to protect human health and the environment," and §104(c)(3) of CERCLA required that by 1989 each state provide the agency with assurances that it has adequate TSD capacity to handle all hazardous wastes expected to be generated in the state for the next 20 years.

Much of the concern over the siting of TSD facilities has concentrated on their location in poor and minority neighborhoods. In 1987, the United Church of Christ Commission on Racial Justice issued a report that found race to be the most significant variable in the location of hazardous waste facilities and that these facilities were concentrated in areas with high minority populations. Toxic Wastes and Race in the United States: A National Report on the Racial and Socio-Economic Character-istics of Communities with Hazardous Waste Sites (1987). This conclusion forms the basis of the environmental justice or environmental racism movement, see R. Bullard, Dumping in Dixie: Race, Class, and Environmental Quality (1990), but the link between racial discrimination and the location of new and expanded facilities is disputed. The initial environmental justice suits, which alleged intentional discrim-ination, did not succeed. See Lazarus, Pursuing "Environmental Justice": The Dis-tributional Effects of Environmental Protection, 87 Nw. U. L. Rev. 787, 834 (1993). A second generation of lawsuits was commenced under Title VI of the Civil Rights Act of 1964, which prohibits discrimination in the distribution of federal or federally financed benefits, including regulatory decisions. President Clinton's 1994 Executive Order No. 12,898, 3 C.F.R. 859 (1995), and EPA guidance allowed plaintiffs to infer a disparate impact from permits resulting in a net increase in pollution. Is the presence of disparate impact arising from the location of a TSD or other facility that generates adverse environmental impacts sufficient to maintain a private right of action for a violation of the Civil Rights Act?

SOUTH CAMDEN CITIZENS IN ACTION v. NEW JERSEY DEPARTMENT OF ENVIRONMENTAL PROTECTION
274 F.3d 771 (3d Cir. 2001)

GREENBERG, Circuit Judge . . .

This matter comes on before this court on appeals by defendant-appellant New Jersey Department of Environmental Protection ("NJDEP") and intervenor-appellant St. Lawrence Cement Co., L.L.C. ("St. Lawrence") from the district court's order granting preliminary injunctive relief to plaintiffs, South Camden Citizens in Action and ten residents of the Waterfront South neighborhood of Camden, New Jersey. Plaintiffs brought this action pursuant to 42 U.S.C. §1983 . . . claiming NJDEP dis-criminated against them by issuing an air permit to St. Lawrence to operate a facility that would have an adverse disparate racial impact upon them in violation of Title VI of the Civil Rights Act of 1964, 42 U.S.C. §§2000d to 2000d-7.

Our opinion focuses on whether, following the Supreme Court's recent decision in Alexander v. Sandoval, 532 U.S. 275 (2000), plaintiffs can maintain this action under section 1983 for disparate impact discrimination in violation of Title VI and its implementing regulations. . . . [W]e hold that an administrative regulation cannot create an interest enforceable under section 1983 unless the interest already is implicit in the statute authorizing the regulation, and that inasmuch as Title VI proscribes only intentional discrimination, the plaintiffs do not have a right enforceable through a 1983 action under the EPA's disparate impact discrimination regulations. Because the district court predicated its order granting injunctive relief on section 1983, we will reverse. . . .

[T]he residents of Waterfront South are predominantly minorities and the neighborhood is disadvantaged environmentally. Waterfront South contains two Superfund sites, several contaminated and abandoned industrial sites, and many currently operating facilities, including chemical companies, waste facilities, food processing companies, automotive shops, and a petroleum coke transfer station. Moreover, NJDEP has granted permits for operation of a regional sewage treatment plant, a trash-to-steam incinerator and a co-generation power plant in the neighborhood. As a result, Waterfront South, though only one of 23 Camden neighborhoods, hosts 20% of the city's contaminated sites and, on average, has more than twice the number of facilities with permits to emit air pollution than exist in the area encompassed within a typical New Jersey zip code.

[St. Lawrence supplied cement materials to the ready-mix concrete industry. It processed ground granulated blast furnace slag (GBFS), a by-product of the steel-making industry, used in Portland cement. In 1998, St. Lawrence wanted to open a GBFS grinding facility on a site it leased in Camden. Community members opposed St. Lawrence's application to NJDEP for construction and operation permits based on environmental justice and air quality concerns. Plaintiffs filed an administrative complaint with EPA and a request for a grievance hearing with NJDEP, alleging that NJDEP's permit review procedures violated Title VI of the Civil Rights Act of 1964 because those procedures did not include an analysis of the allegedly racially disparate adverse impact of the facility. NJDEP did not respond to the grievance hearing request. Instead, it issued St. Lawrence's final air permit.

Plaintiffs then filed a complaint against NJDEP, alleging that its issuance of the permit violated Title VI by intentionally discriminating against them in violation of §601, 42 U.S.C. §2000d. They asserted that the facility's operation under the permit would have an adverse disparate impact on them in violation of §602, 42 U.S.C. §§2000d-1. St. Lawrence intervened. The district court, on April 19, 2001, granted plaintiffs' request for a preliminary injunction (*South Camden I*). It found that §602 and its implementing regulations contained an implied private right of action and remanded to NJDEP for a Title VI analysis.]

South Camden I, however, had a short shelf life. On April 24, 2001, the Supreme Court issued its decision in *Sandoval*, holding that "[n]either as originally enacted nor as later amended does Title VI display an intent to create a freestanding private right of action to enforce regulations promulgated under §602. We therefore hold that no such right of action exists." 121 S. Ct. at 1523. [Instead of dissolving the injunction, the district court allowed plaintiffs to amend their complaint to add a claim to enforce §602 through §1983.] On May 10, 2001, the court issued a supplemental opinion and order continuing the preliminary injunction based on plaintiffs' section 1983 claim and again remanding the matter to NJDEP for a Title VI analysis (*South Camden II*). [The court relied on Powell v. Ridge, 189 F.3d 387 (3d Cir. 1999), in which the court had held that there was a private right of action to enforce a regulation implementing Title VI and that a disparate impact discrimination claim could be maintained under §1983 for a violation of a regulation promulgated pursuant to §602.]

. . . Naturally, in view of *Sandoval*, the overarching legal issue on this appeal is whether plaintiffs can advance a cause of action to enforce section 602 of Title VI and its implementing regulations through section 1983. If they cannot, then the only basis on which they can obtain relief is to demonstrate that the NJDEP engaged in intentional discrimination, a possibility that we do not address on this appeal.

[In *Sandoval*,] the Court held that a private right of action is not available to enforce disparate impact regulations promulgated under Title VI, thus overruling *Powell* at least to the extent that it held to the contrary. [The Court] found that section 602's text and structure did not evince an intent to create a private right of action and that the regulations alone were insufficient to create [one]. Therefore, the Court held that a private right of action was not available to enforce regulations promulgated under section 602. However, inasmuch as the plaintiffs in *Sandoval* did not advance a cause of action under section 1983 to enforce Title VI and its implementing regulations, the majority did not consider whether such an action is available.

Resolution of this issue, therefore, requires us to examine whether disparate impact regulations promulgated pursuant to section 602 may, and if so do, create a right that may be enforced through a section 1983 action.

Section 1983 provides, in relevant part:

> Every person who, under color of any statute, ordinance, regulation, custom, or usage, of any State or Territory or the District of Columbia, subjects, or causes to be subjected, any citizen of the United States or other person within the jurisdiction thereof to the deprivation of any rights, privileges, or immunities secured by the Constitution and laws, shall be liable to the party injured in any action at law, suit in equity, or other proper proceeding for redress.

Therefore, section 1983 provides a remedy for deprivation under color of state law of "any rights . . . secured by the Constitution and laws." In Maine v. Thiboutot, 448 U.S. 1, 6-8 (1980), the Supreme Court . . . held that causes of action under section 1983 are not limited to claims based on constitutional or equal rights violations. Rather, certain rights created under federal statutes are enforceable through section 1983 as well. This rule, however, is limited by two well-recognized exceptions. First, a section 1983 remedy is not available "where Congress has foreclosed such enforcement of the statute in the enactment itself." Wright v. City of Roanoke Redev. & Hous. Auth., 479 U.S. 418, 423 (1987). Second, the remedy is not available "where the statute did not create enforceable rights, privileges, or immunities within the meaning of §1983." Id.

The Supreme Court has established a three-part test to determine whether a federal statute creates an individual right enforceable through a section 1983 action:

> First, Congress must have intended that the provision in question benefit the plaintiff. Second, the plaintiff must demonstrate that the right assertedly protected by the statute is not so "vague and amorphous" that its enforcement would strain judicial competence. Third, the statute must unambiguously impose a binding obligation on the States. In other words, the provision giving rise to the asserted right must be couched in mandatory, rather than precatory, terms.

Blessing v. Freestone, 520 U.S. 329, 340-41 (1997). If a plaintiff satisfies each of these elements, and therefore establishes and identifies a federal right that allegedly has been violated, a rebuttable presumption that the right is enforceable through section 1983 arises. We have found two circumstances, which in harmony with *Wright*, are sufficient to rebut this presumption: where "Congress specifically foreclosed a remedy under §1983, [either] expressly, by forbidding recourse to §1983 in the statute itself, or impliedly, by creating a comprehensive enforcement scheme that is incompatible with individual enforcement under §1983." *Powell*, 189 F.3d at 401. In the former case, the plaintiff's claim must fail. In the latter case, however, the burden shifts to the defendant to "make the difficult showing that allowing a §1983 action to go forward in these circumstances 'would be inconsistent with Congress' carefully tailored scheme.'" Id.

Here, plaintiffs seek to enforce a prohibition on disparate impact discrimination that does not appear explicitly in Title VI, but rather is set forth in EPA regulations. They contend that the regulations are a valid interpretation of Title VI.[6] Section 601 of Title VI provides:

> No person in the United States shall, on the ground of race, color, or national origin, be excluded from participation in, be denied the benefits of, or be subjected to discrimination under any program or activity receiving Federal financial assistance.

42 U.S.C. §2000d. Section 602 provides, in relevant part:

> Each Federal department and agency which is empowered to extend Federal financial assistance to any program or activity, by way of grant, loan, or contract other than a contract of insurance or guaranty, is authorized and directed to effectuate the provisions of section 2000d [Section 601] of this title with respect to such program or activity by issuing rules, regulations, or orders of general applicability which shall be consistent with achievement of the objectives of the statute authorizing financial assistance in connection with which the action is taken.

Id. §2000d-1. Finally, the EPA regulations at issue provide:

> No person shall be excluded from participation in, be denied the benefits of, or be subjected to discrimination under any program or activity receiving EPA assistance on the basis of race, color, [or] national origin. . . .
>   A recipient shall not use criteria or methods of administering its program which have the effect of subjecting individuals to discrimination because of their race, color, national origin, or sex, or have the effect of defeating or substantially impairing accomplishment of the objectives of the program with respect to individuals of a particular race, color, national origin, or sex.

40 C.F.R. §§7.30 & 7.35(b). According to plaintiffs, these statutory provisions and their complementary regulations prohibiting discriminatory impacts in administering programs create a federal right enforceable through section 1983.

This contention raises the question of whether a regulation can create a right enforceable through section 1983 where the alleged right does not appear explicitly in the statute, but only appears in the regulation. . . .

6. We assume without deciding that the regulations are valid, as neither NJDEP nor St. Lawrence timely challenged them in the district court and our analysis does not turn on their validity. That being said, like the Court stated in *Sandoval*, we observe that there does seem to be considerable tension between the section 602 regulations proscribing activities that have a disparate impact and section 601's limitation to interdiction only of intentionally discriminatory activities.

In considering whether a regulation in itself can establish a right enforceable under section 1983, we initially point out that a majority of the Supreme Court never has stated expressly that a valid regulation can create such a right. . . . [The courts of appeals had split on the question of whether a regulation alone may create a right enforceable under §1983.]

. . . To start with, we reiterate that in *Sandoval* the Court made the critical point that "[l]anguage in a regulation may invoke a private right of action that Congress through statutory text created, but it may not create a right that Congress has not." 121 S. Ct. at 1522. Furthermore, . . . the Court's focus in *Wright* was on tying Congress' intent to create federal rights through the statute to the particular federal right claimed. It was of paramount importance that Congress intended to create such a right in the statute, with the regulation then defining the right that Congress already conferred through the statute.

Moreover, it is apparent that in the Court's section 1983 jurisprudence after *Wright* dealing with whether a plaintiff is advancing an enforceable right, the primary consideration has been to determine if Congress intended to create the particular federal right sought to be enforced. . . .

Therefore, we follow *Wright*, in accordance with its actual holding, [and] the teaching of *Sandoval*, . . . and hold that the EPA's disparate impact regulations cannot create a federal right enforceable through section 1983. To the extent, if any, that *Powell* might be thought on a superficial reading to suggest otherwise, in the light of *Sandoval* we cannot regard it as stating controlling law. Since the time of the Supreme Court's decision in *Sandoval*, it hardly can be argued reasonably that the right alleged to exist in the EPA's regulations, namely to be free of disparate impact discrimination in the administration of programs or activities receiving EPA assistance, can be located in either section 601 or section 602 of Title VI.

In reaching our result, we emphasize the following. *Sandoval* made it clear that section 601 proscribes intentional discrimination only. In discussing whether section 602 and its implementing regulations created an implied right of action, the Court first considered whether Congress intended to create a federal right in favor of the plaintiffs. . . . [T]he Court found that there was no evidence of congressional intent to create new rights under section 602. Rather, "§602 limits agencies to 'effectuat[ing]' rights already created by §601." [121 S. Ct. at 1521.]

Inasmuch as the Court found previously that the only right conferred by section 601 was to be free of intentional discrimination, it does not follow that the right to be free from disparate impact discrimination can be located in section 602. In fact, it cannot. . . . [T]he regulations do more than define or flesh out the content of a specific right conferred upon the plaintiffs by Title VI. Instead, the regulations implement Title VI to give the statute a scope beyond that Congress contemplated, as Title VI does not establish a right to be free of disparate impact discrimination. Thus, the regulations are "too far removed from Congressional intent to constitute a 'federal right' enforceable under §1983." Harris v. James, 127 F.3d 993, 1009 (11th Cir. 1997). . . .

We emphasize that the implications of this case are enormous. . . . It is plain that in view of the pervasiveness of state and local licensing provisions and the likely applicability of Title VI to the agencies involved, the district court's opinion has the potential, if followed elsewhere, to subject vast aspects of commercial activities to disparate impact analyses by the relevant agencies. Indeed, we noted in *Powell* that "[a]t least 40 federal agencies have adopted regulations that prohibit disparate-impact discrimination pursuant to [§602]." *Powell*, 189 F.3d at 393. While we do not express an opinion on whether that would be desirable, we do suggest that if it is to happen, then Congress and not a court should say so as a court's authority is to interpret rather than to make the law. . . .

McKEE, Circuit Judge, dissenting: . . .

The issue here, simply stated, is whether §1983 provides an independent avenue to enforce disparate impact regulations promulgated under §602 of Title VI. That is the same question that was posed in *Powell*. We answered it in the affirmative in *Powell*, and the answer was not overturned by the subsequent *holding* in *Sandoval*. . . .

The majority reasons that inasmuch as the *Sandoval* majority did not find the requisite Congressional intent for a private cause of action in the statute there can be no enforceable right under §1983. . . .

However,

> [An enforceable right under §1983] is a different inquiry than that involved in determining whether a private right of action can be implied in a particular statute. In right of action cases we employ the four-factor test [from Cort v. Ash, 422 U.S. 66 (1975)] to determine whether Congress intended to create the private remedy asserted for the violation of statutory rights. The test reflects a concern, grounded in separation of powers, that Congress rather than the courts controls the availability of remedies for violations of statutes. *Because §1983 provides an alternative source of express congressional authorization of private suits, these separation-of-powers concerns are not present in a §1983 case.* Consistent with this view, we recognize an exception to the general rule that §1983 provides a remedy for violation of federal statutory rights only when Congress has affirmatively withdrawn the remedy. [Wilder v. Virginia Hosp. Assoc., 496 U.S. 498, 508 n.9 (1990) (emphasis added).] . . .

NOTES AND QUESTIONS

1. What procedural opportunities to seek redress for alleged discrimination in plant siting did the Supreme Court's decision in *Sandoval* preclude? Why didn't EPA's Title VI regulations provide a basis for the plaintiffs' suit to enjoin NJDEP's permitting of the St. Lawrence facility? See also Save Our Valley v. Sound Transit, 335 F.3d 932 (9th Cir. 2003) (holding that a Department of Transportation regulation prohibiting the recipients of federal funds from taking actions that have the effect of discriminating on the basis of race did not create an individual right that can be enforced under §1983).

What opportunities does Title VI continue to provide for halting the siting of TSD and other pollution-generating facilities after the principal case? Mank, *South Camden Citizens in Action v. New Jersey Department of Environmental Protection*: Will Section 1983 Save Title VI Disparate Impact Suits?, 32 Envtl. L. Rep. 10454 (2002), states that environmental justice advocates can continue to file Title VI administrative complaints with EPA. Accordingly, "EPA still needs to consider how to address environmental justice challenges similar to the South Camden situation." Id. at 10477. Professor Mank asserts that the district court "correctly interpreted EPA's §602 disparate impact regulations to impose an independent duty on [federal funds] recipients to go beyond compliance with existing regulations to examine whether a permit decision will have significantly unjustified disparate impacts on a minority group protected by the statute." Id.

A subsequent effort by the plaintiffs in the principal case to prove a violation of §601 of Title VI due to intentional discrimination by the NJDEP, and to demonstrate an actionable nuisance against St. Lawrence, failed. South Camden Citizens in Action v. New Jersey Dep't of Envtl. Prot., 62 Env't Rep. Cas. (BNA) 1175 (D.N.J. 2006). See generally Lewis, Changing the Bathwater and Keeping the Baby: Exploring New Ways of Evaluating Intent in Environmental Discrimination Cases, 50 St. Louis U. L.J. 469 (2006) (urging courts to look for evidence that government decisionmakers were motivated by an unconscious intent to discriminate).

In Rosemere Neighborhood Ass'n v. EPA, 581 F.3d 1169 (9th Cir. 2009), the court found "a consistent pattern of delay" by EPA in responding to Title VI administrative complaints. For example, "EPA failed to process a single complaint from 2006 or 2007 in accordance with its regulatory deadlines." Id. at 1175. EPA's Office of Civil Rights continues to experience a significant backlog in responding to Title VI complaints. See Hill, A Tale of Two Sections, 29 Envtl. F. 24 (Sept./Oct. 2012).

2. *Environmental Injustice.* The United Church of Christ issued a follow-up to its seminal 1987 report, Toxic Waste and Race at Twenty: 1987-2007 (R. Bullard et al. eds., March 2007). The report concludes that "many of our communities not only face the same problems they did [in 1987], but now they face new ones because of government cutbacks in enforcement, weakening health protection, and dismantling the environmental justice regulatory apparatus." The report finds "clear evidence of racism where toxic waste sites are located and the way the government responds to toxic contamination emergencies in people of color communities." Id. at vii.

3. *The Dormant Commerce Clause and TSD Facility Siting.* Are there other laws that either facilitate or restrict the siting of TSD facilities? The courts have created important limitations on state power to exclude TSD facilities through aggressive use of the dormant Commerce Clause to limit state attempts to impose limitations on all forms of waste imports. See Chapter 2, section F. Section 3009 of RCRA allows state and local government to adopt regulations more stringent than EPA's, but courts have held that RCRA preempts state and local siting policies that in effect amount to a total facility ban. Blue Circle Cement, Inc. v. Board of County Comm'rs, 27 F.3d 1499 (10th Cir. 1994). The court did suggest that a county could justify a total ban under §3009 "if the county consisted only of densely populated residential areas and the hazardous waste activity in fact posed a significant threat to health or safety."

g. Regulation of Nonhazardous Solid Waste

The Solid Waste Disposal Act, whose Subtitle C provisions apply to hazardous waste, also addresses the environmental risks posed by the management of nonhazardous municipal solid waste. The Act finds that land disposal of solid as well as hazardous waste without proper planning and management can threaten health and the environment, that open dumping is harmful to all environmental media and to the public health, and that alternative methods of land disposal are needed to prevent cities from running out of suitable solid waste disposal capacity. §1002(b). The SWDA's objectives therefore include providing technical and financial assistance to state and local governments to develop solid waste management plans, prohibiting future open dumping and requiring the upgrading of existing open dumps, providing guidelines for solid waste management practices, and establishing a cooperative effort among all levels of government and private enterprise to recover valuable materials and energy from solid waste. §1003(a).

These objectives have a far less prescriptive feel about them than do those dealing with hazardous waste management. Congress envisioned state and local governments retaining most of the authority to regulate solid waste management practices; the federal government's role would revolve around the provision of information and financial resources. Subtitle D reflects that allocation of authority. The SWDA requires EPA to adopt suggested guidelines for solid waste management that describe attainable levels of performance and provide minimum criteria for use by the states in defining the practices that constitute the open dumping of solid waste. §1008(a). See also §4004(a) (EPA must issue regulations that distinguish between open dumps and sanitary landfills). EPA also must publish guidelines to assist the states in developing and implementing solid waste management plans. §4002(b). See 40 C.F.R. Part 256.

States must submit their plans for EPA approval. Each state plan must prohibit the establishment of new open dumps and require that all solid wastes be either used for resource recovery or disposed of in sanitary landfills. §4003(a)(2). See also §4005(a) (prohibiting the open dumping of solid or hazardous waste after the promulgation of EPA's §1008(a) criteria). An open dump is a solid waste disposal facility that is neither a sanitary landfill nor a hazardous waste TSD facility. §1004(14). A sanitary landfill is a facility that complies with the design and performance criteria issued by EPA under §4004. §1004(26). The prohibition on open dumping is not enforceable by EPA, but citizen suits may be brought to enjoin open dumping. §4005(a). State plans also must provide for the closing or upgrading of open dumps and, more generally, for whatever combination of resource conservation or recovery and solid waste disposal practices is necessary for sound waste management. §4003(a)(3), (6). EPA must approve a state plan if it satisfies §4003's requirements and provides for plan revisions after notice and public hearing. §4007(a). States with approved plans are eligible for federal financial assistance. §4007(b).

According to EPA's Report on the Environment: 2008 (May 2008), the quantity of municipal solid waste generated in the United States grew by 185 percent between 1960 and 2006, while the U.S. population increased by 66 percent. Per capita municipal solid waste generation increased from 2.7 pounds per person per day in 1960 to 4.6 pounds per person per day in 2006. Since 1990, the amounts of this waste sent to landfills fell from 69 to 55 percent, while the amount recycled rose from 14 to 24 percent. Id. at 4-25.

IX

ENVIRONMENTAL CONTAMINATION LIABILITY AND REMEDIATION

The regulatory programs for the management of toxic substances and hazardous waste discussed in the preceding chapter are primarily prospective in orientation. Inevitably, efforts to comply with regulations designed to ensure proper management of these substances will sometimes fall short, resulting in spills, leaks, or other causes of environmental contamination. Even if statutes such as RCRA succeed in preventing harm from the operation of active waste treatment, storage, and disposal facilities, many inactive or abandoned dump sites will continue to threaten health and natural systems. Sites no longer receiving wastes often are difficult to clean up for several reasons. Some sites are "orphan" sites: no one knows who operated or used them. Others are the work of "midnight dumpers," who used unoccupied land as a waste commons and then disappeared. Some businesses that generated the substances sent to the site, transported those substances to the site, or owned the site at the time of disposal may have gone out of business or into bankruptcy. These factors often make it difficult to identify parties that are capable of financing remediation. Even if it is possible to locate those parties, attempts to allocate responsibility among them may be frustrating. The nature or quantity of wastes present at a site, and the amounts sent or managed by the various identified contributors, may be impossible to establish because records have been lost or destroyed, if any existed at all. It may seem unfair to assign responsibility to a solvent entity whose contribution to the site appears to have been minimal, while assets of more culpable entities do not exist or cannot be reached.

Even if the government can identify and allocate liability among responsible parties with the resources to finance site remediation, it may be difficult to select the appropriate remedy. Remediation may be physically impossible, such as where groundwater has been contaminated with dense, non-aqueous-phase liquids (those with a specific gravity greater than that of water). Where it is not, questions concerning the appropriate extent of remediation abound. Should efforts be made to restore contaminated resources to their precontamination state? What role should cost play in the selection of a remedy? If a multi-million-dollar cleanup technology is capable of reducing the risk of disease attributable to exposure by 99 percent, but simply capping the site can reduce the risk by 95 percent at a fraction of the cost, which remedy should be chosen? The price tag of cleaning up hazardous substance releases is enormous. See, e.g., GAO, EPA's Estimated Costs to Remediate Existing Sites Exceed Current Funding Levels, and More Sites Are Expected to Be Added to the National Priorities List, GAO-10-380 (May 2010).

These kinds of questions are not confined to the contamination of land and groundwater by hazardous chemicals. Oil spills in lakes and oceans present similar legal and practical problems. The principal weapon available to the federal government in its efforts to finance and implement the remediation of sites contaminated by hazardous substances is the Comprehensive Environmental Response, Compensation, and Liability Act (CERCLA), 42 U.S.C. §§9601-9675. CERCLA authorizes EPA to issue orders requiring responsible parties to engage directly in remediation efforts. It also authorizes the government to clean up contaminated sites and to seek reimbursement of its cleanup costs from responsible parties. Although CERCLA creates a strict liability scheme, questions about the fairness of imposing substantial liabilities on parties whose responsibility for site contamination seemed remote have prompted both Congress and the courts to incorporate into this liability scheme principles of causation and fault that have moved the statutory liability scheme closer to the traditional tort law model. The Oil Pollution Act of 1990 (OPA), enacted in response to the 1989 *Exxon Valdez* oil spill, creates a similar remediation and liability structure for oil spills. The explosion of the Deepwater Horizon drilling rig off the coast of Louisiana in April 2010 raised questions about the appropriateness of OPA's liability caps, as well as the government's technical capacity to respond in a timely and effective fashion to massive oil spills. Section D of this chapter addresses liability for oil spills under the OPA.

The first two sections of this chapter provide background information on CERCLA. Section A discusses the history of CERCLA's adoption and amendment, while section B summarizes the statutory scheme and provides an assessment of its impact. Sections C through E analyze the statutory provisions relating to liability for response costs, imminent and substantial endangerments, and natural resource damages, respectively. Section D, on imminent and substantial endangerments, covers not only the CERCLA provisions allowing the government to respond to emergencies resulting from hazardous substance releases that threaten health and the environment, but also the analogous RCRA and OPA provisions relating to government responses to oil spills. That section thus provides a thorough introduction to legal responses to spills and other imminent hazards under three important statutes. Section F covers the regulatory component of CERCLA by focusing on the process of determining cleanup goals. Section G addresses the effect of the discovery of hazardous substances on real estate transactions, under both CERCLA and state law, although earlier portions of the chapter also implicate that material.

A.   THE HISTORY AND PURPOSES OF CERCLA

SUPERFUND AMENDMENTS AND REAUTHORIZATION ACT OF 1986

H.R. Rep. No. 99-253, pt. 1, at 1-2 (1985), reprinted in 1986 U.S.C.C.A.N. 3124-3125

Hazardous waste contamination of the Nation's ground and surface water resources has become perhaps the most significant and troublesome water quality problem facing the country for the remainder of this century. With the ability to render vast quantities of water unfit for use without treatment, toxins that leach and flow [from] thousands of active and abandoned waste sites all across the Nation pose costly and often controversial cleanup and public health problems for government officials at all levels.

During the late 1970s, Federal laws then in existence were found to be inadequate for dealing with the problem of abandoned toxic waste sites such as "Love Canal" in Niagara Falls, New York and the "Valley of the Drums" in Brooks, Kentucky. Special funds in other statutes were simply inadequate for meeting the large costs of cleaning up the thousands of often buried and corroding drums of toxic wastes found at these sites, and so were the laws that would have allowed regulators to hold those responsible for these toxic dumps—the generators, transporters and waste site operators—for the costs of cleaning them up.

On December 11, 1980, the Congress responded to these inadequacies in the Federal laws by enacting the "Comprehensive Environmental Response, Compensation, and Liability Act of 1980" (P.L. 96-510), commonly referred to as the "Superfund" law.

The Origins of CERCLA. CERCLA represents Congress's effort to rectify decades of careless waste disposal practices. The basic idea behind CERCLA is simple: it places responsibility for cleaning up sites on the responsible parties but provides seed money for federal site study and cleanups. The implementation of these concepts, however, has proved anything but simple. Part of the problem stems from the fact that CERCLA was patched together during the last days of the Carter administration. At the last minute, the Senate bypassed the conference procedures and presented the House with a quickly worked-out compromise between the versions being considered by the two legislative bodies. As a result, there is little conventional legislative history. A court commented acerbically that CERCLA is "so badly drafted as to be virtually incomprehensible" and that it resembles King Minos's labyrinth in ancient Crete. See In re Acushnet River & New Bedford Harbor Proceedings Re Alleged PCB Pollution, 675 F. Supp. 22, 26 n.2 (D. Mass. 1987). See also Commander Oil Corp. v. Barlo Equipment Corp., 215 F.3d 321, 326 (2d Cir. 2000) (denigrating "CERCLA's miasmatic provisions"). One court has referred to RCRA and CERCLA as "[t]wo environmental statutes everyone loves to hate." Voggenthaler v. Maryland Square LLC, 724 F.3d 1050, 1055 (9th Cir. 2013).

Implementation Problems. Congress originally anticipated that only a few hundred facilities needed cleanup and that the task could be accomplished relatively quickly by "removing containers or scraping a few inches of soil off the ground." H.R. Rep. No. 99-253, pt. 1, at 54 (1985), reprinted in 1986 U.S.C.C.A.N. 2836. It established a fund of $1.6 billion, originally called the Hazardous Substance Response Trust Fund but more commonly known as the Superfund. The fund was financed by taxes on chemical feedstocks, on certain imported substances from chemical feedstocks, and on domestic and imported petroleum, and by a corporate environmental tax equal to a small percentage of an alternative minimum taxable income in excess of $2 million annually. In addition, the statute authorized the federal government to replenish the fund when it was reimbursed for its cleanup costs in litigation against responsible parties initiated under §107 or in litigation settlements. The initial $1.6 billion fund, however, turned out to be woefully inadequate, even when restocked with litigation recoveries from responsible parties. The number of sites in need of remediation far outstripped what Congress initially anticipated. Instead of the anticipated quick and simple cleanups, CERCLA remediation often involved the pumping and treatment of contaminated groundwater aquifers that lasted for years.

The 1986 and Subsequent Amendments. The Superfund Amendments and Reauthorization Act of 1986 (SARA) increased the trust fund, now formally renamed the Superfund, to $8.6 billion to be spent over five years. Congress added another $5.1 billion in 1990. SARA imposed deadlines on EPA to initiate and implement various phases of remediation at sites on the agency's National Priorities List. It established more detailed criteria for the selection of remedies and provided enhanced opportunities for public participation in the remedy selection process. Congress has amended CERCLA several times since 1986 to mitigate the alleged unfairness of its liability scheme. As indicated below, these amendments clarified the scope of preexisting liability exemptions (such as the lender liability or "innocent landowner" exemptions) or created new ones.

Superfund Financing and the Pace of Cleanup. Congress allowed the special taxes that used to finance the Superfund to expire in 1995 and has refused to reauthorize them. By the end of fiscal year 2003, the Superfund had no tax revenue left. Since then, cleanups have been financed by general revenue that Congress appropriates to the program, by interest earned on amounts in the fund, and by litigation recoveries. Unfortunately, annual congressional funding for the Superfund declined at the same time as cost recoveries in litigation brought by the government did. Cost recovery awards peaked in 2001 at about $562 million, falling to about $110 million in 2004. Schiffer, How Litigation Shaped Superfund, 22 Envtl. F. No. 4 (July/August 2005), at 17, 24.

These developments had two consequences. First, a greater share of the cleanup costs incurred by EPA must now be derived from general revenues, thus shifting a significant share of the responsibility for paying for the cleanup of Superfund sites from industry to the public at large. Second, the pace of cleanups has slowed. The GAO found in 2010 that the limited funds available to EPA under CERCLA were delaying the commencement of and impairing its ability to conduct cleanups at sites posing healthy risks. GAO, EPA's Estimated Costs, *supra.*

B. AN OVERVIEW OF CERCLA

The Cleanup Process. CERCLA authorizes the President (who has delegated his authority to EPA) to respond to hazardous substance releases and recover cleanup costs from parties responsible for creating the problems. Section 104(a)(1) of the Act authorizes EPA to take any response measure consistent with the National Contingency Plan (NCP) that is necessary to protect the public health or welfare or the environment in two situations: (1) whenever a hazardous substance is released or there is a substantial threat of a release into the environment; or (2) whenever there is a release or substantial threat of a release of a pollutant or contaminant that may present an imminent and substantial danger to the public health or welfare. The statute designates certain substances as hazardous by reference to other federal laws. §101(14). EPA may add others to the list if they present substantial danger to the public health or welfare or the environment when released. §102(a).

Response actions may take one of two forms: short-term responses to emergencies such as a spill or leak, called removal actions; and long-term, permanent cleanups, called remedial actions. See §101(23)-(24). EPA may not undertake remedial action unless the state in which the release of hazardous substance occurs has entered into a contract or cooperative agreement with EPA that provides assurances that the state will maintain all future removal and remedial actions. The state also must agree to pay a minimum of 10 percent of the cost of a cleanup. §104(c)(3). A hazardous waste management facility may not receive wastes from a Superfund site unless the facility is in compliance with RCRA. §121(d)(3).

The National Contingency Plan and the National Priorities List. CERCLA requires that EPA issue a national hazardous substance response plan to establish procedures and standards for responding to hazardous substance releases. §105(a). This NCP, published at 40 C.F.R. Part 300, acts as a kind of blueprint for CERCLA cleanups. The NCP must include methods for discovering and investigating facilities at which hazardous substances are located, for evaluating and remedying releases or threats thereof, for determining the appropriate extent of remediation, and for ensuring that remedial actions are cost-effective. Persons in charge of a facility who have knowledge of a release in excess of EPA-designated reportable quantities must notify the government or risk criminal penalties. §103(a)-(b). The NCP includes rules for remedy selection, discussed in section F.2, derived from §121.

The NCP also must include criteria for determining priorities for responding to releases or threatened releases throughout the United States, based on relative risk to public health or welfare or the environment. EPA must use these criteria to compile a National Priorities List (NPL) of response targets, including, to the extent practicable, one facility designated by each state as the one presenting the greatest threat. §105(a)(8); 40 C.F.R. Part 300, Appendix B. EPA has included in the NCP a Hazard Ranking System (HRS) for determining which sites merit inclusion on the NPL; sites that receive a sufficiently high HRS score are placed on the NPL. A site's inclusion on the NPL does not commit EPA to remediation there or impose liability on anyone for the costs of any response taken at the site. Rather, the NPL's purpose is to "identify, quickly and inexpensively, sites that may warrant further action under CERCLA." Eagle-Picher Indus., Inc. v. EPA, 759 F.2d 905, 911 (D.C. Cir. 1985). But, under EPA regulations, only sites on the NPL are eligible to receive money from the Superfund for remediation. 40 C.F.R. §300.425(b)(1). Remedial actions at sites on the NPL account for a small percentage of CERCLA response actions. Between 1983 and mid-2014, EPA listed 1,701 sites on the NPL. As of mid-2014, cleanup remedies were in place at 68 percent of these sites. EPA deemed about 39 percent of NPL sites to be suitable for redevelopment because all necessary long-term protections were in place.

The Superfund. Money from the Superfund may be used to pay costs incurred by the federal government in responding to releases or threatened releases, reimburse private parties for expenditures approved by EPA and incurred in a manner consistent with the NCP, pay for the costs of assessing natural resource damages attributable to hazardous substance releases, and reimburse local governments for carrying out temporary emergency measures. A person who presents a claim to the owner or operator of a facility from which a release occurred and to other responsible parties who is not satisfied within 60 days may seek reimbursement from the Superfund. §112(a). If the United States pays a claim out of the fund, it is subrogated to the claimant's right to recover from responsible parties. §112(c)(1).

Abatement Orders. As an alternative to cleaning up the site by itself or through contractors, the federal government may bring suit in federal district court to require responsible parties to abate an imminent and substantial endangerment due to an actual or threatened release of hazardous substances. The district courts are authorized to grant whatever relief "the public interest and the equities of the case may require." EPA may issue administrative orders to accomplish the same result. §106(a). A person who willfully violates such an order without sufficient cause is subject to fines of up to $25,000 per day of noncompliance. A person who complies with a §106 order is eligible for reimbursement from the Superfund if it can demonstrate that it was not responsible for the release. §106(b).

Cost Recovery and Natural Resource Damage Actions. If EPA expends fund monies for a removal or remedial action instead of using §106 to force responsible parties to perform the cleanup, it may recover its costs from four classes of "potentially responsible parties" (PRPs): (1) current owners or operators of vessels or facilities that contain hazardous substances, (2) owners or operators at the time of disposal, (3) persons who arranged for disposal, and (4) certain persons who transported hazardous substances to the facility at which the release occurred. §107(a). The statute affords a limited range of liability defenses that has expanded over the years. The ground rules for the imposition of §107 liability appear to depart from the standards of liability that apply in more traditional civil litigation such as common law tort actions. Liability is retroactive (i.e., the statute applies to activities that took place before CERCLA's adoption), strict, and in many cases joint and several. The causal link that a CERCLA plaintiff must demonstrate between a PRP's activities and the release that caused the incurrence of response costs is sometimes tenuous. CERCLA also authorizes federal and state agencies to seek recovery for injury to, destruction of, or loss of natural resources linked to hazardous substance releases. See section E.

In certain circumstances, private parties may bring contribution, and sometimes cost recovery actions against PRPs, but they normally may not sue for injuries to public natural resources, and the statute provides no cause of action for personal injuries or property damage. CERCLA includes a citizen suit provision that authorizes litigation against persons alleged to be in violation of statutory or regulatory provisions and against EPA for failure to perform nondiscretionary duties. §310.

Responding to assertions that CERCLA's liability net unfairly and unwisely sweeps too broadly, Congress has whittled away at the scope of response cost and natural resource damage liability. In the Superfund Recycling Equity Act of 1999, Congress created exemptions from arranger liability for the disposal of hazardous substances by certain entities engaged in recycling transactions. 42 U.S.C. §9627. The Small Business Liability Relief and Brownfields Revitalization Act of 2002 exempted from arranger liability entities that sent small volumes of materials to facilities listed on the NPL and certain persons who sent municipal solid waste to such facilities. It also exempted contiguous property owners and bona fide prospective purchasers from owner-operator liability. See CERCLA §107(o)-(r). The 2002 amendments created a program designed to facilitate the cleanup of brownfields and the conversion of such sites to productive use. §104(k). In addition, §113(f)(1) can mitigate potential unfairness by authorizing PRPs held jointly and severally liable to file contribution actions against other PRPs.

Assessments of CERCLA. CERCLA's track record is mixed. On the one hand, according to Senator Baucus of Montana, Superfund's underlying principle that the "polluter pays" "changed our country for the better" by "deterr[ing] pollution[,] . . . encourag[ing] environmental audits and investments in technology that prevent pollution[, and making] . . . everyone realize pollution does carry a price and that polluters must be held accountable."[a] By one account,

> EPA has achieved a high level of success [under CERCLA]. After starting out with little or no practical knowledge of the problems to be addressed, the Agency has, over time, developed institutional capability and expertise, solved problems, improved relationships, and ultimately established a program that operates effectively and performs a critical function in society. Tens of thousands of contaminated sites have been evaluated, short-term removal actions have been taken at several thousand of those sites, and longer term remedial actions are slowly being completed at the most severely contaminated sites. A topic of intense public concern—once dominated by controversy and emotion—has been brought under control, buttressed by sound technical understanding and a general public recognition that actions that should be taken are being taken. [Quarles & Steinberg, The Superfund Program at Its 25th Anniversary, 36 Envtl. L. Rep. 10364, 10365-10366 (2006).]

On the other hand, Senator Baucus conceded that "Superfund has not lived up to its goal of quickly and economically cleaning up toxic dumps" and that it is perhaps "best known for expensive cleanups, excessive delays, and for being a cash cow for lawyers." By one account, "[n]o other environmental statute has been the source of so much controversy—or so much litigation." Quarles & Steinberg, supra, at 10364. The statute's liability system has repeatedly been criticized as both unfair and inefficient. Critics have charged that too much money has been allocated not to cleanup but to "transaction costs," including legal costs incurred by PRPs seeking contribution from other PRPs:

> At a purely practical level, the allocation system is encumbered by the huge evidentiary challenges of determining whose waste went to which site, especially with respect to activities that occurred two, three, four, or five decades earlier, even sometimes dating back to the 19th century. This funding mechanism has raised vast amounts of money to pay for many costly cleanups, but the investigation, negotiation, and litigation it has spawned are notorious. It is not a system one wants to lean on except under absolute necessity. [Id. at 10366.]

Still others complain that too few sites have been cleaned up to justify the billions of dollars thrown at the problem. They have attacked the remedies chosen by EPA as too expensive, inefficient, and inconsistent from site to site. See, e.g., Hamilton & Viscusi, Calculating Risks: The Spatial and Political Dimensions of Hazardous Waste Policy (1999) (criticizing the CERCLA remediation process for failure to consider explicit tradeoffs that balance benefits and costs and supporting more flexible remedy decisions based on comparative risk assessment). Finally, according to some observers, CERCLA helped to depress the market value of older industrial facilities whose prospective buyers feared contamination and resulting liability. Investments were diverted from inner-city industrial areas characterized by chronically high levels of unemployment that could have benefited from redevelopment to undeveloped "greenfield" sites. See generally H.R. Rep. No. 103-582, pt. 1, at 76-77 (1994); S. Rep. No. 103-349, at 4-5 (1994).

---

a. Superfund Reform Act of 1994: Hearings on S. 1834 before the Subcomm. on Superfund, Recycling, and Solid Waste Management, of the Sen. Comm. on Env't and Pub. Works, 103d Cong., pt. 2, at 1 (1994).

The controversy over CERCLA is likely to continue. EPA continues to add new sites to the NPL, and response actions proceed at the sites of newly discovered releases. A significant percentage of Americans still live within four miles of a Superfund site. See generally Symposium, CERCLA at 25: A Retrospective, Introspective, and Prospective Look at the Comprehensive Environmental Response, Compensation and Liability Act on Its 25th Anniversary, 18 Tul. Envtl. L.J. 299 (2005).

The rest of this chapter fleshes out this barebones description of CERCLA and provides an opportunity for you to make your own assessment of CERCLA. It may be useful to return to this section as you proceed through the chapter to refresh your recollection as to how the various components of CERCLA fit together.

C. LIABILITY FOR REMEDIATION OF HAZARDOUS SUBSTANCES

1. Proving a Prima Facie Case for CERCLA Liability

a. Overview

What does the federal government or a state that has incurred costs responding to a release or threatened release of hazardous substances need to show to prevail in a cost recovery action under §107(a)? City of Colton v. American Promotional Events, Inc.-W., 614 F.3d 998, 1002-1003 (9th Cir. 2010), summarized the plaintiff's burden of proof in such an action as follows:

> To establish a prima facie claim for recovery of response costs under section 107(a), a private-party plaintiff must demonstrate: (1) the site on which the hazardous substances are contained is a "facility" under CERCLA's definition of that term, 42 U.S.C. §9601(9); (2) a "release" or "threatened release" of any "hazardous substance" from the facility has occurred, 42 U.S.C. §9607(a)(4); (3) such "release" or "threatened release" has caused the plaintiff to incur response costs[b] that were "necessary" and "consistent with the national contingency plan," 42 U.S.C. §§9607(a)(4) and (a)(4)(B); and (4) the defendant is within one of four classes of persons subject to the liability provisions of Section 107(a).

The United States or a state seeking response cost recovery bears the same burden, except that, as indicated below, it need not show that response costs were necessary and consistent with the national contingency plan.

This section of the chapter addresses each of those elements of a CERCLA prima facie case. The first principal case provides an overview of CERCLA liability and raises several issues elaborated on later in the chapter. The remainder of section C.1 addresses the plaintiff's need to prove that (a) a release or threat of a release (b) of

---

b. Chubb Custom Ins. Co. v. Space Sys./Loral, Inc., 710 F.3d 946 (9th Cir. 2013), held that an insurance company that reimbursed its insureds for the latter's response costs could not bring a cost recovery action against PRPs who owned land next to the insured's contaminated land under a subrogation theory. Payment of an insurance claim does not amount to "incurrence" of response costs for purposes of §107(a), so the insurer is not an appropriate cost recovery plaintiff.

hazardous substances (c) from a facility occurred, and also touches on the kinds of costs that are recoverable in a §107(a) cost recovery action. Section C.2 addresses CERCLA's standard of liability, including available affirmative defenses. Section C.3 identifies the kinds of defendants, or potentially responsible parties (PRPs) who can be held liable. Section C.4 considers how those PRPs held liable can seek reimbursement from other PRPs, either through cost recovery or contribution actions.

NEW YORK v. SHORE REALTY CORP.
759 F.2d 1032 (2d Cir. 1985)

OAKES, Circuit Judge:

This case involves several novel questions about the scope of the Comprehensive Environmental Response, Compensation, and Liability Act of 1980, 42 U.S.C. §§9601-9657 (1982) ("CERCLA"). . . . CERCLA—adopted in the waning hours of the Ninety-sixth Congress, and signed by President Carter on December 11, 1980— was intended to provide means for cleaning up hazardous waste sites and spills, and may generally be known to the public as authorizing the so-called Superfund, the $1.6 billion Hazardous Substances Response Trust Fund, 42 U.S.C. §§9631-9633.

On February 29, 1984, the State of New York brought suit against Shore Realty Corp. ("Shore") and Donald LeoGrande, its officer and stockholder, to clean up a hazardous waste disposal site at One Shore Road, Glenwood Landing, New York, which Shore had acquired for land development purposes. At the time of the acquisition, LeoGrande knew that hazardous waste was stored on the site and that cleanup would be expensive, though neither Shore nor LeoGrande had participated in the generation or transportation of the nearly 700,000 gallons of hazardous waste now on the premises. . . . Apparently relying at least in part on CERCLA, [the district court] directed by permanent injunction that Shore and LeoGrande remove the hazardous waste stored on the property, subject to monitoring by the State, and held them liable for the State's "response costs," see 42 U.S.C. §9607(a)(4)(A). . . .

We affirm, concluding that Shore is liable under CERCLA for the State's response costs. We hold that Shore properly was found to be a covered person under 42 U.S.C. §9607(a); that the nonlisting by the Environmental Protection Agency ("EPA") of the site on the National Priorities List ("NPL"), 42 U.S.C. §9605(8)(B), is irrelevant to Shore's liability; that Shore cannot rely on any of CERCLA's affirmative defenses; but that . . . injunctive relief under CERCLA is not available to the State. . . .

. . . In 1980, while the Senate considered one early version of CERCLA, the House considered and passed another. The version passed by both Houses, however, was an eleventh hour compromise put together primarily by Senate leaders and sponsors of the earlier Senate version. . . .

As explained in F. Anderson, D. Mandelker, & A. Tarlock, Environmental Protection: Law and Policy 568 (1984), CERCLA was designed "to bring order to the array of partly redundant, partly inadequate federal hazardous substances cleanup and compensation laws." It applies "primarily to the cleanup of leaking inactive or abandoned sites and to emergency responses to spills." Id. And it distinguishes between two kinds of response: remedial actions—generally long-term or permanent containment or disposal programs—and removal efforts—typically short-term cleanup arrangements.

CERCLA authorizes the federal government to respond in several ways. EPA can use Superfund resources to clean up hazardous waste sites and spills. 42 U.S.C. §9611.

The National Contingency Plan ("NCP"), prepared by EPA pursuant to CERCLA, id. §9605, governs cleanup efforts by "establish[ing] procedures and standards for responding to releases of hazardous substances." At the same time, EPA can sue for reimbursement of cleanup costs from any responsible parties it can locate, id. §9607, allowing the federal government to respond immediately while later trying to shift financial responsibility to others. Thus, Superfund covers cleanup costs if the site has been abandoned, if the responsible parties elude detection, or if private resources are inadequate. In addition, CERCLA authorizes EPA to seek an injunction in federal district court to force a responsible party to clean up any site or spill that presents an imminent and substantial danger to public health or welfare or the environment. Id. §9606(a). In sum, CERCLA is not a regulatory standard-setting statute such as the Clean Air Act. Rather, the government generally undertakes pollution abatement, and polluters pay for such abatement through tax and reimbursement liability.

. . . [S]tates, like EPA, can sue responsible parties for remedial and removal costs if such efforts are "not inconsistent with" the NCP. Id. §9607(a)(4)(A). . . . Moreover, "any . . . person" who is acting consistently with the requirements of the NCP may recover "necessary costs of response." Id. §9607(a)(4)(B). Finally, responsible parties are liable for "damages for injury to, destruction of, or loss of natural resources, including the reasonable costs of assessing such injury, destruction, or loss resulting from such a release." 42 U.S.C. §9607(a)(4)(C). . . .

Congress intended that responsible parties be held strictly liable, even though an explicit provision for strict liability was not included in the compromise. Section 9601(32) provides that "liability" under CERCLA "shall be construed to be the standard of liability" under section 311 of the Clean Water Act, 33 U.S.C. §1321, which courts have held to be strict liability, and which Congress understood to impose such liability. . . . Strict liability under CERCLA, however, is not absolute; there are defenses for causation solely by an act of God, an act of war, or acts or omissions of a third party other than an employee or agent of the defendant or one whose act or omission occurs in connection with a contractual relationship with the defendant. 42 U.S.C. §9607(b).

Discussion

A.   Liability for Response Costs under CERCLA

We hold that the district court properly awarded the State response costs under section 9607(a)(4)(A). The State's costs in assessing the conditions of the site and supervising the removal of the drums of hazardous waste squarely fall within CERCLA's definition of response costs, even though the State is not undertaking to do the removal. See id. §§9601(23), (24), (25). . . .

1. *Covered Persons.* [Section 9607(a) of] CERCLA holds liable four classes of persons . . . if "there is a release, or a threatened release which causes the incurrence of response costs, of a hazardous substance" from the facility,[16] for, among other things,

---

16. The phrase "from which there is a release, or a threatened release which causes the incurrence of response costs, of a hazardous substance" is incorporated in and seems to flow as if it were a part only of subparagraph (4), but it is quite apparent that it also modifies subparagraphs (1)-(3) inclusive. . . .

"all costs of removal or remedial action incurred by the United States Government or a State not inconsistent with the national contingency plan."

Shore argues that it is not covered by section 9607(a)(1) because it neither owned the site at the time of disposal nor caused the presence or the release of the hazardous waste at the facility. While section 9607(a)(1) appears to cover Shore, Shore attempts to infuse ambiguity into the statutory scheme, claiming that section 9607(a)(1) could not have been intended to include all owners, because the word "owned" in section 9607(a)(2) would be unnecessary since an owner "at the time of disposal" would necessarily be included in section 9607(a)(1). Shore claims that Congress intended that the scope of section 9607(a)(1) be no greater than that of section 9607(a)(2) and that both should be limited by the "at the time of disposal" language. By extension, Shore argues that both provisions should be interpreted as requiring a showing of causation. We agree with the State, however, that section 9607(a)(1) unequivocally imposes strict liability on the current owner of a facility from which there is a release or threat of release, without regard to causation.[17]

Shore's claims of ambiguity are illusory; section 9607(a)'s structure is clear. Congress intended to cover different classes of persons differently. Section 9607(a)(1) applies to all current owners and operators, while section 9607(a)(2) primarily covers prior owners and operators. Moreover, section 9607(a)(2)'s scope is more limited than that of section 9607(a)(1). Prior owners and operators are liable only if they owned or operated the facility "at the time of disposal of any hazardous substance"; this limitation does not apply to current owners, like Shore. . . .

Shore's causation argument is also at odds with the structure of the statute. Interpreting section 9607(a)(1) as including a causation requirement makes superfluous the affirmative defenses provided in section 9607(b), each of which carves out from liability an exception based on causation. Without a clear congressional command otherwise, we will not construe a statute in any way that makes some of its provisions surplusage.[18] . . .

Furthermore, as the State points out, accepting Shore's arguments would open a huge loophole in CERCLA's coverage. It is quite clear that if the current owner of a site could avoid liability merely by having purchased the site after chemical dumping had ceased, waste sites certainly would be sold, following the cessation of dumping, to new owners who could avoid the liability otherwise required by CERCLA. Congress had well in mind that persons who dump or store hazardous waste sometimes cannot be located or may be deceased or judgment-proof. We will not interpret section 9607(a) in any way that apparently frustrates the statute's goals, in the absence of a specific congressional intention otherwise. . . .

---

17. We pause to note the distinction between whether §9607(a) imposes strict liability and whether it requires a showing of causation. That is to say, finding that §9607(a) imposes strict liability does not rebut Shore's causation argument. Traditional tort law has often imposed strict liability while recognizing a causation defense. See W. Prosser, Handbook of the Law of Torts §79, at 517 (1971).

18. The phrase "from which there is a release, or a threatened release which causes the incurrence of response costs, of a hazardous substance" also limits the scope of §9607(a)(1). See *supra* note 16. It is, however, clumsy grammatically, and ambiguous since the absence of a comma after the words "threatened release" and the use of the words "which causes," as opposed to "that causes," leave it uncertain whether there is liability from a release without the incurrence of "response costs." Since response costs were incurred here, the ambiguity is academic for our purposes.

2. *Release or Threat of Release.* We reject Shore's repeated claims that it has put in dispute whether there has been a release or threat of release at the Shore Road site. The State has established that it was responding to "a release, or a threatened release" when it incurred its response costs. We hold that the leaking tanks and pipelines, the continuing leaching and seepage from the earlier spills, and the leaking drums all constitute "releases." 42 U.S.C. §9601(22). Moreover, the corroding and deteriorating tanks, Shore's lack of expertise in handling hazardous waste, and even the failure to license the facility, amount to a threat of release.

In addition, Shore's suggestion that CERCLA does not impose liability for threatened releases is simply frivolous. Section 9607(a)(4)(A) imposes liability for "all costs of removal or remedial action." The definitions of "removal" and "remedial" explicitly refer to actions "taken in the event of the threat of release of hazardous substances."

3. *The NPL and Consistency with the NCP.* Shore also argues that, because the Shore Road site is not on the NPL, the State's action is inconsistent with the NCP and thus Shore cannot be found liable under section 9607(a). This argument is not frivolous. Section 9607(a)(4)(A) states that polluters are liable for response costs "not inconsistent with the national contingency plan." And section 9605, which directs EPA to outline the NCP, includes a provision that requires EPA to publish the NPL. Nevertheless, we hold that inclusion on the NPL is not a requirement for the State to recover its response costs. . . .

. . . [W]e hold that NPL listing is not a general requirement under the NCP. We see the NPL as a limitation on remedial, or long-term, actions—as opposed to removal, or short-term, actions—particularly federally funded remedial actions. The provisions requiring the establishment of NPL criteria and listing appear to limit their own application to remedial actions. . . .

Moreover, limiting the scope of NPL listing as a requirement for response action is consistent with the purpose of CERCLA. The NPL is a relatively short list when compared with the huge number of hazardous waste facilities Congress sought to clean up. And it makes sense for the federal government to limit only those long-term-remedial-efforts that are federally funded. We hold that Congress intended that, while federally funded remedial efforts be focused solely on those sites on the NPL, states have more flexibility when acting on their own.

Finally, we reject Shore's argument that the State's response costs are not recoverable because the State has failed to comply with the NCP by not obtaining EPA authorization, nor making a firm commitment to provide further funding for remedial implementation nor submitting an estimate of costs. . . . Congress envisioned states' using their own resources for cleanup and recovering those costs from polluters under section 9607(a)(4)(A). We read section 9607(a)(4)(A)'s requirement of consistency with the NCP to mean that states cannot recover costs inconsistent with the response methods outlined in the NCP. . . .

4. *Affirmative defense.* Shore also claims that it can assert an affirmative defense under CERCLA, which provides a limited exception to liability for a release or threat of release caused solely by [a third party under §9607(b)(3)]. We disagree. Shore argues that it had nothing to do with the transportation of the hazardous substances and that it has exercised due care since taking control of the site. Who the "third part(ies)" Shore claims were responsible is difficult to fathom. It is doubtful that a prior owner could be such, especially the prior owner here, since the acts or omissions

referred to in the statute are doubtless those occurring during the ownership or operation of the defendant. Similarly, many of the acts and omissions of the prior tenants/operators fall outside the scope of section 9607(b)(3), because they occurred before Shore owned the property. In addition, we find that Shore cannot rely on the affirmative defense even with respect to the tenants' conduct during the period after Shore closed on the property and when Shore evicted the tenants. Shore was aware of the nature of the tenants' activities before the closing and could readily have foreseen that they would continue to dump hazardous waste at the site. In light of this knowledge, we cannot say that the releases and threats of release resulting of these activities were "caused solely" by the tenants or that Shore "took precautions against" these "foreseeable acts or omissions."

B. Injunctive Relief Under CERCLA

Having held Shore liable under CERCLA for the State's response costs, we nevertheless are required to hold that injunctive relief under CERCLA is not available to the State. Essentially, the State urges us to interpret the right of action under section 9607 broadly, claiming that "limiting district court relief [under section 9607] to reimbursement could have a drastic effect upon the implementation of Congress's desire that waste sites be cleaned." Conceding that section 9607 does not explicitly provide for injunctive relief, the State suggests that the court has the inherent power to grant such equitable relief. . . .

The statutory scheme, however, shows that Congress did not intend to authorize such relief. Section 9606 expressly authorizes EPA to seek injunctive relief to abate "an actual or threatened release of a hazardous substance from a facility." Implying the authority to seek injunctions under section 9607 would make the express injunctive authority granted in section 9606 surplusage. In addition, the scope of injunctive relief under section 9607 would conflict with the express scope of section 9606. The standard for seeking abatement under section 9606 is more narrow than the standard of liability under section 9607. Section 9606 authorizes injunctive relief only where EPA "determines that there may be an imminent and substantial endangerment to the public health or welfare or the environment." Section 9607 contains no such limitation. . . .

[The court also held LeoGrande, an officer and shareholder of Shore, personally liable as an owner/operator under §9607(a)(1).]

NOTES AND QUESTIONS

1. Consider how CERCLA's liability scheme differs from common law tort liability. Why did the court reject Shore's efforts to escape liability on the ground that it did not cause the problem that required remediation by the state? Why didn't Shore qualify for the third-party defense? Why didn't the fact that the contaminated site was not on EPL's NPL bar recovery by the state? Why wasn't EPA's prior approval of the cleanup necessary?

2. *Consistency with the NCP.* Who has the burden of proof on the issue of whether response costs were necessary and were incurred in a manner consistent with the NCP? The simple answer is that in a cost recovery action by the United

States or a state, the PRP must prove inconsistency with the NCP to avoid liability. In a private cost recovery action, however, the plaintiff must prove consistency as part of its prima facie case. See United States v. W.R. Grace & Co., 429 F.3d 1224, 1232 n.13 (9th Cir. 2005). How does the text of §107(a) support that difference?

Putting aside the allocation of the burden of proof, when are response costs consistent with the NCP? Minnesota v. Kalman W. Abrams Metals, Inc., 155 F.3d 1019, 1025 (8th Cir. 1998), disallowed a state's cost recovery claim because a state agency "obstinately insisted on employing an untried, high-risk, high-cost remedy" and failed to study the nature and extent of the contamination problem. Compare Raytheon Aircraft Co. v. United States, 590 F.3d 1112 (10th Cir. 2009) (holding that PRP failed to show that EPA's costs in conducting an expanded site investigation were inconsistent with the NCP simply because the government ultimately decided not to list the site on the NPL). Proof that a remedial action was inconsistent with the NCP is not necessarily a complete defense to a §107 cost recovery action, however. To avoid or reduce liability, a PRP must also show that the failure to comply with NCP procedures resulted in the incurrence of avoidable response costs. See United States v. Burlington N. R.R. Co., 200 F.3d 679 (10th Cir. 1999).

May a cost recovery plaintiff seek declaratory relief for liability for future response costs if it has not yet incurred response costs? See City of Colton v. American Promotional Events, Inc.-W., 614 F.3d 998, 1006-1008 (9th Cir. 2010) (describing split of authority and answering no).

b. Release, Hazardous Substance, and Facility

A plaintiff in a §107(a) action must prove it incurred cleanup costs in response to a release or threatened release of hazardous substances from a facility. The following case addresses the meaning of a "release." Although the case relates to the circumstances in which a release triggers reporting obligations under §102(a), not liability in a §107(a) cost recovery action, the court's analysis is nevertheless potentially relevant to the scope of §107(a) liability if a PRP seeks to avoid liability by denying that a release or threatened release has occurred.

FERTILIZER INSTITUTE v. EPA
935 F.2d 1303 (D.C. Cir. 1991)

HENDERSON, Circuit Judge:

. . . CERCLA requires parties to notify the EPA whenever a reportable quantity (RQ) of a hazardous substance is released into the environment. 42 U.S.C. §9603. Additionally CERCLA vests the EPA with authority to determine what constitutes the RQ of any given hazardous substance and thereby enables the EPA to determine what releases must be reported. 42 U.S.C. §9602(a). . . .

[EPA issued final regulations which set RQs for radionuclides (unstable nuclei that release charged particles that are radioactive). In the preamble to the rule, EPA provided its interpretation of what constitutes a "release" of hazardous substances into the environment, thereby triggering the notification requirement. Numerous businesses petitioned for review of the regulations.]

The preamble to the EPA's final rule states in part:

> The Agency considers the stockpiling of an RQ of a hazardous substance to be a release because any activity that involves the placement of a hazardous substance into any unenclosed containment structure wherein the hazardous substance is exposed to the environment is considered a release. An unenclosed containment structure may allow the hazardous substance to emit, escape, or leach into the air, water, or soil. Thus, the placement of an RQ of a hazardous substance in an unenclosed structure would constitute a "release" regardless of whether an RQ of the substance actually volatilizes into the air or migrates into surrounding water or soil. The same rule applies to the placement of material containing radionuclides in tanks or other containment structures outside a building. If the tank or containment structure is not totally sealed off from the environment, the placement into the containment structure of an amount of a hazardous substance that equals or exceeds an RQ constitutes a reportable release. [54 Fed. Reg. at 22,526.] . . .

In the preamble, [EPA also] interprets CERCLA to require notification whenever a hazardous substance is placed into an "unenclosed containment structure." The EPA defines an unenclosed containment structure as "any surface impoundment, lagoon, tank, or other holding device that has an open side with the contained materials directly exposed to the ambient environment." According to this interpretation, therefore, "the placement of an RQ of a hazardous substance in an unenclosed structure would constitute a 'release' regardless of whether an RQ of the substance actually volatilizes into the air or migrates into surrounding water or soil." Id.

The EPA's interpretation of CERCLA's reporting requirement cannot be reconciled with CERCLA's express terms. Rather than defining a release as the movement of a substance from a facility into the environment (as does CERCLA), the EPA defines a release as the placement of a substance into a facility that is exposed to the environment. For the EPA's interpretation to come within CERCLA's meaning, the exposure of a substance to the environment must be equivalent to the release of that substance into the environment. But this is not so. A simple example exposes the flaw in the EPA's analysis: a company could place a non-volatile substance into an open-air storage container and the consequences of the open-air storage would be no different from those that would occur if the company had placed the substance [in] a closed container. Nonetheless, under the EPA's interpretation, the company would have to report the transfer of the substance to the container notwithstanding the non-volatile substance's inability to escape into the air.

Even in the final rule, the EPA cannot escape the inconsistency caused by equating the mere exposure of a substance to the environment to the release of that substance into the environment. At one point the EPA asserts:

> An unenclosed containment structure may allow the hazardous substance to emit, escape, or leach into the air, water, or soil. Thus, the placement of an RQ of a hazardous substance in an unenclosed structure would constitute a "release" regardless of whether an RQ of the substance actually volatilizes into the air or migrates into surrounding water or soil.

54 Fed. Reg. at 22,526. Implicit in this passage is the recognition that the mere exposure of a substance to the environment does not always result in the release of

that substance into the environment. The EPA attempts to gloss over this incongruity by arguing that the placement of a substance into an unenclosed containment structure creates such a great threat of a release that the EPA is justified in treating it as an actual release. This argument, however, is precisely foreclosed by CERCLA. CERCLA provides that the EPA must be notified when a hazardous substance is actually released into the environment. 42 U.S.C. §9603(a). Nowhere in the statute is there any language requiring that the EPA be notified when there is a threatened release. This omission is especially significant given the sections of CERCLA that expressly distinguish between threats of releases and actual releases. See, e.g., 42 U.S.C. §§9604, 9606. These sections give the EPA the authority to act with reference both to releases and to threatened releases. Under these circumstances, we must presume that Congress's failure to subject threatened releases to the reporting requirement was intentional. Accordingly we reject the EPA's claim that the threat of a release from an unenclosed containment structure is sufficient to allow the EPA to require reporting when a reportable quantity of a hazardous material is put in the structure. Under CERCLA's provisions, nothing less than the actual release of a hazardous material into the environment triggers its reporting requirement. . . .

NOTES AND QUESTIONS

1. For purposes of EPA's reporting regulations, what is an unenclosed containment structure? What was EPA's rationale for defining a release to include placement of hazardous substances into such a structure? According to the court, what was the flaw in that reasoning? If EPA reissued its reporting regulations to include within the definition of a release the placement of a volatile substance into an unenclosed structure, would the regulations be valid? What bearing does your answer to that question have on the persuasiveness of the court's "simple example"? Part of the definition of a "release" in §101(22) of CERCLA is "the abandonment or discarding of barrels, containers, and other closed receptacles containing any hazardous substance or pollutant or contaminant. . . ." The court omitted this language when it quoted the definition of a "release." Is this language relevant? If so, which way does it cut? A facility includes an "installation." What does that term mean? See Litgo New Jersey, Inc. v. Commissioner, New Jersey Dep't of Envtl. Prot., 725 F.3d 369, 384-385 (3d Cir. 2013) (rejecting contention that an installation is a process made up of various discrete pieces of machinery that may or may not be located near each other or used together).

To prove a violation of CERCLA's reporting requirements, must a defendant know that a reportable quantity of a hazardous substance has been released, or merely that a hazardous substance has been released? Must that knowledge be actual or may it be constructive? See §103(a); Sierra Club v. Tyson Foods, Inc., 299 F. Supp. 2d 693, 707 (W.D. Ky. 2003).

2. *Releases and Cost Recovery Actions.* Other cases have addressed the scope of the term "release" in the context of §107 cost recovery actions. See, e.g., Westfarm Assocs. Ltd. P'ship v. Washington Suburban Sanitary Comm'n, 66 F.3d 669 (4th Cir. 1995), which held that the movement of perchloroethylene (PCE) through cracks in a public sewer system onto neighboring property was a release, even though the PCE migrated from another person's land after having been previously released there. Suppose that the government discovers that a metal smelting facility shipped

drums of ore contaminated by lead, a hazardous substance under CERCLA, to Mexico to avoid the costs of disposal in the U.S. The government orders the facility to recover the drums by a certain date and dispose of their contents in a permitted RCRA TSD facility. The facility fails to pick up the drums by the agency's deadline. What arguments can the government make that a release has occurred? Is it likely to prevail? See A & W Smelter & Refiners, Inc. v. Clinton, 146 F.3d 1107 (9th Cir. 1998). Compare Pakootas v. Teck Cominco Metals, Ltd., 452 F.3d 1066, 1074-1075 (9th Cir. 2006) (holding that release occurred when hazardous substances leached from metals slag into facility consisting of a portion of the Columbia River, not previously, when metals smelter discharged slag into the river, or when the slag "escaped" into the U.S. where the Columbia River crossed the border between Canadian border).

3. *Hazardous Substances.* Section 101(14)'s definition of a hazardous substance incorporates by reference materials regulated under the Clean Air and Clean Water Acts, RCRA, and TSCA. EPA may designate as hazardous additional substances which, when released into the environment, may present substantial danger to the public health or welfare or the environment. §102(a). Cost recovery actions rarely turn on disputes over whether hazardous substances are present at the site. PRPs typically concede that they are and fight over whether they are responsible for putting them there. Occasionally, however, this issue presents difficulties. See, e.g., Narragansett Elec. Co. v. EPA, 407 F.3d 1 (1st Cir. 2005) (addressing whether ferric ferrocyanide (FFC) was a hazardous substance, even though it was not specifically named in any of the lists incorporated into §101(14) and EPA had never designated it under §102, because the NCP listed cyanides as a hazardous substance, and EPA alleged that FFC qualified as a cyanide).

Must a substance be present in certain minimal concentrations to be regarded as hazardous? In United States v. Alcan Aluminum Corp., 964 F.2d 252 (3d Cir. 1992) (*Alcan Butler*), the court held that the definition of hazardous substances does not include a threshold concentration requirement so that a PRP was liable even though the level of hazardous substances in its emulsion was below that which naturally occurred in the river. The last sentence of §101(14) excludes from the definition of a hazardous substance certain petroleum products. Tosco Corp. v. Koch Indus., Inc., 216 F.3d 886 (10th Cir. 2000), held that the petroleum exclusion did not apply because hazardous substances had commingled with petroleum products in the soil and groundwater. In Wilshire Westwood Assocs. v. Atlantic Richfield Corp., 881 F.2d 801 (9th Cir. 1989), on the other hand, the exclusion applied to unrefined and refined gasoline, even though some of its indigenous components and refining additives had themselves been designated as hazardous under CERCLA.

4. *Facility.* A CERCLA "facility" includes more than the usual image of a leaking dump site. It includes "virtually any place at which hazardous wastes have been dumped, or otherwise disposed of," such as roadsides where hazardous waste was dumped. United States v. Northeastern Pharmaceutical & Chem. Co., 810 F.2d 726, 743 (8th Cir. 1986). See also Pakootas v. Teck Cominco Metals, Ltd., 452 F.3d 1066, 1074 (9th Cir. 2006) (holding that an area in and along the Columbia River contaminated by heavy metals slag was a facility, because contaminated substances had "come to be located" there). Is a publicly owned treatment works a facility? What is the argument that it is not? See Westfarm Assocs. Ltd. P'ship v. Washington Suburban Sanitary Comm'n, 66 F.3d 669 (4th Cir. 1995); Adobe Lumber Co., Inc. v. Hellman, 658 F. Supp. 2d 1188 (E.D. Cal. 2009). Suppose that two cars driven for personal use

collide, causing a hazardous substance spill from one of the cars. Has there been a release from a facility? See §101(9)(B); Emergency Serv. Billing Corp. v. Allstate Ins. Co., 668 F.3d 459 (7th Cir. 2012).

Exactly what does a facility include? In United States v. Township of Brighton, 153 F.3d 307, 313 (6th Cir. 1998), the court held that the "facility" extended beyond the contaminated portion of a dump. While "the bounds of a facility should be defined at least in part by the bounds of the contamination, . . . an area that cannot be reasonably or naturally divided into multiple parts or functional units should be defined as a single 'facility,' even if it contains parts that are noncontaminated." See also PCS Nitrogen Inc. v. Ashley II of Charleston LLC, 714 F.3d 161, 178-179 (4th Cir. 2013) (concluding that the definition of a facility is not predicated on the area targeted for remediation but by the bounds of the contamination). In Sierra Club v. Seaboard Farms, 387 F.3d 1167 (10th Cir. 2004), the court held that a pig-farming operation that consisted of two farms on contiguous sections of land, each with eight buildings, was a single "facility" for purposes of determining whether the facility's emissions exceeded the reportable quantities under §103. The farm was a "site or area where a hazardous substance has . . . come to be located" under §101(9)(B), was managed as one facility, and had a single purpose—producing swine products. Compare New Jersey Tpk. Auth. v. PPG Indus., Inc., 197 F.3d 96, 105 (3d Cir. Nov. 1999) (rejecting argument that entire eastern spur of the New Jersey Turnpike was a single facility).

Problem 9-1

CERCLA excludes from the definition of a facility "any consumer product in consumer use." §101(9). A tanker truck parked at a trucking terminal ruptured, resulting in the release of hazardous industrial chemicals into the environment. The chemicals would have been delivered to a manufacturer for use in its production process had the rupture not occurred. One of the companies whose chemicals escaped from the ruptured tanker cleaned up the spill and then sued the other shippers and the owner of the truck for reimbursement in a CERCLA contribution action. The defendants claim, first, that CERCLA does not apply because it is limited to disposals of hazardous substances at inactive or abandoned waste sites, and, second, that even if the statute is not confined to waste disposal sites, the release here did not occur at a facility because that term excludes consumer products in consumer use. How should the court rule?

c. Recoverable Response Costs

Removal v. Remedial Actions. Section 107(a) authorizes plaintiffs in actions for reimbursement of cleanup costs to recover "all costs of removal or remedial action incurred by the United States Government or a State or an Indian tribe not inconsistent with the [NCP]." The terms "removal" and "remedial actions" are defined at §101(23)-(24). The distinction is significant because the NCP's procedural and substantive requirements are more detailed and onerous for remedial than removal actions. Morrison Enters. v. McShares, Inc., 302 F.3d 1127, 1136 (10th Cir. 2002).

How does one distinguish between a removal and a remedial action? According to one court, the two statutory definitions overlap: "Attempting to untie the Gordian knot of these definitions solely based on their plain meanings is thus unavailing." United States v. W.R. Grace & Co., 429 F.3d 1224, 1239 (9th Cir. 2005). The court deferred to EPA's position in that case that

> the removal/remedial distinction boils down to whether the exigencies of the situation were such that the EPA did not have time to undertake the procedural steps required for a remedial action, and, in responding to such a time-sensitive threat, the EPA sought to minimize and stabilize imminent harms to human health and the environment.

Id. at 1241. Applying the distinction, the court held that the cleanup of a massive, closed asbestos mining site was a removal action because "absent immediate attention, the airborne toxic particles [at the site] would continue to pose a substantial threat to public health." Id. at 1247. Another court opined that "[t]he one consistent thread in the decisions dealing with whether an action is 'remedial' or 'removal' in nature is that 'removal actions generally are immediate or interim responses, and remedial actions generally are permanent responses.'" City of Moses Lake v. United States, 416 F. Supp. 2d 1015, 1022-1023 (E.D. Wash. 2005).

    Morrison Enters. LLC v. Dravo Corp., 638 F.3d 594 (8th Cir. 2011), held that a city's replacement of drinking water wells as part of an ongoing relocation of its water supply system was a remedial action because of its permanent nature. New York v. Next Millennium Realty, LLC, 732 F.3d 117 (2d Cir. 2013), held that installation of a carbon adsorption system to remove volatile organic compounds from groundwater and an aeration system to treat the water before it was collected in a well and pumped into the adsorption system was a removal action. Both systems were designed to address water contamination at the endpoint (the contaminated wells), not permanently remediate the problem by preventing migration from the underlying source of contamination. The court added that neither the cost nor the duration of a project is determinative of whether it is a removal or remedial action.

    Kinds of Recoverable Response Costs. Exactly what kinds of costs qualify as recoverable response costs? One set of issues involves whether EPA's *overhead and oversight costs* are recoverable. When EPA undertakes removal or remedial action under §104(a) of CERCLA, it may recover from PRPs not only the costs incurred directly by private contractors hired by the government to perform the remediation, but also the agency's costs of supervising the contractor's performance. It also may recover in a §107(a) cost recovery action the indirect overhead costs of administering the Superfund program allocated by the agency to a site remediated by the government or its contractors. See, e.g., *W.R. Grace & Co., supra,* at 1249-1250. Sometimes, however, EPA authorizes PRPs to perform cleanups. May the government recover its costs of overseeing a cleanup paid for and conducted by private parties? See §§101(23), (24), 111(c)(8). United States v. E.I. Dupont de Nemours & Co., 432 F.3d 161 (3d Cir. 2005), held that EPA may recover its costs of supervising either a removal action or a remedial action conducted by a PRP pursuant to a unilateral administrative order issued under §106. The court found that the definitions of both removal action in §101(24) and remedial action in §101(25) cover oversight costs. What might its reasoning have been? The court also concluded that recovery of oversight costs is consistent with CERCLA's objectives because EPA's technical expertise is often a key element of a successful cleanup. See also Atlantic Richfield Co. v. American Airlines, Inc., 98 F.3d 564 (10th Cir. 1996). What effects would a contrary decision have on incentives for PRPs to conduct their own cleanups and on the amount of money in the Superfund?

A second set of issues surrounds efforts in private cost recovery actions to recover *medical monitoring costs* by individuals exposed to released hazardous substances, damage to contaminated property, or relocation costs. Most courts have determined that medical monitoring costs are not recoverable. See, e.g., Daigle v. Shell Oil Co., 972 F.2d 1527 (10th Cir. 1992). What language in §101(23)-(24) supports private plaintiffs' right to reimbursement for such costs? Is there a counterargument? The *Daigle* court concluded that long-term health monitoring of the sort requested by the plaintiffs had nothing to do with preventing contact between a "release or threatened release" and the public, because the release had already occurred. The ability to recover property losses resulting from contamination and relocation costs is also limited. See Colorado v. Idarado Mining Co., 916 F.2d 1486, 1499 (10th Cir. 1990); Tanglewood E. Homeowners v. Charles-Thomas, Inc., 849 F.2d 1568, 1575 (5th Cir. 1988).

Finally, the courts have addressed the recoverability of *attorneys' fees* in suits under §107(a). The leading case is Key Tronic Corp. v. United States, 511 U.S. 809 (1994). The answer turned on whether the "enforcement activities" referred to in §101(25)'s definition of "response" included a private party's attorneys' fees associated with bringing a cost recovery action. The starting point for analysis was Alyeska Pipeline Serv. Co. v. Wilderness Soc'y, 421 U.S. 240 (1975), which recognized the general practice of not awarding attorneys' fees to private litigants absent explicit statutory authorization. The Court then held that the reference in §101(25) to "enforcement activity" is not explicit enough to embody private cost recovery under §107. The Court added, however, that an attorney's work, such as identifying PRPs, that is "closely tied to the actual cleanup" may constitute a necessary cost of response, since that kind of work might be performed by nonlawyers such as engineers or private investigators.

The increased difficulty of recovering attorneys' fees (along with other factors, such as a weakening of the joint and several liability standard discussed below, and the limitations imposed on the ability of PRPs to bring contribution actions against other PRPs discussed in section C.4 below) contributed to a reduction of voluntary cleanup activity. Site owners may be willing to initiate cleanup if they are confident of their ability to bring private cost recovery or contribution actions against other PRPs and to recover not only their cleanup costs, but also their litigation costs. If attorneys' fees and court costs are not recoverable, these owners have less incentive to do anything other than wait until the government, through administrative or judicial action, forces them to begin cleanup.

2.   *Standard of Liability*

The forerunner of modern statutory environmental law was the common law tort action. The causes of action available to a plaintiff whose person or property was injured as a result of the polluting activities of another traditionally have been negligence, trespass, nuisance, and strict liability for abnormally dangerous activities. Both Chapter 1, section F, and Chapter 8, section B, address some aspects of the application of tort law to environmental risk. For present purposes, what is relevant is the need for plaintiffs in each of these tort causes of action to demonstrate a central core of elements that includes some demonstration of culpability on the defendant's part. A plaintiff suing in negligence, for example, must show that the defendant had a duty to the plaintiff and that it breached the duty. The duty to refrain from negligent conduct is meant to protect one person from the risk that a legally protected interest will be invaded by harm resulting from hazards created by another. Restatement (Second) of Torts §281, cmt. e. Although trespass to land began as a strict liability cause of action, more recently the courts have tended to regard it as an intentional tort. See, e.g., United Proteins, Inc. v. Farmland Indus., Inc., 915 P.2d 80 (Kan. 1996). To succeed in a private nuisance action, the plaintiff has to prove that any damage suffered was the result of an intentional and unreasonable invasion or an unintentional invasion that is actionable under the rules governing negligence or strict liability actions. Restatement (Second) of Torts §822. Even in an action seeking to impose strict liability for abnormally dangerous activity, a court following the Restatement's approach will "weigh the probability and severity of foreseeable harm, whether the activity is unusual or is in an inappropriate location, and other factors. Thus, fault plays a role in [this] assessment." Farber, Toxic Causation, 71 Minn. L. Rev. 1219, 1223 (1987).

Similarly, the common law required proof of a causal connection between the defendant's acts or omissions and the plaintiff's harm. A defendant is liable in a negligence action only if its negligence was a "legal" or proximate cause of the plaintiff's harm. Restatement (Second) of Torts §430. Negligent conduct is a legal cause of another's harm if the conduct was a substantial factor in bringing about the harm (a cause in fact) and the relationship between the defendant's conduct and the plaintiff's harm is not sufficiently remote as to render the harm unforeseeable. Id. §431. This requirement could pose substantial problems for the plaintiff whose property was damaged by a leaking hazardous waste disposal site. It is not unusual for many companies to dispose of wastes at the same site. If the wastes from these various sources mixed together before the site began leaking, the plaintiff may find it impossible to prove that any particular company's conduct caused all or even an identifiable portion of the contamination.

Situations in which multiple defendants contributed to the plaintiff's harm also raise questions concerning the appropriate allocation of liability. Traditionally, the plaintiff was entitled to recover nothing unless he or she could prove that a particular member of a group of multiple defendants caused the damage and identify the extent of that damage. The Restatement provides that if two or more persons, acting independently, tortiously cause distinct harms or a single harm that can reasonably be apportioned according to the contribution of each, then each defendant is liable only for the portion of the total harm it caused. Restatement (Second) of Torts §881. It is only if multiple defendants tortiously contributed to a single and indivisible harm that each party is jointly and severally liable for the entire harm. Id. §875. Normally, the burden of proving that tortious conduct caused the plaintiff's harm is on the plaintiff. Id. §433B(1). When, however, the conduct of two or more persons combined to bring about harm and one of them seeks to limit its liability on the ground that the harm is apportionable, the burden of proving apportionment is on that defendant. Id. §433B(2).

One of the recurring questions posed in this chapter is how CERCLA's liability system departs from these traditional principles. Must a plaintiff in a §107(a) cost recovery action prove culpability? See §101(32); 33 U.S.C. §1321; Town of Munster v. Sherwin-Williams Co., 27 F.3d 1268, 1272 (7th Cir. 1994). Must the plaintiff prove a causal link between the defendant's acts or omissions and the release that triggered the incurrence of response costs? What role, if any, does foreseeability on the defendant's part play? Is liability joint and several? Consider again *Shore Realty*, the principal case at the beginning of this section, and the following materials.

a.   Strict, Retroactive, and Joint and Several Liability

CERCLA is virtually silent on the standard of liability that applies to cost recovery actions under §107(a), but the courts have interpreted the statute as a sharp departure from the requirements of common law tort litigation. First, "[t]he traditional elements of tort culpability . . . simply are absent from the statute." United States v. Monsanto Co., 858 F.2d 160, 168 (4th Cir. 1988). Section 101(32) defines liability to mean the standard of liability applicable to the oil spill liability provisions of the Clean Water Act, 33 U.S.C. §1321, and the courts have uniformly agreed that this reference reveals Congress's intention to impose strict liability. E.g., United States v. Northeastern Pharmaceutical & Chem. Co., Inc., 579 F. Supp. 823, 844 (W.D. Mo. 1984), aff'd in part, rev'd in part, and remanded, 810 F.2d 726 (8th Cir. 1986).

Second, a §107(a) cost recovery plaintiff need not prove the same kind of causal link between the defendant's activities and the plaintiff's harm traditionally required in tort litigation.

> CERCLA does not require the plaintiff to prove that the defendant caused actual harm to the environment at the liability stage. Harm to the environment is material only when allocating responsibility. . . . Instead, CERCLA focuses on whether the defendant's release or threatened release caused harm to the plaintiff in the form of response costs. If so, and if the other elements [of a prima facie case] are established, the defendant is liable under CERCLA.

Control Data Corp. v. SCSC Corp., 53 F.3d 930, 935 (8th Cir. 1995). As another court put it, "[t]he argument that the government must prove a direct causal link between the incurrence of response costs and an actual release caused by a particular defendant has been rejected by 'virtually every court' that has directly considered the issue." United States v. Hercules, Inc., 247 F.3d 706, 716 n.8 (8th Cir. 2001).

Monsanto held that the government need not prove a nexus between the waste that particular PRPs sent to the site and the resulting environmental harm. Given the synergistic and migratory capacities of leaking chemical waste and the technological infeasibility of tracing waste to its source, requiring a CERCLA plaintiff to "fingerprint" wastes would frustrate the statutory goal of facilitating prompt remediation. A cost recovery plaintiff suing generator PRPs need only show that they sent hazardous substances to the site and that substances like those contained in their wastes were found there. A CERCLA plaintiff must nevertheless show "some connection" between the actions of the defendant and the contamination. The plaintiff will not prevail if it cannot show that hazardous substances generated by the defendant ever arrived at the site of the release. New Jersey Tpk. Auth. v. PPG Indus., Inc., 197 F.3d 96, 105 (3d Cir. 1999). What if a PRP can show that its wastes were removed from the site before any release occurred? The Monsanto court implied that such a PRP would not be liable. Can a generator escape liability by showing that the containers it sent to the site were never breached? Intact drums contribute little if any risk; effectively, there is no "release" from such drums. Percolation of escaped liquid wastes into soil and synergistic interactions of leaked chemicals cause most problems. In B.F. Goodrich v. Betkoski, 99 F.3d 505, 516-517 (2d Cir. 1996), the court rejected the district court's conclusion that a hazardous substance generator is not liable if the substances it sent to the facility would only be released by an intervening force. Are the rules concerning causation the same in a case in which the release occurs at one site and the plaintiff incurs response costs at another site (such as a property adjacent to the site of the release to which hazardous substances have migrated) as in a "one-site" case? See ASARCO LLC v. Cemex, Inc., 2014 WL 2112121 (W.D. Tex. 2014).

Third, CERCLA liability is retroactive in the sense that it applies to activities that took place before the statute's adoption in 1980. Thus, PRPs may be liable for response costs and natural resource damages even if those activities were lawful at the time they occurred. See, e.g., State ex rel. Brown v. Georgeoff, 562 F. Supp. 1300 (N.D. Ohio 1983). Efforts to convince the courts that CERCLA's retroactive liability scheme amounts to a bill of attainder, an ex post facto law, or a violation of the due process rights of PRPs have failed. See, e.g., United States v. Vertac Chem. Corp., 453 F.3d 1031, 1047-1048 (8th Cir. 2006).

As indicated above, the Restatement (Second) of Torts supports the imposition of joint and several liability in certain cases. In the following case, the Supreme Court addressed for the first time whether joint and several liability is available under CERCLA.

BURLINGTON NORTHERN AND SANTA FE RAILWAY CO. v. UNITED STATES
556 U.S. 599 (2009)

Justice STEVENS delivered the opinion of the Court.

In 1980, Congress enacted [CERCLA] in response to the serious environmental and health risks posed by industrial pollution. The Act was designed to promote the "'timely cleanup of hazardous waste sites'" and to ensure that the costs of such cleanup efforts were borne by those responsible for the contamination. These cases raise the questions whether and to what extent a party associated with a contaminated site may be held responsible for the full costs of remediation.

I

In 1960, Brown & Bryant, Inc. (B & B), began operating an agricultural chemical distribution business, purchasing pesticides and other chemical products from suppliers such as Shell Oil Company (Shell). Using its own equipment, B & B applied its products to customers' farms. B & B opened its business on a 3.8 acre parcel of former farmland in Arvin, California, and in 1975, expanded operations onto an adjacent .9 acre parcel of land owned jointly by the Atchison, Topeka & Santa Fe Railway Company, and the Southern Pacific Transportation Company (now known respectively as the Burlington Northern and Santa Fe Railway Company and Union Pacific Railroad Company) (Railroads). Both parcels of the Arvin facility were graded toward a sump and drainage pond located on the southeast corner of the primary parcel. Neither the sump nor the drainage pond was lined until 1979, allowing waste water and chemical runoff from the facility to seep into the ground water below.

During its years of operation, B & B stored and distributed various hazardous chemicals on its property. Among these were the herbicide dinoseb, sold by Dow Chemicals, and the pesticides D-D and Nemagon, both sold by Shell. Dinoseb was stored in 55-gallon drums and 5-gallon containers on a concrete slab outside

B & B's warehouse. Nemagon was stored in 30-gallon drums and 5-gallon containers inside the warehouse. Originally, B & B purchased D-D in 55-gallon drums; beginning in the mid-1960's, however, Shell began requiring its distributors to maintain bulk storage facilities for D-D. From that time onward, B & B purchased D-D in bulk.

When B & B purchased D-D, Shell would arrange for delivery by common carrier, f.o.b. destination.[2] When the product arrived, it was transferred from tanker trucks to a bulk storage tank located on B & B's primary parcel. From there, the chemical was transferred to bobtail trucks, nurse tanks, and pull rigs. During each of these transfers leaks and spills could—and often did—occur. Although the common carrier and B & B used buckets to catch spills from hoses and gaskets connecting the tanker trucks to its bulk storage tank, the buckets sometimes overflowed or were knocked over, causing D-D to spill onto the ground during the transfer process.

Aware that spills of D-D were commonplace among its distributors, in the late 1970's Shell took several steps to encourage the safe handling of its products. Shell provided distributors with detailed safety manuals and instituted a voluntary discount program for distributors that made improvements in their bulk handling and safety facilities. Later, Shell revised its program to require distributors to obtain an inspection by a qualified engineer and provide self-certification of compliance with applicable laws and regulations. B & B's Arvin facility was inspected twice, and in 1981, B & B certified to Shell that it had made a number of recommended improvements to its facilities.

Despite these improvements, B & B remained a "'[s]loppy' [o]perator." Over the course of B & B's 28 years of operation, delivery spills, equipment failures, and the rinsing of tanks and trucks allowed Nemagon, D-D and dinoseb to seep into the soil and upper levels of ground water of the Arvin facility. In 1983, the California Department of Toxic Substances Control (DTSC) began investigating B & B's violation of hazardous waste laws, and the United States Environmental Protection Agency (EPA) soon followed suit, discovering significant contamination of soil and ground water. Of particular concern was a plume of contaminated ground water located under the facility that threatened to leach into an adjacent supply of potential drinking water.

Although B & B undertook some efforts at remediation, by 1989 it had become insolvent and ceased all operations. That same year, the Arvin facility was added to the National Priority List, and subsequently, DTSC and EPA (Governments) exercised their authority under 42 U.S.C. §9604 to undertake cleanup efforts at the site. By 1998, the Governments had spent more than $8 million responding to the site contamination; their costs have continued to accrue.

In 1991, EPA issued an administrative order to the Railroads directing them, as owners of a portion of the property on which the Arvin facility was located, to perform certain remedial tasks in connection with the site. The Railroads did so, incurring expenses of more than $3 million in the process. Seeking to recover at least a portion of their response costs, in 1992 the Railroads brought suit against B & B in the United States District Court for the Eastern District of California. In 1996, that lawsuit was consolidated with two recovery actions brought by DTSC and EPA against Shell and the Railroads.

---

2. F.o.b. destination means "the seller must at his own expense and risk transport the goods to [the destination] and there tender delivery of them. . . ." U.C.C. §2-319(1)(b) (2001). The District Court found that B & B assumed "stewardship" over the D-D as soon as the common carrier entered the Arvin facility.

[After trial, the district court entered judgment for the Governments, holding that both the Railroads and Shell were potentially responsible parties (PRPs) under CERCLA—the Railroads as owners of a portion of the facility under §107(a)(1)-(2), and Shell because it had "arranged for" the disposal of hazardous substances through its sale and delivery of D-D under §107(a)(3).]

Although the court found the parties liable, it did not impose joint and several liability on Shell and the Railroads for the entire response cost incurred by the Governments. The court found that the site contamination created a single harm but concluded that the harm was divisible and therefore capable of apportionment. Based on three figures—the percentage of the total area of the facility that was owned by the Railroads, the duration of B & B's business divided by the term of the Railroads' lease, and the Court's determination that only two of three polluting chemicals spilled on the leased parcel required remediation and that those two chemicals were responsible for roughly two-thirds of the overall site contamination requiring remediation—the court apportioned the Railroads' liability as 9% of the Governments' total response cost. Based on estimations of chemicals spills of Shell products, the court held Shell liable for 6% of the total site response cost. . . .

On the subject of apportionment, the Court of Appeals found "no dispute" on the question whether the harm caused by Shell and the Railroads was capable of apportionment. The court observed that a portion of the site contamination occurred before the Railroad parcel became part of the facility, only some of the hazardous substances were stored on the Railroad parcel, and "only some of the water on the facility washed over the Railroads' site." With respect to Shell, the court noted that not all of the hazardous substances spilled on the facility had been sold by Shell. Given those facts, the court readily concluded that "the contamination traceable to the Railroads and Shell, with adequate information, would be allocable, as would be the cost of cleaning up that contamination." Nevertheless, the Court of Appeals held that the District Court erred in finding that the record established a reasonable basis for apportionment. Because the burden of proof on the question of apportionment rested with Shell and the Railroads, the Court of Appeals reversed the District Court's apportionment of liability and held Shell and the Railroads jointly and severally liable for the Governments' cost of responding to the contamination of the Arvin facility.

. . . We granted certiorari to determine whether Shell was properly held liable as an entity that had "arranged for disposal" of hazardous substances within the meaning of §9607(a)(3), and whether Shell and the Railroads were properly held liable for all response costs incurred by EPA and the State of California. Finding error on both points, we now reverse.

[In Part II of the opinion, the Court held that Shell was liable as an arranger. That portion of the opinion is reproduced at page 954 below.]

III

[Because Shell was not liable at all, the scope of its liability was no longer an issue.] We must, however, determine whether the Railroads were properly held jointly and severally liable for the full cost of the Governments' response efforts.

The seminal opinion on the subject of apportionment in CERCLA actions [is] United States v. Chem-Dyne Corp., 572 F. Supp. 802 [(S.D. Ohio 1983), which] concluded that although the Act imposed a "strict liability standard," id., at 805, it did not mandate "joint and several" liability in every case. Rather, Congress intended the scope of liability to "be determined from traditional and evolving principles of common law[.]" Id., at 808. The *Chem-Dyne* approach has been fully embraced by the Courts of Appeals. See, e.g., United States v. Alcan Aluminum Corp., 964 F.2d 252, 268 (C.A.3 1992); United States v. Monsanto Co., 858 F.2d 160, 171-173 (C.A.4 1988).

Following *Chem-Dyne*, the courts of appeals have acknowledged that "[t]he universal starting point for divisibility of harm analyses in CERCLA cases" is §433A of the Restatement (Second) of Torts. United States v. Hercules, Inc., 247 F.3d 706, 717 (C.A.8 2001). Under the Restatement,

> "when two or more persons acting independently caus[e] a distinct or single harm for which there is a reasonable basis for division according to the contribution of each, each is subject to liability only for the portion of the total harm that he has himself caused. Restatement (Second) of Torts, §§433A, 881 (1976); Prosser, Law of Torts, pp. 313-314 (4th ed. 1971). . . . But where two or more persons cause a single and indivisible harm, each is subject to liability for the entire harm. Restatement (Second) of Torts, §875; Prosser, at 315-316." *Chem-Dyne Corp.*, 572 F. Supp. at 810.

In other words, apportionment is proper when "there is a reasonable basis for determining the contribution of each cause to a single harm." Restatement (Second) of Torts §433A(1)(b).

Not all harms are capable of apportionment, however, and CERCLA defendants seeking to avoid joint and several liability bear the burden of proving that a reasonable basis for apportionment exists. See *Chem-Dyne Corp.*, 572 F. Supp. at 810 (citing Restatement (Second) of Torts §433B) (placing burden of proof on party seeking apportionment). When two or more causes produce a single, indivisible harm, "courts have refused to make an arbitrary apportionment for its own sake, and each of the causes is charged with responsibility for the entire harm." Restatement (Second) of Torts §433A, Comment i, p. 440.

Neither the parties nor the lower courts dispute the principles that govern apportionment in CERCLA cases, and both the District Court and Court of Appeals agreed that the harm created by the contamination of the Arvin site, although singular, was theoretically capable of apportionment. The question then is whether the record provided a reasonable basis for the District Court's conclusion that the Railroads were liable for only 9% of the harm caused by contamination at the Arvin facility.

[The District Court criticized both the Railroads and the government for failing to provide any helpful arguments, leaving the court "to independently perform the equitable apportionment analysis demanded by the circumstances of the case."[9]] . . .

9. As the Governments point out, insofar as the District Court made reference to equitable considerations favoring apportionment, it erred. Equitable considerations play no role in the apportionment analysis; rather, apportionment is proper only when the evidence supports the divisibility of the damages jointly caused by the PRPs. See generally United States v. Hercules, Inc., 247 F.3d 706, 718-719 (C.A.8 2001). As the Court of Appeals explained, "[a]pportionment . . . looks to whether defendants may avoid joint and several liability by establishing a fixed amount of damage for which they are liable," while contribution actions allow jointly and severally liable PRPs to recover from each other on the basis of equitable considerations. See also 42 U.S.C. §9613(f)(1) (providing that, "[i]n resolving contribution claims, the court may allocate response costs among liable parties using such equitable factors as the court determines are appropriate"). The error is of no consequence, however, because despite the District Court's reference to equity, its actual apportionment decision was properly rooted in evidence that provided a reasonable basis for identifying the portion of the harm attributable to the Railroads.

[T]he District Court ultimately concluded that this was "a classic 'divisible in terms of degree' case, both as to the time period in which defendants' conduct occurred, and ownership existed, and as to the estimated maximum contribution of each party's activities that released hazardous substances that caused Site contamination." Consequently, the District Court apportioned liability, assigning the Railroads 9% of the total remediation costs.

The District Court calculated the Railroads' liability based on three figures. First, the court noted that the Railroad parcel constituted only 19% of the surface area of the Arvin site. Second, the court observed that the Railroads had leased their parcel to B & B for 13 years, which was only 45% of the time B & B operated the Arvin facility. Finally, the court found that the volume of hazardous-substance-releasing activities on the B & B property was at least 10 times greater than the releases that occurred on the Railroad parcel, and it concluded that only spills of two chemicals, Nemagon and dinoseb (not D-D), substantially contributed to the contamination that had originated on the Railroad parcel and that those two chemicals had contributed to two-thirds of the overall site contamination requiring remediation. The court then multiplied .19 by .45 by .66 (two-thirds) and rounded up to determine that the Railroads were responsible for approximately 6% of the remediation costs. "Allowing for calculation errors up to 50%," the court concluded that the Railroads could be held responsible for 9% of the total CERCLA response cost for the Arvin site.

[The Ninth Circuit found insufficient data to establish the precise proportion of contamination that occurred on various portions of the Arvin facility or the rate of contamination before B & B's addition of the Railroad parcel. It noted that neither the duration of the lease nor the size of the leased area alone was a reliable measure of the harm caused by activities on Railroads' property, and that the district court had relied on estimates, not detailed records, in apportioning liability.]

Despite these criticisms, we conclude that the facts contained in the record reasonably supported the apportionment of liability. The District Court's detailed findings make it abundantly clear that the primary pollution at the Arvin facility was contained in an unlined sump and an unlined pond in the southeastern portion of the facility most distant from the Railroads' parcel and that the spills of hazardous chemicals that occurred on the Railroad parcel contributed to no more than 10% of the total site contamination, some of which did not require remediation. With those background facts in mind, we are persuaded that it was reasonable for the court to use the size of the leased parcel and the duration of the lease as the starting point for its analysis. Although the Court of Appeals faulted the District Court for relying on the "simplest of considerations: percentages of land area, time of ownership, and types of hazardous products," these were the same factors the court had earlier acknowledged were relevant to the apportionment analysis.

The Court of Appeals also criticized the District Court's assumption that spills of Nemagon and dinoseb were responsible for only two-thirds of the chemical spills requiring remediation, observing that each PRP's share of the total harm was not necessarily equal to the quantity of pollutants that were deposited on its portion of the total facility. Although the evidence adduced by the parties did not allow the court to calculate precisely the amount of hazardous chemicals contributed by the Railroad parcel to the total site contamination or the exact percentage of harm caused by each chemical, the evidence did show that fewer spills occurred on the Railroad parcel and that of those spills that occurred, not all were carried across the Railroad parcel to the B & B sump and pond from which most of the contamination originated. The fact that no D-D spills on the Railroad parcel required remediation lends strength to the District Court's conclusion that the Railroad parcel contributed only Nemagon and dinoseb in quantities requiring remediation.

The District Court's conclusion that those two chemicals accounted for only two-thirds of the contamination requiring remediation finds less support in the record; however, any miscalculation on that point is harmless in light of the District Court's ultimate allocation of liability, which included a 50% margin of error equal to the 3% reduction in liability the District Court provided based on its assessment of the effect of the Nemagon and dinoseb spills. Had the District Court limited its apportionment calculations to the amount of time the Railroad parcel was in use and the percentage of the facility located on that parcel, it would have assigned the Railroads 9% of the response cost. By including a two-thirds reduction in liability for the Nemagon and dinoseb with a 50% "margin of error," the District Court reached the same result. Because the District Court's ultimate allocation of liability is supported by the evidence and comports with the apportionment principles outlined above, we reverse the Court of Appeals' conclusion that the Railroads are subject to joint and several liability for all response costs arising out of the contamination of the Arvin facility. . . .

Justice GINSBURG, dissenting. . . .

As to apportioning costs, the District Court undertook an heroic labor. . . .

The trial court's mode of procedure, the United States urged before this Court, "deprived the government of a fair opportunity to respond to the court's theories of apportionment and to rebut their factual underpinnings—an opportunity the govern-men[t] would have had if those theories had been advanced by petitioners themselves." Brief for United States 41.[3] I would return these cases to the District Court to give all parties a fair opportunity to address that court's endeavor to allocate costs. Because the Court's disposition precludes that opportunity, I dissent from the Court's judgment.

NOTES AND QUESTIONS

1. What guidance did the Court provide to trial courts assessing whether to impose joint and several liability? How typical or atypical is the fact situation in *Burlington Northern* for cases in which PRPs are likely to contest joint and several liability? Compare U.S. Bank Nat'l Ass'n v. EPA, 565 F.3d 199, 208-209 (6th Cir. 2009) (finding that no reasonable trier of fact could have found divisibility between contamination at plant and in well); Board of County Comm'rs of La Plata, Colorado v. Brown Group Retail, Inc., 768 F. Supp. 2d 1092 (D. Colo. 2011) (imposing joint and several liability in sequential ownership case because ownership was not a sufficient ground for apportionment absent evidence of levels of production and volume of solvents used during the ownership of two PRPs). What must an owner or operator at the time of disposal show to justify apportionment—is it enough to show a reasonable basis to apportion the former owner's share of the harm, or must it make such a showing for all of the harm? See PCS Nitrogen Inc. v. Ashley II of Charleston LLC, 714 F.3d 161, 184-185 (4th Cir. 2013). How is the principal case likely to affect the dynamic of CERCLA cost recovery litigation? What effect will the Court's

3. For example, on brief, the United States observed: "[P]etitioners identify no record support for the district court's assumption that each party's contribution to the overall harm is proportional to the relative volume of hazardous substances attributable to it." Brief for United States 45.

approach to joint and several liability have on the degree to which taxpayers foot the bill for EPA's response costs?

According to one assessment, *Burlington Northern* "has not made apportionment any easier for PRPs to achieve," and "courts routinely find facts necessary for reasonable apportionment to be absent from the record." DeGulis & Gable, *Burlington Northern*: CERCLA and Its Ever-Changing, Unpredictable Landscape, 28 Natural Res. & Env't, Spring 2014, at 40, 42. United States v. NCR Corp., 688 F.3d 833 (7th Cir. 2012), for example, distinguished *Burlington Northern*, ruling that the volumes of waste sent by each PRP were not necessarily determinative in cases in which multiple PRPs independently contribute pollution amounts sufficient to require remediation, and that NCR failed to show that the harm was reasonably capable of apportionment. See also PCS Nitrogen Inc. v. Ashley II of Charleston LLC, 714 F.3d 161, 181-183 (4th Cir. 2013) (upholding finding that harm was not divisible based on amount of waste each PRP contributed to the site and amount of soil each PRP caused to be contaminated through secondary disposals, which involve movement or dispersal of existing contamination through earth-moving or construction activities). But cf. NCR Corp. v. George A. Whiting Paper Co., 2014 WL 4755491, *15-18 (7th Cir. 2014) (remanding district court's decision denying contribution because it preselected knowledge as the sole determinative equitable factor and deprived PRP seeking contribution of opportunity to develop evidence concerning other potentially relevant factors, such as relative discharge volumes and extent of voluntary cooperation); United States v. P.H. Glatfelter Co., 2014 WL 4755483, *14 (7th Cir. 2014) (remanding so that district court could consider whether remediation costs necessitated by each party might provide a basis for apportionment).

2. *Joint and Several Liability and Contribution.* Footnote 9 of the majority opinion distinguished between avoidance of joint and several liability and allocation of such liability in a contribution action. Similarly, in a pre–*Burlington Northern* decision, one court observed that the divisibility doctrine is "conceptually distinct" from contribution or allocation of damages. The divisibility inquiry is guided not by equitable considerations (as is the case with contribution) but by principles of causation alone. United States v. Hercules, Inc., 247 F.3d 706 (8th Cir. 2001).

Problem 9-2

For years, Acme Company sent wastes containing heavy metals to the Sparkling Dump Site (SDS). Bilt-More, Inc. and Carson Company sent wastes containing volatile organic compounds (VOCs) for disposal at the site. The wastes were disposed of in shallow lagoons. Releases from the lagoons have resulted in contamination of soil at and adjacent to the SDS with both heavy metals and VOCs. The groundwater in the vicinity of the SDS has been contaminated only with VOCs, because heavy metals are often relatively immobile in soil and have not migrated to the groundwater underneath or adjacent to the site. The remedy chosen by EPA was removal of the contaminated soil and extraction of the groundwater, followed by removal of the VOCs through air stripping, and reinjection of the groundwater into the aquifer. EPA spent $100,000 removing the contaminated soil and $1 million cleaning up the groundwater. EPA sued Acme, Bilt-More, and Carson in a §107(a) cost recovery action, and moved for summary judgment to establish that each defendant is jointly and severally liable for the agency's response costs. Before the district court ruled on the motion, EPA entered a consent decree with Carson in which Carson agreed to pay $100,000 to the agency in return for EPA's dismissal of its §107(a) action against the company. Assuming that Acme and Bilt-More are appropriate PRPs under §107(a)(3), what arguments can each company make to try to limit its liability for EPA's response costs? As counsel for one of the remaining PRPs, what kinds of evidence would you want to develop to support your opposition to EPA's motion?

b. Affirmative Defenses to Liability

Although CERCLA imposes strict liability, §107(b) provides a few affirmative defenses, and some courts have recognized additional equitable defenses. Absent the defenses discussed below, would CERCLA's strict liability and joint and several liability standards remove PRP incentives to act with care?

The "Act of God" Defense. United States v. Alcan Aluminum Corp., 892 F. Supp. 648 (M.D. Pa. 1995), *aff'd*, 96 F.3d 1434 (3d Cir. 1996) (Table), illustrates the limited availability of §107 defenses in general and the "act of God" defense in particular. The court found that no reasonable factfinder could have concluded that a hurricane was the sole cause of the release and resulting response costs, that the effects of the hurricane could have been prevented or avoided "by the exercise of due care or foresight," §101(1), and that heavy rainfall was not an "exceptional" natural phenomenon. See also United States v. W.R. Grace & Co.-Conn., 280 F. Supp. 2d 1149, 1174 (D. Mont. 2003) (presence of asbestos was not an act of God)).

The "Act of War" Defense. In United States v. Shell Oil Co., 281 F.3d 812 (9th Cir. 2002), PRPs unsuccessfully argued that the federal government's requisitioning and regulation of the production of aviation fuel during World War II constituted an act of war under §107(b)(2):

> [T]wo treatises that discuss the issue suggest that "act of war" has a narrow meaning. One suggests the "act of war" defense requires "massive violence." The other suggests that it requires "natural or man-made catastrophes beyond the control of any responsible party." Case law in other contexts also suggests a narrow definition of "act of war." [Id. at 827.]

But cf. In re September 11 Litig., 751 F.3d 86, 92 (2d Cir. 2014) (holding that the terrorist attack on the World Trade Center was an act of war and that "[w]ar, in the CERCLA context, is not limited to opposing states fielding combatants in uniform under formal declarations").

The "Third-Party" Defense. Of much greater practical significance than either of the two preceding defenses is the "third-party" defense of §107(b)(3). The exclusion for persons in a contractual relationship generally precludes lessors, employees, and independent contractors such as transporters from invoking the third-party defense. But see New York v. Fried, 430 F. Supp. 2d 151 (S.D.N.Y. 2006) (refusing to find defense unavailable to landlord who did not cause tenant's release). Acts or omissions of a third party that occurred after dissolution of a contractual relationship do not disqualify a PRP from invoking the third defense, Shapiro v. Alexanderson, 743 F. Supp. 268, 271 (S.D.N.Y. 1990). Some courts have held that the defense is unavailable only if there is a connection between the contractual relationship and the act or omission that resulted in the contamination. New York v. Lashins Arcade Co., 91 F.3d 353, 360 (2d Cir. 1996) (where a purchaser of contaminated property successfully invoked the defense). Compare United States v. Saporito, 684 F. Supp. 2d 1043, 1060-1061 (N.D. Ill. 2010) (defense unavailable because contract was connected to the release).

In Lincoln Properties, Ltd. v. Higgins, 823 F. Supp. 1528, 1542 (E.D. Cal. 1992), the court held that the requirement that the release be "caused solely by" the unrelated third party

> incorporates the concept of proximate or legal cause. If the defendant's release was not foreseeable, and if its conduct—including acts as well as omissions—was "so indirect and insubstantial" in the chain of events leading to the release, then the defendant's conduct was not the proximate cause of the release and the third-party defense may be available.

Under this standard, a county was not responsible for the release into soil and groundwater of PCE introduced into the county's leaking sewer lines by dry cleaners.[c]

Suppose that PCBs are released upstream from the property of a riparian landowner. Does the riparian owner's failure to take affirmative action to prevent the spread of the PCBs preclude it from invoking the "third-party" defense? See Kalamazoo River Study Group v. Rockwell Int'l, 3 F. Supp. 2d 799 (W.D. Mich. 1998). *Saporito, supra,* held that an equipment owner did not exercise due care for purposes of §107(b)(3) merely by including a provision in an equipment lease requiring the user to comply with the law.

The "Innocent Landowner" Defense. The 1986 amendments to CERCLA added a new defense for innocent landowners in §101(35). How does this defense relate to the "third-party" defense of §107(b)(3)?

> [Section 101(35)] is intended to clarify and confirm that under limited circumstances landowners who acquire property without knowing of any contamination at the site and without reason to know of any contamination . . . may have a defense to liability under section 107 and therefore should not be held liable for cleaning up the site if such persons satisfy the remaining requirements of section 107(b)(3). A person who acquires property through a land contract or deed or other instrument transferring title or possession that meets the requirements of this definition may assert that an act or omission of a third party should not be considered to have occurred in connection with a contractual relationship as identified in section 107(b) and therefore is not a bar to the defense. [H.R. Rep. No. 99-962, at 186-187 (1986), reprinted in 1986 U.S.C.C.A.N. 2835, 3279-3280.]

What limits does §101(35)(C) place on the availability of the defense? What effect does sale of property by an "innocent landowner" have on its ability to use the defense? See Westwood Pharmaceuticals, Inc. v. National Fuel Gas Distrib. Corp., 964 F.2d 85, 90-91 (9th Cir. 1992). What is the function of §101(35)(D)?

To prevail in asserting the "innocent landowner" defense, a PRP must show, among other things, that at the time it acquired the facility, it did not know and had no reason to know that any hazardous substance which is the subject of the release or threatened release was disposed of at the facility. §101(35)(A)(i). When does a purchaser have "reason to know"? See §101(35)(B). What other conditions does the statute place upon a PRP seeking to qualify for the "innocent landowner" defense?

---

c. But see Westfarm Assocs. Ltd. P'ship v. Washington Suburban Sanitary Comm'n, 66 F.3d 669 (4th Cir. 1995) (sewer commission was liable because "it had the power to abate the foreseeable release of PCE, yet failed to exercise that power").

See PCS Nitrogen Inc. v. Ashley II of Charleston LLC, 714 F.3d 161, 178-179 (4th Cir. 2013) (holding that PRP did not qualify for innocent landowner defense because it contributed to contamination and failed to exercise due care). In City of Wichita v. Trustees of the APCO Oil Corp. Liquidating Trust, 306 F. Supp. 2d 1040, 1050-1051 (D. Kan. 2003), the court interpreted §101(35)(B) as requiring that an innocent landowner make all appropriate inquiries before purchasing property and lack actual knowledge of the pollution at that time. When the landowner discovers contamination, it must take reasonable steps to control the problem.

What incentives does the defense create for prospective purchasers? EPA issued rules setting standards for conducting all appropriate inquiry into previous ownership, uses, and environmental conditions for purposes of §101(35)(B)(ii) and (iii). 70 Fed. Reg. 66,070 (2005). Prospective landowners who do not conduct such inquiries before or on the date of obtaining ownership may lose their ability to invoke the innocent landowner defense. The same is true for PRPs seeking to qualify for the bona fide prospective purchase or contiguous property owner defenses described below in connection with owner-operator liability. See §107(q)-(r). For a description of what an owner must demonstrate to qualify for each of these defenses, see 70 Fed. Reg. at 66,073-66,074.

Equitable Defenses. At one time, some courts allowed PRPs to assert additional equitable defenses, reasoning that, "because the government in a cost recovery case seeks the equitable remedy of restitution defendants should not be barred from raising equitable defenses." United States v. Iron Mountain Mines, Inc., 812 F. Supp. 1528, 1546 (E.D. Cal. 1992). More recent cases almost uniformly bar the assertion of equitable defenses. E.g., California v. Neville Chem. Co., 358 F.3d 661, 672 (9th Cir. 2004).

Problem 9-3

Allen operated a junkyard on land surrounded by residential property. Among the materials disposed of at the junkyard were used electrical transformers containing PCBs, a toxic chemical. Allen placed the transformers, along with the other junk he received, in an open pit in the ground. When Allen ceased junkyard operations on the site, he covered up the pit with dirt and placed sod over it. Several years later, Allen hired a real estate agent, Walsh, to sell the property. Walsh showed the property to Leonard, who planned to use it for residential purposes after constructing a new house. At that time, Walsh informed Leonard that the land had at some point in the past been used as a junkyard and that local officials had objected to the junkyard operations on several occasions on aesthetic grounds. Leonard did not investigate past uses of the site further.

After Leonard purchased the property, but before he began constructing the house, he noticed that pools of colored liquid formed on a portion of the land during heavy rains. Leonard inquired whether Walsh knew what caused pooling. Walsh said that he did not, but suggested that Leonard hire a chemist from an environmental engineering firm to sample the pools to identify the nature of the liquids. Leonard did so, and found out that the pools contained a combination of water and PCBs. Leonard hired a construction company to excavate the land underneath the pools. The company dug up 50 tons of PCB-contaminated soil. Leonard directed the company to place the soil on large sheets of plastic and to cover the soil piles with more plastic until Leonard could figure out the proper way to dispose of the contaminated soil. Two weeks later, during a heavy rainstorm, the plastic covers blew off the piles and portions of the soil washed onto a neighbor's property. When the neighbor informed the local health department, it requested that EPA investigate. EPA tested the soil, determined that it was contaminated with PCBs, and traced the source of the contamination to Leonard's property. EPA spent $5 million removing the dispersed 50 tons of contaminated soil, excavating other portions of Leonard's property, and removing an additional 50 tons of PCB-contaminated soil discovered during the excavation process.

EPA brought a cost recovery action in federal district court against Leonard, seeking reimbursement of the $5 million in cleanup costs. Leonard asserted two defenses, the "third-party" defense and the "innocent landowner" defense. EPA has moved for summary judgment and a determination that Leonard is liable for the agency's response costs. Should the court grant summary judgment to EPA? If not, what issues of fact would be relevant at trial?

3. Potentially Responsible Parties

a. Owners and Operators

CALIFORNIA DEPARTMENT OF TOXIC SUBSTANCES CONTROL v. HEARTHSIDE RESIDENTIAL CORP.
613 F.3d 910 (9th Cir. 2010)

GOULD, Circuit Judge:

This appeal presents a question of first impression whether "owner and operator" status under the Comprehensive Environmental Response, Compensation, and Liability Act ("CERCLA"), 42 U.S.C. §9607(a)(1), is determined at the time that cleanup costs are incurred or instead at the time that a recovery lawsuit seeking reimbursement is filed. . . .

In 1999, Hearthside Residential Corporation ("Hearthside") bought an undeveloped tract of wetlands known as the Fieldstone Property in Huntington Beach, California. The Fieldstone Property was adjacent to several residential parcels ("Residential Site") that Hearthside never owned or occupied. When Hearthside purchased the Fieldstone Property, it knew that the property was contaminated with polychlorinated biphenyls, or PCBs, a man-made substance considered toxic to humans and animals.

In 2002, Hearthside entered into a consent order with the State of California Department of Toxic Substance Control ("Department") by which Hearthside agreed to remediate the PCB contamination on the Fieldstone Property. The Department determined that the adjacent Residential Site was also contaminated with PCBs, which the Department alleged had leaked onto the Residential Site from the Fieldstone Property. The Department considered Hearthside responsible for investigating and remediating the Residential Site in addition to the Fieldstone Property, but Hearthside disagreed. . . . The Department certified that the Fieldstone Property cleanup was complete on December 1, 2005, and within the same month Hearthside sold the Fieldstone Property to the California State Lands Commission.

[After the Department contracted to clean up the Residential Site, it filed a cost recovery action, seeking reimbursement from Hearthside for the costs of the Residential Site cleanup as the owner of the contamination source at the time of the cleanup. The district court ruled for the Department and Hearthside appealed.]

II

. . . In determining in the first instance when current-ownership status is measured under CERCLA, we observe that the definition of "owner and operator" is silent on the date from which ownership is measured. See 42 U.S.C. §9601(20). Because the plain text of the statute does not admit of a clear answer to this dispute, we look to the statutory context and CERCLA's purposes to determine how Congress intended ownership to be measured.

Considering first the broader context of CERCLA liability, we conclude that the Department's view that ownership is measured at the time of cleanup best aligns with CERCLA's statute of limitations. The parties agree, as they must, that the applicable statute of limitations for a cost-recovery action is triggered (1) at the completion of a "removal" action, or (2) at the initiation of an on-site "remedial" action. 42 U.S.C. §9613(g)(2). Because statutes of limitations are intended in part to protect defendants, it is reasonable to assume that Congress meant the statute of limitations to run against (and protect) the owner of the property at the time cleanup occurs. If Hearthside's argument were adopted as law, then an owner could sell a recently cleaned piece of property to an innocent owner one day before the statute of limitations runs, with the result that the new owner would bear full cleanup liability under CERCLA if a recovery action was later timely filed. Such an unwise and untoward result would undermine the general aim of statutes of limitations to provide notice and predictability to a defendant and to ensure that the defendant is in possession of the evidence needed to defend against the claim. We conclude that Congress's decision to activate the statute of limitations at the time of cleanup is strong contextual evidence that Congress intended the owner at the time of cleanup to be the "current owner" in a subsequent recovery suit.

An analysis of CERCLA's purposes yields the same conclusion—that current ownership is measured at the time of cleanup. First, CERCLA encourages responsible parties to remediate hazardous facilities without delay. *Burlington N. & Santa Fe Ry. Co.*, 129 S. Ct. at 1874. This policy weighs in favor of the Department's position because a landowner that knows it will ultimately be responsible for the cleanup costs has no incentive to delay the completion of that process once it has begun. Conversely, under the view of liability urged by Hearthside, a landowner seeking to avoid liability by transferring the property before a lawsuit is filed has every incentive to delay completing the cleanup process until it has found a buyer; the recovery suit is likely to be filed once cleanup is complete and the total cost is known. Any contrived delay that an owner might employ to find a buyer before the recovery lawsuit is filed would contravene CERCLA's purpose of efficient cleanup, and this consideration favors the Department's view that ownership is determined when cleanup costs are incurred and not when the recovery suit is filed.

Another important purpose of CERLCA is to encourage early settlement between potentially responsible parties and environmental regulators. The importance of settlement within the CERCLA scheme undercuts Hearthside's argument for two reasons.

First, measuring ownership from the date that the recovery lawsuit is filed requires that a recovery lawsuit be filed. A rule that produces a lawsuit in every case is the opposite outcome that CERCLA seeks to promote. Second, one of the most critical elements of a CERCLA settlement is the agreed remedial action plan that the responsible party agrees to undertake. Because the owner at the time of cleanup can help determine the scope of the cleanup and select from among the reasonably effective remedial alternatives, it follows that the same owner should be responsible for the cost of the remediation program that it had the opportunity to influence. CERCLA seeks to include property owners in the technical consulting process, and this policy is best served by a rule that sets current ownership at the time cleanup occurs.

Hearthside contends that the lawsuit-filing date would establish a simple and clear date from which to measure. Hearthside urges that measuring ownership from the time of cleanup would require factual determinations about when cleanup commenced, when cleanup was completed, and when enough response costs were incurred so as to give rise to a recovery cause of action. We agree that in some cases factual determinations may be necessary to determine current ownership.[6] Nonetheless, we are not persuaded that the limited factfinding required to determine when a recovery action accrued is burdensome enough to require a different outcome. As we previously noted, a CERCLA recovery action accrues at the point that recovery costs are incurred, and the statute of limitations runs from the time a removal action is completed or a remedial action is begun on the site. 42 U.S.C. §9613(g)(2). Thus, factual questions surrounding the relevant cleanup dates are a routine and familiar component of CERCLA actions, and courts are well equipped to resolve such factual questions without great difficulty. Given that CERCLA's policies promoting settlement and efficient cleanup support the Department's position, we are not persuaded that the possible necessity of determining the accrual date is sufficient to tip the balance in favor of Hearthside's preferred construction. We hold that current ownership for purposes of liability under 42 U.S.C. §9607(a)(1) is measured from the time the recovery action accrues. Because there is no dispute that Hearthside was the owner of the Fieldstone Property at all times relevant to the remediation of the Residential Site, Hearthside is a current owner under 42 U.S.C. §9607(a)(1). . . .

NOTES AND QUESTIONS

1. What bearing did CERCLA's statute of limitations have on whether current ownership is measured as of the time of the cleanup or the time a cost recovery action is brought? What congressional policies supported the holding that ownership is measured as of the time of the cleanup? What undesirable incentives would a contrary result have created?

2. *What Kinds of Property Interests Qualify as "Ownership"?* Courts interpreting the scope of owner liability under §107(a)(1) and (2) have concluded that, in certain circumstances, a person can qualify as an owner without holding a fee simple in the contaminated facility. May a lessee qualify as an owner? See Commander Oil Corp. v. Barlo Equipment Corp., 215 F.3d 321 (2d Cir. 2000). But cf. City of Los Angeles v.

6. . . . Hearthside owned the Fieldstone Property at the time the Department requested remediation of the Residential Site, as well as during the entire cleanup of the Residential Site by the Department. Therefore, there is no question that Hearthside was the current owner of the Fieldstone Property at the time the Residential Site was remediated. . . .

San Pedro Boat Works, 635 F.3d 440, 452 n.10 (9th Cir. 2011) (suggesting that Congress intended to limit "owner" liability to "individuals possessing all of the proverbial 'sticks in the bundle of rights,' including fee title to the real property"). Suppose a utility has a right-of-way to run a pipeline across property that becomes contaminated with hazardous substances. The contamination did not originate from the pipeline. Is the utility liable as an owner under §107(a)(1)? See Redevelopment Agency of the City of Stockton v. BNSF Ry. Co., 643 F.3d 668 (9th Cir. 2011); Long Beach Unified School Dist. v. Dorothy B. Godwin California Living Trust, 32 F.3d 1364 (9th Cir. 1994). Compare Louisiana v. Braselman Corp., 78 F. Supp. 2d 543 (E.D. La. 1999) (deeming owner of railroad tracks to be an owner at the time of disposal under §107(a)(2) because tracks themselves were a facility contaminated with creosote).

3. *Who Is an Operator*? In Litgo New Jersey, Inc. v. Commissioner New Jersey Dep't of Envtl. Prot., 725 F.3d 369 (3d Cir. 2013), the court rejected the claim that a defendant could not be held liable as a current operator if it only managed remedial activities at the site and could not have caused any of the contamination requiring remediation. Accepting that argument would disregard the distinction between past and present operators and add a causation requirement absent from the statute. In addition, the defendant exercised actual control over pollution-related activities by conducting tests and hiring contractors to perform remediation. This result was not unfair because courts allocate responsibility based on equitable factors and an operator who participated in remediation without interfering with it likely will not be assessed a large share of the remediation costs, and may not be assessed any share at all.

4. *Passive Disposal.* Suppose that A dumps hazardous substances in a pit on property she owns. Before A sells the property to B, she covers the pit with soil and grass. After the sale, B neither manages hazardous substances nor disturbs the land surrounding the pit dug by A. Nevertheless, hazardous substances leak out of the pit into soil and groundwater beneath the pit. Then B sells the property to C. When EPA discovers that groundwater in the vicinity of the property is contaminated, it determines that the pit on C's land is the source of the contamination. EPA cleans up the site and brings a cost recovery action against A, B, and C. Clearly, absent successful invocation of the "innocent landowner" defense of §101(35), C is liable under §107(a)(1) as the current owner of the property. Just as clearly, A is liable under §107(a)(2) as the owner at the time of disposal. But what about B? Is B also liable as a past owner under §107(a)(2)? The answer may turn on the meaning of "disposal" in §107(a)(2). See §101(29). What argument can EPA make that B is indeed liable as an owner at the time of disposal?

The courts have reached conflicting conclusions in cases involving this kind of "passive disposal." In holding a past owner liable on the basis of passive disposal, the court in Nurad, Inc. v. William E. Hooper & Sons Co., 966 F.2d 837 (4th Cir. 1992), relied on a literal interpretation of §101(29), which does not require active human participation. Does this result create desirable incentives for owners such as B? See id. at 845-846. Or does it merely make available to cost recovery plaintiffs more PRPs with potentially deep pockets? United States v. Petersen Sand & Gravel, Inc., 806 F. Supp. 1346 (N.D. Ill. 1992), came out the other way. It did so, in part, based on a comparison of a "release" under CERCLA and a "disposal" under RCRA:

> [I]t is the contextual relationship in the statute between "release" and "disposal" that convinces this court that "disposal" does not contemplate passive migration. A "release" or a threatened "release" is a precondition to the authority to act under CERCLA, and it

is undisputed that a "release" includes the kind of passive migration at issue here. . . . A "release" includes a "disposal," but a "disposal" does not include a "release." In some way, therefore, "release" must be more inclusive than "disposal." Congress could have made operator liability depend on a "release"; instead, Congress designed the entire CERCLA response scheme to activate whenever a "release" occurred, but limited the liability for operators to those who were operators during a "disposal." Some distinction must have been intended, and the so-called innocent owner defense shows that the distinction must have been between active and passive events.

Id. at 1351. What bearing does the innocent landowner defense in §101(35) have on the passive disposal issue? *Petersen Sand & Gravel* indicated that "state common law that protects land purchasers from the intentional failure to disclose hidden defects would also prevent a malevolent owner from carrying out an environmentally irresponsible scheme." 806 F. Supp. at 1353. Carson Harbor Village, Ltd. v. Unocal Corp., 270 F.3d 863 (9th Cir. 2001), contains a thorough review of the cases addressing the passive migration issue.

Courts have addressed the meaning of disposal in other contexts. In Voggenthaler v. Maryland Square LLC, 724 F.3d 1050, 1064 (9th Cir. 2013), for example, the court rejected an operator's claim that it did not dispose of hazardous substances at a dry cleaning facility because it spilled those substances onto the floor rather than directly onto land or into groundwater.

5. *Contiguous Property Owners and Bona Fide Prospective Purchasers.* CERCLA exempts from owner and operator liability certain innocent owners of properties adjacent to contaminated facilities. See §107(q). A person that fails to qualify for the contiguous property owner defense because that person knew or had reason to know that the property was or could be contaminated may nevertheless qualify as a bona fide prospective purchaser (BFPP). See §101(40). A BFPP whose potential liability is based solely on the purchaser's being considered an owner or operator of the facility will not be liable as long as that person does not impede the performance of a response action. §107(r)(1). If there are unrecovered response costs incurred by the United States at a facility owned by a person who is not liable as a BFPP, the United States will have a lien on the facility for the unrecovered response costs if the response action increases the fair market value of the facility above the value that existed before the response action began. §107(r)(2)-(3).

For comparison of the innocent landowner and BFPP defenses, see City of Wichita v. Trustees of the APCO Oil Corp. Liquidating Trust, 306 F. Supp. 2d 1040, 1051-1052 (D. Kan. 2003). See also PCS Nitrogen Inc. v. Ashley II of Charleston LLC, 714 F.3d 161, 180-181 (4th Cir. 2013) (suggesting that the standard of "appropriate care" for a BFPP is higher than the standard of "due care" for an innocent landowner because the former knew of the presence of hazardous substances at the time of purchase, while the latter did not and had no reason to know). For unsuccessful efforts to invoke the BFPP defense, see Voggenthaler v. Maryland Square LLC, 724 F.3d 1050 (9th Cir. 2013) (failure to prevent further harm or make appropriate inquiries); *PCS Nitrogen, supra* (due care not exercised). EPA has issued guidance on what amounts to a prohibited affiliation with other PRPs for purposes of the BFPP and contiguous property owner defenses. See Enforcement Discretion Guidance Regarding the Affiliation Language of CERCLA's Bona Fide Prospective Purchaser and Contiguous Property Owner Protections (Sept. 21, 2011). See also Revised Enforcement Guidance Regarding the Treatment of Tenants Under the CERCLA Bona Fide Prospective Purchaser Provision (Dec. 5, 2012).

Problem 9-4

Suppose that R, a commercial real estate broker, submitted the high bid for property that is the site of an abandoned paint factory that the government had taken over after the owner of the factory defaulted on real estate taxes. After the government provided the tax deed to R, R entered a contract to sell the property to M. When M provided the agreed-upon deposit, R delivered possession to M, but retained legal title as security for payment of the remainder of the purchase price agreed upon in the contract. M never made another payment, leaving R with legal title. EPA discovers that the property is contaminated, cleans it up, and sues R for reimbursement of its response costs under §107(a)(1). If R argues that its mere "legal title" does not make it the owner, and that M is the owner for purposes of §107(a)(1), how should the court rule?

b. Arrangers

Those who send hazardous substances to a facility at which a release later occurs may be liable under §107(a)(3) as persons who "by contract, agreement, or otherwise arranged for disposal or treatment, or arranged with a transporter for transport for disposal or treatment," of those hazardous substances. Moreover, as United States v. Monsanto Co., 858 F.2d 160 (4th Cir. 1988), reveals, the government need not prove a causal nexus between the waste sent to the site by the generator and the resulting environmental harm to render it liable. It is enough if hazardous substances of the same kind as those sent by the generator are present at the facility at the time of the release. What single word in §107(a) supports that result? A question that has engendered more difficulty than the requisite link between the generator and the release is exactly what it means to "arrange for disposal or treatment" of hazardous substances.

SOUTH FLORIDA WATER MANAGEMENT DISTRICT v. MONTALVO
84 F.3d 402 (11th Cir. 1996)

BLACK, Circuit Judge:

[Chemspray and Chemairspray, both of which were allegedly controlled by Juan Montalvo, provided pesticide formulating and aerial spraying services in south Florida. Their businesses were located on the "Chemairspray Site" (or "the Site"), which consisted of two pieces of land. Chemairspray, the company providing spraying services, leased a 10-acre parcel on which it maintained an airstrip. Chemspray owned the adjacent 14-acre plot on which it formulated pesticides from chemicals supplied by chemical manufacturers. Chemairspray contracted with farmers and ranchers throughout south Florida to spray their lands with aerial pesticides and herbicides. Its operations contaminated the Chemairspray Site with pesticide wastes as a result of spills of pesticides on the airstrip and surrounding land during the mixing and loading of pesticides into the applicating tanks of planes. Further contamination resulted from the release of pesticide wastes during the rinsing out of the applicating tanks after spraying runs.

In 1985, the Florida environmental agency sued New Farm, Inc., which had purchased the property leased by Chemairspray, to compel cleanup of the Site. By then, contamination had spread to adjacent lands owned by the South Florida Water Management District (SFWMD). In 1988, New Farm and SFWMD sued Chemairspray, Chemspray, and Montalvo (collectively, "the Sprayers") for response costs under CERCLA. After the Sprayers admitted their liability, the district court found them jointly and severally liable for 75 percent of the costs incurred in cleaning up the Site. As the current owner of the property, New Farm was held liable for the remaining 25 percent. The Sprayers filed a third-party complaint seeking contribution from farmers and ranchers ("the Landowners"), alleging that the Landowners had "arranged for" the disposal of hazardous substances within the meaning of §107(a)(3).]

. . . Since the Sprayers have not alleged the Landowners expressly agreed to dispose of hazardous substances at the Site, the question becomes whether the Landowners, by virtue of their contracting with the Sprayers for aerial spraying services, are parties who "otherwise arranged for" the disposal of hazardous substances.

. . . CERCLA does not define the phrase "arranged for." Congress has left this task to the courts, and the courts have at times struggled with the contours of "arranger" liability under §107(a)(3). When analyzing whether a particular transaction amounted to an arrangement to dispose, courts have focused on various factors. For example, where the transaction involved a sale, courts have asked whether there was a transfer of a "useful" or "waste" product. In several cases, courts have considered whether the defendant intended to dispose of a substance at the time of a transaction. Courts have also looked to whether a defendant made the "crucial decision" to place hazardous substances in the hands of a particular facility. See United States v. A & F Materials Co., 582 F. Supp. 842, 845 (S.D. Ill. 1984). . . .

. . . The Sprayers assert the following supports finding the Landowners "arranged for" the disposal of pesticide wastes at the Chemairspray Site: (1) the Landowners contracted with the Sprayers to have pesticides applied to their property; (2) the Landowners owned the pesticides throughout the application process; (3) the generation of hazardous wastes was a necessary incident to the application process; and (4) the Sprayers acted as the Landowners' agents and/or independent contractors in applying the pesticides and handling the pesticide wastes.[8]

The only link alleged between the Landowners and the Sprayers is the Landowners' contracting with the Sprayers for aerial spraying services. The Sprayers contend this is sufficient to establish liability. . . . We disagree. The Landowners contracted to have pesticides applied to their property. They did not agree to have pesticides and contaminated rinse water spilled onto the Chemairspray Site.

For the Landowners to have "arranged for" the disposal of the pesticide wastes, they must have done more than simply contracted for aerial spraying services. The Sprayers must demonstrate the Landowners took some affirmative act to dispose of the

---

8. . . . The Sprayers have not alleged any basis for an agency relationship beyond the Landowners having contracted for spraying services. Characterizing this act as creating an agency between the parties does not lead to the conclusion the Landowners "arranged for" the disposal of hazardous wastes. While common law principles of agency are relevant in determining CERCLA liability in some instances, see [United States v. Aceto Agric. Chems. Corp., 872 F.2d 1373, 1382 (8th Cir. 1989)], they add nothing to the analysis here. The Sprayers must establish the Landowners "arranged for" the disposal of the pesticide wastes. Whether or not the Landowners' conduct also created an agency/independent contractor relationship is irrelevant.

wastes. The allegations in the Sprayers' complaint do not disclose the Landowners took such an act. The Landowners did not assist the Sprayers in loading the planes or rinsing out the applicating tanks. Indeed, the Sprayers have not even alleged the Landowners knew about the spills at the Site. Nor have the Sprayers alleged the Landowners had either the duty or authority to monitor or control the Sprayers' activities. In other words, there are no allegations from which we can infer the Landowners implicitly agreed to the disposal of these wastes.

The Sprayers analogize this case to the Eighth Circuit's decision in *Aceto* to demonstrate the Landowners effectively controlled the disposal of wastes at the Site. In *Aceto*, the United States and the State of Iowa sued a group of chemical manufacturers under CERCLA to recover costs incurred in cleaning up the site of a pesticide formulation business. The plaintiffs alleged the manufacturers sent raw chemicals to the formulator for mixing and conversion into commercial pesticides. "Inherent" in the formulating process was the generation of hazardous wastes through "spills, cleaning of equipment, mixing and grinding operations, production of batches which [did] not meet specifications, and other means." According to the complaint, the manufacturers specified what pesticides they wanted produced, and retained ownership of the chemicals throughout the formulating process. Once the pesticides had been formulated, they were either shipped back to the manufacturers or forwarded to their customers. Under these circumstances, the Eighth Circuit concluded the plaintiffs in *Aceto* had stated a claim for "arranged for" liability under CERCLA, and upheld the denial of the manufacturers' motion to dismiss.

The service contracted for in *Aceto* bears little resemblance to the service the Landowners purchased in this case. The chemical manufacturers in *Aceto* contracted for formulating services requiring the mixing of active and inactive chemicals according to the manufacturers' specifications. Since the manufacturers provided the chemicals to the formulator, specified what pesticides the formulator was to mix, and retained ownership of the chemicals and pesticides throughout the formulating process, it was possible to infer the manufacturers exercised some control over the formulator's mixing process.

In contrast, the Landowners contracted with the Sprayers to have formulated pesticides sprayed on their property. That the Landowners owned the pesticides during the application process does not, by itself, imply the kind of control over the Sprayers' application procedures that the chemical manufacturers had over the formulator's process in *Aceto*.

In *Aceto*, the mixing and packaging of pesticides "inherently" involved the creation of hazardous wastes such that the manufacturers should have expected the formulator would have to dispose of these wastes as part of the service they were purchasing. The service the Sprayers contracted for—aerial pesticide spraying—does not obviously involve the creation and disposal of hazardous wastes. Granted, the Sprayers have alleged the generation of pesticide wastes was a "necessary incident" to the application process. This may be so, but the Sprayers have not alleged the Landowners knew about this incidental by-product of the service they were purchasing. Whereas it was possible to infer the chemical manufacturers in *Aceto* knew about the creation of hazardous wastes given the service they were being provided, we cannot infer the Landowners had similar knowledge that spraying their crop and pasture lands with pesticides entailed the spilling of pesticides and draining of contaminated rinse water. Without this knowledge, the Landowners cannot be said to have acquiesced to the Sprayers' disposal of the wastes.

... CERCLA liability ... is not boundless. The Sprayers cannot escape the fact they were the parties who spilled the hazardous substances that contaminated the Chemairspray Site. ... Essentially, the Sprayers seek to hold the Landowners liable merely because the Landowners contracted for a service that involved the application of hazardous substances. We think this stretches the meaning of "arranged for" too far.

At the same time, we decline the Landowners' invitation to broadly exclude from CERCLA's reach cases where a plaintiff seeks to hold a defendant liable because the defendant contracted for a service involving the use and disposal of hazardous substances. We emphasize that whether or not a party has "arranged for" the disposal of a hazardous substance depends on the particular facts of each case. ... [W]e conclude the Sprayers have simply not alleged the Landowners had sufficient knowledge of or control over the Sprayers' disposal practices to be held liable under this provision. ...

NOTES AND QUESTIONS

1. What factors induced the court to conclude that the Landowners had not "arranged for" disposal under §107(a)(3)? Must a PRP engage in affirmative acts of disposal to be liable as an arranger? See Redwing Carriers, Inc. v. Saraland Apartments, 94 F.3d 1489, 1506 (11th Cir. 1996). Must it have been physically involved in those acts? Must the defendant have been actively involved in arranging to dispose of the waste to be liable as an arranger? See GenCorp., Inc. v. Olin Corp., 390 F.3d 433, 446-447 (6th Cir. 2004) (stating that a PRP "may not become an arranger through inadvertence"; the alleged arranger must have had "some intent to make preparations for the disposal of hazardous waste," even if the evidence of that intent may be inferred from the circumstances). Must it have had knowledge of the disposal? Must it have had a duty to control the activities that led to the disposal? If so, is arranger liability simply a codification of negligence law? Is such an interpretation consistent with Congress's intention to impose strict liability?

2. How did the court in *Montalvo* distinguish the *Aceto* case? Why was it appropriate to infer knowledge of the creation of hazardous wastes by the chemical manufacturers in *Aceto* but not the Landowners in *Montalvo*? The pesticide manufacturers in *Aceto* argued that they hired Aidex, the company that formulated their pesticides into commercial-grade products, "to formulate, not to dispose," and that they could be held liable as arrangers only if they intended to dispose of a waste. But the Eighth Circuit refused to be bound by the PRPs' characterization of their relationship with the formulator. The court also found it significant that Aidex performed a process on products owned by the manufacturers for the manufacturers' benefit and at their direction. Compare United States v. Hercules, Inc., 247 F.3d 706 (8th Cir. 2001) (finding party to toll conversion agreement liable as an arranger even though it lacked control over the process by which Vertac manufactured dioxin for it, using an ingredient supplied by the party).

3. *Ownership or Possession.* Arrangers are liable under §107(a)(3) based on arrangements to dispose of hazardous substances that they "owned or possessed." In United States v. Vertac Chem. Corp., 46 F.3d 803 (8th Cir. 1995), the court stated that proof of authority to control the handling and disposal of hazardous substances might suffice to impose liability, even absent proof of actual ownership or possession. Similarly, American Cyanamid Co. v. Capuano, 381 F.3d 6, 25 (1st Cir. 2004),

concluded that a broker that arranges for the disposal of hazardous waste by exercising control over the waste may be deemed to be in "constructive possession" of the waste for purposes of arranger liability. GenCorp., Inc. v. Olin Corp., 390 F.3d 433 (6th Cir. 2004), reached the same result. It found constructive possession because, even if the alleged arranger never held title to the plant at which the hazardous substances had been generated, it had an active interest in the plant through its option to buy it. It also had representation on the committee that oversaw the construction, operation, and management of the plant and that approved the design plans, capital appropriations requests, and budgets of the plant (all of which contemplated off-site waste disposal). Can a party that disposes of its own waste qualify as an arranger? See Pakootas v. Teck Cominco Metals, Ltd., 452 F.3d 1066, 1079-1082 (9th Cir. 2006) (stating that §107(a)(3) "does not make literal or grammatical sense as written").

BURLINGTON NORTHERN AND SANTA FE RAILWAY CO. v. UNITED STATES
556 U.S. 599 (2009)

[The facts are described above at page 935 in connection with the Court's treatment of the joint and several liability issue in the case.]

II

. . . In these cases, it is undisputed that the Railroads qualify as PRPs under both §§9607(a)(1) and 9607(a)(2) because they owned the land leased by B & B at the time of the contamination and continue to own it now. The more difficult question is whether Shell also qualifies as a PRP under §9607(a)(3) by virtue of the circumstances surrounding its sales to B & B.

To determine whether Shell may be held liable as an arranger, we begin with the language of the statute. As relevant here, §9607(a)(3) applies to an entity that "arrange[s] for disposal . . . of hazardous substances." It is plain from the language of the statute that CERCLA liability would attach under §9607(a)(3) if an entity were to enter into a transaction for the sole purpose of discarding a used and no longer useful hazardous substance. It is similarly clear that an entity could not be held liable as an arranger merely for selling a new and useful product if the purchaser of that product later, and unbeknownst to the seller, disposed of the product in a way that led to contamination. See Florida Power & Light Co. v. Allis Chalmers Corp., 893 F.2d 1313, 1318 (C.A.11 1990). Less clear is the liability attaching to the many permutations of "arrangements" that fall between these two extremes—cases in which the seller has some knowledge of the buyers' planned disposal or whose motives for the "sale" of a hazardous substance are less than clear. In such cases, courts have concluded that the determination whether an entity is an arranger requires a fact-intensive inquiry that looks beyond the parties' characterization of the transaction as a "disposal" or a "sale" and seeks to discern whether the arrangement was one Congress intended to fall within the scope of CERCLA's strict-liability provisions. See Pneumo Abex Corp. v. High Point, Thomasville & Denton R. Co., 142 F.3d 769, 775 (C.A.4 1998) ("[T]here is no bright line between a sale and a disposal under CERCLA.

A party's responsibility . . . must by necessity turn on a fact-specific inquiry into the nature of the transaction.").

Although we agree that the question whether §9607(a)(3) liability attaches is fact intensive and case specific, such liability may not extend beyond the limits of the statute itself. Because CERCLA does not specifically define what it means to "arrang[e] for" disposal of a hazardous substance, we give the phrase its ordinary meaning. In common parlance, the word "arrange" implies action directed to a specific purpose. See Merriam-Webster's Collegiate Dictionary 64 (10th ed. 1993) (defining "arrange" as "to make preparations for: plan[;] . . . to bring about an agreement or understanding concerning"); see also [Amcast Indus. Corp v. Detrex Corp., 2 F.3d 746, 751 (7th Cir. 1993)] (words "'arranged for' . . . imply intentional action"). Consequently, under the plain language of the statute, an entity may qualify as an arranger under §9607(a)(3) when it takes intentional steps to dispose of a hazardous substance. See [United States v. Cello-Foil Prods., Inc., 100 F.3d 1227, 1231 (6th Cir. 1996)] ("[I]t would be error for us not to recognize the indispensable role that state of mind must play in determining whether a party has 'otherwise arranged for disposal . . . of hazardous substances.'").

The Governments do not deny that the statute requires an entity to "arrang[e] for" disposal; however, they interpret that phrase by reference to the statutory term "disposal," which the Act broadly defines as "the discharge, deposit, injection, dumping, spilling, leaking, or placing of any solid waste or hazardous waste into or on any land or water." 42 U.S.C. §6903(3); see also §9601(29) (adopting the definition of "disposal" contained in the Solid Waste Disposal Act). The Governments assert that by including unintentional acts such as "spilling" and "leaking" in the definition of disposal, Congress intended to impose liability on entities not only when they directly dispose of waste products but also when they engage in legitimate sales of hazardous substances knowing that some disposal may occur as a collateral consequence of the sale itself. Applying that reading of the statute, the Governments contend that Shell arranged for the disposal of D-D within the meaning of §9607(a)(3) by shipping D-D to B & B under conditions it knew would result in the spilling of a portion of the hazardous substance by the purchaser or common carrier. Because these spills resulted in wasted D-D, a result Shell anticipated, the Governments insist that Shell was properly found to have arranged for the disposal of D-D.

While it is true that in some instances an entity's knowledge that its product will be leaked, spilled, dumped, or otherwise discarded may provide evidence of the entity's intent to dispose of its hazardous wastes, knowledge alone is insufficient to prove that an entity "planned for" the disposal, particularly when the disposal occurs as a peripheral result of the legitimate sale of an unused, useful product. In order to qualify as an arranger, Shell must have entered into the sale of D-D with the intention that at least a portion of the product be disposed of during the transfer process by one or more of the methods described in §6903(3). Here, the facts found by the District Court do not support such a conclusion.

Although the evidence adduced at trial showed that Shell was aware that minor, accidental spills occurred during the transfer of D-D from the common carrier to B & B's bulk storage tanks after the product had arrived at the Arvin facility and had come under B & B's stewardship, the evidence does not support an inference that Shell intended such spills to occur. To the contrary, the evidence revealed that Shell took numerous steps to encourage its distributors to reduce the likelihood of such spills, providing them with detailed safety manuals, requiring them to maintain adequate storage facilities, and providing discounts for those that took safety precautions. Although Shell's efforts were less than wholly successful, given these facts, Shell's mere knowledge that spills and leaks continued to occur is insufficient grounds for concluding that Shell "arranged for" the disposal of D-D within the meaning of §9607(a)(3). Accordingly, we conclude that Shell was not liable as an arranger for the contamination that occurred at B & B's Arvin facility. . . .

Justice GINSBURG, dissenting.

Although the question is close, I would uphold the determinations of the courts below that Shell qualifies as an arranger. . . .

That Shell sold B & B useful products, the Ninth Circuit observed, did not exonerate Shell from CERCLA liability, for the sales "necessarily and immediately result[ed] in the leakage of hazardous substances." The deliveries, Shell was well aware, directly and routinely resulted in disposals of hazardous substances (through spills and leaks) for more than 20 years. "[M]ere knowledge" may not be enough, but Shell did not simply know of the spills and leaks without contributing to them. Given the control rein held by Shell over the mode of delivery and transfer, the lower courts held and I agree, Shell was properly ranked an arranger. Relieving Shell of any obligation to pay for the cleanup undertaken by the United States and California is hardly commanded by CERCLA's text, and is surely at odds with CERCLA's objective to place the cost of remediation on persons whose activities contributed to the contamination rather than on the taxpaying public.

NOTES AND QUESTIONS

1. What is the test for imposing arranger liability after *Burlington Northern*? Must the government prove intent? Intent to do what? Is that result consistent with the long-standing interpretation of CERCLA as a statute that imposes strict liability?

2. *The Impact of* Burlington Northern. The extent to which *Burlington Northern* narrows arranger liability is not yet clear. According to some observers, the courts in the kind of "mixed motive" cases referred to in the majority opinion continue to evaluate the usefulness of a product to determine the primary purpose of transactions like those in *Burlington Northern*. See DeGulis & Gable, *supra*, at 41. The results are necessarily fact-dependent. In Team Enterprises LLC v. Western Inv. Real Estate Trust, 647 F.3d 901 (9th Cir. 2011), the court held that a manufacturer of dry cleaning equipment was not liable as an arranger in a contribution action brought by the operator of a dry cleaning business whose use of PCE resulted in groundwater contamination. The court rejected the claim that the manufacturer took intentional steps to dispose of PCE, concluding that, at most, the design of the equipment supplied by the manufacturer to the dry cleaner for recycling PCE back into the dry cleaning process indicated the manufacturer's indifference to the possibility that dry cleaners would pour PCE down the drain. The court refused to infer intent to dispose from the manufacturer's failure to warn the plaintiff about the risk of contamination that would result from improper disposal. Sellers of useful products need not instruct buyers on proper disposal techniques to avoid arranger liability. The court also rejected the claim that the manufacturer had the authority to control and exercised control over the disposal process. The fact that a portion of the manufacturer's instruction

manual directed users to pour wastewater into a bucket was insufficient to establish control because instruction manuals are akin to recommendations, and therefore do not control the actions of the purchaser. Cf. NCR Corp. v. George A. Whiting Paper Co., 2014 WL 4755491, *18-22 (7th Cir. 2014) (holding that paper mill that coated carbonless copy paper with emulsion containing PCBs was not liable as an arranger based on its sale of recycled "broke" to recycling mill because knowledge that the buyer would at some point dispose of the materials was not enough to trigger liability; the mill sold a valuable input for the recycling mills, even though it did not sell a new product, and the mill lacked control over the recycling mill's handling of the broke).

United States v. General Elec. Co., 670 F.3d 377 (1st Cir. 2012), by contrast, held GE liable as an arranger for having shipped scrap insulating material (called scrap Pyranol) containing PCBs to a "chemical scrapper" that used some of the Pyranol as an additive in the manufacture of paints. The court found that the scrap Pyranol was not a useful product, that GE viewed it as waste material, and that any profit GE derived from selling the Pyranol to the scrapper was incidental to the immediate benefit of being rid of an overstock of unusable chemicals. Among the relevant facts were the absence of quality control measures by GE before shipping the Pyranol to the scrapper, GE's decision to excuse payment for Pyranol that the scrapper found too contaminated to be used, and GE's refusal to retrieve the material when asked to do so by the scrapper. The court rejected GE's claim that *Burlington Northern* restricts arranger liability to PRPs with the apparent objective of disposing of hazardous substances or entering an arrangement with a transparent desire to have its hazardous substances enter the environment.

Does *Burlington Northern* affect cases, such as *Montalvo*, that do not involve the sale of a useful product? Celanese Corp. v. Martin K. Eby Constr. Co., 620 F.3d 529 (5th Cir. 2010), interpreted *Burlington Northern* to preclude the argument that a pipeline installer's conscious disregard of its duty to investigate damage it caused to a methanol pipeline with a backhoe amounted to intentional steps to dispose of the methanol so as to trigger arranger liability.

State statutes analogous to CERCLA also authorize joint and several liability. In Department of Envtl. Quality v. BNSF Ry. Co., 246 P.3d 1037 (Mont. 2010), the court refused to follow *Burlington Northern*, holding that a party need not have intended to dispose of a hazardous substance to trigger arranger liability. Noting that §114 of CERCLA preserves state authority to adopt liability laws more stringent than CERCLA, the court concluded that broader arranger liability than CERCLA's best serves the statutory goals of protecting health and the environment and allowing the state environmental agency to most effectively address contamination. Which approach—*Burlington Northern*'s or *BNSY Ry.*'s—do you think is preferable as a policy matter?

3. *Municipal Solid Waste Exemptions.* CERCLA exempts from response cost liability certain persons who sent municipal solid waste to an NPL site. Which persons are eligible for the defense, and under what circumstances? What is municipal solid waste for these purposes? See §107(p).

Problem 9-5

Zeus owns property contaminated by lead that leached into the soil and ground-water from crushed battery casings dumped there over several years. EPA discovered elevated levels of lead in the soil and groundwater underneath and adjacent to the property and incurred response costs in excess of $6 million. Many of the crushed battery casings that contaminated the property were transported to the Zeus site by a battery cracking plant operated by Crackling Batteries Co. (CBC). The CBC plant reclaimed lead from dead lead acid batteries, most of which were from cars. CBC obtained dead batteries from gas stations and auto parts facilities such as the Retail Auto Parts Stores (RAPS). The dead batteries purchased from RAPS were depleted and no longer capable of providing electrical power to cars. CBC purchased the batteries solely for the lead they contained, and the prices CBC paid fluctuated directly with the price of lead.

The batteries CBC purchased required processing before the lead within them could be reused. CBC melted or "guillotined" the top off a battery to remove the lead plates from within it, and then smelted the recovered lead for a variety of new uses, including the manufacture of lead solder, pipe, and shot; sheet and plumber's caulking lead; and ingot lead for battery manufacturers. After CBC removed the lead, it washed and crushed the casings and loaded them into a truck for transportation to the Zeus dump site. Tons of pieces of crushed battery casings were found at the Zeus site. When CBC purchased batteries, it assumed complete ownership and control of them. RAPS relinquished all ownership interest in and control over the batteries and was not directly involved in CBC's transportation, processing, recycling, or disposal activity.

The United States sued Zeus, CBC, and RAPS to recover its response costs. Zeus and CBC settled, but RAPS denied liability. The government's theory is that RAPS is liable as an arranger for disposal. Both parties have filed summary judgment motions on the issue of liability. How should the court rule based on the preceding cases and notes? Suppose that the suit was filed in 2003. Would the result have been different? See §127(e)-(f), added to CERCLA by the Superfund Recycling Equity Act in 1999.

c.   Transporters

Relatively few cases address transporter liability under §107(a)(4). Tippins v. USX Corp., 37 F.3d 87, 94-95 (3d Cir. 1994), concluded that "a person is liable as a transporter not only if it ultimately selects the disposal facility, but also when it actively participates in the disposal decision to the extent of having had substantial input into which facility was ultimately chosen. The substantiality of the input will be a function, in part, of whether the decisionmaker relied upon the transporter's special expertise in reaching its final decision." Prisco v. A & D Carting Corp., 168 F.3d 593 (2d Cir. 1999), held that a private cost recovery plaintiff must prove that a transporter's waste contained a hazardous substance, but not that any material containing such substances transported by a PRP to a facility broke down and released them into the environment.

d.   Lenders and Trustees

The issue of whether a party may become liable under CERCLA even if it is not directly involved in the activities resulting in contamination has arisen in several contexts. One issue involves the extent to which those who lend money to facilities requiring remediation are liable under §107(a). CERCLA includes a "secured creditor exemption" in §101(20)(A), which provides that the term "owner or operator" "does not include a person who, without participating in the management of a vessel or facility, holds indicia of ownership primarily to protect his security interest in the vessel or facility."

The courts disagreed on the scope of the exemption. United States v. Fleet Factors Corp., 901 F.2d 1550 (11th Cir. 1990), took the position that a secured creditor could become liable as an operator under §107(a)(2)

> by participating in the financial management of a facility to a degree indicating a capacity to influence the corporation's treatment of hazardous wastes. It is not necessary for the secured creditor actually to involve itself in the day-to-day operations of the facility in order to be liable—although such conduct will certainly lead to the loss of the protection of the statutory exemption. Nor is it necessary for the secured creditor to participate in management decisions relating to hazardous waste. Rather, a secured creditor will be liable if its involvement with the management of the facility is sufficiently broad to support the inference that it could affect hazardous waste disposal decisions if it so chose. [Id. at 1557-1558.]

The Ninth Circuit, however, ruled that the mere capacity or unexercised right to control facility operations does not take a lender outside the scope of the secured creditor exemption. Rather, "there must be some actual management of the facility before a secured creditor will fall outside the exception." In re Bergsoe Metal Corp., 910 F.2d 668, 672 (9th Cir. 1990).

In 1996, Congress enacted the Asset Conservation, Lender Liability, and Deposit Insurance Protection Act, Pub. L. No. 104-208, 110 Stat. 3009, which added new subsections (E)-(G) to §101(20) of CERCLA. What approach to lender liability do the 1996 amendments reflect? Does the statute codify *Fleet Factors* or *Bergsoe Metal*? See Policy on Interpreting CERCLA Provisions Addressing Lenders and Involuntary Acquisitions by Government Entities, 62 Fed. Reg. 36,424 (1997). When will a foreclosing lender incur liability as an owner or operator?

The 1996 Act also addressed fiduciary liability by adding §107(n) to CERCLA. When and to what extent may fiduciaries incur response cost liability? See Canadyne-Georgia Corp. v. NationsBank, N.A. (South), 183 F.3d 1269 (11th Cir. 1999); Palmtree Acquisition Corp. v. Neely, 771 F. Supp. 2d 1186 (N.D. Cal. 2011). If a deceased person was individually liable as a PRP, do the beneficiaries of a trust created by the deceased's will also become liable as PRPs? See ASARCO LLC v. Goodwin, 756 F.3d 191 (2d Cir. 2014) (concluding that state law governs the question).

Problem 9-6

In 2008, Blanchard purchased a steel manufacturing plant previously owned by Clevenger. To finance the purchase, Blanchard arranged a loan from Downing Savings & Loan. Under the terms of the loan, Downing provided sufficient capital to Blanchard to purchase the site and business and authorized Blanchard to seek additional advances of up to $5 million in working capital. In return, Downing took a security interest in the plant and its assets. Over the next two years, Blanchard applied for and received from Downing $5 million in working capital advances. In January 2011, Blanchard defaulted on its loan payments for the initial loan and the subsequent advances, and Downing foreclosed on its security interest in the plant and its assets.

In February 2011, Downing leased the plant site to Howard for one year. At the same time, Downing sold to Howard all of the plant equipment, inventory, and other assets previously owned by Blanchard. Under the terms of the lease, Howard was responsible for paying all taxes, insurance, mortgage costs, and other maintenance expenses on the plant site. The lease agreement gave Howard a right of first refusal if Downing decided to sell the plant at the expiration of the lease. In February 2012, after Downing's management informed Howard that it intended to sell the property, Howard purchased the plant site from Downing. To facilitate the transaction, Downing financed the mortgage Howard took out on the real property, in exchange for which Downing took a security interest in the land.

The security interest agreement between Downing and Howard gave Downing the right to demand monthly reports from Howard on inventory status and monthly expenditures and receipts. Downing had the right to prohibit Howard from procuring financing from other lenders or executing liens on any of the plant's equipment, the right to approve all major expenses incurred by Howard, including payroll expenditures, the right to approve all contracts entered into by Howard, and the right to inspect the plant facilities on a monthly basis. Downing also retained the right to attend all meetings held by Howard's board of directors and to provide advice to Howard's management on any matters discussed at those meetings.

Between February 2011 and September 2014, Downing's senior loan officer, Reniff, visited the plant site to review Howard's accounts receivables and analyze its inventory and raw materials. During the first year, Reniff made monthly visits to the plant. After that, he visited the plant on a bimonthly basis. Each of the visits took less than a day, during which Reniff toured the plant facilities and spent a few hours in the office reviewing financial records. Reniff attended four meetings of Howard's board of directors during this period. At one meeting, Stafford, Howard's president, discussed with other board members the plant's waste management practices. Shortly thereafter, Howard entered into a contract with Gonder pursuant to which Gonder picked up and removed from the site every six months barrels of liquid waste collected at the plant's loading dock. Reniff reviewed the contract before it was executed but did not communicate with anyone at Howard about it before Stafford signed the contract on behalf of Howard.

In September 2014, during a routine plant inspection, state environmental officials discovered that a variety of hazardous substances had contaminated the plant site. Some of those substances resulted from operations at the plant during Clevenger's and Blanchard's ownership, and some resulted from operations conducted by Howard since February 2011. In particular, the state agency determined that hazardous substances leaked out of the barrels near the loading dock before they were picked up by Gonder.

After being notified of the situation by the state agency, EPA conducted a cleanup at the site and then filed a cost recovery action under §107 against Blanchard, Clevenger, Howard, and Stafford. Clevenger filed an action for contribution against Downing. Downing has filed a motion for summary judgment, claiming that it is protected from liability under the secured creditor exemption. How should the court rule on that motion?

e. Corporate Liability

UNITED STATES v. BESTFOODS
524 U.S. 51 (1998)

Justice SOUTER delivered the opinion of the Court.

. . . The issue before us, under [CERCLA], is whether a parent corporation that actively participated in, and exercised control over, the operations of a subsidiary may, without more, be held liable as an operator of a polluting facility owned or operated by the subsidiary. We answer no, unless the corporate veil may be pierced. But a corporate parent that actively participated in, and exercised control over, the operations of the facility itself may be held directly liable in its own right as an operator of the facility. . . .

[While manufacturing chemicals at a plant in Michigan, Ott Chemical Co. (Ott I) dumped hazardous substances, significantly polluting the site. In 1965, CPC International Inc. (which later changed its name to Bestfoods) incorporated a wholly owned subsidiary, Ott Chemical Co. (Ott II), to buy Ott I's assets in exchange for CPC stock. Ott II continued to pollute its surroundings. The managers of Ott I became officers of Ott II. Some Ott II officers and directors performed duties for both Ott II and CPC. In 1972, CPC sold Ott II to Story, which operated the plant until its bankruptcy in 1977. A state agency subsequently discovered massive chemical contamination of the soil and water at the site. Cordova/California, a wholly owned subsidiary of Aerojet-General Corp., purchased the site from the bankruptcy trustee in 1977. Cordova/California created its own wholly owned subsidiary, Cordova/Michigan, which manufactured chemicals at the site until 1986.

After EPA developed a remedial plan for the site, the United States filed a §107 cost recovery action against CPC, Aerojet, Cordova/California, and Cordova/Michigan, but not Ott I and Ott II, which were defunct. The issue was whether CPC and Aerojet, the parent corporations of Ott II and the Cordova companies, were liable under §107(a)(2). The district court concluded that a parent corporation may incur operator liability both directly, when it operates the facility, and indirectly, when the corporate veil can be pierced under state law. It ruled that a parent is directly liable as an operator under §107(a)(2) if it "actively participat[ed] in and exercis[ed] control over the subsidiary's business during a period of waste disposal," but not on the basis of "mere oversight" of the subsidiary's business in a manner consistent with the investment relationship between parent and subsidiary. Under this test, CPC and Aerojet were liable as operators, based on CPC's selection of Ott II's board of directors, the presence of CPC officials among Ott II's executives, and the significant role in shaping Ott II's environmental compliance policy played by a CPC official, G.R.D. Williams.

In a split decision, the Sixth Circuit reversed in part. The majority acknowledged that a parent company might be directly liable as an operator of a facility owned by its subsidiary: "At least conceivably, a parent might independently operate the facility in the stead of its subsidiary; or, as a sort of joint venturer, actually operate the facility alongside its subsidiary." But it rejected the district court's analysis, concluding that a parent corporation will be liable as an operator based on its control of a subsidiary which owns the facility only when the requirements necessary to pierce the corporate veil under state law are met. According to the court, the liability of the parent as an operator depends on whether its controls over the subsidiary and the extent and manner of its involvement with the facility amount to a sufficient abuse of the corporate form to warrant such piercing. Applying Michigan law, the court held that neither CPC nor Aerojet was liable as an operator, because the parent and subsidiary corporations maintained separate personalities, and the parents did not use the subsidiary corporate form to perpetrate fraud or subvert justice.

The Supreme Court granted *certiorari* "to resolve a conflict among the Circuits over the extent to which parent corporations may be held liable under CERCLA for operating facilities ostensibly under the control of their subsidiaries."[d]]

III

It is a general principle of corporate law deeply "ingrained in our economic and legal systems" that a parent corporation (so-called because of control through ownership of another corporation's stock) is not liable for the acts of its subsidiaries. Douglas & Shanks, Insulation from Liability Through Subsidiary Corporations, 39 Yale L.J. 193 (1929) (hereinafter Douglas). Thus it is hornbook law that "the exercise of the 'control' which stock ownership gives to the stockholders . . . will not create liability beyond the assets of the subsidiary. That 'control' includes the election of directors, the making of by-laws . . . and the doing of all other acts incident to the legal status of stockholders. Nor will a duplication of some or all of the directors or executive officers be fatal." Id. at 196. Although this respect for corporate distinctions when the subsidiary is a polluter has been severely criticized in the literature, nothing in CERCLA purports to reject this bedrock principle, and against this venerable common-law backdrop, the congressional silence is audible. The Government has indeed made no claim that a corporate parent is liable as an owner or an operator under §107 simply because its subsidiary is subject to liability for owning or operating a polluting facility.

But there is an equally fundamental principle of corporate law, applicable to the parent-subsidiary relationship as well as generally, that the corporate veil may be pierced and the shareholder held liable for the corporation's conduct when, *inter alia*, the corporate form would otherwise be misused to accomplish certain wrongful purposes, most notably fraud, on the shareholder's behalf. Nothing in CERCLA purports to rewrite this well-settled rule, either. . . . [T]he failure of the statute to speak to a matter as fundamental as the liability implications of corporate ownership demands application of the rule that "[i]n order to abrogate a common-law principle, the statute must speak directly to the question addressed by the common law," United States v. Texas, 507 U.S. 529, 534 (1993). The Court of Appeals was accordingly correct in holding that when (but only when) the corporate veil may be pierced,[9] may

---

d. Some courts had held that a parent may be held liable for controlling affairs of its subsidiary only when the corporate veil can be pierced, but others had concluded that a parent actively involved in the affairs of its subsidiary may be held directly liable as an operator of the facility, regardless of whether the corporate veil can be pierced.

9. There is significant disagreement among courts and commentators over whether, in enforcing CERCLA's indirect liability, courts should borrow state law, or instead apply a federal common law of veil piercing. Since none of the parties challenges the Sixth Circuit's holding that CPC and Aerojet incurred no derivative liability, the question is not presented in this case, and we do not address it further.

a parent corporation be charged with derivative CERCLA liability for its subsidiary's actions.[10]

IV

A

If the Act rested liability entirely on ownership of a polluting facility, this opinion might end here; but CERCLA liability may turn on operation as well as ownership, and nothing in the statute's terms bars a parent corporation from direct liability for its own actions in operating a facility owned by its subsidiary. As Justice (then-Professor) Douglas noted almost 70 years ago, derivative liability cases are to be distinguished from those in which "the alleged wrong can seemingly be traced to the parent through the conduit of its own personnel and management" and "the parent is directly a participant in the wrong complained of." Douglas, at 207, 208. In such instances, the parent is directly liable for its own actions. The fact that a corporate subsidiary happens to own a polluting facility operated by its parent does nothing, then, to displace the rule that the parent "corporation is [itself] responsible for the wrongs committed by its agents in the course of its business," Mine Workers v. Coronado Coal Co., 259 U.S. 344, 395 (1922), and whereas the rules of veil-piercing limit derivative liability for the actions of another corporation, CERCLA's "operator" provision is concerned primarily with direct liability for one's own actions. It is this direct liability that is properly seen as being at issue here.

Under the plain language of the statute, any person who operates a polluting facility is directly liable for the costs of cleaning up the pollution. See 42 U.S.C. §9607(a)(2). This is so regardless of whether that person is the facility's owner, the owner's parent corporation or business partner, or even a saboteur who sneaks into the facility at night to discharge its poisons out of malice. If any such act of operating a corporate subsidiary's facility is done on behalf of a parent corporation, the existence of the parent-subsidiary relationship under state corporate law is simply irrelevant to the issue of direct liability.

This much is easy to say; the difficulty comes in defining actions sufficient to constitute direct parental "operation." . . . In a mechanical sense, to "operate" ordinarily means "[t]o control the functioning of; run: operate a sewing machine." American Heritage Dictionary 1268 (3d ed. 1992). And in the organizational sense more obviously intended by CERCLA, the word ordinarily means "[t]o conduct the affairs of; manage: operate a business." Id. So, under CERCLA, an operator is simply someone who directs the workings of, manages, or conducts the affairs of a facility. To sharpen the definition for purposes of CERCLA's concern with environmental contamination, an operator must manage, direct, or conduct operations

---

10. Some courts and commentators have suggested that this indirect, veil-piercing approach can subject a parent corporation to liability only as an owner, and not as an operator. See, e.g., Lansford-Coaldale Joint Water Auth. v. Tonolli Corp., [4 F.3d 1209, 1220 (3d Cir. 1993)]; Oswald, Bifurcation of the Owner and Operator Analysis Under CERCLA, 72 Wash. U. L.Q. 223, 281-282 (1994) (hereinafter Oswald). We think it is otherwise, however. If a subsidiary that operates, but does not own, a facility is so pervasively controlled by its parent for a sufficiently improper purpose to warrant veil piercing, the parent may be held derivatively liable for the subsidiary's acts as an operator.

specifically related to pollution, that is, operations having to do with the leakage or disposal of hazardous waste, or decisions about compliance with environmental regulations.

B

With this understanding, we are satisfied that the Court of Appeals correctly rejected the District Court's analysis of direct liability. But we also think that the appeals court erred in limiting direct liability under the statute to a parent's sole or joint venture operation, so as to eliminate any possible finding that CPC is liable as an operator on the facts of this case. . . .

By emphasizing that "CPC is directly liable under section 107(a)(2) as an operator because CPC actively participated in and exerted significant control over Ott II's business and decision-making," the District Court applied the "actual control" test of whether the parent "actually operated the business of its subsidiary," as several Circuits have employed it, see, e.g., Jacksonville Elec. Auth. v. Bernuth Corp., 996 F.2d 1107, 1110 (11th Cir. 1993) (parent is liable if it "actually exercised control over, or was otherwise intimately involved in the operations of, the [subsidiary] corporation immediately responsible for the operation of the facility").

The well-taken objection to the actual control test, however, is its fusion of direct and indirect liability; the test is administered by asking a question about the relationship between the two corporations (an issue going to indirect liability) instead of a question about the parent's interaction with the subsidiary's facility (the source of any direct liability). If, however, direct liability for the parent's operation of the facility is to be kept distinct from derivative liability for the subsidiary's own operation, the focus of the enquiry must necessarily be different under the two tests. "The question is not whether the parent operates the subsidiary, but rather whether it operates the facility, and that operation is evidenced by participation in the activities of the facility, not the subsidiary. Control of the subsidiary, if extensive enough, gives rise to indirect liability under piercing doctrine, not direct liability under the statutory language." Oswald, at 269. The District Court was therefore mistaken to rest its analysis on CPC's relationship with Ott II, premising liability on little more than "CPC's 100-percent ownership of Ott II" and "CPC's active participation in, and at times majority control over, Ott II's board of directors." The analysis should instead have rested on the relationship between CPC and the Muskegon facility itself.

In addition to (and perhaps as a reflection of) the erroneous focus on the relationship between CPC and Ott II, . . . [t]he District Court emphasized the facts that CPC placed its own high-level officials on Ott II's board of directors and in key management positions at Ott II, and that those individuals made major policy decisions and conducted day-to-day operations at the facility. . . .

In imposing direct liability on these grounds, the District Court failed to recognize that "it is entirely appropriate for directors of a parent corporation to serve as directors of its subsidiary, and that fact alone may not serve to expose the parent corporation to liability for its subsidiary's acts." American Protein Corp. v. AB Volvo, 844 F.2d 56, 57 (2d Cir. 1988).

. . . [I]t cannot be enough to establish liability here that dual officers and directors made policy decisions and supervised activities at the facility. The Government would have to show that, despite the general presumption to the contrary, the officers and directors were acting in their capacities as CPC officers and directors, and not as

Ott II officers and directors, when they committed those acts. The District Court made no such enquiry here. . . .

In sum, the District Court's focus on the relationship between parent and subsidiary (rather than parent and facility), combined with its automatic attribution of the actions of dual officers and directors to the corporate parent, erroneously, even if unintentionally, treated CERCLA as though it displaced or fundamentally altered common law standards of limited liability. . . . [Such an approach would essentially create] a relaxed, CERCLA-specific rule of derivative liability that would banish traditional standards and expectations from the law of CERCLA liability. But, as we have said, such a rule does not arise from congressional silence, and CERCLA's silence is dispositive. . . .

We accordingly agree with the Court of Appeals that a participation-and-control test looking to the parent's supervision over the subsidiary, especially one that assumes that dual officers always act on behalf of the parent, cannot be used to identify oper-ation of a facility resulting in direct parental liability. Nonetheless, a return to the ordinary meaning of the word "operate" in the organizational sense will indicate why we think that the Sixth Circuit stopped short when it confined its examples of direct parental operation to exclusive or joint ventures, and declined to find at least the possibility of direct operation by CPC in this case.

In our enquiry into the meaning Congress presumably had in mind when it used the verb "to operate," we recognized that the statute obviously meant something more than mere mechanical activation of pumps and valves, and must be read to contem-plate "operation" as including the exercise of direction over the facility's activities. The Court of Appeals recognized this by indicating that a parent can be held directly liable when the parent operates the facility in the stead of its subsidiary or alongside the subsidiary in some sort of a joint venture. [But] a dual officer or director might depart so far from the norms of parental influence exercised through dual officeholding as to serve the parent, even when ostensibly acting on behalf of the subsidiary in operating the facility. Yet another possibility, suggested by the facts of this case, is that an agent of the parent with no hat to wear but the parent's hat might manage or direct activities at the facility.

Identifying such an occurrence calls for line drawing yet again, since the acts of direct operation that give rise to parental liability must necessarily be distinguished from the interference that stems from the normal relationship between parent and subsidiary. . . . The critical question is whether, in degree and detail, actions directed to the facility by an agent of the parent alone are eccentric under accepted norms of parental oversight of a subsidiary's facility.

There is, in fact, some evidence that CPC engaged in just this type and degree of activity at the Muskegon plant. The District Court's opinion speaks of an agent of CPC alone who played a conspicuous part in dealing with the toxic risks emanating from the operation of the plant. G.R.D. Williams worked only for CPC; he was not an employee, officer, or director of Ott II, and thus, his actions were of necessity taken only on behalf of CPC. The District Court found that "CPC became directly involved in environmental and regulatory matters through the work of . . . Williams, CPC's governmental and environmental affairs director. Williams . . . became heavily involved in environmental issues at Ott II." . . .

We think that these findings are enough to raise an issue of CPC's operation of the facility through Williams's actions, though we would draw no ultimate conclusion from these findings at this point. . . . [The Court remanded, "on the theory of direct operation set out here, for reevaluation of Williams's role, and of the role of any other CPC agent who might be said to have had a part in operating the Muskegon facility."]

NOTES AND QUESTIONS

1. *Parent and Subsidiary Corporations, and Piercing the Corporate Veil.* It is important to distinguish between liability imposed on a parent corporation as a result of its own activities and liability that stems solely from the parent's ownership of another corporation. The Supreme Court in *Bestfoods* described the distinction as one between direct and indirect (or derivative) liability. What is the difference between the two? On remand in *Bestfoods*, the district court found that CPC was not directly liable as an operator. The government failed to prove that G.R.D. Williams, or any other CPC officer or director, engaged in activities that were sufficiently "eccentric" to impose operator liability. The court also rejected the contention that CPC was derivatively liable as a successor to Ott I, because Ott I's acquisition constituted a de facto merger with CPC. Bestfoods v. Aerojet-General Corp., 173 F. Supp. 2d 729 (W.D. Mich. 2001).

In assessing a parent corporation's indirect liability either as an owner or operator, when is it appropriate to pierce the corporate veil? The factors traditionally considered by state courts in deciding whether to pierce the corporate veil include: (1) inadequate capitalization in light of the purposes for which the corporation was organized, (2) extensive control by the parent shareholders, (3) intermingling of subsidiary and parent accounts and property, (4) failure to observe the formalities of separateness, such as separate records, (5) diversion of funds from the subsidiary to the parent, and (6) existence of nonfunctioning officers or directors. New York State Elec. and Gas Corp. v. FirstEnergy Corp., 766 F.3d 212, 224 (2d Cir. 2014), held that a parent was indirectly liable under a veil-piercing theory because it dominated its subsidiaries in such a way as to make them a mere instrumentality of the parent and considered the subsidiaries to be "mere pockets" of the parent. The court also held, however, that the parent was not liable for events that occurred after that domination ended.

Direct liability, as *Bestfoods* indicates, is based on the relationship between the parent and the contaminated site. After *Bestfoods*, when will a parent corporation be directly liable as an operator for CERCLA response costs? In United States v. Kayser-Roth Corp., 272 F.3d 89 (1st Cir. 2001), the court affirmed a lower court finding that a parent was directly liable based on its pervasive control over the subsidiary's environmental affairs. Compare New York State Elec. and Gas Corp. v. FirstEnergy Corp., 766 F.3d 212, 222-24 (2d Cir. 2014) (holding that parent not liable because it did not operate contaminated facility "in the stead of its subsidiary" and did not depart from norms of parental influence); Atlanta Gas Light Co. v. UGI Util., Inc., 463 F.3d 1201 (11th Cir. 2006) (parent not liable as operator). Should the tests for whether a parent corporation is liable as an operator also apply in the context of arranger or transporter liability? See United States v. TIC Inv. Corp., 68 F.3d 1082, 1091-1092 (8th Cir. 1995) (parent corporation is directly liable as an arranger of a subsidiary's off-site disposal practices only if there is "some causal connection or nexus between the parent corporation's conduct and the subsidiary's arrangement for disposal, or the off-site disposal itself").

2. *Successor and Dissolved Corporations.* Courts have imposed operator liability on successor as well as parent corporations. Successor liability doctrine seeks

"to prevent corporations from dying 'paper deaths' only to reemerge having eliminated their environmental liability." United States v. NCR Corp., 840 F. Supp. 2d 1093, 1095 (E.D. Wis. 2011). United States v. General Battery Corp., 423 F.3d 294 (3d Cir. 2005), found that under the prevailing approach to corporate successor liability (referred to as the "mere continuation" test), the successor is not liable for the activities of an acquired corporation unless (1) the successor assumes liability, (2) the transaction amounts to a consolidation or merger, (3) the transaction is fraudulent and intended to provide an escape from liability, or (4) the purchasing corporation is a mere continuation of the selling company. *General Battery* turned on whether there had been a de facto merger, which occurs if (a) there has been a continuation of the enterprise of the seller corporation, (b) there is a continuity of shareholders, (c) the seller corporation ceases its ordinary business operations and liquidates and dissolves as soon as possible, and (d) the purchasing corporation assumes the obligations of the seller ordinarily necessary for the uninterrupted continuation of the seller's normal business operations. The court held the successor liable under that standard. It also held that, after *Bestfoods*, the "substantial continuity" doctrine, which is a more expansive successor liability rule than the mere continuation rule, is untenable as a basis for successor liability under CERCLA. But cf. PCS Nitrogen Inc. v. Ashley II of Charleston LLC, 714 F.3d 161, 173-176 (4th Cir. 2013) (refusing to impose liability under "substantial continuity" test because successor did not assume predecessor's liabilities); K.C.1986 Ltd. P'ship v. Reade Mfg., 472 F.3d 1009, 1022 (8th Cir. 2007) (stating that "there may yet be contexts in which the substantial continuity test could survive").

3. *Corporate Officers and Shareholders.* The courts seem more reluctant to impose CERCLA liability on individuals connected to corporations. Corporate officers apparently will not be held liable, either as operators or arrangers, merely on the basis of their position in the corporate hierarchy. Officers who actively participate in or actually exercise substantial control over hazardous substance management, however, may be liable. See, e.g., United States v. TIC Inv. Corp., 68 F.3d 1082 (8th Cir. 1995) (arranger liability); Sidney S. Arst Co. v. Pipefitters Welfare Educ. Fund, 25 F.3d 417 (7th Cir. 1994) (operator liability). Should corporate officers who control day-to-day corporate activities but not liability-creating conduct be liable? See United States v. USX Corp., 68 F.3d 811 (3d Cir. 1995) (no, although actual knowledge of and acquiescence in a subordinate's decisions may be enough). Likewise, Jacksonville Elec. Auth. v. Bernuth Corp., 996 F.2d 1107 (11th Cir. 1993), established that individual shareholders are liable as operators only when they actually participated in facility operations or in the activities resulting in disposal, or actually exercised control over, or were otherwise intimately involved in the operations of, the corporation operating the facility. But see Carter-Jones Lumber Co. v. LTV Steel Co., 237 F.3d 745 (6th Cir. 2001) (individual shareholder's control of corporation justified piercing of corporate veil and imposing joint and several liability).

Problem 9-7

Blackhawk operated a trucking terminal on the Maggyland site from 1961 to 1971, when it sold the site to Apartments, Inc. In 1973, Apartments, Inc. sold the site to Maggyland Limited, which contracted with Constructor Co. to build an apartment complex. In 1984, Al Adams and Adams, Inc. became general partners in Maggyland Limited, holding a 1 percent interest. Adams was president and majority shareholder of Adams, Inc. At the same time, Lynch Properties, Inc. became a limited partner in Maggyland Limited, holding the other 99 percent. Beginning in 1984, the partners in Maggyland Limited vested day-to-day responsibility for managing the apartment complex in Management Co. The general and limited partners remained responsible for approving rent increases and capital improvements in the apartment complex, which included repaving the parking lot and maintaining natural gas lines on the property. Both of these projects involved movement and dispersal of contaminated soil, although none of the partners knew at the time about the contamination.

While Blackhawk operated its trucking terminal, its trucks routinely carried substances that included asphalt. Its employees dumped unused asphalt into a pit on the site, and hazardous substances, which Blackhawk employees disposed of at the site mixed with the asphalt, creating a black, tar-like substance that oozed from the pit into surrounding soil and groundwater. Some of the hazardous substances at the site resulted from the washing of Blackhawk's trucks. To contain these substances, Blackhawk built levees, using heavy equipment to move earth. The result was the movement of hazardous substances near the levees and mixture of those substances with surrounding soil. Although Blackhawk did not inform Apartments, Inc. of the history of hazardous substance disposal and release when Blackhawk sold the site to Apartments, Inc., the presence of hazardous substances in the area was common knowledge.

In 2014, the state environmental agency responded to complaints from Maggyland Apartment residents that tar-like substances were seeping to the surface at the site. The state agency notified EPA, which discovered tar, asphalt, pesticides, chlorinated benzenes, and polynuclear hydrocarbons in the soil and groundwater at the Maggyland site. The pesticides chlordane and dieldrin were initially sprayed at the site at the direction of Management Co., which was responsible for lawn care at the apartment complex. EPA had registered the two pesticides under FIFRA before the spraying, but it revoked the registrations before 1984. EPA incurred nearly $2 million in response costs removing or containing these contaminants.

EPA has brought an action for reimbursement of its response costs under §107(a) of CERCLA against Blackhawk; Apartments, Inc.; Maggyland Limited; Constructor Co.; Al Adams; Adams, Inc.; Lynch Properties, Inc.; and Management Co. Which of the defendants, if any, should the court hold liable?

4.   Contribution and Private Cost Recovery Actions

Section 113(f)(1) of CERCLA entitles any person to seek contribution from any other person who is liable or potentially liable under §106 or §107. May a person who is not the subject of a prior or pending CERCLA enforcement action bring such a contribution action?

COOPER INDUSTRIES, INC. v. AVIALL SERVICES, INC.
543 U.S. 157 (2004)

Justice THOMAS delivered the opinion of the Court.

Section 113(f)(1) of [CERCLA] allows persons who have undertaken efforts to clean up properties contaminated by hazardous substances to seek contribution from other parties liable under CERCLA. . . . The issue we must decide is whether a private party who has not been sued under §106 or §107(a) may nevertheless obtain contribution under §113(f)(1) from other liable parties. We hold that it may not.

I . . .

After CERCLA's enactment in 1980, litigation arose over . . . whether a private party that had incurred response costs, but that had done so voluntarily and was not itself subject to suit, had a cause of action for cost recovery against other PRPs. Various courts held that §107(a)(4)(B) and its predecessors authorized such a cause of action.

After CERCLA's passage, litigation also ensued over the separate question whether a private entity that had been sued in a cost recovery action (by the Government or by another PRP) could obtain contribution from other PRPs. As originally enacted in 1980, CERCLA contained no provision expressly providing for a right of action for contribution. A number of District Courts nonetheless held that, although CERCLA did not mention the word "contribution," such a right arose either impliedly from provisions of the statute, or as a matter of federal common law. That conclusion was debatable in light of two decisions of this Court that refused to recognize implied or common-law rights to contribution in other federal statutes.

Congress subsequently amended CERCLA in [SARA, enacted in 1986] to provide an express cause of action for contribution, codified as CERCLA §113(f)(1). . . .

SARA also created a separate express right of contribution, §113(f)(3)(B), for "[a] person who has resolved its liability to the United States or a State for some or all of a response action or for some or all of the costs of such action in an administrative or judicially approved settlement." In short, after SARA, CERCLA provided for a right to cost recovery in certain circumstances, §107(a), and separate rights to contribution in other circumstances, §§113(f)(1), 113(f)(3)(B).

II

[Cooper owned and operated four contaminated aircraft engine maintenance sites in Texas until 1981, when it sold them to Aviall. Aviall later discovered that both it and Cooper had contaminated the facilities through leaks and spills of hazardous substances onto the ground and into the groundwater. Aviall notified the Texas Natural Resource Conservation Commission (Commission), which informed Aviall that it was violating state environmental laws, directed Aviall to clean up the site, and threatened to pursue an enforcement action if Aviall failed to do so. Neither the Commission nor EPA took any judicial or administrative measures to compel cleanup by Aviall.

Under the state's supervision, Aviall cleaned up the properties and then sold them to a third party, remaining contractually responsible for the cleanup. After Aviall incurred approximately $5 million in cleanup costs, it sued Cooper in federal district court in Texas, seeking to recover contribution under §113(f)(1). The district court held that §113(f)(1) relief was unavailable to Aviall because it had not been sued under CERCLA §106 or §107. The Fifth Circuit, sitting en banc, reversed, holding that §113(f)(1) allows a PRP to obtain contribution from other PRPs regardless of whether the PRP has been sued under §106 or §107. Three judges dissented.]

970 Chapter IX. Environmental Contamination Liability and Remediation

III

A

Section 113(f)(1) does not authorize Aviall's suit. The first sentence, the enabling clause that establishes the right of contribution, provides: "Any person *may* seek contribution . . . *during or following* any civil action under section 9606 of this title or under section 9607(a) of this title" (emphasis added). The natural meaning of this sentence is that contribution may only be sought subject to the specified conditions, namely, "during or following" a specified civil action.

Aviall answers that "may" should be read permissively, such that "during or following" a civil action is one, but not the exclusive, instance in which a person may seek contribution. We disagree. First, as just noted, the natural meaning of "may" in the context of the enabling clause is that it authorizes certain contribution actions — ones that satisfy the subsequent specified condition — and no others.

Second, and relatedly, if §113(f)(1) were read to authorize contribution actions at any time, regardless of the existence of a §106 or §107(a) civil action, then Congress need not have included the explicit "during or following" condition. In other words, Aviall's reading would render part of the statute entirely superfluous, something we are loath to do. Likewise, if §113(f)(1) authorizes contribution actions at any time, §113(f)(3)(B), which permits contribution actions after settlement, is equally superfluous. There is no reason why Congress would bother to specify conditions under which a person may bring a contribution claim, and at the same time allow contribution actions absent those conditions.

The last sentence of §113(f)(1), the saving clause, does not change our conclusion. That sentence provides: "Nothing in this subsection shall diminish the right of any person to bring an action for contribution in the absence of a civil action under section 9606 of this title or section 9607 of this title." The sole function of the sentence is to clarify that §113(f)(1) does nothing to "diminish" any cause(s) of action for contribution that may exist independently of §113(f)(1). In other words, the sentence rebuts any presumption that the express right of contribution provided by the enabling clause is the exclusive cause of action for contribution available to a PRP. The sentence, however, does not itself establish a cause of action; nor does it expand §113(f)(1) to authorize contribution actions not brought "during or following" a §106 or §107(a) civil action; nor does it specify what causes of action for contribution, if any, exist outside §113(f)(1). Reading the saving clause to authorize §113(f)(1) contribution actions not just "during or following" a civil action, but also before such an action, would again violate the settled rule that we must, if possible, construe a statute to give every word some operative effect.

Our conclusion follows not simply from §113(f)(1) itself, but also from the whole of §113. As noted above, §113 provides two express avenues for contribution: §113(f)(1) ("during or following" specified civil actions) and §113(f)(3)(B) (after an administrative or judicially approved settlement that resolves liability to the United States or a State). Section 113(g)(3) then provides two corresponding 3-year limitations periods for contribution actions, one beginning at the date of judgment, §113(g)(3)(A), and one beginning at the date of settlement, §113(g)(3)(B). Notably absent from §113(g)(3) is any provision for starting the limitations period if a judgment or settlement never occurs, as is the case with a purely voluntary cleanup. The lack of such a provision supports the conclusion that, to assert a contribution claim under §113(f), a party must satisfy the conditions of either §113(f)(1) or §113(f)(3)(B).

Each side insists that the purpose of CERCLA bolsters its reading of §113(f)(1). Given the clear meaning of the text, there is no need to resolve this dispute or to consult the purpose of CERCLA at all. As we have said: "[I]t is ultimately the provisions of our laws rather than the principal concerns of our legislators by which we are governed." Oncale v. Sundowner Offshore Serv., Inc., 523 U.S. 75, 79 (1998). Section 113(f)(1) authorizes contribution claims only "during or following" a civil action under §106 or §107(a), and it is undisputed that Aviall has never been subject to such an action.[5] Aviall therefore has no §113(f)(1) claim.

B

[Aviall argued that, even if it could not bring a contribution action under §113(f)(1), it could recover costs under §107(a)(4)(B), even though it was a PRP. The majority refused to address this issue because it was not properly raised below.]

C

In addition to leaving open whether Aviall may seek cost recovery under §107, we decline to decide whether Aviall has an implied right to contribution under §107. Portions of the Fifth Circuit's opinion below might be taken to endorse the latter cause of action; others appear to reserve the question whether such a cause of action exists. To the extent that Aviall chooses to frame its §107 claim on remand as an implied right of contribution (as opposed to a right of cost recovery), we note that this Court has visited the subject of implied rights of contribution before. We also note that, in enacting §113(f)(1), Congress explicitly recognized a particular set (claims "during or following" the specified civil actions) of the contribution rights previously implied by courts from provisions of CERCLA and the common law. Nonetheless, we need not and do not decide today whether any judicially implied right of contribution survived the passage of SARA. . . .

QUESTIONS

What was the key language in §113(f)(1) used to support the Court's holding? The Fifth Circuit en banc majority had relied on a combination of the first and last sentences of §113(f)(1) to support its conclusion that a PRP may sue for contribution even if it has not already been the subject of an enforcement action under §106 or §107. Can you re-create what that court's argument might have been? How did the Court interpret the last sentence of §113(f)(1)?

Justice Thomas noted that both sides argued that the purpose of CERCLA bolstered their readings of the statutory text, but that the clarity of the text precluded the need to consider statutory purposes. What do you suppose the effect of the Court's holding in the principal case will be on the conduct of the owners of contaminated

---

5. Neither has Aviall been subject to an administrative order under §106; thus, we need not decide whether such an order would qualify as a "civil action under section 9606 . . . or under section 9607(a)" of CERCLA. 42 U.S.C. §9613(f)(1).

sites that have not yet been sued by the government? Is that result consistent or inconsistent with CERCLA's purposes?

UNITED STATES v. ATLANTIC RESEARCH CORPORATION
551 U.S. 128 (2007)

Justice THOMAS delivered the opinion of the Court.

Two provisions of [CERCLA]—§§107(a) and 113(f)—allow private parties to recover expenses associated with cleaning up contaminated sites. In this case, we must decide a question left open in Cooper Industries, Inc. v. Aviall Services, Inc., 543 U.S. 157, 161 (2004): whether §107(a) provides so-called potentially responsible parties (PRPs) with a cause of action to recover costs from other PRPs. We hold that it does.

I

A

Courts have frequently grappled with whether and how PRPs may recoup CERCLA-related costs from other PRPs. The questions lie at the intersection of two statutory provisions—CERCLA §§107(a) and 113(f). Section 107(a) defines four categories of PRPs and makes them liable for [response costs]. Enacted as part of the Superfund Amendments and Reauthorization Act of 1986 (SARA), §113(f) authorizes one PRP to sue another for contribution in certain circumstances.[1]

Prior to the advent of §113(f)'s express contribution right, some courts held that §107(a)(4)(B) provided a cause of action for a private party to recover voluntarily incurred response costs and to seek contribution after having been sued. After SARA's enactment, however, . . . many Courts of Appeals held that §113(f) was the exclusive remedy for PRPs. But as courts prevented PRPs from suing under §107(a), they expanded §113(f) to allow PRPs to seek "contribution" even in the absence of a suit under §106 or §107(a).

In Cooper Industries, we held that a private party could seek contribution from other liable parties only after having been sued under §106 or §107(a). This narrower interpretation of §113(f) caused several Courts of Appeals to reconsider whether PRPs have rights under §107(a)(4)(B), an issue we declined to address in Cooper Industries. After revisiting the issue, some courts have permitted §107(a) actions by PRPs[, but others refused to do so]. Today, we resolve this issue.

B

In this case, respondent Atlantic Research leased property at the Shumaker Naval Ammunition Depot, a facility operated by the Department of Defense. At the site, Atlantic Research retrofitted rocket motors for petitioner United States. Using a high-pressure water spray, Atlantic Research removed pieces of propellant

---

1. Section 113(f)(1) permits private parties to seek contribution during or following a civil action under §106 or §107(a). Section 113(f)(3)(B) permits private parties to seek contribution after they have settled their liability with the Government.

from the motors. It then burned the propellant pieces. Some of the resultant waste-water and burned fuel contaminated soil and groundwater at the site.

Atlantic Research cleaned the site at its own expense and then sought to recover some of its costs by suing the United States under both §107(a) and §113(f). [The Court of Appeals reversed the district court's dismissal of the case, holding that §113(f) does not provide "the exclusive route by which [PRPs] may recover cleanup costs," and that §107(a)(4)(B) provided a cause of action to Atlantic Research.]

II

A

The parties' dispute centers on what "other person[s]" may sue under §107(a)(4)(B). The Government argues that "any other person" refers to any person not identified as a PRP in §§107(a)(1)-(4). In other words, subparagraph (B) permits suit only by non-PRPs and thus bars Atlantic Research's claim. Atlantic Research counters that subparagraph (B) takes its cue from subparagraph (A), not the earlier paragraph (1)-(4). In accord with the Court of Appeals, Atlantic Research believes that subparagraph (B) provides a cause of action to anyone except the United States, a State, or an Indian tribe—the persons listed in subparagraph (A). We agree with Atlantic Research.

Statutes must "be read as a whole." King v. St. Vincent's Hospital, 502 U.S. 215, 221 (1991). Applying that maxim, the language of subparagraph (B) can be understood only with reference to subparagraph (A). The provisions are adjacent and have remarkably similar structures. Each concerns certain costs that have been incurred by certain entities and that bear a specified relationship to the national contingency plan. Bolstering the structural link, the text also denotes a relationship between the two provisions. By using the phrase "other necessary costs," subparagraph (B) refers to and differentiates the relevant costs from those listed in subparagraph (A).

In light of the relationship between the subparagraphs, it is natural to read the phrase "any other person" by referring to the immediately preceding subparagraph (A), which permits suit only by the United States, a State, or an Indian tribe. The phrase "any other person" therefore means any person other than those three. See 42 U.S.C. §9601(21) (defining "person" to include the United States and the various States). Consequently, the plain language of subparagraph (B) authorizes cost-recovery actions by any private party, including PRPs.

The Government's interpretation makes little textual sense. In subparagraph (B), the phrase "any other necessary costs" and the phrase "any other person" both refer to antecedents—"costs" and "person[s]"—located in some previous statutory provision. Although "any other necessary costs" clearly references the costs in subparagraph (A), the Government would inexplicably interpret "any other person" to refer not to the persons listed in subparagraph (A) but to the persons listed as PRPs in paragraphs (1)-(4). Nothing in the text of §107(a)(4)(B) suggests an intent to refer to antecedents located in two different statutory provisions. Reading the statute in the manner suggested by the Government would destroy the symmetry of §§107(a)(4)(A) and (B) and render subparagraph (B) internally confusing.

Moreover, the statute defines PRPs so broadly as to sweep in virtually all persons likely to incur cleanup costs. Hence, if PRPs do not qualify as "any other person" for purposes of §107(a)(4)(B), it is unclear what private party would. The Government posits that §107(a)(4)(B) authorizes relief for "innocent" private parties—for instance, a landowner whose land has been contaminated by another. But even parties not responsible for contamination may fall within the broad definitions of PRPs in §§107(a)(1)-(4). See 42 U.S.C. §9607(a)(1) (listing "the owner and operator of a . . . facility" as a PRP). The Government's reading of the text logically precludes all PRPs, innocent or not, from recovering cleanup costs. Accordingly, accepting the Government's interpretation would reduce the number of potential plaintiffs to almost zero, rendering §107(a)(4)(B) a dead letter. . . .

B

The Government also argues that our interpretation will create friction between §107(a) and §113(f), the very harm courts of appeals have previously tried to avoid. In particular, the Government maintains that our interpretation, by offering PRPs a choice between §107(a) and §113(f), effectively allows PRPs to circumvent §113(f)'s shorter statute of limitations. See 42 U.S.C. §§9613(g)(2)-(3). Furthermore, the Government argues, PRPs will eschew equitable apportionment under §113(f) in favor of joint and several liability under §107(a). Finally, the Government contends that our interpretation eviscerates the settlement bar set forth in §113(f)(2).

We have previously recognized that §§107(a) and 113(f) provide two "clearly distinct" remedies. *Cooper Industries*, 543 U.S., at 163, n.3. "CERCLA provide[s] for a *right to cost recovery* in certain circumstances, §107(a), and *separate rights to contribution* in other circumstances, §§113(f)(1), 113(f)(3)(B)." Id., at 163 (emphases added). The Government, however, uses the word "contribution" as if it were synonymous with any apportionment of expenses among PRPs. This imprecise usage confuses the complementary yet distinct nature of the rights established in §§107(a) and 113(f).

Section 113(f) explicitly grants PRPs a right to contribution. Contribution is defined as the "tortfeasor's right to collect from others responsible for the same tort after the tortfeasor has paid more than his or her proportionate share, the shares being determined as a percentage of fault." Black's Law Dictionary 353 (8th ed. 1999). Nothing in §113(f) suggests that Congress used the term "contribution" in anything other than this traditional sense. The statute authorizes a PRP to seek contribution "during or following" a suit under §106 or §107(a). 42 U.S.C. §9613(f)(1). Thus, §113(f)(1) permits suit before or after the establishment of common liability. In either case, a PRP's right to contribution under §113(f)(1) is contingent upon an inequitable distribution of common liability among liable parties.

By contrast, §107(a) permits recovery of cleanup costs but does not create a right to contribution. A private party may recover under §107(a) without any establishment of liability to a third party. Moreover, §107(a) permits a PRP to recover only the costs it has "incurred" in cleaning up a site. 42 U.S.C. §9607(a)(4)(B). When a party pays to satisfy a settlement agreement or a court judgment, it does not incur its own costs of response. Rather, it reimburses other parties for costs that those parties incurred.

Accordingly, the remedies available in §§107(a) and 113(f) complement each other by providing causes of action "to persons in different procedural circumstances." [Consolidated Edison Co. of N.Y. v. UFI Util., Inc., 423 F.3d 90, 99 (2d Cir. 2005).] Section 113(f)(1) authorizes a contribution action to PRPs with common liability stemming from an action instituted under §106 or §107(a). And §107(a) permits cost recovery (as distinct from contribution) by a private party that has itself incurred cleanup costs. Hence, a PRP that pays money to satisfy a settlement agreement or a court judgment may pursue §113(f) contribution. But by reimbursing response costs paid by other parties, the PRP has not incurred its own costs of response and therefore cannot recover under §107(a). As a result, though eligible to seek contribution under §113(f)(1), the PRP cannot simultaneously seek to recover the same expenses under §107(a). Thus, at least in the case of reimbursement, the PRP cannot choose the 6-year statute of limitations for cost-recovery actions over the shorter limitations period for §113(f) contribution claims.[6]

For similar reasons, a PRP could not avoid §113(f)'s equitable distribution of reimbursement costs among PRPs by instead choosing to impose joint and several liability on another PRP in an action under §107(a). The choice of remedies simply does not exist. In any event, a defendant PRP in such a §107(a) suit could blunt any inequitable distribution of costs by filing a §113(f) counterclaim. Resolution of a §113(f) counterclaim would necessitate the equitable apportionment of costs among the liable parties, including the PRP that filed the §107(a) action. 42 U.S.C. §9613(f)(a) ("In resolving contribution claims, the court may allocate response costs among liable parties using such equitable factors as the court determines are appropriate").

Finally, permitting PRPs to seek recovery under §107(a) will not eviscerate the settlement bar set forth in §113(f)(2). . . . The settlement bar does not by its terms protect against cost-recovery liability under §107(a). For several reasons, we doubt this supposed loophole would discourage settlement. First, as stated above, a defendant PRP may trigger equitable apportionment by filing a §113(f) counterclaim. A district court applying traditional rules of equity would undoubtedly consider any prior settlement as part of the liability calculus. Second, the settlement bar continues to provide significant protection from contribution suits by PRPs that have inequitably reimbursed the costs incurred by another party. Third, settlement carries the inherent benefit of finally resolving liability as to the United States or a State.[8] . . .

Because the plain terms of §107(a)(4)(B) allow a PRP to recover costs from other PRPs, the statute provides Atlantic Research with a cause of action. . . .

QUESTIONS

After *Aviall* and *Atlantic Research*, when may a PRP bring either a cost recovery action under §107(a) or a contribution action under §113(f)(1)? What questions, if any, about the ability of PRPs to recover a fair share of the response costs they have incurred remain unresolved? See Agere Sys., Inc. v. Advanced Envtl. Tech. Corp., 602

---

6. We do not suggest that §§107(a)(4)(B) and 113(f) have no overlap at all. For instance, we recognize that a PRP may sustain expenses pursuant to a consent decree following a suit under §106 or §107(a). In such a case, the PRP does not incur costs voluntarily but does not reimburse the costs of another party. We do not decide whether these compelled costs of response are recoverable under §113(f), §107(a), or both. For our purposes, it suffices to demonstrate that costs incurred voluntarily are recoverable only by way of §107(a)(4)(B), and costs of reimbursement to another person pursuant to a legal judgment or settlement are recoverable only under §113(f). Thus, at a minimum, neither remedy swallows the other, contrary to the Government's argument.

8. Because §107(a) expressly permits PRPs to seek cost recovery, we need not address the alternative holding of the Court of Appeals that §107(a) contains an additional implied right to contribution for PRPs who are not eligible for relief under §113(f).

F.3d 204, 218 (3d Cir. 2010) (describing the relationship between §107 cost recovery claims and §113(f) contribution claims as "sometimes blurry," even after *Atlantic Research*); Kotrous v. Goss-Jewett Co., 523 F.3d 924 (9th Cir. 2008); Yankee Gas Servs. Co. v. UGI Util., Inc., 852 F. Supp. 2d 229, 240 (D. Conn. 2012).[e]

Reread note 6 of the Court's opinion. May a party who has settled and is eligible to file a §113(f) contribution claim also file a cost recovery action under §107(a)? Morrison Enter., LLC v. Dravo Corp., 638 F.3d 594 (8th Cir. 2011), held that §113(f) provides the exclusive remedy for a liable party compelled to incur response costs pursuant to an administrative or judicially approved settlement under §§106 or 107. See also Hobart Corp. v. Waste Mgmt. of Ohio Inc., 758 F.3d 757, 766-768 (6th Cir. 2014) (PRP that has entered into an administrative settlement with the government may only bring a §113(f)(3)(B) contribution action); Bernstein v. Bankert, 733 F.3d 190, 205-206 (7th Cir. 2012) (a plaintiff is limited to a contribution remedy when one is available); Solutia, Inc. v. McWane, Inc., 672 F.3d 1230 (11th Cir. 2012) (PRPs may not file a §107 cost recovery action for costs incurred complying with a consent decree with EPA). Compare United States v. NCR Corp., 688 F.3d 833, 843-844 (7th Cir. 2012) (characterizing the issue as open question). NCR Corp. v. George A. Whiting Paper Co., 2014 WL 4755491, *7-9 (7th Cir. 2014), held that a party that paid response costs after initially being mistakenly designated as a PRP may seek cost recovery from properly designated PRPs under §107(a). The court reasoned that fairness demands some remedy, and contribution was a poor fit because it applies among joint tortfeasors, and the mistakenly designed PRP was never a tortfeasor. The court characterized the cost recovery plaintiff as having made "constructive voluntary" payments, thereby making it eligible to sue under §107(a).

NOTE ON CONTRIBUTION AND PRIVATE COST RECOVERY

More on PRP Options. What options are available to PRPs who wish to pay for a cleanup and then seek at least partial reimbursement from other PRPs? One option is to bring a private cost recovery action under §107(a)(4)(B), the focus of *Atlantic Research*. A second option for a PRP unable to pursue a cost recovery action under §107(a) or a contribution action under §113(f)(1) may be to sue on the basis of an implied federal common law right to contribution for PRPs. Did *Aviall* or *Atlantic Research* address the viability of such an action? A third option is to be sued under §106 or §107 and then bring a §113(f)(1) contribution action against other PRPs.

A fourth possibility is to enter an administrative settlement with EPA or a state. See §113(f)(3)(B); Atlanta Gas Light Co. v. UGI Util, Inc., 463 F.3d 1201 (11th Cir. 2006). What agreements between EPA and PRPs qualify as "settlements" for purposes of §113(f)(3)(B)? See, ITT Indus., Inc. v. BorgWarner, Inc., 506 F.3d 452 (6th Cir. 2007); Responsible Envtl. Solutions Alliance v. Waste Mgmt., Inc., 493 F. Supp. 2d 1017 (S.D. Ohio 2007) (disagreeing on whether administrative orders by consent (AOCs) issued by EPA under §106 qualify). W.R. Grace & Co.-Conn. v. Zotos Int'l, Inc., 559 F.3d 85 (2d Cir. 2009), held that a PRP that has remediated a contaminated site pursuant to an AOC may bring a cost recovery action because §107 is not limited to those who voluntarily remediate a site. Does a consent order settling

---

e. See generally Ferrey, Inverting the Law: Superfund Hazardous Substance Liability and Supreme Court Reversal of All Federal Circuits, 33 Wm. & Mary L. & Pol'y Rev. 633 (2009).

liability under state law trigger a right to bring a §113(f)(3)(B) contribution action? Compare *Consolidated Edison* (cited in *Atlantic Research*) with Trinity Indus., Inc. v. Chicago Bridge & Iron Co., 735 F.3d 131 (3d Cir. 2013). Assuming a contribution action is appropriate, when may it be brought? Bernstein v. Bankert, 733 F.3d 190, 212-213 (7th Cir. 2012), concluded that a §113(f)(3)(B) action is not available until satisfactory performance of a settlement under §122 has occurred.

Resolving Contribution Claims. Section 113(f)(1) provides that, in resolving contribution claims, a federal court "may allocate response costs among liable parties using such equitable factors as the court determines are appropriate." One court likened the process to "trying to figure out what makes Coke taste the way it does." Browning-Ferris Indus. of Ill., Inc. v. Ter Maat, 13 F. Supp. 2d 756, 777 (N.D. Ill. 1998), *aff'd in part, rev'd in part on other grounds*, 195 F.3d 953 (7th Cir. 1999). Most courts agree that liability in a §113(f)(1) contribution action is several, rather than joint and several. Elementis Chromium, L.P. v. Coastal States Petroleum Co., 450 F.3d 607, 612-613 (5th Cir. 2006). But see Browning-Ferris Indus. of Illinois, Inc. v. Ter Maat, 195 F.3d 953, 956 (7th Cir. 1999) (CERCLA does not preclude the imposition of joint and several liability in a contribution action based on equitable considerations).

The factors that courts most frequently use to allocate responsibility in CERCLA contribution actions are the so-called Gore factors. Essentially, "[t]hose parties who can show that their contribution to the harm is relatively small in terms of amount of waste, toxicity of the waste, involvement with the waste, and care, stand in a better position to be allocated a smaller portion of response costs." Control Data Corp. v. SCSC Corp., 53 F.3d 930, 935 (8th Cir. 1995). See, e.g., Lyondell Chem. Corp. v. Occidental Chem. Corp., 608 F.3d 284, 300-301 (5th Cir. 2010) (approving allocation based on volume of waste produced at each facility, weighted by chemical composition). In Boeing Co. v. Cascade Corp., 207 F.3d 1177 (9th Cir. 2000), the court noted that courts may consider factors other than the Gore factors to allocate costs. See also Litgo New Jersey, Inc. v. Commissioner New Jersey Dep't of Envtl. Prot., 725 F.3d 369, 388 (3d Cir. 2013) (courts need not consider each Gore factor and may consider other factors, including the unavailability of the most responsible parties). But in Beazer East, Inc. v. Mead Corp., 412 F.3d 429 (3d Cir. 2005), the court ruled that CERCLA does not allow a court to prioritize the parties' relative contributions of waste, based on the "polluter pays" principle, over their contractual intent to allocate environmental liability among themselves.

What is the role of causation in CERCLA contribution litigation? In *Browning-Ferris, supra*, the Seventh Circuit concluded that liability may be imposed on a contribution defendant on the basis of either "but for" causation or proof that the defendant's activities were a "sufficient condition" of cleanup cost incurrence. "The resulting inquiry thus focuses not only on causation, but also on fault—a negligence concept foreign to the initial determination of responsibility under CERCLA." Nagle, CERCLA, Causation, and Responsibility, 78 Minn. L. Rev. 1493, 1523 (1994). Is it true that, as §107 has been interpreted, the concept of negligence is always foreign to the initial determination of responsibility under CERCLA?

Contribution Protection. Section 113(f)(2) provides that "[a] person who has resolved its liability to the United States or a State in an administrative or judicially approved settlement shall not be liable for claims for contribution regarding matters addressed in the settlement." *Bankert, supra*, held that settling parties are not entitled to contribution protection until they have fully performed all settlement obligations. What language in §113(f)(2) arguably supports that result? Is there a contrary argument? Courts determine the scope of the "matters addressed" in a settlement by referring to the location, time frame, hazardous substances, and cleanup costs covered by the agreement, and whatever other factors bear upon the reasonable expectations of the parties to the settlement and an equitable apportionment of response costs. Akzo Coatings, Inc. v. Aigner Corp., 30 F.3d 761, 766 (7th Cir. 1994). See also American Cyanamid Co. v. Capuano, 381 F.3d 6, 17-18 (1st Cir. 2004) (consent decree requiring that PRP contribute to soil remediation costs did not provide contribution protection for costs of groundwater remediation). *Agere Sys., supra,* held that a PRP protected from a contribution action by §113(f)(2) as a result of a settlement with the United States may bring a contribution action, but not a §107 action, against other PRPs.

What is the effect of a settlement between two private PRPs on a subsequent contribution action? See Boeing Co. v. Cascade Corp., 207 F.3d 1177, 1189-1190 (9th Cir. 2000). United States v. SCA Serv. of Ind., Inc., 827 F. Supp. 526, 531 (N.D. Ind. 1993), held that even though "the text of CERCLA is silent as to whether claims for contribution are barred when private parties settle with other private parties," CERCLA's policy of encouraging settlement supports barring non-settlors from making contribution claims against settlors as it helps reduce amounts spent on legal fees and related costs not directly associated with site remediation. May a settling PRP bring a declaratory judgment action against non-settling PRPs concerning future response costs? See New York v. Solvent Chem. Co., 664 F.3d 22 (2d Cir. 2011) (declaratory relief was available under the Declaratory Judgment Act, 28 U.S.C. §2201(a)).

Private Cost Recovery. Section 107(a)(1)-(4)(B) imposes liability on PRPs for any necessary costs of response incurred by any party other than federal, state, or Indian tribe plaintiffs consistent with the NCP. Suppose that a private cost recovery plaintiff has an independent business reason for cleaning up site contamination (such as a desire to convert the property to a new use). Is it precluded from recovery under this provision? See Carson Harbor Village, Ltd. v. Unocal Corp., 270 F.3d 863, 871-872 (9th Cir. 2001).

Proof of consistency with the NCP is part of the private plaintiff's prima facie case. But see Village of Milford v. K-H Holding Corp., 390 F.3d 926 (6th Cir. 2004) (consistency with the NCP is not required for monitoring and investigation costs). Is that also true for private contribution actions under §113(f)? See Morrison Enter. v. McShares, Inc., 302 F.3d 1127 (10th Cir. 2002) (analyzing the effect of compliance with a state-issued, EPA-approved consent decree). Proof of substantial compliance is sufficient. A private plaintiff's failure to solicit public comment and provide opportunities for public participation may itself demonstrate inconsistency with the NCP. Cf. Regional Airport Auth. v. LFG, LLC, 460 F.3d 697, 707-709 (6th Cir. 2006) (state failed to present preferred alternative to the public for comment).

D. LIABILITY FOR IMMINENT AND SUBSTANTIAL ENDANGERMENTS

Section 104 of CERCLA authorizes EPA to respond to hazardous substance releases and then seek reimbursement of its cleanup costs under §107(a). Sometimes, however, the government would prefer to force responsible parties to conduct the cleanup, especially if the government is short of resources and the health and environmental threats at the site are acute. This section explores the government's power to force private party cleanups under CERCLA and the analogous authority to address imminent hazards under RCRA. The section also addresses the government's power to respond to oil spills, whose potential to threaten health, environmental, and economic interests was starkly illustrated by the 2010 explosion at the Deepwater Horizon drilling rig.

1. *CERCLA Abatement Actions*

EPA's Options. Section 106 of CERCLA authorizes the United States to bring a civil action in federal district court to abate an imminent and substantial endangerment resulting from an actual or threatened release. EPA also may issue administrative orders "as may be necessary to protect public health and welfare and the environment." The government has four different ways to require a PRP to conduct remediation: a settlement approved in a judicial consent decree, a court order after litigation in a §106 action, a settlement reflected in an administrative consent order, and a unilateral §106 administrative order (UAO). The fourth option is attractive because EPA can schedule more cleanups if PRPs, instead of the Superfund, finance them under a unilateral order. An administrative order also permits EPA to specify the precise behavior it expects, as if the PRPs were subject to a regulatory regime.

Civil Abatement Actions. The government's authority under §106(a) both to bring lawsuits and to issue UAOs depends on whether a site presents an "imminent and substantial endangerment to the public health or welfare or the environment." What is the significance of the words "imminent" and "endangerment"? Recall the *Reserve Mining* and *Ethyl Corp.* cases in Chapter 8. Does the "imminent and substantial endangerment" standard merely adopt unchanged the old common law standard for injunctive relief from a prospective nuisance? *Reserve Mining* noted that the common law required "an immediate threat of harm" before a nuisance could be abated. 514 F.2d at 529 n.71. The *Ethyl Corp.* court agreed. 541 F.2d at 20 n.36. In United States v. E.I. du Pont de Nemours & Co., 341 F. Supp. 2d 215, 246-248 (W.D.N.Y. 2004), the court held that EPA need not show that people may be endangered to support a §106 order; possible endangerment to the public welfare or the environment may suffice. Moreover, the endangerment need not be immediate to be imminent. Imminence refers to the nature of the threat rather than the time when the endangerment liability arose. The courts have addressed similar issues under RCRA's imminent hazard section, as the next subsection illustrates.

Section 106 Administrative Orders. A PRP that complies with a UAO may sue for reimbursement from the Superfund if it can show that it is not liable for response costs or that EPA abused its discretion in selecting its preferred remedy. §106(b)(2). The appropriate means for the government to seek compliance in federal district court under §106(b) with an administrative compliance order is to request a declaratory judgment of noncompliance, not a permanent injunction. See United States v. P.H. Glatfelter Co., 2014 WL 4755483, *17-18 (7th Cir. 2014). But if a PRP refuses to carry out a UAO, EPA may seek enforcement in federal district court, fines of up to $25,000 per day of violation, and punitive damages equal to three times the costs incurred by the federal fund as a result of the refusal to carry out the order. §§106(b)(1), 107(c)(3). May punitive damages be assessed in addition to actual response costs? See United

States v. Parsons, 936 F.2d 526 (11th Cir. 1991). United States v. Parsons, 723 F. Supp. 757, 764 (N.D. Ga. 1989), held that financial inability to pay is not a good defense to a §107(c)(3) punitive damage penalty.

Does §106(b) present constitutional problems? In General Elec. Co. v. Jackson, 610 F.3d 110 (D.C. Cir. 2010), the court rejected GE's contentions that the mere issuance of a UAO under §106 triggers a deprivation of property without due process because of the absence of a pre-deprivation hearing. It held that §106 satisfies due process because a PRP may obtain a pre-deprivation hearing by refusing to comply with the UAO and forcing EPA to sue to enforce in federal court.

2. RCRA *Imminent Hazards*

Section 7003(a) of RCRA authorizes EPA to bring suit in federal district court to enjoin activities that may present an imminent and substantial endangerment to health or the environment. EPA also may issue administrative orders "as may be necessary to protect public health and the environment." As a backstop in the event EPA fails to act, §7002(a)(1)(B)—RCRA's citizen suit provision—authorizes any person to sue another person who has contributed or is contributing to hazardous waste management that may present such an endangerment. What constitutes an imminent and substantial endangerment for purposes of these provisions? What kind of relief is available in a citizen suit directed at an endangerment? The next two cases address these questions.

MAINE PEOPLE'S ALLIANCE v. MALLINCKRODT, INC.
471 F.3d 277 (1st Cir. 2006)

Selya, Circuit Judge.

In the teeth of two decades of contrary precedent from four circuits, defendant-appellant Mallinckrodt, Inc. asks us to restrict the role of private citizens in the abatement of imminent and substantial threats to the environment and public health. In support of this entreaty, Mallinckrodt presents a gallimaufry of new, hitherto unconsidered arguments. After careful consideration of this asseverational array, we conclude that our sister circuits have adroitly distilled the meaning of section 7002(a)(1)(B) of the Resource Conservation and Recovery Act (RCRA), 42 U.S.C. §6972(a)(1)(B)—the so-called citizen suit provision. Correctly interpreted, this provision allows citizen suits when there is a reasonable prospect that a serious, near-term threat to human health or the environment exists.[1] In such situations, the provision permits remedies consistent with the scope of a district court's equitable discretion. . . .

[Mallinckrodt owned and operated a chlor-alkali plant on the banks of the Penobscot River in Maine. For years, the Plant (along with other sources) deposited tons of mercury-laden waste into the River. EPA filed an administrative RCRA action against Mallinckrodt to abate the Plant's continuous release of mercury. Pursuant to a

1. We use the phrase "near-term threat" advisedly. It is the threat that must be close at hand, even if the perceived harm is not. For example, if there is a reasonable prospect that a carcinogen released into the environment today may cause cancer twenty years hence, the threat is near-term even though the perceived harm will only occur in the distant future.

1993 consent decree, Mallinckrodt submitted a site investigation report, but EPA and the Maine Department of Environmental Protection (MDEP) disapproved, instructing Mallinckrodt to study the effects of mercury downriver from the Plant. Mallinckrodt made only minimal efforts to do so.

The Maine People's Alliance brought a citizen suit under RCRA §7002(a)(1)(B), alleging that mercury contamination downriver from the Plant "may present an imminent and substantial endangerment to health or the environment." After a bench trial, the district court found that mercury in aquatic systems is susceptible to being transformed by microscopic organisms into methylmercury, a highly toxic substance which attacks the kidneys and the nervous, immune, and reproductive systems. The court determined that Mallinckrodt's disposal activities may have created an imminent and substantial danger. It required Mallinckrodt to finance a study to learn whether mercury contamination in the lower Penobscot adversely affects health or the environment, and if so, to devise a feasible remedial approach. Mallinckrodt appealed.]

This case revolves around the meaning and purport of RCRA §7002(a)(1)(B). . . . The district court read this language as meaning that such suits could be brought to alleviate reasonable medical or scientific concerns. Mallinckrodt urges a more circumscribed interpretation. . . .

An historical perspective illustrates the strength of the current against which Mallinckrodt is swimming. Congress enacted RCRA in 1976. . . . In its original iteration, RCRA §7002 (now codified in pertinent part at 42 U.S.C. §6972(a)(1)(A)) offered citizens the opportunity to bring suit against a polluter only when the polluter was alleged to be in violation of a permit, standard, regulation, condition, requirement, or order issued by EPA. At the same time, RCRA created a cause of action, available exclusively to the EPA Administrator, for cases in which the "disposal of any solid waste or hazardous waste is presenting an imminent and substantial endangerment to health or the environment." RCRA §7003(a). In suits brought under this latter provision, federal district courts were granted broad remedial authority to "restrain" polluters and take "such other action as may be necessary." Id.

Pertinently we think, Congress later loosened the standard for liability under section 7003. This transpired four years later when Congress passed the Solid Waste Disposal Act Amendments of 1980. That legislation amended section 7003 by substituting the words "may present" for the words "is presenting."

. . . [T]he Hazardous and Solid Waste Amendments of 1984 (1984 amendments) . . . introduced a new provision, RCRA §7002(a)(1)(B), into the statutory scheme . . . [which] extended to citizens the right to sue a polluter who may be causing an imminent and substantial endangerment to public health or the environment. . . .

[The court summarized previous judicial interpretation of §7003, concluding that the courts had construed it expansively.] In taking this position, all four courts have emphasized the preeminence of the word "may" in defining the degree of risk needed to support RCRA §7002(a)(1)(B)'s liability standard.

This expansiveness in construing the requisite degree of risk has largely been matched in the courts' assessment of the gravity and immediacy of the threatened harm. With one possible exception, the courts have agreed that the word "substantial" implies serious harm. There has, however, been some reluctance to quantify the needed level of harm more precisely. Imminence generally has been read to require only that the harm is of a kind that poses a near-term threat; there is no corollary requirement that the harm necessarily will occur or that the actual damage will manifest itself immediately.

Mallinckrodt argues that this long line of cases . . . has disregarded the strictures imposed by the adjectives "imminent" and "substantial." We . . . offer our independent judgment on an issue of first impression here (which, as we shortly shall explain, coincides with the result reached by the other courts of appeals that have confronted the question). . . .

Mallinckrodt's textual argument rests on the premise that the courts that heretofore have explicated section 7002(a)(1)(B)'s liability standard have been blinded by the glare of the word "may" and have lost sight of the plain meaning of the words "imminent and substantial." In Mallinckrodt's view, the phrase "may present an imminent and substantial endangerment," when read as a whole, requires a risk of grave harm that is more likely than not to occur. Mallinckrodt deduces this construction from a Rosetta Stone that is part case law and part lexicography.

The word "endangerment," Mallinckrodt says somewhat tautologically, is "the state of being placed in danger." Webster's Third New International Dictionary 748 (1993). In that connection, it defines danger as "exposed to harm" or "peril." Id. at 573. . . . Finally, to give content to the phrase "imminent and substantial," Mallinckrodt invokes case law suggesting that, in other environmental contexts, the unadorned word "endanger" implies a lower standard than that denoted by the phrase "imminent and substantial endangerment." See Ethyl Corp. v. EPA, 541 F.2d 1, 20 n.36 (D.C. Cir. 1976) (en banc); Reserve Mining Co. v. EPA, 514 F.2d 492, 528 (8th Cir. 1975) (en banc).

Mallinckrodt's textual argument makes sense — but only to a point. While the decisions in *Ethyl Corp.* and *Reserve Mining* are some evidence that, as of 1976, the phrase "imminent and substantial endangerment" was thought to denote a heightened standard, the relevant question is how that term was understood in 1984 (when section 7002(a)(1)(B) was enacted). The Senate Report on the 1984 amendments defines the word "endangerment" separately from the phrase "imminent and substantial." See S. Rep. No. 98-284, at 59. Mallinckrodt's criticism fails to account either for that circumstance or for Congress's insertion, in 1980, of the word "may" into section 7003 and its subsequent use in section 7002. That word does not appear at all in the statute considered in *Reserve Mining.* In *Ethyl Corp.*, one of the referenced statutes does use the word "may," but that court did not parse the entire sentence and looked only to the words "imminent and substantial." We also note that statutes referenced in *Ethyl Corp.* and *Reserve Mining* bore the subtitle "Emergency Powers"; in contrast, neither section 7002 nor section 7003 carry such a label.

. . . We conclude, therefore, that Mallinckrodt's textual argument does not carry the day: the interpretive question before us cannot be resolved favorably to Mallinckrodt on the basis of plain meaning alone. . . .

. . . Mallinckrodt asserts that the conventional interpretation of "imminent and substantial endangerment" overlooks RCRA's commitment to a hierarchy of risks in which "imminent and substantial endangerment" ranks at or near the top. This argument builds on the idea that Congress employed relatively lenient risk standards elsewhere in RCRA. Correspondingly, the word "endangerment" is used in other contexts in connection with "imminent danger of death or serious bodily injury." See, e.g., RCRA §3008(e) (defining the crime of "knowing endangerment"). Thus, the decision to require an "imminent and substantial endangerment" must signify a special, harder-to-achieve benchmark.

This argument has some superficial appeal. After all, it is a cardinal rule that courts should strive to interpret statutes as a whole and to give effect to every word and phrase. But the conventional interpretation of section 7002(a)(1)(B) gives full effect to the "imminent and substantial endangerment" language; it merely eschews the mechanical cross-referencing, not mandated by Congress, that Mallinckrodt advocates. That, in itself, should not raise eyebrows: where the various parts of a complicated and multifaceted statutory scheme discuss significantly different topics and function within different paradigms, mechanical cross-referencing, not mandated by Congress, can lead to confusion rather than clarity.

This is such a case. There is no meaningful parallelism between section 7002(a)(1)(B) and the provisions that Mallinckrodt seeks to use as comparators. For example, RCRA §3008(e) is a criminal provision. Given the divergent concerns that drive criminal statutes as opposed to civil remedial statutes, it should not be surprising that the same word may vary in meaning as the context shifts. Indeed, if "endangerment" as defined in section 3008(e) were to mean precisely what it means in section 7002(a)(1)(B), the word "imminent" would be rendered utterly redundant—the statute would, in effect, require an imminent imminence—thus transgressing the very canon of construction that Mallinckrodt labors to invoke. . . .

This brings us to Mallinckrodt's separation-of-powers argument. It asseverates that RCRA's allocation of policymaking authority to EPA is such that the citizen suit provision must be viewed as an "interstitial, emergency-type remedy." Mallinckrodt asserts that this policymaking authority necessarily includes responsibility for setting pollution standards and that, in setting such standards, EPA, consistent with the trade-offs inherent in setting virtually any standard, does not aspire to eliminate all risks.

This assertion is founded on an indisputable verity: the principal responsibility for implementing and enforcing RCRA resides with EPA, not with citizens acting as private attorneys general. See Meghrig v. KFC Western, Inc., 516 U.S. 479, 483-84 (1996). We disagree, however, with Mallinckrodt's contention that the conventional interpretation of section 7002(a)(1)(B)—the interpretation espoused by our sister circuits and by the court below—is inconsistent with this scheme because it allows courts to second-guess EPA's judgments too freely and affords relief based upon harms that EPA has found acceptable.

. . . [A]llowing citizen suits to proceed is not the functional equivalent of allowing courts to hijack EPA's regulatory authority and weave safety standards out of whole cloth. . . .

The fact that courts retain some latitude in this area is not in any sense incompatible with the statutory scheme. There are four different ways that EPA can preempt a citizen suit—and all four require that EPA itself take diligent steps to remedy looming environmental harm. See RCRA §7002(b)(2)(B). That same provision narrowly circumscribes EPA's preemptive power; it states that, when preemption is premised on an EPA order, citizen suits are "prohibited only as to the scope and duration of the administrative order." The short of it is that Congress has told the federal courts that they are not required to steer clear of an area simply because that area might be a focus of future EPA activity. . . .

Insofar as Mallinckrodt theorizes that courts lack the competence to function under the conventional interpretation of RCRA §7002(a)(1)(B), we reject its thesis. To be sure, Mallinckrodt cites case after case for the proposition that forging policy is a task that non-expert, non-accountable judges should not undertake. See, e.g., Chevron U.S.A., Inc. v. Natural Res. Def. Council, Inc., 467 U.S. 837, 866 (1984). Some of these cases suggest that judicial policymaking in the environmental sphere is especially inappropriate because judges lack special competence to interpret complex scientific, technical, and medical data. See, e.g., Safe Food & Fertil. v. EPA, 365 F.3d 46, 49 (D.C. Cir. 2004).

This view sells the federal judiciary short: federal courts have proven, over time, that they are equipped to adjudicate individual cases, regardless of the complexity of the issues involved. Federal courts are often called upon to make evaluative judgments in highly technical areas (patent litigation is an excellent example).[12] Performing that quintessentially judicial function in the environmental sphere is not tantamount to rewriting environmental policy. To the contrary, what the lower court did here— listening to the testimony of expert witnesses, assessing their credibility, and determining whether or not a litigant has carried the devoir of persuasion—is very much within the core competency of a federal district court. . . .

The Senate's discussion of section 7003 in the course of considering the 1984 amendments likewise suggests an expansive view of the provision. The Senate Report [states] that section 7003 is "intended to confer upon the courts the authority to grant affirmative equitable relief to the extent necessary to eliminate any risks posed by toxic wastes." . . . Thus, there is good reason to believe that Congress, intending to create a provision modeled along the lines of section 7003, understood that section as offering much more than emergency authority. . . .

To sum up, the combination of the word "may" with the word "endanger," both of which are probabilistic, leads us to conclude that a reasonable prospect of future harm is adequate to engage the gears of RCRA §7002(a)(1)(B) so long as the threat is near-term and involves potentially serious harm. The language, structure, purpose, and legislative history of the provision will not comfortably accommodate the more restricted reading that Mallinckrodt espouses. While there may be good and wise reasons to adopt a regime in which EPA determinations of environmental liability are exclusive, it is Congress's place, not ours, to construct such a regime. To this date, Congress has not done so.

Given our conclusion that the conventional interpretation of RCRA §7002(a)(1)(B) is correct, the remainder of the liability inquiry falls neatly into place. None of Mallinckrodt's arguments persuade us that the district court either misconstrued this standard or misapplied it to the facts of this case. While an imminent and substantial endangerment requires a reasonable prospect of a near-term threat of serious potential harm, the court below made supportable findings that suffice to bring this case within the compass of that standard. [These included findings that methylmercury is a "highly toxic substance," and that, in an aquatic system, "methylation is a continuous process that can go on for decades."] Based on these and other well-founded findings, the plaintiffs established that the potential risk from mercury is serious and likely to be present here and now. In turn, these findings support a conclusion that, as the district court held, there may be an imminent and substantial endangerment to the lower Penobscot River. No more is exigible. . . .

---

12. Indeed, even on Mallinckrodt's crabbed interpretation of section 7002(a)(1)(B), courts would have to engage in exactly the type of evidence-weighing that Mallinckrodt says is beyond their competence.

NOTES AND QUESTIONS

1. What is the test for relief in a citizen suit under §7002(a)(1)(B) after *Mal-linckrodt*? How did the court respond to the defendant's reliance on statutory text and purposes and legislative history? Does this case also provide guidance on the meaning of an imminent and substantial endangerment under §7003?

2. Other courts have continued to interpret the terms of §7002(a)(1)(B) expansively. Burlington N. & Santa Fe Ry. Co. v. Grant, 505 F.3d 1013 (10th Cir. 2007), explored the meaning of each of the key terms that authorize relief under §7002(a)(1)(B) ("may present," "endangerment," "imminent," and "substantial"). It concluded that it is irrelevant how long contaminants have existed on the property and that proof of harm to a living population is unnecessary. In Cordiano v. Metacon Gun Club, Inc., 575 F.3d 199 (2d Cir. 2009), the court reasoned that imminence requires a showing that a risk of threatened harm is present, that an endangerment is substantial if it is serious, and that an endangerment means a threatened or potential harm, not actual harm. It concluded that an imminent and substantial endangerment requires a reasonable prospect of future harm. In a case decided before *Mallinckrodt*, the court indicated that Congress intended that the courts err on the side of protecting health and the environment in responding to citizen suits under §7002(a)(1)(B). The plaintiff need not show that there is a potential population at risk, quantify the risk posed by the defendant's activities, or show that contaminants are present at levels above those considered acceptable by the state in which the defendant's operations occur. Interfaith Cmty. Org. v. Honeywell Int'l, Inc., 399 F.3d 248 (3d Cir. 2005). See also Estate of Serracante v. Esso Std. Oil (Puerto Rico), 770 F. Supp. 2d 459, 466 (D.P.R. 2011) (use of the word "may" in §7002(a)(1)(B) "was intended to make the provision expansive in order to give courts the tools to 'eliminate any risks posed by toxic waste'"). Compare Crandall v. City and County of Denver, Colo., 595 F.3d 1231 (10th Cir. 2010) (holding that use of propylene glycol, which produces hydrogen sulfide gas, to remove ice from aircraft wings did not amount to an imminent and substantial endangerment); Attorney General of Ok. v. Tyson Foods, Inc., 565 F.3d 769, 777 (10th Cir. 2009) (upholding denial of preliminary injunction in suit to enjoin poultry producers from applying poultry litter to land within river watershed because the state failed to meet even the "low hurdle" in proving an endangerment under §7002(a)(1)(B) of RCRA); Board of County Comm'rs of La Plata, Colorado v. Brown Group Retail, Inc., 768 F. Supp. 2d 1092, 1109-1111 (D. Colo. 2011) (no imminent and substantial endangerment, notwithstanding evidence that solvent levels exceeded applicable regulatory standards, absent evidence of present pathways for exposure and of animals and other living organisms with high mortality rates at and around the contaminated site).

3. *Who Is Liable for an Imminent and Substantial Endangerment?* Who qualifies as a person who "has contributed to or who is contributing to the past present handling, storage, treatment, transportation, or disposal of any solid or hazardous waste which may present an imminent and substantial endangerment" for purposes of §7002(a)(1)(B)? In Hinds Investments, L.P. v. Angioli, 654 F.3d 846 (9th Cir. 2011), the court held that the manufacturer of dry cleaning equipment did not "contribute" to an endangerment resulting from the soil and groundwater contamination resulting from the disposal of chemicals at two dry cleaning stores in shopping malls. The manufacturer was not liable based on the design of the dry cleaning machines and the instructions it provided to businesses purchasing the equipment on how to use the machines. Liability requires active involvement or some degree of control over the

waste disposal process that resulted in the contamination. Neither was proven in that case. Compare Forest Park Nat'l Bank & Trust v. Ditchfield, 881 F. Supp. 2d 949, 973 (N.D. Ill. 2012) ("contribution" requires some causal connection between the defendant's conduct and present site contamination).

4. Why might environmental plaintiffs see RCRA's citizen suit language as more attractive or viable than reliance on CERCLA's provisions, especially where the contamination is to a shared environmental amenity such as a river or lake? Compare the two and assess what prerequisites there are, if any, for litigation under each law. Also, compare the relief each law provides. Commencement of a CERCLA cleanup may reduce the chance of a court's finding a RCRA endangerment. See, e.g., City of Fresno v. United States, 709 F. Supp. 2d 934 (E.D. Cal. 2010).

Environmental laws tend to encourage and reward proactive conduct that reduces pollution and associated risk. However, each law's precise terms can shape when and how a well counseled polluter will take such action. As you read the case that follows, consider whether this Court's conclusion was unavoidable under the law as written and whether the result reached comports with RCRA's stated goals or adds up to sound policy.

MEGHRIG v. KFC WESTERN, INC.
516 U.S. 479 (1996)

Justice O'CONNOR delivered the opinion of the Court.

We consider whether §7002 of [RCRA], 42 U.S.C. §6972, authorizes a private cause of action to recover the prior cost of cleaning up toxic waste that does not, at the time of suit, continue to pose an endangerment to health or the environment. We conclude that it does not.

[In 1988, KFC discovered during the course of construction on one of its "Kentucky Fried Chicken" restaurants in Los Angeles that the property was contaminated with petroleum. KFC spent $211,000 removing and disposing of the contaminated soil to comply with a county health department order. In 1991, it brought a citizen suit under §7002(a) of RCRA to recover its cleanup costs from the previous owners of the property, the Meghrigs. KFC claimed that the contaminated soil had previously posed an "imminent and substantial endangerment" under §7002(a)(1)(B), and that the Meghrigs were responsible for "equitable restitution" of its cleanup costs because, as prior owners, they had contributed to the waste's "past or present handling, storage, treatment, transportation, or disposal." The district court dismissed KFC's complaint, holding that §7002(a) does not authorize either recovery of past cleanup costs or a cause of action for remediation of waste no longer posing an "imminent and substantial endangerment" at the time suit is filed. The Ninth Circuit reversed on both grounds, and the Meghrigs appealed.]

. . . Unlike [CERCLA], RCRA is not principally designed to effectuate the cleanup of toxic waste sites or to compensate those who have attended to the remediation of environmental hazards. . . . RCRA's primary purpose, rather, is to reduce the generation of hazardous waste and to ensure the proper treatment, storage, and disposal of that waste which is nonetheless generated, "so as to minimize the present and future threat to human health and the environment." 42 U.S.C. §6902(b).

Chief responsibility for the implementation and enforcement of RCRA rests with [EPA], see §§6928, 6973, but like other environmental laws, RCRA contains a citizen suit provision, §6972, which permits private citizens to enforce its provisions in some circumstances.

Two requirements of §6972(a) defeat KFC's suit against the Meghrigs. The first concerns the necessary timing of a citizen suit brought under §6972(a)(1)(B): That section permits a private party to bring suit against certain responsible persons, including former owners, "who ha[ve] contributed or who [are] contributing to the past or present handling, storage, treatment, transportation, or disposal of any solid or hazardous waste which *may present* an *imminent* and substantial endangerment to health or the environment." (Emphasis added.) The second defines the remedies a district court can award in a suit brought under §6972(a)(1)(B): Section 6972(a) authorizes district courts "*to restrain* any person who has contributed or who is contributing to the past or present handling, storage, treatment, transportation, or disposal of any solid or hazardous waste . . . , *to order such person to take such other action as may be necessary, or both.*" (Emphasis added.)

It is apparent from the two remedies described in §6972(a) that RCRA's citizen suit provision is not directed at providing compensation for past cleanup efforts. Under a plain reading of this remedial scheme, a private citizen suing under §6972(a)(1)(B) could seek a mandatory injunction, i.e., one that orders a responsible party to "take action" by attending to the cleanup and proper disposal of toxic waste, or a prohibitory injunction, i.e., one that "restrains" a responsible party from further violating RCRA. Neither remedy, however, is susceptible of the interpretation adopted by the Ninth Circuit, as neither contemplates the award of past cleanup costs, whether these are denominated "damages" or "equitable restitution."

In this regard, a comparison between the relief available under RCRA's citizen suit provision and that which Congress has provided in the analogous, but not parallel, provisions of CERCLA is telling. CERCLA was passed several years after RCRA went into effect, and it is designed to address many of the same toxic waste problems that inspired the passage of RCRA. Compare 42 U.S.C. §6903(5) (RCRA definition of "hazardous waste") and §6903(27) (RCRA definition of "solid waste") with §9601(14) (CERCLA provision incorporating certain "hazardous substance[s]," but not the hazardous and solid wastes defined in RCRA, and specifically not petroleum). CERCLA differs markedly from RCRA, however, in the remedies it provides. CERCLA's citizen suit provision mimics §6972(a) in providing district courts with the authority "to order such action as may be necessary to correct the violation" of any CERCLA standard or regulation. 42 U.S.C. §9659(c). But CERCLA expressly permits the Government to recover "all costs of removal or remedial action," §9607(a)(4)(A), and it expressly permits the recovery of any "necessary costs of response, incurred by any . . . person consistent with the national contingency plan," §9607(a)(4)(B). . . . See [also] §9613(f)(1). Congress thus demonstrated in CERCLA that it knew how to provide for the recovery of cleanup costs, and that the language used to define the remedies under RCRA does not provide that remedy.

That RCRA's citizen suit provision was not intended to provide a remedy for past cleanup costs is further apparent from the harm at which it is directed. Section 6972(a)(1)(B) permits a private party to bring suit only upon a showing that the solid or hazardous waste at issue "may present an imminent and substantial endangerment to health or the environment." The meaning of this timing restriction is plain: An endangerment can only be "imminent" if it "threaten[s] to occur immediately," Webster's New International Dictionary of English Language 1245 (2d ed. 1934), and the reference to waste which "may present" imminent harm quite clearly excludes waste that no longer presents such a danger. As the Ninth Circuit itself intimated in Price v. United States Navy, 39 F.3d 1011, 1019 (1994), this language "implies that there must be a threat which is present now, although the impact of the threat may not be felt until later." It follows that §6972(a) was designed to provide a remedy that ameliorates present or obviates the risk of future "imminent" harms, not a remedy that compensates for past cleanup efforts. . . .

Other aspects of RCRA's enforcement scheme strongly support this conclusion. Unlike CERCLA, RCRA contains no statute of limitations, compare §9613(g)(2) . . . , and it does not require a showing that the response costs being sought are reasonable, compare §§9607(a)(4)(A) and (B) (costs recovered under CERCLA must be "consistent with the national contingency plan"). If Congress had intended §6972(a) to function as a cost-recovery mechanism, the absence of these provisions would be striking. Moreover, with one limited exception, . . . a private party may not bring suit under §6972(a)(1)(B) without first giving 90 days' notice to the Administrator of the EPA, to "the State in which the alleged endangerment may occur," and to potential defendants, see §§6972(b)(2)(A)(i)-(iii). And no citizen suit can proceed if either the EPA or the State has commenced, and is diligently prosecuting, a separate enforcement action, see §§6972(b)(2)(B) and (C). Therefore, if RCRA were designed to compensate private parties for their past cleanup efforts, it would be a wholly irrational mechanism for doing so. Those parties with insubstantial problems, problems that neither the State nor the Federal Government feel compelled to address, could recover their response costs, whereas those parties whose waste problems were sufficiently severe as to attract the attention of Government officials would be left without a recovery.

. . . [EPA] (as amicus) . . . joins KFC in arguing that §6972(a) does not in all circumstances preclude an award of past cleanup costs. The Government posits a situation in which suit is properly brought while the waste at issue continues to pose an imminent endangerment, and suggests that the plaintiff in such a case could seek equitable restitution of money previously spent on cleanup efforts. Echoing a similar argument made by KFC, the Government does not rely on the remedies expressly provided in §6972(a), but rather cites a line of cases holding that district courts retain inherent authority to award any equitable remedy that is not expressly taken away from them by Congress. See, e.g., Hecht Co. v. Bowles, 321 U.S. 321 (1944).

RCRA does not prevent a private party from recovering its cleanup costs under other federal or state laws, see §6972(f) . . . , but the limited remedies described in §6972(a), along with the stark differences between the language of that section and the cost recovery provisions of CERCLA, amply demonstrate that Congress did not intend for a private citizen to be able to undertake a cleanup and then proceed to recover its costs under RCRA. As we explained in Middlesex County Sewerage Auth. v. National Sea Clammers Ass'n, 453 U.S. 1, 14 (1981), where Congress has provided "elaborate enforcement provisions" for remedying the violation of a federal statute, as Congress has done with RCRA and CERCLA, "it cannot be assumed that Congress intended to authorize by implication additional judicial remedies for private citizens suing under" the statute. . . .

Without considering whether a private party could seek to obtain an injunction requiring another party to pay cleanup costs which arise after a RCRA citizen suit has been properly commenced, cf. United States v. Price, 688 F.2d 204, 211-213 (C.A.3 1982) (requiring funding of a diagnostic study is an appropriate form of relief in a suit brought by the Administrator under §6973), or otherwise recover cleanup costs paid out after the invocation of RCRA's statutory process, we agree with the Meghrigs that a private party cannot recover the cost of a past cleanup effort under RCRA, and that KFC's complaint is defective for the reasons stated by the District Court. Section 6972(a) does not contemplate the award of past cleanup costs, and §6972(a)(1)(B) permits a private party to bring suit only upon an allegation that the contaminated site presently poses an "imminent and substantial endangerment to health or the environment," and not upon an allegation that it posed such an endangerment at some time in the past. The judgment of the Ninth Circuit is reversed.

NOTES AND QUESTIONS

1. If a cost recovery suit is available under CERCLA, why does it make any difference if reimbursement may not be sought under RCRA? What meaning, if any, did Justice O'Connor attribute to the provision in §7002(a)(1) authorizing the district courts to order the defendant to "take such other action as may be necessary"? Under her reading of the statute, was it necessary to interpret that phrase?

2. What incentives does *Meghrig* create for a property owner who discovers the presence of hazardous waste attributable to the actions of a past generator, transporter, or TSD facility owner? In Avondale Fed. Sav. Bank v. Amoco Oil Co., 170 F.3d 692 (7th Cir. 1999), the court ruled that RCRA's citizen suit provision does not allow an award of restitution for cleanup costs incurred by the current site owner after it filed a citizen suit and that an injunction against the defendant (a former site owner) to prevent off-site contamination was premature because no harm was imminent. In a strong dissent, Judge Wood argued that the restitution ruling creates perverse disincentives for current site owners to mitigate damage by cleaning up contaminated sites pending resolution of a citizen suit. It also creates incentives for defendants to stall, because "the longer the lawsuit runs, the more likely it is that another party will as a practical matter be forced to take it upon itself to clean up the defendants' messes." Id. at 697. What is the likely impact of *Avondale* on the development of brownfields? See also Albany Bank & Trust Co. v. Exxon Mobil Corp., 310 F.3d 969 (7th Cir. 2002) (investigation costs not recoverable in RCRA citizen suit).

3. *Equitable Discretion and Environmental Remedies.* The courts do not always read narrowly the scope of the federal courts' remedial powers in enforcing federal legislation. United States v. Lane Labs-USA Inc., 427 F.3d 219 (3d Cir. 2005), distinguished *Meghrig* in holding that the district courts may order a defendant found to be in violation of the FFDCA to pay restitution to consumers, pursuant to a provision authorizing the courts "to restrain violations" of the Act. The government charged the defendant with inappropriately advertising and promoting its products as effective in the prevention, treatment, and cure of cancer. Characterizing the issue as a "close call," the court stated that, even "[t]hough the [FFDCA] does not specifically authorize restitution, such specificity is not required where the government properly invokes a court's equitable jurisdiction under this statute." Id. at 223. The statute and its legislative history indicated that Congress intended to protect the financial interests of consumers as well as their health. Restitution serves a deterrent function, making it appropriate for the courts to award restitution to prevent further violations. The case differed from *Meghrig* because the latter was a citizen suit, not an enforcement action initiated by the government. The equitable powers of the federal courts are broader

when the public interest is involved, as opposed to a mere private controversy. See also *United States v. Rx Depot, Inc.*, 438 F.3d 1052 (10th Cir. 2006) (holding that an order of disgorgement is permitted under the FFDCA if it furthers statutory purposes).

3. Oil Spills

CERCLA's exclusion of petroleum products from its definition of "hazardous substance," 42 U.S.C. §9601(14), renders CERCLA of little help in the event of an oil spill, although §104(a)'s broad empowerment of the federal government, where "any pollutant or contaminant . . . may present an imminent and substantial endangerment," makes that earlier definitional limitation less disabling. See sections D.1 and D.2 above. Still, neither CERCLA nor the Clean Water Act's provisions addressing liabilities for spills provides a comprehensive regime for addressing massive oil spills.

After the 1989 *Exxon Valdez* oil spill in Alaska revealed gaps and inadequacies in federal and state law for dealing with oil spills, Congress enacted the Oil Pollution Act of 1990 (OPA). The Senate report accompanying S. 686 highlighted the inadequacies of existing oil pollution legislation, including "inadequate cleanup and damage remedies, taxpayer subsidies to cover cleanup costs, third party damages that go uncompensated, and substantial barriers to victim recoveries—such as legal defenses, statutes of limitations, the corporate form, and the burdens of proof that favor those responsible for the spill." 1990 U.S.C.C.A.N. 722, 723. The House bill, H.R. 1465, was passed in lieu of the Senate bill, after incorporating most of the provisions included in S. 686. OPA did not supplant the more limited reach of CERCLA and the Clean Water Act, but added new, more specifically applicable provisions that both expanded and capped liability. It adopted features and many definitions present in both CERCLA and the Clean Water Act. Many of OPA's provisions are clear, but provisions relating to the status of other sources of liability under federal or state law are not. The Deepwater Horizon oil spill that occurred during the spring and summer of 2010 engendered litigation that may eventually clear up many of those statutory uncertainties, but so far it has not. This is in part due to BP's creation of an alternative $20 billion settlement fund that has diverted much of that possible litigation into a venue in which judicial legal clarifications will not occur. Government and private responses to that spill and future spills, and litigation that does end up in the courts, are likely to involve the following key provisions:

Liability. Section 2702(a) of OPA imposes liability on *each* of the responsible parties for discharges of oil into or upon the navigable waters, adjoining shoreline, or the 200-mile Exclusive Economic Zone of the United States. In general, the responsible party is liable for both removal costs and damages. Section 2702(b) enumerates two types of "covered" removal costs and six categories of "covered" damages in addition to specifically identifying which class of claimants may recover for each. The six categories of damages include: natural resources, damage to real or personal property, loss of subsistence use, revenues lost by the United States or state governments, lost profits and lost earning capacity, and increased cost of providing public services during or after cleanup activities. OPA defines the liability established by the statute as only those damages included in §2702(b). Section 2701(5) defines *damages* as "damages specified in section 2702(b) of this title, and includes the cost of assessing these damages." Just as CERCLA does, OPA §2701(17) defines liability as "the standard of liability which obtains under section 1321 of this title," which the accompanying conference report explained had been previously determined to be strict, joint, and several. 1990 U.S.C.C.A.N. 779, 780.

Responsible Parties. Under OPA, a responsible party is defined in §2701(32) as "any person" owning or operating a vessel or facility. Pursuant to §2714(a), the United States Coast Guard "shall" determine the source of the discharge, identify the responsible party, and notify the responsible party of such designation. The language of §2702(a) indicates that there can be multiple responsible parties.

Defenses. The responsible party is completely absolved of "OPA liability" if the discharge is caused *solely* by: "(1) an act of God; (2) an act of war; (3) an act or omission of a third party . . . or (4) any combination of [these]." 33 U.S.C. §2703(a)(2)-(4). However, the defenses are not available if the responsible party failed to report a discharge of oil, cooperate with federal officials in connection with cleanup activities, or comply with a federal removal order issued under subsection (c) or (e) of 33 U.S.C. §1321 (the Clean Water Act's oil spill provision) or the Intervention on the High Seas Act. In a provision echoing CERCLA's language and logic, the third-party defense is narrow because the class of "third parties" is restricted: the defense is unavailable if the third party is an employee or agent of the responsible party or if the third party is in a contractual relationship with the responsible party. Id. §2703(a)(3). Furthermore, to establish a third-party defense, the responsible party has the burden of demonstrating, by a preponderance of the evidence, that it exercised due care in light of all circumstances, took precautions against the third party's foreseeable acts or omissions, provided full cooperation with authorities in connection with removal actions, is in compliance with land use restrictions established for removal actions, and has not impeded any removal actions. Id. §2703(a)(3)(A)-(B), (d)(3)(A)-(D). If an apparently responsible party can overcome these hurdles and demonstrate that it is entitled to a third-party defense, then the "third party or parties shall be treated as the responsible party or parties for purposes of determining liability under [subchapter 1 — Oil Pollution Liability and Compensation]." Id. §2702(d)(1)(A). Although the responsible party has established a third-party defense, it must still pay removal costs and damages, but is later entitled to recover by subrogation from the third party. Id. §2702(d)(1)(B)(ii).

Liability Caps. OPA partially opened the door to greater imposition of liability on responsible parties than provided by preceding law, but it also created the possibility of a liability cap. Section 2704 provides various sorts of caps on "liability under section 2702," with the limits contingent on the category of polluter causing the spill. Under §2704(a)(3), OPA limits oil spill liabilities to "the total of all removal costs plus $75 million." However, §2704(c)(1) eliminates this liability limitation if the incident was proximately caused by the responsible party's gross negligence, willful misconduct, or a violation of federal safety, construction, or operating regulation by the responsible party or its agent, employee, or contractor. In addition, the limitation will be denied if the responsible party fails to report a discharge of oil, cooperate with federal officials in connection with cleanup activities, or comply with a federal removal order issued under subsection (c) or (e) of 33 U.S.C. §1321 or the Intervention on the High Seas Act.

News reports indicate that federal regulators were lax in reviewing drilling proposals and monitoring the BP drilling platform's operations. If you were an attorney for a defendant in the Deepwater Horizon oil spill, what would be the potential significance of an agency informally signing off on, or perhaps simply not objecting to, practices that actually violated existing regulatory requirements?

Furthermore, under §2708(a)(2), the responsible party bears the burden of proof in demonstrating that it is entitled to a limitation of liability. If the responsible party demonstrates that it is entitled to a limitation of liability under §2704, it may assert a claim under §2708 for reimbursement of OPA damages and removal costs against the Oil Spill Liability Trust Fund (the Fund). However, the limitation of liability provisions refer only to liability established by OPA, meaning only the cleanup costs prescribed in §2702(b)(1) and the damages prescribed in §2702(b)(2). This restriction on the liability cap could prove important to construction of related preemption-related provisions discussed below.

The Oil Spill Liability Fund. OPA creates an Oil Spill Liability Trust Fund that is in many respects like the Superfund, at least in Superfund's early days when it was funded by an industry-targeted tax. The OPA fund is administered by the National Pollution Funds Center (NPFC) created under the Coast Guard. The Fund consolidated preexisting federal funds and is currently financed by an 8-cent tax on crude oil or petroleum products imported into the United States. 26 U.S.C. §4611(c)(2)(B)(i). The NPFC is authorized to pay $1 billion per incident and was additionally granted $1 billion in borrowing authority. Id. §9509(d). OPA specifically enumerates the allowable uses of the fund in §2712, principally funding emergency government cleanup activities, and remaining available to pay uncompensated removal costs and damages. Much as CERCLA limits access to the Superfund and cost recovery claims to actions complying with the National Contingency Plan (NCP), OPA removal costs must be consistent with the NCP and the damages must be covered by §2702(b) of OPA.

Damages that Are Recoverable. OPA expanded the range of recoverable damages and allowed entities other than the federal government to recover removal costs. The categories of OPA recoverable claims went further than possible under some states' laws; private claimants may now recover for economic loss unaccompanied by physical injury or real or personal property damage. Id. §2702(b)(2)(E). The law left unclear whether geographical limitations found under much pre-OPA law would apply to OPA claims.

Think about claims that may arise following a spill like the Deepwater Horizon oil spill. What sorts of plaintiff could now prevail who would likely be denied relief under some states' common law? What arguments would you raise in OPA-based litigation if a defendant sought to limit liability to people and businesses near the spill?

OPA's Preemptive and Displacing Effects. Legislators considered and battled over whether OPA should provide an exclusive regime for oil spills. The Senate report accompanying S. 686, available at 1990 U.S.C.C.A.N 722, cited CERCLA and noted how other environmental laws permit states to maintain and enact legislation that is more restrictive than the federal standards. The report clearly stated that the "[f]ederal statute is designed to provide basic protection for the environment and victims damaged by spills of oil. Any state wishing to impose a greater degree of protection for its own resources and citizens is entitled to do so."[f] Although an early House report emphasized uniformity goals, it abandoned that pro-preemption position after the *Exxon Valdez* oil spill. The resulting provisions, as well as early interpretations, appear

---

f. Id. The Senate report acknowledged that in 1990, 24 states had already enacted some form of oil pollution legislation. Id. at 728. Of the 24, 17 of the liability schemes imposed unlimited liability. The Senate, aware of existing state laws imposing unlimited liability, affirmed the state liability scheme as appropriately "based on two widely accepted principles: a polluter should pay in full for the costs of oil pollution caused by that polluter; and, a victim should be fully compensated." Id.

to preserve the possibility of recoveries outside of OPA and above and beyond the federal cap, but portions of a few reported decisions grappling with these provisions find a more displacing or preemptive effect than legislators appear to have anticipated. Look at §§2718 and 2751, with attention to both their language and structure within OPA. Section 2718 (a) and (c) certainly appear to preserve state law authority, with language explicitly preserving "State law, including common law," and allowing "any State" to "impose additional liability or additional requirements." Section 2751 appears at first to preserve admiralty and maritime claims, but includes the opening ambiguous limitation: "Except as otherwise provided in this Act." Generally emphasizing this opening clause, the courts have consistently determined that the maritime savings clause precludes maritime claims for damages for which OPA provides a remedy.[g]

But look at §2718, especially subsections (a) and (c): what arguments can you fashion for preemption or non-preemption if state common law provides compensation for damages of the same sorts provided by OPA? Should state law–based liabilities under such parallel provisions be allowed to exceed the federal cap? What about arguments based on the site of the oil spill and the state of a later victim or a state seeking recovery under state statutory or common law? Can you fashion arguments drawing inferences from the different language used in §2751's maritime law provisions?

Post-enactment interpretations by industry indicate quite uniformly that §2718's savings clause truly preserved state law; oil drilling and shipping operations initially considered closing down operations in states with laws or common law that could create liabilities above and beyond OPA liability. *See* Rockwell, US Pollution Act Might Scare Off UK Carriers, J. Com., Oct. 2, 1991, at 1, available at 1991 WLNR 645222; Unsworth, European Shipowners Dismayed at US Oil Spill Liability Stance, J. Com., July 3, 1991, Maritime, at 1, available at 1990 WLNR 579553. Oil companies complained that profits generated by U.S. markets were not enough to justify taking "a risk of such magnitude that is uninsurable." See Porter, Oil Spill Law: Paying the Piper, J. Com., Nov. 26, 1991, at 1, available at 1991 WLNR 661761. Few companies actually followed through on such threats, perhaps due to responsive insurance markets or the costs of abandoning promising drilling sites. See Deadline Near for Compliance with U.S. Oil Spill Liability Rules, 92 Oil & Gas J. 31, Aug. 1, 1994, available at 1994 WLNR 5285123.

Unfortunately, case law addressing whether state common law and state statutory claims survive OPA's preemptive effect is scarce and conflicting. For example, one federal district court held that OPA does not preempt state common law claims of negligence, trespass, strict liability, and nuisance to recover damages resulting from a discharge of oil. Williams v. Potomac Elec. Power Co., 115 F. Supp. 2d 561 (D. Md. 2000). The court reasoned that a plain reading of §2718(a)-(c) permits states to impose additional liability or requirements relating to the discharge of oil. The court relied on *Locke*, stating that "OPA does not preempt 'state laws of a *scope similar* to the matters contained in Title I of OPA.'" See also St. Joe Co. v. Transocean Offshore Deepwater Drilling Inc., 774 F. Supp. 2d 596, 604 (D. Del. 2011) ("OPA's saving clauses . . . clearly contemplate a concurrent state legal regime"). In contrast, in an unpublished opinion, the Fourth Circuit denied a responsible party's attempt to recover under both

g. See National Shipping Co. of Saudi Arabia v. Moran Trade Corp. of Del. 122 F.3d 1062, 1997 WL 560047 (4th Cir. 1997); Gabarick v. Laurin Maritime (Am.) Inc., 623 F. Supp. 2d 741 (E.D. La. 2009); In re Settoon Towing LLC, 2009 WL 4730971 (E.D. La. Dec. 4, 2009).

state common law and a state statute. National Shipping Co. of Saudi Arabia v. Moran Trade Corp. of Del., 1997 WL 560047, at *3 (4th Cir. 1997). Cf. Mid-Valley Pipeline Co. v. S.J. Louis Constr., Inc., 847 F. Supp. 2d 982 (E.D. Ky. 2012). (OPA preempted oil pipeline's state law claim against sewer pipe owner for indemnification for costs incurred as result of pipeline puncture while pipe owner was performing work near oil pipeline, but not for contribution).

More recently, in a decision involving the Deepwater Horizon spill and turning on construction of several laws including OPA and the CWA, the Supreme Court's *Ouellette* decision (see Chapter 2 for excerpts and discussion), preemption law, and maritime law, the court mostly addressed disputes over removal of claims to federal court. It also, however, included brief and slightly unclear discussion of preemption of oil spill claims rooted in state statutory law. The Fifth Circuit reached a broadly preemptive conclusion, but with a distinction made between state law claims arising where the spill, harm, and plaintiff involve the same state (appearing to remain viable) and a claim under the law of the "affected" state against a "point source" located in another state (held preempted, but also stating claims could be pursued under the "law of the point-source state"). See In re Deepwater Horizon, 745 F.3d 157, 171-174 (5th Cir. 2014). What language in §2718(a) and (c) supports or is in tension with this ruling? The Supreme Court denied a petition for review in 2014. For recent scholarship preceding this decision that discusses the preemption question, see Gignilliat, The Gulf Oil Spill: OPA, State Law, and Maritime Preemption, 13 Va. J. Envtl. L. 385 (2011); Murchison, Liability Under the Oil Pollution Act: Current Law and Needed Revisions, 71 La. L. Rev. 917 (2011).

The Relationship with Clean Water Act §311. Clean Water Act §311 also contains provisions pertaining to oil spill responses. Its provisions generally can be construed to complement OPA, but one area of difference may be sections imposing stronger obligations on the federal government. What provisions of §311 could be read as imposing mandates, rather than merely authorizing action? Consider these provisions in conjunction with the Clean Water Act's citizen suit provision, covered earlier in Chapter 2, section E.1. How might this §311 language be used if the federal government failed to respond decisively to an oil spill? In the *Deepwater Horizon* 2014 decision discussed in the preceding section, the court construed §311(o)'s savings clause narrowly, with substantial weight given to *Ouellette* and preemption law. The provision was inadequate to preserve Louisiana claims under a state wildlife statute. As with the OPA claim, the court distinguished between an all in-state incident and plaintiff and claims involving a spill and different "affected" state. 745 F.3d at 171-174. The court concluded that relief was available under "OPA and the CWA or the law of the point-source."

Oil Spill Prevention. In response to the Deepwater Horizon spill, the Interior Department's Bureau of Ocean Energy Management, Regulation, and Enforcement issued regulations in 2010 to improve drilling safety by strengthening requirements for safety equipment, well control systems, and blowout prevention practices on offshore oil and gas operations, and to improve workplace safety by reducing the risk of human error. The drilling safety regulations strengthen oversight of mechanisms such as the blowout preventers that are designed to shut off the flow of oil and gas. Operators must secure independent, expert reviews of their well design, construction, and flow intervention mechanisms. The workplace safety rule requires operators to set up a Safety and Environmental Management System to reduce human and organizational errors that cause work-related accidents and offshore oil spills. 30 C.F.R. Part 250. The Obama administration imposed a moratorium on deepwater drilling shortly after the explosion, but the capping of BP's well and the adoption of the drilling and workplace safety rules induced it to lift the moratorium six months after the Deepwater Horizon disaster.[h]

E. LIABILITY FOR DAMAGE TO NATURAL RESOURCES

CERCLA authorizes the federal government and the states to recover not only response costs, but also damages for injuries to natural resources resulting from a release of hazardous substances. §107(a)(1)-(4)(C). OPA also allows the federal and state governments and Indian tribes to recover natural resource damages. 33 U.S.C. §§2702(b)(2)(A), 2706. This section focuses on CERCLA, but the OPA provisions raise analogous issues, as section D.3 above indicates.

Interior's Initial Natural Resource Damage Regulations. Section 301(c)(1) required the President to issue natural resource damage assessment regulations. Ohio v. U.S. Dep't of the Interior, 880 F.2d 432 (D.C. Cir. 1989), concerned the validity of a rule measuring damages to natural resources as the *lesser of* (1) restoration or replacement costs or (2) diminution of use values. The state and environmental petitioners claimed that the statute requires damages to be sufficient in every case to restore, replace, or acquire the equivalent of the damaged resources. Interior responded that CERCLA does not establish any floor for damages, instead leaving it up to the agency to decide what the proper measure of damages should be. Although under §107(f)(1) all damages recovered must be spent restoring or replacing the injured resources, Interior argued that the amount recovered from PRPs need not be sufficient to complete the job.

The court explained the significance of this difference of opinion by way of example:

> [I]magine a hazardous substance spill that kills a rookery of fur seals and destroys a habitat for seabirds at a sealife reserve. The lost use value of the seals and seabird habitat would be measured by the market value of the fur seals' pelts (which would be approximately $15 each) plus the selling price per acre of land comparable in value to that on which the spoiled bird habitat was located. Even if, as likely, that use value turns out to be far less than the cost of restoring the rookery and seabird habitat, it would nonetheless be the only measure of damages eligible for the presumption of recoverability under the Interior rule. [Id. at 442.]

The court invalidated the "lesser of" rule. Section 107(f)(1) requires sums recovered by the United States as trustee to be used to restore or replace the injured resources. This mandate, the court concluded, reflects the "paramount restorative

---

h. See Decision Memorandum of Kenneth Salazar, Termination of the Suspension of Certain Offshore Permitting and Drilling Activities on the Outer Continental Shelf (Oct. 12, 2010). See also Hornbeck Offshore Services, L.L.C. v. Salazar, 696 F. Supp. 2d 627 (E.D. La. 2010), *appeal dismissed as moot*, 396 Fed. Appx. 147 (5th Cir. 2010) (invalidating moratorium).

purpose" of the natural resource damage provisions. If the Interior Department were correct that Congress authorized the agency to measure damages by the lesser of restoration costs or diminution in use values, and if the latter would be significantly less than the former in many cases, then Congress would have established a damage assessment and recovery scheme that would be insufficient in most cases to achieve this paramount purpose. The court also relied on the fifth sentence of §107(f)(1), which indicates that restoration costs will not serve as a ceiling on damage recoveries.

Interior tried to justify the "lesser of" rule as economically efficient. It argued that requiring the payment of restoration costs would be a waste of money whenever restoration cost exceeds the use value of the resource. The court did not dispute that Congress intended the natural resource damage provisions to operate efficiently, requiring, for example, that restoration of injured resources take place as cost-effectively as possible. But it found that Interior's argument was based on an assumption that natural resources are fungible goods just like any others, and that the value to society generated by a particular resource can be accurately measured in every case. Congress rejected precisely that assumption because it was skeptical of society's ability to measure the true "value" of natural resources. The court also overturned the regulations' hierarchy of methods for determining use values, which limited damages to the price commanded by the injured resource on the open market, unless the trustee found that the market for that resource was not reasonably competitive. The court directed the agency on remand to consider allowing trustees to derive use values by summing up all reliably calculated use values. It took issue with Interior's decision to limit the role of nonconsumptive values, such as option and existence values, in the calculation of use values.

Industry litigants also attacked the portion of the assessment regulations that governed the measurement of the use value of a damaged resource. The regulations equated lost use value with diminution of the market price when the injured resource is traded in a market. If the damaged resource is not itself traded in a market, but a similar resource is, an appraisal technique could be used to determine lost use value. When neither of these two situations applies, nonmarketed resource methodologies, including contingent valuation (CV), could be used. CV seeks to create a market where none exists by polling people's willingness to pay to benefit from the environmental amenities at issue. Industry charged that CV is too speculative and amounts to little more than ordinary public opinion polling, but the court held that Interior's decision to endorse CV was reasonable.

The Regulations on Remand. In 1994, the Interior Department reissued the regulations on remand from *Ohio*. The regulations allowed trustees to recover the costs of restoration, rehabilitation, replacement, or acquisition of equivalent resources (RRRA) in all cases. Trustees could add to that basic measure of damages the value of the resource services lost to the public from the date of the release to the date RRRA activities are completed. Option and existence values could be used to value damaged resources only if trustees could not calculate use values. In Kennecott Utah Copper Corp. v. U.S. Dep't of the Interior, 88 F.3d 1191 (D.C. Cir. 1996), the court invalidated the provisions that appeared to permit trustees to recover both the cost of restoring the injured resources and the cost of restoring the services provided by those resources. The effect of the decision was to reinstate the pre-1994 approach, which measured the level of restoration of injured resources as the level of services provided by the resources before they were damaged. The court also ruled that CERCLA does not require trustees to choose the most cost-effective restoration option as the measure of damages and that the agency did not err when it failed to adopt a standard to prevent trustees from selecting restoration options whose costs are grossly disproportionate to the value of the injured resource.

The Debate over CV. Those who support the use of CV methodology for assessing natural resource damages contend that it is the only methodology capable of quantifying the inherently subjective nonuse values. CV's critics claim that it lacks reliability, trustworthiness, or a theoretically defensible foundation. Binger et al., Contingent Valuation Methodology in the Natural Resource Damage Regulatory Process: Choice Theory and the Embedding Phenomenon, 35 Nat. Resources J. 443, 444 (1995). They charge that the underlying surveys are entirely hypothetical and that respondents typically lack sufficient information about resource value to make meaningful bids.

Natural Resource Damage Litigation. Relatively few natural resource damage cases have been litigated. The uncertainties involved in predicting judicial receptivity to natural resource damage claims and the complexity of the Interior Department's regulations (which even government lawyers have called a "cookbook for litigation") may be partially responsible. Bourdeau & Jawetz, 25 Years of Superfund Litigation: Progress Made, Progress Needed, 37 Env't Rep. (BNA) 97, 99 (2006).

F.   THE CERCLA CLEANUP PROCESS

1.   An Overview of the Cleanup Process

The courts frequently describe CERCLA's dual goals as adequate remediation of hazardous substance releases that pose threats to public health and the environment (see Figure 9-1) and imposition of liability for the costs of remediation on those responsible for the release. See, e.g., Key Tronic Corp. v. United States, 511 U.S. 809, 815 (1994). When Congress adopted SARA in 1986, it sought to provide more guidance to EPA in its selection of remedies and to increase consistency of cleanups from site to site. Section 121 governs the question of how clean a site must be at the end of remediation. Although this provision, and EPA's implementing regulations and guidance documents, provided greater detail on how to conduct cleanups than the pre-1986 statute, it is generally agreed that §121 has failed to ensure expeditious or efficient cleanups that conform to consistently applied standards.

Section 104(a)(1) of CERCLA authorizes EPA to respond to a release or threatened release of a hazardous substance into the environment or of any pollutant or contaminant that may present an imminent and substantial danger to the public health or welfare. Remedial actions must conform to the cleanup standards adopted pursuant to §121, see §104(c)(4), as well as to the NCP's procedural and substantive dictates. The contents of the NCP are sketched out in §105(a). Section 105(a)(8) requires that EPA devise criteria for determining which releases or threatened releases most urgently demand remedial action, taking into account relative risk to public health or welfare or the environment. Based on these criteria, EPA must include in the NCP a list of sites, known as the national priorities list (NPL), representing the "top priorit[ies] among known response targets." §105(a)(8)(B).

Source: U.S. EPA

Before

The East Ditch, located at the south end of Bowers Landfill, contained discarded tires and debris.

Source: U.S. EPA

During

1993: After excavating soil, the west field was graded and seeded to support wetlands.

Source: U.S. EPA

After

1997: Wetlands that were created during the cleanup flourish with a variety of plants and wildlife.

FIGURE 9-1
A Superfund Success Story: Bowers Landfill, Pickaway County, Ohio, Before, During, and After Remediation

Source: http://www.epa.gov.

For every NPL site, EPA's contractors or PRPs prepare an elaborate study of site conditions and cleanup options called the Remedial Investigation and Feasibility Study (RI/FS) in conformity with agency specifications. The process usually takes at least two years and is expensive ($1 million for a study is not uncommon). Once the RI/FS is prepared, EPA documents its preferred remedy in a record of decision (ROD). EPA affords PRPs an opportunity to negotiate a consent decree under which they can carry out the cleanup dictated by the ROD.

2. *The National Priorities List*

CARUS CHEMICAL COMPANY v. EPA
395 F.3d 434 (D.C. Cir. 2005)

GINSBURG, Chief Judge.

[Carus Chemical Company operated a manufacturing plant on a parcel of land that was part of a larger property known as the Matthiessen & Hegeler Zinc Company Site. The Zinc Company operated a smelter and a rolling mill on the property for more than 100 years. During that time, two large slag piles accumulated at the site, one of which was located adjacent to (and partly in) the Little Vermilion River and partly on Carus's property. EPA placed the entire Matthiessen & Hegeler site on the NPL, based on its belief that the substances in the slag piles posed a threat to human health and the environment. Carus challenged that decision as arbitrary and capricious.]

In order to identify candidates for the NPL, the EPA promulgated the Hazard Ranking System (HRS), a comprehensive methodology and mathematical model the agency uses to "evaluate[] the observed or potential release of hazardous substances" and to "quantif[y] the environmental risks a site poses." Tex Tin Corp. v. EPA, 992 F.2d 353, 353 (D.C. Cir. 1993).

In order to evaluate a waste site using the HRS, the EPA first identifies the "sources" of contamination, the "[h]azardous substances associated with these sources," and the "[p]athways potentially threatened by these hazardous substances." HRS §2.2. The HRS lists four possible pathways: soil exposure, air migration, ground water migration, and the one relevant to this case, surface water migration. For each pathway deemed potentially affected in light of conditions at the site, the agency calculates a score based upon particular "threats." The surface water migration pathway is scored based upon threats to drinking water, to the human food chain, and to the environment. With respect to each pathway and threat to be scored, the HRS calls for the EPA to measure three so-called factor categories: "likelihood of release (or likelihood of exposure)"; "waste characteristics"; and "targets," which may include an individual, a human population, resources, and sensitive environments. The agency's measurements of the first two categories are relevant to this case.

The "[l]ikelihood of release is a measure of the likelihood that a waste has been or will be released to the environment." Id. §2.3. When, as in this case, the EPA determines there has already been a release, it assigns a fixed number for this component of the overall score of the pathway, regardless of the level of that release.

With respect to waste characteristics, the HRS first requires the EPA to "select the hazardous substance potentially posing the greatest hazard for the pathway."

Id. §2.4.1. The agency is then to evaluate persistence, bioaccumulation, and toxicity factors pertaining to that substance (only the last of which features in this case).

For each substance being scored, the agency uses a toxicity factor value between 0 and 10,000, reflecting the potential of that substance to cause adverse health effects. For a single substance there may be multiple toxicity factor values, each corresponding to a route of exposure (e.g., inhalation, ingestion) through which that substance may come into contact with humans. If there are, and if the agency has "usable toxicity data" for more than one such exposure route, then it should "consider all exposure routes and use the highest assigned value, regardless of exposure route, as the toxicity factor value." Id. §2.4.1.1. [EPA places any site with a score greater than 28.50 on a scale of 0 to 100 on the NPL.]

. . . EPA determined that hazardous substances were being released into the Little Vermilion River. Because the observed release was into a river, the agency scored the surface water migration pathway, and because Illinois classified that river as a fishery, the agency scored that pathway for the threat it posed to the human food chain.

Following the method set forth in the HRS, the EPA then assessed the "waste characteristics" of the hazardous substances found at the site, namely, cadmium, copper, lead, nickel, and zinc. Carus's principal dispute is over the EPA's choice, purportedly in compliance with HRS §2.4.1.1, to use the toxicity factor value for cadmium corresponding to the inhalation route of exposure. Plugging this value into the model, the EPA calculated a score of 100 for the pathway and a total score of 50 for the Matthiessen & Hegeler site. [EPA placed the site on the NPL, over Carus's objections.] . . .

Carus raises two separate challenges to the EPA's decision to place the Matthiessen & Hegeler site on the NPL. First, Carus argues the agency wrongly interpreted HRS §2.4.1.1 as requiring it to use a toxicity factor value for cadmium corresponding to a route of exposure (inhalation) unlikely to occur in light of the conditions at the site. Had the agency instead applied the toxicity factor value corresponding to the ingestion route of exposure, Carus maintains, the HRS score for the site would have been below 28.50. Second, Carus contends the sampling data and the documents it submitted during the comment period rendered unreasonable the EPA's reliance solely upon data collected earlier by the Illinois EPA.

A.   The EPA's Interpretation of HRS §2.4.1.1

As the EPA understands HRS §2.4.1.1, and as it applied that regulation in the rulemaking under review, the agency was required to use the toxicity factor value for the inhalation of cadmium even though it was scoring the surface water migration pathway. Carus takes exception to that interpretation, arguing it is nonsensical to read the rule as mandating the use of a toxicity factor value corresponding to an exposure route (inhalation) unlikely to present a threat considering the pathway being scored.

. . . The EPA has consistently interpreted §2.4.1.1 as requiring it to use the highest toxicity factor value for a substance regardless of the most likely route of exposure. Indeed, the protest Carus now advances—that there is no scientific justification for using the toxicity factor value for a route of exposure that is improbable in light of the pathway being scored—was made and rejected when the EPA first issued the regulation. At that time, the agency defended its interpretation of the rule as follows:

> EPA recognizes that toxicity values for substances are route-specific. However, the three pathways . . . receiving a toxicity factor value are substance migration pathways, not human exposure routes. Multiple human exposure routes are possible for each substance migration pathway (e.g., volatile substances in ground water or surface water used for drinking can be inhaled during showering), and, therefore, use of a single route-specific toxicity value is not necessarily appropriate. . . . For this reason, and to avoid the added complexity of route-specific toxicity evaluations, EPA decided to base the toxicity factor on the highest route-specific value (if more than one is available). . . . [T]his may, in a few site situations, overstate toxicity. . . .

. . . [W]e must uphold the EPA's interpretation because it accords both with the text of the regulation and with what we know of the agency's understanding of the rule when it was issued.

As for the former, the regulation reads in relevant part as follows:

> *Toxicity Factor.* Evaluate toxicity for those hazardous substances at the site that are available to the pathway being scored. For all pathways and threats, except the surface water environmental threat, evaluate human toxicity as specified below. . . .
>
> For hazardous substances having usable toxicity data for multiple exposure routes (for example, inhalation and ingestion), consider all exposure routes and use the highest assigned value, regardless of exposure route, as the toxicity factor value.

HRS §2.4.1.1. The EPA's interpretation clearly hews close to the text. The rule first directs the agency to "[e]valuate [the] toxicity" of each hazardous substance "available to the pathway being scored," and then unequivocally requires that, when the substance being scored has "usable toxicity data for multiple exposure routes"—as does cadmium—the EPA "consider all exposure routes and use the highest assigned value, regardless of exposure route."

. . . [Carus claimed that the rule, if read properly,] allows the use of only those toxicity factor values corresponding to routes of exposure the EPA finds are a threat at the site. In support of this interpretation, Carus points to the reference, in the opening sentence of the rule, to the "pathway being scored." According to Carus, this phrase modifies not just the preceding clause of the same sentence but the entire rule, thus requiring the EPA to decide whether exposure via a particular route is likely, considering the pathway being scored, before it uses a toxicity factor value corresponding to that exposure route.

. . . Even if we owed no deference to the agency, however, we would not be persuaded by Carus's alternative reading of the rule. First, the phrase "available to the pathway" plainly limits only the universe of hazardous substances the EPA may use in scoring a pathway; the phrase cannot reasonably be read to limit, as Carus suggests, the universe of toxicity factor values upon which the agency may draw. Second, Carus would read out of the regulation the direction to use the highest toxicity factor value "regardless of exposure route," in contravention of the principle that every word of a legal text should be given effect. . . .

B.   Carus's Submissions to the EPA

Carus also claims the EPA relied upon insufficient and out-dated sampling data obtained by its Illinois counterpart in 1991 and 1993. Carus apparently believes more recent data from samples collected by GeoSyntec Consulting shows the EPA erred in listing the Matthiessen & Hegeler site on the NPL. Before considering this argument we must address two anterior matters.

. . . Carus asserts the documents it submitted to the EPA "establish[ed] risk-based clean-up levels"—whatever that may mean—and "evaluate[d] possible remedial alternatives," both of which contributions the agency apparently failed to consider. Perhaps so, but Carus did and still does nothing to explain how either consideration could have affected the HRS score for the Matthiessen & Hegeler site. Nor does Carus refute the EPA's response that it had no obligation to consider such matters because they are irrelevant to the decision to list a site on the NPL.

In the EPA's response to public comments it explained that the data compiled by GeoSyntec, far from contradicting the data upon which the agency relied, "confirmed the presence of . . . cadmium and lead in soil samples" taken from around the slag piles. The EPA also responded to Carus's claim the GeoSyntec data showed the levels of hazardous substances present in the Little Vermilion River were below applicable limits; the agency explained that an "observed release" of a hazardous substance may be established "[e]ven though levels may be lower than regulatory limits . . . if the measured levels are significantly higher than background levels." In sum, the EPA concluded Carus did not present "any specific comments [showing] that the data used in the HRS scoring [were] incorrect or why [Geosyntec's] data would suggest that the site score is incorrect." Just so. . . .

NOTES AND QUESTIONS

1. Why did EPA place the Mathhiessen & Hegeler site on the NPL? Does it make any sense for EPA to gauge the risk presented by the site, based on a pathway of exposure that was unlikely to occur? How did EPA justify its reliance on the inhalation route of exposure? Why did the court endorse that decision?

2. *Placing Sites on the NPL.* EPA explained the function of the NPL in the preamble to the 1984 version of the NCP:

> The purpose of the NPL . . . is primarily to serve as an informational tool for use by EPA in identifying sites that appear to present a significant risk to public health or the environment. The initial identification of a site on the NPL is intended primarily to guide EPA in determining which sites warrant further investigation designed to assess the nature and extent of the public health and environmental risks associated with the site and to determine what response action, if any, may be appropriate. Inclusion of a site on the NPL does not establish that EPA necessarily will undertake response actions. Moreover, listing does not require any action of any private party, nor does it determine the liability of any party for the cost of cleanup at the site.
>
> In addition, although the HRS scores used to place sites on the NPL may be helpful to the Agency in determining priorities for cleanup and other response activities among sites on the NPL, EPA does not rely on the scores as the sole means of determining such priorities. . . . The information collected to develop HRS scores to choose sites for the NPL is not sufficient in itself to determine the appropriate remedy for a

particular site. After a site has been included on the NPL, EPA generally will rely on further, more detailed studies conducted at the site to determine what response, if any, is appropriate. . . . After conducting these additional studies EPA may conclude that it is not feasible to conduct response action at some sites on the NPL because of more pressing needs at other sites. Given the limited resources available in the [Superfund], the Agency must carefully balance the relative needs for response at the numerous sites it has studied. It is also possible that EPA will conclude after further analysis that no action is needed at the site because the site does not present a significant threat to public health, welfare or the environment. [49 Fed. Reg. 37,070, 37,071 (1984).]

Nevertheless, NPL listing has real-world consequences: "listing a site virtually assures costly clean-up of the site, and . . . this probability in turn has significant immediate consequences for both surrounding property values and the liability of [PRPs]." Board of Regents v. EPA, 86 F.3d 1214, 1217 (D.C. Cir. 1996). See also Mead Corp. v. Browner, 100 F.3d 152, 155 (D.C. Cir. 1996) ("listing drastically increases the chances of costly activity").

Owners of NPL sites have challenged not only the application of the HRS, but the HRS itself. In Eagle-Picher Indus., Inc. v. EPA, 759 F.2d 905 (D.C. Cir. 1985), the court held that the HRS represented a reasonable effort by EPA to reconcile the need for certainty before acting with the need for inexpensive and expeditious procedures for identifying potentially hazardous sites.

3. *Additional Challenges to Placement on the NPL.* EPA has had mixed success in defending its decisions to place facilities on the NPL. In National Gypsum Co. v. EPA, 968 F.2d 40 (D.C. Cir. 1992), the court vacated and remanded an NPL listing because EPA acted arbitrarily in assessing both the site's toxicity and its persistence scores. But in Bradley Mining Co. v. EPA, 972 F.2d 1356 (D.C. Cir. 1992), the D.C. Circuit upheld an NPL listing and rejected the assertion that EPA failed to demonstrate that mercury found in an adjacent lake was caused by mining operations and that it incorrectly calculated the risk that the mercury would contaminate groundwater. See also CTS Corp. v. EPA, 759 F.3d 52 (D.C. Cir. 2014) (rejecting challenges to NPL listing as "methodological nit-picking" and finding that listing decision rested on reliable, site-specific hydrological evidence linking site that had used TCE to groundwater contamination); US Magnesium, LLC v. EPA, 630 F.3d 188 (D.C. Cir. 2011) (upholding listing of plant that produced molten magnesium and rejecting claim that EPA erred in scoring the pathways of exposure under the HRS). See Figure 9-2 for a representation of groundwater contamination and its sources.

4. *The Fate of Love Canal and the Valley of the Drums.* EPA removed the Love Canal landfill site whose discovery was instrumental in the passage of CERCLA from the NPL in 2004. 69 Fed. Reg. 58,322 (Sept. 30, 2004). The site was covered with a 70-acre cap and equipped with a permanent leachate collection and treatment system. EPA indicated that it would continue to engage in annual monitoring and review of institutional controls. The fate of the other site prominent in motivating Congress to adopt CERCLA is less inspiring. In 2008, EPA inspectors found dozens of rusted drums as well as hardened paint sludge on land adjacent to the part of the Valley of the Drums in Kentucky that had been fenced and capped in the 1980s. EPA determined that state officials responsible for maintaining the site failed to take groundwater samples and keep groundwater monitoring wells in operation. See EPA Raises Concern About Original Superfund Site, Greenwire, Dec. 15, 2008.

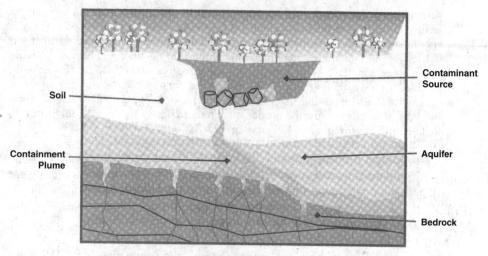

FIGURE 9-2
Contaminated Groundwater

Source: http://www.epa.gov.

3. The National Contingency Plan and Cleanup Standards

Once EPA decides that a site, whether it is placed on the NPL or not, merits remediation, it must determine what kind of cleanup is appropriate. The process of selecting a remedy—the so-called how clean is clean problem—entails consideration of the technical feasibility and implementation costs of alternative remedial possibilities, whether the alternatives adequately address the health and environmental risks posed by the site in its contaminated state, and whether any additional risk reduction benefits likely to accrue from one alternative compared to another are worth the resulting cost increases. In short, the issues that arise in CERCLA remedy selection are precisely the same risk management issues addressed in depth in Chapter 8, which covered an array of approaches to management of the risks presented by exposure to toxic substances.

CERCLA did not originally contain cleanup standards. Instead, it contained only a vague mandate to

> select appropriate remedial actions determined to be necessary . . . which are to the extent practicable in accordance with the national contingency plan and which provide for that cost-effective response which provides a balance between the need for protection of public health and welfare and the environment . . . and the availability of amounts from the [Superfund]. [§104(c)(4).]

Frustrated with the inconsistency of cleanup standards from site to site, Congress adopted §121 of CERCLA in the 1986 SARA legislation to curtail EPA's discretion. Congress sought to strike a balance among (1) technology forcing, (2) the implementation of health-based standards, and (3) cost-effectiveness considerations. The following case expands on how Congress struck that balance.

OHIO v. EPA
997 F.2d 1520 (D.C. Cir. 1993)

Before Mikva, Chief Judge, Edwards and Randolph, Circuit Judges.
Per Curiam: . . .

[According to the court, the NCP is "the means by which EPA implements CERCLA." It "provide[s] the organizational structure and procedures" for responding to releases and threats thereof under §104(a)(1) of CERCLA. 40 C.F.R.§300.1.]

Petitioners, whom we shall call "the States," include both states and private parties contending that EPA's changes to the NCP in 1985 and 1990 are inconsistent with the requirements of CERCLA. The petitions for review . . . [involve] claims that the NCP unlawfully diminishes the level of environmental protectiveness in the remedy selection process and cleanup provisions of CERCLA. . . .

II

The States first challenge several elements of the NCP definition of legally "applicable" or "relevant and appropriate" environmental standards, known as "ARARs." CERCLA does not define ARARs, but the statute does require that remedial actions at Superfund sites result in a level of cleanup or standard of control that at least meets the legally applicable or otherwise relevant and appropriate federal (or stricter state) requirements. 42 U.S.C. §9621(d)(2)(A). The NCP defines "applicable requirements" as follows:

> Applicable requirements means those cleanup standards, standards of control, and other substantive requirements, criteria, or limitations promulgated under federal environmental or state environmental or facility siting laws that specifically address a hazardous substance, pollutant, contaminant, remedial action, location, or other circumstance found at a CERCLA site.

Only those state standards that are identified by a state in a timely manner and that are more stringent than federal requirements may be applicable. 40 C.F.R. §300.5. "Relevant and appropriate requirements" are those substantive requirements that, while not "applicable," nonetheless "address problems or situations sufficiently similar to those encountered at the CERCLA site that their use is well suited to the particular site." Id. . . .

D. Does the NCP Improperly Fail to Apply Zero-Level Maximum Contaminant Level Goals ("MCLGs") as ARARs?

The States challenge EPA's decision that Maximum Contaminant Level Goals ("MCLGs") established under the Safe Drinking Water Act ("SDWA") do not have to be attained for contaminants whose MCLG has been set at a level of zero. . . .

The SDWA is specifically referenced in section 121(d)(2)(A) of CERCLA as one of the federal laws containing ARARs for Superfund cleanups. The SDWA identifies two standards for exposure to contaminants. The first, Maximum Contaminant Level Goals ("MCLGs"), are generally unenforceable goals that reflect the level for a given contaminant at which "no known or anticipated adverse effects on the health of persons occur and which allows an adequate margin of safety." 42 U.S.C. §300g-1(b)(4). Many MCLGs for carcinogens are set at zero. The second type of standards, Maximum Contaminant Levels ("MCLs")—the actual maximum permissible concentration levels under the SDWA—must be set as close as "feasible" to their corresponding MCLGs, taking into account available technology and cost. 42 U.S.C. §300g-1(b)(4)-(5).

While MCLGs are unenforceable under the SDWA, section [121(d)(2)(A)] of CERCLA converts them into enforceable goals. . . . Consistent with this requirement, the NCP generally requires the attainment of MCLGs. When the MCLG for a contaminant has been set at a level of zero, however, the NCP requires only that the MCL be attained. In essence, EPA has made a categorical determination that MCLGs set at a level of zero are never "relevant and appropriate under the circumstances" of a release.

This determination was based on EPA's conclusion "that it is impossible to detect whether 'true' zero has actually been attained." 55 Fed. Reg. 8752 (1990). . . .

The States contend that EPA's decision concerning zero-level MCLGs is inconsistent with CERCLA's mandate that all remedial actions attain MCLGs. This argument ignores the full language of the section, which imposes the requirement "where such goals . . . are relevant and appropriate under the circumstances of the release or threatened release." 42 U.S.C. §9621(d)(2)(A). This language leaves EPA with discretion to determine when MCLGs are relevant and appropriate. . . .

[The court also rejected the states' claim that EPA abused its discretion by concluding that zero-level MCLGs are never relevant and appropriate.] As we understand EPA's scientific analysis, one can never prove a true zero level. If the measuring device indicates zero, this shows only that the device is not sufficiently sensitive to detect the presence of any contaminants. It does not show the total absence of the contaminants. In other words, if one asserts that zero contaminants are present, this can be *falsified* by showing the presence of some detectable level, but it can never be shown to be *true*. EPA chose to set MCLGs for carcinogens at zero under the SDWA because they "are goals which may or may not be practically achievable and the practicality of these goals should be factored into the MCLs," not the MCLGs. 50 Fed. Reg. 46,896 (1985). In contrast, EPA concluded that "ARARs must be measurable and attainable since their purpose is to set a standard that an actual remedy will attain." 55 Fed. Reg. 8752 (1990).

[The states also argued that EPA could and should have selected a method of measurement approximating zero by setting "a goal of achieving the analytical detection limits for specific carcinogens."] That EPA could do this, however, does not mean it is required to do so. Section 121 requires the selection of MCLs where MCLGs are unattainable. That is what the NCP does. That conclusion is reasonable given EPA's discretion to determine when ARARs are relevant and appropriate.

III . . .

A. DOES THE NCP ESTABLISH AN IMPROPER COST-BENEFIT ANALYSIS IN THE REMEDY SELECTION PROCESS?

[Section 121(d)(1) requires the selection of a remedial action "at a minimum which assures protection of human health and the environment," while §121(b)(1) requires the selection of cost-effective actions. Both EPA and the States agreed that §121(d)(1) prohibits EPA from considering cost when it determines the level of protectiveness to be achieved by a remedial action.] The States contend, however, that two provisions in the NCP implicitly authorize the use of cost-benefit analysis, thereby permitting cost to be considered in determining the level of protectiveness to be achieved by a remedial action. In making this argument, the States distort the language of the NCP, which is carefully structured so "that protection of human health and the environment will not be compromised by other selection factors, such as cost." [55 Fed. Reg. 8726.]

The States first point to a provision in the NCP authorizing EPA to balance nine different criteria, including both protection of human health and cost, in selecting a remedy. But while the NCP identifies nine criteria to be used in selecting a remedy, all of the criteria are not given equal weight. Instead, they are divided into three classifications: threshold criteria, primary balancing criteria, and modifying criteria. Under this structure, "[o]verall protection of human health and the environment and compliance with ARARs (unless a specific ARAR is waived) are threshold requirements that each alternative must meet in order to be eligible for selection." 40 C.F.R. §300.430(f)(1)(i)(A). EPA explained in the preamble to the NCP that remedial alternatives "must be demonstrated to be protective . . . in order to be eligible for consideration in the balancing process by which the remedy is selected." 55 Fed. Reg. 8726 (1990). The identification of threshold criteria therefore undermines the States' claim that by listing nine criteria, the NCP permits the level of protectiveness to be affected by cost.

The States also point us to the NCP's definition of "cost-effectiveness," which states that "[a] remedy shall be cost-effective if its costs are proportional to its overall effectiveness." 40 C.F.R. §300.430(f)(1)(ii)(D). The States contend that this language actually authorizes the use of cost-benefit analysis. In making this argument, though, the States ignore the first sentence of the same section of the NCP that they are challenging. It states: "Each remedial action shall be cost-effective, provided that it first satisfies the threshold criteria set forth in §300.430(f)(1)(ii)(A) and (B)." Id. Thus, . . . the NCP explicitly prohibits consideration of costs in the manner complained of by the States.

B. Does the NCP Improperly Fail to Require the Selection of Permanent Remedies to the Maximum Extent Practicable?

The States next argue that the NCP is inconsistent with section 121(b)(1)'s requirement that the President select remedial actions "that utilize[] permanent solutions . . . to the maximum extent practicable." The NCP classifies permanence as one of the five primary balancing criteria, along with reduction of toxicity, mobility, or volume; short-term effectiveness; implementability; and cost. 40 C.F.R. §300.430(f)(1)(i)(B). The States reason that because the selection of permanent remedies "is one of the overarching statutory principles of remedy selection under CERCLA," the other balancing criteria, particularly cost, should play no role in EPA's determination whether a permanent remedy is to be selected. In essence, the States would like permanence to be treated as an additional threshold criterion that must be evaluated independently of cost.

The flaw in the States' argument is in the premise that permanence is an overarching statutory principle. This premise is not supported by the statutory language.

Section 121(b)(1) . . . places as much emphasis on the selection of cost-effective remedies as it does on the selection of permanent remedies. . . . [T]here is nothing in section 121 to suggest that selecting permanent remedies is more important than selecting cost-effective remedies. . . .

. . . Given the statutory requirement to achieve a number of competing goals, EPA's decision concerning how much emphasis to place on the selection of permanent remedies is a reasonable one.

C. Does the NCP Cancer Risk Range Improperly Fail to Protect Human Health and the Environment Without Regard to Cost?

The States next challenge EPA's use of a cancer risk range between 10^{-6} and 10^{-4} in the NCP, arguing that an exposure level greater than 10^{-6} is never appropriate. A 10^{-4} risk subjects the surrounding population to an increased lifetime cancer risk of 1 in 10,000. A 10^{-6} risk subjects the surrounding population to an increased lifetime cancer risk of 1 in 1,000,000. When EPA develops objectives for a remedial action at a site, it selects a remediation goal that "establish[es] acceptable exposure levels that are protective of human health." 40 C.F.R. §300.430(e)(2)(i). EPA attempts to use health-based ARARs to set the goal, but if ARARs are nonexistent or unsuitable for use, EPA establishes the goal based on criteria in the NCP. "For known or suspected carcinogens, acceptable exposure levels are generally concentration levels that represent an excess upper bound lifetime cancer risk to an individual of between 10^{-6} and 10^{-4}. . . ." 40 C.F.R. §300.430(e)(2)(i)(A)(2). The NCP expresses a preference for remedial actions that achieve a level of 10^{-6}[;] however, the ultimate decision depends on a balancing of nine criteria, including cost.

The States contend that by permitting cost to play a role in determining the level of exposure, the cancer risk range fails to meet the requirement in [§121] that remedial actions be "protective of human health." The States' argument necessarily depends, though, on the notion that an exposure level greater than 10^{-6} is not protective of human health. CERCLA requires the selection of remedial actions "that are protective of human health," not as protective as conceivably possible. A "risk range of 10^{-4} to 10^{-6} represents EPA's opinion on what are generally acceptable levels." 55 Fed. Reg. 8716 (1990). Although cost cannot be used to justify the selection of a remedy that is not protective of human health and the environment, it can be considered in selecting from options that are adequately protective. [The court also pointed out that many ARARs, which Congress specifically intended be used as cleanup standards under CERCLA, are set at risk levels less stringent than 10^{-6}.] . . .

NOTES AND QUESTIONS

1. How did the court respond to the states' challenges to the NCP provisions dealing with cost and permanence? CERCLA remedies must be "protective of human health and the environment." §121(b)(1). On what basis did the states contend that the cancer risk range chosen by EPA conflicted with this mandate? Why did the court disagree? Given the text of §121(d)(2)(A), how did EPA justify not establishing MCLGs under the SDWA as ARARs at sites with carcinogenic hazardous substances? For a case in which EPA's choice of a cancer risk level of 10^{-5} rather than 10^{-4} was upheld, see United States v. Burlington N. R.R. Co., 200 F.3d 679 (10th Cir. 1999).

2. *ARARs.* SARA's cleanup standard for remedial actions is tied to "legally applicable" standards adopted under other federal and state environmental laws. The statute, however, does not define which standards or other federal and state laws are "legally applicable." The legislative history indicates that a statutory standard is legally applicable if the statute "subjects to regulation" a hazardous substance, even though the statute does not "apply directly to the situation involved at the hazardous waste site." H.R. Rep. No. 99-253, pt. 5, at 53 (1985). In addition, the cleanup must attain other standards that are "relevant and appropriate" under the circumstances of the release or threatened release. "[W]hat is a 'Relevant and Appropriate' provision of a federal or state environmental statute constitutes a judgmental determination that it would be desirable to comply with such provisions when carrying out the Superfund cleanup but that such provisions do not, as a matter of law, apply to the Superfund site." Whitney, Superfund Reform: Clarification of Cleanup Standards to Rationalize the Remedy Selection Process, 20 Colum. J. Envtl. L. 183, 192 (1995). ARARs are thus not themselves standards but a source of standards. Because neither CERCLA nor the NCP provides across-the-board standards for remedy selection, ARARs must be identified on a site-by-site basis.

There are three different kinds of ARARs: ambient or chemical-specific requirements, performance or action-specific requirements, and location-specific requirements. The first category includes standards that can be expressed as maximum permissible concentrations of particular substances or similar numerical limits. Action-specific requirements are often technology-based requirements derived from statutes such as RCRA with respect to certain kinds of activities at the site of the cleanup. The third category entails restrictions derived from the presence of hazardous substances in sensitive environments, such as wetlands or floodplains. See Whitney, *supra,* at 229.

3. *Institutional Controls.* The NCP allows the use of institutional controls that prevent access to contaminated areas as part of a final remedy "where necessary." 40 C.F.R. §300.430(a)(1)(iii)(D). These controls, however, may not substitute for active response measures as the sole remedy unless active measures are not practicable. In Superfund-financed remedial actions, institutional controls, such as deed and water use restrictions, well drilling prohibitions, and building permits, must be reliable and remain in place after initiation of state maintenance. Id. §300.510(c)(1). May the purchase of contaminated property adjacent to the source of a release qualify as an appropriate institutional control? For criticism of reliance on institutional controls without adequate safeguards, see U.S. Government Accountability Office, Better Financial Assurances and More Effective Implementation of Institutional Controls Are Needed to Protect the Public, GAO-06-900T (2006).

4. *Natural Attenuation.* Are there any circumstances in which the dilution, dispersion, and biodegradation of contaminants without human intervention may suffice as a remedy under §121? Would natural attenuation qualify as "remedial action"? What would the likely reaction of local residents be to the selection of natural attenuation? The National Research Council concluded that natural attenuation is an appropriate and cost-effective remedy for a few types of groundwater contaminants, but not for most common classes of contaminants. See Council Says Natural Attenuation Works; Extensive Data, Public Involvement Needed, 31 Env't Rep. (BNA) 382 (2000).

5. *RCRA Corrective Action.* Contamination may occur not only at inactive dump sites and industrial facilities, but also at active TSD facilities. RCRA authorizes EPA to require corrective action at TSD facilities seeking RCRA permits. See 42 U.S.C.

§6924(u)-(v); Florida Power & Light Co. v. EPA, 145 F.3d 1414, 1416 (D.C. Cir. 1998). EPA faces similar questions in determining the appropriate extent of corrective action as it faces in selecting CERCLA remedies.

G. THE EFFECT OF THE DISCOVERY OF HAZARDOUS SUBSTANCES ON REAL ESTATE TRANSACTIONS

Coupled with the expanded common law duty to disclose material facts in connection with the sale of property, CERCLA has prompted sellers of property to disclose the existence of hazardous wastes. Brokers who misrepresent the condition of the property also may be liable to buyers. Sheehy v. Lipton Indus., Inc., 507 N.E.2d 781 (Mass. App. Ct. 1987). CERCLA-mandated disclosures may have discouraged the development of some brownfield properties. Is the presence of environmental contamination an encumbrance on title that renders title unmarketable? See In re Country World Casinos, 181 F.3d 1146 (10th Cir. 1999).

Due Diligence Investigations. As indicated in section C.2.b, CERCLA includes defenses for innocent landowners and BFPPs. §§101(35), (40), 107(b)(3), (r). Site investigation may help prospective purchasers and lenders avoid purchasing contaminated properties. It also may help them avoid liability under CERCLA and similar state laws if contamination is later found, by enhancing the chances that these defenses will be available. These "due diligence" investigations combine legal and technical assessment of the status of a site's contamination and regulatory compliance. They are routinely performed on sites at which manufacturing has occurred or where substances such as asbestos, lead paint, or urea formaldehyde may have been used. Site assessments must be conducted in a manner consistent with good commercial and customary practices to provide the basis for invocation of the innocent landowner defense. A Phase I environmental site assessment (ESA), which is performed to identify environmental conditions likely to give rise to liability under CERCLA or similar state laws, is composed of four phases: records review, site reconnaissance, interviews with owners and occupants and local government officials, and an evaluation and report stating whether the assessment has revealed evidence of contamination. If the Phase I ESA reveals actual or potential contamination, a further Phase II ESA, composed of site sampling, lab analysis, and recommendations for remediation, may be conducted to assess the nature and extent of contamination.

State Disclosure Laws. The consequences of the presence of hazardous substances on real estate transactions may extend beyond the creation of CERCLA liability for the purchaser who does not qualify for the "innocent landowner" defense. Some states intervene in transactions involving potentially contaminated land. New Jersey's Environmental Cleanup Responsibility Act (ECRA), N.J. Stat. Ann. §§13: 1K-6 to K-14, adopted in 1983, for example, used

> "market forces to bring about the reversal of environmental pollution." Dixon Venture v. Joseph Dixon Crucible Co., 122 N.J. 228, 236-37 (1991). ECRA makes the transfer or the closure of an "industrial establishment" contingent upon compliance with the Act and thereby, internalizes the cost of clean-up within those transactions. [Grand Street Artists v. General Elec. Co., 19 F. Supp. 2d 242, 249 (D.N.J. 1998).]

ECRA required the owners and operators of industrial facilities to investigate the environmental condition of their property before closing or transferring operations. Current site owners were responsible for remediating contamination, even if it was caused by previous owners. See Superior Air Prod. Co. v. N.L. Indus., Inc., 522 A.2d 1025 (N.J. Super. App. Div. 1987). The transferee of property transferred in violation of ECRA could sue a noncomplying transferor to recover the cost of ECRA compliance. New West Urban Renewal Co. v. Westinghouse Elec. Corp., 909 F. Supp. 219, 225 (D.N.J. 1995). A noncomplying owner or operator was strictly liable for all remediation costs. N.J. Stat. Ann. §13:1K-13. Transactions subject to but not in compliance with ECRA could be voided by the buyer, N.J. Stat. Ann. §13:1K-13(a).

Critics charged that ECRA delayed the process and increased the cost of transferring commercial and industrial property, causing some industry to leave the state. Responding to these criticisms, the state legislature adopted the Industrial Site Recovery Act (ISRA), N.J. Pub. L. 1993, c. 139, which amended and renamed ECRA. ISRA still requires the owner or operator of an industrial establishment planning to close or transfer ownership of operations to notify the state Department of Environmental Protection (DEP). The DEP must approve the transfer. But ISRA expanded the exemptions from notification and remediation requirements and established an expedited review process. It also sought to ease the financial burdens of compliance by authorizing insurance and self-guarantees as funding sources. ISRA prompted hundreds of site cleanups, but it may not have induced industrial landowners to engage in more rapid cleanups with fewer litigation-related transaction costs. New Jersey amended ISRA in 2009 to streamline the DEP's oversight of environmental remediation projects and reduce a large case backlog. It also partially privatized the cleanup process. Maro, Note, Outsourcing the Filth: Privatizing Brownfields Remediation in New Jersey, 38 B.C. Envtl. Aff. L. Rev. 159 (2011).

Revitalization of Brownfields. Critics of CERCLA have long complained that the statute's liability scheme creates disincentives to economic development of contaminated property. Developers may fear that the purchase of abandoned contaminated sites would expose them to CERCLA liability. CERCLA thus may create incentives to use undeveloped or "greenfield" sites to avoid liability. Similarly, CERCLA may encourage refusal by lenders to foreclose on contaminated properties, often followed by abandonment of the sites, and a reluctance by purchasers of properties previously devoted to commercial or industrial use to investigate possible contamination due to fear that the information revealed might trigger liability. In those ways, CERCLA may have "helped to deepen the post-industrial economic decline in many city neighborhoods. From an investment and business standpoint, these abandoned properties, or brownfields, became untouchables." Kibel, The Urban Nexus: Open Space, Brownfields, and Justice, 25 B.C. Envtl. Aff. L. Rev. 589, 601 (1998).

The Small Business Liability Relief and Brownfields Revitalization Act of 2002 ordered EPA to establish a program to provide grants to inventory, characterize, assess, and conduct planning related to brownfield sites and perform targeted assessments at those sites. CERCLA §104(k)(2)(A). Brownfield sites comprise real property whose expansion, redevelopment, or reuse may be complicated by the presence or potential release of hazardous substances. §101(39)(A). EPA may make grants to "eligible entities" (local governments, state agencies, or Indian tribes) to investigate and remediate brownfield sites. In allocating grant money among eligible entities, EPA considers the extent to which a grant will facilitate the creation or preservation of greenfields or recreational properties, meet the needs of a community without other funding for environmental remediation and subsequent redevelopment, and facilitate the use or reuse of existing infrastructure. §104(k)(3)(C). It also considers the potential of the proposed project to stimulate economic development and the extent to which a grant would address or facilitate identification and reduction of threats to health and the environment, particularly to minority and sensitive populations. §104(k)(5)(C).

The 2002 amendments bar the federal government from taking enforcement action under §106(a) or §107(a) of CERCLA with respect to eligible response sites at which there is a release or threatened release, and a person is conducting or has completed a response action that complies with the state program. §128(b). An eligible response site is generally one that meets CERCLA's definition of a brownfield site. §101(41). Under certain circumstances, federal enforcement is appropriate even for an eligible response site. §128(b)(1)(B).

CERCLA and Federal Facilities. When a federal agency enters a contract for the sale of real property on which hazardous waste was stored, disposed of, or known to have been released, §120(h)(3)(B) of CERCLA requires that it notify the prospective purchaser and include in the deed a covenant warranting that it will take all necessary remedial action. Hercules, Inc. v. EPA, 938 F.2d 276 (D.C. Cir. 1991), held that notification is required even if the contamination occurred before government ownership. The Community Environmental Response Facilitation Act, Pub. L. No. 102-426, 106 Stat. 2174 (1992), sought to encourage the redevelopment of closed military bases. It requires the federal government to investigate property on which it plans to terminate military operations to determine the likelihood of a release or threatened release of hazardous substances or petroleum products. Deeds for properties covered by the Act must include a covenant warranting that the United States will take any necessary corrective action. §120(h)(4).

X

ENFORCEMENT OF ENVIRONMENTAL LAW

Enforcement is the set of actions that governments or others take to achieve compliance within the regulated community.

U.S. EPA, Principles of Environmental Enforcement, 1-4 (July 15, 1992).

Effective targeting of compliance monitoring and vigorous civil and criminal enforcement play a central role in achieving the goals EPA has set for protection of health and the environment.

U.S. EPA, FY 2014-2018 EPA Strategic Plan 48 (April 14, 2014).

A. INTRODUCTION

EPA has long considered promoting compliance with environmental regulatory requirements to be a critical aspect of environmental governance. The Agency's ongoing commitment to an effective enforcement and compliance program is reflected by EPA's listing "[p]rotecting human health and the environment by enforcing laws and assuring compliance" as one of its five strategic goals in its current Strategic Plan. EPA, Fiscal Year 2014-2018 EPA Strategic Plan 4 (April 10, 2014).

In recent years EPA has periodically revisited its strategies for promoting compliance. It has developed a broader "toolbox" of strategies in an effort to blend traditional civil and criminal enforcement with "compliance assistance" and "compliance incentive" strategies. The Agency explains as follows:

> EPA is working to ensure that government, business, and the public comply with federal laws and regulations designed to protect the environment and human health. We employ several strategies to achieve this goal. Our compliance assurance program provides compliance assistance and incentives, monitors compliance efforts and trends, and enforces against violators. EPA, EPA 2006-2011 Strategic Plan 129 (Sept. 2006).

The agency's strategy of using a combination of tools has been characterized as an integrated approach to compliance assurance. Stoughton et al., Toward Integrated Approaches to Compliance Assurance, 31 Envtl. L. Rep. 11266 (2001).

Circa 2014, the agency is engaged in another initiative to improve compliance, which it labels "Next Generation Compliance." EPA plans to "take advantage of new information and monitoring technologies as well [as] innovative strategies to make rules and permits more effective, enabling EPA, states, and tribes to get better compliance results and tackle today's compliance challenges." FY 2014-2018 Strategic Plan, *supra*, at 48.

This chapter provides an introduction to three key elements of contemporary environmental enforcement. First, it reviews the key actors who engage in the actual work of promoting compliance. Second, it covers the key legal authorities that are available for government officials, as well as citizens, to enforce the law. Finally, the chapter explores some of the recent strategies that EPA and its state partners have developed in their "policy toolboxes" to achieve optimal compliance with environmental regulatory requirements.

B. THE ACTORS

There are four major categories of actors in the environmental enforcement arena: federal officials, state personnel, citizens (individuals as well as environmental nongovernmental organizations, or ENGOs), and regulated parties. We review the roles of each, including some of the areas of overlap and tension.

1. *Federal Officials*

This chapter focuses on the role of the Environmental Protection Agency (EPA) in its capacity as the federal entity primarily responsible for promoting compliance with the major pollution control laws, such as the Clean Water and Clean Air Acts and RCRA. Other agencies, including the Department of the Interior (DOI), also have enforcement responsibilities under various environmental laws, such as the Endangered Species Act, as other chapters reflect. EPA summarizes the alphabet soup of federal agencies involved in different aspects of environmental governance, including environmental compliance, in its 2006-2011 Strategic Plan, reproduced as Figure 10-1:

Department/ Agency	Goal 1: Clean Air and Global Climate Change	Goal 2: Clean and Safe Water	Goal 3: Land Preservation and Restoration	Goal 4: Healthy Communities and Ecosystems	Goal 5: Compliance and Environmental Stewardship
Agriculture	X	X	X	X	X
Army Corps of Engineers	X	X	X	X	X
Commerce	X			X	
Consumer Product Safety Commission	X	X	X	X	X
Defense	X	X	X	X	X
Education	X	X	X	X	X

continued

Department/ Agency	Goal 1: Clean Air and Global Climate Change	Goal 2: Clean and Safe Water	Goal 3: Land Preservation and Restoration	Goal 4: Healthy Communities and Ecosystems	Goal 5: Compliance and Environmental Stewardship
Energy	X	X	X	X	X
Federal Emergency Management Agency		X	X	X	
General Services Administration			X		X
Health and Human Services	X	X	X	X	X
Homeland Security	X	X	X	X	X
Housing and Urban Development	X	X		X	X
Interior	X	X	X	X	X
Justice	X	X	X	X	X
Labor		X		X	X
National Aeronautics & Space Administration	X	X	X	X	X
National Science Foundation				X	X
Nuclear Regulatory Commission	X	X			
Small Business Administration	X	X	X		X
State	X	X		X	
Transportation	X	X	X	X	X
Treasury	X				X
Tennessee Valley Authority		X		X	
U.S. Agency for International Development	X	X		X	
U.S. Trade Representative				X	

EPA, 2006-2011 EPA Strategic Plan: Charting Our Course, Appendix D (Sept. 30, 2006).

FIGURE 10-1
Areas of Coordination Between EPA and Other Federal Agencies

EPA compliance staff have three main responsibilities: (1) determining enforcement priorities and developing the policies to carry them out; (2) conducting enforcement work—inspections, negotiations with regulated parties, administrative enforcement actions, and referral of civil and criminal enforcement cases to the Department of Justice for further action; and (3) authorizing and overseeing the performance of the states in the increasing number of jurisdictions in which states have taken over primary responsibility for implementation of federal environmental programs.

EPA's headquarters enforcement office is known as the Office of Enforcement and Compliance Assurance (OECA). Other EPA headquarters offices play a role in enforcement and promoting compliance, including the "program offices," such as the Office of Water, the Office of Air and Radiation, and the Office of Solid Waste and Emergency Response (OSWER).

EPA's ten regional offices also play an integral role in enforcement. Perhaps surprisingly, there is no uniform structure for how the regions are organized to perform their enforcement and compliance functions; the regional offices have evolved their own structures over the years. John B. Stephenson, former Director of Natural Resources and Environment for the Government Accountability (formerly General Accounting) Office (GAO), testified before Congress in 2006 that EPA's regions "vary substantially in the actions they take to enforce environmental requirements" and that there are "philosophical" differences among the regions in their views about enforcement.[a] Regardless of their structures and philosophical predispositions, the regional offices serve as the primary interlocutors between headquarters (where much of environmental policy, including policy in the enforcement arena, is set) and the states (where, as discussed below, much of the actual implementation work is performed), and they oversee state performance. Further, the regional offices conduct much of EPA's inspection and enforcement activity and they do much of its compliance promotion work.

EPA has the option of bringing cases in court or through its administrative adjudication apparatus. Recent iterations of many of the environmental laws have created or expanded EPA's authority to pursue violators through administrative adjudication (in addition to strengthening its judicial enforcement authorities). See, e.g., CAA §113(d) (enacted as part of the 1990 amendments to allow administrative enforcement actions, with penalties of up to $25,000 per day). Table 10-1 indicates the number of administrative actions EPA brought between FY 1975 and FY 2011.

EPA's consolidated rules of practice, contained in 40 C.F.R. Part 22, govern much of EPA's administrative enforcement work. Agency administrative enforcement cases initially are heard, and decided, by a Presiding Officer. Appeals of Presiding Officer decisions are made to the agency's Environmental Appeals Board (EAB), an entity created within EPA in 1992 for this purpose. The Board generally serves as the final agency decisionmaker, although it has the discretion to refer any case or motion to the EPA Administrator. EAB decisions are subject to judicial review. See, e.g., Pepperell Assocs. v. EPA, 246 F.3d 15, 31 (1st Cir. 2001); City of San Diego v. Whitman, 242 F.3d 1097, 1101 (9th Cir. 2001); 5 U.S.C. §704. For an article on the EAB from an insider, see Firestone, The Environmental Protection Agency's Environmental Appeals Board, 1 Envtl. Law. 1 (1994).

EPA's Office of the Inspector General (OIG) has issued a significant number of reports in recent years on performance in the enforcement and compliance arena.

---

a. Statement of John B. Stephenson, U.S. GAO, Environmental Compliance and Enforcement: EPA's Efforts to Improve and Make More Consistent Its Compliance and Enforcement Activities 2, 3 (June 2006), available at http://www.gao.gov/new.items/d06840t.pdf. The Government Accountability Office revisited this issue, among others, in U.S. GAO, GAO-10-165T Clean Water Act, Longstanding Issues Impact EPA's and States' Enforcement Efforts (2009); U.S. GAO, GAO-10-P-0224, EPA Should Revise Outdated or Inconsistent EPA-State Clean Water Act Memoranda of Agreement (2010).

TABLE 10-1
EPA Administrative Actions by Statute, FY 1975 through FY 2011*

	CAA	CWA/SDWA	RCRA	Totals
FY75	0	738	0	738
FY76	210	915	0	1,125
FY77	297	1,128	0	1,425
FY78	129	730	0	859
FY79	404	506	0	910
FY80	86	569	0	655
FY81	112	562	159	833
FY82	21	329	237	587
FY83	41	781	436	1,258
FY84	141	1,644	554	2,339
FY85	122	1,031	327	1,480
FY86	143	990	235	1,368
FY87	191	1,214	243	1,648
FY88	224	1,345	309	1,878
FY89	336	2,146	453	2,935
FY90	249	1,780	366	2,395
FY91	214	2,177	364	2,755
FY92	354	1,977	291	2,622
FY93	279	2,216	282	2,777
FY94	435	1,841	115	2,391
FY95	232	1,774	92	2,098
FY96	242	998	238	1,478
FY97	391	1,642	423	2,456
FY98	499	1,590	398	2,487
FY99	542	1,390	558	2,490
FY00	379	1,271	3,416	4,049
FY01	341	1,557	306	2,204
FY02	300	1,452	292	2,044
FY03	359	1,806	320	2,485
FY04	461	2,043	387	2,891
FY05	635	2,327	398	3,360
FY06	611	1615	419	2645
FY07	735	1365	422	2522
FY08	628	1567	451	2646
FY09	527	1521	491	2539
FY10	526	1477	399	2285
FY11	549	1393	385	2327

* For FY 1975 through FY 2005, these numbers include administrative compliance orders issued, administrative penalty order complaints, field citations, and HQCAA mobile-source NOVs with penalties. FY 2006 through FY 2011, which are based on the NET FY 2009 and FY 2011 documents, include only administrative compliance orders issued and administrative penalty order complaints. Statistics for FY2010 and FY2011 from the FY 2011 document include only administrative compliance orders issued and administrative penalty order complaints.

Sources: EPA, Annual Report on Enforcement and Compliance Assurance Accomplishments in 1999, Ex. B-5; EPA, National Enforcement Trends—FY 2005; EPA, National Enforcement Trends—FY 2009; EPA, National Enforcement Trends—FY 2011, pp. C-1d, C-2d.

Several have been quite critical of EPA's performance and the performance of the states.[b]

The other major federal agency actor is the U.S. Department of Justice. DOJ's lawyers handle much of the court civil and criminal litigation on behalf of EPA and other federal agencies. In addition to "main Justice" in Washington, D.C., many of the U.S. Attorneys' offices throughout the country play a significant role in civil litigation and criminal prosecutions under the environmental laws. The relationship between the Department of Justice and EPA has not always been free of tension. For a discussion of the allocation of enforcement authority between EPA and the Department of Justice, see Devins & Herz, The Battle That Never Was: Congress, the White House, and Agency Litigation Authority, 61 Law & Contemp. Probs. 205 (Winter 1998). For a summary of DOJ's structure and operations, see Cruden & Gelber, Federal Civil Environmental Enforcement: Process, Actors and Trends (ALI-ABA Course of Study, March 27-28, 2008).

Parts of the executive branch, including the Office of Information and Regulatory Affairs (OIRA), which is located within the Office of Management and Budget (OMB) and reviews EPA regulations, have the potential to become involved in environmental enforcement policy as well. EPA also uses OMB's Program Assessment Rating Tool (PART) to evaluate its performance, including in the enforcement arena.

Congress (including its committees and one of its research arms, the Government Accountability Office) has the capacity to play an important role in enforcement matters on several fronts. For a recent GAO statement that is critical of EPA enforcement, see Statement of John B. Stephenson, *supra*, at 8, 13 (finding significant disparities in regional approaches to enforcement and substantial problems with enforcement data, and concluding that EPA actions have "thus far achieved only limited success and illustrate both the importance and the difficulty of addressing the long-standing problems in ensuring the consistent application of enforcement requirements"). See also U.S. GAO, GAO-08-1111R, Environmental Enforcement: EPA Needs to Improve the Accuracy and Transparency of Measures Used to Report on Program Effectiveness (2008); U.S. GAO, GAO-10-165T, Clean Water Act: Long-standing Issues Impact EPA's and States' Enforcement Efforts (2009); U.S. GAO, GAO-14-80, Clean Water Act Changes Needed if Key EPA Program is to Help Fulfill the Nation's Water Quality Goals (2013)).

Finally, the federal courts are involved at virtually every step of the enforcement process. The courts determine who can sue and be sued, evaluate the validity of the norms or standards allegedly violated, decide whether violations occurred for which liability should attach, and fashion appropriate relief when actionable violations are found.

---

b. See, e.g., EPA, Office of Inspector General Report No. 12-P-0113, EPA Must Improve Oversight of State Enforcement (2011); EPA, Office of Inspector General, Report No. 10-P-0077, EPA Needs to Improve Its Recording and Reporting of Fines and Penalties (2010); EPA, Office of Inspector General, Report No. 08-P-0278, EPA Has Initiated Strategic Planning for Priority Enforcement Areas, but Key Elements Still Needed (2008); EPA, Office of Inspector General, Report No. 2007-P-00023, Better Enforcement Oversight Needed for Major Facilities with Water Discharge Permits in Long-Term Significant Noncompliance (2007).

2.   State Officials

The other major government actors in the environmental enforcement arena are, of course, state officials. As explained in Chapter 1, section C.4, beginning in the 1970s, Congress has adopted a series of laws that have "federalized" environmental law to a significant degree. To a large extent, these laws, the regulations promulgated to implement them, and the cases that have interpreted them represent the corpus of this casebook.

As explained in Chapter 2, in many of these laws (e.g., the Clean Air Act, Clean Water Act, and RCRA), Congress adopted a "cooperative federalism" structure. Under this structure, EPA, while retaining overall responsibility for administering these laws and achieving their purposes, authorizes interested and qualified states to implement them within their respective jurisdictions. In the Clean Water Act, for example, Congress indicates that its intent is to "recognize, preserve, and protect the primary responsibilities and right of States to prevent, reduce, and eliminate pollution." CWA §101(b). Under some laws, EPA is obligated to "delegate" programs to a state to administer once EPA has determined that the state is capable of performing this role. Under most statutes, states achieve delegation by adopting their own versions of federal laws, which the states then administer (including enforce), rather than by implementing the federal law itself.

EPA has authorized states to administer a significant number of environmental programs in recent years. The result is that states have become increasingly important players in the implementation of federal environmental laws. According to R. Steven Brown, the former Executive Director of the Environmental Council of the States (ECOS), the Washington, D.C.–based association of state environmental agencies, "[a] remarkable, and largely unnoticed, change in environmental protection has occurred over the past five to 10 years. The States have become the primary environmental protection agencies across the nation." Brown, The States Protect the Environment, ECOStates (Summer 1999). A 2010 ECOS Report indicates that states operate approximately 96 percent of the major federal delegable environmental programs. This is up from less than 40 percent in 1993.[c]

States that EPA authorizes to administer environmental programs remain subject to federal oversight. EPA's 1986 Revised Policy Framework for State/EPA Enforcement Agreements, revised several times since then, creates a general framework that governs the relationship between EPA and the states. Among other things, this framework establishes criteria that EPA and the states use to assess government performance, and it identifies the circumstances in which EPA may take its own enforcement action in authorized states. In 1995, EPA and the states decided to "reinvent" their relationship by establishing the National Environmental Performance Partnership System (NEPPS), which the Environmental Law Institute (ELI) has described as "the most substantial nation-wide reform in the EPA-state relationship since those relationships were first established over twenty-five years ago." ELI, An Independent Review of the State-Federal Environmental Partnership Agreements 11 (1996). More recently, EPA has been working with the states to implement an

c. Environmental Council of the States, Status of State Environmental Agency Budgets, 2009-2011 (August 2010), available at http://www.ecos.org/files/4157_file_August_2010_Green_Report.pdf; Environmental Council of the States, Report to Congress, State Environmental Agency Contributions to Enforcement and Compliance n.1 (April 2001), available at http://www.ecos.org/files/687_file_ECOS_20RTC_20f.pdf.

approach they have called the State Review Framework, or SRFOECA describes the origins and purposes of the SRF as follows:

> OECA has worked closely with EPA regions, the . . . [ECOS], state media associations and other state representatives to jointly develop a framework and process for conducting reviews of core enforcement programs in the CWA-NPDES, RCRA Subtitle C and the CAA Stationary Sources programs. The goals of the reviews are to promote consistent levels of activity in state and regional enforcement programs, consistent oversight of state and regional enforcement programs, and consistent levels of environmental protection across the country. [EPA, Final FY07 Update to OECA National Program Managers' Guidance 21 (April 2006).]

For GAO reviews of the SRF, see U.S. GAO, GAO-07-883, EPA-State Enforcement Partnership Has Improved, but EPA's Oversight Needs Further Enhancement (2007); U.S. GAO, GAO-12-P-0113, EPA Must Improve Oversight of State Enforcement (2011).

Congress's decision to give EPA overall responsibility for achieving the goals of the federal environmental laws, while requiring or authorizing EPA to delegate primary implementation authority to qualified states and then oversee state performance, has been the source of considerable tension. EPA's head of enforcement during the Clinton presidency indicated that "forging an effective, cooperative relationship with the states on enforcement" was the "most significant" challenge he faced. Mason, Snapshot Interview: Steven A. Herman, 12 Nat. Resources & Env't 286 (1998).

Views differ about the effectiveness of this uneasy partnership. Professor Richard Stewart, in an important early article, suggested that "[t]he success of federal programs has been gravely compromised by . . . dependence upon state and local governments" because of the lack of state buy-in to federal strategies. Stewart, Pyramids of Sacrifice? Problems of Federalism in Mandating State Implementation of National Environmental Policy, 86 Yale L.J. 1196 (1977). On the other hand, Professor Evan Ringquist is one of several political scientists who have highlighted improvements in state capacity and performance: "[M]any states have tossed away their recalcitrant stance toward strong environmental programs, and in many instances state governments, not the 'feds,' are at the forefront in efforts to protect the environment." Ringquist, Environmental Protection at the State Level: Politics and Progress in Controlling Pollution xiii (1993). C. Rechtschaffen & D. Markell, Reinventing Environmental Enforcement and the State/Federal Relationship (2003), examine the effectiveness of the state-federal partnership in the enforcement arena and identify several strategies for strengthening the relationship and improving its performance.[d]

EPA's enforcement office was quite critical of state performance in its 2009 "Clean Water Act Enforcement Action Plan." The agency stated that "[s]tate enforcement response to serious violations . . . is not what it should be"; that there is a "lack of consistency in performance across states"; and that "common issues" include "permit backlogs, [and] failure to identify significant noncompliance, or to take timely and appropriate enforcement." Id. at 3. The agency also observed that "EPA must consistently respond to these issues and press states and ourselves to make the appropriate improvements in order to achieve equitable

d. For GAO recommendations, see U.S. GAO, GAO-10-165T, Clean Water Act: Longstanding Issues Impact EPA's and States' Enforcement Efforts (2009); U.S. GAO, GAO-12-P-0113, EPA Must Improve Oversight of State Enforcement (2011).

protection to the public, a level playing field for competing businesses, and fairness across states in how our environmental laws are enforced." Id. at 8. In fact, EPA indicated its plan to "revisit the division of work with states, many of which are facing near term serious resource problems." Id. at 12.

Challenges that EPA and the states face include a substantial increase in enforcement responsibilities as the size of the regulated community has expanded dramatically in recent years, and significant budgetary pressures. A GAO comment in a 2009 review captures this context to some degree: "Both EPA and state [enforcement] officials told us they found it difficult to respond to new requirements while carrying out their previous responsibilities." U.S. GAO, GAO-10-165T, Clean Water Act: Longstanding Issues Impact EPA's and States' Enforcement Efforts 7 (2009). A 2013 EPA report noted significant concerns about state budgetary pressures: "States continue to struggle with budgets that in most cases are not expected to improve in the near future. Programmatic demands are increasing while resources are decreasing thus making tradeoffs among core program activities difficult. Some regions are concerned that some states may actually begin to give programs back to EPA." EPA, The National Environmental Performance Partnership System: A Review of Implementation Practices 20, EPA 140-R-13-001 (May 2013). EPA's Office of Inspector General offered a recent appraisal in EPA Must Improve Oversight of State Enforcement, No. 12-P-0113 (2011). For scholarly commentary about federal-state challenges in the enforcement arena and options to address them, see, e.g., Hammond & Markell, Administrative Proxies for Judicial Review: Building Legitimacy from the Inside Out, 37 Harv. Envtl. L. Rev. 313 (2013); Markell & Glicksman, A Holistic View of Agency Enforcement, 93 N.C. L. Rev. 1 (2014).

3. *Environmental Nongovernmental Organizations (ENGOs) and Regulated Parties*

Two other groups of actors play significant roles in the enforcement and compliance arena. First, private citizens and nongovernmental organizations play a variety of roles in seeking to promote compliance with the environmental laws. Of greatest significance for this chapter, they act as "private attorneys general" under many of the federal environmental laws. As we discuss in more detail below (see section C.4), most of the major federal environmental laws empower citizens to bring enforcement actions against regulated parties that allegedly are violating environmental requirements. Professor Jeffery Miller explains that

> [n]ot confident that federal and state authorities would fully enforce against violations of the statutes, [Congress] also authorized citizens to enforce through an ingenious new device, the citizen suit provision. The device added members of the interested public, acting as private attorneys general, to the existing federal and state environmental enforcement cadres.

Miller, Theme and Variations in Statutory Preclusions Against Successive Environmental Enforcement Actions by EPA and Citizens, Part One: Statutory Bars in Citizen Suit Provisions, 28 Harv. Envtl. L. Rev. 401, 408-409 (2004).

Citizens are also involved in compliance promotion in other ways. Citizens may bring common law causes of action, such as private nuisance actions, also discussed below (see section C.5), in some circumstances. Citizens also sometimes monitor the performance of individual facilities in various ways, including by serving on "good neighbor committees."[e] Further, citizen groups such as NRDC, US PIRG, and the Environment Working Group have reviewed government and regulated-party performance more systematically. See, e.g., U.S. PIRG Education Fund, Troubled Waters: An Analysis of Clean Water Act Compliance, July 2003-December 2004 (March 2006) (concluding that there is significant noncompliance with the Clean Water Act).

Last, but certainly not least, there are the regulated parties themselves. A significant aspect of the debate in the enforcement and compliance arena these days, in the United States as well as worldwide, involves determining how best to encourage regulated parties to be proactive in managing their operations in a way that minimizes noncompliance, facilitates timely identification of problems when they arise, and promotes timely remediation and other responses. There is a burgeoning interest, for example, in having regulated parties conduct audits and, more generally, develop and implement environmental management systems (EMSs). EPA encourages adoption of EMSs and similar proactive approaches that "improve compliance, prevent pollution, and integrate other means of improving environmental performance." EPA, Position Statement on Environmental Management Systems (EMSs), 71 Fed. Reg. 5664 (2006). EPA's policies to promote self-auditing, discussed in Section D below, are examples.

Thus, while government is clearly part of the solution to the issue of noncompliance, it is widely accepted that the public at large, including environmental and community NGOs, and the regulated community, occupy important parts of this landscape as well, although their appropriate roles remain subject to debate.

Having summarized the roles of some of the major actors in the world of environmental enforcement, we close this section on enforcement actors by returning to the state-federal relationship for a closer look at some of the legal issues that have surfaced. A significant issue in this relationship is when EPA legally may file a lawsuit against a regulated party for alleged violations of environmental requirements if a state agency has already filed a lawsuit or otherwise initiated legal action against the regulated party. A 1999 Eighth Circuit decision, Harmon Indus., Inc. v. Browner, caused considerable consternation among federal officials and some scholars by holding that EPA legally may not file a lawsuit against a regulated party under RCRA if the delegated state agency already has pursued a legal action against that party. An excerpt of that case follows.

HARMON INDUSTRIES, INC. v. BROWNER
191 F.3d 894 (8th Cir. 1999)

HANSEN, Circuit J.

Harmon Industries, Inc. (Harmon) filed this action pursuant to the Administrative Procedure Act, 5 U.S.C. §706 (1994), seeking judicial review of a final decision of

---

e. Lewis & Henkel, Good Neighbor Agreements: A Tool for Environmental and Social Justice, 23 Soc. Just. 134 (Winter 1996), available at http://www.cpn.org/topics/environment/goodneighbor.html.

the United States Environmental Protection Agency (EPA). The district court granted summary judgment in favor of Harmon and reversed the decision of the EPA. The EPA appeals. We affirm.

I. Facts and Procedural Background

Harmon Industries operates a plant in Grain Valley, Missouri, which it utilizes to assemble circuit boards for railroad control and safety equipment. In November 1987, Harmon's personnel manager discovered that maintenance workers at Harmon routinely discarded volatile solvent residue behind Harmon's Grain Valley plant. This practice apparently began in 1973 and continued until November 1987. Harmon's management was unaware of its employees' practices until the personnel manager filed his report in November 1987. Following the report, Harmon ceased its disposal activities and voluntarily contacted the Missouri Department of Natural Resources (MDNR). The MDNR investigated and concluded that Harmon's past disposal practices did not pose a threat to either human health or the environment. The MDNR and Harmon created a plan whereby Harmon would clean up the disposal area. Harmon implemented the cleanup plan. While Harmon was cooperating with the MDNR, the EPA initiated an administrative enforcement action against Harmon in which the federal agency sought $2,343,706 in penalties. Meanwhile, Harmon and the MDNR continued to establish a voluntary compliance plan. In harmonizing the details of the plan, Harmon asked the MDNR not to impose civil penalties. Harmon based its request in part on the fact that it voluntarily self-reported the environmental violations and cooperated fully with the MDNR.

On March 5, 1993, while the EPA's administrative enforcement action was pending, a Missouri state court judge approved a consent decree entered into by the MDNR and Harmon. In the decree, MDNR acknowledged full accord and satisfaction and released Harmon from any claim for monetary penalties. MDNR based its decision to release Harmon on the fact that the company promptly self-reported its violation and cooperated in all aspects of the investigation. After the filing of the consent decree, Harmon litigated the EPA claim before an administrative law judge (ALJ). The ALJ found that a civil penalty against Harmon was appropriate in this case. The ALJ rejected the EPA's request for a penalty in excess of $2 million but the ALJ did impose a civil fine of $586,716 against Harmon. A three-person Environmental Appeals Board panel affirmed the ALJ's monetary penalty. Harmon filed a complaint challenging the EPA's decision in federal district court on June 6, 1997. In its August 25, 1998, summary judgment order, the district court found that the EPA's decision to impose civil penalties violated the Resource Conservation and Recovery Act and contravened principles of res judicata. The EPA appeals to this court.

II. Discussion

A. The Permissibility of Overfiling

When reviewing a federal agency's interpretation of a federal statute, a federal court must defer to the agency's interpretation only if it finds that the agency's interpretation is consistent with the plain language of the statute or represents a reasonable interpretation of an ambiguous statute. We review de novo a district court's findings and conclusions regarding the correctness of an agency's statutory interpretations.

The Resource Conservation and Recovery Act (RCRA) permits states to apply to the EPA for authorization to administer and enforce a hazardous waste program. See 42 U.S.C. §6926(b). If authorization is granted, the state's program then operates "in lieu of" the federal government's hazardous waste program. The EPA authorization also allows states to issue and enforce permits for the treatment, storage, and disposal of hazardous wastes. "Any action taken by a State under a hazardous waste program authorized under [the RCRA has] the same force and effect as action taken by the [EPA] under this subchapter." 42 U.S.C. §6926(d). Once authorization is granted by the EPA, it cannot be rescinded unless the EPA finds that (1) the state program is not equivalent to the federal program, (2) the state program is not consistent with federal or state programs in other states, or (3) the state program is failing to provide adequate enforcement of compliance in accordance with the requirements of federal law. See 42 U.S.C. §6926(b). Before withdrawing a state's authorization to administer a hazardous waste program, the EPA must hold a public hearing and allow the state a reasonable period of time to correct the perceived deficiency. See 42 U.S.C. §6926(e).

Missouri, like many other states, is authorized to administer and enforce a hazardous waste program pursuant to the RCRA. Despite having authorized a state to act, the EPA frequently files its own enforcement actions against suspected environmental violators even after the commencement of a state-initiated enforcement action. See Bryan S. Miller, Harmonizing RCRA's Enforcement Provisions: RCRA Overfiling in Light of Harmon Industries v. Browner, 5 Environmental Law. 585 (1999). The EPA's process of duplicating enforcement actions is known as overfiling. The permissibility of overfiling apparently is a question of first impression in the federal circuit courts. After examining this apparent issue of first impression, the district court concluded that the plain language of section 6926(b) dictates that the state program operate "in lieu" of the federal program and with the "same force and effect" as EPA action. Accordingly, the district court found that, in this case, the RCRA precludes the EPA from assessing its own penalty against Harmon.

The EPA contends that the district court's interpretation runs contrary to the plain language of the RCRA. Specifically, the EPA cites section 6928 of the RCRA, which states that:

> (1) Except as provided in paragraph (2), whenever on the basis of any information the [EPA] determines that any person has violated or is in violation of any requirement of this subchapter, the [EPA] may issue an order assessing a civil penalty for any past or current violation, requiring compliance immediately or within a specified time period, or both, or the [EPA] may commence a civil action in the United States district court in the district in which the violation occurred for appropriate relief, including a temporary or permanent injunction.
>
>   (2) In the case of a violation of any requirement of [the RCRA] where such violation occurs in a State which is authorized to carry out a hazardous waste program under section 6926 of this title, the [EPA] shall give notice to the State in which such violation has occurred prior to issuing an order or commencing a civil action under this section.

42 U.S.C. §6928(a)(1) and (2).

The EPA argues that the plain language of section 6928 allows the federal agency to initiate an enforcement action against an environmental violator even in states that have received authorization pursuant to the RCRA. The EPA contends that Harmon and the district court misinterpreted the phrases "in lieu of" and "same force and effect" as contained in the RCRA. According to the EPA, the phrase "in lieu of" refers to which regulations are to be enforced in an authorized state rather than who is responsible for enforcing the regulations. The EPA argues that the phrase "same force and effect" refers only to the effect of state issued permits. The EPA contends that the RCRA, taken as a whole, authorizes either the state or the EPA to enforce the state's regulations, which are in compliance with the regulations of the EPA. The only requirement, according to the EPA, is that the EPA notify the state in writing if it intends to initiate an enforcement action against an alleged violator.

Both parties argue that the plain language of the RCRA supports their interpretation of the statute. We also are ever mindful of the long-established plain language rule of statutory interpretation as we inquire into the scope of the EPA's enforcement powers under the RCRA. Such an inquiry requires examining the text of the statute as a whole by considering its context, "object, and policy." Pelofsky v. Wallace, 102 F.3d 350, 353 (8th Cir. 1996).

An examination of the statute as a whole supports the district court's interpretation. The RCRA specifically allows states that have received authorization from the federal government to administer and enforce a program that operates "in lieu of" the EPA's regulatory program. 42 U.S.C. §6926(b). While the EPA is correct that the "in lieu of" language refers to the program itself, the administration and enforcement of the program are inexorably intertwined.

The RCRA gives authority to the states to create and implement their own hazardous waste program. The plain "in lieu of" language contained in the RCRA reveals a congressional intent for an authorized state program to supplant the federal hazardous waste program in all respects including enforcement. Congressional intent is evinced within the authorization language of section 6926(b) of the RCRA. Specifically, the statute permits the EPA to repeal a state's authorization if the state's program "does not provide adequate enforcement of compliance with the requirements of" the RCRA. Id. This language indicates that Congress intended to grant states the primary role of enforcing their own hazardous waste program. Such an indication is not undermined, as the EPA suggests, by the language of section 6928. Again, section 6928(a)(1) allows the EPA to initiate enforcement actions against suspected environmental violators, except as provided in section 6928(a)(2). Section 6928(a)(2) permits the EPA to enforce the hazardous waste laws contained in the RCRA if the agency gives written notice to the state. Section 6928(a)(1) and (2), however, must be interpreted within the context of the entire Act. Harmonizing the section 6928(a)(1) and (2) language that allows the EPA to bring an enforcement action in certain circumstances with section 6926(b)'s provision that the EPA has the right to withdraw state authorization if the state's enforcement is inadequate manifests a congressional intent to give the EPA a secondary enforcement right in those cases where a state has been authorized to act that is triggered only after state authorization is rescinded or if the state fails to initiate an enforcement action. Rather than serving as an affirmative grant of federal enforcement power as the EPA suggests, we conclude that the notice requirement of section 6928(a)(2) reinforces the primacy of a state's enforcement rights under RCRA. Taken in the context of the statute as a whole, the notice requirement operates as a means to allow a state the first chance opportunity to initiate the statutorily permitted enforcement action. If the state fails to initiate any action, then the EPA may institute its own action. Thus, the notice requirement is an indicator of the fact that Congress intended to give states that are authorized to act, the lead role in enforcement under RCRA.

The "same force and effect" language of section 6926(d) provides additional support for the primacy of states' enforcement rights under the RCRA when the EPA has authorized a state to act in lieu of it. The EPA argues that the "same force and effect" language is limited to state permits because the words appear under a heading that reads: "Effect of State Permit." The EPA contends that the "same force and effect" language indicates only that state-issued permits will have the same force and effect as permits issued by the federal government. The EPA claims that the district court was incorrect when it applied the "same force and effect" language to encompass the statute's enforcement mechanism. We disagree.

Regardless of the title or heading, the plain language of section 6926(d) states that "[a]ny action taken by a State under a hazardous waste program authorized under this section shall have the same force and effect as action taken by the [EPA] under this subchapter." 42 U.S.C. §6926(d). In this context, the meaning of the text is plain and obvious. "Any action" under this provision broadly applies to any action authorized by the subchapter, and this language is not limited to the issuance of permits. The state authorization provision substitutes state action (not excluding enforcement action) for federal action. It would be incongruous to conclude that the RCRA authorizes states to implement and administer a hazardous waste program "in lieu of" the federal program where only the issuance of permits is accorded the same force and effect as an action taken by the federal government. Contrary to the EPA's assertions, the statute specifically provides that a "[s]tate is authorized to carry out [its hazardous waste program] in lieu of the Federal program . . . and to issue and enforce permits." 42 U.S.C. §6926(b). Issuance and enforcement are two of the functions authorized as part of the state's hazardous waste enforcement program under the RCRA. Nothing in the statute suggests that the "same force and effect" language is limited to the issuance of permits but not their enforcement. We believe that if Congress had intended such a peculiar result, it would have stated its preference in a clear and unambiguous manner. Absent such an unambiguous directive, we will apply a common sense meaning to the text of the statute and interpret its provisions in a manner logically consistent with the Act as whole.

Utilizing a sort of reverse plain language argument, the EPA contends that its approach is logically consistent with the framework of the RCRA. The EPA cites the statute's citizen suit provision for the proposition that limitations on a part[y]'s right to act are expressly stated within the statute itself. See 42 U.S.C. §6972(b)(1)(B). Section 6972(b)(1)(B), provides that "if the [EPA] or State has commenced and is diligently prosecuting a civil or criminal action in a court of the United States or a State," then a private citizen suit is not permitted. Id. The EPA argues that if Congress had intended to limit the EPA's right to file an enforcement action, it would have expressly stated its intention as it did in the citizen suit context. We find the EPA's argument unpersuasive. Section 6972(b)(1)(B) of the RCRA provides the parameters for private litigation. In the course of providing such parameters, Congress apparently found it necessary to delineate exactly when and how a private citizen may initiate a civil action against an alleged environmental violator. In contrast, section 6926 of the RCRA addresses the interplay between federal and state authorization. Section 6926 also contains express language that establishes the primacy of states' enforcement rights once the EPA has granted a state authorization. The mere fact that Congress did not choose to employ the exact same language as contained in an unrelated part of the act does not detract from the plain language used in the state authorization section. Again, Congress provided that the state's program should operate in lieu of the federal program and that the state action should operate with the same force and effect as action taken by the EPA. See 42 U.S.C. §6926(b) and (d). We find the language contained in the state authorization section of the Act to be as unambiguous as the citizen suit provision. In fact, we find it revealing that, under the citizen suit provision, Congress chose to forbid a private citizen from acting if the EPA or a state was diligently pursuing a civil action. See 42 U.S.C. §6972(b)(1)(B). Utilizing the same reverse plain language argument, one can assume that if Congress intended to allow the federal government and the states to initiate competing enforcement actions, it would have chosen the words "and/or" rather than simply "or." The word "or" indicates that Congress did not contemplate competing enforcement actions between the federal government and the states. Thus, when the EPA has authorized a state program, the plain language of the text indicates that primary enforcement powers are vested in the states. See 42 U.S.C. §6926.

Even assuming some ambiguity exists in the statutory language, the primacy of the states' enforcement rights, once the EPA has authorized a state to act, is illustrated further through the RCRA's legislative history. The United States House of Representatives stated after its hearings that, through the RCRA, it intended to vest primary enforcement authority in the states. See H.R. Rep. 1491, 94th Cong., 2d Sess. 24, reprinted in 1976 U.S.C.C.A.N. 6262 ("It is the Committee's intention that the States are to have primary enforcement authority and if at any time a State wishes to take over the hazardous waste program it is permitted to do so, provided that the State laws meet the Federal minimum requirements for both administering and enforcing the law"). The House Report states that although the "legislation permits the states to take the lead in the enforcement of the hazardous wastes [sic] laws[,] . . . the Administrator [of the EPA] is not prohibited from acting in those cases where the state fails to act, or from withdrawing approval of the state hazardous waste plan and implementing the federal hazardous waste program pursuant to . . . this act." 1976 U.S.C.C.A.N. 6269. The House Report also states that the EPA, "after giving the appropriate notice to a state that is authorized to implement the state hazardous waste program, that violations of this Act are occurring and the state [is] failing to take action against such violations, is authorized to take appropriate action against those persons in such state not in compliance with the hazardous waste title." Id. at 6270. The House Report thus supports our interpretation of the statute—that the federal government's right to pursue an enforcement action under the RCRA attaches only when a state's authorization is revoked or when a state fails to initiate any enforcement action.

There is no support either in the text of the statute or the legislative history for the proposition that the EPA is allowed to duplicate a state's enforcement authority with its own enforcement action. The EPA argues that the statute and legislative history support its contention that it may initiate an enforcement action if it deems the state's enforcement action inadequate. The EPA's argument misses the point. Without question, the EPA can initiate an enforcement action if it deems the state's enforcement action inadequate. Before initiating such an action, however, the EPA must allow the state an opportunity to correct its deficiency and the EPA must withdraw its authorization. See 42 U.S.C. §6926(b) and (e). Consistent with the text of the statute and its legislative history, the EPA also may initiate an enforcement action after providing written notice to the state when the authorized state fails to initiate any enforcement action. See 42 U.S.C. §6928(a)(2). The EPA may not, however, simply fill the perceived gaps it sees in a state's enforcement action by initiating a second enforcement action without allowing the state an opportunity to correct the deficiency and then withdrawing the state's authorization.

A contrary interpretation would result in two separate enforcement actions. Such an interpretation, as explained above, would derogate the RCRA's plain language and legislative history. Companies that reach an agreement through negotiations with a state authorized by the EPA to act in its place may find the agreement undermined by a later separate enforcement action by the EPA. While, generally speaking, two separate sovereigns can institute two separate enforcement actions, those actions can cause vastly different and potentially contradictory results. Such a potential schism runs afoul of the principles of comity and federalism so clearly embedded in the text and history of the RCRA. When enacting the RCRA, Congress intended to delegate the primary enforcement of EPA-approved hazardous waste programs to the states. In fact, as we have noted above, the states' enforcement action has the "same force and effect as an action taken by" the EPA. See 42 U.S.C. §6926(d). In EPA authorized states, the EPA's action is an alternative method of enforcement that is permitted to operate only when certain conditions are satisfied. See 42 U.S.C. §6926(b) and (e); 42 U.S.C. §6928(b). The EPA's interpretation simply is not consistent with the plain language of the statute, its legislative history, or its declared purpose. Hence, it is also an unreasonable interpretation to which we accord no deference. Therefore, we find that the EPA's practice of overfiling, in those states where it has authorized the state to act, oversteps the federal agency's authority under the RCRA.

B. RES JUDICATA

As an alternative basis to support its grant of summary judgment, the district court concluded that principles of res judicata also bar the EPA's enforcement action by reason of the Missouri state court consent decree. The EPA argues that the state court judgment has no effect on its enforcement action against Harmon because the two actions lack the elements essential for a finding of res judicata. We review de novo a district court's summary judgment determinations.

Principles of res judicata embodied in the Full Faith and Credit Act, 28 U.S.C. §1738 (1982), see also U.S. Const. art. 4, §1, require federal courts to give preclusive effect to the judgments of state courts whenever the state court from which the judgment emerged would give such an effect. See Hickman v. Electronic Keyboarding, Inc., 741 F.3d 230, 232 (8th Cir. 1984). In this case, we must determine whether Missouri law would give res judicata effect to the consent decree entered between Harmon and the MDNR in Missouri state court.

In Missouri, res judicata requires "(1) [i]dentity of the thing sued for; (2) identity of the cause of action; (3) identity of the persons and parties to the action; and (4) identity of the quality of the person for or against whom the claim is made." Prentzler v. Schneider, 411 S.W.2d 135, 138 (Mo. 1966) (en banc).

In this case, the four Missouri law res judicata requirements are satisfied. In both the state court action and the EPA administrative enforcement action, the parties sought to enforce a hazardous waste program pursuant to the RCRA. In both the state action and the agency action, the complaints named Harmon as the defendant.

In addition, both actions involved the enforcement of regulations based upon identical facts and legal principles. The only dispute is whether the parties are identical.

A party is identical when it is the same party that litigated a prior suit or when a new party is in privity with a party that litigated a prior suit. See United States v. Gurley, 43 F.3d 1188, 1197 (8th Cir. 1994). Privity exists when two parties to two separate suits have "a close relationship bordering on near identity." Id. As the United States and the State of Missouri are not the same party, we must resolve whether their relationship in the enforcement action is nearly identical.

The statutory language of the RCRA provides the framework for the party identity analysis. Pursuant to 42 U.S.C. §6926(b), the federal program operates "in lieu of" the state program. Section 6926(d) of the same statute mandates that "[a]ny action taken by a State under a hazardous waste program authorized under this section shall have the same force and effect as action taken by the [EPA] under this subchapter." 42 U.S.C. §6926(d). As we determined in Part II(A) of this opinion, the plain language of the RCRA permits the State of Missouri to act in lieu of the EPA. When such a situation occurs, Missouri's action has the same force and effect as an action initiated by the EPA. Accordingly, the two parties stand in the same relationship to one another. The EPA argues that it has enforcement interests sufficiently distinct from the interests of the State of Missouri. We explained in *Hickman*, however, that privity under Missouri law is satisfied when the two parties represent the same legal right. As the district court correctly indicated, privity is not dependent upon the subjective interests of the individual parties. In this case, the State of Missouri advanced the exact same legal right under the statute as the EPA did in its administrative action. Accordingly, the identity of the parties requirement is satisfied.

The EPA contends that even if principles of res judicata are satisfied under Missouri law, the doctrine of sovereign immunity precludes applying res judicata to the United States unless the United States was the actual party in the prior lawsuit. Before addressing the merits of the EPA's claim, we note that the EPA did not raise the sovereign immunity defense before the district court. Harmon argues that in failing to raise the issue at the district court level, the EPA has waived its right to assert sovereign immunity on appeal. Sovereign immunity, however, is a jurisdictional threshold matter and it is well-established that questions of subject matter jurisdiction can be raised for the first time on appeal. See DeWitt Bank & Trust Co. v. United States, 878 F.2d 246 (8th Cir. 1989).

Turning to the merits of the EPA's sovereign immunity defense, we conclude that the defense is forestalled by the United States Supreme Court's decision in Montana v. United States, 440 U.S. 147 (1979). In *Montana*, the Supreme Court held that "one who prosecutes or defends a suit in the name of another to establish and protect his own right is as much bound as he would be if he had been a party to the record." 440 U.S. at 154. The Court found in *Montana* that although the United States was not a party to a prior suit, it "had a sufficient laboring oar in the conduct of the state-court litigation to actuate principles of estoppel." Id. at 155. The EPA argues that it had no laboring oar in the State of Missouri's enforcement action. Such an argument ignores the RCRA. Unlike the present case, *Montana* did not involve a statute that authorized the state to proceed "in lieu of" the federal government and "with the same force and effect" as the federal government. In *Montana*, the United States controlled the details of the prior suit directly. In RCRA cases, however, the federal government authorizes the state to act in its place. It cedes its authority to the state pursuant to the authorization plan contained in the statute. See 42 U.S.C.

§6926(b). The "laboring oar" is pulled on much earlier in the process. It occurs at the authorization stage when the EPA grants the state permission to enforce the EPA's interests through the state's own hazardous waste program. After authorization, the state "prosecutes" enforcement actions "in lieu of" the federal government and operates as if it were the EPA. See 42 U.S.C. §6926(b) and (d). Hence, pursuant to *Montana*, the United States must be bound by prior judgments involving state action as authorized by the RCRA. See also United States v. County of Cook, Illinois, 167 F.3d 381, 389 (7th Cir. 1999) (questioning when sovereign immunity to claim preclusion exists); United States v. ITT Rayonier, Inc., 627 F.2d 996, 1002 (9th Cir. 1980) (applying res judicata against the EPA). Accordingly, we find that principles of res judicata as defined by Missouri law foreclose the EPA's enforcement action against Harmon. . . .

III.   Conclusion

For the reasons stated herein, we affirm the judgment of the district court.

NOTES AND QUESTIONS ABOUT THE ACTORS IN ENVIRONMENTAL ENFORCEMENT AND COMPLIANCE

1. *Some Courts Have Disagreed with* Harmon's *Interpretation of RCRA.* In United States v. Power Eng'g Co., 303 F.3d 1232 (10th Cir. 2002), the United States filed a civil enforcement action against a metal refinishing/chrome electroplating business after Colorado had issued an administrative compliance order and an administrative civil penalty order for the same RCRA violations. The Tenth Circuit held that RCRA did *not* preclude the federal enforcement action, disagreeing with the Eighth Circuit in its reading of several key RCRA provisions. The court, finding the statute to be ambiguous, deferred to EPA's view that EPA's authorization of a state permit program does not deprive the federal agency of its enforcement powers. The court also held that the federal enforcement action was not barred by res judicata because the federal and state governments were separate parties and therefore not in privity for res judicata purposes.

2. *Do Different Environmental Statutes Treat "Overfiling" Differently?* Other courts have distinguished *Harmon* and declined to follow it in addressing overfiling under other statutes, such as the Clean Air and Clean Water Acts, on the ground that the statutory language is different. See United States v. Murphy Oil USA, Inc., 143 F. Supp. 2d 1054, 1090-1092 (W.D. Wis. 2001); United States v. LTV Steel Co., 118 F. Supp. 2d 827 (N.D. Ohio 2000); United States v. City of Youngstown, 109 F. Supp. 2d 739 (N.D. Ohio 2000). What is the key language in RCRA §3006 governing the permissibility of "overfiling" by EPA? What is the key language of §3008? What is the key language in the Clean Air and Clean Water Acts? Does this difference in statutory language provide a basis for limiting *Harmon's* holding concerning the validity of federal overfilings to RCRA?

3. What strategies should federal and state enforcement authorities use to foster coordination in the enforcement arena? The governments have developed several mechanisms to enhance coordination. For a 2003 government initiative, see U.S. DOJ and National Ass'n of Attorneys General, Guidelines for Joint State/Federal

Civil Environmental Enforcement Litigation (2003). For a 2013 overview of how the federal pollution control laws are enforced, including a review of the key actors, see Esworthy, CRS Report for Congress, Federal Pollution Control Laws: How Are They Enforced? (2013).

4. There has been a substantial amount of debate in recent years about the theoretical underpinnings of the decision to "federalize" environmental law. Professor Richard Revesz has authored a series of articles that have played an important role in raising such questions, including: Revesz, Rehabilitating Interstate Competition: Rethinking the "Race-to-the-Bottom" Rationale for Federal Environmental Regulation, 67 N.Y.U. L. Rev. 1210 (1992); Revesz, Federalism and Interstate Environmental Externalities, 144 U. Pa. L. Rev. 2341 (1996); and Revesz, Federalism and Environmental Regulation: A Public Choice Analysis, 115 Harv. L. Rev. 553 (2001). Rechtschaffen & Markell, *supra*, review the scholarship pro and con on these issues, as well as some of the constitutional doctrines that have the potential to influence the shape of our cooperative federalism approach. We cover these issues in more detail in Chapter 2.

5. *The Role of Citizen Suits.* Because the major environmental laws allow citizens to file citizen suits as "private attorneys general," numerous questions have arisen concerning the role of such suits vis-à-vis state and/or federal enforcement actions involving the same alleged violator. The Supreme Court in *Gwaltney* (excerpted in section C below) characterized the role of citizen suits as "to supplement rather than to supplant governmental action." Why is supplementation of government enforcement desirable? Professor Plater has argued that the pressures placed on enforcement officials are too substantial to justify exclusive reliance on them as "watchdogs [to] protect us all from marketplace excesses. The backstop enforcement [under the citizen suit provisions] has been a vital credibility factor that drives the bureaucracy's implementation of the law." Plater, The Embattled Social Utilities of the Endangered Species Act—A Noah Presumption and Caution Against Putting Gasmasks on the Canaries in the Coalmine, 27 Envtl. L. 845, 871-872 (1997). The Senate Report cited by the Court in *Gwaltney* stated that citizen suits "perform[] a public service." S. Rep. No. 92-414 (1971), reprinted in 1972 U.S.C.C.A.N. at 3747. But the benefits of citizen enforcement sometimes come with a price. In Hallstrom v. Tillamook County, 493 U.S. 20, 29 (1989), the Court acknowledged the tension between Congress's desire to "encourag[e] citizen enforcement of environmental regulations and [its desire to avoid] burdening the federal courts with excessive numbers of citizen suits." Further, as the Court suggested in *Gwaltney*, citizen suits may undermine government discretion in addressing violations and thereby undercut government's ability to use its entire arsenal of tools to produce results it believes will best promote compliance and desired environmental results. For a discussion of the relationship between citizen suits and government enforcement, see Engstrom, Agencies as Litigation Gatekeepers, 123 Yale L.J. 616 (2013). Section C below reviews the issues that have emerged as this tension has played out in the courts.

C.   THE LEGAL AUTHORITIES

What legal authorities influence how the actors approach their responsibilities or opportunities in the enforcement and compliance arena? Our focus here is primarily on the authorities in the major environmental laws. Each of these laws contains one or more enforcement provisions—provisions that, perhaps most significantly (1) empower government officials to monitor compliance with environmental requirements (via inspections, self-reporting, etc.), and (2) authorize the government to pursue administrative, civil, and/or criminal enforcement in appropriate instances. Many of these laws also contain provisions that authorize citizens to bring legal action in some circumstances. Following our coverage of statutory authorities, we cover the common law doctrines of public and private nuisance briefly.

1.   *The Government's Information-Gathering Authority*

The capacity to monitor compliance is a critical element of our nation's environmental regulatory scheme. EPA's enabling statutes give the agency several tools for performing this responsibility, including the authority to require regulated parties to monitor their own performance and the power to review compliance itself, as Table 10-2 reflects.

The government may demand that regulated entities keep records, install and use specified monitoring equipment, take samples, and submit reports. The best-known of the self-reporting approaches are the CWA's discharge monitoring reports (DMRs). These reports track a party's permitted limits and its actual performance in light of those limits. In many cases, the DMRs on their face reveal whether a regulated party is operating in compliance with its obligations under a permit. Regulated parties must submit these reports to the government. DMRs also are accessible to citizens, and citizens have used them in many cases as the basis for filing citizen suits under the Clean Water Act against the submitters. The *Gwaltney* case, excerpted below, is an example. Congress's 1990 Amendments to the Clean Air Act contain a similar self-reporting requirement that is modeled after the Clean Water Act DMRs. See Van Cleve & Holman, Promise and Reality in the Enforcement of the Amended Clean Air Act, Part I: EPA's "Any Credible Evidence" and "Compliance Assurance Monitoring" Rules, 27 Envtl. L. Rep. 10097 (1997). Congress, also in the 1990 Clean Air Act Amendments, mandates that certain sources of air pollution install continuous emissions monitoring (CEM) systems or their equivalent. CAA §412(a); Reitze & Schell, Self-Monitoring and Self-Reporting of Routine Air Pollution Releases, 24 Colum. J. Envtl. L. 63, 107 (1999); EPA, Technology Transfer Network, Clearinghouse for Inventories and Emissions Factors, Basic Information, http://cfpub.epa.gov/oarweb/mkb/Basic_Information.cfm.

Congress has been fairly creative with some of the tools it has created to encourage identification of violations. It has adopted both bounty provisions that reward individuals who provide information and whistleblower provisions that are intended to protect individuals who do so from retribution from the regulated party. See, e.g., CAA §113(f), CWA §507, and CERCLA §9610(a); Knox v. United States Dep't of Labor, 434 F.3d 721 (4th Cir. 2006); Lewis v. United States DOL, 368 Fed. Appx. 20, 30-32 (11th Cir. 2010) (addressing the CAA whistleblower provision).

TABLE 10-2
Selected Information-Gathering Authorities

CWA	CAA	CERCLA	RCRA
§308(a)(A). Empowers EPA to require the operator of a point source to sample, file reports, and maintain records.	§114. Recordkeeping, Inspections, Monitoring and Entry: Requires owners/operators of emission sources to monitor emissions, keep records, and provide reports. Gives the Administrator a right of entry to these facilities for inspection purposes.	§104(e). Information Gathering and Access: Authorizes the president and his employees to access information and investigate facilities where hazardous substances may be stored, released, or threatened to be released.	§3007. Inspections: Authorizes EPA inspection of facilities where hazardous wastes are or have been generated, stored, treated, disposed of, or transported from.
§308(a)(B). Authorizes EPA inspections.			§3013. Monitoring, Analysis, and Testing: Authorizes the Administrator to investigate if hazardous waste is discovered that may present a substantial threat

EPA's enabling legislation typically empowers EPA to enter regulated premises, copy records, inspect monitoring equipment, and take samples of its own, in addition to requiring regulated parties to track their own performance, as Table 10-2 indicates. Inspections have been characterized as the "backbone" of EPA's compliance monitoring efforts. Reitze & Holmes, Inspections Under the Clean Air Act, 1 The Envtl. Law. 29, 36 (1994). Professor Reitze summarizes EPA's goals for its inspections efforts as follows:

1. assess compliance status and verify proper self-monitoring and reporting;
2. detect and document violations and obtain evidence to support enforcement actions;
3. identify environmental problems and provide information on compliance patterns in the regulated community;
4. perform an oversight function when done by EPA and/or the state reviewing the effectiveness of programs delegated to a state;
5. provide data on the adequacy of programs and the need for additional control;
6. promote compliance through information and technology transfer communicated by inspectors;
7. provide data to support the issuance of permits;
8. provide government agency employees experience and familiarity with industrial processes and facilities;
9. make the source aware of any problems;

10. deter violations; and

11. determine whether compliance orders have been obeyed.

The size of the regulated community far outstrips governments' ability to engage in meaningful monitoring of a significant percentage of regulated parties. One EPA enforcement data base, Enforcement and Compliance History Online (ECHO), http://www.epa-echo.gov/echo/ lists more than 800,000 regulated facilities. EPA itself annually conducts roughly 20,000 inspections, as Table 10-3 reflects (the states conduct the vast majority of government inspections). In its 2014-2018 Strategic Plan the Agency indicates that it expects the annual number of inspections to drop to about 16,000 over the next five years. EPA, Fiscal Year 2014-2018 EPA Strategic Plan 92 (April 10, 2014).

The resulting reliance on regulated party self-monitoring has raised concerns about the credibility and reliability of the data produced through such efforts. See, e.g., U.S. GAO, GAO/RCED-93-21, Environmental Enforcement: EPA Cannot Ensure the Accuracy of Self-Reported Compliance Data (1993).

Government inspection efforts have not fared especially well under scrutiny either. In addition to concerns that not enough inspections are being done, the GAO and OIG have concluded that in some cases the quality of inspections performed is not adequate to evaluate compliance effectively. They also have found that, for numerous reasons, data from inspections are not being reported accurately or in a timely way.[f]

Credible data about levels of compliance, numbers of inspections, and the like are obviously critical to the effort to promote compliance with the law and to understand the effect of such efforts. Unfortunately, our understanding of the state of compliance with environmental requirements is less than complete, at best. As one longtime EPA attorney put it, "there is . . . an obvious need for completely accurate and timely compliance data—something which EPA and the states cannot currently assure." Mugdan, Federal Environmental Enforcement in EPA Region 2, 10 Envtl. L. N.Y. 49, 63 (1999). A December 2005 EPA Office of Inspector General Report concludes that, because of data and other issues, EPA "does not know if compliance is actually going up or down."[g] EPA's enforcement office acknowledges these challenges in a 2009 report, noting that

> EPA lacks nationally consistent and complete information on the facilities, permits, pollutant discharges and compliance status of most NPDES-regulated facilities. This affects the ability of EPA and states to identify violations, target their actions, connect violations to water quality impacts, and to share information with the public. Data problems between EPA and states include data quality, accuracy, and completeness.

f. See, e.g., U.S. GAO, GAO-10-165T, Clean Water Act: Longstanding Issues Impact EPA's and State's Enforcement Efforts (2008); U.S. GAO, GAO-02-712T, Improved Inspections and Enforcement Would Ensure Safer Underground Storage Tanks (2002); EPA, Office of Inspector General Report No. 2001-P-00013, Water Enforcement: State Enforcement of Clean Water Act Dischargers Can Be More Effective, 23-24, 27 (2001); EPA, Office of Inspector General Audit Report No. 2001-P-0006 Enforcement: Compliance with Enforcement Instruments (2001).

g. EPA, Office of Inspector General Report No. 2006-P-0006, EPA Performance Measures Do Not Effectively Track Compliance Outcomes 11 (2005), available at www.epa.gov/oig/reports/2006/20051215-2006-P-00006.pdf.

TABLE 10-3
EPA Regional Inspections

	FY99	FY00	FY01	FY02	FY03	FY04	FY05	FY06	FY07	FY08	FY09	FY10	FY11	FY12	FY13
CAA Stationary	1,406	1,284	1,046	440	491	409	1,745	2,610	2,277	2,325	1,876	2,348	2,346		
CAA CFCs	1,227	579	122	265	255	255	195	226	191	341	242	163	159		
CAA Mobile Source	39	34	8	6	3	801	266	309	475	363	337	364	176		
Asbestos D & R	437	151	325	98	270	276	209	211	233	220	268	206	165		
NPDES Minors	965	1,141	876	1,044	1,221	1,348	1,386	1,720	1,336	1,583	1,401	1,453	1,466		
NPDES Majors	949	640	758	871	565	645	512	794	551	440	488	422	353		
Pretreatment IUS	0	277	273	94	164	158	NR	245	161	166	148	142	112		
Pretreatment POTWs	0	115	134	115	90	135	140	181	125	110	101	78	76		
CWA 311	1,424	1,549	1,269	786	1,141	969	1,159	1,092	980	1,037	1,013	1,034	1,012		
CWA 404	1,079	964	699	643	558	471	453	421	327	355	337	317	345		
EPCRA 313	513	472	321	267	262	298	244	308	268	280	276	262	304		
EPCRA non-313	521	1,366	613	466	725	672	661	620	616	728	693	609	597		
FIFRA	259	799	858	810	338	472	215	344	360	366	346	372	364		
RCRA-HW	2,214	1,746	1,521	1,400	1,643	1,627	1,552	1,874	1,599	1,604	1,585	1,680	1,607		
RCRA-UST	1,482	1,185	1,259	1,080	1,327	1,415	1,216	1,938	2,275	1,866	1,586	2,551	1,574		
SDWA-PWSS	449	488	362	327	228	358	355	71	58	88	83	83	92		
SDWA-UIC	6,880	6,227	5,663	6,218	7,190	8,143	8,416	7,697	7,560	5,859	6,844	6,951	5,863		
TSCA	2,003	1,400	1,453	2,738	2,376	1,792	1,611	2,008	1,662	1,441	1,439	1,368	1,640		
TOTAL	21,847	20,417	17,560	17,668	18,877	20,244	20,335	22,669	21,054	19,172	19,063	20,403	18,251	20,000	18,000

Note: EPA notes that the drop in CAA EPA inspection count for fiscal year 2002 "was due, at least in part, to implementation in that year of a new CAA Compliance Monitoring Strategy (CMS), which changed the definition of a CAA inspection." EPA, National Enforcement Trends—FY 2009,

Source: EPA, National Enforcement Trends—FY 2005, EPA, National Enforcement Trends—FY 2009, EPA, National Enforcement Trends- FY 2011, p. G-1b; EPA, FY 2012 EPA Enforcement & Compliance Annual Results p. 11; EPA, Enforcement Annual Results Numbers at a Glance for FY 2013.

EPA, Office of Enforcement and Compliance Assurance, Clean Water Act Enforcement Action Plan 10 (2009). The GAO notes that while one of EPA's goals is to "obtain accurate data that can be used to determine the extent of state compliance with enforcement standards and the need for corrective actions," "such efforts are still in the early stages, and their success is uncertain and will depend on continued commitment of senior management along with sufficient priority and resources." U.S. GAO, GAO-09-434, Environmental Protection Agency: Major Management Challenges (2009). One of EPA's goals in its Next Generation Compliance initiative is to improve data quality and dissemination.

NOTES AND QUESTIONS ABOUT EPA'S INFORMATION-GATHERING AUTHORITIES

1. *The Fourth Amendment.* In many situations, EPA needs a warrant before it may legally conduct an inspection without a regulated party's consent, but the Supreme Court noted in Marshall v. Barlow's, Inc., 436 U.S. 307, 320 (1978), that "[p]robable cause in the criminal law sense is not required" for an administrative warrant. Instead, the government must show either that reasonable suspicion of a violation exists or that it desires to enter the premises as part of a neutral inspection scheme. Warrants are not needed under certain circumstances, including if the regulated party consents, if an emergency exists, or if the "open field" doctrine applies. In Dow Chem. Co. v. United States, 476 U.S. 227 (1986), EPA made an in-plant inspection of Dow's 2,080-acre Michigan plant to check for air quality violations. The agency decided that a second inspection was necessary and informed Dow that it intended to take aerial photographs of the facility; Dow objected. Rather than obtain a civil search warrant, EPA contracted with a private concern to take sophisticated photographs of the facility. Dow sued, claiming that EPA lacked the authority under §114 of the CAA to engage in site inspections by aerial photography and that, even if it had that authority, the flight and the photographs constituted an unreasonable search of its property in violation of the Fourth Amendment. The Supreme Court held that EPA's statutory "right of entry to, upon, or through any premises" was broad enough to encompass the use of aerial photography. The Court also held that, although Dow had a legitimate expectation of privacy within the interior of its covered buildings, the open areas of the plant did not qualify as a "curtilage" area entitled to protection as a place where the occupants have such an expectation. Instead, the complex was more like an open field, the owner of which is not entitled to an expectation of privacy for activities engaged in there. See generally Tillitt, Note, The Open Fields Doctrine: New Limitations on Environmental Surveillance, 17 Va. Envtl. L.J. 245 (1998).

2. *The Fifth Amendment.* The obligation to maintain and disclose records has been upheld in the context of challenges under the Fourth and Fifth Amendments. Courts have required regulated parties to disclose information even in situations where such records may prove to be self-incriminating. Marchetti v. United States, 390 U.S. 39, 55-57 (1968); United States v. Garcia-Cordero, 595 F. Supp. 2d 1312 (S.D. Fla. 2009), *aff'd*, 610 F.3d 613 (11th Cir. 2010).

3. *Takings.* The Takings Clause has been invoked in connection with government efforts to enter onto property. In Hendler v. United States, 175 F.3d 1374 (Fed. Cir. 1999), EPA installed and operated groundwater monitoring wells on private property in an attempt to mitigate the adverse effects of groundwater pollution originating on an adjacent hazardous waste site. The Federal Circuit concluded that the

property owners were entitled to no damages, holding that the decline in value suffered by the property owners on the portion of their land that suffered a partial physical taking was more than offset by special benefits conferred by the government's cleanup actions, in the form of the elimination of a need for the property owners to engage in a Phase Two investigation of the extent of contamination on its property. The court also affirmed the trial court's conclusion that the retained property suffered no severe damage. Compare Scogin v. United States, 33 Fed. Cl. 568 (1995), where the court held that the government's intermittent use of plaintiff's mooring facility for several weeks to load and unload cleanup equipment was not a taking, that a lease allowing a government contractor to use plaintiff's land in a more substantial manner for remedial purposes after a federal district court ordered him to allow government access was without the plaintiff's consent and therefore did not preclude a taking, and that further proceedings were necessary to determine whether the rental received constituted just compensation. See also Boise Cascade Corp. v. United States, 296 F.3d 1339 (Fed. Cir. 2002) (involving alleged taking under the Endangered Species Act); Seiber v. United States, 364 F.3d 1356 (Fed. Cir. 2004).

4. *FOIA as an Information-Gathering Tool.* Much of the information obtained by the government is available to the public, though there are exceptions to public access contained in FOIA and some of the environmental enabling legislation. See, e.g., Gersh & Danielson v. EPA, 871 F. Supp. 407 (D. Colo. 1994); cf. Miccosukee Tribe of Indians of Fla. v. United States, 516 F.3d 1235 (11th Cir. 2008); Doe v. Browner, 902 F. Supp. 1240 (D. Nev. 1995), *aff'd in part, dismissed in part sub nom.* Kasza v. Browner, 133 F.3d 1159 (9th Cir. 1998).

5. For a case involving a claim that the government violated the CAA whistle-blower provision, 42 U.S.C. §7622, by retaliating against an employee who raised concerns about asbestos in the workplace, see Knox v. United States Dep't of Labor, 434 F.3d 721 (4th Cir. 2006).

6. EPA's use of its inspection authorities under CERCLA has been the subject of considerable litigation. The stakes can be high. The Sixth Circuit upheld a $1.9 million civil penalty against a party for failing to respond adequately to an EPA information request under CERCLA §104(e). United States v. Gurley, 384 F.3d 316 (6th Cir. 2004). Suppose that EPA assumes primary responsibility for a removal action under CERCLA. The agency requests that the owner of the contaminated site provide unconditional access to the agency and its employees for purposes of conducting the cleanup. The site owner responds that EPA may enter the site to undertake the cleanup, but that the owner reserves the right to object on constitutional grounds to the use of any evidence EPA gathers in subsequent criminal proceedings against the owner. The site owner fears that EPA may initiate criminal proceedings under the CAA on the basis of evidence that may become available to it if EPA enters the site. EPA enters the site and completes the cleanup, and then sues the site owner, which it alleges is liable for civil penalties for violating CERCLA's access provisions, §104(e), by refusing to grant unconditional access. Is the site owner liable? See United States v. Omega Chem. Corp., 156 F.3d 994 (9th Cir. 1998). In United States v. Tarkowski, 248 F.3d 596 (7th Cir. 2001), the court affirmed the district court's denial of EPA's request for an order requiring a property owner to allow EPA to enter his property under §104(e) of CERCLA to engage in testing and implement response actions. The district court had found EPA's request for access to be arbitrary and capricious because it was far more extensive than necessary to address the identified threat of contamination, which was minimal. Compare United States v. W.R. Grace & Co., 134 F. Supp. 2d 1182 (D. Mont. 2001) (issuing order allowing EPA immediate access to former vermiculite

mining site under §104(e)); United States v. Martin, 30 Envtl. L. Rep. 20756 (N.D. Ill. 2000) (ordering former site owner to respond to EPA request for information under §104(e) because the agency satisfied the "low threshold" of showing a reasonable basis to believe there may be a release or threat of a release at the site under investigation, and imposing a penalty of $75 a day for past noncompliance).

7. Two commentators have examined quite thoroughly many of the issues associated with obtaining information from regulated parties under the CAA, dividing the issues into nine categories: (1) the identity of the inspectors, (2) types of inspections, (3) how inspections are planned, (4) consensual searches, (5) warrants, (6) pre-entry activity, (7) post-entry activities (chain of custody, inspection of records, etc.), (8) liability of government inspectors, and (9) possible responses to an inspection. Reitze & Holmes, Inspections under the Clean Air Act, 1 Envtl. Law. 29 (1994).

8. EPA and the states have taken a number of steps to encourage regulated parties to be more proactive in uncovering violations, notifying the government, and correcting them. We discuss EPA's self-audit policy and other such initiatives in section D.

2.   The Government's Civil Litigation Authorities

Successful implementation of regulatory controls on activities with the potential to damage the environment ultimately depends on compliance with regulatory

TABLE 10-4
Selected Enforcement Authorities

CWA	CAA	RCRA
§309(a). Compliance orders: Authorizes EPA to issue compliance orders requiring compliance.	§113(b). Civil actions: Authorizes civil enforcement actions, for permanent or temporary injunctive relief, as well as civil penalties up to $25,000/day.	§3008(a) and (g). Compliance orders: Authorizes administrator to issue orders assessing civil penalties of up to $25,000 per day of violation and requiring compliance.
§309(b) and (d). Civil actions: Authorizes the Administrator to file civil actions for injunctive relief and/or payment of penalties of up to $25,000/day.	§113(c). Criminal penalties: Authorizes criminal prosecutions.	§3008(d). Criminal penalties: Authorizes criminal prosecutions.
§309(c). Criminal penalties: Authorizes criminal prosecutions.	§113(d). Administrative assessment of civil penalties: Authorizes Administrator to issue civil penalties of up to $25,000/day, generally with a ceiling on the total penalty that may be imposed.	§3013. Monitoring, analysis, and testing: Authorizes orders that mandate owners or operators of facilities where hazardous waste is found or released that may cause a substantial threat to public welfare to monitor, test, analyze, and report to ascertain the extent of the hazard.
§309(g). Administrative penalties: Authorizes Class I and Class II administrative enforcement penalties for violations, with ceilings on the total penalty that may be imposed.		§7003. Imminent hazard: Authorizes actions in situations that may present an imminent and substantial endangerment.

requirements. Cohen, Empirical Research on the Deterrent Effect of Environmental Monitoring and Enforcement, 30 Envtl. L. Rep. 10245 (2000), and Shimshack, Monitoring, Enforcement, & Environmental Compliance: Understanding Specific & General Deterrence, State-of-Science White Paper 6 (Oct. 2007), review the literature on the relationship between enforcement and corporate compliance. The deterrence-based theory underlying EPA's traditional approach to enforcement is that regulated entities lack strong incentives to comply with costly controls in the absence of a credible threat of enforcement. Compliance is often aided by the knowledge that permit or standard violations will be subject to enforcement actions. What enforcement options are available to the federal government? As Table 10-4 reflects, some statutes contemplate four possible avenues for pursuing alleged violators: (1) the issuance of administrative compliance orders that set timetables for correcting violations; (2) the imposition of administrative civil penalties; (3) the initiation of civil litigation in which the government can request injunctive relief, civil penalty assessments, or both; and (4) criminal prosecution (which is discussed in the next section).

Administrative Compliance Orders. The CAA's civil enforcement provisions typify the options available to EPA under the pollution control laws, though its provisions are unusually elaborate. Assuming that EPA has complied with applicable state notification and waiting requirements, it may issue an order requiring compliance with applicable statutory, regulatory, permit, or SIP provisions. CAA §113(a)(1)(A). Compliance orders must "state with reasonable specificity the nature of the violation and specify a time for compliance which the Administrator determines is reasonable, taking into account the seriousness of the violation and any good faith efforts to comply with applicable requirements." Id. §113(a)(4). Based on concerns that EPA had abused the discretion this provision afforded it to fashion schedules of compliance, Congress amended the statute in 1990 to require that compliance with an administrative order be achieved "as expeditiously as practicable, but in no event longer than one year after the date the order was issued." Id. Administrative compliance orders are nonrenewable. Id.

In the following case, the Supreme Court considered the legality of the CWA's administrative compliance order authority.

SACKETT v. EPA
132 S. Ct. 1367 (2012)

Justice SCALIA delivered the opinion of the Court.

We consider whether Michael and Chantell Sackett may bring a civil action under the Administrative Procedure Act to challenge the issuance by the Environmental Protection Agency (EPA) of an administrative compliance order under §309 of the Clean Water Act, 33 U.S.C. §1319. The order asserts that the Sacketts' property is subject to the Act, and that they have violated its provisions by placing fill material on the property; and on this basis it directs them immediately to restore the property pursuant to an EPA work plan.

I

The Clean Water Act prohibits, among other things, "the discharge of any pollutant by any person," §1311, without a permit, into the "navigable waters," §1344—which the

Act defines as "the waters of the United States," §1362(7). If the EPA determines that any person is in violation of this restriction, the Act directs the agency either to issue a compliance order or to initiate a civil enforcement action. §1319(a)(3). When the EPA prevails in a civil action, the Act provides for "a civil penalty not to exceed [$37,500] per day for each violation." §1319(d). And according to the Government, when the EPA prevails against any person who has been issued a compliance order but has failed to comply, that amount is increased to $75,000—up to $37,500 for the statutory violation and up to an additional $37,500 for violating the compliance order.

The particulars of this case flow from a dispute about the scope of "the navigable waters" subject to this enforcement regime. Today we consider only whether the dispute may be brought to court by challenging the compliance order—we do not resolve the dispute on the merits. The reader will be curious, however, to know what all the fuss is about. In United States v. Riverside Bayview Homes, Inc., 474 U.S. 121 (1985), we upheld a regulation that construed "the navigable waters" to include "freshwater wetlands," themselves not actually navigable, that were adjacent to nav-igable-in-fact waters. Later, in Solid Waste Agency of Northern Cook Cty. v. Army Corps of Engineers, 531 U.S. 159 (2001), we held that an abandoned sand and gravel pit, which "seasonally ponded" but which was not adjacent to open water, was not part of the navigable waters. Then most recently, in Rapanos v. United States, 547 U.S. 715 (2006), we considered whether a wetland not adjacent to navigable-in-fact waters fell within the scope of the Act. Our answer was no, but no one rationale commanded a majority of the Court. In his separate opinion, The Chief Justice expressed the concern that interested parties would lack guidance "on precisely how to read Con-gress' limits on the reach of the Clean Water Act" and would be left "to feel their way on a case-by-case basis." (concurring opinion).

The Sacketts are interested parties feeling their way. They own a 2/3-acre residential lot in Bonner County, Idaho. Their property lies just north of Priest Lake, but is separated from the lake by several lots containing permanent structures. In preparation for constructing a house, the Sacketts filled in part of their lot with dirt and rock. Some months later, they received from the EPA a compliance order. The order contained a number of "Findings and Conclusions," including the following:

> 1.4 [The Sacketts' property] contains wetlands within the meaning of 33 C.F.R. §328.4(8)(b); the wetlands meet the criteria for jurisdictional wetlands in the 1987 "Federal Manual for Identifying and Delineating Jurisdictional Wetlands."
>
> 1.5 The Site's wetlands are adjacent to Priest Lake within the meaning of 33 C.F.R. §328.4(8)(c). Priest Lake is a "navigable water" within the meaning of section 502(7) of the Act, 33 U.S.C. §1362(7), and 'waters of the United States' within the meaning of 40 C.F.R. §232.2.
>
> 1.6 In April and May, 2007, at times more fully known to [the Sacketts, they] and/or persons acting on their behalf discharged fill material into wetlands at the Site. [They] filled approximately one half acre. . . .
>
> 1.9 By causing such fill material to enter waters of the United States, [the Sacketts] have engaged, and are continuing to engage, in the "discharge of pollutants" from a point source within the meaning of sections 301 and 502(12) of the Act. . . .
>
> 1.11 [The Sacketts'] discharge of pollutants into waters of the United States at the Site without [a] permit constitutes a violation of section 301 of the Act, 33 U.S.C. §1311.

On the basis of these findings and conclusions, the order directs the Sacketts, among other things, "immediately [to] undertake activities to restore the Site in accordance with [an EPA-created] Restoration Work Plan" and to "provide and/or obtain access to the Site . . . [and] access to all records and documentation related to the conditions at the Site . . . to EPA employees and/or their designated representatives."

The Sacketts, who do not believe that their property is subject to the Act, asked the EPA for a hearing, but that request was denied. They then brought this action in the United States District Court for the District of Idaho, seeking declaratory and injunctive relief. Their complaint contended that the EPA's issuance of the compliance order was "arbitrary [and] capricious" under the Administrative Procedure Act (APA), 5 U.S.C. §706(2)(A), and that it deprived them of "life, liberty, or property, without due process of law," in violation of the Fifth Amendment. The District Court dismissed the claims for want of subject-matter jurisdiction, and the United States Court of Appeals for the Ninth Circuit affirmed, 622 F.3d 1139 (2010). It concluded that the Act "preclude[s] pre-enforcement judicial review of compliance orders," and that such preclusion does not violate the Fifth Amendment's due process guarantee. We granted certiorari.

II

The Sacketts brought suit under Chapter 7 of the APA, which provides for judicial review of "final agency action for which there is no other adequate remedy in a court." 5 U.S.C. §704. We consider first whether the compliance order is final agency action. There is no doubt it is agency action, which the APA defines as including even a "failure to act." §§551(13), 701(b)(2). But is it *final?* It has all of the hallmarks of APA finality that our opinions establish. Through the order, the EPA "'determined'" "'rights or obligations.'" Bennett v. Spear, 520 U.S. 154, 178 (1997). By reason of the order, the Sacketts have the legal obligation to "restore" their property according to an agency-approved Restoration Work Plan, and must give the EPA access to their property and to "records and documentation related to the conditions at the Site." Also, "'legal consequences . . . flow'" from issuance of the order." For one, according to the Government's current litigating position, the order exposes the Sacketts to double penalties in a future enforcement proceeding.[2] It also severely limits the Sacketts' ability to obtain a permit for their fill from the Army Corps of Engineers, see 33 U.S.C. §1344. The Corps' regulations provide that, once the EPA has issued a compliance order with respect to certain property, the Corps will not process a permit application for that property unless doing so "is clearly appropriate." 33 CFR §326.3(e)(1)(iv) (2011).

The issuance of the compliance order also marks the " 'consummation' " of the agency's decisionmaking process. Bennett, supra, at 178. As the Sacketts learned when they unsuccessfully sought a hearing, the "Findings and Conclusions" that the compliance order contained were not subject to further agency review. The Government resists this conclusion, pointing to a portion of the order that invited the Sacketts to "engage in informal discussion of the terms and requirements" of the order with the EPA and to inform the agency of "any allegations [t]herein which [they] believe[d] to be inaccurate." But that confers no entitlement to further agency review. The mere possibility that an agency might reconsider in light of "informal discussion" and invited contentions of inaccuracy does not suffice to make an otherwise final agency action nonfinal.

---

2. We do not decide today that the Government's position is correct, but assume the consequences of the order to be what the Government asserts.

The APA's judicial review provision also requires that the person seeking APA review of final agency action have "no other adequate remedy in a court," 5 U.S.C. §704. In Clean Water Act enforcement cases, judicial review ordinarily comes by way of a civil action brought by the EPA under 33 U.S.C. §1319. But the Sacketts cannot initiate that process, and each day they wait for the agency to drop the hammer, they accrue, by the Government's telling, an additional $75,000 in potential liability. The other possible route to judicial review—applying to the Corps of Engineers for a permit and then filing suit under the APA if a permit is denied—will not serve either. The remedy for denial of action that might be sought from one agency does not ordinarily provide an "adequate remedy" for action already taken by another agency. The Government, to its credit, does not seriously contend that other available remedies alone foreclose review under §704. Instead, the Government relies on §701(a)(1) of the APA, which excludes APA review "to the extent that [other] statutes preclude judicial review." The Clean Water Act, it says, is such a statute.

III

Nothing in the Clean Water Act *expressly* precludes judicial review under the APA or otherwise. But in determining "[w]hether and to what extent a particular statute precludes judicial review," we do not look "only [to] its express language." Block v. Community Nutrition Institute, 467 U.S. 340, 345 (1984). The APA, we have said, creates a "presumption favoring judicial review of administrative action," but as with most presumptions, this one "may be overcome by inferences of intent drawn from the statutory scheme as a whole." The Government offers several reasons why the statutory scheme of the Clean Water Act precludes review.

The Government first points to 33 U.S.C. §1319(a)(3), which provides that, when the EPA "finds that any person is in violation" of certain portions of the Act, the agency "shall issue an order requiring such person to comply with [the Act], or . . . shall bring a civil action [to enforce the Act]." The Government argues that, because Congress gave the EPA the choice between a judicial proceeding and an administrative action, it would undermine the Act to allow judicial review of the latter. But that argument rests on the question-begging premise that the relevant difference between a compliance order and an enforcement proceeding is that only the latter is subject to judicial review. There are eminently sound reasons other than insulation from judicial review why compliance orders are useful. The Government itself suggests that they "provid[e] a means of notifying recipients of potential violations and quickly resolving the issues through voluntary compliance." It is entirely consistent with this function to allow judicial review when the recipient does not choose "voluntary compliance." The Act does not guarantee the EPA that issuing a compliance order will always be the most effective choice.

The Government also notes that compliance orders are not self-executing, but must be enforced by the agency in a plenary judicial action. It suggests that Congress therefore viewed a compliance order "as a step in the deliberative process[,] . . . rather than as a coercive sanction that itself must be subject to judicial review." But the APA provides for judicial review of all final agency actions, not just those that impose a self-executing sanction. And it is hard for the Government to defend its claim that the issuance of the compliance order was just "a step in the deliberative process" when the agency rejected the Sacketts' attempt to obtain a hearing and when the *next* step will either be taken by the Sacketts (if they comply with the order) or will involve judicial, not administrative, deliberation (if the EPA brings an enforcement action). As the text (and indeed the very name) of the compliance order makes clear, the EPA's "deliberation" over whether the Sacketts are in violation of the Act is at an end; the agency may still have to deliberate over whether it is confident enough about this conclusion to initiate litigation, but that is a separate subject.

The Government further urges us to consider that Congress expressly provided for prompt judicial review, on the administrative record, when the EPA assesses administrative penalties after a hearing, see §1319(g)(8), but did not expressly provide for review of compliance orders. But if the express provision of judicial review in one section of a long and complicated statute were alone enough to overcome the APA's presumption of reviewability for all final agency action, it would not be much of a presumption at all.

The cases on which the Government relies simply are not analogous. In Block v. Community Nutrition Institute, *supra*, we held that the Agricultural Marketing Agreement Act of 1937, which expressly allowed milk handlers to obtain judicial review of milk market orders, precluded review of milk market orders in suits brought by milk *consumers*. Where a statute provides that particular agency action is reviewable at the instance of one party, who must first exhaust administrative remedies, the inference that it is not reviewable at the instance of other parties, who are not *subject* to the administrative process, is strong. In United States v. Erika, Inc., 456 U.S. 201 (1982), we held that the Medicare statute, which expressly provided for judicial review of awards under Part A, precluded review of awards under Part B. The strong parallel between the award provisions in Part A and Part B of the Medicare statute does not exist between the issuance of a compliance order and the assessment of administrative penalties under the Clean Water Act. And in United States v. Fausto, 484 U.S. 439 (1988), we held that the Civil Service Reform Act, which expressly excluded certain "nonpreference" employees from the statute's review scheme, precluded review at the instance of those employees in a separate Claims Court action. Here, there is no suggestion that Congress has sought to exclude compliance-order recipients from the Act's review scheme; quite to the contrary, the Government's case is premised on the notion that the Act's primary review mechanisms are open to the Sacketts.

Finally, the Government notes that Congress passed the Clean Water Act in large part to respond to the inefficiency of then-existing remedies for water pollution. Compliance orders, as noted above, can obtain quick remediation through voluntary compliance. The Government warns that the EPA is less likely to use the orders if they are subject to judicial review. That may be true—but it will be true for all agency actions subjected to judicial review. The APA's presumption of judicial review is a repudiation of the principle that efficiency of regulation conquers all. And there is no reason to think that the Clean Water Act was uniquely designed to enable the strong-arming of regulated parties into "voluntary compliance" without the opportunity for judicial review—even judicial review of the question whether the regulated party is within the EPA's jurisdiction. Compliance orders will remain an effective means of securing prompt voluntary compliance in those many cases where there is no substantial basis to question their validity.

We conclude that the compliance order in this case is final agency action for which there is no adequate remedy other than APA review, and that the Clean Water Act does not preclude that review. We therefore reverse the judgment of the Court of Appeals and remand the case for further proceedings consistent with this opinion.

Justice GINSBURG, concurring.

Faced with an EPA administrative compliance order threatening tens of thousands of dollars in civil penalties per day, the Sacketts sued "to contest the jurisdictional bases for the order." "As a logical prerequisite to the issuance of the challenged compliance order," the Sacketts contend, "EPA had to determine that it has regulatory authority over [our] property." The Court holds that the Sacketts may immediately litigate their jurisdictional challenge in federal court. I agree, for the Agency has ruled definitively on that question. Whether the Sacketts could challenge not only the EPA's authority to regulate their land under the Clean Water Act, but also, at this pre-enforcement stage, the terms and conditions of the compliance order, is a question today's opinion does not reach out to resolve. Not raised by the Sacketts here, the question remains open for another day and case. On that understanding, I join the Court's opinion.

Justice ALITO, concurring.

The position taken in this case by the Federal Government—a position that the Court now squarely rejects—would have put the property rights of ordinary Americans entirely at the mercy of Environmental Protection Agency (EPA) employees.

The reach of the Clean Water Act is notoriously unclear. Any piece of land that is wet at least part of the year is in danger of being classified by EPA employees as wetlands covered by the Act, and according to the Federal Government, if property owners begin to construct a home on a lot that the agency thinks possesses the requisite wetness, the property owners are at the agency's mercy. The EPA may issue a compliance order demanding that the owners cease construction, engage in expensive remedial measures, and abandon any use of the property. If the owners do not do the EPA's bidding, they may be fined up to $75,000 per day ($37,500 for violating the Act and another $37,500 for violating the compliance order). And if the owners want their day in court to show that their lot does not include covered wetlands, well, as a practical matter, that is just too bad. Until the EPA sues them, they are blocked from access to the courts, and the EPA may wait as long as it wants before deciding to sue. By that time, the potential fines may easily have reached the millions. In a nation that values due process, not to mention private property, such treatment is unthinkable.

The Court's decision provides a modest measure of relief. At least, property owners like petitioners will have the right to challenge the EPA's jurisdictional determination under the Administrative Procedure Act. But the combination of the uncertain reach of the Clean Water Act and the draconian penalties imposed for the sort of violations alleged in this case still leaves most property owners with little practical alternative but to dance to the EPA's tune.

Real relief requires Congress to do what it should have done in the first place: provide a reasonably clear rule regarding the reach of the Clean Water Act. When Congress passed the Clean Water Act in 1972, it provided that the Act covers "the waters of the United States." 33 U.S.C. §1362(7). But Congress did not define what it meant by "the waters of the United States"; the phrase was not a term of art with a known meaning; and the words themselves are hopelessly indeterminate. Unsurprisingly, the EPA and the Army Corps of Engineers interpreted the phrase as an essentially limitless grant of authority. We rejected that boundless view, see Rapanos v. United States (plurality opinion); Solid Waste Agency of Northern Cook Cty. v. Army Corps of Engineers, but the precise reach of the Act remains unclear. For 40 years, Congress has done nothing to resolve this critical ambiguity, and the EPA has not seen fit to promulgate a rule providing a clear and sufficiently limited definition of the phrase. Instead, the agency has relied on informal guidance. But far from providing clarity and predictability, the agency's latest informal guidance advises property owners that many jurisdictional determinations concerning wetlands can only be made on a case-by-case basis by EPA field staff.

Allowing aggrieved property owners to sue under the Administrative Procedure Act is better than nothing, but only clarification of the reach of the Clean Water Act can rectify the underlying problem.

NOTES AND QUESTIONS

1. Which statutory and constitutional provisions did the petitioners rely on? What legal authorities did the Court find controlling?

2. What issue under the CWA was at the heart of this dispute? You may find it helpful to refer to Chapter 7 for more detailed coverage of the key CWA jurisdictional issue that is an important part of this case.

3. What effect is *Sackett* likely to have on EPA enforcement strategy under the CWA?

4. Other statutes, such as CERCLA (Chapter 9), the Clean Air Act (Chapter 6), and RCRA (Chapters 8 and 9), give EPA unilateral administrative authority as well. As you have learned throughout the course, sometimes Congress covers the same issues in different ways in different statutes. For example, while the CWA is silent on judicial review of administrative orders, CERCLA explicitly bars pre-enforcement review. Why do you think Congress changed the nature of the tools it gave to EPA in different statutes? What effect is *Sackett* likely to have on EPA's use of its unilateral authority under other statutes? For a collection of essays on *Sackett*, see 42 Envtl. L. 991-1041 (2012).

5. In response to *Sackett,* in a June 2012 Memorandum EPA provided guidance on the use of CWA §309 administrative compliance orders. Mazakas, Acting Director, Office of Civil Enforcement, Use of Clean Water Act Section 209(a) Administrative Compliance Order Authority After *Sackett v. EPA* (June 19, 2012). In a March 2013 Memorandum EPA discussed when language should be included in unilateral administrative enforcement orders notifying the recipient of the opportunity to seek pre-enforcement judicial review. See Shinkman, Director, Office of Civil Enforcement to Regional Counsel, Regions 1-10, Regional Enforcement Division Directors and Regional Enforcement Coordinators (March 2013), available at http://www2.epa .gov/sites/production/files/documents/languageregarding-sackett032113.pdf.

Administrative Civil Penalties. Congress added the power to impose civil penalties without judicial intervention to EPA's arsenal relatively late in the game. Under some of the statutes, such as the CWA and CAA, Congress has started incrementally in the sense that it has created lower penalty ceilings for administrative enforcement than it has established for judicial enforcement. Under the CAA, for example, EPA may issue administrative orders assessing civil penalties of up to $320,000 (with limited exceptions), while the statute does not create a similar ceiling for penalties obtained through civil judicial litigation. CAA §113(d)(1).[h] The Clean Water Act similarly establishes ceilings

---

h. While Congress initially set this limit at $200,000, the Federal Civil Penalties Adjustment Act of 1990 requires periodic adjustments to account for inflation. EPA increased civil penalties to account for inflation again in November 2013. Civil Monetary Penalty Inflation Adjustments Table, 40 C.F.R. §19.4 (2013). 78 Fed. Reg. 66,644 (Nov. 6, 2013).

on penalty amounts recoverable through administrative enforcement that it does not impose for civil litigation. Compare CWA §1319(g) with CWA §1319(d). RCRA does not draw such a distinction; EPA may assess administrative or judicial civil penalties under RCRA of up to $ 37,500 per day of noncompliance. RCRA §3008(a)(3).

The statutes afford EPA considerable discretion in determining the size of a penalty. Under the CAA, EPA must take into account factors that include the size of the business, the economic impact of the penalty on the business, the violator's compliance history and good faith efforts to comply, the duration of the violation, the economic benefit of noncompliance, and the seriousness of the violation. CAA §113(e)(1). See also CWA §309(g)(3); RCRA §3008(a)(3). EPA has developed guidance documents under many of its statutes that elaborate on the approach EPA should take in determining appropriate penalty amounts. See, e.g., EPA, Clean Air Act Mobile Source Civil Penalty Policy for Title II of the Clean Air Act—Vehicle and Engine Emissions Certification Requirements, 3, 11-15 (2009); EPA, Hazardous Waste Civil Enforcement Response Policy (2003). Civil liability under the federal environmental statutes is typically strict liability, and EPA is authorized under statutes such as the CWA to impose civil penalties even in the absence of evidence that a violation caused actual harm to the environment. See, e.g., Kelly v. EPA, 203 F.3d 519 (7th Cir. 2000) (noting, in the course of upholding a civil penalty that EPA imposed for filling in a wetland without a CWA §404 permit, that driving a car without a license is not necessarily dangerous but is nevertheless illegal).

The 1990 CAA amendments authorized EPA inspectors to issue field citations for minor violations. These citations, which have been analogized to traffic tickets, may impose fines of up to $5,000 per day. Congress exempted field citations from APA formal adjudication procedures in an effort to streamline the enforcement process. See CAA §113(d)(3); Miskiewicz & Rudd, Civil and Criminal Enforcement of the Clean Air Act after the 1990 Amendments, 9 Pace Envtl. L. Rev. 281, 314-316 (1992).

Judicial Civil Litigation. As an alternative to administrative enforcement, EPA may pursue alleged violators in federal court. DOJ typically handles such cases on behalf of EPA. Cruden & Gelber, *supra.* The federal district courts have the authority to issue injunctive relief, temporary or permanent, and impose civil penalties based on factors similar to those EPA must consider in calculating administrative civil penalties. See CAA §113(b), (e); CWA §309(b), (d); RCRA §3008(a)(3). The district courts have broad discretion in determining the appropriate penalty amount. The following decision by the Fourth Circuit reviews some of the issues associated with the calculation of penalties.

UNITED STATES v. SMITHFIELD FOODS
191 F.3d 516 (4th Cir. 1999)

Ervin, Circuit J.

Smithfield Foods, Inc. ("Smithfield") appeals a grant of summary judgment in favor of the United States finding Smithfield liable for multiple Clean Water Act violations. Smithfield also challenges the court's imposition of a corresponding $12.6 million civil penalty. . . .

On the penalty issue, Smithfield contends that the district court erred in calculating the penalty, especially with respect to its determination of economic benefit and the denial of "good-faith" credit to Smithfield for its compliance efforts.

For the reasons that follow, we affirm the district court's grant of summary judgment on liability. We remand the penalty determination to the district court with instructions to recalculate the civil penalty as directed by this opinion.

I.

The facts of this case are undisputed and are comprehensively set out in the district court's published opinion, United States v. Smithfield Foods, Inc., 965 F. Supp. 769, 772-781 (E.D. Va. 1997). To properly analyze this case, however, the major events bear repeating. Smithfield owns and operates two swine slaughtering and processing plants, Smithfield Packing Co. and Gwaltney of Smithfield, Ltd. Both plants are located on the Pagan River, a tributary of the James River, in Isle of Wight County, Virginia. The wastewater discharged from these plants is treated in two of Smithfield's facilities, Outfall 001 and Outfall 002. From at least August 1991 to August 1997, treated wastewater was discharged from Outfall 001 into the Pagan River. From at least August 1991 until June 1996, treated wastewater was discharged from Outfall 002 into the Pagan River. Smithfield stopped discharging wastewater into the Pagan River when it successfully connected its plants to the Hampton Roads Sanitation District ("HRSD") system.

A.

Smithfield's wastewater discharges contained numerous pollutants that were regulated under the CWA and thus, could not be discharged into the waters of the United States unless specifically authorized by permit. Permits are governed by the National Pollutant Discharge Elimination System ("NPDES"), under which polluters obtain an NPDES permit to discharge lawfully certain pollutants in specific amounts. See 33 U.S.C.A. §1342. Regulation of NPDES permits is overseen by the Environmental Protection Agency ("EPA"), see 33 U.S.C.A. §1342(a), but locally administered by the Commonwealth of Virginia through its agent, the Virginia State Water Control Board ("the Board"). See 33 U.S.C.A. §§1251(b), 1342(b). The Board is authorized to enforce the CWA subject to the guidance and approval of the EPA. See 33 U.S.C.A. §1319.

Smithfield's discharges were authorized by an NPDES permit ("the Permit") issued in 1986, modified in 1990, and reissued in 1992. The Permit placed restrictions on the amount and concentration of certain pollutants allowed in wastewater released to the Pagan River and required Smithfield to monitor, sample, analyze, and issue reports concerning its discharges. The results of Smithfield's wastewater sampling program were periodically compiled into Discharge Monitoring Reports ("DMRs") and submitted to the Board. . . .

B.

The government filed suit in the United States District Court for the Eastern District of Virginia on December 16, 1996, seeking injunctive relief and penalties for a range of effluent limit violations, submission of false DMRs, submission of late reports, and destruction of records. . . .

The district court held a bench trial . . . in July 1997. The court reviewed evidence and heard from both sides' experts who opined on the proper calculations for each of the factors to be considered under the CWA's penalty statute. In the end, the district court found Smithfield liable for 6,982 days of violations and, after weighing the mitigating and aggravating circumstances, assessed a penalty of $12.6 million. . . .

III.

Smithfield's second major challenge is to the district court's assessment of a $12.6 million penalty. We review the factual findings that formed the basis of the district court's penalty calculation for clear error, but the highly discretionary calculations necessary to award civil penalties are reviewed for abuse of discretion.

The CWA sets out six factors intended to assist courts in determining the appropriate civil penalty. See CWA §309(d), 33 U.S.C.A. §1319(d). Section 309(d) provides that "the court shall consider the seriousness of the violation or violations, the economic benefit (if any) resulting from the violation, any history of such violations, any good-faith efforts to comply with the applicable requirements, the economic impact of the penalty on the violator, and such other matters as justice may require." Id.

These factors are designed to give district courts direction in fashioning penalties for CWA violations, but once applied in a specific case, we have given and will continue to give the district court's final penalty calculation wide discretion. Because of the difficulty of determining an appropriate penalty in a complex case such as this one, we give deference to the "highly discretionary calculations that take into account multiple factors [that] are necessary in order to set civil penalties under the Clean Water Act." Tull v. United States, 481 U.S. 412, 427 (1987).

Although Smithfield contests several of the district court's discretionary decisions, such as the method used to count each violation and the alleged trebling of the penalty, Smithfield's major allegations of error relate to the court's economic benefit calculation and its refusal to grant Smithfield good-faith credit for its compliance efforts. We consider each of these arguments in turn. . . .

B.

Smithfield next argues that the district court erred as a matter of law by allegedly calculating the penalty by trebling the amount of economic benefit calculated. Pointing to the text of the Act, Smithfield contends that, unlike other federal statutes, the CWA does not provide for trebling and therefore the court committed reversible error by assessing a penalty equal to exactly three times the amount of economic benefit calculated. We see no indication that the district court "simply trebled the amount of economic benefit." On the contrary, we find that the district court correctly applied the CWA in assessing Smithfield's penalty.

In calculating the penalty, the district court properly began by determining that the statutory maximum based on Smithfield's violations was $174.55 million. See Smithfield, 972 F. Supp. at 353. Thereafter, the court evaluated two different methods used to assess penalties—the top-down method and the bottom-up method—

and to Smithfield's advantage, chose the bottom-up method.[7] Under the bottom-up method, the court begins with the violator's estimated economic benefit from non-compliance, which here was $4.2 million, and then adjusts up or down based on the court's evaluation of the six factors set out in §309(d). After evaluating and discussing the effect of each of the factors, the court found a $12.6 million penalty appropriate.

When calculating Smithfield's penalty, the district court took into account all six of the statutorily mandated factors and sufficiently detailed its findings as to whether the evidence in each area had a mitigating or aggravating impact on the total penalty. The court properly exercised its discretion in weighing the evidence and determining the credibility of key witnesses and, in doing so, made several decisions that were highly favorable to Smithfield. In the end, however, the court found that Smithfield's thousands of CWA violations warranted a penalty far in excess of the economic benefit calculation.

We find that the court's analysis was complete and in line with what is required under the statute. It is clear from its opinion that the court's exhaustive examination of the facts formed the basis of its final penalty calculation, rather than simply multiplying the economic benefit by three as Smithfield contends.

But even if the court had simply trebled the economic benefit to determine the appropriate penalty, that was within its discretion, as long as it was below the statutory maximum of $174.55 million. As mentioned, the Supreme Court has emphasized that under the CWA, the highly discretionary calculations necessary to assess civil penalties are particularly within the purview of trial judges, see *Tull*, 481 U.S. at 426-427, and we have continually given these determinations wide deference, reviewing them only for abuse of discretion. The government asked for a $20 million penalty, but based on its analysis of the relevant factors, the district court determined that $12.6 million was more appropriate, which is approximately 7.2% of the maximum penalty that could have been assessed. Finding that the court did not abuse its discretion in calculating the penalty, we reject Smithfield's contention that the district court erred as a matter of law in determining the penalty.

C.

Smithfield also argues that the district court erred as a matter of law by failing to give Smithfield credit for certain capital costs incurred and user fees paid when calculating economic benefit.

As one of the six factors the court must use to calculate CWA penalties, economic benefit is assessed to keep violators from gaining an unfair competitive advantage by violating the law. This is accomplished by including as part of the penalty an approximation of the amount of money the violator has saved by failing to comply with its permit. The rationale for including this measure as part of the violators' fine is "to remove or neutralize the economic incentive to violate environmental regulations." As noted in the Senate Report accompanying the 1987

7. As noted by the district court, the CWA does not require the use of either method, however, courts have applied both. See, e.g., Tyson Foods, 897 F.2d at 1142 (using top-down method in which a court begins with the statutory maximum and adjusts downward based on evaluation of §309(d) factors); Hawaii's Thousand Friends v. City & County of Honolulu, 821 F. Supp. 1368, 1395 (D. Haw. 1993) (same). But see United States v. Municipal Auth. of Union Twp., 150 F.3d 259, 265 (3d Cir. 19[8]8) (applying the bottom-up method) (known as "*Dean Dairy*"); Monsanto, 1998 WL 156691, at *16 (same).

amendment adding the economic benefit factor to §309(d), and as recognized by courts, the precise economic benefit a polluter has gained by violating its effluent limits may be difficult to prove, so "[r]easonable approximations of economic benefit will suffice" (referring to S. Rep. No. 50, 99th Cong., 1st Sess. 25 (1985)).

The statute does not define economic benefit and courts have applied different methods to determine the appropriate amount.[10] The district court used the common "cost-avoided" method here whereby economic benefit is measured by determining "the avoided and/or delayed cost of compliance, TTT [using] the weighted average cost of capital (WACC) as a discount/interest rate." The rationale behind this method is that "[w]hen a company delays or avoids certain costs of capital and operations and maintenance necessary for compliance, the company is able to use those funds for other income-producing activities, such as investing that money in their own company." Id.

The cost-avoided method has been utilized elsewhere, and was chosen by the district court in its discretion in part based on the court's evaluation of the credibility of the government's expert witness. The cost-avoided method is not in conflict with the CWA or basic economic principles. On the contrary, it represents a logical method by which a violator in Smithfield's position can be disgorged of any profits it attained through its non-compliance. Finding no fault with the district court's choice to apply the cost-avoided method in this case, we reject Smithfield's claim that its application was in error.

Smithfield further alleges that even under the cost-avoided method, the district court should have given Smithfield credit for (1) capital expenses incurred to build a pretreatment facility and to modify a sludge lagoon in preparation for connecting to HRSD, and (2) future user fees paid that Smithfield claims allowed HRSD to construct the necessary facilities for Smithfield's connection. In support of this argument, Smithfield repeatedly asserts that these are expenses it would have gotten credit for had it built its own direct discharge treatment system.

Smithfield decided to connect to HRSD in 1991 and, from that time until HRSD became available in 1996 and 1997, Smithfield was responsible for complying with its 1992 Permit requirements. Its decision to ignore these requirements in the interim certainly benefited Smithfield financially because, by failing to comply with the 1992 Permit limits, Smithfield avoided the costs of pollution control its competitors were simultaneously incurring by complying with the law. It is these costs that constitute Smithfield's economic benefit.

These capital expenses and user fees can reduce the economic benefit that Smithfield experienced from 1991 to 1996 or 1997 only in so far as they are duplicative of costs Smithfield should have incurred for interim compliance. The building of its pretreatment facility and the paying of user fees for future HRSD use were not costs Smithfield incurred to aid in compliance from 1991 to 1996 or 1997 and, therefore, should not have been credited to Smithfield during the district court's economic benefit calculation. . . .

---

10. In *Dean Dairy*, the Third Circuit calculated a violator's economic benefit by determining that the company would have lost $417,000 per year in revenues from a customer it would have had to drop in order to reduce production enough to comply with its permit. 150 F.3d at 262-267. In most cases, however, the court applies the cost-avoided method applied by the district court in the instant case.

D.

Finally, Smithfield alleges that the district court erred when it failed to give Smithfield credit for its good-faith efforts to comply by connecting to HRSD. Specifically, Smithfield argues that it should have received credit for its efforts to connect to HRSD because, even if it was mistaken, Smithfield believed that connecting to HRSD was the only applicable requirement in the interim.

Section 309(d) of the CWA requires a district court to consider "any good-faith efforts to comply with the applicable requirements" as a mitigating factor in the penalty calculation. 33 U.S.C.A. §1319(d). In practice, a court evaluates the evidence to determine whether the permittee took any actions to reduce the number of violations or attempted to lessen the impact of their discharges on the environment.

In its opinion, the district court began by acknowledging that Smithfield should receive credit for its decision to connect to HRSD when available, a decision that would eventually reduce its discharges to zero. The court went on, however, to focus its inquiry on whether there were any good-faith efforts to comply with the requirements set out in Smithfield's Permits during the relevant period—from 1991 until 1996 or 1997 when Smithfield connected to HRSD. In evaluating the facts presented at trial, the court found little evidence that the defendants made any good-faith efforts to comply because Smithfield did not facilitate its connection to HRSD or mitigate its discharges by treating its wastewater or decreasing its releases of pollutants in the interim.

The court looked beyond these obvious facts, however, for other signs that Smithfield might have tried to mitigate its violations by evaluating Smithfield's other business practices. In doing so, the court found that during the relevant period Smithfield cut back on the number of times it curtailed production to achieve compliance, ignored the advice of its own consultants who pointed out serious deficiencies in the operation and maintenance of Smithfield's existing wastewater treatment plant, and dismissed evidence that its treatment plant employees were inadequately trained. Other than agreeing to connect to HRSD, the court found that Smithfield "apparently believed they could discharge as much and as frequently as they wanted into the Pagan River. . . ."

The district court's finding of liability, with which we agree, was based on the notion that Smithfield impermissibly ignored its explicit obligations under its 1992 Permit by failing to comply with effluent limitations for the entire period between its decision to connect to HRSD and the time the connection was made. It is only reasonable, therefore, that Smithfield's efforts towards connecting to HRSD would not suffice as good-faith efforts to comply with its applicable permit requirements since, during this entire interim period, Smithfield made no effort to heed the specific limits established by its 1992 Permit.

Furthermore, the evidence supports the district court's ruling. The testimony presented at trial and the documentary evidence on which the court relied in making these factual findings illustrate that Smithfield did not make efforts to decrease its violations and, instead, relied on the unreasonable notion that as long as it connected to HRSD within three months of availability, it was unnecessary to comply with the specific effluent limitations listed in its 1992 Permit during the five year interim. Finding that the district court's factual determinations regarding Smithfield's lack of good-faith efforts to comply with applicable requirements were not clearly erroneous, we affirm its findings on this issue.

IV.

For the foregoing reasons, we affirm the district court's grant of summary judgment on liability. We reverse and remand the penalty determination to the district court with instructions to recalculate the civil penalty to the extent required by this opinion.

Affirmed in Part, Reversed in Part, and Remanded. . . .

NOTES AND QUESTIONS CONCERNING THE GOVERNMENT'S CIVIL LITIGATION AUTHORITIES

1. *General Factors EPA Uses to Calculate Penalties.* Many of the statutes contemplate that one of the main factors to be taken into account in determining an appropriate penalty amount is the "economic benefit" the violator gained because of its violations. The notion is that a penalty should be large enough to disgorge the violator's economic benefit, so that the penalty puts the violator in no better shape than competitors that complied with their legal obligations. The other major factor is the "gravity" of the violation. Typically this may be used to increase the amount of a penalty (to ensure that the violator is put in worse shape through the enforcement action than it would be in if it had complied with its obligations).

2. *A Little More Detail on Calculating Economic Benefit.* EPA has developed the BEN computer model to help it to "calculate the economic benefit a violator derives from delaying and/or avoiding compliance with environmental statutes." EPA OECA, BEN User's Manual 1-1 (Sept. 1999). EPA has refined the model over the years. EPA announced revisions to its approach to calculating economic benefit in August 2005. Calculation of the Economic Benefit of Noncompliance in EPA's Civil Penalty Enforcement Cases. 70 Fed. Reg. 50,326 (Aug. 26, 2005). EPA summarizes its methodology for calculating economic benefits as follows:

> BEN calculates the economic benefits gained from delaying and avoiding required environmental expenditures. Such expenditures can include: (1) [c]apital investments (e.g., pollution control equipment), (2) [o]ne-time nondepreciable expenditures (e.g., setting a reporting system, or acquiring land), (3) [a]nnually recurring costs (e.g., operating and maintenance costs). Each of these expenditures can be either delayed or avoided. BEN's baseline assumption is that capital investments and one-time nondepreciable expenditures are merely delayed over the period of noncompliance, whereas annual costs are avoided entirely over this period. BEN does allow you, however, to analyze any combination of delayed and avoided expenditures.
>
> The economic benefit calculation must incorporate the economic concepts of the "time value of money." Stated simply, a dollar today is worth more than a dollar tomorrow, because you can invest today's dollar to start earning a return immediately. Thus, the further in the future the dollar is, the less it is worth in "present-value" terms. Similarly, the greater the time value of money (i.e., the greater the "discount" or "compound" rate used to derive the present value), the lower the present value of future costs. . . .
>
> A violator may gain illegal competitive advantages in addition to the usual benefits of noncompliance. These may be substantial benefits, but they are beyond the capability of BEN or any computer program to assess. Instead BEN asks you a series of questions about possible illegal competitive advantages so that you may identify cases where they are relevant. EPA [BEN User's Manual, at 1-2, 1-3].

EPA has developed a series of other computer models to help in penalty calculation, including ABEL (corporate ability to pay), INDIPAY (an individual's ability to afford costs and civil penalties), MUNIPAY a municipality's or regional utility's ability to pay costs and penalties) and PROJECT (assessing the real cost of a proposed supplemental environmental project). See EPA, Penalty and Financial Models, available at http://www2.epa.gov/enforcement/penalty-and-financial-models. For a discussion of ability to pay, see Fuhrman, Perspectives on the U.S. Environmental Protection Agency's Treatment of Ability-to-Pay Cases, Envtl. Liab. Rep. 131 (April 2009).

3. *Judicial Discretion in Determining Penalty Amounts.* As the principal case reflects, courts have varied in their approaches to determining appropriate penalties. The Third Circuit has approved either the "top down" or "bottom up" approach, United States v. Allegheny Ludlum Corp., 366 F.3d 164, 178 n.6 (3d Cir. 2004), as has the Second Circuit. Catskill Mountains Chapter of Trout Unlimited, Inc. v. City of New York, 451 F.3d 77, 87 (2d Cir. 2006).

4. *A Sampling of Penalty Calculation Issues.* All of the statutes authorize the imposition of penalties for each day of violation. Suppose that an abandoned fish cannery violated its regulatory obligation to notify EPA of its intention to remove asbestos. Three years later, EPA sought civil penalties in federal district court under the CAA. The court regarded the failure to notify as a "continuing violation" and held the company separately liable for each day from the date it should reasonably have given notice to the date state officials learned of the removal. On appeal, the cannery argues that the failure to notify occurred on a single day and it is therefore subject to penalties under CAA §113(b) only for that date. Should the district court's decision be reversed? See United States v. Trident Seafoods Corp., 60 F.3d 556 (9th Cir. 1995). Suppose that a point source violates an effluent limitation that contains a monthly average limitation on discharges. Has it engaged in a violation for one day or 30 days? United States v. Allegheny Ludlum Corp., 366 F.3d 164 (3d Cir. 2004).

5. *Possible Enforcement Sanctions.* EPA may impose a variety of sanctions in addition to penalties. For example, the agency may seek to revoke the violator's authority to operate. RCRA §3008(a)(3). In addition, EPA may prohibit violators from contracting with the government under some circumstances. See, e.g., CWA §508. For an example of a suspension involving BP following the 2010 Deepwater Horizon spill, see EPA Temporarily Suspends BP from New Contracts With Federal Government, 43 Env't Rep. (BNA) 3056 (Nov. 30, 2012).

DOJ sometimes seeks injunctive relief to clean up any damage resulting from the violation's as well as to stop the conduct that violates the law. Cruden & Gelber, *supra,* at 191, 193; Markell, Is There a Possible Role for Regulatory Enforcement in the Effort to Value, Protect, and Restore Ecosystem Services?, 21 J. Land Use & Envtl. L. 553 (2007). What about punitive damages? The Supreme Court has held that the CWA's penalty provisions in §311 do not preempt punitive damages awards in maritime spill cases. Exxon Shipping Co. v. Baker, 554 U.S. 471 (2008).

6. *Possible Defenses to Enforcement.* The target of a government enforcement action has any number of potential defenses available. In addition to the "I did not do it" defense, another defense that occasionally is available is the statute of limitations. How long may the government wait before seeking to enforce the provisions of the environmental laws? The general federal statute of limitations that applies to enforcement actions in the absence of more specific statutory provisions requires

commencement of an "action, suit or proceeding for the enforcement of any civil fine, penalty, or forfeiture" within five years from the date when the claim first accrued. 28 U.S.C. §2462. 3M Co. (Minnesota Mining & Mfg.) v. Browner, 17 F.3d 1453 (D.C. Cir. 1994), held that §2462 applies to civil penalty cases brought before agencies (in this case under TSCA) on the basis that an administrative complaint qualifies as "an action, suit or proceeding" and it is one "for the enforcement of" a civil penalty. The distinction between a one-time and a continuing violation, which arises in the context of civil penalty calculations, is also relevant to the application of the statute of limitations. The relief sought may matter as well. In United States v. Telluride Co., 146 F.3d 1241 (10th Cir. 1998), the Tenth Circuit concluded that §2462 did not apply to the government's request for an injunction requiring the developer to restore the affected wetlands because it did not seek compensation for injury beyond that caused by the defendant, and therefore was not a "penalty" for purposes of §2462. See also United States v. Banks, 115 F.3d 916, 918-919 (11th Cir. 1997) (§2462 applies only to civil penalties, not to claims for equitable relief).

See National Parks Conservation Ass'n, Inc. v. Tennessee Valley Auth., 480 F.3d 410 (6th Cir. 2007), National Parks Conservation Ass'n, Inc. v. Tennessee Valley Auth., 502 F.3d 1316 (11th Cir. 2007), and Sierra Club v. Otter Tail Power Co., 615 F.3d 1008 (8th Cir. 2010), for a circuit split involving the application of the five-year statute of limitations contained in 28 U.S.C. §2462 for a civil penalty action to the obligation to comply with CAA PSD permit and BACT requirements. The Sixth Circuit held that PSD regulations impose an ongoing duty to obtain a PSD permit and apply BACT, while the Eighth and Eleventh Circuits held that there is no ongoing obligation. For example, in *Otter Tail* the Eighth Circuit concluded that "while Otter Tail [the operator of the plant] may have violated [EPA regulations] by failing to apply for PSD permits in the first place, it does not continue to do so by failing to comply with a hypothetical set of operational parameters that would have been developed through the permitting process." 615 F.3d at 1016.

Due process also may provide a defense in some cases. The court in General Elec. Co. v. EPA, 53 F.3d 1324 (D.C. Cir. 1995), refused to fine GE for improper processing of PCBs under TSCA on the ground that GE lacked fair notice of the regulatory interpretation upon which EPA relied in citing the company because the agency's interpretation "is so far from a reasonable person's understanding of the regulations that [the agency] could not fairly have informed GE of [its] perspective." Id. at 1330. The lack of clarity of the regulations was highlighted by the disagreement about their meaning among different divisions of EPA and by EPA's failure to adhere to a consistent interpretation over time. Professor Lazarus suggests that the court in the GE case "created, in effect, a good faith defense based on due process." Lazarus, Meeting the Demands of Integration in the Evolution of Environmental Law: Reforming Environmental Criminal Law, 83 Geo. L.J. 2407, 2528 (1995).

7. Problem 10-1, on page 1072, raises several issues concerning the overfiling issue discussed in *Harmon* and the following notes, and government enforcement, as well as two topics discussed below, citizen suit enforcement (section C.4) and EPA's Self-Audit and Supplemental Environmental Projects (SEPs) policies (section D).

8. *Further Reading.* For a recent book concerning monitoring compliance under the CWA, see D. Earnhart & R. Glicksman, Pollution Limits and Polluters' Efforts to Comply: The Role of Government Monitoring and Enforcement (Stanford Univ. Press 2011). For a series of news articles that addresses water quality concerns and

associated compliance-related issues, see Charles Duhigg, Toxic Waters, N.Y. Times, 2009-1010, available at http://projects.nytimes.com/toxic-waters.

3. *Criminal Liability*

The History of Environmental Criminal Prosecution in a Nutshell. Most of the environmental statutes adopted in the 1970s authorized the imposition of criminal penalties. See Lazarus, Meeting the Demands of Integration in the Evolution of Environmental Law: Reforming Environmental Criminal Law, 83 Geo. L.J. 2407, 2446 (1995). This authority was rarely used during that "environmental decade," and when it was, it tended to be in egregious cases involving intentional activity that resulted in serious environmental harm. The initial push for more widespread criminal enforcement came in 1982, when EPA's General Counsel, responding to charges that the Reagan administration EPA was too soft on corporate polluters, announced that criminal prosecution would play a more important role in the government's enforcement efforts. See Brickey, Environmental Crime at the Crossroads: The Intersection of Environmental and Criminal Law Theory, 71 Tul. L. Rev. 487, 493 (1997). The Justice Department created its Environmental Crimes Unit (later elevated to a Department Section) at about the same time, and it obtained almost 700 guilty pleas and convictions during the next ten years. Id. at 495-496; Brickey, The Rhetoric of Environmental Crime: Culpability, Discretion, and Structural Reform, 84 Iowa L. Rev. 115 (1998). The adoption of the Pollution Prosecution Act of 1990, Pub. L. No. 101-593, 104 Stat. 2954, enhanced EPA's investigatory authority and increased the number of EPA criminal investigators.

Controversy emerged during the 1992 presidential campaign amidst charges that the George H.W. Bush administration's Justice Department declined to prosecute environmental criminal violations or settled for inappropriately lenient sanctions for political reasons. These allegations prompted a series of congressional inquiries into improper political influence as well as an internal review by the Clinton administration's Justice Department. The resulting reports largely exonerated the Department's practices as appropriate exercises of prosecutorial discretion. Lazarus, *supra*, at 2410-2411; Brickey, Crossroads, *supra*, at 496-497.

Criminal Culpability and Environmental Crimes. The increased resort to criminal prosecution raised a series of legal and policy questions, not the least of which is the one at issue in the principal case that follows this introductory material: what degree of culpability must the government prove to convict an individual or corporation of a criminal offense under the environmental statutes?[i] A few provisions of the environmental statutes impose criminal liability for negligent conduct, e.g., CWA §309(c)(1) and CAA §113(c)(4). In United States v. Hanousek, 176 F.3d 1116 (9th Cir. 1999), the court held that criminal liability under the CWA for discharging harmful quantities of oil into navigable waters is triggered by "ordinary" negligence—failure to use reasonable care. The government need not demonstrate that the defendant's actions constituted "criminal

i. See generally Solow & Sarachan, Criminal Negligence Prosecutions Under the Federal Clean Water Act: A Statistical Analysis and an Evaluation of the Impact of *Hanousek* and *Hong*, 32 Envtl. L. Rep. 11153 (2002); Buente & Thomson, The Changing Face of Federal Environmental Criminal Law: Trends and Developments—1999-2001, 31 Envtl. L. Rep. 11340 (2001); Lazarus, *supra*. Section 2.02(2) of the Model Penal Code describes four different criminal states of mind: purposeful, knowing, reckless, and negligent.

negligence," an elevated standard requiring a *gross* deviation from the standard of care that a reasonable person would observe in the situation. Instead, the court held that proof of *ordinary* negligence as defined in tort law was sufficient because it is well established that a public welfare statute (like the CWA) may impose criminal liability upon that lesser standard without violating the Due Process Clause. See also United States v. Hong, 242 F.3d 528 (4th Cir. 2001) (affirming corporate officer's conviction for negligent violation of CWA's pretreatment requirements). The Tenth Circuit (citing the *Hanousek* decision discussed above) held in United States v. Ortiz, 427 F.3d 1278, 1279 (10th Cir. 2005), that the CWA "criminalizes any act of ordinary negligence that leads to the discharge of a pollutant into the navigable waters of the United States."

The so-called knowing endangerment provisions provide for culpability under what is essentially a recklessness standard, imposing severe criminal penalties on persons who knowingly place other persons at imminent risk of death or serious bodily injury. E.g., RCRA §3008(f)(1)(C). For an example of a successful prosecution for violation of RCRA's imminent endangerment provision, see United States v. Hansen, 262 F.3d 1217 (11th Cir. 2001). Many of the federal environmental criminal statutes, however, require proof that the defendant acted knowingly. E.g., CWA §309(c)(2); RCRA §3008(d); CAA §113(c)(1).

The determination of the required standard of culpability is often demanding even in the best of circumstances. "Few areas of criminal law pose more difficulty than the proper definition of the *mens rea* required for any particular crime." United States v. Bailey, 444 U.S. 394, 403 (1980). What makes application of these provisions particularly difficult in the environmental context is that "Congress avoided addressing at all what it meant by the mens rea requirements it enacted." Lazarus, *supra*, at 2454. Thus, "ambiguity abounds in [the] federal [environmental] statutes, especially with respect to the appropriate mens rea in criminal provisions." Id. at 2466. The Conference Committee report on the 1980 amendments to RCRA, for example, states that the Committee did not seek to define "knowing," but left the process of fleshing out the meaning of that term "to the courts under general principles." H.R. Rep. No. 96-1444, at 39 (1980). Two commentators assert that "[e]nvironmental cases decided since late 1998 signal the continuing erosion of the *mens rea*, or scienter, requirements under federal environmental laws." See Buente & Thomson, The Changing Face of Federal Environmental Criminal Law: Trends and Developments — 1999-2001, 31 Envtl. L. Rep. 11340, 11345 (2001).

The principal case that follows considers the application of the "knowing" *mens rea* requirement in the context of a prosecution under the Clean Water Act.

UNITED STATES v. AHMAD
101 F.3d 386 (5th Cir. 1996)

Jerry E. Smith, Circuit Judge: . . .

[In 1992, Attique Ahmad purchased the "Spin-N-Market No. 12," a convenience store and gas station located in Conroe, Texas. The gas station had two pumps, each of which was fed by an 8,000-gallon underground gasoline tank. Ahmad discovered that one of the tanks, which held high-octane gasoline, was leaking. The leak allowed water to enter into the tank and contaminate the gas, preventing Ahmad from selling it. In October 1993, Ahmad hired CTT Environmental Services (CTT), a tank testing company, to examine the tank. A CTT employee told Ahmad that the leak could not be repaired until it was completely emptied, which CTT offered to do. When Ahmad inquired whether he could empty the tank himself, the CTT employee replied that it would be dangerous and illegal to do so. She testified at trial that Ahmad responded, "Well, if I don't get caught, what then?"

In January 1994, Ahmad rented a hand-held motorized water pump from a hardware store, telling an employee that he was planning to use it to remove water from his backyard. Two witnesses testified that they subsequently saw Ahmad pumping gasoline into the street and discharging it into a manhole. Another witness testified that he asked Ahmad what he was doing; Ahmad replied that he was removing the water from the tank. Ahmad dumped about 4,700 gallons of gasoline into the street and the manhole in front of the Spin-N-Market. The gasoline discharged by Ahmad into the street entered a storm drain. The gas flowed through a pipe that empties into Possum Creek, which feeds into the San Jacinto River and eventually into Lake Houston. Several vacuum trucks were required to decontaminate the creek. The gasoline that Ahmad discharged into the manhole flowed through the sanitary sewer system and into the city's sewage treatment plant. When plant employees discovered a 1,000-gallon pool of gasoline in one of the intake ponds, they diverted it into an emergency lagoon. The plant supervisor ordered evacuation of nonessential personnel and called firefighters and a hazardous materials crew to the scene. The fire department determined that the gasoline created a risk of explosion and ordered the evacuation of two nearby schools. No one was injured, but fire officials testified at trial that the discharge created a "tremendous explosion hazard" that could have led to "hundreds, if not thousands, of deaths and injuries" and millions of dollars of property damage.]

Ahmad was indicted for [violating] the [Clean Water Act (CWA) by] knowingly discharging a pollutant from a point source into a navigable water of the United States without a permit, in violation of 33 U.S.C. §§1311(a) and 1319(c)(2)(A) (count one); [and] knowingly operating a source in violation of a pretreatment standard, in violation of 33 U.S.C. §§1317(d) and 1319(c)(2)(A) (count two). . . . At trial, Ahmad did not dispute that he had discharged gasoline from the tank or that eventually it had found its way to Possum Creek and the sewage treatment plant. Instead, he contended that his discharge of the gasoline was not "knowing," because he had believed he was discharging water. . . .

II.

Ahmad argues that the district court improperly instructed the jury on the *mens rea* required for counts one and two. The instruction on count one stated in relevant part:

> For you to find Mr. Ahmad guilty of this crime, you must be convinced that the government has proved each of the following beyond a reasonable doubt:
>
> (1) That on or about the date set forth in the indictment,
> (2) the defendant knowingly discharged
> (3) a pollutant
> (4) from a point source
> (5) without a permit to do so.

On count two, the court instructed the jury:

> In order to prove the defendant guilty of the offense charged in Count 2 of the indictment, the government must prove beyond a reasonable doubt each of the following elements:
>
> (1) That on or about the date set forth in the indictment
> (2) the defendant,
> (3) who was the owner or operator of a source,
> (4) knowingly operated that source by discharging into a public sewer system or publicly owned treatment works
> (5) a pollutant that created a fire or explosion hazard in that public sewer system or publicly owned treatment works.

Ahmad contends that the jury should have been instructed that the statutory *mens rea*—knowledge—was required as to each element of the offenses, rather than only with regard to discharge or the operation of a source. . . .

The language of the CWA is less than pellucid. Title 33 U.S.C. §1319(c)(2)(A) says that "any person who knowingly violates" any of a number of other sections of the CWA commits a felony. One of the provisions that §1319(c)(2)(A) makes it unlawful to violate is §1311(a), which, when read together with a series of definitions in §1362, prohibits the addition of any pollutant to navigable waters from a "point source." That was the crime charged in count one. Section 1319(c)(2)(A) also criminalizes violations of §1317(d), which prohibits the operation of any "source" in a way that contravenes any effluent standard, prohibition, or pretreatment standard. That was the crime charged in count two.

The principal issue is to which elements of the offense the modifier "knowingly" applies. The matter is complicated somewhat by the fact that the phrase "knowingly violates" appears in a different section of the CWA from the language defining the elements of the offenses. Ahmad argues that within this context, "knowingly violates" should be read to require him knowingly to have acted with regard to each element of the offenses. The government, in contrast, contends that "knowingly violates" requires it to prove only that Ahmad knew the nature of his acts and that he performed them intentionally. Particularly at issue is whether "knowingly" applies to the element of the discharge's being a pollutant, for Ahmad's main theory at trial was that he thought he was discharging water, not gasoline.

The Supreme Court has spoken to this issue in broad terms. In United States v. X-Citement Video, Inc., 513 U.S. 64 (1994), the Court . . . reaffirmed the long-held view that "the presumption in favor of a scienter requirement should apply to each of the statutory elements which criminalize otherwise innocent conduct."

Although *X-Citement Video* is the Court's most recent pronouncement on this subject, it is not the first. In Staples v. United States, 511 U.S. 600, 619-20 (1994), the Court found that the statutes criminalizing knowing possession of a machinegun require that defendants know not only that they possess a firearm but that it actually is a machinegun. Thus, an awareness of the features of the gun—specifically, the features that make it an automatic weapon—is a necessary element of the offense. More generally, the Court also made plain that statutory crimes carrying severe penalties are presumed to require that a defendant know the facts that make his conduct illegal.

Our own precedents are in the same vein. In United States v. Baytank (Houston), Inc., 934 F.2d 599, 613 (5th Cir. 1991), we concluded that a conviction for knowing and improper storage of hazardous wastes under 42 U.S.C. §6928(d)(2)(A) requires "that the defendant know factually what he is doing—storing, what is being stored, and that what is being stored factually has the potential for harm to others or the environment, and that he has no permit. . . ." This is directly analogous to the interpretation of the CWA that Ahmad urges upon us. Indeed, we find it eminently sensible that the phrase "knowingly violates" in §1319(c)(2)(A), when referring to other provisions that define the elements of the offenses §1319 creates, should uniformly require knowledge as to each of those elements rather than only one or two. To hold otherwise would require an explanation as to why some elements should be treated differently from others, which neither the parties nor the case law seems able to provide.

In support of its interpretation of the CWA, the government cites cases from other circuits. We find these decisions both inapposite and unpersuasive on the point for which they are cited. In United States v. Hopkins, 53 F.3d 533, 537-41 (2d Cir. 1995), the court held that the government need not demonstrate that a §1319(c)(2)(A) defendant knew his acts were illegal. The illegality of the defendant's actions is not an element of the offense, however. In United States v. Weitzenhoff, 35 F.3d 1275 (9th Cir. 1994), the court similarly was concerned almost exclusively with whether the language of the CWA creates a mistake-of-law defense. Both cases are easily distinguishable, for neither directly addresses mistake of fact or the statutory construction issues raised by Ahmad.

The government also protests that CWA violations fall into the judicially created exception for "public welfare offenses," under which some regulatory crimes have been held not to require a showing of mens rea. On its face, the CWA certainly does appear to implicate public welfare.

As recent cases have emphasized, however, the public welfare offense exception is narrow. The Staples Court, for example, held that the statute prohibiting the possession of machineguns fell outside the exception, notwithstanding the fact that "[t]ypically, our cases recognizing such offenses involve statutes that regulate potentially harmful or injurious items." Staples, 511 U.S. at 607.

Though gasoline is a "potentially harmful or injurious item," it is certainly no more so than are machineguns. Rather, Staples held, the key to the public welfare offense analysis is whether "dispensing with mens rea would require the defendant to have knowledge only of traditionally lawful conduct." Id. at 618. The CWA offenses of which Ahmad was convicted have precisely this characteristic, for if knowledge is not required as to the nature of the substance discharged, one who honestly and reasonably believes he is discharging water may find himself guilty of a felony if the substance turns out to be something else.

The fact that violations of §1319(c)(2)(A) are felonies punishable by years in federal prison confirms our view that they do not fall within the public welfare offense exception. As the Staples Court noted, public welfare offenses have virtually always been crimes punishable by relatively light penalties such as fines or short jail sentences, rather than substantial terms of imprisonment. Serious felonies, in contrast, should not fall within the exception "absent a clear statement from Congress that mens rea is not required." Id. at 618. Following Staples, we hold that the offenses charged in counts one and two are not public welfare offenses and that the usual presumption of a mens rea requirement applies. With the exception of purely jurisdictional elements, the mens rea of knowledge applies to each element of the crimes.

Finally, the government argues that the instructions, considered as a whole, adequately conveyed to the jury the message that Ahmad had to have known that what he was discharging was gasoline in order for the jury to find him guilty. We disagree.

At best, the jury charge made it uncertain to which elements "knowingly" applied. At worst, and considerably more likely, it indicated that only the element of discharge need be knowing. The instructions listed each element on a separate line, with the word "knowingly" present only in the line corresponding to the element that something was discharged. . . .

The obvious inference for the jury was that knowledge was required only as to the fact that something was discharged, and not as to any other fact. In effect, with regard to the other elements of the crimes, the instructions implied that the requisite *mens rea* was strict liability rather than knowledge. . . .

Because the charge effectively withdrew from the jury's consideration facts that it should have been permitted to find or not find, this error requires reversal. . . .

NOTES AND QUESTIONS ABOUT CRIMINAL ENFORCEMENT

1. *"How Far Does 'Knowingly' Travel?"* What was the government's position in *Ahmad*? What stance did the defendant, and ultimately the court, take? What if Ahmad had argued not that he thought the substance he dumped into the sewer was water, but that he did not know that dumping gasoline into the sewer was prohibited by the CWA? Would that argument have provided the basis for a good defense? See the *Hopkins* and *Weitzenhoff* cases, cited in *Ahmad*. For a 2007 Circuit Court decision that provides an overview of the scope of *mens rea* requirements, see United States v. Cooper, 482 F.3d 658, 666 (4th Cir. 2007) (discussing the "customary understanding that *mens rea* requirements do not attach to jurisdictional elements," in a case involving a criminal prosecution and conviction for violation of the CWA). In that case the court noted that the government had to establish that the water into which sewage was discharged was a "water of the United States," but did not have to establish that the defendant knew that it was. Id. at 668.

The rule of lenity dictates that statutory ambiguities be resolved in a criminal defendant's favor to avoid penalizing conduct the defendant could not fairly have known was proscribed. The courts have reversed criminal convictions under the environmental statutes on the basis of this doctrine. See, e.g., United States v. Plaza Health Lab., Inc., 3 F.3d 643 (2d Cir. 1993) (excerpted as principal case in Chapter 7) (holding that a human being was not a point source for purposes of §301(a) of the CWA).

2. *Liability of Responsible Corporate Officers.* The environmental statutes not only subject corporate entities to criminal liability, they also impose liability on responsible corporate officers. E.g., CWA §309(c)(6); CAA §113(c)(6). The Supreme Court endorsed the "responsible corporate officer" doctrine in United States v. Dotterweich, 320 U.S. 277 (1943), upholding the imposition of criminal sanctions under the food and drug laws on a corporate officer on the basis of his position in the corporate hierarchy, even though he had no personal knowledge of the criminal conduct engaged in by other corporate employees. Is the authority to control the illegal activity enough to invoke the doctrine, or must the officer have actually exercised control? See United States v. Iverson, 162 F.3d 1015 (9th Cir. 1998). May an

individual be held criminally liable for violating a CWA permit to which he is not a party? See United States v. Cooper, 173 F.3d 1192, 1201 (9th Cir. 1999).

3. *The Public Welfare Doctrine.* How broad is the public welfare doctrine? The court in *Ahmad* rejected the government's plea to rely on the public welfare doctrine to find the requisite criminal culpability on Ahmad's part. The Supreme Court has concluded that when criminal liability provisions are intended to protect the public welfare by regulating dangerous activities that create a risk of widely distributed harm, and the statute contains no *mens rea* requirement or is otherwise unclear as to what that requirement should be, the courts should assume that the legislature intended to lighten the government's burden of proof on the *mens rea* element of the crime, at least where the punishment is relatively light. Staples v. United States, 511 U.S. 600, 617-618 (1994); United States v. Dotterweich, 320 U.S. 277 (1943).

4. *Civil versus Criminal Enforcement.* As Professor David Ulhmann has noted, "Congress made only limited distinctions between acts that could result in criminal, civil, or administrative enforcement." Uhlmann, Prosecutorial Discretion and Environmental Crime, 38 Harv. Envtl. L. Rev. 159, 162 (2014). This lack of clarity raises the question: when *should* the government initiate criminal as opposed to civil enforcement proceedings? See EPA, Parallel Proceedings Policy Memo (Sept. 24, 2007); U.S. DOJ, Integrated Enforcement Policy, Directive 99-21 (April 20, 1999); U.S. DOJ, Global Settlement Policy, Directive 99-20 (April 20, 1999). Some private practitioners suggest that the federal government has "over-criminalized" environmental law in recent years. See, e.g., Buente & Thomson, *supra.* Others have suggested that the growing criminalization of environmental law, and the lack of predictability about when the government will proceed with a criminal prosecution, have the potential to undermine compliance rather than promote it:

> The disturbing trend toward criminalization of environmental violations continues. EPA criminal investigators are likely to appear in any enforcement effort by EPA. It has reached the point where it is impossible to counsel clients on what kinds of violations will not be treated criminally. While EPA may revel in this lack of predictability, it is becoming more and more difficult for companies, plant managers, and environmental professionals to operate from day to day without fear of being indicted. . . . This atmosphere of fear and unpredictability undermines industry's ability to make intelligent decisions regarding the operation of its facilities and to attract and retain highly competent individuals to run them. In the long run, this will undermine environmental compliance and cause relations between EPA and industry to become increasingly hostile, instead of cooperative, to the detriment of the environment. [Gaynor & Lippard, Environmental Enforcement: Industry Should Not Be Complacent, 32 Envtl. L. Rep. 10488, 10489 (2002).]

Professor Uhlmann, a former DOJ official, has offered a different perspective. Prosecutorial Discretion and Environmental Crime, *supra*; Environmental Crime Comes of Age: The Evolution of Criminal Enforcement in the Environmental Regulatory Scheme, 2009 Utah L. Rev. 1223, 1252. Uhlmann suggests that the void-for-vagueness doctrine and the rule of lenity have mitigated some of the problems with criminalization and that many strategies are available to reduce the risk of overly broad prosecutorial discretion. He concludes that DOJ prosecutors generally have exercised prosecutorial discretion reasonably in deciding which cases to prosecute criminally.

5. *False Statements*. The environmental statutes have separate provisions criminalizing the knowing omission of material information or submission of false material statements or certifications in applications, records, reports, or other documents and the knowing falsification of or tampering with monitoring devices. E.g., CWA §309(c)(4); RCRA §3008(d)(3); CAA §113(c)(2). The government continues to prosecute false statements, tampering, and related offenses. See, e.g., United States v. White, 270 F.3d 356 (6th Cir. 2001); United States v. Fern, 155 F.3d 1318 (11th Cir. 1998). See also Brickey, Rhetoric, *supra*, at 115 (false statement and monitoring charges often accompany alleged substantive violations because defendants file false statements and lie to cover up regulatory noncompliance).

6. For recent discussion of environmental criminal enforcement cases, see Solow & Carpenter's annual surveys, The State of Environmental Crime Enforcement: A Survey of Developments in 2013, Daily Env't Rep. (BNA), April 11, 2014; Daily Env't Rep. (BNA) March 15, 2013; Daily Env't Rep (BNA), Mar. 16, 2012, at 51. For a DOJ review, see Environment & Natural Resources Division, U.S. DOJ, Summary of Litigation Accomplishments: Fiscal Year 2013. DOJ reports that it prosecuted cases against 87 defendants in 2013, and defendants were sentenced to 65 years in jail and $79 million in fines and penalties. Id. at 7.

7. In Southern Union Co. v. United States, 132 S. Ct. 2344 (2012), the Supreme Court held that under the Sixth Amendment it is up to juries, not judges, to make the factual findings necessary to increase a criminal defendant's maximum potential sentence in RCRA cases, applying the Court's opinion in Apprendi v. New Jersey, 530 U.S. 466 (2000). See also Alleyne v. United States, 133 S. Ct. 2151 (2013). In *Southern Union*, the facts at issue involved the number of days the defendant violated RCRA.

4.   *Private Enforcement of Statutory Violations: Citizen Suits*

The federal environmental laws typically allow citizens to bring suit against violators. See, e.g., CWA §505; CAA §304; RCRA §7002. We make two points concerning citizen suits in the first section of this chapter that are worth repeating here. First, citizen suits are intended to "supplement," not displace, government enforcement actions, as the Supreme Court reinforced in its *Gwaltney* decision, excerpted below. Second, despite this "supplemental" role, citizens have been quite active under several statutes in filing suits against violators, especially under the Clean Water Act for violations that violators disclose in their publicly accessible DMRs. May, Citizen Suits and Defenses against Them (2011), http://files.ali-cle.org/thumbs/datastorage/skoobesruoc/pdf/CS028_chapter_10_thumb.pdf, provides statistics on citizen suits in addition to an analysis of the role of such suits. The question of when citizens may sue violators has raised numerous issues and triggered considerable litigation. *Gwaltney* is one of the seminal decisions.

GWALTNEY OF SMITHFIELD, LTD. v. CHESAPEAKE BAY FOUNDATION, INC.
484 U.S. 49 (1987)

Justice MARSHALL delivered the opinion of the Court.

In this case, we must decide whether §505(a) of the Clean Water Act [CWA], also known as the Federal Water Pollution Control Act, 33 U.S.C. §1365(a), confers federal jurisdiction over citizen suits for wholly past violations.

I.

... The holder of a federal NPDES permit [issued under the Act] is subject to enforcement action by the Administrator [of EPA] for failure to comply with the conditions of the permit. ... The holder of a state NPDES permit is subject to both federal and state enforcement action for failure to comply. §§1319, 1342(b)(7). In the absence of federal or state enforcement, private citizens may commence civil actions against any person "alleged to be in violation of" the conditions of either a federal or state NPDES permit. §1365(a)(1). If the citizen prevails in such an action, the court may order injunctive relief and/or impose civil penalties payable to the United States Treasury. §1365(a).

[In 1974, Virginia issued a CWA permit to a predecessor of Gwaltney authorizing the discharge of seven pollutants from the company's meatpacking plant into the Pagan River in Smithfield, Virginia. The permit established effluent limitations, monitoring requirements, and other conditions of discharge. Between 1981 and 1984, Gwaltney repeatedly violated the permit by exceeding applicable effluent limitations for five of the covered pollutants. The last reported violation occurred in May 1984, after Gwaltney installed upgraded waste treatment technology.

Chesapeake Bay Foundation and NRDC notified Gwaltney, EPA, and the Virginia State Water Control Board in February 1984 that they intended to commence a citizen suit under the CWA based on Gwaltney's permit violations. The two nonprofit organizations filed suit in June 1984, alleging that Gwaltney "has violated ... [and] will continue to violate its NPDES permit." They sought declaratory and injunctive relief, civil penalties, and an award of attorneys' fees and costs. The district court granted partial summary judgment for the plaintiffs, finding Gwaltney "to have violated and to be in violation" of the Act. Before the district court reached a decision on the appropriate remedy, Gwaltney moved to dismiss the action for lack of subject matter jurisdiction. It argued that §505(a) requires that a defendant be violating the Act at the time of suit; Gwaltney's last recorded violation occurred several weeks before plaintiffs filed their complaint. The district court denied the motion, concluding that §505 authorizes citizens to bring enforcement actions on the basis of wholly past violations. It held in the alternative that it had jurisdiction under §505 because the complaint alleged in good faith that Gwaltney was continuing to violate its permit at the time suit was filed. The Court of Appeals affirmed.]

II.

A.

It is well settled that "the starting point for interpreting a statute is the language of the statute itself." The Court of Appeals concluded that the "to be in violation" language of §505 is ambiguous, whereas petitioner asserts that it plainly precludes the construction adopted below. We must agree with the Court of Appeals that §505 is not a provision in which Congress' limpid prose puts an end to all dispute. But to acknowledge ambiguity is not to conclude that all interpretations are equally plausible. The most natural reading of "to be in violation" is a requirement that citizen-plaintiffs allege a state of either continuous or intermittent violation—that is, a reasonable likelihood that a past polluter will continue to pollute in the future. Congress could have phrased its requirement in language that looked to the past ("to have violated"), but it did not choose this readily available option.

Respondents urge that the choice of the phrase "to be in violation," rather than phrasing more clearly directed to the past, is a "careless accident," the result of a "debatable lapse of syntactical precision." But the prospective orientation of that phrase could not have escaped Congress' attention. Congress used identical language in the citizen suit provisions of several other environmental statutes that authorize only prospective relief. See, e.g., [CAA §304; RCRA §7002; TSCA §20]. Moreover, Congress has demonstrated in yet other statutory provisions that it knows how to avoid this prospective implication by using language that explicitly targets wholly past violations.[2]

Respondents seek to counter this reasoning by observing that Congress also used the phrase "is in violation" in §309(a) of the Act, which authorizes the Administrator of EPA to issue compliance orders. That language is incorporated by reference in §309(b), which authorizes the Administrator to bring civil enforcement actions. Because it is little questioned that the Administrator may bring enforcement actions to recover civil penalties for wholly past violations, respondents contend, the parallel language of §309(a) and §505(a) must mean that citizens, too, may maintain such actions.

Although this argument has some initial plausibility, it cannot withstand close scrutiny and comparison of the two statutory provisions. The Administrator's ability to seek civil penalties is not discussed in either §309(a) or §309(b); civil penalties are not mentioned until §309(d), which does not contain the "is in violation" language. This Court recently has recognized that §309(d) constitutes a separate grant of enforcement authority: "Section 1319 [§309] does not intertwine equitable relief with the imposition of civil penalties. Instead each kind of relief is separably authorized in a separate and distinct statutory provision. Subsection (b), providing injunctive relief, is

<hr/>

2. For example, the Solid Waste Disposal Act was amended in 1984 to authorize citizen suits against any "past or present" generator, transporter, owner, or operator of a treatment, storage, or disposal facility "who has contributed or who is contributing" to the "past or present" handling, storage, treatment, transportation, or disposal of certain hazardous wastes. 42 U.S.C. §6972(a)(1)(B). Prior to 1984, the Solid Waste Disposal Act contained language identical to that of §505(a) of the Clean Water Act, authorizing citizen suits against any person "alleged to be in violation" of waste disposal permits or standards. 42 U.S.C. §6972(a)(1). Even more on point, the most recent Clean Water Act amendments permit EPA to assess administrative penalties without judicial process on any person who "has violated" the provisions of the Act. Water Quality Act of 1987, §314, Pub. L. 100-4, 101 Stat. 46.

independent of subsection (d), which provides only for civil penalties." Tull v. United States, 481 U.S. 412, 425 (1987).

In contrast, §505 of the Act does not authorize civil penalties separately from injunctive relief; rather, the two forms of relief are referred to in the same subsection, even in the same sentence. 33 U.S.C. §1365(a). The citizen suit provision suggests a connection between injunctive relief and civil penalties that is noticeably absent from the provision authorizing agency enforcement. A comparison of §309 and §505 thus supports rather than refutes our conclusion that citizens, unlike the Administrator, may seek civil penalties only in a suit brought to enjoin or otherwise abate an ongoing violation.

B.

Our reading of the "to be in violation" language of §505(a) is bolstered by the language and structure of the rest of the citizen suit provisions in §505 of the Act. These provisions together make plain that the interest of the citizen-plaintiff is primarily forward-looking.

One of the most striking indicia of the prospective orientation of the citizen suit is the pervasive use of the present tense throughout §505. A citizen suit may be brought only for violation of a permit limitation "which is in effect" under the Act. 33 U.S.C. §1365(f). Citizen-plaintiffs must give notice to the alleged violator, the Administrator of EPA, and the State in which the alleged violation "occurs."§1365(b)(1)(A). A Governor of a State may sue as a citizen when the Administrator fails to enforce an effluent limitation "the violation of which is occurring in another State and is causing an adverse effect on the public health or welfare in his State." §1365(h). The most telling use of the present tense is in the definition of "citizen" as "a person . . . having an interest which is or may be adversely affected" by the defendant's violations of the Act. §1365(g). This definition makes plain what the undeviating use of the present tense strongly suggests: the harm sought to be addressed by the citizen suit lies in the present or the future, not in the past.

Any other conclusion would render incomprehensible §505's notice provision, which requires citizens to give 60 days' notice of their intent to sue to the alleged violator as well as to the Administrator and the State. §1365(b)(1)(A). If the Administrator or the State commences enforcement action within that 60-day period, the citizen suit is barred, presumably because governmental action has rendered it unnecessary. §1365(b)(1)(B). It follows logically that the purpose of notice to the alleged violator is to give it an opportunity to bring itself into complete compliance with the Act and thus likewise render unnecessary a citizen suit. If we assume, as respondents urge, that citizen suits may target wholly past violations, the requirement of notice to the alleged violator becomes gratuitous. Indeed, respondents, in propounding their interpretation of the Act, can think of no reason for Congress to require such notice other than that "it seemed right" to inform an alleged violator that it was about to be sued.

Adopting respondents' interpretation of §505's jurisdictional grant would create a second and even more disturbing anomaly. The bar on citizen suits when governmental enforcement action is under way suggests that the citizen suit is meant to supplement rather than to supplant governmental action. The legislative history of the Act reinforces this view of the role of the citizen suit. The Senate Report noted that "[t]he Committee intends the great volume of enforcement actions [to] be brought by the State," and that citizen suits are proper only "if the Federal, State, and local agencies fail to exercise their enforcement responsibility." S. Rep. No. 92-414, p. 64 (1971). Permitting citizen suits for wholly past violations of the Act could undermine the supplementary role envisioned for the citizen suit. This danger is best illustrated by an example. Suppose that the Administrator identified a violator of the Act and issued a compliance order under §309(a). Suppose further that the Administrator agreed not to assess or otherwise seek civil penalties on the condition that the violator take some extreme corrective action, such as to install particularly effective but expensive machinery, that it otherwise would not be obliged to take. If citizens could file suit, months or years later, in order to seek the civil penalties that the Administrator chose to forgo, then the Administrator's discretion to enforce the Act in the public interest would be curtailed considerably. The same might be said of the discretion of state enforcement authorities. Respondents' interpretation of the scope of the citizen suit would change the nature of the citizens' role from interstitial to potentially intrusive. We cannot agree that Congress intended such a result. . . .

III.

Our conclusion that §505 does not permit citizen suits for wholly past violations does not necessarily dispose of this lawsuit, as both lower courts recognized. The District Court found persuasive the fact that "[respondents'] allegation in the complaint, that Gwaltney was continuing to violate its NPDES permit when plaintiffs filed suit[,] appears to have been made fully in good faith." On this basis, the District Court explicitly held, albeit in a footnote, that "even if Gwaltney were correct that a district court has no jurisdiction over citizen suits based entirely on unlawful conduct that occurred entirely in the past, the Court would still have jurisdiction here." The Court of Appeals acknowledged, also in a footnote, that "[a] very sound argument can be made that [respondents'] allegations of continuing violations were made in good faith," but expressly declined to rule on this alternative holding. Because we agree that §505 confers jurisdiction over citizen suits when the citizen-plaintiffs make a good-faith allegation of continuous or intermittent violation, we remand the case to the Court of Appeals for further consideration.

Petitioner argues that citizen-plaintiffs must prove their allegations of ongoing noncompliance before jurisdiction attaches under §505. We cannot agree. The statute does not require that a defendant "be in violation" of the Act at the commencement of suit; rather, the statute requires that a defendant be "alleged to be in violation." Petitioner's construction of the Act reads the word "alleged" out of §505. As petitioner itself is quick to note in other contexts, there is no reason to believe that Congress' drafting of §505 was sloppy or haphazard. We agree with the Solicitor General that "Congress's use of the phrase 'alleged to be in violation' reflects a conscious sensitivity to the practical difficulties of detecting and proving chronic episodic violations of environmental standards." Brief for United States as Amicus Curiae 18. Our acknowledgment that Congress intended a good-faith allegation to suffice for jurisdictional purposes, however, does not give litigants license to flood the courts with suits premised on baseless allegations. Rule 11 of the Federal Rules of Civil Procedure, which requires pleadings to be based on a good-faith belief, formed after reasonable inquiry, that are "well grounded in fact," adequately protects defendants from frivolous allegations.

Petitioner contends that failure to require proof of allegations under §505 would permit plaintiffs whose allegations of ongoing violation are reasonable but untrue to maintain suit in federal court even though they lack constitutional standing. Petitioner reasons that if a defendant is in complete compliance with the Act at the time of suit, plaintiffs have suffered no injury remediable by the citizen suit provisions of the Act. Petitioner, however, fails to recognize that our standing cases uniformly recognize that allegations of injury are sufficient to invoke the jurisdiction of a court. . . .

Petitioner also worries that our construction of §505 would permit citizen-plaintiffs, if their allegations of ongoing noncompliance become false at some later point in the litigation because the defendant begins to comply with the Act, to continue nonetheless to press their suit to conclusion. According to petitioner, such a result would contravene both the prospective purpose of the citizen suit provisions and the "case or controversy" requirement of Article III. Longstanding principles of mootness, however, prevent the maintenance of suit when " 'there is no reasonable expectation that the wrong will be repeated.' " United States v. W.T. Grant Co., 345 U.S. 629, 633 (1953). In seeking to have a case dismissed as moot, however, the defendant's burden "is a heavy one." [Id.] The defendant must demonstrate that it is *absolutely clear* that the allegedly wrongful behavior could not reasonably be expected to recur." United States v. Phosphate Export Ass'n, Inc., 393 U.S. 199, 203 (1968) (emphasis added). Mootness doctrine thus protects defendants from the maintenance of suit under the Clean Water Act based solely on violations wholly unconnected to any present or future wrongdoing, while it also protects plaintiffs from defendants who seek to evade sanction by predictable "protestations of repentance and reform." United States v. Oregon State Medical Society, 343 U.S. 326, 333 (1952).[6]

Because the court below erroneously concluded that respondents could maintain an action based on wholly past violations of the Act, it declined to decide whether respondents' complaint contained a good-faith allegation of ongoing violation by petitioner. We therefore remand the case for consideration of this question. . . .

NOTES AND QUESTIONS ABOUT CITIZEN SUITS

1. *Continuous and Intermittent Violations and Mootness.* On what basis did the Court in *Gwaltney* conclude that EPA may seek to recover civil penalties for past violations but that private citizens may not? Given that Gwaltney's violations ceased before the filing of the complaint against it, what was the purpose of the Court's remand order? After *Gwaltney*, why can't a permit holder consistently defeat citizen suits by ceasing violations as soon as it receives notice that someone intends to file a citizen suit and repeating the process if violations recur and it receives another notice of an intended suit?

On remand in *Gwaltney*, the Fourth Circuit held that the plaintiff may prevail "either (1) by proving violations that continue on or after the date the complaint is

---

6. Under the Act, plaintiffs are also protected from the suddenly repentant defendant by the authority of the district courts to award litigation costs "whenever the court determines such an award is appropriate." 33 U.S.C. §1365(d). The legislative history of this provision states explicitly that the award of costs "should extend to plaintiffs in actions which result in successful abatement but do not reach a verdict. For instance, if as a result of a citizen proceeding and before a verdict is issued, a defendant abated a violation, the court may award litigation expenses borne by the plaintiffs in prosecuting such actions." S. Rep. No. 92-414, p. 81 (1972), 2 Leg. Hist. 1499.

filed, or (2) by adducing continuing evidence from which a reasonable trier of fact could find a likelihood of a recurrence in intermittent or sporadic violations." Chesapeake Bay Found., Inc. v. Gwaltney of Smithfield, Ltd., 844 F.2d 170, 171-172 (4th Cir. 1988). The same court subsequently upheld the district court's finding of ongoing violations because, at the time the original suit was filed, there was a reasonable likelihood of intermittent or sporadic violations, even though, as it turned out, such violations did not recur. Chesapeake Bay Found., Inc. v. Gwaltney of Smithfield, Ltd., 890 F.2d 690, 693-694 (4th Cir. 1989). What is a sporadic violation? See Sierra Club v. Shell Oil Co., 817 F.2d 1169 (5th Cir. 1987) (given that CWA effluent limitations assume 95 to 99 percent compliance, permit compliance rates above 95 percent do not put a company in violation of an NPDES permit). When should continuing migration of pollutants from past discharges qualify as an ongoing violation? Sierra Club v. El Paso Gold Mines, Inc., 421 F.3d 1133 (10th Cir. 2005) (addressing discharges from a former mining area).

2. *More on Standing.* Steel Co. v. Citizens for a Better Env't, 523 U.S. 83, 105 (1998), held that plaintiffs lacked standing to sue for wholly past reporting violations under EPCRA because the complaint "fails the third test of standing, redressability." Among other things, the Court held that requiring the company to pay EPCRA civil penalties to the Treasury and to reimburse the citizens group's litigation expenses did not satisfy this prong of the standing test. Has the majority's decision significantly impaired the usefulness of citizen suits as a supplement to government enforcement against regulated private entities? Is the decision unique to EPCRA, or does its reasoning apply to other citizen suit provisions as well? See generally *Steel Company Colloquium*, 12 Tul. Envtl. L.J. 1-86 (1998).

We discuss standing in detail in Chapter 3, section A.1, and include there an excerpt of the Court's decision in Friends of the Earth, Inc. v. Laidlaw Envtl. Serv. (TOC), Inc., 528 U.S. 167 (2000), another citizen suit. Standing rulings in cases that are not citizen suits also can affect the scope of citizen suit standing. In Massachusetts v. EPA, 549 U.S. 497 (2007), which is reproduced in Chapter 12, the Court reviewed standing in the context of a challenge by environmental groups and states to EPA's denial of a rulemaking petition to address climate change under the CAA. In a 5-4 decision, the Court held that Massachusetts had standing, in part because the state was "entitled to special solicitude in our standing analysis." Id. at 521. In his dissent, Chief Justice Roberts argued that the Court was "chang[ing] the rule" for standing. Id. at 536. In his view, relaxing standing requirements because a state is seeking review "has no basis in our jurisprudence. . . ." Id.

In Summers v. Earth Island Inst., 555 U.S. 488 (2009), the Court addressed standing in a case in which several environmental organizations challenged a Forest Service rule that provided that projects the Service had categorically excluded from NEPA EIS and EA requirements were also not subject to notice, comment, and appeal procedures. The Forest Service subsequently decided that projects categorically excluded from the EIS and EA requirements included certain fire rehabilitation activities and salvage timber sales because they do not cause a significant environmental impact. As a result, those projects would not be subject to notice, comment, and appeal procedures under the agency's rule. The Court held that the plaintiffs had failed to show injury in fact because they did not identify any application of the regulations (other than an application that had been resolved through a settlement) that "threatens imminent and concrete harm to the interests of their members." Id. at 495. The Court also rejected plaintiffs' argument that they suffered a procedural injury sufficient to create standing, notably that the Service was illegally denying the plaintiffs a congressionally created right to participate. It held that "deprivation of a procedural right without some concrete interest that is affected by the deprivation—a procedural right *in vacuo*—is insufficient to create Article III standing," using language repeated in Justice Kennedy's concurrence. Id. at 496.

In Monsanto Co. v. Geertson Seed Farms, 561 U.S. 139 (2010), the Court found standing in a case in which farmers who did not use a particular genetically engineered type of alfalfa brought a NEPA challenge to an agency action that allowed such alfalfa. The Court concluded that there was a "reasonable probability" that the farmers' crops would be infected by the genetically engineered alfalfa and this was enough to create the required injury in fact.

It remains to be seen what effect the Court's 2013 standing decision in Clapper, Director of National Intelligence v. Amnesty Int'l USA, 133 S. Ct. 1138 (2013), (holding that the plaintiffs lacked standing in a case in the national security arena) may have on environmental cases. *Clapper* is discussed in Chapter 3's coverage of standing.

3. *The Notice Requirement.* What is the effect of failing to provide the requisite prior notice? In Hallstrom v. Tillamook County, 493 U.S. 20 (1989), the Court held that the 60-day notice requirement of RCRA's citizen suit provision, §7002(b), is a jurisdictional prerequisite. Accordingly, when a plaintiff fails to comply with it, the suit must be dismissed. Issues concerning the adequacy of notice have been raised as well. E.g., Friends of the Earth, Inc. v. Gaston Copper Recycling Corp., 629 F.3d 387, 401 (4th Cir. 2011) (reviewing the case law concerning CWA notice requirements and dismissing certain claims of violation because the plaintiffs had failed to identify the alleged violations sufficiently in the notice letter).

4. *The Role of Citizen Suits Revisited: The Issue of Multiple Enforcement Actions.* As noted above, citizen suits play an important role in environmental enforcement but they are considered to play an "interstitial" role and be supplementary to state and federal enforcement, as the Court noted in its *Gwaltney* decision. As might be expected, a legal regime that allows for multiple prospective enforcers (federal and/ or state government enforcers as well as private enforcers), and acknowledges the possibility of suits in different forums (federal judicial and administrative as well as state judicial and administrative forums) opens the door for considerable dispute concerning the viability of citizen suits in different circumstances. For example, what should be the fate of a citizen suit if a local, state, or federal enforcer brings suit, or enters into a settlement with the regulated party for the same alleged violations? When should the citizens be allowed to proceed on a parallel track? When should the citizens' suit be consolidated with the government's suit? When should the citizen suit be dismissed? When are these issues "jurisdictional" versus "claim-processing" in nature? Louisiana Envtl. Action Network v. City of Baton Rouge, 677 F.3d 737 (5th Cir. 2012), discusses the significance of this last distinction and whether the CWA diligent prosecution bar to citizen suits is a jurisdictional limitation on such suits.

Congress has provided limited guidance concerning these issues. For example, the CWA, RCRA and CAA preclude citizen suits if federal or state authorities have commenced and are "diligently prosecuting" their own civil or criminal enforcement action against the alleged violator. See, e.g., CWA §505(b)(1)(B); RCRA §7002(b)(1)(B); CAA §304(b)(1)(B). The CWA also bars citizen suits seeking civil penalties if EPA has filed an *administrative* enforcement action or a state "has commenced and is diligently prosecuting an action under a State law comparable to [§1319(g), EPA's administrative enforcement authority]." §309(g)(6)(A).

The courts have addressed these issues in a wide variety of circumstances. What constitutes "diligent prosecution" for purposes of determining whether a federal or state court or administrative action precludes a citizen suit? In Piney Run Pres. Ass'n v. County Cmm'rs of Carroll County, 523 F.3d 453 (4th Cir. 2008), the Fourth Circuit held that "a CWA enforcement action will be considered diligent where it is capable of requiring compliance with the Act and is in good faith calculated to do so" and determined that the government was engaging in diligent prosecution.

In Paper, Allied-Indus., Chem. and Energy Workers Int'l Union v. Continental Carbon Co., 428 F.3d 1285, 1288 (10th Cir. 2005), the court summarized several of the other appellate courts' decisions concerning *state administrative enforcement actions*, and adopted the Eleventh Circuit's "rough comparability" approach, rather than what it characterized as the "more forgiving" "overall comparability" standard that it indicates the First and Eighth Circuits have adopted. The court held that "three categories of state-law provisions—penalty-assessment, public participation, and judicial review—must be roughly comparable to the corresponding categories of federal provisions." The Eighth Circuit addressed the "comparability" element of §309(g)(6)(A) in Arkansas Wildlife Fed'n v. ICI Am., Inc., 29 F.3d 376, 381 (8th Cir. 1994), holding that a state administrative enforcement action barred a citizen suit. The court reached two conclusions concerning the definition of "comparability." The first is:

> We agree with the reasoning in [North & South Rivers Watershed Ass'n v. Town of Scituate, 949 F.2d 552 (1st Cir. 1991)], that the comparability requirement may be satisfied so long as the state law contains comparable penalty provisions which the state is authorized to enforce, has the same overall enforcement goals as the federal CWA, provides interested citizens a meaningful opportunity to participate at significant stages of the decision-making process, and adequately safeguards their legitimate substantive interests.

The court added, however, that a state statute that seemingly is comparable for the reasons discussed in the preceding quoted language is only "presumptively" so; the plaintiffs have an opportunity to demonstrate that, on the facts of the case, the state did not provide a "meaningful opportunity to participate in the administrative enforcement case." Id. at 382. For a decision holding that a state law is not comparable to EPA's and, therefore, action under the state law did not bar a citizen suit, see McAbee v. Fort Payne, 318 F.3d 1248 (11th Cir. 2003) (applying the "rough comparability" test).

Another issue in this arena is: what are the consequences for a citizen suit if a government enters into a settlement with an alleged violator *after* the citizen files suit? More generally, as the Fifth Circuit noted in Environmental Conservation Org. v. City of Dallas, 529 F.3d 519, 526 (5th Cir. 2008), the CWA is "silent as to which mechanisms may be invoked to dispense with citizen suits . . . that have been properly commenced under [CWA] Section 1365(b)." One environmental advocate suggests that the federal appeals courts "'are beginning to fracture all over' regarding the issue of the impact of a state enforcement action in a case where [proper notice has been provided]." State Consent Orders Can Shield Polluters from Federal Citizen Lawsuits, Group Told, 40 Env't Rep. (BNA) 654 (Mar. 20, 2009). The Second Circuit, in

Atlantic States Legal Found. v. Eastman Kodak Co., 933 F.2d 124, 125 (2d Cir. 1991), held that a citizen suit could not continue after the state entered into a settlement with the defendant, so long as the state settlement "reasonably assures that the violations alleged in the citizen suit have ceased and will not recur." The court held that the state case precluded the citizen suit even though the state did not initiate its enforcement proceeding during the 60-day statutory notice period. The court allowed the citizens to seek recovery of their attorneys' fees on the ground that their action may have helped trigger the state settlement. A year later, the same circuit held that another citizen suit by the same plaintiff was not moot, in a situation in which a local government agency entered into a settlement after the citizen had filed suit and the settlement reasonably assured that the violations would not recur. The court distinguished the two cases on several grounds, including the size of the penalties involved (in the first case, the total penalty was $2 million, while in the latter it was under $10,000) and the identity of the government actors (in the first case it was the state, while in the second it was a local government environmental agency). Atlantic States Legal Found. v. Pan Am. Tanning Corp., 993 F.2d 1017 (2d Cir. 1993). In *City of Dallas, supra*, the Fifth Circuit dismissed a citizen suit as moot following a government settlement approved by a court, "apply[ing] the test that has been endorsed by the Second and Eighth Circuits, under which [the citizens'] claims for relief are moot unless . . . the citizen-suit plaintiff . . . proves that there is a realistic prospect that the violations alleged in its complaint will continue notwithstanding the consent decree." Id. at 528.

5. *The Scope of the Citizen Suit Provisions.* What kinds of alleged violations may form the basis for citizen suits? May a citizen suit be brought under the CWA for alleged violations of state water quality standards? In Northwest Envtl. Advocates v. City of Portland, 56 F.3d 979 (9th Cir. 1995), *reh'g denied*, 74 F.3d 945 (9th Cir. 1996), the court ruled that such a suit was proper, provided the defendant's permit includes an explicit condition that its discharges would not cause violations of water quality standards. Compare Oregon Natural Res. Council v. United States Forest Serv., 834 F.2d 842 (9th Cir. 1987) (citizen suit could not be brought to enjoin alleged violation of state water quality standard by a nonpoint source).

May a suit be brought to enforce state standards that exceed federal minimum requirements? The Second Circuit said no in Atlantic States Legal Found. v. Eastman Kodak Co., 12 F.3d 353, 358-360 (2d Cir. 1993). The Ninth Circuit has considered this issue as well. Community Ass'n for Restoration of the Env't v. Henry Bosma Dairy, 305 F.3d 943 (9th Cir. 2002); Ashoff v. Ukiah, 130 F.3d 409 (9th Cir. 1997).

6. *Citizen Suits to Force Enforcement.* Is a citizen suit to compel EPA to enforce a pollution control requirement against an alleged violator likely to succeed? See Heckler v. Chaney, 470 U.S. 821 (1985), which holds that agency decisions not to take enforcement action are presumptively immune from judicial review.

7. Are there tools besides litigation available to citizens who are concerned that an authorized state is not effectively enforcing its environmental laws? See Hammond & Markell, Administrative Proxies for Judicial Review: Building Legitimacy from the Inside Out, 37 Harv. Envtl. L. Rev. 313 (2013).

8. *The Constitutionality of Citizen Suits.* Miller, The Constitutionality of Citizen Suit Provisions in Federal Environmental Statutes, 27 J. Envtl. L & Litig. 401 (2012), surveys the Supreme Court's decisions concerning the constitutionality of citizen suits and scholarly commentary. He notes that "[c]ritics challenge that citizen suits violate three aspects of Article II: the Vesting Clause, the Appointments Clause, and the Faithful Execution Clause." Id. at 404-405. To date, these critics have not

persuaded the Supreme Court. In his concurrence in *Friends of the Earth, Inc. v. Laidlaw*, 528 U.S. 167 (2000), however, Justice Kennedy stated that "[d]ifficult and fundamental questions are raised when we ask whether exactions of public fines by private litigants, and the delegation of Executive power which might be inferable from the authorization, are permissible in view of the responsibilities committed to the Executive by Article II of the Constitution." Id. at 197.

9. *Attorneys' Fees.* As the Note on Recovery of Attorneys' Fees in Chapter 3 indicates, the ability of public interest groups to recover their attorneys' fees and court costs can be an important inducement to initiate litigation, including citizen suits. Do the environmental laws provide for recovery of such fees? See, e.g., CWA §505(d); CERCLA §310(f); RCRA §7002(e). The Tenth Circuit construed the RCRA attorneys' fee provision in *Browder v. City of Moab*, 427 F.3d 717, 723 (10th Cir. 2005), holding that the plaintiff could recover fees because it prevailed on at least one claim, even though it lost on others, and noting that the district court "retains discretion to adjust the award commensurate with the degree of success obtained." As the Note in Chapter 3 also indicates, *Buckhannon Bd. & Care Home, Inc. v. West Virginia Dep't of Health & Human Res.*, 532 U.S. 598, 600 (2001), rejected the "catalyst" theory, under which a party is a "prevailing party" if its lawsuit brings about a voluntary change in the defendant's conduct. The appellate courts have since addressed whether that conclusion applies under the citizen suit provisions of several environmental statutes. See, e.g., *Southern Alliance For Clean Energy v. Duke Energy Carolinas, LLC*, 650 F.3d 401 (4th Cir. 2011) (approving attorneys' fees for plaintiffs under the CAA attorneys' fees provision, which allows a court to award attorneys' fees "whenever the court determines such award is appropriate," 42 U.S.C. §7604(d), on the ground that the plaintiffs had enjoyed "some success."); *Ohio River Valley Envtl. Coal. v. Green Valley Coal Co.*, 511 F.3d 407, 415 (4th Cir. 2007) (holding that the SMCRA's "whenever appropriate" fee-shifting provision authorizes recovery under the "catalyst theory"). Cf. *Sierra Club v. Hamilton County Bd. of County Comm'rs*, 504 F.3d 634 (6th Cir. 2007) (holding that plaintiff could recover attorneys' fees under the CWA because it was a "prevailing or substantially prevailing party" and not reaching the question of whether the catalyst theory applies under the CWA).

The amount as well as the availability of fee awards is often at issue. In *Pennsylvania v. Delaware Valley Citizens' Council for Clean Air*, 483 U.S. 711 (1987), a plurality of the Court ruled that the CAA citizen suit provision does not permit enhancement of a reasonable "lodestar" fee to compensate for the attorney's risk of not being paid. *City of Burlington v. Dague*, 505 U.S. 557 (1992), established that courts may not enhance fee awards in RCRA or CWA citizen suits above the lodestar amount to reflect the fact that the plaintiff's attorneys were retained on a contingent-fee basis and thus assumed the risk of receiving no payment at all. Are there situations in which an attorney may receive a fee higher than that produced by the lodestar? If so, under what circumstances? See *Perdue v. Kenny A. ex rel. Winn*, 559 U.S. 542 (2010).

Problem 10-1

Chemicals, Inc. (CI), located in a state that EPA has authorized to administer the CWA NPDES program (covered in Chapter 7), has had a NPDES permit since 2000. It never had a violation until 2014. On January 3, 2014, a CI engineer discovered that CI's treatment system is not working properly. The reason for the malfunction is that beginning on January 2, 2014, CI increased its production in order to meet new orders and it therefore began generating more waste. The plant engineer thought that the existing biological treatment system was adequate to treat this expanded volume of waste.

On January 10, 2014, CI informed the state environmental agency (the DEP) by letter of the violation and advised the DEP that the company would take steps immediately to fix the treatment system. The company followed up with a letter on March 1, in which it informed the DEP that while the company thought the problem was an anomaly and would take care of itself, to be safe it would install an upgraded biological treatment unit. The company expressed its commitment to full compliance with the environmental laws and its willingness to work with the DEP to be a model company.

The upgraded biological treatment unit that the company has ordered will cost $100,000, and it will cost an additional $1,000 per month to operate (to buy new biological organisms, etc.). It will take the company until January 1, 2015, to install the equipment and make it operational. The company will pay the $100,000 cost of the equipment on January 1, 2015, when it becomes operational. The company typically gets a 10 percent return on its money.

The penalty for violating the CWA is a maximum of $37,500 for each day a violation continues.

Assume the following facts:

1. In determining an appropriate penalty, the State DEP typically begins by calculating the statutory maximum.
2. The DEP also typically determines the economic benefit of noncompliance. In doing so, it uses EPA's BEN model. The basic methodology is described in the EPA's 1999 BEN User's Manual (this is a paraphrased version of the methodology):

   BEN calculates the economic benefits gained from delaying and avoiding required environmental expenditures. Such expenditures can include (1) capital investments (e.g., pollution control equipment), (2) one-time nondepreciable expenditures (e.g., setting a reporting system, or acquiring land), (3) annually recurring costs (e.g., operating and maintenance costs). Each of these expenditures can be either delayed or avoided. BEN's baseline assumption is that capital investments and one-time nondepreciable expenditures are merely delayed over the period of noncompliance, whereas annual costs are avoided entirely over this period. BEN does allow you, however, to analyze any combination of delayed and avoided expenditures.

   The economic benefit calculation must incorporate the economic concepts of the "time value of money." Stated simply, a dollar today is worth more than a dollar tomorrow, because you can invest today's dollar to start earning a return immediately. Thus, the further in the future the dollar is, the less it is worth in "present-value" terms. Similarly, the greater the time value of money (i.e., the greater the "discount" or "compound" rate used to derive the present value), the lower the present value of future costs.

3. In addition, the DEP generally calculates what it refers to as the "gravity" component of the penalty, based on the seriousness of the violations, good faith efforts to comply, and so forth. Assume that DEP staff have already taken this step and determined that the gravity component of the penalty should be $50,000.

4. The DEP has adopted EPA's 2000 Self-Audit Policy, 65 Fed. Reg. 9618 (2000), and the federal agency's 1998 Supplemental Environmental Projects (SEPs) Policy, 63 Fed. Reg. 24,796 (1998). CI is interested in using one or both of these policies to persuade the DEP to minimize the penalty. Ideally, CI would like to avoid paying any penalty at all.

5. Attorneys for the DEP, CI, and a local citizens group that is concerned about CI's dischargers, Save America's Environment (SAE), are meeting next week to discuss the violations and possible ways to address them. The SAE attorney has notified both the DEP and CI attorneys that it believes a significant penalty is warranted, and that SAE also endorses requiring CI to improve the environmental management of its facility, including changing its production process to reduce its generation of hazardous materials that require treatment. The SAE attorney also has informed the DEP and CI attorneys that SAE is considering filing a citizen suit against CI for its violations.

6. An EPA attorney is planning to attend the meeting as well. EPA has informed the DEP that EPA thinks the violations warrant a penalty, and that EPA may initiate its own judicial enforcement action if the DEP does not resolve the case satisfactorily soon.

Each lawyer should prepare for the meeting by considering the following issues: (1) the maximum potential penalty for CI, (2) the amount of economic benefit that CI has gained through its noncompliance, (3) the extent to which the Self-Audit policy and/or the SEPs policy (the former is excerpted below and both are discussed later in this chapter) should be used to shape the outcome, (4) the issues associated with any lawsuit SAE might bring, (5) the issues associated with any lawsuit EPA might bring, and (6) the strategy each party should pursue during the meeting and thereafter.

5. *Common Law versus Statutory Causes of Action*

In addition to statutory causes of action, either the government or a person may have a cause of action against an entity causing environmental harm, based on common law doctrines such as public and private nuisance. The *Boomer* case, set forth immediately below, is a landmark case in which the court in a common law nuisance action refused to order the closing of a plant responsible for generating air pollution that adversely affected neighboring property. The notes following *Boomer* consider not only alternative approaches to the damages versus injunction question but also the issue of whether judicial receptivity to requests for injunctive relief should differ depending upon whether the substantive source of law is common law or statutory or depending upon the identity of the plaintiff.

BOOMER v. ATLANTIC CEMENT CO.
26 N.Y.2d 219, 257 N.E.2d 870, 309 N.Y.S.2d 312 (1970)

BERGAN, Judge.

Defendant operates a large cement plant near Albany. These are actions for injunction and damages by neighboring land owners alleging injury to property from dirt, smoke and vibration emanating from the plant. A nuisance has been found after trial, temporary damages have been allowed; but an injunction has been denied.

The public concern with air pollution arising from many sources in industry and in transportation is currently accorded ever wider recognition accompanied by a growing sense of responsibility in State and Federal Governments to control it. Cement plants are obvious sources of air pollution in the neighborhoods where they operate.

But there is now before the court private litigation in which individual property owners have sought specific relief from a single plant operation. The threshold question raised by the division of view on this appeal is whether the court should resolve the litigation between the parties now before it as equitably as seems possible; or whether, seeking promotion of the general public welfare, it should channel private litigation into broad public objectives.

A court performs its essential function when it decides the rights of parties before it. Its decision of private controversies may sometimes greatly affect public issues. Large questions of law are often resolved by the manner in which private litigation is decided. But this is normally an incident to the court's main function to settle controversy. It is a rare exercise of judicial power to use a decision in private litigation as a purposeful mechanism to achieve direct public objectives greatly beyond the rights and interests before the court.

Effective control of air pollution is a problem presently far from solution even with the full public and financial powers of government. In large measure adequate technical procedures are yet to be developed and some that appear possible may be economically impracticable.

It seems apparent that the amelioration of air pollution will depend on technical research in great depth; on a carefully balanced consideration of the economic impact of close regulation; and of the actual effect on public health. It is likely to require massive public expenditure and to demand more than any local community can accomplish and to depend on regional and interstate controls.

A court should not try to do this on its own as a by-product of private litigation and it seems manifest that the judicial establishment is neither equipped in the limited nature of any judgment it can pronounce nor prepared to lay down and implement an effective policy for the elimination of air pollution. This is an area beyond the circumference of one private lawsuit. It is a direct responsibility for government and should not thus be undertaken as an incident to solving a dispute between property owners and a single cement plant—one of many—in the Hudson River valley. . . .

The ground for the denial of injunction, notwithstanding the finding both that there is a nuisance and that plaintiffs have been damaged substantially, is the large disparity in economic consequences of the nuisance and of the injunction. This theory cannot, however, be sustained without overruling a doctrine which has been consistently reaffirmed in several leading cases in this court and which has never been disavowed here, namely that where a nuisance has been found and where there has been any substantial damage shown by the party complaining an injunction will be granted.

The rule in New York has been that such a nuisance will be enjoined although marked disparity be shown in economic consequence between the effect of the injunction and the effect of the nuisance.

The problem of disparity in economic consequence was sharply in focus in Whalen v. Union Bag & Paper Co., 208 N.Y. 1, 101 N.E. 805. A pulp mill entailing an investment of more than a million dollars polluted a stream in which plaintiff, who owned a farm, was "a lower riparian owner." The economic loss to plaintiff from this pollution was small. This court, reversing the Appellate Division, reinstated the injunction granted by the Special Term against the argument of the mill owner that in view of "the slight advantage to plaintiff and the great loss that will be inflicted on defendant" an injunction should not be granted. "Such a balancing of injuries cannot be justified by the circumstances of this case," Judge Werner noted. He continued: "Although the damage to the plaintiff may be slight as compared with the defendant's expense of abating the condition, that is not a good reason for refusing an injunction."

Thus the unconditional injunction granted at Special Term was reinstated. The rule laid down in that case, then, is that whenever the damage resulting from a nuisance is found not "unsubstantial," viz., $100 a year, injunction would follow. . . .

Although the court at Special Term and the Appellate Division held that injunction should be denied, it was found that plaintiffs had been damaged in various specific amounts up to the time of the trial and damages to the respective plaintiffs were awarded for those amounts. The effect of this was, injunction having been denied, plaintiffs could maintain successive actions at law for damages thereafter as further damage was incurred.

The court at Special Term also found the amount of permanent damage attributable to each plaintiff, for the guidance of the parties in the event both sides stipulated to the payment and acceptance of such permanent damage as a settlement of all the controversies among the parties. The total of permanent damages to all plaintiffs thus found was $185,000. . . .

This result at Special Term and at the Appellate Division is a departure from a rule that has become settled; but to follow the rule literally in these cases would be to close down the plant at once. This court is fully agreed to avoid that immediately drastic remedy; the difference in view is how best to avoid it.*

One alternative is to grant the injunction but postpone its effect to a specified future date to give opportunity for technical advances to permit defendant to eliminate the nuisance; another is to grant the injunction conditioned on the payment of permanent damages to plaintiffs which would compensate them for the total economic loss to their property present and future caused by defendant's operations. For reasons which will be developed the court chooses the latter alternative.

If the injunction were to be granted unless within a short period—e.g., 18 months—the nuisance be abated by improved methods, there would be no assurance that any significant technical improvement would occur.

The parties could settle this private litigation at any time if defendant paid enough money and the imminent threat of closing the plant would build up the pressure on defendant. If there were no improved techniques found, there would inevitably be applications to the court at Special Term for extensions of time to perform on showing of good faith efforts to find such techniques.

Moreover, techniques to eliminate dust and other annoying by-products of cement making are unlikely to be developed by any research the defendant can undertake within any short period, but will depend on the total resources of the

---

*Respondent's investment in the plant is in excess of $45,000,000. There are over 300 people employed there.

cement industry nationwide and throughout the world. The problem is universal wherever cement is made.

For obvious reasons the rate of the research is beyond control of defendant. If at the end of 18 months the whole industry has not found a technical solution a court would be hard put to close down this one cement plant if due regard be given to equitable principles.

On the other hand, to grant the injunction unless defendant pays plaintiffs such permanent damages as may be fixed by the court seems to do justice between the contending parties. All of the attributions of economic loss to the properties on which plaintiffs' complaints are based will have been redressed.

The nuisance complained of by these plaintiffs may have other public or private consequences, but these particular parties are the only ones who have sought remedies and the judgment proposed will fully redress them. The limitation of relief granted is a limitation only within the four corners of these actions and does not foreclose public health or other public agencies from seeking proper relief in a proper court.

It seems reasonable to think that the risk of being required to pay permanent damages to injured property owners by cement plant owners would itself be a reasonable effective spur to research for improved techniques to minimize nuisance. . . .

Thus it seems fair to both sides to grant permanent damages to plaintiffs which will terminate this private litigation. The theory of damage is the "servitude on land" of plaintiffs imposed by defendant's nuisance. (See United States v. Causby, 328 U.S. 256, 261, 262, 267, where the term "servitude" addressed to the land was used by Justice Douglas relating to the effect of airplane noise on property near an airport.) . . .

JASEN, Judge (dissenting). . . .

I see grave dangers in overruling our long-established rule of granting an injunction where a nuisance results in substantial continuing damage. In permitting the injunction to become inoperative upon the payment of permanent damages, the majority is, in effect, licensing a continuing wrong. It is the same as saying to the cement company, you may continue to do harm to your neighbors so long as you pay a fee for it. Furthermore, once such permanent damages are assessed and paid, the incentive to alleviate the wrong would be eliminated, thereby continuing air pollution of an area without abatement. . . .

This kind of inverse condemnation may not be invoked by a private person or corporation for private gain or advantage. Inverse condemnation should only be permitted when the public is primarily served in the taking or impairment of property. The promotion of the interests of the polluting cement company has, in my opinion, no public use or benefit.

Nor is it constitutionally permissible to impose servitude on land, without consent of the owner, by payment of permanent damages where the continuing impairment of the land is for a private use. This is made clear by the State Constitution (art. I, §7, subd. (a)) which provides that "[p]rivate property shall not be taken for *public use* without just compensation" (emphasis added). It is, of course, significant that the section makes no mention of taking for a *private* use. . . .

I would enjoin the defendant cement company from continuing the discharge of dust particles upon its neighbors' properties unless, within 18 months, the cement company abated this nuisance. . . .

NOTES AND QUESTIONS ABOUT COMMON LAW VERSUS STATUTORY CAUSES OF ACTION

1. Did *Boomer* consider all relevant costs in balancing the equities? Is harm to persons other than the plaintiffs relevant? See Juergensmeyer, Control of Air Pollution Through the Assertion of Private Rights, 1967 Duke L.J. 1126.

2. *Common Law versus Statutory Standards for Injunctive Relief.* Should the relief provided for proven statutory violations be the same as for common law nuisances? The Court in the *Snail Darter* case, TVA v. Hill, 437 U.S. 153 (1978), excerpted in Chapter 5, held that the ESA foreclosed the exercise of traditional judicial equitable discretion and required an injunction preventing completion of the Tellico Dam to save the darter. In Weinberger v. Romero-Barcelo, 456 U.S. 305 (1982), on the other hand, the Supreme Court upheld the district court's refusal to enjoin the Navy from continuing to drop bombs off the coast of Puerto Rico while it applied for a permit under the CWA, even though the activity clearly violated §301(a) of the Act. Distinguishing the *Snail Darter* case, the Court reasoned that issuance of the requested injunction was not the only means of vindicating the statute's purposes. The district court acted well within its traditional equitable discretion, which Congress intended to preserve, by ordering the Navy to apply for a permit but not shutting down training activities in the interim. The reasoning in *Romero-Barcelo* is also evident in Amoco Prod. Co. v. Village of Gambell, 480 U.S. 531 (1987). For two Supreme Court opinions that address the standard for injunctive relief in the NEPA context, see Monsanto Co. v. Geertson Seed Farms, 561 U.S. 139 (2010); Winter v. Natural Res. Def. Council, Inc., 555 U.S. 7 (2008). The Court in *Monsanto*, citing *Romero-Barcelo* for the proposition that an injunction is a "drastic and extraordinary remedy, which should not be granted as a matter of course," held that the existence of a NEPA violation does not create a presumption that "injunctive relief is the proper remedy . . . except in unusual circumstances." 561 U.S. at 157.

3. *Does the Identity of the Plaintiff Matter?* Would it have made any difference if the plaintiff in *Romero-Barcelo* had been the federal government instead of the governor of Puerto Rico and EPA had supported the issuance of an injunction? See footnote 12 of Justice White's opinion in *Romero-Barcelo*. In United States v. Bethlehem Steel Corp., 38 F.3d 862 (7th Cir. 1994), the court stated that the law of injunctions differs when the plaintiff is the government or a "private attorney general" as opposed to a private individual. In the former case, at least where the activity sought to be enjoined may endanger the public health, "injunctive relief is proper, without resort to balancing." Id. at 868. The court upheld an injunction against continued noncompliance with RCRA and the SDWA issued without regard to a balancing of the equities or a finding of irreparable harm.

In United States v. Marine Shale Processors, 81 F.3d 1329 (5th Cir. 1996), the court stated that "a court of equity must exercise its discretion with an eye to the congressional policy as expressed in the relevant statute, but some of *Bethlehem Steel*'s language may tread too closely to the view, rejected in [*Romero-Barcelo*], that a court is 'mechanically obligated to grant an injunction for every violation of law' when the United States is the plaintiff." Id. at 1360. United States v. Massachusetts Water Res. Auth., 256 F.3d 36 (1st Cir. 2001), stated that "[t]he role a court plays in deciding whether to grant a statutory injunction is different than the one it plays when it weighs the equitable claims of two private parties in a suit seeking injunctive relief. . . . [I]n the context of statutory injunctions, the court's freedom to make an independent assessment of the equities and the public interest is circumscribed to the extent that Congress has already made such assessments with respect to the type of case before the court." Id. at 47. The court nevertheless concluded that Congress intended that courts considering alleged violations of the SDWA retain their traditional equitable discretion and that the district court did not exceed its authority by refusing to issue an injunction requiring that a public water system install filtration technology.

4. *The Scope of Judicial Discretion in Fashioning Particular Forms of Injunctive Relief.* In *Boomer*, the court refused to grant an injunction that required the installation of equipment to correct the problem. Should the common law be technology forcing? One of the purported goals of tort law is to force those who cause harm to internalize the resulting costs. It has been suggested that it is fairer to force internalization on those who are in a good position to spread widely the costs of the harm. Does injunctive relief further this goal? See Calabresi, Some Thoughts on Risk Distribution and the Law of Torts, 70 Yale L.J. 499, 534-536 (1961).

More generally, how much discretion does or should a federal district court have in a citizen suit to determine the nature of the relief granted? Suppose that the court finds that the plaintiff has proven that a citizen suit defendant has violated a permit under the Clean Water Act. Is the court limited to ordering compliance or may it mandate the manner of compliance? See NRDC v. Southwest Marine, Inc., 236 F.3d 985, 1000-1002 (9th Cir. 2000). What does EPA think about the scope of a court's injunctive authority? See Memorandum from Susan Shinkman, Director of Office of Civil Enforcement, Securing Mitigation as Injunctive Relief in Certain Civil Enforcement Settlements (2d ed.) (Nov. 14, 2012); Markell, EPA Enforcement: A Heightened Emphasis on Mitigation Relief, 45 Trends 4 (March/April 2014).

5. *What Types of Injuries Are Actionable Under Common Law?* In Curd v. Mosaic Fertilizer, LLC, 39 So.3d 1216 (Fla. 2010), the Florida Supreme Court held that commercial fishermen could bring a common law nuisance-based class action to pursue claims that they had suffered economic losses due to negligent pollution releases that had harmed fishing grounds they used. The court held that the plaintiffs did not need to show that their own property had been damaged. In North Carolina v. TVA, 615 F.3d 291 (4th Cir. 2010), the court reversed a district court ruling that imposed an injunction against the Tennessee Valley Authority (TVA) on the ground that TVA emissions constituted a public nuisance. The district court had ordered TVA to install emission controls and take other actions at several of its electricity generating plants in an effort to reduce emissions from those plants. The Fourth Circuit reasoned as follows:

> The district court's well-meaning attempt to reduce air pollution cannot alter the fact that its decision threatens to scuttle the extensive system of anti-pollution mandates that promote clean air in this country. If courts across the nation were to use the vagaries of public nuisance doctrine to overturn the carefully enacted rules governing airborne emissions, it would be increasingly difficult for anyone to determine what standards govern. Energy policy cannot be set, and the environment cannot prosper, in this way. [Id. at 298.]

Do you agree? What role for the common law is there in a world with an extensive regulatory infrastructure? See the *Ouellette* excerpt in Chapter 1, section G, for consideration of similar issues in the CWA context.

6. *Nuisance and Climate Change*. There have been efforts to use public nuisance to address concerns about climate change. We consider these in Chapter 12. Hammond & Markell, A Primer on Common Law & Related Causes of Action in Climate Change Litigation, in Global Climate Change and U.S. Law (M. Gerrard & J. Freeman eds., ABA 2d ed. 2014), address this issue.

D.   EMERGING ISSUES IN ENVIRONMENTAL ENFORCEMENT AND THE EXPANSION OF THE ENFORCEMENT POLICY TOOLBOX

Much of this chapter focuses on what might be considered "traditional enforcement tools," notably monitoring compliance and civil and criminal enforcement action, including litigation, involving alleged violations. One of the primary purposes of such traditional enforcement is "deterrence," which EPA defines as causing "people [to] change their behavior to avoid a sanction." EPA, Office of Enforcement, Principles of Environmental Enforcement 2-3 (Feb. 1992). The agency has long believed that deterrence must be an important part of an enforcement program and it continues to maintain that position. For example, in its FY 2015 National Program Manager Guidance, EPA's Enforcement Office highlights EPA's "commitment to a strong enforcement program," including "[t]ough civil and criminal enforcement for violations that threaten communities and the environment." Id. at 1.

At the same time, there has been increasing debate about "what works best" in promoting compliance with environmental requirements. See, e.g., Monitoring, Enforcement, & Environmental Compliance: Understanding Specific & General Deterrence (State of the Science White Paper prepared for EPA Oct. 2007) http://www.epa.gov/Compliance/resources/reports/compliance/research/meec-whitepaper.pdf; Silberman, Does Environmental Deterrence Work? Evidence and Experience Say Yes, but We Need to Understand How and Why, 30 Envtl. L. Rep. 10523 (2000). In recent years some members of the regulated community, and many state officials, among others, have increasingly sounded the theme that an approach based on cooperation is more likely to produce compliance in many cases than an approach based on deterrence. C. Rechtschaffen & D. Markell, Reinventing Environmental Enforcement & the State/Federal Relationship (2003). EPA itself has given increasing emphasis in recent years to cooperative approaches. EPA's FY 2007 update to its national enforcement guidance, for example, identifies compliance assistance and compliance incentives (each of which is described below in more detail), as well as traditional enforcement, as tools needed to address environmental risks and noncompliance patterns. EPA, Final FY 07 Update to . . . [OECA] National Program Managers' Guidance 11 (April 2006).

A second overarching issue that has swept the enforcement world involves the debate about what we should be measuring in gauging the effectiveness of enforcement and other compliance promotion efforts. Traditionally, EPA and the states have focused primarily on what some have characterized as "enforcement beans"—the level of government activities, such as the number of inspections conducted, the number of enforcement actions brought, and the amount of penalty dollars sought and collected. Most observers agree that this information has some value, for the reasons that EPA's Michael Stahl has identified:

> These outputs have some virtues as performance measures. They provide a sense of enforcement "presence" and the extent to which deterrence is being used to bring about compliance. They are simple, clear, easily understood, and depict what has been produced for a given level of resources invested. [M. Stahl, Beyond the Bean Count: Measuring Performance of Regulatory Compliance Programs, Pub. Manager 31 (Fall 1999).]

These measures, however, also have significant shortcomings, particularly when used as the exclusive benchmarks for performance, as Stahl also explains:

> [O]utput measures reveal very little about the state of compliance. Is an increase in enforcement outputs good news (i.e., the government was able to identify and correct a higher percentage of noncompliance) or bad news (i.e., noncompliance is increasing)? . . . [O]utput measures do not describe the changes in behavior or other improvements that resulted from government action to ensure compliance. Knowing that [EPA] . . . issued over 2,000 enforcement cases in a year does not give any indication about how many tons of pollutants were removed from the environment from those cases. . . . [O]utput measures say nothing about the extent to which important social objectives or problems are being addressed. Knowing that [OSHA] . . . conducted thousands of inspections in a year does not indicate whether work place injury rates are declining. [Id. at 32.]

Concern that traditional measures of enforcement performance do not provide good metrics for evaluating the effectiveness of such performance has led EPA and the states periodically to revisit the measures used. See, e.g., EPA, National Strategy for Improving Oversight of State Enforcement Performance (Dec. 12, 2013); EPA Performance Measures Do Not Effectively Track Compliance Outcomes, Report No. 2006-P-00006 3 (Dec. 15, 2005), www.epa.gov/oig/reports/2006/20051215-2006-P-00006.pdf (discussing EPA's use of "intermediate outcome" measures (e.g., compliance rates and changes in compliance) and "end outcome" measures (e.g., improved environmental conditions resulting from particular activities) as well as output and input measures); U.S. GAO, GAO-08-1111R, Environmental Enforcement: EPA Needs to Improve the Accuracy and Transparency of Measures Used to Report on Program Effectiveness (2008).

While progress in expanding the range of compliance strategies, and refining measures of performance, has been mixed,[j] these two phenomena have contributed to the emergence of a fairly broad-based desire to expand the toolbox for promoting compliance and to expand the measures used to evaluate performance. These phenomena have made the process of environmental enforcement quite dynamic in recent years. EPA and the states have experimented with a wide variety of compliance promotion strategies, including: (1) compliance assistance approaches, and (2) compliance incentive-based strategies. Most recently, EPA has also launched an initiative that the Agency calls "next generation" compliance. Brief summaries of some of these initiatives are provided below.

---

j. Performance Measures, *supra*; U.S. GAO, GAO-10-165T, Clean Water Act: Longstanding Issues Impact EPA's and States' Enforcement Efforts, 7 (2009).

1. Compliance Assistance

In recent years EPA has highlighted the importance of "compliance assistance," which the agency defines as "providing information and technical assistance to the regulated community to help it meet the requirements of environmental law." EPA Office of Enforcement and Compliance Assurance, Guide for Measuring Compliance Assistance Outcomes 4 (June 2002). EPA characterizes as compliance assistance "activities, tools, or technical assistance that provides clear and consistent information for . . . helping the regulated community understand and meet its obligations under environmental regulations . . . [and] help[ing] the regulated community find cost-effective ways to comply with regulations and/or go 'beyond compliance. . . .'" EPA Office of Enforcement and Compliance Assurance, Guide for Measuring Compliance Assistance Outcomes 4 (Revised October 2007).

EPA groups compliance assistance activities into the following categories: telephone assistance, workshops, presentations, compliance assistance tools, and on-site visits. One of its significant initiatives in this area is the creation of Internet-based Compliance Assistance Centers (www.assistancecenters.net). The primary focus of these centers is to provide compliance assistance to small and medium-sized businesses, local governments, and federal facilities. In FY 2011, the Centers' websites were visited 3,501,256 times and there were 3.5 million user sessions. EPA, Compliance and Enforcement Annual Results 2011 Fiscal Year, available at http://www.epa.gov/compliance/resources/reports/endofyear/eoy2011/programs/compliance.html.

In its June 2002 Guide for Measuring Compliance Assistance Outcomes and in a more focused report, The National Nitrate Compliance Initiative Report, EPA OECA, EPA 300-R-02-003 (Apr. 2002), EPA summarizes one of its compliance assistance initiatives, known as the National Nitrate Compliance Initiative, which involved educating the metal finishing sector about EPCRA §313 requirements (discussed in Chapter 8, section E.2.c) and EPA's audit policy. In late 1999 EPA determined that up to 1,000 facilities (or roughly 40 percent of the covered regulated community) were failing to comply with their reporting obligations under the TRI program for nitrate compounds. EPA considered this widespread reporting failure to be significant because of the inherent risks that nitrates pose (EPA terms them "toxic chemicals that can pose serious risks to human health and the environment") and because, among other things, there had been recent "[c]atastrophic releases" that caused adverse health effects. For example, an incident in Pennsylvania led EPA Region III to issue an emergency order under the Safe Drinking Water Act in June 2000 to provide bottled water to more than 4,000 people because a facility had contaminated local drinking water and more than 21 miles of Connoquenessing Creek with dangerous levels of nitrates.

EPA adopted a "nationally consistent enforcement response" (the National Nitrate Compliance Initiative) to address this widespread noncompliance. EPA first sought to raise awareness about the reporting obligations and the extent of noncompliance by issuing an Enforcement Alert that urged regulated parties to disclose violations under EPA's Self-Audit and Small Business policies (both of which are discussed below). EPA reports that many facilities did so. For the parties that did not pursue voluntary disclosure under these policies following distribution of the Enforcement Alert, EPA followed up by issuing Notice of Opportunity to Show Cause letters that invited these parties either to show EPA that they were not in violation of their reporting obligations or to accept a settlement that included a modest fine and a commitment to report properly in the future. The agency subsequently issued an alternative settlement that included an even more modest penalty and a commitment by the party to undertake a compliance audit of all of its obligations under EPCRA §313. EPA reports that, through this initiative, nearly 600 companies agreed to audit more than 1,000 facilities for EPCRA §313 regulatory obligations (including nitrate reporting). The agency also reports that the initiative increased reporting of nitrate releases from 60 percent to 98 percent. http://www.epa.gov/compliance/incentives/programs/nitratecip.html.

This initiative has features that come within the rubric of "compliance assistance," such as its effort to educate regulated parties about their reporting obligations. It also contains elements, such as promised reductions in penalty amounts for voluntarily reporting and for conducting self-audits, which are in the nature of "compliance incentives." The latter category of EPA strategies to encourage compliance is discussed next.

2. Compliance Incentives

To complement its development of a variety of compliance assistance strategies, EPA has also pursued a number of initiatives referred to as "compliance incentive"–based approaches. EPA has defined compliance incentives as approaches that "encourage regulated entities to voluntarily discover, disclose and correct violations or clean up contaminated sites before they are identified by the government for enforcement investigation or response." EPA, Operating Principles for an Integrated Enforcement and Compliance Assurance Program 8 (Interim Final Nov. 18, 1996).

EPA's "Self-Audit" Policy, Incentives for Self-Policing: Discovery, Disclosure, Correction and Prevention of Violations (2000), excerpted below, is perhaps its best-known compliance incentive policy. The policy is intended to provide incentives for regulated parties to detect, promptly disclose, and expeditiously correct violations. The incentives are of four types. Regulated entities that commit violations but meet the nine conditions in the policy qualify for 100 percent mitigation of the gravity-based component of a civil penalty. Regulated parties that meet all of the conditions except the first (systematic discovery of violations) qualify for a 75 percent mitigation of any gravity-based civil penalty. Further, EPA will not recommend criminal prosecution for regulated parties that disclose violations of criminal law under certain conditions outlined in the policy. Finally, EPA will not routinely request audit reports. In May 2007, EPA reported that since 1995, "more than 3,000 companies have disclosed and resolved violations at over 9,000 facilities under the self-audit policy." EPA, EPA Encourages New Owners of Companies to Disclose Violations, May 15, 2007. During 2011, EPA received disclosures from 458 companies at 855 facilities, which resulted in a reduction of 3,000 pounds of pollution. Coomes, Self-Disclosures Led to Small Pollution Cuts, Compared to All EPA Enforcement Actions, 49 Daily Env't Rep. (BNA) A-3 (March 14, 2012). In 2012, EPA indicated its intent to reduce its investment of resources in implementation of the Self-Audit Policy. The agency suggested that regulated parties had increased their use of such reviews as part of quality management, and that most of the violations disclosed under the Policy were not high priority. Thus, while it appears to be widely accepted that internal compliance reviews are an important feature of effective compliance promotion, the role that government will play in incentivizing such reviews has evolved over the years, and that is likely to continue.

An excerpt from the Self-Audit policy follows.

ENVIRONMENTAL PROTECTION AGENCY, INCENTIVES FOR SELF-POLICING: DISCOVERY, DISCLOSURE, CORRECTION AND PREVENTION OF VIOLATIONS
65 Fed. Reg. 19,618-19,624 (2000)

[Parts I.A and I.B review the history of the Self-Audit policy, which is a revision of EPA's 1995 policy.]

Purpose

... EPA's enforcement program provides a strong incentive for compliance by imposing stiff sanctions for noncompliance. Enforcement has contributed to the dramatic expansion of environmental auditing as measured in numerous recent surveys. For example, in a 1995 survey by Price Waterhouse LLP, more than 90% of corporate respondents who conduct audits identified one of the reasons for doing so as the desire to find and correct violations before government inspectors discover them. . . .

At the same time, because government resources are limited, universal compliance cannot be achieved without active efforts by the regulated community to police themselves. More than half of the respondents to the same 1995 Price Waterhouse survey said that they would expand environmental auditing in exchange for reduced penalties for violations discovered and corrected. While many companies already audit or have compliance management programs in place, EPA believes that the incentives offered in this Policy will improve the frequency and quality of these self-policing efforts.

D.   INCENTIVES FOR SELF-POLICING

... For entities that meet the conditions of the Policy, the available incentives include waiving or reducing gravity-based civil penalties, declining to recommend criminal prosecution for regulated entities that self-police, and refraining from routine requests for audits. . . .

1.   ELIMINATING GRAVITY-BASED PENALTIES

In general, civil penalties that EPA assesses are comprised of two elements: the economic benefit component and the gravity-based component. The economic benefit component reflects the economic gain derived from a violator's illegal competitive advantage. Gravity-based penalties are that portion of the penalty over and above the economic benefit. They reflect the egregiousness of the violator's behavior and constitute the punitive portion of the penalty. . . .

Under the Audit Policy, EPA will not seek gravity-based penalties for disclosing entities that meet all nine Policy conditions, including systematic discovery. ("Systematic discovery" means the detection of a potential violation through an environmental audit or a compliance management system that reflects the entity's due diligence in preventing, detecting and correcting violations.) . . . EPA reserves the right to collect any economic benefit that may have been realized as a result of noncompliance, even where the entity meets all other Policy conditions. Where the Agency determines that the economic benefit is insignificant, the Agency also may waive this component of the penalty.

EPA's decision to retain its discretion to recover economic benefit is based on two reasons. First, facing the risk that the Agency will recoup economic benefit provides an incentive for regulated entities to comply on time. . . . Second, collecting economic benefit is fair because it protects law-abiding companies from being undercut by their noncomplying competitors, thereby preserving a level playing field.

2.   75% REDUCTION OF GRAVITY-BASED PENALTIES

. . . [T]o encourage disclosure and correction of violations even in the absence of systematic discovery, EPA will reduce gravity-based penalties by 75% for entities that meet conditions D(2) through D(9) of the Policy. EPA expects that a disclosure under this provision will encourage the entity to work with the Agency to resolve environmental problems and begin to develop an effective auditing program or compliance management system.

3.   NO RECOMMENDATIONS FOR CRIMINAL PROSECUTION

. . . When a disclosure that meets the terms and conditions of this Policy results in a criminal investigation, EPA will generally not recommend criminal prosecution for the disclosing entity, although the Agency may recommend prosecution for culpable individuals and other entities. . . .

Important limitations to the incentive apply. It will not be available, for example, where corporate officials are consciously involved in or willfully blind to violations, or conceal or condone noncompliance. Since the regulated entity must satisfy conditions D(2) through D(9) of the Policy, violations that cause serious harm or which may pose imminent and substantial endangerment to human health or the environment are not eligible. Finally, EPA reserves the right to recommend prosecution for the criminal conduct of any culpable individual or subsidiary organization.

While EPA may decide not to recommend criminal prosecution for disclosing entities, ultimate prosecutorial discretion resides with the U.S. Department of Justice, which will be guided by its own policy on voluntary disclosures. . . .

4.   NO ROUTINE REQUESTS FOR AUDIT REPORTS

. . . EPA has not and will not routinely request copies of audit reports to trigger enforcement investigations. . . . However, if the Agency has independent evidence of a violation, it may seek the information it needs to establish the extent and nature of the violation and the degree of culpability.

E.   CONDITIONS

Section D describes the nine conditions that a regulated entity must meet in order for the Agency to decline to seek (or to reduce) gravity-based penalties under the Policy. . . .

1.   SYSTEMATIC DISCOVERY OF THE VIOLATION THROUGH AN ENVIRONMENTAL AUDIT OR A COMPLIANCE MANAGEMENT SYSTEM

. . . [T]he violation must have been discovered through either (a) an environmental audit, or (b) a compliance management system that reflects due diligence in preventing, detecting and correcting violations. [Both terms are defined in Section B of the Policy.] . . .

Compliance management programs that train and motivate employees to prevent, detect and correct violations on a daily basis are a valuable complement to periodic auditing. . . . The Agency recognizes that a variety of compliance management programs are feasible, and it will determine whether basic due diligence criteria have been met in deciding whether to grant Audit Policy credit.

As a condition of penalty mitigation, EPA may require that a description of the regulated entity's compliance management system be made publicly available. The Agency believes that the availability of such information will allow the public to judge the adequacy of compliance management systems, lead to enhanced compliance, and foster greater public trust in the integrity of compliance management systems.

2.   VOLUNTARY DISCOVERY

Under Section D(2), the violation must have been identified voluntarily, and not through a monitoring, sampling, or auditing procedure that is required by statute, regulation, permit, judicial or administrative order, or consent agreement. The Policy provides three specific examples of discovery that would not be voluntary, and therefore would not be eligible for penalty mitigation: emissions violations detected through a required continuous emissions monitor, violations of NPDES discharge limits found through prescribed monitoring, and violations discovered through a compliance audit required to be performed by the terms of a consent order or settlement agreement. The exclusion does not apply to violations that are discovered pursuant to audits that are conducted as part of a comprehensive environmental management system (EMS) required under a settlement agreement. In general, EPA supports the implementation of EMSs that promote compliance, prevent pollution and improve overall environmental performance. Precluding the availability of the Audit Policy for discoveries made through a comprehensive EMS that has been implemented pursuant to a settlement agreement might discourage entities from agreeing to implement such a system. . . .

3.   PROMPT DISCLOSURE

Section D(3) requires that the entity disclose the violation in writing to EPA within 21 calendar days after discovery. . . . If a statute or regulation requires the entity to report the violation in fewer than 21 days, disclosure must be made within the time limit established by law. . . .

The 21-day disclosure period begins when the entity discovers that a violation has, or may have, occurred. The trigger for discovery is when any officer, director, employee or agent of the facility has an objectively reasonable basis for believing that a violation has, or may have, occurred. The "objectively reasonable basis" standard is measured against what a prudent person, having the same information as was available to the individual in question, would have believed. It is not measured against what the individual in question thought was reasonable at the time the situation was encountered. . . .

4.   DISCOVERY AND DISCLOSURE INDEPENDENT OF GOVERNMENT OR THIRD PARTY PLAINTIFF

Under Section D(4), the entity must discover the violation independently. That is, the violation must be discovered and identified before EPA or another government agency likely would have identified the problem either through its own investigative work or from information received through a third party. This condition requires regulated entities to take the initiative to find violations on their own and disclose them promptly instead of waiting for an indication of a pending enforcement action or third-party complaint.

Section D(4)(a) lists the circumstances under which discovery and disclosure will not be considered independent. For example, a disclosure will not be independent where EPA is already investigating the facility in question. However, under subsection (a), where the entity does not know that EPA has commenced a civil investigation and proceeds in good faith to make a disclosure under the Audit Policy, EPA may, in its discretion, provide penalty mitigation under the Audit Policy. The subsection (a) exception applies only to civil investigations; it does not apply in the criminal context. Other examples of situations in which a discovery is not considered independent are where a citizens' group has provided notice of its intent to sue, where a third party has already filed a complaint, where a whistleblower has reported the potential violation to government authorities, or where discovery of the violation by the government was imminent. . . .

5.   CORRECTION AND REMEDIATION

Under Section D(5), the entity must remedy any harm caused by the violation and expeditiously certify in writing to appropriate Federal, State, and local authorities that it has corrected the violation. Correction and remediation in this context include responding to spills and carrying out any removal or remedial actions required by law. The certification requirement enables EPA to ensure that the regulated entity will be publicly accountable for its commitments through binding written agreements, orders or consent decrees where necessary.

Under the Policy, the entity must correct the violation within 60 calendar days from the date of discovery, or as expeditiously as possible. EPA recognizes that some violations can and should be corrected immediately, while others may take longer than 60 days to correct. For example, more time may be required if capital expenditures are involved or if technological issues are a factor. If more than 60 days will be required, the disclosing entity must so notify the Agency in writing prior to the conclusion of the 60-day period. In all cases, the regulated entity will be expected to do its utmost to achieve or return to compliance as expeditiously as possible. . . .

6.   PREVENT RECURRENCE

Under Section D(6), the regulated entity must agree to take steps to prevent a recurrence of the violation after it has been disclosed. Preventive steps may include, but are not limited to, improvements to the entity's environmental auditing efforts or compliance management system.

7.   NO REPEAT VIOLATIONS

Condition D(7) bars repeat offenders from receiving Audit Policy credit. Under the repeat violations exclusion, the same or a closely related violation must not have occurred at the same facility within the past 3 years. . . . Examples of notice include a complaint, consent order, notice of violation, receipt of an inspection report, citizen suit, or receipt of penalty mitigation through a compliance assistance or incentive project. . . .

The term "violation" includes any violation subject to a Federal, State or local civil judicial or administrative order, consent agreement, conviction or plea agreement. Recognizing that minor violations sometimes are settled without a formal action in court, the term also covers any act or omission for which the regulated entity has received a penalty reduction in the past. This condition covers situations in which the regulated entity has had clear notice of its noncompliance and an opportunity to correct the problem. . . .

8.   OTHER VIOLATIONS EXCLUDED

. . . Subsection D(8)(a) excludes violations that result in serious actual harm to the environment or which may have presented an imminent and substantial endangerment to public health or the environment. . . . However, this condition does not bar an entity from qualifying for Audit Policy relief solely because the violation involves release of a pollutant to the environment, as such releases do not necessarily result in serious actual harm or an imminent and substantial endangerment. To date, EPA has not invoked the serious actual harm or the imminent and substantial endangerment clauses to deny Audit Policy credit for any disclosure.

9.   COOPERATION

Under Section D(9), the regulated entity must cooperate as required by EPA and provide the Agency with the information it needs to determine Policy applicability. The entity must not hide, destroy or tamper with possible evidence following discovery of potential environmental violations. In order for the Agency to apply the Policy fairly, it must have sufficient information to determine whether its conditions are satisfied in each individual case. . . .

Entities that disclose potential criminal violations may expect a more thorough review by the Agency. In criminal cases, entities will be expected to provide, at a minimum, the following: access to all requested documents; access to all employees of the disclosing entity; assistance in investigating the violation, any noncompliance problems related to the disclosure, and any environmental consequences related to the violations; access to all information relevant to the violations disclosed, including that portion of the environmental audit report or documentation from the compliance management system that revealed the violation; and access to the individuals who conducted the audit or review.

F. OPPOSITION TO AUDIT PRIVILEGE AND IMMUNITY

The Agency believes that the Audit Policy provides effective incentives for self-policing without impairing law enforcement, putting the environment at risk or hiding environmental compliance information from the public. Although EPA encourages environmental auditing, it must do so without compromising the integrity and enforce-ability of environmental laws. It is important to distinguish between EPA's Audit Policy and the audit privilege and immunity laws that exist in some States. The Agency remains firmly opposed to statutory and regulatory audit privileges and immunity. Privilege laws shield evidence of wrongdoing and prevent States from investigating even the most serious environmental violations. Immunity laws prevent States from obtaining penalties that are appropriate to the seriousness of the violation, as they are required to do under Federal law. Audit privilege and immunity laws are unnecessary, undermine law enforcement, impair protection of human health and the environment, and interfere with the public's right to know of potential and existing environmental hazards. . . .

3. "Next Generation Compliance"

A third "emerging" innovation in EPA environmental compliance strategies is still very much "emerging:" EPA's Next Generation Compliance or Next Gen initiative. In an October 2013 article, EPA's Assistant Administrator for the Office of Enforcement and Compliance Assurance (OECA), Cynthia Giles, described EPA's Next Gen initiative as "moving [EPA's] compliance programs into the 21st century." Giles, Next Generation Compliance, The Envtl. F. 22 (Sept.-Oct. 2013).

What is the Next Gen initiative likely to include? One feature Administrator Giles highlights is the idea of simpler and clearer rules that are easier to meet. Giles points to an April 2013 proposed rule that would make it much easier for oil and gas producers to comply with emission control requirements by allowing them simply to buy the necessary air pollution control equipment from a manufacturer that has secured EPA certification rather than requiring that the oil and gas producers field test the equipment independently. She refers to this approach as the use of "rules with compliance built in." Id.

Giles also suggests that a "revolution" in monitoring capacity will be a central feature of Next Gen. Noting that monitoring technologies are "becoming more accu-rate, more mobile, and cheaper," Giles indicates that Next Gen will depend on such technologies, used by regulated parties and citizens as well as government agencies, to produce better information about regulatory compliance issues that need attention. She expresses the expectation that communities with better and more data will press companies to improve performance; that companies may increasingly decide that it is in their best interest to do their own monitoring and share it with the public; and that "[t]hese changes, driven by new technologies, will increase more direct industry and community engagement, and reduce the need for government action." Id. at 24.

A third key feature of Next Gen is significantly increased use of electronic reporting. Administrator Giles paints a dismal picture of current reporting practices and of the need for dramatic improvement:

> [M]uch of the information reported to EPA and states by facilities is still submitted on paper and waits for a government employee to manually enter the data into computer systems. Or, in a time of declining budgets, the paper sits in a corner unopened, until someone has time to examine the data and see if any violations appear likely. This means that important pollutant and violation information can go unnoticed. Errors can be introduced through manual data entry, requiring aggravating and time-consuming correction processes. And far too much time ends up being spent on minor issues while major ones go unaddressed.

Id. at 25. Giles suggests that "e-reporting" is "a solution that saves time and money while improving results." Id.

Giles summarizes the Next Gen vision as follows:

> Just as the Internet has transformed the way we communicate and access information, advances in information and emissions monitoring technology are setting the stage for detecting, processing, and communication capabilities that can revolutionize environmental protection. We are moving toward a world in which states, EPA, citizens, and industry will have real-time electronic information regarding environmental conditions, emissions, and compliance, and we are using what we have learned about compliance to make it easier to comply than to violate. [Id. at 22.]

While EPA's development and implementation of Next Gen are at an early stage, one aspect of the initiative that has begun to attract attention is the agency's decision to reduce the number of inspections it conducts annually and the number of cases it brings. As might be expected, concerns have been raised that such reductions may undermine compliance. As implementation of Next Gen unfolds, it will be worthwhile to monitor public support for this shift in strategies as well as the results it produces.

NOTES AND QUESTIONS CONCERNING THE ENFORCEMENT POLICY TOOLBOX

1. What are the benefits available to a regulated company that voluntarily discloses to EPA its own violations of environmental statutes or regulations? What conditions must a company meet to qualify for the benefits of EPA's audit policy statement? If a company discovers violations during a compliance audit required as part of a binding settlement agreement, is it eligible for the elimination of gravity-based penalties? What if a violation is identified in a compliance certification required to accompany an application for a Title V Clean Air Act permit? Is EPA bound to

adhere to the provisions of the policy statement? In revising the policy in 2000, EPA concluded that it has encouraged voluntary self-policing while preserving fair and effective enforcement, that use of the policy has been widespread, and that users report a high satisfaction rate. EPA lengthened the period during which prompt disclosure must be made from 10 to 21 days. It clarified that a facility in many cases may satisfy the "independent discovery" requirement even where inspections or investigations have commenced at other facilities owned by the same entity. Finally, it indicated that entities that meet all policy conditions except for systematic discovery will not be recommended for criminal prosecution, provided EPA determines that the violation is not part of a pattern or practice of concealment or condoning of environmental violations. EPA extended the 2000 policy in 2008 to new owners. See, e.g., Interim Approach to Applying the Audit Policy to New Owners, 73 Fed. Reg. 44,991 (Aug. 1, 2008).

2. One of the most controversial aspects of EPA's audit policy is its failure to provide a privilege for information discovered during an audit and turned over to the government. Why was EPA unwilling to provide such a privilege? Industry has argued that, absent a privilege, a company could be in a worse position after an audit than before, EPA's policy notwithstanding, if the audit reveals information about noncompliance that the government would not have discovered. Absent a privilege, that information may be used as the basis for enforcement proceedings against the company. Many state legislatures have adopted audit protection laws that make available to companies performing an environmental audit the privilege that EPA refused to provide.

Some state audit protection laws provide immunity from civil or criminal prosecution for any violation voluntarily disclosed to the agency. This immunity goes beyond providing privileged status to information submitted to a state environmental agency as a result of an audit. E.g., Kan. Stat. Ann. §60-3338; Ky. Rev. Stat. Ann. §224.1-040; Ohio Rev. Code Ann. §3745.72.

What effect, if any, should state provisions of this sort have on EPA's willingness to authorize the state to implement a program? Could, and should, EPA withdraw or refuse to approve delegations of permitting authority to states that have adopted such laws? See Beard, The New Environmental Federalism: Can the EPA's Voluntary Audit Policy Survive?, 17 Va. Envtl. L.J. 1, 17-19 (1997); CWA §402(b)(7); CAA §502(b)(5)(E); Inside EPA Weekly Apr. 12, 1996, at 5 (EPA Memo Establishing Criteria for Title V approvals).

3. *EPA's Small Business Compliance Policy and Small Local Governments Compliance Assistance Policy.* EPA issued a Small Business Compliance Policy in April 2000, 65 Fed. Reg. 19,630, on the same day that the agency issued its Self-Audit Policy. The Small Business Policy, as its title suggests, is intended to "promote environmental compliance among small businesses by providing incentives for voluntary discovery, prompt disclosure, and prompt correction of violations." The Policy, which implements the Small Business Regulatory Enforcement Fairness Act of 1996, reduces or waives penalties under certain circumstances for small businesses that disclose and make good faith efforts to correct violations. EPA issued its Small Local Governments Compliance Assistance Policy in 2004. This policy is intended to "promote[] comprehensive environmental compliance among small local governments by establishing parameters within which [a] state[] can reduce or waive" a penalty it otherwise would impose on a small local government, so long as the small government, among other things, uses the state's "comprehensive compliance assistance program."

4. *Supplemental Environmental Projects.* EPA's Supplemental Environmental Projects (SEPs) Policy, 63 Fed. Reg. 24,796 (1998), is another compliance incentive policy that has received considerable attention. EPA defines a SEP as an "environmentally beneficial project that a violator voluntarily agrees to perform, in addition to actions required to correct the violation(s), as part of an enforcement settlement." EPA OECA, Beyond Compliance: Supplemental Environmental Projects 4 (January 2001). Thus, a SEP is an action that is "*in addition* to what is required to return to compliance with environmental laws." Id. at 3 (emphasis added). EPA offers to forgo a portion of a civil penalty as an inducement to regulated parties to agree to a SEP in appropriate instances. In other words, as EPA puts it, "[a]ll else being equal, the final settlement penalty will be lower for a violator who agrees to perform an acceptable SEP compared to the violator who does not agree to perform a SEP." Supplemental Environmental Projects Policy, 63 Fed. Reg. 24,796 (1998). EPA has touted the environmental promise of this enforcement tool, and several commentators have encouraged the use of SEPs as well.[k]

EPA does three things in its SEPs policy. It (1) identifies the types of projects that may qualify as SEPs, (2) explains the "terms and conditions" under which a SEP may become part of a settlement, and (3) addresses the extent of penalty mitigation appropriate for a specific SEP. EPA provides a fairly elaborate methodology for determining how much a penalty should be reduced in exchange for the settling party's agreeing to undertake a SEP. EPA has developed a computer model known as PROJECT to assist in application of the methodology. For a regulated party committing to perform a SEP, the ultimate result in terms of the amount it will be required to pay is that the final settlement penalty must "equal or exceed either: (a) the economic benefit of noncompliance plus 10 percent of the gravity component; or (b) 25 percent of the gravity component only; whichever is greater." 63 Fed. Reg. at 24,801. Thus, like EPA's Self-Audit Policy, excerpted above, the SEPs Policy anticipates that EPA will impose penalties that force the violator to disgorge the economic benefit it gained from the violation; forgiveness or penalty flexibility will come in the "gravity" portion of penalty calculation.

Many states have adopted SEP programs. For a report on these programs, see Bonorris et al., Environmental Enforcement in the Fifty States: The Promise and Pitfalls of Supplemental Environmental Projects, 11 Hastings W.-Nw. J. Envtl. L. & Pol'y 185 (2005). The North Carolina Supreme Court has held that the state's SEP program violates the state constitution. North Carolina Sch. Bds. Ass'n v. Moore, 614 S.E.2d 504 (N.C. 2005).

5. *The Experience with Performance Track.* It seems indisputable that the government's mix of strategies should include a variety of sticks and carrots that create incentives for regulated parties to comply with their legal obligations (and go beyond that) and deter parties from violating their legal responsibilities. EPA's "Performance

k. See, e.g., Markell, EPA Enforcement: A Heightened Emphasis on Mitigation Relief, 45 Trends 4 (March/April 2014); Memorandum from Susan Shinkman, Director of Office of Civil Enforcement, Securing Mitigation as Injunctive Relief in Certain Civil Enforcement Settlements (2d ed.) (Nov. 14, 2012); Memorandum from John Suarez, EPA Assistant Administrator, Expanding the Use of Supplemental Environmental Projects (June 11, 2003); Lloyd, Supplemental Environmental Projects Have Been Effectively Used in Citizen Suits to Deter Future Violations as Well as to Achieve Significant Additional Environmental Benefits, 10 Widener L. Rev. 413 (2004). For a critical appraisal, see Canales, Supplemental Environmental Projects: The Most Affected Communities Are Not Receiving Satisfactory Benefits (June 2006).

Track" program, launched in 2000, was intended to reward "good environmental actors" by "recogniz[ing] and encourag[ing] top environmental performers—those who go beyond compliance . . . to attain levels of environmental performance and management that benefit people, communities, and the environment." EPA, Performance Track Program Guide 2 (Sept. 2005). EPA described the program and the results it produced as follows in its Performance Track Final Progress Report:

> Performance Track was a public-private partnership that encouraged continuous environmental improvement through environmental management systems, community outreach, and measurable results. . . . In partnership with EPA, members voluntarily set measurable goals to improve the quality of our nation's air, water, and land. . . .
>
> Over the life of the program, the combined environmental effort of all Performance Track member facilities has resulted in cumulative reported reductions of many environmental indicators, including reductions in water use by 2.87 billion gallons, greenhouse gas emission reductions of 366,948 metric tons of carbon dioxide equivalent, and conservation of 24,864 acres of habitat. Many of the members' achievements address issues that are not covered by current regulations. [EPA, Performance Track Final Progress Report (May 2009).]

Despite these positive results, in 2009, then-EPA Administrator Jackson announced a halt to the Performance Track program. 74 Fed. 22,742 (May 14, 2009). She announced that EPA intended to focus on the future of EPA environmental leadership programs. Jackson, Next Steps for the National Environmental Performance Track Program and the Future of Environmental Leadership Programs (March 16, 2009).Why did EPA pull the plug on this program? What lessons are there in the program's experience for future environmental leadership initiatives?

6. As this section of the chapter reflects, it is important to monitor agency activities, as well as developments in the law (statutes, regulations, and case law), to understand the direction of, and trends in, environmental enforcement. Two good places to start are EPA's OECA website, http://www2.epa.gov/aboutepa/about-office-enforcement-and-compliance-assurance-oeca, and the website of the Environmental Council of the States (ECOS), an institution created in the early 1990s to serve as the voice of state environmental commissioners in Washington, D.C. ECOS has issued a series of reports that focus on enforcement and compliance, such as State Environmental Agency Contributions to Enforcement and Compliance: 2000-2003 (September 2006). See http://www.ecos.org/section/publications. ECOS's journal, ECOStates, also includes articles on specific strategies for compliance, such as promoting the use of EMSs (environmental management systems).[1]

7. To bring us full circle to the quotes at the beginning of the chapter, a primary purpose of enforcement is to enhance compliance with the environmental laws in order to achieve the goals of these laws. The last section of this chapter makes clear that EPA has attempted to use its enforcement tools creatively to leverage enhanced regulated party compliance, through incentives for self-auditing and similar strategies. It should be obvious, but compliance promotion strategies are not the only driver of

---

1. See, e.g., Habicht, Environmental Management Systems: Local Resource Centers Launched to Advance Environmental Management Systems Within Public Entities, ECOStates, Fall 2002, at 20 (covering EMSs for local governments); Steagall, South Carolina Probes the Relationship Between EMSs and Permitting Decisions, ECOStates, Winter 2006, at 25 (addressing the response to EPA's challenge to incorporate EMS options into the permitting and regulatory structure).

regulated party behavior. Improved regulated party environmental protection strate-gies may yield improved profits in many ways, such as enabling a firm to reduce waste and the cost of waste management, or to bolster its reputation in ways that increase market share and profitability. Effective regulation under the environmental laws depends on an understanding of these profit- and market-oriented forces. For a review of both regulator-created incentives for improved regulated party performance and other incentives for regulated parties to pursue "auditable sustainability and corporate social responsibility" programs, see Hall, The Evolution and New Directions in Envi-ronmental Auditing and Compliance Management Natural Resources and Environ-ment (ABA Fall 2009).

XI

INTERNATIONAL
ENVIRONMENTAL LAW

International environmental law is still a comparatively young field. As recently as 1964, Wolfgang Friedmann, in an influential book about the "changing structure of international law," did not include environmental protection or nature conservation among his "new fields of international law." Wolfgang Friedmann, The Changing Structure of International Law (1964). Today, states have negotiated thousands of treaties on a wide variety of subjects, including protection of the stratospheric ozone layer, prevention of dangerous anthropogenic climate change, mitigation of acid rain, control of hazardous waste exports, regulation of trade in wildlife, protection of wetlands, and prevention of oil pollution.

This chapter examines the role of law in addressing international environmental problems. International law has traditionally been viewed as coming in two general types: *customary norms* arising from the habitual or repeated practice of states, and *treaty norms* contained in binding international agreements. In addition to these two general types of international law are the numerous resolutions, declarations, codes of conduct, and guidelines that have been adopted by international organizations, states, and private groups—sometimes referred to as "soft law."

International environmental law raises a number of general questions that stem from the decentralized nature of the international community:

(1) *Standard setting.* In the absence of an international legislature or an international environmental protection agency, how does the international community establish norms of behavior for states and individuals? Is this best done at the global, regional, or national level? Should the same norms apply to all states, or should different norms apply to different categories of states, based on their historical responsibility and/or current capabilities? For example, should poor, developing states be subject to more lenient standards than industrialized states, as the UN climate change regime provides?

(2) *Acceptance of international standards.* Why do states accept international environmental standards? For example, why would a whaling state such as Japan accept an international moratorium on commercial whaling? Or why would a developing state accept a phase-out of ozone-depleting chemicals? What carrots and sticks should the international community use to encourage acceptance of environmental standards?

(3) *Enforcement of international standards.* How should disputes be resolved about the implementation of international environmental standards? If a state fails to comply with a standard, what enforcement mechanisms are available?

(4) *Effectiveness of international standards.* To what extent are international environmental standards effective? Do they influence state behavior? Do they help ameliorate the environmental problems that they are intended to address?

C. STONE, EARTH AND OTHER ETHICS: THE CASE FOR MORAL PLURALISM
15 (1987)

[Our] animating concern is worldly: What sort of planet will this be? The various possibilities, the conceivable futures, can be thought of as so many filmstrips laid out in front of us, side by side. The first frame of each strip is the same: a "picture" of the entire earth at this moment. But as we move beyond the "near" frames (those depicting our life-times), the films begin to display variances from strip to strip, as the potential futures that they depict diverge. They diverge in the number and variety of human, animal and plant populations that will inhabit the earth. They diverge in the rate at which natural resources are depleted. In some there is more consumption in the near term, and more famine in the far. In some versions the oceans are dead; in others, the atmosphere is gone. There are differences in the world's wealth, both in the aggregate and in its distribution among peoples. There are differences, too, in the sorts of social institutions with which populations are governed: various shades of totalitarianism and democracy.

What futures we can realistically aim for—the range of potential hereafters—can be considered a question of *technology*, within the constraints, principally, of resources.

Which of these accessible futures we ought to select, why one filmstrip might be considered morally preferable to any other: that is a question of *ethics*.

How we arrange our affairs so that the future we choose is the future that becomes reality: that is the question of social institutions, of *law*.

NOTES AND QUESTIONS

1. What do you consider to be the most serious international environmental problems facing the world today? Why do you think these problems are particularly serious? What criteria of seriousness are you using?

2. What makes an environmental problem "international" in character? When are international measures necessary or appropriate?

3. For each of the problems you identified in question 1, what is the nature of the "problem"? What prevents a solution from being reached?

4. What role can international law play in solving environmental problems? Why might states agree to international solutions?

A. A BRIEF INTRODUCTION TO INTERNATIONAL ENVIRONMENTAL LAW

D. BODANSKY, THE ART AND CRAFT OF INTERNATIONAL ENVIRONMENTAL LAW[a]
(2009)

Although international environmental law is a comparatively new field, its rules and standards now fill books—and not short books either. A leading treatise on the principles of international environmental law runs to more than 1,000 densely packed pages, detailing rules of virtually every description on virtually every subject. Not so long ago, international environmental law was considered a narrow specialty within the general field of international law. Today, it has become a field in its own right, with sub-specialties on wildlife law, marine pollution, freshwater resources, climate change, sustainable development, chemicals, and so forth.

The proliferation of international environmental norms is all the more remarkable given the infirmities of the international legal process. International law lacks a legislature to make the law, a judiciary to interpret and apply the law, and an executive to enforce the law. How then, have international environmental norms emerged? What are the obstacles to cooperation, and how has international environmental law addressed them? To what extent do international environmental norms affect behavior and why? What are the means by which they are implemented and enforced? These are the fundamental questions of the international legal process.

Chapter 2: How We Got Here: A Brief History of International Environmental Law

The growth of international environmental law has proceeded in fits and starts, in a pattern familiar to political scientists: a problem is discovered with alarm, often as a result of some dramatic event such as an oil spill; public interest surges, leading to a flurry of new initiatives; environmental responses diffuse to other countries through a process of mimicry; the difficulties and costs of addressing the problem slowly become apparent; people become discouraged, bored, or diverted by the emergence of a new issue; and the earlier issue moves into a more quiescent phase, continuing to be addressed in a routine, low-key manner.[12]

In the emergence of international environmental law, three such cycles or waves can be discerned: (1) a conservationist stage, focusing on the protection of wildlife, stretching from the late nineteenth century through the first half of the twentieth century; (2) a pollution-prevention stage, spanning the so-called environmental revolution of the 1960s and early 1970s, marked by the Stockholm Conference, the establishment of the United Nations Environment Program (UNEP), and the negotiation of numerous multilateral agreements, particularly in the field of marine pollution; and (3) a sustainable development phase, beginning in the mid-1980s with the work of the Brundtland Commission and continuing through the 1992 Earth Summit,

---

a. Excerpted and adapted from Chapters 2, 6, 8, 9, and 10.

12. Anthony Downs, Up and Down with Ecology: The "Issue-Attention Cycle," 28 Public Interest 38 (1972).

the 2002 Johannesburg Summit, and the 2012 Rio+20 Conference. [A listing of major milestones in the development of international environmental law appears in Table 11-1.]

International environmental law had its origins in the conservation and nature protection movement of late nineteenth- and early twentieth-century Europe and North America. Although the conservation movement had a national rather than an international focus, the international dimension of conservation received some attention—in particular, the problems of migratory species (primarily birds) and commercially-exploited species found in common areas such as the oceans (fish, fur seals, and whales). In 1868, a German ornithological meeting proposed the

TABLE 11-1
Milestones in the Development of International Environmental Law

Year	Milestone
1868	German ornithological meeting proposes development of international treaty on bird conservation.
1893	*Behring Sea Fur Seals Arbitration.*
1909	International Boundary Waters Treaty (U.S.-Canada) adopted.
1911	North Pacific Fur Seals Convention adopted.
1916	Migratory Birds Treaty (U.S.-Canada) adopted.
1941	*Trail Smelter* case articulates duty to prevent transboundary pollution.
1946	International Convention for the Regulation of Whaling adopted.
1948	International Union for the Conservation of Nature (IUCN) established (now the World Conservation Union).
1954	International Convention for the Prevention of Pollution of the Sea by Oil (OILPOL) adopted.
1962	Publication of Rachel Carson's *Silent Spring.*
1967	Torrey Canyon oil spill leads to negotiation of Intervention Convention and Civil Liability Convention.
1970	First Earth Day. *Time* magazine names the environment "Issue of the Year."
1972	Stockholm Conference on the Human Environment. United Nations Environment Programme (UNEP) established. World Heritage Convention and London Dumping Convention adopted.
1973	Convention on International Trade in Endangered Species (CITES) and International Convention for the Prevention of Pollution from Ships (MARPOL) adopted.
1976	First UNEP Regional Seas Convention adopted.
1979	Long-Range Transboundary Air Pollution Convention (LRTAP) adopted.
1987	Brundtland Commission Report (*Our Common Future*). Montreal Protocol on Substances that Deplete the Ozone Layer adopted.
1988	*Time* magazine names "endangered earth" "Planet of the Year."
1990	Global Environment Facility (GEF) established. London Amendments to Montreal Protocol adopted.
1992	UN Conference on Environment and Development (Earth Summit). Climate Change and Biodiversity Conventions adopted.
1997	Kyoto Protocol adopted.
1998	Rotterdam Convention on trade in hazardous chemicals adopted.
2001	Stockholm Convention on Persistent Organic Pollutants (POPs) adopted.
2002	Johannesburg World Summit on Sustainable Development.
2012	Rio+20 Conference.
2013	Minamata Mercury Convention adopted.

development of an international treaty on bird protection. The Convention to Protect Birds Useful to Agriculture was ultimately adopted in 1902 by twelve European nations and is widely considered the first multilateral environmental treaty. The 1902 Convention was followed by several bilateral treaties, including the 1916 Migratory Birds Convention between the United States and Canada (represented internationally at the time by Great Britain) and a similar agreement in 1936 between the United States and Mexico.

This initial stage in the development of international environmental law was important, but it had several limitations:

First, its focus of interest was narrow. Although some conservationists advocated nature preservation as an end in itself, early conservation efforts did not reflect a generalized concern about environmental protection or pollution. Instead, the conservation movement's dominant strain was utilitarian and anthropocentric, emphasizing the rational use of natural resources by humans.

Second, in conserving nature, the early conservation movement tended to focus on direct threats—in particular, the hunting of wildlife by humans—rather than indirect threats such as habitat loss, pollution, and the introduction of non-native species.

Third, states adopted conventions in a piecemeal, ad hoc manner, and there was little development of institutions. Even as late as 1940, the Western Hemisphere Convention failed to provide for regular meetings of the parties or any other institutional follow-up. As a result, it became a "sleeping beauty"[20]—its excellent substantive provisions virtually devoid of influence.

Despite the achievements of the conservation movement, the environment remained quite marginal in international affairs as late as 1945, the year the United Nations was established. Significantly, the UN Charter made no reference whatsoever to environmental protection or nature conservation. Nor did states establish a UN specialized agency focused on the environment.

International environmental issues did not come into their own until the late 1960s, as part of a more general upsurge of interest in the environment often referred to as the "environmental revolution." The environmental movement of the 1960s differed from its predecessors in several respects. First, it was a mass movement. Second, it focused on broader issues of pollution, technology, population, and economic growth, rather than just on the conservation of nature. Finally, it moved from the earlier focus on economics and science—on the rational utilization of natural resources—to a more zealous, antiestablishment orientation, part of the new politics of the 1960s.

The first multilateral pollution problem to receive international attention was oil pollution from tankers. Following the *Torrey Canyon* oil spill off the English coast in 1967, maritime and coastal states quickly adopted two conventions to address accidental discharges of oil: one recognized the right of coastal states to intervene, and the other established a liability regime. A series of further tanker accidents helped spur the negotiation of the 1973 International Convention for the Prevention of Pollution from Ships (MARPOL), which addresses not only oil pollution, but also other types of vessel-source pollution, including sewage and garbage.

---

20. Simon Lyster, International Wildlife Law 124 (1985) (characterizing the Western Hemisphere Convention as the "sleeping treaty").

By comparison to marine pollution, transboundary air pollution problems received much less attention initially. Yet it was the Nordic countries' concern about transboundary air pollution, in particular acid rain, that led them to propose an international conference on the environment. The conference was held in Stockholm in 1972 and served as a major catalyst—perhaps *the* major catalyst—in the emergence of international environmental law. The Stockholm Conference was the first UN mega-conference. Everything about it was big: it was attended by 6,000 persons, 114 countries, 400 non-governmental groups, and 1,500 journalists. In addition to the official conference, activist groups organized separate events—an Earth Forum and an even more radical Peoples Forum—popularly dubbed "Woodstockholm."

The Stockholm Declaration sets forth sixteen principles for the preservation and enhancement of the human environment. Most of these principles are seldom cited; the exception is Principle 21, which articulated the responsibility of states to ensure that activities under their jurisdiction and control do not adversely affect other states or areas of the global commons. Principle 21 is now widely regarded as part of international law, a view endorsed by the International Court of Justice.

Another consequence of Stockholm was the UN General Assembly's decision in December 1972 to establish the United Nations Environment Program (UNEP), located in Nairobi, Kenya. Owing in part to opposition by the existing UN specialized agencies, the General Assembly did not give UNEP any management responsibilities. But UNEP has played a significant role in helping to stimulate the development of international environmental law, particularly during the late 1970s and 1980s. Important UNEP initiatives have included its regional seas program, which protects the Mediterranean and Caribbean seas among others, as well as its sponsorship of treaty negotiations to protect the stratospheric ozone layer and to regulate international trade in hazardous wastes. The Stockholm process also led, more indirectly, to the negotiation of several important treaties, including the London Dumping Convention (regulating the dumping of hazardous wastes at sea), the World Heritage Convention, and the Convention on International Trade in Endangered Species (CITES).

The period after Stockholm was generally marked by a downturn of interest in the environment, at least compared to what came before and after. Interest in environmental issues began to revive again only in the mid-1980s, as a result of the discovery of the Antarctic ozone hole in 1985 and the beginning of concern about global warming. The year 1987, in particular, witnessed two seminal events: (1) the adoption of the Montreal Ozone Protocol, which has cut the use of ozone-depleting substances dramatically and is widely considered to be the most successful environmental agreement to date; and (2) the publication of *Our Common Future* by the World Commission on Environment and Development, led by former Norwegian Prime Minister Gro Brundtland (and referred to as the Brundtland Commission), which became a best seller and popularized the concept of sustainable development. By 1988, environmental issues had become so prominent that *Time* magazine named the environment "Newsmaker of the Year." The next several years saw a flurry of activity, including the adoption of the Basel Convention on the Transboundary Movements of Hazardous Wastes in 1989, the London Amendment to the Montreal Protocol in 1990, and agreements between the United States and Canada and among European countries to address the problem of acid rain. The process culminated in the 1992 UN Conference on Environment and Development in Rio de Janeiro (popularly known as the Earth Summit)—one of the largest assemblages of world leaders ever—and the negotiation of the climate change and biological diversity conventions.

The more recent phase in international environmental law differs in important ways from the environmental movement of the 1970s. First, it involves much more complex environmental problems such as climate change and biological diversity, whose solutions may require fundamental economic and social changes rather than a relatively simple pollution-prevention fix.

Second, international environmental issues have assumed a more pronounced North-South dimension. The problems of the 1960s and 1970s, such as vessel-source pollution, ocean dumping, and acid rain, primarily involved industrialized countries. But problems such as climate change and biological diversity cannot be solved by developed countries alone; they require action by developing countries as well. As such, developing countries have played a much more central role in establishing these treaty regimes.

Third, the current generation of environmental problems, such as climate change and loss of biodiversity, involve a high degree of scientific uncertainty. With respect to some issues, such as the dangers posed by genetically modified organisms, it is not clear whether a threat exists at all. As a result, techniques to address uncertainty have gained increasing prominence; of particular importance is the so-called precautionary principle, which urges action against environmental threats even in the face of scientific uncertainties. The shift in emphasis toward precaution is reflected in the transformation of the international regime on ocean dumping in the 1990s from a negative-listing approach, which allowed wastes to be dumped unless a waste was prohibited, to a positive-listing approach, which prohibits dumping unless a substance can be shown to be safe.

The organizing principle of this third phase in the development of international environmental law has been sustainable development, which the Brundtland Commission report defined as "development that meets the needs of the present without compromising the ability of future generations to meet their own needs."[38] It reflects two general themes: integration and long-term planning. First, environmental issues should not be seen as stand-alone items—adding a catalytic converter here or a scrubber there—but as important aspects of economic and social decision-making more generally. Second, sustainable development focuses attention on the issue of intergenerational equity. It requires thinking in a long-term manner about how to manage resources sustainably, so that the resources will be available to future generations.

If the Stockholm Conference was the focal point of the second phase of international environmental law, the Rio Summit filled that role for the third. Like Stockholm, Rio's outputs included a declaration of environmental principles (the Rio Declaration) and a detailed action plan (Agenda 21). But also like Stockholm, its most significant results were not the conference outputs themselves, but the two treaties negotiated in parallel: the UN Framework Convention on Climate Change and the Biological Diversity Convention. Successor conferences were held to mark the ten and twenty year anniversaries of the Rio Summit: the Johannesburg World Summit on Sustainable Development in 2002, and the Rio Conference on Sustainable Development, or Rio+20, in 2012, which promoted the idea of the "green economy," enhanced the role of UNEP, and initiated a process to elaborate sustainable development goals (SDGs).

38. World Commission on Environment and Development, Our Common Future 43 (1987).

Chapter 6: Who's Who in the International Environmental Process

A. States

As the term *inter-national* suggests, international environmental law operates largely as a system of law between states. Although it aims ultimately to change the private behavior that is responsible for most environmental problems, its rules apply primarily to states, and few of these rules create rights or duties for companies, individuals or other non-state actors.

Understanding state behavior is, of course, complex, but a useful starting point is to think of states—like individuals—as rational actors, seeking to advance their own self-interest. Thus, in transboundary pollution cases, downstream states typically favor strong action because they are the ones suffering the ill effects, while upstream states have an interest in continuing to pollute because the environmental damage is an externality. Similarly, with respect to global pollution problems, states have an interest in undertaking collective action, yet each individual state has an interest in free riding, so long as it can do so without penalty.

The assumption that states have identifiable, stable interests that they rationally pursue is incomplete in two ways, however. First, states are motivated not only by self-interest but by normative considerations about what is right or proper to do. That is, they respond to what social scientists have called a *logic of appropriateness* as well as a *logic of consequences*.[14] Second, states are complex entities, with many constituent parts, often with very different interests and beliefs of their own. As a result, we cannot assume that national interests are a given. Instead, interests are often contested and contingent, the outcome of domestic political processes involving complex interactions between different sub-state actors: rival agencies within the executive branches; checks and balances between the executive, legislative and judicial branches; lobbying by business and environmental groups; and public opinion more generally. A state's position on an environmental issue such as climate change, whaling, or genetically-modified organisms emerges from the complex interaction of these sub-state actors—environmental groups raising concerns and creating a demand for public regulation, businesses lobbying officials in the different branches and levels of government, and government actors themselves interacting in a game of bureaucratic politics.

B. International Institutions

In addition to states, international institutions play an important role in the international environmental process. Although international environmental law lacks an institution with general governance functions, a multitude of institutions play significant roles, some global and others regional or bilateral; some focused on a particular issue area such as whaling or forestry and others with a broader mandate; some scientific in orientation and others focused on capacity-building or policy more generally.

In analyzing international institutions, we can array them along a spectrum, based on their degree of autonomy from states. At one extreme, some international institutions serve merely as intergovernmental forums; others operate as autonomous actors.

---

14. James G. March & Johan P. Olsen, Rediscovering Institutions: The Organizational Basis of Politics (1989).

International law uses the concept of "legal personality" to denote the point along this spectrum at which an international institution is considered sufficiently autonomous to have a separate legal existence and to be able to act in its own right for certain legal purposes—asserting claims, entering into treaties, and exercising other implied powers that are necessary for it to fulfill its functions.

The international institution with the broadest competence over environmental issues is UNEP, established as a result of the 1972 Stockholm Conference. In contrast to UN specialized agencies such as the World Health Organization, UNEP lacks a separate treaty basis and instead derives its authority from the UN General Assembly, which created it. UNEP is a comparatively small institution, with a small budget. It has played a largely informational and catalytic role, helping to spur the negotiation of treaties on ozone depletion, biodiversity, and hazardous wastes, and providing secretariat services. The upgrading of UNEP by the Rio+20 conference in 2012, and the transformation of UNEP's Governing Council into a universal body, open to participation by all UN member states, has raised expectations that UNEP may play a larger role in the future.

Perhaps the most distinctive types of international environmental institution are the conferences of parties (COPs) established by most multilateral environmental agreements, which meet on a regular basis and are open to all parties. The decision-making authority and procedures of COPs vary from treaty to treaty. Although none has general legislative power, some have limited authority (usually by a two-thirds or three-quarters majority vote) to adopt new rules that bind all of the treaty parties except those that file a specific objection. In addition, multilateral environmental agreements typically provide for a permanent secretariat—in some cases, an existing institution such as UNEP and in other cases a new one—and some establish specialized bodies to provide scientific advice or to consider issues relating to implementation and compliance.

C. Non-Governmental Organizations (NGOs)

Generally, non-governmental actors exercise influence in one of two ways: either by persuading government decision makers or by changing their calculus of costs and benefits. Most commonly, NGOs exercise their influence with respect to national governments. They lobby their government to support a policy internationally or to implement its international obligations domestically, or they work in alliance with NGOs in other countries to influence foreign states. Most major environmental negotiations are now attended by numerous NGOs, which monitor their own government's positions and statements to guard against potential backsliding and work closely with sympathetic delegations from other countries.

Typically, NGOs take part in international institutions as observers rather than as full participants. But in a few cases, NGOs have a quasi-official status internationally. IUCN, a *sui generis* organization composed of both government agencies and non-governmental groups, is the most prominent example. It initiated the negotiation of the Convention on International Trade in Endangered Species, prepared the first draft of the agreement, continues to be a key source of information about the species that should be protected, and now serves as host of the Ramsar wetlands convention secretariat.

Finally, NGOs may try to influence business through publicity and consumer pressure. In some cases, NGOs have relied on public confrontation. A prominent example was the Greenpeace campaign in 1995 against the sinking of the Brent Spar oil platform by Shell. But, increasingly, NGOs have sought to work in cooperation with industry to develop voluntary codes of conduct. A leading sectoral example is the Forest Stewardship Council (FSC), which NGOs initiated in response to the failure at the 1992 Rio Conference to adopt a binding forest agreement.

D. BUSINESS

Business can play two roles in the international environmental process. First, it can be the object of international regulation—not directly, since international law applies only to states, but indirectly, as the ultimate regulatory target. Second, it can be a subject, actively seeking to shape the development and implementation of international environmental law in either positive or negative ways.

Sometimes companies adopt environmental measures proactively, even before government regulations are adopted. For example, a number of major companies, including British Petroleum, General Electric, and DuPont, have adopted their own, voluntary greenhouse gas emissions targets. Some apparently do so because they believe that a green image will help them in the marketplace and that consumers will reward them through their purchasing decisions. Others may believe that regulation is inevitable and that beginning to adjust now will lower their costs over the long run, or that their actions might help shape the governmental regulations that eventually ensue. And some may reflect the environmental values of the company's leadership. The environmental initiatives of Wal-Mart, for example, seem to be attributable in part to a desire to counteract criticisms of the company's labor practices, thereby improving its image in the marketplace, and in part to the environmental values of the Walton family.

Chapters 8 and 9: International Standard-Setting

The canonical statement of the formal sources of international law—Article 38 of the International Court of Justice Statute—identifies three sources: treaties, custom, and general principles:

- *Treaties* are explicit agreements in writing.
- *Custom* is generated through the regular practice of states, engaged in out of a sense of legal obligation. The rules of diplomatic immunity, for example, evolved over centuries through the repeated interaction of states.
- Finally, *general principles* are norms that reflect fundamental propositions of law, shared by legal systems around the world.

The central difference between treaties on the one hand and custom and general principles on the other is that treaties are the product of a purposive process of negotiation, whereas customary norms and general principles emerge through more diffuse processes. All three are typically classified as "hard law," in contrast to a wide variety of norms that do not qualify as "legal" in character, including resolutions of international organizations, conference declarations, and business codes of conduct. The UN General Assembly, for example, lacks legislative authority, so its resolutions have the status of recommendations. For the same reason, neither the Stockholm

Declaration nor the Rio Declaration on Environment and Development is itself legal in nature; both would have that status only if they were incorporated into a treaty or were deemed to constitute norms of customary international law. And business codes of conduct are developed by non-state actors, without any formal lawmaking authority at all.

A. TREATIES

From the inception of international environmental law, treaties and other forms of negotiated agreements have been the predominant means of achieving international cooperation. According to one recent compilation, states have negotiated more than 450 multilateral environmental agreements and 1,500 bilateral instruments on a wide variety of subjects: protection of the stratospheric ozone layer, prevention of dangerous anthropogenic climate change, mitigation of acid rain, control of hazardous waste exports, regulation of trade in wildlife, protection of wetlands, prevention of oil pollution, and many others.[1] Indeed, in the mid-1990s, environmental treaties were proliferating so rapidly that some worried about "treaty congestion."

Negotiated agreements offer several advantages over more informal mechanisms of international cooperation:

- They enable states to address issues in a purposive, rational manner.
- They promote reciprocity by allowing states to delineate precisely what each party is expected to do.
- Because they have a canonical form, they provide greater certainty about the applicable norms than non-treaty sources of international law.
- Finally, they allow states to tailor a regime's institutional arrangements and mechanisms to fit the particular problem.

Traditionally, treaties were comparatively static arrangements, memorializing the rights and duties of the parties as agreed at a particular point in time. Today, environmental agreements are usually dynamic arrangements, establishing ongoing regulatory processes. The result is that, in most environmental regimes, the treaty text itself represents just the tip of the normative iceberg. The majority of the norms are adopted through more flexible techniques, which allow international environmental law to respond more quickly to the emergence of new problems and new knowledge.

One approach to building a treaty over time that has been used extensively in international environmental law is the "framework convention-protocol approach." Initially, states negotiate a framework convention, which establishes the general architecture of the regime, including, for example, its objective, principles, basic obligations, and institutions. Then, protocols are negotiated that build on the parent agreement through the elaboration of more specific (and costly) commitments.

The framework convention-protocol approach has several rationales. First, it allows states to address a problem in a step-by-step manner rather than all at once. States tend to be willing to join a framework convention because it does not contain stringent obligations. As a result, they can begin to address a problem without waiting

1. Ronald B. Mitchell, International Environmental Agreements Database Project, v.2013.2, iea.uoregon.edu. The database lists more than 1200 multilateral environmental agreements, but this total includes amendments as separate agreements.

for a consensus to emerge on appropriate response measures. For example, when both LRTAP and the Vienna Ozone Convention were adopted, many states remained unconvinced of the need for action. Nevertheless, even skeptical states acquiesced in the adoption of these conventions, since the conventions did not commit them to take any specific actions.

In addition, although framework conventions are themselves weak, they can create positive feedback loops that facilitate the deepening of the regime through the adoption of protocols containing specific substantive commitments. First, the framework convention can help reduce uncertainties and produce agreement about the relevant facts—about who is doing what to whom—by requiring states to submit national reports and by encouraging scientific research and assessments. The institutions established by the framework convention often play a catalytic role in this process by collecting data, providing technical assistance, and issuing reports. Second, the framework convention (and, in particular, the regular meetings of the parties) can help generate normative consensus by providing an ongoing forum for discussion and negotiation, serving as a focal point for international public opinion, and building trust among participants. Finally, when states eventually decide to act, framework conventions increase their capacity to do so by putting in place basic institutions and decision-making processes. The theory is that, once a framework convention is adopted, the international lawmaking process begins to take on a momentum of its own. States that were initially reluctant to undertake substantive commitments, but that acquiesced in the seemingly innocuous process set in motion by the framework convention, will feel increasing pressure not to fall out of step as that process gains momentum.

B. CUSTOM AND GENERAL PRINCIPLES

In contrast to treaties, the two main types of non-treaty norms—customary law and general principles—are not created through purposeful acts of lawmaking and do not have a canonical form. Instead, they emerge through less well-defined, more informal processes and raise a host of theoretical puzzles:

- How do non-treaty norms emerge? To what extent, for example, do customary norms emerge as a result of calculations by states of their rational self-interest? To what extent are they imposed by powerful states? To what extent do they reflect psychological needs for order and regularity?
- Do non-treaty norms have any effect on behavior, and, if so, how and why?
- What does it mean to say that a norm is part of customary international law or is a general principle of law? Where does the "binding" character of these norms come from?
- Finally, should non-treaty norms be followed? Are they legitimate sources of obligation? Do they have any claim to obedience?

Although the concept of customary international law is often viewed as mystifying, the emergence and application of social norms through informal, decentralized processes is a commonplace occurrence. Language provides a good illustration. Every time we speak, we apply a complex set of customary rules of grammar and usage. These rules are not legislated or enforced by any centralized body. Instead, they emerge and evolve through the regular practice of language users and are enforced through a diffuse set of social sanctions.

According to the orthodox account of customary international law, the customary lawmaking process involves two elements: first, consistent state practice and, second, a sense of legal obligation (or *opinio juris*). When many states behave in a consistent manner for a significant period of time, and when this consistent, long-standing practice manifests a belief about what the law requires, then customary international law is created.

C. SOFT LAW

Conference resolutions, business codes of conduct, and the like are not legal norms. Instead, they are usually classified as "soft law." Like hard law, they are normative: they are intended to guide or influence behavior by providing *reasons* for action. The fact that the UN General Assembly, for example, adopted a resolution calling for a moratorium on high seas driftnet fishing is a *reason* to stop using driftnets. The resolution provides a standard of evaluation. Compliance serves as a justification for one's own actions, and violation is a ground for criticism of others. Moreover, like hard law, these non-legal instruments are a social creation; they are the product of identifiable processes of norm-making. From this perspective, soft law does not simply represent the absence of law; it represents a kind of legal purgatory. But, unlike hard law, soft law does not create legally-binding obligations.

Chapter 10: Implementation, Compliance and Effectiveness

Translating policy into action is notoriously difficult. Many policies are characterized, as Richard Elmore once quipped, by "grand pretensions, faulty execution and puny results."[5] Because international environmental law typically aims to control not merely state conduct but private conduct, its implementation poses a particular challenge.

States serve as the primary transmission belt for putting international environmental rules into effect. International environmental agreements generally impose obligations on states and rely on states to implement their commitments. For this reason, the success of treaties such as the Montreal Protocol, the Kyoto Protocol, and the Convention on International Trade in Endangered Species (CITES) depends on the degree to which they are "domesticated." Some treaties spell out the duty to implement explicitly. But even in the absence of any explicit provision, the rule of *pacta sunt servanda*—the foundation of international treaty law—requires states to do whatever is necessary to implement their treaty obligations.

Implementation is not simply a technical, top-down process, involving directives from the government. In practice, it is a political process in which industry groups and environmental organizations all participate to varying degrees. Industry can contribute positively by providing expertise in designing technically feasible and cost-effective approaches, but it may also seek to weaken implementation measures in order to reduce its own adjustment costs. Public participation is also an increasingly integral part of the national implementation process.

5. Richard F. Elmore, Organizational Models of Social Program Implementation, 26 Public Policy 185, 186 (1978).

Treaties vary considerably in how much freedom they give states in the choice of implementation methods. In most cases, international law gives states significant discretion as to the choice of implementation methods. A typical formulation found in many treaties simply requires states to take "appropriate" measures. This allows each state to take into account its own legal system, regulatory culture, and other national circumstances in determining what measures are "appropriate." At the far extreme, treaties establishing an obligation to achieve some overall result, such as the national emissions targets in the Kyoto Protocol, give states almost complete flexibility in determining how they will reach the required outcome—whether by means of taxes, product standards, emission limits, voluntary agreements with industry, subsidies, education, and so forth. At the other end of the spectrum, some agreements set forth quite specific obligations of conduct that leave little discretion. For example, MARPOL requires flag states to prescribe precise rules for the construction and design of oil tankers, and to prohibit and sanction violations of these standards by vessels operating under their authority.

A threshold issue in treaty implementation is whether implementation requires legislation. For a variety of reasons, sometimes the answer is no. A treaty may focus on governmental actions such as reporting, which can be performed by the executive branch on its own authority, without any need for legislative approval. Or, under a country's constitution, treaties may have the force of domestic law directly, making additional legislative implementation unnecessary. Or existing legislation might provide the necessary authority to implement a treaty's obligations. Even when implementing legislation is needed, however, the adoption of legislation is usually only the first step in the implementation process. Most treaties also require various types of administrative implementation, such as further rule-making to give greater specificity to general legislative mandates, monitoring and assessment, preparation of reports, issuance of permits, and the investigation and prosecution of alleged violations.

In contrast to legislative and administrative implementation, judicial implementation of international environmental law is comparatively rare. A notable exception was a Philippines case that applied the principle of intergenerational equity to allow a group of children to challenge timber licenses. [Minors Oposa v. Secretary of Environment and Natural Resources, Supreme Court Reports Annotated (G.R.) No. 101083, (S.C. July 30, 1993), reprinted in 33 I.L.M 174 (1994).]

Even in the absence of international enforcement, many if not most states implement their international environmental obligations almost as a matter of course. Many causal factors help account for this practice of self-implementation: calculations of self-interest, a sense of normative commitment, bureaucratic routines, or pressure (or even litigation) by environmental groups.

NOTES AND QUESTIONS

1. What are the principal differences between the domestic and the international legal processes?

2. How and why might states agree to an international treaty and comply with its terms?

B. TRANSBOUNDARY ENVIRONMENTAL PROBLEMS

It is a truism that pollution does not respect political borders. Merrill, Golden Rules for Transboundary Pollution, 46 Duke L.J. 931, 932 (1997). Traditionally, most pollution was local. But as the nineteenth century progressed and the scale of environmental impacts increased, activities in one state more frequently had environmental effects in another. For example, in the late nineteenth century, the diversion of the waters of the Rio Grande by farmers and ranchers in the United States harmed communities on the Mexican side of the border, leading the United States to articulate the so-called Harmon Doctrine, which provides that a state has the right to do whatever it likes within its own territory, even if its actions cause harm to another state. Similarly, fumes from the Trail Smelter in Canada blew south into Washington State, causing damage to American agricultural communities and leading to a very different result in the *Trail Smelter* arbitration (discussed below).

Today, pollution often travels hundreds or even thousands of miles. A study sponsored by NAFTA's Commission on Environmental Cooperation found that a significant percentage of the dioxin in mothers' breast milk in the Canadian Arctic came from municipal and medical waste incinerators and other sources located outside Canada, in the United States or other countries. Miller, Tracking Dioxins to the Arctic (Fall 2000), available at http://www.cec.org. And in 2006, *The New York Times* reported that pollution from China was now having effects in California. As the *Times* concluded, pollution has become one of China's "lesser-known exports." Pollution from China Casts a Global Shadow, N.Y. Times, June 11, 2006.

Disputes stemming from pollution spillovers are, of course, by no means confined to disputes between countries. In the relatively early days of the United States, the Supreme Court heard several common law cases involving complaints by one state about spillover pollution from another. See, e.g., Georgia v. Tennessee Copper, 206 U.S. 230 (1907); Missouri v. Illinois, 200 U.S. 496 (1906). More recently, Congress has sought to address these issues, and the Supreme Court has had occasion to review Congress's approach. See, e.g., CWA §402(b) and (d); CAA §110(a)(2)(D); Arkansas v. Oklahoma, 503 U.S. 91 (1991) (covered in Chapter 7). Citizens in downstream states have also sought to use domestic courts to obtain recourse for interstate pollution. See, e.g., International Paper Co. v. Ouellette, 479 U.S. 481 (1987). Inter-municipal border wars are not uncommon either. Courts in New York and in other domestic U.S. jurisdictions "have increasingly been faced with deciding . . . inter-municipal feuds." Zarin, Border Wars and SEQRA, Envtl. L. N.Y. 89 (May 2006).

Although these inter-state and inter-municipal disputes have been contentious, transnational pollution problems are even more difficult to address because there are usually no courts with jurisdiction to resolve disputes and no legislature to enact regulatory rules. States are sovereign, and must consent to the jurisdiction of a court or to the regulatory rules specified in a treaty. But upstream states have little reason to do so, since from their perspective the pollution damages are an externality.

Transboundary pollution issues led to some of the earliest developments in international environmental law. In the first half of the twentieth century, pollution of boundary waters was one of the only environmental issues to receive any regular attention, generally on a bilateral basis, as in the treaties the United States negotiated with Canada and Mexico. The pollution damage in the United States from a smelter in Canada led to the *Trail Smelter* arbitration, the first and still one of the only transboundary pollution disputes resolved through adjudication. And concern in the late 1960s among Nordic states about transboundary air pollution, in particular acid rain, led them to propose holding the 1972 Stockholm Conference, which served as a major catalyst in the emergence of international environmental law.

1. The Role of National Courts

Transboundary pollution problems are often similar in kind to the types of local pollution problems litigated in national courts. This suggests the possibility, often overlooked, of using national courts to address transboundary pollution problems. For example, in the *Michie* case, 37 residents of Windsor, Ontario, brought suit in U.S. district court against three American companies for air pollution damage, and eventually reached a large settlement. Michie v. Great Lakes Steel Div., 495 F.2d 213 (6th Cir. 1974). Similarly, in Poro v. Houillieres du Bassin du Lorraine, a German appeals court awarded damages to a German motel owner for injury to its business interests resulting from pollution emitted by a French-owned facility across the border in France.[b]

Consider the following case study and ask yourself, what role could national courts play?

Case Study: Victoria Sewage

For many years, the City of Victoria, British Columbia, has dumped tens of millions of gallons of raw, untreated sewage into the Straits of Juan de Fuca each day. It is the only major city in the region not to treat its sewage. The sewage contains toxic waste, heavy metals, and chemicals, in addition to toilet paper, feces, bacteria, and other refuse. Much of the sewage is carried by currents onto the United States side of the Straits, allegedly endangering the crab, halibut, salmon, cod, squid, oyster, and clam fisheries on the Washington side of the border, as well as lowering the recreational uses and amenities of Olympic Peninsula coastal areas. In a June 13, 2014 letter to British Columbia's premier, Washington State's congressional delegation claimed that untreated pollution from Victoria threatened 67,000 commercial fisheries jobs in Washington. Although Victoria has been planning to build a sewage treatment facility for more than twenty years, the project has been repeatedly delayed due to cost and siting issues, and construction has still not begun. In the meantime, British Columbian officials argue that, because Victoria's sewage is discharged into open waters with rapid currents, it rapidly dissipates and is not a serious threat to the environment, in contrast to U.S. discharges into Puget Sound, a relatively closed body of water.

Attempting to use national courts to address a transboundary pollution problem such as Victoria's sewage would raise a host of issues:

1. What functions should a lawsuit serve? Compensating the victims of past pollution? Or preventing future pollution (for example, through an injunction that required Victoria to build a secondary treatment plant)?

---

b. This case and several others are described in P. Sand, The Role of Domestic Procedures in Transnational Environmental Disputes, in OECD, Legal Aspects of Transfrontier Pollution (1974).

2. Who should be able to bring suit concerning pollution damage in Washington State? Injured individuals or companies? The State of Washington? The United States federal government? Consider the types of damages individuals could claim as opposed to those the state or federal government could claim.

3. Against whom could a case be brought? The City of Victoria or the British Columbian provincial government? Or the Canadian federal government? If the latter, on what theory might Canada be held responsible for the actions of city governments or private companies? What defense might Canada assert?

4. Where could suit be brought? In the country of origin (Canada), where the polluting activity takes place? Or in the victim state (Washington), where the injury occurred? Consider some of the factors that must be relevant in answering this question:

    a. Do U.S. plaintiffs have the right to sue in Canadian courts?

    b. Which court(s) have personal jurisdiction over the potential defendants? Generally, Canadian courts will have jurisdiction over individuals and companies that are located in Canada or are Canadian nationals. In contrast, Washington state courts may have a more difficult time asserting jurisdiction over Canadian defendants.

    c. Which court(s) have jurisdiction over the subject matter of the dispute? Traditionally, Canadian courts have followed the common law doctrine set forth in an 1893 decision of the British House of Lords, British South Africa Company v. Companhia de Moccambique, which held that, in cases of trespass to land, only the courts of the state where the land is situated have jurisdiction. Canadian courts have interpreted this doctrine to preclude claims for compensation for damage to land located in another country.[c] In contrast, U.S. courts generally follow an exception to the *Moccambique* rule, which provides for jurisdiction over lawsuits for damage to foreign property, if the acts that caused the damage occurred within the forum state.

    d. If a Canadian court has jurisdiction and suit could be brought there, what remedies would the court be likely to impose? Money damages for past injuries (which would raise issues of assessment and valuation)? Or injunctions to stop pollution from occurring in the future? Conversely, to what extent would a Washington court's money judgment or injunction be enforceable in Canada?

5. What law applies? Canadian law, U.S. (including Washington State) law, or international law? If a case were brought on a common law cause of action, this choice of law issue might not make a difference, since Canadian and American common law doctrines are broadly similar.[d] Assuming a U.S. statute created a cause of action for water pollution damage, does this law

---

c. See Albert v. Fraser Companies Ltd., 1 D.L.R. 329 (1937) (C.A. N.B.) ("an action founded on trespass to realty in a foreign country whether the title does or does not come into question cannot be tried here").

d. There are also some differences, however. For example, U.S. courts recognize the public trust doctrine, whereas Canadian courts have traditionally not. Moreover, in Canada a defendant may be able to raise the defense of statutory authority more easily, if it is acting pursuant to a permit or license. See generally Environmental Law and Policy in the Canadian Context (A. Greenbaum & A. Wellington eds., 2010).

apply to activities in Canada that cause damage in the United States? And would a Canadian court apply the U.S. law, in particular to activities permitted under Canadian law?

In the 1970s, Western countries attempted to develop international standards regarding many of these questions within the Organization of Economic Co-operation and Development (OECD). The OECD developed principles of non-discrimination and equal right of access to national courts, intended to ensure that states do not apply their law less rigorously to foreign harms than to domestic harms (the principle of non-discrimination) and that international borders do not make a difference in access to remedies for transboundary pollution (the principle of equal access). Under these principles, foreign victims should have equal access in the country of origin to information and notice and to all public authorities, courts, and administrative hearings; and national courts in the country of origin should grant foreigners the same rights and remedies as those enjoyed by nationals.[e]

OECD PRINCIPLES CONCERNING TRANSFRONTIER POLLUTION
(1974)

C. Principle of Non-Discrimination

4. Countries should initially base their action on the principle of non-discrimination, whereby:
   (a) polluters causing transfrontier pollution should be subject to legal or statutory provisions no less severe than those which would apply for any equivalent pollution occurring within their country, under comparable conditions and in comparable zones, taking into account, when appropriate, the special nature and environmental needs of the zone affected;
   (b) in particular, without prejudice to quality objectives or standards applying to transfrontier pollution mutually agreed upon by the countries concerned, the levels of transfrontier pollution entering into the zones liable to be affected by such pollution should not exceed those considered acceptable under comparable conditions and in comparable zones inside the country in which it originates, taking into account, where appropriate, the special state of the environment in the affected country;
   (c) any country whenever it applies the Polluter-Pays Principle should apply it to all polluters within this country without making any difference according to whether the pollution affects this country or another country;
   (d) persons affected by transfrontier pollution should be granted no less favorable treatment than persons affected by similar pollution in the country from which such transfrontier pollution originates.

e. The principle of equal access has also received support from the Council of Europe, Res. (71) 5 of March 26, 1971, and the UN Environment Program's Draft Principles of Conduct in the Field of the Environment for the Guidance of States in the Conservation and Harmonious Utilization of Natural Resources Shared by Two or More States, princ. 14, UNEP Doc. UNEP/GC/101 (1977).

D. *Principle of Equal Right of Hearing*

5. Countries should make every effort to introduce, when not already in existence, a system affording equal right of hearing, according to which:
   (a) whenever a project, a new activity or a course of conduct may create a significant risk of transfrontier pollution and is investigated by public authorities, those who may be affected by such pollution should have the same rights of standing in judicial or administrative proceedings in the country where it originates as those of that country;
   (b) whenever transfrontier pollution gives rise to damage in a country, those who are affected by such pollution should have the same rights of standing in judicial or administrative proceedings in the country where such pollution originates as those of that country, and they should be extended procedural rights equivalent to the rights extended to those of that country.

A number of countries have negotiated bilateral or regional agreements providing for equal access to national courts.[f] Although the United States and Canada do not have such a bilateral treaty, efforts have been made by the private bar and at the state and provincial levels to develop general rules on equal access and non-discrimination. The American and Canadian Bar Associations collaborated to draft a treaty, modeled on the OECD principles, on a regime of equal access and remedies in cases of transfrontier pollution. And in 1982, the Uniform Law Conference of Canada and the U.S. National Conference of Commissioners on Uniform State Law jointly adopted a Uniform Transboundary Pollution Reciprocal Access Act, which has been adopted by several states and provinces, including Ontario. The Uniform Act effectively abolishes the *Moccambique* rule by allowing the state of origin to assert jurisdiction over actions for transboundary damage in a reciprocating jurisdiction (i.e., a state or province in the other country that provides comparable rights of access). The Act also provides that the law of the source state applies and that the plaintiff has the same rights as in cases where the damage occurred in the source state.

f. For example, the 1974 Convention on the Protection of the Environment between Denmark, Finland, Norway, and Sweden provides in Article 3:

(1) Any person who is affected or may be affected by a nuisance caused by environmentally harmful activities in another Contracting State shall have the same right to bring before the appropriate Court or Administrative Authority of that state the question of the permissibility of such activities, including the question of measures to prevent damage, and to appeal against the decision of the Court or Administrative Authority to the same extent and on the same terms as a legal entity of the State in which the activities are being carried out.
(2) The provisions of the first paragraph of this Article shall be equally applicable in the case of proceedings concerning compensation for damage caused by environmentally harmful activities. The question of compensation shall not be judged by rules which are less favorable to the injured party than are the rules of compensation of the State in which the Activities are being carried out.

NOTES AND QUESTIONS

1. If you were contemplating bringing a lawsuit for transboundary water pollution originating in British Columbia, where would you file your suit? Against whom?

2. From a policy standpoint, should international law seek to direct lawsuits to the courts of the source state or the victim state? Or does it matter where the lawsuits are heard?

3. What are the strengths and weaknesses of national courts as a means of addressing transboundary pollution problems?

4. People to Save Sheyenne v. Department of Health, 697 N.W.2d 319 (N.D. 2005), is a North Dakota Supreme Court decision regarding the issuance of a state administrative NPDES permit to discharge water from Devil's Lake into the Sheyenne River, which in turn discharges into the Red River, which flows north across the U.S.-Canadian border into the Canadian province of Manitoba. Manitoba, as well as some U.S. NGOs, opposed the issuance of the permit at the state administrative level, on the ground that the discharge would adversely affect water quality in various ways, and then challenged the permit through the North Dakota court system, up to the North Dakota Supreme Court. The court applied an arbitrary and capricious standard in upholding the state agency's conclusion that the project should be approved despite these concerns. Assume that the permitted discharge from Devil's Lake did cause harm to waters in Canada, as the permit challengers alleged. What recourse should the impacted residents of Canada have had? To what extent should the issuance of a permit by the source state serve as a shield to liability or legal responsibility? What would be the analysis if the affected area were in a state in the United States, rather than in Canada? See International Paper Co. v. Ouellette, 479 U.S. 481 (1987), excerpted as a principal case in Chapter 1.

5. A number of treaties address civil liability for particular types of environmental injuries—in particular, damage from oil spills and nuclear accidents. These treaties address many of the issues raised by transboundary litigation. For example, the 1969 International Convention for Civil Liability for Oil Pollution Damage imposes liability for oil spills on ship owners, gives coastal states exclusive jurisdiction, and provides for enforcement of judgments in the courts of other parties.

6. Despite the OECD principles and the various civil liability conventions, tort recovery for transboundary injuries remains extremely difficult. As Noah Sachs notes:

> The absence of effective remedies is highlighted by the illegal dumping in August 2006 of 528 tons of caustic hazardous waste in villages in the Ivory Coast. The waste was off-loaded by a Greek-owned tanker flying a Panamanian flag and leased by the London branch of a Swiss trading corporation, Trafigura, whose physical headquarters are in the Netherlands. The toxic sludge caused at least eight deaths and dozens of hospitalizations. With the existing barriers to international tort litigation, it is unlikely that injured villagers will receive any monetary compensation from culpable parties. . . .
>
> Suits under domestic law for transboundary environmental damage have been exceedingly difficult to prosecute . . . due to robust and persistent procedural hurdles to transboundary tort litigation. The hurdles include obtaining personal jurisdiction over foreign firms, extraterritorial service of process, the local action rule (which provides that actions in tort for damages to real property must be brought where the property is located), resolving choice of law questions, overcoming motions to dismiss on the grounds of forum non conveniens, deciding whether a defendant's governmental permit is relevant to its tort liability, and enforcing judgments. For pollution that flows across

borders, the locus delicti, or place of the tort, is often hotly disputed. Added to these legal barriers is the practical problem of the expense of bringing suit against a foreign entity and proving its negligence. [Sachs, Beyond the Liability Wall: Strengthening Tort Remedies in International Environmental Law, 55 UCLA L. Rev. 837, 840, 848 (2008).]

7. After many years in which there was relatively little transborder litigation involving the United States and Canada, there are indications the situation may be changing. In Pakootas v. Teck Cominco Metals, 452 F.3d 1066 (2006), the Ninth Circuit held that CERCLA applies to contamination in Washington State resulting from discharges of heavy metals from the Teck Cominco plant in Canada, which was carried by the Columbia River across the border into the United States. The court held that the case did not involve an extraterritorial application of CERCLA—against which there is a presumption in U.S. law—because the leaching of the heavy metal from the slag—the "release" to which CERCLA applies—took place in Washington State and was therefore "entirely domestic." In a December 2012 ruling, the U.S. district court found Teck Cominco liable under CERCLA for dumping nearly 10 million tons of toxic slag into the Columbia River, at least 8.7 million tons of which was transported into Washington State, Pakootas v. Teck Cominco Metals, 2012 WL 6546088 (E.D. Wash., Dec. 14, 2012).[g] The litigation against Teck Cominco is further described in subsection 3 below. In another transboundary pollution case, a Canadian provincial court allowed a lawsuit to proceed against a U.S. utility for mercury pollution from two of the company's coal-fired power plants located in Michigan less than a mile from the border. Edwards v. DTE Energy, Ontario Superior Court of Justice, Doc. No. 298 (Jan. 16, 2008). (Edwards later withdrew his lawsuit, after Michigan announced a new rule to reduce mercury pollution by 90 percent and DTE Energy had made significant efforts to reduce its pollution.) In both cases, the lawsuits were initiated by private parties, under citizen suit provisions of the relevant statutes. See Garcer, Mahoney & Dyck, Cross-Border Litigation Gains Traction in U.S. and Canadian Courts, 20 Envtl. Claims J. 181 (2008).

2. Trail Smelter Arbitration

The *Trail Smelter* case is the seminal case in which an international tribunal has held a state responsible for transboundary pollution and has assessed damages. The case arose in the 1920s from the operation of a giant zinc and lead smelter by the Consolidated Mining and Smelting Company of Canada (Cominco). The smelter, located along the Columbia River about 7 miles north of the U.S. border as the crow flies or about 11 miles following the course of the river, began processing gold in the late 1800s and is now one of the world's largest integrated lead and zinc smelters and refining complexes.

The background of the case is described by Robert Thiel:

To appease B.C. residents of the area, Cominco had built 400-foot stacks at the smelter in the mid-1920s in an attempt to carry the smoke away from Trail. Because mountains surround the valley on the east and west, the giant stacks only succeeded in funneling the emissions southward in diurnal downdrafts through the gorge to northern Stevens County, Washington—scorching fields, orchards, forests and communities near the

g. This opinion was vacated in April 2013 and, as of July 2014, the case was still pending.

town of Northport, a small community about 8 miles south of the border and 18 miles south of Trail.

Outraged over the effects of the fumes on their crops and businesses, Northport residents formed a protective association to obtain compensation from the smelter and, if necessary, intervention by the U.S. State Department. The dispute became acrimonious. Cominco tried to make cash settlements, but was barred from acquiring smoke easements in Washington because of a state constitutional provision prohibiting foreign ownership of land; the Washington residents in turn apparently lacked judicial recourse in British Columbia because the courts there [following the *Moccambique* rule] refused to accept jurisdiction in suits for damage to land located outside the province.

In 1927, the Northport residents and their congressman had convinced the State Department to pressure Ottawa for a resolution. Despite the private nature of the dispute, the two governments agreed in 1928 to refer the dispute to the International Joint Commission [IJC] under the investigation provisions (Article 9) of the [1909] Boundary Waters Treaty.[h] The IJC held hearings and conducted field surveys, and in 1931 it issued a compromise report recommending that the smelter pay $350,000 for damages caused up to 1 January 1932. People in Washington were disappointed by the result. The amount was less than half of their claim, and the IJC had limited its recommended award to actual, observable economic injury to agriculture. It had rejected attempts by the U.S. to show that there had been long-term cumulative effects on soils and forests, and it refused to recognize either the claims of the state for damage to state-owned forests or those of Stevens County for loss of tax revenues. Moreover, the IJC—dividing along national lines in one of the few times in its history—could not agree on any specific remedial measures to be taken by the smelter to curb the pollution, as the U.S. had urged.

The US demanded a better settlement. But the Canadian government stalled on any resolution, in part because Cominco, a subsidiary of the politically-powerful Canadian Pacific Railway, objected to paying even the $350,000 that the IJC had recommended. In exasperation, President Roosevelt sent a letter to Prime Minister Bennett suggesting that "unless a way is found as soon as possible to reach a settlement in this case, real harm may be done to the relations of Canada and the United States in the Far West." Concerned now that the controversy might derail American consent to a treaty on reciprocal tariff reductions, Ottawa finally consented to binding arbitration by a three-member panel. Interestingly enough, the two governments refused to refer the controversy to the IJC for arbitration under Article 10 of the Boundary Waters Treaty,[i] apparently because they had no confidence in the members of the Commission at the time. [R. Thiel, Environmental Cooperation between British Columbia and Washington State 25-27 (LL.M. paper, University of Washington School of Law, May 1997).]

Under the April 15, 1935, agreement between the United States and Canada referring the case to arbitration, the Arbitral Tribunal was to determine:

1. Whether damage caused by the Trail Smelter in the state of Washington has occurred since the first day of January, 1932, and, if so, what indemnity should be paid therefor?

h. Under the Article 9 "reference" provisions of the Boundary Waters Treaty, either government may ask the International Joint Commission to investigate any "differences" between the two governments involving rights, obligations, or interests of the U.S. or Canada along their common frontier. The IJC's conclusions in an Article 9 reference are not decisions and have no binding authority over the two governments.

i. Article 10 of the Boundary Waters Treaty grants authority to the IJC to conduct binding arbitration if both the United States and Canada agree to refer a matter to it.

2. In the event of the answer to the first part of the preceding Question being in the affirmative, whether the Trail Smelter should be required to refrain from causing damage in the State of Washington in the future and, if so, to what extent?
3. In the light of the answer to the preceding Question, what measures or regime, if any, should be adopted or maintained by the Trail Smelter?
4. What indemnity or compensation, if any, should be paid on account of any decision or decisions rendered by the Tribunal pursuant to the next two preceding Questions?

The agreement provided that the Tribunal was to "apply the law and practice followed in dealing with cognate [i.e., similar] questions in the United States of America as well as International Law and Practice," and was to give "consideration to the desire of the High Contracting Parties [i.e., the United States and Canada] to reach a solution just to all parties concerned."

The Tribunal met several times in 1937, inspected the smelter and the damaged areas, and took extensive oral and documentary evidence. On April 16, 1938, it submitted a "final decision" on Question 1 (damages since 1932) and a "temporary decision" on Questions 2 and 3. With respect to Question 1, the United States had presented claims of over $1.8 million divided into seven categories: "(a) cleared land and improvements; (b) uncleared land and improvements; (c) live stock; (d) property in the town of Northport; (e) wrong done the United States in violation of sovereignty, measured by cost of investigation from January 1, 1932, to June 30, 1936; (f) interest on $350,000 accepted in satisfaction of damage to January 1, 1932, but not paid on that date; (g) business enterprises." The Tribunal refused to find damage to livestock, urban property, or business enterprises, and also rejected a claim for intangible injury to United States sovereignty on the grounds that "damages" included only injuries for which pecuniary loss could be proved. It did, however, find that the smelter had caused damages to cleared and uncleared lands in the amount of $78,000 during the period from January 1, 1932, through October 1, 1937. In addition, the Tribunal imposed a temporary pollution abatement regime to allow further study during the following three growing seasons. This study was characterized by the Tribunal as "probably the most thorough study ever made of any area subject to atmospheric pollution by industrial smoke." On March 11, 1941, the Tribunal rendered its final decision.

TRAIL SMELTER ARBITRATION (U.S. v. CANADA)
3 U.N. Rep. Int'l Arb. Awards 1911, 1938 (Trail Smelter Arb. Trib. 1941)

The controversy is between two Governments involving damage occurring, or having occurred, in the territory of one of them (the United States of America) and alleged to be due to an agency situated in the territory of the other (the Dominion of Canada). In this controversy, the Tribunal did not sit and is not sitting to pass upon claims presented by individuals or on behalf of one or more individuals by their Government. . . .

As between the two countries involved, each has an equal interest that if a nuisance is proved, the indemnity to damaged parties for proven damage shall be just and adequate and . . . that unproven or unwarranted claims shall not be allowed. For, while the United States' interests may now be claimed to be injured by the operations of a Canadian corporation, it is equally possible that at some time in the future Canadian interests might be claimed to be injured by an American corporation. . . .

Part Three. [*Prevention of transboundary pollution*]

The second question under Article III of the Convention is as follows:

> In the event of the answer to the first part of the preceding Question being in the affirmative [whether there has been damage], whether the Trail Smelter should be required to refrain from causing damage in the State of Washington in the future and, if so, to what extent?

Damage has occurred since January 1, 1932, as fully set forth in the previous decision. To that extent, the first part of the preceding question has thus been answered in the affirmative. . . .

The first problem which arises is whether the question should be answered on the basis of the law followed in the United States or on the basis of international law. The Tribunal, however, finds that this problem need not be solved here as the law followed in the United States in dealing with the quasi-sovereign rights of the States of the Union, in the matter of air pollution, whilst more definite, is in conformity with the general rules of international law. . . .

As Professor Eagleton puts [it] . . . : "A State owes at all times a duty to protect other States against injurious acts by individuals from within its jurisdiction." A great number of such general pronouncements by leading authorities concerning the duty of a State to respect other States and their territory have been presented to the Tribunal. . . . International decisions, in various matters . . . are based on the same general principle, and, indeed, this principle, as such, has not been questioned by Canada. But the real difficulty often arises rather when it comes to determine what . . . is deemed to constitute an injurious act.

A case concerning . . . territorial relations, decided by the Federal Court of Switzerland between the Cantons of Soleure and Argovia, may serve to illustrate the relativity of the rule. Soleure brought a suit against her sister State to enjoin use of a shooting establishment which endangered her territory. The court, in granting the injunction, said: "This right (sovereignty) excludes . . . not only the usurpation and exercise of sovereign rights (of another State) . . . but also an actual encroachment which might prejudice the natural use of the territory and the free movement of its inhabitants." As a result of the decision, Argovia made plans for the improvement of the existing installations. These, however, were considered as insufficient protection by Soleure. The Canton of Argovia then moved the Federal Court to decree that the shooting be again permitted after completion of the projected improvements. This motion was granted. "The demand of the Government of Soleure," said the court, "that all endangerment be absolutely abolished apparently goes too far." The court found that all risk whatever had not been eliminated, as the region was flat and absolutely safe shooting ranges were only found in mountain valleys; that there was a federal duty for the communes to provide facilities for military target practice and that "no more precautions may be demanded for shooting ranges near the boundaries of two Cantons than are required for shooting ranges in the interior of a Canton."

No case of air pollution dealt with by an international tribunal has been brought to the attention of the Tribunal nor does the Tribunal know of any such case. The nearest analogy is that of water pollution. But, here also, no decision of an international tribunal has been cited or has been found.

There are, however, as regards, both air pollution and water pollution, certain decisions of the Supreme Court of the United States which may legitimately be taken as a guide in this field of international law, for it is reasonable to follow by analogy, in international cases, precedents established by that court in dealing with controversies between States of the Union or with other controversies concerning the quasi-sovereign rights of such States, where no contrary rule prevails in international law and no reason for rejecting such precedents can be adduced from the limitations of sovereignty inherent in the Constitution of the United States.

In the suit of the State of Missouri v. the State of Illinois concerning the pollution, within the boundaries of Illinois, of the Illinois River, an affluent of the Mississippi flowing into the latter where it forms the boundary between that State and Missouri, an injunction was refused. "Before this court ought to intervene," said the court, "the case should be of serious magnitude, clearly and fully proved, and the principle to be applied should be one which the court is prepared deliberately to maintain against all considerations on the other side. (See Kansas v. Colorado, 185 U.S. 125.)" The court found that the practice complained of was general along the shores of the Mississippi River at that time, that it was followed by Missouri itself and that thus a standard was set up by the defendant which the claimant was entitled to invoke. . . .

In the more recent suit of the State of New York v. State of New Jersey concerning the pollution of New York Bay, the injunction was also refused for lack of proof, some experts believing that the plans which were in dispute would result in the presence of "offensive odors and unsightly deposits," other equally reliable experts testifying that they were confidently of the opinion that the waters would be sufficiently purified. The court, referring to Missouri v. Illinois, said: ". . . [T]he burden upon the State of New York of sustaining the allegations of its bill is much greater than that imposed upon a complainant in an ordinary suit between private parties. Before this court can be moved to exercise its extraordinary power under the Constitution to control the conduct of one State at the suit of another, the threatened invasion of rights must be of serious magnitude and it must be established by clear and convincing evidence."

What the Supreme Court says there of its power under the Constitution equally applies to the extraordinary power granted this Tribunal under the Convention. What is true between States of the Union is, at least, equally true concerning the relations between the United States and the Dominion of Canada. . . .

In the matter of air pollution itself, the leading decisions are those of the Supreme Court in the State of Georgia v. Tennessee Copper Company and Ducktown Sulphur, Copper and Iron Company, Limited. Although dealing with a suit against private companies, the decisions were on questions cognate to those here at issue. Georgia stated that it had in vain sought relief from the State of Tennessee, on whose territory the smelters were located, and the court defined the nature of the suit by saying: "This is a suit by a State for an injury to it in its capacity of quasi-sovereign. In that capacity, the State has an interest independent of and behind the titles of its citizens, in all the earth and air within its domain."

On the question whether an injunction should be granted or not, the court said (206 U.S. 230):

> It (the State) has the last word as to whether its mountains shall be stripped of their forests and its inhabitants shall breathe pure air. . . . It is not lightly to be presumed to give up

quasi-sovereign rights for pay and . . . if that be its choice, it may insist that an infraction of them shall be stopped. This court has not quite the same freedom to balance the harm that will be done by an injunction against that of which the plaintiff complains, that it would have in deciding between two subjects of a single political power. Without excluding the considerations that equity always takes into account . . . it is a fair and reasonable demand on the part of a sovereign that the air over its territory should not be polluted on a great scale by sulphurous acid gas, that the forests on its mountains, be they better or worse, and whatever domestic destruction they may have suffered, should not be further destroyed or threatened by the act of persons beyond its control, that the crops and orchards on its hills should not be endangered from the same source. . . . Whether Georgia, by insisting upon this claim, is doing more harm than good to her own citizens, is for her to determine. The possible disaster to those outside the State must be accepted as a consequence of her standing upon her extreme rights.

Later on, however, when the court actually framed an injunction, in the case of the *Ducktown Company* (237 U.S. 474, 477) . . . , they did not go beyond a decree "adequate to diminish materially the present probability of damage to its (Georgia's) citizens." . . .

The Tribunal, therefore, finds that the above decisions, taken as a whole, constitute an adequate basis for its conclusions, namely, that, under the principles of international law, as well as of the law of the United States, no State has the right to use or permit the use of its territory in such a manner as to cause injury by fumes in or to the territory of another or the properties or persons therein, when the case is of serious consequence and the injury is established by clear and convincing evidence.

The decisions of the Supreme Court of the United States which are the basis of these conclusions are decisions in equity and a solution inspired by them, together with the regime hereinafter prescribed, will, in the opinion of the Tribunal, be "just to all parties concerned," as long, at least, as the present conditions in the Columbia River Valley continue to prevail.

Considering the circumstances of the case, the Tribunal holds that the Dominion of Canada is responsible in international law for the conduct of the Trail Smelter. Apart from the undertakings in the Convention, it is, therefore, the duty of the Government of the Dominion of Canada to see to it that this conduct should be in conformity with the obligation of the Dominion under international law as herein determined.

The Tribunal, therefore, answers Question No. 2 as follows: So long as the present conditions in the Columbia River Valley prevail, the Trail Smelter shall be required to refrain from causing any damage through fumes in the State of Washington; the damage herein referred to and its extent being such as would be recoverable under the decisions of the courts of the United States in suits between private individuals. The indemnity for such damage should be fixed in such manner as the Governments, acting under Article XI of the Convention, should agree upon.

Part Four. [Future pollution control regime]

The third question under Article III of the Convention is as follows: "In the light of the answer to the preceding question, what measures or regime, if any, should be adopted and maintained by the Trail Smelter?"

Answering this question in the light of the preceding one, ... the Tribunal now decides that a regime or measure of control shall be applied to the operations of the Smelter and shall remain in full force unless and until modified in accordance with the provisions hereinafter set forth in Section 3, Paragraph VI of the present part of this decision. ...

In order to prevent the occurrence of sulphur dioxide in the atmosphere ... , the operation of the Smelter and the maximum emission of sulphur dioxide from its stacks shall be regulated as provided in the following regime.

I. INSTRUMENTS

The instruments for recording meteorological conditions shall be as follows. ... [Description of instruments omitted.]

II. DOCUMENTS

The sulphur dioxide concentrations indicated by the prescribed recorders shall be reduced to tabular form and kept on file at the Smelter. The original instrumental recordings of all meteorological data herein required to be made shall be preserved by the Smelter.

A summary of Smelter operation covering the daily sulphur balances shall be compiled monthly and copies sent to the Governments of the United States and of the Dominion of Canada. ...

IV. MAXIMUM PERMISSIBLE SULPHUR EMISSION

The following two tables and general restrictions give the maximum hourly permissible emission of sulphur dioxide expressed as tons per hour of contained sulphur. ... [Tables setting forth maximum emissions during growing and non-growing season omitted.]

Part Five. [Compensation]

The fourth question under Article III of the Convention is as follows:

> What indemnity or compensation, if any, should be paid on account of any decision or decisions rendered by the Tribunal pursuant to the next two preceding Questions?

The Tribunal is of opinion that the prescribed regime will probably remove the causes of the present controversy and, as said before, will probably result in preventing any damage of a material nature occurring in the State of Washington in the future.

But since the desirable and expected result of the regime or measure of control hereby required to be adopted and maintained by the Smelter may not occur, ... the Tribunal answers Question No. 4 and decides that ... there shall be paid as follows: (a) if any damages as defined under Question No. 2 shall have occurred since October 1, 1940, or shall occur in the future, whether through failure on the part of the Smelter to comply with the regulations herein prescribed or notwithstanding the maintenance of the regime, an indemnity shall be paid for such damage but only when and if the two Governments shall make arrangements for the disposition of claims for indemnity under the provisions of Article XI of the Convention; (b) if . . . the United States shall find it necessary to maintain in the future an agent or agents in the area in order to ascertain whether damage shall have occurred in spite of the regime prescribed herein, the reasonable cost of such investigations not in excess of $7,500 in any one year shall be paid to the United States as a compensation. . . .

Part Six. [Inspection]

Since further investigations in the future may be possible under the provisions of Part Four and of Part Five of this decision, the Tribunal finds it necessary to include in its report, the following provision:

Investigators appointed by or on behalf of either Government . . . shall be permitted at all reasonable times to inspect the operations of the Smelter and to enter upon and inspect any of the properties in the State of Washington which may be claimed to be affected by fumes. This provision shall also apply to any localities where instruments are operated under the present regime or under any amended regime. Wherever under the present regime or under any amended regime, instruments have to be maintained and operated by the Smelter on the territory of the United States, the Government of the United States shall undertake to secure for the Government of the Dominion of Canada the facilities reasonably required to that effect.

The Tribunal expresses the strong hope that any investigations which the Governments may undertake in the future, in connection with the matters dealt with in this decision, shall be conducted jointly.

NOTES AND QUESTIONS

1. The Trail Smelter Arbitration has been described as "having laid the foundations of international environmental law, at least regarding transfrontier pollution." A. Kiss & D. Shelton, International Environmental Law 45 (2d ed. 2000). What was the outcome of the Trail Smelter Arbitration? What legal test did it articulate and what law did the panel rely upon in formulating this test? What is the precedential effect of the decision, given that it was an agreed-upon process under a bilateral agreement that identified the issues to be decided?

2. Writing in 1991, Peter Sand commented about the *Trail Smelter* case:

One of the many myths of environmental law is the assumption—found in many legal textbooks—that international disputes in this field are settled along the lines of the 1941 Trail Smelter arbitration. Yet over the past 50 years, there have been only two intergovernmental dispute adjudications that could even remotely be compared to Trail Smelter—and even these claims (the 1957 Lake Lanoux arbitration between France and Spain and the 1968 Gut Dam arbitration between Canada and the US) concerned classical questions of water use and flood damage, rather than a genuine environmental problem.

Sand, New Approaches to Transnational Environment Disputes, 3 Int'l Envtl. Aff. 193 (1991). To what extent were the origins of the arbitration atypical? Do you think international arbitration is likely to be used very often in resolving transboundary pollution disputes?

3. The principal holding of the Tribunal was the following: "[U]nder principles of international law, . . . no State has the right to use or permit the use of its territory in such a manner as to cause injury by fumes in or to the territory of another or the properties or persons therein, when the case is of serious consequence and the injury is established by clear and convincing evidence." What type of international law is this principle? Customary law? A general principle? What evidence does the Tribunal give that the principle is a norm of international law?

4. What was the standard of liability applied by the Arbitral Tribunal? Negligence? Strict liability?

5. The Trail Smelter was and is privately owned and caused damage to private property in the United States. Nevertheless, the Tribunal held that "the Dominion of Canada is responsible in international law for the conduct of the Trail Smelter." What was the basis for this holding? Under what circumstances should private activity be "attributable" to the state in which the activity occurred? Should a state be responsible only for acts by its organs or those acting on its behalf, or should it also be responsible for private acts? What duty did Canada breach? And to whom was the duty owed—the United States government or the private landowners in the United States?

6. What did the Tribunal order? Must the smelter stop polluting altogether? Should the United States have pressed for a cessation of all transboundary pollution from the plant?

7. The capital costs of implementing the regime ordered by the Tribunal were estimated at approximately $20 million. Read, The Trail Smelter Dispute, 1 Can. Ybk. Int'l L. 213, 221 (1963).

> Fortunately for the economic life of the south-eastern part of British Columbia, in which the Trail Smelter was the most important factor, it was a private enterprise and not a government department. Notwithstanding the enormous capital expenditure and intermittent interruption of the metallurgical operations imposed, in perpetuity, by the regime of control, the Consolidated Mining and Smelting Company succeeded in selling the products of its smoke abatement programme for substantial profit. In order to comply with the regime, the Company was compelled to remove from the smoke cloud at the stacks more sulphur dioxide than was taken from the stacks of all other smelters of the North American Continent combined.

Id. Who should bear these costs? How can Canada ensure that the Consolidated Mining and Smelting Company will carry out the changes ordered by the Arbitral Tribunal?

8. One commentator has stated, "by far the most difficult part of the case consisted of issues of fact, highly technical in character, and dependent for their solution on scientific experiment and testimony." Reed, *supra*, at 225. For this reason, each government was permitted to designate a scientific expert to assist the Tribunal.

3. The Trail Smelter in the Twenty-First Century—Still a Source of Pollution, but a Different Legal Approach

Despite the precedent-setting decision by the *Trail Smelter* arbitral panel more than 60 years ago, and the attendant focus on pollution problems at the Teck facility, the facility's operations have continued to discharge "vast quantities" of pollutants, "including heavy metal-laden slag and mercury, . . . into the Columbia River." Professor Robinson-Dorn reports that, "as late as 1994 and 1995, the Trail Smelter was discharging more copper and zinc into the Columbia River than the cumulative totals of all permitted U.S. discharges for those materials." In Professor Robinson-Dorn's words, "[b]y any measure, the quantity of hazardous substances discharged from the Trail Smelter is staggering." Robinson-Dorn, The Trail Smelter: Is What's Past Prologue? EPA Blazes a New Trail for CERCLA, 14 N.Y.U. Envtl. L.J. 233, 238-239, 265-266 (2006).

EPA has concluded that large amounts of these pollutants have come to rest in Lake Roosevelt, a designated National Recreation Area that is "one of the most popular recreation areas in Washington State" and that also "lies within the ancestral homelands of the Colville and Spokane Tribes." The lake, which is 135 miles long, extends to about 15 miles from the U.S.-Canadian border. Various environmental studies have shown elevated levels of a wide range of hazardous substances in sediments and fish in Lake Roosevelt, and "that these contaminants pose a risk to aquatic life" and humans. EPA's investigatory efforts, which led the agency to conclude that the lake is severely contaminated and requires attention, were prompted by a Colville Tribe's petition to EPA, requesting that it conduct sampling and other, related work.

This time around, the transboundary pollution from the Trail Smelter has prompted a very different response from the *Trail Smelter* arbitration, involving both a different legal tool (domestic law) and different actors (citizens and native American tribes instead of national governments). Rather than pursuing the Arbitral Panel approach used in the earlier Trail Smelter dispute to hold Canada legally accountable for the environmental and health harms in the United States resulting from the Teck Cominco discharges in Canada, the United States first engaged the company to discuss its voluntarily accepting responsibility for the site and, when that effort foundered, the U.S. EPA acted unilaterally to address the contamination by issuing a CERCLA §106 administrative order in which it directed Teck Cominco to undertake an investigation of the site.

Even though Teck Cominco refused to comply with the order and EPA declined to pursue this noncompliance legally, the matter did not end there. CERCLA §310, like provisions in many U.S. environmental statutes (see Chapter 10), gives citizens the right to sue under certain circumstances, and two American citizens, both members of a local Native American tribe, initiated a domestic U.S. citizen suit under CERCLA §310 against Teck Cominco in an effort to enforce EPA's CERCLA §106 order. First the U.S. District Court, and then the Court of Appeals, upheld the citizens' right to sue Teck Cominco in U.S. courts to enforce EPA's CERCLA order. Pakootas v. Teck Cominco Metals, Ltd., 452 F.3d 1066 (9th Cir. 2006). The state of Washington was supportive of the action, intervening as a plaintiff in the citizen suit. The following quote from the Washington State attorney general captured the state's perspective: "Teck Cominco can't send highly toxic pollution across the Canadian border and then insist that border protects them from liability. They created one big mess here in the U.S., and they should clean it up, not Washington taxpayers." Press Release, Wash. State Office of the Att'y Gen., Washington State Joins Lawsuit to Force Lake Roosevelt Cleanup (Aug. 31, 2004), www.atg.wa.gov/releases/rel_epa_083104.html.

Meanwhile, EPA and Teck Cominco's U.S. subsidiary, which no one has alleged contributed to the contamination of Lake Roosevelt, entered into a settlement agreement that committed Teck Cominco America to undertake particular investigatory work at the site. Settlement Agreement for Implementation of Remedial Investigation and Feasibility Study at the Upper Columbia River Site (June 2, 2006). EPA withdrew its CERCLA §106 administrative order, and the settlement agreement, by its terms, is not based on that order.

As described in Section 1 above, the litigation against Teck Cominco is still ongoing, with a second citizen suit pending, seeking recovery of response costs and natural resource damages resulting from the discharges by Teck Cominco into the Columbia River.

NOTES AND QUESTIONS

1. The U.S. citizen suit litigation to enforce an EPA administrative order against a Canadian company for contamination that originated at its Canadian facility but that has impacted the U.S. environment spawned considerable controversy. One scholar argued that the district court opinion in the *Pakootas* case "turn[ed] . . . principles of sovereignty and international law on their head." Parrish, Trail Smelter Déjà Vu: Extraterritoriality, International Environmental Law, and the Search for Solutions to Canadian-U.S. Transboundary Water Pollution Disputes, 85 B.U. L. Rev. 363, 405 (2005). Do you agree?

2. Do you think transboundary pollution cases are better resolved through international dispute settlement, as in the original *Trail Smelter* arbitration, or through citizen suits in national courts?

3. For very different perspectives on the Trail Smelter litigation, see George, Environmental Enforcement across National Borders, 21 Nat. Resources & Env't No. 1, at 3 (Summer 2006), and Du Bey et al., CERCLA and Transboundary Contamination in the Columbia River, id., at 8 (George represented Teck Cominco in the litigation; Du Bey et al. represented the tribes).

4. The Duty to Prevent Transboundary Pollution—Developments since Trail Smelter

The duty to prevent transboundary harm has been called a "cornerstone" of international environmental law and has been echoed many times since it was first articulated in *Trail Smelter*. Handl, Transboundary Impacts, in Oxford Handbook of International Environmental Law 531, 548 (D. Bodansky et al. eds.) (2007). It reflects the principle of good neighborliness, *sic utere tuo ut alienum non laedas*, which roughly translates as "use your own property so as not to injure that of another."

Perhaps the most important expression of the duty to prevent transboundary harm is Principle 21 of the 1972 Stockholm Declaration on the Human Environment:

> States have, in accordance with the Charter of the United Nations and the principles of international law, the sovereign right to exploit their own resources pursuant to their own environmental policies, and the responsibility to ensure that activities within their jurisdiction or control do not cause damage to the environment of other States or of areas beyond the limits of national jurisdiction.

Stockholm Principle 21 was reiterated, word for word, in Principle 2 of the 1992 Rio Declaration on Environment and Development, with only one change: the words "and developmental" were added between "environmental" and "policies," so that the first half of the principle now reads, "[S]tates have . . . the sovereign right to exploit their own resources pursuant to their own environmental *and developmental* policies. . . ."

One of the most systematic efforts to elaborate the duty of prevention was by the International Law Commission in its *Draft Articles on the Prevention of Transboundary Harm from Hazardous Activities.* The International Law Commission is an official United Nations body, established by the General Assembly, with the mandate to "codify and progressively develop" international law.

INTERNATIONAL LAW COMMISSION, DRAFT ARTICLES ON PREVENTION OF TRANSBOUNDARY HARM FROM HAZARDOUS ACTIVITIES

Report of the International Law Commission on the Work of Its Fifty-Third Session, U.N. Doc. A/56/10, at 153 (2001)

Article 3. Prevention

The State of origin shall take all appropriate measures to prevent significant transboundary harm or at any event to minimize the risk thereof.

COMMENTARY

1. Article 3 is based on the fundamental principle *sic utere tuo ut alienum non laedas*, which is reflected in principle 21 of the Stockholm Declaration. . . .

3. This article, together with article 4, provides the basic foundation for the articles on prevention. The articles set out the more specific obligations of States to prevent significant transboundary harm or at any event to minimize the risk thereof. The article thus emphasizes the primary duty of the State of origin to prevent significant transboundary harm; and only in case this is not fully possible it should exert its best efforts to minimize the risk thereof. The phrase "at any event" is intended to express priority in favor of the duty of prevention. The word "minimize" should be understood in this context as meaning to pursue the aim of reducing to the lowest point the possibility of harm.

4. The present article is in the nature of a statement of principle. It provides that States shall take all appropriate measures to prevent significant transboundary harm or at any event to minimize the risk thereof. The phrase "all appropriate measures" refers to all those specific actions and steps that are specified in the articles on prevention and minimization of transboundary harm. . . . In addition, it imposes an obligation on the State of origin to adopt and implement national legislation incorporating accepted international standards. These standards would constitute a necessary reference point to determine whether measures adopted are suitable.

5. As a general principle, the obligation in article 3 to prevent significant transboundary harm or minimize the risk thereof applies only to activities which involve a risk of causing significant transboundary harm. . . . In general, in the context of

prevention, a State of origin does not bear the risk of unforeseeable consequences to States likely to be affected by activities within the scope of these articles. On the other hand, the obligation to "take all appropriate measures" to prevent harm, or to minimize the risk thereof, cannot be confined to activities which are already properly appreciated as involving such a risk. The obligation extends to taking appropriate measures to identify activities which involve such a risk, and this obligation is of a continuing character. . . .

7. The obligation of the State of origin to take preventive or minimization measures is one of due diligence. It is the conduct of the State of origin that will determine whether the State has complied with its obligation under the present articles. The duty of due diligence involved, however, is not intended to guarantee that significant harm be totally prevented, if it is not possible to do so. In that eventuality, the State of origin is required, as noted above, to exert its best possible efforts to minimize the risk. In this sense, it does not guarantee that the harm would not occur.

8. An obligation of due diligence as the standard basis for the protection of the environment from harm can be deduced from a number of international conventions as well as from the resolutions and reports of international conferences and organizations. The obligation of due diligence was discussed in a dispute which arose in 1986 between Germany and Switzerland relating to the pollution of the Rhine by Sandoz. The Swiss Government acknowledged responsibility for lack of due diligence in preventing the accident through adequate regulation of its pharmaceutical industries.

9. In the *"Alabama"* case, the tribunal examined two different definitions of due diligence submitted by the parties. The United States defined due diligence as:

> [A] diligence proportioned to the magnitude of the subject and to the dignity and strength of the power which is to exercise it; a diligence which shall, by the use of active vigilance, and of all the other means in the power of the neutral, through all stages of the transaction, prevent its soil from being violated; a diligence that shall in like manner deter designing men from committing acts of war upon the soil of the neutral against its will.

The United Kingdom defined due diligence as "such care as Governments ordinarily employ in their domestic concerns." The tribunal seemed to have been persuaded by the broader definition of the standard of due diligence presented by the United States and expressed concern about the "national standard" of due diligence presented by the United Kingdom. The tribunal stated that:

> [The] British case seemed also to narrow the international duties of a Government to the exercise of the restraining powers conferred upon it by municipal law, and to overlook the obligation of the neutral to amend its laws when they were insufficient.

10. In the context of the present articles, due diligence is manifested in reasonable efforts by a State to inform itself of factual and legal components that relate foreseeably to a contemplated procedure and to take appropriate measures, in timely fashion, to address them. Thus, States are under an obligation to take unilateral measures to prevent significant transboundary harm or at any event to minimize the risk thereof. . . . Such measures include, first, formulating policies designed to prevent significant transboundary harm or to minimize the risk thereof and, secondly,

implementing those policies. Such policies are expressed in legislation and administrative regulations and implemented through various enforcement mechanisms.

11. The standard of due diligence against which the conduct of the State of origin should be examined is that which is generally considered to be appropriate and proportional to the degree of risk of transboundary harm in the particular instance. For example, activities which may be considered ultrahazardous require a much higher standard of care in designing policies and a much higher degree of vigor on the part of the State to enforce them. Issues such as the size of the operation; its location, special climate conditions, materials used in the activity, and whether the conclusions drawn from the application of these factors in a specific case are reasonable, are among the factors to be considered in determining the due diligence requirement in each instance. What would be considered a reasonable standard of care or due diligence may change with time; what might be considered an appropriate and reasonable procedure, standard or rule at one point in time may not be considered as such at some point in the future. Hence, due diligence in ensuring safety requires a State to keep abreast of technological changes and scientific developments.

12. It is also necessary in this connection to note principle 11 of the Rio Declaration, which states:

> States shall enact effective environmental legislation. Environmental standards, management objectives and priorities should reflect the environmental and developmental context to which they apply. Standards applied by some countries may be inappropriate and of unwarranted economic and social cost to other countries, in particular developing countries.

13. Similar language is found in principle 23 of the Stockholm Declaration. That principle, however, specifies that such domestic standards are "[w]ithout prejudice to such criteria as may be agreed upon by the international community." The economic level of States is one of the factors to be taken into account in determining whether a State has complied with its obligation of due diligence. But a State's economic level cannot be used to dispense the State from its obligation under the present articles.

14. Article 3 imposes on the State a duty to take all necessary measures to prevent significant transboundary harm or at any event to minimize the risk thereof. This could involve, *inter alia*, taking such measures as are appropriate by way of abundant caution, even if full scientific certainty does not exist, to avoid or prevent serious or irreversible damage. . . .

17. The main elements of the obligation of due diligence involved in the duty of prevention could be thus stated: the degree of care in question is that expected of a good Government. It should possess a legal system and sufficient resources to maintain an adequate administrative apparatus to control and monitor the activities. It is, however, understood that the degree of care expected of a State with a well-developed economy and human and material resources and with highly evolved systems and structures of governance is different from States which are not so well placed. Even in the latter case, vigilance, employment of infrastructure and monitoring of hazardous activities in the territory of the State, which is a natural attribute of any Government, are expected.

18. The required degree of care is proportional to the degree of hazard involved. The degree of harm itself should be foreseeable and the State must know or should

have known that the given activity has the risk of significant harm. The higher the degree of inadmissible harm, the greater would be the duty of care required to prevent it.

NOTES AND QUESTIONS

1. In its 1996 Advisory Opinion on the *Legality of the Threat or Use of Nuclear Weapons*, the International Court of Justice opined that "the existence of the general obligation of States to ensure that activities within their jurisdiction and control respect the environment of others or of areas beyond national jurisdiction is now part of the corpus of international law relating to the environment" (para. 29). Although the Court did not say in its advisory opinion whether the "duty to prevent" is a customary duty or a general principle of international law, its more recent decision in the *Pulp Mills* case characterizes the principle of prevention as a customary rule, and states that the rule

> has its origins in the due diligence that is required of a State in its territory. It is "every State's obligation not to allow knowingly its territory to be used for acts contrary to the rights of other States" (*Corfu Channel* (United Kingdom v. Albania), Merits, Judgment, I.C.J. Reports 1949, p. 22). A State is thus obliged to use all the means at its disposal in order to avoid activities which take place in its territory, or in any area under its juris-diction, causing significant damage to the environment of another State.

Pulp Mills on the River Uruguay (Argentina v. Uruguay), Merits, Judgment of April 20, 2010, para. 101.

2. In 2008, Ecuador initiated a case against Colombia in the International Court of Justice, alleging that the aerial spraying of toxic herbicides by Colombia had "caused serious damage to crops, to animals, and to the natural environment on the Ecuadorian side of the frontier." Ecuador argued that the ICJ had jurisdiction under the 1948 American Treaty on Pacific Settlement of Disputes, to which both Ecuador and Colombia are parties, and which gives the ICJ jurisdiction over all disputes concerning "any question of international law." In September 2013, Ecuador reached a settlement agreement with Colombia, creating a ten-kilometer exclusion zone along the border within which Colombia will not spray, and creating a joint commission tasked to ensure that spraying outside the zone does not drift into Ecuador.

3. Some commentators are skeptical about the usefulness of the principle of prevention in addressing actual transboundary pollution cases. Consider the following analysis:

> Efforts to develop an effective international liability scheme . . . have failed utterly. . . . [A] regime constructed upon custom obscures—without resolving—the differences between the conflicting values states assign to environmental protection. . . . Without codification, . . . the vague customary duties communicate no normative expectations or specific commands, and states can claim that almost any conduct comports with international law. . . .
>
> Notwithstanding the close attention that the international legal community has given the issue of international liability for transfrontier pollution, no operational system for adjudicating liability has emerged. The International Court of Justice (ICJ) has heard

only one dispute of note, the *Nuclear Tests* case, and international arbitration has entertained only a few notable cases. . . . No state even brought suit against the Soviet Union following the 1985 Chernobyl accident, although more than twenty states registered significant increases in radioactivity levels. Moreover, no downstream states sought any remedy under international law against Switzerland for the damages caused by the 1986 Sandoz spill of toxic chemicals into the Rhine River, despite possible Swiss violations of a treaty that provided for arbitration of all disputes. Publicists' efforts at codifying standards of conduct notwithstanding, international liability remains an empty abstraction. . . . [Developments in the Law: International Environmental Law, 104 Harv. L. Rev. 1484, 1492-1501 passim (1991).]

Do you agree with these criticisms of the duty of prevention? If these criticisms are correct, what is the significance, if any, of decisions such as the *Trail Smelter* case and documents such as the Stockholm and Rio Declarations? Do you think they reflect state behavior? Do they have any influence on state behavior?

5. *Operationalizing the Duty to Prevent Through Treaties*

Whether or not states have a duty of prevention under customary international law, transboundary pollution remains common. In practice, states have sought to address it not through customary law but through treaties that articulate more specific limits on particular types of pollution. For example, in the North American context, Canadian complaints about acid rain damages caused by U.S. emissions of sulfur dioxide were ultimately addressed through the 1990 U.S.-Canada Air Quality Agreement. Similarly, in Europe, transboundary air pollution has been addressed through the Long-Range Transboundary Air Pollution Convention (LRTAP), which now has eight protocols that set forth detailed rules limiting pollution from sulphur dioxide, nitrogen oxides (NO_x), volatile organic compounds, heavy metals, and persistent organic pollutants (POPs).

The LRTAP regime illustrates the increasing sophistication of treaties in addressing transboundary harms. Its eight protocols have evolved from the very rudimentary 1985 Sulphur Protocol, which set forth a simple requirement on all parties to reduce their emissions by 30 percent relative to 1980 levels, to the 1994 Sulphur Protocol, which adopts a more sophisticated regulatory approach, basing its emissions reductions on the amounts necessary to avoid exceeding "critical loads" for sensitive ecosystems. The 1994 Sulphur Protocol defines "critical load" as

a quantitative estimate of an exposure to one or more pollutants below which significant harmful effects on specified sensitive elements of the environment do not occur, according to present knowledge. (Article 1.8)

The Protocol requires states to

control and reduce their sulphur emissions in order . . . to ensure, as far as possible, without entailing excessive costs, that depositions of oxidized sulphur compounds in the long term do not exceed critical loads. . . . (Article 2.1)

The Protocol sets forth specific emissions reduction targets for each participating country, calculated to achieve critical loads at the lowest cost. Based on these calculations, the United Kingdom was required to reduce its sulfur emissions by 70 percent from 1980 levels by 2005, France by 77 percent, and Germany by 87 percent (Annex II). The various protocols adopted under LRTAP have now been brought together under the 1999 Gothenburg Protocol, which adopts a comprehensive, multi-gas approach to the problems of acid rain and eutrophication.

6.   *Other Principles Relevant to Transboundary Pollution*

In addition to substantive norms such as the duty of prevention, some scholars contend that customary international law also establishes procedural norms intended to forestall transboundary pollution disputes. These proposed procedural norms include the following:

Duty to assess. The duty to assess is perhaps the most fundamental procedural norm, since only by undertaking a prior assessment does a state know whether an activity may cause transboundary harm. The duty is included in many resolutions and statements of principles relating to transboundary pollution. In 1987, the UNEP Governing Council adopted a decision on *Goals and Principles of Environmental Impact Assessment.* Similarly, Principle 17 of the Rio Declaration states:

> Environmental impact assessment, as a national instrument, shall be undertaken for proposed activities that are likely to have a significant adverse impact on the environment and are subject to a decision of a competent authority.

In its decision in the *Pulp Mills* case, the International Court of Justice found that the practice of "undertak[ing] an environmental impact assessment where there is a risk that the proposed activity may have a significant transboundary impact" has "in recent years . . . gained so much acceptance among States that it may now be considered a requirement under general international law," although the Court went on to say that general international law does not "specify the scope and content" of environmental assessments. *Pulp Mills on the River Uruguay* (Argentina v. Uruguay), Merits, Judgment of April 20, 2010, paras. 204-205. The duty to assess is also set forth in several environmental conventions, most prominently the 1991 Espoo Convention on Environmental Impact Assessment in a Transboundary Context, a regional agreement applicable to Europe.

Duty to notify and inform. If a planned activity appears likely to have transboundary consequences, the state of origin may also have a duty to notify the affected states and provide information. The 1974 OECD Principles Concerning Transfrontier Pollution, for example, provide:

> Prior to the initiation in a country of works or undertakings which might create a significant risk of transfrontier pollution, this country should provide early information to other countries which are or may be affected. . . .[j]

At the 1972 Stockholm Conference, agreement could not be reached on a proposed Principle 20, which would have required states to communicate information

j. See also International Law Association (ILA), Montreal Rules of International Law Applicable to Transfrontier Pollution, article 5 (prior notice).

on activities within their jurisdiction "whenever they believe, or have reason to believe, that such information is needed to avoid the risk of significant adverse effects on the environment in areas beyond their national jurisdiction." Twenty years later, however, countries unanimously adopted the Rio Declaration, which provides:

> States shall provide prior and timely notification and relevant information to potentially affected States on activities that may have a significant adverse transboundary environmental effect. . . . [Principle 19]

Following the Soviet Union's failure to notify other European states immediately of the Chernobyl nuclear accident, states quickly negotiated the Convention on Early Notification of a Nuclear Accident, under the auspices of the International Atomic Energy Agency (IAEA). The Convention was adopted on September 26, 1986, and now has more than 100 parties. It provides in Article 2:

> In the event of an accident specified in article 1 (hereinafter referred to as a "nuclear accident"), the State referred to in that article shall:
>   (a) forthwith notify, directly or through the International Atomic Energy Agency (hereinafter referred to as the "Agency"), those States which are or may be physically affected as specified in article 1 and the Agency of the nuclear accident, its nature, the time of its occurrence and its exact location where appropriate; and
>   (b) promptly provide the States referred to in subparagraph (a), directly or through the Agency, and the Agency with such available information relevant to minimizing the radiological consequences in those States, as specified in Article 5.

Article 5 goes on to specify the exact information to be provided by the state where the accident occurred to other potentially affected states.

The Convention on the Transboundary Effects of Industrial Accidents, 2105 U.N.T.S. 457, adopted in 1992 by the UN Economic Commission for Europe, similarly requires parties to establish an industrial accident notification system, in order to ensure the communication of information needed to counteract transboundary effects.

Duty to consult. In addition to notification, some argue that customary international law also requires the state of origin to consult with potentially affected states, prior to going ahead with an activity that may have transboundary impacts. The *Rio Declaration* provides in Principle 19 that states "shall consult with [potentially affected] States at an early stage and in good faith."

Duty to negotiate. Consultations and negotiations are very similar, and there is no clear line between the two, but the process of negotiation tends to be more active than consultations, implying a concerted effort to reach a mutually agreeable solution. None of the principal resolutions includes a specific duty to negotiate (as opposed to a more preliminary duty to consult).

The object of these procedural duties is unclear. On the one hand, the duty to consult does not appear to include any obligation to reach agreement. But some authorities contend that it implies a duty not to proceed with a project until after a reasonable time for consultation or negotiation. In this regard, the 1974 OECD Principles provide:

> 8. Countries should refrain from carrying out projects or activities which might create a significant risk of transfrontier pollution without first informing the countries which are or may be affected, and, except in cases of extreme urgency, providing a reasonable

amount of time in the light of circumstances for diligent consultation. Such consultations held in the best spirit of co-operation and good neighborliness should not enable a country to unreasonably delay or to impede the activities or projects on which consultations are taking place.

NOTES AND QUESTIONS

1. Professor Knox has offered the following insights concerning the "myth and reality" of transboundary environmental impact assessment (TEIA), and suggests that it might be helpful to consider TEIAs as a form of "nondiscrimination":

The dominant story of transboundary environmental impact assessment in international law has the following elements: (1) customary international law prohibits transboundary pollution; (2) according to the classic version of this prohibition, contained in Principle 21 of the 1972 Stockholm Declaration, states must ensure that activities within their territory or under their control do not harm the environment beyond their territory; (3) to ensure that activities within their jurisdiction will not cause transboundary harm, states must assess the potential transboundary effects of the activities; and (4) to that end, states enter into international agreements requiring them to carry out transboundary environmental impact assessment (transboundary EIA) for activities that might cause transboundary harm.

Despite its popularity, this story is not true. . . . European and North American countries are adopting regional agreements that provide for transboundary EIA. But these agreements do not require transboundary EIA for all activities that might cause transboundary harm, and they do not link it to any hard substantive prohibition against transboundary harm. In short, these agreements do not much resemble the mythic story of transboundary EIA. At the same time, the agreements are not meaningless. They require EIA for certain types of actions, specify the elements an EIA must include, and provide for significant public participation in the EIA process.

What, then, is going on? If transboundary EIA agreements are not designed to end transboundary pollution in accordance with Principle 21, what are they designed to do? One clue is that the agreements were not written on a clean slate. Most countries in North America and Western Europe have already enacted domestic EIA laws, which are limited in scope and lacking in substantive prohibitions but do contain detailed procedural obligations and provide important avenues for public participation. In large part, the regional EIA agreements reflect these domestic EIA laws. In fact, the main way that the agreements extend beyond the domestic laws is by ensuring that states apply EIA without extraterritorial discrimination—that they take extraterritorial effects into account just as they take domestic effects into account, and that they enable foreign residents to have access to the domestic EIA procedures to the same extent as local residents. Another principle in international environmental law describes exactly this approach: the principle of nondiscrimination, which says that countries should apply the same environmental protections to potential harm in other countries that they apply to such harm in their own. Examined closely, each regional transboundary EIA agreement is an application of the principle of nondiscrimination.

The nondiscrimination principle has often been overlooked, cast into shadow by the glow surrounding Principle 21, which is generally considered to be the cornerstone of international environmental law. But Principle 21 suffers from serious weaknesses as a cornerstone of international law, not the least of which is that it does not seem to be a law at all. Perhaps it would be more appropriate to think of it as a capstone that has never been set. Despite limitations of its own, the principle of nondiscrimination may provide a better blueprint for the EIA agreements. [Knox, The Myth and Reality of Transboundary Environmental Impact Assessment, 96 Am. J. Int'l L. 291, 291-292 (2002).]

Which of these approaches is preferable: a Principle 21-like approach that purports to prohibit transboundary harm, or a non-discrimination approach? Which approach is likely to prevail in practice? For a thoughtful analysis of these issues, see Merrill, Golden Rules for Transboundary Pollution, 46 Duke L.J. 931 (1997).

2. Consider the following criticism of procedural duties relating to transboundary pollution:

> In an effort to forestall significant extraterritorial environmental injury and to avoid the confrontational proceedings inherent in a liability regime, international legal analysts have developed rules of state conduct designed to prevent environmental harm *before* the harm occurs. Procedural obligations, including duties to assess potential transboundary harm and to disclose dangerous activities to other nations, have emerged to dislodge the substantive obligation of *sic utere* as the doctrinal bulwark against transnational pollution. Indeed, the recent proliferation of international treaties and charters imposing duties on states to assess transboundary environmental dangers and to inform potentially affected states of dangers signals the move away from ex post determinations of compliance with legal standards of care toward a new regime of procedural requirements. . . .
>
> . . . [S]ubstitution of procedural duties for substantive commands ironically limits the role of international law in environmental protection. In itself, an evaluation of likely environmental hazards affords no direction concerning what courses of action will violate international law. A duty to inform mandates nothing; it provides no guidance about whether and how pollution source states should alter their behavior in light of the new information. Adherence to duties of prior assessment and disclosure will scarcely reduce transboundary pollution. Thus, the shift to procedural obligations renders compliance with international law inconsequential for actually protecting the environment.
>
> The move towards procedural duties may in fact legitimate environmentally hazardous conduct. As procedural duties to assess and inform replace substantive commands to prevent significant transboundary pollution, states may discharge their international obligations simply through the production of assessment and information reports. Procedural duties may give a state an implied license to pollute, as long as procedural technicalities are fulfilled. [Developments in the Law: International Environmental Law, 104 Harv. L. Rev. 1484, 1512-1513 (1991).]

Do you agree with these criticisms? Do the alleged procedural duties relating to transboundary pollution serve any useful function?

C.   GLOBAL ENVIRONMENTAL PROBLEMS

As discussed in Chapter 1, one of environmental law's challenges from its inception has been to establish strategies for governance of "commons" areas. This is certainly true of the international arena. "Global commons" are areas or resources not under the jurisdiction or control of any particular country. Commons resources include the high seas, outer space, the stratospheric ozone layer, the global climate system, and certain land areas such as Antarctica.[k]

---

k. Not all states recognize that Antarctica is a global commons. Seven states have made territorial claims over parts of Antarctica. Several other states (including the United States and

C. STONE, THE GNAT IS OLDER THAN MAN
71-72 (1993)

What distinguishes the cases involving harm to the commons [from transboundary pollution] is that the degraded area lies outside any conventionally recognized jurisdiction. The "no man's land" feature of the commons has distinct implications. To begin with, it introduces distinct problems of monitoring. In the transboundary cases . . . , if Canadian fumes are wafting into the United States, there are presumably local U.S. officials on hand to observe the damage over time. . . . But when the commons are imperiled, things are more complicated. Are significant loadings of heavy metals working their way into the deep seabed, and if so, are the levels dangerous, and who is responsible? To answer these questions about the seabed, even to gather the relevant facts, will typically take some special motivation and effort—perhaps even a multinationally coordinated effort.

Even if the monitors identify substantial and worrisome changes and pin down their source, there are complex obstacles facing anyone seeking to raise a legal challenge. . . . The first obstacle would be one of finding a legal interest that the polluting nation was invading. By themselves, *changes* in the quality of the commons do not necessarily constitute the sort of legal *damage* that would support a strong diplomatic protest, much less a law action. Classic principles of international law incline to conceive of "damage" in terms of affronts to sovereignty. . . .

[N]o claim arising out of common despoliation has yet to be pressed in national or international courts. . . . Hence, if one looks behind the various declarations, principles and proposals and examines the prevailing practices—the law in action—one sees that, aside from a few areas provided for by special treaty, the commons areas are essentially unprotected.

Traditionally, international law has allowed open access to global commons areas such as the high seas and the atmosphere, leading to a tragedy of the commons, as described by Garrett Hardin in his famous essay (see Chapter 1). A central purpose of many multilateral environmental agreements (MEAs) is to limit access to the commons. Today, states have adopted more than 450 MEAs, addressing a huge range of issues including climate change, stratospheric ozone depletion, biodiversity, freshwater resources, oceans, and chemicals. Ronald B. Mitchell, International Environmental Agreements Database Project, v.2013.2, iea.uoregon.edu. Some of the leading MEAs are listed in Table 11-2.

To illustrate the workings of MEAs, this section provides an overview of one such treaty, the Montreal Protocol on Substances that Deplete the Ozone Layer, perhaps the most successful international environmental agreement to date.

Russia) do not recognize the particular claims of the claimant states, but reserve the right to make claims of their own. The 1959 Antarctic Treaty freezes the territorial claims issue by providing that no activity in Antarctica shall be a basis for asserting, supporting, or denying a claim or create any rights of sovereignty in Antarctica.

TABLE 11-2
A Selection of Multilateral Environmental Agreements

Short Title	Title	Date of Adoption	Geographic Scope	Summary
Aarhus Convention	Aarhus Convention on Access to Information, Public Participation in Decision-making and Access to Justice in Environmental Matters	1998	Regional	Procedural rights to promote transparency and participation in national environmental decision making.
Basel Convention	Basel Convention on the Control of Transboundary Movements of Hazardous Wastes and Their Disposal	1989	Global	Prior informed consent regime for exports of hazardous wastes.
Biodiversity Convention	Convention on Biological Diversity	1992	Global	Framework for conserving biological diversity. Biosafety Protocol on genetically modified organisms.
CITES	Convention on International Trade in Endangered Species of Flora and Fauna	1973	Global	Permitting scheme for exports and imports of endangered and threatened species.
Desertification Convention	UN Convention to Combat Desertification in Those Countries Experiencing Serious Drought and/or Desertification, Particularly in Africa	1994	Global	Cooperative framework to encourage and support national action plans to combat desertification.
Espoo Convention	Convention on Environmental Impact Assessment in a Transboundary Context	1991	Regional	Obligations for environmental impact assessments of proposed actions likely to cause a significant adverse transboundary impact.
Kyoto Protocol	Kyoto Protocol to the UN Framework Convention on Climate Change	1997	Global	Binding targets and timetables to reduce greenhouse gas emissions. Allows use of market mechanisms, including emissions trading and Clean Development Mechanism.

TABLE 11-2
(continued)

Short Title	Title	Date of Adoption	Geographic Scope	Summary
LRTAP	Long-Range Transboundary Air Pollution Convention	1979	Regional	Basic framework for addressing transboundary air pollution, with protocols regulating emissions of particular pollutants (sulfur, NO_x, volatile organic compounds, heavy metals).
London Convention	Convention on the Prevention of Marine Pollution by Dumping of Wastes and Other Matter	1972	Global	Permitting scheme for dumping of wastes at sea, establishing "black" (prohibited) and "grey" (regulated) lists of materials. 1996 London Protocol reflects the precautionary approach by adopting a "reverse listing" approach.
MARPOL	International Convention for the Prevention of Pollution from Ships	1973	Global	General framework with regulatory annexes on oil pollution, hazardous substances, sewage, garbage, and air pollution. Oil pollution annex sets forth detailed standards for design and equipment of oil tankers, as well as oil discharge standards.
Montreal Protocol	Montreal Protocol on Substances that Deplete the Ozone Layer	1987	Global	Phaseout schedule for ozone depleting substances.

TABLE 11-2
(continued)

Short Title	Title	Date of Adoption	Geographic Scope	Summary
POPs Convention	Stockholm Convention on Persistent Organic Pollutants	2001	Global	Elimination or restrictions on production and use of listed chemicals.
Ramsar Convention	Convention on Wetlands of International Importance Especially as Waterfowl Habitat	1971	Global	General obligations regarding designation and wise use of wetlands.
Rotterdam Convention	Rotterdam Convention on Prior Informed Consent Procedure for Certain Hazardous Chemicals and Pesticides in International Trade	1998	Global	Prior informed consent regime for exports of pesticides and chemicals.
UNFCCC	UN Framework Convention on Climate Change	1992	Global	Framework of governance for climate change issue.
Whaling Convention	International Convention for the Regulation of Whaling	1946	Global	Detailed regulations on whaling. Indefinite moratorium on commercial whaling.
World Heritage Convention	UNESCO Convention Concerning the Protection of the World Cultural and Natural Heritage	1972	Global	Process for designating world heritage sites. International fund to support world heritage sites in danger.

1. Background on the Ozone Depletion Problem

Ozone is a molecule consisting of three oxygen atoms. At ground level, ozone is considered a pollutant and is one of the main components of smog. But in the stratosphere (the upper part of the atmosphere), ozone plays a beneficial role by shielding the earth from harmful ultraviolet radiation from the sun, which have adverse effects on health (skin cancers, eye cataracts, and immune system suppression), terrestrial ecosystems, aquatic ecosystems, biogeochemical cycles, air quality, and materials.

In 1974, Mario Molina and F.S. Rowland published a paper in *Nature* magazine predicting that chlorofluorocarbons (CFCs)—first developed in the 1930s and widely used at the time in refrigerators, spray cans, and foams—would slowly migrate to the upper atmosphere and chemically react with ozone, thereby depleting the stratospheric ozone layer. Twenty-one years later, in 1995, they were awarded a Nobel

Prize in chemistry for their work on ozone depletion. In addition to CFCs, other ozone-depleting substances (ODS) include (1) halons (used primarily in fire extinguishers); (2) methyl chloroform (used as a solvent), and (3) methyl bromide (used as a fumigant).

Concern about stratospheric ozone depletion grew in the 1970s and 1980s. In the late 1970s, the United States banned aerosol spray cans that use CFCs as a propellant. Internationally, states began to explore ways to collaborate on ozone research and the control of ozone-depleting substances.

2. The Vienna Convention for the Protection of the Ozone Layer

In 1985, a number of states (primarily Western industrialized states) negotiated the Vienna Convention for the Protection of the Ozone Layer, the first international agreement aimed at addressing the ozone problem. At the time, there was still considerable debate about the severity of the stratospheric ozone depletion problem. As a result, states could not reach agreement to reduce the production or consumption of ozone-depleting substances by any specific amount. Instead, the Vienna Convention set forth very general obligations and established a framework for addressing the ozone problem in the future.

VIENNA CONVENTION FOR THE PROTECTION OF THE OZONE LAYER
Vienna, 22 March 1985

Preamble

The Parties to this Convention,

Aware of the potentially harmful impact on human health and the environment through modification of the ozone layer,

Mindful . . . of the precautionary measures for the protection of the ozone layer which have already been taken at the national and international levels,

Aware that measures to protect the ozone layer from modifications due to human activities require international co-operation and action, and should be based on relevant scientific and technical considerations,

Determined to protect human health and the environment against adverse effects resulting from modifications of the ozone layer,

Have agreed as follows. . . .

Article 2: General Obligations

1. The Parties shall take appropriate measures . . . to protect human health and the environment against adverse effects resulting or likely to result from human activities which modify or are likely to modify the ozone layer.

2. To this end the Parties shall, in accordance with the means at their disposal and their capabilities:

(a) Co-operate by means of systematic observations, research and information exchange in order to better understand and assess the effects of human activities on the ozone layer and the effects on human health and the environment from modification of the ozone layer;

(b) Adopt appropriate legislative or administrative measures and co-operate in harmonizing appropriate policies to control, limit, reduce or prevent human activities under their jurisdiction or control should it be found that these activities have or are likely to have adverse effects resulting from modification or likely modification of the ozone layer;

(c) Co-operate in the formulation of agreed measures, procedures and standards for the implementation of this Convention, with a view to the adoption of protocols and annexes;

(d) Co-operate with competent international bodies to implement effectively this Convention and protocols to which they are party.

3. The provisions of this Convention shall in no way affect the right of Parties to adopt, in accordance with international law, domestic measures additional to those referred to in paragraphs 1 and 2 above, nor shall they affect additional domestic measures already taken by a Party, provided that these measures are not incompatible with their obligations under this Convention.

4. The application of this article shall be based on relevant scientific and technical considerations.

Article 5: Transmission of Information

The Parties shall transmit, through the secretariat, to the Conference of the Parties established under article 6, information on the measures adopted by them in implementation of this Convention and of protocols to which they are party in such form and at such intervals as the meetings of the parties to the relevant instruments may determine.

Article 6: Conference of the Parties

1. A Conference of the Parties is hereby established. . . .

4. The Conference of the Parties shall keep under continuous review the implementation of this Convention.

Article 8: Adoption of Protocols

1. The Conference of the Parties may at a meeting adopt protocols pursuant to Article 2. . . .

Article 9: Amendment of the Convention or Protocols

1. Any Party may propose amendments to this Convention or to any protocol. Such amendments shall take due account, *inter alia*, of relevant scientific and technical considerations.

2. Amendments to this Convention shall be adopted at a meeting of the Conference of the Parties. . . .

3. The Parties shall make every effort to reach agreement on any proposed amendment to this Convention by consensus. If all efforts at consensus have been exhausted, and no agreement reached, the amendment shall as a last resort be adopted by a three-fourths majority vote of the Parties present and voting at the meeting, and shall be submitted by the Depositary to all Parties for ratification, approval or acceptance.

4. The procedure mentioned in paragraph 3 above shall apply to amendments to any protocol, except that a two-thirds majority of the parties to that protocol present and voting at the meeting shall suffice for their adoption.

5. Ratification, approval or acceptance of amendments shall be notified to the Depositary in writing. Amendments adopted in accordance with paragraphs 3 or 4 above shall enter into force between parties having accepted them on the ninetieth day after the receipt by the Depositary of notification of their ratification, approval or acceptance by at least three-fourths of the Parties to this Convention or by at least two-thirds of the parties to the protocol concerned, except as may otherwise be provided in such protocol. Thereafter the amendments shall enter into force for any other Party on the ninetieth day after that Party deposits its instrument of ratification, approval or acceptance of the amendments. . . .

Article 10: Adoption and Amendment of Annexes

1. The annexes to this Convention or to any protocol shall form an integral part of this Convention or of such protocol. . . . Such annexes shall be restricted to scientific, technical and administrative matters.

2. Except as may be otherwise provided in any protocol with respect to its annexes, the following procedure shall apply to the proposal, adoption and entry into force of additional annexes to this Convention or of annexes to a protocol:

   (a) Annexes to this Convention shall be proposed and adopted according to the procedure laid down in article 9, paragraphs 2 and 3, while annexes to any protocol shall be proposed and adopted according to the procedure laid down in article 9, paragraphs 2 and 4;

   (b) Any party that is unable to approve an additional annex to this Convention or annex to any protocol to which it is party shall so notify the Depositary, in writing, within six months from the date of the communication of the adoption by the Depositary. . . .

   (c) On the expiry of six months from the date of the circulation of the communication by the Depositary, the annex shall become effective for all Parties to this Convention or to any protocol concerned which have not submitted a notification in accordance with the provision of subparagraph (b) above.

3. The proposal, adoption and entry into force of amendments to annexes to this Convention or to any protocol shall be subject to the same procedure as for the proposal, adoption and entry into force of annexes to the Convention or annexes to a protocol. Annexes and amendments thereto shall take due account, *inter alia*, of relevant scientific and technical considerations. . . .

NOTES AND QUESTIONS

1. What is the function of the Vienna Convention? What did states hope to achieve by negotiating it?

2. What commitments, if any, does the Vienna Convention impose? What other norms or principles does it help establish?

3. What are the requirements set forth by the Vienna Convention for amendments and for adopting and amending annexes? In what ways do the rules for adopting and amending annexes differ from the requirements for amending the Convention? Why do you think these requirements differ?

3. *The Montreal Protocol*

Following the adoption of the Vienna Convention, concern continued to mount about the ozone issue, heightened by the discovery of an "ozone hole" over Antarctica in 1985. In 1987, the parties to the Vienna Convention negotiated the Montreal Protocol on Substances that Deplete the Ozone Layer, which established specific obligations to reduce the consumption and production of specified "controlled substances." Initially, the Montreal Protocol required states to freeze and then reduce their production and consumption of the principal CFCs by 50 percent by the end of the century. In 1990, the Parties to the Montreal Protocol adopted the London Amendments, which required the complete phase-out of most CFCs and halons by the year 2000 and imposed limits on the use of several other ozone-depleting substances. In addition, the London amendments established a Multilateral Fund to provide financial resources to developing countries to help them implement the Protocol, as well as a noncompliance procedure to consider questions raised about whether a state is adequately implementing its obligations under the Protocol. Since the London meeting, the Parties have progressively accelerated the phase-out schedule date for controlled substances, and added additional ozone-depleting substances to the control regime, in amendments and adjustments adopted in 1992 (the Copenhagen Amendment and Adjustments), 1995 (the Vienna Adjustments), 1997 (the Montreal Amendment and Adjustments), 1999 (the Beijing Amendment and Adjustments), and 2007 (the Montreal Adjustments) (see Table 11-3). Today, 96 chemicals are controlled by the Montreal Protocol regime, including CFCs, halons, carbon tetrachloride, methyl chloroform, methyl bromide, and hydrochlorofluorocarbons (HCFCs).

The head of the U.S. delegation to the Montreal Protocol negotiations summarized the significant environmental and financial stakes involved as follows:

The Montreal Protocol . . . mandated significant reductions in the use of several extremely useful chemicals. At the time of the treaty's negotiation, chlorofluorocarbons (CFCs) and halons were rapidly proliferating compounds with wide applications in thousands of products, including refrigeration, air conditioning, aerosol sprays, solvents, transportation, plastics, insulation, pharmaceuticals, computers, electronics, and fire fighting. . . .

[The Montreal Protocol] sounded the death knell for an important part of the international chemical industry, with implications for billions of dollars in investment and hundreds of thousands of jobs in related sectors. The protocol did not simply prescribe limits on these chemicals based on "best available technology," which had been a traditional way of reconciling environmental goals with economic interests. Rather, the negotiators established target dates for replacing products that had become synonymous with modern standards of living, even though the requisite [replacement] technologies did not yet exist. . . . [R. Benedick, Ozone Diplomacy: New Directions in Safeguarding the Planet 1-2 (1991).]

TABLE 11-3
The Montreal Protocol Treaty Regime

1985	Vienna Convention for the Protection of the Ozone Layer
1987	Montreal Protocol to the Vienna Convention
1990	London Amendment and Adjustments to the Montreal Protocol
1992	Copenhagen Amendment and Adjustments to the Montreal Protocol
1994	Vienna Adjustments to the Montreal Protocol
1997	Montreal Amendment and Adjustments to the Montreal Protocol
1999	Beijing Amendment and Adjustments to the Montreal Protocol
2007	Montreal Adjustments to the Montreal Protocol

Benedick attributed the success of the Protocol to a series of factors, including (1) the role of science, (2) the power of public opinion, (3) UNEP's role as facilitator, and (4) the leadership of the United States. Among other things, the United States was the first country to "take regulatory action" to limit the use of CFCs and it also "tenaciously campaigned" for international adoption of a "comprehensive global plan for protecting the ozone layer. . . ." Id. at 6.

Benedick concluded that the Protocol

broke new ground in its treatment of long-term risks and in its reconciliation of difficult scientific, economic, and political issues. . . . [T]he Montreal Protocol was achieved with astonishing rapidity. The signing occurred 13 years after the first scientific hypothesis on the ozone layer was published in 1974—and only nine months after formal diplomatic negotiations began in December 1986. . . . [Id. at 8.]

MONTREAL PROTOCOL ON SUBSTANCES THAT DEPLETE THE OZONE LAYER
Montreal, 16 September 1987

The Parties to this Protocol, . . .

Being Parties to the Vienna Convention for the Protection of the Ozone Layer,

Mindful of their obligation under that Convention to take appropriate measures to protect human health and the environment against adverse effects resulting or likely to result from human activities which modify or are likely to modify the ozone layer,

Recognizing that world-wide emissions of certain substances can significantly deplete and otherwise modify the ozone layer in a manner that is likely to result in adverse effects on human health and the environment, . . .

Aware that measures taken to protect the ozone layer from depletion should be based on relevant scientific knowledge, taking into account technical and economic considerations,

Determined to protect the ozone layer by taking precautionary measures to control equitably total global emissions of substances that deplete it, with the ultimate objective of their elimination on the basis of developments in scientific knowledge, taking into account technical and economic considerations,

Acknowledging that special provision is required to meet the needs of developing countries for these substances, . . .

Considering the importance of promoting international co-operation in the research and development of science and technology relating to the control and reduction of emissions of substances that deplete the ozone layer, bearing in mind in particular the needs of developing countries,

Have agreed as follows: . . .

Article 1: Definitions

. . .

4. "Controlled substance" means a substance listed in Annex A of this Protocol. . . .

5. "Production" means the amount of controlled substances produced minus the amount destroyed by technologies to be approved by the Parties.

6. "Consumption" means production plus imports minus exports of controlled substances. . . .

8. "Industrial rationalization" means the transfer of all or a portion of the calculated level of production of one Party to another, for the purpose of achieving economic efficiencies or responding to anticipated shortfalls in supply as a result of plant closures.

Article 2: Control Measures

1. Each Party shall ensure that for the twelve-month period commencing on the first day of the seventh month following the date of the entry into force of this Protocol, and in each twelve-month period thereafter, its calculated level of consumption of the controlled substances in Group I of Annex A does not exceed its calculated level of consumption in 1986. By the end of the same period, each Party producing one or more of these substances shall ensure that its calculated level of production of the substances does not exceed its calculated level of production in 1986, except that such level may have increased by no more than ten per cent based on the 1986 level. Such increase shall be permitted only so as to satisfy the basic domestic needs of the Parties operating under Article 5 and for the purposes of industrial rationalization between Parties. . . .

3. Each Party shall ensure that for the periods 1 July 1993 to 30 June 1994 and in each twelve-month period thereafter, its calculated level of consumption of the

controlled substances in Group I of Annex A does not exceed, annually, eighty per cent of its calculated level of consumption in 1986. Each Party producing one or more of these substances shall, for the same periods, ensure that its calculated level of production of the substances does not exceed, annually, eighty per cent of its calculated level of production in 1986. However, in order to satisfy the basic domestic needs of the Parties operating under Article 5 and for the purposes of industrial rationalization between Parties, its calculated level of production may exceed that limit by up to ten per cent of its calculated level of production in 1986.

4. Each Party shall ensure that for the periods 1 July 1998 to 30 June 1999, and in each twelve-month period thereafter, its calculated level of consumption of the controlled substances in Group I of Annex A does not exceed, annually, fifty per cent of its calculated level of consumption in 1986. Each Party producing one or more of these substances shall, for the same periods, ensure that its calculated level of production of the substances does not exceed, annually, fifty per cent of its calculated level of production in 1986. However, in order to satisfy the basic domestic needs of the Parties operating under Article 5 and for the purposes of industrial rationalization between Parties, its calculated level of production may exceed that limit by up to fifteen per cent of its calculated level of production in 1986. This paragraph will apply unless the Parties decide otherwise at a meeting by a two-thirds majority of Parties present and voting, representing at least two-thirds of the total calculated level of consumption of these substances of the Parties. This decision shall be considered and made in the light of the assessments referred to in Article 6.

5. Any Party whose calculated level of production in 1986 of the controlled substances in Group I of Annex A was less than twenty-five kilotonnes may, for the purposes of industrial rationalization, transfer to or receive from any other Party, production in excess of the limits set out in paragraphs 1, 3 and 4 provided that the total combined calculated levels of production of the Parties concerned does not exceed the production limits set out in this Article. Any transfer of such production shall be notified to the secretariat, no later than the time of the transfer. . . .

9. (a) Based on the assessments made pursuant to Article 6, the Parties may decide whether: (i) adjustments to the ozone depleting potentials specified in Annex A should be made and, if so, what the adjustments should be; and (ii) further adjustments and reductions of production or consumption of the controlled substances from 1986 levels should be undertaken and, if so, what the scope, amount and timing of any such adjustments and reductions should be. . . .

(c) In taking such decisions, the Parties shall make every effort to reach agreement by consensus. If all efforts at consensus have been exhausted, and no agreement reached, such decisions shall, as a last resort, be adopted by a two-thirds majority vote of the Parties present and voting representing at least fifty per cent of the total consumption of the controlled substances of the Parties.

(d) The decisions, which shall be binding on all Parties, shall forthwith be communicated to the Parties by the Depositary. . . .

10. (a) Based on the assessments made pursuant to Article 6 of this Protocol and in accordance with the procedure set out in Article 9 of the Convention [covering Amendments to the Convention or Protocols], the Parties may decide: (i) whether any

substances, and if so which, should be added to or removed from any annex to this Protocol; and (ii) the mechanism, scope and timing of the control measures that should apply to those substances. . . .

(b) any such decision shall become effective, provided that it has been adopted by two-thirds majority vote of the Parties present and voting.

11. Notwithstanding the provisions contained in this Article, Parties may take more stringent measures than those required by this Article.

Article 3: *Calculation of Control Levels*

For the purposes of Articles 2 and 5, each Party shall, for each Group of substances in Annex A, determine its calculated levels of:

(a) Production by: (i) Multiplying its annual production of each-controlled substance by the ozone depleting potential specified in respect of it in Annex A; and (ii) Adding together, for each such Group, the resulting figures; . . .

(c) Consumption by adding together its calculated levels of production and imports and subtracting its calculated level of exports as determined in accordance with subparagraphs (a) and (b). However, beginning on 1 January 1993, any export of controlled substances to non-Parties shall not be subtracted in calculating the consumption level of the exporting Party.

Article 4: *Control of Trade with Non-Parties*

1. Within one year of the entry into force of this Protocol, each Party shall ban the import of controlled substances from any State not party to this Protocol.

2. Beginning on 1 January 1993, no Party operating under paragraph 1 of Article 5 may export any controlled substance to any State not party to this Protocol.

3. Within three years of the date of the entry into force of this Protocol, the Parties shall, following the procedures in Article 10 of the Convention, elaborate in an annex a list of products containing controlled substances. Parties that have not objected to the annex in accordance with those procedures shall ban, within one year of the annex having become effective, the import of those products from any State not party to this Protocol.

4. Within five years of the entry into force of this Protocol, the Parties shall determine the feasibility of banning or restricting, from States not party to this Protocol, the import of products produced with, but not containing, controlled substances. If determined feasible, the Parties shall . . . elaborate in an annex a list of such products. Parties that have not objected to it . . . shall ban or restrict, within one year of the annex having become effective, the import of those products from any State not party to this Protocol.

5. Each Party shall discourage the export, to any State not party to this Protocol, of technology for producing and for utilizing controlled substances.

6. Each Party shall refrain from providing new subsidies, aid, credits, guarantees or insurance programmes for the export to States not party to this Protocol of products,

equipment, plants or technology that would facilitate the production of controlled substances. . . .

Article 5: Special Situation of Developing Countries

1. Any Party that is a developing country and whose annual calculated level of consumption of the controlled substances is less than 0.3 kilograms per capita on the date of the entry into force of the Protocol for it, or any time thereafter within ten years of the date of entry into force of the Protocol shall, in order to meet its basic domestic needs, be entitled to delay its compliance with the control measures . . . by ten years after that specified. . . . However, each Party shall not exceed an annual calculated level of consumption of 0.3 kg per capita. . . .

2. The Parties undertake to facilitate access to environmentally safe alternative substances and technology for Parties that are developing countries and assist them to make expeditious use of such alternatives.

3. The Parties undertake to facilitate bilaterally or multilaterally the provision of subsidies, aid, credits, guarantees or insurance programmes to Parties that are developing countries for the use of alternative technology and for substitute products.

Article 6: Assessment and Review of Control Measures

Beginning in 1990, and at least every four years thereafter, the Parties shall assess the control measures provided for in Article 2 on the basis of available scientific, environmental, technical and economic information. At least one year before each assessment, the Parties shall convene appropriate panels of experts qualified in the fields mentioned and determine the composition and terms of reference of any such panels. Within one year of being convened, the panels will report their conclusions, through the secretariat, to the Parties. . . .

Article 7: Reporting of Data

1. Each Party shall provide to the secretariat, within three months of becoming a Party, statistical data on its production, imports and exports of each of the controlled substances for the year 1986, or the best possible estimates of such data where actual data are not available.

2. Each Party shall provide statistical data to the secretariat on its annual production (with separate data on amounts destroyed by technologies to be approved by the Parties), imports, and exports to Parties and non-Parties, respectively, of such substances for the year during which it becomes a Party and for each year thereafter. . . .

Article 8: Non-Compliance

The Parties, at their first meeting, shall consider and approve procedures and institutional mechanisms for determining non-compliance with the provisions of this Protocol and for treatment of Parties found to be in non-compliance. . . .

Article 11: Meetings of the Parties

    1. The Parties shall hold meetings at regular intervals. . . .
    2. . . . [O]rdinary meetings of the parties shall be held . . . in conjunction with the meetings of the Conference of the Parties to the Convention. . . .
    4. The functions of the meetings of the Parties shall be to:

        (a) Review the implementation of this Protocol;
        (b) Decide on any adjustments or reductions referred to in paragraph 9 of Article 2;
        (c) Decide on any addition to, insertion in or removal from any annex of substances and on related control measures in accordance with paragraph 10 of Article 2;
        (d) Establish, where necessary, guidelines or procedures for reporting of information as provided for in Article 7 and paragraph 3 of Article 9; . . .
        (h) Consider and adopt, as required, proposals for amendment of this Protocol or any annex and for any new annex. . . .

Design Elements of the Montreal Protocol

Obligations. MEAs use a variety of regulatory approaches to limit the use of the global commons. Some establish "obligations of conduct," which require states to take particular actions. For example, the Convention on International Trade in Endangered Species requires states to establish a permitting system for imports and exports of listed species. Other MEAs establish "obligations of result." For example, the 1985 Sulphur Protocol to LRTAP (discussed above) requires states to reduce their emissions of sulfur dioxide by 30 percent, but leaves it completely up to each state to decide how to achieve that result.

    1. What obligations does the Montreal Protocol impose on parties? Does it establish obligations of conduct or obligations of result?

    2. Why does the Montreal Protocol focus on production and consumption of ozone-depleting substances rather than on emissions? Why does it define consumption in terms of production plus imports minus exports?

Regime Evolution. The Protocol has evolved considerably since it was first adopted in 1987. It regulates many more chemicals than it did initially. The schedule for reducing and eventually phasing out the use of ozone-depleting substances has been continually ratcheted up. A financial mechanism has been created to provide assistance to developing countries (the Multilateral Fund). And a procedure has been established to consider cases of non-compliance (discussed in the next section).

3. How does the Montreal Protocol attempt to ensure that its regulatory measures respond to new scientific information?

4. What is the procedure for strengthening the phase-out schedule of ODS? The procedure for adding additional chemicals to the control regime?

Participation. A basic principle of treaty law is that treaties bind only those states that consent. In this respect, treaties are fundamentally different from statutes, which apply to everyone whether they like a statute or not. As a result, one of the basic tasks of treaty design is to encourage participation. An MEA may set exactly the right environmental standards, but unless states join the regime, it will be ineffective.

5. What incentives does the Montreal Protocol give to countries to join? How does the Montreal Protocol encourage the participation of developing countries in particular? How does it reflect the principle of "common but differentiated responsibilities and respective capabilities"? Which countries are eligible for "Article 5" status?

6. What are the implications of the Protocol for non-parties? What types of restrictions does the Montreal Protocol impose on trade? Identify the categories of products subject to these restrictions.

Implementation. A treaty text, of course, is only the first step in addressing an environmental problem such as stratospheric ozone depletion. To be effective, the treaty must be implemented.

7. Who has the primary task of implementing the Montreal Protocol?

8. How much freedom do states have in deciding how to implement the Montreal Protocol? Identify two or three types of domestic measures that states might use to implement their obligations under the Protocol.

NOTES AND QUESTIONS

1. Benedick notes that the Montreal Protocol imposed "substantial short-term economic costs to protect human health and the environment against unproved future dangers. . . . At the time [that the treaty was negotiated], no measurable evidence of damage existed." The Montreal Protocol thus reflects the so-called precautionary principle, which states that "where there are threats of serious or irreversible damage, lack of full scientific certainty shall not be used as a reason for postponing cost-effective measures to prevent environmental degradation." Rio Declaration on Environment and Development, principle 15.

2. Although the ozone regime is still being phased in by developing countries, and a large black market has developed for banned substances, the international ozone regime has had a significant effect. Former UN secretary-general Kofi Annan described it as "perhaps the most successful international agreement to date." According to the UN Environment Programme, global consumption of CFCs has fallen from 1.1 million tons in 1986 to 35,000 tons in 2006, and 96 percent of all ozone-depleting substances have been phased out globally. Use of ozone-depleting substances has been almost completely eliminated in developed countries, and has fallen by over 80 percent in developing countries. Although the ozone layer will take decades to repair, a 2009 UNEP study concluded that stratospheric ozone is no longer declining and may already be increasing. UNEP, Environmental Effects of Ozone Depletion and Its Interaction with Climate Change, Progress Report, 2009.

3. In NRDC v. EPA, 464 F.3d 1 (D.C. Cir. 2006), the D.C. Circuit held that "the 'decisions' of the Parties—post-ratification side agreements reached by consensus among 189 nations—are not 'law' within the meaning of the Clean Air Act and are not enforceable in federal court. . . . Without congressional action . . . side agreements reached after a treaty has been ratified are not the law of the land; they are enforceable not through the federal courts, but through international negotiations." Id. at 232. What are the possible implications of this decision for implementation of the Montreal Protocol, and for the structure of multilateral agreements more generally?

4. Not all international initiatives in the environmental arena have been as successful as the Montreal Protocol. A comparison of the experience in addressing global warming with ozone depletion provides a good example of this reality. For an interesting analysis of the reasons why the Montreal Protocol has been more successful than other multilateral environmental treaties, including the Kyoto Protocol, see S. Barrett, Environment and Statecraft (2003). In his analysis of the Montreal and Kyoto Protocols, Professor Cass Sunstein suggests considerable similarities between the two:

Of the world's environmental challenges, the two most significant may well be strato-spheric ozone depletion and climate change. At first glance, the problems appear to be closely related. . . . Consider seven similarities between the two problems:

1. Both ozone depletion and climate change have received public recognition on the basis of relatively recent scientific work, theoretical and empirical.
2. Both problems involve the effects of emissions from man-made technologies that come from diverse nations and that threaten to cause large-scale harm.
3. Both ozone-depleting chemicals and greenhouse gases stay in the atmosphere for an extremely long time. Hence the relevant risks are difficult to reverse; even with action that is both immediate and aggressive, the underlying problems will hardly be elimi-nated all at once. . . .
4. No nation is able to eliminate either problem on its own. Indeed, no nation is even able to make significant progress on either problem on its own, certainly not in the long run. Because of the diversity of contributors, both problems seem to be best handled through international agreements.
5. Both problems involve extremely serious problems of international equity. Wealthy nations have been the principal contributors to both ozone depletion and climate change. . . .
6. Both problems present extremely serious problems of intergenerational equity. Future generations are likely to face greater risks than the current generation, and a key question is how much the present should be willing to sacrifice for the benefit of the future. . . .
7. With respect to both problems, the United States is a crucial actor, probably the most important in the world. The importance of the United States lies not only in its wealth and power; it also lies in the fact that the United States has been an extremely sig-nificant source of both ozone-depleting chemicals and greenhouse gases. [Sunstein, Of Montreal and Kyoto: A Tale of Two Protocols, 31 Harv. Envtl. L. Rev. 1 (2007).]

Professor Sunstein also notes, however, that the two protocols have had very different degrees of success:

Notwithstanding these similarities, there is one obvious difference between the two problems. An international agreement, originally signed in Montreal and designed to control ozone-depleting chemicals, has been ratified by almost all nations in the world (including the United States, where ratification was unanimous). . . . Nations are complying with their obligations; global emissions of ozone-depleting chemicals have been reduced by over 95%; and atmospheric concentrations of such chemicals have been declining since 1994. By 2050, the ozone layer is expected to return to its natural level. The Montreal Protocol, the foundation for this process, thus stands as an extraordinary and even spectacular success story. Its success owes a great deal to the actions not only of the United States government, which played an exceedingly aggressive role in producing the Protocol, but to American companies as well, which stood in the forefront of technical innovation leading to substitutes for ozone-depleting chemicals.

With climate change, the situation is altogether different. To be sure, an international agreement, produced in Kyoto in 1997, did go into force in 2005, when Russia ratified it. . . . But numerous nations are not complying with their obligations under the Kyoto Protocol, and the United States firmly rejects the agreement, with unanimous bipartisan opposition to its ratification. Far from leading technical innovation, American companies have sharply opposed efforts to regulate greenhouse gas emissions, and have insisted that the costs of regulation are likely to be prohibitive. Between 1990 and 2004, the United States experienced a decline in emissions of ozone-depleting chemicals, to the point where such emissions are essentially zero. But in the same period, the United States experienced a rapid growth in greenhouse gases. In part as a result, worldwide emissions of greenhouse gases are projected to rise at a rapid rate. An additional complication stems from the fact that developing nations have refused to join the Kyoto Protocol, and it is in those nations that greenhouse gases are increasing most rapidly. In particular, India and China have shown explosive growth in recent years, and China will soon become the leading greenhouse gas emitter in the world.

Given the similarities between the ozone depletion and climate change problems, why do you think the two regimes have had such different degrees of success? Why has the Montreal Protocol been so much more effective than the Kyoto Protocol?

4. Montreal Protocol Noncompliance Procedure

Because the international community lacks both an executive with enforcement powers and a system of compulsory and binding dispute settlement, international agreements have had to develop ad hoc implementation and compliance mechanisms. Such procedures are particularly important for global agreements such as the Montreal Protocol, which are vulnerable to free riding; unless there is some assurance that the main contributors to the problem will comply with their commitments, countries may be reluctant to take actions that cost money and could potentially hurt their competitiveness.

The Montreal Protocol did not itself include a compliance procedure, but provided for the development of such a procedure in Article 8. The procedure was first adopted by the parties on an interim basis in 1990 at the London Conference. It was formally adopted two years later and was subsequently amended by the tenth meeting of the parties in 1998.

MONTREAL PROTOCOL NON-COMPLIANCE PROCEDURE
Report of the 10th Meeting of the Parties, Annex II, UNEP/OzL.Pro.10/9 (1998)

The following procedure has been formulated pursuant to Article 8 of the Montreal Protocol. . . .

1. If one or more Parties have reservations regarding another Party's implementation of its obligations under the Protocol, those concerns may be addressed in writing to the Secretariat. Such a submission shall be supported by corroborating information. . . .

3. Where the Secretariat, during the course of preparing its report, becomes aware of possible non-compliance by any Party with its obligations under the Protocol, it may request the Party concerned to furnish necessary information about the matter. . . .

4. Where a Party concludes that, despite having made its best, bona fide efforts, it is unable to comply fully with its obligations under the Protocol, it may address to the Secretariat a submission in writing, explaining, in particular, the specific circumstances that it considers to be the cause of its non-compliance. The Secretariat shall transmit such submission to the Implementation Committee which shall consider it as soon as practicable.

5. An Implementation Committee is hereby established. It shall consist of 10 Parties elected by the Meeting of the Parties for two years, based on equitable geographical distribution. . . .

6. The Implementation Committee shall, unless it decides otherwise, meet twice a year. The Secretariat shall arrange for and service its meetings.

7. The functions of the Implementation Committee shall be:

(a) To receive, consider and report on any submission in accordance with paragraphs 1, 2 and 4;

(b) To receive, consider and report on any information or observations forwarded by the Secretariat in connection with the preparation of the reports referred to in Article 12 (c) of the Protocol and on any other information received and forwarded by the Secretariat concerning compliance with the provisions of the Protocol;

(c) To request, where it considers necessary, through the Secretariat, further information on matters under its consideration;

(d) To identify the facts and possible causes relating to individual cases of non-compliance referred to the Committee and make appropriate recommendations to the Meeting of the Parties;

(e) To undertake, upon the invitation of the Party concerned, information-gathering in the territory of that Party for fulfilling the functions of the Committee; . . .

8. The Implementation Committee shall consider the submissions, information and observations referred to in paragraph 7 with a view to securing an amicable solution of the matter on the basis of respect for the provisions of the Protocol.

9. The Implementation Committee shall report to the Meeting of the Parties, including any recommendations it considers appropriate. . . . After receiving a report by the Committee the Parties may, taking into consideration the circumstances of the

matter, decide upon and call for steps to bring about full compliance with the Protocol, including measures to assist the Parties' compliance with the Protocol, and to further the Protocol's objectives. . . .

15. The members of the Implementation Committee and any Party involved in its deliberations shall protect the confidentiality of information they receive in confidence. . . .

NOTES AND QUESTIONS

1. What are the key features of the Montreal Protocol noncompliance procedure?

2. Who may initiate noncompliance proceedings? Who do you think has initiated most proceedings thus far?

3. What is the role of the Implementation Committee? Are its decisions binding?

4. What are the penalties, if any, for not complying with the Protocol?

D.   TRADE AND THE ENVIRONMENT

International environmental issues are affected by, and have implications for, many other issue areas: international trade, human rights, and national security, among others. This has led to the development of a series of "law and . . ." subfields within international environmental law. In this section we focus on one of the most controversial of these subfields: trade and environment.

International trade has both positive and negative implications for environmental protection. On the positive side, free trade

- tends to increase income levels, allowing societies to spend more on environmental protection;
- tends to encourage the more efficient use of resources;
- can encourage a process of "upward harmonization," as multinational companies find it efficient to harmonize their practices and products worldwide by disseminating good environmental practices and clean technologies;

Conversely,

- Free trade can encourage a process of "downward harmonization," as industries relocate to countries with lower environmental standards ("pollution havens"), leading to a "race to the bottom."
- Increased levels of trade tend to increase the scale of industrial activity, leading to overexploitation of natural resources and greater pollution.
- Trade in particular products can cause direct harms. For example, trade in endangered species can encourage poaching, while trade in hazardous wastes can cause environmental damage both during the transportation process and in the recipient countries.

The trade-and-environment debate in part concerns these general interconnections between trade and environmental protection, but much of it focuses on a more narrowly defined set of legal issues, concerning the potential restrictions imposed by the international trade regime on both domestic and international environmental measures. For example, can a state impose a tax on electricity based on the amount of carbon dioxide emitted during the generation process? A tax on sales of "gas guzzling" cars? These taxes might not seem to raise trade concerns, but to the extent that they affect domestic and foreign products differently, then they may raise an issue of discrimination. Can a state restrict the imports of tuna or shrimp harvested in ways that harm dolphins or sea turtles? Or can an international treaty limit trade in endangered species or hazardous wastes? Can a state impose duties on imports of carbon-intensive goods from countries that do not participate in the international climate change regime? And, more generally, can states use trade measures as an enforcement tool against countries that violate an international environmental agreement? These are the types of questions that raise concerns among environmentalists that the trade and environmental regimes run at cross purposes. The limitations on citizen participation in the WTO system—and, more generally, the alleged lack of accountability and transparency—have exacerbated these concerns. McRae, Trade and the Environment: The Issue of Transparency, in Greening NAFTA 237 (D. Markell & J. Knox eds., 2003).

1.   Background on the International Trade Regime

Trade agreements have been negotiated at the global level as well as regionally and bilaterally. NAFTA is an example of a regional trade agreement, while the General Agreement on Tariffs and Trade (GATT) is the centerpiece of the global trade regime. In addition to the GATT, the World Trade Organization (WTO) legal system includes several specialized agreements that potentially impact domestic environmental regulation, including the Technical Barriers to Trade (TBT) Agreement, and the Sanitary and Phytosanitary Standards (SPS) Agreement (addressing food and animal safety issues).

The basic rules set forth in the GATT can be summarized as follows:

- States may not impose "quantitative restrictions" on trade—for example, quotas or import bans (Article XI).
- States may impose tariffs on imports, but these tariffs may not exceed the limits specified in the GATT schedule (Article II).
- States may not discriminate between "like products" from different countries—the so-called most favored nation principle (Article I).
- States may not discriminate between "like products" that are imported and domestically produced—the national treatment principle (Article III).

Article XX allows states to make exceptions to these rules for specified purposes, including the protection of human, animal, or plant life or health, and the protection of exhaustible natural resources. It reads in pertinent part:

Article XX: General Exceptions

Subject to the requirement that such measures are not applied in a manner which would constitute a means of arbitrary or unjustifiable discrimination between countries where the same conditions prevail, or a disguised restriction on international trade, nothing in this Agreement shall be construed to prevent the adoption or enforcement by any contracting party of measures: . . .

  (b) necessary to protect human, animal or plant life or health; . . .

  (g) relating to the conservation of exhaustible natural resources if such measures are made effective in conjunction with restrictions on domestic production or consumption. . . .

One of the major sources of the possible conflict between "free trade" and "environmental protection" policies is intuitively easy to grasp. Environmental policies frequently seek to regulate activities (such as the manufacture of products) with adverse effects on human health and the environment, but these regulations, while good for the environment, often hinder free trade, either purposefully or inadvertently, and are therefore open to question from a trade perspective. As Daniel Bodansky and Jessica Lawrence explain,

> [t]he bias towards conflict between the trade and environmental regimes should not be surprising, since at their core, they work in opposite ways. Environmental regulation typically involves "public" governmental intervention in the "private" marketplace to correct perceived market failures, while trade policy represents an attempt to limit government intervention and allow the unimpeded flow of goods. Like the silhouette/vase illusion, in which the same picture can be seen in alternative ways, as either a vase or two faces, conflicts between environmental and trade rules tend to be perceived quite differently, depending on one's starting premises. Environmentalists start from the premise that States have authority to address environmental harms, and view trade rules that limit the permissible forms of environmental regulation as suspect. Trade experts, by contrast, start from the premise that States should refrain from interfering in private transactions and attribute conflicts between the two regimes to environmental rules that hinder trade, which require special justification. Since the WTO dispute settlement system has been the main forum to address trade-and-environment disputes, the trade perspective has predominated in framing the debate. [D. Bodansky & J. Lawrence, Trade and Environment, in The Oxford Handbook of International Trade Law, D. Bethlehem et al. eds., (2009).]

2. *Trade and Environment Disputes*

The first real conflict between the trade and environmental regimes was the *Tuna/Dolphin I* case, decided in 1991. In the *Tuna/Dolphin* dispute, the question was whether the GATT's non-discrimination provisions prohibited the United States from restricting imports of tuna caught in ways that harm dolphins. The GATT panel decision concluding that the U.S. law violated the GATT created significant fears in the environmental community that the GATT threatened the ability of domestic governments to protect the environment.

  The background of the *Tuna/Dolphin* case was as follows: In the Eastern Tropical Pacific (ETP), tuna often swim directly below dolphins, so beginning in the 1950s, when purse seine nets were developed, fishermen have fished for tuna by setting their nets when they spotted dolphins. This is a highly successful strategy for catching tuna, but has led to the "bycatch" and death of many dolphins as well. According to

NOAA estimates, over 6 million dolphins have been killed in the tuna fisheries since the 1950s, the highest known for any fishery.

Beginning in the 1970s, the United States adopted regulations to reduce dolphin killings pursuant to the Marine Mammal Protection Act. Because of concern that foreign boats (which represented an increasing percentage of purse seine fishing vessels) did not operate under similar restrictions, in 1984 Congress added §101(a)(2) of the MMPA, which prohibited imports of tuna caught using fishing techniques that resulted in incidental kills of ocean mammals (including dolphins) in excess of U.S. standards. Specifically, the MMPA barred importation of yellowfin tuna harvested with purse seine nets unless the Secretary of Commerce certified that (1) the government of the harvesting country has a program regulating the taking of marine mammals that is comparable to that of the United States, and (2) the average rate of incidental taking of marine mammals by vessels of the harvesting nation is comparable to, and does not exceed, 1.25 times the average rate of such taking by U.S. vessels during the same period.

In the late 1980s, U.S. environmentalists, concerned that the government was ignoring this MMPA requirement regarding imports, brought suit to require the United States to enforce the MMPA. A court found in their favor and ordered the government to enforce the MMPA. In 1990, the United States imposed an embargo on imports of tuna from Mexico and several other countries. Mexico then challenged the embargo in the GATT.

In its decision, the GATT panel concluded that the U.S. embargo violated the national treatment principle in GATT Article III(4), because the law prevented Mexico from exporting tuna that were "like" U.S.-caught tuna. In the panel's view, tuna produced in ways that kill dolphins are "like" tuna produced in a dolphin-safe manner, and must therefore be treated alike. Products, according to the Panels, are "like" if their characteristics are the same, even if they are produced in different ways. The panel further found that the U.S. law was not justified under Article XX as a "measure relating to the conservation of exhaustible natural resources," because it was aimed at protecting resources outside the United States and Article XX does not cover such extraterritorial measures. Although the panel report was never adopted by the GATT Council, it sparked a huge outcry from environmentalists, who portrayed an out-of-control "GATT-zilla" stomping on the U.S. Congress.

Since the original *Tuna/Dolphin* case, the trade regime has become more receptive to environmental concerns. The 1994 Uruguay Round agreements, which established the World Trade Organization, include several environmental provisions—in particular, the preamble, which recognizes the objective of "sustainable development." And the new WTO Appellate Body, according to Professor John Knox, has "adopted almost every element" of the "moderate environmental proposals" that NGOs have made for reconciling environmental concerns and international trade law. Knox, The Judicial Resolution of Conflicts between Trade and the Environment, 28 Harv. Envtl. L. Rev. 1, 29 (2004). First, in the *Reformulated Gas* case, United States—Standards for Reformulated and Conventional Gasoline, AB-1996-1, Doc. WT/DS2/AB/R (1996), the Appellate Body interpreted Article XX less restrictively, finding that a U.S. law relating to emissions from gasoline fell within the terms of Article XX(g) (although the Appellate Body ultimately concluded that the measures were arbitrary and unjustified and therefore contrary to the chapeau of Article XX). Then, in the *Shrimp/Turtle* case, the Appellate Body ultimately upheld a U.S. ban on imports of shrimp caught in ways that endanger sea turtles, and responded to concerns about the closed nature of the WTO process by allowing an environmental group to file an amicus brief.

The following excerpts from the WTO Appellate Body's 1998 and 2001 decisions in the Shrimp-Turtle dispute focus on two of the significant environmental issues in the GATT, the meaning of the Article XX chapeau (opening paragraph) and Article XX(g).

UNITED STATES—IMPORT PROHIBITION OF CERTAIN SHRIMP AND SHRIMP PRODUCTS
Report of the Appellate Body, AB-1998-4, Doc. WT/DS58/AB/R

[Malaysia, Thailand, India, and Pakistan filed a complaint with the WTO alleging that a U.S. law, Pub. L. No. 101-162, §609 (1989), and associated regulations and judicial rulings, operated to limit the United States' importation of certain shrimp and shrimp products in violation of the GATT. Section 609(b)(1) imposed an import ban on shrimp harvested with commercial fishing technology that could adversely affect sea turtles. Section 609(b)(2) provided that the import ban on shrimp would not apply to harvesting nations that are certified. Certifications would be granted to countries with a fishing environment that does not pose a threat of the incidental taking of sea turtles in the course of shrimp harvesting (e.g., because the relevant species of sea turtle are not present or because the harvesting nation harvests shrimp "exclusively by means that do not pose a threat to sea turtles"). In addition, certifications would be granted to harvesting nations that provide documentary evidence of the adoption of a regulatory program governing the incidental taking of sea turtles in the course of shrimp trawling that is comparable to the U.S. program (which requires U.S. shrimp fisherman to use Turtle Excluder Devices (TEDs) that allow turtles to escape and thereby significantly lower turtle mortality) and where the average rate of incidental taking of sea turtles by their vessels is comparable to that of U.S. vessels. The GATT Panel found that §609 is inconsistent with the GATT, among other rulings. The United States appealed part of the Panel opinion to the WTO Appellate Body.]

111. We turn to the second issue raised by the . . . United States, which is whether the Panel erred in finding that the measure at issue [§609 and the implementing Guidelines] constitutes unjustifiable discrimination between countries where the same conditions prevail and, thus, is not within the scope of measures permitted under Article XX of the GATT 1994. . . .

118. In *United States—Gasoline*, we enunciated the appropriate method for applying Article XX of the GATT 1994:

> In order that the justifying protection of Article XX may be extended to it, the measure at issue must not only come under one or another of the particular exceptions—paragraphs (a) to (j)—listed under Article XX; it must also satisfy the requirements imposed by the opening clauses of Article XX. *The analysis is*, in other words, *two-tiered: first, provisional justification by reason of characterization of the measure under XX(g); second, further appraisal of the same measure under the introductory clauses of Article XX.* (emphasis added). . . .

B. *Article XX(g): Provisional Justification of Section 609*

125. In claiming justification for its measure, the United States primarily invokes Article XX(g). . . .

126. Paragraph (g) of Article XX covers measures:

relating to the conservation of exhaustible natural resources if such measures are made effective in conjunction with restrictions on domestic production or consumption;

1. "EXHAUSTIBLE NATURAL RESOURCES"

127. We begin with the threshold question of whether Section 609 is a measure concerned with the conservation of "exhaustible natural resources" within the meaning of Article XX(g). . . . In the proceedings before the Panel, . . . the [complainants] argued . . . that a "reasonable interpretation" of the term "exhaustible" is that the term refers to "finite resources such as minerals, rather than biological or renewable resources." In their view, such finite resources were exhaustible "because there was a limited supply which could and would be depleted unit for unit as the resources were consumed." . . . For its part, Malaysia added that sea turtles, being living creatures, could only be considered under Article XX(b), since Article XX(g) was meant for "nonliving exhaustible natural resources." It followed, according to Malaysia, that the United States cannot invoke both the Article XX(b) and the Article XX(g) exceptions simultaneously.

128. We are not convinced by these arguments. Textually, Article XX(g) is *not* limited to the conservation of "mineral" or "non-living" natural resources. The complainants' principal argument is rooted in the notion that "living" natural resources are "renewable" and therefore cannot be "exhaustible" natural resources. We do not believe that "exhaustible" natural resources and "renewable" natural resources are mutually exclusive. One lesson that modern biological sciences teach us is that living species, though in principle, capable of reproduction and, in that sense, "renewable," are in certain circumstances indeed susceptible of depletion, exhaustion and extinction, frequently because of human activities. Living resources are just as "finite" as petroleum, iron ore and other non-living resources. . . .

130. From the perspective embodied in the preamble of the *WTO Agreement*, we note that the generic term "natural resources" in Article XX(g) is not "static" in its content or reference but is rather "by definition, evolutionary." It is, therefore, pertinent to note that modern international conventions and declarations make frequent references to natural resources as embracing both living and non-living resources. . . .

131. Given the recent acknowledgement by the international community of the importance of concerted bilateral or multilateral action to protect living natural resources, and recalling the explicit recognition by WTO Members of the objective of sustainable development in the preamble of the *WTO Agreement*, we believe it is too late in the day to suppose that Article XX(g) of the GATT 1994 may be read as referring only to the conservation of exhaustible mineral or other non-living natural resources. Moreover, two adopted GATT 1947 panel reports previously found fish to be an "exhaustible natural resource" within the meaning of Article XX(g). We hold that, in line with the principle of effectiveness in treaty interpretation, measures to conserve exhaustible natural resources, whether *living* or *non-living*, may fall within Article XX(g).

132. We turn next to the issue of whether the living natural resources sought to be conserved by the measure are "exhaustible" under Article XX(g). That this element is present in respect of the five species of sea turtles here involved appears to be conceded by all the participants . . . in this case. The exhaustibility of sea turtles would in fact have been very difficult to controvert since all of the seven recognized species of sea turtles are today listed in Appendix 1 of the Convention on International Trade in Endangered Species of Wild Fauna and Flora ("CITES"). The list in Appendix 1 includes "all species *threatened with extinction* which are or may be affected by trade" (emphasis added).

133. Finally, we observe that sea turtles are highly migratory animals, passing in and out of waters subject to the rights of jurisdiction of various coastal states and the high seas. In the Panel Report, the Panel said:

> . . . Information brought to the attention of the Panel, including documented statements from the experts, tends to *confirm the fact that sea turtles, in certain circumstances of their lives, migrate through the waters of several countries and the high sea* . . . (emphasis added).

The sea turtle species here at stake, i.e., covered by Section 609, are all known to occur in waters over which the United States exercises jurisdiction. Of course, it is not claimed that *all* populations of these species migrate to, or traverse, at one time or another, waters subject to United States jurisdiction. Neither the appellant nor any of the appellees claims any rights of exclusive ownership over the sea turtles, at least not while they are swimming freely in their natural habitat—the oceans. We do not pass upon the question of whether there is an implied jurisdictional limitation in Article XX(g), and if so, the nature or extent of that limitation. We note only that in the specific circumstances of the case before us, there is a sufficient nexus between the migratory and endangered marine populations involved and the United States for purposes of Article XX(g).

134. For all the foregoing reasons, we find that the sea turtles here involved constitute "exhaustible natural resources" for purposes of Article XX(g) of the GATT 1994.

2.   "Relating to the Conservation of [Exhaustible Natural Resources]"

135. Article XX(g) requires that the measure sought to be justified be one which "relat[es] to" the conservation of exhaustible natural resources. In making this determination, the treaty interpreter essentially looks into the relationship between the measure at stake and the legitimate policy of conserving exhaustible natural resources. It is well to bear in mind that the policy of protecting and conserving the endangered sea turtles here involved is shared by all participants . . . in this appeal, indeed, by the vast majority of the nations of the world. None of the parties to this dispute question the genuineness of the commitment of the others to that policy. . . .

137. In the present case, we must examine the relationship between the general structure and design of the measure here at stake, Section 609, and the policy goal it purports to serve, that is, the conservation of sea turtles.

138. Section 609(b)(1) imposes an import ban on shrimp that have been harvested with commercial fishing technology which may adversely affect sea turtles. This provision is designed to influence countries to adopt national regulatory programs

requiring the use of TEDs [Turtle Excluder Devices] by their shrimp fishermen. In this connection, it is important to note that the general structure and design of Section 609 *cum* implementing guidelines is fairly narrowly focused. There are two basic exemptions from the import ban, both of which relate clearly and directly to the policy goal of conserving sea turtles. First, Section 609, as elaborated in the 1996 Guidelines, excludes from the import ban shrimp harvested "under conditions that do not adversely affect sea turtles." Thus, the measure, by its terms, excludes from the import ban: aquaculture shrimp; shrimp species (such as *pandalid* shrimp) harvested in water areas where sea turtles do not normally occur; and shrimp harvested exclusively by artisanal methods, even from non-certified countries. The harvesting of such shrimp clearly does not affect sea turtles. Second, under Section 609(b)(2), the measure exempts from the import ban shrimp caught in waters subject to the jurisdiction of certified countries.

139. There are two types of certification for countries under Section 609(b)(2). First, under Section 609(b)(2)(C), a country may be certified as having a fishing environment that does not pose a threat of incidental taking of sea turtles in the course of commercial shrimp trawl harvesting. There is no risk, or only a negligible risk, that sea turtles will be harmed by shrimp trawling in such an environment.

140. The second type of certification is provided by Section 609(b)(2)(A) and (B). Under these provisions, as further elaborated in the 1996 Guidelines, a country wishing to export shrimp to the United States is required to adopt a regulatory program that is comparable to that of the United States program and to have a rate of incidental take of sea turtles that is comparable to the average rate of United States' vessels. This is, essentially, a requirement that a country adopt a regulatory program requiring the use of TEDs by commercial shrimp trawling vessels in areas where there is a likelihood of intercepting sea turtles. This requirement is, in our view, directly connected with the policy of conservation of sea turtles. It is undisputed among the participants, and recognized by the experts consulted by the Panel, that the harvesting of shrimp by commercial shrimp trawling vessels with mechanical retrieval devices in waters where shrimp and sea turtles coincide is a significant cause of sea turtle mortality. Moreover, the Panel did "not question . . . the fact generally acknowledged by the experts that TEDs, when properly installed and adapted to the local area, would be an effective tool for the preservation of sea turtles."

141. In its general design and structure, therefore, Section 609 is not a simple, blanket prohibition of the importation of shrimp imposed without regard to the consequences (or lack thereof) of the mode of harvesting employed upon the incidental capture and mortality of sea turtles. Focusing on the design of the measure here at stake, it appears to us that Section 609, *cum* implementing guidelines, is not disproportionately wide in its scope and reach in relation to the policy objective of protection and conservation of sea turtle species. The means are, in principle, reasonably related to the ends. The means and ends relationship between Section 609 and the legitimate policy of conserving an exhaustible, and, in fact, endangered species, is observably a close and real one, a relationship that is every bit as substantial as that which we found in *United States—Gasoline* between the EPA baseline establishment rules and the conservation of clean air in the United States.

142. In our view, therefore, Section 609 is a measure "relating to" the conservation of an exhaustible natural resource within the meaning of Article XX(g) of the GATT 1994.

3. "If Such Measures Are Made Effective in Conjunction with Restrictions on Domestic Production or Consumption"

143. In *United States—Gasoline*, we held that the above-captioned clause of Article XX(g),

> . . . is appropriately read as a requirement that the measures concerned impose restrictions, not just in respect of imported gasoline but also with respect to domestic gasoline. The clause is a requirement of *even-handedness* in the imposition of restrictions, in the name of conservation, upon the production or consumption of exhaustible natural resources.

In this case, we need to examine whether the restrictions imposed by Section 609 with respect to imported shrimp are also imposed in respect of shrimp caught by United States shrimp trawl vessels.

144. We earlier noted that Section 609, enacted in 1989, addresses the mode of harvesting of imported shrimp only. However, two years earlier, in 1987, the United States issued regulations pursuant to the Endangered Species Act requiring all United States shrimp trawl vessels to use approved TEDs, or to restrict the duration of tow-times, in specified areas where there was significant incidental mortality of sea turtles in shrimp trawls. These regulations became fully effective in 1990 and were later modified. They now require United States shrimp trawlers to use approved TEDs "in areas and at times when there is a likelihood of intercepting sea turtles," with certain limited exceptions. Penalties for violation of the Endangered Species Act, or the regulations issued thereunder, include civil and criminal sanctions. The United States government currently relies on monetary sanctions and civil penalties for enforcement. The government has the ability to seize shrimp catch from trawl vessels fishing in United States waters and has done so in cases of egregious violations. We believe that, in principle, Section 609 is an even-handed measure.

145. Accordingly, we hold that Section 609 is a measure made effective in conjunction with the restrictions on domestic harvesting of shrimp, as required by Article XX(g).

C. *The Introductory Clauses of Article XX: Characterizing Section 609 Under the Chapeau's Standards* . . .

147. Although provisionally justified under Article XX(g), Section 609, if it is ultimately to be justified as an exception under Article XX, must also satisfy the requirements of the introductory clauses—the "chapeau"—of Article XX. . . .

1. General Considerations

150. We commence the second tier of our analysis with an examination of the ordinary meaning of the words of the chapeau. The precise language of the chapeau requires that a measure not be applied in a manner which would constitute a means of "arbitrary or unjustifiable discrimination between countries where the same conditions prevail" or a "disguised restriction on international trade." . . . In order for a measure to be applied in a manner which would constitute "arbitrary or unjustifiable

discrimination between countries where the same conditions prevail," three elements must exist. First, the application of the measure must result in *discrimination*. . . . Second, the discrimination must be *arbitrary* or *unjustifiable* in character. . . . Third, this discrimination must occur *between countries where the same conditions prevail*. . . .

156. . . . [T]he chapeau of Article XX . . . embodies the recognition on the part of WTO Members of the need to maintain a balance of rights and obligations between the right of a Member to invoke one or another of the exceptions of Article XX, . . . and the substantive rights of the other Members under the GATT 1994, on the other hand. . . . [A] balance must be struck between the *right* of a Member to invoke an exception under Article XX and the *duty* of that same Member to respect the treaty rights of the other Members. . . .

159. The task of interpreting and applying the chapeau is, hence, essentially the delicate one of locating and marking out a line of equilibrium between the right of a Member to invoke an exception under Article XX and the rights of the other Members under varying substantive provisions . . . of the GATT 1994, so that neither of the competing rights will cancel out the other and thereby distort and nullify or impair the balance of rights and obligations constructed by the Members themselves in that Agreement. The location of the line of equilibrium, as expressed in the chapeau, is not fixed and unchanging; the line moves as the kind and the shape of the measures at stake vary and as the facts making up specific cases differ. . . .

2. "UNJUSTIFIABLE DISCRIMINATION"

161. We scrutinize first whether Section 609 has been applied in a manner constituting "unjustifiable discrimination between countries where the same conditions prevail." Perhaps the most conspicuous flaw in this measure's application relates to its intended and actual coercive effect on the specific policy decisions made by foreign governments, Members of the WTO. Section 609, in its application, is, in effect, an economic embargo which requires *all other exporting Members*, if they wish to exercise their GATT rights, to adopt *essentially the same* policy (together with an approved enforcement program) as that applied to, and enforced on, United States domestic shrimp trawlers. . . .

163. The actual *application* of the measure, through the implementation of the 1996 Guidelines and the regulatory practice of administrators, *requires* other WTO Members to adopt a regulatory program that is not merely *comparable*, but rather *essentially the same*, as that applied to the United States shrimp trawl vessels. Thus, the effect of the application of Section 609 is to establish a rigid and unbending standard by which United States officials determine whether or not countries will be certified, thus granting or refusing other countries the right to export shrimp to the United States. Other specific policies and measures that an exporting country may have adopted for the protection and conservation of sea turtles are not taken into account, in practice, by the administrators making the comparability determination.

164. . . . It may be quite acceptable for a government, in adopting and implementing a domestic policy, to adopt a single standard applicable to all its citizens throughout that country. However, it is not acceptable, in international trade relations, for one WTO Member to use an economic embargo to *require* other Members to adopt essentially the same comprehensive regulatory program, to achieve a certain policy goal, as that in force within that Member's territory, *without* taking into

consideration different conditions which may occur in the territories of those other Members.

165. Furthermore, when this dispute was before the Panel and before us, the United States did not permit imports of shrimp harvested by commercial shrimp trawl vessels using TEDs comparable in effectiveness to those required in the United States if those shrimp originated in waters of countries not certified under Section 609. In other words, *shrimp caught using methods identical to those employed in the United States* have been excluded from the United States market solely because they have been caught in waters of *countries that have not been certified by the United States*. The resulting situation is difficult to reconcile with the declared policy objective of protecting and conserving sea turtles. This suggests to us that this measure, in its application, is more concerned with effectively influencing WTO Members to adopt essentially the same comprehensive regulatory regime as that applied by the United States to its domestic shrimp trawlers, even though many of those Members may be differently situated. . . .

166. Another aspect of the application of Section 609 that bears heavily in any appraisal of justifiable or unjustifiable discrimination is the failure of the United States to engage the appellees, as well as other Members exporting shrimp to the United States, in serious, across-the-board negotiations with the objective of concluding bilateral or multilateral agreements for the protection and conservation of sea turtles, before enforcing the import prohibition against the shrimp exports of those other Members. . . .

169. . . . [T]he United States did negotiate and conclude one regional international agreement for the protection and conservation of sea turtles: The Inter-American Convention. This Convention was opened for signature on 1 December 1996 and has been signed by five countries, in addition to the United States, and four of these countries are currently certified under Section 609. . . .

171. The Inter-American Convention . . . provides convincing demonstration that an alternative course of action was reasonably open to the United States for securing the legitimate policy goal of its measure, a course of action other than the unilateral and non-consensual procedures of the import prohibition under Section 609. It is relevant to observe that an import prohibition is, ordinarily, the heaviest "weapon" in a Member's armory of trade measures. The record does not, however, show that serious efforts were made by the United States to negotiate similar agreements with any other country or group of countries before (and, as far as the record shows, after) Section 609 was enforced on a world-wide basis on 1 May 1996. Finally, the record also does not show that the appellant, the United States, attempted to have recourse to such international mechanisms as exist to achieve cooperative efforts to protect and conserve sea turtles before imposing the import ban.

172. Clearly, the United States negotiated seriously with some, but not with other Members (including the appellees), that export shrimp to the United States. The effect is plainly discriminatory and, in our view, unjustifiable. . . . The principal consequence of this failure may be seen in the resulting unilateralism evident in the application of Section 609. As we have emphasized earlier, the policies relating to the necessity for use of particular kinds of TEDs in various maritime areas, and the operating details of these policies, are all shaped by the Department of State, without the participation of the exporting Members. The system and processes of certification are established and administered by the United States agencies alone. The decision-making involved in the grant, denial or withdrawal of certification to the exporting

Members, is, accordingly, also unilateral. The unilateral character of the application of Section 609 heightens the disruptive and discriminatory influence of the import prohibition and underscores its unjustifiability. . . .

176. When the foregoing differences in the means of application of Section 609 to various shrimp exporting countries are considered in their cumulative effect, we find, and so hold, that those differences in treatment constitute "unjustifiable discrimination" between exporting countries desiring certification in order to gain access to the United States shrimp market within the meaning of the chapeau of Article XX.

3.   "ARBITRARY DISCRIMINATION"

177. We next consider whether Section 609 has been applied in a manner constituting "arbitrary discrimination between countries where the same conditions prevail." . . .

180. [W]ith respect to neither type of certification under Section 609(b)(2) is there a transparent, predictable certification process that is followed by the competent United States government officials. . . . [T]here is no formal opportunity for an applicant country to be heard, or to respond to any arguments that may be made against it, in the course of the certification process before a decision to grant or to deny certification is made. Moreover, no formal written, reasoned decision, whether of acceptance or rejection, is rendered on applications for either type of certification. . . . No procedure for review of, or appeal from, a denial of an application is provided.

181. The certification processes followed by the United States thus appear to be singularly informal and casual, and to be conducted in a manner such that these processes could result in the negation of rights of Members. . . . It appears to us that, effectively, exporting Members applying for certification whose applications are rejected are denied basic fairness and due process, and are discriminated against, *vis-à-vis* those Members which are granted certification. . . .

184. We find, accordingly, that the United States measure is applied in a manner which amounts to a means not just of "unjustifiable discrimination," but also of "arbitrary discrimination" between countries where the same conditions prevail, contrary to the requirements of the chapeau of Article XX. The measure, therefore, is not entitled to the justifying protection of Article XX of the GATT 1994. . . .

Following the Appellate Body's decision, the United States tried unsuccessfully to negotiate with several countries about their shrimp fishing practices. In addition, in 1999 the United States made its approach more flexible, issuing its Revised Guidelines for the Implementation of Section 609 . . . , Relating to the Protection of Sea Turtles in Shrimp Trawl Fishing Operations (Revised Guidelines). 64 Fed. Reg. 36,946 (1999). In 2001, Malaysia complained about the revised U.S. guidelines, and the Appellate Body had occasion to review whether U.S. law and practices under this revised regime were consistent with Article XX's chapeau. The following excerpt from the 2001 Appellate Body decision considers this issue.

UNITED STATES—IMPORT PROHIBITION OF CERTAIN SHRIMP AND SHRIMP PRODUCTS
Report of the Appellate Body, AB-2001-4, Doc. WT/DS58/AB/RW

117. The chapeau of Article XX states:

Subject to the requirement that such measures are not applied in a manner which would constitute a means of arbitrary or unjustifiable discrimination between countries where the same conditions prevail, or a disguised restriction on international trade, nothing in this Agreement shall be construed to prevent the adoption or enforcement by any contracting party of measures. . . .

118. The chapeau of Article XX establishes three standards regarding the *application* of measures for which justification under Article XX may be sought: first, there must be no "arbitrary" discrimination between countries where the same conditions prevail; second, there must be no "unjustifiable" discrimination between countries where the same conditions prevail; and, third, there must be no "disguised restriction on international trade." The Panel's findings appealed by Malaysia concern the first and second of these three standards.

119. It is clear from the language of the chapeau that these two standards operate to prevent a Member from applying a measure provisionally justified under a sub-paragraph of Article XX in a manner that would result in "arbitrary or unjustifiable discrimination." In *United States—Shrimp*, we stated that the measure at issue there resulted in "unjustifiable discrimination," in part because, as applied, the United States treated WTO Members differently. The United States had adopted a cooperative approach with WTO Members from the Caribbean/Western Atlantic region, with whom it had concluded a multilateral agreement on the protection and conservation of sea turtles, namely the Inter-American Convention. Yet the United States had not, we found, pursued the negotiation of such a multilateral agreement with other exporting Members, including Malaysia and the other complaining WTO Members in that case. . . .

123. Under the chapeau of Article XX, an importing Member may not treat its trading partners in a manner that would constitute "arbitrary or unjustifiable discrimination." With respect to this measure, the United States could conceivably respect this obligation, and the conclusion of an international agreement might nevertheless not be possible despite the serious, good faith efforts of the United States. Requiring that a multilateral agreement be *concluded* by the United States in order to avoid "arbitrary or unjustifiable discrimination" in applying its measure would mean that any country party to the negotiations with the United States, whether a WTO Member or not, would have, in effect, a veto over whether the United States could fulfill its WTO obligations. Such a requirement would not be reasonable. For a variety of reasons, it may be possible to conclude an agreement with one group of countries but not another. The conclusion of a multilateral agreement requires the cooperation and commitment of many countries. In our view, the United States cannot be held to have engaged in "arbitrary or unjustifiable discrimination" under Article XX solely because one international negotiation resulted in an agreement while another did not. . . .

133. We note that the Panel stated that "any effort alleged to be a 'serious good faith effort' must be assessed against the efforts made in relation to the conclusion of

the Inter-American Convention." In our view, in assessing the serious, good faith efforts made by the United States, the Panel did not err in using the Inter-American Convention as an *example*. In our view, also, the Panel was correct in proceeding then to an analysis broadly in line with this principle and, ultimately, was correct as well in concluding that the efforts made by the United States in the Indian Ocean and South-East Asia region constitute serious, good faith efforts comparable to those that led to the conclusion of the Inter-American Convention. We find no fault with this analysis.

134. In sum, Malaysia is incorrect in its contention that avoiding "arbitrary and unjustifiable discrimination" under the chapeau of Article XX requires the *conclusion* of an international agreement on the protection and conservation of sea turtles. Therefore, we uphold the Panel's finding that, in view of the serious, good faith efforts made by the United States to negotiate an international agreement, "Section 609 is now applied in a manner that no longer constitutes a means of unjustifiable or arbitrary discrimination, as identified by the Appellate Body in its Report."

B.   The Flexibility of the Revised Guidelines

135. We now turn to Malaysia's arguments relating to the flexibility of the Revised Guidelines. . . .

136. Malaysia disagrees with the Panel that a measure can meet the requirements of the chapeau of Article XX if it is flexible enough, both in design and application, to permit certification of an exporting country with a sea turtle protection and conservation programme "comparable" to that of the United States. According to Malaysia, even if the measure at issue allows certification of countries having regulatory programs "comparable" to that of the United States, and even if the measure is applied in such a manner, it results in "arbitrary or unjustifiable discrimination" because it conditions access to the United States market on compliance with policies and standards "unilaterally" prescribed by the United States. Thus, Malaysia puts considerable emphasis on the "unilateral" nature of the measure, and Malaysia maintains that our previous Report does not support the conclusion of the Panel on this point.

137. We recall that, in *United States—Shrimp*, we stated:

> It appears to us . . . that *conditioning access to a Member's domestic market on whether exporting Members comply with, or adopt, a policy or policies unilaterally prescribed by the importing Member may, to some degree, be a common aspect of measures falling within the scope of one or another of the exceptions (a) to (j) of Article XX.* Paragraphs (a) to (j) comprise measures that are recognized as *exceptions to substantive obligations* established in the GATT 1994, because the domestic policies embodied in such measures have been recognized as important and legitimate in character. It is not necessary to assume that requiring from exporting countries compliance with, or adoption of, certain policies (although covered in principle by one or another of the exceptions) prescribed by the importing country, renders a measure *a priori* incapable of justification under Article XX. Such an interpretation renders most, if not all, of the specific exceptions of Article XX inutile, a result abhorrent to the principles of interpretation we are bound to apply (emphasis in Appellate Body decision).

138. . . . [I]t appears to us "that conditioning access to a Member's domestic market on whether exporting Members comply with, or adopt, a policy or policies

unilaterally prescribed by the importing Member may, to some degree, be a common aspect of measures falling within the scope of one or another of the exceptions (a) to (j) of Article XX." This statement expresses a principle that was central to our ruling in *United States—Shrimp*.

139. A separate question arises, however, when examining, under the chapeau of Article XX, a measure that provides for access to the market of one WTO Member for a product of other WTO Members *conditionally*. Both Malaysia and the United States agree that this is a common aspect of the measure at issue in the original proceedings and the new measure at issue in this dispute.

140. In *United States—Shrimp*, we concluded that the measure at issue there did not meet the requirements of the chapeau of Article XX relating to "arbitrary or unjustifiable discrimination" because, through the application of the measure, the exporting members were faced with "a single, rigid and unbending requirement" to adopt *essentially the same* policies and enforcement practices as those applied to, and enforced on, domestic shrimp trawlers in the United States. In contrast, in this dispute, the Panel found that this new measure is more flexible than the original measure and has been applied more flexibly than was the original measure. In the light of the evidence brought by the United States, the Panel satisfied itself that this new measure, in design and application, does *not* condition access to the United States market on the adoption by an exporting Member of a regulatory programme aimed at the protection and the conservation of sea turtles that is *essentially the same* as that of the United States. . . .

143. Given that the original measure in that dispute required "essentially the same" practices and procedures as those required in the United States, we found it necessary in that appeal to rule only that Article XX did not allow such inflexibility. Given the Panel's findings with respect to the flexibility of the new measure in this dispute, we find it necessary in this appeal to add to what we ruled in our original Report. The question raised by Malaysia in this appeal is whether the Panel erred in inferring from our previous Report, and thereby finding, that the chapeau of Article XX permits a measure which requires only "comparable effectiveness."

144. In our view, there is an important difference between conditioning market access on the adoption of essentially the same programme, and conditioning market access on the adoption of a programme *comparable in effectiveness*. Authorizing an importing Member to condition market access on exporting Members putting in place regulatory programmes *comparable in effectiveness* to that of the importing Member gives sufficient latitude to the exporting Member with respect to the programme it may adopt to achieve the level of effectiveness required. It allows the exporting Member to adopt a regulatory programme that is suitable to the specific conditions prevailing in its territory. As we see it, the Panel correctly reasoned and concluded that conditioning market access on the adoption of a programme *comparable in effectiveness*, allows for sufficient flexibility in the application of the measure so as to avoid "arbitrary or unjustifiable discrimination." We, therefore, agree with the conclusion of the Panel on "comparable effectiveness."

145. Malaysia also argues that the measure at issue is not flexible enough to meet the requirement of the chapeau of Article XX relating to "unjustifiable or arbitrary discrimination" because the Revised Guidelines do not provide explicitly for the specific conditions prevailing in Malaysia.

146. We note that the Revised Guidelines contain provisions that permit the United States authorities to take into account the specific conditions of Malaysian

shrimp production, and of the Malaysian sea turtle conservation programme, should Malaysia decide to apply for certification. The Revised Guidelines explicitly state that "[if] the government of a harvesting nation demonstrates that it has implemented and is enforcing a comparably effective regulatory program to protect sea turtles in the course of shrimp trawl fishing without the use of TEDs, that nation will also be eligible for certification." Likewise, the Revised Guidelines provide that the "Department of State will take fully into account any demonstrated differences between the shrimp fishing conditions in the United States and those in other nations as well as information available from other sources."

147. Further, the Revised Guidelines provide that the import prohibitions that can be imposed under Section 609 do not apply to shrimp or products of shrimp "harvested in any other manner or under any other circumstances that the Department of State may determine, following consultations with the [United States National Marine Fisheries Services], does not pose a threat of the incidental taking of sea turtles." Under Section II.B(c)(iii) of the Revised Guidelines (*Additional Sea Turtle Protection Measures*), the "Department of State recognizes that sea turtles require protection' throughout their life-cycle, not only when they are threatened during the course of commercial shrimp trawl harvesting." Additionally, Section II.B(c)(iii) states that "[i]n making certification determinations, the Department shall also take fully into account other measures the harvesting nation undertakes to protect sea turtles, including national programmes to protect nesting beaches and other habitat, prohibitions on the direct take of sea turtles, national enforcement and compliance programmes, and participation in any international agreement for the protection and conservation of sea turtles." With respect to the certification process, the Revised Guidelines specify that a country that does not appear to qualify for certification will receive a notification that "will explain the reasons for this preliminary assessment, suggest steps that the government of the harvesting nation can take in order to receive a certification, and invite the government of the harvesting nation to provide . . . any further information." Moreover, the Department of State commits itself to "actively consider any additional information that the government of the harvesting nation believes should be considered by the Department in making its determination concerning certification."

148. These provisions of the Revised Guidelines, on their face, permit a degree of flexibility that, in our view, will enable the United States to consider the particular conditions prevailing in Malaysia if, and when, Malaysia applies for certification. As Malaysia has not applied for certification, any consideration of whether Malaysia would be certified would be speculation.

149. We need only say here that, in our view, a measure should be designed in such a manner that there is sufficient flexibility to take into account the specific conditions prevailing in *any* exporting Member, including, of course, Malaysia. Yet this is not the same as saying that there must be specific provisions in the measure aimed at addressing specifically the particular conditions prevailing in *every individual* exporting Member. Article XX of the GATT 1994 does not require a Member to anticipate and provide explicitly for the specific conditions prevailing and evolving in *every individual* Member.

150. We are, therefore, not persuaded by Malaysia's argument that the measure at issue is not flexible enough because the Revised Guidelines do not explicitly address the specific conditions prevailing in Malaysia. . . .

153. For the reasons set out in this Report, the Appellate Body: . . .

D.   Trade and the Environment

(b) *upholds* the finding of the Panel . . . that "Section 609 of Public Law 101-162, as implemented by the Revised Guidelines of 8 July 1999 and as applied so far by the [United States] authorities, is justified under Article XX of the GATT 1994 as long as the conditions stated in the findings of this Report, in particular the ongoing serious good faith efforts to reach a multilateral agreement, remain satisfied."

NOTES AND QUESTIONS

1. Consider the following factors:

- The degree to which an environmental measure is specified and applied by a country unilaterally.
- The availability of other less trade-restrictive options to achieve the same environmental objective.
- Whether an environmental measure is intended to protect resources within a country's territory (or resources that have some nexus to the country).
- Whether an environmental measure relates to the processes by which a product is produced or to characteristics of the product itself.
- Whether a measure is supported by scientific evidence.

In the *Tuna/Dolphin* and *Shrimp/Turtle* cases, which of these factors were seen as relevant in determining the compatibility of environmental measures with the GATT? In your opinion, which of these factors should be relevant?

2. What types of changes did the United States make in its regulatory regime between the issuance of the 1998 Appellate Body ruling and the issuance of the 2001 ruling? Why were these changes important to the outcome of the 2001 ruling?

3. What were the major arguments Malaysia and others raised to challenge the legality of the United States' efforts to protect turtles? Why was the Appellate Body not persuaded by these claims?

4. Are the *Tuna/Dolphin* and *Shrimp/Turtle* disputes distinguishable on the facts? Or did the Appellate Body change the law? If the latter, why might a trade institution have become more favorably disposed to environmental concerns?

5. The Mexico-U.S. tuna/dolphin dispute has been back in the news recently. U.S. law prohibits tuna from being labeled "dolphin safe" if the tuna was caught by setting nets on dolphins. In 2008, Mexico initiated a dispute against the United States, alleging that the U.S. labeling scheme violates the WTO Technical Barriers to Trade (TBT) Agreement because it is discriminatory and unnecessary. In May 2012, the WTO Appellate Body agreed that the U.S. labeling scheme discriminates against Mexican tuna. In response, the United States amended its dolphin safe labeling scheme to extend its certification requirements to apply to all oceans, not only the eastern tropical Pacific. Mexico claims that the new rule still discriminates against its tuna fishery, and has initiated compliance proceedings. A final report by the compliance committee is expected in December 2014.

6. In 2009, the European Union banned imports of seal products, except for those produced by indigenous communities. Canada and Norway challenged the ban in the WTO, claiming that the ban discriminates against their sealing industry, by allowing virtually all seal products from Greenland, where most sealing is done by indigenous communities, but almost none from Canada and Norway, where there is little indigenous seal hunting. In its May 2014 opinion, the WTO appellate body took

the same approach as in the *Shrimp/Turtle* case, finding that the EU seals regime could be justified under the substantive provisions of Article XX (in this case, Article XX's "public morals" exception), but that it violated the chapeau's prohibition on "arbitrary or unjustifiable discrimination," because it did not seek to promote animal welfare in indigenous seal hunts.

XII

CLIMATE CHANGE LAW
AND POLICY CHOICES

Climate change is one of the most important, and most debated, issues of our time. The overwhelming consensus of scientific opinion indicates that climate change is occurring; that human (or anthropogenic) activity, especially emissions of greenhouse gases (GHGs), is an important contributor to climate change; and that the impacts of climate change are likely to be significant for human health, the natural environment, and the manner in which people interact with that environment.

We devote the first section of this chapter to a brief overview of climate change science. Section B then reviews the key legal and policy issues and options that the climate change challenge poses. Congress has yet to enact comprehensive legislation that specifically addresses the causes and effects of climate change in the way that other major federal environmental laws address air pollution, water pollution, and hazardous waste management. Nevertheless, many of the key policy choices have already been identified in debates over proposed climate legislation and agency regulatory efforts. Section C discusses the broad array of techniques for addressing climate change that have emerged thus far. Most policy experts agree, for example, that both domestic and international climate mechanisms would ideally impose a price on the use of carbon, either through the adoption of a carbon tax or the implementation of a "cap-and-trade" strategy. The materials in section C consider several leading federal legislative proposals from 2009 and 2010 to illustrate the potential benefits and pitfalls of different strategies for addressing climate change, including possible obstacles to adoption and successful implementation.

Despite Congress's failure to enact comprehensive climate legislation, existing federal, state, and regional laws and agreements already add up to a substantial body of climate law. Section D tackles some of the federalism issues involving allocation of authority to deal with climate change. What role should federal, state, and local law and governments play, especially if a federal climate law is enacted? Section E addresses laws that already aim to mitigate or adapt to climate change, beginning with an analysis of the application of the Clean Air Act (the subject of Chapter 6) to GHG-emitting activities that contribute to climate change. Section E also covers laws at the federal, state, and local levels that seek to promote energy efficiency as a means of reducing GHG levels; laws designed to promote the development of alternative clean energy sources; laws that focus on adaptation risks and responsive strategies; and the application of federal laws covered in earlier chapters (including the National Environmental Policy Act and the Endangered Species Act) to climate-related problems. Section E concludes by considering the role of the common law in efforts to abate GHG emissions that contribute to climate change. Finally, section F analyzes the sometimes halting efforts to address climate change through multilateral international agreements. As these materials indicate, no consensus has emerged yet about the proper allocation of responsibilities among nations or the mix of strategies that the international community should implement.

A. THE SCIENCE OF GLOBAL CLIMATE CHANGE

EPA, ENDANGERMENT AND CAUSE OR CONTRIBUTE FINDINGS FOR GREENHOUSE GASES UNDER SECTION 202(a) OF THE CLEAN AIR ACT; FINAL RULE
74 Fed. Reg. 66,496 (Dec. 15, 2009)

The latest assessment of the [United States Global Climate Research Program (USGCRP)] . . . confirms . . . that current atmospheric greenhouse gas concentrations are now at elevated and essentially unprecedented levels as a result of both historic and current anthropogenic emissions. The global atmospheric carbon dioxide concentration has increased about 38 percent from pre-industrial levels to 2009, and almost all of the increase is due to anthropogenic emissions. The global atmospheric concentration of methane has increased by 149 percent since pre-industrial levels (through 2007); and the nitrous oxide concentration has increased 23 percent (through 2007). The observed concentration increase in these gases can also be attributed primarily to anthropogenic emissions. The industrial fluorinated gases have relatively low concentrations, but these concentrations have also been increasing and are almost entirely anthropogenic in origin.

Historic data show that current atmospheric concentrations of the two most important directly emitted, long-lived greenhouse gases (carbon dioxide and methane) are well above the natural range of atmospheric concentrations compared to at least the last 650,000 years. Atmospheric greenhouse gas concentrations have been increasing because anthropogenic emissions are outpacing the rate at which greenhouse gases are removed from the atmosphere by natural processes over timescales of decades to centuries. It also remains clear that these high atmospheric concentrations of greenhouse gases are the unambiguous result of human activities.

Together the six well-mixed greenhouse gases constitute the largest anthropogenic driver of climate change. Of the total anthropogenic heating effect caused by the accumulation of the six well-mixed greenhouse gases plus other warming agents . . . since pre-industrial times, the combined heating effect of the six well-mixed greenhouses is responsible for roughly 75 percent, and it is expected that this share may grow larger over time. . . .

Warming of the climate system is unequivocal, as is now evident from observations of increases in global average air and ocean temperatures, widespread melting of snow and ice, and rising global average sea level. Global mean surface temperatures have risen by 0.74 °C (1.3 °F) (±0.18 °C) over the last 100 years. Eight of the 10 warmest years on record have occurred since 2001. Global mean surface temperature was higher during the last few decades of the 20th century than during any comparable period during the preceding four centuries. . . .

The scientific evidence is compelling that elevated concentrations of heat-trapping greenhouse gases are the root cause of recently observed climate change. The [Intergovernmental Panel on Climate Change (IPCC)] conclusion from 2007 has been re-confirmed by the June 2009 USGCRP assessment that most of the observed increase in global average temperatures since the mid-20th century is very likely[22] due to the observed increase in anthropogenic greenhouse gas concentrations. Climate model simulations suggest natural forcing alone (e.g., changes in solar irradiance) cannot explain the observed warming.

The attribution of observed climate change to anthropogenic activities is based on multiple lines of evidence. The first line of evidence arises from our basic physical understanding of the effects of changing concentrations of greenhouse gases, natural factors, and other human impacts on the climate system. The second line of evidence arises from indirect, historical estimates of past climate changes that suggest that the changes in global surface temperature over the last several decades are unusual. The third line of evidence arises from the use of computer-based climate models to simulate the likely patterns of response of the climate system to different forcing mechanisms (both natural and anthropogenic).

The claim that natural internal variability or known natural external forcings can explain most (more than half) of the observed global warming of the past 50 years is inconsistent with the vast majority of the scientific literature, which has been synthesized in several assessment reports. Based on analyses of widespread temperature increases throughout the climate system and changes in other climate variables, the IPCC has reached the following conclusions about external climate forcing: "It is extremely unlikely (< 5 percent) that the global pattern of warming during the past half century can be explained without external forcing, and very unlikely that it is due to known natural external causes alone." With respect to internal variability, the IPCC reports the following: "The simultaneous increase in energy content of all the major components of the climate system as well as the magnitude and pattern of warming within and across the different components supports the conclusion that the cause of the [20th century] warming is extremely unlikely (< 5 percent) to be the result of internal processes." . . . The observed warming can only be reproduced with models that contain both natural and anthropogenic forcings, and the warming of the past half century has taken place at a time when known natural forcing factors alone (solar activity and volcanoes) would likely have produced cooling, not warming. . . .

Observations show that changes are occurring in the amount, intensity, frequency, and type of precipitation. Over the contiguous United States, total annual precipitation increased by 6.1 percent from 1901-2008. It is likely that there have been increases in the number of heavy precipitation events within many land regions, even

[handwritten margin note: IPCC climate change Forcing]

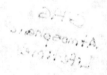

---

22. The IPCC Fourth Assessment Report uses specific terminology to convey likelihood and confidence. Likelihood refers to a probability that the statement is correct or that something will occur. "Virtually certain" conveys greater than 99 percent probability of occurrence; "very likely" 90 to 99 percent; "likely" 66 to 90 percent. IPCC assigns confidence levels as to the correctness of a statement. "Very high confidence" conveys at least 9 out of 10 chance of being correct; "high confidence" about 8 out of 10 chance; "medium confidence" about 5 out of 10 chance. The USGCRP uses the same or similar terminology in its reports. Throughout this document, this terminology is used in conjunction with statements from the IPCC and USGCRP reports to convey the same meaning that those reports intended. . . .

in those where there has been a reduction in total precipitation amount, consistent with a warming climate.

There is strong evidence that global sea level gradually rose in the 20th century and is currently rising at an increased rate. It is very likely that the response to anthropogenic forcing contributed to sea level rise during the latter half of the 20th century. It is not clear whether the increasing rate of sea level rise is a reflection of short-term variability or an increase in the longer-term trend. Nearly all of the Atlantic Ocean shows sea level rise during the last 50 years with the rate of rise reaching a maximum (over 2 mm per year) in a band along the U.S. east coast running east-northeast.

Satellite data since 1979 show that annual average Arctic sea ice extent has shrunk by 4.1 percent per decade. The size and speed of recent Arctic summer sea ice loss is highly anomalous relative to the previous few thousands of years.

Widespread changes in extreme temperatures have been observed in the last 50 years across all world regions including the United States. Cold days, cold nights, and frost have become less frequent, while hot days, hot nights, and heat waves have become more frequent.

Observational evidence from all continents and most oceans shows that many natural systems are being affected by regional climate changes, particularly temperature increases. However, directly attributing specific regional changes in climate to emissions of greenhouse gases from human activities is difficult, especially for precipitation.

Ocean carbon dioxide uptake has lowered the average ocean pH (increased the acidity) level by approximately 0.1 since 1750. Consequences for marine ecosystems may include reduced calcification by shell-forming organisms, and in the longer term, the dissolution of carbonate sediments.

Observations show that climate change is currently affecting U.S. physical and biological systems in significant ways. The consistency of these observed changes in physical and biological systems and the observed significant warming likely cannot be explained entirely due to natural variability or other confounding non-climate factors. . . .

There continues to be no reason to expect that, without substantial and near-term efforts to significantly reduce emissions, atmospheric levels of greenhouse gases will not continue to climb, and thus lead to ever greater rates of climate change. Given the long atmospheric lifetime of the six greenhouse gases, which range from roughly a decade to centuries, future atmospheric greenhouse gas concentrations for the remainder of this century and beyond will be influenced not only by future emissions but indeed by present-day and near-term emissions. Consideration of future plausible scenarios, and how our current greenhouse gas emissions essentially commit present and future generations to cope with an altered atmosphere and climate, reinforces the Administrator's judgment that it is appropriate to define the combination of the six key greenhouse gases as the air pollution.

Most future scenarios that assume no explicit greenhouse gas mitigation actions (beyond those already enacted) project increasing global greenhouse gas emissions over the century, which in turn result in climbing greenhouse gas concentrations. Under the range of future emission scenarios evaluated by the assessment literature, carbon dioxide is expected to remain the dominant anthropogenic greenhouse gas, and thus driver of climate change, over the course of the 21st century. In fact, carbon dioxide is projected to be the largest contributor to total radiative forcing in all periods and the radiative forcing associated with carbon dioxide is projected to be the fastest growing. For the year 2030, projections of the six greenhouse gases show an increase of 25 to 90 percent compared with 2000 emissions. Concentrations of carbon dioxide and the other well-mixed gases increase even for those scenarios where annual emissions toward the end of the century are assumed to be lower than current annual emissions. The radiative forcing associated with the non-carbon dioxide well-mixed greenhouse gases is still important and increasing over time. Emissions of the ozone-depleting substances are projected to continue decreasing due to the phase-out schedule under the Montreal Protocol on Substances that Deplete the Ozone Layer. Considerable uncertainties surround the estimates and future projections of anthropogenic aerosols; future atmospheric concentrations of aerosols, and thus their respective heating or cooling effects, will depend much more on assumptions about future emissions because of their short atmospheric lifetimes compared to the six well-mixed greenhouse gases.

Future warming over the course of the 21st century, even under scenarios of low emissions growth, is very likely to be greater than observed warming over the past century. According to climate model simulations summarized by the IPCC, through about 2030, the global warming rate is affected little by the choice of different future emission scenarios. By the end of the century, projected average global warming (compared to average temperature around 1990) varies significantly depending on emissions scenario and climate sensitivity assumptions, ranging from 1.8 to 4.0 °C (3.2 to 7.2 °F), with an uncertainty range of 1.1 to 6.4 °C (2.0 to 11.5 °F).

All of the United States is very likely to warm during this century, and most areas of the United States are expected to warm by more than the global average. The largest warming is projected to occur in winter over northern parts of Alaska. In western, central and eastern regions of North America, the projected warming has less seasonal variation and is not as large, especially near the coast, consistent with less warming over the oceans. . . .

It has been estimated that unusually hot days and heat waves are becoming more frequent, and that unusually cold days are becoming less frequent, as noted above. Heat is already the leading cause of weather-related deaths in the United States. In the future, severe heat waves are projected to intensify in magnitude and duration over the portions of the United States where these events already occur. Heat waves are associated with marked short-term increases in mortality. Hot temperatures have also been associated with increased morbidity. The projected warming is therefore projected to increase heat related mortality and morbidity, especially among the elderly, young and frail. The populations most sensitive to hot temperatures are older adults, the chronically sick, the very young, city-dwellers, those taking medications that disrupt thermoregulation, the mentally ill, those lacking access to air conditioning, those working or playing outdoors, and socially isolated persons. As warming increases over time, these adverse effects would be expected to increase as the serious heat events become more serious.

Increases in temperature are also expected to lead to some reduction in the risk of death related to extreme cold. Cold waves continue to pose health risks in northern latitudes in temperature regions where very low temperatures can be reached in a few hours and extend over long periods. . . . [T]here is a risk that projections of cold-related deaths, and the potential for decreasing their numbers due to warmer winters, can be overestimated unless they take into account the effects of season and influenza, which is not strongly associated with monthly winter temperature. . . .

Increases in regional ozone pollution relative to ozone levels without climate change are expected due to higher temperatures and weaker circulation in the United States relative to air quality levels without climate change. Climate change is expected to increase regional ozone pollution, with associated risks in respiratory illnesses and premature death. In addition to human health effects, tropospheric ozone has significant adverse effects on crop yields, pasture and forest growth, and species composition. The directional effect of climate change on ambient particulate matter levels remains less certain.

Climate change can affect ozone by modifying emissions of precursors, atmospheric chemistry, and transport and removal. There is now consistent evidence from models and observations that 21st century climate change will worsen summertime surface ozone in polluted regions of North America compared to a future with no climate change. . . .

In addition to the direct effects of temperature on heat- and cold-related mortality, the Administrator considers the potential for increased deaths, injuries, infectious diseases, and stress-related disorders and other adverse effects associated with social disruption and migration from more frequent extreme weather. The Administrator notes that the vulnerability to weather disasters depends on the attributes of the people at risk (including where they live, age, income, education, and disability) and on broader social and environmental factors (level of disaster preparedness, health sector responses, and environmental degradation). The IPCC finds the following with regard to extreme events and human health:

Increases in the frequency of heavy precipitation events are associated with increased risk of deaths and injuries as well as infectious, respiratory, and skin diseases. Floods are low-probability, high-impact events that can overwhelm physical infrastructure, human resilience, and social organization. Flood health impacts include deaths, injuries, infectious diseases, intoxications, and mental health problems.

Increases in tropical cyclone intensity are linked to increases in the risk of deaths, injuries, waterborne and food borne diseases, as well as post-traumatic stress disorders. Drowning by storm surge, heightened by rising sea levels and more intense storms (as projected by IPCC), is the major killer in coastal storms where there are large numbers of deaths. Flooding can cause health impacts including direct injuries as well as increased incidence of waterborne diseases due to pathogens such as Cryptosporidium and Giardia. . . .

According to the assessment literature, there will likely be an increase in the spread of several food and water-borne pathogens among susceptible populations depending on the pathogens' survival, persistence, habitat range and transmission under changing climate and environmental conditions. Food borne diseases show some relationship with temperature, and the range of some zoonotic disease carriers such as the Lyme disease carrying tick may increase with temperature.

Climate change, including changes in carbon dioxide concentrations, could impact the production, distribution, dispersion and allergenicity of aeroallergens and the growth and distribution of weeds, grasses, and trees that produce them. These changes in aeroallergens and subsequent human exposures could affect the prevalence and severity of allergy symptoms. However, the scientific literature does not provide definitive data or conclusions on how climate change might impact aeroallergens and subsequently the prevalence of allergenic illnesses in the United States. . . .

Water resources across large areas of the country are at serious risk from climate change, with effects on water supplies, water quality, and adverse effects from extreme events such as floods and droughts. Even areas of the country where an increase in water flow is projected could face water resource problems from the supply and water quality problems associated with temperature increases and precipitation variability, and could face the increased risk of serious adverse effects from extreme events, such as floods and drought. The severity of risks and impacts is likely to increase over time with accumulating greenhouse gas concentrations and associated temperature increases and precipitation changes.

. . . The most serious potential adverse effects [on coastal areas] are the increased risk of storm surge and flooding in coastal areas from sea level rise and more intense storms. Observed sea level rise is already increasing the risk of storm surge and flooding in some coastal areas. The conclusion in the assessment literature that there is the potential for hurricanes to become more intense (and even some evidence that Atlantic hurricanes have already become more intense) reinforces the judgment that coastal communities are now endangered by human-induced climate change, and may face substantially greater risk in the future. Even if there is a low probability of increasing the destructive power of hurricanes, this threat is enough to support a finding that coastal communities are endangered by greenhouse gas air pollution. In addition, coastal areas face other adverse impacts from sea level rise such as land loss due to inundation, erosion, wetland submergence, and habitat loss. . . .

. . . [C]limate change is expected to result in an increase in electricity production, especially to meet peak demand. This increase may be exacerbated by the potential for adverse impacts from climate change on hydropower resources as well as the potential risk of serious adverse effects on energy infrastructure from extreme events. Changes in extreme weather events threaten energy, transportation, and water resource infrastructure. Vulnerabilities of industry, infrastructure, and settlements to climate change are generally greater in high-risk locations, particularly coastal and riverine areas, and areas whose economies are closely linked with climate-sensitive resources. Climate change will likely interact with and possibly exacerbate ongoing environmental change and environmental pressures in settlements, particularly in Alaska where indigenous communities are facing major environmental and cultural impacts on their historic lifestyles. Over the 21st century, changes in climate will cause some species to shift north and to higher elevations and fundamentally rearrange U.S. ecosystems. Differential capacities for range shifts and constraints from development, habitat fragmentation, invasive species, and broken ecological connections will likely alter ecosystem structure, function, and services, leading to predominantly negative consequences for biodiversity and the provision of ecosystem goods and services.

With respect to food production and agriculture, there is a potential for a net benefit in the near term for certain crops, but there is significant uncertainty about whether this benefit will be achieved given the various potential adverse impacts of climate change on crop yield, such as the increasing risk of extreme weather events. Other aspects of this sector may be adversely affected by climate change, including livestock management and irrigation requirements, and there is a risk of adverse effect on a large segment of the total crop market. For the near term, the concern over the potential for adverse effects in certain parts of the agriculture sector appears generally comparable to the potential for benefits for certain crops. However, the body of evidence points towards increasing risk of net adverse impacts on U.S. food production and agriculture over time, with the potential for significant disruptions and crop failure in the future.

For the near term, the Administrator finds the beneficial impact on forest growth and productivity in certain parts of the country from elevated carbon dioxide concentrations and temperature increases to date is offset by the clear risk from the observed increases in wildfires, combined with risks from the spread of destructive pests and disease. For the longer term, the risk from adverse effects increases over time, such that overall climate change presents serious adverse risks for forest productivity. . . .

. . . [C]limate change impacts in certain regions of the world may exacerbate problems that raise humanitarian, trade, and national security issues for the United States. The IPCC identifies the most vulnerable world regions as the Arctic, because of the effects of high rates of projected warming on natural systems; Africa, especially the sub-Saharan region, because of current low adaptive capacity as well as climate change; small islands, due to high exposure of population and infrastructure to risk of sea-level rise and increased storm surge; and Asian mega-deltas, such as the Ganges-Brahmaputra and the Zhujiang, due to large populations and high exposure to sea level rise, storm surge, and river flooding. Climate change has been described as a potential threat multiplier with regard to national security issues.

NOTES AND QUESTIONS

1. *Judicial Approval.* In Coalition for Responsible Regulation v. EPA, 684 F.3d 102 (D.C. Cir. 2012), *aff'd in part, rev'd in part,* 134 S. Ct. 468 (2013), industry challenged EPA's Endangerment Finding, asserting that scientific evidence did not adequately support it. The court's response focused on EPA's "linchpin finding"—its judgment that the "root cause" of recently observed climate change is "very likely" the observed increase in anthropogenic GHG emissions. Id. at 120. Emphasizing the deference due agency scientific determinations, the court upheld the Finding. It found substantial record evidence that anthropogenic GHG emissions "very likely" caused warming over the last several decades, that anthropogenically induced climate change threatens public health and welfare (including adverse health effects; risks to food production, agriculture, forestry, energy, infrastructure, ecosystems, and wildlife; and increased risks to water resources and coastal areas as a result of expected increases in sea levels). Finally, the court found substantial evidence to support EPA's conclusion that motor-vehicle GHG emissions contribute to climate change and thus to public health and welfare endangerment. The existence of some uncertainty did not vitiate EPA's findings, nor did EPA's failure to quantify either the atmospheric concentration at which GHGs endanger public health or welfare, the rate or type of climate change anticipated to endanger public health or welfare, or the risks or impacts of climate change. This Supreme Court's opinion on appeal, which is excerpted at p.1231 below, did not address this aspect of the case. The uncertainties referred to by the court relate more to the timing, distribution, and extent of local impacts of climate change than to global impacts and trends. See Fischer et al., Robust Spatially Aggregated Projections of Climate Extremes, 3 Nature Climate Change 1033 (2013).

2. *Temperature Trends.* Both the National Oceanic and Atmospheric Administration and the World Meteorological Organization (WMO) of the United Nations have found that the decade ending in 2009 was the warmest since modern measurements began in 1850. 2010 and 2013 were both among the ten warmest years since records began. Special Supplement to the Bulletin of the American Meteorological Society, vol. 95, no. 7 (2014), at 59. 2012 was the hottest year ever recorded in the U.S. More than 34,000 daily record highs were set that year, as compared to only about 6600 record lows. That ratio had been in balance as recently as the 1970s. Gillis, Not Even Close: 2012 Was Hottest Ever in U.S., N.Y. Times, Jan. 9, 2013. Hansen et al., Perception of Climate Change, 109 PNAS no. 37 (Sept. 11, 2012), find that summertime heat extremes covered much less than one percent of the Earth's surface between 1951 and 1980, but now typically cover about ten percent of the land area due to climate change. Global temperatures are now warmer than they have been in at least 4,000 years. See Marcott et al., A Reconstruction of Regional and Global Temperature for the Past 11,300 Years, 339 Science 1198 (2013). Figure 12-1 plots the global mean land-ocean temperature index since 1880. Figure 12-2 reflects temperature trends in the United States during the same period. Both figures use data compiled by NASA. Figure 12-3 depicts the greenhouse effect that has caused temperatures to rise. Figure 12-4 charts projected changes in global temperatures under different greenhouse gas emission control scenarios.

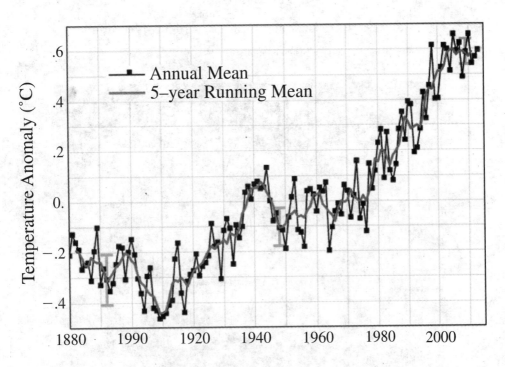

FIGURE 12-1
Global Land—Ocean Temperature Index

Source: GISS Surface Temperature Analysis, http://data.giss.nasa.gov/gistemp/graphs_v3/Fig.A2.gif.

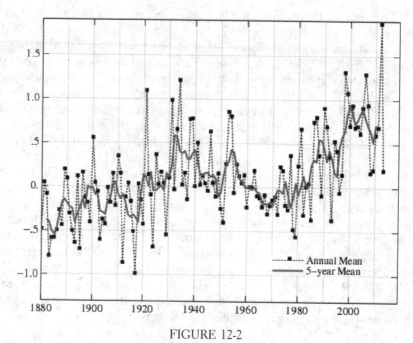

FIGURE 12-2
U.S. Temperature
Continental U.S. annual mean anomalies (°C) vs 1951–1980

Source: http://data.giss.nasa.gov/gistemp/graphs_v3.

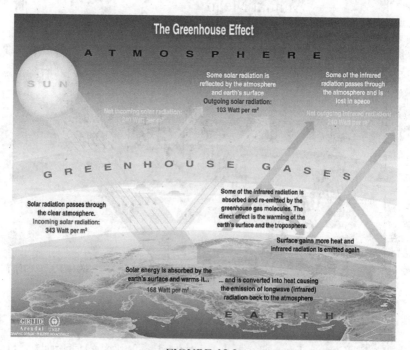

FIGURE 12-3
The Greenhouse Effect

Source: http://yosemite.epa.gov/oar/globalwarming.nsf/content/climate.html (removed)

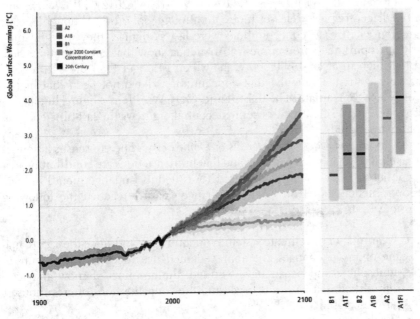

FIGURE 12-4
Scenarios for Past and Possible Future GHG Emissions

Solid lines are multi-model global averages of surface warming (relative to 1980-1999) for the scenarios A2, A1B, and B1, shown as continuations of the 20th century simulations. Shading denotes the ±1 standard deviation range of individual model annual averages. The orange line is for the experiment where concentrations were held constant at year 2000 values. The grey bars at right indicate the best estimate (solid line within each bar) and the likely range assessed for the six SRES marker scenarios. The assessment of the best estimate and likely ranges in the grey bars includes the AOGCMs in the left part of the figure, as well as results from a hierarchy of independent models and observational constraints.

Source: IPCC, Working Group III—Mitigation of Climate Change, Fifth Assessment Report 36 (2014).

U.S. GHG emissions increased by five percent between 1990 and 2012, fell by ten percent between 2005 and 2012, and rose by two percent in 2013. Barboza, U.S. Carbon Emissions Rose 2% in 2013 After Years of Decline, L.A. Times, Jan. 13, 2014; Env't Rep. (BNA) 1616 (May 30, 2014). Declines during this period were driven in part by falling energy demand in the wake of the recession. In 2013, global emissions of GHGs increased by 2.3 percent to record levels. Gillis, Global Rise Reported in 2013 Greenhouse Gas Emissions, N.Y. Times, Sept. 21, 2014. Note that not all GHGs have the same impact on temperatures. Although CO_2 is the GHG emitted in the largest quantities by humans, methane is 21 times more potent on a ton-by-ton basis as a warming agent, and sulfur hexafluoride is 16,300 times more potent than CO_2. Gerrard, Introduction and Overview, in Global Climate Change and U.S. Law 7 (M. Gerrard & J. Freeman eds., 2d ed. 2014).

3. *CO_2 Concentrations.* The WMO reported that atmospheric concentrations of GHGs were at record high levels in 2011, with growth in atmospheric CO_2 increasing

at a steady rate. See WMO Press Release # 965 (Nov. 2012), http://www.wmo.int/pages/mediacentre/press_releases/index_en.html#greenhouse. Although researchers disagree on when CO_2 concentrations were last as high as they were in mid-2013 (nearly 400 ppm), ice core samples in Antarctica show that concentrations have not been that high in at least 800,000 years, which is longer than the entire history of human civilization. It may be that concentrations have not been that high in 15 million years. Freedman, The Last Time CO_2 Was This High, Humans Didn't Exist (May 2, 2013), http://www.climatecentral.org/news/the-last-time-co2-was-this-high-humans-didnt-exist-15938.

4. *Causes and Effects: Consensus or Controversy?* The consensus among scientists that climate change is occurring and that human actions are contributing to it is as strong, if not stronger, than it was when EPA issued its Endangerment Finding. The Intergovernmental Panel on Climate Change (IPCC) reached the following key conclusions in its Fifth Assessment Report:

- "Warming of the climate system is unequivocal, and since the 1950s, many of the observed changes are unprecedented over decades to millennia. The atmosphere and ocean have warmed, the amounts of snow and ice have diminished, sea level has risen, and the concentrations of greenhouse gases have increased."
- "Each of the last three decades has been successively warmer at the Earth's surface than any preceding decade since 1850."
- "Over the last two decades, the Greenland and Antarctic ice sheets have been losing mass, glaciers have continued to shrink almost worldwide, and Arctic sea ice and Northern Hemisphere spring snow cover have continued to decrease in extent (*high confidence*)."
- "The rate of sea level rise since the mid-19th century has been larger than the mean rate during the previous two millennia (*high confidence*)."
- "The atmospheric concentrations of carbon dioxide, methane, and nitrous oxide have increased to levels unprecedented in at least the last 800,000 years. Carbon dioxide concentrations have increased by 40% since pre-industrial times, primarily from fossil fuel emissions and secondarily from net land use change emissions. The ocean has absorbed about 30% of the emitted anthropogenic carbon dioxide, causing ocean acidification."
- "Human influence on the climate system is clear. This is evident from the increasing greenhouse gas concentrations in the atmosphere, positive radiative forcing, observed warming, and understanding of the climate system."
- "Human influence has been detected in warming of the atmosphere and the ocean, in changes in the global water cycle, in reductions in snow and ice, in global mean sea level rise, and in changes in some climate extremes. This evidence for human influence has grown since [the Fourth Assessment Report]. It is *extremely likely* that human influence has been the dominant cause of the observed warming since the mid-20th century."
- "Continued emissions of greenhouse gases will cause further warming and changes in all components of the climate system. Limiting climate change will require substantial and sustained reductions of greenhouse gas emissions."

Summary for Policymakers, in Climate Change 2013: The Physical Science Basis, Contribution of Working Group I to the Fifth Assessment Report of the Intergovernmental Panel on Climate Change 4, 5, 9, 15, 17, 19 (2013). See also U.S. National Climate Assessment, U.S. Global Change Research Program, Climate Change Impacts in the United States 7 (2014) [USGCRP Report] (stating that the "evidence tells an unambiguous story: the planet is warming, and over the last half century, this warming has been driven primarily by human activity"). One organization characterized the science linking human activities to climate change as analogous to the science linking smoking to lung and cardiovascular diseases. The AAAS Climate Science Panel, What We Know: The Reality, Risks and Response to Climate Change 6 (2014).

Not everyone is convinced that human activity is responsible for climate change or that climate change warrants government action. The Nongovernmental International Panel on Climate Change (NIPCC) bills itself as "provid[ing] the scientific balance that is missing from the overly alarmist reports of the [IPCC], which are highly selective in their review of climate science and controversial with regard to their projections of future climate change. . . . In many instances [the IPCC's] conclusions have been seriously exaggerated, relevant facts have been distorted, and key scientific studies have been ignored." NIPCC's bottom line is that "[a]ny warming that may occur is likely to be modest and cause no net harm to the global environment or to human well-being." NIPCC, Climate Change Reconsidered II: Physical Science, Exec. Summary, at 1 (2013), http://climatechangereconsidered.org/#tabs-1-2.

How prevalent are views similar to NIPCC's among climate scientists? According to the Climate Science Panel of Advancing Science, Serving Society, "[b]ased on well-established evidence, about 97% of climate scientists have concluded that human-caused climate change is happening. This agreement is documented not just by a single study, but by a converging stream of evidence over the past two decades from surveys of scientists, content analyses of peer-reviewed studies, and public statements by virtually every membership organization of experts in this field." AAAS, What We Know, *supra*, at 3. Cook et al., Quantifying the Consensus on Anthropogenic Global Warming in the Scientific Literature, Environ. Res. Ltrs. 8 024024 (May 15, 2013), find that, despite widespread public perception that climate scientists disagree over the fundamental causes of climate change, more than 97 percent of peer-reviewed scientific papers published between 1991 and 2011 that expressed a view on those causes attribute climate change to anthropogenic activity. Papers rejecting that link form "a miniucule proportion of the published research, with the percentage slightly decreasing over time." The authors note that 66.4 percent of the papers surveyed expressed no opinion on whether climate change is due to anthropogenic causes. This result is expected in consensus situations, where scientists generally focus on questions that are still disputed or unanswered, not on issues about which there is already agreement.

In 2012, the American Meteorological Society released a statement about the causes and scope of past and anticipated changes in the climate. An Information Statement of the American Meteorological Society (Adopted by AMS Council 20 August 2012), http://www.ametsoc.org/policy/2012climatechange.html. Among other things, the AMS concluded that "[w]arming of the climate system now is unequivocal, according to many different kinds of evidence," and that

> many of the observed changes noted above are beyond what can be explained by the natural variability of the climate. It is clear from extensive scientific evidence that the

dominant cause of the rapid change in climate of the past half century is human-induced increases in the amount of atmospheric greenhouse gases, including carbon dioxide (CO_2), chlorofluorocarbons, methane, and nitrous oxide. The most important of these over the long term is CO_2, whose concentration in the atmosphere is rising principally as a result of fossil-fuel combustion and deforestation. . . . Since long-term measurements began in the 1950s, the atmospheric CO_2 concentration has been increasing at a rate much faster than at any time in the last 800,000 years. Having been introduced into the atmosphere it will take a thousand years for the majority of the added atmospheric CO_2 to be removed by natural processes, and some will remain for thousands of subsequent years.

Oreskes, The Scientific Consensus on Climate Change, 306 Science 1686, 1686 (2004), asserts that "[t]he basic question of what to do about climate change is . . . still open. But there is a scientific consensus on the reality of anthropogenic climate change. Climate scientists have repeatedly tried to make this clear. It is time for the rest of us to listen."

Some have suggested that solar activity is partially responsible for global warming. But some researchers have concluded that total radiation from the sun has decreased since 1985, so that, if anything, one would have expected solar impact to yield falling instead of rising temperatures on the earth. See Lockwood & Frölich, Recent Oppositely Directed Trends in Solar Climate Forcings and the Global Mean Surface Air Temperature, Proceedings of the Royal Soc'y A 1367 (June 8, 2008). See also USGCRP Report, *supra*, at 7 ("Data show that natural factors like the sun and volcanos cannot have caused the warming observed over the past 50 years.").

5. *Ice Sheet Loss and Sea Level Rise.* The IPCC's Fifth Assessment Report quoted above referred to the loss of mass of the Greenland and Antarctic ice sheets. In 2014, scientists reported that early-stage collapse of the West Antarctic ice sheet has already begun and is irreversible, although future social responses to climate change threats may affect the timing of that collapse.[a] Similarly, scientists have determined that the Greenland ice sheet is melting more rapidly than anticipated, and that future sea level rise will be greater than predicted as a result. See Khan et al., Sustained Mass Loss of the Northeast Greenland Ice Sheet Triggered by Regional Warming, 4 Nature Climate Change 292 (2014).

Kemp et al., Climate Related Sea-Level Variations over the Past Two Millennia, 108 PNAS 11017 (2011), finds that sea levels are rising faster than they have in at least 2,100 years. Warming causes sea level rises not only when melting glaciers and ice sheets release additional water into the oceans, but also because warmer water expands in volume. For a pessimistic assessment of our ability to halt sea level rise over the next several centuries, even with deep cuts in GHG emissions, see Meehl et al., Relative Outcomes of Climate Change Mitigation Related to Global Temperature Versus Sea-Level Rise, 2 Nature Climate Change 576 (2012). The authors concluded, however, that aggressive mitigation efforts can slow down sea level rise enough to allow for the adoption of adaptation measures.[b]

---

a. See Rignot et al., Widespread, Rapid Grounding Line Retreat of Pine Island, Thwaites, Smith, and Kohler Glaciers, West Antarctica, from 1992 to 2011, 41 Geophysical Research Ltrs. 3502 (2014); Joughin et al., Marine Ice Sheet Collapse Potentially Underway for the Thwaites Glacier Basin, West Antarctica, 344 Science 735 (2014).

b. Jacob et al., Recent Contributions of Glaciers and Ice Caps to Sea Level Rise, 482 Nature 514 (2012), describe the contributions of melting glaciers and sea ice caps to global mean sea level rise. On the connection between climate change and rising sea levels, see Strauss et al., Surging Seas: Sea Level Rise, Storms, and Global Warming's Threat to the U.S. Coast (2012), http://slr.s3.amazonaws.com/SurgingSeas.pdf. The report includes an interactive map that shows possible sea level rise and water incursion across the U.S. http://sealevel.climatecentral.org.

6. *Climate Change and Public Health.* EPA's Endangerment Finding describes how climate change may affect society, including public health. Figure 12-5 portrays the ways in which human and natural systems may interact as a result of climate change. The USGCRP's Interagency Working Group on Climate Change and Health identified 11 broad human health categories that are likely to be affected by climate change. These include asthma; respiratory and airway diseases; cancer (due to increased duration and intensity of ultraviolet radiation); cardiovascular disease and stroke; foodborne diseases and nutrition; heat-related morbidity and mortality; human developmental effects (due to malnutrition and exposure to toxic contaminants and biotoxins resulting from extreme weather events and increased pesticide use for food production); mental health and stress-related disorders; neurological diseases and disorders; vector-borne and zoonotic diseases; waterborne diseases; and weather-related morbidity and mortality. Interagency Working Group on Climate Change and Health, A Human Health Perspective on Climate Change vi-vii (2010). See also USGCRP Report, *supra*, at 16 ("Climate change threatens human health and well-being in many ways, including through more extreme weather events and wildfire, decreased air quality, and diseases transmitted by insects, food, and water."). Scientists have projected that about ten times more people in the eastern U.S. will die each year from heat waves by 2060 than in 2000. Wu et al., Estimation and Uncertainty Analysis of Impacts of Future Heat Waves on Mortality in the Eastern United States, 122 Envtl. Health Perspectives 130660 (2014). In addition, warming temperatures are projected to increase ozone pollution, which forms as a result of chemical reactions facilitated by warmer air. See Pfister et al., Projections of Future Summertime Ozone over the U.S., 119 J. of Geophysical Research 5559 (2014).

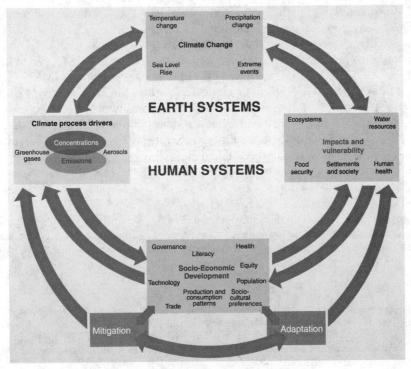

FIGURE 12-5
Earth Systems, Human Systems

Source: IPCC AR4 Synthesis Report, Figure i-1, at 26

These adverse effects have already begun. The 2010 IPCC report found that

> climate change is currently affecting public health through myriad environmental con-
> sequences, such as sea-level rise, changes in precipitation resulting in flooding and
> drought, heat waves, changes in intensity of hurricanes and storms, and degraded air
> quality, that are anticipated to continue into the foreseeable future. In a tally that
> included just four diseases (cardiovascular disease, malnutrition, diarrhea, and malaria)
> as well as floods, the World Health Organization (WHO) estimated 166,000 deaths and
> about 5.5 million disability-adjusted life years (DALYs, a measure of overall disease
> burden) were attributable to climate change in 2000. [A Human Health Perspective
> on Climate Change, *supra*, at 3.]

Warming temperatures have already driven increases in the incidence of Lyme
disease in the U.S. and may spread that and other tick-borne diseases into new areas.[c]
Climate change may even result in the release of long-dormant pathogens as permafrost in the Artic melts.[d] The good news is that the health benefits of climate change
mitigation can offset the costs of reducing GHG emissions. West et al., Co-benefits of
Mitigating Global Greenhouse Gas Emissions for Future Air Quality and Human
Health, 3 Nature Climate Change 855 (2013).

7. *Climate Change and Extreme Weather Events.* According to the IPCC,
"[i]mpacts from recent climate-related extremes, such as heat waves, droughts, floods,
cyclones, and wildfires, reveal significant vulnerability and exposure of some ecosystems and many human systems to current climate variability (*very high confidence*)."
Summary for Policymakers, Climate Change 2014: Impacts, Adaptation, and Vulnerability, Part A: Global and Sectoral Aspects. Contribution of Working Group II to the
Fifth Assessment Report of the Intergovernmental Panel on Climate Change 6 (2014)
[Impacts, Adaptation, and Vulnerability]. The USGRCP concluded in 2014 that
"[s]ome extreme weather and climate events have increased in recent decades, and
new and stronger evidence confirms that some of these increases are related to human
activities." USGCRP Report, *supra*, at 15. Emanuel, Downscaling CMIP5 Climate
Models Shows Increased Tropical Cyclone Activity over the 21st Century, 110 PNAS
12219 (2013), finds that both the frequency and intensity of tropical cyclones will
increase during the twenty-first century as a result of climate change.

U.S. Climate Change Science Program, Synthesis and Assessment Product 3.3,
Weather and Climate Extremes in a Changing Climate, at vi (June 2008), provides
the following synopsis of the likely impact of climate change on extreme weather
events in the United States:

> In the future, with continued global warming, heat waves and heavy downpours are very
> likely to further increase in frequency and intensity. Substantial areas of North America
> are likely to have more frequent droughts of greater severity. Hurricane wind speeds,
> rainfall intensity, and storm surge levels are likely to increase. The strongest cold season

---

c. See Ogden et al., Estimated Effects of Projected Climate Change on the Basic
Reproductive Number of the Lyme Disease Vector, 122 Envtl. Health Perspectives 631 (2014).
See also Patterson, As Earth Warms, West Nile Spreads, The Atlantic, May 9, 2014; Marsa, Hot
Zone—A Warming Planet's Rising Tide of Disaster, Discover Mag. (2010) (discussing the spread of
infectious diseases as a result of climate change).

d. See Legendre et al., Thirty-Thousand-Year-Old Distant Relative of Giant Icosahedral
DNA Viruses with a Pandoravirus Morphology, 111 PNAS 4274 (2014).

storms are likely to become more frequent, with stronger winds and more extreme wave heights.[d]

8. *The Impact of Climate Change on Animals and Plants.* The IPCC's Fifth Assessment Report addressed the impact of climate change on biodiversity:

> Many terrestrial, freshwater, and marine species have shifted their geographic ranges, seasonal activities, migration patterns, abundances, and species interactions in response to ongoing climate change (*high confidence*). While only a few recent species extinctions have been attributed as yet to climate change (*high confidence*), natural global climate change at rates slower than current anthropogenic climate change caused significant ecosystem shifts and species extinctions during the past millions of years (*high confidence*).

Impacts, Adaptation, and Vulnerability, *supra*, at 4. Acidification caused by the ocean's absorption of CO_2 (which may be occurring faster now than it has in the last 300 million years (Hönisch, The Geological Record of Ocean Acidification, 335 Science 1058 (2012)) has increased water corrosivity, "reducing the capacity of marine organisms with shells or skeletons made of calcium carbonate (such as corals, krill, oysters, clams, and crabs) to survive, grow, and reproduce, which in turn will affect the marine food chain." USGCRP Report, *supra*, at 10. See also Wittmann & Pörtner, Sensitivities of Extant Animal Taxa to Ocean Acidification, 3 Nature Climate Change 995 (2013). The National Research Council of the National Academies found in 2013 that among the abrupt changes already underway of most immediate concern are increases in extinction rates of marine and terrestrial species. NRC, Abrupt Impacts of Climate Change: Anticipating Surprises 2 (2013). Further, "[t]he distinct risks of climate change exacerbate other widely recognized and severe extinction pressures," including habitat destruction, invasive species, and unsustainable exploitation of species for economic gain. If unchecked, habitat destruction and fragmentation and overexploitation, "even without climate change, could result in a mass extinction within the next few centuries equivalent in magnitude to the one that wiped out the dinosaurs." Id. at 4. Factoring in climate change, those impacts may occur before 2100. Similarly, Maclean & Wilson, Recent Ecological Responses to Climate Change Support Predictions of High Extinction Risk, 108 PNAS 12337 (2011), conclude that anthropogenic climate change is a major threat to global biodiversity, and that ten percent of species now alive could be extinct by 2100 as a result of climate change.

9. *National Security Risks.* The national security risks posed by climate change, which are referred to in EPA's Endangerment Finding above, have caught the attention of high-level military, national security, and defense officials in the United States, among others. In 2014, the Center for Naval Analyses Military Advisory Board (composed of high-level retired military leaders) warned that the effects of climate change are threat multipliers as well as "catalysts for instability and conflict," including terrorist activities. CNA Military Advisory Board, National Security and the Accelerating Risks of Climate Change 2 (May 2014) (quoted at greater length in section F.3.c below). Similarly, climate change may spur crime rate increases.[e]

d. For discussion of the debate over the possible link between climate change and increased hurricane intensity, see Glicksman, Global Climate Change and the Risks to Coastal Areas from Hurricanes and Rising Sea Levels: The Costs of Doing Nothing, 52 Loyola L. Rev. 1127 (2006).

e. See Ranson, Crime, Weather, and Climate Change, 67 Envtl. Econ. & Mgmt. 274 (May 2014); Hsiang, Quantifying the Influence of Climate on Human Conflict, 341 Science no. 6151 (Sept. 13, 2013).

The nations likely to be hardest hit by climate change include some Southeast Asian and African countries, where "poor governance, corruption, and the influence of vested economic interests" may hamper the ability to deal with climate change stresses. "Large-scale migration from rural and coastal areas into cities and across borders could increase friction between diverse social groups already under stress from climate change." Blair, The Annual Threat Assessment of the U.S. Intelligence Community for the House Permanent Select Committee on Intelligence 39 (Feb. 3, 2010) (written by the Director of National Intelligence). The Maldive Islands are "at risk of complete obliteration" from rising sea levels. Id. African cities probably will face deteriorating living conditions, high unemployment, frequent civil unrest, governmental collapses, and humanitarian crises. Climate change will likely spur a flood of North African refugees seeking access to Europe. The national security implications of climate change are addressed further in section F of this chapter, which deals with climate change and international law.

Professor Sarah Light suggests that the U.S. military has the potential to change societal attitudes about climate change, and therefore affect both behavior and political debate on energy use and climate policy, by linking a reduction in fossil fuel use to the value of promoting national security. She suggests that such an approach would gain traction from "the military's role as an unequivocal validator of climate science" and its current effort to value the costs and intangible benefits to its national security mission of reduced fossil fuel use. See Light, Valuing National Security: Climate Change, the Military, and Society, 61 UCLA L. Rev. 1772, 1778 (2014).

10. *What to Do.* The AAAS Climate Science Panel issued this warning in 2014:

> Earth's climate is on a path to warm beyond the range of what has been experienced over the past millions of years. The range of uncertainty for the warming along the current emissions path is wide enough to encompass massively disruptive consequences to societies and ecosystems: as global temperatures rise, there is a real risk, however small, that one or more critical parts of the Earth's climate system will experience abrupt, unpredictable and potentially irreversible changes. Disturbingly, scientists do not know how much warming is required to trigger such changes to the climate system.

AAAS, What We Know, *supra*, at 4. How should society respond to this and the other risks and impacts described above? The Academies of Science for the G8 + 5 countries issued a statement in 2008 concluding that "progress in reducing global greenhouse gas emission has been slow," and that emissions must eventually be limited to the net absorption capacity of the earth in order to stabilize the climate. That net absorption capacity point "is less than half of current emissions. Immediate large-scale mitigation is required." The statement urged G8 + 5 leaders "to make maximum efforts to . . . commit to these emission reductions." Joint Science Academies' Statement: Climate Change Adaptation and the Transition to a Low Carbon Society 1 (June 2008).

Mitigation efforts are likely to focus on the activities responsible for the greatest percentage of GHG emissions. Figure 12-6 depicts the contributions of various activities, such as fossil fuel consumption, to global anthropogenic GHG emissions. Figure 12-7 portrays how mitigation strategies targeting different sources of GHG emissions may affect efforts to stabilize atmospheric GHG concentrations. Myhrvold & Caldeira, Greenhouse Gases, Climate Change and the Transition from Coal to Low-Carbon Electricity, 7 Envtl. Research Ltrs. 014019 (2012), concluded that "rapid deployment of low-emission energy systems can do little to diminish the climate impacts in the first half of this century. Conservation, wind, solar, nuclear power, and possibly carbon capture and storage appear to be able to achieve substantial climate benefits in the second half of this century; however, natural gas cannot."

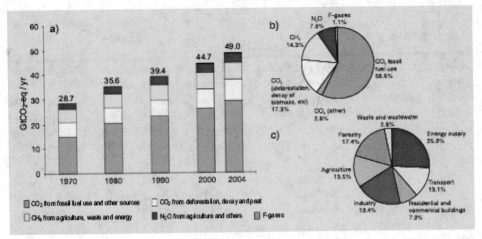

FIGURE 12-6

Global Anthropogenic GHG Emissions

(a) Global annual emissions of anthropogenic GHGs from 1970 to 2004. (b) Share of different anthropogenic GHGs in total emissions in 2004 in terms of CO_2 equivalent. (c) Share of different sectors in total anthropogenic GHG emissions in 2004 in terms of CO_2 equivalent. (Forestry includes deforestation.)

Source: IPCC AR4 Synthesis Report, Figure 2.1, at 36 (2007).

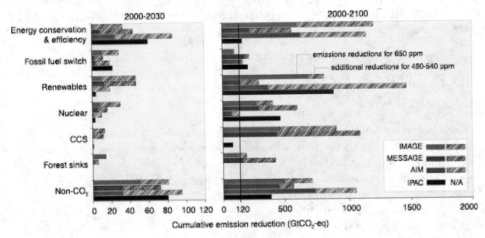

FIGURE 12-7

Illustrative Mitigation Portfolios for Achieving Stabilization of GHG Concentrations

Cumulative emissions reductions for alternative mitigation measures for 2000-2030 (left-hand panel) and for 2000-2100 (right-hand panel). The figure shows illustrative scenarios from four models (AIM, IMAGE, IPAC and MESSAGE) aiming at the stabilisation at low (490 to 540ppm CO_2-eq) and intermediate levels (650ppm CO_2-eq) respectively. Dark bars denote reductions for a target of 650ppm CO_2-eq and light bars denote the additional reductions to achieve 490 to 540ppm CO_2-eq. Note that some models do not consider mitigation through forest sink enhancement (AIM and IPAC) or CCS (AIM) and that the share of low-carbon energy options in total energy supply is also determined by inclusion of these options in the baseline. CCS includes CO_2 capture and storage from biomass. Forest sinks include reducing emissions from deforestation. The figure shows emissions reductions from baseline scenarios with cumulative emissions between 6000 to 7000 GtCO-eq (2000-2100).

Source: IPCC AR4 Synthesis Report, Figure 5.2, at 68 (2007).

Complicating the equation are findings by some scientists that ash and soot particles in the stratosphere help slow global warming. Solomon et al., The Persistently Variable "Background" Stratospheric Aerosol Layer and Global Climate Change, 333 Science 866 (2011). Do these findings suggest that efforts to abate human particulate pollution might be counterproductive? How should policymakers weigh the health risks of exposure to ground-level particulate emissions with the benefits of stratospheric particles at abating warming? Do the findings support one of the methods of geoengineering that have been suggested as a response to climate change—purposefully shooting sulfate aerosol particles into the atmosphere?

What are the costs of failing to address climate change? In a 2014 report, the President's Council of Economic Advisors concluded that although delay can reduce short-term costs, the log-term consequences of delay will be costly in terms of both more extensive climate-related damage and higher costs needed to make more rapid reductions in GHG concentrations. The report found that "delay that results in warming of 3° Celsius above pre-industrial levels, instead of 2°, could increase economic damages by approximately 0.9 percent of global output." Council of Economic Advisors, The Cost of Delaying Action to Stem Climate Change 2 (July 2014). That translates to approximately $150 billion each year. Moreover, "net mitigation costs increase, on average, by approximately 40 percent for each decade of delay." Id. The Council suggested viewing action to address climate change as "climate insurance" to guard against "the most severe and irreversible potential consequences of climate change." Id.

11. *Further Information.* EPA maintains a website with links to scientific studies on which it based its policy decisions concerning climate change. The Hero Database, http://hero.epa.gov.

B.   POLITICAL AND ECONOMIC CHALLENGES

Efforts to prompt political responses to climate science face a remarkable and daunting array of political-economic hurdles. This section analyzes the hurdles to prompting a political response and designing effective policy solutions.

Behavioral Economics Challenges. The uncertain future impacts of climate change and the need for change play almost perfectly into pervasive sorts of cognitive tendencies now well documented in behavioral economics (or "cognitive psychology") scholarship. These tendencies will often make individuals underestimate climate risks and oppose responsive measures that upset settled modes of behavior. Unlike many forms of pollution and environmental harm, GHGs causing climate change are often invisible and ubiquitous. Even dramatic scientific data and geophysical change attributed to climate change require faith that one can appropriately link debated sources of risk to particular resulting phenomena. In addition, many of the most feared resulting changes are at least decades off, and can be predicted with only ranges of probable risk. No single major storm or other climate event can be attributed to climate change, although scientists are confident that in many parts of the world more severe and frequent storms, heat waves, and droughts will result because of it. Thus, linking human contributions to climate change and particular effects is difficult. In addition, responsive actions would require changes in long-established behavior. These attributes of climate change predictably undercut individuals' willingness to accept both the reality of climate change and the costs and possible changes that new legal responses would require.

Most significantly, climate change responses encounter powerful tendencies often captured by the concept of "the status quo bias" and the linked concept of "loss aversion." As explained by Professor Jeffrey Rachlinski, the status quo bias

> makes it difficult for society to undertake reforms to reduce the risk of global climate change. People will be averse to incurring the major economic losses that might be needed to reduce the problem. Loss aversion suggests that if society were not consuming fossil fuels today but could make itself wealthier by beginning to consume them at risk of causing global climate change, it would not do so. That is not the choice that society is making, however. It is choosing whether to incur a loss from the present status quo, rather than choosing to forgo a future gain. Loss aversion might explain the willingness of many countries to freeze, or slightly reduce, their consumption of fossil fuels at 1990 levels while simultaneously refusing to commit to significant reductions in fossil fuel consumption.

Rachlinski, Innovations in Environmental Policy: The Psychology of Global Climate Change, 2000 U. Ill. L. Rev. 299, 308 (2000). Experimental evidence reveals that people are "far more concerned about 'losing' items to which they believe they currently have an entitlement than they are concerned about 'gaining' items for which they never had any expectation of ownership or future ownership." Biber, Climate Change and Backlash, 17 N.Y.U. Envtl. L.J. 1295, 1321-1328 (2009).

These tendencies will play out in the realm of regulatory politics and also link to economic incentives to maintain the status quo.

> Those benefiting from the status quo regulatory setting, as well as regulators who have invested in the status quo either through enactment or implementation efforts, will not only literally have sunk money and effort into that baseline, but they are likely to become attached to it. Regulators and those benefiting from the status quo will require more convincing to change policies than they would to invest in the status quo in the first place. Given predictable entreaties by status quo beneficiaries to retain the status quo, regulators considering a change will likely give inordinate weight to the most frequent and latest lobbying efforts. Simply because a regulatory approach was initially embraced, it will be given a higher value than if offered anew.

Buzbee, Recognizing the Regulatory Commons: A Theory of Regulatory Gaps, 89 Iowa L. Rev. 1, 35 (2003). These tendencies result in policy myopia and, due to the complexity of the underlying science and policy responses, play into frequent human difficulty in assessing unfamiliar and distant risks. Lazarus, Super Wicked Problems and Climate Change: Restraining the Present to Liberate the Future, 94 Cornell L. Rev. 1153, 1156 (2009).

The Ultimate Tragedy of the Commons and Free-Rider Risk Story. Due to the ubiquity of sources contributing to climate change, the substantial profits or benefits inuring to those sources, and the individually small and often unknown resulting harms, GHG emission and resulting climate harms are a near perfect "tragedy of the commons" story, as reviewed and excerpted in Chapter 1. Despite the damages already occurring and predicted for the future, "no single nation has an incentive to reduce its emissions because such reductions will only decrease their own benefits from the commons without successfully preventing the commons' degradation, at least to any appreciable extent." Engel & Saleska, Subglobal Regulation of the Global

Commons: The Case of Climate Change, 32 Ecology L.Q. 183, 190 (2005). Chief Justice Roberts, in his dissent in Massachusetts v. EPA, 549 U.S. 497 (2007) (excerpted in section E.1 of this chapter), used commons tragedy logic not to overcome the tragedy, but to justify lack of judicial involvement to prompt executive action to address climate ills. He argued against granting anyone "citizen suit" standing due to how other nations' pollution increases could render any U.S. response a futile and self-harming gesture. He was concerned that "developing countries such as China and India are poised to increase greenhouse gas emissions substantially over the next century," making U.S. emissions "an increasingly marginal portion of global emissions, and any decreases produced by petitioners' desired standards . . . likely to be overwhelmed many times over by emissions increases elsewhere in the world." Id. at 545 (Roberts, C.J., dissenting). He did not carry the day with this argument, but his concern with how domestic climate mitigation actions could cause harm while providing little or no benefit is a close variant on the tragedy of the commons tale. And the conclusion following from such logic is what Hardin predicted—all nations would rationally just keep on polluting and gaining the benefits of their own polluting activity while bearing only a tiny percentage of the resulting harm caused by everyone. In the aggregate, however, the harms could be substantial. All jurisdictions face an incentive to do nothing and free-ride on the benefits of those jurisdictions that do choose to act, but there is no guarantee any jurisdiction will act individually or collectively to prevent those harms.

   Precommitment Hurdles. Professor Lazarus highlights a related concern. Even if nations start enacting climate legislation, the risk remains that nations will defect and return to their GHG-polluting ways. The mutual fear that nations that act will prove foolish both can prevent nations from entering into climate agreements and undercut investments in carbon markets needed for climate policies to achieve their goals in a cost-effective manner. See Lazarus, *supra.* He therefore suggests "precommitment" strategies to discourage wholesale abandonment of climate regulation efforts.

   Leakage Risks. The risk that controlling GHGs in one jurisdiction may result in market and pollution shifts, thereby undercutting the effectiveness of regulation, is labeled the "leakage" problem. Several forms of leakage could undercut climate efforts. One could result from source category leakage. Professor Robert N. Stavins explains that

> market adjustments resulting from a regulation [can] lead to increased emissions from unregulated sources outside the cap that partially offset reductions under the cap. For example, a cap that includes electricity-sector emissions (and thereby affects electricity prices) but excludes emissions from natural gas or heating oil use in commercial and residential buildings may encourage increased use of unregulated natural gas or oil heating (instead of electric heating) in new buildings.

Stavins, A Meaningful U.S. Cap-and-Trade System to Address Climate Change, 32 Harv. Envtl. L. Rev. 293, 311 (2008). Under "any cap-and-trade system that is not economy-wide," sources not capped will "exploit this incomplete coverage by seeking ways to avoid regulation." Id. This "leakage" can also cross national borders. As Professor Jonathan Wiener has noted,

> restrictions on emissions in Country A could induce emissions-intensive industries to uproot and relocate facilities to unregulated Country B in order to produce their products

at lower cost and export their products to world markets (including back to the regulated country). The extent of this relocation effect depends on the openness to trade and investment flows of the world economy, and on the marginal cost of the emissions constraint relative to the marginal cost of relocating.

Wiener, Think Globally, Act Globally: The Limits of Local Climate Policies, 155 U. Pa. L. Rev. 1961, 1967-1968 (2007). And price effects can also confound regulatory efforts. If jurisdiction A adopts policies reducing energy use to further climate goals, that policy will predictably reduce demand for energy, which in turn should reduce energy prices. With reduced prices, others outside jurisdiction A are likely to increase their energy usage, again defeating climate goals of jurisdiction A's policies. Ostrom, A Polycentric Approach for Coping with Climate Change, World Bank Res. Working Paper 5095 (October 2009). Any climate policies therefore must seek to be as inclusive as possible and include measures to deter or preclude leakage.

Collective Action Coordination Challenges. Even if all nations suddenly decided that climate action had to be taken, policy success would still depend on overcoming the substantial transaction costs inherent in organizing collective negotiations and settling on an effective regulatory response. Jurisdictions and polluters within each jurisdiction will bear different degrees of responsibility for past GHG emissions and anticipated future emissions, as well as asymmetrically experience climate change harms and, sometimes, benefits. The path from agreement that there is a climate change problem to agreement on an effective, broadly binding regulatory response will unavoidably be difficult, perhaps the "largest . . . collective action dilemma . . . the world has ever knowingly faced." Ostrom, *supra*, at 5. In addition, collective action cost disparities by different nations, polluters, and citizens, as covered in Chapter 1 through reference to the work of Mancur Olson, will result in different incentives for involvement and different preferred regulatory responses.

Broad agreement that the pricing of carbon (such as, but not necessarily through, a cap-and-trade–based strategy, which we describe both in Chapter 6, section F, and in the next section of this chapter) as the best means to address climate change, is in part attributable to how it can help overcome many of these formidable political-economic challenges. Less cutting-edge strategies, such as technology-based performance standards, remain part of the climate change regulatory menu due to the relative ease with which such measures could be implemented, modestly expanding the scope of current regulatory approaches. Other regulatory options also need to be assessed with sensitivity to these unavoidable hurdles. The following section turns to the regulatory menu for climate change policy.

C. THE REGULATORY MENU

In light of the scientific background sketched out in section A of this chapter and the political and economic challenges posed by global climate change, what targets of regulation and regulatory design strategies are available to mitigate GHG emissions and thereby reduce anticipated climate change harms? This section begins with a general overview of the principal sources of greenhouse gas emissions and the opportunities for and constraints on mitigating climate change for each. It then provides a more systematic analysis of the tools, regulatory and otherwise, available to governments committed to climate change mitigation. The section concludes with a summary of some of the major bills introduced in Congress during 2009 and 2010 to address climate change by reducing emissions of GHGs. Because no such bill has passed, the discussion is meant to illustrate leading policy options thus far and how the details of various regulatory options might be crafted.

Much of the rest of this chapter is devoted to analysis of the role of government in mitigating and adapting to climate change. Section D addresses federalism issues within the U.S. legal system, section E summarizes the ways in which domestic U.S. legal regimes have begun to address climate change (as well as some of the issues concerning the suitability of those regimes to tackling climate change mitigation and adaptation problems), and section F addresses international responses to climate change.

1.   *Climate Change Mitigation Targets, Opportunities, and Constraints*

In 2010, the National Research Council of the National Academy of Sciences made the following recommendations concerning policy strategies for responding to climate change:

> We thus conclude that there is an urgent need for U.S. action to reduce greenhouse emissions. In response to this need for action, we recommend the following core strategies to U.S. policy makers:
>
> - Adopt a mechanism for setting an economy-wide carbon pricing system.
> - Complement the carbon price with a portfolio of policies to:
>   - ○ realize the practical potential for near-term emission reductions through energy efficiency and low-emission energy sources in the electric and transportation sectors;
>   - ○ establish the technical and economic feasibility of carbon capture and storage and new-generation nuclear technologies;
>   - ○ accelerate the retirement, retrofitting, or replacement of GHG emission-intensive infrastructure.
> - Create new technology choices by investing heavily in research and crafting policies to stimulate innovation.
> - Consider potential equity implications when designing and implementing climate change limiting policies, with special attention to disadvantaged populations.
> - Establish the United States as a leader to stimulate other countries to adopt GHG reduction targets.
> - Enable flexibility and experimentation with policies to reduce GHG emissions at regional, state, and local levels.
> - Design policies that balance durability and consistency with flexibility and capacity for modification as we learn from experience. [National Research Council, Limiting the Magnitude of Future Climate Change 4-5 (2010).]

Similarly, a federal interagency task force identified fifteen technology-based strategies for reducing GHG emissions, as Table 12-1 illustrates:

TABLE 12-1
Key Goals and Technology Strategies

[U.S. *Climate Change Technology Program*] Goal	*15 Technology Strategies*
Reducing emissions from energy end-use and infrastructure	1. Transportation 2. Buildings 3. Industry 4. Electric grid and infrastructure
Reducing emissions from energy supply	5. Low-emission, fossil-based fuels and power 6. Hydrogen 7. Renewable energy and fuels 8. Nuclear fission
Capturing and sequestering carbon dioxide	9. Carbon capture 10. Geologic storage 11. Terrestrial sequestration
Reducing emissions of non-CO_2 greenhouse gases	12. Methane emissions from energy and waste 13. Methane and nitrous oxide emissions from agriculture 14. Emissions of high global-warming potential gases 15. Nitrous oxide emissions from combustion and industrial sources

Source: Committee on Climate Change Science and Technology Assessment, Strategies for the Commercialization and Deployment of Greenhouse Gas Intensity-Reducing Technologies and Practices vii (Jan. 2009).

In a report focused more broadly on regulatory targets and options that should be considered in any climate regulatory regime, regardless of the level of government (including an international agreement), the IPCC, in the IPCC Fourth Assessment Report: Climate Change 2007 Working Group III: Mitigation of Climate Change, surveyed the major possibilities. It noted that changes in lifestyle behavior and consumption patterns can contribute to climate change mitigation. It urged the development of education and training programs to help overcome barriers to the market acceptance of energy efficiency, particularly in combination with other measures; changes in occupant behavior and new technologies to reduce CO_2 emissions related to energy use in buildings; transport demand management through urban planning that reduces the demand for travel and education aimed at reducing car usage and encouraging more efficient driving styles; and industrial management tools such as training and reward systems to reduce energy use. The report also emphasized that the co-benefits from reduced air pollution resulting from GHG emissions reduction efforts may offset a substantial fraction of mitigation costs.

The IPCC also identified various mitigation strategy targets, along with the barriers to effective reliance on those strategies. By sector, these included:

Energy

- Energy infrastructure investments and upgrades in developing and industrialized countries, which can have long-term impacts on GHG emissions due to the long lifetimes of energy plants and other infrastructure capital stock. It is often more cost-effective to invest in end-use energy efficiency improvement than in increasing energy supply to satisfy demand for energy services.
- Efficiency improvement, which can promote energy security, local and regional air pollution abatement, and employment.
- Increased reliance on renewable energy, facilitated by charging higher prices for fossil fuels, and avoidance of higher-priced conventional oil resources such as oil sands, oil shales, heavy oils, and synthetic fuels from coal and gas, all of which can lead to increasing GHG emissions in the absence of carbon sequestration technology, which continues to face technical, economic, and regulatory barriers.

Transportation

- Despite multiple mitigation options in the transport sector, their effect may be counteracted by growth, and consumer preferences (for large and powerful vehicles, for example) tend to work against fuel savings. "Market forces alone, including rising fuel costs, are therefore not expected to lead to significant emission reductions."
- Biofuels, modal shifts from road to rail and to inland and coastal shipping and from low-occupancy to high-occupancy passenger transportation, land use and urban planning, and non-motorized transport all offer opportunities for GHG mitigation.
- Reducing traffic congestion, which provides co-benefits in terms of reduced air pollution.

Building design

- Energy-efficient buildings can not only limit the growth of CO_2 emissions but also improve indoor and outdoor air quality and enhance energy security.
- GHG reductions in the building sector may be constrained (especially in developing countries) by availability of technology, financing, higher costs of reliable information, and limitations inherent in building designs.

Industrial operations

- Most of the potential for GHG emission reductions relates to energy-intensive industries, and full use of available mitigation options is not being made in either industrialized or developing nations.
- Barriers to the full use of available mitigation options include the slow rate of capital stock turnover, lack of financial and technical resources, and the limited capacity of firms, particularly small and medium-sized enterprises, to access and absorb technological information.

Agricultural practices

- This industry can make a significant contribution at low cost to climate change mitigation through increasing soil carbon sinks (which has strong synergies with sustainable agriculture), reducing methane and nitrous oxide emissions, and contributing biomass feedstocks for energy use.
- Mitigation practices must be evaluated for individual agricultural systems and settings.
- The contribution of biomass to mitigation depends on demand for bioenergy from transport and energy supply, water availability, and requirements of land for food and fiber production. Biomass production for energy may compete with other land uses and can have positive and negative environmental impacts and implications for food security.

Forestry

- About 65 percent of the total mitigation potential from these practices is located in the tropics, largely through reducing emissions from deforestation.
- Climate change can affect the mitigation potential of the forest sector and will differ in magnitude and direction for different regions.
- Forest-related mitigation options can have substantial co-benefits, including employment, biodiversity and watershed conservation, renewable energy supply, and poverty alleviation.

Waste mitigation

- Waste minimization and recycling provide important indirect mitigation benefits through energy and materials conservation.
- Lack of local capital and lack of expertise on sustainable technology are constraints in developing countries and countries with economies in transition.

Geo-engineering

- Proposed techniques such as ocean fertilization to remove CO_2 directly from the atmosphere and blocking sunlight by bringing material into the upper atmosphere remain largely speculative and unproven, with the risk of unknown side effects.
- Reliable cost estimates for these options are not available.

QUESTIONS

What does this summary of the IPCC report suggest about the optimal mix of individual consumer choice, the free market, voluntary actions by businesses, and government actions in reducing GHG emissions? What kinds of legal responses can maximize the contributions of each? If government action is needed, at what level should it occur—international (multilateral or bilateral), national, regional, state, or local? Might different regulatory approaches and targets best involve different levels of government? If a substantial research and development component is needed, which level of government is best situated to lead it? If a crackdown on emissions from large, antiquated stationary sources of pollution (especially energy plants) is necessary, how should governmental roles be allocated? Will market-based strategies suffice?

2. Statutory Design Issues

Given the link between GHG emissions and climate change, efforts to mitigate climate change will require reductions in those emissions. Government policymakers will have various options for achieving that goal, ranging from encouraging people to consume less energy produced through the burning of fossil fuels that produce CO_2 emissions to imposing emission controls on GHG emission sources. No single option will suffice. Instead, a mix of strategies implemented at various levels of government is likely to emerge. This section briefly identifies the major alternatives.

Technical and Financial Support. Government can assist efforts to reduce GHG emissions by conducting or funding research on new technologies that lower GHG emissions. As Chapters 6 and 7 above explain, the federal government's initial entry into the field of pollution control took this form. Congress has already enacted legislation to spur the development of GHG emission-reducing technologies. See, e.g., 15 U.S.C. §§2904-2961. The Energy Policy Act of 2005 adopted several "[GHG] intensity-reducing strategies." It requires the President to establish a Committee on Climate Change Technology to coordinate federal climate change technology activities and programs. 42 U.S.C. §13389(b)(1). The Committee must submit to the President a national strategy to promote the deployment and commercialization of GHG intensity-reducing technologies and practices. Id. §13389(c)(1). The Secretary of Energy, in consultation with the Committee, may establish an advisory committee to identify statutory, regulatory, economic, and other barriers to the commercialization and deployment of those technologies and practices in the United States, id. §13389(f)(1), and to develop recommendations for removing those barriers. Id. §13389(g)(1). In addition, the American Recovery and Investment Act of 2009 made more than $16 billion available to the Department of Energy to invest in clean energy technologies, including the development of renewable energy sources such as solar and wind power. Pub. L. No. 111-5, 123 Stat. 140-141 (2009).

One technology that the federal government has sought to develop is carbon sequestration, which involves capturing carbon emissions at the source and storing them in underground reservoirs. In the Energy Independence and Security Act of 2007, Pub. L. No. 110-140, §703, 121 Stat. 1492, Congress ordered the Secretary of Energy to carry out a program to demonstrate technologies for the large-scale capture of carbon dioxide from industrial sources. Among the purposes of the program is to provide information to the states and EPA that will support the development of a regulatory framework for commercial-scale sequestration operations that ensure the protection of human health and the environment. 42 U.S.C. §16293(c)(2)(B)(viii). The legislation requires that the Secretary enter into an arrangement with the National Academy of Sciences to conduct an interdisciplinary study to support the nation's capability to capture and sequester CO_2 from anthropogenic sources. What risk is there that sequestered carbon will escape, creating serious health and environmental risks? How should the legal system address those risks? See Klass & Wilson, Climate Change and Carbon Sequestration: Assessing a Liability Regime for Long-Term Storage of Carbon Dioxide, 58 Emory L.J. 103 (2008).

Another kind of technological fix involves geoengineering, which is referred to in the IPCC report summarized in the previous section of this chapter. Geoengineering involves altering the earth's environment on a large scale to reduce its vulnerability to climate change. Among the possibilities scientists have proposed are reflecting sunlight away from the earth back into space by putting trillions of small lenses in orbit around the earth, by injecting sulfur into the stratosphere, or by laying reflective films over deserts or placing plastic islands in the oceans. Another approach to geo-engineering would be to remove CO_2 from the atmosphere by fertilizing the oceans with nutrients. Some of these geo-engineering options are depicted in Figure 12-8. These ideas have yet to generate broad enthusiasm among scientists specializing in climate control, largely because of doubts about their technical feasibility and uncertainties about unintended adverse consequences. According to Tilmes et al., The Sensitivity of Polar Ozone Depletion to Proposed Geoengineering Schemes, 320 Science 1166 (May 30, 2008), for example, "[a]n injection of sulfur large enough to compensate surface warming due to the doubling of CO_2 would cause a drastic increase in the extent of Arctic ozone depletion during the next century for cold winters and would cause a considerable delay, between 30 and 70 years, in the expected recovery of the Antarctic ozone hole." See also Battersby, Geoengineering Is the Answer to Climate Change. Unless It Isn't, Wash. Post, Nov. 5, 2013.

The American Meteorological Society released a policy statement in 2009 in which it stated that "geoengineering must be viewed with caution because manipulating the Earth system has considerable potential to trigger adverse and unpredictable consequences," and that "[g]eoengineering proposals differ widely in their potential to reduce impacts, create new risks, and redistribute risk among nations." The statement indicated that "it is unlikely that all of the expected climate-change impacts can be managed through adaptation. Thus, it is prudent to consider geoengineering's potential benefits, to understand its limitations, and to avoid ill-considered deployment." The Society recommended enhanced research on the scientific and technological potential for geo-engineering; coordinated study of historical, ethical, legal, and social implications of geo-engineering; and "[d]evelopment and analysis of policy options to promote transparency and international cooperation in exploring geoengineering options along with restrictions on reckless efforts to manipulate the climate system." American Meteorological Society, Geoengineering the Climate System (July 20, 2009). See also Fischer, The Escape Route, Daily Climate (Nov. 12, 2009) (discussing the potential technical and political problems, and the environmental risks, of various geo-engineering options). Is there a risk that the availability of geoengineering technologies will dissuade policymakers from taking steps to mitigate climate change through reductions in GHG emissions? See Lin, Does Geoengineering Present a Moral Hazard?, 40 Ecology L.Q. 673 (2013).

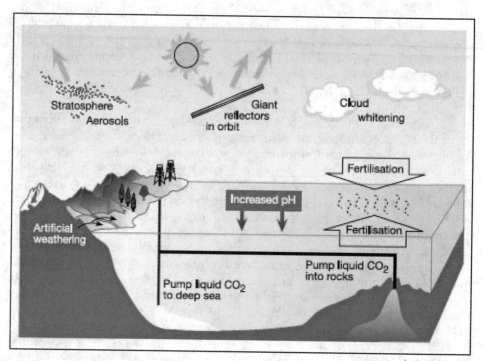

FIGURE 12-8
Geoengineeing Options

Source: http://www.noc.soton.ac.uk/geo-engineering. Reprinted with permission of Prof. Richard Lampit, National Oceanography Centre, UK.

In contrast to reducing CO_2 emissions, some geo-engineering options are projected to be astonishingly cheap and could potentially be undertaken by an individual state or even a rich individual. Given the fact that geo-engineering techniques are likely to affect the entire earth in unpredictable ways, does one nation (or individual) have the right to take action (such as pumping sulfur particles into the air to cool air temperatures) if another objects? What would be the best forum to resolve such disputes?

Economic Incentives. Policymakers can rely on economic incentives, both positive and negative, to encourage desirable and discourage undesirable activities. Tax credits can be used to provide incentives for businesses and homeowners to install energy-saving appliances, insulation, and windows. See, e.g., 26 U.S.C. §1603. To discourage the use of GHG-intensive forms of energy, the government could adopt a tax on carbon production or consumption. Most economists deem a carbon tax to be the simplest and most efficient way to reduce GHG emissions, and some European nations have experimented with it. Stern Review on the Economics of Climate Change (Oct. 2006), a study sponsored by the British government, defines the minimal essential components of an effective strategy to reduce GHG emissions to include the pricing of carbon. In 2009, the California Air Resources Board imposed a fee on GHG emitters (beginning at 12 cents a ton of CO_2 in 2010) to cover the costs of implementing the state's climate change legislation. However, resistance to tax increases of any kind in the United States thus far has prevented any meaningful movement toward the adoption of a carbon tax at the federal level. See generally, Symposium, The Reality of Carbon Taxes in the 21st Century, 10 Vt. J. Envtl. L. 1-179 (2008). As mentioned above and addressed below, a leading policy tool, a cap-and-trade type of regime, harnesses economic incentives and benefits of markets, but hinges as well on regulation imposing caps on aggregate levels of GHGs and, at least initially, allocating limited emission allowances to polluters. For discussion of the cap-and-trade component of a leading state statute to abate GHG emissions, see Ramo, The California Offset Game: Who Wins and Who Loses?, 20 Hastings W.N.W. J. Envtl. L. & Pol'y 109 (2014) (arguing that implementation of California's Global Warming Solutions Act fails to ensure the integrity of offsets or adequately address environmental justice concerns).

Regulatory Standards. Regulation of conduct that results in GHG emissions is an essential part of any comprehensive effort to mitigate climate change. All levels of government have a potential role to play. At the local level, zoning and land use planning can assist in reducing the need to drive from home to work or to shopping areas by clustering homes and businesses within close proximity of one another. Local building codes can require developers to include energy-efficient technologies in new buildings, reducing the amount of energy needed to heat and cool those buildings, and thus the GHG emissions they produce. The federal government also has adopted energy efficiency requirements for federal buildings.

State regulatory standards can take various forms. One approach that nearly half of the states have already taken is to enact renewable portfolio standards requiring that providers of electricity obtain a minimum percentage of their power from renewable sources by a certain date or pay monetary penalties. See, e.g., Duane, Greening the Grid: Implementing Climate Change Policy Through Energy Efficiency, Renewable Portfolio Standards, and Strategic Energy Transmission Investments, 34 Vt. L. Rev. 711 (2010). Some have advocated the adoption of a federal renewable portfolio mandate that would require states to ensure a mix of traditional and renewable energy sources.

Another form of regulation involves imposing limits on the amount of GHGs that various sources are allowed to emit. Ambitious regulation of this kind would set goals that are beyond the reach of current technology in an effort to spur the development of new technologies that do a better job of controlling GHG emissions. Such standards would also increase the cost of burning fossil fuels to produce energy, making alternative sources such as renewables more competitive. Less ambitious technology-based standards would require emissions reductions achievable through the use of the best technology currently available. The California Global Warming Solutions Act of 2006, Cal. Health & Safety Code §§38501-38599, for example, required the State Air Resources Board to adopt a statewide GHG emissions limit, to be achieved by 2020, that is equivalent to the statewide level in 1990. The statute also required the Board to adopt regulations to achieve the maximum technologically feasible and cost-effective emission reductions of GHGs from identified categories of sources. For a summary of the 2006 Act, see http://www.arb.ca.gov/cc/ab32/ab32.htm; see also the *Rocky Mountain Farmers Union* case excerpted in Chapter 2, section F. The federal government has already begun relying on technology-based regulation to reduce GHG emissions. As the section on climate change and the Clean Air Act below indicates, EPA and the National Traffic Highway Safety Administration in 2010 adopted technology-based standards to increase fuel economy and limit GHG emissions from new automobiles. EPA is also developing strategies to impose GHG emissions caps on large stationary sources of GHGs, such as coal-burning electric power plants.

Regulation Combined with Market Mechanisms. Regulatory standards to reduce GHG emissions can be combined with market-based mechanisms and economic incentives. The most popular such approach is the use of a cap-and-trade system. A cap-and-trade system begins with the adoption of an aggregate limit (or cap) on emissions that is designed to achieve a goal such as reducing concentrations of GHGs in the atmosphere to a desired level. The cap is then allocated among regulated sources that emit the pollutant involved. Finally, the system allows regulated sources to buy and sell the right to emit the regulated pollutant, so that sources that retain excess emission allowances by "overcontrolling" may sell their excess allowances to sources having a difficult time meeting their individual emission caps. The basic idea is that cap-and-trade achieves emission reductions in the most efficient way possible because sources that can control cheaply will overcontrol, while sources with high control costs will buy excess allowances generated by others. As section I.2.b of Chapter 6 indicates, the 1990 amendments to the Clean Air Act created a cap-and-trade system for electric utilities as a means of reducing emissions of SO_2 that contribute to acid rain. That program is generally regarded as having successfully reduced acid rain precursors efficiently. The apparent success of the acid rain control program, however, does not guarantee similar results in the climate change context. For one thing, a trading program may work best when it applies wholly or largely to a single industry (electric utilities). GHGs are emitted by virtually every aspect of modern industrial and commercial society.

As indicated below, the most viable, although ultimately unsuccessful, congressional bills seeking to address climate change have centered on a cap-and-trade system for controlling CO_2 and other GHG emissions. The House of Representatives adopted a bill that included an economy-wide cap-and-trade system. American Clean Energy and Security Act of 2009, H.R. 2454, 111th Cong. (2009). The Senate failed to follow suit, however, as opposition developed based in part on the complexity of the system and the fear that transactions under a cap-and-trade system might generate some of the same kinds of speculative instruments and techniques that contributed to a collapse of the mortgage market and the economy in 2008. Some states have joined together to initiate cap-and-trade programs, however. In 2005, seven states in the northeastern and mid-Atlantic regions of the United States signed an agreement to establish binding caps on CO_2 emissions by electric utilities. Under the Regional Greenhouse Gas Initiative (RGGI), the states agreed to reduce emissions by 2.5 percent each year beginning in 2015. By 2019, each state must reduce its annual emissions to 10 percent below baseline levels established in the agreement. Each state will issue an allowance for each ton of CO_2 emitted by electric utilities, but allowances may be bought and sold. Each state would retain 25 percent of its total allowances and sell them to utilities. The revenue would be used to promote energy efficiency and home energy conservation efforts, and to provide rebates for utility consumers. One important question is whether the adoption of a federal cap-and-trade system would include provisions to preempt state programs that already exist.

Although it was released before the economic collapse in 2008, a GAO report found that all of the economists it surveyed agreed that some form of market-based mechanism should be adopted to control GHG emissions. Most of the economists favored either a tax on emissions or a hybrid program relying on both taxes and a cap-and-trade system. See Government Accountability Office, Climate Change: Expert Opinion on the Economics of Policy Options to Address Climate Change, GAO-08-605 (May 2008).

3. Congressional Climate Bills, 2009-2010: Description and Questions for Analysis

During the first two years of the Obama administration, Democrats controlled both houses of Congress, although they were one vote shy of a filibuster-proof majority in the Senate. One of President Obama's campaign pledges was to push the federal government to address climate change. In addition, scientific study after scientific study reconfirmed the reality of climate change. As a result, many policymakers, environmentalists, and climate scientists during 2009 pushed for comprehensive federal climate legislation. Unfortunately, scientific errors that were widely covered in the press empowered climate legislation opponents and climate change skeptics, and international negotiations in Copenhagen ended mostly in disarray except for a last-second informal agreement among many of the world's largest polluters. The lack of an international framework heightened concerns that the United States might commit nationally to climate regulation, causing domestic hardship while other countries failed to act. See section F below. Although several of the most powerful members of the House and Senate championed their own bills, and despite substantial agreement among those bills over basic strategies and regulatory designs, the three leading bills ultimately languished. Since that time, a few new or amended laws directed at other issues, such as transportation, agriculture, and energy, include provisions that regulate some factors contributing to climate change, call for analysis, or relate to climate change adaptation. However, most federal legislative activity since 2010 has had an opposite goal, seeking to reduce or eliminate EPA power to regulate GHG emissions and climate change through the Clean Air Act's existing provisions. Such efforts to take away EPA's existing climate power have thus far failed. Hence, there is of course no guarantee that future proposals or adopted legislation will similarly include a cap-and-trade program as their centerpiece. Nevertheless, the debate over the basic architecture of past proposals illuminates policy choices and questions likely to arise with future federal climate legislation. The discussion below therefore identifies the key bills, summarizes key components, and raises questions for discussion, some of which may relate to GHG emission reduction strategies extending beyond cap and trade.

The first major bill was H.R. 2454, the American Clean Energy and Security Act of 2009, formally proposed by its sponsors, Representatives Henry A. Waxman and Edward J. Markey, on May 15, 2009. It ultimately passed in the House, after significant changes had been made, on June 26, 2009, by a vote of 219-212, with only eight Republicans joining Democrats in support of the bill. On the Senate side, on September 30, 2009, Senators John Kerry and Barbara Boxer introduced S. 1733, the Clean Energy Jobs and American Power Act. After debate, amendments, and filling in of gaps in the initial bill, it was passed by the Senate's Environment and Public Works Committee. S. 1733 was never debated or voted on by the whole Senate. On May 12, 2010, Senators Kerry and Joseph Lieberman introduced another climate bill, the American Power Act. It originally was anticipated to include Republican Senator Lindsey Graham among its backers, but he ultimately declined to co-sponsor a bipartisan bill. Despite efforts to link the BP Deepwater Horizon oil spill (discussed in section C.3 of Chapter 9) and the need for improved energy policy with the bill, and despite some prominent business leaders' signals that they would support a reasonable bill, this bill, too, ultimately fizzled. The failure of these bills was attributed to executive branch and legislative fatigue due to debates over and passage of major economic recovery legislation, health reform legislation, and financial regulatory reform, as well as ongoing wars in Iraq and Afghanistan and high rates of unemployment. In addition, opponents effectively raised doubts and opposition. See E. Pooley, The Climate War (2010), and Lizza, As the World Burns, New Yorker (Oct. 11, 2010), for detailed accounts of battles over climate legislation. Several other bills and amendments also garnered attention but did not pass or gain substantial support.

The three leading climate bills were all massive, thousand-plus-page bills. All three shared several basic attributes: all included provisions mandating or creating incentives for greater efficiency, but they varied in the scope of covered source categories. At least some provisions addressed the power sector, especially coal-burning power plants, transportation, pollutants that act as "super" greenhouse gases, even in tiny quantities, and renewable energy and energy efficiency efforts. The key strategy in all three bills was the creation of a national cap-and-trade market, with the cap declining over time from modest reductions in early years to substantial reductions by 2050. The percentage reduction estimates varied somewhat due to aggregate impacts of all climate-related proposals, but the most aggressive proposals called for reducing emissions by 2050 to only 17 percent of 2005 levels. The House bill and earlier Senate bill (S. 1733) were more comprehensive in defining what sources would come under the cap, while the American Power Act focused more, but not exclusively, on power companies. All three bills also provided for markets in both carbon allowances and "offset credits" generated by conduct that would help alleviate or prevent GHG emissions. The details of what would be a credit-generating offset activity were left to future reports and rulemakings, including means to ensure that claimed offset credits were justified and verifiable. All bills used a combination of subsidies for research and technological innovation and promised distribution of allowances for accomplishment of goals such as development of successful carbon capture and sequestration technologies and greater development of nuclear power. The bills varied and were subject to ongoing debate about whether to supplant EPA's authority to address GHGs under other legislation, especially the Clean Air Act. All required various reports and implementation actions to get the new regulatory regimes rolling, with the Waxman-Markey bill and the Kerry-Boxer bill piling on a remarkable number of reports and pre-implementation steps. Anticipating agencies' failure to complete required studies and issue required reports, the Waxman-Markey bill sought to create a parallel or backup role for the National Academy of Sciences. All also utilized some performance-based standards in addition to market-based strategies. Finally, the bills included provisions empowering regulators to monitor and ensure transparency in any massive new carbon market. The bills differed in their choice of who would serve as the market regulator.

Under all three bills, a substantial number of allowances would be distributed free, with many going to GHG emitters under a "grandfathering" strategy serving to protect the investments of existing polluters. Other provisions distributed allowances via other energy providers to benefit consumers and used allowance allocations to reward valuable innovations and provide incentives to legislatively designated valuable sectors or initiatives. Emission allowances and credits could be freely traded. In addition, by allowing banking of early reductions, polluters could either sell allowances or credits or hold them for their own later use. Offsets were generally subject to greater constraints than were allowances. Under all leading bills, an increasing percentage of allowances would be allocated by auction over time.

Fairly sketchy provisions sought reports and recommendations on strategies for adaptation to climate change. In addition, although an early draft of the Waxman-Markey bill included a citizen suit provision, subsequent bills lacked such a provision. As discussed above, citizen suit provisions are found in all other major U.S. environmental laws enacted after NEPA.

As discussed and summarized in the next section, the leading bills varied somewhat in how they preserved or limited state and local authority to address climate change, but generally they were protective of state and local authority, apart from an initial six-year period of an exclusively federal cap-and-trade market.

QUESTIONS ABOUT THE LEADING CLIMATE BILLS

To what extent are the provisions of these leading bills consistent with reliance on and trust in markets? Does deletion of any provision providing for citizen suit enforcement make sense? Are there attributes of climate change regulation and carbon markets that make citizen suits less valuable or perhaps of greater importance? Why do you think legislators would allocate many allowances by grant rather than by auction? Some economists and policy scholars still think a carbon tax might be preferable to climate legislation centered on a cap-and-trade system. What benefits and risks do you see in reliance on a carbon tax? Which strikes you as more likely to garner legislative and popular support? Can you think of any different strategies for distribution of carbon allowances that might make economic and political sense? Does the allocation of authority between the federal and state governments seem consistent with the allocations found under the other domestic environmental legislation covered in this book? A major challenge for environmental law is to translate environmental goals into implemented reality. How would you assess these bills' prospects, had they been enacted, for timely and effective implementation? Does it make sense for the United States to address climate change in the absence of a multinational agreement that binds all of the world's largest GHG-emitting nations to taking similar action?

D. FEDERALISM ISSUES

As discussed in Chapter 2, the norm for U.S. environmental law has been for federal law to set a regulatory floor but allow states and local governments to take additional and more protective actions. Such regulatory floors typically preserve common law claims, thus preserving the possibility of damages remedies and perhaps even injunctive relief. Many states have been environmental laggards, but others have been innovators, either regulating risks before the federal government or instituting more protective policies. The history of climate change federalism presents an unusual sequence of actions, with states prodding and litigating to force federal climate action, taking their own climate actions before the federal government took meaningful regulatory steps and before federal climate legislation (which Congress still has not adopted), and even acting in concert with other states to take regional actions. Identification of roles for federal, state, and local governments, if a comprehensive federal climate bill is ever enacted, remains a source of debate. This section reviews briefly the history of state and local climate actions, describes the rationales for carving out roles for all three levels of government, and reviews provisions regarding federalism issues contained in the leading federal climate legislative proposals.

The United States today has yet to join and ratify any international climate treaty, as reviewed below in section F. It also has not enacted comprehensive federal climate legislation, despite substantial drafting efforts and movement in committees and one house of Congress during 2009 and 2010. And even under the Clean Air Act's broad protective provisions, EPA took no concrete climate-related steps during the Clinton and Bush administrations until it was sued by Massachusetts and others and ordered to reconsider by the U.S. Supreme Court, as you will read below in the materials on Massachusetts v. EPA. But the nation did not stand still. Existing federal laws apply to discrete aspects of climate change, as section E.4 below indicates. In addition, state and local governments stepped into the breach created by the absence of comprehensive federal legislation, enacting an array of measures to improve energy conservation and address climate change, both individually and through several regional climate regulation regimes. Some actions have had multiple policy goals, such as coordinating efforts to address the causes of climate change, while at the same time pursuing goals of water conservation, reduced health and agricultural harms, and improved air quality. Those state and local climate actions are part of the reason some industries began to revisit long-standing opposition to comprehensive federal climate legislation. These many measures have also influenced the shape of federal legislative proposals.

The following excerpt of a book chapter summarizes recent areas of state and local climate action.

ENGEL & MILLER, STATE GOVERNANCE: LEADERSHIP ON CLIMATE CHANGE
Ch. 29, in Agenda for a Sustainable America 441-457 (J. Dernbach ed., Envtl. L. Inst. 2009)

The prospect of a federal regulatory program poses the question of whether state greenhouse gas programs should be preempted to make way for a more uniform federal program and, if so, to what degree. Given the dramatic leadership of state and local entities in climate policy, this is far from a minor academic question. In this area, as in many others of environmental policy, California and many northeastern states have taken a strong leading role. Further, the development of regional colla-borations on climate change has played an important role and may play an even larger role in the future. Such initiatives include the following:

- *California Global Warming Solutions Act of 2006.* Under this law, California has committed to a 25 percent cut in state greenhouse gas emissions by 2020 (lowering the state's emissions to 1990 levels), and an 80 percent cut below 1990 levels by 2050.
- *California Greenhouse Gas Vehicle Emission Standards.* California has also promulgated the first-in-the-nation vehicle emission standards for greenhouse gases. The California standards must still overcome several legal hurdles before becoming law. . . .

- *Electric Power Generator Standards.* Several states are implementing emission standards related to electric power plants. In both Massachusetts and New Hampshire, existing power plants are required to cap and subsequently reduce carbon dioxide emissions. Oregon and Washington have each passed laws requiring new power plants to reduce their carbon dioxide emissions or purchase offsetting reductions.
- *Renewable Portfolio Standards (RPS).* Twenty-eight states and Washington, D.C., now require that electric utilities generate a certain percentage of their electricity from qualifying renewable technology.
- *Greenhouse Gas Planning Efforts.* Many states have completed or are engaged in the process of planning for greenhouse gas emissions reductions.
- *State-Based Greenhouse Gas Registries.* Related to the state climate action planning process are the many programs now being implemented or developed on the state level to inventory and register state greenhouse gas emissions and emissions reductions on a facility-by-facility and sector-by-sector basis. Climate registries help states to implement their climate mitigation plans by tracking progress toward reaching their targets, encouraging emissions reductions, and providing baseline protection for industries from future mandatory emission reductions.
- *Regional Mitigation Programs.* One of the most promising developments is the collaboration between states on regional programs to mitigate climate change. The most advanced effort is the Regional Greenhouse Gas Initiative (RGGI), a project of northeastern states to establish a carbon dioxide cap-and-trade program applicable to their electric power generation sector. The nine RGGI states—Connecticut, Delaware, Maine, Maryland, Massachusetts, New Hampshire, New Jersey, New York, and Vermont—have adopted a model rule that will ensure that greenhouse gas emissions from the electric power sector are capped at levels present in 2009 (the start date for the program) and reduced by 10 percent by 2019. Perhaps the most important up-and-coming regional collaboration, the Western Climate Initiative, is now being developed by the governors of Arizona, California, New Mexico, Oregon, and Washington, and the premier of the Canadian province of British Columbia.
- *Multi-State Litigation to Reduce Greenhouse Gases.* The states have taken an active litigation posture with respect to compelling reductions in greenhouse gases. The litigation can be divided into two types: (1) litigation against the federal government, specifically the EPA, to compel the federal regulation of greenhouse gas emissions; and (2) common-law actions against individual sources of greenhouse gases seeking emissions reductions. The litigation against the federal government includes Massachusetts v. EPA, filed by Massachusetts and other states and environmental groups against EPA for failure to regulate greenhouse gas emissions from motor vehicles. This is the lawsuit that resulted in the Supreme Court ruling that the Clean Air Act does, indeed, apply to climate change and, thus, that EPA is compelled to determine whether the conditions that mandate regulation—reasonable anticipation of endangerment—were triggered with respect to vehicle greenhouse gas emissions. [This Supreme Court decision is excerpted below.] In Coke Oven Environmental Task Force v. EPA, states and other petitioners [challenged] EPA's failure to include greenhouse gases among the pollutants controlled under the agency's new source performance standards (NSPS) for

steam-generating units operated by electric utilities and other industrial and commercial facilities. Common-law actions include those filed by state attorneys general alleging individual sources of greenhouse gas emissions are contributing to a public nuisance under state and federal law. [Those cases are presented below in section E.3.]

NOTES AND QUESTIONS

1. The dynamic and topsy-turvy reception of state climate efforts is captured well by the fate of California's efforts to regulate GHGs in cars. As Engel and Miller discuss, California had to

> win its effort to obtain a judicial reversal of EPA's denial of a waiver of federal preemption under the federal Clean Air Act. In addition, California [had to] survive a legal challenge filed by the automobile industry claiming that the state's standards are preempted by federal fuel efficiency laws. California . . . also [had to] counter arguments by the U.S. Department of Transportation that California's standards [were] preempted by a federal fuel economy law. Nevertheless, Vermont's law adopting the California vehicle standards recently withstood a vigorous attack on federal preemption grounds.

Id. at 449. Section E.1.c below describes further federal efforts to regulate GHG motor vehicle emissions and the Obama administration's reversal of the Bush administration's opposition to California's initiatives.

2. *State Climate and Energy Laws and Federal Constitutional Challenges.* When a state tries to reduce its energy usage or otherwise reduce its contributions to climate change, it is difficult to craft such laws without impinging on commercial activities outside the state, whether direct or incidental. See section E.2.c's Note on Federalism Obstacles for discussion of cases addressing the constitutionality of several such efforts.

3. *But Does State and Local Climate Activism Make Sense or Result in Good Policy?* The reality that many states and local governments have been active in combating climate change is beyond dispute. The wisdom and efficacy of such actions, however, has very much been a subject of debate. In the absence of a federal bill, most scholars and policymakers see state and local action as a helpful partial step in reducing GHG emissions, testing regulatory approaches, and weakening industry opposition to a federal law due to industry dislike of a changing and perhaps varied set of state regulatory approaches. This is the usual role of state environmental action as a "catalyst" for federal legislation discussed in Chapter 2. The debate over state and local roles is far more pointed in disagreement over how to structure the federalism provisions of proposed (but so far not enacted) national climate legislation. If federal law sets up a national cap-and-trade scheme, under which some portion of the nation's GHG emitters are subject to an annually declining cap on emissions, should additional state and local climate regulation be preempted or "saved" under that national law?

The strongest scholarly voice opposing ongoing state and local climate roles has been Robert N. Stavins of Harvard's Kennedy School. In his view, state and local climate action would be "expensive . . . for residents of those states, who could wind up subsidizing the rest of the country." Stavins, State Eyes on the Climate Policy Prize, 27 Envtl. F. 16 (2010). Stavins asserts that such action would "make no sense," because "it is impossible for regions, states, or localities to achieve greater protection for their jurisdictions through more ambitious actions" since GHGs anywhere contribute equally to climate change. If GHG pollution precluded by a state or local government is subject to "leakage" to another jurisdiction either because pollution sources move or prices drop and demand concomitantly increases, then the active state or local jurisdiction has sacrificed for little or no environmental benefit. Stavins favors the "simplest, cleanest" solution of state and local displacement by a federal climate scheme. Several federal legislators echoed this logic during 2009-2010 debates over a federal bill, with pro-preemption arguments referring to the unacceptable costs of a "patchwork" of state regulations and raising questions about any benefits of allowing such action. In addition, at a more pragmatic level, some influential industry actors appeared to see state preemption as a necessary (although certainly not sufficient) condition for a federal bill to gain support of GHG emitters. For similar arguments, see Stavins, A Meaningful U.S. Cap-and-Trade System to Address Climate Change, 32 Harv. Envtl. L. Rev. 293, 298-299 (2008); Wiener, Think Globally, Act Globally: The Limits of Local Climate Policies, 155 U. Pa. L. Rev. 1961 (2007). Stavins and Wiener are certainly not alone in this view, but an array of scholars have in recent works analyzed the efficacy and legality of state and local climate action and also often addressed why ongoing state and local climate roles might provide value even if a federal climate law were enacted.[a]

Scholarship on climate federalism identifies several reasons to allow state and local climate regulation, even with the enactment of a federal law:

1. *States face different political and physical environments.* A state may simply be more committed to reducing pollution than the nation overall; citizens and politicians may support that extra effort to reduce climate-related pollution,

a. For a sampling of this work, see Adelman & Engel, Adaptive Environmental Federalism, in Preemption Choice, *supra*; Andreen, Federal Climate Change Legislation and Preemption, 3 Envtl. & Energy L. & Pol'y J. 261 (2008); Biber, Cultivating a Green Political Landscape: Lessons for Climate Change Policy from the Defeat of California's Proposition 23, 66 Vand. L. Rev. 399 (2013); Brewster, Stepping Stone or Stumbling Block: Incrementalism and National Climate Change Legislation, 28 Yale L. & Pol'y Rev. 245 (2010); Buzbee, Asymmetrical Regulation: Risk, Preemption, and the Floor/Ceiling Distinction, 82 N.Y.U. L. Rev. 1547 (2007); Buzbee, State Greenhouse Gas Regulation, Federal Climate Change Legislation, and the Preemption Sword, 1 San Diego J. Climate & Energy L. 23 (2009); Carlson, Designing Effective Climate Policy: Cap-and-Trade and Complementary Policies, 49 Harv. J. on Leg. 207 (2012); Carlson, Federalism, Preemption, and Greenhouse Gas Emissions, 37 U.C. Davis L. Rev. 281 (2003); Carlson, Iterative Federalism and Climate Change, 103 Nw. U. L. Rev. 1097 (2009); Engel, State and Local Climate Change Initiatives: What Is Motivating State and Local Governments to Address a Global Problem and What Does This Say About Federalism and Environmental Law?, 38 Urb. Law. 1015 (2006); Glicksman, Nothing Is Real: Protecting the Regulatory Void Through Federal Preemption by Inaction, 26 Va. Envtl. L.J. 5 (2008); Glicksman & Levy, A Collective Action Perspective on Ceiling Preemption by Federal Environmental Regulation: The Case of Global Climate Change, 102 Nw. U. L. Rev. 579 (2008); Kaswan, A Cooperative Federalism Proposal for Climate Change Legislation: The Value of State Autonomy in a Federal System, 85 Denv. U. L. Rev. 791 (2008); Kysar & Meyler, Like a Nation State, 55 UCLA L. Rev. 1621 (2008); Stewart, States and Cities as Actors in Global Climate Regulation: Unitary vs. Plural Architecture, 50 Ariz. L. Rev. 681 (2008); Thomsen & Arroyo, Upside Down Cooperative Federalism: Climate Change Policymaking and the States, 29 Va. Envtl. L. J. 1 (2011); Trisolini, All Hands on Deck: Local Governments and the Potential for Bidirectional Climate Change Regulation, 62 Stan. L. Rev. 669 (2009-2010); Vandenbergh & Cohen, Climate Change Governance: Boundaries and Leakage, 18 NYU Envtl. L. J. 221 (2010-2011).

regardless of the actions of others. This view might be rooted in conceptions of justice, or ethics, or a desire to be a world leader in reducing GHG emissions. In addition, some states may anticipate greater harms from climate change and hence face political pressure to do more to reduce the state's contributions. Such views also often draw on the U.S. Constitution's federalism provisions and the view that whenever possible, state sovereignty and political choices should be respected.

2. *The federal law may prove too weak in goals or as implemented.* A federal climate bill might fall short of what is needed to combat climate change, or for the United States to do its share to reduce global GHG emissions. Federal political opposition or partisan logjams may preclude more federal action, but state political dynamics may support additional action.

3. *State actions would not necessarily be futile.* If states can require reduced GHG emissions and take unused carbon allowances out of circulation, then simple "leakage" movement of pollution or reduced price effects would not inevitably occur. Pollution itself would be, in essence, prevented and those pollution rights retired. Polluters might choose to move their production to more jurisdictions, but pollution costs are among many factors industry considers in choosing locations; leakage is not inevitable.

4. *Federal implementation failures are a great risk.* If necessary steps to implement a federal climate bill do not occur due to simple delay or perhaps litigation challenges, a preemptive federal law could result in no federal climate regulation and no viable state or local venue to push climate regulation goals.

5. *Retaining state and local roles along with federal roles would actually foster market and regulatory stability.* If the federal venue is the only place for climate regulation, then industry derailment of climate implementation could result in no real federal climate regulation, which would also undercut investments in carbon trading and engineering innovations targeted at the rewards of a low-energy economy. In contrast, with state and local governments retaining climate regulatory authority, industry incentives to derail a federal law are reduced, and private investment in carbon markets and green economy innovation would be somewhat protected. Regional, state, and local jurisdictions with laws and initiatives designed to foster energy efficiency and reduce GHG emissions would still provide market rewards for innovations and reduce the risk of a complete loss of carbon trading markets.

6. *With federal, state, and local climate activity, room for interjurisdictional learning is retained.* If the federal government is the only climate actor, then all hope rests with that actor. If state and local governments remain climate players, and can take complementary actions or play roles in implementing and enforcing climate goals, then room remains for both vertical learning (federal-state-local) and horizontal learning (state-state).

7. *With co-pollutants, what would be preempted?* A considerable practical problem for a preemptive federal law would be defining the scope of what would be preempted. Most GHGs are pollutants also regulated for other purposes. Energy efficiency requirements similarly serve many goals in addition to reducing GHG emissions for climate reasons. Large polluters may be denied permits, or subjected to rigorous requirements, for many reasons. Defining in a clear way what would be preempted would be a considerable challenge given the ubiquity of GHG emissions sources and diverse regulatory rationales.

8. *A non-preemptive federal climate law would signal U.S. commitment to climate goals.* Other nations worried about U.S. loss of climate resolve or implementation failures would likely see a non-preemptive federal climate bill as a signal that, regardless of regulatory ups and downs, some U.S. climate progress will continue. This might help other nations enact their own laws or help bring more nations to the table for a new international climate treaty.

Problem 12-1

During 2009-2010 debates over federal climate legislation, preemption emerged as a major issue. The leading bills varied slightly in their language choices, but the key provision in the leading House of Representatives bill (the Waxman-Markey bill, nicknamed after its House sponsors) contained the following provisions:

> Section 861: . . . [N]o state or political subdivision thereof shall implement or enforce a cap and trade program that covers any capped emissions emitted during the years 2012 through 2017. . . . "Cap and trade program" means a system of GHG regulation under which a state or political subdivision issues a limited number of tradeable instruments in the nature of emission allowances and requires that sources within its jurisdiction surrender such tradeable instruments for each unit of GHG emitted during a compliance period. A "cap and trade program" does not include a target or limit on GHG emissions adopted by a state or political subdivision that is implemented other than through the issuance and surrender of a limited number of tradeable instruments in the nature of emission allowances, nor does it include any other standard, limit, regulation, or program to reduce GHG emissions that is not implemented through the issuance and surrender of a limited number of tradeable instruments.

This provision goes on to also state that "cap and trade program" does not include "fleet-wide motor vehicle emission requirements" or other regulation imposing an "average pollution rate" or "lifecycle GHG standard."

Another provision would have amended §116 of the Clean Air Act, 42 U.S.C. §7416, to add a new definition of "standard or limitation respecting control or abatement of air pollution" to include "any provision to cap GHG emissions, require surrender to a state or a political subdivision thereof of emissions allowances or offset credits . . . and require the use of such allowances or credits as a means of establishing compliance with requirements" set by a state or local government.

Analyze these legislative choices, including the amendment to the Clean Air Act. First, where do these provisions ultimately come out on the debate over state and local climate regulatory power under a federal climate bill? Did preemption advocates or state advocates win? Second, fashion policy arguments for and against these provisions, drawing on Chapter 2's materials and the materials above regarding climate federalism.

E.   RESPONDING TO CLIMATE CHANGE

The absence of a comprehensive federal statute on climate change has not left a complete void in federal environmental law relevant to climate change. A 2007

Supreme Court decision, reproduced below, established EPA's authority to regulate GHG emissions under the CAA, and EPA has implemented that authority in several contexts. The federal government also has taken steps to increase energy efficiency and the use of alternative fuels with the goal of reducing GHG emission levels. Other federal laws also may constrain activities that contribute to climate change, including NEPA and the Endangered Species Act (covered in Chapters 4 and 5, respectively). This section addresses efforts to mitigate GHG emissions and adapt to climate change under these and other federal and state laws. It also covers the role of common law litigation in climate change abatement efforts, identifying potential obstacles to successful common law litigation concerning climate change.

1. Regulation Under the Clean Air Act

This section reviews the extent to which EPA is authorized to regulate GHG emissions under the Clean Air Act and what form that regulation has taken or may take.

a. EPA's Authority to Regulate Greenhouse Gas Emissions

Congress has not passed a statute that controls GHG emissions or otherwise deals with climate change mitigation or adaptation. The most likely vehicle for doing so under existing law is the Clean Air Act (CAA). The following materials assess the scope of EPA's authority to tackle climate change under the CAA and highlight some of the issues raised by the agency's climate change–related decisions.

MASSACHUSETTS v. EPA
549 U.S. 497 (2007)

STEVENS, J., delivered the opinion of the Court, in which KENNEDY, SOUTER, GINSBURG, and BREYER, JJ., joined. ROBERTS, C.J., filed a dissenting opinion, in which SCALIA, THOMAS, and ALITO, JJ., joined. SCALIA, J., filed a dissenting opinion, in which ROBERTS, C.J., and THOMAS and ALITO, JJ., joined.

A well-documented rise in global temperatures has coincided with a significant increase in the concentration of carbon dioxide in the atmosphere. Respected scientists believe the two trends are related. For when carbon dioxide is released into the atmosphere, it acts like the ceiling of a greenhouse, trapping solar energy and retarding the escape of reflected heat. It is therefore a species—the most important species—of a "greenhouse gas."

. . . [A] group of States, local governments, and private organizations . . . alleged . . . that the Environmental Protection Agency (EPA) has abdicated its responsibility under the Clean Air Act to regulate the emissions of four greenhouse gases, including carbon dioxide. Specifically, petitioners asked us to answer two questions concerning the meaning of §202(a)(1) of the Act: whether EPA has the statutory authority to regulate greenhouse gas emissions from new motor vehicles; and if so, whether its stated reasons for refusing to do so are consistent with the statute. . . .

I

Section 202(a)(1) of the Clean Air Act, 42 U.S.C. §7521(a)(1), provides:

> The [EPA] Administrator shall by regulation prescribe (and from time to time revise) in accordance with the provisions of this section, standards applicable to the emission of any air pollutant from any class or classes of new motor vehicles or new motor vehicle engines, which in his judgment cause, or contribute to, air pollution which may reasonably be anticipated to endanger public health or welfare. . . .[7]

The Act defines "air pollutant" to include "any air pollution agent or combination of such agents, including any physical, chemical, biological, radioactive . . . substance or matter which is emitted into or otherwise enters the ambient air." §7602(g). "Welfare" is also defined broadly: among other things, it includes "effects on . . . weather . . . and climate." §7602(h).

When Congress enacted these provisions, the study of climate change was in its infancy.[8] In 1959, shortly after the U.S. Weather Bureau began monitoring atmospheric carbon dioxide levels, an observatory in Mauna Loa, Hawaii, recorded a mean level of 316 parts per million. This was well above the highest carbon dioxide concentration—no more than 300 parts per million—revealed in the 420,000-year-old ice-core record.[9] By the time Congress drafted §202(a)(1) in 1970, carbon dioxide levels had reached 325 parts per million.[10]

. . . In 1978, Congress enacted the National Climate Program Act, 92 Stat. 601, which required the President to establish a program to "assist the Nation and the world to understand and respond to natural and man-induced climate processes and their implications," id., §3. President Carter, in turn, asked the National Research Council, the working arm of the National Academy of Sciences, to investigate the subject. The Council's response was unequivocal: "If carbon dioxide continues to increase, the study group finds no reason to doubt that climate changes will result and no reason to believe that these changes will be negligible. . . . A wait-and-see policy may mean waiting until it is too late."

Congress next addressed the issue in 1987, when it enacted the Global Climate Protection Act, note following 15 U.S.C. §2901. Finding that "manmade pollution—

---

7. The 1970 version of §202(a)(1) used the phrase "which endangers the public health or welfare" rather than the more-protective "which may reasonably be anticipated to endanger public health or welfare." Congress amended §202(a)(1) in 1977 to give its approval to the decision in Ethyl Corp. v. EPA, 541 F.2d 1, 25 (C.A.D.C.1976) (en banc), which held that the Clean Air Act "and common sense . . . demand regulatory action to prevent harm, even if the regulator is less than certain that harm is otherwise inevitable."

8. The Council on Environmental Quality had issued a report in 1970 concluding that "[m]an may be changing his weather." Environmental Quality: The First Annual Report 93. Considerable uncertainty remained in those early years, and the issue went largely unmentioned in the congressional debate over the enactment of the Clean Air Act.

9. See Intergovernmental Panel on Climate Change, Climate Change 2001: Synthesis Report, pp. 202-203 (2001). By drilling through thick Antarctic ice sheets and extracting "cores," scientists can examine ice from long ago and extract small samples of ancient air. That air can then be analyzed, yielding estimates of carbon dioxide levels.

10. A more dramatic rise was yet to come: In 2006, carbon dioxide levels reached 382 parts per million, a level thought to exceed the concentration of carbon dioxide in the atmosphere at any point over the past 20-million years. See Intergovernmental Panel on Climate Change, Technical Summary of Working Group I Report 39 (2001).

the release of carbon dioxide, chlorofluorocarbons, methane, and other trace gases into the atmosphere — may be producing a long-term and substantial increase in the average temperature on Earth," Congress directed EPA to propose to Congress a "coordinated national policy on global climate change," and ordered the Secretary of State to work "through the channels of multilateral diplomacy" and coordinate diplomatic efforts to combat global warming. Congress emphasized that "ongoing pollution and deforestation may be contributing now to an irreversible process" and that "[n]ecessary actions must be identified and implemented in time to protect the climate."

Meanwhile, the scientific understanding of climate change progressed. In 1990, the Intergovernmental Panel on Climate Change (IPCC), a multinational scientific body organized under the auspices of the United Nations, . . . concluded that "emissions resulting from human activities are substantially increasing the atmospheric concentrations of . . . greenhouse gases [which] will enhance the greenhouse effect, resulting on average in an additional warming of the Earth's surface."

Responding to the IPCC report, the United Nations convened the "Earth Summit" in 1992 in Rio de Janeiro. The first President Bush attended and signed the United Nations Framework Convention on Climate Change (UNFCCC), a nonbinding agreement among 154 nations to reduce atmospheric concentrations of carbon dioxide and other greenhouse gases for the purpose of "prevent[ing] dangerous anthropogenic [i.e., human-induced] interference with the [Earth's] climate system." [S. Treaty Doc. No. 102-38, Art. 2, p. 5 (1992).] The Senate unanimously ratified the treaty.

Some five years later — after the IPCC issued a second comprehensive report in 1995 concluding that "[t]he balance of evidence suggests there is a discernible human influence on global climate" — the UNFCCC signatories met in Kyoto, Japan, and adopted a protocol that assigned mandatory targets for industrialized nations to reduce greenhouse gas emissions. Because those targets did not apply to developing and heavily polluting nations such as China and India, the Senate unanimously passed a resolution expressing its sense that the United States should not enter into the Kyoto Protocol. President Clinton did not submit the protocol to the Senate for ratification.

II

On October 20, 1999, a group of 19 private organizations filed a rulemaking petition asking EPA to regulate "greenhouse gas emissions from new motor vehicles under §202 of the Clean Air Act." Petitioners maintained that 1998 was the "warmest year on record"; that carbon dioxide, methane, nitrous oxide, and hydrofluorocarbons are "heat trapping greenhouse gases"; that greenhouse gas emissions have significantly accelerated climate change; and that the IPCC's 1995 report warned that "carbon dioxide remains the most important contributor to [man-made] forcing of climate change." The petition further alleged that climate change will have serious adverse effects on human health and the environment. As to EPA's statutory authority, the petition observed that the agency itself had already confirmed that it had the power to regulate carbon dioxide. In 1998, Jonathan Z. Cannon, then EPA's General Counsel, prepared a legal opinion concluding that "CO_2 emissions are within the scope of EPA's authority to regulate," even as he recognized that EPA had so far declined to exercise that authority. Cannon's successor, Gary S. Guzy, reiterated that opinion before a congressional committee just two weeks before the rulemaking petition was filed. . . .

Before the close of the comment period, the White House sought "assistance in identifying the areas in the science of climate change where there are the greatest certainties and uncertainties" from the National Research Council. . . . The result was a 2001 report titled Climate Change: An Analysis of Some Key Questions (NRC Report), which, drawing heavily on the 1995 IPCC report, concluded that "[g]reenhouse gases are accumulating in Earth's atmosphere as a result of human activities, causing surface air temperatures and subsurface ocean temperatures to rise. Temperatures are, in fact, rising."

On September 8, 2003, EPA entered an order denying the rulemaking petition. The agency gave two reasons for its decision: (1) that contrary to the opinions of its former general counsels, the Clean Air Act does not authorize EPA to issue mandatory regulations to address global climate change; and (2) that even if the agency had the authority to set greenhouse gas emission standards, it would be unwise to do so at this time.

In concluding that it lacked statutory authority over greenhouse gases, EPA observed that Congress "was well aware of the global climate change issue when it last comprehensively amended the [Clean Air Act] in 1990," yet it declined to adopt a proposed amendment establishing binding emissions limitations. Congress instead chose to authorize further investigation into climate change. EPA further reasoned that Congress' "specially tailored solutions to global atmospheric issues"—in particular, its 1990 enactment of a comprehensive scheme to regulate pollutants that depleted the ozone layer—counseled against reading the general authorization of §202(a)(1) to confer regulatory authority over greenhouse gases.

EPA reasoned that . . . Congress designed the original Clean Air Act to address local air pollutants rather than a substance that "is fairly consistent in its concentration throughout the world's atmosphere"; declined in 1990 to enact proposed amendments to force EPA to set carbon dioxide emission standards for motor vehicles; and addressed global climate change in other legislation. Because of this political history, and because [of the economic and political repercussions of imposing emission limitations on greenhouse gases], EPA was persuaded that it lacked the power to do so. In essence, EPA concluded that climate change was so important that unless Congress spoke with exacting specificity, it could not have meant the agency to address it.

Having reached that conclusion, EPA believed it followed that greenhouse gases cannot be "air pollutants" within the meaning of the Act. The agency bolstered this conclusion by explaining that if carbon dioxide were an air pollutant, the only feasible method of reducing tailpipe emissions would be to improve fuel economy. But because Congress has already created detailed mandatory fuel economy standards subject to Department of Transportation (DOT) administration, the agency concluded that EPA regulation would either conflict with those standards or be superfluous.

Even assuming that it had authority over greenhouse gases, EPA explained in detail why it would refuse to exercise that authority. The agency began by recognizing that the concentration of greenhouse gases has dramatically increased as a result of human activities, and acknowledged the attendant increase in global surface air temperatures. EPA nevertheless gave controlling importance to the NRC Report's statement that a causal link between the two "'cannot be unequivocally established.'" Given that residual uncertainty, EPA concluded that regulating greenhouse gas emissions would be unwise.

The agency furthermore characterized any EPA regulation of motor-vehicle emissions as a "piecemeal approach" to climate change, and stated that such regulation would conflict with the President's "comprehensive approach" to the problem. That approach involves additional support for technological innovation, the creation of nonregulatory programs to encourage voluntary private-sector reductions in greenhouse gas emissions, and further research on climate change—not actual regulation. According to EPA, unilateral EPA regulation of motor-vehicle greenhouse gas emissions might also hamper the President's ability to persuade key developing countries to reduce greenhouse gas emissions.

[The environmental groups, joined by intervening states and local governments, sought review of EPA's order in the D.C. Circuit. By a 2-1 vote, the panel held that EPA properly exercised its discretion under §202(a)(1) in denying the petition for rulemaking.]

IV

Article III of the Constitution limits federal-court jurisdiction to "Cases" and "Controversies." Those two words confine "the business of federal courts to questions presented in an adversary context and in a form historically viewed as capable of resolution through the judicial process." Flast v. Cohen, 392 U.S. 83, 95 (1968). It is therefore familiar learning that no justiciable "controversy" exists when parties seek adjudication of a political question, when they ask for an advisory opinion, or when the question sought to be adjudicated has been mooted by subsequent developments. This case suffers from none of these defects.

The parties' dispute turns on the proper construction of a congressional statute, a question eminently suitable to resolution in federal court. Congress has moreover authorized this type of challenge to EPA action. See 42 U.S.C. §7607(b)(1). That authorization is of critical importance to the standing inquiry: "Congress has the power to define injuries and articulate chains of causation that will give rise to a case or controversy where none existed before." *Lujan*, 504 U.S., at 580 (Kennedy, J., concurring in part and concurring in judgment). "In exercising this power, however, Congress must at the very least identify the injury it seeks to vindicate and relate the injury to the class of persons entitled to bring suit." Ibid. We will not, therefore, "entertain citizen suits to vindicate the public's nonconcrete interest in the proper administration of the laws." Id., at 581.

EPA maintains that because greenhouse gas emissions inflict widespread harm, the doctrine of standing presents an insuperable jurisdictional obstacle. We do not agree. At bottom, "the gist of the question of standing" is whether petitioners have "such a personal stake in the outcome of the controversy as to assure that concrete adverseness which sharpens the presentation of issues upon which the court so largely depends for illumination." Baker v. Carr, 369 U.S. 186, 204 (1962). . . .

To ensure the proper adversarial presentation, *Lujan* holds that a litigant must demonstrate that it has suffered a concrete and particularized injury that is either actual or imminent, that the injury is fairly traceable to the defendant, and that it is likely that a favorable decision will redress that injury. However, a litigant to whom Congress has "accorded a procedural right to protect his concrete interests,"—here, the right to challenge agency action unlawfully withheld, §7607(b)(1)—"can assert that right without meeting all the normal standards for redressability and immediacy."

When a litigant is vested with a procedural right, that litigant has standing if there is some possibility that the requested relief will prompt the injury-causing party to reconsider the decision that allegedly harmed the litigant. Ibid.; see also Sugar Cane Growers Cooperative of Fla. v. Veneman, 289 F.3d 89, 94-95 (C.A. D.C. 2002) ("A [litigant] who alleges a deprivation of a procedural protection to which he is entitled never has to prove that if he had received the procedure the substantive result would have been altered. All that is necessary is to show that the procedural step was connected to the substantive result").

Only one of the petitioners needs to have standing to permit us to consider the petition for review. We stress here, as did Judge Tatel below, the special position and interest of Massachusetts. It is of considerable relevance that the party seeking review here is a sovereign State and not, as it was in *Lujan*, a private individual.

Well before the creation of the modern administrative state, we recognized that States are not normal litigants for the purposes of invoking federal jurisdiction. As Justice Holmes explained in Georgia v. Tennessee Copper Co., 206 U.S. 230, 237 (1907), a case in which Georgia sought to protect its citizens from air pollution originating outside its borders:

> The case has been argued largely as if it were one between two private parties; but it is not. The very elements that would be relied upon in a suit between fellow-citizens as a ground for equitable relief are wanting here. The State owns very little of the territory alleged to be affected, and the damage to it capable of estimate in money, possibly, at least, is small. This is a suit by a State for an injury to it in its capacity of quasi-sovereign. In that capacity the State has an interest independent of and behind the titles of its citizens, in all the earth and air within its domain. It has the last word as to whether its mountains shall be stripped of their forests and its inhabitants shall breathe pure air.

Just as Georgia's "independent interest . . . in all the earth and air within its domain" supported federal jurisdiction a century ago, so too does Massachusetts' well-founded desire to preserve its sovereign territory today. That Massachusetts does in fact own a great deal of the "territory alleged to be affected" only reinforces the conclusion that its stake in the outcome of this case is sufficiently concrete to warrant the exercise of federal judicial power.

When a State enters the Union, it surrenders certain sovereign prerogatives. . . . See Alfred L. Snapp & Son, Inc. v. Puerto Rico ex rel. Barez, 458 U.S. 592, 607 (1982) ("One helpful indication in determining whether an alleged injury to the health and welfare of its citizens suffices to give the State standing to sue *parens patriae* is whether the injury is one that the State, if it could, would likely attempt to address through its sovereign lawmaking powers.").

These sovereign prerogatives are now lodged in the Federal Government, and Congress has ordered EPA to protect Massachusetts (among others) by prescribing [motor vehicle emission standards under §202(a)(1)]. Congress has moreover recognized a concomitant procedural right to challenge the rejection of its rulemaking petition as arbitrary and capricious. §307(b)(1). Given that procedural right and Massachusetts' stake in protecting its quasi-sovereign interests, the Commonwealth is entitled to special solicitude in our standing analysis.

With that in mind, it is clear that petitioners' submissions as they pertain to Massachusetts have satisfied the most demanding standards of the adversarial process. EPA's steadfast refusal to regulate greenhouse gas emissions presents a risk of harm to

Massachusetts that is both "actual" and "imminent." *Lujan*, 504 U.S., at 560. There is, moreover, a "substantial likelihood that the judicial relief requested" will prompt EPA to take steps to reduce that risk. Duke Power Co. v. Carolina Environmental Study Group, Inc., 438 U.S. 59, 79 (1978). . . .

That [the] climate-change risks [facing Massachusetts] are "widely shared" does not minimize Massachusetts' interest in the outcome of this litigation. See Federal Election Comm'n v. Akins, 524 U.S. 11, 24 (1998) ("[W]here a harm is concrete, though widely shared, the Court has found 'injury in fact.'"). According to petitioners' unchallenged affidavits, global sea levels rose somewhere between 10 and 20 centimeters over the 20th century as a result of global warming. These rising seas have already begun to swallow Massachusetts' coastal land. Because the Commonwealth "owns a substantial portion of the state's coastal property," it has alleged a particularized injury in its capacity as a landowner. The severity of that injury will only increase over the course of the next century. . . . Remediation costs alone, petitioners allege, could run well into the hundreds of millions of dollars. . . .

EPA does not dispute the existence of a causal connection between man-made greenhouse gas emissions and global warming. At a minimum, therefore, EPA's refusal to regulate such emissions "contributes" to Massachusetts' injuries.

EPA nevertheless maintains that its decision not to regulate greenhouse gas emissions from new motor vehicles contributes so insignificantly to petitioners' injuries that the agency cannot be haled into federal court to answer for them. For the same reason, EPA does not believe that any realistic possibility exists that the relief petitioners seek would mitigate global climate change and remedy their injuries. That is especially so because predicted increases in greenhouse gas emissions from developing nations, particularly China and India, are likely to offset any marginal domestic decrease.

But EPA overstates its case. Its argument rests on the erroneous assumption that a small incremental step, because it is incremental, can never be attacked in a federal judicial forum. Yet accepting that premise would doom most challenges to regulatory action. Agencies, like legislatures, do not generally resolve massive problems in one fell regulatory swoop. They instead whittle away at them over time, refining their preferred approach as circumstances change and as they develop a more-nuanced understanding of how best to proceed. That a first step might be tentative does not by itself support the notion that federal courts lack jurisdiction to determine whether that step conforms to law. . . .

. . . Judged by any standard, U.S. motor-vehicle emissions make a meaningful contribution to greenhouse gas concentrations and hence, according to petitioners, to global warming. . . .

While it may be true that regulating motor-vehicle emissions will not by itself reverse global warming, it by no means follows that we lack jurisdiction to decide whether EPA has a duty to take steps to slow or reduce it. See also Larson v. Valente, 456 U.S. 228, 244, n.15 (1982) ("[A] plaintiff satisfies the redressability requirement when he shows that a favorable decision will relieve a discrete injury to himself. He need not show that a favorable decision will relieve his every injury."). . . .

In sum—at least according to petitioners' uncontested affidavits—the rise in sea levels associated with global warming has already harmed and will continue to harm Massachusetts. The risk of catastrophic harm, though remote, is nevertheless real. That risk would be reduced to some extent if petitioners received the relief they seek.

We therefore hold that petitioners have standing to challenge the EPA's denial of their rulemaking petition. . . .

VI

On the merits, the first question is whether §202(a)(1) of the Clean Air Act authorizes EPA to regulate greenhouse gas emissions from new motor vehicles in the event that it forms a "judgment" that such emissions contribute to climate change. We have little trouble concluding that it does. . . . Because EPA believes that Congress did not intend it to regulate substances that contribute to climate change, the agency maintains that carbon dioxide is not an "air pollutant" within the meaning of the provision.

The statutory text forecloses EPA's reading. The Clean Air Act's sweeping definition of "air pollutant" includes "*any* air pollution agent or combination of such agents, including any physical, chemical . . . substance or matter which is emitted into or otherwise enters the ambient air. . . ." §7602(g) (emphasis added). On its face, the definition embraces all airborne compounds of whatever stripe, and underscores that intent through the repeated use of the word "any." Carbon dioxide, methane, nitrous oxide, and hydrofluorocarbons are without a doubt "physical [and] chemical . . . substance [s] which [are] emitted into . . . the ambient air." The statute is unambiguous.[26]

. . . EPA never identifies any action remotely suggesting that Congress meant to curtail its power to treat greenhouse gases as air pollutants. That subsequent Congresses have eschewed enacting binding emissions limitations to combat global warming tells us nothing about what Congress meant when it amended §202(a)(1) in 1970 and 1977. . . .[29]

EPA finally argues that it cannot regulate carbon dioxide emissions from motor vehicles because doing so would require it to tighten mileage standards, a job (according to EPA) that Congress has assigned to DOT. But that DOT sets mileage standards in no way licenses EPA to shirk its environmental responsibilities. EPA has been charged with protecting the public's "health" and "welfare," 42 U.S.C. §7521(a)(1), a statutory obligation wholly independent of DOT's mandate to promote energy efficiency. See Energy Policy and Conservation Act, 42 U.S.C. §6201(5). The two obligations may overlap, but there is no reason to think the two agencies cannot both administer their obligations and yet avoid inconsistency.

---

26. In dissent, Justice Scalia maintains that because greenhouse gases permeate the world's atmosphere rather than a limited area near the earth's surface, EPA's exclusion of greenhouse gases from the category of air pollution "agent[s]" is entitled to deference under [Chevron U.S.A. Inc. v. NRDC, 467 U.S. 837 (1984)]. EPA's distinction, however, finds no support in the text of the statute, which uses the phrase "the ambient air" without distinguishing between atmospheric layers. Moreover, it is a plainly unreasonable reading of a sweeping statutory provision designed to capture "any physical, chemical . . . substance or matter which is emitted into or otherwise enters the ambient air." 42 U.S.C. §7602(g). Justice Scalia does not (and cannot) explain why Congress would define "air pollutant" so carefully and so broadly, yet confer on EPA the authority to narrow that definition whenever expedient by asserting that a particular substance is not an "agent." At any rate, no party to this dispute contests that greenhouse gases both "ente[r] the ambient air" and tend to warm the atmosphere. They are therefore unquestionably "agent[s]" of air pollution.

29. We are moreover puzzled by EPA's roundabout argument that because later Congresses chose to address stratospheric ozone pollution in a specific legislative provision, it somehow follows that greenhouse gases cannot be air pollutants within the meaning of the Clean Air Act.

While the Congresses that drafted §202(a)(1) might not have appreciated the possibility that burning fossil fuels could lead to global warming, they did understand that without regulatory flexibility, changing circumstances and scientific developments would soon render the Clean Air Act obsolete. The broad language of §202(a)(1) reflects an intentional effort to confer the flexibility necessary to forestall such obsolescence. Because greenhouse gases fit well within the Clean Air Act's capacious definition of "air pollutant," we hold that EPA has the statutory authority to regulate the emission of such gases from new motor vehicles.

VII

The alternative basis for EPA's decision—that even if it does have statutory authority to regulate greenhouse gases, it would be unwise to do so at this time—rests on reasoning divorced from the statutory text. While the statute does condition the exercise of EPA's authority on its formation of a "judgment," 42 U.S.C. §7521(a)(1), that judgment must relate to whether an air pollutant "cause[s], or contribute[s] to, air pollution which may reasonably be anticipated to endanger public health or welfare." Put another way, the use of the word "judgment" is not a roving license to ignore the statutory text. It is but a direction to exercise discretion within defined statutory limits.

If EPA makes a finding of endangerment, the Clean Air Act requires the agency to regulate emissions of the deleterious pollutant from new motor vehicles. . . . Under the clear terms of the Clean Air Act, EPA can avoid taking further action only if it determines that greenhouse gases do not contribute to climate change or if it provides some reasonable explanation as to why it cannot or will not exercise its discretion to determine whether they do. To the extent that this constrains agency discretion to pursue other priorities of the Administrator or the President, this is the congressional design.

EPA has refused to comply with this clear statutory command. Instead, it has offered a laundry list of reasons not to regulate. For example, EPA said that a number of voluntary executive branch programs already provide an effective response to the threat of global warming, that regulating greenhouse gases might impair the President's ability to negotiate with "key developing nations" to reduce emissions, and that curtailing motor-vehicle emissions would reflect "an inefficient, piecemeal approach to address the climate change issue."

Although we have neither the expertise nor the authority to evaluate these policy judgments, it is evident they have nothing to do with whether greenhouse gas emissions contribute to climate change. Still less do they amount to a reasoned justification for declining to form a scientific judgment. In particular, while the President has broad authority in foreign affairs, that authority does not extend to the refusal to execute domestic laws. In the Global Climate Protection Act of 1987, Congress authorized the State Department—not EPA—to formulate United States foreign policy with reference to environmental matters relating to climate. See §1103(c), 101 Stat. 1409. EPA has made no showing that it issued the ruling in question here after consultation with the State Department. Congress did direct EPA to consult with other agencies in the formulation of its policies and rules, but the State Department is absent from that list. §1103(b).

Nor can EPA avoid its statutory obligation by noting the uncertainty surrounding various features of climate change and concluding that it would therefore be better not to regulate at this time. If the scientific uncertainty is so profound that it precludes

EPA from making a reasoned judgment as to whether greenhouse gases contribute to global warming, EPA must say so. That EPA would prefer not to regulate greenhouse gases because of some residual uncertainty . . . is irrelevant. The statutory question is whether sufficient information exists to make an endangerment finding.

In short, EPA has offered no reasoned explanation for its refusal to decide whether greenhouse gases cause or contribute to climate change. Its action was therefore "arbitrary, capricious, . . . or otherwise not in accordance with law." We need not and do not reach the question whether on remand EPA must make an endangerment finding, or whether policy concerns can inform EPA's actions in the event that it makes such a finding. We hold only that EPA must ground its reasons for action or inaction in the statute. . . .

Chief Justice ROBERTS with whom Justice SCALIA, Justice THOMAS, and Justice ALITO join, dissenting.

Global warming may be a "crisis," even "the most pressing environmental problem of our time." Indeed, it may ultimately affect nearly everyone on the planet in some potentially adverse way, and it may be that governments have done too little to address it. It is not a problem, however, that has escaped the attention of policymakers in the Executive and Legislative Branches of our Government, who continue to consider regulatory, legislative, and treaty-based means of addressing global climate change.

Apparently dissatisfied with the pace of progress on this issue in the elected branches, petitioners have come to the courts claiming broad-ranging injury, and attempting to tie that injury to the Government's alleged failure to comply with a rather narrow statutory provision. I would reject these challenges as nonjusticiable. . . . This Court's standing jurisprudence . . . recognizes that redress of grievances of the sort at issue here "is the function of Congress and the Chief Executive," not the federal courts. Lujan v. Defenders of Wildlife, 504 U.S. 555, 576 (1992). . . .

The very concept of global warming seems inconsistent with th[e] particularization requirement [of the injury in fact test]. Global warming is a phenomenon "harmful to humanity at large," 415 F.3d, at 60 (Sentelle, J., dissenting in part and concurring in judgment), and the redress petitioners seek is focused no more on them than on the public generally — it is literally to change the atmosphere around the world. . . .

Redressability is even more problematic [than injury in fact]. To the tenuous link between petitioners' alleged injury and the indeterminate fractional domestic emissions at issue here, add the fact that petitioners cannot meaningfully predict what will come of the 80 percent of global greenhouse gas emissions that originate outside the United States. As the Court acknowledges, . . . the domestic emissions at issue here may become an increasingly marginal portion of global emissions, and any decreases produced by petitioners' desired standards are likely to be overwhelmed many times over by emissions increases elsewhere in the world.

Petitioners offer declarations attempting to address this uncertainty, contending that "[i]f the U.S. takes steps to reduce motor vehicle emissions, other countries are very likely to take similar actions regarding their own motor vehicles using technology developed in response to the U.S. program." In other words, do not worry that other countries will contribute far more to global warming than will U.S. automobile emissions; someone is bound to invent something, and places like the People's Republic of China or India will surely require use of the new technology, regardless of cost.

The Court previously has explained that when the existence of an element of standing "depends on the unfettered choices made by independent actors not before the courts and whose exercise of broad and legitimate discretion the courts cannot presume either to control or to predict," a party must present facts supporting an assertion that the actor will proceed in such a manner. *Defenders of Wildlife*, 504 U.S., at 562. The declarations' conclusory (not to say fanciful) statements do not even come close.

No matter, the Court reasons, because any decrease in domestic emissions will "slow the pace of global emissions increases, no matter what happens elsewhere." Every little bit helps, so Massachusetts can sue over any little bit.

The Court's sleight of hand is in failing to link up the different elements of the three-part standing test. What must be likely to be redressed is the particular injury in fact. The injury the Court looks to is the asserted loss of land. The Court contends that regulating domestic motor vehicle emissions will reduce carbon dioxide in the atmosphere, and therefore redress Massachusetts's injury. But even if regulation does reduce emissions—to some indeterminate degree, given events elsewhere in the world—the Court never explains why that makes it likely that the injury in fact—the loss of land—will be redressed. Schoolchildren know that a kingdom might be lost "all for the want of a horseshoe nail," but "likely" redressability is a different matter. The realities make it pure conjecture to suppose that EPA regulation of new automobile emissions will likely prevent the loss of Massachusetts coastal land. . . .

Petitioners' difficulty in demonstrating causation and redressability is not surprising given the evident mismatch between the source of their alleged injury—catastrophic global warming—and the narrow subject matter of the Clean Air Act provision at issue in this suit. The mismatch suggests that petitioners' true goal for this litigation may be more symbolic than anything else. The constitutional role of the courts, however, is to decide concrete cases—not to serve as a convenient forum for policy debates. See Valley Forge Christian College v. Americans United for Separation of Church and State, Inc., 454 U.S. 464, 472 (1982) ("[Standing] tends to assure that the legal questions presented to the court will be resolved, not in the rarified atmosphere of a debating society, but in a concrete factual context conducive to a realistic appreciation of the consequences of judicial action.").

[The Chief Justice referred to *SCRAP*, 412 U.S. 669 (1973), as "the previous high-water mark of diluted standing requirements."] Over time, *SCRAP* became emblematic not of the looseness of Article III standing requirements, but of how utterly manipulable they are if not taken seriously as a matter of judicial self-restraint. *SCRAP* made standing seem a lawyer's game, rather than a fundamental limitation ensuring that courts function as courts and not intrude on the politically accountable branches. Today's decision is *SCRAP* for a new generation.

. . . The good news is that the Court's "special solicitude" for Massachusetts limits the future applicability of the diluted standing requirements applied in this case. The bad news is that the Court's self-professed relaxation of those Article III requirements has caused us to transgress "the proper—and properly limited—role of the courts in a democratic society." [Allen v. Wright, 468 U.S. 737, 750 (1984)] . . .

Justice SCALIA, with whom the Chief Justice, THOMAS, and Justice ALITO join, dissenting. . . .

. . . [T]he statute "condition[s] the exercise of EPA's authority on its formation of a 'judgment.'" There is no dispute that the Administrator has made no such judgment in this case.

The question thus arises: Does anything require the Administrator to make a "judgment" whenever a petition for rulemaking is filed? Without citation of the statute or any other authority, the Court says yes. Why is that so? . . .

. . . The Court . . . with no basis in text or precedent, rejects all of EPA's stated "policy judgments" as not "amount[ing] to a reasoned justification," effectively narrowing the universe of potential reasonable bases to a single one: Judgment can be delayed only if the Administrator concludes that "the scientific uncertainty is [too] profound." The Administrator is precluded from concluding for other reasons "that it would . . . be better not to regulate at this time."[1] Such other reasons—perfectly valid reasons—were set forth in the agency's statement.

When the Administrator makes a judgment whether to regulate greenhouse gases, that judgment must relate to whether they are air pollutants that "cause, or contribute to, air pollution which may reasonably be anticipated to endanger public health or welfare." 42 U.S.C. §7521(a)(1). But the statute says nothing at all about the reasons for which the Administrator may defer making a judgment—the permissible reasons for deciding not to grapple with the issue at the present time. Thus, the various "policy" rationales that the Court criticizes are not "divorced from the statutory text," except in the sense that the statutory text is silent, as texts are often silent about permissible reasons for the exercise of agency discretion. The reasons the EPA gave are surely considerations executive agencies regularly take into account (and ought to take into account) when deciding whether to consider entering a new field: the impact such entry would have on other Executive Branch programs and on foreign policy. There is no basis in law for the Court's imposed limitation. . . .

[Justice Scalia would have deferred to EPA's reasoning that a substance does not qualify as an "air pollutant" "simply because it is a 'physical, chemical, . . . substance or matter which is emitted into or otherwise enters the ambient air.' It must also be an 'air pollution agent.'" He also would have deferred to EPA's view that the Act is directed at air pollution problems that occur primarily at ground level or near the surface of the earth. According to EPA, CO_2 is fairly consistent in concentration throughout the world's atmosphere up to approximately the lower stratosphere.] EPA's conception of "air pollution"—focusing on impurities in the "ambient air" "at ground level or near the surface of the earth"—is perfectly consistent with the natural meaning of that term. . . .

NOTES AND QUESTIONS

1. *Standing.* On what basis did the majority find that Massachusetts satisfied each prong of the constitutional standing test? States may not invoke the "special solicitude" referred to in *Massachusetts* if they assert quasi-sovereign interests. Michigan v. EPA, 581 F.3d 524 (7th Cir. 2009). Cf. North Carolina v. EPA, 587 F.3d 422 (D.C. Cir. 2009) (holding that the state lacked standing to challenge EPA's

[1] The Court's way of putting it is, of course, not quite accurate. The issue is whether it would be better to defer the decision about whether to exercise judgment. This has the effect of deferring regulation but is quite a different determination.

decision to exclude Georgia from the CAA obligation to reduce emissions of ozone precursors because it failed to demonstrate redressability).

Is the case relevant to climate change cases brought by non-state plaintiffs? In Center for Biological Diversity v. United States Interior Dep't, 563 F.3d 466 (D.C. Cir. 2009), the court interpreted *Massachusetts* to create a uniquely expansive set of standing rules for states asserting sovereign interests. The court in Washington Envtl. Council v. Bellon, 732 F.3d 1131 (9th Cir. 2013), *reh'g en banc denied*, 741 F.3d 1075 (9th Cir. 2014), ruled that NGOs lacked standing to support a CAA citizen suit to compel a state agency to regulate GHGs from oil refineries in the state. The NGOs' members alleged recreational, aesthetic, economic, and health injuries linked to climate change. Assuming sufficient injury in fact, the court found no causation or redressability. The plaintiffs' burden on causation was especially high because "there is a natural disjunction between Plaintiffs' localized injuries and the greenhouse effect." Id. at 1143. The causal chain between refinery emissions and localized harm was untenable, given the multitude of independent third parties responsible for climate change. The court distinguished *Massachusetts* not only because the NGOs were not states, but also because the aggregate GHG emissions from U.S. motor vehicles not regulated due to EPA's denial of the petition in *Massachusetts* were much greater than the combined GHG emissions from the five refineries, which made no meaningful contribution to increases in GHG concentrations. Plaintiffs failed to establish redressability absent evidence that regulation of the refineries would reduce the injuries linked to climate change. See also Communities for a Better Env't v. EPA, 748 F.3d 333 (D.C. Cir. 2014), which held that an NGO lacked standing to challenge EPA's refusal to adopt a secondary NAAQS for CO, which it claimed would worsen global warming and displace birds that group members observed for recreational purposes. The group did not show that U.S. CO emissions, at levels allowed by EPA, would worsen warming compared to reduced levels if EPA issued the standard the group sought.

2. *The Merits*. How did the majority respond to each of EPA's justifications for denying the states' petition to regulate under §202(a)(1)? How, if at all, could EPA have justified continued refusal to regulate GHG emissions from motor vehicles on remand? Did the majority improperly ignore, as Justice Scalia charged, the difference between discretion to decide when to make a judgment about whether to regulate GHG emissions and discretion to determine the basis upon which to make such a judgment? Compare WildEarth Guardians v. EPA, 751 F.3d 649 (D.C. Cir. 2014) (holding that EPA properly based denial of petition to regulate GHG emissions from coal mines under CAA §111(b) on limited resources and desire to prioritize by focusing first on source categories with higher GHG emission levels) with Center for Biological Diversity v. EPA, 794 F. Supp. 2d 151 (D.D.C. 2011) (dismissing claim that EPA unreasonably delayed in failing to determine whether GHG emissions from nonroad engines contribute to health endangerment requiring regulation under CAA §213(a)(4), but refusing to dismiss a similar claim concerning GHG emissions from aircraft engines that may be regulated under CAA §231).

State courts also have grappled with whether GHGs qualify as regulated pollutants under state programs implementing the CAA. See, e.g., Longleaf Energy Assocs., LLC v. Friends of Chattahoochee, Inc., 681 S.E.2d 203 (Ga. App. 2009) (holding that CO_2 is not a "regulated [new source review] pollutant" in the CAA's prevention of significant deterioration program).

b. The Endangerment Finding

One year after the decision in *Massachusetts*, EPA responded by publishing an Advanced Notice of Proposed Rulemaking seeking comment on analyses and policy alternatives concerning GHG effects and regulation under the CAA. 73 Fed. Reg. 44,354 (2008). EPA indicated that regulation of GHG emissions from motor vehicles under the CAA might trigger a duty for EPA to regulate smaller stationary sources (including apartment buildings, large homes, schools, and hospitals). But EPA's Administrator, Stephen Johnson, included this statement in the notice:

> I believe the [Notice] demonstrates the [CAA], an outdated law originally enacted to control regional pollutants that cause direct health effects, is ill-suited for the task of regulating global greenhouse gases. Based on the analysis to date, pursuing this course of action would inevitably result in a very complicated, time-consuming and, likely, convoluted set of regulations. These rules would largely pre-empt or overlay existing programs that help control greenhouse gas emissions and would be relatively ineffective at reducing greenhouse gas concentrations given the potentially damaging effect on jobs and the U.S. economy.

Id. at 44,355. The Notice purported not to decide whether GHG emissions from motor vehicles cause or contribute to air pollution which may reasonably be anticipated to endanger public health or welfare for purposes of §202(a)(1). EPA answered that question the next year, after a new administration had taken office.

EPA, ENDANGERMENT AND CAUSE OR CONTRIBUTE FINDINGS FOR GREENHOUSE GASES UNDER SECTION 202(a) OF THE CLEAN AIR ACT; FINAL RULE
74 Fed. Reg. 66,496 (Dec. 15, 2009)

SUMMARY: The Administrator finds that six greenhouse gases taken in combination endanger both the public health and the public welfare of current and future generations. The Administrator also finds that the combined emissions of these greenhouse gases from new motor vehicles and new motor vehicle engines contribute to the greenhouse gas air pollution that endangers public health and welfare under CAA section 202(a). . . .

Pursuant to CAA section 202(a), the Administrator finds that greenhouse gases in the atmosphere may reasonably be anticipated both to endanger public health and to endanger public welfare. Specifically, the Administrator is defining the "air pollution" referred to in CAA section 202(a) to be the mix of six long-lived and directly-emitted greenhouse gases: carbon dioxide (CO_2), methane (CH_4), nitrous oxide (N_2O), hydrofluorocarbons (HFCs), perfluorocarbons (PFCs), and sulfur hexafluoride (SF_6). In this document, these six greenhouse gases are referred to as "well-mixed greenhouse gases." . . .

The Administrator has determined that the body of scientific evidence compellingly supports this finding. The major assessments by the U.S. Global Climate Research Program (USGCRP), the Intergovernmental Panel on Climate Change (IPCC), and the National Research Council (NRC) serve as the primary scientific basis supporting the Administrator's endangerment finding. The Administrator reached her determination by considering both observed and projected effects of greenhouse gases in the atmosphere, their effect on climate, and the public health and welfare risks and impacts associated with such climate change. The Administrator's assessment focused on public health and public welfare impacts within the United States. She also examined the evidence with respect to impacts in other world regions, and she concluded that these impacts strengthen the case for endangerment to public health and welfare because impacts in other world regions can in turn adversely affect the United States.

The Administrator recognizes that human-induced climate change has the potential to be far-reaching and multi-dimensional, and in light of existing knowledge, that not all risks and potential impacts can be quantified or characterized with uniform metrics. There is variety not only in the nature and potential magnitude of risks and impacts, but also in our ability to characterize, quantify and project such impacts into the future. The Administrator is using her judgment, based on existing science, to weigh the threat for each of the identifiable risks, to weigh the potential benefits where relevant, and ultimately to assess whether these risks and effects, when viewed in total, endanger public health or welfare. . . .

Based on the text of CAA section 202(a) and its legislative history, the Administrator interprets the two-part test as follows. . . . First, the Administrator is required to protect public health and welfare, but she is not asked to wait until harm has occurred. EPA must be ready to take regulatory action to prevent harm before it occurs. Section 202(a)(1) requires the Administrator to "anticipate" "danger" to public health or welfare. The Administrator is thus to consider both current and future risks. Second, the Administrator is to exercise judgment by weighing risks, assessing potential harms, and making reasonable projections of future trends and possibilities. It follows that when exercising her judgment the Administrator balances the likelihood and severity of effects. This balance involves a sliding scale; on one end the severity of the effects may be of great concern, but the likelihood low, while on the other end the severity may be less, but the likelihood high. Under either scenario, the Administrator is permitted to find endangerment. If the harm would be catastrophic, the Administrator is permitted to find endangerment even if the likelihood is small.

Third, . . . the Administrator is to consider the cumulative impact of sources of a pollutant in assessing the risks from air pollution, and is not to look only at the risks attributable to a single source or class of sources. Fourth, the Administrator is to consider the risks to all parts of our population, including those who are at greater risk for reasons such as increased susceptibility to adverse health effects. If vulnerable subpopulations are especially at risk, the Administrator is entitled to take that point into account in deciding the question of endangerment. Here too, both likelihood and severity of adverse effects are relevant, including catastrophic scenarios and their probabilities as well as the less severe effects. . . . [V]ulnerable subpopulations face serious health risks as a result of climate change.

In addition, by instructing the Administrator to consider whether emissions of an air pollutant cause or contribute to air pollution, the statute is clear that she need not find that emissions from any one sector or group of sources are the sole or even the major part of an air pollution problem. The use of the term "contribute" clearly indicates a lower threshold than the sole or major cause. Moreover, the statutory language in CAA section 202(a) does not contain a modifier on its use of the term contribute. Unlike other CAA provisions, it does not require "significant" contribution. See, e.g., CAA sections 111(b); 213(a)(2), (4). To be sure, any finding of a "contribution" requires some threshold to be met; a truly trivial or de minimis "contribution" might not count as such. The Administrator therefore has ample discretion in exercising her reasonable judgment in determining whether, under the circumstances presented, the cause or contribute criterion has been met. Congress made it clear that the Administrator is to exercise her judgment in determining contribution, and authorized regulatory controls to address air pollution even if the air pollution problem results from a wide variety of sources. While the endangerment test looks at the entire air pollution problem and the risks it poses, the cause or contribute test is designed to authorize EPA to identify and then address what may well be many different sectors or groups of sources that are each part of—and thus contributing to—the problem. . . .

The Administrator recognizes that the context for this action is unique. There is a very large and comprehensive base of scientific information that has been developed over many years through a global consensus process involving numerous scientists from many countries and representing many disciplines. She also recognizes that there are varying degrees of uncertainty across many of these scientific issues. It is in this context that she is exercising her judgment and applying the statutory framework. . . . [T]his interpretation is based on and supported by the language in CAA section 202(a), its legislative history and case law. . . .

The Administrator finds that emissions of the well-mixed greenhouse gases from new motor vehicles contribute to the air pollution that may reasonably be anticipated to endanger public health and welfare. This contribution finding is for all of the CAA section 202(a) source categories and the Administrator considered emissions from all of these source categories. The relevant mobile sources under CAA section 202 (a)(1) are "any class or classes of new motor vehicles or new motor vehicle engines. . . ." CAA section 202(a)(1). The new motor vehicles and new motor vehicle engines . . . addressed are: Passenger cars, light-duty trucks, motorcycles, buses, and medium and heavy-duty trucks. . . .

NOTES AND QUESTIONS

1. How did the Administrator interpret her task under §202(a)(1)? How did she deal with the uncertainties surrounding the causes and effects of climate change? How did she justify making a finding that a subset of the sources that emit GHGs—the specified kinds of motor vehicles—triggers EPA's regulatory authority under §202(a)(1)?

2. In 2010, EPA denied a series of petitions to reconsider the Endangerment Finding. EPA's Denial of the Petitions to Reconsider the Endangerment and Cause or Contribute Findings for Greenhouse Gases under Section 202(a) of the Clean Air Act, 75 Fed. Reg. 49,556 (Aug. 13, 2010). It summarized its conclusions as follows:

> EPA's analysis of the petitions reveals that the petitioners have provided inadequate and generally unscientific arguments and evidence that the underlying science supporting the Findings is flawed, misinterpreted or inappropriately applied by EPA. . . . The science supporting the Administrator's finding that elevated concentrations of greenhouse gases in the atmosphere may reasonably be anticipated to endanger the public health and welfare of current and future U.S. generations is robust, voluminous, and compelling, and has been strongly affirmed by the recent science assessment of the U.S. National Academy of Sciences. [Id. at 49,556.]

Some members of Congress introduced a resolution that would have disapproved of and nullified the Endangerment Finding, S.J. Res. 26, 111th Cong. (2010), but it did not pass. As indicated in section A above, the court in Coalition for Responsible Regulation v. EPA, 684 F.3d 102 (D.C. Cir. 2012), *aff'd in part, rev'd in part*, 134 S. Ct. 468 (2013), upheld the Endangerment Finding.

c.   EPA Regulation of Greenhouse Gases from Motor Vehicles

Statutory Overview. Efforts to improve fuel efficiency and to reduce air pollutant emissions from mobile sources have a relatively long history. In 1975, Congress enacted the Energy Policy and Conservation Act (EPCA) in response to the 1973-1974 OPEC oil embargo. Congress's announced goal was to "double new car fuel economy by model year 1985" through creation of corporate average fuel economy (CAFE) standards for passenger cars and light trucks. NHTSA, CAFE Overview, Frequently Asked Questions, http://lobby.la.psu.edu/_107th/126_CAFE_Standards_2/Agency_Activities/NHTSA/NHTSA_Cafe_Overview_FAQ.htm. Congress specified that CAFE standards to improve fuel economy must be set at the "maximum feasible level," based on consideration of (1) technological feasibility; (2) economic practicability; (3) effect of other motor vehicle standards of the government on fuel economy; and (4) need of the United States to conserve energy. 49 U.S.C. §32902(a), (f).

Congress amended EPCA by enacting the Energy Independence and Security Act of 2007 (EISA) in order to "require substantial, continuing increases in fuel economy standards." Light-Duty Vehicle Greenhouse Gas Emission Standards and Corporate Average Fuel Economy Standards; Final Rule, 75 Fed. Reg. 25,324, 25,327 (May 7, 2010); 42 U.S.C. §17001 et seq. EISA mandated that the model year (MY) 2011-2020 CAFE standards ensure that the industry-wide average of all new passenger cars and light trucks, combined, be not less than 35 miles per gallon by MY 2020. 49 U.S.C. §32902(b)(2)(A).

Regulatory Efforts. EPA, acting under the CAA, and the Department of Transportation's National Highway Traffic Safety Administration (NHTSA), using its authority under EPCA, have issued three sets of GHG emission standards for different types of motor vehicles, including new cars and light trucks, and medium- and heavy-duty trucks. A fourth set of standards is expected to be proposed in March 2015 and finalized in 2016. A March 2014 Congressional Research Service report summarizes the history of regulatory efforts. McCarthy & Yacobucci, Cars, Trucks, and Climate: EPA Regulation of Greenhouse Gases from Mobile Sources (March 13, 2014) http://www.fas.org/sgp/crs/misc/R40506.pdf. This section briefly reviews these efforts.

Following EPA's issuance of its Endangerment Finding in 2009, EPA and NHTSA issued a joint final rule to reduce GHG emissions and improve fuel economy that applied to MY 2012-2016 cars and light trucks. 75 Fed. Reg. 25,324 (May 7, 2010). The agencies noted that "[f]uel economy gains since 1975 . . . have resulted in saving billions of barrels of oil and avoiding billions of metric tons of CO_2 emissions." 75 Fed. Reg. at 25,327. Yet, despite the relatively long history of CAFE standards, and the progress in reducing emissions they have yielded, mobile sources have been the "fastest-growing" source of U.S. GHGs since 1990. These emissions continue to be a significant source of emissions overall. In 2007, mobile sources emitted 31 percent of all U.S. GHGs. The agencies explained that the rule

> responded to the country's critical need to address global climate change and to reduce oil consumption. EPA is finalizing greenhouse gas emissions standards under the Clean Air Act, and NHTSA is finalizing [CAFE] standards under [EPCA]. These standards apply to passenger cars, light-duty trucks, and medium-duty passenger vehicles, covering model years 2012 through 2016, and represent a harmonized and consistent National Program. Under the National Program, automobile manufacturers will be able to build a single light-duty national fleet that satisfies all requirements under both programs while ensuring that consumers still have a full range of vehicle choices.

Id. The agencies also described the effort as addressing "the urgent and closely intertwined challenges of energy independence and security and global warming. . . . The rules will achieve substantial reductions of GHG emissions and improvements in fuel economy from the light-duty vehicle part of the transportation sector, based on technology that is already being commercially applied in most cases and that can be incorporated at a reasonable cost." Id. at 25,326. With respect to energy independence and security, the agencies explained that "[i]mproving energy security by reducing our dependence on foreign oil has been a national objective since the first oil price shocks in the 1970s. Net petroleum imports now account for approximately 60 percent of U.S. petroleum consumption." Id. at 25,326-25,327.

The agencies also described the link between GHG emission reductions and improved fuel economy:

> The National Program is both needed and possible because the relationship between improving fuel economy and reducing CO_2 tailpipe emissions is a very direct and close one. The amount of those CO_2 emissions is essentially constant per gallon combusted of a given type of fuel. Thus, the more fuel efficient a vehicle is, the less fuel it burns to travel a given distance. The less fuel it burns, the less CO_2 it emits in traveling that distance. While there are emission control technologies that reduce the pollutants (e.g., carbon monoxide) produced by imperfect combustion of fuel by capturing or converting them to other compounds, there is no such technology for CO_2. Further, while some of those pollutants can also be reduced by achieving a more complete combustion of fuel, doing so only increases the tailpipe emissions of CO_2. Thus, there is a single pool of technologies for addressing these twin problems, i.e., those that reduce fuel consumption and thereby reduce CO_2 emissions as well.

Id. at 25,327. EPA and NHTSA estimated that the rule would result in about 960 million metric tons of total CO_2-equivalent emissions reductions and about 1.8 billion barrels of oil savings over the lifetime of vehicles sold in model years (MYs) 2012 through 2016. The combined standards, which become increasingly stringent in each successive model year, are supposed to reduce GHG emissions from the U.S. light-duty fleet for these model years by about 21 percent by 2030 over the level that would have occurred without the rule. Specifically, EPA set national CO_2 emissions standards under §202(a) that require light-duty vehicles to meet an estimated combined average emissions level of 250 grams/mile of CO_2 by MY 2016. NHTSA's standard requires manufacturers to meet an estimated combined average fuel economy level of 34.1 miles per gallon in MY 2016.

In 2012, EPA and NHTSA established GHG emissions for MY 2017-2025 new cars and light trucks. 77 Fed. Reg. 62,624 (Oct. 15, 2012). These regulations are expected to reduce emissions by about 50 percent compared to 2010, and to increase average fuel economy to nearly 50 miles per gallon. McCarthy & Yacobucci, *supra*, at Summary.

For medium- and heavy-duty trucks, EPA and NHTSA have cooperated to set GHG emission standards for MY 2014-MY 2018. 76 Fed. Reg. 57,106 (Sept. 15, 2011). In addition, in February 2014, President Obama directed EPA and NHTSA to develop a second round of standards that will affect these trucks beginning with MY 2019. The agencies are supposed to propose this second round of regulations in March 2015, and to finalize them a year later.[f]

EPA and NHTSA have worked closely with the auto industry in developing regulatory approaches for mobile sources. For example, the agencies adopted the initial joint rule with the support of the industry, which sought and received assurances that it would only have to comply with one set of standards, and not with additional state controls. Section 209 of the CAA, which generally prohibits any state from adopting new vehicle emission standards, authorizes EPA to waive the prohibition for California under certain circumstances. Further, once EPA waives the prohibition for California, other states with air quality that does not meet the CAA's national ambient air quality standards may adopt standards identical to California's. Id. §7507. After initially denying California's petition for a waiver of the §209(a) prohibition to allow it to adopt GHG vehicle emission standards, 73 Fed. Reg. 12,156 (2008), EPA reversed that decision, allowing state enforcement of GHG emission standards for new motor vehicles adopted by the California Air Resources Board in 2004, beginning with the 2009 MY. See California State Motor Vehicle Pollution Control Standards; Notice of Decision Granting a Waiver of Clean Air Act Preemption for California's 2009 and Subsequent Model Year Greenhouse Gas Emission Standards for New Motor Vehicles; Notice, 74 Fed. Reg. 32,744 (July 8, 2009). The auto industry supported the joint EPA-NHTSA rules because California committed to ensure that compliance with the federal standard would be deemed compliance with the state rules. The auto manufacturers agreed not to challenge the joint rule in court and to withdraw litigation against other states that had adopted the California standard. An association of auto dealers challenged the waiver decision, but in Chamber of Commerce of the U.S. v. EPA, 642 F.3d 192 (D.C. Cir. 2011), the court, not reaching the merits, dismissed the challenge on standing and mootness grounds.

While EPA has focused much of its regulatory attention concerning mobile sources on passenger cars, light duty trucks, and medium- and heavy-duty trucks, which account for more than ¾ of all mobile source GHG emissions, EPA has also received several petitions requesting that it set emission standards for a wide variety of other vehicles, including off-road recreational vehicles, marine spark-ignition engines, locomotives, and aircraft. For a review of federal efforts with respect to these sources, see McCarthy & Yacobucci, *supra*, at 10-17, 18.

---

f. White House, Press Office Press Release, Fact Sheet: Opportunity for All: Improving the Fuel Efficiency of American Trucks—Bolstering Energy Security, Cutting Carbon Pollution, Saving Money and Supporting Manufacturing Innovation (Feb. 18, 2014) available at http://www.whitehouse.gov/the-press-office/2014/02/18/fact-sheet-opportunity-all-improving-fuel-efficiency-american-trucks-bol.

d.   Control of Stationary Sources of GHGs

What is the legal impact of EPA's Endangerment Finding and the issuance of the EPA-NHTSA vehicle emission standards for GHGs on other CAA programs? In particular, do these developments set the stage for the adoption of emission standards for stationary sources?

Even before the issuance of either the Endangerment Finding or the EPA-NHTSA rules, EPA issued a rule requiring stationary sources to report their GHG emissions. Mandatory Reporting of Greenhouse Gases, 74 Fed. Reg. 56,260 (Oct. 30, 2009), as amended at 75 Fed. Reg. 57,669 (Sept. 22, 2010). EPA noted that the rule did not reflect a final decisions on whether or how to regulate GHG emissions, but that that the data provided would assist in EPA's assessment of how to address GHG emissions and climate change under the CAA. Eventually, EPA began regulating stationary sources under the CAA, beginning with the Prevention of Significant Deterioration (PSD) permit program, as the following case illustrates.

UTILITY AIR REGULATORY GROUP v. EPA
134 S. Ct. 2427 (2014)

Justice SCALIA announced the judgment of the Court and delivered the opinion of the Court with respect to Parts I and II.

. . . We must decide whether it was permissible for EPA to determine that its motor-vehicle greenhouse-gas regulations automatically triggered permitting requirements under the [Clean Air Act] for stationary sources that emit greenhouse gases.

I. Background

A. STATIONARY-SOURCE PERMITTING

The Clean Air Act regulates pollution-generating emissions from both stationary sources, such as factories and powerplants, and moving sources, such as cars, trucks, and aircraft. This litigation concerns permitting obligations imposed on stationary sources under Titles I and V of the Act. . . .

[The Court described the CAA's PSD permit program.] It is unlawful to construct or modify a "major emitting facility" in "any area to which [the PSD program] applies" without first obtaining a permit. §§7475(a)(1), 7479(2)(C). To qualify for a permit, the facility must not cause or contribute to the violation of any applicable air-quality standard, §7475(a)(3), and it must comply with emissions limitations that reflect the "best available control technology" (or BACT) for "each pollutant subject to regulation under" the Act. §7475(a)(4). The Act defines a "major emitting facility" as any stationary source with the potential to emit 250 tons per year of "any air pollutant" (or 100 tons per year for certain types of sources). §7479(1). It defines "modification" as a physical or operational change that causes the facility to emit more of "any air pollutant." §7411(a)(4).

In addition to the PSD permitting requirements for construction and modification, Title V of the Act makes it unlawful to operate any "major source," wherever located, without a comprehensive operating permit. §7661a(a). . . . The permit must include all "emissions limitations and standards" that apply to the source, as well as associated inspection, monitoring, and reporting requirements. §7661c(a)-(c). Title V defines a "major source" by reference to the Act-wide definition of "major stationary source," which in turn means any stationary source with the potential to emit 100 tons per year of "any air pollutant." §§7661(2)(B), 7602(j).

B. EPA's Greenhouse-Gas Regulations

[In its rulemaking responding to Massachusetts v. EPA, EPA explained that once GHGs are regulated under any part of the CAA, the PSD and Title V permitting requirements would apply to all stationary sources with the potential to emit GHGs in excess of the 100 or 250 tons per year PSD and Title V statutory thresholds. Because GHG emissions tend to be "orders of magnitude greater" than emissions of conventional pollutants, EPA projected that small industrial sources, large office and residential buildings, hotels, large retail establishments, and other small sources not previously regulated under the CAA would be subject to the PSD and Title V programs. The result, EPA said, would be "unprecedented expansion of EPA authority that would have a profound effect on virtually every sector of the economy and touch every household in the land," yet still be "relatively ineffective at reducing greenhouse gas concentrations."

In 2009, EPA issued the Endangerment Finding excerpted at the beginning of section E.2.b of this chapter.] Next, EPA issued its "final decision" regarding the prospect that motor-vehicle greenhouse-gas standards would trigger stationary-source permitting requirements. 75 Fed. Reg. 17004 (2010) (hereinafter Triggering Rule). EPA announced that beginning on the effective date of its greenhouse-gas standards for motor vehicles, stationary sources would be subject to the PSD program and Title V on the basis of their potential to emit greenhouse gases. As expected, EPA in short order promulgated greenhouse-gas emission standards for passenger cars, light-duty trucks, and medium-duty passenger vehicles to take effect on January 2, 2011. 75 Fed. Reg. 25324 (hereinafter Tailpipe Rule).

EPA then announced steps it was taking to "tailor" the PSD program and Title V to greenhouse gases. 75 Fed. Reg. 31514 (hereinafter Tailoring Rule). Those steps were necessary, it said, because the PSD program and Title V were designed to regulate "a relatively small number of large industrial sources," and requiring permits for all sources with greenhouse-gas emissions above the statutory thresholds would radically expand those programs, making them both unadministrable and "unrecognizable to the Congress that designed" them. EPA nonetheless rejected calls to exclude greenhouse gases entirely from those programs. [EPA chose instead to phase in application of the PSD and Title V permit programs by applying them first to sources that emit GHGs in the range of 75,000 to 100,000 tons per year, with possible expansion to sources emitting lower amounts later.

The D.C. Circuit upheld the Endangerment Finding and Tailpipe Rule; held that EPA's interpretation of the PSD permitting requirement as applying to "any regulated air pollutant," including GHGs, was "compelled by the statute"; concluded that PSD permittees must install BACT for GHGs; and held that petitioners lacked Article III standing to challenge the Triggering and Tailoring Rules.]

We granted . . . certiorari but agreed to decide only one question: " 'Whether EPA permissibly determined that its regulation of greenhouse gas emissions from new motor vehicles triggered permitting requirements under the Clean Air Act for stationary sources that emit greenhouse gases.' "

II. Analysis

This litigation presents two distinct challenges to EPA's stance on greenhouse-gas permitting for stationary sources. First, we must decide whether EPA permissibly determined that a source may be subject to the PSD and Title V permitting requirements on the sole basis of the source's potential to emit greenhouse gases. Second, we must decide whether EPA permissibly determined that a source already subject to the PSD program because of its emission of conventional pollutants (an "anyway" source) may be required to limit its greenhouse-gas emissions by employing the "best available control technology" for greenhouse gases. The Solicitor General . . . informs us that "anyway" sources account for roughly 83% of American stationary-source greenhouse-gas emissions, compared to just 3% for the additional, non-"anyway" sources EPA sought to regulate at Steps 2 and 3 of the Tailoring Rule.

We review EPA's interpretations of the Clean Air Act using the standard set forth in Chevron U.S.A. Inc. v. Natural Resources Defense Council, Inc., 467 U.S. 837, 842-843 (1984). . . . The question for a reviewing court is whether . . . the agency has acted reasonably and thus has "stayed within the bounds of its statutory authority." Arlington v. FCC, 133 S. Ct. 1863, 1868 (2013).

A. The PSD and Title V Triggers

We first decide whether EPA permissibly interpreted the statute to provide that a source may be required to obtain a PSD or Title V permit on the sole basis of its potential greenhouse-gas emissions.

1

EPA thought its conclusion that a source's greenhouse-gas emissions may necessitate a PSD or Title V permit followed from the Act's unambiguous language. The Court of Appeals agreed and held that the statute "compelled" EPA's interpretation. We disagree. . . .

The Court of Appeals reasoned by way of a flawed syllogism: Under *Massachusetts*, the general, Act-wide definition of "air pollutant" includes greenhouse gases; the Act requires permits for major emitters of "any air pollutant"; therefore, the Act requires permits for major emitters of greenhouse gases. The conclusion follows from the premises only if the air pollutants referred to in the permit-requiring provisions (the minor premise) are the same air pollutants encompassed by the Act-wide definition as interpreted in *Massachusetts* (the major premise). Yet no one—least of all EPA—endorses that proposition, and it is obviously untenable.

The Act-wide definition says that an air pollutant is "any air pollution agent or combination of such agents, including any physical, chemical, biological, [or] radioactive . . . substance or matter which is emitted into or otherwise enters the ambient air." §7602(g). In *Massachusetts*, the Court held that the Act-wide definition includes greenhouse gases because it is all-encompassing; it "embraces all airborne compounds of whatever stripe." 549 U.S., at 529. But where the term "air pollutant" appears in the

Act's operative provisions, EPA has routinely given it a narrower, context-appropriate meaning.

That is certainly true of the provisions that require PSD and Title V permitting for major emitters of "any air pollutant." Since 1978, EPA's regulations have interpreted "air pollutant" in the PSD permitting trigger as limited to regulated air pollutants—a class much narrower than *Massachusetts'* "all airborne compounds of whatever stripe," 549 U.S., at 529. And since 1993 EPA has informally taken the same position with regard to the Title V permitting trigger, a position the Agency ultimately incorporated into some of the regulations at issue here. Those interpretations were appropriate: It is plain as day that the Act does not envision an elaborate, burdensome permitting process for major emitters of steam, oxygen, or other harmless airborne substances. It takes some cheek for EPA to insist that it cannot possibly give "air pollutant" a reasonable, context-appropriate meaning in the PSD and Title V contexts when it has been doing precisely that for decades.

[The Court identified other instances in which EPA had inferred from context that a generic reference to "air pollutants" under the CAA does not encompass every substance falling within the Act-wide definition. For example, §7411 authorizes EPA to enforce new source performance standards (NSPS) if an existing stationary source undergoes a physical or operational change that increases its emission of "any air pollutant." EPA interprets that provision as limited to air pollutants *for which EPA has promulgated new source performance standards.*]

Massachusetts did not invalidate all these longstanding constructions. That case did not hold that EPA must always regulate greenhouse gases as an "air pollutant" everywhere that term appears in the statute, but only that EPA must "ground its reasons for action *or inaction* in the statute," 549 U.S., at 535 (emphasis added), rather than on "reasoning divorced from the statutory text," id., at 532. . . .

Massachusetts does not strip EPA of authority to exclude greenhouse gases from the class of regulable air pollutants under other parts of the Act where their inclusion would be inconsistent with the statutory scheme. The Act-wide definition to which the Court gave a "sweeping" and "capacious" interpretation is not a command to regulate, but a description of the universe of substances EPA may *consider* regulating under the Act's operative provisions. *Massachusetts* does not foreclose the Agency's use of statutory context to infer that certain of the Act's provisions use "air pollutant" to denote not every conceivable airborne substance, but only those that may sensibly be encompassed within the particular regulatory program. As certain amici felicitously put it, while *Massachusetts* "rejected EPA's categorical contention that greenhouse gases could not be 'air pollutants' for any purposes of the Act," it did not "embrace EPA's current, equally categorical position that greenhouse gases must be air pollutants for all purposes" regardless of the statutory context.[5]

To be sure, Congress's profligate use of "air pollutant" where what is meant is obviously narrower than the Act-wide definition is not conducive to clarity. One ordinarily assumes " 'that identical words used in different parts of the same act are intended to have the same meaning.' " Environmental Defense v. Duke Energy Corp.,

---

5. Our decision in American Elec. Power Co. v. Connecticut, 131 S. Ct. 2527 (2011), does not suggest otherwise. We there held that the Act's authorization for EPA to establish performance standards for powerplant greenhouse-gas emissions displaced any federal-common-law right that might otherwise have existed to seek abatement of those emissions. The authorization to which we referred was that given in the NSPS program of §7411, a part of the Act not at issue here and one that no party in *American Electric Power* argued was ill suited to accommodating greenhouse gases.

549 U.S. 561, 574 (2007). In this respect (as in countless others), the Act is far from a *chef d'oeuvre* of legislative draftsmanship. But we, and EPA, must do our best, bearing in mind the " 'fundamental canon of statutory construction that the words of a statute must be read in their context and with a view to their place in the overall statutory scheme.' " FDA v. Brown & Williamson Tobacco Corp., 529 U.S. 120, 133 (2000). . . . [T]the presumption of consistent usage " 'readily yields' " to context, and a statutory term — even one defined in the statute — "may take on distinct characters from association with distinct statutory objects calling for different implementation strategies." *Duke Energy, supra*, at 574. . . .

In sum, there is no insuperable textual barrier to EPA's interpreting "any air pollutant" in the permitting triggers of PSD and Title V to encompass only pollutants emitted in quantities that enable them to be sensibly regulated at the statutory thresholds, and to exclude those atypical pollutants that, like greenhouse gases, are emitted in such vast quantities that their inclusion would radically transform those programs and render them unworkable as written.[6]

2

Having determined that EPA was mistaken in thinking the Act *compelled* a greenhouse-gas-inclusive interpretation of the PSD and Title V triggers, we next consider the Agency's alternative position that its interpretation was justified as an exercise of its "discretion" to adopt "a reasonable construction of the statute." We conclude that EPA's interpretation is not permissible.

Even under *Chevron*'s deferential framework, . . . an agency interpretation that is "inconsisten[t] with the design and structure of the statute as a whole," University of Tex. Southwestern Medical Center v. Nassar, 133 S. Ct. 2517, 2529 (2013), does not merit deference.

EPA itself has repeatedly acknowledged that applying the PSD and Title V permitting requirements to greenhouse gases would be inconsistent with — in fact, would overthrow — the Act's structure and design. [Among other things,] annual PSD "permit applications would jump from about 800 to nearly 82,000; annual administrative costs would swell from $12 million to over $1.5 billion; and decade-long delays in issuing permits would become common, causing construction projects to grind to a halt nationwide. The picture under Title V was equally bleak. . . . EPA stated that these results would be so "contrary to congressional intent," and would so "severely undermine what Congress sought to accomplish," that they necessitated as much as a 1,000-fold increase in the permitting thresholds set forth in the statute.

Like EPA, we think it beyond reasonable debate that requiring permits for sources based solely on their emission of greenhouse gases at the 100- and 250-tons-per-year levels set forth in the statute would be "incompatible" with "the substance of Congress' regulatory scheme." *Brown & Williamson*, 529 U.S., at 156. [There is] no doubt that the PSD program and Title V are designed to apply to, and cannot

---

6.   During the course of this litigation, several possible limiting constructions for the PSD trigger have been proposed. Judge Kavanaugh argued below that it would be plausible for EPA to read "any air pollutant" in the PSD context as limited to the six NAAQS pollutants. [Others claimed that the relevant pollutants are only those NAAQS pollutants for which the area in question is designated attainment or unclassifiable, or air pollutants with localized effects on air quality.] We do not foreclose EPA or the courts from considering those constructions in the future, but we need not do so today.

rationally be extended beyond, a relative handful of large sources capable of shouldering heavy substantive and procedural burdens. . . .

The fact that EPA's greenhouse-gas-inclusive interpretation of the PSD and Title V triggers would place plainly excessive demands on limited governmental resources is alone a good reason for rejecting it; but that is not the only reason. EPA's interpretation is also unreasonable because it would bring about an enormous and transformative expansion in EPA's regulatory authority without clear congressional authorization. When an agency claims to discover in a long-extant statute an unheralded power to regulate "a significant portion of the American economy," *Brown & Williamson*, 529 U.S.; at 159, we typically greet its announcement with a measure of skepticism. We expect Congress to speak clearly if it wishes to assign to an agency decisions of vast "economic and political significance." Id., at 160; see also Industrial Union Dept., AFL-CIO v. American Petroleum Institute, 448 U.S. 607, 645-646 (1980) (plurality opinion). The power to require permits for the construction and modification of tens of thousands, and the operation of millions, of small sources nationwide falls comfortably within the class of authorizations that we have been reluctant to read into ambiguous statutory text. Moreover, in EPA's assertion of that authority, we confront a singular situation: an agency laying claim to extravagant statutory power over the national economy while at the same time strenuously asserting that the authority claimed would render the statute "unrecognizable to the Congress that designed" it. Since, as we hold above, the statute does not compel EPA's interpretation, it would be patently unreasonable — not to say outrageous — for EPA to insist on seizing expansive power that it admits the statute is not designed to grant.

3

EPA thought that despite the foregoing problems, it could make its interpretation reasonable by adjusting the levels at which a source's greenhouse-gas emissions would oblige it to undergo PSD and Title V permitting. Although the Act, in no uncertain terms, requires permits for sources with the potential to emit more than 100 or 250 tons per year of a relevant pollutant, EPA in its Tailoring Rule wrote a new threshold of 100,000 tons per year for greenhouse gases. . . .

We conclude that EPA's rewriting of the statutory thresholds was impermissible and therefore could not validate the Agency's interpretation of the triggering provisions. An agency has no power to "tailor" legislation to bureaucratic policy goals by rewriting unambiguous statutory terms. . . . It is hard to imagine a statutory term less ambiguous than the precise numerical thresholds at which the Act requires PSD and Title V permitting. When EPA replaced those numbers with others of its own choosing, it went well beyond the "bounds of its statutory authority." *Arlington*, 133 S. Ct., at 1868. . . .

Were we to recognize the authority claimed by EPA in the Tailoring Rule, we would deal a severe blow to the Constitution's separation of powers. . . . The power of executing the laws necessarily includes both authority and responsibility to resolve some questions left open by Congress that arise during the law's administration. But it does not include a power to revise clear statutory terms that turn out not to work in practice.

In the Tailoring Rule, EPA asserts newfound authority to regulate millions of small sources — including retail stores, offices, apartment buildings, shopping centers, schools, and churches — and to decide, on an ongoing basis and without regard for the thresholds prescribed by Congress, how many of those sources to regulate. We are not willing to stand on the dock and wave goodbye as EPA embarks on this multiyear voyage of discovery. We reaffirm the core administrative-law principle that an agency may not rewrite clear statutory terms to suit its own sense of how the statute should operate. EPA therefore lacked authority to "tailor" the Act's unambiguous numerical thresholds to accommodate its greenhouse-gas-inclusive interpretation of the permitting triggers. Instead, the need to rewrite clear provisions of the statute should have alerted EPA that it had taken a wrong interpretive turn. Agencies are not free to "adopt . . . unreasonable interpretations of statutory provisions and then edit other statutory provisions to mitigate the unreasonableness." 2012 WL 6621785, *16 (Kavanaugh, J., dissenting from denial of rehearing en banc). Because the Tailoring Rule cannot save EPA's interpretation of the triggers, that interpretation was impermissible under Chevron.

B. BACT FOR "ANYWAY" SOURCES

. . . We now consider whether EPA reasonably interpreted the Act to require [anyway] sources to comply with "best available control technology" emission standards for greenhouse gases.

1 . . .

Some petitioners urge us to hold that EPA may never require BACT for greenhouse gases—even when a source must undergo PSD review based on its emissions of conventional pollutants—because BACT is fundamentally unsuited to greenhouse-gas regulation. BACT, they say, has traditionally been about end-of-stack controls "such as catalytic converters or particle collectors"; but applying it to greenhouse gases will make it more about regulating energy use, which will enable regulators to control "every aspect of a facility's operation and design," right down to the "light bulbs in the factory cafeteria."

EPA has published a guidance document that lends some credence to petitioners' fears. It states that at least initially, compulsory improvements in energy efficiency will be the "foundation" of greenhouse-gas BACT, with more traditional end-of-stack controls either not used or "added as they become more available." But EPA's guidance also states that BACT analysis should consider options *other than* energy efficiency, such as "carbon capture and storage." EPA argues that carbon capture is reasonably comparable to more traditional, end-of-stack BACT technologies, and petitioners do not dispute that.

Moreover, assuming without deciding that BACT may be used to force some improvements in energy efficiency, there are important limitations on BACT that may work to mitigate petitioners' concerns about "unbounded" regulatory authority. For one, BACT is based on "control technology" for the applicant's "proposed facility," §7475(a)(4); therefore, it has long been held that BACT cannot be used to order a fundamental redesign of the facility. See, e.g., Sierra Club v. EPA, 499 F.3d 653, 654-655 (C.A.7 2007). For another, EPA has long interpreted BACT as required only for pollutants that the source itself emits; accordingly, EPA acknowledges that BACT may not be used to require "reductions in a facility's demand for energy from the electric grid." Finally, EPA's guidance . . . explains that permitting authorities should . . . consider whether a proposed regulatory burden outweighs any reduction in emissions to be achieved, and should concentrate on the facility's equipment that uses the largest amounts of energy.

2

The question before us is whether EPA's decision to require BACT for greenhouse gases emitted by sources otherwise subject to PSD review is, as a general matter, a permissible interpretation of the statute under *Chevron*. We conclude that it is.

The text of the BACT provision is far less open-ended than the text of the PSD and Title V permitting triggers. It states that BACT is required "for each pollutant subject to regulation under this chapter" (i.e., the entire Act), §7475(a)(4), a phrase that—as the D.C. Circuit wrote 35 years ago—"would not seem readily susceptible [of] misinterpretation." *Alabama Power Co. v. Costle*, 636 F.2d 323, 404 (1979). Whereas the dubious breadth of "any air pollutant" in the permitting triggers suggests a role for agency judgment in identifying the subset of pollutants covered by the particular regulatory program at issue, the more specific phrasing of the BACT provision suggests that the necessary judgment has already been made by Congress. The wider statutory context likewise does not suggest that the BACT provision can bear a narrowing construction: There is no indication that the Act elsewhere uses, or that EPA has interpreted, "each pollutant subject to regulation under this chapter" to mean anything other than what it says.

Even if the text were not clear, applying BACT to greenhouse gases is not so disastrously unworkable, and need not result in such a dramatic expansion of agency authority, as to convince us that EPA's interpretation is unreasonable. We are not talking about extending EPA jurisdiction over millions of previously unregulated entities, but about moderately increasing the demands EPA (or a state permitting authority) can make of entities already subject to its regulation. And it is not yet clear that EPA's demands will be of a significantly different character from those traditionally associated with PSD review. In short, the record before us does not establish that the BACT provision as written is incapable of being sensibly applied to greenhouse gases.

We acknowledge the potential for greenhouse-gas BACT to lead to an unreasonable and unanticipated degree of regulation, and our decision should not be taken as an endorsement of all aspects of EPA's current approach, nor as a free rein for any future regulatory application of BACT in this distinct context. Our narrow holding is that nothing in the statute categorically prohibits EPA from interpreting the BACT provision to apply to greenhouse gases emitted by "anyway" sources. . . .

Justice BREYER, with whom Justice GINSBURG, Justice SOTOMAYOR, and Justice KAGAN join, concurring [in Part IIB] and dissenting [from Part IIA]. . . .

These cases take as a given our decision in *Massachusetts* that the Act's general definition of "air pollutant" includes greenhouse gases. One of the questions posed by these cases is whether those gases fall within the scope of the phrase "any air pollutant" as that phrase is used in the more specific provisions of the Act here at issue. The Court's answer is "no." I disagree. . . .

The Tailoring Rule solves the practical problems that would have been caused by the 250 tpy threshold. But what are we to do about the statute's language? The statute specifies a definite number—250, not 100,000—and it says that facilities that are covered by that number must meet the program's requirements. The statute says nothing about agency discretion to change that number . . .

I agree with the Court that the word "any," when used in a statute, does not normally mean "any in the universe." . . . [C]ourts must interpret the word "any," like all other words, in context. As Judge Learned Hand pointed out when interpreting another statute many years ago, "[w]e can best reach the meaning here, as always, by recourse to the underlying purpose, and, with that as a guide, by trying to project upon the specific occasion how we think persons, actuated by such a purpose, would have dealt with it, if it had been presented to them at the time." Borella v. Borden Co., 145 F.2d 63, 64 (C.A.2 1944). The pursuit of that underlying purpose may sometimes require us to "abandon" a "literal interpretation" of a word like "any." . . .

But I do not agree with the Court that the only way to avoid an absurd or otherwise impermissible result in these cases is to create an atextual greenhouse gas exception to the phrase "any air pollutant." After all, the word "any" makes an earlier appearance in the definitional provision, which defines "major emitting facility" to mean "*any* . . . source with the potential to emit two hundred and fifty tons per year or more of any air pollutant." §7479(1) (emphasis added). As a linguistic matter, one can just as easily read an implicit exception for small-scale greenhouse gas emissions into the phrase "any source" as into the phrase "any air pollutant." And given the purposes of the PSD program and the Act as a whole, as well as the specific roles of the different parts of the statutory definition, finding flexibility in "any source" is far more sensible than the Court's route of finding it in "any air pollutant." . . .

From a legal, administrative, and functional perspective—that is, from a perspective that assumes that Congress was not merely trying to arrange words on paper but was seeking to achieve a real-world *purpose*—my way of reading the statute is the more sensible one. For one thing, my reading is consistent with the specific purpose underlying the 250 tpy threshold specified by the statute. The purpose of that number was not to prevent the regulation of dangerous air pollutants that cannot be sensibly regulated at that particular threshold, though that is the effect that the Court's reading gives the threshold. Rather, the purpose was to limit the PSD program's obligations to larger sources while exempting the many small sources whose emissions are low enough that imposing burdensome regulatory requirements on them would be senseless. . . .

An implicit source-related exception would serve this statutory purpose while going no further. The implicit exception that the Court reads into the phrase "any air pollutant," by contrast, goes well beyond the limited congressional objective. Nothing in the statutory text, the legislative history, or common sense suggests that Congress, when it imposed the 250 tpy threshold, was trying to undermine its own deliberate decision to use the broad language "any air pollutant" by removing some substances (rather than some facilities) from the PSD program's coverage. . . .

The Court's decision to read greenhouse gases out of the PSD program drains the Act of its flexibility and chips away at our decision in *Massachusetts*. . . .

Last, but by no means least, a source-related exception advances the Act's overall purpose. . . . The expert agency charged with administering the Act has determined in its Endangerment Finding that greenhouse gases endanger human health and welfare, and so sensible regulation of industrial emissions of those pollutants is at the core of the purpose behind the Act. The broad "no greenhouse gases" exception that the Court reads into the statute unnecessarily undercuts that purpose, while my narrow source-related exception would leave the Agency with the tools it needs to further it. . . .

Justice ALITO, with whom Justice THOMAS joins, concurring in [Parts I and II-A of the majority opinion] and dissenting [from Part II-B].

. . . I believed Massachusetts v. EPA was wrongly decided at the time, and these cases further expose the flaws with that decision. . . .

I do not agree . . . with the Court's conclusion that . . . "anyway sources" . . . must install "best available control technology" (BACT) for greenhouse gases. As is the case with the PSD and Title V thresholds, trying to fit greenhouse gases into the BACT analysis badly distorts the scheme that Congress adopted. . . .

. . . [I]t is curious that the Court, having departed from a literal interpretation of the term "pollutant" in Part II-A, turns on its heels and adopts a literal interpretation in Part II-B. The coverage thresholds at issue in Part II-A apply to any "pollutant." The Act's general definition of this term is broad, and in Massachusetts v. EPA, *supra*, the Court held that this definition covers greenhouse gases. The Court does not disturb that holding, but it nevertheless concludes that, as used in the provision triggering PSD coverage, the term "pollutant" actually means "pollutant, other than a greenhouse gas." . . .

Under the Court's interpretation, a source can emit an unlimited quantity of greenhouse gases without triggering the need for a PSD permit. Why might Congress have wanted to allow this? The most likely explanation is that the PSD permitting process is simply not suited for use in regulating this particular pollutant. And if that is so, it makes little sense to require the installation of BACT for greenhouse gases in those instances in which a source happens to be required to obtain a permit due to the emission of a qualifying quantity of some other pollutant that is regulated under the Act. . . .

The Court's . . . holding that BACT applies to "anyway" sources is [based on] its belief that this can be done without disastrous consequences. Only time will tell whether this hope is well founded, but it seems clear that BACT analysis is fundamentally incompatible with the regulation of greenhouse-gas emissions. . . .

BACT analysis, like the rest of the Clean Air Act, was developed for use in regulating the emission of conventional pollutants and is simply not suited for use with respect to greenhouse gases. I therefore respectfully dissent from Part II-B-2 of the opinion of the Court.

NOTES AND QUESTIONS

1. What were the two issues the Court addressed concerning the application of the PSD and Title V permitting programs to sources emitting GHGs? How did EPA interpret the term "air pollutant" for purposes of §§7479(1) and 7475(a)(4)? Was the majority's interpretation of those provisions in Parts II-A and II-B of the opinion consistent? What did Justice Alito think? How would Justice Breyer have interpreted the permit provisions as they apply to sources not already required to apply for permits as a result of emissions of air pollutants other than GHGs?

2. *The "Deferral Rule."* Center for Biological Diversity v. EPA, 722 F.3d 401 (D.C. Cir. 2013), involved a challenge to EPA's so-called "Deferral Rule," 76 Fed. Reg. 43,490 (July 20, 2011). Under that rule, EPA deferred application of the PSD and Title V permitting programs to stationary sources that emit biogenic CO_2. Biogenic

CO_2 emissions result from the combustion or decomposition of biologically based materials such as landfill waste and forest residue. EPA deferred application of the permitting programs for three years because of uncertainty over the net impact of biogenic sources, which can serve as carbon sinks, on climate change. According to EPA, accounting for the net atmospheric impact of biogenic CO_2 emissions is complex enough to warrant further study. The court vacated the rule, rejecting EPA's reliance on the administrative necessity doctrine. That doctrine, as applied by the D.C. Circuit, requires an agency to adopt the narrowest feasible exemption. EPA rejected a middle-ground approach that would have required biogenic CO_2 sources to obtain permits, but only if they failed to take into account net carbon cycle impacts. The court reasoned that EPA should have explained why it rejected an option that would have reduced emissions from sources exempted from regulation by the Deferral Rule.

3. *Other CAA Provisions and GHGs.* Are the results in *Massachusetts* and *UARG* relevant to EPA's authority and duty to regulate greenhouse gas emissions under §§108 and 109 of the CAA? Could EPA list GHGs as a criteria pollutant under §108(a)(1)? Could an environmental group bring a viable suit to force EPA to list GHGs as a criteria pollutant? See NRDC v. Train, 545 F.2d 320 (2d Cir. 1976), discussed in Chapter 6, section D.1.a. Would it make sense to use the national ambient air quality standards to abate GHG emissions? As Chapter 6 explains, compliance with the NAAQS is measured on a local scale, and the obligations of states and pollution sources often turn on whether the air quality control region in which a source is located has or has not achieved the NAAQS. Reitze, Federal Control of Carbon Dioxide Emissions: What Are the Options?, 36 B.C. Envtl. Aff. L. Rev. 1 (2009), argues that the CAA is a poor vehicle for regulating GHG emissions and reviews other options, including a carbon tax and cap-and-trade systems. Could EPA regulate GHGs as hazardous air pollutants under §112? What finding would EPA have to make to add a GHG to the statutory list of hazardous air pollutants? See §112(a)(2).

The majority opinion in *UARG* refers to possible regulation of GHG emissions under §111's technology-based standards of performance. Does the opinion provide guidance on §111's applicability to GHG-emitting sources? Does it refer to legal or practical obstacles to the adoption of NSPS for GHG-emitting sources? What finding must EPA make to allow it to list and regulate a category of stationary sources? See §111(b)(1)(A). How does this finding compare with the Endangerment Finding that EPA issued for GHG emissions under §202(a)? Would it make sense as a policy matter to regulate GHG emissions under §111 from source categories responsible for a large share of GHG emissions in the United States, such as coal-fired electric utilities?

EPA has issued several proposals to regulate GHG emissions under §111, including proposed NSPS for new electric generating units (EGUs) (79 Fed. Reg. 1430 (Jan. 8 2014)), proposed NSPS for modified and reconstructed EGUs (79 Fed. Reg. 34,960 (June 18, 2014)), and proposed emission guidelines for state regulation of existing EGUs under §111(d) (79 Fed. Reg. 34,830 (June 18, 2014)). EGUs are the largest single U.S. GHG emissions category. If the 50 highest-polluting U.S. power plants were an independent nation, they would be the seventh largest CO_2 emitter in the world. Environment America, America's Dirtiest Power Plants: Their Oversized Contribution to Global Warming and What We Can Do About It 5 (Sept. 2013). Each of EPA's proposals for EGUs raises difficult legal questions. One question is whether EPA may properly define carbon sequestration as the "best system of emission reduction which . . . has been adequately demonstrated" under §111(a)(1), as it has proposed to do for new coal-fired EGUs. Another is whether EPA's regulation of hazardous air pollutants such as mercury from EGUs under §112 bars EPA from requiring state regulation of existing EGUs. See §111(d)(1)(A). A third issue is whether EPA has the authority to issue §111(d) guidelines that entail measures to reduce GHG emissions that extend "beyond the fenceline" of a regulated plant. EPA's §111(d) proposal allows states to meet their GHG emission reduction targets by choosing among several "building blocks," which include not only increasing the efficiency with which power is produced at individual EGUs, but also shifting a greater percentage of the power dispatched within the state from coal to gas-fired units, increasing the extent to which the state's electricity needs are met with renewable or nuclear energy, and reducing demand for electricity.

What would be the economic impacts of EPA's proposals for limiting GHG emissions from EGUs? EPA's proposal for state regulation of existing EGUs would likely produce economic benefits for states with high levels of natural gas production (such as Texas and Oklahoma) and harm coal-producing states. See Center for Strategic and International Studies, Remaking American Power: Preliminary Results (July 24, 2014). One report concluded that the §111(d) proposal's impact on electricity rates "from well-designed CO_2 reduction programs will be modest in the near term, and can be accompanied by long-term benefits in the form of lower electricity bills and positive economic value to state and regional economies." Analysis Group: EPA's Clean-Power Plan: States' Tools for Reducing Costs and Increasing Benefits to Consumers 1 (July 2014).

Is Justice Alito right—given the logistical difficulties in applying the various CAA programs discussed in *UARG* to sources that emit GHGs, is the most rational conclusion that Congress would not have wanted to apply the CAA to GHGs if it had considered that possibility?

2. *Additional Regulation*

The federal, state, and local governments have devised a wide variety of strategies to combat climate change in addition to federal efforts under the Clean Air Act, discussed in the preceding sections. As is the case with much of the material in this chapter, many of these strategies are evolving rapidly, as is their use. This section introduces three such strategies.

a. **Appliance Efficiency**

Like the mobile sources subject to the joint EPA-NHTSA rules discussed in section E.1.c of this chapter, appliances are a major source of energy use (and therefore of GHG emissions). The American Council for an Energy-Efficient Economy (ACEEE) indicates that "American homes use almost 25 percent of the energy consumed in the United States." It suggests that, while there have been significant efficiency gains, many of these gains "are being offset by increases in the number of electronics and appliances in the average home. There are still many large opportunities for improvement, especially in areas such as whole-home performance and systems." ACEEE, http://www.aceee.org/sector/residential; see also E. Shorey & T. Eckman, Appliances and Global Climate Change: Increasing Consumer Participation in Reducing Greenhouse Gases iii (2000) (finding that, because of their substantial electricity consumption, much of it from major home appliances, residences account for about one-fifth of U.S. energy-related GHG emissions).

There has been considerable activity to increase appliance efficiency. For example, Congress has established appliance efficiency standards (or directed relevant agencies to do so) on several occasions, including in the EPCA of 1975, the National Energy Conservation Policy Act of 1978, the National Appliance Energy Conservation Act of 1987 and 1988 Amendments to that Act, the Energy Policy Act of 1992, the Energy Policy Act of 2005, and EISA of 2007. The American Energy Manufacturing Technical Corrections Act, Pub. L. No. 112-210, 126 Stat. 1514 (2012), updated the efficiency standards that apply to appliances such as walk-in freezers, air conditioners, and water heaters.

The Department of Energy (DOE) has completed several rulemakings to establish appliance efficiency standards and has others on tap. Table 12-2 summarizes DOE's rulemaking schedule.

TABLE 12-2
DOE Final Rulemaking Schedule Through January 2013

Product	Final Rule Due Date	Effective Date
Incandescent reflector lamps	June 2009	2012
Linear fluorescent lamps	June 2009	2012
Commercial boilers	July 2009	2012
Refrigerated vending machines	August 2009	2012
Commercial clothes washers	January 2010	2013
BR exempted reflector lamps	January 2010	2013
Small electric motors	February 2010	2013
Direct heating equipment	March 2010	2013
Pool heaters	March 2010	2013
Residential water heaters	March 2010	2013
High-intensity discharge lamps	June 2010	N/A
Residential refrigerators and freezers	December 2010	2013
Microwave ovens—standby power	March 2011	2014
Residential furnaces	May 2011	2015
Fluorescent lamp ballasts	June 2011	2014
Residential clothes dryers	June 2011	2014
Room A/C	June 2011	2014
Residential central A/C and heat pumps	June 2011	2014
Battery chargers	July 2011	2014
External power supplies	July 2011	2014
Residential clothes washers	December 2011	2015
Metal halide lamp fixtures	January 2012	2015
Walk-in coolers and freezers	January 2012	2015
Commercial reach-in refrigerators and freezers	January 2013	2016
Liquid immersed transformers	January 2013	2016
Low-voltage dry-type distribution transformers	January 2013	2016
Residential furnace fans	January 2013	2016

Source: Neubauer et al., Ka-BOOM! The Power of Appliance Standards: Opportunities for New Federal Appliance and Equipment Standards, Executive Summary, http://www.appliance-standards.org/sites/default/files/Ka-BOOM%21%20Executive%20Summary_0.pdf.

The Federal Trade Commission (FTC) administers an "EnergyGuide labeling program" to provide consumers with information on the energy use of appliances. These labels estimate actual energy consumption, provide information as to whether the level of consumption is above or below average for the type of product, and project the estimated yearly operating cost of the product based on the national average cost of electricity. EPA & DOE, Learn More About EnergyGuide, http://www.energystar.gov/index.cfm?c=appliances.pr_energy_guide. The following appliances have EnergyGuide labels: clothes washers, dishwashers, refrigerators, freezers, water heaters, window air conditioners, central air conditioners, furnaces, boilers, heat pumps, and pool heaters. FTC, Consumer Information: Shopping for Home Appliances? Use the EnergyGuide Label, http://www.consumer.ftc.gov/articles/0072-shopping-home-appliances-use-energyguide-label.

Section 137 of the Energy Policy Act of 2005 required the FTC to conduct a rulemaking to examine the effectiveness of current energy efficiency labeling requirements for consumer products covered by EPCA. The FTC's regulations require an operating cost label for most appliances, including refrigerators, refrigerator-freezers, freezers, clothes washers, dishwashers, room air conditioners, and water heaters. Further, the rule requires that the label be affixed to the product in the form of an adhesive label in order to increase the likelihood that the label will remain on the product after purchase and "be available to aid consumers in their equipment purchasing decisions and use of the product." 72 Fed. Reg. 49,948, 49, 956 (Aug. 29, 2007) (codified at 16 C.F.R. Part 305).

Perhaps the best-known labeling program is Energy Star. EPA describes the purposes of Energy Star as: (1) making it easy for consumers to identify and purchase energy-efficient products; and (2) reducing GHG emissions caused by the inefficient use of energy. Energy Star, How a Product Earns the Energy Star Label, http://www.energystar.gov/index.cfm?c=products.pr_how_earn. EPA has developed Energy Star labels for many different kinds of common appliances, such as air conditioners (responsible for five percent of the electricity use in the United States annually) and refrigerators (responsible for eight percent of U.S. residential energy use). ACEEE, http://aceee.org/topics/refrigeration. According to DOE, "[r]esults are already adding up. In 2009, Americans, with the help of Energy Star, saved enough energy to avoid greenhouse gas emissions equivalent to those from 30 million cars—all while saving $17 billion on utility bills." Doe, Energy Star, http://www.energy.gov/energyefficiency/energystar.htm. In May 2011, EPA announced a "Most Efficient" recognition for Energy Star-certified products in seven appliance categories (clothes washers, air-source heat pumps, central air conditioners, furnaces, geothermal heat pumps, refrigerator-freezers, and televisions) that demonstrate "truly exceptional" efficiency.[g]

Many states have also adopted appliance efficiency standards, as Figure 12-9 reflects.

---

g. Ann Bailey, Director, EPA Office of Air and Radiation ENERGY STAR Product Labeling, letter to Energy Star Stakeholders (May 5, 2011). In May 2014, EPA added clothes dryers to the Energy Star label. EPA Press Release, EPA Adds Clothes Dryers to Energy Star Program, Increasing Energy Efficiency of New Appliances (May 2014), http://yosemite.epa.gov/opa/admpress.nsf/596e17d7cac720848525781f0043629e/a20ed0eb81ca520d85257ce50060497d!OpenDocument.

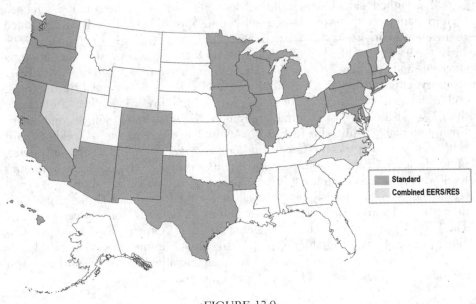

FIGURE 12-9
State Appliance Efficiency Standards
EERS policy approaches by state (as of April 2014).
http://www.aceee.org/files/pdf/policy-brief/eers-04-2014.pdf

b. Building Efficiency

Buildings also are a substantial contributor to GHG emissions. A 2009 EPA report indicates that in 2008 buildings in the United States contributed 38.9 percent of the nation's total CO_2 emissions, including 20.8 percent from the residential sector and 18.0 percent from the commercial sector. Buildings accounted for 74 percent of total U.S. electricity consumption in 2009. Buildings Energy Data Book (March 2012), available at http://buildingsdatabook.eren.doe.gov/docs/xls_pdf/6.1.1.pdf. The average household spends at least $2,000 a year on energy bills— over half of which goes to heating and cooling. EPA, Buildings and Their Impact on the Environment: A Statistical Summary (2009).

"Green building" has become increasingly popular in recent years as a strategy to reduce emissions, energy use, and costs. EPA has defined "green building" as "the practice of creating and using healthier and more resource-efficient models of construction, renovation, operation, maintenance and demolition." EPA, Green Building, http://www.epa.gov/greenbuilding. The federal government and many states have adopted requirements that fall under the umbrella of "green building," and many municipalities have done so as well. There are at least seven "balls" to keep one's eye on in thinking about green building: siting, design, construction, operation, maintenance, renovation, and deconstruction. EPA, Green Building, Basic Information, http://www.epa.gov/greenbuilding/pubs/about.htm. For a treatise-length treatment of green building issues, see The Law of Green Buildings: Regulatory and Legal Issues in Design, Construction, Operations, and Financing (C. Howe & M. Gerrard eds., 2010).

The United States Green Building Council (GBC), launched in 1993, has been an important force in developing green-building approaches. The GBC inaugurated its Leadership in Energy and Environmental Design (LEED) program in 1998. LEED "is a green building certification program that recognizes best-in-class building strategies and practices." USGBC, LEED, http://www.usgbc.org/leed. The LEED rating systems are designed for rating new and existing commercial, institutional, and residential buildings."[h] The rating system has five categories: "Sustainable Sites, Water Efficiency, Energy and Atmosphere, Materials and Resources, and Indoor Environmental Quality." Id. LEED is a "point-based system where buildings earn credits for satisfying specific Green Building criteria. The number of points determines the level of certification." Levels include Certified, Silver, Gold, and Platinum. Kaplow, Does a Green Building Need a Green Lease?, 38 U. Balt. L. Rev. 375, 390 (2009). For a review of developing case law under the federal LEED program, which the authors refer to as "LEEDigation," see Ditfurth & Sakai, Is Going Green Worth It? The Legal Complexities and Challenges to Building "Green" (Environmental Liability, Enforcement & Penalties Reporter, Argent Communications, June 2011).

The federal government has paid considerable attention to "greening" federal and other buildings. Some of the key federal milestones include:

- The Energy Policy Act of 2005 directs the Secretary of Energy to establish federal building energy efficiency performance standards.
- Nineteen federal agencies signed a Federal Leadership in High Performance and Sustainable Buildings Memorandum of Understanding at a White House Summit (2006). http://www.wbdg.org/pdfs/sustainable_mou.pdf.
- An executive order issued by President Bush, Strengthening Federal Environmental, Energy, and Transportation Management, includes federal goals for sustainable design and high-performance buildings. Exec. Order No. 13,423, 72 Fed. Reg. 3919 (Jan. 24, 2007).
- EISA establishes new energy-related requirements and standards for federal buildings. Title IV establishes new energy reduction goals for federal facilities, using 2003 as a baseline, rising from 2 percent as of 2006 to 30 percent by 2015. 42 U.S.C. §8253(a)(1).
- In February 2011, President Obama announced a Better Building Initiative, setting a goal of achieving a 20 percent improvement in energy efficiency by 2020. White House Fact Sheet on Better Building Initiative, February 2011.

The Federal Commitment to Green Building: Experiences and Expectations, a report of the Office of the Federal Environmental Executive, provides a history of federal involvement with green building. Office of the Federal Environmental Executive, The Federal Commitment to Green Building: Experiences and Expectations, available at http://ofee.gov/Resources/Guidance_reports/Guidance_reports_archives/fgb_report.pdf.

Most states have now enacted green building legislation, as have many municipalities. Many of these are based on LEED standards. Some state laws require state buildings to meet "green standards," but do not require the same of private developers. One assessment inventories 137 municipal ordinances that contain green building

---

h. USGBC, LEED Reference Guide for Green Building Operations & Maintenance xii (2009), http://www.gbci.org/Libraries/Credential_Exam_References/LEED-for-Operations-and-Maintenance-Reference-Guide-Introduction.sflb.ashx.

standards for public buildings and 61 ordinances that establish standards for private construction. Sussman, Municipal Green Building Ordinances in the U.S. (Columbia Law School, Center for Climate Change Law, Jan. 2010). Austin, Texas, is credited with introducing the first local "green building" program in 1992. Municipalities have become increasingly sophisticated in developing ordinances. Ordinances cover different types of buildings and tailor requirements depending on different features of the building. For example, municipalities treat different kinds of public buildings differently (e.g., some treat public garages differently from public buildings) and the same is true for private construction (e.g., many treat commercial and residential construction differently). Most ordinances limit their coverage to buildings above a certain size and/or projects over a certain cost. About half of the ordinances limit green building requirements to new construction and "major renovations," typically defined as a renovation that alters or adds more than 50 percent of the gross floor area of a building. Sussman, *supra*.

Several of the "regulatory design" issues we explore elsewhere in the book are present in efforts to "green" buildings. For example, most ordinances include a provision that creates some flexibility in the regulatory scheme by allowing owners to seek an exemption from green building requirements for cost-based reasons (e.g., financial hardship or cost-effectiveness) and/or infeasibility (e.g., required green building materials are not available). Similarly, by drawing lines between different types of buildings (type of use, identity of ownership, size, etc.), the regulatory schemes raise jurisdictional boundaries questions about where these lines should be drawn, just as the regulatory requirements discussed in our coverage of the CAA, the CWA, RCRA and other statutes raise jurisdictional boundaries issues.

c. Renewable Portfolio Standards

Renewable portfolio standards (RPSs) are a mechanism that has been used to shift energy supply from carbon-intensive sources, in this case to renewable sources of energy. In addition to improving energy efficiency (see, e.g., subsections a and b above), increasing use of renewable energy is one of the strategies to reduce GHG emissions.

EPA defines an RPS as a requirement that "electric utilities and other retail electric providers . . . supply a specified minimum amount of customer load with electricity from eligible renewable energy sources." EPA, Renewable Portfolio Standards, http://www.epa.gov/agstar/tools/funding/renewable.html.

The goal of an RPS is to "create[] market demand for renewable and clean energy supplies." Id. Proponents of RPSs have identified a wide range of possible benefits, including the following:

- Environmental improvement (e.g., avoided air pollution, global climate change mitigation, waste reduction, habitat preservation, conservation of valuable natural resources).
- Increased diversity and security of energy supply.
- Lower natural gas prices due to displacement of some gas-fired generation, or a more efficient use of natural gas due to significantly increased fuel conversion efficiencies.
- Reduced volatility of power prices, given stable or non-existent fuel costs for renewables. . . .

- Local economic development resulting from new jobs, taxes, and revenue associated with new renewable capacity.
- Achieves policy objectives efficiently and at a relatively modest cost (ratepayer impacts range from less than 1 percent increases to 0.5 percent savings).
- Spreads compliance costs among all customers.
- Minimizes the need for ongoing government intervention.
- Functions in both regulated and unregulated state electricity markets.
- Provides a clear and long-term target for renewable energy generation that can increase investors' and developers' confidence in the prospects for renewable energy. [EPA, Renewable Portfolio Standards Fact Sheet (2008), available at http://archive.today/58klg.]

While EPA has touted these benefits of RPSs, to date no national RPS has attracted sufficient congressional support to become law. Professor Davies notes that "[f]or more than a decade, debate over a national renewable energy requirement has been mired in congressional deadlock." He reports that more than 25 proposals for an RPS have been introduced in Congress, but none has passed muster in both houses. Davies, Power Forward: The Argument for a National RPS, 42 Conn. L. Rev. 1339 (2010).

States have increasingly ventured into the RPS arena. As of 2012, 29 states, the District of Columbia, and two territories have RPSs, while 8 other states and two territories have established renewable portfolio goals. EPA, Renewable Portfolio Standards, http://www.epa.gov/agstar/tools/funding/renewable.html. Figure 12-10 shows the RPS each state has set and the target date for achieving it.

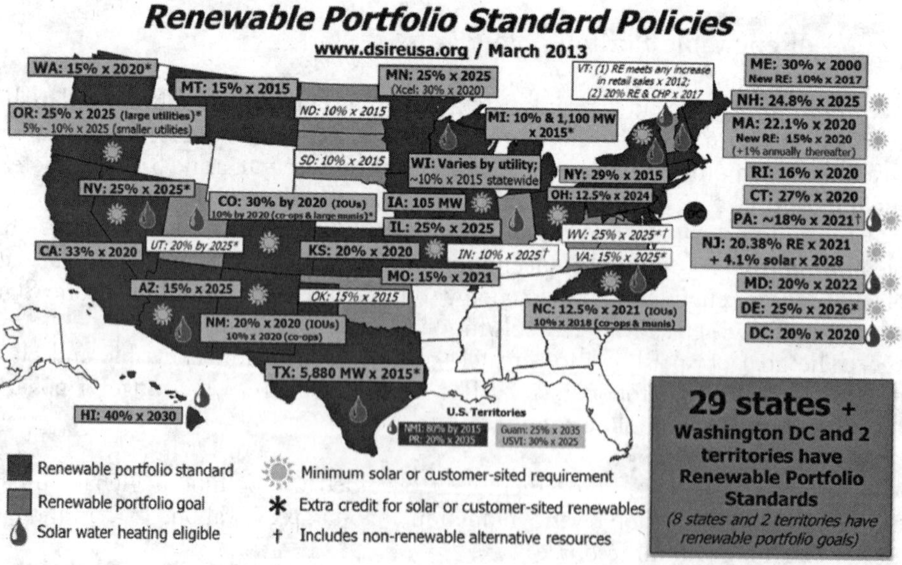

FIGURE 12-10
Renewable Portfolio Standards from Database of State Incentives for Renewable Efficiency (2013) available at http://www.dsireusa.org/documents/summarymaps/RPS_map.pdf

States have taken very different approaches in adopting RPSs in setting goals or targets, defining renewable energy, and establishing timing for meeting goals. As EPA puts it,

> [t]remendous diversity exists among these states with respect to the minimum requirements of renewable energy, implementation timing, and eligible technologies and resources. . . . States have tailored their RPS requirements to satisfy particular policy objectives, electricity market characteristics, and renewable resource potential. Consequently, there is wide variation in RPS rules from state to state with regard to the minimum requirement of renewable energy, implementation timing, eligible technologies and resources, and other policy design details. [EPA, Renewable Portfolio Standards Fact Sheet, *supra*.]

What has been the effect of these efforts to promote use of renewable sources of energy? Renewable energy provided about 13 percent of U.S. total energy needs in 2013. Energy Information Administration, Energy in Brief, http://www.eia.gov/energy_in_brief/article/renewable_electricity.cfm. In 2013, electricity generated by renewable sources came from the following types of renewable energy: hydroelectric power (52 percent), wind (32 percent), biomass wood (8 percent), biomass waste (4 percent), geothermal (3 percent), and solar (2 percent). Id. The amount of renewable energy produced and its percentage of the total energy supply are expected to increase significantly in the future (the latter to 16 percent by 2040). Energy Information Administration, http://www.eia.gov/forecasts/aeo/er/early_elecgen.cfm.

NOTE ON FEDERALISM OBSTACLES

One of the distinguishing features of several of the GHG emission reduction regulatory regimes discussed in this section is that activity is occurring at multiple levels of government. Given the extensive level of state activity, as reflected by the prevalence of state RPSs and in other areas such as those summarized above, it is not surprising that there have been challenges to these activities grounded in constitutionally based federalism principles.

One issue that has received some attention, in the context of regulation of motor vehicles, appliances, and building standards, involves federal preemption. In Metro. Taxicab Bd. of Trade v. City of New York, 615 F.3d 152, 154, 155 (2d Cir. 2010), the court held that federal law (EPCA) preempted New York City's Taxicab & Limousine Commission regulations that "effectively shifted fuel costs from drivers of fleet taxies to fleet owners to incentive the use of hybrid-engine and fuel-efficient vehicles." The goal of the regulation was to require fleet owners, who make vehicle purchasing decisions, to internalize fuel costs by allowing fleet owners to charge more for leases of fuel efficient cars than for non–fuel efficient vehicles. Various fleet owners challenged the regulation because the new lease rates would materially reduce their profits. The court held that EPCA preempted the regulations because the regulations related to fuel economy and therefore "plainly f[e]ll within the scope of the EPCA preemption provision." Id. at 158. In Association of Taxicab Operators v. City of Dallas, 760 F. Supp. 2d 693 (N.D. Tex. 2010), *aff'd*, 720 F.3d 534 (5th Cir. 2013), the court distinguished *Metro. Taxicab Bd.*, holding that the CAA did not preempt a Dallas ordinance that granted "head of the line" privileges at Love Field airport to taxicabs designated as "dedicated compressed natural gas (CNG) vehicles" in an effort to incentivize use of these low-emissions vehicles. The court held that the Dallas ordinance was not a "standard" relating to the control of emissions for purposes of CAA §209 because the ordinance did not force cab drivers to switch to CNG vehicles.

Preemption has also been raised in challenges to green building ordinances and to regulations imposing obligations for appliances. Compare Air Conditioning, Heating & Refrigeration Inst. v. City of Albuquerque, 835 F. Supp. 2d 1133 (D.N.M. 2010) (holding that provisions of Albuquerque's municipal energy code intended to promote "green building" are preempted by federal law) with Air Conditioning & Refrigeration Inst. v. Energy Res. Conservation & Dev. Comm'n, 410 F.3d 492 (9th Cir. Cal. 2005) (rejecting a series of preemption claims concerning California regulations imposing disclosure and other obligations for appliances sold in the state). For in-depth treatment of preemption concerning green building ordinances, see The Law of Green Buildings, *supra*. Gerrard, Federalism Obstacles to Advancing Renewable Energy, N.Y. L.J. (May 8, 2014), surveys other federalism-related issues that have arisen to date, including dormant Commerce Clause claims and claims of impermissible extraterritorial regulation.

In the Energy Policy Act of 2005 and EISA, Congress established a national renewable fuel standard program to combat climate change. See CAA §211(*o*); National Petrochemical & Refiners Ass'n v. EPA, 630 F.3d 145 (D.C. Cir. 2010). Rocky Mountain Farmers Union v. Corey, 730 F.3d 1070 (9th Cir. 2013), *reh'g en banc denied*, 740 F.3d 507 (9th Cir. 2014), excerpted as a principal case in section F of Chapter 2, held that a low carbon fuel standard adopted pursuant to the state's Global Warming Solutions Act of 2006, Cal. Health & Saf. Code §38501, did not discriminate against interstate commerce so as to trigger the dormant Commerce Clause's virtually per se rule of invalidity and did not amount to impermissible extraterritorial regulation. It did not decide whether the standard violated the dormant Commerce Clause under the balancing test of Pike v. Bruce Church, Inc., 397 U.S. 137 (1970), or was preempted by §211(*o*). Minnesota's Next Generation Energy Act was rejected on dormant Commerce Clause grounds in North Dakota v. Heydinger, 2014 WL 1612331 (D. Minn. 2014). Minnesota law sought to preclude or discourage an increase in GHG emissions from its power sector, but the court held that in trying to address the risk that compensatory energy would be imported from other jurisdictions (a form of "leakage" discussed *supra* in section D of this chapter), Minnesota was engaging in unconstitutional extraterritorial regulation of transactions in other states. The court distinguished *Rocky Mountain* in substantial part by contrasting tangible fuels with the "boundary-less nature of the energy grid."

3. Adaptation Risks and Responsive Strategies

Another approach to dealing with the risks posed by climate change involves adaptation. Adaptation is often contrasted with mitigation. Whereas mitigation involves taking steps to reduce the degree of climate change by reducing or eliminating the activities that contribute to it, adaptation involves preparing for the adverse effects of climate change so that they are not as damaging to humans, other species, or the environment. For many years, some of those concerned about climate change were reluctant to focus on adaptation strategies, in part because of the concern that doing so would divert attention from efforts to mitigate or reduce GHG emissions.

But as the consequences of a changing environment have become clearer, the need to adapt to climate change appears increasingly inescapable, regardless of the nature and scope of mitigation efforts. As the IPCC concluded, "[t]here is high confidence that neither adaptation nor mitigation alone can avoid all climate change impacts; however, they can complement each other and together can significantly reduce the risks of climate change." Synthesis Report of the IPCC Fourth Assessment Report, The Summary for Policymakers (2007), http://www.ipcc.ch/publications_and_data/ar4/syr/en/spms5.html. In a 2011 report, the National Research Council highlighted the need for both as well:

> Aggressive emissions reductions would reduce the need for adaptation, but not eliminate it. Climate change is already happening, and additional changes can be expected for all plausible scenarios of future greenhouse gas emissions. Prudent risk management demands advanced planning to deal with possible adverse outcomes—known and unknown—by increasing the nation's resilience to both gradual changes and the possibility of abrupt disaster events.

Committee on America's Climate Choices, National Research Council, America's Climate Choices 3 (The National Academies Press 2011). See also U.S. Global Change Research Program, The Third National Climate Assessment: Climate Change Impact in the United States 5 (2014) (noting that "both [mitigation and adaptation] response activities are necessary to limit the magnitude and impacts of global climate change on the United States.")

This section provides a brief overview of the concept of adaptation. It also summarizes some of the adaptation efforts to date. There is considerable ferment at all levels of government, and in the private and public NGO sectors, to improve understanding of adaptation challenges and to respond. As the U.S. Global Change Research Program noted in its 2014 report, "the implementation of adaptive actions is still nascent." Id. at 6. The "law" of climate change adaptation is very much still emerging as well. For more in-depth review of the legal issues, see The Law of Adaptation to Climate Change (M. Gerrard & K. Kuh eds., ABA 2012); Markell & Ruhl, An Empirical Assessment of Climate Change in the Courts: A New Jurisprudence or Business as Usual?, 64 Fla. L. Rev. 15 (2012).

As indicated above, adaptation involves adjusting, or adapting, to changes in climate. A more eloquent definition is that adaptation is an "adjustment in natural or human systems in response to actual or expected climatic stimuli or their effects, which moderates harm or exploits beneficial opportunities." Intergovernmental Panel on Climate Change, Glossary, http://www.ipcc.ch/publications_and_data/ar4/wg2/en/annexessglossary-a-d.html.

Some changes in climate may be beneficial, at least for certain components of society in limited locales for limited periods of time. Professor Jason Johnston, for example, suggests that likely changes in climate will lead to "increased agricultural productivity, reduced deaths and disease due to cold weather, and increased value from warm weather recreational pursuits." Johnston, Climate Change Confusion and the Supreme Court: The Misguided Regulation of Greenhouse Gas Emissions under the Clean Air Act, 84 Notre Dame L. Rev. 1 (2008). One study predicts a four percent increase in annual agricultural profits within the United States. Dechenes & Greenstone, The Economic Impacts of Climate Change, 97 The Am. Econ. Rev. 354 (2007), available at http://papers.ssrn.com/sol3/papers.cfm?abstract_id=564722.

These beneficial effects, however, are likely to be dwarfed by projected changes in climate that will raise significant concerns for the long-term future well-being of humans and other species and that therefore will motivate efforts to adapt to such changes. The United Nations Framework Convention on Climate Change, analyzed in section F of this chapter, indicates that climate change is likely to "increas[e] risks to human health, inundat[e] low-lying areas, chang[e] extreme weather events, alter[] water supplies, [and] chang[e] crop yields and ecosystems," among other impacts. UNFCCC, An Overview of Investment and Financial Flows Needed for Adaptation, in Adaptation to Climate Change 96 (E. Schipper & I. Burton eds., 2007), reprinted in the Earthscan Reader on Adaptation to Climate Change (E. Schipper & I. Burton eds., 2009). EPA's report, Climate Change Indicators in the United States, 2014, provides thirty indicators of the likely effects and causes of climate change. EPA summarizes some of the adverse effects on ecosystems as follows:

> Changes in the Earth's climate can affect ecosystems by altering the water cycle, habitats, animal behavior—such as nesting and migration patterns—and the timing of natural processes such as flower blooms. Changes that disrupt the functioning of ecosystems may increase the risk of harm or even extinction for some species. While wildfires occur naturally, more frequent and more intense fires can significantly disrupt ecosystems, damage property, put people and communities at risk, and create air pollution problems even far away from the source.
>
> While plants and animals have adapted to environmental change for millions of years, the climate changes being experienced now could require adaptation on larger and faster scales than current species have successfully achieved in the past, thus increasing the risk of extinction or severe disruption for many species.

Id. at 84. The U.S. Global Change Research Program provides another review of adverse impacts and adaptation challenges in its Third National Climate Assessment in 2014, *supra*.

The price tag of attempts to adapt to changes in climate runs into the billions of dollars. A 2009 report estimates that water and wastewater systems in the United States face climate adaptation costs that could approach $1 trillion through 2050. National Association of Clean Water Agencies and Association of Metropolitan Water Agencies, Confronting Climate Change: An Early Analysis of Water and Wastewater Adaptation Costs (2009), available at http://www.amwa.net/galleries/climate-change/ ConfrontingClimateChangeOct09.pdf. For a 2014 assessment of the effects of climate change on various aspects of the American economy, see Gordon, Risky Business Project, Risky Business: The Economic risks of Climate Change in the United States (June 2014).

"Climate changes and their associated impacts [are likely to] vary greatly from location to location." Pew Global Commission on Climate Change, Climate Change 101: Adaptation, at 6 (Jan. 2011); U.S. Global Change Research Program, *supra*, at 11 (noting that "[o]bserved and projected climate change impacts vary across the regions of the United States."). EPA's Climate Change Indicators in the United States, 2014 (3d ed.) reviews some of the variations to date in changes in temperature, precipitation, and other aspects of climate. To provide three examples: (1) some parts of the U.S. have experienced more warming than others; (2) while many parts of the U.S. have experienced increases in precipitation, others, including Hawaii and parts of the Southwest, have experienced decreases; and (3) sea level rise relative to the land has "risen the most along the Mid-Atlantic coast and parts of the Gulf coast, where some stations registered increases of more than 8 inches between 1960 and 2013," while sea level has "decreased relative to land in parts of Alaska and the Northwest." Id. at 28, 34, 45. Concerning sea level rise in particular, EPA elaborates that "[t]he Atlantic coast is particularly vulnerable because of low elevations and sinking shorelines"; it notes that the loss of coastal land "can affect a large number of people" because of the significant population that lives along the Atlantic coast and also put coastal ecosystems at risk. Id. at 52. Because climate change is expected to have significant, and significantly different impacts, depending on location, there is no single answer to the question of how best to meet adaptation challenges; instead, policymakers and others will need to draw on different tools and strategies to match the particular challenges they face.

As indicated above, there has been an enormous amount of activity in the adaptation arena in recent years. The rest of this section provides a brief overview of this activity. Even though much of the activity has occurred at the state and local level, our focus is primarily on federal initiatives, with a particular focus on recent Executive Orders and efforts by EPA.

In a 2009 report, the GAO provided what arguably is a mixed picture concerning the state of federal adaptation efforts. The report noted that "there is no coordinated national approach to adaptation;" "no single entity is coordinating climate change adaptation efforts across the federal government . . . ;" and the federal government's emerging adaptation activities are carried out in an ad hoc manner and are not well coordinated across federal agencies, let alone between state and local governments. But the report also noted that broad adaptation efforts had begun. For example, CEQ had begun to "coordinate the federal response to climate change in conjunction with the Office of Science and Technology Policy, NOAA, and other agencies." In addition, the U.S. Global Change Research Program, the coordinator of federal research on climate change, "has developed a series of 'building blocks' that outline options for future climate change work, including science to inform adaptation." The GAO also reported that a variety of federal agencies had "begun to take action," largely in an ad hoc way, to promote adaptation. GAO, Climate Change Adaptation: Strategic Federal Planning Could Help Officials Make More Informed Decisions, GAO-10-175T 2-3 (2009) (hereinafter GAO Report 10-175T).

In a October 2009 Executive Order, President Obama directed federal agencies to participate in an Interagency Climate Change Adaptation Task Force, which was charged with developing a U.S. strategy for adapting to climate change. Exec. Order No. 13,514, 74 Fed. Reg. 52,117 (Oct. 8, 2009). The Task Force issued an interim strategy report in March 2010, in which it highlighted the need to build resilience, the need to engage all sectors of society in the effort, and the importance of local government efforts in particular because of the variation in challenges:

> Adaptation and resilience will require a set of thoughtful, preventative actions, measures and investments to reduce the vulnerability of our natural and human systems to climate change impacts. This will require new approaches and preparation, especially at the local level as regional impacts differ greatly. Adaptation and resilience will require action from all segments of society—the public sector, local to Federal government, the private sector, the nonprofit sector and individuals. This challenge provides Federal, Tribal, State, and local governments with significant opportunities for innovation.

The Task Force issued a final progress report in October 2010 and then a follow-up report in 2011. Progress Report of the Interagency Climate Change Adaptation Task Force: Recommended Actions in Support of a National Climate Change Adaptation Strategy (Oct. 5, 2010); Progress Report of the Interagency Climate Change Adaptation Task Force (Oct. 28, 2011). In the 2011 report, the Task Force focused on five key adaptation areas in particular: (1) integrating adaptation into federal government planning and activities; (2) the importance of enhancing the capacity of local communities to build resilience; (3) improving access to science for decisionmaking; (4) safeguarding natural resources in the context of a changing climate; and (5) the need for bilateral and multilateral adaptation activities to account for risks from climate change. Id. at iv. It noted that the federal government "is only one part of a broader effort that must include multiple levels of government and private and non-governmental partners throughout the country." Id. at 7. Further, it highlighted the importance of such partnerships, noting that "most adaptive actions will occur at the local level." Id. at 8.

In June 2013, President Obama issued The President's Climate Action Plan. The President's Climate Action Plan (June 2013), available at http://www.whitehouse .gov/sites/default/files/image/president27sclimateactionplan.pdf. This Plan addressed adaptation as well as mitigation issues. In November 2013, the President issued an executive order, Preparing the United States for the Impacts of Climate Change. Exec. Order No. 13,653, 78 Fed. Reg. 66,817 (Nov. 6, 2013). The Order established four policy priorities:

> The Federal Government must build on recent progress and pursue new strategies to improve the Nation's preparedness and resilience. In doing so, agencies should promote: 1) engaged and strong partnerships and information sharing at all levels of government; 2) risk-informed decisionmaking and the tools to facilitate it; 3) adaptive learning, in which experiences serve as opportunities to inform and adjust future actions; and 4) preparedness planning. [Id. §1.].

The Order directed implementation of several interagency/intergovernmental initiatives. For example, it established an Interagency Council on Climate Preparedness and Resilience, which would be comprised of senior officials from a wide variety of federal agencies, and co-chaired by the Chair of CEQ, to facilitate progress on these priorities. Id. §6. The Council is intended to build upon the work of the Interagency Climate Change Adaptation Task Force discussed above, the existence of which ended thirty days after the first meeting of the Council. Id. §6(f)). The Order also created a State, Local, and Tribal Leaders Task Force on Climate Preparedness and Resilience. This Task Force was charged with providing recommendations by November 2014 to the President and Council "for how the Federal Government can . . . support State, local, and tribal preparedness for and resilience to climate change." Id. §7.

As is the case for several agencies, EPA has undertaken several adaptation initiatives. It issued an initial policy statement on climate change adaptation in 2011, Policy Statement on Climate-Change Adaptation (June 2, 2011), available at http://www.epa .gov/climatechange/Downloads/impacts-adaptation/adaptation-statement.pdf, and an updated policy statement in June 2014. Policy Statement on Climate Change Adaptation (June 26, 2014), available at http://www.epa.gov/climatechange/Downloads/ impacts-adaptation/adaptation-statement-2014.pdf. In February 2013, EPA issued a

Draft Climate Change Adaptation Plan for the agency, available at http://www.epa.gov/climatechange/pdfs/EPA-climate-change-adaptation-plan-final-for-public-comment-2-7-13.pdf. In the draft plan, EPA identified ten steps it will take to integrate climate adaptation planning into its operations. In November 2013, EPA issued 17 draft Program and Regional Adaptation Plans for public comment. The latter 17 plans, developed by the agency's Regional and Program offices, discuss how each will address climate change as part of the agency-wide plan. EPA, Adaptation Implementation Plans (2013), available at http://www.epa.gov/climatechange/impacts-adaptation/fed-programs/EPA-impl-plans.html. EPA's June 2014 Policy Statement states that "together, these plans provide a roadmap for how the EPA will continue to implement the agency's programs, serving all communities that are facing climate-related challenges and working with them to protect human health and the environment even as the climate changes." Further, Administrator McCarthy directed that EPA "immediately implement" the following seven actions to promote better adaptation practices:

- modernize EPA financial assistance programs to encourage climate-resilient investments;
- provide information, tools, training and technical support for climate-change preparedness;
- implement priority actions identified in the EPA's Climate Change Adaptation Plan and the Implementation Plans;
- focus on the most vulnerable people and places;
- measure and evaluate performance;
- continue agency planning for climate change related risk;
- coordinate with other federal agencies;

EPA, Policy Statement on Climate Change Adaptation (2014), available at http://epa.gov/climatechange/Downloads/impacts-adaptation/adaptation-statement-2014.pdf.

For two specific EPA initiatives to address adaptation, see EPA's National Water Program Climate Change 2012 Strategy: Response to Climate Change, which discusses the water program's plans for adapting to anticipated changes to water resources; and the Office of Research and Development's (ORD) Global Change Impacts & Adaptation, which discusses various types of vulnerability to climate change and options for adaptation that would help to bolster resilience capacity in the face of these changes. For two of the many assessments with a natural resource focus, see Center for Climate and Energy Solutions, Impacts and Adaptation Options in the Gulf Coast (June 2012); GAO, Climate Change: Various Adaptation Efforts Are Under Way at Key Natural Resource Management Agencies, GAO-13-253 (May 2013). For an assessment with an energy focus, see GAO, Climate Change, Energy Infrastructure Risks and Adaptation Efforts, GAO-14-74 (Jan. 2014).

While we do not focus on them in detail, many states and municipalities have developed various strategies to promote adaptation. See, e.g., California Natural Resources Agency, 2009 California Climate Adaptation Strategy (2009) (integrating local land use planning with climate adaptation planning, among other things); New York Department of Environmental Conservation, New York State Climate Action Plan Interim Report (2010); Wisconsin Department of National Resources and Nelson Institute for Environmental Studies, Wisconsin's Changing Climate: Impacts and Adaptation (2011); Washington State Department of Ecology, Integrated

Climate Response Strategy (2012); and Massachusetts Executive Office of Energy and Environmental Affairs, Massachusetts Climate Change Adaptation Report (2011). A 2011 New York City report on climate change includes creation of an intergovernmental task force to manage the adaptation process, one example of a municipal focus on adaptation. City of New York, PlaNYC: A Greener, Greater New York 157 (2011) [hereinafter NYC Plan]. President Obama's 2013 Executive Order highlights the potential value of "vertical coordination" of efforts, as does the GAO in its 2013 report, Future Federal Adaptation Could Better Support Local Infrastructure Decision Makers, GAO 13-242 (April 2013).

While initiatives to facilitate adaptation to climate change are ongoing on multiple levels, the picture of what is occurring will undoubtedly look very different in a few years than it does today. A California Climate Change Center report suggests that there may be common methodological approaches that can be tailored to individual situations, suggesting that it is important to "[m]ainstream[] adaptation"—i.e., to "us[e] or creat[e] mechanisms that allow decision-makers to integrate future climate risks into all relevant policy interventions, planning, and management." California Climate Change Center, Preparing for the Impacts of Climate Change in California: Opportunities and Constraints for Adaptation 24 (2006), available at http://www.energy.ca.gov/2005publications/CEC-500-2005-198/CEC-500-2005-198-SF.PDF. The variability in climate change impacts suggests the value of tailored approaches. The multiplicity of agencies (vertically and horizontally) involved in different aspects of adaptation is likely to pose significant coordination challenges to effective governance. Despite significant effort expended to date, "designing adaptation projects or policies and their implementation remain a challenge for policy-makers and practitioners alike." Schipper & Burton, *supra*.

4. Climate Change and Other Aspects of Environmental Law

Two of the statutes covered elsewhere in the casebook, NEPA (Chapter 4) and the Endangered Species Act (Chapter 5), have already been used in efforts to address climate change concerns. They are likely to be used increasingly in the future. In this section, we sample some of the issues that have arisen.

a.   NEPA and Climate Change

As the text covers in detail in Chapter 4, NEPA is a "look before you leap" approach to regulation that requires reviews of the environmental impacts of projects as part of the project review/approval process in situations in which there is a "major federal action significantly affecting the quality of the human environment."

As one might expect, those concerned about climate change have argued that NEPA encompasses the obligation to consider climate change as a possible impact associated with particular types of projects. There has been a fair amount of activity by federal agencies to consider the appropriate role of NEPA in addressing climate change concerns; the courts have weighed in on several occasions as well.

In February 2010, the CEQ issued draft guidance on NEPA and climate change. Nancy H. Sutley, Draft NEPA Guidance on Consideration of the Effects of Climate Change and Greenhouse Gas Emissions (Feb. 18, 2010). Three of the highlights from this guidance are:

(1) CEQ does not propose that climate change assessments be a "new" component of NEPA analysis, "but rather [that they be treated] as a potentially important factor to be considered within the existing NEPA framework." Id. at 11.

(2) Not all NEPA analyses need to address climate change concerns. "[W]here a proposed Federal action . . . would be anticipated to emit GHGs to the atmosphere in quantities that the agency finds may be meaningful, it is appropriate for the agency to quantify and disclose its estimate of the expected annual direct and indirect GHG emissions. . . ." On the other hand, "[m]any agency NEPA analyses to date have found that GHG emissions from an individual agency action have small potential effects. Emissions from many proposed Federal actions would not typically be expected to produce an environmental effect that would trigger or otherwise require a detailed discussion in an EIS." Id. at 2, 3.

(3) "Where an agency determines that an assessment of climate issues is appropriate, the agency should identify alternative actions that are both adapted to anticipated climate change impacts and mitigate the GHG emissions that cause climate change."

Id. at 11. The guidance raised a host of issues, but in 2014, CEQ announced that it would not finalize the guidance.

Individual agencies have taken steps to integrate climate change considerations into their NEPA analyses. The Forest Service, for example, has issued a series of guidance documents on climate change considerations at both the planning and project levels. According to the agency, the guidance documents "frame climate change with two fundamental challenges: how our management may influence climate change mainly through incremental changes to global pools of greenhouse gases and how climate change may affect our forests and grasslands. These guidance documents will be dynamic and adaptive as we discover more about climate change science, its application to adaptation and mitigation strategies, and appropriate analysis at the unit and project scales." U.S. Forest Service, Climate Change Land Management & Project Planning, http://www.fs.fed.us/emc/nepa/climate_change. Other agencies, such as the Bureau of Land Management, are in the process of preparing guidance documents on how to address climate change in NEPA documents. See Department of the Interior, Climate Change Adaptation Plan: Interim Plan 22 (2014). See also U.S. Department of Transportation Climate Adaptation Plan: Ensuring Transportation Infrastructure and System Resilience 17 (2014) (describing a similar commitment by the Federal Motor Carrier Safety Administration). For "a systematic analysis of how the Environmental Impact Statements (EISs) required under NEPA, and under state law NEPA analogs, treat the issue of climate change," see Columbia Law School, Center for Climate Change Center, NEPA and Climate Change, www.law.columbia.edu/centers/climatechange/resources/eis.

The courts have weighed in on the role of NEPA in addressing climate change. Markell & Ruhl, An Empirical Survey of Climate Change Litigation in the United States, 40 Envtl. L. Rep. 10644, 10649 (July 2010), noted that litigation involving alleged NEPA violations relating to climate change typically involves environmental NGOs arguing that a federal agency should not be able to take an action because of inadequate NEPA analysis of the effects of the proposal on climate change (or the effects of climate change on the viability of the proposal). http://www.climatecase chart.com.

The impacts of climate change are relevant to agency initiatives concerning energy use. In Center for Biological Diversity v. National Highway Traffic Safety Admin., 538 F.3d 1172 (9th Cir. 2008), for example, the court invalidated on NEPA grounds an agency rule that established fuel economy standards for light trucks. The court found that the CAFE standard "will affect the level of the nation's greenhouse gas emissions and impact global warming." In support of this finding, the court stated that

> NHTSA does not dispute that light trucks account for a significant percentage of the U.S. transportation sector, that the U.S. transportation sector accounts for about six percent of the world's greenhouse gases, and that "fuel economy improvements could have a significant impact on the rate of CO_2 accumulation in the atmosphere," which would affect climate change. . . . [Id. at 1214.]

The court held that the agency violated NEPA in numerous ways. The agency's environmental assessment (EA) failed adequately to consider the cumulative impact of the rule on GHG emissions. While acknowledging that climate change is "largely a global phenomenon" and "includes actions that are outside of the agency's control," the court held that these features of climate change do "not release the agency from the duty of assessing the effects of *its* actions on global warming within the context of other actions that also affect global warming." Id. at 1217 (citing 40 C.F.R. §1508.7 and other sources). The court concluded that "[t]he impact of greenhouse gas emissions on climate change is precisely the kind of cumulative impacts analysis that NEPA requires agencies to conduct." Id. It also ruled that NHTSA failed to justify its FONSI and remanded the case for the agency to prepare a revised EA or to develop an EIS.

In other cases, courts have concluded that agencies met their NEPA duties in light of the uncertainties of climate change impacts or the minimal impacts individual projects were likely to have on climate change. In Center for Biological Diversity v. Kempthorne, 588 F.3d 701 (9th Cir. 2009), for example, NGOs challenged the issuance by the Fish and Wildlife Service of regulations allowing non-lethal takes of polar bears and walruses in the course of oil and gas activities in and along the Beaufort Sea. The groups challenged the agency's FONSI, arguing that the regulations' effects on bears and walruses was highly uncertain, given that climate change was already adversely affecting the animals. The court upheld the FONSI, concluding that it made reasonable predictions based on available data. See also Barnes v. U.S. Dep't of Transp., 655 F.3d 1124 (9th Cir. 2011) (because increased GHG emissions resulting from construction of new airport runway were such a small percentage of U.S. and global emissions, uncertainty did not require preparation of EIS). Cf. Hapner v. Tidwell, 621 F.3d 1239 (9th Cir. 2010) (Forest Service adequately considered impact of prescribed burning project on climate change in proportion to its significance, given that small amount of land involved would have meaningless impact on climate change).

For a comprehensive listing of NEPA cases involving climate change issues, see Climate Change Litigation in the U.S., http://www.climatecasechart.com. The case law will continue to evolve concerning the nature and extent of agency obligations to assess climate impacts on a project-specific and cumulative basis.

b. The Endangered Species Act and Climate Change

As discussed in more detail in Chapter 5, the ESA is intended to protect endangered and threatened species. Climate change may affect implementation of ESA §4 (listing, designation of critical habitat, and formulation of recovery plans), §7 (the "no jeopardy" provision), and §§9 and 10 (the "take" and "incidental take" provisions), at a minimum. A revealing example of the relevance of climate change to ESA listing decisions relates to polar bears.

ENDANGERED AND THREATENED WILDLIFE AND PLANTS; DETERMINATION OF THREATENED STATUS FOR THE POLAR BEAR (URSUS MARITIMUS) THROUGHOUT ITS RANGE; FINAL RULE
73 Fed. Reg. 28,212 (May 15, 2008)

Finding

We have carefully considered all available scientific and commercial information [concerning] past, present, and future threats faced by the polar bear. . . . [W]e recognize that polar bears evolved in the ice-covered waters of the circumpolar Arctic, and are reliant on sea ice as a platform to hunt and feed on ice-seals, to seek mates and breed, to move to feeding sites and terrestrial maternity denning areas, and for long-distance movements. The rapid retreat of sea ice in the summer and overall diminishing sea ice throughout the year in the Arctic is unequivocal and extensively documented in scientific literature. Further extensive recession of sea ice is projected by the majority of state-of-the-art climate models, with a seasonally ice-free Arctic projected by the middle of the 21st century by many of those models. Sea ice habitat will be subjected to increased temperatures, earlier melt periods, increased rain-on-snow events, and shifts in atmospheric and marine circulation patterns.

Under Factor A ("Present or Threatened Destruction, Modification, or Curtailment of its habitat or range"), we have determined that ongoing and projected loss of the polar bear's crucial sea ice habitat threatens the species throughout all of its range. Productivity, abundance, and availability of ice seals, the polar bear's primary prey base, would be diminished by the projected loss of sea ice, and energetic requirements of polar bears for movement and obtaining food would increase. Access to traditional denning areas would be affected. In turn, these factors would cause declines in the condition of polar bears from nutritional stress and reduced productivity. As already evidenced in the Western Hudson Bay and Southern Beaufort Sea populations, polar bears would experience reductions in survival and recruitment rates. The eventual effect is that polar bear populations would decline. The rate and magnitude of decline would vary among populations, based on differences in the rate, timing, and magnitude of impacts. However, within the foreseeable future, all populations would be affected, and the species is likely to become in danger of extinction throughout all of its range due to declining sea ice habitat. . . .

Regulatory Implications for Consultations Under Section 7 of the Act

When a species is listed as threatened under the Act, section 7(a)(2) provides that Federal agencies must insure that any actions they authorize, fund, or carry out are not likely to jeopardize the continued existence of any listed species or result in the destruction or adverse modification of designated critical habitat. Furthermore, under the authority of section 4(d), the Secretary shall establish regulatory provisions on the take of threatened species that are "necessary and advisable to provide for the conservation of the species" (16 U.S.C. 1533(d)). . . .

The significant cause of the decline of the polar bear, and thus the basis for this action to list it as a threatened species, is the loss of arctic sea ice that is expected to continue to occur over the next 45 years. The best scientific information available to us today, however, has not established a causal connection between specific sources and locations of emissions to specific impacts posed to polar bears or their habitat.

Some commenters to the proposed rule suggested that the Service should require other agencies (e.g., the Environmental Protection Agency) to regulate emissions from all sources, including automobile and power plants. The best scientific information available today would neither allow nor require the Service to take such action.

First, the primary substantive mandate of section 7(a)(2)—the duty to avoid likely jeopardy to an endangered or threatened species—rests with the Federal action agency and not with the Service. The Service consults with the Federal action agency on proposed Federal actions that may affect an endangered or threatened species, but its consultative role under section 7 does not allow for encroachment on the Federal action agency's jurisdiction or policy-making role under the statutes it administers.

Second, the Federal action agency decides when to initiate formal consultation on a particular proposed action, and it provides the project description to the Service. The Service may request the Federal action agency to initiate formal consultation for a particular proposed action, but it cannot compel the agency to consult, regardless of the type of action or the magnitude of its projected effects.

Recognizing the primacy of the Federal action agency's role in determining how to conform its proposed actions to the requirements of section 7, and taking into account the requirement to examine the "effects of the action" through the formal consultation process, the Service does not anticipate that the listing of the polar bear as a threatened species will result in the initiation of new section 7 consultations on proposed permits or licenses for facilities that would emit GHGs in the conterminous 48 States. Formal consultation is required for proposed Federal actions that "may affect" a listed species, which requires an examination of whether the direct and indirect effects of a particular action meet this regulatory threshold. GHGs that are projected to be emitted from a facility would not, in and of themselves, trigger formal section 7 consultation for a particular licensure action unless it is established that such emissions constitute an "indirect effect" of the proposed action. To constitute an "indirect effect," the impact to the species must be later in time, must be caused by the proposed action, and must be "reasonably certain to occur" (50 CFR 402.02

(definition of "effects of the action")). . . . [T]he best scientific data available today are not sufficient to draw a causal connection between GHG emissions from a facility in the conterminous 48 States to effects posed to polar bears or their habitat in the Arctic, nor are there sufficient data to establish that such impacts are "reasonably certain to occur" to polar bears. Without sufficient data to establish the required causal connection—to the level of "reasonable certainty"—between a new facility's GHG emissions and impacts to polar bears, section 7 consultation would not be required to address impacts to polar bears.

NOTES AND QUESTIONS

1. *Listing and Delisting.* In re Polar Bear Endangered Species Act Listing and §4(d) Rule Litig., 794 F. Supp. 2d 65 (D.D.C. 2011), upheld the listing, rejecting claims that, on the one hand, the FWS should not have listed the bear at all and, on the other, that it should have listed the bear as endangered, not threatened. On the second set of issues, the court deferred to the agency's conclusion that the scientific evidence did not indicate that the bear was on the brink of extinction. The district court's rejection of the claim that the FWS should not have listed the bear at all was affirmed on appeal. In re Polar Bear Endangered Species Act Listing and Section 4(d) Litig., 709 F.3d 1 (D.C. Cir. 2013). The appellate court concluded that none of the seven reasons the challengers advanced for why polar bears were not even threatened had merit. The court's overarching response was that the challengers failed to undercut the FWS's principal justification for listing—that the bear depends on sea ice for survival, sea ice is declining, and climatic conditions have reduced and will continue to reduce dramatically the extent and quality of Arctic ice to a degree sufficient to jeopardize bear populations. Compare Colorado River Cutthroat Trout v. Salazar, 898 F. Supp. 2d 191 (D.D.C. 2012) (upholding determination that listing was not warranted, and rejecting claim that the FWS should have considered the impact of climate change due to absence of sufficient evidence in the record that climate change affected the trout).

Another listing case is Greater Yellowstone Coal., Inc. v. Servheen, 665 F.3d 1014 (9th Cir. 2011), in which the court refused to allow the FWS to delist a grizzly bear population on the basis of the absence of data showing a population decline due to whitebark pine loss, to which climate change has contributed. The court invalidated the delisting because the FWS provided no data indicating that whitebark pine declines would not threaten the grizzly population, and considerable data showing a relationship between pine seed shortages, increased bear mortality, and decreased female reproductive success pointed in the opposite direction. Climate change also may affect critical habitat designation. See, e.g., Alliance for Wild Rockies v. Lyder, 728 F. Supp. 2d 1126, 1139 (D. Mont. 2010) (rejecting claim that FWS should have included unoccupied habitat to compensate for anticipated future habitat loss due to climate change).

2. *Section 7.* Climate change may affect the application of §7's mandate that agencies avoid taking action that jeopardizes listed species or adversely affects their critical habitat. See, e.g., Center for Biological Diversity v. Salazar, 804 F. Supp. 2d 987, 1008 (D. Ariz. 2011) (invalidating biological opinion based on FWS's failure to consider the impact of climate change on species affected by the Army's proposed groundwater withdrawals); NRDC v. Kempthorne, 506 F. Supp. 2d 322, 357 (E.D.

Cal. 2007) (concluding that biological opinion was not based on the best available science because the FWS failed to analyze information that climate change would adversely affect listed fish species and its habitat)

   3. *Taking Prohibition*. Climate change is also potentially relevant to §9's "take" prohibition. As the *Sweet Home Chapter* case excerpted in Chapter 5 indicates, significant habitat modification may qualify as a take. Is it possible that a court will conclude that a substantial GHG emitter violates the "take" prohibition? What arguments exist in support of and against this position? The relationship between climate change and the take prohibition was at issue In re Polar Bear Endangered Species Act Listing and §4(d) Rule Litig., 818 F. Supp. 2d 214 (D.D.C. 2011). The take prohibition of §9(a)(1)(B) applies on its face only to endangered species. Section 4(d), however, authorizes the FWS to issue "such regulations as [it] deems necessary and advisable to provide for the conservation" of threatened species. The agency's default position is that the take prohibition applies to threatened species to the same extent as to endangered species. After the FWS listed polar bears as threatened, however, it adopted a "special rule" refusing to apply the take prohibitions to activities occurring outside the range of the species that may incidentally impact polar bears. The court found that decision to be consistent with the ESA, although it invalidated the §4(d) rule due to NEPA noncompliance. The environmental plaintiffs argued that that the FWS cannot effectively provide for the conservation of the polar bear without addressing GHG emissions (which occur outside the current range of the bear), given that the FWS itself expected them to lead to a significant decline of the bear's sea ice habitat. The court, however, deferred to the FWS's conclusion that §4(d) is neither useful nor appropriate to alleviate the threat to polar bears from climate change caused by GHG emissions. After conducting a NEPA analysis, the FWS reissued the §4(d) rule for the polar bear. 78 Fed. Reg. 11,766 (Feb. 20, 2013).

   4. For in-depth analysis of the impact of climate change on ecosystems and adaptation of wildlife in connection with the ESA, see http://www.epa.gov/climate-change/impacts-adaptation/ecosystems.html. For more on climate change and the ESA, see Ruhl, Climate Change and the Endangered Species Act: Building Bridges to the No-Analog Future, 88 B.U. L. Rev. 1 (2008).

5. *Common Law Remedies*

   Common law–based strategies of the kind surveyed in Chapter 1 are another obvious tool for those concerned about climate change and wanting the legal system to address it. In fact, the legal scholarship exploring the promise of common law litigation to address climate change has come fast and furious over the past few years. For analysis of the role of common law litigation, see generally Symposium, Civil Litigation as a Tool for Regulating Climate Change, 46 Val. U. L. Rev. 357-500 (2012). For a collection of the extensive, and rapidly growing, number of articles, see Kysar, What Climate Change Can Do About Tort Law, 41 Envtl. L. 1 (2011). We review the evolution of common law doctrines in Chapters 1, 8, and 10, and highlight in this section some of the issues that are likely to arise in connection with efforts to use common law doctrines to address climate change.

   Despite the attention common law approaches have received, their use to date has been quite limited. In their 2010 survey of climate change litigation, Professors Markell and Ruhl found that less than ten percent of the cases dealing with climate change that have been filed as of December 31, 2009 are based on common law doctrines. Markell & Ruhl, An Empirical Assessment of Climate Change in the Courts: A New Jurisprudence or Business as Usual?, 64 Fla. L. Rev. 15 (2012).

Some commentators have been very supportive of common law litigation and optimistic about its prospects. Others have expressed a much more skeptical view. Professor Kysar, for example, suggests that tort law "seems fundamentally ill-equipped to address the causes and impact of climate change." He concludes that, because they are "[d]iffuse and disparate in origin, [and] lagged and latticed in effect, anthropogenic greenhouse gas emissions represent the paradigmatic anti-tort, a collective action problem so pervasive and so complicated as to render at once both all of us and none of us responsible." He anticipates that "[i]n all likelihood, courts will agree with commentators that nuisance and other traditional tort theories are overwhelmed by the magnitude and the complexity of the climate change conundrum." As a result, "tort law is unlikely to play a substantial role in the ultimate effort to reduce greenhouse gas emissions, compensate climate change victims, or otherwise implement legal responses to the global warming problem." Kysar, *supra*, at 3-4.

The availability of the common law may well depend on developments in other branches, such as congressional statutory enactments and agency regulation. In the meantime, some of the major issues the courts have begun to confront include justiciability, standing, personal jurisdiction over defendants, preemption/displacement, the type and levels of proof necessary to meet elements of the different causes of action (e.g., causation), and the extent of liability, including the role of joint and several liability. A 2011 Supreme Court opinion, excerpted below, closed the door to some, but by no means all, common law causes of action.

AMERICAN ELECTRIC POWER CO. v. CONNECTICUT
131 S. Ct. 2527 (2011)

JUSTICE GINSBURG delivered the opinion of the Court.

We address in this opinion the question whether the plaintiffs (several States, the city of New York, and three private land trusts) can maintain federal common law public nuisance claims against carbon-dioxide emitters (four private power companies and the federal Tennessee Valley Authority). As relief, the plaintiffs ask for a decree setting carbon-dioxide emissions for each defendant at an initial cap, to be further reduced annually. The Clean Air Act and the Environmental Protection Agency action the Act authorizes, we hold, displace the claims the plaintiffs seek to pursue.

ISSUE

I

In Massachusetts v. EPA, 549 U.S. 497 (2007), this Court held that the Clean Air Act authorizes federal regulation of emissions of carbon dioxide and other greenhouse gases. "[N]aturally present in the atmosphere and . . . also emitted by human activities," greenhouse gases are so named because they "trap . . . heat that would otherwise escape from the [Earth's] atmosphere, and thus form the greenhouse effect that helps keep the Earth warm enough for life." 74 Fed. Reg. 66499 (2009). Massachusetts held that the Environmental Protection Agency (EPA) had misread the Clean Air Act when it denied a rulemaking petition seeking controls on greenhouse gas emissions from new motor vehicles. Greenhouse gases, we determined, qualify as "air pollutant[s]" within the meaning of the governing Clean Air Act provision (quoting §7602(g)); they are therefore within EPA's regulatory ken. Because EPA had authority to set greenhouse gas emission standards and had offered no "reasoned explanation" for failing to do so, we concluded that the agency had not acted "in accordance with law" when it denied the requested rulemaking. Id., at 534-535 (quoting §7607(d)(9)(A)).

Responding to our decision in *Massachusetts*, EPA undertook greenhouse gas regulation. In December 2009, the agency concluded that greenhouse gas emissions from motor vehicles "cause, or contribute to, air pollution which may reasonably be anticipated to endanger public health or welfare," the Act's regulatory trigger. §7521(a)(1); 74 Fed. Reg. 66496. The agency observed that "atmospheric greenhouse gas concentrations are now at elevated and essentially unprecedented levels," almost entirely "due to anthropogenic emissions"; mean global temperatures, the agency continued, demonstrate an "unambiguous warming trend over the last 100 years," and particularly "over the past 30 years." Acknowledging that not all scientists agreed on the causes and consequences of the rise in global temperatures, EPA concluded that "compelling" evidence supported the "attribution of observed climate change to anthropogenic" emissions of greenhouse gases. Consequent dangers of greenhouse gas emissions, EPA determined, included increases in heat-related deaths; coastal inundation and erosion caused by melting icecaps and rising sea levels; more frequent and intense hurricanes, floods, and other "extreme weather events" that cause death and destroy infrastructure; drought due to reductions in mountain snowpack and shifting precipitation patterns; destruction of ecosystems supporting animals and plants; and potentially "significant disruptions" of food production.[2]

EPA and the Department of Transportation subsequently issued a joint final rule regulating emissions from light-duty vehicles, see 75 Fed. Reg. 25324 (2010), and initiated a joint rulemaking covering medium- and heavy-duty vehicles, see id., at 74152. EPA also began phasing in requirements that new or modified "[m]ajor [greenhouse gas] emitting facilities" use the "best available control technology." §7475(a)(4); 75 Fed. Reg. 31520-31521. Finally, EPA commenced a rulemaking under §111 of the Act to set limits on greenhouse gas emissions from new, modified, and existing fossil-fuel fired power plants. Pursuant to a settlement finalized in March 2011, EPA has committed to issuing a proposed rule by July 2011, and a final rule by May 2012. See 75 Fed. Reg. 82392.

II

The lawsuits we consider here began well before EPA initiated the efforts to regulate greenhouse gases just described. In July 2004, two groups of plaintiffs filed separate complaints in the Southern District of New York against the same five major electric power companies. The first group of plaintiffs included eight States and New York City, the second joined three nonprofit land trusts; both groups are respondents here. The defendants, now petitioners, are four private companies and the Tennessee Valley

---

2. For views opposing EPA's, see, e.g., Dawidoff, The Civil Heretic, N.Y. Times Magazine 32 (March 29, 2009). The Court, we caution, endorses no particular view of the complicated issues related to carbon-dioxide emissions and climate change.

Authority, a federally owned corporation that operates fossil-fuel fired power plants in several States. According to the complaints, the defendants "are the five largest emitters of carbon dioxide in the United States." Their collective annual emissions of 650 million tons constitute 25 percent of emissions from the domestic electric power sector, 10 percent of emissions from all domestic human activities, and 2.5 percent of all anthropogenic emissions worldwide.

By contributing to global warming, the plaintiffs asserted, the defendants' carbon-dioxide emissions created a "substantial and unreasonable interference with public rights," in violation of the federal common law of interstate nuisance, or, in the alternative, of state tort law. The States and New York City alleged that public lands, infrastructure, and health were at risk from climate change. The trusts urged that climate change would destroy habitats for animals and rare species of trees and plants on land the trusts owned and conserved. All plaintiffs sought injunctive relief requiring each defendant "to cap its carbon dioxide emissions and then reduce them by a specified percentage each year for at least a decade."

π claims

Relief sought

The District Court dismissed both suits as presenting non-justiciable political questions, citing Baker v. Carr, 369 U.S. 186 (1962), but the Second Circuit reversed. On the threshold questions, the Court of Appeals held that the suits were not barred by the political question doctrine, and that the plaintiffs had adequately alleged Article III standing.

Turning to the merits, the Second Circuit held that all plaintiffs had stated a claim under the "federal common law of nuisance." For this determination, the court relied dominantly on a series of this Court's decisions holding that States may maintain suits to abate air and water pollution produced by other States or by out-of-state industry. See, e.g., Illinois v. Milwaukee, 406 U.S. 91, 93 (1972) (*Milwaukee I*) (recognizing right of Illinois to sue in federal district court to abate discharge of sewage into Lake Michigan).

App. Holding #1

The Court of Appeals further determined that the Clean Air Act did not "displace" federal common law. In Milwaukee v. Illinois, 451 U.S. 304, 316-319 (1981) (*Milwaukee II*), this Court held that Congress had displaced the federal common law right of action recognized in *Milwaukee I* by adopting amendments to the Clean Water Act. That legislation installed an all-encompassing regulatory program, supervised by an expert administrative agency, to deal comprehensively with interstate water pollution. The legislation itself prohibited the discharge of pollutants into the waters of the United States without a permit from a proper permitting authority. *Milwaukee II*, 451 U.S., at 310-311 (citing §1311). At the time of the Second Circuit's decision, by contrast, EPA had not yet promulgated any rule regulating greenhouse gases, a fact the court thought dispositive. "Until EPA completes the rulemaking process," the court reasoned, "we cannot speculate as to whether the hypothetical regulation of greenhouse gases under the Clean Air Act would in fact 'spea[k] directly' to the 'particular issue' raised here by Plaintiffs." . . .

App Holding #2

III   STANDING   *4:4 court split*

The petitioners contend that the federal courts lack authority to adjudicate this case. Four members of the Court would hold that at least some plaintiffs have Article III standing under *Massachusetts*, which permitted a State to challenge

1266 Chapter XII. Climate Change Law and Policy Choices

EPA's refusal to regulate greenhouse gas emissions; and, further, that no other threshold obstacle bars review.[6] Four members of the Court, adhering to a dissenting opinion in *Massachusetts*, or regarding that decision as distinguishable, would hold that none of the plaintiffs have Article III standing. We therefore affirm, by an equally divided Court, the Second Circuit's exercise of jurisdiction and proceed to the merits.

IV

A

"There is no federal general common law," Erie R. Co. v. Tompkins, 304 U.S. 64, 78 (1938), famously recognized. In the wake of *Erie*, however, a keener understanding developed. See generally Friendly, In Praise of Erie—And of the New Federal Common Law, 39 N.Y.U. L. Rev. 383 (1964). *Erie* "le[ft] to the states what ought be left to them," id., at 405, and thus required "federal courts [to] follow state decisions on matters of substantive law appropriately cognizable by the states," id., at 422. *Erie* also sparked "the emergence of a federal decisional law in areas of national concern." Id., at 405. The "new" federal common law addresses "subjects within national legislative power where Congress has so directed" or where the basic scheme of the Constitution so demands. Environmental protection is undoubtedly an area "within national legislative power," one in which federal courts may fill in "statutory interstices," and, if necessary, even "fashion federal law." Id., at 421-422. As the Court stated in *Milwaukee I*: "When we deal with air and water in their ambient or interstate aspects, there is a federal common law." 406 U.S., at 103.

Decisions of this Court predating *Erie*, but compatible with the distinction emerging from that decision between "general common law" and "specialized federal common law," Friendly, *supra*, at 405, have approved federal common law suits brought by one State to abate pollution emanating from another State. See, e.g., Missouri v. Illinois, 180 U.S. 208, 241-243 (1901) (permitting suit by Missouri to enjoin Chicago from discharging untreated sewage into interstate waters); Georgia v. Tennessee Copper Co., 240 U.S. 650 (1916) (ordering private copper companies to curtail sulfur-dioxide discharges in Tennessee that caused harm in Georgia). See also *Milwaukee I*, 406 U.S., at 107 (post-*Erie* decision upholding suit by Illinois to abate sewage discharges into Lake Michigan). The plaintiffs contend that their right to maintain this suit follows inexorably from that line of decisions.

Recognition that a subject is meet for federal law governance, however, does not necessarily mean that federal courts should create the controlling law. Absent a demonstrated need for a federal rule of decision, the Court has taken "the prudent course" of "adopt[ing] the readymade body of state law as the federal rule of decision until Congress strikes a different accommodation." United States v. Kimbell Foods, Inc., 440 U.S. 715, 740 (1979). And where, as here, borrowing the law of a particular State would be inappropriate, the Court remains mindful that it does not have creative power akin to that vested in Congress. See Missouri v. Illinois, 200 U.S. 496, 519 (1906) ("fact that this court must decide does not mean, of course, that it takes the place of a legislature"); cf. United States v. Standard Oil Co. of Cal., 332 U.S. 301,

---

6. In addition to renewing the political question argument made below, the petitioners now assert an additional threshold obstacle: They seek dismissal because of a "prudential" bar to the adjudication of generalized grievances, purportedly distinct from Article III's bar.

308, 314 (1947) ([characterizing Congress as] "the primary and most often the exclusive arbiter of federal fiscal affairs").

In the cases on which the plaintiffs heavily rely, States were permitted to sue to challenge activity harmful to their citizens' health and welfare. We have not yet decided whether private citizens (here, the land trusts) or political subdivisions (New York City) of a State may invoke the federal common law of nuisance to abate out-of-state pollution. Nor have we ever held that a State may sue to abate any and all manner of pollution originating outside its borders.

Distinction based on agency state v. Private citizens and political subdivisions

The defendants argue that considerations of scale and complexity distinguish global warming from the more bounded pollution giving rise to past federal nuisance suits. Greenhouse gases once emitted "become well mixed in the atmosphere," 74 Fed. Reg. 66514; emissions in New Jersey may contribute no more to flooding in New York than emissions in China. The plaintiffs, on the other hand, contend that an equitable remedy against the largest emitters of carbon dioxide in the United States is in order and not beyond judicial competence. And we have recognized that public nuisance law, like common law generally, adapts to changing scientific and factual circumstances. *Missouri*, 200 U.S., at 522 (adjudicating claim though it did not concern "nuisance of the simple kind that was known to the older common law"); see also *D'Oench, Duhme & Co. v. FDIC*, 315 U.S. 447, 472 (1942) (Jackson, J., concurring) ("federal courts are free to apply the traditional common-law technique of decision" when fashioning federal common law).

We need not address the parties' dispute in this regard. For it is an academic question whether, in the absence of the Clean Air Act and the EPA actions the Act authorizes, the plaintiffs could state a federal common law claim for curtailment of greenhouse gas emissions because of their contribution to global warming. Any such claim would be displaced by the federal legislation authorizing EPA to regulate carbon-dioxide emissions.

HOLDING

B

"[W]hen Congress addresses a question previously governed by a decision rested on federal common law," the Court has explained, "the need for such an unusual exercise of law-making by federal courts disappears." *Milwaukee II*, 451 U.S., at 314 (holding that amendments to the Clean Water Act displaced the nuisance claim recognized in *Milwaukee I*). Legislative displacement of federal common law does not require the "same sort of evidence of a clear and manifest [congressional] purpose" demanded for preemption of state law. Id., at 317. "'[D]ue regard for the presuppositions of our embracing federal system . . . as a promoter of democracy,'" id., at 316, does not enter the calculus, for it is primarily the office of Congress, not the federal courts, to prescribe national policy in areas of special federal interest. *TVA v. Hill*, 437 U.S. 153, 194 (1978). The test for whether congressional legislation excludes the declaration of federal common law is simply whether the statute "speak[s] directly to [the] question" at issue. *Mobil Oil Corp. v. Higginbotham*, 436 U.S. 618, 625 (1978); see *Milwaukee II*, 451 U.S., at 315.

when Congress adopts a law that touches on the subject matter of a question that was previously an exercise of lawmaking by federal courts, the need for court lawmaking disappears

We hold that the Clean Air Act and the EPA actions it authorizes displace any federal common law right to seek abatement of carbon-dioxide emissions from fossil-fuel fired power plants. *Massachusetts* made plain that emissions of carbon dioxide qualify as air pollution subject to regulation under the Act. And we think it equally plain that the Act "speaks directly" to emissions of carbon dioxide from the defendants' plants.

Section 111 of the Act directs the EPA Administrator to list "categories of stationary sources" that "in [her] judgment . . . caus[e], or contribut[e] significantly to, air pollution which may reasonably be anticipated to endanger public health or welfare." §7411(b)(1)(A). Once EPA lists a category, the agency must establish standards of performance for emission of pollutants from new or modified sources within that category. §7411(b)(1)(B); see also §7411(a)(2). And, most relevant here, §7411(d) then requires regulation of existing sources within the same category. For existing sources, EPA issues emissions guidelines; in compliance with those guidelines and subject to federal oversight, the States then issue performance standards for stationary sources within their jurisdiction, §7411(d)(1).

The Act provides multiple avenues for enforcement. See *County of Oneida*, 470 U.S. 226, 237-239 (1985) (reach of remedial provisions is important to determination whether statute displaces federal common law). EPA may delegate implementation and enforcement authority to the States, §7411(c)(1), (d)(1), but the agency retains the power to inspect and monitor regulated sources, to impose administrative penalties for noncompliance, and to commence civil actions against polluters in federal court. §§7411(c)(2), (d)(2), 7413, 7414. In specified circumstances, the Act imposes criminal penalties on any person who knowingly violates emissions standards issued under §7411. See §7413(c). And the Act provides for private enforcement. If States (or EPA) fail to enforce emissions limits against regulated sources, the Act permits "any person" to bring a civil enforcement action in federal court. §7604(a).

If EPA does not set emissions limits for a particular pollutant or source of pollution, States and private parties may petition for a rulemaking on the matter, and EPA's response will be reviewable in federal court. See §7607(b)(1); *Massachusetts*, 549 U.S., at 516-517, 529. As earlier noted, EPA is currently engaged in a §7411 rulemaking to set standards for greenhouse gas emissions from fossil-fuel fired power plants. To settle litigation brought under §7607(b) by a group that included the majority of the plaintiffs in this very case, the agency agreed to complete that rulemaking by May 2012. The Act itself thus provides a means to seek limits on emissions of carbon dioxide from domestic power plants–the same relief the plaintiffs seek by invoking federal common law. We see no room for a parallel track.

C

The plaintiffs argue, as the Second Circuit held, that federal common law is not displaced until EPA actually exercises its regulatory authority, i.e., until it sets standards governing emissions from the defendants' plants. We disagree.

The sewage discharges at issue in *Milwaukee II*, we do not overlook, were subject to effluent limits set by EPA; under the displacing statute, "[e]very point source discharge" of water pollution was "prohibited unless covered by a permit." 451 U.S., at 318-320. As *Milwaukee II* made clear, however, the relevant question for purposes of displacement is "whether the field has been occupied, not whether it has been occupied in a particular manner." Id., at 324. Of necessity, Congress selects different regulatory regimes to address different problems. Congress could hardly preemptively prohibit every discharge of carbon dioxide unless covered by a permit. After all, we each emit carbon dioxide merely by breathing.

The Clean Air Act is no less an exercise of the legislature's "considered judgment" concerning the regulation of air pollution because it permits emissions until EPA acts. See Middlesex County Sewerage Authority v. National Sea Clammers Assn., 453 U.S. 1, 22, n.32 (1981) (finding displacement although Congress "allowed some continued dumping of sludge" prior to a certain date). The critical point is that Congress delegated to EPA the decision whether and how to regulate carbon-dioxide emissions from power plants; the delegation is what displaces federal common law. Indeed, were EPA to decline to regulate carbon-dioxide emissions altogether at the conclusion of its ongoing §7411 rulemaking, the federal courts would have no warrant to employ the federal common law of nuisance to upset the agency's expert determination.

EPA's judgment, we hasten to add, would not escape judicial review. Federal courts, we earlier observed, can review agency action (or a final rule declining to take action) to ensure compliance with the statute Congress enacted. As we have noted, the Clean Air Act directs EPA to establish emissions standards for categories of stationary sources that, "in [the Administrator's] judgment," "caus[e], or contribut[e] significantly to, air pollution which may reasonably be anticipated to endanger public health or welfare." §7411(b)(1)(A). "[T]he use of the word 'judgment,'" we explained in *Massachusetts*, "is not a roving license to ignore the statutory text." 549 U.S., at 533. "It is but a direction to exercise discretion within defined statutory limits." EPA may not decline to regulate carbon-dioxide emissions from power plants if refusal to act would be "arbitrary, capricious, an abuse of discretion, or otherwise not in accordance with law." §7607(d)(9)(A). If the plaintiffs in this case are dissatisfied with the outcome of EPA's forthcoming rulemaking, their recourse under federal law is to seek Court of Appeals review, and, ultimately, to petition for certiorari in this Court.

Indeed, this prescribed order of decisionmaking—the first decider under the Act is the expert administrative agency, the second, federal judges—is yet another reason to resist setting emissions standards by judicial decree under federal tort law. The appropriate amount of regulation in any particular greenhouse gas-producing sector cannot be prescribed in a vacuum: as with other questions of national or international policy, informed assessment of competing interests is required. Along with the environmental benefit potentially achievable, our Nation's energy needs and the possibility of economic disruption must weigh in the balance.

The Clean Air Act entrusts such complex balancing to EPA in the first instance, in combination with state regulators. Each "standard of performance" EPA sets must "tak[e] into account the cost of achieving [emissions] reduction and any nonair quality health and environmental impact and energy requirements." §7411(a)(1), (b)(1)(B), (d)(1); see also 40 C.F.R. §60.24(f) (EPA may permit state plans to deviate from generally applicable emissions standards upon demonstration that costs are "[u]nreasonable"). EPA may "distinguish among classes, types, and sizes" of stationary sources in apportioning responsibility for emissions reductions. §7411(b)(2), (d). And the agency may waive compliance with emission limits to permit a facility to test drive an "innovative technological system" that has "not [yet] been adequately demonstrated." §7411(j)(1)(A). The Act envisions extensive cooperation between federal and state authorities, see §7401(a), (b), generally permitting each State to take the first cut at determining how best to achieve EPA emissions standards within its domain, see §7411(c)(1), (d)(1)-(2).

It is altogether fitting that Congress designated an expert agency, here, EPA, as best suited to serve as primary regulator of greenhouse gas emissions. The expert agency is surely better equipped to do the job than individual district judges issuing ad hoc, case-by-case injunctions. Federal judges lack the scientific, economic, and technological resources an agency can utilize in coping with issues of this order. See generally Chevron U.S.A. Inc. v. Natural Resources Defense Council, Inc., 467 U.S. 837, 865-866 (1984). Judges may not commission scientific studies or convene groups of experts for advice, or issue rules under notice-and-comment procedures inviting input by any interested person, or seek the counsel of regulators in the States where the defendants are located. Rather, judges are confined by a record comprising the evidence the parties present. Moreover, federal district judges, sitting as sole adjudicators, lack authority to render precedential decisions binding other judges, even members of the same court.

Notwithstanding these disabilities, the plaintiffs propose that individual federal judges determine, in the first instance, what amount of carbon-dioxide emissions is "unreasonable," and then decide what level of reduction is "practical, feasible and economically viable." These determinations would be made for the defendants named in the two lawsuits launched by the plaintiffs. Similar suits could be mounted, counsel for the States and New York City estimated, against "thousands or hundreds or tens" of other defendants fitting the description "large contributors" to carbon-dioxide emissions.

The judgments the plaintiffs would commit to federal judges, in suits that could be filed in any federal district, cannot be reconciled with the decisionmaking scheme Congress enacted. The Second Circuit erred, we hold, in ruling that federal judges may set limits on greenhouse gas emissions in face of a law empowering EPA to set the same limits, subject to judicial review only to ensure against action "arbitrary, capricious, . . . or otherwise not in accordance with law." §7607(d)(9).

V   *Relief in state courts*

The plaintiffs also sought relief under state law, in particular, the law of each State where the defendants operate power plants. The Second Circuit did not reach the state law claims because it held that federal common law governed. See International Paper Co. v. Ouellette, 479 U.S. 481, 488 (1987) (if a case "should be resolved by reference to federal common law[,] . . . state common law [is] preempted"). In light of our holding that the Clean Air Act displaces federal common law, the availability *vel non* of a state lawsuit depends, *inter alia,* on the preemptive effect of the federal Act. Id., at 489, 491, 497 (holding that the Clean Water Act does not preclude aggrieved individuals from bringing a "nuisance claim pursuant to the law of the source State"). None of the parties have briefed preemption or otherwise addressed the availability of a claim under state nuisance law. We therefore leave the matter open for consideration on remand.

For the reasons stated, we reverse the judgment of the Second Circuit and remand the case for further proceedings consistent with this opinion. . . .

JUSTICE SOTOMAYOR took no part in the consideration or decision of this case.

JUSTICE ALITO, with whom JUSTICE THOMAS joins, concurring in part and concurring in the judgment.

I concur in the judgment, and I agree with the Court's displacement analysis on the assumption (which I make for the sake of argument because no party contends otherwise) that the interpretation of the Clean Air Act adopted by the majority in *Massachusetts v. EPA*, 549 U.S. 497 (2007), is correct.

NOTES AND QUESTIONS

1. What are the jurisdictional implications of Part III of the Court's decision?

2. Why would the federal common law of nuisance be displaced if EPA chose not to regulate? What would be the effect, if any, on the allocation of federal decisionmaking authority over GHG emissions if Congress adopted a statute blocking EPA's authority to regulate those emissions under the CAA for two years? What if Congress adopted a statute permanently stripping EPA of its authority to regulate GHG emissions under the CAA? Can you fashion an argument that such a bill would (or would not) allow federal judges to apply federal common law in a suit such as the principal case?

3. What issues does the Court's opinion leave open? For a general review, see Markell & Hammond, Civil Remedies, in Global Climate Change and U.S. Law (M. Gerrard & J. Freeman eds., ABA 2d ed., 2014). For two circuit court assessments, see Bell v. Cheswick Generating Station, 734 F.3d 188 (3d Cir. 2013) (holding that the CAA does not preempt *state* common law claims and, in doing so, distinguishing *AEP*); Native Village of Kivalina v. ExxonMobil Corp., 696 F.3d 849 (9th Cir. 2012) (holding that the CAA displaced *federal* common law nuisance claim against oil, energy, and utility companies whose emissions allegedly contributed to climate change that induced melting of permafrost on which the Village was located).

4. In Alec L. v. Jackson, 863 F. Supp. 2d 11 (D.D.C. 2012), five citizens and two organizations sued various government agency officials for their alleged violation of the federal public trust doctrine (PTD) because of their purported failure to reduce GHG emissions sufficiently to reduce global atmospheric CO_2 levels to less than 350 parts per million during the twenty-first century. The plaintiffs claimed that the defendants breached their fiduciary duty under the PTD to protect the atmosphere as a "commonly shared public trust resource." The plaintiffs did not allege violation of any specific federal statute or constitutional provision. The district court granted the defendants' motion to dismiss on the jurisdictional ground that the plaintiffs' PTD claim did not raise a federal question because the claim was grounded in state common law. Relying on the principal case, the court also reasoned that "even if the [PTD] had been a federal common law claim at one time, it has subsequently been displaced by federal regulation, specifically the Clean Air Act." Id. at 15-16. The district court denied reconsideration of its decision, Alec L. v. Perciasepe, 2013 WL 2248001 (D.D.C. 2013), and the D.C. Circuit affirmed, holding that the PTD is a matter of state law and therefore the federal courts lacked subject matter jurisdiction. Alec L. ex rel. Loorz v. McCarthy, 561 Fed. Appx. 7 (D.C. Cir. 2014).

F. INTERNATIONAL ISSUES

TABLE 12-3
Key Dates in the Development of the International Climate Change Regime

1988	Toronto Conference recommends goal of reducing global emissions by 20 percent by 2005.
	UN General Assembly declares climate change a "common concern of mankind."
	Intergovernmental Panel on Climate Change (IPCC) established by UN Environment Programme (UNEP) and World Meteorological Organization (WMO).
1990	UN General Assembly establishes intergovernmental negotiating committee (INC) to negotiate framework convention on climate change.
	IPCC issues First Assessment Report (FAR), estimating that global mean temperature likely to increase by 0.3° C per decade under business-as-usual scenario.
1992	INC adopts United Nations Framework Convention on Climate Change (UNFCCC); opened for signature at Rio Conference on Environment and Development.
1994	UNFCCC enters into force.
1995	First Conference of the Parties (COP-1) adopts Berlin Mandate, initiating Kyoto Protocol negotiations.
	IPCC adopts Second Assessment Report (SAR), concluding that "balance of evidence suggests . . . a discernible human influence on global climate."
1997	Kyoto Protocol adopted by COP-3.
1998	COP-4 adopts Buenos Aires Plan of Action (BAPA), initiating negotiation of detailed rules for implementing Kyoto Protocol.
2001	COP-7 completes BAPA negotiations and adopts Marrakesh Accords, setting forth detailed rules for Kyoto Protocol.
	IPCC issues Third Assessment Report (TAR), finding that "most of the observed warming over the last 50 years is likely to have been due to the increase in anthropogenic greenhouse gas concentrations."
2005	Kyoto Protocol enters into force.
2007	Bali Action Plan initiates negotiations on post-2012 climate change regime.
	IPCC issues Fourth Assessment Report (AR4), concluding that "warming of the climate system is unequivocal."
2009	Copenhagen Accord negotiated at COP-15, establishing process for states to pledge national commitments and actions.
2010	COP-16 adopts Cancun Agreements, formalizing the main elements of Copenhagen Accord.
2011	COP-17 adopts Durban Platform, initiating negotiations on post-2020 climate change regime.
2012	COP-18 adopts Doha Amendment, extending Kyoto Protocol through 2020.

The climate change problem is intrinsically international, as Table 12-3 illustrates, both in its causes and in its effects. U.S. emissions, for example, account for less than a quarter of the global total. As a result, even if the United States (or any other individual country) were to become "carbon neutral," with zero emissions, this would not solve the climate change problem if other countries continued to emit. Similarly, climate change has global effects, so every country in the world has a stake in the outcomes of the international regime.

Although most economic models suggest that the benefits of taking action against climate change exceed the costs, the climate change issue has several features that make it extremely difficult to address both nationally and internationally:

- *High stakes.* The issue implicates virtually every part of a country's economy— energy production, transportation, even agriculture. So it is as much an economic and development issue as an environmental issue. Moreover, policies to reduce emissions threaten powerful and entrenched economic interests, which benefit from continued use of fossil fuels.
- *High uncertainties.* Both the benefits and costs of taking action against climate change are uncertain. Although most scientists believe that the consequences of climate change will be severe—perhaps even catastrophic—substantial uncertainties persist about how much warming will occur and the likely damages. Similarly, economists give widely different estimates of the costs of reducing emissions.
- *Distant time horizon.* Climate change is a long-term problem. It requires societies to undertake potentially costly actions now to avert damages that are not only uncertain, but, to a significant degree, far off in the future.
- *Divergent state interests.* The costs and benefits of reducing emissions are likely to vary widely from state to state, depending on a state's energy resources and vulnerability to climate change, so states have very different perceived interests. Some states may think they have nothing to gain from reaching agreement, either because the costs of action will fall particularly hard on them (this is true of oil-producing states) or because they could benefit from climate change.

Historically, Western countries have contributed the bulk of greenhouse gas emissions. But this is rapidly changing, with the dramatic growth of emerging economies such as China, India, and Brazil. China overtook the United States as the world's biggest emitter almost a decade ago, and most of the increase in greenhouse gas emissions over the next century is expected to occur in developing countries.

NOTES AND QUESTIONS

1. Developing countries now account for more than half of global GHG emissions, but their emissions per capita are still very low compared to Western countries. In allocating the burden of taking action to combat climate change, should we focus on historical responsibility? Current capabilities? Per capita emission levels? Emission reduction opportunities (as measured, for example, by marginal costs of abatement)? Some other criterion? Some combination of these criteria?

2. International law has traditionally depended on consent. Given divergent state interests regarding climate change, could an international climate change agreement leave every state better off—that is, could it result in what economists refer to as a "Pareto improvement"? If so, how? If a state refuses to consent to a climate change agreement, should other states be allowed to use coercion—for example, through the application of trade measures—against the dissenting state?

1. The UN Climate Change Regime

Although the general theory of greenhouse warming has been understood since the end of the nineteenth century, an international regime to address the problem began to develop only in the late 1980s, due to improved scientific knowledge, promotion of the issue by scientists and environmentalists, and an upswing in public concern about global environmental issues generally. The first intergovernmental response came in 1988, when the World Meteorological Organization (WMO) and the UN Environment Programme (UNEP) created the Intergovernmental Panel on Climate Change (IPCC) to provide a scientific and policy assessment of the problem. Two years later, the UN General Assembly established an Intergovernmental Negotiating Committee (INC) to develop a framework convention on climate change. The INC negotiated the UN Framework Convention on Climate Change (UNFCCC) in little more than fifteen months, finalizing the text on May 9, 1992, shortly before the beginning of the Earth Summit (discussed in Chapter 11).

a. The UN Framework Convention on Climate Change

UN FRAMEWORK CONVENTION ON CLIMATE CHANGE
1771 U.N.T.S. 107 (May 9, 1992)

The Parties to this Convention,

Acknowledging that change in the Earth's climate and its adverse effects are a common concern of humankind,

Concerned that human activities have been substantially increasing the atmospheric concentrations of greenhouse gases, . . .

Noting that the largest share of historical and current global emissions of greenhouse gases has originated in developed countries, that per capita emissions in developing countries are still relatively low and that the share of global emissions originating in developing countries will grow to meet their social and development needs, . . .

Noting that there are many uncertainties in predictions of climate change, particularly with regard to the timing, magnitude and regional patterns thereof, . . .

Recognizing further that low-lying and other small island countries, countries with low-lying coastal, arid and semi-arid areas or areas liable to floods, drought and desertification, and developing countries with fragile mountainous ecosystems are particularly vulnerable to the adverse effects of climate change,

Recognizing the special difficulties of those countries, especially developing countries, whose economies are particularly dependent on fossil fuel production, use and exportation, as a consequence of action taken on limiting greenhouse gas emissions, . . .

Determined to protect the climate system for present and future generations,

Have agreed as follows:

Article 2: Objective

The ultimate objective of this Convention and any related legal instruments that the Conference of the Parties may adopt is to achieve . . . stabilization of greenhouse gas concentrations in the atmosphere at a level that would prevent dangerous anthropogenic interference with the climate system. Such a level should be achieved within a time frame sufficient to allow ecosystems to adapt naturally to climate change, to ensure that food production is not threatened and to enable economic development to proceed in a sustainable manner.

Article 3: Principles

In their actions to achieve the objective of the Convention and to implement its provisions, the Parties shall be guided, *inter alia*, by the following:

1. The Parties should protect the climate system for the benefit of present and future generations of humankind, on the basis of equity and in accordance with their common but differentiated responsibilities and respective capabilities. Accordingly, the developed country Parties should take the lead in combating climate change and the adverse effects thereof.

2. The specific needs and special circumstances of developing country Parties, especially those that are particularly vulnerable to the adverse effects of climate change, and of those Parties, especially developing country Parties, that would have to bear a disproportionate or abnormal burden under the Convention, should be given full consideration.

3. The Parties should take precautionary measures to anticipate, prevent or minimize the causes of climate change and mitigate its adverse effects. Where there are threats of serious or irreversible damage, lack of full scientific certainty should not be used as a reason for postponing such measures, taking into account that policies and measures to deal with climate change should be cost-effective so as to ensure global benefits at the lowest possible cost. To achieve this, such policies and measures should take into account different socio-economic contexts, be comprehensive, cover all relevant sources, sinks and reservoirs of greenhouse gases and adaptation, and comprise all economic sectors. Efforts to address climate change may be carried out cooperatively by interested Parties.

4. The Parties have a right to, and should, promote sustainable development. Policies and measures to protect the climate system against human-induced change should be appropriate for the specific conditions of each Party and should be integrated with national development programmes, taking into account that economic development is essential for adopting measures to address climate change.

5. . . . Measures taken to combat climate change, including unilateral ones, should not constitute a means of arbitrary or unjustifiable discrimination or a disguised restriction on international trade.

Article 4: Commitments

1. All Parties, taking into account their common but differentiated responsibilities and their specific national and regional development priorities, objectives and circumstances, shall:

   (a) Develop, periodically update, publish and make available to the Conference of the Parties . . . national inventories of anthropogenic emissions by sources and removals by sinks of all greenhouse gases not controlled by the Montreal Protocol, using comparable methodologies to be agreed upon by the Conference of the Parties;

(b) Formulate, implement, publish and regularly update national and, where appropriate, regional programmes containing measures to mitigate climate change by addressing anthropogenic emissions by sources and removals by sinks of all greenhouse gases not controlled by the Montreal Protocol, and measures to facilitate adequate adaptation to climate change; . . .

(f) Take climate change considerations into account, to the extent feasible, in their relevant social, economic and environmental policies and actions, and employ appropriate methods, for example impact assessments, formulated and determined nationally, with a view to minimizing adverse effects on the economy, on public health and on the quality of the environment, of projects or measures undertaken by them to mitigate or adapt to climate change;

(g) Promote and cooperate in scientific, technological, technical, socio-economic and other research, systematic observation and development of data archives related to the climate system. . . .

2. The developed country Parties and other Parties included in Annex I commit themselves specifically as provided for in the following:

(a) Each of these Parties shall adopt national policies and take corresponding measures on the mitigation of climate change, by limiting its anthropogenic emissions of greenhouse gases and protecting and enhancing its greenhouse gas sinks and reservoirs. These policies and measures will demonstrate that developed countries are taking the lead in modifying longer-term trends in anthropogenic emissions consistent with the objective of the Convention, recognizing that the return by the end of the present decade to earlier levels of anthropogenic emissions of carbon dioxide and other greenhouse gases not controlled by the Montreal Protocol would contribute to such modification . . . ;

(b) In order to promote progress to this end, each of these Parties shall communicate . . . detailed information on its policies and measures referred to in subparagraph (a) above, . . . with the aim of returning individually or jointly to their 1990 levels these anthropogenic emissions of carbon dioxide and other greenhouse gases not controlled by the Montreal Protocol. . . .

(d) The Conference of the Parties shall, at its first session, review the adequacy of subparagraphs (a) and (b) above. Such review shall be carried out in the light of the best available scientific information and assessment on climate change and its impacts, as well as relevant technical, social and economic information. Based on this review, the Conference of the Parties shall take appropriate action, which may include the adoption of amendments to the commitments in subparagraphs (a) and (b) above . . . ;

(f) The Conference of the Parties shall review, not later than 31 December 1998, available information with a view to taking decisions regarding such amendments to the lists in Annexes I and II as may be appropriate, with the approval of the Party concerned. . . .

3. The developed country Parties and other developed Parties included in Annex II shall provide new and additional financial resources to meet the agreed full costs incurred by developing country Parties in complying with their obligations under

Article 12, paragraph 1. They shall also provide such financial resources, . . . needed by the developing country Parties to meet the agreed full incremental costs of implementing measures that are covered by paragraph 1 of this Article and that are agreed between a developing country Party and the international entity or entities referred to in Article 11. . . .

5. The developed country Parties and other developed Parties included in Annex II shall take all practicable steps to promote, facilitate and finance, as appropriate, the transfer of, or access to, environmentally sound technologies and know-how to other Parties, particularly developing country Parties, to enable them to implement the provisions of the Convention. . . .

7. The extent to which developing country Parties will effectively implement their commitments under the Convention will depend on the effective implementation by developed country Parties of their commitments under the Convention related to financial resources and transfer of technology. . . .

Article 7: *Conference of the Parties*

1. A Conference of the Parties is hereby established.

2. The Conference of the Parties, as the supreme body of this Convention, shall keep under regular review the implementation of the Convention and any related legal instruments that the Conference of the Parties may adopt, and shall make, within its mandate, the decisions necessary to promote the effective implementation of the Convention. . . .

4. . . . [O]rdinary sessions of the Conference of the Parties shall be held every year unless otherwise decided by the Conference of the Parties.

Article 11: *Financial Mechanism*

1. A mechanism for the provision of financial resources on a grant or concessional basis, including for the transfer of technology, is hereby defined. It shall function under the guidance of and be accountable to the Conference of the Parties. . . .

2. The financial mechanism shall have an equitable and balanced representation of all Parties within a transparent system of governance. . . .

5. The developed country Parties may also provide and developing country Parties avail themselves of, financial resources related to the implementation of the Convention through bilateral, regional and other multilateral channels.

Article 12: *Communication of Information Related to Implementation*

1. In accordance with Article 4, paragraph 1, each Party shall communicate to the Conference of the Parties, through the secretariat, the following elements of information:

(a) A national inventory of anthropogenic emissions by sources and removals by sinks of all greenhouse gases not controlled by the Montreal Protocol, to the extent its capacities permit, using comparable methodologies to be promoted and agreed upon by the Conference of the Parties;

(b) A general description of steps taken or envisaged by the Party to implement the Convention. . . .

2. Each developed country Party and each other Party included in Annex I shall incorporate in its communication the following elements of information:

(a) A detailed description of the policies and measures that it has adopted to implement its commitment under Article 4, paragraphs 2(a) and 2(b); and

(b) A specific estimate of the effects that the policies and measures referred to in subparagraph (a) immediately above will have on anthropogenic emissions by its sources and removals by its sinks of greenhouse gases during the period referred to in Article 4, paragraph 2(a). . . .

Article 17: Protocols

1. The Conference of the Parties may, at any ordinary session, adopt protocols to the Convention. . . .

Article 18: Right to Vote

1. Each Party to the Convention shall have one vote, except as provided for in paragraph 2 below. . . .

Annex I and Annex II Countries

ANNEX I

Australia, Austria, Belarus*, Belgium, Bulgaria*, Canada, Czechoslovakia*, Denmark, European Economic Community, Estonia*, Finland, France, Germany, Greece, Hungary*, Iceland, Ireland, Italy, Japan, Latvia*, Lithuania*, Luxembourg, Netherlands, New Zealand, Norway, Poland*, Portugal, Romania*, Russian Federation*, Spain, Sweden, Switzerland, Turkey, Ukraine*, United Kingdom of Great Britain and Northern Ireland, United States of America

ANNEX II

Australia, Austria, Belgium, Canada, Denmark, European Economic Community, Finland, France, Germany, Greece, Iceland, Ireland, Italy, Japan, Luxembourg, Netherlands, New Zealand, Norway, Portugal, Spain, Sweden, Switzerland, United Kingdom of Great Britain and Northern Ireland, United States

*Countries that are undergoing the process of transition to a market economy.

Note: Turkey was deleted from Annex II by an amendment that entered into force 28 June 2002.

NOTES AND QUESTIONS

1. What are the basic functions of the UNFCCC? Is it likely to lead to emissions reductions? If so, how?

2. Which countries or groups of countries do you think pushed for inclusion of which provisions of the UNFCCC? Which provisions, for example, reflect the views of the European Union? The United States? Developing countries? Oil-producing states? What other categories or groups of countries, if any, are identified in the UNFCCC? What special provisions relate to them?

3. The preamble of a treaty is often used to set forth basic principles or concepts. In the case of the UNFCCC, the agreement also contains specific articles entitled "objective" and "principles." What is the purpose of each of the paragraphs in the preamble? What do Articles 2 and 3 add?

4. The chapeaux of Article 4.1 frames the enumeration of commitments that follows with the language "taking into account the [Parties'] common but differentiated responsibilities and respective capabilities and their specific national and regional development priorities, objectives and circumstances." What is the effect of this language on the commitments set forth in Article 4.1?

5. The UNFCCC recognizes the principle of "common but differentiated responsibilities and respective capabilities." Which commitments in the UNFCCC are "common"? Which are "differentiated"? What commitments do developed countries have under the UNFCCC? Developing countries? What is the effect of Article 4.7 on the obligations of developing countries?

6. During the negotiations, the European Union pushed for mandatory targets for emission reductions, while the United States opposed the inclusion of "targets and timetables." Which side was successful? Read Article 4.2 carefully. Does it reflect a targets-and-timetables approach?

7. What institutions are established by the UNFCCC? What are the powers of the Conference of the Parties (COP)? Can it make legally binding decisions?

8. How does the UNFCCC try to ensure that the climate change regime develops in response to new circumstances and new knowledge? What are the various mechanisms by which development can take place?

9. The UNFCCC is open for signature by any state. Today, it has 196 parties, including virtually every country in the world. Why do you think so many countries have joined? Given the fact that just 20 countries account for more than 80 percent of global greenhouse gas emissions, does it make sense to address the climate change issue in a global forum with 196 parties? Or would it be preferable to address the issue in a smaller forum, limited to the "big emitters"?

10. The first Bush administration actively participated in negotiating the UNFCCC, and the United States ratified the agreement in October 1992, making it one of the first countries to do so. Why do you think the United States was so supportive? If the UNFCCC were to come before the Senate today, do you think the Senate would give "advice and consent" to ratification?

b. The Kyoto Protocol

At the first Conference of the Parties (COP-1) held in 1995, states reviewed the adequacy of UNFCCC Article 4.2 (pursuant to Article 4.2(d)), concluded that the commitments were inadequate, and adopted the Berlin Mandate, authorizing a new round of negotiations to "take appropriate action for the period beyond 2000, including the strengthening of the commitments of . . . Annex I Parties . . . through the adoption of a protocol or another legal instrument." The Berlin Mandate negotiations had the goal of setting "quantified limitation and reduction objectives within specified time-frame" for the emissions of Annex I (developed country) Parties—i.e., targets and timetables. But it specifically excluded "any new commitments" for non-Annex I (developing country) Parties. Over the next two years, the Ad Hoc Working Group on the Berlin Mandate (AGBM) negotiated the Kyoto Protocol, which was adopted by COP-3 on December 10, 1997.

The Kyoto Protocol imposed quantitative emissions targets for developed countries for a five-year (2008-2012) "first commitment period." These emissions targets varied from country to country. For example, the European Union was required to reduce its emissions by 8 percent relative to 1990 levels and Japan by 6 percent. (The U.S. reduction target would have been 7 percent had it joined the Protocol.) In 2012, the parties to the Kyoto Protocol adopted an amendment establishing a second commitment period, which runs through 2020. Pursuant to the Berlin Mandate, the Protocol has not imposed any emission reduction targets on developing countries.

The Protocol allows developed country parties to meet their emission targets using several "flexibility mechanisms." Pursuant to Article 4, the EU member states were allowed to create an emissions "bubble" and meet their 8 percent reduction target collectively. In addition, parties may engage in emissions trading pursuant to Article 17, and may receive credits for emission reduction projects undertaken in developing countries under the Clean Development Mechanism (CDM) (pursuant to Article 12). Parties have complete freedom in their choice of domestic policy instruments to achieve their targets, and may "bank" unused emissions allowances if they emit less than their targeted amount (Article 3.13). The Protocol also provides for a detailed system of reporting and review (Articles 5 and 8) and for the establishment of a compliance system (Article 18).

KYOTO PROTOCOL
2303 U.N.T.S. 148 (Dec. 10, 1997)

Article 3

1. The Parties included in Annex I shall, individually or jointly, ensure that their aggregate anthropogenic carbon dioxide equivalent emissions of the greenhouse gases listed in Annex A do not exceed their assigned amounts, calculated pursuant to their quantified emission limitation and reduction commitments inscribed in Annex B and in accordance with the provisions of this Article, with a view to reducing their overall emissions of such gases by at least 5 per cent below 1990 levels in the commitment period 2008 to 2012. . . .

3. The net changes in greenhouse gas emissions by sources and removals by sinks resulting from direct human-induced land-use change and forestry activities, limited to afforestation, reforestation and deforestation since 1990, measured as verifiable changes in carbon stocks in each commitment period, shall be used to meet the commitments under this Article of each Party included in Annex I. . . .

4. . . . The Conference of the Parties serving as the meeting of the Parties to this Protocol [hereinafter CMP] shall, at its first session or as soon as practicable thereafter, decide upon modalities, rules and guidelines as to how, and which, additional human-induced activities related to changes in greenhouse gas emissions by sources and removals by sinks in the agricultural soils and the land-use change and forestry categories shall be added to, or subtracted from, the assigned amounts for Parties included in Annex I, . . .

7. In the first quantified emission limitation and reduction commitment period, from 2008 to 2012, the assigned amount for each Party included in Annex I shall be equal to the percentage inscribed for it in Annex B of its aggregate anthropogenic carbon dioxide equivalent emissions of the greenhouse gases listed in Annex A in 1990 . . . multiplied by five. . . .

8. Any Party included in Annex I may use 1995 as its base year for hydrofluorocarbons [HFCs], perfluorocarbons [PFCs] and sulphur hexafluoride [SF_6], for the purposes of the calculation referred to in paragraph 7 above.

9. Commitments for subsequent periods for Parties included in Annex I shall be established in amendments to Annex B to this Protocol, which shall be adopted in accordance with the provisions of Article 21, paragraph 7. The CMP shall initiate the consideration of such commitments at least seven years before the end of the first commitment period referred to in paragraph 1 above.

10. Any emission reduction units, or any part of an assigned amount, which a Party acquires from another Party in accordance with the provisions of Article 6 [on joint implementation] or of Article 17 [on emissions trading] shall be added to the assigned amount for the acquiring Party.

11. Any emission reduction units, or any part of an assigned amount, which a Party transfers to another Party in accordance with the provisions of Article 6 or of Article 17 shall be subtracted from the assigned amount for the transferring Party.

12. Any certified emission reductions which a Party acquires from another Party in accordance with the provisions of Article 12 [Clean Development Mechanism] shall be added to the assigned amount for the acquiring Party.

13. If the emissions of a Party included in Annex I in a commitment period are less than its assigned amount under this Article, this difference shall, on request of that Party, be added to the assigned amount for that Party for subsequent commitment periods. . . .

Article 5

1. Each Party included in Annex I shall have in place, no later than one year prior to the start of the first commitment period, a national system for the estimation of anthropogenic emissions by sources and removals by sinks of all greenhouse gases not controlled by the Montreal Protocol. . . .

2. Methodologies for estimating anthropogenic emissions by sources and removals by sinks of all greenhouse gases not controlled by the Montreal Protocol shall be those accepted by the Intergovernmental Panel on Climate Change and agreed upon by the Conference of the Parties at its third session. . . .

Article 8

1. The information submitted under Article 7 by each Party included in Annex I shall be reviewed by expert review teams. . . .

2. Expert review teams shall be coordinated by the secretariat and shall be composed of experts selected from those nominated by Parties to the Convention and, as appropriate, by intergovernmental organizations. . . .

3. The review process shall provide a thorough and comprehensive technical assessment of all aspects of the implementation by a Party of this Protocol. The expert review teams shall prepare a report to the CMP, assessing the implementation of the commitments of the Party and identifying any potential problems in, and factors influencing, the fulfillment of commitments. . . .

4. The CMP shall adopt at its first session, and review periodically thereafter, guidelines for the review of implementation of this Protocol by expert review teams. . . .

6. Pursuant to its consideration of the information referred to in paragraph 5 above, the CMP shall take decisions on any matter required for the implementation of this Protocol.

Article 9

1. The CMP shall periodically review this Protocol in the light of the best available scientific information and assessments on climate change and its impacts, as well as relevant technical, social and economic information. . . . Based on these reviews, the CMP shall take appropriate action.

2. The first review shall take place at the second session of the CMP. Further reviews shall take place at regular intervals and in a timely manner.

Article 12

1. A clean development mechanism is hereby defined.

2. The purpose of the clean development mechanism shall be to assist Parties not included in Annex I in achieving sustainable development and in contributing to the ultimate objective of the Convention, and to assist Parties included in Annex I in achieving compliance with their quantified emission limitation and reduction commitments under Article 3.

3. Under the clean development mechanism:

(a) Parties not included in Annex I will benefit from project activities resulting in certified emission reductions; and

(b) Parties included in Annex I may use the certified emission reductions accruing from such project activities to contribute to compliance with part of their quantified emission limitation and reduction commitments under Article 3. . . .

4. The clean development mechanism shall be subject to the authority and guidance of the CMP and be supervised by an executive board of the clean development mechanism.

5. Emission reductions resulting from each project activity shall be certified by operational entities to be designated by the CMP on the basis of:

(a) Voluntary participation approved by each Party involved;

(b) Real, measurable, and long-term benefits related to the mitigation of climate change; and

(c) Reductions in emissions that are additional to any that would occur in the absence of the certified project activity. . . .

7. The CMP shall, at its first session, elaborate modalities and procedures with the objective of ensuring transparency, efficiency and accountability through independent auditing and verification of project activities.

8. The CMP shall ensure that a share of the proceeds from certified project activities is used to cover administrative expenses as well as to assist developing country Parties that are particularly vulnerable to the adverse effects of climate change to meet the costs of adaptation.

9. Participation under the clean development mechanism . . . may involve private and/or public entities. . . .

Article 17

The Conference of the Parties shall define the relevant principles, modalities, rules and guidelines, in particular for verification, reporting and accountability for emissions trading. The Parties included in Annex B may participate in emissions trading for the purposes of fulfilling their commitments under Article 3. Any such trading shall be supplemental to domestic actions for the purpose of meeting quantified emission limitation and reduction commitments under that Article.

Article 18

The CMP shall, at its first session, approve appropriate and effective procedures and mechanisms to determine and to address cases of non-compliance with the provisions of this Protocol, including through the development of an indicative list of consequences. . . . Any procedures and mechanisms under this Article entailing binding consequences shall be adopted by means of an amendment to this Protocol.

Article 21

7. . . . . [A]ny amendment to Annex B shall be adopted only with the written consent of the Party concerned.

Article 25

1. This Protocol shall enter into force on the ninetieth day after the date on which not less than 55 Parties to the Convention, incorporating Parties included in Annex I which accounted in total for at least 55 per cent of the total carbon dioxide emissions for 1990 of the Parties included in Annex I, have deposited their instruments of ratification, acceptance, approval or accession. . . .

Annex A:

Greenhouse gases

Carbon dioxide (CO_2)
Methane (CH_4)
Nitrous oxide (N_2O)
Hydrofluorocarbons (HFCs)
Perfluorocarbons (PFCs)
Sulphur hexafluoride (SF_6)

Annex B:

quantified emission limitation or reduction commitment (percentage of base year or period)

Australia 108	Liechtenstein 92
Austria 92	Lithuania 92
Belgium 92	Luxembourg 92
Bulgaria 92	Monaco 92
Canada 94	Netherlands 92
Croatia 95	New Zealand 100
Czech Republic 92	Norway 101
Denmark 92	Poland 94
Estonia 92	Portugal 92
European Community 92	Romania 92
Finland 92	Russian Federation 100
France 92	Slovakia 92
Germany 92	Slovenia 92
Greece 92	Spain 92
Hungary 94	Sweden 92
Iceland 110	Switzerland 92
Ireland 92	Ukraine 100
Italy 92	United Kingdom of Great Britain and Northern Ireland 92
Japan 94	United States of America 93
Latvia 92	

HEPBURN, CARBON TRADING: A REVIEW OF THE KYOTO MECHANISMS

Annual Review of Environmental Resources 32: 375-393 (2007)

3.1. Conceptual Underpinnings

The three Kyoto Protocol "flexibility mechanisms" are designed to enable emission reductions to occur in the cheapest locations across the globe. The first mechanism, emissions trading, can occur between countries with binding targets, so that countries can meet their domestic targets by purchasing credits from other countries that have exceeded their targets. The largest implementation of emissions trading to date has been the EU ETS [Emissions Trading System]. Second, the CDM [Clean Development Mechanism] is a project-based mechanism that allows credits from emission reduction projects in poorer countries to be used by rich countries to meet their own commitments under the Kyoto Protocol. Third, JI [Joint Implementation] is also a project-based mechanism that enables countries with binding targets to get credit from projects carried out in other countries with binding targets.

All three mechanisms rest on the Coasian solution for the tragedy of the commons—privatize the commons and trade the resulting property rights. . . . [W]ith environmental assets, under some relatively straightforward conditions, economic theory implies that an ETS will deliver emission reductions at least cost to society. There is evidence to support this assertion from experience in other environmental and non-environmental contexts. . . .

3.2. International Emissions Trading and the Carbon Markets

Article 17 of the Kyoto Protocol allows Annex B countries to "participate in emissions trading for the purposes of fulfilling their commitments," provided that trading is supplemental to domestic action. This allows nation states who would not otherwise meet their commitments to purchase units from other states in the form of

- Assigned amount units (AAUs), the unit assigned directly to nation states under the Kyoto Protocol
- Certified emission reductions (CERs) from project activities under the CDM
- Emission reduction units (ERUs) from JI projects
- Removal units on the basis of land use, land-use change and forestry (LULUCF) activities.

    . . . .

3.4. The Clean Development Mechanism

Under Article 12 of the Kyoto Protocol, the CDM was established to help non-Annex I countries in "achieving sustainable development" and to provide Annex I countries with an alternative mechanism for complying with their targets. The CDM does this by allowing Annex I governments or private entities to accrue CERs from project activities in non-Annex I countries. . . . CERs are only created if all parties give their voluntary approval and if the emissions reductions are real, measurable, and additional.

The process for putting together a project under the CDM requires the project developer to satisfy a number of procedural stages. These hurdles can involve relatively high transaction costs, although there are simplified procedures for small-scale projects. Projects are proposed in a formal Project Design Document, which presents detailed information, including a study of what would have occurred without the project (the "baseline"), . . . a monitoring and verification plan to determine the quantity of emissions reduced that are "additional" to the status quo, coupled with an estimate of expected emission reductions. . . .

Typical projects to date have included renewable energy projects (wind, smaller-scale hydro, renewable biomass) and the capture [and] destruction of damaging greenhouse gases such as methane, nitrous oxide, and hydrofluorocarbons. . . .

3.5. Joint Implementation

JI under article 6.1 of the Protocol allows the transfer or acquisition of ERUs between Annex I states, which are also engaged in emissions trading. . . . JI processes have similar processes and institutions to the CDM. Sellers of ERUs are primarily from Russia and Eastern Europe, whereas the buyers are primarily Western European countries with tighter Kyoto targets. . . .

NOTES AND QUESTIONS

1. The Kyoto Protocol emissions targets reflect a "comprehensive approach" to climate change. They cover emissions of a basket of six gases (carbon dioxide, methane, nitrous oxide, and three trace gases), and allow countries to receive credits for removal of carbon dioxide from the atmosphere due to reforestation and certain other carbon "sink" activities, such as forest management.

2. Article 3 of the Protocol establishes an elaborate compliance equation to determine whether parties have met their emissions targets. Study Article 3 and try to piece together the various parts of this equation.

3. The Kyoto Protocol negotiations were followed by five additional years of negotiations to develop the detailed rules for implementing Kyoto, which were adopted in 2001 by COP-7 in the so-called Marrakesh Accords. Identify the areas in the Kyoto Protocol that required further elaboration by the COP.

4. The Marrakesh Accords paved the way for ratification and entry into force of the Protocol, which occurred in 2005. As of July 2014, the Kyoto Protocol had 192 parties. A notable exception is the United States. Prior to the Protocol's adoption in December 1997, the U.S. Senate adopted a non-binding resolution by a vote of 95-0, stating that the United States should not join any agreement that would result in "serious harm" to the U.S. economy or that mandated emission reduction commitments for developed countries but did not do the same for developing countries within the same compliance period. Byrd-Hagel Resolution, S. Res. 98, July 25, 1997. President Clinton signed the Kyoto Protocol, but never submitted it to the Senate for advice and consent to ratification, and President Bush repudiated the Protocol early in his administration.

5. Although the United States has rejected the Kyoto Protocol, the Protocol reflects many U.S. ideas, including a market-based approach that allows countries to meet their commitments through emissions trading and through emission reduction projects in developing countries (under the Clean Development Mechanism). What are the advantages and disadvantages of a market-based approach? Do you agree with critics that the Kyoto Protocol's "flexibility mechanisms" are ethically suspect, since they allow rich, developed countries to buy their way out rather than to reduce their own emissions? Are purchases of emissions "allowances" similar to buying "indulgences" from the Catholic Church during the Middle Ages?

6. The Kyoto Protocol has numerous critics. For example, David Victor has criticized Kyoto's targets-and-timetables approach in the following terms:

> The Kyoto diplomats made hasty promises that some countries, notably the United States, quickly abandoned as unrealistic. Others, such as Canada, balked in response. Still others, such as Russia, were allowed to make Kyoto promises so diluted that they required no real effort to honor. Of the major economies, only the European nations and Japan actually made (and have so far honored) promises that required much effort; but those countries are a relatively small and shrinking part of the warming problem. [David Victor, Plan B for Copenhagen, 461 Nature 342 (Sept. 17, 2009).]

7. In 2012, the parties to the Kyoto Protocol adopted the Doha Amendment, which established a second commitment period running from 2012-2020. But a number of states that had accepted first commitment period targets declined to accept new emission reduction targets for the second commitment period, including Japan, Russia, and Canada. As a result, the Doha Amendment encompasses only a small number of states, including the members of the European Union, Norway, Switzerland, and Ukraine.

c. Copenhagen Accord

In 2007, the parties to the UNFCCC adopted the Bali Action Plan, which initiated negotiations to develop a "comprehensive outcome" addressing the post-2012 period (to complement the negotiations on the Kyoto Protocol's second commitment period). The Bali Action Plan negotiations were set to conclude at the Copenhagen Conference in December 2009, which was attended by more than 120 heads of state, making it one of the largest gathering of world leaders in history. But what emerged from the Copenhagen Conference was not a new legal agreement, but rather a political agreement, negotiated by 28 countries (including all of the major economies), primarily at the head-of-state level. The breakthrough on the Accord reportedly came in the final hours of the conference, at a small meeting between President Obama, Chinese Premier Wen Jiabao, Indian Prime Minister Singh, and Brazilian President Lula.

Due to objections by a handful of states (led by Sudan, Venezuela, Bolivia, and Cuba), the Copenhagen Conference was unable to adopt the Accord. Instead, the conference merely "took note" of it, leaving its status unclear within the UNFCCC process. It was not until the following year that the political deal struck in Copenhagen was formalized in the UNFCCC process, through the adoption at COP-16 of the Cancun Agreements. In contrast to Copenhagen, where a group of countries (albeit small) objected to adoption, in Cancun only a single state (Bolivia) objected and the chair simply noted the objection and then gaveled the decision through. The Cancun Agreements reiterate all of the key elements of the Copenhagen Accord and, through formal adoption by the parties, put them on a firmer legal footing within the UNFCCC process. More than 130 countries (representing more than 85 percent of global emissions) associated themselves with the Accord, and more than 80 have submitted national pledges to limit their greenhouse gas emissions, as provided in paragraphs 4 and 5 of the Accord.

COPENHAGEN ACCORD
(2009)

The Heads of State, Heads of Government, Ministers, and other heads of the following delegations present at the United Nations Climate Change Conference 2009 in Copenhagen: [list of countries associating themselves with the Accord]. . . .
Have agreed on this Copenhagen Accord which is operational immediately.

1. We underline that climate change is one of the greatest challenges of our time. We emphasize our strong political will to urgently combat climate change in accordance with the principle of common but differentiated responsibilities and respective capabilities. To achieve the ultimate objective of the Convention . . . , we shall, recognizing the scientific view that the increase in global temperature should be below 2 degrees Celsius, on the basis of equity and in the context of sustainable development, enhance our long-term cooperative action to combat climate change. . . .

2. We agree that deep cuts in global emissions are required according to science, . . . with a view to reduce global emissions so as to hold the increase in global temperature below 2 degrees Celsius. . . . We should cooperate in achieving the peaking of global and national emissions as soon as possible, recognizing that the time frame for peaking will be longer in developing countries and bearing in mind that social and economic development and poverty eradication are the first and overriding priorities of developing countries and that a low-emission development strategy is indispensable to sustainable development.

3. Adaptation to the adverse effects of climate change and the potential impacts of response measures is a challenge faced by all countries. Enhanced action and international cooperation on adaptation is urgently required. . . . We agree that developed countries shall provide adequate, predictable and sustainable financial resources, technology and capacity-building to support the implementation of adaptation action in developing countries.

4. Annex I Parties commit to implement individually or jointly the quantified economy wide emissions targets for 2020, to be submitted in the format given in Appendix I by Annex I Parties to the secretariat by 31 January 2010. . . . Delivery of reductions and financing by developed countries will be measured, reported and verified in accordance with existing and any further guidelines adopted by the Conference of the Parties, and will ensure that accounting of such targets and finance is rigorous, robust and transparent.

5. Non-Annex I Parties to the Convention will implement mitigation actions, including those to be submitted to the secretariat by non-Annex I Parties in the format given in Appendix II by 31 January 2010. . . . Least developed countries and small island developing States may undertake actions voluntarily and on the basis of support. . . . Mitigation actions taken by Non-Annex I Parties will be subject to their domestic measurement, reporting and verification the result of which will be reported through their national communications every two years. Non-Annex I Parties will communicate information on the implementation of their actions through National Communications, with provisions for international consultations and analysis under clearly defined guidelines that will ensure that national sovereignty is respected. Nationally appropriate mitigation actions seeking international support will be recorded in a registry along with relevant technology, finance and

capacity building support. Those actions supported will be added to the list in Appendix II. These supported nationally appropriate mitigation actions will be subject to international measurement, reporting and verification in accordance with guidelines adopted by the Conference of the Parties.

6. We recognize the crucial role of reducing emission from deforestation and forest degradation and the need to enhance removals of greenhouse gas emission by forests and agree on the need to provide positive incentives to such actions. . . .

7. We decide to pursue various approaches, including opportunities to use markets, to enhance the cost-effectiveness of, and to promote mitigation actions. . . .

8. Scaled up, new and additional, predictable and adequate funding as well as improved access shall be provided to developing countries, in accordance with the relevant provisions of the Convention, to enable and support enhanced action on mitigation, including substantial finance to reduce emissions from deforestation and forest degradation (REDD-plus), adaptation, technology development and transfer and capacity-building, for enhanced implementation of the Convention. The collective commitment by developed countries is to provide new and additional resources . . . approaching USD 30 billion for the period 2010-2012 with balanced allocation between adaptation and mitigation. . . . In the context of meaningful mitigation actions and transparency on implementation, developed countries commit to a goal of mobilizing jointly USD 100 billion dollars a year by 2020 to address the needs of developing countries. This funding will come from a wide variety of sources, public and private, bilateral and multilateral, including alternative sources of finance. . . .

10. We decide that the Copenhagen Green Climate Fund shall be established as an operating entity of the financial mechanism of the Convention. . . .

12. We call for an assessment of the implementation of this Accord to be completed by 2015, including in light of the Convention's ultimate objective. This would include consideration of strengthening the long-term goal referencing various matters presented by the science, including in relation to temperature rises of 1.5 degrees Celsius.

NOTES AND QUESTIONS

1. Compare the approach taken by the Copenhagen Accord with that of the Kyoto Protocol. What are the main differences?

2. What issues regarding the post-2012 climate regime did the Copenhagen Accord resolve and what issues did it leave open for future negotiations?

3. Many people criticized the Copenhagen Accord because it was a political agreement rather than a legally binding instrument. Do you think this matters? If so, in what ways do you think the Copenhagen Accord would have been more effective if it had been adopted as a legal agreement?

d. Durban Platform

In December 2011, the Durban Conference of the Parties adopted the Durban Platform, which launched a new round of negotiations to develop a "protocol, another legal instrument, or an agreed outcome with legal force under the UN Framework

Convention on Climate Change applicable to all Parties." The new negotiations began in 2012 and are scheduled to end in 2015, with the new instrument to be effective from 2020.

ESTABLISHMENT OF AN AD HOC WORKING GROUP ON THE DURBAN PLATFORM FOR ENHANCED ACTION
Decision 1/CP.17, December 2011

The Conference of the Parties,

Recognizing that climate change represents an urgent and potentially irreversible threat to human societies and the planet and thus requires to be urgently addressed by all Parties, and acknowledging that the global nature of climate change calls for the widest possible cooperation by all countries and their participation in an effective and appropriate international response. . . .

Noting with grave concern the significant gap between the aggregate effect of Parties' mitigation pledges in terms of global annual emissions of greenhouse gases by 2020 and aggregate emission pathways consistent with having a likely chance of holding the increase in global average temperature below 2 °C or 1.5 °C above pre-industrial levels,

Recognizing that fulfilling the ultimate objective of the Convention will require strengthening of the multilateral, rules-based regime under the Convention. . . .

2. . . . [D]*ecides* to launch a process to develop a protocol, another legal instrument or an agreed outcome with legal force under the Convention applicable to all Parties, through a subsidiary body under the Convention hereby established and to be known as the Ad Hoc Working Group on the Durban Platform for Enhanced Action. . . .

4. *Decides* that the Ad Hoc Working Group on the Durban Platform for Enhanced Action shall complete its work as early as possible but no later than 2015 in order to adopt this protocol, another legal instrument or an agreed outcome with legal force at the twenty first session of the Conference of the Parties and for it to come into effect and be implemented from 2020. . . .

5. *Also decides* that the Ad Hoc Working Group on the Durban Platform for Enhanced Action shall plan its work in the first half of 2012, including, inter alia, on mitigation, adaptation, finance, technology development and transfer, transparency of action and support, and capacity-building. . . .

6. *Further decides* that the process shall raise the level of ambition and shall be informed, inter alia, by the Fifth Assessment Report of the Intergovernmental Panel on Climate Change, the outcomes of the 2013-2015 review and the work of the subsidiary bodies. . . .

7. *Decides* to launch a workplan on enhancing mitigation ambition to identify and to explore options for a range of actions that can close the ambition gap with a view to ensuring the highest possible mitigation efforts by all Parties. . . .

NOTES AND QUESTIONS

1. The Durban Platform decision establishes two workstreams. Workstream 1 aims to negotiate a new instrument that would be adopted in 2015 and would apply from 2020. Workstream 2 aims to raise the level of ambition of parties' actions in the period through 2020.

2. What parameters does the Durban Platform establish for the 2015 agreement? How does its approach compare with the Kyoto Protocol?

3. What do you think should be the main elements of the 2015 agreement? Do you think the 2015 agreement should look more like the Kyoto Protocol or the Copenhagen Accord? Or should it take a different approach from either one?

2.   Using Other Regimes to Address Climate Change

Although the UNFCCC remains the locus of activities to combat global warming, other regimes have taken or are considering measures to limit greenhouse gas emissions.

Ozone Regime. Ozone-depleting substances (ODS), as well as some potential substitutes for ozone-depleting substances, are also greenhouse gases. There are thus strong synergies between the ozone and climate change regimes. On the one hand, the ozone regime can assist the climate change regime by phasing out ozone-depleting substances that are also greenhouse gases, such as hydroclorofluorocarbons (HCFCs). But it can also undermine the climate change regime by encouraging substitutes that are potent greenhouse gases. Under the ozone regime, for example, hydrofluorocarbons (HFCs) are encouraged as substitutes for ODS, because they have no effect on the ozone layer. But under the climate change regime, HFCs are restricted because they are potent greenhouse gases, many thousand times more powerful, molecule for molecule, than carbon dioxide.

On balance, the positive effect of the ozone regime in limiting global warming has significantly outweighed the negative effect. Indeed, one study estimates that the existing controls on ozone-depleting substances under the Montreal Protocol have reduced CO_2-equivalent (CO_{2eq}) emissions by roughly four times more than the Kyoto Protocol. Vedlers et al., The Importance of the Montreal Protocol in Protecting Climate, 104 PNAS 4814 (Mar. 20, 2007). Another study calls the Montreal Protocol "the most successful climate treaty to date." Molina et al., Reducing Abrupt Climate Change Risk Using the Montreal Protocol and Other Regulatory Actions to Complement Cuts in CO_2 Emissions, 106 PNAS 20616 (Dec. 8, 2009).

Recognizing the potential synergies between the ozone and climate change regimes, the parties to the Montreal Protocol adopted an amendment in September 2007 accelerating the phase-out schedule of HCFCs. HCFCs came into widespread use in the 1990s as a substitute for chlorofluorocarbons (CFCs), which are banned under the Montreal Protocol. But HCFCs are themselves ozone-depleting substances (albeit to a much lesser degree than CFCs) and also contribute to global warming. So phasing them out has a dual benefit. The accelerated phase-out schedule will provide up to 16 Gt (gigatons, or billions of metric tons) of CO_2 equivalent in climate mitigation by 2040, more than the Kyoto Protocol's first commitment period.

More recently, some countries have proposed regulating and phasing out the use of HFCs under the Montreal Protocol, to avoid their use as substitutes for HCFCs. An HFC phase-out under the Montreal Protocol would encourage countries to leapfrog HFCs to more climate-friendly alternatives. Nevertheless, some developing countries have objected, arguing that HFCs are already controlled under the Kyoto Protocol and are not themselves ozone-depleting substances, so they fall outside the scope of the Montreal Protocol.

Aircraft Emissions. The Kyoto Protocol regulates emissions within a country's territory, but does not regulate emissions from international transport by air or sea (sometimes referred to as "international bunkers"). Instead, Article 2.2 provides that Annex I parties shall pursue "limitation or reduction of emissions of greenhouse gases . . . from aviation and marine bunker fuels, working through the International Civil Aviation Organization [ICAO] and the International Maritime Organization [IMO], respectively."

ICAO is the UN specialized agency addressing international civil aviation. Although it has traditionally focused on aviation safety, it established a Committee on Aviation Environmental Protection (CAEP) in 1983 and a Group on International Aviation and Climate Change (GIACC) in 2008.

International aviation is estimated to contribute only about one to two percent of global CO_2 emissions, but as much as five percent of the total greenhouse effect, due to its role in cloud formation. Moreover, it is one of the fastest-growing sectors. Despite increases in fuel efficiency, emissions from civil aviation doubled between 1990 and 2006 and are projected to quadruple by 2050 due to increased travel. According to some estimates, these increases could be cut in half through a combination of operational practices, improved engines, and lower-carbon fuels.

At a high-level ICAO meeting held in October 2009, states agreed to a goal of improving global fuel efficiency by 2 percent annually, and established a process to develop a framework for the use of economic instruments, such as emissions trading, for emissions from civil aviation. But, frustrated with the slow progress of work in ICAO, the European Union attempted in 2012 to unilaterally extend its emissions trading system to emissions from flights landing in or departing from EU member states. Under tremendous pressure from the United States, China and India, the European Union backed down, agreeing in late 2012 to suspend extension of its emissions trading system to international civil aviation. In return, ICAO announced the formation of a high-level group to develop recommendations on the creation of a global market-based mechanism to address emissions from international civil aviation.

Maritime Emissions. Emissions from international shipping account for about 2.7 percent of global greenhouse gas emissions. Although maritime transport is already the most carbon-efficient mode of transport, the shipping industry estimates that it could improve its overall carbon efficiency by 50 percent through better ship design, more efficient operational practices, and use of lower-carbon fuels.

The International Maritime Organization (IMO) is ICAO's counterpart for maritime transport. An existing IMO treaty—the International Convention for the Prevention of Pollution from Ships (MARPOL)—addresses air pollution in Annex VI. In 2011, the IMO adopted an amendment to MARPOL Annex VI that regulates the energy efficiency of ships. The amendment was adopted by a vote of 49 in favor, 5 against, and 2 abstaining, with Brazil, China, and Saudi Arabia among those voting against the amendment. As a study prepared for the Pew Center on Global Climate Change concluded,

> The MARPOL Annex VI amendment is significant in several ways. First, it sets forth the first mandatory standards for a sector relating to greenhouse gas emissions. Second, its regulations apply uniformly, with no differentiation between vessels flagged in developed and developing countries . . . . Third, the amendment's adoption by a majority vote represents the first time that a decision relating to climate change has been taken over the objection of a significant group of countries.
>
> Countries that voted against the . . . amendment are free to opt out, but their ships will still need to meet the standards if they wish to call on ports of states that accept the

amendment. Moreover, it is likely that shipbuilders will comply with the new standards for all new ships, regardless of where a ship is expected to be flagged, since failure to comply with the standards will lower the potential resale value of a ship. For these reasons, the new MARPOL standards are expected to be applied universally to all new ships, even if some countries legally reserve to the amendment. [D. Bodansky, Multilateral Climate Efforts Beyond the UNFCCC 7-8 (2011).]

NOTES AND QUESTIONS

1. The UNFCCC regime is based on the principle of common but differentiated responsibilities and respective capabilities (CBDR). In contrast, ICAO and IMO have traditionally set uniform standards for international aviation and maritime transport, because of the international nature of the shipping industry. The Montreal Protocol imposes the same limits on ODS for developed and developing countries, but gives developing countries a 10-year grace period within which to comply. Some developing countries have argued that the principle of CBDR should apply to whatever climate change measures are adopted by the Montreal Protocol, ICAO or IMO. Do you agree?

2. In contrast to the UNFCCC, which operates by consensus, MARPOL allows decisions to be made by a three-quarters majority vote. As noted above, the 2011 MARPOL Annex VI amendment was adopted by a vote of 49-5-2. A related debate over whether to include the principle of CBDR in the terms of reference for a new expert group on market-based measures was also resolved on a majority basis. Saudi Arabia reportedly complained about the "tyranny of the majority trampling a significant maritime minority," while the United States referred to "the dose of poison that is CBDR." Do you think decisions on climate change mitigation actions should be decided by majority vote or consensus? Does the use of majority voting pose any potential problems? If you were representing the United States, would you support adoption of a three-quarters majority-voting rule in the UNFCCC?

3. In September 2011, the Pacific Island State of Palau announced that it would seek an advisory opinion from the ICJ on "the responsibilities of States under international law to ensure that activities carried out under their jurisdiction or control that emit greenhouse gases do not damage other States." UN Press Conference on Request for ICJ Advisory Opinion, Feb. 2, 2012. Although some countries have expressed support for the Palau initiative, it has languished in the General Assembly. Do you think an ICJ advisory opinion would be helpful in addressing climate change? If the ICJ were to give an advisory opinion finding that states have an international obligation to ensure that their greenhouse gas emissions do not harm other states, what effect, if any, do you think this would have on state behavior? What influence would it have on the UNFCCC negotiating process?

3. Climate Change and . . .

a. Trade

M. SELL, CLIMATE CHANGE AND ENERGY
Trade and Environment: A Resource Book (IISD 2007)

Dealing with climate change is fundamental to economic activity in all its forms—how we produce, use and trade energy and goods. Emissions of carbon dioxide . . . [are] a side effect of most production processes. Therefore, climate change mitigation measures have implications for most WTO agreements in some form or other. . . .

Energy Subsidies and Taxation

Governments use taxes and tax breaks to provide incentives to energy producers and users to become climate friendly. A carbon tax can be applied in various ways: as an excise tax on consumption, . . . on energy inputs, [or] . . . on energy production processes . . . [The WTO] requires that [a carbon] tax be applied equally to domestic and foreign products that are similar or "like." As a general rule, the WTO has not distinguished goods on the basis of how they are produced. . . . Countries implementing climate policy could argue that similar goods with similar end use produced in different ways are "unlike." However, this has yet to be done, and would require either the judgment of a dispute settlement panel, or an agreement between WTO Members, to recognize the distinction. A carbon tax on production methods could possibly also be defended as an environmental exception under GATT Article XX. . . .

Border Tax Adjustments

As countries choose different energy paths in the short to medium terms, some will be facing higher costs up front. Countries taking on carbon reduction commitments may experience some negative competitiveness effects, and there have been calls . . . for the use of border tax adjustments (BTAs) to offset such competitiveness effects with regard to countries that are not limiting their emissions. . . . The WTO allows Members to apply border tax adjustments. However, the legality of applying a border tax adjustment based on a product's implicit carbon content is still undecided and BTAs are controversial.

G. HUFBAUER & J. KIM, THE WORLD TRADE ORGANIZATION AND CLIMATE CHANGE: CHALLENGES AND OPTIONS
Peterson Inst. for International Economics (2009)

In the absence of parallel commitments, and given the resistance by India and China to accept binding emission targets, some developed countries . . . harbor fears that their own stringent GHG-control programs will put domestic firms at a severe disadvantage in global markets. This will lead to the "leakage" of production and jobs to firms located in countries that do not adopt equivalent controls. . . .

Among the mitigation and adaptation policy options that countries have introduced or considered, several may have trade implications. For example, product or performance standards (e.g., labeling requirements or energy efficiency standards) could easily be operated as technical barriers to imports. . . .

In the absence of clearer guidelines than now exist, it is difficult to predict whether various policy options would be compatible with WTO rules. For example, it remains uncertain whether border adjustments are allowable for carbon taxes or permits that are based on energy consumed or carbon emitted, either in making a product or inputs to the product. It is also unclear whether the Agreement on Technical Barriers to Trade (TBT) would allow standards and labeling requirements based on production and processing methods (PPMs) that do not affect the physical characteristics of the product.

The prior record of panel and Appellate Body decisions on these and other climate-related questions is sparse. If the rule book is filled out through case-by-case litigation, it could be years before an overall framework is established. Moreover, case outcomes may depend heavily on how disputed measures are designed and implemented, making for a pretty complicated rule book.

NOTES AND QUESTIONS

1. In what ways could the trade regime play a constructive role in combating climate change? In what ways could the trade and climate change regimes conflict?

2. Should states that have adopted measures to control their own greenhouse gas emissions be allowed to impose trade measures on imports from states that have failed to implement comparable controls? If so, on what basis are trade measures permissible? Should they be designed only to internalize the climate change externalities caused by manufacturing the imported goods? Or can they be imposed in a more punitive way, to induce states to join the international climate change regime or to penalize states for noncompliance?

b. Human Rights

Over the last several years, interest has grown tremendously in the subject of climate change and human rights. Litigators have begun to bring claims asserting that climate change is responsible for human rights violations. The UN Human Rights Council has adopted several resolutions on climate change, which recognize that the adverse effects of climate change have a range of direct and indirect implications for the effective enjoyment of human rights. The UN High Commissioner for Human Rights has produced a report on the subject. Report of the Office of the U.N. High Commissioner for Human Rights on the Relationship Between Climate Change and Human Rights, U.N. Doc. A/HRC/10/61 (Jan. 15, 2009). In 2010, the parties to the UNFCCC adopted a decision in Cancun emphasizing that "parties should, in all climate change related actions, fully respect human rights." Decision 1/CP.16, FCCC/CP/2010/7/Add.1. And in March 2012, the UN Human Rights Council established an Independent Expert on the issue of human rights obligations relating to the environment, who will examine climate change, among other issues.

Proposals to treat climate change as a human rights problem raise many fundamental questions:

- Theoretically, what does it mean to conceptualize climate change in human rights terms? How would a human rights approach differ from treating climate change as an environmental, economic, or scientific problem?

- Descriptively, what does human rights law say about climate change and, conversely, what does climate change law say about human rights?
- Normatively, does it make sense to approach climate change as a human rights issue? What are the pros and cons?

INTERNATIONAL COUNCIL ON HUMAN RIGHTS, CLIMATE CHANGE AND HUMAN RIGHTS: A ROUGH GUIDE
2008

[C]limate change is already undermining the realisation of a broad range of internationally protected human rights: rights to health and even life; rights to food, water, shelter and property; rights associated with livelihood and culture; with migration and resettlement; and with personal security in the event of conflict. Few dispute that this is the case.

Moreover, the interlinkages are deep and complex. The worst effects of climate change are likely to be felt by those individuals and groups whose rights protections are already precarious. This is partly coincidence. As it happens, the most dramatic impacts of climate change are expected to occur (and are already being experienced) in the world's poorest countries, where rights protections too are often weak. But the effect is also causal and mutually reinforcing. Populations whose rights are poorly protected are likely to be less well-equipped to understand or prepare for climate change effects; less able to lobby effectively for government or international action; and more likely to lack the resources needed to adapt to expected alterations of their environmental and economic situation. . . .

The construction of an international climate change regime too has rights implications. Mitigation policies have clear human rights dimensions. On one hand, any strategy (or mix of strategies) that is successful at global level will tend to determine the long-term access that many millions of people will have to basic public goods. On the other, choices made in the shorter-term—such as whether and where to cultivate biofuels or preserve forests—will affect food, water and health security and, by extension, the cultures and livelihoods of numerous particular persons in particular places.

Adaptation policies will raise comparable human rights concerns. Adaptation may be reframed as a compensatory or corrective response to potential or actual climate change-related human rights violations. . . . At the same time, adaptation actions can themselves affect human rights—such as, for example, if communities or individuals are forcibly removed from disaster or flood-prone areas, or, less forcibly, expected to conform to new economic policy imperatives (by adopting different cash crops or energy sources, for example).

Despite the obvious overlaps outlined above, the mainstream climate change literature and debate has, until very recently, given little or no attention to human rights concerns. . . .

What explains this mutual disinterest? The primary cause appears to be a kind of disciplinary path-dependence. The study of climate change began among meteorologists, became firmly entrenched in the physical sciences, and has only gradually—if inevitably—reached into the social sciences. The basic orientation has remained preeminently, though not solely, economic. Climate change negotiations have centered on consensus-driven welfare-based solutions, approaches that have historically thrived independently of and in parallel to human rights. . . .

In addition, experts in either discipline might identify plausible reasons for doubting that a "human rights approach" would assist the formation of effective policies to address climate change. Listed below are five such reasons.

The rights at issue are difficult to enforce. Climate change generally (if not exclusively) affects categories of human rights that have notoriously weak enforcement mechanisms under international law—social and economic rights, the rights of migrants, rights protections during conflicts. . . . In the absence of strong enforcement institutions, either at national or international level, it is not immediately obvious what human rights can add to a policy discussion that is already notably welfare-conscious, even if focused on the general good rather than on individual complaints.

Extraterritorial responsibility is hard to establish. Under human rights law, a person's government ordinarily has the primary duty to act when rights are violated. In the context of climate change, however, responsibility for impacts in the most vulnerable countries often lies not with the government nearest to hand, but with diffuse actors, both public and private, many of whom are located far away. Human rights law does not easily reach across international borders to impose obligations in matters such as these.

Local accountability is hard to establish. Although countries that lack economic resources and infrastructure are least likely to be major emitters of greenhouse gases, they are most likely to suffer devastating effects of climate change—effects whose human consequences will be worsened by their low capacity to adapt. . . . If a government cannot be held accountable for failing fully to protect those rights in the ordinary course, it will surely be even harder to hold it responsible for circumstances it did not create.

Emergency conditions limit the application of human rights law. The most severe climate change impacts will be catastrophic—drought, floods, famines, mass migration, wars—and will affect large numbers of people. . . . International human rights treaties and most national constitutions typically allow for the suspension ("derogation") of many human rights in times of emergency. . . . Human rights, traditionally conceived as a bulwark against expansive state discretion, become less relevant as *legal* tools at such times (although their rhetorical force may increase). Indeed, many human rights traditionalists might be expected to oppose climate change action on precisely the grounds that it will empower government, both nationally and internationally, at the expense of individuals.

Rights may conflict. Human rights protect others besides those who are potentially harmed by climate change. Economic actors are also rights-holders and it is foreseeable that some of them will invoke the human right to property or peaceful enjoyment of their possessions to prevent or reduce action on climate change. The right to property has been given a broad interpretation by international tribunals and could be asserted by those who have been licensed to act in ways that harm the environment. Other human rights claims too—such as to culture, or freedom of religion, or family reunion—may bring individuals into conflict with climate change policies. All of these rights, like other rights, may be limited for the public good, and struggles can be expected over exactly where the line should be drawn in such cases.

The above objections are not negligible. But they nevertheless rely, perhaps excessively, on a *legalist* vision of human rights that, if frequently effective, is not necessarily definitive. . . .

As harms due to climate change are increasingly felt, it is very likely that many of those affected will turn to the hard law language of human rights for protection.

Indeed, this is already happening. However, human rights can be articulated in registers other than law. In approaching climate change, a case might be made for a less legalist application of human rights principles to the climate change field, in favour of an approach better suited to the immense policy challenges that lie ahead. Five potential benefits of such a policy orientation are identified below.

Human rights prioritise harms to actual persons. . . . In a debate necessarily steeped in scenarios and probabilities, human rights law requires that hard lines be drawn where possible. The important questions about impact scenarios would then be: *who*, precisely, is likely to suffer *what* and *why*? Human rights standards provide thresholds of minimum acceptability. . . .

Accountability. The human rights preoccupation with accountability might be helpful in constructing a climate regime. . . . Accountability mechanisms of some sort will be needed to underpin any functional climate regime, because compliance will be vital to credibility. . . . The incorporation of human rights assessments in policy projections could . . . help to determine who is accountable for what, and how accountability should be attributed.

Focus on the most vulnerable. Human rights analysis and advocacy have always paid particular attention to those who are on the margins of society as a result of poverty, powerlessness, or systemic discrimination. It is widely acknowledged that social and economic vulnerability greatly increases the risk of suffering from the impacts of climate change. . . . A human rights focus can redirect attention to people who are otherwise likely to be ignored or unheard. . . .

Procedural guarantees. Various doctrines of procedural or process rights have evolved within human rights law, many of which have been adopted in international environmental law. In principle these can help those harmed by climate change to influence policies that affect them, and can assist policymakers to understand and take account of public needs.

Taken together, these strengths suggest that human rights could play a valuable role during climate change negotiations and when implementing policies, particularly in ethically fraught areas. Human rights supply not only legal imperatives, but also a set of internationally agreed values around which common action can be negotiated and motivated. They provide a language of minimum thresholds, legally defined, about which there is already widespread consensus. . . .

NOTES AND QUESTIONS

1. Are you persuaded that climate change should be addressed as a human rights issue? Why or why not?

2. What are the main differences between a human rights approach to climate change and the approach of the UNFCCC regime?

3. In 2005, a group of Alaskan Inuit submitted a petition to the Inter-American Commission on Human Rights, asserting that climate change is causing violations of their rights to life, health, culture, and subsistence. Do you think that human rights litigation offers a promising approach to addressing the climate change problem? What would be the effect of a ruling by a human rights body that global warming is resulting in human rights violations?

c. National Security

In 2007, the United Kingdom brought the issue of climate change before the UN Security Council, arguing that since the climate change issue "threatens the peace and security of the world, this has to be the right place to address it." The UK Foreign Minister, Margaret Beckett, warned that climate change could cause migration on a "massive scale," due to flooding, drought, disease, and famine. As she argued, "Climate change is [a] security issue but it is not a narrow matter of national security. . . . This is about our collective security in a fragile and interdependent world."

NATIONAL SECURITY AND THE ACCELERATING RISKS OF CLIMATE CHANGE
CNA Corporation (2014)

CNA's Military Advisory Board (MAB) first addressed the national security implications of climate change in our 2007 report—*National Security and the Threat of Climate Change*. We gather again as a group of 16 retired Generals and Admirals from the Army, Navy, Air Force, and Marine Corps to re-examine climate change in the context of a more informed, but more complex and integrated world, and to provide an update to our 2007 findings.

As we identified in our 2007 report . . . , the projected effects of climate change ". . . are threat multipliers that will aggravate stressors such as poverty, environmental degradation, political instability, and social tensions—conditions that can enable terrorist activity and other forms of violence." We remain steadfast in our concern about the connection between climate change and national security.

In many areas, the projected impacts of climate change will be more than threat multipliers; they will serve as catalysts for instability and conflict. In Africa, Asia, and the Middle East, we are already seeing how the impacts of extreme weather, such as prolonged drought and flooding, are posing security challenges to these regions' governments. We see these trends growing and accelerating. . . .

When it comes to thinking about how the world will respond to projected changes in the climate, we believe it is important to guard against a failure of imagination. . . .

Rising temperatures across the middle latitudes of the world will increase the demand for water and energy. These growing demands will stress resources, constrain development, and increase competition among agriculture, energy production and human sustenance. In light of projected climate change, stresses on the water-food-energy nexus are a mounting security concern across a growing segment of the world. . . .

The projected impacts of climate change . . . not only affect local communities but also, in the aggregate, challenge key elements of our National Power. Key elements of National Power include political, military, economic, social, infrastructure, and information systems. The projected impacts of climate change could be detrimental to military readiness, strain base resilience, both at home and abroad, and may limit our ability to respond to future demands.

NOTES AND QUESTIONS

1. In response to the UK initiative, the United States argued that climate change is already being addressed in other forums. More recently, in 2013, Russia and China vetoed efforts by Pakistan and the United Kingdom to hold a formal session on climate change and international security. The Pakistan-UK effort was supported by small island states, but most developing states sided with Russia and China. Do you think the UN Security Council is the appropriate place to discuss the climate change issue? What advantages and disadvantages does it have as compared to, say, the UNFCCC process?

2. The Ugandan president, Yoweri Musaveni, has characterized climate change as "an act of aggression by the rich against the poor." Do you think there is an analogy between climate change and military aggression? Or is this merely inflammatory rhetoric?

3. Overall, are you persuaded that climate change is a national security issue, rather than simply an environmental or energy issue? For further discussion of the national security implications of climate change, see the end of section A of this chapter.

TABLE OF ACRONYMS

ACEEE	American Council for an Energy-Efficient Economy
ACM	Asbestos-containing materials
ACRS	Advisory Committee on Reactor Safeguards
AEC	Atomic Energy Commission
AFO	Animal feeding operation
ALJ	Administrative law judge
AMC	American Mining Congress
ANILCA	Alaska National Interest Lands Conservation Act
APA	Administrative Procedure Act
API	American Petroleum Institute
AQCR	Air quality control region
AQRV	Air quality–related value
ARARs	Applicable or relevant and appropriate requirements
ARRA	American Recovery and Reinvestment Act
BACT	Best available control technology
BADT	Best available demonstrated technology
BAPA	Buenos Aires Plan of Action
BART	Best available retrofit technology
BAT	Best available technology
BATEA	Best available technology economically achievable
BCT	Best conventional technology
BLM	Bureau of Land Management
BNA	Bureau of National Affairs
BO	Biological opinion
BOD	Biological oxygen demand
BoR	Bureau of Reclamation
BPCTCA	Best practicable control technology currently available
BPJ	Best professional judgment
BPT	Best practicable technology
CAA	Clean Air Act
CAEP	Committee on Aviation Environmental Protection
CAFE	Corporate average fuel economy
CAFO	Combined animal feeding operation
CAIR	Clean Air Act Interstate Rule
CASAC	Clean Air Scientific Advisory Committee
CATX	Categorical exclusion
CBA	Cost benefit analysis

CBDR	Common but differentiated responsibilities
CEC	Commission for Environmental Cooperation
CEM	Continuous emission monitoring
CEQ	Council on Environmental Quality
CEQA	California Environmental Quality Act
CER	Certified emission reduction
CERCLA	Comprehensive Environmental Response, Compensation, and Liability Act
CFCs	Chlorofluorocarbons
CFR	Code of Federal Regulations
CITES	Convention on International Trade in Endangered Species
CMA	Chemical Manufacturers Association
CO	Carbon monoxide
CO_2	Carbon dioxide
CO_{2eq}	Carbon dioxide-equivalent
COP	Conference of the Parties
CRA	Comparative risk assessment
CRP	Conservation Reserve Program
CRS	Congressional Research Service
CSO	Combined sewer overflow
CV	Contingent valuation
CWA	Clean Water Act
CZMA	Coastal Zone Management Act
DEIS	Draft environmental impact statement
DMA	Diversity maintenance area
DMR	Discharge monitoring report
DO	Dissolved oxygen
DOI	Department of the Interior
DOT	Department of Transportation
DQA	Data Quality Act
DSP	Dominant social paradigm
EA	Environmental assessment
EAJA	Equal Access to Justice Act
ECOS	Environmental Council of the States
ECRA	Environmental Cleanup Responsibility Act
EDF	Environmental Defense Fund
EGU	Electric generating unit
EIP	Economic incentive program
EIS	Environmental impact statement
ELI	Environmental Law Institute
EMS	Environmental management system
ENGO	Environmental nongovernmental organization
EPA	Environmental Protection Agency
EPCA	Energy Policy and Conservation Act
EPCRA	Emergency Planning and Community Right-to-Know Act
ERC	Emission reduction credit

ERU	Emission reduction unit
ESA	Endangered Species Act or environmental site assessment
ESD	Environmentally sustainable development
ETS	Environmental tobacco smoke
FAA	Federal Aviation Administration
FACA	Federal Advisory Committee Act
FCCC	Framework Convention on Climate Change
FDA	Food and Drug Administration
FEIS	Final environmental impact statement
FEMAT	Forest Ecosystem Management Team
FFC	Ferric ferrocyanide
FFDCA	Federal Food, Drug, and Cosmetic Act
FHWA	Federal Highway Administration
FIFRA	Federal Insecticide, Fungicide, and Rodenticide Act
FIP	Federal implementation plan
FLPMA	Federal Land Policy and Management Act
FOE	Friends of the Earth
FOIA	Freedom of Information Act
FONSI	Finding of no significant impact
FTC	Federal Trade Commission
FWPCA	Federal Water Pollution Control Act
FWS	Fish and Wildlife Service
GAO	Government Accountability Office
GATT	General Agreement on Tariffs and Trade
GHG	Greenhouse gases
GIACC	Group on International Aviation and Climate Change
GIS	Geographic information systems
GPA	Global Programme of Action
GSA	General Services Administration
HC	Hydrocarbons
HCFCs	Hydrochlorofluorocarbons
HCP	Habitat conservation plan
HEW	Department of Health, Education, and Welfare
HHS	Department of Health and Human Services
HMTUSA	Hazardous Materials Transportation Uniform Safety Act
HRS	Hazard Ranking System
HSWA	Hazardous and Solid Waste Amendments
HUD	Department of Housing and Urban Development
ICAO	International Civil Aviation Organization
I&M	Inspection and maintenance
IMO	International Maritime Organization
INC	Intergovernmental Negotiating Committee
IPCC	Intergovernmental Panel on Climate Change
IQA	Information Quality Act

ISRA	Industrial Site Recovery Act
ITC	Interagency Testing Committee
LAER	Lowest achievable emission rate
LDR	Land disposal restriction
LEED	Leadership in Energy and Environmental Design
LEV	Low-emission vehicle
LID	Low impact development
LRTAP	Long-Range Transboundary Air Pollution Convention
LULU	Locally undesirable land use
LULUCF	Land use, land-use change and forestry
MARPOL	International Convention for the Prevention of Pollution from Ships
MCL	Maximum contaminant level
MCLG	Maximum contaminant level goal
MEA	Multilateral environmental agreement
MGP	Manufactured gas plant
MIS	Management indicator species
MTBE	Methyl tertiary butyl ether
MTD	Maximum tolerated dose
MUSYA	Multiple-Use Sustained Yield Act
MWC	Municipal waste combustor or municipal waste combustion
NAAEC	North American Agreement on Environmental Cooperation
NAAQS	National ambient air quality standard
NAFTA	North American Free Trade Agreement
NAPAP	National Acid Precipitation Assessment Program
NAS	National Academy of Sciences
NCCP	Natural Community Conservation Plan
NCI	National Cancer Institute
NCP	National Contingency Plan
NEP	New environmental paradigm
NEPA	National Environmental Policy Act
NESHAP	National emission standard for hazardous air pollutant
NFMA	National Forest Management Act
NGO	Nongovernmental organization
NHTSA	National Highway Traffic Safety Administration
NIH	National Institutes of Health
NIMBY	Not in my backyard
NIOSH	National Institute for Occupational Safety and Health
NJDEP	New Jersey Department of Environmental Protection
NMFS	National Marine Fisheries Service
NOAA	National Oceanic and Atmospheric Administration
NO$_x$	Nitrogen oxides
NPDES	National Pollutant Discharge Elimination System
NPDWR	National primary drinking water regulation

NPFC	National Pollution Funds Center
NPL	National Priorities List
NPS	Nonpoint source pollution
NRC	National Research Council or Nuclear Regulatory Commission
NRDC	Natural Resources Defense Council
NSPS	New source performance standards
NSR	New source review
NWF	National Wildlife Federation

O_3	Ozone
O & G	Oil and grease
ODS	Ozone-depleting substance
OECA	Office of Enforcement and Compliance Assurance
OECD	Organisation of Economic Co-operation and Development
OIG	Office of Inspector General
OIRA	Office of Information and Regulatory Affairs
OPA	Oil Pollution Act
ORVR	On-board refueling vapor recovery
OMB	Office of Management and Budget
OSH	Occupational Safety and Health
OSHA	Occupational Safety and Health Administration
OSWR	Office of Solid Waste and Emergency Response
OTA	Office of Technology Assessment
OTAG	Ozone Transport Assessment Group

PAH	Polycyclic aromatic hydrocarbon
PCBs	Polychlorinated biphenyls
PCE	Perchloroethylene
PEL	Permissible exposure limit
PM	Particulate matter
PMN	Premanufacture notification
POPs	Persistent organic pollutants
POTW	Publicly owned treatment works
PPA	Pollution Prevention Act
PPM	Parts per million
PRP	Potentially responsible party
PSD	Prevention of significant deterioration

QA/QC	Quality assurance/quality control
QALYs	Quality adjusted life years

RACM	Reasonably available control measures
RACT	Reasonably available control technology
RCRA	Resource Conservation and Recovery Act
RFA	Regulatory Flexibility Act
RFG	Reformulated gasoline
RGGI	Regional Greenhouse Gas Initiative

RI&FS	Remedial investigation and feasibility study
RMRR	Routine maintenance, repair, and replacement
ROD	Record of decision
RPA	Reasonable and prudent alternative
RPS	Renewable portfolio standard
RQ	Reportable quantity
RRRA	Restoration, rehabilitation, replacement, or acquisition
SAB	Scientific Advisory Board
SAFETEA-LU	Safe Accountable, Flexible, Efficient Transportation Equity Act: A Legacy for Users
SARA	Superfund Amendments and Reauthorization Act
SDWA	Safe Drinking Water Act
SEC	Securities and Exchange Commission
SEP	Supplemental environmental project
SEPA	State environmental policy act
SFIP	Sector Facility Indexing Project
SIP	State implementation plan
SO_x	Sulfur oxides
SPA	Slag processing area
SRF	State Revolving Fund
SWANCC	Solid Waste Agency of Northern Cook County
SWDA	Solid Waste Disposal Act
SWMU	Solid waste management unit
TCLP	Toxicity characteristic leaching procedure
TCM	Transportation control measure
TCP	Transportation control plan
TEIA	Transboundary environmental impact assessment
TMDL	Total maximum daily load
TRI	Toxic Release Inventory
TRPA	Tahoe Regional Planning Agency
TSCA	Toxic Substances Control Act
TSD	Treatment, storage, and disposal
TSDF	Treatment, storage, and disposal facility
TSP	Total suspended particulates
TSS	Total suspended solids
TTHMs	Total trihalomethanes
TVA	Tennessee Valley Authority
UAO	Unilateral administrative order
UIC	Underground injection control
UNDP	United Nations Development Program
UNEP	United Nations Environment Program
UNFCCC	United Nations Framework Convention on Climate Change
USC	United States Code
USDA	United States Department of Agriculture
USEPA	United States Environmental Protection Agency
USGCRP	United States Global Climate Research Program

USGRCP	United States Global Change Research Program
USGS	United States Geological Survey
UST	Underground storage tank
VOCs	Volatile organic compounds
WHO	World Health Organization
WMC	Watershed Management Council
WMO	World Meteorological Organization
WRP	Wetlands Reserve Program
WTE	Waste-to-energy
WTO	World Trade Organization

TABLE OF CASES

Principal cases are indicated by italics. Alphabetization is letter-by-letter (e.g., "Aircraft Owners" precedes "Air Pollution").

INDEX